New International Dictionary of New Testament Theology

New International Dictionary of New Testament Theology

ABRIDGED EDITION

Verlyn D. Verbrugge

Formerly titled *The NIV Theological Dictionary of New Testament Words*

ZONDERVAN.com/
AUTHORTRACKER
follow your favorite authors

To my parents
who instilled in me a love of the Scriptures

New International Dictionary of New Testament Theology: Abridged Edition
Copyright © 2000 by The Zondervan Corporation

Formerly titled: *The NIV Theological Dictionary of New Testament Words*

Requests for information should be addressed to:

Zondervan, *Grand Rapids, Michigan 49530*

Library of Congress Cataloging-in-Publication Data

New international dictionary of New Testament theology/ [edited by] Verlyn D. Verbrugge.—Abridged ed.
        p. cm.
    "Formerly titled: THE NIV theological dictionary of New Testament words." Includes indexes
        ISBN-13: 978-0-310-25620-5
        ISBN-10: 0-310-25620-8 (alk. Paper)
        1. Bible. NT.—Theology—Dictionaries. 2. Greek language, Biblical—Glossaries, vocabularies, etc.. I. Verbrugge, Verlyn
D. II. NIV theological dictionary of New Testament words.
    BS2397 .N48
    225.3—dc22

                                                                                                                    2003021824

This edition printed on acid-free paper.

Printed in the United States of America

09 10 11 12 • 11 10 9 8 7 6 5 4

Contents

Introduction

This book is an abridgment of the popular *New International Dictionary of New Testament Theology*, edited by Colin Brown. This four-volume set is itself a translation of a German work, *Theologisches Begriffslexikon zum Neuen Testament*, published in the 1960s and early 1970s and edited by Lothar Coenen, Erich Beyreuther, and Hans Bietenhard.

But the present work is much more than an abridgment. The arrangement of the material as it occurs in *NIDNTT* has been completely revamped and new entries have been added. Let me explain.

1. *NIDNTT* is arranged according to English topics. Sometimes an English category is linked to a single Greek word, but many times two or more Greek words are discussed, all of which have nuances of the English word. This abridgment has rearranged the material so that each Greek word is discussed in its own place in Greek alphabetical order. As I examined the *NIDNTT*, it became apparent to me that there was often little discussion of the interrelationship of Greek words within a particular semantic field. That is, rather than being a discussion of semantic domains, *NIDNTT* is a discussion of individual Greek words that have been grouped together according to English meaning. It therefore made as much sense to discuss these words in their sequence in the Greek alphabet. (Note that this is the method used in the *New International Dictionary of Old Testament Theology and Exegesis*, edited by Willem VanGemeren and published by Zondervan in 1997.)

That does not mean that readers no longer have access to the discussions of other Greek words with similar English meanings, since (like *NIDOTTE*) at the end of many entries are cross-references to other Greek words. For example, the *NIDNTT* entry "Death, Kill, Sleep" discusses four Greek words and their cognates: *apokteinō, thanatos, katheudō,* and *nekros*. At the end of each of these words in this abridgment is a cross-reference to the other three words. You are encouraged to look up all four of these words if you want to make a thorough study of this English topic.

2. In this abridgment, each of the Greek words has a number, according to the Goodrick-Kohlenberger numbering system. This numbering system (similar but superior to Strong's) was introduced in *The NIV Exhaustive Concordance*, published in 1990 (available now as *Zondervan NIV Exhaustive Concordance*) and edited by Edward W. Goodrick and John R. Kohlenberger III. (The same numbering system forms the basis of *The Greek-English Concordance to the New Testament* and *The Exhaustive Concordance to the Greek New Testament*.) Thus, if you use the New International Version (NIV), you can look up an English word in the *Exhaustive Concordance*, find its corresponding GK number, and turn to that number in this abridgment for a discussion of that word. An easier means of finding GK numbers is *The NIV English-Greek New Testament*, by William D. Mounce. This book contains the running text of the NIV with Greek words rearranged underneath the English words, together with parsing information and the GK number of each word.

If you use a reference work that has Strong's numbers, conversion charts are available in the back of the present work.

3. Even though the initial lexical paragraph of each entry in this abridgment has Greek words written in Greek letters (always followed by transliteration), the rest of the entry uses only transliteration. Therefore you can read and understand this theological dictionary even if you do not know Greek. And you can easily find the cross-reference entries as well, since these too are cited both by Greek transliteration and by GK number.

4. Some material is obviously deleted in any abridgment. So what has been deleted from *NIDNTT*? (a) As a matter of policy, all references to secondary literature, including the extensive bibliographies, have been eliminated. These references only went as far as the mid-1970s (when the four-volume set was published), so these scholarly references are dated. If you want to know which works were consulted for any particular article in *NIDNTT*, you can go to the larger work for that information.

(b) *NIDNTT* also contained a number of full-length articles on specific topics, such as "Revelation in Contemporary Theology" and "Infant Baptism: Its Background and Theology." These articles fit more in the category of systematic theology than that of biblical exegesis; in addition, they too are dated. Thus, they have been eliminated.

(c) Some articles of *NIDNTT* discussed the pros and cons of various interpretations of particular passages of Scripture. In general I have eliminated these discussions and simply given the conclusions. Also, in *NIDNTT* the editors made various additions to certain German original articles in order to make their content more palatable to evangelical Christians; sometimes these added comments even contradicted the original. In this abridgment, each article is a homogenous whole rather than a hybrid and is written from a thorough evangelical perspective.

(d) The discussion of the history of a particular word in classical Greek has usually been abbreviated more substantially than the rest of the original article. The important thing for the exegete to know is how a particular word was used in Hellenistic Greek, not what its presumed root meant nor how it was used in Homer, Hesiod, Plato, Aristotle, and the like. Furthermore, sometimes the authors of *NIDNTT* went into long discussions of Old Testament theology that had little or nothing to do with the particular Greek word being discussed; these too have been significantly shortened.

(e) In a good number of cases, the same Greek word was discussed under more than one English category, usually with virtually identical information in both places. Such multiple entries have been merged into a single entry.

5. The present work is more than an abridgment, however. It became apparent to me as I was working on this material that there were significant New Testament Greek words with deep theological significance that were omitted from the present work. For example, while *NIDNTT* contains a lengthy article on *ginōskō*, to know (*1182*), it has no discussion of two other Greek words that are also translated "know": *epistamai* (*2179*) and *oida* (*3857*). The present work now has entries for all three of these words. To give one more

example: There is no discussion of the verb *hypotassō* (submit, be subject to, *5718*) in *NIDNTT*, but anyone wanting to study the words used in the New Testament regarding the relationship of husbands and wives in Ephesians 5:21–33 or between slaves and masters in 1 Peter 2:18 will need to study this word. Thus, I have added *hypotassō* to this abridgment and discussed its meaning.

6. One final note on Bible versions and translations. All direct Scripture translations have been made to correspond to the NIV unless otherwise noted. Regarding the Old Testament, especially the LXX, all the references given are those of the English Bible, with differences between English versification and LXX versification noted when necessary. In the book of Psalms, however, where most chapters and many verses vary by one between English translations and the LXX, only the English chapter and verse numbers are given. Finally, if a particular Greek word occurs in the LXX and has no corresponding word in the Hebrew Bible or the NIV translation, the LXX reference is given and then is so noted.

This book would not have seen the light of day if it had not been for the help of others, to whom I am deeply grateful. Britt Dennison of Zondervan New Media arranged to have the present *NIDNTT* keyed so that he could make this book available on CD-ROM. Nancy Wilson developed the necessary macros to convert the CD-ROM material into a usable format for me to work on, and she designed the present work and did the typesetting. Stan Gundry, vice-president and editor-in-chief at Zondervan, gave me as senior academic editor the assignment of abridging *NIDNTT* and encouraged me as I argued for its rearrangement in GK number order. A special word of thanks must be given to Bob Buller of Loveland, Colorado, who edited and proofread this entire abridgment after me and offered invaluable help in making it clearer and more focused.

I pray that this present work will serve interpreters of God's Word to understand better the message of the New Testament and so help them in their preaching and teaching to give guidance to God's people for many years to come.

Verlyn D. Verbrugge
Easter, 2000

Abbreviations

1QH	*Hodayot, Thanksgiving Hymns*	e.g.	for example
1QM	*Milḥamah, War Scroll*	Eng.	English
1QpHab	*Pesher Habakkuk*	Ep. Jer.	Epistle of Jeremiah
1QS	*Rule of the Community, Serek Hayyaḥad*	Eph.	Ephesians
1QSa	*Rule of the Congregation* (Appendix a to 1QS)	Esd.	Esdras
		esp.	especially
1QSb	*Rule of the Blessings* (Appendix b to 1QS)	Est.	Esther
11QMelch	*Melchizedek*	Exod.	Exodus
4QFlor	*Florilegium, Midrash on Eschatology*ᵃ	Ezek.	Ezekiel
4QpPs 37	*Pesher Psalm 37*	Ezr.	Ezra
A	LXX, Codex Alexandrinus	fem.	feminine
ʾAbot R. Nat.	*ʾAbot of Rabbi Nathan*	fig.	figurative(ly)
acc.	accusative	fut.	future
act.	active	Gal.	Galatians
Add. Est.	Additions to Esther	gen.	genitive
adj(s).	adjective(s)	Gen.	Genesis
adv.	adverb	Gk.	Greek
ANE	ancient Near East	Hab.	Habakkuk
Ant.	Josephus, *Jewish Antiquities*	Hag.	Haggai
aor.	aorist	Heb.	Hebrew(s)
Apoc. Ab.	*Apocalypse of Abraham*	Hel.	Hellenistic
Apoc. El.	*Apocalypse of Elijah*	Herm. *Mand.*	Shepherd of Hermas, *Mandate*
Apocr.	Apocrypha	Herm. *Sim.*	Shepherd of Hermas, *Similitude*
app.	approximate(ly)	hiph.	hiphil
Aram.	Aramaic	Hos.	Hosea
art.	article	Ign. *Eph.*	Ignatius, *To the Ephesians*
Assum. Mos.	*Assumption of Moses*	Ign. *Magn.*	Ignatius, *To the Magnesians*
b.	Babylonian Talmud	Ign. *Phld.*	Ignatius, *To the Philadelphians*
B	LXX, Codex Vaticanus	Ign. *Rom.*	Ignatius, *To the Romans*
B. Bat.	*Baba Batra*	Ign. *Trall.*	Ignatius, *To the Trallians*
Bar.	Baruch (Apocrypha)	imperf.	imperfect
Bar.	*Baruch* (Pseudepigrapha)	impers.	impersonal(ly)
Barn.	*Barnabas*	ind.	indicative
Bel.	Bel and the Dragon	intrans.	intransitive(ly)
Ber.	*Berakot*	Iren., *Haer.*	Irenaeus, *Adversus haereses* (*Against Heresies*)
ca.	circa		
CD	Cairo Genizah copy of the *Damascus Document*	Isa.	Isaiah
		Jas.	James
cent.	century	Jdg.	Judges
cf.	confer, compare	Jdt.	Judith
ch(s).	chapter(s)	Jer.	Jeremiah
Chr.	Chronicles	Jn.	John
cl./CL	classical	Jon.	Jonah
Clem.	Clement	Jos.	Joshua
Clem. Alex., *Strom.*	Clement of Alexandria, *Stromata* (*Miscellanies*)	*Jub.*	*Jubilees*
		Jud.	Judaism
Col.	Colossians	*J.W.*	Josephus, *Jewish War*
Cor.	Corinthians	Ki.	Kings
d.	died	*L.A.E.*	*Life of Adam and Eve*
Dan.	Daniel	Lam.	Lamentations
dat.	dative	Lat.	Latin
dep.	deponent	*Leg.*	Philo, *Legum allegoriae* (*Allegorical Interpretation*)
Deut.	Deuteronomy		
Dial.	*Dialogue With Trypho*	*Let. Aris.*	*Letter of Aristeas*
Did.	*Didache*	Lev.	Leviticus
Eccl.	Ecclesiastes	lit.	literature, literal(ly)

Lk.	Luke	*Rab.*	*Rabbah*
LXX	Septuagint	Rev.	Revelation
m.	Mishnah	Rom.	Romans
Macc.	Maccabees	S	LXX, Codex Sinaiticus
Mal.	Malachi	Sam.	Samuel
masc.	masculine	*Sanh.*	*Sanhedrin*
Matt.	Matthew	sec.	section
Mek. Exod.	Mekilta Exodus	Sem.	Semitic
Mic.	Micah	*Shab.*	*Shabbat*
mid.	middle	*Sheb.*	*Shebiʿit*
Mk.	Mark	*Sheqal.*	*Sheqalim*
MS(S)	manuscript(s)	*Sib. Or.*	*Sibylline Oracles*
MT	Masoretic Text	sing.	singular
Nah.	Nahum	Sir.	Sirach
Ned.	*Nedarim*	Song	Song of Songs
Neh.	Nehemiah	subj.	subject, subjective
neut.	neuter	subst.	substantive
niph.	niphal	Sus.	Susanna
nom.	nominative	Sym.	Symmachus's Gk. translation of the OT
NT	New Testament	*T. Ab.*	*Testament of Abraham*
Num.	Numbers	*T. Ash.*	*Testament of Asher*
Obad.	Obadiah	*T. Benj.*	*Testament of Benjamin*
obj.	object(ive)	*T. Dan*	*Testament of Dan*
Odes Sol.	*Odes of Solomon*	*T. Iss.*	*Testament of Issachar*
Ohal.	*Ohalot*	*T. Jos.*	*Testament of Joseph*
OT	Old Testament	*T. Jud.*	*Testament of Judah*
Pal.	Palestine(an)	*T. Levi*	*Testament of Levi*
par.	parallel, parallels	*T. Naph.*	*Testament of Naphtali*
part.	participle	*T. Reu.*	*Testament of Reuben*
pass.	passive	*T. Sol.*	*Testament of Solomon*
Pent.	Pentateuch	*T. Zeb.*	*Testament of Zebulun*
perf.	perfect	*Tanḥ.*	*Tanḥuma*
pers.	person(al)	*Tg. Isa.*	*Targum Isaiah*
Pesiq. Rab.	*Pesiqta Rabbati*	*Tg. Onq.*	*Targum Onqelos*
Pet.	Peter	Theod.	Theodotion's Gk. translation of the OT
Phaedr.	*Phaedrus*	Thess.	Thessalonians
Phil.	Philippians	Tim.	Timothy
Phlm.	Philemon	Tob.	Tobit
pl.	plural	Tit.	Titus
plupf.	pluperfect	trans.	translation, transitive(ly)
Pr. Man.	Prayer of Manasseh	vb(s).	verb(s)
prep.	preposition(al)	voc.	vocative
preps.	prepositions	Wis.	Wisdom of Solomon
pres.	present	*y.*	Jerusalem Talmud
pron	pronoun	*Yebam.*	*Yebamot*
Prov.	Proverbs	Zech.	Zechariah
Ps.	Psalm(s)	Zeph.	Zephaniah
Pss. Sol.	*Psalms of Solomon*		
rab.	rabbinic		

Transliteration

Hebrew

Letters

א	*ʾ*	ו	*w*	כ	*k*	ע	*ʿ*	שׂ	*ś*
ב	*b*	ז	*z*	ל	*l*	פ	*p*	שׁ	*š*
ג	*g*	ח	*ḥ*	מ	*m*	צ	*ṣ*	ת	*t*
ד	*d*	ט	*ṭ*	נ ן	*n*	ק	*q*		
ה	*h*	י	*y*	ס	*s*	ר	*r*		

Vowels

ַ	*a*	ֵ	*ē*	ֹ	*ō*	ְ	*e*
ָ	*ā*	ֵי	*ê*	וֹ	*ô*	ֲ	*a*
ָה	*â*	ִ	*i*	ֻ	*u, ū*	ֱ	*e*
ֶ	*e*	ִי	*î*	וּ	*û*	ֳ	*o*

Greek

Letters

α	*a*	ζ	*z*	λ	*l*	π	*p*	φ	*ph*
β	*b*	η	*ē*	μ	*m*	ρ	*r*	χ	*ch*
γ	*g*	θ	*th*	ν	*n*	σ, ς	*s*	ψ	*ps*
δ	*d*	ι	*i*	ξ	*x*	τ	*t*	ω	*ō*
ε	*e*	κ	*k*	ο	*o*	υ	*u, y*		

Special Characters

γγ	*ng*	γξ	*nx*	ῥ	*rh*
γκ	*nk*	γχ	*nch*	῾	*h*

A *alpha*

5	ἀββά

ἀββά (abba), father (5).

OT 1. In Aram. ʾabbā is originally, like the feminine equivalent ʾimmā, a word derived from baby language (like our "dada"). Already in the pre-Christian era the word underwent a considerable extension of meaning, replacing not only the older form of address common to biblical Heb. and Aram., ʾābî, my father, but also the Aram. terms for "the father" and "my father." In other words, ʾabbā as a form of address to one's father was no longer restricted to children but was also used by adult sons and daughters. The childish character of the word ("daddy") thus receded, and ʾabbā acquired the warm, familiar ring that we may feel in such an expression as "dear father."

2. Nowhere in the entire wealth of devotional literature produced by ancient Jud. do we find ʾabbā used as a way of addressing God. The pious Jew knew too much of the great gap between God and humanity (Eccl. 5:1) to be free to address God with the familiar word used in everyday family life. The literature of rab. Jud. contains only one indirect example of ʾabbā used in reference to God (*b. Taanith* 23b).

NT abba occurs in the NT only 3x: Mk. 14:36; Rom. 8:15; Gal. 4:6. In each case it is used in calling on God in prayer. In the other Gk. literature of early Christianity abba is found only in quotations of these passages.

1. It seems clear from the Gospel tradition—indirectly confirmed in Rom. 8:15 and Gal. 4:6 (see below)—that Jesus addressed God in his prayers as "my Father." In so doing, he made use of the warm, familiar term ʾabbā, used in the everyday life of the family. The only exception is the cry of dereliction from the cross (Mk. 15:34 par.), which is a quotation from Ps. 22:1.

(a) The invocation ʾabbā is expressly attested in the Markan text of Jesus' prayer in Gethsemane (Mk. 14:36). But in the other prayers of Jesus recorded by the Evangelists (→ patēr, 4252), there is good reason to argue that the Aram. ʾabbā underlies, either directly or indirectly, the various Gk. versions of his invocation of the Father.

(b) This use, unthinkable for the pious Jew, of the familiar term ʾabbā in prayer denotes the unique relationship of Jesus to God. It expresses not only his attitude of trust and obedience toward the Father (Mk. 14:36 par.), but also his incomparable authority (Matt. 11:25–27 par.).

2. The early church took over the use of ʾabbā in prayer. Note esp. Rom. 8:15 and Gal. 4:6, where Paul may have been thinking of the Lord's Prayer. In the oldest version of this prayer (Lk. 11:2–4), the invocation reads patēr, "[dear] Father," and suggests ʾabbā as the Aram. original. Thus, when Jesus gave his disciples the Lord's Prayer, he gave them authority to follow him in addressing God as ʾabbā and so granted them a share in his status as Son (cf. Jn. 1:12). Accordingly, Paul sees in the invocation "Abba" clear evidence of our adoption as sons through Christ and of the eschatological possession of the Spirit (Rom. 8:14–17; Gal. 4:4–7). The fact that the church, like Jesus, may say "Abba" is a fulfillment of God's promise: "I will be a Father to you, and you will be my sons and daughters" (2 Cor. 6:18; cf. 2 Sam. 7:14; also *Jub.* 1:24–25).

See also *patēr*, father (4252).

11	Ἀβραάμ

Ἀβραάμ (Abraam), Abraham (11).

OT The name derived either from the Babylonian *Abam-rāmā*, he loves the Father (i.e., God) or from the Aram. lengthening of the Canaanite name *Âb-rām*, the Father (i.e., God) is exalted. The popular etymology of the Heb. ʾabrāhām (Gen. 17:4–5) makes the name signify "father of a multitude."

1. The tradition of Gen. 11:27–25:11 depicts Abraham as the first of the so-called patriarchs, the ancestor of the later people of Israel. Admittedly, he continues to have the second place in the OT behind the patriarch Jacob, as is already indicated by the name Israel, which Jacob received and which was applied to the nation (→ *Israēl* [2702]), *Iakōb* [2609]). But a profound and far-reaching significance was attached to Abraham.

(a) Abraham stands for the prophetic experience of Israel. He is not only called a "prophet" (Gen. 20:7; cf. 15:13–16), he was also tested as a prophet (22:1), to see whether in his person God's people would esteem God enough to be willing to offer human sacrifice. Abraham held to the word of his God almost to the point of killing his only son. God then released him and the people of Israel, because he loves faithfulness and not sacrifice.

(b) Abraham was the recipient of a promise of land, which steadily grew despite the scanty beginnings. His life constantly appeared threatened by the lack of a son and heir (Gen. 15:2–3), and the latter was only born when Sarah was past the age of childbearing (18:1–15). In the panoramic perspective of the Pentateuch the theme of the land is not brought to fulfillment but looks towards fulfillment with the dying Moses (Deut. 34). Yet insofar as the land was never merely a physical possession but was constantly seen as a spiritual heritage (representing freedom, peace, and well-being in and with God), later Israel remained profoundly conscious of the fact that it still looked for the ultimate fulfillment of the promise to Abraham.

(c) The making of the covenant in Gen. 17 develops this theme and ensures that the land promised as a *possession* to Abraham and his posterity is not understood in a nationalistic way as personal property, but as the place of worship appropriate to the creator of the world (Gen. 1). In Gen. 17 the message is formulated that enabled Israel to survive even the terrible situation of national collapse and the far from glorious period of reconstruction under Persian rule.

(d) This insight was decisively influenced by the declaration that Abraham was called so that "all peoples on earth will be blessed through [him]" (Gen. 12:3). This declaration stands in the context of the promise of the land that looks forward to the kingdom of David (15:18) and relates these words, with their ring of power politics, to an antinationalistic perspective. Humankind, including Israel and the patriarchs, had fallen prey to the desire to be like God (3:5), to the mysterious couching of sin before the door of the heart (4:7), and to the need to establish a name for itself in a single kingdom (11:1–9). But the Lord of the world made a new beginning with Abraham, the man who unconditionally remained true to the promise (of the land) despite its meager fulfillment.

Alongside the instances where Abraham is mentioned in Gen., there is the particularly important and oft-repeated expression, esp. in Deut., "the land that the LORD swore he would give to your fathers—to Abraham, Isaac and Jacob" (cf. Deut. 1:8; 6:10; 9:5, 27; 29:13; 30:20; 34:4). Amid the despair of the exile, this expression denotes the fixed point on which election depended: a solemnly attested promise of God that made it possible for the Israelites after the loss of the land and in the anxiety of being remote from God (Isa. 63:15–64:11; cf. esp. the complaint of 63:16!) to accept their sin as sin, because they understood God as the one who is dependable. Thus Abraham is the ancestor to whom the promise was the basis of his life; God counted this to him as righteousness (Gen. 15:6).

2. The special position of Abraham, already foreshadowed in this development, reached its highest expression in Jud. Because of Abraham's election, all who confess themselves as his descendants have a place in the coming kingdom of God. Rab. Jud. saw Abraham's life as a series of acts of obedience; according to it, Abraham had kept the whole law. By contrast, Hel. Jud., esp. Philo, stressed his trust in God's promises, esp. those about the final judgment and the kingdom of God, and attributed the beginnings of belief in a world to come to his time.

NT 1. Since Abraham was the ancestor of Israel, the descent of Jesus from him became of great importance for the proclamation of Jesus as the Messiah. It underlined the continuity in God's saving activity both for his people and the world (cf. the genealogy in Matt. 1:1–17).

2. (a) For the Jews in general it was a special title of honor to be known as "children of Abraham" (Matt. 3:9; Lk. 3:8), for according to the popular belief, Abraham's merits guaranteed Israel a share in the kingdom of God—an idea John the Baptist attacked. According to him, to be descended from Abraham was in itself of no value. Only those who set their hearts and minds on the coming kingdom of God, brought forth the true fruit of repentance, and by baptism anticipated the final judgment had any right to hope for a place in the kingdom. God could raise up from stones children for Abraham. That is why Jesus considered it so important to search for the lost sheep of Israel. He healed a "daughter of Abraham" (Lk. 13:16), cured the woman with an issue of blood who had been excluded from the community (8:43–48), and caused salvation to come to the house of Zacchaeus as "a son of Abraham," although he had been living outside the Mosaic law (19:9).

When Luke records that the apostles addressed their hearers as descendants of Abraham and mentions the God of Abraham, Isaac, and Jacob, he intends his readers to understand how aware the apostles were of their loyalty to the faith of their ancestors and how strenuously they had sought to win Jesus' people despite their unwillingness (Acts 3:12–13, 25; 13:26).

(b) "Abraham's side" (Lk. 16:22) means the pouch above the girdle made by pulling up the garment slightly. It suggests special care, as that of a mother loving her child whom she carries in the folds of her dress over her breast, or the place of honor at table beside Abraham (cf. Jn. 13:23). Jud. frequently expected intercession by Abraham, who lives with God (Lk. 16:22–31), as well as by Isaac and Jacob. The Jewish belief that those who have lived with God (e.g., the patriarchs) must remain alive after death was shared by Jesus, who justified it by saying that where God is, there also must be life (cf. Matt. 22:32; Mk. 12:26–27; Lk. 20:37–38.). The one who lives with God can die but cannot cease to live. It is from this angle that we must understand the resurrection of Jesus.

3. When Paul explains Abraham's importance, he is concerned above all with justification (righteousness) by faith. His exposition both in Gal. 3:6–20 and Rom. 4:1–13 is not a deductive proof in the strict sense. Rather, in the light of the revelation of Christ, Paul recognizes that Scripture had long before spoken of justification by faith.

(a) The details of the apostle's arguments about Abraham were partly determined by the ideas of his Judaizing opponents, who maintained that Moses' law was the definitive revelation that brought salvation. It followed that Abraham must have lived by it, even before it had been revealed at Sinai. By contrast, Paul maintains in Gal. that anyone who wishes to live by the works of the Mosaic law is under a curse (Gal. 3:10), since it implies that people must earn their salvation. Such persons do not permit God to be the God who alone can give humankind that which is good without qualification and save them (Rom. 7; cf. Gen. 3). As Paul sees it, Scripture shows clearly that Abraham was justified not by works of the law but by faith (Rom. 4:3; Gal. 3:6; cf. Gen. 15:6).

Scripture even foresaw the placing on an equal footing of the lawless pagan and the pious Jew through faith (Gal. 3:6–9), because faith excludes every basis for human honor. The Mosaic law was given to reveal that sin, in the last analysis, is directed against God and not against human beings. It thus prepared us for the recognition that our only hope is in God (3:24) and that Jesus is the promised offspring of Abraham (3:16–17). By abrogating the law, God opened to everyone the possibility of living by faith and so sharing the heritage of Abraham in all its fullness.

(b) In Rom. 4 these thoughts are expressed with even greater clarity. Abraham had nothing to boast about, for it was faith that was reckoned to him for righteousness (4:1–3). No one can earn wages from God (4:4–8; cf. Ps. 32:1–2). Following methods of rab. argument, Paul maintains that God's blessing does not result from circumcision, which Jud. regarded as a sign of the fulfillment of God's law and of turning away from transgression (Rom. 4:9–12). Abraham was, after all, justified before he was circumcised. Circumcision was simply a seal of the righteousness by faith reckoned to the Gentile Abraham. Hence Abraham is the father of believers who come from the Gentiles (4:16).

Paul then adds another example of Abraham's faith (Rom. 4:18–22). Just as we are dead before God and have nothing to hope for, so Abraham and Sarah's procreative power was dead. But trust in God created and creates new life. The point of comparison is the deadness, the lack of any prerequisite conditions, not the willingness to yield oneself.

Paul's view of obedience in faith was not always accepted in the early church. Jas. 2:14–26 pointedly shows that Pauline concepts were misused even by Christians. For some only the relationship of the soul to God was important; the deeds of our transient bodies were considered to be relatively unimportant. Against such a view it was necessary to stress that faith expresses itself in works and that faith will be judged, as with Abraham, by the way it works itself out in life.

4. This false security with which Jews and Judaizers alike deluded themselves by appealing to Abraham contributed in great measure to this attitude. The way in which it hindered faith in Jesus is the background to the discussion about Abraham in Jn. 8:30–40, 48–59. The first section (8:30–40) makes it clear that the newly found faith of the Jews was not genuine but only superficial, for they were not doing the works of Abraham (8:39–40). Abraham relied solely on God's liberating word, but they wished to silence that word when it stood before them incarnate in Jesus. They thought that descent from Abraham guaranteed their freedom, whereas in fact only Jesus and holding fast to his word could give them true freedom.

The second section of the discussion (Jn. 8:48–59) begins with the Jews' suggestion that Jesus was demon-possessed when he proclaimed himself as God's word. When Jesus promised eternal life to those who kept his word (8:51), he was, according to the Jews, blaspheming God. To them, he was a mortal man like Abraham and the prophets, who had died (8:52). But Jesus is greater than Abraham in the sense of being more than human. God had given him authority to grant eternal life. Jesus went on to say that Abraham had called himself happy in that he should see the day of God's word (Jesus) (8:56). Then comes the vital sentence: "Before Abraham was born, *I am*" (8:58). The Word of God was, is, and ever will be. Hence Jesus is truly eternal, but Abraham lived and died.

5. The descendants of Abraham in Heb. 2:16 are presumably all who live by faith as did Abraham—i.e., all who believe in Christ. In Heb. 6:13, Abraham is presented as a model of the believing patience and perseverance that obtain the promise (see also 11:8–12, 17–19). Salvation, however, does not come from Abraham and his descendants (7:2, 4–10). They remain its recipients. Abraham recognized one greater than himself, Melchizedek. In the same way, the Levitical priests were only temporary, for they too, as descendants of Abraham, gave tithes to Melchizedek. Hence the one who has been proclaimed a priest forever after the order of Melchizedek must be greater.

See also *Sarra*, Sarah (*4925*); *Hagar*, Hagar (*29*); *Isaak*, Isaac (*2693*).

12	ἄβυσσος

ἄβυσσος (*abyssos*), abyss, pit, underworld (*12*).

CL & OT 1. In cl. Gk. *abyssos* is an adj. meaning bottomless, unfathomable. Used by itself with the noun *gē* (earth) understood, it means a bottomless place, hence abyss. In late Gk. the word stood for the primal deep, the primal ocean, the realm of the dead, the underworld.

2. *abyssos* occurs about 25x in the LXX, mostly to translate Heb. *tᵉhôm*, the primal ocean (Gen. 1:2), "deep" waters (Ps. 42:7), and the realm of the dead (Ps. 71:20). Rab. Jud. also maintained the meaning primal flood for *tᵉhôm*. The word also stands for the interior of the earth, where bodies that cause uncleanness are found.

NT In the NT *abyssos* is the prison for demons (Lk. 8:31; Rev. 9:1–2). It is closed, but the smoke of subterranean fires rises from it (9:1–2). It is ruled by a prince—not Satan but Apollyon (9:11). Weird creatures emerge from it (9:3–11), including "the beast" (11:7; 17:8). Satan is bound in it for the thousand-year reign of Christ (20:1, 3). Rom. 10:7–8, following Ps. 107:26, uses it to describe the realm of the dead. It is impossible for the living to descend into the *abyssos*.

See also *hadēs*, Hades, the underworld, the realm of the dead (*87*); *geenna*, Gehenna, hell (*1147*); *katōteros*, lower (*3005*); *tartaroō*, sent to Tartarus, hell (*5434*).

14 (*agathoergeō*, do good), → *19*.

16 (*agathopoieō*, do good), → *19*.

17 (*agathopoiia*, doing good), → *19*.

18 (*agathopoios*, doing good, one who does good), → *19*.

19	ἀγαθός

ἀγαθός (*agathos*), good (*19*); ἀγαθοεργέω (*agathoergeō*), do good (*14*); ἀγαθοποιέω (*agathopoieō*), do good (*16*); ἀγαθοποιός (*agathopoios*), doing good, one who does good (*18*); ἀγαθοποιΐα (*agathopoiia*), doing good (*17*); ἀγαθωσύνη (*agathōsynē*), goodness, uprightness, generosity (*20*).

CL & OT 1. As an adj. in cl. Gk. *agathos* means serviceable, good, excellent. The subst. *to agathon* and the pl. *ta agatha* mean the good or good things that evoke a state of well-being; these may be material, intellectual, moral, or religious, depending on one's ideal for life. (a) In Gk. philosophy the concept of the good plays a major role. For Plato the idea of the good is the all-embracing, highest, and indeed dominant idea or form. The good is the power that preserves and supports, in contrast to evil, which spoils and destroys. Aristotle applied the good as a formal concept to the totality of human relations. In his *Ethics* he defines the goal of all action as the attainment of some form of good.

(b) In Hel. thought the ancient humanistic attitude to life was shattered and the predominant meaning of the concept of good once again became religious. According to the Hermetic writings, the salvation brought about by the deity (i.e., deification) is the good. Thus God is the good, for he alone is free from attachment to the material. In Hel. Jud., Philo names moderation, fear of God, and wisdom as the highest possessions by means of which the soul finds the way to God, the highest good.

2. In the Hebrew Bible the concept of the good is indissolubly linked with personal faith in God. The good is always a gift from God and is thus outside the control of human strength (Gen. 3:5). God is the one who is good. This realization is further developed within the OT in the course of a deepening relationship of individuals to God (e.g., Ps. 23:6; 34:10; 84:11). The LXX often translates *tôb* by *to agathon* and thus approaches the Hel. outlook. God becomes a person's highest good, and human beings become the recipients of this good in the sense that they acquire a right to "good" treatment, as long as they regard God as their highest good.

3. That God is the one who is good is made clear in his saving dealings with his chosen people, in his giving of the Mosaic law (Deut. 30:15; Prov. 28:10), in the historical events of the exodus from Egypt (Exod. 18:9), and in the conquest of Canaan (Num. 10:29–32). The Israelites found renewed reason for praising God as the one who is good by realizing that everything that comes from him is good, whether it be his work in creation (Gen. 1:18, 31 [note, however, that *kalos* is used here]), his word (Isa. 39:8), or his Spirit (Ps. 143:10), even if appearances seem to say the opposite (Gen. 50:20).

The constant tension between God's promises and their incomplete fulfillment was bearable for Israel because they recognized that God's promises in all their temporal fulfillments always look beyond themselves towards a final, eschatological fulfillment. The good that God has promised his people will come to its real fulfillment in salvation in the end times (see, e.g., Isa. 52:7; Jer. 32:41 = LXX 39:41).

Recognition of the goodness of God could not be taken away from the remnant even by hard, shattering, historical events like the exile. Yet Yahweh's goodness, his benevolent action in history, had been temporarily withdrawn from Israel. Wisdom literature contains striking expression of the way in which God's people saw their own limitation without illusion in the presence of the incomprehensible God. They recognized the uncertainty of all life's values and the vanity of existence (Eccl. 3:12; 5:17), and they saw clearly one's inability to achieve good (7:20 = LXX 7:21). But in the last analysis even this skepticism could not destroy the knowledge of the goodness of God.

Postexilic Jud. and rab. theology also held firmly to the fact that God is good. God's goodness brings salvation. It is revealed in his law, which is good. In carrying out God's law, human beings can now themselves do good and be good. Nevertheless, essential goodness can only be realized in one's personal relationships with God and one's fellow human beings (Mic. 6:8; *kalos* in the LXX).

4. The people at Qumran radicalized this unshaken confidence that good could be achieved into a strict asceticism and linked it with the command to hate forever the sons of wickedness. But here too—as consistently throughout the OT—it is the newly emerging songs of praise that are the genuine expressions of the sect's piety. They begin and end with the praise of God and his benevolent actions even in the midst of need and oppression. What stands out is what has been asserted in every period of Israel's history and expressed most completely in the Psalms (e.g., Ps. 16:2; 118:1), namely, that God himself is the one who is really and exclusively good.

NT *agathos* occurs 102x in all the different types of NT writings (Gospels, Acts, and letters) except Rev. (where *kalos* does not occur either). The compounds formed with *poieō* are rare; *agathoergeō* occurs only twice (Acts 14:17; 1 Tim. 6:18); *agathōsynē* occurs 4x.

1. Jesus clearly reaffirms the OT statement about God's essential goodness: "No one is good—except God alone" (Mk. 10:18; cf. Matt. 19:17; Lk. 18:19). But this does not prevent a natural application of the predicate "good" to the moral differences among human beings, who do good as well as evil (Matt. 12:35; 25:21; cf. Lk. 6:45; 19:17), an application that includes within it the goodness of God (e.g., Matt. 5:45; 22:10).

But this admission of normal differences and the demand for works of love (see Matt. 5:16, where *kalos* is used instead of *agathos*, and 25:31–45) must not be separated from Jesus' preaching as a whole. Jesus calls sinners to repentance. In this connection it is impossible to ignore the call: "Unless your righteousness surpasses that of the Pharisees and the teachers of the law, you will certainly not enter the kingdom of heaven" (5:20); "be perfect . . . as your heavenly Father is perfect" (5:48).

2. Jn. 5:29 proclaims judgment according to works. But this statement too has to be seen within the context of Jesus' whole message (cf. 10:27–29; 15:5–8). It is only in Christ that we receive a new opportunity of existence. Insofar as we receive a share in God's goodness, we also can pass on good to others by doing good. According to

10:11, 14, Jesus is the good (*kalos*) shepherd who lays down his life and makes available the eternal good of redemption (here *kalos* is a synonym for *agathos*). In 1:46 the skeptical question posed, "Can anything good (*agathon*, i.e., salvation) come from [Nazareth]?" is most likely the utterance of a man who could not conceive of the Messiah coming from such an insignificant place as Nazareth.

3. Paul takes up the message of the Synoptic Gospels. He too acknowledges the relative difference between good and evil people. Within God's sustaining order of things, for example, civil authorities have as their task to maintain law and order and punish evildoers, not those who do good (Rom. 13:1–4). The concept *agathopoios* is similar: "Those who do right" will receive praise from the authorities (1 Pet. 2:14).

But the distinction that is justified among human institutions breaks down before God. The natural self is irretrievably in bondage to the powers of sin and death and has no right to claim the attribute "good." Even for those who are fanatical observers of the Mosaic law, which is good, it only works death for them (Rom. 7:18–24; cf. 3:20; 6:23; Gal. 3:10–13). But through redemption in Christ goodness overflows to the believer: "We know that in all things God works for the good of those who love him" (Rom. 8:28).

In Christ believers are created for good works (Eph. 2:10) and receive a good conscience (cf. Acts 23:1; 1 Tim. 1:5, 19). This also underlies the urgent exhortations to bear fruit in good works (Col. 1:10), to seek to do good (1 Thess. 5:15), and to do it to everyone (Rom. 15:2; 16:19; Gal. 6:6, 10). Likewise, in several places believers are exhorted to "goodness" (*agathōsynē*; see Gal. 5:22; Eph. 5:9; cf. Rom. 15:14). Paul uses *agathoergeō* in 1 Tim. 6:18 to encourage the wealthy to do good.

Those who do good and "seek glory, honor and immortality" will receive eternal life (Rom. 2:7). Paul also maintains the concept of judgment according to works (2 Cor. 5:10; Gal. 3:10), though comparison with Rom. 8:31–39 is not intended. The gift and the task of the new life are kept in tension, with both aspects fully emphasized.

4. In the remaining NT writings *agathopoieō*, to do good, is used only in 1 Pet. 2:15, 20; 3:6, 17; 3 Jn. 11; and in Lk. 6:9, 33, 35. *agathopoiia*, doing good, is employed only in 1 Pet. 4:19. Such right action is the visible proof that a person has really and gratefully grasped the new opportunity for existence as one's own. In 1 Pet. 3:16, 21, we read of the good conscience that the believer ought to demonstrate to the pagan.

In contrast, Heb. 9:11 and 10:1 lay their emphasis on future, eschatological gifts (cf. 1 Pet. 4:19). In the present age there is a permanent tension between God, who is good and who gives good gifts, and reality, characterized by sin and death, in which the Christian's life is caught up. It is in this perspective that the promise of Phil. 1:6 stands and has meaning: "He who began a good work in you will carry it on to completion until the day of Christ Jesus." Therefore the warning of Gal. 6:9 also holds good: "Let us not become weary in doing good [*kalos*], for at the proper time we will reap a harvest if we do not give up."

See also *kalos*, good, beautiful, noble (*2819*); *chrēstos*, pleasant, kind, good (*5982*).

20 (*agathōsynē*, goodness, uprightness, generosity), → *19*.

21 (*agalliasis*, exultation, great joy), → *22*.

22	ἀγαλλιάω

ἀγαλλιάω (*agalliaō*), exult, rejoice greatly, be overjoyed (*22*); ἀγαλλίασις (*agalliasis*), exultation, great joy (*21*).

CL & OT 1. *agalliaō*, exult, shout for joy, and the corresponding noun *agalliasis*, exultation, are found only in the LXX, the NT, and writers dependent on them. They are later formations derived from the cl. Gk. *agallō* and *agallomai*, to adorn, glorify, revere, boast, enjoy. This is the basic human emotion of joy.

2. In the LXX *agalliaō* and *agalliasis* indicate the festive joy that expresses itself publicly over God's acts of salvation in the past and present (e.g., Ps. 32:11). The significance of these words soon extended beyond the sphere of public worship. *agalliaō* came to express both corporate and individual attitudes of thankful joy before God (cf. Ps. 9:14; 16:9; 21:1; 31:7; 35:27; 92:4), not only for past experiences of God's salvation, but for his faithful dealings that are still future (cf. Hab. 3:18), because they are ensured by Yahweh. The rejoicing embraces even the created universe, the silent witness to God's mighty acts (e.g., the heavens, earth, mountains, islands), which all join in the jubilation (Ps. 19:5; 89:12; 96:11; 97:1). Even God joins in (Isa. 65:19).

Under the prophets during and after the exile, Israel's rejoicing in God, even in wretched situations, broadened out to include anticipatory gratitude for final salvation and messianic joy (Isa. 61; cf. esp. v. 10). It was in this eschatological direction that the Heb. attitude of thanks and praise reached its profoundest expression (cf. Ps. 126:2, 5; Isa. 25:9).

3. (a) Loud, exultant rejoicing over God's acts of salvation in the past, present, and future continued as characteristic of the theology and the piety of rab. Jud. The whole aim of the Jew's life was to glorify God.

(b) By contrast, the Qumran community held that the day of salvation had already begun. In praise and prayer (esp. 1QH; 1QS 10:11) they rejoiced in God, who in his mercy had granted them salvation and given them insight into his secrets.

NT 1. In the NT *agalliaō* occurs 11x and *agalliasis* 5x. In the OT exultant rejoicing arises from gratitude and unshakeable trust in the God who has helped and is still helping his people Israel. He will do away with all want and distress in his final act of deliverance at the coming of Messiah. In the NT the rejoicing turns to the God who now in Jesus Christ has already inaugurated the age of salvation and will gloriously complete it on Christ's return.

(a) In the Gospels there is jubilation even before the coming of Jesus. Zechariah sang for joy when the forerunner of the Lord was born (Lk. 1:14; cf. vv. 67–79), and even the child in Elizabeth's womb shared in the rejoicing (1:44). Jesus spoke of devout Israelites who for a short time rejoiced in the light of John the Baptist (Jn. 5:35). In her song of praise Mary rejoiced that she had been granted a place in God's saving purpose (Lk. 1:47).

Jesus, the one who brought salvation, not only called on people to rejoice but joined in himself. The Beatitudes conclude with the exhortation: "Rejoice and be glad [*agalliaō*], because great is your reward in heaven" (Matt. 5:12; cf. Lk. 6:23). Jesus rejoiced because the time of salvation was at hand; it was revealed to babes but at the same time, since it also involved judgment, it was hidden from the wise (Lk. 10:21; cf. Matt. 11:25). Even Abraham rejoiced that he had a part in the day of salvation (Jn. 8:56).

The early church regarded itself as the elect of the last days because of God's saving work in Jesus Christ. It made his cross, resurrection, and future return the basis of its rejoicing, and thus interpreted David's joy Christologically (Acts 2:26; cf. Ps. 16:10). The Philippian jailer rejoiced with his whole family because he had come to faith and had been incorporated into the saved community through faith and baptism (Acts 16:34). When the early church believers broke bread, they sang with joy as they anticipated the Parousia of the risen Christ (Acts 2:46).

(b) Paul does not use this word group, but he is no stranger to the idea. He expresses it partly through the vb. *kauchaomai*, to boast (→ *kauchēma*, *3017*).

(c) In Heb. 1:9 God himself addresses Christ in the words of Ps. 45:7: He anoints his Son with "the oil of joy," i.e., with consecrated oil as used at joyous feasts. In Jude 24 the church bows in praise before the one who is able to present us before his glorious presence "with great joy." Peter calls on the church to look away from its sufferings in the last days, for they are insignificant in comparison with the rejoicing that will break forth at the end of time (1 Pet. 1:6, 8; 4:13). In Rev. believers are summoned by a voice that cries, "Let us rejoice and be glad [*agalliōmen*] and give him glory!" (19:7).

2. *agalliasis* thus becomes the characteristic attitude of the NT church, whose public worship is full of joy, and of the individual Christian. We feel joy through the salvation achieved by Jesus Christ in the past, personally experienced in the present, and confidently expected in the future. Looked at in this way, the sufferings of the present are alleviated. For even though they weigh heavily on us, we have good reason to rejoice.

See also *euphrainō*, gladden, cheer (up) (*2370*); *chairō*, be glad, rejoice (*5897*).

23 (agamos, unmarried), → *6004.*

26	ἀγαπάω

ἀγαπάω (*agapaō*), to love (*26*); ἀγάπη (*agapē*), love (*27*); ἀγαπητός (*agapētos*), loved, beloved (*28*); φιλόστοργος (*philostorgos*), tenderly loving, affectionate (*5816*); ἄστοργος (*astorgos*), without natural affection (*845*).

CL & OT 1. Cl. Gk. has a number of words for "to love"—the most important being *phileō*, *stergō*, *eraō*, and *agapaō*. (a) *phileō* (→ *5797*) is the most general word for love or regard with affection. This vb. denotes the attraction of people to one another who are close together, both inside and outside the family; it includes concern, care, and hospitality, as well as love for things in the sense of being fond of something.

(b) *stergō* means to love, feel affection, esp. of the mutual love of parents and children. It is also used of the love of a people for their ruler, the love of a tutelary god for the people, and even of a dog for its master. It is less common for the love of husband and wife and does not occur in the NT, apart from the compounds *astorgos* (Rom. 1:31; 2 Tim. 3:3) and *philostorgos* (Rom. 12:10).

(c) The vb. *eraō* and the noun *erōs* denote the love between man and woman, which embraces longing, craving, and desire. Sensual ecstasy leaves moderation and proportion far behind, and the Gk. tragedies knew the irresistible power of Eros—the god of love bore the same name—that forgot all reason, will, and discretion.

There was also a more mystical understanding of *erōs*, whereby the Gks. sought to go beyond normal human limitations in order to attain perfection. The fertility cults, of course, glorified the generating Eros in nature, and the mystery religions had rites intended to unite participants with the godhead. Here spiritual and psychical unity with the god came into the foreground more and more, however much erotic pictures and symbols were used. Plato and Aristotle sought to raise spiritual love above the physical. For them *erōs* was the striving for righteousness, self-possession, and wisdom; it was the embodiment of the good, the way to attain immortality.

(d) Though the vb. *agapaō* appears frequently in Gk. lit., the noun *agapē* is a late word. Only one reference has been found outside the biblical and related lit., in a papyrus document that gives the goddess Isis the title *agapē*. *agapaō* is colorless as a word, appearing frequently as a synonym with *eraō* and *phileō* and meaning to be fond of, treat respectfully, be pleased with, welcome. When, on rare occasions, it refers to someone favored by a god, it is clear that, unlike *eraō*, it is not our longing for worth that is meant, but a generous move by one for the sake of the other. Such a notion is expressed above all in the way *agapētos* is used, mostly of an only child to whom all the love of the parents is given.

2. In the LXX *agapaō* is the preferred word to translate the Heb. vb. *'āhēb*. The noun *agapē* finds its origin here to translate the corresponding Heb. noun (the vb. occurs far more frequently than the noun). The vb. can refer to both persons and things and denotes both human relationships with each other and God's relationship with us.

(a) Love and hate represent two of the basic polarized attitudes to life. The phenomenon of love in the OT is experienced as a spontaneous force that drives one to something or someone over against itself. *agapē* means the vital urge of the sexes for one another (cf. Hos. 3:1; 4:18; Jer. 2:25; Ezek. 16:37). The powerful perception of marital love as an enriching gift derives both from Gen. 2:18–24 and esp. from Song of Songs, which celebrates the strength of passionate love: "Love is as strong as death, its jealousy unyielding as the grave. Its burns like blazing fire, like a mighty flame" (Song 8:6).

(b) The blood relationship with father and mother and the spiritual bond between friends is also described by *agapē*. Heb. does not distinguish between the ideas conveyed by *eraō* and *agapaō*. Thus, the friendship love of Jonathan and David for one another is expressed in terms of a communal fellowship deeper than love for a woman (2 Sam. 1:26; cf. 1 Sam. 18:1, 3; 20:17 in A).

(c) In a further sense, love lies at the root of social community life: "Love your neighbor as yourself" (Lev. 19:18). Love in this context means devotion towards one's neighbors for their sake, accepting them as brothers and sisters and letting them come into their own. This aspect is illustrated by social legislation that is esp. concerned with the rights of aliens (19:34), the poor (cf. 25:35), and orphans.

3. The word love in the OT is used less commonly and with greater caution to describe the relationship between God and human beings. In this respect the OT contrasts with Gk. lit. in being far removed from any mystical thinking. In the OT humanity can never ascend to God; rather, all human thought, feeling, action, and worship are a response to a previous movement by God. Thus, the LXX prefers the simpler word *agapē* to the more loaded *erōs*.

(a) At the beginning of the OT stands not only the God who loves, but also the God who elects and who acts directly in nature for the sake of his people, with whom he has made a covenant (Exod. 24). The great deeds of Yahweh are the deeds of his history with his people, such as the exodus, the gift of the land, and the Torah. Righteousness, faithfulness, love, and grace are some of the concepts embodied in such actions. The people reply with jubilation, praise, and obedience.

God's judgment and grace permeate the entire OT. God holds to his covenant, despite Israel's frequent relapses, which draw God's wrath on them. The only ground for this is to be found in his electing grace and love (e.g., Hos. 11:1). Statements concerning this devotion of God to his people reach the level of suffering love (cf. Isa. 53, where such love is prophesied of the coming Servant of the Lord).

(b) The prophets elaborated on the theme of God's love as the main motif of his electing work. It was an enormity of unique proportions for Hosea, surrounded by the Canaanite world of sexual fertility cults and love feasts, to represent the relationship between Yahweh and his people as that of a deceived husband and a prostitute. Yet, despite the fact that Israel had broken the covenant and thus become an adulteress, Yahweh wooed back his faithless wife, the godless covenant people, with an inconceivable love (cf. Hos. 2:19–20).

Besides using this picture of marriage, Hosea also used the picture of a father to describe Yahweh's unfathomable love for Israel, whom he loved in Egypt and drew to himself with bonds of love (11:1–4). But Israel turned away. So Hosea pictured the struggle going on inside Yahweh himself as that between the jealous wrath of a deceived father and his glowing love (see 11:8–9). This description by Hosea of the passionate and zealous love of God is unprecedented in its boldness. The Godness of God does not express itself in destructive power, but in tender and compassionate love, which precedes any responsive human love and suffers through the faithlessness of his people (6:4).

The later prophets took over, with modifications, Hosea's picture of love and the theme of the beloved. Jeremiah spoke of Israel's first love in the desert and of its growing cold in the promised land (2:1–8). But Yahweh's love is everlasting (31:3 = LXX 38:3), and he will help the degenerate people again (cf. 3:6–10; 31:4). In Isa. 54:4–8 it is not the wife who has left her husband but Yahweh who has left his young bride, to whom he now again turns in compassion. One can even speak of Yahweh's political love, recognized in the return of the exiles from Babylon (43:4).

(c) Deut. expresses similar ideas. But whereas in the prophets Yahweh's love is the sole and incredible basis for his future actions in saving his lost people, the allusions to Yahweh's electing love in Deut. always provide the ground for exhorting Israel to love God and to follow his directing (Deut. 7:6–11). This theme is summarized in 6:5: "Love the LORD your God with all your heart and with all your soul and with all your strength." Such love for God is realized in keeping the covenant law (Exod. 20:6; Deut. 10:12–13) and in loving one's neighbor (Lev. 19:18; cf. 19:34 as an example).

4. (a) In Hel. and rab. Jud. *agapē* became the central concept for describing God's relationship with his people and vice versa. God loves his people through every distress. Proof of his love is the Torah, and the believer reciprocates God's love by obeying his law, emulating God's zealous compassion, and remaining true to him, even to the point of martyrdom (4 Macc. 13:24; 15:3). Loving one's neighbor is the chief commandment to the pious Jew. There are even examples of commands to help one's enemy.

(b) The Qumran community believed it had been chosen in God's love, but this love referred only to the children of light. God loves the angel of light and hates all who belong to the company of Belial. There is an often repeated command: "Love everyone whom God elects, hate everyone he hates" (1QS 1:3–4; cf. Matt. 5:43–47). Since God's love is not conceived as having universal application, even love for one's neighbor is restricted to members of the sacred community.

NT 1. (a) In the NT love is one of the central ideas that express the whole content of the Christian faith (cf. Jn. 3:16). God's activity is love, which looks for a reciprocal love from people (1 Jn. 4:8, 16).

(b) It is significant that *stergō* occurs only 3x in the NT, once in the compound *philostorgos*, loving with devotion, in a section in which Paul emphasizes the need for love in the church by piling up words for love: "Be devoted to one another in brotherly love" (Rom. 12:10). *stergō* also occurs in Rom. 1:31; 2 Tim. 3:3 in the compound *astorgos*, heartless, without love. Moreover, *erōs* and *eraō* do not occur at all. The reason for this is presumably that the anthropocentric way of thinking that is bound up with these words does not correspond with the NT approach.

phileō, on the other hand (→ *5797*), appears frequently, both by itself and in compound words. But it remains a more limited and colorless word. The main emphasis of this word group is on love for people who are closely connected, either by blood or by faith (e.g., Jn. 11:36; 15:19; 16:27).

agapaō and *phileō* are used synonymously in Jn. 3:35 and 5:20 (cf. 16:27) of the Father's love for the Son, and in 21:15–17, when Jesus asks Peter whether he loves him and in Peter's reply. In 1 Cor. 16:22 *phileō* is clearly used of love for the Lord Jesus: "If anyone does not love the Lord—a curse be on him. Come, O Lord!"

(c) By contrast, *agapē* and *agapaō* are used in nearly every case in the NT to speak of God's relationship with us—not unexpectedly, in view of the OT usage. Where *agapē* is obviously directed toward things (cf. Lk. 11:43), the very use of the vb. *agapaō* is intended to make it plain that love here is directed to the wrong ends, i.e., not toward God. Thus the vb. is used of misdirected love in Jn. 3:19 (love of darkness), 12:43 (love of human glory), and 2 Tim. 4:10 (love of the present age).

In the case of the noun *agapē* there is no corresponding negative usage in the NT. It is always in the sense of the love of God, either subj. gen. (i.e., God's love of us) or obj. gen. (i.e., our love of God), or in the sense of the divine love for other human beings that the presence of God evokes. This brings *agapē* close to concepts like faith, righteousness, and grace, all of which have their point of origin in God alone.

2. (a) In the Synoptic tradition the main emphasis falls on the preaching of the kingdom of God and of the new way of life that breaks

in with Jesus himself. God sends his beloved (*agapētos*) Son, to whom to listen is to be saved (Mk. 1:11; cf. 9:7; Lk. 3:22; see also Ps. 2:7; Isa. 42:1). *agapētos* also figures in the Christological interpretation of Isa. 42:1 in Matt. 12:18. Jesus' activity among us reveals the mercy and love of God: Jesus himself is the one who truly loves, and he takes to himself the poor, the sick, and sinners. The word *agapē* is not found in the passion narrative, though the underlying thought of mercy and love as the way God intends to redeem lies clearly in the background.

The Sermon on the Mount is best understood when the Beatitudes are seen in the first instance as statements by Jesus about himself (Matt. 5:3–11; cf. Lk. 6:20–22; → *makarios, 3421*). Jesus is the first to keep the radical demands of discipleship and so fulfill the law. The command to love one's enemies (Matt. 5:44; cf. Lk. 6:27), the word of forgiveness from the cross (Lk. 23:34), and the promise to the criminal on the cross (23:43) all fit into the same pattern.

(b) In the Synoptics love for God is based on the twofold summary of the law (Matt. 22:34–40; cf. Lk. 10:25–28). Here too, through God's mercy, grows the new reality of love revealed in Jesus' ministry. His followers enter and share this and so fulfill the demands of the Sermon on the Mount. Discipleship, however, also involves suffering, and when disciples suffer, they are recognized by God (Matt. 10:37–39; 25:31–40). This demand indicates the hardship love has to face; it can only succeed in this world by way of suffering. If love cost God what was most dear to him, the same applies to us.

(c) This approach provides a different interpretation for loving one's neighbor. It is God's love, creating the new realities among humankind, that is itself the basis and motivation for love between people. Note again the twofold command to love as a summary of the law (Matt. 22:37–40; Mk. 12:29–31). The second half, love for one's neighbor, is also quoted in Rom. 13:9; Gal. 5:14; Jas. 2:8. Jesus decisively stepped over the boundaries of Jewish and rab. tradition in his radical command to love one's enemies (Matt. 5:43–48; Lk. 6:27–28, 32–36). Jesus, the Son of God, loves those who crucify him; in fact, he dies for them. Jesus' interpretation of the command to love in the parable of the Good Samaritan implicitly extends love to include everyone (Lk. 10:37; cf. 7:47).

3. (a) Paul stands entirely in the line of OT tradition when he speaks of God's love. *agapē* is for him electing love. Rom. 11:28 shows in particular how this word in Paul's thought links up with the Israelite election tradition (cf. 9:13–26). The "called" are the *agapētoi* ("loved," Rom. 1:7; cf. Col. 3:12). As in the OT, the motive for the election is God's love, which can also be rendered by *eleos*, mercy (→ *1799*). This love becomes a revealing activity in Christ's saving work (Rom. 5:8; 8:35–39). The circle of guilt, wrath, and judgment is broken through, for in Jesus Christ God appears as love. Indeed this love is predicated of Jesus Christ himself (e.g., Gal. 2:20; Eph. 5:2; 2 Thess. 2:13).

The contrasting concept in Paul is *orgē*, wrath (→ *3973*). Human beings under the law find themselves on a direct road leading to God's judgment; from this destiny God in his electing love rescues those who believe (1 Thess. 1:10). If God's action can be defined as love (cf. 2 Cor. 13:11, 14), then the great love song of 1 Cor. 13 is not merely a chapter of ethics, but a description of all God's activity. In place of the word "love" we can put the name of Jesus Christ. This does not mean that God becomes the "good Lord" who lets anything pass, for there is still the possibility in unbelief of judgment to come. But God's righteousness is realized in the fact that the beloved Son stands in the place of the unrighteous (cf. 2 Cor. 5:18–21).

The electing love of God is also in the background of Eph. 5:22–33, where the relationship between husband and wife is compared with the love of Christ for the church. There are two points of contact here. On the one hand, there is the election of Israel (cf. Rom. 9); the church is the called-out body, the new Israel, which has come to faith in Christ. On the other hand, there is the OT picture of marriage, dating from the time of Hosea, with the implication of a relationship of fidelity and covenant love. What is true for the Christian community is true also for the individual and for marriage. God's love is able to overcome every kind of difficulty and infidelity.

Certainty of salvation consists in knowing that God's loving activity is stronger than any other power, including death (Rom. 8:37–39; 1 Cor. 15:55–57). The resurrection is the crowning act of God's love, in which is displayed his victory over these forces (cf. 2 Cor. 5:16–21).

(b) A believer is a sinner who is loved by God. When one realizes this, one enters the sphere of God's love and becomes loving. Hence, as in the OT, so also in Paul love for God and love for one's neighbor derive from God's own love. This love of God is poured into our hearts by the Spirit (Rom. 5:5; 15:30). Human response to God's saving act is described by Paul most often as faith or knowledge, but also as *agapē* (cf. 1 Cor. 8:3; Eph. 3:19; 6:23; 1 Tim. 1:14). Through the Spirit, knowing God and being known by him become the same thing. The same applies to being loved by, and loving, God (Rom. 8:37; cf. Gal. 4:9). Those loved by God become active in love (Gal. 5:6; 1 Thess. 3:6). Thus love is part of the fruit of the Spirit (Gal. 5:22).

Paul's formula "in Christ" speaks of the existence of a believer in the sphere of God's love. When I am "in Christ" or Christ is "in me," this love has taken hold of me and is making me, a believing person, into a loving person (cf. Gal. 2:20; 1 Tim. 1:14; cf. also 2 Cor. 5:14 with v. 17). The law has been fulfilled because Jesus is love and has died for sinners. Insofar, therefore, as Christians love one another, they too fulfil the law. *agapē* is also a reflection of what is still to come (1 Cor. 13:9, 12–13).

4. (a) In John, God's nature and activity are illustrated with particular clarity by his use of *agapē*. That partly arises from the fact that *agapē* is used here more frequently than in Paul in its absolute form—i.e., as a noun with no gen., or as a vb. with no obj. God is essentially love (1 Jn. 4:8), and his purpose right from the beginning has been one of love. The love of the Father for the Son is the archetype of all love. This fact is made visible in the sending and self-sacrifice of the Son (Jn. 3:16; 1 Jn. 3:1, 16). For us to "see" and "know" this love is to be saved. God's primary purpose for the world is his compassionate and forgiving love, which asserts itself despite the world's inimical rejection of it. In God's *agapē* his glory is simultaneously revealed (cf. Jn. 12:16, 23–28). The believer, taken up into this victory, receives life (cf. Jn. 3:36; 11:25–26; 1 Jn. 4:9).

(b) Whereas Paul describes the way we turn to God as faith, John's term is *agapē*. The relationship between Father and Son is one of love (Jn. 14:31). In this relationship believers are included (14:21–24; 15:9–10; 17:26). They are to love Father and Son with an equal love (8:42; 14:21–24; 1 Jn. 4:16, 20). The continual oscillation between the subj. and obj. of love in John shows that the Father, the Son, and the believers are all united in the one reality of divine love; the alternative is death (1 Jn. 3:14–15; 4:7–8). John's typical phrase "remain in" can refer equally to Jesus or to love (Jn. 15:4–10; 1 Jn. 4:12–16).

(c) In John, love for other human beings is grounded even more clearly than in Paul in the love of God (Jn. 13:34; 1 Jn. 4:21). Love is a sign and a proof of faith (1 Jn. 3:10; 4:7–21). Without love for other believers there is no relationship with God. In this connection John takes up the command to love (Jn. 13:34; 15:12, 17; 2 Jn. 5). To love is to keep the law (Jn. 14:23–24).

5. (a) Love found expression for itself in early Christian circles by way of the kiss of fellowship, which was a regular part of the worship of the congregation (Rom. 16:16). In 1 Pet. 5:14 it is called the "kiss of love," though no details of this rite are known.

(b) *agapē* also denotes an early Christian ceremony known as the "love feast." In 1 Cor. 11 it is linked with a celebration of the Lord's Supper. Later it became separated from the Lord's Supper and was celebrated in its own right (cf. Jude 12; perhaps also 2 Pet. 2:13). This common meal had its central significance in celebrating and displaying the special fellowship that believers shared in their *agapē*. It also seems certain that this service provided an opportunity for congrega-

tions to give practical expression to their love in generous social action (cf. Acts 6:1–6).

See also *phileō*, be fond of, love (*5797*).

27 (*agapē*, love), → *26*.

28 (*agapētos*, loved, beloved), → *26*.

29	Ἁγάρ

Ἁγάρ (*Hagar*), Hagar (*29*).

OT Hagar was Abraham's concubine and the mother of Ishmael. The two OT stories about her (Gen. 16:1–16; 21:8–21) recount the hostility of Sarah, the expulsion of Hagar, and Ishmael's ultimate home in the desert. They reflect the conviction that Israel was related to the warlike Bedouin peoples of Palestine and seek both to explain the connection and give the reason for the Ishmaelites' wild way of life. Their status as children of the slave-concubine is clearly inferior.

NT In the NT, Paul makes allegorical use of this inferiority to urge the superiority of the new covenant (Gal. 4:21–31). Hagar and her son represent the bondage of the old Jewish dispensation, which is in stark contrast to the new freedom experienced by those for whom Isaac, as son of the free woman, is the allegorical prototype. The Hagar of the allegory represents Sinai, because Sinai is in Arabia, where Hagar lived.

See also *Abraam*, Abraham (*11*); *Sarra*, Sarah (*4925*); *Isaak*, Isaac (*2693*).

32 (*angelia*, message), → *33*.

33	ἀγγέλλω

ἀγγέλλω (*angellō*), announce (*33*); ἀγγελία (*angelia*), message (*32*); ἀναγγέλλω (*anangellō*), report, announce, proclaim (*334*); ἀπαγγέλλω (*apangellō*), report, announce, proclaim (*550*); διαγγέλλω (*diangellō*), make known, proclaim (far and wide) (*1334*); ἐξαγγέλλω (*exangellō*), proclaim, report (*1972*); καταγγέλλω (*katangellō*), proclaim (*2859*); καταγγελεύς (*katangeleus*), proclaimer (*2858*); προκαταγγέλλω (*prokatangellō*), announce, proclaim beforehand, foretell (*4615*).

CL & OT 1. (a) In cl. Gk. the vbs. of this group are largely interchangeable; the simple *angellō* is predominant. Regarding the compounds, *apangellō* tends to be a more official word than *anangellō*. *di-*, *ex-* and *katangellō* often indicate an elevated, ceremonious style of proclamation, though *exangellō* can emphasize the secret nature of what is being told, sometimes in the sense of gossip. *katangellō* can denote making a claim concerning oneself. The noun *angelia* can mean either message or command. The one who conveys the message is the *katangeleus*, herald.

(b) In general, these words refer to the activity of a messenger who conveys a message given to him either orally or in writing, and who in this way represents the sender of the message. The content of the message may be private family news or news concerning political events: war, victory or defeat of an army, the solemn proclamation of a ruler, or the accession of an emperor. Good news (*angelia agathē*) is also called *euangelion* (gospel, → *2295*).

(c) Just as the messenger who brings the news stands under the special protection of the gods, so too his message can acquire a sacred significance. This is esp. true where it is associated with the cultic veneration of rulers and gods: e.g., where the messenger solemnly proclaims the successful completion of a sacrifice that brings blessing or the approach of a ceremonial procession. He proclaims the manifestation of a god, announces the reign of a new king, or recounts the mighty deeds of his god or emperor.

2. (a) In the LXX *angellō* appears 5x and means to announce. In contrast, *anangellō* and *apangellō* occur frequently in the sense of report, announce (e.g., Gen. 9:22; 37:5), proclaim (e.g., Ps. 19:1;

51:15), speak out openly (e.g., Gen. 12:18; 1 Sam. 9:19), and instruct (e.g., Deut. 24:8). *diangellō*, *exangellō*, and *katangellō* seldom occur in the LXX—9x, 12, and 3x, respectively.

(b) The OT is clear that where the lordship of the divine ruler is proclaimed and his mighty deeds made known, no room is left for proclaiming the lordship of other gods. The power of the Lord God is declared to all the world (Exod. 9:16; Ps. 64:9), as is his righteousness (Ps. 22:30–31), faithfulness (30:9), wondrous deeds (71:17), and steadfast love (92:2). He himself, the Lord, proclaims what is to come (Isa. 42:9; cf. 46:10), which idols cannot do (44:7–20).

(c) It is primarily the prophets, God's chosen messengers, who make known his saving acts among his people and in all the earth (Isa. 12:5), who proclaim his will (Mic. 6:8), and who announce what is to come (this last notion comes strongly into focus in intertestamental writings). In Hag. 1:13 and Mal. 3:1 a prophet is even called *angelos* (angel, messenger, → *34*). Proclamation or announcement takes place at the behest of Yahweh or in the knowledge of his acts of salvation.

NT 1. In the NT *angellō* occurs only once (Jn. 20:18) and *angelia* 2x (1 Jn. 1:5; 3:11). The compounds occur more frequently, meaning simply to relate or speak: *anangellō* (14x; e.g., Acts 14:27), *apangellō* (45x; e.g., Matt. 2:8; 28:11), and *katangellō* (18x; e.g., Rom. 1:8). The other derivatives occur infrequently in the NT: *prokatangellō* (Acts 3:18; 7:52), *diangellō* (Lk. 9:60; Acts 21:26; Rom. 9:17), *exangellō* (1 Pet. 2:9), and *katangeleus* (Acts 17:18).

2. Usually the words in this group mean proclamation in a special, technical sense: making known God's activity, his will to save. This proclamation, the authority of which is derived from its ultimate source, enters deeply into the life of the messenger and makes total demands on him. When used in this way, these terms can scarcely be distinguished in meaning from *euangelizō*, proclaim (good news; → *euangelion*, 2295). Note 1 Jn. 1:5, for example: "This is the message [*angelia*] we have heard from him and declare [*anangellō*] to you: God is light; in him there is no darkness at all," as well as Lk. 9:60: "Let the dead bury their own dead, but you go and proclaim [*diangellō*] the kingdom of God."

(a) John uses the words of this group exclusively in a theologically pregnant sense, whereas *euangelizō* and *kēryssō* (preach, → *3062*)—words often used in the Synoptic Gospels, Acts, and Paul—do not appear in his writings. John also prefers *martyreō*, to bear witness (→ *martyria*, *3456*); what has already happened and been experienced is the subj. of witness. According to the Samaritan woman's words in Jn. 4:25, when the Messiah comes, "he will explain [*anangellō*] everything to us." Note too the prediction of Jesus regarding the coming Spirit: "He will tell [*anangellō*] you what is yet to come" (16:13). In these passages it is not so much a matter of a proclamation of an event or the heralding of a new age that is already dawning in the Messiah, as it is the revealing, the reporting, of "that which was from the beginning" (1 Jn. 1:1). Believers may go forward with confidence into the darkness of the future, because the full truth of the Word will one day be revealed to them by the Spirit.

The content of the announced message in Jn. is both information, or reminder, of the saving event and commandment. *angelia* can be thus rendered as message or command in 1 Jn. 1:5; 3:11. The difference between this and the dynamic, dramatic announcement of the new age, which is conveyed by *kēryssō* and *euangelizō*, is made clear in 1:2–3: "We proclaim [*apangellō*] to you the eternal life, which was with the Father and has appeared to us. We proclaim [*apangellō*] to you what we have seen and heard, so that you also may have fellowship with us." The message is that God is light (1:5), and therefore believers must not walk in darkness (cf. 1:7) but in love.

(b) Luke and Paul use the words of the *angellō* word group in a variety of senses, ranging from the simple sense of giving notice (Acts 21:26, *diangellō*), informing (2 Cor. 7:7, *anangellō*), to the more theologically significant giving a report (e.g., Acts 14:27; 15:4), to the special meaning of command (Acts 17:30), confess (1 Cor.

14:25), proclaim, (e.g., Acts 4:2; 13:5; 26:20; cf. also 1 Pet. 2:9), and finally to the solemn, liturgical type of proclamation that results from the sacred celebration of the Lord's Supper: "For whenever you eat this bread and drink this cup, you proclaim [*katangellō*] the Lord's death until he comes" (1 Cor. 11:26). The proclaiming here refers probably both to the symbolic action of breaking the bread and pouring out the wine and to the recital of the passion narrative during the Lord's Supper.

Luke and Paul, in contrast to John, are dealing with the proclamation of a completed event or the announcement of one in the future. The subj. of the proclamation is new to the hearers (Acts 4:2; 16:17; 1 Cor. 9:14) and becomes operative by being proclaimed (Acts 13:38; 1 Cor. 2:1).

(c) The message of Christ is the message of the risen one. *apangellō* becomes, in the resurrection narratives of the Gospels, a technical term for witness to the resurrection (Matt. 28:8, 10–11; Mk. 16:10, 13; Lk. 24:9; Jn. 20:18 [*angellō*]). The word is here used in its original sense: A messenger conveys the news, which he or she has received directly beforehand from the sender of the message (the risen one, Matt. 28:10; Jn. 20:18; angels, Lk. 24:6–10). It is no coincidence that Luke uses the same word in his account of Jesus' transfiguration (9:36), in that the disciples do not pass on to anyone the message that they have seen Jesus transfigured.

(d) Jesus is proclaimed as the one in whom the prophetic promises (cf. *prokatangellō* and *katangellō* in Acts 3:18, 24; 7:52) have found fulfillment. Paul opened the Scriptures and explained "that the Christ had to suffer and rise from the dead. 'This Jesus I am proclaiming [*katangellō*] to you is the Christ,' he said" (Acts 17:3). It is not surprising, then, that the commission to proclaim is itself backed by a variety of OT quotations (e.g., Rom. 9:17, cf. Exod. 9:16; Rom. 15:21, cf. Isa. 52:15).

See also *kēryssō*, announce, make known, proclaim (aloud) (*3062*).

34	ἄγγελος

ἄγγελος (*angelos*), angel, messenger (*34*); ἀρχάγγελος (*archangelos*), archangel (*791*); ἰσάγγελος (*isangelos*), like an angel (*2694*).

CL & OT Cl. Gk. uses *angelos* for a messenger or ambassador in human affairs, who speaks and acts in the place of the one who has sent him. He is under the protection of the gods.

1. (a) In the OT angels are heavenly beings, members of Yahweh's court, who serve and praise him (Job 1:6; cf. Isa. 6:2–3). Yahweh is their creator, and angels never became autonomous or had cults dedicated to them in Israel. Sometimes they appear in warlike contexts (e.g., Gen. 32:1–2; cf. Jos. 5:13–15). They witnessed the creation of the world (Job 38:7), but as created beings they are not without fault (4:18; cf. 15:15). They can be mediators of revelation (Zech. 1:9, 11–19; 2:2–5; cf. Ezek. 40:3). Also mentioned are "destroying angels" (Ps. 78:49) and "the destroyer" (Exod. 12:23).

Special kinds of angels are the cherubim, who show traits of both men and animals (Gen. 3:24; Ezek. 1:5–12; 10:19–22; 11:22; Ps. 18:10 [Heb. 11]), and the seraphim, who have six wings (Isa. 6:2). In Dan. angels appear as powerful intermediate beings with personal names: archangels, watchers, and angels of the nations. Millions surround God's throne (cf. 4:13, 17; 7:10; 8:16; 9:21; 10:5–6; 12:1).

(b) We should distinguish these from "the angel of the LORD." He is a heavenly being given a particular task by Yahweh, behind whom the angel's personality entirely disappears. Hence it is wrong for the one to whom the angel has appeared to try and fathom his nature (or name, cf. Jdg. 13:17–18). This angel almost always appears to help either Israel or an individual, and he is virtually a hypostatic appearance of Yahweh (Exod. 14:19; Num. 22:22; Jdg. 6:11–24; 2 Ki. 1:3–4). Only in 2 Sam. 24:16–17 do we find him opposing Israel. Sometimes it is impossible to distinguish between Yahweh and his angel.

2. In later Jud. popular belief in angels greatly increased. Provided that they were not regarded as independent and no angel cult formed, belief in angels was considered an extension of OT piety. Angels represented Yahweh's omniscience and omnipresence, formed his court and attendants, and were his messengers. They were linked with the stars, elements, natural phenomena, and powers, which they ruled as God's representatives. The individual had a guardian angel, and national guardians were set over the peoples, including Michael over Israel (Dan. 10:13, 21; 12:1). Groups of angels included archangels, powers, dominions, thrones, lords, and authorities.

In the scrolls of the Qumran community angels are a feature of a cosmic dualism. God has created two kingdoms, light and darkness, and each has a prince (*sar*) or angel set over it (→ *daimonion, 1228*). Under these princes are all human beings and other angelic beings (also called princes or spirits). The angels of light are often called "sons of heaven" or "sons of God." The "disobedient heavenly watchers" have fallen, and God has judged the angels. In the last days war between God and his heavenly warriors and the sons of darkness will scourge the earth.

NT *angelos* is found 175x in the NT. It is used of men only 6x (Matt. 11:10; Mk. 1:2; Lk. 7:24, 27; 9:52; Jas. 2:25). In general the Jewish concepts of the OT are taken over. Angels are representatives of the heavenly world and God's messengers. When they appear, the supernatural world breaks into this one. Because God is present in Jesus, his way on earth is accompanied by angels (Matt. 1:20; 2:13, 19; 28:2, 5; Mk. 1:13; Lk. 1:19; 2:9, 13; 22:43; Jn. 1:51; cf. Acts 1:10). At his coming again they will be at his side (Matt. 13:49; 16:27; 25:31; 2 Thess. 1:7). As Son of God, Jesus stands indisputably above the angels (Mk. 13:27; Heb. 1:4–14).

The concept of the guardian angel occurs in Matt. 18:10 as an expression of God's love for the "little ones" (cf. Acts 12:15). Angels are mediators of God's judgment (12:23). They act on behalf of the apostles (5:19; 12:7–11) and make God's will known to them (8:26; 10:3–8; 27:23–24).

In Paul Christ dominates the angels (Eph. 1:20–21; Phil. 2:9–11). No creature or elemental angel can separate us from the love of God (Rom. 8:38; cf. Gal. 4:3). The apostle attacked gnostic veneration of angels because it obscured the recognition of Christ's unique position as mediator (Col. 1:15–20; 2:18; cf. Rev. 19:10; 22:8–9). But he recognized various categories of angels (Rom. 8:38–39; 1 Cor. 15:24; Eph. 1:21; Col. 1:16). Angels took part in the giving of the Mosaic law at Sinai (Gal. 3:19; cf. Acts 7:53; Heb. 2:2); they take an interest in the fate of people (Lk. 15:10) and the apostles (1 Cor. 4:9).

Angels surround God's throne and fill the heavenly world with songs of praise (Rev. 5:11; 7:11). They mediate revelation, give visions (1:1; 10:1–11; 14:6–11; 17:1), and carry out God's judgments (7:1; 8:2–3; 9:1, 13; 11:15; 12:7–9; 14:15, 17–20; 15:1, 6–7; 18:1–2; 19:17; 20:1–3). On the other hand, Satan also has angels (Matt. 25:41; 2 Cor. 12:7). Peter (1 Pet. 3:19–20; 2 Pet. 2:4) and Jude (6) speak of the fall of the angels. "The angels of the churches" (Rev. 1:20; 2:1; etc.) are probably angels and not pastors.

archangelos (archangel) is found in the NT only in 1 Thess. 4:16 and Jude 9. The concept, however, may also be found in Rev. 8:2, 7–8, 10, 12; 9:1, 13; 11:15. The only names given are Gabriel (Lk. 1:19) and Michael (Jude 9; Rev. 12:7).

isangelos, like an angel, is found only in Lk. 20:36 (cf. Matt. 22:30; Mk. 12:25). The word describes the condition of those who have been raised from the dead, who are no longer subject to the natural conditions of earthly life, including marriage.

See also *Cheroub*, cherub (*5938*).

ἅγιος (*hagios*), holy, sacred (*41*); ἁγιάζω (*hagiazō*), make holy, consecrate, sanctify (*39*); ἁγιασμός (*hagiasmos*), holiness, consecration, sanctification (*40*); ἁγιότης (*hagiotēs*), holiness (*42*); ἁγιωσύνη (*hagiōsynē*), holiness (*43*).

CL & OT 1. In its origin, *hagios* is related to *hazomai*, which means to stand in awe of the gods or one's parents, to respect. *hagios* can be applied to the shrine of Aphrodite, an oath, the gods, and even certain people. Most of its derivatives are late and occur chiefly in the LXX. In contrast to *hieros* (→ *2641*), this word expressed not something holy in and of itself, but the challenge to worship that issues from the holy.

2. In the LXX this word group serves predominantly to translate Heb. *qādôš* and its derivatives. The decisive element in the OT concept of the holy is not so much the awesome divine power. Rather, through certain places, objects, or occasions people enter into direct contact with the divine power. The basic idea is not that of separation (though this is favored by many scholars), but the positive thought of encounter, which inevitably demands certain modes of response (e.g., Ps. 24:3–4). *hagios* is a concept that posits ethical values. This ethic is the expression of the holiness of Yahweh in a world of both similar and different sacred practices. For example, sexual intercourse is in no way immoral. But compared with sacred practices, it is a profane act that therefore makes one impure for coming into contact with the holy (1 Sam. 21:4–6; cf. Exod. 19:15).

3. (a) The vb. *hagiazō*, to make holy, sanctify, is used more uniformly in the context of its setting than the noun and the adj. A man had to sanctify himself after he had been temporarily excluded from the life of the community by uncleanness (2 Sam. 11:4) or when he came into contact with God (e.g., via theophany, Exod. 19:10–24.; holy war, 1 Sam. 21:5; family sacrifice, 1 Sam. 16:5). One could also sanctify people (1 Sam. 7:1, to the priesthood) or things (1 Ki. 8:64; cf. Jos. 6:19) and thus place them at God's disposal. As Num. 6:1–21 shows, the case of the Nazirite is a special form of consecration.

(b) The OT makes reference to various things that are holy: e.g., bread (1 Sam. 21:4) or sacrificial flesh (Jer. 11:15). The psalmist speaks of various things as holy: Yahweh's temple (e.g., Ps. 5:7), his hill (3:4; 15:1), Zion (2:6), heaven (20:6), the height from which he hears (102:19), and his throne (47:8). Yahweh himself is terrible and holy (99:3). None of the gods is holy as he is, for none casts down the exalted and raises the humble as he does (1 Sam. 2:2).

4. (a) The use of *hagios* is vividly illustrated in Isa. After the thrice-repeated "holy" of the heavenly attendants Isaiah acknowledges himself to be a man of unclean lips, whereupon his guilt is taken away and his sin covered (Isa. 6:3–7). The prophecies of Isa. frequently contain the expression "the Holy One of Israel," which is used esp. in two contexts in earlier parts of Isa. (i) Instead of leaning on the Holy One of Israel, the people have relied on horses and chariots (31:1; cf. 10:20; 30:15). (ii) The sinful people, laden with guilt, have despised the Holy One of Israel (1:4; cf. 30:12–13) and will thus be smitten by him. But in Isa. 40–55, the Holy One, who is the Creator of the world and the Lord of the nations (40:25), will redeem Israel out of slavery like a kinsman (43:14). He was sufficiently removed from his people to punish them without bias, but he is also sufficiently powerful, after the punishment, to create something utterly new. Therefore nations will run to the Holy One of Israel, because he will glorify Israel (55:5).

(b) Another aspect of holiness occurs in the Deuteronomic formula "the holy people." Insofar as the people are holy to Yahweh, their God (Deut. 7:6; 14:2, 21; 26:19), the formula explains their separation from the practices and cult objects of foreign religions (e.g., 7:5; 14:21). The whole Torah is what distinguishes Israel from the foreign nations. Deut. 26:18–19 declares that through keeping the whole Torah Israel will become a people holy to Yahweh. The underlying thought here finds expression in the Holiness Code (Lev. 17–26). Note esp. Lev. 11:44, "Be holy, because I am holy" (cf. 19:2; 20:7).

(c) Jeremiah made little use of the word group. Note, however, Jer. 1:5, where Yahweh consecrated Jeremiah from his mother's womb to be a prophet to the nations. The words occur more frequently in Ezek. Special mention should be made of the phrase to show oneself holy before someone, which generally refers to the house of Israel (i.e., Judah). The clearest example is Ezek. 36:23. Yahweh's name has been profaned through the scattering of the people, and the exiles have contributed to its further profanation. But when Yahweh gathers his people from the four corners of the earth, he will manifest himself in them before all the nations as the Holy One, and the nations will come to acknowledge that he is Yahweh.

5. By far the most extensive occurrences of the word group are to be found in the cultic, ritual texts of the OT (Exod. 25–Num. 10; Ezek. 40–48; cf. also parts of 1 and 2 Chr.). (a) Everything that belongs to the realm of the cultus is holy—such as holy occasions (e.g., the great feasts, New Moons, Sabbaths, Year of Jubilee) and holy objects that serve the cultus (e.g., temple, tent and ark, altars and their equipment, firstfruits, anointing oil, incense). In the ritual of the oath, holy water is used (cf. Num. 5:17). The temple has holy money (1 Chr. 29:2–9, 16); the priests have holy garments (Exod. 28:2–43); the high priest has a breastplate with the inscription "HOLY TO THE LORD" (28:36 = LXX 28:32).

Sometimes holiness can be thought of almost physically: It is transferred by contact (Exod. 29:37; 30:29), and improper contact can be fatal (Num. 4:15, 20). Thus, it is the duty of everyone who takes part in the cultus to be pure (to sanctify oneself). Whoever is unclean must quickly take steps to purify himself. There are also holy people (priests, Levites, Nazirites) and the holy anointing of the Davidic kings (Ps. 89:20; cf. 1 Sam. 24:6). A distinction can be drawn between the holy and the holiest (e.g., the Most Holy Place in the tabernacle and temple). The sense of this distinction, however, is less a gradation of the holiness that derives from God than a gradation of human dealings with the Holy One.

(b) Three additional details should be noted. (i) Occasionally the term *hagioi*, holy ones, saints, stands for heavenly companions of God (e.g., Zech. 14:5). (ii) Only rarely are the members of the holy nation called saints or holy ones. (iii) On only three occasions is Yahweh's Spirit called holy (Ps. 51:11; Isa. 63:10–11).

6. (a) Intertestamental Jud. introduced no real innovations into this scheme of holiness, apart from the fact that the Scriptures were now also called holy (1 Macc. 12:9). This change was revolutionary, for from now on the Scriptures were to form the new pivotal point for the system of holiness in Jud., thereby replacing the temple. This process was, admittedly, only completed in the rab. writings with their belief in the Holy Spirit as the Spirit who speaks in the Scriptures. Hence, those who obeyed the Torah were in particular regarded as holy, and holiness focused more and more on daily life.

(b) An important feature was the slow development of the term "the saints" for the members of the Jerusalem cultic community (e.g., Wis. 5:5; 18:9).

(c) In the book of *1 Enoch* a new theme develops that qualifies the righteous as holy, who will be vindicated in due course (48:8–9, cf. v. 7).

(d) In Qumran the community saw itself as the eschatological, priestly community of the saved, in which the ordinances of purification that were originally obligatory only for the priests were made binding for all the members. The concept of holiness plays a big part in the Qumran texts. The community described itself as "the saints of his people" (e.g., 1QM 6:6), God's "holy people" (1QM 14:12), "men of holiness" (1QS 8:13, etc.), and the "remnant of holiness" (1QS 8:21). Thus there prevailed at Qumran a priestly concept of holiness in which the temple cult was replaced by special ways of obedience to the Torah, such as washing, cultic meals, and esp. observance of the religious calendar (1QS 9:3ff.).

NT 1. In general, two facts stand out regarding *hagios* in the NT. (a) God is seldom described as holy (Jn. 17:11; 1 Pet. 1:15–16; Rev.

4:8; 6:10), and Christ is only once called holy in the same sense as God (Rev. 3:7; cf. 1 Jn. 2:20). The concept of holiness is determined rather by the Holy Spirit, the gift of the new age. (b) The proper sphere of the holy in the NT is not the cultus but the prophetic. The sacred no longer belongs to things, places, or rites, but to manifestations of life produced by the Spirit. As time went on, however, use was made of the holy priesthood of all the saints. Hence cultic conceptions of holiness were again taken up in the early church.

2. (a) A number of passages reflect the framework of OT tradition: God's name is called holy (Lk. 1:49), as is his covenant (Lk. 1:72), his angels (Mk. 8:38; Lk. 9:26; Acts 10:22; Jude 14; Rev. 14:10), his attendants (Eph. 2:19; Col. 1:12; 1 Thess. 3:13; Rev. 18:20), the prophets (Lk. 1:70), and the Scriptures (Rom. 1:2), esp. the Torah (Rom. 7:12).

(b) The Synoptic tradition introduces the NT emphasis. Jesus is addressed by demons as "the Holy One of God" (Mk. 1:24; Lk. 4:34). This expression indicates that Jesus was endowed at his baptism with the Holy Spirit and was driven into the desert for forty days by the Spirit, like an ancient prophet or a Nazirite, before he performed his first miracle (Mk. 1:21–26). We probably find the same concept in Lk. 1:35: "So the holy one to be born will be called the Son of God." As Samson was a holy one of God from his mother's womb (Jdg. 13:7), Jesus was holy from his conception, i.e., filled by the Holy Spirit (cf. Mk. 6:20 of John the Baptist).

A somewhat different, but analogous, idea is evident in Acts 4:27 (cf. 3:14), where Jesus is called God's "holy servant." The inhabitants of Jerusalem rejected him, as they had always denied and killed the prophets in the past (7:51–52). In all these cases holy means belonging to and authorized by God. Hence, resisting Jesus is equivalent to resisting God.

(c) The first petition of the Lord's Prayer contains the words: "Hallowed be your name" (Matt. 6:9; Lk. 11:2). The vb. *hagiazō* appears only here and at Matt. 23:17, 19 in the Synoptic Gospels. This expression here (perhaps based on an ancient Aramaic prayer) means not only to reverence and honor God but also to glorify him by obeying his commands. This petition and the next one ("your kingdom come") are a cry from the depths of distress. From a world enslaved by evil, death, and Satan, the disciples are to lift their eyes to the Father and cry out for the revelation of his glory and kingdom, knowing in faith that he will grant it. The goal for which the Christian prays is not the sanctification of the world through God, but the sanctification of God through the world (cf. Matt. 5:48; also Num. 14:21; Isa. 11:9; Hab. 2:14).

3. (a) In Paul's letters those who name Jesus as their Lord are called *hagioi*, saints. This is not primarily an ethical expression but a concept parallel to "called" (Rom. 1:7; 1 Cor. 1:2), "chosen" (Rom. 8:33; Col. 3:12), and "faithful" (Col. 1:2); it implies association with the Holy Spirit. Christ is their sanctification as well as their righteousness and redemption (1 Cor. 1:30), and thus the one in whom they become holy to the true God (see 1 Cor. 6:11; cf. 2 Thess. 2:13; 1 Pet. 1:1–2). The power to do so comes from the risen Christ, who operates according to the Spirit of holiness (Rom. 1:4). Holiness is a condition of acceptance at the Parousia and of entering the inheritance of God's people (Acts 20:32; 26:18; Col. 1:12). In all these cases holiness implies a relationship with God that is expressed not primarily through the cultus but through the fact that believers are "led" by the Holy Spirit (Rom. 8:14). As in the OT, holiness demands behavior that rightly responds to the Holy Spirit.

(b) Sanctification is like a growing fruit that results in eternal life (Rom. 6:19–22; cf. 1 Thess. 4:3–7). Spiritual worship is the offering of oneself as a living, holy sacrifice, acceptable to God (Rom. 12:1). An essential aspect of sanctification is love for all the saints (Eph. 1:15), sharing with them in need (Rom. 12:13), and not profaning the sacred by bringing disputes with fellow believers before secular authorities (1 Cor. 6:1–2). In Paul's judgment, a non-Christian marriage partner does not profane the Christian. Rather, the non-

Christian partner is sanctified by the Christian, just as the children of the marriage are also sanctified (1 Cor. 7:14). Because it is God himself who sanctifies (1 Thess. 5:23), bearing fruit unto sanctification is all the more important (Rom. 6:22; cf. Phil. 2:12–16).

4. (a) Heb. presents a highly specialized aspect of holiness. Christ, as the high priest, is the one who sanctifies his people (2:11; 13:12) and officiates in a sanctuary not made with hands (8:2; 9:24). The division of Israel's earthly sanctuary (*ta hagia*) into the Holy Place and Most Holy Place (9:2–3) shows that ultimate access to the sanctuary has not yet been achieved. But Christ has entered the true, heavenly sanctuary once for all with the gift of his blood and has achieved eternal redemption (9:12; 10:14). His self-offering makes obsolete the animal sacrifices of the temple. By the will of God "we have been made holy through the sacrifice of the body of Jesus Christ once for all" (10:10).

But, Heb. goes on to warn us, "since we have confidence to enter the Most Holy Place" (10:19), we must not defile the blood of the covenant, through which we have been sanctified; "for we know him who said, 'It is mine to avenge; I will repay,' and again, 'The Lord will judge his people'" (10:30; cf. Deut. 32:35–36). Therefore we are to strive for peace with everyone and for the holiness without which no one can see God (12:14). Conversely, holy fellow believers (3:1) are to recognize the discipline that God applies as a help, for God disciplines in order that we may win a share in his holiness (*hagiotēs*, 12:10; cf. Prov. 3:11–12).

(b) This concept is particularly developed in 1 Pet. To the idea of "the sanctifying work of the Spirit" (1:2) there is added the blunt warning, "As obedient children, do not conform to the evil desires you had when you lived in ignorance. But just as he who called you is holy, so be holy in all you do; for it is written, 'Be holy, because I am holy'" (1:14–16; cf. Lev. 19:2). This theme is continued in 1 Pet. 2:5: "You also, like living stones, are being built into a spiritual house to be a holy priesthood, offering spiritual sacrifices acceptable to God through Jesus Christ" (cf. 2:9–10). Thus the dynamic of the outpouring of the Spirit is here restated in terms of the holy functions of the priesthood.

(c) Believers are again seen as priests in Rev. 1:6; 5:10; 20:6. But Rev. also depicts the future abode of Christians as the holy city, the new Jerusalem (21:2, 10; 22:19). The most significant feature of ancient Jerusalem was the fact that it contained the temple, the focal point of meeting between God and humankind. But in the new Jerusalem there is no temple, "because the Lord God the Almighty and the Lamb are its temple" (21:22). These pictures present both a continuity with the divinely appointed institutions of Israel and a radical break. The historical institutions in Israel are now obsolete. Yet the use of the concepts of priest, temple, and holy city in this dynamic and spiritual way affords a perspective to the suffering, persecuted church to see its situation and role in terms of God's historical purposes for his people.

(d) In the Fourth Gospel the adj. *hagios* is used only of the Father (Jn. 17:11), the Spirit (1:33; 14:26; 20:22), and the Son (6:69). This latter passage occurs in Jn.'s account of Peter's confession. In Jn. Peter does not confess Jesus as the Christ (cf. Matt. 16:16; Mk. 8:29; Lk. 9:20; though cf. Jn. 1:41; 4:25; 7:41; 11:27; 20:31), with all its Jewish overtones, but as the "Holy One of God." This expression is rare, occurring elsewhere in the NT only in the address of the demoniac at Capernaum (Mk. 1:24; Lk. 4:34). The fact that John uses the epithet "holy" elsewhere only of the Father and the Spirit sets Jesus with God and not humankind. The expression "the Holy One" occurs in the only instance of *hagios* in the Johannine letters: "But you have an anointing from the Holy One, and all of you know the truth" (1 Jn. 2:20). The reference is evidently to the Holy Spirit, but the context links this closely with the Father and the Son (cf. 2:22–27).

The vb. *hagiazō* occurs 4x in Jn. and is absent from the Johannine letters. In the first instance it denotes the special consecration of Jesus to do the will and work of the Father (Jn. 10:36). The other three

occur in Jesus' high priestly prayer: "Sanctify them by the truth; your word is truth. . . . For them I sanctify myself, that they too may be truly sanctified" (17:17, 19). In the background here is the use of *hagiazō* in the LXX for the sanctifying of priests (e.g., Exod. 28:41; 29:1, 21) and sacrifices (e.g., 28:38; Num. 18:9). In context here it surely refers to Jesus' own sacrificial death, which he does for the sake of his disciples. The ultimate goal of his cross is that they might be set apart for God and thus be able to live according to God's truth.

See also *hieros*, holy (*2641*); *hosios*, holy, devout, pious (*4008*).

42 (*hagiotēs*, holiness), → *41*.

43 (*hagiōsynē*, holiness), → *41*.

48 (*hagneia*, purity, chastity, propriety), → *54*.

49 (*hagnizō*, purify), → *54*.

50 (*hagnismos*, purification), → *54*.

51	ἀγνοέω

ἀγνοέω (*agnoeō*), not know, be ignorant (*51*); ἀγνόημα (*agnoēma*), error (*52*); ἄγνοια (*agnoia*), ignorance (*53*); ἀγνωσία (*agnōsia*), lack of knowledge (*57*); ἄγνωστος (*agnōstos*), unknown (*58*).

CL & OT *agnoeō* means not to know and is used against the full background of the Gk. concept of knowledge (→ *ginōskō*, *1182*). It does not refer merely to something not grasped by the mind, but can also mean to make a mistake or be in error. Similarly, *agnoēma* (Heb. 9:7 is its only NT occurrence) is used not merely for error but also for an offense done in ignorance. *agnoia* similarly refers not only to not knowing, but also to ignorance or lack of education. The positive opposites are *gnōsis* ("knowledge") and *sophia* (→ *5053*). The Stoics considered ignorance to be the root of all evil and sometimes identified the two. If someone was living without knowledge, it was either because that person had not received the revelation or had refused it.

In legal settings *agnoia* means ignorance of the law (e.g., Lev. 22:14). The LXX uses *agnoia* concretely in the sense of *agnoēma*, also meaning (unintentional) guilt, offense, error (e.g., 5:18). *agnōstos* means both unknowable and unknown.

NT 1. (a) *agnoeō* means first not to understand, in the sense of not being able to grasp something (Mk. 9:32; Lk. 9:45, in each case of a passion prediction by Jesus).

(b) It also means not to know, not to be informed (e.g., 2 Pet. 2:12, where the godless blaspheme in matters they do not know). It is esp. prominent in the phrase "I do not want you to be unaware," i.e., uninformed (Rom. 1:13; 11:25; 1 Cor. 10:1; 12:1; 2 Cor. 1:8; 1 Thess. 4:13), always with the address "brothers." Through this expression Paul stresses his desire to end his readers' lack of knowledge. *agnoeō* is used also in the formula "or don't you know?" (Rom. 6:3; cf. 7:1), with the force of failing to realize. Here a present knowledge is presupposed that implies a need to respond to the gospel.

These passages never mean merely a lack of intellectual knowledge that can be removed by a neutral statement of facts. Rather, *agnoeō* is used in the OT sense. This lack of knowledge can be removed only by knowledge intimately linked with recognition and acceptance by God.

(c) *agnoeō* denotes ignorance that leads one astray. In 1 Tim. 1:13 Paul, looking back on his past, says, "I was shown mercy because I acted in ignorance and unbelief." Ignorance marked out Paul's life, leading him astray, until his conversion to the Christian faith, which included proper knowledge. The same shade of meaning is found in Heb. 5:2 where, using OT language, the author contrasts unintentional sins with deliberate ones. *agnoeō* is expanded here from unknowing to unwanted, so that it denotes sins for which there is atonement in contrast to those for which there is none.

(d) *agnoeō* means also a failure to know in the sense of a disobedient closing of the mind to the revealing word of God (Acts 13:27;

Rom. 10:3). This is not simply a lack of knowledge, but a false understanding. Ignorance and disobedience are here used as parallels; ignorance is the guilty turning away from the revelation of God in Jesus Christ. The guilty ignorance of the Jews can only be dealt with by God himself as he forgives and reveals himself in the gospel. This passage reflects the OT link between knowledge and right conduct. One should probably include 1 Cor. 14:38 in this connection. To reject a command is to reject God, with the implied corollary that this involves nonrecognition by not only Paul but by God himself.

(e) Finally, *agnoeō* means to be unknown. In 2 Cor. 6:9 Paul says that he is "unknown," i.e., to the world, for he is not included among its great ones. On the other hand, he is well known to God and the church (see also Gal. 1:22).

2. (a) In Acts 3:17 *agnoia* is used in the juridical sense of the LXX. The guilt of the Jews is, from the viewpoint of the subj., a sin arising from ignorance. On the other hand, the Stoic-Jewish sense is found in the other cases of its use, among them being some that betray gnostic usage (→ *ginōskō*, *1182*). Acts 17:30, for example, refers to heathenism (cf. 14:16; Rom. 3:25). Since the period of humankind before the decisive revelation of God in Christ was characterized by ignorance, "God overlooked such ignorance, but now he commands all people everywhere to repent" (Acts 17:30).

(b) *agnōstos* in Acts 17:23 means simply unknown in the inscription "TO AN UNKNOWN GOD" on an altar at Athens. Paul addressed the Athenians as those who had until then honored the unknown God without their being aware of it, but he was now proclaiming this God as the revealed God, the true and only God, the God of the OT and of salvation history. Paul's mention of ignorance was not intended to justify or excuse the pagans; it was to introduce them to God's saving purposes and to lead them to the joy of repentance.

See also *aisthēsis*, experience (*151*); *ginōskō*, know, understand, comprehend, recognize (*1182*)).

52 (agnoēma, error), → *51.*

53 (agnoia, ignorance), → *51.*

54	ἀγνός

ἀγνός (*hagnos*), pure, holy (*54*); ἀγνίζω (*hagnizō*), purify (*49*); ἀγνεία (*hagneia*), purity, chastity, propriety (*48*); ἀγνισμός (*hagnismos*), purification (*50*); ἀγνότης (*hagnotēs*), purity, sincerity (*55*); ἀγνῶς (*hagnōs*), sincerely (*56*).

CL & OT 1. In cl. Gk. *hagnos* originally meant that which inspires (religious) awe. It refers primarily to an attribute of deity, then to things having some relation to the deity. It thus comes to mean holy, in the sense of pure. Ritual purity is in mind here, e.g., avoidance of blood-guilt or of touching corpses. Since to the primitive mind sexual intercourse also makes a person ritually unclean, *hagnos* came to mean chaste. This cultic term was then transferred to the sphere of morality and is frequently used in the Hel. period in the sense of innocent, morally faultless.

From *hagnos* came the vb. *hagnizō*, to purify (by means of expiatory rites), and the noun *hagnismos*, purification; both words are limited to the cultic sphere. *hagneia* is used of cultic purity, chastity, purity of mind. *hagnotēs* (unknown outside the NT) means purity, moral blamelessness.

2. (a) In the LXX *hagnos* occurs 11x (the word normally used for cultic purity is *katharos*, → *2754*). In distinction from *hagios* (holy, set apart for God, → *41*) and *katharos*, the nuance of *hagnos* is one of integrity (e.g., Ps. 12:6; Prov. 20:9). It is significant that *hagnos* is found chiefly in the wisdom literature.

(b) More common in the LXX is the vb. *hagnizō*, which describes measures taken to achieve eligibility for the cult. Whereas *hagios* always includes the thought of the power and might of that which is holy, *hagnizō* expresses the removal of what is not seemly (e.g., Exod. 19:10, washing of garments; Num. 6:3, abstinence from alcohol), esp.

in the sense to purify oneself from sin or uncleanness (e.g., Num. 8:21; 19:12). Likewise, *hagneia* refers to ritual purity (e.g., Num. 6:2–21; 2 Chr. 30:19; 1 Macc. 14:36).

NT 1. In the NT only *hagnizō* and *hagnismos* (only at Acts 21:26) occur in their proper meaning, ritual purification—in connection with the Jews before the Passover (Jn. 11:55) and with Paul's vow in Jerusalem (Acts 21:24–26; 24:18). In Jas. 4:8; 1 Pet. 1:22; 1 Jn. 3:3, on the other hand, *hagnizō* refers to moral purification.

hagnos occurs only in NT letters, where Hel. influence is noticeable. It means: (a) chaste (2 Cor. 11:2; Tit. 2:5); (b) innocent with regard to something (2 Cor. 7:11); and (c) morally pure, upright—said of Christ (1 Jn. 3:3), of a Christian's behavior (Phil. 4:8; 1 Tim. 5:22; 1 Pet. 3:2), and of wisdom (Jas. 3:17). The adv. *hagnōs* refers to sincerity in Christian service (Phil. 1:17); the noun *hagneia* denotes moral purity and blamelessness (1 Tim. 4:12; 5:2).

2. This survey of the *hagnos* word group in the NT shows that the original significance (i.e., ritual purity) no longer has a great part to play. This is understandable, since it was only the Jewish-Christian community in Jerusalem that clung to the temple cult and thus observed the ordinances connected with it (Acts 3:1; 21:18–26). To all the Gentile churches, ritual purification meant little or nothing, for nowhere in the NT—apart from the apostolic decree (Acts 15:28–29), which was intended to make it possible for Gentile and Jewish Christians to live together in mixed churches—are cultic regulations for Christians to be found.

Purification gains a new meaning in the NT, however, for these words are used to express the moral purity demanded of Christians. The starting point is the fact that Christ is *hagnos*, pure, i.e., without sin (1 Jn. 3:3). Because of this, those who belong to him should also be pure. Through his sacrificial death Christ has not only made the normal sacrifices of the temple cult unnecessary, but he has also exposed their real meaning. Purity and integrity are, moreover, not merely human virtues; they indicate the relation of a person to God. Therefore, this word group is no longer the preferred means of referring to sexual purity or abstinence; the NT word for that is *enkrateia* (self-discipline, → *1602*).

See also *katharos*, clean, pure (*2754*).

55 (hagnotēs, purity, sincerity), → *54.*

56 (hagnōs, sincerely), → *54.*

57 (agnōsia, lack of knowledge), → *51.*

58 (agnōstos, unknown), → *51.*

59 (agora, market), → *60.*

60	ἀγοράζω

ἀγοράζω (*agorazō*), buy (*60*); ἀγορά (*agora*), market (*59*); ἀγοραῖος (*agoraios*), frequenting the market (*61*); ἐξαγοράζω (*exagorazō*), redeem (*1973*).

CL & OT Originally any place of public assembly, the *agora* became identified with the marketplace, a center of community life regularly used for political meetings, judicial hearings, and esp. for trade. The derived adj. *agoraios* (lit., belonging to the *agora*) could be used in a good sense to describe those who did business in the marketplace, but more frequently it applied to loafers who hung around the *agora* looking for excitement or trouble. *agorazō* came to mean buy in the marketplace, thence buy in general. In Hel. times it was also in common use as a term for buying slaves. *exagorazō* could be applied to the redeeming of slaves.

In the LXX *agora* describes the trading activity of Tyre (Ezek. 27:12–22). A girl seeks her lover there (Song 3:2), and Eccl. 12:4 uses the shut doors of the *agora* as a figure for deafness. *agorazō* normally refers to commercial purchase (e.g., Gen. 41:57; Neh. 10:31). Dan. 2:8 preserves an interesting use of *exagorazō*, where the Babylonian astrologers attempt to evade their fate by gaining (buying) time.

NT *agora* is used 9x in the Synoptics, 2x in Acts. It serves as a place for children to play (Matt. 11:16 par.), an employment exchange (20:3), a center of public life where the Pharisees love to be conspicuous (23:7 par.), and a focal point of Jesus' healing ministry (Mk. 6:56). Paul found himself on trial in the Philippian *agora* (Acts 16:19) and seized evangelistic opportunities among the crowds in Athenian *agora* (17:17). Acts 17:5 refers to the *agoraioi*, the marketplace rabble-rousers; the same word reappears in 19:38 with a semitechnical sense of court sessions (*agoraioi hēmerai*).

agorazō is found 25x in the NT with its usual commercial meaning, mostly in the Gospels (e.g., Matt. 13:44; Lk. 22:36), though 5x it describes the buying (redeeming) of Christians. This clearly reflects the contemporary terminology of the slave market. In 1 Cor. 6:20; 7:23 (cf. Rev. 14:3) the emphasis is not the freedom of the redeemed but their new status as slaves of God, bought with a price to do his will. Hence the sheer effrontery of heretics "denying the sovereign Lord who bought them" (2 Pet. 2:1). The price Christ paid for his people (his blood) is spelled out in Rev. 5:9.

exagorazō also means redeem in Gal. 3:13; 4:5, where the idea of escaping from the consequences of breaking God's law is added. This word also occurs 2x to express the different idea of (lit.) "redeeming the time (*kairos*)" (Eph. 5:16; Col. 4:5), which probably means buy up intensively; i.e., snap up every opportunity that comes.

See also *pōleō*, sell (*4797*).

61 (agoraios, frequenting the market), → *60.*

66 (agrielaios, wild olive), → *1778.*

67 (agrios, of the field, wild), → *69.*

69	ἀγρός

ἀγρός (*agros*), field (*69*); ἄγριος (*agrios*), of the field, wild (*67*).

CL & OT In secular Gk., *agros* typically denotes a piece of cultivated land, but it can also mean the countryside as distinct from the town or village. Similarly, the adjective *agrios* sometimes describes trees, animals, or crops to be found "in the fields," but more often it has the sense of "wild." In this latter sense it is frequently applied figuratively to people (savage, fierce) and to things and circumstances (cruel, harsh).

Most of the above usages are found in the LXX. Any piece of land under cultivation is an *agros* (e.g., Exod. 8:13; Ruth 2:2). At the same time *agros* describes the untilled open country beyond the town or village boundary (e.g., Deut. 22:27; 1 Sam. 30:11), where the traveler might expect to meet a wild animal (Hos. 13:8; cf. Jer. 14:5). Such beasts are naturally *agrios*, wild (Job. 6:5; Ps. 80:13). The adj. is not applied figuratively to people in the LXX or other Jewish writings, but it can describe a "malignant" ulcer (Lev. 21:20; Deut. 28:27) or "wild" waves (Wis. 14:1).

NT *agros* occurs 35x in the Gospels, 18 of which refer to land under cultivation or destined for it (e.g., Matt. 13:24; Lk. 14:18; cf. Acts 4:37). *agroi* can also mean countryside, where farmhouses may be found (Lk. 9:12). Otherwise (though cf. Matt. 27:7–8, 10), the reference is to the countryside (e.g., Mk. 15:21). The adjective *agrios* is used in its lit. sense ("wild" honey, i.e., honey "found in the open field," Mk. 1:6) and fig. to describe the "wild" waves of the sea (Jude 13).

See also *gē*, earth, world (*1178*); *kosmos*, adornment, world (*3180*); *oikoumenē*, earth (*3876*); *chous*, soil, dust (*5967*).

70	ἀγρυπνέω

ἀγρυπνέω (*agrypneō*), keep oneself awake, be awake, keep watch, guard, care (*70*); ἀγρυπνία (*agrypnia*), wakefulness (*71*).

CL & OT In cl. Gk. *agrypneō* means to lie awake, be watchful; the noun *agrypnia* means sleeplessness, usually accompanied by watch-

fulness. In the LXX the vb. occurs 11x, usually with the meaning watch (e.g., Job 21:32; Ps. 102:7; 127:1). The noun occurs in the LXX only in the Apocr. (once in 2 Macc. 9x in Sir., e.g., Sir. 31:1–2, 20 = LXX 34:1–2, 20).

NT In the context of his eschatological discourse, Jesus charged his disciples to be on the alert (Mk. 13:33; Lk. 21:36). A similar charge is repeated in Eph. 6:18 at the climax of the discourse on the Christian's armor: Believers must "keep alert" because the spiritual forces of evil continually threaten their moral and spiritual lives. In Heb. 13:17 the author urges obedience to church leaders because "they keep watch over you as men who must give an account." *agrypnia* occurs in the pl. in 2 Cor. 6:5 and 11:27, where it refers to Paul's "watching" or "sleepless nights" endured for the sake of the church.

See also *grēgoreō*, watch, be on the alert, be watchful (*1213*); *tēreō*, preserve, keep (*5498*); *phylassō*, guard, preserve, keep (*5875*).

71 (agrypnia, wakefulness), → *70.*

74	ἀγών

ἀγών (*agōn*), fight (*74*); ἀγωνίζομαι (*agōnizomai*), fight (*76*); ἀνταγωνίζομαι (*antagōnizomai*), fight against (*497*); ἐπαγωνίζομαι (*epagōnizomai*), fight for (*2043*); καταγωνίζομαι (*katagōnizomai*), conquer, defeat (*2865*); συναγωνίζομαι (*synagōnizomai*), fight along with, help (*5253*); ἀγωνία (*agōnia*), agony, anxiety (*75*).

CL & OT 1. In cl. Gk., *agōn* (from *agō*, drive, lead) can mean gathering, gathering place, or a struggle or fight (in war, politics, or law; also in a sporting contest). *agōnizomai* has the same shades of meaning even when compounded with various prepositions. *agōnia* has higher style ranges in meaning, from effort to anxiety. In Cynic and Stoic diatribes the outlook and terminology of the stadium is used for exercise in virtue and for life's moral struggle.

2. In stark contrast to the above stands OT Jud., to which this range of concepts is alien. In the LXX *agōn* occurs almost exclusively in the Apocr. (15x, particularly 2 and 4 Macc.) and translates a Heb. word only in Isa. 7:13, where God rebukes Ahaz for contending (NIV "try the patience") with him. *agōnizomai* likewise appears only in the Apocr., and its compounds are altogether absent. On the other hand, 4 Macc. 12:15 speaks of the struggle for virtue (*aretēs*), Sir. 4:28 of the struggle for truth, and Wis. 4:2 of moral striving. It is also used frequently for military conflict.

The suffering of the martyrs that took place in the hippodrome is also described in Macc. in the imagery of the stadium. Expressions like *agōn theios*, divine struggle, or *hieroprepēs*, holy struggle (4 Macc. 17:11; 11:20), indicate that, just as the games were held in honor of a deity, the sufferings and deadly combats of the martyrs were considered to be to the glory of God. These ideas had a powerful influence on early Christianity, esp. in Heb. and Rev.

NT 1. In the Gospels *agōnizomai* occurs only 2x: Jn. 18:36, of Jesus' servants, who would fight for him with weapons; and Lk. 13:24, "Make every effort to enter [salvation] through the narrow door." The remaining occurrences of this word group are predominantly in the writings of Paul, a native of a Hel. city who used technical terms from the stadium.

The prep. compounds of *agōnizomai* are only used 4x, but without any change of meaning (Rom. 15:30; Heb. 11:33; 12:4; Jude 3). In Lk. 22:44 *agōnia* may mean effort, fear, excitement, alarm, or anxiety. This Gethsemane passage (cf. Heb. 5:7) should not be translated "as he fought with death" (which imports the meaning of the English word "agony" but which is not in the original), but rather "as he was afraid" or "as he was concerned for victory" in face of the approaching battle on the cross.

2. The transforming power of the Christian faith shows itself also in a language that reverses in a positive sense realities like the

cross and slavery (which seem completely negative to the natural self). It also draws into its range of imagery things such as spiritual armor and contending against unseen spiritual forces (cf. Eph. 6:10–18). In addition to Paul in Eph. and the Pastoral Letters, Heb. and Lk. also find a place for the image of a fight. Three groups of ideas can be distinguished:

(a) *agōn* emphasizes the conscious application of one's powers for the achievement of a goal. Jesus encourages us to strive to enter the kingdom through the narrow door (Lk. 13:24, here *agōnizomai*). Paul's work is not merely the fulfillment of an obligation but an *agōn*, which is linked with *kopos* (burden) and *ponos* (hardship) (see Col. 1:29; 1 Tim. 4:10). What matters is the highest, imperishable, and only rewarding goal, the *brabeion* (prize). Therefore, not only supreme effort but also supreme renunciation are demanded.

According to 1 Cor. 9:24–27, everyone who competes must go "into strict training." This does not mean a kind of asceticism, which keeps the body in submission out of contempt for it. Rather, the Christian exercises discipline by having his or her body under control and directing it toward a goal in accordance with one's own will. For this, godly exercise (1 Tim. 4:7–8) is necessary. This is the race, the good fight, which Paul has himself completed (2 Tim. 4:7) and which he recommends to Timothy (1 Tim. 6:12).

(b) The obj. of this *agōn*, however, is not primarily the perfection of the individual, i.e., a private salvation, but the spread of the gospel. That is, the apostles strive for the salvation of God's elect, "that we may present everyone perfect in Christ" (Col. 1:28). So we are always dealing with an *agōn hyper*, a struggle for, on behalf of, others (Rom. 15:30; Col. 2:1–2; 4:12), which takes place above all in prayer. In prayer we can intercede for someone else and make this cause and suffering our own (Rom. 15:30; Col. 4:3; 1 Thess. 5:25; 2 Thess. 3:1; Heb. 13:18).

The proclamation of the divine message leads to conflict with opponents (2 Cor. 7:5; Heb. 12:3–4). But in the last analysis the adversaries against which we struggle are not human but "the rulers . . . the authorities . . . the powers of this dark world . . . the spiritual forces of evil in the heavenly realms" (Eph. 6:12).

(c) This struggle through suffering is particularly expressed by the prep. *syn*. The compounds *synagōnizomai* and *synathleō* (Rom. 15:30; Phil. 1:27; 4:3) do not just convey the bearing of the same conflict as the apostle (Phil. 1:30), but a suffering with Christ while looking up to him (Heb. 12:1–4), "sharing in his sufferings" (Phil. 3:10), being "poured out like a drink offering on the sacrifice and service coming from your faith" (Phil. 2:17; cf. 2 Tim. 4:6), and completing "what is still lacking in regard to Christ's afflictions, for the sake of his body, which is the church" (Col. 1:24). Therefore, the *agōn* with all its sufferings brings joy to the Christian, the joy of the team that is indebted to its captain for the victory.

See also *athleō*, compete (*123*); *brabeion*, prize (*1092*); *thriambeuō*, lead to a triumphal procession (*2581*); *nikaō*, be victorious (*3771*).

75 (agōnia, agony, anxiety), → *74.*

76 (agōnizomai, fight), → *74.*

77	Ἀδάμ

Ἀδάμ (*Adam*), Adam (*77*).

OT Adam (probably from the common Sem. root *'dm*, [to be red], Heb. *ᵃdāmâ*, the red arable soil in contrast to the lighter colored desert) is a collective term for humankind, people. A single person is called *ben-'ādām* (lit., son of man). *'ādām* is the ordinary Heb. word for a human being.

Adam as a proper name is found in the OT only in Gen. 4:25; 5:2–5; 1 Chr. 1:1 (possibly also Gen. 2:20; 3:17, 21). Only Gen. 2–3 is of importance for the use of Adam in the NT, which tells how, in spite of the goodness of God's creation, humanity experienced evil and death.

When God created heaven and earth, he formed the man out of the earth and breathed the breath of life into him (Gen. 2:7; cf. Ps. 104:29–30). Hence human beings are entirely dependent on God. Without his sustenance they are only a pile of earth.

To give the first man an understanding of his true nature, God brought him the animals to be named, at which time he realized that they could not be a real partner for him. This prepared him for the creation of woman as his partner. A human being is really human only when he or she is with other human beings. This occurs above all in the mutual relationship of husband and wife.

The first human beings were allotted a place to live in, a garden containing the tree of life, where uninterrupted life with God was to be found. There was also the tree of the knowledge of good and evil. The fact that the first couple was not allowed to approach it and take of its fruit suggests that though evil existed, God desired at first to spare them the knowledge of all that it involved, for only God himself could overcome it.

But then the cleverest of the animals (the serpent) attacked humankind at its most vulnerable spot. It suggested that God was leaving them foolish and ignorant so that he might not lose his unique authority. The result of Adam and Eve's transgression (→ *parabasis*, sin, *4126*) was not that God was no longer God, but that human beings experienced evil—first subjectively in the experience of shame (3:7), then objectively through death and God's curse. Evil affected the relationship of humans and animals (3:15, "enmity"), woman and childbirth, one's work, and personal relationships (3:16–19).

NT 1. In Pauline theology Adam as a type is important (see 3 below). The name Adam is found 9x in the NT. Jude 14, quoting *1 Enoch 1:9*, mentions Enoch as the seventh from Adam, the first man. In Lk. 3:38 Adam is mentioned last in the genealogy as "the son of God." Luke wishes to affirm that Adam, and with him the whole human race, is of divine origin (cf. Acts 17:28). His purpose is probably to show that Jesus is the revealer for all humanity and not only for Jews. Jesus reveals what was intended by Adam, as the representative of humankind. Note too that Jesus is the only one after Adam who is said to be of divine origin (Lk. 1:34–35).

2. A different question is in view in 1 Tim. 2:13–15 when it says that Adam was formed first, then Eve; and Adam was not deceived, but the woman was deceived and became a transgressor. Paul's main point in this section is that Eve was the one who succumbed to the blandishments of the serpent.

3. In Rom. 5:12–21; 1 Cor. 15:20–22, 45–49, Paul sets out the contrast between the old and new ages, between humanity under sin and under salvation, by a typological parallelism of Adam and Christ, where Adam is the type and Christ the antitype (→ *typos*, image, *5596*).

(a) The transgression of God's commandment brought about a loss of trust in both God and other human beings (see Gen. 3). Thus, Paul writes, "Sin entered the world through one man" (Rom. 5:12, → *hamartia*, sin, *281*). The thought here is not that of the transmission of sin by physical inheritance, but of the creation of a situation of mutual mistrust that no one can avoid. Hence, sin permeates the whole of humanity.

(b) Death is not the natural result of sin but God's judgment on it (Rom. 6:23). Hence death came through sin to all human beings (5:12), or put more briefly, "In Adam all die" (1 Cor. 15:22).

(c) Before the giving of the Mosaic law, human beings did not sin as Adam did (Rom. 5:14). In contrast to Adam and those under the law, they had no express commandment. They died because they had sinned, but there was no exact bookkeeping. Sin takes on the explicit character of transgression and disobedience directed against God in the light of the law (Rom. 7:7–11). To that extent Adam typifies fallen humanity before God.

(d) Adam is also a type of that which is to come—the age to come, the kingdom of God (Rom. 5:14). The sentence, "For as in Adam all die, so in Christ all will be made alive" (1 Cor. 15:22; cf.

Rom. 5:14–19), means that humanity, which has lost its real life through sin, is typified by Adam. The Risen One is the personal agent of new life, for he represents the beginning of the general resurrection of the dead (1 Cor. 15:20). In Jewish thought this was linked with the beginning of the new creation, the forgiveness of sins (cf. Rom. 4:25; 1 Cor. 15:17). This creates for all the possibility of being freed from the compulsion to sin, the root of which is mistrust of God.

The Risen One is the beginning of a new humanity, for he accepted the validity of God's sentence of judgment, allowing God to be God. He put his trust in him alone and expected from him nothing but what was good. In so doing, he undid humanity's basic sin, that of Adam (Gen. 3).

(e) When Paul speaks of Jesus as Adam's antitype, he uses the idea of "the second man" (1 Cor. 15:45–49). The term suggests the true, original man who came into the world to impart the saving truth by which he himself lived. Whatever personalities Jud. may have expected in the last days, Jesus as the Risen One exceeded all expectations, for in his individual person he represented the general resurrection, and with it the advent of the kingdom of God, the new creation, and the forgiveness of sins (1 Cor. 15:24–26; Col. 1:18).

Paul may have used this picture to express to the Greeks and the Hel. world the message proclaimed to Palestinian Christians of the resurrection, the advent of the kingdom of God, and the forgiveness of sins. The Greeks conceived of salvation as the truth, the "idea" that lies behind the world and has been obscured by the transitory, vain world of appearances. Therefore, only the original man can bring about the true being of humanity, for he incorporates the original purpose of God for humankind. But this true man, Paul says, is not Adam but Christ. As the original man revealed in the resurrection, Jesus can make the new creation a reality for the Greeks.

4. Paul insists on the corporeality of the resurrection body. Resurrection does not mean that the spiritual element in human beings is now with God. What makes us sinners is not the fact that we exist in "flesh" as transient beings, but that we live "according to the flesh" (→ *sarx*, flesh, *4922*). That is, we allow ourselves to be determined by that which is transitory in our lives. Hence, resurrection is not without a body. The corporeality given to humanity at creation is not that given at the resurrection. The original man is not merely the simple original picture of humankind; the concept is eschatological. The Risen One brings us a new and for us unknown existence with God (1 Cor. 15:44–54.). Hence the new creation is more than a mere restoration of the original; it brings into being something new and until now unknown.

See also *eikōn*, image (*1635*); *anthrōpos*, man, human being (*476*); *Heua*, Eve (*2293*).

80 (adelphē, sister), → 81.

81	ἀδελφός

ἀδελφός (*adelphos*), brother (*81*); ἀδελφή (*adelphē*), sister (*80*); ἀδελφότης (*adelphotēs*), brotherhood (*82*); φιλάδελφος (*philadelphos*), loving one's brother or sister (*5790*); φιλαδελφία (*philadelphia*), love for brother or sister (*5789*); ψευδάδελφος (*pseudadelphos*), false brother (*6012*).

CL & OT 1. *adelphos* (a compound word from *delphys*, womb, and *a*, not; hence one out of the [same] womb) was originally used for brother in the physical sense, while *adelphē* was a sister. The masc. pl. covered all the children of a family. Soon it came to signify all close relatives, such as nephew, brother-in-law, etc. Later it metaphorically came to mean companion, friend. In the addressing of letters, *adelphos* was also applied to a fellow official or a fellow member of a society. Members of a religious group could call each other brothers. In some elements in Gk. philosophy, brotherhood was understood from the standpoint of a universal humanity.

2. *adelphos* in the LXX is similarly used for a physical brother and *adelphē* for a physical sister (Gen. 4:8–11; 12:13; 44:20). Gen. 29:12 (NIV relative) indicates that it could be applied to other relatives as well. Examples also occur of *adelphos* being used for fellow Israelites (i.e., ancestors of Jacob's sons; see Ps. 22:22). In Exod. 2:11 Moses' fellow Hebrews are called brothers (NIV "his own people"; cf. Gen. 16:12; Deut. 2:4). In Gen. 19:7 Lot calls the Sodomites brothers.

Hosea uses the words son and brother in his picture of God's relationship to his people (Hos. 1:10–2:1[Heb. 2:1–3]). Here we see the transference of brother from physical to spiritual relationships. Deut. 15:1–11 demands love for the poor brother; here brother and neighbor become synonymous. In the command to love (Lev. 19:17–18), brother and neighbor are used interchangeably. The difference between *plēsion* (neighbor) and *adelphos* in the OT is that the latter includes blood relationship. In religious use there is little difference.

3. In Qumran texts, brother refers only to members of the Qumran community, which considered itself the true Israel. They could hate all others. The rabbis made a stricter distinction between brother and neighbor. The former was any adherent to Jud. (including proselytes), while neighbor was a non-Israelite inhabitant of the land.

NT 1. The same variety of uses for *adelphos* (343x) and *adelphē* (25x) occurs in the NT as in the OT. This fact creates the differences of interpretation concerning the brothers and sisters of Jesus (Mk. 6:3 par.; 3:31–35 par.; Jn. 7:5; Acts 1:14; 1 Cor. 9:5). Were they children of Joseph from an earlier marriage (Orthodox interpretation), close relatives of Jesus (Roman Catholic interpretation), or later children of Joseph and Mary (general Protestant interpretation)?

2. *adelphos* sometimes means fellow Israelites in the NT (e.g., Acts 2:29; 3:17; 22:1). In Rom. 9:3 Paul defines them as "brothers . . . according to the flesh" (lit. trans.). Note that Paul does not use *adelphoi* when speaking to a Gentile audience (Acts 17:22). Christians are the new people of God (2 Cor. 6:16–18; Heb. 8:8–12; 1 Pet. 2:9–10). Hence the word *adelphos* was applied to fellow Christians (Acts 15:32–33, 36). The decision of the apostolic council explicitly applied the term to Gentile Christians (15:23).

The NT uses the terminology of the family of God (cf. Gal. 6:10) far more commonly than that of the people of God. God is the Father. Through faith in Jesus Christ Christians become his sons and daughters (cf. Rom. 8:14; 2 Cor. 6:18; Gal. 3:26; → *huios*, *5626*) or his children (Jn. 1:12–13; Rom. 8:16–17; → *teknon*, *5451*). All this makes intelligible the use of *adelphos* as a title for a brother in the faith. The children of God are his household (Eph. 2:19).

The coming of Jesus underlines the sharp distinction between relationship to God and relationship by birth. Jesus, for example, pointed up the tension in his own life (Mk. 3:31–35 par.; 13:12–13 par.) and demanded that, if need be, one should leave one's natural family for the new community (10:28–31 par.; Lk. 14:26).

Jesus is the one and only natural Son of God. But he is also the firstborn brother of believers (Rom. 8:29), "the firstborn over all creation" (Col. 1:15), and "the firstborn from among the dead" (1:18; cf. Rev. 1:5). In his humiliation he became the brother of believers (Heb. 2:11–12, 17). Thus, Jesus can speak of his disciples as his brothers (Mk. 3:33–35 par.). Yet even as brother he remains Lord. So Paul calls himself the *doulos*, slave, of Christ, and the *adelphoi* he entitles *syndouloi*, fellow slaves (Col. 1:7; 4:7).

3. Because Jesus became our brother, we are brothers of one another. The ruling principle in this brotherhood is *agapē* (love, → *26*; cf. esp. 1 Jn.), a uniquely Christian perspective. When Paul addresses Christians as *adelphoi* (pl.), he prefers to add *agapētoi*, beloved (1 Cor. 15:58; Phil. 4:1). The spiritual community is based on the love of God, which creates a new reality from God among humankind.

Love as typified in natural relationships is sometimes expressed by *philia* (→ *5797*). Note esp. its use in compound terms like *philadelphos*, "love as brothers" (1 Pet. 3:8), and *philadelphia*, "brotherly love" (Rom. 12:10). It has been attracted to the superior concept of *agapē* and, applied to love among people, has become a synonym of it. The same is true of the concept *adelphotēs*, brotherhood (1 Pet. 2:17; 5:9).

The professing Christian who does not obey God, esp. the command to love his or her brother, is still walking in the dark (1 Jn. 2:9). Anyone spreading false teaching or accepting it is a *pseudadelphos*, false brother (2 Cor. 11:26; Gal. 2:4). By one's actions one excludes oneself from fellowship with God and no longer belongs to his family.

4. It should be noted that the NT demands love for the brother and love for the neighbor equally. This means that the two terms are considered synonymous as far as their claim on us is concerned. But we can make a distinction with regard to the object of love. Those passages that demand love for one's neighbor (*plēsion*, → *4446*) look directly or indirectly to Lev. 19:18. This presumes that love is to extend beyond the circle of those to whom one is linked by physical or spiritual relationship. Since in Matt. 5:43–48 the command to love includes one's enemies, any limits one may give to *adelphos* are transcended. The scope of human love is as wide as the scope of God's salvation.

See also *plēsion*, neighbor (*4446*); *hetairos*, companion, friend (*2279*).

82 (adelphotēs, brotherhood), → *81.*

87	ᾅδης

ᾅδης (*hadēs*), Hades, the underworld, the realm of the dead (*87*).

CL & OT 1. *hadēs* occurs in Homer as the proper name of the god of the underworld; in the rest of Gk. lit. it stands for the underworld as the abode of the dead, who lead a shadowy existence there. After Homer it can mean the grave, death. Only gradually did the Greeks also attach to this concept the ideas of reward and punishment. The good and the righteous were rewarded in *hadēs*, while the wicked and the godless received a variety of punishments.

2. In the LXX *hadēs* occurs more than 100x, most of them to translate Heb. *šeʾôl*, the underworld that receives all the dead. It is a land of darkness, in which God is not remembered (Job 26:5–6; cf. 10:21–22; Ps. 6:5; 30:3, 9; 115:17; Prov. 1:12; 27:20; Isa. 5:14). The dead are cut off from him and outside his activity in history (Ps. 88:3–5). In death there is no proclamation or praise (Isa. 38:18; cf. Ps. 88:11). The dead are unclean and therefore, in contrast with surrounding religions, Israel's dead enjoyed no sacral worship. Necromancy was expressly forbidden (Deut. 18:11). No Israelite comforted himself or herself with the hope of one day being reunited with the departed. The shades themselves suffer under their decay (Job 14:21–22).

By contrast, *šeʾôl* not only lies on the border of life in the beyond but also penetrates the circle of the living on every side—through illness, weakness, imprisonment, oppression by enemies, and death. Thus the psalmist acknowledges that he has already in a sense been in *šeʾôl* but has been rescued by Yahweh. Wherever the voice of Yahweh is not heard or he abandons a person, the reality of death and *šeʾôl* begins (Job 12:24–25). Dying, therefore, is not merely a biophysical process; it is the ending of one's life relationship with Yahweh. Nevertheless, Yahweh's power does not cease at the frontier of *hadēs* (Ps. 139:8; Amos 9:2). Only exceptionally in the OT did faith (Job 14:13–22) or poetic imagination (Isa. 14:9–20; Ezek. 32:20–32) concern itself with the realm of the dead. There are isolated hints of hope beyond death (cf. Job 19:25–27; Ps. 49; 73:23–28; Dan. 12), where the possibility of resurrection appears.

2. In rab. Jud., under Persian and Hel. influence, the doctrine of the immortality of the soul appeared, and this altered the concept of *hadēs*. The earliest attestation of this doctrine is *1 Enoch* 22: Reward and punishment begin, after death, in *hadēs*. According to Josephus, this was the position of the Pharisees and the Essenes, in contrast to that of the Sadducees. A later view states that the souls of the righteous, after death, enter heavenly blessedness, while the souls of the ungodly are punished in *hadēs*. Thus, *hadēs* has lost its role as the resting place of all souls and become a place of punishment for the ungodly.

NT 1. In the NT *hadēs* occurs 10x (only in Matt., Lk., Acts, and Rev.). Hades lies within the earth, so that one has to go down to it (Matt. 11:23; Lk. 10:15). It is a prison (*phylakē*, 1 Pet. 3:19; Rev. 20:7; → *5871*). Like a city or town it has gates (Matt. 16:18) and is locked with a key that Christ holds in his hand (Rev. 1:18). Those gates will never imprison any who belong to the messianic community. In Rev. 20:13–14 Hades is personified; at the resurrection it must give up its dead. Thus, it is not an eternal but only a temporary place or state. According to Acts 2:27, 31 and Lk. 16:23, 26, all the dead are in Hades. According to other passages, however, only the spirits of the ungodly are there (1 Pet. 3:19; Rev. 20:13–14).

2. Jesus has risen to an eternal life (Heb. 7:16). He has conquered the power of death and the devil (2:14) and is Lord both of the dead and of the living (Rom. 14:9). According to the NT, Hades cannot affect the church (Matt. 16:18–19; 1 Pet. 3:19–22; 4:6; Rev. 1:18). Any Christian who dies is united with Christ (2 Cor. 5:8; Phil. 1:23)—even though that person is naked (i.e., without a body, 2 Cor. 5:2–3), in the heavenly Jerusalem (Heb. 12:22), under the heavenly altar (Rev. 6:9), or before God's throne (7:9; 14:3). Christ preached to the spirits in prison (1 Pet. 3:19–20; 4:6). His saving work embraces the dead, and nothing is beyond his grace.

3. The fact that in the NT there is no description of the geography of the beyond must be connected with this emphasis on the all-embracing dominion and grace of Christ. This is in sharp contrast to descriptions in certain rab. and Christian writings, down to Dante's *Divine Comedy*. Perhaps, however, it was the silence of the NT about these details that excited the curiosity of the pseudo-pious and led to dissatisfaction with placing one's hope in Christ alone. Yet another factor contributing to this expansion was the substitution of the Gk. doctrine of the immortality of the soul in place of the NT doctrine of the resurrection of the dead (1 Cor. 15).

See also *abyssos*, abyss, pit, underworld (*12*); *geenna*, Gehenna, hell (*1147*); *katōteros*, lower (*3005*); *tartaroō*, sent to Tartarus, hell (*5434*).

88 (adiakritos, unwavering, impartial), → *1359.*

89	ἀδιάλειπτος

ἀδιάλειπτος (*adialeiptos*), unceasing, constant (*89*); ἀδιαλείπτως (*adialeiptōs*), unceasingly, constantly (*90*).

CL & OT Both the adj. and the adv. are comparatively rare in cl. Gk. In the LXX only the adv. occurs and then exclusively in the Maccabean literature (1 Macc. 12:11, 2 Macc. 3:26; 9:4; 13:12; 15:7; 3 Macc. 6:33). It is also found in other intertestamental sources.

NT In Rom. 9:2 Paul describes "unceasing" anguish of heart for the Jews, for whose sake he could wish himself accursed and cut off from Christ (9:3). For although they are descended from Israel and have all God's promises, they are not truly of Israel. Paul's yearning for the salvation of Israel may be compared with Jesus' concern for Jerusalem (Matt. 23:37–39). In 2 Tim. 1:3 *adialeiptos* is used of Paul's constant remembrance of Timothy in his prayers.

The adv. *adialeiptōs* is likewise only found in the Pauline literature. In 1 Thess. 1:2 it is used of Paul's continual prayers for the Thessalonian Christians (cf. also Rom. 1:9). Likewise, Paul thanks God constantly for the response of the Thessalonians to the word of God (1 Thess. 2:13) and urges them to pray unceasingly (5:17).

See also *menō*, remain (*3531*).

90 (adialeiptōs, unceasingly, constantly), → *89.*

92 (adikeō, do wrong, commit injustice, deal unjustly, injure), → *94.*

93 (adikēma, unjust deed, a wrong), → *94.*

94	ἀδικία

ἀδικία (*adikia*), wrongdoing, unrighteousness, injustice (*94*); ἀδικέω (*adikeō*), do wrong, commit injustice, deal unjustly, injure (*92*); ἀδίκημα (*adikēma*), unjust deed, a wrong (*93*); ἄδικος (*adikos*), unjust (*96*); ἀδίκως (*adikōs*), unjustly (*97*).

CL & OT 1. (a) *adikeō* and its derivatives occur often in Gk. lit. As the initial *a* (alpha privative) indicates, they denote the opposite of the positive concepts *dikē*, *dikaiosynē*, and *dikaios* (→ *dikaiosynē*, righteousness, *1466*)—i.e., the unjust are the opposite of the just. The vb. *adikeō* means to commit an injustice; with an obj., deal unjustly with someone, injure, harm; in the pass., suffer injustice. The noun *adikēma* denotes the individual unjust deed. Unjust deeds can also be described as *adikia*, but this noun is used esp. for the concept of injustice. *adikos* is the adj. of both nouns, but it has a more general meaning of wrong, useless, not of a right nature.

(b) The meaning of words in this group are usually dependent on how justice is perceived at a certain time. *adikos* covers all that offends against morals, custom, norms, or decency (*dikē*), all that is unseemly, unspeakable, or fraudulent. What is "unjust" is not measured by laws laid down in writing, as is the case with *anomos*, lawless (→ *nomos*, law, *3795*).

(c) *adikia*, however, is frequently rooted in legal thinking. It is a synonym of *parabasis* (transgression, → *4126*) and can refer also to particular crimes such as theft, fraud, incest, etc. In lists of vices *adikia* is used as a general description of a wide range of things.

(d) These words are also used in a religious context. *adikeō* can mean the neglect of one's duties toward the gods. The unjust do not match up to the claims of the deity and are thus guilty before him. They offend *eusebeia*, reverence for God (→ *sebō*, revere, worship, *4936*).

2. (a) The LXX uses these words to translate a variety of Heb. equivalents (e.g., *adikeō* translates 24 different Heb. words). The adj. *adikos*, often used as a noun, and the adv. *adikōs* usually represent a word meaning deceit, fraud, lie (Ps. 63:11; Prov. 6:17; Jer. 5:31). *adikēma* is rare in the LXX and means an unjust act committed against the law or an offense against God (e.g., Lev. 16:16; Jer. 16:17). By far the most common of these words in the LXX is *adikia* (ca. 250x), which represents 36 different Heb. words; it usually means offense, guilt, punishment; in some cases perversity, wickedness (e.g., Hos. 10:13); violent act, injustice (e.g., Ps. 7:16); and lie (e.g., 119:104).

(b) The fact that *adikia* occurs mostly in the sing. shows that attention is focused not on the individual act but on the whole phenomenon of transgression. Sin in ancient Israel was above all an offense against the sacral order of divine justice (1 Sam. 3:13–14). As such, it affected the community, whose existence was intimately connected with the preservation of divine justice. Hence, sin in the OT is regarded as a phenomenon of theological and social import, as something that destroys the community. For that reason the covenant people must purge evil from their midst (cf. Lev. 16:21–33; 17:4, 9).

An offense that incurs guilt sets in motion a process of destruction whose effects recoil on the offender as well as the community unless the fateful connection of deed and consequence is broken (Gen. 4:13; Num. 32:23). The offense is, in the first place, regarded objectively as a harmful event even if it is committed in error (Gen. 20:3–7; 1 Sam. 14:24–45). These harmful effects can only be checked by the punishment of the offender, by the vicarious slaying of an animal, or by the offering of an atonement offering.

3. In the later OT writings and in Judaism *adikia* tended to be limited to the concrete individual act, but it was extended to apply to all people. In this context it is significant that occasionally the LXX translates *šeqer*, lie, by *adikia* (Ps. 52:3; 119:29, 69; 144:8, 11). Philo and Josephus mention *adikos* and *asebēs* in the same breath. Just as *dikaios* is prominent in Philo's teaching on virtue, so *adikos* is prominent in his teaching about wickedness. Jewish apocalyptic regarded the whole period before the coming of the Messiah as the "world of unrigh-

teousness" (*1 Enoch* 48:7), which the Messiah will destroy (91:5–13; *Pss. Sol.* 17:29, 36).

NT 1. (a) *adikeō* occurs only 28x in the NT, mostly in Acts and Rev. It means to act unjustly, harm in relation to other people (e.g., Matt. 20:13; Acts 7:24, 26, 27; Gal. 4:12). In Rev. it has things as its objects (6:6; 9:4). The pass. used with the meaning to suffer injustice is always found in the context of relations between human beings (Acts 7:24; 1 Cor. 6:7–8; 2 Cor. 7:12). *adikēma* occurs 3x. In Acts 18:14 and 24:20 it denotes a criminal act; in Rev. 18:5 it is parallel to *hamartia* and is used in relation to God. *adikia* is virtually limited to Lk.'s and Paul's writings, while *adikos* is occasionally used absolutely (e.g., Matt. 5:45; Lk. 18:11). Both of these denote behavior that does not conform to the moral norm. The adv. *adikōs* occurs only in 1 Pet. 2:19.

(b) These concepts become more theologically significant in contexts where they are contrasted with *dikaios*, just, and *dikaiosynē*, righteousness, justice (Acts 24:15; Rom. 3:5; 1 Pet. 3:18) or with *alētheia*, truth (e.g., Jn. 7:18; Rom. 1:18; 2:8). The NT's use of these words shows that we are dealing with commonly accepted categories of injustice, whose meaning in each case we discover only through a close examination. Hence we must seek to learn the meaning of each individual passage from its context or from what qualifies it or is contrasted with it.

2. *adikia* and *hamartia* (sin, → *281*) convey the most important concepts in the NT doctrine of sin. Of these *adikia* is, as in the LXX, the less specific and more varied in its nuances of meaning. The definition in 1 Jn. 5:17 juxtaposes the two. *hamartia* is the main idea; *adikia* probably means unjust deeds and injustice among human beings, which are not to be regarded as mortal sins but are to be forgiven.

In comparison with *hamartia*, *adikia* describes more powerfully the outwardly visible characteristics of that which stands under the power of sin. Hence, in the parable of the unjust steward, mention is made of "worldly wealth" (Lk. 16:9; lit., "mammon of unrighteousness"), in Jas. 3:6 of the injustice perpetrated by the tongue, and in Lk. 18:1–8 of the "unjust" judge.

3. (a) Paul never uses *hamartia* in Rom. 1:18–32, where he discusses various sins of the Gentiles, only *adikia* and *asebeia*. God's wrath rests on those who as his creatures should have known him and honored him (Rom. 1:18, 21, 25; 2:8). In 1:29 *adikia* is a comprehensive term at the start of a list of vices. Similarly, 1 Cor. 6:1 contrasts the unrighteous (i.e., Gentiles who do not yet recognize righteousness through faith and have thus fallen victims to their *adikia* and God's wrath) with the saints; the former will not inherit the kingdom of God (1 Cor. 6:9).

(b) The criterion for unrighteousness is God's righteousness (Rom. 3:5, 26; 9:14), which discloses human unrighteousness (3:5). The gulf opened by the contrast of God's righteousness and human unrighteousness is bridged by Christ, who as the righteous one stands in our place (3:24; 2 Cor. 5:21; cf. also 1 Pet. 3:18). A new division of the righteous and the unrighteous has appeared because the truth has been received (Rom. 1:18; 2:8).

Just as *adikia* was often used in the OT to mean lie, falsehood, so also Paul and John use *adikia* in contrast to *alētheia* (truth, → *237*; Jn. 7:18). The consequence of faith in Christ is not merely the elimination of sin as a power but also conversion to a life in righteousness (2 Thess. 2:9–12). Within the community there is no longer any place for legal litigation, so Paul in 1 Cor. 6:1–11 warns the Corinthians to cease from it and to prefer suffering unjustly (cf. 1 Pet. 2:19). The basis of this is that Christians are controlled by love (1 Cor. 13:6). A preoccupation with one's rights, which can lead to fighting against and suing a neighbor, is shattered by the love of one's neighbor and one's enemy. This idea, which is a continuation of the OT command to love one's neighbor (Lev. 19:13–18), goes back to Jesus himself (Matt. 5:43–48).

4. (a) This fundamental vision of the Christian life likewise shines through in later NT writings. In 2 Tim. 2:19 Paul warns the community that unrighteousness is incompatible with calling on God's name. Heb. 8:12 picks up the message of Jer. 31 regarding God's forgiving love in the new covenant and gives it a Christological interpretation, for Christ makes forgiveness for unrighteousness possible (1 Jn. 1:9).

(b) In 2 Pet. 2 the apostle emphasizes the final judgment and the condemnation of the *adikoi* (2:9, 13, 15).

(c) The ungodly world is judged in the apocalyptic final judgment described in Rev. This book frequently uses *adikeō* for judicial actions performed against human beings and things (2:11; 6:6; 7:2–3; 9:4, 10, 19; 11:5 [2x]; cf. 22:11).

See also *hamartia*, sin (*281*); *parabasis*, overstepping, transgression (*4126*); *paraptōma*, transgression, trespass, false step, sin (*4183*).

96 (*adikos*, unjust), → *94*.

97 (*adikōs*, unjustly), → *94*.

99 (*adokimos*, not standing the test, worthless, disqualified, unfit), → *1511*.

104 (*adynateō*, to be impossible), → *1539*.

105 (*adynatos*, powerless, impotent), → *1539*.

106 (*adō*, sing), → *6046*.

109 (*azymos*, unleavened, made without yeast), → *2434*.

| *113* | ἀήρ | ἀήρ (*aēr*), air (*113*). |

CL & OT According to cl. concepts, *aēr*, air, filled the space between the earth and the moon. The Greeks considered it impure and was thus the home of the spirits.

NT *aēr* appears 7x in the NT. It is used (a) for the space above us (Acts 22:23; 1 Thess. 4:17; Rev. 16:17); (b) in idioms: beat the air (1 Cor. 9:26), speak into the air (14:9); (c) in connection with God's judgments (the smoke from the abyss [→ *abyssos*, *12*] darkens it and the sun [Rev. 9:2]; an angel pours his bowl of wrath into it [16:17]).

Since the air fills the space between heaven and earth, it is the place where Christ meets the church at the Parousia (1 Thess. 4:17). Satan is the evil spirit who rules "the kingdom of the air" (Eph. 2:2; cf. 6:12) and is at work in the godless. That is, the evil spirits are subservient to the ruler of the realm of darkness.

See also *daimonion*, demon, evil spirit (*1228*); *ekballō*, expel, send out (*1675*); *diabolos*, devil (*1333*).

114 (*athanasia*, immortality), → *2505*.

| *119* | ἀθετέω | ἀθετέω (*atheteō*), set at naught, reject (*119*). |

CL & OT In cl. Gk. *atheteō* means to set aside a treaty or promise, to break faith, and in general to deny and do away with what has been laid down.

In the LXX *atheteō* is frequently used for breaking faith with God and other human beings, and for profanely disregarding and abusing something holy (e.g., God's sacrifice, 1 Sam. 2:17; God's law, Ezek. 22:26).

NT In the NT, the word is used for acts of irreligion: rejecting God (1 Thess. 4:8), his command (Mk. 7:9), his purpose (Lk. 7:30), Jesus Christ (Lk. 10:16; Jn. 12:48), God's grace (Gal. 2:21), Moses' law (Heb. 10:28), one's first faith (1 Tim. 5:12), and "dominion" (Jude 8)—probably the authority of Christ in his ministers. Exceptions to this meaning occur in Mk. 6:26; 1 Cor. 1:19; Gal. 3:15.

See also *katargeō*, abolish, nullify (*2934*); *exoutheneō*, reject with contempt (*2024*).

| *123* | ἀθλέω | ἀθλέω (*athleō*), compete (*123*); ἄθλησις (*athlēsis*), contest (*124*); συναθλέω (*synathleō*), contend with (*5254*). |

CL & OT The word group *athlēsis*, *athleō*, *synathleō* is used for sporting contests. It may, however, be used metaphorically of anything requiring effort.

NT Of the four NT passages that contain forms of *athleō* (2 Tim. 2:5; *synathleō* Phil. 1:27; 4:3; *athlēsis* Heb. 10:32), three are connected with suffering. In the Heb. passage the accompanying *theatrizomenoi* indicates the crowd of spectators who are present at the abuse and torture, as in 4 Macc. 17:14–17.

See also *agōn*, fight (*74*); *brabeion*, prize (*1092*); *thriambeuō*, lead to a triumphal procession (*2581*); *nikaō*, be victorious (*3771*).

124 (*athlēsis*, contest), → *123*.

125 (*athroizō*, gather together), → *5251*.

130 (*Aigyptios*, Egyptian), → *131*.

| *131* | Αἴγυπτος | Αἴγυπτος (*Aigyptos*), Egypt (*131*); Αἰγύπτιος (*Aigyptios*), Egyptian (*130*). |

OT In the LXX, *Aigyptos* translates Heb. *miṣrayim*, a word of uncertain meaning. The significance of Egypt in the OT may be surveyed under seven heads. (1) It is first of all part of God's world. In Gen. 10:6, 13, *miṣrayim* (LXX, *Mesrain*) appears as an ancestral or eponymous figure for Egypt and the Egyptians, securing them their place in God's world among the families of the earth. At the opposite extreme from the Euphrates, the Nile of Egypt was an outermost bound of the lands covenanted with Abraham (Gen. 15:18). Culturally, Egypt was a land of great antiquity (cf. Isa. 19:11), known for luxurious products such as fine linen (Prov. 7:16; Ezek. 27:7) and dashing chariots and steeds (1 Ki. 10:28–29; Song 1:9). Though it was a powerful country, it was subject to God's summons (Zech. 14:18–19). The sweeping onset of her annual Nile flood was used as a symbol of devastating judgment on Israel (Amos 8:8; 9:5).

(2) Egypt was a place of refuge and sojourn. After Bethel (cf. Gen. 12:8), Abraham, pressed by famine, sought deliverance not from God but in Egypt (12:10–13:1). From there he brought Hagar, by whom he and Sarah sought a human solution to their childlessness (Gen. 16). In due time (cf. 15:13–14), Egypt was the divinely provided refuge for Israel's family (Gen. 37; 39–50) through Joseph (45:7–8; 50:20).

(3) In OT tradition, Egypt became above all else "the land of slavery," from which God saved Israel by his might and wonders (Exod. 20:1) at the exodus (Exod. 1–15). This deliverance was recalled in the desert (Exod. 23; 32; Lev. 11:45; 25:38; etc.) and impressed Israel's foes (Jos. 9:9; 1 Sam. 4:8; 6:6). Forever after it reechoed down the centuries as a major starting point for Israel as a nation. The psalmists sang of it (e.g., Ps. 78:12, 43, 51; 80:8; 106:7, 21), and the prophets swelled the chorus (e.g., Jer. 2:6; Ezek. 20; Dan. 9:15; Hos. 12:9, 13; Amos 2:10; 9:7; Hag. 2:5). Israel came forth from Egypt as God's "son" (Hos. 11:1).

(4) Egypt further became a symbol of spiritual bondage, e.g., of servitude to idolatry in future exiles (Hos. 8:13 and 9:3 in a context of Assyrian threat), although it would not again be the place of exile of the whole Hebrew nation (11:5). Future deliverances for Israel were to be measured by the Egyptian deliverance (Isa. 11:11; Hos. 11:11; Zech. 10:10).

(5) After the exodus period, Egypt's role in the OT varies— occasionally an ally (1 Ki. 3:1) or a refuge (1 Ki. 11:40; Jer. 26:21–23), sometimes an outright foe (1 Ki. 14:25–26; 2 Ki. 23:33–34), but above all as a snare, an object of misplaced confidence for help (e.g., 2 Ki. 17:4). Trust in Egyptian "strength" rather than in God's provi-

sion led to new forms of bondage (cf. Isa. 30–31; Jer. 2:18, 36; 37:5, 7; 41:17; 42–44; Ezek. 17:15; 23; Hos. 7:11, 16; 12:1).

(6) The Lord pronounced judgment on Egypt by his word through Isaiah (Isa. 19–20), Jeremiah (Jer. 46), Ezekiel (Ezek. 29–32), and even Joel (3:19), because of pride, self-assertion, and attacks on the covenant people.

(7) But Egypt was also to know restoration and divine healing. Along with Assyria and Israel it was to become God's people (cf. Isa. 19:19–25) and never again be a snare or be exalted over other nations (cf. Ezek. 29:13–16).

NT In the NT, Egypt's roles correspond to those in the OT. (1) At Pentecost, along with others, Egyptians heard God's works proclaimed in their own tongue (Acts 2:10). God was offering them salvation.

(2) Deliverance from Egypt at the exodus remained a paradigm of God's saving power (see Acts 7; 13:17), and Israel's subsequent unfaithfulness after the exodus was a paradigm of human sin (see Acts 7:39; Heb. 3:16; 8:9; Jude 5).

(3) Just as Israel and his family were divinely sustained in Egypt (Gen. 45:5, 7), from where God later called forth Israel as his "son" (Hos. 11:1), so the infant Jesus was taken into refuge in Egypt by divine command (Matt. 2:13), and from there he came forth in final fulfillment of Hosea's words (Matt. 2:15, 19) (→ *plēroō, 4444*).

(4) Egypt is also a symbol of worldliness and materialism. The author of Hebrews, in his account of the heroes of faith, recalls how Moses rejected Egypt's blandishments of rank and material treasures in favor of God's call to deliver his people (11:24–27). This theme of rebel worldliness in opposition to God finds focus also in Rev. 11:8, where the bodies of faithful slain lie in the street of a city "figuratively called Sodom and Egypt." Finally, Paul draws from Gen. 16 the example of Hagar/Ishmael and Sarah/Isaac to illustrate human legalistic devising and divine promise and fulfillment, and to make clear the distinction between law and grace. The former is born of human self-will, under law; the latter is the heir of promise, God's gift from above (Gal. 4:21–31).

132 (aidios, eternal), → *172.*

133	αἰδώς

αἰδώς (*aidōs*), modesty, reverence, respect (*133*).

CL & OT 1. (a) In cl Gk. the noun *aidos*, related to the vb. *aideomai*, to have respect for, stand in awe of, means awe, reverence, modesty. In contrast to *hybris*, pride, *aidos* signifies a respect for the established sacred institutions (e.g., home, marriage, laws of hospitality) or for the privileges of certain people (e.g., king, priest, orator). It also connotes fear of any damage or change to existing circumstances.

(b) At a later period *aidos* became an independent concept in individual ethics, signifying the Greeks' sense of self-esteem, honor, or shame. *aidos* in this sense came to be associated with *sōphrosynē*, prudence, discipline, and *eleutheria*, freedom, as the attitude of the worthy person. This word is limited in use to the language of the elite and to the ethics of the aristocracy in a society divided by a class system.

2. Heb. possesses no equivalent for *aidōs*. The word is found in the LXX only at 3 Macc. 1:19 in the sense of modesty and in 4:5 for reverence for age. The vb. *aideomai* occurs 7x in the LXX (5x in Macc.), meaning to stand in awe or show respect.

NT In the NT *aidōs* occurs only in 1 Tim. 2:9, where Paul writes that women should behave "with decency and propriety." The background of Greek and Stoic ethics is unmistakable, and the context (2:10) makes it clear moderation in dress is not being stressed here as much as "good deeds" as the true adornment of a woman. The noun also occurs in variant texts of Heb. 12:28, where it denotes reverence toward God.

See also *aischynē*, modesty, shame, disgrace, ignominy (*158*).

135	αἷμα

αἷμα (*haima*), blood (*135*).

CL & OT 1. Early on *haima* is used physiologically as the bearer of life and the life force. It is a prerequisite for both in human and animal life. It can also metaphorically denote lineage. Since blood is the seat of life, "shedding blood" becomes a synonym for "kill." Blood guilt had to be atoned for by blood.

haima gained special importance in cultic usage, for it was the most important element in sacrifices. Sacrificial blood was regarded as having strengthening and cleansing power. Greeks and Romans had blood sacrifices for the dead; originally blood was poured over the dead, then later onto the funeral pyre, and finally into the grave and on the grave mound.

Various blood rituals involving the drinking or sprinkling of blood, often including human blood, were employed esp. in magical rites to bring rain, welfare, love, or harm. The drinking of blood, esp. that of a killed enemy, brought strength and gave the gift of prophecy. In a blood covenant human blood was collected in drops in a cup and drunk in wine by all participants.

2. Like the classical world, the OT sees blood as the seat of life (Gen. 9:4; Lev. 17:11, 14; Deut. 12:23). God is the sole Lord of all life. He is sovereign over the blood and life of humankind (cf. Ezek. 18:4). Hence he avenges the shedding of innocent blood (Gen. 9:5; cf. Jer. 51:35–36 = LXX 28:35–36).

Animal blood also belongs to God. It is holy, and its consumption is forbidden on pain of death (Lev. 3:17; 7:26–27 = LXX 7:16–17; 17:10, 14; Deut. 12:23; 1 Sam. 14:32–34). The blood of the sacrificial animals is given back to God, being poured out at the base of the altar. It was used for sprinkling the altar (Exod. 29:16; Lev. 3:2), the high priest (Exod. 29:21), and the tabernacle veil (Lev. 4:6; Num. 19:4). Sacrificial blood also has power for atoning (Lev. 16:6, 15–19; 2 Chr. 29:23–24), purifying (Lev. 14), and sanctifying (Exod. 29:20–21) people. It belongs to the making of the covenant (24:6–8). Blood put on the doorposts protected the firstborn from death (12:22–23).

Later Jud. continued this understanding of blood. The idea of the holiness of blood esp. lived on. The expression *sarx kai haima*, flesh and blood, is a typical description of humankind in this period.

NT *haima* is found 97x in the NT. It is used for human blood, both lit. (Mk. 5:25; Lk. 13:1; Jn. 19:34) and fig. (i.e., shed blood, Matt. 23:35); in the combination *sarx kai haima*, flesh and blood (5x); for the blood of animals in general (Acts 15:20, 29; cf. Lev. 17) and the blood of sacrificial animals in particular (12x in Heb.); theologically most important, for the blood of Christ, where it is linked directly 25x with the saving significance of the death of Jesus; and as an apocalyptic sign (9x).

1. *haima* as human blood (Jn. 19:34) is the bearer of life (see NIV text note on Jn. 1:13). The expression shedding blood refers to a person's violent death at the hand of others (Rom. 3:15). This idea is to be understood in Heb. 12:4, "You have not yet resisted to the point of shedding your blood." In the same way the blood of Jesus can refer to his violent death, of which Judas (Matt. 27:4), Pilate (27:24) and Israel (27:25; Acts 5:28) are guilty.

God alone is the Lord of all life. Since he controls the blood and life of humanity, he avenges innocent human blood (Gen. 9:5), esp. the blood of the martyrs, of prophets and righteous men (Matt. 23:30, 35; Lk. 11:50–51), and of saints and witnesses to Jesus (Rev. 6:10–11; 16:6–7; 17:6; 18:24; 19:2) who lost their lives for the sake of God's word. Blood can denote the entire person in God's sight, for which each individual will have to give account to God. When Paul said, "Your blood be on your own heads" (Acts 18:6) and "I am innocent of the blood of all men" (20:26), he was looking back to Ezek. 3:17–19: Paul had fulfilled his task of proclaiming the gospel, and the Ephesians were solely answerable to God for their life both now and in eternity.

2. The expression *sarx kai haima*, flesh and blood, characterizes humanity's weakness and transitoriness and, ultimately, slavery to sin and death. Fear of death (Heb. 2:14–15) is an important sign of our fallen state as creatures (as "flesh and blood"). In our natural state we cannot share God's glory, for "flesh and blood cannot inherit the kingdom of God" (1 Cor. 15:50).

The severe limitations of human knowledge are bound up with one's incapacity as a result of sin. Only God has infinite powers of knowledge and revelation. Therefore, true knowledge of God is possible only by his own self-revelation. "This was not revealed to you by man (lit., flesh and blood), but my Father in heaven" (Matt. 16:17). This means the final abandonment of all effort to base the divine revelation on human authority (Gal. 1:16). Christians are engaged in a battle of faith with hostile powers, which are "not ... flesh and blood" (Eph. 6:12). Hence we cannot find weapons in our own psychological or moral powers, but must turn to God for aid.

3. The NT took over from the OT the concept of sacrificial blood. Heb. 9:7, 12–13, 18–22, 25; 10:4; 11:28; 13:11 mention the sacrificial blood of animals, which serves as a type of the superior blood of Christ, the NT antitype. Jesus' death has a reconciling significance, and his sacrificial blood brings forgiveness and sanctification, establishes peace with God, and provides the foundation of fellowship with him.

In practice the sacrifice was carried out by the *haimatekchysia*, the shedding of blood. This word is found in the NT only in Heb. 9:22 and cannot be found in non-Christian usage. In context, it refers primarily to the making of the covenant at Sinai (Exod. 24:5–8) and specifically to the killing of the sacrificial animal. Probably the word also includes pouring out blood at the base of the altar (29:12; Lev. 4:7, 18, 25, 30, 34; 8:15; 9:9), throwing it against the altar (Exod. 24:6; Lev. 1:5, 11; 9:12), and throwing it on the people of Israel (Exod. 24:8; Heb. 9:19). In Heb. 11:28 the pouring (or sprinkling) of the blood refers to the Passover sacrifice (Exod. 12:7, 13, 22–23). The OT gave typological expression to the power of the blood to remove sin and save. The NT sees in the death of Christ the ultimate significance and fulfillment of this idea.

Occupying a central position in NT thought is the blood of Jesus Christ (1 Pet. 1:2), the blood of Jesus (Heb. 10:19; 1 Jn. 1:7), the blood of Christ (1 Cor. 10:16; Eph. 2:13; Heb. 9:14), the blood of the Lord (1 Cor. 11:27), the blood of the Lamb (Rev. 7:14; 12:11). It derives its meaning from the sacrifices of the Day of Atonement (Lev. 16). It is sacrificial blood that Christ, in perfect obedience to God (Rom. 5:19; Phil. 2:8; Heb. 5:8), shed on the cross (Heb. 9:12–14). In his suffering and death Jesus offered the true sacrifice for the removal of sins and reconciliation with God.

By his blood Christ also ransomed and freed the church, the new people of God, from the power of the devil and other evil powers (Acts 20:28; Eph. 1:7; 1 Pet. 1:18–19; Rev. 5:9; 12:11). That blood justifies all who appropriate for themselves his sacrificial death (Rom. 3:25; 5:9) and cleanses them from their sins. God blots out the entire guilt of those who confess their sins to him in faithful trust (1 Jn. 1:7–10; Rev. 1:5; 7:14). Thus, it is possible to have a clear conscience before God (Heb. 9:14; 10:22; 13:18).

In the OT reconciliation and purification were two different, though related, actions. Reconciliation resulted from the bringing of the sacrificial blood into the Most Holy Place on the Day of Atonement; purification could be achieved at any time in the year outside the Most Holy Place. Both are given in the NT in the salvation through the blood of Christ.

In Jesus' blood lies the power for sanctification (Heb. 13:12). It also gives us access to God (Eph. 2:13, 18; Heb. 10:19), and we receive assurance of faith, confidence in prayer, and a changed life (1 Pet. 1:13–23). As the "blood of the covenant" (Matt. 26:28; Mk. 14:24; 1 Cor. 11:25; Heb. 10:29; 13:20), it is the basis of the new divine order, guaranteeing the promises of the new covenant (Jer. 31:31–34).

Blood is sometimes used fig. for the atoning work of Christ (Jn. 6:53–56; Rev. 19:13), the part being used for the whole saving act and work of Jesus (Eph. 1:7). In most of the passages that have been cited, however, one cannot simply substitute the death of Christ for the blood of Christ. Rather, the blood means the *application* of Jesus' death to the individual. This is clearly indicated in the phrase "the sprinkled blood" (Heb. 12:24). In the OT community reconciliation was carried out visibly with the blood of an animal. In the NT church it is an invisible spiritual reality through the blood of Jesus (1 Pet. 1:2; Heb. 9:13–14; 10:22). As believers appropriate the blood of Jesus, the power of his sacrificial death becomes theirs in all its effects.

4. Blood (and its color, red) symbolically express the eschatological terrors on earth and in heaven in the last days. Here too are direct links with the OT. The NT takes over from Joel the prophecy of the change in the moon's color (2:31[MT 3:4]; cf. Acts 2:20; Rev. 6:12). Similarly, blood and fire are used to picture war (Joel 2:30 [MT 3:3]; cf. Acts 2:19; Rev. 8:7). The change of water to blood refers to eschatological catastrophes (Exod. 7:17–21; Rev. 8:8; 11:6; 16:3–4). The blood of grapes, in the OT a metaphorical expression for wine (Gen. 49:11; Deut. 32:14), becomes a picture of the great judgment on the nations (Rev. 14:19–20; cf. Isa. 63:2–3), when God will destroy all powers opposed to Christ at the end of history.

136 (haimatekchysia, shedding of blood), → *135*.

139 (ainesis, praise), → *140*.

140	αἰνέω

αἰνέω (*aineō*), to praise (*140*); αἶνος (*ainos*), praise (*142*); αἴνεσις (*ainesis*), praise (*139*); ἐπαινέω (*epaineō*), praise (*2046*); ἔπαινος (*epainos*), praise (*2047*).

CL & OT 1. In cl. Gk. *aineō* meant to mention (esp. honorably and so to praise), and to vow, promise, or simply say. The noun *ainos* meant a saying that is esp. pregnant with meaning or is cleverly phrased, needing explanation. Thus, it also came to mean proverb, story, fable; praise, eulogy. The compound verb *epaineō* meant to approve, sanction; also to praise, give a public mark of esteem. The corresponding noun *epainos* meant praise, approval, agreement, song of praise (about a person; for a deity *hymnos*, song, hymn, was used; → *5631*).

2. The LXX uses *aineō* to translate the Heb. *hālal*, chiefly in the piel (e.g., 1 Chr. 16:4, 36; Isa. 62:9; cf. Ps. 18:3), though it translates other Heb. vbs. as well. Likewise, *epaineō* chiefly stands for *hālal* (e.g., Gen. 12:15; Jdg. 6:20; Ps. 10:3). The noun *ainesis* is relatively common in the LXX, while *ainos* and *epainos* are rare.

The LXX uses *aineō* only in the sense to praise. There is, however, a striking variation as regards the Heb., where *hillēl* is used in secular contexts (e.g., in Gen. 12:15, of a beautiful woman; in 2 Sam. 14:25, of a handsome man; in Ps. 10:3, of praise by the wicked; in Jdg. 16:24, of the praise of Dagon). The LXX tends to avoid *aineō* in its rendering of such passages, keeping it for the regular praise of God in proper worship, esp. in Ps. 146; 150. *epaineō* and *epainos* are used for the praise of God by his people, and also for praise among human beings.

NT 1. *aineō* occurs 8x in the NT (Lk. 2:13, 20; 19:37; Acts 2:47; 3:8, 9; Rom. 15:11 [quoting Ps. 117:1]; Rev. 19:5). *ainos* occurs only in Matt. 21:16 (quoting Ps. 8:2) and Lk. 18:43, *ainesis* only in Heb. 13:15. We find the usage of the LXX carried through rigorously; both vb. and noun are used only of the praise of God. The compounds *epaineō* and *epainos* are used for both God and human beings.

2. In contrast to cl. Gk., this word group in the NT does not mean praise for a special achievement; it is applied to the whole person and not merely to specific acts. The manner in which *epainos* and *epaineō* are used shows clearly that ultimately only God can give this recognition in his saving verdict on the day of judgment (Rom. 2:29; 1 Cor. 4:5; 1 Pet. 1:7). At the present time, however, an individual may receive praise from the church (2 Cor. 8:18), the apostle (1 Cor. 11:2, 17, 22), and authorities appointed by God (Rom. 13:3–4; 1 Pet. 2:14).

3. This word group is preferred where it is a question of the formal praise of God in thanksgivings, prayers, and hymns (Matt. 21:16; Lk. 2:13, 20; 18:43; 19:37–38; Acts 2:47; 3:8–9; Rom. 15:11; Eph. 1:3–6; Phil. 1:11). This praise is given in the present, but it reaches its full development in the new creation (Phil. 1:11; Rev. 19:5). *ainesis* occurs in the expression "sacrifice of praise" (Heb. 13:15), where the Christian's sacrifice is contrasted with Jewish sacrifices.

See also *eucharistia*, thanksgiving (*2374*).

141 (ainigma, riddle, indistinct image), → *4130*.

142 (ainos, praise), → *140*.

145	αἱρέομαι

αἱρέομαι (*haireomai*), choose (*145*); αἵρεσις (*hairesis*), sect, school, party, group (*146*); αἱρετικός (*hairetikos*), factious, heretical, heretic (*148*); αἱρετίζω (*hairetizō*), choose (*147*); διαιρέω (*diaireō*), distribute, divide (*1349*); διαίρεσις (*diairesis*), allotment, division (*1348*).

CL & OT 1. *haireō* (act.) is found frequently in cl. Gk. in the sense of take, seize, grasp, understand. But the mid. *haireomai*, take for oneself, seize for oneself, choose for oneself, is also commonly used. The noun *hairesis* denotes (a) taking, acquisition, conquest; (b) choice; (c) aspiration, inclination; and (d) purposeful decision or resolve. Thus it always contains an element of action and personal decision.

The adj. *hairetikos* describes someone who is capable of choice. *hairetizō* is an intensive form, meaning to choose someone. The derivative *diaireō* means to take apart or divide in order to differentiate (i.e., to distinguish, separate), then also to allocate. The noun *diairesis* similarly means dissection, distribution, allocation, and classification. As in the case of *hairesis*, the emphasis is on the action and only secondarily on the effect.

In later cl. writers and esp. in Hel. Gk., *hairesis* denotes the teaching or the school of a particular philosopher with which a person identifies by one's own choice. A school of philosophy, which gathered around the authoritative figure of its teacher, was defined by its dogmas, to which the followers assented. Plato used *dihairesis* as a term for the dialectic method, as employed for the purpose of classifying words.

2. This word group appears infrequently in the LXX. This may be due to the character of the OT concept of election, which was not based on the pattern of free, political choice or of complete freedom to choose a set of teachings or an outlook on life. *haireomai* occurs 11x and means choose, prefer, delight in. *hairesis* occurs 5x and denotes a freewill offering or free choice. More frequent is the intensive form *hairetizō*, choose, which is often used with *eklegomai* for God's act of choosing (cf. 1 Chr. 28:4, 6, 10; Ps. 25:12; 119:30). The sense of adoption is also present in some examples (Hag. 2:24; Mal. 3:17). *diaireō* is found chiefly in the sense of classify, apportion (cf. Gen. 32:7; Jos. 18:5; 1 Chr. 24:3–5; Ezek. 37:22). The noun *diairesis* usually means distribution, part, division (e.g., 1 Chr. 27:1–15), or even clan (Jdg. 5:16).

3. The writings of Philo and esp. those of Josephus contain a specific development of these nouns. *hairesis* was used to describe both Gk. schools of philosophy and the religious groups within Jud.— the Essenes, the Sadducees, and the Pharisees. The Heb. equivalent in rab. Jud. is *mîn*, which denotes a member of a sect (*hairetikos*), not the sect itself. The meaning of the word then underwent a decisive change, being used more often for a heretical sect in a bad sense. This change, which came around A.D. 100, eventually led to *mîn* being used not to distinguish between groups within the Jewish community, but to designate people of other faiths, e.g., Christians or gnostics. These people stood outside the believing community and were thus considered outside the sphere of salvation.

NT 1. In the NT *haireomai* occurs only 3x, always in the mid. voice. At Phil. 1:22 and Heb. 11:25 it has the weakened meaning of prefer.

Here it overlaps in meaning with *thelō* (→ *2527*) and *boulomai* (→ *1089*). *thelō* expresses more a sovereign decision with clear, resolute intent, whereas *boulomai* means a wish and desire based on asserted authority.

In 2 Thess. 2:13 *haireomai* has a specialized biblical meaning not found in cl. Gk., elect someone to something (here, God's election of the church to salvation). In this sense of God's elective decision, it is to be distinguished from *eudokeō*, have good pleasure (→ *2305*), which expresses God's sovereign choice, and *klēroō* (→ *klēros* [*3102*]), which promises to the chosen, as those called, their appointed destiny. *eklegomai* (→ *1721*), on the other hand, emphasizes the selective aspect of the choice, and *dechomai* (→ *1312*), acceptance and reception on the ground of God's good pleasure.

2. The NT meaning of *hairesis* follows the usage in Hel. Gk. and Jud. In Acts, where 6 of the 9 examples are found, it refers to the parties of the Pharisees and Sadducees as groups within the Jewish community (5:17; 15:5; cf. 26:5). From the Jewish point of view, Christians too are described as belonging to a sect, that of the Nazarenes (24:5; cf. 24:14; 28:22).

Because of its universal character, the Christian church did not view itself as a *hairesis*, i.e., a private, unauthorized school or party. Hence in Gal. 5:20 *haireseis* is listed as one of the works of the sinful nature. Justification for this is provided in 1 Cor.: Anyone who splits the church or breaks it up into parties is dividing Christ, whose body is the church (1 Cor. 1:10–13; 11:18–19; cf. 12:27). Paul draws a distinction between *haireseis* and *schismata*. Whereas the latter denotes splits in the church brought about by personally motivated disputes, *haireseis* add to the division an eschatological aspect. The ruinous *haireseis* are caused by activities of false teachers, who deny Christ (cf. 2 Pet. 2:1).

In contrast to cl. Gk., *hairetikos* is used in biblical Gk. for the adherents of a *hairesis*, i.e., a heretic. In Tit. 3:10 we see the church's procedure for disciplining heretics, following principles stated in Matt. 18:15–20 and 2 Jn. 10.

3. *diaireō* should be translated in the NT to divide, distribute (e.g., Lk. 15:12: "He divided his property between them"). In 1 Cor. 12:11 Paul speaks of the distribution of spiritual gifts, which the Spirit apportions to the members of the church as he wills. The noun *diairesis* occurs in the NT only in 1 Cor. 12:4–6 (3x), where it refers to the manifold nature of the gifts of the Spirit and their distribution among the members of the body in the unity of the single grace of God.

See also *eklegomai*, pick out for oneself, choose (*1721*).

146 (hairesis, sect, school, party, group), → *145*.

147 (hairetizō, choose), → *145*.

148 (hairetikos, factious, heretical, heretic), → *145*.

149	αἴρω

αἴρω (*airō*), to raise up, take away (*149*); ἐπαίρω (*epairō*), to lift up, take up (*2048*).

CL & OT 1. In cl. Gk. *airō* means to raise up or carry. When a ship raised its sail, it was ready to start out; thus the vb. came to mean to set sail or, more generally, to start out. The vb. was also used in the sense of raising someone's courage. Later it developed the additional meaning of to kill (i.e., to lift up and take away one's life, put an end to). *epairō* had a more metaphorical meaning of to arouse a person's emotions, to excite; also, to magnify, exalt.

2. Both of these words occur frequently in the LXX. *airō* often means simply to lift up and carry (e.g., Lev. 10:4–5; Jos. 3:3, 6). But it also had theological significance, as in lifting up one's hands (Ps. 28:2; 119:48), one's eyes (123:1) or one's soul (25:1) to the Lord, or in taking away, forgiving sins (1 Sam. 15:25; 25:28). *epairō* is essentially a synonym of *airō* (e.g., lift up one's eyes, Gen. 13:10; lift up one's hands, Ps. 134:2; cf. esp. 24:7, 9, which uses both *airō* and

epairō in parallel). Note, however, that Isa. 6:1 uses *epairō* when Isaiah sees the Lord exalted on his throne.

NT 1. *airō* is used 101x in the NT. In most cases, it simply means pick up, take away, carry (e.g., Matt. 14:12, 20; Mk. 2:3). In Jn. 19:15, the crowd calls for Pilate to take Jesus away and crucify him. In Rev. 10:5 an angel raises his right hand to swear an oath.

But *airō* also has fig. uses similar to the LXX. In Jn. 11:41, Jesus lifts up his eyes and prays to God (note how this verse uses the same vb. for taking away the stone from the tomb of Lazarus), and in Acts 4:24 the early Christians raise their voices in prayer to God. In Col. 2:14 Paul emphasizes that Jesus has taken away or removed our sins by nailing them to the cross, and John points out how the Son of God appeared "so that he might take away our sins" (1 Jn. 3:5). This is probably also the meaning of John the Baptist's affirmation about Jesus as the Lamb of God "who takes away the sin of the world" (Jn. 1:29).

Another specialized use of *airō* occurs in Matt. 16:24; Mk. 8:34; Lk. 9:23, where Jesus invites and challenges us to deny ourselves, "take up" our cross, and follow him. Our Lord calls us to a dedicated discipleship, even if it means martyrdom.

2. *epairō* occurs 19x in the NT. Similar to *airō*, it can denote crying out (lifting up one's voice, Lk. 11:27; Acts 2:14), seeing (lifting up one's eyes, Lk. 16:23; 18:13), and praying (lifting up one's hands to the Lord, 1 Tim. 2:8). Jesus "lifted up his hands" and blessed his disciples (Lk. 24:50), after which he was "taken up" into heaven (Acts 1:9).

151	αἴσθησις	αἴσθησις (*aisthēsis*), experience (*151*); αἰσθητήριον (*aisthētē-*

rion), organ of sense, faculty (*152*).

CL & OT 1. *aisthēsis* in cl. Gk. means perception by the senses (in contrast to knowledge through rational deduction), experience, sensation; in an ethical context it means judgment.

2. In the LXX *aisthēsis* is used predominantly in the wisdom literature, esp. meaning knowledge, wisdom, true insight; it frequently includes ethical discrimination and decision. *aisthētērion* is the organ where such discrimination is made (cf. Jer. 4:19). This insight stands in contrast to inexperience (Prov. 1:4), lack of discipline (12:1), and folly (15:7).Wisdom brings true knowledge of God (2:3–6), which begins with "the fear of the LORD" (1:7).

NT In the NT *aisthēsis* and *aisthētērion* are each used only once. In Phil. 1:9 Paul places "insight" (*aisthēsis*) and "knowledge" (*epignōsis*, → *ginōsko*, *1182*) side by side as two of love's expressions and functions. Knowledge is directed primarily toward God; discernment is necessary for human relationships, where it must distinguish between good and evil and judge accordingly (cf. esp. 1:10).

Heb. 5:14 says of "the mature" that they have their faculties (*aisthētēria*) "trained . . . to distinguish good from evil." The concrete organ of sense has here become virtually a habitual ability. It is a spiritual gift, however, that must be developed.

See also *ginōskō*, know, understand, comprehend, recognize (*1182*); *agnoeō*, not know, be ignorant (*51*).

152 (*aisthētērion*, organ of sense, faculty), → *151.*

153 (*aischrokerdēs*, greedy for base gain), → *158.*

154 (*aischrokerdōs*, greedy for money), → *158.*

155 (*aischrologia*, foul talk), → *158.*

156 (*aischros*, ugly, shameful, base, disgraceful), → *158.*

157 (*aischrotēs*, ugliness, wickedness), → *158.*

158	αἰσχύνη	αἰσχύνη (*aischynē*), modesty, shame, disgrace, ignominy (*158*);

αἰσχύνομαι (*aischynomai*), be ashamed, be put to shame, be disgraced, be confounded (*159*); ἀνεπαίσχυντος (*anepaischyntos*), not to be ashamed (*454*); ἐπαισχύνομαι (*epaischynomai*), be ashamed (*2049*); καταισχύνω (*kataischynō*), to dishonor, disgrace, put to shame; pass. to be dishonored, be disappointed (*2875*); αἰσχρός (*aischros*), ugly, shameful, base, disgraceful (*156*); αἰσχρότης (*aischrotēs*), ugliness, wickedness (*157*); αἰσχροκερδής (*aischrokerdēs*), greedy for base gain (*153*); αἰσχροκερδῶς (*aischrokerdōs*), greedy for money (*154*); αἰσχρολογία (*aischrologia*), foul talk (*155*).

CL & OT 1. (a) In cl. Gk. *aischynō* occurs almost exclusively in the mid. or pass. with the meaning to feel shame, be ashamed, or to be confounded, be disconcerted. *epaischynomai* is a strengthened form of the mid., and *kataischynō* of the act. and pass. meanings of *aischynō*. The noun *aischynē* has the subj. sense of modesty (understood as fear of what is *aischron*, ugly) and the obj. sense of shame (that which results from an *aischron*, shameful deed). *aischynē* is mainly a sociological concept; it exposes a person to the ridicule of society, which he or she tries to escape by being ashamed.

(b) *aischros* is used lit. and fig. in the sense of base (e.g., base gain). *aischrotēs* means ugliness.

2. (a) In general the LXX uses *aischynō* to mean to put to shame; *aischynē* means shame. This group of words is found most frequently in Isa., Jer., and Ps.; the emphasis is not on the sociological, but on the theological, aspect of *aischynō*. Frequently Yahweh is the implied or the stated subj. of *aischynō*, as may be seen from the pass. construction used as a circumlocution for God (cf. Isa. 1:29; 20:5; Jer. 2:26). The psalmists pray for (cf. Ps. 6:10; 35:26; 40:15) and the prophets foretell (Isa. 1:29; 41:11; Jer. 2:26) Yahweh's judgment, which will put their enemies and the ungodly to shame (Ps. 40:14; 83:16–18). Thus in the OT *aischynō* refers primarily to the obj. ruin of evildoers or of the whole nation (cf. 69:4–7, 19–20).

(b) In the sexual sense *aischynō* is found frequently in Ezek. (16:36–37; 23:10, 18) and in the normative statement in Gen. 2:25, "The man and his wife were both naked, and they felt no shame." Here shame in the body is the most primitive expression of the feeling of guilt, the sign of a lesion going through one's bodily nature and casting doubt on the unity of body and spirit. This disturbance results from an act of disobedience against Yahweh, and Adam and Eve react to the obj. loss of innocence, and the innermost disturbance of their relationship with God, by the feeling of shame (3:7).

NT This group of words is found much less often in the NT than in the LXX. The noun and vb. together occur only 11x, *aischros* 4x, *epaischynomai* 11x, *kataischynō* 13x, *aischrotēs* and *aischrologia* once each, and *aischrokerdēs* 2x. NT usage is closer to that of the LXX than that of cl. Gk.

1. (a) Mk. 8:38 and Lk. 9:26 use *epaischynomai* in the sense of to be ashamed. The point of reference is not, however, a virtue or vice, but one's confession of Christ. Being ashamed, i.e., submitting to fear of human ridicule, is rejected as conduct because it denies the eschatological and universal authority of the Son of Man (cf. 2 Tim. 1:8, 16; 1 Pet. 4:16).

(b) In a similar way to the prophets (cf. Jer. 8:9), Paul speaks in 1 Cor. 1:27 of God as actively putting to shame, i.e., nullifying, the wise and the powerful, while he chooses what is foolish and weak in the world, i.e., gives it standing and worth. Through the cross of Christ glory and shame have undergone an exchange of values. Similarly in Rom. 5:5, Paul affirms (lit.): "Hope does not put to shame," i.e., it does not rest on something that does not exist and hence will never disappoint us; instead, it rests on God's promises (cf. 8:24–25).

Rom. 1:16 uses *epaischynomai* as part of an early Christian confession. The negative phrase, "I am not ashamed," means positively, "I confess." The statement is not psychological but rather forensic: With the gospel I will not be put to shame. Paul takes up the same thought in a pass. form at 9:33, in a quotation from Isa. 28:16: The believer "will never be put to shame," i.e., his or her existence is secured (cf. also 1 Pet. 2:6). It is the apostle's continual concern that he should not be put to shame in his missionary work (2 Cor. 7:14; 9:4), i.e., that he not work in vain (cf. Gal. 2:2; Phil. 2:16; 1 Thess. 3:5). In 2 Tim. 2:15 it is Paul's wish that Timothy should not be ashamed of (*anepaischyntos*) the gospel but should rightly handle the word of truth. As in the OT, so in Paul's use of *kataischynō*, the primary meaning is obj., to be put to shame; human feelings of shame are the subj. side of the coin.

(c) The author of Heb. uses *epaischynomai* with reference to God's saving activity: Christ is not ashamed to call human beings his brothers and sisters (2:11), and God is not ashamed to be called their God (11:16). Christ even takes the public shame (*aischynē*) of death on the cross upon himself (12:2).

2. *aischynē* in the NT means shame suffered or self-inflicted (2 Cor. 4:2; Jude 13). Phil. 3:19 and Rev. 3:18 use *aischynē* with a sexual sense. *aischros*, disgraceful, is found in the NT chiefly in the phrase *aischron estin*, "it is a disgrace" (1 Cor. 11:6; 14:35; Eph. 5:12). Peter uses *aischrokerdē* (an adv. meaning greedy for money) to encourage "shepherds" to serve the church because they want to, motivated neither by guilt nor greed (1 Pet. 5:2). Finally, *aischrologia*, foul talk (Col. 3:8), and *aischrokerdēs*, greedy for base gain (1 Tim. 3:8; Tit. 1:7), are found listed in catalogues of sins.

See also *aidōs*, modesty, reverence, respect (*133*).

159 (*aischynō*, be ashamed, be put to shame, be confounded), → *158*.

160	αἰτέω

αἰτέω (*aiteō*), ask, ask for, demand (*160*); αἴτημα (*aitēma*), request, demand (*161*); ἀπαιτέω (*apaiteō*), demand back (*555*); ἐξαιτέω (*exaiteō*), ask for, demand (*1977*); παραιτέομαι (*paraiteomai*), ask for, request, excuse, refuse, decline (*4148*).

CL & OT 1. In cl. Gk. the basic meaning of *aiteō* is to ask or demand; mid., to ask (or desire) for oneself. The noun *aitēma*, therefore, means the thing asked for, in the sense of a request, desire, or demand. *apaiteō* intensifies the idea of demanding, usually in the sense of demanding back. *exaiteō* means to ask for oneself, while *paraiteomai*, because of the sense attaching to the prefix *par-*, means to ask to be released from an obligation, to present one's apologies.

2. The Heb. equivalent for asking, wishing, requesting for oneself is *šāʾal* (Deut. 10:12; Jdg. 5:25; 1 Sam. 12:13; Job 31:30; etc.). Used with reference to God, it approximates closely the idea of prayer and is often associated with thanksgiving for answered prayer (e.g., 1 Sam. 1:20; Ps. 105:40). In legal language it can mean to examine (Deut. 13:15), consult. *šāʾal* is rendered by *aiteō* generally when the desire is for something specific (e.g., Exod. 3:22; Jos. 14:12; Jdg. 5:25; 1 Sam. 12:17); Hannah asks for herself a son from Yahweh and Eli promises her "what you have asked of him" (1 Sam. 1:17). Similarly in Ps., whenever *aiteō* expresses a promise of answered prayer, it concerns a specific request (e.g., Ps. 2:8; 21:4; 27:4).

NT 1. In the NT *aiteō* and *aiteomai* occur 70x. It generally means to request, ask (for oneself). (a) On a human level the mid. form (*aiteomai*) is almost always used in addressing superiors (e.g., Matt. 14:7; 27:20; Lk. 23:23; Acts 9:2) and thus has an official flavor. In general, the act. form of the vb. (*aiteō*) has no special nuances. Only in Matt. 5:42 does *aiteō* have a trace of unpleasantness: to demand something unpleasant, or at least to ask in a way that the other person feels unpleasant (hence it can almost be translated here "accost"). Jesus emphasizes that his followers should respond even to requests such as these. The ethical implications should be noted: I am to overcome my reluctance and open both heart and hand to the person making the request, for the request is nothing less than God calling me to open my heart to him.

(b) In those passages where a request is made to God, no difference in meaning is discernible between the act. and mid. forms of

the vb. Such requests are supplicatory prayers (cf. Matt. 21:22), though in the NT other words can also be used (see the cross-reference entries at the end of this article). It is striking that *aiteō* is never used of Jesus' own requests and prayers, but always *deomai* or *erōtaō* (e.g., Lk. 22:32; Jn. 14:16; 16:23–26). This is presumably because *erōtaō* usually relates to asking a question and retains the flavor of intimate conversation.

(c) Wherever the NT speaks of requests made to God, it emphasizes that such requests are heard by God (cf. Matt. 6:8; 7:7–11; 18:19; 21:22; Mk. 11:24; Jn. 14:13–14; 15:7, 16; 16:23–24, 26; Jas. 1:5; 1 Jn. 3:22; 5:14–15). This fact encourages us to pray with certainty. If there is doubt in our hearts, prayer dies.

What is the basis for this certainty? In Matt. 7:8 the fact that requests are heard is stated as a basic principle of the kingdom of God: "Everyone who asks receives." On the basis of this principle, Jesus says: "Ask and it will be given to you" (7:7). The ultimate foundation of this principle is given in 7:9–11 (cf. also 6:8; Jn. 15:16; 16:23, 26–27; Col. 1:9–12): God is the Father who loves his own more than an earthly father loves his child and who therefore cannot permit their requests to be unavailing, but gives them what they need. In other words, certainty is based on God's fatherly goodness and love. Moreover, God is a living God who hears and sees and has a heart full of compassion.

As God deals with us, so should we deal with our neighbors and respond to their requests (Matt. 5:42). We are to give to them because we experience afresh every day the generosity and fatherly goodness of God.

(d) The NT repeatedly makes the point that the prayer that God hears must be the right kind of prayer. This is alluded to in Matt. 7:7–8, where the vbs. seek (*zēteō*, *2426*) and knock (→ *krouō*, *3218*) are used in parallel with ask. Frequently in the Bible, seeking has God as its obj. It denotes a God-oriented attitude on our part. True prayer must be in keeping with the nature of him to whom it is addressed, in which case our requests will be well-pleasing to God and according to his will (cf. 1 Jn. 5:14). To ask from God means to ask from him something right and good (Matt. 7:11). Lk. interprets this specifically as asking for the Holy Spirit (11:13). In other places true prayer is described as asking in faith (Matt. 21:22; Jas. 1:5–6). In prayer we are never to forget whom we are addressing: the living God, the Almighty One with whom nothing is impossible, and from whom therefore all things may be expected.

To doubt God is to do him an injustice, for it belittles his deity, misjudges his character, and therefore receives nothing from him (Jas. 1:7). True prayer is bound up with faith. Various Johannine passages expand the idea of asking in faith: Jesus' words must remain in us (Jn. 15:7); we must keep his commands and do what pleases him (1 Jn. 3:22); and we must ask in Jesus' name (Jn. 14:13–14; 15:16; 16:24, 26). Since such prayer is heard and since I can be certain of that fact, the result is joy (16:24). Matt. 18:19 may be relevant here: United prayer by several disciples indicates that all selfish desires have been renounced, for selfish prayer is false and receives nothing from God (Jas. 4:3; cf. Mk. 10:35).

2. When the obj. of *aiteō* is a subordinate person, it easily assumes the meaning to require, demand (Lk. 1:63; Acts 16:29); this is also true when a creditor demands back from a debtor goods given on loan or trust (predicated of God in Lk. 12:48). In 1 Pet. 3:15, "give an answer" (regarding the Christian's hope) means to demand proof of its truth and credibility, or simply to demand information.

This meaning throws light on the implications lying behind the Jews' demand for "signs" (1 Cor. 1:22; → *sēmeion*, *4956*). Those who take this attitude set themselves above God and call him to account; they are demanding that God should justify himself in relation to what he had done in Christ. It is little wonder that Jesus denied their request (Matt. 16:1–4, though *erōtaō* is used here).

3. (a) The noun *aitēma* occurs in its nonreligious sense in Lk. 23:24. In its religious sense, i.e., when addressed to God, it means a

request and esp. any individual request viewed in relation to its content (e.g., Phil. 4:6; 1 Jn. 5:15).

(b) The compound vb. *apaiteō* often carries the intensified meaning to demand, but is used particularly in the sense of reclaiming either stolen goods (Lk. 6:30b) or goods loaned out for a limited period (12:20, where God requires back a person's life).

(c) *exaiteō* occurs only in Lk. 22:31 in the sense of to demand that someone (Peter) be handed over. This demand was made by Satan to Peter's master, namely, God himself, with the alleged purpose of testing the genuineness and steadfastness of Peter's faith, but with the ulterior motive of bringing about his downfall.

(d) In Mk. 15:6 *paraiteomai* means to ask for someone's release, while in Lk. 14:18–19 it means to ask for one's own release (from the obligation of accepting an invitation). Should the obligation be considered intolerable, then the vb. can mean to refuse, decline (e.g., Acts 25:11, regarding the Roman death penalty; Heb. 12:19, 25, regarding God and his word) or to reject (e.g., 1 Tim. 4:7; 5:11; 2 Tim. 2:23). In Tit. 3:10, church disciplinary measures are in view. The act of rejection here acquires an official character, though whether it refers to official excommunication or merely to the breaking off of fellowship remains an open question.

See also *gonypeteō*, fall on one's knees, kneel down before (*1206*); *deomai*, ask, request, beseech, beg (*1289*); *proseuchomai*, to pray, entreat (*4667*); *proskyneō*, worship, do obeisance to, prostrate oneself, do reverence to (*4686*); *erōtaō*, ask, ask a question, request (*2263*); *krouō*, knock (*3218*); *entynchanō*, meet, turn to, approach, petition, pray, intercede (*1961*).

161 (aitēma, request, demand), → 160.

162	αἰτία

αἰτία (*aitia*), ground, cause, reason, charge (*162*); αἴτιος (*aitios*), responsible, guilty (*165*); αἰτίωμα (*aitiōma*), charge (*166*); ἀναπολόγητος (*anapologētos*), inexcusable (*406*); ἀναίτιος (*anaitios*), innocent (*360*); ἀνέγκλητος (*anenklētos*), blameless, irreproachable (*441*).

CL & OT 1. In cl. Gk. *aitia* means the ground or motive of a thought or action, in a causal sense the origin or occasion of a thing, event, or phenomenon. Nevertheless, *aitia* is seldom used in a good or neutral sense. Usually it carries the sense of charge, accusation, blame, indicating the responsibility and guilt that attaches to an act. Likewise *aitiōma*, a word not found before Acts but occurring in cl. Gk. in the form *aitiama*, means a charge against a wrongdoer. *aitios* means culpable, responsible. The compound adj. *anapologētos* is used in the same context to indicate the hopelessness of a case for the defense at law; it is found in the 2nd century B.C. with the meaning without excuse.

2. The LXX uses *aitia* consistently. It occurs over 21x, mostly in the Apocr. (esp. 1–4 Macc.). Apart from 4 Macc. 1:16, where the philosophical concept of causation dominates, the LXX uses deal with some event that belongs to the darker side of life: e.g., fighting (2 Macc. 4:42), idolatry (Wis. 14:27), death (18:18; 1 Macc. 9:10), sensual pleasure (Sus. 14). In Gen. 4:13, Cain cries out: "My punishment [*aitia*] is more than I can bear." The culpable act and the punishment as its inevitable consequence are for him causally related. Job 18:14 contains an aphorism on the inescapable destiny of the wicked to be smitten by a fatal disease (the LXX here differs from the MT, using *aitia* in its description of death as a kind of majestic stroke of fate). Prov. 28:17 concludes that "a man tormented by the guilt [*aitia*] of murder" will go to the grave wandering in insecurity.

3. *aitios* is used 7x in the LXX: 6x in the Apocr., where it means having become guilty, and at 1 Sam. 22:22, where David declares that he is "responsible for the death" of a family of priests. *anapologētos* and *aitiōma* do not occur in the LXX.

NT 1. *aitia* occurs 20x in the NT. Some texts use the word in a purely causal sense, stating the reason why something happens. Thus the woman with an issue of blood gives Jesus the reason why she touched him (Lk. 8:47). Peter inquires the reason for the visit by Cornelius's men (Acts 10:21). Timothy's mother and grandmother serve as a "reason" for a special reminder by Paul (2 Tim. 1:6). Similar uses are found in 2 Tim. 1:12; Tit. 1:13; Heb. 2:11. The noun *aitios* is used in Heb. 5:9 in a positive sense of Christ as the "*source* of eternal salvation for all who obey him."

2. *aitia* is also used in connection with legal charges and accusations brought against someone. At Matt. 19:3 the Pharisees ask whether divorce is lawful for "every reason," as though it were the inevitable consequence of such causes, whereas Jesus' answer makes possible a new beginning for the disordered marriage. In 19:10, however, *aitia* means a case or "situation." Possibly there is an allusion here to a concurrent discussion on the connection between marriage and discipleship, which presented a choice between a wife and the Lord (cf. 1 Cor. 7:32–35).

In Acts 22:24; 23:28; 25:18, 27, Luke writes about Paul's trials and is concerned to bring to light the ground of the charges against him or to show that they cannot be established. Acts 25:7 uses for such unprovable allegations the noun *aitiōma*, accusation (here only in the NT). *aitios* is used in a similar sense in the story of the disturbance led by Demetrius (Acts 19:40); there is danger that a charge will be laid against the city because of the disorder, for which no satisfactory "account" can be given.

3. A third grouping of NT texts has to do with the occasion for a death sentence. (a) The inscription on the cross specified the "charge" on which Jesus was condemned to death (Matt. 27:37; Mk. 15:26). This indicated to the onlookers that his execution was inevitable because of his claim to kingship. The Gospels, however, testify to a deeper necessity than the immediate human factors, for Jesus' death sprang from the purpose of God. In Acts 13:28 this "proper ground" of death is mentioned in a speech of Paul and is described as unjustified in terms of human justice.

(b) In the report of the trial before Pilate (into which are interwoven many legal ideas), Pilate pronounces his repeated conclusion that he can find no guilt in Jesus deserving death (*aitia* in Jn. 18:38; 19:4, 6; *aitios* in Lk. 23:4, 14, 22). Hence in the Gospel accounts the crowd, by demanding the death of an innocent man, is all the more culpable.

(c) Acts 28:18 uses *aitia* twice, first for the charge made against Paul of committing a capital crime. Since, however, there was insufficient reason (*aitia*) for the accusation, the Romans wished to save him from unjust condemnation to death.

4. Paul uses *anapologētos* twice in Romans to mean the state of having no excuse in a legal sense. In the light of eschatology, the ungodly are "without excuse" as they stand before God's destroying wrath (Rom. 1:20). No one is able, under any circumstances, to make an "excuse" to God (2:1). Everyone, whether Jew or Gentile, deserves death; therefore, as the argument of Rom. 2 continues, we are totally dependent on God's free grace and goodness in Jesus Christ. He took our sentence of death on himself and by this means truly "excused" us. The theological emphasis given to the theme that Christ *had to* suffer is a logical counterpart to the ideas associated with this group of words (cf. Mk. 8:31; 9:12; Lk. 24:26–27; → *dei, 1256*).

5. The adj. *anaitios*, innocent, is used in Matt. 12:5, 7 to describe the guiltless condition of priests who "desecrate" the Sabbath by serving in the temple. *anenklētos* means blameless, irreproachable, and is spoken of Christians who will be presented blameless by Christ on the day of the Lord (1 Cor. 1:8; cf. Col. 1:22). A blameless life is also required of Christian leaders (1 Tim. 3:10; Tit. 1:6–7).

See also *elenchō*, bring to light, expose, convict, punish (*1794*); *enochos*, guilty, subject to, liable to (*1944*); *amemptos*, blameless (*289*).

165 (aitios, responsible, guilty), → 162.

166 (*aitiōma*, charge), → 162.

168 (*aichmalōsia*, captivity), → 171.

169 (*aichmalōteuō*, capture, put in prison), → 171.

170 (*aichmalōtizō*, capture, take captive), → 171.

171	αἰχμάλωτος

αἰχμάλωτος (*aichmalōtos*), captive, prisoner of war (*171*); αἰχμαλωτίζω (*aichmalōtizō*), capture, take captive(*170*); αἰχμαλωτεύω (*aichmalōteuō*), capture, put in prison (*169*); αἰχμαλωσία (*aichmalōsia*), captivity (*168*); συναιχμάλωτος (*synaichmalōtos*), fellow prisoner (*5257*).

CL & OT 1. In cl. Gk. *aichmalōtos* means lit. one caught by the spear; hence it denotes a person taken as a prisoner of war. The vb. *aichmalōtizō* means to take as a prisoner of war, to take prisoner; *aichmalōteuō*, to lead away into captivity.

2. (a) *aichmalōtos* occurs 25x in the LXX and usually means to lead off as captive (Num. 21:29; Isa. 14:2) or go into exile (5:13; Amos 6:7). The noun *aichmalōsia* is far more frequent (130x) and means imprisonment, prisoner, banishment, exile. Usually it refers to the Babylonian exile or the exiles (e.g., Isa. 45:13; Jer. 1:3; Ezek. 1:1–2). *aichmalōteuō* (45x) and *aichmalōtizō* (23x) mean to lead into captivity.

(b) Originally Israel had no experience of prisoners of war. The holy war waged under Yahweh's orders required the complete annihilation of the enemy (e.g., Jos. 6:17–21; 1 Sam. 15:3). Gradually, however, changes took place, and the victors began to sell prisoners as slaves (1 Sam. 15:8–9). Women were often regarded as part of the booty (Gen. 34:29; Num. 31:9; Deut. 21:10–14).

(c) The problem of prisoners crops up esp. with the exile, when entire groups of the Israelite population were deported by Assyria and Babylon. For the Israelites the horror of captivity did not merely lie in their being given up into the hands of those ill-disposed toward them. Rather, banishment from their own land meant above all the loss of their claim to that well-being promised by Yahweh as a pledge of his covenant. To live in a foreign and hostile land was tantamount to being cut off from fellowship with the creator and guarantor of their own existence (cf. Ps. 137:1–6). These people knew that captivity and banishment were a punishment inflicted by an angry God (Ps. 78:61–62; Jer. 15:2).

NT 1. This group of words occurs only 12x in the NT. In representing deportation by the Gentiles as God's final punishment (Lk. 21:24), NT apocalyptic echoes the OT's horror at the idea of captivity. It is significant that Lk. 4:18 (quoting Isa. 61:1) explicitly includes the freeing of prisoners among Jesus' various saving acts. The NT understands the freedom that Jesus brings as both facilitating and improving human relations and reconciling humankind with God.

In two OT quotations *aichmalōsia* occurs in a modified sense (Eph. 4:8 quotes Ps. 68:18; Rev. 13:10 adapts Jer. 15:2). Jer. 15:2 was a message of judgment directed to Jerusalem, but in the case of the church Christians may be called to suffer captivity for their faith. However, they must not resort to force of arms, as Peter did in Gethsemane. In 2 Tim. 3:6 *aichmalōtizō* means capture, gain control over.

2. Reflecting on his Christian struggle against sin, Paul writes that he sees a principle at work in him that makes him "a prisoner of the law of sin" at work within him (Rom. 7:23). By contrast, Paul's concept of the new life as an exclusive union with the Lord allows him to use *aichmalōtizō* of the service of Christ: "We take captive every thought to make it obedient to Christ" (2 Cor. 10:5; cf. 2:11; 3:14; 4:4).

3. Paul refers to the imprisonment he shares with various Christians when he calls those esp. close to him *synaichmalōtoi*, fellow prisoners (Rom. 16:7; Col. 4:10; Phlm. 23).

See also *desmios*, bind (with bonds) (*1300*); *doulos*, slave (*1528*); *libertinos*, freedman (*3339*).

172	αἰών

αἰών (*aiōn*), aeon, age, life span, epoch, long time, eternity (*172*); αἰώνιος (*aiōnios*), without beginning or end, eternal, forever (*173*); ἀΐδιος (*aidios*), eternal (*132*).

CL & OT 1. The Gk. word *aiōn*, perhaps derived from *aei*, always, does not consider time so much from the point of view of an abstract period as from the point of view of the time in which one has lived. In Homer *aiōn* is often parallel with *psychē*, soul, life; in other poets it denotes a life span or generation. Thence it can mean the time that one has already lived or will live, i.e., it can relate to both past and future. It thus appeared appropriate to later philosophers to use the word both for the dim and distant past and for the far future, eternity.

In Plato, *aiōn* is developed to represent a timeless, immeasurable, and transcendent super-time, an idea of time in itself. Plutarch and the Stoics appropriate this understanding, and from it the Mysteries of Aion, the god of eternity, could be celebrated in Alexandria. In Hel. philosophy the concept of aeons contributed toward a solution of the problem of the world order. The aeons were assumed to be mediating powers that bridge the infinite qualitative distinction between God and the world. They are an emanation of the divine *plērōma*, the fullness of the divine being (→ *plēroō*, to fulfill, *4444*). As differing levels of being of the divinity, they rule the various historical periods, which follow one another in a perpetual circular movement. The thought of personal divine aeons was widespread in the speculation of the ancient Orient.

2. (a) *aiōn* occurs over 450x in the LXX, over 100 in Ps. alone. It is the LXX equivalent for Heb. *ʿôlām*, a long time or duration, which is also used as an adv. meaning forever, for all time. This fact is not, however, due to this later speculative development in the meaning of the word, but to the primary meaning of life span. This is clearly shown by the way in which the LXX uses the two adjs. *aiōnios* (ca. 160x) and *aidios*, both meaning eternal. The latter word, a term of steadiness and unalterability stemming from the syncretism of Hel., Egyptian, and Oriental thought, is found only in Wis. 7:26 as a predicate of wisdom and in 4 Macc. 10:15. By contrast, the frequent occurrence of *aiōnios* in both OT and NT shows that we are concerned here with a characteristically biblical concrete idea that must be understood in relation to the whole duration of a person's life.

The OT *ʿôlām*, duration, must always be distinguished from moment, for which *regaʿ* is used (*chronos*, → *5989*; cf. Isa. 54:7–8). For the point of time of a unique event, the word *ʿēt* (*kairos*, → *2789*; cf. Mic. 5:3) is available. If *ʿôlām/aiōn* in the OT thus denotes the time of life, one cannot begin to explain it from those passages in which it is remote antiquity that is regarded as *ʿôlām*. Rather, it is a case, in the first instance, of an extent of time, e.g., for which a slave is obligated (Exod. 21:6; Deut. 15:17), for which Samuel is consecrated to the temple service (1 Sam. 1:22), and for the priestly service of the sons of Aaron (Exod. 29:9). In all these cases it extends throughout a person's whole life, but is also limited to it. All this comes to an end with the death of the person concerned.

(b) This is also the case in statements made of generations (e.g., Exod. 32:13; 40:15; Ps. 18:50) or of the whole nation (Jos. 4:7; Jdg. 2:1). With the decline of these entities the time here indicated is also ended, without this appearing as a particularly noticeable break, since it was indeed "their" time.

This provides us with the simplest explanation of the so-called eternity formulae: e.g., "Praised be Yahweh the God of Israel, from eternity to eternity [*apo tou aiōnos kai heōs tou aiōnos*]" (1 Chr. 16:36, lit. trans.). Israel is summoned to constant thanksgiving and praise (16:34), linked with the continuing of the nation in its generations. In fact, "eternal" and "for a thousand generations" stand in parallel in 16:15. The formula "from eternity to eternity" is thus best derived from the other formula "to eternity to the generations [*eis ton aiōna eis tas geneas autōn*]" (Exod. 40:15, lit. trans.; cf. Isa. 13:20). The formula thus regains its true sense in that even here it is not a question of an eternity conceived of in abstract and infinite terms, but in terms of one's life and praise in relation to God. The content of God's eternal promises is never an abstract unchangeability, but a mutual relationship with human beings (cf. 1 Sam. 2:30; 3:13–14): As long as it is intact, it is eternal, but it can fall to pieces.

(c) Even the great promises, which are established forever, are not simply timelessly and irrevocably valid. They remain bound to their living point of reference in the living God (e.g., in 1 Ki. 9, the eternity of the temple is bound to God's living presence; 2 Sam. 7 refers to the eternity of the Davidic monarchy). Human life is limited (Gen. 6:3); it cannot therefore be the ground of endless duration. But because the eternal God lives (cf. the polemic against the dead idols in Isa. 40 and 44), his action and his salvation are eternal (45:17), his covenant endures (55:3), and his will is incontestable (Exod. 12:14–24; 27:21).

(d) This explains why *ʿôlām* is able not only to designate subsequent and future time (Gen. 13:15; Exod. 14:13, Deut. 13:16; 23:3, 6; 29:29; Jos. 8:28; Mic. 4:7) but also remote antiquity (Gen. 6:4; Deut. 32:7; Mic. 5:2). All time is related to the action in history of the living God (Joel 2:1–11). It is true that there are tendencies in the later portions of the OT toward abstract concepts of eternity (Ps. 9:5; 21:4; cf. Sir. 1:2), and there are even passages in the Apocr. that speak of an eternity entirely removed from time (with Prov. 8:23 as the point of departure). But it remains significant that in the OT *ʿôlām/aiōn* always retain the relatedness of time to life. The idea that the time in which human beings live is not eternity and that eternity is the "time" in which God lives does not correspond with the OT conception.

3. This sense of the word is also continued in the older Jewish apocalyptic writings (e.g., *1 Enoch*) and in the Dead Sea Scrolls. The word *ʿôlām* pales increasingly until it becomes an epithet for everything connected with God and his heavenly world—angels, the final judgment, the blessings of salvation, even the pious.

It is only in the rab. Jud. at the turn of the era and in the apocalyptic lit. of the 1st cent. A.D. (e.g., 2 Esd.) that one finds a new use of *ʿôlām*, which exhibits a spatial significance as well as a temporal one. Under the influence of Persian thought, the OT statements concerning primal and final time (Isa. 24–27; Joel 2) are systematized into a doctrine of the two worlds (aeons), whose only remaining common factor is that God is the Lord of this world as of that, the Lord of this age as of that. They are related antithetically, for this age is the time of unrighteousness, sin, and pain. But when the age to come supersedes this one, all this will come to an end, since there will then be a new earth, where the righteous will live.

The NT affinity of the terms *aiōn*, aeon, and *kosmos*, world (→ *3180*), is also based on this idea. The expected Messiah either brings in the future age himself, or "the days of the Messiah" are thought of as an interim period, which are followed by the new age. This is reflected in the terms "this age" and "the age to come."

NT 1. In the NT the noun *aiōn* occurs over 100x, the adj. *aiōnios* 70x, and *aidios* only 2x (Rom. 1:20 of the unchangeable power and deity of God; Jude 6 of the eternal chains of the fallen angels). *aiōn* has the following meanings: (a) A long time, duration of time, where both a specifically limited period of time as well as an unlimited period can be meant; it is chiefly linked with a preposition. The meaning "eternity" is only appropriate with certain qualifications, since the OT idea of time, which predominantly conditions the NT, does not regard eternity as the opposite of temporality.

(b) An age, epoch, era (of the world), especially in Matt. with reference to the end of the world (13:39; 28:20). This denotes the course of world events. It is also used in the pl. with this meaning (e.g., Heb. 9:26; 1 Cor. 10:11). The underlying idea is that the world runs its course in a series of successive ages.

(c) Occasionally we see a meaning of *aiōn* in the spatial sense, probably going back to the influence of Jewish apocalyptic (e.g., Mk. 4:19; 1 Cor. 2:6; esp. (pl.) Heb. 1:2; 11:3).

2. The simple grammatical evidence of the use of *aiōn* in the NT points back to two sources: the OT and Jud. influenced by Persian thought. The prepositional use of *aiōn* in the NT (more than 60x) does not elucidate the connection between *aiōn*, time, and life for the reader as well as its use in the OT. It is true that even here one can scarcely deny the connection (*eis ton aiōna* means "never" in 1 Cor. 8:13; "forever" in Lk. 1:55), but, insofar as a preposition precedes it, one can only consider the designation of "antiquity" or the "far future" as the essential NT use of the word.

(a) The meaning of antiquity (with prepositions *apo*, from, *pro*, before, *ek*, from) is rare. It occurs in Lk. always in the context of statements that God has from of old spoken through the prophets (Lk. 1:70; Acts 3:21; 15:18), and—as all three passages make clear—through the primal prophet Moses (cf. Lk. 24:27). It is also found in Jn. 9:32 in the sense of "never since the world began [*ek tou aiōnos*]." In 1 Cor. 2:7; Eph. 3:9; Col. 1:26; and esp. Jude 25 the meaning verges on pretemporal eternity.

(b) The same shift of meaning can also be seen in the far more widely attested statements about the future, which are uniformly linked only with *eis*, into (and generally with the sing. of *aiōn*). It is further clear that passages such as Matt. 21:19; Mk. 3:29; Lk. 1:55; Jn. 13:8; and 1 Cor. 8:13 are speaking of a future within time that is linked with the duration of that to which reference is made. Yet the statements of the Johannine writings, which cannot always be pinned down with absolute certainty of meaning (e.g., Jn. 4:14; 6:51, 58; 8:35, 51–52; 1 Jn. 2:17; 2 Jn. 2), Heb., where the meaning is clear (e.g., 1:8, quoting Ps. 110:4; Heb. 5:6; 6:20), and naturally those cases where *aiōn* is used in the pl., all reveal a strong inclination to conceive of a timeless, post-temporal, eternity.

These uses stand in theological (Jn.), Christological (Heb.), or doxological contexts (pl. statements, e.g., Rom. 1:25; 11:36). As in the OT, these statements reveal the background conviction that God's life never ends, i.e., that everything belonging to him can also never come to an end. So it comes about that even where the conception of the age is intensified (e.g., *eis tous aiōnas tōn aiōnōn*; lit., "to the eternity of eternities"), the connection with the basic meaning of *aiōn* as life span is still not lost. What appertains to the living God is "eternal." But one must not forget that this God is also the final judge, so that even perdition must be called *aiōnios* (Matt. 18:8; 25:41, 46; Mk. 3:29; 2 Thess. 1:9; Heb. 6:2; Jude 7).

3. It is quite a different matter with the use of the word *aiōn* occurring as a noun (40x). This must be seen against the background of Jewish apocalyptic lit. The word serves as the principal term for the NT's understanding of its history and eschatology. This meaning of *aiōn*, age, occurs throughout the NT.

(a) For the Synoptics, the most important fact is that the kingdom of God has dawned. If details are taken over from apocalyptic, then it is only in order to say that the present age is approaching its end because the kingdom of God has come. The contrast between the two ages is scarcely discernible; it merely serves to throw into relief the different nature of the course of the world under the reign of Christ. His return and the resurrection of the dead follow on his own resurrection. The new age has dawned with Jesus. The period until the Parousia enables the Christian community to proclaim the gospel.

Matt. displays the fullest and most vivid conception of the aeons in the sense of distinguishing between two successive worlds of space and time, for here alone is found the typical distinction between "this age" and "age to come" (12:32). In answer to the question concerning the time of the end of the world and the signs of the messianic future (24:3), Matt. is able to give a clear reply, not only in the subsequent apocalypse (chs. 24–25, here without the word *aiōn*), but even more clearly in the interpretation of the parable of the wheat and the weeds (13:36–43, cf. 13:49). But this is vastly different from, e.g., the conceptions in Qumran: There is no final battle and no dualism of different worlds, rulers, and subjects. The Son of Man is Lord; the devil may well be able to bring ruin, but he is no real counterpart to the Son of Man. The world is and remains God's creation. The aeons are not authorities in their own right, nor are they emanations of God or his delegates.

(b) Paul also makes use of apocalyptic concepts in his eschatology. He uses *aiōn* to designate the course of the world apart from Christ and under the control of sin (Gal. 1:4, Christ "rescued us from the present evil age"; cf. Rom. 12:2). Satan is admittedly "the god of this age" (2 Cor. 4:4), and the present world is dominated by evil, demonic powers. But against the power of darkness is ranged the victorious kingdom of Christ (cf. Col. 1:13).

It is clear from Paul's confrontation with his opponents in Corinth that he understands the course of the world from the perspective of Jewish apocalyptic. The enthusiast group believed that, with baptism, they had already reached the goal of redemption and the resurrection from the dead (1 Cor. 15:12–24; cf. 2 Tim. 1:18). The Corinthian pneumatists replaced future eschatological expectation with a present eschatology; final salvation had already come to them. Paul, too, could stress that the fullness of time (Gal. 4:4) and the new creation has already begun (2 Cor. 5:17), in which Christ has delivered his church from the present evil age (Gal. 1:4). But in 1 Cor. 15:20–28, by contrast, his starting point is that the rule of Christ has not yet achieved its final goal; and later Eph. 1:21 maintains that this age still persists and that the future one is still awaited.

Thus Paul does not develop any systematic doctrine of aeons, nor does the rest of the NT. The ages are interlocked. Eschatology is determined solely by the revelation of Christ, with Christ as the turning point of time. With him the *now* of salvation has arrived (cf. Rom. 3:21; Col. 1:26). For the believer, the present age (1 Cor. 1:20; 3:18; 10:11) belongs to the past. The proper antithesis to this age is God himself, his righteousness, and his kingdom.

(c) In Heb. this age is called "the present time [*kairos*, → 2789]" (9:9) and the new age "the time [*kairos*] of the new order" (9:10). The equation of *aiōn* and *kosmos* (1:2; 9:26; 11:3) probably originates in Jewish linguistic usage, but it can also be evidenced in Gnosticism. The frequent pl. *aiōnes*, meaning world (in the spatial rather than the temporal sense), goes back to the conception of the various layers of the world frame or of a multiplicity of world systems. Four and even seven aeons can be found in Jewish writings.

Yet despite the adoption of many Hel. linguistic and conceptual elements, Heb. holds fast to the primitive Christian eschatological proclamation. It knows the sequence of two ages (which in Heb. are Christologically defined), for the end of the ages (9:26) has come because Christ has appeared in order to abolish sin by the sacrifice of himself. The present age is defined by sacrifice and the first tent, while the new age is concerned with God's working in the heavenly sanctuary. There Christ has already instituted the priestly ministry, and the Christian community is already on the way there (9:8–15; cf. 10:19; 13:14). The new age reaches out from the heavenly world into the present time. Even if hidden, it is already present (6:5).

(d) In 2 Pet., by contrast, the author develops a distinctly futurist eschatology. Even though the mighty Parousia of Jesus Christ (1:16) and entrance into his eternal kingdom (1:11) are expressly mentioned, interest is directed rather to the future blessings of salvation—the reward of the righteous, participation in the divine nature (1:4). The letter concentrates on the proclamation of the end time, the certainty of judgment (2:4–10; 3:5–10), the dissolution of the existing order (3:11–12), and the promise of "a new heaven and a new earth, the home of righteousness" (3:13). The letter closes with the doxology: "To him be glory both now and forever [lit., to the day of eternity]! Amen" (3:18).

4. The expression "eternal life," corresponding to the basic meaning of *aiōn* as defined by the OT, should be understood primarily as life that belongs to God. From the book of Dan. on, "eternal life" is an expression of the longed-for eschatological blessings of salvation, life in the age to come (cf. Dan. 12:2). In the Synoptics (e.g., Matt. 18:8; 19:16, 29; 25:41, 46), Paul's letters (e.g., Rom. 2:7; 5:21; Gal. 6:8;

1 Tim. 1:16; 6:12), and Jude 21, there is a temporal understanding of eternal life (→ *zōē*, 2437). This is a life that is awaited in the future along with the resurrection of the dead, just as the term can be used in Jud. alternately with the kingdom of God (cf. Matt. 25:34; 1 Cor. 6:9–10) to denote salvation.

Jn. understands eternal life in relation to Christ through faith and love and in keeping the commands of Christ (e.g., Jn. 3:15–16, 36; 4:14, 36; 17:2–3). The word "eternal" here indicates a definite quality: It is a different life from the old existence typified by hate, sin, pain, and death. Eternal life does not therefore just begin in the future; it is already the possession of those who have entered fellowship with Christ. Thus 3:15 speaks of having eternal life in the present. But there is also a temporal sense, so that eternal (*aiōnios*) indicates the quantity of this life: Because it belongs to Christ, who himself is the life (14:6), it has no end. It will not cease even at death (8:51; 11:25–26). One must also observe that the NT does not use the phrase "eternal death," because the idea of eternity is so closely connected with life that the negation of eternal life can also only be understood as the experience of ruin.

5. Surveying the usage of the word *aiōn*, aeon, and the connected eschatology, one can establish that, with all the varied accentuations, the NT speaks of eternity in the categories of time. Any dualism between two world systems is thus foreign to it. The world is and remains God's creation, and Christ is the Lord of the worlds, even if his lordship is hidden. Thus, the expression *ho mellōn aiōn*, the age to come, is used with great caution. It is "today" that stands in the center of the statements, and what is coming is only relevant in view of the respective present. Everywhere the NT exercises conscious discretion in the face of events of which knowledge is forbidden (Matt. 24:37–44; 1 Thess. 5:1–3). This is also a warning to Christians today not to speculate about God's mystery.

See also *kairos*, time, esp. a point of time, moment (*2789*); *chronos*, time, period of time (*5989*); *hōra*, hour, time, point of time (*6052*).

173 (aiōnios, without beginning or end, eternal, forever), → *172*.

174 (akatharsia, uncleanness), → *2754*.

176 (akathartos, unclean), → *2754*.

177 (akaireomai, have no time, no opportunity), → *2789*.

178 (akairōs, untimely, ill-timed, inopportune), → *2789*.

179 (akakos, guileless, innocent), → *2805*.

180	ἄκανθα

ἄκανθα (*akantha*), thorn (*180*); ἀκάνθινος (*akanthinos*), thorny, of thorn (*181*).

CL & OT 1. In cl. Gk. *akantha* denotes a thorn tree or bush as well as any prickle, whether of plant, animal (e.g. porcupine), or fish. The adj. means thorny, made of thorn wood, and is even used of "thorny questions."

2. The LXX uses *akantha* with literal reference in Exod. 22:6; Jdg. 8:7, 16; Song 2:2. But the symbolic is never far away. Literal and symbolic combine in Gen. 3:18 (= LXX 3:19), where the growth of thorns symbolizes the new perversity of nature after Adam and Eve sinned. The main figurative uses are for affliction (Ezek. 28:24) and that which is hazardous, full of difficulty (Prov. 15:19), painful, or out of place (26:9). "Thorns for grapes" typifies disappointed and blighted hopes (e.g., Isa. 5:2, 4, LXX only) and looks back to Gen. 3:18 as its origin. Thorns are the wild growth that comes when cultivation ceases (Isa. 5:6), not only physically but spiritually and religiously (e.g., Isa. 34:13; Hos. 10:8).

NT The literal meaning blends with symbolic in Jesus' "crown of thorns" (Matt. 27:29; Mk. 15:17; Jn. 19:5): He is not only in intense suffering but bearing the fruit of the curse of Gen. 3:18. Thorns are the enemy of growth (Matt. 13:7) and spiritually are specified as the anxious care typical of this world, the deceptive allure of riches, and all manner of desires (13:22; Lk. 8:14). They evidence failure to respond to God's Word and reveal an unregenerate heart (Heb. 6:8).

See also *tribolos*, thistle (*5560*); *skolops*, thorn (*5022*).

181 (akanthinos, thorny, of thorn), → *180.*

182 (akarpos, unfruitful, fruitless), → *2843.*

184 (akatakalyptos, unveiled), → *2821.*

185 (akatakritos, without a trial, uncondemned), → *3210.*

186 (akatalytos, indestructible), → *3395.*

189	ἀκαταστασία

ἀκαταστασία (*akatastasia*), disorder, revolution (*189*); ἀκατά-στατος (*akatastatos*), restless, unstable (*190*).

CL & OT In cl. Gk. this word generally has a political meaning, referring primarily to the disorder, anarchy, or confusion that can result from a variety of disruptions in the state. *akatastatos*, by contrast, has the much more psychological meaning of being restless, unsettled. The LXX uses *akatastasia* in Prov. 26:28 to denote the ruin caused by a flattering mouth and a lying tongue. In a similar vein, Tob. 4:13 speaks of "great confusion" that is brought about as a result of giving in to the sin of pride (here, by refusing to take a wife from among one's own people). The related adj., *akatastatos*, addresses the city of Jerusalem in a state of restlessness, tossed by the storms of life (Isa. 54:11).

NT 1. *akatastasia* occurs 5x in the NT. It can mean, as in cl. Gk., political instability. In his eschatological discourse, Jesus predicts the coming of wars and "revolutions" as one sign of the end of this age (Lk. 21:9). Disturbances also resulted as Paul spread the gospel in the Greco-Roman world. On more than one occasion he was imprisoned after his enemies had caused "riots" (2 Cor. 6:5; cf. Acts 16:16–24) in their opposition to the apostle.

2. But the NT also uses this word to refer to disruption among human beings in general and esp. in the church. In Jas. 3:16, the author stresses that if we harbor envy and selfishness in our hearts, it will result in "disorder" in our relationships with others and in other sorts of evil practices. Paul expresses a fear that if he returns to Corinth, things will erupt into a total state of disarray because of the hard feelings between himself and some of the believers in Corinth. One of the words he uses to describe this potential situation is *akatastasia*, disorder (2 Cor. 12:20).

3. Finally, *akatastasia* has a liturgical connotation in 1 Cor. 14. In that chapter Paul is dealing with the problem of spiritual gifts, esp. that of tongues and prophecy. He does not want glossolalia to get out of hand in the church, and he endorses prophecy as superior to speaking in tongues. But even in prophecy it can happen that several people feel led to utter a prophecy at the same time. Thus the apostle encourages those who have that gift to wait their turn and insists that the prophecies that are uttered must be evaluated by the prophets. His final conclusion to this issue is a general statement about God: "For God is not a God of disorder but of peace" (14:33; see also *eirēnē*, peace, *1645*).

4. *akatastatos* is used in Jas. 1:8 to describe someone who continually doubts the will and power of God; such a person is double-minded and "unstable" in all that he or she does. The same word is used later in this book to denote one of the features of the tongue, that it is "restless" and capable of great evil (3:8). No one is able to tame the tongue.

190 (akatastatos, restless, unstable), → *189.*

192	Ἀκελδαμάχ

Ἀκελδαμάχ (*Hakeldamach*), Akeldama (*192*).

This place name is found only in Acts 1:19, where it refers to a field that Judas purchased with the thirty pieces of silver and where he presumably committed suicide. It can be identified with the field purchased by the priestly authorities (Matt. 27:3–10), the two being linked by the popular designation of the place as "Field of Blood."

Problems surround several aspects of this matter.

1. The acquisition of the field. Matthew's account (27:7) says that the priests made the purchase, whereas Acts 1:18 makes Judas the purchaser. Since Matt. 27:3 associates Judas's contribution with the condemnation of Jesus and records that he took immediate steps to relieve himself of the accursed money, we ought to understand Acts as merely intending to make a direct link between that which was paid to Judas and the purchase of the field. In this regard, the priests were but his agents.

2. The relation of Akeldama to the death of Judas. Matt. explains that the name "Field of Blood" arose from the use of blood money in its purchase. Acts does not absolutely require more than this; it does not specify that Judas's suicide took place there; at most it offers the circumstance of his death as additional justification for such a repellent nomenclature. In any event Judas's suicide became notorious through the grim details as recorded in Acts. After his hanging, the body fell—before or after death, or perhaps in the actual death throes of the unfortunate man.

198 (akoē, hearing, a thing heard, message, report, rumor), → *201.*

199	ἀκολουθέω

ἀκολουθέω (*akoloutheō*), follow (*199*); ἐξακολουθέω (*exakoloutheō*), follow (*1979*); ἐπακολουθέω (*epakoloutheō*), follow (*2051*); παρακολουθέω (*parakoloutheō*), accompany, understand (*4158*); συνακολουθέω (*synakoloutheō*), follow (*5258*).

CL & OT 1. *akoloutheō* means go somewhere with someone, accompany, follow, and (with hostile intentions) pursue. It developed a metaphorical meaning: follow the drift, understand. Substantival forms meaning disciple or discipleship also occur. Among the Stoics *akoloutheō* had philosophical connotations. To follow nature or God is the basic direction of the philosophical life.

2. The cl. Gk. meanings continue in the LXX. Elisha wants to follow Elijah as his servant (1 Ki. 19:20). Usually the words have no theological force (e.g., Ruth 1:14). There are no OT precedents for the more specific NT usage of *akoloutheō*; it never speaks about becoming like God, only obeying him.

2. In rab. Jud. the words describe the relationship of a pupil to a teacher of the Torah. The pupil who subordinates himself to a rabbi follows him everywhere, learning from him and serving him. His obligation to serve is an essential part of learning the Mosaic law. The goal of such learning and training is a complete knowledge of the Torah and the ability to practice it in every situation.

NT 1. The restricted use of these words in the NT is important. (a) *akoloutheō* appears almost exclusively in the Gospels. The compound vbs. are used less and are not usually applied to people, except for *synakoloutheō*, accompany (Mk. 5:37; 14:51; Lk. 23:49).

(b) Following does not always involve being a disciple. When the Synoptics speak of crowds following Jesus (cf. Matt. 4:25; 8:1; 21:9; Mk. 10:32), they use the word in a neutral sense.

(c) The word has special significance when it refers to individuals. On Jesus' lips it often appears as an imperative, as when he calls disciples to follow him (Matt. 9:9 par.; 8:22 par.; 19:21 par.; Jn. 1:43; 21:19–22). Those called do follow (e.g., Lk. 5:11). *akoloutheō* is thus the call to intimate discipleship of the earthly Jesus. Jn. hints at its spiritual implications for fellowship with the Exalted One (esp. Jn. 12:26). In Rev. 14:4 *akoloutheō* denotes those who have shared in the lot of suffering of the slaughtered and exalted Lamb.

2. *akoloutheō* in the Synoptics connotes going behind. This fact supports the idea of an affinity with the teacher-pupil relationship of the rabbis. But there are characteristic differences between the disciples of Jesus and those of the rabbis.

(a) Jesus did not wait for voluntary followers. He called people with divine authority as God called the prophets in the OT (Mk. 1:16–18 par.; Matt. 8:22).

(b) Jesus did not call his followers to master certain traditions. He pointed them instead to the future dawn of the kingdom of God (Lk. 9:59–60). To be a disciple of Jesus was a calling to help in the service of the kingdom (Mk. 1:15). Those called shared in his authority. They were sent to the same people (cf. Matt. 15:24 with 10:5–6), with the same message (cf. Matt. 4:17 with 10:7), to do the same mighty deeds (Mk. 3:14–15). They will sit with him on the throne to judge (Matt. 19:28; Lk. 22:30).

(c) One who takes up the new calling gives up an old one. This is not an oppressive precondition, however; it follows self-evidently (Mk. 1:16–20; Matt. 9:9). Note the rich young ruler (Mk. 10:17–22) who could not free himself from his old ties. Even the disciple who is already following Jesus is not exempt from the danger of making new reservations in the life of discipleship (cf. Matt. 8:21–22 par.).

(d) Since the disciple cannot expect any better fortune than one's Lord (cf. Matt. 10:24–25), readiness for suffering becomes a part of discipleship: "If anyone would come after me, he must deny himself and take up his cross and follow me" (Mk. 8:34; cf. Matt. 10:38). To take up one's cross means being ready for death (→ *stauros*, 5089). Readiness to suffer is only made possible through self-denial, which consists in freedom from oneself and from all forms of personal security.

3. John takes over Synoptic phraseology (Jn. 1:43) but tends to see it more within the framework of his total vision. Jesus appeared as light and life in a world of death and darkness. Anyone who follows him (8:12) walks in the light and is saved. Thus, following Jesus means accepting his revelation (cf. Jn. 12:44). People's lives find a new purpose as they are directed into the true life. To follow the call of the Shepherd (10:4, 27) means both safety in Christ and fellowship in suffering with him (12:26), which in turn means exaltation with him (12:32).

4. The rest of the NT expresses fellowship with Christ in such words as Paul's concept of being in Christ or in his idea of imitation (→ *mimeomai*, 3628) of Christ.

See also *mathētēs*, learner, pupil, disciple (3412); *mimeomai*, imitate, follow (3628); *opisō*, behind, after (3958).

201	ἀκούω

ἀκούω (*akouō*), hear, listen, attend, perceive by hearing (201); ἀκοή (*akoē*), hearing, the ear, a thing heard, message, teaching, report, rumor (198); ἀκροατής (*akroatēs*), hearer (212); εἰσακούω (*eisakouō*), obey, pass. to be heard (1653); ἐπακούω (*epakouō*), listen to, hearken to(2052); ἐπακροάομαι (*epakroaomai*), listen attentively (2053); παρακούω (*parakouō*), fail to hear, take no heed (4159); παρακοή (*parakoē*), disobedience (4157); ἐνωτίζομαι (*enōtizomai*), pay attention to, hear (1969).

CL & OT 1. (a) In cl. Gk. *akouō* refers primarily to the perception of sounds by the sense of hearing. The person or thing heard is in the acc.; the person from whom something is heard is in the gen. or uses the preps. *apo*, *para*, or *ek*. Hearing, however, covers not only sense perception but also the apprehension and acceptance by the mind of the content of what is heard. The related noun *akoē* means the sense of hearing, the act of hearing, the organ of hearing (the ear), and the content of hearing (the message).

(b) Hearing plays a part in every religion. The general tendency of the Gk. and Hel. world, however, was to stress seeing the divinity. Nevertheless, the idea that the gods hear and listen is not foreign to paganism.

2. In the LXX *akouō* or *akoē* stands consistently for Heb. *šāmaʿ* and shares the shades of meaning of that vb. Here too the primary meaning is sense perception by the human ear. But apprehension is immediately involved as soon as one receives a statement, piece of news, or message (Gen. 14:14). Such apprehension demands listening

(4:23; 23:11), understanding (11:7; 42:2), and acceptance of the thing heard. Hence, *šāmaʿ* and *akouō* acquired the meaning obey. The *akouō* compounds also occur in the LXX for *šāmaʿ* with little difference in meaning.

3. (a) In biblical revelation hearing has much greater significance than in the Gk. or Hel. world. For God meets human beings through his Word, and we are charged with hearing that Word. This does not, of course, exclude God's revelation in the visible sphere. For example, God revealed himself to Moses in the burning bush (Exod. 3:1–6); and in the vision that constituted his call, Isaiah saw Yahweh in the temple surrounded by seraphim singing his praises (Isa. 6:1–7). But, as in most cases of the visible revelation of God's commission, here each visible revelation was linked with a verbal prophetic mission, which had to be heard and followed. Likewise, the visions that are frequently described in the prophetic writings (e.g., Amos 7–9; Jer. 1:11–19) require interpretation. Here too seeing and hearing form a unity.

(b) Moses, with whom "the LORD would speak . . . face to face" (Exod. 33:11), lived in the memory of his people as the model bearer of the divine, verbal revelation. The Decalogue given to him (Exod. 20:1–17; Deut. 5:6–21) is introduced by the solemn "Hear, O Israel" (Deut. 5:1). This command also stands as an urgent warning before the command to love God (Deut. 6:4–5).

The prophetic revelation presupposed that the content of God's will was already known (Mic. 6:8). As bearers of the divine revelation, the prophets warned the people, the nations, and even heaven and earth to hear God's word, which was coming through themselves (Isa. 1:2, 10; Jer. 2:4; 7:2; 9:20 = LXX 9:19; Mic. 1:2). But equally we hear the prophets complaining that Israel had not heard the voice of its God and was unwilling to do so (Hos. 9:17; Jer. 7:13; Ezek. 3:7). Thus the pre-exilic prophets in particular became preachers of judgment. God lets his judgment fall on a people who will not hear, nor is he himself any longer willing to hear this people (Isa. 1:15; cf. Ezek. 8:18). In the catastrophes that overtook Israel, culminating in the destruction of Jerusalem and the Babylonian captivity, the postexilic prophets saw God's judgment on the people for their unwillingness to hear (Zech. 7:8–14).

The end result of the exile was that Israel became the people of the law, who sought to render the obedience they owed to God by the painstaking fulfillment of his will down to the last detail. For this reason the most important part of the tradition was the Torah, the law, contained in the Pentateuch. These five books contain a strong emphasis on the relation between hearing and doing (Exod. 19:5, 8; Deut. 28:1; 30:11–14). As the divinely commissioned bearers of revelation, the prophets stood beside the Torah at the center of religious faith. "The Law and the Prophets" is in the NT a comprehensive description of the OT writings. To hear them is the task of the pious Israelite (cf. Matt. 5:17–20; 22:40; Lk. 16:29).

(c) The tendency to listen to the law was strengthened in Jud. by the rise of synagogues with their regular Sabbath worship. The synagogue became the focal point of the Jewish communities beyond the borders of Palestine. The recitation of the Shema (consisting of parts of Deut. 6:4–9; 11:13–21; and Num. 15:37–41) had a fixed place in their worship. In addition, the pious Jews recited daily the Shema as an obligation of faith and witness. In principle any suitably qualified member of the community could expound the Torah in the synagogue services. Yet the formation of a class of expositors, called rabbis, is understandable. Their expositions of Scripture were handed down orally until they were fixed in writing in the Mishnah and later the Talmuds (2d cent. A.D. and later). Thus, hearing acquired even greater significance in Jud., esp. since in the rab. view the time of revelation was over.

4. Just as people hear God, God hears them. This is the major way whereby the living God differs from idols, which have ears but do not hear (e.g., Ps. 115; 135:17; Wis. 15:15). Thus the psalmists pray, "Give ear to me and hear my prayer" (Ps. 17:6; cf. 31:2; 86:1; etc.). And in

the figurative sense the OT often speaks of the "ears" of God, who hears what people say (Num. 12:2), such as their cry for help as well as their grumbling (Exod. 3:7; Num. 14:27).

Not only does God hear prayer, he also answers it. This too can be expressed by *šāmaᶜ* and *akouō* (Ps. 30:10). But in these cases we more often find the LXX using the compounds *eisakouō* and *epakouō*, which are particularly frequent in the language of prayer (e.g., Ps. 3:4; 20:1, 6, 9; Isa. 49:8). *enōtizomai*, pay attention to, hear, is derived from *ous*, ear. Thus, the OT contains a whole range of statements in which pious Israelites express their certainty that God hears and answers prayer. It is put particularly beautifully in Ps. 94:9: "Does he who implanted the ear not hear?" On the other hand, guilt can step between God and humankind and make his ear deaf, so that he does not hear (Isa. 59:1–2).

NT 1. The NT use of *akouō* (more than 400x) follows the cl. Gk. and OT uses. The noun *akoē* (24x) denotes the sense of hearing (1 Cor. 12:17), the act of hearing (Rom. 10:17; 2 Pet. 2:8), the ear (esp. the pl.; cf. Mk. 7:35; Acts 17:20), and a message or report (Rom. 10:16; 1 Thess. 2:13; Heb. 4:2). Hence the "hearing of faith" (lit. trans. of Gal. 3:2, 5; cf. Rom. 10:17) is the apostolic message that has faith as its content and is spoken and received as God's word (1 Thess. 2:13).

Of the compounds, *eisakouō* (5x) is used of God hearing (Lk. 1:13; Acts 10:31) and of people hearing (i.e., obeying; 1 Cor. 14:21, in dependence on Isa. 28:11–12). *parakouō* (3x) means fail to hear, leave unheeded in Mk. 5:36; in Matt. 18:17 it means refuse to hear, be disobedient. The noun *parakoē* (3x), disobedience, refers to Adam's disobedience to God (Rom. 5:19), to the Corinthians' disobedience to Paul (2 Cor. 10:6), and to human disobedience to the word of God spoken through angels (Heb. 2:2). *enōtizomai* (used once) means "listen carefully" in Acts 2:14. The rare word *epakroaomai* (used once) means to listen to (Acts 16:25), while the related noun *akroatēs* (4x), listener, occurs in Rom. 2:13; Jas. 1:22, 23, 25, where the hearer of the law (or of the word) is contrasted with the doer.

2. (a) The many shades of meaning of *akouō* become apparent when we ask the theological question *how* one hears the NT message. The content of this message is Jesus Christ, the Messiah promised under the old covenant. To those who believe in him are given the fullness of salvation and a new revelation that surpasses that of the OT. This revelation, which has been manifested in Christ, is perceived not just through hearing but also through seeing (Lk. 2:20; Jn. 1:14; Acts 4:20; 1 Jn. 1:1; see also *horaō*, *3972*). Jesus pronounced a blessing on the eyes and ears of those who became witnesses of the salvation longed for by the godly of former generations (Matt. 13:16–17; Lk. 10:23–24). To those sent to him by the imprisoned Baptist Jesus said: "Go back and report to John what you hear and see" (Matt. 11:4). Alongside his words stand Jesus' mighty acts.

(b) Not only Jesus' earthly appearance but also the events of Easter and Pentecost are perceived by hearing *and* seeing. Paul's crucial vision of Christ (1 Cor. 15:9) is amplified by Acts 22:14–15: He was to be a witness of what he had "seen and heard." The Gospels testify that seeing the risen Christ is bound up with hearing the apostolic commission to be witnesses (Matt. 28:18–20; Mk. 16:15; Lk. 24:46–49; Jn. 20:21; cf. Acts 1:8). The events of Pentecost were perceived originally through seeing and hearing (Acts 2:33; cf. also 2 Cor. 12:1–6). Hearing also plays an important part in the visions of Rev. (e.g., 1:10; 5:11, 13). Nevertheless, the mystery of our salvation is unfathomable; what God has prepared for those who love him, no eye has seen and no ear heard, nor has any human heart conceived (1 Cor. 2:9).

(c) The message of Christ is grounded in a revelatory event, rooted in the OT (Rom. 1:2). Receipt of the Christian message requires faith. But faith presupposes hearing, and this in turn rests on preaching (Rom. 10:14–19; cf. Deut. 32:21; Ps. 19:4). On the other hand, as Jn. 20:29 implies, seeing is not a necessary condition for faith.

(d) The NT does not distinguish between Jesus' word and that of the apostles in the sense that "he who listens to you listens to me" (Lk.

10:16; cf. Matt. 10:40; Jn. 13:20; Gal. 4:14). The apostles are fully authorized witnesses of Jesus. The word Jesus spoke has been reliably handed on by those who heard it (Heb. 2:3). To hear the message is to hear Christ and to hear the word of truth (Eph. 1:13; 4:20–21) or the word of God (Acts 13:7, 44).

3. Like the OT, the NT connects hearing and doing. In the Sermon on the Mount Jesus expounds God's will revealed in the Mosaic law and expresses his authority, which marks his essential difference from the teachers of the law (Matt. 7:28–29; Mk. 1:22). Thus, in the parable that concludes this sermon the Lord compares the man who *hears and does* his word with a man who builds his house on rock (Matt. 7:24–27). In Lk. 11:28 Jesus pronounces a blessing on those who hear and keep (→ *phylassō*, *5875*) his word. Jn. 10:16, 27 refer to the sheep who hear Jesus' voice and follow it.

In Rom. 2:13 Paul contrasts the doers of the law with the hearers (*akroatai*, pl. of *akroatēs*). The mere hearers are unbelieving Jews, who do not let the Mosaic law point them to Christ; the doers are believing Gentiles who demonstrate that the works of the law are written in their hearts (2:14–15; cf. Jer. 31:33). Similarly, in Jas. 1:22–23 the doers of the word are contrasted with the hearers. The NT understands faith not merely as hearing but as obeying.

In Mk. 12:29–30 (par. Matt. 22:34–40)—in response to a question by a teacher of the law, "Of all the commandments, which is the most important?" (Mk. 12:28)—Jesus cites the Shema, which includes the command to love the Lord above all (see OT section, above). To the Shema he adds of his own accord a second commandment, drawn from Lev. 19:18: "'Love your neighbor as yourself.' There is no commandment greater than these [two]" (Mk. 12:31). Lk. 10:25–37 also brings together Deut. 6:5 and Lev. 19:18, though here Jesus gives it in response to a question from a lawyer about inheriting eternal life. Jesus goes on to discuss the practical outworking of the Mosaic law expressed in the parable of the good Samaritan. These incidents imply that hearing the law is never enough; doing must follow.

4. (a) Hearing the word does not always lead to faith, i.e., to the acceptance of God's Word (Mk. 4:16; Lk. 8:13). Understanding must be added to hearing if the sown seed of the Word is to bear fruit (Matt. 13:23; 15:10). The contrary attitude, which does not understand the Word and will not accept it, eventually results in hardening (→ *sklēros*, *5017*). Thus we find repeatedly in the NT, esp. with respect to the Jewish nation, references to the sentence of hardening pronounced in Isa. 6:9–10 (cf. Matt. 13:13–15; Acts 28:27; Rom. 11:8). In Jn. the Jews are plainly told that such hearing is in reality no hearing (5:37; 8:43). This is what Stephen meant when he described the judges at his trial as having "uncircumcised hearts and ears," and their subsequent behavior bore out the accusation (Acts 7:51, cf. 57). Even Jesus' disciples were not protected against failure to hear and understand (Mk. 8:17–18).

A contrast to this hardening is presented by the receptivity of those whose ears God has opened (Isa. 50:5), and who keep his Word in a pure and good heart (Lk. 8:15). It is only to this kind of hearing that the mystery of the kingdom of God is revealed (Matt. 13:11). But although such hearing and understanding are God's gift, human activity is by no means excluded. We see this in the numerous and varied calls for attention (e.g., "He who has ears, let him hear," Matt. 11:15; cf. also 15:10; Mk. 4:24; Rev. 2:7, 11, 17, 29; 3:6, 13, 22).

(b) Jn. 5:25, 28 deals with hearing at the time of consummation; the dead will hear the voice of the Son of God and awaken either to life or to judgment. The raising of Lazarus, whom Jesus called out of his grave with a loud voice (11:43), anticipates this final event.

5. Less is said in the NT about God's hearing than in the OT. The "ears" of God are mentioned twice in quotations from the OT: Jas. 5:4 (cf. Isa. 5:9); 1 Pet. 3:12 (cf. Ps. 34:16). Rev. 9:20 adopts from the OT the statement that idols do not hear. God hears the godly who do his will (Jn. 9:31), and believers may be confident that God hears their prayers when they are in accordance with his will (1 Jn. 5:14). Stephen's speech (Acts 7:34, quoting Exod. 3:7) refers to Israel's being

heard in Egypt. *epakouō* occurs in the NT only in the quotation of Isa. 49:8 (2 Cor. 6:2). *eisakouō* is used in the NT in the sense of hearing and answering only in the pass. In Lk. 1:13 and Acts 10:31 it refers to the hearing of the prayers of Zechariah and Cornelius. In Matt. 6:7 Jesus criticizes those who, like the Gentiles, hope to succeed in making their prayers heard by the multiplication of words. On several occasions Jesus expresses the certainty that God hears prayer (Matt. 7:7–12; Lk. 11:5–13; Jn. 16:23–24).

Heb. 5:7 deals with God's hearing of Jesus' prayers (esp. his prayer in Gethsemane, cf. Matt. 26:36–46). Heb. sees the answer to these prayers in Jesus' exaltation as "the source of eternal salvation for all who obey [*hypakouō*, → *5634*] him" as high priest after the order of Melchizedek (Heb. 5:9). This confirms the assurance, expressed in the story of Lazarus, that God always heard and answered Jesus (Jn. 11:41). Correspondingly, Jesus always heard God as his Father, and as mediator passed on the revelation he heard from his Father (8:26, 40; 15:15). Christ's relationship with his Father has its deepest roots in this mutual hearing.

See also *hypakouō*, listen, obey (*5634*).

202 (akrasia, licentiousness, lack of self-control), → 1602.

203 (akratēs, uncontrolled, unbridled), → 1602.

212 (akroatēs, hearer), → 201.

213 (akrobystia, foreskin, uncircumcision), → 4362.

214 (akrogōniaios, lying at the extreme corner, cornerstone or capstone), → 1224.

224 (alazoneia, boastfulness), → 5662.

225 (alazōn, boastful), → 5662.

229	ἄλας

ἄλας (*halas*), salt (*229*); ἀλυκός (*halykos*), salty (*266*); ἀλίζω (*halizō*), to salt, season with salt (*245*); ἄναλος (*analos*), saltless, insipid (*383*); συναλίζω (*synalizō*), to assemble with, eat (salt) with (*5259*).

CL & OT 1. (a) In. cl. Gk. *halas* (more commonly *hals*) essentially means salt; poetically, the sea; proverbially, to have eaten salt together, i.e., be old friends, enjoy hospitality. *halizō* means to supply with salt; to salt food; to collect, assemble, as military forces. *halykos* means salty; *analos*, without salt, unsalted; *synalizō*, to bring together, collect; eat (salt) with, i.e., eat at the same table.

(b) The domestic and medicinal value of salt both as condiment and preservative was as universal in the ancient world as it is today. Salt on sacrifices probably is related to the primitive idea of sacrifice as the meal of a god, but the association of salt with the deity also balanced the notion of spoilage and corruption commonly linked with demons. Lasting alliances were made by eating bread and salt or salt alone. Several ancient authors also refer to salt's ability to improve the productivity of the soil.

2. In the LXX the Heb. vb. *mālaḥ*, to salt, is translated by *halizō*, and the corresponding noun *melaḥ* by *hals* or *halas*. *halykos* occurs only in reference to the Dead Sea (e.g., Num. 34:3). The main source of salt in Palestine was from the so-called Hill of Salt, which stretched for about seven miles along the SW corner of the Dead Sea. Salt was also obtained by evaporation of water in salt pits in the same area (cf. Zeph. 2:9; 1 Macc. 11:35) and from the incrustation of marshes along the shore (Ezek. 47:11). Salt was seen as a necessity for a people whose diet relied heavily on vegetables (Ezr. 7:22; Sir. 39:26). The commercial value of salt is illustrated by references to taxation (e.g., 1 Macc. 10:29). Salt was also used to preserve fish and meat (Bar. 6:28 = Ep. Jer. 6:28). Rubbing a newborn baby with salt (Ezek. 16:4), still practiced among Arabs, may have been to preserve life or to drive away evil spirits.

The impressive scene of desolation around the Salt (Dead) Sea formed a natural boundary (Num. 34:3) and offered a perpetual

reminder of the ability of large quantities of salt to destroy vegetation (Deut. 29:23) and leave an area uninhabitable (Jer. 17:6). Sowing an enemy city with salt after its capture (Jdg. 9:45) may not have involved using massive quantities to render the ground useless for cultivation. Rather, token amounts could be sprinkled as a sign of cursing the city with infertility and barrenness. The miracle of healing carried out by Elisha (2 Ki. 2:19–22) at the beginning of his ministry made use of the symbolism of salt staying corruption and death.

Small amounts of salt sprinkled on fodder were beneficial as an antiseptic for animals (Isa. 30:24), and a light application on soil to improve its quality for crop bearing was well known. To eat someone's salt, i.e., bread, was to enjoy that person's hospitality, while to eat the salt of the palace (Ezr. 4:14) meant being on the royal payroll (cf. the word "salary," derived from Lat. *sal*, salt). But the uppermost thought behind the expression is that of loyalty in the relationship of employee to employer. In a similar way, the salt of the covenant (Lev. 2:13) refers to the solemn and irrevocable character of the relationship between God and his people—hence the custom of salting sacrifices (Exod. 30:35; Ezek. 43:24).

NT 1. (a) Salt is mentioned in six NT passages. In Matt. 5:13 commentators usually take salt to be a preservative, but the context ("of the earth") may suggest rather the stimulating property of salt as a fertilizer. Jesus came not to keep the world from spoiling but to save it (Jn. 3:17) and to provide life in abundance (10:10). There is only one instance in the LXX of salt being used to prevent spoilage, a reference to the priests' wives salting down the priestly portion of sacrificial meat for later use by their families (Bar. 6:28 = Ep. Jer. 6:28).

Matt. 5:13, therefore, is probably best translated, "You are salt *for* the soil," balanced in parallelism with 5:14, "You are light for the world." Although one cannot see salt that has been added to food, it can be tasted. Salt is noticed by the tongue and light by the eye; in both cases the user is gratified. A city on a hill cannot be hidden, even at night, because of its lights. Salt in food, or its absence, cannot be kept from the eater's knowledge. Note that it is not the Jewish teachers of the law who are the salt and light, but Jesus' disciples. Moreover, savorless salt and a covered lamp are useless; thus, the Christian disciple who fails to be stimulating and bright in the work that God wants done is good for nothing.

(b) The stability of sodium chloride as a chemical compound has raised a problem about salt being said to be liable to lose its quality of saltiness. But Jesus is likely referring to one of the impure salts of Palestine in everyday use, which could and did lose their savor through physical disintegration or through being mixed with wind-blown gypsum dust. Thus, "*if* the salt loses it saltiness" should perhaps be translated as *whenever*, since what follows is not a contrary to fact condition but a real possibility.

2. (a) Mk. 9:49 presents interpretive difficulties because there are three major textual readings. The best attested reading is, "everyone will be salted with fire." Other MSS have, "for every sacrifice will be salted with salt" (Lev. 2:13); still others, a combination of both readings. Interpretation of this verse is at best uncertain. The secondary textual reading may be right in interpreting "salted with fire" as a reference to the Christian disciple being seasoned with salt, as were the OT sacrifices. This can take place through trials (1 Pet. 1:7, 4:12; cf. 1 Cor. 3:13), and everything contrary to God will be purged away. The self-sacrifice metaphor in Mk. 9:42–50 is appropriate to a situation of suffering in which the principle of sacrifice is severely tried. Taken this way, Jesus' teaching is a challenging pronouncement on suffering, which sheds light on the experience of the church in Nero's Rome (possibly the context for this Gospel).

(b) The organic union of Mk. 9:49 and 9:50 has been questioned, esp. since the latter saying occurs in a different context in Matt. 5:13 and Lk. 14:34. Matthew and Luke use the vb. *mōrainomai* ("lose saltiness," also meaning "become fools") rather than Mk.'s "become unsalty" (*analos*). If there is a relationship between savorless and foolish and between salt and wisdom, then "have salt in yourselves" may have a similar meaning to what it does in rab. writings with regard to instruction to disciples by teachers in order to become wise. In Mk. 9:50 eschatological wisdom is meant, i.e., the wisdom of disciples lived out in their religious attitude, faith, and conduct, keeping in mind the last events to come (Matt. 10:16; Eph. 5:15–16). These events provide the organic link between Mk. 9:49 and 50.

(c) How does the last phrase of Mk. 9:50 ("be at peace with each other") fit in? This is probably an example of two Gk. imperatives in conditional parataxis, linked by the consecutive *kai* ("and"): "If you have salt in yourselves [i.e., learn wisdom together], *then* you will be able to maintain peace with one another." Note in the context that the disciples have been arguing about who would be greatest (9:34). But salt made those who ate at the common table friends, and there should be no quarrelling among friends. Such a covenant was inviolable.

(d) A reference to ancient practices throws light on the unity and meaning of Mk. 9:42–50 as a whole. Amputation of the hand was known in biblical times (Deut. 25:12). Ancient peoples in general cut off a guilty person's hands or feet in cases of theft, robbery, or forgery. Similarly, the eye was taken for adultery (cf. Gen. 19:11; Job 31:1; Matt. 5:29–30). (Recent movements in some Islamic countries have revived this practice.) Punishment by amputation was considered humane in an age when the death penalty was common for theft, robbery, sedition, and even adultery. In such cases, the stump had to be cauterized, or else gangrene would set in. Salt was a primitive treatment for wounds, including injuries left after amputation.

In other words, Jesus may be using a metaphor encouraging his followers to avoid the supernatural fire of the next world by applying a symbolic fire in this. If salt is a medicament for damaged tissue, then Jesus is calling us to symbolic amputation to this life; in this way we will not only avoid the circumstances whereby actual amputation might result but will also avoid the fire to come.

3. Lk. 14:25–34 is a discourse on the need for persistent whole-heartedness in following Jesus. That takes precedence even over the family. Anyone who lays down his or her cross has no further testimony. Anyone who leaves a house roofless is a laughingstock. The one who sues for peace before a battle starts is beaten without a struggle. Salt that has lost its flavor is like all these—good neither for a fertilizer nor for the manure pile.

4. In Col. 4:6 Paul states that a Christian's speech should always be gracious, "seasoned with salt." Salt gives flavor to discourse and recommends it to the palate (cf. Job 6:6), and this may be the primary idea of the metaphor here. Salt also preserves from corruption and renders wholesome. Eph. 4:29 carries similar ideas: "Do not let any unwholesome speech come out of your mouth but only what is helpful for building up others according to their needs, that it may benefit those who listen." But salt in Col. 4:6 can also be understood as a metaphor for wisdom (cf. above discussion): "Your talk should always be with grace; it should be wise, and you should learn how to answer everyone."

5. *halykos* occurs only at Jas. 3:12. In nature it is impossible for both saltwater and fresh to come from the same spring. It ought to be just as unnatural for the tongue of the Christian to pour out curses as well as blessings.

6. The only occurrence of *synalizō* in the NT (Acts 1:4) poses difficulties, both textual and interpretive. But seeing that having salt together was a euphemism for eating together, the NIV is probably correct in translating it, "while he was eating with them." That the resurrected Jesus did take food with his disciples is affirmed in Lk. 24:41–43 (cf. Acts 10:41), to convince them of the reality of his presence.

| 230 | ἀλείφω | ἀλείφω (*aleiphō*), anoint (*230*). |

CL & OT In the ancient Near East, anointing gained special significance in early times. The cleansing and strength-giving properties of ointments and oils were applied not only for purposes of purification, bodily hygiene, and beautification, but also to treat wounds and cure diseases. The healing properties were linked with magic, for every ailment was associated with the power of gods or demons.

Anointing acquired a further significance, which may be traced to these magical ideas, when practiced at the institution of an official or vassal king in Egypt or a priest in Babylon. Here the action indicates obligation and honor as well as protection for the one who is anointed (→ *chriō*, 5987). Trees, idols, and even weapons were anointed.

Anointing in the OT is close in its uses and in its significance to practices outside Israel. In the LXX *aleiphō* is normally used for anointing for the care of the body or for beauty's sake (Ruth 3:3; 2 Chr. 28:15; Dan. 10:3; Jdt. 16:8). Anointing by a host is a mark of care and honor for one's guest (Ps. 23:5, though a different Gk word is used here). It is omitted during a period of mourning (2 Sam. 14:2; cf. 12:20). In Ezek. 13:10–16 *aleiphō* is used for whitewashing. Occasionally this word is synonymous with *chriō*.

NT In the NT *aleiphō* occurs only 9x. In contrast with the more important word *chriō*, it refers to the physical action of anointing, performed exclusively on people. Ointments used are olive oil, or the more expensive myrrh, and balsam. On the theological significance of anointing in the NT, three ideas may be distinguished.

1. In the Sermon on the Mount (Matt. 6:17), Jesus commands all who fast also to anoint themselves with oil. This is seen as a normal expense for personal hygiene and a general expression of joy, which should be continued during the fast. Only what is done secretly before God and not before other people has true worth.

2. The background of Lk. 7:38–50 is the Jewish custom of anointing the head of a guest (cf. also Jn. 12:3). Jesus here exposes the Pharisee who failed to show him this honor and who now has to watch Jesus receive it at the hands of a humble woman whom the Pharisee would regard as one of the lost. Here anointing becomes an expression of faith and its omission an expression of unbelief.

3. Anointing a sick person with oil (Mk. 6:13; Jas. 5:14; cf. Lk. 10:34) reminds us of the anointing of the sick elsewhere in the ancient world. Medicinal properties were attributed to the anointing. The healings performed by the disciples or elders of the church were accompanied by anointing, and it took place in the context of preaching and prayer. Healing, and thus anointing also, came to be seen as a visible sign of the beginning of God's reign.

See also *chriō*, anoint, 5987.

| 237 | ἀλήθεια | ἀλήθεια (*alētheia*), truth, sometimes faithfulness (*237*); ἀληθής (*alēthēs*), true, sincere, real, correct, faithful, trustworthy, genuine (*239*); ἀληθινός (*alēthinos*), genuine, real, true, valid, trustworthy (*240*); ἀληθῶς (*alēthōs*), truly, certainly, indeed, in very truth (*242*); ἀληθεύω (*alētheuō*), to speak the truth (*238*). |

CL 1. (a) In Homer *alētheia* is usually used in contrast to telling a lie or withholding information. However, this is not his only meaning. For example, he uses the word to describe a woman who is careful, honest, accurate, or reliable.

(b) In Gk. history writers *alētheia* most often stands for truth in opposition to falsehood.

(c) This usage also persists in later Hel. writers, such as Epictetus (who contrasts telling the truth with deceiving flatteries) and Philo (who writes that the evil spies who spied out the promised land preferred deceit to truth).

(d) Josephus uses *alētheia* in several different senses. (i) Truth is that which corresponds to the facts of the matter. (ii) Truth is also proved to be such by historical events; e.g., the words of a prophet are proved true. (iii) *alēthēs* is used in the sense of "genuine" or "real."

2. The use of *alēthēs* in Gk. philosophical texts has its own unique emphases. (a) Parmenides asks about the nature of real being and

draws a contrast between the way of truth and the way of seeming. Change belongs only to the material world, which is the realm of mere appearance. There can be no change in what really exists. Hence truth, in contrast to appearance, belongs to the extrahistorical realm of the changeless.

(b) The Sophists held a different view. Protagoras, for example, wrote about wind, which may seem warm to one person and cool to another. It is not necessary, he urged, to say that one view is true and the other false. Each may be true for the person concerned. In this way Protagoras comes near to the modern notion of existential truth.

(c) Plato rejects this view. (i) If "true" and "false" are only relative to the individual, then as soon as someone says that the philosophy of Protagoras is false for him, it is therefore false. Falsehood, for Plato, is a matter of deception. It conceals reality. By contrast, the divine and divinity are free from falsehood. God is true in deed and word and neither changes himself nor deceives others. Plato thus returns to the earlier view of Parmenides, that truth stands in contrast to appearance and to change, although he goes further in locating it in the realm of eternal ideas. (ii) At the same time, Plato also uses *alētheia* and *alēthēs* in more ordinary ways. *alētheia* sometimes means simply "the facts of the matter" and can stand in contrast to legend.

(d) Aristotle takes us closest to the view of truth found in modern propositional logic. He distinguishes between the genuine proposition, which is either true or false, and sentences such as pleas or commands. Logically, a true proposition entails the denial of its contrary. He also argues that the truth of a proposition consists in corresponding with facts. Often, however, Aristotle uses the actual word *alētheia* in its ordinary, everyday sense without philosophical content.

(e) Philo uses *alētheia* in ordinary ways. As a Jewish theologian he speaks of "true doctrine." But as a speculative writer influenced by Platonism he also contrasts truth with mere appearance. He also sees the truth of God manifested in historical events.

3. (a) *alēthinos* frequently means real or genuine, but it may also mean simply truthful. (b) The adv. *alēthōs*, truly, varies in force from context to context. At its weakest it may simply mean indeed or certainly. But it may sometimes be used more solemnly to mean in very truth. (c) The vb. *alētheuō* usually means to speak the truth, though it can also mean to prove true or (in the pass.) to be fulfilled.

OT 1. (a) The Heb. word that is the nearest equivalent to *alētheia* is *ᵓᵉmet*. The LXX generally translates this word either as *alētheia* or as *pistis*, faith, faithfulness (→ *4411*). Similarly, Eng. versions sometimes render *ᵓᵉmet* as "truth," sometimes as "faithfulness." Indeed, many OT scholars claim that for Heb. writers the notion of truth is close to faithfulness in meaning, suggesting the idea of stability, firmness, or reliability. They use etymology to strengthen this conclusion (*ᵓᵉmet* being derived from the root *ᵓmn*, to be firm). But such a method of determining meaning can be misleading and simplistic, esp. since words get their meaning more from context than from etymology.

(b) Although *ᵓᵉmet* is translated as both *alētheia* and *pistis*, this does not mean that these two words are interrelated in meaning; this may simply be a case of the same word having two different meanings. That is, *ᵓᵉmet* means truth in some contexts, faithfulness in others. To use an analogy: Just because we use the Eng. word "taste" to mean taste by eating as well as taste in aesthetics does not mean there is a connection between aesthetics and enjoying food. If there is a connection between truth and faithfulness, it is not because of etymology but because God is said to act both faithfully and with integrity; otherwise said, he acts faithfully in accordance with his spoken word. Hence believers may lean confidently on God and find him faithful.

(c) When *ᵓᵉmet* is used in the sense of faithfulness, it frequently occurs in parallelism with the word *ḥesed*, steadfast love. This conjunction of these two words can have different nuances, according to context. For example, when Abraham's servant Eliezer asks Bethuel and Laban to show *ḥesed* and *ᵓᵉmet* to Abraham (Gen. 24:49), he is probably requesting them to act with honesty and integrity. Earlier in

the same chapter, however, when he first meets Rebekah, Eliezer praises God, "who has not forsaken his *ḥesed* and *ᵓᵉmet*," meaning that God has remained loyal and faithful to his covenant promises to Abraham (24:27).

Characteristically, it is in Ps. that both praise and prayer are offered repeatedly on the basis of God's faithfulness. Over half of the occurrences of *ᵓᵉmet* in the book have this meaning (e.g., 25:10; 57:3; 115:1). God's steadfast love is manifested as an expression of his faithfulness, and his faithfulness endures forever (117:2). But it would be a mistake to infer from these examples that *ᵓᵉmet* always means reliability in a theological sense, rather than simply "truth" in contrast to deceit or falsehood. For example, *ᵓᵉmet* in 119:43 almost certainly means "word of truth" (cf. NIV; *logon alētheias* in LXX; cf. also 43:3; 45:4).

(d) *ᵓᵉmet* is used in contrast to deceit or falsehood in a number of places. In Gen. 42:16 Joseph wishes to establish whether the brothers have told the truth. In Exod. 18:21, Moses selects men of truth, those who hate a bribe, to help him with the burden of administration. The emphasis here rests on honesty and integrity—their ability to make judgments on the basis of truth. In 1 Ki. 17:24 the widow acknowledges the truth of Elijah's word after he restored her son to life.

(e) In wisdom lit., *ᵓᵉmet* is sometimes used in the sense of faithfulness (Prov. 3:3; 16:6), but more often against the background of a contrast between truth and falsehood or deception. When Wisdom says, "My mouth speaks what is true" (8:7), the point is that she will not deceive the one who embraces her. In 12:19 truthful lips are set in contrast to a lying tongue, and the whole passage attacks lies, deceit, and false witness (12:17–22; cf. also 22:21; 23:23).

(f) The prophets also use *ᵓᵉmet* in the sense both of faithfulness and of truth in contrast to falsehood. In Isa. 43:9, the nations are to come together as a judicial assembly to determine whether the claim of Yahweh or that of the pagan gods is true. The claim is reliable only if it accords with the facts of the matter. In Isa. 59:14–15, the complaint that truth is lacking may be alluding to Israel's unfaithfulness, but the real cause of complaint is "uttering lies" (59:13b; cf. also Jer. 9:5; Zech. 8:16–17).

2. Let us now sum up what the OT has to say about *ᵓᵉmet*. (a) In the vast majority of contexts truth is not an abstract and theoretical concept. Certainly it is never located, as it is in Plato, in some timeless, extrahistorical realm. The God of Israel reveals his truth not only in his words but also in his deeds, and this truth is proved in practice in the experience of his people. Similarly, people express their respect for truth not in abstract theory, but in their daily witness to their neighbors and their verbal and commercial transactions. It is not surprising, then, to find in the OT what would nowadays be called an existential view of truth. But it is not *only* existential truth. Note how Ps. 119:105 sees God's law as a lamp that shows the believer the true state of affairs.

(b) Such truth is firm and can be relied on. But this insight is not arrived at on an exclusively theological basis. Certainly a believer may confidently rely on God because of his covenant faithfulness. But this particular use of *ᵓᵉmet* does not lie behind every occurrence of the word. The Hebrews recognized the *logical* truth that others also recognized, that a true word can be relied upon because it accords with reality, and that both for a God of truth and for a person of truth, word and deed are one. Those who call on God "in truth" (Ps. 145:18) do so honestly.

3. (a) In the Apocr., *alētheia* is used mostly (though not always) to mean truth in contrast to falsehood. In 1 Macc. 7:18 the real issue is the deceitful use of words. In Sir. 7:20 the servant works reliably indeed, but the main point is that he is "true," in the sense of being honest. In Tob. 7:10 truth is used of giving a true report. However, sometimes *alētheia* does duty for *ᵓᵉmet* in the sense of faithfulness (*pistis*), esp. when a writer alludes to earlier OT writings. Thus in Wis. 15:1 the writer declares, "You, our God, are kind and true [*alēthēs*]," probably in paraphrase of Exod. 34:6. Here the word probably means faithfulness, because the sense of Exod. 34 is too clear to be lost.

(b) Truth is esp. prominent in the Dead Sea Scrolls, most of all in the Thanksgiving Hymns. God is the God of truth (1QH 15:26); the phrase "truth of God" also occurs (1QS 11:4; 1QM 4:6; cf. 1QS 3:7). Truth is emphasized as a quality of moral behavior. Entrance into the Qumran community is a conversion to truth (1QS 6:15), and the initiates bind themselves to the precepts of truth by oath (1:11–15). They are now within the sphere of influence of the spirit of truth (3:24). The community are "true witnesses to justice" (8:6).

NT 1. *Synoptic Gospels and Acts*. The words in this group occur only 23x in the Synoptic Gospels and Acts (out of a total 183x). (a) On the lips of Jesus these words occur only in Lk. 4:25; 9:27; 12:44; 16:11; 21:3. In most of these the forms (lit.) "the truth is" or "truly I tell you" serve to introduce a solemn statement and are presumably Lk.'s translation into Gk. of the characteristic *amēn* formula used elsewhere by Jesus.

(b) At the same time the isolated occurrences of *alētheia* and *alēthēs* in the Synoptics do not exhaust what we may infer about Jesus' attitude to truth. (i) Negatively, many of his sayings attack hypocrisy or, more generally, any discrepancy between word and deed or between word and reality (e.g., Matt. 23:2–3, 23–24; Lk. 11:46). The Jewish leaders display attitudes that are untruthful and deceitful, based on a contrast between word and deed. (ii) Positively, Jesus' own words always accord with his deeds and with actuality. He preaches grace to the outcast; thus, he eats with tax collectors and sinners. He is Messiah in word, proclaiming the advent of God's kingdom; therefore he is also Messiah in deed, demonstrating the advent of the kingdom by works of power. Jesus' life of integrity culminates in the cross.

(c) Other occurrences of *alētheia* and *alēthēs* in the Synoptic Gospels and Acts either have the sense of truth in contrast to falsehood, concealment, or deception, or else refer to honesty or sincerity. In Matt. 22:15–16 (cf. Mk. 12:14), the Pharisees seek to trap Jesus with their questions and introduce this query with the words, "We know you are a man of integrity [*alēthēs*] and that you teach the way of God in accordance with the truth [*alētheia*]." The point here is that Jesus will not conceal the truth through any fear of consequences. He is honest in stating his views.

The same meaning of *alētheia* occurs in Mk. 5:33, when the woman with a flow of blood who touched Jesus in the crowd tells "the whole truth," i.e., conceals nothing about what she has done. However, in 12:32, to speak "right" (*alētheia*) is simply to state the facts of the matter accurately or correctly (cf. also Acts 26:25).

(d) *alēthinos* occurs in the Synoptics only in Lk. 16:11: "Who will trust you with true riches?" Here the meaning is clearly that of "genuine" or "real."

2. *Paul's letters*. (a) One of Paul's most distinctive uses of *alētheia* in the NT is his use of the phrase "the truth" to characterize the gospel itself. Although this is most prominent in the Pastorals, this meaning already occurs in Gal. and perhaps in 2 Thess. In Gal. 2:5 Paul declares that what is at issue in his conflict with the Judaizers is "the truth of the gospel." In Paul's judgment, enticement to compromise the gospel is an enticement to compromise the truth, and vice versa. To give way is to deny the truth, both in the sense of his own integrity and in the sense of the actual situation in salvation history as it now is. Hence, in 5:7 "the truth" is synonymous with the gospel itself or (more probably) that which is real: "Who . . . kept you from obeying the truth?"

(b) Paul also uses *alētheia* in a broader sense to mean God's revelation of his will or even of his being, either through the law or, at one point, through creation. This use is characteristic of Rom. 1–2. Human beings by their wickedness "suppress the truth" (1:18) and exchange the truth about God for a lie (1:25). Hence there will be wrath for those who do not obey the truth (2:8). The law itself, by contrast, is "the embodiment of knowledge and truth" (2:20). The truth at issue here is not primarily the truth of the gospel, but the rejection of the truth about God as creator and judge. The Gentile world has not willfully rejected

gospel truth, but it has willfully suppressed what may be seen about God and his sovereign claims from creation (1:20).

(c) Truth in Paul often stands in contrast to lying or deception. Indeed, together with Wis. 13–14, Paul inherits the traditional Heb. prophetic view that divine truth stands in contrast to idolatry, precisely because idolatry is a deception and delusion (cf. Rom. 1:25). Paul uses *alētheia* in a thoroughly natural sense when he asserts, "I speak the truth in Christ—I am not lying" (9:1) and "everything we said to you was true" (2 Cor. 7:14). Practical integrity is as important to Paul as it was to Jesus. For both, truth becomes a matter of correspondence between word and deed.

(d) These two aspects of *alētheia* are brought together in a striking way in 2 Cor. On the one hand, Paul is accused of vacillation and change and asserts his own concern for the truth in the sense of an honesty or integrity in which word and deed correspond. Indeed, he urges, it is the false apostles who need artificial commendation. But the apostle has also been accused of veiling his gospel. Again he urges that it is not he but his opponents who tailor the gospel message to conform to human expectations and demands. He renounces disgraceful, underhanded ways and refuses to tamper with God's word, but "by setting forth the truth plainly we commend ourselves to every man's conscience in the sight of God" (2 Cor. 4:2). Side by side with this emphasis on speaking the truth, Paul stresses his unity of word and conduct (see 6:4–7).

(e) Paul believes in the power of truth. Truth exposes lies (Rom. 3:4, where divine truth exposes human falsehood for what it is). Love of the truth can even lead to salvation (2 Thess. 2:10), although this does not mean mere theoretical truth, but commitment to the truth as this is expressed in the gospel. To encounter the truth as it is in Jesus leads on to transformation of life, which enables the believer to turn away from old deceits (Eph. 4:21–22). Thus, in 2 Cor. 6:7 "truthful speech" occurs in parallel with "the power of God" and "weapons of righteousness." Paul does not use the weapons of power politics or psychological pressure, but with honest integrity speaks and acts in truth and righteousness (cf. also Eph. 6:14, where truth is part of the Christian's armor).

(f) Truth is demanded of Christians as a corollary of their union with Christ and status as a new creation. In 1 Cor. 5:8 the believer celebrates the festival of new life with "sincerity and truth," banishing all impurity and deception or dishonesty, just as the Jews banished the old leaven from their houses at Passover. The new life is to be untarnished, free from anything that spreads corrupting influences by virtue of its impurity or duplicity. The same idea occurs in Eph. 4:25, with more explicit reference to falsehood. Because the believer has put on the new nature (4:24), Paul insists that everyone must "speak truthfully to his neighbor, for we are all members of one body." In 1 Cor. 13:6, Paul probably means that love is brave enough to face the truth. It has nothing to conceal.

(g) The Pastoral Letters reflect a distinctive outlook, although they develop a trend we have already seen in Gal. and Rom. Truth is essentially the revealed truth of the gospel message. Note that in these letters, the problem of false doctrine looms as large as it did earlier in Gal. To become a Christian is "to come to a knowledge of the truth" (1 Tim. 2:4; cf. 2 Tim. 3:7). By contrast, the great danger under attack is that people will listen only to teachers who "turn their ears away from the truth and turn aside to myths" (2 Tim. 4:4); such people "have been robbed of the truth" (1 Tim. 6:5). "The truth" in the Pastorals, esp. in the sense of Christian revelation, is wholesome and sound.

(h) The verb *alētheuō* occurs only 2x in the NT, both times in Paul. In Gal. 4:16 Paul exclaims, "Have I now become your enemy by telling you the truth?" Here the irony has the most point if truth means the facts of the gospel as they really are, in contrast to the deceptions of Paul's opponents. Even if *alētheuō* is understood to mean little more than "to proclaim the Christian message," the contrast between Paul and his opponents loses its point if this is not specifically a truth proclamation that hides nothing from the hearer. In Eph. 4:15 Paul commands Christians to speak the truth in love. *alētheuō* here probably entails integrity of life in addition to truthful speech.

(i) The adjective *alēthinos* occurs only once in Paul, where "to serve the living and true God" (1 Thess. 1:9) has its characteristic meaning of real or genuine. The real God stands here in contrast to idols or so-called gods. The adv. *alēthōs* also occurs only once in Paul. In 2:13 the Thessalonians received the message of Christ not as mere human words, but "as it actually [genuinely] is, the word of God."

3. *Jn.'s writings.* Considerations about word frequency alone suggest the importance of truth in Jn.'s writings, which contain nearly half the occurrences of *alētheia* (45x), 17 out of 26x for *alēthēs*, and 23 out of 28x for *alēthinos*. The discussion should not be whether Jn. reflects a Gk. or Heb. view of truth, but what is the nature of the concept of truth Jn. reflects. Jn. uses this word group regularly in the sense of reality in contrast to falsehood or mere appearance.

(a) Special attention must be given to the phrase "full of grace and truth" in Jn. 1:14 (cf. 1:17). Many scholars find the background to this in Exod. 34:6, that the Lord God abounds "in love [*ḥesed*] and faithfulness [*ʾemet*]." Certainly the Exod. 34 background of seeing God is appropriate to Jn.'s thought (cf. Jn. 1:14–18), but what Jn. stresses here is not the covenant faithfulness of God, but that in Christ, the Logos, we can see God in his genuine actuality and reality (cf. 1:17). The law does indeed constitute a witness to God, as does Moses, but the reality itself is encountered in Christ.

(b) There can be no doubt that sometimes in Jn. *alētheia* and *alēthēs* mean simply truth in contrast to falsehood. In Jn. 4:18 the woman of Samaria speaks the truth about her marital status. In 10:41 it is affirmed that everything that John the Baptist said about Jesus is true. The statement "I tell you the truth: It is for your good that I am going away" (16:7) dispels any suspicion that the words may have been tailored to provide some illusory comfort. In 1 Jn. a liar is one who does not speak the truth (2:4; cf. 2:21, 27). To err from the truth is to be deceived (1:8). The notion of witness is prominent in Jn.'s Gospel, and much is made of the fact that the witness to Christ is true (5:31–32). But the notion of a witness that is true rather than false leads to the question of the validity of that witness and thereby to the use of *alētheia* in the sense of validity.

(c) The debate about truthful witness is developed more fully in Jn. 8:13–58, where the issue is validity of the witness. The witness to Jesus Christ is valid because there is no higher court of appeal than God himself. The witness of those who judge "by human standards" (8:15) is not necessarily dishonest (though cf. 9:41), but such testimony is untrue in the sense that it is invalid. Valid witness depends on revelation.

(d) One of the most important uses of *alētheia* and *alēthēs* in Jn. is to convey the idea of reality in contrast to whatever the situation may seem to look like on the surface. (i) The clearest example of this is the use of the adj. *alēthēs* to mean "real." Thus, in 6:55 Jesus says that his flesh is real food, his blood real drink. This real food gives more lasting satisfaction and nourishment than other things people call food. (ii) Those who worship God in spirit and in truth (4:23–24) are not those who worship in sincerity. Jesus does not criticize the Samaritans for lacking sincerity. Rather, true worship is that which accords with reality, which people grasp on the basis of revelation. That is why it is associated with the Holy Spirit.

(e) Special attention should be given to the phrase "doing the truth" in Jn.'s writings. This phrase combines an allusion to the way of Christian revelation with an additional reference to the contrast between truth and falsehood. Thus in Jn. 3:21 the statement, "Whoever lives by [does] the truth comes into the light, so that it may be seen plainly that what he has done has been done through God," cannot simply refer to the one who lives up to his or her aspirations faithfully. Rather, the phrase emphasizes that the one who practices a Christian faith and life will have nothing to hide. In 1 Jn. 1:6 the author similarly combines the notion of truth as revelation with truth in contrast to falsehood. A tension between profession of faith and actual practice is inconsistent with Christian revelation and also in principle self-contradictory. Hence if we claim to have fellowship with God but walk in darkness, "we lie and do not live by [do] the truth."

(f) There are several passages in Jn. in which the meaning of *alētheia* or *alēthēs* is too broad to be equated with any of the five categories discussed above. (i) One of the most important of these is Jn. 14:6, where Jesus declares, "I am the way and the truth and the life. No one comes to the Father except through me." The way leads to the Father; that is primary, and "the truth" describes the way. Nevertheless, as the truth Jesus is also the goal of our search, for "anyone who has seen me has seen the Father" (14:9). So when Jesus declares that he *is* the truth, a number of ideas are combined. First, truth is not abstract or suprahistorical but revealed in the actual personal life of the Word made flesh. Second, Christ is also the truth because he is the revelation of God and thus his own witness is valid. Third, truth also stands in opposition to deception or falsehood. In the case of divine revelation, this means that Christ is both truth and reality.

(ii) The same range of meaning probably applies to the assertion "your word is truth" in Jn. 17:17. The context is the distinctiveness of the community of believers as over against the world. The community is holy, for it belongs to God and is founded on his Word. However, the very word on which the community depends for its existence and consecration is also a word of commission that sends it out into the world (17:18). In both respects, this word from God is valid, effective, in no way false; it accords with reality. Thereby the community's sanctification is assured and its commission validated.

(iii) In Jn. 8:44–45, the truth spoken by Jesus is set in contrast to the lie spoken by the devil. The devil does not hold "to the truth, for there is no truth in him." Here truth is primarily contrasted with falsehood or deception. There is doubtless an allusion here to the deception by the serpent in Gen. 3:4–5. The implication is that by opposing the truth of Jesus (here, also in the sense of the authentic divine revelation), Jesus' enemies are actually doing the devil's work. The devil also seduces us away from reality and life.

(iv) By contrast, the Spirit of God is the Spirit of truth (Jn. 14:17; 15:26; 16:13; cf. 1 Jn. 4:6; 5:6). It is striking that this phrase is repeated in no less than three of the five Paraclete sayings. The Paraclete (*paraklētos*, → *4156*) can be understood as a prosecuting counsel who exposes (*elenchō*, → *1794*) the facts of the matter (Jn. 16:8; NIV "convict"). The Spirit places the Christian community in the light of judgment that belongs, strictly speaking, to the last day. Hence, his verdict is absolutely valid and does not need to be modified by fresh knowledge. One other idea, however, must be added. The Spirit of truth, as Paraclete, continues the work of Jesus as Paraclete, whereby proponents of truth and falsehood are shown up to be what they are (cf. Jesus' self-proclaimed task as bearing witness to the truth, 18:37). Falsehood is exposed in all its seductive deception as a lie. The truth is shown to be reality, based on God's revelation (cf. 14:6 again).

(g) In Jn.'s writings *alēthinos* often has its characteristic meaning of genuine, real. In Jn. 1:9, Jesus is the real light, in contrast to John the Baptist. This "light" exposes a person to the light of judgment. True, John the Baptist did indeed expose people's actions and called them to repentance, but the *real* crisis of division, which brings to light the direction in which people are going, is Jesus Christ. We have already seen that "true worshipers" (4:23) are those whose worship is based on reality, not on human aspiration. In 6:32 Jesus tells his hearers that whereas Moses gave Israel bread from heaven, God now gives them the real bread, to which the manna merely pointed—Jesus himself. Similarly in 15:1 Jesus is the real vine, worthy of the name. Israel as vine was unproductive and wild; real fruitfulness is to be found only in Christ.

Nevertheless, *alēthinos* may also have the same range of meaning as *alēthēs*. It may denote a true saying (Jn. 4:37) or true judgment (8:16). Sometimes the two senses merge, as when the meaning is primarily or partly, though not exclusively, that of real, genuine, e.g., "the only true God" (17:3).

It is difficult to determine how narrowly or otherwise we should interpret the meaning of *alēthinos* in Rev. God is "him who is holy and true" (3:7), "the faithful and true witness" (3:14). Note also: "Just and true are your ways" (15:3); "true and just are your judgments" (16:7); "these are the true words of God" (19:9); "these words are trustworthy and true" (21:5; cf. 6:10; 19:2; 22:6). It must not be forgotten that Rev. uses only *alēthinos* and never *alēthēs* or even *alētheia*. Hence it would be unwise to try to draw too clear-cut a distinction between them. In Hel. lit. *alēthinos* is used of divine beings to mean "that which truly exists," and this may well form part of the meaning in Rev. But God is also true in contrast to the deceits and falsehoods of idolatry and the Antichrist. The martyrs and faithful believers may also rely on his truth.

(h) The adv. *alēthōs* occurs 7x in Jn., once in 1 Jn., but not in Rev. Sometimes it is used in the sense of real or genuine, as an adverbial equivalent to *alēthinos*. Thus Nathanael is (lit.) "really an Israelite" (Jn. 1:47); that is, he is a man really worthy of the name. Usually, however, the adv. is used in the sense of truly or indeed.

4. *Other NT writings.* (a) In 1 and 2 Pet. we find "the truth" or "the way of truth" used as in the Pastorals virtually as a synonym for the truth of the gospel. Christians are those who have become obedient to the truth (1 Pet. 1:22); false prophets and false teachers deny Christ and thereby cause others to revile the way of truth (2 Pet. 2:2).

Sometimes true means in accordance with the facts of the matter. Thus, "the true grace of God" (1 Pet. 5:12) means the grace that the readers have proved true in their experience and that was based on reality and not delusion. A true proverb (2 Pet. 2:22) states truth as it is in the light of experience.

(b) At first sight "the word of truth" in Jas. 1:18 seems to mean simply the message of the gospel. But the context suggests that what is at issue here is that God acts reliably and consistently. God does not tempt us to sin (1:13–16), and with him is no shadow due to change (1:17). Because of this reliability, his word is the word of truth. To wander from the truth (5:19) may also seem to mean to turn away from the gospel. But once again the term here is broader, meaning the right path. In what sense does selfish ambition lead one to "deny the truth" (3:14)? Most likely James is warning his readers that selfish ambition and arrogance lead people to put considerations about their own status even above those that concern the truth. Often lies stem from a concern to defend or assert the claims of one's own status in the eyes of others.

(c) The reference in Heb. 10:26 to receiving "the knowledge of the truth" certainly means knowledge of the truth of the gospel. But *alētheia* here also underlines the absoluteness and finality of the Christian message. If a person turns his or her back on that which is the truth, indeed there is nothing else. *alēthinos* occurs 3x in Heb. In 8:2; 9:24 it describes "the true tabernacle." Like Jewish apocalyptic writers the author contrasts the heavenly sanctuary as it existed in the mind of God and the earthly tabernacle, which reflected this heavenly reality. *alēthinos* in 8:2 and 9:24 bears its characteristic meaning of genuine or real. In 10:22 a true heart means one that is honest and without deceit.

238 (alētheuō, to speak the truth), → 237.

239 (alēthēs, true, sincere, real, faithful, trustworthy, genuine), → 237.

240 (alēthinos, genuine, real, true, valid, trustworthy), → 237.

242 (alēthōs, truly, certainly, indeed, in very truth), → 237.

245 (halizō, to salt, season with salt), → 229.

248 (allassō, to change, exchange), → 2904.

251 (allēgoreō, speak allegorically), → 4130.

252	ἀλληλουϊά

ἀλληλουϊά (*hallēlouia*), hallelujah (*252*).

OT The best explanation for the Heb. word *halᵉlû-yāh* is that it is composed of two elements: the 2d pers. pl. masc, piel imperative of the root *hālal*, to praise; and the abbreviated form of the divine name *yāhweh* as *yāh*. The vb. is used widely of secular (e.g., Gen. 12:15) and religious (e.g., Jdg. 16:24) praise, and in its usage combines the notions of admiration, adulation, and rejoicing. The fact that *halᵉlû-yāh* is followed immediately by *halᵉlû ʾeth-yāhweh* (e.g., Ps. 148:1) suggests that from early days it had become a recognized shout of praise to the Lord.

Praise is offered to Yahweh for his works in creation (e.g., Ps. 104), his deliverance in the exodus and his patience in the desert days (105; 106), his universal rule through the Melchizedek priest-king (110), and his eschatological purpose to make the whole world at the end what his chosen people are now (145–150).

NT This word occurs only in Rev. 19:1, 3, 4, 6 and reflects the LXX usage (which transliterated the word rather than translated it). The heavenly hosts praise the Lord for his victory over the "great prostitute," ascribing to him salvation, glory, and power.

See also *amēn*, amen (*297*); *hōsanna*, Hosanna (*6057*).

254 (allogenēs, foreign), → 259.

257	ἄλλος

ἄλλος (*allos*), other (*257*); ἄλλως (*allōs*), otherwise (*261*); ἕτερος (*heteros*), other (*2283*); ἑτέρως (*heterōs*), differently (*2284*).

CL & OT 1. In cl. Gk. *heteros* and *allos* have essentially the same meaning: another, other. They will often introduce a new person, thing, or group. Originally *heteros* had the notion of the other of two options or groups, though this distinction is not rigidly kept.

2. In the LXX *allos* refers to that already mentioned in contrast to others and can even render a demonstrative pron. *heteros* had a personal connotation and was used to translate words like man, neighbor, brother. *allos* is used about 100x, *heteros* about 250x.

NT In the NT there is little distinction between *heteros* (98x) and *allos* (155x). The use seems to depend mostly on author's preference (e.g., Lk. prefers *heteros*). The polemic factor is one of the reasons why *allos* is found so frequently in 1 and 2 Cor.

1. (a) Both words are used to denote another person, thing, or group; e.g., *allos* (Matt. 5:39; 12:13; Jn. 5:32); *heteros* (Lk. 5:7; 23:40). *tē hetera* can mean the next day (Acts 20:15; 27:3). (b) The same use is found in the pl. (e.g., Matt. 20:3, 6; Lk. 10:1; Jn. 7:12; 9:16; Acts 2:13). (c) In enumerations (Matt. 13:5, 7–8; Lk. 8:6–8) and in contrasts (Heb. 11:35–36) *heteros* and *allos* are used interchangeably. (d) Used as a noun, *ho heteros* has the force of a neighbor whom God has put in my way (Rom. 2:1; 13:8; 1 Cor. 10:24; Gal. 6:4).

2. These words become important theologically when they express a more or less qualitative difference, external or internal (e.g., Mk. 12:32; 1 Cor. 3:11; 2 Cor. 1:13). Jesus appeared to his disciples after his resurrection "in a different form" (Mk. 16:12), so that they did not recognize him (cf. Lk. 24:16; Jn. 20:15). At his transfiguration "there came another appearance on his face" (Lk. 9:29, lit. trans.). In 1 Cor. 15:39–41 Paul reflects on various kinds of flesh in his discussion of the resurrection body. Matt. 11:3 implies a question whether the Messiah must be some other person besides Jesus.

(a) The interpretation of Acts 2:4 ("in other [*heteros*] tongues") raises the question of whether the gift of tongues at Pentecost was a form of ecstatic utterance or whether the disciples were in fact speaking other languages, which they presumably did not know before (→ *glōssa*, tongue, language, speech, *1185*). The mistaken presumption of some of the onlookers that "they have had too much wine" (2:13) suggests that this was ecstatic speaking in tongues (as in 10:46; 19:6; 1 Cor. 12:10, 30; 14:1–4). Yet Luke also writes that visitors from various parts of the Roman empire were asking in amazement: "Are not all these men who are speaking Galileans? Then how is it that each of us hears them in his own native language?" (Acts 2:7–8).

(b) The story of Pentecost is a preparation for the apostles' missionary preaching and pictures the outpouring of the Spirit in a twofold manner: the speaking in tongues as a sign of the outpouring of the Spirit as prophesied by Joel 2:28–32 (cf. Acts 2:17–21), showing the last days have now come; and the proclamation of the word of God (Peter's Pentecost sermon in 2:14–36). At Pentecost the gospel was proclaimed to Jews and proselytes in Jerusalem—an event that marks the beginning of the fulfillment of Acts 1:8 and forms the transition to Peter's missionary preaching.

Note, however, that the perception that these are all Galileans comes from the onlookers. It is not impossible that among the hundred and twenty or so followers (Acts 1:15) were those who already knew some of the languages mentioned (e.g., Simon of Cyrene, Matt. 27:32; cf. Acts 2:10; and "men from Cyprus and Cyrene," 11:20). Note too that there were various synagogues in Jerusalem, including some that catered to people of the Diaspora (cf. 6:9). If so, the miracle of Pentecost may be that those filled with the Spirit were now preaching Jesus Christ boldly and with confidence in their own native language. It may also be significant that the emphasis in Acts 2 is not on the speaking of these languages but on the hearing by the audience (2:8, 11).

(c) In 2 Cor. 11:4 and Gal. 1:6–9, Paul stresses the uniqueness of the salvation offered by his gospel. "A different gospel" would not be the gospel, any more than another spirit can be the Holy Spirit. Such a gospel as the teaching of the Judaizers, which insisted on circumcision for Gentile converts, is thus no gospel. To Paul such a demand involves a matter of principle concerning the basis of salvation. To attempt to fulfill the demands of the law in order to be saved puts forward a righteous act by human beings as needed for salvation. The whole theme of Gal. treats the issues involved with the choice of the free grace of God in Christ versus salvation by human endeavor. The "gospel" of this latter alternative is anathema to Paul (Gal. 1:8; → *anathema*, *353*).

(d) In Rom. 7:23 "another law," i.e., the carnal egoistic urge, as a tool of the law of sin, fights against the good law of God, which the mind agrees with (cf. 7:25).

3. Phil. 3:15 contains the only NT instance of the adv. *heterōs*, differently. Paul seems to be arguing here against enthusiasts who claimed perfection and special revelations for themselves. He takes up their slogan and applies it to Christians. Those who are truly "perfect" (*teleioi*; → *telos*, *5465*) or mature are, in fact, those who know that they are imperfect and need to press on to what lies ahead (3:12–13). They have not yet reached their goal and do not yet possess "the prize for which God has called [them] heavenward in Christ Jesus" (3:14). The practical conclusion is given in 3:15: "All of us who are mature should take such a view of things. And if on some point you think differently, that too God will make clear to you." This last point is presumably directed at the claim to special revelations. Paul is confident that by being realistic and patient, they will grow in insight.

4. Several Gk. words are related to *allos*, such as *allotrios*, strange, alien, hostile (*259*); *allogenēs*, foreign (*254*); and *allophylos*, foreign (*260*); for these words → *allotrios* (*259*).

259	ἀλλότριος

ἀλλότριος (*allotrios*), adj., belonging to another, strange, alien, hostile; noun, a stranger (*259*); ἀλλογενής (*allogenēs*), foreign (*254*); ἀλλόφυλος (*allophylos*), alien to the race, hence from a Jewish standpoint a Gentile, heathen (*260*); ἀπαλλοτριόω, *apallotrioō*, alienated (*558*).

CL & OT 1. In cl. Gk. *allotrios* (from *allos* [another]) means another, strange, foreign, alien to people or land, hence unsuitable and even hostile. *apallotrioō* means to alienate, estrange. *allogenēs* (from *allos* and *genos* [race]) means foreign, strange. *allophylos* (from *allos* and *phylē* [tribe]) means alien to the race, strange.

2. In the LXX, *allotrios* translates different Heb. words and means foreign, alien (e.g., Gen. 31:15; Lev. 10:1; Deut. 14:21; 15:3; 32:16). Sometimes *allogenēs* is used with a similar meaning (e.g., Exod. 29:33;

Lev. 22:10; Num. 16:40; Joel 3:17). Aliens are still foreigners (Exod. 12:43–49), though they have certain rights and duties in the community.

NT 1. *allotrios* occurs parabolically in Matt. 17:25 in the discussion of the propriety of paying the half-shekel temple tax (cf. Exod. 30:11–16; 38:26). Jesus asks whether kings take tribute from their own sons or "from others." Peter replies, "From others"; to which Jesus says, "Then the sons are exempt." However, he counsels payment of the tax to avoid giving offense. The incident implies that Jesus' disciples are "sons of God" and that the Jews are in fact "others."

In Lk. 16:12 *allotrios* ("someone else's property") stands parallel to "worldly wealth" (v. 11; → *mamōnas*, *3440*). Money and possessions belong to another person. The implication is that they do not belong to the disciple, who is instead a steward of such things. In Jn. 10:5 the sheep, who belong to the shepherd and follow him, do not recognize the voice of a stranger. The implication is that Jewish (and other would-be) teachers are strangers disowned by the true flock of God, whereas Jesus is the true shepherd, known and followed by the true people of God.

In Acts 7:6 (referring to Gen. 15:13), the *gē allotria* ("a country not their own") is the land of Egypt, whereas Palestine is the homeland of Israel. But for Abraham even the promised land was a foreign country (Heb. 11:9) because it was not his true, heavenly home. Therefore, he lived in tents, and by it testified that he was a stranger in this world.

Christians are servants of Christ. Therefore, they should not judge "someone else's" servant (Rom. 14:4). Paul refuses to boast of the work or methods that "others" have done (2 Cor. 10:15–16), because he will not adorn himself with borrowed plumage. He will not even preach in a place where others have already been at work, refusing to build on a foundation laid by someone else (Rom. 15:20). Timothy is warned not to be hasty in laying hands on a man and entrusting him with a ministry. Otherwise, he might participate in the sins "of others" and be called to account for them (1 Tim. 5:22). The Jewish high priest entered the Holy Place with blood "that is not his own" (Heb. 9:25); Jesus, however, brought his own blood into the heavenly sanctuary. In Heb. 11:34 *allotrios* occurs in the expression "routed foreign armies."

2. *apallotrioō* occurs only in Eph. 2:12; 4:18; Col. 1:21—in each case as a passive part. translated "excluded," "separated," or "alienated." Before their conversion, Paul's readers were not citizens of Israel, the chosen people of God. They stood—like the heathen now—outside God's covenant and promises and were thus subject to wrath. They did not know God and lived in sin. Since they have now become Christians, they are not to return to their sinful state.

3. *allogenēs* occurs only in Lk. 17:18. The grateful Samaritan who returns to give thanks after being healed of his leprosy is called a "foreigner," for he is not a Jew. *allophylos* occurs only at Acts 10:28. Jews were forbidden to have fellowship with any "Gentile" (lit., "someone from another nation"), for the heathen were ceremonially unclean and such association would make a Jew unclean. In Christ, however, these barriers of the law have been abolished.

See also *diaspora*, dispersion (*1402*); *xenos*, foreign; stranger, alien (*3828*); *parepidēmos*, staying for a while in a strange place; stranger, resident alien (*4215*); *paroikos*, stranger, alien (*4230*).

260 (*allophylos*, alien to the race; a Gentile), → *259*.

261 (*allōs*, otherwise), → *257*.

263 (*alogos*, irrational, without speech), → *3364*.

266 (*halykos*, salty), → *229*.

279 (*hamartanō*, to sin), → *281*.

280 (*hamartēma*, a sin, transgression), → *281*.

281	ἀμαρτία

ἀμαρτία (*hamartia*), sin (*281*); ἀμάρτημα (*hamartēma*), a sin, transgression (*280*); ἀμαρτάνω (*hamartanō*), to sin (*279*); ἀμαρτωλός (*hamartōlos*), adj., sinful; noun, a sinner (*283*); ἀναμάρτητος (*anamartētos*), without sin (*387*).

CL & OT 1. (a) In cl. Gk. *hamartanō* originally meant to miss the mark, not share in something, be mistaken. The Gk. view of a mistake was intellectually oriented, so that *hamartanō* is the result of some *agnoia*, ignorance. The cognate noun is *hamartia*, mistake, failure to reach a goal (chiefly a spiritual one). The result of such action is *hamartēma*, failure, mistake, an offense committed against friends or one's own body. From these words developed the adj. and noun *hamartōlos*, the thing or person that fails.

(b) In the Gk.-speaking world the noun *hamartēma* prevailed over the vb. *hamartanō*. Aristotle placed it between *adikēma* (injustice) and *atychēma* (misfortune), as an offense against the prevailing order, but one without an evil intention. *hamartia* became a collective term with a relatively indefinite sense: offending against right feeling. It can mean anything from stupidity to law-breaking, anything that does not conform to the dominant ethic, to the respect due to social order and the *polis*.

(c) The Gk. view of guilt finds its deepest expression in conjunction with the fateful infatuation of the human being as cl. tragedy depicts it. Guilt is not just an action, but a reality rooted in one's innermost being. Guilt is the cause of suffering. Guilt and fate are inextricably interwoven.

(d) In its attempt to escape the determinism of fate, Hellenism severed the connection between guilt and fate through various rites and gnosis in the mystery religions. In addition, the concept of guilt was intellectualized and rationalized in the Stoa; it could be surmounted through better understanding and correct behavior. Both views work from the presupposition that a human being is basically good.

2. (a) In the LXX the two words *hamartia* and *adikia* (injustice, → *94*) represent almost the whole range of Heb. words for guilt and sin. *hamartia* and its cognates particularly represent the Heb. words *ḥaṭṭāʾt*, lapse, sin, and *ʿāwôn*, guilt, sin as a conscious deviation from the right way. The vb. *hamartanō* corresponds to that semantic range of the nouns. *hamartōlos* usually means evildoer, lawless one.

(b) Unlike the NT, the OT has no primary, general word for sin. Yet sin, over and above the guilt of the individual, was clearly recognized as a reality that separates human beings and the nation of Israel from God. Yahweh himself is the yardstick for right and wrong. His covenant with the people, his commandments and law, his word spoken by chosen servants all express his normative will. Sin is an estrangement from God and thus brings harm and punishment on itself.

(c) The OT's view of sin is the negative reverse side of the idea of the covenant, and thus is often expressed in legal terms. The nation's history is often depicted as a history of apostasy, of punishment, of Yahweh's gracious intervention, and of returning.

Gen. 3–11 provides a clear example of the OT idea of sin, depicting in masterly fashion humanity's independent and self-sufficient behavior. Sin spreads in a series of fresh outbreaks, starting with the fall of Adam into sin in Gen. 3 and leading on to fratricide (4:1–8), the song of Lamech (4:23–24), to the apex of evil in the world before the flood (6:1–6), and finally to the building of the tower of Babel (11:1–9). The tendency to depart from the order given by God and to establish oneself in one's own position and to go one's own way is seated in the heart (Gen. 6:5; 8:21).

(d) Sin is both a falling away from a relationship of faithfulness to God and disobedience to his commands and law. The former is described as unfaithfulness to God's covenant (Hos. 2; Jer. 3:10), while the latter is a violation of God's word (1 Sam. 15:23–26; Ps. 78). In both cases God's people shut themselves off from fellowship with him and become God-less (cf. Jer. 2:29).

(e) The sin of the individual cannot be separated from that of the nation. The earlier OT writings concentrate on the nation's history of recurrent apostasy (Jdg. 2:6–3:6); later traditions put more emphasis on the fate of the individual (Ps.; Job).

3. (a) Sin is universal. No one can exist in the presence of God's holiness (Isa. 6:1–7). His accusation is against the people as a whole (Hos. 12). The universality of sin is esp. emphasized in Gen. 6:5; 8:21; Isa. 64:6–7. This view forms a starting point for a doctrine of original sin, but nowhere in the OT is this teaching given any systematic formulation. The consequence of sin is death (Gen. 2:17). If that does not happen at once, it is due to God's sovereign grace, in which he delays the consequence of destruction and does not allow punishment and judgment to be his last word. Rather, God makes them the basis of renewal, as in the cases of Noah (Gen. 6–9) and the new covenant (Jer. 31; Ezek. 37). The rebellious can only hope for God's mercy until at last they hear the message of the servant of God, who, although without sin, bears the sins of others (Isa. 53).

(b) The various OT sacrifices, including the great day of atonement ritual described in Lev. 16, were designed to cover sin. But forgiveness of sins is linked with confession of guilt (cf. Gen. 50:17; 2 Sam. 12:13; Ps. 51).

4. In Jewish thinking the concept of sin was more strongly oriented toward the law, even as it became more superficial under the influence of speculative and casuistic thinking. Gentiles do not know God's commands and are therefore all sinners. For the religious Jew the essence of sin was above all the transgression of God's laws and commandments. Idolatry, unchastity, and bloodshed were regarded as unforgivable sins. The possibility of atonement for sins committed unintentionally was found in sacrifice, purificatory rites, good works, suffering, and martyrdom. As to the question of the origin of sin, Judaism found the answer in Adam and Eve or the fallen angels (Gen. 6:1–6). The consequences of sin are sickness, death, and eternal damnation. The religious had their sights fixed on the possibility of sinlessness, their examples being Abraham, Moses, Elijah, and Enoch. The complete removal of sin was expected in the messianic kingdom.

NT Following the prominent use of *hamartanō* and its cognates in the LXX, the NT uses them as the comprehensive expression of everything opposed to God. The Christian concept of sin finds its fullest expression and its deepest theological development in Paul and John. *hamartia* occurs 173x (64x in Paul, 25x in Heb., and 17x each in Jn. and the Johannine letters); *hamartanō* occurs 42x (7x each in Rom. and 1 Cor., 10x in the Johannine letters and 3x in Jn.). *hamartēma* occurs only 4x and refers to the individual sinful act (e.g., 1 Cor. 6:18); it is used in the context of forgiveness (Mk. 3:28; Rom. 3:25), and in Mk. 3:29 it is used of the unpardonable sin. The adj. *anamartētos* occurs only in Jn. 8:7 and means without actual sin. *hamartōlos*, sinful, is the usual adj. (47x); used as a substantive, its nuances follow those of *hamartia*.

1. (a) Jesus used the OT and Jewish concept of sin that was familiar in the world around him. This becomes clear from the fact that in the Synoptic Gospels *hamartia* and *hamartēma* are found almost exclusively in the context of the forgiveness of sins. *hamartanō* is frequently used absolutely, i.e., in its usual and familiar sense (cf. Matt. 18:15; Lk. 17:3–4). The use of the nouns chiefly in the pl. shows that the dominant idea is that of individual faults committed against the law or one's fellow human beings. The sinner is the one who does not abide by the law and the Pharisaic interpretation of it. As a result, the sinner is put on the same level as the tax collector (Matt. 9:10; Mk. 2:15–16) and is likened to the Gentile or the ungodly (Matt. 26:45; Mk. 14:41; Lk. 6:32–34). The combination "adulterous and sinful generation" in Mk. 8:38 implies that sin separates one from God; hence repentance and forgiveness are necessary.

(b) Jesus' preaching went beyond the Jewish concept of sin when, as in the Sermon on the Mount, he radicalized the law and set up his coming and his person as a new standard that brought about a new state of affairs (Matt. 7:21–23; 12:31; Mk. 3:28–35; Lk. 12:10). This is true even though these passages do not often explicitly mention sin. The new situation is disclosed by Jesus' mixing with sinners. Jesus comes to sinners, not to the righteous (Matt. 9:13; Mk. 2:17; Lk. 5:32).

He pronounces the poor blessed (Matt. 5:2–11) and calls the burdened to him (11:28).

In connection with this mission Jesus is called "a friend of . . . 'sinners'" (Matt. 9:10–11; 11:19). His fellowship with sinners is particularly prominent in Luke (Lk. 7:36–50; 15:1–32; 18:9–14; 19:1–10). Jesus' remarks about the Pharisees in Matt. 23:1–36; Mk. 12:37–40; Lk. 20:45–47 make it esp. clear that with his coming the criterion for distinguishing righteous from sinful has been altered. Those who according to Jewish legal standards were reckoned righteous are shown to be sinful before God in view of their self-righteousness and their rejection of Jesus.

(c) In the passion narrative, esp. in the account of the Last Supper, Jesus' whole life and preaching are seen clearly from the perspective of the cross (Matt. 26:28). Jesus replaces ritual atonement with the sacrifice of his own life. Here the righteous and unrighteous alike are seen to be sinners. This insight is anticipated in Peter's cry in Lk. 5:8 ("Go away from me, Lord; I am a sinful man!") and is summed up in the evangelists' overall interpretation of Jesus' mission as the one who will save his people from their sins (Matt. 1:21; Lk. 1:77). Thus baptism, which John the Baptist viewed in terms of repentance (Mk. 1:4), takes on a new meaning. Both baptism and forgiveness of sins are grounded by the apostles in the death and resurrection of Jesus (Jn. 20:23; Acts 2:38; 5:31; 10:43).

2. (a) Paul's primary statements about sin are found in Rom. 1–8, but it is striking that *hamartia* and its cognates scarcely occur in 1:18–3:20. Here Paul speaks about both Jews and Gentiles, who alike fall short when they are confronted with God's righteousness. As a result of our unbelief and unrighteous acts, we all fall under God's wrath. The law (*nomos*, → 3795) produces knowledge of sin, but not mastery of it (Rom. 3:20; 5:20; 7:7–12; Gal. 3:22). The law is not thereby invalidated (Rom. 3:31), but rather serves to lead us to faith in Christ (Gal. 3:23–25). God's righteousness cannot be attained by the way of the law. Law–sin–death: that is the fateful road we all tread without Christ and without faith. Adam is an example of this (Rom. 5:12–21). Through his sin he brought death into being, both for himself and for the entire human race (cf. Rom. 1:32; 6:16; 7:5–11; 8:13; 1 Cor. 15:56).

It is only when one comes to know Christ that the full power of sin is disclosed. Those who struggle against God's Spirit are imprisoned in the flesh (*sarx*, → 4922), which, as God's enemy, produces sin and death. Spirit and flesh fight against one another in a person under the law (Rom. 7:13–25; cf. Gal. 5:16–26). Paul almost always uses *hamartia* in the sing., implying that sin is almost a personal power acting in and through humanity (Rom. 5:12, 21; 6:6, 17; 7:9–23). The same is also true of *sarx* (Gal. 5:19, 24) and *thanatos* (death, → 2505; Rom. 6:9b). This vivid way of putting things contributed, along with Paul's statements on the universality of sin since Adam (Rom. 5), to the church's doctrine of original sin.

(b) Jesus Christ, as the counterpart of Adam (1 Cor. 15:45), has by his coming broken this circle. He took on himself the curse of the law in place of all human beings (Gal. 3:10–14). He endured death (Rom. 5:8; 6:3–10; 1 Cor. 15:3) and dealt with sin by bearing it (Rom. 8:1–4). He himself became sin (2 Cor. 5:21) in order to establish God's righteousness (Rom. 5:11; 11:15; 2 Cor. 5:18–19; → *katallassō*, to reconcile, 2904). Through his victory, Jesus overpowered the law, sin, and death, replacing them by righteousness and life.

The way of the law, which Paul himself had earlier tried to walk, does not lead to life but rather to death. Paul saw in his own persecution of Christ and the Christians *the* sin of his life (1 Cor. 15:9; 1 Tim. 1:15). But God's grace opened up a new way (Rom. 5:15; 1 Cor. 15:10–11), the way of faith (Rom. 3:21–30). Abraham, who became righteous through faith (Rom. 4), serves as a type of this new way.

Christ's reconciling death has taken place for us once for all (Rom. 3:25–26; 5:8), so that those who believe receive peace with God (5:1–5). Through baptism believers are taken up into the Christ-event. By dying and rising with Christ, they are torn from the domin-

ion of death in order to participate in Christ's new life (6:1–11). This indicative is immediately followed by an imperative, that Christians are now to free themselves from the bondage of sin in order to enter the service of righteousness (6:12–18). The freedom to put oneself at the disposal of the Spirit is realized in love (Gal. 5:13–26; cf. Rom. 8:9–17). As a result, all self-righteousness as well as all confidence in the self is excluded (Rom. 10:3; 1 Cor. 1:18–31). Thereafter, all that does not arise from faith and so from union with the living Christ is sin (Rom. 14:23).

(c) Thus we have two strands in Paul's teaching on sin. (i) All human beings are subject to the power of sin, from which they can be redeemed only through God's once-and-for-all act of reconciliation in Jesus Christ. (ii) God calls everyone to turn to this new righteousness in faith, to be servants of Christ instead of servants of sin, and then to walk in the Spirit or in Christ. It is the juxtaposition and interweaving of these two strands that shows the depth and seriousness of sin as a ruling power and the greatness of God's act of grace, and that at the same time gives the reason for our responsibility for faith and actions.

3. (a) In the Johannine literature the concept of *hamartia* is set within the context of the Christ-event. Jesus came into the world (Jn. 1:1–14) and bore its sin as the Lamb of God (1:29; 1 Jn. 3:5). He himself was without sin, but he shed his blood for the sin of the world—i.e., for those imprisoned in their alienation from God (1 Jn. 1:7; 2:2; 4:10; Rev. 1:5). Any will or power that opposes Jesus is sin. This was clear in the case of Judas Iscariot (Jn. 6:70–71; 19:11), but also in the way the Jews reacted to Jesus (8:44–47). They supposed Jesus to be a sinful human being, but they were the ones who were sinful, since they did not recognize him as the Redeemer (9:16–41). Here sin is equated with unbelief, and people are faced with a decision for or against Jesus (15:22–24). Through belief or unbelief people decide either for life or for death (8:24; 9:41; 16:8–9). Thus by his coming Jesus exposed sin as such (15:22–24) and, insofar as he brought life, stripped the prince of this world of his power (12:31; 16:11).

(b) Sin is seen as the opposite of love in 1 Jn. (3:1–10). It is true that purification from sin has taken place through Christ (1:7) and that sin is an impossibility for those born of God (3:8–9), but no one can consider himself or herself sinless or dispense with forgiveness (1:8). On the contrary, Christ forgives our sins when we confess them (1:9). Thus 1 Jn. also preserves the tension between Christ's redemptive act, ethics, and human actions. The test lies in one's love of fellow believers (1:9; 4:7; cf. 1:4; 2:7; 3:10). However, 1 Jn. also knows of the serious mortal sin, by which Jn. probably means apostasy and idolatry (5:16–21).

4. Hebrews seeks to show that Jesus became a human being in every sense (2:14), even to the point of being tempted (4:14–16; 5:7–8), yet he yet remained free from sin (4:15). Heb. deals with sin in the context of sacrifice. Christ as the true high priest (7:25–27) offered himself once and for all for our sin, replacing the repeated sin offerings of the OT. Jesus is the unique sacrifice that makes the offering of further sacrifices superfluous (10:4–10, 18); they are replaced by the possibility of forgiveness through faith (11:1–40). Jesus' unique sacrifice liberates us once and for all from sin; his example helps us in our struggle against the peril of continuing in sin (12:1–4). For those who fall away from the faith, eternal judgment is waiting (6:4–6; 10:26–31). This is the sin that excludes further repentance.

5. The letter of James warns of lust that produces sin and death (1:15) and of the danger of failing to act on the knowledge provided by faith (4:17). At the same time, James exhorts his readers to confess their sin, knowing that God will forgive them (5:15–20).

6. In his first letter, Peter cites Isa. 53 to encourage his readers to stand firm in the midst of suffering by taking as our example him who once suffered for us and thereby redeemed us from our sins (1 Pet. 2:21–25; 3:18; 4:1).

See also *adikia*, wrongdoing, unrighteousness, injustice (*94*); *parabasis*, overstepping, transgression (*4126*); *paraptōma*, transgression, trespass, false step, sin (*4183*).

283 (*hamartōlos*, adj., sinful; noun, a sinner), → *281*.

289	ἄμεμπτος

ἄμεμπτος (*amemptos*), blameless (*289*); ἀμέμπτως (*amemptōs*), blamelessly (*290*); μέμφομαι (*memphomai*), find fault (*3522*); μεμψίμοιρος (*mempsimoiros*), fault-finding (*3523*); μέμψις (*mempsis*), reason for complaint (*3524*).

CL & OT 1. In cl. Gk. *amemptos* usually means blameless, without reproach. It may be used of persons or things. On occasion *amemptos* was used with the connotation "content," in the sense that one is not characterized by blaming others. The vb. *memphomai* means to blame, find fault with. With the dat. and acc. of the person it may connote the idea of regarding someone as blameworthy. The adj. *mempsimoiros* characterizes one who is apt to find fault, while *mempsis* indicates the ground of, or reason for, complaint or blame.

2. (a) In the LXX *amemptos* can mean clean, pure, perfect, complete, righteous, and possibly straight, upright. In parallelism with *katharos* (clean) in Job 11:4, it describes the blamelessness of Job's character (see also 1:8). In 15:14 this word occurs in parallelism with *dikaios* (righteous; cf. also 22:3). It occurs in Wis. 10:5, 15; 18:21 in the sense of moral purity. The adv. *amemptōs* occurs in an LXX addition to the Heb. text of Est. 3:13 in the sense of honorable, with regard to Artaxerxes' well-intentioned efforts to unify his empire.

(b) In Job 33:10 *mempsis* is parallel with the phrase "considers me his enemy." The sense is that of reason for complaint. In 39:7 the same word describes the shouts of a driver to the wild donkey, connoting the idea of scolding or censuring. In 15:15 (A); 33:23; Wis. 13:6 the word connotes fault or blame.

NT 1. (a) *amemptos* occurs in the NT in the sense of moral purity in Lk. 1:6, where it describes Zechariah's blamelessness with regard to the commandments of the Lord. In Phil. 3:6 Paul uses the word to describe his standing as a Pharisee with regard to the law of God; he was not guilty of disobedience. The word occurs in a similar sense in 2:15 to describe the moral purity of those believers who do not grumble or question; they are further described as "pure" (*amōmos*). In 1 Thess. 3:13 Paul expresses his desire that the Thessalonian Christians be "blameless" at the Parousia (cf. Matt. 25:34–40). This blamelessness is the result of their abounding love one for another (1 Thess. 3:12). *amemptos* is applied to the first covenant in Heb. 8:7 in a negative sense. If there had been "nothing wrong" with it, there would have been no need for another one.

(b) The related adv. *amemptōs* occurs in 1 Thess. 2:10 to describe Paul's activity among the Thessalonians in regard to there being no cause for censure or blame on his part, and in 5:23 to denote the effect of the total work of sanctification at the Parousia.

2. The vb. *memphomai* has the basic connotation of blame or finding fault. In some later MSS of Mark 7:2 it is used to express the reaction of the Pharisees to those disciples who were eating with unwashed hands: They were open to blame because they were guilty of violating Jewish tradition.

In Rom. 9:19 Paul uses *memphomai* in a rhetorical question on a matter of human responsibility that occurs in an exposition of the sovereignty of God: "Why does God still blame us?" This vb. clearly connotes guilt or blameworthiness here, for Paul argues that God's sovereignty does not free sinners of guilt before God.

In Heb. 8:8 *memphomai* occurs with the dat. of the pers. in a sense similar to the above but in contrast to *amemptos* (8:7). The Sinaitic covenant is described as not being faultless (*amemptos*). It has fault in that the people to whom it was given did not keep it, for "God found fault [*memphomenos*] with" them (8:8). It is not that the

intrinsic nature of the commandments was changed, but rather the mode of reception of the covenant (8:8–12, quoting Jer. 31:31–34).

3. *mempsimoiros* (lit., finding fault with one's lot [*moira*]) occurs only in Jude 16, where it describes a grumbler or malcontent.

See also *aitia*, ground, cause, reason, charge (*162*); *elenchō*, bring to light, expose, convict, punish (*1794*); *enochos*, guilty, subject to, liable to (*1944*).

290 (*amemptōs*, blamelessly), → *289*.

291 (*amerimnos*, free from concern), → *3533*.

294 (*ametameletos*, not to be regretted, irrevocable), → *3564*.

295 (*ametanoētos*, impenitent), → *3567*.

296 (*ametros*, without measure), → *3586*.

297	ἀμήν

ἀμήν (*amēn*), amen (*297*).

OT 1. Amen is a transliteration of the Heb. *ʾāmēn*, derived from *ʾāman*—show oneself dependable (niph.); know oneself to be secure, have faith (hiph.)—it means certain, true.

The Heb. word was used 30x in the OT (trans. by *amēn* 3x, by *genoito* 23x) on solemn occasions to confirm a curse or adjuration by identifying oneself with it, to accept a blessing, or to associate oneself with a doxology. To say "amen" confirms a statement by someone else. In Num. 5:22 the woman suspected of adultery confirmed the priest's adjuration with a double "Amen" (*genoito*). In Deut. 27:15–26 the people give a twelvefold confirmation (*genoito*) to the curses pronounced against certain transgressors of the Mosaic law (see also Neh. 5:13 [*amēn*]; Jer. 11:5 [*genoito*]). Since God himself is a witness of such confirmation, he is called in Isa. 65:16 "the God of [the] amen" (lit. Heb.; LXX and NIV "the God of truth").

The doxologies at the end of the first four books of the Psalms (41:13; 72:19; 89:52; 106:48) are closed by "Amen"(Heb.; LXX *genoito*). Neh. 8:6 (cf. also 1 Chr. 16:36) shows it to be the people's expression of response. By declaring "Amen" the people affirm that which has been said as certain, positive, valid, and binding.

2. In rab. sources amen is found only as a confirmatory and emphatic answer to what has been said by another. Those saying "Amen" to a prayer or doxology made it their own. In a similar manner, saying "Amen" to an adjuration, blessing, or curse made it binding on oneself. Jews were to say "Amen" to any doxology. Those who said "Amen" properly would be richly rewarded by God. Amen is seldom found at the end of a prayer.

When someone joined the Qumran community, the priests repeated doxologies to God's glory and blessed all who belonged to God's portion, while the Levites cursed all who belonged to Belial's portion. All those entering the covenant answered these doxologies, blessings, and curses with a double "Amen."

NT Amen is found 129x in the NT. In the Gospels it is found only in the mouth of Jesus, generally in the phrase, "Amen, I say to you...." Sometimes Luke translates an original amen by *alēthōs* ("truly," 9:27; 12:24; 21:3) or *epʾ alētheias* ("in truth" 4:25). John has a double amen 25x, either for liturgical reasons or to strengthen the amen. By introducing his words in this way, Jesus labeled them as certain and reliable and made them binding on himself and on his hearers. They expressed his majesty and authority.

Amen appears in the other NT writings at the close of prayers and doxologies in order to strengthen and confirm them (Rom. 1:25; 9:5; 11:36; 16:27; Eph. 3:21; Heb. 13:21). Anyone hearing a thanksgiving in a worship service answers it with "Amen." Hence that element must be expressed in a language he or she understands (1 Cor. 14:16). In the NT letters it is assumed that the congregation will answer with an amen (Rom. 15:33; Gal. 6:18; Rev. 1:7).

In Rev. 7:12 amen stands at the beginning and end of a doxology, and in 19:4 it is linked with "Hallelujah." In 22:20 the church answers a divine "surely" with its amen and so endorses the promise. When Christ calls himself "the Amen" in 3:14 and affirms that he is "the faithful and true witness" (virtually a trans. of amen), he is taking up Isa. 65:16 (LXX). In 2 Cor. 1:20 Paul sees all the promises of God fulfilled and guaranteed in Christ.

See also *hallēlouia*, hallelujah (*252*); *hōsanna*, Hosanna (*6057*).

299 (amiantos, undefiled, pure), → *3620.*

303	ἀμνός

ἀμνός (*amnos*), lamb (*303*); ἀρήν (*arēn*), lamb (*748*); ἀρνίον (*arnion*), lamb (*768*).

CL & OT *amnos* denotes a lamb as distinct from *probaton*, sheep. In the LXX and NT both *amnos* and *arēn* are used; *arnion* is no longer a diminutive. *amnos* in the OT is used chiefly in passages of a cultic and sacrificial character. Lambs are presented at the sanctuary as burnt offerings and sacrifices (Lev. 9:3; Num. 15:5) to atone for sin and to cleanse people—either as a whole or as individuals (e.g., lepers, Lev. 14:10).

At the annual Passover feast each family was to kill and eat a lamb without blemish, a male a year old, in memory of the exodus from Egypt (Exod. 12:5 in A). At the exodus event itself the blood of the lamb was smeared on the doorframes and lintels of Jewish houses (cf. 12:7, 13, 23). In his prophecy of the new temple Ezek. mentions lambs as gifts for the Sabbath-offering and the feast-offering (Ezek. 46:4, 11).

In Isa. 53:7 the patiently suffering Servant of the Lord is compared with a lamb being led to the slaughter but remaining silent as though before shearers. Here for the first time a person is spoken of as fulfilling the function of a sacrificial animal. Acts 8:32 sees in this passage a reference to the "good news of Jesus" (Acts 8:35).

NT 1. In the NT Jesus is described 4x as *amnos*. In Jn. 1:29, 36, John the Baptist describes Jesus, whom he has baptized, as "the Lamb of God"—not merely *like* a lamb, but *as* the Lamb of God. John further describes this lamb as one "who takes away the sin of the world." This links the phrase with Isa. 53:6 about the Servant of the Lord on whom God "has laid . . . the iniquity of us all."

If "lamb" stands for "offering," then the Baptist's statement becomes clear: No offerings brought by human beings can take away the sin of the world, but God himself provides an offering, which does indeed take it away. He gave his only Son and did not spare him (cf. Rom. 8:31–32, perhaps an echo of Gen. 22). Jn. 1:29 must be seen against the background of Jesus' baptism (1:32–34), when he publicly identified himself with sinners and their lot. The eschatological time of salvation has begun.

Two other NT passages stress other aspects of Jesus' being compared to a lamb: Acts 8:32 stresses his patient suffering, while 1 Pet. 1:19 emphasizes the sinlessness and perfection of his sacrifice.

2. *arēn* occurs once in the NT, where Jesus says the disciples will be as defenseless as lambs among wolves (Lk. 10:3; Matt. 10:16 uses *probaton*, → *4585*).

3. In Jn. 21:15 Christ exhorts Peter: "Feed my lambs [*arnia*]." The only other places where *arnion* occurs is in Rev. (29x). The Judge of all the earth is the one who died for us, and even as sovereign Lord he still bears the marks of his passion (Rev. 5:6). In 5:6, 8, 12–13, Christ is seen in this twofold aspect. He is the Lord, the one who opens the seals and who is to be worshiped. At the same time he is "the Lamb, who was slain," having redeemed people of all races to God by his blood and made them a kingdom and priests (5:9–10). He is both *arnion* and *leōn*, lion (→ *3329*).

The eschatological wrath from which kings, rulers, free persons, and slaves all wish to hide is "the wrath of the Lamb" (Rev. 6:16). In ch. 7 the blood of the Lamb has cleansing power. The robes of the martyrs were cleansed not by their martyrdom but by the blood of the

Lamb, who is worshiped as God (7:10). Rev. 19:7, 9 speaks of the marriage of the Lamb, the church being the bride. The twelve apostles are called "apostles of the Lamb," and God and the Lamb illumine the new Jerusalem (21:14, 23).

See also *probaton*, sheep (*4585*); *poimēn*, shepherd (*4478*).

306	ἄμπελος

ἄμπελος (*ampelos*), vine, grapevine (*306*); ἀμπελουργός (*ampelourgos*), vinedresser, gardener (*307*); ἀμπελών (*ampelōn*), vineyard (*308*); οἶνος (*oinos*), wine (*3885*); οἰνοπότης (*oinopotēs*), wine drinker (*3884*); οἰνοφλυγία (*oinophlygia*), drunkenness (*3886*).

CL & OT 1. In cl. Gk. and in the LXX *ampelos* means a vine (e.g., Gen. 40:9–10; 49:11; Isa. 24:7). *ampelōn* means vineyard (Gen. 9:20; Deut. 20:6). *ampelourgos*, a rare term in the LXX, means a vineyard worker (2 Ki. 25:12; Jer. 52:16). *oinos* means wine in cl. Gk. and mostly translates Heb. *yayin*, wine.

2. Viticulture is one of the oldest forms of agriculture (cf. Gen. 9:20–21). The twin themes of the vine and wine both as symbols of fertility and well-being and as causes of debauchery and shame run throughout Scripture. Grape-growing was an important part of OT economy. As with other crops, the owner was not permitted to reap the vineyard twice in one harvest; gleanings were to be left for those who lacked possessions (Lev. 19:10; Deut. 24:21). Vineyards were to lie fallow every seventh year (Exod. 23:10–11; Lev. 25:3–7) and were not to be sown with other plants (Deut. 22:9).

3. (a) The symbolism of Israel as a vine is found in Ps. and prophetic books. Ps. 80:8–13 asks why Yahweh has allowed his vine, Israel, to be ravaged. Isa. 5:1–7 uses ancient vineyard practice in a fig. sense; Israel is the vineyard, Yahweh the gardener, and a harvest of wild grapes comes instead of ripe, juicy grapes (cf. also Jer. 2:21). The infidelity of Israel as a spreading vine is reproached in Hos. 10:1. The wood of the vine is good for nothing but fuel (Ezek. 15:1–8; cf. 19:10–14); its ceasing to bear fruit is a symbol of judgment. In 17:1–10 "the seed of [the] land" (Zedekiah) is planted by "a great eagle" (Nebuchadnezzar) and becomes "a low, spreading vine," but it will be transplanted by another eagle (Hophra). This allegory closes with the question whether the transplanted vine will survive when the east wind strikes it.

(b) In Ps. 128:3 the wife of him who fears Yahweh "will be like a fruitful vine within your house." The abundance of vineyards is a sign of Yahweh's favor (Hos. 2:15). Superabundance at the grape harvest will characterize the end times (Amos 9:13; cf. Joel 2:24; 3:18; Zech. 10:7). In Sir. 24:17 the vine is a symbol of wisdom.

4. Wine is often mentioned in lists of produce (e.g., Gen. 27:28; Deut. 7:13; 11:14; 18:4). Because of its color it can be called the "blood of the grape" (Deut. 32:14; Sir. 39:26; cf. Isa. 63:3; Rev. 14:20). The misuse of wine brings numerous evils, beginning with the nakedness of Noah and the curse of Canaan (Gen. 9:20–27). Those whose lives are in the grip of wine are denounced by the prophets (Isa. 5:11, 22; 28:7; Mic. 2:11; Hab. 2:5). Priests were forbidden to drink wine when engaged in their duties (Lev. 10:9; Ezek. 44:21). Similarly, Prov. has numerous warnings against inordinate love of wine (e.g., 20:1; 21:17). The Nazirites took vows never to drink wine or the products of the grapevine (Num. 6:3; cf. Jdg. 13:4, 7, 14), and the Rechabites abstained both from wine and from building houses (Jer. 35:6–7 = LXX 42:6–7).

But wine was also part of daily life and was often safer to drink than water. Wine was drunk at feasts and was an honored gift (cf. 1 Sam. 25:18; 2 Sam. 16:1). It was an article of trade (2 Chr. 2:8–10, 15). It is praised by the psalmist as gladdening the human heart (Ps. 104:15). Libations of wine were also used in sacrifice, both to false gods (Deut. 32:37–38) and to Yahweh (Exod. 29:40; Lev. 23:13).

5. In the prophets judgment is expressed under the symbolism of wine: The wicked will be forced to drain the cup and will not be able to stand (Ps. 60:3); the wine harvest (Joel 3:13) and the treading of the grapes (Isa. 63:2–6) are pictures of judgment.

NT 1. Vineyards often feature in Jesus' parables. (a) In Lk. 13:6–9 the center of interest is the fig tree, which is planted in a vineyard (*ampelōn*) and tended by a caretaker (*ampelourgos*), who pleads for it to be spared one more year after three successive years of failure to bear fruit. If it fails then, it will be cut down. The parable pictures judgment on the Jewish people in the light of their failure to respond to the preaching of Jesus (cf. 13:5b). The ultimate disaster came with the Jewish War and fall of Jerusalem in A.D. 70.

(b) Matt. 20:1–16 records the parable of the workers in the vineyard. Each worker receives a denarius regardless of how long he has worked. Two meanings are possible for this parable. It may be teaching God's sovereign grace that, in contrast with the grumbling attitude of the Pharisees, welcomes latecomers and sinners into the kingdom (cf. the three parables in Lk. 15). But note that the parable follows Jesus' response to Peter's declaration of having left all to follow Jesus (Matt. 19:27). Jesus replies that the disciples will sit on twelve thrones judging the twelve tribes of Israel and will inherit eternal life (19:28–29). Thus, this parable may be encouraging the disciples not to be proud and self-seeking but to accept whatever they receive as God's gift.

(c) The parable of the two sons, the first refusing to work in the vineyard but then going and the second promising but not actually going (Matt. 21:28–32), has a similar theme to the parable of the lost son in Lk. 15:11–32. Here again the first-last theme recurs: Tax collectors and prostitutes go into the kingdom of God before hypocrites.

(d) This is followed by the parable (or perhaps allegory) of the wicked tenants, which is a Christological restatement of Isaiah's parable of the vineyard (Matt. 21:33–46; Mk. 12:1–12, Lk. 20:9–19; cf. Isa. 5:1–7). The tenants (the Jewish nation) have killed servants (the prophets down to John the Baptist) sent by the owner (God) to get his fruit. By killing the heir (Jesus), they believe the vineyard will be theirs to use as they wish. But the owner will put the tenants to death and replace them with "other tenants, who will give him his share of the crop at harvest time" (Matt. 21:41), i.e., a new people of God.

(e) Jn. 15:1–11 contains Jesus' great description of himself as the true vine, the Father as the gardener, and the need of the disciples to remain in him in order to bear fruit. This is more precisely defined in terms of Jesus' words remaining in them (15:7) and of their remaining in his love (15:9), which means keeping his commandments (15:10). All this is said that the joy of Jesus may be in them to the full (15:11). Whereas Israel was the vine or the vineyard in the OT, the vine is now narrowed down to Jesus himself; the only way for the branches to live and flourish is to remain in him. Paul uses a similar picture in the olive tree from which the natural branches have been removed and those of a wild olive grafted in (Rom. 11:17–24; → *dendron*, *1285*; *elaion*, olive tree, *1778*).

2. (a) Wine is generally understood lit. in the NT and never in a cultic sense. John the Baptist abstained from drinking wine (Lk. 1:15), perhaps following a Nazirite vow. Jesus, by contrast, was accused of being "a glutton and a drunkard [*oinopotēs*]" (Matt. 11:18–19). Jesus justifies his refraining from fasting on the grounds that the presence of the bridegroom is a time for festivity; but when the bridegroom is taken away, the disciples will then fast (Matt. 9:14–17; Mk. 2:18–22; Lk. 5:33–38). The saying has not only messianic implications but hints of Jesus' death. Lk. 5:39 adds: "No one after drinking old wine wants the new, for he says, 'The old is better.'" Jesus here warns against the attitude of his opponents, who stick to the old and familiar, thinking that they know that the old is better simply because it is old.

(b) The NT maintains a similar attitude to wine as the OT. On the one hand, it is one of God's gifts of creation to be enjoyed. Paul exhorts Timothy to drink a little wine for his stomach's sake (1 Tim. 5:23), and wine is a means of healing in Lk. 10:34. On the other hand, to refrain from drinking wine may be necessary for the gospel, so as not to make a fellow believer stumble (Rom. 14:21). Moreover, drunkenness (*oinophlygia*) is a characteristic Gentile way of life (1 Pet. 4:3), and Jesus and Paul both warn against it (Lk. 21:34; Eph. 5:18). Elders and deacons must not be drunkards (1 Tim. 3:3, 8; Tit. 2:3).

(c) There is an outward correspondence between the symptoms of drunkenness and of being filled with the Spirit. Note how Paul exhorts the Ephesians not to be drunk on wine (as perhaps some were) but to be Spirit-filled (Eph. 5:18). At Pentecost the bystanders made a contrasting mistake, concluding that the disciples were filled with new wine, whereas in fact they were filled with the Spirit (Acts 2:13).

(d) Jesus' first miracle was that of turning water into wine at a wedding (Jn. 2:1–11). The story is symbolic not only of Jesus' transforming power, but also of the new age foretold in the OT, in which wine would be present in abundance.

(e) *oinos* is not mentioned in the accounts of the Last Supper, but Jesus did say that he would not drink of the fruit of the vine until he drank it new in the kingdom of God (Matt. 26:29; Mk. 14:25). Elsewhere the consummation is pictured in terms of an eschatological meal (cf. Matt. 8:11; 22:1–14).

(f) Wine is often mentioned in Rev., but only once lit. (18:13), where it is a commodity that cannot be sold in the days of judgment. In 14:10; 16:19; 19:15 it pictures the wrath of God, recalling OT imagery on wine and the cup of God's wrath. Rev. 14:8 celebrates the fall of Babylon, "which made all nations drink the maddening wine of her adulteries" (cf. 17:2; 18:3). Here the debauching effects of wine are descriptive of worldly passion that will be requited by the wine of God's wrath.

307 (*ampelourgos*, vinedresser, gardener), → *306*.

308 (*ampelōn*, vineyard), → *306*.

318 (*amōmētos*, unblemished), → *441*.

320 (*amōmos*, unblemished, blameless), → *441*.

326	ἀναβαίνω

ἀναβαίνω (*anabainō*), go up, mount up (*326*); καταβαίνω (*katabainō*), descend (*2849*); μεταβαίνω (*metabainō*), pass over (*3553*).

CL & OT 1. *bainō*, the root word of *anabainō*, though absent from the NT, means to go, walk. *anabainō* indicates movement up toward a destination: to go up, ascend, grow up. The spatial meaning predominates: One climbs a mountain, mounts a platform, or goes upstairs. If the destination is a holy place, the going up involves performance of some cultic act. The mystic is promised ascent to the world of the gods, heaven, or Olympus.

2. In the LXX *anabainō* is used particularly of going up the mountain of God, the sanctuary, and Jerusalem (Exod. 34:4; 1 Sam. 1:3; 2 Ki. 19:14). In Gen. 28:12, Jacob's dream pictured a ramp or stair-like pavement, which, in accordance with the ancient concept of the world, led up to the gate of heaven. This was the place where intercourse between the earth and the upper divine world took place. God's messengers were going up and down, doing God's commands or supervising the earth. In Jon. 2:7 descent into the underworld signifies condemnation and death, while ascent signifies pardon and life.

NT 1. *anabainō* occurs 82x in the NT. It retains the basic spatial sense of climbing a mountain or going up to Jerusalem for the Passover (Lk. 2:4; 18:10; Jn. 7:8–10; Acts 3:1; Gal. 2:1). It stands in contrast to *katabainō* (81x), which reverses the spatial direction. *anabainō* occasionally denotes the growth of plants (Matt. 13:7); fig. it can denote the rise of ideas (Lk. 24:38; 1 Cor. 2:9 ["conceived"]) and the ascent of prayers to God (Acts 10:4).

2. The specific cultic connotation fades in the Synoptics behind a more general spiritual meaning. When Jesus came up out of the water of the Jordan after his baptism, he received the Spirit (Matt. 3:16). When he climbed a mountain, his ascent was the prelude to some action on his or God's part (Matt. 5:1; 14:23; 15:29; Mk. 3:13; Lk. 9:28).

3. Jn. uses *anabainō* as a fixed expression for the ascent of the Son of Man (similarly Acts 2:34; Rom. 10:6–7; Eph. 4:8). In this sense the vb. is complemented by *katabainō*, descend. These con-

cepts describe a movement that originates from heaven and is directed toward the earth, or vice versa. The stress is not on some kind of journey to heaven; the decisive element is Jesus' going from and to God.

Christ, as the preexistent Logos, bridges the gulf between heaven and earth and becomes a man (Jn. 3:13; cf. Prov. 30:4; Jn. 6:33, 38, 41–42). Then, after his elevation on the cross he ascends "to where he was before" (Jn. 6:62). His descent reveals the Father's love; his ascent, God's sovereign power. In his descent Jesus is the revealer; in his ascent, the perfecter through whom his people receive God as Father (Jn. 20:17). In his descent and ascent he bridges the gulf between God and the world, between light and darkness.

The Son stands in a permanent relationship to the Father, which is described with the help of the vision of the ascending and descending angels (Jn. 1:51; cf. Gen. 28:12). Thus, in the earthly presence of the Son of Man, descent and ascent are repeated, in that his thoughts are derived from the Father and his acts are directed to the Father.

4. (a) Jn. uses *metabainō* to describe the passage from death to life. As Jesus crosses the frontier in his elevation on the cross, so human beings do in the obedience of faith. The believer passes over into the risen Christ's sphere of life (Jn. 5:24; 13:1; 1 Jn. 3:14).

(b) In addition to the spatial uses noted above, *katabainō* also denotes the eschatological arrival of the Lord at his second coming and the descent of the heavenly Jerusalem (1 Thess. 4:16; Rev. 3:12; 21:2, 10). But already God's good and life-giving gifts are coming down to us, above all his trustworthy word, so "that we might be a kind of first-fruits of all he created" (Jas. 1:17–18). Similarly Jesus is the living bread that has come to us from God himself and has been made a present reality (Jn. 6:50, 58).

5. The ascent and descent of Christ in Eph. 4:8–11 calls for special attention. Paul refers to this motif in connection with a discussion of unity and gifts in the church. In 4:8 he alludes to Ps. 68:18: "This is why it says: 'When he ascended on high, he led captives in his train and gave gifts to men.'" There are two main differences from Ps. 68. The latter is in the 2d pers. sing. rather than 3d sing., and it refers to receiving rather than giving gifts. In Ps. 68 this verse most likely suggests the return of warrior Yahweh from a war and the voluntary or enforced gifts given to him. (Note, however, that the idea of giving rather than receiving gifts is supported by the Syriac version of the OT and the Targum, where the passage is interpreted of Moses' ascent of Sinai to receive God's law.)

How should we understand the alterations Paul gives to Ps. 68:18? Eph. 4:8 is probably best regarded not as a direct OT quotation of a prophecy regarding the bestowal of gifts but as an interpretative gloss on the Ps., explaining what God is doing *now* in contrast with the situation described in the Ps. The introductory words, "it says" occur again in Eph. 5:14, introducing a quotation not to be found in Scripture. It is possible that "Scripture" should be supplied as the unexpressed subj. (as in Rom. 10:11), with the idea that God (or the Spirit) is interpreting for the church now what was said in a different context in the OT. This Ps. must now be read in the light of the descent and ascent of Christ, which has brought about a reversal of the situation in which the victors received gifts from the vanquished. That is, the victor gives gifts.

Paul's argument in Eph. 4:9–10 goes on to state that the words "he ascended" imply that Christ "also descended to the lower, earthly regions"—possibly a reference to his incarnation. The ascent is fulfilled in his resurrection and ascension (cf. Phil. 2:8), the ultimate purpose of which is that he might "fill the whole universe" (Eph. 4:10; cf. 1:23; Col. 2:9). The gifts that are then enumerated as a result of that ascension might at first sight appear as anticlimactic: apostles, prophets, evangelists, pastors and teachers (Eph. 4:11). But in the context of the argument, God's ultimate purpose for humankind is growth in personal maturity in Christ (4:12–16). These gifts are directly related to that growth, for they carry on the ministry of Christ to the church (cf. 4:7).

See also *anō*, above, upward (*539*); *ouranos*, heaven (*4041*).

329 (anablepō, look up [at], see again), → *1063.*

331 (anaboaō, cry out), → *1066.*

334 (anangellō, report, announce, proclaim), → *33.*

335 (anagennaō, cause to be born again, bear again), → *1164.*

| 336 | ἀναγινώσκω |

ἀναγινώσκω (*anaginōskō*), read (*336*); ἀνάγνωσις (*anagnōsis*), reading (*342*).

CL & OT 1. *anaginōskō* is a compound derived from *ginōskō*, recognize, know (*1182*). Originally *anaginōskō* had an intensive force (know exactly) but came to mean read, read aloud (in the cl. world anyone reading alone always did so aloud). In legal orations *anaginōskō* was often used to call the court secretary to read documents. *anagnōsis* means reading, reading aloud, esp. in meetings or before a court.

2. The cultic reading of the divine commandments was an early practice at the great Israelite festivals (Exod. 24:7; cf. Jos. 24:25). At that time the main incidents in Israel's history were probably also recounted (Exod. 15:1–18; Jdg. 5). Jer. substituted a reading of his oracles for a prophetic sermon he was not allowed to give (Jer. 36:5–10 = LXX 43:5–10). Ezra's reading of the Mosaic law had to be supplemented by a Levitical explanation (Neh. 8:8). There was also private reading of and meditation on the Scriptures (Deut. 17:18–20; cf. Ps. 1:2; Isa. 30:8).

3. Jewish synagogue worship had a reading from the Torah on the Sabbath, all festivals, the New Moon, fast days, Mondays, and Thursdays, and a reading from the Prophets on the Sabbath, festivals, and fasts. Any member of the congregation could read (Lk. 4:16–17). In the LXX God's command to the prophets to proclaim the word (Jer. 3:12; 11:6; etc.) was translated by *anaginōskō*, thereby implying reading in a service or some public place.

NT In the NT *anaginōskō* occurs 32x; *anagnōsis* 3x. Normally, reading the OT is meant, as in the Synoptics and in Acts 8:28; 13:15, 27; 15:21; 2 Cor. 3:14–15. It is used also for the reading of a letter (Acts 15:31; 2 Cor. 1:13; 3:2), esp. in a service (Col. 4:16; 1 Thess. 5:27).

Jesus held that an intensive reading of Scripture was necessary for theological discussion, as indeed for all knowledge of God—hence his frequent reproach, "Have you never read?" (Mk. 2:25; 12:10; etc.). But, as Paul argued in 2 Cor. 3:14–15, there was a veil over the minds of the Jews. They did not rightly understand the OT, for their reading took place without conversion to Christ (3:16) and so without the Spirit (3:17). Without the illumination of the Spirit one cannot understand the Scriptures (1 Cor. 2:14), which are a witness of Christ (cf. Jn. 5:39; → *graphē*, *1210*).

The NT letters were from the first intended to be read in Christian services (1 Thess. 5:27). They were not confined to the local church to which they were addressed (Col. 4:16). Ultimately, reading these letters ranked equally with reading the OT.

See also *biblos*, book (*1047*); *epistolē*, letter (*2186*).

337 (anankazō, compel, force), → *340.*

338 (anankaios, necessary), → *340.*

339 (anankastōs, by compulsion), → *340.*

| 340 | ἀνάγκη |

ἀνάγκη (*anankē*), compulsion (*340*); ἀναγκαῖος (*anankaios*), necessary (*338*); ἀναγκάζω (*anankazō*), compel, force (*337*); ἀναγκαστῶς (*anankastōs*), by compulsion (*339*).

CL & OT 1. The words based on the stem *anank-* denote in varying gradations every form of outward or inward pressure exerted on human beings. For the Greeks *anankē* was the power that determined all reality, the principle dominating the universe. At various times they ascribed a divine character to it; Plato even ranked it higher than the gods. We are under a constraint because of our natural being; the final limitation of our existence by death is part of this compulsion.

2. In the OT the naturalist outlook of the Gk. world is replaced by a historical one. *anankē* translates Heb. words that denote the afflictions and distresses of illness, persecution, enmity, etc., which were often understood by Israelites to indicate God's alienation from them (cf. its use in such passages as 1 Sam. 22:2; Job 7:11; 15:24; 36:19; Ps. 107:6, 13, 19, 28; Tob. 4:9; 2 Macc. 6:7; 15:2; 4 Macc. 5:13, 16, 37; 6:9, 24). In the last resort, Yahweh alone can save one from *anankē* (Ps. 25:17). He will raise up the great "distress [→ *thlipsis, 2568*] and anguish [*anankē*]" on the day of his wrath (Zeph. 1:15), a conception that had powerful effect on the thought of postexilic Jud.

NT In the NT the noun *anankē* occurs 17x, the adj. *anankaios* 8x, and the vb. *anankazō* 9x—mostly in Paul's letters. *anankazō* describes a compulsion that does not rely on an outward force (Matt. 14:22; Lk. 14:23; Acts 28:19; Gal. 2:3). The adj. *anankaios* refers once to "close" friends to whom one is bound (Acts 10:24), but otherwise means necessary. In Acts 13:46 this necessity is to be understood analogously to *dei* (cf. Lk. 24:7, 26; Acts 1:16, 21; → *1256*) as an exposition of the concept of salvation history that is sustained by a belief in God's providence governing the processes and events of history.

The noun *anankē* often denotes compulsion (Lk. 14:18; cf. 1 Cor. 7:37). In Phlm. 14 and 2 Cor. 9:7 constraint is contrasted with free will. The law involves all kinds of legal necessities (Heb. 7:12; 9:16, 23), of which one (the daily sacrifice the high priest offers for himself and the people) is no longer necessary on account of Christ's unique sacrifice (9:25–26). The thought of providence in the history of salvation is found in passages such as Matt. 18:7; Rom. 13:5; and 1 Cor. 9:16.

Without being confined to any particular phase of salvation history, *anankē* is used almost as an alternative to *thlipsis* to describe the tribulations that continually recur and break in on believers from the outside (1 Cor. 7:26; 2 Cor. 6:4; 12:10; 1 Thess. 3:7). It is against this background that Lk. 21:23 should be understood: "There will be great distress [*anankē*] in the land" (Lk. omits the relative clause of Mk. 13:19 and changes *thlipsis* to *anankē*; cf. Matt. 24:21). *anankē* here does not mark the end of the aeon, only that of Jerusalem (cf. Lk. 21:20), and with this the times of salvation for the Gentiles begin (21:24).

See also *dei*, it is necessary, one must (*1256*); *opheilō*, owe, be indebted to (*4053*); *prepō*, be fitting, seemly or suitable (*4560*).

342 (anagnōsis, reading), → 336.

344 (anadeiknymi, show clearly, reveal), → 1259.

345 (anadeixis, commission, manifestation), → 1259.

348 (anazaō, come to life again), → 414.

353	ἀνάθεμα

ἀνάθεμα (*anathema*) cursed, accursed (*353*); ἀνάθημα (*anathēma*), votive offering (*356*); ἀναθεματίζω (*anathematizō*), execrate, lay a curse on (*354*); κατάθεμα (*katathema*), that which is devoted to the deity and hence accursed thing (*2873*); καταθεματίζω (*katathematizō*), curse (*2874*).

CL & OT 1. *anathema* means lit. that which is set up (from *ana* [up] and *tithēmi* [place]). From this several meanings evolved: consecrated gift, offering (set up in the temple of the deity); what is handed over (to the wrath of the gods); what is dedicated (to destruction); and what has fallen under the power of a curse or ban.

2. The LXX uses *anathema* regularly to translate the Heb. *ḥērem*, ban (cf. Num. 21:3; Jos. 6:17; 7:12; Jdg. 1:17; Zech. 14:11). What is banned (persons or things) is directly given up to God and so cannot be redeemed (Lev. 27:29). The OT recognizes the destruction or annihilation of what has been banned, mostly by fire (27:29; Deut. 13:16–17; Jos. 10:28–40). But also it may be assigned in some instances to the priests for their maintenance or disposal (Num. 18:14; Ezek. 44:29).

3. Besides the understanding of the ban as dedication, the ban can also be punishment (Lev. 27:29). Those who appropriate to themselves what has been banned or refuse to accept the *anathema* in all its extent come under the power of the ban themselves (Deut. 7:26; cf. 1 Ki. 20:42). Likewise, when an offense against the sacred covenant is suspected (Jdg. 21:11) or punishment by God is spoken of (e.g., Zech. 14:11; cf. *ḥērem* in Isa. 34:2, 5; 43:28; Jer. 50:21, 26; Mal. 3:24), *anathema* occurs as punishment.

4. Ezr. 10:8 distinguishes between a ban on all belongings and personal exclusion from the community. Ban and excommunication are always measures. Those excommunicated are exiled from the community and so from the sphere of salvation, but they are not directly given over to God and destroyed.

NT 1. The old form *anathēma* is found only in Lk. 21:5, where it means consecrated gift. Such gifts offered in the temple are votive offerings that were often costly (2 Macc. 2:13; cf. Jdt. 16:18–19).

2. Paul takes over a restricted use of *anathema* from the LXX: the cursed thing, what has been dedicated to destruction. (a) Paul's Jewish kinship is not abolished by his membership in the church of Jesus Christ. He is even willing to come under the curse (*anathema*), that is, to be annihilated by God and delivered to eschatological judgment, in order to save Israel (Rom. 9:3). Paul speaks here in the prophetic style of the OT (cf. Exod. 32:32).

(b) In 1 Cor. 12:3 Paul distinguishes between ecstasy that is the work of the Spirit of God and ecstasy that issues from demonic influence. Persons in ecstasy who pronounce an *anathema* on Jesus (i.e., who uttering the ban deliver the man Jesus to annihilation by God) cannot possibly speak by the Holy Spirit; they have become the mouth and instrument of demonic powers.

(c) Most likely the curse formula in 1 Cor. 16:22, like other formulas at the end of 1 Cor., stems from the liturgy of the Lord's Supper. The *anathema* calls on those participating to test their faith before the meal so that anyone unworthy may be excluded (cf. 11:28). The formula "a curse be on him" pronounces for a specific case the sentence that comes from God and delivers the offender to the punishment of God.

(d) Paul uses *anathema* in the same sense in Gal. 1:8–9: Anyone who preaches a false gospel is delivered to God for destruction. It is not an act of church discipline in the sense of excommunication; rather, the curse exposes a culprit to the judicial wrath of God.

3. In this act of being handed over to God lies the theological meaning of the consecrated gift and the ban curse. Just as the consecrated gift is a sign of submission (cf. 1 Ki. 10:25), of atonement for wounded honor (Gen. 12:16; 20:16), and of reconciliation (32:14–15), so a person sentenced by *anathema* is delivered up to the judgment of God. At the same time, hope of a last-minute change of mind is not discounted. On the contrary, it is emphasized (cf. 1 Tim. 1:20).

4. *anathematizō* means bind with an oath or curse and thus confirm an agreement that has been made (Acts 23:12, 14; cf. Deut. 13:15; 20:17). In the LXX this vb. means carry out the ban (Num. 21:2–3; Deut. 13:15; 20:17; Jos. 6:21). But it also may mean spread a curse over, execrate. In Mk. 14:71 it is simply curse—the same meaning as *katathematizō* in Matt. 26:74. *katathema* (Rev. 22:3) is essentially the same as *anathema* and denotes what has been delivered up to God, what has a curse laid on it.

See also *kakologeō*, speak evil of, revile, insult (*2800*); *katara*, curse, malediction (*2932*); *rhaka*, empty-head, fool (*4819*).

354 (anathematizō, execrate, lay a curse on), → 353.

356 (anathēma, votive offering), → 353.

360 (anaitios, innocent), → 162.

363 (anakainoō, renew), → 2785.

364 (anakainōsis, renewal), → 2785.

365 (anakalyptō, uncover, unveil), → 2821.

398	ἀνάπαυσις

ἀνάπαυσις (*anapausis*), rest (*398*); ἀναπαύω (*anapauō*), give rest; mid. rest, take one's rest (*399*); ἐπαναπαύομαι (*epanapauomai*), rest, take one's rest, rely on (*2058*); καταπαύω (*katapauō*), bring to rest, rest, stop, resting (*2924*); κατάπαυσις (*katapausis*), rest, place of rest (*2923*).

CL & OT 1. In cl. Gk. *anapauō* in its act. form means to make to cease, bring to an end; to rest (trans.), make to halt, refresh. In mid. and pass. it means to cease, take rest from, recover, come to rest; later also, to die. *katapauō* means to stop, put an end to; with reference to persons, to hinder, depose, kill; also to appease, calm. *anapausis* means repose, relaxation, a rest from something.

2. The concept of rest is important in the OT, esp. in connection with the idea of Yahweh giving his people rest from their many enemies. The vb. *nûaḥ* is frequently used for to come to rest, e.g., of an army or swarms of locusts. In the religious realm the use was extended to the idea of God's Spirit resting on human beings and things (Num. 11:25; Isa. 11:2), the resting of God's hand (25:10), and resting in the grave (Job 3:17).

Probably the most important use theologically is that of the hiph. of *nûaḥ*, in the sense of to give rest to (Isa. 14:3; 28:12), usually with Yahweh as subj. He gives rest to his people by the provision of the promised land and the conquest of their enemies (Deut. 3:20; 12:10; 25:19; Jos. 1:13, 15; 21:44). Typical of the concrete and this-worldly hopes of the OT faith in Yahweh is this promise of peace in the land, where Judah and Israel will dwell securely, "each man under his vine and fig tree" (1 Ki. 4:25).

The idea of the Sabbath rest (Heb. *šabbāṭ*; LXX *anapausis* or *katapauō*) gained special significance for Israel. The first creation narrative accounts for this by referring to Yahweh's rest on the seventh day of creation (Gen. 2:2–3; Exod. 20:11). The Sabbath rest was by no means confined to the religious, worshiping community or to a privileged class; male and female slaves, aliens, and even cattle are included in the instructions about the day of rest devoted to Yahweh (Exod. 16:23, 25; 20:10). Along with the curse of work (Gen. 3:17–19), God's people are given the blessing of rest, in which to rejoice in their God and his works.

anapausis is used in intertestamental Jud. to refer to the rest promised to the disciples of wisdom—the refreshment that comes from the possession of wisdom given by God (cf. Sir. 6:28; 24:7; 30:17; 51:27).

NT 1. In the NT *anapauō* means to take one's rest in the normal bodily sense (Matt. 26:45; Mk. 14:41), to calm someone who has become disturbed (Matt. 11:28), and to refresh by giving pleasure, comfort, or compensation (1 Cor. 16:18; 2 Cor. 7:13; Phlm. 7, 20). This may come about through Christian love, fellowship, or action. Jesus called his disciples to come apart and rest for a while in body and spirit because of the many who were coming and going (Mk. 6:31). Unclean spirits also seek rest (Matt. 12:43; Lk. 11:24), but self-reformation only makes the last state worse than the first, for the spirit returns with seven other spirits more evil than himself. Matt.'s account of this saying applies it to contemporary Jud.: "That is how it will be with this wicked generation" (Matt. 12:45c).

In Rev. the meaning of *anapauō* is extended to signify rest from hardship and affliction in the eschatological consummation (6:11; 14:13). The four living creatures praise God without rest (*anapausis*, 4:8); by contrast, those who worship the beast have no rest from torment (14:11).

The concept of rest receives a key development in Matt. 11:28–30. Everyone—whether under the law (Jews) or far off from God (Gentiles)—whose life lacks peace and security is called to become a disciple of Jesus. Only here does one find true rest: not the invulnerability and calm of the Stoic, but peace, contentment, and security in God the Father, revealed by Jesus.

2. The concept of rest is esp. important in Heb. (which uses *katapausis* and *katapauō*). Joshua had been called to bring God's people into their rest in the promised land (Heb. 4:8); that rest is regarded as having been fulfilled only in a limited sense and is linked up with the true rest of God on the seventh day (4:4; cf. Gen. 2:2; also Heb. 3:11 [= Ps. 95:11], 18; 4:1, 3, 5, 10–11). The thought of this letter here shows a similarity to the interpretation given in some passages of Deut. to the fulfillment of the promise made to the people. This fulfillment is not a guarantee of permanent rest but gives rise to new promises, which accompany God's people on their way through history and are realized in topical events (cf. Deut. 5:33; 12:10; Heb. 4:1–11). In Heb., God's new covenant people are exhorted to claim the ancient promise of God's rest, available to them in Jesus Christ, and to lay hold of it in hope, by faith in Christ as Lord.

3. In 1 Pet. 4:12–19 Christians are urged not to give occasion for just punishment on their part. They may, of course, experience suffering, but they are to rejoice insofar as they suffer for Christ's sake and even share in his sufferings (4:13). Indeed, suffering of this kind may be taken as a sign of being owned by God: "If you are insulted because of the name of Christ, you are blessed, for the Spirit of glory and of God rests [*anapauō*] on you" (4:14). This passage recalls Jesus' own promise about the blessedness of being persecuted for righteousness' sake (Matt. 5:11; Lk. 6:22).

Peter may be directing this passage against certain individuals in the early church who taught that those who truly enjoy the gifts of the Spirit are exempt from suffering (cf. Paul's thorn in the flesh, 2 Cor. 12:1–10). This teaching is countered by arguing almost the opposite; i.e., not that possession of the Spirit makes suffering inevitable, but that if one suffers for the sake of Christ, it is a sign that the Spirit rests on the believer.

Note the connection here between Christ and the Spirit: The Spirit is the Spirit of Christ (cf. 1 Pet. 1:11). In addition, the Christ who lived and died in history (1:19; 2:21–25; 3:18) is present to believers through the Spirit both before and after Christ's coming (1:10–12; 3:8), and indeed it is the Spirit who made Christ alive after his death (3:18; cf. 1:13). The believer's life should be lived for Christ (1:3–9; 3:16; 5:1). The Spirit is bestowed esp. on the persecuted; note Jesus' saying in Matt. 10:19–20 and the comment about Stephen, who "saw the glory of God, and Jesus standing at the right hand of God" (Acts 7:55).

Peter uses OT imagery in 1 Pet. 4:14 to show that the glory that manifested itself in the pillar of cloud and in other ways in the OT (cf. Exod. 33:9–10; 40:34–35; Isa. 40:1–7; Hag. 2:7) is now a present reality in the life of the persecuted Christian (cf. 1 Pet. 1:7; 5:4; also 2 Cor. 4:17; Col. 3:4). His wording seems to be inspired also by Isa. 11:2: "The Spirit of the LORD will rest [*anapauō*] on him—the Spirit of wisdom and of understanding, the Spirit of counsel and of power, the Spirit of knowledge and of the fear of the LORD" (cf. Isa. 42:1; 48:16; 61:1; Jn. 1:32; 16:13; 1 Cor. 1:30; Eph. 1:17–18). What was first applied to the servant of Yahweh and then to Christ is here applied to the believer, for the believer belongs to Christ through the Spirit and shares in his suffering and life.

4. *katapausis* occurs outside Heb. only at Acts 7:49, where Stephen, quoting Isa. 66:1, states: "Heaven is my throne, and the earth is my footstool. What kind of house will you build for me, says the LORD? Or where will my resting place be?" The context in Acts 7 is a polemical attack on the notion of God being tied to the temple. The vb. *katapauō* also occurs only in Acts outside of Heb., where Paul and Barnabas attempt to "keep the crowd" of Lystra from offering sacrifices to them (Acts 14:18).

5. *epanapauō* is a late and rare word. In Lk. 10:6 it is linked with the disciples' greeting of peace as they go upon their evangelistic mission: "When you enter a house, first say, 'Peace to this house.' If a man of peace is there, your peace will rest on him; if not, it will return to you" (Lk. 10:5–6). This greeting was no mere formality. In the context of the mission it was decisive as to where the recipients stood in relation to Jesus. But even where it was spurned, it would not be made void, for it would return and remain with those who brought this peace in all its fullness.

In Rom. 2:17 *epanapauō* means to rest on, i.e., "rely on," the Mosaic law. In context Paul is addressing Jews who rely on formal adherence to the law and fail to see that their actions are at variance with it and that they are condemned by it.

399 (anapauō, give rest, mid. rest, take one's rest), → 398.

404 (anapiptō, recline, sit down), → 3111.

405 (anaplēroō, fill up), → 4444.

406 (anapologētos, inexcusable), → 162.

411 (anaseiō, stir up, incite, excite), → 4940.

414	ἀνάστασις

ἀνάστασις (*anastasis*), resurrection (*414*); ἐξανάστασις (*exanastasis*), resurrection (*1983*); ἀνίστημι (*anistēmi*), raise, intrans. rise (*482*); ἐξανίστημι (*exanistēmi*), raise up, awaken, intrans. rise (*1985*); ἀναζάω (*anazaō*), come to life again (*348*).

CL & OT 1. In cl. Gk. the vb. *anistēmi*, when used trans., means to make to stand up, awaken, rouse (of persons lying down or sleeping); its meaning was widened to include appointing to an office or task. When used intrans. it could mean stand up, rise, appear, with the connotation of a revolt or political uprising. Esp. with the part., *anistēmi* could express the beginning of an action, e.g., of a conference. In post-Homeric Gk. it was also used of things, such as to set up or repair statues, altars, and the like. Occasionally it means to get well. *exanistēmi* has the same meaning. *anastasis* and *exanastasis* have the intrans. meaning of getting up, rising up (also from the dead).

The doctrine of the transmigration of the soul into some other body was a philosophical doctrine in ancient Greece; it was a characteristic doctrine of the Pythagoreans and found its cl. expression in Plato. Evidence of a belief in direct translation to the heavenly abode is more rare. Some myths included such a story about Ganymedes (who was carried off to become the cup-bearer of Zeus), Menelaus, and Apollonius of Tyana.

In his *Phaedo* Plato defends the idea of the soul's immortality in the course of a dialogue between Socrates and his friends prior to the former's execution by drinking poison. Socrates does not fear death because of the immortality of the soul, which he defends on the basis of the Platonic doctrine of forms, the eternal realities behind our transient, physical world. The soul possesses a certain likeness to the forms, so that when the body dies the soul goes on. It is an essential feature of the soul to partake in life; thus, at death the soul retires elsewhere.

Plato sets out his doctrine of the transmigration of souls in the myth of Er at the end of his *Republic*. Er, a soldier, is killed in battle, but after several days there are no sign of decay, and he returns to life

on the funeral pyre to report what he has seen in the beyond. At death the soul goes to a spot to be judged. Er sees the just souls ascending to a thousand years of happiness; the unjust tell of a thousand years of travail on the earth, where they have been sent as punishment, each soul receiving tenfold retribution for the evil it has done. The very wicked are cast forever into Tartarus (→ *tartaroō*, *5434*), where they receive terrible torture. After spending seven days by a meadow, the soul journeys to a place where it must choose the next form of its life.

There was a strong tradition in Gk. thought that denied the possibility of resurrection, although some passages do entertain the idea of resurrection as an isolated miracle. Evidently the physician Aesclepius enjoyed the reputation of being able to raise the dead. Note Acts 17:31–32, which records how Paul's preaching of the resurrection at Athens elicited skeptical amusement, and 17:18, where the Athenians believed that Paul was preaching two new gods whom they had never heard about: *Iēsous* (Jesus) and *Anastasis* (Resurrection).

2. (a) The older portions of the OT seem to contain no statements of a recognizable hope of resurrection from the dead. Death is the definite end, the destruction of human existence (Gen. 3:19; Job 30:23). This concept is not invalidated by the accounts of isolated individuals returning to life: the widow's son in Zarephath (1 Ki. 17:17–22), the Shunammite's son (2 Ki. 4:18–37), and the man thrown hurriedly into Elisha's grave (13:20–21). That Enoch (Gen. 5:24) and Elijah (2 Ki. 2:11) did not die but were snatched away from earth before their death was a proclamation of the power of death to destroy life and the general lack of hope beyond it.

Some suggest that Job 19:25–27 teaches a doctrine of resurrection, but the interpretive difficulties in this passage should not be overlooked. First, the Heb. of 19:26b–27a can be read either as an affirmation ("I will see God; I myself will see him," so NIV) or as a wish ("I would see God; I want to see him myself"). If the latter is correct, then Job is stating his desire for a face-to-face meeting with God before he dies (cf. 13:15–24), which he deems far better than a postmortem vindication of his case by some unnamed defense attorney (19:25). Second, Job has already declared that physical death is the end of one's existence (14:7–22), so it is unlikely that he would now affirm the opposite. Thus, although one might argue that 19:25–27 *allows* for a doctrine of the resurrection, one should not conclude that it *teaches* such a belief.

(b) The lack of a clearly defined doctrine of resurrection is confirmed by statements in Ps. in which prayer is made for salvation and preservation from the domain of death (which destroys life), but *not from a death that has already been experienced*. Thus the author of Ps. 88 prays to be delivered from Sheol (Heb. *šeʾôl*; Gk. *hadēs*; → *87*) and Destruction (Heb. *ʾabaddôn*; Gk. *apōleia*, → *724*), where the dead are evidently cut off from Yahweh (88:5, 10–11). Conversely, those who have been saved by Yahweh sing of salvation in the same or similar terms (30:2–3, 11; 86:12–13; 103:1, 3–5; Isa. 38:17).

The salvation referred to in Ps. 16:10 appears to be this-worldly, although it also points beyond the grave: "because you will not abandon me to the grave, nor will you let your Holy One see decay." Some scholars see no mention of a life after death in Ps. 16, whereas others do. Without doubt, both Peter and Paul see this passage as a prediction of the resurrection of Jesus from the dead, which is the ultimate fulfillment of the psalm (Acts 2:25–28, 31; 13:35).

Another passage deserving attention is Ps. 49:15: "But God will redeem my life from the grave; he will surely take me to himself." Some suggest that the psalmist expects to be taken to heaven in a way similar to Enoch or Elijah, though others seriously doubt this. It is probably best to exercise the same caution here as earlier. Ps. 49 does not teach a clear doctrine of resurrection, though it does envisage an ongoing life with Yahweh in which the believing Israelite is saved from the power of Sheol.

A similar thought is probably expressed in Ps. 73:24: "You guide me with your counsel, and afterward you will take me into glory." As with Ps. 49, the psalmist does not use any special vb. implying resurrection, and "glory" probably means honor and prosperity in this life. Still, the psalmist's language is odd if he is referring to this life only, for he speaks of God as receiving him somewhere, not only of his bestowing material blessings on him. Earlier the psalmist declares his enjoyment of fellowship with God, and if God is to receive him, it must presumably be to future fellowship after death.

In sum, all we can say is that the psalms give glimpses of the hope of a blessed existence after death. They do not, however, reflect on what part of an individual survives death, such as one's soul or spirit.

(c) Outside of Ps., Deut. 32:39 (part of the Song of Moses) and 1 Sam. 2:6 (part of the Song of Hannah) proclaim that Yahweh kills and makes alive. Note esp. the latter passage: "The LORD brings death and makes alive; he brings down to the grave and raises up." Although a full-blown doctrine of the resurrection is not included here, these songs both stress the extraordinary power of the God of Israel, who can freely dispose of life, bestow it, withdraw it, and then give it again. The main point of these passages is a simple assertion that the living God can intervene in one's darkest hour.

3. The connection between the living God and the continuation of life for those who are his forms the premise of Jesus' interpretation of Exod. 3:6 in his debate with the Sadducees over the resurrection and the problem case of levirate marriage. In Mk. 12:26–27, Jesus states: "Now about the dead rising—have you not read in the book of Moses, in the account of the bush, how God said to him, 'I am the God of Abraham, the God of Isaac, and the God of Jacob'? He is not the God of the dead, but of the living. You are badly mistaken!" (cf. par. Matt. 22:31–32; Lk. 20:37–38). The Sadducees, of course, regarded death as extinction. But if God is unable to deliver people from the ultimate disaster—death—then his promise of protection is of little value. These Jewish leaders failed to appreciate the essential link between God's covenant faithfulness and the resurrection. Jesus is also confounding the Sadducees here (for whom every *word* of the Torah possessed validity) by using their own methods of exegesis against them.

4. The two OT passages dealing with translation to heaven without dying require further comment. (a) Enoch differs from the rest of the antediluvian patriarchs mentioned in Gen. 5 in one key way: "Altogether Enoch lived 365 years. Enoch walked with God; then he was no more, because God took him away" (5:23–24). Heb. 11:5 regards Enoch as an example of faith that is pleasing to God, which was the cause of his translation. The LXX uses the vb. *metatithēmi*, to change the position of, convey to another place, for the Heb. *lāqah*, take, which is followed by the author of Heb.

Considerable Jewish lit. grew up to supply elaborate details of Enoch's translation. The most important such work, *1 Enoch*, exists in its entirety only in Ethiopic (hence the frequent title *Ethiopic Enoch*). The work purports to contain revelations to Enoch on such topics as the origin of evil, angels and their destinies, Gehenna, and paradise (cf. Jude 14–15, which quotes *1 Enoch* 1:9). Yet another work, *2 Enoch* (*Slavonic Enoch*) has the title "The Book of the Secrets of Enoch" in some MSS; it is not clear whether *2 Enoch* is a Jewish work or a Christian reply to *1 Enoch*. A third book attributed to Enoch, *3 Enoch* (*Hebrew Enoch*), is a Jewish, possibly anti-Christian, work dating from the Christian era. All three books provide elaborate details about Enoch's life and departure that are wanting in the OT account.

Enoch is also mentioned in *Jub.* 4:17 as "the first among men that are born on earth who learned writing and knowledge and wisdom." Elsewhere Enoch is seen as a type of the righteous man: "Enoch pleased God and was taken up, an example of repentance to all generations" (Sir. 44:16). This thought is amplified in Wis. 4:10–15, which stresses Enoch's innocence in the midst of wickedness and points out that "while living among sinners [he was] taken up." Philo likewise includes speculations about Enoch and his translation to heaven. In short, what in Gen. 5:21–24 began as a cursory statement regarding Enoch's life and translation developed in later Jud. into a view of Enoch as a model of wisdom and righteousness, culminating in elaborate theories of how he was taken away.

(b) The translation of Elijah is described in 2 Ki. 2:1–15; he is taken up into heaven by a whirlwind and by a chariot and horses of fire (2:11). The description of Yahweh here in terms of chariots and horsemen may emphasize his power, as opposed to Israel's need in this very area (cf. 2 Ki. 13:7; Ps. 20:7). The whirlwind may be compared with the manifestations of Yahweh's power in the elements in 1 Ki. 18:38, 45; 19:11–14, and possibly also with the motif of Baal as the rider of the clouds. A subsequent search fails to find Elijah's body (2 Ki. 2:16–18), and Elisha succeeds him. The end of no other OT prophet is described in these terms. Again the vb. *lāqah* is used for this removal of Elijah from earth.

The only safe conclusions one can draw from these two accounts is that both Elijah and Enoch enter Yahweh's presence at the end of their earthly lives and that Yahweh himself takes the initiative. In neither case is death mentioned. Rather, Yahweh's power is manifested through their avoidance of death.

5. A number of prophetic passages are also relevant to this discussion. (a) Hos. 6:1–2, for example, states: "Come, let us return to the LORD. He has torn us to pieces but he will heal us; he has injured us but he will bind up our wounds. After two days he will revive us; on the third day he will restore us, that we may live in his presence." The historical background of this passage is the Syro-Ephraimite War (735–734 B.C.; cf. 2 Ki. 15; 18; Isa. 7–8), and the passage constitutes a call to national repentance and faith in Yahweh for restoration, using the language of healing after being stricken for apostasy. Perhaps Hosea is consciously using the language and idioms of Baal worship polemically against the Baals. If so, Hosea's point is that it is Yahweh, not the Baals or their cults, who will restore Israel to health and vitality.

(b) Hos. 13:14 declares: "I will ransom them from the power of the grave. I will redeem them from death. Where, O death, are your plagues? Where, O grave, is your destruction?" Paul takes up the phrasing of 13:14b to celebrate the resurrection of the dead: "When the perishable has been clothed with the imperishable, and the mortal with immortality, then the saying that is written will come true: 'Death has been swallowed up in victory' [Isa. 25:8]. 'Where, O death, is your victory? Where, O death, is your sting?'" (1 Cor. 15:54–55).

In context, Hosea's words do not refer to the resurrection hope of the individual but to Yahweh's power over the death and the destruction of the nation in history. They testify to the extraordinary power of Israel's living God, before whom the dominion of death must yield. When Paul uses this passage, he is not basing an argument for individual resurrection on this particular Scripture, but he is writing freely, in scriptural language, of the ultimate victory of Christ over death. To be more precise, Paul makes use of OT testimonia (strings of OT texts), following a Jewish pesher style of exegesis, to interpret the meaning of the original passage in the light of the point he is making. In this sense, Hosea's words find their ultimate fulfillment in the resurrection, where people are ransomed from the grave and redeemed from death.

(c) Isa. 26:19 expresses a fleeting confidence in the resurrection of Israel: "But your dead will live, their bodies will rise. You who dwell in the dust, wake up and shout for joy. Your dew is the dew of the morning; the earth will give birth to her dead." Under the assumption (as most commentaries make) that Yahweh is the speaker here, this passage clearly teaches a belief in the resurrection, though the focus of this belief is more national than individual. Isa. 25:8 contains a similar perspective: "He will swallow up death forever. The sovereign LORD will wipe away the tears from all faces; he will remove the disgrace of his people from all the earth. The LORD has spoken."

(d) Ezekiel's vision of the valley of dry bones (Ezek. 37) has often been understood as a prediction of the resurrection. In a vision Yahweh asks the prophet whether dry bones can live (37:3). Ezekiel replies that Yahweh alone knows. Then Yahweh commands Ezekiel to prophesy to the bones, promising to cause sinews and flesh to come on them and breath to enter them so that they live (37:4–6). The prophet does so, and what is promised comes about (37:7–11). The prophet is then given the interpretation: "'This is what the Sovereign

LORD says: O my people, I am going to open your graves and bring you up from them; I will bring you back to the land of Israel. Then you, my people, will know that I am the LORD, when I open your graves and bring you up from them. I will put my Spirit in you and you will live, and I will settle you in your own land. Then you will know that I the LORD have spoken, and I have done it, declares the LORD'" (37:12–14).

The background of this passage includes the fall of Jerusalem, the capture of the temple, and the exile, which had left the Israelites saying: "Our offenses and sins weigh us down, and we are wasting away because of them. How then can we live?" (Ezek. 33:10). In this context, then, the vision of the valley of dry bones is one of national restoration. Ezekiel is probably basing his view of Yahweh's creative power on Gen. 2:7, and the vision he sees derives from the countless corpses scattered on the battlefield in the wake of Nebuchadnezzar's armies. The prophet is not concerned with the resurrection of individual dead people as such, although the symbolism used undoubtedly raised the question of renewal of life for those who have died.

(e) Dan. 12:2 is the only OT verse that manifests a clear and undisputed reference to the resurrection of the dead. The context describes a great tribulation, Michael arising to take charge of God's people, and a book containing the names of all those to be delivered: "Multitudes who sleep in the dust of the earth will awake: some to everlasting life, others to shame and everlasting contempt." Dan. 12 is concerned only with a resurrection within Israel: some to salvation and others to condemnation. But this passage did lend itself to the doctrine of the resurrection that became championed by the Pharisees in the NT. To them, justice required resurrection, for only that doctrine provides the answer to the problem of the death of the most faithful servants of the living God.

6. The lit. of the intertestamental period exhibits a variety of beliefs about the afterlife and resurrection. (a) Jesus ben Sirach, writing about 180 B.C., had no conception of resurrection or life after death and thus held a position comparable with that of the Sadducees in the time of Christ. Sheol is the ultimate abode of the dead. It is devoid of pleasure (Sir. 14:16), a place of darkness (22:11), endless sleep (46:19), silence (17:27–28), and corruption (10:11). No one can praise God there (18:28). There is no return from death (38:21), which is a state of eternal rest (30:17). The only immortality known to Sirach is a good name (39:9; 41:11–13; 44:8) or the perpetuation of one's name in one's children (11:28; 46:12).

(b) However, 2 Macc. describes in resurrection terms the hope of the martyrs of Israel in their struggle against Antiochus Epiphanes (see esp. 2 Macc. 7:9, 11, 14, 22–23, 29; 12:43). Thus an elder named Razis tore out his entrails rather than fall into the hands of the Greeks. He flung his bowels at the crowds, "calling upon the Lord of life and spirit to give them back to him again" (2 Macc. 14:46).

(c) The Apocalypse of Baruch (*2 Bar.*) was written late in the 1st or early in the 2d cent. A.D. as a reflection on the tragedy of the destruction of Jerusalem in A.D. 70. One's only hope lies in the world to come. For the author the dead will be raised in exactly the same form (50:2). They will thus be recognizable (50:3–4). After that they will be changed and glorified so as to inhabit a world that does not die; the wicked are changed only to be tormented (51:3–6). This book makes resurrection dependent on adherence to the practice of the law.

(d) The book of 2 Esdras, also written ca. A.D. 100, describes the coming of the Messiah. After an interim kingdom of four hundred years, all the dead will be raised and the Lord will sit on his throne of judgment, where he will reward people according to what they have done. The two possible places to go to are "the pit of torment" and "the place of rest," "the furnace of hell [Gehenna; → *geenna, 1147*]" and "the paradise of delight" (2 Esd. 7:32–36). The nations will also be raised for judgment (7:37–43). The saved are those who "keep the law of the Lawgiver perfectly" (7:89). The face of the righteous in the resurrection will "shine like the sun" (7:97).

(e) The resurrection of righteous Israelites (though not of others) is implied in *1 Enoch* 90:33. The wicked have no hope of rising from

their beds (46:6), but the righteous will be raised as the chosen of the Elect One, the heavenly Son of Man (51:1–3). The nature of the resurrection is described in 62:13–16; 103:4, though the message is not consistent. The first passage speaks of resurrection in terms of a transfigured body, the second as a reshaped soul.

(f) The Qumran community expected a grand final conflict between the sons of light and the sons of darkness, but they do not seem to have been much concerned about the fate of the dead. Their view seems more in line with an immortality of the soul rather than a resurrection of the body. The sect clearly shared a belief in some form of future life. According to Josephus, the Essenes (a group similar to those at Qumran) believed in both the resurrection of the body and the immortality of the soul.

(g) In the main, later Talmudic lit. accepted the idea of resurrection, the coming to life of the dead. In *b. Sanh.* 90b, the Sadducees ask Gamaliel where in Scripture was the evidence that the Holy One brings the dead to life. Gamaliel replied by citing from the Law Deut. 31:16, from the Prophets Isa. 26:19, and from the Hagiographa Song 7:10. But the Sadducees are not satisfied, and Gamaliel finally quotes Deut. 11:9, claiming that the promise of the land "to them" implied resurrection of the dead.

7. Neither the OT nor the intertestamental lit. has a uniform eschatological expectation. In various places there is the growing belief that because Yahweh lives, his faithful people will also live. The nature of such an existence is rarely defined, although there is an implied continuity of identity. While Sheol is depicted as the ultimate end of a person, some writings begin to suggest a richer and more worthwhile survival in another world and even to propose a resurrection to life on earth.

Many suggestions have been offered as to the source of this new thinking (many of them linked with other ancient religions), but it seems best to relate the development of this doctrine to progressive revelation in Scripture. The idea of an afterlife has its deepest root in an awareness of the living God himself: Because Yahweh lives and is the covenant God of Israel, his people, one can expect an ongoing and living relationship with him. This awareness developed over the course of Israel's history.

NT 1. Both *anistēmi* (used 107x in the NT) and *anastasis* (42x) are found in the NT in general senses not connected with resurrection. (a) The vb. is used of raising up children for a deceased brother in a levirate marriage (Matt. 22:24; cf. Gen. 38:8), of rising to speak (Matt. 26:62) or read Scripture (Lk. 4:16). It is also used with the meaning of appear or come, e.g., a king (Acts 7:18), a priest (Heb. 7:11, 15), accusers (Matt. 12:41; Mk. 14:57; Lk. 11:32), a questioner (10:25), and an enemy rising up against someone (Mk. 3:26; Acts 5:36; 6:9). There is also the weakened meaning indicating the beginning of an action expressed by another vb., i.e., rise, set out, get ready (Matt. 9:9; Mk. 2:14; 7:24; 10:1). In fact, most instances of *anistēmi* do not refer to the resurrection; this is the opposite of what occurs with *egeirō*, to raise up (→ *1586*).

(b) Luke uses *anastasis* in 2:34 ("This child is destined to cause the falling and rising of many in Israel") to draw attention almost at the outset of his Gospel to the role of Jesus in God's purposes and to his divisive effect within Israel, a fact borne out by the succeeding narrative. In the case of this noun, however, most uses of it do refer to the resurrection.

2. The richest theological meaning of *anistēmi* and *anastasis* in the NT centers around the doctrine of the resurrection of the dead. Thus used, the root becomes virtually synonymous with *egeirō*. At first sight, there seems little difference between these two word groups. Closer study shows that *egeirō*, esp. in the pass., is used predominantly for what happened at Easter, i.e., the raising of the crucified Jesus to life, while *anistēmi* and *anastasis* refer more often to the raising of people during Jesus' earthly ministry and to the eschatological and universal resurrection (1 Cor. 15:25–26 makes the difference

between the two clear, although the Eng. does not always make it sufficiently clear that two different roots are being used).

The intrans. meaning predominates with both verbal stems, and Christ is almost always the subj. of both (except in 1 Cor. 15). When the trans. meaning is used, God is usually the subj. and Christ the obj. In other words, the general rule in the NT is that God's action on and through Christ is expressed by *egeirō*, while *anistēmi* expresses, as it were, what happens in the realm of human experience.

3. Of central importance for the NT are statements about Jesus' resurrection, including his predictions (e.g., Mk. 8:31; 9:9, 31; 10:34) and the testimony by Mary Magdalene (Matt. 28:8, 10) and the disciples (e.g., Acts 1:22; 2:31; 4:33). Through an act of God, the dead and buried Lord was raised to life again (cf. Acts 2:31, 34; Eph. 5:14) with a body that was new and material, not identical with the old but not merely visionary (cf. Jn. 20–21). He appeared to his disciples in a form that could be seen and felt (Lk. 24:16, 31, 39; Jn. 20:27; Acts 1:2, 9; cf. 1 Jn. 1:1–3), though he might not always permit the latter (Jn. 20:17). Although Jesus possessed the light and spirit body of the new age, he maintained normal human fellowship with his disciples by eating and drinking with them (Lk. 24:29–30, 42–43; Jn. 21:12–13; Acts 1:4; 10:41).

The disciples' testimony was not based on their observation of the actual event of Jesus' resurrection, which no one saw (note that in Matt. 28:4 the guards fainted), but on their meetings with the Risen One (Acts 1:22). The fact that Jesus did not remain among the dead but was alive (Lk. 24:5) gave the disciples, who until then had vacillated, the certainty that they had to do with the Lord, God's Son (Rom. 1:4). Jesus' resurrection thus became the sign of God's triumph over the power of sin and death. It had cancelled the fall of Adam and all the human slavery that had resulted from it, for the Crucified One had entered God's glory as the first among many. This is the foundation of all Christian hope and preaching (1 Pet. 1:3; 1 Cor. 15); it also explains why baptism is the sign of salvation (Rom. 6:5; 1 Pet. 3:21).

Jesus incorporates "the resurrection and the life" (Jn. 11:25) in the mystery of his person. In other words, the resurrection, which Jews had regarded as something only in the future, begins at the point where he appears and sets his Spirit to work. Anyone who is linked to him by faith and who has been possessed by his power experiences the beginning of the transition from this transient age to the new one, to the liberation from sin and death (Phil. 3:10). This is testified to in the Lord's Supper (Jn. 6:54). Hence, faith may be interpreted as a dying and rising again with Jesus (Rom. 6:11).

4. Although John gives us a concept of resurrection as something apparently already realized, it is only the beginning. In 2 Tim. 2:18 Paul expressly rejects the idea that the general resurrection of the dead has already taken place in the resurrection of Jesus; the contexts of Col. 2:13 and Eph. 2:6 do not suggest it either. The general resurrection, one of the fundamentals of the Christian faith (Lk. 14:14; 2 Cor. 5:10; Heb. 11:35), was taught by Jesus (Jn. 6:39–40, 54). It meant the resurrection of the body, not just a continuation of being or a reawakening of the soul. Moreover, it was linked with judgment (Heb. 6:2). This doctrine, a key point of contention to the gospel message, was rejected by the Sadducees (Matt. 22:23), who claimed that the resurrection was not taught in the Torah. It was equally rejected by the Greeks, because the teaching was too materialistic for their spiritualized thinking (Acts 17:18, 32; 1 Cor. 15:12).

5. Concerning the term *resurrection*, as in Jewish apocalyptic, two lines of thought are discernible with respect to the scope of its effects. Besides the general resurrection as depicted in Matt. 25:31–46; Rev. 20:11–15 (which is linked with the return of Christ and the separation of the good and bad), the NT also speaks of a prior "resurrection of the righteous" (Lk. 14:14), of the dead in Christ (1 Thess. 4:16; perhaps also 1 Cor. 15:23–24, where *to telos* may mean "the rest" rather than "the end"). In Rev. 20:4–6, the dead in Christ who have come to life in "the first resurrection" are said to reign for a thousand years; the remainder of the dead appear before the throne of God for the first time on the day of final judgment (20:11–15). (For interpretations of the millennium → *chilias*, *5942*).

While it is true that, in the general resurrection, individual identity persists in spite of death, so that all will stand before God in their complete being, one notes a fuller language used with respect to believers. They will be "like the angels" (Lk. 20:36), free of all human impulses, including sexual ones (Matt. 22:30; 24:38). They will also be like Jesus, for they will "see him as he is" (1 Jn. 3:2). We must remember that the analogy of seed and harvest has only a superficial resemblance to the process of resurrection. God gives a body as he wills (1 Cor. 15:38), and he alone guarantees the identity of the person.

6. In Phil. 3 Paul describes how he, in order to gain Christ, considers as "rubbish" all the things in which he had previously gloried as a Jew (3:8). His desire is to have a righteousness not of his own, but "that which is through faith in Christ" (3:9); his goal is "to know Christ and the power of his resurrection [*anastasis*] and the fellowship of sharing in his sufferings, becoming like him in his death, and so, somehow, to attain to the resurrection [*exanastasis*] from the dead" (3:10–11). It is debated whether *exanastasis* simply means *anastasis*, as is normally the case, or whether Paul is alluding to an earlier transformation and the church's being lifted up to be with Christ (cf. 1 Thess. 4:17; Rev. 20:4). This cannot be answered in any conclusive way.

The background in Phil. 3 may be a polemical confrontation with perfectionists who were claiming that knowledge of the heavenly Lord was all important and that believers were already raised with Christ to new life (cf. Phil. 3:12–16; also 1 Cor. 15:12; 2 Tim. 2:18). To counteract this, Paul insists that the only way to enter into the power of Christ's resurrection is by being willing to share in his sufferings and so become like him in his death. The last phrase is clearly baptismal (cf. Rom. 6:1–11; 2 Cor. 4:7–15; Col. 2:12, 20; 3:1; 2 Tim. 2:11). Paul's reference to knowing "the power of his resurrection" (Phil. 3:10) suggests a present experience. Yet in 3:11 Paul testifies to the hope that completely conforming to our Lord (3:21) will come at the time of the resurrection, which will complete God's saving plan for his people. Thus, the phrase *ei pōs* ("somehow") is not an expression of doubt about the reality of Paul's resurrection but about the way in which it will be his, i.e., by martyrdom in the near future or by some other means at a more distant time.

7. The vb. *anazaō*, come to life again, is rare in cl. Gk. Paul uses it in Rom. 7:9 to describe how the law (esp. the command not to covet) provoked *and* condemned sin: "Once I was alive apart from law; but when the commandment came, sin sprang to life and I died." Paul is arguing that the law identifies sin for what it is (7:7). But sin uses the law in an attempt to justify itself, by assuming that one can actually fulfill the law (7:8–11). This is a deception, and it results in killing the person concerned (7:11), because failure to keep the law brings condemnation. *anazaō* is also used of the prodigal son after his return: "For this son of mine was dead and is alive again" (Lk. 15:24, cf. 32).

See also *egeirō*, wake, rouse, raise up (*1586*).

416 (anastauroō, crucify), → *5089*.

418	ἀναστρέφω

ἀναστρέφω (*anastrephō*), to overturn, turn back, turn round; fig. behave, conduct oneself, live (*418*); ἀναστροφή (*anastrophē*), turning back; fig. way of life, conduct, behavior (*419*).

CL & OT 1. In cl. Gk. *anastrephō* means trans. to upset, turn upside down; intrans. to turn back, turn round. It eventually took on the fig. meaning of human behavior, i.e., to conduct oneself, live in a particular way. *anastrophē* denotes a turning round or a turning movement; then fig. way of life, conduct. In Gk. inscriptions one's *anastrophē* can be termed good, praiseworthy, blameless, fearless, etc.

2. The LXX uses *anastrephō* 80x for Heb. *šûb*, to turn round, return, and 8x for *hālak*, to walk; only in 1 Ki. 6:12; Prov. 8:20; 20:7 does the fig. sense of walking (in God's commands, in righteousness, etc.) apply.

anastrophē occurs only in the Apocr. (3x) and only with the fig. meaning of one's conduct of life (Tob. 4:14; 2 Macc. 5:8; 6:23).

NT In the NT the vb. occurs only 9x, the noun 13x—mostly in 1 and 2 Pet. and Heb. The lit. sense of the vb. occurs in Acts 5:22; 15:16; otherwise only the fig. meaning is found.

1. (a) Since both noun and vb. are neutral terms, they can designate a pre- or non-Christian (Jewish, Gal. 1:13; heathen, Eph. 2:3) way of life as well as a Christian one (2 Cor. 1:12). The determining factor of a person's life can be an ethical value system or one's faith (cf. Gal. 1:13). Lack of any moral obligation leads to an unbridled manner of life, where a person follows only his or her desires (1 Pet. 1:14; 2 Pet. 2:7) and finally is destroyed (Eph. 4:22).

(b) Turning to Christ implies a turning away from one's previous way of life, for which Christ frees and enables that person. The main point is to translate knowledge into practice. By faith and baptism we are introduced into the domain of power of Jesus Christ; we live "in Christ" and thus in a new fellowship with God. The knowledge of our earlier perversity (cf. 2 Cor. 6:14–16; Gal. 1:13; Eph. 2:1–3; 4:22; Col. 1:21; 3:1–17) helps us to set aside the old, makes us conscious of the new, and frees us for a new life of obedience, piety, and holiness (2 Cor. 1:12; 1 Pet. 1:15, 17; 3:16). This new conduct can itself assume exemplary significance (1 Tim. 3:15; 4:12) and be crowned by an appropriate end of life (Heb. 13:7). Such Christian conduct, however, is threatened by a double danger: reversion to heathen modes of conduct (2 Pet. 2:18) and legalism (cf. 1 Tim. 4:12 in the context of 4:1–3).

2. The word group has particular significance in the paraenesis of 1 Pet. Here the present, in which Christians live in the world "as aliens and strangers," is seen as a time of testing for faith (1 Pet. 2:11–12). The exhortation to live in a Christian way is grounded in having been called out by a holy God, in invoking the Father, who is also judge of all and cannot be bribed, and in the sacrificial death of Jesus, understood as a ransom "from the empty way of life [*anastrophē*]" handed down from one's ancestors (1:15–18). A way of life in conformity with Christ is also important because we live under the critical eyes of a heathen environment, so it serves as a witness to them (2:12; 3:1, 16).

See also *hodos*, way, road, highway, way of life (*3847*); *peripateō*, go about, walk (*4344*); *poreuomai*, go, to journey, to travel, to walk (*4513*).

419 (anastrophē, way of life, conduct, behavior), → 418.

422	ἀνατέλλω

ἀνατέλλω (*anatellō*), to rise, cause to rise (*422*); ἀνατολή (*anatolē*), rising sun, east (*424*).

CL & OT 1. In cl. Gk. *anatellō* means to rise, come to light. It was used esp. of the rising of the sun or moon. As a result, the related noun *anatolē* came to mean the east, since that is the direction in which the sun rises.

2. In the LXX *anatellō* can simply mean to rise or sprout, as of plants (Isa. 44:4; cf. 61:11; Jon. 4:8). In Gen. 3:18 God tells Adam that thorns and thistles will sprout up from the earth as a result of his sin. In 2 Sam. 10:5 the vb. is used of the growing of beards and in Jdg. 9:33; 2 Sam. 23:4 of the rising of the sun. *anatellō* occurs in several messianic prophecies: In Num. 24:17, a star will rise out of Jacob. In Isa. 60:1, the glory of the Lord will soon rise in Israel. In Mal. 4:2 the sun of righteousness will rise with healing in its wings. Note esp. Zech. 6:12, where God promises to send "the Branch" (*anatolē*), who will "branch out [*anatellō*]" from his place" (cf. also 3:8 = LXX 3:9; Jer. 23:5). As in cl. Gk. *anatolē* in the LXX often means the rising of the sun, thus also east.

NT 1. *anatellō* occurs 9x in the NT. In most places it refers to the rising of the sun (e.g., Matt. 5:45; 13:6). But 2 Pet. 1:19 likely alludes to Num. 24:17, where the messianic bearer of light will arise in our hearts. In Heb. 7:14, the author (probably alluding to the "Branch" metaphor of the OT) writes that Jesus descended (i.e., sprouted) from the tribe of Judah, not Levi. Matt. 4:16, a quotation of Isa. 9:2, uses *anatellō* instead of the LXX's *lampō* for to dawn.

2. *anatolē* in the NT usually denotes the east (e.g., the place from which the Magi came, Matt. 2:1–2; cf. also 2:9; Lk. 13:29; Rev. 7:2). Zechariah, in his song in Lk. 1, uses this word in a specialized sense as a designation for the Messiah (1:78). He is probably alluding to the promise of the coming star of Num. 24:17 or to the coming light in Isa. 60:1 (although "the Branch" in Jer. 23:5; Zech. 3:8; 6:12 may also be in view).

424 (anatolē, rising sun, east), → 422.

433 (anapsyxis, refreshing), → 6034.

434 (anapsychō, to refresh, cheer), → 6034.

435	ἀνδραποδιστής

ἀνδραποδιστής (*andrapodistēs*), slave-dealer, kidnapper (*435*).

CL & OT *andrapodistēs* derives from the verbal idea of catching human beings (*andra*) by the foot (*pod-*) and selling them into slavery. It does not occur in the LXX, though the cognate *andrapodon* (slave) is used in 3 Macc. 7:5.

NT In 1 Tim. 1:9–10 Paul refers to those who disregard God's law in general and break God's laws in particular. Among those named are *andrapodistai*, slave-dealers or kidnappers (cf. Exod. 21:16; Deut. 24:7), who are guilty of breaking the eighth commandment. This term may include those who break into Christian homes to carry off any belonging to the Way (Acts 9:1–2). By extension, it may also refer to those who by false teaching (1 Tim. 1:3–7) drag away believers from their rightful place before God and rob them of their liberty in Christ.

See also *lēstēs*, robber, highwayman, bandit, revolutionary (*3334*); *sylaō*, plunder, rob (*5195*); *apostereō*, rob, defraud, deprive (*691*); *spēlaion*, cave, den (*5068*).

437 (andrizomai, behave in a manly way), → 467.

441	ἀνέγκλητος

ἀνέγκλητος (*anenklētos*), not accused, without reproach, blameless, irreproachable (*441*); ἄμωμος (*amōmos*), unblemished, blameless (*320*); ἄσπιλος (*aspilos*), spotless, without blemish (*834*); ἀμώμητος (*amōmētos*), unblemished (*318*).

CL & OT 1. In cl. Gk. *anenklētos* means a person or thing against which no accusation can be made, being free of guilt. Its meaning changed from the original sense to that of respectability without reproach. In the LXX it is only found at 3 Macc. 5:31.

2. *aspilos*, spotless, is not found in the LXX. *amōmos*, faultless, is used esp. in legal OT texts (e.g., Exod. 29:1; Lev. 3:1, 6; Num. 6:14) of sacrificial animals that were free from blemish, but also in Ps. in a moral sense. *amōmētos*, unblemished, is in origin a term of praise, almost equivalent to *anenklētos*.

NT 1. *anenklētos*, not accused, without reproach, takes on theological ideas in the NT. (a) In 1 Tim. 3:10; Tit. 1:6–7, in a discussion on qualifications for deacons or elders, Paul stresses the need to be beyond reproach, in the ordinary sense of common respectability. Thus, in addition to spiritual qualifications, ordinary standards of decency also become preconditions of office in the church, for the sake of the church's good name in the world.

(b) This word has its original, legal sense in 1 Cor. 1:8 and Col. 1:22. In the former, God promises to keep believers firm to stand blameless or innocent on the judgment day. This blamelessness is not an ethical quality, as if it is the Christian's own achievement, but follows from holding fast to fellowship with Jesus to the end (1:9).

Col. 1:22 also speaks of judgment. It is Christ's reconciling word, which has been achieved by his death, that forms the basis of our blamelessness. Alongside *anenklētos*, Paul uses *amōmos*, faultless, a word drawn from the language of Jewish ritual (cf. Eph. 5:27; Phil. 2:15; 1 Pet. 1:19). Through faith in Jesus Christ we are delivered from well-merited accusation (Col. 1:22–23), so that we can appear blameless before him (cf. Rom. 8:33–34).

2. *amōmētos* occurs in 2 Pet. 3:14, where the author exhorts us to live blamelessly until the great day of the Lord comes, even if troubles come our way. Such a lifestyle is possible only if we are at peace with the Lord through Jesus Christ (cf. Rom. 5:1).

3. *amōmos* means unblemished in the cultic sense of free from defects; hence Christ is described as "a lamb without blemish [*amōmos*] or defect [*aspilos*]" (1 Pet. 1:19). He "offered himself unblemished [*amōmos*] to God" (Heb. 9:14). *amōmos* is used in the moral and religious sense of blameless of the Christian community (Eph. 1:4; 5:27; Phil. 2:15; Rev. 14:5; cf. Jude 24). For *amiantos*, → *mianō*, to defile, *3620*.

See also *aretē*, virtue (*746*).

445 (*anektos*, bearable, tolerable, endurable), → *462*.

446 (*aneleēmōn*, merciless), → *1799*.

447 (*aneleos*, without pity), → *1799*.

449 (*anemos*, wind), → *847*.

451 (*anexeraunētos*, unsearchable), → *2236*.

454 (*anepaischyntos*, not to be ashamed), → *158*.

455 (*anepilēmmptos*, above reproach, without blame), → *3284*.

462	ἀνέχομαι

ἀνέχομαι (*anechomai*), bear, endure (*462*); ἀνοχή (*anochē*), delay, limited period, restraint, forbearance (*496*); ἀνεκτός (*anektos*), bearable, tolerable, endurable (*445*).

CL & OT 1. In cl. Gk. *anechomai* occurs both in an active and deponent form. It means (with an obj.) to hold up, honor, hold back; (without an obj.) to stand out, persevere, endure. The mid. deponent form predominates in the NT and other Gk. literature.

2. In the LXX *anechomai* translates several Heb. roots, all of which express the idea of restraining some action or emotion. Such statements can refer to human beings (Gen. 45:1) or to God (Isa. 1:13; 42:14). The pressure building up behind such restraint can cause it to burst forth with dire results. There is a tendency to portray God as exercising restraint, while human beings give way to the vehement reaction, such as crying out in anguish at the silence and inaction of God (63:15; 64:12). *anochē* occurs only in 1 Macc. 12:25, where it refers to an armistice or an "opening" to reenter the land.

NT 1. (a) In the NT *anechomai* occurs 15x, mainly in Paul (10x), but with little consistency of usage. Its meaning is difficult to determine because of its frequent use in formal phrases and in passages that go back to an earlier tradition. In Col. 3:13 its proximity to a catalogue of five virtues is significant, but the pres. part. is intended to qualify the final item enumerated in the list, namely, *makrothymia* (patience; → *3429*): (lit.) "Put on then ... patience, forbearing one another...." The pers. obj. ("one another") indicates a characteristic aspect of NT usage. When forbearance is exercised, virtue is no longer self-centered; rather, an essential part of a Christian's calling is the service of others (cf. also Eph. 4:2, "bearing with [*anechomai*] one another in love").

(b) In love there is mutual forbearance; hence Paul's plea to the Corinthians: "Put up with a little of my foolishness" (2 Cor. 11:1). The apostle appears to them as weak and insignificant, without any of the outward marks of apostolic authority borne by the "super-apostles" (11:5). But he *is* an apostle and, as such, a bearer of the truth of Christ; Christ bears the Corinthians in his love, so they should bear with Paul.

The strong theological content of mutual forbearance becomes apparent here. When the believers in Corinth are admonished or instructed, they are to accept the message as from its divine source, from the God who is longsuffering toward them (cf. 2 Tim. 4:3). There is a play on the vb. throughout 2 Cor. 11 in the contrast drawn with the way the Corinthians are already "putting up with" false teachers (11:4, 19–20) but want to dispense with Paul.

(c) *anechomai* in 1 Cor. 4:12 should be construed as having a pers. obj., by analogy with the surrounding vbs. In other words, Paul does not simply "endure" when persecuted; he is longsuffering toward his persecutors. Paul's words are certainly reminiscent of Jesus' teaching in Matt. 25:35.

(d) In Acts 18:14 the vb. is used as a technical legal term for receiving an accusation on the part of Gallio, the proconsul of Achaia, who says, "If you Jews were making a complaint about some misdemeanor or serious crime, it would be reasonable for me to listen [*anechomai*] to you."

(e) The only occurrence of the vb. in the Synoptic Gospels is in the question of Jesus: "O unbelieving and perverse generation ... how long shall I stay with you? How long shall I put up [*anechomai*] with you?" (Matt. 17:17; Mk. 9:19; Lk. 9:41). The occasion is the disciples' failure to cast out a dumb spirit afflicting an epileptic boy. These words express Jesus' exasperation at the blindness of those who refused to accept God's presence and power in him.

(f) In 2 Thess. 1:4 the vb. refers to enduring afflictions: "Therefore among God's churches we boast about your perseverance and faith in all the persecutions and trials you are enduring [*anechomai*]." By contrast, 2 Tim. 4:3 and Heb. 13:22 refer to Christian teaching and exhortation. In the former passage the allusion is to the fickleness of those who "will not put up with" sound teaching; in the latter the author wants his readers to "bear with" his word of exhortation.

2. The noun *anochē* occurs only in Rom. 2:4 and 3:25, where it refers to the "tolerance" or "forbearance" of God. The religious Jew is not exempt from judgment just because he or she is a member of God's chosen people. Anyone who thinks that is showing contempt for God's kindness, "tolerance," and patience (Rom. 2:4). Later on Paul explains that "in his forbearance" God left the sins committed before the coming of the Messiah unpunished, while awaiting his arrival. That is, God restrained his wrath until he openly displayed his righteousness in Christ and brought to an end the period of the Mosaic law.

Apart from the fact that in the NT *anochē* is used only of God, there is no clear-cut distinction between *anochē* and *makrothymia* (→ *3429*). Yet certain nuances are detectable. *makrothymia* is undoubtedly less active and vigorous and may be translated patience. It also has stronger eschatological overtones, looking forward to God's final judgment, whereas *anochē* denotes the period of God's gracious forbearance with particular reference to Israel and the period up to the cross of Christ.

3. The adj. *anektos* (bearable, tolerable) occurs in the comparative form in Jesus' pronouncement on the Jewish cities that had rejected him. It will be "more bearable" for Tyre and Sidon (Matt. 11:22; Lk. 10:14; cf. Isa. 23; Ezek. 26:2–28:24; Joel 3:4; Amos 1:9–10; Zech. 9:2–4) and Sodom and Gomorrah (Matt. 10:15; 11:24; Lk. 10:12; cf. Gen. 19; Isa. 1:9) in the day of judgment. Note the paradox that these places mentioned in the OT were notorious centers of wickedness, whereas the places in Galilee on which Jesus pronounces judgment (e.g., Korazin and Bethsaida) are relatively insignificant. There is an implicit claim that Jesus' appearance is more crucial than any prophetic pronouncement, and thus the guilt of rejection is all the greater.

See also *kartereō*, be strong, steadfast, persevere (*2846*); *makrothymia*, patience, longsuffering (*3429*); *hypomenō*, be patient, persevere, endure, be steadfast (*5702*).

464 (*anēthon*, dill), → *3303*.

467	ἀνήρ

ἀνήρ (*anēr*), a man (*467*); ἀν-δρίζομαι (*andrizomai*), behave in a manly way (*437*).

CL & OT 1. In cl. Gk. *anēr* has all the meanings known in the LXX and the NT: (a) a man, in contrast to a woman; (b) husband, also bridegroom; (c) adult and warrior; (d) manliness; also gentleman, hero; (e) humankind, as genus (see esp. *anthrōpos*, 476).

2. *anēr* is used to translate a number of Heb. words used in the OT. The man is lord of the wife (Gen. 3:16). He alone is competent in legal and cultic proceedings (Exod. 23:17; 34:23, → *arsēn*, 781; 1 Sam. 1:3–4, → *anthrōpos*, 476). But alongside this typically oriental and patriarchal way of life, one can find allusions to men's responsibilities to women (cf. Deut. 20:7; 21:14; 22:13–19; 24:5; see also *gynē*, 1222).

NT 1. As in cl. Gk., *anēr* in the NT can mean: (a) man in contrast to woman (Matt. 14:21; 1 Cor. 11:3–15); it is a typical form of address in Acts 15:7, 13 and elsewhere; (b) husband (Mk. 10:2, 12 [cf. Matt. 19:3, 9]; Rom. 7:2–3; Eph. 5:22–33; Tit. 1:6) or a betrothed person (cf. Matt. 1:19; 2 Cor. 11:2; Rev. 21:2); (c) adult (1 Cor. 13:11; cf. Jas. 3:2); (d) manliness, including maturity and dignity (Lk. 23:50; Acts 6:3, 5); (e) humankind, as a genus (Lk. 5:8; Jas. 1:20).

Paul often uses *anēr* to distinguish man from *gynē* (e.g., 1 Cor. 7:1–16). Lk. uses it in the more general meaning of *anthrōpos* (e.g., Lk. 11:31; 19:7; Acts 2:5).

2. The organization and leadership of the Christian community in the NT was largely male-oriented, just as Jesus' circle of the Twelve comprised only men. But the man did not receive his special position because of some sort of natural fitness. It came rather from Christ, by whom he was honored and whom he was called upon to reflect (1 Cor. 11:7). In the sequence God—Christ—man—woman (1 Cor. 11:3–15), each one is the "head" of the following, and, conversely, each member is the reflected splendor of the preceding one (→ *doxa*, 1518).

This qualification of the man, however, does not indicate preferential status but special task and responsibility. For before God, man and woman are on the same level (see Gal. 3:28; cf. 1 Pet. 4:7). This establishment of the equality of the sexes before God is something new and worthy of note in Christianity. It throws into sharp relief the distinction between the Christian view and the otherwise widespread contempt for women in the ancient world.

When Christ and man are put in parallel in Eph. 5:25 and 28 (cf. also Col. 3:19; 1 Pet. 3:7), the point of comparison is the responsibility of the man to love his wife in the same way as Christ loves his church, i.e., with a life of total, selfless, self-sacrificial devotion. The exhortation to "be men of courage" (*andrizomai* in 1 Cor. 16:13) is a summons similar to being on one's guard and standing firm in the faith (also in that verse). It is a powerful form of demand aimed at the whole community: Their ultimate goal should be to become "a perfect man [*andra teleion*]" (Eph. 4:13 KJV; "mature," NIV).

3. *anēr* is used in the sense of husband in the phrase "husband of one wife," which occurs in the Pastoral Letters as one of the qualifications for bishops (1 Tim. 3:2), deacons (3:12), and elders (Tit. 1:6). Some view the phrase to mean "married only once" (cf. NRŠ). While such an interpretation may agree with later developments in the church, the view that a man should not have more than one living wife seems to fit the first-century situation better. On the one hand, it excludes polygamy, which did occur in the first century and in this respect would meet the OT norms for marriage. On the other hand, it also excludes divorcees who had remarried, since the first wife was still regarded as the wife despite the divorce (cf. Mk. 10:11; Lk. 16:18b).

The converse of this phrase occurs in 1 Tim. 5:9 in the case of the enrollment of widows, who must be (lit.) "the wife of one husband." To refuse to help widows who had been "married more than once" (NRŠ) seems unjust, esp. in cases of levirate marriage (→ *gameō*, 1138). But this ruling is understandable if we see the situation as a woman's not having been involved in divorce or a polygamous mar-

riage (cf. NIV, "faithful to her husband"). It should be remembered too that this passage is not concerned about welfare in general and the Christian's attitude to anyone in need, but with those *within* the church who have a claim on church resources. Elsewhere Paul advises remarriage in case of need (1 Cor. 7:8–9, 39–40).

See also *anthrōpos*, human being (*476*); *arsēn*, male (*781*).

473 (*anthrōpareskos*, one who tries to please people), → *743*.

474 (*anthrōpinos*, human), → *476*.

476	ἄνθρωπος

ἄνθρωπος (*anthrōpos*), human being (*476*); ἀνθρώπινος (*anthrōpinos*), human (*474*).

CL & OT 1. In cl. Gk. *anthrōpos* means a human being, sometimes a male person. The fem. equivalent is woman, often in a contemptuous sense. The adj. *anthrōpinos* means human, belonging to humanity. *anthrōpos* is contrasted to beasts and to gods. In a contemptuous sense, it can mean a slave. There is also a voc. usage that has undertones of reproachfulness: "Man!"

2. (a) The Heb. words corresponding to *anthrōpos* are ʾādām, ʾîš, and ʾᵉnôš. ʾādām is human nature as contrasted with God (1 Sam. 15:29) and with animals (Gen. 1:26). In its generic use it includes both men and women (cf. Gen. 1:27). ʾîš occurs in Gen. 2:24; ʾᵉnôš often signifies the aspect of weakness, mortality (cf. Ps. 8:5).

In both Gen. 1:1–31 and 2:4b–24, the creation of humankind is the high point. One's humanity resides in the life one has been given (2:7b) in correspondence to God (1:27a). A person is deemed worthy to be spoken to by God and is given a task (1:28; 2:15–17). Through disobedience humankind falls victim to death. ʾādām, a word connected with ʾādāmâh, earth, now no longer simply alludes to one's creatureliness (2:7) but also to one's transitoriness (3:19).

3. The OT is not acquainted with anything corresponding to the Gk. division of a human being into two or three parts, consisting of *nous, psychē*, and *sōma* (mind, soul, and body). The following concepts indicate, in rough outline comparison, different aspects of a person, always seen as a whole. They do not represent different parts.

(a) Flesh (Heb. *bāśār*), often indicating transitoriness (Ps. 78:39). (b) Spirit (Heb. *rûah*) denotes a person as a living being (146:4). (c) Soul (Heb. *nepeš*) denotes a person as life bound up with one's body (1 Sam. 19:11b), as an individual (Deut. 24:7a; Ezek. 13:18–19). The soul is neither preexistent nor immortal, for it is the whole person (Gen. 2:7). (d) Heart (Heb. *lēb*) is the essential, inner person as opposed to outward appearance (1 Sam. 16:7b; Job 12:3).

4. (a) A pessimistic conception of humankind is found in some places in wisdom literature (e.g., Job 14; Eccl.). These concepts are radicalized in Qumran texts, where the transitoriness and sinfulness of human beings are presented in a wide variety of formulations.

(b) Another branch of Jud. reveals the development to a body-soul dualism (4 Macc. 2:21–22), which in Hel. Jud. led to an attitude of loathing for the body (2 Esd. 7:88, 100). According to Josephus, there was widespread belief that redemption is the liberation of the soul from the body. The image of God in us is restricted to the *nous*, mind or reason.

(c) This dualistic view of humanity in the Hel. world is found esp. in Gnosticism, an early form of which certain sections of the NT seem to combat (e.g., John).

NT In the NT, as in the OT, the question about humankind is that concerning sin and redemption. Abstract definitions find no place here. Humanity differs from animals and plants (Matt. 4:19; 12:12; 1 Cor. 15:39; Rev. 9:4), from angels (1 Cor. 4:9; 13:1), from Christ (Gal. 1:12; Eph. 6:7), and from God (Matt. 7:11; 10:32–33; Mk. 10:9; Jn. 10:33; Acts 5:29; Phil. 2:7). *anthrōpos* is used in order to belittle in Jas. 1:7 (with reference to Jesus in Matt. 26:74; Jn. 19:5). Jesus is called *anthrōpos* in respect of his true humanity in Phil. 2:7 and 1 Tim. 2:5. Jesus' own self-designation was "the Son of Man" (see under *huios*, *5626*). *kata anthrōpous* (1 Pet. 4:6) and *kata anthrōpon* (Rom. 3:5; 1 Cor. 3:3; 15:32)—lit., "according to men, in a human fashion"—are used as common synonymous phrases for *anthrōpinos*, human (Rom. 6:19; 1 Cor. 10:13). Sometimes *anthrōpos* can mean a male person (see Matt. 11:8; 19:5; 1 Cor. 7:1).

The NT is not interested in an isolated, self-contained anthropology any more than the OT. Statements about humanity are always partly theological pronouncements. The emphasis in this word is on our creatureliness (as distinct from other creatures and from God), on our being addressed and chosen by God, on our transitoriness and disobedience, and on our being subject to the wrath and grace of God. The unity and equality of humankind are not postulates of abstract ideas; they are realized in the Christian community (Gal. 3:28; cf. Rom. 3:22, 29; 10:12; Jas. 2:1–9). Through Christ the "one new man" (Eph. 2:15) comes into being. At the same time new differentiations come to light through God's electing activity in Christ (Matt. 20:16) and through the variety of the gifts of the Spirit in the church (1 Cor. 12).

1. *The Synoptics.* Human beings owe God obedience and service without any prior claim to reward (Lk. 17:17–19). Jesus' universal call to repentance assumes that all are sinners (Matt. 6:12; Mk. 1:15; cf. Matt. 5:45; 9:13; Lk. 15:7). At the same time, God puts great value on human beings (Matt. 6:26b; 10:29–30), even as sinners (Lk. 15). One's vocation is to be a child of the Father and to be perfect like him (Matt. 5:45, 48). The expression in Lk. 2:14 relates to human beings as recipients of the divine favor (cf. Lk. 3:22), i.e., the elect messianic community.

2. *Paul.* (a) The old self without Christ, i.e., the unconverted person, is either devoted to the law (Rom. 2:17–29) or in rebellion against it (1:18–20); such an individual perverts knowledge of God and in so doing becomes perverted himself or herself (1:21–32). Alongside statements about one's responsibility stand those about one's incapability (cf. the inexcusability in 2:1 with the inability to do good in 7:18–19). This is a tension that Paul sees removed only in God and overcome in Christ (Phil. 2:12b–13). Through Christ, "the new man" and "the last Adam" (Rom. 5:9–21; 1 Cor. 15:21–22, 45–49), we become free. We become "a new creation" (2 Cor. 5:17; cf. Eph. 4:22–24; Col. 3:1–4:6).

Baptism signifies the death of the "old self" with Christ (Rom. 6:6). Through incorporation into the body of Christ we are born as a new people (→ *palingenesia*, *4098*). To the "new self" is directed the imperative to be what Christ has made us (Eph. 4:22–5:21; Col. 3:9–17; cf. Rom. 6:6–14). It is not in our natural capacities to become this; it comes about through being renewed in Christ and in living out this new life. Rom. 8:1–17 depicts this in terms of being led by the Spirit. Paul distinguishes further between the inner and outer self (2 Cor. 4:16), that is, between our essential being (often expressed in terms of the heart) and our outward appearance.

(b) Paul has several other important anthropological concepts. (i) *sōma* (→ *5393*), body, is not only the physical body but the whole person, the self, the "I" (see Phil. 1:20; also cf. 1 Cor. 15:44 with Phil. 3:21).

(ii) *sarx* (→ *4922*), flesh, occasionally synonymous with *sōma*, speaks of the transience of humankind (2 Cor. 4:10–11). It furthermore signifies one's sinful nature (Rom. 8:1–14; 1 Cor. 15:50).

(iii) *psychē* (→ *6034*), soul, denotes a person as a living being (2 Cor. 12:15). In 1 Cor. 15:44 Paul relates its existence to this life as contrasted with the next: "It is sown a natural body [*sōma psychikon*], it is raised a spiritual body [*sōma pneumatikon*]."

(iv) *pneuma* (→ *4460*), spirit, in some passages overlaps in meaning with that of *sōma* and *psychē* and refers to the inner self. It can resemble the modern concept of self-consciousness (cf. Rom. 8:16, where the Spirit is said to bear witness with our spirit that we are children of God).

(v) From Gk. thought, and found primarily in Paul, are: *nous* (→ *3808*) mind, which focuses attention on a human being as a conscious, rational being; and *syneidēsis* (*5287*), conscience. Rom. 2:15 refers to the conscience of the Gentiles and its role in their knowledge of God.

3. *John.* Johannine statements view humanity as prey to the *kosmos*, the world in opposition to God, and therefore missing the real self (→ *pseudomai*, *6017*, on Jn. 8:41–47; 1 Jn. 1:10; 2:22; 5:10; Rev. 2:2). The coming of Jesus confronts human beings with a decision: either to remain the way we are or to be born again (Jn. 3:3–8). This decision demonstrates whether we are "of the world" or "from God" (cf. Jn. 8:47 and 1 Jn. 4:5 with Jn. 5:24; 6:44, 65; 12:32). There is, however, no depreciation of matter here (see Jn. 1:14). On the contrary, the whole person is made free through Jesus (Jn. 8:31–36) and thus gains life (5:24; 11:25–26).

4. *The NT and Modern Psychology.* Biblical psychology is practical rather than scientific, but it is understandable in its context. Thus, since strong emotion frequently affects the lower parts of the body from the solar plexus down, the bowels (→ *splanchnon*, *5073*) is the term used where we today, in equally popular terms, would speak of the heart (e.g., 2 Cor. 6:12; 7:15; Phil. 1:8; Phlm. 7, 12). At the opposite extreme *nous* is the mind, intellect, or understanding (e.g., Rom. 12:2; 1 Cor. 14:19). *kardia* (*2840*), heart, stands somewhere between the two; it is sometimes emotional, though less warm than *splanchna* (e.g., Rom. 1:24; Jas. 3:14), and sometimes it represents the inner set of one's life pattern, including volition (e.g., 2 Cor. 4:6; 9:7; Eph. 4:18).

Thus the NT seizes on common sense terms to describe centers of emotion, feeling, volition, and comprehension. The Bible is concerned not with theory, but with bringing every single part of the person into an effective whole through the Holy Spirit's giving of continuous life to the human *pneuma*, spirit (e.g., Jn. 3:6; 1 Cor. 2:10–16). The human being is seen as a whole being, and whatever touches one part affects the whole.

There is nothing in NT teaching that runs counter to sound contemporary psychological practice, but the NT stresses the importance of a relationship with God as necessary for the full maturity of the human being in himself or herself as well as in relation to others in church and in society.

See also *anēr*, a man (*467*); *arsēn*, male (*781*).

478	ἀνθύπατος

ἀνθύπατος (*anthypatos*), proconsul (*478*).

Consul was originally the title of the two chief magistrates of the Roman republic. Holders of the office were of senatorial rank and served for one year in Rome before going to administer in the provinces. The office was somewhat modified in the empire, when even children could be given the title.

Luke uses this word in Acts 13:7–8, 12; 18:12; 19:38, where he shows civil power exercising its legitimate authority in an appropriate manner.

See also *Kaisar*, Caesar, emperor (*2790*); *hēgemōn*, leader, commander, chief (*2450*).

482 (anistēmi, raise; intrans. rise), → *414.*

485 (anoētos, unintelligent, foolish), → *3808.*

486 (anoia, folly), → *3808.*

487	ἀνοίγω

ἀνοίγω (*anoigō*), open (*487*); ἄνοιξις (*anoixis*), opening (*489*); διανοίγω (*dianoigō*), open, explain (*1380*).

CL & OT 1. In cl. Gk. *anoigō* means to open, remove that which obstructs. Fig. it can mean to reach the high seas. The vb. can be used trans. (to open a door, a place, an object, a part of the body) and intrans. (to open; partly in the pass. sense of to be opened).

2. In the LXX *anoigō* can mean to open the mouth (Ezek. 3:27); one's eyes and ears (e.g., Gen. 21:19; Isa. 35:5; 37:17); a container (e.g., a bag, box, vessel, or grave; Exod. 21:33; Jdg. 4:19; Ps. 5:9), a window, door, or gate (1 Sam. 3:15; 2 Ki. 13:17; Isa. 22:22; 26:2); or a book (Neh. 8:5). If the act of opening is related to human beings, God is often the subj.; objects include the womb (Gen. 29:31), mouth (Exod. 4:12, 15; Num. 22:28), eyes (Gen. 21:19; Isa. 35:5), ears (Isa. 50:5), or God's hands (Ps. 145:16).

NT In the NT *anoigō* is found 78x, esp. often in the Johannine literature. Following the LXX pattern the vb. is usually trans. and only rarely intrans. (Jn. 1:51; 1 Cor. 16:9; 2 Cor. 6:11). The sole occurrence of *anoixis* (Eph. 6:19) has a trans. meaning in Paul's request for prayer "that whenever I open my mouth [lit., in the opening of my mouth], words may be given me so that I will fearlessly make known the mystery of the gospel."

Objects of the vb. *anoigō* include (as in the LXX) the mouth (Matt. 5:2; Lk. 1:64; Acts 8:35; 10:34; 18:14), eye (Matt. 9:30; Jn. 9:10, 14; 10:21; Acts 9:8, 40), ear (Mk. 7:35), a door (Acts 12:10, 14; 14:27; 1 Cor. 16:9; 2 Cor. 2:12; Rev. 3:20), a place (Matt. 3:16), or a scroll (Rev. 5:2–5). If we leave aside those passages where "to open the mouth" means to begin to speak (e.g., Matt. 5:2; 13:35), which reflects a Semitic idiom (cf. Job 3:1; 33:2; Dan. 10:16), the vb. is used mostly with a theological sense: It is God himself who opens.

1. In Paul's writings *anoigō* occurs in his quotation of Ps. 5:9 in Rom. 3:13a, in the catena of quotations demonstrating that human beings are all guilty sinners: "Their throats are open graves." In 2 Cor. 6:11 Paul writes: "We have spoken freely to you [lit., our mouth is open to you], Corinthians, and opened out hearts wide [*platynō*, make wide] to you." Paul has kept no secrets back from the Corinthians, and he yearns for them.

Apart from these references, Paul uses God as the subj. of opening. He opens a door for Paul to do fruitful and effective missionary work (1 Cor. 16:9; 2 Cor. 2:12; Col. 4:3; cf. Acts 14:27; Rev. 3:8). Note that he never uses *anoigō* with Christ as subj.

2. Rev. 3:20 speaks of our opening the door to Christ: "Here I am! I stand at the door and knock. If anyone hears my voice and opens the door, I will come in and eat with him, and he with me." The underlying idea here is the kingdom of God seen as a feast (Isa. 25:6–9; Matt. 8:11; 22:1–14; Mk. 13:29; 14:25; cf. also the idea of a judge standing at the doors in Jas. 5:9). There are also promises of feeding on Christ himself (Jn. 6:35–40, 48–58) and living with him (Jn. 14:2–3, 23). Rev. 3:20 is in a letter addressed to the lukewarm church at Laodicea, but the sing. subj. invites individual response.

Elsewhere in the writings of Jn. God is the one who opens. He opens heaven (Jn. 1:51; Rev. 19:11), the temple (Rev. 11:19), and the holy tent of heaven (15:5). On his authority an angel opens the abyss of the underworld (9:2). But the exalted Lord has the authority to open the way of access to God. Note the beginning of the letter to the church at Philadelphia: "The words of him who is holy and true, who holds the key of David. What he opens no one can shut, and what he shuts no one can open. . . . See, I have placed before you an open door that no one can shut" (3:7–8). Reference to "the key of David" (→ *kleis*, *3090*) recalls God's promise to Eliakim (Isa. 22:22), who was given authority to open and shut. Here in Rev. the metaphor is construed as access to God and eternal life, as in Rev. 1:18: "I was dead, and behold I am alive for ever and ever! And I hold the keys of death and Hades" (cf. also Matt. 16:19).

In Rev. 5:2–9 it is the exalted Lord, the slain Lamb who has ascended to the throne, who alone is worthy to open the scroll with the seven seals that contains the record of God's plan in history in the last days. The earthly Jesus is here equal with God. The Fourth Gospel contains a counterpart to this in the fact that Jesus opens the eyes of the blind, which is something God alone can do (see Jn. 9; 10:21). He

is also the shepherd for whom "the watchman opens the gate . . . and the sheep listen to his voice" (10:3).

3. In Matt. 2:11 the Magi open their treasures. Elsewhere in Matt. Jesus opens the eyes of the blind (9:30; 20:33; cf. Mk. 7:35). As in Jn., opening in Matt. is implicitly or explicitly the act of God. He opens the heavens at the baptism of Jesus (Matt. 3:16), symbolizing the favor and openness of God to Jesus and confirming the action. To those who knock, the kingdom of heaven will be opened (7:7; cf. 7:13–14). But to those who do not come at the hour of opportunity, the door of the kingdom will not be opened (25:11). Here it is the eschatological Lord who is speaking and who thus has the authority of God to open and shut. Matt. 27:52 refers to the opening of the tombs and the raising of the dead at the moment of Jesus' death.

4. In the writings of Lk. *anoigō* is esp. associated with the concept of time. At the right time, Zechariah opens his mouth (Lk. 1:64), and the heavens open *after* Jesus' baptism (3:21). The public ministry of Jesus begins when Jesus enters the synagogue at Nazareth, opens the book of the prophet Isaiah, reads from Isa. 61:1–2, and identifies himself with the one on whom the Spirit of the Lord rests (Lk. 4:17). Jesus is the one who opens and closes the door of the kingdom (13:25) and the one to whom the servants must be ready to open (12:36).

The sayings about asking, knocking, and opening in Lk. 11:9–10 are rounded off by the promise of the Spirit: "If you then, though you are evil, know how to give good gifts to your children, how much more will your Father in heaven give the Holy Spirit to those who ask him!" (11:13). He follows this with the Beelzebub controversy concerning the power and authority by which Jesus acted (11:14–26). These references suggest that the ability and authority to open ultimately rest with God.

Acts 8:32 quotes Isa. 53:7: "As a lamb before the shearer is silent, so he did not open his mouth." This is interpreted Christologically by Philip to the Ethiopian eunuch. Acts 9:8, 40 refers to the opening of physical eyes, but 26:18 uses the metaphor spiritually in an account of Paul's commission to the Gentiles: "to open their eyes and turn them from darkness to light, and from the power of Satan to God." The words recall the mission of the servant (Isa. 42:6, 17), and in the light of Lk. 4:17 constitute an extension of Jesus' own mission.

Peter's vision of the great sheet containing clean and unclean animals (signifying God's inclusion of the Gentiles in his people) descends from heaven. The fact that heaven is opened in order to let down the sheet (Acts 10:11) signifies the divine origin of the vision. Several passages in Acts refer to the opening of doors. In 5:19, 12:10, and 16:26–27, prison doors are opened by divine agency. This contrasts with the doors closed by humans, either to imprison the apostles (5:23) or to keep Peter from entering John Mark's mother's house (12:14, 16). God also opens the door of faith, as Paul reports to Antioch how God "had opened the door of faith to the Gentiles" (14:27).

5. *dianoigō* occurs 8x in the NT. It is used in the expression (lit.) "every male that opens the womb [i.e., every firstborn male] will be called holy to the Lord" (Lk. 2:23; cf. Exod. 13:2, 12). In this passage the infant Jesus is being presented in the temple and sacrifices are being offered for him. The same vb. is used in Stephen's vision just before his martyrdom, when he saw "heaven open and the Son of Man standing at the right hand of God" (Acts 7:56). As elsewhere, the open heaven signifies God's acceptance and blessing of the one who sees heaven open, and it confirms the rightness of this person's actions.

The imperative of *dianoigō*, "Be opened," is given as a translation of *Ephphatha* (Mk. 7:34; cf. v. 35) in the healing of the deaf and dumb man. This is not a meaningless magical formula but an intelligible performative utterance.

In Lk. 24:31 *dianoigō* is used of opening the eyes in the sense of understanding (cf. Gen. 3:5, 7; 2 Ki. 6:17) in the self-disclosure of the risen Christ to the two disciples at Emmaus. At the moment of recognition, he vanishes from physical sight. In Lk. 24:32 the same vb. refers to understanding the significance of the Scriptures in relation to Jesus as the Christ (cf. also 24:45). Lk. uses the word again of Paul's missionary work among the Jews at Thessalonica, "explaining [*dianoigō*] and proving that the Christ had to suffer and rise from the dead. 'This Jesus I am proclaiming to you is the Christ,' he said" (Acts 17:3). In each instance human beings needed help in order to see Christ. Both one's understanding and the Scriptures require opening.

See also *kleis*, a key *(3090)*.

488 (anoikodomeō, rebuild), → *3868.*

489 (anoixis, opening), → *487.*

490 (anomia, wickedness, lawlessness), → *3795.*

491 (anomos, lawless, unlawful), → *3795.*

492 (anomōs, apart from the law), → *3795.*

495 (anosios, unholy), → *4008.*

496 (anochē, delay, limited period, restraint, forbearance), → *462.*

497 (antagōnizomai, fight against), → *74.*

498 (antallagma, what is given or taken in exchange), → *2904.*

500 (antapodidōmi, give back, repay, return, requite), → *625.*

501 (antapodoma, repayment, requital, recompense), → *625.*

502 (antapodosis, repaying, reward, recompense), → *625.*

505	ἀντί

ἀντί (*anti*), for, because of, instead of *(505)*.

CL & OT The root sense of *anti* is over against, opposite. Thus, the prep. naturally came to denote equivalence (for), exchange (for the price of, in return for), and substitution (instead of). Exod. 21:23–25, for example, uses *anti* for equivalence in the famous *lex talionis* ("life for life, eye for eye..."). But the prevailing sense in the LXX, as in nonbiblical Gk., is substitutionary exchange. Abraham offers up the ram as a burnt offering instead of (*anti*) his son Isaac (Gen. 22:13). Judah offers to remain in Egypt instead of (*anti*) Benjamin as a slave to Joseph (44:33). Lamenting the death of his son Absalom, David says, "If only I had died instead of [*anti*] you" (2 Sam. 18:33).

NT 1. *Equivalence.* Jesus quotes the *lex talionis* in Matt. 5:38 and carries it one step further: Rather than seeking for equivalence in injury, we should love and forgive our enemies. In 1 Cor. 11:15 Paul's point is *not* that a veil is superfluous for a woman, since nature has given her hair *in place of* a covering; rather, from the general fact that "long hair is given to her [to serve] as [*anti*] a covering," he infers that the long hair of a woman shows the appropriateness of her being covered when she prays or prophesies in the Christian assembly.

2. *Exchange.* In return "for [*anti*] evil" Christians are not to do evil back (Rom. 12:17; 1 Thess. 5:15); when insulted believers are not to return insults (1 Pet. 3:9). Also, Esau exchanged his birthright for the price of a meal (Heb. 12:16).

3. *Substitution.* The half-shekel tax alluded to in Matt. 17:24 was regarded as redemption money (cf. Exod. 30:12) that released the donor from hypothetical slavery or absolved the donor from divine anger. Thus, when Jesus commanded Simon Peter to give the collectors the shekel he would find in the fish's mouth "for [*anti*] my tax and yours," Matt. probably wants his readers to understand the redemption tax as a substitutionary offering designed to release the giver from obligation. Archelaus reigns over Judea in place of (*anti*) his father Herod (Matt. 2:22; cf. also Lk. 11:11; Jas. 4:15).

4. *Special uses.* (a) In Jn. 1:16 *charin anti charitos* ("one blessing after another"; lit., "grace for grace," KJV) denotes a perpetual and rapid succession of blessings, as though there were no interval between the arrival of one blessing and the reception of the next. Alternatively,

the notion of the replacement may be prominent here, as if the blessings of "old" grace are being replaced by those of "new" grace (sometimes taken to refer to the spiritual presence of the Holy Spirit in place of the physical presence of Christ).

(b) When the author of Heb. observes that Jesus endured the cross "for [*anti*] the joy set before him" (12:2), the meaning of the prep. phrase could be (i) "in exchange for" or "as the price for" the joy that was in prospect for him, i.e., that of seeing "the light of life" (Isa. 53:11); or (ii) "instead of" the joy of continued fellowship in God's immediate presence, which lay within his grasp. The second alternative seems preferable in light of the use of *prokeimai* ("set before") in Heb. 6:18; 12:1 (cf. 2 Cor. 8:12) to denote a present reality, the prevailing substitutionary sense of *anti*, the absence of any hint of bargaining between Jesus and God or of personal advantage as a motive of Jesus for his suffering, and the parallel in Heb. 11:25–26 with reference to Moses.

(c) Finally, "for [*anti*] many" in Mk. 10:45 (also Matt. 20:28) should be linked not with the vb. "give" but with *lytron* (ransom, i.e., "a ransom in the place of many"). The life of Jesus, surrendered in a sacrificial death, brought about the release of forfeited lives. He acted on behalf of the many by taking their place. As with *hyper* ("on behalf of," → *5642*) in 1 Tim. 2:6 ("for all"), the notions of exchange and substitution are both present. It is not sound hermeneutics to appeal to a contestable "wider" sense of *anti* (i.e., "on behalf of") in Matt. 17:27 (or Gen. 44:33) as the key to the proper understanding of *anti* in this passage, where the customary sense of the prep. (i.e., exchange and/or substitution) gives an unobjectionable meaning and the term *lytron* is applied to a human life.

508 (antidikos, enemy, opponent), → *2398.*

515	ἀντιλέγω

ἀντιλέγω (*antilegō*), speak against, contradict, object *(515)*; ἀντιλογία (*antilogia*), argument, opposition *(517)*.

CL & OT 1. *antilegō* has the basic meaning of to speak against or contradict someone. But it can also have a stronger meaning of actively opposing someone. Similarly, *antilogia* can mean a controversial discussion but also a rebellion.

2. Isa. 22:22 uses *antilegō* in a messianic passage; it reads lit. in the LXX: "I will give the glory of David to him and he will rule, and there will be no opposing person." Isa. 65:2 is quoted in Rom. 10:21 about God's people being a disobedient and "obstinate" people, though earlier the prophet says that he has not been "rebellious" (Isa. 50:5). *antilogia* is used in Num. 20:13; 27:14; Ps. 81:7; 106:32 for Meribah (Heb. word meaning quarrelling). The word is also used several times in OT legal material for disputes (Exod. 18:16; Deut. 17:8; 19:17), though the contentions can be other than legal in nature (Ps. 18:43; 31:20; 55:9).

NT 1. *antilegō* occurs 11x in the NT. It refers once to the disagreement between the Pharisees and the Sadducees about the resurrection (Lk. 20:27) and to the severe objections that the Jews had to Paul's preaching (Acts 13:45). The vb. is used in the Jewish legal challenge against Jesus as someone who opposes Caesar (Jn. 19:12) and later in the legal proceedings against Paul (Acts 28:19). In a Christian setting, *antilegō* is used of heretics who oppose sound teaching (Tit. 1:9). Note also how the aged Simeon prophesies that the son of Mary and Joseph will be "a sign that will be spoken against" (Lk. 2:34).

2. *antilogia* is used 4x in the NT. Heb. 6:16 says that an oath puts an end to "argument," 7:7 that there is no argument that a lesser person is blessed by a greater. In 12:3, Jesus endured "opposition" from sinful people. In Jude 11 the word is used of Korah's rebellion.

517 (antilogia, argument, opposition), → *515.*

518 (antiloidoreō, abuse or revile in turn), → *3366.*

519 (antilytron, ransom, ransom price), → *3389.*

531 (antitypos, copy, image, antitype), → *5596.*

| 532 | ἀντίχριστος |

ἀντίχριστος (*antichristos*), Antichrist (*532*); ψευδόχριστος (*pseudochristos*), false Christ (*6023*).

The words *antichristos* and *pseudochristos* are first found in the second half of the 1st cent. A.D. and are creations of Christian literature. The prep. *anti* originally meant "in the place of" and then "against." It indicates a fundamental, dualistic opposition of a kind familiar in Hellenism (both contemporary with the NT and later in the expression *antitheos*, anti-God). The compound with *pseudo*, false, gives the word the ethical connotation of being false or deceptive.

OT The background of this word is to be found in Jewish apocalyptic literature, which was especially interested in calculating and describing the end of this age, the coming of the Messiah (→ *Christos*, *5986*), and the setting up of the kingdom of God. Dan. 7–12, the earliest expression of this type of literature, was influential. Apocalyptic brings together eschatological expectations of Jewish prophecy (e.g., Isa. 26; 35; Jer. 5:1–7:34; Ezek. 37–48), classical theories about the ages (→ *aiōn*, *172*), and explanations and veiled judgments on contemporary political events. Examples of pre-Christian apocalyptic writings are the *Testaments of the Twelve Patriarchs* and most of the *1 Enoch*.

Regular features of this literature are the birth pains of the Messiah, the dissolution of the old age, and the transition to the new age with all its terrors (including plagues, diseases, wars, earthquakes, and signs in the heavens; see 2 Esd. 4:48–5:8; 6:21; *1 Enoch* 80:4–8; 99). Human apostasy will increase, and all the powers of evil will arm themselves under the leadership of Satan against God and his people. Satan, through his personification, is the rival of the Messiah, who is either the forerunner or the central figure of the kingdom of God. The greater the tribulation, the more fervently the Messiah was awaited by the godly.

The typical example of such personification is King Antiochus IV Epiphanes (reigned 175–164 B.C.). Some scholars see him in Dan. 8:23ff. His desecration of the Jerusalem temple with an altar to Zeus and the sacrifice there of a pig was considered to be an "abomination of desolation" (→ *bdelygma*, *1007*) and his reign to be the breaking in of the anti-God. In *Assum. Mos.* 6ff., traits of his personality have clearly been united with those of Herod the Great to form an anti-God figure. Such traits were also seen in Caligula, the Roman emperor (reigned A.D. 37–41), who wished to erect a statue of himself in the temple.

NT If we base our thoughts only on the NT, one thing is certain: All that is said of the Antichrist is essentially negative in relation to the picture of the Christ. It gives the dark background against which Christ's victory and kingdom shine out the more brightly. The actual word is found only 5x (in 1 and 2 Jn.). But outlines of the Antichrist can also be found unmistakably in Matt. 24; Mk. 13; Lk. 21; 2 Thess. 2:3–12; and Rev.

1. Mk. 13:14 speaks of "the abomination that causes desolation" (cf. Dan. 9:27; 12:11). It is personified, for the neut. word "abomination" is followed by a masc. part. Also mentioned (Mk. 13:21–22) are false prophets (*pseudoprophētai*) and those who falsely claim to be the Christ (*pseudochristoi*). These may all apply to the Antichrist, the opponent of God in all his disguises and masks. No distinction need really be made between sing. and pl.

2. In 2 Thess. 2:3–4, Paul speaks of "the man of lawlessness," who exalts himself "over everything that is called God or is worshiped" and who takes his seat in the temple of God. Jesus will annihilate him with the breath of his mouth (2:8).

3. Rev. gives the fullest picture of the Antichrist and his war against the church. Here too the word is missing, but everything said in ch. 13 about the two beasts clearly contains the traits of a personified power opposed to God, which is in fact a blasphemous parody of the Christ (→ *thērion*, *2563*). The details of this figure include traits

from Dan. 7:7–12, 23–25. On an eschatological interpretation, everyone who deceives and persecutes the church and blasphemes the Christ is no doubt intended. In both cases the conqueror is Christ.

4. In the Johannine letters (1 Jn. 2:18, 22–23; 4:3; 2 Jn. 7), teachers of false doctrines are called "antichrists." They claimed special fellowship with and love for God (cf. 1 Jn. 1:5–6; 2:4–5; 5:1–2), but they denied that Jesus is the Christ and that he became a man (4:2–3). Moreover, they apparently did not take sin seriously (cf. 3:6–10). Here the deception does not come from outside but from inside the church. Members of the church had become servants of the Antichrist.

537 (*anypokritos*, unfeigned, genuine), → *5693*.

| 539 | ἄνω |

ἄνω (*anō*), above, upward, up (*539*); ἄνωθεν (*anōthen*), from above (*540*); κάτω (*katō*), below, downward, down (*3004*).

CL & OT 1. *anō*, meaning above, upward, earlier in time, can describe land or mountains in contrast to the sea, or the sky and heaven in comparison with the earth, or even the earth in contrast to the underworld.

2. Jud. emphasized strongly the contrast between above and below, i.e., between heaven as God's sphere and the earth as humanity's sphere. Yet there is a parallelism between what exists above and what exists and happens on earth. As heaven cannot exist without the twelve constellations, earth cannot exist without the twelve tribes. Similarly, God studies the Torah in heaven as people do on earth. In this case, that which is above is prior in time.

Stimulated by Hel. ideas, Philo worked out an extensive speculation on above and below, though this did not prove significant either for Jud. or the NT. Philo saw the upper and lower worlds as divided into levels. The lowest level is the material, and on the highest God stands. The sky forms a spiritual material, the transitional level between the upper and lower worlds.

NT 1. The NT contains no cosmological speculations that set God and the world in radical opposition, attributing created reality to some other deity. God is the Maker and Lord of the entire world. Nevertheless, a distinction is drawn between the holy God and the sinful world.

Jesus looked "up" (*anō*), i.e., toward heaven, where God lives according to the ancient world concept (Jn. 11:41; cf. Acts 2:19). In contrast to his enemies who are "from below [*katō*]," from this sinful world, he is "from above [*anō*]," from God, to whom he will return (Jn. 8:23).

In Gal. 4:25–26 is a reference to "Jerusalem that is above," which is free and is the mother of Christians, in contrast to the present Jerusalem, which, with her children subject to the Mosaic law, is in slavery.

The "heavenward" call toward which Paul presses is the call of God in Jesus Christ (Phil. 3:14). Correspondingly, Paul encourages his readers to "set [their] minds on things above" (Col. 3:1–2). This is more narrowly defined by a reference to the fact that "Christ is seated at the right hand of God" (3:1).

2. The meaning of *anōthen* in Jn. 3:3, 7 has been a matter of debate among scholars. It can mean that a person must be born "again," but it can also mean that one must be born "from above." Perhaps we do not need to choose between the two, for when we are born from above (i.e., born of the Spirit of God), we experience rebirth (i.e., we are born again).

See also *anabainō*, go up, mount up (*326*); *ouranos*, heaven (*4041*).

540 (*anōthen*, from above), → *539*.

| 545 | ἄξιος |

ἄξιος (*axios*), of like value, fit, worthy, worth (*545*); ἀξίως (*axiōs*), worthily, in a manner worthy of, suitably (*547*); ἀνάξιος (*anaxios*), unworthy (*396*); ἀναξίως (*anaxiōs*), unworthily (*397*);

ἀξιόω (*axioō*), consider or think worthy, make worthy (*546*); καταξ-ιόω (*kataxioō*), deem worthy, consider worthy (*2921*).

CL & OT 1. In cl. Gk. *axios* meant originally tipping or balancing the scales. Two entities, either of the same or of different (*anaxios*) weight, are compared. The meaning of *axios* is then extended to cover the relationship between persons or things that correspond (or do not correspond) to one another—that is, fit, appropriate. Since this relation of fitness implies corresponding worth, *axios* comes finally to mean worthy or worth. The adv. *axiōs* is esp. used in this sense. *anaxios* is the negative form, not suitable, unworthy. The vb. *axioō* means to think worthy, think suitable, or to request, ask. *kataxioō* has the same meaning, intensified: to deem worthy.

2. This group of words has no great significance in the LXX. *axios* often means deserving. In Prov. 3:15 it has the notion of comparison: "Nothing you desire can compare with [wisdom]." In relation to God, *axios* becomes a quality belonging to the zealous keeper of the law, who uses personal worthiness as the foundation for a claim on God (2 Macc. 7:20; 4 Macc. 17:8–12).

NT 1. In contrast to the Jewish concept of merit, the prodigal son makes it clear that no one can make a claim on the father (God): "I am no longer worthy to be called your son" (Lk. 15:19, 21; cf. Jn. 1:27; Acts 13:25). The Capernaum centurion, who in the Jewish view deserved Jesus' help because he had built a synagogue, did not consider himself worthy for Jesus to be troubled with him, but simply asked Jesus to say a word of healing for his servant (Lk. 7:7). Instead, it is the grace of God in the gospel that imparts worth and makes one worthy of fellowship with him. On the other hand, Jesus teaches that, "Anyone who does not take his cross and follow me is not worthy [*axios*] of me" (Matt. 10:38)

In Lk. 20:35; Acts 5:41; and 2 Thess. 1:5 the undeserved gift of salvation is expressed by *kataxioō*. Our worth before God is decided by whether we come into contact with the message of Christ and obey it.

2. In the NT letters *axios* frequently has the meaning of fitting, in accord with. This is esp. evident in the use of the adv. *axiōs* in exhortations that demand a right lifestyle in accord with the gospel of Christ (Phil. 1:27), the Lord (Col. 1:10; 1 Thess. 2:12), or our calling (Eph. 4:1). In a similar vein, Paul warns in 1 Cor. 11:27 against celebrating the Lord's Supper "in an unworthy manner" (*anaxiōs*). Paul is not requiring a particular moral quality in the participants; rather, he is looking for a manner of life that accords with the gospel, namely, mutual love (cf. 11:17–34).

axios can also describe the value of human actions. A much-quoted proverb says, "The worker deserves his wages" (1 Tim. 5:18; cf. also Matt. 10:10; Lk. 10:7; 1 Cor. 9:14). Sinners do things for which they deserve (*axios*) to die (Rom. 1:32), but Paul's enemies can find nothing in his behavior deserving death, with which to accuse him (Acts 25:11, 25). Christians are worthy to be clothed in white in the age to come (Rev. 3:4).

At Rom. 8:18 Paul uses *axios* in its original sense of a comparison between two entities: "Our present sufferings are not worth comparing" to our future glory.

3. At Rev. 4:11 *axios* is used with reference to the exalted Lord. No one is worthy of such glory and honor as God (because of creation, 4:11) and the Lamb (because of Christ's sacrificial death, 5:12). In the end, the Lamb alone is worthy to be entrusted by God with the execution of his plans of salvation and of kingship (5:2, 4, 9).

See also *artios*, suitable, complete, capable, sound (*787*); *orthos*, upright, straight, right (*3981*).

546 (*axioō*, consider or think worthy, make worthy), → *545*.

547 (*axiōs*, worthily, in a manner worthy of, suitably), → *545*.

548 (*aoratos*, invisible), → *3972*.

550 (*apangellō*, report, announce, proclaim), → *33*.

555 (*apaiteō*, demand back), → *160*.

557 (*apallassō*, set free, release), → *2904*.

558 (*apallotrioō*, alienated), → *259*.

560 (*apantaō*, meet), → *2918*.

561 (*apantēsis*, meeting), → *2918*.

562	ἅπαξ

ἅπαξ (*hapax*), once (*562*); ἐφά-παξ (*ephapax*), once for all (*2384*).

CL & OT 1. In cl. Gk. the fundamental meaning of *hapax* includes numerical singularity and completeness that needs no additions. In the LXX *hapax* generally means once or one time (e.g., Gen. 18:32; Exod. 30:10; Ps. 62:11), or once and for all (e.g., 1 Sam. 26:8). In Hag. 2:6 the prophet says that Yahweh will shake the earth, sea, and dry land once more (*hapax*), implying the need for readiness and watching in view of the coming of the messianic kingdom.

NT 1. *hapax* is found 14x in the NT. It means once in contrast to twice, thrice, etc. (2 Cor. 11:25; Phil. 4:16; Heb. 9:7), and once in the sense of an event that cannot be repeated. It is so used of the sacrificial death of Christ (Heb. 9:26–28; 1 Pet. 3:18), of what the OT sacrifice did not do (Heb. 10:2), of God's saving activity (Jude 3, 5), and of the coming judgment (Heb. 12:26 = Hag. 2:6). With the uniqueness and finality of Jesus' saving work the NT writers contrast the uniqueness and finality of human reaction, either in faith or in unbelief.

The derivative *ephapax* (not found in pre-Christian writings) means "at the same time," i.e., together, in 1 Cor. 15:6. It is used 4x more (Rom. 6:10; Heb. 7:27; 9:12; 10:10), where it refers to the once-for-all sacrificial death of Christ.

2. The theological importance of both terms lies in the fact that they stress the historical nature of God's revelation. Just as God revealed himself to Israel in history when he brought them out of Egypt, so he revealed himself to his covenant people once for all, unrepeatably, and finally, in Christ. This is of decisive importance in confronting those religions where salvation is an ideal concept, based on the mere idea of deity and divorced from history (as in Gnosticism).

In contrast to the situation of the OT covenant people, Heb. argues that in view of the once-for-all sacrificial death of Jesus, we are now in the end time (*ephapax*, Heb. 10:10; *heis*, 10:12, 14, → *1651*). The author draws a contrast between the single, complete act of Christ and the repeated sacrifices of the old covenant, which are temporary and imperfect since they had to be repeated every year. Otherwise those who brought these sacrifices and worshiped God through them would have ceased to bring them. As mere shadows of the future and perfect sacrifice of Christ, they served merely to bring sins to mind (10:3) and so to point to the one who is to come.

This indicates that the very nature and purpose of the OT sacrificial system were not to purify once for all but to point to the final sacrifice and purification in Jesus, who is both the sacrifice and high priest. Just as human beings finally die and face the judgment, so Jesus' giving himself in death to put away sins is final (Heb. 9:26–28). This sacrifice distinguishes the activity of the Son from that of the earthly high priest with his temporal sacrifice and with its limited validity, offered daily for himself and the people.

The author of Heb. sees the death of Christ as the once-and-for-all sacrifice and the resurrection and ascension of Christ in terms of the high priest entering the Most Holy Place on the Day of Atonement (Heb. 9:12; 10:12; cf. Lev. 16). In the OT the high priest did this on an annual basis. After sacrificing, he entered the Most Holy Place with the blood of the sacrifice on behalf of God's people. But Christ has entered the immediate presence of God through his heavenly exaltation by his own blood to represent his people before God and obtain for them *eternal* salvation (cf. 9:14; 10:19–25).

In Rom. 6:10 Paul writes: "The death [Christ] died, he died to sin once for all [*ephapax*]; but the life he lives, he lives to God." The statement comes at the climax of a discussion of the problem of antinomianism. If we are saved by "the gift that came by the grace of the one man, Jesus Christ" (5:15), and not because of anything that we have done, then why not go on sinning that grace may abound (6:1)? Paul replies that baptism implies baptism into Christ's death (6:3) and that just as he was raised by the glory of the Father, we too should walk in the newness of life (6:4). The whole purpose of his death was to free us from the enslavement of sin (6:5–9). This he has done once for all, and now he lives to God (6:10). "In the same way, count yourselves dead to sin but alive to God in Christ Jesus" (6:11).

The finality and unrepeatability of the historic act of salvation is paralleled by the finality of personal salvation. If it is frittered away, it is also unrepeatable: "It is impossible for those who have once [*hapax*] been enlightened . . . if they fall away, to be brought back to repentance" (Heb. 6:4–6). Warnings against apostasy occur throughout Heb. (cf. 3:1–4:16; 6:1–20; 10:26–39; 12:1–29; 13:9–14, 22).

Jude 3 urges its readers "to contend for the faith that was once for all [*hapax*] entrusted to the saints." Faith here means an orthodox body of beliefs that the church adheres to. The source of this teaching is ultimately God himself, but it is mediated by the apostles and other human agents (cf. Jude 17 with Lk. 1:2; Acts 16:4). The emphasis on a body of truth as opposed to heretical doctrines is more pronounced in later NT writings, such as the Pastoral Letters (cf. 1 Tim. 1:3; 4:6; 2 Tim. 2:2; 4:3–4; Tit. 1:9), though from the start we see evidence of the gospel as an authoritative message handed down in the church (e.g., Acts 2:42; Rom. 16:17; 1 Cor. 11:2, 23; 15:1–3; Gal. 1:23; 6:10).

Jude 5 goes on to remind readers that they "already [*hapax*] know" many of the truths of Scripture, such as the story of the exodus but also the deaths of the rebellious people in the desert, and uses this story to warn them against apostasy (cf. Heb. 6:4–6). The similar illustration in 1 Cor. 10:5 and Heb. 3–4 suggests that the use of the exodus generation formed part of common Christian instruction.

See also *heis*, one (*1651*); *monos*, alone, only (*3668*).

563 (aparabatos, unchangeable), → *4126.*

564 (aparaskeuastos, unprepared), → *2941.*

565 (aparneomai, deny, disown, renounce), → *766.*

569	ἀπαρχή

ἀπαρχή (*aparchē*), the gift of the firstfruits, offering, gift (*569*).

CL & OT In cl. Gk. *aparchē* is a technical term that denotes firstfruits of any sort (e.g., of natural products or livestock) that were sacred to the deity and had to be consecrated to it before the whole could be used for oneself. In religious contexts there is also occasional mention of the offering of individual people to lifelong service in the sanctuary or of whole groups to the deity. Later *aparchē* included the payment of regular taxes in the secular sphere.

2. In the LXX *aparchē* translates initially the Heb. word meaning firstfruits—that is, the offering of the firstfruits of natural products, such as wine and grains, that were consecrated to Yahweh, the giver of fruitfulness (Num. 18:12; Deut. 18:4; 26:2, 10; 2 Chr. 31:5). *aparchē* also translates the Heb. word for contribution, offering, which denotes the contribution of natural products or money to the cult for the priests and Levites (Exod. 25:2–3; Deut. 12:11, 17; 2 Chr. 31:10, 12, 14), also understood as a thank offering to Yahweh. This practice is supported by the Israelite belief in creation: Yahweh is the glory and owner of human, animal, and plant life. The gift of the firstfruits of everything living belongs to him (Exod. 23:19; Num. 18:15).

NT 1. In the NT *aparchē* occurs only 9x, mostly in Paul. In Rom. 11:16 Paul takes up the thought of Num. 15:17–21: "If the part of the dough offered as firstfruits is holy, then the whole batch is holy; if the root is holy, so are the branches." Admittedly, there is a certain difference between the OT example and Paul's use of it. In the case of the Israelites, the rest of the dough could be put to secular use.

Paul's point is that since the patriarchs (the root; cf. 11:28) are holy, the nation as a whole is consecrated. Thus, by means of this exegesis, he guarantees the role of the entire nation of Israel in salvation history.

2. *aparchē* has a similar fig. sense in Rom. 16:5, where Paul speaks of Epenetus as the firstfruits (i.e., the first convert) of the province of Asia. Similarly, in 1 Cor. 16:15 the household of Stephanas is called the firstfruits of Achaia. The same idea is found in a variant reading of 2 Thess. 2:13, where "from the beginning" (Gk. *ap' archēs*) is read as *aparchēn* (firstfruits; see NIV text note).

More generally, James addresses his readers as the firstfruits of God's creation: "He chose to give us birth through the word of truth, that we might be a kind of firstfruits of all he created" (Jas. 1:18). Christians are considered here as the firstfruits of the new created order that supersedes the old Israel. In Rev. 14:4 the 144,000 are similarly so described "as firstfruits to God and the Lamb."

3. Rom. 8:23 reverses the OT relationship between giver and receiver: "Not only so, but we ourselves, who have the firstfruits of the Spirit, groan inwardly as we wait eagerly for our adoption as sons, the redemption of our bodies." Here it is not God but believers who receive the firstfruits. The Holy Spirit given to believers is seen as the first installment and guarantee of the final redemption of our bodies.

4. In 1 Cor. 15:20 *aparchē* is used in connection with the resurrection: "But Christ has indeed been raised from the dead, the firstfruits of those who have fallen asleep." The assertion follows Paul's reflections on the drastic consequences for believers if there were no resurrection from the dead (15:12–19)—both preaching and faith, for example, would be empty (15:14). But Christ has indeed been raised, and his resurrection is a guarantee of our resurrection. The thought is further developed in 15:23 in relation to the eschatological order of resurrection life: "But each in his own turn: Christ, the firstfruits, then, when he comes, those who belong to him."

See also *thyō*, to sacrifice, slaughter, kill, celebrate (*2604*).

570 (hapas, all, the whole), → *4246.*

572 (apataō, trick, deceive), → *4414.*

573 (apatē, deception, trickery, deceitfulness), → *4414.*

574 (apatōr, fatherless), → *4252.*

575	ἀπαύγασμα

ἀπαύγασμα (*apaugasma*), radiance, effulgence, reflection (*575*); αὐγάζω (*augazō*), shine forth, illuminate, see (*878*); αὐγή (*augē*), dawn, daybreak (*879*); διαυγάζω (*diaugazō*), to shine through, dawn (*1419*).

CL & OT *apaugasma* is found only in Hel. writers, where it means either radiance (in the act. sense) or reflection (in the pass. sense). It is not attested before Wisdom of Solomon. Philo uses it to say that what God breathed into Adam was "an effulgence" [*apaugasma*] of his blessed nature. The only LXX text is Wis. 7:25–26, where divine wisdom is hailed as "a reflection [*apaugasma*] of eternal light . . . and an image [*eikōn*, → *1635*] of his goodness." In this setting wisdom is hypostatized as a source of light, whose shining forth (*apaugasma*) can be understood as reflection.

NT *apaugasma* derives from *augazō*, to shine forth, or to illuminate (cf. 2 Cor. 4:4). The vb. *diaugazō*, to shine through, dawn, occurs in 2 Pet. 1:19. The cognate noun *augē*, radiance, is found in Acts 20:11 and means dawn or daybreak, i.e., when the sun shines forth.

The only NT use of *apaugasma* is in Heb. 1:3, where the Son of God is referred to as "the radiance [*apaugasma*] of God's glory." This verse stands in a doxological, possibly hymnic tribute to the cosmic Christ, who is described as either the radiance of the divine glory (as sunlight conveys the brightness and intensity of the sun) or as God's reflection (as the moon reflects the light of the sun). The act. sense of "radiance" is preferable to "reflection" (cf. NIV). But either way, the verse is a piece of wisdom Christology that interprets Christ as the supreme and final revelation of the Father.

See also *eidōlon*, image, idol (*1631*); *eikōn*, image, likeness, form, appearance (*1635*); *charaktēr*, stamp, representation, outward appearance, form (*5917*); *hypodeigma*, proof, example, model (*5682*); *hypogrammos*, outline, copy, example (*5681*); *typos*, type, pattern (*5596*).

577 (apeitheia, disobedience), → *4275.*

578 (apeitheō, be disobedient), → *4275.*

579 (apeithēs, disobedient), → *4275.*

585 (apeirastos, without temptation, untempted), → *4280.*

587 (apekdechomai, wait, wait eagerly), → *638.*

588 (apekdyomai, undress, strip), → *1544.*

589 (apekdysis, laying aside), → *1544.*

592 (apeleutheros, freedman), → *1800.*

594 (apelpizō, expect back), → *1828.*

598 (aperitmētos, uncircumcised), → *4362.*

599 (aperchomai, go away, depart), → *2262.*

601 (apisteō, disbelieve), → *4411.*

602 (apistia, unbelief), → *4411.*

603 (apistos, unbelievable, faithless, unbelieving), → *4411.*

605	ἁπλότης

ἁπλότης (*haplotēs*), simplicity, sincerity, uprightness (*605*); ἁπλοῦς (*haplous*), single, simple, sincere (*606*); ἁπλῶς (*haplōs*), sincerely, generously (*607*); διπλοῦς (*diplous*), double (*1487*); δίψυχος (*dipsychos*), double-minded (*1500*).

CL & OT 1. In cl. Gk. *haplotēs* and *haplous* mean singleness, single (opposite of *diplous*, double). In addition to this numerical meaning grew a positive ethical connotation for the word group, so that *haplotēs* came to mean straightness, openness, speaking without a hidden meaning. This meaning grew over time, but the meaning based on intellectual outlook diminished in importance, so that *haplous* came to mean simple, silly.

2. In Judaism and the LXX we find the basic meaning of single (e.g., Wis. 16:27). *haplous* also means unambiguous, clear. The wise, who accept God's commands wholeheartedly, have a clear walk in their lives (*haplōs*, Prov. 10:8–9). David gave God his silver and gold in singleness of heart (1 Chr. 29:17). When *haplous* is used in the context of human relationships of giving, it implies goodness, kindness, and generosity, understood as a quality of the heart (Prov. 11:25). *diplous* occurs in such passages as Exod. 16:5, where the Israelites are told to pick up twice as much manna on the sixth day, and 22:4, where a thief must pay back double what he has taken.

NT 1. This word group is infrequent in the NT. *haplotēs* generally means personal wholeness, undividedness, and hence uncomplicated simplicity. Paul, using the picture of devotion of a bride to one man (2 Cor. 11:2–3), shows the completeness of human surrender to Christ. The basis of such a demand is Christ's complete self-surrender for us (cf. 2 Cor. 5:14–20). Hence, a similar personal integrity should be a mark of the Christian in his or her dealings with others.

Paul viewed the collection made by one church for another as a true expression of a unity transcending the local church. So *haplotēs* receives a universal connotation (2 Cor. 8:2; 9:11, 13) and means a oneness of heart, generosity. Generous giving within the local church (Rom. 12:8) is also an expression of unity within the body of Christ (cf. 12:4). But unity should also be internal, for Eph. 6:5 and Col. 3:22 instruct slaves to obey their masters "with sincerity of heart."

2. In Matt. 6:22; Lk. 11:34, in a parable of Jesus, *haplous* denotes singlehearted devotion and service to Christ. But if we serve Christ with a view to our own advancement, our lives will be filled with darkness.

3. *haplōs* occurs in Jas. 1:5 in a reference to God who gives "generously," to show the undividedness and honesty of his giving in contrast to the inner division of the one who doubts, who is "double-minded" (*dipsychos*, 1:8; → *psychē*, soul, *6034*).

4. *diplous* is found in 1 Tim. 5:17, where Paul states that a teaching elder is worthy of double honor. In Rev. 18:6, God promises to pay Babylon back double for her sins.

606 (haplous, single, simple, sincere), → *605.*

607 (haplōs, sincerely, generously), → *605.*

608	ἀπό

ἀπό (*apo*), from, away from (*608*).

CL In general *apo* (from) in cl. Gk. denotes motion from the edge or surface of an object, while *ek* (out, out of; → *1666*) denotes motion from within going out. But in Hel. Gk. the distinction between these two was becoming blurred, so that the meaning of these two words overlaps considerably. Note, for example, how Lk. uses *apo* at least 10x with *exerchomai* (to go out; in most cases, this construction refers to the casting out of demons).

NT 1. *General meanings.* In the NT both *apo* and *ek* are used in the following senses: (a) temporal (e.g., *apo*, Matt. 11:12; *ek*, Jn. 9:1); (b) causal (*apo*, Matt. 18:7; *ek*, Jn. 4:6); (c) instrumental (*apo*, Matt. 11:19; *ek*, Lk. 16:9); (d) adverbial (*apo*, 2 Cor. 1:14; *ek*, 9:7); (e) to denote place of origin (*apo* and *ek* together, Jn. 1:44; 11:1); (f) to denote membership (*apo*, Acts 12:1; *ek*, 6:9). Such overlapping of function makes one hesitate to distinguish between "out of [*ek*] the water" in Mk. 1:10 and "out of [*apo*] the water" in Matt. 3:16, as though Matt. reflects a later tradition of baptism by affusion rather than by immersion (the Markan tradition).

2. *Notable instances.* (a) In 1 Cor. 11:23, Paul records what he received "from [*apo*] the Lord." The phrase here can mean either that the Lord Jesus was the ultimate origin of a tradition that reached Paul in reliable form through other apostles, or that Jesus was the immediate source of the tradition. The prep. does not tend to either possible interpretation, although "received" (*paralambanō*, → *lambanō*, 3284) and "passed on" (*paradidōmi*, see 4140) were technical terms for the transmission of tradition.

(b) The typical Gk. prep. for personal agency is *hypo* (by, → 5679). When *apo* is used for agency, it generally denotes less immediate and indirect causation (though this nuance cannot be pressed in all cases). In such cases *apo* may be rendered "at the hands of" (e.g., 2 Cor. 7:13), "by the will of" (e.g., Rev. 12:6), or "as a result of " (9:18). This is esp. relevant in Jas. 1:13a, where a view is expressed of God as the ultimate cause of temptation but not directly as the tempter. James begins by stating: "Let nobody say when he is tempted, 'I am being tempted by circumstances and influences that come from God or are permitted by him.'" However, the following rebuttal of this sentiment (lit., "he himself tempts no one," 1:13c) shows that a direct divine temptation is also in mind.

(c) Heb. 5:7 says that Jesus offered up fervent prayers during his time on earth and he "was heard because of [*apo*] his reverent submission [*eulabeia*]." *apo* here could mean that Jesus was heard and thus delivered from an anxious dread (of death), but most likely *apo* here is causal (cf. the use of *eulabeia* [fear, awe; → 2325] in 12:28 and the related vb. *eulabeomai* in 11:7).

(d) The remarkable phrase in Rev. 1:4 ("peace to you from him who is, and who was, and who is to come"), where the words after *apo* are in the nom. rather than the gen., has been given various explanations: e.g., the result of the seer's reverence for the divine name, a paraphrase of the indeclinable tetragrammaton YHWH ("he who is"), and a nom. apposition originally preceded by four dots standing for the tetragrammaton.

614 (apoginomai, die), → *1181.*

617 (apodeiknymi, prove, appoint, demonstrate, exhibit), → *1259.*

618 (apodeixis, proof, demonstration), → *1259.*

620 (apodekatoō, give a tenth part, collect a tithe), → *1281.*

621 (apodektos, acceptable, pleasing), → *1312.*

622 (apodechomai, admit), → *1312.*

625	ἀποδίδωμι

ἀποδίδωμι (*apodidōmi*), give away, give up, give back, sell, give back what is due, recompense (*625*); ἀνταποδίδωμι (*antapodidōmi*), give back, repay, return, requite, pay back in his own coin (*500*); ἀνταπόδοσις (*antapodosis*), repaying, reward, recompense (*502*); ἀνταπόδομα (*antapodoma*), repayment, requital, recompense (*501*).

CL & OT 1. In. cl. Gk. *apodidōmi* means primarily to give up, render, give back. In the mid. it means to sell. Hence it acquired the specific meaning of giving something up that one must give up because of an obligation (thus, to pay out a wage). This gives the word the technical sense to render, requite, in both good and bad senses. *antapodidōmi* and its derivatives express this meaning of the word in the Hel. period.

2. (a) In the OT act and consequence are linked like cause and effect, such as sowing and harvest (e.g., Job 4:8; Prov. 22:8; cf. Gal. 6:7–9). The idea of a personal judge and recompenser is present here insofar as God is the one who maintains this order and allows an action to return upon a doer (cf. 1 Sam. 26:23–24; 2 Sam. 16:8). Thus, he avenges wrongdoing (Jer. 15:15). The most important Heb. term for recompense is *šālam* in the piel, which means to restore, repay, pay damages (cf. Exod. 22). In legal usage it means to requite, because the judge repays a claim that a person has earned by action either on the good side (reward) or on the bad (punishment; see esp. Prov. 19:17; cf. 2 Sam. 3:39; Ps. 62:12; Jer. 25:14; 50:29).

(b) The idea of recompense is found first and foremost in the negative sense of God's punishment for the disobedience of Israel as a nation. (Ezekiel was the first to declare that no individual will die on account of another's sin; Ezek. 18.) God punishes his people for their unfaithfulness to the covenant between him and his people. The Deuteronomic History (Jdg.–2 Ki.; cf. Deut. 28) finds in the recompense of God the key to understanding the history of Israel (cf. esp. Jdg. 2:6–23).

3. The OT regarded fellowship with God as a free gift, which had come to the people by grace in their deliverance from Egypt and the bestowal of the land of Canaan. But in the intertestamental period the idea of recompense came to be related exclusively to the Jewish law. The latter was no longer anchored in the historic event of the old covenant; it was no longer a set of instructions on how to remain within the grace of the covenant. It became an absolute norm, according to which each person's actions were assessed and by means of which one hoped to attain to salvation (which is seen as other-worldly and future). Recompense was now not simply the punishment of faithlessness and apostasy; it also determined who has succeeded in reaching the height of fellowship with God through personal good works. This legalistic understanding of recompense leads the LXX to translate the Heb. equivalents into the legal terms *antapodidōmi*, to requite, and *antapodoma*, requital.

NT 1. In the NT *apodidōmi* occurs 48x. The whole range of the word is represented: to hand over (Matt. 27:58), give or pay back (Matt. 18:23–34; Lk. 4:20), sell (Acts 5:8, mid.), pay what has been agreed (Matt. 20:8), perform what one has sworn to do (5:33), and then esp. to forgive. *antapodidōmi* (7x) fits into the same pattern; it emphasizes the character of what is given in return. *antapodoma* and *antapodosis* are used in reference to the divine recompense (Rom. 11:9; cf. Lk. 14:12) at the final judgment (Col. 3:24).

2. *apodidōmi* has its home in the NT expectation of judgment and punishment. The NT concept of recompense can best be illustrated from Mk. 8:38: "If anyone is ashamed of me and my words in this adulterous and sinful generation, the Son of man will be ashamed of him when he comes in his Father's glory with the holy angels." As in the OT, what determines our fate on the last day is our attitude to the Lord (i.e., Jesus Christ). This is the meaning of the parable of the last judgment in Matt. 25:31–46. (Note, of course, that this attitude is expressed in our relationships with our neighbors.) The decisive factor is whether we are true to Jesus and his word, whether we confess him or reject him (cf. Heb. 10:26–30). The NT, like the OT, thinks in terms of a covenant already established and expects recompense to operate against those who withdraw from Jesus Christ.

3. This gives us the background of the NT use of *apodidōmi*. All people are responsible to the heavenly judge, whether they are Christians or unbelievers (Rom. 2:6; cf. 1 Cor. 3:13–15; 2 Cor. 5:10). *apodidōmi* does not imply an evaluation of human works on the basis of some inherent moral worth in the works themselves (Matt. 16:27; Rom. 2:6; 2 Tim. 4:14; Rev. 22:12). The works are rather the expression either of opposition to Christ (and subsequent rejection) or of allegiance to him and to the new covenant.

Esp. instructive is Rev. 20:11–15. All are judged according to their works as recorded in books (v. 12). When it comes to the book of life (vv. 12, 15), however, the pattern of recompense is no longer carried through consistently. Believers are withdrawn from the judgment. Through election they have a righteousness that leads to life. For them the recompense consists of the "inheritance" God gives (cf. Col. 3:24). Since recompense comes with final judgment, Christians are forbidden to take vengeance in the present age (Rom. 12:17; 1 Pet. 3:9; cf. 1 Thess. 5:15).

See also *kerdos*, gain (*3046*); *misthos*, pay, wages, reward (*3635*); *opsōnion*, wages, payment (*4072*).

627 (apodokimazō, reject, declare useless), → *1511.*

628 (apodochē, acceptance, approval), → *1312.*

629 (apothesis, putting off, removal), → *1544.*

631 (apothēsaurizō, lay up treasure), → *2565.*

633 (apothnēskō, die), → *2505.*

635 (apokathistēmi, reestablish, restore), → *640.*

636	ἀποκαλύπτω

ἀποκαλύπτω (*apokalyptō*), uncover, disclose, reveal (*636*); ἀποκάλυψις (*apokalypsis*), disclosure, revelation (*637*).

CL & OT 1. In cl. Gk. the vb. *apokalyptō*, unveil, denotes the disclosure of previously hidden things; the noun *apokalypsis*, disclosure, revelation, is only used from the 1st cent. B.C. on, predominantly in a religious sense. The religious and theological use of both words is rare in the Gk.-Hel. world. There is no sense in secular Gk. of revelation in the NT sense of the word. God has not left himself without a witness among the heathen (Acts 14:17), but even if they had the ability to recognize an invisible power and godhead from the works of God, they have perverted this knowledge through worship of idols (Rom. 1:18–23). If there is a reality behind heathen idol worship, it is the reality of demonic powers (1 Cor. 10:20).

2. (a) The noun *apokalypsis* occurs in the LXX only in 1 Sam. 20:30 for *ʿerwâ*, nakedness, and 3x without Heb. equivalent (Sir.11:27; 22:22; 42:1). The vb. *apokalyptō* (80x) almost without exception represents forms of the Heb. vb. *gālâ*, in particular the niph., to strip, and piel, expose, uncover. In Gen. 8:13, it is used of removing the roof of the ark; elsewhere it often refers to the exposure of the otherwise covered sex organs for the purpose of sexual union (e.g., Lev. 18:6–19). The goal of the uncovering is thus not distant observation, but entrance to the most intense form of encounter that can involve an individual.

This picture was most notably taken up by Ezek. in order to characterize Israel's guilty and corrupt state (e.g., 13:14; 16:36–37, 57).

In a fig. but still everyday use, *apokalyptō* means to reveal, make known. It is thus used of human speech in Jos. 2:20; 1 Sam. 20:2, 13; 22:8, 17; and of human plans in 1 Macc. 7:31. The noun *apokalypsis* is used in Sir. 22:22 and 42:1 in a secular sense for the revelation or publication of secrets. Perhaps there is theological significance in 11:27; at the end of one's life "one's deeds are revealed." Here the thought may be of God's judgment.

(b) *apokalyptō* is found relatively rarely in the LXX with a theological significance. In the story of Balaam's prophetic experience (Num. 22:31; 24:4, 16), God opened the prophet's inner eye and presented him with a true view of reality that did not accord with the wishes of Balak, who wanted him to curse Israel. God gave Balaam knowledge of the Most High so that he could hear and speak his word. In a time when revelations were rare, God revealed himself to Samuel (1 Sam. 3:1, 7); Samuel's prophetic authority is grounded in a series of further revelations (3:21). In 9:15 and 2 Sam. 7:27, Samuel and David are able to hear God's instructions and promises. "Open my eyes that I may see wonderful things in your law," prays the psalmist (Ps. 119:18). To his servants the prophets, God reveals his divine plan (Amos 3:7; for additional aspects of God's revealing, see Ps. 98:2; Isa. 52:10; 53:1; Sir. 1:6).

3. (a) For most of Jud. at the time of Jesus the content of divine revelation was set down in Scripture. New prophecy was extinct. Consequently the *apokalyptō* word group rarely occurs in Jud. apart from the LXX. There were the ideas that the Messiah would give a new exposition of the law and that he would give a new Torah. The Dead Sea Scrolls, however, indicate that there were Jewish circles with a continuing consciousness of prophetic revelation and illumination (e.g., 1QH 1:21; 5:9; 6:4).

(b) In this connection, Jewish apocalyptic lit. describes how God had entrusted holy men of antiquity with revelations of the last things, the coming of the Messiah and his kingdom, the resurrection of the dead, the judgment, and so on. Determinative for such apocalyptic thought is the contrast between the two worlds, the present age and the age to come. Linked with assertions concerning the future are all kinds of portrayals of the heavenly world and speculations about the constellations and the course of history. It is also a typical apocalyptic motif for an angel to appear as a mediator of revelation. Apocalyptic lit. also penetrated into early Christianity.

NT 1. *apokalyptō* occurs 26x in the NT, and *apokalypsis* 18x. Most of these are in Paul's writings (cf. also Matt., Lk., 1 Pet., and Rev.). The noun always has theological significance; the vb. is found in Lk. 2:35 in an everyday sense (of thoughts being revealed). On the borderline of secular-theological usage is the aphorism of Matt. 10:26: "There is nothing concealed that will not be disclosed" (cf. Mk. 4:22, where *phaneroō* is used as a synonym; Lk. 8:17 uses *phaneros*; → *epiphaneia*, appearance, *2211*). By contrast with the LXX, the prevailing significance of *apokalyptō* in the NT is religious and theological.

2. A theological understanding of the NT revelation is first oriented around the content and only secondarily around the act and event of the revelation. Nevertheless, the latter must also be considered. As in the OT eyes and ears were opened by God, so in the NT there is a becoming visible, an appearance of God or Christ (2 Tim. 1:10; Tit. 2:11; 3:4) or a speaking by God (Heb. 1:1–2). God's revelation must become perceptible in the earthly world. In accordance with this, the apostles preach what they have heard and seen and have even touched with their hands (Acts 4:20; 1 Jn. 1:1).

The content of this seeing is Jesus Christ, the Word become flesh, the Word of life (Jn. 1:14; 1 Jn. 1:1). The disciples are called blessed because they have been allowed to hear and see what was denied to many prophets, what the righteous longed for, and what angels themselves long to see (Matt. 13:16; Lk. 10:23–24; 1 Pet. 1:12). To hear and see in this way, and in faith to perceive the glory of God (Jn.

11:40), are distinguished from the hearing and seeing of unbelief, which in truth is no hearing or seeing at all (in this connection Isa. 6:9–10 is cited 6x in the NT: Matt. 13:13–15; Mk. 4:12; Lk. 8:10; Jn. 12:39–41; Acts 28:26–27; Rom. 11:8).

The knowledge of a new revelation of God surpassing the previous one is characteristic of the attitude of faith of NT Christians. The earlier revelation given to the prophets is a pointer to Christ and the gospel (Rom. 1:2; 1 Pet. 1:11–12). But when unbelieving Jews read the OT, a veil lies over their hearts, which can only be removed when they are converted to Christ (2 Cor. 3:14–16).

3. (a) In the Synoptic Gospels Jesus is the bearer of divine revelation. Simeon describes Jesus as "a light for revelation to the Gentiles" (Lk. 2:32; cf. Isa. 42:6). Jesus further confronts us as revealer in the words of Matt. 11:25–27, where he praises the Father and Lord of the world for giving his revelation not to the wise and understanding but to babes. Knowledge of God through the old covenant has been surpassed; thus it can be regarded as only the first step towards the knowledge that the revelation of Jesus mediates.

(b) Although in Jn.'s Gospel the noun is lacking and the vb. occurs only in 12:38 (in a quotation of Isa. 53:1), the theme that Jesus is the mediator of the divine revelation is expounded even more powerfully than in the Synoptics (the word "to reveal" is primarily *phaneroō* [e.g., 1:31; 2:11; 3:21; cf. 1 Jn. 1:2; 2:19, 28]). He is the only Son who has made the Father known (Jn. 1:18), and he speaks what he has heard from his Father (3:32; 8:26; 15:15).

(c) The central content of the revelation is Christ himself. The Father in heaven revealed to Peter who Jesus is—"this was not revealed . . . by man" (Matt. 16:17). The disciples are to declare openly what has been revealed to them and what Jesus has said to them (10:26–27). Thus, in the disciples' preaching the event of revelation is continued: The one who hears the disciples hears Jesus himself (Lk. 10:16). In Jn.'s Gospel Jesus promises his disciples the Spirit of truth, who will teach them everything and lead them into the full truth (Jn. 14:26; 15:26; 16:13).

4. (a) This foregoing is important for understanding Paul. He, too, is aware of himself as a bearer of divine revelation. He stresses that Christ works and speaks through him (Rom. 15:18; 2 Cor. 13:3). From Christ Paul received his apostolic commission (Rom. 1:5), which is grounded in the fact that he has seen the resurrected Lord (1 Cor. 9:1; 15:8). Thereby he belongs to the circle of Easter witnesses and apostles (15:11).

The authority with which Paul attacks the heresy threatening the Galatians is founded on the revelation of the resurrected Christ. He insists that he did not receive his gospel from other humans, but God revealed (*apokalyptō*) his Son in him (Gal. 1:16). To the Thessalonians Paul stresses that the gospel they received from him is "not . . . the word of men, but . . . the word of God" (1 Thess. 2:13). In 1 Cor. 2:10 the Holy Spirit appears as the author of what "God has revealed" to the apostle (cf. also Rom. 16:25; Eph. 3:5). The NT does not draw a distinction between the message of Jesus and the apostolic word, as if only the former is a revelation of God's word (cf. Lk. 5:1; 8:21 with 1 Cor. 14:26; Col. 1:25). That is, early Christianity accepted both the words of Jesus transmitted in the Gospels and the apostolic writings into the canon and gave both recognition as divine revelation.

(b) The word *apokalypsis* is not confined in Paul to the foundation message of Christ. In Gal. 2:2 Paul reports that he traveled to Jerusalem to the apostolic council on the basis of a "revelation"; i.e., he undertook the journey on the basis of divine direction, although we are not given any more exact details of the way he received it. In 2 Cor. 12:1–7 (cf. also 1 Cor. 14:6) Paul refers to his own "visions and revelations." In this connection he also mentions the word that the exalted Lord spoke to him: "My grace is sufficient for you, for my power is made perfect in weakness" (2 Cor. 12:9).

Still, however important these revelations were for the apostle's personal faith and life, we must distinguish them from the basic revelation of Christ. Such a revelation can be shared by other Spirit-filled

Christians (1 Cor. 14:26, 30; Phil. 3:15). This explains Paul's prayer that God might give the Ephesians "the Spirit of wisdom and revelation" (Eph. 1:17). For the Spirit who guides the disciples into all truth opens up the understanding of revelation that is given them in the words of Jesus and of the apostles (cf. 2:18; also Jn. 16:13).

(c) Alongside the revelation through words stands revelation through God's acts. Paul is thinking of this when he speaks, from the standpoint of a man imprisoned under the law, of the message of faith that is to be revealed. The thought there is not only of the message itself but also of its content, the salvation event in Christ (Gal. 3:23). In the gospel is disclosed God's great gift of salvation—the "righteousness of God," through which sinners are justified (Rom. 1:17; 3:21).

This revelation, of course, contrasts with another: the revelation of God's wrath, which falls on sinful humanity and allows it to sink even deeper into sin (Rom. 1:18–32; cf. 2:5). This revelation is anticipated by the gospel and the cross of Christ, which show both God's love for sinners and his enmity against sin. In 1 Cor. 3:13 Paul speaks of the purifying fire that will be revealed on the day of the Lord. Preceding that day (2 Thess. 2:2), however, will be the revelation of the anti-Christian power that seizes control of the sanctuary of God, which the Lord will then destroy (2:3, 6, 8).

This advent is the day when "our Lord Jesus Christ [will be] revealed," when he appears in the fullness of his power (1 Cor. 1:7; 2 Thess. 1:7). With it is linked the revelation of the sons of God in their heavenly glory, which will cause them to forget the sufferings of the time (Rom. 8:18–19). Whenever Peter uses the *apokalyptō* word group (apart from 1 Pet. 1:12), he has this end revelation in view. The revelation of Christ is the revelation of his glory, in which Christians who are now led through suffering and manifold temptations will also have a share. They should therefore set all their hope on this salvation and grace (1:5–9, 13; 4:13; 5:1).

Such an *apokalypsis* is also the great theme of Rev. (cf. 1:1), which ends its vision of the future with the prayer: "Amen. Come, Lord Jesus" (22:20). The hope of this eternal future is a part of the Christian belief in revelation that cannot be surrendered.

See also *epiphaneia*, appearance, revelation (*2211*); *dēloō*, reveal, make clear, explain, give information, notify (*1317*); *chrēmatizō*, impart a revelation, injunction, or warning (*5976*).

637 (apokalypsis, disclosure, revelation), → *636*.

638	ἀποκαραδοκία

ἀποκαραδοκία (*apokaradokia*), eager expectation (*638*); ἐκδέχομαι (*ekdechomai*), expect, wait for (*1683*); ἐκδοχή (*ekdochē*), expectation (*1693*); ἀπεκδέχομαι (*apekdechomai*), wait, wait eagerly (*587*); προσδέχομαι (*prosdechomai*), receive, welcome (*4657*); προσδοκάω (*prosdokaō*), wait for, look for, expect (*4659*); προσδοκία (*prosdokia*), expectation (*4660*).

CL & OT *apokaradokia* does not occur in pre-Christian Gk., but the simple vb. *karadokeō* (wait for) does. With the prefix *apo-* the vb. suggests to anticipate something longingly but anxiously. For more on the root *dechomai*, to accept, → *1312*.

NT 1. *apokaradokia* only occurs 2x in the NT. In Phil. 1:20 Paul expresses eager expectation that Christ will be exalted in him. Rom. 8:19 ascribes to creation an intense longing for the revelation of God's children, who alone know that the creation has been subjected to decay "in hope" (→ *elpis*, *1828*). Hope does not remove the tension from *apokaradokia*, but it frees it from fear and uncertainty. By contrast, *ekdochē* (Heb. 10:27–28) and *prosdokia* (Lk. 21:26; Acts 12:11–12) are only used of fearful anticipation.

2. (a) *ekdechomai* means await, wait for. It occurs 6x, of which three refer to ordinary waiting (Acts 17:16; 1 Cor. 11:33; 16:11) and one has a fig. use (Jas. 5:7, of the farmer who waits for the fruit of the fields). The other two refer to eschatological waiting (Heb. 10:13; 11:10): Christ, seated at the right hand of the Father, is waiting for the

moment when his enemies will be made his footstool (cf. Ps. 110:1); Abraham was waiting for the city with sure foundations (a picture of heaven as a world of blessedness and perfect communion with God).

(b) *apekdechomai* (8x) means to wait eagerly for something. That expectation is directed toward the returning Lord (Phil. 3:20), who will transform our bodies; toward our entry into the full riches of sonship through the resurrection of the body (Rom. 8:23); and toward righteousness in the last judgment (Gal. 5:5). Since human and non-human creation share equally in the effects of the fall and in salvation, creation's anticipation of freedom from the curse of death is directed toward the time when God's children will enter into glory (Rom. 8:19). Aware of the nature of hope (8:24), they wait in patient endurance while suffering in the present age (v. 25).

(c) *prosdechomai* refers either to persons (meaning to admit someone to a place or into a community) or to things (meaning to accept something). This vb. occurs 14x in the NT and means mostly to wait. Where it refers to expectations of faith it denotes the messianic expectation of Israel (of Simeon and Anna in Lk. 2:25, 38, who were waiting for the salvation of Jerusalem) and the eschatological goal of salvation (resurrection, Acts 24:15; mercy in the judgment, Jude 21; the incomparable glory that will come with the epiphany, Tit. 2:13).

3. *prosdokaō*, to wait, look for someone or something, occurs 16x. In Matt. 11:3 it appears in the Baptist's question about the expected Messiah. In 24:50 it is used of Jesus' Parousia, which will come unexpectedly. In 2 Pet. 3:13 *prosdokaō* identifies the goal of expectation as "a new heaven and a new earth, the home of righteousness," and in 3:12 as the arrival of "the day of God." Those who wait "speed its coming" through their holy conduct (3:11–12).

See also *elpis*, expectation, hope (*1828*).

639 (apokatallassō, reconcile), → *2904*.

640	ἀποκατάστασις

ἀποκατάστασις (*apokatastasis*), restoration (*640*); ἀποκαθίστημι (*apokathistēmi*), reestablish, restore (*635*).

CL & OT 1. (a) In cl. Gk. the vb. *apokathistēmi* meant originally to restore to a previous state, then generally to restore. In a literal and non-religious context, it was used for giving back something lent or the restoration of a sick person; later, more generally, the renewing of the world. *apokatastasis*, derived from the vb., means the reestablishment of a former state, restoration. Here again it occurs chiefly in secular contexts, such as the improvement of a road or the reconstitution of a city's affairs.

(b) These words developed a specialized use in connection with astronomical and cosmological speculation in the Hel. age. Ancient, and esp. Stoic, thought imagined the course of the universe in terms of an infinite series of cyclical cosmic periods, of which the *apokatastasis* was always the final stage of the old period and the point at which the new one began. In Stoicism and the Hermetic literature, the concept of *apokatastasis* could be associated with political expectations. The neo-Platonism of the post-Christian era applied this concept anthropologically to the soul of an individual—the repeated entry of the immortal soul into the mortal body through reincarnation, with a view to being cleansed from matter and reattaining its original condition.

2. Only the vb. is found in the LXX, usually to translate the root *šûb*: in the qal meaning to turn back, return; in the piel to bring back; and most frequently hiph. to bring back, restore. In nonreligious contexts *apokathistēmi* takes on a wide range of meanings: e.g., Abraham paying money to Ephron (Gen. 23:16), a stone being rolled from the mouth of a well (29:3), a man being reinstated in his office (41:13), and water flowing back (Exod. 14:26–27).

2. More important is the use of the word in the prophets. While *apokathistēmi* is found but rarely in the preaching of the early prophets (e.g., Hos. 2:3; 11:11; Amos 5:15), it has a special theological signif-

icance in the announcement of eschatological salvation in exilic and postexilic prophecy. Yahweh will bring Israel back from exile into his own land (Jer. 16:15; 23:8; 24:6). Ezekiel draws a parallel between the restoration of Israel and her beginnings (16:55), and Mal. 4:6 prophesies of a returned Elijah who will turn the hearts of fathers and sons toward each other again. Thus in the LXX, *apokathistēmi* becomes more and more the term for the eschatological, and in part messianic, hopes of Israel for restoration of her former state.

3. This tendency grew stronger in the last few centuries B.C. Here *apokathistēmi* acquires at times a specifically political character. In Dan. 4:33–34 it is used of Nebuchadnezzar's recovery of power and dominion, while 1 Macc. 15:3 speaks of the plans of Antiochus VII to regain control of the kingdom of "our fathers" and to reestablish the former state of affairs. Josephus used *apokatastasis* in describing the return of the Jews from exile, while Philo linked this idea with the mystical one of the restoration of the soul.

NT 1. In the NT the vb. is found 8x (mostly in the Synoptic Gospels). (a) In Mk. 3:5 (par. Matt. 12:13; Lk. 6:10) and Mk. 8:25 the original nonreligious meaning of *apokathistēmi* is found in connection with the healing of the sick: a hand or a blind man's sight is restored, i.e., healed. Note also Heb. 13:19 ("so that I may be restored to you soon," i.e., that I may come to you soon), which also goes back to ordinary Gk. usage.

(b) Mk. 9:12 (par. Matt. 17:11) alludes to Mal. 4:5–6. In his discussion with his disciples about the Messiah, Jesus counters their political messianic hopes, which center on the figure of a revived Elijah who "restores all things," by referring to the fate of the Son of Man, who "must suffer much and be rejected." Thus, the Jewish political Messiah associated with *apokathistēmi* is transformed into the doctrine of the suffering Son of Man, so this meaning of the vb. recedes.

A similar tendency may be seen in Acts 1:6–8. To the question of the disciples, still conceived in terms of a political Messiah, "Are you at this time going to restore the kingdom to Israel?" Jesus replies by forbidding reckoning and calculation and points to the promised gift of the Spirit. In other words, in the era of the church it is not political control that matters, but the interim kingdom of the Spirit and of power.

2. (a) *apokatastasis* occurs only once in the NT, in Peter's sermon from the temple portico (Acts 3:21). He calls on the people to repent so that their sins may be blotted out and that God may send Christ back to them: "He must remain in heaven until the time comes for God to restore everything, as he promised long ago through his holy prophets." This sentence accords with the eschatological messianic hope of OT prophecy and Judaism. The restoration of all things does not mean the conversion of all humanity, but the universal renewal of the earth. It emphasizes the objective side of the coming age, the permanent condition of a renewed world.

(b) In the early church Origen used Acts 3:21 as the basis for a theory of the Apokatastasis, i.e., the doctrine of the restoration of all created things. Central to this is the view that God's work of salvation has as its aim the removal of all the disorder in creation that has resulted from sin, i.e., the medical, political, and cosmic restoration of all created things to the harmony of one, all-embracing order of being. In the history of Christian thought, this thinking has led to universalism, though evangelical Christianity has never accepted universal salvation as a teaching of the Scriptures.

See also *hilaskomai*, propitiate, expiate, be gracious (*2661*); *katallassō*, reconcile (*2904*).

648 (apokryptō, hide), → *3221.*

649 (apokryphos, hidden), → *3221.*

650	ἀποκτείνω

ἀποκτείνω (*apokteinō*), kill (*650*); τελευτάω (*teleutaō*), come to an end, die (*5462*); τελευτή (*teleutē*), end, euphemism for death (*5463*).

CL & OT 1. *apokteinō* in cl. Gk. expresses any kind of violent ending to one's life. It can thus mean kill, have put to death, murder, and execute. *teleutaō* originally had the general meaning of bring to an end (e.g., one's work), come to an end; hence also die.

2. *apokteinō* is found over 150x in the LXX. It refers to homicide (Gen. 4:8), penal execution (Exod. 32:27), or the carrying out of mass killing in a holy war (Num. 31:7–8; 1 Sam. 15:3). It also occurs in prophetic visions of judgment (Amos 4:10; 9:1; Ezek. 23:10). *teleutaō* means simply die, with no distinction as to whether the death is from natural causes (e.g., Exod. 1:6) or is sudden and violent (19:12; 21:16–17; Amos 9:10).

NT 1. *apokteinō*, kill, occurs 74x in the NT, especially in the four Gospels. The vb. nearly always refers to the violent killing of God's messengers, whether in direct narrative (Matt. 14:5; cf. Mk. 6:19), in parables (Mk. 12:5–8 par; cf. Matt. 23:37 par.), or prophetically with reference to the disciples (Matt. 24:9). Its use in the three Synoptic passion predictions (Mk. 8:31; 9:31; 10:34; par.) is of central significance; the person who is to be killed is the Son (cf. 1 Thess. 2:15). In Jn. *apokteinō* is usually combined with *zēteō*, seek, or *bouleuō*, plan (e.g., Jn. 7:1, 19–25; 11:53).

Jesus' followers also come within the scope of the threat of being killed (Acts 21:31; 23:12–14). This is indicated especially in Rev. 6:11 (cf. also 11:7), though the vb. is used in this book more often of the execution of God's judgment (see 6:8; 9:15–18; 19:21). Metaphorically, Eph. 2:16 declares that by his death Jesus has "killed" the hostility between Jew and Gentile and thus brought about reconciliation. In Rom. 7:11 sin as a power is said to kill a person by means of the commandment. In 2 Cor. 3:6 the meaning is the same: *gramma*, letter, is said to kill in contrast to the life-giving Spirit.

2. The noun *teleutē* occurs only in Matt. 2:15 for the death of Herod. *teleutaō* is used 11x in the NT (3x in OT quotations: Matt. 15:4; Mk. 7:10; 9:48). In Matt. 9:18 and Jn. 11:39 it refers to dead persons who are raised to life by Jesus; the vb. is used in order to emphasize that Jairus's daughter and Lazarus have really died. The vb. is also used of the death of Herod (Matt. 2:19), in the parable of the seven brothers who died (22:25), and in historical allusions to the deaths of David, Jacob, and Joseph (Acts 2:29; 7:15; Heb. 11:22). The dominant word for die in the NT, however, is *apothnēskō* (→ *thanatos, 2505*).

See also *thanatos*, death (*2505*); *katheudō*, sleep (*2761*); *nekros*, dead, dead person (*3738*).

655 (apolambanō, receive, get back), → *3284.*

660 (apollymi, destroy), → *724.*

661 (Apollyōn, Apollyon, Destroyer), → *724.*

664	ἀπολογέομαι

ἀπολογέομαι (*apologeomai*), defend, make defense (*664*); ἀπολογία (*apologia*), defense (*665*).

CL & OT In cl. Gk. these words are used primarily in a legal setting, where one defends oneself in a court of law against specific charges. A speech of defense is called an *apologia*. *apologeomai* is used in Jer. 12:1 for the prophet as he brings a case before the Lord. In 31:6 (= LXX 38:6) the vb. denotes the watchmen who cry out on the hills of Ephraim. The noun does not occur in the OT (but cf. Wis. 6:10).

NT 1. *apologeomai* occurs 10x in the NT, *apologia* 8x. The predominant meaning is legal, esp. in the defenses Paul makes after his arrest in Jerusalem (vb.: Acts 24:10; 25:8; 26:1–2, 24; noun: 22:1; 25:16; cf. 2 Tim. 4:16). In Phil. 1:7, 16, Paul indicates how the judicial process became an opportunity for him to preach the gospel.

2. Paul also uses this word group in his struggle to defend himself before the Corinthians, who were siding with his opponents and against the apostle (1 Cor. 9:3; 2 Cor. 12:19).

3. Christians should always be ready to defend their faith against any who oppose it or even just inquire about it (1 Pet. 3:15). In a legal setting, Jesus indicates that his followers may have to defend themselves before kings and judges; yet they do not need to worry, since words will be given to them by himself (Lk. 21:14) or by his Spirit (12:11).

665 (*apologia*, defense), → *664*.

666 (*apolouō*, wash, wash away), → *3374*.

667 (*apolytrōsis*, redemption, deliverance, release), → *3389*.

668 (*apolyō*, set free, release, pardon, let go, send away, divorce), → *687* and *3395*.

675 (*apoplanaō*, go astray, wander away), → *4414*.

678 (*apopnigō*, strangle), → *4465*.

684 (*aposkiasma*, shadow, darkness), → *5014*.

686 (*apostasia*, rebellion, state of apostasy, defection), → *923*.

687	ἀποστάσιον

ἀποστάσιον (*apostasion*), decree of divorce (*687*); ἀπολύω (*apolyō*), set free (*668*).

CL & OT 1. In cl. Gk. *apolyō* means set free, release, free from; it can be used of releasing prisoners or freeing a person from legal charges. It also means dismiss, occasionally used of dismissing a wife. *apostasion* refers to the relinquishment of a property upon sale.

2. Both words are rare in the LXX. *apolyō* is used in a variety of senses, including divorce (1 Esd. 9:36). *apostasion* occurs 4x with reference to a deed of divorce (Deut. 24:1, 3; Isa. 50:1; Jer. 3:8). OT law allowed divorce if a man found "something indecent" in his wife, but forbade it to a man who had been compelled to marry a girl whom he had raped (Deut. 22:28–29). The penalty for a wife who was discovered not to be a virgin was death (22:13–21), and the penalty for both partners in a case of adultery was death (22:22). In general divorce was frowned upon, but cases did occur (Mal. 2:14–16). After the exile Jewish men who had married foreign wives were required to put them away (Ezr. 9–10; Neh. 13:23–27).

NT 1. In the NT *apolyō* has the cl. Gk. meaning release a prisoner (Mk. 15:6–15 par.; cf. Matt. 18:27); set free from disease (Lk. 13:12); acquit (6:37); send people away (Mk. 6:36, 45; 8:3, 9); dismiss from the duties of life, allow to die (Lk. 2:29). It is esp. used of divorcing a wife (Matt. 1:19; 5:31–32; 19:3, 7–9; Mk. 10:2, 4, 11–12; Lk. 16:18). *apostasion* means divorce (Matt. 5:31; 19:7; Mk. 10:4).

2. Divorce was an accepted fact of life in NT times. A husband was at liberty to put away his wife, provided that he followed the proper legal process of granting her a notice of divorce. But the grounds on which a husband might divorce his wife were disputed between the two rab. schools of Shammai and Hillel (teachers in 1st cent. B.C.), who allowed divorce only for adultery or for marital incompatibility, respectively.

The teaching of Jesus in Mk. 10:1–12 affirms that God's purpose in creation was that husband and wife should become one flesh and that divorce is inconsistent with God's will (10:6–9). Jesus admitted that Moses allowed divorce, provided that proper legal forms were followed. But this concession was allowed only "because your hearts were hard" (10:5)—i.e., either because of human obstinacy towards the law of God or in order to bring such obstinacy out into the open. What is not clear is how this teaching should affect the Christian attitude toward legislation in a non-Christian society or how the church should treat Christians involved in divorce (see, however, Jn. 7:53–8:11).

In the ensuing discussion (Mk. 10:11–12), Jesus explains why divorce is wrong by defining it in terms of adultery: A man who divorces his wife and remarries is committing adultery against his first wife. Jesus was going beyond the existing Jewish view of adultery as an offense against a husband. He insists here that the wife is on the

same level as a husband. The same principle is applied in 10:12 (cf. Luke 16:18a) to a wife who divorces her husband (as was possible in the Roman world, but not among Jews) and remarries; remarriage after divorce is adultery. Lk. 16:18b stresses that the man who marries a divorcée commits adultery against her first husband, thus stating that the existing Jewish understanding of adultery must be applied to remarriage as well.

Matt. 19:9 agrees with Mk. 10:11 but adds the caveat, "except for marital unfaithfulness" (→ *porneuō*, 4519). This exception pertains to the issue of remarriage and follows the rule of Shammai by allowing for remarriage only if a wife has been guilty of adultery. An alternative view is that the adultery in question is misconduct on the part of a betrothed woman before the consummation of her marriage, in which case Jewish law demanded that the wedding should not proceed (cf. Matt. 1:18–25; note how Joseph proceeded to marry Mary only upon a divine revelation that she was free from adultery).

A further form of Jesus' teaching appears in Matt. 5:32, where he states that a person who divorces his wife (again, "except for marital unfaithfulness") is responsible for making her and her second husband commit adultery against him.

3. Paul gives a similar teaching. Only after the death of a person's partner is one allowed to remarry (Rom. 7:1–3). He repeats the command of Jesus that husband and wife should not separate from each other; if, however, they do separate, they should not remarry (1 Cor. 7:10–11). In cases where only one partner has become a Christian, the Christian should not regard this as a reason for divorce. (This issue arises perhaps because of a fear that there was something unholy about union between a believer and an unbeliever.) The marriage bond itself is not a cause of defilement, since the unbelieving partner and any children are "sanctified" by the believing partner (7:14). However, if the unbelieving partner seeks a separation, the Christian should allow it. What is not clear is whether in such a case the Christian partner was free to remarry.

See also *chōrizō*, divide, separate (*6004*).

690	ἀποστέλλω

ἀποστέλλω (*apostellō*), send (*690*); ἐξαποστέλλω (*exapostellō*), send out (*1990*); πέμπω (*pempō*), send (*4287*); ἀπόστολος (*apostolos*), envoy, ambassador, apostle (*693*); ἀποστολή (*apostolē*), apostleship (*692*); ψευδαπόστολος (*pseudapostolos*), false apostle (*6013*).

CL & OT 1. (a) In cl. Gk. *apostellō* means send away, send off. Where a delegation for a particular purpose is involved, the cause for sending is often stressed through this word. Since the envoy has full powers and is the personal representative of the one sending him, a close connection is established between the sender and the recipient. The other verb for send, *pempō*, stresses the mere fact of sending. In popular Stoic philosophy the idea of the envoy's authority to represent his master acquires a religious significance. A Cynic peripatetic teacher considered himself an envoy sent by Zeus. Hence *apostellō* is also a technical term denoting divine authorization.

(b) *apostolos* (derived from *apostellō*) first meant a cargo ship or the fleet sent out. Later it denoted a commander of a naval expedition or a band of colonists sent overseas. In the papyri it could mean an invoice or even a passport. Josephus uses the word for a group sent on a mission. All its usages have two ideas in common: a commission, and being sent overseas.

2. The LXX uses *apostellō* and *exapostellō* about 700x, almost exclusively to render *šālaḥ*, stretch out, send (*pempō* occurs only 26x). The translators rightly realized that the Heb. vb. does not describe the mere act of sending so much as its essential purpose, the authorization of the messenger (cf. Jos. 1:16; 1 Ki. 5:8; 2 Ki. 19:4). Hence two conclusions may be drawn: (a) The LXX, following the Heb. text, uses *apostellō* to denote not the institutional appointment of someone to an office, but the authorization of that person to ful-

fill a particular function or a task that is normally clearly defined. (b) If the sending is linked with a task in the use of *apostellō*, the stress falls on the sender, that is, the one who gives his authority to the one sent. In the story of Isaiah's call, the messenger is not even named (Isa. 6:8).

3. The Jewish legal institution of the *šālîaḥ* is important for NT exegesis. What has been said above of the use of *apostellō* applies equally to the *šālîaḥ*. The term does not denote a continuing office, but the exercise of a function limited in scope and duration by a definite commission and terminating on its completion. Rab. Jud. in Jesus' time recognized the function of a messenger as the proxy or representative of the one who had given him the commission (cf. 1 Sam. 25:40–41; 2 Sam. 10:4, 6). The *šālîaḥ* acted with full authority for someone else. The leader in synagogue prayer was the *šālîaḥ* of the community. Rabbis were sent as representatives of the Sanhedrin for inspections and collections, at home and in the Diaspora.

But these representatives were not missionaries. Jud. in NT times did not know of officially sent out missionaries. Thus, *šālîaḥ* could not be used of those trying to win others for Judaism. Strangely enough, the word *šālîaḥ* is not applied to the prophets in spite of Isa. 6:8, though to have done so would have been an easy deduction from their position as messengers. Certain great men of the past (e.g., Moses, Elijah, Ezekiel) are called God's *šᵉlûḥîm* (pl.) because of the mighty acts performed through them.

NT A. *apostellō* is used 132x in NT; *exapostellō*, 13x; *pempō* occurs as a virtual synonym esp. in Jn. (32x) but also in Lk. and Acts (10x and 11x). John's use of *apostellō* and *pempō* side by side without any obvious difference seems to stress the purely functional aspects of the term in contrast to the institutional concepts already being attached to *apostolos* (see below), and also to underline more strongly the authority of the Lord who sends (cf. Jn. 4:34; 7:16; 14:24 with 5:36; 7:29; 17:21, 25).

B. 1. In contrast to the LXX (which uses the noun *apostolos* only in 1 Ki. 14:6, where the Lord commissions the prophet Ahijah with a hard message for Jeroboam's wife), the frequent occurrence of this noun in the NT (80x) is striking. It always has the general sense of messenger, and particularly as the fixed designation of a definite office, the primitive apostolate.

(a) With the exceptions of Lk. 11:49 and Acts 14:14, Luke applies *apostolos* expressly to the Twelve. They had been called by the historical Jesus to their office (Lk. 6:13) and had been with him throughout his ministry from the time of John's baptism. The risen Lord had met them in various appearances (Lk. 24:36–51; Acts 1:3), so they had the best possible knowledge of what Jesus had said. Before the ascension they had received the promise of the Spirit (Acts 1:4) and the command to evangelize (1:8). At Pentecost (Acts 2) they were made bearers of the Spirit, the great authorities of early Christianity who, based in Jerusalem, guarded the true tradition that went back to Jesus.

According to Luke, there could be no other independent authorities beside the apostles. They had to make or confirm every important decision. They commissioned the Seven (6:6), resolved theological disputes (15:1–31), and began the mission to the Gentiles (10:1–11:18). Except in 14:14, Luke never calls Paul an apostle. He clearly did not fulfill the preconditions for the office of an apostle that were fulfilled by the Twelve. According to Luke's account, the gap left in the circle of the Twelve by Judas's betrayal was closed by the election of Matthias (1:16–28).

(b) It is remarkable that such a fundamental concept as *apostolos* should appear rarely in the other three Gospels. In Jn. 13:16 *apostolos* cannot be understood as an office, for here it obviously means no more than messenger. In Matt. 10:2 the term is found at the head of the list of the Twelve before they are sent out (cf. Mk. 3:14), and in Mk. 6:30 they are called by this name when they return. Both remind us of the *šālîaḥ* concept.

(c) The Pauline letters are the oldest source of information about the technical use of *apostolos* and *apostolē* in the NT. The following

features and assumptions emerge from Paul's understanding of the office of apostle in his debates with his opponents:

(i) The call and commissioning to lifelong service of an apostle is not through any human being "but by Jesus Christ and God the Father" (Gal. 1:1; cf. Rom. 1:5; 1 Cor. 1:1; 2 Cor. 1:1). It comes about through meeting with the risen Lord (1 Cor. 9:1; 15:7; Gal. 1:16), who himself gives his apostle the message of the gospel (1 Cor. 11:23; 2 Cor. 4:6; Gal. 1:12). The apostle delivers it as Christ's "ambassador" (2 Cor. 5:20).

(ii) In contrast with the Jewish *šālîaḥ*, the call to apostleship is bound with the duty of mission among the Gentiles (Rom. 11:13; cf. 10:15; 1 Cor. 1:17; Gal. 2:8). Presumably the apostles were originally sent out two by two (Gal. 2:1, 9; cf. Mk. 6:7; Lk. 10:1; Acts 15:36–40). Special signs and wonders attend their work (2 Cor. 12:12; cf. Rom. 15:19). Their task is primarily to preach and not to baptize (1 Cor. 1:17).

(iii) Suffering is an inescapable part of the apostle's service (1 Cor. 4:9–13; 15:30–32; 2 Cor. 4:7–12; 11:23–29).

(iv) Like the prophets, apostles have a special insight into the mystery (→ *mysterion, 3696*) of Christ (1 Cor. 4:1; Eph. 3:1–6).

(v) Paul gives no suggestion that his special position as an apostle exalts him above the church and distinguishes him from the others with spiritual gifts (1 Cor. 12:25–28; cf. Eph. 4:11; Rom. 1:11–12). His spiritual gifts are there to fulfill definite functions in the church (→ *charis, 5921*). His authority is not derived from some special quality within himself (2 Cor. 3:5) but from the gospel itself in its truth and power to convict (Rom. 15:18; 2 Cor. 4:2). That is why Paul takes pains to make it clear when he is giving his own opinion (1 Cor. 7:10, 12).

(vi) Paul met the risen Lord as last of the apostles (1 Cor. 15:8); if we are to take "last of all" absolutely, then there was no possibility of continuing the apostolate by calling others to it.

It is not completely clear whom Paul reckoned as apostles in a technical sense. Paul certainly belonged to their number (affirmed 14x in his letters), as did Peter (Gal. 1:18–19), Junias, Andronicus (Rom. 16:7), and Barnabas (cf. Acts 14:14 with Gal. 2:1, 9, 13). Some doubt whether he considered James, the Lord's brother, to be an apostle, as the *ei mē* ("only") of Gal. 1:19 is ambiguous. It is uncertain if he included Silvanus (2 Cor. 1:19; 1 Thess. 1:1; 2 Thess. 1:1).

At any rate, Paul never applies the title of apostle to the Twelve as a defined group. When Paul calls Titus, Epaphroditus, and others "representatives [lit., apostles] of the churches" in 2 Cor. 8:23 (cf. Phil. 2:25), he is clearly not using *apostolos* as a technical term for a member of the Christian apostolate. In other words, we cannot be certain whether the characteristics Paul attributes to the apostles are necessarily applicable to the NT apostle as such.

(d) Light is thrown on the question whether we can equate the Twelve with the apostles by the fact that only in Rev. 21:14 are they expressly called that in the other NT writings. In Heb. 3:1 the title is given to Jesus.

(e) It is clear then that, apart from the general meaning of messenger or envoy, two differing concepts lie behind the NT use of *apostolos*. We must ask the questions: Where did the idea and institution of Christian apostleship come from? When did the Twelve begin to bear the name *apostolos*? What is the relation between their apostleship and that of Paul? What was the origin of the differing concepts of Paul and Luke? If the circle of apostles in the time of Paul was obviously wider than that of the Twelve, how was the title attributed and even confined to them? These questions may not be answered by questioning the textual accuracy of our sources or by a false harmonization, which may involve the elimination of certain passages from consideration.

2. NT scholars have offered various attempts to trace the sources of the concept of apostleship and the reasons for its varied forms, often by using the results of investigation in the history of religion and in the historic background and development of the period.

(a) For a long time scholarship was dominated by the view that both linguistically and functionally Christian apostleship was derived from the Jewish institution of the *šālîaḥ*. After a period for hearing and learning, Jesus appointed his disciples as apostles by sending them out and setting them to active work (Matt. 10:1–5; Mk. 6:7–11; Lk. 9:10). In other words, the apostolate was originally not an office but a commission. Later it was renewed and modified by the risen Lord, and the apostles were now called for life as missionaries to an authoritative position as Spirit-empowered witnesses of the resurrection. The apostle Paul forms an exception to this rule, and he felt compelled to establish his apostleship.

But it is impossible to prove exegetically, except perhaps from Luke, that Jesus transmitted the office of apostle to the Twelve, either during his earthly activity or immediately after his resurrection.

(b) A second view claims that the Twelve were instituted as apostles by the historical Jesus but that apostleship was not limited to these men. Paul considered himself as an apostle like the rest; the apostles are essentially the foundation-laying preachers of the gospel. Any limitation of the apostles to the Twelve occurred after Paul's death. But if this is so, how are we to understand the commissioning of the Twelve by the historical Jesus? And was the apostolic circle later limited to the Twelve or transferred to them? Did Paul coin the formula "apostle of Jesus Christ," or did he take it over and become responsible for its establishment as a technical term?

(c) Other scholars see no relationship between the concept of *šālîaḥ* (which does not even occur before A.D. 140 and is a juridical term) and *apostolos* (which has a religious connotation, is eschatological in character, is lifelong, and has the missionary charge). Rather, they argue that the notion of apostleship derived from Jewish gnostic circles, where it was used as a title for redeemer figures or heavenly emissaries. Paul developed the title, which was then quite naturally extended to others among the Twelve, as tradition increasingly identified them with the leadership of the Gentile mission. But this view fails to explain why, when the title of apostle came to be applied to the Twelve, all the others who had previously been called apostles lost their status. Moreover, at best Paul came into contact with Gnosticism only late in his life. This view also virtually requires Acts to be dated in the 2nd cent.

(d) Still other scholars suggest, on the one hand, that it is perhaps best to admit a darkness lying over the beginnings of the primitive Christian apostolate. If we take the growth of the canon seriously, we must recognize that the concepts of the apostolate vary in NT writings.

On the other hand, we should note that the missionary commission was an essential part of the primitive Christian apostolate. If we remember that the Twelve were tied to Jerusalem by their eschatological role as representatives of the twelve tribes of Israel, it is unlikely that Jesus, either before or after his resurrection, appointed them as apostles in the sense in which that authoritative office was later understood. How could a circle of disciples with such authority have lost its power by the time of the apostolic council (Acts 15), which contains no reference to "the Twelve"?

The starting point for understanding the technical term *apostle* must be the meaning of the vb. *apostellō*. Already in secular Gk. "to send" was used as a technical term for a divine authorization, and its substantive was used, admittedly rarely, with the meaning messenger. Since the Hel. churches most likely would not have understood the concept of the *šālîaḥ*, the Gentile Christians understood *apostolos* as a divinely sent messenger. If we consider too that the LXX uses this term for the mission of the prophets, OT prophecy also served as a positive basis for the special concept of apostleship in the early church. If that is so, the early church chose, as it so often did, an unfamiliar word, seldom used in the secular language, with little ready-made content, in order to fill it with one expressing its own conceptions.

Missionaries specially called by the Lord, then, bore this title. It was soon applied to Peter, the only disciple (at least known to us) active in missionary work. Paul was included in this circle because of his special commission from the risen Lord. After his time, when the Twelve became more and more regarded as the only legitimate bearers of the message of Jesus as the Christ and believers became convinced that they had been the initiators of the mission to the Gentiles, the title *apostolos* (primarily through Luke's influence) was gradually transferred to the whole circle of the Twelve, indicating their role as guarantors of the legitimate tradition.

(e) The above hypotheses (representing, in general, European scholarship) draw a sharp distinction between the picture in Luke–Acts and that in the Pauline writings and other Gospels. Scholars in the English-speaking world, while recognizing Luke's special interests, are less inclined to see such a conflict of attitudes. Luke's neglect to make explicit reference to the "Twelve" at the Jerusalem council (Acts 15) is probably due to his taking their identity for granted in the light of his previous identification of the Twelve as apostles (Lk. 6:12–16; Acts 1:13–26). We should note too the collegiate character of church leadership that Acts consistently depicts (1:13–26; 6:2–6; 8:14–17; 11:1–18; 13:1–4).

Moreover, Acts certainly does not play down the call and commissioning of Paul, which it records no less than 3x (Acts 9:1–19; 22:1–21; 26:2–18). We would hardly expect Paul to be given the title *apostolos* at his conversion. Nevertheless, the Lord reveals to Ananias that Paul is "my chosen instrument to carry my name before the Gentiles and their kings and before the people of Israel" (9:15), and Luke's account of Paul's words contain the vbs. *exapostellō* ("Go; I will send you far away to the Gentiles," 22:21) and *apostellō* ("I am sending you to [the Gentiles] to open their eyes and turn them from darkness to light," 26:17–18). Moreover, in encountering the risen Christ on the Damascus road, Paul fulfilled a basic qualification for apostleship, that of being "a witness . . . of his resurrection" (1:22) (though he did not fulfill the other condition, that of being a follower of Jesus in his earthly ministry). In short, the picture that Acts paints is not that Paul was not an apostle, but that he was an apostle extraordinary, which is precisely what Paul himself says in his letters (1 Cor. 9:1–6; 15:5–9; Gal. 1:12–17).

Moreover, Luke is certainly careful to point out that Paul is equal in power and authority to Peter. Note how every significant event that transpired with Peter in the first half of Acts also transpires with Paul in the second half. Both preach similar messages (2:4–36; 13:16–41), heal a cripple (3:1–10; 14:8–10), appear before Jewish authorities (3:5–21; 22:30–23:10), perform miracles by proxy (5:15; 19:11–12), receive a beating (5:40; 16:22–23), oppose a sorcerer (8:14–24; 13:6–12), heal an older man (9:33–34; 28:7–8), raise a dead person (9:36–42; 20:7–10), receive a vision concerning the Gentile mission (10:9–23; 11:1–18; 22:17–21; 26:13–18), and are miraculously released from prison (12:3–11; 16:22–28). And while Acts presents the Jerusalem apostles as a closely knit body working separately from Paul (e.g., 8:14; 9:27; 15:2; 16:4), it does speak of Paul and Barnabas as "apostles" (14:4, 14).

The difference of emphasis between Luke and the other Evangelists is also less sharp than may appear at first sight. *apostolos* occurs in Matt. 10:2 (= Lk. 6:13) and Mk. 6:30 (= Lk. 9:10). Luke's Gospel uses the term only 4x more, of which 11:49 may simply mean one sent by God, and the other occasions are patently synonyms for the disciples (17:5 [cf. 17:1]; 22:14; 24:10). The use of the word in all four Gospels appears to be the application of a term familiar at the time of writing but which was not necessarily current at the time when the incidents described happened. All four Gospels give accounts of the call of the disciples (Matt. 10:2–4; Mk. 3:16–19; Lk. 6:13–16 [cf. Acts 1:13]; Jn. 1:35–43). In all four (but especially Matt.) the disciples are called the Twelve. During the earthly ministry of Jesus they figure as learners (→ *mathētēs*, 3412). And in all four they are sent as witnesses to the risen Christ (Matt. 28:16–20; Mk. 16:7 [cf. 3:14]; Lk. 24:46–49 [cf. Acts 1:8]; Jn. 20:21–23, 30–31; 21:15–19, 24).

Finally, one thing is certain. The NT never betrays any understanding of the apostolate as an institutionalized church office, capable of being passed on. The adoption and transformation of the concept of apostleship by the early church had an important and possibly decisive influence in preventing the disintegration of the witness to Christ and maintaining the continuity of its tradition down to the time when the canon of the NT was fixed. It was due to the office of the apostolate that the link with the crucified and the exalted Lord was preserved.

3. In 2 Cor. 11:13 Paul calls those who oppose his authority and ministry in Corinth "false apostles" (*pseudapostolos*). Scholars have debated whether these are the same as the "super-apostles" of 11:5, though most tend to agree that they are not. If anything, the "super-apostles" is a somewhat tongue-in-cheek term Paul uses for the original twelve apostles, perhaps because his opponents are using that expression. Paul makes clear that the latter are false apostles, agents of Satan, "masquerading as apostles of Christ."

691	ἀποστερέω

ἀποστερέω (*apostereō*), rob, defraud, deprive (*691*).

CL & OT 1. In cl. Gk. *apostereō* means refuse to pay a debt or return property or money deposited with another for safekeeping; defraud; become a defaulter; withdraw from a person or thing; in logic, to draw a negative conclusion.

2. In Exod. 21:10 a husband who takes a second wife is warned not to "deprive" the first of food, clothes, or her conjugal rights. Mal. 3:5 threatens judgment against those who "defraud" wage earners.

NT In Mk. 10:19 Jesus quotes the commandment *mē aposterēsēs* ("do not defraud") to the rich young ruler. Although no OT commandment is written in precisely this way, these words are probably intended to summarize the tenth commandment, for one who covets what belongs to another has in his or her heart already deprived that person of it.

In 1 Cor. 6 Paul censures the Corinthians for engaging in lawsuits with one another before secular courts. As those who should know the law of love and presumably Christ's teaching in Matt. 5:39–48, they ought rather to accept being cheated (1 Cor. 6:7) and certainly not actively defraud others (6:8). Similarly, James assails those who have "failed to pay" their workers (5:4).

Paul uses the verb again in 1 Cor. 7:5. Because a married couple belong to each other, an attempt by one partner to spiritualize the marriage amounts to fraud, a withholding of what is due. Sexual abstention can be lawful only if it is by mutual consent, for a good purpose (prayer is Paul's example), and as a temporary measure. In 1 Tim. 6:3–5 Paul assails those who teach that an outward show of religion can be made a means of gain. Such people are depraved in mind and "robbed of" the truth they once knew.

See also *lēstēs*, robber, highwayman, bandit, revolutionary (*3334*); *sylaō*, plunder, rob (*5195*); *andrapodistēs*, slave dealer, kidnapper (*435*); *spēlaion*, cave, den (*5068*).

692 (apostolē, apostleship), → *690.*

693 (apostolos, envoy, ambassador, apostle), → *690.*

695 (apostrephō, turn away from), → *2188.*

697 (aposynagōgos, put out of the synagogue), → *1711.*

700 (apotithēmi, put off), → *1544.*

701 (apotinassō, shake off), → *1759.*

706	ἀποτρέπω

ἀποτρέπω (*apotrepō*), mid. turn away from, avoid (*706*); ἐκτρέπω (*ektrepō*), pass. turn away from, avoid (*1762*).

CL & OT 1. Both verbs occur more in cl. Gk. than in biblical Gk. *apotrepō* is commonly used fig. (in the act. voice) of dissuading, deter-

ring, or diverting a person from a course of action and (in the mid. and pass. voices) of avoiding danger or rejecting truth; *ektrepō* often denotes a literal turning aside, as of a tributary from a river or a person from a road.

2. *apotrepō* occurs only in the Apocr, where it refers to such matters as averting reproofs (Sir. 20:29), relinquishing pleasures (4 Macc. 1:33), or diverting people from their intents (3 Macc. 1:23). *ektrepō* occurs only in Amos 5:8 (God turns darkness into morning).

NT 1. In Heb. 12:13 the author encourages the disheartened to make straight paths for their feet "so that the lame may not be disabled [*ektrepō*], but rather healed." Minor injuries ("the lame") were to be bound up ("healed"), so that major injuries (such as total disability) would be avoided. In other words, *ektrepō* here carries its technical medical sense of "disabled" (as in Hippocrates) rather than its general sense of "turn away."

2. In 2 Tim. 3:5b Paul enjoins Timothy (and indirectly the church at Ephesus) to have "nothing to do with" (*apotrepō*) any persons who are characterized by the vices he lists in 3:2–4, for they have a form of godliness but deny its power (3:5a). Such people are to be denied church membership as much as the quarrelers of 2:23–26.

3. *apotrepō* in 2 Tim. 3:5 is virtually synonymous with *ektrepō* in 1 Tim. 6:20, where Timothy is told to "turn away from godless chatter" and the subtle and endless distinctions that belong to "what is falsely called knowledge." Those who give their attention to such matters wander from the faith (6:21).

4. In the remaining three uses of *ektrepō* in the Pastoral Letters, the idea of doctrinal or ethical deviation is uppermost. As a result of neglecting the Christian triad of love, a good conscience, and sincere faith, the false teachers "have . . . turned to" useless talk (1 Tim. 1:6). Paul warns Timothy that the time is coming when people will find a crowd of teachers to satisfy their craving for novelty; such people reject the truth and "turn aside to myths" (2 Tim. 4:4). Already some widows have become busybodies and gossips (1 Tim. 5:13) and "turned away" to become Satan's servants (5:15)—perhaps an allusion to immorality.

709 (apopheugō, flee from, avoid), → *5771.*

718 (aproskopos, without offense, giving no offense, blameless), → *4682.*

719 (aprosōpolēmptōs, unbiased), → *4725.*

721	ἅπτω

ἅπτω (*haptō*), to touch (*721*).

CL & OT 1. In Homer *haptō* in the act. means to fasten to, take hold of, kindle. It occurs more frequently in the mid. *haptomai*, to touch, eat (i.e., touch food), attack (i.e., touch with hostility). In cl. Gk. it is used also for sexual relationships with women and can mean as well to seize, attack, concern oneself with, and finally understand. Stories are told how the god of healing, Asclepius, healed miraculously by a touch.

2. (a) Occasionally the LXX uses *haptō* (more usually *haptomai*) for touching (or not touching) persons and things that have been made particularly sacred (e.g., the tree of knowledge of good and evil [Gen. 3:3]; Mount Sinai [Exod. 19:12]) or, in contrast, things through which one became unclean (e.g., unclean animals [Lev. 11:8]; corpses [Num. 19:11]; tombs [19:16]). More than external and superficial contact is implied in Gen. 20:6, for the issue there is sexual intimacy. In 2 Sam. 5:8 and Zech. 2:8 *haptomai* means to kill or attack. (b) An angel touched Jacob's thigh and made him limp (Gen. 32:25); another angel touched Daniel and raised him up from his deep sleep (Dan. 8:18). (c) God himself can touch us, either to change our hearts (1 Sam. 10:26) or to afflict us with illness (2 Ki. 15:5) or distress (Job 19:21).

NT 1. In the NT the act. *haptō* is found 4x for the lighting of a lamp (Lk. 8:16; 11:33; 15:8) or a fire (Acts 28:2). The mid. *haptomai* is used of sexual relations in 1 Cor. 7:1, of the touching of unclean foods in Col. 2:21 (cf. Matt. 15:11), and of not touching unclean, idolatrous things in 2 Cor. 6:17 (quoting Isa. 52:11). In Lk. 7:39 we see the difference between Jesus and the crowd, for he does not shrink from the touch of an unclean woman. After his resurrection Jesus forbade Mary to touch him (Jn. 20:17), i.e., to "hold on to" him.

2. (a) The most frequent use of *haptomai* (30x) is in the Synoptic reports of Jesus' acts of healing. Isa. 6:5–7 was fulfilled in Jesus once for all. The Lord touched a leper so that he blotted out his impurity (Mk. 1:40–42). In healing a deaf man with an impediment in his speech, Jesus put his fingers into his ears, spat, touched his tongue, and said to him, "*Ephphatha*" (Mk. 7:33–34).

(b) The stories of healing in Mk. 1:41; 3:10–11; 6:56 involve touch. Because the sick realized that "power was coming from [Jesus]" (Lk. 6:19), they pushed forward to touch him (Mk. 3:10), his garment (Matt. 9:20–21; Mk. 5:27–30, Lk. 8:44–45), or even its fringe (Matt. 14:36; Mk. 6:55–56). Those who in faith touched even his clothes became well, for whether they knew it or not they had touched the form of glory and life.

Most notable here is the woman with the bleeding problem. Jesus does not know at first who has touched him, only that power has gone forth from him (Mk. 5:30; Lk. 8:45–46). It should be remembered that a woman's menstrual flow was regarded as a source of uncleanness (Lev. 15:19–24; 2 Sam. 11:4), which precludes sexual intercourse (Lev. 15:19, 24; 18:19; Ezek. 22:10). A discharge of longer duration causes everything the woman touches to be unclean (Lev. 15:25–30). Hence, the woman is not only physically ill but debarred from normal human relationships. She knows that to touch anyone under these circumstances is out of the question, but she acts in true and simple faith. Those who do not believe touch Jesus only superficially (Mk. 5:31) and do not experience his power. Those whom Jesus touches of his own volition share in his divine power (Mk. 9:27), and God himself turns to them.

(c) Also significant in the stories of Jesus are the mothers who bring their children to Jesus so that he may touch them, bless them, and pray over them (Matt. 19:13–15; Mk. 10:13–16; Lk. 18:15–17).

724	ἀπώλεια

ἀπώλεια (*apōleia*), destruction (*724*); ἀπόλλυμι (*apollymi*), destroy (*660*); Ἀπολλύων (*Apollyōn*), Apollyon, Destroyer (*661*).

CL & OT 1. As a trans. vb. *apollymi* means (a) lose (e.g., father, spouse, courage, life); or (b) annihilate (e.g., a crowd of people in war), destroy, kill. The mid. intrans. form means (a) disappear, get lost, be lost; or (b) die, go to ruin through financial disaster or violence. *apōleia* means destruction, downfall, annihilation. *apollyōn* means the destroyer and contains a pun on *Apollōn*, the god of plagues. The ideas conveyed by this group of words usually involve injury (of a violent nature), destruction, or the end of earthly existence.

2. In the LXX *apollymi* usually means be lost, perish, or destroy. It can be used of the destruction of a city, a group of people, or a tribe (cf. Num. 16:33; 32:39; 33:52). Of great importance are the requirements of the Holiness Code, which warn transgressors of the law, such as those who make child sacrifices to Molech and those who are sorcerers, that they will be "cut off" by stoning from God's covenant people (Lev. 20:3, 5, 6).

The exhortations at the end of Deut. confront the nation with the alternatives of receiving the blessing of a long life for obedience or the curse of extinction for disobedience (e.g., Deut. 28:20; 30:18). Thus, *apōleia* involves not only exclusion from belonging to Yahweh, but also destruction and loss of life. Although in most OT writings *apōleia* is understood in the sense of earthly death, later texts occasionally link the words of this group with *hadēs*, the underworld (→ 87), and *thanatos*, death (Prov. 15:11; 27:20; cf. Job 26:6; 28:22, → 2505).

3. Jewish apocalyptic lit. of the intertestamental and NT periods speaks of an eschatological destruction of the world, sometimes conceived in terms of a conflagration. The ungodly will perish along with the world.

NT 1. *apollymi* occurs 90x and *apōleia* 18x in the NT. Lk. 15:4, 8 uses *apollymi* for the losing of a sheep and a coin; similarly, the mid. refers to the state of being lost (15:4, 6, 24, 32). *apollymi* has the sense of kill, destroy (a person) in Matt. 2:13; 27:20; Mk. 3:6 par.; 9:22; 11:18 par. The vb. has an impers. obj. in Paul's quotation of Isa. 29:14 at 1 Cor. 1:19: "I will destroy the wisdom of the wise." The mid. can also have the sense of die or perish: with reference to things (food in Jn. 6:12, 27; gold in 1 Pet. 1:7; heaven and earth in Heb. 1:11; world in 2 Pet. 3:6), or to people (Matt. 26:52; Mk. 4:38 par.; Lk. 13:3, 5, 33; 1 Cor. 10:9–10). Finally, *apōleia* usually means ruin, destruction (Matt. 7:13; Rom. 9:22; Phil. 1:28; Rev. 17:8), though occasionally it means waste, squandering (Mk. 14:4 par.).

2. The theological use of these words is prominent in the three parables of Lk. 15, portraying the human condition of being lost. People without God are like lost sheep (cf. Ps. 119:176), doomed to perish unless rescued by the shepherd. Jesus is pictured as this shepherd (cf. Jn. 10:11–16), who has come "to seek and to save what was lost" (Lk. 19:10). He is commanded not to lose those whom the Father has given him (Jn. 6:39; 18:9). Those who endeavor to secure their life by self-effort will lose it, while those who lose it for Christ's sake and the gospel's by giving themselves to him (cf. Matt. 8:19–22; 16:24) will keep it (10:39; Mk. 8:35 par.; Lk. 17:33; Jn. 12:25). For with him is life; "whoever believes in him shall not perish but have eternal life" (Jn. 3:16).

3. The specific theological sense of these words in the NT is brought out by Jn. and Paul. Just as *sōtēria* (salvation) and *zōē aiōnios* (eternal life) connote sure and lasting salvation or eternal life (Jn. 10:28), so *apollymi* and *apōleia* mean definitive destruction for all eternity (1 Cor. 1:18; cf. 2 Cor. 2:15; 4:3). It is the fate awaiting those who do not come to repentance (2 Pet. 3:9; cf. Matt. 13:3, 5), who reject love of the truth (2 Thess. 2:10), who go on the broad way "that leads to destruction" (Matt. 7:13), or who are enemies of the cross of Christ (Phil. 3:18–19). Judas (Jn. 17:12) and the Antichrist (2 Thess. 2:3) are described as two people "doomed to destruction."

4. *Apollyōn* (only in Rev. 9:11) is given as a translation of *ᵓabaddôn* (cf. Job 26:6; 28:22; Ps. 88:11; Prov. 15:11). It refers to the angelic king of the underworld, the prince of the scorpions, the Destroyer.

See also *olethros*, destruction, ruin (*3897*); *phtheirō*, destroy, ruin (*5780*); *exaleiphō*, wipe away, blot out (*1981*).

725 (ara, curse), → 2932.

736	ἀργύριον

ἀργύριον (*argyrion*), silver (*736*); ἄργυρος (*argyros*), silver (*738*); ἀργυροῦς (*argyrous*), made of silver (*739*); ἀργυροκόπος (*argyrokopos*), silversmith (*737*).

CL & OT The Gk. word derives from the adj. *argos*, shining, white, and occurs first in Homer. While the word denotes anything silver, it often has the significance of money. In the LXX *argyrion* occurs frequently in the OT, often in connection with gold. Silver was less plentiful in ancient Babylon and Egypt. The Bible mentions it early on as a medium of exchange (Gen. 23:15), and this use predominates in the OT. But it was also used for jewelry (Exod. 3:22; Song 1:11) and was sometimes fashioned into an idol (Jdg. 17:3). Mining for silver is mentioned in Job 28:1, and because it was rarely found in pure form, it regularly needed refining, whereby the dross was burned away in a hot fire and the pure silver remained. The OT refers to this process as symbolic of God's refining process in human hearts, so that he can make them pure and valuable to his service (Ps. 12:6; 66:10; Isa. 48:10; Zech. 13:9; Mal. 3:3; cf. Dan. 11:35; 12:10).

NT The NT frequently uses words in this word group. *argyrion* occurs 20x; *argyros*, 5x; *argyrous*, 3x, and *argyrokopos*, once.

Silver was used far more frequently than gold (→ *chrysos*, *5996*) in the NT world as an exchange of currency. Undoubtedly this was because silver was seen as not worth as much as gold. When Peter and

John encountered a crippled man while they were entering the temple, Peter said, "Silver or gold I do not have" (Acts 3:6). Peter did not have money to give to this man, but he did have the power of Jesus to make him walk. Similarly, when Jesus sent out the Twelve on their mini-mission journeys, he instructed them not to take "any gold or silver or copper in your belts" (Matt. 10:9; cf. Lk. 9:3); rather, they were to be dependent on the people with whom they stayed for physical needs. When Judas bargained with the Jewish authorities about a price for betraying Jesus, he was given thirty silver coins (Matt. 26:15; 27:3–9). Note that the NIV translates *argyrion* as "money" more than half of its occurrences in the NT (e.g., Matt. 25:18, 27; 28:12, 15).

Like gold, silver was also used as a precious metal for a wide variety of purposes, both decorative and religious. It could be used as a commodity in its own right (Rev. 18:12), for valuable articles in one's home (2 Tim. 2:20), and for idols (Acts 17:29; 19:24; Rev. 9:20). In connection with this last item, a riot erupted at Ephesus when the association of silversmiths, led by Demetrius, realized that their business of making silver shrines of the temple to Artemis in Ephesus was suffering because of the success of Paul's preaching of the gospel (Acts 19:23–40).

As with any worldly possession, silver or gold can easily become an object of coveting (Acts 20:33). It has no lasting value; the only thing that makes life worth living is the "precious blood of Christ, a lamb without blemish or defect," which has redeemed us (1 Pet. 1:18–19). James points out the temporary nature of silver and how it can become "corroded" and thus lose its value (Jas. 5:3). When the apostle Paul uses picturesque language to refer to building fruitful, enduring lives on the foundation of the church, which is Jesus Christ, he talks about using "gold, silver, costly stones," in contrast to those who build with elements that will not stand the test of God's fire of judgment, "wood, hay or straw" (1 Cor. 3:12). This last reference points to the metaphorical use in the Bible of the refining process of silver (see OT, above).

737 (*argyrokopos*, silversmith), → *736*.

738 (*argyros*, silver), → *736*.

739 (*argyrous*, made of silver), → *736*.

742 (*areskeia*, the desire to please), → *743*.

743	ἀρέσκω

ἀρέσκω (*aresko*), strive to please, accommodate, please (*743*); ἀρεστός (*arestos*), pleasing (*744*); ἀρεσκεία (*areskeia*), the desire to please (*742*); εὐάρεστος (*euarestos*), acceptable, pleasing (*2298*); εὐαρεστέω (*euaresteo*), please (someone), take pleasure in (*2297*); ἀνθρωπάρεσκος (*anthropareskos*), one who tries to please people (*473*).

CL & OT 1. In cl. Gk. *aresko* denotes the pleasure that human beings or the gods derive from something. From the vb. are derived the adjs. *arestos*, pleasant, *euarestos*, pleasing, content, and *areskeia*, pleasure, grace.

2. (a) Formations peculiar to the LXX are *euaresteo*, find pleasure, be content, and *anthropareskos*, someone who seeks to please people (only in Ps. 53:5, a mistranslation of a Heb. word meaning "he who encamps against you"; it also occurs in *Pss. Sol.* 4:7, 8, 19).

(b) *aresko* occurs 60x in the LXX, *arestos* 33x, as a translation of good, right. The former is often a part of the expression, "It will please God . . ." (Num. 23:27; cf. also Mal. 3:4). A word may be said to please someone, meet with approval—e.g., the king and the assembly (2 Chr. 30:4), the king and his commanders (1 Macc. 6:60).

(c) *areskeia* is found only in Prov. 31:30; *euarestos* only in Wis. 4:10; 9:10. The vb. *euaresteo* occurs 14x, generally for the Heb. word meaning to walk (with God; e.g., Gen. 5:24, where the Heb. stresses that "Enoch walked with God," whereas the LXX says that "Enoch pleased God").

NT 1. In the NT *aresko* is found 17x (14x in Paul). (a) Paul's use of the vb. 3x in Rom. 15:1–3 is noteworthy. He charges the self-styled "strong" Christian with being concerned about pleasing himself, i.e., being self-centered (15:1); instead everyone should seek to please one's neighbor, to build that person up (15:2). This does not mean pleasing others in the sense of looking for approbation and recognition from them (cf. Eph. 6:6), but doing God's will in the form of loving one's neighbor—esp. a weak fellow believer. The basic direction of Christian conduct is grounded in the attitude of Christ (Rom. 15:3), who did not live to please himself. Rather, he assumed the attitude of the OT servant of God (Ps. 69:9), who submitted himself in obedience toward God.

(b) *aresko* in Paul is thus a term that characterizes an attitude to life. He knows this from his own experience. Through his conversion he was freed from concern about pleasing other people, for he stood under the Lord's command. Now, therefore, he seeks to please God and Christ, not human beings (see 1 Thess. 2:4). Aligning himself with Christ and the goal set by him of saving everyone, Paul seeks to "please everybody in every way," that they may be saved (1 Cor. 10:33; cf. also Rom. 12:17–18; 1 Cor. 9:22, though the vb. is not used in these verses). The Christian congregation must also see how they can please God (1 Thess. 4:1).

(c) In 2 Tim. 2:4 Paul adopts the picture of the soldier used elsewhere in Hel. moral teaching (cf. 1 Cor. 9:7; Phil. 2:25; Phlm. 2). A soldier on active service does not get involved in civilian life but aims to please his commanding officer. A believer must therefore not be diverted from his or her work for Christ by concern about earthly welfare. Similarly, the unmarried man who is not tied by marital considerations can direct all his energy into gaining Christ's approbation and recognition (1 Cor. 7:32). On the other hand, "those controlled by the sinful nature cannot please God" (Rom. 8:8). The Jews who put Jesus and the prophets to death "displease God and are hostile to all men" (1 Thess. 2:15).

2. *arestos*, pleasing, occurs 4x in the NT. In Acts 12:3 the execution of James is said to have been pleasing to the Jews. Elsewhere God is the object of the pleasing. In Acts 6:2 the expression "it would not be right [i.e., before God]" uses this adj. In Jn. 8:29, Jesus says that he always does what pleases God, i.e., what is consonant with his will. Because Christians keep God's commandments and do what pleases him, they receive from him in prayer whatever they ask (1 Jn. 3:22).

3. *euarestos*, pleasing (8x in Paul and once in Heb.), also has God or Christ as its object (except for Tit. 2:9, though even here, God is in the picture of slaves as they try to please their masters; cf. Eph. 6:6). Children are to obey their parents, because "this pleases the Lord" (Col. 3:20). Paul thanks the Philippians for their gift, which is a "sacrifice, pleasing to God" (Phil. 4:18). The Christians in Rome must offer their bodies as sacrifices, "holy and pleasing to God" (Rom. 12:1; cf. v. 2). Believers exist "to please" God (2 Cor. 5:9). Anyone who serves Christ in righteousness, peace, and joy in the Holy Spirit "is pleasing to God" (Rom. 14:18). Therefore, we must pray that God may work in us through Christ "what is pleasing to him" (Heb. 13:21).

4. *euaresteo*, please, occurs 3x in Heb. In 11:5–6 the author takes up the Enoch story of Gen. 5:24. Enoch "pleased God" as a believer (cf. comments above about the use of *euaresteo* in this verse in the LXX); without faith no one can "please God" (11:6). In the Christian life acts of love are "sacrifices" with which "God is pleased" (13:16).

5. *areskeia* occurs only in Col. 1:10. Paul prays that the Colossians may be filled with the knowledge of God's will and with wisdom so that they may walk worthily of the Lord and "please him in every way."

6. *anthropareskos* occurs only in Paul's rule to slaves (Eph. 6:6; Col. 3:22), who must obey their masters not only to "win their favor," but out of reverence for the Lord.

See also *eudokeo*, be well pleased, regard favorably, take delight in (*2305*).

744 (*arestos*, pleasing), → *743*.

| 746 | ἀρετή |

ἀρετή (*aretē*), virtue (*746*).

CL & OT 1. (a) In cl. Gk. *aretē* was used with reference to things, animals, human beings, and gods. It could connote the excellent quality of arms or horses. Homer speaks of the *aretē* of the gods and demonstrations of their power. This religious usage goes into the Hel. period. Usually, however, the reference is to human qualities: e.g., *aretē* of feet, in fighting, or of the mind. Thus *aretē* is used of the whole person, of both physical and spiritual abilities. It can describe quality of women or courage of men.

(b) The meaning of *aretē* as virtue is limited in the case of Socrates, who used it to describe not general human qualities that are outwardly apparent, but inner morality. He made *aretē* into something based on one's striving for the good and suggested that virtue may be learned.

Plato saw *aretē* as conditioned by the soul, and in his doctrine of the soul he developed the sequence of the four classic virtues: *sophia*, wisdom; *andreia*, courage; *sōphrosynē*, prudence; and *dikaiosynē*, justice. This scheme of the four cardinal virtues is taken over by the wisdom lit. and Cicero.

In contrast to the psychology of Plato, Aristotle regarded *aretē* as the permanent pattern of behavior in a person, depending on one's qualities and decisions. He distinguished between ethical (practical) virtues (e.g., courage, temperance, and generosity) and dianoetic virtues (e.g., insight, wisdom, knowledge, and art). *aretē* is defined as the mean between two extremes.

The Stoics emphasized the agreement between the virtues and human nature; to live according to nature means to live according to virtue. They serve no outside purpose, such as the interests of the state or of the gods, but are an end in themselves, bringing the goal of happiness.

2. (a) The Heb. language has no word corresponding to *aretē*. The only places where this word occurs in the canonical books of the LXX are Isa. 42:8, 12; 43:21; 63:7; Hab. 3:3, where it means praise of Yahweh, praiseworthy deed; and Zech. 6:13, where it refers to the majesty of Joshua, the priestly messiah-designate.

(b) *aretē* is often mentioned in the books of Macc., esp. 4 Macc., where it often means the martyrs' loyalty to the faith, which they kept until death (7:22; 9:8, 18). In 2 Macc. 6:31 the martyrdom of Eleazar is called a memorial of his *aretē* (cf. 4 Macc. 1:8, 10). At the same time, we find the Gk. concept of *aretē* as courage (2 Macc. 15:17), manliness (4 Macc. 17:23), cleverness (1:2), or reason (1:30). Gk. influence can be detected also in Wis. 5:13, where virtue is contrasted with wickedness, and in 4:1, where it is linked with immortality. In 8:7 the four Platonic cardinal virtues are named.

NT *aretē* does not play a crucial part in the vocabulary of the NT, where it appears only 5x. More important are the catalogues of virtues (and vices), in which the virtues of the Christian (and vices of the non-Christian) are spelled out.

1. In 1 Pet. 2:9 and 2 Pet. 1:3 it is God's *aretē* that is mentioned. Since 1 Pet. 2:9 is a citation of the LXX of Isa. 43:21, the acc. pl. *aretas* should be rendered as praiseworthy acts. These are to be proclaimed by God's people. More Gk. thought may be recognized in 2 Pet. 1:3–4, which mentions, along with *aretē*, *doxa* (glory) and *dynamis* (power). *aretē* here means God's attribute of perfection, which through its manifestations of power has granted gifts to us by which we are to become partakers of the divine nature (cf. Matt. 5:48). In the background here is the Gk. idea of the relatedness of divine nature and human nature (cf. also Acts 17:28).

2. Phil. 4:8 and 2 Pet. 1:5 speak of human virtue. In both cases *aretē* forms part of a series in a comprehensive list of virtues, and both series have parallels in cl. lit. *aretē* is used here as in 4 Macc. but is a general term for good and correct behavior in Christians.

3. The connection between individual words for various NT virtues and corresponding lists in non-Christian Gk. lit. is indisputable,

even though *aretē* is not used. Note how Paul speaks unreservedly about "what is good" (Rom. 12:9) or about "whatever is right, whatever is pure, whatever is lovely" (Phil. 4:8) as the goal Christians ought to strive to attain. The earliest church was thus fully aware of good qualities in the heathen and brought conscience (Rom. 2:14) and virtue into its Christian proclamation.

Nevertheless, we should not overlook the differences between Stoic and Christian lists of virtues, or between the Gk. and NT concepts of virtue. The Platonic scheme of the four cardinal virtues does not appear in the NT catalogues. Instead, all the Christian virtues are brought under the main concepts of love (Gal. 5:22; Eph. 4:32–5:2; Col. 3:12) or of faith (Eph. 4:2–5; 2 Pet. 1:5) and are controlled by these. Nor does the NT know the Aristotelian distinction between practical and theoretical virtues. It stresses rather the totality of our actions, both as practical acts and as expressions of obedience.

Finally—and this is of great importance—the Stoic's view of a person being autonomous in one's virtues is foreign to the NT. Here the virtues are the fruit of the Spirit (Gal. 5:22–23), subservient to mutual love and the glorification of God. Hence, the NT virtues are seen as gracious gifts of the divine Spirit; they are the actions and the marks of God's new creation.

See also (*anenklētos*), not accused, without reproach, blameless, irreproachable (*441*).

748 (*arēn*, lamb), → *303*.

749 (*arithmeō*, to number), → *750*.

| 750 | ἀριθμός |

ἀριθμός (*arithmos*), number (*750*); ἀριθμέω (*arithmeō*), to number (*749*).

CL & OT 1. (a) In cl. Gk. *arithmos* denotes a quantity, total, number, amount (e.g., of gold). It can also mean the assessment of numbers, i.e., count, muster, and then a troop or military unit. Where *arithmos* is understood as quantity as opposed to quality, it can mean the virtual embodiment of what is worthless (e.g., "number of words" can mean "empty words"). Occasionally *arithmos* has the sense of code, cipher.

(b) In popular and religious Hel. thought, *gematria* (the process of encoding a word by adding together the numerical value of its component letters) gained popularity. The decoding of a gematrical number was only possible for the initiated.

2. In the LXX *arithmos* most commonly means number (e.g., Gen. 34:30; Exod. 16:16). It can also mean measure (Ps. 39:4), sum, or total (Num. 1:49; 1 Chr. 7:5; Isa. 34:2). In 2 Chr. 17:14 it has the idea of enrollment.

2. In rab. and Jewish Hel. literature, gematria is also found as an exegetical method and for solving problems. *Tg. Onq.*, for example, replaces the information in Num. 12:1 that Moses took a "Cushite" (heathen) wife by the information that the woman was "lovely to look at," since both words produce the numerical value 736.

NT 1. *arithmos* occurs only 18x in the NT (10x in Rev.); *arithmeō*, 3x. By and large, the noun simply means "number" (e.g., Rom. 9:27; Rev. 20:8) and is used for numerical details (e.g., Jn. 6:10, untranslated in the NIV; Acts 4:4; Rev. 5:11; 7:4). The meaning in Lk. 22:3 is perhaps "company" (i.e., lit. "Judas . . . being among the company of the Twelve"). Jesus uses *arithmeō* when he says that the hairs of our head are numbered, showing God's incredible care in our lives (Matt. 10:30; Lk. 12:7); the vb. is also used for the great multitude in Rev. 7:9 that "no one could number."

2. In Rev. 13:17–18 *arithmos* denotes a code or cipher for the number 666. Doubtless we have here a functional gematria, which puts into code the name of the person intended. The context speaks pictorially of a "beast" (→ *thērion*, 2563), which has traditionally been understood as the Antichrist. "The number of the beast," which

is stated as being a "man's number," shows that behind the beast and its number is concealed a human figure known to the hearers and readers of the text of that time. This excludes all attempts to decode the number that do not relate to a human figure. Note, of course, that the text does not make it explicit whether one is to use the Gk. or Heb. alphabet for interpreting the number, though the text itself is in Gk.

Of the many attempts at interpretation, the consonantal Heb. script for "Caesar Nero" (*qsr nrwn* = 100 + 60 + 200 + 50 + 200 + 6 + 50 = 666) has some probability. This solution is all the more attractive in that, combined with Rev. 17:11 ("the beast who once was, and now is not"), it may refer to the legend of *Nero redivivus*, so that the Antichrist is thus being painted in the colors of the hated Nero. That this legend story is also known from Jewish apocalyptic lit. supports this. But no definitive interpretation of 13:17–18 can be given.

3. As the process of gematria has shown, numbers in the ancient world do not merely indicate quantities but also qualities. Some numbers possess an almost fixed symbolic meaning. This is esp. true in the NT of four, seven, and twelve. For more on such numbers, see one, *heis* (1651); two, *dyo* (1545); three, *treis* (5552); four, *tessares* (5475); five, *pente* (4297); seven, *hepta* (2231); eight, *oktō* (3893); ten, *deka* (1274); twelve, *dōdeka* (1557); forty, *tesserakonta* (5477); seventy, *hebdomēkonta* (1573); and a thousand, *chilias* (5942).

4. Care must be taken not to attribute theological significance to the use of particular numbers when it is unclear that such significance was intended. Many cases are best treated as literal or rhetorical or round-number approximations.

Yet some cases are less obvious. In Matt. 1 the genealogy of Jesus is schematized into sequences of fourteen, which is double seven. The enumeration here is selective and cannot be treated as being exhaustive. It is therefore reasonable to suppose that the generations listed have been chosen with some purpose in mind, though we do not know whether that purpose was theologically significant or simply rhetorical or mnemonic.

The total of 153 fish in Jn. 21:11 is another debatable instance. Several church fathers opted for a symbolic interpretation. Some modern scholars have explained the figure by gematria or as a "triangular" number, following Augustine. But perhaps it is best just to take the number literally. Ancient sources do suggest the practice of counting a catch of fish in order to share them among the participating fishermen. Note that John elsewhere gives precise numbers where it is superfluous to look for a symbolic meaning (e.g., 46 in 2:20; 38 in 5:5), and Jn.'s constant emphasis on witness belies the esoteric.

There is no doubt, of course, that numbers are often used symbolically in Rev. It is surely significant, for example, that there were *seven* churches in Asia being addressed. Yet note that the choice of seven is in part dictated by geographical particularities, for the seven cities mentioned were the most efficient centers of communication for the churches of the province.

754	ἀριστερός

ἀριστερός (*aristeros*), left, left hand (754); εὐώνυμος (*euōnymos*), left (hand) (2381).

CL & OT 1. In cl. Gk. *aristeros* meant the opposite of *dexios* (→ 1288), that is, left (as opposed to right). The fem. by itself (with *cheir* understood) denoted the left hand or left side. Derivative meanings include clumsy and unlucky, foreboding. *euōnymos* (a combination of *eu* and *onoma*) etymologically meant honorable, of good name. For some reason very early this word became a euphemistic synonym of *aristeros*.

2. Both *aristeros* (e.g., Gen. 14:15; 24:49) and *euōnymos* (e.g., Exod. 14:22, 29; Num. 20:17) occur in the OT. Significance is attached to which hand Jacob used in blessing the sons of Joseph in Gen. 48:14. The left is a symbol for folly and ill fortune in Eccl. 10:2.

NT In general the NT avoids these words' sinister connotations and uses them for the left hand or side. Regarding *aristeros* Paul speaks of having "weapons of righteousness in the right hand and in the left" (2 Cor. 6:7) in his defense of his ministry. James and John use the expression *ex aristerōn* in expressing their desire for the chief places at the right and left hand of Jesus in his kingdom (Mk. 10:37). Lk. 23:33 mentions the two malefactors crucified on the right and left of Jesus. *euōnymos* is used in the same contexts in Mk. 10:40 and 15:27 (cf. Matt. 20:21, 23; 27:38). This word also has a neutral sense in Acts 21:3 (NIV "south") and Rev. 10:2. But *euōnymos* does have a pejorative sense in Matt. 25:33, 41 in the parable of the sheep and the goats; those who are judged are placed on the judge's left.

See also *dexios*, right, right hand, right side (1288); *cheir*, hand (5931); *epitithēmi*, to put on, lay on (2202).

757 (*arketos*, enough, sufficient, adequate), → 758.

758	ἀρκέω

ἀρκέω (*arkeō*), be enough, suffice, be adequate; pass. be satisfied or content with (758); ἀρκετός (*arketos*), enough, sufficient, adequate (757); αὐτάρκεια (*autarkeia*), sufficiency, contentment (894); αὐτάρκης (*autarkēs*), self-sufficient, independent, content (895).

CL & OT 1. In Homer *arkeō*, to suffice, be sufficient, pass. be satisfied, had the meaning to give protection, ward off, have power, help. Later it means to suffice, satisfy. The adj. *arketos* does not occur until the 1st cent. A.D. and means sufficient; the noun *autarkeia* denotes a sufficiency of means, competence, such as that enjoyed by an independent, self-supporting person. Similarly, *autarkēs* means self-sufficient, hence strong, and is frequently found with the vb. *einai*, to be, in the sense of to be satisfied.

In the moral philosophy of Stoicism the ability to be content became the essence of all the virtues. To practice this virtue was to acquiesce wisely in that which suited one's nature. Stoics prided themselves in becoming independent of things and relying on themselves or in submitting to the lot meted out by the gods.

2. The LXX makes little use of this word group. In Num. 11:22 *arkeō* means be sufficient; in 1 Ki. 8:27, contain, be sufficient for; in Prov. 30:15 [= LXX 24:50]; 2 Macc. 5:15; Wis. 14:22; 4 Macc. 6:28, to satisfy. But OT piety knows more about contentment than this mere incidence of words might imply (cf. Ps. 73:23–28; 131; Hos. 12:8–9; 13:6).

NT 1. The words in this group are not widely used in the NT. *arkeō* expresses the idea that something is sufficient (e.g., oil, Matt. 25:9; bread, Jn. 6:7); it also describes the attitude of mind that is satisfied or content with what is available (Heb. 13:5), with food and clothing (1 Tim. 6:8), or with wages (Lk. 3:14).

2. *arketos*, enough, is used as an adjectival predicate in Matt. 6:34; 10:25; 1 Pet. 4:3. In 2 Cor. 9:8, Paul uses *autarkeia* to show the Corinthians that if they give from the heart, they will have "all that [they] need," i.e., God will richly bestow on them the necessities of life. The mark of *autarkeia* is no longer autonomy and self-sufficiency but freedom to give to others; we are not to live exclusively for ourselves. In 1 Tim. 6:6 Paul uses the same word to say that contentment, when linked with godliness, is great gain.

3. (a) Such an attitude of contentment presupposes in the NT the trust and confidence that God's children have in their heavenly Father. Since they are secure in his love, they can be content with what they have, because it is allotted to them by God himself. In his promises, he undertakes to watch over his people all their lives (Heb. 13:5). Such confidence banishes anxiety about the future because the future, like the present, is provided for by God (Matt. 6:34). His children are delivered from anxiety about themselves so that they may be free to care for others.

(b) In Phil. 4:11 Paul describes his own attitude: He has learned, in whatever state he is, to be content (*autarkēs*). Such contentment springs from complete readiness to accept whatever God gives. The apostle makes no distinction between the necessary and the superfluous, but simply gives thanks for everything. He can accept both abundance and want as part of his life, and he gives thanks that he has received both as a gift, together with God's gracious forgiveness and quickening power. As an example of this attitude we should note Paul's thorn in the flesh. He exercises contentment here and requests no more than God is graciously pleased to give. This thorn serves as a repeated reminder to Paul that he is utterly dependent, in all that he does, on the enabling power of his Lord (2 Cor. 12:1–10).

4. The scope of this word group becomes clear in Jn. 14:8. Philip claims that if he and the other disciples were shown the Father, then "that will be enough [*arkeō*] for us." Jesus answers that their true need, like that of all people, is in fact more limited: It is sufficient to see Christ, for those who see him also see the Father. Christ's revelation of God is the most comprehensive and complete revelation conceivable to anyone.

See also *hikanos*, enough, worthy, able, competent, qualified (*2653*).

762 (Harmagedōn, Armageddon), → 4483.

766	ἀρνέομαι

ἀρνέομαι (*arneomai*), refuse, deny, dispute, disown, disregard (*766*); ἀπαρνέομαι (*aparneomai*), deny, disown, renounce (*565*).

CL & OT *arneomai* means deny, refuse, reject; its opposite is *didōmi*, grant, give. Regarding a matter needing clarification, the vb. means dispute, contest; its opposite is *homologeō*, agree, assent to. Later *arneomai* developed the meaning disown, renounce. It is in this sense that the originally intensive form *aparneomai* is mostly used in the NT.

In Gen. 18:15 *arneomai* means dispute, deny; *aparneomai* (Isa. 31:7) means reject. In the Apocr. *arneomai* has the sense of refuse (Wis. 12:27; 16:16; 17:10) and renounce (4 Macc. 8:7; 10:15).

NT 1. *arneomai* occurs 33x in the NT and *aparneomai* 11x. In addition to the senses of refuse (Heb. 11:24) and deny (Jn. 1:20), the vbs. have the specific sense of disown in relation to Jesus Christ.

2. Denial and rejection of Jesus Christ can be the result of ignorance (Acts 3:13–14, cf. v. 17). Generally, however, *arneomai* means that one falls back from a previous relationship with him into unfaithfulness (2 Pet. 2:1; Jude 4). This is the meaning of Peter's denial (Mk. 14:30, 68, 70). In 1 Jn. 2:22–23, certain heretics were denying that Jesus was the Messiah. The opposite of denying Jesus Christ is holding fast (Rev. 2:13) or being faithful (2:10) to him. Used absolutely, *arneomai* can mean to abandon fellowship with the Lord (2 Tim. 2:12).

Denial of Jesus is not only a matter of the lips; it is failure in discipleship. At a time of suffering there is particular danger of denying the Lord (Rev. 2:13; 3:8; cf. 2 Tim. 2:11–12). The motive for denial is usually fear of others, fear of suffering ridicule or persecution, or anxiety about what others will think.

3. Denial of Christ is also present where one refuses to fulfill one's responsibility before God (1 Tim. 5:8). Moreover, denial of God on our part will be met by a denial of us on God's part (Lk. 12:9; 2 Tim. 2:12). For denial is a rejection of God's offer of salvation and a conscious renunciation of his grace. God, however, "cannot disown himself" (2 Tim. 2:13); he remains true to his own nature.

4. To follow him who "made himself nothing" (Phil. 2:7) implies to deny oneself and take up one's cross (Matt. 16:24; Mk. 8:34; Lk. 9:23; → *stauros*, 5089). Interpreted in the light of Peter's denial, this means to say no to oneself and to surrender oneself totally, even if it means dying a martyr's death. But the connection with Paul's remarks about being buried with Christ (Rom. 6:4–5) and being crucified with Christ so that he lives in us (Gal. 2:20) should not be overlooked. Self-

denial is not therefore a legalistic demand, but the way forward into life "in Christ."

768 (arnion, lamb), → 303.

771 (harpagē, robbery, plunder, greediness, rapacity), → 773.

772 (harpagmos, robbery, prize, booty), → 773.

773	ἁρπάζω

ἁρπάζω (*harpazō*), snatch, seize (*773*); ἁρπαγμός (*harpagmos*), robbery, that of which someone is robbed, prize, booty (*772*); ἁρπαγή (*harpagē*), robbery, plunder, greediness, rapacity (*771*); ἅρπαξ (*harpax*), rapacious, ravenous, a robber, swindler (*774*); μετατίθημι (*metatithēmi*), to transfer, change the position of, change, turn away (*3572*).

CL & OT 1. In cl. Gk. *harpazō* is related to Lat. *rapio*, seize, snatch, and means to snatch, seize, carry off, rob, plunder, ravish. *harpagmos* means both robbery, rape, and the thing of which a person is robbed, a prize to be grasped.

2. *harpazō* in the LXX means to take away, rob (e.g., Lev. 6:4; 19:13; Jdg. 21:23; Ps. 7:3; Isa. 10:2; Mic. 3:2), tear (in pieces) (e.g., Gen. 37:33; Ps. 22:13; 104:21; Amos 3:4). In Ps. 50:22, Yahweh, facing an apostate people, is compared to a lion rending his prey in pieces.

Only once in the LXX does *harpazō* have the meaning rapture, being caught up: Wis. 4:11, apparently referring to Enoch and Elijah, says that they "were caught up" (*metatithēmi* is used elsewhere in the LXX and in cl. Gk.; e.g., Gen. 5:24; Wis. 4:10; Sir. 44:16; 49:14). The translation of Enoch (Gen. 5:24) appears frequently in Jewish lit.; thus, it is important to discuss what is meant by the rapture in Gen. 5:24. Enoch, because his life pleased God, was taken directly into God's presence without first going to Sheol (→ *hadēs*, 87). The manner in which this took place is not mentioned (cf. Heb. 11:5, where *metatithēmi* is used). Elijah was taken directly into God's fellowship in a fiery chariot (2 Ki. 2:11–12; for further discussion, → *anastasis*, 414).

NT 1. (a) *harpazō* is found 14x in the NT. As in cl. Gk. and the LXX, it can mean steal, carry off, drag away (Matt. 12:29; Jn. 10:12). It also means to lead away forcibly (Jn. 6:15; 10:28–29; Acts 23:10; Jude 23). It is used of the Spirit's carrying someone away in Acts 8:39; 2 Cor. 12:2, 4; 1 Thess. 4:17; Rev. 12:5.

(b) We must distinguish in the NT between movement from one place on earth to another and being caught up into a supernatural world. (i) Following the baptism of the Ethiopian eunuch, "the Spirit of the Lord suddenly took Philip away" (Acts 8:39). This should be taken spatially and really. It has close links with 2 Ki. 2, even in verbal details (cf. esp. 2:12). But it may also be compared with the Spirit driving Jesus into the desert after his baptism (cf. Matt. 4:1; Mk. 1:12; Lk. 4:1).

(ii) But 2 Cor. 12:2–10 is based on a different concept. There Paul tells of an experience between just God and himself, in which he was "caught up into the third heaven." He is not even sure how to explain it, but this rapture gave him a high degree of ecstatic experience. There he hears "inexpressible things," which leaves an indelible impression on him. Still, in contrast to his opponents, Paul knew that he had not reached final perfection in his rapture, for that would have made faith unnecessary. Moreover, because he was uncertain what to make of the experience, he was reluctant to write about it.

(c) In 1 Thess. 4:17 Paul deals with the final rapture into the fellowship of the redeemed at the last day. He addresses this topic because some members of the Thessalonian church had questions about the fate of believers who had already died. Paul answered this concern through the certainty of resurrection. Christians who are still alive when Jesus returns on the clouds of heaven will not die but will be taken up directly into the fellowship of those who have already been raised. They will meet the Lord Jesus in the air; the language is that of contemporary Jewish apocalyptic (On the view that *paralambanō* in Matt. 24:40–41; Lk. 17:34–35 refers to the same event, → *lambamō*, to take, *3284*.)

(d) In Rev. 12:5 the male child (representing Jesus) is "snatched up" to God to escape the persecution of the dragon; this is the expression in picture language of incidents like that recorded in Matt. 2:13–18.

(e) On the use of *harpazō* in Matt. 11:12, → *bia*, force, *1040*.

2. The noun *harpagmos* is found only in Phil. 2:6, where Paul refers to Jesus Christ, "who, being in very nature God, did not consider equality with God something to be grasped [*harpagmon*], but made himself nothing." This sentence occurs in what was probably an early Christian hymn (2:5–11). *harpagmos* most likely means a thing seized, like the spoil, booty, or prize of war. It denotes that which Christ refused to seize and hang on to for himself, namely, his being equal with God. He had every right to do so, of course, since he was God and shared God's throne. But he chose to empty himself (→ *kenoō*, *3033*) and took the form of a servant, which in turn provides the pattern for Christian conduct.

3. In Heb. 10:34, *harpagē* means robbery, plunder, namely, the forcible confiscation of Christian property. In Matt. 23:25; Lk. 11:39 it denotes the root cause of something that is plundered, namely, greed. Jesus charges the Pharisees with hypocrisy, i.e., having a clean outside but inside being filled with greediness. Elsewhere Jesus describes the greed of the Pharisees, who "devour widows' houses" (Lk. 20:47), i.e., betraying the financial trust that widows placed on them to manage their affairs after a husband's death and finding ways to take all their property.

4. *harpax* means rapacious, ravenous—of wolves (Matt. 7:15); and as a noun, a robber (Lk. 18:11; cf. 1 Cor. 5:10–11; 6:10).

774 (*harpax*, rapacious, ravenous, a robber, swindler), → *773*.

775	ἀρραβών

ἀρραβών (*arrabōn*), first installment, down payment, deposit, pledge, earnest (*775*).

CL & OT *arrabōn* is a legal concept borrowed from Sem. languages. It is rare and means (1) an installment with which one secures a legal claim on a thing as yet unpaid for; (2) an earnest, an advance payment, by which a contract becomes legally valid; and (3) in one passage (Gen. 38:17–20) a pledge. In each case a payment is involved by which a person guarantees further payment to the recipient.

NT *arrabōn* occurs 3x in the NT, all of them related to the Holy Spirit. Eph. 1:14 interprets the other two: The Spirit is the present earnest of our future inheritance, guaranteeing our complete, final salvation, i.e., eternal communion with God. This statement, as in 2 Cor. 1:22, is probably associated with baptism. In the sealing (→ *sphragis*, *5382*) of the believer through baptism, the Holy Spirit is given to the human heart as an earnest. The future reality represented by this earnest appears in 2 Cor. 5:5 as the "house" expected from heaven, which will one day replace the present "tent," our earthly body (5:1–4). This is similar to Paul's emphasis on our having "the firstfruits of the Spirit" (Rom. 8:23; → *aparchē*, *569*). The present reality of the Spirit is a sign and pledge of that which is to come.

In all three NT passages, however, the *arrabōn* should not be understood to imply that, in giving the earnest of the Spirit, God is legally our debtor. Even the installment of the Spirit remains a free, undeserved gift of God to us.

See also *dōron*, gift, present (*1565*); *korban*, corban, gift (*3167*).

779 (*arrōstos*, sick, ill), → *3798*.

780 (*arsenokoitēs*, male homosexual, pederast, sodomite), → *781*.

781	ἄρσην

ἄρσην (*arsēn*), male (*781*);
θῆλυς (*thēlys*), female (*2559*);
ἀρσενοκοίτης (*arsenokoitēs*), male homosexual, pederast, sodomite (*780*).

CL & OT 1. In cl. Gk. *arsēn* means male as opposed to female, *thēlys* (which with the art. can mean woman).

2. *arsēn* occurs 54x in the LXX. It appears in the phrase "male and female" in Gen. 1:27, regarding the creation of male and female in the image of God (cf. also 5:2; 6:19–20; Lev. 12:7; note that in Gen. 7:2–3, 9, 15–16; Lev. 3:1, 6, *arsēn* can refer to the male of an animal species). Male is referred to apart from female in passages such as Gen. 17:14, 23 (the institution of circumcision as the covenant sign); Exod. 1:16–18, 22; 2:2; 12:5 (the Passover lamb had to be a male without blemish); Mal. 1:14 (in connection with sacrifice); Lev. 18:22; 20:13 (in condemnation of homosexual practices); and Num. 1:2 [= LXX 1:3]; 3:40 (in the census of the people).

The references to male and female correspond to those of man and woman generally in the OT. On the one hand, there is a recognition in Gen. of the divinely instituted parity in that man and woman together constitute the image of God, and of their complementary roles in the transmission of life in both the human and the animal realm. On the other hand, there are certain roles (e.g., in receiving the covenant sign, in the priesthood, and in certain sacrifices) that only the male may fill.

NT 1. Matt. 19:4 refers to the creative act in Gen. 1:27 in connection with divorce. Jesus' reply to the Pharisees takes it as the major premise for his teaching on marriage: "At the beginning the Creator 'made them male [*arsēn*] and female [*thēlys*].'" This leads to the minor premise quoted from Gen. 2:24: "For this reason a man will leave his father and mother and be united to his wife, and the two will become one flesh" (Matt. 19:5). The conclusion is drawn: "So they are no longer two, but one. Therefore what God has joined together, let man not separate" (19:6).

2. In Lk. 2:23 Jesus' parents offered the sacrifice prescribed for males in Exod. 13:2, 12.

3. Paul's use of *arsēn* exhibits a tension between the creation ordinances and their abolition in the gospel age. By contrast, the ungodly have abolished the creation ordinances for perverted sexual relations in a way that can only bring judgment.

(a) In Rom. 1:27 *arsēn* is used 3x to denote (homo)sexual perversion as a result of worshiping the creature rather than the Creator. Because human beings have put something else in the place that properly belongs only to God, natural male-female relationships have been altered. Paul also uses the noun *arsenokoitēs* (a male homosexual, pederast, sodomite) as one who is excluded from the kingdom (1 Cor. 6:9) and condemned by the Mosaic law (1 Tim. 1:10; cf. Gen. 19; Lev. 18:22, 29; 20:13; Deut. 23:17).

(b) Gal. 3:28, by contrast, asserts that in Christ Jesus "there is neither Jew nor Greek, slave nor free, male nor female." This, however, is not a call to abolish all earthly relationships. Rather, it puts these relationships in the perspective of salvation history. As Paul goes on to say, "If you belong to Christ, then you are Abraham's seed, and heirs according to the promise" (Gal. 3:29; cf. also Rom. 10:2). All who are in Christ have the same status before God, but they do not necessarily have the same function. In the context of the circumcision question in Gal., the assertion is doubly relevant, for women could not receive the sign that Judaizers were insisting as a prerequisite for full salvation. There may also be an underlying Adam-typology in the passage, in that some rabbis asserted that Adam was originally androgynous.

4. Rev. 12:5, 13 takes up the imagery of Isa. 66:7 and Ps. 2:9 in the vision of the dragon's attack on the woman with the male child: "She gave birth to a son, a male child, who will rule all the nations with an iron scepter. . . . When the dragon saw that he had been hurled to the earth, he pursued the woman who had given birth to the male child." Whereas the child is here clearly Christ, the woman represents both the mother of Jesus and the church, whose other offspring are now pursued by the dragon.

See also *anēr*, a man (*467*); *anthrōpos*, human being (*476*); *gynē*, woman (*1222*).

785 (*arti*, now, just, immediately), → 2789.

---

787   ἄρτιος

ἄρτιος (*artios*), suitable, complete, capable, sound (*787*); καταρτίζω (*katartizō*), put in order, restore, make complete, prepare (*2936*); καταρτισμός (*katartismos*), preparation, equipment (*2938*); κατάρτισις (*katartisis*), being made complete, completion (*2937*); προκαταρτίζω (*prokatartizō*), get ready, arrange in advance (*4616*); ἐξαρτίζω (*exartizō*), finish, complete, equip, furnish (*1992*).

CL & OT 1. In cl. Gk. *artios* means suitable, appropriate, fitting a situation or requirements; hence also normal, perfect, sound in physical, intellectual, moral, and religious respects. In mathematics it describes what is straight and denotes even numbers (in contrast to *perissos*, odd). *katartizō* means put in order, restore, furnish, prepare, equip. *katartismos* and *katartisis* mean restoration.

2. The LXX uses *katartizō* 19x for various Heb. vbs. It is used for completing the building of the wall and temple by the postexilic community (Ezr. 4:12–13, 16; 5:3, 9, 11; 6:14). Other meanings of the vb. include: to set up, establish, in a literal sense (Ps. 8:2; 74:16); to hold one's steps fast to Yahweh's paths (17:5); to equip (40:6); and to restore (68:9). Frequently Yahweh is the subj. of sentences that refer to his work of establishing and founding. *artiōs* is used in the LXX only as a temporal adv. meaning until now (2 Sam. 15:34).

NT Of this group of words only *katartizō* is used with any frequently in the NT (13x), while *artios* (2 Tim. 3:17), *katartisis* (2 Cor. 13:9), and *katartismos* (Eph. 4:12) occur only once each.

1. At Matt. 4:21; Mk. 1:19, *katartizō* has the secular sense of repairing fishing nets. The NT also uses the vb. for to prepare (Matt. 21:16 [Ps. 8:2]; Rom. 9:22; Heb. 10:5 [Ps. 40:6]), to form (Heb. 11:3), and to equip (13:21; 1 Pet. 5:10). God is the subject of sentences that express his power to strengthen and establish.

2. Of particular importance are those passages in which *artios* and its derivatives are used in connection with the preparation and equipment of believers and the church for the service of God and their fellow believers. *artios* occurs in 2 Tim. 3:17 with the perf. pass. part. of *exartizō*, where it describes the OT Scriptures as an indispensable, God-given guide for equipping believers for every good work. So too in Eph. 4:12, *katartismos* refers to the preparation of the church for works of service, so that we may become mature believers (cf. 4:13).

artios and *katartismos* thus have not so much a qualitative meaning as a functional one. This standard hortatory use of *artios* and its derivatives arises from the fact that all imperatives are founded on the one indicative, i.e., the firm promise of salvation. The life of the saints is to correspond to God's free grace, which is itself the standard to which they are to aspire. It is on this ground that in 2 Cor. 13:11 and Gal. 6:1, *katartizō* can mean to restore; in 1 Thess. 3:10, to make up, to put in a fit state. *katartisis* in 2 Cor. 13:9 also comes into this category, where it refers to the restoration and perfection of the church.

3. At 2 Cor. 9:5 *prokatartizō* is used of arranging or gathering and making ready Paul's collection for Jerusalem; at Acts 21:5 *exartizō* means that "our time was up."

See also *axios*, of like value, fit, worthy, worth (*545*); *orthos*, upright, straight, right (*3981*).

---

788   ἄρτος

ἄρτος (*artos*), bread, loaf (*788*).

CL & OT Early on *artos* designated bread baked from various kinds of flour. Together with meat it was the most important form of food. Originally, Israelite bread was made from barley flour mixed with broad beans, lentils, and the like. Later, wheat bread became more common, but only the better off could afford it. Both forms of bread were made from ground grains to which yeast was normally added. It was baked on a griddle (Lev. 2:5) or in clay ovens (Hos. 7:4, 6–7). The flat loaves were about half an inch thick and could be as much as twenty inches in diameter.

When there were unexpected guests (Gen. 19:3) or when people were busy as at harvest time (Ruth 2:14), bread was baked from unleavened dough, or the grain was simply eaten roasted. Because the latter kept almost indefinitely, it was taken on sudden journeys (cf. 1 Sam. 17:17). The use of unleavened bread is linked especially with the exodus from Egypt (Exod. 12:8, 11, 34, 39). The annual observance of the Feast of Unleavened Bread (12:14–20; 13:3–10) meant the cultic representation of that rescue.

In the Israelite sacrificial system, flour or bread found a place as gifts in the grain offering (cf. Lev. 2). The twelve loaves of "the bread of the Presence" were placed on a special table in the sanctuary (Exod. 25:30; 1 Chr. 28:16). They were of unleavened bread and were placed as an offering before Yahweh.

In the early rab. period, the head of the house took the loaf from the table and pronounced a blessing. His guests answered, "Amen." He then gave a piece of bread to each guest but ate first himself. Jesus also offered a blessing at mealtime, as is suggested both in the accounts of the feeding of the five and four thousand (Mk. 6:41 par.; 8:6 par.) and of the Last Supper.

NT Since bread was such a staple, it was often used as a synonym for food and the support of life in general. The prodigal son in the far country remembers that his father's paid servants "have bread enough and to spare" (NIV, "have food to spare," Lk. 15:17). To eat bread means to have a meal (cf. Isa. 65:25); to break one's bread for the hungry means to feed and care for them (58:7, 10); not to eat another's bread without paying means to work with one's own hands (2 Thess. 3:8); to eat no bread and drink no wine means to live as an ascetic (Lk. 7:33). The fourth petition of the Lord's Prayer (Matt. 6:11) is concerned with all our bodily and spiritual needs. In quoting Deut. 8:3, "Man does not live on bread alone," Jesus was referring to material things in general, to which he opposed the life-sustaining power of God's word (Matt. 4:4).

The miracles of the feeding of the five thousand (Matt. 14:13–21 par.) and of the four thousand (15:32–39 par.), where a few loaves and a couple of fish fed many people, show that Jesus, the messianic Lord, gives the true bread of life (see Jn. 6:25–28, which follows the miracle). Behind the concept of the bread of life lies the ancient widespread desire for a food that would impart everlasting life (cf. 6:34). Jesus' answer was: I am what you are asking for; those who want to share in this eternal life must know that I myself am the bread and that I will give it to those who come to me. In saying this, Jesus opposes all others who claim to be or to have the bread of life.

For comments about bread in the Lord's Supper (Mk. 14:22 par.; Acts 2:42; 1 Cor. 10:16; 11:23), → *deipnon*, 1270.

See also *epiousios*, daily (*2157*); *manna*, manna (*3445*).

791 (*archangelos*, archangel), → 34.

792 (*archaios*, old, ancient), → 794.

---

794   ἀρχή

ἀρχή (*archē*), beginning, cause (*794*); ἄρχω (*archō*), to begin, to rule (*806*); ἄρχων (*archōn*), ruler, prince (*807*); ἀρχηγός (*archēgos*), ruler, leader (*795*); ἀρχαῖος (*archaios*), old, ancient (*792*).

CL & OT 1. In Gk. philosophy *archē* denotes the starting point, the first cause, and power, authority, or rule. The vb. *archō* commonly means be the first (to do something), begin by doing something, rule (as leader). Its part. *archōn* means ruler, prince; *archēgos* has a similar meaning. The adj. *archaios* denotes that which has been from early times; hence old, ancient.

When one spoke of the beginning (*archē*) in Gk. philosophy, the end (*telos*) was also in view. Since the beginning, the first cause of all that is, comes out of the infinite, so the end will also lose itself in the infinite. Gradually, *archē* developed its meaning from the underlying cause to the underlying laws that determine the development and progress of the cosmos.

2. The LXX uses this word group to translate over 30 Heb. words. (a) The vb. *archō* usually indicates the beginning of an action (e.g., Gen. 6:1; Deut. 1:5). This usage has no theological coloring.

(b) The concept of a beginning in time that is dominant in the vb. can be seen in an even more specialized sense in the noun *archē*, when it is used to translate Heb. ʿôlām, a distant time (Jos. 24:2; Isa. 63:16, 19), or qedem, antiquity, of old (e.g., Hab. 1:12; Ps. 74:2; Mic. 5:2). So used, it does not mean only the distant past in time, but the state that once was, the beginning of a nation or of the world. The adj. *archaios*, old, has more or less the same range of meaning (→ *palai, 4093*).

(c) The meaning of foremost or highest rank is found alongside the temporal meaning. This comes from its rendering of Heb. rōʾš, head, with its wide range of nuances, thus forcing *archē* to take on a wide range of meanings (e.g., Jer. 22:6, summit; Num. 1:2, census; Exod. 12:2, first [months]; 1 Ki. 21:9, 12 = LXX 20:9, 12, prominent [place]; → *prōtos, 4755*). The connotations of beginning and highest rank sometimes come together (e.g., Ps. 111:10, where the fear of the Lord is the *archē sophias* ["beginning of wisdom"]).

(d) From the Heb. rōʾš, *archē* takes on the meaning of command or the military unit command (Jdg. 9:34; 1 Sam. 11:11). The element of ruling is particularly clear when it is used to render memšālâ, rule, dominion (Gen. 1:16; Jer. 34:1 = LXX 41:1; Mic. 4:8).

(e) This lies behind the relatively unambiguous use of *archōn* (450x) and *archēgos* (34x) as a translation for rōʾš when it means a political or military leader, or a head of a family (e.g., Num. 25:4; 30:1 = LXX 30:2; 1 Chr. 8:6, 28; Neh. 11:3). *archōn* also is used for śar, holder of authority and power, leader (e.g., Gen. 12:15; Jdg. 8:3), and nāśîʾ, head of a tribe, patriarch (e.g., Num. 2:3, 5, 7; Ezek. 7:27), while *archēgos* denotes an elected charismatic leader in time of need (Heb. qāṣîn, Jdg. 11:6). Thus, *archēgos* refers more to the actual exercise of power and *archōn* more to the authority behind it. *archōn* can also extend to the celestial beings who represent the nations in the world of spirits and who in great measure are hostile to God's people (Dan. 10:13; cf. 7:27, *archē*).

NT The NT uses this word group in much the same way as secular Gk. They esp. denote a first point in time and indicate an area of authority.

1. (a) *archē* (55x in NT; 18x in the Johannine Gospel and letters) can mean beginning, commencement (Mk. 1:1; 13:8; Heb. 3:14). In Heb. 5:12; 6:1, it carries the meaning of groundwork, elementary teaching. The phrases apʾ *archēs* and ex *archēs* denote the first point in time, its occasion being determined from the context (e.g., "the beginning" of Jesus' activity, Lk. 1:2; cf. Jn. 15:27; 16:4). Jesus knew "from the beginning" whether someone believed (Jn. 6:64); John points to the command to love that the church had "since the beginning" (1 Jn. 2:7; cf. 2:24; 3:11; 2 Jn. 5–6); the devil was a murderer and liar "from the beginning" (Jn. 8:44; cf. 1 Jn. 3:8); Mk. 13:19 and 2 Pet. 3:4 look back to the beginning of the world. Acts 11:15 thinks of the first days of the church in Jerusalem, and Phil. 4:15 of the beginning of Paul's missionary activity.

(b) Jn. 1:1 implies something before time, i.e., not a beginning within time, but an absolute beginning, which can be affirmed only of God, of whom no temporal categories can be predicated. The Logos (Word) is in the strictest sense preexistent before the world began, and so before time began (cf. also 1 Jn. 1:1; 2:13–14).

(c) In Col. 1:18 *archē* may mean first cause or perhaps firstfruits (cf. *aparchē, 569*), in the sense of Christ as the firstfruits and the first-born from the dead. Paul may be calling Christ here the First Cause of creation, but it is equally possible that his existence before time is meant (cf. also Rev. 21:6; 22:13).

(d) *archē* can mean power, authorities, rulers (cf. Lk. 12:11; 20:20; Tit. 3:1, where it is linked with *exousia*, authority, and refers to the civil [Roman] or religious [Jewish] authorities). Persecution may

come from the leaders of the synagogues (Lk. 12:11). Tit. 3:1 calls for obedience to the civil powers and the authorities in general.

(e) In some NT passages *archē* means an angelic power. As in early rab. Jud., the world and all its manifestations and powers are regarded as under the control of angels and guided by them. While various categories of supernatural, heavenly beings are recognized (e.g., *archai, dynameis, exousiai*, cf. Col. 1:16), the NT sees no importance in working out their levels or specific functions. Rather, it stresses that they have been created through Christ and for him. Accordingly, Christ's reconciling act embraces the whole cosmos (1:20).

Christ is the head of every *archē* and *exousia* (Col. 2:10; cf. Phil. 2:10–11). These evil rulers and authorities, ruled by the devil (Eph. 6:12), brought him to the cross without recognizing him (1 Cor. 2:8); but on the cross Christ disarmed them, robbing them of their might (Col. 2:14–15). By his resurrection Christ was exalted to God's right hand above all these powers (Eph. 1:20–21). Nothing can now separate believers from the love of God (Rom. 8:38–39).

It is striking that the mystery (→ *mystērion, 3696*) of the call of the Gentiles to Christian faith should be made known to the principalities and powers in the heavenly places through the church (Eph. 3:10). This mystery has a cosmic meaning that reaches out into the spiritual world. In the end times, when God's kingdom will be established, Christ will destroy every *archē, dynamis*, and *exousia* (1 Cor. 15:24).

2. *archō* is found 86x in the NT. In the act. it means be the first, rule (Mk. 10:42; Rom. 15:12); in the mid., begin, commence. Often it occurs in an idiom that serves as a formal introduction to a speech or action (e.g., "he began to say . . . ") and can thus be left untranslated.

archō has its full meaning in Lk. 3:23: Jesus was about thirty years old when he began his work. Similarly, it marks a temporal beginning in Matt. 16:21 and in Lk. 24:27, where the resurrected Jesus explains the Scriptures, beginning with Moses and the Prophets. In 1 Pet. 4:17 judgment comes first to the household of God and then to the others.

3. *archaios* occurs 11x in the NT. The people of an older generation are called *hoi archaioi*, i.e., ancestors (Matt. 5:21). Some thought that Jesus was one of the prophets "of long ago" (i.e., who had lived in OT times and had come back to life; Lk. 9:8, 19). Mnason of Cyprus was an *archaios mathētēs*, a disciple who had known Jesus from the first days of the church (Acts 21:16). The "ancient world" (2 Pet. 2:5) is the world before the flood. Satan is "that ancient serpent"—alluding to the Eden story (Gen. 3)—who was active at the beginning of the world and of human history (Rev. 12:9; 20:2). Those who are in Christ are a new creation, in whom the "old," earthly nature with its sinful existence has passed away (2 Cor. 5:17).

4. *archēgos* (4x in the NT) is applied only to Jesus. (a) He is prince or "author of life" (Acts 3:15). The expression here means that Jesus Christ brings people to new life (cf. Jn. 1:4). God raised up Jesus, who had been murdered on the cross, and exalted him to his right hand as *archēgos* (Acts 5:31), i.e., "as Prince" (and Savior). The expression is parallel to 2:36: God has made Jesus *kyrios* (Lord) and Christ.

(b) Heb. 2:10 speaks solemnly of Christ as *archēgos tēs sōtērias* ("author of . . . salvation"; cf. 5:10; 6:20). Moreover, because Christ has himself reached the goal, he is not only the "author" but also the "perfecter" (*teleiōtēs*) of salvation (12:2).

5. *archōn* has several referents in the NT. (a) It is found 37x meaning ruler, prince. Only in Rev. 1:5 is it used of Christ, where (cf. Ps. 89:27) he is called the *archōn* of the kings of the earth (cf. Phil. 2:11; Rev. 19:16; → *kyrios, 3261*). Otherwise, the *archontes* are those who rule over the nations (Matt. 20:25; cf. Mk. 10:42). In Acts 4:25–26 (cf. Ps. 2:1–2) Herod and Pilate, both *archontes*, cooperated at the crucifixion of Jesus.

(b) *archōn* is also used to denote the synagogue authorities (e.g., Matt. 9:18, 23; Lk. 8:41), the lay members of the Sanhedrin (e.g., 23:13, 35; Jn. 3:1), members of the highest Jewish authorities (7:26, 48; Acts 3:17; 4:5, 8), and the high priest (23:5). Exod. 2:14 is quoted in Acts 7:27: An Israelite refused to recognize Moses as his ruler, or as one set in authority over him. In Lk. 14:1 it refers to a "prominent Pharisee." In Acts 14:5 Jewish and Gentile authorities are hostile to the apostle. Paul and Silas were dragged before the *archontes* of Philippi (16:19). In his teaching about the state Paul says that the authorities (*archontes*) are not a cause of fear to those who do good (Rom. 13:3).

(c) In addition evil spirits can be called *archontes* (→ *daimonion*, *1228*). The Pharisees accused Jesus of driving out demons by the power of the *archōn* of the demons, meaning Beelzebub as the *diabolos* (Matt. 9:34; 12:24; cf. 10:25; Mk. 3:22; Lk. 11:15). Satan, prince (*archōn*) of this world (cf. Eph. 2:2), has been judged (Jn. 16:11) and cast out of heaven through the death and exaltation of Jesus (12:31). He tries in vain to get hold of Jesus and destroy him (14:30). The whole of the present world is under *archontes*, who are on their way to destruction (1 Cor. 2:6). They have a wisdom that contrasts with the wisdom of God. It is these *archontes* who crucified Christ (2:8).

795 (archēgos, ruler, leader), → *794.*

796 (archieratikos, high-priestly), → *2636.*

797 (archiereus, high priest), → *2636.*

799 (archipoimēn, chief shepherd, over-shepherd), → *4478.*

801 (archisynagōgos, ruler of the synagogue), → *1711.*

802 (architektōn, master builder), → *5454.*

803 (architelōnēs, chief tax collector), → *5468.*

806 (archō, begin, rule), → *794.*

807 (archōn, ruler, prince), → *794.*

810 (asaleutos, unshakable, firm, enduring), → *4888.*

812	ἄσβεστος

ἄσβεστος (*asbestos*), inextinguishable, that which is not or cannot be quenched (*812*).

CL & OT 1. In cl. Gk. this word means unquenchable, though its meaning is extended to signify ceaseless. As a noun it was used of unslaked lime and subsequently of plaster. Later, fireproof asbestos fibers were made into fire-resistant clothing.

2. In the LXX *asbestos* occurs only in Job 20:26. It apparently translates a Heb. phrase meaning not blown upon or unfanned.

NT *asbestos* occurs only 3x in the NT. In Matt. 3:12 and Lk. 3:17 it is part of the teaching of John the Baptist regarding the coming Messiah, that he will burn up "the chaff with unquenchable fire." In Mk. 9:43 the word refers to the unquenchable fires of hell. Fire was the most powerful destructive force known in the ancient world, and the NT use of *asbestos* implies utter and complete destruction of whatever is rejected by God as unsuitable or unworthy.

See also *sbennymi,* quench, extinguish, quell (*4931*).

813 (asebeia, impiety, godlessness), → *4936.*

815 (asebēs, godless, impious), → *4936.*

816	ἀσέλγεια

ἀσέλγεια (*aselgeia*), licentiousness, debauchery (*816*); ἀσωτία (*asotia*), dissolution, profligacy (*861*); ἀσώτως (*asotōs*), dissolutely, wildly (*862*).

CL & OT 1. In cl. Gk. *aselgeia* denotes licentiousness in lifestyle, which can mean excess in areas such as food or sex. *asotia* had an original nuance of incurable but usually meant those who by their manner of life destroy themselves. This word is often linked with other vices, esp. those characterized by a wild and undisciplined life. It is esp. used of the person who is reckless and wasteful of his or her resources.

2. *aselgeia* does not occur in the OT (but cf. Wis. 14:26; 3 Macc. 2:26). *asotia* occurs only in Prov. 28:7, where a person who lives a dis-

solute lifestyle brings dishonor to his or her father (see also 2 Macc. 6:4). In Prov. 7:11 the related *asotos* describes a wanton, flighty woman who never stays home but is out looking for wild excitement.

NT 1. *aselgeia* occurs 10x in the NT, mostly in vice lists, where it is often linked with other sexual sins (e.g., Rom. 13:13; 2 Cor. 12:21; Gal. 5:19; 1 Pet. 4:3). According to Jesus, it is one of the vices that destroys a person from within (Mk. 7:22). *aselgeia* was one of the chief sins of Sodom and Gomorrah (2 Pet. 2:7) and is characteristic of godless paganism (Eph. 4:19; Jude 4).

2. *asotia* occurs 3x in the NT, *asotōs* once. The latter word describes the "wild living" of the prodigal son as he wasted his wealth. *asotia* is used to describe wild and disorderly conduct rather than extravagance. In Eph. 5:18, Paul writes that drunkenness leads to "debauchery." The children of those chosen to be elders are not to be "wild" and disobedient (Tit. 1:6). In 1 Pet. 4:4 *asotia* is one of a number of words that describe the wanton lifestyle of pagans, who make fun of the sober and moral choices of the believer.

819	ἀσθένεια

ἀσθένεια (*astheneia*), weakness, sickness, disease, timidity (*819*); ἀσθενής (*asthenēs*), without strength, weak (*822*); ἀσθενέω (*astheneō*), to be powerless, weak (*820*).

CL & OT 1. In cl. Gk. this group of words conveys the meaning of powerlessness, weakness, lack of strength. It relates primarily to bodily weakness, e.g., sickness, though it can also express other sorts of weakness, such as the frailty of woman, the weakness of human nature, or economic weakness (poverty). Only rarely is it used for lack of conviction, moral weakness.

2. (a) In the LXX *astheneia* occurs only 7x. In the Pentateuch *asthenēs* occurs only 2x (Gen. 29:17, Leah's weak eyes; Num. 13:18 = LXX 13:19, on whether the Canaanites are strong or weak). The remaining books likewise use *asthenēs* infrequently. These words can mean sickness (e.g., Dan. 8:27), but also human weakness (Jdg. 16:7, 11, 17), social insignificance (6:15), and political weakness (2 Sam. 3:1).

(b) *astheneō* acquires a specific character in prophetic lit. It is found chiefly in prophecies of judgment, describing in a fig. sense the people who have rebelled against Yahweh and who will therefore stumble and fall (Jer. 6:21; 18:15; Hos. 4:5; 5:5; Nah. 2:5; 3:3).

(c) In Ps. and in the wisdom lit., *astheneō* can express the stumbling of the ungodly and of enemies (Ps. 9:3; 27:2; cf. Job 28:4). Words in this group may also be used for human poverty and human wretchedness (Ps. 6:2; 31:10; Prov. 21:13; 22:22). Theodotion is esp. fond of using *astheneō*.

NT 1. The Gospels and Acts tend to use the words in this group for bodily weakness or sickness (e.g., Matt. 10:8; Lk. 13:11; Jn. 4:46; Acts 9:37). The pres. act. part. can be used as a noun meaning a sick person (Jn. 5:7), usually pl. (e.g., Mk. 6:56; Jn. 6:2).

2. In Paul, the words in this group undergo theological reflection and are developed in relation to our sinful nature, to Christology, and to ethics. (a) In Rom. 6:19 Paul refers to being "weak in your natural selves" (lit., "weakness of the flesh [*sarx*, → *4922*]"), i.e., natural human weakness. Rom. 8:26 defines *astheneia* as human powerlessness over against God, needing the help of the Spirit's power. In 1 Cor. 15:43, *astheneia* stands opposite to "power" (*dynamis*, → *1539*).

In Rom. 8:3 Paul develops the concept of weakness further by associating it with the law, which is powerless because it is "weakened by the sinful nature [*sarx*]." That is, our inability to do what is good demonstrates a weakness in the law. Paul does not use weakness here in the sense of a relative quantity, but of an absolute one: incapability. His strongest formulation comes at Rom. 5:6, where he equates being powerless (lit., being weak) with being ungodly and being sinners (see 5:8; cf. Heb. 4:15; 7:28).

(b) Paul introduces another train of thought in seeing weakness as the place where God's might can be exhibited. In the course of arguing against his opponents in Corinth, the apostle unfolds his theology of the cross. In the crucified one the "weakness of God" comes to light, which to human eyes appears to be powerlessness and folly (1 Cor. 1:25, 27; cf. 2 Cor. 13:4). But since God has demonstrated his power in weakness (i.e., in the death of Christ) by raising him from the dead (2 Cor. 13:4), it is in the very sufferings of his followers that God's creative, life-giving power is revealed. Paul regards his own weakness as a mark of discipleship and fellowship in Christ's sufferings (1 Cor. 2:2–3; 4:10). At the same time the power of God is at work in weakness amid the conditions of suffering and alienation. Thus Paul concludes that he would rather boast of his weakness (2 Cor. 11:30; 12:5, 9–10; 13:9), for God's "power is made perfect in weakness" (12:9).

(c) Paul also uses this word group to distinguish between the strong (Rom. 15:1) and the weak (14:1) in faith. Paul is probably taking up catchwords or familiar slogans used by groups within the churches of Corinth and Rome (cf. Rom. 14:1–15:13; 1 Cor. 8:10). Those known as the "weak" have a weak conscience (1 Cor. 8:7) and have not yet reached a full knowledge of the faith (8:11). Thus, they abstain from meat and perhaps wine (Rom. 14:2), esp. from meat offered to idols (1 Cor. 8:7), observe certain special days (Rom. 14:5), and evidence ascetic and legalistic tendencies. The strong, by contrast, know that nothing is unclean in itself (Rom. 14:14), since they know only one Lord, from whom all things come (1 Cor. 8:6). Hence, they will eat anything (Rom. 14:2), even meat offered to idols (1 Cor. 8:1), and they regard all days alike (Rom. 14:5).

Although Paul regards himself as belonging to the "strong" (Rom. 14:14; 15:1; 1 Cor. 8:4), he stresses the importance of strong and weak living together in love (1 Cor. 8:1–3) before their common Lord (Rom. 14:6–8). The strong should not place a stumbling block (Rom. 14:13, 20; 1 Cor. 8:9) in the way of the weak or cause them offense (Rom. 14:13), thus troubling their conscience (1 Cor. 8:13), leading them astray (Rom. 14:21, 23; 1 Cor. 8:10), and bringing about their ruin (Rom. 14:21; 1 Cor. 8:11; cf. the OT use of this word group for stumbling and falling).

3. *asthenēs* also has a general sense of weakness. In 1 Pet. 3:7 women are spoken of as "the weaker partner," and Paul's personal appearance in Corinth is described as weak (2 Cor. 10:10). General human weakness is the subject of the epigrammatic saying in Matt. 26:41: "The spirit is willing, but the body [*sarx*] is weak." Gal. 4:9 should probably also be included here: The "basic principles [*stoicheion*, → 5122] of the world" (4:3) are described as "weak and miserable," i.e., disarmed and therefore powerless (cf. Col. 2:14). Economic weakness in the sense of need, poverty, is likely meant in Acts 20:35, so that the wealthy are to help the needy ("weak"), for "it is more blessed to give than to receive."

See also *nosos*, illness, sickness (3798); *malakia*, weakness, softness, sickness (3433); *paralytikos*, paralytic (4166).

820 (astheneō, to be powerless, weak), → *819.*

822 (asthenēs, without strength, weak), → *819.*

828 (askeō, practice something, engage in), → *1602.*

832 (aspazomai, greet), → *2330.*

833 (aspasmos, greeting), → *2330.*

834 (aspilos, spotless, without blemish), → *441.*

843	ἀστήρ

ἀστήρ (*astēr*), star (843); ἄστρον (*astron*), star, constellation (849).

CL & OT 1. The lit. use of *astēr* and *astron* is found in cl. Gk. writers and the LXX. In the OT, the stars, like the sun and moon, are God's creation (Gen. 1:16). Both cl. writers and the LXX refer to stars as indicating time (by their appearance) and having a fixed order as well as

light and beauty. The most frequent use of *astēr* and *astron* in the LXX is in reference to their incalculable number, usually with the descendants of the patriarchs in mind (cf. Gen. 15:5; 22:17; 26:4; Exod. 32:13; Deut. 1:10; 10:22; 28:62).

2. The fig use of *astēr* and *astron* is also common in Gk. lit. and the LXX. Most frequent is the application to an illustrious person. In the LXX, those "who lead many to righteousness" will shine "like the stars for ever and ever" (Dan. 12:3). Often similes employ the beauty or glory of the stars (e.g., 1 Chr. 27:23; Wis. 7:29; Sir. 50:6). Obad. 4 speaks of pride as setting one's nest among the stars; in a similar way Isa. 14:12 refers to *Heōsphoros* (NIV: "morning star"), who in his proud heart will ascend above the stars of God and make himself like the Most High (14:13; cf. 2 Macc. 9:10).

In Num. 24:17, an *astron* is prophesied to come forth out of Jacob, a man out of Israel who will rule in victory. This text was understood messianically at Qumran but was not utilized in the NT, unless possibly in Rev. 22:16. This text may also be behind the Magi's decision to go to the land of Israel when they saw the "star in the east" (Matt. 2:1–2, 9). Along similar lines, *astron* was applied to Simon Bar Kokhba (whose name in Aram. means "Son of a Star"), the leader of the Jewish rebellion against the Romans in A.D. 132.

3. Astrology and the worship of the stars are known both in Gk. writers and the LXX. Although the stars are sometimes personified in the LXX (e.g., Jdg. 5:20; Ps. 148:3; Bar. 3:34), a strong stance is taken against astrology and the worship of the stars (Deut. 4:19; Isa. 47:13; Jer. 8:2; Amos 5:26).

4. The imagery of darkened stars is associated with suffering and judgment in the LXX (Job 3:9; 9:7; Eccl. 12:2; Wis. 17:5). The failure of the stars to give light becomes standard apocalyptic language used to describe historical and eschatological judgment (Isa. 13:10; Ezek. 32:7; Joel 2:10; 3:15). Occasionally the imagery varies, referring to stars falling, the host of heaven rotting away, and the skies being rolled up like a scroll (Isa. 34:4; cf. Dan. 8:10).

NT 1. Both *astēr* and *astron* are found in the NT; the difference between the two is stylistic (e.g., Lk.–Acts uses only *astron*, Rev. *astēr*). These two words occur 28x in the NT, only some of which are literal: Acts 27:20 (as guides to navigation at sea); 1 Cor. 15:41 (where *astēr* occurs 3x to refer to differing orders of glory); Heb. 11:12 (fig. of Abraham's innumerable descendants); Acts 7:43 (where Stephen alludes to the worship of stars in the OT period).

2. Unique to the infancy narrative of Matt. is the story of the Magi and the *astēr* that led them to Bethlehem (2:1–12). The ancient world often associated the birth of a great ruler with extraordinary phenomena in the heavens. Whether in Matt. we have to do with a miraculous star or something natural (e.g., the conjunction of planetary bodies, such as the conjunction of Jupiter and Saturn in 7 B.C., or a supernova) is uncertain. The Magi were experts in esoteric knowledge, persons for whom astrology was important (→ *mageia*, magic, 3404). Theologically viewed, the star was a sign of the dawning of the new and glorious era of the kingdom that the birth of the King inaugurates.

3. (a) The metaphorical use of *astēr* is frequent in the NT, esp. in Rev. Seven stars are mentioned 5x in Rev. 1–3. These stars are held in the right hand of the one who discloses himself to John in a vision (1:16, 20; 2:1; 3:1). In 1:20 the mystery is explained: The stars are "the angels of the seven churches" (the seven lampstands symbolize the seven churches). The number seven probably derives from the common seven-branched candelabra of Israel, if not from the symbolic perfection of the number itself. The seven stars may also be linked to the sovereignty symbolized in the ancient world by the seven planets. Whatever the case, the point is that true sovereignty, as opposed to the sovereignty claimed by the Roman emperors, lies with Christ and his people.

(b) The symbolism of the "morning star" in Rev. 2:28 and 22:16 is likewise difficult to understand. Although it can be related to the words of Num. 24:17, more probably it alludes to the morning star Venus, with the connotation not only of beauty but of daybreak, and also of sovereignty and victory (attested in Roman times). In Rev. 2:28, then, we may also understand the morning star given to the faithful as symbolic of sovereignty or rule.

(c) Further fig. use of *aster* is found in the crown of twelve stars worn by the woman of Rev. 12:1, where the stars symbolize the twelve tribes of Israel. Jude 13 speaks of ungodly and heretical persons as "wandering stars" destined to an eternal darkness.

4. Stars are associated with the sun and moon in the apocalyptic imagery of eschatological judgment. In contrast to the LXX, where the darkening of the stars is common, only Rev. 8:12 in the NT refers to this. Elsewhere the NT speaks of stars falling from the sky (Matt. 24:29; Mk. 13:25; cf. Lk. 21:25), a phenomenon mentioned only 2x in the LXX. What is symbolized here is an event of great significance. If, as is probable, this language alludes to the fall of Jerusalem in A.D. 70, the theological continuity with and anticipation of the final eschatological judgment is not to be missed.

Further use of the falling stars imagery is found in Rev. At the opening of the sixth seal the stars fell to the earth "as late figs drop from a fig tree when shaken by a strong wind" (6:13). The blowing of the third trumpet announces the falling of "a great star, blazing like a torch . . . from the sky," which has the name Wormwood and makes bitter a third of the waters (8:10–12). At the fifth trumpet another star falls "from the sky to the earth" (9:1). Finally, the tail of the dragon "swept a third of the stars out of the sky and flung them to the earth" (12:4).

In the apocalyptic language about the sun, moon, and stars a recurrent question concerns how literally it is to be understood. One may debate the possibility of these luminaries being literally darkened, but not that the stars fall to earth. These statements about the stars underline the fig. nature of apocalyptic language. The real meaning of this language is theological. In the NT we move into the era of fulfillment prior to the consummation of God's purposes. Momentous events have occurred and are yet to occur—all of which are part of the same fabric of judgment and blessing and call for the most exalted language.

See also *hēlios*, sun (2463); *selēnē*, moon (4943).

844 (astēriktos, unstable), → 5114.

845 (astorgos, without natural affection), → 26.

847	ἀστραπή

ἀστραπή (*astrapē*), lightning (847); ἄνεμος (*anemos*), wind (449); βρέχω (*brechō*), to rain (1101); βροχή (*brochē*), rain (1104); βροντή (*brontē*), thunder (1103); εὐδία (*eudia*), fair weather, a good day (2304); ἶρις (*iris*), rainbow (2692); λαῖλαψ (*lailaps*), a tempestuous wind (3278); νεφέλη (*nephelē*), cloud (3749); νότος (*notos*), south wind (3803); ὄμβρος (*ombros*), rainstorm (3915); ὁμίχλη (*homichlē*), mist, fog (3920); ὄψιμος (*opsimos*), late (rain) (4069); πρόϊμος (*proïmos*), early (rain) (4611); ῥιπίζω (*rhipizō*), blow (4847); ὑετός (*hyetos*), heavy shower (5624); χάλαζα (*chalaza*), hail (5898); χιών (*chiōn*), snow (5946).

CL & OT Note that the basic cl. Gk. definitions are given in the NT section.

In neither Gk. nor Heb. is there a word corresponding to our word weather, but the ancients used a variety of words with which they discussed aspects of weather, and clearly some of those aspects mattered to them. In general the Gks. related meteorological phenomena to the gods. For example, the gods might use clouds for concealment when watching a battle on earth or when making love on a mountaintop, or they might use them as chariots. Note too that Iris ("rainbow") is the messenger goddess, and Nephele ("cloud"), the mother of the Centaurs.

There is much more than this in the OT, where God uses the weather to set forth his purposes. Note Deut. 11:13–17, where Yah-

weh says that if the people love him and serve him, he will give them rain; but if they worship other gods, he will withhold rain, the land will give no fruit, and the people will perish (cf. Lev. 26:4; 1 Ki. 17:14; Ps. 68:9; Jer. 5:24; Amos 4:7). Such a link between the people's religious life and the weather is often found. Great deliverances like that under Deborah and Barak are due to storms (Jdg. 5:20–21; cf. Jos. 10:11). Note Ps. 148:8: "lightning and hail, snow and clouds, stormy winds that do his bidding."

Phenomena such as clouds are associated with theophanies (e.g., Exod. 19:9; 24:16; 34:5; Lev. 16:2; Ps. 97:2). God makes the clouds his chariot and the winds his messengers (104:3–4; cf. Isa. 19:1). The coming day of the Lord is "a day of clouds and blackness" (Joel 2:2). The lightning is God's weapon (2 Sam. 22:15; Ps. 144:6) and the thunder his voice (Job 37:5; cf. Ps. 77:18; 104:7). He is often pictured as sending the wind or using it (e.g., Exod. 10:13, 19; 15:10; Num. 11:31), sometimes as the instrument of his wrath (Ezek. 13:13).

NT 1. *astrapē* means lightning, beam of light. In the OT *astrapē* is God's weapon, brilliantly lighting up the world (Ps. 77:18); it is also connected with rain (Jer. 10:13). In the NT it denotes the suddenness and the visibility of the coming of the Son of Man (Matt. 24:27; Lk. 17:24) and occurs in comparisons—e.g., Satan's fall (10:18) or an angel's face (Matt. 28:3). *astrapē* occurs 4x in Rev. (4:5; 8:5; 11:19; 16:18), each time linked with other phenomena (voices, thunders, earthquake, and/or hail), proving that God is judge.

2. *anemos* normally denotes the winds that blow on the earth. This is the most common use of *anemos* in the NT (e.g., the winds that beat against the houses built on rock and on sand in Matt. 7:25, 27; the great storm that shipwrecked Paul in Acts 27:4, 7, 14–15). Jesus is supreme over the elements, as becomes clear from his stilling of the storm (Matt. 8:26–27; Mk. 4:37, 39; Lk. 8:23–25) and his walking on the sea (Matt. 14:24–32; Mk. 6:47–51). God is in control of the winds, for in Rev. angels hold back the four winds so they will not blow on the earth (7:1). The word is used fig. of "every wind of teaching" (Eph. 4:14), where someone not well established in the faith may depart quickly from sound doctrine.

3. *brochē*, rain (cf. *brechō*, to rain) is normally used for precipitation from the clouds; fig. it denotes what comes on human beings in abundance. In the NT there are two fig. uses: "Fire and sulfur rained down" on Sodom (Lk. 17:29), and the sinful woman "wet" (lit., "rained on") Jesus' feet with her tears (Lk. 7:38, 44). Jesus uses the fact that God makes rain fall on the just and the unjust to teach the universality of his love (Matt. 5:45). Rain is here symbolic of God's gifts in general. God is in control of rain, for Elijah prayed that it might not rain and it did not (Jas. 5:17). With this we should class the power of the two witnesses to prevent rain (Rev. 11:6).

4. *brontē* means thunder. In the NT it is used for a mighty voice on a number of occasions (Jn. 12:29; Rev. 6:1; 10:3–4; 19:6). In Rev., thunder is linked 4x with lightning (4:5; 8:5; 11:19; 16:18). The one other fig. use of *brontē* is Mk.'s explanation of the name "Boanerges . . . Sons of Thunder," which is applied to the sons of Zebedee (Mk. 3:17). Precisely why James and John receive this name is uncertain (though cf. 10:35–40; Lk. 9:51–55).

5. *eudia* is derived from *eu* and *Dios*, genitive of *Zeus*, to give the meaning "a good sky" and thus "fair weather." Its only NT use is Matt. 16:2, where it refers to the ability of the Pharisees and Sadducees to predict the coming of good weather as contrasted with their inability to discern what is more important, "the signs of the times."

6. *iris* means rainbow; fig. it denotes a halo or the iris of the eye. The Gks. personified the rainbow as the messenger goddess Iris. In the OT the rainbow appears as a sign of God's covenant that he will no longer send floods to destroy the earth (Gen. 9:13; note, however, that the LXX uses *toxon* [hunter's bow, reflecting the Heb. word], not *iris*). The LXX uses *iris* once only for the name of a plant (Exod. 30:24). In the NT the word occurs only in Rev. 4:3; 10:1. The first refers to a rainbow (or halo) around God's throne, "resembling an emerald"; the sec-

ond refers to a strong angel robed in a cloud with a rainbow round his head. In both places the rainbow symbolizes the permanence of God's covenant and his will to be gracious to us.

7. The word *lailaps* is a tempestuous wind, whipping up so great a storm that the boat begins to fill (Mk. 4:37) and the disciples are in danger (Lk. 8:23). In 2 Pet. 2:17 this word refers to certain false teachers, who are likened to mists driven by a *lailaps*.

8. *nephelē* means a cloud or cloud mass. In the NT clouds are most often associated in some way with Jesus (though cf. Lk. 12:54; 1 Cor. 10:1–2; Jude 12). The Synoptics tell of the cloud at Jesus' transfiguration, which is plainly linked with the presence of God and from which the heavenly voice greets Jesus as "my Son, whom I love" (Matt. 17:5; Mk. 9:7; Lk. 9:34–35). At his ascension a cloud receives Jesus out of the sight of the disciples (Acts 1:9). When Jesus comes again at the Parousia there will be clouds (Matt. 24:30; 26:64; Mk. 13:26; 14:62; Lk. 21:27; 1 Thess. 4:17; Rev. 1:7). In Rev. 14:14–16, a reaper is sitting on a cloud at the judgment.

9. *notos* means the south wind (see Lk. 12:55; Acts 27:13; 28:13), but also south as a direction (Lk. 13:29; Rev. 21:13) and land to the south (Matt. 12:42; Lk. 11:31).

10. *ombros* signifies a rainstorm (cf. Lk. 12:54, only place in NT).

11. *homichlē*, mist or fog, is used of false teachers, who are compared to mists driven around by a strong wind and have nothing substantial about them (2 Pet. 2:17).

12. *opsimos* simply means late, but it was commonly used in the LXX with *proïmos* to indicate the late (and early) rains. In Palestine the *proïmos* is important to get the crops started and the *opsimos* to mature the grain before the dry season starts. Both words occur only in Jas. 5:7 in the NT.

13. *rhipizō*, to blow (of winds), occurs only in Jas. 1:6, where James likens the doubter to a wave blown about by winds; the thought is that of instability.

14. *hyetos* denotes a heavy shower in contrast to *ombros* (continuous rain). In the NT it is once used of rain as unpleasant (Acts 28:2); otherwise it is a gift of God (14:17), given in response to prayer (Jas. 5:18). It is linked with his blessing (Heb. 6:7) and is withheld in fulfillment of his purpose for his witnesses (Rev. 11:6).

15. Hail (*chalaza*) occurs in the NT only in Rev. It follows the blowing of the first trumpet (8:7), is one of the phenomena following the opening of the ark of God's covenant in heaven (11:19), and is the last of the horrors that followed the pouring out of the seventh bowl (16:21). The violence of a mighty hailstorm is a suitable picture of God's power and underlines the truth that his judgments are irresistible.

16. Snow (*chiōn*) is used in the NT only as a way of indicating whiteness. It is the color of the angel's robe (Matt. 28:3) and the head and hair of the glorious Lord (Rev. 1:14).

849 (*astron*, star, constellation), → *843*.

852 (*asynetos*, senseless, foolish), → *5304*.

854	ἀσφάλεια

ἀσφάλεια (*asphaleia*), firmness, certainty, security (*854*); ἀσφαλής (*asphalēs*), firm, sure, safe, secure (*855*); ἀσφαλίζω (*asphalizō*), guard (*856*); ἀσφαλῶς (*asphalōs*), securely (*857*).

CL & OT 1. In cl. Gk. *asphaleia* means security against stumbling, assurance from danger, certainty, the convincing nature of an argument, and a security or pledge as a technical legal term. *asphalēs* means immovable, steadfast, unshaken, and the vb. *asphalizō* means to secure, safeguard, and even to arrest.

2. In the OT *asphaleia* occurs 19x. It denotes the security that the Lord promises his people (Lev. 26:5; Deut. 12:10; cf. Prov. 8:14). It is also used of the foundations of the earth (Ps. 104:5). The word is used 6x in 2 Macc. (e.g., 3:22; 4:21), where it means security. Similar nuances occur for other words in this word group (e.g., the vb. is translated "I will uphold you with my righteous right hand" in Isa. 41:10).

NT *asphaleia* is used in a physical sense in Acts 5:23 ("we found the jail securely locked"). It is used fig. of the "certainty" of the things in which Theophilus has been instructed (Lk. 1:4). It denotes "safety" in 1 Thess. 5:3, where Paul is warning against a false sense of security. *asphalēs* is translated "safeguard" in Phil. 3:1. The adv. *asphalōs* denotes securely in the sense of being "under [secure] guard" in Mk. 14:44 (cf. also Acts 16:23). It is used fig. in the sense of being "assured" of the truth about who Christ is in Acts 2:36. *asphalizō* means to guard or make secure (the tomb of Jesus) in Matt. 27:64–66 and to fasten in Acts 16:24.

See also *bebaios*, sure (*1010*); *themelios*, foundation (*2529*); *kyroō*, confirm, ratify (*3263*).

855 (*asphalēs*, firm, sure, safe, secure), → *854*.

856 (*asphalizō*, guard), → *854*.

857 (*asphalōs*, securely), → *854*.

861 (*asōtia*, dissolution, profligacy), → *816*.

862 (*asōtōs*, dissolutely, wildly), → *816*.

867	ἀτενίζω

ἀτενίζω (*atenizō*), look at a person or thing intently, gaze on, observe (*867*).

CL There is little cl. use of this word that goes beyond the normal use in the senses listed above. In the Hel. period it was used in connection with magical activity. The word appears only 2x in the LXX, once with a fig. meaning (to "look diligently" to help those constructing the temple, 1 Esd. 6:28) and once lit. (3 Macc. 2:26).

NT *atenizō* occurs 14x in the NT. In each use it seems to emphasize the intensity of the look. When Jesus read from Isa. 61 in his hometown synagogue, all eyes were "fastened on him" (Lk. 4:20). When Peter was trying to avoid identification with Jesus after his arrest, he found himself scrutinized by a servant girl (22:56). In Acts 1:10 the disciples gaze at their ascending Lord (cf. also 3:12; 6:15; 7:55; 10:4; 11:6; 23:1). In 2 Cor. 3:7, 13, *atenizō* describes the way the Israelites would have stared at Moses' radiant face, had it not been hidden by the veil.

Three times *atenizō* is used in connection with a miracle (Acts 3:4; 13:9; 14:9). Peter "looked straight at" the crippled man in 3:4 and called for his attention (though the actual healing in 3:6–8 does not include any reference to eye contact). In 14:9 Paul looks directly at a crippled man, apparently to determine if he has faith. Only in 13:9 is the look directly incorporated in a context of cursing. It is not stated or implied, however, that anything like an evil eye is employed in the curse.

See also *horaō*, see (*3972*); *kollourion*, eye salve (*3141*); *blepō*, look at, see (*1063*); *theatron*, theater, place of assembly, a spectacle (*2519*).

869 (*atimazō*, dishonor, treat shamefully), → *5507*.

871 (*atimia*, shame, dishonor, disgrace), → *5507*.

872 (*atimos*, despised, dishonored), → *5507*.

878 (*augazō*, shine forth, illuminate, see), → *575*.

879 (*augē*, dawn, daybreak), → *575*.

889	αὐξάνω

αὐξάνω (*auxanō*), grow, cause to grow, increase (*889*); αὔξησις (*auxēsis*), growth, increase (*890*); ὑπεραυξάνω (*hyperauxanō*), grow abundantly (*5647*); προκοπή (*prokopē*), progress, advancement, furtherance (*4620*); προκόπτω (*prokoptō*), go forward, advance, make progress, prosper (*4621*).

CL & OT 1. In cl. Gk. *auxanō* means to cause to grow, to cause to increase. Trans. it is used esp. for natural growth, such as that of fruits, but also for increase and advancement in respect and power. The mid.-pass. can also mean to be exalted, glorified, or praised. The noun *auxēsis* means growth. *hyperauxanō* means to grow abundantly, plentifully, or extravagantly. *auxanō* is also used for the waxing of the moon and the sun. No specific philosophical or religious significance for this word stands out in the Gk. world, but *prokoptō* and *prokopē* in Stoic philosophy and in Philo denote ethical advance.

2. In the LXX *auxanō* means to be or make fruitful, plentiful. God is mainly the subj. of the process of causing growth (Gen. 17:20; 35:11; cf. Jer. 3:16; 23:3). It is frequently linked with *plēthynō*, to fill, multiply, and occurs in the original creation mandate, later renewed, to be fruitful and multiply (Gen. 1:22, 28; 9:1, 7; cf. 17:6). In the parabolic promise of Isa. 61:11 the process of growth is not viewed as something automatic. The point of the comparison is the difference between the first state and the last. The surprising thing is that the beginning and end stages are completely different. Where previously there was nothing, God's creative will becomes effective: He creates righteousness and praise. Sir. 43:8 speaks of the waxing of the new moon.

NT 1. Natural growth is alluded to directly only in Lk. 1:80 and 2:40, where the child Jesus is said to grow physically and in the Spirit.

2. (a) *auxanō* features in the parable of the sower (Mk. 4:8), the parable of the mustard seed (Matt. 13:32; Lk. 13:19), and the saying about the lilies of the field (Matt. 6:28). The picture of plantlike growth illustrates the coming of the kingdom through the gospel in the face of all opposition. God is the one who causes to grow that which he himself sows through Jesus or through his servants (cf. also 1 Cor. 3:6–7; 2 Cor. 9:10).

(b) In Paul's letters *auxanō* is not used in relation to the doctrine of justification but belongs to paraenesis. Only God can cause the church to grow (1 Cor. 3:5–11). Only by remembering its foundation or origin, which is Jesus Christ (1 Cor. 3:11), can the church truly grow (→ *themelios*, 2529). The thought here is not solely of numerical increase but also of maturity and the consolidation of the community in Christ from which good works naturally grow (2 Cor. 9:6–11).

(c) Eph. 2:20–22 does not contradict the picture of 1 Cor. 3:11, where the apostles and prophets are said to be the foundation on which the building grows, for Eph. 2:20 identifies Jesus Christ as "the chief cornerstone" (cf. Ps. 118:22; Matt. 21:42; Mk. 12:10–11; Lk. 20:17; Acts 4:11; 1 Pet. 2:7; → *gōnia*, 1224). Moreover, the church was by this time uniquely dependent on the witness of the apostles and prophets for the preaching about Christ. Thus, the growth of the church derives ultimately from Jesus Christ, who also holds the building together (cf. Eph. 2:20–21 with 1:5–7, 10; 2:10; 4:15–16).

Growth does not mean that the gospel calls people into some kind of extrahistorical existence. Because Christians are placed in the fellowship of the people of God, they are placed in a historical process that is determined by the promise of the worldwide rule of Christ. The existence together of Jews and Gentiles as children in the presence of the Lord of the church opens up a new dimension for the church as it grows into a single structure, a structure that continues to grow in personal holiness in Christ.

(d) Paul also uses the concept of a growing body to picture growth in the church (Eph. 4:15–16; Col. 2:19). Eph. 4:15–16 shows the way that this growth is to take place. When truth is spoken in love and love takes effect, the church grows into Christ, the one head. According to Col. 1:6, all growth springs from the gospel. As people are moved by the gospel, they grow in knowledge of God (Col. 1:10–11) and in grace (cf. 2 Pet. 3:18).

3. The NT can also speak of growth in faith (2 Cor. 10:15; 2 Thess. 1:3). Faith is conditioned by one's personal circumstances as well as by God's saving acts in history. It is brought about and renewed by the Word, the living Christ himself. But it undergoes transformation in the life of the Christian. Believers have their own particular history in relation to their Lord. They live between the "no longer" and the "not yet."

The decision that leads to baptism admittedly takes place only once, but faith needs to be constantly renewed (cf. Rom. 14:1; 1 Thess.

3:10). Faith grows out of the obedience of believers in the fellowship of the Christian community (2 Thess. 1:3; cf. Phil. 1:25–26). It leads to a more effective witness in the world (2 Cor. 10:15–16). Quantitative and qualitative growth are closely connected. The final goal of growth in faith is the day of Christ (Phil. 1:6). Growing faith always works outward, bringing fruit and bearing witness (2 Cor. 10:15; 2 Thess. 1:3).

4. In Acts growth is an important word for the missionary activity of the community (6:7; 12:24; 19:20). Acts 7:17 ("the number of our people in Egypt greatly increased") provides a clear reminder of OT salvation history. The experience of Israel (Exod. 1:7) is eschatologically applied to the Christian community (Acts 12:24).

5. The expression in Jn. 3:30, "He must become greater; I must become less," probably derives from the ancient linguistic usage of increasing or decreasing in esteem or importance. John the Baptist points to his Lord and withdraws his own light so that the one to whom he points may be seen.

6. *auxanō* is distinguished from the noun *prokopē* (Phil. 1:25; 1 Tim. 4:15) and the vb. *prokoptō* (Lk. 2:52; Rom. 13:12; Gal. 1:14; 2 Tim. 2:16; 3:9, 13), meaning advance, progress, in that in the NT the former occurs exclusively in a positive sense. It has thus more positive theological associations, for not every "advance" is also "growth." Note, for example, Paul's testimony of his advance in Judaism beyond people of his own age, illustrated by his zeal for persecuting the church (Gal. 1:13–14).

See also *pleonazō,* become more or great, grow, increase (*4429*).

890 (*auxēsis*, growth, increase), → *889*.

894 (*autarkeia*, sufficiency, contentment), → *758*.

895 (*autarkēs*, self-sufficient, independent, content), → *758*.

896 (*autokatakritos*, self-condemned), → *3210*.

912 (*aphesis*, release, pardon, cancellation, forgiveness), → *918*.

914 (*aphtharsia*, incorruptibility, immortality), → *5780*.

915 (*aphthartos*, imperishable, incorruptible, immortal), → *5780*.

918	ἀφίημι

ἀφίημι (*aphiēmi*), let go, cancel, remit, leave, forgive (*918*); ἄφεσις (*aphesis*), release, pardon, cancellation, forgiveness (*912*); πάρεσις (*paresis*), letting pass, passing over (*4217*).

CL& OT 1. In cl. Gk. *aphiēmi* (*apo*, from, and the vb. *hiēmi*, to put in motion, send) denotes the voluntary release of a person or thing over which one has legal or actual control. With a pers. obj., it means to send forth, send away (of a woman, to divorce), to leave, dispatch; with an impers. obj., to loose (e.g., a ship into the sea; to end a meeting), to discharge (e.g., arrows), to give up. In its fig. sense the vb. means to let alone, permit, neglect, give up, even to lose one's life. The legal use is important: to release from a legal bond, to acquit, to exempt (from guilt, obligation, or punishment). The noun *aphesis* means release, pardon, or remission. None of these meanings is found in a religious sense.

2. The LXX uses *aphiēmi* in such cl. Gk. senses as to let go (Jdg. 3:1), leave, give up (9:9, 11, 13, all only in A), leave behind (2 Sam. 15:16; 20:3), allow (16:10), leave over (Ps. 17:14), and release in the year of release (Deut. 15:2). It is seldom used in the sense forgive. Where it is, it usually renders the Heb. *nāśāʾ*, to release from guilt or punishment (e.g., Gen. 18:26; Ps. 32:1, 5; Isa. 33:24), or *sālaḥ*, to forgive, pardon (e.g., Lev. 4:20–35; Num. 14:19; Isa. 55:7). Sometimes it stands for *kipper*, to cover, make atonement (Isa. 22:14). The one who forgives is God (though cf. Gen. 50:17). Through that act, the destroyed relationship between God and his people is reconstituted.

aphesis occurs about 50x in the LXX; 20 are in Lev. 25 and 27 (for the Year of Jubilee [release]) and 5 in Deut. 15:1–9 (for release from debts in the Year of Jubilee). It is also used of the release of captives and slaves (Isa. 61:1; Jer. 34:8, 15, 17 = LXX 41:8, 15, 17; Ezek. 46:17).

Only once does *aphesis* perhaps have the sense of forgiveness (Lev. 16:26), though even here it may simply have the sense of send away, release.

In other words, these words, which in the NT are central to the issue of forgiveness, are not used in the LXX to convey that concept. Israel experienced God's grace of forgiveness largely in the context of OT worship; various terms were used to express the idea (e.g., washing, cleansing, covering).

3. *Forgiveness in the OT.* A number of preexilic Psalms (e.g., Ps. 25:11; 65:3; 78:38; 79:9) and passages in the prophets (e.g., Isa. 6) show a significant degree of reflection on the consciousness of sin and forgiveness. Sin is opposition to God, grounded in the inmost part of one's nature. It can only be brought to an end by a gracious gift of God (cf. Ps. 65:3–5).

Already in the Pentateuch we find references to sacrifices for sin and forgiveness (e.g., Exod. 32:11–14; 43:6). Sacrifices for atonement and forgiveness were instituted at the time of Moses and the exodus. Israelites did not think of sin in the abstract, but as a localized sphere arising out of transgression. It could not simply be forgotten; rather, it had to be dealt with by expiatory ritual, by which God broke through the continued outworking of the act and, as in Lev. 16, passed it on to the animal and so removed the guilt (Lev. 16:20, 22; cf. 17:11). The essential point is that God alone is the one who frees and forgives in all acts of atonement. However, not every sin could be atoned for and so forgiven by rites of atonement (e.g., offenses against the law of circumcision, Gen. 17:14; against the laws of the Sabbath and the Passover, Exod. 12:15; Num. 9:13).

In Isa. 40–55 the prophet recognizes that atonement by means of the blood of animals is not enough. Moreover, he sees that in the situation of the exile expiatory ritual will disappear. In the coming Servant of God Isaiah heralds the one on whom the sin of Israel and of the other nations will be laid, and through whom God will bring about an all-embracing atonement and forgiveness of sin (Isa. 53; cf. 55:6–13).

4. *Judaism. aphiēmi* and *aphesis* are found as terms for forgiveness in Josephus and Philo. However, a tension appears between this and the forgiving goodness of God that is associated in the OT with his righteousness (cf. Ps. 143:11). This is especially apparent in Josephus. The idea of one's working together with God and God's justice causes this Jewish historian to turn forgiveness into leniency on God's part. Where there is confession of sin and a change of mind, God is ready to be reconciled and hence to remit punishment. But this kind of forgiveness does not mean that evil is overcome and sin removed.

Rab. Judaism developed a thoroughgoing system of casuistry, in which God's forgiveness is catalogued. A distinction is made between (a) forgiveness of sins in this world by virtue of repentance and propitiatory sacrifices (e.g., on the great Day of Atonement); (b) forgiveness of sins in the world to come by means of expiation in the fire of Gehenna, or by means of divine grace; and (c) forgiveness of sins, or preservation from sins, in the messianic age. In connection with the latter, it is said that the Messiah will gain forgiveness for Israel on the grounds of his intercession and sufferings (*Tg. Isa.* 53:4ff.), but there is nowhere a reference to the Messiah forgiving sins by virtue of his own authority. God alone has the right to forgive sins. As in the OT, however, there are unforgivable sins (e.g., blasphemy against the name of God).

5. *Qumran.* There are a number of passages (e.g., 1QS 2:8, 16; 3:6–12; 11:3; CD 2:3–4; 3:18) that speak of God's forgiveness. In addition to a strong consciousness of election and mission, every single member of the community had a marked sense of sin and worthlessness. This awareness and at the same time knowledge of election by God was emphasized by a strong insistence on sin and forgiveness and with it a confession of utter dependence on God's grace. Forgiveness at Qumran was not tied to bloody rites of propitiation; rather, it was obtained by those who saw the error of their ways and turned from it in humility and a right spirit. Those who did not repent sincerely, but clung to Belial (Satan), excluded themselves from forgiveness and thus from the new covenant.

NT 1. *aphiēmi* occurs 143x in the NT. Of these 47 occur in Matt., 34 each in Mk. and the Lucan writings, and 15 in Jn. This leaves only 13x in the rest of the NT. In most instances *aphiēmi* denotes the original senses of to let, dismiss, divorce, release, leave, leave behind, or abandon. Only 45x does it bear the sense to forgive. Of these 45x, it is used occasionally in a secular sense (Matt. 18:27, 32), but usually in the religious sense (e.g., Matt. 12:32 par.)—e.g., forgiveness of sins (Mk. 2:5, 7, par.; Lk. 7:47–49), debts (Matt. 6:12), or trespasses (Mk. 11:25–26; Matt. 6:14–15).

aphesis, by contrast, occurs 17x in the NT, of which 15 have the sense of forgiveness (cf. Mk. 1:4 par.; Matt. 26:28; Lk. 1:77; Acts 2:38; Heb. 9:22), and 2 release from captivity (Lk. 4:18). In Paul's writings, *aphesis* occurs only in Eph. 1:7 and Col. 1:14.

paresis, passing over, letting go unpunished, occurs only at Rom. 3:25. There are, in addition, further circumlocutions for forgiveness (some of them echoing OT ritual language), such as *kalyptō*, to cover (→ *2821*); *airō*, to take away, cancel (e.g., Jn. 1:29; → *149*); *apolouō*, to get oneself washed (→ *louō, 3374*). In Paul the idea is expressed in more precise theological terms: *dikaioō*, to justify (→ *dikaiosynē, 1466*); and *katallassō*, to reconcile (→ *2904*).

2. (a) The mere fact that we are sinners has destroyed our relationship with God (→ *hamartia, 281*), so forgiveness takes the central place in Christian proclamation as the means whereby this relationship is restored. It stands as the action of God in the face of human sin and is based on Christ's work (Col. 1:14; Eph. 1:7), whose power to forgive sins is made known in preaching (Lk. 24:47; Acts 10:42–43; 13:38), baptism (cf. Acts 2:38; Rom. 6:1–4), and the Lord's Supper (Matt. 26:28; cf. Jn. 6:53–58). The OT proclamation of forgiveness is here taken up and preached afresh as the fulfillment in Christ of what was promised of the old covenant (Jer. 31:34; 33:8) in the eschatological present (cf. Lk. 1:77; 4:18–21). The Synoptic Gospels and Acts often use the phrase "forgiveness of sins" (cf. Mk. 1:4–5 par.; Acts 5:31). The terms preferred by the other NT writers—such as redemption (*apolytrōsis*), reconciliation (*katallagē*), justification (*dikaiōsis*)—concentrate more on the work of Christ.

(b) According to Mk. 10:45 par., the preaching of Jesus reached its climax in the forgiveness brought by him (Matt. 18:21–35; Lk. 4:18–21; 15:11–32). It appears as the activity appropriate to him (Mk. 2:7, 10, par.; Lk. 7:49). In Mk. 2:1–12 par. (the healing of the paralytic), we see forgiveness taking, despite all the objections, the place it is to occupy in the activity of Jesus as the one proper essential work he has come to do. Jesus' attitude to notorious sinners underlines his preaching by action (Lk. 7:36–50; 19:1–10).

(c) Forgiveness includes both making of no account the sin that has been committed (Mk. 2:5 par.; cf. Jn. 8:11) and the acceptance of the sinner (Lk. 15:20–32; cf. also Col. 1:13–14, which speaks of deliverance from the dominion of the powers and transference to Christ's kingdom), to whom a new life is given and with it the promise of eternal life (Matt. 5:43–48; Lk. 23:43; Jn. 14:19b). Early Christian preaching shows that this acceptance is at the same time an acceptance into the church. It therefore includes a share in the forgiveness that is continually pronounced there, because it is continually needed (Matt. 18:18; cf. 16:19; Jn. 20:23).

Forgiveness is closely associated with the death of Jesus on the cross (cf. Jn. 3:16; Rom. 8:32; Heb. 9:22). As the "Lamb of God," he takes away the sin of the world (Jn. 1:29; cf. 1 Pet. 2:21–24). In the Lord's Supper reference is made to the reconciling effect of Jesus' death in the words "blood of the covenant . . . poured out . . . for the forgiveness of sins" (Matt. 26:28). In 1 Cor. 15:17 it is linked to the resurrection of Jesus (cf. Rom. 4:25; 14:9; 2 Cor. 5:15b; cf. also Acts 5:31).

(d) Repentance (*metanoia*, → *3567*) and confession of sins (Mk. 1:15; Acts 2:38; 5:31; 1 Jn. 1:9) are not "works" offered up to God.

Rather, they are the acceptance, brought about by God himself, of his verdict on the "old self" and an openness to his word of deliverance (cf. Acts 19:18). Nor can the readiness of a person to forgive a fellow human being, with which the divine declaration of forgiveness is closely linked (Matt. 6:12 par.; 14–15; Mk. 11:25; Lk. 6:37), be regarded as a meritorious precondition. It belongs to the new life that has been given by Christ. Where this has been received, it is the natural, daily sign of the forgiven sinner's gratitude.

This process is demonstrated negatively by the example of the wicked servant (Matt. 18:32–35). The passages cited from the Sermon on the Mount are also directed at those who have already received God's forgiveness, in whom gratitude is to be expected, showing itself in one's imitation of Christ and his forgiveness (cf. Col. 3:13; Eph. 4:32). One's forgiveness of a debtor (Matt. 6:12 par.) and even of an enemy (Matt. 5:38–48; Rom. 12:19–21) comes about as the consequence of God's forgiveness in Christ.

(e) As noted above, in Paul the terms *aphiēmi* and *aphesis* virtually disappear (cf. Rom. 4:7). This is because the proclamation of forgiveness appears there as a systematized doctrine. The fact that forgiveness is not merely a remission of past guilt, but includes total deliverance from the power of sin and restoration to fellowship with God, is expressed by Paul in his doctrine of justification (cf. Rom. 3:21–28; 4:22, 25; Gal. 3:6–9) and of reconciliation (of the sinner, Rom. 5:10–11; 2 Cor. 5:18; of the world, Rom. 11:15; 2 Cor. 5:19) with God. These have taken place in Christ as God's own free act and form the center of the gospel. Forgiveness takes place because God gives himself completely in the sacrifice of his Son (Rom. 8:32; 2 Cor. 5:21) and so gives a person a share in his own righteousness (Rom. 3:21–28). Thus, "in Christ" we become pardoned sinners (Rom. 8:1) and new creatures (2 Cor. 5:17).

(f) The task of proclaiming this message of forgiveness is given to the church, which carries it out in preaching, in the personal declaration of forgiveness to individuals, and in the rites of baptism and the Eucharist. The last of these is not a case of mere reference to and repetition of something past. Each celebration of the Lord's Supper is a fresh act of proclamation, coming from Christ himself to the concrete situation of the present (1 Cor. 11:26). The validity of forgiveness is grounded in the authority given by Christ to the church (Matt. 18:18; cf. 16:19; Jn. 20:23; cf. also 1 Jn. 5:16) and always remains conditional on obedience to him.

Moreover, forgiveness comes about through the renewed realization of forgiveness in the real situations of everyday life, with their call to decision, and not in some timeless application. This prong is shown by the commission to retain sin along with the commission to forgive sins (*krateō* used rather than *aphiēmi*, Jn. 20:23; cf. Matt. 18:18; 16:19). Without this, forgiveness would be in danger of being trivialized. In this connection see Acts 5:1–11; 1 Cor. 5:1–5; Heb. 6:4; 10:26–27; 1 Jn. 5:16–17.

923	ἀφίστημι

ἀφίστημι (*aphistēmi*), trans. cause to revolt, mislead; intrans. go away, withdraw, depart, (*923*); ἀποστασία (*apostasia*), rebellion, state of apostasy, defection (*686*).

CL & OT 1. In cl. Gk. *aphistēmi* means trans. to put away, remove: (a) in a spatial sense; (b) from a condition or relationship; or (c) from association with a person. It also means to turn someone against a person, to cause to revolt. Intrans. it means to remove oneself, go away; withdraw from, give up; fall away. From it are derived the nouns *apostasis* (later *apostasia*), revolt, apostasy; *apostatēs*, deserter, political rebel; and *apostasion*, a legal term for handing over at the time of purchase, also used of a bill of divorce (Deut. 24:1, 3; Matt. 5:31; 19:7; Mk. 10:4).

2. In the LXX words of this group occur more than 250x, rendering about 40 different Heb. words. They are of special interest theologically when used to translate forms of *māʿal*, to act unfaithfully

or against the law (2 Chr. 26:18; 28:19, 22); *pāšaʿ*, to rebel, transgress (21:8, 10); and *mārad*, to rebel, revolt (Gen. 14:4; Jos. 22:18). The meaning of *aphistēmi* is like that in cl. Gk.: removal in a spatial sense (Gen. 12:8), separation of persons (1 Sam. 18:13; Ps. 6:8), withdrawal from a relationship (Num. 8:25) or from a state (Prov. 23:18; Isa. 59:9), and political revolt (Gen. 14:4; 2 Chr. 21:8, 10; Ezek. 17:15).

A meaning not found in cl. Gk. is the use in religious contexts: God departs from people (Jdg. 16:20; 2 Ki. 17:18; 23:27) and withdraws his gifts (Num. 14:9, protection; 2 Sam. 7:15, steadfast love; Isa. 59:11, 14, salvation and righteousness). The underlying cause is our own willful departure from God (Deut. 32:15; Jer. 2:5; 3:14) and scorn of his gifts (Num. 14:31; Neh. 9:26). This rebellion expresses itself in the cultic worship of other gods (Deut. 7:4; 13:10, 13; Jdg. 2:19 A) and in ethical behavior of disobedience toward God (Ezek. 33:8 A; Dan. 9:9–11). Against this background we should understand exhortations to resist sin (Exod. 23:7; Ps. 119:29; Isa. 52:11).

3. At Qumran the act of turning away from the community and its rules was condemned as apostasy. The literature of the sect sets down a two-year period of repentance for the apostate member who wanted to return (1QS 7:18ff.), but anyone who had belonged to the community for more than ten years was completely excluded if he became guilty of apostasy (1QS 7:22ff.).

NT 1. In the NT this group of words is found only in Luke, Paul, and Heb. 3:12. On the word *apostasion*, bill of divorce, also part of this word group, → 687.

2. *aphistēmi* occurs in the spatial sense in Lk. 2:37 ("she never left the temple"). More often it refers to the separation of people: holding back from carrying out a punishment (Acts 5:38; 22:29), Mark's withdrawal from helping Paul in his work (15:38), the departure of the Christians from the Jewish synagogue (19:9), and the disappearance of supernatural beings from human presence (Lk. 4:13; Acts 12:10; 2 Cor. 12:8). In Lk. 13:27 (citation of Ps. 6:8) believers are warned against unfruitful discipleship. Those who fail to grasp the present hour of grace may one day find themselves separated forever from the Lord. In 2 Tim. 2:19 *aphistēmi* refers to moral behavior: "Everyone who confesses the name of the Lord must turn away from wickedness." Acts 5:37 uses the word for political defection.

3. Of theological importance is falling away in the religious sense. In Acts 21:21 (cf. 2 Macc. 5:8) Paul is accused of leading the Diaspora Jews astray by teaching them to disregard the OT law. The absolute use of *apostasia* in 2 Thess. 2:3 is a common expression in Jewish apocalyptic, with its prophecy of a period of apostasy shortly before the appearance of the Messiah (*1 Enoch* 5:4; 93:9). Paul locates this event in an anti-Christian period directly preceding the return of Christ. In 1 Tim. 4:1 he states that some will "abandon the faith" in the last days in terms of falling into false, heretical beliefs.

Lk. 8:13 probably refers to apostasy as a result of eschatological temptation. Here are people who have come to believe, who have received the gospel "with joy." But under pressure of persecution and tribulation arising because of the faith, they break off their relationship with God. According to Heb. 3:12, apostasy consists in an unbelieving and self-willed movement away from God.

aphistēmi thus connotes the serious situation of becoming separated from the living God, after a previous turning toward him, by falling away from the faith. It is a movement of unbelief and sin.

See also *piptō*, fall (*4406*).

926 (*aphomoioō*, make like, similar), → 3927.

928 (*aphorizō*, separate, set apart, appoint), → 3988.

932 (*aphrosynē*, lack of sense, folly, foolishness), → 3702.

933 (*aphrōn*, foolish, senseless), → 3702.

940 (*acharistos*, ungrateful), → 2374.

950 (*apseudēs*, guileless, truthful), → 6017.

952	ἄψινθος

ἄψινθος (*apsinthos*), wormwood (952).

CL & OT *apsinthos* refers to some variety of the plant group *Artemisia*, of which several varieties occur in Palestine. All of them have a bitter taste. *apsinthion* (a neut. form) occurs in Aquila's translation of Prov. 5:4; Jer. 9:15; 23:15, but the word group appears nowhere else in the LXX.

NT *apsinthos* should be understood lit. in Rev. 8:11: "The name of the star is Wormwood. A third of the waters turned bitter [lit., became wormwood), and many people died from the waters that had become bitter." It is part of a vision of judgment on the ungodly world.

The problem with this use of *apsinthos* is that it both refers to the name of a star and then describes the water into which the star fell. Obviously the water became bitter and the name of the star is connected with this bitterness. In Rev., however, the water causes death, whereas wormwood, while bitter, is not known to be poisonous. The author may have in mind a genuinely poisonous substance, other than the wormwood we know. Or he may be using a way of speech clearly evident in antiquity, whereby bitterness and poison were connected. Perhaps John is reasoning from the bitterness of the taste to the bitterness of the results. This fits in also with the fact that in the OT wormwood is used of God's punishment of the wicked, including their death; e.g., "This is what the LORD Almighty, the God of Israel, says: 'See, I will make this people eat bitter food and drink poisoned water'" (Jer. 9:15; cf. 23:15).

B *beta*

<table>
<tr><td>956</td><td>Βαβυλών</td></tr>
</table>

Βαβυλών (*Babylōn*), Babylon (*956*).

CL & OT 1. (a) We do not know when Babylon was founded. The earliest known reference, from the time of Shar-kali-sharri of Akkad (*c.* 2500–2290 B.C.), is to Bab-ilim, gate of god, which appears to be a popular etymology of a pre-Sem. name, Babila. The Gk. form expresses the later pl. variation Bab-ilani, gate of the gods.

(b) The town had little historical importance prior to Hammurabi (18th cent. B.C.), who made it the cultural leader of the Near East. This was partially due to making Marduk the city god of Babylon, and so the head of the Sumerian-Akkadian pantheon of some 1,300 deities. It brought all the religious traditions into one system. Babylon made great advances, independently of Greece, in philology, medicine, mathematics, and astronomy (cf. Dan. 1:4, 17).

(c) Babylon regained political power during the time of the Chaldean kings (625–539 B.C.), the most important of whom was Nebuchadnezzar (605–562). Its immense riches came from its far-reaching commercial traffic.

2. Gen. 10:8–12 traces back the concept of world dominion to Babylon, after which it passed to Assyria. In 11:1–9 the architecture of the giant temple of Babylon is stigmatized as the expression of human pride that wishes to storm heaven.

3. As a result of the exile we find four types of statements concerning Babylon. (a) The king of Babylon is Yahweh's instrument for the destruction of Judah and its allies (Jer. 25:9; 27:6–7). He bears Yahweh's sword in his world conquest (Ezek. 30:24–25). Judah will be destroyed because of its harlotry with Assyria and Babylon, in view of the introduction of their cults when on friendly terms with them (23:11–32).

(b) Toward the end of the exile, the downfall of Babylon and the deliverance of the exiles were proclaimed (Isa. 47; 48:12–16a, 20–22; 21:1–10; Jer. 50; 51). In this connection the total desolation of Babylon in war was expected.

(c) Isa. 13 expects the eradication of sinners and the destruction of tyranny to coincide with the destruction of Babylon, and 14:1–23 mocks Babylon as a fallen power, the end of which will bring peace and salvation to all peoples. Here Babylon appears as a type of the power that opens to those who are evil every possibility in the world. When it falls, they perish. As the later chapters of Isa. show, the polemic against Babylon exceeded in seriousness anything that had gone before.

(d) Contrary to expectation, Babylon was not destroyed, and the freeing of the exiles did not mark the opening of a new era of salvation. Dan. 2 and 7 speaks of four world powers that eliminated one another: Babylon, Media, Persia, and Greece. The destruction of the last of them would be followed by a final kingdom of salvation.

NT 1. The mention of Babylon in Acts 7:43 picks up OT threads: The Babylonian exile happened as punishment for Israel's persistent idolatry. According to Matt. 1:11, 17, the second phase of Israel's history ended with the exile. After the passing of fourteen more generations (as in the previous two periods), the fulfillment of all God's promises was to be expected—esp. the promise of Jesus, the Messiah.

Babylon in 1 Pet. 5:13 (seen against the background of Jewish parallels) most likely refers to Rome. The significance of this name, which is probably more than a mere disguise, is as follows: As the Jews once lived in exile in Babylon, so the Christians now live as exiles in the world; they are strangers in the dispersion (1 Pet. 1:1), attacked with hate by a totalitarian world that seeks to have its own way (cf. 4:12–18; 5:8–9).

2. The most important references to Babylon are in Rev. 14:8; 16:19; 17:1–19:10, which links up with Isa. 13 and 14. Here Babylon is the type of worldly power in rebellion against God and the antitype of the heavenly Jerusalem (21:1–22:5). In the last analysis history consists in the great struggle of worldly power against the rule of Christ. As Christ is killed and passes on his way through death to resurrection and redemption, the powers of this world continually manifest their might, riches, and abominations. But in the end they will be conquered by the slaughtered Lamb on the throne.

Babylon the Great has some of the features of historic Rome. Like Rome, she sits "on many waters" (17:1) and has seven hills (cf. 17:4, 9). She wears a fillet with a name, as worn by Roman harlots (17:5). The description of the woman riding on the beast (17:3–4) recalls pictures of oriental gods and goddesses, esp. Cybele of Rome.

<table>
<tr><td>958</td><td>βάθος</td></tr>
</table>

βάθος (*bathos*), depth (*958*); βαθύς (*bathys*), deep (*960*).

CL & OT 1. (a) In cl. Gk. *bathos* denotes the extension of a thing in any spatial dimension (downward, horizontal, or even upward). In military usage it indicates the number of men standing behind one another. Used fig. *bathos* expresses the completeness, intensity, or greatness of an object or human quality (wisdom, understanding, soul) as well as its inscrutability and hiddenness. The derived adj. *bathys* has the same shades of meaning as the noun.

(b) Hel. and esp. gnostic religion took up the fig. meaning in speaking of the depth of deity and of God as depth. God was thought of primarily as apersonal, not as Thou or He.

2. (a) In the LXX *bathos* is rarely used lit., though it does refer to the sources of rivers (Job 28:11; Zech. 10:11;) and the depths of the sea (Wis. 10:19). In its fig. sense it always denotes that which is separated from God. *bathos* thus stands for the inner need of a person troubled by guilt and sin (Ps. 130:1) and the external need of pressing circumstances (Ps. 69:2, 14). It also expresses the most extreme separation from God (the depths of the sea, Jon. 2:4; Mic. 7:19) in passages where the frontier between lit. and fig. meanings is fluid. In Ezek. *bathos* means the underworld (cf. Ezek. 26:20; 31:14, 18; 32:18–19, 24), which also expresses separation from God.

(b) It is significant that although Heb. *tᵉhôm* is generally translated the deep (e.g., Gen. 1:2), the LXX does not render it *bathos* but *abyssos* (→ *12*). While *bathos* always contains the idea of separation from God, *abyssos* suggests a final, terrible, and mysterious depth.

NT 1. *bathos* appears 8x in the NT; the adj. *bathys*, 4x. The lit. sense of *bathos* occurs only in the Synoptics: depth of soil (Matt. 13:5), the depth of the sea (Lk. 5:4). In 2 Cor. 8:2 it denotes "extreme poverty."

2. Rom. 11:33 and 1 Cor. 2:10 speak of the depth of God or the depth of the knowledge of God. This refers to the unfathomable nature of his ways and judgments in contrast to the superficiality of human insight. But it also suggests a richness of the ways and means available to God to pursue his plan of salvation. It is important that God is not reduced here to an impersonal it. He is not described as the ultimate ground of all being, but as the one who has revealed himself in Jesus Christ, in whom are hid the ultimate mysteries.

3. Similarly, in Eph. 3:18 *bathos* expresses the comprehensiveness of God's grace and of Christ's love. Christian faith should not be satisfied with the fragmentary or the superficial.

4. In Rom. 8:39 *bathos* is linked with *hypsōma* ("height," cf. Isa. 7:11) and clearly describes some kind of power that oppresses humanity. In astrology *bathos* is the part of heaven below the horizon, from which the stars rise. Powers emanating from the stars are perhaps

intended here. What is theologically decisive is the statement that even these powers have been defeated by the power of God's love in Jesus Christ—a statement of great relevance even today.

5. In Lk. 24:1; Jn. 4:11; Acts 20:9, *bathys* has a somewhat lit. meaning: "very early" in the morning, a "deep" well, and a "deep" sleep. But Rev. 2:24 is of theological significance. Here Jesus refers to the "deep secrets" of Satan as promoted by "that woman Jezebel" (2:20). These involve participation in the immorality and ungodliness of this world. To plunge into such depths does not mean control over these powers but surrender to them and the loss of salvation.

See also *hypsos*, high (*5737*); *hypsoō*, exalt, raise (*5738*).

960 (*bathys*, deep), → *958*.

966	βαπτίζω

βαπτίζω (*baptizō*), dip, immerse, baptize (*966*); βάπτω (*baptō*), dip (*970*); βαπτισμός (*baptismos*), dipping, washing (*968*); βάπτισμα (*baptisma*) baptism (*967*); βαπτιστής (*baptistēs*) baptizer, Baptist (*969*).

CL & OT 1. In secular Greek *baptō* means dip, dye, draw (water). *baptizō* is an intensive form of *baptō*, meaning dip, cause to perish (as by drowning a man or sinking a ship). For ritual washings, in general *louō*, wash (the whole body), *niptō*, wash or rinse (parts of the body), and *rhainō*, sprinkle, were used.

2. In the LXX *baptō* usually translates the Heb *ṭābal*, dip (13x). *baptizō* occurs only 4x, translating *ṭāba* only in 2 Ki. 5:14, where it is used in the mid. of Naaman's sevenfold immersion in the Jordan. The use of *baptizō* in the story of Naaman may have been decisive for its later use in the mid. to signify taking a ritual bath for cleansing.

It seems that *baptizō*, both in Jewish and Christian contexts, normally meant immerse and that even when it became a technical term for baptism, the thought of immersion remains. The metaphorical uses of the word in the NT appear to take this for granted, such as the prophecy that the Messiah will baptize in Spirit and fire (Matt. 3:11), the "baptism" of the Israelites in the cloud and the sea (1 Cor. 10:2), and Jesus' death as a baptism (Mk. 10:38–39; Lk. 12:50). The Pauline representation of baptism as burial and resurrection with Christ is consonant with this view.

3. The Jewish baptizing sects (including Qumran) do not appear to have used *ṭābal* and *baptizō* for their lustrations. It is doubtful whether these lustrations should in any sense be classed with baptism, seeing that they were repeated often while baptism is received only once; nevertheless, it does seem as if a novice's first lustration had the character of initiation into full membership of the community. Note too that these lustrations were accompanied by penitence and submission to God's will and were thus viewed as effective for the cleansing of moral impurity.

4. A Gentile convert to Judaism at the beginning of the Christian era was required to receive circumcision, undergo a ritual bath, and offer a sacrifice. The Heb. and Aram. word *ṭābal* is used for this so-called "proselyte baptism." The few references to this event in Gk. lit. employ *baptō*, not *baptizō*. The extent to which proselyte baptism influenced the baptism of John and early Christian baptism is a much-debated question, esp. since the earliest references to it belong to the latter half of the 1st cent. A.D. Note that the decisive event for proselytes was circumcision, not baptism. The Christian understanding of baptism in terms of dying and rising is determined by its character as a baptism into the Messiah, who died and rose and thereby inaugurated the "age to come."

NT 1. John's baptism is universally described in the NT by the vb. *baptizō*; this is also true of Christian baptism throughout the NT. *baptō* occurs 4x (Lk. 16:24; Jn. 13:26 [2x]; Rev. 19:13), and only with the meaning dip. Of the noun forms *baptismos* occurs only 4x; *baptisma* occurs 19x and refers to John's baptism, Christian baptism, or the baptism (death) that Jesus had to undergo. John himself is often called *baptistēs*, the baptizer (12x, only in the Synoptics).

2. *The baptism of John.* John's baptism, which was a "baptism of repentance for the forgiveness of sins" (Mk. 1:4), had two focal points: It marked the "turn" (repentance) of a Jew to God, associating a person with the penitent people and assuring that person of forgiveness and cleansing, and it anticipated the messianic baptism with Spirit and fire, assuring the penitent one a place in the kingdom (cf. Matt. 3:11). Isa. 4:2–5 and Mal. 3:1–6 suggest that this messianic baptism was symbolic of a universal judgment that would refine God's people and fit them for the kingdom, but that would consume the wicked.

3. *Jesus' baptism and the command to baptize.* Christian baptism is rooted in the redemptive action of Jesus. His submission to the baptism of John (Mk. 1:9) demonstrated his solidarity with sinful humanity. The divine approval it received (1:10–11) showed it to be the initiation of the movement of salvation. The authorization of baptism during Jesus' ministry (Jn. 4:1–2) was provisional. The command to baptize belongs in the resurrection era, after redemption was achieved, universal authority was given to the risen Lord, and the mission of the church to the world began (Matt. 28:18–20).

4. *The early church.* (a) Baptism seems to have accompanied the proclamation of the gospel from the beginning of the church's mission (Acts 2). Baptism required repentance (2:38) and was administered "in the name of Jesus Christ," i.e., in relation to Jesus Christ and with the use of his name, so that the baptized called on the name of Christ (22:16) even as the name was called over them, signifying to whom they belonged (cf. Jas. 2:7). It was "for the forgiveness of . . . sins" and with a view to receiving the Holy Spirit (Acts 2:38). Variations from this norm (notably 8:14–17; 10:44–45; 19:1–6) reflect the variety of circumstances and of experiences of the Spirit in a period of transition.

(b) Paul's interpretation of baptism in Gal. 3:27 is significant. Baptism is "into Christ" (a shorthand expression for "into the name of Christ"); it relates believers to Christ in such a way that they are "in Christ" (cf. 3:26). From this basic view flow the other features of baptism that appear in Paul.

- Baptism "into Christ" is baptism "into his death" (Rom. 6:3–4); it relates believers to Christ's redemptive action, so that Christ's death on Golgotha was their death; it entailed an end ("death") to the life of estrangement from God and the beginning of life in Christ.
- Baptism into Christ is baptism into the church, for to be in Christ is to be a member of the body of Christ (Gal. 3:27–29; 1 Cor. 12:13).
- Baptism into Christ is baptism into the Spirit of Christ (1 Cor. 12:13), for the Spirit and Christ are inseparable (Rom. 8:9–11; 2 Cor. 3:17).
- Baptism into Christ involves a life after the pattern of Christ's dying to sin and rising for righteousness (Rom. 6:4; cf. the baptismal ethics of Col. 3:3–13).
- Baptism into Christ is for life in the kingdom to be revealed in the day of Christ (2 Cor. 1:22; Eph. 1:13; 4:30).

This eschatological relation of baptism explains the adoption by the church of the custom of baptizing the living for the dead (cf. 1 Cor. 15:29), that the latter might share in the kingdom of God. The practice cannot be reconciled with Paul's proclamation and was used by him only as part of a polemic against those who denied the resurrection.

Baptism into Christ is subordinate to the gospel of Christ (1 Cor. 1:17). Paul as an apostle usually left it to others to administer (1:14–16). This is not to minimize baptism but to clarify its function. It embodies the gospel of grace and the occasion for confessing it. Confessional declarations in the NT letters may have originated as baptismal confessions (e.g., Rom. 10:9; Phil. 2:6–11; Eph. 4:4–6; Col. 1:13–20).

(c) The relation between "washing" and the "word" is reflected in Eph. 5:26 (cf. 4:5). In harmony with this, 1 Pet. 3:21 defines baptism as "the pledge [or response, cf. NIV note] of a good conscience toward God." In this context the power of the resurrection becomes known (baptism "saves you by the resurrection of Jesus Christ").

In Jn 3:3–5 and Tit. 3:5 baptism is associated with regeneration (→ *gennaō, 1164*). In both passages the operation of the Spirit is in the foreground. In Tit. 3:5 (a baptismal hymn?) the pertinent clause should be rendered, "He saved us through the washing characterized by the regeneration and renewal wrought by the Holy Spirit," while Jn. 3:3–5 affirms the necessity of a new beginning from God ("from above," see NIV note) through submission to baptism and the recreative work of the Holy Spirit. Through the lifting up of Jesus on the cross (3:14–15) and the sending of the Holy Spirit (3:8; cf. 7:39), the two "baptisms" have been brought together.

(d) In Acts and the NT letters baptism appears as a divine-human event. Both elements are given due weight. (i) *Divine.* Since baptism signifies union with Christ (Gal. 3:27), all that Christ did for humankind in his redeeming acts is joined with baptism in the apostolic writings: union with Christ (Rom. 6:1–5; Col. 2:11–12), forgiveness of sins and cleansing from sins (Acts 2:38; 22:16), bestowal of the Spirit (2:38; 1 Cor. 12:13), membership in the body of Christ (12:13; Gal. 3:27), renewal by the Spirit (Tit. 3:5), and the promise of the kingdom of God (Jn. 3:5). (ii) *Human.* In order to receive these benefits of Christ and his saving grace, human beings must exercise faith. This joining of divine action and human faith within the context of baptism implies two things: that God's gracious gift to the faithful belongs to the context of baptism, and that his gift in baptism is only to those with faith (see esp.1 Pet. 3:21).

A word of caution is, however, required. Acts demonstrates that all statements about the action of God in baptism must allow for divine freedom in bestowing salvation and the Spirit. At Pentecost, for example, the Spirit was poured out on a company of men and women who had not received *Christian* baptism (i.e., baptism in the name of Jesus), and we do not know how many of them had received any other baptism. The complicated phenomena regarding baptism and the Spirit in the stories of the Samaritan believers (Acts 8:14–17), Cornelius and his company (10:44–48), and the Ephesian "disciples" (19:1–6) doubtless were not solitary in the early church. Life is more complex than formulations of doctrine, and God is able to meet every variation from the norm.

5. *Infant baptism.* The belief that the apostles commanded the baptism of infants as well as of responsible persons is attested as early as Origen (3d cent. A.D.). Apart from some notable exceptions, it became the unquestioned conviction of Christendom until the present century. The rise of the critical study of the Bible caused a widespread change of opinion, so that by 1940 the majority of NT scholars agreed that in the apostolic age baptism was administered to believers only.

This revised view was contested in the 1950s and 1960s, above all by O. Cullmann and J. Jeremias. It was maintained that the traditional arguments for the apostolic institution of infant baptism are vindicated by sound theology and by modern biblical and archaeological research. For example, that household baptisms (Acts 11:14; 16:33; 18:8) included infants is strengthened by the contention that the term *oikos* (house) had gained an almost technical significance among Jews and had special reference to little children. The terminology of Jewish proselyte baptism is perhaps suggested in 1 Cor. 7:14, with the presumption that the Jewish customs of baptizing young children of proselytes was accepted by the primitive church. The saying of Jesus concerning little children and the kingdom of God (Mk. 10:14) has been given form-critical evaluation: The story is said to reflect the *Sitz im Leben* of a church seeking to answer the question, "Should we baptize our children?" and the answer is implied, "Yes, bring them to baptism as they were once brought to Jesus." This conclusion is supported by the contention that the command "Do not hinder them" reflects an early liturgical use of the term in baptism (→ *kōlyō, 3266*).

The Reformed view of the one covenant with its continuing sacraments, stressing the close relation between circumcision and baptism, is supported by typological exegesis, hinted at in 1 Cor. 10:1–6 (where baptism is seen as symbolized by the passing through the Red Sea) and Col. 2:11–12. Evidence from early Christian burial inscriptions is given as proof of the baptism of infants in the earliest church.

These views have met with differing reactions. Some consider the rise of infant baptism to be no earlier than the close of the 2d cent. A.D. Others believe that infant baptism is excluded from the horizon of the apostolic writers, not only because of the lack of explicit reference, but also by their equation of the gift of baptism with the gift of faith. Moreover, according to the NT, baptism imparts to the baptized not only a blessing but esp. Christ and his full salvation. This is comprehensible only in a milieu where baptism and personal conversion are inseparable (cf. Acts 2:41; 16:33).

6. (a) *baptismos*, dipping, immersion, represents Jewish ritual cleansing (by immersion) of vessels in Mk. 7:4; in Heb. 9:10 it refers to the purification of persons. Presumably this reflects the Jewish usage of the term. Among Greek-speaking Jews this word was probably used for proselyte baptism. In Heb. 6:2, "instruction about baptisms" (*baptismoi*) denotes instruction about the contrast between Christian baptism and all other religious washings.

(b) The word *baptisma* appears for the first time in the NT. Since its earliest use is for the baptism of John, it may have been coined by John's disciples, though it is more likely a Christian innovation that was then referred back to John's baptism. It seems that *baptisma* was formed on the analogy of its Heb. equivalent, *ṭᵉbîlâ*, in order to express the Christian conviction that baptism was a new thing in the world, differing from all Jewish and pagan purificatory rites.

See also *louō*, wash (*3374*); *niptō*, wash (*3782*).

967 (*baptisma*, baptism), → *966*.

968 (*baptismos*, dipping, washing), → *966*.

969 (*baptistēs*, baptizer, Baptist), → *966*.

970 (*baptō*, dip), → *966*.

975 (*barbaros*, barbarian, foreigner, non-Greek), → *1818*.

976 (*bareō*, load, burden, weigh down), → *983*.

977 (*bareōs*, heavily, with difficulty), → *983*.

983	βάρος

βάρος (*baros*), weight, burden (*983*); βαρύς (*barys*), heavy, burdensome, weighty, important, fierce (*987*); βαρέω (*bareō*), load, burden, weigh down (*976*); βαρέως (*bareōs*), heavily, with difficulty (*977*); βαρύτιμος (*barytimos*), very expensive or precious (*988*); ἐπιβαρέω (*epibareō*), to burden (*2096*); καταβαρέω (*katabareō*), to burden, weigh down (*2851*); φορτίον (*phortion*), burden, load (*5845*); φορτίζω (*phortizō*), burden, load (*5844*).

CL & OT *baros* in cl. Gk. and Hel. usage means a weight or burden; the adj. *barys* means heavy. The vb. *bareō* means load, burden, weigh down. The diminutive *phortion* (from *phortos*) means a load or burden carried by an animal or person, hence also cargo. All these words came to be used interchangeably.

In the LXX *baros* and *bareō* occur only rarely; *barys* is more frequent. The adv. *bareōs* in conjunction with *akouō* (hear) denotes being heavy of hearing (Isa. 6:10; cf. Matt. 13:15; Acts 28:27). Isaiah is called to prophesy and make the heart of the people calloused, their ears dull (heavy), and their eyes shut; "otherwise they might see with their eyes, hear with their ears, understand with their hearts, and turn and be healed."

NT 1. (a) *baros* is used in Matt. 20:12 of the burden of daily toil. The Jerusalem council desired to lay no greater burden on the Gentile Christians than that they should abstain from meat sacrificed to idols, from blood, from what had been strangled, and from sexual immorality (Acts 15:28–29). Teaching in Rev. 2:24 is also described as a burden. In 2 Cor. 1:8; 5:4, Paul speaks of being burdened (*bareō*; NIV "pressure" in 1:8) by persecution on the one hand and the general human condition on the other; these are overcome by confidence in God, who raises the dead, and by hope of ultimate triumph. *bareō* is used of eyes heavy with sleep (Matt. 26:43; Lk. 9:32), of being weighed down with dissipation and drunkenness (21:34), and of the church being burdened by unnecessary financial demands (1 Tim. 5:16).

(b) Affliction prepares for us "an eternal glory that . . . outweighs (*baros doxēs*) them all" (2 Cor. 4:17). Paul's use of *baros* here may be influenced by the fact that weight and glory in Heb. come from the same root, *kbd*. In Gal. 6:2 Paul encourages his readers to bear one another's burdens—to come to the aid of one another, if overtaken by a fault. Such joint bearing does not do away with the personal responsibility of Christians, however, for everyone also has to bear his or her own load (*phortion*, 6:5) before God. In 1 Thess. 2:7, *baros* denotes the weight of authority that Paul might have exerted at Thessalonica, had he so wished. It also denotes the financial burden he spared them by working to support himself (2:9, *epibareō*).

(c) While *bareō* is used in the NT only in the pass., compounds are used in the act.: *epibareō* (2 Cor. 2:5; 1 Thess. 2:9; 2 Thess. 3:8) and *katabareō* (2 Cor. 12:16). Both mean to burden.

2. (a) The adj. *barys* occurs only 6x in the NT. In Acts 20:29 false teachers who break into the church are described as weighty (fierce, savage) wolves, of whom the church must beware. In 25:7 the Jews brought weighty charges against Paul. The apostle's opponents at Corinth sneered at his weighty (*bareiai*) letters (2 Cor. 10:10).

(b) Both the burden of suffering and the burden of the Mosaic law figure in the teaching of Jesus, the latter esp. in his discussions with the teachers of the law and the Pharisees. Matt. 23:4 (*phortia barea*, heavy loads) and Lk. 11:46 (*phortizete . . . phortia*, lit. burden with burdens) speak of the heavy burdens that the hypocrites lay on people without themselves touching them with a finger. They stress the multiplicity of external commandments and fail to consider "the more important matters (*ta barytera*) of the law—justice, mercy and faithfulness" (Matt. 23:23; cf. Mic. 6:8).

Compared with this yoke under which Judaism stood, Jesus' "yoke (*zygos*, → 2433) is easy and [his] burden (*phortion*) is light." For that reason he calls to himself all who are weary and burdened (*phortizō*) (Matt. 11:28–30). There are, it is true, commands for Jesus' disciples, but they are not heavy, for Jesus is yoked with those who heed this call. In the words of 1 Jn. 5:3, "his commands are not burdensome (*bareiai*)," for the commands are the enactment of love.

See also *kopos*, trouble, difficulty, labor (*3160*).

987 (*barys*, heavy, burdensome), → 983.

988 (*barytimos*, very expensive or precious), → 983.

989 (*basanizō*, to torture, torment), → 992.

990 (*basanismos*, torturing, torment), → 992.

991 (*basanistēs*, torturer), → 992.

992	βάσανος

βάσανος (*basanos*), torture, torment (*992*); βασανίζω (*basanizō*), to torture, torment (*989*); βασανισμός (*basanismos*), torturing, torment (*990*); βασανιστής (*basanistēs*), torturer (*991*).

CL & OT 1. In cl. Gk. *basanos* signified originally a means of testing, esp. for gold; then torture as a means of examination, and finally torment generally.

2. In the LXX two-thirds of the occurrences of this word group (the vb. 30x, the noun 40x) are found in 4 Macc. (e.g., 4:26; 5:6; 6:5, 10–11, 27, 30) and in the wisdom lit. (e.g., Wis. 3:1), where it means torment or torture (esp. of Jewish martyrs). In other words, it is a typical word formation of the Hel. epoch. In early Christian lit. it was used of the torture of Christian martyrs. Elsewhere in the OT *basanos* denotes means of reparation for guilt (1 Sam. 6:3–4, 8, 17), shame or disgrace

(Ezek. 16:52, 54), a cause of sin or misfortune (3:20; 7:19), or God's punishments (16:52, 54, of Jerusalem; 32:24, 30, of the heathen nations).

NT 1. In the NT the words in this group occur a total of 22x. (a) *basanos* in Matt. 4:24 is the physical afflictions of the sick that Jesus healed; in Lk. it refers to the torment that the rich man suffered (16:23) in Hades, the "place of torment" (16:28).

(b) The vb. *basanizō*, to torment, oppress, is used of the servant of the centurion from Capernaum who was tormented by his sickness (Matt. 8:6). The demons were afraid that Jesus would torment them (8:29; Mk. 5:7; Lk. 8:28). The disciples on the sea were hard pressed by the wind and waves (Matt. 14:24; Mk. 6:48). In 2 Pet. 2:8 the apostle depicts how righteous Lot felt his soul tortured by his observation of the dissolute activities of the people of Sodom. The vision of Rev. 12:2 mentions the "pain" of the mother of the Christ child, about to give birth. Elsewhere in Rev. *basanizō* is used of the torments that are the consequence of divine judgment (9:5; 11:10; 14:10; 20:10).

2. The word *basanismos* occurs 6x in Rev. It is used of the torments that are occasioned after the fifth trumpet by the eschatological locusts (9:5). In 14:11 those who worship the beast are threatened by the angel with eternal torment, while 18:7, 10, 15 deal with the *basanismos* that the prostitute Babylon, i.e., the anti-Christian city under God's judgment, must undergo.

3. *basanistēs* is used of jailers who torture the unforgiving servant in Jesus' parable (Matt. 18:34).

See also *mastigoō*, whip, flog, scourge, chastise (*3463*); *ōdinō*, to travail as in giving birth (*6048*); *talaipōreō*, experience distress, endure hard labor (*5415*).

993 (*basileia*, kingship, kingly rule, kingdom), → 995.

994 (*basileios*, royal), → 995.

995	βασιλεύς

βασιλεύς (*basileus*), ruler, king (*995*); βασιλεία (*basileia*), kingship, kingly rule, kingdom (*993*); βασιλεύω (*basileuō*), to be king, rule (*996*); συμβασιλεύω (*symbasileuō*), share the rule (*5203*); βασίλειος (*basileios*), royal (*994*); βασιλικός (*basilikos*), royal, kingly (*997*); βασίλισσα (*basilissa*), queen (*999*).

CL & OT 1. (a) In cl. Gk. *basileus* was originally a general term for a ruler. In Homer it denoted a hereditary, legitimate ruler whose power is traced back to Zeus. Thus Odysseus was a *basileus* in Ithaca. After monarchy had given place to the rule of an aristocracy, and then in various Gk. cities one noble set himself up as monarch, a new term came into being, *tyrannos*, i.e., one who has gained the rule by illegitimate means. After the "slaying of the tyrants" (514 B.C. in Athens), *tyrannos* took on a negative meaning, and the term *basileus* reemerged as the title of a just and legal ruler.

(b) The Hel. concept of divine kingship is derived from the political traditions of the Macedonian monarchy and the overshadowing personality of Alexander the Great (356–323 B.C.). The Hel. idea of divine kingship surfaced again in the Roman emperor cult. As a result, Augustus (63 B.C.–A.D. 14) was able to comprehend in his own person the *imperium* as a single whole, a unification for which there was neither national nor cultural precedent. The effect of the confession "Jesus is Lord," used by Christians, was to destroy this vital ideology of the Roman *imperium*. This led to the persecution of Christians during the first three centuries.

(c) The abstract noun *basileia* originally denoted the fact of being king, the position or power of the king, and it is best translated office of king, kingly rule. Besides this meaning came a second meaning, which emphasized the geographical aspect of *basileia*, the area over which a king reigned: his kingdom.

(d) The vb. *basileuō* means to become or be king, to reign. *symbasileuō* expresses the idea of ruling with. The adjs. *basileios* and *basilikos* both express that which appertains to a king, i.e., royal. Finally, in Hel. times the fem. term for king (i.e., queen) was *basilissa* (superseding the Attic forms *basilis* and *basileia*).

2. In the LXX the words of this root are frequent, mostly as translations of the Heb. root *mālak*, to be king, reign. The term *basileus* appears frequently in almost all OT books and esp. in the historical writings. The words are used first and foremost for earthly kings and their secular government, and only secondarily of Yahweh's kingship. This means that the concept of Yahweh's kingly rule can only be presented in connection with the Israelite monarchy.

(a) Every nation with whom Israel came into contact after the conquest had a king. The Israelites, however, did not adopt monarchy as an institution until relatively late. Rather, they continued for two centuries as a sacred confederation of tribes with a central sanctuary. Israel's initial hesitation to adopt the institution of monarchy is bound up with the concept of the holy war, which Yahweh himself conducted on Israel's behalf (Exod. 14:14; Jos. 23:10; Jdg. 7:22). Yahweh was seen as commander in chief of the Israelite army and as the one to whom the land unconditionally belonged.

(b) Israel's constant harassment by the Philistines provided the surface reason for the introduction of the monarchy, but the OT records a tension in its institution. According to 1 Sam. 9:1–10:16; 11:1–11, 14–15, Yahweh approved the concept, in view of his people's request, by telling Samuel to anoint Saul the Benjaminite king (9:16; cf. also the laws in Deut. 17:14–20). But there was also a questioning of the monarchy as a threat to the theocratic lordship of Yahweh. Note esp. 1 Sam. 8:1–22a; 10:17–27, where the people's request of Samuel, "Appoint a king to lead us, such as all the other nations have," receives Yahweh's answer, "They have rejected me as their king" (8:5, 7). That is, the monarch was seen both as Yahweh's gift and as his rival.

3. Of decisive significance for the Judahite monarchy was the religious ratification it received through Nathan's prophetic promise to David (2 Sam. 7:1–11b, 16). The house of David was promised everlasting duration (7:16). Because of this Davidic covenant, the right of David's hereditary successors to the kingdom of Judah was never called into question. The dynasty was assured of continuance despite the ups and downs of its history. By contrast, the monarchy of the northern kingdom never achieved the stability of the Davidic dynasty. In the north, the most powerful and charismatic leader became king.

Another feature of Judah's theology of kingship, in contrast to the Egyptian concept of a king who is divine by nature, was the adoption of the ruler as Yahweh's son. This was celebrated at a festival of enthronement and hymned in royal psalms (e.g., Ps. 2:7; 45:7; 110:1). However, the less the kings of Judah measured up to the standards set forth in the theology of kingship, the more strongly did the expectation of an eschatological messianic king develop, who would finally fulfill the prophecy of Nathan and the associated concepts of kingship (Amos 9:11–15; cf. Gen. 49:8–12). Isaiah in particular, a prophet with close associations with Judah's king, prophesied of a branch of David who would bring in a new era of righteousness and peace (Isa. 11:1–9; 9:2–7; cf. also Mic. 5:2–5; Jer. 23:5–6; Ezek. 17:22–24).

4. The kingship of Yahweh is not addressed much in the wisdom literature, in the oral teaching of the prophets, or in many of the historical narratives. It is frequent, however, in the hymns of the Psalter (the so-called enthronement psalms); the later prophetic writings, including the prophecies against the nations in Jeremiah (e.g., 46:18; 48:15; 51:57); and in the narrative parts of Daniel.

(a) One of the earliest examples of the title *king* being used of Yahweh is Isaiah 6:5, "My eyes have seen the King, the LORD Almighty." It is no coincidence that this title for Yahweh appears during a vision that came to Isaiah in the central sanctuary at Jerusalem, because the idea of "God Most High" had been associated with the title king (cf. Gen. 14:18–19). The divine title *melek* (Heb. king) brought with it a claim to universal authority, which found expression esp. in lordship over the pantheon of gods. Yahweh's kingship has a cosmic dimension: He is the creator of the world (cf. Ps. 24:1; 93:1; 95:3–5);

"the LORD Most High [is] the great King over all the earth" (47:2); he is the king of the nations (cf. 47:3; 99:2; Jer. 10:7).

(b) In addition to this concept of Yahweh's *being* king, we find the dynamic concept of Yahweh *becoming* king. This finds expression especially in the enthronement psalms in the cry (lit.) "Yahweh has become King!" (Ps. 47:8; 93:1; 96:10; 97:1; 99:1; Eng. versions have "the LORD reigns" for this Heb. perf.). The inseparability of the two concepts "Yahweh is King" and "Yahweh has become King" is esp. evident in the later chapters of Isaiah. Yahweh is "Jacob's King" or "Israel's King" (41:21; 44:6). Put in the context of announcing the new exodus, a herald now brings to the city of Jerusalem the message: "Your God reigns [has become King]" (52:7).

(c) In the OT's messianic theology, the lordship of Yahweh is combined with the hoped-for lordship of the Messiah. Thus Isaiah was the first to use the royal title for Yahweh and almost always related it to the currently reigning son of David. Even the messianic prince of the future is for Isaiah no autocrat, but one who is appointed and receives his office from God (9:7; 11:1–2). The rule of the future, messianic son of David is thus a delegated exercise of authority, representing the kingly rule of Yahweh.

5. *basileia* (Heb. *malkût*) means kingdom, reign; the reference is to power rather than to locality. The word in the OT usually refers in a purely secular sense to political kingdoms (cf. 1 Sam. 20:31; 1 Ki. 2:12; 1 Chr. 12:23; 2 Chr. 11:17; Dan. 9:1). There are, however, occasional references to God's rule as his *basileia* or *malkût*, kingship, which he is presently exercising (Ps. 103:19; 145:11–13; Dan. 4:3 = LXX 3:33). This is analogous to the use of *basileus* or *melek*, king, as an epithet of Yahweh.

In later texts Yahweh's kingship is interpreted in an eschatological sense. The recognition begins to emerge of a kingdom of Yahweh at the end of time that breaks through all national barriers. One day Yahweh will rule over the whole earth. His throne will be in Jerusalem, and all nations will make their pilgrimage to Zion to worship him (Isa. 24:23; Zech. 14:9). This coming kingdom of Yahweh is always presented as immanent.

In Dan. 7, this eschatology is elevated to a transcendent level in the concept of the kingdom of the "son of man" (7:13–14) and the kingdom of "the people of the Most High" (7:27). The son of man is an individual (7:14) who represents the Most High (7:27), just as the king of Judah represented the people. In other words, when power is committed to him, it is at the same time being given to the saints of the Most High. This transfer takes place within the heavenly realm, so that the earthly empires symbolized by the four beasts are replaced by the transcendent rule of the saints of the Most High represented by the son of man. We have already here the most important elements of apocalyptic.

6. (a) The expression "kingdom of heaven" owes its origin to the endeavor of rab. Judaism to find an alternative for the divine name in the phrase *kingdom of Yahweh*. Kingdom of heaven is thus an expression that implies the essential idea that God rules as King. Since it is not evident in this world, it is necessary to choose for or against it by a decision of will. The opportunity to accept or reject the kingdom will, however, come to an end when Yahweh reveals himself at the end of time.

(b) There is a tension in Judaism between the expectation of the Messiah as a nationalistic, Israelite king at the end of time, and the hope of the eschatological revelation of the kingdom of God. In the last days the Messiah will come, ascend the throne of Israel, and subject all the nations of the earth to himself. Not until then will the hitherto hidden kingdom of heaven emerge from the transcendent realm. But there is in Judaism no inner connection between the coming of the national messianic king and the coming of the rule of God. This is further confirmed by the fact that the people of Israel receive no mention in statements concerning the kingdom of God. Membership within the nation can no longer be a determining factor when a personal decision before God is required.

(c) The Apocr. in general follow the OT pattern of thought about the kingdom of God. In some places, however, we may detect Hel. influence. Thus the LXX can identify the *basileia* with the four cardinal virtues (4 Macc. 2:23), and in Wis. 6:20 we read, "The desire for wisdom leads to a kingdom." This shift to an ethical meaning is completed by Philo, where the content of the *basileia* is the rule of the sage, seen as the true king. Thus, the eschatological character of the term as used in the OT was lost.

NT In the NT *basileia* is used more frequently than *basileus* and *basileuō*. Words from this root occur chiefly to the Synoptic Gospels. In Matt. and Lk.–Acts they play a positively decisive role. The two nouns are used only occasionally in Jn., the Pauline letters, and the other NT letters, but they come to the fore again in Rev. By contrast, the vb. *basileuō* appears only occasionally in the Synoptic Gospels, more often in Rev. But it has its maximum theological significance in Paul (Rom. and 1 Cor.).

1. basileus *and* basileuō *in the NT.* The NT follows closely the precedent set by the OT and Judaism in giving to God and Christ alone the full right to the title *king*. Human kings, by contrast, are generally regarded as of limited importance.

(a) The earthly kings referred to are frequently those who set themselves against God and his Christ: Pharaoh (Acts 7:10; Heb. 11:23, 27), Herod the Great (Matt. 2:1–3; Lk. 1:5), Herod Antipas (Matt. 14:9), Herod Agrippa I (Acts 12:1, 20), Herod Agrippa II (25:13–14), Aretas (2 Cor. 11:32), and the Roman emperor (1 Tim. 2:2; 1 Pet. 2:13; Rev. 17:9–18). These rulers are called "kings of the earth" (Matt. 17:25; Acts 4:26; Rev. 1:5), "kings of the Gentiles" (Lk. 22:25), or "kings of the whole world" (Rev. 16:14).

Just as the OT is at variance with oriental views of divine kingship, so the NT is opposed to Hel. and Roman ideas of this kind. The earthly king is not an incarnation of the deity, since no one but God or the Messiah can occupy such a position. Thus in Rev., in sharp contrast to the presumptuous claims to divinity of Domitian, only God is recognized as "King of the ages" (15:3) and only Christ as the "King of kings" (17:14; 19:16). The "kings from the East" (16:12) are a rod in God's hand, and he will destroy them at the last day if they do not submit to him (17:2–14; 19:18–21; 21:24).

(b) Only David and Melchizedek receive a positive assessment in the NT as earthly kings: David, because as the king chosen by God (2 Sam. 7) he is the forefather of Jesus Christ (cf. Matt. 1:6; Acts 13:22); Melchizedek, because as the priest-king of Salem (Gen. 14:18) he is the OT type of the high priesthood of Christ (Heb. 7:1–3).

(c) Jesus, "who as to his human nature was a descendant of David" (Rom. 1:3; cf. Matt. 1:6) is the messianic Son of David, King of the Jews, or King of Israel. These titles are used principally in the section of the Gospels portraying his trial before Pilate (Matt. 27; Mk. 15; Lk. 23; Jn. 18–19), exclusively on the lips of Jesus' Jewish opponents, of Pilate, and of his soldiers. Note, for example, the many references to "king of the Jews" (Mk. 15:2, 9, 18, 26, to cite only Mk.'s references). Like the soldiers on guard (Lk. 23:37), the rulers of the people mocked as they passed by, "Let this Christ, this King of Israel, come down now from the cross, that we may see and believe" (Mk. 15:32).

If it is true, as the Roman inscription on the cross makes probable, that Jesus was condemned on a charge of claiming to be the messianic king of Israel, and if this claim is never found on the lips of Jesus in the Gospels, presumably the basis of the charge is to be found largely in the way Jesus behaved. It is unlikely, in other words, that the Jewish leaders were acting out of pure malice in accusing Jesus of being a claimant to the throne or that Pilate had no other intention in ordering the inscription on the cross than to make mock of Jewish messianism (cf. Jn. 18:36–37). Rather, note that Jesus himself saw his miracles of healing, his casting out of demons, and his preaching of the gospel to the poor as the fulfillment of Isaiah's prophecies (Isa. 29:18–19; 35:5–6; 61:1–2), and accordingly as messianic events (Matt. 11:2–6; Lk. 4:16–27).

Moreover, his two principal actions during the last days at Jerusalem—the entry into Jerusalem (Matt. 21:1–9; Mk. 11:1–10; Lk. 19:28–38; Jn. 12:12–19) and the cleansing of the temple (Matt. 21:12–13; Mk. 11:15–19; Lk. 19:47–48)—make it clear that Jesus knew himself to be the fulfiller of messianic prophecies (for OT allusions in these narratives cf. 2 Ki. 9:13; Ps. 118:26; Isa. 62:11; Zech. 9:9; and Exod. 30:13; Lev. 1:14; Isa. 56:7; Jer. 7:11).

It is also demonstrable that Jesus was confronted during his ministry with the question of whether or not he was the Messiah, as, for instance, in connection with the feeding of the five thousand, when the people wanted "to make him king" (Jn. 6:15). Similarly, John the Baptist used a term for the Messiah that was not common among the Jews, "the one who was to come," when he asked whether Jesus was that person (Matt. 11:3; Lk. 7:19–20). Jesus did not respond to the question directly with an open declaration of his messiahship. Instead, he pointed to the fulfillment of Isaiah's prophecies in veiled language that challenged the hearer to make up his or her mind (Matt. 11:5; Lk. 7:22). The fact that Jesus saw himself to be the king of the Jews and Messiah of his people, and yet concealed it in this way, is his "messianic secret" (→ *Christos*, 5986).

The same point is brought out by the short answer of Jesus, recorded in the Gospels, to Pilate's question whether he was the king of the Jews: "It is as you say" (Matt. 27:11; Mk. 15:2; Lk. 23:3). Only once did Jesus openly reveal this messianic secret: in the trial before the Sanhedrin (Matt. 26:57–75; Mk. 14:53–72; Lk. 22:54–71). To the high priest's question, "Are you the Christ?" he replied unequivocally with the statement, "I am . . . and you will see the Son of Man sitting at the right hand of the Mighty One and coming on the clouds of heaven" (Mk. 14:62; cf. Matt. 26:64; Lk. 22:69).

In Acts and the writings of Paul, there is no mention of "King of Israel" or "King of the Jews." Nevertheless, it can be seen from a passage like Acts 17:7 that Christians in Thessalonica were being denounced by the Jews for confessing allegiance to Jesus as another king. There is a certain irony in the way the Jews accused Christians of opposing the quasi-divine claims of the Roman emperor. However, it is basically true to say that with the application of the messianic title *Christ* to Jesus, the proclamation of Jesus as king of Israel faded eventually into the background, giving way to a soteriological message that focused on his cross and resurrection (cf. Rom. 4:25; 1 Cor. 15:3–4).

(d) In Exod. 19:6, the people of God share in his kingship: "You will be for me a kingdom of priests and a holy nation" (cf. Isa. 61:6). This thought is applied to Christian believers in Rev. 1:6 and 5:10 (*basileia* is used in both cases). The former passage refers to believers in the present time; the latter is part of the "new song" of the saints before the Lamb. The same thought occurs in 1 Pet. 2:9: "But you are a chosen people, a royal [*basileion*] priesthood, a holy nation, a people belonging to God, that you may declare the praises of him who called you out of darkness into his wonderful light." This verse accords with Rev. 5:10, where the glorified saints "will reign on the earth" (cf. 1:6).

The vb. *basileuō*, reign, is used of the reign of believers in Rom. 5:17 (in contrast to the reign of death, cf. 5:14, 17, 21; cf. also the reign of sin, 6:12), in 1 Cor. 4:8 (here ironically of the lordly behavior of the Corinthians, which falls short of true reigning), and in Rev. 20:4, 6; 20:5 (of the reign of the saints on earth and in glory). For the idea of reigning expressed in other terms, see Eph. 2:6; 2 Tim. 2:12; Jas. 2:5.

(e) *basilissa*, queen, occurs only 4x in the NT. Matt. and Lk. both record the saying about the Queen of the South in the context of the sign of Jonah (Matt. 12:42; Lk. 11:31; cf. 1 Ki. 10:1–10; 2 Chr. 9:1–12). She serves as an example of the lengths to which a non-Jew might go in seeking wisdom. Gentiles thus have all the more reason to leave their ways, for in Jesus the Galilean preacher is "one greater than Solomon." In Acts 8:27 the Ethiopian eunuch is described as the treasurer of "Candace, queen of the Ethiopians." He too was a seeker, who had come "to Jerusalem to worship." The episode is all the more pointed in the light of the persecution by the Jews that had just scattered the Jerusalem church (8:1), the eunuch's study of Scripture (Isa. 53:7–8; Acts 8:32–33), and the fact that he was a eunuch. By contrast Babylon, who plays the queen, is judged (Rev. 18:7).

2. *basileia in the NT.* (a) For an earthly, human king there is an earthly, human kingdom. In this sense *basileia* means, according to context, the office of king (e.g., Lk. 19:12, 15; Rev. 17:12) and also the area governed, domain (e.g., Matt. 4:8; Lk. 4:5; Mk. 6:23; Rev. 16:10). In almost all these passages the earthly kingdoms seem to stand in contrast to the kingdom of God, since they are subject to the god of this world, Satan (Matt. 4:8). In Matt. 12:26 there is even explicit mention of the *basileia* of the devil.

(b) The kingdom of God (usually changed to kingdom of heaven in Matt., though cf. 12:28; 19:24; 21:31, 43) is an expression of central importance only within the Synoptic tradition.

(c) In order to understand Jesus' proclamation of the kingdom of God, it is best to start with those passages that deal with the coming of the kingdom of God in the near future. Mk. 1:15 records the theme of Jesus' preaching in a pregnant sentence: "The kingdom of God is near" (cf. Matt. 3:2; 5:17; Lk. 17:20–21; 21:31). Jesus did not preach that there was already a kingdom of God to which one must confess allegiance but that the rule of God was coming.

Just as summer is known to be near when the fig tree puts out leaves, so the events of the present reveal that God's rule will soon break in on the world (Matt. 24:32–33; Mk. 13:28–29; Lk. 21:29–31). It is to this sudden, unexpected, imminent irruption of the kingdom of God that Jesus' parables of the Parousia point: the sudden coming of the flood (Matt. 24:37–39; Lk. 17:26–27), the unexpected entrance of the burglar (Matt. 24:43–44; Lk. 12:39–40), the surprise of the doorkeeper and the servant at the homecoming of their master (Matt. 24:45–50; cf. Lk. 12:42–46), and the sudden arrival of the bridegroom (Matt. 25:1–13). "I tell you the truth, some who are standing here will not taste death before they see the kingdom of God come with power" (Mk. 9:1).

For Jesus the advent of the kingdom was so imminent that he vowed not to "drink again of the fruit of the vine until the kingdom of God comes" (Lk. 22:18). The Parousia of the Son of Man will take place even before the disciples have finished proclaiming the kingdom of God in Israel (Matt. 10:23). From these references it may be concluded that Jesus proclaimed the imminent advent of the kingdom of God within the lifetime of his hearer.

(d) Although for Jesus the realization of God's rule is still in the future, its urgent proximity already casts its shadow over the present: "If I drive out demons by the Spirit of God, then the kingdom of God has come upon you" (Matt. 12:28; cf. Lk. 11:20). The casting out of demons reveals that the devil has been bound by one stronger than he (Matt. 12:29; Mk. 3:27; Lk. 11:21). The disarming of Satan, an event the Jews expected in the end time, has taken place (10:18); in the works of Jesus the kingdom of God is already a present reality.

To the Pharisees' question when the kingdom of God was coming, Jesus can therefore answer, "The kingdom of God is among you" (Lk. 17:20–21; not as NIV, "is within you"). Because the kingdom is already present, the friends of the bridegroom cannot fast (Mk. 2:19; cf. Matt. 9:15; Lk. 5:34), and it is the Father's good pleasure to give Jesus' disciples the kingdom (12:32). With the appearance of John the Baptist, the new era has begun and is already present (cf. Matt. 11:12–13; Lk. 16:16).

(e) Jesus insists that the verdict to be passed on to people in the final judgment is already determined by the attitude they adopt to himself in the present age: "Whoever acknowledges me before men, I will also acknowledge him before my Father in heaven" (Matt. 10:32; cf. Lk. 12:8). Those who hear and do Jesus' words will survive the eschatological crisis. The unrepentant cities, on the other hand, will be condemned, because in spite of the miracles done in them by Jesus they did not repent (Matt. 11:21–24). Jesus himself will appear as the eschatological judge (25:31) and will disown those who merely say, "Lord, Lord" (7:22–23; cf. Lk. 13:27); he will plead before the Father the cause of those who have confessed him (Matt. 10:32; cf. Lk. 12:8). One's final destiny is decided by the attitude adopted to Jesus' words and actions (Matt. 7:24–27; cf. Lk. 6:47–49), in other words, by one's attitude to Jesus himself. After all, Jesus' view of the kingdom of God is inextricably bound up with his person.

Thus Jesus preached the kingdom of God neither solely as a present reality (also known as "consistent eschatology") nor exclusively as a future event (futuristic eschatology). Rather, he was aware that the future rule of God was present in his actions and in his person. He spoke, therefore, of the future kingdom, which would suddenly dawn, as already realizing itself in the present. His eschatology is, therefore, an "already but not yet" eschatology.

3. *The kingdom of God in the preaching of Jesus.* (a) According to Jesus, the kingdom of God is totally in the hands of God. We can, therefore, neither hasten its coming by doing battle with God's enemies (as the Zealots hoped) nor force it to appear by scrupulous observation of the law (as the Pharisees hoped). We can only await its coming with patience and confidence, as in the parables of the mustard seed (Matt. 13:31–32; Mk. 4:30–32), the yeast (Matt. 13:33), and the seed growing secretly (Mk. 4:26–29).

(b) This kingdom is coming in the form of a cosmic catastrophe (Lk. 17:26; Mk. 13:26; 14:62), ushered in by the appearance of the Son of Man. Jesus thus aligned himself, not with the concept of an earthly, nationalistic messiah, but with the apocalyptic tradition in Judaism and its expectation of the Son of Man. Although he clearly used apocalyptic imagery (e.g., the heavenly feast in the kingdom of God, Matt. 8:11; Mk. 14:25), he rejected all attempts to predict the time of the end (13:28–34).

(c) Jesus upheld the OT doctrine of election (Matt. 10:6) with the associated belief that God wants to reach the entire world through the nation of Israel. This is not to say that Israel has a special claim on God's favor. Indeed, Israel is in danger of being put to shame by the heathen on the day of judgment (12:42; Lk. 11:31). The kingdom will be taken from Israel and given to the Gentiles (Matt. 21:43). God will cast the sons of the kingdom (Israel) into outer darkness (8:12; cf. Lk. 13:28). But Jesus promised the Twelve, as the representatives of a new Israel, the office of judges and rulers in the future kingdom of God (Matt. 19:28; Lk. 22:28–30; cf. Mk. 10:35–45).

(d) A person can receive the kingdom only as a child (Mk. 10:15; Lk. 18:17; cf. Matt. 18:3; Jn. 3:3) and must wait for it (Mk. 15:43; Lk. 23:51). Particularly frequent is the metaphor of entering the kingdom of God (Matt. 5:20; 7:21; 18:3; 19:23–24; 23:13; Jn. 3:5). Such entry in the fullest sense lies in the future (Matt. 25:34; Mk. 9:43–47), but the presence of the kingdom of God in the person of Jesus faces the individual with a clear-cut, yes-or-no decision (cf. Matt. 5:30; 7:24–27; 18:8–9; Mk. 9:43–48; Lk. 9:62). When a decision is made, it involves a readiness for sacrifice, which may mean self-denial to the point of being hated by one's own family (Matt. 10:17–22, 37). Yet this decision produces overwhelming joy at the greatness of God's gift (cf. the parables of the hidden treasure and the pearl of great price, Matt. 13:44–46).

(e) The kingdom of God is transcendent and supernatural; it comes from above, from God alone. When it does, the hungry will be filled and the sad will be comforted (cf. the Beatitudes of Matt. 5:3–10; Lk. 6:20–22). It requires us to love our enemies (Matt. 5:38–42; Lk. 6:27–28, 32–36) and to be as free from care as the birds of the air and the lilies of the field (Matt. 6:25–33; Lk. 12:22–31). Here again Jesus himself, in whom alone the future kingdom of God is present, is the one whose words and deeds attest the presence of the kingdom—the proof of which is in his seeking out the company of tax collectors and sinners, offering them fellowship and promising them forgiveness of sins.

As the king invites beggars and the homeless to his feast (Matt. 22:1–10), as the father's love receives back again the lost son (Lk. 15:11–32), as the shepherd goes out after the lost sheep (15:4–7), as the woman searches for the lost coin (15:8–10), as the master out of the goodness of his heart pays the workers hired at the last hour a full day's pay (Matt. 20:1–15), so Jesus offers to the poor in spirit the promise of forgiveness, "for theirs is the kingdom of heaven" (5:3). Only sinners can appreciate the remission of sins through God's goodness(cf. Matt. 9:12; Mk. 2:17; Lk. 5:31).

4. *The kingdom of God and the kingdom of Christ outside the preaching of Jesus.* (a) Jesus spoke primarily of the kingdom of God, though he also made references to "my kingdom" (e.g., Lk. 22:30; Jn. 18:36). After his resurrection the church, convinced that he had been exalted to the status of Lord (Acts 2:36; Phil. 2:9–11), introduced a Christological emphasis in the preaching of the kingdom. The apostles thus continued the inseparable connection between Jesus and the kingdom.

In 2 Tim. 4:18, Paul speaks of the confidence of being delivered from every kind of evil and of being brought "safely to [the Lord's] heavenly kingdom" (cf. 2 Tim. 4:1; 2 Pet. 1:11). The inseparable connection between the person of Jesus and the presence of God's kingdom is expressed most clearly when Jesus Christ himself becomes an equivalent for "kingdom of God," as is shown by the following sample comparisons. Whereas Joseph of Arimathea was waiting for "the kingdom of God" (Mk. 15:43), believers are awaiting "the Lord Jesus Christ" (Phil. 3:20). Whereas Jesus' message may be summed up as "the kingdom of God is near" (Mk. 1:15), James says, "The Lord's coming is near" (Jas. 5:8). In Samaria Philip preached "the good news of the kingdom of God and the name of Jesus Christ" (Acts 8:12; cf. 28:31).

The phrase "kingdom of Christ" and the equation of "kingdom of God" with Jesus Christ are thus the result of the changeover from an implicit to an explicit Christology. Jesus' proclamation of the kingdom of God was in no way displaced in the early church as it preached Jesus. The postresurrection Christology, in which Jesus Christ is the center of the kerygma, is rather the outcome of the realization that the kingdom of God is present only in the person of Jesus Christ, so that one can only properly speak of the kingdom of God by speaking of Jesus Christ.

(b) The kingdom of God has only a peripheral place outside the Synoptics. In its place we find the Christological kerygma of the cross and resurrection of Jesus, the expectation of the Parousia, the resurrection of the dead, and the use of terms such as *life* and *righteousness*. Is there a sequence from Jesus' preaching of the kingdom to the Christological kerygma and the Pauline doctrine of justification-righteousness?

A survey of the synonyms used in the Synoptic tradition for "kingdom of God" is illuminating. Matt. 6:33 says that we are to seek God's "kingdom and his righteousness." In a single passage we find the expressions "to enter life" (Mk. 9:43, 45) and "to enter the kingdom of God" (9:47). Following the question of the rich young man, "What must I do to inherit eternal life?" (10:17), Jesus remarks to his disciples, "How hard it is for the rich to enter the kingdom of God!" (10:23). Likewise, the phrase "to inherit eternal life" (10:17) has a counterpart in "take your inheritance, the kingdom prepared for you" (Matt. 25:34). Paul says in Rom. 14:17: "the kingdom of God is ... righteousness, peace and joy in the Holy Spirit." Thus, when Paul declares that the righteousness of God consists in justifying "the wicked" (4:5), he is taking up the central concern of Jesus' preaching of the kingdom, namely, the promise of salvation to sinners.

The futurist eschatology in the preaching of Jesus is likewise retained in the expectation of his Parousia and the general resurrection of the dead. Pauline theology, which is a development of Christology, contains, like the preaching of Jesus, both a present and a future element, since the crucified and risen one is also the one who is coming again. By tying salvation to the person of Jesus and by developing Christology along the lines of soteriology, pneumatology, and eschatology, Paul has maintained a consistent and legitimate extension of Jesus' preaching of the kingdom of God, although he has adapted this to the postresurrection situation as regards the cross and resurrection.

(c) Evidence that the kingdom of Jesus Christ is the same as the kingdom of God is also demonstrated in that both expressions are found together, sometimes God being named first, sometimes Christ. Thus it is equally acceptable to speak of "the kingdom of Christ and of God" (Eph. 5:5), and of "the kingdom of our Lord and of his Christ" (Rev. 11:15). The rule of Christ and the rule of God are, in other words, identical. When the rule of Christ has become established, it is taken up into the rule of God (5:10; 20:4, 6; 22:5); at the end of time Christ hands back to the Father the kingdom he has received from him (1 Cor. 15:24–28).

996 (basileuō, to be king, rule), → *995.*

997 (basilikos, royal, kingly), → *995.*

999 (basilissa, queen), → *995.*

1001 (baskainō, bewitch), → *3404.*

1002 βαστάζω

βαστάζω (*bastazō*), carry, bear, endure (*1002*); δυσβάστακτος (*dysbastaktos*), difficult to carry (*1546*).

CL & OT In cl. Gk. *bastazō* means to lift up and carry away. It can have a fig. meaning to endure or suffer; also, to exalt, extol. In the LXX this vb. is used primarily in a physical sense. In Jdg. 16:30 (except A), Samson pushes with all his might to break down the pillars of the Philistine temple. In Ruth 2:16, Boaz instructs his workers to "pull out" extra stalks of grain for Ruth to glean. In 2 Ki. 18:14, Hezekiah agrees to turn over or "pay" to the Assyrians whatever they ask, if they will only withdraw from his land. A fig. sense occurs in Job 21:3, where Job asks his friends to "bear" with him as he speaks.

NT 1. *bastazō* occurs 27x in the NT. Fewer than half of the uses refer to physically carrying something (e.g., a jar of water, Lk. 22:10; a coffin, 7:14). The word is used for Jesus carrying his own cross (Jn. 19:17) and for Paul being carried by the soldiers as they rescued him from the mob in Jerusalem (Acts 21:35). *bastazō* can even be used to describe carrying a child in the womb (Lk. 11:27).

2. More important is the fig. use. In three places, this word group is used to express the burden of the law on the Jews. Matt. 23:4 and Lk. 11:46 use *dysbastaktos* to describe the heavy burdens that the Jewish leaders placed on the people, while Peter insists that neither they nor their fathers have been able to bear (*bastazō*) such a heavy yoke (Acts 15:10). In Matt. 8:17, the author cites his own trans. of Isa. 53:4 to the effect that Jesus, the servant of God, carried our diseases (as demonstrated in his miracles). The church at Ephesus has "endured" hardships for Christ's sake (Rev. 2:3), and Paul bears in his body the marks of Jesus (Gal. 6:17). In fact, Jesus instructs all of us to carry our cross and follow him (Lk. 14:27).

3. God told Ananias that he had chosen Paul to "carry" the name of Jesus before Gentiles (Acts 9:15); perhaps the implication is that Paul's mission work would involve much suffering and endurance. Paul exhorts believers to fulfill the law of Christ by bearing each other's burdens (Gal. 6:2), though he also admits that we each have our own individual burdens to carry (6:5). In a similar vein, Paul instructs the strong in faith to "bear with" the weaknesses of the weak (Rom. 15:1) rather than insisting on their own rights in areas of Christian freedom.

1007 βδέλυγμα

βδέλυγμα, in the phrase τὸ βδέλυγμα τῆς ἐρημώσεως (*to bdelygma tēs erēmōseōs*), the abomination of desolation (*1007*).

CL & OT The phrase *to bdelygma tēs erēmōseōs* occurs in Mk. 13:14 and its parallel, Matt. 24:15. It is taken from the LXX of Dan. 12:11 and appears with slight variations in Dan. 9:27; 11:31; and 1 Macc. 1:54. In Dan. the Heb. expression signifies "the abomination that causes (spiritual) desolation," i.e., it creates either a horror in the mind of the beholders or an objective condition of spiritual devastation. In the OT an abomination denotes chiefly something that is abominable to God, esp. objects offensive in the light of the ceremonial law; hence, it frequently describes idolatrous objects (see Ezek. 5:11). Some have argued that the phrase "abomination that causes desolation" originated as a typical Jewish term of contempt for a heathen deity. In 1 Macc. 1:54, Antiochus Epiphanes (reigned 175–164 B.C.) caused a pagan altar to be erected on the great altar in the Jerusalem temple; this altar is described as "the abomination of desolation." The temple of God was thus turned into a heathen temple. The command to render such worship, in Jerusalem and beyond, led to the Maccabean revolt.

NT In Mk. 13:14 the desolating abomination appears to be well known to the readers, so no further explanation is given. Many exegetes, observing that "abomination" is neut. in gender, but the participle "standing where it does not belong" is masc., have concluded that the abomination is the Antichrist, who steps into the place reserved for God (cf. 2 Thess. 2:4; note, however, that in Matt. 24:15 the participle is a neuter, so that the possible reference to the Antichrist applies only in Mk. 13:14). If the term *Antichrist* be extended to mean a power that sets itself against God, it could be employed in this context, but the later developed doctrine, such as appears in Rev. 13 and 17, should not be read into Mk. 13:14. To Jesus the term *abomination* probably connotes idolatry of some sort.

Luke paraphrases Jesus' words by the expression "Jerusalem being surrounded by armies" (Lk. 21:20). It is possible that this is closer to Jesus' intention than is commonly recognized, for the Roman armies affixed idolatrous images to their ensigns, which were set in the ground at night and accorded worship. By agreement with the Jews, these ensigns were never brought into the Roman fortress in Jerusalem. But if they were set in the holy place, that could only be as a result of brute force, and it would entail war to the death. The "abomination" would thus bring about the desecration of the city and sanctuary and would lead to destructive warfare, so bringing to pass the fulfillment of the prophecy of Jesus in Mk. 13:2.

The use of the expression "abomination that causes desolation" for the desecration and ultimate destruction of the temple and city indicates that Jesus viewed such an event in the light of the day of the Lord, as the OT prophets before him, and above all Daniel, in his references to that abomination.

1010 βέβαιος

βέβαιος (bebaios), sure (*1010*); βεβαιόω (bebaioō), confirm (*1011*); βεβαίωσις (bebaiōsis), confirmation (*1012*).

CL & OT In cl. Gk. *bebaios* means firm, durable, reliable; and in the legal sphere, valid, legal. *bebaioō* similarly means make firm, strengthen, confirm; also, guarantee. *bebaiōsis* means establishing, confirmation, or (in legal language) guarantee (valid confirmation of a legal act). In the LXX this word group rarely occurs and usually has the same meaning as in cl. Gk. (e.g., Ps. 119:28, where it means to strengthen).

NT In the NT the words in this group occur 18x (7x in Heb. alone). They connote validity, i.e., the confirming evidence of the divine Word (Mk. 16:20; Heb. 2:2–3) and of the gospel (Phil. 1:7). Here the NT has adopted the technical sense that these words had acquired in the legal sphere. This word group can also denote that a thing is firm and reliable because it has a firm foundation. Thus one's hope and confidence are firmly secured, as by an anchor, when the object of trust is God's Word (cf. Heb. 6:16, 19).

1. (a) The promises of God, the Word of God, and the gospel are absolutely certain to be fulfilled because they have been legally confirmed by God through an oath (Heb. 6:16–20) and so form the foundation of the faith (*eis bebaiōsin* is a recognized Gk. legal term for a

guarantee). God's promise stands secure, and believers may depend on it. God has given the promise "by grace" to those who believe, not on the basis of the Mosaic law, so the promise is "guaranteed" (Rom. 4:16). It depends for its validity and efficacy on God alone; that is what makes it sure.

Another reason for the confirmation or legal validation of God's promises to the fathers is given in Rom. 15:8: Jesus Christ has himself given them this legal validation. His whole life was one of "service" to the Jews and the Gentiles in order to make God's promises sure for them. He showed them how all the promises of God were fulfilled in him and thus proven true. He thereby made evident "God's truth" and faithfulness, which form the ultimate basis for our confidence and certainty in the foundations of faith. God's promise is compared in Heb. 9:15 with a will that comes into force when the person who issued it dies (9:17). This throws a special light on the death of Jesus.

(b) Rather than God's promise, it is often the *logos*, the word (of God), that is described by these words as trustworthy. Heb. 2:2 states that if the message declared by angels (i.e., the OT law) was sure, impregnable, and valid, so that "every violation and disobedience received its just punishment," how much more is the word that comes from the Lord, who is so much "superior to" angels (1:4). For God himself has borne witness to that word and has confirmed it by "signs, wonders and various miracles" (2:4). In Mk. 16:20, the validity of the word (of the disciples) was confirmed by "signs that accompanied it." These signs indicate that the living Lord himself is speaking and working through his witnesses; their witness is therefore true and reliable.

If God's truth and faithfulness are the primary basis for the validity of his Word and thus for the whole of the Christian's assurance concerning his or her faith, then these subsequent signs are a less important confirmation of one's confidence in God's promises. According to 2 Pet. 1:19, "we have the word of the prophets made more certain," because it has been confirmed by divine actions and manifestations from the heavenly world, namely, at the transfiguration of Jesus. These experiences (like the Easter experiences) strengthened the disciples' confidence in the absolute reliability and validity of the Word of God.

(c) This use of this word group leads also to the sense of witnessing and witness (to the gospel), as in 1 Cor. 1:6; Phil. 1:7; and Heb. 2:3. Here there is also the idea that God's Word is so sure and reliable that it must be believed when it is preached. Thus the idea drawn from the legal sphere, that God's Word is here and is now made valid by the witness that is borne to it, is often present.

2. (a) The believer's assurance about salvation is to be understood on this basis of the legal foundation and validity of God's Word and promise. Often the two meanings are directly related to one another (cf. Heb. 6:16 and 6:19; 1 Cor. 1:6 and 1:8; 2 Pet. 1:10 and 1:19). The certainty of the believer's hope is inextricably rooted in the legal validity of God's Word. This is worked out impressively in Heb. 6:19. Since God's promise is unchangeable and his oath (6:16) valid (God does not lie!), the believer's hope is firm and assured, like a ship that is firmly anchored.

(b) Because of this, the whole position of the Christian gains an element of assurance and certainty. It is God himself who establishes believers or makes them firm in Christ (2 Cor. 1:21; cf. 1 Cor. 1:8), who seals them with the Holy Spirit. Such people are "strengthened in the faith" (Col. 2:7). Likewise, the author of Hebrews insists that our hearts are "strengthened by grace, not by ceremonial foods" (13:9).

See also *themelios*, foundation (*2529*); *asphaleia*, firmness, certainty (*854*); *kyroō*, confirm, ratify (*3263*).

1011 (*bebaioō*, confirm), → *1010*.

1012 (*bebaiōsis*, confirmation), → *1010*.

1015 (*Beelzeboul*, Beelzebub, Beelzebul), → *1333*.

1016 (*Beliar*, Belial, Beliar), → *1333*.

1018 (*belos*, arrow, dart), → *4483*.

1033	Βηθλέεμ

Βηθλέεμ (*Bēthleem*), Bethlehem (*1033*).

OT This is the modern Beit Laḥm, a town in the Judean hill country five miles southwest of Jerusalem. The Heb. *bêt leḥem* means "house of bread." Ephrath was likely the surrounding district, hence the distinctive form "Bethlehem Ephrathah" (Mic. 5:2). Another Bethlehem was part of Zebulun (Jos. 19:15) and was situated some seven miles northwest of Nazareth in NT Galilee. The NT refers only to the Judean town.

Prior to the monarchy Israel's hold on this part of the Judean hills was insecure (cf. 2 Sam. 23:14). Israelite tribal tradition remembered the town as the birthplace of the Levite who ultimately founded the sanctuary at Dan (Jdg. 17:7) and of the concubine whose death fomented an intertribal war (19:1). Two texts link the town with Rachel's burial place (Gen. 35:19; 48:7; cf. 1 Sam. 10:2). Bethlehem remained one of Judah's smaller towns (Mic. 5:2), though according to the Chronicler, it was rebuilt or fortified by Rehoboam (2 Chr. 11:6). The postexilic lists of exiles indicate a small community there (Ezr. 2:21; Neh. 7:26).

Bethlehem's permanent theological significance rests exclusively in its claim to be David's birthplace (1 Sam. 16:4; 17:12, 15; 20:6, 28). This claim is integral to the story of Ruth, which links both Ruth and her family with Bethlehem (1:22) and with David himself (4:22). With the development of an eschatological theology, in which a Davidic Messiah was central, it was naturally held that Bethlehem would be his place of origin. In intertestamental literature the Judean origins of a Messiah are regularly affirmed, though Bethlehem itself does not figure with any prominence.

The crucial OT text for NT theology is clearly Mic. 5:2, one of the foundation stones for Christian messianic interpretation. This text stresses the contrast between the numerical insignificance of Bethlehem's population and its theological importance as the place from which, like David of old, Israel's ideal ruler would come.

NT Matt. identifies Bethlehem as the birthplace of Jesus (2:1) and as the place to which the Magi are directed (2:5, 8). The main purpose here is to show the fulfillment of Mic. 5:2 in predicting where the Messiah would be born (→ *plēroō*, *4444*). This quotation is just one element in a substantial network of OT texts that are interpreted and elaborated in Matt. 1–2. In the context of Matthean theology as a whole, Jesus' birth at Bethlehem conveys the fact that he is Messiah (→ *Christos*, *5986*).

In Luke this specialized Jewish interest is absent, for he draws no explicit theological conclusion from Jesus' birth at Bethlehem. Yet Luke does adhere firmly to this tradition of Jesus' birth there (Lk. 2:15). The description of the census (2:1–3) is Luke's means of showing how Jesus, a Galilean, came to be born at Bethlehem.

1037	βῆμα

βῆμα (*bēma*), judgment seat (*1037*).

CL & OT 1. In cl. Gk. *bēma* can mean step or stride, as in walking. It is also used as a platform for a public speaker and, in legal contexts, denotes the place where litigants stood for trial.

2. In the LXX *bēma* occurs in Deut. 2:5 in the sense of a unit of measure. Here the Lord affirms to Moses that he will not allow the people of Israel to take any territory belonging to the descendants of Esau, "not even enough to put your foot on" (lit., "not even a *bēma* of a foot," cf. Deut. 11:24; Jos. 1:3, where a similar idea without *bēma* occurs). In Neh. 8:4 and 1 Esd. 9:42 the word denotes the wooden platform on which Ezra stood to read from the book of the law. In Sir. 19:30 the word occurs in the pl. in the sense of the steps of a person, i.e., one's manner of walking that reveals one's character.

NT 1. In the NT *bēma* occurs once in the sense of step as a unit of measure (Acts 7:5). There is it translated "foot of ground," i.e., a small area (cf. Deut. 2:5).

2. The word is used most frequently of the platform on which was placed a seat for an official. In Acts 12:21 it is the platform from which orations were made; in Matt. 27:19; Jn. 19:13; Acts 18:12, 16–17; 25:6, 10, 17, the seat where civil officials held session to hear certain legal cases and to render judgment. Thus Jesus was brought before Pilate's *bēma*, and the Jews at Corinth accused Paul before the tribunal of Gallio. Later Paul appeared before the *bēma* of Festus at Caesarea.

3. The word is used 2x in Paul's letters, in both cases with regard to divine judgment. Rom. 14:10 speaks of "God's judgment seat," and 14:11 cites Isa. 45:23 as confirmation that all will appear before it. The emphasis here is on the role of the litigant before the *bēma*: "So then, each of us will give account of himself to God" (Rom. 14:12). In 2 Cor. 5:10 Paul speaks of "the judgment seat of Christ," stressing that Christ will judge everyone (cf. Matt. 16:27; 25:31–46). Here the emphasis falls on the judgment rendered: "that each one may receive what is due him for the things done while in the body, whether good or bad."

Note the reversal of roles that takes place: Jesus, who appeared before a human judgment seat and suffered unjust judgment, will one day sit in righteous judgment over the unjust. But Paul reminds his readers that believers are not exempt from this judgment. Although we are reconciled (cf. 2 Cor. 5:20–21) and justified (Rom. 5:1; 8:1), we still must give account and have our work tested (cf. 1 Cor. 3:13–15).

See also *krima*, dispute, decision, verdict, judgment (*3210*); *paradidōmi*, deliver up, give up, hand over (*4140*); *katadikazō*, condemn (*2868*).

1040	βία

βία (*bia*), force, violence (*1040*); βιάζω (*biazō*), to use force or violence (*1041*); βιαστής (*biastēs*), a violent man (*1043*); βίαιος (*biaios*), violent (*1042*).

CL & OT 1. In cl. Gk. *bia* means bodily strength, force, might. The vb. *biazō* is rare in the act., but in the mid. expresses the idea of forcible action in deed and word. Trans. it means to violate, rape; intrans. to use force, enforce one's will; pass. to suffer violence. *biastēs* means a violent person and carries a derogatory sense.

2. (a) The LXX uses *bia* infrequently. Occasionally God's power is described as *bia* (Isa. 28:2; 30:30), and in the LXX of Ezek. 44:18 the new order of priests is said to be without power. *bia* also occurs in Exod. 14:25; Neh. 5:14–15, 18; Est. 3:13 [S¹ only]; Isa. 17:13; 52:4; 63:1; Dan. 11:17; Hab. 3:6; Wis. 4:4; 5:11; 7:20.

(b) *biazō* occurs 18x in the LXX, always with the idea of forcible action: to urge (using friendly constraint; e.g., Gen. 33:11; Jdg. 13:15–16 [A]; 19:7; 2 Sam. 13:25, 27), to rape (Deut. 22:25, 28), and to break through (Exod. 19:24).

NT 1. In the NT *bia* occurs only in Acts (3x) and denotes force or violence (cf. also *biaios*, "violent [wind]," in 2:2). Thus in 27:41 it refers to the force of waves smashing a ship. In 21:35 the author records the violence of the mob threatening Paul, while in 5:26 Peter and the apostles are arrested, but the Jewish leaders do "not use force," for fear of the crowd. In every case of *bia* the violence is a potential threat to human lives.

2. These passages in Acts may give us an insight into *biazō* in Lk. 16:16: "The Law and the Prophets were proclaimed until John. Since that time, the good news of the kingdom of God is being preached, and everyone is forcing his way [*biazō*] into it" (cf. Matt. 11:12). Some take this passage to mean that everyone acts against the kingdom of God with violence. This would imply a background of persecution, such as Lk. describes in Acts; that is, ever since the kingdom of God has been

preached, violence has been used against it. Note the context in Lk., where Jesus is replying to mockery of the Pharisees. However, basing their argument on Lk.'s use of *eis* (into) rather than of *pros* or *epi* (against) as the preposition that goes with "it" (i.e., the kingdom of God), most exegetes consider the meaning to be that everyone presses his or her way into the kingdom of God.

Matt. 11:12 contains a parallel passage, but its interpretation is also difficult: "From the days of John the Baptist until now, the kingdom of heaven has been forcefully advancing [*biazō*], and forceful men [*biastēs*] lay hold [*harpazō*] of it." To take *biazō* here (a mid./pass. form) as a mid. gives the unlikely meaning that the kingdom of heaven uses force, it coerces. To take it as intrans. gives a more probable interpretation: The kingdom of God accomplishes its purpose mightily, and those who violently press toward it seize (upon) it. But this translation is also unsatisfactory, since it depicts the kingdom as "suffering violence" in a good sense, with people pressing toward it and striving vehemently to grasp it, whereas *biazō* usually denotes hostile action.

The best interpretation of Matt. 11:12, therefore, is the one that takes *biazō* as pass. in an unfavorable sense: The kingdom of heaven suffers violence, and violent men assault it, meaning either that they place hindrances in its way or that it is forcibly introduced. Perhaps Matt. has in the background here the accusation leveled at Jesus that he had sought to snatch at equality with God (cf. Phil. 2:6; → *harpazō*, seize, *773*). If so, then Matt. 11:12 is saying that it is not Jesus but the persecutors who are laying violent hands on the kingdom of heaven.

If this interpretation is correct, the allusion may be to the assault of Satan and evil spirits against the kingdom or to Herod's assault on John the Baptist. Or perhaps in Matt.'s mind are the Zealots, who were trying to bring in the Davidic kingdom by using force against the Romans, or even Jewish antagonists, who continued to persecute Christians. The context suggests that the fate of John the Baptist is uppermost in Jesus' thoughts. But his warning does not preclude the other suggestions.

See also *ischys*, strength, power, might (*2709*); *keras*, horn (*3043*); *kratos*, power, might, rule (*3197*).

1041 (biazō, to use force or violence), → *1040.*

1042 (biaios, violent), → *1040.*

1043 (biastēs, a violent man), → *1040.*

1046 (biblion, book), → *1047.*

1047 βίβλος

βίβλος (*biblos*), book (*1047*); βιβλίον (*biblion*), book (*1046*).

CL & OT 1. *biblos* is derived from an older form *byblos*, which meant the papyrus plant, or its fibrous stem, that was exported to Greece through the port of Byblos in Syria. From there it came to mean any material used in writing, such as a clay tablet, leather, parchment. From there developed the meaning scroll, book, writing, letter, order. In Koine Gk. *biblos* is often replaced by its diminutive *biblion*. Eventually these words came to denote an ancient holy book (cf. the magical books in Acts 19:19). Josephus and Philo call the Heb. Scriptures *hierai bibloi*, holy books.

2. In the LXX *biblos*, or more commonly *biblion*, translates Heb. *sēper*, and its meaning is fixed by OT usage. It is used for anything that has been written. Examples are a war diary (Exod. 17:14; cf. Num. 21:14), a law book (Deut. 17:18; cf. Exod. 24:7), a private letter (2 Sam. 11:14), a divorce document (Deut. 24:1, 3; cf. Mk. 10:4), a land register (Jos. 18:9), and various chronicles of the kings (1 Ki. 15:31). There is a religious connotation only insofar as Yahweh is a witness of what has been written and watches over its fulfillment, esp. in cases of contracts.

3. In the sing. these words are used for individual OT writings (1 Chr. 27:24; Tob. 1:1), in the pl. for groups of writings (Dan. 9:2; 1 Macc. 12:9). Important in this connection is their use in the sing. for

the book of the law, the Torah. This usage springs undoubtedly from the fact that the Torah was written on a special scroll. Since this scroll contains God's holy will, *biblion* became in the LXX a solemn expression for the book of the law (Deut. 28:58; cf. Jos. 1:8). Various later books stood beside the Torah and the other OT writings, but by the end of the first cent. A.D. the canon was closed.

4. Various other "books" are mentioned in Jewish writings, esp. apocalyptic. The book is here a picture of God's eternal purposes for the future of his people, his world, or his creatures. There is the book of the divine plan (cf. Ezek. 2:8–10), the book of life (cf. Exod. 32:32–33; Isa. 4:3; Dan. 12:1; *Jub.* 19:9), the book of human history (Ps. 40:7; 139:16), and the book of judgment (Isa. 65:6; Dan. 7:10; *1 Enoch* 89:61–64). These books express God's sovereign will and work in history.

NT 1. The NT uses *biblion* 34x, *biblos* only 10x (though they are interchangeable). Particularly noticeable are the 23 occurrences of *biblion* in Rev. OT usage reappears in Matt. 1:1, "a record (*biblos*) of the genealogy" (cf. Gen. 5:1), and Matt. 19:7; Mk. 10:4, "a certificate (*biblion*) of divorce" (cf. Deut. 24:1, 3). Both words are used for the Torah (Gal. 3:10; Heb. 9:19) or for other books of the OT canon (cf. Mk. 12:26; Lk. 3:4; 4:17; 20:42; Acts 1:20; 7:42). The writer of the Fourth Gospel also calls his work a *biblion* (Jn. 20:30; cf. 21:25).

Book is used in a special way in Rev.: the book in which all the things revealed are to be written (1:11); the book sealed with 7 seals, which contains the plan for the world in the last days (5:1–9); the book of life, in which are found the names of those who are to enter eternal life (13:8; 20:15; cf. Phil. 4:3); and the books of judgment (Rev. 20:12). While this is the language of apocalyptic, it has been given a new force and significance.

2. The books of the Bible contain a message that awakens and demands faith. Only where this message is believed are they rightly read and understood (Jn. 20:30–31). But when John speaks of his book in this connection, he is not necessarily using the word with any theological significance.

It is otherwise in Rev. As in Jewish apocalyptic, the *biblion* contains divine decrees concerning what will happen in the world and among God's people until the return of Christ, who will ultimately triumph over every power that is opposed to God. In contrast to Jewish apocalyptic, however, the seer John passes on a prophetic message under his own name to the contemporary churches known to him. He wants to provide comfort and warning (cf. Dan. 12:4, 9; Rev. 1:11).

Rev. 5:1–9 speaks of a scroll like that in Ezek. 2:9–10. It is written on both sides and sealed with 7 seals, presumably a deed and probably a will, and contains God's eschatological plan. The history of God's dealings with the world has already been decided. Only one, the crucified and exalted Christ, is worthy to break the seals and to make God's plans a reality and to fulfill them. Confession of Christ is decisive for the concept of history in Rev.

The end time is the time of judgment. In this context Rev. takes up once more the pictures of the book of life and the books of judgment (20:12). The names of those who will be preserved from judgment are contained in the book of life (cf. Lk. 10:20; Phil. 4:3). They are the conquerors (Rev. 3:5), or those who have been predestined "from the creation of the world" (17:8). But that does not mean that predestination makes the call to obedience unnecessary, for a name can be blotted out of the book of life. Human victory and divine predestination are here linked, just as are faith as a gift and as a personal decision.

See also *anaginōskō*, read (*336*); *epistolē*, letter (*2186*).

1050 βίος

βίος (*bios*), life (*1050*); βιόω (*bioō*), live (*1051*); βίωσις (*biōsis*), way of life (*1052*); βιωτικός (*biōtikos*), pertaining to life (*1053*).

CL & OT 1. In cl. Gk. *bios* denotes life in its concrete outward manifestations. It is used generally for "lifetime" or "duration of life," and specifically for an individual's way of life. Aristotle gave an ethical meaning to the term, such as a political life or a contemplative life. Later *bios* acquired the concrete meaning of livelihood, trade, or wealth (cf. *biōtikos*, pertaining to life, everyday).

2. The LXX adopts mainly the temporal meaning of *bios*, i.e., the duration of life. That meaning is clearest in Job, where it occurs 13x. A person's lifetime, in all its wretchedness, is compared to forced labor (7:1), a shadow (8:9), vanity (7:16), and sorrow (15:20). Wisdom, by contrast, promises the godly length of life (Prov. 3:2), which is a gift she holds in her right hand (3:16), while the godless are punished with a short life (Wis. 2:1, 4, 5). In Song 8:7 *bios* means wealth, and in Prov. 31:14 food.

In 4 Macc., Hel. influence replaces the temporal meaning of *bios* with an ethical meaning. The author describes a way of life that is true to the Mosaic law (5:36; 7:15): upright (1:15), pleasant (8:23), and even divine (7:7). In Wis. 4:9; 5:4 *bios* means conduct.

NT 1. *bios* is surprisingly rare in the NT, occurring only 11x (*bioō* only once, 1 Pet. 4:2). It has a clearly temporal meaning (duration of life) only in a variant reading of 1 Pet. 4:3; *bioō* in the previous verse denotes living one's earthly life. In 1 Tim. 2:2 and 2 Tim. 2:4 it has the more general sense of living one's everyday life.

2. The NT uses *bios* 6x in the concrete, somewhat external sense of wealth, fortune, or possessions. In Mk. 12:44 and Lk. 21:4 the poor widow puts "all she had to live on" into the treasury, while Lk. 15:12, 30 tells of the prodigal son wasting his inherited "property." Real love shows itself in sharing one's "material possessions" with a fellow believer in need (1 Jn. 3:17).

3. Paul uses *biōsis* to describe his manner of life as a Pharisaic Jew (Acts 26:4). The meaning of *bios* as "manner of life" occurs seldom in the NT. "The pride of life" (lit. trans. of 1 Jn. 2:16) refers to ostentatious living, and in Lk. 8:14 there is an allusion to "life's worries." The reason why this Gk. conception of *bios* is not adopted by the NT is that we should not conduct our lives for ourselves; rather, we must live in the service of others.

See also *zōē*, life (*2437*).

1051 (*bioō*, live), → *1050*.

1052 (*biōsis*, manner of life), → *1050*.

1053 (*biōtikos*, pertaining to life), → *1050*.

1056 (*blastanō*, sprout, shoot forth), → *1285*.

1059	βλασφημέω

βλασφημέω (*blasphēmeō*), slander, defame, blaspheme (*1059*); βλασφημία (*blasphēmia*), slander, defamation, blasphemy (*1060*); βλάσφημος (*blasphēmos*), slanderous, blasphemous, a blasphemer (*1061*).

CL & OT 1. In cl. Gk. *blasphēmeō* means to speak harm, bring into ill repute, slander, blaspheme; it refers to a strong expression of personal defamation. *blasphēmia* (an action noun) means profane language or slander, defamation, by which another person is damaged. *blasphēmos* expresses the quality of the action or the doer. False representations of a deity—e.g., in anthropomorphic terms— can be described as blasphemy; so too can doubts about the deity's authority.

2. Words in this group appear only 22x in the LXX, most frequently in 2 Macc. They are always either directly or indirectly against the majesty of God; with a few exceptions (e.g., Isa. 66:3; Wis. 1:6; Sir. 3:16), they refer to the reviling of the people of Israel by heathen enemies. Thus in a comparison with the king of Assyria, Yahweh is written off as powerless, reviled (2 Ki. 19:4, 6, 22); when Israel is under attack, Yahweh is blasphemed (2 Macc. 8:4; 9:28; 10:4, 34); the Edomites rejoice over Jerusalem's fall and in so doing blaspheme Yahweh (Ezek. 35:12–13).

In Isa. 52:5 the lament of the rulers over the continual despising of God's name through the exile is the basis for Yahweh's saving intervention (cf. 52:6). The God of Israel is not as a rule a source of hope and help, or even of fear, for the heathen; this fact alone is enough to earn them the title of blasphemers (Dan. 3:29). Surprisingly, perhaps, the LXX does not use this vb. in Lev. 24:16 for someone who blasphemes the name of the Lord; rather it refers to (lit.) "anyone who names the name of the Lord." In Jewish circles, even to name Yahweh's name was considered blasphemy. This applies not only to Israelites but also to the nations, whose blasphemy may be requited by God with death (cf. *blasphēmeō* in 2 Ki. 19:6; *blasphēmos* in 2 Macc. 9:28).

3. (a) The concept of blasphemy is found elsewhere in the OT where the technical terms are lacking. It is blasphemy to make false, irreverent use of God's name: "You shall not misuse the name of the LORD your God, for the LORD will not hold anyone guiltless who misuses his name" (Exod. 20:7; cf. Deut. 5:11). Similarly, the king or priest was not to bring discredit on his sacred office (1 Sam. 2:27–36; 3:13; 2 Sam. 12:14), oppose God's chosen (Num. 16:30), break the covenant (Deut. 31:20; Isa. 1:4), or doubt Yahweh's power either in judgment or salvation (Num. 14:11, 23; 20:10–12; 2 Ki. 18:30–35; Isa. 5:24; 10:8–12). Blasphemy is closely linked to cursing. Job's wife and Satan expected Job to curse God and thus blaspheme (Job 1:11; 2:5, 9). But his friends regarded his protestations of innocence as blasphemy (15:2–6; 34:35–37).

(b) In numerous OT passages the innocent appear to reproach Yahweh, but this is not regarded as blasphemy. It is more a confession of faith and of utter dependence on him to act (e.g., Exod. 5:22; Num. 11:11–15; Jos. 7:7; Isa. 38:13; Jer. 12:1–4; 15:15–18; 20:7–10; Lam. 3:10–11). By contrast, genuine blasphemy merits death and is punished by human judges (Lev. 24:10–16; 1 Ki. 21:13) or by God himself (Exod. 20:7; Num. 16:30; 2 Macc. 9:4, 12). The forms of the penalties suggest the extermination of the guilty party.

NT Words of the *blasphēmeō* group are found in the NT 56x (the vb. 34x). As in the OT and in rab. Jud., the terms are used in the NT in a religious sense, i.e., with direct or indirect reference to God (except for Jude 9). Blasphemy against God amounts to words or conduct injurious to his honor and holiness.

1. This sin against God's majesty can consist of blasphemy against God's person (Acts 6:11; Rev. 13:6; 16:11, 21), against his name (Rom. 2:24; 1 Tim. 6:1; Rev. 16:9), against his word (Tit. 2:5), or against his angels (2 Pet. 2:10–12).

Since Jesus claims for his words and actions messianic authority and assumes rights and powers (e.g., to forgive sins, Lk. 5:21) that, in the view of the religious Jews and teachers of the law, belong to God alone, he is regarded in these circles as a blasphemer (Matt. 9:3; Mk. 2:7; Jn. 10:36). The sentence of death against him is therefore based, among other things, on a charge of blasphemy (Matt. 26:65; Mk. 14:64). In 1st-cent. Jud., blasphemy was still an offense deserving death. According to *m. Sanh.* 7:5, a blasphemer is not culpable unless he pronounces the divine name itself (cf. Lev. 24:10–16); the judges were to rend their garments on hearing the evidence. Jesus' *egō eimi* ("I am") in Jn. 8:58 was apparently understood as a claim to the divine name, whereupon the Jews took up stones to stone him (8:59).

2. From a NT point of view, the real blasphemers are those who deny the messianic claims of Jesus and therefore revile and mock him. Some such people were at the cross, who "hurled insults [*blasphēmeō*]at him . . . saying, 'You who are going to destroy the temple and build it in three days, save yourself! Come down from the cross, if you are the Son of God!'" (Matt. 27:39–40). Those who impugn the dignity of the one sent by God commit an offense against God himself.

3. Since the church of Christ and its members bear witness by their existence to Christ himself, they too undergo the abuse that was directed against their Lord (1 Pet. 4:4; Rev. 2:9). Thus Paul suffers as Christ's disciple (Acts 13:45; 18:6) the persecutions he had previously inflicted on Christians (1 Tim. 1:13). To revile the church that bears

Christ's name can be to mock Christ and thus, indirectly, to blaspheme against God.

4. Christians for their part must take care that they do not, by their conduct, give cause for blasphemy against God or his word (1 Tim. 6:1; Tit. 2:5). Indeed, the behavior of Christ's disciples (even toward each other) should contribute to the glory of the Father (cf. Matt. 5:16). This is probably the sense in which we should interpret NT lists of sins, which typically contain prohibitions of blasphemy (Eph. 4:31; Col. 3:8; 1 Tim. 6:4; 2 Tim. 3:2). Blasphemy is mentioned in them as characteristic of the heathen and of apostate Christians. By contrast, Rom. 2:24 adapts the LXX of Isa. 52:5, which blames Israel for reviling God's name by living a hypocritical life.

5. The sin of blasphemy, including blasphemy against the Son of Man, can be forgiven; only blasphemy against the Holy Spirit is unforgivable (Matt. 12:31–32; Mk. 3:28–29; Lk. 12:10). This statement has been the subject of much discussion. Among the many attempts at exegesis, the most convincing is the suggestion that the person committing this sin is one who recognizes that the Holy Spirit is working through Jesus but who consciously and deliberately ascribes this work to the devil instead. Such a person is declaring war on God. This is what the context suggests, since Jesus' enemies cannot deny that God's Spirit is working through Jesus because of an exorcism he has just performed (Matt. 12:22), so they accuse him of casting out demons by Beelzebub, the prince of demons (12:24; → *diabolos*, devil, *1333*).

Thus, blasphemy here is much more serious than simply taking the divine name in vain, which a believer may have done before coming to repentance and faith. One of the prime works of the Spirit is leading a person to salvation in the name of Christ (cf. Rom. 8:15–16). Resisting the Holy Spirit's call, therefore, and remaining in hardened unbelief is tantamount to blasphemy against the Spirit. Thus, those who might be tormented by fear that they may have committed the unforgivable sin show by their very concern that they have not committed it.

6. Another passage that has been the subject of debate is Jude 9: "But even the archangel Michael, when he was disputing with the devil about the body of Moses, did not dare to bring a slanderous accusation [*blasphēmia*] against him, but said, 'The Lord rebuke you!'" In v. 7 the false teachers are compared with the people of Sodom and Gomorrah and in v. 8 are accused of polluting their own bodies, rejecting authority, and reviling the celestial beings (probably angels). Presumably an archangel was sent by God to bury the body of Moses after his death (Deut. 34), and Satan did his best to prevent this, claiming as lord of the material order that the body was his and possibly accusing Moses of murdering the Egyptian (cf. Exod. 2:12). The point of the observation is that even the archangel Michael did not respond with like reviling but committed the responsibility for rebuking Satan to God, using an imprecation found in Zech. 3:2.

Perhaps in the background here is notion that we should be very careful, both in uttering a curse and in reviling, not to challenge a power too great for us to cope with. Note what Jude 10 says: "Yet these men speak abusively against [*blasphēmeō*] whatever they do not understand; and what things they do understand by instinct, like unreasoning animals—these are the very things that destroy them" (cf. 1 Cor. 2:7–16). That is, the unspiritual not only fail to understand but even blaspheme God in the process. Thus the sense may be comparable with blasphemy against the Holy Spirit in the Gospels. There may also be the sense here in which the believer should leave judgment to God (cf. Rom. 12:19; cf. Deut. 32:35).

7. *blasphēmos*, abusive, slanderous, blasphemous, occurs at Acts 6:11; 2 Tim. 3:2; 2 Pet. 2:11; and as a noun, blasphemer, at 1 Tim. 1:13.

See also *katalaleō*, speak evil of, rail at, slander (*2895*); *loidoreō*, insult, abuse, revile (*3366*); *oneidizō*, insult, denounce, rebuke (*3943*).

1060 (*blasphēmia*, slander, defamation, blasphemy), → *1059*.

1061 (*blasphēmos*, slanderous, blasphemous, a blasphemer), → *1059*.

1063	βλέπω

βλέπω (*blepō*), look at, see (*1063*); ἀναβλέπω (*anablepō*), look up (at), see again (*329*); ἐμβλέπω (*emblepō*), look, look at, look in the face, consider (*1838*).

CL & OT 1. (a) In cl. Gk. *blepō*, see, is near to *horaō* (→ *3972*) in meaning but gradually came to be used less frequently. Originally *blepō* applied only to the function of the eyes, seeing, looking, watching. It later came to mean to look at, view, look into; also to give heed to, pay attention to something. Fig. it can mean observe, notice.

(b) The use of *anablepō*, to look up, see again, goes far back into cl. times. In the LXX it almost always means simply to look up, but Is. 42:18 has the sense connected with blindness, "Look [*anablepō*], you blind, and see [aor. of *horaō*]." The idea of recovery of sight is described as early as Herodotus and in an inscription from the temple of Asclepius.

NT 1. *blepō* occurs 132x in the NT. In general it simply refers to the capacity to see (Matt. 12:22; Lk. 7:21). Otherwise it can mean to watch, look at, look into (Matt. 5:28; Rev. 5:3–4). It also represents intellectual functions such as attending, paying attention to (Mk. 13:33; 1 Cor. 1:26), heeding something (2 Cor. 10:7), or being careful. Fig. it can mean to perceive or observe (Rom. 7:23; Heb. 2:9).

2. *anablepō* occurs 24x in the NT. The generic meaning to look up is found in several passages (e.g., Mk. 16:4; Lk. 19:5; 21:1). Jesus looked up to heaven when giving thanks for the bread to be multiplied for the crowd (Matt. 14:19; Mk. 6:41; Lk. 9:16) and when healing the deaf man in Mk. 7:34. The man whose vision was restored by a double touch of Jesus looked up after the first touch (8:24). The vb. means to see again in Jesus' message to John the Baptist about his messianic works (Matt. 11:5; Lk. 7:22). In Acts 9:12, 17, 18, it refers to the restoration of Saul's vision. Jn. 9:11, 15, 18 describes the healing of the man born blind by using *anablepō*, although obviously the prefix *ana-* cannot mean "again" here, since the man had never been able to see.

3. (a) The NT uses of *emblepō* (12x) are generally straightforward, usually signifying a look of interest, love, or concern. Jesus "looked" at the rich young man and loved him (Mk. 10:21). He later "looked" at the disciples as he discussed an important issue (Matt. 19:26; Mk. 10:27). A servant girl who thought Peter may have been associated with Jesus "looked closely" at him (14:67). When Jesus applied the parable of the vineyard, he "looked directly" at his audience (Lk. 20:17). In the poignant passage about Peter's meeting with Jesus after the denial, Jesus "looked straight at" him (Lk. 22:61).

(b) On one occasion *emblepō* describes the perception of a formerly blind man after a second healing touch by Jesus (Mk. 8:25). Conversely, Saul was unable to see (*emblepō*) after his exposure to the light on the road to Damascus (Acts 22:11; cf. 9:8, which uses the simple *blepō*). It is uncertain whether the usage of *emblepō* in Jn. 1:36, 42 implies some sort of special insight or perception. Since John sometimes varies his vocabulary without special meaning (and conversely, may employ one word with several levels of meaning), one must be careful when attributing a spiritual meaning to a word. In this case, however, the significance of the recognition may justify understanding a similar significance in *emblepō*.

See also *horaō*, see (*3972*); *kollourion*, eye salve (*3141*); *atenizō*, look at a person or thing intently, gaze on (*867*); *theatron*, theater, place of assembly, a spectacle (*2519*).

1066	βοάω

βοάω (*boaō*), call, shout, cry out (*1066*); ἀναβοάω (*anaboaō*), cry out (*331*); βοή (*boē*), cry, shout (*1068*).

CL & OT *boaō* means cry out, call out (e.g., Gen. 39:14; Isa. 36:13; 1 Macc. 13:45). In many contexts it is expressive of the extremities of human needs and joys. Both *boaō* and *anaboaō* can be used for calling out in distress (e.g., Num. 20:16; Jdg. 10:10). The noun *boē*, occurs, among other places, in Exod. 2:23 and 1 Sam. 9:16. In each case the cry of God's people in their affliction does not go unheeded by God.

The OT gives numerous warnings about abusing the needy so that they cry out to God (Exod. 22:22–27; Deut. 24:15; Job 31:38; Mal. 3:5). There is also an extended use of the idea of crying in the sense of a murder crying out for justice and retribution (e.g., Gen. 4:10). If the victim is dead, the deed itself is an accusing witness.

Crying is used in the context of the coming salvation promised in Isa. 40:3, which refers to the triumphant return of the exiles from Babylon through the deserts, led by the Lord himself. In the next stanza the prophet is told to cry of the transitoriness of humankind compared with the word of God (40:6, 8). Isa. 54:1 refers to crying aloud for joy—a passage that recalls the increase of the nation despite adverse circumstances.

NT The same range of reference is found in the NT, where the Isa. passages are seen as finding their fulfillment in events attending the coming of Christ. *boaō* is used in Mk. 15:34 for Jesus' cry of anguish (*anaboaō* in Matt. 27:46). This cry uses the words of Ps. 22:1 to express the desolation of a sense of abandonment by God. Taken at face value, the words suggest that Jesus experienced the desolation that the people of God experienced throughout their history. But there is an irony in the situation. For this was *the* Son of God experiencing the desolation, and it was at the hands of God's people. Some commentators hold that the cry was not one of despair but that of a righteous sufferer trusting in God's protection and expecting vindication (cf. Ps. 22:22–31).

boaō is used of evil spirits leaving a person (Acts 8:7), of the sick (Lk. 9:38; 18:38), and of the shouts of a crowd (Acts 17:6; 25:24). Crying to God is a form of prayer that God answers (Lk. 18:7). The vb. also occurs in the quotation from Isa. 40:3 that all four Evangelists apply to John the Baptist (Matt. 3:3; Mk. 1:3; Lk. 3:4; Jn. 1:23). His is the voice that cries, and his message is a Christological interpretation of Isa. 40:3. The preparation of the desert for the coming of the Lord is a type of the preparation of God's people for the coming of the Lord in the person of Jesus Christ. In Gal. 4:27, Paul applies Isa. 54:1 to the joy of freedom found in the church.

boē is used only in Jas. 5:4 for the cry of the oppressed.

See also *krazō*, cry aloud (*3189*).

1068 (*boē*, cry, shout), → *1066*.

1069 (*boētheia*, help, assistance), → *1070*.

1070	βοηθέω

βοηθέω (*boētheō*), to help, assist (*1070*); βοήθεια (*boētheia*), help, assistance (*1069*); βοηθός (*boēthos*), helpful, helper (*1071*).

CL & OT 1. In cl. Gk. *boētheō* means to go to the assistance of, help. The noun often has a military connotation of an auxiliary or allied troop going to help fellow soldiers in battle.

2. The LXX often uses this word group in military contexts (e.g., 2 Sam. 18:3; 1 Ki. 1:7). But when all is said and done, Israel's real helper is Yahweh, as the stone named Ebenezer was to indicate (1 Sam. 7:12). The psalms are filled with recognition of the Lord as Israel's helper (Ps. 18:2; 19:14 [rock]; 79:9; 118:7), and God's people should go nowhere else for aid (60:11; Isa. 10:3; 31:1).

NT 1. *boētheō* occurs 8x in the NT, *boētheia* 2x, and *boēthos* only once. A physical use of the noun occurs in Acts 27:17, where the sailors passed "helps" (i.e., "ropes") under the ship to hold it together during the storm. Five instances of the vb. are in the imperative, three of which are calls uttered to Jesus for help (Matt. 15:25; Mk. 9:22, 24). In Paul's vision at Troas, a man from Macedonia asks him to "come over . . . and help us" (Acts 16:9), which initiated his mission in Macedonia and Greece. The other call for help came from the Asian Jews who were trying to lynch Paul in the Jerusalem temple (21:28).

2. Just as the OT called on God as Israel's helper, so in the NT believers recognize Jesus as their helper (cf. Heb. 13:6, quoting Ps. 118:7). In Jesus the Son of God we "may receive mercy and find grace

to help us in our time of need" (Heb. 4:16), and he can help us in our temptations, since he too has been tempted (2:18).

1071 (*boēthos*, helpful, helper), → *1070*.

1083 (*botanē*, plant), → *3303*.

1087 (*boulē*, will, resolve, purpose), → *1089*.

1088 (*boulēma*, will, intention, purpose), → *1089*.

1089	βούλομαι

βούλομαι (*boulomai*), to will, wish, want, desire (*1089*); βουλή (*boulē*), will, resolve, purpose (*1087*); βούλημα (*boulēma*), will, intention, purpose (*1088*); ἐπιβουλή (*epiboulē*), plot, plan (*2101*).

CL & OT 1. In cl. Gk. *boulomai* meant originally to prefer, favor, then to want, elect, decide. It is synonymous with *(e)thelō* (→ *2527*). In Hel. Gk. *boulomai* occurs the less frequently of the two. *boulē* denotes an intention, a deliberation, as well as the result of a deliberation in a sense of a decision, resolution, or edict. From this *boulē* developed the meaning of an assembly of people who had power to make decisions. A later word is *boulēma*, describing the will more as a purpose, intention, or tendency.

2. (a) *boulomai* occurs over 100x in the LXX, the same as with *thelō*. Different translators tended to prefer one over the other. Thus *boulomai* is found more frequently in Exod., 1 Sam., and Job. It means to like, want (Isa. 1:11), find pleasure in (2 Sam. 24:3), desire (Job 13:3). It can express the varied nuances of general human volition, but is also commonly used for the will of God (e.g., 1 Sam. 2:25; Isa. 53:10).

(b) *boulē* also occurs over 100x in the LXX, this time in contrast with *thelēma* (49x). It denotes one's consideration that precedes a decision (e.g., Deut. 32:28). It can even be found in the sense of wisdom (Prov. 2:11; 8:12). The "Spirit of counsel," i.e., of considered reflection, is a gift of God (Isa. 11:2). The word can also mean advice, whether good (Gen. 49:6; 1 Ki. 12:8) or foolish (Ps. 1:1; Isa. 19:11). As in cl. Gk., it can denote the council as a political institution (1 Macc. 14:22) or the resolution of an assembly (3 Macc. 7:17). Above all, *boulē* can designate the will or purpose of God (e.g., Ps. 33:10–11; 73:24), which is trustworthy and reliable (Isa. 25:1). His purpose includes Israel's salvation (14:26).

(c) The divine will and purpose plays a special role in the Dead Sea Scrolls. The elect community must perform God's will (1QS 9:13, 23), and nothing takes place apart from that will (1QH 1:8; 10:9). It is the irrevocable prerequisite for every insight into right action (14:13).

NT 1. (a) As in Hel. Gk. generally, the NT tends to use *thelō* rather than *boulomai* (207x versus 37x), though they are virtually interchangeable. *boulomai* generally denotes conscious volition, a decision of the will. Such volition presupposes the possibility of freedom of decision. (i) It denotes human volition (1 Tim. 2:8; 5:14; Tit. 3:8), usually without any theological significance (e.g., Mk. 15:15; Acts 12:4; Jas. 4:4). (ii) But it also denotes the volition of God (Lk. 22:42; Heb. 6:17; Jas. 1:18), Jesus (Matt. 11:27), or the Holy Spirit (1 Cor. 12:11). (iii) It can designate a wish determined by personal inclinations (Acts 25:22; Phlm. 13; 1 Tim. 6:9).

(b) As a rule, *boulē* (12x) refers to the free decision of the will, which is prepared to carry it out. It can refer either to human decisions (e.g., Lk. 23:51; Acts 27:12, 42) or to the counsel or purpose of God (e.g., Lk. 7:30; Acts 2:23; 4:28; Eph. 1:11; Heb. 6:17). *epiboulē* (4x in the NT) is a synonym and refers onlys to human plots against Paul (Acts 9:24; 20:3, 19; 23:30).

(c) *boulēma* (3x), in contrast to *boulē*, stresses the will more as mental direction and should be translated as intent, intention (Acts 27:43; Rom. 9:19; 1 Pet. 4:3).

2. Theological significance is found esp. where this word group speaks of the counsel, intention, or will of God (or Jesus or the Holy Spirit). It is always a case of an unalterable determination.

(a) In Lk.'s writings *boulomai* and *boulē* elucidate vital aspects of Lk.'s Christological proclamation as the fulfillment of God's purpose. Lk. 10:22 ("those to whom the Son chooses to reveal him") shows the indivisible unity between Father and Son. Jesus' death on the cross is part of "God's set purpose" or "will" foretold in Scripture (Acts 2:23; 4:28, both *boulē*). Despite this will, however, the Jewish leaders are not absolved from the fact that they crucified him. The Jews did not realize that the promises given to David in Ps. 16:10 point beyond him to God's plan with Jesus (Acts 13:34–37; cf. also 2:25–36).

It is one's attitude to the humiliated and crucified one that decides to whom the revelation will be disclosed. "To whom the Son chooses to reveal him" (Lk. 10:22) means, therefore, that with respect to knowledge of God, all human willing here reaches its limits. But note that this is not a rule of arbitrary predestination here, but rather a conscious awareness of the revealed will of God. Lk. 22:42 makes it clear that Jesus, in unity with the Father, carries out only the divine will: "Father, if you are willing [*boulomai*], take this cup from me; yet not my will [*thelēma*], but yours be done."

Paul stresses in Acts 20:26–31 that in spite of threatening heresies, he had testified to "the whole will [*boulē*] of God" (20:27), namely, God's gracious approach to sinners in the sacrifice of his Son (20:28).

(b) In the rest of the NT this word group is used only 7x for the will and purpose of God. In Rom. 9:19, when Paul refers to the Gentiles' relationship to the will of God, he makes use of *boulēma* (the opponent gives the excuse, "Who resists his will?"); in 9:18, however, where he himself speaks as a believer of the double will of God, he uses *thelō*. Since *boulēma* expresses more an intention, which is often found to be dark and impenetrable, this word takes on the tone of arbitrary willfulness or caprice in the mouth of an opponent.

In 1 Cor. 12:11 Paul points out that all gifts in the community derive from the one Spirit of God, apportioned "just as he determines." In Eph. 1:11 *boulē* means the purpose of God; that is, in Christ, God "works out everything in conformity with the purpose [*boulē*] of his will [*thelēma*]." In the context of 1:3–5 Paul is stressing that the purpose of divine election precedes the act of the historical election of Israel. Heb. 6:17 uses *boulē* similarly for the unalterable purpose of God. Peter stresses in 2 Pet. 3:9 that God's promise to send Jesus back is firm, despite its seeming delay; his will is the salvation of all. In Jas. 1:18, our rebirth is the choice of God's saving will.

See also *thelō*, wish, want, desire, will, take pleasure in (*2527*).

1092	βραβεῖον

βραβεῖον (*brabeion*), prize (*1092*); βραβεύω (*brabeuō*), award prizes, judge, rule (*1093*); καταβραβεύω (*katabrabeuō*), decide against, condemn (*2857*).

CL & OT 1. The noun *brabeion*, victor's prize (which could be wreaths made of olive, laurel, ivy, pine, flowers, palm branches, or myrtle; fixed money prizes; oil or barley; shields as gifts of the deity; accompanying rights throughout the home cities), is a technical term from the world of ancient sports. *brabeuō* denotes the function of the umpire, but was also used metaphorically to mean lead, determine, rule. Just as *brabeus*, umpire, can have the meaning of prince, *brabeion* is also used with the sense of scepter.

2. Heb. lacks the idea of the prize. Despite the LXX's use of the imagery of the fight, it does not make use of *brabeion*. *brabeuō* appears in the LXX only in Wis. 10:12, where Wisdom was the umpire at Jacob's struggle with the angel (see Gen. 32:24–30).

NT To be accurate, *brabeuō* (only in Col. 3:15) should be translated: "Let the peace of Christ decide as umpire in your hearts." It is striking that Paul also uses in Col. the word *katabrabeuō*, withhold the victor's prize (2:18); it stands parallel in meaning to the *krinō* (judge) of Col. 2:16.

In 1 Cor. 9:24–27 and Phil. 3:10–14 (both of which contain *brabeion*), extraordinary emphasis is placed on the determination with which a contest is to be pursued. Paul instructs believers to run vigorously with purpose, "not . . . aimlessly," in order to obtain the victor's prize (1 Cor. 9:26), which the Christian obtains only with effort—perhaps even requiring the sacrifice of one's life (cf. Phil. 2:16–17)—and through *koinōnia*, sharing in the suffering of Christ (cf. 3:10). This process has nothing to do with ethical perfection; Christians have entered the race (1 Cor. 9:24), are mature (*teleioi*, Phil. 3:15), and have been made Christ's own only through faith in him (3:9, 12). The "prize" in Phil. 3:14 means participation in the resurrection of the dead—not, of course, in the general resurrection of the good and evil, but probably the so-called first resurrection at Christ's return on the clouds before his thousand-year reign (1 Cor. 15:23; 1 Thess. 4:14–17; Rev. 20:6).

See also *athleō*, compete (*123*); *agōn*, fight (*74*); *thriambeuō*, lead in a triumphal procession (*2581*); *nikaō*, be victorious (*3771*).

1093 (*brabeuō*, award prizes, judge, rule), → *1092*.

1100 (*brephos*, unborn child, embryo, baby, infant), → *4090*.

1101 (*brechō*, to rain), → *847*.

1103 (*brontē*, thunder), → *847*.

1104 (*brochē*, rain), → *847*.

1106 (*brygmos*, gnashing), → *1107*.

1107	βρύχω

βρύχω (*brychō*), gnash (*1107*); βρυγμός (*bryg-mos*), gnashing (*1106*).

CL & OT 1. In cl. Gk. *brychō* is used for the act of eating noisily or greedily as well as for the act of gnashing the teeth. It is also used metaphorically in the sense of the eating away of a disease. The noun *brygmos* connotes a biting and a gnashing of the teeth.

2. In the LXX *brychō* occurs in poetic literature, where the gnashing of the teeth is a demonstration of anger (Job 16:9; Ps. 35:16; 37:12; 112:10) or perhaps of mocking (Lam. 2:16). *brygmos* in Prov. 19:12 denotes the wrath of a king. In Sir. 51:3 the noun means biting, for the writer gives thanks to God for deliverance from "grinding teeth about to devour me."

NT In the NT *brychō* is used only once (Acts 7:54), where it describes the angry reaction of those listening to Stephen's speech. The noun *brygmos* always occurs in the expression "there will be weeping and gnashing of teeth" (Matt. 8:12; 13:42, 50; 22:13; 24:51; 25:30; Lk. 13:28)—a description of the condition of the wicked in their future existence. The association of this word with *klauthmos* ("weeping," → *klaiō*, *3081*) and the figure of torment that accompanies the expression in Matt. 13:42, 50 suggests that the gnashing of the teeth reflects extreme suffering and remorse.

See also *klaiō*, weep (*3081*); *koptō*, strike (*3164*); *lypeō*, inflict pain (*3382*); *pentheō*, be sad, grieve, mourn (*4291*); *stenazō*, to sigh, groan (*5100*).

1109	βρῶμα

βρῶμα (*brōma*), food (*1109*); βρῶσις (*brōsis*), eating, consuming, food (*1111*); βρώσιμος (*brōsimos*), edible (*1110*); γάλα (*gala*), milk (*1128*).

CL & OT *brōma* and *brōsis* both mean food and the process of eating. Rarely is each used in a fig. sense (e.g., the food of immortality). In the LXX both words usually mean food, rarely eating as a process (e.g., Jer. 15:3). God, who has assigned food to both humans and animals (Gen.

1:29–30; 2:16; 9:3), also looks after his people's food throughout their history (cf. Gen. 41:35–49; Ps. 78:18, 30). The food God gives is an expression of the righteousness he has also given (Joel 2:23 LXX).

NT *brōma* occurs in the NT 17x, both lit. (e.g., Matt. 14:15; Mk. 7:19; Rom. 14:15, 20) and fig. (e.g., Jn. 4:34; 1 Cor. 3:2; 10:3). *brōsis* (11x) denotes the act of eating (e.g., Rom. 14:17; 1 Cor. 8:4; 2 Cor. 9:10), as the synonym of *brōma* both lit. (Heb. 12:16; cf. Matt. 6:19 with the idea of consuming rust) and fig. (Jn. 4:32; 6:27, 55).

1. Lit. use. In the NT, as in the OT, food is a gift from God. We should ask for it daily (cf. Matt. 6:11) and receive it thankfully (cf. 1 Tim. 4:4). Ascetic and ritual tendencies, which classed certain foods as taboo, are rejected by the NT as false teaching (Col. 2:16–17; 1 Tim. 4:3–7; Heb. 13:9). No food is unclean as such (Mk. 7:18–19; cf. Acts 10:14–15), and no food possesses any special significance for our relationship to God (1 Cor. 8:8; cf. 6:13). The kingdom of God is realized not in eating or drinking but in righteousness, peace, and joy in the Holy Spirit (Rom. 14:17).

But Christians can be commanded to avoid a particular food (e.g., meat offered to idols) if a fellow Christian by eating will be plunged into a conflict of conscience (Rom. 14:15, 20; 1 Cor. 8:13). Out of love for that tempted believer for whom Christ died, the "strong" Christian must be willing to forego a particular food.

2. Fig. use. (a) *brōma* is used in contrast to *gala*, milk, in 1 Cor. 3:2, to contrast the basics of the faith with deeper teachings. Since faith involves a process of maturing, "infants" in the faith cannot yet "digest" the deepest truths of divine wisdom. The "spiritual food" referred to in 10:3 is the manna that miraculously kept the Israelites alive when naturally grown food was lacking. This food is interpreted typologically with reference to the Lord's Supper (→ *pinō*, *4403*).

(b) In Jn. 4:32 Jesus startlingly describes the work he did in fulfillment of his Father's commission as the food (*brōsis*) on which he lived. His whole life constituted a revelation that did not have its origin in himself but that he received from his Father. *brōsis* is mentioned three more times in Jn. in connection with feeding on Christ as "food that endures to eternal life" (Jn. 6:27). His flesh is "real food" (6:55), for he is the bread of life. To eat this bread is another way of describing what it is to believe in Jesus (6:35).

See also *peinaō*, hunger (*4277*); *geuomai*, taste, partake of, enjoy, experience (*1174*); *esthiō*, eat (*2266*); *pinō*, drink (*4403*).

1110 (brōsimos, edible), → *1109.*

1111 (brōsis, eating, consuming, food), → *1109.*

1117 (bōmos, [pagan] altar), → *2604.*

Γ *gamma*

| 1120 | Γαβριήλ |

Γαβριήλ (*Gabriēl*), Gabriel (*1120*).

OT The name comes from the root *geber* (man or strong) together with *ʾēl* (God). This suggests two meanings: man of God or God is strong. In the OT Gabriel appears only in Daniel, where as a heavenly messenger he makes his appearance as a man (Dan. 8:16, 9:21), in order to reveal the future by interpreting a vision (8:17) and to give understanding and wisdom to Daniel himself (9:22).

Jewish intertestamental texts (esp. in the various books of Enoch) display much more interest in Gabriel. Particularly noteworthy is his position at God's left hand and his authority over all powers. His functions extend beyond those in Daniel to intercession and destruction of the wicked.

NT In the NT Gabriel appears only in the Lukan birth narrative, where he is the angelic messenger announcing the births of John (1:11–20) and Jesus (1:26–38). As the one who comes from the immediate presence of God, he brings reassurance to Mary of her standing in God's sight (1:30).

| 1126 | γαζοφυλάκιον |

γαζοφυλάκιον (*gazophylakion*), treasure room, treasury (*1126*).

CL & OT In cl. Gk. *gazophylakion* means a treasury. The word is used a number of times in the canonical books of the LXX for living quarters (Neh. 3:30; 13:7) or for a room or chamber connected in some way with the temple (2 Ki. 23:11; Neh. 10:38–39 = LXX 10:37–38; 13:4–5; Ezek. 40:17); once it is used for the royal treasury of a pagan king (Est. 3:9). In the Apocr. it refers either to the sacred or the royal treasury (e.g., 1 Macc. 3:28; 14:49; 2 Macc. 3:6, 24, 28, 40; 4 Macc. 4:3, 6).

NT There are no references in the NT to the temple treasury where valuables were stored. In Mk. 12:41, 43 and Lk. 21:1, *gazophylakion* refers to one of the thirteen trumpet-shaped collection boxes in the temple, into which the Jews (including the widow lady noticed by Jesus) threw coins. These were marked to indicate the use to which the funds were put. Jn. 8:20 refers to the *gazophylakion* as the place where Jesus taught in the temple precincts; he was probably standing in the Court of the Women, where the collection boxes were placed.

1128 (*gala*, milk), → *1109*.

| 1138 | γαμέω |

γαμέω (*gameō*), marry (*1138*); γάμος (*gamos*), wedding (*1141*); γαμίζω (*gamizō*), give in marriage (*1139*); γαμίσκω (*gamiskō*), give in marriage (*1140*).

CL & OT 1. (a) In cl. Gk. *gamos* means wedding, marriage, consummation of marriage, or the wedding feast. The vb. *gameō* means to marry, celebrate a wedding, have sexual relations. *gamizō* and *gamiskō* are later forms, meaning give (a daughter) in marriage.

(b) Even though we find traces of polygamy and polyandry in the Gk. myths, monogamy predominated in the Gk. world. Morality within marriage was strict, at least on the part of the wife. She was to be faithful and inviolable, a good mother and manager of the home. But the man had greater freedom. He could have concubines or relations with prostitutes. Adultery in the Gk. states was severely punished, esp. in the case of the woman.

In the Hel. period marriage morals had become looser. There was much prostitution in the towns, esp. in ports such as Corinth. Certain cults had introduced sacred prostitution. Sexual relationships with priestesses became part of the cult and granted a sharing in the divine; it was referred to as sacred marriage.

2. *gameō* and *gamos* are infrequent in the LXX. In the OT proper, *gamos* occurs only at Gen. 29:22; Est. 2:18; 9:22 (but cf. 1:5 in the LXX); in the Apocr., *gamos* is used 17x. The OT law contains no prescribed form of marriage ceremony. Nevertheless, marriage was important. In the genealogies (e.g., Gen. 5) marriage and the begetting of children (esp. males) are the most important features mentioned. Even though from Abraham down to the kings there is evidence for polygamy (e.g., Gen. 16:1–16; 25:6; 29:21–30; 1 Sam. 18:27; 25:42–43; 2 Sam. 3:2–5), monogamy occupies the central position (see esp. Gen. 1:26–28; 2:18–24). The royal law in Deut. demands that the king "must not take many wives, or his heart will be led astray" (17:17; cf. 1 Ki. 11:1–11).

In the OT marriage is clearly regarded from the husband's standpoint and serves above all for the generation of offspring (cf. Gen. 1:28). To achieve this end a man might take another wife (cf. 16:1–16, of Abraham; Deut. 25:5–10, of levirate marriage; but note Lev. 20:21). At the same time the wife is to be loved and taken seriously as a partner (Gen. 2:23–24); in 2:18 she is described as a "helper." The partnership continues in the Fall and in the problems of sexuality created by it (ch. 3).

3. Adultery was outlawed in the OT and subject to severe punishment (Exod. 20:14; Lev. 18:20; 20:10; Deut. 5:18; 22:22–27). Even if committed unwittingly, adultery is hateful to God (Gen. 20:3–7). Adultery was a feature of paganism, but God's people were to be different in sexual practices and marriage.

In the OT divorce depended solely on the man (cf. Deut. 24:1–4; Jer. 3:8). The many laws about various sexual offenses show how the elemental power of sexuality, which threatens family and society, should be restrained and directed into the channels willed by God. One of the chief concerns was the problem of marriages with foreigners, which were forbidden (Deut. 7:3–4; 20:16–18; Ezr. 9–10; but cf. 21:10–14), though earlier cases of such marriages are exemplified (Gen. 41:45; Exod. 2:21; Num. 12:1; 2 Sam. 11:3). Heathen marriages undermined allegiance to Yahweh, esp. in the case of Solomon (1 Ki. 11:1–11).

4. If adultery was a violation of the divine law and thus an offense against the covenant, participation in the Canaanite fertility rites was an offense against both marriage and God. Hosea was the first to express the people's apostasy as prostitution and a breach of the marriage bond between God and Israel (Hos. 1–2; cf. Isa. 50:1; Jer. 2:2, 10, 25; 3:1–25; Ezek. 16, 23). Hosea's own act of marrying a prostitute at God's command (Hos. 1:2) was symbolic of Yahweh's relationship with Israel. It was God's mercy, stretching far beyond all law, that caused him not to annihilate or cast off his people as the law of marriage demanded, but to turn to them again in spite of all Israel's disloyalty and even to promise them a new covenant.

5. The Mosaic law restricted marriage and sexual intercourse to only those partners and times approved by God (Lev. 18:6–18). The Israelite was forbidden to have sexual intercourse with any close female relative. Intercourse during menstruation was prohibited, as was adultery, homosexual practices, and defilement with animals (18:19–33). Certain of these offenses were punishable by death (Deut. 27:20–23), others by problems such as childlessness (Lev. 12:6–18; 20:19–21; but cf. Gen. 38).

Certain prohibitions were attached only to the priesthood. The high priest was permitted to marry only a virgin selected from his own people (Lev. 21:13–14), and priests were forbidden to marry prostitutes and divorced women (21:7). Num. 36:5–9 contains a prohibition against an heiress marrying outside her own tribe (cf. Tob. 7:10).

A man falsely accusing his new bride of not being a virgin could be fined one hundred shekels, whipped, and compelled to take her as his wife (Deut. 22:13–19). But if his accusation proved true, the woman was to be stoned to death (22:20–21). A man who raped a virgin already engaged was liable to the death penalty (22:25–27). But in the case of a woman not pledged to marriage, the man was to take her as his wife and pay the girl's father fifty shekels (22:28–29).

6. The so-called levirate marriage (from Lat. *levir*, brother-in-law) refers to the marriage of a man to his deceased brother's widow when he died childless. The widow was not to remarry outside the family, and the unmarried brother was to perform the duties of a husband to her to raise up children to the deceased, so as to perpetuate his name in Israel. If the man refused, the woman was entitled to subject him to public disgrace before the elders (Deut. 25:5–10). The OT contains two instances of levirate marriage: the story of Onan in the patriarchal period (Gen. 38:8–10), and the story of Ruth offering herself to Boaz, who married her as a near kinsman to her deceased husband.

7. No restrictions on the age of marriage are given in the OT, though early marriage is sometimes spoken of with approval (Prov. 2:17; 5:18; Isa. 62:5). During the patriarchal age the bridegroom's father was to secure a bride for his son (Gen. 24:3; 38:6; Exod. 2:21; but cf. Gen. 21:21, where a mother does so). The selection of the bride was followed by formal betrothal, confirmed by oaths and a dowry (Gen. 34:12; Exod. 22:16; 1 Sam. 18:25). The marriage feast could last as long as seven or even fourteen days (cf. Jdg. 14:12; Tob. 8:19).

The fact that Jacob was permitted to take Laban's other daughter, Rachel, seven days after taking Leah, suggests that polygamy was openly countenanced. The OT Heb. expression for marrying was (lit.) "to take a wife" (cf. Num. 12:1; 1 Chr. 2:21). The bridegroom normally took the bride from her father's house to his own or his father's. Companions attended the groom (Jdg. 14:11). He was preceded by singers or musicians (Gen. 31:27; Jer. 7:34; 16:9; 1 Macc. 9:39) and accompanied by torch-bearers or lamp-bearers (2 Esd. 10:2; Jer. 25:10; cf. Matt. 25:7; Rev. 18:23). The bride awaited the groom with her maidens, whereupon the whole party returned to the groom's home (Song 3:11; cf. Matt. 25:6). A newly betrothed and married man was exempt from military service for a year (Deut. 20:7; 24:5).

8. There is evidence of polygamy in Palestine in NT times. Herod the Great (37–4 B.C.), for example, had ten wives. The ongoing practice of levirate marriage evidently led to polygamy, which was countenanced by the school of Shammai but not by that of Hillel. The practice of taking a second wife, if there was dissension with the first, was often due to the high price fixed in the marriage contract for divorce.

9. The Essenes by and large condemned marriage, although one order of Essenes allowed it so as to propagate the race. At Qumran, 1QSa permitted marriage on reaching maturity (i.e., age twenty). In the main, however, total renunciation meant complete holiness, esp. in a priestly sect.

NT 1. The use of the *gamos* word group in the NT can hardly be distinguished from that in cl. Gk. Marriage was taken for granted. Hence, *gameō* (e.g., Mk. 6:17; Lk. 14:20) and *gamos* (Jn. 2:1–2) can be used without any theological connotation. Yet the NT deals with questions concerning the relationship of husbands and wives far more frequently than the use of this word group might suggest. Sexual offenses are fundamental offenses against marriage. Note how often such sins are repeatedly mentioned in lists of offenses (e.g., Rom. 13:13; 1 Cor. 6:9).

2. Marriage as an institution is clearly presupposed in the NT. It is based on God's commandment, esp. as noted in the creation story (e.g., Matt. 19:4–5; Mk. 10:6–7; 1 Cor. 6:16; Eph. 5:31). Though the NT essentially looks on marriage from the man's standpoint (as the head, cf. 1 Cor. 11:3; Eph. 5:23), the OT traditions are so transcended that the man's special rights fall away, and the shared life of husband

and wife stands in the foreground (cf. 1 Cor. 7:3; Eph. 5:21–33; Col. 3:18–19). The NT attacks both divorce and sexual impurity. In 1 Tim. 4:3 Paul criticizes false teachers who forbade marriage. An unbroken marriage is assumed as something self-evident for the Christian (Matt. 5:27–31; 19:9; Mk. 10:11–12; Lk. 16:18; 1 Cor. 7:10–16; 1 Thess. 4:4; 1 Tim. 3:2, 12; Heb. 13:4).

3. (a) In the Sermon on the Mount Jesus is, as it were, a second Moses, the lawgiver of the eschatological era. In his instructions he speaks about the seventh commandment (Matt. 5:27–28; cf. Exod. 20:14; Deut. 5:18). In the dawning kingdom of God adultery is a sin that shows that one's heart is attached to oneself, not to God. In God's sight the lustful eye and the desiring thought are reckoned as the completed act. The story about the woman taken in adultery (Jn. 7:53–8:11) shows Jesus, the Judge, as the Savior who is prepared to forgive this sin. Thereby he shows himself to be the sovereign Lord of creation, of its order, and of the law.

(b) The Sermon on the Mount also addresses divorce (Matt. 5:31–32). Deut. 24:1 in principle permitted divorce, but the rabbis disagreed as to the grounds that justified it (Matt. 19:3). Jesus prohibited divorce (Mk. 10:2–12), granting it only on the grounds of immorality (Matt. 5:32; 19:9; → *porneuō*, 4519). The issue of divorce also surfaces in 1 Cor. 7:10–11.

(c) The practice of levirate marriage is presupposed in the question of the Sadducees concerning the marital status in the resurrection of a woman who had married seven brothers, each dying childless (Matt. 22:22–33; Mk. 12:18–27; Lk. 20:27–38). Jesus' reply rebuked the Sadducees for not knowing the Scriptures or the power of God. For in the resurrection one's present marital relationships are transcended and the dead raised are like the angels (Matt. 22:30, Mk. 12:25; Lk. 20:36). God is the God of the living.

(d) The question concerning eunuchs (Matt. 19:12) must also be understood eschatologically. The exigencies of the times call for celibacy from those who have the gift. Such people should voluntarily renounce marriage in order better to serve God (i.e., "because of the kingdom of heaven"). Marriage is only provisional in the light of the coming kingdom (cf. 1 Cor. 7:1–9, 26–29).

4. Both in the OT and among Jesus' contemporaries a wedding was the occasion for a festive meal. Hence *gamos* can also mean the wedding feast (see Jn. 2:1–11). In Matt. 22:1–14 Jesus uses a royal wedding feast as a parable. As background here we have the parallelism of God and the king, the concept of the eschatological feast (cf. Isa. 25:6), the picture of the marriage feast of the Messiah with his people, and the prophetic picture of marriage as representing the relationship between Yahweh and Israel. Earthly marriage will be superseded by the union of God with his people. As Messiah, Jesus is the true bridegroom (→ *nymphē*, 3811). The decisive factor is sharing his feast (Matt. 25:1–13; cf. Lk. 12:36–40). The marriage feast of the Lamb (Rev. 19:7–9) means the final union of the triumphant Christ with his own.

5. (a) Arising out of questions in the Corinthian church, Paul warns against various kinds of sexual immorality (1 Cor. 6:18–20) and then deals with marriage itself (ch. 7). He appeals to Jesus and rejects divorce (7:10; cf. Mk. 10:9–12). Paul also sees marriage as secondary when compared to faith, going so far as to recommend celibacy as a special gift in the light of the near end (1 Cor. 7:1, 7; cf. Matt. 19:12). Marriage, like all worldly activity, stands under the *hōs mē* ("as if not," 1 Cor. 7:29–31); that is, those with spouses should live as if they had none.

This is the standpoint from which the question of mixed marriages with unbelievers is handled (1 Cor. 7:12–16). The unbelieving partner is to decide whether it is to continue; the Christian partner should be prepared to let it continue. The consecration of such a mixed marriage by the believing partner is to be understood as a real power, for here grace is stronger than the unbelief of the heathen partner. It is the means of bringing the children within the covenant relationship, for otherwise they would be unclean. It may also lead to the salvation of the unbelieving partner.

The meaning of 1 Cor. 7:36–38 is unclear. Some take it to refer to a couple living together ascetically in so-called spiritual marriage, to whom Paul gives permission later to enter into full physical union. It seems more likely, however, that the passage refers to a father (or guardian) who did not wish to offend custom by not marrying off his daughter at the usual age. The verb *gamizō* (a synonym of *gamiskō*) occurs in the NT only in Matt. 22:30; 24:38; Mk. 12:25; Lk. 17:27; 20:34–35; 1 Cor. 7:38. Except in the last passage it clearly means to give in marriage. The NIV and NRSV, however, put the first interpretation in the text; the NIV puts the second in a note.

(b) Paul also saw marriage as a picture of our relationship with God. In Rom. 9:25 he quotes Hos. 2:23, alluding to the names of Hosea's children (Not Love and Not My People; cf. Hos. 1:6–10). For despite these names Yahweh will have mercy on his people and restore them. Paul sees in this promise grounds for the inclusion of Gentiles among the people of God. He uses the picture of marriage in 2 Cor. 11:2 to warn against apostasy. It is reversed in Eph. 5:22–33. Because Christ is the bridegroom of the church, marriage should be held holy. In 5:32 the marriage relationship is described as a mystery, symbolic of the relationship of Christ to the church. It is all the more reason why husbands and wives should love one another.

The picture of marriage lies also behind the expression "adulterous generation" (Matt. 12:39; 16:4; Mk. 8:38). Jesus is probably alluding to the people's attitude to God here. "That woman Jezebel" (Rev. 2:20–25) and "the great prostitute" (17:1) are pictures of the great apostasy from God, who is the great Husband and Lord. The former passage alludes to the wife of King Ahab, who served Baal and sought the life of Elijah (1 Ki. 16:31; 18:4, 13; 19:1–2). The church at Thyatira must not tolerate those who practice and teach things characterized by Jezebel. Regarding Rev. 17:1, the great prostitute is identified as Babylon, who typifies the world.

See also *moicheuō*, commit adultery (*3658*); *nymphē*, bride (*3811*); *koitē*, bed, marriage bed, intercourse (*3130*); *hyperakmos*, past the peak, begin to fade; be overpassionate (*5644*).

1139 (gamizō, give in marriage), → 1138.

1140 (gamiskō, give in marriage), → 1138.

1141 (gamos, wedding), → 1138.

1147 γέεννα	γέεννα (geenna), Gehenna, hell (1147).

OT The word *geenna* does not appear in the LXX or Gk. literature. It is the Gk. form of the Aram. *gêhinnām*, which in turn goes back to the Heb. *gê hinnōm*. This term originally denoted a valley lying to the south of Jerusalem, "the valley of the son [or sons] of Hinnom" (Jos. 15:8; 18:16; Isa. 66:24; Jer. 32:35). Child sacrifices were offered in this valley (2 Ki. 16:3; 21:6), for which reason Josiah desecrated it (2 Ki. 23:10); and it will be the place of God's judgment (Jer. 7:32; 19:6–7).

Jewish apocalyptic assumed that this valley would become the hell of fire (*1 Enoch* 27:1–2; 54:1–6; 56:3–4; 90:26–27). Hence, *geenna* came to be applied to the eschatological hell in general, even when it was no longer localized at Jerusalem. In time *geenna* became simply the place of punishment and so attracted the corresponding ideas about Hades (→ *hadēs*, 87). *geenna* thus became a temporary place of punishment (until the final judgment).

At the end of the first cent. A.D. or the beginning of the second, a doctrine of a fiery purgatory arose among the rabbis. All those in whose cases merit and guilt are equally balanced go to *geenna*, where they are purified and, if they do penance, inherit paradise. Alongside this was the concept of an eschatological *geenna* judgment, limited in time, after the last judgment.

NT In the NT *geenna* was a preexistent entity and a fiery abyss (Matt. 25:41; 13:42, 50, all referring to the "eternal fire"). It was the place of eternal punishment after the last judgment (23:15, 33; cf. 25:41, 46;). Body and soul are judged in it (Mk. 9:43, 45, 47–48). It must be distinguished from Hades, which houses the souls of the dead *before* the last judgment. The same fiery punishment will overtake Satan and the demons, the beast from the abyss, the false prophet, death, and Hades (Matt. 8:29; 25:41; Rev. 19:20; 20:10, 14–15). In contrast with later Christian writings and ideas, the NT does not describe the torments of hell, nor does it contain the idea that Satan is the prince of *geenna*, to whom sinners are handed over for punishment.

See also *abyssos*, abyss, pit, underworld (*12*); *hadēs*, Hades, the underworld, the realm of the dead (*87*); *katōteros*, lower (*3005*); *tartaroō*, sent to Tartarus, hell (*5434*).

1149 (Gethsēmani, Gethsemane), → 1778.

1151 γελάω	γελάω (gelaō), laugh (1151); καταγελάω (katagelaō), laugh

at, mock (*2860*); γέλως (gelōs), laughter (*1152*).

CL & OT 1. (a) In cl. Gk. this word group covers a wide range of meanings—from joyous laughter to ridicule and scorn. The compound *katagelaō* is an intensification, meaning either laugh loudly or sneer. The words were applied not only to humans but also to the gods. Merry laughter was a divine characteristic that often featured in theophanies.

(b) Three categories of humor and irony in the cl. Gk. world are of interest by comparison and contrast with the biblical presentation. (i) *Gk. comedy.* The production of a combination of comedies and tragedies in connection with the festival of Dionysus continued well into the NT era. The plots of the comedies included fantasy and burlesque, and the satirical element was strong. Prominent men in society were parodied, and even mythology and theology were treated with great irreverence. Still, although the gods were made to appear foolish and cowardly, the reality of their power was assumed. Moreover, the religious humor should be understood not as laughing at the gods, but rather as taking part in their joy.

(ii) *The dramatic irony of the tragedies.* The themes of classical tragedy most often concerned the relation of humans to the powers controlling the universe and how these powers determined their destiny. Frequently the audience was given a glimpse behind the scenes and could foresee the course of events.

(iii) *Socratic irony.* Socrates, as portrayed by Plato, was a teacher of philosophy who employed humor to great effect as a means of education. He often said less than he thought, confessing his own ignorance, and by means of relentless ironical questions forced his disciples to abandon their self-confident opinions.

2. (a) In the LXX *gelaō* and *gelōs* usually translate Heb. words with the radicals *ṣḥq* or *śḥq*. The Heb. words generally denote true or supposed superiority toward another expressed in scorn or laughter (e.g., 2 Chr. 30:10; Job 12:4; Ps. 52:6; Prov. 1:26; Eccl. 7:6). They are rarely used for religious joy (but cf. 2 Sam. 6:5, 21; 1 Chr. 13:8; Ps. 126:2). In Gen. 17:17; 18:12, 13, 15, the contrast is between laughter and belief. In Prov. 10:23 *gelōs* is the mark of a fool. Laughter is rarely attributed to God (Ps. 2:4; 37:13; 59:8; cf. Prov. 1:26), and then only to express his absolute superiority over the ungodly, who will not accept him as God even though they are nothing beside him.

(b) Certain exceptions, however, should be noted. (i) In Gen. 21:6 laughter appears to refer to two different things: a God-given joy for Sarah ("God has brought me laughter") and a human scornful skepticism ("everyone who hears will laugh with [over] me"). The LXX gives the whole clause a positive meaning by substituting *synchairō* (rejoice with) in the second clause. (ii) In Job 29:24 the positive meaning of the Heb.—"I smiled at them"—is interpreted by the LXX to refer to ridicule. (iii) In Ps. 126:2 laughter is associated with the joy of the time of salvation.

(c) The above conclusions should not be taken to indicate that the OT is humorless. Scholars are divided on this question, some regarding humor, i.e., playfulness, as inappropriate to the seriousness of the subjects treated. It must be conceded that the assessment of humor is a subjective process; for example, if Nebuchadnezzar's madness in Dan. 4 is regarded by some as humorous, the dividing line between tragedy and comedy is a narrow one.

Yet there is a general consensus about the existence of certain types of humor in the OT. (i) *Lighthearted portrayal of people and situations*: e.g., the characterization of Jacob and Esau (Gen. 25:27–34); Jacob meeting his match in Laban (29:15–30); the story of Balaam (Num. 22); Abimelech's death at the hands of a woman (Jdg. 9:50–54); David being dressed in armor (1 Sam. 17:38).

(ii) *Extensive use of wordplay.* Names are often seen as significant. In Gen. 25:26 "Jacob" suggests "following at the heel" in order to supplant (cf. Gen. 27:36; Jer. 9:4). The prophets' words include many bitter puns. "The Sovereign LORD showed me . . . a basket of ripe fruit [*qayis*]. . . . Then the LORD said to me, 'The time is ripe [*qēs*] for my people Israel'" (Amos 8:1–2; cf. also Isa. 5:7; Hos. 8:7; 12:11).

(iii) *Quiet educational humor.* This is best illustrated by the book of Proverbs, where the teacher gently teases his disciples and makes sinners look ridiculous (e.g., Prov. 6:9–10; 19:24; 27:15). It is also possible to understand Ecclesiastes in this way (cf. Eccl. 3:16–22).

(iv) *Dramatic irony.* This is used to good effect in the story of Joseph (Gen. 42:6–45:4) and is present throughout Job. Insofar as the reader is admitted beforehand into the knowledge of God's activity in Job, it might even be called divine irony.

(v) *Prophetic irony of varying degrees, from mild sarcasm to bitter satire.* This is used on the one hand with the intent of giving God's people a true awareness of their rebellion against him: e.g., Samuel's descriptions of kingship (1 Sam. 8:10–18; cf. the ironic words of God himself in Job 40:6–14). On the other hand, ironic scorn and ridicule are hurled at other nations and their gods, who have dared to challenge the God of Israel: e.g., Elijah's taunts at the prophets of Baal (1 Ki. 18:27), Isaiah's mockery of idols and those who make them (Isa. 44:9–20), and the comical picture of the arrival of the king of Babylon in Sheol (14:3–21). When this reaches the point of simple exultation over the weakness and downfall of one's enemies, as in Nahum, there does not appear to be much humor in it.

3. Rab. literature in general maintained the majesty of God. Thus, the rabbis seldom speak of his laughter. The OT verses noted above where God is said to laugh were considered a surprising phenomenon; the rabbis even repointed the vb. in Ps. 2:4 to say that God will make his enemies the objects of mutual derision. Yet this has no bearing on the rab. attitude toward humor in general. Talmudic literature makes a wide use of humor. Satan, for example, is shown in a ridiculous light. The main characteristics of rab. humor are self-irony and educative humor, but never humor for its own sake.

NT 1. The incidence of the *gelaō* word group follows the usage of the OT rather than cl. Gk. *gelaō* usually does not denote joy or true humor (but cf. Lk. 6:21). As with *paizō* (play, make sport) or *empaizō* (ridicule, mock), it is associated with irreverence. In the account of Jairus's daughter, for example, *katagelaō* is the scornful, superior laughter of those who ridiculed Jesus, believing he could do nothing about someone already dead (Matt. 9:24; Mk. 5:40; Lk. 8:53). This story illustrates the power of God in Jesus over our ultimate enemy, death, and at the same time the emptiness of unbelief.

In Jas. 4:9 *gelōs* denotes activity that is inappropriate because it is engaged in by sinners: "Grieve, mourn and wail. Change your laughter to mourning and your joy to gloom" (cf. Eccl. 2:2; 7:2–6; Tob. 2:6; Sir. 21:20; 27:13). This verse may reflect the Sermon on the Plain: "Blessed are you who weep now, for you will laugh. . . . Woe to you who laugh now, for you will mourn and weep" (Lk. 6:21b, 25b). The laughter in 6:21b is associated with salvation joy, with no thought of triumph over enemies (→ *klaiō*, 3081), but in 6:25b laughter denotes a mockery of things spiritual. Lk.'s thought may be influenced by Ps. 126:1–2: "When the LORD brought back the captives to Zion, we were

like men who dreamed. Our mouths were filled with laughter, our tongue with songs of joy." For joy in the NT, → *chairō*, 5897.

2. One can isolate various categories of humor in the NT. (a) *The humor of Jesus in the Synoptics.* Jesus has a sense of the comic in the situations of daily life: e.g., a man rushing out of the temple and leaving his offering behind (Matt. 5:23–24), a man trying to take a splinter out of someone's eye when he has a log in his own (7:3–5), or the idiotic attitude of a man who does not prepare against robbery unless he knows a thief is coming (24:43). Jesus also uses wordplays (e.g., *Petros . . . petra* ["Peter . . . rock" in 16:18]), exaggeration (the two debt loads in 18:23–35), and paradox ("whoever wants to save his life will lose it," 16:25). Many of the questions Jesus directed at his opponents have an ironical ring (9:5; 12:12; 21:25). There is also irony in the way he takes well-known concepts and gives them a different meaning (e.g., 9:13, where "righteous" means "self-righteous"). Matt. 23 is comparable with the biting irony of the OT prophets.

(b) *Divine irony.* John's Christology, which so markedly presents a human Jesus and an eternal Christ in the same person, introduces into the Gospel a certain type of dualism and hence a special kind of irony. Words and ideas carry two senses at the same time (cf. Jn. 1:36; 2:19–22; 4:32; 6:20; 11:50; 12:7), and this enigma is highlighted by questions that reveal people's failure to understand Jesus' words and deeds (cf. 2:18, 20; 3:4; 4:11). To a certain extent all the Gospel writers make use of this motif, esp. in the Passion narratives (cf. the widespread use of the title "king" in questions, accusations, taunts, and the inscription over the cross).

(c) *Lighthearted portrayal of people and situations.* Note the gently humorous description of Zacchaeus in Lk. 19:1–6, Peter's reactions in Jn. 13, the escape from prison in Acts 5:17–32, and Peter's being left knocking at the door in 12:12–16.

(d) *The humor of Paul.* Paul, a Pharisee, enjoyed scholarly argumentation, and there is considerable humor and irony in the tussles he has with his opponents. He poses paradoxical questions (Rom. 3:29; 6:1; 7:7; Gal. 2:17) and uses humorous illustrations (e.g., the pottery and the potter in Rom. 9:20–23 [cf. Isa. 29:16; 45:9]; the protest of the different parts of the body in 1 Cor. 12:14–26). He also uses wordplays (e.g., "not busy . . . busybodies" in 2 Thess. 3:11; the name of the runaway slave Onesimus, whose name means useful or beneficial [Phlm. 11]). Finally Paul speaks of himself in humorous terms. He is a nervous and unimpressive speaker (1 Cor. 2:3), a laughingstock in the arena (4:9). Moreover, his boasting turns out to be a list of his sufferings and weaknesses (9:15–18; 2 Cor. 10:1–13:4).

(e) *Humor in the other NT books.* Note James's humorous similes: the double-minded man (Jas. 1:6–8), the rudder and the fire (3:1–6), and the idiotic statement, "keep warm and well fed" (2:16).

3. Although humor and irony are not dominant in the Bible, they are more theologically significant than scholars have usually allowed. Every good teacher knows that one's words must be spiced with humor and irony if they are to rivet attention, esp. of those who are reluctant to listen. True humor is not the self-security of arrogance but the consciousness of being master of the situation. God, while condemning mocking that is a sign of rebellion against him, cannot help seeing the ridiculous and comical aspects of the revolt and fighting of helpless creatures bent on frustrating his purposes. Laughter can also be seen as a humble reaction to the amazing and ridiculous fact of our being recipients of God's honor and blessing. Jesus came with a joyful message, and though he took the opposition seriously, he was profoundly conscious that the victory lay with God— hence his lighthearted humor.

Certainly irony is written into the basic facts of redemption: God promised a childless man who was "as good as dead" (Heb. 11:12) that he would be father of a nation; he chose not a great and powerful nation to serve his purposes, but a small one that was despised and often at the mercy of its powerful neighbors; the climax of the world's rejection of God—the cross—was in fact the means he used to redeem the world (1 Cor. 2:6–8); hence Christians know that they are strongest when most aware of their weaknesses (2 Cor. 12:10). Biblical theology has irony in its very essence.

1152 (gelōs, laughter), → *1151.*

1153 (gemizō, to load), → *1154.*

1154	γέμω

γέμω (*gemō*), to load, be full (*1154*); γεμίζω (*gemizō*), to load (*1153*).

CL & OT 1. In cl. Gk. *gemō* (used only in pres. and imp.) and *gemizō* were used of loading a ship or animals and of being full, e.g., a harbor with craft. These words are found in an extended sense also: full of truth, evil, over-boldness, disproportion, and ugliness.

2. In the LXX *gemō* and its cognates are used only 10x, in the sense of bearing spices or gold (Gen. 37:25; 2 Chr. 9:21), loading beasts (Gen. 45:17), and being full (Ps. 10:7 = LXX 9:28; Amos 2:13).

NT Of the 20x these vbs. occur in the NT, most convey the sense of filling an object with something. In a metaphorical sense, they can denote filling with something intangible and usually uncomplimentary, such as being full of greed and other sins (Matt. 23:25; Lk. 11:39), of cursing and bitterness (Rom. 3:14; cf. Ps. 10:7), of God's wrath (Rev. 15:7), of abominations (17:3–4), and of seven plagues (21:9).

See also *perisseuō*, be more than enough, abound, excel (*4355*); *plēthos*, number, multitude, crowd (*4436*); *plēroō*, fill, complete, fulfill, accomplish, carry out (*4444*); *chortazō*, to feed, fatten, fill (*5963*); *chōreō*, have or make room, give way, go (*6003*).

1155	γενεά

γενεά (*genea*), generation, family, clan, race, age (*1155*); γενεαλογία (*genealogia*), genealogy, family tree (*1157*); γενεαλογέω (*genealogeō*), trace descent (*1156*); ἀγενεαλόγητος (*agenealogētos*), without genealogy (*37*).

CL & OT *genea*, derived from the root *gen-*, means birth, also (noble) descent, then descendants, family, race (i.e., those bound together by a common origin). Those born at the same time constitute a generation. In the LXX *genea* is almost always the translation of *dôr* and means generation; the whole history of Israel is often regarded as a work of God extending through many generations.

NT *genea* occurs 43x in the NT, mainly in the Gospels and Acts; its compounds are rare.

1. The basic meaning of *genea* relates to the OT sense referred to above. It occurs 4x in the context of Christ's genealogy (Mt. 1:17). The remote past is denoted (as in OT, cf. Isa. 41:4) by the phrase *apo geneōn*, "for . . . generations" (Col. 1:26; cf. Acts 15:21). The unending future is similarly expressed by a familiar LXX phrase, *eis geneas kai geneas* (lit., "to generations and generations"; Lk. 1:50; Eph. 3:21; cf. Lk. 1:48). Acts 13:36 refers to David's generation, and Acts 14:16 and Eph. 3:5 to earlier generations.

genealogia occurs only in 1 Tim. 1:4 and Titus 3:9, alluding specifically to the practice of searching back through one's family tree in order to establish ancestry. Presumably those doing this were Jews who, starting out from OT and other genealogies, were propagating all kinds of "Jewish myths," perhaps pre-Christian gnostic speculations. It is also possible that Ebionites were using similar arguments to attack the doctrine of the miraculous birth of Jesus circulating in the Christian church (cf. the genealogies in Matt. 1 and Lk. 3).

In Gen. 14 Melchizedek is introduced, in contrast to typical OT manner, without any statement regarding his ancestry. For that reason he is described in Heb. 7:3 as *agenealogētos* (cf. 7:6); that is, he had no natural ancestry like other human beings. The author of Heb. goes on to relate this priest-king to Jesus via Ps. 110:4, as someone who had a unique genealogy. The author is not attempting to call in question,

however, the genuine humanity of Jesus (cf. 2:9, 14–18); rather, he is stressing our Lord's true divinity.

2. Acts 8:33 is a quotation of Isa. 53:8. The passage is interpreted Christologically, but the precise interpretation is not easy to grasp. But it does seem certain that "generation" (NIV, "descendants") is used here in its genealogical sense.

3. Almost all remaining NT *genea* passages use the phrase "this generation." The OT does not know this stereotyped phrase in its NT sense, though Gen. 7:1 ("this generation" and Ps. 12:7 ("such people"; cf. Deut. 1:35) come close. In the NT passages the demonstrative "this" has a pejorative character; that is, it refers to a class of people who stand over against the children of light and are described as "unbelieving" (Mk. 9:19), "unbelieving and perverse" (Matt. 17:17), "adulterous and sinful" (Mk. 8:38; cf. Matt. 12:39), "wicked" (Lk. 11:29), "corrupt" (Acts 2:40), and "crooked and depraved" (Phil. 2:15). The Song of Moses may have had a certain influence on the wording (cf. Deut. 32:5, 20). In these passages the temporal, "genealogical" element is absent.

4. In Matt. 24:34; Mk. 13:30; Lk. 21:32 (which also use "this generation" and describe it as passing away), the temporal, genealogical element does seem to be present, though it is of secondary importance. By using this phrase, Jesus appears to set a time limit for certain events, which raises the question: Which events are they?

(a) Mk. 13 has the character of a farewell discourse, not that of an apocalypse. This type of address occurs frequently in the literature of pre-Christian Judaism as well as elsewhere in the NT. Its essential and recurring features are warnings about future apostasy and persecution, a promise of coming redemption, and an exhortation to watchfulness.

(b) The main historical element in the above references is the tradition according to which Jesus announces the coming destruction of Jerusalem (e.g., Mk. 13:1–4, 14–20). Note that in the Lukan parallel (21:20–24), Lk. seems to interpret Jerusalem as the embodiment of the people of Israel, whose hearts God had hardened in judgment while the "times of the Gentiles" are being fulfilled (i.e., the time when salvation comes to the Gentiles; cf. Acts 28:24–28; Rom. 11:25–26). These times will come to an end with the coming of the kingdom of God, the Son of Man, and the day of the Lord (perhaps even within his own lifetime; cf. Lk. 18:8; 21:34–36).

(c) Only by such considerations can the phrase "this generation" in Mk. 13:30 and its parallels be explained. In Matt. it has the temporal sense of *this* specific generation; thus, it might appear as if Jesus expected the end of this age to occur in connection with the judgment on Jerusalem at the end of that first generation (→ *aiōn, 172*). But in view of what happened in A.D. 70 and its theological relation to the preaching of Paul, Lk. understood *genea* as a *class of people*, not as a generation in the first century. Since what we can hypothesize about Matt. and Lk.'s sources implies that they did not seem to link the judgment on Jerusalem and the end of the world, and since Mk. 13 in general (esp. 13:13, 24) has an indefinite and open ring, we must conclude that Jesus himself was ambiguous on this issue in his farewell discourse. But the evangelists were not copyists; they were witnesses who, led by the Spirit, testified to the word they had heard and brought it to bear on their own times.

(d) The events referred to in Matt. 24:34; Mk. 13:30; Lk. 21:32 have generally been taken to refer to cosmic events associated with the second coming of Christ. But if these events were expected within the first generation of Christians, were Jesus or the evangelists mistaken? Not at all. The failure of events to materialize can be attributed to a gracious postponement by God of the catastrophe as well as to a telescoping of events, comparable with seeing a mountain range at a distance. That perspective makes the mountains appear to stand close together, and indeed relatively speaking they do stand close together. But the closer one approaches the mountains, the more one sees distinctions among them.

We should also note that insufficient attention has been paid to the prophetic language in the passage as a whole. Here, as in the OT, the imagery of cosmic phenomena is used to describe *this-worldly* events, namely, historical acts of judgment. The following passages are significant, not least because of their affinities with the present context: Isa. 13:10 (predicting doom on Babylon); 34:4 (referring to "nations" and "peoples" in 34: 1, but esp. Edom in 34:5–17); Ezek. 32:7 (on Egypt); Amos 8:9 (on the northern kingdom of Israel); Joel 2:10 (on Judah). The cosmic imagery draws attention to the divine dimension of the event in which the judgment of God is enacted.

The use of Joel 2:28–32 in Acts 2:15–21 provides an instance of the way in which such prophetic cosmic imagery is applied to historical events in the present (cf. also Lk. 10:18; Jn. 12:31; 1 Thess. 4:16; 2 Pet. 3:10–13; Rev. 6:12–17; 18:1). Other OT passages relevant to the interpretation of the present context include Deut. 30:4; Isa. 19:1; 27:13; Dan. 7:13; Zech. 2:6; 12:10–14; Mal. 3:1. In view of this, Mk. 13:24–30 may be interpreted as a prophecy of judgment on Israel in which the Son of Man will be vindicated. Such a judgment took place with the destruction of Jerusalem, the desecration of the temple, and the scattering of Israel—all of which happened within the lifetime of "this generation." This disintegration of Israel as the people of God coincides with the inauguration of the kingdom of the Son of Man. But the final judgment will not take place until the Parousia, of which the events of the first century are a figure. Such an interpretation fits the preceding discourse and the introductory questions of the disciples (Mk. 13:1–4 par.).

1156 (*genealogeō*, trace descent), → *1155*.

1157 (*genealogia*, genealogy, family tree), → *1155*.

1161 (*genesis*, birth, origin), → *1181*.

1164	γεννάω

γεννάω (*gennaō*), beget, become the father of, bear (*1164*); ἀναγεννάω (*anagennaō*), cause to be born again, bear again (*335*).

CL & OT 1. *gennaō* is a causal form of *ginomai*. Like *tiktō*, *gennaō* is used of begetting by the father and bearing by the mother. In NT times *gennaō* also means come into being or produce in a metaphorical sense (cf. Gal. 4:24, of partners in a covenant; 2 Tim. 2:23, of quarrels). The compound *anagennaō* means cause to be born again.

2. In the LXX *gennaō* is used chiefly for Heb. *yālad*, bear, bring forth. It is never used in those passages that speak of Israel as God's firstborn (Exod. 4:22; 23:4) or God as Israel's father. The OT sharply dissociates itself from pagan procreation myths. Israel is Yahweh's people not by natural procreation but by election.

3. Two passages in Ps. speak of the begetting of the king-messiah by God: Ps. 2:7 and 110:3 (only in LXX). Though the idea that the king was the "son of God" was current in the ANE, the OT was unique in that each successive king was adopted and/or declared to be a son when he ascended the throne. The relationship was confirmed, on a historical basis, at each new accession. The connection of the Ps. passages with the prophecy of Nathan (2 Sam. 7) is extensive.

The line of Christological interpretation in the NT starts here (cf. Matt. 22:43–44; Mk. 12:36–37; Lk. 20:42–43; Acts 4:25; 13:33; 1 Cor. 15:25; Heb. 1:5, 13; Rev. 2:27). The absence of physical procreation is shown by the reference to the "seed of David," which is used in the sing. collectively of David's posterity. The tension between human parentage and the role of God appears in accounts of Jesus' birth and descent (Matt. 1:16; cf. 1:1, 6, 20; Lk. 1:33b, 35b; cf. 3:23–38).

4. In Pal. Jud. the thought of God's begetting occurs only in connection with messianic expectation. In all rab. literature there is only one reference that applies Ps. 2:7 to the Messiah. This silence is apparently due to the rabbis' opposition to the Christian church, which had applied Ps. 2 to Jesus' sonship.

NT *gennaō* occurs 97x in the NT. However, there is significant difference between this word and others that are used: *tiktō* (bring forth, bear; → *5503*), *apokyeō* (give birth, bear, in the NT only fig., Jas. 1:15,

18), *ōdinō* (suffer birth pains, Gal. 4:19, 27; Rev. 12:2). The meaning of *gennaō* must be determined by context in both its active and passive forms, since it is used both of a father and a mother. It is also used in a fig. sense.

1. Various passages apply the term to God, who is said to have begotten someone. (a) Ps. 2:7 is quoted in Acts 13:33 and Heb. 1:5; 5:5 (the latter two relate Ps. 2:7 to Ps. 110 and 2 Sam. 7:14). Jesus Christ is the true Son and God's King. He has fulfilled what the Israelite kings left unfulfilled. As the crucified and risen one, he has assumed the office of the Lord's anointed as the truly anointed one. Strikingly, the NT does not apply Ps. 2:7 to Jesus' birth narratives; thus, a physical, sexual begetting is precluded. Acts 13:33 applies the words "today have I begotten you" (lit.) to Jesus' resurrection.

It is not easy to determine the precise significance of "today" in Heb. 1:5; 5:5. One thing is clear, however: This begetting by God goes beyond the OT understanding of adoption. The Heb. passages are concerned with the declaration and proclamation of what the Son already is. Jesus' sonship denotes the mystery of the incarnation of God.

(b) The Johannine writings use the expression *gennaō ek* (be begotten of) to describe the origin of the believer. Believers know that their true existence does not belong to this world; their beginning and end are in God through Jesus Christ. In the dialogue with Nicodemus the references to being "born again" mean that humans must receive a new origin, exchanging the old nature for a new one (Jn. 3:3, 5, 6, 7, 8). This idea expresses the same essential idea as being born "of God" (1 Jn. 3:9; cf. 2:29; 4:7) and being born "from above" (*anōthen*, Jn. 3:3, 7; cf. NIV note), which John describes as an act of God (1:12–13). Jn. attributes this to the work of the Spirit (3:5–8), and only such persons can see the kingdom of God (3:5).

2. Paul uses *gennaō* in 1 Cor. 4:15 and Phlm. 10 of his relationship with his converts. He could even speak of being in labor (*ōdinō*) or suffering birth pains until Christ is formed in them (Gal. 4:19). The same thoughts lie behind those passages that speak of Paul's "son" in the faith (1 Cor. 4:17; 1 Tim. 1:2; 2 Tim. 2:1; cf. 1 Pet. 5:13).

Rab. Jud. spoke in a similar way of winning proselytes (→ *prosēlytos*, *4670*). The command to be fruitful (Gen. 1:28; 9:7) was sometimes taken to mean that Israelites had to win others to their faith. The idea of new birth through conversion to Jud. was common among the rabbis. Paul's language in the above passages seems to have adopted Jewish ideas.

3. The vb. *anagennaō* occurs only in 1 Pet. 1:3, 23, where it means born again. Its meaning is similar to *gennaō* in Jn. 3:3–4 (see also *palingenesia*, *4098*). Through the preached word of the living God (1 Pet. 1:23), believers have been called by God into a new life, which is summed up as "living hope" (1:3) and "love" (1:22). New birth is not something a person can take up and dispose of at will; it is only possible by God's "great mercy" (1:3) and "power" (1:5). Believers stand under the indicative: God "has given us new birth into a living hope through the resurrection of Jesus Christ from the dead" (1:3). At the same time, however, they stand under the imperative: "Set your hope fully on the grace to be given you when Jesus Christ is revealed" (1:13). Those born again realize that separation from the old aeon has taken place. The decisive factor that makes rebirth possible is God's act in the resurrection of Jesus Christ.

See also *ginomai*, be born, become, happen (*1181*); *ektrōma*, miscarriage (*1765*); *palingenesia*, rebirth, regeneration (*4098*); *tiktō*, bring forth, bear, give birth to (*5503*); *eugenēs*, well-born, noble in descent or character (*2302*).

1174	γεύομαι

γεύομαι (*geuomai*), taste, partake of, enjoy, experience (*1174*).

CL & OT *geuomai* means to taste; fig. to partake of, enjoy, experience. In the LXX the word occurs in the fig. sense only in Job 20:18; Ps. 34:8 ("Taste and see that the LORD is good"); Prov. 31:18. For a lit. sense, see Gen. 25:30; 1 Sam. 14:24, 29, 43; Jon. 3:7.

NT 1. In the NT *geuomai* occurs 15x. Taste is used in a lit. sense in Matt. 27:34; Jn. 2:9; Acts 10:10; Col. 2:21. The Colossian church was distracted by a "philosophy" (2:8) that had elements of Jewish traditions merged with those of paganism, one of which was service to "the basic principles of the world" (2:20)—probably angelic powers in charge of the universe. Part of that service to these powers involved adherence to certain Jewish ritual laws. Paul questions why these people are still acknowledging such powers when Christ has gained victory over them: "Why . . . do you submit to its rules: 'Do not handle! Do not taste! Do not touch!'?" (2:20–21). Such regulations have no value in promoting godliness or Christian piety.

The parable of the great banquet concludes with the pronouncement: "I tell you, not one of those men who were invited will get a taste of my banquet" (Lk. 14:24). Here Jesus himself is speaking through the master in the parable, rejecting those who rejected his invitation to the banquet on account of worldly concerns. The lit. sense of "taste" symbolizes participation in the messianic banquet, the kingdom of God.

2. In a fig. sense, 1 Pet. 2:3 ("You have tasted that the Lord is good") takes up the words of Ps. 34:8. The readers are urged to put away malice, deceit, hypocrisy, envy, and slander (2:1) and to grow up to maturity, for they have been "born again" (1:23; 2:2).

Ps. 34:8 may also be reflected in Heb. 6:4–6 (a passage notoriously difficult to interpret), where the author states that it is impossible to bring back to repentance those who, among other things, "have tasted the heavenly gift [and] . . . who have tasted the goodness of the word of God." It is difficult to say precisely what the "heavenly gift" is (some suggestions include the forgiveness of sins, the gift of salvation, the Holy Spirit, or Christ himself). In any case, the Christians being addressed have already experienced something of the world to come. If this is so, this passage then is an instance of the characteristic tension between the "already" and the "not yet" in the life of the Christian.

In Heb. 2:9 Christ died so that "he might taste death for everyone." His death is an act of salvation. His condemnation as a sinner does not spare us from physical death, but it does take away our fear of death, for through it the power of eternal destruction has been broken (cf. 2:14–15). Note Jn. 8:51–52: "I tell you the truth, if anyone keeps my word . . . he will never taste death." The promise of Mk. 9:1 and Lk. 9:27 that some "will not taste death before they see the kingdom of God" probably anticipates three fulfillments: the transfiguration of Jesus (which took place immediately after this saying), his resurrection, and the coming of the Son of Man in judgment on Jerusalem.

See also *peinaō*, hunger (*4277*); *brōma*, food (*1109*); *esthiō*, eat (*2266*); *pinō*, drink (*4403*).

1178	γῆ

γῆ (*gē*), earth, world (*1178*); ἐπίγειος (*epigeios*), earthly (*2103*).

CL & OT *gē* is the earth or world; the land in contrast to water; also, as part of the earth, a piece of land, a field with arable soil. The meaning "land," as the area controlled by a single state, emerged by analogy alongside these natural meanings. In ancient Gk. mythology *gē* and *ouranos*, sky, are among the oldest deities.

The LXX uses *gē* more than 2,000 times. Neither in the LXX nor in the NT is there any thought of divinity about it. The earth is part of God's creation (cf. Gen. 1:1–2).

NT The NT uses *gē* 250 times, particularly in the Gospels, Acts, and Rev. It is first of all the soil in which the sower sows his seed (cf. "because the soil [*gē*] was shallow," Matt. 13:5). One can sit down on the earth (Mk. 8:6); it stands in contrast to water (Matt. 14:24). All land taken together has a boundary ("the Queen of the South . . . came from the ends of the earth," Matt. 12:42; the witnesses of the resurrected Jesus were to go "to the ends of the earth," Acts 1:8). The angels of

judgment stood "at the four corners of the earth," controlling "the four winds of the earth" (Rev. 7:1; cf. Matt. 24:31). Christ will be, as was Jonah when he was in the fish in the midst of the water, "in the heart of the earth" (Matt. 12:40). In all these passages the earth is something created.

1. The historical use of the term occurs wherever it is used in a political sense, e.g., the land of Judah (Matt. 2:6), the land of Israel (2:20), the land of Midian, and the land of Egypt (Acts 7:29, 36). It is frequently difficult to decide whether a passage is speaking of a particular country (esp. the land of Israel) or of the populated earth as a whole (→ *oikoumenē*, *3876*). With our modern view of the world we are inclined to think globally and universally. However, the NT can use "the earth" in a particularistic way to refer to (lit.) "all the tribes of the land" (Matt. 24:30; Rev. 1:7; cf. Zech. 12:10–14). Yet the remarkable expression "from the ends of the earth to the ends of the heavens" (Mk. 13:27) means the whole earth, expressed here by joining two OT phrases (Deut. 13:7; Ps. 19:6).

2. Both earth and heaven are God's creation. Yet the earth is the scene of the imperfect (Heb. 8:4–5), of sin (Mk. 2:10; Rev. 17:5), and of death (1 Cor. 15:47). Hence Christians are to set their minds on things that are above, not on things that are on earth (Col. 3:2). Heaven and earth (i.e., the present sinful order) will eventually pass away (Matt. 5:18; 24:35; 2 Pet. 3:10), which means experiencing God's judgments. In so doing, they will make way for "a new heaven and a new earth" (2 Pet. 3:13; Rev. 21:1). Redemption extends to the furthest corner of the physical realm. That the meek will inherit the earth is the promise of Christ (Matt. 5:5); this earthly kingdom is the same as the kingdom of heaven, the coming redeemed creation (Rom. 8:21).

3. *epigeios* (7x in the NT) means lit. "on the earth," but it can also be linked with the dualism of heaven and earth and so mean earthly (1 Cor. 15:40; 2 Cor. 5:1; Phil. 3:19).

See also *oikoumenē*, earth (*3876*); *agros*, field (*69*); *chous*, soil, dust (*5967*); *kosmos*, adornment, world (*3180*).

1181	γίνομαι

γίνομαι (*ginomai*), be begotten, be born, become, come about, happen (*1181*); ἀπογίνομαι (*apoginomai*), die (*614*); γένεσις (*genesis*), birth, origin (*1161*).

CL & OT 1. *ginomai* (cl. Gk. *gignomai*) has several shades of meaning: come into being, be produced (of things), take place (of events), become.

2. In the LXX, *ginomai* also occurs as a substitute for forms of *einai* (to be). The construction *kai egeneto . . . kai* ("and it happened . . . and" [Gen. 4:8; etc.]) renders the Heb. construction (*wayᵉhî . . . wa-*, "and it came to pass that . . ."). *apoginomai* (the prefix *apo* means from) means go away, cease, depart, i.e., die (no occurrences in the LXX). *genesis* (origin, birth), a cognate of *ginomai*, occurs numerous times in the LXX, most notably as the title of Genesis.

NT 1. *ginomai* is used in the NT in a variety of connections and has no special religious or theological meaning. (a) It means be born (Gal. 4:4); grow (of fruit, Matt. 21:19); arise, happen (of various occurrences, 8:26; Acts 6:1; 12:18); be made, be done (Jn. 1:3; Matt. 11:21); become something (Mk. 1:17). It is frequently used in Lk. and Acts in the construction *kai egeneto . . . kai* (lit., "and it happened that . . ."; "and it came to pass that . . ."; cf. above). Paul uses the strong negation *mē genoito* (lit., "let it not be, by no means"; e.g., Rom. 3:4; 6:2).

(b) *ginomai* may also stand for *einai* (to be, e.g., Matt. 10:16; Mk. 4:22). With the gen. it denotes origin or membership (Lk. 20:14; 2 Pet. 1:20). With the dat. of the person it denotes belonging to (Rom. 11:5).

2. *apoginomai* occurs only in 1 Pet. 2:24: "He himself bore our sins in his body on the tree, so that we might die (*apogenomenoi*) to sins and live for righteousness." It thus stands in contrast to living. It denotes the change that has come about in the lives of believers through Christ's death and resurrection, which makes a rebirth possible (→ *gennaō*, *1164*; cf. Rom. 6:8, 11).

3. *genesis* means birth in Matt. 1:18 and Lk. 1:14. It also means created life or being. It is used in this sense in Jas. 1:23: He "is like a man who looks at his face (lit., the face of his created life [or natural being, *genesis*]) in a mirror."

Two other passages require closer examination. (a) Matt. begins his Gospel this way: "A record of the genealogy (*genesis*) of Jesus Christ the son of David, the son of Abraham." The formula goes back to an OT model, where *genesis* introduces a genealogy or family register (Gen. 2:4; 5:1; 11:10), or a family story (6:9; 37:2). The genealogies and family stories often overlap. Most likely in Matt. it functions as the title of the family register of Matt. 1:2–17 (note 1:18, which introduces the birth narrative).

(b) Jas. 3:6 contains the expression *trochon tēs geneseōs*, which has been translated as "wheel of life," "course of . . . life" (NIV), "cycle of nature" (NRSV). The passage describes the tongue as "a world of evil," capable of corrupting the whole body and setting the whole course of one's life on fire. The expression seems somewhat related to the Orphic idea of the perpetual recurrence of nature, though it seems less a philosophical expression and more a euphemism for the ups and downs of life.

See also *gennaō*, beget, become the father of, bear (*1164*); *ektrōma*, miscarriage (*1765*); *palingenesia*, rebirth, regeneration (*4098*); *tiktō*, bring forth, bear, give birth to (*5503*); *eugenēs*, well-born, noble in descent or character (*2302*).

1182 γινώσκω

γινώσκω (*ginōskō*), know, come to know, understand, comprehend, perceive, recognize (*1182*); γνῶσις (*gnōsis*), knowledge (*1194*); γνώμη (*gnōmē*), opinion, judgment (*1191*); γνωρίζω (*gnōrizō*), make known (*1192*); ἐπιγινώσκω (*epiginōskō*), know, understand, recognize (*2105*); ἐπίγνωσις (*epignōsis*), knowledge, recognition (*2106*); γνωστός (*gnōstos*), known, intelligible, acquaintance (*1196*).

CL 1. In cl. Gk. *ginōskō* has a wide range of meanings. (a) Basically it means to notice, perceive, or recognize a thing, person, or situation through the senses, esp. sight. This leads to an intelligent ordering in the mind of what has been perceived in the world of experience. Thus the vb. also means to experience, learn, get to know. The noun *gnōsis* also expresses the act of knowing through experience.

(b) Occasionally *ginōskō* means to distinguish, for experiencing different things may lead to this.

(c) Familiarity leads to personal acquaintance. Hence *ginōskō* can also mean to know in a personal way, to understand, and even to judge. *gnōsis* too is repeatedly found with the meaning knowledge, insight, and *gnōmē* with that of insight, reflection, and judgment or opinion.

(d) *ginōskō* may be used to express a relationship of trust between persons, i.e., to recognize as a friend, love as a friend. Perhaps to know in Hel. Gk., meaning to have sexual relations with, is derived from this.

(e) Knowledge of situations can be reached by reflecting, judging, and investigating, i.e., by logical thought processes.

(f) Since verdicts in criminal and civil courts were based on a weighing of given facts, they could be expressed by *ginōskō* in the pass., meaning to be judged.

(g) The object of knowledge may be a concrete object or an idea in the mind. Esp. in philosophy speculative cognition plays a great part. The goal of philosophical knowledge is seeing—seeing the lasting and real, which can be seen only by the eyes of the soul. With *ginōskō* there is always the implication of grasping the full reality and nature of an object under consideration. It is thus distinguished from mere opinion (*dokeō*, *1506*), which may grasp an object inadequately or even falsely.

2. The above uses of *ginōskō* and its derivatives are also found in Hel. Gk. In addition, however, we find a growing use of the terms, based on a fairly loose link with the language of Gk. philosophy. They appear in the widely different systems of thought and conceptual

schemes influenced by syncretism, which have been bracketed together under the title of Gnosticism. It lies beyond the scope of this article to survey all of gnostic thought, but certain features of Gnosticism may be mentioned.

(a) In Hel. culture people adopted a new attitude toward the world, which involved doubt about arriving at the truth concerning the world and reality along rational lines. Humans experience the world and history as an impenetrable fate, which they cannot influence and to which they are handed over like powerless slaves. The world is more a prison than a home. Hence, humans yearn for freedom and escape from the compulsion imposed on them in an alien world. One way of escape lies in *gnōsis*—not a mental penetration of things by logical thought, but from outside the universe, from a divine source. It comes through revelation given in grace. The means by which one can acquire knowledge of this other reality include sacramentalism, magic, mysticism, and semiphilosophical speculation.

(b) *gnōsis* is primarily one's knowledge of oneself, of one's true nature, which would explain the inharmonious relationship of one's manner of existence on earth and in history. It shows a person the way back to salvation through a knowledge of past, present, and future.

(c) A gnostic myth tells "the tragic history of the soul." The soul began as divine, but as the result of a primeval fall was exiled and fettered to matter, which is hostile to God. That is why human beings cannot feel at home in the cosmos, for this cosmos and the God of the soul have nothing in common. Hence, humans are plagued by a vague, hopeless longing to leave the world. The less one has been lost to the cosmos, the stronger is this longing. If one has surrendered completely to the cosmos, no hope of salvation remains. The process of salvation begins when, as a result of an external "call," this longing is replaced by instruction about the unknown God out there. If the call is heard, nothing prevents the divine soul from returning to the divinity and being deified.

(d) All this leads to a gnostic attitude toward life that is itself termed *gnōsis*. It expressed itself in a feeling of superiority over all non-gnostics—in Christian Gnosticism, over all mere believers. Gnostics are the only ones who really know God, and the true self is not part of the cosmos. Moral rules are either the demands of cosmic powers intended to reduce humans to slavery or purely human values. Whether by asceticism or libertinism, the gnostic seeks to scorn these values and become free from worldly ties.

OT In the OT, as with the common Gk. attitude, knowledge is derived through the senses; the thing to be known must present itself to the senses and so let itself be known. Hence we find vbs. of hearing and seeing parallel to vbs. of knowing (e.g., 1 Sam. 14:38; Isa. 41:20; cf. Exod. 16:6–7; Deut. 33:9).

1. In the LXX the *ginōskō* word group mainly renders words formed from the Heb. root *yādaʿ*, which has a wide range of meaning. It can mean (a) to notice, observe, experience (e.g., Gen. 3:7; Jdg. 16:20; Eccl. 8:5). (b) It also then means to distinguish between certain things. (c) Knowledge passed on by a third party gives the meaning of know by learning (Prov. 30:3). (d) Experience becomes a reality in a relationship based on familiarity with the person or thing known. The use of *yādaʿ* in wisdom literature is an example of this. Knowledge can be obtained by observing the world and life as the work of God, which in turn leads to an upright life before God (Prov. 2:6; Eccl. 8:17).

(e) Knowledge can result in technical ability, i.e., to know how to do something (1 Ki. 7:14; cf. Gen. 25:27; Isa. 47:11). (f) In certain circumstances observation and resultant action (or failure to act) become closely linked. Hence, *ginōskō* (*yādaʿ*) also means to concern oneself with, care for, trouble oneself with (e.g., Ps. 1:6, 37:18; cf. Prov. 27:23). (g) To know can also mean to have sexual relations with (Gen. 4:1; 19:8). (h) To know another person "face to face" means to have a personal and confidential relationship with another person (e.g., Deut. 34:10). When God knows a people (Amos 3:2), he chooses or elects them (cf. Num. 16:5). This knowledge is gracious and loving, but it demands a personal response. (i) The distinctiveness of the OT concept of knowledge is clearly seen in passages that speak of our knowledge of God.

2. Knowledge of God is always linked with God's acts of self-revelation. Note the formula, "And you [or they] will know that I am the LORD" (54x in Ezek., and elsewhere), which is always linked with the proclamation of some specific act by Yahweh (e.g., Ezek. 6:7, 13, 14; 7:4; 11:10–12; cf. also Exod. 6:7; 7:5, 17; 1 Ki. 20:13, 28 [= LXX 21:13, 28]; Isa. 45:3, 6–7). In 2 Ki. 5:15, Naaman the Syrian comes to a knowledge of the God of Israel through the healing of his leprosy. In Sir. 36:4–5, God is asked to reveal himself to the nations, that they too may recognize that there is no other God beside Yahweh.

The testimony to God's past actions and signs grounded in salvation history are capable of bringing about knowledge of Yahweh (Exod. 31:13; Ezek. 20:12–20). Such knowledge in the OT is not concerned with the speculative question of the being of God, but with a personal knowledge of the God who, working in grace and judgment, has turned to humanity. To know him means to enter into the personal relationship that he himself makes possible.

Israel's intimate relationship with God required that the nation's conduct correspond to God's actions. The command "Be still, and know that I am God" (Ps. 46:10) does not mean that the nations attacking Yahweh's city should undergo a purely religious conversion to Yahweh. Rather, they should abandon their rebellion in recognition of Yahweh's rule in history. In the rhetorical questions of Jer. 22:15–16, knowledge of God is clearly interpreted as doing justice and righteousness, esp. to the poor and needy. Similarly, in Hos. 4:1–2 knowledge of Yahweh is directly related to specific behavior: Lack of faithfulness and disloyalty to the covenant are bound up with lack of knowledge of God. The result is a breakdown of human relationships.

Thus, while the Gks. were concerned with detached knowledge and a speculative interest in the metaphysical nature of things, the OT regards knowledge as something that arises from a personal encounter. As Israel continually inquired into God's revelation in the past, present, and future, they discerned the purposes and demands of God in worship and in conduct.

3. (a) The confrontation between Hel. Jud. and polytheism led to the development of a semidogmatic concept of the knowledge of God. It meant above all knowing that there was one God and combating the claims of heathen deities as gods. Since rab. lit. warns against speculations about what was before creation, Jud. was obviously involved in controversy with the gnostics.

(b) There are, to be sure, some contacts between the OT and the Hel.-gnostic concepts of knowledge; in both, knowledge of God comes by revelation. In the latter, however, the place of history is consistently denied, whereas in the former the knowledge of God is inseparably bound up with his revelation in time and space.

(c) In the intertestamental period Qumran texts show a development of the OT concept of knowledge. Knowledge is one of the most important fruits of salvation enjoyed by pious members of the sect. God himself is the "God of knowledge" (cf. 1QS 3:15), i.e., the God who possesses all knowledge and from whom alone a person can acquire knowledge. There are many objects of human knowledge. Of these the "secrets" or "hidden things" are frequently mentioned, by which the sect meant the revealed secrets of creation, history, and the last days; in this we see the affinity of Qumran teaching with later apocalyptic. Alongside this the knowledge of God's will as revealed in the Torah plays an important part. On it depended a person's reception and place in the community (1QS 2:22).

NT 1. *Survey of use and meaning in the NT. ginōskō* is found 221x, of which 87x are in the Johannine literature, 50x in Paul, and 44x in Lk.-Acts; *epiginōskō* occurs 44x. *gnōsis, gnōrizō,* and *epignōsis* occur 29x, 25x, and 20x respectively. The verbal adj. *gnōstos* is found 15x; *gnōmē* (predominantly in Paul and Rev.) 9x.

In a large number of cases we have the general and popular use of the words as outlined above: to hear of (Mk. 5:43; Jn. 4:1; Phil. 1:12), notice (Matt. 16:8; Mk. 6:33 *epiginōskō*; 13:28–29), feel (5:29–30), recognize (Matt. 7:16; Lk. 24:16, both *epiginōskō*; Jas. 2:20) learn, know (Lk. 12:47–48; Jn. 1:48; 21:17), understand (Mk. 4:13), find out (Jn. 13:35; 15:18; 1 Jn. 2:3, 5), distinguish (1 Cor. 14:7), and know how to (Matt. 16:3).

The noun *gnōmē* is by and large found only in the usual meaning of opinion, judgment. Thus, in 1 Cor. 7:25 the opinion of the apostle is clearly distinguished from a "command of the Lord," but it is still authoritative (cf. 7:40). In Rev. 17:13 it occurs in the phrase "one purpose." In Acts 20:3 Paul "decided" to return through Macedonia.

2. *The influence of OT usage.* The universal use of the LXX in the early church ensured a linguistic continuity between the OT and NT. But the revelation of God in Jesus Christ gave a new stress to the OT concept of knowledge. Where it expresses a personal relationship between the one who knows and the one known, the NT concept of knowledge is clearly taken from the OT. This applies to sexual relations (Matt. 1:25; Lk. 1:34) as well as to Christ's statement in Matt. 7:23, "I never knew you," i.e., I never had anything to do with you. The statement in 2 Cor. 5:21 that Christ (lit.) "knew no sin" does not mean that he had no intellectual knowledge of sin but that Jesus had no personal truck with sin. Similarly, Rom. 7:7 should be paraphrased: "As a human I would have had no intimate dealings with sin had it not been for the law" (cf. 3:20).

ginōskō has also the sense of know personally in 2 Cor. 5:16. The meaning of this verse is the subject of much controversy: Did Paul know the earthly Jesus? In 2 Cor. 5:11–21 Paul is involved in controversy with opponents who were attacking him personally and his claim to be an apostle. They maintained he was lacking in visible spiritual qualities to authenticate his claim to be an apostle (5:13). They probably charged him with being a braggart who commended only himself (cf. 5:11–12). Part of Paul's defense is the reference to Christ's death "for all," through which "all died" (5:14–15), including the person with supposed, visible, spiritual qualities.

As a consequence of all dying with Christ (2 Cor. 5:14), Paul says, "we know no one after the flesh" [lit. trans.]; instead, we know people according to the visible demonstration of the Spirit and power. In order to show how obvious this is, Paul inserts the statement that should be clear to all, in 5:16b: "Though we once regarded Christ in this way" (i.e., the visible Christ as he was on earth), "we do so no longer" (i.e., we have to do now only with the invisible, risen Christ in whose service we stand). Because Christ died and was raised for all, he is the invisible Lord of all, and his lordship is externally inescapable. Thus both Paul and his claims to apostleship, in common with all else that has died with Christ, are not subject to judgment by external and the normal visible standards. "In Christ" only the new creation is of value. The old has passed away and a new order has begun. In light of this argument, it is clear that Paul in 2 Cor. 5:16 is neither affirming nor denying that he knew the earthly Jesus personally. Equally it has no bearing on the meaning of the historic Jesus for Paul.

(a) We find the influence of the OT most clearly in those contexts where the vb. means to give recognition to. In 1 Cor. 16:18 Paul writes regarding colleagues who have rendered devoted service, "Such men deserve recognition [*epiginōskete*]." In 1 Cor. 4:19 Paul tells the Corinthians that when he comes, he "will find out" the power and nature of his arrogant enemies in Corinth. In Matt. 17:12 Jesus speaks of the scribes' failure to "recognize" John the Baptist as Elijah come again, so that they "have done to him everything they wished."

Phrases such as "know God's righteous decree" (Rom. 1:32), "know the law" (7:1), and "know his will" (2:18) do not imply a mere theoretical knowledge, but the recognition that it applies to the person individually and demands obedience. The Pharisees' remark that "this mob . . . knows nothing of the law" (Jn. 7:49) implies that the common people would not have gone after Jesus if they had really known and obeyed the Mosaic law. But in recording it, Jn. sees an unconscious irony in the Pharisees' own failure to see where the law was pointing them (cf. 7:42, 51 with 5:39–40.; 11:49–53). Note also the juxtaposition of "the knowledge of God" and being "obedient to Christ" in 2 Cor. 10:5.

Even where Paul borrows the concept of knowledge held by the Hel. popular philosophy, he recasts it. In Rom. 1:28, what concerns Paul is the question whether knowledge of God is personal. If such acknowledgment that manifests itself in living obedience is refused, God's judgment is inevitable. The statement in 1:21 that those who knew God had become futile in their thinking must have appeared as a contradiction in terms to Hel. thought; one's futility was a result of *not* knowing God (cf. Wis. 13:1; *agnoeō, 51*). Paul, however, considered that the knowledge of God necessarily included proper glorification and gratitude. Hence, the heathen who rejected God reduced this knowledge to mere intellectual activity, and what they considered wisdom was in fact nothing but folly (Rom. 1:22–23). True recognition of God, however, is a gift of God; it is based on his revelation (1 Cor. 13:8–12; 14:6; cf. Lk. 1:7; 2 Pet. 1:5).

Nevertheless, in apparent contradiction to its gift-like character, knowledge in the NT involves the ready will of the person who receives it. Through disobedience and ingratitude one can fail to appropriate it. Hence, the exhortations in the NT are calls to grasp that gift and use it rightly (e.g., 1 Cor. 14:27; Eph. 5:5; Jas. 1:3; 5:20). In 2 Cor. 8:9–15 we find a striking example of the outworking of knowledge in practical behavior. Here the knowledge of "the grace of our Lord Jesus Christ, that though he was rich, yet for your sakes he became poor, so that you through his poverty might become rich" (8:9) finds expression in the collection for Jerusalem, which Paul was urging. Knowledge in the sense of recognition is thus linked with the practical behavior of the one who knows and involves a way of life (Col. 1:9–10) that brings credit to the one known.

(b) We also find typical OT usage in the NT in the case of God's knowledge. This refers to his loving, electing knowledge of humankind (cf. 2 Tim. 2:19, quoting Num. 16:5; also 1 Cor. 13:12; Gal. 4:9). God's knowledge in Rom. 11:33 includes his whole activity, which embraces Gentiles and Jews alike. His knowledge is eternally valid for his creatures and triumphs over guilt and disobedience.

(c) There are, however, passages where *ginōskō* implies theological and theoretical knowledge. This overtone cannot be immediately derived from OT usage. Matt. 13:11 and Lk. 8:10 speak of a hidden knowledge granted only to the disciples concerning "the secrets of the kingdom of God." Such knowledge made them authoritative interpreters of the parables. Col. 2:2 also refers to understanding knowledge of God, but this knowledge is described as a "mystery" that is not open to all, but only to the saints to whom God has proclaimed his secret (1:26).

But even the knowledge of theological truths (e.g., of a particular teaching about baptism) has as its object obedience that expresses itself in life (Rom. 6:6). The express purpose of such knowledge mentioned is "that we should no longer be slaves to sin."

3. *The use of the word-group in the NT controversy with Gnosticism.* A number of contemporary scholars see evidence of a conflict with Gnosticism in a variety of NT passages. We should first note that the extant sources of Gnosticism are substantially later than the NT. Certain gnostic ideas appear to be indebted to the NT itself. Moreover, the extant texts display a wide variety of beliefs that make it impossible to treat Gnosticism as if it were a homogeneous belief system. Yet there were people in NT times who vaunted their superior knowledge (1 Cor. 1:18–2:16; 8:1; cf. Col. 2:8; 1 Tim. 4:7; 6:20). In such passages we see incipient tendencies that later flowered into Gnosticism.

The NT writers found themselves in conflict with traveling preachers who had their own version of the apostolic message. Timothy was expressly warned against the "godless chatter and the opposing ideas of what is falsely called knowledge [*gnōsis*]" (1 Tim. 6:20). Similarly, Rev. 2:24 mentions opponents who claim to have learned

"Satan's so-called deep secrets." There is much in Paul's letters (esp. 1 and 2 Cor.; Phil. 3:2–21; Col. [esp. 2:4–23]), in the Johannine lit., and in Jude that can be understood against the background of an antignostic controversy. Has the understanding of knowledge in these NT writers been influenced by their gnostic opponents, and if so how?

(a) Paul. In his discussion of the use of food offered to idols Paul quotes the claim: "We know that we all possess knowledge [*gnōsis*]" (1 Cor. 8:1). *gnōsis* cannot refer merely to knowledge about food here; rather, the important thing is the possession of *gnōsis*. The one who has this *gnōsis* claims to know the true being of God and his own originally divine being (cf. 2 Cor. 13:5). Such a person recognizes the nonreality of the universe and its earthly relationships and regulations, and thus finds no problem in eating food offered to idols (cf. Phil. 3:19a; Rev. 2:20) or in immorality (1 Cor. 6:12–20; Phil. 3:19b; cf. Rev. 2:20). For such a one the question of resurrection is irrelevant (1 Cor. 15:12), as is even the historical, earthly Jesus (1 Cor. 12:3; Phil. 3:18). Christian Gnosticism applied the dualism of spirit and matter to its Christology, which was always docetic.

Paul, however, measures this gnostic knowledge with the yardstick of love: "Knowledge puffs up, but love builds up" (1 Cor. 8:1b). Gnostics with their knowledge were interested only in themselves and their claim to a superior freedom loosed from all earthly ties. Love, on the other hand, is concerned with building up the church, i.e., with the salvation of others in the fellowship of Jesus Christ (including the weak, who do not possess this knowledge [1 Cor. 8:7, 9], and with outsiders and unbelievers [14:23]).

The knowledge claimed by the Corinthians is thus unacceptable to Paul. "The man who thinks he knows something does not yet know as he ought to know" (1 Cor. 8:2). This may be compared with 15:34, where Paul says that some people are "ignorant of God." In view of this, Paul is compelled to explain what he understands by knowledge. He finds it possible to express knowledge only passively, as a being known (cf. Gal. 4:9). This being known, however, is not the counterpart of some previous active comprehension of God by us, but rather of our loving God (cf. 1 Cor. 8:3). Full and real knowledge of God is ultimately part of the eschatological promise and expectation (13:12).

Paul rejected the gnostic anticipation of the end times, in which being known by God and the perfect knowledge of God come together by simply disregarding existence on earth and in the body (cf. 2 Tim. 2:18b). For Paul the whole stress lay on God's having known us before time. In short, being known by God involves election. If there is any human knowledge of God, it is the mediated knowledge of God as he revealed himself in the life and work of Christ. It is the Spirit-given "knowledge of the glory of God in the face of Christ" (2 Cor. 4:6). Prior to the end we can know God only as we know Jesus Christ (Phil. 3:10; cf. Col. 2:2–3), and only if we acknowledge him as the Lord (Phil. 3:8). Such an acknowledgment is the counterpart to being known by God. Thus love for God is the counterpart of having been known by God (1 Cor. 8:3).

Love for God, however, takes shape in a new obedience to the Lord Jesus Christ and in being free from the lordship of sin (cf. Phil. 3:10 with Rom. 6:3–13), in fellowship with Christ's sufferings, and in strenuous service by the resurrection power of Christ while one presses on to the promised resurrection from the dead (Phil. 3:10). At present such knowledge is only fragmentary (1 Cor. 13:12), but it looks to fulfillment. The Corinthian gnostics in their pride did not want anything of this knowledge. Hence, Paul ironically demanded of them to "acknowledge that what I am writing to you is the Lord's command" (1 Cor. 14:37). In the light of all this it is clear that Paul's polemics remain essentially within the limits of the OT concept of knowledge. At the same time he amplifies and works out this concept Christologically.

(b) John. It can be argued that John's statements about knowledge are spoken in the context of a gnostic thought world. For example, the very fact that knowledge can represent a mutual and inner fellowship between Jesus and his own as well as between Jesus (the Son) and God (the Father) (Jn. 10:14–15), may point to a gnostic background.

Describing knowledge as fellowship is possible if the one who knows, the messenger of God who mediates the knowledge, and the utterly transcendent God who is to be known are all personally equal. Knowledge of God includes knowledge of the one he has sent and becomes coterminous with eternal life (Jn. 17:3), another gnostic thought. This knowledge, which brings salvation, is possible only through the ability to know him who is true (1 Jn. 5:20).

This reflection of Johannine language on the terminology of Gnosticism is understandable if one realizes that the recipients of the Christian message and its opponents influenced the form in which it was expressed. John's purpose is to speak to gnostics, so he uses their language. This does not make the gospel a myth or John a gnostic.

One can say that John has given the gnostic myth an entirely new orientation. The gnostic understood knowledge as self-knowledge, through which one came to realize that one was not only a stranger in the universe but also divine. A person thus experienced deliverance from the world and history alike. For John, knowledge is of a personal reality that stands over against humanity. This "other reality" is God, mediated by revelation. Since "no one has ever seen God" (Jn. 1:18), there can be no immediate knowledge of God or direct fellowship with him. But God may be known in the one he has sent, his Son. The Son is not, like the savior in Gnosticism, a mythological figure. Rather, he bears the historical name Jesus. He is the Word become flesh (1:14; 1 Jn. 1:1–4). Those who see Jesus see the Father (Jn. 14:9; 12:45). Those who know him will know the Father also (14:7). Hence, fellowship with God can come only through fellowship with Jesus (10:14–15).

Fellowship between Jesus and those who are his, made effective by mutual knowledge, does not imply, as in Gnosticism, the deification of humanity and removal from the world and history. In Jn., knowledge gains its form from the one God and his revelation in history through historical channels. In other words, true knowledge is obtained by fellowship with the historical Jesus. Moreover, by sending his Son, God revealed his love to his own (Jn. 17:23; 1 Jn. 4:9–10) and to the world (Jn. 3:16). The Son loved his own according to the measure of his Father's love for him (15:9; 17:26). Moreover, just as the Son demonstrated his love for the Father by obeying his commands (14:31), so those who know him demonstrate their knowledge by keeping God's commands (1 Jn. 2:3–6), above all that of loving fellow believers (4:7–8; cf. 2:7–11), and by not sinning (3:6).

Thus *ginōskō* has a double application: It means knowing the love of God shown in the sending of his Son (Jn. 17:8; 1 Jn. 3:16), and the obedience of love based on it (1 Jn. 4:6). Such knowledge is already eternal life here and now (Jn. 17:3), because it is a life in history derived from God's historical revelation. In view of all this, John's concept stands out as deliberately and diametrically opposed to that of Gnosticism. The striking equation of faith and knowledge in the relationship of humanity to God is also part of the polemic against Gnosticism, which at the very least depreciated faith in contrast to knowledge. While 17:3 attributes eternal life to knowledge, 3:36 attributes it to faith. Moreover, gnostic self-satisfaction, which is concerned only with one's own salvation, is opposed by John's emphasis on the existence of the church in brotherly love (13:35) and unity (17:21–23).

4. *Later developments.* (a) In the Pastorals, *epignōsis* receives a special stamp through the controversy with Gnosticism. In Paul's earlier letters and in John's writings, church doctrine was still under development in the controversy with Gnosticism. In the Pastorals, however, a definite doctrinal tradition is evident, and all entanglement with "godless myths and . . . tales" (1 Tim. 4:7) is forbidden. Hence, gnostic terminology has been largely eliminated and replaced by other terms.

gnōsis is regarded in these letters as a technical term for the gnostic heresy (1 Tim. 6:20), and *epignōsis* takes its place when reference is being made to Christian knowledge (2:4; 2 Tim. 2:25; 3:7; Tit. 1:1). It has an intellectual, semidogmatic stress. Knowledge of God's truth is of equal importance with experiential profession of the Lord. Hence,

conversion to the Christian faith can be described almost technically as coming to a knowledge (*epignōsis*) of the truth (1 Tim. 2:4; 2 Tim. 3:7; cf. 1 Tim. 4:3; 2 Tim. 2:25; Tit. 1:1; Heb. 10:26).

(b) In 2 Pet. *epignōsis* is used in a similar theoretical, technical way in connection with God's call. Knowledge here is of the orthodox tradition, of the church's doctrinal teaching (1:2, 3, 8; 2:20), which must become effective in a corresponding way of life. In contrast to the Pastorals, however, *gnōsis* has a good sense in 2 Pet. (cf. 1:5–6; 3:18).

See also *aisthēsis*, experience (*151*); *agnoeō*, not know, be ignorant (*51*); *epistamai*, know, understand (*2179*); *oida*, know (*3857*).

| 1185 γλῶσσα | γλῶσσα (*glōssa*), tongue, language, speech (*1185*); ἑτερόγλωσσος |

(heteroglōssos), speaking a foreign language, of alien speech (*2280*).

CL & OT 1. In cl. Gk. the noun *glōssa*, tongue, language, speech, originally meant the tongue of humans and animals in the physiological sense. Fig. *glōssa* stands for the faculty of speech, utterance, and also language, dialect.

2. In the LXX *glōssa* (also *glōtta*) means the tongue as the physical organ in humans and animals in 100 out of 160x (e.g., Jdg. 7:5; Job 5:21); fig. it denotes the faculty of speech, language (Gen. 11:7). In the poetic and prophetic books of the OT and in Sir., the tongue is esp. the organ of sinful humanity—the tool of falsehood and evil, of arrogance and godlessness (Ps. 140:3; Isa. 3:8). Sins of the tongue are like a sword or bow and arrows (Ps. 57:4), or like a poisonous snake (140:3). "The tongue has the power of life and death" (Prov. 18:21); thus, one should keep it from evil (Ps. 34:13) and use it instead to intercede for justice and truth (35:28; 37:30) and to praise God (51:14; 126:2).

NT In the NT use of *glōssa* (50x) the chief theological emphasis lies in Acts and 1 Cor. 12 and 14; the tongues of fire that rested on the disciples (Acts 2:1–4) are a picture of the baptism with fire of the Holy Spirit, and the speaking "in other tongues" is a sign of the working of the Spirit (1 Cor. 12:10, 28). For the rest, the NT use of the word links on to that of the LXX (often in quotations: e.g., Rom. 3:13, quoting Ps. 5:9), whereby *glōssa* characterizes the tongue as a part of the body (Lk. 16:24; Rev. 16:10), as the organ of speech (Lk. 1:64; Jas. 1:26; 1 Jn. 3:18), and as language (Acts 2:11). In Rev., *glōssa* is used 7x in the summary phrase "every tribe and language [*glōssa*] and people and nation" (5:9; 7:9; 10:11; 11:9; 13:7; 14:6; 17:15) to denote the totality of peoples and nations in God's eyes.

1. The tongue as the organ of speech reveals one's inmost self. Thus it can be subject to demonic binding (Mk. 7:33, 35). Under the power of the evil one sin is revealed in many various ways through the tongue (cf. Jas. 1:26; 3:5–6, 8; 1 Pet. 3:10). But even here Jesus proves his saving power. The renewing power of the Holy Spirit is made manifest with the tongue, and by it people praise God and confess his name (cf. Phil. 2:11).

2. The phenomenon at Pentecost of speaking in tongues (or glossolalia, a word of Gk. origin but not found in the NT) is regarded in the NT as a fulfillment of OT prophecies (Acts 2:16–21 [Joel 2:28–32]; 1 Cor. 14:21 [Isa. 28:11–12]) and as a mark of the dawning of the age of salvation. Paul is also aware of ecstatic manifestations in Hellenism (1 Cor. 12:2).

(a) Paul quotes Isa. 28:11–12 in 1 Cor. 14:21 ("men of strange tongues" [*heteroglōssos*]) and applies the prophecy to glossolalia, which unbelievers do not understand. In Isa.'s original prophecy, Yahweh threatens his people, who have failed to respond to his word as delivered to them in their own language by Isaiah, with the foreign speech of the Assyrian invader. In 1 Cor. 14 Paul draws an analogy between the event of Isa.'s day and the enthusiasm for glossolalia in the Corinthian church. Certain members of the Corinthian congregation felt impelled by the Holy Spirit to give voice to inarticulate and enthusiastic prayer, praise, and thanksgiving in the Spirit (14:14–17). But since this phenomenon was not understood by others, it did not contribute to the edification and strengthening of the congregation (14:5) and was thus discouraged. Indeed, it might even be regarded as a judgment on the community (14:21). Prophecy was far better, since outsiders could understand what was going on, be convicted of sin, repent, and come to Jesus (14:24–25).

Paul did not forbid speaking in tongues (1 Cor. 14:39b); indeed, he himself practiced it freely (14:18). But he urgently exhorted examination, discipline, and restraint (14:14–17). In congregational gatherings, speaking in tongues should only occur if accompanied by interpretation (i.e., by a person discerning the message spoken in tongues), so that the church would be edified (14:26–28). Paul nowhere intimates that glossolalia is an indispensable proof of the reception of the Spirit or that it raises those members who have received it to a higher level of Christian living. Speaking in tongues must never contribute to the exaltation or self-assertion of pious people, but be used only to the glory of God.

(b) According to Lk.'s account in Acts 2, the bestowal of the Spirit in Jerusalem was linked with speaking "in other tongues" as together the disciples proclaimed God's great deeds (Acts 2:4, 11). At the same time, the Holy Spirit caused many to understand this proclamation in their own language. God was reversing what had happened at the tower of Babel. When later in Caesarea the first Gentiles received the Holy Spirit and became members of Christ, they also shared in this gift of grace by praising God "in tongues" (10:46; cf. also 19:6).

(c) These two sections of the NT are undoubtedly of different kinds: In Jerusalem, Luke describes the speaking in tongues as a preaching of the gospel directed to people in foreign languages or at least dialects; in Caesarea, Ephesus, and Corinth, however, it was praise and worship addressed to God in inarticulate tones. What is common is the conviction that these phenomena are rooted in the work of the Holy Spirit and are intended to glorify and praise God.

See also *logos*, word, utterance, meaning (*3364*); *rhēma*, word, utterance, thing, matter, event, case (*4839*).

1191 (gnōmē, opinion, judgment), → *1182.*

1192 (gnōrizō, to make known), → *1182.*

1194 (gnōsis, knowledge), → *1182.*

1196 (gnōstos, known, intelligible, acquaintance), → *1182.*

| *1197* γογγύζω |

γογγύζω (*gongyzō*), complain, grumble, murmur (*1197*); γογγυσμός (*gongysmos*), complaining, grumbling (*1198*); γογγυστής (*gongystēs*), grumbler (*1199*); διαγογγύζω (*diagongyzō*), mutter, murmur (*1339*).

CL & OT 1. In cl. Gk. *gongyzō* is an onomatopoeic word, meaning to mutter, usually with a connotation of expressing dissatisfaction.

2. In the LXX *gongyzō* occurs 16x and *diagongyzō* 11x. In general these words are applied to the Israelites who grumbled against their leaders (Moses and Aaron), and ultimately, therefore, against the Lord (e.g., Exod. 16:7; 17:3; Num. 14:27; Ps. 106:25). In Isa. 29:24, complaining is set over against learning obedience.

NT 1. *gongyzō* occurs 8x in the NT and *diagongyzō* 2x. Jesus' enemies often grumbled and muttered against him, as when he went into the home of Zacchaeus (Lk. 19:7) or when he called himself the bread of life (Jn. 6:41, 43). In 7:32 (cf. 7:12) *gongyzō* does not carry as much of a negative connotation, since the people were "whispering" among themselves that Jesus might be the Messiah (as seemed evident from his miraculous signs).

2. In the early church, the Hel. Jews "complained" that the Judean Jewish widows were receiving better treatment (Acts 6:1); this led to seven leaders being chosen to handle the daily distribution of food. In

1 Cor. 10:10, Paul warns Christians not to grumble against the Lord as the Israelites did; if they do, a similar judgment awaits them. Both Paul (Phil. 2:14) and Peter (1 Pet. 4:9) instruct us to offer Christian service to one another without grumbling or complaining. To be a grumbler is, instead, characteristic of a heretic (Jude 16).

1198 (gongysmos, complaining, grumbling), → *1197.*

1199 (gongystēs, grumbler), → *1197.*

1200 (goēs, sorcerer, juggler), → *3404.*

1205 (gony, knee), → *1206.*

| *1206* γονυπετέω |

γονυπετέω (*gonypeteō*), fall on one's knees, kneel down before (*1206*); γόνυ (*gony*), knee (*1205*).

CL & OT 1. In the Gk. world, slaves kneeled before their masters and suppliants before the gods, but this practice was usually expressed by *proskyneō* and *hiketeuō*, not by *gonypeteō*.

2. The Oriental ceremony of kneeling appeared in Israel only when its kings adopted the style of other monarchs and demanded similar tokens of servility (1 Chr. 29:20). At the same time, however, there is evidence that the widespread custom of kneeling before the gods was also adopted, so that falling prostrate was a sign of submission and homage, of humility and awe before Almighty God (Ps. 95:6). The OT looks forward to the same practice in the messianic age of salvation (Isa. 45:23).

NT 1. Apart from Heb. 12:12 (cf. Isa. 35:3), *gony* occurs in the NT only in phrases that mean to bend the knee, kneel before. (a) Such activity expresses awe before a superior or homage before a king, i.e., recognition of a king's might and sovereignty (mockingly in Mk. 15:19, where the phrase occurs in parallel with *proskyneō*; → *4686*), the adoration and veneration due to God alone and not to any idol (Rom. 11:4), the recognition of God as the supreme judge (14:11), or the acknowledgment that Jesus is Lord of all (Phil. 2:10).

(b) To fall on one's knees is esp. meaningful in Lk. 5:8, where it expresses the humble attitude of a man who, having received Christ's abundant grace, recognizes both his sinful and lost condition and the unmerited nature of the gift. Falling down before Jesus is here a sign of repentance and faith (cf. also Jn. 9:38).

(c) In other passages falling on one's knees is simply a gesture associated with prayer, emphasizing its earnestness and urgency (e.g., Lk. 22:41; Acts 7:60; 9:40).

2. The simple vb. *gonypeteō* occurs 4x, esp. to intensify the urgency of a request or question (Matt. 17:14; Mk. 1:40; 10:17). In Matt. 27:29 it is used in a mocking sense.

See also *aiteō*, ask, ask for, demand (*160*); *deomai*, ask, request, beseech, beg (*1289*); *proseuchomai*, to pray, entreat (*4667*); *proskyneō*, worship, do obeisance to, prostrate oneself, do reverence to (*4686*); *erōtaō*, ask, ask a question, request (*2263*); *krouō*, knock (*3218*); *entynchanō*, meet, turn to, approach, petition, pray, intercede (*1961*).

1207 (gramma, letter, document), → *1210.*

| *1208* γραμματεύς |

γραμματεύς (*grammateus*), scribe, clerk, secretary, biblical scholar, teacher of the law of Moses (*1208*); νομικός (*nomikos*), expert in Jewish law, lawyer (*3788*).

CL & OT 1. In cl. Gk. *grammateus* (derived from *gramma*, letter of the alphabet) is the title given to officials at Athens and elsewhere, from secretary and registrar to clerk. A *grammateus saphēs*, lit. accurate writer, means a scholar.

2. (a) For the most part, *grammateus* translates two Heb. roots. *šōṭēr* refers to an officer or an overseer (Exod. 5:6), the seventy elders (Num. 11:16), army administrative officers (Deut. 20:5), and magis-

trates (1 Chr. 23:4). *sōpēr* was used for the royal private secretary (2 Sam. 8:17), the military scribe who kept the muster rolls (Jer. 37:15 = LXX 44:15), and one skilled in the law of Moses (Ezr. 7:6; Neh. 8:1).

(b) In ancient Israel the writing art was preserved as a craft by certain families. Ezek. 9:2 offers a glimpse of an ancient scribe's appearance. Among the Kenites were families of scribes living at Jabez (1 Chr. 2:55). Such scribal schools trained suitable priests and Levites, who in turn instructed the people in the law on the great feast days and made legal judgments (Deut. 33:10). The most noted of scribes was the priest Ezra, who sought the law of the Lord, both to practice it and to teach its decrees in Israel (Ezr. 7:6, 10). In the latter respect he is the prototype of the scribes of later times, who were professional interpreters of the law. Moreover, Ezra's priestly lineage symbolized the close connection between the priesthood and official interpretation of the law, a connection that existed probably until the 2d cent. B.C.

During the monarchy, Levitical scribes were needed in the fiscal organization of temple operations. They recorded the priestly assignments (1 Chr. 24:6) and were involved in temple repairs (2 Ki. 12:10; 2 Chr. 34:13). Since the furnishing of written copies of the Torah and other parts of Scripture was a Levitical responsibility (Deut. 17:18; Jer. 8:8), Jehoshaphat's reforms (2 Chr. 17) are probably associated with scribes. At least one "writing prophet" employed an amanuensis (Jer. 36:4, 18, 32). A scribe also probably drew up the deed of sale in Jer. 32:10–12, since the document was entrusted to Baruch before witnesses.

Government scribes served in various ways, from giving the king counsel (1 Chr. 27:32) to mustering the army (2 Ki. 25:19). If David's cabinet is listed in order (2 Sam. 8:16–18; 1 Chr. 18:15–17), the king's scribe ranked below the military commander, recorder, and high priest, but above the palace priests. By Josiah's reign Shaphan the scribe precedes the recorder as well as the governor of the city (2 Ki. 22:3–13; 2 Chr. 34:8–21). The high status of Shaphan's family is evident from the careers of his son Ahikam and grandsons Gedaliah (master of the palace, later governor of Judea under the Babylonians) and Micaiah (chief minister of state under Jehoiakim, Jer. 36:11). Such royal scribes apparently kept offices at the palace (36:12), which illustrates their importance in the Judean government.

(c) The scribal profession received considerable impetus by the return of the Jews from exile, when the need arose to copy, study, and expound the Scriptures to make them the basis of national life. Thus the finest age of the *sōp^erîm* apparently spanned the two centuries between the only bearers of the title in that period whose names we know: Ezra (ca. 398 B.C.) and Ben Sira (ca. 180).

Ben Sira's portrait of the *grammateus* reveals how the position of teacher was becoming less closely associated with the temple, though he retains a positive attitude toward the cult and stresses the privileges of the priesthood (Sir. 7:29; 35:6; 45:6–26). Proud of his profession, Ben Sira lauds the perfect scribe in 38:24–39:11. The scribe, schooled in Torah and religious wisdom, understands the implications of both the written law and oral tradition (39:6). Thus he enters on the heritage of the prophets (who include the lawgiver Moses, 46:1). He invites the untaught to his school (51:23), though he carefully preserves the scribe's claim to exclusiveness by seeking to bar peasants and artisans from the study of wisdom (38:25–34).

The scribe's learning makes him an important figure (Sir. 39:4), able to administer justice among the people. They regard him as esp. pious on account of his knowledge of the revealed will of God. Ben Sira claims to teach in his own name (50:27), a new development. Stressing the personality of the teacher most likely indicates that Hel. individualism was gaining significance among the Jewish people. Nevertheless, the scribe soft-pedaled the notion of his being a wisdom teacher in favor of the reputation of being one learned in the Scriptures (39:1, 7–8).

(d) During the Maccabean revolt a company of scribes, now a numerous and independent group, sought a conference with the Seleucid-appointed high priest Alcimus and the Seleucid general Bacchides

(1 Macc. 7:12–14). Although this conference ultimately cost them their lives (7:16), the incident illustrates the continuing association between scribes and the priesthood. By NT times scribal rules and practices had acquired binding authority among the orthodox and were imposed on proselytes in addition to the plain sense of the written Torah.

NT 1. *grammateus* occurs 63x in the NT. In Acts 19:35 the word has a secular use, denoting the town clerk at Ephesus. Otherwise, it always has its Jewish meaning of one learned in Torah, rabbi, teacher of the law. *nomikos*, lawyer, occurs 9x. Tit. 3:13 mentions a certain Zenas as a *nomikos*, though it is not clear whether he was an expert in Jewish or Roman law. Elsewhere in the NT, *nomikos* means a Jewish expert in Mosaic law (Matt. 22:35; Lk. 7:30; 10:25; 11:45–46, 52; 14:3; but cf. Tit. 3:9).

2. Judging by the frequency of their appearance in the Synoptic Gospels, those identified by the term *grammateus* were clearly influential. Far from being simply clerks or copyists, they were teachers of the law (Matt. 7:29; Mk. 1:22) or lawyers; some were members of the Sanhedrin (Matt. 16:21; cf. 26:3). These men devoted themselves to several fields. (a) They studied and interpreted the Jewish law, which was both civil and religious, and determined its application to the details of daily life; decisions of the great scribes became the oral law or tradition. (b) They studied the Scriptures generally in regard to historical and doctrinal matters; i.e., "Elijah must come first" (Matt. 17:10) is attributed to scribal teaching. (c) Each noted scribe attracted around him a group of disciples (Matt. 7:29; Mk. 1:22) and a developed system of teaching of his own (Matt. 17:11; Mk. 8:11). (d) On occasion, they proselytized outsiders to the faith (Matt. 23:15).

The Synoptic Gospels show teachers of the law as active on their own account, either as individuals (4x) or as groups (16x), and in association with the priestly Sadducean party (Matt. 2:4; 21:15) or the Pharisees (mentioned together 19x, esp. in Matt. 23). When they are linked with Pharisees, usually "teachers of the law" takes precedence, probably because they were the scholars of the party. When necessary, a Pharisee could be more precisely identified as *nomikos* and *nomodidaskalos* (e.g., Gamaliel, Acts 5:34). These scholars were the leaders of what became rab. Judaism. Rabbis formed a closed order. Only a fully qualified scholar, who by ordination had received the official spirit of Moses mediated by succession (cf. Matt. 23:2), could legitimately be called a *grammateus*.

3. The elevated reputation of the rabbis among the people (Matt. 23:6–7; Mk. 12:38–39) rested on their knowledge of the law and oral traditions, but also of secret doctrines concealed by an esoteric discipline. Sociologically, the rabbis were the successors of the prophets, i.e., those who knew the divine will and proclaimed it in instruction, judgment, and preaching. It was they who decided what was required, in all details of conduct, in order to give practical effect to the law. This was necessary, since biblical Heb. was no longer widely understood. The teachers of the law were not individuals of wealth or property; yet this was a responsibility that gave them powerful influence, not only in the council of elders, but over public opinion as well.

Prominent rabbis, as leaders of the Pharisaic communities, formed one of the three parties in the Sanhedrin, and as such they took part in the prosecution and condemnation of Jesus (Matt. 26:57). Matt. is more specific about the Pharisees being the ones who hounded Jesus, whereas Mark often includes the teachers of the law (e.g., Mk. 2:16; 3:22; 12:35). The latter were also associated with the rulers and the elders in the persecution of Peter and John (Acts 4:5) and the martyrdom of Stephen (6:12).

At the end of the Sermon on the Mount, Matt. notes the astonishment of the crowd at the authoritative manner in which Jesus taught, "not as their teachers of the law" (Matt. 7:29). The teachers argued from Scripture and tradition, often quoting older authorities to support their claims. Jesus, by contrast, spoke with freshness, directness, and in his own name: "I say to you." In sharp contrast to rab. exposition, with its dependence on the tradition of the elders, here was the disturbing activity of a prophet directly authorized and commissioned by God.

4. Some teachers of the law apparently accepted Christ's teaching (Matt. 8:19), but most were prejudiced against him. They challenged Jesus about his disobedience to traditional practices under the law and found fault with much that Jesus and his disciples said and did (Matt. 21:15), such as eating with those who ignored the traditions (Mk. 2:16) or without first ritually washing their hands (Matt. 15:1–2; Mk. 7:5). They were affronted by Jesus' apparent blasphemy when he claimed to forgive sins (Matt. 9:3; Mk. 2:6–7; Lk. 5:21). Ignoring the miracles of healing, they demanded some other authenticating sign from God (Matt. 12:38).

For his part, Jesus attacked these teachers of the law for their misuse of "Corban" (Matt. 15:1–20; Mk. 7:1–23), for their spiritual blindness in failing to recognize him (Matt. 12:38–42; Lk. 11:16, 29–32), for ascribing his actions to Satanic inspiration (Matt. 12:24–32; Mk. 3:22–30; Lk. 11:15–22), and for their self-seeking desire for popularity (Matt. 23:5–7; Mk. 12:38–40; Lk. 20:46–47). As a by-product of the effort of study, teachers of the law came to be noted for their abilities in business and administration. This led to their being appointed as trustees for widows and orphans (cf. 2 Esd. 2:20–21), which led to the temptation to live comfortably on "expenses," thus earning a rebuke from Jesus for swallowing up the victims' estates (Mk. 12:40; Lk. 20:47).

Jesus conceded that the teachers of the law sat "in Moses' seat" (Matt. 23:2), i.e., that it was their business to teach God's will as revealed in the law of Moses. But he warned the people and his disciples not to follow their example, for they did not practice what they preached. Jesus then pronounced seven woes on the teachers of the law and the Pharisees (Matt. 23:13–36) for obscuring the real issues of belief and conduct behind casuistry and hypocrisy, making it virtually impossible for people to fulfill God's law.

5. Teachers of the law who were also Pharisees sided with Paul regarding the doctrine of the resurrection (Acts 23:9). Paul, himself an ordained teacher of the law (deduced from his part in capital punishment, 26:10), saw a fulfillment of Isa. 29:14 in the Jewish theologians' rejection of the preaching of the cross; he asks: "Where is the scholar [*grammateus*]?" (1 Cor. 1:19–20).

6. In the early church the Christian *grammateus* continued as a scholar and instructor in God's law (cf. Matt. 13:52; 23:34), so that Mosaic law was not abolished but reapplied for the needs of the Christian church. Matthew's Gospel, esp. in its proofs from Scripture, reveals a Christian *grammateus* at work.

See also *nomos*, law (*3795*).

1210	γραφή

γραφή (*graphē*), writing, in the NT always of Scripture (*1210*); γράφω (*graphō*), write (*1211*); γράμμα (*gramma*), letter, document (*1207*); ἐγγράφω (*engraphō*), write in, record (*1582*); ἐπιγραφή (*epigraphē*), inscription, superscription (*2107*); ἐπιγράφω (*epigraphō*), inscribe, write (*2108*); προγράφω (*prographō*), write before(hand), set forth publicly (*4592*).

CL & OT 1. (a) Originally, the root *graph-* meant to scratch on, engrave, with reference to reports, letters, lists, and instructions. The materials could be stone, wood, metal, wax, or leather. From the time of Herodotus this root was used generally in the normal sense of to write, and later to prescribe, order. From the practice of handing in a written accusation, *graphō* came to mean in judicial language to accuse.

(b) The passive forms *gegraptai* and *gegrammenon* mean that which is laid down in writing, the valid norm, esp. in the legal sphere. *engraphō* usually means to enter officially in documents or lists.

(c) The noun *graphē* originally carried the verbal sense of the act of writing, drawing, or painting; then the concrete sense of writing, inscription, letter, indictment; in Plato, the written law; in papyri of the 3d cent., a list.

(d) *gramma* means the product of the action, esp. where contrast with the spoken word is stressed; the ability to write; also individual letters of the alphabet as well as papers, letters, documents. The pl. *grammata* is used in the sense of elementary knowledge, then lit., learning. The concept of "holy writings" or "holy scriptures" became important in the Hel. period. The authority of the written word led to explanatory commentaries, such as those on the writings of Homer.

2. (a) The vb. *graphō* occurs about 300x in the LXX, almost always for *kātab*, to write. *graphē* (approximately 50x) always stands for (holy) writing, written decree, types of script (of different languages), letter. Only once (2 Chr. 24:27) is it used for *midrāš*, commentary. *gramma* (26x) has the meaning of writing, document, letter, book.

(b) The 22 letters of the Hebrew alphabet (all consonants) were carved (Exod. 32:16) or painted (Deut. 27:3, 8; Jos. 8:32) on stones, scratched or written with ink on potsherds, carved or painted on wood (Deut. 6:9; Ezek. 37:16), and later written primarily on leather or papyrus (Isa. 8:1). They were also taught in the schools (cf. Isa. 28:9–10). With the spread of the Aramaic language, the Aramaic alphabet (the so-called square character) gained predominance in Israel. By the time of the second temple it found general acceptance.

(c) The purposes of writing can be diverse. The OT mentions books (Jos. 8:34; 10:13), letters (2 Sam. 11:14–15; 2 Ki. 10:1, 6; 2 Chr. 32:17), lists (Jos. 18:8–9), deeds of purchase (Jer. 32:10–12), bills of divorce (Deut. 24:1, 3), sentences and decrees (1 Sam. 10:25; Est. 8:8; 9:23; Ps. 149:9), and divine commandments (Deut. 17:18; 27:3; 31:9). The words of Jeremiah were written down by his disciple Baruch, at his master's dictation (Jer. 36:4, 18, 32).

3. (a) The most important act of writing in the OT concerns the laws of God. The central part of this law, the Decalogue, was written, according to the biblical narrative, by God himself, on stone tablets that he had prepared (Exod. 24:12; 31:18; 32:16; Deut. 4:13; 5:22; 9:10). Moses was involved in writing down the Decalogue and the book of the covenant when he was on the mountain the second time (Exod. 34:1a, 4, 27–28).

Apart from this central issue related to the giving of the commandments, other passages state that God himself writes things. He keeps a book in which he writes those who commend themselves to him and from which he can also blot them out again (Exod. 32:32). He also writes his law in human hearts (Jer. 31:33; cf. Deut. 6:6).

The writing of God's law was so important that Israel was commanded not only to pass it on by word of mouth, but individually and lit. to write it on the doorposts of their houses and on pieces of parchment tied to their foreheads and arms (Deut. 6:8–9; cf. Prov. 3:3). The written word served as a reminder and a witness (Exod. 17:14; Deut. 6:8; Hab. 2:2). The power inherent in the written word can even have physical effects (e.g., Num. 5:23–24). When the written word is disobeyed, it can at a future date be used as a witness against evildoers (Isa. 30:8); but where it has been fulfilled, it can become a pledge (Deut. 27:3).

(b) The written word carries great authority, which is invoked by later generations (2 Ki. 14:6; 2 Chr. 23:18; Ezr. 3:2; Neh. 10:34; 2 Macc. 10:26). Even noncanonical books are referred to in the Bible (2 Sam. 1:18; frequently in Ki. and Chr.). In other citations and allusions within the Bible we can see the beginnings of the interpretation of Scripture. Thus 1 and 2 Chr. are in part a revision of previous books in a new style and for a new audience. The prophets likewise speak God's word to Israel by referring to his traditional promises and commands, interpreting them afresh for a changed situation.

(c) During Josiah's reform in 621 B.C. (2 Ki. 23:24–25), Deut. was rediscovered in the temple by Hilkiah, the priest. After the destruction of the temple and the exile, Ezra put the "Law of the God of heaven" (Ezr. 7:21), most likely the Pentateuch, into operation among the Jews (3:2; 7:6–26; 10:3; cf. Neh. 8:1–13:28). He bore the title of *sôpēr*, scribe (→ *grammateus*, *1208*), as a secretary of state at the Persian court. In the period that followed, the Scriptures were collected and set in order; nevertheless, disagreements about the canonicity of certain books (Ezek., Song, Prov., Eccl., Est.) continued into the 1st cent. A.D. Around A.D. 80, at Jamnia, the number of books was fixed at 24, divided into three groups: the Torah (Law), the Prophets, and the Writings (cf. Lk. 24:44; see also *kanōn*, canon, *2834*).

The Scriptures were now formally constituted into a canon. The reading of them was, along with prayer, the central part of the worship service from the time of Ezra on. Indeed, it appears that the reading out of the law gave the motivation for the first meetings for worship, where the word of God was heard (Neh. 8). Already in the pre-Christian period, the reading of a portion of the Mosaic law was followed by a passage from the prophetic books (cf. Lk. 4:17; Acts 13:15), which was supposed to relate to the passage from the law or to the meaning of the day. Exposition was added, a kind of sermon, which had an important function in the service.

(d) The need to translate the Heb. passages being read arose when Aramaic superceded Heb. as the everyday language. Similarly, God's Word had to be translated so members of the Gk.-speaking Diaspora could understand it. Thus, next to the reader would stand an interpreter who gave an explanatory translation, which led to the development of written Targums in many languages.

The most significant of all these translations is the Septuagint (LXX), a Gk. translation that began in the 3d cent. B.C. in Alexandria with the Pentateuch and was probably completed in the 2d cent. The LXX became the Bible of the Christians. Most segments within Jud. had the same Bible and the same historical situation as their basis, but they drew different conclusions from it, following their doctrines and experience. Consequently, there arose side by side many legitimate possibilities for claiming Israel's history and interpreting the Bible.

4. (a) In Philo and Josephus, the most important writers of the Jewish-Hel. era, we again find the whole range of meaning covered by the words in the *graphē* word group. Philo uses the phrase "Holy Scripture" (sing. and pl.) esp. often to refer to the Bible. In his works this Jewish scholar attempts to bring the Jewish Bible into harmony with Gk. philosophy. Philo offers a lit. exposition for beginners, but this only forms a foundation for an allegorical interpretation, which reveals the true meaning of Scripture. Philo's writings exercised greater influence on the church fathers than on later Jud. In Josephus's historical work *The Antiquities of the Jews*, the traditional text of Scripture is paraphrased to cover the biblical period.

(b) In the Qumranic community, which has left a relatively large library, writing and the written word were of special importance. A wide range of different subjects were recorded in the writing room at Qumran. Much can be learned about their expectation of an imminent end from the symbolic inscriptions on their military equipment.

The residents of Qumran presupposed a canon of holy Scripture, which served as the foundation of the new covenant (1QS 7:1; CD 5:2–3; 7:15–18). The study of this was continued even by night, when scholars relieved one another in shifts. The range of books regarded as holy Scripture was wider than those of the canon adopted later by the Pharisees. For example, *T. Levi* 14:1 and *T. Naph.* 4:1 (both revered by the Qumran community) cite *1 Enoch* as *graphē*. Other books regarded by the community as Scripture are a "Book of Time Divisions by Jubilees and Weeks" (CD 16:3–4), a "Book of Meditation" for priests and judges (10:6), and a "Rule of His Time" (1QM 15:5).

Through living with the Bible, the members of the Qumran communities came to see the events of their day as foreshadowed and predicted in Scripture; proof texts are thus used with the formula "as it is written" (1QS 5:15, 17; 8:14; CD 1:13; 5:1f.; 7:19). This is more obvious in their biblical commentaries. A text will be cited from the Bible, which they regard as inspired; then "its interpretation" follows. The latter is based not on literal or historical considerations, but on an application to the present, which is veiled in mystery and revealed only to students who have the Holy Spirit (1QH 14:12–13; 16:1–16). This is

referred to as *pesher* exegesis. Paraphrases in the style of a Targum or midrash are also found. The community's own psalms are likewise full of echoes of the Bible.

(c) In the literature of Pharisaic Jud., *kātab* and its derivatives are frequently used of the writing of testaments, bills of divorce, and other documents, but particularly for the writing of biblical scrolls and phylacteries (cf. Deut. 8:4–9; 11:13–21), which required great care. It is a matter of importance that at the New Year God writes people's names in his book for life or death, which is the origin of the traditional Jewish New Year wish.

In the schools of the Pharisees, importance was attached to making children learn writing while still young, then read and memorize the text of the Bible, and finally its interpretation. In the extended midrash, the meaning for the present day is unfolded to cover the entire Scriptures. The meaning of a passage was sought in a democratic, didactic discussion and fixed in each case by the majority as far as it related to making a norm for living.

NT 1. (a) In the NT the vb. *graphō* occurs 191x, about half of which refer to the Bible. In about 70 cases there is an introductory formula, which is followed by a Bible citation. Among the various verbal forms, particles, and adverbs used, several characteristic features may be singled out. The formula *kathōs gegraptai*, "as it is written" (used in the Synoptics, Rom., and 1 and 2 Cor.), is used for setting down a norm. Luke has a preference for *gegrammenon*, and esp. for *panta ta gegrammena*, "all/everything that is written" (Lk. 18:31; 21:22; Acts 13:29, each time in connection with "carry out" or "fulfill"; → *plēroō*, to fill, fulfill, *4444*). John prefers the perf. part. *estin gegrammenon*, "[it] is written" (6:31, 45; 10:34; 12:14), by which he emphasizes the permanence of the written word.

Parallel to the use of *graphō* in the NT is often that of *legō*, to say, which can be used, as in Pharisaic Jud., to express the directness with which the Scripture addresses us. Matt. typically uses the formula *hina plērōthē*, "that it might be fulfilled," and constantly adds *to rhēthen*, what was said (e.g., Matt. 1:22; 2:15, 17, 23; 4:14; 8:17). John also links *plēroō*, to fulfill, with *logos*, word, or *graphē*, writing. Citations of Scripture in Heb. are usually introduced by verbs of saying or have no introduction formula.

In another 17 uses of *graphō*, there follows no direct quotation of the OT, but a general allusion to the Scriptures (nearly always as a whole). More than half of these are in the Synoptic Gospels (cf. also Acts 13:29) and present (with the exception of Lk. 21:22) the suffering, death, and resurrection of the Son of Man, and John as his forerunner (Mk. 9:13), as events prophesied in the OT. John sees the Scriptures as pointing directly to Jesus (Jn. 1:45; 5:46). Passages of this category in Paul (Rom. 4:22–24; 15:4; 1 Cor. 9:10; 10:11; also 5:6) emphasize in a way similar to the exegetical methods of Qumran the relevance of the ancient Scriptures for the community of the present.

Only here and there is *graphō* used in a secular sense. Jesus wrote in the sand (Jn. 8:6, 8). Paul wrote sentences in his own hand, esp. at the end of his letters, in order to authenticate their contents (Gal. 6:11; 2 Thess. 3:17; Phlm. 19; also 1 Cor. 16:21; Col. 4:18). Zechariah wrote his son's name on a writing tablet (Lk. 1:63). In the parable of the unjust steward the debtors' bills are written differently (16:6–7). Also mentioned in the NT are a letter of commendation, a letter to the governor, and the intention to write something to the emperor (Acts 18:27; 23:25; 25:26). The vb. *epigraphō* is used of an altar inscription in Athens (Acts 17:23), in a quotation of Jer. 31:33 (Heb. 8:10; 10:16, though the LXX has *graphō*), and with regard to the names of the twelve tribes of Israel that will be "written" on the gates of the new Jerusalem (Rev. 21:12). The noun *epigraphē* is used of the inscription on an imperial coin (Matt. 22:20; Mk. 12:16; Lk. 20:24) and on the cross (Mk. 15:26; Lk. 23:38).

(b) With the use and interpretation of the canonical Scriptures for teaching purposes, an independent tradition came into being, a tradition that acquired a new authority of its own simply because it was in a written form. According to Col. 4:16 and 1 Thess. 5:27, Christian writings were read in services. Hence, the act of writing came sometimes to be emphasized, and certain writers made reference to their own writing in order to assure the church of their love (e.g., 2 Cor. 2:4), to guarantee the truth of the message (Lk. 1:3–4; Phil. 3:1; 1 Jn. 2:21; 5:13; Rev. 19:9), to remind (Rom. 15:15; 2 Pet. 3:1), to exhort (1 Cor. 4:14; 5:9, 11; 1 Pet. 5:12), to testify (Jn. 21:24; 1 Pet. 5:12), and to stimulate faith (Jn. 20:30–31).

graphō has great importance in Rev. As elsewhere in apocalyptic, the written word here acquires a directly sacramental character. Those who want to attain the promises of the book must, therefore, read (aloud) and hear this writing without adding or taking away anything (1:3; 22:18–19). As far as the letters to the seven churches are concerned, they are dictated to John by the Son of Man himself (1:10–19; 2–3). The apocalypse sealed with the seven seals is written within and without (5:1). The Lamb's book of life contains the names of those who will be saved (13:8; 20:15; 21:27). The Messiah riding on a white horse has a mysterious name, and also the title of King and Lord written on him (19:12, 16). The great prostitute likewise has a mysterious name written on her (17:5).

The two protagonists—the Lamb and the beast—mark their followers on the hand and forehead, where the Jews carried their phylacteries, which contained the confession of God's uniqueness (Rev. 13:16; 14:1; 22:4; cf. Deut. 6:4, 8). Those who persevere do not accept the mark of the beast; they receive rather a stone on which is written a new name (Rev. 2:17; 20:4). Just as the gates of the new Jerusalem have the names of the twelve tribes inscribed on them, so also the names of God, the Son of Man, and the holy city are written on the temple pillars (3:12; 21:12).

(c) In connection with the vb. *engraphō* we encounter the concept, universal in Jud., of the heavenly book, in which the names of the faithful are inscribed (Lk. 10:20; → *biblos*, book, *1047*); then also the picture of an inscription written by God on human hearts as an assurance of his love. Similarly, Paul sees the church as a letter of Christ, not written with ink (2 Cor. 3:2; → *epistolē*, letter, *2186*). The prophecy about the commandments written on human hearts and minds (Jer. 31:33) was important to all Jews (cf. Heb. 8:10; 10:16).

(d) Paul says that before the Galatians' very eyes Jesus Christ "was clearly portrayed" (*prographō*) as crucified (Gal. 3:1). Elsewhere, this vb. means "have already written" (Eph. 3:3), "written about long ago" (Jude 4), and "written in the past" (Rom. 15:4).

(e) The noun *graphē* is used 50x in the NT, nearly always absolutely in either the sing. or pl. and exclusively of holy Scripture. The sing. may refer to an individual passage (Mk. 12:10; Lk. 4:21; Jn. 13:18; Acts 8:32; Rom. 11:2; Jas. 2:8, 23) or Scripture as a whole (Jn. 20:9; 2 Tim. 3:16; 2 Pet. 1:20). The pl. *hai graphai*, the Scriptures, designates collectively all the parts of Scripture (e.g., Matt. 21:42; Mk. 14:49; Lk. 24:27, 32, 45; Jn. 5:39; Acts 17:2, 11; 2 Pet. 3:16). Matt. 26:56 refers to "the writings of the prophets."

At times Scripture is qualified: *graphai hagiai*, "Holy Scriptures" (Rom. 1:2); *graphai prophētikai*, "the prophetic writings" (16:26). In 2 Tim. 3:14–15, Paul urges Timothy, a convert from Judaism (Acts 16:1–3), to continue in the study of "the holy Scriptures" as a basis for his Christian life and work. Scripture is *theopneustos*, inspired, God-breathed (2 Tim. 3:16–17, → *pneuma*, spirit, *4460*).

(f) *gramma* is used 14x in the NT. It occurs 8x (in the pl.) in a concrete sense, with a marked leaning toward the secular and the legal. It can mean letters of the alphabet (Gal. 6:11), written information (Acts 28:21), a debtor's bill (Lk. 16:6), and learning (Jn. 7:15; Acts 26:24), which for Jews implies knowledge of the Scriptures; it also can designate the writings of Moses (Jn. 5:47) and, generally, the holy Scriptures (2 Tim. 3:15).

The other 6x *gramma* is used in a transferred sense, placed parallel to *nomos* (law) and contrasted with *pneuma* (spirit). The tendency to make a contrast between *gramma* and *pneuma* (already established in cl. Gk. and in Jer. 31:31–33) was developed by Paul into a system

(Rom. 2:27, 29; 7:6; 2 Cor. 3:3, 6, 7). The following scheme exhibits the juxtaposition of ideas set out in these passages that contrast the Jewish use of Scripture with the reality of life in Christ and the Spirit.

gramma	*pneuma*
letter	spirit
written on stone tablets	with the Spirit on tablets of flesh
law	freedom
circumcision (in the flesh)	circumcision (of the heart)
old	new
death	life

The detailed and consistent application of the contrast clearly shows that we have here a polemical scheme.

2. (a) "Scripture" in the NT is generally identical with the Greek version of the Hebrew Bible, the LXX. Sometimes, however, known pseudepigrapha (e.g., Jude 14–15 cites *1 Enoch* 1:9) and unknown texts (e.g., Jn. 7:38; Jas. 4:5) are quoted. Moreover, specifically Christian writings are also given an equal authority. In 1 Tim. 5:18, for example, Deut. 25:4 is cited as "Scripture," then followed by a known saying of Jesus (cf. Lk. 10:7). Here we may see the beginnings of a development in which the words of Jesus became authoritative in their own right alongside the old holy writings.

The same can also be said for what Paul wrote. In 2 Pet. 3:15–16, Peter evidently places Paul's apostolic writings on a par with the OT: "Bear in mind that our Lord's patience means salvation, just as our dear brother Paul also wrote you with the wisdom that God gave him. He writes the same way in all his letters, speaking in them of these matters. His letters contain some things that are hard to understand, which ignorant and unstable people distort, as they do the other Scriptures, to their own destruction."

(b) In the holy Scriptures God promised the good news beforehand through his prophets (Rom. 1:2); now in the day of salvation they are being or have been fulfilled (e.g., Matt. 26:54, 56; Lk. 4:21; Jn. 13:18; 19:24, 28, 36). Scripture cannot be annulled or broken (Jn. 10:35; cf. Matt. 5:17). Scripture is frequently personified so that, as it were, it speaks (Jn. 7:42; Rom. 9:17; Gal. 4:30; Jas. 2:23; 4:5) and can be inquired of (Acts 17:11). It foresees and prophesies (Gal. 3:8; 2 Pet. 1:20), judges, gives encouragement (Rom. 15:4; Gal. 3:22), and can be the subj. of faith (Jn. 2:22). The Scripture can even become a means by which people can be made perfect (2 Tim. 3:16–17). It is an object of investigation and is read and interpreted (Matt. 21:42; Lk. 24:27, 32; Jn. 5:39). It can be used to prove and confute (Acts 18:28), but it can also be twisted (2 Pet. 3:16).

3. (a) The first Christians were Jews living among Jews. For them, therefore, as for all other Jews, the Bible was "holy Scripture," the foundation, rule, and goal for faith and life. In it they encountered the living Word of God, experienced by means of interpretation as a personal message—at first handed down in this form by word of mouth and preserved intact by amazing powers of memory. At various times and for various reasons, the oral tradition was collected and committed to writing, which became an abiding sign and a testimony that could be experienced afresh by each succeeding generation.

This constant process of appropriating Scripture did not happen without sharp tensions: between Scripture and actual life, and between various interpretations made by particular groups. Each group saw Scripture in the light of its own historical experience, while at the same time their experience of history was molded by the biblical word. Since all Jewish communities believed the interpretation of Scripture to be the work of the Holy Spirit, its results were regarded as revealed truth, having the same dignity as the original. Thus there arose, in addition to the Heb. Bible, the Mishnah on the one hand and the NT on the other, which with its Christology was analogous and at the same time superior to the OT.

(b) Methods of interpretation can be discovered by a study of the Bible quotations. The variations in the cited texts are hardly coincidental. Interpreters used textual variants and altered, shortened, or lengthened texts in the style of a midrash; quotations from different contexts were sometimes linked together under one heading because of similar words. NT citations of the OT sometimes show similarities to forms of the text that were later used by Theodotion, Aquila, and Lucian as the basis of their translations. Finally, Aram. Targums are similar to texts used by Paul and Matthew.

4. The various quotations of the OT in the NT are not incidental ornament but its very foundation. The NT is built on authoritative texts from the Heb. Bible. There is often a flowing transition from the allusion into citation; and citations without introduction are found alongside others that have an introductory formula (i.e., "Scripture says," "Moses said," "Isaiah wrote," or the like. Specifically Christian interpretation is shown esp. in those statements that point to the fulfillment of Scripture). This emphasis on the biblical text was important for the Jews as a starting point in missionary endeavors and was taken over by Christians in their mission to the heathen.

(a) Proof from Scripture gained special force and development in the conflict with Jud. It was the principal tool of apologetics. Jewish opposition to Christian preaching led Matthew in particular to include direct quotations of Scripture. The birth and passion narratives esp. were linked with the OT, since it was here that the greatest conflict arose. By means of evidence from Scripture, discouragement and doubt concerning Jesus' suffering and death could be dispelled and hostile attacks repelled. What had happened to the Lord Jesus was for Christians neither a chance event nor a catastrophe, but God's purpose from of old.

(b) This typical use of evidence from Scripture, with its testimony to the fulfillment of promise, emphasizes not only the continuity but also the break between the old era and the new. Jesus' coming gave the Scriptures a new importance for Christians, since it revealed a meaning hitherto unrealized. The NT writers saw the events of Jesus' life mapped out beforehand in the OT. In fact, it was not merely from oral tradition that the believing community composed its life of Jesus, but also "according to the Scriptures," which were understood as having been written for his sake and for their own.

(c) The NT presents a state of continual tension. On the one hand, it emphasizes strongly the authority of the Hebrew Bible (or the LXX); on the other hand, it allows this authority to fade into the background before the claims of the gospel. Understanding the unity existing within the tension is expressed particularly in typology. Here there is seen in the fulfillment of a promise, the promise of a still greater fulfillment. The historical value of types such as Adam, Abraham, Moses, Elijah, the temple, and the sacrifices does not have to dissolve because these have been overshadowed by Christ. This leads to a new goal to which God leads his people along the course of history.

1211 (graphō, to write), → 1210.

| 1213 | γρηγορέω |

γρηγορέω (*grēgoreō*), watch, be on the alert, be watchful (*1213*).

OT *grēgoreō* is a late pres. found in Hel. Gk. It is formed from the perf. of *egeirō* (rouse, stir; → *1586*). In the LXX it means stand (Neh. 7:3) or watch (Jer. 5:6; 31:28 [= LXX 38:28]; Lam. 1:14).

NT Followers of Christ are exhorted to be watchful and alert, either to dangers or for opportunities. In Matt. 24:42–43; 25:13; Mk. 13:34–35, 37; Lk. 12:37; 1 Thess. 5:6, 10; Rev. 3:2–3; 16:15, this word is set in an eschatological context, in which believers must live carefully because they do not know the day or the hour of the Lord's return. In Matt. 26:38, 40–41; Mk. 14:34, 37–38, Jesus instructs Peter, James, and John to keep watch with him while he goes away to pray to the Father in the Garden of Gethsemane. In Paul's speech to the Ephesian elders (Acts 20:31), he admonishes them to watch out for false prophets (wolves), who will seek to infiltrate the church with heresy. The use of *grēgoreō* in 1 Cor. 16:13; Col. 4:2; 1 Pet. 5:8 denotes a

more general watchfulness on the part of Christians, esp. against the wiles of the devil.

See also *tēreō*, preserve, keep (*5498*); *phylassō*, guard, preserve, keep (*5875*); *agrypneō*, keep or be awake, keep watch, guard (*70*).

1214 (gymnazō, exercise, train), → 1218.

1215 (gymnasia, exercise), → 1218.

| 1218 | γυμνός |

γυμνός (*gymnos*), naked (*1218*); γυμνάζω (*gymnazō*), exercise, train (*1214*); γυμνασία (*gymnasia*), exercise (*1215*); γυμνότης (*gymnotēs*), nakedness (*1219*).

CL & OT 1. *gymnazō* as a trans. vb. means to train someone; as an intrans. vb. it means to do gymnastics. Since athletics were performed naked, we can easily understand why the vb. was developed from *gymnos*, naked, poorly dressed; (fig.) unveiled, bare. *gymnotēs* means nakedness; (fig.) barrenness; *gymnasia* means exercise. In Gk. philosophy *gymnos* and *gymnotēs* are used to describe the state of the soul separated from the body.

2. In the LXX *gymnos* is found in the sense of extreme helplessness (Isa. 58:7; Ezek. 16:22). This helps us understand its fig. use in Job 26:6. Even the realm of the dead cannot hide itself from God but is manifest to him in its complete helplessness. *gymnotēs*, nakedness, is found only in Deut. 28:48. In parts of Jewish apocalyptic *gymnos* is a major concept meaning without a covering for the body.

NT 1. The NT use of the *gymnos* word group is the same as in cl. Gk. (a) *gymnos* is found 15x and varies in meaning from completely naked (Mk. 14:52) to forcibly stripped (Acts 19:16) and inadequately dressed (Matt. 25:36, 38, 43–44). In Jn. 21:7 Peter put his outer garment on so as not to stand *gymnos* before Jesus. The fig. use, unveiled, revealed, is found in Heb. 4:13; 1 Cor. 15:37; 2 Cor. 5:3; Rev. 3:17; 16:15.

(b) *gymnotēs* in a material context means nakedness, bareness, extreme poverty (see Rom. 8:35; 2 Cor. 11:27). It can be extended to mean spiritual poverty (Rev. 3:18).

(c) *gymnazō*, train, is used only metaphorically in the NT, in 1 Tim. 4:7; Heb. 5:14; 12:11; 2 Pet. 2:14.

(d) *gymnasia* is found only in 1 Tim. 4:8 with the meaning of training, exercise, where Paul attacks a mistaken asceticism.

2. *gymnos* is the only word in this group with theological importance. (a) No one can hide from God's Word (Heb. 4:13). It completely lays bare, and nothing can be hidden.

(b) In 1 Cor. 15:37 Paul compares the "naked grain" (NEB, i.e., seed), which is sown in the earth, with the plant that emerges. Paul saw here a symbol of the resurrection. Just as new plant life springs up from the naked, seemingly dead, grain, so God causes the resurrection body to come into being through the death of the earthly body. The continuity between the old and the new body is historical rather than material.

(c) In 2 Cor. 5:3 *gymnos* means without a body covering. As to theological interpretation, there are three possibilities. (i) Paul assumes that between death and the coming of Christ there is an intermediate state marked by "nakedness," i.e., existence without a body. Paul would gladly have avoided this state by being alive at the time of the Parousia, when the redeemed then living will have the heavenly body put on over the old one (→ *dynō, 1544*).

(ii) *gymnos* may express the fate of the unredeemed, who do not receive a body of glory.

(iii) Some scholars see Paul as combating gnostic concepts in Corinth. The gnostics denied that they had, or even wanted, a "heavenly dwelling" (2 Cor. 5:2). Their goal was to be unclothed of every form of body. Paul did not see bodilessness as the goal of redemption, for it would rob him of communion with God. He longed for the new heavenly dress, so that the unclothing (i.e., death) would end in a new existence in a God-given body.

(d) *gymnos* can mean inner poverty (Rev. 3:17; 16:15).The same is true of *gymnotēs* in 3:18.

See also *dynō*, set, dress (*1544*); *himation*, garment (*2668*).

1219 (*gymnotēs*, nakedness), → *1218*.

1220 (*gynaikarion*, a little woman), → *1222*.

1221 (*gynaikeios*, female), → *1222*.

1222	γυνή

γυνή (*gynē*), woman (*1222*); γυναικάριον (*gynaikarion*), a little woman, contemptuously a silly woman (*1220*); γυναικεῖος (*gynaikeios*), female (*1221*).

CL & OT 1. In cl. Gk. *gynē* denotes a woman, female being. This word may be set in contrast with a man (→ *anēr*, *467*), goddess, wife, fiancée, mistress, maid, or female among animals. In the Gk. world the attitude to women extended from a striking disrespect for woman (in Athens) through the moderately esteemed status of the Dorian woman to the pronounced high estimate of women in Sparta. The Hel. environment of the NT shows in its great diversity strong parallels to the general Oriental picture in which, as compared with the OT, the cultic significance of women is often in evidence (e.g., in sacral prostitution).

2. (a) In the LXX *gynē* usually stands for the Heb. *ʾiššâ*. In Heb. society the woman was subject to the authority of a man (father, brother, husband), and her worth and honor lay in bearing children (cf. Deut. 25:5–10; → *gameō*, marry, *1138*); childlessness was a curse (Gen. 29:21–30:24). Polygamy, though evident (e.g., Abraham, David, Solomon), was an encumbrance. Excluded from all official cultic business (1 Sam. 1:3–5; cf. Exod. 23:17), the Heb. woman tended to bow readily to idolatry, though she could also take a deeply spiritual lead in the worship of Yahweh (cf. 1 Sam. 1:9–19; 2:1–11).

In contrast to much of the rest of the Oriental (religious) world, she could be recognized as an individual and as a person standing side by side with men. The former point finds its highest expression in the story of Ruth, the Moabitess, and Esther, the queen of Persia. The latter point is presented in the creation account of humanity as male and female (Gen. 1:27–28; cf. 2:18–25). Note too that wisdom is personified as a woman (e.g., Prov. 8:1–3; Wis. 7:12–30).

(b) In one sense, under OT law the wife was no more than a possession. She could be coveted, like an ox or donkey (Exod. 20:17; Deut. 5:21). Even Ruth, whose character stands out, was finally *bought* along with the field that Boaz redeemed (Ruth 4:5, 10). Although women were members of covenant Israel, they could not receive circumcision. A father or husband could nullify a woman's vows (Num. 30). A husband had the right to divorce his wife (Deut. 24:1–4), but the wife had no similar reciprocal rights. The woman required monthly purification (Lev. 15:19–31) and remained impure twice as long after the birth of a daughter than after a son (12:2–5). In the synagogues women began to be segregated from men from the 3d cent. B.C. on.

In cases of marriage the father's consent was essential, although note that Rebekah was consulted (Gen. 24:58). Failure to produce an heir was a mark of reproach (cf. Ps. 127:3–5; 128:3–6; Isa. 54:1–4), which finds classic expression in the stories of Sarah and Hannah. In both cases the sons who were born according to the promise of Yahweh (Isaac and Samuel) became his instruments of salvation for his people.

(c) On the other side, Deut. 24:5 prescribes that a man should not be eligible for military service for a period of one year after taking a wife (though even here the emphasis falls on the man's happiness). In the OT the price of the bride became a dowry (Gen. 34:12; Exod. 22:16–17). Num. 27:1–7 shows awareness of a daughter's right of inheritance. A wife differed from material possessions in that she could not be sold.

From time to time in Israelite history women played a significant part in politics, sometimes for good, sometimes for ill (e.g., Jdg. 4:4–10; 1 Ki. 1:11–31; 21:5–14; 2 Ki. 11:1–3). They could even be prophetesses (e.g., Miriam in Exod. 15:20; Deborah in Jdg. 4:4; 5:1–31; Huldah in 2 Ki. 22:14–20). The contexts make it clear that both Deborah and Huldah were married at the time.

NT In the NT *gynē* means a woman, female being (Matt. 9:20; Lk. 13:11), or wife (Matt. 5:31–32; 1 Cor. 7:2–16); it can also mean someone engaged to be married (Matt. 1:20, 24). In the voc. *gynai* is common as an address (e.g., Matt. 15:28; Jn. 2:4; 19:26). Besides *gynē* is *thēlys*, female (→ *arsēn*, male [*781*]). *gynaikarion*, a diminutive of *gynē*, little woman, is used only once and denotes a "weak-willed" woman (2 Tim. 3:6); *gynaikeios*, female, occurs in 1 Pet. 3:7.

1. *Women in the Gospels*. (a) *The parables*. Several of Jesus' parables deal with women (Matt. 13:33, the woman and the yeast; Lk. 15:8–10, the lost coin; Matt. 24:40–41, the women at a mill). In the first two, the woman represents the action of God the Father. In the latter it counterbalances the men in the field, indicating that men and women have the same status in relation to salvation. Lot's wife illustrates the dire need for wholehearted commitment (Lk. 17:32; cf. Gen. 19:26); it is not without significance that this allusion draws on the action of a woman to illustrate a danger that can happen to men. Jesus follows this teaching immediately by the parable of the persistent widow, who keeps petitioning an unjust judge and gains vindication (Lk. 18:1–8). The parable of the wise and foolish virgins illustrates the need to be ready for the coming of the Son of God by both men and women (Matt. 25:1–3).

(b) *Healing*. Jesus gave proof of his compassion and power by healing both women and men: e.g., Peter's mother-in-law (Matt. 8:14–15), Jairus's daughter and the woman with the persistent flow of blood (9:18–26), and the Syro-Phoenician woman's daughter (15:21–28). The widow of Nain's son was raised to life out of compassion for his mother (Lk. 7:11–17). In Jn. 11:1–44 Lazarus was raised in response to his sisters, Mary and Martha.

(c) *Followers of Jesus*. Jesus' call went out to any on society's list of rejected people, including women, on whom he conferred a new dignity. Even in Jesus' infancy Lk. places the faith of Anna alongside that of Simeon (Lk. 2:25–38). While there was no woman disciple (perhaps because the disciples were a counterpart to the twelve sons of Jacob), we do find women as a significant element among Jesus' followers; they were more prominent than the men in their love, care, and courage after the crucifixion (Matt. 27:55–28:10; Mk. 15:40–16:8; Lk. 23:49–24:11). In fact, Jesus received financial support for his ministry from several prominent women (8:1–3). Jesus spoke to women in public; unconcerned about Jewish rules, he even taught them (Mary in 10:38–42; the Samaritan woman in Jn. 4:7–27).

Mary Magdalene or Mary of Magdala is one of the most prominent women who followed Jesus. Jesus had cast out "seven demons" from her (Lk. 8:2); she apparently found a new beginning in him and became a devoted follower. Women, perhaps surprisingly (since women could not be legal witnesses in Jewish society), were the first to the tomb on Easter Sunday and were the first to witness Jesus after his resurrection (Matt. 28:9; Jn. 20:10–18). (For Mary, the mother of Jesus, → *mētēr*, *3613*.)

On more than one occasion, women anoint Jesus. Mary of Bethany, the sister of Martha, anoints Jesus' feet and wipes them with her hair (Jn. 11:2; 12:3). In Mk. 14:3–9, a woman in the house of Simon the leper anoints Jesus' head during the last week of his life. Jesus commends this woman in spite of the disciples' criticism of the waste of the perfume. Jesus sees this anointing as anticipating his death and sees in it also a messianic message. The title "Christ" means the "anointed one" (→ *Christos*, *5986*), and Jesus emphasizes the intrinsic connection between his messiahship and his death (cf. Matt. 16:13–23). He was anointed at the beginning of his ministry by the Spirit (Lk. 4:18); now he receives this unprecedented anointing at the hands of a woman at the beginning of his passion.

(d) *The sayings of Jesus*. If Jesus' parables and actions lift women to a status equal to that of men, and if in the Gospel narratives certain women stand out, the sayings of Jesus make it clear that it is not because of their gender that women or men are important. Rather, it is their relationship with Jesus that matters. When told of the presence of his mother and brothers, Jesus replies, "Here are my mother and my brothers! Whoever does God's will is my brother and sister and mother" (Mk. 3:34–35; cf. Matt. 12:46–50; Lk. 8:19–21; Jn. 15:14). In reply to the woman in the crowd who called out, "Blessed is the mother who gave you birth and nursed you," Jesus answers, "Blessed rather are those who hear the word of God and obey it!" (Lk. 11:27–28). Note also Jesus' reference to the widow of Zarephath (Lk. 4:25–26; cf. 1 Ki. 17:18–24), the story of the widow's mite (21:1–4), and the woman taken in adultery (Jn. 8:1–11; though not in the best MSS, most regard this incident as an authentic tradition).

In Matt. 21:31–32 Jesus asserts that prostitutes and tax collectors will enter the kingdom of heaven before the religious leaders, for they repented at John the Baptist's preaching. While Jesus does not condone their sin, this saying illustrates how the social outcasts find not only acceptance but also places of honor in the kingdom. A tacit witness to this is the genealogy of Matt., which includes the names of four women, all of whom were involved in sexual irregularity: Tamar (Matt. 1:3; cf. Gen. 38), Rahab (Matt. 1:5; cf. Jos. 2:1), Ruth (Matt. 1:5; cf. Ruth 3:6–18), and Bathsheba, the wife of Uriah (Matt. 1:6; cf. 2 Sam. 11:2–5). In addition, Mary herself was suspected by Joseph of having had sexual intercourse with another man (Matt. 1:18–21).

2. *Paul and Acts.* (a) *The status of women.* In Gal. 3:28 Paul asserts forthrightly that in Christ "there is neither Jew nor Greek, slave nor free, male [*arsēn*, → *781*] nor female [*thēlys*], for you are all one in Christ Jesus." To enter the Christian community means to join a society in which traditional male-female roles are discarded in favor of equality. God in Christ restores the original balance within the image of God that he intended when he created man and woman.

In Eph. 5:25, Paul stresses that a man should love his wife as Christ loves the church. He greets at least seven women by name in the Roman congregation (Rom. 16:6, 12, 15), and the letter was probably carried by Phoebe, a deacon of the church of Cenchrea (16:1–2). As a rabbi, Paul should hardly have deigned to address women where no men were present, but he did so unhesitatingly at Philippi (Acts 16:13).

The question arises as to whether there is a tension between this strand of Paul's teaching and a hierarchical view of woman's subordination to man in 1 Cor. 11:2–16; 14:34–35; 1 Tim. 2:11–15; and Tit. 2:4–5. In the first of these passages, Paul develops a hierarchical doctrine of headship. Although *kephalē* (head, → *3051*) can mean ruler or superior authority, it can also mean source (e.g., the source of a river). Since 1 Cor. 11:12 reflects Gen. 2, where man is said to be the source of woman, this may also be the point in 1 Cor. 11:3. In 1 Tim. 2:11–15 Paul's premise is the ontological priority of the male, on the basis of which he does not permit women "to teach or to have authority over a man" (2:11). It is a valid question whether this is principle is universally normative or a specific command in the light of some unknown situation in Ephesus.

Most important in Paul is his understanding of the relationship of husband and wife in marriage. At first sight, he may appear to teach an uncompromising subordinationism in such passages as Eph. 5:22: "Wives, submit to your husbands as to the Lord" (cf. Col. 3:18). But one should note the context for this instruction: "Submit to one another out of reverence for Christ" (Eph. 5:21; → *hypotassō*, submit, *5718*). Moreover, the marriage relationship is reciprocal in that husbands are to love their wives (cf. also 1 Cor. 7:1–14). He uses three principles: loving one's wife as oneself (Eph. 5:28), reflecting the second great commandment (Matt. 22:39; cf. Lev. 19:18); the one-flesh doctrine of marriage (Eph. 5:31; cf. Gen. 2:24); the pattern of Christ's love for the church (Eph. 5:25, 32; cf. Col. 3:19). In other words, the headship does not consist in authoritarianism. Rather, it is expressed in self-

giving, that is, in taking the form of a servant (cf. Mk. 10:45; Phil. 2:7); this includes a husband's headship.

(b) *The ministry of women.* Even before Pentecost women were among those who "joined together constantly in prayer" with the disciples (Acts 1:14; cf. 12:12). The first convert at Philippi was Lydia, who was baptized with her household (16:14–15), and women evidently played an important role in that church's life (Phil. 4:2). At Thessalonica and Berea, women were among the prominent members of the church (Acts 17:4, 12). As a believer the woman is an *adelphē*, sister (→ *adelphos*, brother, *81*). Among Paul's fellow workers with the apostles were Priscilla, the wife of Aquila (18:2, 26; Rom. 16:3–4), and Phoebe, "a servant [or deacon, *diakonos*; → *diakonia*, servant, *1355*] of the church in Cenchrea" (Rom. 16:1). This use of *diakonos* may suggest an order of women deacons in the early church, parallel to men as deacons (see esp. the use of this word in 1 Tim. 3:8–11). If so, their role was not that of oversight but of service to the saints (cf. Dorcas in Acts 9:36–39). The house of Mary, the mother of John Mark, served as a place of meeting for the church (Acts 12:12).

Regarding the veiling of women in Corinth (1 Cor. 11:1–16) and Paul's instruction for women to keep silent in the churches (14:33b–36) there has been much debate. While some see Paul as inconsistently adopting a rab. attitude here, others see these rulings as valid primarily in the social, cultural, educational, and church setting of his time, which no longer obtains today. One thing is certain: There was variety and flexibility of ministry in the NT in the light of the needs of the situation, and the gifts needed for ministry were given to both men and women (1 Cor. 11:1–11). Note (in addition to the individuals mentioned above) the four daughters of Philip, who prophesied (Acts 21:9).

3. *Peter.* The injunctions to wives and husbands in 1 Pet. 3:1–7 are comparable with those in Eph. 5:21–33 and Col. 3:18–19. Wives are to be submissive to their husbands, and character rather than outward adornment should be their true beauty. But reciprocally, husbands are to be considerate of their wives and remember that they are fellow heirs of the grace of God.

4. *Hebrews.* In the great chapter on faith, women are singled out as examples among the great heroes of the OT. They include Sarah, who received power to conceive (11:11); Rahab the prostitute, who did not perish with the others in Jericho because she received the spies (11:31); and the women who "received back their dead, raised to life again" (11:35; cf. 1 Ki. 17:17–24; 2 Ki. 4:25–37).

5. *Revelation.* In the letters to the seven churches the church at Thyatira is accused of tolerating "that woman Jezebel, who calls herself a prophetess [and] . . . misleads my servants into sexual immorality and the eating of food sacrificed to idols" (2:20). Elsewhere, women constitute an important symbol in this book (cf. 9:8; 12:1, 4, 6, 13–17; 14:4; 17:3, 4, 6–10, 18; 19:7; 21:9).

In Rev. 12 the vision of the woman clothed with the sun, with the moon under her feet, wearing a crown of twelve stars, and giving birth to a son, recalls the story of Mary giving birth to Jesus and escaping from Herod with the infant Jesus into Egypt (cf. Matt. 2:1–23). But the image of the woman also represents the community of God's people (cf. Isa. 54:5; Jer. 3:6–10; Ezek. 16:8; Hos. 2:19–20; 2 Esd. 9:38–10:59). The OT often uses birth and nurture imagery in its description of Yahweh's relationship with his people (Isa. 49:21; 50:1; 66:7–11; Jer. 4:31; Hos. 4:5; Mic. 4:9–10; Bar. 4:8–23).

In Rev. 21:2–3, the church is pictured as the new Jerusalem, coming like a bride from heaven for her husband (the bride is the wife of the Lamb, 21:9). This thought resumes in the picture of the marriage supper of the Lamb (19:7–9). By contrast Babylon, the symbol of godless civilization, is a prostitute who has by now been judged (17:1–18).

See also *mētēr*, mother (*3613*); *parthenos*, maiden, virgin (*4221*); *chēra*, widow (*5939*).

1223 (Gōg, Gog), → *4483.*

1224 γωνία

γωνία (*gōnia*), corner (*1224*); ἀκρογωνιαῖος (*akrogōniaios*), lying at the extreme corner, cornerstone or capstone (*214*).

CL & OT 1. In cl. Gk. *gōnia* simply means corner. Theological interest lies esp. in the expression *kephalē* [head, → *3051*] *gōnias* in Ps. 118:22: "The stone the builders rejected has become the capstone." This psalm, performed at the temple gates (118:19–20, 26–27), perhaps at the time of one of Israel's great festivals, celebrates the victory and salvation that Yahweh gives in his righteousness (118:10–21) and Yahweh's steadfast love (118:1–4, 28–29) in the face of distress (118:5–9). The stone mentioned here is one of the most important parts of the building: either a large cornerstone that binds together two rows of stones, esp. in the foundations, or the keystone, which completes an arch or structure.

2. *akrogōniaios* has the same meaning. It occurs first in Isa. 28:16: "So this is what the Sovereign LORD says: 'See, I lay a stone in Zion, a tested stone, a precious *cornerstone* for a sure foundation; the one who trusts will never be dismayed.'" This saying comes in the context of the prophet's pronouncement of woe on Israel's unbelieving nobles, who have evidently made a treaty with Egypt, invoking the protection of pagan gods in order to be saved from the Assyrian armies. Isaiah denounces this as a "covenant with death" (28:15), which will be of no help "when an overwhelming scourge sweeps by." The scheming politicians should have known better than to pin their hopes on such flimsy shelter. True refuge is available only in the building Yahweh has founded in Zion, the cornerstone of which is faith and which is built in accordance with justice and righteousness (28:16–17a). Isaiah is probably thinking here of Yahweh's purposes for the Davidic monarchy, with the promises he sees attached to it.

NT 1. (a) *gōnia* is used in Matt. 6:5 of a street corner in Jesus' warning not to be "like the hypocrites, for they love to pray standing in the synagogues and on the street corners to be seen by men. I tell you the truth, they have received their reward in full." Here Jesus' criticism is not directed at the practice of prayer but at ostentatious displays of public prayer.

(b) In Acts 26:26, Paul reminds Festus that King Agrippa knows what has happened to Paul, "because it was not done in a corner," i.e., in secret. In Rev. 7:1 the seer sees four angels standing at the "four corners" of the earth; the ANE regarded the world as a quadrilateral (cf. Jer. 49:36, "four winds"). Rev. 20:7–9 recalls Ezek. 38–39 and describes how Satan leads forth Gog and Magog, the Gentile hosts, from the four corners of the earth to do battle against the holy city. This struggle ends with the destruction of these powers that are hostile to God.

2. *kephalē gōnias* occurs 5x, all of them derived from Ps. 118:22. The cornerstone as the most important stone in the foundation is laid first. Because of its position it could be "a stone that causes men to stumble and a rock that makes them fall" (1 Pet. 2:8, an allusion to Isa. 8:14). The *kephalē gōnias* here certainly means the cornerstone (probably also Matt. 21:42; Mk. 12:10; Lk. 20:17; Acts 4:11).

The point of the NT statements about the cornerstone is the same. The builders who have rejected the stone are the Jewish nation and its leaders. They have rejected Christ, but through his death and resurrection God has made this same Christ into the cornerstone of a new building, the church (cf. Matt. 16:18; 1 Cor. 3:9–17; 14:12, where the church is also compared to a building). According to 1 Pet. 2:8, what applies to Jewish leaders also applies to all who do not accept the message of Christ. But if Jesus is for unbelievers the cause of their judgment (i.e., the stone of offense and the rock of stumbling), he is for Christians the "living Stone—rejected by men but chosen by God and precious to him" (2:4). This description of Christ as the cornerstone thus expresses powerfully the truth that our eternal destiny is decided in him.

3. *akrogōniaios* occurs in the NT only in Eph. 2:20 and 1 Pet. 2:6. In both passages the saying of Isa. 28:16 is given a Christological interpretation. This messianic view of the passage is visible already in Rom. 9:33 and was widely held in early Christianity (→ *petra*, rock, *4376*). The juxtaposition in Eph. 2:20 of "foundation" and "cornerstone" shows that the apostle has the Isa. passage in mind. The foundation on which the new community is built is the apostles and prophets; the cornerstone is Jesus Christ. On this foundation the community grows into a holy temple in the Lord, into whom Christians, through the Holy Spirit, are also built (cf. also 1 Cor. 3:11, where Christ is spoken of as the foundation [*themelios*, → *2529*] of the church). Jesus Christ is the living stone chosen by God and precious. Christians need to join him in order to be themselves built as "living stones" (1 Pet. 2:5) into the spiritual house, the church.

Δ delta

1227 (*daimonizomai*, be possessed by a demon), → *1228*.

| *1228* δαιμόνιον |

δαιμόνιον (*daimonion*), demon, evil spirit (*1228*); δαιμονιώδης (*daimoniōdēs*), of the devil (*1229*); δαίμων (*daimōn*), demon (*1230*); δεισιδαιμονία (*deisidaimonia*), reverence for the divinity, religion, superstition (*1272*); δεισιδαίμων (*deisidaimōn*), superstitious, religious (*1273*); δαιμονίζομαι (*daimonizomai*), be possessed by a demon (*1227*).

CL & OT 1. *daimōn* denotes superhuman power, god, destiny, and demon. In popular belief the world was full of demons, beings between gods and humans that could be appeased or controlled by magic, spells, and incantations. They were first of all spirits of the dead, esp. the unburied, then ghosts that could appear in varying forms (esp. at night). Demons lived in the air near the earth. Their work could be seen in the disasters and miseries of human fate. Through natural catastrophes they shook the cosmos. Above all they made people sick or insane. In some systems of Hel. philosophy, whole hierarchies of demons were drawn up. Philo considered angels and demons to be of the same nature, but angels kept their distance from the earth.

daimonion is the adj. derived from *daimōn* and is used as a noun meaning the divine. It expresses that which lies outside human capacity. In popular belief *daimonion* was used as a diminutive of *daimōn*.

2. Although these words appear rarely in the LXX, traces of the general popular belief are found in the OT (1 Sam. 28:13; Isa. 8:19). Necromancy was forbidden in Israel (Lev. 19:31; Deut. 18:11; 1 Sam. 28:9), as were sacrifices to evil spirits (Lev. 17:7) and all types of magic. Worship of demons is mentioned, however, in connection with Israel's idolatry (Deut. 32:17; 2 Chr. 11:15; Ps. 106:37).

The OT often combats pagan ideas about demons. For example, although the surrounding nations looked on the sun, moon, and stars as demons and worshiped them, the OT simply calls them "lights" (Gen. 1:14). Calamities and evil are attributed to God (1 Sam. 16:14; 2 Sam. 24:1), not demons. The mediator between God and humankind is the angel of Yahweh, not demons.

In the LXX *daimōn* occurs only in Isa. 65:11 (and then only in S); *daimonion* is found 19x. According to Ps. 96:5, all the gods of the nations are *daimonia* (cf. Deut. 32:17; Ps. 106:37; Isa. 65:3; Bar. 4:7). Tob. 6:7, 13–14 holds that an evil spirit can gain power over a person and kill him or her.

3. Judaism. (a) Rab. Jud. abandoned the reserve of OT piety. Belief in demons became widespread, though the Jews never felt themselves as strongly threatened by them as did their neighbors. The scribes believed strongly in the existence of demons and had many names for them. Numerous myths developed about demons being the result of sexual relations between fallen angels and women (cf. Gen. 6:1–4). Others thought that some of the generation of the Tower of Babel were turned into demons.

According to many rabbis, the demons are spirits, but they have bodily organs such as wings. They can propagate themselves and appear in various forms. They are innumerable and fill the world. They have access to heaven, where they can discover God's counsels. They live both in the air and on earth, preferably in deserts, ruins, and impure places (e.g., cemeteries). Although they belong to Satan's kingdom, God gives them authority to inflict the punishments imposed on sinners. Their power began in the time of Enosh (Gen. 4:26) and will end in the days of the Messiah. God's people could be protected from them by God and his holy angels, God's Word, keeping the commandments, amulets, and exorcisms.

(b) Pseudepigrapha. The commonest name for a demon is "spirit" (unclean, evil); Gen. 6:1–4 gives their origin. They are sometimes called Satan's angels. They lead people astray into magic, idolatry, war, conflict, and bloodshed (cf. Jas. 3:15). They also tempt human beings to penetrate into hidden secrets. Numerous myths developed about them and their activities. They are bound at the place of condemnation, but a remnant is at the disposal of Mastema, the lord of the spirits, to lead people astray and to harm them.

(c) Qumran. The Qumran documents present a cosmological dualism mitigated by monotheism. Two spirits are subordinate to God: Michael, the spirit (angel) of light; and Belial (Satan), the spirit (angel) of darkness. Angels of destruction serve under Belial and execute God's temporal and eternal judgments on evildoers. Those angels walk according to the laws of darkness and tempt human beings to transgress God's law. In the final eschatological battle Belial and his angels will be defeated by the sons of light.

NT In the NT *daimōn* occurs only in Matt. 8:31. Otherwise we find *daimonion* (63x) or *pneuma akatharton*, evil (unclean), spirit. Angels and demons are opposites. The fear of demons disappears because of faith in the triumph of Jesus Christ.

Since demons lie behind sorcery, witchcraft is rejected (Gal. 5:20; Rev. 9:20–21; 18:23; 21:8; 22:15). Heathen worship brings people into contact with demons (1 Cor. 10:20–21), for they stand behind paganism (Rev. 9:20). Demons are active today (Eph. 6:12) and teach their wisdom (Jas. 3:15); they will be especially active in the last days (1 Tim. 4:1; Rev. 16:13–14). Thus it is important to discern the spirits (1 Cor. 12:10; 1 Jn. 4:1). The demonic powers are destined for judgment (Matt. 8:29; 25:41; 2 Pet. 2:4; Jude 6).

Demons are subordinate to Satan and are his angels (Mk. 3:20–27; Eph. 2:2). They have power to do evil and can cause illness (Lk. 13:11, 16; cf. Acts 10:38; 2 Cor. 12:7). They can enter people, take possession of them, and change their personalities (Mk. 5:2–10). Because the kingdom of God was present in Jesus, he broke the power of the demons (Matt. 12:28) through his word of command (→ *ekballō*, *1675*). Demons had superhuman knowledge; they knew Jesus and their own fate (Matt. 8:29; Jas. 2:19). Jesus' enemies reproached him by insisting he had a demon (Jn. 7:20; 8:48–49, 52; 10:19–21). In his answer Jesus claimed that he honored the Father (8:49).

daimoniōdes occurs only in Jas. 3:15, where the author says that envy and selfish ambition are of the devil. *deisidaimonia* means reverence for the gods, superstition, religion. In the NT it is found only in Acts 25:19, where it means religion. Festus told Agrippa and Bernice that the Jews had certain disputes about their *deisidaimonia* and a certain Jesus. The adj. from this noun, *deisidaimōn*, reverent before gods, superstitious, religious, is found only in Acts 17:22, where Paul describes the Athenians as being religious. *daimonizomai*, be possessed by a demon, is used 13x in the Gospels, but most often in Matt. and Mk.

See also *aēr*, air (*113*); *ekballō*, expel, send out (*1675*); *diabolos*, devil (*1333*).

1229 (*daimoniōdes*, of the devil), → *1228*.

1230 (*daimōn*, demon), → *1228*.

1235 (*daktylos*, finger), → *5931*.

| *1253* Δαυίδ |

Δαυίδ (*Dauid*), David (*1253*).

OT In Israel, judgeship and kingship were two forms of the same theocratic ideal, in that Yahweh was both Judge and King. Thus, the divine rebuke occasioned by Israel's request for a king did not arise from the fact that monarchy as such betokened a decline from the theocratic principle, but from the fact that a permanent institution such as kingship meant that the people were not walking in confidence that Yahweh would continue to provide leadership for them. It was in this sense that they had rejected him from being king (1 Sam. 8:7); pressed by a new Ammonite threat (12:12), they were tiring of the demands of the way of faith and wanted the security of an institutionalized system.

God, however, condescended to human needs and failings and turned the monarchy into a high and noble institution, culminating especially in the reign of King David (see 1 Sam. 16–1 Ki. 2; 1 Chr. 11–29). After David had established his throne, he considered that the time for the Deuteronomic ideal of building a temple had arrived (cf. Deut. 12:10 with 2 Sam. 7:1). This was, however, forbidden him. Yet Nathan's oracle of prohibition turned into an oracle of hope: Far from David's building Yahweh a house, Yahweh would build the house of David (2 Sam. 7:11). From this prophecy of an unbroken succession of Davidic kings came the vision of the ideal kingship, focused in a single expectation.

At what point did this anticipation of an ideal messianic king arise? Presumably after the shortcomings of those kings who followed David, beginning with Solomon. Such a hope naturally arose while the promised line was still in existence, not after the Davidic line had run out into the arid sands of the exile. The Psalms clearly show a hope running beyond the dimensions of any actual king (e.g. Ps. 2; 72), and we are surely correct if we see them as taking their origin from the focal points of the reign of an actual king but consciously reaching forward to the realization of what he was failing to be.

The expectation centered around the following elements: the qualities of his kingly person and rule (e.g., Isa. 11:1–9), his universal sway (e.g., Ps. 72; Isa. 9:7), and the priestly dimension of his kingship (Ps. 110; Zech. 3:8–10; 6:12–13), even to the extent of performing the priestly rite of substitutionary sacrifice (Isa. 52:13–53:12). The OT also gives evidence of what must be called the mystery of the person of the expected king. Three examples must suffice: (a) He is a shoot from Jesse's stock, but he is also the root from which Jesse springs (Isa. 11:1, 10); (b) he can be addressed as "God" (Ps. 45:6) and yet receive anointing from "God, your God" (45:7; cf. Heb. 1:8–9); (c) he is born in David's line and yet has the title "mighty God" (Isa. 9:6–7).

NT Within the NT the life of David is alluded to in Matt. 12:3; Mk. 2:25; Lk. 6:3; Acts 2:29, 34; 7:45; 13:22, 36; Heb. 11:32. His authorship of certain psalms is asserted in Acts 1:16; 2:25; 4:25; Rom. 4:6; 11:9; Heb. 4:7. But the NT's main interest appears in those places where Jesus is connected directly with David and where Davidic concepts are applied to Jesus.

1. The ancestry theme (Matt. 1:1–17; Lk. 1:27, 32; 2:4, 11; 3:31; Rom. 1:3; 2 Tim. 2:8) stresses two things. (a) Jesus' ancestry (i.e., as a descendant of David) demonstrates the reality of his humanity, so that both the miracle and the power of his resurrection shine out (cf. the development of this theme in Heb. 2:5–18). (b) The reality of Jesus' descent from David makes him the repository of the promises vouchsafed to but never secured by his famous ancestor (Lk. 1:69; Jn. 7:42; Acts 2:29–35; 13:34–37; 15:16).

2. By the time of Jesus, messianism in Davidic terms had developed to where it was common knowledge and could even be used by non-Israelites in hopes of securing a favor (e.g., Matt. 15:22). The general acceptance of the terminology of the Davidic hope is seen in the greetings given to Jesus (e.g., Matt. 21:15; Mk. 11:10; see section "The Son of David" under *huios*, *5626*). This theme is especially apparent in the descriptions of the royal Christ of Rev. as the possessor of Davidic authority (Rev. 3:7), as David's root (5:5), and as both David's root and descendant (22:16).

The most complete description of Jesus' self-consciousness on this point is his question to the scribes and Pharisees how the expected Messiah could be both David's Son and David's Lord (Matt. 22:41–45; Mk. 12:35–37; Lk. 20:41–44). To Jesus, David, the inspired author of Ps. 110, saw a descendant on his throne appointed by Yahweh, who was also his "Lord." How can the same person, Jesus asked, be derived from David (and hence dependent on him) and also his Lord and thus superior?

Jesus, of course, deliberately shunned any ascription of kingship as it was defined in his day. His reply to Pilate in Jn. 18:37 is most pointed: Jesus could not deny being a king, yet he could not accept the political ambitions and half-understandings linked with earthly kingship. Therefore, he wanted the religious leaders to face up to the mystery inherent in the expectations they professed and to learn to reform their thinking, first in the light of the total OT revelation of the Messiah, and second in the light of that revelation as illumined, explained, and fulfilled in Jesus.

1255 (deēsis, a request, entreaty), → *1289.*

1256 δεῖ	δεῖ (*dei*), it is necessary, one must (*1256*).

CL & OT 1. In cl. Gk. *dei* and *deon estin*, it is necessary, one must, both denote a compulsion of some undefined sort. Since the impers. verb form does not name the originator of the compulsion, the precise meaning is dependent on the context for the force that evokes the necessity. The coercive power can be someone's will, laws of the state, or even an evil spell. By far the most powerful and comprehensive force is Fate, which determines the necessities of human, historical, and cosmic life. Even the gods are subject to Fate. This led, esp. in Hellenism, to an anxiety-filled and fatalistic approach to life.

2. Heb. does not have a word corresponding to *dei*, since the Gk. notion of a necessity that works in the manner of fate is foreign to Israel. The OT picture of God is a complete contrast, conceiving him as a personal will powerfully active in history, who claims for himself the lives of individual people. Through the introduction of the notion of *dei* into the LXX, the OT understanding of God was influenced by Hellenism, though *dei* was itself transformed by the underlying OT idea of the necessity of the divine will.

Alongside its nontheological usage (e.g., 2 Ki. 4:13–14) *dei* is found esp. in the context of the Mosaic law and of apocalyptic expectation. In the LXX of Lev. 5:17, the cultic prohibitions are called (lit.) "the commands of the LORD concerning those things that one must not do." This impers. formulation makes it possible for the personal claims of Yahweh's will to retreat into the background (cf. Prov. 22:14a).

dei in the LXX most commonly translates the Heb. infin. (construct) with the prep., "in order to." In this way final or future statements receive a slightly deterministic reinterpretation. Note, for example, Dan. 2:28: God has revealed "what must take place" (LXX *dei*), whereas the Aram. reads "what will happen in days to come" (cf. 2:29).

NT In the NT forms of *dei* are used with surprising frequency (101x), mostly in the Gospels (but esp. Lk.-Acts, 40x). But *dei* is freed from traditional Gk. associations even more decisively than in the LXX. By being connected with God's saving work, *dei* is charged with new meaning. The concept of *dei* plays a distinct role in three contextual areas: (1) eschatological-apocalyptic expectation; (2) the salvation history interpretation of the way of Jesus; and (3) the context of the Christian life.

1. *Apocalyptic contexts. dei* as an apocalyptic term refers to the cosmic drama that will inevitably break in upon the world. But it is not a matter of some unalterable fate. Rather, it is a necessity determined by the divine will. Jesus' so-called eschatological discourses announce a coming time of war, hunger, and great distress: "Such things must happen" (Mk. 13:7; cf. Matt. 24:6; Lk. 21:9; cf. Dan. 2:28 in the LXX). The universal preaching of the gospel must also occur before the end comes (Matt. 24:14; Mk. 13:10).

Rev. 1:1 is also based on Dan. 2:28: "The revelation of Jesus Christ, which God gave him to show his servants what must soon take place" (cf. 4:1; 22:6). With this "must" of judgment and salvation belong the individual acts of the final apocalyptic drama: The enemies of God's witnesses must be killed (11:5), the monster of the last days must remain a little while (17:10), and Satan must be loosed for a little while (20:3) before the ultimate victory of the Lamb (22:3).

Paul too is aware of eschatological necessity, such as the final judgment (2 Cor. 5:10), the transformation at the general resurrection of the dead (1 Cor. 15:52–53), and the reign of Christ, "until he [God] has put all his enemies under his feet" (15:25).

2. *Jesus' life and way as salvation history.* Through his use of *dei* Lk. expresses in many instances the fact that Jesus' way was not the result of chance or accident, but of the saving will of God, which made the history in Jesus' life salvation history. A divine necessity expressed by *dei* requires the twelve-year-old Jesus to be in his Father's house (Lk. 2:49). In his interpretation of the OT law Jesus' *dei* conflicts with the *dei* of the rabbis (13:14, 16, the healing on the Sabbath day). Justice and love are the divine *dei* of the Torah (11:42). Jesus' preaching is directed by the divine will (4:43; 13:33), as is his road to suffering (9:22; 17:25).

Lk. also does not depict the end of Jesus' life as the tragic failure of a prophet but rather presents his death and resurrection as necessary saving acts of God: "Did not the Christ have to suffer these things and then enter his glory?" (Lk. 24:26; cf. 24:7; Acts 3:21). The Scriptures, in other words, must be fulfilled (Lk. 24:44). The will of God, manifested and recorded in the OT, attained in Christ its complete fulfillment and exposition; this is what Lk. intends to say through his use of the divine *dei* regarding the way of Jesus.

In the other Gospels *dei* refers primarily to the death of Jesus as a divine necessity (Matt. 16:21; Mk. 8:31; Jn. 3:14)—the necessary fulfillment of the Scriptures (Matt. 26:54; Jn. 20:9).

3. *The life of the Christian.* The divine *dei* covers not only the past history of Jesus and future eschatological events; it also embraces the present life of Christians. Esp. in Acts human beings are implicated in God's saving activity. Paul is not the only one to be led in God's plan from the days of his conversion to his journey to Rome (cf. Acts 9:6, 16; 19:21; 23:11; 27:24), for God's saving will applies to everyone: "There is no other name under heaven given to men by which we must be saved" (4:12).

Jn. 3:7 designates regeneration as a divine "must" for human beings. Moreover, the entire Christian life is subordinated to the will of God; thus, *dei* is found in the paranetic material of the NT: in the exhortation to persistent prayer (Lk. 18:1; Jn. 4:24; Rom. 8:26), to live in a way that is pleasing to God (1 Thess. 4:1), to discipleship (2 Thess. 3:7), and to living a peaceable life (2 Tim. 2:24).

See also *anankē*, compulsion (*340*); *opheilō*, owe, be indebted to (*4053*); *prepō*, be fitting, seemly or suitable (*4560*); *chreia*, need, necessity, lack, want (*5970*).

1257 (*deigma*, example), → *1259*.

1258 (*deigmatizō*, expose to public disgrace), → *1259*.

| 1259 δείκνυμι |

δείκνυμι (*deiknymi*), show, explain, prove (*1259*); δειγμα-τίζω (*deigmatizō*), expose, make an example of (*1258*); παραδειγμα-τίζω (*paradeigmatizō*), expose to public disgrace, make an example of (*4136*); δεῖγμα (*deigma*), example (*1257*); ἀναδείκνυμι (*anadeiknymi*), show clearly, reveal (*344*); ἀνάδειξις (*anadeixis*), commission, manifestation (*345*); ἀπόδειξις (*apodeixis*), proof, demonstration (*618*); ἀποδείκνυμι (*apodeiknymi*), prove, appoint, demonstrate, exhibit (*617*); ἐνδείκνυμι (*endeiknymi*), show, display (*1892*); ἔνδειξις (*endeixis*), demnonstration, proof (*1893*).

CL & OT *deiknymi*, to demonstrate, show, occurs in cl. Gk., inscriptions, and papyri. *deigmatizō* (to expose, exhibit, make public) does not occur as often as *paradeigmatizō*. The prefix *para-* has an intensive force, so the vb. came to mean to expose to public disgrace, make a public example of someone, make oneself infamous or a sorry spectacle. In the papyri, however, one finds examples of a good sense, such as following an illustrious example.

In the LXX *deiknymi* occurs as a translation for a variety of Heb. vbs. Although it has a normal secular sense, it acquires a theological significance when Yahweh shows something, such as his showing Abraham the land promised to him (Gen. 12:1; cf. also God showing in 41:28; Exod. 25:9, 40 [= LXX 8, 39]; Ps. 60:3; 78:11; Amos 7:1, 4, 7).

paradeigmatizō means primarily to expose people publicly by executing them (e.g., Num. 25:4; see also Ezek. 28:17; Dan. 2:5; 3 Macc. 7:14; and Mordecai's prayer in the Gk. additions to Esther, following 4:17).

NT 1. In the NT *deiknymi* has various senses. (a) It can mean point out, make something or someone known to someone. Satan, for example, showed Jesus the kingdoms of the world (Matt. 4:8; Lk. 4:5). Jesus instructed a cured leper to show himself to the priest (Matt. 8:4; Mk. 1:44; Lk. 5:14). Moses was shown a pattern of the tabernacle Israel was to build (Heb. 8:5; cf. Exod. 25:40). The risen Christ showed his hands and side to his disciples (Jn. 20:20). Thomas asked Jesus to show the Father to the disciples (Jn. 14:8–9), whereas Paul showed the Corinthians the most excellent way, the way of love (1 Cor. 12:31). John received visions that the Lord showed him (Rev. 1:1; 4:1; 21:9–10; 22:1, 6, 8).

(b) The vb. can also mean to explain, prove. James challenges believers to prove their faith by their deeds (Jas. 2:18; cf. 3:13). Jesus "began to explain" to his disciples the way of suffering that lay before him (Matt. 16:21). The vision Peter received demonstrated that the Gentiles were to be admitted to the church (Acts 10:28).

2. (a) *deigmatizō* means to expose, make an example of. Joseph did not want to expose Mary to public disgrace, even though he thought she may have committed adultery while they were engaged (Matt. 1:19). Jesus, by his death and resurrection, "made a public spectacle" of the powers and authorities (Col. 2:15). *paradeigmatizō* occurs in Heb. 6:6, where those who turn their backs on Christ are, through that act of denial, crucifying him again and "subjecting him to public disgrace." Conversely, Sodom and Gomorrah serve as a warning, specifically "an example [*deigma*] of those who suffer the punishment of eternal fire" (Jude 7).

(b) *anadeiknymi* means to show clearly, reveal. In Acts 1:24, the apostles asked God to show clearly through the casting of lots who was to be the successor to Judas. In Lk. 10:1, Jesus "appointed" the seventy-two. *anadeixis* typically means commissioning, installation, but in the NT it is used only of the manifestation or public appearance of John the Baptist to Israel (Lk. 1:80).

(c) *apodeixis* appears only at 1 Cor. 2:4, where Paul writes that his message and preaching did not come with clever worldly means of persuasion, "but with a demonstration of the Spirit's power [lit., Spirit and power]." Some take this verse to refer to the convicting force of the Holy Spirit *in* the apostolic preaching, while others see it as a reference to the signs and wonders that accompanied Paul's preaching and could be seen in the growing Corinthian church. The apostle does acknowledge such phenomena in his own ministry (2 Cor. 12:12).

(d) *apodeiknymi* occurs 4x in the NT. In Acts 25:7 it means simply to prove (charges). In 2 Thess. 2:4 Paul prophesies that the man of lawlessness will "proclaim" himself to be God. In 1 Cor. 4:9 Paul claims that God "has put us apostles on display" in the role of condemned men in the arena. The amphitheater is the context here, implying not only that God appoints death for the apostles but that he also displays them publicly in this role. The Stoics used this context to picture the philosopher heroically standing out in the midst of troubles, but Paul seems rather to stress the humiliation involved in suffering for others. In Acts 2:22 the powerful deeds that Jesus of Nazareth performed demonstrate or "accredit" him as God's chosen Messiah.

(e) *endeiknymi* occurs 11x in the NT. In Rom. 2:15, the Gentiles show by their conscience that they have a sense of God's law imprinted on their hearts. Paul uses the same vb. in Rom. 9:17, 21 with God as the subject, where he notes how God displayed his power by raising up Pharaoh and by bearing patiently the objects of his wrath. According to Eph. 2:7, God has shown his incomparably great grace in Christ Jesus (cf. 1 Tim. 1:16). We too are called to demonstrate Christian virtues in our lives (Tit. 3:2; Heb. 6:10–11). *endeixis* occurs 4x in the NT. Twice Paul states how God demonstrated his justice through Jesus' sacrifice of atonement (Rom. 2:25–26). In 2 Cor. 8:24 he calls on the Corinthians to show proof of their love in participating in the collection.

See also *tekmērion*, proof (*5447*).

1268 (deipneō, eat, dine), → *1270.*

1270	δεῖπνον

δεῖπνον (*deipnon*), a main meal, dinner, supper, banquet (*1270*); δειπνέω (*deipneō*), eat, dine (*1268*); τράπεζα (*trapeza*), table (*5544*).

CL & OT 1. (a) In ancient religions eating and drinking were mostly formal meals, i.e., acts of public or private fellowship linked with the sacred. Families, clans, and religious fellowships received a share in divine power through the common meal, which represented their union with the deity. The origin of the sacred character of the meal is connected with magic, according to which the divine is embodied in material things. The thought that deity was contained in every plant led to the idea that the deity possessed a life-giving power, which was received directly by those who shared the meal.

(b) *deipnon* in the sense of a cultic meal was part of the living vocabulary of Hel. religion, in which it played an important role. Participants believed they were sitting at the god's table (cf. 1 Cor. 10:21, "the table of demons") and that through the meal they entered into fellowship with the deity. They thus became partners or sharers (cf. 10:20).

2. (a) The word *deipnon* does not play a significant role in the LXX. Until 4 Macc. 3:9 it occurs only in Dan., where it means delicacies (1:8, 13, 15, 16) and bread (5:1). The vb. *deipneō* occurs only in Prov. 23:1; Dan. 11:27; Tob. 7:8; 8:1. *trapeza* appears over 75x in the LXX, with reference to the table holding the bread of Presence in the tabernacle or temple (Exod. 25:23–30; 7:48), a table in front of a couch (Ezek. 23:41), the "table" of judgment that God prepares for carrion-eating animals to enjoy (39:20), and, most frequently, a dining table (1 Sam. 20:29, 34; 1 Ki. 2:7; Ps. 23:5; Dan. 1:5; Sir. 14:10; 29:26).

OT festivals and sacrifices are often connected with cultic meals and can be described as eating and rejoicing before the Lord (Deut. 12:7). Table fellowship binds a person to God and takes place before God (Exod. 18:12; 24:11). A meal often played a role in the conclusion of a secular covenant (Gen. 26:30; Jos. 9:14–15), at which Yahweh was present as an unseen guest. Jacob and Laban sealed their peace treaty with a meal (Gen. 31:46, 54; see also Exod. 18:12; Jdg. 9:26–41; 1 Sam. 11:15; 1 Ki. 1:25, 41–49). Table fellowship meant the granting of forgiveness (2 Sam. 9:7; 2 Ki. 25:27–30), protection (Jdg. 19:15–21), and peace (Gen. 43:25–34). The breaking of table fellowship was the most detestable of crimes (Ps. 41:9; Jer. 41:1–2).

(b) The Passover meal (→ *pascha*, 4247) originated in Israel's nomadic period. A year-old lamb or kid (Exod. 12:5) was killed by the head of the household on 14 Nisan at sundown (12:6). Its blood was smeared on the doorframes, its flesh roasted and eaten by the family during the night of 14–15 Nisan (12:8–9). After Josiah's reform (621 B.C.), the killing of the Passover lambs and the Passover meal took place in Jerusalem (2 Ki. 23:21–23; cf. Deut. 16:5–7). The Jewish Passover meal in the time of Jesus recalled the sparing of the houses marked with the blood of the Passover lambs and the redemption out of slavery in Egypt. At the same time it looked forward to redemption in the future, of which the redemption from Egypt was the pattern.

(c) Joining in table fellowship meant sharing in Yahweh's blessing. This was signified by the prayer at the beginning and the thanksgiving at the end of a meal. The head of the household took the bread and spoke over it the benediction on behalf of all those present. Then he broke the bread and gave each at the table a piece. In this way every participant in the meal received a share of the benediction. A benediction also followed the meal. The head of the household took a cup of wine, the "cup of blessing" (cf. 1 Cor. 10:16), and pronounced a prayer of thanksgiving on behalf of all present. Then everyone drank from the cup of blessing in order to receive a part of that benediction.

(d) Isa. 25:6–8 (cf. 65:13) refers to a bountiful eschatological feast that Yahweh will provide "for all peoples," when sorrow and death are things of the past. This feast, with the attendant removal of "the sheet that covers all nations," is linked closely with the Lord's Supper, esp. in Lk.'s version.

3. The residents at Qumran participated daily in a cultic meal. A priest presided and pronounced the benediction over the bread and the wine at the beginning of the meal. Reference was made to an eschatological meal with the Messiah in which bread would be eaten and new wine drunk.

NT 1. *The NT sources.* The expression "the Lord's Supper" (*kyriakon deipnon*) occurs only in 1 Cor. 11:20. In meaning it is closely related to the phrase the "Lord's table [*trapeza kyriou*]" (10:21). Both passages indicate that the word "Lord" (→ *kyrios*, 3261) is firmly established in the tradition and terminology of the Lord's Supper (10:22; 11:27, 31–32). The institution of this supper has been handed down in four forms (Matt. 26:26–29; Mk. 14:22–25; Lk. 22:15–20; 1 Cor. 11:23–25), each with somewhat different wording. Many scholars believe the variations represent to some extent the liturgical text entrusted to the writer by his own community.

(a) 1 Cor. 11:23–25 is older than any of the others, reproducing perhaps the form of words current in the Christian community at Damascus, where Paul first experienced Christian fellowship in the mid-30s (Acts 9:19; Gal. 1:17); he traces this form back to Jesus and notes that he had passed it on to the Corinthians (1 Cor. 11:23). Matt.'s version is generally considered to be an expanded form of Mk.'s. Ancient MSS of Luke have a shorter version (omitting Lk. 22:19b, 20), but most scholars see this as less authentic. A comparison with Paul and Mk. suggests that Lk.'s text is a conflation of Paul's and Mk.'s. Thus we are left with Mk. 14:22–25 and 1 Cor. 11:23–25 as the oldest forms.

(b) In addition to the fourfold record of the Lord's Supper, we must also take into consideration: (i) 1 Cor. 10:16, a commentary on the Lord's Supper; (ii) 11:26, an explanatory comment by Paul; (iii) 11:27–28; 16:20, 22; Rev. 22:17–21, all perhaps parts of the introductory liturgy to the early Christian celebration of the Lord's Supper; (iv) Acts 2:42, 46; 20:7, 11, which recount the daily celebration of the Lord's Supper ("breaking of bread"); and (v) Jn. 6:51–58, with Jesus' saying about the bread: "This bread is my flesh, which I will give for the life of the world" (6:51c).

2. *The historical roots.* (a) The Lord's Supper in the early church was certainly not just the continuation of the disciples' daily table fellowship with the earthly Jesus. Yet it is related to the accounts of Jesus eating with his disciples as well as with tax collectors and sinners (Matt. 9:10–13; Mk. 2:13–17; Lk. 5:27–32), and to the accounts of the feeding of the five thousand (Matt. 14:13–21; Mk.6:30–44; Lk. 9:10–17; Jn. 6:1–13) and the four thousand (Matt. 15:32–39; Mk. 8:1–10). Esp. the meals with tax collectors and other despised people (Lk. 15:1–2; 19:5–6) are parabolic actions—Jesus' word of forgiveness coming to life in events.

(b) The Lord's Supper in the early church, with its joy at present table fellowship with the exalted Jesus, is also related in some way to the table fellowship of the risen Jesus with his disciples after Easter. That is, the church's celebration of eschatological meals has roots in the meals shared during Jesus' postresurrection appearances (Lk.

24:30–31, 35, 43; Jn. 21:13; Acts 10:41). However, this connection should not be pressed too far, for when the risen Jesus ate and drank with his disciples, he was doing something extraordinary that could not be repeated. Note, for example, that the appearances of the risen Jesus were limited to the original witnesses (1 Cor. 15:5–8).

Thus, the table fellowship enjoyed at the Lord's Supper cannot be separated either from Jesus' last meal with his disciples or from the risen Lord's table fellowship with his followers. The retrospective look at Jesus' saving death (Mk. 14:22–25) was an essential constituent of the Lord's Supper from the first.

3. *The words of institution.* (a) There is a general consensus on the following points: (i) As already mentioned, Mk. 14:22–25 and 1 Cor. 11:23–25 are the two oldest forms of the words of institution. (ii) Behind these lies an original Aram. (or Heb.) form, which has not been preserved. (iii) While there are differences in wording between Paul and Mk., they are minor compared to the overall unity of the passages. In Mk. the saying about the bread runs, "Take it; this is my body" (14:22); the saying about the cup, "This is my blood of the covenant, which is poured out for many" (14:24). In Paul the saying about the bread runs, "This is my body, which is for you" (1 Cor. 11:24); the saying about the cup, "This cup is the new covenant in my blood" (11:25).

The main difference between the two is a certain asymmetry in Paul, for he does not have, "This is my blood" to parallel "This is my body." Many scholars hold, therefore, that Mk., for liturgical reasons, made parallel what was originally asymmetrical, so that the body and blood are identified as the two parts of the crucified Lord. Others, however, insist that the Pauline-Lukan form can be derived, according to the principles governing the handing down of tradition, from Mk.

4. *The setting of the words of institution.* The account of the institution, regardless of its form, appears in the NT in the setting of the Passover meal and the coming passion of our Lord. (a) That passion began with the betrayal by Judas, which led to Jesus' arrest, trial, and violent death (Mk. 9:31; 14:21; cf. 14:41)—note esp. Paul's "the Lord Jesus, on the night he was betrayed, took bread" (1 Cor. 11:23). The vb. used in the passion narrative, *paradidōmi* ("to betray, be delivered up," → *4140*), should be understood in the context of the salvation history of God, who "gave [his Son] up [also *paradidōmi*] for us all" (Rom. 8:32; cf. 4:25). Both Mk. and Paul, therefore, have in their salvation history the theme of God's substitutionary delivering up of the Lord Jesus for us.

(b) The Synoptics agree that Jesus' Last Supper was a Passover meal (Matt. 26:17–19; Mk. 14:12, 14, 16; Lk. 22:7, 11–12, 15). According to them, Jesus was crucified on the day of the Passover. But according to Jn., the Passover lambs had not yet been eaten when Jesus was accused before Pilate (Jn. 13:1; 18:28); Jesus' crucifixion took place on "the day of Preparation of Passover Week" (19:14). Various explanations have been given for this difference. We do know that there were different calendars followed in the first century by different groups of Jews, and perhaps Jesus followed a calendar different from the religious leaders. Or, since Jesus knew that he would not be alive on the Friday evening and since he "eagerly desired to eat this Passover" with his disciples before he suffered (Lk. 22:15), he resolved to eat it with them twenty-four hours earlier. Provision was made in the OT for the observance of the Passover on a day other than the usual one in a case of necessity (cf. Num. 9:10–11; 2 Chr. 30:2–3, 13, 15).

5. *The Lord's Supper and the liturgy of the early church.* (a) Acts 2:42 describes a liturgy of early Christian worship. After teaching, there followed closely the Lord's Supper ("breaking of bread"), which was concluded with "prayer." Perhaps the "fellowship" in this verse refers to a common meal that preceded the Lord's Supper. The accompaniment of the Lord's Supper with a meal is assumed in 1 Cor. 11:20–22.

(b) Parts of the introductory liturgy to the celebration of the early Christian meal may be found in 1 Cor. 11:26–29; 16:20, 22; Rev. 22:17–21. Many scholars believe that Paul, in 1 Cor. 16:20, 22, is citing a series of liturgical phrases that originate in the introductory liturgy of the Lord's Supper—the invitation to the holy kiss, the anathema ("curse") against those who do not love the Lord, and the *marana tha* ("Come, O Lord"). The anathema excluded the unworthy from the Lord's Supper; to strengthen this warning, there followed the prayer for the Lord's presence in *marana tha* (cf. Rev. 22:20). The call "Come, O Lord" is also reflected in the "until he comes" of 1 Cor. 11:26.

6. *The principal theological ideas of the Lord's Supper.* (a) A theological interpretation of the Lord's Supper must begin with the Last Supper. Most likely Jesus' reference to "body" is a euphemism for himself. The words "This is my body" (Mk. 14:22c) mean, therefore, "This is myself; with this bread I am giving myself." If so, it means that the disciples receive a share in Jesus' surrender of himself.

(b) This self-surrender of Jesus is included in the words over the cup, "This is my blood . . . which is poured out for many" (Mk. 14:24). There are frequent references to the shedding of blood in the OT (e.g., Gen. 9:6) and the NT (e.g., Matt. 23:35), where it denotes a violent death or the surrender of one's life. The pouring out of Jesus' blood, therefore, means that his life is surrendered as a substitutionary, atoning death for "many" (cf. Mk. 10:45; 1 Cor. 15:3, which interpret the death of Jesus in the context of Isa. 53:11–12). In short, Jesus' self-surrender (the saying over the bread) is his substitutionary death for the many (the saying over the cup).

(c) The eschatological perspective in Mk. 14:25 (about Jesus' not drinking wine until he drinks it again in the kingdom of God) gives the Lord's Supper a future reference. Jesus is placing his disciples within the sphere of God's coming reign (→ *basileia*, 993). Jesus' substitutionary atoning death for many makes them participants in the sovereignty of God breaking in among humanity. In the form of an oath, Jesus promises the consummation of salvation and assures his disciples that this will be his last meal with them before that time. When salvation has been fully realized, Jesus will once again break the blessed bread for his people and pass around the cup of blessing.

(d) The words of institution in the Lord's Supper are linked to the concept of covenant. The phrase "blood of the covenant" echoes Exod. 24:8 (cf. Zech. 9:11; Heb. 9:20; 10:29; 13:20) and makes a typological reference to the covenant blood sprinkled at Sinai. Just as the covenant at Sinai was confirmed by the blood of sacrificial animals, the "new covenant" (Lk. 22:20; 1 Cor. 11:25; cf. Jer. 31:31–34) is made effective through the blood of Jesus. The substitutionary death of Christ is superior to all the sacrifices of the old covenant because it inaugurates the covenant of salvation.

This new covenant is a covenant of the forgiveness of sins. Note the statement that Jesus' blood is poured out "for the forgiveness of sins" (Matt. 26:27–28; cf. Exod. 24:8; Jer. 31:31–34). The Lord's Supper is a present expression of that forgiveness.

(e) Paul's view of the Lord's Supper is further expressed in 1 Cor. 10:17: "Because there is one loaf, we, who are many, are one body," i.e., the body of Christ as a community. Here Paul is concerned with the relationship between the Lord's Supper and the church, both of which are vitally linked to the body of Christ. For Paul the Christological concept of the body implies the ecclesiastical one as well. That is, since the celebration of the Lord's Supper symbolizes and actualizes the one body of Christ, any Lord's Supper that does not achieve real table fellowship (11:20) is an abuse. This was, in part, Paul's answer to the Corinthian abuses, which perhaps arose when some in Corinth conceived the Lord's Supper as granting the individual participant the food of immortality.

(f) Jn.'s Gospel uses the pair of terms "flesh" and "blood" in the theology of the Lord's Supper, as well as the double notion of *eating* the flesh and *drinking* the blood (Jn. 6:51, 53–56). This made a close connection between the elements in the meal and the components of the person of Christ. However, these two phrases must not, according to Jn., be misunderstood in a literal or even sacramental sense, for

6:63 clearly shows that Jn. has in mind the personal presence of Christ spiritually through his word, and his self-offering in word and sacrament through faith (6:35, 47, 54). If so, the reference to eating the flesh, etc., is thus in an anti-docetic setting and is intended to emphasize the reality of the Incarnation. For John "eating the flesh" and "drinking the blood" of the Son of Man is the continuing sign of participation in his life by faith.

Note too that Jn. 6 is not directly about the Lord's Supper; rather, the Lord's Supper is about what Jn. 6 describes—namely, the eating and drinking that means belief in Christ (6:35), which is "eternal life" (6:54) and which is described as remaining in Jesus (6:56). Eternal life and remaining in Christ are central to faith and to one's relationship with Jesus; they are not confined to a sacramental meal but belong to the essence of one's day-to-day relationship with Christ. In presenting this discourse and in the absence of an account of the institution of the Lord's Supper, Jn. is, in effect, saying that the entire Christian life should be characterized by this kind of feeding on Christ and that this is what the sacramental meal of the church is really about.

See also → *pascha*, Passover (*4247*).

1272 (deisidaimonia, reverence for the divinity, religion), → *1228.*

1273 (deisidaimōn, superstitious, religious), → *1228.*

1274	δέκα

δέκα (*deka*), ten (*1274*).

NT 1. Ten, as the decimal base, is naturally common, esp. in round numbers and approximations, as well as in its large multiples (1 Cor. 4:15; 14:19; Rev. 5:11; etc.). The most noteworthy usages are in Rev.

2. The "ten days" of Rev. 2:10 most likely denote a short, or perhaps prolonged but limited, period of tribulation. The phrase is commonly referred back to Dan. 1:12–15, though it is unclear whether this allusion would have been readily perceived in Smyrna. An interesting Apocr. parallel might be seen in the ten generations of *Sib. Or.* 4:45–87, which is probably close to Rev. in time and place.

3. Rev. refers to a dragon and a beast with seven heads and ten horns (12:3; 13:1; 17:3, 7, 12, 16). The beast has ten royal diadems on its horns (13:1), and the horns represent kings (17:12). The image is evidently derived from Dan. 7:24, where the horns stand for ten kings of the fourth world kingdom, though it is differently used in Rev. The number here may stand for the universal extension of the power of these kings.

See also *dekatos*, a tenth part, tithe (*1281*).

1281	δέκατος

δέκατος (*dekatos*), tenth (fem. sing., tithe) (*1281*); ἀποδεκατόω (*apodekatoō*), give, collect a tithe or tenth (*620*); δεκατόω (*dekatoō*), collect or pay a tithe, tenth (*1282*).

Cl & OT 1. In cl. Gk. *dekatos* means a tenth (cf. *deka*, ten, *1274*). The Eng. word "tithe" is related to the word "tenth." There are examples in Gk. literature of a tithe being a sacred matter, a sacrifice due to the deity: e.g., Agamemnon conquered Mycenae and dedicated a tenth to the gods. On conquering the Etruscans, the Liparians were said to have dedicated a tithe of the spoils at Delphi.

Instances of the vb. *dekatoō* are lacking in cl. Gk. and the papyri. It was probably coined to match the technical religious term *dekatē* (fem. form of *dekatos*), tithe, which outside Jewish circles denoted esp. the tenth part of the spoils of battle that Gks. regularly dedicated to some god. *apodekatoō* is found only in biblical Gk.

2. In the LXX *apodekatoō* (6x) and *dekatoō* (only in Neh. 10:37) mean either to pay tithes or receive tithes (depending on voice); *dekatē* means tithe (9x; the more common form *dekatos*, tenth, appears over 100x).

In the OT, *dekatos* takes on a specific theological meaning. (a) *Overview.* A tithe was considered that part of the whole that a worshiper owed to God for the support of his sanctuary and its priests. The Hebrews were obligated to tithe their crops and livestock (Lev. 27:30–33), paying their tithes to the Levites (Num. 18:20–24) or (later) to the descendants of Levi who served as priests (cf. Heb. 7:5). Payment was made in Jerusalem (Deut. 12:5–6, 11, 17–18) or each third year in their home communities (14:28–29; 26:12). The Levites themselves had to give one tenth of this tithe to the priests (Num. 18:26, 28; Neh. 10:38–39).

(b) *Origin.* When and why the tenth was chosen for the "sacred tax" is unclear, though the custom was widespread in the ancient world. It was not confined to Semitic peoples but included Indo-European peoples as well.

Perhaps a tenth was adopted as a result of the ancient system of counting by tens, a system made easy by the ten fingers and toes. But the tithe may also have been selected because of the views about numbers that the ancients had. Not only was ten a favorite round number (cf. Gen. 31:7), but seemingly it was also a sacred number made up of two other specially sacred numbers—three and seven. Note the many times in the OT in which the number ten figures in holy matters: e.g., the clauses "and God said," "and God saw," "and God blessed," in Gen. 1 occur ten, seven, and three times respectively, hardly a coincidence; there are ten patriarchs mentioned before the flood (Gen. 5) and ten after it (11:10–30); ten was used in measuring Noah's ark (6:15) and frequently in measuring and furnishing the tabernacle (Exod. 26).

(c) *The tithe in other cultures.* Although the tithe formed an important part of Israelite culture, it was nevertheless not unique to Israel. Sometimes it was a strictly political matter, a tax paid by the people to their king or one imposed on conquered nations by the conqueror. More often, however, it was a combination of the secular with the sacred. In Babylon during the reign of Nebuchadnezzar II, a tithe from the land was paid to the temple by everyone, including the king, while Babylonian kings took a tithe of all imports. Persian satraps also demanded a tithe of imports. Cyrus, the Persian king, made his soldiers give a tenth of their spoils to Zeus.

(d) *Tithing in the OT.* The concept of the tithe in the OT seems to have developed as time went on. Early in the record Abram gave Melchizedek a tenth of everything (Gen. 14:20), but this was spoils of war, not the produce of the land. There is no mention of any law demanding this of Abram, nor is there any explanation as to why he gave it. Jacob vowed to give a tithe to God (28:22); this too was apparently a spontaneous thought, a promise to thank God conditional on God's prospering him and bringing him back home again safely. There are no details on how this tithe would be given or who would receive it in God's behalf.

The tithe is perhaps alluded to in the so-called Book of the Covenant (Exod. 21:1–23:19), in the laws governing the giving of the firstfruits of the land (23:16, 19; 34:22–26). The first of the crop, and presumably the best, was sacrificed to God, probably in recognition that all things belong to him (Deut. 26:10). This gift of firstfruits may be the forerunner of the tithe, with the tithe being introduced to fix precisely the amount of firstfruits to be brought. But this question about the relation of the firstfruits to the tithe cannot be answered unequivocally, for biblical texts seem both to equate them (Deut. 26:1–15) and to distinguish between them (Neh. 12:44).

The OT describes various aspects of the tithe, and it is not always clear how the various parts fit together. (i) From the beginning the tithe of the land's produce—seed, fruit trees, and the like—was recognized as belonging in some unique way to the Lord. It was "holy to the LORD" (Lev. 27:30–32). Annually a person was required to bring his tithe—a personal offering of grain, wine, oil, etc.—to some designated place and eat it there with his sons, daughters, servants, and the Levites who happened to be present (Deut. 12:6–7, 11, 17). If the journey to this place was too far, the tithe could be exchanged for money and the money spent there on whatever the appetite craved. There the offerer with his household and the Levite was to eat before the Lord and rejoice (14:22–29; cf. 15:19–23).

(ii) Every third year, however, the tithe was not taken away from home and consumed by the offerer in some distant place but was stored up within local communities and used to meet the material needs of Levites, aliens, orphans, and widows in and around that community (Deut. 14:28–29; 26:12).

(iii) What is more difficult to harmonize is the biblical command that the people give their tithes to the Levites and priests (rather than consume them). The Levites and priests received no land by which to support themselves, so their maintenance and that of the sanctuary had to come from the people's gifts. Thus, in Num. 18:21 God instructs the people to give to the Levites "all the tithes in Israel as their inheritance." The Levites themselves were to oversee the collection of the tithes from all the rural towns, and the priest, Aaron's descendant, accompanied them on their rounds. From that tithe the Levites gave a tenth to the priest (18:28; Neh. 10:32–39), and in return the Levites and the priest served in the sanctuary. How this relates to the first aspect discussed above is uncertain. Since the tithe could be a substantial amount, perhaps the tithe feast used only a small portion of the tithe, with the rest being given for the Levites and the priests.

(iv) On more than one occasion Israel neglected its obligation with regard to the tithe, so that the Levites were forced to leave the sanctuary in order to support themselves by tilling the soil. As a result, the sanctuary fell into disrepair. Reforms took place under Hezekiah (2 Chr. 31:5–6), Nehemiah (Neh. 13:12), and Malachi (Mal. 3:8, 10), and the people once more gave their proper tithe, the sanctuary was restored, and the priests and Levites were able to give themselves wholly to the law once again.

(e) *The tithe in Hel. Jud. and beyond.* The tithe in the period of Hel. Jud. was still the chief source of income for the priests and Levites, though, as in the OT, since it was left to the conscience of the taxpayer, it often was not paid. On occasion, therefore, according to Josephus, greedy high priests made sure they received their due by sending bands of desperados to take the tithe right from the threshing floors. In the late pre-Christian and early Christian centuries the tithe was augmented by a type of poll tax for the support of the temple and its ministers: An annual half-shekel tax (Matt. 17:24; cf. *m. Sheqal.*; → *statēr*, stater [a silver coin worth four drachmas], *5088*) was collected not only from the Jews in Palestine but from those of the Diaspora as well. After the destruction of the temple the rabbis still stressed the importance of tithing. They viewed it as one of the three elements by means of which Israelites could escape the lot of the wicked.

(f) *Meaning of the tithe.* Underlying the tithe is the fundamental idea that "the earth is the LORD's, and everything in it" (Ps. 24:1). Thus, for Israel to give a tenth was to acknowledge in a tangible way the Lord's ownership of the land and its produce. Hence, Judah's failure in this was tantamount to robbing God (Mal. 3:8, 10), not of the material things themselves—these already belonged to God (Ps. 50:10)—but of the recognition that these material things were exclusively his. One's possessions were to be seen as gifts given by God, the proper response to which was gratitude. Tithing, then, was also an expression of thanks to and faith in God for his generosity (cf. Gen. 28:20–22).

Moreover, tithing in Israel supported the Levites and priests and provided the poor with food. Tithing was viewed, therefore, as God's way of involving his people in his own redemptive activity, in his own immense concern for the poor and destitute. Just as God had shared his blessings with his people, so those who received them must share them with the less fortunate. Hence, religious leaders repeatedly reminded the Israelites of the importance of tithing: To give the tithe would bring divine blessing; to withhold it, divine cursing (Mal. 3:8, 10).

NT 1. *The tithe in the NT.* Since the tithe played such an important part in the OT and in the Jud. of NT times, it is surprising that never

once is tithing mentioned in any of the instructions given to the church. Jesus mentions the teachers of the law and Pharisees who tithe, but he never commands his disciples to do so. In fact, the only three NT uses of *apodekatoō* occur in Jesus' criticism of the Pharisees (Matt. 23:33; Lk. 11:42; 18:12). The self-righteous Pharisee of Jesus' parable (Lk. 18:9–14) suggests that by tithing all sorts of income he has gone beyond the OT law and so has put God in his debt. The classic example of the Pharisees' zeal about tithing (to the neglect of "the more important matters of the law—justice, mercy and faithfulness") was their care to tithe even common garden plants used as condiments or medicinal herbs, a practice presumably not required by the Mosaic law (cf. Lev. 27:30–32; Deut. 14:22–23).

Likewise, the writer to the Heb. refers to Abraham's tithes (*dekatos*, in the form *dekatē*, tithe) to Melchizedek (hence also Levi's to Melchizedek through Abraham, 7:2, 5), but he never suggests his readers should follow this example. Paul writes about sharing material possessions to care for the needs of the poor (1 Cor. 16:1–3; 2 Cor. 8–9; Eph. 4:28) and to sustain the Christian ministry (1 Cor. 9). He urges and commends generosity (2 Cor. 8:1–5; 9:6), but not once does he demand, as a command from God, that any specific amount be given.

Paul, however, did demand (*diatassō*, → *tassō, 5435*) of his churches that a collection (*logeia*, → *3356*) be taken "for God's people," i.e., for the Christians in the mother church at Jerusalem (1 Cor. 16:1–3; 2 Cor. 8:4; 9:1, 12). Since *logeia* can mean a collection of taxes as well as voluntary contributions collected at worship for charity, some have argued that Paul's choice of this unusual word implies a sort of required tax, similar to the poll tax paid annually by Jews. Yet all of Paul's other words for the collection (*charis*, grace, 1 Cor. 16:3; *koinōnia*, fellowship, 2 Cor. 8:4; *diakonia*, service, 2 Cor. 8:4; 9:1; *eulogia*, praise, blessing, 2 Cor. 9:5), as well as his explicit teaching on the subject (Rom. 15:25–28; 2 Cor. 8–9), argue against such a position.

Christians are to give, not a required amount, but as they have decided in their own hearts (2 Cor. 9:7) and as God has prospered them (1 Cor. 16:2). We must remember that we are slaves (Rom. 6:16; 1 Cor. 7:22; Eph. 6:6; 1 Pet. 2:16; → *doulos, 1528*) of Christ, that neither we nor our possessions are our own to use as we like (cf. 1 Cor. 6:20), that we are stewards responsible for our master's goods (1 Pet. 4:10), and that we will someday account for what we have done with these goods (Rom. 14:12). Our model is Christ and his generosity (2 Cor. 8:9). Hence, our giving must not be done with reluctance or compulsion (9:7), nor is it limited to an annual tithe. Rather it must be done cheerfully, voluntarily, systematically, and generously (1 Cor. 16:1–2; 2 Cor. 9:6–9).

In sum, the NT writers maintain an eloquent silence on tithing, emphasizing rather: (1) the need for spontaneous generosity (Lk. 21:4; Acts 11:28–30; 2 Cor. 8:1–3, 7; 9:5–10; Eph. 4:28; 1 Tim. 6:18; Heb. 13:16; Jas. 2:15–16) in response to God's limitless giving (2 Cor. 8:8–9; 9:15; 1 Jn. 3:17); (2) the need for individual decision (1 Cor. 16:2; 2 Cor. 9:7; cf. Acts 11:29) apart from external pressure (2 Cor. 8:8; 9:5, 7); (3) the blessedness of giving (Acts 20:35); and (4) the consequence of giving as being the glory of God or Christ (2 Cor. 8:19; 9:12–13).

2. *Tithing in the early church.* The writings of the early church fathers do not contain the common words for tithing, though giving continued to be an important part of early Christian worship. Irenaeus considered tithing to be a Jewish law not required of Christians, who should give without external constraint. Origen viewed tithes as something that Christians should far exceed in their giving. What guides and propels the believer is God's goodness and the inner compulsion of the Holy Spirit.

Presumably through voluntary giving, the early church was able to supports its pastors and elders (cf. 1 Cor. 9:3–11; 1 Tim. 5:17–18). Later, however, tithing was reintroduced as a means of supporting the church, based on such passages as Matt. 10:10; Lk. 10:7; 1 Cor. 9:3–4. Eventually, the power of civil law required what instruction failed to accomplish, so that by A.D. 785, people were taxed for the support of the church whether they liked it or not.

1282 (dekatoō, collect or pay a tithe, tenth), → *1281.*

1283 (dektos, acceptable, welcome, favorable), → *1312.*

1285 δένδρον	δένδρον *(dendron),* tree *(1285);*

φυτεία *(phyteia),* plant *(5884);* ἔμφυτος *(emphytos),* implanted *(1875);* βλαστάνω *(blastanō),* sprout, shoot forth *(1056);* ῥίζα *(rhiza),* root *(4844);* ῥιζόω *(rhizoō),* take root *(4845);* ἐκριζόω *(ekrizoō),* uproot *(1748);* κλάδος *(klados),* branch *(3080);* κλῆμα *(klēma),* branch *(3097);* φύλλον *(phyllon),* leaf *(5877);* ἐγκεντρίζω *(enkentrizō),* to graft *(1596).*

CL & OT 1. (a) In cl. Gk. many of these words, apart from their lit. use in agricultural contexts, carry a fig. and even a philosophical or cosmological sense. They are often associated with people or families: e.g., *phyteuō,* to plant, of a father begetting children; *blastanō,* of children being born.

(b) *rhiza* esp. has a wide range of meanings. It is used for the foundation of the earth and the foot of a mountain. It is also regularly used for that from which other things spring, i.e., the root of evil or good and the stock of a race or family. The soul is the head or origin. The earth is the origin of all things.

2. Because of the frequency with which they are combined, our discussion on the OT will consider this group of words as a whole. The main focus will be on the application of this word group to people and nations.

(a) *Miscellaneous uses.* (i) Both *dendron* and *xylon* (→ *3833*) are regularly used to denote idolatrous worship (e.g., Isa. 57:5; Jer. 2:27; Ezek. 6:13), esp. of Asherah poles (cf. Deut. 16:21; Isa. 27:9). *xylon* carries a much wider range of meanings in the LXX than in the NT and is often used as a synonym for *dendron.*

(ii) The planting words are often used fig. to denote promises of God's blessing, wrath, and providence. Through Ezek. comes the promise that all kinds of trees for food will grow; their leaves will not wither nor fail (47:12; cf. Ps. 1). In this context the vine and the fig tree (→ *sykē, 5190*) represent one's personal security (Mic. 4:4; cf. 1 Ki. 4:25; Zech. 3:10 = LXX 3:11). There is personal disaster when Yahweh strikes "their vines and fig trees" (Ps. 105:33; cf. Jer. 5:17; Hos. 2:12).

(iii) Both *dendron* and *xylon* are used in the expression "the tree of life." Apart from Gen. 2:9; 3:22, 24 *(xylon),* however, references are confined to Prov. The fruit of the righteous is the tree of life (11:30); a desire fulfilled is a tree of life (13:12); a gentle tongue is a tree of life (15:4).

(b) *Trees and plants as parables of people.* Several recurring themes are found in passages where trees and plants are used as parables of people. (i) Sometimes the tree or plant is a picture of the individual (e.g., a ruler [Jdg. 9:8]; a godly man [Ps. 1:3; Jer. 17:7–8]; Job [Job 19:10]). It can also represent the proud and arrogant man (Isa. 2:13, the cedar and oak). The tree can also represent mighty nations other than Israel: Assyria (Ezek. 31:3–4); Nebuchadnezzar and Babylon (Dan. 4:10–34); Moab (Jer. 48:32). All these trees are under God's control (Ezek. 17:24).

But most frequently Israel is pictured as a tree (usually the vine, though other trees are used as well). In Ezek. 17:5–10, Israel is a vine planted by the king of Babylon. But in the last analysis Israel is God's own planting: a vine (Ps. 80:8–9; Isa. 5:1; Ezek. 19:10); the shoot of God's own planting (Isa. 60:21; *phyteuma);* a tree (Isa. 65:22; *xylon);* a poplar, olive, cedar, and vine (Hos. 14:5–6).

(ii) Three further observations may be made here. In Hos. 14:8 the picture changes, for God himself is the tree (a cypress). Whatever fruit Israel produces comes ultimately from him. Second, nowhere in the OT is Israel pictured directly as a fig, though this is implicit, since God requires good figs as well as good grapes (Jer. 24:1–2; 8:13; cf. Mic. 7:1). Finally, chosen servants of God may be called to represent

Yahweh in the work of planting. Thus Jeremiah's prophetic ministry is described as one of uprooting *(ekrizoō)* and planting *(kataphyteuō).*

(iii) Israel is a people planted in good soil. The importance of the ground where a tree is planted is a frequent thought. Water and fertile soil (Ezek. 17:6, 8) are necessary (Job 14:7–9). Yahweh has provided the right soil (2 Sam. 7:10; Isa. 5:1–2; Ezek. 19:10). He himself is the soil. If the root is not planted in him, the fruit fails or is poisonous.

(iv) Where there is a root, there is hope of a new beginning after catastrophe. With this thought Job contrasts the life of a human being with that of a tree (Job 14:7–12). The notion of root and branch or root and fruit signifies totality, usually spoken in the context of totality of destruction (cf. Job 18:16; Amos 2:9). Nebuchadnezzar is reassured that after his coming downfall, the stump of the roots will be left in the earth (Dan. 4:15, 26).

(v) *rhiza* is occasionally related to the future hope in the OT. It is used in connection with the holy remnant. "A remnant . . . will take root below" (2 Ki. 19:30). The servant of the Lord is seen as a young plant and "like a root out of dry ground" (Isa. 53:2). *rhiza* also occurs in connection with the messianic hope. In Isa. 11:1 it refers to the house of Jesse itself; hope lies in the shoot or branch (cf. 60:21). In 11:10, however, it is the *rhiza* itself that springs from the house of Jesse and is identified with the Messiah. The thought of the Messiah as the root continued into Jud., although there was preference elsewhere to speak of the Messiah as the branch (Isa. 4:2; Jer. 23:5; 33:15; Zech. 3:8; 6:12). The OT never speaks of Abraham as the root, though the thought is implicit (Isa. 41:8; 51:2; cf. Ps. 105:6).

(vi) The vitality of the tree is evidenced by the growth of leaves, fruit, and spreading branches (Ps. 1:3; 80:10–11; Ezek. 31:5; Hos. 14:6).

(vii) The branches that shelter birds and animals are a metaphor for a mighty kingdom offering protection to its vassals (Ezek. 17:23; 31:6; Dan. 4:21–22).

(viii) The tree is assessed by its fruit, and its fate is often a picture of Yahweh's judgment. Despite assiduous care the vine, Israel, brought forth only wild grapes (Isa. 5:4). When Yahweh wanted to gather grapes, there were no grapes on the vine or figs on the fig tree (Jer. 8:13). The cedar and forest (Assyria) is cut down (Ezek. 31:12; Isa. 10:34). The vineyard (Israel) is made a waste (5:6). The oak (Israel) is felled (6:13). Apart from a few gleanings, the olive tree (Israel) is stripped (17:6). In the exile the vine (Judah) is plucked up and transplanted (Ezek. 19:12–13).

(ix) The vb. *enkentrizō* is used only once in the LXX with the meaning of to goad or spur on (Wis. 16:11). But the thought of grafting into the tree of Israel is found in the teaching of the rabbis (*b. Yebam.* 63a). In Philo, Jewish proselytes were regarded as grafted into the tree whose root was Abraham.

NT 1. *Miscellaneous uses.* (a) The NT frequently draws on illustrations from nature. Note the reference to the signs of the times in Matt. 16:1–3. The natural world also shares with humanity the results of God's blessing or wrath (Rev. 7:1, 3; 8:7; 9:4).

(b) The NT refers to the tree of life *(xylon,* → *3833)* in Rev. 2:7; 22:2, 14, 19 and to the cross as a tree *(xylon)* in Acts 5:30; 10:39; Gal. 3:13; 1 Pet. 2:24. But everywhere else the word for tree is *dendron.*

2. *Trees and plants as parables of people.* These words are esp. significant when applied to people, and the OT concepts referred to above provide a framework for understanding. (a) Individuals are pictured as trees, though the references are largely to Jewish opponents: the Pharisees (Matt. 3:10; 12:33; Lk. 6:43–44), false prophets (Matt. 7:17), the ungodly and scoffers (Jude 12). In Matt. 15:13 the Pharisees are called plants *(phyteia)* that God has not planted (cf. 13:24–25).

The old Israel is also pictured as a tree. Matt. 21:33–34; Mk. 12:1–2; Lk. 20:9–10 use the vineyard with God as the planter *(phyteuō;* → *sperma,* seed, *5065).* The fig tree *(sykē)* in Mk. 11:12–13 is probably Israel. But *dendron* also symbolizes the new community of

Israel. The kingdom is like a mustard seed becoming a tree (Matt. 13:32; Lk. 13:18–19). It has insignificant origins, but its branches now extend far and wide, offering protection for all who live in it (cf. Dan. 4:21–22; Ezek. 17:23; 31:6). The church is like the branches of a vine, which is Christ (Jn. 15:1–2).

There is a strong organic connection between the old and the new trees. In Mk. 12:1–2, God is still the planter of the vineyard, but he does not destroy it. He replaces one set of tenants by another. In Rom. 11:17–18 the olive tree stands for both the old and the new communities, and the root is the same. Jesus Christ is also the one who plants. He is the sower (cf. Matt. 13:37), and his followers must do the same (1 Cor. 3:6; 9:7). The gospel preached is "the word planted [*emphytos*] in you, which can save you" (Jas. 1:21). But whereas the apostles plant the word, the Son of Man plants people (Matt. 13:38).

(b) Good soil is necessary. Mk. 12:1–2 and Lk. 13:6–7 speak of the care given by God to ensure the right soil. The new Israel likewise is planted in good soil, rooted (*rhizoō*) in the love of Christ (Eph. 3:17; Col. 2:7). But in the teaching of Jesus human hearts also represent the soil. Good soil is the heart that hears, understands, holds fast, and yields fruit (Matt. 13:23; Mk. 4:20; Lk. 8:15; cf. Jas. 1:21).

(c) *rhiza* is used in a variety of contexts. (i) It is used as a metaphor for source or origin. The love of money is the root of all kinds of evil (1 Tim. 6:10). Heb. 12:15 warns against allowing a root of bitterness to spring up, preventing believers from attaining to the grace of God and causing trouble and defilement. (ii) The root guarantees the life of the tree (Rom. 11:16, 18); without roots a plant dies (Mk. 4:6, 17). (iii) Jesus Christ is described as the root three times (Rom. 15:12; Rev. 5:5; 22:16; Isa. 11:1, 10 is clearly in mind). In Rom. 11:17–18 Paul perhaps adopts the Jewish thought of Abraham as the root of Israel, but we must understand this passage in the light of Gal. 3:6–7, where sharing Abraham's faith determines our relationship to him, and to be in Christ is to be a child of Abraham (3:29).

(d) The fruit (*karpos*, → 2843) evidences the quality of the tree. Character may be gauged from conduct (Matt. 3:8; 7:16–17; Lk. 3:8; 6:43–44). In Matt. 12:33–34 the fruit is the Pharisees' words of condemnation of Jesus. In 21:33–46 the parable of the wicked tenants in the vineyard is accompanied by two other parables, the two sons (21:28–32) and the marriage feast (22:1–14). The fruit required is the acceptance of Jesus' authority and invitation. In Jn. 15:1–2 the fruit required from the branches (*klēma*) is love, obedience, and prayer. It cannot be produced without complete dependence on the vine, which is Jesus Christ himself.

(e) Fruitlessness leads to destruction. The trees are cut down (Matt. 7:19). The plants are uprooted (15:13; cf. Jude 12). In Rom. 11:19 branches are broken off. In the parable of the fig tree in Lk. 13:6–9, there is a temporary stay of execution to allow one final chance for the nation of Israel to bear the fruit of repentance (cf. 13:5). The cursing of the fig tree carries this scene one step further (→ *sykē*, 5190, for a discussion of this incident). The time of reckoning is drawing near, and Israel will be judged shortly on how the nation has responded to the mission and message of Jesus.

(f) In Rom. 11:16–17 Paul uses the picture of grafting (*enkentrizō*). The process referred to is sometimes said to be untrue to actual practice, where a wild olive (*agrielaios*) becomes a cultivated olive (*kallielaios*) by engrafting it on a cultivated olive. However, the *agrielaios* may have been an oleaster, and the practice of such grafting in order to rejuvenate an unproductive olive was not unknown in the ancient world. Gentiles who are now members of God's people are the *agrielaios*. Perhaps the tension between Paul's picture and approved horticultural practice is intended to underline the miraculous nature of this work of God, which is contrary to nature.

For Paul the grafted branches are not proselytes but Gentile Christians as a body. The thrust of the passage is to illustrate what God has done by incorporating the Gentiles into his covenant people through Christ. But this passage also contains a warning to the Gentiles, lest they fall into arrogance and fail to acknowledge humbly their

dependence. They are supported by the root (11:18), and they should not write off unbelieving Jews. After all, if the root is holy, so are the branches (11:16); moreover, God has power to graft in again the natural branches.

See also *sperma*, seed (*5065*).

1288	δεξιός

δεξιός (*dexios*), right, right hand, right side (*1288*).

CL & OT 1. In cl. Gk. *dexios* means right (opposite to left); the fem. form by itself often meant the right hand (with *cheir* understood) or the right side. The right hand symbolized power, success, and loyalty. Its subsidiary meanings are skillful (opposite of clumsy) and lucky. The fem. pl. could mean contract because of the handshake that sealed it.

In the OT God's right hand is often spoken of symbolically, especially in the Psalms. It provides support (18:35) and victory (118:15). It even expresses God's omnipresence (139:10). The place at a person's right hand is important as a place of honor (1 Ki. 2:19; Ps. 45:9). Ps. 110:1 is esp. significant in the light of its frequent use in the NT. The king of Israel, placed by Yahweh at his right hand, is honored as God's coregent, who by war and victory will overthrow the enemies of Israel, and thus of God.

NT 1. *dexios* occurs 54x in the NT, most of which are in line with the word in cl. Gk. For the right hand sealing an agreement see Gal. 2:9. The angel in the tomb was sitting on the right side (Mk. 16:5). In the final judgment those who are chosen are summoned to the right hand of the Son of Man (Matt. 25:31–34).

2. The main theological use of *dexios* occurs in connection with Ps. 110:1 (quoted or referred to indirectly in the NT 19x). This psalm was probably interpreted messianically already in pre-NT times. Jesus expounded it in Mk. 12:35–37 (par. Matt. 22:41–46; Lk. 20:41–44). For the Jews the Messiah was God's eschatological, political coregent, who would establish a visible kingdom of God on earth. Jesus rejected the political aspects of messiahship and was guarded in his attitude to the title "Son of David." But he did consider himself to be the fulfillment of this verse.

The context in Matt. and Mk. is esp. significant, for Jesus' question to the Pharisees about the Messiah immediately follows a lawyer's question to Jesus about which commandment is the greatest. Jesus replied by citing Deut. 6:4–5 and Lev. 19:18 (see Matt. 22:37–39). He went on to ask whose son the Messiah was. The Pharisees responded with the traditional, "The son of David." Jesus then replied, quoting Ps. 110:1: "How is it then that David, speaking by the Spirit, calls him 'Lord'?" (Matt. 22:41–43). That is, in addition to Yahweh, whom we are commanded to serve and worship with our whole being, there is another Lord who has the same title and sits at Yahweh's right hand. The Pharisees cannot answer Jesus' question, so he pronounces judgment on the teachers of the law and the Pharisees (Matt. 23), whose teaching and practice have caused them to miss the significance of God's Word.

At his trial (Mk. 14:62; par. Matt. 26:64; Lk. 22:69), although unarmed and ridiculed, Jesus solemnly declared that he was "the Son of Man," who would sit "at the right hand of the Mighty One" (cf. Dan. 7:13, combined with Ps. 110:1). With this unheard-of claim he demanded recognition that God exercises his power in radically different way from that of the world. God works under and indeed by means of the greatest human powerlessness. The one who will come in judgment at the right hand of God's throne (→ *thronos*, 2585) is the Lamb who was slain (Rev. 5:6).

3. The early church clearly saw Jesus as seated at God's right hand. This is pictured in various ways. Rom. 8:34 lays emphasis on the priestly function of Jesus at God's right hand as our heavenly intercessor. Col. 3:1 stresses Christ's position at God's right hand and our being hidden "with Christ in God" (3:3) as a motivation for living a

moral life on this earth. Eph. 1:20 and 1 Pet. 3:22 underline the essential meaning of Jesus' coregency.

For Heb. esp. Jesus' sitting at God's right hand is not the exercise of worldly power but the reign of the one who has offered himself as a sacrifice and has therefore been exalted above all angels (1:3, 13). This self-sacrifice, which led to his exaltation, is the unchangeable source of all the blessings of salvation toward which the tired Christian community must hasten (12:2). But Jesus' sitting at God's right hand does not yet mean the immediate defeat of all his enemies. This is reserved for the eschatological consummation (10:12; cf. 1 Cor. 15:25).

4. A polemical motive is added in Acts. The proclamation of Jesus sitting at God's right hand (2:34) and his exaltation to that position (2:33; 5:31) becomes a word of judgment on the Jews and their pride in the Mosaic law. The one they killed is the Messiah! Stephen saw Jesus *standing* at God's right hand (7:55–56). That he is standing rather than sitting indicates that he has the role of witness for Stephen's defense. Jesus appears before God as a witness (*martys*; → *martyria*, *3456*) on behalf of his own witnesses on earth.

See also *aristeros*, left, left hand (*754*); *cheir*, hand (*5931*); *epitithēmi*, to put on, lay on (*2202*).

1289 δέομαι

δέομαι (*deomai*), ask, request, beseech, beg (*1289*); δέησις (*deēsis*), a request, entreaty (*1255*); προσδέομαι (*prosdeomai*), need (in addition or further) (*4656*); ἱκετηρία (*hiketēria*), supplication (*2656*); ἔντευξις (*enteuxis*), petition, prayer (*1950*).

CL & OT 1. In cl. Gk. the basic meaning of the *deomai* word group is to lack, be in need of, from which developed the meaning to request, beseech.

2. (a) In the LXX *deomai* is used with the meaning to beseech, beg for favor (e.g., Jacob's request of the angel in Hos. 12:4; cf. Esther's request of the king in Est. 8:3 [S]). A suppliant can plead with God for mercy (1 Ki. 8:33–47; Ps. 30:8; 141:1). But *deomai* in the LXX can also mean to appease, placate. The person praying attempts to placate God's anger by his entreaties (Exod. 32:11; 1 Ki. 13:6; Zech. 8:21). Such a prayer can be accompanied by an offering (1 Sam. 13:12) or associated with confession of sin (Dan. 9:18).

(b) The noun *deēsis* in the LXX means supplication (e.g., 1 Ki. 8:28, 30; Ps. 6:9; 28:2, 6), cry of lamentation (e.g., 17:1; 61:1), or cry for help (e.g., 34:15; 39:12). It is used only for calling on God in prayer, often standing alongside *proseuchē*, prayer (e.g., 1 Ki. 8:38, 45; Ps. 6:9; → *proseuchomai*, pray, *4667*).

NT 1. In the NT *deomai* occurs 22x, always with the meaning to ask, beseech, beg. (a) It is used in a general sense as a courtesy formula, without any particular obj. (cf. the English phrase "I beg you"; e.g., Acts 8:34; 21:39; 26:3).

(b) In some passages *deomai* is used in its full sense of making earnest entreaty, even imploring. There is a warmth, an attractiveness, about it (e.g., 2 Cor. 5:20; 8:4; 10:2; Gal. 4:12).

(c) In all other cases *deomai* has the religious sense of beseeching Jesus or God. The requests made are specific, arising out of real need and expecting definite help of an external or a spiritual nature (e.g., Lk. 5:12; 10:2). In some passages (e.g., 9:38), the reason for the request is given. In 1 Thess. 3:10 one sees how even an external request may be directed to a spiritual end.

Prayer should be made to God for forgiveness (Acts 8:22), to bring in God's harvest (Lk.10:2), and for ability to stand on the last day (21:36). In some passages, *deomai* is used absolutely, i.e., without God specifically mentioned as direct obj. In such cases, of course, the direct obj. has to be supplied.

(d) If the request is made not in one's own interest but on behalf of someone else, then *deomai* means to intercede (e.g., Acts 8:24; Rom. 1:10). Intercession is often the visible and practical expression

of the heartfelt affection and fellowship that exist among Christians (e.g., 2 Cor. 9:14; Eph. 6:18; Phil. 1:4; 2 Tim. 1:3). Paul highly valued such intercession and expected great things from it (e.g., 2 Cor. 1:11; Phil. 1:19).

In Jas. 5:16, the same point is sharpened by the phrase "the prayer of a righteous man" (i.e., of a believer whose life bears out his or her faith) and the adj. qualifying *deēsis* ("effective"). This comes about when the prayer involves dynamic fellowship and genuine conversation with God—which in itself is a gift from God. This is exemplified by Elijah (5:17; cf. 1 Ki. 17:1; 18:1). Similarly, 1 Pet. 3:12 (quoting Ps. 34:16) says that the prayer of the "righteous" is heard by God.

(e) Whenever the request is addressed to God, *deomai* naturally assumes the meaning of to pray and can often be so translated (similarly *deēsis*, prayer). This is esp. the case when no content is stated (e.g., Acts 10:2; Heb. 5:7, where the noun stands alongside *hiketēria*, entreaty, petition). Thus, as in the OT, *deomai* and *deēsis* often occur with *proseuchē* or other synonyms (e.g., Rom. 1:10; Eph. 6:18; Phil. 4:6 [with *aitēma*]; 1 Tim. 2:1 [with *enteuxis*]). Prayer is an important evidence of true Christian faith (2:1). It is the mark of a Christian (5:5; cf. Acts 9:11). Even Jesus prayed (Heb. 5:7; cf. Lk. 22:44) and made intercession (22:32).

2. *prosdeomai* occurs only in Acts 17:25, meaning to be in need of. In this word the original sense of *deomai* reappears, and Lk. uses it here to underscore the self-sufficiency and complete independence of God, who is highly exalted above all.

See also *aiteō*, ask, ask for, demand (*160*); *gonypeteō*, fall on one's knees, kneel down before (*1206*); *proseuchomai*, to pray, entreat (*4667*); *proskyneō*, worship, do obeisance to, prostrate oneself, do reverence to (*4686*); *erōtaō*, ask, ask a question, request (*2263*); *krouō*, knock (*3218*); *entynchanō*, meet, turn to, approach, petition, pray, intercede (*1961*).

1296 (derō, beat), → *3463.*

1297 (desmeuō, bind [with bonds]), → *1300.*

1299 (desmē, bundle), → *1300.*

1300 δέσμιος

δέσμιος (*desmios*), prisoner (*1300*); δεσμεύω (*desmeuō*), bind (with bonds) (*1297*); δέσμη (*desmē*), bundle (*1299*); δεσμός (*desmos*), bond, tether, imprisonment (*1301*); δεσμωτήριον (*desmōtērion*), prison (*1303*); δεσμώτης (*desmōtēs*), prisoner (*1304*); δεσμοφύλαξ (*desmophylax*), prison warden (*1302*); σύνδεσμος (*syndesmos*), that which binds together, bond, fetter (*5278*).

CL & OT 1. In cl. Gk. the root *desm-* conveys the basic meaning of bind. *desmeuō* means to bind together, chain up. A *desmē* is a bundle tied together. *desmios* means one who is in chains or in prison. *desmos* at first meant chain, and later imprisonment, custody. *desmōtērion* is a prison, *desmōtēs* a prisoner, and *desmophylax* a prison warden. *syndesmos* can mean either a chain that holds one or a binding that holds things together. All these words are used in a physical sense.

2. The lit. sense of words in this group dominates in the LXX: Sheafs are bound together (Gen. 37:7, *desmeuō*); a donkey is tied to a vine (49:11, *desmeuō*); Joseph is thrown into prison by Potiphar (39:22, *desmōtērion*); Samson is bound with cords (Jdg. 15:13–14, *desmos*). Because many in OT times suffered from the humiliation inflicted by chains and bondage, liberation from these was part of the salvation that awaited them: e.g., "Say to the captives, 'Come out,' and to those in darkness, 'Be free!'" (Isa. 49:9; cf. 42:7). The hymn of praise sung by those who have been freed recalls Israel's servitude in Egypt: "He brought them out of darkness and the deepest gloom, and broke away their chains" (Ps. 107:14; cf. 116:16 = LXX 115:7).

3. As with *zygos*, yoke (*2433*), *desmos* can refer to our true relationship with God, to the bond and covenant between him and us. Hosea speaks of the cords of divine love with which Yahweh seeks to

bind his people to himself (Hos. 11:4), while Jeremiah complains of the godless nation that had torn off Yahweh's cords (Jer. 2:20; 5:5).

NT In the NT *desmos* occurs 18x and *desmios* 16x, chiefly in the Synoptic Gospels and in Paul's writings. Once again the lit. sense is more conspicuous than the spiritualized. The other words in this group occur infrequently, most often in a lit. sense (cf. Matt. 11:2; 13:30; Lk. 8:29; Acts 5:21, 23; 16:23, 26 27, 36; 22:4) in the context of prison, prisoners, and jailers.

1.The Gerasene demoniac tore his chains apart (Lk. 8:29). Pilate customarily released a prisoner at the festivals (Matt. 27:15–16). An earthquake broke the shackles of the prisoners in the jail at Philippi (Acts 16:25–27). Above all, *desmos* is mentioned in connection with Paul's path of suffering. In his farewell address to the Ephesian elders he speaks of the "prison and hardship" that await him in Jerusalem (20:23). Luke describes Paul's arrest in detail (21:18–36) and calls him *ho desmios Paulos*, "Paul, the prisoner" (23:18; cf. 25:14, 27; 28:17). But Luke also stresses that Paul was unlawfully imprisoned (23:29; 26:31), showing the apostle as a prototype of the suffering of the innocent martyr.

2. In his prison letters Paul sometimes calls himself "a prisoner of Christ Jesus" (Phlm. 1, 9; cf. Eph. 3:1; 4:1). In Phil. he connects his imprisonment with Christ and his gospel (Phil. 1:7, 13–14, 17), noting that it has helped to further the spread of the gospel. On the one hand, people in the prison and elsewhere know that he is wearing his chains for Christ's sake; on the other hand, because he is in prison, the rest of the believers venture to proclaim the gospel of Christ more fearlessly (1:12–18).

3. Occasionally *desmos* occurs in a fig. sense. The dumbness (Mk. 7:35) or paralysis (Lk. 13:16) of a person can be called a fetter with which he or she is bound. This bondage is not only physical; rather, the NT often saw its underlying cause in demonic powers. Eph. 4:3 speaks of peace and Col. 3:14 of love as a *syndesmos*, i.e., a divine bond that binds believers together (cf. Hos. 11:4) and sets them free. Ultimately, however, the Head (Christ) holds his church together (Col. 2:19). People can also be bound (*desmeuō*) by legalistic demands (Matt. 23:4) or be held captive to sin (*syndesmos*, Acts 8:23).

See also *aichmalōtos*, captive, prisoner of war (*171*); *doulos*, slave (*1528*); *libertinos*, freedman (*3339*).

1301 (*desmos*, bond, tether, imprisonment), → *1300*.

1302 (*desmophylax*, prison warden), → *1300*.

1303 (*desmōtērion*, prison), → *1300*.

1304 (*desmōtēs*, prisoner), → *1300*.

1305	δεσπότης

δεσπότης (*despotēs*), lord, master (of a house), owner (*1305*); οἰκοδεσπότης (*oikodespotēs*), the master of a house (*3867*); οἰκοδεσποτέω (*oikodespoteō*), be master of a house, rule one's household (*3866*).

CL & OT 1. In cl. Gk. *despotēs* means (a) master of a house (who had absolute authority over his household); (b) master as opposed to slave; (c) owner; (d) ruler over subject peoples (transferred to the field of politics). *despotēs* often involves harshness and caprice, while *kyrios* (*3261*) emphasizes more strongly the idea of the legality with which someone acts. *oikodespotēs*, master of a house, became an astrological term in cl. Gk.; the planets were *oikodespotai* in particular signs of the Zodiac; in this context *oikodespotēsis* meant the predominance of a planet.

2. *despotēs* occurs only about 60x in the LXX, far less than *kyrios*. It expresses the arbitrary, unlimited exercise of power without any real conditions, This was foreign to Israel's concept of God, who experienced his lordship in his gracious, saving actions in history. Where *despotēs* is used (esp. in later writings), it emphasizes God's omnipotence (cf. Isa. 1:24; 3:1; Jer. 4:10; 15:11; Jon. 4:3; Dan. 9:8, 15–19;

Wis. 6:7; Sir. 23:1; 36:1 = LXX 33:1). *oikodespotēs* does not occur in the LXX.

NT 1. In the NT *despotēs* occurs 10x. (a) God is addressed in prayer 3x as *despotēs* (Lk. 2:29; Acts 4:24; Rev. 6:10 [possibly alluding to Zech. 1:12]).

(b) *despotēs* occurs 2x with reference to Christ: 2 Pet. 2:1 (Christ the Master bought us—the background is the metaphor of the redemption of slaves) and Jude 4. In both passages the term is used in opposition to heretical ideas. The false teachers deny that Jesus is *despotēs*; the canonical authors emphasize here not Jesus' divine nature but his right to command and exercise influence and power.

(c) *despotēs* as earthly lords in the sense of owners occurs in 1 Tim. 6:1–2; Tit. 2:9 (in contrast to slaves; cf. Eph. 6:5; Col. 3:22); 1 Pet. 2:18 (in contrast to servants). Slaves are exhorted to be obedient to their masters in order that the faith may not be brought into disrepute by their disobedience. The word has a metaphorical sense in 2 Tim. 2:21 as master of the house. Those who purify themselves from false teaching are instruments for noble use, consecrated and useful to the *despotēs*; here Christ is to be understood as the *despotēs*.

2. *oikodespotēs* occurs 12x in the NT, esp. in Matt. (13:27, 52; 20:1, 11; 21:33; 24:43; cf. Lk. 14:21; 22:11), where it means the owner of a house or land, or a master who rules over his household. In Mk. 14:14 the owner of the house where Jesus intends to observe the Passover is called *oikodespotēs*. In Matt. 24:43, if the *oikodespotēs* had known when the thief was coming, he would have been watching. In the parable of Lk. 13:25–30 Jesus is the *oikodespotēs*, who will shut the door on those who come late; this term depicts him as the Lord of the kingdom.

In the context of Matt. 10:25, Jesus' opponents have apparently abused him and called him Beelzebub (cf. 9:34). How much more will the members of his household (i.e., his disciples and followers) be exposed to abuse? Here *oikodespotēs* is used in parallel with "teacher" and "master" (10:24–25) and characterizes the relationship between Jesus and the disciples as one of imitation of suffering.

3. *oikodespoteō* occurs only in 1 Tim. 5:14, where Paul gives directions to younger women to marry and "manage their homes."

See also *kyrios*, lord, master, owner, Lord (*3261*).

1312	δέχομαι

δέχομαι (*dechomai*), take, receive, accept (*1312*); δεκτός (*dektos*), acceptable, welcome, agreeable, favorable (*1283*); ἀποδέχομαι (*apodechomai*), admit (*622*); ἀποδοχή (*apodochē*), acceptance, approval (*628*); ἀπόδεκτος (*apodektos*), acceptable, pleasing (*621*); εὐπρόσδεκτος (*euprosdektos*), acceptable, pleasant, welcome (*2347*); δοχή (*dochē*), reception, banquet (*1531*); εἰσδέχομαι (*eisdechomai*), take in, receive, welcome (*1654*).

CL & OT 1. (a) In cl. Gk. the basic meaning of *dechomai* is to accept or receive. Letters, presents, and offerings are the principal objects. It can also be used in the sense of to receive words, i.e., to hear, understand; also to accept persons, i.e., offer hospitality. Human beings are generally the subject, who can accept things even to the point of enduring blows of fate. Rarely is the subj. a godhead who receives sacrifices and prayers. The corresponding noun *dochē* means primarily a receptacle; fig., reception of people, a meal for guests. *dektos* or *dekteos* indicates that which one can accept; also agreeable, welcome, favorable.

(b) *apodechomai* strengthens the positive significance of the simple vb. in the sense of welcoming, approving, agreeing, valuing. The common Hel. noun *apodochē* correspondingly means acceptance, approbation, approval. The verbal adj. *apodektos* has a similar meaning to *dektos*, i.e., acceptable, agreeable, pleasing. As with *ek-* or *apekdechomai*, it has the meaning of to expect or wait for (→ *apokaradokia*, eager expectation, *638*).

2. (a) In the LXX, apart from everyday usage (e.g., Gen. 33:10, accept gifts), *dechomai* denotes primarily the readiness to receive and

accept the divine word (e.g., Deut. 33:3; Jer. 9:20) and action (Zeph. 3:7). In Jer. and Zeph. it occurs in the negative declarations of judicial prosecution: Israel has not accepted Yahweh's correction (Jer. 2:30; 5:3; 7:28; Zeph. 3:2) and will therefore have to endure the divine judgment (Jer. 25:28 = LXX 32:28; cf. Hos. 4:11). *dechomai* thus obtains the further meaning of involuntary and necessary submission to disaster.

(b) *eisdechomai*, on the other hand, is found largely in prophetic announcements of salvation. Yahweh will regather his scattered people and receive them again into fellowship with him (Jer. 23:3; Ezek. 20:34; Hos. 8:10; Mic. 4:6; Zeph. 3:19–20).

(c) Occasionally, *dechomai* and *dektos* occur in priestly passages, in the so-called declaratory formula: "It is not acceptable." By this means priests made known the acceptance or rejection of an offering for Yahweh (Lev. 22:19–25). The decision about a gift's acceptance or rejection or repudiation in the mouth of the priest embraces a divine judgment as to whether the person bringing the offering is acceptable to Yahweh.

(d) In wisdom lit. *dechomai* characterizes the intellectually open and receptive life of the pious: The wise accept the words of wisdom (Prov. 4:10), heed commands (10:8), and receive insight (21:11). The word *dektos* gains a noncultic and ethical stamp in wisdom literature: "To do good is the beginning of the right way; that is more acceptable to God than to present sacrifices" (16:5 LXX; cf. Sir. 2:5; 3:17).

NT 1. In the NT the *dechomai* word group is found mainly in the Synoptic Gospels and in Paul, who also uses the compounds frequently. As in the ancient world and esp. in Jud., so in the NT hospitality plays a large role. Because of their wandering existence, Jesus, Paul, and the other apostles were dependent on the hospitality of others. Lk. mentions from time to time the friendly reception Jesus and Paul had among the people and in the congregations (Lk. 8:40; Acts 18:27; 21:17, *apodechomai*), just as Jesus and Paul willingly accepted those who approached them (Lk. 9:11; Acts 28:30). Paul thanks his congregations for their hospitality (Gal. 4:14; 2 Cor. 7:15) and exhorts them to be ready to accept others as well (Col. 4:10).

2. (a) Acceptance of disciples and apostles is not, however, simply a matter of an unwritten humanitarian law. On the contrary, Jesus' messenger represents his message and person: "He who receives you receives me, and he who receives me receives the one who sent me" (Matt. 10:40; cf. Lk. 9:48; 10:16; Jn. 13:20). The apostles' continuation of Jesus' mission means that the hospitality they are offered represents acceptance of Jesus and thus of God.

But Christ not only meets people through his messengers, he also confronts his church incognito in every unfortunate individual in need of help: "Whoever welcomes one of these little children in my name welcomes me" (Mk. 9:37; cf. Matt. 18:5; Lk. 9:48). God is being accepted or rejected in the sphere of everyday life by how we treat children and others.

(b) Thus, *dektos*, *apodektos*, and *euprosdektos* have lost their cultic content, as was already the case in wisdom lit. The offering pleasing to God now is the sacrifice of the individual life for daily service in the world (Rom. 15:16; Phil. 4:18; cf. Rom. 12:1). *apodektos* is used in 1 Tim. 2:3 and 5:4 to express what is acceptable to God: intercession for rulers, who also come within the scope of God's salvation, and the duty of children to parents. *dektos* occurs in Lk. 4:19 (cf. Isa. 61:2); Lk. 4:24; Acts 10:35; 2 Cor. 6:2 (cf. Isa. 49:8); and Phil. 4:18. *euprosdektos* is found at Rom. 15:16, 31; 2 Cor. 6:2; 8:12; 1 Pet. 2:5.

3. In the early Christian communities the phrase "to receive [*dechomai*] the word" became a technical term for the believing acceptance of the gospel (Lk. 8:13; Acts 8:14; 11:1; 17:11; 1 Thess. 1:6; 2:13); objects of this vb. can also be the kingdom of God (Mk. 10:15), grace (2 Cor. 6:1), and love of the truth (2 Thess. 2:10). Faith is the affirmative acceptance of God's rule, as a child accepts a gift (Mk. 10:15; cf. Matt. 18:3).

4. The Hel. word *apodochē* occurs only in a kerygmatic formula: "Here is a trustworthy saying that deserves full acceptance: Christ

Jesus came into the world to save sinners" (1 Tim. 1:15; cf. also 4:9). There remains the application of Isa. 61:2 in Lk. 4:19, that with the coming of Jesus the acceptable (*dektos*) time of salvation has begun (cf. 2 Cor. 6:2).

See also *lambanō*, take, receive (*3284*).

1313 δέω	δέω (*deō*) bind, tie (*1313*).

OT *deō* is used in the LXX mainly for Heb. *ʾāsar*, but only in a literal sense, never with the fig. sense of binding with an oath. It is mainly used for tying up humans (cf. Samson in Jdg. 15–16) or animals (2 Ki. 7:10 A). Love can be said metaphorically to bind (Song 7:5).

NT In the NT, *deō* is often used for tying up or securing an animal (Mk. 11:2) or a person (Matt. 14:3; Acts 9:2). In Col. 4:3 Paul's being bound is an expression of the mystery of Christ, a sign that even in the greatest affliction God's power is at work (cf. 2 Tim. 2:9).

deō is used symbolically in Acts 20:22, where Paul sees his plans and travels bound by the Spirit of God. This binding controls his actions like a command that he cannot avoid. The verb is also symbolic in Rom. 7:2 and 1 Cor. 7:27, 39, where it is used for the binding of husband and wife to each other.

The binding in Matt. 16:19 and 18:18 denotes both teaching authority (to determine what is forbidden) and disciplinary power (to place under a ban)—"binding and loosing" were technical terms in rab. Jud. These passages in Matt. are concerned with the judicial function exercised by Peter and the disciples. Wherever the message entrusted to them is rejected, it inevitably binds people to their unforgiven guilt to await the coming judgment (cf. Jn. 12:47–48). The authority given to the disciples is, therefore, fundamentally different from the authority claimed by rab. casuistry. Christian proclaimers do not know in the last analysis who have been loosed or bound by their message, for this rests alone with the divine Judge (for more on Matt. 16:18–19, → *kleis*, key, *3090*).

In Matt. 13:30, the harvest is a picture of the judgment, and the binding of the weeds symbolizes condemnation (cf. also 22:13–14). Binding should not be confused with mistaken efforts to create a pure messianic community here and now by separating out sinners. The best illustration of Matt. 16:19 and 18:18 is probably 10:12–15, where people who refuse to listen to God's saving message are handed over to him for judgment.

1316 (dēlos, clear, plain, evident), → *1317*.

1317 δηλόω	δηλόω (*dēloō*), reveal, make clear, explain, give information, notify (*1317*); δῆλος (*dēlos*), clear, plain, evident (*1316*).

CL & OT 1. *dēloō* means to announce, make manifest, explain, set forth. It takes on the meaning of to interpret, clarify in Stoic philosophy. Later Hel. writers use it for the publication of divine secrets, such as those declared by an angel. It is not possible to differentiate precisely between *dēloō* and the other Gk. synonyms for this concept (see end of this entry).

2. *dēloō* has a secular sense in Jos. 4:7; Tob. 10:8. But primarily in the LXX it designates divine revelation. God makes known his name (Exod. 6:3), his purposes (33:12), his ways (1 Ki. 8:36; 2 Chr. 6:27), his mysteries (Dan. 2:28–30), and his covenant (Ps. 25:14). *dēloō* can also denote the revelation of God's power (Jer. 16:21) and glory (2 Macc. 2:8). The word is found frequently in Dan. 2 (14x out of 39x in LXX), occasionally in the sense of expounding, interpreting (2:5–47; 7:16).

NT *dēloō* occurs 7x in the NT, *dēlos* 3x. The vb. bears the everyday sense of making known in 1 Cor. 1:11 and Col. 1:8. *dēlos* in Matt. 26:73; 1 Cor. 15:27; Gal. 3:11 is also nontheological. In 1 Pet. 1:11 *dēloō* leads into the sphere of faith, where Peter states that the prophets tried to find out the time and circumstances concerning the Messiah, to which the Spirit at work in them "was pointing." According to 2 Pet. 1:14, the Lord "made clear" to Peter the nearness of his end.

In Heb. 9:8, the Holy Spirit revealed that the way into the sanctuary did not become visible as long as the first tent (the Jewish tabernacle) was standing, and that only with Christ, the high priest of the good things to come (8:11), did the fulfillment appear. Heb. 12:27 offers a spiritual interpretation of Hag. 2:6. The future shaking of created things spoken of here is an allusion to the everlasting kingdom, which is not transitory. In 1 Cor. 3:13 Paul deals with the final revelation of the day of judgment, which will reveal the true character and value of human works "by fire." *dēloō* here expresses not the imparting of knowledge, but God's final active revelation.

See also *apokalyptō*, uncover, disclose, reveal (*636*); *epiphaneia*, appearance, revelation (*2211*); *chrēmatizō*, impart a revelation, injunction, or warning (*5976*).

| 1321 | δημιουργός | δημιουργός (*dēmiourgos*), maker (*1321*). |

CL & OT *dēmiourgos* in cl. Gk. denoted magistrates and workmen, especially skilled handworkers. Beginning with Plato, the word also referred to the activity of God in creating the universe. The word group is scarcely used in the LXX (see Wis. 15:13; 2 Macc. 4:1; 10:2). Josephus and Philo both apply the word to God as the one who not only created but also fashioned the universe.

NT The virtual absence of *dēmiourgos* from the NT is not without significance. In Heb. 11:10 it is used of God as the *technitēs* and *dēmiourgos* of the heavenly city. The writer here uses a fine, rhetorical phrase to stress the excellence and abiding quality of the heavenly city as one built on firm foundations by God himself. In later Christian writing the word became more common; it also played a considerable role in Gnosticism, where the "demiurge" was used to explain the origin of the evil, material universe.

See also *katabolē*, foundation, beginning (*2856*); *ktisis*, creation (*3232*).

| 1322 | δῆμος | δῆμος (*dēmos*), people, populace, crowd, popular assembly |

(*1322*); ἐκδημέω (*ekdēmeō*), leave one's country, emigrate, take a long journey (*1685*); ἐνδημέω (*endēmeō*), be at home(*1897*); ἀποδημέω (*apodēmeō*), go on a journey, be away, be absent (*623*); δημόσιος (*dēmosios*), public (*1323*).

CL & OT 1. (a) In cl. Gk. *dēmos* means chiefly the people, popular assembly, population. The word often refers to the people in contrast to the king, the nobility, or the powerbrokers and landowners. In this kind of context *dēmos* could have a derogatory sense, though it could also have a feeling of pride insofar as it referred to free, self-governing citizens. The term diminished in importance in view of the imperialism and expansionism of the Hel. and Roman empires.

(b) The vb. *endēmeō* means to be in the homeland, at home, while the vb. *ekdēmeō* means to go abroad, go out of the country, travel.

2. In the LXX the word *dēmos* is found about 110x, chiefly to translate *mišpāḥâ*, family, clan, i.e., a smaller grouping within the whole people or tribe. In 1 and 2 Macc. there are a number of references to the *dēmos* of the Jews (e.g., 1 Macc. 8:29; 14:20–25; 2 Macc. 11:34).

NT 1. In the NT *dēmos* appears 4x, all in Acts. In 12:22 it refers to the pagan people who were present at the audience that Agrippa I gave to the representatives of Tyre and Sidon, and who flattered him in a blasphemous fashion. In 17:5 it is uncertain whether the group before which the apostles were brought in Thessalonica is the popular assembly or simply the throng of people who were present. In 19:30, 33, it

is clearly a crowd that is meant, not a legal assembly (cf. 19:39; note esp. 19:33, where *dēmos* is parallel with *ochlos*, → *4063*).

2. *ekdēmeō* and *endēmeō* are found in the NT only in 2 Cor. 5:6–9, where Paul plays with these words (3x each). The apostle longs for the fulfillment of Christ's work and his Parousia (4:18; 5:10), when he will receive a new body (1 Cor. 15:43–44, 48–53). In 2 Cor. 5 he contrasts two realms of existence: the this-worldly, present, earthly life, and the otherworldly, future, heavenly life. In the present time he, like everyone, has an earthly body: "We are at home in the body" (5:6). That means, however, that he is not living with Christ, i.e., in the heavenly sphere of existence; he is thus "away from the Lord" (5:6); that is, he is not among the true *dēmos* to which he belongs.

The clear and visible evidence of this is the earthly body in which Paul lives. Only in faith, which is a gift of God, a guarantee (2 Cor. 5:5) of the world to come, can the gap between this world and that other world—i.e., the present and the future—be bridged, and even then not visibly (5:7). For this reason faith produces the desire and longing to be with Christ and to enjoy full fellowship with him. This will happen only when one "is away from the body" and goes to be "at home with the Lord" (5:8). The present is thus marked by the combination of "already" and "not yet": We as Christians are not yet perfect or with Christ, but we live by faith with the certain hope that the consummation will come, at which time we will be united with Christ. Until then, however, whether "we are at home in the body or away from it" and with the Lord, we should strive to please Christ (5:9).

3. *apodēmeō*, to go out of the country, to travel, is found 6x in the NT, all in Synoptic parables. Matt. 21:33 (Mk. 12:1; Lk. 20:9) tells of a householder who rented out his vineyard to tenants and went out of the country. In the parable of the talents the man who is about to go out of the country gives his property to his servants to manage (Matt. 25:14) and "[goes] on his journey" (25:15). In these two parables *apodēmeō* represents God's absence and the fact that he has given his people an autonomy and responsibility of which they will have to give account.

In the parable of the lost son the younger son took his share of the inheritance and "set off [*apodēmeō*] for a distant country" (Lk. 15:13). The vb. here represents the action of going away from God. In the context of 15:1, it characterizes the kind of life led by the "tax collectors and 'sinners,'" who "were all gathering around to hear [Christ]."

4. *dēmosios* means public, i.e., belonging to the state (Acts 5:18). In the dat. form it is used as an adv., publicly (16:37; 18:28; 20:20).

See also *ethnos*, nation, people, pagans, Gentiles (*1620*); *laos*, people (*3295*); *ochlos*, (throng of) people, crowd, mob (*4063*); *polis*, city, city-state (*4484*).

1323 (*dēmosios*, public), → *1322*.

1324 (*dēnarion*, denarius, a day's wage), → *5088*.

| 1328 | διά | διά (*dia*), through (with gen.), on account of (with acc.) (*1328*). |

CL In cl. Gk. this prep. generally means passing through and out from, when followed by a word in the gen. case, and on account of, for the sake of, when followed by a word in the acc.

NT In Hel. Gk. and the NT *dia* acquires a variety of nuances it usually did not have in cl. Gk.

1. *Means or instrument.* From the local sense of *dia* developed the instrumental sense, which marks that *through* which an action passes before its accomplishment. In the phrase "faith expressing itself through [*dia*] love" (Gal. 5:6), love is the means by which faith becomes visibly operative or effective. Thus, Paul's view of the interrelationship of faith and good deeds is similar to that of James (Jas. 2:14–26). Likewise, at his judgment seat Christ will recompense us for both good and bad actions that have been "done while in [*dia*; lit.,

through the instrument of] the body" (2 Cor. 5:10). In 5:18, Paul emphasizes that God is the reconciler and Christ the divinely appointed means (using *dia*) of reconciliation (cf. Rom. 5:11; Col. 1:20). In 1 Cor. 8:6 Christ is portrayed as the mediator of creation ("through [*dia*] whom all things came and through [*dia*] whom we live").

2. Attendant circumstances. dia can also express the circumstances that accompany an action or state; in this function the prep. overlaps with *en* (→ *1877*). Note the interchange of these two in Rom. 4:11, where the NIV translates "while he was still uncircumcised" for (lit.) "in [*en*] uncircumcision" and "have not been circumcised" for (lit.) "through [*dia*] uncircumcision." One cannot, therefore, insist from the prep. *dia* that Timothy received his gift through Paul's hand; it can equally be understood that he received his gift from God at the same time that Paul (and possibly others) laid hands on Timothy (2 Tim. 1:6; cf. also 1 Tim. 4:14). "By [*dia*] faith" in 2 Cor. 5:7 also probably belongs to this category of accompanying circumstances.

3. Cause or ground. dia can also mean "on account of," "because of." In some cases *dia* as means and *dia* as cause are juxtaposed. For example, Heb. 2:10 makes a reference to "God, for [*dia* followed by an acc.; because of] whom and through [*dia* followed by a gen.; by means of] whom everything exists" (cf. a similar juxtaposition in 1 Cor. 11:9).

4. Purpose. There is no unanimity among NT scholars as to whether *dia* can have a sense of purpose, but in several places it approaches this sense. For example, Jesus says in Mk. 2:27 that "the Sabbath was made for [*dia*] man," i.e., for the purpose of serving human needs not met during the rest of the week (cf. also *dia* in Matt. 14:2; Jn. 11:42; 12:30; Rom. 11:28).

The alleged instances most often cited are Rom. 3:25; 4:25, although it is questionable to use a meaning of purpose here since it is so infrequent, if used at all. In Rom. 3:25, Paul seems to be observing that the outcome of God's provision of Christ as a propitiatory sacrifice was the demonstration of his own righteousness, a righteousness that needed vindication because in his patience God had not exacted the full and proper penalty for sins committed previously. That is, the phrase *dia tēn paresin* probably means "on account of his passing over," not "with a view to his forgiving."

The matter is more complex in Rom. 4:25 ("he was delivered over to death for [*dia*] our sins and was raised to life for [*dia*] our justification"). The parallelism here would suggest that *dia* be taken in the same sense in each instance, yet a causal sense is difficult in 4:25b (i.e., "and was raised to life *because of* our justification"). Three solutions may be mentioned (in ascending order of probability). (i) *dia* denotes purpose in both clauses: "in order to deal with" (4:25a; cf. 1 Cor. 15:3); "in order to effectuate" (Rom. 4:25b). (ii) *dia* is causal in 4:25a ("because of"; cf. the LXX of Isa. 53:12,) but denotes purpose in 4:25b ("in order to achieve"). (iii) *dia* is causal in both clauses: "because of [the need to atone for] our sins" (4:25a); "because of [the need to achieve] our justification" (4:25b).

1330 (diaballō, accuse, bring charges with hostile intent), → *1333.*

1333	διάβολος

διάβολος (*diabolos*), adj., slanderous; noun, slanderer, the devil (*1333*); διαβάλλω (*diaballō*), accuse, bring charges with hostile intent (*1330*); Βεελζεβούλ (*Beelzeboul*), Beelzebul, Beelzebub (*1015*); Βελιάρ (*Beliar*), Beliar, Belial (*1016*); Σατανᾶς (*Satanas*), the Adversary, Satan (*4928*).

CL & OT 1. *diaballō* means to throw over or across, divide, set at variance, accuse, bring charges, slander, deceive. From the vb. is derived the noun *diabolos*, slanderer, accuser, devil. It is hardly found outside the NT and LXX.

2. In the LXX *diabolos* occurs 22x (13x in Job 1–2). Except for Est. 7:4 and 8:1, it is always a translation of Heb. *śāṭān*, which is also transcribed 3x in the LXX simply as *satan* (1 Ki. 11:14, 23a, 25b).

śāṭān, however, is also translated by other Gk. words. In the OT *śāṭān* refers to an adversary or wicked opponent; it rarely denotes the devil in the later sense of the word (i.e., an evil spiritual being opposing God). For example, in 1 Sam. 29:4 it is used of a potential saboteur in the ranks; in 1 Ki. 11:23, 25 it denotes the leader of a faction and later Syrian king Rezon (but see also Ps. 109:6, where the LXX gives *diabolos*). *śāṭān* is also used of the angel who stood in Balaam's way (Num. 22:22, 32).

It is in the prologue to Job that Satan first appears as a heavenly being who accuses the righteous to God's face (the public prosecutor in heaven!). He similarly appears in Zech. 3:1–2. The word is first used as a personal name in 1 Chr. 21:1, where Satan entices David to undertake the census of the people.

3. (a) In intertestamental Jud. the devil is often identified with the "evil inclination" and with the "angel of death." He now has a clearly evil character. As in the OT, he is the accuser of human beings before God. The fall of the angels plays a large role (linked with Gen. 6:1–6; → *1 Enoch* 86:1–88:3; *Jub.* 5:1–12). The impure spirits who deceived Noah's grandsons are children of "the Watchers" (19:28). The majority of these spirits were destroyed, but a tenth remained, and with these Mastema is able to carry out his purpose among humankind (10:8). For the rest, the demons stand alongside Satan in their own right, while he functions as the sole accuser before God.

Satan tries above all to disrupt the relationship between God and Israel, but he also tries to separate the rest of humankind from God. It is only later traditions that state that Satan had been an angel of high rank. The rabbis allowed that human beings had free will, to enable them to keep the law and to ward off the evil inclination or Satan.

(b) In the writings of Qumran Belial appears as the name of the evil spirit, the angel of darkness. He lives in the hearts of his followers, the "sons of darkness" (1QS 1:10) and rules in the preacher of apostasy (CD 12:2). The enemies of the righteous are filled with "guiles of Belial" (1QH 2:16–17; 6:21; 7:4). Fornication, riches, and defilement of the temple are the "three traps of Belial" (CD 4:15). Belial threatens the world and the righteous (1QH 3:29, 32; 5:39), but God protects his righteous ones (1QM 14:9). Belial and his followers are solemnly cursed (1QS 2:4–9; 1QM 13:4–5). In the last days, after the Qumran community has cut itself off from the rest of the people, Belial is let loose against Israel (CD 4:13). At the end of the final war, the "sons of darkness," who constitute Belial's army (1QM 1:1, 13), will be destroyed (11:8–9).

4. *Beelzeboul* is an indeclinable noun. The origin and meaning of this name are not entirely clear. In 2 Ki. 1:2–3 *baʿal zᵉbûb*, lord of the flies, appears to be god of Ekron. *Beelzeboul* may be derived from *baʿal zᵉbûl*, lord of the heights—i.e., of heaven—but more likely it comes from *baʿal zibbûl* (from post-OT Heb. *zebel,* manure, dung; *zibbûl* meaning an idolatrous sacrifice)—lord of the idol, which is equated to dung.

NT 1. In the NT *diabolos* occurs 37x, *Satanas* 36x, *Beelzeboul* 7x. In addition, there are the following names: the enemy (→ *echthros,* 2398), the evil one (→ *ponēros,* 4505), the prince (*archōn,* → *archē,* beginning, 794) of this world, the adversary (*antidikos,* which is a literal translation of the OT *śāṭān,* 1 Pet. 5:8; → *echthros,* 2398). *diaballō* is used only in Lk. 16:1 of the unjust steward who was (justly) accused of and denounced for embezzlement.

2. Matt. 25:41 refers to the angels of the devil. In the account of Jesus' temptation (Matt. 4:1–11; Lk. 4:1–13), the devil arrogates to himself the position of a lord of the world, hoping by this transference of title to deter Jesus from his way. Appropriately he is called the "prince of this world" in Jn. 12:31; 14:30; 16:11. The residence of the devil is not hell; rather, the eternal fire is prepared for the devil and all his angels (Matt. 25:41). As in the OT, he has access to God in order to accuse humankind (Jn. 12:31; 16:11). Hence, Jesus prays for the faith of his disciples and teaches them to pray for deliverance from the evil one (Matt. 6:13).

According to Lk. 10:18, Jesus saw Satan's downfall. This follows the joyful return of the seventy-two, who tell Jesus: "Lord, even the demons submit to us in your name" (10:17). Rev. 12:5, 7–12 links this fall of Satan with Jesus' appearance and his ascension into heaven. In 12:9 *diabolos* and *Satanas* stand side by side as words of equal significance and weight, while in 12:8 this figure is described as a dragon (*drakōn*, → *1532*) or serpent (*ophis*, → *4058*), and in 12:10 as accuser (*katēgōr*; → *katēgoros*, *2991*). This breaks up the dualistic view of the world held in Qumran: Jesus has defeated and disarmed the devil and can thus rob him of his plunder, i.e., Jesus is able to heal those who are demon-possessed (Matt. 12:27–29).

But even though Satan has been thrown out of heaven, this does not prevent him from being able to act. The unbelieving Jews are of their father, the devil (Jn. 8:44). Peter is addressed as "Satan" because he tried to turn Jesus back from his way of suffering obedience (Matt. 16:23). Satan also entered Judas as he was preparing to betray Jesus (Lk. 22:3; Jn. 13:27). Satan can but does not necessarily stand behind illness (Lk. 13:16; cf. Acts 10:38; 2 Cor. 12:7). In the parable of the sower, "the evil one" (Matt. 13:19), "Satan" (Mk. 4:15), or "the devil" (Lk. 8:12) snatches the saving word from human hearts lest they believe and are saved.

A person who tries to impede God's word of salvation can also be called *diabolos*. For instance, in the parable of the wheat and the weeds (Matt. 13:24–30), the presence of "evil" in the community is explained through the activity of an "enemy." The parable teaches that there is no such thing as an absolutely pure church; the church on earth will inevitably be a mixed body. Separation is the special task of the eschatological judge. On "evil" or "the evil one" in the Lord's Prayer, → *ponēros*, evil (*4505*).

3. (a) In Paul's letters *diabolos* occurs 8x (Eph. 4:27; 6:11; 1 Tim. 3:6–7, 11; 2 Tim. 2:26; 3:3; Tit. 2:3) and *Satanas* 10x (Rom. 16:20; 1 Cor. 5:5; 7:5; 2 Cor. 2:11; 11:14; 12:7; 1 Thess. 2:18; 2 Thess. 2:9; 1 Tim. 1:20; 5:15). In 2 Cor. 6:15 Paul makes use of the name Belial, found in the writings of Qumran. Paul attributes many misfortunes and difficulties to the work of Satan. The thorn in the flesh is a "messenger of Satan" sent to bruise him (2 Cor. 12:7). Satan wants to outwit Paul (2:11). To prevent Paul from making his journey (1 Thess. 2:18), Satan can change himself into an angel of light and with this disguise disseminate impure thoughts through those he sends out (2 Cor. 11:14). He tempts Christian communities (1 Cor. 7:5; 2 Cor. 2:11). He is wily and deceitful (Eph. 6:11), sets traps (1 Tim. 3:7; 2 Tim. 2:26), and is encountered in calamity and sin as the ruler of the air (Eph. 2:2).

(b) In 1 Cor. 5:5 the notorious sinner is to be excluded from the congregation and given over to Satan "so that his sinful nature may be destroyed." Interpretations on the meaning of this verse abound. Perhaps behind these disciplinary instructions stands the Jewish conception of Satan as master of destruction and as executor of the divine wrath, from whose control becoming a member of the congregation secured freedom, and into whose control the culprit is now thrown back. But Paul's language here may also reflect the LXX of Job 2:6, where the Lord delivered Job into Satan's hand, not to kill him but to test him. In any case, the intended result of this process is to make it possible for the spirit of this man to be ultimately saved. Accordingly, Hymenaeus and Alexander are handed over to Satan to be punished and dissuaded from their blasphemies (1 Tim. 1:20).

4. The devil's area of activity is primarily the non-Christian world (Acts 26:18; cf. 2 Cor. 6:16), and hence magic is bound up with him (Acts 13:10). An apocalyptic story, presumably originating from the *Assumption of Moses* and telling of an attack of the devil on the archangel Michael, is presupposed in Jude 9 (→ *blasphēmeō*, revile, *1059*). Acts 5:3; Rev. 2:9–10; 20:7 also speak of Satan's fight against the Christian community.

5. At the time of the end Satan will send the Antichrist (2 Thess. 2:3–12; the beast of Rev. 13:17). Matt. 25:41; Rev. 20:10 (cf. 1 Jn. 3:8; Heb. 2:14); and possibly Rom. 16:20 speak of the destruction of the devil at the end. Angry and violent, he realizes that until then he only

has a little time and rages wildly against God's people (Rev. 12:12, 16–17). On the binding of Satan in Rev. 20 → *chilias*, thousand, *5942*.

6. Our help against temptation and the tricks of the devil is the armor of God (Eph. 6:11, 16), a determined turning to God (Jas. 4:7), and a sober and alert faith. This alone will cause the devil to lose his power, although he paces about like a roaring lion, irritated and dangerous (1 Pet. 5:8). The ultimate reason for his defeat, however, is the "blood of the Lamb" (Rev. 12:11), that is, the victory of Jesus through his death on the cross.

7. The NT contains no speculations about the origin or nature of the devil. Satan is also not equated with the evil inclination or with the angel of death. Indeed, death and the devil are distinguished (Rev. 20:10, 14), though Satan has power over death (Heb. 2:14).

8. In Jn.'s writings are occasional references to the role of the devil in the early history of Genesis 3 (Rev. 12:9; cf. Jn. 8:44; 1 Jn. 3:8). Jewish exegesis interpreted the serpent as the devil. Thus, the devil is a sinner right from the beginning (1 Jn. 3:8) and has been a murderer from the beginning (Jn. 8:44b). He does not have a share in the truth; when he lies, he speaks on his own account (8:44c).

But it is noteworthy here that dependence on the power of the devil can show itself both in actions and decisions. The effects of this are expressed in John by means of the predicative statements of descent and relationship. One who sins belongs to the devil, like Cain (1 Jn. 3:8, 12); or he is a devil himself, like Judas, the betrayer (Jn. 6:70). Hence, the children of God can stand over against the children of the devil (1 Jn. 3:10). Jesus' enemies are called children of the devil, i.e., those who share his nature and behavior (Jn. 8:44). When "young men" succeed in defeating the evil one (1 Jn. 2:13–14), it is a gift of Christ (cf. Jn. 17:15).

9. *Beelzeboul* in the NT is the name of a chief demon. Jesus' enemies accuse him of being possessed by him (Mk. 3:22; cf. Matt. 9:34; 12:24; Lk. 11:15; cf. also Matt. 10:25; 12:27; Lk. 11:18–19 for further use of the name). Similar charges persist in Jewish sources, ascribing Jesus' works to magic (e.g., *b. Sanh.* 43a; cf. 107b; *b. Soṭah* 47a). In reply Jesus reminds his accusers that if that were so, Satan and his kingdom would be divided, since he would be fighting against himself. That would be good news, signaling his end. Jesus follows up these comments with the parable of binding the strong man (Mk. 3:23–30; cf. Matt. 12:25–37; Lk. 11:17–23). Satan is the strong man who is enslaving people through sin, demon-possession, sickness, and death. Jesus' casting out of demons means that one stronger than Satan has come, restraining his activity and releasing the enslaved.

Note that by substituting "Satan" for "Beelzebub" in his reply in Mk. 3:23, Jesus puts this controversy in the perspective of a direct confrontation with Satan. Since it is unlikely that Satan fights against himself, this means that Jesus is certainly not casting out demons by the prince of demons. After all, there is much evidence that Satan continues his work. Some people are possessed by demons, and it is the mission of Jesus and his disciples to cast them out (cf. Mk. 3:15). Moreover, Satan is active among those who oppose Jesus and attribute the work of the Holy Spirit (3:29) to Beelzebub.

1334 (*diangellō*, make known, proclaim [far and wide]), → *33*.

1339 (*diagongyzō*, mutter, murmer), → *1197*.

1343 (*diadēma*, diadem, crown), → *5109*.

1346 (*diazōnnymi*, tie or gird around), → *2439*.

| *1347*   διαθήκη | διαθήκη (*diathēkē*), covenant (*1347*). |

CL & OT 1. *diathēkē* in cl. Gk. means will or testament. It denotes an irrevocable decision, which cannot be altered or canceled. A prerequisite of its effectiveness before the law is the death of the disposer. Hence *diathēkē* must be clearly distinguished from *synthēkē*, agreement, in which two partners accept reciprocal obligations.

2. In the LXX *diathēkē* occurs 270x for Heb. *berît*, covenant. (a) It may denote a covenant between two friends (1 Sam. 18:3), which was regarded as having legal force (20:8); a covenant between two rulers, fixing their spheres of interest (Gen. 21:25–32; 26:26–29; 1 Ki. 5:12) or terms of peace (20:34 = LXX 21:34); a covenant between two kings, which included their peoples. Two tribes could also make a covenant (Jos. 9:15–16). Linguistically, the LXX could have used *syntheke* in these examples.

(b) The situation was somewhat different when a king made a covenant with his subjects (2 Ki. 11:4) or when a group became subjects of a leader (1 Sam. 11:1). The covenant made by Abner with David (2 Sam. 3:12–13) was intended to make all Israel (3:21) subject to David, not merely Abner.

(c) Yahweh's covenants with Noah (Gen. 6:18), Abraham (2 Ki. 13:23), and David (Jer. 33:21) are similar. Here the covenant extends explicitly to their descendants (Gen. 9:8–9; 15:18; cf. 2 Sam. 7:12–16), and the covenant with Abraham extends to Israel (Exod. 6:4–5). But in Jer. 50:5 (= LXX 27:5) the covenant can also be interpreted as a covenant of Israel with its God. Ezek. 16:8 speaks of a covenant with Jerusalem. There are exceptional usages of *diathēkē*, such as Yahweh's covenant with day and night (Jer. 33:25, not in LXX) and Jerusalem's with death (Isa. 28:14–18).

3. Since all these covenants were expressed by the same word, the Jews must have felt some unity behind them. Neither the relationship of the covenant partners nor the contents of the covenant agreement provided this, but there was a common pattern in how a covenant was made. There were six vital elements in such a ceremony: (a) the preamble, mentioning the names of the partners; (b) a preliminary history of the relationship of those entering the covenant; (c) a basic declaration about the future relationship of the partners; (d) details of the new relationship; (e) an invocation of the respective gods worshiped by both sides, who would act as witnesses; (f) a pronouncement of blessings and curses for keeping or breaking the stipulations of the covenant.

4. In Israel's covenant with Yahweh, the preamble is suggestive of the way in which Yahweh introduces himself (cf. Exod. 20:2, which, as in the covenant formula, is followed by a survey, however brief, of past events). This may be the source of Israel's unique interest in its history, which is seen as Yahweh's history, and hence covenant or salvation history. The third element reflects the thought that found its clearest expression in Isa. as the proclamation of salvation, the promise of divine faithfulness and peace (Isa. 54:10; 55:3). Since this promise cannot be revoked, God has proclaimed himself bound and has renounced all arbitrariness. This lays the basis for the gospel of grace.

When we compare these covenant promises of Isa. and those in Jer. 31 with the formula of the Sinai covenant, we realize that the details mentioned in 3(d) should not be understood as a condition to be first fulfilled, which would be followed by a reward for achievement. Rather, they are the regulations for the new life that God's covenant initiates (cf. Gen. 9:9; 15:13–16; Jer. 31:31). As in Deut. 26, Israel's reflection on its past history and the law belong together as instruction for its new life.

5. The relationship of the partners in the covenant is expressed by *hesed*, God's covenant loyalty (NIV unfailing love). This concept is understood in 1 Sam. 20:8 as protective action. Both partners—Yahweh and the covenant people—face one another in the *berît*. They are thus in a partnership, so they both share in the covenant meal (Gen. 31:54; Exod. 24:9–11), which thereby strengthens the fellowship of those involved.

The covenant did have a place in the cultus (Ps. 50), though the covenant and its renewal were not purely cultic acts (cf., e.g., Jos. 8:30–35; 24:24). The covenant belonged essentially to the daily life of the twelve tribes. The cultus could not guarantee the continuance of an intact, everlasting covenant. Yahweh alone, as founder of this covenant, could guarantee its continuance and with it the cultus in its

true meaning. Only he could renew the covenant broken by human disobedience.

There is an essential continuity of the covenant concept throughout Scripture. Note the words of Jeremiah, for example, who links covenant and personal application of God's law: "'This is the covenant I will make with the house of Israel after that time,' declares the LORD. 'I will put my law in their minds and write it on their hearts; I will be their God, and they will be my people'" (31:33). Here is the same divine upholding of the covenant that is found elsewhere in the OT. The covenant relationship is summed up in the promise, "I will . . . be your God, and you will be my people" (Lev. 26:12; cf. Jer. 7:23; 11:4; 30:22; 32:38; 2 Cor. 6:16; Heb. 8:10; Rev. 21:3).

6. The Qumran community attributed great importance to the covenant. They considered that the promise of the new covenant (Jer. 31:31–34) had been fulfilled in their midst and called themselves "the new covenant in the land of Damascus" (CD 6:19). While the Sinaitic covenant was for the whole people, the Qumran covenanters considered themselves to be its holy remnant, the pure community of the age of salvation. This explains their strict rules for receiving new members and their commitment to keeping the Mosaic law as it was expounded by the community.

NT While "covenant" is found almost 300x in the OT, it occurs only 33x in the NT. Almost half of these instances come in quotations from the OT, and another 5 clearly look back to OT statements. The few independent cases are almost exclusively in Heb., rarely in Paul and Acts, and never in the Johannine writings. In the three cases where the standard Gk. meaning of "will" plays a part (Gal. 3:15; Heb. 9:16–17), it is easy to recognize the intention of helping the Greeks to understand the OT concept.

These statistics are, however, misleading. The covenant question in the NT cannot be answered solely from the passages where the word is used. It involves a whole complex of theological ideas, including covenant terminology. There are three groups of issues: the question of the Lord's Supper, Paul's question about the relationship of the Christian church to Israel as the people of God, and the covenant in Heb.

1. In all four NT passages dealing with the Lord's Supper, *diathēkē* plays an important part: Matt. 26:28; Mk. 14:24; Lk. 22:20 (omitted in some MSS); 1 Cor. 11:25. The word is used only in connection with the cup (Paul and Lk. add the adj. "new"). The use of the formula "the blood of the covenant" with "is poured out" clearly alludes to the covenant blood of the OT (cf. Exod. 24:5–8) and with it the covenant Yahweh made with Israel. This means that the work of Jesus was, according to his own word, a taking up and fulfilling of the covenant statements of the OT (cf. also Jer. 31:31–34).

If the word *diathēkē* does not appear as often as one might expect, the reason is that the underlying thought has been taken over in the sayings about the kingdom of God. Linguistically, we can see this most clearly in Lk. 22:29 in the phrase *diatithemai . . . basileian*, "confer . . . a kingdom," which uses the same formula as "establish a covenant" in the LXX. The new covenant and the kingdom of God are correlated concepts.

Just as in the old covenant curse and blessing played a role, so also in the new covenant: The blessing is obviously the blessing of forgiveness of sins and membership in the kingdom; hints of a curse are found in 1 Cor. 11:27–32. Just as one could keep the old covenant only if one knew its ordinances, so in the Lord's Supper repetition is expressly intended to produce remembrance (11:25).

2. It is not easy to formulate Paul's attitude to Israel as the people of God. (a) The apostle can use only the word "mystery" (*mystērion*, → *3696*) for the Jewish rejection of Jesus and their enmity to the gospel (Rom. 11:25). He does so in "great sorrow and unceasing anguish" (9:2). He is so deeply moved by this subject that his delineation of the righteousness of God given through Christ (Rom. 1–8) leads to an analysis of the inexplicable hardening of Israel, which nevertheless

will lead to salvation in God's will (Rom. 9–11, esp. 11:11–16). This account reaches its climax in praise of the unfathomable depths of the divine action (11:33–36). In it Paul insists that Israel's rejection and unfaithfulness cannot cancel God's covenant. He also knows that the fellowship between Israel and the church cannot be removed, because it is based on the unity of the one who calls. In other words, God's people from now on include the church and Israel.

(b) In light of this, Paul concludes that a part of Israel has been temporarily hardened (Rom. 11:25), which has happened through God's will. God promised Israel that sin would be completely blotted out and that all obstacles between God and humanity would be removed. This is the force of the quotation from Isa. 59:20–21 in Rom. 11:26–27. It is, therefore, obvious that the fulfillment of this covenant promise is still to be awaited with regard to the remnant of Israel, so long as the hardening still exists.

(c) To make this clearer still, in Gal. 3:15 Paul examines the Gk. concept of a will, which cannot be annulled. If that is so with a human will, how much less can God's covenant with Israel be annulled (3:17), through which Israel received such incomparable privileges (Rom. 9:4–5) and of which Paul the Christian can boast again and again (Rom. 11:1; 2 Cor. 11:22; Phil. 3:5)?

Since God's covenant with Abraham, which consists of the free promise, came into force (Gal. 3:16), something that was added later (Rom. 5:20)—the law (Gal. 3:17)—cannot narrow this promise or annul it. We as humans will never be able to use the law of God in order to establish our own righteousness. Left to our own power, we cannot keep the law; sin is too deep-rooted in our hearts. Rather, we are saved only by God's free grace through Christ's atoning death. As far as the law is concerned, it "was put in charge to lead us to Christ" (3:24). The one who clings to the law remains a slave child (4:25). Christians, however, are children of the promise (4:26–28) and thus free, and they belong to Christ without any distinctions (3:26–28).

3. In Heb. we find a fully developed covenant theology (*diathē-kē* occurs 17x). Since the high priestly office of Christ is the prevailing concept of Christology in this book, it expresses the new covenant in a cultic setting, which reflects the author's concern for such issues as purification, sanctification, sacrifice, atonement, and blood. He clearly contrasts the old and new covenants. The new is the better covenant (cf. 7:22). Its guarantor and mediator is Christ (8:6; 12:24), who through his death has brought redemption from the sins of the old covenant (9:5).

Against this background the author interprets the prophetic promise of Jer. 31:31–34, twice quoted (8:8–12; 10:16–17). By the promise of the new covenant the old has been declared obsolete by God and is ready to vanish (8:13). This does not mean that it has been completely ruled out, but that it has been overtaken and fulfilled by the new. In Christ the pattern (*typos*, 8:5) or reality (*eikōn*, 10:1) of God's one covenant has become apparent. The new covenant is founded on better promises (8:6; 9:15), but like the old covenant it is a covenant in blood (10:29; 12:24; 13:20). It is not, however, the blood of a sacrificial animal, but the blood of the sacrificer himself, the high priest, Jesus (9:13–15; 10:12–14). Hence, Christ's death was essential, for only through the death of the testator does his will become operative in law (9:16–17).

Seeing that the forgiveness of sins and the renewal of the human heart promised in Jer. 31:31–34 has become a reality in Christ (Heb. 10:16–23), the old covenant is explained as "a shadow of the good things that are coming" (10:1). With the coming of the new covenant, the old has been annulled in the sense that it has become obsolete and superfluous. At the same time, the writer of Heb. uses words from the old covenant (e.g., Ps. 95:7–8; see Heb. 3:7, 15; 4:7) to warn his readers against deliberate, conscious sin, for there is a point beyond which a person cannot return. We must make sure, therefore, not to harden our hearts in unbelief.

See also *engyos*, guarantor (*1583*); *mesitēs*, mediator, guarantor (*3542*).

1348 (*diairesis*, allotment, division), → *145.*

1349 (*diaireō*, distribute, divide), → *145.*

1354 διακονέω

διακονέω (*diakoneō*), serve, support, serve as a deacon (*1354*); διακονία (*diakonia*), service, office, aid, support, distribution (of alms etc.), office of a deacon (*1355*); διάκονος (*diakonos*), servant, deacon (*1356*); ὑπηρέτης (*hypēretēs*), servant, helper, assistant (*5677*); ὑπηρετέω (*hypēreteō*), serve, render service, be helpful (*5676*).

CL & OT 1. In cl. Gk. *diakoneō* first meant to wait at tables; this was expanded to mean to care for household needs, then to serve generally. The first meaning involved personal subjection, which was considered unworthy and dishonoring for a free man. But when used in the third sense it could denote service for a cause, e.g., for the good of the community or for a god. As such it was an honorable task, a fitting occupation for a free man. In general the voluntary giving of oneself in the service of one's fellow human being is alien to Gk. thought. The highest goal before a person was the development of one's own personality.

The derivative noun *diakonia* expresses the occupations implied by the vb. and means service, office. *diakonos* denotes the person carrying out the task—a waiter at a table, and later a servant in general.

2. Even though the OT has the concept of service and contains the commandment to love one's neighbor (Lev. 19:8), and although Israel knew charitable acts (as did the ANE generally), *diakoneō* does not occur in the LXX. The instances of *diakonos* are used exclusively for court servants (Est. 1:10; 2:2; 6:1, 3) and torturers (e.g., 4 Macc. 9:17). *diakonia* is used only in Est. 6:3, 5 and 1 Macc. 11:58. Instead of this word group in cultic contexts, we find the word groups *douleuō* (→ *1526*), *latreuō* (→ *3302*), and *leitourgeō* (→ *3310*).

3. (a) *diakoneō* is found in both Philo and Josephus. Although Jud. at the time of Jesus practiced social responsibilities (e.g., to the poor), this was done mainly by alms, not by service (cf. Lk. 10:30–35). Lowly service (e.g., waiting at tables) was beneath the dignity of a free man (cf. 7:44–46). There was, however, organized care for the poor in terms of giving food. Moreover, there were common meals and alms. In the Diaspora, synagogues often set up a committee of seven for its service.

(b) Josephus writes that the Essenes served each other. He mentions regular contributions for the needy, poor, and aged (→ *ptōchos*, poor, *4777*). Service to the poor and common meals, the latter possibly with eschatological connotations (1QSa 2:17–22), belonged to the fulfilling of righteousness and the expectation of the kingdom. The community's holding its goods in common had a temporary counterpart in the Jerusalem church (Acts 2:44).

NT 1. *diakoneō* occurs 37x in the NT, primarily in the Gospels and Paul's letters. *diakonia* occurs 34x, mostly in Acts and Paul's letters. *diakonos* (29x) is a predominantly Pauline concept, though it also appears in the Gospels.

(a) *diakoneō* occurs with the meaning of serving at a table in Matt. 8:15; Lk. 4:39; 10:40; Acts 6:2. It has the sense of service to individuals in Matt. 4:11; 25:44; 27:55; Mk. 1:31; 15:41; Lk. 8:3; 2 Tim. 1:18; of service to the church in Heb. 6:10; 1 Pet. 4:10–11. It is used specifically of the work of deacons in 1 Tim. 3:10, 13; in connection with the offering for the Jerusalem saints in Rom. 15:25; 2 Cor. 8:19–20; as an expression for the proclamation of the gospel in 2 Cor. 3:3; 1 Pet. 1:12; as an expression of Jesus' giving up of himself for others through suffering and death in Matt. 20:28; Mk. 10:45; of the voluntary self-humiliation of the disciple in Lk. 22:26–27; and of a person's following Christ in Jn. 12:26.

In other words, the concept extends beyond the limits of its former sphere of meaning. The eschatological saying in Lk. 12:37 points to a radical change in the previously held values. This is also true of

22:27, linked with the previous verse in which Jesus' humility becomes the norm for the life of the disciples.

(b) *diakonia* means table service in Lk. 10:40 and Acts 6:1. It is used in a general sense for loving service in 1 Cor. 16:15 and Rev. 2:19; for loving service through the making of a collection in Acts 11:29; 12:25; Rom. 15:31; 2 Cor. 8:4; 9:1, 12–13 (where the grace of Christ is clearly seen as the basis and motive); for the proclamation of the word and the Christian mission in Acts 6:4; 20:24; 21:19; 2 Cor. 11:8; 2 Tim. 4:11; for all services in the Christian community in Eph. 4:12; for service by angels in Heb. 1:14; and for ministry in the church in 2 Cor. 3:7–8; 4:1; 5:18; 6:3; Col. 4:17; 2 Tim. 4:5. Every service and every office, however, finds its meaning in the organic unity of the body of Christ (Rom. 12:7; 1 Cor. 12:5).

(c) *diakonos* has as its primary meaning the one who serves at table (Matt. 22:13, where there is an eschatological note; Jn. 2:5, 9). It means a servant in a wider sense in Matt. 20:26; Mk. 10:43, and a helper in Eph. 6:21; Col. 4:7. Esp. in Paul, the word receives a specifically Christian sense; e.g., a servant of the new covenant (2 Cor. 3:6), of righteousness (11:15), of Christ (11:23; Col. 1:7; 1 Tim. 4:6), of God (2 Cor. 6:4), of the gospel (Eph. 3:7; Col. 1:23), and of the church (1:25). Christ himself is called a *diakonos* in Rom. 15:8 (of Israel). In Rom. 13:4 the secular ruler is called a servant of God.

In Phil. 1:1 and 1 Tim. 3:8–13, *diakonos* is used of a man holding the office of deacon in the church; the same title is applied to a woman, Phoebe, in Rom. 16:1 (the same office may be intended by 1 Tim. 3:11). Sometimes *diakonos* is replaced by *hypēretēs* (e.g., Lk. 1:2; Acts 26:16; 1 Cor. 4:1). Elsewhere in the NT *hypēretēs* means the (armed) servant of someone in authority (e.g., Matt. 26:58; Jn. 18:3, 12, 18, 22). The vb. *hypēreteō*, serve, render service, occurs in Acts 13:36 (of David serving God); 20:34 (of Paul tending to his own needs); 24:23 (of Paul's friends tending to his necessities).

2. The NT meaning of *diakoneō* is derived from the person of Jesus and his gospel. It becomes a term denoting loving action for brother or sister and neighbor, which in turn is derived from divine love; it also describes the outworking of *koinōnia*, fellowship.

When Jesus served his disciples and humanity in general, he was demonstrating God's love as God willed it. "I am among you as one who serves" (Lk. 22:27; cf. Jn. 13:1–15), and "The Son of man did not come to be served, but to serve" (Matt. 20:28). Jesus washed his disciples' feet as an example (Jn. 13:15) to challenge the disciples; the leader among them was to be as one who serves (Lk. 22:26; cf. Matt. 20:26). Each person should serve with the gift God has given him or her (1 Pet. 4:10). Anyone who gives food to the hungry, shelters the homeless, clothes the naked, or visits the sick and imprisoned (Matt. 25:35–36) is serving Christ himself. The service done to Jesus on earth, esp. by women (cf. Lk. 7:44–50; 8:3), will not be forgotten (Mk. 14:9).

3. The fellowship of the common or shared meal, which involved serving at tables (Acts 6:1), remains basic for the understanding of *diakonia* in the NT. We should think of the breaking of bread in private homes, of the love feasts in which the rich shared with the poor (cf. 1 Cor. 11:17–34), and of the house churches that had devoted themselves to *diakonia*, like that in the house of Stephanas (1 Cor. 16:15). This service, in which possessions were used for others, is the principal and foundational element of fellowship in the NT church (2 Cor. 9:13; cf. Acts 4:32–37; 2 Cor. 9:7). This service also extended from the local church to churches elsewhere that needed help (Acts 11:29; 12:25; 2 Cor. 8:3–4; 9:1–5). The spiritual and physical *diakonia* of giving and receiving took place in acknowledgment of Christ's sacrifice (2 Cor. 8:9; 9:12–15).

Such service edifies the whole body of Christ (Eph. 4:12), which is why Paul calls the charismatic gifts *diakoniai* (1 Cor. 12:5), services that form part of an organic whole. *diakonia* can also be used for each particular spiritual gift (Rom. 12:7), just as the deacon is one among all the others who serve.

Paul expanded the concept of *diakonia* even further. He saw the whole of salvation (i.e., God's service in Christ for and among

humankind) expressed in the *diakonia* of the apostles. Already in the OT there was a divine *diakonia* ("ministry"), but it was expressed in the law and therefore brought death and condemnation (2 Cor. 3:7, 9). In Christ, however, the service of the Spirit, of righteousness, of reconciliation has begun (3:8–9), and this service has been entrusted to the apostle, who as Christ's ambassador proclaims, "Be reconciled to God" (2 Cor. 5:20). Hence, the term *diakonia* is used as a technical term for the work of proclaiming the gospel (Rom. 11:13; 2 Cor. 4:1; cf. 2 Tim. 4:5). Even more, the whole church becomes a body for service in the world (Eph. 4:1–16).

4. (a) The difference between this word group and *doulos* (slave, → *1528*) is important for one's understanding of *diakonos*. *doulos* stresses almost exclusively the Christian's complete subjection to the Lord; *diakonos* is concerned with a believer's service for the church and fellow believers, whether this is accomplished by serving at tables, with the word, or in some other way. The *diakonos* is one who serves on Christ's behalf and continues this service for the outer and inner self; such people are concerned with the salvation of others.

Hence, Paul can see himself as a *diakonos* of the gospel (Eph. 3:7; Col. 1:23), a servant through whom the believers in Corinth had come to faith in Christ (1 Cor. 3:5), a servant of the new covenant (2 Cor. 3:6), a servant of Christ (11:23), a servant of God (6:4), and a servant of the church (Col. 1:25). In this connection Paul was also concerned with the collection (2 Cor. 8:4; 9:1, 12–13) for the poor among the saints in Jerusalem.

(b) Paul likewise refers to his various companions and helpers, who stood with him in the work of proclaiming the gospel, as *diakonoi* (Eph. 6:21; Col. 1:7; 4:7) or, more often, *synergoi*, fellow workers (Rom. 16:3, 9, 21; 2 Cor. 8:23; Phil. 2:25; 4:3; Col. 4:11; 1 Thess. 3:2).

(c) Acts 6:1–6 also belongs in this context, though only *diakoneō* and *diakonia* are used. The Seven, who are placed alongside the apostles, took over the care of the poor in the church because the Hellenists complained that their widows were neglected in the daily distribution of food. However, they doubtless had spiritual functions as well, qualities that emerged when this particular ministry was terminated (cf. Stephen in 6:8–7:60 and Philip in 8:9–40; 21:8).

(d) The work of a deacon finally developed into a special office, whose beginnings can be traced already in the NT (cf. Phil. 1:1; 1 Tim. 3:8–13). In the course of the church's history the office developed a standardized form, though its precise form is not clear from the NT. Nor does it seem to have been universal in the church. Originally all the various functions exercised in the church could be called "services" or ministries (1 Cor. 12:5). Hence, the various office-bearers (apostle, prophet, etc.; cf. Eph. 4:11–12) were *diakonoi* of the church (cf. 1 Cor. 3:5; Col. 1:25). But in the more specialized sense the concept of service was narrowed down to the material care of the church, which was closely linked with the office of the bishop (e.g., 1 Tim. 3:1–7, 8–13).

This means that for the *diakonos* there was always a task for spirit and body expressed by one's role in public worship, care of the poor, and administration. Service of God and of the poor were, after all, a unity, as the *agape*, the common meal often preceding the Lord's Supper, implied. Originally it was obvious that all were servants, standing in a fellowship of service, but the concept was increasingly eroded by the growth of a hierarchy with its different grades. The *diakonos* was retained in the Orthodox Church, but the diaconate became merely a transitional stage on the way to the priestly office in the Roman Catholic and Episcopalian Churches.

(e) The NT also recognizes the work of the female deacon, but her role is left undefined (Rom. 16:1; perhaps also 1 Tim. 3:11). This office is increasingly recognized in churches today. In the NT, this office seems closely connected with that of the widow (→ *chēra*, 5939).

5. In Rom. 13 Paul urges obedience to the secular ruler, even though he is not a believer, "for he is God's servant [*diakonos*] to do you good. But if you do wrong, be afraid, for he does not bear the sword for nothing. He is God's servant [*diakonos*], an agent of wrath to bring punishment on the wrongdoer" (Rom. 13:4; cf. 1 Pet. 2:13–17; also Matt. 22:15–22; Mk. 12:13–17; Lk. 20:20–26).

See also *latreuō*, serve (*3302*); *leitourgeō*, serve (*3310*); *doulos*, slave (*1528*).

1355 (*diakonia*, service, aid, distribution [of alms], office of deacon), → *1354*.

1356 (*diakonos*, servant, deacon), → *1354*.

1359	διακρίνω

διακρίνω (*diakrinō*), make a distinction, judge, render a decision; doubt, waver (only in NT) (*1359*); διάκρισις (*diakrisis*), distinguishing, quarrel (*1360*); ἀδιάκριτος (*adiakritos*), unwavering, impartial (*88*).

CL & OT *diakrinō* (a form of *krinō*) has the basic meaning of judge, make a distinction, distinguish; separate, divide; render a decision, dispense justice. The noun *diakrisis* means separation, division; interval, judgment; and quarrel, struggle.

In the LXX *diakrinō* means primarily judge (e.g., Exod. 18:16; 1 Ki. 3:9; 1 Chr. 26:29), distinguish, make a distinction (4 Macc. 1:14); also dispense justice. The meaning take issue, to enter into judgment, is also attested (Ezek. 20:35, 36; Joel 3:2). The meaning to judge can be intensified to mean examine (Job 12:11; 23:10) and choose (9:14; 15:5). *diakrisis* is found only in 37:16, where it means clouds (this may be a mistake in translation by the translator).

NT 1. *diakrinō* is found 19x in the NT. In 3 instances it means to judge: the appearance of the sky, but not the signs of the times (Matt. 16:3), oneself (1 Cor. 11:31), and prophetic words (14:29). Twice it refers to God, who makes no distinction between Jews and pagans (Acts 15:9; cf. 11:12). The idea of making differentiating evaluation is found in 1 Cor. 4:7; 11:29; Jas. 2:4. As a legal technical term, *diakrinō* is found only in 1 Cor. 6:5, of dispensing justice between two believers (cf. Ezek. 34:17, 20). The vb. is used 2x in the mid. in the sense of take issue with, contend with: the circumcision party with Peter (Acts 11:2), and Michael with the devil (Jude 9).

2. *diakrinō* takes on the further meaning of doubt 8x (cf. the similar use of *distazō* in Matt. 14:31; 28:17). In Rom. 14:23 doubt appears as a lack of faith and thus as sin. Jas. 1:6–8 relates this to prayer: One must ask in faith, whereas one who asks in doubt is a divided person who lacks the power of hope. Matt. 21:21 and Mk. 11:23 teach that a faith that does not doubt can move mountains. A comparison with Matt. 17:20, where Jesus expresses the same idea with "because you have so little faith," shows that doubt is akin to faintheartedness. In Rom. 4:20 *diakrinō* comes close to disbelief: "[Abraham] did not *waver* through unbelief regarding the promise of God." Faith involves the promises of God; doubt is thus a lack of trust in those promises. According to Acts 10:20, if Peter hesitated (*diakrinō*), he would be failing to trust the Spirit, who was sending him on the road to Cornelius. Jude encourages us to be merciful "to those who doubt" (Jude 22).

Strictly speaking, doubt in the NT is directed against hope and confidence. Such doubt always arises in confrontation with the gospel, in that the possibility of doubt only exists where the gospel can be heard or seen. Doubt in the NT is an affair of the believer rather than of the unbeliever, although doubt can certainly lead to unbelief.

2. *diakrisis* is used in the sense of distinguishing: of spirits (1 Cor. 12:10), of good from evil (Heb. 5:14). In Rom. 14:1 it means quarrel or passing judgment. The noun is not found in the NT in the sense of doubt.

3. *adiakritos*, unwavering, impartial, occurs only in Jas. 3:17. Part of wisdom that comes from God is to be impartial in our relationship with other believers.

1360 (*diakrisis*, distinguishing, quarrel), → *1359*.

1363 (*dialegomai*, discuss), → *1368*.

1364 (*dialeipō*, to leave off, cease), → *3309*.

1367 (*diallassomai*, become reconciled), → *2904*.

1368	διαλογίζομαι

διαλογίζομαι (*dialogizomai*), ponder, consider, reason (*1368*); διαλογισμός (*dialogismos*), thought, opinion, reasoning, consideration, argument (*1369*); διαλέγομαι (*dialegomai*), discuss (*1363*).

CL & OT 1. The meaning of *dialegomai* in cl. and Hel. Gk. is expressed by the Eng. word dialogue; it means hold a conversation. Philosophers used this word for conversation with teaching as its object: One debates and in so doing learns. The vb. *dialogizomai*, to consider, think through, is closely linked with it, as is the noun *dialogismos*, weighing, consideration, thought, discussion.

2. The LXX uses *dialegomai* to translate Heb. *dābar*, to speak, both of God and human beings speaking; it is also used with the meanings of to negotiate with someone, make a speech, sometimes to dispute, strive, contend. The related *dialogizomai* means to think, account, consider (e.g., 2 Sam. 14:14; Ps. 10:2 = LXX 9:23; 140:8). This vb. can be used neutrally, but more often has the depreciatory sense of harbor ill designs, intrigue (35:20; 36:4). *dialogismos* means thought, plan, purpose (e.g., 40:5; 94:11; 139:2; Isa. 59:7); it often denotes perverse, vain thinking that contemplates destruction (Ps. 94:11) and is turned against both God (Isa. 59:7; Jer. 4:14) and the pious (Ps. 56:5). We see this esp. in Ben Sira's picture of the fool's *dialogismos* as a wheel constantly turning round its axle (Sir. 33:5 = LXX 36:5). But the word is also used for God's profound (Ps. 92:5) and wonderful (40:5) thoughts.

NT 1. In the NT, *dialogizomai* and *dialogismos* are always used with a slightly depreciatory connotation. The thoughts of the human heart do not necessarily lead, as the Gks. thought, to a knowledge of the truth (cf. 1 Cor. 1:21–25), but are evil (Matt. 15:19; Mk. 7:21), full of doubt and suspicion (2:6, 8; Lk. 5:22; 6:8), full of greed (12:17; 20:14), moved by the passing moment (3:15), concerned with the superficial (Matt. 16:7–8; Mk. 8:16–17), and often sly (Matt. 21:25; Mk. 11:31). The decision humans made about Jesus shows what they really are and think (Lk. 2:35; cf. 2:34). Jesus unmasks his disciples' ambitious thoughts (Mk. 9:33–34; Lk. 9:46–47) and brings the attitude of faith to light through the example of the child (cf. Lk. 9:48).

In Rom. 1:21 Paul says that as a result of rejecting God, people became "futile" in their thinking; in 14:1 he speaks of "disputable matters" in how to live the Christian life (cf. 1 Tim. 2:8). According to 1 Cor. 3:20 we read that "the thoughts of the wise are futile," and in Phil. 2:14 we read of arguing (*dialogismos*) that is the germ of apathy.

2. *dialegomai* in Mk. 9:33–34 and Jude 9 means to argue, fight with words; but in Heb. 12:5 it is used of God's speaking through fatherly discipline. In Acts 17:2, 17; 18:4, 19; 19:8–9; 20:7, 9; 24:12, 25, the word refers to Paul's reading and exposition of the OT, activities that were, in theory at least, permitted to every adult male in a synagogue (cf. Lk. 4:16–21). Here the vb. becomes a technical term for Paul's teaching in the synagogue and approaches the idea of preaching, though it may have included dialogue and questions.

See also *dokeō*, trans. think, believe, consider; intrans. seem, appear (*1506*); *logizomai*, reckon, think, credit (*3357*).

1369 (*dialogismos*, thought, opinion, reasoning, argument), → *1368*.

1370 (*dialyō*, break up, dissolve, disperse), → *5025*.

1371 (*diamartyromai*, charge, adjure, bear witness to), → *3456*.

1374 (*diamerizō*, divide, separate), → *3532*.

1375 (*diamerismos*, division), → *3532*.

1378 (*dianoēma*, thought), → *3808*.

1379 (*dianoia*, understanding, intelligence, mind, thought), → *3808*.

1380 (*dianoigō*, open, explain), → *487*.

1398 (*diaseiō*, shake violently, intimidate), → *4940*.

1399 (*diaskorpizō*, scatter, disperse, waste), → *5025*.

1401 (*diaspeirō*, scatter), → *5025*.

1402	διασπορά

διασπορά (*diaspora*), dispersion (*1402*).

CL & OT 1. *diaspora* (derived from *diaspeirō*, disperse; → *skorpizō*, *5025*) means dispersion. The word was first used in the LXX and occurs almost entirely in Jewish and Christian literature.

2. *diaspora* occurs 12x in the LXX. It has three different meanings: (a) the event or state of the dispersion of the Jews among the heathen nations (Deut. 28:25; Jer. 34:17 [= LXX 41:17]); (2) the community of those so dispersed (Ps. 147:2; Isa. 49:6; 2 Macc. 1:27; *Pss. Sol.* 8:28); (3) the place or country where the scattered Jews now live (Judith 5:19).

3. Although *diaspora* became a technical term for the scattering of the Jews, it is remarkable that it is never used in the LXX to translate the Heb. terms *gōlâ* and *gālût*, which denote their being led away into captivity and the exile. The Gk. words used for these words tended to have hard, negative ideas, suggesting captivity in a foreign country. *diaspora*, by contrast, is more neutral.

The change to *diaspora* reflects an evolution of Jewish thought. After wars of conquest, foreign rulers deported masses of Jews in order to break their military strength. The first large Jewish *diaspora* was in Babylonia, where Nebuchadnezzar deported a section of the vanquished (2 Ki. 24:14–16; 25:11–21) and where the majority of Jews remained even after the edict of Cyrus allowing them to return. The original deportation was seen as God's punishment (Jer. 17:1–4; Ezek. 12:15). But this outlook gradually dissipated, and out of the exile there grew communities of Jews who lived there of their own volition. Through the preaching of the prophets a more positive attitude toward the situation emerged (cf. Isa. 60; Hag. 2:6–9; Zech. 8:20–23): Through this dispersion God intended to bring all nations to himself (cf. esp. Isa. 40–66). Thus, the *diaspora* provided the motivation for the almost worldwide missionary activity among the Jews.

NT In the NT *diaspora* occurs only 3x. It is used of both the Jews and the church. Jn. 7:35 speaks of the dispersion of the Jews among the Greeks (cf. Deut. 30:4; Ps. 147:2). Jas. 1:1 and 1 Pet. 1:1 are theologically more significant. Peter directs his letter to "God's elect, strangers in the world, scattered (*diaspora*) throughout Pontus, Galatia, Cappadocia, Asia and Bithynia" (1 Pet. 1:1); James, to "the twelve tribes scattered (*diaspora*) among the nations" (Jas. 1:1). If these letters were written to Gentile Christians, this word has a special significance. The apostles see in Christians dispersed throughout the world a parallel to the Jewish dispersion. The true homeland of Christ's followers is not the place where they happen to live. It is in heaven (cf. Phil. 3:20), the Jerusalem that is above (cf. Gal. 4:26). On earth they are always strangers, living as aliens (→ *paroikos*, *4230*). They are like God's seed that is sown far and wide, whose fruit will be apparent at the great ingathering (cf. Matt. 24:31).

See also *allotrios*, alien, hostile (*259*); *xenos*, foreign; stranger, alien (*3828*); *parepidēmos*, staying for a while in a strange place; stranger, resident alien (*4215*); *paroikos*, stranger, alien (*4230*).

1407 (*diasōzō*, bring safely through, save, rescue), → *5392*.

1408 (*diatagē*, ordinance, direction), → *5435*.

1411 (*diatassō*, command, order), → *5435*.

1419 (*diaugazō*, to shine through, dawn), → *575*.

1422	διαφέρω

διαφέρω (*diapherō*), carry through; be different, valuable (*1422*); διάφορος (*diaphoros*), different, superior (*1427*).

CL & OT 1. In cl. Gk. *diapherō* has a trans. meaning to carry through or across. Intrans. it means to differ, be different from; sometimes, to excel or surpass.

2. *diapherō* seldom occurs in the LXX and usually with the intrans. meaning. The beasts in Daniel's vision are different from each other (7:3). There is no difference between the wrath of a king and the roar of a lion (Prov. 20:2). If someone loudly blesses a neighbor early in the morning, it is no different from a curse (27:14). *diaphoros* likewise means different (e.g., Lev. 19:19; Deut. 22:9; Dan. 7:7, 19 [the last two in Theod.]).

NT 1. *diapherō* has a trans. meaning 3x in the NT. In concern for his Father's house, Jesus refused to allow anyone "to carry" anything connected with business through the temple (Mk. 11:16). After the preaching of Paul and Barnabas, the word of God "spread" (lit., was carried) through the region (Acts 13:49). The people on the ship headed for Rome "were . . . driven" by the wind and seas for fourteen days and nights (27:27).

2. More important are the intrans. meanings (10x). Believers are of much more value to the Father than birds (Matt. 6:26; 10:31) or sheep (12:12). That is, to God human life is more important than anything else. As Paul reflects on the issue of the old and new covenants, he uses the analogy of an heir when that person is a child and when he is grown up. Until an heir comes of age, he is no different from a slave (Gal. 4:1) but is required to live according to law. But when he grows up, he is free from the laws of his father.

3. Paul writes that God has dispensed "different" (*diaphoros*) gifts according to his grace (Rom. 12:6). Heb. uses *diaphoros* to stress the superiority of Jesus' name (1:4) and ministry (8:6).

1425 (*diaphtheirō*, spoil, destroy, ruin), → *5780*.

1426 (*diaphthora*, destruction, corruption), → *5780*.

1427 (*diaphoros*, different, superior), → *1422*.

1434 (*didaktikos*, skillful in teaching), → *1438*.

1435 (*didaktos*, taught), → *1438*.

1436	διδασκαλία

διδασκαλία (*didaskalia*), teaching, instruction (*1436*); διδαχή (*didachē*), teaching (*1439*).

CL & OT 1. The noun *didaskalia* denotes the activity of a teacher. The word also occurs with a pass. meaning, i.e., doctrine (that which is taught). *didachē*, derived directly from the verbal stem of *didaskō*, means instruction or doctrine imparted by teaching.

2. (a) In the LXX *didaskalia* occurs only 4x. In Prov. 2:17; Sir. 24:33; 39:8, it denotes the law considered as the will of God, while in Isa. 29:13 it means human doctrines, which by their very multiplicity are to be distinguished from the one will of God. The reason for the rarity of *didaskalia* in the LXX lies in the fact that its primary meaning in cl. Gk. is intellectual teaching with a view to knowledge, whereas Israel saw teaching as meaning the law of God, to which the only appropriate response was obedience.

(b) *didachē* is found only in the title of Ps. 60, "for teaching." The Heb. equivalent of *didachē* is *talmūd*, study (see, e.g., *m. Abot* 6:2).

NT In the NT *didachē* occurs 30x, the majority of which are in the Gospels and Acts. *didaskalia* occurs 21x, most of them in the Pastoral Letters.

1. (a) Jesus' preaching is called *didachē* (Mk. 1:22, 27), without any further details being given as to its content (cf. Mk.'s use of *didaskō*, to teach, → *1438*). Mk. sees Jesus' teaching as having a close connection with his miracles, which are proof, so to speak, of the divine authority behind the teaching. In 11:18 Jesus' authoritative teaching is given as the reason for the scribes' plot to kill him, while in 12:38 *didachē* is extended to cover his polemic against the scribes.

(b) Matt. uses *didachē* in 7:28 to describe the Sermon on the Mount (chs. 5–7), a portion of which is Christ's exposition of the law (cf. 22:33). Matt. also uses this word for the teaching of the Pharisees and Sadducees (16:12).

(c) In Acts *didachē* is used for the early Christian preaching and appears in a variety of phrases: e.g., "the apostles' teaching" (Acts 2:42), "the teaching about the Lord" (13:12), "new teaching" (17:19); these expressions denote the testimony of the apostles to Christ (cf. 1:21). Exposition of the Mosaic law, which Matt. describes as *didachē*, is no longer considered part of the teaching.

(d) Jn.'s use of *didachē* in Jn. 7:16–17 (cf. 18:19) points in the same direction. Jesus' message is described as teaching that comes from the Father. This message becomes in 2 Jn. 9–10 the "teaching of Christ."

(e) In Rom. 6:17; 16:17 Paul uses *didachē* to refer to the whole of his apostolic teaching. In 1 Cor. 14:6, 26 the word denotes one of several types of "edifying speech," all contrasted with speaking in tongues. In the Pastoral Letters, *didachē* seems to have become a given body of doctrine that is to be inculcated (2 Tim. 4:2; Tit. 1:9). This is indicated elsewhere by the fact that "teaching" is referred to as *parathēkē*, that which has been entrusted (1 Tim. 6:20; 2 Tim. 1:12, 14), and *didaskalia* (see below).

(f) *didachē* in Heb. 6:2 probably also means a specific set of doctrines ("instruction about baptisms," etc.), while in 13:9 the writer describes the teachings of his opponents as *didachē* (cf. Rev. 2:14, 15, 24).

(g) To summarize: In the NT *didachē* denotes Christ's message (with his call to repentance and faith) and the early Christian preaching in the widest sense. It is striking that no explicit distinction is made between a fixed body of doctrine (handed down by tradition) and the message preached at any given time. The fact that the early church, at a relatively early stage, possessed a more or less fixed body of doctrine is indicated by the brief confessions of faith quoted by Paul, even though he himself may not yet have viewed them as sacrosanct. The material collected in the Sermon on the Mount points in the same direction. Such compilations led to such works as *The Teaching of the Twelve Apostles* (often called the *Didache* [cf. 2:1; 6:1; 11:2]), which were regarded as authoritative teaching.

2. This development can be observed in the use of *didaskalia* as well. (a) The phrase *didaskalias . . . anthrōpōn* (lit., "teachings of men") is applied to the teachings of the scribes and Pharisees in Matt. 15:9; Mk. 7:7 (quoting Isa. 29:13). The same text from Isa. is in view in Col. 2:22, which describes the doctrines of the false teachers in Colosse. Similarly, 1 Tim. 4:1 refers not only to the spirits of seduction and error but also to "things [doctrines] taught by demons."

(b) In all other places in the NT, *didaskalia* is in the sing. In Rom. 12:7 it means the teaching office, and in 15:4 it describes the function of Ps. 69:9, quoted in Rom. 15:3, namely, to provide Christians with instruction. In Eph. 4:14 Christians wavering in spiritual discernment are said to be "blown here and there by every wind of teaching."

(c) The Gospels and Paul's other letters, with their limited use of *didaskalia* (6x), form a contrast with the Pastoral Letters, where the word occurs 15x. In 1 Tim. 1:10; 2 Tim. 4:3; Tit. 1:9; 2:1, the word is qualified by the word "sound" and means that relatively fixed "orthodoxy" that the churches have received and that is their duty to preserve against heresy. The same fixed doctrinal tradition is called in 1 Tim. 6:3 "godly teaching," in 4:6 "good teaching," and in 4:16 simply "doctrine" (cf. 2 Tim. 3:10). The word denotes the activity of teaching in 1 Tim. 4:13 (cf. 5:17; Tit. 2:7). In 2 Tim. 3:16 we learn that the Scripture, inspired by God (i.e., the OT), is profitable for (among other things) "teaching." Finally, in Tit. 2:10 slaves are told that their behavior should "make the teaching about God our Savior attractive" (cf. 1 Tim. 6:1).

See also *didaskō*, teach (*1438*); *didaskalos*, teacher, master (*1437*); *katēcheō*, inform, instruct (*2994*); *paideuō*, bring up, instruct, train, educate (*4084*); *paradidōmi*, to deliver, hand down (*4140*).

1437 διδάσκαλος

διδάσκαλος (*didaskalos*), teacher, master (*1437*); νομοδιδάσκαλος (*nomodidaskalos*), teacher of the law (*3791*); καλοδιδάσκαλος (*kalodidaskalos*), teaching what is good (*2815*); ψευδοδιδάσκαλος (*pseudodidaskalos*), false teacher (*6015*); ἑτεροδιδασκαλέω (*heterodidaskaleō*), teach a different, i.e., heretical, doctrine (*2281*).

CL & OT 1. *didaskalos* is widely used in cl. Gk. in the sense of teacher or tutor. The word covers all those regularly engaged in the systematic imparting of knowledge or technical skills: the elementary teacher, the tutor, the philosopher, even the chorus master, who has to conduct rehearsals of poetry for a public performance. Since a teacher's activity is confined to specific areas, *didaskalos* is often more closely defined by the subj. taught. In this connection it is interesting that Socrates did not want to be known as a teacher, for virtue was not something that could be taught. Epictetus, on the other hand, recommended himself as a teacher for those striving after perfection.

2. (a) In the LXX *didaskalos* occurs only 2x: in Est. 6:1, where it denotes a reader, and in 2 Macc. 1:10, which refers to Aristobulus, head of the Egyptian Jewish community, who dedicated an exposition of the Pentateuch to King Ptolemy Philometor. This second usage shows a new nuance to this word, for its roots lie in Palestinian Jud. and in the Heb. vb. *limmad* (piel of *lāmad*), to teach. Not just the word but the whole Gk. notion of teacher is foreign to the OT insofar as the latter is more concerned with obedience than with the imparting of information (→ *didaskō*, to teach, *1438*).

(b) The situation is different in the Qumran texts, where *môreh* (Heb. word for teacher) occurs more frequently, though usually with some qualifying phrase like "of righteousness" (e.g. 1QpHab 1:13; 2:2; CD 1:11; 20:32). The title Teacher of Righteousness probably refers to the founder of the sect, who taught the true understanding of the Torah.

Other Heb. terms for teacher are *maśkîl*, instructor (e.g., 1QS 3:13; 9:12, 21), and *rab*, teacher of the law (from which the term *rabbî* [lit., "my teacher"] is derived). A Jewish rabbi at the time of Christ had the task of expounding the Torah and of giving rulings in matters of the law. He had pupils who studied his exposition and his rulings and were in duty bound to respect and obey him as their teacher. In the 1st cent. A.D., *rabbî* became the exclusive word for an officially appointed teacher of the law.

(c) Philo's usage conforms to that of cl. Gk. He uses *didaskalos* not only of Moses but also of God himself. In both cases he regards a teacher as one who imparts knowledge, not as one who lays ethical demands before others.

NT In the NT *didaskalos* occurs 59x, most of them in the Gospels. The word refers to Jesus 41x, of which 29x represent a direct form of address. In the Gospels *didaskalos* also applies to John the Baptist (Lk. 3:12), Nicodemus (Jn. 3:10), and the Jewish teachers of the law (Lk. 2:46). Elsewhere in the NT, it denotes the teachers of the church (Acts 13:1; 1 Cor. 12:28; Eph. 4:11; Jas. 3:1). In 1 Tim. 2:7 and in 2 Tim. 1:11 Paul calls himself *didaskalos*, a term that he uses alongside *kēryx*, herald (→ *kēryssō*, to preach, *3062*), and *apostolos*, apostle (→ *693*).

1. *Jesus as teacher.* (a) The voc. form *didaskale*, master, teacher, applied to Jesus (e.g., Matt. 8:19; Mk. 9:17, 38; Lk. 10:25) or to John the Baptist (Lk. 3:12), is merely the translation of the Heb. *rabbî* (cf. Jn. 1:38; 20:16, where this is made explicit; cf. also Mk. 9:5; 11:21). Jesus had all the marks of the rabbi: He was asked to give rulings on disputed questions of the law (Lk. 12:13–14) and on doctrinal issues (Mk. 12:18–34); he also had pupils. The later conditions for a rabbi, namely, study and ordination, were not binding in the time of Jesus.

Matt. tends not to use the vocative *didaskale* in places where Mk. has it; when he does use it, it comes from the lips of Jesus' opponents or from outsiders. Perhaps Matt. discards this title for Jesus because, being in sharp conflict with the Jewish rabbis, he wishes to avoid the too-frequent ascription of that title to Jesus. Moreover, Matt. tends to use titles for Jesus that are Christological in content (see also *rhabbi, 4806*). Mk. and Lk. use *didaskalos* for the most part quite spontaneously and without attaching to it any Christological significance.

(b) In addition to its use in the voc., *didaskalos* is often used absolutely in the Gospels to denote Jesus (e.g., Matt. 9:11; 17:24). It occurs in the saying in Matt. 10:24–25 ("A student is not above his teacher"), where Jesus describes the relationship between him and his followers, and in 23:8, where he admonishes his disciples not to call anyone *rhabbi*, for they have only one teacher, Jesus; he above all others is *the* Teacher, whose authority continues even after his death (cf. Jn. 3:2; 11:27–28; 13:13–14, where *didaskalos* is used with other Christological titles).

2. *The teaching office in the early church.* In 1 Cor. 12:28 *didaskalos* is mentioned as the third charismatic office of a triad (alongside apostles and prophets). Those holding this office had the task of explaining the Christian faith to others and of providing a Christian exposition of the OT. Later Paul adds a fourth office—that of the *euangelistēs*, evangelist (Eph. 4:11), but in both cases the teacher is appointed to a particular church (cf. Acts 13:1, where the *didaskaloi* are mentioned together with the prophets). Jas. 3:1, warning against too strong an influx into the teaching office (which the writer himself appears to hold), points out that the failures of teachers will incur severe penalties in the judgment. Heb. 5:12 refers to Christians who ought long since to have been "teachers," but who instead need to be taught again the first principles of the faith. In 2 Tim. 4:3 the word appears to be applied, ironically, to false teachers.

3. The following compounds may be noted. (a) *nomodidaskalos*, teacher of the law, is found only in Christian writings. In 1 Tim. 1:7 it is used of false teachers who desire to be teachers of the law but who are without understanding and have fallen into vain discussion. They evidently occupied themselves with myths and endless genealogies (1:4). In Acts 5:34 the term describes the Pharisee Gamaliel, who "was honored by all the people" and urged the other leaders to leave the apostles alone, suggesting that if the Christian movement was from God, they could not stop it (5:38–39). In Lk. 5:17 it denotes the Pharisees.

(b) *kalodidaskalos*, teaching what is good, is found only in Tit. 2:3, where it is a description of what the older women in the church ought to be.

(c) *pseudodidaskalos*, false teacher, occurs only at 2 Pet. 2:1, where such men are seen as counterparts to the false prophets of old. They will secretly bring destructive heresies and even deny the Master who bought them, but they will bring swift judgment on themselves.

(d) *heterodidaskaleō* means to teach a different, i.e., heretical, doctrine. It occurs only 2x in the NT. Timothy is urged to remain at Ephesus and "command certain men not to teach false doctrines any longer" (1 Tim. 1:3). These people were evidently the same as those who aspired to be *nomodidaskaloi* in 1:7. In 6:3 the test of such a teacher is whether he agrees with "the sound instruction of our Lord Jesus Christ and . . . godly teaching." The character of those who do not is delineated in 6:4–10.

See also *didaskō*, teach (*1438*); *didaskalia*, teaching, instruction (*1436*); *katēcheō*, inform, instruct (*2994*); *paideuō*, bring up, instruct, train, educate (*4084*); *paradidōmi*, to deliver, hand down (*4140*).

1438	διδάσκω

διδάσκω (*didaskō*), teach (*1438*); διδακτός (*didaktos*), taught (*1435*); διδακτικός (*didaktikos*), skillful in teaching (*1434*).

CL & OT 1. In cl. Gk. *didaskō* occurs frequently. In the act. it means to teach, inform, instruct, demonstrate, prescribe; in the pass. to be instructed, be taught; in the mid. to learn for oneself, to think out, to master. The word is used typically for the relationship between teacher and pupil, instructor and apprentice. What is taught may be not only knowledge, opinions, or facts but also artistic and technical skills, all of which are to be systematically and thoroughly acquired by the learner through the activity of a teacher. The word is not found describing an activity of the gods until the 1st century B.C., when the goddess Isis is said to cause people to be instructed in the things of religion and culture.

2. In the LXX *didaskō* occurs about 100x, most commonly in Deut., Job, Ps., Prov., and Jer. But in contrast to cl. Gk., the word here does not usually denote the communication of knowledge and skills (e.g., 2 Sam. 22:35), but chiefly instruction in how to live (e.g., Deut. 11:19; 20:18), the subject matter being the will of God. God's ordinances and judgments are to be learned, understood, and obeyed. They may be taught by God himself (4:1, 10, 14), by fathers in the teaching of their children (11:19), or by the godly, who know God's will. The fact that the LXX never uses *didaskō* for the preaching of the prophets is a result of the close link between teaching and the law.

3. (a) The use of words for teaching in Qumran documents largely corresponds to that of the LXX. What is taught are the requirements of God's will (1QS 9:13; 1QH 2:17), the laws of the covenant (1QSa 1:7; 1QM 10:10), and requirements for battle (10:2; 14:6).

(b) In rab. Jud., as indeed in the later portions of the OT (e.g., 2 Chr. 17:7–9), teaching is again used for the communication of God's will concerning our relationship to him or our fellow human beings, this will being discerned through the interpretation of the law. The Heb. word for teaching (*limmad*, a piel vb. form) is used as a specialized term for the translation of the Torah into concrete directions for the life of the individual. Hence, it is best regarded as pronouncing a scholarly opinion on the basis of scriptural interpretation.

NT In the NT *didaskō* occurs 97x. The meaning is almost always to teach or instruct, though the purpose and content of the teaching can be determined only from each individual context.

1. *Jesus' teaching work according to the Gospels.* It is the unanimous testimony of the Synoptic writers that Jesus "taught" publicly—i.e., in synagogues (Matt. 9:35; 13:54), in the temple (26:55; Mk. 12:35; Lk. 21:37), or in the open air (Matt. 5:2; Mk. 6:34; Lk. 5:3). Only Lk. 4:16–21 gives details concerning the outward form of his teaching, namely, his standing to read a portion from the Prophets, then sitting to expound it (the normal Jewish and rab. custom). *didaskō* is used 13x absolutely as a comprehensive term for Jesus' preaching (e.g., Mk. 2:13; 6:6; 10:1; 12:35; 14:49).

While Jesus was on earth, he taught about God, his kingdom, and his will—all themes of contemporary Jud. He differed from his rab. counterparts not in his subject matter but in the radical way in which he handled these subjects, consistently applying all he said to concrete situations in our human lives and involving himself personally in the subjects under discussion. Instead of giving merely theoretical teaching about God, his providence, his grace, or his wrath, Jesus showed God's goodness and wrath at work in concrete situations (e.g., Lk. 15:1–32). Instead of speculating on the kingdom of God, he announced its nearness (Mk. 1:15) and so issued a call to repentance and a change of behavior (Matt. 5:21–48; Mk. 7:15). And instead of inculcating the type of legal casuistry that sought to ensure salvation, he told his hearers: "So in everything, do to others what you would have them do to you" (Matt. 7:12).

(a) *Mark.* In Mk. 4:2 Jesus' teaching consists of parables regarding the kingdom of God, a kingdom whose nearness has already been summarized as the essence of his preaching (1:14–15). In 2:13 *didaskō* describes his confrontation with contemporary Jewish legalism; in 10:1–12 and 12:14–34 the vb. introduces examples of Jesus giving his ruling on controversial matters, while in 11:17 and 12:35–36 the subj. of his teaching is a passage from the OT. Mk. attaches importance to the link between teaching and doing (6:2, 34). In other words, Mk. uses *didaskō* not only in the sense of teaching, i.e., giving practical instructions or rulings on the basis of scriptural interpretation, but also in the sense of preaching the kingdom of God and the gospel.

(b) *Luke*. Lk. frequently adopts Mk.'s use of *didaskō* and, where he does so, uses it in senses similar to those of Mk. This applies also to passages where the vb. is peculiar to Lk. (6:6; 11:1; 12:12; 13:26; 23:5). His view of what Jesus taught emerges most clearly from his account of Jesus in the temple (chs. 20–21), where the subjects are the law, future events, and matters concerned with Christology. The main thrust in Lk. is the nearness of God's kingdom. Lk. 4:16–21 provides an example of Jesus' work during his ministry: He reads Isa. 61:1–2 and points to himself as the fulfillment of the prophetic promise. Now is the period of salvation, which is already manifest (4:21) in his miracles; they are part of the teaching itself.

(c) *Matthew*. Like Lk., Matt. also retains the basic sense of *didaskō*: to teach, preach. As regards content, however, Matt. 5:2, 19 and 28:20 are noteworthy. In Matt. 5:2–3 (the beginning of the Sermon on the Mount), Jesus is shown teaching his disciples; hence it is they whose righteousness must exceed that of the teachers of the law (5:20). For Matt., Jesus is the teacher of the church, who supersedes the Sinaitic revelation and its rab. interpretations ("you have heard that it was said") in order to lay a new foundation ("but I tell you").

After Jesus' death, Peter guarantees this foundation (Matt. 16:18), holding the office of the keys, which to the Jews meant the office of a teacher. The foundation guaranteed by him is no new law, but the fulfillment of the old, now freed from rab. distortions. Only now does the original intention of the law become clear (19:8: "from the beginning"). These two verses (16:18; 19:8) throw light on 5:19: Those who live without the Torah live without righteousness. The follower of Jesus is called not to lawlessness but to a superior righteousness, the foundation of which is the law and Christ's interpretation of it. This is why, after his resurrection, this interpretation must be passed on through teaching (28:20).

(d) *John*. *didaskō* occurs 10x in the Gospel of Jn. (6:59; 7:14, 28, 35; 8:2, 20, 28; 9:34; 14:26; 18:20) and 3x in 1 Jn. (2:27). In most cases, Jesus himself is the subject of the vb., while the theme of the teaching is always the message of Jesus as the one who reveals God; it is a message that demands faith and is recognized as the true message from God only by those who believe. The same is true in 1 Jn. 2:27, where the author encourages the church and alludes to their "anointing," which bestows on them the Holy Spirit, the source of all knowledge (1 Jn. 3:24; cf. Jn. 14:25). Hence those who have the anointing need no further instruction: they know the truth already (cf. 1 Jn. 2:21). One of the three instances in the NT of *didaktos*, taught, occurs in Jn. 6:45 in the quotation from Isa. 54:13, where those who come to Jesus are seen as fulfilling the prophecy, "They will all be taught by God." It is God himself who draws people to Jesus.

2. *The disciples' teaching*. (a) The Synoptic Gospels speak not only of the teaching carried out by Jesus but also of that undertaken by his disciples (Matt. 28:20; Mk. 6:30). In Lk. 12:12 the Holy Spirit is promised as teacher (cf. Jn. 14:26).

(b) In Acts what is taught is the resurrection from the dead (4:2), "the word of the Lord" (5:42; 15:35), or the message about Jesus (4:18; 5:28; cf. 18:25). In 15:1 is a reference to some who were "teaching" circumcision, and in 21:21 Paul is said to have been charged with teaching apostasy from Moses; in both cases the teaching arises from the normal Jewish practice of discussing the law.

In several places in Acts (e.g., 4:2), *didaskō* is linked with *katangellō*, to preach, proclaim, or with *euangelizō*, to proclaim the good news (15:35). However, if only because of the rhetorical character of these pairs of words, any distinction here between "teaching" and "preaching" seems inadmissible (see esp. 18:11, 25; 28:31). The context of these passages is the postresurrection message of salvation (cf. 1:1; 4:18; 5:21, 25, 28, 42; 11:26; 15:1, 35; 20:20), and it is, therefore, salvation as understood by the postresurrection church that forms the subj. matter of *didaskō* in Acts. Conversely, Paul is accused of teaching the Jewish people to forsake Moses, the customs of the Jews, the temple, the people, and the law (21:21, 28). Luke regards the essence

of this salvation as having become manifest in Jesus (Lk. 4:16–21; Acts 1:21–22).

(c) Paul uses *didaskō* 16x (e.g., Rom. 2:21; 12:7; 1 Cor. 4:17; 11:14; Gal. 1:12). His earlier life had been governed by the traditions of the fathers (Gal. 1:14), which were "taught." In Rom. 2:21 he uses *didaskō* in the Heb. sense of *limmad* when he asks the Jew: "You, then, who teach others, do you not teach yourself?" Rom. 12:7 refers to the church office of the *didaskalos*, teacher, whose task it is to expound the principles of the faith (cf. 1 Cor. 4:17; → *1437*). In Gal. 1:12 *didaskō* means to hand on a tradition. Paul's language is noteworthy in 1 Cor. 11:14, where he speaks of nature teaching; this idea may have a Stoic background. The use of *didaktos* in 1 Cor. 2:13 is similar to Jn. 6:45 (see above).

(d) A different nuance occurs in those letters ascribed to Paul that some scholars regard as non-Pauline. In 2 Thess. 2:15 ("hold to the teachings we passed on to you, whether by word of mouth or by letter"), the reference is to 1 Thess. and to (more or less fixed) oral traditions. Here, therefore, *didaskō* no longer means to hear the message in a concrete situation but to receive and keep teaching handed down (reminiscent of the teaching methods used by the rabbis). *didaskō* also occurs in Eph. 4:21, where the phrase "[you] were taught in him," like the previous phrase to "know Christ," refers to the conversion of those who are being addressed (cf. Col. 2:7).

It is difficult to determine the meaning of *didaskō* in Col. 1:28 and 3:16. But the reference is probably to the practical exhortation required of all members of the church. The phrase "with all wisdom," which qualifies *didaskō* in both passages, probably has to do with the manner rather than the content of the teaching.

(e) In the Pastoral Letters, it is Timothy's right and duty to teach (1 Tim. 4:11; 6:2); in 2 Tim. 2:2 teaching is the task of those who meet certain requirements, while in 1 Tim. 2:12 women are debarred from teaching. In all these passages what is taught is assumed to be "good" or "sound" doctrine (*didaskalia*, → *1436*), which is passed on and preserved. The emphasis here falls on handing it on. In Tit. 1:11 *didaskō* refers to false teachers, who, for the sake of gain, are teaching Jewish myths and human commands. The sole instances of *didaktikos*, skillful in teaching, occur in 1 Tim. 3:2 and 2 Tim. 2:24, where it is listed among the qualifications of bishops and God's servants.

(f) Closely related to the usage of the word in the Pastoral Letters is its use in Heb. In 5:12 the author reproaches his readers with the fact that, although they should already have been teachers of others, they need to be taught afresh the first principles of God's Word (i.e., the basic Christian doctrines cited in 6:1–3). In 8:11 the word occurs in the quotation of Jer. 31:31–34, where the knowledge of God, which doubtless is also knowledge of his will, is the subj. of the teaching.

(g) The two occurrences of *didaskō* in Rev. (2:14, 20) refer to the activity of false teachers in Pergamum and Thyatira, respectively.

See also *didaskalos*, teacher, master (*1437*); *didaskalia*, teaching, instruction (*1436*); *katēcheō*, inform, instruct (*2994*); *paideuō*, bring up, instruct, train, educate (*4084*); *paradidōmi*, to deliver, hand down (*4140*).

1439 (didachē, teaching), → *1436*.

1440 (didrachmon, a double drachma, two-drachma coin), → *5088*.

1443 (didōmi, give, grant), → *1565*.

1449 (diermēneutēs, interpreter, translator), → *2257*.

1450 (diermēneuō, translate, interpret, explain), → *2257*.

1451 (dierchomai, go through, come through), → *2262*.

1455 (diēgeomai, tell, describe), → *2007*.

1456 (diēgēsis, narrative, account), → *2007*.

1465 (dikaios, upright, just, righteous), → *1466*.

| 1466   δικαιοσύνη |

δικαιοσύνη (*dikaiosynē*), righteousness, uprightness (*1466*); δίκαιος (*dikaios*), upright, just, righteous (*1465*); δικαιόω (*dikaioō*), justify, vindicate, treat as just, acquit, pronounce or treat as righteous, make or set free from (*1467*); δικαίωμα (*dikaiōma*), regulation, requirement, commandment, righteous deed (*1468*); δικαίως (*dikaiōs*), justly, in a just manner, uprightly (*1469*); δικαίωσις (*dikaiōsis*), justification, vindication, acquittal (*1470*).

CL 1. All the words in this group derive from *dikē* (justice, punishment, → *1472*). Dike was the daughter of Zeus, who shared in his government of the world. Zeus made a difference between animals and human beings: To the former he gave a *nomos* (law, i.e., that they should devour each other), while to the latter, in order to make human life possible, he gave *dikē*, justice, whose implacable enemy is *bia*, violence. In its basic religious sense, therefore, and in common with all things divine in Gk. religion, *dikē* is an elemental cosmic force that humans recognize as superior to themselves. It is not a standard imposed on the world by God but something inherent in the very nature of being and related to living together in society.

Later *dikē* was also regarded as punishment or as the goddess of punishment who pursued wrongdoers. In the arguments that preceded the creation of the city-state, *dikē* and its derivatives were first of all battle cries; later they became concepts basic to the whole ideas of the *polis*. Of overriding importance here was the idea that justice prevails when everyone does what is fitting for him or her.

For Plato *dikaiosynē* is basic to the structure of the state and the human soul; it is the chief of human virtues for Aristotle. To these philosophers, it was right and proper to accept the existence of utterly diverse social ranks with their accompanying degrees of power and to take upon oneself that which befitted one's own station. In other words, *dikē* acquired the status of the axiomatic, unshakable foundation of all human life.

2. Hence, the righteous person (*dikaios*) was originally someone whose behavior fit into the framework of society and who fulfilled rightful obligations toward the gods and one's fellow human beings. The observance of such obligations set this individual apart from the unrighteous. Hybris and uncivilized behavior were out of keeping with the character of a righteous person; thus, the term *dikaia zoē* ("righteous life") was applied to a civilized way of life, i.e., one that, unlike barbarism, adhered to the rules of an orderly society. Later the meaning was extended to cover the idea of conforming to a given standard. *dikaion* was particularly common as a neut. noun in the sense of "that which is [legally and ethically] right." It came to mean a legal claim.

3. (a) The noun *dikaiosynē* denotes the quality of the righteous individual but is also in itself the standard that a judge is required to uphold, the condition he seeks to restore. Thus it is *impartial* justice, one of the four cardinal virtues, along with *phronēsis* (prudence), *sōphrosynē* (temperance), and *andreia* (fortitude).

(b) The derivative vb. *dikaioō* means to put right (e.g., the law on violence); to demand as a right, regard as being right, pass sentence; also to give someone one's due, either in the sense of to punish or to declare righteous, justify.

4. Two other nouns derive from the same stem. *dikaiōma* means right action; judgment (either of condemnation or acquittal); ordinance, decree; legal documents, credentials. *dikaiōsis* means condemnation, punishment; acquittal; just claim; discretion, judgment as to what is just or unjust.

OT In the LXX the noun *dikaiōma* often means ordinance or statute. It translates the Heb. *ḥōq* or *ḥuqqâ* some 70x, and *mišpāṭ* 38x. Apart from this, the *dikaios* word group predominantly translates words belonging to the Heb. *ṣdq* word group. *diakaiosynē* normally renders the Heb. *ṣᵉdāqâ* and less frequently *ṣedeq*. The adj. *dikaios* occurs some 180x for *ṣaddîq*. The vb. *dikaioō* is used 22x to translate *ṣādaq*. Most of these words also occasionally translate other Heb. roots.

1. Righteousness in the OT is not a matter of actions conforming to a given set of absolute legal standards, but of behavior in keeping with the relationship between God and humans. Thus the righteousness of God appears in his God-like dealings with his people, i.e., in redemption and salvation (Isa. 45:21; 51:5–6; 56:1; 62:1). His righteous acts are extolled from the earliest times (Jdg. 5:11; 1 Sam. 12:7; Ps. 103:6; Isa. 45:24 = LXX 45:25). Those who long for redemption call on God's righteousness, i.e., they plead for his intervention (Ps. 71:2; 143:11). Israel's enemies, on the other hand, discover that God's righteousness is the root of their downfall (Isa. 41:10–11; 54:17). For Israel's sake, even the land may be restored through the gift of God's righteousness (Isa. 32:15–20; Hos. 10:12; Joel 2:23). Dwelling in the land, Israel enjoys God's righteousness (Ps. 24:5).

2. In the preexilic period, little is said about individual righteousness; the main concern is that people should remain within national righteousness. Access to it is denied to any whose life falls short of God's standards (Ps. 15; 24:3–6), God's righteousness being, in effect, salvation per se. On a purely human level, judgment is pronounced not in terms of "the guilty person is justly punished," but rather "acquitting the innocent and condemning the guilty" (Deut. 25:1; lit., "the just man is made just and the guilty man made guilty").

In general before the exile, a person's righteousness is not so much in relation to God as in relation to fellow humans; this behavior is regulated on the one hand by human relationships (e.g., between family members [Gen. 38:26]; between the king and one of his officers [1 Sam. 24:15]), and on the other hand by God's law (Zeph. 2:3). Amos 5:4–6, 14 and Hosea testify generally to a concern for righteousness before God through interpersonal relationships.

The exile marks a turning point, and thereafter the OT has no hesitation in speaking of the devout person's righteousness before God. Before the exile the pledge of God's presence among the people was their free, independent possession of the land, with his righteousness covering both the people and the land they owned. But afterward, God's pledge is his law, which provides clear terms of reference for righteousness among his people, and at the same time the framework within which a person may share in Yahweh's righteousness. Hence, when the psalmists refer to themselves as "righteous" (e.g., Ps. 119), they are appealing to their membership of that nation that Yahweh has permitted to partake of his righteousness, for, as the religion of Israel had long since made clear, God alone can pronounce a person righteous.

Such a claim on the part of a psalmist is, therefore, an act of testimony. The fact that an individual joins in public worship is evidence that he or she is not cut off from the righteousness of God. Moreover, the law is considered easy to keep, so by claiming to be righteous people are joyfully acknowledging the law to be the wellspring of their daily lives. Here and there, however, a note is already heard that one's own righteousness counts for nothing in God's eyes (Job 4:17; Ps. 143:1) and that everyone is dependent on his mercy alone (Dan. 9:18). Consequently, in the intertestamental period "righteousness" takes on increasingly the character of "goodness," which counterbalances the impartial judgment of God.

3. Outside specifically theological contexts, the Heb. root *ṣdq* is used in connection with weights and measures, indicating conformity to the proper standards (Lev. 19:36; Deut. 25:15; Ezek. 45:10), and correct sacrifices that have been offered in accordance with the prescribed ritual (Deut. 33:19; Ps. 4:6; 51:21). A righteous person in the law is one who is "in the right" (cf. Exod. 23:7; 1 Sam. 24:17; Ezek. 16:52).

The standard of righteousness must be seen against the wider background of the covenant relationship with Yahweh. His righteousness implies the same kind of appropriate conduct that in Israel upholds the law by means of judicial procedure. God's righteousness in the Psalms is a divine attribute, occasionally personified. "The LORD loves righteousness and justice" (Ps. 33:5); that is, Yahweh loves to perform righteous and just deeds (cf. 99:4; Jer. 9:24) and is concerned about upholding righteousness and justice. In some contexts righteousness amounts to deliverance (Ps. 22:31), salvation (69:27), victory (Isa. 41:2), righteous help (Ps. 71:24), healing (40:10), and perhaps even reward (106:31). Negatively, it means punishment of the wicked (119:75).

Because the nation found its focus in the king, it depended on him for its right-ordering and well-being; thus the king has a special place in maintaining righteousness in Israel (cf. 2 Sam. 15:1–6; Ps. 72; Amos 2:6–7; 5:12–15; Mic. 3:1–2). Within Yahweh's righteousness there is a place for punishment and deliverance. Thus, in the destruction of Jerusalem the city confesses: "The LORD is righteous, yet I have rebelled against his command" (Lam. 1:18). Nevertheless, Yahweh may still deliver Israel, giving sentence in his favor because of the character of Yahweh himself (Isa. 46:12–13; cf. 51:5–8, 17).

Isa. 56–59 begins with the call: "Maintain justice and do what is right, for my salvation is close at hand and my righteousness will soon be revealed" (56:1). Righteousness is the key to national recovery (58:8–14; cf. 60:17, 21) and will ultimately spread to the nations (61:10–11). This righteousness depends on Yahweh's gift (46:12–13; 50:9; 52:13–53:12), but it calls for a corresponding righteousness in the national and individual lives of the people (cf. Deut. 6:20–25; 24:13).

4. *dikaios* is used in the Apocr. as in the rest of the LXX, except that there are no instances of the meaning "in the right" and "innocent." "Righteous" is applied to God, human beings, and actions (Tob. 3:2; 14:9; Wis. 2:10; 3:1; Sir. 10:23); the meaning "just" occurs at Wis. 12:15; 2 Macc. 9:18. In the pseudepigraphal *Pss. Sol.*, *dikaios* denotes the upright who trust in God and keep his law, as distinct from sinners (2:34; 3:4–8; 15:6). When applied to God it describes his attitude in discriminating between the upright and the sinner (2:10, 18, 32, 34; 5:1; 8:8; 9:2; 10:5). It is also applied to the Messiah in this sense (17:32).

dikaiosynē in the Apocr. is the righteousness or righteous conduct that makes a person acceptable to God (Tob. 12:9; 14:11; Wis. 1:15). It denotes God's righteousness in discerning good and evil and saving the good and punishing evil (5:18; 12:16). In 15:3 knowledge of God constitutes righteousness. In Sir. 42:2 *dikaioō* means to do justice to, punish, and in 7:5; 10:29; 13:22 it means to recognize or declare to be right or righteous. The vb. also occurs in the passive, meaning to be declared innocent or to acquit and even accept (18:22).

5. In rab. Judaism righteousness was identified with conformity to the law. Many of the OT laws, esp. the ceremonial ones, were no longer relevant as they stood, but according to the rabbis, they were intended to train God's people in obedience and to provide a way for them to acquire merit in his sight. The passion for obedience was transformed into a striving for merit, to ensure one's part in God's kingdom. Acts of charity and mercy were considered esp. meritorious, the former (*ṣᵉdāqâ*) comprising anything that could be done by material expenditure (e.g., feeding the hungry, clothing the naked, giving drink to the thirsty), while the latter were those requiring a moral effort (e.g., mourning with mourners; visiting those who were sick or in prison; cf. Matt. 25:35–36). However, there are many passages in rab. literature that show the power of trusting in God, quite apart from meritorious works.

Few qualified for the designation "a righteous man." It was believed that no one, not even the patriarchs Abraham, Isaac, and Jacob, could achieve righteousness apart from God's grace, but that (as it were) "God helps those who help themselves." In the day of judgment merits will be weighed against demerits. Should there be an even balance, some maintained that the persons concerned will go to hell, emerging later when purification is complete, while others believed that God will make use of his own great riches and of the merits of the righteous.

6. The Qumran community seems to have been deeply aware of its own guilt and of the transitoriness of life; hence, we read recurring appeals to justification by God: "Righteousness, I know, is not of man, nor is a perfect walk of the son of man. To the most high God belong deeds of righteousness; but the way of man will not stand, save by the spirit which God created for him" (1QH 12:30–31). But as impressively like Paul as such statements appear at first sight, it should be

noted that righteousness is based not simply on the law (as it is in Jud. generally), but on the radical doctrines of the Teacher of Righteousness. The "sons of righteousness" are those who follow their Teacher's doctrine, and the justifying grace of God is seen essentially in the fact that this doctrine of radical legal piety has been revealed.

NT The NT uses the words of this group in many different ways. The adj. *dikaios* occurs in almost all NT books, while its related words are predominantly Pauline, occurring with particular frequency in Rom. It will make for greater clarity if we examine the usage of each writer.

1. *Matthew. dikaios* is applied to Christ (27:19), to righteous people (e.g., 1:19; 5:45; 9:13), and to things (20:4; 23:35). *dikaiosynē* occurs at 3:15; 5:6, 10, 20; 6:1, 33; 21:32; and *dikaioō* at 11:19; 12:37.

Matt.'s doctrine of righteousness is central to his message. Even the work of John the Baptist is described in these terms, for John came to show people "the way of righteousness" (Matt. 21:32), calling all Israel to repentance and baptism. In insisting that no one had any claim on God (3:9), John was acting in the name of God, who was even then bringing in his kingdom. In order "to fulfill all righteousness" (3:15), Jesus submitted to John's baptism. Those who hunger and thirst after righteousness are blessed (5:6), for whether they live according to the law or not (1:19), their one desire is that God may justify them.

In the light of such righteousness, Jesus was esp. concerned to address sinners rather than the righteous (Matt. 9:13), who believed they had no need of it. Admittedly, he did not dispute the righteousness of such people (in the sense that they have formally fulfilled the law; cf. 10:41; 13:17; 23:29). The conflict with the Pharisees and teachers of the law who fancied that they were in the way of righteousness (23:27–28) arose only because they could not see their righteousness as the free gift of God and so did not submit to John's baptism (21:32). They grumbled because God's calling was in the nature of a free gift and had nothing to do with just rewards (20:13–15). They adopted a holier-than-thou attitude toward others, but Jesus taught that separation between the wicked and the righteous is reserved for the final judgment of God (13:49).

In teaching this, however, Jesus was not seeking to soften the demands of God's revealed will; on the contrary: "Unless your righteousness surpasses that of the Pharisees and the teachers of the law, you will certainly not enter the kingdom of heaven" (Matt. 5:20). Jesus intensified the law or repealed it (5:21–48), depending on the character and work of God, who loves his enemies and therefore sends rain on the just and the unjust (5:44–45).

Should the practice of such righteousness bring about a conflict with the letter of the law, then the blessed are those who, like Jesus himself, are persecuted for righteousness' sake (5:10). "Seek first [God's] kingdom and his righteousness," Jesus exhorts (6:33). But this righteousness is not to be displayed before human eyes (6:1); to do so is to seek a reward not from God but from people—as do the Pharisees, who, like whitewashed tombs, appear righteous in the eyes of other people, but within (and so in God's sight) are full of unclean thoughts (Matt. 23:27–28).

2. *Luke.* The adj. *dikaios* is applied to Christ (Lk. 23:47; Acts 3:14; 7:52; 22:14), to people (Lk. 1:6, 17; 2:25; 14:14; Acts 10:22; 24:15), and to things (Lk. 12:57; Acts 4:19). The adv. *dikaiōs* occurs in the Gospels only at Lk. 23:41, in the remark of the penitent thief who recognized that he and the other thief were suffering justly but that Jesus had done no wrong. The noun *dikaiōma* occurs at 1:6 with regard to Zechariah and Elizabeth, who observed "all the Lord's commandments and regulations blamelessly." The noun *dikaiosynē* occurs at 1:75; Acts 10:35; 13:10; 17:31; 24:25; the vb. *dikaioō* at Lk. 7:29, 35; 10:29; 16:15; 18:14; Acts 13:38–39.

Lk. uses this word group to show that Christianity is the legitimate development of Jud., the latter being a religion receiving status by the Romans as a *religio licita*. Hence, special mention is made of devout observers of the Jewish law (*dikaioi*) who came into contact with Jesus: e.g., Zechariah and Elizabeth, Simeon, Joseph of Arimathea (Lk. 1:6; 2:25; 23:50), to whom is added the Roman centurion Cornelius (Acts 10:22; cf. 10:35).

The beginning of Lk.'s Gospel is marked by references to Jewish hopes regarding the return of Elijah, who will turn the disobedient to the wisdom of the righteous (Lk. 1:17), and to similar hopes of a life whose characteristics will be righteousness and holiness (1:75). Lk. sees this returning Elijah in the person of John the Baptist; tax-gatherers and public sinners were justified before God (7:29) by being baptized by John, while the teachers of the law and the Pharisees deceived themselves into thinking they could pass themselves off as righteous (20:20), or indeed that they were already righteous (16:15). This is vividly portrayed in the parable of the Pharisee and the publican (18:9–14).

But in heaven there is more joy over one repentant sinner than over ninety-nine righteous (Lk. 15:7). Lk. does not deny that there is joy in heaven over the righteous, but the greatest joy is over those who turn from sin. The wonderful thing about Jesus is that by his word he makes new life possible for those who are so depraved and sinful as to suffer social and religious ostracism (5:32); this applies not only to Jews but to Gentiles as well (Acts 10:22, 35). Jesus himself is thus the exemplar of a righteous person. His righteousness is openly recognized by the Roman centurion at Jesus' death (Lk. 23:47), after which it becomes fundamental to Christian preaching (Acts 3:14; 7:52; 22:14). As the "Righteous One" (3:14), Jesus was raised by God from the dead, in advance of the general resurrection of the righteous and the unrighteous (24:15), and has been commissioned to judge the whole world in righteousness (17:31).

3. *Mark.* Apart from Mk. 2:17 (cf. comments on Lk. 5:32), the only instance of this word group in Mk. is the use of the adj. at 6:20 to describe Herod's reluctance to have John the Baptist executed on account of Herodias, "because Herod feared John and protected him, knowing him to be a righteous and holy man." The usage is in line with Jewish concepts of righteousness, but the general absence of the word group is indicative of Mk.'s tendency to avoid technical language.

4. *John.* The adj. *dikaios* is applied to the Father by Jesus in his high priestly prayer (Jn. 17:25; see also 1 Jn. 1:9; Rev. 16:5), to Jesus (1 Jn. 2:1, 29; 3:7), and to humans (Rev. 22:11). It applies to Jesus' just judgment (Jn. 5:30); the Jews are likewise urged to "make a right judgment" (7:24). The noun *dikaiosynē* occurs only at Jn. 16:8, 10; 1 Jn. 2:29; 3:7, 10; Rev. 19:11; 22:11; *dikaiōma* occurs at Rev. 15:4; 19:8.

(a) The two instances of *dikaiosynē* in Jn.'s Gospel are used in a significant passage: The Paraclete will "convict the world of guilt in regard to sin and righteousness and judgment" (Jn. 16:8). Jesus is seeking to explain that righteousness will be manifested by his returning to the Father (16:10), for it is not to be found in the world itself; the Father alone is its source and fountainhead. Jesus must therefore go away from his disciples in order that their hopes might not be set on him in any "this-worldly" fashion but might be centered on the Father, with whom the Son is one.

(b) Two mutually exclusive spheres are described in 1 Jn.: "Dear children, do not let anyone lead you astray. He who does what is right is righteous, just as he [Christ] is righteous. He who does what is sinful is of the devil, because the devil has been sinning from the beginning" (1 Jn. 3:7–8; cf. 3:10). In other words, a person can belong only to one of these two spheres (cf. 2:29). Since only one person is completely righteous (i.e., Jesus, 2:1), and only one has sinned from the beginning (3:8), it is crucial whose side we are on, i.e., whether we recognize and confess our sin (1:8–2:2) or not.

(c) *dikaiosynē* is used of the rider on the white horse, Christ, who is called "Faithful and True. With justice he judges and makes war" (Rev. 19:11). In the concluding visions of Rev., there is a great separation between the righteous and the evildoers (22:11; cf. Dan. 12:9–10).

5. *Paul.* Paul applies the adj. *dikaios* to God (Rom. 3:26), Christ (2 Tim. 4:8), human beings (Rom. 1:17; cf. Gal. 3:11; 1 Tim. 1:9; Tit.

1:8), and things (Rom. 7:12; Eph. 6:1; Phil. 1:7; 4:8; Col. 4:1; 2 Thess. 1:5–6). The noun *dikaiosynē* occurs in numerous places in his letters, as does the vb. *dikaioō*. *dikaiōma* occurs in Rom. 1:32; 2:26; 5:16; 8:4; and the only instances of *dikaiōsis* in the NT are in Rom. 4:25; 5:18. The adv. *dikaiōs* occurs in 1 Cor. 15:34; 1 Thess. 2:10; Tit. 2:12. Paul thus makes the most frequent use of this word group and gives it its widest range of meanings.

Of all NT writers, Paul establishes the closest connection with the OT when speaking of God's righteousness and God's justification of sinners. God's righteousness is essentially his covenant dealings with his people, who are thereby constituted a new humanity, a new Israel comprising both Jews and Gentiles. This divine righteousness is revealed by the fact that God's purposes are not foiled by human sin; rather, God remains almighty as both Lord and Savior in spite of human rebellion. Since sin has been so radically dealt with, the demarcation between Israel and the Gentiles can be swept away so that the new people of God may come into being.

The transgression and unbelief of the one man (Adam, Gen. 3) brought unbelief and sin into the world (Rom. 5:12), with the result that all humans fall under God's condemnation. But now the righteous act (*dikaiōma*) of the one man (Christ), his absolute trust in him who justifies the ungodly, has defied the curse of sin by bringing into the world the possibility of trust in God. The result, at the appearing of Christ, will be the acquittal (*dikaiōsis*), the declaring righteous, of all who are members of the new humanity (5:16–19). The following strands of teaching may be distinguished:

(a) No one can be justified by the works of the law, on the basis of perfect obedience to it (Rom. 3:20, 28; Gal. 2:16; 3:11). Indeed, Christ would not have had to die if *dikaiosynē* were by the law (Gal. 2:21; cf. 3:21). Henceforth, those who want to be justified by obeying the law show that they have fallen from grace (5:4). Through Christ the law has lost its absolute validity (Rom. 10:4), for by its own standards, he who knew no sin was made sin for us (2 Cor. 5:21).

Rom. 2:13 seems to contradict this by stating that "those who obey the law ... will be declared righteous," not those who hear the law (cf. 10:5). But it was precisely in the matter of *doing* the law that Israel had failed (9:31), for people can only do the will of God when they are grasped by God's righteousness and completely taken up by it. Otherwise sin usurps the law (Rom. 7), and we are powerless against it because sin is not primarily evil deeds or inclinations but striving for our own righteousness and justification (10:3). Hence, only those who have died to sin are justified (6:7) and can do God's will (6:10).

(b) From this Paul concludes that we can be justified only by faith in Christ (Rom. 3:26, 28; 5:1; Gal. 2:16), i.e., by trusting utterly and only in God's grace, which by definition must be a free gift (Rom. 3:24). Jews and Gentiles are justified in the same way: the circumcised (Israel) on the ground of their faith and the uncircumcised (the Gentiles) because of their faith (Rom. 3:30; cf. Gal. 3:8). Here Paul appeals to the testimony of Scripture concerning Abraham, who trusted in the God who justifies the ungodly (Rom. 4:5, 9, 11; Gal. 3:6).

Similarly, in the light of the transition between Rom. 3:20 and 3:21, *dikaiosynē* in the latter passage must mean the manner in which God justifies sinners through faith in Christ. The outcome of this righteousness of God is therefore being "justified freely by his grace" (3:24). The same theme is taken up in 3:25–26, which may be paraphrased as follows: "God put forward Christ Jesus as a propitiation [→ *hilaskomai*, to reconcile, *2661*] by his sacrificial death, which becomes a reality through faith. This took place to show his righteousness, because in the time of his forbearance he passed over [→ *anechomai*, endure, *462*] former sins; it was to prove that he himself is righteous, that he might be just and the justifier of him who lives by faith in Jesus Christ."

Christ's atoning work is viewed from three different aspects. (i) It is experienced as a reality only by faith, since it was Christ's faith in him who justifies the ungodly (Phil. 2:8) that enabled him to be "made sin," i.e., treated as ungodly. To faith, therefore, Christ's atonement is something objectively real. (ii) The sacrificial death of Christ atones for sin because it is proof of God's righteousness, i.e., it was not intended to atone for Christ's alleged offense of blasphemy, but to procure justification for all believers (cf. 1 Cor. 1:30). (iii) This justification anticipates Christ's return in that it is already revealed; it enables God to be just, for he does not plunge us into sin so that we may experience his grace (see Rom. 3:5–8), but, in spite of the alienation between God and us, God enables us even now to exercise believing trust and thereby to enter into newness of life (Rom. 5:17).

(c) Since believers have died with Christ to sin and are now justified (Rom. 6:7), they live only for God (6:11). This is expressed by the phrase "slaves to righteousness" (6:18). Paul can thus speak of being subject to God's righteousness (10:4). All such phrases are but variations on the theme of the Christian's belonging exclusively to God. Similarly, Paul can speak of the service of righteousness (2 Cor. 3:9; 11:15) and of its weapons (Eph. 6:10–17), since the righteousness of God is the way in which he reveals himself and the only way in which he can be approached (Rom. 1:16–17).

(d) As the resurrection anticipates the universal manifestation of God's kingdom, in the same way righteousness at the present time (Rom. 3:26) anticipates the final revelation of God's righteousness at the Parousia of Christ, for believers "by faith ... eagerly await through the Spirit the righteousness for which we hope" (Gal. 5:5; cf. 2:17; Rom. 5:19). Otherwise, however, Paul always speaks of believers as having been justified, that is, in the past tense. The connecting link between present and future righteousness is the fact that, while we have already become a people for God's own possession, he is still at enmity with the world as a whole (cf. "all men" in 5:18).

Hence, the justification of the individual springs entirely from that of "the many" (Rom. 5:19), so that it is not we who possess righteousness but righteousness that possesses us; we are its servants (6:18; 2 Cor. 3:9). Our justification both comes from and extends into the future.

(e) In the Pastorals righteousness is spoken of as a virtue (1 Tim. 6:11; 2 Tim. 2:22; Tit. 1:8; 2:12). Similarly, Scripture is profitable for "training in righteousness" (2 Tim. 3:16), and the law is considered to be only for the lawless and the profane, not for the righteous, who by their virtues far surpass the law (1 Tim. 1:9). Thus, "the Lord, the righteous Judge" (cf. Rev. 19:11), will award the "crown of righteousness" to his apostle when the latter has finished his course (2 Tim. 4:7–8). The preaching of virtue is made possible, however, by our being "justified by his [Christ's] grace" (Tit. 3:7), for God "saved us, not because of righteous things we had done, but because of his mercy" (3:5).

6. *The letter to the Hebrews.* The adj. *dikaios* occurs at Heb. 10:38 in a quotation from Hab. 2:4: "My righteous one will live by faith" (also at Heb. 11:4; 12:23). *dikaiosynē* occurs at 1:9 (quoting Ps. 45:7); 5:13; 7:2; 11:7, 33; 12:11; *dikaiōma* at 9:1, 10. (a) Righteousness "comes by faith" in the invisible God (11:7; cf. 11:4, 33–34). God's discipline (*paideia*; → *paideuō*, to discipline, *4084*) leads to this righteousness (12:11), and God has prepared a place in heaven for those made perfectly righteous (12:23). The Son, as the antitype of Melchizedek, is the "king of righteousness" (7:2; cf. 1:8–9). The "regulations" of the old covenant, esp. those relating to the sacrificial system, are described as *dikaiōma* (9:1), further characterized as "external regulations" (9:10), i.e., those of a temporary nature.

(b) Although Heb. does not use the vb. *dikaioō*, relates faith directly to the invisible God (ch. 11), and draws many examples from the OT, there are certain parallels with Pauline thought. For Paul likewise tries to show that his understanding of salvation is entirely in line with that of the OT. The burden of the argument of Rom. 4 is to show from the examples of Abraham and David that justification under the old covenant was, in fact, by faith (cf. Gal. 3:15–18 with Heb. 6:13–15). Similarly, Paul's teaching on Jesus' propitiatory death is paralleled in Heb. by the argument that Jesus as our perfect high priest has offered himself in sacrifice, fulfilling the Day of Atonement ritual and thus inaugurating the new covenant (Heb. 7–10).

The new element in Heb. is the way in which the theme of the Day of Atonement ritual is carried through, so that believers have their sins dealt with and gain access to God through Jesus' sacrificial act on the cross and his exaltation (see esp. Heb. 10:19–22; cf. Lev. 16). The whole argument of Heb. 9–10 leads to the climax that Jesus has opened the new sanctuary in the temple of his body.

The writer applies this teaching with respect to the need for patience, which he supports by quoting from Hab. 2:3–4: "He who is coming will come and will not delay. But my righteous one [*dikaios*] will live by faith. And if he shrinks back, I will not be pleased with him" (Heb. 10:37–38). The prophet Habakkuk lived in the latter part of the seventh cent. B.C., at a time of oppression, crying out for vindication of divine righteousness. Yahweh replied by telling him to be patient, for the oppressor would reap due judgment, and the righteous would be preserved by their loyal trust in God. In the LXX version of Hab., the words have a slightly different emphasis because of the change from the Heb. "his" to the Gk. *mou* ("my"). Depending on where the *mou* is placed, the text reads either, "The righteous one will live by faith in me" or, "My righteous one will live by faith[fulness]" (*pistis* [faith, → *4411*] can mean either "faith" or "faithfulness").

Regardless of which of these options is correct, the interpretation in Heb. focuses on one individual, God's chosen one, and on *pistis*. Does the author mean that God's righteous one will live in faithfulness, or that the chosen righteous one will gain life by his or her faith? Perhaps the author of Heb. is ambiguous so that he intends it to be read in both ways. For in living by faith one becomes faithful in the sense of being loyal to the promises of God, enduring temptation and hardship. This is, in fact, the theme of Heb. 11, with its many examples of faith that enabled the heroes of faith to endure.

Hab. 2:4 is quoted and interpreted twice by Paul as he lays the foundation for his doctrine of justification by faith. In Rom. 1:16–17 Paul declares that the gospel is "the power of God for the salvation of everyone who believes" and that righteousness comes to those who have faith; he supports his assertions by quoting Hab. 2:4: "The righteous will live by faith." In Gal. 3:11 Paul argues: "Clearly no one is justified before God by the law, because, 'The righteous will live by faith'" (cf. Phil. 3:9, where the same thought occurs without quoting Hab. 2:4). It seems entirely possible that this OT verse was current as a testimonium in early Christian times and that both Paul and the author of Heb. used it independently, each giving a slightly different emphasis to it.

7. *James.* The adj. *dikaios* occurs in Jas. 5:6 with reference to "innocent men" and in 5:16 that "the prayer of a righteous man is powerful and effective." *dikaiosynē* is found at 1:20 (living in anger does not bring about a "righteous life"); 2:23 (quoting Gen. 15:6; cf. Rom. 4:3; Gal. 3:11); and Jas. 3:18 (people who live in peace produce "a harvest of righteousness"). The vb. *dikaioō* also occurs 3x, all in Jas. 2 with reference to the question of whether a person is justified by what one does or by faith: in 2:21, with reference to Abraham and his sacrifice of Isaac; in 2:25, with reference to Rahab and her hiding of the spies; and in 2:24, where James draws the conclusion: "You see that a person is justified by what he does and not by faith alone."

There has been a considerable debate about whether James is contradicting Paul. But the context of James is different from the context in which Paul makes his remarks. Paul is arguing about whether one must keep certain stipulations of the law in order to become righteous with God. To this the answer is no. But James envisions a situation in which the rich, content with their own "spirituality," are indifferent to the starving and ill-clad (Jas. 2:14–18), and in which church members see no inconsistency between spirituality and slander (Jas. 3:1–16). If faith makes no difference in a person's life, it is questionable whether that person has the faith that is necessary to be saved. As Paul testifies regarding the moral laxity and complacent attitudes in Corinth, more is needed in the Christian life than some nondescript attitude of faith. It may be significant that the apostle makes no reference to justification by faith in 1 or 2 Corinthians.

James, in other words, is essentially working with a different definition of faith. For him, faith means either notional assent to a doctrine or uncritical acceptance of an attitude without asking about its practical implications; even demons have this sort of faith (Jas. 2:19). Faith is not the wholehearted trust and self-commitment of which Paul speaks. Similarly, the works that justify a person in James are not the works envisaged by Paul. For Paul, works denote human attempts to procure favor with God by one's own efforts in obeying the law. With James works denote the response of a believer as he or she works out faith in daily life. Note esp. the word "alone" in Jas. 2:24: "You see that a person is justified by what he does and not by faith *alone*." James' position complements rather than contradicts Paul.

In both Paul and James *dikaioō* means to pronounce righteous. In the case of James it concerns evidence that can be seen by others, whereas in Paul it is the eschatological verdict pronounced by God on the undeserving. Paul bases his argument on Gen. 15:6, where Abraham believes God's promises and is declared righteous. Although James quotes the same passage, he illustrates his point not from that passage but from the subsequent story of the offering of Isaac (Jas. 2:21; cf. Gen. 22:1–14). This enables him to draw the conclusion: "You see that his faith and his actions were working together, and his faith was made complete by what he did" (2:22); thus, "as the body without the spirit is dead, so faith without deeds is dead" (2:26). A bare and lifeless faith is like a corpse; still, the deeds that animate faith are not the self-righteous acts that supposedly accrue merit with God but the responses of the faithful to God's living word (cf. Abraham and Rahab).

8. *1 and 2 Peter.* The adj. *dikaios* occurs in 1 Pet. 3:12 (quoting Ps. 34:16); 3:18; 4:18 (quoting Prov. 11:31); 2 Pet. 1:13; and 2:7–9 (cf. Gen. 19:16, 29). The adv. *dikaiōs* occurs in 1 Pet. 2:23, which explains that the suffering Christ "entrusted himself to him who judges justly." The noun *dikaiosynē* occurs 2x in 1 Pet. and 4x in 2 Pet. Christ bore our sins on the tree "so that we might die to sins and live for righteousness" (1 Pet. 2:24); "but even if you should suffer for what is right, you are blessed" (3:14). Peter opens his second letter with a reference to "those who through the righteousness of our God and Savior Jesus Christ have received . . . faith" (2 Pet. 1:1). In 2:5 he speaks of Noah as "a preacher of righteousness," and 2:21 describes the Christian faith and life as "the way of righteousness." Finally in 3:13 we read: "But in keeping with his promise we are looking forward to a new heaven and a new earth, the home of righteousness."

There is the sense in which a righteous person is a member of the righteous community, but in none of these passages is the notion a bare formality. Righteousness takes its character from God himself (1 Pet. 2:23; cf. Rev. 16:5), and salvation is grounded in righteousness (1 Pet. 3:18) that finds its expression in right behavior (2:24; cf. 3:12; 4:18). Those who are called to suffer for righteousness' sake are blessed (3:14), and in so doing live out the righteousness of Christ. Thus, the Christian faith and way of life can be called "the way of righteousness" (2 Pet. 2:21), and the goal of life is described in terms of righteousness (3:13).

1467 (*dikaioō*, justify, vindicate, acquit, pronounce righteous), → *1466*.

1468 (*dikaiōma*, regulation, requirement, righteous deed), → *1466*.

1469 (*dikaios*, justly, in a just manner, uprightly), → *1466*.

1470 (*dikaiōsis*, justification, vindication, acquittal), → *1466*.

1472	δίκη

δίκη (*dikē*), justice, punishment, vengeance (*1472*); ἐκδικέω (*ekdikeō*), execute justice, punish, avenge (*1688*); ἔκδικος (*ekdikos*), avenger (*1690*); ἐκδίκησις (*ekdikēsis*), vengeance, recompense, punishment (*1689*).

CL & OT 1. (a) In cl. Gk. the noun *dikē* is the name of the goddess of just punishment. In legal language, the word means justice, a judi-

cial case, a legal decision, vengeance, or punishment. Along with the later word *dikaiosynē* (righteousness, → *1466*), *dikē* is one of the basic concepts in the Gk. legal world.

(b) The vb. *ekdikeō* means avenge or punish. Later, in the papyri, it means to decide a case, work as an advocate, defend or help someone to obtain legal rights. An *ekdikos*, therefore, is an avenger, and *ekdikēsis* means vengeance, recompense.

2. (a) In the LXX *dikē*, justice, vengeance, punishment, occurs 38x, of which 21x have no Heb. equivalent. It can be used of Yahweh's intervention to exact vengeance and punishment on his own people (Lev. 26:25; Amos 7:4). But it can also be used of his intervention against his enemies (Deut. 32:41). Other passages emphasize God's intervention to ensure justice for the person offering prayer (Ps. 9:4–5; 35:23; 43:1; 74:22) and for the poor (140:12). In the Apocr. *dikē* means justice (Wis. 1:8), vengeance (18:11), and punishment (cf. 2 Macc. 8:11).

(b) Through the LXX's use of *ekdikeō*, several different concepts of justice are brought into contact with one another. The OT's message of a justice that communicates God's will to individuals and the OT's judicial procedure, which is carried out solely with God's authority, are translated by a legal terminology that was previously neutral and secular. The OT took the thought embodied in Deut. 32:35 seriously, leaving vengeance to God (cf. Gen. 4:15; 2 Ki. 9:7; Ps. 37:28; 58:10; 79:10, the last two with *ekdikēsis*). Hos. 9:7 refers to the day of vengeance (*ekdikēsis*).

3. (a) In the OT punishment and judgment go together. Sodom and Gomorrah provide a classical instance of Yahweh's punishment of a notoriously wicked pagan city (Gen. 19; cf. Lk. 17:29, 32; Rom. 9:29). This event is often mentioned (e.g., Deut. 29:23; 32:32; Isa. 1:9–10; Jer. 23:14; Ezek. 16:46–56; Amos 4:11). Amos announced God's punishment of the surrounding nations for their crimes against humanity (Amos 1–2), but this culminates in the announcement of God's punishment of his people for their sin of idolatry (3:14) and for crimes committed against fellow Israelites (4:1; 5:7–15). The prophets construed foreign invasions as punishment for Israel's sin, culminating in the destruction of the northern kingdom in 722 B.C. (2 Ki. 15–17) and the exile of large sections of the population of Judah in 597 and 587 B.C. (2 Ki. 23–25).

(b) On an individual level the Mosaic legislation specified a range of punishments for crimes both against God and against human beings. God expected his people to obey him and to lead a holy life, based on his law. The following are crimes against God: idolatry, punishable by death (Deut. 13:10–16); infant sacrifice (cf. 2 Ki. 21:6, 16), which was involved in the worship of Molech and Canaanite idols (Deut. 18:10–11); blasphemy (Exod. 20:7; 22:28; Lev. 19:12; 24:11–23; Deut. 5:11); false prophecy (18:20–22); and violation of the Sabbath (Exod. 20:8–11; 31:13–17; Num. 15:32–36). Whereas offenses committed inadvertently could be atoned for (Lev. 16; Num. 15:27), stubbornness was punishable by being cut off from the people, i.e., death (15:30–31; Deut. 17:8–12).

(c) Civil crimes included murder, which was punishable by death (Gen. 9:6; Exod. 21:12; Num. 35:31), though those who had killed accidentally might flee to cities of refuge (35:6–25). The law provided for execution by the nearest able-bodied male relative of the deceased, "the avenger of blood" (35:19). But under the monarchy the king seems to have assumed jurisdiction (2 Sam. 14:7, 11; 1 Ki. 2:34). In the case of unsolved murder, ritual and sacrificial provision was made lest the land remain polluted (Deut. 21:1–9). Second-degree murder with no clearly specified penalty was recognized (Exod. 21:22–25).

The penalty for criminal assault resulting in serious injury was stated in terms of the *lex talionis*, i.e., the same injury must be inflicted on the offender: "life for life, eye for eye, tooth for tooth, hand for hand, foot for foot, burn for burn, wound for wound, bruise for bruise" (Exod. 21:23–25; cf. Lev. 24:19–20; Deut. 19:21). The OT here is establishing a principle of equity so that punishments fit the crimes. Assault on one's parents was deemed serious enough to be punishable by death (Exod. 21:15). Serious injuries to slaves by their masters entitled the slaves to manumission (21:26–27). For robbery, provision was made for restitution plus punitive damages (22:1, 3, 4; Lev. 6:2–7; 19:13).

(d) The Mosaic law did not allow religious prostitution, and prostitution in general was opposed. Sodomy and homosexuality were punishable by death (Lev. 18:22, 29; 20:13), as were carnal relations with animals (18:23; 20:15). All crimes of immorality were grievous offences against God and adversely affected the community. Remarriage of one's previously divorced wife would cause the land to sin (Deut. 24:4). Adultery committed by betrothed or married persons was punishable by stoning (Lev. 20:10; Deut. 22:23–24). There was, however, no set penalty for fornication. Rape sometimes carried the death penalty (22:23–27); in other cases the man was to take an unbetrothed virgin as a wife by paying fifty shekels to her father (22:28–29). Polygamy was countenanced, but there were certain forbidden degrees of marriage, and incest constituted a capital crime (Lev. 18:7–18; 20:11–21). Intercourse during menstruation brought ritual uncleanness (18:19; 20:18; cf. 15:24).

(e) The fifth commandment laid down the decree: "Honor your father and your mother, so that you may live long in the land the LORD your God is giving you" (Exod. 20:12; cf. Lev. 19:3; Deut. 5:16). Not only was assault on one's parents a capital offense, but so was cursing (Exod. 21:15, 17; Lev. 20:9; Deut. 21:18–21). Kidnapping (which in ancient times was done in order to sell the victim as a slave) carried the death penalty (Exod. 21:16; Deut. 24:7). False accusation and perjury carried the same penalty as that required for the accused crime (19:19).

(f) Cases of torts (i.e., wrongs dealt with by personal actions rather than by public prosecution) were judged by the elders of a town sitting by the gate (cf. Ruth 4). Such cases included damage to crops and vineyards from straying cattle or fire (Exod. 22:5–6), injury to livestock (21:33–36; Lev. 24:18, 21), or injury to persons from livestock (Exod. 21:28–32).

(g) Stoning is the most frequently mentioned form of capital punishment in the OT. Perhaps it was used in cases affecting the community at large because it involved the maximum participation of the community, including the prosecuting witnesses (Deut. 17:7; cf. Lev. 20:2–5, 27; 24:15–16; Num. 15:32–36). In the case of murder, death by the sword is prescribed (35:19, 21). Death by burning was prescribed for certain sexual offenses that involved prohibited degrees of intercourse (Lev. 20:14; 21:9). Execution by hanging on a tree involving the public exposure of the victim involved particular shame (Deut. 21:22–23; cf. Jos. 10:26–27).

(h) Scourging to a maximum of forty stripes is stipulated in Deut. 25:1–3. It was apparently a penalty for one who unjustly accused his wife of unchastity before marriage (22:18). Imprisonment seems to have been restricted to detention prior to trial (though cf. Jer. 37:15–16). Monetary fines are mentioned in Exod. 21:22, 30–31; 22:1–4; Deut. 22:18–19, 29. Enslavement was the penalty for a thief who could not repay damages (Exod. 22:3) or for nonpayment of debts (2 Ki. 4:1; Neh. 5:5; Amos 2:6). Exod. 21:2 lays down a maximum of six years in the case of an Israelite. Voluntary slavery is discussed in Lev. 25:39–43.

NT 1. In the NT *dikē* only occurs 3x, of which 2 are found in the context of the expectation of the final judgment (→ *krima*, 3210). In 2 Thess. 1:9, Paul uses *dikē* of the punishment of eternal destruction meted out to those who oppress the community, and Jude 7 uses the fire of Sodom and Gomorrah "as an example of those who suffer the punishment of eternal fire." Acts 28:4 tells how the Maltese supposed that Paul, who had been attacked by a snake, was a murderer whom *dikē* (perhaps the Gk. goddess; cf. NIV, "Justice") "has not allowed . . . to live."

2. *ekdikeō* occurs 6x in the NT; *ekdikēsis*, 9x; *ekdikos*, 2x. (a) Lk. 18:3, 5 uses the vb. and 18:7–8 the noun in the secular sense. The

widow in the parable of the unjust judge is seeking "justice" against her adversary. Also, *ekdikēsis* in Acts 7:24 denotes earthly justice taken by Moses into his own hand. Note also 2 Cor. 7:11, where *ekdikēsis*, punishment, and *apologia*, vindication—two terms from criminal law—occur together; Paul's sharp intervention against an offender produced just punishment. Similarly, the apostle makes known in 10:6 his readiness to punish every act of disobedience.

(b) *ekdikos*, avenger, in Rom. 13:4 designates an office, for this passage contains a remarkable collection of expressions derived from the language of secular government. God gives to the office of avenger the power it needs. This perspective is in line with OT thinking that a political institution needs to have authority conferred on it. This applies both to the kings of Israel and to other kings to whom Yahweh has given power (cf. Exod. 22:28; 1 Sam. 15:1; 2 Sam. 1:14; 1 Ki. 19:15–16; Prov. 8:15; Isa. 10:5–19). Peter in 1 Pet. 2:13–17 confirms this theme (cf. Jn. 19:11; Tit. 3:1).

(c) *ekdikeō* and its derivatives are used primarily in the NT with the sense of vengeance. These occurrences appear mostly in OT quotations or phrases and express God's vengeance. Sometimes this vengeance is mentioned in connection with the coming day of judgment (e.g., 2 Thess. 1:8, which uses motifs from Isa. 66:15: God's vengeance on his enemies is compensation for those who suffer persecution; cf. also Lk. 21:22).

The use of *ekdikeō* in Rev. 6:10; 19:2 likewise deals with the last judgment. The first records the anguished questioning and petition of Christian martyrs for vengeance, i.e., for the final judgment. This is not fulfilled immediately; there is a short delay. Hence vengeance, purged of all human malice, is left to God; its execution is first proclaimed in 19:2 (cf. 2 Ki. 9:7), once the number of fellow servants and brothers is complete (6:11).

(d) While Rev. makes persecutors and unbelievers the recipients of vengeance, the author of Heb. 10:30, quoting Deut. 32:35, warns the Christian community itself about God's vengeance (cf. also 1 Thess. 4:6). His vengeance is a serious matter, and we must acknowledge that he is just. Paul recalls Lev. 19:18 and Deut. 32:35 when he says that vengeance is God's prerogative (Rom. 12:19–20). Instead of seeking vengeance, the Christian community must love its enemies. Those who do so heap "burning coals on [the] head" of their enemy; i.e., they bestow on such people the fruit of grace, love, and peace (cf. Prov. 25:21–22; Matt. 5:44; Lk. 6:27). But God will one day uphold his right for vengeful judgment.

See also *kolasis*, punishment (*3136*).

1503 διώκω

διώκω (*diōkō*), run after, pursue, persecute (*1503*); ἐκδιώκω (*ekdiōkō*), drive away, persecute severely (*1691*); καταδιώκω (*katadiōkō*), search for, hunt for (*2870*); διωγμός (*diōgmos*), persecution (*1501*); διώκτης (*diōktēs*), persecutor (*1502*).

CL & OT 1. In cl. Gk. *diōkō* means lit. to chase, pursue, drive away; fig. to pursue something zealously, try to achieve something, prosecute.

2. (a) In the LXX *diōkō*, along with *ekdiōkō* and *katadiōkō*, is used primarily of pursuit by hostile soldiers (Exod. 15:9) or by anyone with hostile intent (Gen. 31:23). The word occurs with some regularity in psalms of individual lament (e.g., Ps. 7:1, 5; 31:15; 35:3; cf.

Jer. 15:15; 20:11), where the oppression referred to causes the psalmist to suffer, even though active persecution in the narrow sense is not part of the picture. (b) The LXX also uses *diōkō* in exhortations to pursue a goal, such as social righteousness (Deut. 16:20), peace (Ps. 34:14), and right living that honors God (Prov. 15:9). *diōgmos* occurs in a primarily negative sense in the LXX (Prov. 11:19; Lam. 3:19; but cf. 2 Macc. 12:23), while *diōktēs* does not appear at all.

NT *diōkō* in the NT occurs 45x, of which 30 refer to persecution (cf. the use of *diōgmos* [10x] and *diōktēs* in 1 Tim. 1:13) In 1 Thess. 2:15 the compound *ekdiōkō* likewise means to persecute. The fig. meaning of this vb. as pursuing a particular way of life is found only in NT letters (Phil. 3:12, 14). *diōkō* (Lk. 17:23) and *katadiōkō* (Mk. 1:36) can also mean to run after, follow.

1. *Persecution.* (a) God's messengers meet persecution. This was already the experience of the OT prophets (Matt. 5:12; Acts 7:52) and will be that of Jesus' disciples (Matt. 5:11–12, 44; 10:23). In this they are like their Lord (Jn. 5:16; cf. 15:20: "If they persecuted me, they will persecute you also"). Paul, once a persecutor of the church (1 Cor. 15:9; Gal. 1:13, 23; Phil. 3:6; 1 Tim. 1:13, using *diōktēs*), experienced this same connection (Gal. 5:11; 2 Tim. 3:11). In 2 Tim. 3:12 he writes that being a Christian is always linked with persecution.

(b) Christ himself is being persecuted whenever a Christian experiences it (Acts 9:4–5; 22:7–8; 26:14–15). According to Jn. 15:18–25, persecution is caused by the world's hatred of God and his revelation in Christ (cf. also Matt. 10:22; Mk. 13:13; Lk. 21:17; Rev. 12:13). Paul sees behind it the contrast between the hostility of the natural self against God and thus also against the person led by God's Spirit (Gal. 4:29). Hence persecution may be a sign that one is on God's side. Thus Jesus calls those blessed "who are persecuted because of righteousness" (Matt. 5:10–12).

(c) There is the danger of corrupting the message in order to avoid persecution (Gal. 6:12). Thus, Christians are challenged to maintain their faith during such times. They must meet the hatred of their persecutors by a word of blessing (Rom. 12:14).

(d) In persecution Christians experience the help, strength, and saving power of Christ (Rom. 8:35–39; 2 Cor. 4:7–12; 12:10). Paul set an apostolic example by enduring it patiently (1 Cor. 4:12). It is a special reason for giving God thanks when believers endure persecution with faith (2 Thess. 1:3–4).

2. *Pursuit of Christian objectives.* The fig. meaning of *diōkō* shows more strongly than does *zēteō* (seek, → 2426) that there are certain things the Christian must strive after, such as hospitality (Rom. 12:13), mutual peace (14:19; Heb. 12:14; 1 Pet. 3:11), holiness, love (1 Cor. 14:1), doing good (1 Thess. 5:15), and righteousness (1 Tim. 6:11; 2 Tim. 2:22). These are lasting objectives in the life of faith, which has as its goal the attaining of the resurrection from the dead. Paul presses on toward this goal like the runner set on winning the victor's prize (Phil. 3:12–14), though any credit belongs to "God's mercy" (Rom. 9:16).

See also *thlipsis*, oppression, affliction, tribulation (*2568*).

1504	δόγμα

δόγμα (*dogma*), decree, ordinance, command, doctrine, dogma (*1504*); δογματίζω (*dogmatizō*), decree, ordain (*1505*).

CL & OT *dogma* (from *dokeō*, think, suppose) means opinion, conclusion, belief. From the noun comes the intensive vb. *dogmatizō*, to lay down as an opinion, decree. In the LXX *dogma* and *dogmatizō* can mean public decree or edict (Est. 4:8 in S[3] only; Dan. 2:13), a divine ordinance of the Mosaic Law (3 Macc. 1:3), and a community decision (2 Macc. 15:36).

Philo and Josephus understood the Mosaic law as a system of holy tenets, the *dogmata* of a divine philosophy; they were superior to any doctrines of Gk. philosophy.

NT 1. Lk. 2:1 uses *dogma* for the political decree of Caesar Augustus concerning the census. This edict served God's plan of salvation in having the Messiah born at Bethlehem. The Jews at Thessalonica accused Jason of aiding Paul and Silas in "defying Caesar's decrees" (Acts 17:7).

2. Acts 16:4 uses *dogmata* for the decisions of the Jerusalem Council that were binding on the whole church and were to be delivered to the Gentile churches. These stipulations ran the risk of turning the gospel of Christ into a legalistic religion. But they were in fact decrees proclaiming liberty within the area of social interaction among believers. This verse lays the foundation for the use of the word "dogma" for ecclesiastical decrees, requiring intellectual assent.

3. Eph. 2:15 uses *dogmata* for the individual "regulations" of the Mosaic law; Col. 2:14 uses the word for the "regulations" leveled against humankind, which God has nailed to the cross. In 2:20–21 the apostle forbids the church to allow regulations regarding food and cleanliness to be imposed upon it. Here the vb. *dogmatizō* is translated: "Why . . . do you submit to its rules?"

See also *entolē*, command, order (*1953*); *parangellō*, give orders, command (*4133*); *keleuō*, command, order (*3027*).

1505 (*dogmatizō*, decree, ordain), → *1504*.

1506	δοκέω

δοκέω (*dokeō*), trans. think, believe, suppose, consider; intrans. seem, appear (*1506*).

CL & OT 1. In cl. Gk. *dokeō* trans. means to believe, think, hold, assume, conclude; intrans. to assume an appearance, appear; hence, give an impression, pose as.

2. *dokeō* occurs app. 70x in the LXX, generally with the same meanings as in cl. Gk. It can mean to say, think, account (e.g., Gen. 38:15; Prov. 27:14). Most of the references are in the noncanonical writings (esp. 2 and 3 Macc.) or passages where *dokeō* does not translate a Heb. word (e.g., Tob. 3:15; Wis. 3:2; 12:27; 1 Macc. 8:26, 28; 15:20). Occasionally we find the sense of desire, wish (e.g., Jdt. 3:8). The most usual meaning is to seem, appear.

NT 1. *dokeō* occurs 62x in the NT, with more than one sense. (a) In Lk. 8:18 Jesus warns us to listen carefully: "Whoever has will be given more; whoever does not have, even what he thinks [*dokeō*] he has will be taken away from him" (cf. Mk. 4:24). The phrase expresses the illusory state of those who think they have a tangible and permanent security. Jn. 5:45 conveys the challenge to give up an existing opinion, while 2 Cor. 11:16 speaks of an opinion that cannot yet be reached. In Matt. 3:9 John warns the Jews not to think that their position as children of Abraham makes a significant difference before God. (b) The meaning to conclude is found esp. in Acts (e.g., 15:22, 25, 28).

2. (a) In Gal. 2:2, 6, 9, Paul calls the Jerusalem apostles by the part. of *dokeō*, i.e., those who matter, the recognized authorities; in 2:9 he refers to those recognized as pillars or leaders, i.e., James, Peter, John. This is not necessarily an ironic point here, for this expression is often found of a recognized authority in extrabiblical lit. (b) In passages like 1 Cor. 8:2, however, the expression "the man who thinks" means an opinion based on self-deception.

3. Noteworthy is the question formed with the impers. *dokei*, i.e., *ti dokei hymin*, "What do you think?" found in Jn. 11:56 as well as various passages in Matt. (e.g., 18:12; 21:28; 22:42). It demands an answer that will commit the one questioned, unlike all mere opinions. Note that this is the question placed by the high priest before the Sanhedrin (26:66) so as to provoke them to pass a judgment on Jesus.

See also *dialogizomai*, ponder, consider, reason (*1368*); *logizomai*, reckon, think, credit (*3357*).

1507 (*dokimazō*, test, accept as proved, approve), → *1511*.

1508 (*dokimasia*, test), → *1511*.

1509 (*dokimē*, the quality of being approved, hence character), → *1511*.

1510 (*dokimion*, testing, means of testing; adj. genuine), → *1511*.

1511	δόκιμος

δόκιμος (*dokimos*), tested, approved, genuine, esteemed (*1511*); δοκιμάζω (*dokimazō*), test, accept as proved, approve (*1507*); δοκιμασία (*dokimasia*), test (*1508*); δοκίμιον (*dokimion*), testing, means of testing, adj. genuine (*1510*); ἀδόκιμος (*adokimos*), not standing the test, worthless, disqualified, unfit, reprehensible (*99*); ἀποδοκιμάζω (*apodokimazō*), reject, declare useless (*627*); δοκιμή (*dokimē*), the quality of being approved, hence character (*1509*).

CL & OT 1. In cl. Gk. *dokimos* means trustworthy, reliable, approved, recognized. It is used as a technical term for genuine, current coinage, but also applied to persons enjoying general esteem. *adokimos* means untested, not respected. The derived vb. *dokimazō* means to test, pronounce good, establish by trial, recognize, while *apodokimazō* means to disapprove of, reject, blame.

2. The LXX uses *dokimos* only to recognize coins as valid currency (e.g., Gen. 23:16; 1 Ki. 10:18). Hence, worthless money or metal is called *adokimos* (Prov. 25:4; Isa. 1:22). *dokimazō* is most often used in the expression to test something for genuineness by fire. It is transferred to God, who tests human beings. In Ps. the prayer that God may test the one who is praying (17:3; 26:2; 139:1, 23) is an expression of complete trust. In the prophets, however, God's threat of testing becomes equivalent to judgment (Jer. 9:7; Zech. 13:9).

NT In the NT *dokimos* is used mostly by Paul in the sense of recognized, approved, accepted (Rom. 14:18; 16:10; 1 Cor. 11:19; 2 Cor. 10:18); correspondingly *adokimos* means worthless, rejected, in the sense of not having stood the test (Rom. 1:28; 1 Cor. 9:27; 2 Cor. 13:5; 2 Tim. 3:8; Tit. 1:16). *dokimazō* can mean interpret, examine, test (e.g., Lk. 12:56; 1 Cor. 3:13; 11:28; 2 Cor. 13:5; Gal. 6:4; 1 Jn. 4:1). The result of testing is either *dokimazō*, recognize, approve (Rom. 14:22; 1 Cor. 16:3; 2 Cor. 8:22; 1 Thess. 2:4) or *apodokimazō*, repudiate, reject (Matt. 21:42; Heb. 12:17; 1 Pet. 2:4). *dokimē* is found with the act. meaning of a test by means of instructions or tribulations (2 Cor. 2:9; 8:2), and with the pass. meaning of the result of the testing of faith (Rom. 5:4; 2 Cor. 9:13; 13:3; Phil. 2:22). *dokimion* is used for the means of testing in Jas. 1:3. In 1 Pet. 1:7 faith is purified as gold in the fire proves genuine.

1. All to whom God's grace has been entrusted must keep themselves in it (cf. Lk. 19:12–27). Passages that speak of testing, trial, recognition, and rejection are addressed only to members of the church. Heb. 6:8 speaks of those who by their falling away from God have become incapable of returning and hence of bearing the fruit of repentance and faith. They are thus *adokimos*, rejected (cf. also 12:17), for they have crucified "the Son of God all over again" (6:6). We find a virtual reversal of this process in passages like Matt. 21:42 and 1 Pet. 2:4, 7, which use *apodokimazō*. The stone (Jesus) that the builders (the Jewish spiritual leaders) found unsuitable and rejected (crucified), in God's eyes was found worthy to become the cornerstone.

2. What matters in testing is that we use God's gifts aright. Timothy, to whom the word of truth has been entrusted, is to show himself as an approved worker (2 Tim. 2:15) by faithful preaching. By contrast, those who do not honor God according to the knowledge granted them, who "did not think it worthwhile" (*dokimazō*) to know him, are given over to a "depraved" (*adokimos*) mind (Rom. 1:28) and to improper conduct as a punishment. Here we see how closely linked *dokimazō* is with *peirazō* (→ *peirasmos*, temptation, *4280*). Both groups of words are concerned with testing. With *dokimazō* the stress falls on a positive result in which that which is tested passes and is recognized as genuine, but *peirazō* tends to be more negative and means a temptation to evil, in which lusts (Jas. 1:14), want and affliction (1 Cor. 10:13), or Satan himself (1 Thess. 3:5) entice one to fall.

3. God himself tests and passes judgment on the day of judgment. Paul declares in 1 Cor. 3:13 that all service for the church and all the fruit borne by it are subjected to God's testing and verdict in the fire of judgment. The determining factors will be whether faith was created (3:5) and the church built up (3:16). Those who have stood the test in faith (Jas. 1:12) will receive eternal life as the victor's crown.

4. This test is taking place already in this life. God even now shows himself as the tester of human hearts (1 Thess. 2:4). Thus, the whole of a Christian's life is subject to the testing scrutiny of God. All depends on our being found as "approved in Christ" (Rom. 16:10). Paul submitted himself to God's judgment, not to that of human beings (1 Cor. 4:3–5; 9:27), even though we can and should recognize when someone has stood the test (2 Cor. 13:3; Phil. 2:22). The content and goal of Paul's pastoral care of the individual and community is that they should be found obedient (2 Cor. 2:9).

5. That one has stood the test is manifested in various ways. (a) By a serious effort to know God's will. The gift of the Holy Spirit enables a person to recognize God's will (Rom. 12:2) and to test what is well-pleasing to him (Eph. 5:10; Phil. 1:10) and what is best (1 Thess. 5:21). The gift of testing and distinguishing of the spirits (1 Jn. 4:1) is also part of the Christian's duty.

(b) By loyalty to God. *peirazō*, *dokimazō*, and *epiginōskō* are used side by side in 2 Cor. 13:5, so as to move the Corinthians to the crucial task of testing their own faithfulness. If Christ dwells in us, we cannot and may not be *adokimos*; for if we are, our being Christians is futile.

(c) By loving one's neighbor. In his instructions on the collection (2 Cor. 9:13), Paul writes that because of the Corinthians' proving themselves in this service, many will praise God; thereby he shows that such service that is concerned with the needs of the Christian community is part of the testing of faith working in love.

(d) By holding fast to hope in the midst of tribulation. The church is exposed to attacks from within and without, from Satanic powers and godless people. It lives by faith, not by sight. In this position willed by God it maintains its living hope by remaining under God's hand, by the overflowing of the riches given by God and of the goodness created by the Spirit to others (2 Cor. 8:2), by patience (Jas. 1:2–3), and by overcoming temptations (1 Pet. 1:6–7).

See also *peirasmos*, test, trial, tempting, temptation (*4280*).

1517 (*doma*, gift), → *1565*.

1518	δόξα

δόξα (*doxa*), radiance, glory, repute (*1518*); δοξάζω (*doxazō*), praise, glorify (*1519*); ἔνδοξος (*endoxos*), honored, glorious (*1902*); ἐνδοξάζομαι (*endoxazomai*), honor, glorify (*1901*); συνδοξάζω (*syndoxazō*), glorify together (*5280*); κενόδοξος (*kenodoxos*), desirous of praise, conceited, boastful (*3030*); κενοδοξία (*kenodoxia*), desire for praise, conceit, vanity, illusion (*3029*).

CL & OT 1. This word group affords one of the clearest examples of change in the meaning of a Gk. word as it came under biblical influence. The basic meaning of *doxa* in secular Gk. is opinion, conjecture. It ranges from the opinion about a person or thing to the valuation placed on one by others, i.e., repute, praise. The vb. *doxazō* means think, imagine, suppose, magnify, praise, extol (see also *dokeō*, *1506*).

2. The concepts of *doxa* and *doxazō* were transformed in the LXX, where the meaning "opinion" does not occur; the meanings praise and honor are shared with secular Gk. *doxa* is seldom used for the honor shown to a human being (for this *timē* is employed); it is often used for the honor and praise given to God (e.g., Ps. 29:1; Isa. 42:12). Above all, *doxa* expresses God's glory and power (Ps. 24:7–10; 29:3; Isa. 42:8).

3. Behind this new meaning lies the Heb. concept of *kābôd*, glory, honor, which the LXX represents by *doxa*. When it is used of God, it does not mean God in his essential nature, but the glorious

revelation of his person. Characteristically, *kābôd* is linked with verbs of seeing (Exod. 16:7; 33:18; Isa. 40:5) and appearing (Exod. 16:10; Deut. 5:24; Isa. 60:1). We may recognize this *kābôd* in creation (Ps. 19:1; Isa. 6:3), but it expresses itself above all in salvation history (i.e., in God's great acts, Ps. 96:3) and in his presence in the sanctuary (Exod. 40:34–35; 1 Ki. 8:10–11; Ps. 26:8). In 1 Sam. 4:21–22 the loss of the ark of God to the Philistines meant that "the glory has departed from Israel." In the last days a full manifestation of the *kābôd* was expected, in order to bring salvation to Israel (Isa. 60:1–2; Ezek. 39:21–22) and to convert the nations (Ps. 96:3–9; Zech. 2:5–11).

4. The intertestamental period demonstrated a strong interest in the heavenly world. The concept of glory is not confined, as in the OT, to God's self-revelation. It is also applied to the realities of heaven: God, his throne, and the angels. In the language of liturgy and hymns, glory may be used as an epithet applied to almost any concept linked with God. For example, Adam in Paradise possessed glory but lost it through the fall. Thus, humans could share in God's glory. In Qumran it was expected that the elect would "inherit all the glory of Adam" (1QH 4:15; cf. CD 3:20).

NT 1. *doxa* is found 166x times in NT, *doxazō* 61x. The meaning of these words continues the LXX usage and the underlying Heb. *kābôd*, so that the ideas of opinion and conjecture are not found. (a) The meanings honor, fame, repute, and (for the vb.) honor and praise belong to general Gk. usage. The specifically biblical connotation may be seen in expressions such as giving glory to God (Lk. 17:18; Acts 12:23; Rom. 4:20; Rev. 4:9; 11:13) and "for the glory of God" (1 Cor. 10:31), in the so-called doxologies (Lk. 2:14; 19:38; Rom. 11:36; Gal. 1:5; Eph. 3:21; Phil. 4:20; 1 Tim. 1:17), and in application to Christ (Rom. 16:27; 2 Tim. 4:18; Heb. 13:21; 1 Pet. 4:11; 2 Pet. 3:18; Jude 25). The highest duty of humankind is to glorify and praise God in worship, word, and act (Matt. 5:16; Rom. 1:21; 1 Cor. 6:20; 10:31).

(b) When applied to humans or earthly powers with the meaning of splendor, radiance, glory, *doxa* reflects OT usage (e.g., Matt. 4:8; 6:29; 1 Pet. 1:24).

(c) *doxa* in the sense of God's glory, majesty, and power is preeminently the inheritance of OT usage. God is "the God of glory" (Acts 7:2), "the glorious Father" (Eph. 1:17, lit., "the Father of glory"), and "the Majestic Glory" (2 Pet. 1:17). The expression "the glory of God [or the Father]" is frequent (e.g., Acts 7:55; Rom. 1:23; 6:4; Rev. 15:8). God's power is sometimes linked with his glory (Col. 1:11; 2 Thess. 1:9; Rev. 5:13; 19:1). The concept is also applied to Christ— to his earthly life (Lk. 9:32; Jn. 1:14; 2:11; 2 Cor. 2:8), his exalted existence (Lk. 24:26; Jn. 17:5; Rom. 8:17 [*syndoxazō*]; 1 Tim. 3:16), his return (Matt. 16:27; Mk. 8:38; Tit. 2:13; 1 Pet. 4:13), and his preexistence (Jn. 12:41; 17:5). The vb. *doxazō* is used in a corresponding sense, especially in Jn. (e.g., 7:39; 11:4; 12:16; 13:31–32; 17:1).

(d) The NT also contains evidence of the concept that had been widespread since Ezekiel, that angels and other heavenly beings are endowed with glory. This is found in manifestations from heaven, where stress is laid on the visible light (Lk. 2:9; 9:31; Acts 22:11; Rev. 18:1). It is carried a step further when angelic powers are called *doxai* in Jude 8 (cf. 2 Pet. 2:10).

(e) When Paul speaks of the glory of the first man (1 Cor. 11:7) and explains the shining of Moses' face as the shining of glory (2 Cor. 3:7–18; cf. Exod. 34:30), he is also using Jewish concepts. Equally of Jewish origin is the idea that believers share in the glory (Jn. 17:22; Rom. 8:30; 2 Cor. 3:18) or will do so (Rom. 8:17–18, 21; Phil. 3:21; Heb. 2:10; 1 Pet. 5:1, 4, 10). The Christian hope is "the hope of glory" (Col. 1:27).

3. The other forms of the word group need only brief mention. *syndoxazō* (only in Rom. 8:17), be glorified together with someone, has essentially the same meaning as 1(e). *endoxazomai* (only 2 Thess. 1:10, 12) is synonymous with *doxazō*. The adj. *endoxos* (4x) means glorious; it can be linked with God or human beings (Lk. 7:25; 13:17;

1 Cor. 4:10; Eph. 5:27). *kenodoxos* (only Gal. 5:26) and *kenodoxia* (only Phil. 2:3) express the vain desire for honor. This meaning is not unknown in secular Gk., but it is in Christian lit. that those words first find wider usage.

4. For the Greeks fame and glory were among the most important values in life. Rabbis also had a high esteem for a person's honor. In Matt. 6:2, however, Jesus censures a piety that looks for honor from others; such an attitude is incompatible with faith (Jn. 5:44). Paul, following Jesus' example (Jn. 5:41; 8:50; cf. Heb. 5:4–5; 2 Pet. 1:17), did not seek glory from human beings (1 Thess. 2:6). Rather, he voluntarily accepted dishonor (2 Cor. 4:10; 6:8), strove to carry out his service to the honor of the Lord (2 Cor. 8:19–21), and looked to the praise Christ would give him as reward on his day (Phil. 2:16; 1 Thess. 2:19–20). Paul's statement that in the final judgment the righteous will receive "glory, honor and immortality" refers to eternal life itself (Rom. 2:7, cf. 2:10).

5. The glory of this world is depreciated in the light of eschatology, although Jesus could also recognize the glory of the creation (Matt. 6:29; Lk. 12:27). In the NT glory means the divine eschatological reality or manner of existence. Salvation lies in humanity and nature having a share in this ultimate manner of existence. The thought in the NT that the eschatological glory will take believers as well as the entire creation up into itself through a new creation or transfiguration is a development beyond the OT (Rom. 8:18, 21; 1 Cor. 15:43; 2 Cor. 3:18; 4:17; Phil. 3:21; Col. 3:4; 1 Pet. 5:1; but cf. Isa. 66:19, 22).

This concept does not, however, cancel the link with the OT *kābôd*. For glory manifests itself in the NT, just as in the OT, in the operation of God's power and salvation in "salvation history." It appears above all in Christ and his work of salvation (Lk. 9:29–35; Jn. 1:14; 2:11; 2 Cor. 4:4, 6), in believers (Jn. 17:22; 2 Cor. 3:18; Eph. 1:18; 3:16; Col. 1:11), and indeed already in the old covenant (2 Cor. 3:7–11).The presence of this "personal" *doxa* of God in Christ means the presence of salvation (Jn. 1:14; 17:22; 2 Cor. 4:4, 6).

Glory with its transforming power is operative even now among believers (Rom. 8:30; 2 Cor. 3:18) through the resurrection of Christ and our fellowship with him, who is "the firstfruits of those who have fallen asleep" (1 Cor. 15:20).

6. The transfiguration of Jesus (Matt. 17:1–8; Mk. 9:2–8; Lk. 9:28–36) corresponds in the Synoptics to the continuing possession of *doxa* in Jn., though only in Lk. 9:32 is *doxa* used with reference to Jesus. The transfiguration is a parallel on a higher plane to Moses' meeting with God on Mount Sinai (Exod. 24:15–18; 33:18–34:35). However, it is not to be understood, as in the case of Moses, as merely a reflection caused by temporary contact with the heavenly world, but rather as a revelation of the glory that Jesus possessed continually but not openly. At his Parousia Jesus will be revealed in his glory and power (Matt. 19:28).

See also *timē*, price, value, honor (*5507*).

1519 (doxazō, praise, glorify), → *1518.*

1522 (dotēs, giver), → *1565.*

1524 (doulagōgeō, to bring into slavery), → *1528.*

1525 (douleia, slavery), → *1528.*

1526 (douleuō, be subject, serve), → *1528.*

1527 (doulē, female slave), → *1528.*

| 1528 δοῦλος |

δοῦλος (*doulos*), slave (*1528*); δουλεία (*douleia*), slavery (*1525*); δουλεύω (*douleuō*), be subject, serve (*1526*); δουλαγωγέω (*doulagōgeō*), to bring into slavery (*1524*); δούλη (*doulē*), female slave (*1527*); δοῦλος² (*doulos²*), adj. enslaved, in slavery (*1529*); δουλόω (*douloō*), become a slave (*1530*); σύνδουλος (*syndoulos*), fellow servant (*5281*).

CL & OT 1. In cl. Gk. times, personal freedom was a prized possession. To be independent of others and to manage one's own life was the essence of such freedom. Humans found their true worth in being conscious of themselves and in the free development of their potential. Because *douleuō* involved the abrogation of one's own autonomy and the subordination of one's will to that of another, the Greeks felt revulsion and contempt for a slave; subordination in service was debasing and contemptible.

This group of words is shown in a favorable and honorable light only in the phrase "to serve [*douleuō*] the laws." The idea of serving the gods appears first in the Cynic Stoics. Along similar lines, a Stoic wise man so excused himself from all obligation to serve the community (cf. the Stoic concept of world citizenship) that he made himself a free servant of his neighbor.

2. (a) In the OT the primary word for servant is *ʿebed* (pl. *ᵃbādîm*). In the main, two different Gk. words are used to translate this Heb. word: *doulos* and *pais* (→ *4090*). Of the 800 or so occurrences of *ʿebed* in the Heb. OT, *pais* is used 340x, *doulos*, 327x. In general in the LXX, *doulos* denotes someone in enforced bondage, while *pais* denotes the free servant of the king (e.g., 2 Sam. 11:24; 15:15). This latter usage in court circles led to the frequent use of *ʿebed*, servant, as a humble self-designation (Gen. 33:5, *pais*).

(b) Slaves from foreign nations often came to the Israelites via war (cf. Num. 31:7–12; Deut. 20:10–15; 1 Ki. 20:39; 2 Chr. 28:8–9). Some were presented to the tabernacle or temple (Num. 31:32–47; Jos. 9:23–27; Ezr. 8:20), others to military leaders (Deut. 20:10–14; 21:10; Jdg. 5:30). But most belonged to the king, and slaves were an important part of the Israelite economy under the monarchy (1 Ki. 9:21).

From earliest times right up to the revolt of A.D. 70, Hebrews could possess slaves from among their own people (e.g., Exod. 21:2; Jer. 34:8–11). A Hebrew was forcibly sold as a slave by a court if he could not make good the value of stolen goods, since he could not pay his debts (Exod. 21:2), or because he or she sold himself or herself because of poverty (Deut. 15:12; 2 Ki. 4:1; Neh. 5:1–5). In all cases, such slavery was normally limited to six years (but cf. Exod. 21:5–6; Deut. 15:16–17). The OT law regulates the protection of slaves (Exod. 21:2–11; Lev. 25:39–55; Deut. 15:12–18). Slaves played a full part in cultic life (circumcision, Gen. 17:12–13; Sabbath, Exod. 20:10; sacrifice, Deut. 12:18; Passover, Exod. 12:44).

(c) The memory of Israel's experiences in their captivity in Egypt, "the land of slavery [LXX *douleia*]" (Exod. 13:3, 14) lingered on and was the primary source of this root's essential meaning and its emphasis on being a slave, i.e., a repressive or at least dependent form of service under the complete control of a superior. Israel's recollection of Egyptian bondage determined (Deut. 15:12–15) the treatment of fellow Hebrews mentioned above (see Exod. 21:2).

3. (a) The religious use of the idea of slave was probably influenced by court practice. *douleuō* is the usual LXX word for worship in this context (Jdg. 2:7; 2 Chr. 30:8). As in the rest of the ancient Near East, although in contrast to ancient Gk. ideas, worshipers of God in the OT styled themselves as his servants. They thus gave expression to his awesomeness and to their duty to serve God, placing themselves under his protection.

(b) In contrast to other Sem. cultures, however, only rarely is the bestowal of a name used to designate this belonging to God—e.g., Obadiah, whose name means "servant of Yahweh" (1 Ki. 18:3–16). Just as one humbly referred to oneself as "your servant" when addressing the king (e.g., 2 Sam. 9:8), so those who prayed to God frequently designated themselves as "servant" (e.g., Ps. 19:11, 13; 31:16; 86:2, 4; 119:17, 23, 38, 49). Yahweh can also ascribe to someone the title "my servant" (e.g., Job 1:8; in such references in the LXX, sometimes *doulos* is used and sometimes *pais*). The worth of a *doulos* stood or fell with one's knowledge of Yahweh and relations with him. Hence, although *doulos* retained the element of unconditional subjection to another, it lost the character of abject baseness. As a result of God's special election, *doulos* became a title of honor (Ps. 89:3).

4. (b) The Heb. designation *ʿebed* (servant) is used of Moses (Jos. 1:1–2), Joshua (24:29), the patriarchs (Exod. 32:13; Deut. 9:27), and David (1 Ki. 8:24–26; 14:8). Even Nebuchadnezzar is called a servant of Yahweh (Jer. 25:9). Similarly, Job, who has even less connection with the people of Israel, receives the title of "servant" in the prologue and epilogue of the book (Job 1:8; 2:3; 42:7–8). From Ezekiel's time on, the sing. *ʿebed* is used of the people of Israel (Ezek. 28:25; 37:25), and Isa. uses the pl. of the whole body of Israelites (Isa. 54:17). In Isa. 56:6 proselytes too are called those who "serve" (*douleuō*) God.

(b) The "servant of God" expression in the OT can be divided into two main traditions. (i) In 2 Sam. 3:18 the king (David) is Yahweh's servant, whose special function lies in saving the people from all its enemies (cf. also Ezek. 34:23–24; 37:24–25; Hag. 2:23; Zech. 3:8). (ii) The prophets, who are the authoritative messengers of God's word (1 Ki. 18:36), impose God's will on the people, and set historical processes in motion, are Yahweh's "servants" (e.g., Amos 3:7).

(c) Most prominent in Isa. are four passages known as the "servant songs": Isa. 42:1–9; 49:1–7; 50:4–9; 52:13–53:12. Some scholars, on the basis of 49:3, have identified this servant as the people of Israel collectively. Others find a movement within these songs from a collective to an individual identification of this servant. An individual interpretation of the songs is supported by 49:5–6, which sets the servant over against the people. Some suppose him to be a prophet because of his peculiarly prophetic traits (ear, 50:4–5; mouth, 49:1–2), while others, because he establishes justice (42:1, 3–4), releases prisoners (42:7; 49:9), and wields a sword (49:2), see him as a king. Such extreme language can never have been applied to a living or dead person. In other words, the servant represents someone who is yet to come—Israel's Messiah.

NT 1. *doulos* occurs 124x, of which 30 are in Paul, 30 in Matt., and 26 in Lk. *douleuō* occurs 25x, of which 17 are in Paul. *douloō* (8x, mostly in Paul) is a synonym for *douleuō*. (a) In order to appreciate the nuances of meaning in the NT, we must first see what its attitude is to the position of the slave in society, esp. as seen in Jesus' parables. Occasionally, slaves are put in positions of responsibility and command (Matt. 24:45). But a slave owed his master exclusive and absolute obedience (8:9); "no one can serve [*douleuō*] two masters" (6:24). A slave's work earned neither profit nor thanks; he was only doing what he owed (Lk. 17:7–10). The master could use his unlimited power over his slave for good (Matt. 18:27) or for unmerciful punishment, if the slave was guilty of some fault (18:34; 25:30).

The NT resists our contemporary verdict on slaves as a contemptible lower class, by its use of *doulos* in Jesus' parables to describe the relation of all people to God. It finds nothing objectionable in the division of society into master and servant, free and bond. Note too how the NT repeatedly calls slaves to be obedient to their masters in all things—even to unmerciful ones (Eph. 6:5; Col. 3:22; 1 Tim. 6:1; Tit. 2:9; cf. 1 Pet. 2:18). Paul recognizes Philemon's right to Onesimus as his possession, even if Philemon's position shows something of the tension existing between the status quo and faith in the one master, the Lord Jesus Christ (cf. 1 Cor. 7:20–24). Note 1 Cor. 7:21b: "if you can gain your freedom, do so." However, for Paul the main point is freedom in Christ (7:22f–24).

(b) The sociological problems of this state of affairs are mitigated by the fact that God's revelation in Jesus Christ shows that all are in the relentless grip of a completely different sort of slavery. Outside the sphere of Christ's rule all human beings are "slaves of sin" (Rom. 6:17, cf. 6:16). This *douleia* (slavery) can consist of a miserably meticulous observance of the letter of the law in the hope of gaining salvation (cf. Rom. 7:6, 25), of a slavish adoration of the mediating cosmic powers (Gal. 4:3, 8–9), of a frenzied horror of death (Heb. 2:15), or of the service of the belly (Rom. 16:18) and one's lusts (Tit. 3:3). This means in general that "everyone who sins is a slave to sin" (Jn. 8:34).

One cannot free oneself from this servitude of sin by one's own efforts or change masters by one's own decision. Only those whom the Son sets free are really free (Jn. 8:36). Christ's redemption frees one for obedient service under the command of him as Lord (Rom. 12:11; 14:18; Col. 3:24) and leads one into the service of righteousness in the new Spirit-given nature (Rom. 6:18, *douloō*; 7:6). Paul regards himself, called to his office as an apostle, in a special way as a *doulos* of Christ Jesus (Rom. 1:1; Gal. 1:10; Phil. 1:1).

Paul also uses the word *doulos* to refer to the office of some of his colleagues, such as Epaphras (Col. 4:12). In this titular sense *doulos* is closest in sense to *diakonos* (servant), a word Paul uses frequently of the apostolic service of witness (cf. Col. 4:7, "minister [*diakonos*] and fellow servant [*syndoulos*]"; → *diakoneō*, serve, *1354*). Here, as elsewhere, the distinctive thing about the concept of the *doulos* is the subordinate, obligatory, and responsible nature of one's service in exclusive relation to one's Lord. At the same time, all who are called to freedom must serve (*douleuō*) one another in love (Gal. 5:13). Paul made himself a servant of all (1 Cor. 9:19, *douloō*); in the service of the gospel (Phil. 2:22) he is the *doulos* of the community for Christ's sake (2 Cor. 4:5). He who would be first in Christ's community must be its *doulos* (Matt. 20:27).

2. This last evaluation of slavery is only excelled by the dignity given to it insofar as the Lord Jesus took upon himself the title of *doulos*. Christ divested himself and took on "the very nature of a servant [*doulos*]" (Phil. 2:7). This statement shows the theological significance of this group of words. In becoming a human being, the preexistent Lord takes on the form of a slave. When Christ took on this form, he entered into full solidarity with humankind in its subjection to sin, law, and death. As servant, he was subject to the law (Gal. 4:4) and bore its curse (3:13). He took on a form "in the likeness of sinful man" (Rom. 8:3) and thus made himself a brother of the human race, "who all their lives were held in slavery [*douleia*] by their fear of death" (Heb. 2:15). The form of the *doulos* most precisely describes Jesus Christ's incarnation as the deepest self-abasement.

3. The Lord's form as a *doulos* unmasks the nature of the unredeemed person's life as *douleia*. This slavery is that of sin, i.e., obsession with the illusion that we can make or maintain our own lives and freedom in our own power. That which the Greeks regarded as the highest form of freedom (cf. above) becomes in the NT the source of abject bondage. We obstinately wave God's help aside and busy ourselves in running our own lives in our own strength, trusting in our own resources and falling into the grip of fear (Rom. 8:15; Heb. 2:15). We make use of the law and the powers of this world to create our own righteousness and are enslaved under the curse of the law (Gal. 3:13), being "slaves to those who by nature are not gods" (4:8). Since every attempt to liberate ourselves ensnares us further, our *douleia* is complete and is not restricted, as in gnostic dualism, to the level of matter and the body.

4. Jesus Christ alone redeems humankind from slavery to sin with the price of his death. The metaphor of sacral manumission is here united with the idea of a change of masters. Believers "have been set free from sin and have become slaves to righteousness" (Rom. 6:18; cf. also 6:19, where Paul uses the alternate word *doulos* [*1529*] to contrast our former slavery to sin with our present slavery to righteousness; see also 6:22). In other words, our manumission from bondage of a supposed independence does not lead to a new independence. Rather, the one manumitted is set free for "the obedience that comes from faith" (1:5), which he or she offers to the Lord Jesus Christ as a slave (12:11; 14:18; Col. 3:24; cf. Rom. 7:6; 1 Thess. 1:9). In fact, our servitude to Christ demands that we make our bodies our slaves (*doulagōgeō*; 1 Cor. 9:27) so we might not forfeit the prize for which we labor.

Yet this new relationship of master and servant is not dominated by "a spirit that makes you a slave again to fear"; rather, believers have "received the Spirit of sonship" (Rom. 8:15). However, this freedom of God's children must not become an occasion "to indulge the sinful nature"; rather, we must "serve [*douleuō*] one another in love" (Gal. 5:13). This sort of service of love to one's neighbors is rooted in Christ's love in taking the form of a servant (note how the exhortations of Phil. 2:1–4 are causally related to 2:5–11). As a *doulos*, Jesus showed his love to his disciples by washing their feet (the duty of a slave), "that you should do as I have done for you" (Jn. 13:15). The nature of Christ's loving work thereby prevents any separation between serving God and serving one's neighbor.

5. Hence, those who want to be first in Jesus Christ's community must be its slaves (Matt. 20:27). It is understandable, then, in light of this dialectical concept of Christian freedom as a *douleia* after the pattern of the Redeemer, that the sociological question of the freedom of slaves did not appear a pressing one in the NT. Christians were aware of the indelible distinction between master and slave. However, the liberating knowledge of the common service that both had to one heavenly Master (Eph. 6:9) was normative.

Master and servant must be subject to this Lord, because in their mutual treatment of each other they join themselves to that community whose rule is love. It is thus not left to one's individual choice to decide whether or not to subject oneself to others in the community. It is precisely the concept of *douleuō*, in contrast to that of *diakoneō* (serve), that emphasizes the obligatory character of service to God and to one's neighbor as the duty of all those set free by Jesus Christ.

See also *aichmalōtos*, captive, prisoner of war (*171*); *desmios*, prisoner (*1300*); *diakoneō*, to serve (*1354*); *libertinos*, freedman (*3339*).

1529 (doulos², adj. enslaved, in slavery), → *1528.*

1530 (douloō, become a slave), → *1528.*

| 1532   δράκων |

δράκων (*drakōn*), dragon (*1532*).

CL & OT *drakōn* denotes dragon, snake, giant sea creature, or serpent. In many myths the *drakōn* is a picture of the primeval power of chaos, whose defeat at the hands of a god enabled the world to come into being. Such concepts may lie behind several OT passages: God killed "the gliding serpent" or "the monster" (Job 26:13; Ps. 74:13–14); someday God will kill "the gliding serpent" in the sea (Isa. 27:1); monsters or serpents live in the sea (Job. 7:12; Ps. 148:7; Amos 9:3). In calling Pharaoh a monster, Ezek. 29:3; 32:2 typifies the attitude of the OT to the mythological worldview. It praises the fact that Yahweh has removed all threats to his people in the past and will continue to do so. That is why the LXX, in the account of the signs by which Moses was to confirm his call, translates snake by *drakōn*, so as to give greater glory to God's action (Exod. 7:9–12).

NT In the NT *drakōn* is found only in Rev., where it is used exclusively as a synonym for Satan (see 12:9; 20:2; cf. Gen. 3:1–15). In Rev. 12 the dragon has 7 heads and 10 horns (cf. Dan. 7:7–8). It has power in heaven, so that its tail sweeps down a third of the stars. Demons are subordinate to it. It stands by the woman who is about to give birth to the man child so that it may devour him but is defeated by Michael and his angels and is cast down to earth together with its demons (12:7–9). There it persecutes the woman and tries to drown her in a flood of water from its mouth (12:13–17).

On earth the dragon gives its power and its throne to the "beast" (which, like the dragon, has 7 heads and 10 horns). The beast causes the inhabitants of the world to worship the dragon (13:2, 4). The dragon is thrown into the abyss by an angel for a period of a thousand years (i.e., a millennium, 20:2–3; → *chilias*, *5942*), so that it can no longer deceive the nations. When the thousand years are past, it is released and collects Gog and Magog for the final battle against God's people; it is defeated and thrown into the lake of fire (20:8, 10). The consummation of Christ's victory will be the elimination of Satan.

See also *ophis*, snake, serpent (*4058*).

1536 (dromos, course, race), → *4513.*

1538 (dynamai, to be strong enough to, be able to), → *1539.*

| 1539 δύναμις |

δύναμις (*dynamis*), power, might, strength, force, ability, capability, deed of power, resources (*1539*); δύναμαι (*dynamai*), to be strong enough to, be able to (*1538*); δυνάστης (*dynastēs*), a ruler, sovereign (*1541*); δυναμόω (*dynamoō*), strengthen (*1540*); ἐνδυναμόω (*endynamoō*), strengthen (*1904*); δυνατός (*dynatos*), powerful, strong, mighty, able (*1543*); δυνατέω (*dynateō*), be strong, able, strong enough (*1542*); ἀδυνατέω (*adynateō*), to be impossible (*104*); ἀδύνατος (*adynatos*), powerless, impotent (*105*).

CL & OT 1. In cl. Gk. *dynamis* means ability to achieve, physical strength; then troops, fighting forces, and political power. This word also figures in the realm of nature, e.g., in the power of heat and cold and the healing power of certain plants and elements. In Hel. times the word took on metaphysical connotations. The Stoics, for example, equated the all-pervading creative force with God. The gnostics honored God as the Almighty and hoped for redemption through their incorporation into the heavenly powers, often through magic. Sick people looked for healing through the power of the god Asclepius.

2. In the LXX *dynamis* generally means military forces (e.g., Exod. 15:4; Deut. 11:4). It can also stand for the power of a ruler (e.g., Jdg. 8:21) or of God (e.g., Ps. 68:28). The pl. was used to translate *ṣᵉbāʾôt* in the phrase "Yahweh Sabaoth," i.e., the Lord of the heavenly hosts (e.g., Ps. 46:7, 11; 48:8). Yahweh is in control of the transcendent powers; autonomous powers of nature and magic are pushed into the background. His might is primarily revealed at the level of history and to a particular people. The proof of God's power, so fundamental for Israel, was the miraculous deliverance by the Lord's hand at the Red Sea (Deut. 3:24).

The subsequent theological struggle with Canaanite religion led to an emphasis on God's activity in nature and his power over it; the most comprehensive demonstration of that power is his creation of the world (cf. Jer. 27:5; 32:17). On the basis of the nation's experience, individuals can also praise God as their refuge and "strength" (2 Sam. 22:31–40; Ps. 46:1). God's power, at work in the believer, is the Spirit (Mic. 3:8, *dynasteia*). God is Spirit, not flesh; he far transcends the whole creation (cf. Isa. 31:3–4).

3. Jewish apocalyptic lived in the expectation of the divine judgment of the world in the near future; his people hoped to see a display of the might of which they currently experienced so little. The writings from Qumran foresaw the triumph of God's power and might in the war of the children of light against the children of darkness. The end of the age brings the conclusive and world-embracing demonstration of God's mighty deeds (1QM 11:1–12:5). In this, God's power is expressed through both human fighters and the mighty angels. The Messiah too will be a victorious warrior and will be the instrument of God's final demonstration of power (*Pss. Sol.* 17:24, 42–43, 51). In some Jewish writings, "power" serves as a circumlocution for the name of God. Wisdom is described as a mirror of the power of God (Wis. 7:25–26).

NT The noun *dynamis* (119x) is esp. frequent in Paul's letters. *dynamoō* (2x) and *dynateō* (3x) are rare, but the vb. *dynamai*, to be able (expressing possibility or capability), occurs 210x. The compound verb *endynamoō* is used 7x. The adj. *dynatos* occurs 32x, whereas the noun *dynastēs* (ruler) occurs 3x, twice in reference to secular rulers (Lk. 1:52; Acts 8:27) and once with reference to God (1 Tim. 6:15). The adj. *adynatos* (powerless) occurs 10x, the vb. *adynateō*, 2x.

1. *The Synoptic Gospels and Acts*. Here *dynamis* denotes the power of God, the heavenly powers (in the pl.), miraculous power (in the pl., mighty deeds, miracles), and the power that brings salvation to completion.

(a) Mary confesses that God is the "Mighty One" (Lk. 1:49, *dynatos*), probably in response to the angel Gabriel, who affirmed that with God nothing is impossible (*adynateō*, 1:37); Jesus himself used the reverential circumlocution of "the Mighty One" to refer to God (Mk. 14:62). All his work is supported by the knowledge of the almighty power of God: "With God all things are possible" (Matt. 19:26; Mk. 10:27; Lk. 18:27; in contrast to *adynatos* [impossible] in all three; cf. 14:35). At the end, his power is declared preeminently in the resurrection of the dead (Mk. 12:24).

(b) The NT also speaks of "powers," i.e., cosmic, spiritual powers that can appear in person (Rom. 8:38; Eph. 1:21; 1 Pet. 3:22). Significantly, superhuman representatives of evil are also credited with having power, but it is always pointed out either that their power has already been broken or that it will shortly be abolished (cf. Matt. 12:29; Mk. 3:27; Lk. 10:19; 11:22; 1 Cor. 15:24; 2 Thess. 2:9; Rev. 13:2; 17:13–14). It is fundamental for the proclamation of the good news that, in and through Christ, those things to which both the OT and Jud. looked forward have taken place, namely, God's demonstration of power in the last days and his triumph over the rise of evil.

(c) Christ was powerful in speech and action (Lk. 24:19). His miracles are called *dynameis* (e.g., Acts 2:22), because in them God's rule on earth began to have a powerful effect, and the fight against the devil was carried out on the level of human existence (Matt. 12:22–30; Mk. 6:2, 5; Lk. 19:37; Acts 10:38). Jesus is the "more powerful" one (Mk. 1:7, *ischys*, → *2709*), who, as God's representative, subdues the strong man, i.e., the devil. His miracles were done by a "power" within himself (Mk. 5:30; 6:14). Lk. links this God-given power with the Holy Spirit (Lk. 1:35; 4:14; Acts 10:38). These miracles, therefore, demonstrate that Jesus is the Messiah, the one anointed with the Spirit (Acts 2:22; 10:38). By the power of this same Spirit bestowed on the apostles (Acts 4:7; 6:8), they performed great "miracles" (*dynameis* in 8:13; 19:11). The apostles' authoritative preaching (4:33; cf. 6:8–10) was proof of a supernatural power.

(d) All these proofs of the Spirit and of divine power, of course, are only recognized as such where there is faith. They cannot take place in an area of unbelief (Mk. 6:5). But the final demonstration of Christ's power will be both public and irresistible. This will be at the time of his return (Matt. 24:32; Mk. 13:28; Lk. 21:29), when the kingdom of God will be consummated "with power" (Matt. 24:30; Mk. 9:1; 13:26). Believers already have a share in this final demonstration of God's power, which is why no limits are put to their actions, since all things are possible for them (Mk. 9:23; cf. *adynateō* in Matt. 17:20).

2. *John's Gospel and Revelation*. (a) *dynamis* does not occur in the Gospel of Jn., because here the messianic activity of Jesus is based on God's sending of his Son and on the unity of will between Father and Son. The Son "can [*dynamai*] do nothing" without the Father (5:19, 30); his miracles are signs (20:30; → *sēmeion*, *4956*) that reveal the divine power of Jesus. Conversely, the inability of humans to believe in Jesus and to enter the sphere of God's reality is due to their imprisonment in the world of darkness (3:3; 8:43; 14:17). Only election (6:44) and rebirth (3:5) secure their release.

(b) Rev. sees the saints in a vision praising Christ, who, by his enthronement in heaven (→ *thronos*, *2585*), has crowned his redeeming work on earth. Admittedly, it is God who is worshiped in the hymns of praise for his "glory and honor and power [*dynamis*]" (Rev. 4:11; cf. 7:12; 19:1), but the exalted Christ is also worthy to receive such sovereign power on the grounds of his sacrificial death (5:12; 12:10). For it was through Christ that God broke the power of evil rulers of the world (13:2); Christ made possible the victorious culmination of God's sovereign rule (11:17; 12:10). John's visions of the Son of Man are given a Christological interpretation (cf. 13:1–14 with Dan. 7) and are polemically contrasted with Roman world domination and the Caesar cult.

3. *Paul*. Paul lays a greater emphasis on the present experience of the revelation of God's power, which he understands primarily in terms of the power that raises the dead in the last days and the new creativity of the Holy Spirit. This power of God was evident in Christ, the Risen One; as the now Exalted One, he is the bearer and the mediator of this same power. Admittedly, God's invisible power can be deduced from the works of creation (cf. Rom. 1:20). But it is the resurrection of Jesus that represents the central proof of God's might (cf. 1:4; 1 Cor.

5:4; 2 Cor. 13:4; Phil. 3:10). With the resurrection belongs the exaltation (Eph. 1:20–21), whereby Christ became the "power of God" (1 Cor. 1:24). Paul uses *endynamoō*, to strengthen, to describe this work of the exalted Christ in the lives of individual believers in Phil. 4:13 (also Eph. 6:10; 1 Tim. 1:12; 2 Tim. 2:1; 4:17). In Christ's mediating work is a double revelation of God's power: the Word that brings salvation and the Holy Spirit who creates and makes new.

(a) The gospel is effective as the "power of God" that brings salvation (Rom. 1:16; 1 Cor. 1:18), for the preacher speaks in Christ's power (2 Tim. 1:8–9; cf. 4:17). It announces the love of God, whom we would otherwise fear as the condemning judge of the world; this love was visibly proved on the cross when Christ died for us while we were still sinners (Rom. 5:8). Believers see, through the gospel, that the OT promises have now come into force; they discover in the process the previously announced gospel of God in OT prophecy (Rom. 1:2).

(b) The natural self does not have the power to please God or to fulfill the law (cf. Rom. 8:7–8; Gal. 3:21). In our weakness we even experience the law to be a power that misleads us into sin (cf. Rom. 5:20; 1 Cor. 15:56). But as believers, like the risen Lord, we live in the power of God and of Christ (2 Cor. 6:7; 13:3–4; also Eph. 1:19). It is not obedience to the law but the love of Christ that protects us from the cosmic powers (Rom. 8:38–39). The kingdom of God is experienced in power, in sharp contrast to mere words (1 Cor. 4:19–20) and exterior piety (2 Tim. 3:5). Because God's power is intended for the glorification of Christians, there is a close link between it and his glory (→ *doxa*, *1518*; cf. Rom. 1:4 with 6:4).

(c) Paul also connects the power of God with the Holy Spirit, who is the power of the resurrection and of the life in the new aeon as well as the power that works signs and wonders (Rom. 15:19; 1 Cor. 12:10, 28; Gal. 3:5), which also vindicate Paul's apostleship (2 Cor. 12:12). *dynamis* therefore denotes here the Spirit insofar as he is revealed in the mighty works of those gifted with the Spirit (cf. 1 Cor. 2:13, 15; 3:1; 14:37; Gal. 6:1). The Spirit, as the power of Christ, realizes the authority of the heavenly Lord in the earthly community. For Paul, to be in Christ (e.g., Rom. 5:1; 1 Cor. 1:30) and to be in the Spirit (e.g., Rom. 8:11, 14–16; 1 Cor. 2:4, 12–16) are one and the same thing. The two thoughts are brought together in Eph. 2:18.

The Spirit has power to purify and judge the church (1 Cor. 5:4). He strengthens it and trains it in patience so that its members are kept in faith until judgment day (cf. Eph. 3:16–17; Col. 1:11; 2 Thess. 1:11–12). Since the Spirit is the representative of the exalted Lord, he cannot be manipulated like the power of magic in the hands of a magician (cf. Acts 8:18–20). On the contrary, his supernatural origin and his characteristic as the power of God is proved by the fact that in weak human beings he is powerful (2 Cor. 12:9–10). From the human point of view, God chose weak and unworthy things to be objects of his demonstrations of might (1 Cor. 1:27): e.g., Paul, the former persecutor of Christians, and the social nonentities of Corinth.

(d) The greatest proof of this law of divine action and the justification of the despised Christian way of life is to be found in the cross. Christ died on the cross in weakness, having renounced all claims to power, and he now lives by the power of God (2 Cor. 13:4). The same is true of Christians: They are weak, but that is the very reason why God's power equips them for life with Christ. Accordingly, God's work in a believer is contrary to human expectations. Paul, though in prison, is able to say that he can do all things through the One who makes him strong (Phil. 4:13). The strong in Christ, for their part, are to regard themselves as under obligation to serve their weaker brothers and sisters. Thus they will avoid the danger of forgetting that the strength they have is not their own but has been given them by Christ. Thus they will not misuse their freedom for their own ends (Rom. 15:1).

(e) By the power of God, Christians are assured of future perfection. The present inner transformation, which has already begun, will be followed by the visible and total transformation of the body for

eternal life. This will take place when we are raised from the dead by the same divine power that raised Jesus (1 Cor. 6:14; cf. 2 Cor. 4:14). Christ will then change us by his power and so will change our lowly earthly bodies to be like his own glorified body (Phil. 3:21). On this account, the Christian hope is based on the resurrection and knows the power that was made visible when Christ was raised from the dead (Phil. 3:10; cf. 1 Cor. 4:19–20).

4. The adj. *adynatos*, powerless, impotent, is used of the helpless lame man at Lystra, crippled from birth (Acts 14:8), who was healed in response to Paul's command to stand on his feet. In Rom. 15:1 this word is used as a noun in the contrast: "We who are strong [*dynatos*] ought to bear with the failings of the weak [*adynatos*]" (cf. a related contrast in Matt. 19:26; Mk. 10:27; Lk. 18:27).

In Heb. 6:4 *adynatos* denotes the impossibility of restoring those who commit apostasy, and also the impossibility of God ever proving to be false (6:18). In 10:4 this word asserts that it is impossible for the blood of bulls and goats to take away sin. This stands in contrast with the fact that without faith it is impossible to please God (11:6).

See also *exousia*, freedom of choice, right, power, authority (*2026*); *thronos*, throne, seat (*2585*); *ischys*, strength (*2709*).

1540 (dynamoō, strengthen), → *1539.*

1541 (dynastēs, a ruler, sovereign), → *1539.*

1542 (dynateō, be strong, able, strong enough), → *1539.*

1543 (dynatos, powerful, strong, mighty, able), → *1539.*

1544 δύνω

δύνω (*dynō*), set, dress (*1544*); ἐκδύω (*ekdyō*), undress (*1694*); ἀπεκδύομαι (*apekdyomai*), undress, strip (*588*); ἀπέκδυσις (*apekdysis*), laying aside (*589*); ἐνδύω (*endyō*), dress, clothe (*1907*); ἔνδυμα (*endymā*), clothes (*1903*); ἐπενδύομαι (*ependyomai*), put on over (*2086*); ἀποτίθημι (*apotithēmi*), put off (*700*); ἀπόθεσις (*apothesis*), putting off, removal (*629*).

CL & OT In cl. Gk. as well as in LXX and Jud., *dynō* (also *dyō*) often refers to the going down of the sun; fig. these vbs. mean put on, arm oneself (e.g., with strength). *ekdyō* means undress (oneself), extract oneself from, escape. *endyō* means to clothe or dress (oneself), put on (e.g., a garment, weapon), and fig. assume qualities, virtues.

NT 1. *dynō* is found only in Mk. 1:32; Lk. 4:40, both times of the setting of the sun.

2. *ekdyō* has a lit. meaning (stripping a person of his or her clothes) in Matt. 27:28, 31; Mk. 15:20; Lk. 10:30. The fig. meaning occurs in 2 Cor. 5:4; Paul uses it without an obj. in the sense of undressing oneself, losing the garment of the body: "We do not wish to be unclothed." Three general lines of interpretation may be traced (see also *gymnos*, *1218*).

(a) Paul longed for Christ's return before his death, because death would bring with it an intermediate, bodiless state (*gymnos*), an existence in nakedness. In other words, Paul did not wish to lose his garment (i.e., his body) through death, but instead to be further clothed at the Parousia. Note, however, that elsewhere Paul indicates he was looking forward to fellowship with Christ in the intermediate period (Phil. 1:23).

(b) Paul did not want to lose the garment of his body, because its loss is the fate of the unbelievers, who lose their earthly body in death and receive no heavenly body.

(c) Paul was combating a gnostic group in Corinth. The gnostics longed to be freed from the covering of the body. Note esp. how Paul is not stressing being unclothed, but being further clothed. At the same time, evidence for Gnosticism in the 1st cent. is slim at best.

3. *apotithēmi* is used fig. in the NT for the laying aside of carnal qualities (Rom. 13:12; Eph. 4:25), even one's whole being insofar as it lies under the power of the former age. Paul encourages us to "put off your old self" (Eph. 4:22; cf. Col. 3:9) and to "put on the new self"

(*endyō*, Eph. 4:24; Col. 3:10; cf. Rom. 6:4–5; Gal. 3:27). In 1 Pet. 3:21 *apothesis* is used for the removal of dirt; in 2 Pet. 1:14, for putting off the earthly body (i.e., death).

4. (a) *apekdyomai* is found in Col. 2:15 and 3:9. In the latter the obj. is a thing: "You have taken off your old self." Paul stresses with this vb. that it is a complete putting off and putting away, which makes falling back into the former manner of life impossible. *apekdyomai* in Col. 2:15 has the force of undressing, rendering powerless (the mid. is being used as an act.). God has "disarmed [undressed] the powers and authorities." Behind this verse lies an oriental custom. When someone in high office was deposed, he had to put off the robes of his office. In the same way God stripped the powers of their honors and gave their power to the one to whom it alone belonged, Christ.

(b) *apekdysis* occurs only in Col. 2:11, where it is used metaphorically. Paul uses it to describe the true circumcision, "not . . . a circumcision done by the hands of men but . . . the circumcision done by Christ." It consists of "the putting off of the sinful nature," which the Christian experiences in baptism, and baptism is being buried with Christ (2:12).

5. *endyō* is used 28x in the NT and *endyma* 8x. Jesus uses the noun in his challenge to us to consider that life is more than food and the body more than clothes (Matt. 6:25, 28; Lk. 12:23). The angel at the resurrection was wearing brilliant apparel (Matt. 28:3). Alongside the lit. meaning of the vb. (Matt. 27:31), *endyō* is often used fig. (a) One can put on spiritual armor (Rom. 13:12; Eph. 6:11), Christian virtues (Col. 3:12; 1 Thess. 5:8), and the spiritual, resurrection body (1 Cor. 15:53).

(b) One can also put on Christ (Rom. 13:14; Gal. 3:27). This is done both by baptism and faith. If we regarded this purely formally, Paul's linguistic usage might suggest an approximation to the rituals of the mystery religions, in which initiates sought to identify themselves with the gods by putting on ritual garments. In fact, however, Paul is concerned with a new relationship of one's personality with Christ. For him putting on Christ means sharing Christ's nature. He also writes of the putting on of the new self (Eph. 4:24; Col. 3:10), which is identical with Christ (cf. Gal. 2:20).

(c) *endyō* is used absolutely in 2 Cor. 5:3: "when we are clothed." Paul did not desire to be freed from having a body but wished to put on a new, spiritual body. This being clothed takes place at the Parousia.

5. *ependyomai* is found only in 2 Cor. 5:2, 4. Paul longs to have his heavenly body put on over his present one. The mid. is used with a pass. sense.

See also *gymnos*, naked (*1218*); *himation*, garment (*2668*).

1545 δύο	δύο (*dyo*), two (*1545*); δίστομος (*distomos*), double-edged (*1492*).

NT 1. The word *dyo* occurs some 135x in the NT, but few are of real importance. Two is the smallest expression of plurality and naturally points to alternatives or contrasts (cf. Matt. 6:24; 21:28; 24:40–41). Emissaries often traveled in pairs (cf. Matt. 21:1; Mk. 6:7). "Two or three" is a frequent approximation for a very few (e.g., Matt. 20).

2. In Jn. 8:17 Jesus refers to the OT principle that "the testimony of two men is valid" (cf. Num. 35:30; Deut. 17:6; 19:15). He uses it to demonstrate that he himself and the Father are the two who bear witness to him. There are several other NT references to the need for two or three witnesses (Matt. 18:16; 2 Cor. 13:1; 1 Tim. 5:19; Heb. 10:28). Perhaps this same motif can be traced elsewhere in Gospel events (e.g., Jesus' transfiguration [Matt. 17:1; Mk. 9:2; Lk. 9:28]; Jesus' prayer in Gethsemane [Matt. 26:37; Mk. 14:33]; Jesus' conversation with the two on the way to Emmaus [Lk. 24:13]).

3. The only significant usage of the simple number two in Rev. is in 11:4–11, where again the theme is witness. The imagery goes back to Zech. 4:2–3, 11–14. In Rev. 11:6, however, the two witnesses have powers corresponding to those of Moses and Elijah, who are not named, but represent the testimony of the Law and the Prophets.

4. In Rev. 1:16 a sharp, two-edged (*distomos*) sword proceeds from the mouth of the risen Christ (cf. 2:12, 16). The language recalls Isa. 11:4; 49:2, but is applied to the need of Christians at Pergamum, who faced judicial execution by the Roman authority. The double edge on this sword describes a Roman weapon, and the Roman proconsul wielded the power of the sword. But here Christ holds the ultimate executive and judicial authority. The sword is later associated with "the Word of God" (19:13; 15; cf. Eph. 6:17; Heb. 4:12).

1546 (*dysbastaktos*, difficult to carry), → *1002*.

1554 (*dysnoētos*, hard to understand), → *3808*.

1557 δώδεκα	δώδεκα (*dōdeka*), twelve (*1557*).

CL & OT 1. The number twelve gets its symbolic meaning from the twelve months; it is thus also originally an astronomical number.

2. The OT, however, does not seem to be aware of this. The number twelve is found almost exclusively for the number of the tribes of Israel (e.g., Num. 1:4–49; 10:14–28; 13:2–15; 26:4–63; 34:13–28). Even after the dissolution of the united monarchy, the OT people of God continued to understand itself as the twelve tribes of the people of Israel (cf. 1 Ki. 18:31; Ezr. 8:35; Ezek. 47:13; 48:1–35). The number twelve in Scripture primarily denotes the people of God in its totality. In Jewish apocalyptic writings an astral-theological usage of the number twelve turns up (e.g., *1 Enoch* 76:1–14; 82:11), alluding to the twelve tribes.

NT 1. The thought of the twelve tribes as the people of God is alive in the NT, not only as historical reminiscence (Acts 7:8), but also when Paul, before Agrippa, counts himself as a member of the twelve tribes and appeals to the promises made to them, which apply to him (Acts 26:7, *dōdekaphylon*; cf. also Phil. 3:5). The circle of "the Twelve" (e.g., Matt. 10:1–2, 5; 11:1; 19:28; 20:17; 26:14, 20; Lk. 8:1; 9:12; Jn. 6:67; 20:24; Acts 6:2; 1 Cor. 15:5) is to be seen against this background of the twelve tribes, since it owes its existence to a particular calling by the earthly Jesus (see also *mathētēs*, disciple, *3412*; *apostolos*, apostle, *693*).

In view of the presence of the kingdom of God among the disciples (i.e., Jesus himself), their commission (Mk. 3:14–15) points them primarily to the lost sheep of the old twelve tribes of the house of Israel (Matt. 10:6; 15:24), though they also have a representative function in the post-Easter church. Thus the NT people of God can be addressed in Jas. 1:1 as "the twelve tribes scattered among the nations" (cf. 1 Pet. 1:1), whereby the continuity of salvation history is maintained.

2. There is an echo of the astral-religious significance of the number twelve in Rev. 12:1, in the vision of a woman clothed with the sun, wearing a crown with twelve stars on her head. But the woman is here only the symbol of the daughter of Zion. The twelve stars of the crown signify the twelve tribes, the OT people of God (cf. Gen. 37:9–10), from whom the Messiah comes and to whom also belong all who confess the name of Jesus (Rev. 12:17). Correspondingly, the NT people of God, composed of Jews and Gentiles, is described in 7:4–8 in the 12 x 12,000 (or 144,000) sealed from the tribes of Israel (cf. also 14:3). Thus the number 144,000 does not denote a numerical limitation of those sealed; rather, it symbolizes the final perfection of God's people. Note that when John *sees* this crowd, as opposed to hearing their number, he sees "a great multitude that no one could count, from every nation, tribe, people and language" (7:9).

The number twelve in the description of the new Jerusalem (Rev. 21:12–27) is used as an expression of its glory, which is sufficient for the eschatological people of God. The church in heaven is the completion of the twelve tribes of the OT (21:12–13) and the twelve apostles of the NT (21:14).

3. In other respects twelve is used simply in its numerical sense (e.g., Matt. 9:20; Mk. 5:42; 8:19; Lk. 2:42; Acts 19:7; 24:11).

1561 (*dōrea*, gift), → *1565*.

1562 (*dōrean*, as a present, gratis), → *1565*.

1563 (*dōreomai*, give, present), → *1565*.

1564 (*dōrēma*, present), → *1565*.

1565	δῶρον

δῶρον (*dōron*), gift, present (*1565*); δωρεά (*dōrea*), gift (*1561*); δωρεάν (*dōrean*), as a present, gratis (*1562*); δωρέομαι (*dōreomai*), give, present (*1563*); δώρημα (*dōrēma*), present (*1564*); δίδωμι (*didōmi*), give, grant (*1443*); δόμα (*doma*), gift (*1517*); δότης (*dotēs*), giver (*1522*).

CL & OT 1. *dōron* is from *do-*, the same root as *didōmi*. All the words in this group revolve around the idea of a present, gift, or bestowal. *dōrean* (acc. of *dōrea*) is used adverbially in the sense of gratis, undeservedly, as a present. *dōron* (and *dōrea*) denotes esp. a complimentary gift. As a gift from the gods, it can also mean dispensation. As a gift to the gods, *dōron* denotes a consecrated gift. It can also mean tax, tribute, or bribe.

2. The LXX uses *dōron* with the following main meanings: (a) a present given to another person (Gen. 24:53; 32:13); (b) tribute, booty (Jdg. 3:15, 17–18; 5:19); (c) bribe (Exod. 23:7–8; Deut. 16:19); (d) most frequently, the cultic meaning of offering (esp. in Lev. and Num.; e.g., Lev. 1:2–3, 10, 14; Num. 5:15; 6:14), usually with the vb. *prospherō*, to bring, offer; (e) a gift brought to God in recognition of his greatness and power (Ps. 68:29; 72:10; Isa. 18:7); (f) a gift from God (Gen. 30:20). *dōrēma* appears in the LXX only in Sir. 34:21 (= LXX 31:18), and then only in some MSS.

3. *dōreomai* is rare in the LXX. It has the sense of "giving" (a) from one person to another (Est. 8:1; Prov. 4:2), (b) from people to God (Lev. 7:15 = LXX 7:5), and (c) from God to people (Gen. 30:20). Much more frequent is *didōmi*, which as a rule renders the Heb. *nātan*, to give (likewise used in this threefold way).

4. *dōrea* occurs in the LXX usually in the adverbial acc. form, *dōrean*. It means (a) for nothing (i.e., without payment, Exod. 21:2, 11; without recompense, Gen. 29:15), (b) without cause (1 Sam. 19:5; 25:31), or (c) in vain (Ezek. 6:10; Mal. 1:10).

NT 1. (a) In the NT *dōron* (19x) stands once for a human gift (Rev. 11:10; cf. Matt. 7:11; par. Lk. 11:13, *doma*) and once for the divine gift (Eph. 2:8). For the latter, *dōrea* is found more often (Jn. 4:10; Acts 2:38; Rom. 5:15, 17; Eph. 4:7; Heb. 6:4). Rom. 5:16 and Jas. 1:17 have *dōrēma* (in the latter together with *dosis*). All other uses of *dōron* denote an offering to God (e.g., Matt. 5:23–24; 23:18–19; Mk. 7:11; Heb. 5:1; 9:9; 11:4; note esp. Matt. 2:11, where it is the gift of adoration by the Magi. The occasional combination with *prospherō*, to bring, offer, underlines the connection with the OT sacrificial system (→ *thyō*, *2604*).

(b) *didōmi* (415x) is found in all the nuances of presenting, giving, bestowing, granting, etc., both (i) among people (Matt. 7:11a; Acts 20:35) and (ii) by God (Matt. 7:11b; 1 Jn. 4:13; Rev. 2:7, 17). The meaning to offer also occurs (Lk. 2:24), while a metaphorical meaning (i.e., to allow or provide) is found in such passages as Mk. 10:37; Acts 13:20.

(c) *dōrean* (9x) has the threefold meaning common in the OT: (i) gratis, for nothing (Matt. 10:8; Rom. 3:24; 2 Cor. 11:7); (ii) without cause (Jn. 15:25, OT quotation from Ps. 35:19; 69:4); (iii) in vain (Gal. 2:21).

2. *dōron* and *didōmi* as cultic terms are found in contexts where the subject matter is the regular offering (Matt. 5:23–24; 8:4; Lk. 2:24). Some passages emphasize, in keeping with OT prophecy, that religious offerings are no substitute for obedience to God's will (e.g., Matt. 15:5; Mk. 7:11; cf. Isa. 1:10–17; Mic. 6:6–8). The problem of the sacrificial cult is faced squarely in Heb. (e.g., Heb. 5:1–10; 8:3–4), where a contrast is drawn between the merely temporary OT system with its offerings (*dōron* and *thysia*) made by human beings and the final, once-for-all offering of Christ (7:26–28; 9:25–28; 10:10–14).

3. This opens up the NT teaching that God is a God who gives and that his giving is seen supremely in the redeeming work of Christ. (a) There are general statements to the effect that God "gave" his Son (Jn. 3:16) and verses where Jesus is referred to as "the gift of God" (*dōrea*, 4:10). The statement that Christ "gave himself" for all people or for our sins appears as a creedal formula in Gal. 1:4; 1 Tim. 2:6.

(b) Other references point specifically to Jesus' death on the cross: e.g., Jesus gave his life as a ransom for many (Mk. 10:45 par.). Similarly, Lk.'s account of the Last Supper (Lk. 22:19) speaks of Christ's body "given for you."

(c) This gives to Christians the assurance of belonging forever to the church of Christ. Jn. in particular sees the basis for this assurance in the fact that the church has been given to Christ by God (Jn. 10:28–29; cf. 17:6–12). Moreover, to belong to this church means to share in the gift of eternal life (10:28; cf. 3:14–17; 11:25–26; 17:3).

(d) In Paul the gift motif is incorporated into his preaching of the free and unmerited grace of God (cf. *dōrean*, Rom. 3:24), which declares sinners justified without works (→ *dikaiosynē*, 1466). *dōrea* or *dōrēma* (Rom. 5:15–17; 2 Cor. 9:15), taken together with *charisma*, sums up the whole of God's saving work of pardon, justification, and reconciliation (cf. also Eph. 2:8).

(e) God is praised as the giver of all good gifts in general (Jas. 1:17; cf. Matt. 7:11). All who call on him for his gifts can do so with the utmost confidence (7:7). The one great gift he has given to his church is his Spirit (Lk. 11:13; 2 Cor. 1:22; 5:5; 1 Thess. 4:8). In the church, all other "gifts" (usually *charisma*, → *charis*, 5921) are the results of this one gift (Rom. 12:3–8; 1 Cor. 12:1–11).

(f) *doma*, gift, occurs only at Matt. 7:11; Lk. 11:13; Eph. 4:8; Phil. 4:17.

4. Those who have received Christ as a free gift respond to the double command to love God and their neighbor (Matt. 22:37–40) by a twofold giving. (a) They give themselves to God (cf. 2 Cor. 8:5). According to the NT, this is the only legitimate "offering" that can and should be brought to God (e.g., Rom. 12:1). It includes the "sacrifices" of word and deed (Heb. 13:15–16; 1 Pet. 2:5) and may mean even laying down one's life for Christ (Phil. 2:17).

(b) Believers give themselves to other people in love, as required by the "new command" (Jn. 13:34). This shows itself in the first instance within the church, where the giving should be a reflection of God's giving. To give simply and without ulterior motives (Rom. 12:8) is the way in which God gives (Jas. 1:5).

See also 2 Cor. 9:7 on God's love for the cheerful giver (*dotēs*, found only here in the NT); Mk. 12:41–44 = Lk. 21:1–4 (Jesus' verdict on the poor widow's gift); and the precepts of the Sermon on the Mount (Matt. 5:42; cf. Lk. 6:38). Christians, having received the gift of the gospel, are concerned to pass this gift on to others. This is giving in its profoundest sense (Rom. 1:11; 1 Thess. 2:8; cf. Matt. 10:8b).

See also *arrabōn*, down payment, pledge, earnest (*775*); *korban*, corban, gift (*3167*).

E *epsilon*

<table>
<tr><td>1573 ἑβδομήκοντα</td><td>ἑβδομήκοντα (hebdomēkonta), seventy (1573); ἑβδομηκοντά-</td></tr>
</table>

κις (*hebdomēkontakis*), seventy-seven (*1574*).

OT The captivity of Judah in Babylon was to last seventy years (Jer. 25:11), and in Dan. seventy weeks are appointed as the period in which messianic redemption will be accomplished (9:24). Seventy elders were appointed to assist Moses (Num. 11:16).

NT Two NT passages call for brief comment. Jesus commends forgiveness until "seventy-seven times," i.e., without limit (Matt. 18:22). In contrast to Gen. 4:24 (*hebdomēkontakis*), unlimited vengeance has given place to unlimited forgiveness.

In Lk. 10:1 Jesus sends out seventy (or seventy-two, according to some MSS) disciples, denoting an outreach to the entire world. The textual evidence for or against *dyo* (two) added to seventy is finely balanced. In either case symbolic meaning has been attached to the figure. Note that the nations enumerated in Gen. 10 total seventy in the Heb., seventy-two in the LXX (see also *hepta*, seven, *2231*).

1574 (*hebdomēkontakis*, seventy-seven), → *1573*.

1578 (*Hebraios*, Hebrew [noun]), → *2702*.

1579 (*Hebrais*, Hebrew [fem. adj.]), → *2702*.

1581 (*engizō*, approach, come near), → *1584*.

1582 (*engraphō*, to write in, record), → *1210*.

<table>
<tr><td>1583 ἔγγυος</td><td>ἔγγυος (engyos), guarantor (1583).</td></tr>
</table>

CL & OT *engyos* is derived from the vb. *engyaō*, pledge, engage. As an adj., it means offering surety and so becomes a noun meaning guarantee or guarantor. The *arrabōn*, pledge (→ *775*), applied to things, whereas *engyos*, surety, guarantee, may be applied to persons. The *engyos* guaranteed that a legal obligation would be carried out. In many religions people called on a god to act as the guarantor when an oath was taken.

NT *engyos* is found in the NT only in Heb. 7:22, though it has an obvious par. in 8:6, where *mesitēs*, mediator (→ *3542*), stands. Heb. 7:22 is to be linked with 7:20, which shows that the usual procedure for an oath has been reversed, for humans have not named God as guarantor, but God has placed the man Jesus as guarantor for the new divine dispensation (*diathēkē*, → *1347*), which has the promise (8:6) as its content. Compare here Paul's statements that the Holy Spirit has come to us on earth as the pledge [*arrabōn*, → *775*] of our redemption [2 Cor. 1:22; 5:5; Eph. 1:14]. Heb. makes a similar point, i.e., that after Jesus had offered the vicarious sacrifice of himself, he ascended to God in heaven, where he now acts as the guarantor and representative of those who are still on earth awaiting the rest promised to the people of God (4:9).

This role of Christ can hardly be taken to mean that he is a guarantor before God for our faith and obedience. He is rather a guarantee to those who believe God's promise and know that it has been accomplished in Christ, though they do not yet see its fulfillment. This guarantee is anchored as our hope (6:19) in Jesus' twofold and unrepeatable work: his offering up of himself (7:27) and his entrance into the true, heavenly sanctuary (9:12). Through it our sanctification (10:10) has been accomplished once for all. In this way Christ links our future perfection with his already achieved perfection.

See also *diathēkē*, covenant (*1347*); *mesitēs*, mediator, guarantor (*3542*).

<table>
<tr><td>1584 ἐγγύς</td><td>ἐγγύς (engys), near (1584); ἐγγίζω (engizō), approach, come</td></tr>
</table>

near (*1581*); μακράν (*makran*), far (*3426*).

CL & OT 1. In cl. Gk. *engys* means: (a) near (in space), near by; (b) near in time; (c) with numbers, nearly; (d) related or similar; (e) in the fig. sense of intellectual proximity. The vb. *engizō* is mostly intrans., meaning to approach, to come near (occasionally "to the gods").

2. (a) In the LXX *engys* sometimes denotes the approval of Yahweh in his drawing near to his people (a distinctive characteristic of the God of Israel; see Ps. 34:13; cf. Deut. 4:7 [*engizō*]). God's nearness is experienced above all in Israelite worship (cf. Ps. 145:18). Later on in Jud. this same word marked out the Israelite as distinct from non-Israelites, and within Israel the righteous as distinct from the godless. "To come near" also became a technical expression for recruiting a proselyte.

(b) In the spatial sense *engizō* is frequently found in phrases that describe approach to holy places (e.g., Exod. 3:5). Only the priests who conform to the requirements of the cultic prescriptions can draw near Yahweh's sanctuary (Lev. 21:23; Ezek. 40:46). This vb. can also denote more generally participation in worship (Eccl. 4:17; Isa. 29:13) or a devout attitude of nearness to God (Ps. 119:169; Hos. 12:6).

(c) As an indication of time, this word group expresses the imminent approach of the day of the Lord. In opposition to the way of thinking that saw that day in the far distance (cf. the quotations in Isa. 5:19; Ezek. 12:22, 27; Amos 6:3), the prophets proclaimed its nearness. This day always brings with it the impending judgment (Isa. 13:6; cf. Ezek. 7:7; 30:3; Joel 1:15; 2:1; Zeph. 1:7, 14), which occasions darkness and terror. Only the later chapters of Isa. announce the approach of a new age that will bring forth salvation and righteousness (46:13; 50:8; 51:5; 56:1).

(d) The pair of words "the near and the far" (Deut. 13:7; Isa. 33:13; 57:19; Ezek. 6:12) is a description of totality, embracing all.

NT 1. Both *engizō* and *engys* occur most frequently in the historical books of the NT. In the *spatial* sense, the adj. *engys* is used a greater number of times than the vb. *engizō*. In Acts and Jn. *engys* has almost exclusively a local meaning (e.g., Jn. 19:20; Acts 1:12). At times the vb. serves to indicate both place and motion (e.g., "as they approached Jerusalem," Mk. 11:1). These two words are more frequently used with a temporal meaning: e.g., the hour of Jesus' passion "is near" (Matt. 26:45); "the end of all things is near" (1 Pet. 4:7); the Passover was near (Jn. 2:13).

2. (a) The theological understanding of *engizō*, to come near, in the Synoptics is linked with Isaiah's proclamation of salvation: The kingdom of heaven has drawn near (e.g., Matt. 4:17; Lk. 10:9, 11; cf. CL & OT 2[c]). Behind this vb. stands the thought of the divine promise and preparation. The perf. *ēngiken* (the most frequently used tense of this vb.) thus expresses the end of God's time of preparation. His kingdom *has* drawn near; in the proclamation and work of Jesus it *is* already here in the present. Corresponding to this vb. is the negative formulation *ou makran*, not far, which expresses the overcoming of the separation between God and humankind (e.g., Mk. 12:34).

(b) *engys* and *engizō* are also used in the context of the awaited apocalyptic end time and the return of the Son of Man. Lk. in particular awaits the future of the all-embracing kingdom of God. The desolation of Judea and cosmic catastrophes will announce the dawn of the end of the world: "Even so, when you see these things happening, you know that the kingdom of God is near" (Lk. 21:31; cf. 21:28). The connection between the dawn of the kingdom in the coming of

Jesus and the awaited coming of the Son of Man to establish the reign of God is brought out by Matt. and Mk. Apart from this, both use *engizō* only in connection with the fate of Jesus (e.g., Matt. 21:1; 26:46).

3. Whereas in the Synoptics the vb. is used in both the perf. and fut. tenses, expressing the consequent tension between the "already" and "not yet," Paul relates these terms exclusively to the fut. In Rom. 13:12 and Phil. 4:5, the prospect of the approaching day and the coming Lord provide the basis for the admonitions to Christians to live a life full of hope. In the non-Pauline letters, the word group similarly refers to the near return of Christ and the imminent end of all things (Heb. 10:25; Jas. 5:8; 1 Pet. 4:7). Thus *engizō* in the NT designates almost exclusively the drawing near of God and of his salvation. Only Heb. 7:19 and Jas. 4:8 speak of a human drawing near to God.

See also *eschatos*, last, end (*2274*); *telos*, end, goal (*5465*).

1586	ἐγείρω

ἐγείρω (*egeirō*), wake, rouse, raise up (*1586*); ἔγερσις (*egersis*), awakening, i.e., resurrection (*1587*); ἐξεγείρω (*exegeirō*), raise, raise up (*1995*); συνεγείρω (*synegeirō*), raise with (*5283*).

CL & OT 1. In cl. Gk. the words in this group are synonymous with the *anastasis* word group (→ *414*). Thus the vb. when trans. means to waken, lift up, erect, stimulate; when intrans. awake, get up, stand up. When used of persons, it denotes those who are awakened from sleep, lethargy, or unconsciousness, and are stimulated to action or revolt. The noun means (trans.) a waking up, an establishing; (intrans.) a waking, a standing up, a recovery (i.e., from illness). The meaning of resurrection from death in our understanding of the term is not found.

2. The LXX use of this word group normally corresponds to Gk. idiom. It means rise up, awake, arouse, or stand up (e.g., Gen. 41:4, 7; Jdg. 2:16, 18; Dan. 8:18). That it is synonymous with *anistēmi* may be seen from Gen. 38:8 and 2 Sam. 7:12, where *anistēmi* is used both for human beings and God, while in Isa. 45:13a *egeirō* is used in a similar expression. At the same time, already in LXX we see a modification of the verbal connotation through its use for the raising of the dead and the work of God's Spirit in humankind (→ *anastasis*, *414*).

NT 1. Generally speaking, this word group has the same meaning in the NT as in cl. Gk. and the LXX. *egersis* is found only once (Matt. 27:53), in connection with the resurrection of Jesus; elsewhere the *anastasis* word group is used. *egeirō* occurs 143x, often as an introduction to action (e.g., Matt. 1:24; 2:14; 8:26; 25:7) or for the appearance of characters on the stage of history (e.g., 24:7, 11, 24). *exegeirō* occurs only 2x—once for God's raising up Pharaoh to display his sovereign purposes, and once for the resurrection of our bodies (1 Cor. 6:14). *synegeirō* occurs 3x, all of which refer to our being raised with Christ in his resurrection (Eph. 2:6; Col. 2:12; 3:1; cf. also Rom. 6:4–6).

2. A survey of the cases in which *egeirō* is used with the meaning awaking to life at first creates the impression that the line of development seen in the OT and Jewish apocalyptic has been further developed (→ *anastasis*, *414*). In several cases, people regarded by doctors as dead are reported to be brought back to life by Jesus. He took the hand of Jairus's daughter, for example, and caused her to get up and walk (Mk. 5:41); his command to "get up" was expressed by the imperative of *egeirō*. The same is true of the widow's son outside the gate of Nain (Lk. 7:14; but cf. Jn. 4:50 [the official's son]; 11:43 [Lazarus], where this vb. is not used). Jesus had full authority to raise the dead to life.

Jesus made it clear that (for him) the dead persons were not dead but only asleep. All four Gospels indicate that death can set no bounds to Jesus' activity, for the life that proceeded from him stripped death of its power. The spectators' laughter at such a statement about sleeping (Mk. 5:40) serves only to stress the extraordinary and incomprehensible nature of this life-giving power. What the Jews at best

considered possible, apart from their belief in final resurrection (see Jn. 11:24), was that someone might be preserved from dying in the first place, even as in the OT: "Could not he . . . have kept this man from dying?" (11:37). But now God, the Lord over life and death, stood in person before them.

3. This brings us to the heart of the concept, which has to do with the raising of Jesus. The letters of the NT never use *egeirō*, except in Phil. 1:17, in any sense but that of resurrection from the dead. It is used so often in Rom. and in 1 and 2 Cor. that it must have been a dominant element in Paul's preaching. In fact, Paul explains in 1 Cor. 15 that God's breaking into history in Jesus' resurrection is the decisive factor in the gospel, the means by which we are saved, without which all faith would be vain. Witnesses are adduced for the truth of the event; they were those to whom Jesus had "appeared" (15:5–8).

For the preacher of the gospel, the resurrection is the touchstone of its truth. One who disputes or denies the resurrection makes God a liar and faith a hollow mask (1 Cor. 15:14–17). The heart of our faith is, after all, faith "in him who raised Jesus our Lord from the dead" (Rom. 4:24), and his Spirit lives in those who believe, giving life to our mortal bodies (8:11; cf. 2 Cor. 4:14). It is Jesus' resurrection that has removed our sins (1 Cor. 15:17) and broken the power of death (Rom. 6:4, 9, in connection with baptism). One should note that Jesus' coming back to life is not described only with God as actor but also with Jesus, for, as Jesus said (though *egeirō* is not used here): "The reason my Father loves me is that I lay down my life—only to take it up again. . . . I have authority to lay it down and authority to take it up again" (Jn. 10:17–18). While the resurrecting power issues from God, it belongs to the Son also, who is of one being with the Father.

4. This is seen most clearly in the case of the final resurrection, when it is normally left open as to who raises the dead—Christ or God. Paul writes simply: "The dead will be raised," i.e., will rise (1 Cor. 15:52; cf. Matt. 11:5). It is, however, clear that the resurrection of the dead is inseparably linked with the resurrection of Christ; it is based on it and follows from it (1 Cor. 15:13–17). Except in 1 Cor. 15 the *anastasis* group is normally used. In 1 Cor. 15:42–44 Paul contrasts the difference between now and then by the contrasts "perishable" and "imperishable," "dishonor" and "glory," "weakness" and "power," "natural" and "spiritual." The power to raise the dead is transferred from God to Jesus, and is promised by him to his disciples (Matt. 10:8).

See also *anastasis*, resurrection (*414*).

1587 (*egersis*, awakening, i.e., resurrection), → *1586*.

1590 (*enkainizō*, make new, consecrate), → *2785*.

1591 (*enkakeō*, become tired, lose heart), → *2805*.

1592	ἐγκαλέω

ἐγκαλέω (*enkaleō*), accuse(*1592*); ἔγκλημα(*enklēma*), accusation, charge(*1598*) .

CL & OT Deriving from *kaleō*, call, *enkaleō* in secular Gk. meant first to demand as one's due, then to make a claim or bring an accusation against someone, usually in a context of legal proceedings. *enklēma* corresponds to this developed meaning, and signifies a charge or indictment. The notion of accusation appears in the LXX in Zech. 1:4.

NT In the NT, Lk. uses *enkaleō* in its regular classical sense (Acts 19:38, 40; 23:28, 29; 26:2, 7). The only theological use of the word is in Rom. 8:33, where Paul dispels apprehensions lest Satan or someone else should succeed in impeaching God's elect at judgment day. *enklēma* is used of the charge against Paul in Acts 23:29; 25:16.

1593 (*enkataleipō*, to abandon, desert), → *3309*.

1595 (*enkauchaomai*, boast), → *3017*.

1596 (*enkentrizō*, to graft), → *1285*.

1598 (enklēma, accusation, charge), → *1592.*

1600 (enkopē, hindering, hindrance), → *1601.*

1601	ἐγκόπτω

ἐγκόπτω (*enkoptō*), hinder, thwart (*1601*); ἐγκοπή (*enkopē*), hindering, hindrance (*1600*).

CL & OT The vb. *enkoptō* originally meant to knock in or cut into. The meaning hinder arose out of its military use. During a retreat the road might be cut into (i.e., broken up), in order to delay the pursuing enemy. The noun *enkopē*, therefore, denoted a temporary hindrance, later a permanent impediment. Neither vb. nor noun occurs in the LXX.

NT The noun occurs once in the NT (1 Cor. 9:12), the vb. 5x. Both words indicate something that hinders progress in the realm of faith or in the Christian life, bringing it to a standstill—if not permanently, at least for the moment.

If Paul allowed himself to receive money from the churches he was working with, he felt the proclamation of the gospel would be considerably hindered (1 Cor. 9:12). Thus, he waived his right to earn a living by preaching, which in itself could not be contested. Again, Paul's mission in Rome was only delayed by the fact that he had to complete projects he had begun in other places (Rom. 15:22). Paul wanted to go to Thessalonica, but the visit was repeatedly hindered by Satan (1 Thess. 2:18). Unfortunately, it is not possible to determine what hindrances Paul classified as Satan's work. It may have been an illness (2 Cor. 12:7; cf. Phil. 2:25–30) or the machinations of the Jews (1 Thess. 2:15–16).

In Gal. 5:7 the Christian life is compared to a race, the running of which was hindered by false teachers. The true way of faith was endangered by sectarian, legalistically inclined Jewish Christians, who were threatening to destroy the unity of the church (4:17).

Insufficient knowledge can also act as a hindrance to one's prayers (1 Pet. 3:7). The trouble here is that, under the influence of prevailing pagan custom, husbands were tending to despise their wives instead of recognizing them as partners. The passage has nothing to do with the common prayers of married couples, nor with marriage as a hindrance to prayer. Similar concepts of hindering occur in 1 Cor. 11:20–29 and 13:1 (where the vb. is not used). In the former it is a selfish lack of brotherly consideration that prevents the proper celebration of the Lord's Supper, and in the latter a lack of love that hinders effective preaching.

The meaning of *enkoptō* in Acts 24:4 is a matter of debate. The NIV, NASB, and several other translations use "weary." However, the basic meaning of *enkoptō* makes good sense: "in order not to hinder you further [i.e., by a long speech from carrying out of your administrative duties]." "Burden," "delay," or "detain" (NRSV) are also possible translations.

See also *kōlyō*, hamper, hinder, prevent, forbid (*3266*).

1602	ἐγκράτεια

ἐγκράτεια (*enkrateia*), self-control, self-restraint (*1602*); ἐγκρατής (*enkratēs*), master of oneself, self-controlled (*1604*); ἐγκρατεύομαι (*enkrateuomai*), have control over oneself, abstain (*1603*); ἀκρασία (*akrasia*), licentiousness, lack of self-control (*202*); ἀκρατής (*akratēs*), uncontrolled, unbridled (*203*); ἀσκέω (*askeō*), practice something, engage in (*828*).

CL & OT 1. *enkrateia* and *enkratēs* contain the root *krat-*, which means power or control. *enkratēs* thus denotes someone who has power in the physical or intellectual sense (the opposite being *akratēs*). *enkrateia* is used absolutely of having power over oneself—i.e., perseverance or self-control (the opposite being *akrasia*). From *enkratēs* comes the vb. *enkrateuomai*, abstain from something. The Gk. philosophers considered *enkrateia* as a chief virtue, a sign of human freedom to moderate one's desires, esp. sexual desire and enjoyment of food and drink. *askeō* originally meant exert oneself, esp. in the sense of work or physical exercise. Later it came to mean tame the passions, esp. sexual desire.

2. In the LXX *enkrateia* occurs 3x (Sir. 18:15 [S], 30; 4 Macc. 5:34), where it means abstinence from excess. *enkratēs* (11x) and *enkrateuomai* (3x) denote that one is in control of something (cf. Gen. 43:31; 1 Sam. 13:12; Sir. 6:27). *askeō* occurs only in 2 Macc. 15:4. Apart from occasional fasting, asceticism is not practiced in the OT.

NT 1. The *enkrateia* word group (including *akrasia* in Matt. 23:25; 1 Cor. 7:5; and *akratēs* in 2 Tim. 3:3) is attested only 10x in the entire NT. *askeō* appears only in Acts 24:16 ("strive"). This statistical survey does not, however, allow us to say that there are no traces of asceticism in the Gospels. Lk. in particular underlines an ascetic trait, esp. with regard to possessions, though without using these words (cf. Matt. 5:3–12 with Lk. 6:20–23; Matt. 25:34–40 with Lk. 14:14). But viewed as a whole, asceticism in the sense of renunciation of possessions, sexual activity, and food is not a part of Jesus' teaching in the Gospels. It is only demanded where something stands in the way of following him (cf. the story of the rich young ruler, Matt. 19:21).

2. In Acts 24:25 *enkrateia* is found alongside righteousness and judgment as a theme of Paul's proclamation. "Self-control" may here be an allusion to the marriage of the procurator Felix, which was the result of adultery. But it may also simply be an expression of an ascetic tendency that Lk. continues in Acts (cf. 2:44–45; 4:32).

3. In 1 Cor. 7 Paul affirms sexual asceticism for himself and regards it as desirable, though not compulsory, for the members of the congregation (7:1). But he does not turn marriage and sexual intercourse into a sin (cf. 7:5, 28); it is better to remain within marriage than to aggravate suppressed drives through compulsory abstinence (cf. 7:9: "if they cannot control themselves" [*enkrateuomai*]). Though marriage is a concession to human drives and celibacy (7:7) is preferable (esp. in the expectation of the imminence of the end of the world), Paul elsewhere sees marriage as a picture of the relationship between Christ and his church (Eph. 5:21–33). Here Paul wants to save the Corinthians from hardships that being married involves in the final catastrophe (1 Cor. 7:25–26). They are to be free in their service of the Lord.

enkrateia is an aspect of the fruit of the Spirit (Gal. 5:23). Self-control is here a positive behavior that is set over against the fornication (*porneia*), impurity, debauchery, and idolatry that the sinful nature produces (5:19–20). *enkrateia* must be received as the gift of the Spirit in one's commitment to the gospel. Whether *enkrateia* in 5:23 refers only to one's sexual side or is meant more comprehensively is disputed.

4. Tit. 1:8 (*enkratēs* in a list of virtues) and 2 Tim. 3:3 (*akratēs* in a list of vices) do not betray an ascetic attitude in the Pastoral Letters. Rather, these letters see marriage as a healthy ordinance of life willed by God, in contrast to some of Paul's opponents (1 Tim. 4:1–3; 5:14–15; Tit. 2:3–5). Part of the intention of the catalogue of vices in 2 Tim. 3:1–5, with its affirmation of marriage, is to warn against the dissolution of marriage and against a false self-gratification in the last days. Furthermore, note how elders in a congregation should be chaste (Tit. 1:8), married to one woman (1:6; cf. 1 Tim. 3:2).

5. *enkrateia* occurs 2x in 2 Pet 1:6 in a list that characterizes the attitudes desired of believers in the post-apostolic period: faith, virtue, knowledge, self-control (*enkrateia*), patience, godliness, and love for all people. The list exhibits the process by which faith comes alive and becomes fruitful in love. *enkrateia* here means having power over oneself, not on the basis of some supposed self-realization, but on the basis of knowledge that comes from faith (1:5–6).

See also *sōphrosynē*, prudence, self-control (*5408*).

1603 (enkrateuomai, have control over oneself, abstain), → *1602.*

1604 (enkratēs, master of oneself, self-controlled), → *1602.*

1609 (egō, I; in expression *egō eimi*), → *1639.*

1612 (*hedraios*, firm, steadfast), → 2529.

1613 (*hedraiōma*, foundation), → 2529.

1618 (*ethnikos*, heathen, Gentile), → 1620.

1619 (*ethnikōs*, like the Gentiles), → 1620.

1620	ἔθνος

ἔθνος (*ethnos*), nation, people, heathen, pagans, Gentiles (*1620*); ἐθνικός (*ethnikos*), heathen, Gentile (*1618*); ἐθνικῶς (*ethnikōs*), like the Gentiles (*1619*).

CL & OT 1. In cl. Gk. *ethnos* (derived from *ethos*, custom) means a group with common customs, a clan; and then crowd, people. The word came to have a derogatory sense of common people or foreigners (in contrast to Greeks.). Its tone approaches *barbaros*, non-Gk., barbarian. Later *ethnos* was used to describe subject peoples.

2. (a) *ethnos* appears in the LXX about 1,000x (mostly in pl.); in the majority of cases it stands for the Heb. *gôy* and the pl. *gôyim*. Where mention is made of many peoples, esp. non-Israelites, *ethnē* is used, never *laoi* (e.g., Exod. 19:5–6). There is thus a contrast between *laos*, i.e., Israel as the chosen people (→ 3295), and *ethnē*, the Gentiles—though the sing. *ethnos* can be used to refer to Israel as God's people (e.g., Exod. 19:6; Deut. 26:5; Ps. 106:5 [in parallelism with *laos*]; cf. Exod. 32:10; Num. 14:12).

(b) Israel is a people for God's own possession (Exod. 19:5), while the rest of humanity is called the *ethnē*, the nations (Deut. 4:27; 18:9). A typical passage is Exod. 33:13, where *ethnos* is the multitude that by Yahweh's grace becomes his people (*laos*). The contrast is just as stark in Deut. 7:6: Yahweh has separated the *ethnē* over the earth and fixed their bounds. But Jacob as Yahweh's portion has become the *laos* of God (Deut. 32:8–9 LXX). Nevertheless, Yahweh is seen as King over the nations (Jer. 10:7, lacking in the LXX). This is the point behind Gen. 10, where the emphasis is not on the unity of humanity derived from common ancestors, but on nations divided according to clans and languages.

The Gentiles are first of all Israel's neighbors, some of whom live in Palestine itself (Jdg. 3:1). They entice Israel into idolatry, who then fall away from Yahweh. Thus we often read of the "detestable practices of the nations" (e.g., 1 Ki. 14:24; 2 Ki. 16:3). In the face of Israel's sin, the nations become the means and instruments of God's judgment (Hos. 8:10; Amos 9:9). But if they overreach themselves and go beyond the commission given them by Yahweh, they incur judgment themselves (Isa. 8:9; 10:5). Nevertheless, the Gentile Cyrus is called God's anointed and becomes the savior of Israel (Isa. 45:1–7).

A universalizing tendency in the LXX can be detected in Dan. 9:6, where the prophets are said to have reached every people on earth. Over against the world empires stands the kingdom of God (4:34). In the end time the nations will come to Mount Zion and there share in salvation (cf. Isa. 2:2–4; 25:6–8; Mic. 4:1–3; Zech. 8:20–23). The nations await the Messiah (Gen. 49:10 LXX). Thus the negative evaluation of the Gentile world is, in the last analysis, not lasting and permanent. Even in the present the name of Yahweh is to be glorified among all the Gentiles (Ps. 18:49; 46:10).

3. (a) In *Jub.* 10:22 the origin of the nations is traced to human sin (cf. Gen. 11), whereas in 2 Esd. 3:7, 12 they are said to have arisen naturally (though after the fall), because God gave humankind the blessing of fertility.

(b) In rab. Jud., the non-Israelite *gôy* is a stranger to God and far from him. The Gentiles are themselves to blame for this state of affairs, for they were offered the Torah, but rejected God's instruction. They are thus condemned to hell, with no hope of salvation, and have no part in the world to come. Only in exceptional cases is a share in the coming perfect world promised to pious Gentiles. God is the creator of all, but he loves Israel alone.

As individuals, Gentiles have been given up to every possible vice (e.g., idolatry, immorality). In Jewish eyes they are unclean. If in exceptional instances they do something good, God rewards them at once, in order to avoid having to reward them in the world to come. The punishment for their sins is delayed by God until the measure is full; then judgment falls on them. A great turning point will come in the messianic age, when the nations who have made Israel their subjects (esp. Rome) will be destroyed by the Messiah and end up in hell. Nations who have had no contact with Israel will be subjected to the Messiah, who will rule the world.

Some rabbis taught that the Gentiles will then be given access to the blessings of salvation. The Messiah is the light of the Gentiles, and many will join Israel as proselytes. But the political catastrophes of A.D. 66–70 and 132–135 created great bitterness among the Jews. Thus, the view arose that the messianic age will allow no more proselytes. Only a person who joins Israel during the time of his or her sufferings can be a proselyte.

(c) In the pre-Christian era and up to A.D. 70, the Jews (esp. Hel. Jews) carried out a strong missionary activity or, to be more precise, proselytism (cf. Matt. 23:15). These efforts were moderately successful (cf. the many half or full proselytes whom Paul met in the Jewish Diaspora). Once again, the position changed after A.D. 70; from then on the making of proselytes declined greatly. Those who wanted to become proselytes had to come of their own initiative. An added difficulty arose in A.D. 135, when Emperor Hadrian prohibited people from becoming Jews. It was at this point that the Christians got their great opportunity, even though the church was not always distinguished from Jud.

(d) At Qumran the attitude to Gentiles is completely negative. The Gentile nations are idol worshipers, without God, and enemies of God. God commits the judgment of all nations into the hands of his chosen ones, and the nations will reap the reward of their wickedness. It will be the Qumran people themselves, the "sons of light," who will carry out this work of punishment and destruction, and the wealth of the nations will be brought in through the gates of Jerusalem. God's people can take comfort from the fact that God will never again allow his people to be destroyed by the hand of the nations.

NT In the NT *ethnos* occurs 162x (43x in Acts, 54x in Paul's letters). It is used about 40x in quotations from the OT. The *ethnē* often mean all peoples (cf. Matt. 24:9; 28:19; Mk. 11:17; Lk. 21:24; Rom. 15:11).

1. (a) In 14 places, the Jewish people are called *ethnos* (e.g., Lk. 7:5; 23:2; Acts 10:22); this is true esp. in Jn.'s Gospel, apparently because they set themselves against faith in Jesus Christ (Jn. 11:48, 50–52; 18:35). In other places, however (e.g., Acts 26:23), a clear distinction is drawn between *laos*, the people of Israel, and the *ethnē*, Gentiles.

(b) *ethnē* clearly refers to Gentiles in Matt. 4:15 (cf. Isa. 9:1); 20:25; Lk. 21:24; Acts 4:25 (cf. Ps. 2:1–2); 7:7; 13:19; Rom. 1:5; Gal. 3:8; Rev. 10:11; 14:8; 15:3–4.

2. In about 100 instances *ethnos* is used in contrast to the followers of Jesus (though occasionally Paul calls Gentile Christians *ethnē* (e.g., Rom. 11:13; Gal. 2:12). Jesus' disciples must pray differently from the *ethnē* (Matt. 6:32) and not be anxious like them (Lk. 12:30). Gentiles are mentioned alongside Samaritans (Matt. 10:5). Jesus teaches the future salvation of the Gentiles, although he was sent only to the Jews (Matt. 8:10–11; 15:24). Gentiles will tread Jerusalem down "until the times of the Gentiles are fulfilled" (Lk. 21:24). One of the horrors of the end time will be the rising of nation against nation (Matt. 24:7).

3. The distinction between Jews and Gentiles is spoken of chiefly in Acts and the NT letters, i.e., in the missionary documents of the NT. God is not the God of the Jews only, but also of the Gentiles (Rom. 3:29; Rev. 15:3–4); but the Gentiles do not know God (1 Thess. 4:5) and are led astray to idols (1 Cor. 12:2). They do not know the law of God and do not keep it (Gal. 2:15); they live in the futility of their minds (Acts 14:16; Eph. 4:17). Although the word *ethnos* is not used, the Gentiles are meant in Rom. 1:18–32, where Paul speaks of those

who do not know God, have fallen into idolatry, and have therefore been given up by God to all kinds of evil. Nevertheless, there are *ethnē* who fulfill the requirements of the law (2:14–15). The Gentiles begin life outside the call of God and outside the salvation of God's people (Eph. 2:11–12). Jews and Gentiles are alike in rejecting the cross (1 Cor. 1:23).

4. (a) Israel is the people whom God has appointed to be his own possession and for service to him; the Gentiles are outside this unique relationship. By God's own act, however, this difference has been overcome; the Messiah has come in the person of Jesus, so that now even those born Gentiles have a share in God's covenant and salvation. Thus Peter discovers that a God-fearing Gentile is acceptable to God and that the Holy Spirit can come on a Gentile (Acts 10:35, 45; 11:1, 18; cf. Eph. 2:11–12, 17–22).

(b) Paul is in a special way "the apostle to the Gentiles" (Rom. 11:13), in the face of Jewish opposition (1 Thess. 2:16). To him has been entrusted the mystery (→ *mystērion*, *3696*) that the Gentiles are called to Jesus Christ apart from the law (Rom. 1:5; Gal. 1:16; 2:7–9; cf. Eph. 3:1–13). This is not to say that Paul denies the prior claim of the Jews. In fact, Paul strongly emphasizes it (e.g., Rom. 1:16). Israel is and remains God's people and thus possesses all the gifts and titles that mark it out as different (9:4–5).

The relationship of Jews to Gentiles is given extensive treatment in Rom. 9–11 (cf. also Eph. 2–3). Those Gentiles who have come to faith in Jesus Christ have been grafted into the rich olive tree (Rom. 11:17; → *elaion*, *1778*) and are supported by it. Consequently, there can be no division between Christians and Gentiles. The Pauline churches consist both of born Jews and born Gentiles, and both belong to God's people by faith in Jesus Christ. They are children of Abraham by virtue of their faith (Rom. 4:16–17, cf. Gal. 3:7, 13–14, 26–29). Salvation has come to them through the unbelief of Israel (Rom. 11:11), and the failure of the Jews has meant riches for the Gentiles (11:12). As the apostle to the Gentiles, Paul seeks to save as many Gentiles as possible, in order ultimately to win the Jews for the gospel (11:13–14). When the full number of the Gentiles has come in, Israel too will turn to Christ (11:11–12, 25).

(c) Evidence of Jewish priority is apparent in the record of Acts, where Paul preaches to the Gentiles only after the Jews have rejected the gospel (Acts 13:46; 18:6; 19:9; 28:17–28). The question of the mission to the Gentiles as carried out by Paul was discussed and settled at the so-called Council of Jerusalem (Acts 15).

6. According to Rev., Christ has ransomed a church for himself out of every nation and has made them his kingdom and priests (Rev. 5:9–10; cf. Exod. 19:6). Along with the chosen of Israel is an innumerable multitude from the Gentiles (7:9). The exalted Christ will rule the nations with a rod of iron (12:5) and will give authority to "him who overcomes" to do so (2:26–27). He will strike the nations with the sword in his mouth (19:15). In the time of the two witnesses, the temple court is given over to the Gentiles (11:2). All nations will see the dead bodies of these witnesses (11:9). The beast has authority over all nations and peoples whose name is not written in the book of life (13:7–8). The eternal gospel will be preached to all nations (14:6).

As for the harlot Babylon, "all the nations" have drunk "the maddening wine of her adulteries" and have been deceived by her sorcery (Rev. 14:8; 18:3, 23). In the judgments of God, "the cities of the nations" will fall (16:19). During the millennium Satan is unable to deceive the nations (20:3; → *chilias*, thousand, *5942*), but will do so again as soon as he is freed (20:8). In God's new world, the *ethnē* walk in the light of the new Jerusalem and bring their treasures into the new city (21:24, 26).

7. *ethnikos* (adv. *ethnikōs*) means national, foreign, like a Gentile; as a noun it means Gentile. The adj. appears only 4x in the NT, the adv. once. Gentiles salute only their brothers; any of Jesus' disciples who behave in that way make themselves like an *ethnikos* (Matt. 5:47). In prayer the disciple is not to heap up empty phrases as the Gentiles do (6:7). Those who refuse to listen to a rebuke by the church

cut themselves off and join Gentiles and unrepentant tax-collectors (18:17). In Antioch Peter had eaten with Gentile Christians and so transgressed the Jewish ritual regulations, thus living *ethnikōs*, like the Gentiles; Paul argues that he thus can no longer force Gentile Christians to observe the law (Gal. 2:14). Membership in God's people is now determined by fellowship in Christ by faith, which unites Jewish and Gentile Christians.

See also *dēmos*, people, populace, crowd, popular assembly (*1322*); *laos*, people (*3295*); *ochlos*, (throng of) people, crowd, mob (*4063*); *polis*, city, city-state (*4484*).

1621 ἔθος	ἔθος (*ethos*), usage, custom (*1621*); εἴωθα (*eiōtha*), custom (*1665*); ἦθος (*ēthos*), custom, way of life (*2456*).

CL & OT 1. In cl. Gk. *ethos* means tradition, usage, custom. Used with various preps. it means "according to principles" or "in the usual way." The related word *ēthos* is a more abstract term, similar to the English word *ethos*.

2. (a) In the LXX *ethos* (8x) has the sense of popular custom, esp. in connection with feasts. In the Apocr. the word always refers to a tradition within a given class or nation: e.g., giving presents to members of the royal family (1 Macc. 10:89), the custom of the ancestors (2 Macc. 11:25; 4 Macc. 18:5), or customs relating to execution (2 Macc. 13:4). Even when a tradition is reversed, the resulting custom can come to be ethically and legally binding (4 Macc. 18:5; Wis. 14:16).

(b) *ēthos* occurs 7x and ordinarily conveys the idea of basic human motives or attitudes (4 Macc. 1:29; 2:7, 21; 5:24), a frame of mind (13:27), or a manner of life resulting from certain ethical or psychological impulses (e.g., Sir. Prol. 27; 20:26).

(c) *eiōtha* (a 2d perf. of *ethō*) occurs in the LXX only in 4 Macc., with reference to a main principle or thesis of a rhetorical argument (cf. Num. 24:1; Sir. 37:14 for other forms of this vb.).

NT In the NT *ethos* occurs 12x, *eiōtha* 4x, and *ēthos* only once. The range of meaning extends from religious custom to personal habit, although no hard and fast distinctions can be drawn. Some passages merely give objective information on customs or traditions, while others reflect the clash of early Christian teaching and practice with the way of life found in Jud.

In the Gospels *ethos* is variously qualified as the custom of the priesthood (Lk. 1:9), the custom relating to Passover and to education of sons (2:42; when a son reached the age of 12, his father introduced him to the requirements of God's law by taking him to the three great feasts), Jewish burial custom (Jn. 19:40), or Christ's personal custom of teaching daily in the temple and spending the night near the Mount of Olives during feast days (Lk. 22:39).

ethos also occurs in Acts, where it is an important word in early Christian polemic. In 15:1 we read of the confrontation between Jewish and Gentile Christians over the necessity of circumcision (note the appeal to the custom of Moses [cf. Lev. 12:3]); both Stephen (Acts 6:14) and Paul (26:3; 28:17) were accused of altering the customs delivered by Moses or the fathers. The apostle himself appealed to Roman legal custom (25:16) in one of his defenses. The Roman slave owners at Philippi appealed to Roman political and religious law against what they conceived to be Jewish customs and religious propaganda (16:21; Romans were forbidden to become proselytes of Jud., even though it was a *religio licita*).

As far as *eiōtha* is concerned, Jesus and Paul both had a personal custom of visiting the synagogue on the Sabbath (Lk. 4:16; Acts 17:2). Jesus customarily taught the crowds whenever they gathered around him (Mk. 10:1). Pilate apparently established a custom of releasing a Jewish prisoner annually during the Passover (Matt. 27:15).

Finally, the use of *ēthos* and *ethos* shows something of the internal dangers facing the early Christian church. The church is doomed if it allows itself to be infected by the immoral habits of the surrounding world (*ethos*, 1 Cor. 15:33). Here Paul cites the saying from the 4th cent. comedy *Thais* by Menander, "Bad company corrupts good character." Heb. 10:25 states that for some people nonattendance at public worship had already become a habit (*ethos*), an attitude of indifference that the church must seek to overcome in light of the imminence of the day of judgment.

See also *nomos*, law, norm (*3795*); *stoicheion*, elements, rudiments (*5122*).

1624 (*eidea*, appearance), → *1626*.

1626	εἶδος

εἶδος (*eidos*), form, outward appearance, sight (*1626*); εἰδέα (*eidea*), appearance (*1624*).

CL & OT 1. In cl. Gk. *eidos* denotes appearance, visible form, stressing a link between the visible appearance and reality. One who praises the *eidos* of a woman refers not only to her outward beauty but to her true character. The word is used in Plato for the Forms or Ideas that are the existing realities behind our world. The modern distinction between the external and the internal, the visible and the invisible, and the outward form and essential content is inappropriate and foreign to this aspect of Gk. thought. For Aristotle, the *eidos* was different from Plato's view; it was the expression of the essence in visible form.

2. In the LXX *eidos* (54x) denotes the outward appearance of the whole being (cf. Gen. 29:17; Isa. 53:2–3), not merely the outer shell behind which something quite different can be supposed. God conversed *en eidei* with Moses (Num. 12:8); this means that Moses saw the glory of the Lord. *eidea* (5x) refers to the fact that Seth bore his father Adam's "likeness" (Gen. 5:3) or to the "appearance" of an individual (2 Macc. 3:16, where the high priest's appearance betrayed his anguish).

NT 1. *eidos* occurs only 5x in the NT (twice each in Paul and Lk., once in Jn.). "Avoid every kind of evil" in 1 Thess. 5:22 may go back to Job 1:1, 8. *eidos* in this case simply means "kind" or "type."

2. In 2 Cor. 5:7 Paul declares that "we live (walk) by faith, not by sight (*dia eidous*)." At the present time we live by faith and not by what we can see with our eyes. The interpretation of this word here is difficult, however, because *eidos* does not normally mean "sight" but visible form. There may, therefore, be more here. If, as seems apparent, "we" is to be understood as the subj. of both halves of the sentence, the verse may be contrasting the present time as the sphere of faith and the coming future time, in which we will have a visible form to observe. Some argue that 5:7b may also be taken to refer to the visible form of the Lord: We now walk by faith (*dia pisteōs*), but the Lord does not walk in visible form. Against this view, however, is the fact that it requires a sudden, implicit change of subj., for which there is no warrant in the text.

3. In his account of Jesus' baptism, Lk. says that the Holy Spirit descended on Jesus "in bodily form (*eidos*) like a dove" (Lk. 3:22; cf. Mk. 1:10; Matt. 3:16). This account stresses the reality of what happened. Similarly, Lk. uses *eidos* in his account of Jesus' transfiguration: "As he was praying, the appearance (*eidos*) of his face changed" (Lk. 9:29; cf. Matt. 17:2; Mk. 9:2; cf. also *eidea* with regard to the resurrected Jesus in Matt. 28:3). But no special tendency in Lk.'s writing can be deduced from this.

4. Jn. 5:37 contains the statement: "You (Jews) have never heard his voice nor seen his form (*eidos*)." This is contrasted with the first half of the verse: "The Father who sent me has himself testified concerning me" (cf. also 5:38). Part of the OT witness is that God cannot be seen in visible form (cf. Deut. 4:12), although this inability to see God physically was never intended as a reproach. Similarly, this is not the meaning of the reproach implicit in this verse. It means rather that the Jews have not obeyed God by believing in Jesus as God's Son (cf. 5:38). There may also be a further implication that Jesus has in fact

heard the voice of the Father and seen his "form," so that he has a unique authority and relationship with the Father (cf. the whole argument in 5:17–47).

See also *morphē*, form, outward appearance, shape (*3671*); *schēma*, outward appearance, form, shape (*5386*); *hypostasis*, substantial nature, essence, confidence (*5712*).

1627 (*eidōleion*, temple of an idol), → *1631*.

1628 (*eidōlothytos*, meat offered to idols), → *1631* and *2604*.

1629 (*eidōlolatrēs*, idolater, worshiper of idols), → *1631*.

1630 (*eidōlolatria*, idolatry, worship of idols), → *1631*.

1631	εἴδωλον

εἴδωλον (*eidōlon*), image, idol (*1631*); εἰδωλόθυτος (*eidōlothytos*), meat offered to idols (*1628*); εἰδωλεῖον (*eidōleion*), temple of an idol (*1627*); κατείδωλος (*kateidōlos*), full of idols (*2977*); εἰδωλολάτρης (*eidōlolatrēs*), idolater, worshiper of idols (*1629*); εἰδωλολατρία (*eidōlolatria*), idolatry, worship of idols (*1630*).

CL & OT 1. Homer uses *eidōlon* for the phantoms and shades in Hades. It can also mean any unsubstantial form, an image reflected in a mirror or water, an image or idea in the mind. It was not generally used in cl. Gk. for the images of the gods (→ *eikōn*, *1635*).

2. *eidōlon* refers without exception in the LXX to the images of the heathen gods and the deities represented by them. (To express the image of God in humankind, *eikōn* is used.) *eidōlon* reflects Jewish contempt for heathen polytheism. *eidōleion* is a contemptuous expression for the temples of heathen idols (1 Esd. 2:10; Bel 9; 1 Macc. 10:83). Similarly, *eidōlothytos* means meat offered to idols (4 Macc. 5:2).

The prohibitions against making *eidōla* and serving other gods are linked already in the Decalogue (Exod. 20:3–4; Deut. 5:7–8). The depreciation of images based on these prohibitions leaves its traces everywhere in the OT. This does not imply, however, that there is no reality behind this idolatrous worship. Idols are abominations, behind which stand demonic powers (Deut. 32:16–17, 21). Anyone who comes into contact with these powers will move God to wrath.

Israel often succumbed to the temptation to open the doors to these powers, esp. when the rise of the Assyrian and Babylonian empires gave the impression that their gods were more powerful than the God of Israel (Isa. 36:19–20). Jer. 44:15–19 and Ezek. 8 give graphic pictures of how widely heathen idol worship had spread throughout Israel. The prophets insisted that the misfortune that had overtaken the people was God's punishment for falling away from Yahweh and compromising with the heathen cultus (Isa. 10:11; Jer. 9:13–16; Ezek. 8:17–18). The call to repentance combined a demand for just treatment of one's neighbor (Isa. 1:15–17; Hos. 4:1–3; Amos 5:14–15) with the demand to turn away from false gods (Hos. 14:8).

The prophets never grew tired of stressing to the people how impotent and vain (→ *mataios*, *3469*) were pagan idols (1 Chr. 16:26; Ezek. 8:10), for they are merely the creation of human hands and cannot hear, see, or do anything (Jer. 14:22; Hos. 8:4–5; 13:2; Hab. 2:18–19). The sharpest polemic against such images occurs in Isa. 40:18–20; 44:9–20; 46:1–2. The making of the idols is described in language that renders them ludicrous, and the power of Yahweh, who molds history, stands in contrast with them (Isa. 45–48). He will destroy the false gods (Jer. 10:10–15; Ezek. 6:4–6, 13; Mic. 1:7), and people will throw away their idols on the day of God's judgment (Isa. 2:18–20).

NT 1. The NT continues the usage of the LXX, though it also contains new word formations. In Acts 17:16 it is said that Athens was *kateidōlos* ("full of idols"). We also find the compounds *eidōlolatrēs*, idolater (7x), and *eidōlolatria*, idolatry (4x), based on a linkage with *latreia*, service or worship of God (cf. Rom. 9:4).

2. The NT continues the OT's condemnation of the worship of false gods. The fact that this word group is not found in the Gospels

suggests that the controversy had ceased to be of importance in Palestine. But as soon as the apostolic preaching moved into the non-Jewish, Hel. world, it immediately revived. For example, turning to "the living and true God" (1 Thess. 1:9) was impossible without a turning away "from idols" and pagan worship. Their retention was a sign of lack of repentance (Rev. 9:20).

Paul's arguments in Rom. 1:18–32 are particularly concerned with this controversy. He shows himself a Jew in his stress on the nothingness of the idols, but he recognizes the demonic powers behind them to which one subjects oneself when participating in the heathen cult. That is why *eidōlolatria* is one of the serious sins against which Christians must repeatedly be warned (1 Cor. 5:10–11; 10:7, 14). It is frequently mentioned in lists of sins (cf. Gal. 5:19–21; Eph. 5:5; Col. 3:5; Rev. 21:8).

3. From this basic attitude toward idols it follows that Christians were prohibited from eating the meat of animals offered in heathen sacrifice. According to Acts, the apostles were unanimous that Gentile Christians should refrain from sacrificial meat (Acts 15:20, 29; 21:25), a decision justified by reference to Jewish practice (15:21). In this matter, therefore, Jews and Christians were basically in agreement.

In 1 Cor. 8 and 10 the practical problems that sprang from this attitude are examined in detail. In ch. 8 Paul argues with those in Corinth who believed that the eating of such meat was harmless, since they knew that the false gods had no real existence anyway (1 Cor. 8:1–6). Paul agrees that idols have no real existence (8:4), but he expects that those who realize this will, out of love, show consideration to those who do not; they must not do anything to influence these weaker believers to eat such meat (8:9–13).

Paul gives the underlying reasons for his attitude in 1 Cor. 10. Basing his argument on Deut. 32:17, he explains that demons stand behind the idols. Fellowship with Christ, which Christians enjoy in the Lord's Supper, excludes communion with these powers, and believers should not challenge the Lord. If they do, they will bring down judgment on themselves (10:7–10, 14–22). Christians are under no obligation to inquire fearfully whether meat bought in the market (generally near the temple) or served at a meal came from a sacrifice. But if someone pointed out that it was sacrificial meat, then, out of regard for that person's conscience, Christians ought not to eat it, even if their own conscience (perhaps on the strength of Ps. 24:1) permitted it (1 Cor. 10:25–30).

See also *eikōn*, image, likeness, form, appearance (*1635*); *charaktēr*, stamp, representation, outward appearance, form (*5917*); *apaugasma*, radiance, effulgence, reflection (*575*); *hypodeigma*, proof, example, model (*5682*); *hypogrammos*, outline, copy, example (*5681*); *typos*, type, pattern (*5596*).

1635 εἰκών

εἰκών (*eikōn*), image, likeness, form, appearance (*1635*).

CL & OT 1. *eikōn* is derived from *eoika*, which means to be similar, like. The word means an image (of a painting, statue, figure on a coin, figure of a god), comparison, likeness, representation, simile. In Gk. thought an image shares in the reality of what it represents. The essence of the thing appears in the image; e.g., the god is himself present and operative in his image.

2. In the OT images were strictly prohibited (Exod. 20:4; Deut. 27:15), whether as a false god or as a representation of Yahweh. An image was not the full reality and would only confuse Israel's relationship with the true God (Deut. 4:16; 2 Ki. 11:18). Among Israel's neighbors the image of a god served as a means of controlling the god. It was a source of power in the priest's hand in his dealings with the deity. In the Babylonian exile Israel learned to mock the making of idols (Isa. 40:19–20) but also to be terrified by them (Ezek. 7:20; 8:5; 16:17; 23:14). Both lines of thought can be traced in Dan. 2–3.

In contrast, Israel's relationship with God was based on his covenant and word. Religious images reveal nothing of his nature.

Only human beings can be called the "image" of God (Gen. 1:26–27). The goal of the image of God in humankind is dominion over the world. The idea of the fall marring the image of God is implied in Wis. 2:23 (cf. Wis. 13–15). Some aspects of the image remain, however, such as rationality, for even after the fall human beings are referred to as being in God's image (Gen. 9:6).

NT In Matt. 22:20; Mk. 12:16; Lk. 20:24, *eikōn* is used of the emperor's image on a denarius. Pious Jews hated these coins, both because of their implied breach of the second commandment and because they bore the image of a foreign ruler.

In Rev. the image of the beast (13:14) is a cultic image, and worship of it means apostasy. The classical world knew of images of the gods that spoke and moved.

In Heb. 10:1 *eikōn* signifies the true form of the good things to come that has appeared in Christ, in contrast to the law, which is a mere shadow of these things. In 2 Cor. 4:4 and Col. 1:15 Christ is said to be the *eikōn* of God, but there is no difference here between the image and the essence of the invisible God, for in Christ we see God (cf. Jn. 14:9). By participating in Christ humankind has once again gained God's image (Rom. 8:29) as it was intended to be, and in communion with Christ we are transformed into his image. Paul can speak of this transformation as a present happening (2 Cor. 3:18; Col. 3:10) and also as a future, eschatological event (1 Cor. 15:49; cf. Phil. 3:21).

See also *eidōlon*, image, idol (*1631*); *charaktēr*, stamp, representation, outward appearance, form (*5917*); *apaugasma*, radiance, effulgence, reflection (*575*); *hypodeigma*, proof, example, model (*5682*); *hypogrammos*, outline, copy, example (*5681*); *typos*, type, pattern (*5596*).

1639 εἰμί

εἰμί (*eimi*), to be (*1639*); ἐγώ (*egō*), I (*1609*).

CL & OT This entry focuses exclusively on the expression *egō eimi*, I am.

1. The *egō eimi* formula does not occur in cl. Gk., and there are scarcely any relevant parallels in later periods. But in the wider context of the ancient Near East, an emphatic "I am" style can be demonstrated. For example, in ancient India we read: "I am Kaksivat . . . I compel Kutsa . . . look at me!" The Mandaean analogies are esp. interesting: "I am the life, that was from of old. . . . I am the glory, I am the light"—though Christian influence cannot be excluded here.

2. The mere Heb. words that translate "I am" occur frequently in the OT and are not an exclusively religious formula. But certain "I am" formulae are noteworthy. Esp. important are those self-presentations in which Yahweh makes himself known as the saving God of the fathers (Gen. 15:7; 17:1; 28:13; 35:11; cf. also the opening of the Decalogue, "I am the LORD your God, who . . ." [Exod. 20:2]). Most important is the *egō eimi ho ōn* (lit., "I am the existing One") in the LXX of Exod. 3:14.

This self-presentation was necessary in the polytheistic world of the ancient Orient; it sought to secure the trust of the recipient of the revelation in this one God alone. Yahweh is the one who acts in history. Frequently in Ezek. is the phrase, "[You/they] will know that I am the LORD" (e.g., Ezek. 33:29; 36:36; 37:6, 13; 39:28). In the OT this expression means something like, "I am the Absolute." The clearest expression of this power of Yahweh over nature and history is in Isa., where Yahweh declares: "I am the LORD, who has made all things, who alone stretched out the heavens, who spread out the earth by myself" (Isa. 44:24); "I am the first and I am the last; apart from me there is no God" (44:6; cf. 43:11; 45:5, 22).

NT 1. In Jn. the "I am" sayings occur as a fixed formula. (a) These expressions have a formal structure: It begins with *egō eimi* ("I am") and is followed by a concrete noun and a qualifying adj. or prep. phrase (e.g., "I am the light of the world"; "I am the good shepherd"). Whether the "I" should be considered the subj. or predicate is a matter of debate. That is, is Jesus answering the question, "Who are you?" (hence, "I am *the good shepherd*"), or the question, "Who is the good shepherd?" (hence, "*I am* the good shepherd")? The former seems preferable.

(b) A further question is the meaning of the visual picture in the pronouncement. Are we dealing with parables, metaphors, or allegories when Jesus says, "I am the good shepherd"? If so, then Jesus is comparing himself with a shepherd and his followers with sheep. Or is Jesus the genuine embodiment of the shepherd and his followers the sheep (cf. Jn.'s frequent use of "true" in such passages as 1:9; 4:23, 37; 7:28; 8:16; 15:1)? If so, then Jesus *is* the shepherd in the fullest sense of the term, and this divine truth applies to no one else but him. The second option offers the better interpretation (see [d]).

(c) The OT and Jud. supplied the raw material for the use of some nouns (e.g., "the light," "the door," "the shepherd," "the vine") in these formulae. See, for example, Ps. 23:1: "The LORD is my shepherd" and 27:1: "The LORD is my light and my salvation."

(d) Jesus is "the bread of life" in that he is what he gives (Jn. 6:35, 41, 48, 51). This bread of life, i.e., Jesus himself, provides eternal life (6:47). It comes from heaven (6:51), and access to it is through faith (6:47). Jesus is "the light of the world" (8:12); in following him one has the light of life. In contrast to all others Jesus is "the door" (10:7, 9), for he alone gives access to salvation. The saying about "the good shepherd" (10:11) has the same meaning: Jesus gives his life for the sheep and saves them. He knows his sheep, and they know him. Anyone who has questions about the resurrection should turn to Jesus, for there is no resurrection outside of his person (11:25). Anyone who asks where, what, or who is "the way and the truth and the life" (14:6) will not only find an explanation in Jesus' teaching but discover that Jesus himself is that which these terms refer to. Finally, Jesus is "the true vine" (15:1, 5); between him and ourselves there exists a real union.

(e) Note should also be taken of the unaccompanied "I am" saying in Jn. 8:58. In Jesus' conversations with his enemies, he suggested that he had seen Abraham (8:57). When they objected, Jesus replied with the strong statement, "Before Abraham was born, I am!" Through this statement he linked himself with Yahweh as the great "I AM" of the OT (esp. Exod. 3:14b). The Jews certainly understood his saying that way, since they picked up stones to kill him, presumably for blasphemy (see Lev. 24:10–16); but since Jesus' hour had not yet come, he slipped "away from the temple grounds" (Jn. 8:59).

2. (a) In the Synoptics, the account of Jesus walking on the water (Matt. 14:22–23; Mk. 6:45–52) suggests a theophany in the tradition of the OT. The phrase "he was about to pass by them" (Mk. 6:48c) is reminiscent of Yahweh's passing before Moses on Mount Sinai (Exod. 33:18–23) or before Elijah on Mount Horeb (1 Ki. 19:11–13). Meanwhile, the disciples in the boat are in a state of panic, thinking they see a ghost (Mk. 6:49). Jesus replies: "Take courage! It is I [*egō eimi*]. Don't be afraid!" (6:50). Only this self-revelation of Jesus convinces them of the reality of the appearance.

Each of the six antitheses of the Sermon on the Mount (Matt. 5:21–48) distinguishes Jesus' message from what was said to the Israelites of old by the provocative formula, "but I [*egō*] tell you" (5:22, 28, 32, 34, 39, 44). This formula marks Jesus as the lawful and true expositor of the Torah. In contrast to the teachers of the law with their abbreviations and casuistic distortions, Jesus goes back to the original meaning of the Torah, to the will of God.

In Mk. 13:6 (cf. Matt. 24:5; Lk. 21:8) Jesus warns against people who will arise in his name and lead many astray by using the words *egō eimi*. Here the early church separated itself from those who unlawfully claimed the authority of Jesus. Only Jesus has the right to use those words.

Jesus, at his examination before the Sanhedrin, answered the high priest's question, "Are you the Christ, the Son of the Blessed One?" with the words *egō eimi*, "I am" (Mk. 14:61–62). In the early church there was clearly discussion about the identity of the Messiah

(cf. Jn. 1:20) and Jesus. Jesus answered that question in the affirmative. The Jewish leaders knew what Jesus was saying, for they considered it blasphemy and promptly condemned him to death.

Finally, the risen Christ led his disciples to recognize his identity with the crucified Jesus through the use of the *egō eimi* formula. When they had difficulty believing the one standing in their midst was really the Jesus whom they had known, he showed them his hands and feet and said, "It is I myself!" (Lk. 24:39). And just before his ascension, Jesus promised his disciples: "Surely I am [*egō eimi*] with you always" (Matt. 28:20).

(b) In Rev. the *egō* of Christ's sayings and the *egō* of the pronouncements of God occur side by side. In fact, sometimes the same *egō eimi* sayings can appear on the lips of both Christ and God. In Rev. 1:8 God is the subject of the sentence, "I am the Alpha and the Omega . . . who is, and who was, and who is to come," while in 1:17–18 the Son of Man speaks, "I am the First and the Last. I am the Living One." "The First and the Last" corresponds to "the Alpha and the Omega"; both verses are derived from Isa. 44:6. The most complete identification of Christ and God is expressed at the end of Rev. The subject of the sentence in 21:6, "I am the Alpha and the Omega, the Beginning and the End," is God; in 22:13 Jesus is the one who says, "I am the Alpha and the Omega, the First and the Last, the Beginning and the End." No one can contest the identity of God with Jesus here.

1644 (eirēneuō, live in peace, have peace, keep peace), → 1645.

1645	εἰρήνη

εἰρήνη (*eirēnē*), peace (*1645*); εἰρηνεύω (*eirēneuō*), live in peace, have peace, keep peace (*1644*); εἰρηνικός (*eirēnikos*), peaceable, peaceful (*1646*); εἰρηνοποιός (*eirēnopoios*), peacemaker (*1648*); εἰρηνοποιέω (*eirēnopoieō*), make peace (*1647*).

CL & OT 1. In cl. Gk. *eirene* denotes peace as the antithesis to war or the condition resulting from a cessation of war. It is the state of law and order that gives rise to the blessings of prosperity. It can also mean peaceful conduct, although peaceableness toward others is generally rendered by *philia* (love, friendship) or *homonoia* (unity, concord). Not until the Stoics does peace occur (though infrequently) in the sense of spiritual peace. *eirēneuō* means to live in peace, have peace, sometimes to bring about peace. *eirēnikos*, peaceful, embraces everything relating to peace. The compounds *eirēnopoieō*, to make peace, establish peace, and *eirēnopoios*, peacemaker, when they occur, bear the sense of political pacification by force of arms.

2. (a) In the LXX *eirēnē* is almost invariably used to translate the Heb. *šālôm*, which occurs nearly 250x in the OT. The well-being that comes from God is regularly expressed by *eirēnē*. This Gk. word also corresponds to several other Heb. words that embrace the general meaning of rest, safety, freedom from care, and trustfulness.

Unlike the cl. Gk. meaning of *eirēnē*, the Heb. *šālôm* is the opposite not so much of war as of any disturbance in the communal well-being of the nation (cf. 2 Sam. 11:7). Hence, in the LXX *eirēnē* also acquires the sense of general well-being, the source and giver of which is Yahweh alone. Note the name of the place of Gideon's altar—"The LORD is Peace" (Jdg. 6:24). *eirēnē*, coming as it does from God, is close to the idea of salvation (cf. Ps. 85:10). When God withdraws his peace, mourning inevitably take its place (Jer. 16:5).

(b) Throughout the Heb. OT, *šālôm* covers well-being in the widest sense of the word (Jdg. 19:20); prosperity, even in reference to the godless (Ps. 73:3); bodily health (38:3; Isa. 57:19); contentedness on going to sleep (Ps. 4:8) and at death (Gen. 15:15); good relations between nations and people (Jdg. 4:17; 1 Ki. 5:26 = LXX 5:12; 1 Chr. 12:17–18); and salvation (Jer. 29:11= LXX 36:11; cf. 14:13). Participation in this peace means sharing in the gifts of salvation, while expulsion from it means the end of prosperity (Lam. 3:17). *šālôm* also has a close association with righteousness (cf. Isa. 48:18).

(c) The concept of peace is found at the climax of the blessing in Num. 6:24–26, where it sums up all the other blessings and is closely associated with the presence of Yahweh: "The LORD bless you and keep you; the LORD make his face shine upon you and be gracious to you; the LORD turn his face toward you and give you peace" (Num. 6:24–26). *šālôm* is ultimately the gift of Yahweh (Gen. 28:21; 41:16; Lev. 26:6; Jdg. 18:6; 1 Chr. 22:9; cf. 12:19; 23:25).

(d) The proclamation of peace is a theme of the OT prophets (e.g., Isa. 9:5–6 = LXX 9:6–7; 26:12; 45:7; 48:18, 22; 52:7; 53:5; Jer. 6:14; 8:11, 15; Ezek. 34:25; 37:26; Nah. 2:1 = LXX 1:15; Zech. 6:13; 8:10–19; 9:10). Jeremiah esp. preached that Yahweh withdraws his *šālôm* in judgment (e.g., Jer. 12:12; 14:19; 16:5; 25:37 = LXX 32:22). The theme of Yahweh as the giver of peace figures prominently in the Psalms (e.g., Ps. 4:8; 29:10–11; 37:11; 55:18; 119:165; 122:6–8); it also occurs in Prov. 3:2, 17, 23 and Job 5:24; 15:21; 25:2.

(e) After the destruction of Jerusalem (597 and 587 B.C.) the promise of peace became central to the prophetic message. The false prophets of salvation had been utterly discredited (Jer. 6:14; 8:11; Ezek. 13:10, 16). In Isa. the divine covenant of peace (54:10) comes to be viewed eschatologically: righteousness, splendor, salvation, and glory (Isa. 62:1–2) are all expected to be manifest at the end. The created world will again be made whole (11:6–9; 29:17–24; 62:1–9), for God will create new heavens and a new earth (65:17–19; cf. Rev. 21:1–4). This coming of the day of salvation is linked with the Prince of Peace (Isa. 9:5–6), who as God's anointed (61:1–2) is the founder of the kingdom of peace.

3. (a) The *šālôm* of Yahweh underlies the whole concept of peace in the rab. lit., but it is enlarged both in the God-human relationship and on the human plane. The phrase for "to greet" means "to ask after (someone's) peace," i.e., to wish it for someone. *šālôm* becomes the essence of the salvation expected by the Jews. Among the rabbis the role of the peacemaker is similar to that in the NT, though the motive is not so much positive love for one's neighbor as the desire to get rid of all that hinders *šālôm*.

(b) Similarly in the Pseudepigrapha, *eirēnē* implies salvation, which includes the cessation of war, but can also mean withholding judgment. The concept of peace becomes introverted in Philo and signifies peace of mind, though this is not divorced from the external and objectively verifiable state of peace. He also regards inward peace as being victory over temptation and lust.

(c) The Qumran community considered itself to be the eschatological community of the saved; its members had already entered into the enjoyment of eschatological peace. There are references to eternal peace (1QS 2:4), the superabundance of peace (4:7), peace without end (1QH 7:15–16), lasting peace (15:15), and peace without limit (18:30). Yet the community saw itself as still in the midst of conflict against Belial and the sons of darkness. God, however, has engraved the covenant of peace (= salvation) for all eternity with the stylus of life (1QM 12:3).

NT *eirēnē* is found 92x in the NT, 25x in the Gospels. Christ's farewell discourses in Jn. contain the word 6x, each one denoting Christ's gift to his disciples (Jn. 14:27 [2x]; 16:33; 20:19, 21, 26). The vb. *eirēneuō* appears 3x in Paul; *eirēnopoios* and *eirēnopoieō* each occurs once, and *eirēnikos* 2x.

1. Both in form and content *eirēnē* stands firmly in the OT tradition. Peace is, of course, the opposite of war (Lk. 14:32; Acts 12:20). In Lk. 11:21; Acts 24:2 it denotes external security. In 1 Cor. 14:33, peace is the opposite of disorder in the church. *eirēnē* is also used for harmony among human beings (Acts 7:26; Gal. 5:22; Eph. 4:3; Jas. 3:18) and for messianic salvation (Lk. 1:79; 2:14; 19:42). Hence the word can describe both the content and the goal of all Christian preaching, the message itself being called "the gospel of peace" (Eph. 6:15; cf. 2:17; Acts 10:36).

In other words, the biblical concept of peace is primarily that of wholeness. This divinely wrought reality exercises a powerful influence in the present world, although it still awaits final fulfillment. Soteriologically, peace is grounded in God's work of redemption.

Eschatologically it is a sign of God's new creation, which has already begun. Teleologically, it will be fully realized when the work of new creation is complete. Only in a secondary sense does peace describe human and divine-human relationships, in which case it refers to a psychological state arising from sharing in the all-embracing peace of God.

2. (a) As opposed to *akatastasia*, disorder (→ *189*), peace is an order established by God as the God of peace (1 Cor. 14:33; cf. also Rom. 15:33; 16:20; Phil. 4:9; 1 Thess. 5:23; Heb. 13:20). The wideranging scope of salvation is shown by the fact that peace is linked with love (→ *agapē*, *27*) in 2 Cor. 13:11 and with grace (*charis*, → *5921*) in the introductions (e.g., Rom. 1:7; 1 Cor. 1:3; 1 Pet. 1:2; Rev. 1:4; cf. 2 Jn. 3; Jude 2) and closings (Rom. 16:20; cf. 2 Cor. 13:11; Gal. 6:16; 1 Thess. 5:23; 2 Pet. 3:14; 3 Jn. 14) of NT letters. It is linked with life (Rom. 8:6) and is in contrast with tribulation (→ *thlipsis*, *2568*).

Peace comes "from him who is, and who was, and who is to come" (Rev. 1:4; cf. Heb. 7:2, where Melchizedek is a type of the king of peace). The Gospel of Jn. insists that this peace differs not only quantitatively but also qualitatively from that of the world (Jn. 16:33) in that it is given by Christ himself. "Peace in heaven and glory in the highest" (Lk. 19:38; cf. 2:14) also form part of the expected salvation. Peace, if it is to exist at all, must be all-embracing.

(b) Christ is the mediator of peace. He brings in the kingdom of God and is the bearer of reconciliation (Lk. 2:14; Rom. 5:1; Col. 1:20). Indeed, he himself is peace (Eph. 2:14–18), as is Yahweh in the OT. Peace is described as "the peace of Christ" (Col. 3:15), which is maintained through communion with him (Jn. 16:33; Phil. 4:7; 1 Pet. 5:14). While Jn. stresses Christ's gift of peace to his disciples (14:27), Jesus stresses that his disciples are to pass peace on to others. If it is refused, it returns to the disciples (Matt. 10:13; Lk. 10:5–6). Peace may go unrecognized (Lk. 19:42) or be forgotten and obscured (Rom. 3:17). But if there is a conflict between personal well-being and God's peace, then the former must be surrendered, or else there will be disharmony instead of peace (Lk. 12:51–53). There is no room for false peace.

3. Peace, in the sense of wholeness both for humankind and the world (2 Cor. 5:17; Gal. 6:15), brings a newness to human relationships. Hence the injunction: "Be at peace with each other" (Mk. 9:50) and with all people wherever possible (Rom. 12:18). The kingdom of God is righteousness and peace (14:17) in the sense of establishing a just harmony among human beings. The church is built up in peace and in the joy of the Holy Spirit (14:17, 19) because it is God who causes peace to rule in our hearts, to reign in the Christian community (Col. 3:15), and to make itself known as the fruit of the Spirit (Gal. 5:22). God in Christ has come "telling the good news of peace" (Acts 10:36, possibly alluding to Isa. 52:7).

4. In 2 Tim. 2:22 and Heb. 12:14, peace in the sense of concord and harmony is to be pursued not only in the church but among people generally, so far as is possible. Matt. 5:9 states the beatitude: "Blessed are the peacemakers, for they will be called sons of God." The word *eirēnopoios*, used only here in the NT, is an adj. meaning making peace. It is perhaps related to 5:48: "Be perfect [*teleioi*, → *telos*, *5465*], therefore, as your heavenly Father is perfect." The disciple who brings the wholeness and maturity that comes from God alone and that is intimately bound up with his presence is one who brings peace in the fullest sense. Such a person is a child of God fulfilling the destiny and title of Israel (cf. Hos. 1:10; Wis. 2:13, 18).

5. In Heb 12:11, the adj. *eirēnikos* expresses "a harvest of righteousness and peace" that springs from being disciplined. This leads to the exhortation to "make every effort to live in peace with all men and to be holy" (12:14). Such a lifestyle is in contrast to "godless ... Esau" (12:16; cf. Gen. 25:29–34), who, by trading his birthright, showed a failure to seek peace and holiness (Heb. 12:14). In Jas. 3:17 *eirēnikos* is associated with wisdom: "But the wisdom that comes from heaven is first of all pure; then peace-loving...."

6. The vb. *eirēnopoieō* is found only at Col. 1:20, where it refers to the cosmic scope of the reconciling death of Christ: "For God was pleased to have all his fullness dwell in him, and through him to reconcile to himself all things, whether things on earth or things in heaven, by making peace [*eirēnopoieō*] through his blood, shed on the cross" (1:19–20). The Gk. aor. tense used here is perhaps better translated as "having made peace," since it refers to the historic event of the cross (cf. 2:13–15).

7. In at least one place (Rom. 15:13) peace is to be understood as a power that, together with joy, can pervade the whole person: "May the God of hope fill you with all joy and peace as you trust in him, so that you may overflow with hope by the power of the Holy Spirit." This peace is neither the Stoic's withdrawal from the world nor a pious flight into spirituality and mystical contemplation. It is the joyful assurance of sharing the peace of God as one goes through life and looks to eternity.

1646 (*eirēnikos*, peaceable, peaceful), → *1645*.

1647 (*eirēnopoieō*, make peace), → *1645*.

1648 (*eirēnopoios*, peacemaker), → *1645*.

1650 εἰς   εἰς (*eis*), into, for the purpose of (*1650*).

CL & OT In cl. Gk. *eis* generally meant motion *into* something (*pros* expressed motion toward something; → *4639*). In a similar vein, *eis* was used with impers. objects and *pros* with the personal. Also, *eis* was usually strictly differentiated from *en* (in, → *1877*), which denoted a static resting within something. But Hel. Gk. (including the LXX) manifests a general tendency to confuse the categories of linear motion ("to, into") and punctiliar rest ("in"). The confusion was in both directions: *eis* denoting position (e.g., Gen. 37:17a; Jos. 7:22) and *en* implying movement (e.g., Exod. 4:21; Tob. 5:5). The obsolescence of the dat. case in Gk. meant the disappearance of *en* from the modern Gk. vernacular, where only *eis* (with the acc.) is found.

NT 1. *General usage.* Since the NT uses *eis* either for movement into something or for static position (some authors interchange *eis* and *en* more than others), we must avoid two dangers: to treat these two preps. as everywhere synonymous, or always to insist on a distinction between them.

One significant text in this respect is Jn. 1:18, where John writes about the only Son of God residing "at [*eis*] the Father's side [or bosom]." The general imagery suggests a deep and affectionate intimacy between the Father and the Son. What, then, is the import of *eis*? Some scholars give it a dynamic sense (i.e., movement toward or into), even going so far as to see the doctrine of eternal generation here. Others see *eis* as both static and dynamic. The prevailing view among grammarians and commentators today, however, is that *eis* is simply a synonym for the more classically correct *en* (i.e., a static sense of the word). Any notion of dynamic interpersonal relationship found here stems from "side" and "Father," not from the prep. *eis*.

2. *Purpose.* *eis* often expresses metaphorical direction, i.e., goal or purpose. Note Col. 1:16, where "for [*eis*] him" indicates that Christ is the ultimate goal of creation as well as the one through (→ *dia*, *1328*) whom creation took place. *eis* can also mark the divine appointment of believers "for eternal life" (Acts 13:48), or of unbelievers "stumbling" over the Stone because of their rejection of salvation, as they were destined "for" (1 Pet. 2:8).

3. *Result.* It is also generally recognized now that *eis*, on occasion, expresses a result (e.g., its use with an infinitive in Rom. 1:20; 7:5; 12:2; 2 Cor. 8:6; Gal. 3:17; Phil. 1:10; Heb. 11:3; Jas. 3:3). Note the result use of *eis* in Rom. 10:10: "For it is with your heart that you believe and are justified [lit., for, *eis*, justification]." If the result sense of *eis* is recognized in 12:2, Paul's point is not that the aim of the transformation of one's character is to discern God's will, but rather

that the Christian's ability to ascertain God's will naturally results from the renewal of the mind.

Often the categories of purpose (sec. 2) and result merge, for a result may be a *designed* consequence. Thus, it is sometimes impossible to determine what is intended (e.g., in the phrase "to [*eis*] the glory of God" in 2 Cor. 4:15; Phil. 1:11; 2:11).

4. *Special uses.* (a) One passage long debated by scholars is the use of *eis* in the LXX of Gen. 15:6 ("Abram believed the LORD, and he credited it to him as [*eis*] righteousness"), which is quoted in Rom. 4:3, 9, 22; Gal. 3:6; Jas. 2:23. With regard to Paul's usage, the verse has been interpreted in several ways: Righteousness was imputed to Abraham on the basis of his faith (cf. 1 Macc. 2:52; Rom. 9:30; 10:6; Heb. 11:7); Abraham's faith was reckoned as a substitute for law-based righteousness; or Abraham's faith in God was the equivalent of righteousness.

(b) The prep. *eis* is used with the vb. *baptizō* (to baptize). In Matt. 3:11 ("I baptize you with water for [*eis*] repentance") and Acts 2:38 ("be baptized ... for [*eis*] the forgiveness of your sins"), a few scholars argue for a causal sense of the prep. Better options, however, are that *eis* in Matt. 3:11 denotes the purpose or result of baptism, or perhaps it has temporal significance (i.e., while confessing or repenting of sin). Or, since elsewhere John's baptism is termed a "baptism of [i.e., relating to, marked by] repentance" (Mk. 1:4; Lk. 3:3; Acts 13:24; 19:4), *eis* may simply mean "in relation or reference to." Similarly, in Acts 2:38 forgiveness of sin may be the purpose or result of repentance and baptism, or else forgiveness is regarded as conceptually (but not necessarily chronologically) connected with baptism.

In 1 Cor. 12:13 (baptism "by one Spirit into [*eis*] one body"), *eis* denotes the purpose and effect of Spirit baptism; alternately, the baptized may be conceived of as entering into the body of Christ that already exists. To be baptized "into" the death of Christ (Rom. 6:3b) is to participate in all of the saving benefits of his death to sin (6:10) or to submit to a water baptism that relates to his death.

In several passages we read about baptism "into [*eis*] the name" of Jesus. Most likely *eis* here denotes a transference of ownership, as when money is paid "into the account of" a certain person. That is, the one being baptized passes into the possession of the Triune God (Matt. 28:19) or of the Lord Jesus (Acts 8:16; 19:5; cf. 1 Cor. 1:13, 15) and comes under his control and protection.

Being baptized "into [*eis*] Christ" (Rom. 6:3a; Gal. 3:27) probably means being baptized into the body of Christ, the church (so that to be baptized into Christ = to put on Christ [3:27b] = to be in Christ [3:28]). But the phrase may also describe a believer's entry into personal union and communion with Christ (i.e., into fellowship with Christ).

(c) Finally, *eis* occurs 45x with the vb. *pisteuō* (believe; → *pistis*, faith, *4411*). This is a characteristically Johannine idiom (only 8x is it used outside Jn.'s Gospel and 1 Jn. [Matt. 18:6; Acts 10:43; 14:23; 19:4; Rom. 10:14; Gal. 2:16; Phil. 1:29; 1 Pet. 1:8]). It seems clear that, for John, believing *eis* is intimately connected with believing "in the name" (see Jn. 1:12; 2:23; 3:18; 1 Jn. 5:13). The latter phrase probably means "believe in the person of," though it can also imply a transfer of ownership, resulting in a new allegiance.

At a minimum, *eis* after *pisteuō* introduces the object of faith or the direction of faith. In addition, the phrase depicts the commitment of oneself to the person of Christ, something more than an intellectual acceptance of his message or a recognition of the truth about Christ. The two aspects are related. Since the person of Christ is the essence of the message that is proclaimed and accepted, to truly accept that message is to accept him. To believe *that* naturally becomes to believe *in* (cf. Jn. 20:31; Rom. 10:9–11).

1651 εἷς   εἷς (*heis*), one (*1651*); ἑνότης (*henotēs*), unity (*1942*).

CL & OT 1. In pre-Socratic nature philosophy *to hen*, the one (neut. of *heis*), refers to the ultimate unity of being, eternity; the nontransient, simple being. Parmenides described being as a sphere, perfect in itself and uniform, simple and excluding all peculiarities.

The Sophists applied these fundamental concepts to ethics. Since all being is absolutely identical, value judgments become impossible. Socrates opposed these doctrines and posited an abiding unity that, over against the change and multiplicity of opinions, would be recognized by all. The basis for such universally recognized demands is universally valid concepts. Plato taught a world of ideas in which reality increases until it reaches its peak on the highest incorporeal idea of the One as the good, divine, world intellect. For the Stoics, all existence is ultimately a unity; the divine penetrates everything and manifests itself in diversity, creating order and furnishing a unitary law. The human soul is by its nature one with the world soul.

In Gnosticism, the divine world of life, light, and spirit is original and remains by nature one. In a precosmic catastrophe, pieces of it were broken off and handed over to the evil, the dark, and the many (i.e., the creation of the world). The goal of the cosmic drama is the return of all the scattered fragments of the spiritual and divine into the unity of God.

2. The comparable Heb. terms are *ʾeḥād* (masc.) and *ʾaḥat* (fem.), meaning: (a) one (Gen. 1:9); (b) the first (2:11; 8:5); (c) the one . . . the other (Exod. 18:3–4); (d) one after the other (Isa. 27:12); (e) one with another (Ezek. 33:30); (f) one to another (Job 41:16); (g) anyone (Gen. 26:10); (h) one and the same (27:45); and (i) the only one (Isa. 51:2).

The unity of God is particularly stressed in Deut. 6:4. A lit. trans. of the Heb. is: "Yahweh our God, Yahweh one"; the LXX translates this, "[The] Lord our God is one [*heis*] Lord" (cf. NIV: "The LORD our God, the LORD is one"). These words form the *Shema*, i.e., the daily Jewish confession of the unity of God, the basic creed by which it separates itself from paganism and idolatry. Some parts of the OT speak of the existence of other gods (e.g., Exod. 15:11; 1 Sam. 26:19 [ironic]). Explicit monotheism became increasingly dominant from the 7th cent. B.C. on (e.g., 1 Ki. 8:60; Jer. 2:11; esp. Isa. 41:29; 43:10; 44:8). But the unique reality of God was firmly anchored in the faith of Israel from the beginning. This forms the basis for the call to unity among the people (Mal. 2:10). In rab. Jud. "the One" became a surrogate for God.

NT 1. *Survey of* heis *in the NT*. (a) As a simple numeral. (i) One (e.g., Matt. 5:41; Jn. 9:25): One thing can be decisive (Mk. 10:21); the plagues of judgment come on one day (Rev. 18:8); there is one sacrifice of Christ (Heb. 10:12, 14; cf. *hapax*, once, *562*). The one who repents is more valuable than the ninety-nine who do not need to repent (Lk. 15:7). (ii) The one . . . the other (e.g., Matt. 24:40–41). (iii) Every one (e.g., 1 Cor. 12:18–19). (iv) One by one (e.g., Mk. 14:19). (v) The first (e.g., Matt. 28:1). (vi) Alone (Mk. 2:7). Note that *heis* can stand parallel to *monos*, only (→ *3668*; e.g., Mk. 2:7 [*heis*]; Lk. 5:21 [*monos*]).

(b) The one God and Father. The *Shema* (Deut. 6:4; see above) is quoted in Mk. 12:29. Jas. 4:12 declares, "There is only one Lawgiver and Judge." In warning against the temptation to exalt oneself to positions only God can occupy, Matt. writes that we have only "one Father" in heaven and "one Teacher, the Christ" (Matt. 23:8–10). The uniqueness of God is asserted over against idols in the controversy about eating meat offered to idols (1 Cor. 8:4–6). This means that "for us there is but one God, the Father, from whom all things came and for whom we live; and there is but one Lord, Jesus Christ, through whom all things came and through whom we exist" (8:6). Therefore, idols have no real existence (8:4). Still, on grounds of love and expediency Paul urges the Corinthians not to eat meat that has been first offered to idols.

Eph. 4:3 urges unity and peace in the church on the grounds of the unity of God: "There is one body and one Spirit—just as you were called to one hope when you were called—one Lord, one faith, one baptism; one God and Father of all, who is over all and through all and in all" (Eph. 4:4–6). In 1 Tim. 2:5 Paul writes a parenthetical reminder that "there is one God and one mediator between God and men, the man Christ Jesus." There is a unity in the human race that derives from our common origin from God, who created the world (Acts 17:24): "From one man he made every nation of men" (17:26).

There is one abiding will of God (Matt. 5:17–18), and in conformity with that will there is one church composed of Jews and Gentiles. One of the main themes of Rom. is to demonstrate the continuity of the divine purposes revealed in the OT in the light of the work of Christ and the inclusion of the Gentiles: "There is only one God, who will justify the circumcised by faith and the uncircumcised through that same faith" (Rom. 3:30).

(c) One Christ. In addition to Jesus Christ's being our only teacher and mediator, the NT also testifies that he is one with the Father (Jn. 10:30; 17:11, 21–23). He is also the one shepherd with one flock (Jn. 10:14–16).

(d) One Spirit. Paul bases his teaching on the multiplicity of gifts in the church and the necessity of order and harmony in their use on the unity of the Spirit, who is the giver of these gifts (1 Cor. 12:9, 11, 13). Jews and Gentiles are no longer alien in Christ, "for through him we both have access to the Father by one Spirit" (Eph. 2:18; cf. also the "one Spirit" in 4:4). The word *henotēs*, unity, occurs only in Eph., where it expresses the unity of the church in maturity, based on the divine unity: "Make every effort to keep the unity of the Spirit through the bond of peace" (4:3); "until we all reach unity in the faith and in the knowledge of the Son of God and become mature" (4:13).

(e) The one church of the one Lord. (i) There is a unity of believers with their Lord. There is also a unity of husband and wife that comes about through sexual intercourse; for this reason a believer should not be joined to a prostitute (1 Cor. 6:16; cf. Gen. 2:24; Matt. 19:5; Eph. 5:31). The believer's union with Christ is not physical but spiritual: "But he who unites himself with the Lord is one with him in spirit" (1 Cor. 6:17; cf. the marriage analogy of Christ and the church in Eph. 5:28–33; Rev. 21:2).

(ii) In Heb. 2:11, "out of one" (lit.; NIV, "the same family") points to the closest possible unity of believers with Jesus, which is here uniquely expressed in terms of "brothers" in the quotation in 2:12 from Ps. 22:22. There is also a unity of believers in the body of Christ (1 Cor. 12:12–13; Gal. 3:28; Col. 3:15) through and in the Holy Spirit (Eph. 4:4). Our unity in the one Lord causes the wall of partition between Jews and Gentiles, broken down at the cross, to be abolished once and for all; now there exists instead only one, new people of God in Christ (Eph. 2:13–16). This is a particular emphasis in Jn. (see 11:52; 17:11, 21, 23). Those who are made one have a common life (Acts 4:32; Rom. 15:6; 1 Cor. 12:26; Gal. 6:2; Phil. 2:2). Conversely, those who are in rebellion against God have one purpose and will against him (Rev. 17:13).

2. *The theological meaning of* heis *in the NT*. Unity in the NT is always seen from the standpoint of Christ, in whom alone is salvation (Acts 4:12). In Gk. and Roman philosophy the unity of God and the world was demanded by educated reason. In the OT the unity of God is a confession derived from God's revelation. The decisive advance in the NT is the basing of the unity and uniqueness of God on the unique revelation through the one man Jesus Christ, the Revealer and Lord (1 Cor. 8:4–6; 1 Tim. 2:5–6).

That is why Paul, after saying in 1 Cor. 8:4 that there are no real idols in the world and that there is no God but one, can recognize in the following sentence that there are in fact many gods and lords. But (and this is the justification for the original statement) these gods have no reality and are therefore only "so-called gods." They have no claim to lordship over us. We know this because there is one Lord Jesus Christ (8:6).

This truth is expressed esp. clearly in Jn. 10:30, which should not be interpreted to mean that the oneness of Jesus with the Father consists of the joining of two persons or beings who were formerly separated. We must rather understand it in the light of Jn. 14:9: "Anyone who has seen me has seen the Father." No one can speak of God unless he or she is speaking concretely of Jesus. The unity of the Spirit is based on Jesus as well (Eph. 4).

"The one man, Jesus Christ," is decisive for the salvation of "the many" (Rom. 5:15). He died for all the one, decisive death (Jn. 11:50, 52; 2 Cor. 5:14). The obedient death of this one man is interpreted by the "much more" of Rom. 5:17. The one man Adam became a curse for humanity "because all sinned" (5:12); by way of contrast, the one man Jesus Christ brought righteousness and life for all (5:17).

The foundation and continuity of the church's unity are grounded in him as the one shepherd of the one flock (Jn. 10:14–16). Paul expresses this fact through his picture of the one body, in which the members are linked and are mutually dependent. The several members cannot live in diversity without the one head (1 Cor. 12). The counterpart to this in Jesus' high priestly prayer in Jn. 17 is the concept of mutual indwelling, where Jesus prayed "that all of them may be one . . . that they may be one as we are one: I in them and you in me" (17:21–23).

See also *hapax*, once (*562*); *monos*, alone, only (*3668*).

1653 (eisakouō, obey, pass. to be heard), → *201.*

1656 (eiserchomai, come in, enter), → *2262.*

1658 (eisodos, entrance, access), → *3847.*

1665 (eiōtha, custom), → *1621.*

| 1666 ἐκ | ἐκ (*ek*), out, out of (*1666*). |

CL Originally *ek* signified an exit "from within" something. Consequently, it came to denote origin, source, derivation, or separation. The prep. was thereby also used of the material out of which something is made, the country of one's origin, and a person with whom a connection is severed. In Hel. Gk. *ek* and *apo* began overlapping in usage (→ *apo*, from, *608*).

NT 1. The NT continues many of the basic nuances of *ek* in cl. Gk. In Matt. 27:29 *ek* denotes the material out of which something is made, in Acts 23:34 the country of one's origin, and in Jn. 17:15 a person with whom a connection is to be severed. But in the stereotyped use of *ek* plus a noun preceded by an article (e.g., *hoi ek pisteōs,* "those who believe," lit., "those of faith," Gal. 3:7, 9), the notion of belonging is more prominent than that of origin.

The frequently used phrase *ek (tou) theou* (lit., "[out] of God") can depict (a) the agency of God in effecting spiritual regeneration (e.g., Jn. 1:13; 1 Jn. 3:9; 4:7; 5:1, 4, 18a), corresponding to the role of the male in the act of physical procreation (cf. Matt. 1:18); or (b) God as the source of Jesus' teaching (Jn. 7:17), the giver of the Holy Spirit (1 Cor. 2:12a) and spiritual gifts (7:7), the source of both physical (11:12b) and spiritual (2 Cor. 5:18) life, the one who empowered Paul to carry out his divine commission (3:5b), the architect of believers' resurrection bodies (5:1), and the one true source of love (1 Jn. 4:7).

2. *Notable uses.* (a) In Jn. 15:19 (2x); 17:14, 16, Jesus refers to living in the world but not "belonging to the world" (lit., "of [*ek*] the world"). Christians must live in the world but must not display its characteristics.

(b) Rom. 1:3–4 refers to two successive stages of Christ's existence, not to two coexisting states. With respect to human descent (cf. 9:5), Jesus Christ was born (lit.) "out of [*ek*] the seed of David." His installation as Son of God in power, performed by the Holy Spirit, took its rise "by [*ek*, i.e., as a result of] his resurrection from the dead." Further, Paul views the resurrection of all believers as ideally achieved in Christ's resurrection (cf. 1 Cor. 15:20, 23; Col. 1:18). The inclusive category, "the resurrection of the dead," includes the first determinative instance, "his resurrection from the dead."

(c) Many proposals have been made in regard to the meaning of the phrase *ek pisteōs eis pistin* ("by faith from first to last"; lit., "out of [*ek*] faith into [*eis*, → *1650*] faith") in Rom. 1:17. Suggestions include: from the faith of the preacher to the faith of the hearer; from God's faithfulness to human faith; from smaller to greater degrees of faith; from faith as a starting point to faith as a permanent condition. But it seems best to construe *ek* as indicating not a source or starting point ("from faith") but a basis or means ("by faith," as in Hab. 2:4), with the *eis pistin* either intensifying the effect (as in NIV, quoted above) or denoting the goal of God's impartation to us of a righteous status ("leading to faith"). On either of these latter views, faith is portrayed as the vital and perpetual characteristic of Christian experience.

(d) Two different preps. are used in Rom. 3:30: God will justify the Jews "by [*ek*] faith" and the Gentiles "through [*dia*; → *1328*] that same faith." Many commentators have sought a distinction between the two preps. But if any distinction is intended, it is formal, not substantial: God justifies the Jew as a result of faith and the Gentile on the same ground (i.e., by means of that same kind of faith). Note that both prep. phrases may mean "through faith" or "by faith," since both can express either effective means or efficient cause. Elsewhere Paul can use *ek* or *dia* to denote the immediate means of justification or salvation (*ek*: Rom. 1:17; 3:26; 5:1; *dia*: 3:22, 25; Gal. 3:26; Eph. 2:8; cf. a change from *dia* to *ek* in Rom. 3:26 [on this, → *dia, 1328*]; Gal. 2:16). Above all, any suggestion of two distinct means of justification undermines Paul's earlier insistence that there is no difference between Jew and Gentile with respect to sinfulness (Rom. 3:22–23) or the ultimate ground (= grace) and means (= redemption) of justification (3:24).

(e) Without the wider context of 2 Cor. 10–13, one would be tempted to translate 13:4, "he was crucified in [*ek*; i.e., a condition of physical] weakness," but *ek* probably bears a causal sense: "because of [his weakness]." The "weakness" Paul suggests is not physical or moral, but the "weakness"—in human eyes—of nonretaliation or nonaggressiveness (cf. 10:1–2, 10–11; 11:20–21, 30; 12:9–10; 13:4b, 9–10). But in such weakness, divine power comes to full strength (12:9).

1672 (hekatontarchēs, centurion), → *4483.*

| 1675 ἐκβάλλω | ἐκβάλλω (*ekballō*), drive out, expel, send out, take out (*1675*). |

CL & OT *ekballō* can mean drive out from a place (see Gen. 3:24), divorce (Lev. 21:7), and forcibly expel one's enemies (Exod. 34:24; Jdg. 6:9). By the 1st cent. A.D. this word could be used in a favorable sense, send out.

NT *ekballō* is used 81x in the NT, with a wide range of meanings. The slave wife Hagar is cast out (Gal. 4:30; cf. Gen. 21:10). A disciple of Jesus is thrown out of the synagogue (Jn. 9:34–35). The name of Christ is rejected (Lk. 6:22). While Jesus rejects no one who comes to him (Jn. 6:37), Diotrephes excludes Christians from the church (3 Jn. 10). The taking out of a splinter (Matt. 7:4) and the removal of an eye (Mk. 9:47) imply the use of force. But the vb. can also have a positive sense: the Spirit's sending Jesus into the desert (1:12), sending out reapers (Matt. 9:38 par.), and bringing out treasures (13:52).

The word has a theological bearing only in connection with casting out demons (cf. Matt. 7:22; 8:16 par.; 9:34; 12:26–27; 17:19 par.; Lk. 13:32). While the pagans and Jews of the NT world tried to drive out the demons by magic and exorcism, Jesus needed only his word of command (Matt. 8:16). Because he possessed the authority of God (cf. Mk. 1:24 par.), demons had to yield to his power. Jesus also gave his disciples authority to cast out demons (Matt. 10:1, 8). His dominion over these powers was a sign that the kingdom of God had come in his person (12:22–28).

See also *aēr*, air (*113*); *daimonion*, demon, evil spirit (*1228*); *diabolos*, devil (*1333*).

1683 (ekdechomai, expect, wait for), → *638.*

1685 (ekdēmeō, leave one's country, emigrate), → *1322.*

1688 (ekdikeō, execute justice, punish, avenge), → *1472.*

1689 (*ekdikēsis*, vengeance, recompense, punishment), → *1472.*

1690 (*ekdikos*, avenger), → *1472.*

1691 (*ekdiōkō*, drive away, persecute severely), → *1503.*

1693 (*ekdochē*, expectation), → *638.*

1694 (*ekdyō*, undress), → *1544.*

1699 (*ekzēteō*, seek, search for), → *2426.*

1700 (*ekzētēsis*, be amazed, useless speculation), → *2426.*

1701 (*ekthambeō*, be amazed, alarmed), → *2512.*

1702 (*ekthambos*, utterly astonished), → *2512.*

1703 (*ekthaumazō*, be greatly amazed), → *2512.*

1705 (*ekkathairō*, clean out), → *2754.*

1709 (*ekklaō*, break off), → *3089.*

1711	ἐκκλησία

ἐκκλησία (*ekklēsia*), assembly, meeting, congregation, church (*1711*); συναγωγή (*synagōgē*), assembly, synagogue (*5252*); ἀρχισυνάγωγος (*archisynagōgos*), ruler of the synagogue (*801*); ἀποσυνάγωγος (*aposynagōgos*), put out of the synagogue (*697*).

CL 1. (a) *ekklēsia*, derived from *ekkaleō* (call out), denotes the popular assembly of the competent citizens of a *polis*, city-state (in Athens, they met 30–40x a year, more in times of emergency). Decisions were made on suggested changes in the law, on appointments to official positions, and on every important question of internal and external policy (contracts, treaties, war and peace, finance). To these was added, in special cases (e.g., treason), the task of sitting in judgment, which normally fell to regular courts. The *ekklēsia* opened with prayers and sacrifices to the gods. Every citizen had the right to speak and propose matters for discussion; a decision was valid only if it won a certain number of votes.

(b) Thus, *ekklēsia* was clearly characterized as a political phenomenon, rooted in the constitution of the democracy. The scope of its competence varied in the different states. In only three known cases was this word used for the business meeting of a cultic guild.

2. In contrast to *ekklēsia*, *synagōgē* exhibited a wide breadth of usage. It denoted the collecting of things (books, letters, possessions, fruit at harvest) and people (including troops). The word found its most clearly defined meaning in the activities of the guilds, used for their regular, mostly festive assemblies, which were almost without exception cultic fellowships. It also denoted their business meeting and (rarely) the guild itself. The use of *synagōgē* for a specific place of assembly originated within Jud.

OT 1. In the LXX *ekklēsia* occurs about 100x, mostly for the Heb. *qāhāl* (though this Heb. root is translated by other words as well, such as *synagōgē*, *ochlos*, crowd, or *plēthos*, multitude). By contrast, *synagōgē* appears (225x) as the usual translation for Heb. *ʿēdâ*, congregation (which is never translated by *ekklēsia*).

2. (a) *qāhāl* means a summons to an assembly and the act of assembling. What assembles is the *ʿēdâ*, the *ʿām* (people), Israel, Judah, the elders, or the princes. This breadth of usage indicates that the decisive meaning of the word is to be determined from the noun, not from the vb. Who make up the *qāhāl*? In the earliest strata of the OT, the word stands primarily for the summons to war of all the men capable of bearing arms (Gen. 49:6; Num. 22:4; verbal form in 2 Sam. 20:14; 1 Ki. 12:21). To a certain extent, the soldiers represent the people (the *ʿām*), but occasionally the word stands for the whole congregation of the people (Num. 16:33).

In Deut. *qāhāl* means primarily the congregation summoned by Yahweh to conclude the covenant with him at Sinai (Deut. 9:10; 10:4). They are bound by the rules he has given, and their participation in his covenant is maintained by obedience. Thus, *qāhāl* could also have a religious element alongside that of a special, solemn assembly.

In the subsequent period (Jos. to 2 Ki.), the word lost once again its strictly religious character (e.g., 1 Ki. 8:65; 12:3) and came to mean simply the general assembly of the people; it included women and perhaps even children in Jer. 44:15 and in postexilic passages such as Ezr. 10:1; Neh. 8:2. In Ezek. (15x), it is used without religious significance for the mustering of the army and even refers to nations other than Israel (17:17, Egypt; 27:27, Tyre; 32:22, Assyria). The LXX understandably translates it not by *ekklēsia* but by *synagōgē* or *ochlos*.

In Chr. (32x), *qāhāl* appears both in a representative sense for the assembly of Israel's leaders summoned by the king to make decisions, which may be either religious (1 Chr. 13:2, 4) or political (29:10), and for the crowd gathered for sacrifice and worship (e.g., 2 Chr. 20:5, 14; 30:2, 4). This crowd (gathered in the temple) is also designated *qāhāl* in Ps. (e.g., 22:22; 89:5; 149:1)—though 26:5 refers to a *qāhāl* of evildoers.

(b) The primary word for the assembly of God's people is *ʿēdâ*, which occurs in the Pent. (109x; 82x in Num. alone), the prophets (only at Jer. 6:18; 30:20; Hos. 7:12), and 10x in Ps. This word is related to the root *yāʿad*, appoint. It implies, therefore, an appointed place and/or time when resolutions are made before Yahweh. It is not difficult to see that the significance of this root agrees closely with the deuteronomistic use of *qāhāl*. The reference to time is clear in Exod. 9:5 and 1 Sam. 13:8, 11, which have a word derived from the stem, *môʿēd*, appointed time, assembly, appointed festival.

The *ʿēdâ* can be defined as the expression coined for the people (*ʿām*) gathered before the *ʿōhel môʿēd*, the Tent of Meeting (Exod. 33:7–11). The people were the people of the covenant and thus of the Mosaic law. In the desert narratives this *ʿēdâ* is divided up into tribes, clans, and families, led by elders, heads, and princes. The word expresses a concept of corporateness, in which the stress falls not on the total of individuals, but on the unity of the fellowship.

The *ʿēdâ* appears to have been constituted with the divine command to leave Egypt and to celebrate the Passover (its first occurrence is Exod. 12:3). It is Israel that travels through the desert, that rebels, and that experiences God's help (Exod. 16:1–35; Num. 20:1–29). But Israel is also the witness of God's revelation and receiver of his commands (Exod. 34:31–32; 35:1). Israel offers sacrifices (Lev. 4:13–21) and can become guilty through the sin of individuals (10:6). But Israel also keeps watch over the maintenance of the covenant to the point of carrying out its sentences (see 24:14, 16; Num. 15:35–36). In preserving Israel's purity, the priests play an important role as representatives and mediators to God (cf. Lev. 4:13–21; 8:3–13; 9:5–7; Num. 3:7; 8:9, 20; 15:22–26).

But *ʿēdâ* means not only the community centered in the cult or the law (Num. 35:12, 24). In the sense of *ʿām* it also represents the community as a people. It is the *ʿēdâ* that receives and deplores the report of the spies (13:26; 14:1–10). It is to the *ʿēdâ* that the troops returning from battle (31:12–14) and the leaders of the people (Jos. 9:18–21) have to justify themselves. Still, the *ʿēdâ* itself does not wage war, but appoints forces to do it (cf. Num. 31:3–6). Otherwise, however, the word in practice covers the people as a community in all its functions.

On the other hand, the *ʿēdâ* is not bound to a particular land or place. The generation of the desert did not yet have a specific place, and the generation of the exile had it no longer. The tent and the ark were the symbols and the source of that obedience to the law that so strongly characterized the postexilic community. For this reason, in contrast to *qāhāl*, *ʿēdâ* never refers to any people other than Israel and clearly needs no other special qualification: only 4x is the name of Yahweh added.

(c) The above differences become clear from those passages in which both words occur in the same context (e.g., Exod. 12:1–6; 16:1–3; Num. 14:1–7; 20:1–8). *ʿēdâ* is the unambiguous and permanent term for the covenant community as a whole, while *qāhāl* is the ceremonial expression for the assembly that results from the covenant. It can also stand for the regular assembly of the people on secular (Num.

10:7; 1 Ki. 12:3) or religious occasions (Ps. 22:25), as well as for a gathering crowd (Num. 14:5; 17:12).

3. Where *ekklēsia* is used in the LXX for *qāhāl*, it indicates the assembly of the people or a judicial assembly (e.g., Deut. 9:10; 23:3–8; Jdg. 21:5, 8; Mic. 2:5), i.e., a political body (e.g., the returned exiles Ezr. 10:8, 12; Neh. 8:2, 17). It also indicates, especially in Chr., the assembly of the people for worship (e.g., 2 Chr. 6:3; 30:2, 4, 13, 17; cf. Joel 2:16). Still, even in these cases *ekklēsia* is only used where it is a question of the people as God's assembly, characterized by having answered Yahweh's call. Admittedly the word is used esp. where the historic greatness of Israel is implied and avoided where it could be a merely political claim. Perhaps that is why, in legal passages regulating the life of the community, *qāhāl* is translated by *synagōgē*.

synagōgē, on the other hand, apart from its general use as assembly, place of assembly, and the mustering of troops, was clearly used to denote the religiously defined community of Yahweh. It took over none of the usual Gk. terms for cultic assemblies but was a word without previous associations. Hence, we can understand why in the Pent. *qāhāl* was also translated by *synagōgē*. This choice of word could give expression to the fact that the present community had been given the law or that the laws were regularly read in public worship. Thus *synagōgē* is at the same time a reminder of the great events of salvation history and of the promises to Israel (cf. Num. 14:7–9). The term also acquired eschatological significance from its context (Isa. 56:8; Ezek. 37:10).

4. At Qumran, *qāhāl* occurs only seldom, and then for the summoned assembly of the community. *ʿēdâ*, on the other hand, serves both as a designation for the unified congregation and for the remnant of Israel. It also appears as a word for the elect. But we also read in Qumran documents of the congregation of Belial, of wickedness, of scoffers, etc. This reflects the struggle between true and false congregations, which can be decided only by obedience to Yahweh.

NT 1. The origin of the Jewish synagogue is somewhat of a mystery, though many scholars think it started during the time of the exile, when what held the Jews together as a people was their common bond in their Scriptures. During NT times, the synagogue was the regular place where Jews everywhere in the Roman world met for worship and teaching. It was the place where the apostle Paul regularly began his ministry in a new city (e.g., Acts 13:14; 14:1;17:1–2). The official whose duty it was to take care of the physical arrangements for the worship services was the *archisynagōgos*. Toward the end of the first century, it appears as if Christians were no longer welcome in the synagogue. Whatever process that may have been used to "evict" them is perhaps anachronistically reflected in the *aposynagōgos* of Jn. 9:22; 12:42; 16:2.

2. (a) It is striking that Jesus' followers did not describe their meetings and community as a *synagōgē* (except for Jas. 2:2), for that word would have been natural for a group that sprang from Jewish roots and, at least in the beginning, counted itself a part of Jud. *synagōgē* occurs in the NT (apart from Jas. 2:2; Rev. 2:9; 3:9) only in the Gospels and Acts. It describes either the meeting place of the local Jewish community or the congregation itself (often the word carries both meanings).

Acts 6:9 mentions that Stephen's opponents came from the "Synagogue of the Freedmen (as it was called)—Jews of Cyrene and Alexandria as well as the provinces of Cilicia and Asia." There were several synagogues in Jerusalem, no doubt formed according to the country of origin of the members. Rev. 2:9 and 3:9 describe the Jewish assembly as a whole as "a synagogue of Satan." Their claim to be a congregation of God, the true Israel, is disputed and the title claimed for the Christians.

The polemic of Jn., Acts 6, and Rev. suggests why the early church avoided *synagōgē* as a term to describe itself: This term came to be regarded as the symbol of the Jewish legal religion. Once the law of Moses effectively took central place in Jewish life and liturgy (cf.

Matt. 23:2), the idea of the synagogue must have seemed so rigid to Christians that they separated from it in favor of a reformed Christian assembly. A word with such connotations could not be used to describe a fellowship and an event, at the center of which was the proclamation of a gospel of freedom from law and of salvation available only through faith in Jesus Christ.

(b) What is immediately striking about *ekklēsia* is that, except for Matt. 16:18 and 18:17, the word is absent from the Gospels. The fact that Luke uses the word 23x in Acts suggests that he consciously avoided using it for the group belonging to the period of Jesus' earthly activity. By far the majority of occurrences of the word appears in Paul's letters (62x out of 114x). It is Paul in particular who shaped this concept.

3. *The primitive community*. The absence of the word *ekklēsia* from the Gospels cannot be explained by saying that at the time of their writing the concept was not in current use, since the Gospels received their literary form contemporary with or later than Paul's letters. One can say with certainty that all the early Christian writers used *ekklēsia* only for those fellowships that came into being after the crucifixion and resurrection of Jesus. Though Jesus himself called together the Twelve, he did not found the *ekklēsia* as such in his own lifetime.

But equally clearly a consciousness of the church arose as early as the primitive Christian community. Its roots lie in the fact that some of the disciples became witnesses of resurrection appearances and were commissioned to bear the news that the time of salvation had dawned. In other words, the concept of the church developed through the consciousness of being in the eschatological situation created by the resurrection appearances (cf. 1 Cor. 15:3–11). The early Christian *ekklēsia* understood itself as the herald of the lordship of Christ, which was already being realized in their midst. But the church was also aware that it was still part of this age and was therefore not identical with the *basileia*, the kingdom of God.

4. *Paul's letters*. (a) When Paul speaks of the *ekklēsia*, which he does in individual letters with different emphases, his starting point is the proclamation of Christ. When people receive the salvation message in faith, Christ becomes present and real in their experience. The *ekklēsia* appears as the event in which God fulfills his election through his personal call (Rom. 8:29–30). For this reason he can speak of the *klētoi*, the called, when he means the Christian community (e.g., Rom. 1:6–7; 1 Cor. 1:2).

For the same reason Paul addresses his letters to Thessalonica to the *ekklēsia* of the Thessalonians *en theō patri*, in God the Father (1 Thess. 1:1–2; 2 Thess. 1:1–2), a formula that links the idea of the church as event with that of the local church. It is not difficult to recognize the basic idea of the OT *qāhāl*. But the *ekklēsia* of the Thessalonians also introduces the claim that the call of God, which has gone out through the apostle and other preachers in the form of the offer of reconciliation (cf. 2 Cor. 5:19–20), has brought together this assembly. It represents for this place God's new creation.

It is not only the church's origin that lies with God. The *ekklēsia* can only be understood in relation to the Lord as the *ekklēsia tou theou*, the congregation of God (1 Cor. 1:2; 11:16, 22; 15:9; 2 Cor. 1:1; Gal. 1:13; 1 Thess. 2:14; 2 Thess. 1:4). Only Gal. 1:22 and Rom. 16:16 have the qualifying *en Christō*, in Christ, or *tou Christou*, of Christ.

(b) The fact that *ekklēsia* has the nature of an event does not, however, exclude the factor of continuity. The church expresses itself in permanent forms and institutions, where the Lord will continue to make his presence real. Coming together (*synagō*) must be reckoned an essential element in *ekklēsia* (cf. 1 Cor. 11:18). Hence the *ekklēsia* should be thought of in purely concrete terms.

Paul never uses the word *ekklēsia* to express an invisible body—a concept that arose in the context of hypocrisy and deceit. The church fathers who developed this concept insisted that those who belong to God are visible to him alone. The idea recalls 2 Tim. 2:19: "The Lord knows those who are his." It extends to the church, in other words, what Paul said of Israel, that they are not all Israel who belong to

Israel, but only "the children of the promise" (Rom. 9:6–8). It recognizes the danger, which church members are warned against, of reaping corruption through sowing to the flesh (Gal. 3:7; cf. Rom. 8:12–13). Thus, while the precise application of invisible to the word *ekklēsia* may be missing, the concept of an invisible church is present (cf. Matt. 13:24–43; 25:31–46; Heb. 2:3; 3:7–4:14; 6:1–12; 10:26–39; 12:12–28).

The *ekklēsia* has its location, existence, and being within definable geographical limits. The apostle thus writes of "the church of God in Corinth" (1 Cor. 1:2; 2 Cor. 1:1), indicating both that it belongs to the people of that place and has a new and different quality. Those who are drawn into the *ekklēsia* live in the sphere of power of the new creation (2 Cor. 5:17). But they are not removed from their position in the social order. They remain Israelites, Romans, slaves, freedmen, etc. (cf. 1 Cor. 7:17–24). But these differences lose the divisive power that prevents unity and fellowship (cf. Gal. 3:27–29). Thus, those counted among the "saints," as Paul calls the members of the *ekklēsia* (1 Cor. 1:2; Phil. 1:1; → *hagios*, 41), are those whom the Lord calls, to whom he gives faith, and whose participation in the new life is indicated by baptism (Rom. 6:3–4).

(c) Paul best expressed his understanding of the Christian community by calling it a body (*sōma*, cf. Rom. 12:1–5; 1 Cor. 12:12–27; → *5393*). The fact that the Christian community is a body, and the body of Christ at that (1 Cor. 12:27), takes up the spatial idea. Belonging to Christ means becoming like a limb, part of an organism in which each unit has its own special function and gift (→ *charis*, *5921*), to be exercised in mutual giving and receiving.

There is no gradation according to importance in the *ekklēsia*. Rather, it embraces gifts of leadership and organization, as well as of healing, speaking in tongues, and the discernment of spirits (Rom. 12:4–8; 1 Cor. 12:14–31). These are all manifestations of the working of the one Spirit, i.e., of the presence of the exalted Lord in this his body. Their development and orderly growth requires Christian community life (1 Cor. 14:33).

Paul did not intend to secure this reality by means of a rigid system of offices. The exercise of the gifts must be thought of concretely. Paul understands *ekklēsia* as the living, assembled congregation. Only in meeting and living together can love, described in 1 Cor. 13 as the supreme gift, be made real, just as it is only in this way that the other God-given gifts can be acknowledged and used. The situation at Corinth appears to be prior to the general adoption of institutionalized offices, such as bishop and elder (see Phil. 1:1; Acts; the Pastoral Letters). But even in 1 Tim. 3:15 the congregation is accorded greater intrinsic value than the office-holders, for it is the congregation that is the *oikos theou*, the house of God.

(d) The fact that the *ekklēsia* in the full sense exists in several places at once arises out of the concreteness of Paul's concept, for it points to the present manifestation of the expected rule (kingdom) of the crucified Christ (→ *basileus*, 995). This is why *ekklēsia* occurs so frequently in the pl., whether it refers to the different congregations in an area (e.g., 1 Cor. 16:1; Gal. 1:2, 22), to a number of churches, or to all of them (e.g., Rom. 16:16; 1 Cor. 7:17; 14:33–34).

The fact that small groups in individual houses are called churches (Rom. 16:5; 1 Cor. 16:19; Phlm. 2; cf. Col. 4:15) indicates that neither the significance of the place nor the numerical size of the assembly determines the use of the term. What counts is the presence of Christ among them (cf. Gal. 3:1), Christ's revelation of himself to them (cf. 1 Cor. 3:4–10), and faith nourished by him. Hence, the collections for Jerusalem (1 Cor. 16:1; 2 Cor. 8:19) are not an expression of respect for the superiority of the Jerusalem church, but an expression of fellowship under the one Lord.

(e) While *ekklēsia* generally refers to its particular local form, there is nevertheless *one ekklēsia*. The passages that make this clear are those in which Paul recalls the time when he still persecuted the church (1 Cor. 15:9; Gal. 1:13; Phil. 3:6). There is one church because the Lord of the church is one. Baptism seals the relationship with

Christ, and in the Lord's Supper those who are in Christ experience their corporate nature. These are particular events, tied to particular places, and yet at the same time they are related to the body of Christ in its totality. Therefore, despite differences of detail, there can exist not only the one faith, but beyond that, common rules and even ordinances (1 Cor. 7:17; 11:16; 14:40; 16:1), laid down and enforced by the authority of the apostle.

(f) In Col. and Eph., the church as body (*sōma*) is developed in terms of the relationship of the members to the head (*kephalē*, Col. 1:18). Those who have been rescued by the Father out of the realm of the powers of darkness and transferred into the kingdom of the Son become a part of this body (1:13). They share in redemption and the forgiveness of sins and have entered the peace that Christ has created (Col. 1:20; cf. Eph. 2:12–22). The reconciliation achieved by Christ in his death and announced by his messengers is the beginning of the *ekklēsia*, in terms both of chronology and of relative significance. The *sōma* of the *ekklēsia* thus becomes a way to describe the sphere towards which Christ's lordship is directed.

Eph. develops this thought in the assertion that through the *ekklēsia* the wisdom of God is made known even to the cosmic powers (Eph. 3:10; 4:8–10). They have lost their influence (Col. 2:14–15, 20), for Christ, who in any case stands over them, has reconciled heaven and earth (Eph. 1:20–21; Col. 1:15–20). The emphasis in Eph. falls on the mystical unity of the body (esp. Eph. 4:3–13). It serves as a picture of growth to maturity (4:13; Col. 2:19). A sharp contrast is now made between the head and the body—the Lord stands over against his church, which is completely dependent upon him.

The concept also takes on an organizational aspect, related to the role of offices (cf. Eph. 4:11). What was earlier to be the concern of the whole congregation is now the responsibility of specific officials: to equip the saints to carry out their duty (4:12).

5. *Matthew and Luke*. (a) From the context, *ekklēsia* in Matt. 18:17 is to be understood as the number of those living and meeting in one place. Matt. is interested in tracing the outlines of an order for the new community. This suggests that *ekklēsia* is used here in the OT sense of *ʿēdâ*, synagogue.

The interpretation of Matt. 16:18 is more difficult. Does the "I will build," for example, refers to Jesus' lifetime or to the period after his death? In general, it is best to see the future tense as referring to the period after Jesus' death. Jesus is not speaking here of a church coming into being at this moment. Rather, *ekklēsia* here is the eschatological assembly of the true people of God. The statement that "the gates of Hades (i.e., the powers of death) will not overcome it" has its foundation in the fact that this community is linked to the risen Christ as victor over death.

(b) For Luke the period of the church is a particular segment of salvation history between Jesus' resurrection and return. This follows directly from the use he makes of the word. While *ekklēsia* is completely absent from his Gospel, he uses the term 23x from Acts 5:11 onwards (but not in Acts 2).

(c) In Acts, as in Paul, *ekklēsia* indicates first of all Christians living and meeting in a particular place: e.g., the early community in Jerusalem (5:11; 8:1; 11:22; 12:1, 5), the church at Antioch (13:1), and elsewhere. Acts 20:28 characterizes the *ekklēsia* as *ekklēsia tou theou*, the church of God, an idea that may be understood throughout. It becomes this through the Spirit, who incorporates individual members into the church. It is the Spirit who moves and equips the church (1:5, 8; 2:4–21; cf. 4:31–37) and for whose sake it is attacked and persecuted (7:55–60).

In Acts too the *ekklēsia* is ultimately one. Admittedly, it appears only as it gathers in particular places (cf. 14:27), but it always implies the totality. As in the OT (cf. 7:38, which refers to Israel in the desert period), the *ekklēsia* is those who follow the call of God and come together (cf. *synagō* in 14:27); yet even when their meeting is over, they retain their quality of *ekklēsia*. It is one throughout the world, yet is at the same time fully present in every individual assembly. Luke can use the sing. to refer to the church at large (8:3) as well as to "the church throughout Judea, Galilee and Samaria" (9:31).

6. *The Johannine writings.* (a) Jn. focuses attention on the fact that in this world of death and unbelief, which cannot recognize the Lord (Jn. 1:10; 14:17), people can still experience birth from above (3:3 –21; cf. 1:12–13) and pass from death to life. Unlike Acts, with its households and local groups, Jn. always refers to individuals who come to this faith and knowledge.

The application to Jesus of Jewish concepts for the eschatological people of God (e.g., vine, 15:1–8; shepherd and flock, 10:1–18) shows Jesus to be the one revealer and fulfiller. Jn. draws attention to the unbridgeable gulf between faith and unbelief and recognizes that only God can bring a person to Jesus (6:44; 17:2). This emphasis on the individual is balanced by Jesus' command to mutual love (13:34–35), without any organizational forms and terms coming into view. Allegiance has long ago been determined by God (10:1–6; 26–30; 17:6), so even coming together in unity can only be his work (17:21).

(b) In Rev., however, *ekklēsia* (as in Acts) means the congregation that has grown up, exists, and meets in a particular place. Until 22:16, all the references occur in the letters of chs. 2 and 3 or in the vision of the seven lampstands (1:4, 11, 20; i.e., the seven *ekklēsiai* in Asia). In 22:16, the exalted Jesus speaks to the churches through his angel. The references in 3 Jn. 6, 9, 10 are all to a local Christian assembly.

7. *James and Hebrews.* Jas. 5:14, which deals with the elders of the *ekklēsia*, uses the word in the technical sense for a local congregation organized according to the pattern of a Jewish synagogue; Heb. 2:12 cites Ps. 22:22 (Heb. *qāhāl*) and means the cultic festival gathering. Heb. 12:23 is different. Here the word occurs in a series of eschatological terms taken from Jewish tradition: Believers are qualified as "the church of the firstborn, whose names are written in heaven." Entrance into this "church" is understood as entering into fellowship with "righteous men made perfect" and with "Jesus the mediator of a new covenant." It is not here a question of the description of a group, but of the characterization of the eschatological event (the service of worship).

8. There remains the question of other terms used to denote the Christian community, particularly in writings in which *ekklēsia* is absent or rare.

(a) The Gospels frequently (e.g., 68x in Matt.; 58 x in Jn.) use *mathētēs*, disciple, to refer to Jesus' followers. In the NT (it is absent from the LXX), it occurs primarily in the pl. The word originally denoted those who were devoted to the teaching of a master and were committed to passing it on. Since *mathētēs* does not occur outside the Gospels and Acts, we have a stratum of tradition in which the corporate concepts for the Christian community have not yet been formulated. It belongs to the period of the first gathering of people around the earthly Jesus, and in Acts around the exalted Jesus, thought of as present in the Spirit.

(b) It is different with the pl. *hoi hagioi*, the saints, which occur 4x in Acts (always in narratives about Paul) and 38x in Paul for the members of the churches. The saints are also called the elect (Rom. 1:7; 1 Cor. 1:2), those who have been sanctified by God. The word indicates the true Israel and was probably first used for the original congregation in Jerusalem (Acts 9:13; 1 Cor. 16:1) and then for Christians in general.

(c) This conviction led Peter to use a whole series of Jewish expressions shaped by the OT. The letter is addressed to "God's elect, strangers" (1 Pet. 1:1), who are called to be *hagioi*, holy (1:15), and already "believe in God" (1:21). They are described as "a chosen people, a royal priesthood, a holy nation, a people belonging to God" (2:9)—all of which reflect OT language. The Christian community is nothing new; it is to be understood as the fulfillment of the promises and hopes given to Israel. They come together as living stones in a spiritual house (2:5–8) and serve one another with different gifts as God's grace is revealed in them (4:10). In the process, the OT order of elders

seems to have been taken over (cf. 5:1–4; → *presbyteros*, 4565). In all this, according to the terminology of shepherd and flock, Christ stands at the head as chief shepherd, i.e., as Messiah.

(d) The members of the congregation are also called *adelphoi*, brothers (→ *81*). The term occurs most frequently in Paul (96x), but also in Acts, the Johannine letters, Jas., and Heb.

See also *synagō*, gather (*5251*).

1719 (eklampō, shine forth), → *3290.*

1721	ἐκλέγομαι

ἐκλέγομαι (*eklegomai*), pick out for oneself, choose (out) (*1721*); ἐκλεκτός (*eklektos*), chosen (out) (*1723*); ἐκλογή (*eklogē*), picking out, election, selection (*1724*).

CL 1. In cl. Gk., words in this word group refer to the election and/or selection of persons or things. *eklogē* is sometimes used of the general conscription of men for military service or the selection of individual soldiers from the army for a particularly difficult or glorious mission. *eklegomai* and *eklogē* are esp. used in a political sense, for the election of people to perform a certain task or administer a certain office (e.g., the elders of the *polis*). Such election placed a responsibility on the elected person, usually to act with a concern for the well-being of the other members of the community.

2. The words may be applied to objects. *eklegomai* is used to denote a decision in favor of what is intellectually or aesthetically good, or the selection of esp. treasured passages from lit. *eklogē* can also refer to the requisition of material (e.g., ships) or the levying of official tribute and taxes. In every case a part has been claimed from a greater quantity by an independent act of decision for a particular purpose.

3. Certain Stoic writers use this word for a single person's free decision between two or more possibilities with respect to one's manner of life, livelihood, or use of material goods.

OT 1. (a) The noun *eklogē* does not occur in the LXX, primarily since there is no comparable Heb. noun. The fact that only verbal forms are found results in an emphasis not on the action but on the person who chooses and the one chosen (*eklektos*). The act. form of *eklegō* occurs only 10x, especially in the books of Ki. and Chr. The mid. *eklegomai* nearly always renders forms of the Heb. vb. *bāhar*, choose, select, prefer. This Heb. vb. has roughly the same range of meanings as the Gk. vb. (see Isa. 40:20, where it denotes one's choice of suitable material for an idol; Gen. 6:2, the carefully considered choice of a wife; 13:11, Lot's choice of the part of the land that seemed to him most favorable).

In Prov. the niph. of *bāhar* portrays one object as desirable in comparison to another, e.g., a devout and obedient life before God as preferable to gold and silver (Prov. 8:10, 19; 16:16). The vb. is also used for the people's election of a king (1 Sam. 8:18). The part. *bāhûr* and the adj. *bāhîr* can describe specially chosen elite troops (cf. Jdg. 20:15–16; 1 Sam. 24:2; 2 Chr. 25:5) or particularly suitable material (Exod. 14:7). *bāhar* (translated with *eklegō*) also refers to the basic religious decision of choosing between Yahweh and other gods (Jos. 24:15), or between life in God's temple and life in the world of evildoers (Ps. 84:10).

(b) In the majority of cases where *bāhar* (and thus *eklegō*) is found, God is the one who chooses. In Deut., besides the people whom God has singled out for a special mission (4:37; 7:7; 14:2), the referent is above all the one place God has appointed for his people as a center for worship and for sacrifices (cf. 16:6–7; 18:5–6; 26:2). In 1 Ki. (cf. 11:13, 32; 14:21) and 2 Chr. (cf. 6:34, 38; 12:13), this is defined more closely as Jerusalem, the city of David. David himself is also described as chosen (1 Ki. 8:16; 11:34). In the cultic sphere we find God's choice of the priests (Deut. 18:5; 1 Sam. 2:28; 1 Chr. 15:2; 16:41). Saul and David were chosen by God as kings (1 Sam. 10:24;

16:8–10; 2 Sam. 6:21). Finally, the later chapters of Isa. refer to God's choice of his Servant (Isa. 43:10) and of Jacob and Abraham (41:8).

2. This emphasis on God's action is further strengthened by the fact that the part. *bāḥûr*, which points to the quality of the object, is not used of Israel as the chosen people; instead, the adj. *bāḥîr* is used (in Gk., *eklektos* is used for both words). This means theologically that the OT is concerned with not drawing attention to the importance or status of the nation. Rather, God chooses freely out of grace, not because of human merit. *bāḥîr* (cf. 2 Sam. 21:6; Ps. 105:43; Isa. 42:1; 65:22 = LXX 65:23) also indicates that the purpose of that choice is some commission, and that such election can only meaningfully retain its validity in the fulfillment of that service. The whole outlook of Deut., as well as that of Isa., sees in this activity of God the creation among the nations of a new, different type of community, whose purpose is to show God's sovereign acts and grace and the seriousness of his demands.

The doctrine of election is thus an indissoluble part of the knowledge of God's holiness, uniqueness, and unconditioned sovereignty. It expresses the total claim he makes in keeping with these aspects of his nature. This line of thought reaches its climax in the passages of Isa. that speak of God's servant (*pais theou*, → *4090*), who appears as God's agent in the redemption of all humanity. God's election is not based on human qualifications, nor does it create a position of privilege. Hence, it can only be maintained meaningfully where it leads to a response of love for God, obedience, and the kind of life presupposed by the commandments. It is not a goal already reached, but a beginning that has to be confirmed. Thus, we find a warning that God may reject again those whom he has drawn to him in this way (cf. 1 Sam. 16:1; Jer. 14:19).

3. There is, however, a danger of thinking and speaking of those who are chosen, their qualifications, and the difference between them and other people, as if it belonged to an elite who deserved preference by reason of their struggles, sufferings, stricter discipline, or greater self-sacrifice. Rab. theology, and even more so apocalyptic (→ *mystērion*, *3696*), effected such a transformation in the interpretation of suffering in connection with the Servant passages in Isa. They saw proof of election in unyielding resistance in times of affliction. Therefore, utmost importance came to be attached to the possession and knowledge of the Torah as a basis for belief in election, giving Israel an advantage over others (cf. 2 Esd. 5:23–27). This was expressed particularly in thoughts of vengeance, which also influenced this line of thought (cf. *1 Enoch* 62:11–15).

Election thus became a status and privilege that could be recognized and achieved by means of dubious merits. It was a continuation of these ideas when the OT teaching about the difference between the true, spiritual Israel and mere political and physical membership of the people, esp. in the context of resistance to Hellenistic "infiltration," led the devout to separate themselves off into exclusive groups. Inevitably this brought the concept of individual election further to the fore. This is esp. apparent in the Qumran texts (e.g., 1QS 4:22; 8:1–15), in which consciousness of being chosen led not only to a feeling of superiority over other nations and over the ungodly but also to a direct hatred for those who have been rejected (1:3–4). Certain aspects of Pharisaic piety, such as their contempt for the common people (*ʿam hāʾ āreṣ*), are also expressive of such an attitude (→ *Pharisaios*, *5757*).

NT 1. In the NT, the vb. *eklegomai* and the part. *eklektos* (used as a subst.) each occur 22x, relatively seldom in comparison with the LXX. The noun *eklogē*, not found in the LXX, is found 7x, chiefly in Paul.

(a) Matt. and Mk. use *eklektos* in the pl. in the context of eschatological sayings. This use is clearly in the same sense as Jewish tradition, according to which the object of election is a body of people, even though it is spoken of as many individuals (cf. also the *genos eklekton* in 1 Pet. 2:9). The sing. is applied to Jesus Christ in Lk. 23:35 and 1 Pet. 2:4, 6. It is used once (Rom. 16:13) of an individual church

member. It occurs also in 2 Jn. 1 and 13 with *kyria* or *adelphē*, but the references there are hardly to individual persons, but rather to churches.

(b) Of the 22 uses of *eklegomai*, always mid. (most of them in Lk. and Acts), the subj. of the vb. may be grouped under four heads. (i) In 4 places in Acts (6:5; 15:22, 25; possibly 1:24) the vb. indicates appointment by the church to a particular office. (ii) Lk. 14:7 describes the self-esteem in which human beings indulge when they choose special seats at table. (iii) In Lk. 10:42 Mary's decision to devote herself exclusively to the words of Jesus is described by saying that she has chosen the good part (cf. 1 Sam. 15:22). (iv) In all other cases, it is used in connection with God's or Christ's work of election. John consistently represents Christ as the agent of election (Jn. 6:70; 13:18; 15:16, 19); in Lk. 6:13 Luke speaks of Jesus' selection of the Twelve.

(c) The noun *eklogē* is used unambiguously and exclusively for God's act of election: in Rom. 9:11; 11:5, 7, 28, each time with reference to Israel; in 1 Thess. 1:4 and 2 Pet. 1:10, where the church is reminded that God's election is the basis of her existence; and in Acts 9:15, the only case in which the meaning is slightly different, for Paul is described in the words of the exalted Lord as a *skeuos eklogēs*, a vessel of election—i.e., an instrument by means of which God operates and makes effective his choice.

2. If we concentrate on those passages in which God is the subject, we should note first what is said about the circumstances and purpose of God's elective activity, and then about the unique position given to Christ or attributed to him. It is necessary to speak in these terms since all the statements about election arose as a result of reflection on the part of these witnesses to God's work *after* they had encountered him and been added to the church. It was then that they began to face the question of where the fundamental starting point lay on their own road to faith, and of what was the foundation of a church that was able to survive temptation and persecution.

In other words, NT writers were asking themselves whether faith and discipleship were the fruit of human temperament and human decision, or whether the secret lay elsewhere as to how an obedient response came to be made to the call that went out through the preaching of the gospel. Statements about election are thus an attempt to express the truth that the existence of a people of God can be explained only on the basis of God's plan, will, and action, and not from a series of human resolves.

The problem is presented most clearly in Matt. 22:14, where we find added to a parable the epigrammatic saying: "Many are invited (*klētoi*), but few are chosen (*eklektoi*)." Historical experience offers a surprising result, for not all to whom God shows favor actually arrive at the goal of this call. This saying of Jesus directs attention to two facts: (1) Between the first stage and the last God is active in relation to humankind; and (2) arrival at this goal is based solely on God's gracious choice.

3. In Rom. 9–11 Paul, whose whole outlook on life has been shaken to the roots, wrestles with this problem as it relates to Israel's position before God in view of her rejection of Christ. Paul comes to the conclusion that Israel is counted as God's chosen people because of a free decision of God, dependent not on any conditions, but solely on the one who elects. The nation continues to enjoy God's love in election, not because of blood descent, but because of God's promise (Rom. 9:11–12; 11:28). Since election was a free act of God's grace, not all have in fact reached the goal (cf. Matt. 22:14). But although the majority have gone astray, there remains a remnant (Rom. 11:5, 7). Moreover, God does not abandon his aim, even though for the time being all seems lost. The interval during which Israel rejects God's purpose serves rather to extend the horizon of his grace to the Gentiles (Rom. 11:28–32).

In Paul's speech in Acts 13:17, he likewise draws attention to the choice of Israel through the patriarchs. Luke also gives expression to the Pauline thought of Rom. 11 in Peter's address in Acts 15:7. This is the only passage in which *ta ethnē*, the nations or Gentiles (→ *1620*), are expressly named as the object or sphere of operation of God's elective activity. The barrier is now broken down; salvation is available to all. This does not mean, of course, that the mystery of God's electing grace has been fathomed. It is based on a plan, yet it is not an automatic process that one can predict. It is the action of God in history that is always open to modification.

4. Is there any discernible reason for God's activity of selecting those whom he chooses? As before, Luke hints at the answer in his Gospel. In the story of the Transfiguration, where the heavenly voice bears witness to the greatness of Jesus (Lk. 9:35), Lk. uses *eklelegmenos*, chosen, where the other Synoptics have *agapētos* (cf. Matt. 17:5; Mk. 9:7). In other words, the whole elective activity of God reaches its culmination in his Son, who abstains in his behavior from every attempt to assert himself. Jesus is God's Chosen One. The ultimate goal of all previous election was to prepare the way for him to be revealed.

If we add to this the teaching of 1 Pet., we find that through Jesus is revealed also the lack of understanding among humanity in general and even among God's own people. The possibility of recognizing God's work in and through Jesus is closed to them. It is the one rejected and cast out by humankind (cf. 3 above) whom God makes his chosen cornerstone (1 Pet. 2:4, 6; cf. Ps. 118:22; Isa. 28:16). The consequences of being God's chosen one becomes apparent in his life.

5. It is on this cornerstone, Christ, that God builds up his church from the nations. At the same time the continuity of the covenant is assured in him. As humans are called by election, the church comes into being as the body of Christ, the new *genos eklekton* (1 Pet. 2:9), the chosen race. Wherever we read of the election of the church (e.g., 1 Thess. 1:4), the underlying thought is that of the basis of its existence in Christ. It is significant how seldom this is mentioned in the NT. Generally, its existence is attributed directly to God's grace.

However, in the "little apocalypse" (Mk. 13 par.) and Lk. 18:7, the church is spoken of as the elect (*eklektoi*). This appears in the context of the persecution believers are to endure, the suffering they are to bear in the course of discipleship, and the protection they will be given by God, who entirely for their sake will go so far as to shorten the time (Mk. 13:20 par.). Only their belonging to Christ will protect the church's members from judgment and condemnation (Rom. 8:33).

With direct reference to the apostles but also as an example of what is true of disciples generally, John shows Christ as the one who chooses and puts God's election into effect. In Jn. 6:70; 13:18; 15:16, 19, Jesus is the explicit subj. (with an emphatic *egō*, I) of *eklegomai*. Lk. 6:13 likewise refers to Jesus' choice of the apostles (see also Acts 1:24). The Chosen One of God is God's agent of choice. In Christ, God's favor has already been bestowed on us, and it comes to us effectively in the call that goes out and invites us through Christ.

6. As to what underlies God's choice, the NT is clear that he bestows favor upon human beings and joins them to himself solely on the basis of his own free decision and his love, which are not dependent on any temporal circumstances. This is the deeper meaning of Eph. 1:4, where the expression "before the creation of the world" is not to be understood in a purely temporal sense. Rather, it refers to a decision rooted in the depths of God's nature, like his *prognōsis* (foreknowledge) or *prothesis* (purpose). (Cf. the chain of verbs in Rom. 8:29–30, whose tense suggests that all these actions are already past.) In any case, what is revealed of God's work of election runs across all the usual human standards. With majestic independence he passes by those who are worthy of respect (or have they scornfully rejected his call?) and presents as his elect the poor (Jas. 2:5), the weak, the foolish, and the despised of this world (1 Cor. 1:27–28).

Does this result in a pure community of the elect? As far as their character in God's eyes is concerned, yes. But the question attributed to Jesus in Jn. 6:70 gives food for thought. Among the company of the elect there is a devil! Is it possible to fall from grace? Certainly the assurance of election must never be allowed to turn into a false sense of security. As early as 1 Thess. 1:4, but stated more clearly in Col. 3:12 and 2 Pet. 1:10, we find the reminder of the manifestation of

God's grace linked with an imperative, an exhortation also to live in it, to prove oneself as one whom God has sanctified. Only when faith is lived out is election evident (cf. Tit. 1:1). We can only really speak of election when we also give due weight to what Jn. emphasizes, but which is always implicit: the commission to fruit-bearing service, obedience, and a God-fearing and God-trusting life.

1723 (eklektos, chosen out), → *1721.*

1724 (eklogē, picking out, election, selection), → *1721.*

1725 (eklyō, become loose, become weary, become weak), → *3395.*

1729 (eknēphō, become sober, come to one's senses), → *3768.*

1733 (ekpeirazō, put to the test, try, tempt), → *4280.*

1738 (ekpiptō, fall off or from, lose one's way), → *4406.*

1742	ἐκπλήσσω

ἐκπλήσσω (*ekplēssō*), amaze, astound (*1742*).

CL & OT The root meaning of *ekplēssō* is to strike out or expel. The vb. is found with this sense in cl. Gk., but it occurs far more frequently with its derived meaning of astound or amaze. Among the sources of amazement expressed by this vb. in nonbiblical lit. are fear, desire, love, joy, and pleasure. In Eccl. 7:16 (= LXX 7:17) this vb. means "be appalled" in the sense of "be destroyed." In Wis. 13:4 it is used with reference to those who are ignorant of the true God and are "amazed" at the powerful deeds of false gods (here fire, wind, and the luminaries). This vb. is also used to describe the amazement that pagans felt when God's people willingly underwent martyrdom (2 Macc. 7:12; 4 Macc. 17:16; cf. 8:4).

NT *ekplēssō* occurs 13x in the NT, though only once outside the Gospels (and then in Acts). It is always found in the pass. ("be amazed"). In most cases it expresses the astonished reaction of uncommitted onlookers to Jesus' teaching (e.g., Mk. 1:22 par.; 6:2 par.); once it refers to a demonstration of his healing power (Lk. 9:43). Only Luke names individuals as the subject of this vb.: Mary and Joseph are amazed to find the boy Jesus sitting among the temple teachers (2:48), and the proconsul Sergius Paulus is "amazed at the teaching about the Lord" (Acts 13:12).

See also *ekstasis*, distraction, confusion, astonishment, terror, trance, ecstasy (*1749*); *mainomai*, rave, be mad (*3419*).

1743 (ekpneō, breathe out), → *4460.*

1748 (ekrizoō, uproot), → *1285.*

1749	ἔκστασις

ἔκστασις (*ekstasis*), distraction, confusion, astonishment, terror, trance, ecstasy (*1749*); ἐξίστημι (*existēmi*), trans. drive out of one's senses, confuse, astound; intrans. lose one's mind, be amazed (*2014*).

CL & OT In cl. Gk. *ekstasis* originally meant a change of location, then metaphorically confusion, terror, madness. The specific meaning ecstasy, in which consciousness is partially or entirely nonoperative through the work of a divine power, is found esp. in Philo. The vb. *existēmi* means confuse, terrify; in the mid. lose one's wits.

Neither vb. nor noun is used in the LXX with the specific sense of ecstasy (for such states *prophēteuō* [→ *4736*] is used). *ekstasis* often means confusion, terror, madness (Deut. 28:28; 1 Sam. 11:7; 14:15; Jer. 5:30 [S]; Zech. 12:4). *existēmi* in the act. sense occurs in Exod. 23:27; Jdg. 4:15; 8:12 with the same force as in secular Gk. The mid. *existamai* means lose one's wits in Isa. 28:7, but the meaning of be terrified, be frightened is more common (e.g., Ezek. 26:16; 27:35).

Ecstatic phenomena are found in the OT, such as the ecstasy of the elders in the desert (Num. 11:24–29) and the description of Balaam's trance condition (24:4). The ecstatic character of the early Israelite prophetic bands is described in 1 Sam. 10:5–6, 10; 19:20–24.

When at times prophets are said to be mad (2 Ki. 9:11; Hos. 9:7) or drunken (Isa. 28:7; Jer. 23:9), prophecy and ecstasy are linked. Israelite prophets claimed their visions as divine messages (cf. Jer. 23:16–17). False prophets also appeared in Israel and neighboring countries as ecstatics and visionaries (e.g., the prophets of Baal on Mount Carmel, opposed by Elijah, in 1 Ki. 18:28). Ecstasy, visions, and the claim to an oracle are not infallible signs that distinguish the true from the false prophet; only the message will do that. In the intertestamental period prophecy gradually died out.

NT In the NT *ekstasis* and *existēmi* express human reaction of astonishment to the wonderful acts of God (Mk. 2:12; 5:42; Lk. 5:26; Acts 3:10), as do *thaumazō* and related expressions (→ *thauma*, *2512*). The act. of *existēmi* occurs in Lk. 24:22 and Acts 8:9, 11, with the meaning terrify, amaze.

The statement of Jesus' relatives about him can be understood in the specific sense of ecstasy (Mk. 3:21), which would mean that he was taken to be an ecstatic. More likely, however, they were saying he was out of his mind, for the Gospels contain no ecstatic traits in Jesus' life of faith and prayer.

According to Acts 10:10; 11:5; 22:17, the visions seen by Peter in Joppa and Paul in Jerusalem occurred during a trance (*ekstasei*). Acts also records speaking in tongues, recognizing in it the work of the Holy Spirit (10:44, 46; 11:15, 17; 19:6), though without using words of this group to refer to it. But in 1 Cor. 14 Paul clearly regards this phenomenon as ecstatic (cf. 12:23). Paul even states in 12:18 that he was no stranger to speaking in tongues. This verse and Acts 22:17 suggest that the visions and revelations of 2 Cor. 12:2–7 were ecstatic experiences. The same may be true of John (Rev. 1:10; 4:1–2). If so, he was seized by the Spirit and carried up to heaven, just as Paul was in 2 Cor. 12:2, 4.

Paul's reticence in 2 Cor. 12 and his sober evaluation of speaking in tongues in 1 Cor. 14:19 show that one must not overrate the importance of ecstasy for the early church. Paul did not regard his initial vision of Christ on the road to Damascus as ecstatic (1 Cor. 9:1; 15:8; Gal. 1:16). The strong spiritual consciousness that meets us in the NT is founded on the certainty that the church has been given a new revelation in Christ, transcending all that has gone before. The examples of ecstatic pious experiences must be seen as a result, not as the cause, of this faith.

See also *mainomai*, rave, be mad (*3419*); *ekplēssō*, amaze, astound (*1742*).

1759	ἐκτινάσσω

ἐκτινάσσω (*ektinassō*), shake out, shake off (*1759*); ἀποτινάσσω (*apotinassō*), shake off (*701*).

CL & OT 1. In cl. Gk. *ektinassō* means shake out, as in cleaning clothes; search thoroughly, make a disturbance. *apotinassō* means shake off.

2. (a) *ektinassō* occurs 21x in the LXX. The Lord shook off the Egyptians in the midst of the sea, i.e., out of their chariots as they turned to flee (Exod. 14:27; Ps. 136:15). Neh. sealed an oath taken by the priests by shaking out his lap, symbolizing that anyone breaking the promise would be cursed by a life of homeless wandering, emptied of all his possessions (5:13). Fig. this word can express weakness: e.g., shaken off as easily as a locust (Ps. 109:23). Captive Jerusalem is told to stand up and shake herself free from the dust of despair in captivity and from the Gentiles (Isa. 52:2).

(b) In 1 Sam 10:2 *apotinassō* denotes how Saul's father ceased to be concerned about the lost animals. In Lam. 2:7 *apotinassō* means abhor, reject: The Lord has disowned, cast off, his sanctuary.

NT 1. (a) In commissioning the Twelve, Jesus tells them that where their message is not accepted, they are to "shake the dust off" (*ektinassō*, Matt. 10:14; Mk. 6:11; *apotinassō*, Lk. 9:5) their feet, a ges-

ture of abandonment. No trace of association with the house or city is to remain; these inhabitants are thus branded as no better than the heathen outside the covenant. Many Jewish travelers shook off the dust of Gentile territory from their sandals and clothes before reentering the promised land. Once the apostles have discharged their responsibilities to preach, those rejecting the gospel will suffer judgment, heavier even than that inflicted on Sodom and Gomorrah. The fate of those cities is often an OT type of fearful retribution for aggravated sin (Deut. 29:23; Isa. 13:19; Jer. 49:18; 50:40; Amos 4:11; Zeph. 2:9).

(b) Paul also follows Jesus' advice and makes use of the same dramatic symbolism when the Jews stir up opposition to his preaching in Pisidian Antioch (Acts 13:51) and when he makes his final break from the synagogue in Corinth (18:6).

2. *apotinassō* is used in its lit. sense to describe Paul's action in shaking the snake from his hand after the shipwreck on Malta (Acts 28:5).

See also *seiō*, shake, cause to quake, agitate (*4940*); *saleuō*, shake, cause to waver, unsettle, drive away (*4888*).

1762 (ektrepō, pass. turn away from, avoid), → *706*.

1765	ἔκτρωμα

ἔκτρωμα (*ektrōma*), miscarriage (*1765*).

CL & OT *ektrōma* is connected with the vb. *ektitrōskō*, to have a miscarriage. It is found esp. in medical language to denote a premature still birth. It occurs in the LXX in the suggestion that an untimely still birth would have been preferable to life (Job 3:16; Eccl. 6:3), and in the appearance of an aborted fetus (Num. 12:12).

NT In the NT the word occurs only in 1 Cor. 15:8, where Paul describes his encounter with the risen Christ: "Last of all he appeared to me also, as to one abnormally born (*tō ektrōmati*)." The definite art. (*tō*) in this passage draws attention to this birth as something singular and even shocking; it is softened only by the addition of the word "as" (*hōsperei*). The words "to me also" stand at the end of the Greek sentence in a place of emphasis and contrast Paul with the other apostles.

In the interpretation of this verse, 15:9 is decisive. Here Paul alludes to his unworthiness to be called an "apostle" (a title of honor), because he formerly persecuted the church. If *ektrōma* is thus understood not as premature birth but as still birth, the significance of Paul's choice of the word lies in his joyful gratitude that God chose him to be an apostle despite his utterly reprobate life as a former persecutor.

ektrōma was probably a term of abuse. It might refer to Paul's physique or infirmities, to which there are numerous allusions in his writings (e.g., 1 Cor. 2:3; 4:10; 2 Cor. 11:30; 12:7–10; Gal. 4:13–14). It might contain a hint that Paul was still too much influenced by the law and was not as spiritual as his opponents in Corinth (cf. 1 Cor. 2). There may be in it the suggestion that Paul was still an embryo believer, lacking the same period of "gestation" that the other apostles had. (These suggestions are not necessarily mutually exclusive.)

But Paul's words must also be understood in the context of the argument of 1 Cor. 15. Paul is concerned in 15:3–7 with the proof of Jesus' resurrection, based on his appearances to the apostles and to others. Referring to his own encounter with Christ on the Damascus road, Paul writes (lit.), "Last of all, as to the *ektrōma*, he appeared also to me" (1 Cor. 15:8; cf. 9:1; Gal. 1:16; Acts 9:3–6; 22:4–16; 26:9–18). The thought of the risen Christ's appearance to him leads immediately to the thought of his apostleship (1 Cor. 15:9), which some questioned (9:1). After all, Paul was a former persecutor of the church. Moreover, he lacked the two qualifications that were laid down when the other apostles considered a replacement for Judas: He had not been a disciple of Jesus in his earthly ministry, and he was not a witness like them of Jesus' resurrection (Acts 1:21–22).

Against this, Paul claimed to receive his apostleship directly from the risen Lord, whom he had seen (cf. the above references). Admittedly, he had not known the earthly Jesus and his encounter had happened after the ascension. Nevertheless, Paul insisted that he had encountered the risen Christ and received his apostleship directly from him. As such, the description of him as the aborted one may be triply apt. As a person Paul was not as acceptable as others. He was premature in the sense that he had not served the period of discipleship like the Twelve and had become an apostle at his conversion. But above all, he had encountered Christ as "one abnormally born"—sometime after the resurrection appearances to the others had ceased.

See also *gennaō*, beget, become the father of, bear (*1164*); *ginomai*, be born, become, happen (*1181*); *palingenesia*, rebirth, regeneration (*4098*); *tiktō*, bring forth, bear, give birth to (*5503*); *eugenēs*, well-born, noble in descent or character (*2302*).

| 1772 ἐκχέω | ἐκχέω (*echeō*), pour out (*1772*); ἐκχύννομαι (*ekchynnomai*), |

pour out (*1773*); σπένδω (*spendō*), pour out (a drink offering) (*5064*); πρόσχυσις (*proschysis*), pouring or sprinkling (of blood) (*4717*).

CL & OT 1. The simple form *cheō*, pour, is still in use in cl. Gk., but compounds (esp. *ekcheō*, pour out) gradually displace it. *ekcheō* is used of pouring liquids, sometimes with the idea of draining. It can also be used with regard to scattering solid objects and, metaphorically, for squandering money. *ekchyn(n)ō* is a Hel. Gk. form.

2. In the LXX *ekcheō* is a general word for pour, often used in purificatory rites (Exod. 30:18; Num. 19:17). It occurs esp. in the pouring or shedding of blood—either in sacrifices or, more frequently, in murder (cf. Gen. 9:6; 37:22; Deut. 19:10; 1 Sam. 25:31; Ps. 13:3). It is also used of pouring out offerings, generally of water, to Yahweh (e.g., Jdg. 6:20; 1 Sam. 7:6) or to other gods (e.g., Isa. 57:6). The technical term for offering libations (of wine) is *spendō* (Exod. 25:29 = LXX 25:28; 30:9; Num. 4:7; 28:7).

Among nonliteral uses, a common expression is to pour out anger on someone, as in God's acts of judgment (e.g., Ps. 79:6; Ezek. 7:8). People can also pour out their soul, i.e., their complaint, before God (1 Sam. 1:15; Ps. 142:2). One special use is the promise that God will pour out his Spirit on the human race (Joel 2:28–29; cf. Ezek. 39:29; Zech. 12:10). A Jewish inscription uses *ekcheō* of shedding the blood of an innocent martyr.

NT 1. *ekcheō* is used in the lit. sense in Matt. 9:17; Lk. 5:37 (of wine running out); Jn. 2:15 (of money "scattered"); Acts 1:18 (of Judas's bowels being "spilled out").

2. The use of shedding blood as a synonym for murder or martyrdom occurs in Matt. 23:35; Acts 22:20 (both *ekchynnomai*); Rom. 3:15; Rev. 16:6. Heb. refers to the sprinkling or pouring of blood in the OT sacrificial ritual with *proschysis* (Heb. 11:28; cf. Exod. 12:22) and *haimatekchysia* (Heb. 9:22; → *haima*, blood, *135*). The latter is found exclusively in Christian writings, but cf. *ekchysis haimatos*, pouring out of blood (1 Ki. 18:28; Sir. 27:15).

3. These two OT senses of shedding blood—murder or martyrdom and sacrifice—come together in the crucial words of Jesus in the institution of the Lord's Supper, "This is my blood of the covenant, which is poured out [*ekchynnomai*] for many" (Mk. 14:24; cf. Matt. 26:28); Lk. 22:20 reads, "This cup is the new covenant in my blood, which is poured out [*ekchynnomai*]for you." Jesus is both a martyr, an innocent victim of murder, and a sacrifice "for many."

Several OT passages are alluded to in these words; two are esp. important. "This is my blood of the covenant" echoes Exod. 24:8, the sacrificial offering that instituted the old covenant of Sinai, which is now being replaced (as Jer. 31:31–34 predicted) with a new covenant, sealed by Jesus' sacrificial death. "For many" points to Isa. 53:11–12, where the "many" are to be made righteous by the death of God's Servant bearing their sin; he is said in Isa. 53:12 to have "poured out his

life unto death." Thus, the pouring out of Jesus' blood introduces us into a new covenant relationship with God.

4. Paul takes up the pouring of libations as a metaphor for his approaching martyrdom in his use of *spendō* in Phil. 2:17 and 2 Tim. 4:6. The libation is not, like the blood sacrifices, an atoning offering, but an expression of dedication to God.

5. The more metaphorical uses of pour in the OT are also echoed in the NT. The pouring out of God's fury provides the imagery of the seven bowls of God's wrath poured out in Rev. 16, where *ekcheō* occurs 9x. More characteristically, God's love is "poured out" in the hearts of believers (Rom. 5:5), and this has been done by the bestowal of the Holy Spirit, who is several times said, following Joel 2:28–29, to have been "poured" on those who receive Christ (Acts 2:17–18, 33; 10:45; Tit. 3:6).

1773 (*ekchynnomai*, pour out), → *1772*.

1777 (*elaia*, olive tree, olive), → *1778*.

| 1778 ἔλαιον | ἔλαιον (*elaion*), olive (oil) (*1778*); ἐλαία (*elaia*), olive tree, |

olive (*1777*); ἐλαιών (*elaiōn*), olive orchard (*1779*); ἀγριέλαιος (*agrielaios*), wild olive (*66*); καλλιέλαιος (*kallielaios*), cultivated olive (*2814*); Γεθσημανί (*Gethsēmani*), Gethsemane (*1149*).

CL & OT 1. *elaion* refers to the oil of the olive, the most commonly used oil in the ancient world. It was a regular part of the diet of most Mediterranean peoples and was also used as fuel for lamps and medicine. The Greeks also used it for anointing the body after bathing and before wrestling and other sports.

2. In the LXX *elaion* was normally olive oil, though it could also denote a fragrant ointment compounded from various spices with olive oil as its base. Oil was a basic agricultural product of Palestine and a staple element in the diet (1 Ki. 17:12–16; cf. the common formula "grain, new wine and oil," e.g., Deut. 7:13; 11:14). It was also used cosmetically (2 Sam. 14:2; Ps. 104:15), esp. at banquets (Ps. 23:5; cf. Amos 6:6), and so is sometimes a symbol for joy (Ps. 45:7; cf. Isa. 61:3).

A fragrant oil was used to anoint the priests. Anointing with oil became a symbol of investing with authority, whether as priest (Exod. 29:7; cf. 40:15), king (1 Sam. 10:1; 16:1, 13; 1 Ki. 1:39), or (on at least one occasion) prophet (cf. 19:16). Oil was used in the consecration of the tabernacle and its vessels (Exod. 40:9; Lev. 8:10). In temple ritual it was mixed with grain offerings and used in ritual anointing (e.g., Lev. 2:1–16; 5:11; 6:15, 21). It also provided fuel for the lamps (Exod. 27:20; Lev. 24:2). The prophets frequently refer to oil (Isa. 41:19; 61:3; Jer. 31:12; 40:10 = LXX 47:10; Hos. 2:5, 8, 22; Joel 1:10; Mic. 6:7, 15; Hag. 2:12 = LXX 2:13), esp. Ezek. (e.g., 16:9, 13, 18–19; 23:41). Oil is mentioned in Ps. (e.g., 45:7; 92:10; 141:5) and Prov. (21:17; cf. 5:3; 21:20).

elaia and *elaiōn* mean both the olive tree and its produce. The olive tree matures slowly, so that to grow olives and enjoy their fruit was a common picture of a settled and prosperous condition. The fruitfulness of the olive makes it a suitable metaphor for those who enjoy God's blessing (Ps. 52:8; 128:3), esp. Israel (Jer. 11:16; Hos. 14:6 = LXX 14:7; Hab. 3:17). *Gethsēmani* is a transliteration of Aram. *gaṯ šᵉmānê*, oil press.

NT 1. Most of the practical uses of the olive and its oil mentioned in the OT reappear in the NT. Jas. 3:12 mentions the olive as a crop; its oil as an item of commerce appears in Lk. 16:6; Rev. 18:13 (cf. Matt. 25:9). For its use as fuel for lamps, see Matt. 25:3–8.

The injunction in Rev. 6:6 to spare the oil and wine even though there is to be a famine of grain is probably an echo of the standard OT formula, the "grain, new wine and oil"; only one-third of the produce is to be affected while the rest is spared, as in the following vision ("a fourth of the earth," 6:8) and in the plagues introduced by the seven trumpets in chs. 8–9. It may also be significant that while grain is an annual crop, olives and vines take much longer to recover from devastation; it is, therefore, a temporary famine, not total destruction. This point is reinforced by the highly inflated price of wheat and barley, which are necessities more basic than oil and wine. A "quart of wheat" was generally regarded as the amount of food that a working man would eat in a day, and a denarius was a day's wage for a laborer (cf. Matt. 20:2–13; Mk. 6:37; Jn. 6:7). Thus an entire day's wages would be spent on wheat alone.

2. Matt. 6:17 (*aleiphō*, anoint, → 230) suggests that the cosmetic use of oil was still normal in Palestine. In Lk. 7:46 it is expected that the host would anoint his guest at a banquet; the Pharisee's neglect of this simple courtesy is contrasted with the woman's lavish use of the much more expensive *myron*, oil of myrrh.

The use of anointing with oil as a symbol of joy and honor in Ps. 45:7 is taken up in Heb. 1:9 with reference to Christ, no doubt with the thought of his "anointing" for his messianic task (for which see Lk. 4:18; Acts 4:27; 10:38).

3. The medicinal use of oil on an open wound (cf. Isa. 1:6) is seen in Lk. 10:34 and is in line with widespread ancient practice. The NT also mentions the practice of anointing with oil in miraculous healing (Mk. 6:13; Jas. 5:14), although its effect here is not so much medicinal as it is symbolic—probably a symbol of the protection and blessing of God on the patient (→ *aleiphō*, 230).

4. The olive tree (*elaia*) is used 2x as a symbol in the NT. (a) The two witnesses of God in Rev. 11:4 are described as "the two olive trees and the two lampstands that stand before the Lord of the earth." This is an allusion to Zech. 4:2–14, where the two olive trees whose oil feeds the golden lampstand represent "the two who are anointed to serve the Lord of all the earth" (4:14, normally taken to be Zerubbabel and Joshua, whose combined leadership was the channel of God's power to enable Israel to live up to its calling). The two witnesses in Rev. 11 symbolize the faithful witness of the church, esp. Christian martyrs, and the point of the allusion to Zech.'s vision is that their faithful witness, in the power of the Spirit (cf. Zech. 4:6), is the channel of God's power to fulfill his purpose in a hostile world.

(b) In Paul's famous allegory in Rom. 11:17–24, the olive tree represents the people of God. The cultivated olive (*kallielaios*) is Israel, from which some of the branches were broken (many Jews rejected Christ and so lost their place as God's people), while shoots of wild olive (*agrielaios*) grafted into their place represent the inclusion of Gentiles into the people of God. Eventually, however, God is able to graft the natural branches back into their own stock (Jews who "do not persist in unbelief" will be restored, and thus "all Israel will be saved," 11:23, 26). The stock remains the same; it is only in the branches that changes take place. Israel, the people of God, remains a continuous entity, but its membership is subject both to the exclusion of native Israelites and the inclusion of the alien stock of Gentile believers.

Some commentators remark that Paul's theology is better than his knowledge of horticulture. But while modern agriculturists look askance at the attempt to graft the wild olive onto the cultivated olive, this is independently attested in ancient times as a device to rejuvenate an unproductive olive. Philo applied a similar figure of speech to Israelites and proselytes. Where Paul does, quite consciously, go beyond nature is in his comment that after branches have been cut off, "God is able to graft them in again" (Rom. 11:23). This is the miracle of God's grace.

5. The Mount of Olives (or Olivet) is the ridge on the east side of Jerusalem, across the Kidron Valley, on which olive orchards still grow. It must be crossed by a traveler entering Jerusalem from the east and so is mentioned in the accounts of Jesus' triumphal entry into Jerusalem (Matt. 21). Its commanding view of the temple area accounts for Jesus' lament there over Jerusalem's impenitence (Lk. 19:29–44) and his teaching there on the approaching ruin of the temple (Matt. 24:1–3).

Somewhere on this ridge Jesus and his disciples spent the nights of his last week (Lk. 21:37), probably in the place known as Gethse-mane, to which they went after the Last Supper (Mk. 14:26, 32) and which was their regular rendezvous (Jn. 18:1–2). Gethsemane was the scene of Jesus' final commitment to his redemptive suffering as well as of his arrest. It was also on this Mount that Jesus ascended to heaven (Lk. 24:50–51; Acts 1:12); Acts 1:11, taken with Zech. 14:4, has led to the conclusion that it will also be the scene of his return.

1779 (elaiōn, olive orchard), → *1778.*

1781 (elassōn, smaller, younger), → *3625.*

1788 (elachistos, very small, the least), → *3625.*

1790 (eleaō, show mercy), → *1799.*

1791 (elegmos, conviction, reproof, punishment), → *1794.*

1792 (elenxis, conviction, rebuke, reproof), → *1794.*

1793 (elenchos, proof, evidence, conviction, reproof), → *1794.*

1794 ἐλέγχω

ἐλέγχω (*elenchō*), bring to light, expose, set forth, convict, convince, punish, discipline (*1794*); ἔλεγχος (*elenchos*), proof, evidence, conviction, reproof, correction (*1793*); ἐλεγμός (*elegmos*), conviction, reproof, punishment (*1791*); ἔλεγξις (*elenxis*), conviction, rebuke, reproof (*1792*).

CL & OT 1.(a) *elenchō* originally meant blame, insult; then test, examine, inquire into a matter. Plato and Aristotle used it of the logical exposition of the facts of a matter for the purpose of refuting an opponent's argument. Thus the word developed its principal meaning of convince, refute. In Stoicism the basic concept was applied to philosophical ethics. Philo and Josephus spoke of the correction that people receive from their own consciences, the Logos, the truth, or God. *elenchō* eventually acquired a sense that brought it near to *paideuō*, to teach (→ *4084*).

(b) The noun *elenchos* has a similar variety of meanings: proof, conviction, correction, reproof. The nouns *elegmos* and *elenxis*, common in the LXX and the NT, are found chiefly in the Hel. period and have as a rule the meaning of conviction or correction.

2. In the LXX *elenchō* is used in the great majority of cases to mean to bring to account, to correct; *elenchos* generally means rebuke, correction. Words of this group are found in this sense mainly in the later books of the OT (Job, Ps., Prov.) and in the Apocr. (Wis., Sir.). *elegmos* is used in Isa. 37:3; 50:2 with the meaning rebuke, reproach, disgrace. At Num. 5:18–19, 23–24, 27, the LXX translates the "water of bitterness" used in the ordeal by the phrase *hydōr tou elegmou*, water of conviction. *elenxis* occurs only at Job 21:4; 23:2, where it means concern, complaint.

3. (a) The historical books occasionally use *elenchō* in secular contexts: Because of a dispute about a well, Abraham complained to Abimelech, the king of Gerar (Gen. 21:25); in the quarrel between Jacob and Laban, the kinsmen were to judge who was in the right (31:37). In these cases *elenchō* refers to the clarification of a practical point at dispute, not an intellectual question.

(b) In prophetic proclamation *elenchō* has a legal character, as seen from its use alongside words for righteousness and judgment. The task of the priests to pronounce judgment and give advice is clearly presupposed (Ezek. 3:26; Hos. 4:4; cf. Isa. 29:21; Mal. 2:7). In a negative sense, the prophetic message of judgment spoke of divine reproof and the coming day of punishment (Jer. 2:19; cf. Hos. 5:9). Positively, the prophets proclaimed salvation in terms of justice for the poor (Isa. 11:3–4) and the healing instruction Yahweh would give to the nations (Isa. 2:4; Mic. 4:3).

(c) This word group comes into its own in the poetic lit., chiefly in the sense of correction and punishment. The psalmist prays for preservation from divine punishment (Ps. 6:1), yet the correction that comes from Yahweh or from just people is regarded as a help and benefit (141:5; cf. Job 5:17). In proverbial wisdom, while the ungodly neither accept or deserve correction, the wise are grateful for it, for they recognize in it God's love (Prov. 3:11–12; 9:7–8; cf. 29:15). As may be seen from the repeated parallel use of *elenchō* and *paideuō* (e.g., 3:11–12), or *elenchos* and *paideia* (e.g., 6:23), this word group comes close to the Stoic ideal of education and character training. The godly are trained by correction and discipline to follow the right path in life (6:23; 5:12–13; 19:25; Sir. 18:13).

4. On grounds of the command in Lev. 19:17, "Rebuke your neighbor frankly," correction played an important part in Jud., both as a command to love one's neighbor and as a task that earns merit. It had a special importance in the Qumran texts. One who observes a fellow member transgressing the law must censure him, at first before witnesses (CD 7:2). If this correction achieves nothing, the case must be brought before the whole community, which then proceeds to punish the sinner (1QS 3:6).

NT 1. The words of this group are found in the NT in the Gospels (especially Jn.) and in the later letters (esp. the Pastorals). In Jn. *elenchō* means, as in the prophetic warnings of judgment, to reveal and convict of sin. It is the negative, reverse side of God's saving work of revelation (Jn. 3:20; 16:8; cf. also Eph. 5:13; Jude 15). Examples of what is revealed are sin, righteousness, and judgment (Jn. 8:46; 16:8–11), an illegitimate marriage (Lk. 3:19), and deeds of ungodliness (Jude 15).

2. *elenchō* is found particularly often in hortatory passages (e.g., Eph. 5:13). The Pastoral Letters assign to the leader of the community the task of rebuking church members (1 Tim. 5:20; 2 Tim. 4:2; Tit. 2:15) and of convicting opponents of their error (1:9, 13). The corresponding activity is called *elegmos* in 2 Tim. 3:16 and *elenxis* in 2 Pet. 2:16. Mention should also be made of the instructions about church order in Matt. 18:15–17, where Jesus says that erring church members should first be told privately of their fault, then in the presence of several witnesses, and, if this be fruitless, before the whole church (cf. the procedure at Qumran).

3. It may be seen from the citation of Prov. 3:11–12 at Heb. 12:5 and Rev. 3:19 that the Hel. concept of education has found its way into the NT. In both cases *elenchō* and *paideuō* are used in parallel.

4. The interpretation of *elenchos* in Heb. 11:1 presents difficulties. Its meaning here can be deduced only from its context, in the definition of faith given in this chapter. The sentence falls into two parallel parts. *elenchos* strengthens *hypostasis*, and *pragmata ou blepomena*, things not seen, explains *elpizomena*, things hoped for. The concepts are Hel. in character. The purpose of the statement is not so much to encourage subjective assurance of faith, as if faith could give the status of reality to what lies in the future. It is rather to secure a link with objectivity.

Thus, *elenchos* should not be interpreted subjectively (as if it denoted absence of doubt), in a hortatory sense (as if it meant correction), or even in an intellectual sense (meaning evidence). Rather, it should be understood in its context in the theology of Heb. in a strictly theological sense, as referring to conviction about the power of the future world promised by God, which is here described in the language of secular Gk. as "things not seen" (see also *hypostasis*, 5712). Heb. 11:1 would then mean: "But faith is the pledge of things hoped for, the conviction of things we cannot see."

See also *aitia*, ground, cause, reason, charge (*162*); *enochos*, guilty, subject to, liable to (*1944*); *amemptos*, blameless (*289*).

1795 (eleeinos, pitiful), → *1799.*

1796 (eleeō, feel compassion, show mercy or pity), → *1799.*

1797 (eleēmosynē, charity, alms), → *1799.*

1798 (eleēmōn, merciful, compassionate), → *1799.*

1799 ἔλεος

ἔλεος (*eleos*), compassion, mercy, pity (*1799*); ἐλεέω (*eleeō*), feel compassion, show mercy or pity (*1796*); ἐλεήμων (*eleē-*

mōn), merciful, compassionate (*1798*); ἐλεεινός (*eleeinos*), pitiful (*1795*); ἐλεάω (*eleaō*), show mercy (*1790*); ἐλεημοσύνη (*eleē-mosynē*), charity, alms (*1797*); ἀνέλεος (*aneleos*), without pity (*447*); ἀνελεήμων (*aneleēmōn*), merciless (*446*).

CL & OT 1. In cl. Gk. *eleos* means compassion, pity, mercy—the emotion that arises when one sees another person's affliction. It is the reverse of envy at someone else's good fortune. Behind it may be an element of fear that we will someday suffer in the same way ourselves. *eleos* is also a technical term for the conclusion of a defendant's speech, in which the accused tried to awaken the compassion of the judges. In one of history's most famous cases, Socrates refused to conform to this pattern and ended up having to drink the hemlock. The derived noun *eleēmosynē* originally meant the same as *eleos* but was then applied to an act of kindness as a result of compassion. It then obtained the specialized meaning of a gift to the poor; it finds its earliest use in the LXX (Dan. 4:24).

aneleos, meaning unmerciful, without compassion, is not found in cl. Gk. (*anēleēs* was used). *aneleēmōn* also means without compassion. *eleeinos* is mainly used of a person's passive condition as evoking compassion, hence pitiable, distressing. *eleeō* means to have compassion, be sorry for, be merciful, sympathize with. The cry *eleē-son* ("have mercy") was addressed to the gods.

2. *eleos* and its derivatives are found nearly 400x in the LXX. The relevant Heb. concepts, which are legal in nature, thus betray a different background of thought from the predominantly psychological one in Gk. (a) *ḥesed* (the Heb. word most often translated by *eleos*) means proper covenant behavior, the solidarity that the covenant partners owe one another. The covenant may be between equals or by one who is stronger than his partner. In either case it may result in one person giving help to the other in his need. Thus, the connotations of *eleos* meaning *ḥesed* may stretch from loyalty to a covenant to kindness, mercy, pity.

This is esp. the case when *eleos* is linked with *oiktirmos* (→ *3880*; e.g., Ps. 25:6; Isa. 63:15; Hos. 2:21 = LXX 2:19; Zech. 7:9). Because of Yahweh's superiority as the partner in the covenant who remains faithful, his *eleos* was understood for the most part as a gracious gift. He promised it at the making of the covenant, and he constantly renewed it. Hence Israel requests *eleos* from him, including the mercy of forgiveness, when it broke the covenant (e.g., Num. 14:19; cf. Exod. 34:9; Jer. 3:12). In such cases, the stress is not on the basic attitude in *eleos* but on its manifestation in acts.

(b) The Heb. *ṣᵉdāqâ* (normally translated *dikaiosynē*, righteousness, → *1466*) is also rendered sometimes by *eleēmosynē* (e.g., Isa. 1:27). Just as Yahweh enforces his covenant law mercifully, so *eleēmosynē* may be used for human kindness, charity, and even for alms when these conform to the pattern of this law.

NT *eleos* and its derivatives are found 78x in the NT, mostly in Paul (25x) and Luke-Acts (20x).

1. In the Synoptics *eleeō* is found mainly in the narratives (though see Matt. 5:7; 18:33; Lk. 16:24). The noun *eleos*, by contrast, usually occurs in reports of speech (though see Lk. 1:58). (a) The vb. denotes the divine mercy of Jesus Christ, expressed in the context of human misery as he sought to heal people. Jesus answered the cry for help, "Have mercy on me" (Matt. 9:27; 15:22; 17:15; Mk. 10:47–48; Lk. 17:13), from sick people or from relatives of the demon-possessed (Matt. 15:22; 17:15) by healing them. On one occasion he commanded a man from whom he had driven out demons to tell people at home how the Lord had had mercy on him (Mk. 5:19).

Normally on these occasions Jesus is addressed by the messianic title "Son of David," though the title "Lord" (*kyrios*, → *3261*) or "Teacher" (*didaskalos*, → *1438*) is also used (cf. Matt. 17:15 with Mk. 9:17; Lk. 9:38). This makes the cry, "Lord, have mercy," a confession of faith in the divine authority of Jesus.

(b) Mercy from one person to another is expressed by *eleeō* or *eleēmōn* 2x in Matt. and once in Lk., but in each case the motivation is clearly God's mercy. In Matt. 5:7 "the merciful" (*eleēmōn*) are promised God's mercy—the vb. is pass. to avoid using God's name. In the parable of the unforgiving servant (18:23–35) the demand for mercy (18:33) is based on the limitless compassion of his master (18:27, 35; → *splanchnon, 5073*). In Luke 16:24, the suffering rich man, who had been merciless during his life, calls on Abraham with the same words for mercy as are used only in calling on God.

(c) In Matt.'s and Lk.'s used of *eleos*, a reference, often direct, to the OT is noticeable. In his controversies with the Pharisees Jesus bears witness to the sovereign mercy of God, which seeks a response not in ritual detail but in solidarity through action with the lowly and hungry (Matt. 9:13; 12:7; cf. 1 Sam. 15:22; Hos. 6:6). In his "woes" leveled against them Jesus includes the charge that in their interpretation of the law the Pharisees have shifted the main stress from "justice, mercy and faithfulness" to a more casuistic formalism (Matt. 23:23; cf. also Lk. 10:37). Lk.'s two great songs in Lk. 1 announce one of his main themes—that the covenant loyalty of God, promised in the OT and shown throughout the history of Israel, will reach its climax in the gracious self-humiliation of God to the humble in the event of Christ (1:50, 54, 72, 78). These two songs are filled with OT quotations and allusions.

(d) Matt. reports Jesus' criticism of hypocrites' attempts to obtain public praise and acknowledgment by openly giving alms to the needy (*eleēmosynē*, see Matt. 6:1–4). Lk. 11:41 and 12:33 both lay down the giving away of one's possessions to the poor as a pattern for Jesus' followers. In Acts Tabitha (9:36) and Cornelius (10:2) are both singled out for their charity and thus become recipients of singular blessing. The former was perhaps a Hel. Jewess, a resident of Joppa. She fell sick and died (9:37), but was restored through Peter. Cornelius, a centurion of the Italian Cohort at Caesarea and a "devout and God-fearing" man (10:2), had his prayers and alms come up before God (10:4, 31). God sent Peter to preach to him, and he received the Holy Spirit and became the first Gentile into the church (10:44–48).

In his defense before Felix, Paul identifies his bringing of alms for the poor as the purpose of his last journey to Jerusalem (Acts 24:17). In 3:1–8 Peter did not have monetary alms for the crippled man but ended the man's time of begging and imperfect mercy by the full mercy brought in the name of Jesus Christ (3:6).

2. *Paul.* (a) Paul regarded himself as one who "was shown mercy" in order that he might become an apostle (1 Tim. 1:13, 16); "by the Lord's mercy" he had been made trustworthy (1 Cor. 7:25). In view of the wide-scale rejection of the gospel by Israel, Paul tried in his letter to the Romans to make clear that God's free mercy did not contradict his covenant loyalty (Rom. 9:15–16, 18; 9:15 quotes Exod. 33:19). God's plan of salvation for both Jews and Gentiles (Rom. 9:23–24; 11:30–32; 15:9) is based on his mercy (*eleos*), not on good works (Eph. 2:4–9; Tit. 3:5). Hence Paul admonishes believers to pass on the mercy they have experienced (2 Cor. 4:1) and to do so cheerfully (Rom. 12:8). Thus, mercy becomes one of the signs by which a disciple can be known (cf. Jas. 3:17), while being "ruthless" (*aneleēmōn*) is the lowest rung in the downward ladder of Rom. 1:29–32.

(b) Paul and other NT writers (2 Jn. 3; Jude 2), in their confidence in God's gracious giving, greet their readers at the beginning (1 Tim. 1:2; 2 Tim. 1:2) or end (Gal. 6:16) of their letters with a prayer for the mercy of God and of Jesus Christ—mostly combined with "grace" and "peace." God's mercy can heal (Phil. 2:27); it is a present gift for the "household" (2 Tim. 1:16) and the final, future gift ensuring salvation (1:18). Paul proclaims the Christian hope of a future resurrection of an imperishable body by contradicting the group in Corinth that affirmed that the bodily resurrection was already past; he describes those who confine hope only to this life as "to be pitied more than [*eleeinoteroi*] all men" (1 Cor. 15:19).

3. *Other NT Writings.* (a) Peter begins by praising God's mercy (1 Pet. 1:3), by which Christians have been given "new birth into a living hope through the resurrection of Jesus Christ from the dead" (cf. Eph. 2:4; 1 Cor. 15:19). As in Rom. 9:25–26, Peter praises the enlarge-

ment of God's mercy to take in the Gentiles (1 Pet. 2:10) by using Hosea's words (Hos. 2:23).

(b) James impressed on an indolent church that mercy shown here on earth has its bearing on the final judgment, and that "judgment without mercy" (*aneleos*, only here in the NT) awaits the one who has shown no mercy (2:13; cf. Matt. 18:33–34; 25:40, 45; Lk. 16:24–25).

(c) Jude, after mentioning the love of God believers have experienced and their expectation of a final merciful judgment by Jesus Christ, urges his readers to exercise a discriminating mercy to those around them (Jude 21–23).

(d) Rev. 3:17, like 1 Cor. 15:19, convicts the church at Laodicea of its "pitiful" (*eleeinos*) condition in spite of its earthly riches, and places it under the judgment of Christ, which alone is valid.

(e) Heb. uses the high priest in the OT and his functions on the great day of atonement (Lev. 16) as a type pointing to Christ, who is greater than any high priest and who exercises a "merciful" understanding (2:17; cf. 4:15). In this way he gives the despairing church confidence to draw near the throne of grace to find mercy (4:16).

See also *oiktirmos*, compassion, pity (*3880*); *splanchnon*, inward parts, hence as the seat of emotion, the heart, love (*5073*).

1800 ἐλευθερία

ἐλευθερία (*eleutheria*), freedom, liberty (*1800*); ἐλεύθερος (*eleutheros*), free, independent, not bound (*1801*); ἐλευθερόω (*eleutheroō*), to free, set free (*1802*); ἀπελεύθερος (*apeleutheros*), freedman (*592*).

CL *eleutheria* means freedom, independence. This way of speaking arose in contrast to the bondage of slaves. Similarly, *eleutheros* means free, not bound, of free birth, being one's own master. Later the noun and adj. were occasionally used to denote the mental attitude that made use of freedom. It could be used in the good sense of being in control of oneself, magnanimous, generous. But it could also be used in the less frequent and negative sense of being reckless or unrestrained. The adj. *apeleutheros* follows the original sense and denotes a freedman, i.e., one who was not free by birth. The vb. *eleutheroō* means to free, set free, although not exclusively in relation to slaves. It could refer to freeing someone from any bond that prevented him or her from acting freely.

1. In secular Gk. *eleutheros* had primarily a political sense. The *eleutheros* is the full citizen who belonged to the *polis*, the city-state, in contrast to the slave, who did not enjoy full rights as a citizen. Freedom consisted in one's right to participate in public debates over civic matters and decide about one's own affairs within the *polis*. Aristotle considered freedom to be the essential good of the *polis*.

But in order to preserve that freedom, the law (*nomos*) was required as the principle of order. Freedom and law were thus not contradictory. They belonged together and qualified each other. The constant danger was a rejection of the law in the name of a misconceived freedom that was purely arbitrary, because it was willing to grant itself more freedom than it was willing to grant others. This idea of freedom was also naturally applied to relations between states, which gave rise to the idea of sovereignty.

2. In Stoic philosophy this political idea of freedom was transformed by the collapse of the *polis*. Freedom was understood in a philosophical and religious sense. For the Stoic, humanity in the final analysis is not in control of external things, such as the body, money, honor, and political freedom. To the Stoics, therefore, *eleutheria* meant withdrawal from the apparent reality of this world. It was a deliberate surrender to the law and rule of the cosmos, or the deity that ruled the cosmos. This meant that humans must free themselves from whatever bound them too closely to the world: passions (such as anger, anxiety, and pity) and the fear of death. Freedom required one to be so adjusted and detached as to live in complete harmony with the cosmos or the

gods. This freedom must be perpetually renewed through constant struggle and unending effort.

3. The mystery religions had their own answer to the question of freedom. Through cultic rites, initiates were freed from this hopeless world and obtained a part in the destiny of the deity.

OT 1. In the LXX, *eleutheria* and its cognates are used primarily in the context of slavery (e.g., Exod. 21:2, 5, 27; Lev. 19:20; Deut. 15:12–13) and prisoners of war (21:14). It is striking that the specific word is not found in connection either with the liberation of Israel from Egypt or their return from exile. The political use of *eleutheria* is apparently foreign to the LXX. As the forced labor during Solomon's reign suggests, under the monarchy the Israelites were not free subjects, but were the king's slaves. Only a few privileged men stood out as truly free.

This is not the way it should have been, however. Yahweh was Lord over his people, and through his laws he promised protection for the helpless and weak, including slaves. An enslaved Israelite, for example, could never become another's permanent property (Deut. 15:13–18). After six years the slave was to be set free without payment being made to the owner (Exod. 21:2–4). Yet Jer. 34:8–16 indicates that there were those in Israel who wanted to follow the pattern in the surrounding nations of keeping slaves for life. Because of these social injustices, Jer. derisively proclaimed to Israel "'freedom' to fall by the sword, plague and famine" (34:17; cf. Amos 2:6–16).

2. However, the conclusion should not be drawn from the narrow range of meaning of the *eleutheria* word group that the *issue of freedom* did not exist for Israel. Rather, Israel's political freedom was a part of the redeeming and saving acts of God. Freedom for Israel meant being set free by Yahweh, as, for example, from bondage in Egypt (cf. Exod. 20:2; Deut. 7:8). Thus it was identical with redemption. It was not given by nature but was always experienced as the gracious gift of God.

The fact that Israel, even as a political entity, existed on the basis of this act of liberation has several consequences. (a) The gift of freedom remained bound to the one giving it. Desertion of Yahweh had the necessary consequence of loss of freedom. This is shown by the era of the judges, which was an age of falling away from Yahweh, followed by slavery, repentance, and liberation (Jdg. 2:10–3:6). The history of the northern and southern kingdoms was similar. The Assyrian conquest was the result of the godlessness of the northern kingdom (2 Ki. 17:7–23), just as the Babylonian captivity resulted from the godlessness of the southern kingdom (2 Ki. 21:10–15; 22:19–20; 23:25–27).

(b) God's acts are fundamental to communal human life. According to the Decalogue, God wanted his people to live in freedom in all aspects of their life. This high regard for freedom was extended to the stranger (Exod. 22:21; 23:9; Lev. 19:33–34) and to the slave. The escaped slave was even to be afforded protection from his former master (Deut. 23:15–16).

(c) The struggle to preserve this freedom played a repeated and significant role in the message of the prophets, who developed it in their own particular ways (e.g., Isa. 1:23; 10:1–4; Jer. 7:5–6; Amos 2:6–7; 4:1; Mic. 3:1–3). Enslavement by the nobility of whole strata of society that were originally free was a breach of divine law. The promise was given to those bound that the Messiah would come "to proclaim freedom for the captives and release from darkness for the prisoners" (Isa. 61:1).

3. By the time of Jesus, freedom was understood predominantly in an external, political sense (cf. the typical misunderstanding in Jn. 8:33). Freedom movements with a religious basis were repeatedly formed to implement the promised freedom by force against the pagan secular authorities. The best known of these were the Maccabees in the 2d cent. B.C., who wanted to ensure religious freedom through political freedom, and the Zealots at the time of Jesus (cf. Acts 5:37; 21:38).

NT 1. (a) In the NT *eleutheria* occurs 11x, *eleutheros* 23x, *eleutheroō* 7x, and *apeleutheros* only at 1 Cor. 7:22. These words are found chiefly in Paul (esp. in Rom. 6–8; 1 Cor. 7–10; Gal. 2–5) and Jn. 8:32–36.

(b) NT usage exhibits some interesting nuances. *eleutheria* is never used in the secular sense of political freedom. From this it may be inferred that the recovery of Israel's political freedom no longer played a role in the thinking of the NT writers. Jesus was no political messiah. The NT also dissociates itself from the idea of freedom as power to do with oneself and one's life whatever one wants. Rather, *eleutheria* is to be seen in the light of "the glorious freedom of the children of God" (Rom. 8:21) that takes place through Christ (Gal. 2:4; 5:1). It is present only "where the Spirit of the Lord is" (2 Cor. 3:17). When Jas. 1:25 and 2:12 speak of "the law that gives freedom," *eleutheria* means the new way of life in which one lives in accordance with God's will. Even the vb. *eleutheroō* is used in the NT exclusively for the act that occurs or has occurred through Jesus: "The truth will set you free" (Jn. 8:32; cf. Rom. 6:18, 22).

On the other hand, *eleutheros* has primarily the secular sense of being free in contrast to being a slave (Gal. 3:28; Eph. 6:8; Col. 3:11; Rev. 6:15) or being independent with respect to a law (Rom. 7:3). Gal. 4:22–23 is therefore used with a double meaning and leads in 4:26, 31; 5:1 to the specifically NT idea of being free in Christ. The characteristic of this free person is not the contrast with the slave but the fact that, as a free person, one is at the same time Christ's slave (1 Cor. 9:19; 1 Pet. 2:16; cf. Paul's self-designation in Rom. 1:1; Phil. 1:1). The *apeleutheros kyriou* ("the Lord's freedman") is at the same time the *doulos Christou* ("Christ's slave"; 1 Cor. 7:22).

2. (a) What does freedom mean? In contrast to the secular Gk. mind, the NT sees every human as basically unfree (Jn. 8:39; Rom. 6:20; 2 Pet. 2:19). We are unable to free ourselves and order our lives as though we are not in bondage. Our perennial efforts to take ourselves in hand, however we attempt it, lead to the greatest bondage in which we miss what we were meant to be (Matt. 16:25; Jn. 12:15). Our true freedom does not consist of the unfettered power to direct our lives, either in a political or in a Stoic sense. It lies rather in life with God, lived as he originally intended it (Rom. 6:22; Gal. 5:1, 13; 1 Pet. 2:16). We only gain this as we deny ourselves (Matt. 16:24).

Paradoxically, those who are free do not belong to themselves (1 Cor. 6:19; 9:19; 1 Pet. 2:16). They belong to him who has set them free (Rom. 6:18, 22; Gal. 5:1), "who died for them and was raised again" (2 Cor. 5:15). The NT idea of freedom thus follows from the OT. The gift of freedom is bound to the giver: "All things are yours . . . and you are of Christ, and Christ is of God" (1 Cor. 3:21–23). The realm of this freedom even extends to the supernatural powers and rulers that are robbed of their authority, because they have been conquered by Christ and can no longer separate us from Christ (Rom. 8:38; 1 Cor. 15:24; Gal. 4:3, 9). The impenetrable horizon becomes transparent in the light of this freedom.

(b) What are humans freed from? In our natural state we are subject to the powers of this age (→ *aiōn*, 172; cf. Matt. 17:18; Lk. 13:16; Eph. 6:12; 1 Pet. 5:8). The NT idea of freedom goes far beyond that of the OT in that it sees true freedom as liberation from those powers that suppress true humanity: sin (Jn. 8:31–36; Rom. 6:18–22; 8:2–11), Satan (Matt. 12:22; Lk. 13:16; Eph. 6:12), law (Rom. 7:3–6; 8:3; Gal. 2:4; 4:21–31; 5:1–13), and death (Rom. 6:20–23; 8:21). It is a liberation from the "old self" (Rom. 6:6; Eph. 4:22; Col. 3:9).

Sin in the NT is not a single act that with time will disappear. It has a permanent bondage for those who lend themselves to it (2 Pet. 2:19). They are no longer free to serve God but are compelled to sin. Yet there is no magical insurance against sin. Believers are called to a constant struggle with sin (e.g., Rom. 6:12, 19; 1 Cor. 6:18–19; Eph. 6:10–18). They are exposed to the tempter (2 Cor. 2:11; 1 Thess. 3:5) and remain sinful. Side by side with the indicative statement that "we died to sin" (Rom. 6:2) stands the imperative not to let sin reign in us (6:12) but instead to live in Christ to God (6:11). These statements are not in contradiction. The imperative follows from the indicative. As liberation from the compulsion to sin, *eleutheria* (Rom. 6:18) opens up the hitherto impossible possibility of serving God (cf. Jas. 1:25; 2:12).

The OT law declared God's irrevocable intention of leading us to life in fellowship with him (Rom. 7:10; 10:5). But in fact it had the opposite effect, because it prompted us more than ever to sin (5:20; 7:7–13) and revealed our profound godlessness (Gal. 3:19). Hence, no one can stand in righteousness before God's law (Rom. 3:19–23). What was to point us to salvation became a curse to us (7:10; Gal. 3:10). Christ, however, has freed us from this curse (3:13).

Yet the fact that we can be free from the law does not mean that the law is completely set aside (Matt. 5:17; Rom. 3:31; 6:15). It remains for believers the expression of God's holy will (7:12, 14; cf. Matt. 5:18–19), which now finds fulfillment in love (Jn. 13:34–35; Gal. 5:13–14). But it is no longer the impossible way to life. As a way of salvation, the law had its end in Christ (Rom. 10:4). Those who live in servitude under the law (Gal. 4:3) can through Christ (4:5) live as children and heirs (4:7). Therefore, anyone who tries to resurrect the law as a way of salvation by trying to fulfill its demands stands under a curse (1:8–9; 3:1–5; 5:11–15).

Death is the harvest we reap from a life under sin and the law (Rom. 6:21, 23; 7:10–11, 23–24; 1 Cor. 15:56). Death has a double meaning in that it denotes death in time and in eternity (Rom. 8:6). Just as Rom. 6 presents freedom from sin and Rom. 7 freedom from the law, Rom. 8 follows the sequence by presenting freedom from death (cf. 1 Cor. 15:26). The thought here, as in the case of these other powers, is not their utter abolition, but liberation from the inevitability of their compulsion and claim. Christians must die, but for us the sting of death has been removed (1 Cor. 15:55) because we know of the resurrection of Christ as the pledge of our own resurrection. Freedom from death means that God has promised us a future in Christ beyond our own death. Nothing more can stand between us and God (Rom. 8:38–39); we are liberated from fear of death.

(c) The means of freedom. The liberation of believers does not lie within the realm of our own capacities. For this reason there is in the NT no summons to contend for freedom. It has already been given through what Christ has done for us (Gal. 5:1). Only the Son, because of his sacrifice on the cross (3:13), can open up the possibility of existence in *eleutheria* (Jn. 8:36). It becomes a reality for us when we open our lives to the call of the gospel (2 Cor. 5:20–21) and believe in Christ and his Word (Jn. 8:31–32; Rom. 10:13–15). The Bible's message of freedom summons us from the only possible way of life open to us (living according to human standards and thinking) to live instead according to the Spirit (Rom. 8:12–13; Gal. 6:8). True freedom exists only where the Holy Spirit works in us as the principle of life and where we do not block his working (Rom. 8:1–11; 2 Cor. 3:17; Gal. 5:18).

(d) The goal of freedom. Freedom can be misused "as a cover-up for evil" (1 Pet. 2:16). This occurs when freedom is misunderstood in the Gk. sense of being master of all our decisions. This leads to libertinism or antinomianism instead of serving our neighbors (Gal. 5:13–14). Those who are truly free show their freedom in being able to serve God (1 Thess. 1:9), righteousness (Rom. 6:18–22), and their fellow human beings (1 Cor. 9:19; Jas. 1:25). "Christ's love compels us" to this sort of life (2 Cor. 5:14). Those who are free become servants of Christ (Rom. 1:1; 1 Cor. 7:22; Phil. 1:1). As Luther put it, "A Christian is a perfectly free lord of all, subject to none. A Christian is a perfectly dutiful servant of all, subject to all." The ultimate decisive factor in living this way is to live in love (1 Cor. 13). The deeper we penetrate into the "perfect law that gives freedom," the more free we become for such action (Jas. 1:25; 2:12).

(e) The demand for political freedom. Political freedom plays a subordinate role in the NT. Jesus swept aside all misunderstanding here. He and his kingdom do not live by external freedom. If they did, it would not have been so readily abandoned (Jn. 18:36). Even when Jesus stresses his earthly authority (Matt. 28:18), he draws no conclusions about claims for political freedom. He disappointed all the Jewish expectation of a political messiah. The kind of freedom he

preaches is that which comes through returning to the Father (Matt. 4:17; Lk. 24:47; Jn. 8:34–36).

For Christians, freedom is no longer a highest good, which, if need be, justifies resort to war and force. We know of a freedom in Christ in which we can live even as the world and the human race remain unchanged, although it is often hidden among sufferings (Jn. 8:31, 38; Rom. 8:18–23).

At the same time, the fact cannot be ignored that within the church, as with the prophets, there was a move towards freedom in the sense of equal rights for all. The old distinctions that reflected the environment of the ancient world between the free and the slave (cf. Phlm.) and the behavior of men and women (1 Cor. 14:34) still remained. However, in the final analysis such distinctions are invalid (Gal. 3:28; 1 Cor. 12:13; Col. 3:11). The freedom granted by God was given to operate above all in the communal life of the people of God. The Christian church is the community of the truly free (Gal. 4:21–31).

1801 (eleutheros, free, independent, not bound), → *1800.*

1802 (eleutheroō, to free, set free), → *1800.*

1803 (eleusis, coming, advent), → *2262.*

1817 (Hellas, Greece), → *1818.*

1818 Ἕλλην	Ἕλλην (*Hellēn*), a Greek (*1818*); Ἑλλάς (*Hellas*), Greece (*1817*);

Ἑλληνικός (*Hellēnikos*), Greek (*1819*); Ἑλληνίς (*Hellēnis*), a Greek woman (*1820*); Ἑλληνιστής (*Hellēnistēs*), a Hellenist (*1821*); Ἑλληνιστί (*Hellēnisti*), adv. Greek, in the Greek language (*1822*); βάβαρος (*barbaros*), barbarian, foreigner, non-Greek (975).

CL & OT 1. *Hellēn* refers to a Gk., as opposed to a *barbaros* (non-Greek; lit., barbarian). Gk. mythology contains the mythological genealogies that invented a hero, Hellen, son of Deucalion (there is also a tradition that he is a son of Zeus), father of the Doric and Aeolian tribal heroes. The opposition between Gk. and non-Gk. was one of culture and not religion. In the period after Alexander the Great, especially in the East, all who had adopted the Gk. language, culture, and way of life were counted as "Greeks," even though they were of a different ethnic origin.

2. In the LXX *Hellēn* is sometimes used for Heb. *yāwān* or *yᵉwānîm* (actually the Ionians; Dan. 8:21; 10:20). The experiences of the Jews under Antiochus IV Epiphanes resulted in the word *Hellēn* taking on the additional shade of meaning "hostile to the Jews" (e.g., 2 Macc. 4:36; 11:2; cf. *Hellēnikos* in 4:10, 15; 6:9; 11:24; 13:2). It thus had the overtone of pagan. In this way *Hellēn*, originally a term of respect, was surrendered to the language of religious contempt, since Jews began from belief in the one God, whereas the Greeks, in their contempt for the Jews, began from philosophical culture.

Elsewhere in the LXX words in this group are found in Isa. 66:19; Jer. 46:16 = LXX 26:16; 50:16 = LXX 27:16 (in both cases the Heb. is different); Ezek. 27:13; Joel 3:6; Zech. 9:13; Dan. 11:2; 1 Macc. 1:1, 10; 8:9, 18; 3 Macc. 3:8; 4 Macc. 8:8; 18:20.

3. The world that Christianity entered was characterized by the pervading influence of Gk. culture, esp. in the eastern part of the Roman empire. The conquests of Alexander the Great and his policy of Hellenization, continued by his successors, caused the Gk. language and ways to become the decisive cultural factor. Gk. cities arose everywhere, including Syria and Palestine, bursting the old tribal groupings of the native peoples. The upper strata in these cities spoke Gk., which became the language of trade and was widely understood in Palestine. Just how far the process of Hellenization had gone can be seen in the case of the Jews of Alexandria in Egypt, for whom a Gk. translation of the Bible, the LXX, had to be made in the 3d cent. B.C. Many of these people no longer understood or spoke their ancestral Heb. or Aram. tongue.

Philo of Alexandria (ca. 20 B.C.–ca. A.D. 50) was a Hellenistic philosopher and writer who sought to restate Jewish belief in terms of

Gk. philosophy. He developed an allegorical method of interpreting the OT, which saw Gk. philosophical ideas embodied in the history and institutions of Israel. In his system he accorded a central place to the Logos (Word) as the creative power that orders the world and the intermediary that enables people to know God. Numerous other Jewish authors also used Gk. language and thought forms to proclaim and spread as missionaries Jewish belief in God and the Mosaic law. Chief among these was Flavius Josephus (ca. A.D. 37–ca. 100), who wrote his celebrated history of the *Jewish War* (ca. 77) and his *Antiquities of the Jews* (ca. 94) with a view to gaining Roman sympathies.

One discovers in 1 Macc. an account of the heavy inroads of the Gk. spirit and attitude toward life into the Jerusalem priesthood. There was even a risk of losing fundamental religious tenets, and many were prepared to apostatize from their fathers' faith in God and turn from the law. This and the violent and clumsy attempts at Hellenization made by Antiochus IV Epiphanes (d. 163 B.C.) provoked a reaction in the circles loyal to the law, which resulted in the Maccabean movement (cf. 2 Macc. 6–8). Soon, however, the Maccabees themselves became Hellenized. Thus, even the ranks of pious Jews, loyal to the law, were penetrated by Gk. thought, teaching, and myths. The rabbis understood Gk. and were acquainted with Gk. lit. The numerous Gk. loanwords in the Talmud and Midrash are evidence of the cultural supremacy of Greece even among Jews.

NT In the NT *Hellas*, Greece, occurs only in Acts 20:2. *Hellēn*, a Gk. person, occurs 26x. *Hellēnis* is found in Acts 17:12, where it refers to Gk. women in Thessalonica, and in Mk. 7:26, where it describes the Syrophoenician woman; she was probably a Gk. by birth who happened to live in the province of Syria and in the area of Phoenicia. *Hellēnikos*, Gk. (adj.), occurs only in Rev. 9:11 (the word "language" should be supplied). *Hellēnisti* means "in Gk."; the title on Jesus' cross was written in Aram., Latin, and Gk. (Jn. 19:20). The officer who rescued Paul from the mob was surprised to discover that Paul understood Gk. (Acts 21:37). *Hellēnistēs* refers to a person who speaks Gk. and lives as a Gk. (Acts 6:1; 9:29). In 9:29 it refers to a group of Jews in Damascus who sought to kill Paul, and in 6:1 to Gk.-speaking Jewish Christians who were not Greeks at all.

1. In Jn. 7:35 the Jews wonder if Jesus intends to go to "where our people live scattered among the Greeks [*Hellēnes*], and teach the Greeks." In Jn. 12:20–22 the same word refers to Gk.-speaking proselytes (→ *prosēlytos*, *4670*), not pagans, for they wanted to worship in the temple; they wanted to see Jesus. This gives rise to a prospect of the mission to the Gentiles, for which Jesus' death is a prerequisite. Gk.-speaking Jewish Christians first preached the gospel to the Greeks (Acts 11:20). This was advanced above all by Paul and his companions (17:4; 19:10; etc.). Whenever the Jews refused his message, Paul turned to the Greeks. Yet of the "islanders" on Malta to whom Paul ministered after his shipwreck, Luke uses the word *barbaros* (Acts 28:2, 4).

Jews and Greeks lived everywhere side by side, with the result that mixed marriages took place. From one of these came Timothy (Acts 16:1). Paul was accused of taking Greeks into the temple and thus defiling it (21:28). Sometimes the word *Hellēn* can also mean a proselyte (14:1; 17:4).

2. The expression "Jews and Greeks," which occurs esp. in Paul's writings, can stand for the whole of humanity (1 Cor. 1:24; 10:32; 12:13; Gal. 3:28; Col. 3:11). The Jews are mentioned first as an expression of their privileged place in salvation history (Rom. 3:1–2; 9:4–5). But God is just as much God of the Greeks as of the Jews (10:12). Paul was set aside in a special way to exercise his apostolic ministry among the Greeks (Rom. 1:14; cf. *ethnos* [→ *1620*] in Gal. 1:16; 2:9; Eph. 3:6–7; 1 Tim. 2:7). Not all pagans were *Hellēnes*, for alongside them Paul refers also to "non-Greeks" (*barbaros*, Rom. 1:14) and to "barbarian [and] Scythian" (Col. 3:11). *barbaros* in 1 Cor. 14:11 ("foreigner") refers to someone who speaks a language not commonly understood (hence probably not Gk.). The *Hellēnes* were characterized

by their seeking wisdom, which made the cross of Christ seem folly to them (1 Cor. 1:22–23).

The picture painted by Paul in Rom. 1:18–32 of the Greeks (1:16) or the heathen (→ *ethnos*, *1620*) is a gloomy one. Nevertheless, God directs his message as much to them as to the Jews (Rom. 1:16; 2:9, 3:9). If a Gk. does good and fulfills what the law requires, he or she will receive honor like the Jew (2:9–10, 14–16; cf. Jer. 31:33–34). Since the Greeks were all pagans from the beginning, the concepts pagan and Gk. are interchangeable, when contrasted with that of the Jew (cf. Rom. 3:29–30 with 1 Cor. 1:22–24); thus, the Greeks figure here as the foremost representatives of the pagan world. The church in Corinth was given the warning not to offend "Jews, Greeks or the church of God" (1 Cor. 10:32). The non-Christian population of Corinth fell into the two first-mentioned groups, alongside which the church now stood as a new people.

In this new people of God (→ *laos*, *3295*), differences of origin are removed. God, who in reality had always been the God of the Greeks (Rom. 10:12), although they did not recognize him, has now become consciously and in fact their God, in that they have believed in Jesus Christ and through the Holy Spirit have been baptized into one body (1 Cor. 12:13). Whoever has been baptized into Jesus Christ is God's child and has put on Christ, whether Jew or Greek, so those who are born *Hellēn* now belong to the offspring of Abraham (Gal. 3:26–29). Being a Greek or Jew belongs to the old self, which has to be put away along with all its evil characteristics (Col. 3:11; cf. 3:5–10, 12–13).

1819 (Hellēnikos, Greek), → *1818.*

1820 (Hellēnis, a Greek woman), → *1818.*

1821 (Hellēnistēs, a Hellenist), → *1818.*

1822 (Hellēnisti, adv. Greek, in the Greek language), → *1818.*

1827 (elpizō, expect, hope), → *1828.*

1828	ἐλπίς

ἐλπίς (*elpis*), expectation, hope (*1828*); ἐλπίζω (*elpizō*), expect, hope (*1827*); ἀπελπίζω (*apelpizō*), expect back (*594*); προελπίζω (*proelpizō*), hope in advance (*4598*).

CL & OT 1. In cl. Gk. *elpis* is a general word for the anticipation of future events of all kinds, of good (hope) or evil (fear). Thus it means not only hope, but also expect, suppose, think. Living hope as a fundamental religious attitude was unknown in Gk. culture. In the final analysis people had to stand without hope before the hostile forces of guilt and death.

2. (a) In the LXX, *elpizō* primarily translates Heb. vbs. of trusting (→ *pistis*, *4411*). Hoping as an act occurs in promises and exhortations, but mostly as a confession of assurance, especially in Ps.

(b) Of 146 OT passages in which vbs. or nouns describe hope, half do so in a secular sense. In these it is an expectation combined with certainty and tension, directed toward some definite desired object or event lying in the future. What characterizes the judgment of this hope is that in many passages, despite its personal intensity, the hope is described as futile. Prov. emphasizes, for example, that a fool's hope will come to nothing (11:7).

(c) Hope in God is often the subject of the OT even where specific words do not occur. In formal structure it resembles secular hope, but is essentially different in content, basis, and effects. In many passages the faithful of Israel name Yahweh as the object and guarantor of hope: e.g., "You have been my hope, O Sovereign LORD" (Ps. 71:5). Jeremiah spoke of Yahweh as the "hope of Israel" (Jer. 14:8; 17:13). People wait for his name (Ps. 52:9), his word of forgiveness (130:5), his arm (Isa. 51:5), and his salvation (Gen. 49:18).

In eschatological passages the content of the hope is not expressed in abstract terms but in the form of a vision. For this reason words of hope seldom occur there (but see Isa. 25:9; 42:4; 51:5; Hab. 2:3). The horizon of hope in the OT stretches far beyond what most witnesses could see in terms of personal hope for their individual lives. It embraces Yahweh's coming in glory, his reign over a new earth, the conversion of Israel and the nations, and the new covenant, based on the forgiveness of sins.

An important element in the maintenance of a true hope was the struggle of the Lord's prophets against false prophets, with their false hope and dreams of salvation. Throughout her history so frequently marked by judgment, Israel repeatedly looked to God for the continuation of his gracious dealings with them (cf. Ps. 40:1; Isa. 40:31; Jer. 31:17; Hos. 12:7). Such hope was a gift of God (Ps. 62:5; Jer. 29:11). Wherever, humanly speaking, the future seemed a dead end, prophets of judgment such as Hosea, Jeremiah, and Ezekiel opened up the divine perspective of a new beginning (cf. Jer. 29:1–14; 31:31–34; Ezek. 36:37; Hos. 2).

(d) As a subjective attitude, the hope of faith, like secular hope, is a concrete personal expectation. It looks forward confidently, although not without tension. Yahweh knows and brings to pass what the future holds, so hope attains unparalleled assurance in the realm of revelation. Everything at present may run counter to the promise, but the one who hopes trusts God not to disappoint the hope awakened through his word (Ps. 42:5; Isa. 8:17; Mic. 7:7).

Hand in hand with confident anticipation of God's gracious dealing goes submission to his sovereign rule. The time and manner of fulfillment are left to him. Therefore, hope and the fear of God are often parallel (e.g., Ps. 33:18; 147:11; cf. Prov. 23:17–18). To those who fear the Lord a future and hope are promised, and they can endure anxiety while waiting. They demonstrate new strength (Isa. 40:31) by overcoming temptation and actions directed toward the hoped-for future. During the siege, for example, Jeremiah bought a field to bear witness to the word of God that houses, fields, and vineyards would again be purchased (Jer. 32:6–15).

2. Intertestamental Jud. is characterized by a variety of eschatological expectations, directed toward the coming of the Messiah and the restoration of the kingdom of Israel. These hopes were often disappointed. Men rose with messianic claims and set the enthusiasm of the people ablaze, but sooner or later all these movements collapsed. This explains the pessimistic streak that accompanied the eschatological expectations of the rabbis. God's kingdom could only come when Israel was completely obedient to the law. But who could really say what complete obedience was? This made the individual's personal hope uncertain as well, for who could say that God was really pleased with him or her?

The community of Qumran, by contrast, continued to affirm that there was hope, founded on God's saving actions. Nevertheless, this hope was valid only for the elect of God. In Hel. Jud. the messianic hope retreated behind the idea of the immortality of the soul (see esp. Philo).

NT 1. Remarkably, *elpizō* and *elpis* play no great role in the Gospels. Only the vb. appears, once each in Matt. (12:21 = Isa. 42:4) and Jn. (5:45), and 3x in Lk. (6:34; 23:8; 24:21), in the sense of subjective expectation. The main emphasis on hope is found in the Paul's writings (19x out of 31 for the vb.; 36x out of 53 of the noun). In Acts both vb. (2x) and noun (8x) are used particularly of the "hope of Israel," which is interpreted as hope in the resurrection.

apelpizō means to cease to hope, to give up hope, to doubt. In the NT it occurs only in Lk. 6:35. Here, however, we have a departure from the usual meaning; it means expecting to get something in return. *proelpizō*, to hope before, occurs only in Eph. 1:12. The "before" means either the hope Jewish Christians had before the influx of Gentile Christians or the messianic hope the Jews had prior to Christ's coming.

2. In the NT words in this word group never indicate a vague or a fearful anticipation, but always the expectation of something good. In many passages *elpis* denotes not a personal attitude but the objec-

tive benefit of salvation toward which hope is directed (Gal. 5:5; Col. 1:5; Tit. 2:13). Where the vb. or noun is used absolutely the reference is usually to the eschatological fulfillment (e.g., Rom. 8:24; 12:12; 15:13; Eph. 2:12).

3. All NT witnesses agree that through the coming of the promised Messiah the situation described in terms of hope in the OT has been fundamentally altered. In Christ the promised day of salvation has broken in as God's great "today." What was previously future has now become present for believers: justification, a personal relationship with God, the indwelling of the Holy Spirit, and a new people of God comprising both Israel and the nations. Since the "today" of salvation is only apparent by faith, it acquires a double aspect: to the "now" one has to add "not yet" (1 Jn. 3:2), to the "having" and "being in Christ" one must add hope in and looking for him.

4. Hope is so fundamental that a Christian can be described as having been reborn to a "living hope" (1 Pet. 1:3). In paganism there were ideas of a metaphysical future, but no hope providing comfort and freedom from the fear of death (Eph. 2:12; 1 Thess. 4:13). The significance of *elpis* is further clarified by the fact that, along with *pistis* (faith) and *agapē* (love), it forms part of the early Christian triad (see, e.g., 1 Cor. 13:13; 1 Thess. 1:3). None of the three can exist without the others; all three are rooted in Christ. Faith without hope, for example, is empty and futile (1 Cor. 15:14, 17).

5. The essential features of NT hope are given decisive shape by three factors. (a) As to its *content*, hope is never egocentric but always centered on Christ and on God. Its heart is not the blessing of the individual but the universal kingly rule of God, who will be "all in all" (1 Cor. 15:28). More specifically, the content of *elpis* is defined as: salvation (1 Thess. 5:8), eternal life (Tit. 1:2; 3:7), righteousness (Gal. 5:5), resurrection in an incorruptible body (Acts 23:6; 24:15; 1 Cor. 15:52–56), seeing God and being conformed to his likeness (1 Jn. 3:2–3), and the glory of God (Rom. 5:2; cf. 2 Cor. 3:12; Col. 1:27).

(b) As to hope's *basis*, it does not rest on one's own good works but on God's gracious work in Jesus Christ, who is therefore called "our hope" (1 Tim. 1:1; cf. Col. 1:27). This Christ is no stranger to the community of hope but the one whom believers recognize as the crucified and risen Lord and whose presence they know through the Spirit. Along with the gift of his Son God assures us that that he will give us everything through faith in him (Rom. 8:32). Because Christ has risen as the "firstfruits," we will also rise (1 Cor. 15:20–23). The Coming One is the Exalted One, whom God has already set over all things and given to the church as its head (Eph. 1:22).

(c) As to its *nature*, hope is a gift of the Father's grace (2 Thess. 2:16), like faith, and it is therefore aroused through the message of salvation (Col. 1:23). The goal of hope in all its riches gives enlightenment (Eph. 1:18), and hope unites those who have been called (4:4). Through the Holy Spirit we receive a superabundance of hope (Rom. 15:13), for God's Spirit is given to us as the firstfruits of all that we will receive (8:23); his indwelling in believers is the guarantee of their resurrection (8:11).

6. One cannot separate hope as a subjective, personal attitude from its objective content, since hope is not a theoretical knowledge about a promised future salvation but a function of a living faith. (a) It is always a confident, sure expectation of divine saving actions. Hope looks at the coming city of God; faith gives certainty to our hope (Heb. 11:1; → *hypostasis*, *5712*). In Rom. 4:18 Abraham's faith is presented as hope "against all hope"—i.e., against what human judgment of the future declared as impossible, Abraham set his hope through God's promise. Like faith, NT hope carries unconditional certainty within itself. Therefore, confessions of hope can be introduced by words of certainty, such as "we believe" (Rom. 6:8), "I am convinced" (8:38), "[I am] confident" (Phil. 1:6). Certain that God's promises of salvation will be realized, the Christian glories in this hope (Rom. 5:2; cf. Heb. 3:6).

(b) Like faith and hope, love and hope are also essentially related in the NT. If 1 Cor. 13:7 states that love "always hopes," Col. 1:4–5 speaks of "the love you have for all the saints . . . that spring[s] from the hope that is stored up for you in heaven." NT hope extends both heart and vision. The church feels solidarity with the whole creation as it groans and hopes for the redemption of the body (Rom. 8:20–23).

(c) NT hope demonstrates its living character by the steadfastness with which it waits (→ *hypomenō*, 5702), patiently bearing the tension between our present as we walk by faith (2 Cor. 5:7) and our future manner of life (cf. Rom. 8:25; 1 Thess. 1:3). This waiting is something active, for it involves overcoming (Rev. 2:7, 11, 17, etc.). Although the waiting may be painful, this too is reckoned positively, as labor that announces rebirth (Matt. 24:8). Thus those who hope are comforted and confident (2 Cor. 5:8; 1 Thess. 4:18; 2 Thess. 2:16).

(d) To this context belongs the fundamental renunciation of all calculations of the future, a humble recognition of our limited knowledge, and submission to the life to which we have been appointed. The goal of our hope calls us to "watch and pray." It motivates us to personal purity (1 Jn. 3:3) and spurs us on to holy living (2 Cor. 5:8–9; Heb. 12:14). Hope requires us to hold fast our confession without wavering (Heb. 10:23) and to be ready to give an answer to anyone who asks about our hope (1 Pet. 3:15). Finally, NT hope is a joyful waiting (Rom. 12:12), which gives courage and strength. It protects the inner self as a helmet protects the head (1 Thess. 5:8). As a ship is safe when at anchor, our life is secured by the hope that binds us to Christ, our great high priest, who has entered the sanctuary on our behalf (Heb. 6:18–19).

See also *apokaradokia*, eager expectation (638).

1838 (emblepō, look, look at, look in the face, consider), → *1063.*

1842	Ἐμμανουήλ

Ἐμμανουήλ (*Emmanouēl*), Immanuel (*1842*).

OT The name Immanuel, which occurs in Isa. 7:14 and 8:8, means (lit.) "God [is] with us" (Heb. ʿimmānû ʾēl). In the context of the time of Isaiah and Ahaz the name was given to a child not yet conceived, with the promise that the danger threatening Israel from Syria and Samaria would pass "before the boy knows enough to reject the wrong and choose the right." Thus, the child and its name were a sign of God's gracious, saving presence among his people.

The name Immanuel can have either a minimum or a maximum significance. It could be a general statement that the birth and naming of the special child will indicate that the good hand of God is on the Israelites. Or it could be a divine name meaning that God's presence with them is to be found in the child. In justification of the latter interpretation is the name of the child in Isa. 9:6, whom we may fairly regard as the same person. One of his names there is Mighty God.

NT Matt. 1:21–23 describes the angel's promise to Joseph about the son conceived in Mary by the Holy Spirit, the son who is to be called "Jesus, because he will save his people from their sins," in fulfillment of Isa. 7:14. This does not necessarily mean that Isaiah prophesied a virgin birth, for *parthenos* (→ 4221) could be used of women other than virgins (e.g., Gen. 34:3); similarly the Heb. ʿalmâ could mean a young woman married or single (Gen. 24:43; Exod. 2:8; Song 1:3; 6:8). That question rests on the interpretation of verses other than Matt. 1:23 (e.g., Matt. 1:18–20; Lk. 1:34–35).

The name Immanuel is not applied to Jesus elsewhere in the NT. The point of Matt. 1 is to see in Jesus' birth a saving act of God, comparable with the birth of the first Immanuel. Both births signify God's presence with his people through a child. But whereas the earlier event in Isaiah's day was regarded at the time as having decisive significance, in the light of the coming of Jesus the birth of that child in the time of Isaiah proves to be merely the anticipation of the truly decisive saving act and presence of God when Jesus was born (→ *plēroō*, 4444). "God with us" is another way of saying that Jesus is the Son of God; that child is God come to earth.

See also *theos*, God (2536); *kyrios*, Lord (3261).

1844 (emmenō, stay or remain in, persevere, abide by), → *3531.*

1850 (empaizō, mock, ridicule), → *3943.*

1853 (emperipateō, go about, walk), → *4344.*

1855 (empimplēmi, fill full, fill up, satisfy), → *4444.*

1863 (empneō, to pant), → *4460.*

1864 (emporeuomai, trade), → *4797.*

1871 (emphanēs, visible), → *1872.*

1872	ἐμφανίζω

ἐμφανίζω (*emphanizō*), reveal, make known (*1872*); ἐμφανής (*emphanēs*), visible (*1871*).

CL & OT 1. In cl. Gk. *emphanizō* means to manifest, exhibit; pass. to become visible. The word also connotes the ideas of making plain, declaring, or explaining. The adj. *emphanēs* connotes the idea of visible, open, manifest.

2. (a) In Est. 2:22 *emphanizō* means to say or tell. The sense is that of making known or revealing the ways of God in Exod. 33:13, while in Isa. 3:9 the vb. indicates that certain people manifest or display their sin. In Exod. 33:18 it means to show or exhibit.

(b) Isa. 2:2 and Mic. 4:1 describe the exalted position of the mountain of the house of the Lord over the other mountains. *emphanēs* here is probably used in the sense of conspicuous or manifest. In Isa. 65:1 the adj. occurs in a phrase that the Lord manifested himself to those who did not ask for him. In Exod. 2:14 *emphanēs* denotes how Moses became aware of the fact that his murder of the Egyptian had become known.

NT 1. (a) In the NT *emphanizō* occurs 5x in the sense of declare, inform. In Acts 23:15 it is used in a legal context, where a group of forty men, in a plot against Paul, ask the Sanhedrin to "petition" the commander under pretense of presenting a case against the apostle (cf. also 25:2, 15). In 23:22 the word describes the act of a nephew of Paul who disclosed information to the commander about the plot against his uncle.

(b) In Heb. 11:14 the word *emphanizō* has the sense of show or manifest. Those who acknowledge their transience on the earth demonstrate that they are seeking a homeland.

(c) *emphanizō* occurs 4x in the sense of appear. In Matt. 27:53 risen saints appeared in Jerusalem after the resurrection of Christ. In Jn. 14:21–22 Jesus says he will show himself to his followers but not to the world. Here the vb. connotes a manifestation to the spiritual faculties rather than to the senses. In Heb. 9:24 the verb is used of Christ's appearance in the presence of God.

2. The adj. *emphanēs* is used 2x in the NT. In Acts 10:40 it refers to the post-resurrection appearance of Christ, who made himself manifest to certain witnesses. In Rom. 10:20 the word occurs in a quotation from Isa. 65:1: "I revealed myself to those who did not ask for me." This verse illustrates both the fulfillment of OT prophecy and the consistency of God in receiving the Gentiles, whereas Israel, as ever, has remained disobedient (Rom. 10:21; cf. Isa. 65:2).

See also *lampō*, shine (3290); *lychnos*, lamp, light (3394); *phainō*, shine (5743); *phōs*, light, brilliance, brightness (5890).

1875 (emphytos, implanted), → *1285.*

1877	ἐν

ἐν (*en*), in, on, (*1877*).

CL & OT *en* takes the dat. case. In cl. Gk. its primary meaning was locative, to denote the place in which something was situated. By the time of Hel. Gk., it was by far the most common prep. and served a wide variety of purposes. It encroached on the territory of such preps. as *eis* (into; on this, → 1650), *dia* (both with gen. and acc.), *meta, syn,* and *kata*. In the LXX it was the usual prep. used to translate the Heb. *b^e* (which occurs more than 15,000x).

It may seem remarkable, therefore, that in modern Gk. this prep. is no longer used. But the ultimate disappearance of *en* from the language is related to two facts: (a) the disappearance of the dat. case, a process completed by the 10th century, and (b) the diversified use of *en* in Hel. Gk. A principle of language development seems to be that the more a particular linguistic form is employed, the more it is subject to weakening and ultimate collapse.

NT   1. *en* is the most frequent prep. in the NT (over 2700x). Three factors that contributed to its extended NT usage are LXX usage (see above), the increasing imprecision of the dat., and the influence of distinctively Christian ideas, such as "in Christ."

2. Because of its wide variety of usage, *en* often leaves the exegete with ambiguities. For example, what does "all in all" mean in 1 Cor. 15:28 (cf. Eph. 1:23; Col. 3:11)? Does it express God's unchallenged supremacy in the universe, his indwelling of all members of the redeemed community, or something else? The prep. is of no help in deciding this issue, since it is too imprecise. Often all the exegete can do is to reduce the number of possible meanings of *en* by examining the context.

3. *en* often has a fig. sense in the NT, denoting the sphere within which an action occurs or the element or reality in which something is contained or consists. Phrases such as "in the Lord," "in (the) Spirit," "in the body," "in faith," and "in truth" indicate states in which God's people live and act. In Eph. 6:1 and Col. 3:20, for example, children's obedience to their parents should be *en kyriō* ("in the Lord"), i.e., arising from Christian motives. Similarly, the Christian widow is free to remarry (1 Cor. 7:39), but only *en kyriō* (lit., "in the sphere of the Lord"); i.e., she may marry only a fellow Christian. In Gal. 1:16, where Paul is describing how he received his gospel, he writes that God revealed "his Son in [*en*] me." Paul is here stressing the inward and intensely personal character of God's revelation to him of the risen Jesus (though one can also simply translate the phrase "to me," cf. NRSV).

4. Of considerable theological importance is "causal *en*" (usually regarded as a subdivision of "instrumental *en*"), where *en* means "on account of, because of." For example, in Rom. 5:3 Paul mentions that believers can rejoice "in [their] sufferings." Taking the apostle's theology of suffering into account, the most likely understanding of this verse is that believers can rejoice "because of their suffering" (for other examples of causal *en*, see Matt. 6:7; Jn. 16:30; Acts 7:29; 24:16; Rom. 1:21, 24; 1 Cor. 4:4; 7:14; 2 Cor. 12:5, 9; Phil. 1:13; Col. 1:21; cf. LXX examples in Deut. 24:16; 2 Sam. 3:27; Ps. 31:10; 42:9).

5. The most theologically rich use of *en* is Paul's *en Christō* ("in Christ"). *en* here has various nuances, of which the most important are: (a) union with Christ (Rom. 8:1; 2 Cor. 5:17, 21); (b) sphere of reference, a meaning virtually synonymous with being a Christian (Rom. 16:7; 2 Cor. 12:2; Phil. 3:3); (c) instrumentality (Rom. 3:24; 2 Cor. 3:14); (d) cause (1 Cor. 15:22; Col. 2:10); (e) location (Rom. 8:39; Phil. 2:5); and (f) authoritative basis (1 Thess. 4:1).

John also uses this formula, though he has a different nuance in his writings. He expresses the idea of personal co-inherence (Jn. 6:56; 14:20; 15:4–5; 1 Jn. 3:24; 4:13, 15–16), patterned on the archetype of divine co-inherence (Jn. 10:38; 14:10–11, 20; 17:21, 23). That is, not only are we in Christ but he is in us, just as he is in the Father and the Father is in him. Paul, it is true, does refer to Christ as being in us (cf. Rom. 8:10; 2 Cor. 13:5; Col. 1:27), but more frequently he speaks of the Spirit indwelling us (Rom. 8:9, 11; 1 Cor. 6:19; 2 Tim. 1:14).

One important use of *en Christō* occurs in 2 Cor. 5:19. Does Paul mean that "God lived in Christ" and in that position was reconciling the world to himself? Or is Paul using a periphrastic construction, namely, that God was reconciling the world to himself "through Christ"? Both of these embody Pauline sentiments, but grammatical considerations tend to favor the first option. A functional Christology presupposes and finds its ultimate basis in an ontological Christology.

Not only was Christ God's agent in effecting reconciliation (Rom. 5:10–11; 2 Cor. 5:18; Col. 1:19–22); he also mediated the divine presence, thus giving validity to his reconciliatory sacrifice. God was in Christ and therefore acted through Christ (cf. Jn. 14:10b, "the Father, living in me . . . is doing his work").

6. *en* is also used with *baptizō*, to baptize (→ *966*). Generally this has a local sense: e.g., "in the Jordan River" (Matt. 3:6), "in the desert region" (Mk. 1:4), "at Aenon" (Jn. 3:23), and "in the cloud and in the sea" (1 Cor. 10:2). *en hydati* (lit., "in water") denotes the element in which the baptized were "immersed" or with which they were "drenched" (Matt. 3:11; Jn. 1:26, 31, 33; cf. the simple dat, *hydati* in Lk. 3:16; Acts 1:5; 11:16). So also with (*en*) *pneumati* (*hagiō*) (lit., "in the [Holy] Spirit"), which is generally contrasted with (*en*) *hydati* (Matt. 3:11; Lk. 3:16; Jn. 1:33; Acts 1:5; 11:16), believers are either immersed "in" the Spirit or drenched "with" the Spirit. Personal agency with the vb. *baptizō* cannot be expressed by a simple dat. or by *en* with the dat.; rather, it is always expressed with *hypo* (→ *5679*) with the gen.

Thus, it seems likely that "[*en*] one Spirit" in 1 Cor. 12:13 means not "by one Spirit" but "in [or with] one Spirit." Note also that in the sayings about John the Baptist regarding Spirit baptism, it is always Jesus who is the baptizer, never the Spirit. Moreover, 12:13b ("we were all given the one Spirit to drink") suggests an inward participation in the Spirit to which a preceding outward immersion in the Spirit corresponds. The Holy Spirit is both around (12:13a) and within (12:13b; cf. Eph. 5:18).

7. *en* is used 4x with *pistis* (faith, → *4411*; see Eph. 1:15; Col. 1:4; 1 Tim. 3:13; 2 Tim. 3:15). The prep. phrase here likely marks out the sphere or realm in which faith is operative, thus specifying the actual object of faith. For example, Col. 1:4 may be paraphrased "your faith (that rests) in Christ Jesus" or "your faith experienced in fellowship with Christ Jesus." In Mk. 1:15, the only clear case where *en* follows the vb. *pisteuō* (to believe), the expression simply means to believe in the truth of the gospel.

1892 (*endeiknymi*, show, display), → *1259*.

1893 (*endeixis*, demonstration, proof), → *1259*.

1897 (*endēmeō*, be at home), → *1322*.

1901 (*endoxazomai*, honor, glorify), → *1518*.

1902 (*endoxos*, honored, glorious), → *1518*.

1903 (*endyma*, clothes), → *1544*.

1904 (*endynamoō*, strengthen), → *1539*.

1907 (*endyō*, dress, clothe), → *1544*.

1918 (*energeia*, working, operation, action), → *2237*.

1919 (*energeō*, to work, be active, effect something), → *2237*.

1920 (*energēma*, activity, experience), → *2237*.

1921 (*energēs*, active, effective, powerful), → *2237*.

1922 (*eneulogeō*, bless), → *2330*.

1923 (*enechō*, hold fast, be subject to), → *1944*.

1926 (*enthymeomai*, reflect, consider), → *2596*.

1927 (*enthymēsis*, thought, reflection), → *2596*.

1936 (*ennoia*, thought, knowledge, insight), → *3808*.

1937 (*ennomos*, under law, orderly), → *3795*.

1940 (*enoikeō*, live in, dwell in), → *3875*.

1941 (*enorkizō*, adjure, cause someone to swear), → *3923*.

1942 (*henotēs*, unity), → *1651*.

1944	ἔνοχος

ἔνοχος (*enochos*), guilty, subject to, liable to (*1944*); ἐνέχω (*enechō*), hold fast, be subject to (*1923*).

CL & OT 1. In cl. Gk. *enochos* means hold fast, be subject to. It is frequently used as a technical legal term: A person is made liable or subject to a certain penalty under the law. The forum (law court, laws, humans, or gods) before which one is guilty or liable is usually referred to in the dat. Frequently, *enochos* is also used with the gen. of a crime or its punishment.

2. The LXX has *enochos* 21x in the same sense as secular Gk. It is used primarily to refer to a person who is liable to death because of some serious sin, such as manslaughter, adultery, sodomy, incest (Gen. 26:11; Exod. 22:2 = LXX 22:3; Lev. 20:9–27; Num. 35:27; Deut. 19:10). In Isa. 54:17 *enochos* is used of those who incur guilt by engaging in a legal dispute with Israel. In Ezek. 14:4, 7, *enechō* is used in the sense of being entangled (cf. 3 Macc. 6:10).

NT 1. *enochos* occurs 10x in the NT, following the above pattern. In Matt. 5:21–22 [4x], the respective courts before which a lawbreaker is arraigned are referred to in the dat. or *eis* with the acc.: *krisis*, local court; *synedrion*, supreme national court; *gehenna*, hell. The lesser or greater degree of guilt is reflected in the nature of the court and the severity of the punishment.

2. Jas. 2:10 uses *enochos* of lawbreakers. Every sin, however insignificant it may appear, makes the doer "guilty of breaking all of [the law]" and therefore liable to judgment.

3. In the accounts of the trial of Jesus in Matt. and Mk., the death sentence is pronounced using the term *enochos*. The high priest regards the evidence of blasphemy as conclusive in Jesus' case and declares him "worthy of death" (Matt. 26:66; cf. Mk. 14:64).

4. Heb. 2:15 explains the significance of the death of Jesus, which frees those who were "held" in slavery (i.e., to the devil and to death). In 1 Cor. 11:27 Paul concludes that those who take the bread and wine in an unworthy manner become "guilty of sinning against the body and blood of the Lord." The Lord gave himself up to death for the sake of his people; their opposite action, loveless behavior toward fellow believers (cf. Matt. 5:21–22), results in guilt. Here too *enochos* is used of a matter of life and death. Similarly, Mk. 3:29 uses *enochos* with a gen. of the penalty: Anyone who blasphemes against the Holy Spirit is "guilty of an eternal sin."

5. *enechō* appears 3x in the NT, in each case (as in the LXX) with a negative application of the meaning "held." Herodias "nursed" a grudge against John the Baptist (Mk. 6:19); the teachers of the law "opposed" Jesus (Lk. 11:53); and the Galatians were letting themselves be "burdened" again with a yoke of slavery (i.e., the law).

See also *aitia*, ground, cause, reason, charge (*162*); *elenchō*, bring to light, expose, convict, punish (*1794*); *amemptos*, blameless (*289*).

1945 (entalma, precept, rule), → *1953.*

1946 (entaphiazō, prepare for burial), → *2507.*

1947 (entaphiasmos, laying out for burial), → *2507.*

1948 (entellō, to command, give orders), → *1953.*

1950 (enteuxis, petition, prayer), → *1289.*

1952 (entimos, respected, honored, valuable, precious), → *5507.*

1953 ἐντολή

ἐντολή (*entolē*), command, commandment, order (*1953*); ἐντέλλω (*entellō*), to command, give orders, order (*1948*); ἔνταλμα (*entalma*), precept, rule (*1945*).

CL & OT 1. *entolē* and *entellō* occur in cl. Gk. to denote instructions given by a person of high social standing to a subordinate. At an early date these words were also used of the commands of God, in a way similar to the royal or imperial decrees.

2. The vb. occurs 400x in the LXX; *entolē*, 244x. Both words are most concentrated in the Pentateuch (esp. in Deut.). The vb. is also frequent in Jer. and the noun in Ps. 119. It translates words derived from the root *ṣwh*. *entalma* is found only 4x (Job 23:11–12; Isa. 29:13; 55:11).

(a) The Heb. *ṣiwwâ* (Pi'el) means to order, direct, summon a person or thing to a place or task. Yahweh appoints a king over his people (1 Sam. 13:14; cf. 2 Sam. 6:21)and gives his angels protective charge over his own (Ps. 91:11). He decrees victories for Israel (Ps. 44:4) and orders things to be done (Exod. 4:28). Alternatively, when the vb. is linked with a negative, God forbids certain actions (Gen. 2:16; 3:11, 17).

(b) *miṣwâ* is used mostly of divine commands. Ps. often speak of "your commands." In other words, the command of God is something known.

(c) Other Heb. roots translated by this Gk. word group are *pqd*, to entrust something to someone (2 Chr. 36:23), call to account, punish (wickedness, Isa. 13:11)—God is the subject; *dbr*, speak, command—Yahweh or his representative(Moses, Deut. 18:18; Joshua, Jos. 4:12) issues the command; and *ḥqq*. This last one merits special attention. *ḥōq, ḥuqqâ* means lit. what is established, carved, fixed in writing, and thus a statute (e.g., Deut. 6:24; 16:12; 28:15). These statutes are handed down and experienced, and God's covenant, law, justice, and commands are thus realized. Disregard of the divine statutes brings the punishment of Yahweh (1 Ki. 11:11). In one case God refers to Israelite worship practices as "rules [*entalma*] taught by men" (Isa. 29:13; but cf. the LXX of 55:11 for a positive use of this word).

(d) *entolē* is rarely used for Heb. *tôrâ* (law). In such cases it has the secondary sense of the summary of God's commands and thus the normative law of God for Israel (Deut. 17:19; 2 Ki. 21:8; 2 Chr. 30:16).

3. In Qumran literature (where these Heb. roots appear), one discovers that the Qumran sect was concerned with the literal, scriptural keeping of the commands of the Pentateuch and the prophets, which would differentiate them from the more lax attitude of the Jerusalem priesthood. Moses' law is preserved through constant learning and remembrance in daily living. Observance of this normative pattern is also decisive as to whether one will stand in the impending last judgment.

4. The Jud. of the synagogues suffered from an atomistic ethic that fragmented everything into individual demands and acts. The OT Apocr. and Pseudepigrapha maintained the usage and sense of the OT and LXX. Josephus assimilated his ideas of *entolē* to Roman thinking and used it in a legal rather than a theological sense.

Jud. at the time of Jesus lived in a tension. On the one hand, Jews attempted to create a comprehensive list of basic commandments, the obligation of the *halakah* (the transmission in a kind of catechism of ethical rules) to observe in a casuistical system. On the other hand, they also tried to distinguish between the more and the less important commandments (cf. Matt. 22:34–40; Mk. 12:29–30; Lk. 20:39–40). The theological problem in Jud. lay in the lack of an authoritative, prophetic message that could apply the law in terms of commandments that were valid for the contemporary situation.

NT In the NT *entolē* occurs 67x; *entellō*, 14x; *entalma*, 3x. These are concentrated chiefly in the Gospels and in Paul.

1. According to the Synoptic Gospels, Jesus' teaching entered the divisive discussion of the commandments. Nevertheless, he refused to participate in casuistry or set up a hierarchical scale that would distinguish between the least, and therefore dispensable, commands (cf. Matt. 5:19) and a single, great command that would unify the entire law. Jesus refused to play off the command to love God against the command to love one's neighbor (cf. 22:36, 38).

Jesus also refused to let a clear command of God be rendered void by human ordinances, even under the pretext of a supposed love of God that had priority. He denounced these human statutes as "your tradition" (Matt. 15:3), "rules taught by men" (*entalma*, Matt. 15:9; Mk. 7:7), and "the tradition of men" (7:8). Instead, Jesus taught that love of God and love of humankind were inseparable. Beside the first great commandment, there is a "second . . . like it. . . . All the Law and the Prophets hang on these two commandments" (Matt. 22:39–40; cf.

Mk. 12:31). By relating the commandment to its original sense of an offer of life springing from the love of God, it is possible both to love God and one's neighbor in gratitude.

This is shown by numerous examples in the teaching of Jesus. The rich young ruler was challenged to surrender all his goods to the poor in order to live by the daily care of God as he followed Jesus (Matt. 19:16–30; Mk. 10:17–31; Lk. 18:18–30). God's original ordinance of monogamous marriage was designed to further the joy of marriage, not to sanction a casuistical approach to divorce (Matt. 19:7; Mk. 10:3, 5; cf. Deut. 24:1). Both the context and the parable of the good Samaritan (Lk. 10:25–37) show Jesus' loving attitude to his legalistic opponent. Through encounter with the love of God, the shattered unity of love for God and love for and service to one's fellow human being is restored (cf. Lk. 10:27, 29).

Jesus brought word and action into a unity. He stood in contrast to his opponents, who burdened people with commands (Matt. 11:28–30; 23:4; cf. Lk. 11:46), and displayed a regal and prophetic authority over the commands of God. He showed this in the antitheses of the Sermon on the Mount (Matt. 5:21–48) and in his attitude to the Sabbath (Mk. 2:23–27). Jesus did not set aside the law; rather, he rose above the discussion of the commandments and the bondage into which we get when we administer them by pointing us to the Giver of the Law (Matt. 5:48; cf. 5:17).

Jesus completely fulfilled God's command to abandon self for others (Matt. 26:39; Mk. 14:36; Lk. 22:42; cf. Phil. 2:8; Jn. 19:30). Hence, the Johannine writings can rightly speak of "a new command" (Jn. 13:34). The missionary commission speaks of doing all that Jesus told us (Matt. 28:20; cf. Acts 1:2, 8). Paul emphasized serving God's law by the power of the Spirit (Rom. 7:25; cf. 7:1–24; 8:2).

The remaining Synoptic passages with *entolē* and *entellō* have meanings discussed under the OT section. The parents of John the Baptist observed "all the Lord's *commandments* and regulations" (Lk. 1:6). The women among Jesus' followers rested on the Sabbath "in obedience to the commandment" (23:56). Jesus commanded his disciples not to speak about his transfiguration (Matt. 17:9; cf. Mk. 9:9).

2.(a) The rabbis taught that God's law was the best means available to subdue one's evil inclination. In contrast, Paul developed the sharpest antithesis to this (Rom. 7:7–25). For him, the Spirit of God is the only power that subdues evil inclinations. He testifies to the revelatory function of God's law in unveiling sin's power. True, "the law is holy, and the commandment is holy, righteous and good" (7:12), and it "was intended to bring life" (7:10). However, it resulted in bringing about "covetous desire" (7:8), which brought in its train sin and death (7:9–10). In fact, the commandment can even provoke one to sin (7:11; cf. 5:20).

The service of the law, therefore, is ultimately beneficial, because its leads us to see our powerlessness before sin and the hopeless and fatal character of our struggle. That is, anyone set under the law is obligated to carry it on by himself or herself against the personal power of sin (7:24). When we realize we cannot measure up to its demands, we are driven to the saving power of the gospel of Jesus Christ (7:25; 8:1–4). The teaching of Paul, the servant of the risen Christ, is thus in line with the teaching of Jesus. Our Lord has abolished "in his flesh the law with its commandments and regulations" (Eph. 2:15). The accumulation here of the synonyms *nomos* (→ *3795*), *entolē*, and *dogma* (→ *1504*) graphically portrays how they have all been swept away by Christ.

There is no basic contradiction, then, when Paul urges us to keep "God's commands" (1 Cor. 7:19; cf. Matt. 19:17). Faith that works through love (Gal. 5:6) and the "new creation" (6:15) provide the necessary presuppositions for keeping God's commands. On this basis, 1 Cor. 7:19 repudiates Christian libertinism. Eph. 6:2 endorses the fifth commandment to "honor your father and mother" (cf. Exod. 20:12). Rom. 13:9 sees the command to "love your neighbor as yourself" (Lev. 19:8) as a summary of all the commands of the second part of the Decalogue. Paul's imperative is grounded in the preceding indicative of Christ's saving work and the power of the Spirit given to us.

On several occasions Paul uses *entolē* to denote mandates he has given in his authority as an apostle. Col. 4:10 cites instructions concerning Barnabas (cf. Acts 17:15), while 1 Cor. 14:37 stresses that what he is writing is a command of the Lord and will be as such recognized by those who are spiritual. Paul charges Timothy to "keep this command without spot or blame" (1 Tim. 6:14; cf. 6:20), but the false teachers at Colossae were to be resisted because they were trying to enforce rules "based on human commands" (*entalma*, Col. 2:22).

(b) In agreement with Paul, Heb. systematically expounds the theme of the superiority of the heavenly, royal high priesthood of Christ over the Levitical priesthood. It demonstrates how a "former regulation (*entolē*) is set aside because it was weak and useless" (7:18). It is superseded by a better hope (7:19; cf. Rom. 7:7–10) and by "the power of an indestructible life" (Heb. 7:16).

3. (a) In Jn. *entolē* and *entellō* are used primarily in relation to Jesus, God's only Son, the revealer (Jn. 8:5; 11:57 offer two exceptions). Just as the Father's commands to Jesus (15:10) constitute one command (12:49–50), so Jesus speaks now of his command(s) (13:34; 14:15, 21; 15:10). These commands can really be reduced to one essential command, the command to love (15:12).

The basic relationship established by the commandment is what the Father has given to the Son (10:18; 12:49–50; 15:10). There is no conflict between the authority given to the Son and his free decision and active obedience (cf. 10:17–18; 14:31), nor is there a conflict with the words and actions of the Son (12:49). The command of the Father is eternal life (12:50)—not because anyone can fulfill it and thus gain eternal life, but because the fulfillment of this command by the Son means eternal life for the world. By keeping the Father's commands, the Son shows his love for the Father (14:31) and remains in his Father's love (15:10). This love is not a mystical love; it is active in history (3:16). It means the Father's giving of his Son and the self-giving of the Son for the disciples (14:9; 15:12–14).

The historical expression of the Son's love does not end with those who accept that love. Rather, receiving that love provides the basis, conditions, and possibility of extending this love to others (Jn. 13:34). It must be practiced; it is therefore the one new command (cf. 15:12), although historically and ethically it is by no means new. Still, it excludes both legalism and antinomianism (13:35; cf. Lk. 10:25–37; Rom. 13:9; 1 Cor. 7:3–4, 19). To abide in Jesus' command is to abide in his love, just as his abiding in the Father's command means to abide in the Father's love (15:10).

(b) Usage of these terms in Jn.'s letters is essentially the same as in the Gospel. Keeping the command is equated with keeping the word (1 Jn. 2:4–5, 7). However, here it is no longer the Son himself who proclaims the command. Rather, the discussion is about the command of God the Father, presumably the command to love as cited in the Gospel. The situation of the author and the recipients of these letters suggests a conflict with an antinomian docetism that evidently disputed both Christ's person and the need for spiritual believers to submit to an ethic binding on all. This necessitated further explanation of the commandment. "This is his command: to believe in the name of his Son Jesus Christ, and to love one another as he commanded us" (1 Jn. 3:23; cf. Gal. 5:6; 1 Cor. 7:19).

The idea of the Father's command can also be given a new meaning: "I am writing you a new command; its truth is seen in him and you, because the darkness is passing and the true light is already shining" (1 Jn. 2:8). Thus, the command to love is now the "old command." "I am not writing you a new command, but an old one, which you have had since the beginning" (2:7; cf. 2 Jn. 5–6). Here the word old (*palaian*) means known of old, as opposed to the enthusiastic, new doctrine of the docetic gnostics.

This command, long observed in the churches, provides the ground for certainty that all prayers are answered by God (1 Jn. 3:22). In 1 Jn. 4:21 the twofold command of the OT and the Synoptics (cf. Mk. 12:28–34) is formulated as a single command that comes from Jesus: "He has given us this command: Whoever loves God must also love his brother." Again the stress falls on brotherly love. But there is a corollary: "This is how we know that we love the children of God: by loving God and carrying out his commands" (5:2). Moreover, overtones of Jesus' invitation in Matt. 11:28–30 and the certainty of victory in 1 Jn. 2:8 may be heard in 1 Jn. 5:3–4.

(c) In the same certainty of victory, Rev. testifies to present opposition (12:17), patience, and ultimate victory (14:12; 22:14). This is the lot of those who keep God's command and bear witness to Jesus.

4. Libertine groups in the churches are attacked even more strongly in 2 Pet. than 1 and 2 Jn. Certain opponents have turned their backs "on the sacred command that was passed on to them" (2 Pet. 2:21). Peter here refers to the entire Christian teaching, but above all to the ethical practices described in this verse as "the way of righteousness" (cf. Prov. 21:16; Job 24:13; Matt. 21:32). The sole defense against libertinism is to recall OT prophecy and "the command given by our Lord and Savior through your apostles" (3:2). Both verses understand Jesus as the proclaimer of a new law and Christian doctrine as the summary of it.

5. Finally, the hortatory passages of the Apostolic Fathers present a picture of a new legalism. The scheme of a two-ways doctrine (see esp. *Barn.* 19ff.; cf. Herm. *Mand.*) promises eternal punishment to those who do not hear or keep Christ's commandments, whereas those who do keep the commandments are promised eternal life. Ignatius exhorted the church to submit themselves to the bishop and to his commands (Ign. *Trall.* 13:2). He praised them because they were united in the commandments of Christ (Ign. *Rom.* preamble) and were "adorned from head to foot in the commandments of Jesus Christ" (Ign. *Eph.* 9:2).

See also *dogma*, decree, ordinance, command (*1504*); *parangellō*, give orders, command (*4133*); *keleuō*, command, order (*3027*).

| 1961 | ἐντυγχάνω |

ἐντυγχάνω (*entynchanō*), meet, turn to, approach, petition, pray, intercede (*1961*); ὑπερεντυγχάνω (*hyperentynchanō*), plead, intercede (*5659*).

CL & OT In cl. Gk. *entynchanō* means to approach or appeal to someone. It is found in the papyri in the sense of appealing to someone against a third person. Since petitions may be addressed to God, it has also the sense of to pray. Apart from Dan. 6:13 (= LXX 6:12), neither vb. occurs in the OT (but see Wis. 8:20; 16:28; 1 Macc. 8:32; 10:61, 63, 64; 11:25; 2 Macc. 2:25; 4:36; 6:12; 15:39; 3 Macc. 6:37). *hyperentynchanō* is first found in the NT.

NT *entynchanō* is used of Paul's appeal to the emperor in Acts 25:24. In Rom. 11:2 it denotes Elijah's pleading with God against Israel (cf. 1 Ki. 19:10). It is twice used of Christ's continuing intercession at the right hand of God (Rom. 8:34; Heb. 7:25); this intercession is grounded in his death, resurrection, and ascension.

These vbs. are also used of the Holy Spirit, who "himself intercedes [*hyperentynchanō*] for us with groans that words cannot express ... [and who] intercedes [*entynchanō*] for the saints in accordance with God's will" (Rom. 8:26–27). This refers in some way to Christian prayer. Even a believer's prayer life exists only by God's grace. During times of spiritual weakness, the Spirit himself helps us by interceding for us.

What is most debated in Rom. 8:26–27 is the meaning of the "groans that words cannot express" (NRSV, "sighs too deep for words"). The noun used here is *stenagmos* (→ *stenazō*, to sigh, groan, *5100*). Does this refer to glossolalia (speaking in tongues)? Scholars are divided over the issue. Any interpretation of this passage must reckon with the fact that in 8:22–23, the vb. *stenazō* occurs: The entire creation groans [*systenazō*, to groan together] under the effects of sin, and "we ourselves, who have the firstfruits of the Spirit, groan [*stenazō*] inwardly as we wait eagerly for our adoption as sons, the redemption of our bodies." In other words, there are times in the life of every

believer when the effects of sin become oppressive to our hearts and words do not come into our minds as we cry out to God. But at such times God himself, through the Spirit, becomes our advocate.

Paul is not promoting a pietistic sense of raising us above our own strength in order to bring us near to God. The Spirit does not free us from earthly things but as our proxy brings our needs to God in ways that we cannot express ourselves. The groans are a sign of the church's solidarity with the rest of the creation. The presence of the Spirit is only the firstfruits of the full reality of our adoption as God's children, the redemption of the body (Rom. 8:23). The reference to our body, which in the Gk. is sing., may refer to the corporate body of the church (cf. 12:4–5) or to the physical body; perhaps the two ideas may coalesce here.

Later in Rom. Paul defines worship in terms of presenting the body "as living sacrifices, holy and pleasing to God" (12:1). He then goes on to explain what this means in terms of not being conformed to the world, the renewal of the mind, proving the will of God, the exercise of gifts in the body of Christ, and daily living in a world ruled by pagan authorities (12:3–13:7). These references indicate how the worship described in ch. 8 is to be complemented. It involves the dedication of the whole person to God in a way that is rational, embracing the whole mind, and practical, reaching out into daily living in the church and in the world (→ *latreuō*, serve, *3302*).

See also *aiteō*, ask, ask for, demand (*160*); *gonypeteō*, fall on one's knees, kneel down before (*1206*); *deomai*, ask, request, beseech, beg (*1289*); *proseuchomai*, to pray, entreat (*4667*); *proskyneō*, worship, do obeisance to, prostrate oneself, do reverence to (*4686*); *erōtaō*, ask, ask a question, request (*2263*); *krouō*, knock (*3218*).

1964 (*enybrizō*, despise, insult), → *5615*.

1969 (*enōtizomai*, pay attention to, hear), → *201*.

1972 (*exangellō*, proclaim, report), → *33*.

1973 (*exagorazō*, redeem), → *60*.

1977 (*exaiteō*, ask for, demand), → *160*.

1979 (*exakoloutheō*, follow), → *199*.

| 1981 | ἐξαλείφω |

ἐξαλείφω (*exaleiphō*), wipe away, blot out (*1981*).

CL & OT *exaleiphō*, from *aleiphō* (anoint, rub with oil; → *230*), means lit. plaster, whitewash; metaphorically, wipe out, cancel, or destroy. In the LXX it carries both these meanings. The lit. sense plaster appears in Lev. 14:42, 43, 48; in its metaphorical sense, it denotes God's judicial work of wiping out life (Gen. 7:23) and the memory of offenders (Exod. 17:14; Deut. 9:14), and of erasing names from the book of life (Exod. 32:32–33); it also denotes God's gracious work of obliterating sins (Ps. 51:9; 109:14; Isa. 43:25).

NT *exaleiphō* appears 5x in the NT as a metaphor for obliterating sins (Acts 3:19), erasing names from the book of life (Rev. 3:5; cf. Exod. 32:32–33), wiping away tears (Rev. 7:17; 21:4), and canceling a bond of debt (Col. 2:14). The image implied here is probably that of smoothing the surface of a wax tablet for writing. The bond in Col. 2:14 is our obligation as God's creatures to keep his law on pain of death, which becomes a death warrant as soon as we sin.

See also *apōleia*, destruction (*724*); *olethros*, destruction, ruin (*3897*); *phtheirō*, destroy, ruin (*5780*).

1983 (*exanastasis*, resurrection), → *414*.

1985 (*exanistēmi*, raise up, awaken; intrans. rise), → *414*.

1987 (*exapataō*, trick, deceive), → *4414*.

1990 (*exapostellō*, send out), → *690*.

1992 (*exartizō*, finish, complete, equip, furnish), → *787*.

1995 (*exegeirō*, raise, raise up), → *1586*.

2001 (exeraunaō, search out), → *2236.*

2002 (exerchomai, go out, come out), → *2262.*

2003 (exesti, it is permitted, possible, proper, or even lawful), → *2026.*

2007	ἐξηγέομαι

ἐξηγέομαι (*exēgeomai*), explain, expound, interpret, tell (*2007*); διήγησις (*diēgēsis*), narrative, account (*1456*); διηγέομαι (*diēgeomai*), tell, describe (*1455*).

CL & OT 1. In some cl. writers *exēgeomai* means to lead or to govern. It can also mean to dictate or to prescribe, as when Plato speaks of "what the law prescribes." Plato also uses this word for expound or interpret, such as his reference to expounding the intentions of the lawgiver and expounding the poets. Finally, the Gk. historians use this word simply to mean tell or relate. *diēgēsis* means narrative or narration, sometimes with the added idea of fullness of detail. Likewise, *diēgeomai* means to describe or tell, sometimes with the force of setting out something in detail.

2. In the LXX *exēgeomai* mainly has the sense of recounting, telling, or declaring. Thus it is used of telling a dream (Jdg. 7:13), describing a miracle (2 Ki. 8:5), and declaring the Lord's glory among the nations (1 Chr. 16:24). In 1 Macc. 3:26 it introduces the telling of the story of a battle, and in 2 Macc. 2:13 the reporting of events. Josephus uses this vb. to denote interpretation or exposition. He speaks of two rabbis who give expositions or are interpreters of the laws. Philo uses words from this word group to refer to expositions of Scripture.

3. In the LXX *diēgeomai* occurs many more times than *exēgeomai* as the regular word used for to tell, recount, or declare. Thus, Abraham's servant tells Isaac all that he has done (Gen. 24:66); Jacob tells Laban of his family (29:13); and Saul is told about the men of Jabesh (1 Sam. 11:5). *diēgeomai* is also used for the telling of God's wonderful works (1 Chr. 16:9; Ps. 105:2; 145:5); on one occasion it denotes complaining to God (55:17). *diēgēsis* occurs infrequently in the LXX. In Hab. 2:6 it refers to telling a parable against someone. It occurs 7x in Sir. in the sense of godly discourse (6:35; 27:11), speech or conversation (9:15; 38:25), or a story (22:6) or saying (39:2). It is used at the beginning and end of the *Letter of Aristeas* to describe the narrative that the book tells.

NT 1. In the NT *exēgeomai* occurs once in Jn. and 5x in Lk.–Acts. Jn. 1:18 has considerable theological importance: "No one has ever seen God, but God the One and Only, who is at the Father's side, has made him known" (*ekeinos exēgēsato*). Two aspects of this vb.'s meaning in cl. Gk. and the OT may help in understanding what this text means. (a) The basic force of the vb. in Jn. 1:18 is simply that of speaking about things hidden in God. That is, the Logos makes known or declares the invisible God. (b) Since this word was used in a technical sense for the interpretation of the will of the gods by religious professionals, perhaps Jn. is also saying that Jesus is the one who makes known the will of God. The incarnate Word brings from the heart of God a revelation both for Jew and for Greek (cf. also Heb. 1:1–2).

2. In Lk.–Acts *exēgeomai* always means to relate or to tell. Cleopas and his companion relate what happened on the road to Emmaus (Lk. 24:35), and Cornelius relates his vision to his servants (Acts 10:8). In the remaining three passages in Acts people relate what God has done (15:12, 14), sometimes in great detail (21:19).

3. *diēgeomai* occurs 8x in the NT, meaning to tell, describe, or declare. Witnesses tell what happened to a demoniac (Mk. 5:16); the apostles tell Jesus what they have done (Lk. 9:10; cf. Mk. 9:9; Acts 9:27; 12:17; Heb. 11:32). The demoniac who is cured must declare how much God has done for him (Lk. 8:39). Once (Acts 8:33) the word occurs in a quotation of the LXX of Isa. 53:8 to mean declare or describe.

4. The noun *diēgēsis* is used in the sense of narrative or account in the much-discussed prologue of Lk. (1:1). Lk. has "many" prede-

cessors whose work he describes as attempts "to draw up an account" of the words and deeds of Jesus. Many see this verse as a comment on the origins of the Gospels. Most have argued that Lk.'s predecessors are Mk. and Q, but to limit it to these two can hardly be an adequate interpretation of the word "many." When all is said and done, however, what Lk. says here about the sources for his Gospel remains a mystery.

See also *epilyō*, explain, interpret, settle, solve (*2147*); *hermēneuō*, explain, interpret, translate (*2257*).

2014 (existēmi, drive out of one's senses, confuse; lose one's mind, be amazed), → *1749.*

2016 (exodos, departure, exit), → *3847.*

2017 (exolethreuō, destroy utterly), 3897.

2018 (exomologeō, promise, confess, praise), → *3933.*

2019 (exorkizō, charge under oath, exorcise), → *2020.*

2020	ἐξορκιστής

ἐξορκιστής (*exorkistēs*), exorcist (*2020*); ἐξορκίζω (*exorkizō*), charge under oath, exorcise (*2019*).

CL & OT 1. In cl. Gk., *exorkizō* occurs infrequently and often means the same as *exorkoō*, bind someone by oath, administer an oath. But the vb. can also mean to exorcise an evil spirit.

2. *exorkizō* is found in the LXX only at Gen. 24:3 and 1 Ki. 22:16, where it means to swear, curse. In neither of these is there any question of exorcism. The only example of what can be termed exorcism in the OT is that of Saul, when he was afflicted by "an evil spirit from the LORD" (1 Sam. 16:14). Yahweh permitted some spirit to afflict Saul, which was temporarily exorcised by David's playing of the harp.

NT 1. This word group is rare in the NT. *exorkistēs* occurs only at Acts 19:13, where it means one who drives out an evil spirit, and *exorkizō* only at Matt. 26:63, where it means to adjure, implore. In the NT the usual vb. for driving out spirits (→ *daimonion*, demon, *1228*) is *ekballō*, to cast out (→ *1675*). But the phenomenon of exorcism was much more widespread in the ancient world than the infrequent use of this noun and vb. suggest. This article deals with exorcism in the general sense of any form of such expulsion.

2. (a) During Jesus' ministry some afflicted people had symptoms different from ordinary human diseases. The NT refers to them as under the influence of one or more evil spirits. If we wish to regard some of these situations as what we call today mentally ill (e.g., schizophrenics), we still have the difficulty of understanding their immediate cure by a word of command in a way unmatched by modern psychotherapists. Some demon-possessed people, it is true, manifested recognizable illnesses and disabilities such as epilepsy (Matt. 17:14–18; Mk. 9:14–26; Lk. 9:37–43), and deafness and dumbness (Mk. 9:17, 25; cf. also Matt. 9:32–33; Lk. 11:14).

Present-day descriptions of illness are mainly descriptions of symptoms. Demon possession is the description of a cause. In such cases a person's psyche is affected not simply by some past event, but by the influence of an evil spirit. Nothing is said of how a spirit gains control in the first place, but possession reoccurs when the personality is merely cleaned up without being renewed and occupied by God's Spirit (Matt. 12:44–45; Lk. 11:25–26). This puts some responsibility for healing on the person.

A clear indication of demon-possession is what the spirits say when face to face with Jesus, calling him "the Holy One of God" (Mk. 1:24), "the Son of God" (3:11), "Son of the Most High God" (5:7). Yet Jesus exorcised them and refused to accept their testimony as legitimate preaching of the gospel (1:34; 3:11–12).

(b) The spirits who possess people belong to Satan's kingdom (Matt. 12:26–27) and consequently face ultimate destruction (Mk. 1:24) in the abyss (Lk. 8:31; cf. Matt. 8:29). There are grades of possessing spirits. Jesus, for example, spoke of one kind that needed intensive prayer before it could be cast out (Mk. 9:29). The argument about casting out by Beelzebub turns on the superiority of one spirit (i.e., the Holy Spirit) over another (Matt. 12:23–32; → *diabolos*, devil, *1333*).

3. (a) Jesus commands with absolute authority an evil spirit to come out directly (Lk. 4:36). His power is "the finger of God" (11:20) or "the Spirit of God" (Matt. 12:28). The word of command is "come out" (Mk. 1:25), with the addition once of "never enter . . . again" (9:25), or simply "Go" (Matt. 8:32). The disciples were given authority to cast out in the name of Jesus (Lk. 10:17; Acts 16:18; cf. Matt. 7:22; Acts 19:13).

(b) Mary Magdalene is named with other women as "cured of evil spirits and diseases" (Lk. 8:2). Seven demons are said to have come out of Mary. An unusual factor in the exorcism of the Canaanite woman's daughter (Matt. 15:21–28; Mk. 7:24–30) is that she was freed at a distance without any audible command. The only other distant exorcism, though of a different kind, occurred when handkerchiefs were taken from Paul and applied to the sufferers (Acts 19:12). A demon-possessed girl followed Paul and Silas, declaring that they were preachers of God's salvation; Paul cast out the spirit (16:16–18).

(c) When exorcisms took place, there was sometimes a final show of violence (Mk. 1:26; 9:26) or defiance if the spirit refused to come out (Acts 19:16). Once exorcised, the spirit was like a traveler in a barren land, still looking for the relief of repossessing a victim (Matt. 12:43–45; Lk. 11:24–26). It is not easy to understand the exorcism in Matt. 8:28–34; Mk. 5:1–17; Lk. 8:26–37. The "Legion" of demons asked permission to enter a group of pigs, and Jesus allowed this. Did the demons intentionally drown their new hosts, and, if so, what did they expect to gain thereby (cf. Matt. 17:15)? Perhaps there was danger in releasing a host of demons into the crowd.

4. Apart from the Gospels and Acts, there is no other case of exorcism in the NT. Perhaps the gift of distinguishing between spirits (1 Cor. 12:10) refers to exorcists. Deceiving spirits inspired false prophets (1 Jn. 4:1–2) and were to be tested and exposed by what they said of Jesus Christ, but apparently they were not exorcised (cf. 1 Cor. 12:3).

5. In a few places in the NT, exorcisms are referred to that are not based on the name of Jesus. One such may be the unattached exorcist who "was not one of us" (Mk. 9:38; Lk. 9:49), though he may have been a believer who chose not to leave home. Jesus spoke of successful exorcists who at the judgment would be told, "I never knew you" (Matt. 7:22–23). Jesus also admits that certain Jewish exorcists did cast out demons (Matt. 12:27; Lk. 11:19).

The sons of Sceva appear to have had some success as *exorkistēs* until they used the name of Jesus as a magical formula (Acts 19:13–16). The evil spirit whom these sons were trying to exorcise jumped on them and overpowered them, so that they fled the house naked. It is a tribute to the effectiveness of Christian exorcism that the name of Jesus does occur in early magical formulae.

See also *omnyō*, swear an oath (*3923*).

2022 (*exoudeneō*, reject), → *2024*.

2024 ἐξουθενέω

ἐξουθενέω (*exoutheneō*), reject with contempt (*2024*); ἐξουδενέω (*exoudeneō*), reject (*2022*).

NT These words occur 12x in the NT. Christ is the obj. of contempt in Mk. 9:12 (*exoudeneō*) and the despised "stone" in Acts 4:11 (*exoutheneō*, citing Ps. 118:22, but not from the LXX [cf. Mk. 8:31; Lk. 17:25]).

See also *katargeō*, abolish, nullify (*2934*); *atheteō*, set at naught, reject (*119*).

2026 ἐξουσία

ἐξουσία (*exousia*), freedom of choice, right, power, authority, ruling power, a bearer of authority (*2026*); ἐξουσιάζω (*exousiazō*), have the right or power, exercise authority (*2027*); κατεξουσιάζω

(*katexousiazō*), exercise authority over, tyrannize (*2980*); ἔξεστι (*exesti*), 3d pers. sing. of ἔξειμι (*exeimi*), used impers. in the sense: it is permitted, possible, proper, or even lawful (*2003*).

CL & OT 1. In cl. Gk., *exousia* (derived from *exesti*) denotes unrestricted possibility or freedom of action; hence power, authority, right of action. From the noun comes *exousiazō*, to exercise one's rights, have full power of authority; and *katexousiazō*, an infrequent word meaning exercise, or misuse, of the authority of one's office.

(a) By contrast with *dynamis*, where strength is based on inherent physical, spiritual, or natural powers and is exhibited in powerful deeds and natural phenomena, *exousia* denotes the power that may be displayed in the areas of legal, political, social, or moral affairs. For instance, it refers to the right of a king, a father, or a tenant to dispose as he wishes, or to the authorization of officials or messengers. The word is thus used only of people; it cannot be applied to natural forces.

(b) *exousia* does not necessarily require enforcement; it can simply rest or even be delegated to someone else. When it is illegally seized, it denotes despotic rule. In further derived meanings, it can denote the office appropriate for the authority and (in the pl.) office-holders and "the authorities."

2. In the LXX *exousia* occurs somewhat infrequently (70x); the vb. is also rare. It is most commonly found in the Apocr., with the meaning of permission to do something (Tob. 2:13 S only). The book of Dan. is important as background material for the NT use of the word, where *exousia* means dominion, power, with reference even to the whole world. The authority of the human world rulers originates from the supernatural realm; it is delegated by God, the Lord of history. He whose rule is eternal (Dan. 4:34) installs and removes kings (cf. 2:21) and can take the dominion away from them all (7:12).

Human government is provisional at best and opposed to God. Therefore, at the end of the times, the "son of man" will be enthroned to symbolize the rule of God's mercies. He will be invested with might, glory, and sovereign authority to rule all nations. His dominion is an everlasting dominion, which never passes away (Dan. 7:14). This kingdom will belong to "the saints, the people of the Most High," the true Israel of the last days (7:27). They will receive kingly power, and "all rulers will worship and obey him [the Most High]." The NT sees this passage of Dan. as fulfilled in Jesus as the Messiah.

3. Josephus and Philo follow the general Gk. usage but stress the aspect of authoritative, ruling power. It is a basic premise for Josephus that the power of the world's governments is not gained without God and that no one can escape from his power. In Qumran writings, the powers of the devil and darkness will be destroyed at the end by the kingdom of the archangel Michael and by the Israel he represents (1QM 17:7–8).

NT In the NT *exousia* appears 102x, most frequently in Lk., 1 Cor., and Rev. It is used in a secular sense meaning power to give orders (Lk. 7:8; 19:17; 20:20), in a concrete sense meaning jurisdiction (23:7), and in the pl. meaning officials, authorities (12:11). In Rom. 13:1, the "authorities" that exist should be understood as state officials, not (as some suggest) angelic powers.

In the NT both *exousia* and *dynamis* are related to the work of Christ, the consequent new ordering of cosmic power structures, and the empowering of believers. Both words are brought together in Lk. 9:1. Whereas Jesus' *dynamis* has its foundation in his being anointed, his *exousia* is founded on his being sent. *exousia* is that power, authority, and freedom of action that belong to God himself, to a commission in the last days, and to Christians in their eschatological existence.

1. *God's* exousia. (a) God's authority is linked with his role as the one who controls world history and is Judge of the world. By his own authority, he has fixed the dates and times of the end (Acts 1:7). He has the power to consign people to eternal ruin (Lk. 12:5). The absolute freedom of God finds its expression in his predestination:

Paul compares God with a potter, who can do what he likes with the clay (Rom. 9:21; cf. Isa. 29:16; 45:9; Jer. 18:6; Wis. 15:7).

(b) God can delegate this authority, as he did to the angel who punishes at the judgment (Rev. 6:8; cf. also 9:3, 10, 19). By way of contrast, the heavenly powers (*exousiai*) are scarcely taken into consideration in this eschatological event. They are generally mentioned along with the *archai* (→ *archē*, 794) and have the same significance as the *dynameis* (Eph. 1:21; 3:10; Col. 1:16; 2:10; → *dynamis*, 1539). Because of Christ's exaltation, they have been subjected to him (Eph. 1:21; 1 Pet. 3:22).

But the opposition has not yet been completely broken; this means that the Messiah's rule must continue for the time being (1 Cor. 15:24). The natural self stands under the domination of darkness and the lordship of the devil (Acts 26:18; Col. 1:13). Satan appears, in fact, to have increased power; he is called the "prince [ruler] of this world" (Jn. 12:31; 14:30; 16:11), even "the god of this age" (2 Cor. 4:4). The devil, like God, can delegate his rule over the world to others, e.g., to the Antichrist (cf. Rev. 13:2, 4, 12). He even tempted Jesus with such an offer (Lk. 4:6). Nevertheless, the devil's power is allotted him by God; his activity fits into God's plan and is therefore under God's control (22:53). Note how Jesus announces his downfall (Jn. 12:31; 16:11).

2. *The* exousia *of Jesus*. (a) The work of the earthly Jesus announces that the devil and the demons have been deprived of their power; the one who has been sent by God has the authority to destroy the devil's works (1 Jn. 3:8) and to snatch people from his rule. Exorcism is therefore attributed to the authority of Jesus (Lk. 4:36), which he can also pass on to his sent-out disciples (Matt. 10:1; Mk. 3:15; 6:7; Lk. 9:1; 10:19). Jesus acted with God's authority when he forgave a man his sins and confirmed the power of his word by a healing miracle (Matt. 9:2–8; Mk. 2:3–12; Lk. 5:18–26).

Jesus' commission from God to save people brought him into collision with the law as the Pharisees understood it. Jesus rejected the literalistic understanding of the letter of the law (Matt. 12:10, 12; Mk. 3:4; Lk. 14:3; Jn. 5:10). His authority could be seen in his teaching, which provoked astonishment (Matt. 7:29; Mk. 1:22, 27; Lk. 4:32), because he did not teach as the Jewish teachers did. The latter were guided by tradition (Matt. 7:29), whereas Jesus, the anointed one, not only received his words from God's mouth but also spoke with the unique authority of the Son, who alone knows the Father and who alone can reveal him (Matt. 11:27; Lk. 10:22; cf. Jn. 3:35; 10:15; 13:3; 17:25). The cleansing of the temple (Matt. 21:12–13; Mk. 11:15–17; Lk. 19:45–46; Jn. 2:13–17) also presupposes a consciousness of messianic authority.

(b) In Jn.'s Gospel, Jesus' authority is based on the fact that he is the Son and that he has been sent (cf. Jn. 17:2); he has also been given the authority to judge at the end of time (5:27). But as in the Synoptics, Jesus seeks to save people rather than to judge them (3:17). His power is not forcible domination, but absolute freedom to be a servant to the world. He has the *exousia* to give his life and to take it again (10:18). Jesus' sacrifice opens the way for believers to come to the Father (3:16; 14:6). Those who receive him and believe in his name are given *exousia* to become children of God (1:12).

(c) As a result of Jesus' resurrection, he received all power in heaven and on earth (Matt. 28:18). This fulfilled Dan.'s vision of the enthronement and granting of power to the Son of Man (cf. Dan. 7:14). But now, in place of the collective "saints of the Most High" (7:27) stands Christ. Further, God's power is not realized by violently subjugating the nations but by spreading the gospel, winning the world to faith in Christ. Hence it is the church, not Israel, that outwardly expresses the reign of the Messiah on earth (Acts 1:6–8). The disarming of the evil one through the cross and the exaltation of Christ must be preached as good news to all the world. The exalted Lord thus sends out his messengers and empowers them for service in the gospel (Matt. 28:18–20).

Analogous with Jesus' earthly ministry and in accord with the contents of the Easter message, Christ's apostles received power to confer the Holy Spirit (Acts 8:19; 19:6; but cf. 2:38; 10:44–48) and to build up rather than to destroy (2 Cor. 10:8; 13:10). Because of his spiritual ministry as a servant in the church, an apostle has "the right" (*exousia*) to have his physical needs looked after by the church (1 Cor. 9:4–6; 2 Thess. 3:9).

3. *The* exousia *of believers*. The authority of a Christian believer is founded on the rule of Christ and on the disarming of all powers. It implies both freedom and service. Christians are free to do anything (1 Cor. 6:12; 10:23) because the law, as a prohibitive barrier, has been broken down through Christ's redeeming act and because we have received the Spirit of freedom (2 Cor. 3:17). Nothing is any longer under the rule of the powers. In practice, however, this theoretically unrestricted freedom is governed by what is helpful to other Christians and to the congregation as a whole. Since God's work of complete redemption has not yet been consummated, believers must be sensitive to and take into account both their own Christian lives, still linked with the sinful nature and the old self, and the consciences of weaker believers (1 Cor. 10:28, 31–33), and not plunge into unbridled freedom as if the resurrection has already taken place (2 Thess. 2:1–2).

It is just such an unrestrained use of one's freedom that can precipitate a Christian into a new servitude. Hence we must not let anything be our master. "'Everything is permissible [*exestin*] for me' — but not everything is beneficial. 'Everything is permissible [*exestin*] for me' — but I will not be mastered [from *exousiazō*] by anything" (1 Cor. 6:12; cf. 10:23–24). While there may be truth in these slogans from the libertines at Corinth, Paul insists that it is not the whole truth. It is all too possible to use our freedom to "be burdened again by a yoke of slavery" (Gal. 5:1; → *eleutheria*, 1800).

See also *dynamis*, power, might, strength, force (*1539*); *thronos*, throne, seat (*2585*); *ischys*, strength (*2709*).

2027 (*exousiazō*, have the right or power, exercise authority), → 2026.

2037 (*heortazō*, celebrate a festival), → 2038.

2038   ἑορτή

ἑορτή (*heortē*), festival, feast (*2038*); ἑορτάζω (*heortazō*), celebrate a festival (*2037*).

CL & OT 1. In cl. Gk. since the time of Homer, *heortē* has denoted a festival. The Gks. celebrated festivals during the change of the seasons and the high points of the year's work from seedtime to harvest (fertility festivals), also for family events and the relationship between the individual and the community (family and tribal festivals). These festivities were almost always associated with certain deities and named after them. In addition to local festivals, there was an increasing number that were general throughout Greece. Later important political events were also given festivals (memorial feasts), e.g., the battle of Marathon and the victory of Salamis.

Processes that were natural in origin were often exaggerated to excess in festivals, such as immoderate indulgence in wine-drinking and love. Preparation for such feasts included fasting, washings, and changes of clothing. The festival itself was celebrated with prayer and song, music and dancing, processions, sacrifice, sport, games, and competitions. Hostilities were usually interrupted during a festival. Gods appeared and entertained or were entertained by their worshipers. In the end all festivals were variations of a fertility religion, which sought by magical means to further conception, growth, and life in plants, animals, and human beings.

2. The ancient farming and city culture of Canaan possessed a wealth of religious cults honoring gods such as El, Dagon, and Baal, goddesses such as Asherah, and later Egyptian and Babylonian deities. These cults were full of fertility rites, which attributed to sexual processes a religious potency. The constant temptation of Israel aris-

ing from fascination with these cults is clear, particularly in 1 and 2 Ki. On the whole, however, Israel, unlike Greece, withstood the temptation.

Israel had regular festivals, based on an agricultural economy. These are outlined in the Pentateuch (e.g., Lev. 23; Num. 28:9–29:39; Deut. 16:1–17). Every seven days brought the Sabbath, a day on which important decisions and work were avoided. In the spring the Israelites celebrated the Passover (→ *pascha, 4247*) and the Feast of Unleavened Bread, which celebrated Israel's exodus from Egypt. During this time the first agricultural festival, that of Firstfruits (the beginning of the wheat harvest), was also celebrated. The end of the wheat harvest saw the Feast of Weeks (which eventually also commemorated the making of the covenant and the giving of the commandments on Mount Sinai), and the Feast of Tabernacles was held at the end of the wine harvest (commemorating also Israel's journey through the desert).

Sabbaths and the feasts of pilgrimage were celebrated "to the LORD" (cf. Exod. 16:23, 25). The prophets sought to prevent Israel from relapsing into mere ritualism and heathenism in its feasts. By threatening (Amos 8:10; Mal. 2:3) and scolding (Amos 5:21; Isa. 1:13–14), they aimed to make room for God's commandments and their fulfillment along with and indeed within the sacrificial rites. Whenever it became impossible for the people to carry on the sacrifices God had ordained, the Sabbath became the most important festival for Israel, representing both a witness to outsiders and a sign of the covenant (cf. Exod. 31:12–18).

3. There were also individual and family celebrations (circumcision, marriage, and burial), national ones (accession and victory celebrations), local festivals, and occasions like a festival of sheep-shearing. In addition to Sabbath days, importance was attached to celebrating the new moon, when a day of rest was kept and special sacrifices were offered. Two further important religious festivals were held in the autumn: the New Year (Rosh Hashanah) on the first day and the Day of Atonement on the tenth day of the month Tishri (Lev. 23:26–32; Num. 29:1–11). After the exile arose the festival of Purim, associated with the book of Est. The Apocr. tells of the desecration of the feasts and the temple (1 Macc. 1:39, 45; 2 Macc. 6:6–7), the reconsecration of the temple, and the establishment of the Feast of Hanukkah (Dedication), to commemorate this event (1 Macc. 4:36–41; 2 Macc. 10:1–8).

Because different groups followed somewhat different calendars (e.g., lunar calendar vs. solar calendar), there were often slight variations on when certain festivals were celebrated.

NT 1. In the early Christian church the propriety of celebrating the festivals together with the whole of the Jewish people was never questioned. Jesus and Paul went regularly to the synagogues on the Sabbath in order to pray, read, or teach (cf. Mk. 1:21; Lk. 4:16; Acts 16:13), and the disciples and the churches took part in the pilgrim festivals. It is thus not surprising that allusions to the Jewish festival calendar find their way into the NT (e.g., 1 Cor. 5:7–8; Gal. 5:9; Col. 2:16–17). Pagans who had to give up their form of festival celebrations in order to become Christians could be taken along to the widely known Jewish festivals, whose historical background was in agreement with the spiritual and moral values that pervaded them.

2. What is tacitly assumed in the Synoptics becomes a main theme in Jn.'s Gospel: Jesus is not merely a Jew among Jews; rather, he represents the true Israel. Therefore, he demonstrates in his life, suffering, and death the proper festal celebration. Through him the meaning of the traditional festivals returns with a new, final significance and is offered afresh to the Jews in this renewed form. Weaving into his Gospel the fabric of the recurring festivals of Israel, Jn. presents Jesus' discourses on the true meaning of these festivals with himself as the center. It is significant that 17 of 25x the word *heortē* occurs in the NT are found in this Gospel.

John makes references to three Passover celebrations. (a) The Passover at the beginning of his Gospel, with its record of the cleans-

ing of the temple (2:12–22), sounds a note of messianic hope. At Passover time multitudes of people thronged together, seeking bringers of salvation, messiahs. (b) In the second Passover (Jn. 6) the bread motif is emphasized: The bread of slavery becomes the bread of freedom. This chapter is an exposition on the words "bread" and "flesh." The Christian sacrament of the Lord's Supper is a substitute for the Passover sacrifice. (c) In the account of the third Passover (Jn. 12ff.) the messianic motif is again stressed, though in contrast to his attitude at the feast of the previous year Jesus now accepts the acclamation of the people (12:12–15; cf. 6:15). His ceremonial entry into Jerusalem occurs on the very day on which the Passover lambs were selected to be slaughtered, the day before the evening of the festival.

Thus the entire Gospel of Jn. points with unmistakable symbolism to the fact that Jesus is in truth the Lamb of God, who will be sacrificed for Israel. He dies on the day and at the hour when Israel kills the lambs, and (in contrast to those crucified with him, but like the Passover Lamb, cf. Exod. 12:46) no bone of his body is broken (Jn. 19:31–36; cf. also 1:29–36; 1 Cor. 5:7; 1 Pet. 1:19; Rev. 5:6, 9, 12). This lamb symbolism in Jn. 12 and 19 forms a setting for the Passion discourses of chaps. 14–16.

Other festivals are mentioned in the Gospel of John as well. Most likely the "feast of the Jews" in 5:1 refers to the Feast of Tabernacles. The next year's Feast of Tabernacles is mentioned in 7:2. Later that same year, Jesus was present in the temple for the Feast of Dedication (10:22–29; cf. 1 Macc. 4:36–59).

3. In spite of the fact that the Christian festivals were rooted in Jewish tradition, differences and conflicts soon appeared. Paul writes severely against feast days that imply recognition of astral and other natural powers instead of the one God (Gal. 4:8–11; Col. 2:8–17; cf. Rom. 14:5–8). Moreover, for the apostle the significance of all feasts, whether Jewish or pagan, has been superseded by Christ. He does not reject celebrations as such, but he does require celebration of the right kind.

A similar situation is found in the Sabbath controversy of the Gospels. Jesus took part in the debates of the Jewish schools of thought on the question of rightly keeping the Sabbath. Jesus was criticized by those who held stricter views, but in answer he justified his actions on biblical grounds in the manner of his times (cf. Matt. 12:1–12 par.).

4. Along with the general adoption of the Jewish festivals by the early Christian communities, special Christian festivals began to develop, although in the NT we find only a beginning of these. In addition to the Sabbath services, Christians had special gatherings on the first day of the week in memory of the redemption brought about by the resurrection of the Lord (Acts 20:7; 1 Cor. 16:2). Toward the end of the 1st cent. this day came to be called the "Lord's day" (Rev. 1:10). The fact that the two days (seventh and first) followed one another soon led to a conscious contrasting of the two (Ign. *Magn.* 9:1; *Barn.* 15:9; *Did.* 14:1). In the following centuries, when the days of the week came generally to be given the names of the ancient pagan planet gods, the name "Lord's day" was changed to "Sunday," which earned for the Christians the accusation that they were sun worshipers.

It was not until the end of the 2d cent. that Passover became the Christian Easter, and one hundred years later still that the Feast of Weeks became the Christian Pentecost. In the 4th cent., Ascension Day was introduced between these two special days as a purely Christian festival. The last of the great Christian festivals to appear was Christmas, around A.D. 335 in Rome. Of the many dates suggested, December 25 prevailed, perhaps celebrated in opposition to a sun cult festival around the time of the winter solstice. It is noteworthy that the date is not far removed from that of the Jewish Hanukkah festival. Both were in part known as a festival of lights.

Christians in every age have celebrated festivals, for such celebrations draw attention to historical realities. They have their basis in an appreciation of time and the refusal simply to accept continuous repetition without a break. Like the commandments, the festivals of Israel were also at first accepted without question by Jewish Christians. In the end they had to be forcibly excluded from the Jewish religious community as heretics, since for them Jesus Christ had become increasingly the real meaning of the ancient feasts, and it was through him that they regarded themselves as permanently linked to all Israel.

See also *pascha*, Passover (*4247*).

2039 ἐπαγγελία

ἐπαγγελία (*epangelia*), announcement, promise (*2039*); ἐπαγγέλλομαι (*epangellomai*), announce, proclaim, promise, profess (*2040*); προεπαγγέλλω (*proepangellō*), announce before, promise before (*4600*); ἐπάγγελμα (*epangelma*), announcement, notification, promise (*2041*).

CL & OT 1. (a) The words in this group are derived from the root *angel-*, like *euangelizō* and *euangelion* (gospel, → *2295*). In cl. Gk. they were originally synonymous with other words from the same root (e.g., compounds of *angellō*, report, *33*): *epangellomai* means to announce, proclaim; *epangelia*, announcement, report. In the context of state proclamations they denote summoning. In legal usage the noun means notification of a charge. In the mid. the vb. means to announce one's accomplishments or to take up a moral position.

(b) The nearest point of contact to the NT usage of these words is the meaning to announce an intention, offer to do something, promise. It is significant that when they are used in this sense, it is never the gods who promise something to human beings, but only vice versa. In this connection, the word often carries the specific sense of a promise of money. In the Hel. world, *epangelia* became a technical term for a free-will payment, gift, or endowment.

2. (a) *epangelia* occurs only 6x in the LXX, though the OT is familiar with the concept of promise and fulfillment. The entire OT is the story of what God said and then did as a result of his promises. In some cases the fulfillment is clearly recorded (e.g., Jos. 23:14: "Not one of all the good promises the LORD your God gave you has failed. Every promise has been fulfilled" [cf. also 21:45]). But generally the fulfillment appears as a partial or token fulfillment, which does not reveal the whole of the divine plan. Hence Israel is compelled in every new situation to reinterpret the old promises and is called to new expectancy by new proclamations of salvation (→ *logos*, word, *3364*).

Basic to the theme of Israel's existence under promise is God's triple promise to Abraham of a land, a great nation, and blessing in Gen. 12:1–3. Gen. develops the promise of the nation through the story of Isaac, the wanderings of Abraham and his descendants, and the covenant theme (Gen. 17). Jer. 31:31–34 records the promise of a new covenant at a time of national collapse, when the whole idea of surviving in the promised land was problematic. The central idea of the new covenant is that of the law written on the heart (cf. also Ezek. 18:1–32; 36:26–38, which couple a new spirit and new heart with national restoration).

The teaching of the prophets consists of promises of judgment and grace, culminating in the promises of the Servant Songs of Isaiah (Isa. 42:1–4; 49:1–6; 50:4–9; 52:13–53:12). The promises of return from exile and sustenance in calamity of the later chapters of Isa. renew the exodus theme (cf. Exod. 2:24–25; 12:1–42; 15:1–18; Isa. 40:1–31; Hos. 11:1). But as in Gen. 12:3, there is also a theme of blessing that extends beyond Israel, so that Yahweh promises that the servant will be "a light for the Gentiles" (Isa. 49:6). As early as Isa. 2:2–4 and Mic. 4:1–3 there is the prophecy of the nations flowing to the mountain of the house of the Lord so that they may learn the ways of Yahweh in peace and righteousness.

(b) The OT records various vows made by the righteous. But while the Law and the Prophets demand faithfulness in personal dealings (Exod. 20:15–16; Deut. 27:19; Hos. 4:1–2; Mic. 6:8), human promises are ultimately secondary to God's promises. He alone can both promise and fulfill, for he alone knows and overrules the future.

(c) Jewish writers in the Gk. language adopt Hel. usage. Thus they use *epangellomai* in the ordinary sense of promise (e.g., money,

1 Macc. 11:28). But they also prepare the way for Paul's use of *epangelia* for God's activity. In 3 Macc. 2:10 God promises to answer prayer.

(d) With the appearance of apocalyptic lit., interest is strongly attracted to the world to come (e.g., 2 Esd. 7:119). At the same time assurance of salvation is considerably dampened by the doctrine that crucial to being eternally saved is strict observance of the law.

NT 1. (a) *epangellomai*, to promise, is found 15x in the NT, but only 4x is it used of human promises (Mk. 14:11; 1 Tim. 2:10; 6:21; 2 Pet. 2:19). Most occurrences are in Paul's letters, Heb., and Jas.

(b) *proepangellō* means to announce beforehand, promise beforehand. It occurs 2x in the NT: In Rom. 1:2 Paul refers to the gospel of God that he promised beforehand in the old covenant through his prophets; and in 2 Cor. 9:5 Paul speaks of the "generous gift" for the poor in Jerusalem that the Corinthians have promised in advance.

(c) *epangelia* (52x) is used only once in a secular sense (Acts 23:21); it is used absolutely 33x, most of them in Paul; the sing. form is predominant, but the pl. occurs 11x. As in cl. Gk., *epangelia* in the NT can refer either to form or to content, though the distinction is not always clear.

(d) *epangelma* is a synonym of *epangelia*. It is used only 2x, both in 2 Pet. Peter is trying to stir up hope for Christ's return at a time when it is flagging, and he stresses God's promised creation of a new heaven and earth (3:13). Since this consummation will bring with it a share in eternal life and a partaking of his divine power, the author calls the promises that point to it "very great and precious" (1:4).

(e) Though these words seldom occur in the Gospels (only Mk. 14:11, which speaks of the promise of money to Judas, and Lk. 24:49, which refers to the promise of the Spirit), the Gospels frequently reflect on the continuity between God's message in the OT and his word now, often using the vb. *plēroō* (fulfill, *4444*). Note, for example, Lk. 4:21: "Today this scripture [Isa. 61:1–2] is fulfilled in your hearing." Thus in spite of the absence of the term *epangelia*, the Gospels (esp. Matt.) deal extensively with promise and fulfillment.

2. (a) In Lk.–Acts, the giver of the promise is God alone (Acts 7:5)—"the God of glory" (7:2) or the "Father" (Lk. 24:49; Acts 1:4). The promise provides insight into his plan of salvation and carries with it the future realization of that plan, so that its fulfillment is a creative act (Acts 13:32–33).

(b) The recipients of the promise are "our fathers" (Acts 13:32), esp. Abraham (7:17), Israel as the covenant people (13:23), Jesus' disciples (Lk. 24:49; Acts 1:4), the hearers of Peter's sermon at Pentecost with their children, and those living far away from Jerusalem (2:38–39). It is through Israel that the Gentiles first hear the promise.

(c) The content of the promise is the historical sending of Jesus as Savior (Acts 13:23, 32–33; 26:6). Because he, the crucified and risen one, has earned the forgiveness of sins, all who turn to him in faith and are baptized in his name receive the Holy Spirit, the promised gift of God in the last days (2:38–40).

(d) By being fulfilled, the promise becomes the good news, the gospel (*euangelion*, → *2295*). Acts 13:32 uses the vb. *euangelizō*, to bring good news, to describe Paul's testimony to the fulfillment of the promise.

3. Paul is the one who gives the most emphatic testimony that the *epangelia* is a gift of God's free grace. God alone has the absolute power to fulfill his word of promise (Rom. 4:21). He is the God "who gives life to the dead and calls things that are not as though they were" (4:17); he is the God "who does not lie" (Tit. 1:2).

(a) In his struggle against mixing the gospel with Jewish legalism, Paul thought through the question of the relation between God's law and his promises, his demands and his bountiful grace. In answer to the Jewish theory that humanity can enjoy the promised salvation only on the basis of prior fulfillment of all the duties required by the law, Paul set out in antithetical form three basic insights afforded by the gospel. (i) It is not the law that makes us recipients of the word of promise and its fulfillment, but justifying grace (Rom. 4:13). Since the law cannot enable a person to do God's will, the law and the promise are in reality opposites (Gal. 3:18, 21–22).

(ii) Law and promise can neither limit nor supplement one another, since the law demands works, whereas faith is not a human work or a legalistic achievement. If those who make the law into a way of salvation were able by doing so to become "heirs," then faith would be null and the promise void (Rom. 4:14).

(iii) The example of Abraham shows that the law cannot be a condition for the reception of the promise or for salvation. The promise given to him is the characteristic pattern of all other promises. It was given centuries before the revelation of the Mosaic law, and the law must not be interpreted as an added clause by means of which God invalidates his promises, as a human being might add a clause to a will. Thus Paul uses the picture of a *diathēkē*, will, covenant, in Gal. 3:15–18, to emphasize the irrevocability of God's promises.

(b) For Paul it is fundamental that all God's promises have been given his "Yes" in Christ (2 Cor. 1:20). The sending of Jesus and all he did is God's active ratification of all his promises of salvation. Christ's ministry to Israel demonstrated God's truthfulness and took place in order to confirm the promise given to the patriarchs (Rom. 15:8). By dying in our place under the curse with which the law threatens every transgressor, he prepared the way for the sending of the Holy Spirit. He died "in order that the blessing given to Abraham might come to the Gentiles through Christ Jesus, so that by faith we might receive the promise of the Spirit" (Gal. 3:14). Strictly speaking, the Holy Spirit is here spoken of as the promised gift of salvation (cf. Eph. 1:13–14). In view of the close association of the Holy Spirit with eternal life, it is not surprising that in Tit. 1:2 "eternal life" is mentioned as the substance of the promise.

(c) Historically, Israel was the first to receive the promise, while the Gentiles stood outside it (Eph. 2:12). In Gal. 3:16 Paul interprets the "seed" of Abraham in the sing. as referring to one individual, Christ. He is the universal heir, whereas believers are "co-heirs with Christ" (Rom. 8:17). But since it is not physical descent from Abraham but faith in Jesus Christ that makes us entitled to the inheritance, believers from among the Gentiles are also "heirs together with Israel … and sharers together in the promise in Christ Jesus" (Eph. 3:6).

4. (a) In the book of Heb., the question of the relation of law to promise plays no part; faith itself is in danger. Doubt is expressed as to whether the promises will be fulfilled at all. The purpose of the letter is therefore to call its readers to hold fast to the promises and to testify to God's faithfulness to his word.

(b) The writer has in mind "a great cloud of witnesses" (12:1) who have testified to their faith both by divine intervention in their lives and by personal steadfastness. These saints lived out their lives on the basis of the divine promises. The author mentions specific men and women of faith in the early history of Israel—such as Abraham (6:12–20; 7:6; 11:8–19), Isaac (11:20), Jacob (11:21), and Rahab (11:31)—who experienced the promised help of God. In 4:1–9 the example of Israel in the desert stresses that unbelief makes fulfillment of the promises impossible (cf. Ps. 95:11).

(c) The content of the promises mentioned in Heb. is the blessing of many descendants (6:14), rest (4:9–11), and the new covenant (8:1–10:18), which on the basis of the remission of sins holds out the prospect of "the promised eternal inheritance" (9:15). At the same time Heb. emphasizes that in the old covenant the promises neither were nor could be completely fulfilled. In the final analysis they are interpreted in terms of the gospel and therefore refer to complete salvation in Christ (cf. 4:2). Thus the writer declares in 11:39 that the whole cloud of witnesses who came before Christ did not receive "what had been promised." For this reason he ascribes to the patriarchs an understanding of the promise that looks far beyond historical foreshadowing and partial fulfillments to an eternal consummation (11:10–16).

The author uses the keyword *kreittōn*, better (12x), to describe the superiority of the new covenant to the old. Christ is the mediator of a superior covenant, "founded on better promises" (8:6). Jeremiah's promise of a new covenant (Jer. 31:31–34) is cited twice, indicating that by the better promises we should understand full forgiveness, deep knowledge of God, and a Spirit-worked obedience to his commandments (Heb. 8:8–12; 10:16–17). The content of the promises also includes all the other aspects of eternal salvation, such as the unshakeable kingdom (12:28), the future city (13:14), and the Sabbath rest for the people of God (4:9).

The new covenant has been brought into operation by the death of Jesus. This means that the fulfillment of the promises is drawing steadily nearer: "You see the Day approaching" (10:25; cf. 10:37). It is thus all the more necessary to remain steadfast, not to cast away one's confidence, and to "hold unswervingly to the hope we profess, for he who promised is faithful" (10:23; cf. 6:11–12). After all, God swore to these promises with an oath (6:13).

2040 (*epangellomai*, announce, promise, profess), → *2039*.

2041 (*epangelma*, announcement, notification, promise), → *2039*.

2043 (*epagōnizomai*, fight for), → *74*.

2044 (*epathroizō*, be gathered even more), → *5251*.

2046 (*epaineō*, praise), → *140*.

2047 (*epainos*, praise), → *140*.

2048 (*epairō*, to lift up, take up), → *149*.

2049 (*epaischynomai*, be ashamed), → *158*.

2051 (*epakoloutheō*, follow), → *199*.

2052 (*epakouō*, listen to, hearken to), → *201*.

2053 (*epakroaomai*, listen attentively), → *201*.

2058 (*epanapauomai*, rest, take one's rest, rely on), → *398*.

2061 (*epanorthōsis*, correcting, restoration, improvement), → *3981*.

2063 (*eparatos*, accursed), → *2932*.

2086 (*ependyomai*, put on over), → *1544*.

2088 (*eperchomai*, come, come along, approach), → *2262*.

2089 (*eperōtaō*, ask), → *2263*.

2090 (*eperōtēma*, question, request, appeal), → *2263*.

2093 ἐπί	ἐπί (*epi*), on, at (*2093*).

CL Basically denoting position *on* something that forms a support or foundation, *epi* is the opposite of *hypo* (under, → *5679*) and differs from *hyper* (above, → *5642*) in implying actual rest on some object. In this primary local sense of on, upon, *epi* is followed by the gen., the dat., or the acc., often without distinction in meaning.

NT 1. *epi* has a versatility of use matched only by *en*. From the simple spatial meaning of *epi* there naturally developed a multitude of derived senses, so that it may express addition (Lk. 3:20; 2 Cor. 7:13), superintendence (Rom. 9:5), cause or basis (Acts 3:16; 1 Tim. 5:19), circumstance (Rom. 8:20; 1 Cor. 9:10), and purpose or destination (Gal. 5:13; Eph. 2:10). Of special interest is the use of *epi* (with the acc.) to denote the recipients of various spiritual blessings or experiences, such as a trance (Acts 10:10), the word of God (Lk. 3:2), the kingdom of God (Matt. 12:28), the Holy Spirit (Acts 10:45; Tit. 3:6), the power of Christ (2 Cor. 12:9), or the grace of God (Lk. 2:40).

2. *epi to auto*. In the LXX this prep. phrase means "together" or "at the same place" (e.g., 2 Sam. 2:13; Ps. 2:2; 34:3). It has the sense of "together" in Acts 4:26 (quoting Ps. 2:2) and Matt. 22:34. In Acts 2:47 the phrase seems to be a quasi-technical expression denoting the union of the Christian fellowship. That *epi to auto* and *en ekklēsia* are

sometimes synonymous, signifying "in church fellowship," seems evident from the parallelism at 1 Cor. 11:18 and 20. The togetherness of the early Christians was expressed principally in their meeting for public worship "in church fellowship" or "in the assembly."

3. Rom. 5:12 has a significant use of *epi* in the phrase *eph' hō*. Interpretation of this verse falls into two main groups: that which construes *hō* as a relative pronoun (whose antecedent is either "death" or "one man"), with *epi* meaning "in" or "because of"; and that which treats *eph' hō* as a conjunction, "on the ground of the fact that" or "because." The former is less probable, since elsewhere in Paul (e.g., 2 Cor. 5:4; Phil. 3:12; 4:10), *eph' hō* is conjunctional, whatever its precise nuance. In light of Paul's linking of Adam and his descendants through his Adam-Christ analogy (cf. Rom. 5:18–19; 1 Cor. 15:22), he probably means that "death spread to all because all sinned" (either actually in Adam's primal transgression or in their federal representative, Adam), or "death spread to all because all [since the time of Adam] have sinned."

Similarly, *eph' hō* in 2 Cor. 5:4 has a causal sense: We groan in our human tent "because we do not wish to be unclothed but to be clothed with our heavenly dwelling." The origin of that groaning or sighing, i.e., a sense of frustration under the limitations of a flesh-dominated body, is in a yearning (5:2) or wish (5:4) for the acquisition of a spiritual body (cf. 1 Cor. 15:44), which arises because God has given us the Spirit as the pledge of the resurrection transformation (2 Cor. 5:4b, 5).

4. In 1 Pet. 2:24a, two translations have been offered for "on [*epi*] the tree." Christ bore our sins while his body was located on the cross, and in his body Christ bore our sins upon the cross. The second of these is the preferred translation. Note that Peter is probably alluding here to Deut. 21:23, where *epi* is followed by "tree" in the gen. case. In 1 Pet. 2:24a, however, *epi* is followed by an acc. This change of case suggests a change in nuance from Deut., from location to means or instrument. If this interpretation is correct, then the vb. "bore" (*anapherō*, → *pherō*, bear, 5770) does not mean offer in sacrifice but has the nontechnical sense of "carry up." The picture is not of Christ as a priest and the cross as an altar but of Christ as the sin-bearer (cf. Jn. 1:29) and the cross as the place where sin was destroyed (cf. Col. 2:14–15).

5. After the vb. *baptizō* (to baptize), there is probably little difference between "in the name of Jesus" with the prep. *en* (Acts 10:48; → 1877) or *epi* (2:38). It refers either to the candidate's confession of faith in the name of Jesus (cf. 22:16) or to the administrant's acting on the authority of Christ or his invocation of the name of Jesus during the baptismal rite.

6. With the vb. *pisteuō* (to believe), *epi* occurs 5x with the dat. case (4x with a pers. obj.: Rom. 9:33; 10:11; 1 Pet. 2:6 [all quoting Isa. 28:16]; 1 Tim. 1:16; once with an impers. obj., Lk. 24:25). When used with a pers. obj. *epi* denotes placing reliance on a person who affords a firm support or a solid foundation. *epi* also occurs 7x with the acc. case after *pisteuō* (Matt. 27:42; Acts 9:42; 11:17; 16:31; 22:19; Rom. 4:5, 24; cf. Wis. 12:2) and once after *pistis* (faith, Heb. 6:1; → 4411). The meaning in these verses seems to be the notion of turning away from former objects of devotion that brought disappointment to a new personal object of faith in whom one has confidence.

2096 (*epibareō*, burden, be a burden to), → *983*.

2101 (*epiboulē*, plan, plot), → *1089*.

2103 (*epigeios*, earthly), → *1178*.

2105 (*epiginōskō*, know, understand, recognize), → *1182*.

2106 (*epignōsis*, knowledge, recognition), → *1182*.

2107 (*epigraphē*, inscription, superscription), → *1210*.

2108 (*epigraphō*, inscribe, write), → *1210*.

2116 (*epieikeia*, mildness, forbearance, gentleness, graciousness), → *4558*.

2117 (*epieikēs*, mild, yielding, gentle, kind, forbearing), → *4558*.

2118 (*epizēteō*, seek after, strive for, search for, want), → *2426*.

2120 (*epithesis*, laying on [of hands]), → *2202*.

2121 (*epithymeō*, desire, want), → *2123*.

2123	ἐπιθυμία

ἐπιθυμία (*epithymia*), desire, lust (*2123*); ἐπιθυμέω (*epithymeō*), desire, want (*2121*); ἐπιποθέω (*epipotheō*), long for, crave, desire (*2160*); ἐπιπόθησις (*epipothēsis*), longing (*2161*); ἐπιπόθητος (*epipothētos*), long for (*2162*); ἐπιποθία (*epipothia*), longing (*2163*).

CL & OT From the basic meaning of being excited about something (cf. *thymos*, urge, passion), *epithymia* and *epithymeō* in cl. Gk. meant to have an impulse, desire. *epithymia* developed ethically bad connotations because, like the other three passions (fear, pleasure, and sorrow), desire results from a false evaluation of the possessions and evils of this life.

In the LXX each word occurs about 50x. Both are used for human aspirations in general, such as a morally indifferent desire (Deut. 12:20–21), a praiseworthy desire (Gen. 31:30; Isa. 58:2), and an evil desire (Num. 11:4; 11:34; Deut. 9:22). If the tenth commandment (Exod. 20:17) forbids covetous desire, it is because God wants from us not merely obedience in acts but also in words, thoughts, and even wishes. He desires love from the whole heart (Deut. 6:5).

NT 1. *epithymia* occurs 38x and *epithymeō* 16x (mostly in Lk. and Paul's letters). The noun has a neutral or good sense only in Lk. 22:15; Phil. 1:23; 1 Thess. 2:17; perhaps Rev. 18:14. Often the vb. is used in a good sense; only in Paul and Matt. 5:28 does it have a bad connotation. Where the terms are used in a neutral or good sense, they express strong desire (cf. Matt. 13:17; Lk. 15:16; Phil. 1:23; 1 Thess. 2:17; Heb. 6:11).

2. Theologically, those passages are more important where *epithymia* is used in a bad sense of evil desire or lust. (a) In Matt. 5:28 *epithymeō* refers to sexual desire and lust; in Mk. 4:19 *epithymia* is used of the desire for all kinds of other goods and values of this world, such as riches. It is clear from both passages that Jesus considered *epithymia* a sin with a highly destructive power. It chokes the word (Mk. 4:19) and can break a marriage (Matt. 5:28). For Jesus, evil desires, just like evil deeds, flow out of and betray an evil heart that has separated itself from God.

(b) Paul sees *epithymia* as an expression of sin that rules a person. Its driving power is *sarx*, the sinful human nature that has turned from God (cf. Eph. 2:3). *epithymia* seeks gratification (Gal. 5:16) and urges us to act. When all is said and done, it expresses a deeply rooted tendency to find the focus of one's life in oneself and to trust oneself. The power of the "old self" (Eph. 4:22) is seen in *epithymia*.

Desires can find their expression in every direction: sexual desire, material enjoyment, or coveting another's possessions (cf. Rom. 1:24; Gal. 5:16–21; 1 Tim. 6:9; Tit. 3:3). Desires can enslave us. Those who allow themselves to be driven by desires are under the reign of sin (Rom. 6:12; Eph. 2:3; 2 Tim. 3:6; Tit. 3:3). When we become slaves of such allurements and temptations (Eph. 4:22), the heart comes under their control. Only a life turned to God's will, subject to him, and determined by him presents the opposite picture (Rom. 6:12–14; Eph. 4:22–24; Tit. 2:12–14).

Since there is something primitive and instinctive in human desire, Paul maintains that it is recognized as what it really is when the law speaks to it (as in the command, "Do not covet"). This command causes desire to become conscious sin (Rom. 7:7–8), which flagrantly contradicts God's law. God's answer to human desire is the Spirit. Those who walk by the Spirit have the power to resist desire (Gal. 5:16; cf. Rom. 8:9–15), because the Spirit replaces sinful desire as the determining power in life (Eph. 4:23).

When Paul speaks of desire and longing in a good sense, he uses *epipotheō* (cf. Rom. 1:11; 2 Cor. 5:2; 9:14), *epipothēsis* (2 Cor. 7:7, 11), and *epipothia* (Rom. 15:23). This word group is used 13x in the NT.

(c) In Johannine writings, the origin of desire is traced to "the world" (1 Jn. 2:16–17) and ultimately comes from the devil (Jn. 8:44; → *diabolos*, *1333*). World here means the sphere of enmity to God and Christ. The devil entices us with "the cravings of sinful man, the lust of his eyes and the boasting of what he has and does" (1 Jn. 2:16), i.e., with allurements that appeal to the senses. He awakens hatred in us and a tendency to lie, for he is "a murderer from the beginning" and "the father of lies" (Jn. 8:44). Since desire originates from the world, it is transient like this world. Those who build their lives on it will "pass away" with it; those who are led by the will of God will abide forever (1 Jn. 2:17).

(d) In the Catholic Letters *epithymia* is either neutral or shows the same trend as in Paul and John. It represents the sinful nature and its passions (1 Pet. 2:11; 2 Pet. 2:10). It is related to other lusts of the senses in their desire for the material and to drunkenness, carousing (1 Pet. 4:3), and debauchery (2 Pet. 2:18). It is a power that entices and lures us, so as to bring us under its domination (Jas. 1:14; 1 Pet. 1:14; 2 Pet. 2:18). *epithymia* promises us complete freedom but in reality enslaves us. When that happens, it "gives birth" to sinful action, which makes us guilty before God, and leads to death (Jas. 1:15). We must always be attentive to the dangers of *epithymia* and turn from it. We can conquer it if we consistently live "for the will of God" (1 Pet. 4:2).

See also *hēdonē*, pleasure (*2454*); *oregō*, strive (*3977*).

2126 (*epikaleō*, call, appeal to), → *2813*.

2129 (*epikataratos*, cursed), → *2932*.

2138 (*epilambanomai*, lay hold of, grasp, catch), → *3284*.

2146 (*epilysis*, explanation, interpretation), → *2147*.

2147 ἐπιλύω

ἐπιλύω (*epilyō*), explain, interpret, settle, solve (*2147*); ἐπίλυσις (*epilysis*), explanation, interpretation (*2146*).

CL & OT 1. In cl. Gk. *epilyō* may mean to loose, untie, or release. This meaning does not occur in the NT, but appears again in the 2d cent. A.D. and later. *epilysis* can mean release from fear. In the papyri the word is used for the "discharge" of an account. Writers of the 1st and 2d centuries A.D. use *epilyō* or *epilyomai* to mean explain, interpret, or solve a problem, or perhaps to confute an accusation. The noun *epilysis* often, but not always, means interpretation, such as of an oracle or a dream. Most often it means the explanation of something obscure, although in the specialized contents of medicine and magic it can mean a change of dressing or a magic spell.

2. *epilyō* and *epilysis* occur in Aquila's version of the Gk. OT to mean the interpretation of dreams (Gen. 40:8; 41:8, 12). Josephus uses the vb. in the sense of solving a problem: Solomon grasps the problems set by the Queen of Sheba and solves them quickly. Similarly, Philo describes how the president of the community discusses questions arising from Scripture and solves a problem passage.

NT In the NT the vb. *epilyō* occurs 2x (Mk. 4:34; Acts 19:39) and the noun *epilysis* once (2 Pet. 1:20).

1. The broad meaning of *epilyō* in Mk. 4:34 seems clear: Jesus explained or expounded the parables privately to his disciples. Perhaps the simplest explanation is that *epilyō* refers to the translation of parabolic speech into straightforward discourse, of which Mk. 4:14–20 furnishes one example. While in the case of the crowd Jesus was mainly concerned with initial *response*, in the case of the disciples he was also concerned with *instruction*. Important also in understanding this text may be the concept of "the secret (*mystērion*, → *3696*) of the kingdom of God" in 4:11. Although the crowds do understand that Jesus is talking about the kingdom, his *epilysis* to the disciples concerns the relation of the kingdom *to his own person*.

2. In Acts 19:39, *epilyō* means to solve a problem or settle a dispute. The immediate linguistic context is decisive for this meaning: A question can only be "settled," and a problem can only be "solved."

Thus the town clerk of Ephesus tells the citizens that the regular or statutory assembly will "settle" any further question that they raise in regular session (note the meaning in Josephus and Philo).

3. The meaning of *epilysis* in 2 Pet. 1:20 ("No prophecy of Scripture came about by the prophet's own interpretation") is controversial. The NIV adopts the position of many older commentators by understanding *epilysis* to refer to the biblical prophet's activity; that is, to what was in his mind as he wrote. The word *ginetai* (→ *1181*) in this verse is thus taken to denote origin ("comes from"). This interpretation anticipates the thought of 1:21 that "prophecy never had its origin in the will of man, but men spoke from God as they were carried along by the Holy Spirit." The difficulty with this interpretation is that it is not in harmony with the ordinary force of *epilysis*.

Many commentators therefore take *epilysis* to denote the interpretation of previously written Scripture. But if so, does *idias epilyseōs* mean "private" in contrast to Spirit-inspired or "private" in contrast to that of the Christian community? If the former, then the passage, together with 3:16, suggests that certain false teachers had been guilty of misusing OT prophecy. Thus Peter is saying that just as the prophets themselves were led by the Spirit (2 Pet. 1:21), so no reader can "interpret" prophecies without the guidance of the Spirit. More likely, however, "private interpretation" should be understood to mean arbitrary exegesis on the basis of personal whim, without reference to others in the Christian community. That is, the author is here condemning arbitrary exegesis of the OT.

See also *exēgeomai*, explain, expound, interpret, tell (*2007*); *hermēneuō*, explain, interpret, translate (*2257*).

2152 (*epimenō*, stay, remain, continue [in]), → *3531*.

2155 (*epiorkeō*, swear falsely, commit perjury, break one's oath), → *3923*.

2156 (*epiorkos*, perjured, perjurer), → *3923*.

2157 ἐπιούσιος

ἐπιούσιος (*epiousios*), daily (*2157*).

Epiousios, daily, is linked with *artos* in the fourth petition of the Lord's Prayer. Apart from this petition it is found only once in a papyrus of the 5th cent. A.D., where its meaning is far from certain. Hence the interpretation of the word has been a matter of controversy from early times, though "daily" is found already in the 2d cent. Four possibilities emerge.

1. The term is derived from *hē epiousa hēmera*, the next day (cf. Acts 7:26), *epiousa* being the part. of *epeimi*, approach. In that case *epiousios artos* means bread for tomorrow. Matt. 6:34 would seem to contradict this meaning: "Do not worry about tomorrow." But the use of *epiousa* in Prov. 27:1 shows that the expression does not necessarily mean tomorrow, but can indicate the coming day in general, which could be today. Hence, some translate Matt. 6:11 and Lk. 11:3 "bread for the coming day."

2. Origen suggested we should understand it as *arton epi tēn ousian*, the bread necessary for existence. Since Origen's mother tongue was Gk., we cannot deny the linguistic possibility of his interpretation (cf. Prov. 30:8). It reminds us of Exod. 16:4, where the Israelites were to gather only so much manna as they needed for the day. Thus, Jesus instructs the disciples to pray daily for the bread needed for life.

3. Some take the first option but reinterpret it in terms of the final consummation. The morrow that Jesus had in mind is not the next day, but the great morning of the final fulfillment, when Jesus with his disciples will eat the bread of life in eternity (Matt. 26:29; Lk. 22:30; Rev. 2:17). Jesus is asking his disciples to pray for this bread. The church fathers similarly linked the fourth petition with the Christ who imparts himself in the Lord's Supper as "the bread of life" (Jn. 6:35). However, although these gifts for salvation may be included in

the fourth petition, in the light of Matt. 6:25–34 we cannot doubt that Jesus was thinking first of all of earthly bread.

4. Other scholars believe that Matt. chose the unknown *epiousios* to bring out a special stress in the Aram. underlying this petition—the presumed word *leyômāʾ*, which had a double meaning that could be expressed in Gk. only by combining two terms: (*artos*) *epiousios* (bread) in so far as it is needed for the day, and *sēmeron*, for today. Thus, this petition is not merely a constant reminder to the disciples of God's fatherly faithfulness, but also that in the new age, which has already begun, prayer for provision for a longer period should no longer concern them.

See also *artos*, bread, loaf (*788*); *manna*, manna (*3445*).

2158 (*epipiptō*, fall on), → *4406*.

2160 (*epipotheō*, long for, crave, desire), → *2123*.

2161 (*epipothēsis*, longing), → *2123*.

2162 (*epipothētos*, long for), → *2123*.

2163 (*epipothia*, longing), → *2123*.

2170 (*episkeptomai*, view, inspect, visit), → *2176*.

2172 (*episkēnoō*, take up one's abode with), → *5008*.

2173 (*episkiazō*, overshadow, cover), → *5014*.

2174 (*episkopeō*, oversee, care for), → *2176*.

2175 (*episkopē*, visitation, office as overseer), → *2176*.

2176 ἐπίσκοπος

ἐπίσκοπος (*episkopos*), overseer, guardian, bishop (*2176*); ἐπισκέπτομαι (*episkeptomai*), view, inspect, visit, afflict (*2170*); ἐπισκοπέω (*episkopeō*), take care, oversee, care for (*2174*); ἐπισκοπή (*episkopē*), visitation, affliction, position or office as an overseer or bishop (*2175*).

CL & OT 1. This group of words (formed from the root *skep-* [look] with the prefix *epi* [at, on]) denotes the activity of looking at or paying attention to a person or thing. It stresses active and responsible care for what is seen. The vb. can mean observe, superintend, watch over, scrutinize. The noun *episkopos*, overseer, was first used to describe a deity as the one who kept watch over a country or people, esp. over the keeping of treaties and the markets. But the title was also given to those who had a responsible position in the state, such as officials sent from Athens to dependent states to ensure order or to fix their constitutions. The word was later extended to religious communities, where the *episkopoi* were those responsible for external relationships.

2. (a) In the LXX this word group mostly translates variants of the root *pāqad*, take care of, look for, investigate, inspect. *episkopeō* is used only 5x, while *episkeptomai* is found 150x, of which 49 are in Num.. There the vb. gained the meaning appoint for supervision, commission (cf. the prayer in Num. 27:16).

(b) These words are also used for God's watching over and solicitous care for the land (Deut. 11:12), his elect people (Ruth 1:6; Ps. 80:14; Zeph. 2:7), and individuals (e.g., Sarah, Gen.21:1). It expresses his loyalty to the covenant and his mercy. In the prophets (esp. Jer.) it can mean visit in the sense of afflict or punish (cf. Exod. 32:34), for when God sees sin, he must judge his people to bring them to repentance.

(c) The LXX coined the subst. *episkepsis* and *episkopē* to represent *pequddâ* or *peqûdâ*, the "number" of men from each tribe who could serve in the army (Num. 1:21, 23, 25, etc.; cf. 1 Chr. 24:3) and the visitation of God in judgment, either in the course of history or in the day of Yahweh (cf. Job 7:18; Jer. 11:23; 23:12).

3. *episkopos* can mean overseer, officer, governor (2 Chr. 34:12; Neh. 11:9, 14, 22). It is used once of God (Job 20:29). In some cases (e.g., Num. 31:14; Jdg. 9:28) particular persons in a position of authority are *episkopoi*, but the word can also denote the exercise of power and those who exercise it (e.g., Isa. 60:17). For the various offices in Israel and their relationship to one another, → *presbyteros* (*4565*).

NT 1. This word group is markedly less common in the NT than in the LXX. *episkopeō* is found only in Heb. 12:15 and possibly 1 Pet. 5:2. In the former passage it describes the effort Christians should make to see that they remain in divine grace.

2. *episkeptomai* occurs 11x (7x in Lk.–Acts; also in Matt. 25:36, 43; Heb. 2:6; Jas. 1:27). (a) This vb. is used in Heb. 2:6 (Ps. 8:4) and often in the Lukan writings for the loving care of God. He has chosen out of all the nations a people for himself (Acts 15:14), whom he has visited in blessing (Lk. 1:78; 7:16) and redeemed (1:68; → *lytrōsis*, *3391*). In Heb. 2:6 the writer expresses his wonder that God should create and care for humankind.

(b) *episkeptomai* is used in Acts 6:3 for the church's selection of seven men to serve, in 7:23 for Moses' concern for his people, and in 15:36 for Paul's proposal to return to the churches in Asia Minor to care for their converts. In Jas. 1:27, believers show religious service to God by caring for widows and orphans. Note too Jesus' comments in Matt. 25:36, 43: Those who suffer or are in prison represent the Lord himself; the decision we make regarding them indicates our salvation or condemnation.

(c) All these uses stress the same loving care, showing with a heart moved to action. The OT meaning of visitation for punishment is lacking for this word. God's visitation took place once for all on the cross.

3. (a) Earlier uses of *episkopos* reach their climax in 1 Pet. 2:25, where Jesus as the exalted Christ is described as "the Shepherd (*poimēn*) and Overseer (*episkopos*) of your souls." It is no accident that *episkopos* is here linked with *poimēn*, for these two thoughts are already connected in the OT (Num. 27:17) and again in the NT (Acts 20:28). Oversight means loving care and concern, a responsibility willingly shouldered; it must never be used for personal aggrandizement. Its meaning is to be seen in Christ's selfless service, which was moved by concern for the salvation of the human race.

(b) It is significant that, as the growing band of disciples became a church, they hesitated to apply the title of *episkopos* to designate an office. Gk. usage may have had materialistic overtones connected with this word, and OT associations may have been reminiscent of authoritarian oversight. Its application to oversight in the church is to be seen in the context of the application of all Christ's work to the church. In other words, titles of offices in the NT are essentially titles that apply first to Christ.

The need for pastoral oversight to keep the church in the way of faith was originally a duty binding on all members, as it apparently still was in Heb. 12:15. But eventually oversight became the task of a special office. The change is somewhat reflected in Acts 20:28, which focuses on the duties of the hearers to the church. Already the church is a clearly defined group ("flock") over whom the *episkopoi* watch. No doubt, this title is to be distinguished from that of apostle and prophet, and perhaps too from that of teacher (→ *didaskō*, *1438*), for overseers were linked to a specific place and church. But at first it was probably synonymous at least with that of shepherd (*poimēn*) and elder (*presbyteros*) and the ideas associated with them. The use of *diakonos* (→ *diakoneō*, *1354*) was also not yet fixed.

4. *episkopē* (overseer) is first used in 1 Tim. 3:1 to designate a defined office to which one could aspire. It is striking how attention here shifts from the duties of the office (as in Acts 20) to the personal qualities needed for it: personal discipline, a well-ordered family, gifts of teaching and personal relationships, and a good name in the non-Christian world. The development of the episcopal office marks the transition from the missionary era of the church with its charismatic gifts to an institution with a permanent character. After the death of the apostles, the expanding church felt a need for a form of church government that would ensure continuity.

See also *presbyteros*, older, elder, presbyter (*4565*).

| 2179 ἐπίσταμαι | ἐπίσταμαι (*epistamai*), know, understand (*2179*) |

CL & OT 1. In cl. Gk. *epistamai* means to know or understand, sometimes to know how to do something. In some writers it denotes being assured of something or even believing. The present part. can refer to someone who is knowing, wise, or skillful (as in war).

2. In the LXX this word refers primarily to what someone knows on the basis of observation or inner awareness, whether that person is God (e.g., Exod. 4:14; Isa. 37:28; Jer. 17:16; Ezek. 11:5) or a human being (Exod. 9:30; Num. 20:14; Job 38:20; Ezek. 28:19). But the word can also refer to specific knowledge that one has received from God (Num. 24:16; Isa. 41:20) or to knowledge of the future that one surmises on the basis of observing the present (Deut. 31:27). In Prov. 9:13 the woman Folly is described as one who does not know.

Jer. 1:5 uses *epistamai* for the divine foreknowledge of God, that even before the prophet was born, the Lord knew him and planned for him to be a prophet. Jeremiah answers using the same word, "Ah, Sovereign LORD . . . I do not know how to speak; I am only a child" (1:6). The Lord then responds by giving the prophet words in his mouth (1:9). The vb. later becomes important in Jeremiah's message that the priests, who were responsible for the religious leadership of the people, "did not know me [Yahweh]" (2:8). Ezek. on one occasion uses *epistamai* to refer to knowledge that God alone is aware of (37:3).

NT 1. In general in the NT, *epistamai* is limited to the knowledge that a person receives by observation or by hearing some information. It is used parallel with *oida* in Mk. 14:68 and Jude 10. The guild of which Demetrius was leader all knew that they were making a good income from the silver shrines of Artemis that they sold (Acts 19:25). King Agrippa was "familiar with" the events concerning Jesus (26:26), and the citizens of Jerusalem knew that Paul had at one time been an ardent persecutor of Christians (22:19).

2. *epistamai* can also take on theological nuances in the NT. Abraham launched out in faith when God called him, "even though he did not know where he was going" (Heb. 11:8). By contrast, a person who teaches false doctrines simply in order to make a good living is filled with pride and "understands nothing" about the true teaching of our Lord Jesus Christ (1 Tim. 6:4). Jas. uses the vb. to stress that everything we do should be linked with the prayer that it be God's will, for we "do not even know what will happen tomorrow" (4:14).

See also *phronēsis*, way of thinking, frame of mind, intelligence, good sense (*5860*); *nous*, mind, intellect, understanding, reason, thought (*3808*); *synesis*, faculty of comprehension, understanding, insight (*5304*); *ginōskō*, know (*1182*); *oida*, know, understand (*3857*).

2182 (*epistellō*, inform or instruct by letter, write), → *2186*.

2185 (*epistērizō*, strengthen), → *5114*.

| 2186 ἐπιστολή | ἐπιστολή (*epistolē*), letter (*2186*); ἐπιστέλλω (*epistellō*), inform or instruct by letter, write (*2182*). |

CL & OT 1. *epistellō* means send, announce, order, generally in writing. Hence, what is transmitted (originally a military or administrative order) is called *epistolē*. With the spread of Hel. culture a whole range of letters developed: private letters of an intimate nature, open letters (e.g., didactic letters of philosophers), and artistic letters (aesthetic treatises in letter form). Traveling philosophers and their pupils often carried letters of recommendation. Gk. letters followed a fixed pattern: the sender (nom.) to the recipient (dat.), greetings (*chairein*); they usually end with a short farewell greeting.

2. Preexilic letters are only briefly quoted in the OT—usually rulers' letters to other rulers or their subjects. They involve conspir-acy (2 Sam. 11:14–15; 1 Ki. 21:9–10; 2 Ki. 10:1–6), mockery (19:10–13), homage (20:12), and prophetic oracle (2 Chr. 21:12–15). Naaman carried a letter of recommendation (2 Ki. 5:6).

A wider range of epistolary lit. appears in later OT writings. Because of the occupation of the land after the exile, political correspondence with the foreign rulers was necessary (cf. Ezr. 4:7–6:12; Add. Est. 13:1–7; 1 Macc. 10:3, 7, 17–20; 11:29–37; 12:5–23; etc.). The Diaspora resulted in religious letters and instructions being sent to those in exile (see Jer. 29:4–23).

NT *epistolē* occurs 24x in the NT; *epistellō* 3x. Of the 27 books of the NT, 21 are clearly letters. In addition, epistolary style as a literary form can be found in Lk. 1:3–4; Acts 1:1; 15:23–29; 23:26–30; Rev. 1:10–11.

1. Most early Christian writings took the form of occasional lit. The problems of the missionary churches, which found themselves in constant tension with their political and religious surroundings, needed explanations. Moreover, after a lengthy absence the missionary wanted to remind his converts of his message, to reaffirm it, and to develop it. Moreover, conflict about tradition and doctrine (even heresy) required responses, and there was the increasing need felt for church order. Thus, letters played a decisive role in carrying the young church through a period of outward and inward danger. Eventually these letters were assembled in collections (cf. 2 Pet. 3:16).

2. Paul gave the NT letters their original form. He was not motivated by any stylistic reasons but by his Christian message. The standard Gk. preface (cf. Acts 15:23; 23:26; Jas. 1:1) was expanded: *chairein* was replaced by an explicit greeting according to the Oriental pattern (e.g., *charis hymin*, grace be with you). An expanded preface often prepared readers for the contents of the letter (cf. Rom. 1:1–7; Gal. 1:1–5). It was followed by thanksgiving, prayer, and an assurance of remembrance (Rom. 1:8–12; Phil. 1:3–11; 1 Thess. 1:2–10); when necessary, this changed to blame and warning (Gal. 1:6–9). Similarly, the short farewell greeting became a full prayer for blessing. Paul dictated his letters (Rom. 16:22), but often penned the closing sentences himself as a sign of authenticity (1 Cor. 16:21; Gal. 6:11; Phlm. 19).

3. Paul's letters arose from situations in his churches and were written for particular circles of readers (cf. 1 Cor. 16:5–9). They often answered questions raised by the church (esp. 1 Cor.). They are molded throughout by the *kerygma* and Paul's apostolic office. Hence, they are public, official letters, designed to be read in church services as well as passed on (1 Thess. 5:27) (Philemon is an exception).

epistolē is found only once in a metaphorical sense (2 Cor. 3:2–3), but this instance is of great importance. When one thinks of the technique of dictating a letter at that time—slow writing on rough papyrus with thick ink, while the thought of the one dictating outran the pace of the scribe—the passage suggests the interweaving of two pictures, one derived from what had already been written, the other from what had formed itself in the author's mind.

The former picture, "you yourselves are our letter," refers back to the practice of Paul's enemies just mentioned (traveling prophets claiming to be Christians but propagating their own views). They obtained letters of recommendation from the churches to establish their competence (3:5), so that they might be paid accordingly (2:17). Paul rejected them brusquely. His competence came from God, and that was only for service (3:6). The local church itself in its spiritual and historical existence is his letter of recommendation, composed by the exalted Lord and written with the Spirit of God, with the freedom experienced and lived out under Christ's lordship (3:17). Paul was only the secretary (3:3), through whose help a church had come into existence (5:17).

This introduces the second picture: The letter is "written on our hearts . . . not on tablets of stone, but on tablets of human hearts" (3:2–3). Looking back to Ezek. 11:19 and Jer. 31:31–34, Paul prepares for the theme of the section immediately following: the contrast between the letter (the old covenant apart from the Spirit) and the Spirit (the new covenant in the Spirit). The church's attestation of the new covenant lies in its spiritual existence, in which the gospel of the cross puts an end to all self-glorification and unbridled speculation. In it the Crucified and Exalted One is alone Lord and is awaited as the coming Judge (1 Cor. 2:2; 2 Cor. 5:10, 15).

In other words, 2 Cor. 3:2–3 is concerned with what Calvin called the inner testimony of the Holy Spirit (cf. 1 Cor. 2:14–16). If one reads the letter, that is, the church, unspiritually, one merely establishes the external fact of its existence. In fighting the fight of faith, the church is deprived of all tangible security and proof. It is a conflict between life and death, salvation and destruction (2 Cor. 2:15–16). Paul's polemic gained its seriousness and its clarity from his realization of this fact.

See also *biblos*, book (*1047*); *anaginōskō*, read (*336*).

2188	ἐπιστρέφω

ἐπιστρέφω (*epistrephō*), turn, turn around, turn back, be converted (*2188*); στρέφω (*strephō*), turn, change (*5138*); ἀποστρέφω (*apostrephō*), turn away from (*695*); ἐπιστροφή (*epistrophē*), conversion (*2189*).

CL & OT 1. The three vbs. *strephō, apostrephō,* and *epistrephō* were used trans. and intrans.; all share the meaning of turn, turn to, turn oneself around. They describe a largely intentional turning of the body or thoughts to a person or thing. *strephō* has more the sense of turn over, turn around, transform; *epistrephō* means turn towards, return, and derivatively be converted (i.e., change one's mind and behavior).

2. Behind *epistrephō* in the LXX lies the Heb. *šûb*, which occurs ca. 1050x and means turn around, return (qal); bring back, restore (hiph.). It appears with a theological meaning of be converted, change one's behavior by returning to God ca. 120x.

Conversion in the OT is turning from evil (Jer. 18:8) to the Lord (Mal. 3:7). People can, however, be so permeated by evil (Hos. 5:4) that they resist such turning (2 Chr. 36:13). Note that when people do return, it is because they have first received the heart to do so from God (Jer. 24:7). God uses the prophets to help to bring about conversion (Neh. 9:26; Zech. 1:3–4).

Those who refuse to return to God experience his wrath in drought (Amos 4:6–8), captivity (Hos. 11:5), destruction (1 Ki. 9:6–9), and death (Ezek. 33:9, 11). Those who return to God receive forgiveness (Isa. 55:7), remission of punishment (Jon. 3:9–10), fertility and prosperity (Hos. 14:5–7), and life (Ezek. 33:14–16). The historical books of the OT always call for the return of Israel as a body, but the prophets, esp. Jer. and Ezek., stress the conversion of the individual. They look forward to the new covenant, when God will give a new heart and spirit (Jer. 33:31–34; Ezek. 11:19; 18:31; 36:26–27; 37:14). The conversion of the people as a whole will take place in the messianic age (Deut. 4:30; Hos. 3:5; cf. Mal. 4:5–6).

3. Rab. Jud. accepted this OT tradition. A condition for admittance to the Qumran community was conversion, i.e., turning from all evil and turning to Moses' law. Hel. Jewish circles also knew the concept of religious conversion. Those who turn to Yahweh are forgiven; they do not continue in sin but keep the commandments of God.

NT 1. *epistrephō* is found 36x in the NT, half of which have its secular meaning of turning, returning, turning away (cf. Matt. 10:13; 2 Pet. 2:22), while the other half have its theological meaning of conversion (cf. Mk. 4:12 par.; Lk. 1:16–17; 22:32; Acts 15:19; 2 Cor. 3:16; Jas. 5:19–20). Unlike the LXX, the vb. is often synonymous with *metanoeō*. Only in Matt. 18:3 and Jn. 12:40 does *strephō* have a theological meaning (be converted); likewise *apostrephō* only in Acts 3:26. The noun *epistrophē* is found only in 15:3.

2. (a) The call to conversion means a fundamentally new turning of the human will to God, a return home from blindness and error to the Savior of all (Acts 26:18; 1 Pet. 2:25). *epistrephō* is not con-

cerned primarily with what a person turns from (the old life), but with turning to Christ and through him to God (cf. Jn. 14:1, 6) and so to a new life. Conversion involves a change of lords. One who until then has been under the lordship of Satan (cf. Eph. 2:1–2) comes under the lordship of God; he or she comes out of darkness into light (Acts 26:18; cf. Eph. 5:8).

Conversion and surrender of one's life to God involve faith in Jesus Christ (Acts 11:21) and result in the forgiveness of sins (3:19; 26:18). Conversion leads to a fundamental change of one's entire life (26:20)—a new outlook and new objectives. The converted serve God alone with a clear conscience (14:15; 1 Thess. 1:9; cf. Heb. 9:14).

(b) *epistrephō* involves a complete transformation (→ *morphē, 3671*) of one's existence under the influence of the Holy Spirit. The vb. *metamelomai*, however (→ *3564*), expresses the feeling of repentance of sin, which need not involve turning to God. *metanoeō* (→ *3567*) is much closer to *epistrephō*, though *epistrephō* has a wider meaning, for it always includes faith.

See also *metamelomai*, change one's mind, regret, repent (*3564*); *metanoia*, change of mind, conversion (*3567*); *prosēlytos*, proselyte (*4670*).

2189 (*epistrophē*, conversion), → *2188*.

2190 (*episynagō*, gather together), → *5251*.

2191 (*episynagōgē*, gathering together), → *5251*.

2198 (*epitagē*, order, injunction), → *5435*.

2199 (*epitassō*, command, order), → *5435*.

2202	ἐπιτίθημι

ἐπιτίθημι (*epitithēmi*), to put on, lay on (*2202*); ἐπίθεσις (*epithesis*), laying on (of hands) (*2120*).

CL & OT 1. This entry deals mainly with the phrase *epitithēmi tēn cheira* or *tas cheiras*, to lay the hand or hands on someone or something. Miraculous healings, performed through the laying on of hands, are attributed in Hel. lit. to Asclepius, Zeus, and other gods and wise men. The phrase with the noun, *epithesis tōn cheirōn*, the laying on of hands, occurs only in Philo and the NT.

2. (a) *epitithēmi tas cheiras* has two main associations in the LXX. The more frequent use is the one that describes how a sacrificer lays his hand on the head of a sacrificial animal. The meaning of this action is clearly seen in the ritual for the great Day of Atonement (Lev. 16), where the laying on of hands symbolizes the transference of guilt to the scapegoat. To drive out the goat meant to drive out sin itself. In other sacrifices the laying on of hands (often in Lev.) symbolizes Israel's committing to Yahweh their sin and evil and allowing him to destroy it.

(b) Though more rare, the laying on of hands can also be an act of blessing (Gen. 48:18). It is no doubt closely related to the ritual of laying on of hands on the occasion of one's installation to an office (Num. 27:18, 23). This ritual denotes that a particular quality of the one who performs the act passes that to the one on whom hands are laid. The two passages that took on the greatest significance for rab. Jud. were those dealing with Moses' appointment of Joshua as his successor (Num. 27:15–23; Deut. 34:9). In the former, by means of the laying on of hands Moses invested Joshua with his authority; in the latter, his spirit of wisdom. The Jews saw here the model and origin of their own ordination practice, which they viewed as handing on the spirit of Moses from the present teacher to the pupil.

NT 1. (a) *epitithēmi tas cheiras* occurs 20x in the NT, mostly in connection with miracles of healing (Matt. 9:18; Mk. 5:23; 6:5; 7:32; 8:23; Lk. 13:13; Acts 28:8) performed by Jesus and the apostles as signs that the messianic age has already dawned. The expression also appears in Matt. 19:13, 15 to denote a gesture of blessing the children brought to Jesus, which symbolized the gracious offer of a share in the kingdom of God made to those who are not of age, i.e., to such as approach God with the attitude of children.

(b) Acts 8:17–19; 9:17; 19:6 (possibly also 1 Tim. 5:22) belong in the context of baptism. The Holy Spirit is given to those who are baptized and have the apostles' hands laid on them, although the possibility of some sort of ordination cannot be excluded. Two passages take us directly into the sphere of Jewish ordination: Acts 6:6, where the seven Hellenists are appointed to serve in the daily distribution to their section of the community; and 13:3, where Paul and Barnabas are authorized, commissioned, and sent out to a specific missionary task.

2. The noun expression *epithesis tōn cheirōn* occurs 4x in the NT. It is used once in connection with baptism (Acts 8:18). On another occasion it denotes one of the elementary doctrines of Christianity (Heb. 6:2). Twice (1 Tim. 4:14; 2 Tim. 1:6) it denotes the rite by which Timothy was ordained. According to these two passages, Timothy had conferred on him, through the laying on of hands by the elders or Paul, the gifts needed for leading the congregation: preaching the Word and teaching or refuting false teachers.

3. It is striking that in every passage where the laying on of hands appears in connection with ordination or sending out for a particular service, it is always carried out by people who at that moment possess different gifts. In Acts 6:6 the laying on of hands for serving tables is performed by the apostles; in 13:3 for the missionary task, by prophets and teachers; in 1 Tim. 4:14, by the elders; and in 2 Tim. 1:6, by Paul. The NT does not seem to recognize the power of ordination as being restricted to a particular office, e.g., that of the apostles.

We should note also the close connection between the laying on of hands and intercessory prayer. This suggests that there is no thought of a human transfer of a particular quality necessary for office from one office-bearer to another, as if succession is occurring. The idea that the gifts needed for ministry are at someone's disposal is contradicted by Peter's clash with Simon Magus (Acts 8:18–24). It is God himself who equips his servants with his gifts and sends them out; this happens through the prayer of the church. The laying on of hands bears witness to the church's conviction that their prayers, founded on God's promises, have been heard.

See also *dexios*, right, right hand, right side (*1288*); *aristeros*, left, left hand (*754*); *cheir*, hand (*5931*).

2203	ἐπιτιμάω

ἐπιτιμάω (*epitimaō*), rebuke (*2203*); ἐπιτιμία (*epitimia*), censure (*2204*).

CL & OT The vb. in cl. Gk. means to honor, censure, penalize, and raise in price. The noun can mean penalty, value, honor, and respect.

In the LXX, people rebuke (e.g., Gen. 37:10) but should not do so (Ruth 2:16), unless they have judicial, paternal, or fraternal authority (Eccl. 7:5 = LXX 7:6; cf. Prov. 17:10). But God does have the right to rebuke, not only human beings or his enemies (Ps. 9:5; 76:6), but also the created order (106:9) and Satan (Zech. 3:2 = LXX 3:3).

NT 1. The vb. is found frequently in all three Synoptic Gospels, implying disapproval, but not exaction of a concrete penalty. The sense of censure or rebuke will suit all instances, but more precise definition is possible. (a) People rebuke one another as a sign of disapproval: The disciples rebuked those who presented children to Jesus (Mk. 10:13 par.), the crowd rebuked the blind man who sought Jesus (10:48 par.), Peter rebuked Jesus for his passion prediction (8:32 par.), and the Pharisees asked Jesus to rebuke the disciples (Lk. 19:39). In each instance Jesus disapproves of the rebuke, though he himself is free to deliver a rebuke (to Peter, Mk. 8:33; to the Sons of Thunder, Lk. 9:55). Note, however, that the situation of one brother rebuking another and the rebuke by the penitent thief do not receive adverse comment (Lk. 17:3; 23:40).

(b) Sometimes Jesus rebukes in order to repress, when he casts out demons (Mk. 1:25; 9:25), dispels a fever (Lk. 4:39), or stills a storm (Mk. 4:39). Jesus is here depicted as Lord of all on the model of Yahweh (Ps. 106:9) and as the bringer of salvation, for demons flee at his command.

(c) At Mk. 3:12; 8:30 and par., Jesus rebukes in the sense of forbidding what might happen if the disciples or cured demoniacs start publishing his deeds as Lord of all. Jesus does not want anyone to make known his deeds until he has finished his ministry of dying on the cross. In 2 Tim. 4:2, rebuking is a function of the authoritative Christian teacher, alongside preaching, convincing, and exhorting; note also Jude 9, where the archangel Michael upbraids Satan with "the Lord rebuke you" (cf. Zech. 3:2).

2. The noun *epitimia* appears only in 2 Cor. 2:6, where it refers to censure or even punishment meted out by the church in congregational discipline.

See also *noutheteō*, warn, advise (*3805*); *parakaleō*, summon, invite, exhort, encourage (*4151*).

2204 (epitimia, censure), → *2203.*

2205	ἐπιτρέπω

ἐπιτρέπω (*epitrepō*), allow, permit (*2205*); ἐπιτροπή (*epitropē*), charge, commission (*2207*).

CL & OT 1. In cl. Gk. *epitrepō* means to entrust something to a person, bequeath, then also permit or allow. In general, this word denotes official authority: A person in charge gives instructions or permission to someone under his authority to do something.

2. This vb. rarely occurs in the LXX, the noun only in 2 Macc. 13:14. In Gen. 39:6 Joseph is entrusted with (or given charge over) Potiphar's entire household. In Est. 9:14, the king gives permission for Haman's sons to be hung on gallows. In the LXX of Job 32:14, Elihu charges the three friends of Job with having given permission to Job to speak in the way he has. Finally, in 2 Macc. 13:14 *epitropē* refers to Judas's commitment to God's "decision," whatever the outcome, in his battle against the Seleucids.

NT 1. *epitrepō* occurs 18x in the NT, *epitropē* only once (Acts 26:12). Behind all uses lies the notion of authority, though on different levels. On a human level, Pilate gives Joseph permission to take Jesus' body down from the cross and to bury it (Jn. 19:38). Paul asks for and receives permission to address the Jews (Acts 21:39–40), and Agrippa gives Paul permission to address him (26:1). Later, Paul was permitted to live under house arrest in Rome (28:16) rather than in some prison.

2. Matt. 19:8; Mk. 10:4 refer to the divorce permission of Moses in the OT law (Deut. 24:1–4; for more on this, → *apostasion*, decree of divorce, *687*; *chōrizō*, divide, separate; be divorced, *6004*).

3. Jesus was a person from whom permission was sought. Two would-be followers asked for his permission, the one to bury his father and the other to say farewell to his family before following Jesus (Matt. 8:21; Lk. 9:59, 61). Jesus, however, did not accept either of these excuses as sufficient grounds for withholding discipleship. The legion of demons sought permission from Jesus to enter into swine (Mk. 5:13; Lk. 8:32) before leaving the man in whom they were living. Consistently, Jesus manifested power over evil spirits.

4. In two of the most debated passages of the NT, Paul indicates that he does not permit women to exercise authority over men in the church (1 Cor. 14:34; 1 Tim. 2:12). Whether Paul wrote this for cultural reasons or because of absolute principles cannot be decided on contextual grounds.

5. "If the Lord permits" (1 Cor. 16:7; cf. Heb. 6:3) seems to be a standard phrase that a person might use to indicate his or her dependence on God and his will (cf. Jas. 4:15, "If it is the Lord's will," which uses the vb. *thelō*, to wish, desire, will, *2527*).

2207 (*epitropē*, charge, commission), → 2205.

2210 (*epiphainō*, show, appear), → 2211.

2211	ἐπιφάνεια

ἐπιφάνεια (*epiphaneia*), appearance, revelation (*2211*); ἐπιφαίνω (*epiphainō*), show, appear (*2210*); ἐφίστημι (*ephistēmi*), appear, stand beside (*2392*); ἐπιφανής (*epiphanēs*), powerful, splendid, terrible (*2212*); φανερός (*phaneros*), visible, clear, open, evident (*5745*); φανερῶς (*phanerōs*), openly (*5747*); φανερόω (*phaneroō*), reveal, make known, show, manifest (*5746*); φανέρωσις (*phanerōsis*), revelation, manifestation, disclosure (*5748*); φαντάζω (*phantazō*), make visible (*5751*).

CL & OT 1. (a) In cl. Gk. *epiphaneia*, derived from *phainō*, to appear (cf. *phōs*, light, *5890*), originally denotes outward appearance or mode of appearance; then also, fig., glorious appearance, i.e., esteem, distinction, majesty. Later it came to express the sensation that a person or thing causes, so that by the time of Jesus, the word had almost become a technical term for the appearance of an otherwise hidden deity.

(b) Since appearances of a divinity occur principally in the temple, the whole narrative section of the Temple Chronicle of Lindos is entitled *epiphaneiai*. The epiphany of a god is celebrated as the feast of his birth, of his accession, of extraordinary happenings worked by him that reveal his power, or of his return from a foreign land.

(c) Since *epiphaneia* describes the powerful intervention of the gods, rulers who were regarded as divine kings applied the adj. *epiphanēs* to themselves (cf. Antiochus Epiphanes in 1 Macc. 1:10).

2. (a) In the LXX *epiphainō* is the chief rendering of Heb. ʾôr (hiph.), to cause to shine, though it also translates other Heb. vbs. It occurs in the Aaronic blessing (Num. 6:25) and associated passages (Ps. 31:16; 67:1; 80:3, 7, 19; 118:27). Always it is Yahweh's marvelous rescuing and redemptive vindication of his people in the sense of the OT theophany that is meant.

(b) *epiphanēs* is the LXX rendering of Heb. *nôrāʾ* (niph. part. of *yārēʾ*, to fear), terrible, fearful (Jdg. 13:6; Joel 2:11, 31; Hab. 1:7; Mal. 1:14). The LXX apparently confused derivatives of *yārēʾ* with derivatives of *rāʾâ*, to see (or even ʾôr, to illuminate) and so introduced an element of the terrible into the concept of this Gk. word. This becomes esp. clear in the translation of the expected "great" and/or "dreadful" day of the Lord (Joel 2:11, 31 [cf. Acts 2:20]; Mal. 4:5) by *megalē* and *epiphanēs*. By introducing through the LXX the element of the terrible into the epiphany concept, the expectation of God's appearance in the end times meant that words from this group could designate the double outcome of salvation history—fear and dread for unbelievers, glory for believers.

3. This word group is found esp. in 2 Macc. *epiphaneia* here denotes the intervention of God (3:24; 14:15; esp. 15:27) in the sense of an OT theophany; 3 Macc. 2:19 and 6:4, 9, go back to the OT usage corresponding with Num. 6:25. The adj. *epiphanēs* can describe both the "Lord" (2 Macc. 15:34; 3 Macc. 5:35), the God of Israel, and also the sanctuary of Dionysus (2 Macc. 14:33).

NT 1. By and large, *epiphaneia* and *epiphainō* occur in the Pastoral Letters, Paul's latest writings in the NT. *epiphaneia* is used with a twofold meaning for the visible appearance of Jesus Christ on earth. (a) It occurs with reference to the appearance of the Lord on earth at the end of history. According to 2 Thess. 2:1–12, the coming of the "man of lawlessness" will precede the visible appearance of the Lord Jesus. In fact, this man is already at work (2:7), but his coming (2:9) is being presently impeded by some undisclosed power (2:6–7). The Lord Jesus will destroy him "by the splendor [*epiphaneia*] of his coming [*parousia*]" (2:8). *epiphaneia* and *parousia* (→ 4242) are to be understood here as a hendiadys, *epiphaneia* stressing the powerful and effective action of the returning Christ, and *parousia* accentuating more strongly the fact of his reappearance.

The decisive factor at the return of the Lord is what he will do. His appearance, the judgment, and the final establishment of his kingdom belong inextricably together. The awaited judgment day of the Lord will be both terrible and glorious (cf. Acts 2:20). Because of the double possible outcome in salvation history, the need to stand one's ground in the fight of faith must be stressed (note how the thought of 1 Tim. 6:12 precedes that of 6:14, where *epiphaneia* occurs). Those who love the Lord long "for his appearing" (2 Tim. 4:8). The stress laid on Christ's powerful action in the designation of his return derives ultimately from the fact that the Lord Jesus can be called both "God and Savior" (Tit. 2:13) in connection with his expected *epiphaneia*, even though the NT is restrained in its application of "God" to Jesus Christ.

(b) Christians also applied *epiphaneia* to the visible earthly appearance of their Savior in his incarnation (2 Tim. 1:10). *epiphainō* (apart from Acts 27:20) is used in the NT solely of Jesus' earthly appearance, whether with a forward (Lk. 1:79) or a backward (Tit. 2:11; 3:4) look. To see God's powerful revelation shining in Jesus' servant form is not a judgment of one's reason, but a judgment exclusively of faith, for outside faith the revelation of God is not visible.

(c) The vb. *ephistēmi* (predominantly used by Luke) can sometimes mean simply to come upon someone (e.g., Lk. 10:40; Acts 4:1). But it can also be used of the appearance of the angel of the Lord (Lk. 2:9; Acts 12:7) or even of the Lord himself (Acts 23:11). In 1 Thess. 5:3 the vb. is used of the sudden coming of eschatological woes.

2. (a) The early church prayed to the no longer and not yet visible Lord, who is nevertheless believed in as present and active, to reveal himself (1 Cor. 16:22; Rev. 22:20; cf. Num. 6:25). Their thought was not that of seeing him, but of his intervention and of a growing certainty that strengthens faith.

(b) In pregnant usage this word group is found in the Bible only in the context of the revelation of Yahweh in the OT and of Jesus Christ in the NT. To speak of revelation in the fullest biblical sense is to speak of Jesus Christ, our Savior. The words are never employed in connection with revelation in creation. The words accordingly do not belong to a theory of knowledge that is independent of history but to NT soteriology. The mighty saving intervention of God has already occurred, but its fulfillment will take place only at the appearance of Jesus Christ. Thus, believers live in the tension of being already reconciled but not yet redeemed (Rom. 8:23). In other words, they live in hope.

3. (a) Regarding the related words, the adj. *phaneros*, visible, clear, evident, is not usually a technical theological term, although it is used in important theological contexts. It stresses what is visible to the sight. It is used in connection with the messianic secret (Mk. 3:12), wherein Jesus charges his disciples not to make him known. Nevertheless, his name does become known (6:14). *phaneros* is also used in Jesus' declaration that in general we can do nothing in secret that will not be made manifest (Mk. 4:22; Lk. 8:17).

In Acts 4:16 the Jewish leaders are compelled to acknowledge that the apostles, Peter and John, have performed a notable deed in healing the lame man in the temple and that this was manifest to all who lived in Jerusalem. Similarly, that Paul's imprisonment was for Christ became "clear throughout the whole palace guard" (Phil. 1:13). These instances imply that God's truth will become visible and evident in God's good time, whether we try to hasten it or hinder it. *phaneros* also has a nontechnical sense in Acts 7:13, where Stephen refers to Joseph's making himself known to his brethren.

Rom. 1:19 declares that what may be known about God "is plain" to people in the natural order. In 2:28 those who are Jews "outwardly" (*phaneros* is used; lit., "in the open"), i.e., by possessing circumcision and making a formal profession of the law, are contrasted with those who are Jews inwardly, who have true, spiritual circumcision of the heart (2:29). Paul is arguing that genuine membership of God's people does not consist of possessing the outward marks of covenant membership; there must also be the inner spiritual reality. Yet where this is absent, as in the case of unbelieving Jews, it does not nullify the faithfulness of God (3:1–4, 31; cf. Ps. 51:4). God plans to use even the unbelief of the Jews to his glory, and he wills their inclusion among his people by grafting them back through their turning to him on a massive scale (Rom. 9:1–11:36).

In the day of the Lord the works of all people—including believers—will come to light (1 Cor. 3:13; cf. 14:25; Mk. 4:22; Lk. 8:17). Indeed, the present dissensions within the church make it manifest who are genuine (1 Cor. 11:19). In Gal. 5:19–23 Paul draws attention to the self-evident character of the works of the sinful nature as contrasted with the fruit of the Spirit. Timothy is exhorted to practice the duties of his ministry so that his progress may be evident to all (1 Tim. 4:15). Similarly, the believer's attitude to sin makes it plain that he or she is a child of God (1 Jn. 3:10).

(b) The adv. *phanerōs* means openly, publicly, so that everyone can see (Mk. 1:45; Jn. 7:10). In Acts 10:3 it can be translated "distinctly" or "plainly."

(c) The vb. *phaneroō*, reveal, make known, manifest, occurs 49x in the NT. (i) In Mk. 4:22 it has the character of a proverbial saying. Elsewhere, it occurs in the Synoptics only in the longer ending of Mk. (16:12, 14).

(ii) This vb., however, occurs frequently in Jn., virtually as a synonym for *apokalyptō*, reveal (→ *636*). John the Baptist came baptizing with water so that Jesus Christ "might be revealed to Israel" (Jn. 1:31). The miraculous sign at the wedding in Cana "revealed his glory, and his disciples put their faith in him" (2:11). Those who do evil, hate the light and do not come to it; "but whoever lives by the truth comes into the light, so that it may be seen plainly that what he has done has been done through God" (3:21).

Jesus' brothers urge him to go to Jerusalem and "show [himself] to the world" (Jn. 7:4). But those words betray a lack of faith (7:5), and Jesus rejects their counsel, for his time has not yet come. Jesus explains the blindness of the man blind from birth on the grounds that it is not the blind man who sinned or his parents, but "that the work of God might be displayed in his life" (9:3). In his high priestly prayer Jesus declares: "I have revealed you to those whom you gave me out of the world" (17:6). In 21:1, 14, *phaneroō* is used of Jesus' revelation of himself to his disciples.

The vb. also figures prominently in 1 Jn. In Jesus "the life appeared; we have seen it and testify to it, and we proclaim to you the eternal life, which was with the Father and has appeared to us" (1:2). By contrast the action of unbelievers in quitting the community makes it clear that they were not truly of the community (2:19). In 2:28 the vb. is used of the coming of Christ. The letter proceeds to develop the tension between the two appearances of Christ and the implications this has for believers: "Dear friends, now we are children of God, and what we will be has not yet been made known. But we know that when he appears, we shall be like him, for we shall see him as he is" (3:2). Jesus has "appeared" to take away sin (3:5) and to destroy the works of the devil (3:8). Finally, God has "showed his love among us" by sending his Son so "that we might live through him" (4:9; cf. Jn. 3:16).

In Rev. 3:18 the church at Laodicea is counseled to buy white garments from the risen Christ to keep the shame of its nakedness from being made manifest. In 15:4 the song of those who have conquered celebrates the holy God and the fact that "all nations will come and worship before you, for your righteous acts have been revealed."

(iii) Paul uses *phaneroō* and *apokalyptō* as synonyms (cf. Rom. 1:17 and 3:21 on the revelation of the righteousness of God in Christ; Eph. 3:5 and Col. 1:26 on the revelation of the mystery hidden for ages). In Rom. 1:19 and 1 Cor. 4:5 *phaneroō* has the sense of make visible. The former passage refers to the revelation of God's "eternal power and divine nature" in the creation (Rom. 1:20); the latter refers to the coming judgment when God "will expose the motives of men's hearts." For Paul this has the practical implication that he will not pronounce judgment before the time, being content to leave it to God,

and equally he does not wish to have premature commendation for the same reason.

Paul uses *phaneroō* 9x in 2 Cor., esp. in polemical contexts. He uses it of the revelation that comes about through his preaching (2:14; 11:6). His own apostolic way of life is itself a paradoxical revelation of Christ, in a way comparable to Christ's own way of life. For human beings naturally expect God to manifest himself in success. But in fact it is the opposite. Paul's apostolic way has been one of affliction and suffering, always carrying "around in our body the death of Jesus, so that the life of Jesus may also be revealed in our body" (2 Cor. 4:10; cf. 4:11). By contrast, the existence of believing men and women in the church shows "that you are a letter from Christ" (3:3), vindicating Paul's apostleship in contrast with the letters of accreditation vaunted by his opponents.

Paul also uses *phaneroō* for the appearance of everyone before the judgment seat of Christ (2 Cor. 5:10–11). Moreover, "what we are is plain to God" (5:11a), and Paul hopes it is also plain to his readers (5:11b). In 7:12 Paul declares that his intention in writing as he did was so that the Corinthians could see how devoted he was to them. Despite his lack of eloquence Paul expresses the hope that his apostleship and devotion to Christ have been made "perfectly clear" to them (11:6).

Revelation takes place in proclamation (Rom. 16:25–27; Col. 1:25–26; 4:4). In Eph. 5:13 Christian conduct is seen in terms of light. The thought of revelation is further developed in terms of mystery hidden for ages but now revealed in Christ (Col. 1:26; 3:4; 4:4; cf. Eph. 3:5–6; 6:19).

In 1 Tim. 3:16 Paul takes up the theme of mystery in his quoting of an early Christian hymn, one phrase of which is that Christ Jesus "appeared in a body." *phaneroō* here refers to the incarnation (cf. Rom. 1:3–4 and the use of the vb. elsewhere for the incarnate ministry of Jesus in Jn. 1:31; Heb. 9:26; 1 Pet. 1:20; 1 Jn. 1:2; 3:5, 8) and possibly also his entire earthly ministry right up to the ascension. The same vb. also describes the significance of the incarnation in 2 Tim. 1:10, where Paul outlines the purpose of Jesus Christ's appearing. The incarnation is also in mind in the other reference to the vb. in the Pastoral Letters, but it is mediated by proclamation: "At his appointed season he brought his word to light" (Tit. 1:3).

(iv) The vb. occurs 2x in Heb. 9, but with somewhat different meanings. In 9:26 it refers to Jesus' incarnation, his appearance "at the end of the ages," the purpose of which was to offer a sacrifice for sins that supersedes the OT sacrifices and the Day of Atonement ritual. Christ's manifestation is unique and unrepeatable. Conversely, the author earlier argued that the structure of the tabernacle (and by implication the temple) and the prohibition of all but the high priest from entering the inner sanctuary are proof of the incompleteness of the old covenant: "The Holy Spirit was showing [*dēloō*] by this that the way into the Most Holy Place had not yet been disclosed [*phaneroō*] as long as the first tabernacle was still standing" (9:8).

(v) The vb. also occurs 2x in 1 Pet., again referring to the two manifestations of Christ in his historical life and at his second coming: He "was revealed in these last times for your sake" (1:20); and "when the Chief Shepherd appears, you will receive the crown of glory that will never fade away" (5:4).

(d) The noun *phanerōsis*, revelation, manifestation, occurs only 2x in the NT. In 1 Cor. 12:7 it describes the gifts of the Spirit: "Now to each the manifestation of the Spirit is given for the common good." In 2 Cor. 4:2 it is used in connection with Paul's preaching in a reply to accusations, where he insists that he has been "setting forth the truth plainly" (cf. this use with 2 Cor. 5:10–11 and the use of the vb. generally in 2 Cor. [see above]). Probably the background here is that of the law court, where this vb. was used of appearances in court.

(e) The vb. *phantazō*, make visible, occurs only in Heb. 12:21 of Moses on Sinai: "The sight [part. of *phantazō*] was so terrifying that Moses said, 'I an trembling with fear'" (cf. Deut. 9:19). For the related word *phantasma*, → *mageia*, magic, *3404*.

See also *apokalyptō*, uncover, disclose, reveal (*636*); *dēloō*, reveal, make clear, explain, give information, notify (*1317*); *chrēmatizō*, impart a revelation, injunction, or warning (*5976*).

2212 (*epiphanēs*, powerful, splendid, terrible), → *2211*.

2215 (*epiphōneō*, call out, shout), → *3189*.

2224 (*epoikodomeō*, build on something, build further), → *3868*.

2226 (*eponomazō*, call by a name, give a surname), → *3950*.

2227 (*epopteuō*, observe), → *3972*.

2230 (*epouranios*, heavenly), → *4041*.

2231 ἑπτά

ἑπτά (*hepta*), seven (*2231*); ἑπτάκις (*heptakis*), seven times (*2232*).

CL & OT 1. The qualitative significance attaching to the number seven (*hepta*) throughout the history of religions can be explained from the original amazement felt at the regularity of the passage of time in seven-day periods, consonant with the four phases of the moon, and secondarily from other astronomical observations. Since for primitive humanity there was no linear time sequence and human beings could only apprehend time as a period, seven became the symbol of the fulfilled and perfectly completed period. Philosophical speculations concerning the meaning of the number seven were known from Greece.

2. For the Israelites, seven was the symbol of perfection. The OT adopted the symbolic imagery of this number in various ways: the completion of creation in seven days (Gen. 1:1–2:4a); seven-day feasts are fulfilled times (Lev. 23:6, 34); sprinkling of blood, seven times repeated (*heptakis*), brought Israel complete purification (16:14, 19); Yahweh promised Cain sevenfold, i.e., comprehensive, vengeance (Gen. 4:15); Yahweh sees everything with seven eyes (Zech. 4:10); one of the marks of the fulfillment of the age of salvation is a sevenfold increase in the sun's illuminating power (Isa. 30:26). In Prov. seven can virtually signify all (26:16, MT only).

A multiple of seven stands for a round figure, comprising the whole (Gen. 46:27—70 in MT, 75 in LXX; Jdg. 20:16). In the table of the nations in Gen. 10, seventy (7 x 10) nations are enumerated (cf. *1 Enoch* 89:59–60). Perhaps this concept lies behind Lk. 10:1–17, where some MSS. report that Jesus sent out seventy disciples aimed at the nations of the world (NIV reads "seventy-two"; see also *hebdomēkonta*, seventy, *1573*). Seventy was also determinative of the name *Septuagint*, the translation of the OT into Gk. for the seventy nations of the world (cf. *Let. Aris.*, with its legend that the LXX was the work of seventy Jewish elders).

NT 1. In the NT letters the number seven and its derivatives occur only with reference to the OT: Rom. 11:4 (cf. 1 Ki. 19:18); Heb. 4:4 (cf. Gen. 2:2); Heb. 11:30 (cf. Jos. 6:1–21). In Rom. 11:4 Paul adduces from 1 Ki. 19:18 that in his time there is already a Christian remnant of Israel, which represents the full total of Israel as dawn heralds the day (Rom. 11:16). In Mk. 12:18–23 the Sadducees imagine a case where an infertile woman is involved in a levirate marriage (Deut. 25:5–6) until she has had seven husbands.

2. Someone possessed by seven "spirits" (Matt. 12:43–45) or by "seven demons" (Lk. 8:2) is totally possessed. In Matt. 18:21 Peter inquires concerning the limits of forgiveness: "up to seven times?" Here the seven has numerical significance. But Jesus replies that forgiveness has to take place "seventy-seven times," i.e., totally and without limit (18:22; cf. Lk. 17:4).

3. Despite all the individual differences, the genealogical trees of Jesus in Matt. and Lk. are both orientated around the number seven. Matt. 1:17–28 has three groups of fourteen (7 x 2) generations: from Abraham to David, from David to the deportation to Babylon, and from then to Christ; Jesus begins the seventh seven. Lk. 3:23–38 cites seventy-seven ancestors of Jesus. Both evangelists are obviously inter-

ested in the fulfillment of history in the person of Jesus Christ—of salvation history (Matt.) and world history (Lk.). In other respects Matt. shows a predilection for the number seven as a scheme for the arrangement of his gospel (e.g., seven parables in ch. 13; seven woes in ch. 23). It is the stylistic expression of his theology of fulfillment.

4. Of all NT writings, Rev. uses the number seven most frequently. It is directed to seven churches of Asia, symbolic of all churches (1:4, 11). Then there are seven spirits (1:4; 4:5; 5:6), seven seals (5:1), the Lamb with seven horns and eyes (5:6), seven angels with seven trumpets (8:2–6), seven thunders (10:3–4), seven angels with seven bowls of wrath (15:1–16:21), etc. The number seven denotes in general the final eschatological appearance of God, encompassing everything. Correspondingly, on the side opposed to God, there is a final action that seeks to withstand the power of God (e.g., the dragon with seven-crowned heads, 12:3; etc.).

In fact, the number seven plays an important part in the entire structure of Rev. The book consists of seven series of visions, each in turn consisting of seven items. Some have attempted to relate these seven visions to the seven days of creation in Gen. 1. In the idealist interpretation of this book, these seven series of visions are not consecutive, but each one looks at world history from the ascension of Christ to the consummation from a different standpoint and gradually builds up to the end of history and the new creation.

2232 (*heptakis*, seven times), → *2231*.

2236 ἐραυνάω

ἐραυνάω (*eraunaō*), search (*2236*); ἐξεραυνάω (*exeraunaō*), search out (*2001*); ἀνεξεραύνητος (*anexeraunētos*), unsearchable (*451*).

CL & OT 1. In cl. Gk. *ereunaō* (the earlier form of *eraunaō*) and *exereunaō* denoted tracking by animals, then (in the human sphere) to trace out, examine, search out, e.g., in connection with a house search, a judicial hearing, and esp. a scientific, philosophical, and religious investigation. *anexereunētos* means unsearchable, unfathomable.

2. (a) In the LXX *ereunaō* means seek, search thoroughly; it is used for Laban's angry search for his missing household gods (Gen. 31:35) and for a plundering search of houses (1 Ki. 20:6 = LXX 21:6), but also for the quest for wisdom and discernment (Prov. 2:4 *exereunaō*) and the contrite examination of one's way of life (Lam. 3:40 *exereunaō*). God and his thoughts cannot be searched out (Jud. 8:14).

(b) Philo says that humans can by searching penetrate the innermost being of God. He also uses the word to describe learned investigation of the thought and exegesis of the OT. The Qumran sect searched the Scriptures in order to fathom God's will.

NT 1. The NT use of *eraunaō* (6x) and *exeraunaō* (once) resembles that of cl. Gk. In Jn. 5:39 and 7:52, *eraunaō* refers to the Jewish penetrating examination of Scripture in order to obtain its meaning—presumably in the law (cf. 5:16, 45). The form *eraunate* in 5:39 should be understood as ind. ("you search"), not imperative ("search!"); the Jews search the Scriptures, but they are preoccupied with words and think that by merely fulfilling the letter they can ensure themselves eternal life. This very searching, however, blinds them to the pointers of true life proclaimed by the OT Scriptures. A preconceived attitude and approach to the study of the law led to the Jews' rejection of Jesus (7:52), in whom alone is life.

2. In 1 Pet. 1:10–11, *exeraunaō* and *eraunaō* refer to the prophets' eager searching and reflection over the information revealed to them by the Spirit; it must be sharply distinguished from *prophēteuō* (to prophesy; → *prophētēs*, prophet, *4737*).

3. An OT concept appears in Rom. 8:27 and Rev. 2:23, that God searches human hearts (cf. 1 Sam. 16:7; 1 Ki. 8:39; Ps. 7:9). While God searches the depths of human hearts, his judgments on them are unfathomable (Rom. 11:33, *anexeraunētos*). Only the Spirit of God working in a human being is able to search for knowledge of that which is still

hidden in the depths of God (1 Cor. 2:10; cf. Matt. 11:25; 13:11; 16:17; Eph. 3:3, 5). In 1 Cor. 2:9 Paul takes up Isa. 64:4: Where the Spirit searches, the barrier to all autonomous human search falls; through the Spirit, we are able to get a grasp of the "the deep things of God."

See also *heuriskō*, find, discover (*2351*); *zēteō*, seek (*2426*).

2237	ἐργάζομαι

ἐργάζομαι (*ergazomai*), to labor, be active, work, bring about (*2237*); ἔργον (*ergon*), deed, action, achievement, work, thing, matter (*2240*); ἐργασία (*ergasia*), work, practice, business (*2238*); ἐργάτης (*ergatēs*), someone who does something, worker (*2239*); κατεργάζομαι (*katergazomai*), to produce, accomplish (*2981*); ἐνέργεια (*energeia*), working, operation, action (*1918*); ἐνεργέω (*energeō*), to work, be active, effect something (*1919*); ἐνεργής (*energēs*), active, effective, powerful (*1921*); ἐνέργημα (*energēma*), activity, experience (*1920*); εὐεργεσία (*euergesia*), kindness, a good deed, well-doing (*2307*); εὐεργετέω (*euergeteō*), do work, benefit, show kindnesses (*2308*); εὐεργέτης (*euergetēs*), benefactor (*2309*); συνεργός (*synergos*), working together with, fellow worker, assistant (*5301*); συνεργέω (*synergeō*), to work together, cooperate, aid (*5300*).

CL & OT 1. (a) In cl. Gk. *ergon* denotes a deed or action. It can refer to a specific occupational or official activity (e.g., agriculture or the military profession); it eventually had the weakened meaning of thing, matter. The vb. *ergazomai* has the basic meaning to work, to be engaged in something. Used trans. it means to create, produce, perform, process. *ergasia* can mean labor, occupation, arrangement, work, or business. *ergatēs* generally indicates someone who does something, a worker as the member of a class (e.g., slave) or occupational group (e.g., farm workers).

(b) *energeia* denotes activity; *energeō* means to be active, be at work; trans. to effect or do something. *energēs* means active, effective; *energēma*, that which is effected, a deed.

(c) Also belonging to this word group are *euergesia*, good deed, well-doing; *euergeteō*, to do good; *euergetēs*, which became in Greco-Roman culture an honorary title given to generous people, esp. kings; *synergos*, a fellow worker, assistant; *synergeō*, to work together, cooperate.

(d) Early in cl. Gk. times, work is described as having moral value; those who work hard receive commendation from the gods, whereas laziness is a disgrace. Humans show themselves fit for society by their *ergon*. In Plato *ergon* is closely related to virtue (→ *aretē*, *746*). In Aristotle the task of *aretē* is to bring to perfection the *ergon* of an organ (e.g., the seeing of an eye). One's deeds can be called good, lovely, bad, evil, unjust, etc.

2. (a) In the LXX this word group has the whole range of meaning of the cl. Gk. uses. What is new is conditioned by Israel's particular faith in God. *ergon* is used at the beginning of the LXX to describe the work of the divine creator (Gen. 2:2–3). God accomplishes his work through his word (→ *logos*, *3364*). A frequent phrase found in Heb. poetry for God's work is "the works of your hands," which embraces heaven, earth, and human beings (e.g., Ps. 8:6; 138:8; cf. Isa. 29:23). *ergon* is also used for the acts of Yahweh in history, through which he demonstrates his covenant faithfulness (cf. Ps. 95:9); sometimes it means miracle (e.g., Sir. 48:14). But God's deeds can also be judgment (e.g., Isa. 28:21).

(b) When *ergon* relates to what human beings do, it gives expression esp. to three major theological ideas. (i) In most places it has a positive meaning; it can describe the accomplishment of a task laid on people by God (cf. Gen. 2:15). Cultic actions, such as offering sacrifices, are deeds of religious worth (Num. 8:11). But also in everyday life work that fulfills God's law is judged positively (cf. Exod. 20:9–10). This applies both to one's ordinary sphere of work (cf. Deut. 2:7; 14:29; Ps. 90:17) and to particular acts of obedience (e.g., righteousness in Ps. 15:2).

(ii) In conjunction with the fall, *ergon* denotes work as trouble, a burden, and a curse (cf. Gen. 3:17–19; 4:12; 5:29). This idea is esp. alive in Hel. Jud., where human works are seen as essentially sinful (1 Esd. 4:37; 2 Esd. 7:119).

(iii) In still other places in the LXX, *ergon* has the meaning of a bad, reprehensible deed, which brings separation from God, i.e., sin (e.g., Job 11:11). It is not so much here a matter of a particular wicked act but the sinful nature of actions that are alienated from God (cf. Prov. 11:18; Isa. 59:6).

(c) *energeia* is used 8x in the LXX, primarily for the work of divine or demonic powers (e.g., Wis. 7:17, 26; 2 Macc. 3:29).

(d) Jud. developed the view of human works as necessary in order to fulfill the law and therefore do righteousness. The way to godliness is prescribed by a multiplicity of regulations related to such things as the Sabbath or ritual cleansings. But since not everyone follows this path in all its details, a distinction is made between the righteous and average devout individuals. This distinction led to the notion of reward and punishment through divine judgment, in that God will some day recompense humans according to their deeds. The godless will then receive their punishment, whereas the righteous can die without fear.

NT *ergazomai*, to work, occurs 41x in the NT; *ergon*, work, 169x; *ergasia*, business, 6x; and *ergatēs*, worker, 16x; *katergazomai*, to produce, accomplish, 22x. These basic meanings have not changed from cl. Gk. In referring to the actions of believers, *ergon* can be used synonymously with *karpos*, fruit (*2843*). The noun *ergon* can be used as an object of *ergazomai*, to work a work (e.g., Matt. 26:10), of *poieō* (→ *4472*), to do a work (e.g., 23:3, 5), and in one place of *prassō* (*4556*), to do a deed (Acts 26:20).

1. (a) In the Synoptics *ergazomai* sometimes denotes activity in general (e.g., Matt. 21:28), the performing of some work (e.g.. 26:10). *ergatēs* can denote someone who works for wages (20:1, 2, 8), also a witness standing in Christ's service and sent into the world (9:37–38; Lk. 10:2), but also an evildoer, who will not stand in the judgment (13:27). In contrast to the Pharisees, whom Jesus censures for doing works "for men to see" (Matt. 23:5), the deed of the woman who anointed him is called "a beautiful thing [*ergon*]" (26:10). Jesus encourages his disciples to let their light so shine before others "that they may see your good deeds and praise your Father in heaven" (5:16). At the same time, the Synoptics stress that no one has legal claims before God for remuneration for one's deeds (cf. Lk. 17:10; cf. Matt. 20:1–16). *ergon* is related to the work of Christ in Matt. 11:2; Lk. 24:19.

(b) Jn. uses this word group to illustrate the unique activity of Jesus, which is bound up with the working of God: "My Father is always at his work ... and I, too, am working" (5:17 cf. 4:34; 17:4). Jesus' working fulfills his divinely appointed mission (cf. 5:36; 9:4; 10:25), which aims to awaken faith in him as the one sent to reveal God (cf. 6:29). Jesus' miracles also serve this end (14:11; → *sēmeion*, sign, *4956*). Those who believe in Jesus are given the promise that they will do even greater works than him (14:12). Works done "through God" (3:21) contrast with "deeds [that are] evil" (3:19), which are committed in alliance with the devil (8:41, 44).

(c) Paul takes up more the contemporary Jewish understanding of work as those acts required by God's law. He stresses, by way of a blunt antithesis, that it is humanly impossible to achieve righteousness in God's sight; rather, a right relation with God can only be received by grace through Jesus Christ, who is "the end of the law so that there may be righteousness for everyone who believes" (Rom. 10:4). Paul is concerned with understanding the true significance of faith, of which Abraham is adduced as an example (Rom. 4:1–25; Gal. 3:6–18). This insight into the process of salvation forms the center of Pauline theology (cf. Rom. 3:20–28; 4:6; 9:12, 32; Gal. 2:16; 3:2, 10).

Nevertheless, Paul does have passages in which works receive a positive significance. Just as Paul knows of a law of Christ besides the law that condemns (cf. 1 Cor. 9:21; Gal. 6:2), so he speaks of positive deeds besides "the deeds of darkness" or "the acts [*erga*] of the sinful nature" (Gal. 5:19). Missionary work, for instance, appears as a "work of the Lord" (1 Cor. 16:10), which Christ works through the apostles (cf. Phil. 1:6). Indeed, Paul puts to the Corinthians the rhetorical question, "Are you not the result of my work in the Lord?" (1 Cor. 9:1). In the sphere of ethics, Paul upholds the validity for Christians of the imperative to do good to everyone (Gal. 6:10). Believers are to work out their salvation with fear and trembling (Phil. 2:12; cf. Eph. 6:13). Good deeds are esp. stressed in the Pastoral Letters (1 Tim. 5:10, 25; 6:18; Tit. 1:16; 2:7, 14; 3:8, 14).

Paul also writes of good works in the context of the final judgment, when God "will give to each person according to what he has done" (Rom. 2:6). Not only will the works of the heathen be judged, but those of Christians as well. While our deeds do not determine our entrance into heaven, they do play a role in the reward we receive (1 Cor. 3:11–15; cf. Rom. 14:10; 2 Cor. 5:10).

(d) While Paul stresses faith as the decisive factor, James emphasizes works, extolled in the law of liberty (1:25). Without works faith is dead (2:17); it is only through works that faith is perfected (2:22, 24). Note that James is writing against a dead orthodoxy that considers mere confession of faith sufficient for salvation. In his own way he thus helps to describe the field of tension in which God's saving activity seeks to awaken us to faith, to whose structural elements belong obedience, hope, and love.

2. (a) *energeia*, working, action, occurs 8x in the NT; *energeō*, to be active, 21x; *energēma*, deed, 2x; *energēs*, effective, 3x. This subgroup refers, as a rule, to the working of God (e.g., 1 Cor. 12:6; Eph. 1:11; Phil. 2:13) or of his antagonist, Satan (2 Thess. 2:9), who is also ultimately subject to God (2:11); in 2 Cor. 4:12, Paul refers to death as an active, working power. Prominence is given to the efficacious power of God by which he raised Jesus Christ (Eph. 1:20; Col. 2:12). This power is at work in Christ (Phil. 3:21), in the Holy Spirit (1 Cor. 12:11), and in God's Word (Heb. 4:12). By it the apostles are equipped for their office (Eph. 3:7; Col. 1:29). The members of the body of Christ also come to share in it (Eph. 4:16; cf. 1 Cor. 12:10).

(b) *euergetēs* occurs only in Lk. 22:25, where it has the sense of an honorary title. Jesus' disciples are not to allow themselves to be called "Benefactors," as are the rulers of the world (cf. Matt. 23:8–12); rather, they are called to serve (Lk. 22:26). *euergeteō*, to do good, occurs only in Acts 10:38, referring to the good deeds of Jesus to which his apostles testify. *euergesia* is used 2x: in Acts 4:9 it denotes the healing of a sick man by the apostles; in 1 Tim. 6:2, the desired attitude of a Christian master to his slaves.

(c) *synergeō*, to work together, is found 5x; *synergos*, fellow worker, 13x. In Rom. 8:28 Paul seizes on a Jewish maxim that for those who love God, "God works for [their] good"; this will include their suffering and pain. Jas. 2:22 speaks of the necessity of faith working together with good deeds.

Otherwise, these words refer to the missionary situation. Mk. 16:20 reports that the Lord worked with the disciples, confirming their word by the accompanying signs. This ratificatory accompanying work of God is the decisive element in all missionary activity, although it does require cooperation on the part of God's servants. Paul formulates it thus: "We are God's fellow workers" (1 Cor. 3:9; cf. 2 Cor. 6:1). The content of apostolic cooperation is outlined in 1 Thess. 3:2 ("in spreading the gospel of Christ"); Col. 4:11 ("for the kingdom of God"); 3 Jn. 8 ("for the truth"); and 2 Cor. 1:24 ("for your joy").

See also *poieō*, do, make (*4472*); *prassō*, accomplish, do (*4556*).

2238 (*ergasia*, work, practice, business), → *2237*.

2239 (*ergatēs*, someone who does something, worker), → *2237*.

2240 (*ergon*, deed, action, work, thing, matter), → *2237*.

2244 (*erēmia*, desolate place, desert, wilderness), → *2245*.

2245 ἔρημος	ἔρημος (*erēmos*), abandoned, solitary, desolate, deserted

(*2245*); ἐρημία (*erēmia*), desolate place, desert, wilderness (*2244*); ἐρημόω (*erēmoō*), lay waste, devastate, make desolate, depopulate (*2246*); ἐρήμωσις (*erēmōsis*), devastation, desolation, destruction (*2247*).

CL & OT 1. In cl. Gk. *erēmia* denotes a desolate area. *erēmōsis*, devastation, is first found in the LXX. The vb. *erēmoō* can mean to set free, hand over, leave alone. A desert in the ancient world was not only land without water and vegetation and therefore uninhabited, but could also be an area that was laid waste and depopulated, an abandoned settlement. The ancient Greco-Roman world awaited the revelation of the divinity in a lonely spot, and it feared the desert as the habitat of demons.

2. (a) In the LXX *erēmos* occurs 345x. It usually translates Heb. *midbār*, desert (which also means steppe, grassland, e.g., Gen. 37:22). More than a third of the uses of *erēmos* are in the Pentateuch, since Exod. to Deut. recount Israel's wandering in the desert. *erēmia*, by contrast, is used only 7x in the LXX. The vb. *erēmoō*, to devastate, occurs 60x in the LXX, used almost exclusively of punitive destruction of houses, cities, and lands (e.g., Isa. 6:11; 54:3; Ezek. 26:19). *erēmōsis*, devastation, is found app. 20x.

(b) The desert in the OT has a double aspect: It is the place where Yahweh reveals himself, but it is also the abode of demons, who threaten humans with impurity, sickness, and death. (i) The positive valuation is represented by the many theophanies in the desert. An angel strengthens Elijah with nourishment in a desert as he flees from Jezebel (1 Ki. 19:4–6). God's appearance at Horeb (Exod. 3:1–4:17; 1 Ki. 19:11–18) or Sinai (Exod. 19) is not only a mountain but also a desert theophany. Israel's forty years of wandering in the desert was counted as a time of particular closeness to Yahweh (e.g., Hos. 9:10). The references to Yahweh's faithfulness at this time (and Israel's unfaithfulness: Ps. 78:15–19; 95:7–11; Ezek. 20) are frequent in the OT. Hope of eschatological salvation is also linked with speculations involving the desert (Isa. 40:3; Jer. 31:2 = LXX 38:2; Ezek. 34:25; Hos. 2:14–23).

(ii) At the same time the desert is a place of deadly danger, of separation from God, and of demonic powers (Deut. 8:15; cf. Num. 21:4–9; Isa. 30:6). Yahweh's terrifying east wind, like all winds conceived in personal terms, comes out of the desert (Hos. 13:15). The scapegoat is chased into the desert (Lev. 16:10, 21–22). Desert demons take possession of the ruins of Babylon (cf. Isa. 13:21–23) and Edom (34:13–15). Contemporary desolation and misery are seen as devastation (1:7; 54:3; Jer. 2:15; Ezek. 19:13). The drying up of water esp. characterizes the transformation into desert (Isa. 44:27; 51:10; Ezek. 29:10; 30:12). For Daniel's use of *erēmōsis* appearing in the temple in Jerusalem (Dan. 8:13), → *bdelygma*, abomination, *1007*.

(iii) In God's promises for the future, Israel will some day find salvation in the desert (cf. Ezek. 34:25; Hos. 2:14). When that happens the desert will become arable land, water will flow in it, roads will be opened, and desolated towns will be rebuilt (e.g., Isa. 32:15–16; 35:5–6; 41:18; 58:12; Ezek. 36:10, 33–38). Where roads are constructed through the desert (Isa. 43:19), Yahweh's lordship has dawned. God's victory over his enemies and the enemies of his people is thus also a victory over the desert.

NT 1. (a) In the NT words in this group occurs 60x, mostly in the Gospels and Acts. The NT estimation of the desert is similar to that of the OT and Jud. Israel's forty years of wandering in the desert is seen as a momentous fact of God's historical activity (Jn. 3:14; 6:31, 49; Acts 7:30–44; 13:18; 1 Cor. 10:5; Heb. 3:8, 17), and the idea that end-time movements begin in the desert is still alive (Matt. 24:26; Acts 21:38). The apocalyptic flight of the woman into the desert (Rev. 12:6, 14) is to be explained from the high regard in which Israel's time in the desert was held, and it simultaneously attests to the expectation that the Messiah will come from the desert (cf. Hos. 11:1; Matt. 2:15).

The youthful John the Baptist is hidden in the desert (Lk. 1:80) and then begins his work there (Matt. 3:1). As in Jud., prophets belong in desert places and on mountains, as was proper for ascetics; thus, Heb. 11:38 localizes the miscellaneous heroes of faith in deserts, mountains, and caves. Linking up with the desert wanderers and desert dwellers of the OT, the new Israel is able to understand itself, by way of antitype, as the wandering people of God.

(b) Insofar as Jesus' significance is described as prophetic and messianic, the desert also has its place. He comes forth like Moses in the desert (Acts 3:22–23; 7:37; cf. Deut. 18:15), even surpassing him, although he is Moses' antitype (cf. Heb. 3:1–6). Jesus' infant flight into Egypt (Matt. 2:13–15, 19–21) renders possible the arrival of the Messiah from Egypt through the desert (cf. Hos. 11:1). It is in the desert that Jesus defeats Satan's temptation (Matt. 4:1–11; Lk. 4:1–13), and there he miraculously feeds his followers (Matt. 14:13; Mk. 6:32). Several times Jesus lingers in the desert to pray and fast (cf. Mk. 1:35, 45)—not only to come close to God, but also to break the power of the demons. The desert is still a favorite place for visions (Rev. 17:3; cf. Acts 8:26). Perhaps that is why Paul sought out the Arabian desert (Gal. 1:17), though it may also have been simply to escape from the clutches of his opponents.

2. The desert is qualified negatively where the sin and failure of the desert generation is noted (Acts 7:41–43; 1 Cor. 10:5; Heb. 3:8, 17). Demonic dangers threaten in the desert (2 Cor. 11:26; cf. Lk. 15:4), for that is where demons (cf. Matt. 12:43) and madmen (Lk. 8:29) live. As in the OT, the ruin (*erēmoō*) of houses, cities, and land is considered to be accomplished by demonic powers carrying out God's judgment of punishment (Matt. 12:25; Lk. 11:17). The idolatrous city of Babylon (= Rome) will be brought "to ruin" (Rev. 17:16; 18:17, 19) by punishing demons (18:2); again, OT models are in the background. On the NT use of "the abomination that causes desolation" (Matt. 24:15; Mk. 13:14), → *bdelygma*, abomination, *1007*.

See also *oros*, mountain, mountain chain or region (*4001*); *Sina*, Sinai (*4982*).

2246 (*erēmoō*, lay waste, devastate, make desolate, depopulate), → *2245*.

2247 (*erēmōsis*, desolation), see *2245*; for the phrase *to bdelygma tēs erēmōseōs*, the abomination of desolation, → *1007*.

2255 (*hermēneia*, interpretation, translation), → *2257*.

2257	ἑρμηνεύω

ἑρμηνεύω (*hermēneuō*), explain, interpret, translate (*2257*); ἑρμηνεία (*hermēneia*), interpretation, translation (*2255*); μεθερμηνεύω (*methermēneuō*), translate (*3493*); διερμηνεύω (*diermēneuō*), translate, interpret, explain (*1450*); διερμηνευτής (*diermēneutēs*), interpreter, translator (*1449*).

CL & OT 1. (a) In cl. Gk. *hermēneuō* may mean to explain, expound, or interpret, though it often means little more than to speak or speak plainly. Similarly, the noun *hermēneia* often means interpretation, but sometimes means little more than communication or speech.

(b) Closely related to the meaning of "speech" in general, *hermēneuō* and *hermēneia* are also used in the quasi-technical sense of "articulation" or "expression" of thoughts in words. Thus Xenophon refers to the "power of expression" that makes teaching and the formulation of laws possible. Plato speaks of expressing (or perhaps expounding) the laws in word.

(c) The other main meaning of *hermēneuō* is to translate, mainly used in writers from the 1st cent. on. The vbs. *diermēneuō* and *methermēneuō* have this same sense.

2. In the LXX the usual meaning of *hermēneuō* is to translate. In Ezra 4:7 it represents the Heb. *targēm*: A writing is made in Aram., then also a translation (see NIV note). In the prologue to Sir., the noun *hermēneia* and the vb. *methermēneuō* refer to a translation from Heb. into Gk., although in 47:17 *hermēneia* refers to "interpretations" along-

side songs, proverbs, and parables. *diermēneuō* occurs only in 2 Macc. 1:36, where it should probably be translated "means."

The use of these words to mean "translate" occurs in Josephus and in Philo. But *hermēneia* is used in Philo in the quasi-technical sense of articulating thoughts in words. For example, Philo speaks of reproducing something in actual words and of how the image of the divine word articulates the invisible light. In one passage of Philo about Moses and Aaron, *hermēneia* occurs twice: Aaron is to be Moses' "spokesman"; God will give to Moses the capacity to express thought in words.

3. A purely lexicographical study of *hermēneuō* cannot take account of the notion of midrash in Jud. However, a broader discussion of the semantic field of "hermeneutics" would not be complete without at least briefly mentioning it. Midrash in Jud. represents both the procedure of interpreting and the result of interpretation. It thus involves investigation, analytical study, midrashic interpretation, and exposition; and then the conveying of the results arrived at. In midrashic lit., interpretation may sometimes proceed by means of specific hermeneutical rules, such as the seven rules formulated by Hillel (ca. 30 B.C.), later expanded to thirty-two in the 2d cent. A.D.

NT 1. More than half of the 20 occurrences of *hermēneuō* and related words in the NT mean "translate" in a fairly straightforward sense. In the pass. *methermēneuō* always means "is translated" or "means." Thus Immanuel means "God with us" (Matt. 1:23); the Aram. transliteration "*Talitha, koum*" means "Little girl . . . get up" (Mk. 5:41); Golgotha means a skull (15:22); Messiah means Christ (Jn. 1:41); rabbi means a teacher (1:38); and so on (Mk. 15:34; Acts 4:36; 13:8). The pass. of *hermēneuō* can be used in the same way (Jn. 1:42; 9:7; Heb. 7:2), as can *diermēneuō* (Acts 9:36).

An interesting point arises, however, in connection with Jn. 9:7. Siloam does not strictly mean "sent," although the word in the Heb. (*šilōah*, Isa. 8:6) is related to the word for "send" (*šālah*). *hermēneuetai* here means something broader than "is translated." Siloam conveys the thought expressed by "sent," which is an important key word for Jn. The same can be said of Heb. 7:2. Melchizedek means king of righteousness (Heb. *melek*, king; *ṣedeq*, righteousness) only in the broad sense that the name expresses the thought inspired by the language. We have already noted this kind of meaning for *hermēneuō* in other writers, esp. Philo. The main point about most of the passages in which *hermēneuō* means translate, however, is the concern of the Evangelists that this language should be intelligible to outsiders or non-Jews.

2. In Lk. 24:27 *diermēneuō* means to expound or interpret. Beginning with the Pentateuch and the Prophets, Jesus expounded the OT in terms of his own person and mission. Lk.–Acts suggests that this involved esp. such passages as Isa. 53:7–12 (Lk. 22:37; Acts 8:32, 33; cf. Mk. 9:12). Such expounding is parallel to Christ's opening the Scriptures in Lk. 24:32. In the light of Jesus' finished work, OT passages that hitherto had expressed only promise can now be "interpreted" in terms of fulfillment. The OT is seen not simply as an end in itself, but also as a tradition of conceptual and historical paradigms of God's acts that reach their climax in the coming of Christ (cf. 1 Cor. 10:11). Thus, while the OT interprets the coming of Christ, Christ also interprets the OT. Hence the Christian interpretation of Isa. 53, for example, can never remain merely "Jewish."

3. The remaining 7 uses of *diermēneuō, diermēneutēs,* and *hermēneia* all relate to the interpretation of speaking in tongues (1 Cor. 12:10, 30; 14:5, 13, 26, 27, 28). It is tempting to imagine that this takes the form of "translating" otherwise unintelligible speech. But if speaking in tongues is, as Paul seems to imply (14:14), subrational and preconceptual, it does not provide communicable concepts that may then be "translated" into the native language of the community. Conversely, if glossolalia were already rational and conceptual, it is difficult to see why the speaker could not "interpret" his or her own

utterances to the church. In at least four places, however, Paul makes it clear that often the interpreter is different from the one speaking in tongues (1 Cor. 12:10; 14:5, 13, 28).

Furthermore, ecstatic utterance is usually addressed to God rather than to the congregation (1 Cor. 14:2; cf. 14:16). Presumably, then, *hermēneia* in these verses is an intelligible description of the preconceptual mood or attitude that is expressed in tongues. If this is so, it is conceivable that Paul's injunction to the ecstatic to pray for the capacity to interpret his own utterance is tantamount to short-circuiting the place of tongues in public worship altogether (14:13). At the very least, Paul views tongues as being primarily a private affair between a human and God (14:2–6, 16, 19, 23, 28), but by way of concession allows a maximum of two or three ecstatic utterances in public on condition that someone is present who can interpret them (14:27–28). The basic principle expressed in these passages is the importance of rationality and intelligibility in public worship. Only that which is intelligible can build up the church.

4. We cannot leave a study of this word without saying something about the interpretation of Scripture. In the history of Christian thought up to the present, the study of hermeneutics has taken two distinct forms. (a) Traditionally, hermeneutics has involved the attempt to formulate general rules for the interpretation of biblical texts. But this approach encounters two difficulties. (i) It has become increasingly recognized in the light of biblical criticism that different types of biblical lit. require methodologies of their own. For example, methods used in the interpretation of Jesus' parables must be different from those employed in interpreting Heb. poetry or parts of the Pauline letters. The few general principles that can be universally applied to all types of biblical lit. tend to be so basic as to be obvious—e.g., the need to pay attention to the linguistic context, the historical situation, the literary genre, and the purpose of the writer.

(ii) Nowadays, it is also more widely appreciated that the process of understanding a text is not simply a matter of observing certain hermeneutical rules. Such observance may admittedly constitute a necessary precondition for the correct interpretation of a text, but it does not of itself initiate genuine understanding. It is the recognition of this latter difficulty that leads to a second understanding of the task of hermeneutics.

(b) If the interpreter is to understand a text adequately and correctly, due account must be taken of one's own subjectivity. One's presuppositions, cultural orientation, and psychological capacities shape one's understanding of the text. Some of these presuppositions may act as a barrier to understanding, yet it is more important to note that they also serve as an indispensable point of contact with the subject matter of the text, at least at the commencement of the ongoing process of understanding.

One special aspect of the problem of the relation between the interpreter and the text is that of historical distance. This problem can be illustrated with reference to Bultmann's proposals about demythologizing. He contends that belief in miracles is bound up with a 1st-cent. worldview. But we should also argue that the attitude of modern secular scientists toward miracles equally reflects their own historical position as products of a materialistic, science-oriented culture in the 20th cent. The problem of historicity, therefore, is a two-way issue and concerns the horizons of the modern interpreter as well as those of the text.

In practice the task of hermeneutics is first to recognize and accept the problem of "distance" between the interpreter and the text and then to disentangle what the text actually says from any presuppositions about what at first it merely *seems* to say in the absence of due critical reflection. The interpreter must not read his or her own ideas into the text. Next, the horizons of the interpreter and the horizons of the text must be brought into a relationship of active engagement and dialogue until the two sets of judgments, or of questions and answers, become eventually fused into one.

This hermeneutic endeavor takes full account of the subjectivity of the interpreter, but without losing sight of the primacy of the text

itself. The term *hermeneutical circle* may be misleading, for in the hermeneutical movement between text and interpreter, genuine progress will be achieved towards a fusion of horizons, provided that there is both critical reflection and a humble listening to the text. It is clear that the hermeneutical problem is a genuine and important one, and it would be a mistake to avoid it by arguing that the interpretation and application of Scripture are exclusively the work of the Holy Spirit. The same might be said about the need for any theological study.

See also *exēgeomai*, explain, expound, interpret, tell (*2007*); *epilyō*, explain, interpret, settle, solve (*2147*).

2262	ἔρχομαι

ἔρχομαι (*erchomai*), come, appear (*2262*); ἔλευσις (*eleusis*), coming, advent (*1803*); εἰσέρχομαι (*eiserchomai*), come in, enter (*1656*); ἀπέρχομαι (*aperchomai*), go away, depart (*599*); παρεισέρχομαι (*pareiserchomai*), come in, step in (*4209*); περιέρχομαι (*perierchomai*), wander (*4320*); προέρχομαι (*proerchomai*), go forward, advance, proceed (*4601*); προσέρχομαι (*proserchomai*), go to, approach, accede to (*4665*); συνέρχομαι (*synerchomai*), come together, assemble (*5302*); διέρχομαι (*dierchomai*), go through, come through (*1451*); ἐξέρχομαι (*exerchomai*), go out, come out, get out (*2002*); ἐπέρχομαι (*eperchomai*), come, come along, approach (*2088*); παρέρχομαι (*parerchomai*), go by, pass by, pass (*4216*); ἥκω (*hēkō*), have come, be present (*2457*).

CL & OT *erchomai*, a common Gk. word, means come or go, mostly in the lit. sense. It is used metaphorically in a temporal sense: *erchontai hēmerai*, days are coming (e.g., 1 Sam. 2:31; 2 Ki. 20:17), and also of destruction that comes on people (Prov. 1:26; 6:15). The rare noun *eleusis* denotes arrival (used in the NT only in Acts 7:52, of the coming of Jesus). *hēkō* is virtually a synonym for *erchomai*.

In the LXX the words are used mainly in a literal sense. But coming may have a religious significance. A person may come to sacrifice (1 Sam. 16:2, 5) and to worship and praise God before the sanctuary (Lev. 12:4; 1 Ki. 8:42; Ps. 100:2, 4). The heathen also go into the house of their god (2 Chr. 32:21).

In a metaphorical sense, prayer and supplication (2 Chr. 30:27; Ps. 88:2; 119:170) and human cries (Exod. 3:9; Ps. 102:1) are said to come before God. References to the coming of the Gentiles to Israel and thus to God are bound up with messianic expectation (Isa. 60:5–6; 66:18; Jer. 16:19; Hag. 2:7–8).

OT writers frequently mention God's coming in judgment. But he also comes as Deliverer (Ps. 50:3–4, 15; Isa. 35:4; Zech. 14:5–7), as the Savior who feeds his flock, as the Redeemer who takes away the sin of Jacob, and as the One who brings light to Jerusalem (Isa. 40:10–11; 59:20; 60:1). The hope of God's coming is bound up with messianic expectation. The Messiah will come as the king of peace (Zech. 9:9) and as the one who has been blessed in the name of the Lord (Ps. 118:26). Dan. 7:13 speaks of the coming of "one like a son of man" (→ *ho huios tou anthrōpou* under *huios*, *5626*).

NT 1. The NT use of *erchomai* and *hēkō* follows cl. Gk. usage. The original, spatial meaning is dominant. But it merges into a religious meaning. Coming to Jesus (Jn. 1:39, 47) leads to discipleship. There are the same overtones in the coming of the wise men from the East (Matt. 2:2), which is also of the coming of the heathen. It points to their entry into the kingdom of God (cf. 8:11; Rom. 11:25). The metaphorical sense of events coming in time also occurs, esp. in eschatology: The days or hour are coming when . . . (e.g., Matt. 9:15; Mk. 2:20; Jn. 2:4); the fullness of time comes (Gal. 4:4), as does faith (3:23, 25), wrath (Eph. 5:6), and judgment (Rev. 18:10).

2. The addition of various prefixes to *erchomai* to form compounds gives a wide range of meaning. Usage here generally agrees with cl. Gk. and the LXX.

(a) *aperchomai* means go away (Mk. 1:35; 6:46; 14:39). It is also used metaphorically of going away from Jesus (Jn. 6:66; Jude 7) and of "the first heaven and the first earth" and "the old order of things" passing away (Rev. 21:1, 4).

(b) *dierchomai* means go or pass through (Acts 14:24; 15:3, 41; etc.). It is used of death coming "to all men" (Rom. 5:12) and of Jesus as the great high priest passing through the heavens (Heb. 4:14).

(c) *eiserchomai*, come in, enter, is used of entering the temple or synagogue (Lk. 1:9; 4:16). It is used metaphorically of entering the kingdom, life, and rest (Matt. 18:3; Heb. 3:11, 18).

(d) *exerchomai*, go out, come out, spread, is used mostly in a lit. sense (e.g., Matt. 14:14). But it is also used metaphorically of the coming forth of the Messiah (2:6), of news spreading (9:26), of the issuing of an emperor's decree (Lk. 2:1), and of demons going out of a person (Mk. 1:25–26). In Johannine language it is used of Jesus' coming forth from God (Jn. 8:42; 13:3).

(e) *eperchomai*, come along, approach, is an intensive form of *erchomai*. It is used in a lit. sense (Acts 14:19), in a hostile sense (Lk. 11:22), and in a neutral sense of the coming ages (Eph. 2:7). It denotes the coming of an imminent evil (Lk. 21:26; Jas. 5:1) and of the Spirit (Lk. 1:35; Acts 1:8).

(f) *parerchomai*, go by, pass by, is used locally (Mk. 6:48; Lk. 18:37) and temporally (Mk. 14:35). It also has the meaning of transgress (Lk. 15:29).

(g) *pareiserchomai* is used of the coming in of the law (Rom. 5:20), which had a subordinate purpose in God's plan of salvation, and of false brothers who had slipped into the church at Jerusalem (Gal. 2:4).

(h) *perierchomai*, wander, is used of Jewish itinerant exorcists (Acts 19:13), the going around from house to house of young widows (1 Tim. 5:13), and the roaming around of persecuted witnesses to the faith (Heb. 11:37).

(i) *proerchomai*, go forward, advance, proceed (Acts 20:5; 2 Cor. 9:5), is used in a metaphorical sense of the precursor of Christ (Lk. 1:17).

(j) *proserchomai*, go to, approach, is used mostly lit. (e.g., Matt. 5:1). Heb. 4:16 speaks of drawing near to the throne of grace; 10:22 and 11:6 speak of the believer's drawing near to God in a way that far exceeds the prerogative of the high priest.

(k) *synerchomai*, come together, assemble, can refer to the gathering of a crowd or local church; it can also mean come together in the sense of sexual union (Matt. 1:18).

3. (a) The idea of coming has a theological significance in relation to the coming of Christ and the coming of God and his kingdom. The Synoptic Gospels present Jesus as having come to preach the gospel, not to destroy the Mosaic law but to fulfill it, to call sinners to repentance, not to bring peace but a sword, and to cast fire on the earth (Matt. 5:17; 9:13; Mk. 1:38–39; 2:17; Lk. 5:32; 12:49). The Son of Man has come to give his life a ransom for many and to seek and save the lost (Matt. 20:28; Mk. 10:45; Lk. 19:10).

Jn. bears witness to Jesus as the light of the world (Jn. 1:9; 3:19; 8:12), who came to give to those who belong to him life in all its fullness (10:10). He did not come to judge the world but to save it and to bear witness to the truth (12:46–47; 18:37). He has come from God in the name of the Father (5:43; 8:42; 16:28).

John the Baptist went before him (Lk. 1:17). He too had come and was indeed the Elijah who was to come again (Matt. 11:14, 18; 17:10; Mk. 9:11; cf. Mal. 4:5). John pointed to one mightier than himself who would come (Matt. 3:11; Mk. 1:7; Lk. 3:16).

(b) The coming of Jesus in the flesh (1 Jn. 4:2) gave rise to the doubt that even the imprisoned John entertained: "Are you the one who was to come, or should we expect someone else?" (Matt. 11:3). Jesus will come again in power and glory on the clouds of heaven (24:30; 26:64 par.). Christ will come as judge (16:27; 25:31; Rom. 2:6; 14:10; 2 Cor. 5:10). The strength of the Christian hope is shown by the prayer cry *Marana tha* (1 Cor. 16:22)—"Come, O Lord!" (cf. Rev. 22:20).

Prayer for the coming of the Lord is bound up with prayer for the coming of the kingdom of God (Matt. 6:10; Lk. 11:2). False prophets, messiahs, and even the Antichrist will precede the coming of Christ (Matt. 24:24; Mk. 13:22–23; 2 Thess. 2:3–9; 1 Jn. 2:18). The day and hour of this coming is known only by the Father (Matt. 24:36; Mk. 13:32; Acts 1:7). The Lord will come like a thief in the night (Matt. 24:42–43; Lk. 12:39; 1 Thess. 5:2). Therefore, the disciples must be awake (Matt. 24:44; 25:13).

(c) The Fourth Gospel sees Easter and Pentecost in the light of the coming of Jesus and the Spirit. Jesus will not leave his disciples as orphans, but will return to them as the Living One. The Father and the Son will come and make their home with them (Jn. 14:16–21). Jesus promises help through the coming of the *paraklētos* (14:16, 26; 15:26; 16:7; cf. 16:12–15; 1 Jn. 2:1; → 4156), who will bear witness to Jesus and lead the disciples into all truth.

(d) We are now called to come to this Lord, who has come and who will come again. Jesus refers to this in the parable of the great supper (Matt. 22:1–14; Lk. 14:15–24). But people can refuse to come. In the last analysis, in other words, our response to this invitation is the work of God's grace (Jn. 6:37, 44).

See also *katantaō*, come to, arrive at (*2918*); *mellō*, be about to, intend, propose (*3516*).

2263	ἐρωτάω

ἐρωτάω (*erōtaō*), ask, ask a question, request (*2263*); ἐπερωτάω (*eperōtaō*), ask (*2089*); ἐπερώτημα (*eperōtēma*), question, request, appeal (*2090*).

CL & OT 1. In cl. Gk. *erōtaō* means to ask, ask a question. *eperōtaō* means to consult a person or to put a question. Later Gk. used it technically for putting a formal question at a meeting or in the process of making a contract. It may even mean to accept the terms of a treaty. In religious contexts both vbs. can mean to put a question to an oracle or a god. The noun *eperōtēma* can mean a question put to another person or to someone in authority for a formal, binding answer.

2. In the LXX *erōtaō* commonly means ask (e.g., Gen. 24:47, 57; Exod. 3:13; Isa. 41:28). *eperōtaō* is used for the same idea (e.g., Gen. 24:23; 26:7; Isa. 19:3), including inquiry of God (e.g., 65:1). *eperōtēma* occurs only in Theodotion's version of Dan. 4:14 and in Sir. 33:3.

NT 1. *erōtaō* occurs 63x in the NT; it commonly means to ask, inquire. Jesus' questions and counterquestions were part of his teaching method, designed to expose the person concerned to the implications of one's own questions or make someone reflect on one's attitudes (e.g., Matt. 16:13; 19:17; 21:24). It is also used of the theological questions put by the disciples (Mk. 4:10; Lk. 9:45; Acts 1:6). Jn. 16:23 implies that in the future salvation there will be no need to ask Jesus any more questions. Asking implies imperfect knowledge, which will be overcome by perfect fellowship with Jesus (cf. 16:30; cf. 16:5, 19). Conversely, Jesus does not need to ask questions, for he knows already what is in a human being (2:25).

In Jn. asking is characteristic of the doubting, contentious questions of the Jews (e.g., Jn. 1:19, 21, 25). But it may be compared with the question of the Greeks (12:21) and with those of Jesus, who asks things for his disciples of the Father (14:16; 17:9, 15, 20). The vb. is used of the efficacy of intercession by believers for one another in 1 Jn. 5:16. This use extends to the believer a sense of the vb. that in Jn. is otherwise applied to Jesus. In 2 Jn. 5 it describes the action of the author in begging his readers to follow love (cf. v. 6). In Acts 1:6 it means to ask (a question). Elsewhere it generally means to request: of the disciples to Jesus (Matt. 15:23; Lk. 4:38), of the Jews to Pilate (Jn. 19:31), and in Lk.'s writings of invitations (Lk. 7:36; 11:37; Acts 10:48; 18:20).

2. *eperōtaō* is nearly as common (56x) and is most frequent in the Gospels. The basic sense is to ask—i.e., synonymous with *erōtaō* (e.g., Matt. 16:1; Mk. 9:32; Lk. 2:46; 1 Cor. 14:35). However, certain nuances of meaning may be detected in some passages.

(a) *Seeking*. The Pharisees and Sadducees, traditionally enemies, join together to ask for a sign that might accredit Jesus with popular authority (Matt. 16:1). In Rom. 10:20, Paul quotes Isa. 65:1 regarding those who "did not seek" (→ *zēteō*, *2426*) him and who "did not ask" (*eperōtaō*) for him. This verse in Isa. applies to Yahweh's willingness to be found by disobedient Israel, even though Israel did not seek him. Paul applies this principle to the Gentiles, who in times past did not seek Yahweh but now have found him through faith in Christ, whereas Israel remains disobedient and estranged. To them Isa. 65:2 still applies.

(b) *Probing*. In debate the opponents of Jesus ask probing questions, to which an answer must be given, and Jesus put counterquestions (Matt. 22:46; Mk. 11:29; Lk. 6:9).

(c) *Questioning an authority*. Several passages imply that a questioner is approaching an authority higher than himself. On feast days and Sabbaths the temple Sanhedrin informally received questions and stated their traditions, and on one such occasion the boy Jesus put questions to the temple elders (Lk. 2:46). In a similar sense, the disciples dared not question Jesus about a passion prediction (Mk. 9:32), and the Corinthian wives were to ask their husbands at home about church matters (1 Cor. 14:35).

3. The noun *eperōtēma* is found in the NT only at 1 Pet. 3:21 in respect of baptism: "This water symbolizes baptism that now saves you also—not the removal of dirt from the body but the pledge [*eperōtēma*] of a good conscience toward God." If "pledge" is an accurate meaning here, it denotes a statement of faith given by the one being baptized in answer to a formal question. This person should make such a statement with a clear conscience. Possibly it also means that baptism itself is a prayer to God for a good conscience. Or again, it may mean the answer by God to a such a question, i.e., the granting of a clear conscience toward God (cf. Heb. 10:19–25).

See also *aiteō*, ask, ask for, demand (*160*); *gonypeteō*, fall on one's knees, kneel down before (*1206*); *deomai*, ask, request, beseech, beg (*1289*); *proseuchomai*, to pray, entreat (*4667*); *proskyneō*, worship, do obeisance to, prostrate oneself, do reverence to (*4686*); *krouō*, knock (*3218*); *entynchanō*, meet, turn to, approach, petition, pray, intercede (*1961*).

| 2266 | ἐσθίω | ἐσθίω (*esthiō*), eat (*2266*). |

CL & OT 1. Along with drinking, eating is necessary to maintain physical life. On a physical level there are two extremes in eating: gluttony and asceticism. Beyond the physical, people have sought to commune with the deity through sacramental meals and foods and so obtain a share in the immortal powers of life or even in the deity itself.

2. All food is understood in the OT as the gift of God, whether it is cultivated by human beings or grown naturally (Deut. 14:4). This places humankind under obligation to God and under his command (Gen. 3:2–3). Thus, abstinence from or consumption of certain foods (2:17; Lev. 7:23–27 = LXX 7:13–17) are tests of human obedience. Disobedience can bring punishment (Gen. 3:6, 17). But in general, the satisfaction of one's need of food is traced to God (Ps. 22:26); not having enough to eat or being unable to eat (102:4, 9–10) are evidences of God's anger and punishment (cf. Hos. 4:10).

The righteous and the devout do not need to worry about food (Ps. 127:2; Isa. 3:10; cf. Matt. 6:25), for their relationship with God is in order (Eccl. 9:7). After the meal God should be praised (Deut. 8:10) and not forgotten (6:11–12). Since eating is not something we should do in isolation but as an expression of our relationship with God, we must share our bread with the hungry (Isa. 58:7; cf. Lk. 16:19–25). One can eat and drink to God's glory (Exod. 24:11; cf. 1 Cor. 10:31) and make ritual sacrifices of food to him (Lev. 2:3, 6, 9–16). Isa. 22:13 describes the irresponsible behavior of those who care for nothing but eating and drinking (cf. Matt. 24:38; Lk. 12:19; 1 Cor. 15:32).

NT 1. The various traditions about John the Baptist (Matt. 11:18; Mk. 1:6; 2:18) recount that he fasted and lived abstemiously. The Gospels recount how Jesus cultivated table fellowship with others (e.g., Pharisees, Lk. 7:36) as well as with his disciples (Mk. 14:18). The complaint that Jesus was eating with tax collectors and sinners is met in Mk. 2:16–17 by the statement that Jesus had not come to call the righteous but sinners (→ *pinō*, *4403*). Esp. important in Luke is the fact of the disciples' eating with Christ after he had risen from the dead (Lk. 24:30–31, 35, 41–43; Acts 1:4; 10:41).

The mode of life of the early Christian church was by no means ascetic. Believers had joyful common meals (Acts 2:46), and ritual prohibitions were rejected (Gal. 2:12). Table fellowship symbolized fellowship in general. Even Luke's account of the Parousia retains the significance of table fellowship in the kingdom of God (Lk. 14:15; 22:30). The stories of the feedings in Mk. 6:34–44 and 8:1–9 are part of the miracle stories that glorify Jesus' power and greatness.

2. Eating is discussed in the context of mission insofar as the missionary is entitled to support (1 Cor. 9:14; cf. Matt. 10:10; Lk. 10:7). The command to work belongs among the exhortations to the church, for whoever will not work should not eat (2 Thess. 3:10).

3. Eating and drinking became a problem in Corinth, where certain groups sought to prove their strength and freedom by deliberately participating in sacrifices to idols (1 Cor. 10:14–20). Paul had to point out that one can have communion either with God or with idols and demons, but not both; they are mutually exclusive (10:20–22). A further question was the permissibility of buying in the marketplace and eating meat sacrificed to idols. Paul answered this question in the affirmative (10:25), but with the proviso that one has to take into account "weak" believers (1 Cor. 8:9–13; 10:32; cf. Rom. 14:1–15:6).

Even the Lord's Supper gave rise to a crisis in Corinth, for in the absence of the apostle certain irregularities endangered the common meal (the love feast) that preceded the Lord's Supper (1 Cor. 11:17–34). The more well-to-do members of the church apparently came early with food and gorged themselves on it. When the poorer people and slaves arrived, there was little food left, so that "one remains hungry, another gets drunk" (11:21). Such lack of love set a most inappropriate context for the Lord's Supper and thus desecrated the unifying body and blood of the Lord. In other words, these abuses indicated a failure of the church in Corinth to understand itself at the Lord's Supper as the body of Christ (cf. 6:15; 10:16; 11:29; 12:27). In the common celebration of the Lord's Supper, all the members of the church, rich and poor alike, ought to take part in love.

4. (a) Jn. raises other questions. The true bread that comes down from heaven (Jn. 6:32) is Jesus himself (6:35, 48). Eating of him as the bread of life means believing in him and so receiving eternal life (6:47–51). This section has traditionally been interpreted as an allusion to the sacrament of the Lord's Supper, when we symbolically "eat the flesh of the Son of Man and drink his blood" (6:53, cf. 54–56).

(b) The eating of the little scroll in Rev. (10:9–10; cf. Ezek. 3:1–3) means the real appropriation of the revelation, the content of which (cf. ch. 12ff.) is described as "sweet" (denoting victory) and "sour" (symbolizing struggle).

5. It is not clear what the "altar" in Heb. 13:10 refers to. The author is here contrasting those who adhere to the old covenant with those who believe in Jesus. The latter draw spiritual sustenance from the sacrifice of Christ, which is not available to the former. There may also be an allusion here to the Lord's Supper.

See also *peinaō*, hunger (*4277*); *brōma*, food (*1109*); *geuomai*, taste, partake of, enjoy, experience (*1174*); *pinō*, drink (*4403*).

| 2274 | ἔσχατος | ἔσχατος (*eschatos*), (adj.) extreme, last, least; (as neut. noun), |

end; ἐσχάτως (*eschatōs*), finally (*2275*).

CL & OT 1. (a) In cl. Gk. the adj. *eschatos* (a superlative form derived from the prep. *ek/ex*, out of, away from) spatially meant the place furthest away (the utmost ends of the earth); temporally, the last events of a series; materially, the extreme (mostly the lowest place in order of rank). Substantively, *to eschaton* meant the end in spatial and temporal respects; it could also be used as an adv., like *eschatōs*, to mean "finally."

(b) In Gk. thinking *eschatos* often designates the end point of a continuously conceived succession of circumstances. In qualitative respects *eschatos* designates an extreme positive or negative intensification (e.g., the greatest injustice or extreme danger). In Aristotle the term denotes the conclusion of a logical path of thought. As the expression of order of rank among human beings, *eschatos* means the opposite of *prōtos* (first). The temporal dimension is the least developed sense of *eschatos*. Gk. thought, for example, has no developed eschatological understanding of time, i.e., one directed toward a future goal or end of the historical process.

2. The very different historical understanding of existence in the OT is immediately apparent in that of its 150x in the LXX, *eschatos* has local significance only in isolated cases (e.g., Deut. 28:49; Isa. 48:20; 49:6; Jer. 6:22). Its use is predominantly in the temporal sense to mean last, finally, outcome, end. In the historical books the word plays no real role, apart from the characteristic and stereotyped phrase "from beginning to end" (cf. 2 Chr. 16:11; 20:34; 25:26). On the other hand, *eschatos* features particularly in prophetic and apocalyptic expectations of the future.

(a) A number of prophets use the formula "in the last days" (lit., "at the end of the days"; e.g., Isa. 2:2; Hos. 3:5; Mic. 4:1; cf. Jer. 23:20; 49:39 = LXX 25:18; Ezek. 38:16). This indicates the future-directed thinking of the prophets, which pointed Israel's self-understanding— until then largely orientated around past events—in a new direction. Moreover, the context in which this formulation is found reveals that the prophets do not think of "the end of the days" as a renewed historical time span, the final or end time.

It is noteworthy that this formula is mostly encountered in announcements of salvation. Eschatological time will be stamped by Yahweh's saving activity. Yahweh will make it possible for his people to turn back (Hos. 3:5). He will destroy his enemies (Jer. 23:20; 30:24 = LXX 37:24). The nations will come to Jerusalem and receive instruction from Israel (Isa. 2:2–4; Mic. 4:1–5). Salvation will penetrate "to the ends of the earth" (Isa. 48:20; 49:6). However much the individual pictures of salvation presented by the various prophets differ, the expectation of a comprehensive age of salvation at the end of time brought in by Yahweh himself is common to them all.

(b) Apocalyptic literature contains numerous allusions to the end of the days (e.g., Dan. 2:28, 45; 10:14; 2 Esd. 6:34; *2 Bar.* 6:8). Such literature is distinguished from the prophetic expectation by the progression from the more simple pictures of the future into the realm of the visionary, allegorical, and other-worldly. A certain element of calculation concerning the final times is discernible (Dan. 8:19–25; 10:14; 12:5–12; 2 Esd. 14:5). According to the apocalyptic outlook, dramatic battles will take place between various world powers. There will be cosmic catastrophes in the end times before Yahweh establishes his transcendent, imperishable kingdom (cf. esp. Dan. 2:3–45; 7:17–27). The end of this world signifies the beginning of the coming one (2 Esd. 6:7; 7:113).

3. The formula "the end of the days" is also found in the Dead Sea Scrolls (e.g., 1QpHab 2:5–6; 9:6; CD 4:4; 6:11). The calculating tendency of apocalyptic has hardened into a rigid deterministic understanding of the final time. It is the fixed and predetermined time of divine visitation (1QS 3:18, 23; CD 8:2–3), when the godless and wickedness will be annihilated, but the righteous and truth will live forever (1QS 4:18–23; 1QH 6:30–31). It is not the saving character of the final times that stands in the foreground—as it does in the prophets— but the day of disaster, judgment, and vengeance (1QS 10:18–21; CD 19:5–16). Only a small community of elect (4QFlor 3:19) will be saved.

NT As in the LXX, the spatial aspect of *eschatos* in the NT fades into the background. True, in Acts (1:8; 13:47), as in Isa., the spatial for-

mula "to the ends of the earth" has a universal eschatological significance. More important are the material overtones of the least and lowest (e.g., Lk. 14:9), frequently in the antithesis of *prōtos* and *eschatos* (e.g., Mk. 9:35). But in the NT, the chief stress falls on the temporal dimension of *eschatos*. In contrast to past periods of time, Jesus has come "in these last days" (Heb. 1:2). *eschatos* also contrasts the final future of God with the present (e.g., Jn. 11:24).

1. The Synoptic Gospels record 4x this maxim from Jesus: "Many who are first will be last, and many who are last will be first" (Matt. 19:30; 20:16; Mk. 10:31; Lk. 13:30). This aphorism possibly meant originally something like: "How quickly one's fortunes can change overnight." But in the mouth of Jesus it undergoes an eschatological radicalization as the conclusion of a discussion concerning the rewards of discipleship (Mk. 10:28–31 par.). In society, kings, rulers, and nobles are first; slaves and outcasts are the last. In the coming kingdom age, however, this precedence will be reversed, as God stands on the side of those who are the last and lowest on earth. To them, like the poor followers of Jesus, the kingdom of God is promised, whereas those who regard themselves as its first candidates are excluded (Matt. 8:11–12; Lk. 13:28–30). Jesus' followers are given the commission of realizing now in the present this eschatological reversal. Thus, Jesus answers the disciples' disputes about seniority with the reminder: "If anyone wants to be first, he must be the very last, and the servant of all" (Mk. 9:35).

2. (a) Both the way of life and the proclamation of Paul are in accord with this instruction of Jesus. He counters the Corinthian enthusiasts by saying that God has paraded the apostles as the lowest of men, like those condemned to death, a spectacle and the scum of the world (1 Cor. 4:9–13; cf. 15:8, where with the thought of negative quality is linked the significance of the chronological conclusion of the list of witnesses).

(b) Within the framework of Paul's Adam–Christ typology (cf. Rom. 5:12–21; 1 Cor. 15:21–22), the apostle contrasts in 15:45 the first man (Adam) with Christ ("the last Adam"). Adam and Christ are not here thought of as individual persons, but each as representative of a whole humanity. The "last Adam" therefore does not mean the last person either numerically or chronologically, but Christ as the new, the second representative of a new humanity created in his image. Paul therefore understands the risen Christ, the creator of life, as the eschatological prototype of God's new humanity. With his resurrection the final time has already begun.

(c) The letters of other authors confirm that this idea belonged to early Christian eschatology generally. In Heb. 1:2 the prophetic expectation of the final times, expressed in the formula "in these last days," relates to the present time of the early Christians, in which God "has spoken to us by his Son." With the enthronement of Jesus as Son and as Lord of creation the turning-point of the ages has come. Peter also speaks of Christ as "revealed in these last times" (1 Pet. 1:20; cf. also Mk. 12:6), and John makes the recipients of his letter emphatically aware that they are living in "the last hour" (1 Jn. 2:18). The characteristics of the final time, now dawned, include the outpouring of the Spirit (Acts 2:17; cf. Joel 2:28–32), the growth of moral corruption (2 Tim. 3:1–9), and the appearance of scoffers (2 Pet. 3:3; Jude 18) and antichrists (1 Jn. 2:18).

(d) The term *eschatos* does not, however, serve merely to denote the new time that began with the coming of Jesus. It also refers to the final, consummative action of God that is still to come. In 1 Cor. 15:23–28 Paul expresses the chronological sequence of the future events of the final times. In this scheme death is chronologically the last and physically the hardest enemy to be destroyed before the final goal (→ *telos*, 5465) of God is reached (15:26–28).

3. Only in Jn.'s Gospel is explicit allusion found to the "last day" (6:39–40, 44, 54; 11:24; 12:48). The expression takes up and continues the prophetic exposition of the "day of Yahweh." The decisive mark of the "last day" is the resurrection of the dead. The judgment of unbelievers (12:48) represents the negative side of this. Thus in the

expectation of the end in Jn.'s Gospel, as in the eschatological proclamation of the OT prophets, what stands in the foreground is not judgment but all-embracing salvation.

4. Rev. presents a vision of the "seven last plagues," through which the divine wrath is discharged (15:1; 21:9). But note that the climax of this vision is not in the annihilation of enemies, but in the song of praise to the Lamb (15:3–4; 19:7–8; 21:22).

Also in Rev. is found the formula "the first and the last" as a self-designation of the exalted Christ (1:17; 2:8; 22:13). This goes back to the description of God in Isa. 41:4; 44:6; 48:12. This formula belongs essentially to the synonymous phrases "the Alpha and the Omega" (Rev. 1:8; 21:6; 22:13) and "the Beginning and the End" (22:13). The application of these divine predicates to the exalted Christ means the ascription to him of a rank equal with God in the attribution of his functions of Creator and Perfecter.

See also *engys*, near, (*1584*); *telos*, end, goal (*5465*).

2275 (eschatos, finally), → *2274*.

2278	ἐσώτερος

ἐσώτερος (*esōteros*), inner; with art., the inner shrine (*2278*).

CL & OT *esōteros* is an adj. in the comparative state, used to describe things as being further in the interior, more inward, or more intimate. In the LXX it is used as the prep. within (e.g., the inner shrine of the tabernacle or within the curtain [Exod. 26:33; Lev. 16:2, 12, 15], also the innermost part of the cave where David and his men hid [1 Sam. 24:4], and as an adj. describing doors, gates, porches, etc., in the palace-temple complex (e.g., 2 Chr. 4:22; Ezek. 8:3).

NT As an attributive adj. *esōteros* describes the inner cell of the prison in Philippi where Paul and Silas were kept (Acts 16:24). The subst. form with the art. is used metaphorically for the heavenly Most Holy Place, which Jesus has entered for us (Heb. 6:19). It corresponds to the inner shrine of the tabernacle, the place of the invisible presence of the God of Israel.

2279	ἑταῖρος

ἑταῖρος (*hetairos*), comrade, companion, friend (*2279*).

CL & OT The noun *hetairos* means "one who is linked to another" in some fashion, determined only by the context. The link may be military, religious, political, or simply friendship. It is often used of peers or in reference to inferiors: e.g., pupils associated by virtue of sharing a teacher, or soldiers linked together and addressed by a superior officer.

In the LXX *hetairos* commonly translates *rēaʿ* (friend) and its cognates, but twice represents *ḥābēr* (associate, companion: Song 1:7; 8:13). Philo uses the term of friends and companions, while Josephus applies it not only to soldiers and junior officials, but also to bad company. In the Jerusalem Talmud *ḥābēr* is applied to qualified teachers who for some reason have not yet been ordained as official rabbis. At Qumran, the same Heb. word group refers to anyone in the community.

NT *hetairos* is found only 3x in the NT, all in the vocative (Matt. 20:13; 22:12; 26:50). In each case, the person speaking is addressing an inferior who has insulted him in some way, though the words are without malice. Moreover, the speaker and the person addressed are in some sort of relationship. In the two parables the speaker has the last word; in the climactic incident Jesus suffers at the hands of his betrayer, yet the impression is unfailingly transmitted that Jesus is still in control of his destiny (cf. Matt. 26:53; Jn. 10:17–18).

See also *adelphos*, brother (*81*); *plēsion*, neighbor (*4446*).

2280 (heteroglōssos, speaking a foreign language, of alien speech), → *1185*.

2281 (heterodidaskaleō, teach a different, i.e., heretical, doctrine), → *1437*.

2282 (heterozygeō, be unevenly yoked, fig. be mismated), → *2433*.

2283 (heteros, other), → *257*.

2284 (heterōs, differently), → *257*.

2286 (hetoimazō, get ready, hold in readiness), → *2289*.

2288 (hetoimasia, state of readiness, preparation), → *2289*.

2289	ἕτοιμος

ἕτοιμος (*hetoimos*), ready, prepared (*2289*); ἑτοίμως (*hetoimōs*), readily (*2290*); ἑτοιμάζω (*hetoimazō*), get ready, hold in readiness (*2286*); ἑτοιμασία (*hetoimasia*), state of readiness, preparation (*2288*); προετοιμάζω (*proetoimazō*), prepare beforehand (*4602*).

CL & OT 1. In cl. Gk. this word group denotes preparation, both in the act. sense (make ready) and in pass. (readiness, ability). Only in Homer is it found with a religious sense, in connection with preparation for sacrifice.

2. In the LXX these words chiefly translate *kûn* (esp. niph. and hiph.); the principal meanings are to establish, set up, make, prepare, get ready. (a) Though used in a secular sense, they can have a religious meaning in connection with the Passover (2 Chr. 35:4, 6), sacrificial animals (Num. 23:1, 29), the ark (1 Chr. 15:1; 2 Chr. 1:4), and the temple (31:11).

(b) These words are also used for the divine activity of creation, preparation, and establishing. (i) God has established the heavens (Prov. 3:19; 8:27), founded the earth upon the waters (Ps. 24:2), and established the mountains (65:6). He prepares rain (147:8), provides food for his creatures (65:9), and concerns himself with their destiny (Gen. 24:14, 44).

(ii) God's creation and providence extend also to his acts of salvation in history. He has established Israel to be his people forever (2 Sam. 7:24) and sworn that he will bring them into a land appointed for them (Exod. 23:20; Ezek. 20:6). Therefore, he creates food for them (Ps. 78:19–20) and, despite their unbelief and their enemies, leads them into the sanctuary that his own hands have prepared (Exod. 15:17). Moreover, he sets up the kings of Israel (esp. David) and establishes their rule (Ps. 89:4; cf. 2 Sam. 7:12; 1 Chr. 14:2; 17:11).

(iii) God does all this because his faithfulness is established in the heavens (Ps. 89:2). There he has set up his throne from the beginning (93:2; 103:19), founded on righteousness and justice (89:14). He has established it for judgment (9:7); for the judgment day he has prepared a sacrifice (Zeph. 1:7–8).

(c) This all-embracing work of God in creating and providing for his people does, however, demand self-preparation and readiness on our part. The people and Moses are called on to prepare themselves (ritually) for the revelation of God at Sinai (Exod. 19:10–11, 15; 34:2). The prophets challenge Israel to prepare to meet their God (Amos 4:12; cf. Mic. 6:8; 2 Chr. 27:6). This involves the preparation of the heart (Sir. 2:17; cf. Ps. 57:7; 108:1; Sir. 2:1; 18:23).

NT 1. In the NT the noun *hetoimasia* occurs only once (Eph. 6:15), but the vbs. *hetoimazō* and *proetoimazō* between them appear 42x, and the adj. and adv. 20x. When used with reference to objects, the meaning corresponds with that in the OT, though the words of this group are not used with reference to God's creation and providence in nature, and in a cultic setting only with reference to the Passover (e.g., Matt. 26:17, 19). Apart from their secular meaning, they connote God's activity of provision in terms of the history of salvation and one's self-preparation and readiness.

2. In his song of praise Simeon declares: "My eyes have seen your salvation, which you have prepared in the sight of all people" (Lk. 2:30–31; cf. 3:6; Isa. 52:10). The world is unable in its own light to recognize the salvation present in Jesus; God has prepared it for those who love him (1 Cor. 2:9). By his free elective grace, God makes "the riches of his glory known to the objects of his mercy, whom he

prepared in advance for glory" (Rom. 9:23). Jesus comforts his disciples by saying, "I am going [to my Father's house] to prepare a place for you" (Jn. 14:2–3).

Peter likewise encourages the Christians undergoing trials in Asia Minor by telling them that they "are shielded by God's power until the coming of the salvation that is ready [*hetoimos*] to be revealed in the last time" (1 Pet. 1:5). He also writes them that God is "ready to judge the living and the dead" (4:5). The invitation, "Come, for everything is now ready" (Lk. 14:17; cf. Matt. 22:4, 8; Jn. 7:6), has gone out, but many have proved unworthy. No one, however, can glory in his or her own works, "for we are God's workmanship, created in Christ Jesus to do good works, which God prepared in advance for us to do" (Eph. 2:10; cf. 2 Tim. 2:21).

3. To this sphere, which is marked out by God's work of preparation arising from his free elective choice, belong also the statements about our own self-preparation and readiness. The OT call, "In the desert prepare the way for the LORD" (Isa. 40:3), is applied in the NT to John the Baptist (Matt. 3:3; Mk. 1:3; Lk. 3:4), who by his preaching of repentance prepares the way for the coming of the Lord to his people.

The Lord who has come is also the Lord who is coming, like a thief in the night or like a bridegroom to his wedding. The church is thus exhorted to be "ready" for his coming (Matt. 24:44; Lk. 12:40). Only those virgins who are ready when he arrives will be let in (Matt. 25:10). The servant who has made nothing ready despite the knowledge of his master's will stands condemned (Lk. 12:47). The church too must be *ready* "to do whatever is good" (Tit. 3:1), "to give an answer to everyone" (1 Pet. 3:15; cf. Eph. 6:15), and "to punish every act of disobedience" (2 Cor. 10:6). The apostle Paul notes his own readiness not only to be imprisoned but even to die for the Lord Jesus in Jerusalem (Acts 21:13).

See also *kataskeuazō*, make ready, prepare, build, equip, furnish (*2941*); *zōnnymi*, gird (*2439*).

2290 (hetoimōs, readily), → *2289.*

2293	Εὕα

Εὕα (*Heua*), Eve (*2293*).

OT Gen. 3:20 derives the name Eve from the fact that she was the "mother of all the living." The first creation narrative tells of the creation of man and woman together in the image of God (1:27). In the second narrative (2:18–25), woman was formed from man to be his helper. In Gen. 3 it is the woman who heeds the blandishments of the serpent and eats the forbidden fruit before giving some to her husband. It is only after the fall that the name Eve is mentioned. She is mentioned as the mother of Cain (4:1) and Abel, but not elsewhere in the OT.

NT Eve is mentioned by name in 2 Cor. 11:3 and 1 Tim. 2:13. The latter passage alludes to Gen. 2–3 in support of Paul's argument why he does "not permit a woman to teach or to have authority over a man" (1 Tim. 2:12), for the Gen. story depicts Adam being formed first and the woman being deceived first. For Paul the story is symbolic of the role of the sexes in life in general and that of the church. In 2 Cor. 11:3 the deception of Eve by the serpent is seen as an example of how Christians may be led astray.

See also *Adam*, Adam (*77*); *gynē*, woman (*1222*).

2294 (euangelizō, bring or announce good news, proclaim, preach), → *2295.*

2295	εὐαγγέλιον

εὐαγγέλιον (*euangelion*), good news, gospel (*2295*); εὐαγγελίζω (*euangelizō*), bring or announce good news, proclaim, preach (*2294*); εὐαγγελιστής (*euangelistēs*), proclaimer of glad tidings or of the gospel, evangelist (*2296*); προευαγγελίζομαι (*proeuangelizomai*), announce the good news beforehand (*4603*).

CL & OT 1. (a) The words in this word group are derived from *angelos*, messenger (→ *34*), or *angellō*, to bear a message, announce (→ *33*). In cl. Gk. a *euangelos*, messenger, is someone who brings a message of victory or other political or personal news that causes joy. In the Hel. period the word also meant one who announces oracles. Similarly, the vb. *euangelizomai* means to speak as a messenger of gladness, to proclaim good news; and, where it is used in a religious sense, to promise. But the vb. is often found with its original sense weakened to make it synonymous with *angellō*.

(b) The noun *euangelion* means: (i) the reward received by a messenger of victory (since his good news brings relief to the recipients, he is rewarded); (ii) the message itself—chiefly a technical term for a message of victory, but also used of political and private messages bringing joy. Such messages are seen as gifts from the gods. When they are received, sacrifices are offered to the gods out of gratitude, but also in order to hold the gods to their gift. (iii) It is mainly in connection with oracles (i.e., the promise of some future event) and in the imperial cult that *euangelion* acquires a religious meaning. In this latter sphere news of a divine ruler's birth, coming of age, or enthronement, as well as his speeches, decrees, and acts, are glad tidings that bring long-hoped-for fulfillment to the longings of the world for happiness and peace. It is not difficult to trace a connection between this religious use of *euangelion* in the Hel. world, esp. in the imperial cult, and its use in the NT.

2. (a) At the same time the OT roots of the NT concept of *euangelion* must not be ignored. In the LXX *euangelion* never appears in the sing. form. The pl. means reward for good news (2 Sam. 4:10). Occasionally *euangelia*, a form unknown in the NT, also appears in the sense of glad tidings (e.g., 2 Sam. 18:20, 22).

(b) More significant is the fact that the vb. *euangelizō*—not found frequently elsewhere and limited to a few writings—comes to stand for the Heb. *biśśar*, to announce, tell, publish (e.g., 1 Ki. 1:42; Jer. 20:15). This vb. is used in Ps. 40:9; 68:11; 96:2; Isa. 52:7, to herald Yahweh's universal victory over the world and his kingly rule. With his enthronement (cf. Ps. 96 as an enthronement psalm) and return to Zion (cf. Isa.) a new era begins. The one who brings "good tidings" (*euangelizomenos*, Isa. 40:9; 52:7) announces this new era of world history and inaugurates it by his mighty word. Peace and salvation have now come; Yahweh has become king; his reign extends over the whole world (Ps. 96:2–10).

This "'gospel' is effective speech, a powerful saying, a word that brings its own fulfillment. In the mouth of his messengers God himself speaks, and his word is accomplished; he commands and it is done (cf. Ps. 33:6, 9). The act of proclamation is itself the dawn of the new era. Hence it is easy to understand the special significance that attaches to the messenger of the good news. With his arrival on the scene and the delivery of his message, salvation, redemption, and peace become a reality (cf. Isa. 61:1).

3. Rab. Jud. kept alive the concept of the messenger of good tidings. He was variously expected: as an unknown figure, as the forerunner of the Messiah, or as the Messiah himself. The content of his message was already familiar from Isa. and was thus no longer of primary interest. The important thing about him was rather his coming and the fact that by his proclamation he would usher in the era of salvation. Everything depended on his appearance and proclamation (cf. *Pesiq. Rab.* 36).

Here we may make the same observation as was made concerning OT usage. The eschatological event finds expression in the Heb. vb. (*biśśar* means to preach the message of coming joy) and esp. the participial noun (*mᵉbaśśēr*, the eschatological messenger of joy), but not in the noun *bᵉśôrâ*, good news. This fact suggests that the NT term *euangelion* is derived from Gk. usage rather than Heb., or more precisely from the language of the imperial cult. The main difference is in the content of the *euangelion*.

NT 1. Although the vb. *euangelizō* and the noun *euangelion* are important NT terms, the two words are found with varying degrees of frequency in its various writings. *euangelizō* is found only once in Matt. (11:5); in Lk.–Acts, on the other hand, it occurs 25x, in Paul 21x. The vb. is not found in Mk., but the noun occurs there 8x, and 4x in Matt.; Luke uses the noun only 2x (Acts 15:7; 20:24), but Paul uses it 60x. Both are virtually absent from the Johannine writings. It would be a mistake, however, to assume that because certain NT writings do not use the vb. or noun, the thought expressed by them is lacking. In Johannine writings, for instance, the concept is expressed by words such as *martyreō*, to witness, and *martyria*, witness (→ *3456*).

2. According to Matt. 24:14; 26:13; Mk. 1:15; 8:35; 10:29; 13:10; 14:9 (cf. also Matt. 4:23; 9:35; Mk. 1:1, 14), Jesus used *euangelion* (or, the Aram. word underlying it). Perhaps he used it to indicate that the words of messianic expectation in Isa. 35 and 61 are fulfilled in his words and actions (cf. Matt. 11:5; Lk. 7:22, where "the good news is preached" is *euangelizontai*; see also 4:18). But if so, they are fulfilled in a way that will disappoint (Matt. 11:6) the expectations popularly attached to the messenger of glad tidings in Isa. (i.e., political liberation and destruction of Israel's enemies). Certainly the answer in Matt. 11:5–6 to the Baptist's question means that the glad tidings awaited since Isa. are now being proclaimed and are already effective.

There is no doubt that Jesus saw his message of the coming kingdom of God (Mk. 1:14), which was already present in his words and actions, as good news: "Blessed are your eyes because they see, and your ears because they hear" (Matt. 13:16). This message of joy is no longer to be separated from the messenger who brings it, and this messenger is Jesus himself (cf. Matt. 5:1–2; Lk. 11:20). Moreover, he is also its subject, the one of whom the message tells. It was thus consistent for the early church to take up the term *euangelion* to describe the message of salvation connected with the coming of Jesus.

3. Paul solidified the term *euangelion* in the vocabulary of the NT, though its use preceded him. His frequent use of this word absolutely (at least 23x) suggests that he was taking over phraseology already familiar to his readers. Perhaps in the early churches this terminology had developed by analogy out of that associated with the "gospel" of the imperial cult, though in conscious opposition to the latter. In the missionary outreach, the message of salvation through Jesus Christ came into conflict with the political message because of its universal claims. It was inevitable that OT statements and ideas, esp. from Isa., would become linked with this Hel. terminology.

In Paul *euangelion* becomes a central concept of his theology. It means the familiar good news: that God has acted for the salvation or redemption of the world in the incarnation, death, and resurrection of Jesus (cf. the development of these ideas in confessional formulae in Rom. 1:1–4; 1 Cor. 15:3–7). Insofar as this event is promised in the OT, the OT belongs to the gospel (→ *proeuangelizomai* in Gal. 3:8). However, *euangelion*, as used by Paul, does not mean only the content of what is preached, but also the act, process, and execution of the proclamation. Content and process of preaching are one. They are not separated in thought (Rom. 1:1), apart from when they are set close alongside each other (1 Cor. 9:14, 18). For in the very act of proclamation the content of the *euangelion* becomes reality and brings about the salvation it contains.

The action of proclamation is denoted not only by the vb. *euangelizō* (as in 1 Cor. 1:17), but also by *euangelion* used as a noun of action. Thus in 2 Cor. 8:18 *euangelion* means preaching of the gospel. Similarly, the gen. in the phrases gospel "of God" or "of Christ" (e.g., Rom. 1:1; 15:16; 1 Cor. 9:12; 2 Cor. 2:12) should be taken as both obj. and subj.: Christ or God is both the content and author of the gospel. It is difficult to make a clear distinction here, since Paul sometimes stresses the one aspect and sometimes the other.

Wherever it is proclaimed, this gospel is charged with power. It creates faith (Rom. 1:16–17; Phil. 1:27), and brings salvation, life (Rom. 1:16; 1 Cor. 15:2), and judgment (Rom. 2:16). It reveals God's righteousness (1:17), brings the fulfillment of hope (Col. 1:5, 23), intervenes in the lives of people, and creates churches. Since this gospel

is no human invention (Gal. 1:11), but rather God or Christ is himself speaking through his messengers, the apostles, the gospel is closely associated with the apostolate (2 Cor. 10–13; cf. also Gal. 2:7–8). Just as in Isa. 40:9; 52:7; and Nah. 1:15 the heralds and watchmen on the walls proclaim the coming of God, so the messengers proclaim the gospel (Rom. 10:15).

Paul was conscious of having been called to bring the gospel esp. to the Gentiles (Rom. 1:1; Gal. 1:16) and so to carry the eschatological event beyond the borders of Israel (Rom. 15:19). His whole activity was *euangelizesthai* (1 Cor. 1:17). As one who shares in the blessings of the gospel (9:23), he could thus speak of "my/our gospel" (e.g., Rom. 16:25; 2 Cor. 4:3). By this he meant the one gospel that was preached in Jerusalem (Gal. 1:6–9; 2 Cor. 10:13–16) but that had now broken out of the bounds of the Jewish law and become the gospel for the Gentiles, freed from the law (Rom. 1:15; Gal. 1:16; 2:7–8). Paul's opponents, by contrast, have "a different gospel" (2 Cor. 11:4; Gal. 1:6–10). But since apostleship and preaching the gospel belong together, every attack on Paul and his apostleship is an attack on the gospel and vice versa. To preach the gospel is not to commend oneself, but to commend the Lord (2 Cor. 4:5, 10:18; Gal. 1:10).

4. In Paul's later writings, these same uses continue. The *euangelion* was entrusted to him as a preacher, apostle, and teacher (2 Tim. 1:10–11). Its message of Jesus Christ—descended from David and risen from the dead (2:8)—is not limited to a single, past event but is experienced as a word charged with power in the present so that it cannot be fettered by human chains (2:9). It brings peace (Eph. 2:17; 6:15) and draws together those who are near and those who are far off (i.e., Gentiles and Jews, 3:1–9). It gives salvation (1:13) and has "brought life and immortality to light" (2 Tim. 1:10). In 1 Pet., the *euangelion* is not a human word but the word of God (1:12); it produces rebirth and new life (1:23–25).

5. In a similar manner, in the Synoptic Gospels, *euangelion* is the name given to the good news of the saving event in Jesus Christ as preached in the church. The separate Evangelists do, however, have different emphases when it comes to detail.

(a) Mk. stands close to the Pauline use of *euangelion*, always using it absolutely (except at 1:1, 14). Mk. and Paul see Jesus Christ as both content and author of the gospel. Wherever it is proclaimed, he is present and at work—present to such a degree that what is done for the gospel's sake is done for Jesus' sake as well (8:35; 10:29). The content of this gospel is the history of Jesus with its individual events (cf. 14:9). Mk. does not record these events merely out of historical interest, but rather uses the narrative about Jesus in order to express what the gospel is: the message of salvation through the suffering Son of Man, whose hidden glory as Son of God did not become apparent except (in a limited way) to his followers. Mk. therefore sets *euangelion* as a kind of title over his whole book (1:1, "The beginning of the gospel about Jesus Christ, the Son of God"); this means that these stories are not merely reports about Jesus, but the good news in which Jesus is proclaimed as the living Lord and in which he himself addresses the readers of Mk., bringing about and strengthening faith (1:15).

(b) Matt. and Lk. are dependent on Mk. but modify his ideas. Matt. never uses the word without further qualifying it as "the good news of the kingdom" (4:23; 9:35) or "this gospel" (26:13; cf. 24:14). In so doing he has shifted the emphasis. In the foreground now is the idea of Jesus as the bringer and proclaimer of the gospel. The content of the gospel is now chiefly the teaching in which Jesus instructs his disciples (4:23; 9:35; 24:14). But insofar as the church passes on this gospel, Jesus himself is also its content (see esp. 24:14; 26:13).

(c) In Lk.'s writings the term *euangelion* is found only at Acts 15:7 and 20:24. Possibly this reflects Lk.'s particular scheme, according to which the era of Jesus must be distinguished from the era of the church, and so too the preaching of Jesus from that of the apostles. Thus he can describe as *euangelion* the apostolic preaching, but not the preaching of Jesus. Particularly instructive in this context is the alteration of *euangelion* in Mk. 10:29 to *basileia* in Lk. 18:29.

This suggestion is not upset by the fact that Lk. has a special predilection for the vb. *euangelizō*, which has almost become a technical term for proclamation. Note how he uses this vb. interchangeably with other vbs. of proclamation, such as *kēryssō* (cf. Lk. 4:18, 43–44; 9:2, 6), *katangellō* (Acts 13:5, 38; 15:35–36; 16:17; 17:18, 23; 26:23), and *didaskō* (Lk. 20:1). Moreover, Lk. generally qualifies this oral proclamation by a phrase like "kingdom of God" (4:43; 8:1) or "Jesus" (Acts 5:42; 8:35; 11:20). Thus Lk. can also describe the Baptist's activity as *euangelizō* (Lk. 3:18), although he explicitly stresses that the kingdom of God was not proclaimed until after the Baptist (16:16).

6. However varied may be the emphasis and development of the term *euangelion* in the NT, the reference is always to the oral proclamation of the message of salvation and never to something fixed in writing, such as a book or a letter. The NT knows only the gospel; the pl. "the Gospels" is a contradiction of its nature. Nevertheless, from the 2d cent. on reference is made to the Gospels, meaning the written Gospels (cf. Iren., *Haer.* 3.11.8; cf. 3.1.1; Clem. Alex., *Strom.*, 1.136.1). This is the outcome of a development that can be traced back to Mk., who associated *euangelion* with his written stories about Jesus, though he did not identify the two. His introductory phrase in Mk. 1:1 (see above) clearly does not mean that in what follows he is writing a biography of Jesus. This identification did, however, take place at a later stage as a result of a historicizing tendency that is already evident in Matt. and Lk. Hence, "gospel" came to be used as a description of a book, and consequently the pl. form *ta euangelia* became possible as a collective term for these reports.

7. *euangelistēs* is a term for one who proclaims the *euangelion*. This word, which is rare in non-Christian lit. but common in early Christian writings, is found in the NT only at Acts 21:8 (of Philip), Eph. 4:11 (as one of God's ministry gifts to the church), and 2 Tim. 4:5 (of Timothy). In these passages the *evangelist* is distinguished from the *apostle*. This is esp. obvious in the case of the evangelist Philip, whose activity had to be ratified by the apostles Peter and John (Acts 8:14–15). The term thus clearly refers to people who carry on the work of the apostles in preaching the risen Christ. But it is difficult to decide whether *euangelistēs* refers to an office or simply to a specific activity.

2296 (euangelistēs, proclaimer of the gospel, evangelist), → 2295.

2297 (euaresteō, please [someone], take pleasure in), → 743.

2298 (euarestos, acceptable, pleasing), → 743.

2302	εὐγενής

εὐγενής (*eugenēs*), well-born, noble in descent or character (*2302*); νόθος (*nothos*), born out of wedlock, unable to register a valid claim to ancestry (*3785*).

CL & OT From Homer on, *eugenēs* meant well-born, of noble descent. It is also used of things: animals of good pedigree, and (later) plants of good stock. *nothos* means born out of wedlock (though Athenian writers used it when one parent was not a citizen). It had the general derivative meaning of spurious, counterfeit, both of people and things.

The LXX uses *eugenēs* in Job 1:3 to translate *gādôl*, where it means well-favored, wealthy, esp. in this world's goods. *eugenēs* is also used in 2 Macc. 10:13; 4 Macc. 6:5; 9:13, 23, 27; 10:3 15, typically with reference to nobility of character as demonstrated through one's willingness to undergo martyrdom.

NT The NT also uses *eugenēs* sparingly. It means high-born in Lk. 19:12 and in 1 Cor. 1:26 (where it forms a third category with "wise" and "influential"). Acts 17:11 uses it of the Jews at Berea, who were of "more noble character" than the Thessalonians, for they "received the message" with complete alacrity of mind (*prothymia*) and tested what they heard by Scripture.

nothos only occurs at Heb. 12:8, where it denotes those unable to make an accredited claim to being children of God.

See also *gennaō*, beget, become the father of, bear (*1164*); *ginomai*, be born, become, happen (*1181*); *ektrōma*, miscarriage (*1765*); *palingenesia*, rebirth, regeneration (*4098*); *tiktō*, bring forth, bear, give birth to (*5503*).

2304 (eudia, fair weather, a good day), → 847.

2305	εὐδοκέω

εὐδοκέω (*eudokeō*), be well pleased, regard favorably, take delight in (*2305*); εὐδοκία (*eudokia*), good will, good pleasure, favor, wish, desire (*2306*).

CL & OT 1. In cl. Gk. *eudokeō* means to be well pleased or content, to approve; in the pass. to be favored, i.e., prosper. The goal of the Epicurean philosophy of life is to be content.

2. (a) In the LXX *eudokeō* occurs over 60x. It means to take pleasure in, enjoy, decide on, choose, and denotes a passionate and positive volition. The godly rejoice over the sanctuary (1 Chr. 29:3; Ps. 102:14) and in the works of truth (1 Esd. 4:39). The people and priests decided on Simon as leader (1 Macc. 14:41). The older advisors pleaded with Rehoboam to be kind to the people and to please them (2 Chr. 10:7). With a negative, *eudokeō* means to spurn (Hab. 2:4).

(b) Yahweh takes pleasure in his people (Ps. 44:3; 149:4), esp. in those who are godly (2 Sam. 22:20) and who fear him (Ps. 147:11). The psalmist prays that it may please Yahweh to deliver him (40:13). But Yahweh has no pleasure in one's physical strength (147:10) or in anyone who does evil (Mal. 2:17). A penitent mind is more pleasing to him than a sacrifice (Ps. 51:16–19; Jer. 14:12).

(c) The LXX formed the noun *eudokia* from the vb. It occurs 26x. *eudokia* can denote both human will or pleasure (cf. Ps. 141:5; Sir. 9:12) and the divine good pleasure or blessing (e.g., Ps. 5:12; 51:18). Sir. esp. displays the tendency to use *eudokia* to describe God's good pleasure, gracious will, and activity (e.g., 1:26; 11:17; 15:15).

3. (a) The formula "to do God's good pleasure" occurs frequently among the rabbis. The expression "well-pleasing in God's sight," stemming from courtly language, is also common. The formula "may it be pleasing in [God's] sight" means "may it be [God's] will." This corresponds with the expression Jesus used in Matt. 11:26 ("this was your good pleasure"; cf. Matt. 18:14; Lk. 10:21; 12:32).

(b) At Qumran we find expressions such as "all the sons of [God's] good pleasure" (1QH 4:33; 11:9) or of "the elect of [the divine] good pleasure" (1QS 8:6). "Good pleasure" here is a term related to election. The word expresses not human good will, but God's elective pleasure.

NT 1. *eudokeō* occurs 21x in the NT; *eudokia*, 9x times. The vb. has human beings as the subject 7x, the noun 2x. For example, the congregations of Macedonia decided to make a collection for the parent community of Jerusalem (Rom. 15:26–28). Paul considered it preferable to be away from the body and be at home with the Lord (2 Cor. 5:8). He took pleasure in his weakness for the sake of Christ (12:10). He was ready to share not only the gospel with the church at Thessalonica but his own self (1 Thess. 2:8). He decided to stay behind in Athens alone (3:1). All who find pleasure in unrighteousness will be judged (2 Thess. 2:12). In Rom. 10:1 Paul says that it is his heart's wish and prayer that the Jews may be saved. During Paul's time in prison, some people preached Christ out of jealousy and rivalry, but others because they were well disposed toward Paul (Phil. 1:15).

2. (a) In all other passages *eudokeō* and *eudokia* refer to God's purpose, resolve, and choice. God is "not pleased" with sacrifices (Heb. 10:6, 8; cf. Ps. 40:6–8 in LXX) and with those who shrink back (Heb. 10:38; cf. Hab. 2:4). Christ does God's will by offering himself as a sacrifice and so gains God's good pleasure. It is God's purpose to give the kingdom to the little flock (Lk. 12:32). God "was pleased" to reveal Jesus Christ to Paul (Gal. 1:15) and to save believers by the folly of the preaching of the cross (1 Cor. 1:21). God "was not pleased" with the majority of the Israelites in the desert period and destroyed

them (10:5). God decided that all the fullness of the Godhead should dwell in Christ (Col. 1:19).

(b) At the baptism of Jesus God's voice sounded out from heaven: "This is my Son, whom I love; with him I am well pleased" (Matt. 3:17; cf. Mk. 1:11; cf. Gen. 22:2; Ps. 2:7). This voice resounded with the same words at Jesus' transfiguration (Matt. 17:5; cf. 12:18). Here, too, it is a case of God's choice and determination, by which he has installed Jesus as Messiah. *eudokia* in 11:26 describes the transcendent purpose of God.

(c) The best-known place in the NT where *eudokia* occurs is Lk. 2:14, in an expression that corresponds to that of Qumran (see above). The phrase refers to people "on whom [God's] favor rests," i.e., those whom God has elected in order to bring to salvation in Christ. The message of the angels to the shepherds of Bethlehem proclaims that God has sent his Messiah to earth. For this he is glorified in heaven; the effect on earth is divine "peace" (→ *eirēnē*, 1645). We are not dealing here with human goodwill. Rather, we are dealing with God's sovereign and gracious will, which elects for itself a people for salvation and sanctification.

(d) In Phil. 2:13 Paul summons the congregation to work out their salvation in fear and trembling, because God is at work in them, inspiring "to will and to act according to his good purpose [or, for his own chosen purpose]." God has chosen believers and continues to work in them so that his elective purpose reaches its goal. The passage brings together the sovereignty of God and the responsibility of humankind.

In Eph. 1:5, 9, *eudokia* is synonymous with "will," "purpose," and "plan." Believers have a place in God's eternal will and election, which have salvation and holy living as their goal. God's free grace is the central point of these statements. The concise formulation in the prayer of 2 Thess. 1:11 ("that ... he may fulfill every good purpose of yours") likewise means that God's elective purpose is directed toward the conduct of Christians. Paul prays that God's will may be done and reach its goal.

2306 (eudokia, good will, good pleasure, favor, wish), → *2305.*

2307 (euergesia, kindness, a good deed, well-doing), → *2237.*

2308 (euergeteō, do work, benefit, show kindnesses), → *2237.*

2309 (euergetēs, benefactor), → *2237.*

2311 (eutheōs, at once, immediately), → *2789.*

2317 (euthys, at once, immediately), → *2789.*

2320 (eukaireō, have opportunity), → *2789.*

2321 (eukairia, favorable opportunity, the right moment), → *2789.*

2322 (eukairos, opportune), → *2789.*

2323 (eukairōs, when convenient), → *2789.*

2325 εὐλάβεια

εὐλάβεια (*eulabeia*), fear, awe, piety (*2325*); εὐλαβής (*eulabēs*), devout (*2327*); εὐλαβέομαι(*eulabeomai*), to reverence, to be afraid (*2326*).

CL & OT 1. The *eulabeia* word group originally denoted caution, discretion, and later reverence. The meanings fear and reverence are found in early Christian lit. From the basic meaning of *eulabeia* there evolved the additional idea of fear, dread, anxiety.

2. In the LXX the vb. occurs frequently. The original meaning of *eulabeomai*, to take care, is recognizable in Deut. 2:4; Sir. 18:27; 26:5. But the meaning to fear predominates in the LXX (e.g., Exod. 3:6; 1 Sam. 18:15, 29). In Hab. 2:20 it denotes the awesome reverence that all the earth should have before Yahweh. It is frequently found in combination with *phobeomai*, from which it cannot be sharply distinguished. But *eulabeomai* can also mean to trust, seek or take refuge, honor (e.g., Nah. 1:7; Zeph. 3:12). *eulabeomai* thus approaches the

idea of devoutness. The adj. *eulabēs* means devout, godly; the noun *eulabeia* can mean fear (Jos. 22:24; Wis. 17:8) or circumspection (Prov. 28:14).

NT 1. *eulabēs*, devout, God-fearing, occurs 4x in the NT. This adj. describes the piety of Simeon in Lk. 2:25 and Ananias in Acts 22:12. In 2:5 the witnesses from the Jewish Diaspora on the day of Pentecost are described as "God-fearing" (cf. also the "godly men" who buried Stephen in 8:2).

2. *eulabeia* occurs in the NT only in Heb. 5:7 and 12:28. In 5:7 Jesus was heard for his "reverent submission" to God (cf. 5:8). The raising of Jesus from the dead was God's answer to his Son's supplication in the days of his flesh (cf. Phil. 2:8–11). In Heb. 12:28, the understanding of *eulabeia* as fear is suggested by 12:29 (cf. Phil. 2:12, "fear and trembling"), but the idea of devoutness is equally possible (NIV, "reverence").

3. The vb. *eulabeomai* is found in the NT only in Acts 23:10 (as a variant reading to *phobeomai*, which has the same meaning, fear) and in Heb. 11:7, where it denotes the attitude of "holy fear" in Noah while he was building the ark.

See also *sebō*, to reverence, worship (*4936*).

2326 (eulabeomai, to reverence, to be afraid), → *2325.*

2327 (eulabēs, devout), → *2325.*

2328 (eulogeō, speak good of, praise, bless), → *2330.*

2329 (eulogētos, praised, blessed), → *2330.*

2330 εὐλογία

εὐλογία (*eulogia*), fine speaking, praise, blessing (*2330*); εὐλογέω (*eulogeō*), speak good of, praise, bless (*2328*); εὐλογητός (*eulogētos*), praised, blessed (*2329*); ἐνευλογέω (*eneulogeō*), bless (*1922*); ἀσπάζομαι (*aspazomai*), greet (*832*); ἀσπασμός (*aspasmos*), greeting (*833*).

CL 1. The *eulogeō* word group is compounded from the adv. *eu*, well, and the root *log-*, speak (word), and thus means to speak well. (a) Applied to form, speaking well refers to its aesthetic appeal, the attractive presentation of what one is saying. (b) Applied to content, speaking well expresses praise and extolling. This praise can be of things or persons, including praise of the gods (obj. gen.). In such a context *eulogeō* comes close to the meaning of *eucharisteō*, thank (→ *eucharistia*, 2374). One cannot ascribe to the Gk. gods a specific activity of blessing.

2. The etymology of *aspazomai* is obscure. It originally expressed liking and welcoming, respect and love for persons and things. Later, its application was limited to the act of greeting as opposed to the word of greeting (cf. *chaire*, hail!). It included offering one's hand, embracing, kissing, and genuflection. Correspondingly, the subst. *aspasmos* means first embrace, love, then greeting, visit.

OT In the LXX this word group is common (*eulogeō* occurs 450x), most often translating forms of the root *bārak* (bless). Such words are particularly common in Gen., Deut., Ps., and Tob. In order to understand the OT concept of blessing, we must deal not only with the *bārak*/*eulogeō* groups of words but also with texts that describe the blessing without using this terminology.

1. Basically *bārak* means endow with beneficial power, which involves both the process of endowing and the condition of being endowed. Hence, blessing originally involved a self-contained beneficial force that one could transmit to another; it stood in contrast to the destructive power of cursing (→ *kataraomai*, curse, 2933).

2. In the OT (esp. Gen. 12–36) one can find elements of the ideas and customs of blessing that were common in the ANE religions. (a) A blessing becomes effective because words, along with actions ratifying them, are invested with beneficial power (e.g., "you are blessed," Gen. 26:29). The actions that accompany the pro-

nouncement of a blessing have a symbolic significance—such as laying on hands (Gen. 48:13–18), raising hands or arms (Exod. 17:11), kissing or embracing (Gen. 48:10), touching clothes (2 Ki. 2:13–14), or placing the hand under the thigh (Gen. 24:9; 47:29).

(b) The imparted blessing works unconditionally and irrevocably. It is permanent and can neither be revoked nor rendered ineffective (Gen. 27:33; 2 Sam. 7:29).

(c) The blessing does not have its original setting in the sacral context of the cult, but in that of the family bonds of kinship.

(d) There are different occasions for blessing: a greeting (when one meets or leaves) (Gen. 47:7–10), and at climactic points in life—such as birth (Ruth 4:13–14; cf. Lk. 2:34), marriage (Gen. 24:60), and death (48:1–22; 49:28–33). Note esp. the blessing of the heir, by which the head of a family, before his death, conveyed his power chiefly to his firstborn son and thus passed it on to the next generation (27:1–40; 48:1–49:28).

(e) Anyone can impart a blessing or a curse. But some people were esp. endowed with a power to bless and curse, e.g., Melchizedek (Gen. 14:18–20), the seer Balaam (Num. 22), charismatic leaders like Joshua (Jos. 6), and later prophets and priests.

(f) In earlier times blessing had a mutual character. Not only did the mighty bestow a blessing on their inferiors (e.g., Melchizedek on Abraham, Gen. 14:18–20), but also the inferiors on the mighty (e.g., Jacob on Pharaoh, 47:7–10). Human beings reply to the blessings of a deity by blessing him, i.e., by recognizing his power in praise.

(g) The blessing works by producing fertility in people (Gen. 24:34–36) and in livestock and lands (30:25–43). It works vertically in the continued growth of succeeding generations, and horizontally in peace, security from enemies, good fortune, and well-being for a tribe or group (expressed comprehensively in the concept *šālôm*, well-being).

3. (a) The story of Balaam (Num. 22–24) demonstrates Yahweh's power to bless. Balak, king of Moab, apprehensive of an Israelite invasion into his land, called on the pagan soothsayer Balaam to help by cursing the foe (22:1–6). The point of the story is that Yahweh, Israel's God, is the master of the power to pronounce blessing. Balaam is deprived of his own innate powers and may only bless, not curse, at Yahweh's command (22:12, 31, 38; 23:3–5).

(b) The pronouncements of the blessing in the Balaam story (Num. 23:7–10, 18–24; 24:3–9, 15–24) have their true home in the formal pronouncements of blessing and cursing (cf. Gen. 9:24–26; 49; Deut. 28; 33). Blessing belongs to the language of the seer. It differs from the prophetic promise of salvation in the way it depicts salvation. It portrays the earthly well-being of the people or the land (see, e.g., Num. 24:5–6).

(c) The decisive incident of the historical understanding of the blessing in Israel's history occurs in the prologue to the story of the patriarchs (Gen. 12:1–3). The text contains a threefold command and a sixfold promise. (i) In the threefold command (12:1), Abraham must depart from his land, his tribe, and his family; he must break off his settled way of life, in order to travel on towards a vaguely indicated destination.

(ii) In the sixfold promise the root *bārak* occurs 5x. The blessing becomes an object of Yahweh's promise for future times. In Gen. 12:2–3 a son is not specifically named as the blessing promised to Abraham. Rather, the blessing is the great nation and the great name that this nation will obtain (fulfilled during the time of David and Solomon (cf. 2 Sam. 7:9). Genesis, however, takes up the tradition of the promise of a son or a posterity in the patriarchal stories (cf. Gen. 26:24) as what was necessary for the blessing to reach its fulfillment.

The final clause is the most comprehensive: "All tribes of the earth can obtain blessing in you" (alternate trans. of 12:3b; cf. 18:18; 28:14). This sentence is to be understood in the context of Gen. 1–11, which mentions 5x a curse on the human race (3:14, 17; 4:11; 5:29; 9:25). In contrast, 12:3b sets before "all tribes of the earth" a history of blessing. It includes liberation from vain toil (3:17), wandering

(4:11–12), base servitude (9:25), and the destructive chaos of the nations (11:1–9). Thus, Gen. 12:1–3 spans the histories of patriarchs, nation, and humanity with a promise of blessing.

4. (a) After Israel's settlement in Canaan, a lengthy struggle began over whether the Canaanite fertility gods (the Baals) or Yahweh (the God of promises who brought Israel out of Egypt) was to be honored as bestower of blessing. The fierceness of this clash is esp. apparent in the accounts of the prophet Elijah (1 Ki. 17–19). Yahweh is victorious and is confessed as Lord of the land. His continued activity in bestowing blessing in the promised land of Canaan adds a new element to his actions in history.

(b) This understanding of blessing is expressed in Deut. Here the whole nation receives the gifts of civilized society as blessings from Yahweh's hand (Deut. 28:3–7; cf. 7:13–16). Yahweh's blessing is expressed here in this-worldly terms. In contrast to the concept of blessing in Gen. 12:2–3; 15:1–6; 18:18; 26:24, Deut. does not speak of blessing in the form of an unconditional promise, but in conditional sentences: "*If* you fully obey the LORD your God and carefully follow all his commands . . . all these blessings will come upon you" (Deut. 28:1–2; cf. 28:15–16). The blessing is thus an element in the covenant between Yahweh and Israel. As Yahweh fulfils his covenant obligations in blessing, so Israel is bound to keep the covenant.

The reverse side of this conditional blessing is the curse that attends Israel's failure to keep its obligations. That is the significance of the command of Deut. 11:29 to set the blessing on Mount Gerizim and the curse on Mount Ebal. The two possibilities between which Israel must choose (30:19) are developed at length in ch. 28.

(c) Besides Yahweh, the real bestower of blessing, there are also individual people or groups who mediate blessing: kings, prophets, and priests. The role of the king in mediating blessing is not as prominent in Israel as, e.g., in Egypt. But the promise given by Nathan (2 Sam. 7:16) shows that the Davidic kingship conveys blessing. The first temple at Jerusalem is consecrated with a twofold act of blessing by Solomon before and after the prayer of consecration (1 Ki. 8:14, 55). The extent to which the king was seen as bringing blessing is particularly clear in the messianic texts that speak of a new king who will bring his nation the blessings of well-being and peace (cf. Isa. 9:6–7; 11:1–16).

Part of the task of the early prophets was to intercede for Yahweh's blessing on the nation (Elijah in 1 Ki. 18:41–45; Elisha in 2 Ki. 6:24–7:1; Amos 7:1–6). The later literary prophets proclaimed well-being in the form of a future activity of Yahweh, which they portrayed as an earthly salvation. It is seen as a messianic kingdom of peace (Isa. 11; Zech. 9:9–10), a quiet and prosperous life (Mic. 4:3–4; Zech. 9:17), prosperity (Isa. 55:1–5), the destruction of enemies (27:1), and universal well-being (65:17–25).

5. (a) Blessing also plays an important part in Israelite worship. That is apparent in the consecration of Solomon's temple (1 Ki. 8:14, 55). The temple as the holy precinct is the true place for the mediation of blessing to the nation and the land. The blessing was bestowed at the close of worship on the members of the cultic community as they returned to their houses (cf. *bārak* in Ps. 65; 115:12–15; 128; 129:8; 132; etc.). The community responded by praising Yahweh, using the same word, *bārak* (see 18:47; 28:6; 66:20; 68:20; 124:6; etc.).

(b) The theology of blessing in the priestly tradition presupposes the institutions of the cult. The bestowal of blessing is a privilege of the Levitical priests. Lev. 9:2–23 tells of the first pronouncement of the priestly blessing at the end of the first service of sacrifice in the tabernacle. It is confirmed by the appearance of Yahweh's glory. Num. 6:24–26 records the wording of the priestly blessing, to be pronounced at the end of every act of worship: "The LORD bless you and keep you; the LORD make his face shine upon you and be gracious to you; the LORD turn his face toward you and give you peace." This rhythmic blessing falls into three parts, each of which describes Yahweh's blessing and cites his promises—protection, grace, and well-being (Heb. *šālôm*).

(c) While the concept of blessing in Num. 6 is related to the cultic community, the blessing pronounced in Gen. 1:28 embraces all creation: "Be fruitful and increase in number; fill the earth and subdue it" (cf. 1:22). Ultimately, God intends all humanity to be blessed.

6. (a) The dramatic dialogues in Job show the limitations of the OT teaching about blessing. There can be no mechanical application of the theology of blessing of Deut., the theology upheld by Job's friends, for it does not square with the reality of Job's sufferings (cf. also Ps. 73; the skepticism of the Preacher in Eccl.). Yahweh's blessing is no longer primarily experienced in the present but is awaited in the promised *eschaton*.

(b) In rab. Jud. pronouncements of blessing and praise are widespread. The first tractate of the Mishnah, *Berakoth*, includes numerous praises introduced with the formula "Praised be the Lord." The rabbis knew of appropriate praises for the most widely varied situations of daily and cultic life.

(e) The texts of the Qumran community include hymns of praise, some of which begin with the formula "Praised are you, Lord." The extant fragments of the Blessings Scroll (1QSb) contain blessings for priests and other persons.

NT Compared with the fundamental significance of blessing in the OT, the NT gives less prominence to both the concept and the act. The group of words associated with the root *eulog-* occurs 67x in the NT. This group is most frequent in Lk., the major Pauline letters, and Heb.

1. The aesthetic sense of *eulogia* found in cl. Gk. is alluded to in a deprecatory fashion in Rom. 16:18: "Such people are not serving our Lord Christ, but their own appetites. By smooth talk and flattery (*eulogia*), they deceive the minds of native people."

2. (a) Far more often (40x) the root has the meaning praise, extol. The adj. *eulogētos* means blessed, praised. This usage derives from the basically secular Gk. meaning, speak well of someone, and from the LXX translation of the OT form of praise of God, "Blessed (i.e., praised) be Yahweh." In this context it takes on a doxological character. Zechariah's hymn (Lk. 1:68) and some letters (2 Cor. 1:3; Eph. 1:3; 1 Pet. 1:3) begin with the formula "Praise be to . . . God (the Lord)." Another form of doxology occurs as a short interjection of praise in Paul's letters (Rom. 1:25b; 9:5; 2 Cor. 11:31). It is expanded as a hymn in Rev. (5:13b; 7:12).

(b) The greeting of a superior was expressed not by the doxological adj. *eulogētos* but by the perf. part. pass. of *eulogeō: eulogēmenos*. This expresses not only praise and greeting but recognition that God has blessed the person concerned. Jesus, for example, is greeted with this cry in his triumphal entry (Mk. 11:9 par.; cf. Ps. 118:26). This form of greeting also welcomes the coming of God's kingdom, initiated with the Messiah's coming (Mk. 11:10). It is also applied to Mary, the mother of the Messiah (Lk. 1:42).

(c) The Jewish custom of offering praise on various occasions in everyday life and in worship is also attested in the NT writings (Lk. 1:64; 2:28–29, 34; 24:53; 1 Cor. 14:16; Jas. 3:9–10). According to the Synoptics, Jesus pronounced a blessing as a prayer at table before and after meals (Mk. 6:41 par.; 8:7; 14:22–23; Lk. 24:30). As the parallelism of *eulogeō* and *eucharisteō* (→ *eucharistia*, *2374*) in Mk. 8:6–7; 14:22–23 shows, the blessing at meals gives thanks to the Creator for his material gifts.

3. Where the *eulogia* word group occurs with the special sense of bless or blessing (28x), the NT is oriented more toward the theology of blessing in the OT than toward that of later Jud. But the NT presents no special theology of blessing. It refers to it incidentally as something familiar to its readers.

(a) In the Synoptics the idea of blessing is significant in three pericopes: (i) the blessing of the children, (ii) Jesus' commissioning of the Twelve, and (iii) the departure of the risen Jesus from his followers.

(i) In laying his hands on the children and blessing them (Mk. 10:13–16 par.), Jesus did nothing unusual. On the contrary, he acted like a Jewish father or rabbi. Note that his activity is not limited to adults; it also includes children and so embraces people at all stages of life.

(ii) The context of the commissioning in Matt. 10:1–16 shows that the instructions to greet houses (10:12, *aspazomai*) refers to the greeting of blessing (cf. 10:13, "peace"). As in Jesus' own ministry, the disciples have a twofold task: to preach the kingdom of God and to heal (10:7–8a). They are sent out as evangelists and bearers of blessing, like Jesus' own mission. Acts also shows the complementary activities of the apostles in proclaiming salvation by word and deed. There blessing does not reach its fullness until the missionary preaching has given way to the regular building up of churches. It is, therefore, not surprising that blessing is not as often spoken of in the NT as in the OT.

(iii) Behind the risen Christ's benediction in Lk. 24:50–51 lies the custom of blessing given at departure. The departing Lord shares with his church the power of his blessing, through which he remains bound to it. Its content is the presence of the exalted Lord with his church (see Matt. 28:20; cf. Gen. 26:3).

(b) Of NT writers Paul uses the concept of blessing most deliberately and gives it its new Christological form. (i) In Gal. 3:8 he cites Gen. 12:3b: "All nations will be blessed through you." The fulfillment of the blessing promised to Abraham is now seen as God's redeeming act in Christ. The gift of the blessing is no longer that of a great nation or of the fruitfulness of the land, but the promised Spirit of Christ (3:14). The common ground between the quotation from Gen. and Paul's interpretation is that both the promised blessing and its fulfillment in Christ should reach all nations (3:8, 14). In 3:8–14 Paul so interprets the relation of blessing and curse that, through Christ's taking to himself the curse of the Mosaic law in his death (3:13), believers of all nations now receive the blessing of God's redemption in Christ (3:14; cf. Eph. 1:3; Acts 3:25–26).

(ii) The phrase *eulogias Christou* (Rom. 15:29) does not mean an act of blessing but the effect of the preaching of Christ in the church. Paul is certain that his coming to Rome will further the growth of the community.

(iii) The connection between blessing and gifts (cf. Gen. 33:11) is shown esp. in 2 Cor. 9:5–6. Paul calls the collection he has been making for the community at Jerusalem a *eulogia*, a generous gift. The Corinthian church should contribute ungrudgingly (*ep' eulogiais*), not grudgingly, so that through this gift God's blessing may be given tangible expression in the Jerusalem church.

(c) Heb. makes fullest use of the OT concept of blessing found in the stories of the patriarchs (e.g., 6:7–8). It frequently alludes to or paraphrases OT benedictions: 6:14 (Abraham, cf. Gen. 22:16–17); 7:1–7 (Melchizedek, cf. Gen. 14:18–20); 11:20 (Isaac, cf. Gen. 27:27–40); 11:21 (Jacob, cf. Gen. 48:15–16). The book's purpose in telling these examples is stated in 6:12: "to imitate those who through faith and patience inherit what has been promised." The parallelism of blessing and promise shows that blessing here means eschatological well-being (cf. also Matt. 25:34).

(d) Finally, there are the paraenetic texts on blessing: Lk. 6:27–28; Rom. 12:14; 1 Cor. 4:12; 1 Pet. 3:9. Here Jesus' disciples are exhorted to meet the curses or reproaches of their enemies with the opposite, blessing. Blessing here means simply a friendly disposition toward one's enemies. The commandment to love one's enemies replaces the *lex talionis* (cf. esp. 1 Pet. 3:9). What Paul formulated Christologically is here developed in paraenesis. The opposition of blessing and cursing is abolished. Since Christ has taken the curse upon himself (Gal. 3:13), Christians can only be exhorted to bless (Rom. 12:14).

See also *makarios*, blessed, happy (*3421*).

2335 (eunouchizo, castrate), → *2336*.

2336 εὐνοῦχος	εὐνοῦχος (*eunouchos*), eunuch (*2336*); εὐνουχίζω (*eunouchizo*), castrate (*2335*).

CL & OT This word seems to be a Sem. loanword, denoting primarily a guardian of the harem, an office that was normally held by castrated men. Sometimes when *eunouchos* is used of a high official of state (cf. Acts 8:27), it is no longer clear whether it is literally a eunuch or whether it has become a mere title. The term is also used for castrated animals and plants that do not bear seed. The vb. *eunouchizō* denotes the act of castration.

Almost half the OT occurrences of this word are in Est. Where no stress seems intended, the Heb. word used here (*sārîs*) is probably simply a title of a court official (cf. the use of this word elsewhere in the OT, e.g., Potiphar in Gen. 39:1). Etymologically *sārîs* has nothing to do with castration. If it acquired the meaning of a eunuch, it was because many court officials fell into this class.

The eunuch was excluded from the community of Israel (cf. Deut. 23:1). This separated Israel from the fertility cults of its neighbors, which practiced both sacred prostitution and self-castration to the glory of the deity. In the last days the eunuch, who had been excluded, will find a place in God's salvation (Isa. 56:3–5).

Rab. Jud., like the OT, rejected castration, primarily because of the command to marry (see Gen. 1:28). It differentiates, however, between those who are sterile because of physical malformation and those who have been made eunuchs.

NT The treasurer of Queen Candace is called a eunuch (Acts 8:27), but perhaps it should not be taken literally (cf. OT usage). If he really was a eunuch, his conversion could be seen as a fulfillment of Isa. 56:3–5. Since the resurrection of Jesus the age of salvation and of the Messiah was dawning, and so such persons could be received into the community of salvation. The treasurer would have been a semi-proselyte; as a eunuch he could not be a full proselyte. The gospel was offered to the half-proselyte and any others who were until then excluded from the community of salvation (→ *prosēlytos*, *4670*).

The vb. *eunouchizō* is found twice linked with *eunouchos* in Matt. 19:12, where three types of eunuchs are described: (1) those who are such from birth, because of corporal malformation, (2) those who have been made such by others, (3) those who made themselves eunuchs "because of the kingdom of heaven." Jesus is clearly speaking not merely of celibacy, but also of unfitness for marriage, esp. for physical reasons. Under the first two headings Jesus adopts the division accepted by the rabbis. Only the third category presents something new, showing that the real stress falls here. Physical inability by nature or castration is intended in the first two, but this is improbable in the third. There were those who took it lit. in the early centuries of the church (e.g., Origen), though he later clearly rejected a lit. understanding of the passage.

Perhaps Jesus is here reacting against a slander spoken against him and his disciples. Because he was unmarried he was perhaps accused of being a eunuch (cf. the charge in Matt. 11:19, "a glutton and a drunkard"). Jesus answers by referring to the kingdom of God. One's joy in it can be so great that one is prepared for the sake of the kingdom to renounce everything else—under some circumstances even marriage.

2338 (*euodoō*, to lead along a good road, succeed), → *3847*.

2347 (*euprosdektos*, acceptable, pleasant, welcome), → *1312*.

2351	εὑρίσκω

εὑρίσκω (*heuriskō*), find, discover (*2351*).

CL & OT 1. In cl. Gk. *heuriskō* means to find, discover, whether by searching or chance discovery. It is used lit. of searching for and finding something, and fig. of finding oneself (mid.) and of making an intellectual discovery (e.g., a law of nature). It can also mean to fetch, obtain, and to acquire, procure for someone.

2. In the LXX *heuriskō* is also used in a lit. and a fig. sense. The objects of finding can be either things (Gen. 31:35) or persons (e.g., Saul, 1 Sam. 10:21). In theological contexts its objects are God (e.g., Isa. 55:6), grace (Gen. 18:3; Exod. 33:13; Num. 11:11), and mercy (Gen. 19:19; Jdg. 6:17). The OT can even refer to finding life (Prov. 21:21) and rest (Sir. 11:19). In most passages in which the combina-

tion of seeking (→ *zēteō*, *2426*) and finding occurs, God is the one who can or should be sought and found (Isa. 55:6; 65:1; cf. Prov. 8:17; Jer. 29:13 = LXX 36:13; Wis. 13:6). Wisdom, too, as the knowledge of God, can be found (Prov. 14:6), although this notion was contested by Job in his inexplicable suffering (Job 28:12–13).

Seeking and finding God happens in prayer (Isa. 55:6) and hearing (Jer. 29:12–13 = LXX 36:12–13), in calling and answering; prayer leads in its turn to the return of the godless, who alter their way of life (Isa. 55:7) and through God's forgiveness are led to recognize that God's ideas and ways (55:8) are not the same as theirs. We must also remember that when God is found, he discloses himself to us and lets himself be found (55:6; Jer. 29:14 = LXX 36:14).

NT 1. (a) The range of meaning of *heuriskō* in the NT is the same as in the LXX. One can accidentally find things (e.g., a treasure, Matt. 13:44; leaves, 21:19) or encounter people (22:9; Jn. 1:41, 45). The apostle can find "children walking in the truth" (2 Jn. 4). There will be those who seek death as an escape in the final affliction but will not find it (Rev. 9:6). What is most important is whether we are "found . . . in the book of life" (20:15).

(b) *heuriskō* has a theological significance in Jn. 1:41: "We have found the Messiah" (cf. 1:45). This human finding is matched by God's free giving (6:39; 17:12, 22; 18:9). The three lost and found parables of Lk. 15 express an element of joy over the lost that is found (15:7, 10, 23).

The God who meets us in Jesus Christ seeks and finds the lost (Lk. 15:6, 8–10). He acts like a conscientious shepherd (15:1–6; Jn. 10:9) and like a forgiving father (Lk. 15:20, 22–24, 32). This being lost and being found again can be represented by the ideas of death and coming to life (15:24, 32). This divine finding, which is a creative act, is matched by returning on our part, by repentance (15:7, 10, 21), and by living out one's life to the full.

(c) It is understandable that the use of the pass. construction is particularly frequent, not so much with the meaning of find oneself—be found (Lk. 17:18; Acts 8:40)—as with that of being found out, show oneself. Followers of Christ no more want to be found a sinner (Gal. 2:17) or a false witness (1 Cor. 15:15) than the pious Jew wants to show himself to be fighting against God (Acts 5:39). The former are concerned with being found to be faithful stewards (1 Cor. 4:2), to be in Christ (Phil. 3:9), and to be worthy (Rev. 5:4), blameless (2 Pet. 3:14), and established in the faith (1 Pet. 1:7). What matters is the manner of life that the returning Lord finds in his servants (responsibility for one's neighbor, Matt. 24:46; faith, Lk. 18:8; watchfulness, Matt. 25:1–13; wise stewardship, 25:14–30).

It is also possible to speak of seeking and finding, or not finding, fault. The latter is the case with the question of Jesus' guilt during his trial (Lk. 23:4, 14, 22; Jn. 18:38; 19:4, 6; Acts 13:28; cf. also 1 Pet. 2:22, where Isa. 53:9 is quoted with a Christological interpretation). But it also applies to the trials in which his disciples, Peter and John (Acts 4:21), and later Paul (23:9; 24:20), were involved. Paul can "find" a certain state of affairs in his relationship to the law (Rom. 7:21), and the church at Ephesus can discover false people in their ranks (Rev. 2:2). The meaning of acquire is found in Heb. 9:12, that Christ has gained for us eternal redemption.

2. *heuriskō* frequently appears in the NT with *zēteō* (used lit., Matt. 12:43; Jn. 7:34; 2 Tim. 1:17; used fig., Matt. 7:7–8; Acts 17:27; Rev. 9:6; used in a parable, Matt. 13:45–46). Even where *zēteō* does not explicitly occur, *heuriskō* usually implies some sort of preliminary act before finding (e.g., 10:39; 11:29; Lk. 23:4). Passages like Matt. 13:44, which clearly refer to an accidental finding, are in the minority. The NT puts the stress less on the manner and way in which it is possible to find than on what is found (e.g., Jn. 1:41, see above). It is presupposed that a seeking took place prior (Matt. 7:7; Lk. 11:9). What one strives for and finds is by nature a gift (Heb. 4:16). It is also presupposed that by our way of life we will show ourselves to be followers of Jesus Christ (cf. Phil. 2:8 with 3:9).

3. The natural self primarily seeks to hold on to natural life in the sense of an instinct for self-preservation. We are able to find our lives, but only through death for Jesus' sake (cf. Matt. 16:25; Mk. 8:35; Lk. 9:24; Jn. 12:25–26). The real thing that is to be found is the kingdom of God (Matt. 13:44–46), "the road that leads to life" (7:14), "rest" (Matt. 11:29; cf. Isa. 28:12; Jer. 6:16)—which the unclean spirit cannot find (Matt. 12:43; Lk. 11:24)—and "favor [grace] with God" (Lk. 1:30; cf. Acts 7:46; Heb. 4:16).

Jesus is depicted as the one who finds faith (Matt. 8:10) or does not find it (cf. Lk. 18:8). He wants to find people who believe in him and his message. Where Jesus does find faith, those in whom it resides find the way to life and thus to a new way of life (Phil. 2:5–11).

See also *zēteō*, seek (*2426*); *eraunaō*, search (*2236*).

2354 (*eusebeia*, devoutness, piety, fear of God, religion), → *4936*.

2355 (*eusebeō*, reverence, be devout), → *4936*.

2356 (*eusebēs*, God-fearing, devout, pious), → *4936*.

2357 (*eusebōs*, godly, in a godly manner), → *4936*.

2359 (*eusplanchnos*, tenderhearted, compassionate), → *5073*.

2370	εὐφραίνω

εὐφραίνω (*euphrainō*), gladden, cheer (up) (*2370*); εὐφροσύνη (*euphrosynē*), joy, gladness, cheerfulness (*2372*).

CL & OT 1. *euphrainō* in cl. Gk. means, in the act. to cheer, gladden a person; in the mid. and pass. to make merry. *euphrosynē* means merriment, joy, good cheer. Such joy stems largely from events and situations that give rise to communal rejoicing, such as a banquet. Philosophers also use the word for introspective and spiritual joy.

2. (a) In the LXX *euphrainō* occurs more frequently than *chairō* and is not sharply distinguished from *agalliaō* (→ *22*). It occurs in Deut., the Deuteronomistic historical works, and esp. Ps., Lam., Eccl., and Isa. In the Apocr. Sirach uses it frequently. The distribution is similar with *euphrosynē*. The word is clearly the appropriate expression for the joy of the believing community expressed at cultic celebrations or sacrificial feasts.

(b) Joy can also be that of the heart of an individual, esp. in response to God's help in situations of need (cf. Ps. 13:5). *euphrainō* is used alongside *agalliaō* to express the joy in which even the heavens and the earth participate (Ps. 96:11; 97:1), God also rejoicing with them (Isa. 65:19). Joy is a feature of God's eternal world. Festive joy at the great communal feasts—the human enjoyment of eating, drinking ,and bodily refreshment—becomes a vivid picture of our joy in the coming kingdom.

(c) For the rest a wide diversity of usage can be found: joy as an emotion (e.g., Ps. 16:11), joy in someone or something (2 Sam. 1:20; Eccl. 11:9), joy in God (Neh. 8:10–12; Ps. 33:21), joy in God's word (Ps. 119:74; Jer. 15:16), and joy in the time of salvation (Isa. 35:10; 55:12).

3. In rab. Jud. joy is still of great importance. Joy in God's law now occupies a large place. The festivals, esp. Passover and the Feast of Tabernacles, are joyous occasions. In Qumran, salvation is seen as already present, and there is rejoicing over God's redemptive gifts (cf. 1QM 12:13; 13:12–16; 1QH 11:23; 18:14–16; CD 20:33).

4. Philo's piety is esp. marked by *euphrosynē*. Taking festive joy as his starting point, he finds joy merely in seeking God. God himself radiates joy by means of the Logos.

NT In the NT the word *chairō* (→ *5897*) is the preferred word for joy. *euphrainō* occurs 14x (5 of which are in OT quotations).

1. In line with the OT, the words are clearly connected with the rejoicing found at a festive banquet. *euphrainō* thus denotes in the NT the joy of the festive company. In Lk. 12:19; 16:19, it refers to eating, drinking, and enjoying oneself. This is what a person without God sees as supremely worthwhile and what material possessions are thought to be for. But emphasis on the joy wrought by God is a peculiar feature of Lk.'s writings. Thus 15:23, 32, contains an invitation to make merry over the return of the lost son, while the elder son enviously desires a similar joyous feast for himself (15:29).

Acts 14:17 speaks of joy in the gifts of nature as being God's gifts in creation. Acts 2:26, 28, applying Ps. 16:8–11 to the resurrection, speaks of joy in the presence of God. On the other hand, Acts 7:41 refers to the shameless rejoicing of Israel when worshiping before the golden calf (cf. Exod. 32:4, 6).

2. In Rom. 15:10 and Gal. 4:27 Paul, influenced by OT quotations, uses this word group. In Rom. 15:10 he sees the fulfillment of Deut. 32:43—rejoicing that the message of Christ has now come to the Gentiles. Similarly in Gal. 4:27 (quoting Isa. 54:1), the call to rejoice is applied to the Jerusalem that is above, the church of the new covenant. Likewise in Rev. 12:12 and 18:20, based on OT quotations (cf. Isa. 44:23; 49:13; Jer. 51:48; not Rev. 11:10, however), eschatological rejoicing is expressed by *euphrainō*. Insofar as such joy often appears in the NT under the figure of a joyous feast and that Jesus himself, when on earth, did not hesitate to join in the festivities of the common meal, *euphrainō* is in full accord with the joyous message of the gospel.

See also *agalliaō*, exult, rejoice greatly, be overjoyed (*22*); *chairō*, be glad, rejoice (*5897*).

2372 (*euphrosynē*, joy, gladness, cheerfulness), → *2370*.

2373 (*eucharisteō*, be thankful, thank), → *2374*.

2374	εὐχαριστία

εὐχαριστία (*eucharistia*), thanksgiving (*2374*); εὐχαριστέω (*eucharisteō*), be thankful, thank (*2373*); εὐχάριστος (*eucharistos*), thankful (*2375*); ἀχάριστος (*acharistos*), ungrateful (*940*).

CL & OT 1. *eucharistia* comes from the root *chair-/char-*, the main words of which express the feeling of joy (→ *chairō*, to rejoice, *5897*; *charis*, grace, *5921*); the initial *eu* is an adv. meaning well, rightly, properly. Thus *eucharistia* means a thankful attitude, an expression of gratitude, thanksgiving. The adj. *eucharistos* means pleasant, well-behaved, or thankful. The vb. *eucharisteō* means to be thankful, owe thanks, give thanks.

2. The word group is only once represented in the OT canonical books (Prov. 11:16, where the adj. translates Heb. *ḥēn*, charming, graceful). In the Apocr. the vb. is found 6x (e.g., Wis. 18:2; 2 Macc. 1:11; 10:7), the noun 4x (e.g., Wis. 16:28; Sir. 37:11). Both are used for thanks from one person to another and from humanity to God.

(a) In 2 Macc. 12:31 the Maccabean army thanks certain heathen people for the kindness shown the Jews living in Scythopolis. In Add. Est. 16:4, certain officials withhold the gratitude that they owe to their benefactor, the Persian king. According to Sir. 37:11, experience shows that one should not consult with a grudging person about gratitude.

(b) Reasons for thankfulness to God are salvation from oppression by enemies and persecution (2 Macc. 1:11; 3 Macc. 7:16), but also being put to the test, which is seen as an opportunity for God to work out his salvation in preservation (Jdt. 8:25). Wis. 18:2 records the thanks of the holy ones for their preservation from guilt toward those who abuse them. Wis. 16:28 advises people to begin the day before dawn with thanksgiving.

NT 1. Of the 38x *eucharisteō* occurs in the NT and the 15x for *eucharistia*, Paul uses the vb. 24x, the noun 12x. *eucharistos* is found only in Col. 3:15, and *acharistos* only in Lk. 6:35; 2 Tim. 3:5. The noun and vb. are almost exclusively reserved in the NT for thanksgiving to God. Only 3x (Lk. 17:16; Acts 24:3; Rom. 16:4) are they used for thanks to humans; the first and last instances are to be understood in the context of spiritual action, while in Acts 24:3 we have an example of respectful Jewish speech.

2. These words are common in the opening sections of Paul's letters. Whatever detailed admonition and criticism may follow, the apostle usually writes of his thankfulness to God for those to whom he is

writing: for their faith and its influence "all over the world" (Rom. 1:8; cf. 2 Cor. 1:11), for the harmony between faith and love in action (Eph. 1:15–16; Col. 1:3–4; 1 Thess. 1:2–3), for the grace given to the church (1 Cor. 1:4), for sharing in the gospel (Phil. 1:3, 5), for God's work of election (2 Thess. 2:13), and for steadfastness in hope (1 Thess. 1:2–3).

3. When Paul exhorts his readers to thanksgiving, he normally uses the noun. This word is always used absolutely; it marks out thanksgiving and the showing of gratitude as basic and lasting elements of the Christian life (cf. *eucharisteō* in Eph. 5:20; Col. 3:17; 1 Thess. 5:18). No petition and intercession can be made without simultaneous thanksgiving (Phil. 4:6; Col. 2:7; 4:2; 1 Tim. 2:1). A life based on thanksgiving (Eph. 5:4) is the converse of an evil life.

4. The vb. is found in Matt. 15:36; Mk. 8:6; Acts 27:35; Rom. 14:6; 1 Cor. 10:30; and the noun in 1 Tim. 4:3 in the technical sense of the benediction before a meal, according to Jewish custom, beginning with the words, "You are blessed, Yahweh our God, King of the universe." The vb. is found also in the words of institution of the Lord's Supper—with both bread and wine in Lk. 22:17, 19, with the bread only in 1 Cor. 11:24 (though 11:25 "in the same way" implies it for the wine), with the wine only in Matt. 26:27; Mk. 14:23 (but the use of *eulogeō*, to bless, with the bread is an equivalent; → *eulogia*, blessing, *2330*). Hence, during the 2d cent. *eucharistia* became the general name for the whole service of the Lord's Supper (the Eucharist).

We have prayers of thanksgiving quoted in Lk. 18:11–12 (the self-satisfied Pharisee) and Jn. 11:41–42 (Jesus at the tomb of Lazarus). The word is used absolutely in 1 Cor. 14:16–17 for a prayer of thanksgiving in a tongue.

5. Apart from the introductions of his letters, Paul often mentions praise for general and specific gifts of grace: for increasing grace (2 Cor. 4:15), for a share "in the inheritance of the saints in the kingdom of light" (Col. 1:12), for reception of the word preached as the word of God (1 Thess. 2:13), and for the gift of tongues (1 Cor. 14:18). For all that, in 1 Cor. 14:18 (cf. 1:14) there is a depreciatory note when he speaks about his thanksgiving, so as to deflect the interest of his readers to the true building up and unity of the church. Paul's collection would awaken thanksgiving to God among those who received it (2 Cor. 9:11–12).

6. Both noun and vb. can mean the thanksgiving of the doxologies in the apocalyptic hymns (Rev. 4:9; 7:12; 11:17).

See also *aineō*, to praise (*140*).

2375 (eucharistos, thankful), → *2374.*

2376 (euchē, prayer, oath, vow), → *4667.*

2377 (euchomai, request, vow), → *4667.*

2379 (eupsycheō, to cheer), → *6034.*

2380 (euōdia, fragrance, aroma), → *4011.*

2381 (euōnymos, left [hand]), → *754.*

2384 (ephapax, once for all), → *562.*

2392 (ephistēmi, appear, stand beside), → *2211.*

2397 (echthra, enmity), → *2398.*

| 2398 | ἐχθρός |

ἐχθρός (*echthros*), hostile, hated, enemy (*2398*); ἔχθρα (*echthra*), enmity (*2397*); ἀντίδικος (*antidikos*), enemy, opponent (*508*).

CL & OT In cl. Gk. *echthros* in the pass. sense means hated, hateful; in the act. sense, hostile, enemy, opponent. *antidikos* was originally an opponent in a trial.

In the LXX *echthros* occurs more than 450x, usually to designate enemies in military conflicts, the nations with which one is in a state of war (1 Sam. 29:8; Nah. 3:11, 13), or one's personal enemies (Exod. 23:4; Num. 35:23; Ps. 5:8; 13:2, 4). In the case of Israel's enemies it is not a matter merely of national enemies in the normal sense. Since Israel is God's people, its enemies are also God's enemies (Exod. 23:22; Jos. 7:8). When God's people fall away from him, his enemies can be found within Israel itself (Isa. 1:24). The ungodly are the enemies of the righteous (Ps. 5:8–12; 55:3) and of God (37:20). Hope for the future centers on deliverance from one's enemies and on their destruction (Num. 24:18; Ps. 110:1–2; 132:18; Isa. 62:8; Mic. 5:9).

NT 1. In the NT *echthros* (occurring 32x) is first of all someone's personal enemy (Rom. 12:20; Gal. 4:16). The NT also reflects OT usage in that the coming of the era of salvation implies deliverance from one's enemies (Lk. 1:71, 74). In the prophecies concerning Jerusalem, enemies will besiege and destroy the city (19:43). Enemies rise against the two eschatological witnesses (Rev. 11:5, 12). The enemies of the cross of Christ will come to grief (Acts 13:10; Phil. 3:18). Enemies of Christ are referred to in those passages where Ps. 110:1 is cited as a prophecy of Christ (Matt. 22:44; Mk. 12:36; Lk. 20:43; Acts 2:35; 1 Cor. 15:25; Heb. 1:13; 10:13). In 2 Thess. 3:15 the reference is to someone disobeying Paul's instructions; fellowship is to be broken off, but this person is not to be regarded as an enemy.

Satan also can be described as *echthros* (Matt. 13:24–39; Lk. 10:19) and even *antidikos* (1 Pet. 5:8). Possibly here the thought is that of accuser in the final judgment (cf. Zech. 3), for *antidikos* is found elsewhere in the NT only in the sense of opponent in the law court (Matt. 5:25; Lk. 12:58; cf. 18:3).

Since the natural human rebels against God in thought and action, such a person is an *echthros* in relation to God (Rom. 5:10; Col. 1:21). According to Rom. 11:28, those Jews who do not yet believe are "enemies" for the Gentiles' sake. Because of their stubbornness and unbelief, God's salvation has come to the Gentiles.

When in Matt. 5:43–44 the command to love one's neighbor is contrasted with a call to hate one's enemy, the reference can hardly be to any OT passage (but cf. Ps. 31:6a; 139:21–22). We can compare Jesus' comments here to certain regulations of the Qumran community. Those who belonged to this community undertook a vow to "love all that he [God] has chosen and hate all that he has rejected" (1QS 1:3); and further, to "love all the sons of light, each according to his lot in God's community, and hate all the sons of darkness, each according to his guilt, in God's vengeance" (1QS 1:9–11). Josephus also reports that the Essenes had to swear to hate the unrighteous and to support the just. In contrast, Jesus calls us to love our enemies.

2. *echthra*, hate, enmity, existed between Herod Antipas and Pilate (Lk. 23:12), but as a result of their common action against Jesus this turned into friendship. In the catalogue of sins in Gal. 5:19–21 *echthra* is explicitly named as one of the "acts of the sinful nature" (5:20). The "sinful mind" is *echthra* against God (Rom. 8:7, "hostile to God"). Christ, however, has brought peace, in that he has through his cross removed that hostility as well as the hostility between Jews and Gentiles (Eph. 2:14, 16).

See also *miseō*, hate (*3631*).

| 2400 | ἔχω |

ἔχω (*echō*), have (*2400*); μετέχω (*metechō*), share, participate in (*3576*); μετοχή (*metochē*), sharing, participation (*3580*); μέτοχος (*metochos*), partaking, sharing, a partner, companion (*3581*).

CL & OT 1. *echō* means to have or hold in a wide range of senses: possess, keep, have, hold; aor. acquire, take into possession; intrans. keep, hold oneself. Thus the connection between the subj. and obj. of *echō* can denote a wide range of personal, material, and metaphorical meanings. Sometimes the subj. and obj. can exchange places (i.e., in Gk. one may say "he has a sickness" or "a sickness has him"). Moreover, the word can denote entry into any one of these conditions: to attain to, get hold of, come by.

metechō means to share or participate, with an obj. in the gen. The noun *metochē* means sharing, participation, and the adj. *metochos* likewise means sharing.

Two aspects of these words are theologically significant: There is the rational and material sense of having, and there is the enthusiastic sense of having, as being possessed, or mystical sharing. Various writers speak of *daimonion echein* (to have a demon), which acted in people. Later the idea broadened out into the pantheistic and mystical having of the divine One. In later philosophy it was no longer said that a person had *nous* or *logos* (reason). Instead, one was said to participate (*metechō*) in them. Plato used *metochē* (participation) to express the relationship of particular things to the Idea or Form. The lower and relative participates in the higher and absolute.

2. Heb. has no special word for *echō*. It uses instead a circumlocution, such as saying that something is in the hands of someone. *echō* is used to translate over 50 different Heb. expressions. It occurs more than 500x in the LXX, though many are in passages that have no Heb. original. It is the same with the compounds *metechō*, *metochē*, and *metochos*—words appearing only in later writings of the OT.

The theological significance of the words in this group is to be derived from the broader context of the Heb. Bible. At the heart of the OT message stands the confession that God has chosen his people, that they are his possession. The reverse is also true: He is his people's God (Ps. 33:12; 144:15; cf. Hos. 2:21–25). Therefore, there are to be no other gods beside him (Exod. 20:2–6). Because Yahweh is the God of his people, he is strength, rock, fortress, and Savior of the individual (e.g., Ps. 18:3; 27:1). Hence, Israel's confession: "Our God is a God who saves" (68:20; cf. 73:25). God is specifically the inheritance of the Levites (e.g., Deut. 10:9; Ezek. 44:28).

The relationship described through these concepts provides the basis for what the NT describes in its theological use of the idea of having. Paul, for example, clearly refers to this when he wrote that Israel had the law and boasted of it (Rom. 2:20, 23; cf. 10:2). Israel had "the adoptions as sons . . . the divine glory, the covenants, the receiving of the law, the temple worship and the promises . . . the patriarchs, and from them is traced the human ancestry of Christ " (Rom. 9:4–5). But Israel did not have the fulfillment of all this in Christ.

NT The distribution of *echō* in the NT has the same broad range of meaning as in cl. Gk. and the LXX. The following aspects are theologically significant.

1. *echō* is used as an expression for possession and relationship. The phrase *daimonion echein* (to have a demon), which occurs in cl. Gk., also occurs in the Synoptics (Matt. 11:18; Lk. 7:33). But the demon is only mentioned in the context of Jesus' lordship over it. For that reason the reproach that he had Beelzebub (Satan), i.e., that he was possessed by him, is absurd and blasphemous (Mk. 3:22, 30; cf. Jn. 7:20; 8:48; 10:20–21). It may be compared with the expression *akatharton pneuma echein*, to have or be possessed by an evil spirit (e.g., Mk. 7:25; cf. Lk. 4:33).

The NT also has such statements as to have children, sons, brothers, a wife, etc. The lame man at the pool of Bethesda says, "I have no one to help me into the pool" (Jn. 5:7). Similarly Paul: "I have no one else like [Timothy]" (Phil. 2:20; cf. 1:7). *Echō* is also used absolutely for sexual intercourse (Matt. 14:4).

Having is used in a theologically significant way in those passages in which a relationship with God is involved. The Jews claimed to have God as their father (Jn. 8:41). Similarly, Paul instructs, "Masters, provide your slaves with what is right and fair, because you know that you also have a Master in heaven" (Col. 4:1). This relationship between God and humans is further defined by Christ. Believers have him as their advocate with the Father (1 Jn. 2:1) and as their high priest (Heb. 4:14; 8:1; 10:19–21). Those who despise him already have a judge (Jn. 12:48).

2. As in the OT, this having fellowship with God is characterized not by human striving, but by God's promises and gift. This was also the ground of salvation in the OT. To have salvation is to have it through Jesus Christ: "Whoever hears my word and believes him who sent me has eternal life" (Jn. 5:24). This thought is stressed by Heb., Paul, and esp. Jn.

Jn. does this in his own special way. "He who has the Son has life; he who does not have the Son of God does not have life" (1 Jn. 5:12; cf. Jn. 3:15–16, 36; 2 Jn. 9). A person can know of God, talk about him, and even claim to have him, as the false teachers do, and still not have him. Here *echō* is the expression for genuine fellowship with God and true faith in its fullest and deepest sense. To "have fellowship" with one another and with Christ (1 Jn. 1:6–7) is to "know" him (2:3) and to "live" in him (2:6). These polemically intended words all refer to the same thing.

Jn.'s opponents see this fellowship with God as a mystical mastering of God. For Jn. this is possible only through the Son of God, who has become flesh. It comes through the witness of the Holy Spirit, whom Christians have (1 Jn. 2:20, 27; 5:10). Those who do not have the witness of the Father and his word living in them do not know God and have no life (Jn. 5:38–40). But those who stand in a personal relationship to the historical Jesus through the Spirit have the Father and life (1 Jn. 1:1–3; 4:13–16). To this also belong confession (4:2, 15), abiding in the doctrine of Christ (2 Jn. 9), and keeping his word and commandments (1 Jn. 2:3–6).

In this way Jn. takes up the prophetic message of John the Baptist, which saw the promised time of salvation break in with Christ. This is a theme that links Jn. with the Synoptics and Paul. For example, now in the present believers have peace with God (Rom. 5:1), redemption through his blood (Eph. 1:7; Col. 1:14), and access to God's gracious purpose in salvation (Eph. 3:12). Now is the day of salvation (cf. 2 Cor. 6:2).

3. Paul strongly emphasizes this theme in a different way. To participate in salvation is to be in Jesus Christ through his Spirit. It is a spiritual having: "If anyone does not have the Spirit of Christ, he does not belong to Christ" (Rom. 8:9). To have the Spirit means to be led by the Spirit (8:14). The believer is no longer his or her own (1 Cor. 6:19; cf. 3:16); he or she is Christ's slave (Rom. 1:1; 1 Cor. 7:22). This also means that to have the Spirit and to be bound to this Lord is to have this treasure in earthen vessels (2 Cor. 4:7) and to bear continually in our bodies the dying of Jesus (2 Cor. 4:10–12). Although the Spirit is the pledge and firstfruits (→ *arrabōn*, 775; Rom. 8:23; 2 Cor. 1:22; 5:5), the believer remains on this side of the barrier of death, which Christ has already broken through. But as the pledge of future resurrection glory, he gives us the certainty (Rom. 8:11) that one day our earthly house will be destroyed (2 Cor. 5:1) and we will participate in this glory.

Here lies the point of contrast between Paul and the enthusiasts in Corinth, who claimed that they already had the resurrection glory (1 Cor. 4:8, 10; 15:12). Paul opposed this with the gospel of the cross (1 Cor. 1:17, 23). In opposition to the self-seeking grandeur of "knowledge" that destroys, Paul stressed love, which builds up (8:1). Love is also opposed to libertinism (10:23–24; 13:2). For the sake of the gospel Paul had to bear much suffering, including bearing the dying of Christ in his own body (2 Cor. 4:10). But in this suffering he also received great strengthening and comfort (2 Cor. 1:5).

4. This having is to be understood neither as a permanent possession nor as absolution from obedience. This is underlined by the use of *metechō* in Paul and Heb. To share in *dikaiosynē* (righteousness, justification) puts the whole of one's life under obligation and excludes *anomia* (lawlessness, 2 Cor. 6:14). To be in Christ leaves no room for sin. Participation in the Lord's Supper rules out participation in pagan sacrifices, and vice versa (1 Cor. 10:17, 21). *metechō* is used virtually as a synonym for *koinōneō* (→ *3126*). In Heb. the concern is above all with sharing in the sufferings and patience of Christ. Those who "share in Christ" (Heb. 3:14; cf. 6:4) are thus called to patient endurance in persecution and to holding fast to the true faith, so that they may not lose their share in future glory. To be sharers in discipline (12:8) is in fact a sign of being a true child, for the Lord disciplines those whom he loves (12:6; cf. Prov. 3:12).

5. Just as all spiritual having comes under the lordship of the present and coming Lord, so is also the possession of all material

goods: "What do you have that you did not receive?" (1 Cor. 4:7). For all earthly goods God has to be asked in the right attitude (Jas. 4:2), and their use has to be seen in the light of eschatology. Paul is one who has nothing and yet possesses all things (2 Cor. 6:10). Therefore, he urges the Corinthians to have as if they did not have (1 Cor. 7:29–31). It is not simply that for the sake of future glory they are to break loose from all possessions. Such possessions are to be given to those in need (Eph. 4:28). Participation with God and with one another is now already a fact through the Holy Spirit, who establishes us in sonship, obedience, love, and hope.

See also *koinōnia*, communion, fellowship (*3126*).

Z zeta

2409 (zaō, live), → *2437.*

2412 (zestos, boiling, hot), → *6037.*

2414 (zeugos, a pair), → *2433.*

2419 ζῆλος

ζῆλος (*zēlos*), zeal (*2419*); ζηλόω (*zēloō*), to be zealous (*2420*); ζηλωτής (*zēlōtēs*), a zealot (*2421*).

CL & OT 1. In cl. Gk. *zēlos* denotes an emotional going out to a person, idea, or cause. Where the goal is good, it means eager striving, competition, enthusiasm, and even praise, glory. Where the goal is bad, it means jealousy, ill will, envy. Accordingly, *zēlōtēs* can denote a person seeking to reach good goals or a jealous, envious individual. Likewise, *zēloō* can mean to be zealous or to be jealous.

2. (a) The word group is found mostly in the later portions of the LXX (e.g., Prov. 6:34), where it often means zeal directed to God or passionate readiness for service controlled by God's will, i.e., by the law (e.g., 1 Ki. 19:10, 14; Ps. 69:9). The concept of striving for ethical perfection (Philo's use of the word) does not appear in the LXX.

(b) More frequent are passages that speak of God's zeal, sometimes translated jealousy. In Exod. 20:5 God calls himself *zēlōtēs* and cites two directions for his zeal: He turns it against the evildoers to punish them (i.e., *zēlos* connotes God's wrath; Num. 25:11; Deut. 29:20); but to those who fear him, it manifests itself as mercy (Isa. 63:15). As Lord of history, God displays his *zēlos* for his own people against heathen nations (e.g., 2 Ki. 19:31; Isa. 9:7; 26:11; Ezek. 36:6; 38:19). But he also manifests *zēlos* at Israel's unfaithfulness, which is often presented as adultery (Ezek. 16:38; 23:25–27).

(c) The OT usage continued in Jud. of the NT era. Qumran texts speak of God's zeal, which is expressed in his righteous judgments. The rabbis, however, hesitated to speak of God's zeal or jealousy, for they shied away from anthropomorphisms.

NT 1. *zēlos* occurs 16x in NT, *zēlōtēs* 8x; and *zēloō* 11x. Both good and bad senses of the word group occur. (a) The bad sense of jealousy is found in Acts 7:9 (of Joseph's brothers); 5:17; 13:45; 17:5 (of the Jews' jealousy of the apostles' success). Jealousy is a deadly danger to the continued existence of a church (1 Cor. 3:3; 2 Cor. 12:20; Jas. 3:16). A Christian should not show jealousy but must walk by the Spirit (Gal. 5:16, 20) and deal lovingly with others (Rom. 13:13). The NT also expresses a critical attitude toward the Jewish zeal for the law (cf. Rom. 10:2). Thus Paul rejects his earlier being "zealous for the traditions of [his] fathers" (Gal. 1:14), which had caused him to become a persecutor of the church (Acts 22:3; Phil. 3:6).

(b) But zeal in itself is not rejected. Paul rejoices that godly grief has produced repentance and zeal in the Corinthians (2 Cor. 7:11), and he explicitly calls us to be zealous for service to Christ (Tit. 2:14), who himself was zealous for God (Jn. 2:17). He praises the missionary zeal that surrounds others with good (Gal. 4:18; cf. 2 Cor. 11:2). Paul esp. instructs us to "eagerly desire" the gifts of the Spirit (1 Cor. 12:31; 14:1, 39), which is rightly used in a love that is free from jealousy (1 Cor. 13:4). Finally, the NT endorses a positive zeal for the welfare of others (2 Cor. 7:7; 9:2) and for doing what is right (1 Pet. 3:13), but here too love must take precedence over zeal.

2. In the NT era, there were several resistance groups against the Romans—from those led by Judas the Galilean (6 B.C.) to defenders of the fortress Masada (A.D. 74); *zēlōtēs* is a generic word for all these groups. Judas interpreted the first commandment to mean that none but God should be honored as king or Lord; thus, payment of taxes to the emperor should be rejected. The Zealots observed the Sabbath strictly, demanded circumcision even of the heathen, and had rigorous requirements for cleanliness. They willingly suffered martyrdom for their beliefs.

Jesus' disciple named Simon (Lk. 6:15; Acts 1:13) is called a *zēlōtēs*; i.e., he had presumably at one time been a Zealot. He is likely the same as "Simon the Cananaean" (Matt. 10:4; Mk. 3:18, NRSV), where *ho kananaios* probably translates Aram. *qanʾān*, zealot, i.e., *zēlōtēs*. The presence of a former Zealot among Jesus' disciples does not imply, as some have argued, his endorsement of the movement, and to interpret the cleansing of the temple (e.g., Matt. 21:12–17; cf. Jn. 2:13–17) as an act of resistance against Rome goes beyond the evidence. Note too how Jesus' teaching on paying taxes to Caesar (e.g., Mk. 12:13–17) repudiates Zealot ideals, as does his attitude toward the Sabbath (e.g., 2:23–3:5) and ceremonial washing (e.g., 7:15).

See also *spoudē*, zeal (*5082*).

2420 (zēloō, to be zealous), → *2419.*

2421 (zēlōtēs, a zealot), → *2419.*

2422 (zēmia, damage, disadvantage, forfeit, loss), → *3046.*

2423 (zēmioō, suffer damage, loss, forfeit), → *3046.*

2426 ζητέω

ζητέω (*zēteō*), seek (*2426*); ἐκζητέω (*ekzēteō*), seek, search for (*1699*); ἐπιζητέω (*epizēteō*), seek after, strive for, search for, want (*2118*); ζήτημα (*zētēma*), question, controversy (*2427*); ζήτησις (*zētēsis*), investigation, argument, discussion, debate (*2428*); ἐκζήτησις (*ekzētēsis*), useless speculation (*1700*).

CL & OT 1. In cl. Gk. *zēteō* has the general meaning of to seek. It became a technical term for striving after knowledge, used esp. for philosophical investigation. Occasionally *zēteō* was used as a legal term for a judicial investigation. *ekzēteō* and *epizēteō* emphasize the basic meaning of seek, investigate, strive. Apart from that, *ekzēteō* can refer to scientific investigation and *epizēteō* to legal searching or claims. The noun *zētēsis* could be used as a technical term for philosophical investigation.

2. The LXX uses *zēteō* some 400x and means to seek, aspire, demand, ask; the less frequent compounds *ekzēteō* and *epizēteō* denote an inquiry, investigation, or asking of questions. (a) *zēteō* can refer to nonreligious processes: Joseph sought his brothers (Gen. 37:16); Saul looked for the runaway female donkeys (1 Sam. 10:2, 14); Pharaoh sought to kill Moses (Exod. 2:15; cf. 4:19). The phrase "to seek the life of" is regularly used of the intent to kill (e.g., 1 Sam. 24:10; 25:29; 26:20; 1 Ki. 19:10, 14; Jer. 11:21). This OT seeking entails an activity that involves the whole person. People in the ANE regarded seeking as having an emotional and volitional element.

(b) When applied fig. to one's relationship to God, *zēteō* and its compounds denote the conscious turning of the Israelites to their God with all their being, or that of Yahweh to his people. The prophets frequently reproach the Israelites that they have not sought God (Isa. 9:13; 31:1; Jer. 10:21) and warn the rebellious people to seek their God, i.e., to be obedient to him (Deut. 4:29; Isa. 55:6; Jer. 29:13–14 = LXX 36:13–14). Esp. the Ps. (e.g., 24:6; 27:8; 83:16; 105:3–4) and 2 Chr. (e.g., 7:14; 11:16; 15:12; 18:4, 7) refer to seeking the Lord, seeking God, or seeking the face of the Lord. These expressions define what willing obedience to Yahweh means, though they also allude to cultic occasions like worship and prayers. To seek God thus acquires the meaning to seek after God where he is to be found, e.g., in the temple and in worship.

(c) Passages that refer to God's seeking are fewer but very important. Like a shepherd, God will seek his people who have wandered away and will gather them (Ezek. 34:12–16). Hence, the theological use of *zēteō* in the LXX serves to express the reciprocal covenant relationship between Yahweh and Israel.

(d) In Philo, philosophical thinking and questions of the intellect are connected with the seeking of the heart to form a unique synthesis.

NT 1. In the NT *zēteō* occurs 117x, mostly in the Gospels and in Paul's letters. Its range of meaning embraces the cl. Gk. and OT elements. Thus, *zēteō* in the NT refers to following and seeking something (Lk. 15:8) and to probing ideas and reflections (Mk. 11:18; 14:1, 11), as well as judicial enquiry (Jn. 8:50b). It can also mean anything from deliberate striving and desiring (Matt. 6:33; 1 Cor. 10:33) to asserting one's claims (Mk. 8:12). *ekzēteō* occurs only 7x in the NT and has an intensive sense (Lk. 11:50–51; Acts 15:17; Rom. 3:11; Heb. 11:6; 12:17; 1 Pet. 1:10). *epizēteō* occurs 13x and has a similar intensive force (e.g., Matt. 6:32; 16:4; Lk. 4:32; Acts 12:19; Rom. 11:7; Heb. 11:14). *ekzētēsis*, useless speculation, occurs only at 1 Tim. 1:4.

2. A parable tells of a merchant looking for beautiful pearls (Matt. 13:45) or of a housewife hunting through her home to find a drachma (Lk. 15:8). The passion narratives report that Judas sought for an opportunity to betray Jesus (Matt. 26:16; Mk. 14:11; Lk. 22:6). The use of *zēteō* here implies an act of the will.

3. Like the prophets, Jesus called on his hearers to seek God, i.e., to put their life at the disposal of God's will and rule: e.g., "But seek first [God's] kingdom and his righteousness, and all these things [about which you worry] will be given to you as well" (Matt. 6:33; cf. 7:7–8; Lk. 11:9–10; 12:31). According to Jn.'s Gospel, the Jews opposed this call by seeking Jesus' life (5:18; 7:1, 19; 8:37) and by trying to establish their own glory (5:44; 7:18).

4. Paul gives the clearest statement of the contrast between one's self-assertion and one's seeking of God in his discussion of Israel's rebuke for wanting to establish its own righteousness (Rom. 10:3); he sets over against it the way of faith that seeks to attain to righteousness in Christ (Gal. 2:17). Similarly, he censures his opponents who look "out for [their] own interests" (Phil. 2:21), while he ventures to assert of himself that he does not seek his own advantage (1 Cor. 10:33; cf. 13:5, where he states that love does not seek its own interests). Once again, the human will is involved.

5. Paul acknowledges the nations' search for God in Acts 17:27, and in 1 Cor. 1:22 he refers to Gk. questioning and striving after wisdom. In the NT the Gk. concept of *zētēsis* comes to mean an argument, battle of words, or dispute (Jn. 3:25; Acts 15:2; 25:20). Such disputes do not promote the faith or build up the Christian community, but are linked to strife, envy, and slander (1 Tim. 6:4; 2 Tim. 2:23, Tit. 3:9). The related word *zētēma* is limited in the NT to points of religious controversy, either within the Jewish community (Acts 18:15; 23:29) or within the church (15:2).

6. Finally, God's seeking must be mentioned. It includes both God's claim to the fruits of obedience (Lk. 13:6), to true worship (Jn. 4:23), and to faithful stewardship (1 Cor. 4:2) and the dedicated pursuit of the Son of Man, whose mission it is to seek the lost and rescue them (Lk. 19:10).

See also *heuriskō*, find, discover (*2351*); *eraunaō*, search (*2236*).

2427 (*zētēma*, question, controversy), → *2426*.

2428 (*zētēsis*, investigation, argument, discussion, debate), → *2426*.

2433	ζυγός

ζυγός (*zygos*), yoke, balance (*2433*); ζεῦγος (*zeugos*), a pair (*2414*); ἑτεροζυγέω (*heterozygeō*), be unevenly yoked, fig. be mismated (*2282*); συζεύγνυμι (*syzeugnymi*), yoke together, join together (*5183*); σύζυγος (*syzygos*), yokefellow, comrade, possibly wife (*5187*).

CL & OT 1. In cl. Gk. *zygos* has two meanings: (a) the yoke that beasts or slaves wear (means the same); the cognate vb. *zeugnymi* means to unite, bind; (b) a beam of a weighing balance or the balance itself (which resembles a yoke).

2. (a) The OT expressly forbids yoking together different kinds of animals (Deut. 22:10; note the context, which forbids mixing of crops, animals, and material). In Lev. 19:19, the noun *heterozygos* may refer to not allowing different species of animals to mate together.

(b) The OT knows both meanings of *zygos*. (i) It often denotes a yoke, the shaped piece of wood on the necks of working animals (e.g., Num. 19:2). But the noun was widely used fig., e.g., as a term for bondage (Lev. 26:13) or the burdensome servitude of the nation (*zeugos*, 1 Ki. 12:19–21). In this sense *zygos* became a symbol of political suppression (2 Chr. 10:4, 9–14). To this meaning belongs the yoke that Jer. wore as an acted-out parable, summoning Israel to submit to Nebuchadnezzar (27:2–11 = LXX 34:2–11). In breaking Jer.'s yoke, the prophet Hananiah proclaimed salvation from the foreign rule of Babylon (28:2–11 = LXX 35:2–11), a prophecy that was not fulfilled (28:13–17 = LXX 35:13–17). Liberation from enforced subjection is part of messianic prophecy (Isa. 9:3 = LXX 9:4; 10:27).

(ii) It can also mean scales, balances (e.g., Lev. 19:36; Isa. 40:12, 15). Yahweh requires true scales and honest dealings among people. But he also weighs human beings in his balances and finds them wanting (Ps. 62:9; Dan. 5:27). Job desires his calamities to be weighed in the balances (Job 6:2). In the background stands the idea of scales as a symbol of justice and Yahweh as the ultimate judge (31:6).

(iii) *zygos* receives an additional fig. meaning in the LXX in wisdom lit. Sir. 51:25–26, for example, instructs the reader to bring one's neck under the yoke of wisdom. This denotes an invitation to accept the Torah, for wisdom at this period was identified with the law. Jer. describes Israel's true relationship with Yahweh as a yoke that the wayward shake off (2:20; 5:5; the latter verse defines this relationship as knowledge of Yahweh and his law). Hel. Jud. identifies the yoke with the Torah, that one should submit oneself to Yahweh's will. This sort of burden marks out Israel from all other peoples.

(c) *zeugos* means a span holding a pair of animals together and hence also a pair (1 Ki. 19:19, 21; 2 Ki. 5:17; Job 1:3).

(d) *zeugnymi* means to bind (1 Sam. 6:7, 10; 2 Sam. 20:8); *syzeugnymi* occurs only in Ezek. 1:11, 23 and means to entwine, touch.

NT 1. *zygos* occurs only 6x in the NT. (a) Only in Rev. 6:5 does it mean a balance or scales, which the rider of the black horse has in his hand. The vision symbolizes inflation and scarcity, causing hardship among the lower classes but not seriously affecting the wealthy.

(b) In 1 Tim. 6:1 Paul addresses "all who are under the yoke of slavery," exhorting them to yield to the existing social order by showing respect to their masters. Slaves are not to take the law into their own hands and free themselves from servitude, but are to serve their masters (esp. believing ones) even better (6:2).

(c) Jesus' invitation in Matt. 11:29–30 recalls the language of the wisdom tradition: "Take my yoke upon you and learn from me, for I am gentle and humble in heart, and you will find rest for your souls. For my yoke is easy and my burden is light" (cf. Prov. 8:1–11; 9:5; esp. Sir. 51:25–26). Those who come to Jesus come to one who upholds the law (Matt. 5:17–18), but also to one whose interpretation of the law is in no sense a bondage. He is the one in whom the prophecies of the law and the prophets are fulfilled (cf., e.g., 1:22–23; 2:6, 15; 4:13–26). He is the bearer of salvation and the one in whom the kingdom of God and redemption have come (4:17; 12:28).

(d) In his speech to the Jerusalem council Peter asks the circumcision party why they want to put "on the necks of the disciples a yoke that neither we nor our fathers have been able to bear?" (Acts 15:10). He is probably taking up the Jewish language about the yoke of the law and interpreting it as a yoke of bondage. It is true that the devout Jew did not consider the yoke of the law as a burden (cf. Jn.

8:33). Yet the way the law was understood was not in fact a liberating experience (cf. Matt. 5:20; 6:2–18; 23).

(e) In Gal. 5:1, Paul likewise alludes to Jewish views about the yoke of the law, which he denounces as a yoke of slavery: "It is for freedom that Christ has set us free. Stand firm, then, and do let yourselves be burdened again by a yoke of slavery." Many Jews understood the law, esp. the law of circumcision, as something to be fulfilled as a condition of divine acceptance and salvation. The apostle saw this notion as fundamentally at variance with the redemptive death of Christ (3:10–14) and the Spirit-led life (5:18); the Christian life is based on grace and promise, and those who do not live by the promises of God are not children of God but slaves (4:28–31). Thus, he calls on his readers to take hold of their freedom in Christ and to walk by the Spirit (5:1–26).

2. The adj. *syzygos* (lit., yoked together) can mean yokefellow, comrade, and even wife. The identity of the "loyal yokefellow" in Phil. 4:3 is not clear. It may be a proper name (Syzygos), refer to Epaphroditus (cf. 2:25–30), or be some other person known to the Philippians but no longer to us.

3. *zeugos* means a yoke of two animals (Lk. 14:19) and a pair (2:24; cf. Lev. 5:11).

4. The vb. *zeugnymi*, to join, occurs as a variant reading in Mk. 10:9. Otherwise the compound *syzeugnymi* is used (see Matt. 19:6). Both vbs. are found in cl. Gk. and Josephus of marital union (→ *chōrizō*, to separate, divorce, *6004*).

5. In 2 Cor. 6:14 Paul uses *heterozygeō*, alluding probably to the yoking of different kinds of animals in Lev. 19:19; Deut. 20:20. What Paul means in this section is a matter of debate. The RSV interprets the injunction as a warning against mixed marriages: "Do not be mismated with unbelievers," which is not impossible (cf. the temple imagery used in 2 Cor. 6:16, which is used in 1 Cor. 6:18 as an argument against sexual immorality). But the whole context and argument of 2 Cor. 6:14–7:1 look beyond mixed marriages to idolatry and defilement in general. Thus, Paul does not want believers to get involved in *any* partnership with unbelievers where they might be tempted to give up their Christian moral standards.

This is not a Christian version of the Qumran insistence on separation from the world and disobedient Israel. Christians are to remain in the world, but they are not to be a party to idolatry and moral defilement. They are to seek to win the world but must not allow their faith to be compromised, esp. by pagan idolatry and the sexual mores of unbelievers (1 Cor. 5:1; 6:12–20; 10:14–23). The church is the community of God's elect, separate from the world (1:1–9). The outward shape of the world is passing away (7:29–31), and believers will some day judge the world (6:2–3).

| 2434 | ζύμη | ζύμη (*zymē*), yeast (*2434*); ζυμόω (*zymoō*), ferment (*2435*); ἄζυμος (*azymos*), unleavened, made without yeast (*109*). |

CL & OT 1. Leaven, in fermenting grain, is *not*, strictly speaking, yeast, but old, sour dough (stored and then used as a fermentation agent by adding juices), which was hidden in the new dough in order to permeate it and give it lightness. In the Roman state cult the Flamen Dialis was not permitted to come into contact with leaven because it sours and corrupts.

2. *zymē* is used in the LXX in cultic contexts concerned with regulations for feasts and sacrifices (e.g., Exod. 12:15, 19; Deut. 16:3). It was used in the peace and wave offerings (*zymitēs*, Lev. 7:13 = LXX 7:3), but was forbidden in the cereal offerings consumed by fire (2:11; 6:17). In the ritual of Passover and the Feast of Unleavened Bread all yeast was cleansed out from every Jewish home annually, and they ate only unleavened bread from that evening and the following seven days (Exod. 12:14–20), commemorating the Exodus from Egypt (12:34, 39). This process also served a hygienic purpose in breaking any chain of infection established by successive use of sour yeast.

3. Leaven was given different meanings in rab. tradition: a metaphor for human restraints on obeying God, and the Torah with its power to lead Israelites who observe it back to God. Philo allegorized it to mean not only swelling arrogance and pretension but also complete (spiritual) nourishment and blissful joy.

NT 1. *zymē* and *zymoō* appear in the Synoptic Gospels and in Paul. Each instance is in a literary figure, whose meaning varies from context to context.

(a) *Parable.* In Matt. 13:33; Lk. 13:21, the hidden but persistent expansion of the kingdom of God is compared to leaven hidden in dough until it permeates the whole lump. It ties in with the preceding parable of the mustard seed, which denotes enormous expansion from something minute. No indication is given of the significance of the dough, whether it is meant to refer to the culture of society or to the world as a whole.

(b) *Metaphor.* In Mk. 8:15 leaven is an attribute of the Pharisees and of Herod, of which the disciples are to beware. Matt. 16:11–12, in a warning against Pharisees and Sadducees, interprets the metaphor as their "teaching," and Lk. 12:1, in a warning against Pharisees alone, as "hypocrisy."

(c) *Proverb.* In 1 Cor. 5:6 and Gal. 5:9 Paul uses the words, "A little yeast works through the whole batch of dough." Proverbial in form, though not found outside Paul as a proverb, these words may have been associated in the Christian church with Jesus' parable of the yeast (cf. above). In 1 Cor. the proverb symbolizes the notion that the pride the Corinthians are expressing in their toleration of an open transgressor will inevitably work its way through the entire community. In Gal. the imagery refers to the influence of false teachers on the understanding of the congregation.

(d) *Type.* In 1 Cor. 5:7 Paul exhorts the community to "get rid of the old yeast." This is an injunction either to expel the offender (5:13) or to divest themselves of their "boasting" about associating with the transgressor. The grounds for the command are that Christ as the Passover Lamb has been sacrificed and that their church festivals are to be kept by expelling yeast ("malice and wickedness") and by partaking of bread without yeast ("sincerity and truth").

This type recalls the Passover ritual and the Christian identification of Christ with the Passover lamb (Jn. 19:14, 31; 1 Pet. 1:19). Just as the Jews removed all yeast before eating the Passover, so believers are to cast out wickedness because the Passover sacrifice has already taken place, whereby they are accepted and made new by God (1 Cor. 6:11). As occurs so often in Paul, the Christian imperative is based on the indicative (cf. also Rom. 6; 1 Cor. 6:19–20; Col. 2:20–4:1).

2. Apart from the uses of *azymos* in 1 Cor. 5:7–8, this word occurs in the NT in the pl. form *ta azyma*, meaning the Feast of Unleavened Bread. This was originally a harvest festival (Exod. 23:14–17) celebrated in the month Abib. It became part of the Passover ritual, set for 15–21 Nisan. The Jews regularly equated the Passover with the Feast of Unleavened Bread (cf. Ezek. 45:21; Lk. 22:1).

2435 (zymoō, ferment), → *2434.*

| 2437 | ζωή | ζωή (*zōē*), life (*2437*); ζάω (*zaō*), live (*2409*); συζάω (*syzaō*), live with (*5182*); ζῷον (*zōon*), living creature (*2442*); ζωογονέω (*zōogoneō*), procreate, give life to, keep alive (*2441*); ζωοποιέω (*zōopoieō*), make alive, give life to (*2443*); συζωοποιέω (*syzōopoieō*), make alive with (*5188*). |

CL 1. In cl. Gk. life refers in the first place to that living quality of nature that is shared by humans, animals, and plants. For the Gks., therefore, life belongs to the category of natural science. What causes life is the *psychē* (soul). Just as *psychē* and *zōē* belong together in Gk. thought, so do *psychē* and *sōma* (body); natural life is made up of the components soul and body.

Not only each individual but also the whole universe is thought of as a living organism or as a world with a soul. Even the gods are considered to be living creatures (zōa), having bipartite natures analogous to the human body and soul. A third component to human life is the reason, mind, or understanding (nous), which is a divine element that enters human life from outside, enhancing it beyond one's natural life.

2. Two trends are visible in the history of Gk. philosophy: True life is progressively divorced from concrete, everyday events and transferred to a supernatural, divine world; and life is increasingly seen as something tangible, "scientific," so that *true* human life manifests itself not so much in the continuum of historical events as in discontinuous moments of ecstatic vision, totally divorced from history.

(a) Among the Stoics the slogan "to live according to nature" implied life that is virtuous or lived according to reason, which enables the person, who is otherwise "dead," to fulfill the purpose of his or her existence. The Stoics idealized withdrawal from the outward bustle of the world to the cultivation of one's own inner life.

(b) Neo-Platonism differentiated between life in this world and life beyond this world. Humans possessed natural life, but life that is perfect and true can be found only in the one divine realm of the One. The way to this true life leads via negation of the body and cleansing from all earthly things. In other words, life is an upward ascent.

(c) Gnosticism, by contrast, saw life as a descent. Life is essentially divine, something indestructible and immortal. In the human world this pure life is intermingled with matter, being imprisoned in the body. Hence, one must break free from this prison in order to enjoy, at least temporarily, the ecstatic vision. This true life is attained on earth only in fleeting moments of ecstasy; its full enjoyment is reserved for the future, when matter reunites with the divine world.

OT 1. The OT Israelites viewed life as something thoroughly natural, vital, and pertaining to this world. The Gk. division of life into body, soul, and reason was alien to them. It is true that soul (e.g., Jos. 10:28) or flesh (e.g., Gen. 6:13) can be used in place of life, but this is an example of the synthetic approach, where a part can represent the whole. In those passages where the life is said to be the blood (Lev. 17:11, 14; cf. Gen. 9:4; Deut. 12:23), this should be understood not as a scientific statement; rather, its aim is to draw attention to the fact that life is not ours to dispose of.

The Israelites did not think of life as a topic for scientific analysis, but primarily as duration—as the days of one's life granted a person by Yahweh, Lord of life (Gen. 25:7; 47:28; cf. Deut. 32:39). Long life was considered a divine blessing promised to the obedient (Gen. 15:15; 25:8; Deut. 5:16; 30:19; Prov. 3:1–2). The power of death invades human life in the form of sickness, hatred, or loneliness (Ps. 18:5–6; 33:19; 56:13; 116:8).

The ideal life for an Israelite was one of personal involvement— a life expressed, e.g., by hunger and thirst (e.g., Jdg. 15:18–19), hatred and love (e.g., Gen. 24:27), desires and lusts (e.g., 1 Sam. 1; 2 Sam. 13). The sheer vitality, concreteness, and diversity of life were a source of the utmost delight (1 Ki. 3:11–14; Job 2:4; Prov. 3:16); life was synonymous with health, well-being, and success (Ps. 56:13; Prov. 2:19; Eccl. 9:9; Mal. 2:5). An essential feature of life was attendance at the sanctuary, where the worshiper joined in fellowship with the living in praising Yahweh, the Creator of life, and was even granted the occasional privilege of gazing on him, albeit indirectly (Exod. 33:18–23; Ps. 27:4; 65:5; 84:5; 142:7). Only in extreme despair was there any thought of death, which puts an end to a life that was intolerable (Jer. 20:14–18; Job 3:11–12).

2. Yahweh is to be praised as the author of life (Ps. 36:9; 139:13–16; Jer. 17:13). Gen. 2:7 states that he formed the first man from the dust of the ground and breathed divine breath into his lifeless body so that he became a living being. The distinction here is between body and life. The whole physical, emotional, and intellectual life of humankind stems from God. If God withdraws his breath of life, then a human crumbles to dust (Job 34:14–15; Ps. 104:29–30).

Human trials and tribulations—toil and failure, shame and fear, pains of childbirth—were caused by humanity's fall into sin (Gen. 3). The divine punishment is not so much death as the shortening of one's life span (6:3) or experiencing the various trials of life. These are the discords that mar human existence, the original harmony of life having been broken.

3. The Israelite view of life is expressed most clearly in Deut. At the feast of covenant renewal, the worshiping community is confronted by the word of Yahweh with a choice between life and death (Deut. 30:1–20). The obedient are promised blessing, prosperity, and life, while the disobedient can expect nothing but curse, adversity, and death (30:15, 19). The living power of God's Word extends even to one's physical existence: "Man does not live on bread alone but on every word that comes from the mouth of the LORD" (8:3; cf. 32:47; Lev. 18:5).

4. In the same manner the prophets call Israel back to Yahweh; this is Israel's only chance of life, threatened as it is with imminent disaster (Amos 5:4, 14). Isa. laments over the scoffers among the people who have entered into a covenant with death (28:15). Jer. sets the way of life and of death once more before a faithless Israel (21:8), who has forsaken the source of life (2:13; 17:13). Ezek. stresses repeatedly that the righteous will live, while the godless must die (3:18–21; 14:20; 18:4, 9, 13, 17, 20–23; 33:11; 37:5). Here the gift of natural life becomes an integral part of the covenant: Obedience leads to prosperity and blessing, while the transgressor forfeits the right to live.

Jer.'s distinction between the two ways is taken up in wisdom lit., where Wisdom offers to guide us along the pathway to life, while the ways of folly lead to death (e.g., Prov. 2:18–19; 3:2, 18; 4:4, 10, 22; 6:23; 8:35).

5. In Ps. Yahweh is portrayed as the one who gives life and delivers from death (e.g., 16:11; 27:1; cf. 31:4–5). The godly, however, sometimes find that their expectations of long life and prosperity are contradicted by their day-to-day experiences. Hence, elsewhere true life is seen as arising from fellowship with Yahweh: "Your love is better than life" (63:3). Life is here viewed metaphorically in terms of spirituality that seeks refuge and finds satisfaction in fellowship with Yahweh (16:5, 9–11; 23; 36:8–12). In Ps. 73, the assurance of Yahweh's nearness and the sense of security it brings give the worshiper a hope beyond death: "My flesh and my heart may fail, but God is . . . my portion forever" (73:26).

6. To a large extent, rab. Jud. adopted the OT view of life, but under Hel. influence true life was increasingly seen as the gift of eternal life, life without end (4 Macc. 7:19; 15:3; 16:25; 17:12; 18:19). Hence, as in the NT, eternal life could be referred to simply as zōē (e.g., *Pss. Sol.* 15:15). From the Maccabean period on, belief in resurrection and eternal life became widespread among Jewish theologians.

In Hel. Jud., belief in the resurrection of the dead was largely replaced by the doctrine of the immortality of the soul. Earthly life lost significance (Wis. 4:8–9) or was even regarded as the prison of the soul; the act of dying gained increasing significance (2 Macc. 8:21; 4 Macc. 15:12), and true life (i.e., life that is immortal) was transferred to the world beyond (15:3; *Pss. Sol.* 3:16).

By contrast, the usage found in Qumran texts is similar to that of the OT, the only new feature being the rather formal association of life with the blessings of salvation (1QS 3:7; 4:7; 1QH 2:20, 31; 9:66; 1QM 1:9; 12:3; CD 3:20).

NT 1. The noun zōon, apart from its use in Heb. 13:11; 2 Pet. 2:12; Jude 10 (all of which mean animals), is confined in the NT to Rev., where it refers to the four living creatures by the heavenly throne. zōogoneō refers to the giving or preserving of life, including physical life (e.g., the physical life of Moses in Acts 7:39).

2. The NT teaching contains elements of OT, Jewish, and Gk. origin. (a) The OT view of life is recalled most strongly in the Synoptics. Natural life is regarded as a priceless possession (cf. Mk. 8:37). Jesus frequently exercised his power in order that the sick or dying might live

(5:23; cf. Jn. 4:47–53), or even to restore to earthly life those already dead (Mk. 5:35–43; Lk. 7:11–15; Jn. 11:1–44). Life is regarded as something dynamic, but at the same time bounded and transient (Acts 17:28; Jas. 4:14). It is no merely natural occurrence, but an event that can succeed or fail (Lk. 15:13; 2 Tim. 3:12). True life depends on the word of God (Matt. 4:4, quoting Deut. 8:3), while to live away from God is described as being dead (Lk. 15:24, 32).

The basic necessities of life, such as food and clothing, are to be gratefully received as gifts of the Creator (Matt. 6:25–34; Lk. 12:15). God, who can kill and make alive (Matt. 10:28; Rom. 4:17), is the undisputed Creator of life (Acts 17:25); he is the living God (Matt. 16:16; 26:63) and the God of the living (Matt. 22:32; Mk. 12:27; Lk. 20:38).

(b) Over against the present life stands the life to come (Mk. 10:30; 1 Tim. 4:8). It is described as "eternal life" (Matt. 19:16; Mk. 10:17; cf. "life and immortality" in 2 Tim. 1:10). One attains this as a gift from God, who raises the dead (Matt. 22:31–32). The fact that the future life is occasionally referred to by the use of *zōē* alone indicates that such life is regarded as real and true (18:8–9; Mk. 9:43, 45). There is no implication here, however, of a devaluation of earthly life. On the contrary, our relationship to God's will in this present life determines our destiny in the life to come (Matt. 19:16; Lk. 10:25). Matt. 7:13–14 (cf. Lk. 13:23–24) takes up the idea of the two ways found in Deut. 30:19; Jer. 21:8. This close relationship between the present life and future life is expressed in the parable of the last judgment (Matt. 25:31–46): The disobedient will suffer eternal punishment, while the righteous enter eternal life (25:46).

3. (a) Paul's view of life is deeply affected by the resurrection of Christ from the dead (1 Cor. 15:4), which has proved the power of divine life over death (Rom. 14:9). Christ is the embodiment of God's living power, conquering death and raising the dead (2 Cor. 13:4). Life means Christ's everlasting life.

Through his resurrection Christ, the last Adam, has become the author of a new life for humankind (Rom. 5:12–21; 1 Cor. 15:20–22). In that resurrection, Christians are "made . . . with Christ" (Eph. 2:5; Col. 2:13). The life of Christians is thus not their own life but the life of Christ; he lives in them (Gal. 2:20; Phil. 1:21), and they live the life of Christ (2 Cor. 4:10). Their life is justified by Christ (Rom. 5:18), and by his life they will be saved (5:10). The life of Christ is mediated to Christians by the word of life (Phil. 2:16; cf. 2 Tim. 1:10; Tit. 1:2–3) and by the creative power of the life-giving Spirit (Rom. 8:2, 6, 10–11; 1 Cor. 15:45).

(b) The new Spirit-wrought life of believers (Rom. 6:4) does not try to escape from everyday life into Stoic indifference and asceticism. Rather, Christians are to serve their fellow human beings responsibly, in whatever historical situation they find themselves. Since they no longer live for themselves (Rom. 14:7; 2 Cor. 5:15) but for God (Rom. 6:10–11) and Christ (14:8; 2 Cor. 5:15), their lives show positive, tangible results (Gal. 5:25–26) as they follow in the footsteps of Christ and take up his cross (2 Cor. 4:9–10). Hence, Paul can make the paradoxical statement: We are "regarded as . . . dying, and yet we live on" (6:9), since life comes from and through death. Not living for oneself means having an attitude of love for others (Rom. 13:8–10; cf. 14:11–21).

(c) In the believer's new life there is a tension between present and future, between the indicative and the imperative (Gal. 5:25). The new life exists already but has not yet been fully manifested (Col. 3:3–4). Christ's resurrection is the pledge of our own future resurrection to an eternal life, where death and all the imperfections of the present creation will be over (Rom. 8:18–21; cf. 1 Cor. 15:22).

The new life points forward to eternal life when the last enemy, death, is vanquished (Rom. 6:22; 1 Cor. 15:26, 28; Gal. 6:8). Paul depicts the transition from temporal to eternal life in terms of cosmic drama, miraculous transformation, and rapture (1 Cor. 15:20–28, 35–44, 51–57; 1 Thess. 4:13–17). This future life will be a bodily life (1 Cor. 15:35–49; 2 Cor. 5:1–10), which involves seeing face to face

(1 Cor. 13:12; 2 Cor. 5:7), entering into the fullness of righteousness, peace, and joy (Rom. 14:17), being glorified (2 Cor. 3:8–9; cf. Rom. 8:17), but above all living with Christ forever (*syzaō*, 2 Tim. 2:11; cf. Rom. 6:8; Phil. 1:23; 1 Thess. 4:17).

4. (a) Jn. presents the Word as being eternal life even before his incarnation. He has lived eternally with God and for the benefit of humanity (Jn. 1:4; 1 Jn. 1:1–2); i.e., he is the source of divine life and power both in the old and the new creations. In his incarnation he is the revelation of God. He not only brings eternal life by his word (Jn. 6:68; 10:28; 12:50; 17:2); he himself *is* the true life (1 Jn. 5:20), as his various "I am" sayings indicate: "I am the bread of life" (Jn. 6:35, 48), "the resurrection and the life" (11:25), "the way and the truth and the life" (14:6). The preexistent Son of the eternal Father has been sent into the world to give life to humans both by his word and in his own person (6:33; 10:10; 1 Jn. 4:9).

(b) The life of God is received by faith. Those who believe in the Son have life (1 Jn. 5:12)—eternal life (Jn. 6:40, 47); they have already passed from death to life (5:24; 1 Jn. 3:14). This eternal life expresses itself in love (Jn. 15:9–17) and joy (16:20–24). Brotherly love is the criterion of true life: "We know that we have passed from death into life, because we love our brothers" (1 Jn. 3:14).

5. Rev. combines the Son of Man tradition (1:13) with the figure of a slain Lamb: "I am the First and the Last. I am the Living One; I was dead, and behold I am alive for ever and ever! And I hold the keys of death and Hades" (1:17–18; cf. 4:9–10). Whereas the Gospel of Jn. concentrates on the present life, Rev. concerns itself primarily with the life to come. In the vision of the new Jerusalem, the pictures of the tree of life and the water of life, familiar from the story of the Garden of Eden (Gen. 2:9–17), reappear as symbols of the fullness of life in the new city of God (Rev. 21:6; 22:1–14, 17, 19). The vision of the new heaven and the new earth is the most wide-ranging in its promises: The last enemy, death, will be vanquished, and our eternal life with God will be utter perfection (21:3–4).

See also *bios*, life (*1050*).

2438 (*zōnē*, girdle, belt), → *2439*.

2439 ζώννυμι	ζώννυμι (*zōnnymi*), gird (*2439*); ζώνη (*zōnē*), girdle, belt (*2438*);

διαζώννυμι (*diazōnnymi*), tie or gird around (*1346*); περιζώννυμι (*perizōnnymi*), gird with, gird around (*4322*).

CL & OT 1. In cl. Gk. the vbs. in this group refer to girding oneself or someone else. The noun *zōnē* can mean girdle or money belt, purse (cf. Mk. 6:8).

2. (a) Generally speaking, the OT uses these words in the same way as cl. Gk. The girdle (*zōnē*), made of linen or leather, served to tuck in the long skirts of one's robe, in order to give greater freedom of movement. Hence the putting on of a girdle acquired the particular meaning of making oneself ready to go (2 Ki. 4:29); to lay aside one's girdle means, correspondingly, to rest. A person in authority wore a girdle as part of his finery (Isa. 22:21), an officer as his badge of rank. A richly embroidered girdle formed part of the vestments of the high priest (Exod. 28:4, 39–40 = LXX 35–36; 29:9; Lev. 8:7, 13; 16:4). A golden girdle, worn around the breast, was an angel's mark of distinction (Dan. 10:5; cf. Rev. 15:6). A broad leather girdle was used as armor, to protect the lower part of the body (1 Sam. 25:13); thus, the expression "everyone who wears the girdle" means "the men fit for war."

(b) A metaphorical use occurs in Isa. 11:5, which looks forward to the new David as an ideal king, the Messiah, of whom it is said: "Righteousness will be his belt." *perizōnnymi* is used fig. in Ps. 65:6 (Yahweh has "armed [himself] with strength"); 18:32, 39 (Yahweh "arms me with strength"); and 30:11 (Yahweh "clothed me with joy").

NT 1. The NT continues the same use of these words. *diazōnnymi* occurs in a direct sense in Jn. 21:7, where Peter girds himself with his outer garment because he does not wish to meet the Lord improperly dressed, and *perizōnnymi* in Lk. 17:8, where a servant girds himself in order to serve his master. In Jn. 13:4–5 Jesus changes his clothes in preparation for performing the task of a slave.

2. In some passages the vbs. in this group have, as in the LXX, the special meaning of making oneself ready to depart, i.e., to get moving, stand in readiness. Thus in Acts 12:8 Peter is commanded to prepare himself to leave prison, and in Jn. 21:18 this same vigorous Peter, who is well able to gird himself and make himself ready to go, is told that when he is old another will make him ready for a journey and determine the destination of his life (probably an allusion to his martyrdom). In Lk. 12:35 (echoing Exod. 12:11), the church is challenged to live unfettered by the world, in expectation of the Lord's coming, in readiness to depart (cf. 1 Cor. 7:29–31). In Matt. 10:9, the disciples are not to secure themselves financially by taking extra money in their "belts" (*zōnē*), but to leave everything to God's provision.

3. According to Mk. 1:6, John the Baptist did not wear over his clothing the linen girdle customary among nomads, but a leather one (cf. 2 Ki. 1:8). His appearance is like that of Elijah (cf. Mal. 3:1; 4:5), the forerunner of the Messiah. His clothing does not indicate hostility to culture or asceticism but is to be explained in terms of desert typology. John's garb proclaimed his conscious prophetic calling. In Acts 21:11 Agabus (like the prophets of the OT; cf. Isa. 20:2; Jer. 13:1–11) carried out a symbolic action with Paul's girdle (a long cloth worn about the waist), to indicate his impending arrest. In the vision of Rev. 1:13, the golden girdle marks the exalted Christ as the true high priest, as does his long robe (cf. Exod. 28:4).

4. *perizōnnymi* is used in a metaphorical sense in Eph. 6:14: Believers are to put on God's "truth" like a military girdle, which will protect them from the attacks of the evil one.

See also *hetoimos*, ready, prepared (*2289*); *kataskeuazō*, make ready, prepare, build, equip, furnish (*2941*).

2441 (*zōogoneō*, procreate, give life to, keep alive), → *2437*.

2442 (*zōon*, living creature), → *2437*.

2443 (*zōopoieō*, make alive, give life to), → *2437*.

H *eta*

2450 ἡγεμών

ἡγεμών (*hēgemōn*), leader, commander, chief (*2450*); ἡγέομαι (*hēgeomai*), lead, consider (*2451*).

This word can refer to the emperor or a provincial governor (cf. Matt. 10:18; Mk. 13:9; Lk. 21:12; 1 Pet. 2:14), particularly the procurators in Judea—Pilate (Matt. 27:2, 11, 14–15, 21, 27; 28:14; Lk. 20:20), Felix (Acts 23:24, 26, 33; 24:1, 10), and Festus (26:30). In Matt. 2:6 it means more generally "ruler." In 1 Pet. 2:13–14 believers are expected to honor political authority.

The related vb. *hēgeomai* is used 7x as a participial substantive to denote a ruler or leader (Matt. 2:6; Heb. 13:7, 17, 24). Elsewhere, however, the vb. means to consider, think (e.g., 2 Cor. 9:5; Phil. 2:3, 6, 25; 1 Tim. 6:1).

See also *Kaisar*, Caesar, emperor (*2790*); *anthypatos*, proconsul (*478*).

2451 (*hēgeomai*, lead, consider), → *2450*.

2454 ἡδονή

ἡδονή (*hēdonē*), pleasure (*2454*); φιλήδονος (*philēdonos*), lover of pleasure (*5798*).

CL & OT *hēdonē* is from the same root as *hēdys*, sweet, pleasant, pleasing. Originally it meant something pleasant to the taste, and then pleasant generally. It occurs in an extended sense as feelings of pleasure, enjoyment. Finally, it came to mean desire for pleasure. When regarded as a gift of nature, *hēdonē* was considered good.

In Hel. times a distinction was made between higher and lower *hēdonai*—those of the mind and soul and those of the body. Then the concept was confined to its ethically bad elements, and it was used in contrast to *chara*, joy, and *aretē*, virtue. The Stoics used it for pleasure of the senses, esp. sex, and then for unrestricted passions. Those who let themselves be ruled by *hēdonē* missed the purpose of life.

In Num. 11:8 *hēdonē* means (good) taste, a quality in a thing that gives someone pleasure (see also Prov. 17:1; Wis. 7:2; 16:20). It is not until 4 Macc. (10x) and esp. Philo, who uses *hēdonē* as the power in revolt against *logos*, that the word is used in a primarily negative sense. *hēdonē* is a root of all evil impulses and can bring only trouble and pain. Rab. writings have repeated warnings against the "evil impulse" (*yēṣer hā-rāʿ*), which makes a person reluctant to study the Torah.

NT 1. In the NT *hēdonē* is found only 5x—all in later books and all with a bad connotation. The desire for pleasure fills those estranged from God. They live out their own irresistible desire for pleasure, become separated from God, and end up being slaves of the *hēdonai*. Only God can deliver them (Tit. 3:3–7). 2 Pet. 2:13–15 gives a picture of those who have given themselves over to their *hēdonai*, showing how they have become the victims of these destructive powers.

2. People estranged from God are not the only ones threatened by the insatiable desires of the impulses (Tit. 3:3). Christians also remain exposed to this power. Even prayer can be misused as a means to satisfy our passions (Jas. 4:3). If we give way to them, we become entangled in perpetual dissatisfaction and find ourselves in a chaotic condition (4:1). The NT lists of vices picture clearly the characteristics and results of *hēdonē*—ranging from unrestrained sexuality through lack of self-discipline to a self-centered indifference to one's fellow human beings.

3. The dangers that unchecked impulses have for faith are seen most clearly in the interpretation of the parable of the sower (Lk. 8:14). When *hēdonē* asserts its mastery, faith dies, choked among the thorns.

4. This process is seen clearly in those who entangle themselves in false teaching, lead others astray, and become victims of moral self-destruction (see 2 Tim. 3:1–5, where this is a characteristic of "the last days"; Paul uses *philēdonoi*, lovers of pleasure, in contrast to *philotheoi*, lovers of God).

5. We must never confound *hēdonē* with the desire for true joy (*chara*), which is never rejected by the NT. Joy is satisfied by communion with God, often even in the midst of suffering and persecution (cf. Jas. 1:2).

See also *epithymia*, desire, lust (*2123*); *oregō*, strive (*3977*).

2455 (*hēdyosmon*, mint), → *3303*.

2456 (*ēthos*, custom, way of life), → *1621*.

2457 (*hēkō*, have come, be present), → *2262*.

2460 Ἠλίας

Ἠλίας (*Ēlias*), Elijah (*2460*); Heb. *ʾēlîyyâhû* or *ʾēlîyyâ* (Yah(u) is God).

OT 1. The OT account of Elijah is found in 1 Ki. 17–2 Ki. 2. Elijah came from Tishbe in Transjordan and was active as a prophet in the northern kingdom of Israel in the first half of the 9th cent. B.C. He prepared for Jehu's revolution, which destroyed the dynasty of Omri because it had favored Canaanite culture and religion. Elijah took a stand that in Israel Yahweh's claims alone should be recognized and that faith in Yahweh should remain free from all Canaanite influences.

Elijah preached that Yahweh guided the fortunes of humanity and nations. The forces of nature (e.g., the drought in 1 Ki. 17, for which the Baal cult had no explanation) were also under Yahweh's sovereignty and served to carry out his purposes. Yahweh demanded the rule of law and justice and watched over the ethical and legal norms for life in the nation of Israel, to which the king also was subject. Yahweh, not Baal, had power over life and death. From this Elijah deduced Yahweh's claim to sole obedience from his people.

Yahweh revealed his character not merely in catastrophic expressions of his rage but also in the silence (cf. "a gentle whisper" [1 Ki. 19:12]). He worked quietly, hardly recognizable behind events (cf. "the gently flowing waters of Shiloah" [Isa. 8:6]). Elijah cast the old faith in Yahweh in a new mold and placed it on a new foundation. This justifies the tradition that placed him beside Moses. Mal. 4:5–6 presents Elijah as a figure of the messianic age. He prepares the way for God, purifies the priests, and creates peace.

2. Three parallel concepts of Elijah's return were developed in intertestamental and rab. Jud.: (a) Elijah belonged to the tribe of Gad, and he would prepare the way for God and deliver Israel in the last days. (b) Elijah belonged to the tribe of Benjamin, and he would be the forerunner of the Messiah. (c) Elijah belonged to the tribe of Levi, and he would be the high priest of the messianic age.

According to these traditions, Elijah was sinless and so obtained eternal existence. Thus, Elijah was the intercessor for Israel in heaven. He was also the one who rescued from greatest need. In post-NT times we find the idea that he was the heavenly scribe who made a record of the acts of human beings and esp. kept a register of Israelite marriages. He accompanied the souls of the dead into the other world.

Sir. 48:10 expects that Elijah will have the task of restoring the tribes of Israel, which in Isa. 49:6 is one of the tasks of the Servant of the Lord. Elijah thus receives a messianic function. It was widely believed that Elijah was a forerunner of the Messiah, proclaiming the coming days of salvation, fighting against the Antichrist, introducing the Messiah, and sometimes anointing him. Since Mal. 3:1; 4:5–6 were combined with 2:4, the Jews anticipated Elijah as the eschatological high priest, who would restore pure doctrine and a pure community and clear up controversies in doctrine, law, and difficult passages of Scripture. Hence many points in Jud. were left open. One awaited the coming of Elijah, who would decide such matters.

According to the Targum, God would gather the Diaspora through Elijah and Moses. A midrash on Ps. 43 says there are two deliverers: Elijah of the tribe of Levi, and the Messiah of the house of David (cf. the expectation at Qumran that in the messianic age there would be a priestly Messiah beside the Messiah from the tribe of Judah).

NT Elijah is mentioned 29x in the NT. Lk. 4:25–26; 9:54; Jas. 5:17; and Rev. 11:6 refer to the historical details of his life. The statement in Jas. 5:17 that the drought lasted three and a half years is based on Palestinian tradition; this verse stresses the power of prayer by quoting the example of Elijah. Lk. 4:25–26 is a threat by Jesus that it might please God to offer salvation to the Gentiles to the exclusion of Israel. In Lk. 9:54 Jesus rejects the suggestion that he should act like Elijah, for his task was to save, not to destroy.

In Mk. 15:34 par., Jesus prayed in the words of Ps. 22:1 on the cross. This prayer was misunderstood by those standing by as a call to Elijah to help, since Elijah was the helper in need (15:35–36). Since Elijah did not intervene, Jesus' messianic claim could be considered a failure.

According to the NT, some expected Elijah to come before the dawn of the end (Matt. 17:10; Mk. 9:11). Some wondered whether John the Baptist was Elijah (Jn. 1:21, 25); others thought that Jesus himself was Elijah who had returned (Mk. 6:15 par.; 8:28 par.). Mk. 9:11 expresses the Jewish expectation of Elijah as forerunner of the Messiah and restorer. The argument of the scribes was that since Elijah had not come, Jesus could not be the Messiah. Rev. 11:3 shows that the restoration was expected to come by the preaching of repentance.

Jn. 1:21, 25 states that John the Baptist personally refused to accept that he was the eschatological Elijah. In Jesus' perspective, however, the appearance of John fulfilled the expectation of the coming of Elijah (see Mk. 9:11–13 par.; Matt. 11:10–14 par.). Matt. 11:14 ("if you are willing to accept it") shows that this was a new and unusual verdict. He meant that there was to be no pure, direct embodiment of Elijah in person, but also that the promise was fulfilled. It meant also that Jesus did not take the restitution in a political or national sense, but in a religious one through repentance and forgiveness. Jesus saw his own fate foreshadowed in that of the Baptist (Mk. 9:13). The early church accepted Jesus' verdict and thereby confessed Jesus' messiahship (Mk. 1:2; Lk. 1:16–17, 76).

Elijah appeared with Moses at Jesus' transfiguration (Mk. 9:4–5 par.). Apocalyptic tradition knew of two forerunners of the Messiah, normally Enoch and Elijah (both of whom had been raptured). But in Rev. 11:3–6 they are Moses and Elijah. When Moses and Elijah appear at Jesus' transfiguration, it is an announcement of the beginning of the end time. According to Mk. 9:12–13 and Rev. 11:3–10, Elijah is a suffering figure. That he appears at Jesus' transfiguration points to Jesus' coming sufferings and confirms his prediction of suffering (Mk. 8:31–32; Lk. 9:31).

Paul refers to the OT story of Elijah in Rom. 11:2–5. He had gained the conviction from 1 Ki. 19:10, 14, 18 that also in Elijah's time God had separated for himself an elect, holy remnant, who in Paul's time were those Jews who believed on Jesus as Messiah.

2461	ἡλικία

ἡλικία (*hēlikia*), age, life span, stature (*2461*).

CL & OT In cl. Gk. *hēlikia* had a range of meanings: (1) the relative age in life of a person, (2) the years of discretion as an expression of manliness (*en hēlikia*, come of age), (3) a generation, and (4) height, stature, size of body.

In the LXX *hēlikia* is found only with the first two meanings, mostly in 2, 3, and 4 Macc. In Jud., as in antiquity generally, there was great respect for the older men (Lev. 19:32) because they had wisdom and understanding (Job. 15:10, Sir. 6:34–35; 25:4–6). Elders accordingly exercised a leading role among the people.

NT In the NT *hēlikia* doubtless means stature in Lk. 19:3. But normally it has the first two meanings above (e.g., Heb. 11:11, age; Jn. 9:21, 23, maturity). The three following points are of importance:

1. A human being cannot influence the physical age he attains; it is a gift of the Creator. Hence in Matt. 6:27 and Lk. 12:25 *hēlikia* means age or span of life. No amount of worrying is able to lengthen a person's life by a trifling measure of time.

2. Lk. 2:52 says that Jesus "grew in wisdom and stature." The use of the vb. "grew" (*prokoptō*, i.e., make progress) makes it probable that *hēlikia* is used here in the fig. sense of growing up to maturity, to full manhood.

3. The word is found in a metaphorical sense in Eph. 4:13, "to the measure of maturity [*hēlikia*] of the fullness of Christ" (lit. trans.). Maturity is that through which a person is to be distinguished from a child (cf. 4:14), who is tossed about and easily influenced. The measure of the maturity implies a goal that has been set. But here this goal is not for the individual believer but for the church, which is built up as the body of Christ (4:12). Each member contributes his or her measure of effectiveness (4:16) according to the measure of the grace given to each (4:7). The goal, however, is that all should arrive at the unity of faith and knowledge of the Son of God (4:13a) (→ *plēroō*, fullness [*4444*]). Only then will the whole body be like a mature person (4:13).

2463	ἥλιος

ἥλιος (*hēlios*), sun (*2463*).

CL & OT 1. In cl. Gk. *hēlios* usually refers to the sun, the most conspicuous of the heavenly bodies. Occasionally fig. uses of *hēlios* are found. The conspicuous character of the sun, its fundamental importance to life and esp. agriculture, and its daily journey across the sky all readily explain the nearly universal worship of the sun in primitive societies. Frequently the sun is personified into a god: e.g., Shamash in Mesopotamia, Helios in the Greek world, Sol Invictus in the Roman world.

2. (a) The use of *hēlios* in the LXX is similar to that of cl. Gk. The most common use is to mark time, whether of the day, by reference to its rising, setting, and midday heat, or of the season. Another important use is the specialized "under the sun," by which Eccl. designates life in the real world. Both the LXX and Gk. lit. use the rising of the sun to designate the direction east. The permanence of the sun and its fixed order are sometimes stressed. Throughout the LXX the sun is understood to be the creation of God, the greater light made to rule the day (Gen. 1:16).

(b) In the OT the sun can take on a fig. meaning in referring to excellence, permanence, beauty, or strength (Jdg. 5:31; Ps. 89:36; Song 6:10 = LXX 6:9; Wis. 7:29; Sir. 23:19; 26:16; 50:7). It is also associated with righteousness (Wis. 5:6).

(c) The OT clearly stands against the widespread practice of the worship of any heavenly bodies, strictly forbidding any reverence for the sun, moon, and stars (Deut. 4:19; 17:3; cf. 2 Ki. 23:5, 11; Jer. 8:2; Ezek. 8:16). We come near to a personification of the sun in Mal. 4:2: "But for you who revere my name, the sun of righteousness will rise with healing in its wings." This may reflect the representation of the sun as a winged disk common in the art of the ANE.

(d) A specialized group of references in the LXX, which are esp. important to the background of the NT, may be described as apocalyptic in tone. (i) Although the judgment oracles of the prophets refer to anticipated judgment in history, they also foreshadow the divine wrath of final judgment. Most frequent is a reference to a darkening of the sun as a prelude to or an accompaniment of divine judgment. In some passages an impending historical judgment is in view: Isa. 13:10

(Babylon); Ezek. 32:7 (Egypt); Joel 2:10, 31; 3:15; and Mic. 3:6 (Jerusalem). But there is a tendency for this language to shade into a description of the eschatological day of the Lord. Moreover, judgment may be indicated by other irregularities: e.g., the sun does not rise (Job 9:7); it stands still (Hab. 3:11); it goes down at noon (Amos 8:9) or while yet day (Jer. 15:9); it shines at night (2 Esd. 5:4). In their contexts these passages refer to shame, sorrow, and confusion.

(ii) In the eschatological blessing that follows judgment, "the sun will no more be your light by day . . . for the LORD will be your everlasting light" (Isa. 60:19).

(iii) By contrast, indicative of the incomparable glory of the promised new reality, "the sunlight will be seven times brighter, like the light of seven full days" (Isa. 30:26). This is fig. language for judgment and blessing. There are few parallels in classical lit. since the framework of eschatological expectation is lacking.

NT 1. The NT continues the ordinary usage of *hēlios* as the marker of time (Mk. 1:32; 16:2; Eph. 4:26) and direction (Acts 27:20; Rev. 7:2, 16:12) and as the source of scorching heat (Matt. 13:6; Mk. 4:6; Jas. 1:11; Rev. 7:16; 16:8). Consistent with the OT idea of "life under the sun," Jesus teaches that the Father in heaven "causes his sun to rise on the evil and the good" (Matt. 5:45). In his argument concerning the nature of the resurrection body, Paul speaks of the contrasting glory of the sun, moon, and stars (1 Cor. 15:41). Paul's judgment on Elymas causes a blindness that makes him unable to see the sun (Acts 13:11).

2. The NT often has a fig. use of *hēlios*. In the transfiguration narrative of Matt. 17:2, Jesus' face is said to have "shone like the sun." John's vision of Christ similarly describes his face as "like the sun shining in all its brilliance" (Rev. 1:16). The description of the mighty angel of 10:1 likens his face to the sun. The angel who announces the great supper of God in 19:17 is described as "standing in the sun." The woman of Rev. 12 (probably to be identified with the Zion of Isa. 66:7–16), who gives birth to the child destined to rule all nations, is portrayed as "clothed with the sun" (Rev. 12:1). Jesus teaches in Matt. 13:43 that "the righteous will shine like the sun in the kingdom of their Father." The light from heaven that Paul saw on the Damascus Road was "brighter than the sun" (Acts 26:13).

3. Apocalyptic references to *hēlios* are frequent in the NT and depend on the same imagery as in the OT. (a) Most obvious, signifying God's wrath in judgment, are various references in Rev. At the opening of the sixth seal "the sun turned black like sackcloth" (6:12); at the blowing of the fourth trumpet "a third of the sun was struck" so that its light was diminished by a third (8:12); at the fifth trumpet the sun was darkened "by the smoke from the Abyss" (9:2). Note also the saying of Jesus in the Synoptics that "the sun will be darkened" (Matt. 24:29; Mk. 13:24) or, less precisely, that there will be signs in the sun (Lk. 21:25). These words clearly have an eschatological ring to them, although their primary reference is probably to the historical event of the fall of Jerusalem.

The same issue confronts us in the quotation of Joel 2.28–32 in Acts 2:17–21. How can one understand "the sun will be turned to darkness," etc. (Acts 2:20), as it stands in the context? Certainly the main meaning is the eschatological fulfillment experienced in the reception of the Holy Spirit at Pentecost. Perhaps Peter regarded the second half of the quotation (Acts 2:19–20) as simply symbolic for the inauguration of the eschatological age. Furthermore, Peter and his listeners may have associated the failing of the sun's light at the time of the crucifixion (Lk. 23:45; cf. Matt. 27:45; Mk. 15:33) with the prophecy of Joel. It is, however, consistent with the meaning of this language elsewhere (in both OT and NT) to understand Acts 2:19–20 as referring to coming judgment. The point is that the last days have begun. Warnings and the call to repentance are therefore timely (2:38, 40; 3:19, 23). Salvation is available to those who call on the name of the Lord (2:21; cf. 4:12).

(b) Like the LXX, the NT also uses *hēlios* in describing the glorious aspect of eschatology, here as exhibited in the city coming down out of heaven, the new Jerusalem. That city is of such splendor that there is no need of the sun (Rev. 21:23). God's servants there will not "need the light . . . of the sun, for the Lord God will give them light" (22:5).

(c) It is worth noting that whereas most of the references to *hēlios* in the LXX are lit. rather than fig. or apocalyptic in character, in the NT the reverse is true. This is of course explained by the eschatological orientation of the NT. Moreover, there is a theological connection between God's blessings and his judgments, whereby earlier blessings may typify eschatological blessing and earlier judgments may typify eschatological judgment. So magnificent is the kingdom inaugurated by Christ at his first advent that it may rightly be characterized in language that, strictly speaking, refers to the consummation (e.g., Luke 4:18; 7:22; 10:18, 24). In the same way, the fall of Jerusalem as a judgment sign connotes the eschatological judgment and points proleptically to the end times; thus, it may be described in the boldest of language (e.g., the darkening of the sun).

See also *selēnē*, moon (*4943*); *astēr*, star (*843*).

| 2465 | ἡμέρα |

ἡμέρα (*hēmera*), day (*2465*).

CL & OT 1. In cl. Gk. *hēmera* can denote the period of twenty-four hours, in which case it includes the night, or it may exclude the night. But it can also mean a much longer period of time, including a lifetime or even time generally.

2. In the OT, like years and months (e.g., Exod. 2:2; 2 Ki. 17:1), days serve as a division of time (Gen. 1:5–2:2; Jos. 6:3), the Heb. word being almost invariably *yôm*. The day can include the night, in which case it begins with the evening (Gen. 1:5), or else be distinguished from the night (Isa. 34:10). The word may indicate a particular day (Gen. 4:14, today; Job 3:1, birthday) or (in the pl.) a period of time (Gen. 6:3, lifetime; 8:22, so long as the earth remains; Ps. 90:4, a thousand years; Isa. 60:20, days of mourning; Jdg. 17:10, a year). Certain days have a special character—such as six days of the week as days of work, while the seventh day is the Sabbath, the day of rest (Exod. 20:9–10). A day in the temple courts is better than a thousand elsewhere (Ps. 84:10). Human beings have no power over the day of death (Eccl. 8:8).

3. Those passages that speak of "the day of the LORD" are esp. important theologically. But the phrase has various meanings. Originally the day of Yahweh was a day of joy (assumed in Amos 5:18, 20; cf. Zech. 14:7). The prophets, however, reinterpreted this popular idea of a day of salvation and proclaimed it instead as a day of unrelieved judgment (cf. Joel 1:15; 2:2; Amos 5:18, 20). The event in view may be a political (Ezek. 34:12) or a cultic one, or it may be *the* great eschatological event (e.g., Isa. 2:11–12, 17; Amos 8:9), the latter often described in cosmological language (Joel 3:14; Zeph. 1:15).

In many cases it is difficult to distinguish the one from the other. The day of Yahweh can mean the fall of Jerusalem and so belong to the past (Lam. 1:21) or, as in the eschatological passages mentioned above, still be future. It can be imminent (Ezek. 7:7), so that the hearers should give heed to the prophetic message (Mic. 1:2). Yet no time scale may be indicated (Isa. 24:21). It may even be regarded (by the sinner, at least) as a long way off (Amos 6:3; 9:10). This shows that the prophets' preaching of this day cannot be isolated from concrete situations but must always be seen to have taken place in a particular historical context.

The day of the Lord figures prominently in oracles of judgment against foreign nations (Isa. 13:6; Ezek. 30:3; Joel 3:14; Obad. 15), though Israel too may be the object of judgment (Isa. 2:12; Ezek. 13:5; Joel 1:15; 2:1, 11; Amos 5:18, 20; Mal. 4:5). There is no set technical expression for this day of the Lord. It may be referred to as "the day of disaster" (Jer. 46:21 = LXX 26:21), "the day of calamity" (Hab. 3:16), "the day of your fall" (Ezek. 26:18; 27:27; 32:10), "a bitter day" (Amos 8:10), "the evil day" (6:3), etc. But it can also be a day of salvation: the day "when the LORD binds up" (Isa. 30:26), "the day I cleanse" (Ezek. 36:33), "the day the LORD gives you relief" (Isa. 14:3), etc. Similarly, the prophets can use the pl. ("the days are coming, when . . .") in both oracles of judgment (e.g., Isa. 39:6; Jer. 7:32; 9:24 = LXX 9:25; 19:6) and salvation (30:3= LXX 37:3; 31:27, 31, 38= LXX 38:27, 31, 38; Amos 9:13).

In general, therefore, the day of the Lord involved a breaking into history in a spectacular fashion. Moreover, though judgment may be nigh, usually a golden age lay beyond it, which may be presented as being near or far. But nowhere is this day brought about by human achievement or the policies contrived by human beings.

The golden age, usually described in apocalyptic language, has a universal character (cf. Isa. 11:6; 65:17, 21; Mic. 4:4). Sometimes the nations are depicted as serving Israel (Isa. 60:10–16; 61:5; Dan. 2:44; 7:27), or Israel's king as holding universal sway (Ps. 2:8–9; 72:8–11; Mic. 5:2, 4; Zech. 9:9–10). Jer. 3:17 declares that only universal submission to God can eliminate that which militates against well-being. The thought of the Gentiles sharing the faith of Israel also comes into the prophetic vision (Ps. 22:27; 96:1–3; Jer. 16:19–21; Zeph. 3:10; Zech. 2:11; 8:22–23). Such universalism related it to the mission of Israel. Note how the Gentiles are envisaged in the books of Ruth and Jon. as included in God's universal concern. The figures of the Son of man, the suffering servant, the Messiah, and the idea of the kingdom of God all converge on the day of the Lord.

4. The Hebrews had no word for time in the abstract and similarly had no corresponding expressions for past, present, and future. Rather, the Heb. *yôm* is often qualified by a genitival phrase, an infinitive, or a relative clause. Thus there could be a *yôm* of salvation experienced in a variety of past events: the day of Israel's election (Deut. 9:24; Ezek. 16:4–5); the day of the plagues on Egypt and other days connected with the saving events of the exodus (Exod. 10:13; 12:17; Num. 11:32); the day of the dedication of the tabernacle (9:15); the day of the giving of the law (Deut. 4:10); the day of victory over the Amorites (Jos. 10:12).

Out of such expressions arose a variety of stock phrases, such as "since the day the Israelites came up out of Egypt" (Jdg. 19:30; cf. 1 Sam. 8:8; 2 Sam. 7:6; Ps. 78:42; Isa. 11:16; Jer. 7:22; 11:4; 31:32 = LXX 38:32; 34:13 = LXX 41:13; Hos. 2:17 = LXX 2:15). This day provided the model for speaking of another past day of salvation experienced in the return from exile (Hag. 2:15, 18–19 = LXX 2:16, 19–20; Zech. 4:10; 8:9), and what was true corporately for Israel could similarly be applied to the individual (Ps. 18:18; 20:1–2; 59:16; 77:2; 138:3; 140:7; Lam. 3:57).

But days could also be remembered as a day of judgment (Num. 32:10; 2 Chr. 28:6; Ps. 78:9; 95:8; 137:7; Isa. 9:3, 13 = LXX 9:4, 14; Lam. 1:12; 2:1 = LXX 2:2; Obad. 11, 14; Zech. 14:3). Whereas in some of these instances *yôm* is a literal day, in others it denotes a concrete time that was longer and was characterized by a specific event.

In this connection we can note that the two Gen. creation narratives both use *yôm* and the corresponding Gk. *hēmera*: the seven-day narrative (Gen. 1:5, 8, 13–14, 16, 18–19, 23, 31; 2:2–4a) and the one-day creation and fall narrative (2:4b–3:24). *yôm/hēmera* occurs in 2:17 regarding the tree of knowledge of good and evil: "for when [lit., in the day that] you eat of it you will surely die." This should not be understood in a literal sense of physical death within twenty-four hours. Rather, it brought a change in the human condition that affects humanity all the *days* of their life (3:14, 17).

Various attempts have been made to harmonize the Gen. narratives with a modern scientific view of the world, such as the view that the six days of Gen. 1 correspond to geological eras. But these place a considerable strain on both scientific theory and the biblical text. Even if the days of Gen. 1 correspond to geological eras, it does not help to harmonize 2:4b, which locates the creation of humanity "in the day that the LORD God made the earth and the heavens" (NRSV), seemingly prior to the planting of the garden of Eden. It seems best, therefore, to recognize Gen. as prescientific, symbolically represent-

ing the origin of the world from God in its order and relative autonomy. Exod. 20:11 views the six creation days followed by a rest day in Gen. 1 as a divine pattern for human activity in explaining the commandment concerning the Sabbath.

The present day may be characterized by laments and distress (e.g., 2 Ki. 19:3; Ps. 20:9; 86:7; Isa. 37:3; 61:2), but also by salvation (49:8). There is, however, a gnomic use of the word "day," esp. in teachings that have to do with popular wisdom and in cultic regulations. In the latter *yôm/hēmera* refers to a "today" that is continually repeated and hence continuously present (e.g., Exod. 20:8; 31:15; 35:3; 40:2; Ps. 20:9; 37:19; Prov. 11:4; Eccl. 7:15 = LXX 7:16; 9:9; 11:9; 12:1).

5. In addition to the above expressions, the OT contains adverbial expressions of time such as "on that day" (201x, of which 89 refer to the past, 112 to the future) and "today" (217x). An analysis of all these passages leads to the conclusion that the function of the references to the day of the Lord, whether in the past or the future, is to illuminate the present "today." Authors use past revelatory events to shed light on and give exhortations for living in the present. The day of Yahweh is not so much a final day of history as a day of Yahweh's decisive action in which what is happening in the present is brought to a final resolution. In fact, there can be more than one day of the Lord, but only those days actively become his day when he manifests himself in judgment and/or salvation (cf. Ps. 95:8; Jer. 28:9; Ezek. 33:33; Mal. 3:1, 3, 19–21).

In the apocalyptic writings, however, the idea is transformed. The future is increasingly abstracted from the present and has an epoch of its own. Thus, Zech. 14:21 depicts the future more in terms of a state of being than a decisive event (cf. Isa. 61:2–3; Dan. 7).

The OT writers saw time as both quantitative and qualitative. The quantitative approach provides the framework of continuity, allowing for the interconnectedness of specific events. The qualitative approach sees history as a succession of unique experiences. This view of time stands in contrast with that of the Egyptians, for whom time was an endless, meaningless continuum, caught in a perpetual seasonal pattern of alteration. But in Israel Yahweh was Lord of past, present, and future. It is the qualitative approach that gives the historical event its theological significance.

In events of the annual cult rituals the qualitative and quantitative views of time intersect. In the Passover, for example, this cultic practice could lead to a cyclical attitude to life characterized by the performance of established rites. But the whole purpose of the rite is to summon the Israelite to reflect on that day in the past in which God's people were brought out of Egypt (Exod. 13:3–10). And the exodus becomes a paradigm for a future day of the Lord as well.

6. Apocalyptic and later Jud. carried the idea of the future day further, with eschatology now becoming part of the doctrine of the last things and developing strong apocalyptic. The questions are asked: How long will this age last? When can we expect the new age? (2 Esd. 4:33, 35; cf. Mk. 13:4). The messianic age will be preceded by a time of tribulation, subdivided into twelve shorter periods (*2 Bar.* 27) and marked, among other things, by unrighteousness and licentiousness (2 Esd. 5:2–13; cf. Matt. 24:12). The new age will be heralded by signs (*2 Bar.* 25:4; cf. Mk. 13:24), and "the end" (*2 Bar.* 29:7–8; cf. Mk. 13:7) will be the transition to the days of the Messiah, when judgment gives way to wisdom, sinlessness, and life (*1 Enoch* 5:8–9).

The days of the Messiah were expected to bring in renewal, a righting of wrongs, and the restoration of all that had been lost through Adam's transgression. Thus, the nations that had oppressed Israel will be destroyed, while Israel's boundaries will be fully restored in the new temple (though on this point there was not unanimity). Israel will be rich to a degree hitherto unknown. Both human beings and nature will increase in fruitfulness. Sinful desires and the devil himself will be destroyed. The Holy Spirit will be poured out. Sickness and death will be removed and the dead will arise.

7. The Qumran texts regard the date of the eschatological day as being already fixed (1QM 13:14). It will bring the annihilation of those who do not keep the commandments (CD 8:1–3); it will be the day of God's visitation, the day of vengeance (1QS 10:19), when evildoers will be destroyed. There will be a battle with fearful carnage (1QM 1:9) as the sons of light war against the sons of darkness (1:11). God will then be praised (18:5–8), and on the day of judgment those who are willing to be added to the elect will be saved (14:7–15).

NT 1. The resurrection narratives contain striking expressions of time: "on the third day" (1 Cor. 15:4; cf. Matt. 16:21; Lk. 9:22) or "after three days" (Mk. 8:31; 9:31; cf. 10:34; also Hos. 6:2).

The situation is similar with regard to the space of forty days, which already has OT significance, for both Moses and Elijah fasted forty days and nights (Exod. 34:28; 1 Ki. 19:8). The length of Jesus' fast (Matt. 4:2) seems linked with these and other OT passages (cf. Deut. 8:2–3, 15–16). Note how the story of Jesus' temptation alludes to the desert temptation of Israel in the quotations from Deut. 8:3 (Matt. 4:4; Lk. 4:7), Deut. 6:16 (Matt. 4:7; Lk. 4:12), and Deut. 6:13 (Matt. 4:10; Lk. 4:8). There is the further parallelism between Jesus and Moses: Deut. 9:18 (cf. also the giving of the Sermon on the Mount afterward); 34:1–4; and Ps. 91. Jesus, in other words, recapitulates the experiences of Israel, particularly the desert generation.

2. (a) The expectation of the last day is found throughout the NT: Synoptics (e.g., Matt. 10:15; 12:36; Mk. 13:32; Lk. 10:12), John (Jn. 6:39; cf. also 1 Jn. 4:17), Acts (17:31), Paul's letters (Rom. 2:5; 13:12; Eph. 4:30; 2 Tim. 1:12), general letters (2 Pet. 3:12; Jude 6), and Rev. (9:6). The phraseology varies: e.g., that day (2 Tim. 4:8), the last day (Jn. 6:39–40), the day of wrath (Rev. 6:17), the day of judgment (2 Pet. 2:9), the day of the Lord (1 Thess. 5:2), the day of the Son of Man (Lk. 17:24), the day of Christ (Phil. 2:16), the great day of God (Rev. 16:14), or simply the day (1 Cor. 3:13). The pl. is also common (e.g., 2 Tim. 3:1; 2 Pet. 3:3; Rev. 9:6; 10:7).

(b) There are differing statements as to when the last day takes place. Paul teaches that an apocalyptic day is still to come (Rom. 2:5; 2 Cor. 1:14), yet at the same time he regards himself as already involved in the eschatological event. Not only does he take over the existing tradition of the nearness of the last day (Rom. 13:12), but he also calls on his readers to walk "as in the daytime" (13:13), "now" being the day of salvation (2 Cor. 6:2). In other words, the present and the future ages are intertwined. With the *parousia* (→ *4242*) being delayed, the imminent day of Rom. 13:12 is separated out from the remote "last day" (e.g., 2 Pet. 3:8). The suddenness of the last day is taught in various places of the NT (e.g., Lk. 21:34–35; 1 Thess. 5:2, 4; 2 Pet. 3:10). The date is unknown (Matt. 24:42; 25:13; Mk. 13:32). As in the apocalyptic tradition, a period of tribulation and catastrophe will precede the last day (cf. Mk. 13; 2 Tim. 3:1; Rev. 2:10).

(c) What will happen on that last day? God (Acts 17:31) or Christ (1 Cor. 1:8; Phil. 1:6, 10; cf. 2 Cor. 5:10) will judge the world and reward each one according to his or her deeds (Rom. 2:5). A separation will then come between those who are to enter the kingdom and those who are to be cast out; i.e., in this present age the church is still a mixed body (cf. Matt. 25:34, 41). The dead will be raised (Jn. 11:24; cf. 1 Cor. 15:52). Thus the last day becomes a day of fear (Matt. 10:15) and of joy (Lk. 6:23; 21:28; 2 Tim. 4:8).

The message of the last day is not confined to the future, however, but has a definite application to the present. Paul regards the present church as being his glory on the last day (2 Cor. 1:14; Phil. 2:16). Its members are to conduct themselves even now as if living on that day (Rom. 13:13) and as answerable to God when that day comes (Matt. 25:31–46). They must be watchful since its date is unknown (24:42) and it will come suddenly (1 Thess. 5:1–6).

3. The futurity of the last day (Matt. 25:13) does not alter the fact that the exalted Lord is even now with his church (28:20). In Jn. the *paraklētos* (→ *4156*) is the representative of Christ (cf. Jn. 16:5–15 with 16–28). A certain duration of time is indicated by phrases such

as "every day" (Matt. 26:55; Mk. 14:49; Acts 2:46; 3:2; 1 Cor. 15:31), "day after day" (Heb. 7:27; 10:11), "day by day" (2 Cor. 4:16). This present time, although it merges even now with the age to come (1 Cor. 15:20–26; 2 Cor. 4:16), is still characterized by tribulation (Rom. 8:36; 1 Cor. 15:31–32; 2 Cor. 11:28).

See also *marana tha*, maranatha (*3448*); *parousia*, presence, appearing, coming, advent (*4242*).

2477	Ἡρῳδιανοί

Ἡρῳδιανοί (*Hērōdianoi*), Herodians (*2477*).

NT Although, as their name implies, the Herodians were presumably supporters of the house of Herod, little is known about them. They are twice reported in the Gospels as joining forces with the Pharisees in efforts to destroy Jesus. In Mk. 3:6 it was the direct outcome of the Sabbath healing of the man with the withered hand in a Galilean synagogue. In Matt. 22:16 and Mk. 12:13 the question was jointly raised about paying taxes to Caesar.

The Herodians were probably not members of Herod's domestic staff, for the Pharisees would hardly have allied themselves with such people, thus implying equal status. Nor were they court officers, for court officers did not inquire of any beneath them as to the legality of taxes. The Herodians, therefore, likely refers not to an organized party but to those of a particular political outlook—supporters of the house of Herod—and thus also of Roman power.

It seems most probable that the Herodians arose during the rulership not of Herod the Great but of Antipas, who apparently adopted the name Herod after the deposition of Archelaus. Antipas rebuilt Sepphoris, demolished by Varus in 4 B.C., and founded Tiberias on the west shore of the Sea of Galilee. As a cautious experiment, Antipas brought in Jewish officials to govern both cities, each with a regular Gk. constitution. Thus Antipas proved he could depend on the loyalty of the Jewish upper classes, who filled the offices in councils and magistracies.

Antipas's quarrel with Pilate, whatever its origin, no doubt caused his stock to rise among the populace, for there was widespread dissatisfaction with Pilate's rule. The rule of Roman procurators had originated in the desire of the Jews not to suffer another Herod the Great. But when they found that procuratorial rule was even less bearable, there was an upsurge of general support for the house of Herod in the person of Antipas. That support was in part given expression by the appearance in his reign of the Herodians, who as a group probably included not only the official aristocracy that Antipas had created, but other Jews of influence and standing. The Pharisees were no friends of the Herods, but for them to ally with the Herodians in the tribute money incident is understandable. Both parties were seeking to get rid of Jesus as a potential troublemaker, whose activities would sooner or later cause the Romans to intervene and thereby threaten the Jewish establishment.

But why did the Pharisees turn to the Herodians in the incident of the healing of the man with the withered hand in the synagogue on the Sabbath? The issue, on the surface at least, involved the Torah, but the Herodians were more concerned with political than religious issues. Indeed, they were probably not even present at the service described in Mk. 3:6, since the Pharisees went out of the synagogue to take counsel with the Herodians. Most likely this meeting took place since the Herodians were the only political party available in Galilee. After all, the aristocratic party of the Sadducees was based only in Jerusalem (→ *Saddoukaios, 4881*). The Herodians were undoubtedly not interested in the religious question involved in Jesus' apparent breach of the Sabbath, but they were concerned with preventing trouble that might lead to disturbances and so threaten the political and social order. If Jews began to suspect that Jesus might be the Messiah, there would indeed be political unrest, for any messianic claim conflicted with the Herodians' hopes for the restoration of their rule in Judea.

2483 (*hēsychazō*, be quiet, be silent, rest), → *2484*.

2484	ἡσυχία

ἡσυχία (*hēsychia*), quiet, quietness, rest, silence (*2484*); ἡσυχάζω (*hēsychazō*), be quiet, be silent, rest (*2483*); ἡσύχιος (*hēsychios*), quiet (*2485*).

CL & OT 1. In cl. Gk. *hēsychia* is used of the quietness of peace (as opposed to war), relief from pain, a place of solitude, and the life of tranquillity. The adj. *hēsychios* describes a quiet disposition. *hēsychazō* commonly denotes a cessation of speech, work, or conflict, a calming of oneself, or the imposition of silence.

2. In the LXX *hēsychia* can refer to freedom from war (1 Chr. 4:40; 22:9), the stillness of night (Prov. 7:9), and the tranquillity of life (11:12; Ezek. 38:11; 1 Macc. 9:58). The vb. *hēsychazō* is often used of the peace that follows war (e.g., Jdg. 3:11, 30; 2 Ki. 11:20), of refraining from speech (Neh. 5:8; Job 32:6), of ceasing from a course of action (32:1), and of relaxation (37:8).

NT 1. In Lk.'s writings *hēsychazō* denotes resting from work on the Sabbath day (Lk. 23:56), ceasing an effort to convince (Acts 21:14), and silencing potential opposition (Lk. 14:4; Acts 11:18). *hēsychia* in Acts 22:2 portrays the silence that descended on the agitated Jerusalem crowd when they heard Paul address them in Aram.

2. In 1 Thess. 4:11 Paul exhorts the Thessalonians to aim at leading an unobtrusive life of tranquillity (*hēsychazō*). Moreover, they are to avoid the disorderliness of busybodies and to attend to their business with quietness (*hēsychia*) and earn their own living (2 Thess. 3:12). Any eschatological excitement (cf. 2:1–2) that produces corporate turmoil or individual laziness is here repudiated.

3. In the Pastoral Letters, Paul urges Christians to pray for conditions that will permit "peaceful and quiet [*hēsychios*] lives" (1 Tim. 2:2), free from outward disturbance. He enjoins women to listen "in quietness [*hēsychia*]" to the instruction given in the church and to show the necessary deference to their teachers (2:11). The public exposition of Scripture was outside a woman's proper domain of service (though cf. Tit. 2:3–5), as was any exercise of ecclesiastical authority over a man. In the church a woman was to remain silent (*hēsychia*, 1 Tim. 2:12).

4. Peter insists that a woman's adornment should not be external but inward, "the unfading beauty of a gentle and quiet [*hēsychios*] spirit" (1 Pet. 3:4), a spirit that calmly bears disturbances created by others and that itself does not create trouble.

See also *echos¹*, sound, noise, report (*2491*); *sigaō*, to be quiet, be silent (*4967*); *siōpaō*, to be quiet, be silent (*4995*); *phimaō*, to quiet, muzzle (*5821*); *phōnē*, sound, noise, voice, language (*5889*).

2485 (*hēsychios*, quiet), → *2484*.

2490 (*ēcheō*, make a sound), → *2491*.

2491	ἦχος¹

ἦχος¹ (*echos¹*), sound, noise, report (*2491*); ἠχέω (*ēcheō*), make a sound (*2490*); ἦχος² (*echos²*), roaring (*2492*).

CL & OT 1. In cl. Gk. *echos* denotes the sound of words, of letters, or of a voice. It can, like *ēcheō*, be used of an echo and, in a medical sense, of ringing noises in the ears. The vb. *ēcheō* can describe the clanging of a metal shield or the chirp of a grasshopper.

2. In the LXX *echos* occurs 25x, and *ēcheō* 22x. Both words generally denote inarticulate sounds, such as the blast of the trumpet (Exod. 19:16; Ps. 150:3), the roaring of water (46:3; Isa. 17:12), or the tumult of a city or military camp (Ruth 1:19; 1 Sam. 4:5).

NT 1. *echos* occurs 4x in the NT. It denotes the roaring of the sea and the waves (Lk. 21:25), a sound (*echos*) from the sky like a violent blast of wind (Acts 2:2), a trumpet blast (Heb. 12:19), and (metaphorically) a rumor spread throughout a region (Lk. 4:37).

2. In 1 Cor. 13:1 we find the only NT use of *ēcheō*. Paul suggests that to exercise any spiritual gifts, including glossolalia, without love (i.e., without an interpretation that all can understand and benefit from, cf. 14:5–12, 19) is as unedifying as "a resounding [*ēcheō*] gong or a clanging cymbal" that might be heard in pagan worship.

See also *hēsychia*, quiet, quietness, rest, silence (*2484*); *sigaō*, to be quiet, be silent (*4967*); *siōpaō*, to be quiet, be silent (*4995*); *phimaō*, to quiet, muzzle (*5821*); *phōnē*, sound, noise, voice, language (*5889*).

2492 (*echos²*, roaring), → *2491*.

Θ *theta*

2498 θάλασσα

θάλασσα (*thalassa*), sea, lake (*2498*).

CL & OT 1. In cl. Gk. *thalassa* denotes the ocean, the open sea.

2. Mostly the LXX uses *thalassa* for sea, but it does not differentiate between the open sea and inland lakes. The Mediterranean (Jos. 1:4) and the Red Sea (Exod. 23:31) are called *thalassa*, but so are the Dead Sea (Gen. 14:3) and the Lake of Gennesaret (Kinnereth, Num. 34:11). (a) In accord with the general conception of the ancients, the OT pictures the earth as disk-shaped, surrounded by sea (Gen. 1:6–10) or water (→ *hydōr*, *5623*). Itself a creation of God (Ps. 104:24–26), water once covered the whole earth (Gen. 1:2), but Yahweh drove it back and put it in check (1:9–10). God has founded his earth firmly on the seas and rivers (Ps. 24:2).

(b) Because of its relation to chaos (Gen. 1:2, → *abyssos*, abyss, *12*), the sea becomes the embodiment of disaster. In the sea the power of water hostile to God and humans opposes the people of Israel (cf. Ps. 46:3–4; 65:8). The sea is the habitat of the dragon, who is God's enemy (Job 7:12; cf. Dan. 7; Rev. 13:1).

(c) But the sea trembles before Yahweh (Hab. 3:8), who fights and vanquishes its demonic monsters, leviathan, and the dragon (Ps. 74:13–14; Isa. 27:1). Yahweh is the Lord of the sea (cf. Neh. 9:6; Isa. 50:2), and he can command an annihilating flood to liberate the earth in judgment from a humanity that has lapsed into wickedness (Gen. 6–8). Indeed, Yahweh uses the sea in order to drown his enemies (Exod. 14:23, 28; 15:1). Conversely, the pious experience Yahweh's help amid dangers of water and fire (Ps. 18:17; Isa. 43:2).

(d) In Jud., the sea retains its threatening role, only now demonic powers are named even more clearly as having command over the sea. With the victory of Yahweh over the sea, the power of chaos in primeval time (Sir. 43:23), Jud. expected the destruction of the might of the sea monsters by God in the end time, whereas the waters of the sea and rivers will rage against the godless (Wis. 5:22).

NT 1. As in the OT, open sea and inland lake are not differentiated in the NT. The Mediterranean Sea (Acts 10:6, 32), the Red Sea (7:36; 1 Cor. 10:1), and the Sea of Galilee (Matt. 4:18) are all called *thalassa*. Only Lk. deliberately calls the Lake of Gennesaret (Galilee) a *limnē*, an inland lake (→ *3349*).

2. The cosmological role of the sea is essentially the same as in the OT. God is the creator of the tripartite world—heaven, earth, and sea (Acts 4:24; 14:15; Rev. 10:6; 14:7). The "sea of glass" (4:6; 15:2) is the transparent surface of the vault of heaven with the heavenly ocean, which was thought to be the source of rain; the fire of this sea (15:2) is the lightning of the heavenly thunderstorm, here probably understood as judgment. The scene of victors standing on the heavenly sea recalls Israel's song of triumph over Egypt by the Red Sea (Exod. 15).

3. The sea also threatens life in the NT (e.g., Lk. 21:25; Acts 28:4; 2 Cor. 11:26) and so belongs on the side of that which opposes God. Rev. esp. extends Jewish apocalyptic traditions in its conception of the sea as a personal power (Rev. 7:2–3) that will be overcome in the last days; it will have to surrender its dead (20:13) and will then cease to exist (21:1). The sea is also the home of demonic beasts (13:1). In the plagues of the final times, the water of the sea will be turned into blood (8:8; 16:3).

4. Like the open sea, the Sea of Galilee is also controlled by demonic powers, which, together with the storm (cf. Jas. 1:6; Rev. 7:1), try to destroy Jesus' disciples. But the wind and the sea must obey Jesus' authoritative word (Matt. 8:23–27; Mk. 4:35–41; Lk.

8:22–25). Jesus' walking on the sea (Matt. 14:22–33; Mk. 6:45–52) may be understood as a victory over the demonic powers localized in the water (cf. also the drowning of the Gadarene pigs in Matt. 8:32; Mk. 5:13; Lk. 8:33). Water is a favored locality for a theophany (cf. the call of the first disciples at the Sea of Galilee, Matt. 4:18–22; Mk. 1:16–20; cf. also Matt. 17:24–27). There also seems to be a symbolic meaning in the sea when Peter, Andrew, James, and John are given a magnificent catch of fish (Lk. 5:1–11; Jn. 21:1–11); Jesus uses this miracle to depict a fruitful mission field.

See also *pēgē*, spring, source (*4380*); *hydōr*, water (*5623*); *kataklysmos*, a deluge, flood (*2886*); *Iordanēs*, the river Jordan (*2674*); *limnē*, lake (*3349*).

2501 (*thambeō*, be astounded, amazed), → *2512*.

2502 (*thambos*, astonishment, fear), → *2512*.

2505 θάνατος

θάνατος (*thanatos*), death (*2505*); θανατόω (*thanatoō*), kill (*2506*); ἀθανασία (*athanasia*), immortality (*114*); θνήσκω (*thnēskō*), die (*2569*); ἀποθνήσκω (*apothnēskō*), die (*633*); συναποθνήσκω (*synapothnēskō*), die together with someone (*5271*); θνητός (*thnētos*), mortal (*2570*).

CL 1. *thanatos* means the act of dying or the state of death. But it is also used of mortal danger, the manner of death, and the death penalty. Similarly, *thanatoō* means put someone to death, kill, and lead into mortal danger. Living creatures subject to death are described as *thnētos*, mortal. Humans are called *thnētoi*, mortals, in contrast to the gods, who possess *athanasia*, immortality. Only in exceptional cases are human beings elevated as heroes into the number of the immortal gods.

thnēskō, die, and *apothnēskō*, expire, denote the act of dying. Where a reference is to a death shared with others we find the compound form *synapothnēskō*, die with someone.

In the Hel. period the words *thanatos*, *thanatoō*, *thnēskō*, and *apothnēskō* are also used metaphorically of intellectual and spiritual death.

2. For the Gks., death meant the end of living activity, even if the soul found a place in the realm of the dead. Death is the common destiny of everyone; its negative side is occasionally made evident, when death is personified as a demon or monster from the underworld. Since Gks. had no doctrine of creation, death did not pose for them the question "Why?" Realization of the inevitability of death found its normal consequence in the demand to enjoy life to the full (cf. the maxim in 1 Cor. 15:32, "Let us eat and drink, for tomorrow we die"). A gentle death after a long life was a great blessing, but the ancients also found comfort in death as a release from the futilities of life.

3. A way of overcoming the agony of death appears in the notion that a person lives on in one's children. Epitaphs and great funeral monuments also help to keep alive the memory of the deceased, thereby making death tolerable.

A special characteristic of the Gks. was to make death a part of life by regarding it as an act of human achievement. It was important to die gloriously, either in fighting courageously or by facing death without fear. In such cases, death was regarded as a fine thing. Gk. philosophers had various reflections on the process of dying and the meaning of death.

4. Occasionally one finds a belief in the immortality of the soul. Plato, for example, discusses it at length and gives it a philosophical basis as the corollary of a moral view of personality. In death the soul is freed from the body, the immortal from the mortal. Plato even has

a doctrine of the transmigration of souls, which is connected with rewards and punishments for actions in life. The Stoics in general rejected personal immortality; in death, the individual soul becomes submerged in the divine universal soul, which permeates the cosmos.

OT All the words in the *thanatos* group are found in the LXX, though *athanasia*, immortality, occurs only in late writings (Wis., 4 Macc.). The way in which they are used is not much different from that in cl. Gk.

1. (a) Death means the final end of one's existence (2 Sam. 12:15; 14:14). Humans have been taken from the ground, and to dust they return (Gen. 3:19). Once the soul has descended to Sheol (→ *hades*, 87), no further life can come to it. This is evident in the frequent complaints that death brings with it separation from Yahweh, the source of life (Ps. 6:5; 30:9; 88:5, 10–12; Isa. 38:11). We have no option but to accept the common lot of death (Gen. 3:19; Sir. 14:18–19; 41:1–4).

If God allows us to die old and full of days, so that we achieve in this life what is possible for us, we may be thankful and content (Gen. 15:15; Ps. 91:16). True, we may sigh over the transience of life (90:3–6) and speak in our prayers of the snares of death and of descent into hell (116:3, 8), but death does not become in itself an object of fear. What is to be feared is an evil or early death, which indicates God's punishment for human guilt. For God punishes individuals by death in order to cleanse the community of his people of evildoers (cf. Deut. 13).

(b) The OT does not contain a concept of original sin or inherited death as a consequence of sin. Death in the abstract is not linked to divine punishment. Adam was threatened with *early* death as a punishment for a definite act of disobedience (Gen. 2:17, "when you eat of it you will surely die"). Even in Ps. 90, which refers back to the story of the fall and reflects on the connection between sin and death, it is primarily the fleeting nature of life that is attributed to human sin (cf. also Ps. 14:2; 51).

(c) Since an individual can lead life only as a member of the people of Yahweh, the idea does not occur to anyone that death may be brought about as an act of heroism. Even where the individual becomes keenly aware of the burdensomeness of life, committing suicide would be a denial of life. When Saul killed himself after the death of his sons and defeat in battle in order to avoid falling into the hands of the Philistines, there is no suggestion that this is a heroic ending to his life (1 Sam. 31; cf. 2 Sam. 17:23).

(d) Only occasionally is Yahweh seen as the Lord of Sheol (Ps. 139:8). Total confidence may be placed in him, even in the face of death (73:23–28).

2. (a) After the exile the concepts of the people and the covenant of Yahweh were given a new meaning. There was an individualization of the relationship with God (Jer. 31:29–34; Ezek. 18:2–32). This meant that for the Jews of the last few centuries before Christ, death posed a difficult problem. It was increasingly looked on as something inappropriate to human destiny. Writers stressed that Adam's sin brought death into the world: "You laid upon him (Adam) one commandment of yours; but he transgressed it, and immediately you appointed death for him and for his descendants" (2 Esd. 3:7).

(b) Where death is thus regarded as something brought on humankind in the course of history, the way is open to reflect on the possibility that God will overcome sin and death. Thus in Jewish apocalyptic we find the concept of a kingdom of God at the end of time, in which sin has been conquered and death has lost its power. The hope of a resurrection (→ *anastasis*, 414), first found in Isa. 26:19 and Dan. 12:2, further makes possible a faith that even for earlier generations death will be overcome by a divine act of new creation. The righteous will enter into eternal life, the unrighteous into eternal death (2 Esd. 7:31–44).

(c) There is also an increasing use of the language of death in a figurative sense. Death takes place whenever Israel, or (beginning with Ezek.) the individual Israelite, breaks away from God (Ezek. 18:21–32). Here it is the breaking off of fellowship with God, which is seen as death, just as its enjoyment is seen as life.

3. With the changes of spiritual emphasis that characterized the Hel. period, strongly dualistic ideas began to find their way into Jud. Thus the soul came to be regarded as immortal (Wis. 3:4; 4:1; 15:3). It remains in heavenly places, awaiting the resurrection (*1 Enoch* 102–104; 2 Esd. 7:88–99)—except for those writers who abandoned the concept of resurrection and held that an eternal, bodiless existence began immediately after death (4 Macc. 16:13; 17:12).

Another effect of Gk. influence was the way that Jewish martyrs saw their death as heroic, so that it was extolled as glorious (4 Macc. 10:1) and virtuous (2 Macc. 6:31). Josephus has the Jewish commander Eleazar encourage the Jews in the fortress of Masada to choose death rather than surrender to the Romans. If it is impossible to live with honor, one ought to die bravely. The choice of such a death leaves behind it admiration, and those who fall fighting for liberty must be regarded as fortunate.

NT In the NT *thanatos*, death, occurs 120x: in the Gospels, mostly with reference to the death of Jesus; in Paul, mainly of human death. *thanatoō*, kill, occurs 11x; *thnētos*, mortal, 6x, all in Paul. *apothnēskō*, die, is used 112x in the NT. In the Synoptic Gospels it is rarely used of the death of Jesus; in Paul, however, this use is frequent because of the confessional formula, "Christ died for our sins" (1 Cor. 15:3; cf. Rom. 5:8). *synapothnēskō*, die together with someone, occurs in Mk. 14:31; 2 Cor. 7:3; 2 Tim. 2:11; only in the last instance does it have a Christological reference. *athanasia*, immortality, occurs 3x (1 Cor. 15:53–54; 1 Tim. 6:16).

1. The NT view of death is in direct continuity with the old Jewish view. Humans are *thnētos*, mortal; they live in the shadow of death (Matt. 4:16; Heb. 2:15). God, the source of all life, is the only one to whom immortality belongs (1 Tim. 6:16). Death is seen as the death of an individual, and relativizing death by a reference to the continuing life of a community is foreign to NT thought.

(a) This being the case, importance is attached to the question of what causes death. The answer to this question is summed up by Paul: "The wages of sin is death" (Rom. 6:23). On the basis of this view, the devil can be regarded as the one who has power over death (Heb. 2:14), though, of course, it is God himself who can destroy both body and soul in hell (cf. Matt. 10:28; Rev. 2:23). For the NT the question as to the cause of death is a theological one. Death is universal, and it points to the universality of human guilt and our need of redemption. Where we turn our backs on God, we cut ourselves off from the root of life and become subject to death.

If we dedicate our lives to earthly things, over which we exercise control, we cut ourselves off from the source of true life. In our progress toward death we catch sight of the basic condition of life: We live as sinners *in* death. Death is thus the power dominating our lives and to that extent is a present reality. "Spiritual" death and "physical" death, inextricably bound up together, constitute the reality of a life in sin. Thus the sinner cries: "Who will rescue me from this body of death?" (Rom. 7:24).

(b) It is Paul who, among the NT writers, reflects most on the connection between guilt and one's mortal destiny. After pointing out that all without distinction have fallen into sin and thus become subject to death (Rom. 1–4), and that they are called to life in Christ, he goes on in 5:12–21 to develop these themes with the help of Adam–Christ typology. The life that has been brought about by Christ forms an analogy to the fact that "sin entered the world through one man [Adam], and death through sin" (Rom. 5:12; cf. 1 Cor. 15:21–22). But death is not simply a fate we have inherited, "because all sinned." That is, death is a punishment for each person's own sin. On the other hand, salvation and life, i.e., victory over death, do not come as a result of our own efforts, but only through an act of God's grace coming from outside us and appropriated by us.

In our rebellion against God, we seek to find life through our own works; consequently, whenever we avail ourselves of the law as a means of salvation, we find death instead. Therefore, law, sin, and death are on the same level: "The sting of death is sin, and the power of sin is the law" (1 Cor. 15:56). Accordingly, for those who try to find life on the basis of law, death becomes a present reality (see Rom. 7:9–10).

If death is the consequence of human sin, then why are nonhuman living creatures likewise subject to mortality? To this Paul replies that the "creation" has been subjected, not by its own will but as a result of human sin, to futility and impermanence. It now waits to be set free from death, together with the "children of God" (Rom. 8:19–22). Thus, Paul does not regard even death in nature as a "natural" phenomenon.

(c) From all that we have said, it is evident that in the NT death is regarded not as a natural process, but as a historical event resulting from the sinful human condition. Death is a power that enslaves one in the course of this life (Heb. 2:15). The possibility of removing the horror of death by means of intellectual insight concerning its inevitability or through a heroic act of dying is excluded in NT thought.

2. Statements about Jesus' death on the cross form the central point of the salvation story in the NT (→ *stauros*, *5089*). They are usually found in connection with statements about his resurrection and the justification or new life of those who believe.

(a) Pre-Pauline confessions stated "that Christ died for our sins according to the Scriptures, that he was buried, that he was raised on the third day according to the Scriptures, and that he appeared ..." (1 Cor. 15:3–5), and also that "he was delivered over to death for our sins and was raised to life for our justification" (Rom. 4:25). Jesus died our human death (Phil. 2:7–8; Heb. 2:14), and this death is for us, i.e., for our advantage (Mk. 10:45; 14:24; Rom. 5:6–8; 1 Thess. 5:10; Heb. 2:9–10). His death overcomes the law (Rom. 7:4; cf. Gal. 2:21), sin (2 Cor. 5:21; Col. 1:22), and our own death (Rom. 5:9; 2 Tim. 1:10; Heb. 2:14–15; Rev. 1:17–18). It is to make manifest this victory that the death of Jesus, the risen, present, and coming One (1 Cor. 11:26; 2 Cor. 5:14–15), is proclaimed, in order that his death may not have been in vain (Gal. 2:21).

(b) The gospel of victory over death is expressed in different ways. For example, Jesus' death was a propitiatory sacrifice that removes the guilt of sin (Rom. 3:25–26; 1 Cor. 11:24–25; cf. also Eph. 1:7; 1 Pet. 1:18–19). Here the OT ideas of the covenant sacrifice (Mk. 14:24; Heb. 13:20) and the Passover sacrifice (1 Cor. 5:7) also find a place. Christ's death was also a substitutionary sacrifice (2 Cor. 5:21) and a ransom—a concept originating in the laws of slavery, but strongly metaphorical in its Christological use (cf. Mk. 10:45; Gal. 3:13; 2 Pet. 2:1).

(c) John, in contrast to the pre-Pauline and Pauline tradition, places emphasis not on the death of Jesus as such, but on the whole event of his coming into this world of death. His death on the cross is the highest expression of the incarnation of the Logos. At the same time, when seen as an exaltation, it is a divine token of the general victory over death (Jn. 12:33; 18:32).

(d) God breaks the power of sin by identifying himself with us in the death of Jesus. Since he offers his own self as a basis for life, we are freed from compulsion to commit the primal sin of self-righteousness. We are acquitted (justified, Rom. 4:24), brought into a proper creaturely status (new creation, 2 Cor. 5:17), and given new life with Christ (Eph. 2:4–5).

3. The NT accords special importance to the defeat of death (or law or sin), accomplished through the death of Jesus and to the corresponding promise of life already present. (a) Note, for example, Rom. 6:10–11: "The death he died, he died to sin once for all; but the life he lives, he lives to God. In the same way, count yourselves dead to sin but alive to God in Christ Jesus" (cf. also Gal. 2:19–20; Col. 2:20). These passages tell us that where Christ's death on the cross has been overcome, where a person has given up to death his or her "old self"—i.e., the desire to find life independently by one's own efforts—there Christ is experienced as the power and wisdom of God (cf. 1 Cor. 1:23–24). True life is life that comes by God's grace. It begins with faith in Christ.

(b) John expresses essentially the same concept: "I tell you the truth, if anyone keeps my word, he will never see death" (Jn. 8:51; cf. also 5:24). "We know that we have passed from death to life, because we love our brothers" (1 Jn. 3:14). Freedom from death, in the sense of spiritual death as a result of sin, gives to those who know they have been accepted by God the freedom to give themselves without reserve to their neighbors.

(c) In the Synoptics the defeat of death is demonstrated especially by miracle stories, particularly the raising of the dead. Faced with death, Jesus says: "Don't be afraid; just believe" (Mk. 5:36). He can thus say to his disciples, "Follow me, and let the dead bury their own dead" (Matt. 8:22). Such sayings are consistent with viewing freedom from sin as deliverance from death and the beginning of real life lived by grace.

(d) The defeat of death here and now for the Christian has a natural corollary in the final subjection of the unbeliever to death. For the apostle's preaching is to one "the smell of death; to the other, the fragrance of life" (2 Cor. 2:16).

4. If death is the result of sin, if we have been delivered from the power of sin and death (Rom. 6:13), and if we are now new creatures (2 Cor. 5:17), why does physical death continue to reign over us? The NT gives various answers to this question.

(a) For Paul physical death links with the dialectic of the "already" and the "not yet." The idea that death is the "last enemy" (1 Cor. 15:26) and has yet to be swallowed up in victory (15:54–55) appears side by side with the believer's song of triumph: "Thanks be to God! He gives us the victory through our Lord Jesus Christ" (15:57). We have received the Spirit as a pledge of eternal life, yet we await the redemption of our bodies (Rom. 8:23; 1 Cor. 15:53). The expectation of this victory over death takes the concrete form of a belief in the resurrection of the dead, which has already begun with the resurrection of Jesus (1 Cor. 15:12–21). Thus, hope in God who gives life to the dead (Rom. 4:17) becomes an integral part of our faith (2 Cor. 5:1–10; Rom. 5:1–5).

This thought is developed at the Christological level, where Christians learn to regard their suffering and death, through faith, as suffering and dying with Christ. In the very experience of suffering and death Paul finds fellowship with God, and thus also assurance of salvation and of eternal life (Rom. 8:36–39; 2 Cor. 4:11–12; Phil. 1:20). In this sense he can regard death as simply a laying aside of the mortal body. "For to me, to live is Christ and to die is gain" (Phil. 1:21).

(b) John does not give extensive consideration to the death of a believer. He concentrates on the present tense of salvation and all but ignores the connection between death and the traditional doctrine of judgment and resurrection (but see Jn. 5:28–29). Since believers have passed through the judgment and already have eternal life, they will not die for all eternity (10:28). Hence, in 14:2–3 Jesus speaks of our being taken up into the "rooms" of his Father's house, presumably at the time of death.

(c) In the later writings of the NT, the emphasis on the present experience of salvation becomes progressively replaced by a strong moral interpretation of the Christian faith, with the result that physical death ceases to be a problem for the Christian. We must all die on account of our sins, only to find grace at the final judgment. Thus, it is easy to understand how the concept arose of a second death for those who are condemned: "He who conquers will not be hurt at all by the second death" (Rev. 2:11; cf. 20:13–14).

(d) The different traditions have in common the conviction that death does not separate believers from God, but rather leads them into fellowship with the suffering and dying Christ and thus to the source of all life. "If we live, we live to the Lord; and if we die, we die to the Lord. So, whether we live or die, we belong to the Lord" (Rom. 14:8; see also 8:38; Jn. 12:24–26; Phil. 1:20; 1 Thess. 4:13–14; Rev. 14:13).

See also *apokteinō*, kill (*650*); *katheudō*, sleep (*2761*); *nekros*, dead, dead person (*3738*).

2506 (thanatoō, kill), → 2505.

2507 θάπτω

θάπτω (thaptō), bury (2507); τάφος (taphos), tomb (5439); ταφή (taphē), burial (5438); ἐνταφιάζω (entaphiazō), prepare for burial (1946); ἐνταφιασμός (entaphiasmos), laying out for burial (1947); μνῆμα (mnēma), tomb (3645); μνημεῖον (mnēmeion), memorial, tomb (3646) ; συνθάπτω (synthaptō), be buried with (5313).

CL & OT 1. *thaptō* in cl. Greek means to give someone a proper burial. *taphos* and cognates (derived from *thaptō*) mean funeral rites and, later, tomb; *taphē* is burial, funeral, or place of burial. *entaphiazō* and *entaphiasmos*, both rare, apply to instances of inhumation or embalming. *mnēma* and *mnēmeion*, derived from *mnaomai* (be mindful of), mean tomb.

Both burial and cremation were widespread in antiquity. In the NT period cremation was almost universal among the Romans, but inhumation again became prevalent in the 2d century. In the Semitic East burial was dominant. It is questionable how much religious significance should be attached to differences in the manner of disposal of the dead, though in some cases, as in Egypt, preservation of the body was seen as all-important, as indispensable to the afterlife. Otherwise, the emphasis was often more on the proper care and guardianship of the tomb as a cultic place.

2. In the LXX *taphos*, *mnēma*, and *mnēmeion* can all mean tomb, with no real difference. *taphē* can mean both tomb and burial. In Gen. 50:2, 3, 26 *entaphiazō*, *taphē*, and *thaptō* translate the same Heb. root *ḥānaṭ* (to embalm) in speaking of the embalming of Jacob and Joseph in Egypt. Elsewhere *thaptō* means bury.

Inhumation or placing in caves or rock sepulchers was the universal Jewish practice in all periods. Tombs were the communal possession of a family (Gen. 23:4; etc.); there a dead person "was gathered to his people" (25:8; etc.). The cremation of Saul and his sons (1 Sam. 31:12) was exceptional, and such treatment may be regarded as a shameful abuse (cf. Amos 2:1) or a solemn punishment (Jos. 7:25). The law required burial of an executed criminal on the same day (Deut. 21:23), and care was taken to bury enemies slain in battle (1 Ki. 11:15; etc.). To be denied burial was a shameful indignity (Deut. 28:26; 1 Ki. 13:22).

3. It was common in NT times to practice secondary burial, placing the bones in "ossuaries" that were stored in extended family sepulchers. Scrupulous care was taken to let none be unburied. Rab. interpretation of Deut. 21:23 insisted that burial be completed, if possible, on the day of death.

NT 1. The NT uses the same three interchangeable words for tomb as in the LXX. *mnēmeion* occurs 40x, *mnēma* 8x, and *taphos* 7x.

2. In Matt. 23:27 Jesus likens the scribes and Pharisees to "whitewashed tombs" (cf. Lk. 11:44). It was the custom to chalk graves on 15 Adar, lest those inadvertently walking over them incur pollution before the Passover (cf. Jn. 11:55; 18:28). In Matt. 23:29–31, Jesus alludes to the Pharisees' scrupulosity in embellishing the tombs of prophets whom their forebears had rejected and killed. The contrast is between their fastidious outward observance of cleanliness and the evil of their inward motives (cf. Rom. 3:13; also Acts 23:3).

3. As to NT burial traditions, the duty fell on the family or closest associates of the deceased (Matt. 8:21; 14:12; Mk. 6:29; Lk. 9:59–60). It was carried out with the utmost possible speed (Acts 5:5–10). It was deemed a good work to make special provision for the burial of strangers (Matt. 27:7–8). In Rev. 11:9 the two witnesses are subjected to the indignity of lying dead and unburied for three and a half days. The fullest accounts of funeral practice are the narratives of Lazarus (Jn. 11) and of Jesus himself.

4. When Jesus arrived in Bethany after Lazarus had died, he had been in the tomb four days (Jn. 11:17). The lapse of time is significant.

It was the custom for mourners to visit the dead for the first three days, after which the progress of decomposition was thought to be irreversible. Hence the action of Jesus demonstrated his absolute mastery over death. This episode polarized reactions to Jesus and pointed to his own resurrection.

5. Joseph of Arimathea's decision to bury Jesus was an act both of obedience to the Jewish law and of devotion to one whom he had feared to acknowledge in his life. Deut. 21:22–23 instructs that someone hung on a tree should not remain there all night but be buried the same day, so that the land be not defiled, for such a one is accursed.

Nicodemus brought an enormous quantity of myrrh and aloes for the burial (Jn. 19:39). This evidently accorded with usual practice (cf. 11:44), except that the sheer quantity of spices represented a costly act of devotion to Jesus, resembling that of Mary (12:2–11). Jesus there applied her gift to the theme of his burial (*entaphiasmos*, Jn. 12:7; cf. Matt. 26:12; Mk. 14:8). Note also the significant gift of myrrh to the baby Jesus (Matt. 2:11), early seen as symbolizing burial and the expectation of resurrection. Unlike the Egyptians, the Jews did not embalm, but myrrh and other aromatic spices represented the preservation of the body, and this to the Jewish mind was the prerequisite of resurrection.

6. The burial of Jesus plays a part in early Christian preaching as authenticating his death and resurrection (1 Cor. 15:4), both of them foreshadowed in the Scriptures. The words of Ps. 16:10 ("You will not . . . let your Holy One see decay") were esp. applied to the risen Christ, not to David, for the latter's body was in a tomb and had seen decay (Acts 2:27–31; 13:35–37). The focal burial text (Deut. 21:22–23) also recurs in a new application, which avers the treatment of the sin-bearing Jesus as under its curse (cf. Acts 5:30; 10:39; 13:29; Gal. 3:13; 1 Pet. 2:24).

This emphasis on Jesus' burial contrasts with a disinterest in the actual tomb. All four Gospels describe the discovery of the empty tomb, but the subject is not mentioned in 1 Cor. 15, the earliest surviving testimony to the resurrection. That same chapter, however, insists strongly on the relevance of eyewitness testimony; Paul argues that the literal and theological aspects of the resurrection are inseparable. The truth of Christ's resurrection cannot be divorced from an event to whose objectivity such testimony was relevant.

7. In Rom. 6:4 and Col. 2:12 burial (*synthaptō*, be buried with) is used as a figure of baptism. The disciple is identified with the Master in death, burial, and risen life.

2509 (*tharreō*, be of good courage, take heart), → 2510.

2510 θαρσέω

θαρσέω (tharseō), be of good courage, take heart (2510); θαρρέω (tharreō), be of good courage, take heart (2509).

CL & OT Both vbs. mean be of good courage, take heart. The imperative form *tharsei*, *tharseite*, take heart, is common in cl. Gk. The dominant form in the LXX is *tharseō*. It is consistently used to translate the command, "Fear not." Whether it is Moses' exhortation to the people overcome with fear (Exod. 14:13; 20:20), Elijah's words of comfort to the widow in Zarephath threatened with death by starvation (1 Ki. 17:13), or prophetic encouragement to the nation or to Jerusalem (Zeph. 3:16; Hag. 2:5 = LXX 2:6; Zech. 8:13, 15), comfort and encouragement arise from overcoming fear and are based on confident hope in God's help and promises.

NT 1. The companions of blind Bartimaeus address him with the expression *tharsei*, take heart (Mk. 10:49), because Jesus was calling him and offering help. Elsewhere the imperative is found only in the mouth of Jesus. The paralytic whose sin Jesus forgives is to be of good cheer (Matt. 9:2), as is the woman with an issue of blood whom he heals (9:22). When the disciples are frightened by his appearance on the lake, Jesus' word of comfort (*tharseite*) is strengthened by *mē phobeisthe*, fear not (Matt. 14:27). In the farewell discourses of the Fourth Gospel, Jesus commands his disciples, whom he is leaving behind in a world full of tribulation: "Take heart! I have overcome the world" (Jn. 16:33). In Acts 23:11 a similar word of comfort is given by the risen Lord to Paul in prison.

2. In 2 Cor. 7:16 Paul uses *tharreō* to express the confidence he has in the Corinthian church. In 10:1–2 the same word is used of the boldness with which he is determined to face those who oppose him in Corinth. In 5:6, 8 he uses this vb. to speak of the confidence that fills his heart. In his life of suffering he is supported by the assurance that he has an eternal home with the Lord. Heb. exhorts its readers to a similar confidence in the face of a pagan environment hostile to them (13:6).

See also *paramytheomai*, encourage, cheer up, console (*4170*).

2512	θαῦμα

θαῦμα (*thauma*), object of wonder, wonder, marvel, miracle (*2512*); θαυμάζω (*thaumazō*), be astonished, wonder at, be surprised (*2513*); θαυμάσιος (*thaumasios*), wonderful, remarkable (*2514*); θαυμαστός (*thaumastos*), wonderful, marvelous, astonishing (*2515*); ἐκθαυμάζω (*ekthaumazō*), be greatly amazed (*1703*); θαμβέω (*thambeō*), be astounded, amazed (*2501*); ἐκθαμβέω (*ekthambeō*), be amazed, alarmed (*1701*); ἔκθαμβος (*ekthambos*), utterly astonished (*1702*); θάμβος (*thambos*), astonishment, fear (*2502*); θορυβέω (*thorybeō*), throw into disorder, pass. be troubled, distressed (*2572*); θόρυβος (*thorybos*), commotion, uproar, turmoil (*2573*); θορυβάζω (*thorybazō*), cause trouble, pass. be troubled, distressed (*2571*).

CL & OT 1. The word group associated with *thauma* designates that which by its appearance arouses astonishment and amazement. Synonymous with these is the word group associated with *thambos*, astonishment, dread, and *thambeō*, frighten. The compounds *ekthambeō*, terrify, and *ekthambos*, terrifying, terrified, are intensive. Examples of *thaumazō* as a human reaction to the working of a deity in the revelation of its divine power is found throughout Gk. religion, beginning with Homer.

2. In the LXX *thaumazō* occurs primarily in Job, Isa., and Sir., often in conjunction with *prosōpon*, face; it means to lift up the countenance, show favor toward, be partial (Job 13:10; Prov. 18:5). According to Deut. 10:17; 2 Chr. 19:7, God is not partisan. In a more general sense *thaumazō* denotes a friendly disposition that readily grants requests (e.g., Gen. 19:21), takes into consideration (Deut. 28:50), and is highly favored (2 Ki. 5:1). In this kind of usage, the element of fear is not included. Elsewhere, however, *thaumazō* means to be petrified with fear (e.g., Lev. 26:32; Job 21:5; Ps. 48:5; Jer. 4:9). On occasion the idea of astonishment passes over to that of horror. Human reaction to God's activity can be astonishment (e.g., Job 42:11) mingled with fear and horror (e.g., 21:5).

The adjs. *thaumastos* and *thaumasios* are found chiefly in Ps. and Sir. Daniel prays to the awesome and fear-inspiring God (Dan. 9:4 in Theodotion). God is awe-inspiring among his holy ones (Ps. 68:35); he is marvelous in the execution of his deeds, both in creation and history (cf. 9:1; 26:7; 71:17; 86:10); in 106:22 the miracles of God in the land of Ham and his "awesome deeds" at the Red Sea are compared. In 118:23–24 the rejected stone becomes the capstone, which "is marvelous in our eyes"; in the NT this is applied to Christ (cf. Matt. 21:42; Mk. 12:10–11; Lk. 20:17; Acts 4:11; 1 Pet. 2:7).

NT 1. In the NT *thauma* occurs only 2x: in the phrase "[it is] no wonder" (2 Cor. 11:14) and in Rev. 17:6, "I was greatly astonished." *thaumasios* is found only in Matt. 21:15 for the "wonderful things" of Jesus. The adj. *thaumastos* occurs 6x: twice (Matt. 21:42; Mk. 12:11) in the quotation of Ps. 118:23–24 concerning the "marvelous" thing about the stone the builders rejected (see above). In 1 Pet. 2:9 the light to which God has called Christians is "wonderful." In Jn. 9:30 the man healed by Jesus describes as "remarkable" the attitude of the Jews

who refused to acknowledge where Jesus had come from. (For Rev. 15:1, 3, see below.) *thaumazō* occurs the most frequently (43x).

The word group related to *thambos* is comparatively rare in the NT (Mk. 1:27; 9:15; 10:24, 32; 14:33; 16:5–6; Lk. 4:36; 5:9; Acts 3:10–11). There is a similar number of instances of *thorybos* (Matt. 26:5; 27:24; Mk. 5:38; 14:2; Acts 20:1; 21:34; 24:18) and *thorybeō* (Matt. 9:23; Mk. 5:39; Acts 17:5; 20:10). Matt. 26:5; 27:24; Mk. 14:2 are concerned with disturbances in the nation that could arise from action taken against Jesus. Matt. 9:23 and Mk. 5:38–39 report the din in Jairus's house following the death of his little girl. According to Acts 17:5, the Jews in Thessalonica throw the town into an uproar in order to disrupt Paul's missionary work. In 20:1 *thorybos* denotes the silversmiths' riot in Ephesus (19:23–32), and in 21:34 the riot among the people of Jerusalem (21:30–32) that leads to Paul's imprisonment.

2. In the Synoptics *thaumazō* describes the amazement people experienced at Jesus' healing activity and miraculous power, such as in the healing of the Gerasene demoniac (Mk. 5:20), the cursing of the fig tree (Matt. 21:20), and the healing of a mute demoniac (Matt. 9:33; Lk. 11:14; cf. Matt. 15:31). In Matt. 9:33 the impression is put into words: "Nothing like this has ever been seen in Israel!" In the story of the storm on the sea note how closely astonishment and fear belong together: Matt. speaks of astonishment (8:27), Mk. of being terrified (4:41), and Lk. combines both (8:25; cf. 9:43).

thaumazō does not always include an element of fear. In Lk. 11:38 the Pharisees express amazement at Jesus' disregard for the Jewish purificatory prescriptions. Otherwise, however, *thaumazō* and *thambeō* or *ekplēssō* (→ *1742*) are closely related in the Gospels.

In Nazareth the people are "amazed" at the gracious words Jesus uses (Lk. 4:22), though this does not stop them from trying to kill him (4:29). According to Mk. 9:15, even the sight of Jesus is enough to produce "wonder" (*ekthambeō*). On the way to Jerusalem Jesus' followers are filled with fear and astonishment at his persistence (10:32, *thambeō*). Hence, it is appropriate to ask whether the amazement to which Jesus' discussion with the Pharisees gives rise when they question him concerning tax for the emperor may not have contained an element of fear (Matt. 22:22; Mk. 12:17; Lk. 20:26). Do the Gospel writers postulate such an inkling of divine presence on the part of Pilate when they record he was amazed that Jesus did not defend himself against his accusers (Matt. 27:14; Mk. 15:5)?

There are two reports of Jesus' being surprised: at the faith of the Capernaum centurion (Matt. 8:10; Lk. 7:9) and at the unbelief of the people in Nazareth (Mk. 6:6). A case of Jesus' being distressed (*ekthambeō*) occurs in Gethsemane (Mk. 14:33).

Lk.'s infancy narrative (Lk. 1–2) uses *thaumazō* 4x. Zechariah's long delay in the temple, together with his loss of speech, surprises the people (1:21–22); they take it as an indication that something extraordinary has happened. The same is true when the child born to Zechariah and Elizabeth is given the name John by his father (1:63). The Christmas message of the shepherds arouses amazement (2:18), as does the encounter of Jesus' parents with Simeon and his words in the temple (2:33). Lk.'s Easter narrative uses the same word 2x. In 24:12 Peter is amazed at what has happened; in 24:41 the disciples are unable to believe for joy and astonishment when Jesus appears to them. The appearance of the angels at the grave is also frightening (*ekthambeō* in Mk. 16:5–6).

3. In the Fourth Gospel, *thaumazō* denotes the amazement that the Jews feel in seeing Jesus' knowledge of Scripture without his having received formal instruction (Jn. 7:15); he replies (7:16) by pointing out that his teaching comes from the Father, who has sent him. In 7:21 Jesus notes the surprise of the Jews to a miracle he has performed on the Sabbath (7:23). Jesus' works will inevitably provoke astonishment: "For the Father loves the Son and shows him all he does. Yes, to your amazement he will show him even greater things than these" (5:20). To Nicodemus Jesus directs the challenge, "You should not be surprised" (3:7). Nicodemus is not to take offense at the initially unintelligible language concerning the new birth; rather, he is to open

his heart to it in faith (cf. 5:25–28; also 1 Jn. 3:13, where Christians should not be surprised at the hatred of the world).

4. According to Acts 2:7, when the Spirit was poured out the assembled crowd of Jews are "utterly amazed" (*thaumazō*). "Wonder [*thambos*] and amazement [*ekstasis*, → *1749*]" fill the crowd at Peter's healing of a man crippled from birth (3:10; cf. 3:12). For the Sanhedrin an object of astonishment is the boldness of Peter and John and the fact that they are "unschooled, ordinary men" (4:13). Elsewhere the word occurs in Acts when OT stories are related (7:31; cf. Exod. 3:3) or quoted (Acts 13:41; cf. Hab. 1:5).

5. In the NT letters (apart from 2 Cor. 11:14, cf. above), two passages should be noted. In Gal. 1:6 Paul expresses amazement that the Galatians have so quickly allowed themselves to be won over to another gospel; this leads into a debate concerning the Galatian teachers of false doctrine. In 2 Thess. 1:10, the Lord will come in order to be glorified among his saints (cf. LXX of Ps. 68:35) and "to be marveled at" (*thaumazō*) among those who believe in him. In Jude 16 the author notes how some people "flatter" others in order to gain advantage over them.

6. In Rev. *thaumazō* occurs 4x (13:3; 17:6–8). Rev. 13:1–3 reports that at the emergence of the beast from the sea, the embodiment of the anti-Christian power, "the whole world was astonished and followed the beast" (13:3). This astonishment leads to adoration of the beast and the power behind him, namely, the dragon. The astonishment in 17:8 also refers to this adoration. The model for this apocalyptic picture is the cult of the Roman Caesars. The astonishment of the seer in 17:7, however, is different; this concerns the mystery of "Babylon the great," which is drunk with the blood of the saints and of the witnesses of Jesus (13:5–6).

Further, Rev. 15:1 speaks of a "great and marvelous [*thaumastos*] sign." The seer sees seven angels bringing the seven final plagues that consummate the divine judgment of wrath. But before this event of terror happens, he catches a glimpse of the multitude who have conquered and who sing the song of Moses and of the Lamb (15:2), part of which is a praise of the "great and marvelous [*thaumasta*] . . . deeds" of God (15:3).

See also *sēmeion*, sign, wonder, miracle (*4956*); *teras*, miraculous sign, prodigy, portent, omen, wonder (*5469*).

2513 (*thaumazō*, be astonished, wonder at, be surprised), → *2512*.

2514 (*thaumasios*, wonderful, remarkable), → *2512*.

2515 (*thaumastos*, wonderful, marvelous, astonishing), → *2512*.

2517 (*theaomai*, behold), → *3972*.

2518 (*theatrizō*, to bring on stage, make a show of, publicly expose), → *2519*.

2519	θέατρον

θέατρον (*theatron*), theater, place of assembly, a spectacle (*2519*); θεατρίζω (*theatrizō*), to bring on stage, make a show of, publicly expose (*2518*).

CL Theaters were common in the ancient world since the 6th cent. B.C. There is literary and archaeological evidence of theaters in a number of cities, used for religious, dramatic, and civic events.

NT The theater was a natural place for the citizens of Ephesus to seize Paul's companions, Gaius and Aristarchus, during the riot over Paul's success in that city (Acts 19:29). It had a capacity of around 25,000 people. While the gathering is properly called an "assembly" in 19:32, 41 (*ekklēsia*, → *1711*) , it was an impromptu assembly.

This word can also designate a play or spectacle itself. Thus Paul employs *theatron* in 1 Cor. 4:9 to describe the apostles as those who are spectacles, as in a theater. In this imagery the theater is the whole universe. Heb. 10:33 uses the vb. *theatrizō* to convey a similar idea: Believers are exposed to public ridicule and shame.

See also *horaō*, see (*3972*); *kollourion*, eye salve (*3141*); *blepō*, look at, see (*1063*); *atenizō*, look at a person or thing intently, gaze on (*867*).

2521 (*theios*, divine), → *2536*.

2522 (*theiotēs*, deity), → *2536*.

2525 (*thelēma*, will, intention), → *2527*.

2526 (*thelēsis*, will), → *2527*.

2527	θέλω

θέλω (*thelō*), wish, want, desire, will, take pleasure in (*2527*); θέλημα (*thelēma*), will, intention (*2525*); θέλησις (*thelēsis*), will (*2526*).

CL & OT 1. In cl. Gk. *thelō* (originally *ethelō*) means to be ready, be inclined, desire, have in mind, will, and esp. to will in the sense of compelling. The noun *thelēma*, used rarely, denotes intention, wish, and then chiefly will.

2. In the LXX *thelō*, like *boulomai* (→ *1089*), occurs over 100x (often of an aspect of God's character). It means to take pleasure in, delight in (e.g., Ps. 18:19; Ezek. 18:23), will, be willing (Deut. 10:10). Negatively, it means to refuse (Gen. 37:35). *thelēma* (44x) stands mainly for the divine good pleasure (Ps. 40:8; Jer. 9:23 = LXX 9:24; Mal. 1:10), but also for the will of God (Ps. 103:7; Isa. 44:28). When *thelēma* is used of human beings, it can denote a wish (Ps. 107:30) or the human will.

NT *thelō* occurs 207x in the NT and *thelēma* 62x. Many uses of the vb. have a general sense of willing, desiring (e.g., Matt. 20:21; 26:17), finding pleasure in (e.g., Mk. 12:38), or claiming (2 Pet. 3:5). *thelēma*, by contrast, only rarely has a general sense (e.g., 1 Cor. 7:37; 16:12).

1. (a) In Paul's letters *thelō* and *thelēma* are often used to describe God's will, esp. as the ultimate source of salvation in Christ. Christ's act of self-sacrifice for the sake of our sins is "according to the will of our God" (Gal. 1:4). By this act we are called to be his children (Eph. 1:5) in accord with his comprehensive saving will (1:9); God works all things in conformity with his will, esp. his election of Israel and now his inclusion of Gentiles into the church (1:11). God's will here denotes his eternal and providential saving will, to which Paul owes his apostleship (cf. 1 Cor. 1:1; 2 Cor. 1:1).

(b) The exegesis of Rom. 9:14–32 has caused interpreters difficulties. How are the human will and God's will related to each other? Note that Paul does not go into the question of human responsibility here (cf. for this 10:16–21), nor should we attempt to understand this passage by rational analysis. Paul is emphasizing that it is not human volition that is decisive for God's action; rather, God's saving will is the precondition for all human volition. The freedom of divine compassion is not dependent on human exertion or on human resistance (cf. 9:17). God accomplishes his will in history precisely in that he harnesses both the obedient and the obdurate into his saving plan (9:18). It is God's will to make known his compassion precisely in patience and wrath (9:22). The ultimate goal of his will is in fact not the "objects of his wrath"; rather, it is the "objects of his mercy" (9:22–23). The goal of his will is that all human beings should be helped and come to the knowledge of the truth (1 Tim. 2:4).

(c) The fact that the ultimate intention of God's will is the revelation of his glory in Christ is stressed esp. in Col. 1:27. God is moving toward the point when the mystery of his saving will is to be unveiled for believers in the Christ event. Even if this will, for the time being, has been correctly apprehended only by believers, yet it is still directed toward the redemption of all (1 Tim. 2:4). The NT church does not acknowledge a double predestination in God's will, whereby from the beginning one section of humanity has been arbitrarily excluded from salvation.

Understanding God's saving will is for the believer the precondition of a right attitude and right behavior in the age of salvation, which has already dawned. Those who are unwise and lack understanding miss the insight into the divine will and corresponding behavior (Eph. 5:17–18). Paul elaborates this with particular sharpness in Rom. 2:17–24 with regard to Jewish teachers of the law. They think they know God's will from the law and are able to guide the blind. But the very contradiction between their teaching and behavior betrays the fact that they have not yet understood God's will. For Christ is the daybreak of the new age, and this requires a renewal of the mind (12:2), i.e., thinking transformed by the bestowal of the Spirit. Whatever in God's will is good, well-pleasing, and perfect should lead us to appropriate behavior (12:2).

(d) (i) Where Paul uses *thelō* with religious significance in referring to humans, it is linked with vbs. of doing. Since believers no longer resist God's will, God becomes the one acting in us. Willing and working become his gifts to us (Phil. 2:13). All human volition and behavior are thus to take place out of obedience to God and in accord with his saving will (cf. 1 Cor. 7:36; 2 Cor. 8:10–11). But where Spirit and flesh are still at variance with one another, i.e., where the Spirit has not yet fully gained acceptance, willing does not turn into doing (Gal. 5:17).

(ii) There is considerable disagreement over the contrast between volition and action in Rom. 7:15–23. According to many interpreters, the contrast is that we as humans would like to fulfill God's will that confronts us in the law, but we repeatedly fall short of that will because we are bound to the sinful nature. In our own strength, we cannot overcome this fragmentation; we can only do so when, according to God's promise, we come under the law of the Spirit, who gives freedom and life in Jesus Christ (8:2). Other interpreters, however, place the discrepancy between what we as individuals deep down really want and what actually results. The split is not in our consciousness, but in the fact that we do the opposite of what we want.

It should, however, be remembered that Rom. 7:7–13 has reached the conclusion that sin works death in one through the good. This may suggest that Paul is speaking of the unredeemed person, whose radical failure is disclosed only when he or she comes to faith.

(e) Paul often uses *thelō* to declare to his congregations what he as their apostle wishes: e.g., "I wish" or "I would like" (1 Cor. 7:7, 32; 14:5; Gal. 3:2); "I do not want you to be unaware [or ignorant]" (Rom. 1:13; 1 Cor. 10:1); "I want you to realize" (11:3). In many places this vb. assumes the weight of apostolic authority.

2. Jn. uses *thelō* and *thelēma* to stress that Jesus, the one sent by God, does not act according to his own will but according to the will of the Father at work in him (Jn. 5:30; 6:38). He is entirely the bearer of the Father's will (4:34). That will is that Jesus, as the Savior, does not lose those appointed for life (6:39) and that those so appointed take hold of salvation in Jesus (6:40). Salvation is impossible as a human action (3:8), but it is divinely possible. The Son gives life to whom he wills (5:21; cf. 6:27, 57). The sole criterion for establishing the legitimacy of the revealer is the doing of his will (7:17; 9:31; 1 Jn. 2:17). But ethics does not take precedence over faith here. Rather, the doing of God's will refers to the faith to which proof is given in obedience.

3. (a) In the Synoptic Gospels and Acts, this word group is found only rarely for the will of God. In Matt. 7:21; 12:50, we meet the same the formula as in Jn., "whoever does the will of my Father." But here again one must not distinguish a will of God concerned with ethics and another one concerned with a saving purpose. There is only one all-embracing will of God with which alone corresponds an equally comprehensive attitude to life by the believer. So, too, the third petition in the Lord's Prayer (Matt. 6:10), like the prayer in Gethsemane (26:39, 42; Mk. 14:36, Lk. 22:42), is not to be understood as an acquiescent accommodation to some unalterable power, but as an active affirmation that helps to realize the divine willing (his saving plan) and leads toward the goal of doing the divine will.

4. The interpretation of Ps. 40:6–8 in Heb. 10:5–10 corresponds with Jn.'s thinking concerning God's will and its fulfillment in the work of the one who has been sent. The author of Heb. sees Ps. 40:6–8 as a dialogue between the preexistent Christ and God. The principle

of Christ's coming into his world and of the determination of his earthly life is thus presented as the exclusive fulfillment of God's will (Heb. 10:7, 9), including the presentation of his own life as a sacrifice (10:10) through which God's will has been so completely fulfilled that a transformation of humankind in sanctification has become possible (13:21). This transformation is the doing of God's will in undivided obedience (10:36). According to 1 Pet. 3:17; 4:2, 19, this obedience may include suffering.

See also *boulomai*, to will, wish, want, desire (*1089*).

2529	θεμέλιος

θεμέλιος (*themelios*), foundation (*2529*); θεμελιόω (*themelioō*), lay the foundation, pass. be founded (*2530*); ἑδραῖος (*hedraios*), firm, steadfast (*1612*); ἑδραίωμα (*hedraiōma*), foundation (*1613*).

CL & OT 1. *themelios* was probably originally an adj. that went with *lithos*, stone; it is linguistically connected with the vb. *tithēmi*, place, stand, lay down. Hence it means that which is placed beneath, a foundation or base—both in the lit. sense (e.g., foundations of a house, city, or building) and in a metaphorical sense (e.g., in philosophical thought, the basis of a system of thought). Similarly, the vb. *themelioō* means to lay the foundation.

A similar meaning is conveyed by the adj. *hedraios* (derived from *hedra*, seat, chair), which generally means firm, unshakeable, stable. Thus, *hedraios* is used in much the same way as *themelios* in questions about absolute certainty and the ultimate basis of all existence (esp. by Plotinus). The reference is always to something secure and permanent in itself.

2. When the OT speaks of a basis and foundation, it is never in the Gk. philosophical sense of ultimate, self-sufficient existence. The OT speaks of the foundations of houses (1 Ki. 7:9–10; Jer. 51:26 = LXX 28:26) and cities (Amos 1:4–14), as well as of the mountains (Deut. 32:22; Ps. 18:7), the earth (Prov. 8:29; Isa. 24:18; Mic. 6:2), and the heavens (2 Sam. 22:8). Even in the last examples, foundations are here certainly to be understood in a lit. sense, in keeping with the ancient conception of the universe. The important point is that these foundations are not secure in themselves, but are laid and sustained by God (Prov. 8:29; cf. Isa. 14:32; Job 9:6) and are capable of being destroyed again (Deut. 32:22; Ps. 18:7; Lam. 4:11). The foundations of all things can tremble at a theophany (Ps. 18:7, 15), which calls into question at the same time the permanence and stability of the earth's foundations.

3. Of particular importance for the theological meaning of the term *foundation* is Isa. 28:16 (cf. 54:11). Here Yahweh himself will lay the foundation and cornerstone for Israel in Zion. The image of a new building is certainly not intended to point to a future great new city, but to the establishment in the city of God of a people of God who live by faith. Zion is to become a center of pilgrimage for the nations (cf. Isa. 2:2–3; Mic. 4:1–2). Not until much later (cf. Eph. 2:20; 1 Pet. 2:4–8) is the foundation stone (Isa. 28:16) seen to refer to the Messiah.

NT In the NT *themelios* occurs 15x and extends throughout the NT. It does not differ from cl. Gk. usage in its meaning. The vb. *themelioō* is used 5x; *hedraios* occurs only 3x in Paul (1 Cor. 7:37; 15:58; Col. 1:23), and *hedraiōma* once (1 Tim. 3:15, in the same sense as *themelios*). Lk. uses *themelios* only in the lit. sense of the foundation of a building (Lk. 6:48–49; 14:29). In Heb. 11:10 and Rev. 21:14, 19, it refers to the foundations of the future city of God. Paul uses the noun and vb. only in a fig. sense.

1. (a) The image of a house and house building (→ *oikos*, *3875*, and *oikodomeō*, *3868*) is occasionally used in the NT as a picture of how people govern and order their lives, as they found and build it (Matt. 7:24–25). Those who have the words of Jesus as the foundation are securely based. This also applies to the Christian community, the church. It is a "spiritual house" (Eph. 2:20–22; 1 Tim. 3:15; 1 Pet. 2:5), which Jesus himself plans to build (cf. Matt. 16:18) by his Spirit and Word. Just as the foundation is of decisive importance in build-

ing a house, so it is with the church. This foundation is Jesus Christ (1 Cor. 3:11), on which Paul has set the church (3:10) and on which further building must proceed (3:12–15). But whatever is built, Christ must remain the basis.

(b) Insofar as this foundation only comes to us through the proclamation of the apostles and prophets, they can themselves be described as *themelios*, "Christ Jesus himself as the chief cornerstone" (Eph. 2:20). In the same way, in Matt. 16:18 Peter is called the rock on which the church will be built. The church thus lives from what God has done in Jesus and what is proclaimed by the apostles.

2. Where the church rests on such a foundation, she can herself conversely be described as the foundation of the truth (1 Tim. 3:15; *hedraiōma*). For it is she who protects and preserves the truth in her confession (3:16), in the fight against enemies within and without. Similarly in 2 Tim. 2:19, the foundation is formed not only by God's act in Christ but, arising out of this, by the fact that the church puts away from herself all unrighteousness (cf. 2:20–21).

3. As is evident from the simile of building a house, Paul makes a fundamental distinction between two separate tasks of the preacher. The first is to lay the foundation (missionary proclamation, evangelism); the second is to build up the church (1 Cor. 3:10). His own task is primarily the former of these (Rom. 15:20; cf. 2 Cor. 10:16); he does not intend to build further where someone else has already laid the foundation.

4. In addition to these ecclesiological uses, these words can also be applied to individual Christians. The steadfastness to which they are called (*hedraios*, 1 Cor. 15:58) depends entirely on their relationship to the Lord, which is grounded in faith (*hedraios*, Col. 1:23) and love (*themelioō*, Eph. 3:17). There may, however, be also an allusion here to the church, for in both contexts it is mentioned as the body of Christ or by the expression "in Christ" (Col. 1:18; Eph. 3:21).

5. A completely different use is found in Heb. 6:1, where *themelios* means the basic doctrines of the Christian faith. The distinction made here is between the groundwork, which every Christian has to know, and further insights, which come to those who are prepared to study the Scriptures in greater depth. *themelios* is thus used to distinguish between the relative importance of various items of Christian teaching.

See also *bebaios*, sure (*1010*); *asphaleia*, firmness, certainty (*854*); *kyroō*, confirm, ratify (*3263*).

2530 (*themelioō*, lay the foundation, pass. be founded), → *2529*.

2535 (*theopneustos*, God-breathed, inspired by God), → *4460*.

2536	θεός

θεός (*theos*), God (*2536*); θεῖος (*theios*), divine (*2521*); θειότης (*theiotēs*), deity (*2522*); θεότης (*theotēs*), deity, divinity (*2540*).

CL & OT 1. (a) Gk. religion was polytheistic. The gods were represented in anthropomorphic form as personal beings who exercised a determining influence on the world and fate of human beings, but who themselves were dependent on a superior fate. Since they were not creator-gods, they were not considered as outside the universe and transcendent. The influence of the gods was not universal, but was limited by their natures and attributes. From Aeschylus, on the different gods came increasingly to be identified one with another. Their convergence into one divine being was prepared by the pre-Socratic thinkers and the ideas of classical tragedy.

(b) The Gk. philosophical understanding of god was nonpersonal. Philosophers sought the origin of all things and the principle that shaped the world. In the process of philosophical reflection, the divine forms were spiritualized and finally replaced by general concepts such as "world reason," "the divine," and "being," which influenced and formed the world as powers, giving it meaning and creating order.

In Hel. syncretism the various Gk. and non-Gk. divinities were equated as a result of the recognition that behind the diverse names stood the same entities. Not infrequently these tendencies led to the honoring of one godhead as the divine All. This development reached its height in Neo-Platonism, where the divine is the universal One, which has no obj. existence or personality. It is Being itself, manifested through a series of hypostases and emanations in the world.

2. By contrast, the religion of the OT and Jud. is monotheistic and personal. (a) In the OT the words *ʾēl*, *ʾelôah*, and *ʾelōhîm*, from related roots, are generic designations of God. *ʾēl* is a word common to all Semitic languages for god and also as the proper name for a particular god. For the patriarchs, *ʾēl* was the only God, whom they honored on the basis of his revelation. He appears as *ʾēl ʿelyôn*, "God Most High" (Gen. 14:18–22); *ʾēl rōʾî*, "the God who sees" (16:13); *ʾēl ʿôlām*, "the Eternal God" (21:33); *ʾēl bêt-ʾēl*, "God of Bethel" (31:13; Bethel means "house of God"); *ʾēl ʾelōhê yiśrāʾēl*, "God, the God of Israel" (33:20); and *ʾēl šadday*, "God Almighty" (e.g., 17:1; 28:3; Exod. 6:3).

ʾelōhîm, though pl. in form, is seldom used in the OT to mean "gods." In Israel the pl. is understood as the pl. of fullness: Elohim is the God who really, and in the fullest sense of the word, is God.

(b) The origin and meaning of the divine name *Yahweh* is somewhat uncertain. Most likely the name is connected with the verbal root *hwy* or *hwh*, to be. The OT gives an interpretation of this name at the theophany of the burning bush (Exod. 3:13–15). After Moses asked God's name in order to be able to give it to the people of Israel, "God said to Moses, 'I AM WHO I AM [*ʾehyeh ʾašer ʾehyeh*]. This is what you are to say to the Israelites: "I AM has sent me to you." ' God also said to Moses, 'Say to the Israelites, "The LORD [*yhwh*; i.e., Yahweh], the God of your fathers—the God of Abraham, the God of Isaac and the God of Jacob—has sent me to you." This is my name forever, the name by which I am to be remembered from generation to generation.'"

There has been considered debate as to the translation and meaning of the words *ʾehyeh ʾašer ʾehyeh*. This is reflected in the NIV note: "Or *I WILL BE WHAT I WILL BE.*" Of the various suggestions about the meaning of this name, the best perhaps is the phrase, "I am he who exists." That is, Yahweh is the God whom Israel must recognize as really existing. In the context of Exod. the revelation of the divine name is a proclamation to Israel of the one with whom they have to do. God is calling his people out of Egypt and promises to be with Moses for that purpose.

The proclamation of the Decalogue begins with the words: "I am the LORD [Yahweh]" (Exod. 20:2; cf. Deut. 6:5), and the first commandment requires exclusive worship and service to this God (Exod. 20:3, cf. 5). When Moses sought God's presence, he was not permitted to see God's face but nevertheless received the reply: "I will cause all my goodness to pass in front of you, and I will proclaim my name, the LORD [Yahweh], in your presence. I will have mercy on whom I will have mercy, and I will have compassion on whom I will have compassion" (33:19). The God who thus revealed himself to Moses and to Israel was distinct from the deities of Egypt and Canaan, with their fertility rites concerned with the cycle of nature. He remained a mystery, yet he was graciously active in the history of his people.

Exod. 3 does not give a new name to God for the first time but rather the explanation of a name known already but now identified as that of the saving God of Israel. Although Israel did not work out a metaphysical doctrine of time, the idea of God as "he who is" is paralleled by numerous other statements about God in the OT (Ps. 90:1–2; 102:27; Isa. 41:4; 48:12). The thought of time is also bound up with that of Yahweh's ongoing presence (Jos. 3:7; Isa. 49:6, 26).

The Heb. name *yhwh ṣebāʾôt*, "LORD Almighty" (KJV, "LORD of hosts"), occurs some 279x. The "hosts" in question most likely relate either to the earthly armies of Israel or to the celestial armies of spirits and angels. This expression is found most frequently in the prophets, for whom Yahweh was above all a warrior God. It refers to the totality of forces over which Yahweh rules. In the LXX the expression is usually translated by *kyrios pantokratōr* (Lord Almighty) or *kyrios sabaōth*. The term *pantokratōr* is taken up in the NT by 2 Cor. 6:18;

Rev. 1:8; 4:8; 11:17; 15:3; 16:7, 14; 19:6, 15; 21:22; *Sabaōth* occurs in Rom. 9:29 (cf. Isa. 1:9) and Jas. 5:4.

The name of Yahweh was combined with various Heb. verbs to form proper names: e.g., Jehoiachin (Yahweh establishes), Jonathan (Yahweh gives), and Joshua (Yahweh is salvation). Joshua is the Heb. form that underlies the name of Jesus.

The form *Jehovah* arose out of a misunderstanding that also resulted in the reluctance of pious Jews to pronounce the divine name (ca. 300 B.C.). Any time they came to *yhwh* in the Heb. text, they uttered the word *ᵃdōnay* ("my Lord"). In the MT the divine name was written with the consonants of *yhwh* and the vowels of *ᵃdōnay* as a reminder to say the latter whenever the word was read. The LXX reflects the Jewish reluctance to pronounce the divine name and puts the word *kyrios* ("Lord") in its place. The NIV and other Eng. versions also reflect the practice by using LORD (in small capital letters) whenever *yhwh* is in the OT text.

The fact that Israel's God is both higher than and over all other gods is first given full expression in Isa. 40:25. The God of Israel is the Lord of all, whose sovereign power fills all the earth (6:3). There are no gods apart from him (41:4; 42:8; 43:10–13; 45:3, 6; 48:11). Jeremiah strongly supported the proposition that the gods of the heathen are no gods at all (2:11).

3. The OT contains no all-embracing definition of God. But it does make an extensive range of statements that testify to the being of God and have their basis in the divine revelation. Nor does the OT attempt to prove the existence of God; rather, it merely assumes that God is (e.g., Gen. 1:1). He is the first and the last (Isa. 41:4; 44:6; 48:12), the eternal, the almighty, and the living one, the creator of heaven and earth (e.g., Gen. 1:1); he is the Lord, who guides the destinies of the nations, but who has made Israel a people for his own possession (Exod. 19:5–6). Israel stands under his protection. Yahweh leads, guides, and gives Israel his promises. But he is also the commanding God, who makes his will known and expects obedience. The history of Israel is the history of God with this people. Thus Israel's belief in God is founded on a theology of history.

The OT expresses a conception of God as personal, that God is capable of all the emotions that a person can have, such as love, anger, compassion, and repentance. But even if human characteristics can be attributed to him, he cannot be compared with any human being (Hos. 11:9). The transcendent God, who dwells in light where no one can approach, is exalted above time and space and is therefore unique in his Godhead, not to be portrayed or localized (cf. Exod. 20:4). He is the eternal king (Isa. 52:7), who rules over all the kingdoms of the world (37:16).

The most fundamental feature of God's being is expressed by the word "holy." He is "the Holy One" (Isa. 40:25; Hos 11:9; Hab. 3:3). But the holy, transcendent God steps out of his concealment through his word and his acts of revelation and repeatedly communicates with his people in demonstrations of power and glory. This holy God is just in all he does (cf. Ps. 7:11). He is the judge who condemns unrighteousness and to whom humankind must answer.

But the OT also testifies to God's grace and forgiving mercy (e.g., Exod. 34:6; Ps. 103:8). He is called Father in the OT—the father of the people of Israel (Exod. 4:22–23; Deut. 32:6; Isa. 63:16; Jer. 31:9 = LXX 38:9; Hos. 11:1). He comforts the pious (Job 15:11), blesses them, and helps them (Ps. 45:7; 90:1; 94:22). In particular he takes up the cause of the poor and needy, widows, and orphans (146:9; Isa. 49:13). Through a personal relationship between God and his people is created an I–Thou relation between God and individual believers, who can turn to him in prayer for all their needs. Therefore, already in the OT God is not just a dreaded enemy of humanity; he makes it possible for people both to trust and love him, because he himself loves his chosen people.

4. Intertestamental Jud. confessed the one God in unswerving loyalty and fought passionately against pagan polytheism. But it saw the one God working in a multitude of mediatorial and angelic beings.

Dualistic concepts were introduced in apocalyptic writings. The rabbis laid great stress on avoiding the name of God, using instead a system of substitute terms: e.g., "heaven," "the Lord" (*ᵃdōnay*), and later "the Name." In addition there were abstract terms like "glory," "power," and "the Holy One, blessed be he."

5. The residents of Qumran took over a cosmological dualism—e.g., God and Belial, light and darkness. To this corresponds the anthropological opposition of flesh and spirit, the pious and the godless, sons of light and sons of darkness. However, the dualism of the two spirits that rule the world is subordinated to the fundamental OT idea of God as the creator of all things. For he created the spirits of light and of darkness, which lie at the basis of his working (1QS 3:25; cf. 3:19–26).

The Qumran doctrine of God stands out as being rigidly deterministic. God's actions are determined by a fixed plan (1QS 3:15; 11:11–12; 1QH 18:22). Nothing happens apart from his will (1QS 3:15; 11:17, 19; 1QH 1:20; 10:9), for all authority is in his power. God's hand leads the individual at all times, and his just rebuke accompanies all perversity (9:32–33). A person can only speak because God opens the mouth (11:33). God created the righteous for eternal salvation and lasting peace, but the "perverse" for the time of his wrath (14:15–33). The "lot" of Belial will result in eternal destruction (1QM 1:5); all "men of lies" will be destroyed (1QH 4:20–21).

6. Philo attempted to link the OT idea of Yahweh with the Platonic-Stoic idea of God. In speaking of Israel's God, he distinguishes between *ho theos* (the good Creator) and *ho kyrios* (the kingly Lord of the world). Philo also makes extensive use of the philosophical concept of *to theion*, the divine. God is fully transcendent and the active power in everything. He produces out of himself the original, typical ideas and forms them into the visible world. The Word is his mediator for creation and revelation.

NT The NT rests firmly on the OT foundation in its doctrine of God, but its emphases are new. God is now near, the Father of Jesus Christ, who justifies freely by his grace (cf. Paul's concept of the righteousness of God). His action in election bursts all claims to exclusiveness. But it is the same God who reveals himself as in the OT and whose plan of salvation, there promised, comes to fulfillment.

1. *The one God.* (a) *theos* is the most frequent designation of God in the NT. Belief in the one, only, and unique God (Matt. 23:9; Rom. 3:30; 1 Cor. 8:4, 6; Gal. 3:20; 1 Tim. 2:5; Jas. 2:19) is an established part of Christian tradition. Jesus himself made the fundamental confession of Jud. his own and expressly quoted the Shema (Deut. 6:4–5; see Mk. 12:29–30; cf. Matt. 22:37; Lk. 10:27). This guaranteed continuity between the old and the new covenants. The God whom Christians worship is the God of the fathers (Acts 3:13; 5:30; 22:14), the God of Abraham, Isaac, and Jacob (Acts 3:13; 7:32; cf. Matt. 22:32; Mk. 12:26; Lk. 20:37), the God of Israel (Matt. 15:31; Lk. 1:68; Acts 13:17), and the God of Jesus Christ (2 Cor. 1:3; Eph. 1:3; 1 Pet. 1:3).

Just as God once made Israel his people, so now he has chosen those who believe in Christ as an elect race and a holy people for his possession (Acts 15:14; 20:28; Heb. 11:25; 1 Pet. 2:9). Faith is in him (Rom. 4:3; Gal. 3:6; Tit. 3:8; Heb. 6:1; Jas. 2:23; 1 Pet. 1:21), hope is on him (Acts 24:15; Rom. 4:18; 2 Cor. 3:4; 1 Pet. 3:5), and prayer is to him. The community of Jesus may have no false gods beside him, whether money (Matt. 6:24), the "belly" (Phil. 3:19), or the cosmic powers (Gal. 4:8–11). They must serve him alone, do his will, and remain faithful to him.

(b) Confession of the one God appears in Eph. 4:6 in an expanded form ("one God and Father of all, who is over all and through all and in all"), which glorifies the omnipresence of the rule of God. Similar formulae, referring now to God, now to Christ, occur in Rom. 11:36 and 1 Cor. 8:6.

(c) The one God is the living and only true God (Rom. 3:30; Gal. 3:20; 1 Thess. 1:9; 1 Tim. 1:17; 2:5; Jude 25; cf. Jn. 17:3). He is the God whom the heathen do not know (1 Thess. 4:5). It is true that

Paul acknowledges the existence of "so-called" gods, who have authority as demonic powers over the heathen, but for Christians there is only one God (1 Cor. 8:5–6). Even if the honor and power of the gods do not belong to the *stoicheia* (→ *5122*) that the Galatians previously worshiped, they can still intrude divisively between the young congregation and their God (Gal. 4:8–9).

This one God is called "our God" (Acts 2:39; 2 Pet. 1:1; Rev. 4:11; 7:12; 19:5). The individual believer, like Paul, can speak personally of him as *his* or *her* God (Rom. 1:8; 2 Cor. 12:21; Phil. 1:3; 4:19; Phlm. 4). Belief in the one God involves turning away from all heathen ways. Therefore in missionary preaching testimony to God is linked with a struggle against the worship of false gods (Acts 14:15; 17:24–25; 19:26).

(d) The NT letters and especially Acts give a partial picture of the excesses of the NT world and their local religious expressions. Paul was painfully impressed in Athens by the many figures of gods and shrines that he saw as he went through the city (Acts 17:16, 23). Just how strongly the cult of Artemis dominated the religious life of Ephesus is clear from 19:23–41. Here things came to a head in a violent clash when silversmiths who derived great profit from making little models of the temple of Artemis felt their economic existence threatened by Paul's preaching. The significance of sacrificial meals in the heathen cultus at Corinth is indicated in 1 Cor. 8:1–7. Magic also played an important part in Hel. times (see Acts 8:9; 13:6; 19:13–16). In Ephesus, as a result of the powerful testimony of the Christian message of salvation, books of magic were publicly burned (19:19).

Those converted to the true and living God had been freed from bondage to false gods (1 Thess. 1:9). But for many Christians the fascinating power of the heathen cults had not entirely lost its force. Therefore Paul explained to the Corinthians, "I do not want you to be participants with demons" (1 Cor. 10:20), for the heathen present their sacrifices to demonic beings and not to God.

2. *The transcendent God.* (a) God is the creator, sustainer, and Lord of the world (Acts 17:24; Rev. 10:6), the master builder of all things (Heb. 3:4). He exercises his lordship from heaven, for heaven is his throne and earth his footstool (Matt. 5:34; 23:22; Acts 7:49). He is the Almighty, with whom nothing is impossible (Mk. 10:27). No one can hinder, let alone destroy, his work (Acts 5:39; cf. 2 Tim. 2:9). He is the highest (Mk. 5:7; Lk. 1:32; Acts 7:48; 16:17; Heb. 7:1), the great king (Matt. 5:35), the king of the nations (Rev. 15:3).

(b) Prayer is a powerful witness to belief in the transcendent God, for prayer is directed to God who lives in heaven (Matt. 6:9; cf. Jn. 17:1). At present satanic and demonic powers still oppose God's rule on earth. Therefore the congregation of Jesus prays for the full revelation of his kingdom (Matt. 6:10a), for the full accomplishment of his will on earth as in heaven (6:10b), and for the hallowing of his name (6:9). In Jesus the kingdom of God (→ *basileia*, *993*) has already broken in; it has been demonstrated by his powerful and wonderful acts. He has broken into Satan's realm and driven out demons by the "finger of God" (Lk. 11:20); but only the age to come will bring the full establishment of God's kingdom. Then Christ will conquer all powers opposed to God (1 Cor. 15:24; 2 Thess. 2:8; Rev. 21:8, 27). When he has completed this his last task, God will be "all in all" (1 Cor. 15:28).

3. *The personal character of God.* (a) We must not imagine God as possessing a limiting form. Nevertheless, we are only capable of speaking about him in concepts that belong to our categories of thought. Moreover, if the personal character of God is ignored or restricted, the meaning of revelation is drastically changed. A depersonalized God is not the God of the NT.

The God to whom the NT testifies is the God who speaks and acts; he reveals himself through word and deed. He works in sovereign, absolute power (Jn. 5:17). He makes his will known in commands and brings everything to the goal he has determined. After he had spoken in the old covenant in many ways to the fathers through the prophets, he has spoken in these last days "to us" through the Son, who reflects his glory and bears the very stamp of his nature (Heb. 1:1–3). In the preaching of the Word he addresses everyone personally and receives into his fellowship all who believe in Jesus.

(b) It belongs to the personal character of God that he is Spirit (Jn. 4:24). Activities of the Spirit and of power proceed from him. The Spirit of God descended on Jesus at his baptism (Matt. 3:16; cf. 12:18). Filled by this Spirit, he worked as the Messiah sent by God. Through the Spirit of God he cast out the evil spirits (12:28). Christians are characterized by having not the spirit of the world, but the Spirit who is from God (1 Cor. 2:12), for the natural self does not understand anything that comes from the Spirit of God (2:14–15). Only the spiritual person is capable of knowing God (2:11) and of penetrating the depths of God. God has revealed his secret wisdom to believers through his Spirit (2:10), who lives in them and thus becomes the formative power of their being (2:11).

Still, in this age limits are imposed on a believer's knowledge. God's "judgments" are "unsearchable" and his "paths beyond tracing out" (Rom. 11:33). But mysteries hidden in God from the beginning of time have now been made known through the proclamation of salvation. The apostolic ministry testifies to the world of the unfathomable riches of Christ. Through the Christian community the knowledge about God's manifold wisdom has penetrated as far as the cosmic powers (Eph. 3:8–10). Paul saw himself as the custodian of "the secret things of God" (1 Cor. 4:1).

In 1 Cor. 6:11 the apostle explains that the Spirit of God (in conjunction with the name of the Lord Jesus Christ) has washed, sanctified, and justified believers. Through the divine Spirit working in them they are no longer in the realm of the flesh but in that of the Spirit. Hence they live according to the Spirit (Rom. 8:4–14).

True confession of Christ is brought about by the Spirit of God (Rom. 10:9; 1 Cor. 12:3; cf. Matt. 16:17). In situations of suffering he gives the word that is necessary for the defense of and witness to the gospel (10:20). The Spirit rests on those who are abused on account of the name of Christ (1 Pet. 4:14).

(c) The personal character of God finds special expression in the confession of God as Father. Jesus' relationship with God is essentially determined by his Father–Son relationship. As God's "one and only" Son, he is bound to God in a special way, as Jn.'s use of the *monogenēs* (lit., "of one kind") is intended to show (cf. Jn. 1:14, 18; 3:16, 18; 1 Jn. 4:9). In prayer Jesus called God "*Abba*, Father" (Mk. 14:36) or "Father" (Matt. 11:25–26; Lk. 23:24; Jn. 11:41; 17:1, 5, 11). Jesus also gave his disciples the right to approach God as "Father" (Matt. 6:9; Lk. 11:2). In the quiet room at home the individual may pray personally to his or her Father (Matt. 6:4, 6, 18). The name "Father" is applied to God in illustrations and parables (e.g., Lk. 15:11–32). As Father, God is the God who is near, to whom we can turn in believing trust with all our petitions. He receives his creatures with fatherly goodness and surrounds them with his care (Matt. 6:26–32; 10:29–31).

The NT letters use the solemn, confessional formula "the God and Father of our Lord Jesus Christ" (Rom. 15:6; 2 Cor. 1:3; Eph. 1:3; Col. 1:3; 1 Pet. 1:3). In Christ believers are related to God as children. His Spirit testifies to them that they are God's children (Rom. 8:16), so in prayer they too may cry "*Abba*, Father" (Rom. 8:15; Gal. 4:6). This is a gift of grace procured through the Spirit of God's Son.

The idea of the children of God takes on a special coloring in 1 Jn. Here the statements are no longer determined, as in Paul, by the concept of adoption, of being received into the place of a child, but by that of begetting (→ *gennaō*, *1164*). Christians are God's children because they have been begotten by God (1 Jn. 3:9; cf. 2:29; 4:7). This means that the origin of their new being is to be found solely in God (4:4). True fellowship with God is possible only when Christians abide in God and when God abides in them (4:16). But since God is love, this means abiding in love. Out of this deep, inner relationship with God arises a completely new, concrete, ethical obligation: love of the brethren, which must lead to practical aid (3:16–17).

4. *The attributes of God.* (a) The NT has no fixed, systematically ordered doctrine of the attributes of God. But there is a wealth of allusions, esp. in expressions of prayer and faith and in descriptions of divine acts. More rare than in the OT but nevertheless present are allusions to the holiness of God (Jn. 17:11; 1 Pet. 1:15; Rev. 3:7; 4:8; 15:4), his (present and future) wrath (Rom. 1:18; 2:5; 9:22; Eph. 5:6; 1 Thess. 1:10; Rev. 6:17; 11:18; 14:10), and his glory (Acts 7:2; Rom. 1:23; 6:4; Eph. 3:16; 1 Thess. 2:12; Tit. 2:13; Rev. 15:8; 21:11, 23). Only once is God called *teleios*, in the sense of moral perfection (Matt. 5:48). Paul strongly emphasizes the faithfulness of God (Rom. 3:3; 1 Cor. 1:9; 10:13; cf. 2 Cor. 1:18). God abides by his promises and fulfills them (Rom. 9:6–8). He does not lie (Heb. 6:18; cf. Tit. 1:2); he is utterly true, and his testimony is absolutely valid (Jn. 3:33).

(b) God is the eternal (Rom. 16:26) and only wise God (16:27). He is described as invisible (1:20; Col. 1:15–16; 1 Tim. 1:17; Heb. 11:27) and immortal (Rom. 1:23; 1 Tim. 1:17). In 1 Tim. 1:11 and 6:15 he is called by an attribute taken over from Hel. Jud., the "blessed" God. The doxology in 1 Tim. 6:15–16 is reminiscent of the prayers of the Hel. synagogue. It confesses God in solemn words as "the only Ruler, the King of kings and Lord of lords, who alone is immortal and who lives in unapproachable light, whom no one has seen or can see."

Paul's description of God in his speech at the meeting of the Areopagus (Acts 17:24) also betrays Hel. influence. God created the world and everything in it. The Lord of heaven and earth does not dwell in temples made by human hands. Nor is he served by human hands, as though he needs anything, since he himself gives to all beings life, breath, and everything else. Though some of these expressions may sound strange today, Paul was concerned to testify to the true and living God in terms that were relevant to his day. This is the God whom the heathen of Athens worshiped, more unconsciously than consciously, and to whom they had erected an altar with the inscription "TO AN UNKNOWN GOD" (Acts 17:23). The apostle even pressed into his service the words of two Greek poets (17:28): "In him [God] we live and move and have our being" (Epimenides), and "we are his offspring" (Aratus).

In this connection, Paul held that humanity had a natural awareness of God that was consonant with the revelation of God in the OT and Christian experience. Human beings do not arrive at such a conclusion as the result of a metaphysical proof. Rather, they are born with this awareness, and reflection on the finite character of the natural order should be sufficient to tell them that God is not to be identified with anything or anyone within that order (Acts 14:17; Rom. 1:19ff., 32; possibly 2:12–16).

(c) A central concept in Paul's theology is the righteousness of God (Rom. 1:17, 21–22; 9:30; 10:3; 2 Cor. 5:21; Phil. 3:9). It is a judging but also a saving righteousness. God is just when he condemns sinful humanity. But he is equally just when he bestows his forgiving grace on those who believe in Christ and in the salvation procured through him. For Christ's sake, in whom God himself offered the atoning sacrifice for the guilt of humanity, he does not count their sins against them but pronounces them righteous. Thus the righteousness of God forms the foundation of Paul's doctrine of justification.

(d) Because God is the initiator of salvation, both he and Christ are called *sōtēr*, savior (1 Tim. 1:1; 2:3; 4:10; Tit. 1:3; 2:13; 3:4; → *5400*). God sent his Son into the world (Gal. 4:4) and delivered him to death for us (Jn. 3:16; 1 Jn. 4:10; cf. Rom. 8:32). This saving act of God is proclaimed through the word of the cross, understood by believers as God's power and God's wisdom (1 Cor. 1:18, 24).

Paul calls the whole message of salvation, declared to the world, the "gospel of God" (Rom. 15:16; 1 Thess. 2:2; 1 Tim. 1:11; cf. also 1 Pet. 4:17). It brings salvation to everyone who believes (Rom. 1:16; cf. 1 Cor. 2:5). At the same time the offer of salvation is universal. God desires that everyone should be saved and come to the knowledge of the truth (1 Tim. 2:4), for his saving grace has appeared to all (Tit. 2:11).

The power of God is not only at work in the gospel; it has demonstrated itself from the beginning of creation (Rom. 1:20). That same power raised Christ from the dead (Acts 2:24, 32; Rom. 8:11; 10:9) and thereby ushered in the new creation of humankind and of the universe. Believers even now experience the transcendent fullness of God's power (2 Cor. 4:7), his mighty strength (Eph. 1:19; 3:20). Hence the apostle prays that they may be continually built up through the Spirit, according to the riches of his glory, with power in the inner self (3:16). The ultimate aim of faith, knowledge, and love is to be filled with all the fullness of God (3:19).

(e) The saving power of the divine being is expressed in a series of genitives that are connected with the noun God. God is "the God of peace" (Rom. 15:33; 16:20; 1 Cor. 14:33; Phil. 4:9; 1 Thess. 5:23; cf. Heb. 13:20), "the Father of compassion and the God of all comfort" (2 Cor. 1:3; cf. Rom. 12:1), "the God of all grace" (1 Pet. 5:10, cf.12; Eph. 1:7), and "the God of love" (2 Cor. 13:11).

(f) The full depth of God's being is expressed in the statement: "God is love" (1 Jn. 4:8). His love embraces the lost world, which has turned away from him. It is the decisive reason for his saving and redeeming activity. He has proved his love by giving up his Son to death in order that all who believe on him may have eternal life (Jn. 3:16). Above all his love is for the individual believer: God loved us (1 Jn. 4:10), and we are dearly loved by God (Col. 3:12). All real love has its origin in God (1 Jn. 4:7). Whoever does not love has not known God (4:8). The love of God is poured out in our hearts through the Holy Spirit (Rom. 5:5). It is the highest spiritual gift, without which all the other *charismata* are meaningless (1 Cor. 13).

5. *God and Christ.* The uniqueness of Jesus Christ as the Son of God is most fully developed in Jn. and the NT letters. (a) "As to his human nature [he] was a descendant of David" (Rom. 1:3; cf. Matt. 1:1–17; Lk. 3:23–38; Acts 2:30; 2 Tim. 2:8), and he was "declared with power to be Son of God by his resurrection from the dead" (Rom. 1:4). The allusion here is to the divine decree of Ps. 2:6–8.

According to the developed Christology of Jn. 1:1, Christ already existed before his earthly existence as the divine Word (→ *logos, 3364*) with God. Thus he came from God (3:2; 13:3; 16:27–28). It was God himself who sent him into the world at the time that he had determined in order to carry out his saving purposes (Gal. 4:4–5). He came with divine authority; God was with him (Jn. 3:2). He is the image of the invisible God (Col. 1:15); in him "the fullness of the Deity lives in bodily form" (2:9). Because he has come from God, he alone is capable of bringing a true message from God (Jn. 1:18). He is therefore the only trustworthy revealer. He and the Father are one (10:30; 14:10; 17:11, 21); whoever sees him sees God (12:45; 14:9).

(b) There is not only a oneness of being between God and Jesus Christ, but also a complete harmony in speech and action. The words Jesus speaks are words he has heard from the Father (Jn. 14:10); the works he performs are the works of God (9:4). They serve to reveal the divine glory and therefore glorify God (17:4). This is expressed particularly in Jesus' "I am" statements, which in the OT are self-revelations of God himself. Jesus is the light (8:12; cf. 1:4, 8–9; 9:5), the life (14:6), the truth (14:6), the living bread (6:48; cf. 6:51–58, 63), and the only way to God (14:6). Rev. also has divine "I am" statements, such as "I am the First and the Last" or "I am the Alpha and the Omega," which come both from the mouth of God and from that of the eternal Christ (Rev. 1:8, 17; 21:6; 22:13). Clearly in the NT faith in God is closely bound up with faith in Christ.

(c) But Jesus Christ does not usurp the place of God. His oneness with the Father does not mean absolute identity of being. In his preexistent being Jesus was in the form of God, but he did not cling tenaciously to his equality with God (Phil. 2:6). Rather, he emptied himself (→ *kenoō, 3033*). In his earthly existence he was obedient to God, even unto death on the cross (2:8). He is the mediator, but not the originator, of salvation (2 Cor. 5:19; Col. 1:20; Heb. 9:15), the Lamb of God, who takes away the sins of the world (Jn. 1:36). After completing his work on earth, he was raised to God's right hand (Eph. 1:20;

1 Pet. 3:22) and invested with the honor of the heavenly *kyrios*, Lord (Phil. 2:9–10). Although coordinated with God, he remains subordinate to him (cf. 1 Cor. 15:28). This is true also of his position as eternal high priest in the heavenly sanctuary (Heb. 9:24; 10:12–13; cf. Ps. 110:1). He represents us before God (cf. also Rom. 8:34).

(d) A few NT texts equate the Son of God with God himself. In Rom 9:5, after Paul has expounded the position of Israel in salvation history and has emphasized as a special advantage the fact that Christ, according to the flesh, stems from this people, he adds a relative clause that runs lit., "who is over all God blessed forever. Amen." The NIV translates it appropriately as a reference to Christ: "Christ, who is God over all, forever praised. Amen." Though this translation is disputed by some scholars, to treat this doxology instead as directed to God the Father does not follow the form of doxologies elsewhere in the LXX and the NT. Moreover, the assertion of Christ's Lordship is in accord with Paul's teaching elsewhere (Rom. 1:4; 10:9; 14:9; Eph. 1:20, 23; Phil. 2:9–11; Col. 1:18–19; cf. Acts 2:36; Heb. 1:2–4).

Jn. 1:1 declares: "In the beginning was the Word, and the Word was with God, and the Word was God." Though groups such as the Jehovah's Witnesses draw theological significance from the fact that *theos* in the third phrase of this verse lacks an article, a correct understanding of Gk. grammar demonstrates that definite nouns in a predicate nominative position preceding the verb "to be" regularly lack the article (Colwell's Rule). The context of this verse clearly shows that *theos* in this verse is definite.

In Jn. 1:18 a number of very good MSS read *monogenēs theos* ("the only God") instead of *ho monogenēs huios* ("the only Son"; see NIV text and note). The unusualness of such a reading gives strong grounds for accepting its authenticity, thus further affirming the deity of the Word.

Jn. 20:28 contains the unique affirmation of Thomas addressing the risen Christ as God: "My Lord and my God." The statement marks the climax of this Gospel. God has become visible for Thomas in the form of Jesus. The climax of 1 Jn. occurs in the confessional formula of 5:20, which asserts the full identity of Christ and God: "We know also that the Son of God has come and has given us understanding, so that we may know him who is true. And we are in him who is true—even in his Son Jesus Christ. He is the true God and eternal life." The last phrase may also be translated: "This [Christ] is the true one, God and eternal life."

Finally, Tit. 2:13 speaks clearly of believers waiting for "the blessed hope—the glorious appearing of our great God and Savior, Jesus Christ." The title "great God" is firmly rooted in Jud., and it may seem surprising to have that title ascribed to Jesus. Yet that is precisely what a careful analysis of the Gk. text suggests (the Granville Sharp Rule; cf. also "our God and Savior Jesus Christ" in 2 Pet. 1:1 and "our Lord and Savior Jesus Christ" in 3:18).

(e) Jesus' cry of desolation recorded in Matt. 27:46 and Mk. 15:34 ("My God, my God, why have you forsaken me?"; cf. Ps. 22:1) has sometimes raised problems for Christology. It was at times felt that the words imply an abandonment of Jesus by God, which is incompatible with belief in his divinity and denotes a lack of trust on Jesus' part. Nevertheless, Matt. and Mk. did not shirk to record it. This cry expresses Jesus' sense of utter desolation, such as he had not even experienced at his temptation or in Gethsemane. His faithfulness to God's will had led him to the point where that will had to be done without the conscious awareness of God's presence. This was the experience of the psalmist, and in recording the cry the Evangelists saw a further fulfillment of Ps. 22, even though they did not use a typical "fulfillment" formula (e.g., "as it is written") here.

The suggestion made by some scholars that the Evangelists deliberately put that cry into the mouth of Jesus, perhaps in the light of Ps. 22, raises more problems than it solves, for it is incredible that the church would have invented an utterance that seems to go back on all Jesus had taught. The cry reveals the anguish Jesus felt in being utterly rejected by friend and foe alike and in dying the most excruciating

death. We should also understand this cry in the light of Mk. 14:36 and Paul's interpretation of Jesus' death in 2 Cor. 5:21 and Gal. 3:13.

The parallels with Ps. 22 may, however, be pursued even further. Some scholars cite parallels in Christian writings in which the quotation of a single text of Scripture implied that the entire section was to be kept in view. In Ps. 22 the psalmist survives his immediate desolation and ends up praising God in the congregation (22:22). All the ends of the earth will remember and turn to the Lord (22:27). Dominion belongs to the Lord, and he rules over the nations (22:28). Posterity will serve him and proclaim his deliverance to a people yet unborn (22:30–31). If the earlier part of Ps. 22 may be seen as being fulfilled in Jesus' death, the latter may be said to find fulfillment in the revelation of the risen Christ and his commission to his followers to evangelize (Matt. 28:16–20).

6. *God and the church.* (a) The community of believers is called the "church of God" (Acts 20:28; 1 Cor. 1:2; 10:32; 15:9; 2 Cor. 1:1; Gal. 1:13; 1 Thess. 2:14; 1 Tim. 3:15; → *ekklēsia*, *1711*). It consists of those who are chosen by God and called to be saints (Rom. 1:7) and who have received all the gifts of salvation and grace. They have peace with God (Rom. 5:1), for they have been reconciled through Christ (2 Cor. 5:18). As the beginning of God's new creation (5:17), they are his workmanship, created in Christ Jesus for good works (Eph. 2:10). God works in them both to will and to accomplish (Phil. 2:13) and gives them assurance of the completion of their salvation (Rom. 5:2, Phil. 3:21). At Christ's return he will give life to their mortal bodies (Rom. 8:11) and a share in his glory and in eternal life.

(b) The church is the temple of God (1 Cor. 3:16; 2 Cor. 6:16; Eph. 2:21), God's holy building into which all believers are placed as living stones (1 Pet. 2:4–5), the dwelling of God in the Spirit. Christians are members of God's household (Eph. 2:19, 21); they form his new people (1 Pet. 2:9), the body of Christ (1 Cor. 12:27). In him believers have a share in the fullness of the being of God and Christ (Eph. 1:23; Col. 2:10). The community stands under God's protection. It is hidden in him, for God is on its side (Rom. 8:31). Thus no power is capable of separating it from God's love (8:38–39).

Paul emphasizes strongly that the church of God consists of Jews and Gentiles. This is because Christ has reconciled Jews and Gentiles to God into one body through the cross (Eph. 1:22–23; 2:11–16). Whoever receives the word of reconciliation (2 Cor. 5:19) and believes in Christ has free access to the Father (Eph. 2:18). In God's people of the new covenant racial and national differences are removed.

7. *The Trinity.* The NT does not contain the word *trinity* (a word coined by Tertullian) or *homoousios* (a word used in the Nicene Creed to denote that Christ was *of the same substance as* the Father). But the NT does contain a fixed, three-part formula in which "God," "the Lord Jesus Christ," and "the Holy Spirit" are mentioned together (2 Cor. 13:14; cf. 1 Cor. 12:4–6). The Father, Son, and Holy Spirit appear together as one "name" in the baptismal formula in Matt. 28:19. Note too the triadic form of "one God and Father," "one Lord," and "one Spirit" in Eph. 4:4–6. In Gal. 4:4–6 God first sends the Son and then the Spirit of his Son to continue the work of Jesus on earth.

Regarding two-part formulae, God and Christ are closely connected in 1 Cor. 8:6 as "one God, the Father . . . [and] one Lord, Jesus Christ," as well as in 1 Tim. 2:5 as "one God and one mediator between God and men." In this connection Matt. 23:8–10 should also be mentioned, where Jesus draws the disciples' attention to the fact that they have "one Master" (himself) and "one Father . . . in heaven." In such statements two facts—that God and Christ belong together but that they are distinct—are equally stressed.

A close relationship also exists between Christ and the Holy Spirit. Thus Paul can say outright that "the Lord is the Spirit" (2 Cor. 3:17). In Jn.'s Gospel the Holy Spirit, while having a certain independence, is bound to the exalted Christ (Jn. 16:14). Christ and the Holy Spirit are in an interchangeable relationship.

Finally on two-part formulae, in Acts 5:3–4 Peter clearly states that lying to the Holy Spirit and lying to God are one and the same.

8. *Pagan deities.* It is unlikely that the average Gk. and Roman took the old gods and goddesses seriously, but tradition and superstition led people to altars, shrines, and images. The multiplicity of altars at Athens moved Paul to describe the Athenians as *deisidaimonesterous* (Acts 17:22), a word that could mean superstitious but that Paul intended in a more positive sense, "very religious." But note also that in 1 Cor. 10:20 Paul equated pagan deities with demons.

The following Gk. deities are named in the NT. (i) *Zeus and Hermes.* At Lystra, after an outstanding miracle of healing, Barnabas and Paul were treated as heavenly visitants, the dignified Barnabas as Zeus, and Paul, the talker, as Hermes (Acts 14:8–18). (ii) *Ares.* At Athens Paul was taken to the Areopagus, or Hill of Ares, where speakers were allowed to hold forth and where the Athenian Council met (17:19). (iii) *Artemis.* Her temple at Ephesus was one of the wonders of the ancient world, and Paul's successful preaching roused the makers of silvershrine souvenirs (19:21–41). (iv) *Hades.* In cl. Gk. this god's name came to stand for his kingdom of the underworld; in the NT this word is used of the place where the dead go (→ *hadēs*, 87).

Three Canaanite gods appear in quotations from the OT: Baal (Rom. 11:4; cf. 1 Ki. 19:18), and Molech and Rephan (Acts 7:43; cf. Amos 5:26, NIV note).

9. *theios* occurs 3x in the NT. With the art., *to theion* means "the divine being" in Acts 17:29. As an adj., it means divine and is used with power and nature in 2 Pet. 1:3–4. *theiotēs* means "divine nature" (Rom. 1:20): "God's invisible qualities—his eternal power and *divine nature*—have been clearly . . . understood from what has been made." *theotēs*, deity, divinity (Col. 2:9), is used as an abstract noun for *theos* in connection with the incarnation: "For in Christ all the fullness of the *Deity* lives in bodily form."

See also *Emmanouēl*, Immanuel (*1842*); *kyrios*, Lord (*3261*).

2537 (*theosebeia*, fear of God, reverence for God, devoutness), → *4936.*

2538 (*theosebēs*, devout, God-fearing), → *4936.*

2540 (*theotēs*, deity, divinity), → *2536.*

2542 (*therapeia*, service, treatment), → *2543.*

2543	θεραπεύω

θεραπεύω (*therapeuō*), heal, cure (*2543*); θεράπων (*therapōn*), servant (*2544*); θεραπεία (*therapeia*), service, treatment (*2542*).

CL & OT 1. In cl. Gk. *therapeuō* means to serve, to be in service to (a superior); thus also to serve in the sense of venerating the gods, to care for (e.g., as a doctor), whence finally to cure, usually by medical means.

2. The LXX frequently uses *therapōn* to mean attendant, servant. The use of the vb. seems imprecise, even haphazard. In addition to the meaning serve, it can mean to sit (Est. 2:19; 6:10), to appease (Prov. 19:6), and to seek (29:26).

NT *therapeuō* occurs 43x in the NT, almost all of which appear in the Synoptics and Acts. Except for Acts 17:25, the vb. means exclusively to heal. Thus, in the NT *therapeuō* never has the meaning to serve (though cf. *therapeia* in Lk. 12:42, "servants" and *therapōn* in Heb. 3:5, "servant"). The cultic usage for the worship of God is found only in Acts 17:25, where Paul concludes, based on God as the Creator of the world and the Lord of heaven and earth, that he does not dwell in temples made by humans and that no one can give him anything. Nevertheless, he still accepts service from human beings.

1. Only in Lk. 4:23 (in the proverb "Physician, heal yourself") and in 8:43 ("no one could heal" the woman with the flow of blood) does *therapeuō* denote healing by ordinary medical means. Otherwise the vb. describes the miraculous healings of Jesus and his disciples.

(a) The Gospels present Jesus' work in terms of teaching and miracles (Matt. 4:23–24; 9:35; Lk. 6:18). Healing plays an essential part in his miraculous work, but it must be seen in the context of his teaching if it is to be understood correctly. This is esp. clear in Matt., where the great collection of Jesus' teaching (Matt. 5–7) and of his miracles (chs. 8–9) are enclosed between two almost identical verses, 4:23 and 9:35 (Jesus taught "in their synagogues, preaching the good news of the kingdom, and healing [*therapeuō*] every disease and sickness"). This emphasizes Christ's twofold task of teaching and healing.

As Jesus repeatedly heals the sick (e.g., Matt. 4:24; 12:15; 14:14; 15:30), he is fulfilling OT prophecies (8:16–17; cf. Isa. 53:4). The healings do not prove Jesus to be the Christ, but viewed against their OT background, they form part of his act of obedience and thus a necessary element in his messianic work. This conviction lies behind the many summaries (e.g., Matt. 4:24; Mk. 1:34; 3:10) of his miracles that emphasize that all who turn to Jesus find healing. This is why he has power to heal on the Sabbath (Matt. 12:10; Mk. 3:2; Lk. 6:7; 13:14). In taking up the cause of the helpless, Jesus proves himself to be the Servant of God (Matt. 8:7; 19:2).

(b) In Mk. 6:5–6 there is the remarkable statement that in Nazareth Jesus "could not do any miracles." It is clear from most of the detailed accounts of healing that faith on the part of those concerned was already present before they were healed by Jesus (cf. Matt. 8:8–10, 13; 9:27–30; 15:21–28; Lk. 8:43–48). Thus, after the disciples' failure to heal the lunatic boy (Matt. 17:16), the father confidently turned to Jesus for help, and his faith was vindicated, for the lad was healed (17:18). Healing is faith's reward, because faith is confident that even when people have done their utmost and failed, the power of God in Christ is inexhaustible. Thus healing does not initiate faith but assumes it (cf. Mk. 6:5–6). It is not that faith is the power that effects the miracle; it is rather preparedness for the miracle. At the same time, however, we may never tie faith so closely to miracles that it is an absolute requirement. Note, for example, the healing of the servant of the high priest's ear in the Garden of Gethsemane (Lk. 22:51). The root cause of healing lies in the heart of the healer, Jesus.

(c) Christ healed not only bodily infirmities but also cast out demons (e.g., Matt. 8:16; Mk. 1:34; 3:10–11; Lk. 4:40–41), revealing his messianic claims. Satanic powers are subject to his power and word, and by exercising power over the demons, he was utterly different from the ordinary exorcists of his time. In these miracles we glimpse the splendor of Christ the King.

(d) Jesus also gave his disciples a share in his healing power (Matt. 10:1, 8; Mk. 6:13; Lk. 9:1, 6). They entered into his work not only in the sense of teaching his doctrine, but in the sense of being empowered for the same messianic works he himself performed. For this, implicit faith is required (Matt. 17:16–21), the faith by which the early church experienced the enabling Christ in its midst (cf. Acts 5:16; 8:7). In the healings performed by the disciples the church was given a token of the active presence of its exalted Lord.

2. In sum, the NT stories of healing are not told in order to "prove" the messiahship of Jesus by demonstrating his power over natural laws. The real miracle is his victory over forces struggling for mastery over this cosmos. Although the healing miracles, in common with all the miracles in the Gospels, are repeatedly given prominence as outworkings of the Lord's power (cf. Matt. 14:14; 19:2), they are not regarded as having any importance in their own right.

See also *iaomai*, cure, restore (*2615*); *hygiēs*, healthy, well (*5618*).

2544 (*therapōn*, servant), → *2543.*

2545 (*therizō*, reap, harvest), → *2546.*

2546	θερισμός

θερισμός (*therismos*), harvest (*2546*); θερίζω (*therizō*), reap, harvest (*2545*); θεριστής (*theristēs*), reaper, harvester (*2547*).

CL & OT 1. This word group in cl. Gk. is commonly used in the lit. sense of reaping or gathering food crops. It is also used metaphorically, frequently in proverbs that highlight the inevitable moral consequences of prior actions. *therizō* also occurs in the extended sense of cutting off or destroying human adversaries.

2. In the LXX *therismos* means either the process of harvesting a crop (Exod. 34:22) or the produce reaped (Isa. 16:9). *therizō* is commonly used in the extended sense of reaping the fruit of a prior deed, either good (Job 5:26) or evil (4:8), or of gaining a reward through persistent effort (Ps. 126:5).

The harvest theme is symbolically used in the OT of a time of divine appointment in general (Jer. 8:20) or of temporal judgments in particular: e.g., on Ethiopia (Isa. 18:4–5), Babylon (Jer. 51:33 = LXX 28:33), Judah (Hos. 6:11), and Israel (Isa. 17:5). The richly descriptive harvest imagery portrays judgmental acts of God in justice and vengeance. A people ripened by sin are compared to a harvest prepared for the sickle of divine retribution. First cut down, then bound in bundles, threshed, and winnowed, the grain is gathered in the storehouse while the chaff is consumed by fire. A few OT prophets looked beyond the temporal horizon of divine judgment to the general harvest that would consummate this present age. Joel 3:13 foresees the ingathering of the end-time harvest of the nations. Isa. 27:12 expands the imagery so that the divine threshing process will separate Israel (grain) from the nations (chaff).

3. The figure of the world as a ripened field ready for harvest was taken up in Jewish apocalyptic lit. The end of this present evil age, which is to be consummated in a holocaust of judgment, is like a harvest in which good and evil fruit is reaped. The ethical maxims of Philo make frequent use of the sowing-reaping motif.

NT 1. The primary meaning of *therismos* (13x in the NT) is the process or time of gathering ripened crops, particularly grain (Matt. 13:30; Mk. 4:29; Jn. 4:35). *therizō* (21x; e.g., Matt. 6:26; Jas. 5:4) is used of reaping a cultivated crop and, in the case of grain, of threshing, winnowing, and storing the produce. *theristēs*, the agent who harvests a crop, is used only in Matt. 13:30, 39.

2. The notion of harvesting a ripened crop provided Jesus and the NT writers with a powerful image for explaining various facets of the divine economy. (a) The *therismos* group occurs in the Synoptics in the sense of the increase of one's labor generally. In the parable of the talents (Matt. 25:24, 26) and pounds (Lk. 19:21–22), the master and the nobleman, respectively, are accused of unjustly appropriating the fruit (→ *karpos*, *2843*) of others' work.

(b) Jesus developed the basic harvest imagery into the notion of the potential fruit of the Christian mission. Predisposed by God for reception of the gospel, humans are likened to a crop of fully ripened grain ready for harvest (Matt. 9:37–38; Lk. 10:2). With a note of urgency Jesus, "the Lord of the harvest," enjoins his followers, the reapers, to gather the ripened harvest before it perishes in the field. Jn. acknowledges that in the work of the kingdom the spiritual harvester reaps the labors of faithful planters who went before (Jn. 4:36–38). Both sower and reaper may anticipate due rewards for faithful performance of their appointed tasks.

(c) The harvest imagery also depicts the judgmental aspects of the kingdom, i.e., the preservation of the righteous and the punishment of evildoers. Using the figure of winnowing grain John the Baptist affirms of Jesus: "His winnowing fork is in his hand, and he will clear his threshing floor, gathering his wheat into the barn and burning up the chaff with unquenchable fire" (Matt. 3:12).

(d) Jesus used the harvest imagery to emphasize the eschatological aspects of the divine judgment. In the parable of the seed growing secretly (Mk. 4:29), the decisive event in the life of the kingdom is the reaping of a spiritual harvest with sharpened sickle. Jesus uses *therismos* as a symbol of the final separation between the righteous (the wheat) and the wicked (the weeds) in the parable of the weeds (Matt. 13:24–30); the granary is the Father's eternal kingdom. The vision of the Son of Man (cf. Mk. 13:26–27; Rev. 1:13) reaping earth's ripened harvest in judgment with his angels (14:15–16) recapitulates the teaching of the OT and Jesus on the subject.

See also *sperma*, seed (*5065*); *karpos*, fruit (*2843*).

2547 (*theristēs*, reaper, harvester), → *2546*.
2548 (*thermainō*, warm), → *6037*.
2549 (*thermē*, heat), → *6037*.
2555 (*theōreō*, watch), → *3972*.
2559 (*thēlys*, female), → *781*.

2563	θηρίον

θηρίον (*thērion*), wild animal, beast (*2563*).

CL & OT In cl. Gk. *thērion* usually means a wild animal, occasionally an animal kept at pasture. From Plato on it came to be used metaphorically as a derogatory term for people of a "bestial" type: beast, monster.

In the LXX *thērion* designated a wild animal. The *thērion* is an enemy of humans (Gen. 3:14–15; 9:2, 5; 37:20). In warnings of God's judgment the ravages of wild beasts are listed along with other troubles (Lev. 26:22; Deut. 32:24; Jer. 12:9; 15:3). The devouring of human corpses by beasts is regarded as the height of shame (2 Sam. 21:10; cf. Gen. 40:19). In the days to come full harmony between humanity and beast, which existed in Paradise, will be restored (Lev. 26:6; Isa. 35:9; Ezek. 34:25; Hos. 2:20 = LXX 2:18).

In Dan. 7 *thērion* refers to world powers, seen as supernatural, beast-like figures. They arise from the chaos that is hostile to God (water) and represent the sort of political powers with which the Jewish people had to deal throughout the centuries. The coming of the Son of Man will put an end to them.

NT 1. *thērion* (45x in the NT) occurs in lists of living creatures (Acts 11:6; Jas. 3:7), in a catalogue of plagues (Rev. 6:8), and as a description of the Cretans (Tit. 1:12). In Mk. 1:13 the wild beasts emphasize the horror and human desolation of the desert; possibly they are also intended as an allusion to the messianic return of the Paradise era, with its state of peace between humankind and beast.

2. This word appears 38x in Rev., particularly in chs. 13–19. The beast and the false prophet, representing powers opposed to God, join the dragon to form the satanic trinity (16:13). From their mouths issue three foul demonic spirits like frogs, who gather the world rulers at Armageddon for battle. The beast in 11:7 combines characteristics of all four beasts in Dan. 7, dreadfully intensified. It originates in the realm of chaos (11:7; 13:1), is given authority by the "dragon" (13:2, 4), has the attributes of beasts of prey (11:7), and executes its claims to total power with ruthless force (13:7–8, 15).

As the Antichrist the beastly monster caricatures the Lamb (with its wound, 13:3, 14 [cf. 5:6]; its horns, 13:1 [cf. 5:6]; world dominion, 13:2 [cf. 5:5]; and worship, 13:4 [cf. 5:8–14]). It also apes the title of God (17:8, 11; cf. 1:4). "Another" beast (13:11), otherwise called "the false prophet" (16:13; 19:20; 20:10), furthers the plans of the first beast by its propaganda of working miracles (13:13), erecting an image (*eikōn*, 13:14), and branding people with a mark (*charagma*, 13:16–17). Although to outward appearances a lamb, it speaks like a dragon (13:11; cf. Matt. 7:15). The final victory over these beastly powers will belong to Christ and his church (Rev. 15:2; 19:19–20).

2564 (*thēsaurizō*, store up, gather, save up, reserve), → *2565*.

2565	θησαυρός

θησαυρός (*thēsauros*), treasure box, chest, storeroom, treasure (*2565*); θησαυρίζω (*thēsaurizō*), store up, gather, save up, reserve (*2564*); ἀποθησαυρίζω (*apothēsaurizō*), lay up treasure (*631*).

CL & OT 1. In cl. Gk. *thēsauros* means a treasure chamber, storage room, granary; also treasure. Early in recorded history temples were built with treasure chambers, where gifts and taxes in kind and money could be stored. The practice appears to have spread from Egypt to Greece. Collecting boxes were also known (cf. 2 Ki. 12:10). *thēsaurizō* is used similarly in the sense of storing up treasure or putting it in safekeeping.

2. Jos. 6:19, 24 (= LXX 6:18, 23) mentions the "treasury" of the Lord in connection with the holy war and the ban (cf. 1 Ki. 7:51; 14:26); in 1 Ki. 14:26 and 15:18 "the treasures of the temple of the LORD and the treasures of the royal palace" are carried off to Egypt. Later, besides the common usage of treasure (Prov. 10:2), we find reference to treasures in or from heaven (Job 38:22 ["storehouses of the snow"]; Jer. 50:25 = LXX 27:25 ["arsenal . . . weapons of his wrath"]). In Isa. 33:6, "the fear of the LORD is the key to [Zion's] treasure," which is defined as "salvation and wisdom and knowledge."

Isa. 45:3 refers to "the treasures of darkness" (i.e., treasures that are hidden away), which God will give to Cyrus so that he may have a true knowledge of Yahweh, the God of Israel. The prophet is perhaps contrasting earthly treasure for which human beings work and fight with the treasure that Yahweh alone gives. We should be as eager to search for the fear of the Lord and the knowledge of God as people do for buried treasures (Prov. 2:4–5).

3. In rab. Jud. good works (e.g., almsgiving) are a treasure stored up as a reward in the world to come, while the interest is enjoyed in this world. The rabbis sometimes spoke of the treasure from which the scribe draws and of the treasure house of eternal life, i.e., the place where the souls of the dead are stored up.

NT The NT continues both the cl. Gk. meaning of *thēsauros* (18x) and its usage in OT and rab. lit. The vb. *thēsaurizō* occurs 8x. The concept often involves the paradoxical transformation of earthly values. What is treasured by humans is of no enduring worth in God's sight, and real treasure involves earthly poverty.

1. (a) In Matt. 2:11 the "treasures" that the Magi open to the infant Jesus are gifts of gold, incense, and myrrh. In 12:35 the heart is compared with good things "stored up," out of which a good person brings forth good. The picture is either that of a storehouse or a treasure chest. As the context suggests, Jesus' words here constitute a warning against the hypocrisy of appearing to speak good, whereas in fact one intends evil.

(b) In the Sermon on the Mount Jesus tells his disciples: "Do not store up [*thēsaurizō*] for yourselves treasures [*thēsauros*] on earth, where moth and rust destroy, and where thieves break in and steal. But store up [*thēsaurizō*] for yourselves treasures [*thēsauros*] in heaven. . . . For where your treasure [*thēsauros*] is, there your heart will be also" (Matt. 6:19–21; cf. Lk. 12:21, 33–34). The idea of treasures in heaven is a Jewish notion. The nature of this treasure is not defined, although the following sayings warn against double-mindedness, trying to serve God and Money (→ *mamōnas*, 3440), and anxiety about food and clothing—culminating in the injunction: "But seek first his kingdom and his righteousness, and all these things will be given to you as well" (Matt. 6:33).

Clearly, Jesus outlines a contrast between worldly possessions and spiritual good. In view of the proximity of this section to the Lord's Prayer (Matt. 6:9–13) and the saying about the kingdom in 6:33, we should understand this treasure primarily in terms of the kingdom of heaven (cf. 13:44). On a human side this is understood in terms of doing God's will; on God's side it involves God's reign and gracious provision for his children. But the treasure is not some form of accumulated spiritual capital; it is the realization of a gracious personal relationship with the Father and with one's fellow human beings in the kingdom of God. What is worth possessing is not material things that perish but personal acceptance by God and by others. In a similar vein, Paul instructs believers not to put our hope in earthly wealth but in God and to share what we have; in this way we will "lay up treasure" (*apothēsaurizō*) for ourselves for the coming age.

(c) The teaching about treasure is further exemplified by the story of the rich young ruler, to whom Jesus said: "If you want to be perfect, go, sell your possessions and give to the poor, and you will have treasure in heaven. Then come, follow me" (Matt. 19:21; cf. Mk.

10:21; Lk. 18:22). This saying makes explicit an implicit point in the background of the earlier sayings: Not only is the treasure to be seen in the light of the coming end time, it is also connected with following Jesus.

(d) Matt. 13:44 states that "the kingdom of heaven is like treasure hidden in a field. When a man found it, he hid it again, and then in his joy went and sold all he had and bought that field." Important here is both the overpowering joy that the kingdom brings and the wholehearted self-sacrifice it causes one to make. According to rab. teaching, if a worker lifted a treasure in the course of his work, the find belonged to the master. But in this parable the man does not lift it until he is the actual owner of the field, and he is prepared to go to any lengths permitted by the law to obtain it. Note also the following parable of the pearl of great price (13:45–46).

(e) The parable of the rich fool (Lk. 12:16–21) presents the converse of Jesus' positive teaching about treasure. It describes a man who did, in fact, store up earthly possessions. "But God said to him, 'You fool! This very night your life will be demanded of you. Then who will get what you have prepared for yourself?' This is how it will be with anyone who stores up [*thēsaurizō*] things for himself but is not rich toward God" (12:20–21). Lk. presents the parable in conjunction with Jesus' refusal to intervene in a family feud over possessions. He warns of greed, for "a man's life does not consist in the abundance of his possessions" (12:15). Lk. follows this story with Jesus' teaching on anxiety about food and clothing and on laying up treasure in heaven (cf. above).

(f) *thēsauros* in the sense of treasure chest occurs in Matt. 13:52 at the conclusion of Matt.'s account of seven parables. In response to the disciples' affirmation that they have understood, Jesus said: "Therefore every teacher of the law who has been instructed about the kingdom of heaven is like the owner of a house who brings out of his storeroom [*thēsauros*] new treasures as well as old." The contents of the treasure chest is not simply the teaching but the teaching as the occasion for appropriating the kingdom.

2. (a) Paul uses *thēsaurizō* in his instructions to the Corinthians about the collection for the poor believers in Jerusalem, setting aside whatever amount each one wants and storing it up until Paul arrives (1 Cor. 16:2). He uses the same word again in 2 Cor. 12:14, where he declares that "children should not have to save up [*thēsaurizō*] for their parents, but parents for their children." The apostle is speaking here of his forthcoming visit and his determination not to be a burden to them. Paul regards himself as their father (cf. 1 Cor. 4:15), and hence he feels under obligation to support them.

(b) In Rom. 2:5 the vb. is used fig. in addressing the Jews who by their hardened hearts "are storing up" God's wrath against themselves for the day of judgment. There is an ironic contrast here, for the Jews are presuming on "the riches [*ploutos*, → 4458] of [God's] kindness, tolerance, and patience" (2:4)—reflecting the Jewish conception of treasure stored up in the world to come as a reward for good works.

(c) Paul uses the noun *thēsauros* 2x, both with a Christological connotation. In 2 Cor. 4:7 he compares the treasure of God's gift in Christ to the believer with the bodily existence of those who receive it: "But we have this treasure in jars of clay to show that this all-surpassing power is from God and not from us." This treasure of "the knowledge of the glory of God in the face of Christ" has just been defined in a manner recalling the creation of light (2 Cor. 4:6; cf. Gen. 1:3; Ps. 112:4). The treasure is thus revealed but at the same time hidden by the vessel that contains it and the outward circumstances of the believer's life.

Col. 2:3 also speaks of treasure Christologically: "in whom are hidden all the treasures of wisdom and knowledge." As in 2 Cor. 4, the treasure is linked with revelation and knowledge (cf. Col. 2:2). But the hiddenness refers to Christ, who, although it might not appear so to earthly sight, is nevertheless "the image of the invisible God," in whom "God was pleased to have all his fullness dwell" (1:15, 19), and who is now with God (3:3). Jesus Christ is like a hidden treasure, for which a searcher should be willing to wager everything to find. Jesus is the only place where wisdom and knowledge may be found.

3. In Heb. 11:26, the author writes that Moses "regarded disgrace for the sake of Christ as of greater value than the treasures [*thēsauros*] of Egypt, because he was looking ahead to his reward." The main exegetical question here is the phrase "for the sake of Christ." Is the author giving a veiled reference to the belief that Jesus, long before his incarnation, accompanied the Israelites through the desert (cf. 1 Cor. 10:4)? Perhaps. But "[the] Christ" here can be translated "the anointed one" (→ *Christos, 5986*). OT texts such as Ps. 89:50–51; 105:15 suggest that the people of God are God's anointed. In other words, what Moses preferred to the treasures of Egypt was the lot of God's people as his anointed firstborn, for he believed God's promises to them (cf. Heb. 11:27).

Thus in this context Israel is God's son, as God through Moses reminded Pharaoh when he demanded their release: "Israel is my firstborn son" (Exod. 4:22). It was with the lot of Israel that Moses identified himself. This interpretation has the advantage of being compatible with all the other instances of faith in Heb. 11 drawn from OT history, none of which are given a specific Christological interpretation. The reproach, abuse, or stigma that was the lot of the Israelites thus anticipates the reproach that falls on those who follow Christ. The same act of faith is required to prefer suffering, in the light of God's promises, to material gain.

4. Jas. 5:3 takes up the thought about treasure expressed in the teaching of Jesus: "Your gold and silver are corroded. Their corrosion will testify against you and eat your flesh like fire. You have hoarded wealth [*thēsaurizō*] in the last days." This text spells out the judgment awaiting those who are preoccupied with earthly treasure. There is an irony here. For while the people concerned thought that they were storing up treasure, they were, in fact, storing up judgment (cf. Rom. 2:5).

5. In 2 Pet. 3:7 we see a further idea of storing up judgment. Pet. applies this idea to the whole world order: "By the same word the present heavens and earth are reserved [*thēsaurizō*] for fire, being kept for the day of judgment and destruction of ungodly men." Although in general the NT refers to a judgment of fire as applying only to God's enemies (e.g., Rev. 20:14–15), Pet. speaks of a fiery destruction of the present heaven and earth. Still, the Bible is filled with varying images of judgment, the new creation, regeneration, and the new heaven and earth. Perhaps the specific image of fire is drawn from Jewish apocalyptic writings (e.g., 2 Esd. 13:10–11; *Sib. Or.* 2:187–213; 3:83–92; 4:171–182; 5:155–161; → *pyr*, fire, *4786*).

See also *mamōnas*, money, wealth, property (*3440*); *peripoieō*, save for oneself, acquire, gain possession of (*4347*); *ploutos*, wealth, riches (*4458*); *chrēma*, property, wealth, means, money (*5975*).

2567 (thlibō, press upon, oppress, afflict), → *2568*.

2568	θλῖψις

θλῖψις (*thlipsis*), oppression, affliction, tribulation (*2568*); θλίβω (*thlibō*), press upon, oppress, afflict (*2567*); στενοχωρία (*stenochōria*), straits, distress, affliction, difficulty (*5103*); στενοχωρέω (*stenochōreō*), crowd, cramp, confine, oppress (*5102*).

CL & OT 1. In cl. Gk. *thlibō* means press, squeeze, crush. A fig. use, meaning oppress (external) and grieve, vex (internal), is common. Some Stoics referred to the pressures of life, which the true Stoic must and can overcome. The noun *thlipsis*, oppression, distress, affliction, is linked with the vb. It is occasionally found coupled with *stenochōria*, which is used to express a narrow place, hence being pressed by inner and outer difficulties.

2. In the LXX *thlipsis* usually denotes need, distress, and affliction, depending on context (e.g., war, exile, and personal hostility). As in cl. Gk. it is sometimes linked with *stenochōria* (e.g., Deut. 28:53, 55, 57; Isa. 8:22; 30:6) as well as with other words of fear and pain. *thlipsis* in the LXX is often the oppression that belongs of necessity to the history of Israel and that was regarded by the faithful as part of salvation history. There is a connection between oppression (Exod. 3:9) and deliverance (3:10). Even when the oppression is a punishment, its purpose is deliverance (Neh. 9:27; Hos. 5:14–6:2).

The eschatological nature of oppression is often stressed (cf. Hab. 3:16; Zech. 1:15). Dan. 12:1 speaks of "a time of distress such as has not happened from the beginning of nations" until the writer's own time. But here also deliverance from trouble is referred to, and this expresses the faith and hope of the faithful in Israel. "A righteous man may have many troubles, but the LORD delivers him from them all" (Ps. 34:19; cf. 37:39). This was the unshakeable conviction of the faithful, who were able to pray: "Though you have made me see troubles, many and bitter, you will restore my life again" (71:20).

3. Jud. also knew of the troubles of the people that it expected in the end time and described in detail in various apocalypses (*1 Enoch, 2 Esd., 2 Bar.*).

NT *thlipsis* is used 45x in the NT, *thlibō* 10x, always fig. (apart from Matt. 7:14—the narrow road leads to life; Mk. 3:9—the crowd crushes Jesus). *stenochōria* is found 4x (Rom. 2:9; 8:35; 2 Cor. 6:4; 12:10), *stenochōreō* 3x (2 Cor. 4:8; 6:12). The usage of these words in the NT is clearly the same as in the OT. The following cases are of importance.

1. *thlipsis* has an eschatological significance for the church (cf. esp. the quotation of Dan. 12:1 in Matt. 24:21 and Mk. 13:19). The tribulation stands in the closest connection with the Son of Man (Matt. 24:30) of Dan. 7:13 and the birth pangs of the Messiah (Matt. 24:8). This tribulation belongs to the period of catastrophes before the final salvation, and it is characterized by leading astray, hate, political strife, and catastrophes of nature. The same thought is to be found in Rev., not merely in 2:22 and 7:14 (cf. 3:10), where the "great tribulation" is referred to, but also in 1:9, where "suffering" is once again linked with Dan. 2:28 and 7:13.

2. A second element is expressed by the phrase "Christ's afflictions" (Col. 1:24). The OT statement about the many troubles of the righteous (Ps. 34:19) is esp. applicable to the truly righteous one, Jesus Christ (Acts 3:14–15). Jesus himself insists that he "must" suffer (e.g., Mk. 8:31; Lk. 24:26). "What is still lacking" in Col. 1:24 is not only a question of the afflictions left over for the church, but also of the afflictions that the Lord suffered in his unique suffering (1:20, 22), with which the church knows itself to be linked in its own affliction. Passages like 2 Cor. 1:5 (cf. 1:4, 6) and 4:10 (cf. 4:8) allow us to infer that the thought of such afflictions was implicit in the proclamation of the passion of Christ.

3. In the light of the two preceding concepts we can understand believers' afflictions. (a) Believers are implicitly included in the eschatological afflictions. They are exposed to tribulations (Matt. 24:9), esp. hatred, betrayal, and death. It is above all the time of leading astray (cf. 24:4–5, 11, 24), the time of testing (→ *peirasmos, 4280*).

(b) Col. 1:24 makes it clear that Christians experience these afflictions in solidarity with Christ's passion. Only so can they be rightly explained and endured (cf. 2 Cor. 1:4–6; 4:8–11; Phil. 3:10; 1 Pet. 4:13). Precisely for this reason tribulation and all other distress cannot separate us from Christ (Rom. 8:35). Because we suffer with him in these distresses, we will be glorified together with him (8:17; cf. 8:37).

(c) The connection of *thlipsis* with the eschatological and Christological tribulations, both of which are divine "necessities," makes it probable that the tribulations of Christians are also conditioned by this "must." Note Jn. 16:33: "In this world you will have trouble"; Acts 14:22: "We must go through many hardships to enter the kingdom of God." It is perhaps most clearly expressed in 1 Thess. 3:3, where Paul writes that he had sent Timothy to exhort the church "that no one would be unsettled by these trials. You know quite well that we were destined for them." Paul had expected nothing else for his own life (3:4; cf. Acts 20:23) and had experienced it in full measure in his missionary work (e.g., 2 Cor. 6:4–10; 11:16–12:10; Phil. 1:17; 4:14). But it caused him joy, not grief (Rom. 5:3; cf. Jas. 1:2–3).

(d) Various NT churches experienced tribulation: Jerusalem (Acts 11:19), Corinth (2 Cor. 1:4), Thessalonica (1 Thess. 1:6; 3:3), and Macedonia generally (2 Cor. 8:2). But these afflictions are determined, as far as believers are concerned, by their goal in God's plan of salvation. They are therefore never purposeless, but produce hope (Rom. 5:3–5). Just as a woman who has given birth to a child no longer remembers the anguish in her joy (Jn. 16:21), so believers may have sorrow (16:22) and tribulation (16:33), but Jesus encourages us to "take heart." Believers know God's righteousness, which repays with affliction those who cause affliction and grants rest to the afflicted (2 Thess. 1:6–7).

See also *diōkō*, run after, pursue, persecute (*1503*).

2569 (*thnēskō*, die), → 2505.

2570 (*thnētos*, mortal), → 2505.

2571 (*thorybazō*, cause trouble, pass. be troubled, distressed), → 2512.

2572 (*thorybeō*, throw into disorder, pass. be troubled, distressed), → 2512.

2573 (*thorybos*, commotion, uproar, turmoil), → 2512.

2579 (*thrēskeia*, service of God, religion), → 3302.

2580 (*thrēskos*, pious), → 3302.

2581	θριαμβεύω

θριαμβεύω (*thriambeuō*), lead to a triumphal procession (*2581*).

CL & OT 1. This vb. is derived from the noun *thriambos*, originally a hymn sung at the ceremonial processions in honor of the god Dionysus. In the 2d cent. B.C. it took on the meaning to celebrate a triumph or to lead someone in a triumphal procession. In the Hel. environment of the NT, *thriambeuō* meant the triumphal procession of a ruler, which his defeated enemies had to follow. Prisoners provided a spectacle laid on by the victor. Censers were also carried in the triumphal processions and spread a festive perfume.

2. This word does not occur in the LXX.

NT *thriambeuō* only appears twice in the NT: 2 Cor. 2:14 and Col. 2:15, on both occasions in the trans. sense, to lead in a triumphal procession.

1. Col. 2:15 presents God as the triumphant victor: Jesus' journey to the cross is God's triumphal procession. Through Jesus' death and resurrection the spiritual authorities and powers opposed to God have been disarmed and defeated. God, as it were, leads them like prisoners in his triumphal procession.

2. In 2 Cor. 2:14, Paul himself is led in triumph as one whom God has defeated, who as the servant of Jesus Christ is at all times and in all places a part of God's triumphal procession. The apostle understands his missionary task as the work of a slave, who puts the power of the divine victor on show and by his proclamation spreads the perfume of the knowledge of God—to some for life, to others for death (2:14–17).

See also *athleō*, compete (*123*); *agōn*, fight (*74*); *brabeion*, prize (*1092*); *nikaō*, be victorious (*3771*).

2585	θρόνος

θρόνος (*thronos*), throne, seat (*2585*).

CL & OT 1. In cl. Gk. *thronos* originally meant a chair with an attached footstool; it denoted a place of honor, such as the master of a house might use, though it could also be offered to guests and bards. Under Lat. influence, this word came to mean the seat of a god and

could also then be used metaphorically, as in the pl. *thronoi*, for power. To be seated on the throne was a sign of regal or divine majesty.

2. (a) The concept of the royal throne derives from the Orient. Sitting on a throne denotes the unique exaltation of the absolute ruler, his superiority over against those subject to him. It is his sole right to sit on the throne; the suppliant or servant stands before him. Only when the king sits on the throne does he take his power. The magnificent ornamentation of a throne indicates his divine dignity; at its sides, to the right and left, stand attendant heavenly beings such as cherubim as pictorial symbols of ruling power (cf. 1 Ki. 10:18–20). The earthly ruler was honored as a son of the god or even (as in Egypt) as the incarnation of the divine.

(b) Since the king was originally also the judge, his throne was both a visible symbol of regal power (2 Sam. 3:10; 14:9) and of justice (Ps. 122:5). The throne was thus a constant factor over against the changing bearers of power. In this way, Nathan's promise of the permanence of the Davidic rule (2 Sam. 7:13) was linked with "the throne" (cf. also 1 Chr. 28:5; 29:23). This formed the primary link with the later hope of the everlasting throne of the Messiah.

3. In the OT the throne represents God's power and righteousness. This can never be simply identified with the king's power, however much the ANE court style was taken over. The Israelite king stood in an adoptive relationship with Yahweh as his "Son" (Ps. 2:7). Jer. specified Jerusalem as God's throne (3:17), but also Israel (14:21). Ezek., in his great vision of the future, saw the new temple as the abode of the divine throne (43:7), while in Isa. 66:1 heaven is said to be Yahweh's throne (cf. 6:1; 14:13).

The special nature of the divine kingship is seen in the throne vision of Isa. 6:1–13, but most clearly in Ezek. 1:4–28. Here Yahweh's kingly power is seen under the symbolism of transcendent creatures, representing the world rule of their Lord. They each have four faces, representing God's omnipresence, and face the world, while above their outspread wings (1:22) stands the vault of heaven, which keeps the destroying floods away from the creation (cf. Gen. 1:6–7). It is above this world—inaccessible to humans—that God's throne is seen, surrounded by an unearthly brightness. The throne of the "Ancient of Days" in Dan. 7:9 probably has a similar significance (cf. Ps. 97:2) The other thrones mentioned there are probably for the assessors or the jury in the court proceedings.

4. The hidden nature and dynamic of Israel's throne theology is revealed by the rite of Yahweh's ceremonial enthronement (cf. Ps. 24; 93; 96–99). Yahweh's kingship is not an inactive representation, but a fight that has just been won (see esp. Ps. 93; also 46; 89:7–14). In Israel's enthronement ritual, which may have been part of the New Year Festival, the ark of the covenant represented the throne of God: Yahweh was depicted as present, though invisible, "enthroned between the cherubim" (99:1), which were on both sides of the ark.

NT 1. The NT adds little to these OT concepts. In Rev. the throne plays a dominant role. The word occurs there 47x, over against 15x in the rest of the NT. In Matt. 5:34, Jesus speaks of heaven as God's throne and for that reason forbids us to swear by it. The promise to Nathan is alluded to in Lk. 1:32, with extended reference to the messianic throne (2 Sam. 7:12, 16; cf. also Acts 3:20–21). Note too such phrases as "glorious throne" (Matt. 19:28; cf. 25:31; 1 Sam. 2:8) and "throne of grace" (Heb. 4:16). The latter is the antitype to the "atonement cover [*hilastērion*, → *hilaskomai*, *2661*]" in the earthly sanctuary.

2. A striking point in the NT is that the Son of Man sits on the divine throne of judgment (Heb. 12:2). Matt. 19:28 even promises such ruling authority to the twelve apostles, as judges with him over Israel. In Matt. 25:31–46, the Son of Man judges the world from "his throne in heavenly glory" entirely on his own. A pictorial tension exists between these statements and those (following Ps. 110:1) that view the Messiah sitting at the right hand of God, but there is no material contradiction.

3. (a) In Heb. the throne of Jesus is not merely a throne of justice, but also a "throne of grace" (4:16). Because of the incarnation of our heavenly high priest and his perfect life, we can approach this throne "with confidence" and find mercy and grace.

(b) In Col. 1:15–20, generally considered to be a baptismal hymn, thrones are mentioned along with "powers . . . rulers . . . [and] authorities." This list denotes various groups of angels who belong to the council of the heavenly throne (cf. 1 Ki. 22:19). Within the compass of the hymn, this enumeration declares that Christ's creative power not only embraces what is visible, the earth, but also what is invisible, the world of angels.

4. (a) The picture of the throne in Rev. is based on Ezek. and is developed esp. in ch. 4. The throne there signifies the transcendent majesty of God. The "sea of glass, clear as crystal" (Rev. 4:6) is the vault of heaven (as in Ezek. 1). but the twenty-four elders on their thrones are new (Rev. 4:4). They are the heads of the heavenly court council. They represent the old and new Israel—the heads of the twelve tribes together with the twelve apostles. Their function is like that of the heavenly beings. They constantly adore "him who sits on the throne" (4:10), before whom they fall down and cry: "You are worthy, our Lord and God, to receive glory and honor and power, for you created all things, and by your will they were created and have their being" (4:11).

(b) A new factor appears in Rev. 5:6–9. "In the center of the throne," as the divine judgment of the world begins, appears the one who is to carry it out—"a Lamb, looking as if it had been slain" (cf. 5:12). Christ, in highest glory, is here pictured in terms of complete defenselessness. Nowhere is the paradox of the NT revelation of Christ shown so clearly as here. God's power is, from a human point of view, total powerlessness. Christ carries out the judgment in, and as, a self-sacrifice. The one who sits on the throne was a human, who turned power into service and brotherhood. To him, at the end of time, the whole creation pays its homage (5:13).

(c) Opposing this Christian throne as seen by faith is the throne of the Antichrist, who proclaims his power and demands submission (Rev. 13:4–8; cf. 2 Thess. 2:4). This throne, too, speaks of dominion—not of the Lamb, but of the dragon (Rev. 13:2). But his dominion succumbs to the wrathful judgment of the Lamb (16:10). The throne of the Lamb is ultimately triumphant. From it flows the river of the water of life in the new Jerusalem (22:1).

See also *dynamis*, power, might, strength, force (*1539*); *exousia*, freedom of choice, right, power, authority (*2026*); *ischys*, strength (*2709*).

2592 (*thymiama*, incense), → *3337*.

2593 (*thymiatērion*, censer, altar of incense), → *3337*.

2594 (*thymiaō*, burn incense), → *3337*.

| 2596 | θυμός |

θυμός (*thymos*), passion, anger, rage (*2596*); θυμόω (*thymoō*), pass. become angry (*2597*); ἐνθυμέομαι (*enthymeomai*), reflect, consider (*1926*); ἐνθύμησις (*enthymēsis*), thought, reflection, idea (*1927*).

OT There is virtually no distinction in the LXX between *thymos* and *orgē* (→ *orgē*, *3973*).

NT *thymos* occurs only 18x in the NT. In general it means anger, wrath, rage.

1. In Heb., Lk., Acts, and the Pauline writings (apart from Rom. 2:8), *thymos* refers to human anger. The pl. may denote outbursts of anger or even passions. As in the LXX it often stands alongside *orgē* without any perceptible distinction of meaning (e.g., Eph. 4:31; Col. 3:8). It is also linked with *eris* (quarreling), *zēlos* (jealousy), *eritheia* (selfish ambition) in 2 Cor. 12:20 and Gal. 5:20. These are dangers into which even the church might fall. On the other hand, some people were filled with rage at the teaching of Jesus (Lk. 4:28) and Paul (Acts 19:28).

All this has its origin in the old human nature (Gal. 5:19–20; Eph. 4:31; Col. 3:8–9) and can only be overcome in the power of the

Spirit, who renews the heart (Eph. 4:23; Gal. 5:16, 18, 22, 25), and creates a new nature (Eph. 4:24).

2. In Rom. 2:8 *thymos* (with *orgē*) describes the divine anger, although God's name is not mentioned. The divine anger will be revealed at the final judgment (2:5) in those whose hearts are hardened and who do not obey the truth (2:8), but do evil (2:9).

In Rev. *thymos* denotes almost exclusively divine anger (e.g., 15:1, 7; 16:1). The picture of the cup of God's wrath is a striking expression, derived from the OT (cf. Jer. 25:15–28), of the divine judgment (14:10; 16:19; 19:15) that human beings must, as it were, drink. It brings eternal ruin. Similar to this are the expressions the "winepress of God's wrath" (14:19) and the "bowls filled with the wrath of God" (15:7; 16:1).

3. Of the vbs. derived from *thymos*, *thymoō*, become angry, occurs in the NT only in Matt. 2:16, and *enthymeomai*, reflect, consider, only in Matt. 1:20; 9:4. The noun *enthymēsis*, consideration, reflection, is always in the negative sense of bad or foolish thoughts (9:4; 12:25; Acts 17:29; Heb. 4:12). Except in Acts 17:29 the contexts suggest hidden, secret thoughts that one prefers not to reveal but that God in his omniscience perceives and brings to light.

See also *orgē*, anger, *3973*.

2597 (*thymoō*, become angry), → *2596*.

| 2598 | θύρα |

θύρα (*thyra*), door, entrance (*2598*).

CL & OT 1. In cl. Gk. *thyra* denotes a door of a house and occasionally, by metonymy, the house itself. The phrase "at the door(s)" can indicate nearness of place or time: To be "at the door" of a king or other influential person means to be paying court to or seeking benefit from that person. The noun can also be used for any entrance, lit. or metaphorical.

In the LXX *thyra* denotes an opening, doorway, or gate, and fig., any aperture (e.g., an animal's jaws, human lips).

NT 1. In the NT *thyra* is used lit.: (a) the door of a house or room (e.g., Matt. 6:6; 25:10; Mk. 1:33; 2:2; Acts 5:9); (b) the door of the temple (Acts 3:2; 21:30); (c) prison doors (5:19, 23; 12:6) that miraculously open to liberate apostles, proof that the gospel cannot be hindered by bonds or imprisonment; (d) the entrance to a cave tomb (Matt. 27:60; Mk. 16:3); and (e) the opening in a stone enclosure (Jn. 10:1–2).

2. *thyra* is also used fig. (a) The phrase "before" or "at the door" indicates nearness in time or place (Matt. 24:33; Mk. 13:29; Jas. 5:9; cf. also Acts 5:9).

(b) The image of the open door denotes an opportunity for the spread of the gospel. God opens a door for the message of salvation (Col. 4:3), giving the missionary a field in which to work (1 Cor. 16:9; 2 Cor. 2:12), and he opens a door of faith to Gentiles by offering them the possibility of believing in Christ (Acts 14:27). By contrast, the closed door (Matt. 25:10; Lk. 13:25; cf. Rev. 3:7) carries a sense of judgment.

(c) The narrow door in Lk. 13:24 (cf. Matt. 7:13–14, where *pylē* is used) denotes the entrance into the kingdom of God, and the shutting of that door indicates irrevocable loss of an opportunity. According to Rev. 3:8, the exalted Christ alone has the authority to grant access to his kingdom. Rev. 3:20 is best understood in an eschatological setting: The returning Savior seeks fellowship with a disciple in a festal meal; the door is opened by obedience and faith. Only once does the NT expressly refer to the door of heaven (4:1), although this metaphor may underlie other passages that speak of opening and shutting the sky or heavens (Lk. 4:25; Rev. 11:6).

(d) In the "I am the door [NIV, gate]" sayings in Jn. 10:7, 9, Jesus is the gate to the sheep, the door whereby the genuine shepherd approaches the flock. In 10:9 the image is that of the gate through which the sheep go in and out; i.e., Jesus is the gate for the sheep to go into the fold, the gate leading to salvation and life (cf. 14:6), an idea perhaps indebted to a messianic interpretation of Ps. 118:20. The image of Jesus as the gate to salvation appears early in patristic exegesis (Ign. *Phld.* 9:1; *Herm. Sim.* 9.12.1).

See also *pylē*, gate, door (*4783*).

2599 (*thyreos*, shield), → *4483*.

2602 (*thysia*, sacrifice, offering, act of offering), → *2604*.

2603 (*thysiastērion*, altar), → *2604*.

2604	θύω

θύω (*thyō*), to sacrifice, slaughter, kill, celebrate (*2604*); θυσία (*thysia*), sacrifice, offering, act of offering (*2602*); θυσιαστήριον (*thysiastērion*), altar (*2603*); προσφορά (*prosphora*), offering, the act of offering, the offering that is brought (*4714*); προσφέρω (*prospherō*), offer, sacrifice (*4712*); εἰδωλόθυτος (*eidōlothytos*), a thing sacrificed to idols (*1628*); ὁλοκαύτωμα (*holokautōma*), whole burnt offering (*3906*); βωμός (*bōmos*), (pagan) altar (*1117*).

CL 1. In cl. Gk. *thyō* has the basic meaning to sacrifice, though originally in connection with the smoke offering it meant to smoke, offer a smoking or a burnt sacrifice. Because sacrificial animals or portions of animals—and humans also—were burnt, *thyō* assumed the meaning to slaughter for cultic ends. The noun *thysia* signifies the ritual of sacrifice as well as the sacrificial animal or any sacrificial gift.

2. *prosphora* originally meant bringing, presenting. It was used of income, revenue, and the offering of sacrificial gifts, then in particular an offering of food, esp. in the form of a gift of grain. For the act of offering, the vb. *prospherō* was used. From Sophocles on, in connection with making an offering in the form of a gift, the expression came to indicate total submission to the deity.

OT 1. *Principal sources*. Many passages in the OT exhibit the wide-ranging significance that sacrifice acquired in Israel. The main sources are the Mosaic legislation (e.g., Exod. 20:22–23:33; 34; Lev. 1–7; 16; Deut. 12–26), though sacrifices are also outlined in Ezek. 40–48. The OT presents a variety of interrelated ideas. Note too that the notion of sacrifice was not unique to Israel but was widespread in the ancient Near East (cf., e.g., Lev. 20:2–5; Deut. 18).

2. *Cultic sites*. The offering of sacrifice was localized at a cultic site that centered on the altar (Heb. *mizbēaḥ*, place of sacrifice). The LXX is the first place where the corresponding Gk. noun *thysiastērion*, sacrificial table, altar, occurs (419x); its use remains confined to Jewish and Christian lit. *thysiastērion* is always used for altars dedicated to God, such as the altar on which Abraham intended to offer Isaac (Gen. 22:9–10), the altar of burnt offering (Lev. 4:7), and the altar of incense (Exod. 30:1; 40:5). For altars of foreign gods *bōmos* (high place) is used in the LXX, even though *mizbēaḥ* was sometimes used for pagan altars in the MT (e.g., Exod. 34:13; Num. 3:10). This distinction is reflected in the NT in Paul's use of *bōmos* for the altar to the unknown god in Acts 17:23.

The patriarchs built their own altars and offered sacrifice without recourse to priesthood: e.g., Noah (Gen. 8:20); Abraham (12:6–8; 13:18; 22:9); Isaac (26:25); Jacob (33:20; 35:1–7); Moses (Exod. 17:15). Some altars were made of earth (Exod. 20:24). The altar built by Elijah on Mount Carmel consisted of twelve uncut stones representing the twelve tribes (1 Ki. 18:31–32). Altars were also built by Joshua (Jos. 8:30–31 = LXX 9:2), Gideon (Jdg. 6:24–31), and David (2 Sam. 24:18–25). Solomon's bronze altar for burnt offerings was probably a new one (1 Ki. 8:22, 54, 64; 9:25; 2 Chr. 4:1); it was 20 cubits square and 10 cubits high and stood in the inner court.

Within the Holy Place in the tabernacle was a miniature altar of incense, overlaid with gold (Exod. 30:1–10). Only Aaron and the high priests had access to this altar for burning incense morning and evening and for making atonement once a year on the Day of Atonement. The

horns of the altar were projections that were smeared with the blood of the sacrifice (29:12; 30:10; Lev. 4:7). On the large altar the victims were tied to the horns (Ps. 118:27). Offenders might cling to them for safety (1 Ki. 2:28). In Ezekiel's vision of the temple no incense altar is mentioned, but the altar of burnt offering is described in detail (43:13–17).

The temple that was rebuilt after the exile was provided with altars. Antiochus Epiphanes removed the golden altar in 169 B.C. (1 Macc. 1:21), and two years later surmounted the altar of burnt offering with the abomination of desolation (1:54). The Maccabees built a new altar and restored the altar of incense (4:44–49). In the time of Herod the altar of burnt offering was a pile of uncut stones approached by a ramp.

3. *Types of sacrifice*. The OT describes various forms of sacrifice, named according to the occasion and form of the gift. The Heb. noun *zebaḥ* is the generic term for sacrifice. It is used for sacrifices in which the flesh is eaten, e.g., feasts at altars (1 Sam. 2:13) and the yearly sacrifice (1:21).

(a) The *ḥaṭṭāʾt* is generally rendered "sin offering." In this sacrifice the blood of the animal is not used on the person. The rites for the healed leper (Lev. 14) and the consecration of the priest involve this sacrifice and the daubing by blood, but the blood is taken from a different sacrifice. The priest purges the sanctuary by means of a sin offering on behalf of those who have polluted it. Unrepented impurities cannot be so purged (Num. 15:27–29) but must be dealt with by the Day of Atonement ritual (→ *hilaskomai*, make atonement, *2661*).

Repentance is a precondition of the sin offering (Lev. 4:22–23, 27–28). This sacrifice covers the inadvertent violation of prohibitive commandments (4:2, 13, 22, 27), but not the neglect of performative commandments. The type of animal offered is related to the social and economic position of the offender: a bull for the high priest and community, a male goat for a chief, and a female of the flock for a common Israelite (cf. Lev. 4:2–21; 9:2–3, 15; 16:5, 11; Num. 15:22–26). The very poor could offer birds or flour (Lev. 5:7–13). Where more than one kind of sacrifice is offered, the sin offering take precedence, because the altar must first be purged before other gifts may be offered (cf. Lev. 5:8 with Num. 6:14–17).

(b) The *ʾāšām* is generally translated "guilt offering." It was to be offered, together with a fine, for unwitting trespass in any holy thing (Lev. 5:15; cf. also ch. 27). Cases where the guilt offering has to be made include reparation by a Nazirite for desecrating his hair and vow (Num. 6:1–12), the desecration of Israel by foreign nations (Jer. 2:3), and the desecration of Israel by mixed marriages (Ezra 10:19). Lev. 5:17–19 prescribes the guilt offering for unwitting sins in order to avoid divine retribution. It was also to be offered in cases of a breach of faith (6:1–7; Num. 5:6–10); the guilty party must express repentance in confession.

Isa. 53:10–11 declares that the servant of Yahweh is made a "guilt offering" and will "bear [the] iniquities" of the people. In other words, the servant of Yahweh takes over the role of the animal in the guilt offering by offering his own life. In the NT Jesus' self-giving as a *lytron*, ransom (Matt. 20:28; → *3389*), recalls this passage.

(c) The *ʿōlâ* is the "burnt offering." For this the LXX has *holokautōma* and *holokautōsis*. The entire beast or fowl was laid on the altar, except the skin (Lev. 7:8) and those parts that could not be washed clean (1:9–17), and it was consumed by fire. The animal had to be a male without defect from the herd or flock (1:3, 10; 22:18–19) or, if necessary, a fowl (1:14–17; 5:7; 12:8; 14:22; 15:14–15, 29–30; Num. 6:10–11). A lamb was offered by individuals (Lev. 12:6; Num. 6:14) and by the nation with the sheaf-waving (Lev. 23:12) and also daily at the morning and evening sacrifices (Num. 28:1–10; cf. 2 Ki. 16:15; Ezra 3:5; Neh. 10:33; Ezek. 46:13, 15).

The atoning character of the burnt offering is made explicit in Lev. 1:4 and is implied in certain rituals (9:7; 14:20). The OT refers to human burnt offerings made to other gods (2 Ki. 3:27; Jer. 19:5); human sacrifice is condemned in the OT (Lev. 18:21; 20:1–5; Deut.

12:31; 18:10; 2 Ki. 23:10; Jer. 32:35; Ezek. 20:25–26; Mic. 6:7). Abraham was prepared to offer Isaac as a burnt offering, though God drew his attention to a ram instead (Gen. 22:2, 13).

(d) The Heb. noun *minḥâ* (LXX *thysia*) means a gift or present (Gen. 32:14, 19, 21–22; Jdg. 6:18), tribute (3:15–18; 2 Sam. 8:2, 6), and an offering made to God of any kind, esp. of grain (Gen. 4:3–5; Num. 16:15; 1 Sam. 2:17, 29; Isa. 1:13). The sacrifices of Cain and Abel are both described by this same word; it is the context that indicates that Abel's offering of the firstlings of his flock and their fat portions (Gen. 4:3) was acceptable to God rather than Cain's offering of the fruit of the ground. But Cain's decisive sin was resenting God with an impenitent heart (4:6–7), which in turn led to the murder of his brother and his attempted cover-up (4:8–9).

(e) The *šᵉlāmîm* is frequently translated as "fellowship offering" or "peace offering." This was a thank offering, votive offering, or freewill offering (cf. Lev. 7:11–16; 19:5–8; Deut. 27:7). The ritual is prescribed in Lev. 3. The offerer lays his hand on the animal's head and kills it. The priest throws the blood on the altar and round it. The entrails are removed and the fat burnt as a pleasing odor to Yahweh. Certain parts of this offering went to the priest and the rest was eaten by the offerer (7:15–16). It was mainly a private and family sacrifice, but was offered in public at Pentecost (23:19) and at the consecration of priests (9:4).

(f) Several other cultic rites are noted in the OT. The *nesek* ("drink offering") consisted of wine (Gen. 35:14; Lev. 23:37; Num. 29:39). It is mentioned in connection with the morning offering (Exod. 29:41; Num. 28:8) and with other offerings (6:15, 17; 15:5, 7, 10; 1 Chr. 29:21; 2 Chr. 29:35; Ezek. 45:17).

The "memorial offering" (*ʾazkārâ*), a term associated with the meal offering (Lev. 2:2, 9, 16; 6:8; Num. 5:26), denotes the frankincense burned for the bread of the Presence (Lev. 24:7). A meal offering could be used as a sin offering and a memorial by the very poor (5:12). The bread of the Presence was to be set on the table in the sanctuary at all times before Yahweh (Exod. 25:30). It was an expression of the covenant, being offered with fire and frankincense. In 1 Sam. 21:1–6 David and his men ate this bread, which act Jesus appeals to in the NT in order to justify the disciples' plucking grain on the Sabbath (Matt. 12:1–8).

The "wave offering" (*tᵉnûpâ*) was waved at the high priest's ordination (Exod. 29:26). The Levites were also offered as a wave offering (Num. 8:11, 13, 15, 21). The offering was so called because it was waved, signifying that the sacrifice was Yahweh's.

4. *Purpose of sacrifice.* What is the fundamental idea behind a sacrifice? Various theories have been advanced, such as to provide food for God. Although this may have been in the minds of some Israelites because of influence from Canaanite religion, it was trenchantly denounced by the psalmist in Ps. 50:8–15. An alternative view that sacrifice releases the life force of the animal through its death (an animist interpretation) cannot be sustained in light of a detailed examination of the passages concerned.

At the root of sacrifice is a profound awareness in humans of a need for a source of power outside themselves. In its deepest form it represents an awareness of the need to be reconciled and to commit oneself without reserve to the God who offers reconciliation and who is worthy of total commitment. The variety of sacrifices in the OT expresses the varied aspects of this need and the divine provision made for them under the old covenant. With the death of Christ the NT writers see the sacrifices of the OT superseded.

A number of passages in the prophets denounce mere sacrificial ritual (Isa. 1:11–31; Jer. 6:20; 7:21–22; Hos. 6:6; Amos 5:21–27; Mic. 6:6–8). Right conduct and obedience are stressed over against such ritual. What is most important is not the act of sacrifice but the heart of the worshiper (cf. esp. 1 Sam. 15:22). In Hos. 6:6 (cf. Matt. 9:13; 12:7) Hos. offers a statement of priorities by means of hyperbole: "For I desire mercy, not sacrifice, and acknowledgment of God rather than burnt offerings." Isa. condemned not only vain offerings, new

moons, and Sabbaths but also prayer (1:13–15; 29:13) that is not made with the right inner attitude. The same focus on moral righteousness, in contrast to mere ritual, is also found in Ps. (e.g., 40:6–8; 50:8–15) and in wisdom lit. (cf. Prov. 15:8; 21:3, 27).

5. *Sacrifice in the postexilic period.* Sacrifice was restored soon after the return (Ezra 3:2–7). Darius authorized not only the rebuilding of the temple but provision for the temple worship (6:9–10). Thus, the second temple remained the center for Israelite religion (6:17; 7:17; 8:35; 10:19). The Jerusalem temple was destroyed in A.D. 70, and with it sacrificial rites died out. But already in NT times the growth of synagogue worship, esp. in the Diaspora, was displacing sacrificial ritual, which could only be participated in at Jerusalem. The Qumran community had already cut itself off from the temple, replacing material sacrifices with obedience to the Torah and the praise of God.

NT *thyō* and its cognates are found in various NT writings. The vb. *thyō* occurs 14x, the vb. *prospherō* 47x (esp. Matt. and Heb.), the noun *thysia* 28x (more than half in Heb.), and *thysiastērion* 23x. These words retreat into the background in the writings of John and Paul. Examination of the context of these passages reveals how far the NT writers have dissociated themselves from OT worship. Even the allusions to the altar in the visions of Rev., which formally lean heavily on the imagery of the OT, exhibit a new interpretation of the concept of sacrifice.

1. *Synoptic Gospels.* Jesus does not reject the temple worship practices any more than the prophets. Rather, he directs his polemic against attempts to evade God's radical demand of love through ritual and hair-splitting observance of the law. In the Sermon on the Mount priority is given to reconciliation, but not to the exclusion of formal worship (see Matt. 5:23–24). Doing one's utmost to seek reconciliation among human beings is the sine qua non of true worship.

Hos. 6:6 is cited twice in Matt. In Matt. 9:12–13 the Pharisees complain that Jesus is guilty of defilement by eating with tax collectors and sinners. In reply Jesus says: "It is not the healthy who need a doctor, but the sick. But go and learn what this means, 'I desire mercy, not sacrifice.' For I have not come to call the righteous, but sinners." Jesus' message here is in line with his previous teaching in the Sermon on the Mount (5:23–24). "Sacrifice," as the highest form of Israelite worship, stands for the keeping of the Mosaic law, which itself demanded separation from anything that defiles as a prerequisite for worship. The greater includes the less. To Jesus, what defiles is not what the Pharisees presume, i.e., formal association with sinners, but the heart that lacks mercy.

Jesus appeals to Hos. 6:6 again when his disciples are criticized for plucking the ears of grain on the Sabbath (Matt. 12:7). Here too "sacrifice" stands for the observance of the religious prescriptions of the law, and the principle is the same. Humane considerations take precedence over formal observance of the letter of the law. In addition, someone greater than the temple is here (12:6), and "the Son of Man is Lord of the Sabbath" (12:8).

In a series of woes pronounced on the scribes and Pharisees Jesus condemns the practice of swearing not only by the temple but also by the gold of the temple (Matt. 23:16–17) and by the altar and the sacrifice (23:18–22). The scribal rulings operated on the principle that oaths by the most holy things are to be avoided, because they are as binding as oaths made in God's name. But oaths made by less holy things are less serious and thus less binding. Jesus sweeps such rulings aside as chicanery. We should not make an oath at all unless we intend to keep it (cf. 5:33–37). In all this Jesus is not rejecting sacrifice and the temple as such; rather, he is putting them in perspective.

All four Gospels record Jesus' cleansing of the temple (Matt. 21:10–17; Mk. 11:15–17; Lk. 19:45–47; Jn. 2:13–17). In the Synoptics it occurs as a symbolic act after Jesus' entry into Jerusalem during the last week of his ministry. It represents his coming into his own and God's purging judgment on his own house. Jn. likewise sets the account before the Passover but places it before his narrative of Jesus' public ministry. In the Synoptic account Jesus adopts words from an eschatological proclamation of Isa. (56:7) and from Jer.'s denunciation of the temple (7:11): "It is written ... 'My house shall be called a house of prayer,' but you are making it a 'den of robbers'" (e.g., Matt. 21:13).

Jesus' action is also a fulfillment of Mal. 3:1–3 and thus a messianic sign. The purification of Jerusalem and the temple was part of Jewish expectation (cf. *Pss. Sol.* 17:30). In Jn. 2:17, "His disciples remembered that it is written: 'Zeal for your house will consume me'" (cf. Ps. 69:9). The Ps. itself adds: "and the insults of those who insult you fall on me." This may well be implied in Jesus' action; the attitude of humans to the temple expresses their attitude toward God. Jn.'s narrative then compares the Jerusalem temple with the temple of Jesus' body—both of which are the dwelling place of God. And in both cases the attitude of the Jews of Jesus' day showed how oblivious they were to the presence of God among them.

Lk. 2:24 refers to the offering made by Joseph and Mary on behalf of their infant son (cf. Lev. 12:2–8), which because of their poverty consisted of two birds. Lk. 13:1 mentions the blood of those Galileans that Pilate had mingled with their sacrifices. In this connection Jesus rebutted the inference that anyone who so suffered must have been esp. guilty of sin: "I tell you, no! But unless you repent, you too will all perish" (13:3).

The guilt of those who reject God's servants is expressed in the saying that "upon you will come all the righteous blood that has been shed on earth, from the blood of righteous Abel to the blood of Zechariah son of Berekiah, whom you murdered between the temple and the altar" (Matt. 23:35; cf. Lk. 11:51). Not only are these the first and last victims of murder in the Heb. OT (Gen. 4:8; 2 Chr. 24:21); they were also murdered in connection with sacrifice.

The *holokautōma* (burnt offering) is mentioned in Mark's account of the two greatest commandments. The teacher of the law acknowledges that Jesus is right, then adds that loving God "is more important than all burnt offerings and sacrifices" (12:33).

2. *Acts.* Stephen's speech in Acts 7 similarly adopts a negative attitude toward sacrifice. The first allusion is to the sacrifice to the golden calf (7:41; cf. Exod. 32:4, 6); the second cites Amos 5:25 on the absence of sacrifice in the desert wanderings (Acts 7:42–43). Stephen draws the conclusion that Israel's failure to worship God in a spiritual way resulted in God's giving Israel over to paganism.

There is a distinct note of futility in the reference to a pagan altar in the account of Paul's address in the meeting of the Areopagus: "Men of Athens! I see that in every way you are very religious. For as I walked around and looked carefully at your objects of worship, I even found an altar [*bōmos*] with this inscription: TO AN UNKNOWN GOD. Now what you worship as something unknown I am going to proclaim to you" (Acts 17:23). This is the only use of the word *bōmos* (the LXX word for pagan altars) in the NT.

The apostle Paul continued to make occasional offerings himself. Acts 21:26 (using *prospherō* and *prosphora*) tells how Paul joined four men who had evidently undertaken a Nazirite vow (cf. Num. 6:1–21; Acts 18:18) in their purification rites and paid their expenses. By associating himself with them in their vow, Paul was consistent with his principle of being "all things to all men" in order to win them to Christ (1 Cor. 9:22). Whereas Paul repudiated the extension of circumcision to the Gentiles, he nevertheless kept the law among Jews. Similarly, Acts 24:17–18 reports how Paul made offerings (*prosphoras*) and was purified in the temple.

3. *Paul's letters.* In his letters Paul takes over the Jewish-Christian interpretation of the death of Jesus, which saw its saving efficacy in terms of OT sacrificial language. In urging moral purity to the Corinthians, Paul writes: "Get rid of the old yeast that you may be a new batch without yeast—as you really are. For Christ, our Passover lamb, has been sacrificed [*thyō*]" (1 Cor. 5:7; → *pascha*, Passover, *4247*). Rom. 3:25 describes Jesus' death as a *hilastērion*, propitiation (→ *hilaskomai*, make atonement, *2661*).

Rom. 15:16 sums up the grace of Paul's calling " to be a minister of Christ Jesus to the Gentiles with the priestly duty of proclaiming the gospel of God, so that the Gentiles might become an offering [*prosphora*] acceptable to God, sanctified by the Holy Spirit." Here the Gentile Christians are the offering and Paul the priest of the Diaspora Jews (cf. Isa. 66:20).

In Phil. 4:18 Paul describes the gifts sent by the Philippians as "a fragrant offering [*osmē*, → *4011*], an acceptable sacrifice [*thysia*], pleasing to God." In 2:17 he sees his own impending martyrdom in similar terms: "But even if I am being poured out like a drink offering on the sacrifice [*thysia*] and service coming from your faith, I am glad and rejoice with all of you" (cf. 1:19–26). The use of *thysia* here and the fact that Paul was in prison expecting the possibility of execution suggest that he was thinking of his death not as a propitiatory sacrifice, but as a freewill offering for the sake of the church.

In Rom. 12:1 Paul sees the Christian life as a sacrifice: "I urge you, brothers, in view of God's mercy, to offer your bodies as living sacrifices [*thysia*], holy and pleasing to God—this is your spiritual act of worship." The life of the believer, not ritual, is now the true sacrifice of the people of God. In Eph. 5:2 Paul urges his readers to "live a life of love, just as Christ loved us and gave himself up for us as a fragrant offering [*prosphora*] and sacrifice [*thysia*] to God." In short, Christ's death is an atoning sacrifice, offered by pouring out his blood.

In Corinth there was an acute problem over whether Christians should eat meat that had been sacrificed to idols. The term *eidōlothytos* (Acts 15:29; 21:25; 1 Cor. 8:1, 4, 7, 10; 10:19; Rev. 2:14, 20) refers to meat sacrificed according to the rites of the locality and thus offered to a pagan deity, part of which was burned on an altar, part eaten at a solemn meal in the temple, and part sold in the market. The eating of such meat was condemned by the Jerusalem council. The church of Pergamum was accused of allowing people to eat it and of practicing immorality. From the Jewish standpoint it was unclean and therefore forbidden.

For Christians this issue raised the question of whether eating such meat implied some kind of allegiance to or communion with a pagan deity. The "strong" at Corinth said that they could do it with good conscience and impunity (cf. 1 Cor. 4:4, 10; 8:1–2). But weak believers who did so had a guilty conscience about it. Paul replies that Christians should be guided by love rather than any vaunted knowledge; he himself says he will not eat such meat if it causes others to stumble (8:1–13). Although all things come from God (8:4–6), Christians should be guided by concern for the consciences of others, not by what they feel in their own conscience (8:10–13). Moreover, to participate knowingly in something offered to demons (10:20) is to be a partner with demons, and as such is incompatible with partaking of the Lord's table (10:19–22). On the other hand, when Christians are unaware of any demonic associations, they may eat the meat (10:23–30) but should do everything to the glory of God (10:31–11:1).

Between these two passages in 1 Cor. Paul deals with the question of freedom and the Christian worker's right to upkeep. Alluding to Deut. 18:1, he asks in 1 Cor. 9:13: "Don't you know that those who work in the temple get their food from the temple, and those who serve at the altar [*thysiastērion*] share in what is offered on the altar?"

4. *Hebrews.* The central theme of Heb. is the way in which, through Christ, believers enter into the reality of which the OT institutions represent only an anticipation, one of which is the OT sacrificial system. The noun *thysia* and the vb. *prospherō* occur frequently. The function of the high priest is defined in terms of offering gifts and sacrifices for sin (5:1; cf. 8:3). But Jesus, "unlike the other high priests ... does not need to offer sacrifices day after day, first for his own sins, and then for the sins of the people. He sacrificed for their sins once for all when he offered himself" (7:27). And again: "Christ was sacrificed [*prospherō*] once to take away the sins of many" (9:28).

The gifts and sacrifices of the earthly tabernacle could not "clear the conscience of the worshiper" (9:9). Their very repetition shows that they "can never take away sins. But when this priest [Jesus] had offered for all time one sacrifice for sins, he sat down at the right hand of God" (10:11–12; cf. the use of *prosphora*, offering, in 10:14 and 18). The earthly tabernacle is but a copy of the heavenly one. "It was necessary, then, for the copies of the heavenly things to be purified with these sacrifices, but the heavenly things themselves with better sacrifices [*thysia*] than these" (9:23). In keeping with the symbolism of the Day of Atonement ritual (cf. Lev. 16), Christ is seen by his resurrection and ascension as entering the inner sanctuary once and for all "to do away with sin by the sacrifice of himself" (9:26; cf. 10:1).

Heb. 10:5–10 sees the coming of Christ anticipated in Ps. 40:6–8. The Ps. is cited in the LXX version, which reads "a body you prepared for me" in place of the MT "my ears you have pierced." Four different sacrifices are mentioned here: "sacrifice" [*thysia*], "offering" [*prosphora*], "burnt offerings" [*holōkautōma*], and "sin offerings." The spiritual principles underlying these sacrifices are fulfilled and transcended in the perfect and voluntary self-sacrifice of Christ. Unlike the purificatory rites of the old covenant, which required constant repetition, Christ's offering effects the sanctification of believers once and for all (5:10). Only "if we deliberately keep on sinning after we have received the knowledge of the truth, no sacrifice [*thysia*] for sins is left" (10:26; cf. 3:12; 6:4–8; 10:29; 12:25–29). This denotes contempt of the most flagrant kind, like the Israelites who rebelled and thus failed to enter the promised land.

Heb. 11:4 locates the essential difference between the sacrifices of Cain and Abel (Gen. 4:3–10) in the fact that Abel's offering [*thysia*] was given "by faith." The sacrifices that yet remain for believers are those of praise and proper living: "Through Jesus, therefore, let us continually offer to God a sacrifice [*thysia*] of praise—the fruit of lips that confess his name. And do not forget to do good and to share with others, for with such sacrifices [*thysia*] God is pleased" (13:15–16). The linking of praise with practical living shows that such sacrifice extends beyond liturgical worship.

This passage is set in the context of a reminder that we have no lasting city on earth (Heb. 13:14). The writer earlier presented Christ's death in terms of the Day of Atonement tabernacle ritual but now argues, "We have an altar [*thysiastērion*] from which those who minister at the tabernacle have no right to eat. The high priest carries the blood of animals into the Most Holy Place as a sin offering, but the bodies are burned outside the camp. And so Jesus also suffered outside the city gate to make the people holy through his own blood" (13:10–12). The allusion is to the Day of Atonement animals (Lev. 16:27). Here the word "altar" is used by metonymy for "sacrifice." The saying is comparable with speaking of Christ as a *hilastērion* (Rom. 3:25).

The Jews possess both a visible altar and a visible city, Jerusalem, but not the spiritual reality. They also have material sacrifices in contrast to the spiritual sacrifices of praise and deed (Heb. 13:16). The "we" in question must mean "we Christians" (cf. 8:1) in contrast to the Jews, who cling to the material sacrifices of the temple ritual. Those who do so have no right to feed on Christ. The absence of a visible altar (13:10) compares with the absence of a visible city (13:14).

5. *1 Peter.* The theme of the sacrifice of the Christian is taken up in 1 Pet. 2:5, where the apostle exhorts us "like living stones, [to be] built into a spiritual house to be a holy priesthood, offering spiritual sacrifices [*thysia*] acceptable to God through Jesus Christ." This priesthood, which also includes being a holy nation, is defined in terms of declaring "the praises of him who called you out of darkness into his wonderful light" (2:9; cf. Exod. 19:5–6). By Christ's death believers of all nations are constituted the new people of God and the new priesthood of God.

In 1 Pet. 1:18–19 Peter understands the death of Christ as a ransom in sacrificial terms, which provides the basis for the Christian life: "You know that it was not with perishable things such as silver or gold that you were redeemed from the empty way of life handed down to you from your forefathers, but with the precious blood of Christ, a lamb without blemish or defect" (see also *lytron*, ransom, *3389*). The writer has in mind here both the perfect Passover lamb (cf. Exod. 12:5; 29:1; Lev. 22:17–25) and the lamb led to the slaughter in Isa. 53:7 (cf. 52:3).

6. *Altars.* In addition to the reference to *thysiastērion* noted above, altars are mentioned in several other NT passages. Zechariah received tidings of the birth of his son, John the Baptist, from an angel of the Lord standing "at the right side of the altar of incense" (Lk. 1:11). Rom. 11:3 alludes to Elijah's complaint: "Lord, they have killed your prophets and torn down your altars; I am the only one left, and they are trying to kill me" (cf. 1 Ki. 19:14). The saying forms part of Paul's argument about the remnant and the people of God. God has not rejected his people, even though it may seem as if there are no godly people remaining. Just as God kept for himself seven thousand who had not bowed the knee to Baal, so he keeps a remnant today. But it is by grace and not works (Rom. 11:4–6). Still, Jas. 2:21 asks: "Was not our ancestor Abraham considered righteous for what he did when he offered his son Isaac on the altar?"

The remaining passages referring to altars occur in Rev. The souls of the martyred saints are under the altar, crying out for vengeance (6:9–10). Their sacrifices are in no sense atoning, but neither were all the OT sacrifices. The prayers of the saints have a sacrificial character: "Another angel, who had a golden censer, came and stood at the altar. He was given much incense to offer, with the prayers of all the saints, on the golden altar before the throne" (8:3). The mingling of incense indicates symbolically the hallowing of the prayers from a source outside human beings, without which their prayers would not be acceptable to God. The action of the angel in taking fire from the altar and throwing it on earth (8:5) is a sign that the prayers are answered in the judgments that befall the earth (cf. 6:9–10).

The judgment that comes "from the horns of the golden altar that is before God" (Rev. 9:13) again indicates the divine judgment in answer to the cries of the saints. The miniature golden altar of incense stood within the Holy Place of the tabernacle (Exod. 30:1–10). Similarly, in Rev. 14:18 and 16:7 judgment comes from the altar.

In Rev. 11:1 John is told to "measure the temple of God and the altar, and count the worshipers there." He is not, however, to measure the court outside the temple, which is given over to the nations, who will trample the holy city for forty-two months (11:2). The measuring symbolizes setting the holy places apart from that which is profane and which will be subject to tribulation and judgment. The sanctuary symbolizes God's people, and they will come through the tribulation (cf. also Ezek. 40:5; 42:20; Zech. 2:1). Just as the sealed will come to no ultimate harm, so the sanctuary, which represents the true church sanctified by God himself, will be safe when God's wrath falls on the holy city.

See also *aparchē*, the gift of the firstfruits, offering, gift (*569*).

2606 (thōrax, breastplate), → 4483.

I iota

2609	Ἰακώβ

Ἰακώβ (*Iakōb*), Jacob (*2609*); Ἰάκωβος (*Iakōbos*), James (*2610*).

OT Jacob (Heb. *ya*ᶜ*akōb*) was the second son of Isaac and Rebekah and the grandson of the patriarch Abraham. He was favored by his mother, while Isaac was partial to his other son, Esau. Early in his life Jacob obtained the birthright due his brother Esau by giving him some "red stew" in return for the birthright (Gen. 25:30). According to the Deuteronomic legislation, the right of the firstborn included a double portion of the paternal estate (Deut. 21:17), and most probably involved leadership of the clan as well (Gen. 27:29). The subterfuge by which Jacob obtained the blessing of Isaac was initiated and encouraged by Rebekah (27:5–17). The blessing itself (27:27–29) apparently had the validity of a last will and testament.

Jacob's deception led to his flight to the home of his uncle Laban. As he stopped for the night at Luz, Jacob had a dream of a ladder reaching to heaven (Gen. 28:10–17). In the dream the Lord spoke to him, reiterating the promise given earlier to Abraham (12:7; 13:15–16; 15:17–21; 17:1–8; 24:7). Not only did the reiteration of the promise include the affirmation that the land would belong to the descendants of the patriarchs (28:13), but that they and their descendants would be the vehicle by which God's favor would extend to the Gentiles (28:14).

Jacob's dramatic encounter with the Lord led to his calling the site Bethel (i.e., "house of God"), and that site continued to be known as Bethel throughout the OT. Jacob was hired by Laban and in return for fourteen years of labor he received Laban's two daughters—first Leah, then Rachel—as his wives. Leah became the mother of Reuben, Simeon, Levi, Judah, Issachar, and Zebulun.

Rachel, however, did not bear children immediately and, in keeping with the prevailing custom, gave her maid, Bilhah, as a concubine to her husband. Bilhah became the mother of Dan and Naphtali. At length Rachel gave birth to two sons, Joseph and Benjamin. Jacob also had two sons, Gad and Asher, by Zilpah, Leah's maid.

Relations between Jacob and Laban became strained partly because of Jacob's increase in wealth (Gen. 31:1–2), and Jacob left with his family. When he heard this, Laban pursued Jacob. When he reached his son-in-law, he berated him for several things, including the alleged theft of the family gods (31:30), which, in reality, Rachel had taken and secreted in the camel's saddle. The possession of the family gods designated the one who had them the right to the paternal estate. After a mutual agreement that they would not again interfere with one another, Jacob resumed his journey.

In a dramatic event at the river Jabbok Jacob wrestled with a man whom he identified as God (Gen. 32:30). It was during this experience that his name was changed to Israel (*Israēl*, → *2702*). He named the site of the encounter Peniel ("face of God"). As he continued, Jacob encountered Esau (33:1–4). A reconciliation was effected by the two brothers, which seems to have been an enduring one.

After an unfortunate experience with the people of Shechem (Gen. 34), Jacob returned to Bethel, but not before he had all the images of foreign deities removed from his household. After the images were buried under an oak at Shechem, the Lord appeared to Jacob and the terms of the Abrahamic covenant were again affirmed. On the journey from Bethel, Jacob suffered the loss of his wife Rachel, who died while giving birth to Benjamin (35:16–18). This tragedy was soon followed by the death of his father Isaac (35:29) and the banishment of his son Joseph to Egypt (Gen. 37).

Joseph rose to power in Egypt, and his wisdom and foresight led to his overseeing the storage of food in Egypt. This propitious act enabled the Egyptians to have provisions while many in the surrounding areas were ravaged by famine. When the famine struck Canaan, Jacob sent his sons to Egypt to obtain food. He kept his youngest son Benjamin with him, however. Alleging that they were spies, Joseph required them to bring Benjamin to Egypt to prove their word and, hence, their innocence.

After his brothers brought Benjamin to Egypt, Joseph identified himself as their brother and arranged to have Jacob brought to Egypt as well. Jacob lived in Egypt for seventeen years. When he was near death, he exacted from Joseph the promise that he would be buried in Canaan. He adopted Joseph's sons, Ephraim and Manasseh (Gen. 48:1–6), and pronounced a blessing on them as well as on his own sons (48:8–49:27). Jacob died at age 147 and was buried with his ancestors in the cave of Machpelah (50:1–13).

The name Jacob became an eponym for Israel and occurs frequently with that connotation in the OT (Num. 23:7, 10, 23; Ps. 14:7; Isa. 48:20; Amos 3:13). The patriarch Jacob is frequently cited in connection with the acts of God on his behalf. God is described as the God of Abraham, Isaac, and Jacob (Exod. 3:6, 15), and the covenant given to the patriarchs is cited in the same connection (2 Ki. 13:23). Malachi assured the people that the love shown by God to Jacob had not been withheld from them with the words, "I have loved Jacob, but Esau I have hated" (Mal. 1:2–3).

Iakōbos (James) is the Hellenized form of *Iakōb*.

NT 1. In the NT *Iakōb* denotes both the patriarch Jacob and the legal father of Jesus (Matt. 1:2, 15–16; Lk. 3:34). NT writers make several allusions to events in Jacob's life. Jn. 4:5–6, 12 refers to a plot of ground that Jacob gave to Joseph, which was the site of Jacob's well (Gen. 33:19; 48:22). Stephen mentions several events in the life of Jacob (Acts 7:8, 12, 14). The writer of Heb. cites Jacob as a recipient, like his grandfather Abraham, of God's promises (11:9), as an example of faith (11:21), and as someone who conspired to get the birthright from his brother Esau (12:16–17; Esau's selling of his birthright is cited as an example of reckless godlessness).

In Rom. 9:6–13 Paul talks about the events surrounding the birth of Jacob and Esau in a passage explicating the fact that God's work of election is not based on works (9:11). Paul here refers to the purposes expressed in the words God spoke before the births of the two brothers, "the older will serve the younger" (Gen. 25:23). He quotes Mal. 1:2–3 in this connection as well. Allusion is made to Jacob's dream at Bethel in Jn. 1:51, where Christ transfers the image of the ladder to himself.

"The God of Abraham, Isaac and Jacob" is an expression that occurs in the NT. Peter used this phrase in connection with "the God of our fathers" in speaking to Jews (Acts 3:13). Jesus used a somewhat expanded formula to illustrate that God was the God of the living (Matt. 22:32; Mk. 12:26; Lk. 20:37). Stephen used the appellation "the God of Jacob" in his defense (Acts 7:46), which may reflect Ps. 132:5.

Jacob is mentioned along with the patriarchs Abraham and Isaac in Matt. 8:11, where their fellowship in heaven is the reward of the people of faith. Jacob is used as an eponym of the Jewish nation in Lk. 1:33 and Rom. 11:26 (the latter being a free quotation from Isa. 59:20).

2. There are several people in the NT with the anglicized name James (*Iakōbos*). (a) One of the sons of Zebedee, who became a disciple of Jesus, was named James (Matt. 4:21). Together with his brother John (who were called "Sons of Thunder" [Mk. 3:17]) and Peter, they formed the inner circle of Jesus' disciples. James and John sought high places when Jesus established his kingdom (Mk. 10:35–

40); Jesus promised them suffering instead. Shortly after the establishment of the NT church, James was executed by Herod Agrippa I (Acts 12:2).

(b) Another one of Jesus' disciples was called "James son of Alphaeus" (Matt. 10:3). Nothing more is known about him from the NT besides his name.

(c) In the Gospels, James, the brother of Jesus (cf. Gal. 1:19), is mentioned by name only (e.g., Matt. 13:55; Mk. 6:3). He did not accept the authority of Jesus during Jesus' lifetime (Jn. 7:5), but after his death and resurrection (perhaps as a result of a personal appearance from the resurrected Jesus, 1 Cor. 15:7), he became a believer (Acts 1:14). Eventually he became the leader of the church in Jerusalem (Acts 12:17; 15:13; 21:18; Gal. 2:9). Paul calls him one of the apostles in Gal. 1:19. Most scholars think that James was a child of Joseph and Mary, though a few scholars suggest he was the son of Joseph from a previous marriage or else a cousin of Jesus (taking *adelphos*, brother, in a general sense of relative). There is little doubt that this James is the one who authored the letter of James in the NT (Jas. 1:1).

See also *Israēl*, Israel (*2702*); *Ioudaia*, Judea (*2677*).

2610 (*Iakōbos*, James), → *2609*.

2611 (*iama*, healing), → *2615*.

2615 ἰάομαι	ἰάομαι (*iaomai*), cure, restore (*2615*); ἴασις (*iasis*), healing

(*2617*); ἴαμα (*iama*), healing (*2611*); ἰατρός (*iatros*), physician (*2620*).

CL & OT 1. *iaomai*, to cure, restore, is used in the lit. sense as a medical term, and also fig., to free from an evil, such as ignorance or some intellectual shortcoming; also to heal psychological illnesses. Likewise the nouns *iasis* and *iama*, healing, and *iatros*, physician, are used both lit. and metaphorically.

(a) The various types of medical treatment throughout human history can be properly understood only when one is acquainted with the ideas that have been held regarding the causes of sickness. Apart from external injuries, where the cause is obvious, sicknesses in the ancient world were not simply physiological phenomena, the causes and nature of which could be investigated and therefore possibly cured. Originally, sicknesses were ascribed to attacks by external forces (e.g., gods, demons, sin, guilt, magical powers such as a curse, etc.). To bring about a cure a number of methods were employed: exorcisms (to cast out demons), various magical practices (the earliest beginnings of medicine), influences based on suggestion, or prayers and offerings, in an attempt to appease the deity. Both the sickness and its cure, therefore, were believed to arise from the intervention of a superior will.

As early as the 3d cent. B.C., the science of medicine reached its first flowering among the ancient Egyptians. But the honor of having set medical science on an empirical basis belongs esp. to the Gks. Already in Homer's time physicians were esteemed, esp. those of Egypt. The oath of Hippocrates (born 460 B.C.) is a remarkable testimony to the fact that, as medicine in Greece came into its own, there gradually arose a specific code of ethics among physicians.

(b) It remains true, however, that in the ancient world no clear line of demarcation can be drawn between rational and magical ideas of reality. Thus, the relationship between the origins of medicine as a rational science and "supernatural" healings attributed to superior powers is inextricably involved. Thus we constantly find that among different peoples special healing deities were worshiped (e.g., Apollo, Asclepius, Imhotep, Tammuz). Temple-like edifices were built to them and used as healing centers (e.g., the Asclepeion of Cos), where priests acted as physicians and ran what can only be described as a healing business. All kinds of offerings were presented, not merely to obtain a cure, but also as thanksgiving for miraculous cures already obtained. In the ancient world there were numerous accounts of miraculous healing, often embellished to the point of being grotesque.

Kings were originally chief priests as well and as such had the gift of healing. It is thus no surprise to read that Emperor Vespasian healed the blind and lame by his touch and with the use of spittle.

2. In the LXX , it is characteristic of faith in Yahweh that he alone is the source of all healing ("I am the LORD, who heals [*iaomai*] you," Exod. 15:26; cf. 2 Ki. 5:7). To turn to a physician (let alone another deity) for healing could on occasion mean distrust of Yahweh and an offense against the first commandment (2 Ki. 1; 2 Chr. 16:12). As sicknesses come from Yahweh himself, he is the only one who can bind up and heal (Job 5:18). For the same reason the OT makes little distinction between external ills with an obvious cause (e.g., injuries sustained through accident, in war, etc.) and other ills arising from within. In every aspect of life humans are dependent on Yahweh alone. This does not mean that demons have nothing to do with sickness. Rather they are thought of as being in God's service (cf. Exod. 12:23; Hab. 3:5).

This view of sickness and healing as marks of Yahweh's visitation or of his renewed favor often brings a devout man into grievous inward conflict (cf. Job and Ps., e.g., Ps. 38; 51; esp. 88). This could lead to a deep questioning of Yahweh when the malady was felt to be undeserved (Job 9:17–23; Ps. 73:21–22). Yet the devout turned in prayer, lament, and thanks to God alone as the only one who could grant healing (30:3; 103:3; cf. Wis. 16:12).

In spite of this radical attitude to sickness and healing, some passages do indicate the use of medical treatment (e.g., 1 Ki. 17:21; 2 Ki. 4:34; 5:13–14; 20:7), though the means used by the prophets are seldom "medical" as we understand the word. These are miraculous cures, carried out in reliance on the healing power of Yahweh.

The priest in Israel was not a healer. His function was restricted to that of a medical officer of health, who ascertained whether healing had taken place (Lev. 13–14). In later works, where the work of a physician is regarded in a positive light, he is God's servant in the strictest sense. It is God who appoints him and through prayer grants him wisdom for his work (Sir. 38:1–2, 9–14). An important element in the OT understanding of sickness and healing is the idea that bodily sickness is closely connected with sin and therefore a manifestation of God's anger against specific transgressions (e.g., Ps. 32:1–5; 38:3–8). Healing then becomes a picture of forgiveness, of God's mercy, of his nearness (e.g., Ps. 30:3; 41:4; 103:3; Isa. 6:10).

3. In Jud., too, medicine was generally held in considerable suspicion, although we do read of rabbis who were also physicians. The Jews also shared ideas that were widespread in relation to miraculous healings. Incantations, invocations, and other practices played a large role. With few exceptions, the rabbis themselves do not appear in tradition as miraculous healers.

NT 1. In the NT *iaomai* occurs 26x; *iasis*, 3x; *iatros*, 6x; *iama*, 3x (all in 1 Cor. 12). Apart from *iama*, this word group occurs chiefly in the Synoptic Gospels and esp. in Lk. The use of *iaomai* corresponds in the Gospels and in Acts to that of *therapeuō* (→ *2543*). Hence, the remarks made under *therapeuō* on the theological assessment of healing miracles apply here also. The cures done by Jesus and his disciples are signs of the incoming kingdom of God (Lk. 9:2, 11, 42; Acts 10:38) and the fulfillment of OT prophecy (cf. Isa. 35:3–6; 61:1–2).

This is not to deny that the NT shares the view of sickness common at that time (cf. Lk. 13:11; Acts 12:23). As we noted above, the miraculous cures of Jesus are not without parallels in the extrabiblical world. But even though the NT records of healing show all the familiar features of other ancient healing/miracle stories (e.g., the helplessness of physicians, Mk. 5:26–29; the instantaneous nature of the miracle, Lk. 8:47), the NT accounts are simple and straightforward. They do not aim to glorify some miracle worker or even miracles as such. Rather, the historical account is still very much in mind, and such events are viewed in the light of Christ's message. Farce, magic, and sensationalism are absent.

The healings done by Jesus are determined by his word and by faith (e.g., Matt. 8:8, 13; 15:28; Lk. 7:7). They are therefore fundamentally different from other healings in the ancient world. Jesus also breaks through a typical Jewish doctrine of retribution (i.e., that every sickness must be caused by a certain sin; cf. Jn. 9:2–5), without thereby denying the basic connection between sin and sickness (e.g., Jn. 5:13–14; cf. Jas. 5:16). The focal point of all these healings is not the miracle but the healer himself, who reveals his uniqueness and his sense of mission and whose authoritative preaching has brought in the dawn of the new age (cf. Lk. 6:19; Acts 10:38).

2. In 1 Cor. 12 *iama*, healing, occurs 3x as Paul enumerates various spiritual gifts. All the apostles received the gift of healing as well as a commission to preach the gospel. But Paul makes it clear that healing can also be carried out by other individuals whom God has endowed with that spiritual gift. The gift of healing is one function among others, all of which are coordinated with one another in the church as the body of Christ.

See also *therapeuō*, heal, cure (*2543*); *hygiēs*, healthy, well (*5618*).

2617 (*iasis*, healing), → *2615*.

2620 (*iatros*, physician), → *2615*.

2625 (*idios*, one's own, [pl.] possessions, property), → *4347*.

2626	ἰδιώτης

ἰδιώτης (*idiōtēs*), layman, unlettered, uneducated, unskilled (*2626*).

CL & OT 1. In cl. Gk. *idiōtēs* means: (a) a private person as opposed to an occupant of a public office, or an individual citizen of the totality of citizens; (b) a layperson as opposed to an expert (e.g., a priest or philosopher), an unlettered person; (c) an outsider as opposed to one who "belongs."

2. *idiōtēs* occurs in the LXX only in Prov. 6:8b (in a section not in the Heb.). It denotes a common person in contrast to a king. The rabbis transliterated the word and used it for a private person as opposed to the king, a layperson as opposed to an expert, or a human as opposed to God.

NT In the NT *idiōtēs* occurs 5x. In Acts 4:13 it is used of the apostles as unlettered, uneducated men. Similar is 2 Cor. 11:6, where Paul says he is "not a trained [*idiōtēs*] speaker," though he insists he does have knowledge.

The *idiōtai* in 1 Cor. 14:16 are all those who do not possess the gift of tongues and who, since they do not understand what is said when this gift is exercised, cannot join in the Amen to the church's thanksgiving. Similarly, in 14:23–24, the same word refers to those who "do not understand" the concept of speaking in tongues because they are unbelievers who attend Christian meetings only occasionally. For their sakes, Paul urges that public worship should be intelligible.

2627 (*idou*, see! look! behold!), → *3972*.

2632 (*hierateia*, priestly office), → *2636*.

2633 (*hierateuma*, priesthood), → *2636*.

2634 (*hierateuō*, hold the office or perform the service of a priest), → *2636*.

2636	ἱερεύς

ἱερεύς (*hiereus*), a priest (*2636*); ἀρχιερεύς (*archiereus*), high priest (*797*); ἀρχιερατικός (*archieratikos*), high-priestly (*796*); ἱερωσύνη (*hierōsynē*), priestly office, priesthood (*2648*); ἱερατεία (*hierateia*), priestly office (*2632*); ἱεράτευμα (*hierateuma*), priesthood (*2633*); ἱερατεύω (*hierateuō*), hold the office or perform the service of a priest (*2634*); ἱερουργέω (*hierourgeō*), perform holy service, act as a priest with regard to something (*2646*).

CL & OT 1. All the words in this word group are formed from the adj. *hieros*, holy (→ *2641*). According to the Stoic Zeno, the priest, versed in chastity and godliness, must be in concord and harmony with nature (viewed as divine). For the Stoics "the wise man alone" is therefore a priest.

2. The LXX uses *hiereus* to trans. Heb. *kōhēn*, priest. The development of the priesthood in the OT depends much on the view one takes of the dating of the OT books and the sources behind them. In the context of the various scholarly reconstructions, the following comments are generally accepted.

(a) The task of the priest in Israel seems not to have been originally sacrificial service, but speaking on behalf of Yahweh (cf. 1 Sam. 14:36–42) and instruction in the Torah (Deut. 27:9–10; 31:9–13). After all, sacrifices could be offered by the head of a family (cf. Gen. 8:20; 31:54; Exod. 12:21). Moses' father-in-law, Jethro the priest of Midian (Exod. 2:18–22; 3:1), offered burnt offerings and sacrifices at Sinai. He held a fellowship meal with the elders of Israel and advised Moses in the regulations of sacral law (Exod. 18:12–26).

(b) The descendants of Levi became the priestly class (Exod. 32:25–29; Deut. 33:8–11), although not every Levite served as a priest (Jdg. 19:1). The Levites enjoyed a particularly close relationship to Yahweh (Deut. 10:9). In point of law they stood close to aliens in possessing no land, but they did belong to the tribal system and had certain "towns to live in, with pasturelands for [their] livestock" (Josh. 21:2; cf. entire ch.). The high priesthood belonged to the clan of Aaron.

(c) In the premonarchic period priests are found primarily in connection with a sanctuary (e.g., the shrine of the Ephraimite Micah in Jdg. 17). At the sanctuary of the ark in Shiloh, Eli's family carried out the priestly duties, which consisted of offering sacrifices and burnt offerings and oracular prophecy (1 Sam. 1:3; 2:27–28).

(d) The flourishing temple cult in Jerusalem at the time of the monarchy gave rise to organized priesthoods (1 Ki. 4:2–5; cf. 12:26–31), which quickly gained recognition over against the local sanctuaries (2 Ki. 10:11, 19–21; 11:1–12). Local priests did not cease to exist, though they were often involved in pagan worship. Among other things, Josiah's reform "did away with the pagan priests appointed by the kings of Judah to burn incense on the high places of the towns of Judah" (2 Ki. 23:5); Josiah reestablished the worship of Yahweh as centered in the temple.

(e) In exilic times a clearer distinction was made between the priests and Levites as two divisions of the tribe of Levi. According to Ezek. 44:15, the Zadokites put forward their claim to the high-priestly offices. They derived their origin from Zadok, a pre-Davidic priest of Jerusalem, who was traced back through the family of Eli at Nob to that of Eli at Shiloh (2 Sam. 8:17; 1 Chr. 24:3).

(f) The postexilic reconstruction demanded Zadokite origin for the chief priests, Aaronic descent for the ordinary priests, and Levitical parentage for the temple servants (cf. 1 Chr. 24). In addition to those offering sacrifices, a growing body of experts in the Scriptures, ordained by Ezra (Neh. 8), soon overshadowed the priesthood.

(g) At the time of Jesus a social gap divided the chief priests (who formed an elite group and received power from the Romans to rule the people) from the ordinary priests. The latter formed twenty-four divisions of service in four to nine family groups (1 Chr. 24; cf. Lk. 1:5, 8). The divisions performed their service in the temple in turn, a week at a time. For the rest of the time the priests carried out a profession in the surrounding land. They could pass expert judgment on questions of ritual purity and often undertook the reading and exposition of the Torah in synagogue worship. Priestly rank was hereditary.

(h) At Qumran the Zadokite priesthood, deprived of its powers by the Hasmoneans, constituted itself as the priestly salvation community of the last days (1QS 5:2, 9; CD 3:21–4:2). Its founder, the "Teacher of Righteousness," was a Zadokite priest (4QpPs 37 3:16), while his opponent, the "wicked priest" (1QpHab 8:8), is perhaps the high priest Jonathan (152–143 B.C.). The priests took precedence in the community. The chief priest of the last days is ranked above the Messiah (1QSa 2:11–21). The purificatory prescriptions for priests were applied to all members of the community.

3. Regarding the high priest, *archiereus* occurs only 5x in the canonical books of the LXX, but 41x in the Apocr. (a) The postexilic office of high priest was until 172 B.C. in the possession of the

Zadokites. Since the nation lacked an independent political head, he also had political powers. Out of this arose tensions (e.g., between the high priest Eliashib and Nehemiah, Neh. 13:4–9, 28) and tendencies toward Hel. customs (2 Macc. 4:12–15). Power struggles for this office gave Antiochus IV (Epiphanes) several opportunities from 175 B.C. on to fill the position. It was against this that the Maccabean uprising was directed. In Jerusalem the Hasmonean Jonathan (a member of an ordinary priestly family) usurped the office of high priest in 152 B.C. (1 Macc. 10:20–21). The Hasmoneans held it against the protests of the Pharisees until 37 B.C. Then Herod and the Romans arbitrarily installed and deposed twenty-eight high priests until A.D. 70.

(b) At the time of Jesus the high priest was the highest representative of the people. He could take over the offering of the sacrifice at any time; he had the first choice of the parts of the sacrifice, the leadership of the priesthood, and the chief seat in the Sanhedrin (→ *synedrion*, *5284*). His greatest task was the absolution of the community on the Day of Atonement.

(c) The esteem of the high-priestly office led to a widespread Jewish expectation of an eschatological high priest alongside the kingly Messiah.

4. Melchizedek, who in Gen. 14:18 is called "king of Salem" and "priest of God Most High," holds a unique place in the biblical record (cf. Ps. 110:4). See further, *Melchisedek, 3519*.

5. *hierōsynē* (1 Chr. 29:22; Sir. 45:24; 1 Macc. 2:54) goes back to the basic meaning of priestly office. Josephus and Philo both testify to its high esteem. Josephus himself possessed this office.

6. *hierateia* is the word used for priesthood in the LXX (e.g., Exod. 29:9; 40:15; Jos. 18:7; 1 Sam. 2:36; Neh. 7:64; 13:29). In Num. 3:10 and 18:1 it denotes the priestly service, but more frequently simply the priestly office. By their investiture and anointing (Exod. 29:9; 40:15), in accord with divine instruction (Num. 25:13; Neh. 13:29; Sir. 45:7), Aaron's descendants have an eternal *hierateia*.

7. Exod. 19:6 speaks of Israel as "a kingdom of priests." This suggests that all Israelites were to have access to Yahweh and that the nation was to serve as priests for the rest of the world. The LXX translates this phrase by *basileion hierateuma* ("kingly priesthood") and stresses that Israel is called from among the nations to priestly service for God (cf. Isa. 61:6).

NT 1. In the NT *hiereus* refers mainly to the Levitical priests; in Heb. also to Christ and in Rev. to Christians. The word occurs 31x.

(a) Jesus had strikingly few dealings with the priesthood. When he sent healed lepers to the priests for confirmation of their healing (Matt. 8:4; Mk. 1:14; Lk. 5:14; 17:14), he was respecting their authority and acting in accordance with the law (cf. Lev. 13:49; 14:2–3). Lk. 10:31 is reminiscent of the prophetic critique of a merely external cult. In Matt. 12:1–8 (also Mk. 2:23–28; Lk. 6:1–5), Jesus declared his freedom over against cultic precepts. In the light of Lev. 24:9; Num. 28:9–10; Deut. 23:25; 1 Sam. 21:1–6; Hos. 6:6, not only was plucking grain on the Sabbath permitted, but Jesus as the Son of Man is Lord of the Sabbath.

Only in Lk. 1:5, 8; Acts 6:7 are priests found in a positive relationship to the salvation event. In Zechariah the priesthood is taken into the service of the immediate preparations for salvation through the promised Messiah. Lk. 1:8 provides the only NT instance of *hierateuō*. The addition of a large number of priests from the lower classes to the Jerusalem congregation (Acts 6:7) does not appear incredible in view of the social contrast with the priestly aristocracy.

(b) In Rev. 1:6 and 5:10 (cf. 20:6) Christians are called "a kingdom and priests" and thus have been picked out from humanity for the service of God. The promise of Exod. 19:6 is thus fulfilled, but the new order knows no temple, since God himself is now the temple (21:22).

(c) The thought of Exod. 19:6 is also taken up in 1 Pet. 2:9: "But you are a chosen people, a royal priesthood, a holy nation, a people belonging to God, that you may declare the praises of him who called you out of darkness into his wonderful light." This concept of priest-

hood embraces the idea of access to God in intimate knowledge and the prophetic role of priesthood in proclaiming the knowledge of God. It complements Peter's earlier idea of offering spiritual sacrifices: "You also, like living stones, are being built into a spiritual house to be a holy priesthood, offering spiritual sacrifices acceptable to God through Jesus Christ" (2:5). In both cases the priesthood of all believers is seen to supersede that of the Jewish priesthood. This is, in fact, the concept of Exod. 19:6.

(d) In Rom. 15:16 Paul describes his gracious calling "to be a minister [*leitourgos*] of Christ Jesus to the Gentiles with the priestly duty [*hierourgeō*] of proclaiming the gospel of God, so that the Gentiles might become an offering acceptable to God, sanctified by the Holy Spirit." The context suggests that this letter itself is a summary of Paul's priestly ministry (cf. 15:15). God's saving purpose is for both the Jewish nation and Gentiles. Salvation is grounded on grace received by faith (chs. 1–8), and Jew and Gentile are on the same footing. Chs. 9–11 consider God's purposes for the Jewish nation. The idea of the self-offering of the individual's life (12:1) is paralleled by that of the Gentiles. Just as the OT priest presented the sacrifice to Yahweh, so Paul, as the apostle to the Gentiles (cf. 1:5; also Acts 9:15; 22:21; 26:17–18; Gal. 2:8–9), is the one who has the special task of bringing them to God.

This offering, which would otherwise be unclean, is made acceptable by the sanctifying work of the Holy Spirit (cf. Rom. 15:16 with 8:2–27). In the background of Paul's thought may be Isa. 66:20, where the Diaspora Jews are an offering that the Gentiles will bring to Jerusalem, though here the roles are reversed. A similar concept is recorded in Phil. 2:17. Paul is in prison and awaiting possible execution (cf. 1:12–14, 17–26) and can envisage his own death as an offering for the sake of the church: "Even if I am being poured out like a drink offering on the sacrifice and service coming from your faith, I am glad and rejoice with all of you."

(e) Although the words "priest" and "high priest" do not occur in Jn. 17, Jesus' prayer here is sometimes referred to as his high-priestly prayer. The chapter represents his prayer for his people prior to his arrest and execution. Note 17:19, where Jesus says: "For them I sanctify [*hagiazō*] myself, that they too may be truly sanctified." The vb. *hagiazō* was used in the LXX for the sanctifying of priests (e.g., Exod. 28:41; 29:1, 21) and of sacrifices (e.g., 28:38; Num. 18:9; → *hagios*, holy, *41*). The notion of sanctifying through death for the sake of the people may reflect the Day of Atonement ritual carried out by the high priest (Lev. 16).

2. *archiereus* occurs only in the Gospels (83x), Acts (22x), and Heb. (17x). In the Gospels and Acts it refers to the chief priests opposed to Jesus; in Heb. it has a Christological and soteriological significance, for Jesus is depicted as the true high priest.

(a) In the Gospels and Acts the high priest is mentioned as the president of the Sanhedrin in the trials of Jesus and his followers (e.g., Matt. 26:62; Acts 5:21, 27; 23:1–5). Often the pl. "chief priests" occurs, denoting the holders of the higher priestly offices (e.g., Matt. 21:45–46; Jn. 12:10; Acts 5:24; 25:2). The priestly aristocracy thus appears as a closed group who staged persecutions and condemnations. Their combined act with the "elders" and the "teachers of the law" is interpreted as being ordained by God (e.g., Matt. 16:21; 20:18; → *dei*, it is necessary, one must, *1256*).

Looked at historically, it may well have been Jesus' cleansing of the temple (e.g., Mk. 11:18; Jn. 2:13–17) as an attack on the carefully preserved temple administration of the chief priests that was the decisive factor in their hostility against him. Perhaps too their arrangement with the Romans, who gave them their power, aroused fears that the Romans might take measures against Jesus and his followers on their own account (11:48). Note the prophetic remark of the high priest Caiaphas that one man should die to save the nation (11:50). Jn.'s observation is an ironical comment on what to Caiaphas was sheer political realism: "[Caiaphas] did not say this on his own, but as high priest that year he prophesied that Jesus would die for the Jewish nation, and not only for that nation but also for the scattered children of God, to bring them together and make them one" (11:51–52).

Caiaphas is mentioned in the NT at Matt. 26:3, 57; Lk. 3:2; Jn. 11:49; 18:13–14, 24, 28; Acts 4:6. His successor, according to Josephus, was "Jonathan the son of Ananus," who is commonly identified with the Annas of the NT. According to Jn. 18:13, Caiaphas was the son-in-law of Annas, who had been deposed as high priest in A.D. 15. Lk. dates the public ministry of John the Baptist "during the high priesthood of Annas and Caiaphas" (3:2). As the head of a powerful family, Annas continued to exert considerable influence, which is evidenced by the fact that he procured appointment to the office for five of his sons.

(b) In Acts 22:30–23:10, during Paul's interrogation before the Sanhedrin, the high priest Ananias commanded that Paul should be struck on the mouth. Paul responded by lashing out at him, calling him a "whitewashed wall." When those who stood by were shocked that Paul would speak that way to a high priest, the apostle apologized (based on Exod. 22:28) and admitted he did not know this man was the high priest. His failure to recognize the high priest is perhaps due to Paul's possible failing eyesight or to a change of high priest since his last visit to Jerusalem. The interrogation broke up in disorder when Paul played off the Pharisees and Sadducees against each other.

Ananias appeared in person to support the renewed charges before Felix at Caesarea five days later (Acts 24:1). This Ananias had been appointed high priest in A.D. 48 but was sent to Rome in A.D. 52 to answer charges of cruelty. He was acquitted by Claudius through the efforts of Herod Agrippa II. An unscrupulous man, Ananias was a typical powerful Sadducee. Because of his collaboration with the Romans he was hated by the nationalists and was murdered at the outbreak of the Jewish war in A.D. 66.

(c) While high-priestly functions are attributed to Christ in the NT outside Heb., such as intercession (Jn. 17:19; Rom. 8:34; 1 Jn. 2:1) and the opening of access to God (Rom. 5:2; Eph. 2:18; 1 Pet. 3:18), only Heb. offers a fully developed high-priestly Christology. The author of this NT book interprets the suffering and the present work of Christ as a high-priestly service. Alongside the title *archiereus*, Christ also, on the basis of Ps. 110:4, bears the title *hiereus*. But the interest is really focused on the high-priestly rank of Christ. The thought of a high-priestly self-sacrifice, prominent in Heb., is new. The writer develops the concept of the priesthood of Christ as the antitype of the Levitical priesthood, and does so in respect of structure, scriptural basis, bearer, service, place, and time.

(i) *Structure.* Every high priest, who stands as a representative of humans before God (Heb. 5:1), must be founded on his solidarity with humanity in their susceptibility to sin (5:2) and on divine calling (5:4). Of the duties of the high priest Heb. is interested only in the sacrificial service (5:1; 8:3), and primarily in his double service on the Day of Atonement (2:17; cf. Lev. 16)—the slaughter of the sacrificial animal (Heb. 9:22) and his entry with the sacrificial blood into the Most Holy Place (9:7). The goal of this high-priestly service is to render access to God by blotting out the guilt of one's sins (4:16; 7:18–19, 25; 10:1, 19, 22).

(ii) *Scriptural basis.* The fact and significance of the priesthood of Christ are grounded on Ps. 110:4 (cf. Heb. 5:6) and Gen. 14:17–24 (Heb. 7:1–10). Following an exegetical tradition of Hel. Jud., Heb. interprets Jesus according to the historical figure of Melchizedek (see also *Melchisedek*, *3519*). This man was not tied to any descent and is therefore seen as eternal (7:3). He is also superior to the Levitical priesthood, since Melchizedek blessed Abraham, the ancestor of the Levites, and received a tithe from him (7:5–10).

All this prefigures the priesthood of the Son who is addressed in Ps. 110 (cf. Heb. 7:3). It is grounded, moreover, on a divine oath (Ps. 110:4), whereas the Levitical priesthood rested on legal ordinance (Heb. 7:11, 20–21). The OT law (7:16), however, can only install men in their weakness as high priests (7:23, 28). God's oath, by contrast, in which resides the "power of an indestructible life" (7:16), entrusts

to Jesus the Son of God, who has overcome all weakness, an unalterable priesthood (*hierōsynē*; 7:24 cf. 5:7–10; 7:28).

(iii) *The bearer.* The weakness of the Levitical priesthood lies in its sinfulness (Heb. 5:3; 7:27). Although Jesus became a human being in every respect (2:17), he did not sin (4:15; 9:14); only such a high priest can act for us (7:26), for he alone can atone.

(iv) *Service.* The Levitical priestly service is inadequate, since for an atoning sacrifice it must have recourse to animal blood. This only effects an external purification, not the eradication of the guilt of sin from the conscience (Heb. 9:13–14). On the contrary, it is only the necessity of continually renewed sacrifices that actuates a consciousness of sin (10:1–4). But Christ, through his self-sacrifice, has effected once for all the liberation of the conscience from all sin (9:14, 26) and thus opened the way to God (10:19–22).

(v) *Place.* The Levitical priestly service is imperfect, since its nature is earthly and it takes place in an earthly sanctuary (Heb. 9:1). According to Exod. 25:40, the tabernacle is the shadowy replica of the heavenly sanctuary, in which Christ officiates as high priest (Heb. 8:2, 5; 9:11, 24). The heavenly sanctuary is perfect, "true," because it is "not a part of this creation" (8:2; 9:11). To that extent not only Christ's entrance into heaven, but also the death he suffered on earth, is heavenly high-priestly service. He is a high priest forever but is first proclaimed as such on the basis of his sacrificial death (5:10).

(vi) *Time.* The words "covenant" and "promise" (Heb. 8:6–13; 10:16–17) bring a historical moment into the contrast between the earthly, Levitical high priesthood and the heavenly high priesthood of Christ. The latter sets the former aside (7:18–19). Moreover, the unique self-sacrifice of Christ marks the arrival of the end (already prophesied in the OT) of the cult as an atoning institution (10:5–10, 18). Christians know only the sacrifice that is left for humans—that of praise, confession, and service (13:15–16).

(d) The high-priestly Christology of Heb. does not serve speculative but paraenetic interests. Heb. encourages believers in Jesus to hold fast to their confession by giving a new emphasis both to Jesus' historical work and to his present significance at God's right hand. Thus Jesus' death on the cross represents the high-priestly self-sacrifice of the eternal Son of God, surpassing all other sacrifices and valid once and for all. His exaltation is seen as the entrance of the perfect high priest into the heavenly and true sanctuary and as his continual intercession for believers. Christ, therefore, as the eternal and heavenly high priest, now gives to those who hold firm to their confession of him a present guarantee of immediate access to God and a future guarantee of entrance into the lasting heavenly world.

2638 (hierothytos, devoted, sacrificed to a divinity), → 2641.

| 2639 ἱερόν | ἱερόν (*hieron*), temple (*2639*). |

CL & OT 1. The expression *to hieron* is the neut. form of the adj. *hieros*, holy, used as a noun. In cl. Gk. *to hieron* and its pl. *ta hiera*, the holy things, can denote sacrifice; the pl. can also refer to cultic objects. *to hieron* can mean a consecrated grove, any place of sacrifice, or the inner part of the place of worship, the *temenos* (→ *naos*, *3724*). Polybius uses *to hieron* of the Jerusalem temple, and both Jewish and Christian writers frequently use the word for pagan shrines (e.g., Ezek. 27:6; 28:18 LXX of Tyre; 1 Macc. 10:84; 11:4 of Dagon).

2. (a) *LXX terminology.* In the canonical writings of the OT, the LXX uses *to hieron* only in Chr. to denote the Jerusalem temple (1 Chr. 9:27; 29:4; 2 Chr. 6:13; cf. also a mistranslation in Ezek. 45:19). However, it does occur in the Apocr. (e.g., 1 Esd. 1:8; 5:44; 8:18, 81; 1 Macc. 15:9; 2 Macc. 2:9; 3 Macc. 3:16; 4 Macc. 4:3). The reason for its general absence from the canonical writings is its associations with idolatry, coupled with the fact that the Heb. OT uses the following more general terms to denote the temple. (i) *bayit*, the ordinary word for house, can be used for the temple of a god (Dagon, 1 Sam. 5:2) and

the house of God (Exod. 23:19; 34:26; Jdg. 18:31; 1 Ki. 6:5; Isa. 2:2; 38:22; Ezek. 41:7–14).

(ii) *hêkāl*, meaning a great house, is used for a palace (e.g., 2 Ki. 20:18; Isa. 39:7) as well as the temple at Jerusalem (e.g., 1 Ki. 6:3, 5, 33; Ezr. 3:6, 10; Ps. 18:6; Isa. 6:1; Hag. 2:15, 18; Mal. 3:1). Note too the expression "your holy temple" (Ps. 5:7; Jon. 2:4) and "his holy temple" (Ps. 11:4; Mic. 1:2; Hab. 2:20), which uses this word.

(iii) *qōdeš*, meaning holiness, can mean the Holy Place, esp. in the tabernacle or tent of meeting (e.g., Exod. 26:33; 28:29, 35, 43; Lev. 4:6; 16:23; Num. 4:12). The Holy Place of the temple corresponds to that in the tabernacle (1 Ki. 8:8, 10; Ezek. 41:21, 23; Dan. 8:13; 9:26). In some passages this expression may stand for the temple as a whole.

(iv) The related word *miqdāš* means sacred place, sanctuary: e.g., in Moab (Isa. 16:12), Bethel (Amos 7:9, 13), Jerusalem (Lam. 1:10); it can also designate the tabernacle (Exod. 25:8) or the temple (Ezek. 45:3–4, 18). In some places this word is qualified (e.g., *miqdāš yhwh*, "sanctuary of the LORD," Num. 19:20; Jos. 24:26; 1 Chr. 22:19; Ezek. 48:10).

(v) *māqôm* means place, e.g., God's place (Isa. 26:21; Jer. 7:12; Hos. 5:15; Mic. 1:3), Jerusalem as God's special place (1 Ki. 8:30; 2 Ki. 22:16), Shechem (where God appeared to Abraham, Gen. 12:6), or holy places (28:11, 19; Deut. 12:2; 2 Sam. 7:10).

(b) *Background.* The OT refers to numerous holy places and shrines before the building of Solomon's temple. The tower of Babel suggests the existence of some form of temple (Gen. 11:4). The patriarchs encountered Yahweh at various places, generally building an altar or pillar to commemorate the occasion (cf. 22:9; 28:22). During Israel's desert period, the tabernacle provided a meeting place for Yahweh and his people (Exod. 33:7–11). Various local shrines were recognized in the period of the judges, such as Shechem (Jos. 8:30–35; 24:1–27) and Shiloh (1 Sam. 1:3). The Canaanite deities had their own temples, such as the house of Dagon (1 Sam. 5:5) and of the Ashtoreths (1 Sam. 31:10).

David was conscious of a discrepancy between his own lifestyle, having built a palace for himself, and provision for the worship of Yahweh (2 Sam. 7:2). Although David had succeeded in consolidating the kingdom, Yahweh told David through Nathan that he did not need a building erected by humans, for he was the one who enabled them to do things. Nevertheless, Yahweh would provide a house (7:13). But since David was a man of blood, he was not permitted to build the temple; this would fall to his son Solomon (7:12–17), though David did collect material and treasure and bought the site for it, the threshing floor of Araunah the Jebusite (2 Sam. 24:18–25; 1 Chr. 21:25; 22:2–19).

(c) *Solomon's temple.* The building began in Solomon's fourth year and was completed seven years later (1 Ki. 6–8; 2 Chr. 3–5). The location was in the area now covered by the Moslem shrine known as the Dome of the Rock. Phoenician craftsmen were employed in its building (1 Ki. 5:10, 18; 7:13–14), and it shared architectural features common to Phoenician and Canaanite buildings. There apparently was an inner and outer courtyard (cf. 6:36; 7:12). The bronze altar for burnt offerings stood in the inner court (8:22, 64; 9:25). Between this and the porch was the bronze basin (7:23–26). West of the porch, behind bronze doors, stood the Holy Place, where the ordinary rites were performed. It had latticed windows (6:4) and contained the golden incense altar, the table for the bread of the Presence, the five pairs of lampstands, and the instruments of sacrifice.

The inner sanctuary was a perfect cube of twenty cubits, containing the ark of the covenant. The latter was a receptacle for the Ten Commandments, the manna, and Aaron's rod (Exod. 25:16, 21–22; 40:20; Deut. 10:1–5; 31:9; Jos. 24:26; Heb. 9:4–5). It served as the meeting place where Yahweh revealed his will (Exod. 25:22; 30:36; Lev. 16:2; Jos. 7:6). It was here that the high priest appeared on behalf of the people with the sacrificial blood on the annual Day of Atonement (Lev. 16; → *hilaskomai*, to reconcile, *2661*).

According to Exod. 37:1–9, the ark was made at Sinai by Bezalel according to the pattern given to Moses. It played a crucial part in the crossing of the Jordan (Jos. 3–4), the fall of Jericho (ch. 6), and subsequent history in the conquest of Canaan (Jdg. 2:1; 20:27; 1 Sam. 1:3; 3:3). Its loss to the Philistines signaled the loss of Yahweh's presence in Israel, but it also led to plagues for the Philistines (1 Sam. 4:1–7:2). David brought the ark to Jerusalem (2 Sam. 6; cf. 15:24–29). It was placed in Solomon's temple with great ceremony (1 Ki. 8:1–11; cf. 2 Chr. 35:3). Jer. anticipated an age without its presence (3:16). The ark was destroyed with the fall of Jerusalem at the hands of the Babylonians in 587 B.C. and was not replaced in the second temple.

Shishak of Egypt plundered the temple in the reign of Solomon's son, Rehoboam (1 Ki. 14:26), and later kings, including Hezekiah, used its treasure to purchase allies and pay tribute to invaders (15:18; 2 Ki. 16:8). Idolatrous kings introduced the symbols of pagan deities (16:10–18; 21:4; 23:1–12). By the time of Josiah (ca. 640 B.C.) the temple had fallen into considerable disrepair (2 Ki. 22:4–6), and restoration was financed by collecting money from worshipers. Jer. warned against abuse of the temple and false reliance on it as a guarantee of the divine presence (7:4, 11). It was looted and sacked by Nebuchadnezzar (2 Ki. 25:9, 13–17; cf. Dan. 5:2–3, 23), though Israelites continued to offer sacrifices there after its destruction (Jer. 41:5).

(d) *Ezekiel's vision of a temple.* During the exile the prophet Ezek. received a vision of a new temple (see Ezek. 40–43). Its dimensions are somewhat different from those of Solomon's temple, and the vision includes a description of the surrounding area, with gates fortified to prevent the inclusion of non-Israelites.

(e) *The second temple.* The returning exiles brought with them the vessels looted by Nebuchadnezzar and authorization from Cyrus of Persia to rebuild the temple (ca. 537 B.C.; cf. Ezra 1; 3:2–3, 8–13). There was no ark. Instead of Solomon's ten lampstands, a seven-branched candelabrum stood in the Holy Place with the table for the bread of the Presence and the incense altar. These were taken as spoil by Antiochus IV Epiphanes (ca. 175–164 B.C.), who set up a pagan altar or statue in its place (1 Macc. 1:54). Some three years later the Maccabees removed the pollution and replaced the temple furniture (4:36–59). They also turned the temple into a fortress, which later in 63 B.C. for three months withstood the siege of Pompey.

(f) *Herod's temple.* In an attempt to conciliate the Jews, Herod began a massive rebuilding of the temple in 19 B.C. The main structure was finished within ten years, though work went on until A.D. 64 (cf. Jn. 2:20). The temple area was dominated by the fortress of Antonia at the northwest corner, which formed the residence of the procurator and also housed the Roman garrison (cf. Lk. 13:1; Acts 21:31–35). The outer court was surrounded by a portico. Solomon's Colonnade (Jn. 10:23; Acts 3:11; 5:12) was on the east side. The Jewish teachers of the law held their schools and debates in the colonnades (Mk. 11:27; Lk. 2:46; 19:47), and the merchants and moneychangers had their stalls there as well (Lk. 19:45–46; Jn. 2:14–16).

The inner area was surrounded by a balustrade that separated it from the court of the Gentiles. This inner area contained three courts: the court of women, the court of Israel, and the priests' court, in which stood the altar outside the temple proper (cf. Matt. 23:35). At the Feast of Tabernacles men could enter the latter. The altar was of unhewn stone. The temple was destroyed in the Jewish War in A.D. 70.

NT As the focal point of Jewish religion, the temple figures prominently in the NT, esp. in the light of Jesus' associations with it. It was the place of God's presence, glory, revelation, and meeting with his people. Jesus' actions in connection with the temple had a parabolic character, signifying God's presence with his people for those with eyes to see. Its destruction epitomized God's judgment on the Jewish people for their rejection of him in the person of Jesus. At the same time it signified the end of the old covenant and its supersedure by the new.

1. *The infancy narratives in Lk.* Lk. 2:22–52 preserves two groups of stories that center on the temple as the focal point of the divine presence. Jesus' parents brought him to the temple to make the customary offering (in their case, the form permitted for the poorest sections of the community, 2:24; cf. Lev. 12:2–8). In so doing, they showed as devout Jews due reverence for the law and respect for the temple. Corresponding to this, Simeon and Anna represent the godly remnant of Israel, who seek Yahweh in the temple and who are thus granted a revelation of his Messiah (Lk. 2:25–38). Note also Lk.'s account of the circumstances attending the birth of John the Baptist (1:5–80). His father, Zechariah, was a priest, and the revelation of God's purposes in giving him a son came as he was burning incense in the temple (1:8–23).

In short, in Lk.'s infancy narratives the temple is the place where the godly remnant of Israel wait on God and where they receive revelations of God's saving purposes—first in the birth of John the Baptist and then in the birth of Jesus.

2. *The temple as the scene of Jesus' ministry.* (a) Lk. relates as one of Satan's temptations for Jesus to make a spectacular display by casting himself down from the top of the temple (Lk. 4:9–12). This temptation is based on a perverted interpretation of Ps. 91:11–12, which Jesus meets with Deut. 6:16: "Do not put the Lord your God to the test." The fact that Jesus answers the temptation in this manner indicates that he has no need to vindicate his divine vocation in this way. He is conscious of his divine calling, and that is sufficient. He can trust the Father to vindicate him in whatever way the Father chooses.

(b) Throughout Jesus' public ministry, the temple remains to Jesus the focal point of meeting God and worshiping him. The contrasting attitudes of Jud. are epitomized in the temple. For example, both the Pharisee and the tax collector pray in the temple, the former pleading his own righteousness and the latter confessing his need and crying out for mercy (Lk. 18:10–14). A similar contrast in Jewish piety is exhibited in the story of the widow's two small copper coins (Mk. 12:41–44), which Jesus considers worth more than the gifts of the rich. This incident occurs in the last week of Jesus' ministry, which is deliberately set in the temple as the place of revelation and worship; it is immediately followed by Jesus' prophecy of the destruction of the temple, occasioned by the disciples' remark about its "massive stones" and "magnificent buildings" (13:1).

(c) Jesus' messianic entry into Jerusalem (Matt. 21:1–9; Mk. 11:1–10, Lk. 19:28–38; Jn. 12:12–19) leads directly to his entry into the temple and his cleansing of it (Matt. 21:10–17; Mk. 11:15–19; Lk. 19:45–48; cf. Jn. 2:13–17). Jesus does not go there simply because Jews happen to be gathered there or because he wants to do things openly. This is not merely a prophetic denunciation of commercialism (Mk. 11:17). Rather, Jesus is acting in judgment as God himself would act, driving out the money changers and those who sold animals and birds for sacrifice. It is an attempt to restore the true function of the temple as a house of prayer and place where God will be known. This last point is made clear by the fact that Jesus proceeds to teach daily in the temple (Matt. 26:55; Mk. 14:49, Lk. 22:53). But his action results in the decision of the religious authorities to destroy him. Their counteraction is thus a repudiation of God's summons.

In Jn. the cleansing of the temple is placed at the beginning of his account of Jesus' public ministry. Some have suggested that Jesus cleansed the temple twice. Others, however, argue that Jn.'s placement of the story here represents a thematic ordering of his material rather than a chronological one. It is followed by a discussion of the sign of Jesus' authority—the destruction and raising of the temple of Jesus' body (Jn. 2:18–22), the believing response of some (2:23–25), the discussion on rebirth with Nicodemus (3:1–15), and the teaching on coming to the light so that one's deeds may be seen to have been wrought by God (3:16–21). The cleansing is preceded by the Johannine prologue (1:1–18), the witness of the Baptist (1:19–34), the call of the disciples (1:35–51), and the miracle at Cana (2:1–11), revealing the transforming power of Jesus.

(d) Jesus describes the tabernacle as "the house of God" (Matt. 12:4) in answer to the Pharisees' challenge on the legality of plucking ears of grain on the Sabbath (cf. 1 Sam. 21:2–7; Hos. 6:6). In the course of his reply Matt. records Jesus as saying, "I tell you, something greater than the temple is here" (Matt. 12:6, lit. trans.). This "something" may be the community of the disciples, who with Jesus constitute the corporate Son of Man (12:8). Or it may be the kingdom of God effectively present in the eschatological community or the believing remnant of God's people. Many scholars, however, relate the phrase to Jesus himself as God's new temple (cf. Jn. 2:21).

(e) In his final week of public ministry Jesus also denounces the practice of swearing by, among other things, the temple or any part it (Matt. 23:16–22; cf. 5:33–37). To swear by any part of the temple (which in rab. teaching was less binding than swearing by God himself) is in fact to introduce duplicity into one's dealings. Rather, one's word should be binding, and note that the God who sanctifies the temple also sanctifies its several parts. Therefore, any such oath is tantamount to swearing by God himself.

(f) On the question of the temple tax (Matt. 17:24–27), → *statēr*, stater (a silver coin worth four drachmas), *5088*.

3. *The destruction of the temple.* In two groups of passages Jesus discusses the coming destruction of the temple. In the first group he refers to the temple of his body (Matt. 26:61; 27:40; Mk. 14:57–58; 15:29–30; Jn. 2:18–22; cf. Acts 6:14). Already Jesus' own person is superseding the material temple as the dwelling place of God, where God and humans meet.

In the second group Jesus prophesies the physical destruction of the Jerusalem temple (Matt. 24:1, 15; Mk. 13:2–3, 14; Lk. 21:5–6, 20). The cause of the destruction is the rejection by the Jewish leaders and the people as a whole of God's summons to them in the person of Jesus. For Jesus' coming to Jerusalem and visitation of the temple has failed to find the response of penitence, faith, and commitment. God's people have rejected him, and the destruction of the temple will be his judgment on them, a symbol of the termination of the divinely appointed covenant relationship. It is anticipated by Jesus' cursing of the fig tree (Matt. 21:18–19; Mk. 11:12–14). The sign will be "the abomination that causes desolation" (Matt. 24:15–22; Mk. 13:14–20; Lk. 21:20–24).

Judas's casting the rejected pieces of silver into the temple (Matt. 27:5) indicates the permanent defilement of the sanctuary by the death of Jesus. The rending of the temple veil on Jesus' death (Matt. 27:51; Mk. 15:38; Lk. 23:45) shows us that access to God is now by Christ's death.

4. *The temple in Acts.* The death and resurrection of Jesus do not mean a repudiation of the temple or of Israel for the early church. The sermons of Acts addressed to Jews lay the guilt for Jesus' death squarely with the Jewish leadership (cf. Acts 2:23; 3:13–14; 4:10–11; 5:30; 7:52; 10:39; 13:27–29), but they all hold out the invitation to repentance, faith, and a return to God. God has not yet finally rejected his ancient people. Similarly, the temple is still the divinely appointed place of worship, though now in the context of Christian fellowship (2:46; 3:1–10). As late as 22:17 Paul has a revelation of the risen Lord while praying in the temple.

The apostles taught there as Jesus did (5:12, 20–21). As a Jew, Paul respected the rites and customs of the temple, bringing the offering of Nazirite purification (21:26; 24:6, 12, 18; 25:8; 26:21). His attitude is to be understood in the context of his determination to be all things to all people in order to save some (1 Cor. 9:19–23). So long as the temple stood, judgment had not fallen on the nation. Indeed, the early church was essentially Jewish Christian. Only after Peter's vision was the church opened up to Gentile believers (Acts 10). Nevertheless, a note of criticism regarding the temple begins to be heard in Stephen's speech (7:44–50) and indirectly in Paul's Areopagus address (17:24).

5. *The temple in the NT letters.* Where the Christian community is called the temple of God, the word *naos* (→ *3724*) is used. *to hieron*

occurs only in 1 Cor. 9:13, where Paul uses Deut. 18:1 to claim monetary support for Christian workers on the basis of the OT pattern that those employed in temple service received food for their work. Heb. uses the pl. phrase *ta hagia* ("the holy things," → *hagios*, holy, *41*) for the sanctuary in connection with its discussion of the Day of Atonement ritual as a type of Christ's priestly work (Heb. 9:24–25; cf. 13:11; Lev. 16). *oikos theou*, "God's household," occurs in 1 Tim. 3:15 (cf. Heb. 3:6; 10:21; 1 Pet. 4:17).

See also *naos*, temple, shrine, sanctuary (*3724*).

2640 (hieroprepēs, befitting a holy person or thing), → *2641*.

2641	ἱερός

ἱερός (*hieros*), holy (*2641*); ἱεροπρεπής (*hieroprepēs*), befitting a holy person or thing (*2640*); ἱεροσυλέω (*hierosyleō*), rob temples (*2644*); ἱερόσυλος (*hierosylos*), temple robber (*2645*); ἱερόθυτος (*hierothytos*), devoted, sacrificed to a divinity (*2638*).

CL & OT 1. In cl. Gk. *hieros* is that which is determined, filled, or consecrated by divine power. In contrast to *hagios*, holy, *hosios*, devout, pious, and *semnos*, revered, august (→ *sebō*, *4936*), all of which contain an ethical element, *hieros* denotes what is holy in and of itself, quite apart from any ethical judgment. It is not used of the gods themselves, but of what belongs to their sphere, what they have sanctified, and what has been consecrated to them.

Among objects described as holy are the head of Zeus and his bed, the abode of the gods (the snowy regions of Olympus), the scales of Kronos, the bow of Hercules, and the chariot of Achilles. The gods themselves sanctified such things as the light, the air, night and day, the earth, fruitful ground, and cities like Pergamum, Thebes, and Athens. Similarly, people are said to be *hieroi* because they possess a trait that comes from the gods. For example, kings are *hieroi* since they received their sovereignty from the gods. From the time of Augustus (63 B.C.–A.D. 14) the Roman emperor was addressed by the title *hieros*. Not only his person but everything connected with him came to be counted as *hieros*, because it had been sanctified by the gods.

2. (a) The thought of consecration to the gods leads into the realm of the cultus, which was the decisive general factor in determining the meaning of *hieros*. Even if everything that is called *hieros* does not belong directly to the cultus, it nevertheless remains associated with it. For example, when the choruses in the theater are called *hieroi*, it is because they convey a divine message; noncultic songs consecrated to the gods are *hieroi*, and the circle in which justice is administered is called *hieros*. Again, *hieros* can be used of people, esp. of those who have been initiated into the mysteries.

(b) *ta hiera* (lit., the holy things) denotes above all the sacrifice, occasionally the sacrificial animal, and the omens that accompanied the sacrifice. However, *ta hiera* was more typically used for cultic objects (images, vestments, sacred utensils, etc.), actions, and the cultus itself.

(c) *to hieron* has predominantly the meaning of sanctuary, cultic center (→ *2639*).

3. *hieroprepēs*, befitting the sacred, *hierosyleō*, rob a temple or commit sacrilege, and their derivatives need no further explanation. *hierothytos* means devoted, offered to a god, or sacrificed; it is a specifically cultic term. The pl. *ta hierothyta* means the sacrifice or sacrificial flesh. For *hiereus*, priest, and *archiereus*, high priest, chief priest, → *hiereus*, *2636*.

4. In the LXX most of the words in the *hieros* word group go back to the Heb. *kōhēn* (in form, the part. of *kāhan*, to be a priest, serve as priest). *hieros* did not fit the Jewish concept of holiness prevailing at the time of the trans. of the LXX, because it meant what is holy in and of itself apart from any ethical element, whereas since the exile only what conformed to the Torah could, to the Jewish mind, be holy. Even the temple in Jerusalem was not generally called *to hieron* until the Apocr. (though cf. 1 Chr. 9:27; 29:4; 2 Chr. 6:13). These words could, however, be used for the priest and his activities (→ *hiereus*, priest, *2636*).

NT 1. Most of the words in the group occur only rarely in the NT. *hierothytos* (only in 1 Cor. 10:28) is the meat that was slaughtered in the pagan cult. The fact that some Christians continued to eat it, knowing its origin, caused questions of conscience at Corinth, which Paul attempted to resolve by directing the church to the glory of God and concern for others (10:31–11:1).

2. *hieroprepēs*, befitting a holy person or thing, worthy of reverence (only in Tit. 2:3), corresponds with a preference for the solemn and cultic in the Pastorals. In this verse, the older women in the congregation should conform to propriety in their behavior.

3. *hieros*, sacred, holy, occurs in 2 Tim. 3:15 in a solemn context of a reference to "the holy Scriptures" (similar to what is found in Philo and Josephus). Although the word was otherwise not popular, it could be used more easily of the Scriptures because they possessed a sacred quality all their own. In a comparison (1 Cor. 9:13) Paul uses *ta hiera* in its usual sense of sacred actions (NIV, "temple").

4. *hierosylos* means temple robber, one who commits sacrilege against a temple. In Acts 19:37 Paul and his companions are defended by the town clerk of Ephesus against such a charge. The apostle was accused of teaching that "man-made gods are no gods at all" and therefore of undermining both trade and the temple of Artemis (19:26–27). The related vb., *hierosyleō*, rob temples (Rom. 2:22), apparently alludes to a problem frequently aired in rab. discussion. To what extent was it permissible to do business in pagan temple utensils and property, although they were ritually unclean? Under certain circumstances such dealings were allowed, if they contributed to the damaging of the pagan cult. Paul seems to be rejecting such devious practices. The verse may also allude to the practice of some Jews of removing gold and silver idols from shrines for private profit.

5. For *to hieron*, temple (almost without exception, Herod's temple), → *2639*. The most important difference between *to hieron* and *naos* (→ *3724*) is that the former is never spiritualized. It always means the structure with its walls, gates, porticos, courts, and buildings.

See also *hagios*, holy, sacred (*41*); *hosios*, holy, devout, pious (*4008*).

2642 (Hierosolyma, Jerusalem), → *2647*.

2644 (hierosyleō, rob temples), → *2641*.

2645 (hierosylos, temple robber), → *2641*.

2646 (hierourgeō, perform holy service, act as a priest), → *2636*.

2647	Ἰερουσαλήμ

Ἰερουσαλήμ (*Ierousalēm*), Jerusalem (*2647*); Ἰεροσόλυμα (*Hierosolyma*), Jerusalem (*2642*); Σιών (*Sion*), Zion (*4994*).

CL & OT 1. *Ierousalēm* and *Sion* are proper nouns, unknown in early cl. Gk. The form *Hierosolyma* was used for the city in the Roman province of Judea and *Hierosolymitēs* for an inhabitant of Jerusalem. Hel. Jud. took advantage of this rendering of the Heb. name to liken it to Gk. *hieros*, holy, in order to distinguish the city as the "holy city" of Jud.

2. (a) The Israelites found Jerusalem as the name of a Canaanite city-state of the Jebusites (cf. Jos. 10:1) and took it over. The name means something like "foundation of Salem," i.e., of a god who, according to Ugaritic texts, embodied the twilight. His sanctuary was in this settlement, which originally was situated on the hill Zion. In later history Jerusalem was the name of the whole of the expanding settlement. After David had seized it, the city was also called the City of David. The name of the city in Jdg. 19:10–11 and 1 Chr. 11:4 is Jebus, derived from the proper noun Jebusite.

(b) The etymology of the name Zion (Heb. *ṣiyyôn*) cannot be explained with certainty. It does derive from Canaan's pre-Israelite period and represents a description of the terrain, a geographical name. From the earliest times Zion was the name of the southeast hill, site of the original Jebusite fortress and of the ancient Canaanite settlement of Jerusalem (Jos. 10; Ezek. 16:2–5).

3. (a) In the OT *yᵉrûšālayim* occurs 660x and *ṣiyyôn* 154x. The LXX transcribes the Heb. original as *Ierousalēm* (fem.), in the Apocr. occasionally as *Hierosolyma* (neut. pl.). Inhabitants of this city are described in the canonical OT with a noun plus *Ierousalēm* (e.g., "dwellers in [inhabitants of] Jerusalem" in Isa. 5:3; Zech. 12:10); in the Apocr. we read *Hierosolymitēs* ("Jerusalemite," e.g., Sir. 50:27; 4 Macc. 4:22; 18:5).

(b) As a neutral city, belonging to neither Judah nor Israel and yet lying exactly between the two territories, Jerusalem was an ideal capital for David. Since he captured it with an army of mercenaries, it remained independent (cf. 2 Sam. 5:6–10). The bringing of the ark of Yahweh into Jerusalem (2 Sam. 6) was a decisive act for the further significance of the city, for it then became the central cultic sanctuary of all Israel. Even after the northern kingdom's break with the south, Jerusalem retained its central theological significance for all Israel (1 Ki. 12:27–28). Yahweh of hosts, who once was enthroned above the ark (2 Sam. 6:2), now "dwells on Mount Zion" (Isa. 8:18), on the "mountain of the LORD's temple" (Isa. 2:2–3; Mic. 4:1–2).

Jerusalem, as the royal capital, became the center of the political kingdom. As "the holy city" (Isa. 48:2; 52:1), it became more and more the focus of theocratic hopes. Both historical experience and theological reflection strengthened the idea of the inviolability and indestructibility of the temple city (cf. 2 Ki. 18–19; 2 Chr. 32; Isa. 36–37; Jer. 7:4). During the exile, it was the embodiment of every longing (Ps. 137). Soon the name of the city was linked with eschatological expectations (Jer. 31:38–40): Jerusalem would become the focus for the whole world, to which all the Gentiles would stream (3:17), and would then be called "a house of prayer for all nations" (Isa. 56:7). In all this complex of ideas Jerusalem and Zion frequently occur together.

(c) When the prophets spoke about the conditions they observed in Jerusalem, however, a different picture emerges. Jerusalem had fallen away from God and become a prostitute. The worship of idols and disregard of God's commands were rife in the city. Hence, they announced God's judgment on the city (e.g., Isa. 32:9–14; Jer. 6:22–30)—judgment that was sure to come because the corrupt people would not turn and repent (4:3–4). Foreign peoples and kings would carry out that judgment, which would result in a cleansed and purified Jerusalem (Isa. 40). It was Yahweh's intention to do good to Jerusalem once again (Zech. 8:15), and at the end of the age the city "will be holy; never again will foreigners invade her" (Joel 3:17).

The eschatological Jerusalem was always conceived, however, as an improved, renewed earthly city, never as supernatural and heavenly. Thus, the nations could go on pilgrimage to it and accept a new way of life (Isa. 2:2–4) by turning to Yahweh (Jer. 3:17). From Jerusalem streams of blessing would pour out into the world (Ezek. 47:1–12). From this holy city Yahweh would reign over the whole world (Isa. 24:23; Jer. 3:17).

4. The name *Siōn* was at first not used by the Israelites. When the prophets and poets took up the name, they extended or shifted its meaning. On the one hand, Zion together with Jerusalem could be applied to the whole expanded city, and Zion could be equated with Judah (e.g., Ps. 69:35; Jer. 14:19) or even with Israel (Isa. 46:13). On the other hand, Zion was no longer reckoned as the southeast hill but included the northeast hill with its temple buildings (cf. Ps. 2:6; 20:2). Yahweh is God on Zion (99:2; 135:21), and the Lord of hosts lives on Mount Zion (Jer. 8:19).

5. (a) The use of the names in Jud. does not differ from that of the OT. Jerusalem/Zion was the beloved city, toward which one turned one's face during the daily times of prayer (cf. Dan. 6:10). One went there on pilgrimage, whenever possible, at the great festivals (cf. Acts 2:5), and one wanted to die and be buried there. Huge sums of money flowed to Jerusalem from the Diaspora as temple tax.

(b) Eschatological ideas were also formed. Alongside the concept that the earthly city would be the scene of Yahweh's victory (2 Esd. 13:25–38; *Sib. Or.* 3:663–704) there developed in apocalyptic lit. a belief in the heavenly, preexistent Jerusalem (2 Bar. 4:2–7), which

would descend to earth at the end of the age (2 Esd. 10:27, 54; 13:36). The new Zion/Jerusalem will be of unimaginable beauty (Tob. 13:16–17), inhabited by vast multitudes (*Sib. Or.* 5:251–68) and ruled over by God himself (3:787).

NT 1. In the NT the name Jerusalem occurs 139x. As in the LXX we meet the two forms *Ierousalēm* (76x) and *Hierosolyma* (63x). The name *Siōn* occurs only 7x in the NT, mostly in quotes from the OT (only Heb. 12:22 and Rev. 14:1 use it independently).

2. (a) In the Synoptics and Acts Jerusalem frequently denotes simply the city. However, a theologically significant idea is often linked to this geographical name. To the theocratically minded Jew Jerusalem was God's choice to be the focus of the world. Yahweh, who alone rules, exercised his sovereignty there through two institutions: the priesthood (which performed the sacrifices) and the scribes or rabbis (who knew and expounded the Scriptures). Thus, Jerusalem was "the city of the great King" (Matt. 5:35; cf. Ps. 48:2), where the temple stood, in which the only valid sacrificial service was maintained.

(b) Because Jerusalem had this theocratic significance, it played a decisive role in the events of Jesus' passion. Jesus had to go to Jerusalem in order to fulfill his mission there at the center of the Jewish world (Matt. 16:21; Lk. 9:31, 51). There Jesus confronted the priests as functionaries of the cult (cf. Lk. 19:45–48) and the scribes as keepers of the Mosaic tradition (Matt. 23). It is significant that Jerusalem was the place where Jesus suffered, died, was buried, and rose again. His sacrifice made sense and was effective only in Jerusalem (Mk. 10:33–34). What a paradox that the sacrifice was rejected by the theocratic institutions while being accepted by God.

3. Jerusalem is esp. important in the theology of Lk. He begins and ends his Gospel with activities in Jerusalem and in its temple (Lk. 1:5–25; 24:53); Acts continues in this direction. Jesus' disciples, to whom he appeared after his resurrection, remained at his express command in Jerusalem (Lk. 24:49, 52), waiting for the outpouring of the Holy Spirit (Acts 1:4; 2:1–4). In accordance with their commission they proclaimed the divine events to all peoples, beginning from Jerusalem (Lk. 24:47; Acts 5:20–21). The city remained central to God's people. The so-called apostolic council, for example, gathered within its walls (Acts 15:1–33; cf. 21:18).

4. One must mention, however, another concept in the Synoptics that corresponds to the OT prophetic message of Jerusalem as the evil city. It kills God's messengers (Matt. 23:37–39). A prophet is nowhere more in danger than in Jerusalem (Lk. 13:33). The city does not recognize what belongs to its peace (19:42). Its inhabitants have not wanted to be gathered (Matt. 23:37). Therefore, it comes under judgment (Lk. 19:43–44), which will be carried out by means of foreign peoples (21:20). Jerusalem will be destroyed (Matt. 23:38; Lk. 21:24), so that the discerning should weep (Lk. 23:28–31).

This judgment on Jerusalem begins when the temple veil is torn in two (Matt. 27:51) at Jesus' death and the graves outside the city are opened (27:52–53). But something new arises from the ruins. Jesus will return to the destroyed city and be greeted with a cry that welcomes the Messiah (Matt. 23:39, citing Ps. 118:26).

5. (a) In Jn. Jerusalem is not only the scene of the passion but also the place where Jesus reveals his glory, since many deeds and miracles take place there. Jn. alone records that Jesus frequently came from Galilee to Jerusalem (2:13–17; 5:1–2; 7:1–10; 12:12–15).

(b) Paul was born at Tarsus (Acts 21:39; 22:3), but most likely Jerusalem was the scene of his boyhood and upbringing. For him as well, Jerusalem is the center of Christendom, but in a different sense from the Synoptics and Acts. The gospel went out from Jerusalem (Rom. 15:19) and has brought into being a new unity between Gentiles and Jews, the *ekklēsia* (cf. Eph. 2:14). Paul emphasizes his agreement with the apostolic council in Jerusalem (Gal. 2:1–10). But he does not view this as the highest authority. If he seeks out the apostles (cf. Gal. 1:18–20), it is out of brotherly love and respect; for they preceded him chronologically (1:17–18). But he received his commission and instructions, like the others, from the Lord himself (1:1; 2:2).

Because Gentile Christians have received a share in the spiritual blessings of the original church in Jerusalem, it was natural for Paul that these churches should "share with them [that is, the Jerusalem church] their material blessings" in the form of financial help (Rom. 15:27). We should view Paul's collection as the legitimization of the Gentile Christian churches toward Jerusalem and the external documentation of the interdependence of Gentile Christianity and the original Jerusalem church (cf. also 2 Cor. 8:14–15; 9:12).

(c) Rev. describes Jerusalem (without mention of the name) as the historical scene of the passion (11:8), itself involved in the events of the end. As the wicked city ("which is figuratively called Sodom and Egypt," 11:8), it will be trampled on, while the temple and those who worship in it will be saved (11:1–12; cf. Lk. 21:24). In Rev. 14:1 the OT name for the temple hill, Mount Zion, occurs.

6. Apart from the topographical uses of the name indicated so far, there also occurs in the NT the idea of the heavenly Jerusalem. (a) In Gal. 4:26 Paul speaks of "Jerusalem that is above," which, according to an allegorical interpretation, is the free woman who gave birth to believers. In Jewish apocalyptic tradition heavenly Jerusalem was the preexistent place where God's glory was always present. For Paul it was also the place of freedom from the law. This "Jerusalem that is above" forms a sharp contrast to "the present city of Jerusalem," which is called the mother of unbelievers (4:25).

(b) Heb. 12:22 speaks of "the heavenly Jerusalem," within which Mount Zion is situated. This is the place to which believers have come through their relationship with Jesus and the new covenant.

(c) In Rev. 3:12; 21:2 the "new Jerusalem" is described as a heavenly city. At the end of the age it will descend from heaven as the bride of the exalted Christ and receive as its citizens all those who have been marked as conquerors (3:12). This beautiful city (21:2, 10–11) is of vast extent (21:12–16), but one thing is absent from it: the temple, "because the Lord God Almighty and the Lamb are its temple" (21:22). This view forms a contrast with Jewish expectations in which the temple will mark the focal point of heavenly Jerusalem.

2648 (hierōsynē, priestly office, priesthood), → *2636.*

2652	Ἰησοῦς

Ἰησοῦς (*Iēsous*), Jesus (*2652*).

OT *Iēsous* is the Gk. form of the OT Jewish name *Yēšûaʿ*, arrived at by transcribing the Heb. and adding a nom. -*s* to facilitate declension. *Yēšûaʿ* (Joshua) seems to have come into general use about the time of the Babylonian exile in place of the older *Yᵉhôšuaʿ*. The LXX rendered both the ancient and more recent forms of the name uniformly as *Iēsous*. Joshua the son of Nun, who was Moses' successor and completed the occupation of the promised land by the tribes of Israel, appears under this name (cf. Exod. 17:8–16; Num. 11:27–29; Deut. 31:3, 7–8, 23; 34:9; book of Joshua). The name means "Yahweh is help" or "Yahweh is salvation" (cf. the vb. *yāšaʿ*, help, save).

Among Palestinian Jews and also among the Jews of the Diaspora the name Jesus was fairly widely distributed in the pre-Christian period and in the early part of the Christian era. Note Jesus ben Sirach, the author of the book of Sirach in the Apocr. (cf. Sir. 50:27). The name Jesus occurs in the writings of Josephus (1st cent. A.D.) no less that 19x, including "Jesus the so-called Christ" (*Ant.* 20.9.1). The name also occurs in numerous nonliterary Jewish texts, among them inscriptions on graves and ossuaries from the area of Jerusalem.

NT 1. The NT also shows the name Jesus widely spread among the Jews at the time of Jesus of Nazareth and his disciples. Thus, in Lk.'s genealogy of Jesus (3:29) it is borne by one of his ancestors, without the fact being noted as anything extraordinary. Col. 4:11 mentions a Jewish Christian man named Jesus, who also had a second, non-

Semitic name, Justus. Moreover, the OT Joshua appears in the NT as *Iēsous* (Acts 7:45; Heb. 4:8).

Some text traditions of the NT show a tendency to no longer use the name Jesus (e.g., the Western text of Acts 13:6). The motive here is clearly deep reverence for the name Jesus; no one other than Jesus could have the name of "the author and perfecter of our faith" (Heb. 12:2). This reverence led rapidly to the almost general renunciation on the part of Christians of its further secular use.

But it is no less significant that by the end of the 1st cent. Jesus had become uncommon as a personal name among Jews as well. In its place the OT name *Yᵉhôšuaʿ* reappeared, with *Iasōn* as the Gk. equivalent. Talmudic Jud. soon accustomed itself, when it was obliged to name Jesus of Nazareth, to referring to him as *Yešû* and not as *Yēšûaʿ*. Although the reason for this may lie in the purely external fact that the Christians referred to their Lord as *Yešû*, it is also an expression, not only of Jewish antipathy, but also of how far this name had become unique to the Christians.

2. According to the NT, Jesus' name was determined by heavenly instruction to the father (Matt. 1:21) and the mother (Lk. 1:31). Matt. also gives an interpretation of the name Jesus: to "save his people from their sins." This interpretation is certainly linked with the meaning of the Heb. name *Yᵉhôšuaʿ* (see above). In Matt. 1:21, of course, perhaps under the influence of Ps. 130:8, salvation is defined as forgiving the people's sins. What was formerly reserved for God is attributed to Jesus.

The same understanding of the name Jesus and a corresponding testimony probably lies behind Lk. 2:11, where the angel of the Lord on the night of Jesus' birth announced Jesus to the shepherds as *sōtēr*, Savior (cf. 1:77). In this regard one should not overlook the fact that Lk. particularly emphasizes Jesus as the Savior of sinners (cf. Lk. 15). In these texts, therefore, we have an early Christology, with a similar theological approach as in Phil. 2:9. The name Jesus already contains what is later fulfilled in the title "Lord," applied to the risen and glorified Jesus of Nazareth for the salvation of all humanity.

See also *Nazarēnos,* Nazarene, from Nazareth (*3716*); *Christos,* Christ (*5986*); *Christianos,* Christian (*5985*).

2653	ἱκανός

ἱκανός (*hikanos*), enough, worthy, able, competent, qualified (*2653*); ἱκανότης (*hikanotēs*), ability, competence (*2654*); ἱκανόω (*hikanoō*), enable, make sufficient, qualify (*2655*).

CL & OT 1. In cl. Gk. *hikanos,* found only from the time of the Gk. tragic poets on, conveys the idea of attaining a fixed goal, realizing a set purpose, and means adequate, sufficient, large enough, or numerous enough.

2. (a) In the LXX *hikanos* generally means sufficient, enough: what craftsmen need for their work (Exod. 36:7); a brother's need of help (Lev. 25:25–28); and what is needed to ward off hunger (Prov. 25:16), to offer a sacrifice (Lev. 5:7), or to bring down divine judgment (Obad. 5). Here then it is no longer a result being assessed as to whether it reaches a given standard; the whole reference is to a person and his or her needs. The sense of the word has shifted from that of obj. measurement (to suffice, be enough) to the personal idea of to need, stand in need of.

(b) It is also striking that the LXX translates the Almighty God not only by the word *pantokratōr*, but also by *ho hikano*, the sufficient one. Perhaps this arose because of a misreading of the Heb. word for Almighty (*šadday*). Note that the Heb. word for sufficiency or need is *day* and for "who" is sometimes *še*. If *šadday* is divided into *še* and *day*, it then means "one who is sufficient" (see LXX of Ruth 1:20–21; Job 21:15; 31:2; 40:2 = LXX 39:32; Ezek. 1:24). Yahweh does not have to conform to some external standard or ideal; rather, he himself sets the standard for himself and hence also for his creation.

NT 1. The NT use of the *hikanos* word group comes largely from the language of Hellenism and Hel. Jud. By far the most instances (27 out

of 39x) occur in Lk.'s writings, where *hikanos* almost always means much, considerable, applied either to time (e.g., Lk. 8:27) or numbers (e.g., Acts 11:24); nothing of theological importance arises here except in the difficult saying of Christ concerning the two swords (Lk. 22:38).

Having originally sent his apostles forth on their preaching mission without any external means of protection (cf. Lk. 22:35), Jesus now urges them to show courage and endurance in the face of trials. The swords of 22:38 are not intended for use, as Lk. 22:49–51 indicates. Rather, the apostles are to have the courage of "sword-bearers," men who are ready to risk their lives for a cause. Since Jesus perceives that this is their intention, he says, "That is enough."

2. Almost all other instances of *hikanos* in the NT occur in Paul. Taken in connection with Matt. 8:8 and Mk. 1:7, they indicate the development of an early Christian language of confession: I am not worthy, nor is anyone worthy (2 Cor. 2:16; 3:5), to be an apostle (1 Cor. 15:9), to be a minister of the new covenant (2 Cor. 3:6), or to serve Christ (Mk. 1:7). I am not worthy of his presence (Matt. 8:8), which transforms me into his likeness (cf. 1 Cor. 11:1). It is entirely of God's grace that we are able to do anything (2 Cor. 3:5–6; Col. 1:12: *hikanotēs* and *hikanoō*).

By contrast, 2 Tim. 2:2 clearly indicates that in the later NT period certain gifts, esp. faithfulness, made some more competent to teach than others. But this in no way obscured the conviction that the Christian's sufficiency is always the gift of God. Paul, who is thoroughly conversant with Gk. usage where *hikanos* means considerable (e.g., of numbers, 1 Cor. 11:30), follows the LXX in its use of the word to translate Heb. *day*, need. A Christian's own worth is meaningless when it comes to one's sufficiency before God. Works acceptable to God are not those performed for God, but only those that he himself requires and that the Christian therefore receives from his hand (cf. Exod. 4:10–12).

See also *arkeō*, be enough, suffice, be adequate (758).

2654 (*hikanotēs*, ability, competence), → 2653.

2655 (*hikanoō*, enable, make sufficient, qualify), → 2653.

2656 (*hiketēria*, supplication), → 1289.

2661	ἱλάσκομαι

ἱλάσκομαι (*hilaskomai*), propitiate, expiate, conciliate, make gracious, be gracious (2661); ἵλεως (*hileōs*), gracious, merciful (2664); ἱλασμός (*hilasmos*), propitiation, propitiatory sacrifice (2662); ἱλαστήριον (*hilastērion*), that which expiates or propitiates, means of propitiation, atonement cover (2663).

CL & OT 1. (a) In cl. Gk. the adj. *hileōs* originally meant cheerful, joyous; then later, gracious, benevolent. It was chiefly used of rulers or gods. *hilaskomai* (mid. deponent) has a causative meaning: to make gracious, appease; the aor. pass. *hilasthēnai* should be translated in an intrans. mid. sense: to let oneself be appeased, to have mercy. The subj. is generally a human and the obj. a deity; the setting is usually a cultic act by which a deity is appeased. If a human is the obj., the vb. means to conciliate or bribe. The noun *hilasmos* is rare in cl. Gk. and found mainly in late lit. It denotes the action by which a deity is to be propitiated. *to hilastērion* is the neut. adjectival noun from *hilastērios*; on Gk. inscriptions it means a propitiatory gift for the gods.

(b) The basic idea behind *hilasmos* is a human effort to dispose in one's favor the awful and frequently calamitous power of the dead, of demons, and of the gods, and to strengthen one's own power by the assistance of supernatural forces. This presupposes some knowledge of the threat posed to human existence by the envy, punishment, and baseless anger of the all-powerful gods. The propitiation of deities is accomplished by means of cultic acts, including human or animal sacrifice, purificatory rites, prayers, and dances.

In later, more enlightened times the power of the gods lost some of its terror, so that the significance of propitiatory rites diminished.

In Stoicism cultic rites are replaced by the moral person, who keeps in line with the will of the deity through ethical behavior.

2. (a) In contrast to cl. Gk. usage, *hileōs* with *eimi* or *ginomai* in the LXX means to be or become gracious, translating primarily the Heb. vb. *sālaḥ*, to forgive (15x; e.g., 1 Ki. 8:30, 34, 36; 2 Chr. 6:21; Jer. 5:1). *hileōs* occurs in the LXX only as a predicate of God.

(b) The vb. *hilaskomai* occurs only 11x in the LXX, always in a mid. or pass. sense and always with Yahweh as subj. It means to have mercy; 7x it translates the Heb. *sālaḥ*, to forgive (e.g., 2 Ki. 5:18; Ps. 25:11). But in six of these passages there is implicit or explicit mention of divine wrath (Exod. 32:14, cf. 32:11; 2 Ki. 24:3–4; Ps. 78:38; 79:9; Lam. 3:42; Dan. 9:19, Theod., cf. 9:16).

(c) The compound *exhilaskomai* occurs 105x in the LXX, mostly for the Heb. vb. *kipper*, to cover, propitiate, atone. Occasionally this vb. has the sense of purify (of objects, e.g., Ezek. 43:20, 22, 26) or entreat favor (e.g., of a person, Zech. 7:2; 8:22; Mal. 1:9). But in most cases the subj. of *exhilaskomai* is a human (the priest) and the obj. God, and the process is a cultic act. In Sir., sin is the obj. (e.g., 20:28), and the subj. is either God (5:6; 34:19 = LXX 31:19) or a human (3:3, 30; 20:28). In a noncultic sense, Gen. 32:20 and Prov. 16:14 clearly use *exhilaskomai* in the sense of appeasing anger.

(d) The LXX uses *hilasmos* (10x) to translate derivatives of the Heb. vb. *kipper* (piel), to cover over, pacify, propitiate, which describe the process of propitiation (sacrificial propitiation in the cult, e.g., Lev. 25:9; Num. 5:8).

(e) The LXX uses *hilastērion* 20x for Heb. *kappōret*, which may be rendered propitiatory or mercy seat, or atonement cover (e.g., Exod. 25:17–22; 31:7; 35:12; Lev. 16:2, 13–15; Num. 7:89). It designates the slab of gold placed on top of the ark of the testimony, on which were two cherubim, whose outstretched wings came together and formed the throne of Yahweh. When the high priest entered the Most Holy Place on the Day of Atonement (Lev. 16), this holiest place had to be enveloped in a cloud of incense. Then the blood of the sin offering of atonement was sprinkled on and before the *hilastērion*.

3.(a) Sacrificial rites were widespread throughout the ancient world. In some OT writings the notion of propitiating an angry deity receives emphasis (e.g., 1 Sam. 26:19; cf. also Gen. 8:20–21; 2 Sam. 24:17–25). Yahweh needs to be propitiated because of human sin (cf., e.g., Isa. 43:22–25).

(b) The Israelite concept of propitiation can therefore be understood only against the background of the OT doctrine of sin (→ *adikia*, 94). An offense (even if unwitting) against Yahweh's covenant laws gives rise to objective guilt (cf. 1 Sam. 14:2–44), which sets in motion a destructive force whose disastrous effects fall of necessity as punishment on the miscreant and his or her affairs. This chain of sin and disaster can be halted only by Yahweh, who diverts the evil effect of a misdeed from the doer to an animal, which dies in his place—the classic example being the ritual of the scapegoat given to Azazel on the Day of Atonement (Lev. 16:20–22).

In this act, the subject who brings about the atonement is Yahweh. The priests function merely as his representatives in the cultic action (cf. Exod. 28:38; Num. 18:22–23), while the wrongdoer or the sinful people are the recipients of the atonement. According to the OT, life is carried in the blood, and thus blood acts as the means of atonement (Lev. 17:11; cf. 17:14; Gen. 9:4; Deut. 12:23; see below).

4. In discussing reconciliation and atonement scholars have drawn a distinction between propitiation and expiation. In propitiation the action is directed toward God or some other offended person, and the underlying purpose is to change an attitude of wrath into one of favor. In expiation, however, the action is directed toward that which has caused the breakdown in the relationship; the defilement of an offensive act is removed through some act of expiation.

(a) The writers of the OT did not manifest a crude pagan idea of propitiating a capricious and malevolent deity. Nor did they share a common quasi-mechanistic view of life in which the effects of sin could be nullified by resorting to the appropriate rite as an antidote.

There is a personal dimension that affected both the offending and the offended parties, which means that, when an *offense* has to be expiated, the action must be taken because the *personal relationship* between the parties requires it. That is, expiation has, as it were, the effect of propitiation; the sin that may have brought about God's wrath is expiated.

(b) A closer examination of the significance of blood in the OT further supports the idea of propitiation. Key here is Lev. 17:11: "For the life of a creature is in the blood, and I have given it to you to make atonement for yourselves on the altar; it is the blood that makes atonement for one's life" (cf. the related prohibition in 17:14; also Deut. 12:23). In many OT passages (e.g., Gen. 9:5–6; Num. 35:19; 2 Sam. 23:16–17; Ps. 72:14), blood means death rather than life. As long as the blood circulates in the animal or human being, there is life. When it no longer circulates, death ensues.

Taken in isolation, it is possible to construe certain passages that deal with atonement (e.g., Exod. 30:10; Lev. 16:27; 17:11) as offering the life of the victim. But it is equally possible to understand them as offering the *death* of the victim, whose life has been taken away. In various passages where atonement is effected by some means other than the cultus, it is the termination of life that brings about the atonement. In the original Passover, for example, the blood of a slain animal was the means of averting destruction (Exod. 12:13); a substitute death had taken place for the death of the firstborn. Note too how Moses sought atonement for the sin of the people by asking Yahweh to blot him out of God's book (Exod. 32:30–32; cf. also Deut. 21:1–9; 2 Sam. 21:3–4).

In the case of sacrifice within the cultus, atonement is effected not simply by offering the blood but by the offering of the whole sacrifice (Ezek. 45:17). Different parts of the slain animal could be associated with atonement: e.g., the head (Lev. 1:4) and the burning of the fat (4:26). In some cases where atonement is spoken of, blood appears to be excluded altogether (e.g., Exod. 29:33; Lev. 10:17–18). In other places atonement is connected with ceremonies like the pouring of oil on the head of a cleansed leper (14:18, 29), the offering of incense (Num. 16:46), and the scapegoat (Lev. 16:10).

In other words, where blood is mentioned in the OT, the thought that is uppermost is not the blood itself but the shedding of the blood, as a symbol of the termination of life; and where blood is linked with sacrifice or atonement, the thought is that of the death of the victim. Such acts are not arbitrary but are required because Yahweh is who he is.

NT In view of the frequent occurrence of cultic terms using this word group in the LXX, it comes as a surprise to find how rarely the NT uses these words. Each of the four terms is used only twice, so that the whole group of words appears only 8x in the NT (3x in Heb.).

1. (a) *hileōs* appears in Matt. 16:22 as a negative exclamation in Peter's rebuke of Jesus when the latter told him of his impending death at Jerusalem: "Never, Lord! . . . This shall never happen to you!" The Gk. translated "Never, Lord" is *hileōs soi, kyrie* (lit., "gracious to you, Lord"); the words to be supplied or understood are *eiē ho theos* (i.e., "may God be"). For biblical parallels see Gen. 43:23; 2 Sam. 20:20; 1 Chr. 11:19.

(b) Heb. 8:12 comes at the end of a quotation from Jer. 31:31–34: "For I will forgive [lit., be gracious to, *hileōs*] their wickedness and will remember their sins no more." It concludes an argument that the new covenant has been inaugurated by Christ, that this is the covenant foretold by Jer., and therefore that "by calling this covenant 'new,' he had made the first one obsolete" (Heb. 8:13).

2. (a) It is striking that *exhilaskomai*, the primary vb. in the LXX, does not occur in the NT. The aor. pass. of *hilaskomai* is used in Lk. 18:13 in the tax collector's prayer in the temple: "God, have mercy on me, a sinner"; the thought is similar to that of Ps. 79:9, where the same vb. is used. It can be rendered as both "be propitious" and "be merciful." The tax collector felt the need for a forgiveness that only God himself could bestow—and he cries out for mercy.

Jesus' rejoinder is contained in Lk. 18:14: "I tell you that this man, rather than the other [the Pharisee], went home justified before God" (on justification, → *ikaiosynē*, 1466). The Pharisee's attitude in Jesus' parable was not atypical of attitudes within Judaism. In the Talmud one rabbi was said to be confident that his righteousness was sufficient to exempt his whole generation from judgment. If the saved numbered only "a hundred, I and my son are among them; and if only two, they are I and my son" (*b. Sukkah* 45b). Similarly, in terms of performing acts understood as constituting righteousness, Paul declared himself "as for legalistic righteousness, faultless" (Phil. 3:6). According to Paul, justification is by faith related to the saving act of Christ on the cross (Rom. 3:20–27).

In sum, the parable in Lk. 18:9–14 focuses on two aspects: From a human side, what matters is a heartfelt turning to God, which simply casts oneself on God's mercy; on God's side, human self-righteousness is of no avail, but God has mercy on the ungodly who turn to him for mercy.

(b) Heb. 2:17 takes up the cultic ritual of the Day of Atonement: "For this reason he [Jesus] had to be made like his brothers in every way, in order that he might become a merciful and faithful high priest in service to God, and that he might make atonement [*hilaskomai*] for the sins of the people" (cf. Lev. 16:14–17). Note the NIV footnote here, "and that he might turn aside God's wrath, taking away the sins of the people." Jesus is portrayed as a faithful high priest (cf. 1 Sam. 2:35) who atones for the sins of the people. His death and exaltation are interpreted in terms of the annual Day of Atonement ritual, which is seen as a type of Jesus' reconciling work and which is thus rendered obsolete by the fulfillment that comes with Jesus.

The author here points out that Jesus stands as a high priest in the service of God. While there is no explicit reference to appeasement of an angry deity and God is not said to be the recipient of the atonement, when we look at this passage against the wider background of personal relations with Yahweh in the OT or the more specific background of the Day of Atonement ritual, the reason why guilt has to be dealt with lies in the character of God himself, who is angry with our sins and requires a substitute sacrifice. He is both the provider and the recipient of the reconciliation.

3. The noun *hilasmos* occurs only in 1 Jn. "He is the atoning sacrifice [*hilasmos*] for our sins, and not only for ours but also for the sins of the whole world" (2:2). "This is love: not that we loved God, but that he loved us and sent his Son as the atoning sacrifice [*hilasmos*] for our sins" (4:10). Note again the NIV footnote in both of these verses, that Jesus is "the one who turns aside God's wrath." The decision whether to translate *hilasmos* by "expiation" (RSV; note that the NRSV uses "atoning sacrifice") or "propitiation" must be decided against the background of the considerations already discussed (see OT section). But as with other OT and NT passages concerning reconciliation, it is not a matter of applying some impersonal antidote. The question at issue is our personal relationship with God and that which hinders this relationship must be dealt with for God's part just as much as for ours (cf. 1 Jn. 1:5–10; 4:7–10, 13–21).

In 1 Jn. 1, the author outlines what it is that makes atonement for our sins—the death of Christ: "But if we walk in the light, as he is in the light, we have fellowship with one another, and the blood of Jesus, his Son, purifies us from all sin" (1:7). Jesus' death (referred to by the word "blood") is the basis on which we are purified whenever we confess our sins: "If we confess our sins, he is faithful and just and will forgive us our sins and purify us from all unrighteousness" (1:9). Jn. does not set out the need for a *hilasmos*. For him it is self-evident in the light of the character of God and the coming judgment (4:17). Note also that atonement is not regarded as something that we do to God, but rather as an expression of God's love for us (4:10).

4. (a) In the description of the ark of the covenant located in the Most Holy Place of the tabernacle, Heb. 9:1–5 calls the top of it the *hilastērion*, i.e., "the atonement cover" or "the mercy seat" (Heb. 9:5a;

cf. Exod. 25:18–22; 37:7–9). This, as noted above, is the word used in the LXX.

(b) The interpretation of Rom. 3:25 has been the subject of significant debate. It stands at the center of Paul's statement of God's righteousness in the face of human sin. Gentiles stand condemned apart from the law (1:18–32; cf. 2:12); Jews are condemned by the law (2:1–3:20). "But now a righteousness from God, apart from law, has been made known, to which the Law and the Prophets testify. This righteousness from God comes through faith in Jesus Christ to all who believe. There is no difference, for all have sinned and fall short of the glory of God, and are justified freely by his grace through the redemption that came by Christ Jesus. God presented him as a sacrifice of atonement [*hilastērion*], through faith in his blood" (3:21–25).

What does *hilastērion* mean here? In spite of objections, it seems best to relate this to the Day of Atonement ritual as described in Lev. 16. Paul is suggesting here that what the atonement cover meant for the removal of sins in the OT ritual, Christ is the new covenant equivalent, the antitype of the OT type. In other words, Christ now occupies the place that the *hilastērion* occupied in the OT—the central place where atonement occurs that restores the relationship between God and his people.

We must not forget that the overall context for Rom. 3:21–25 is 1:18–3:20, which begins: "The wrath of God is being revealed from heaven against all the godlessness and wickedness of men who suppress the truth by their wickedness" (1:18). Somewhere, somehow, that wrath needs to be propitiated, and the apostle affirms that it is through the "atoning sacrifice" of Christ that this indeed takes place. In sum, therefore, Jesus Christ is the person whom God has set forth or "presented" as a propitiatory sacrifice, and we can receive the benefits of that sacrifice through faith in the atoning power of his blood.

See also *apokatastasis*, restoration (*640*); *katallassō*, reconcile (*2904*).

2662 (hilasmos, propitiation, propitiatory sacrifice), → *2661.*

2663 (hilastērion, that which expiates or propitiates, atonement cover), → *2661.*

2664 (hileōs, gracious, merciful), → *2661.*

| 2668 | ἱμάτιον |

ἱμάτιον (*himation*), garment (*2668*).

CL & OT 1. In cl. Gk. *himation* (technically a diminutive of *heima*) means garment, article of clothing.

2. (a) In the LXX *himation* means both the outer garment and clothes as a whole. Clothes were often torn as a mark of sorrow (Jdg. 11:35). Because of what happens to clothing, it is easy to see that a garment can become a symbol of the transient (Isa. 50:9; 51:6, 8) as well as of God's salvation and protection (61:10; cf. Gen. 3:21).

(b) In the rab. writings clothing is used as a metaphor for repentance, the fulfilling of the commandments, good works, and the study of the Torah, which one wraps oneself in as a garment or armor. In *1 Enoch* the garment is used as a symbol of salvation.

NT *himation* is used 60x in the NT. It is used lit. for clothing in general (cf. Matt. 27:31; Acts 9:39), and more esp. for the outer garment (cf. Matt. 9:20–21; Jn. 19:2). It is also used fig. or parabolically (Mk. 2:21; Heb. 1:11; cf. Matt. 22:11–12, *endyma*).

1. Sometimes what was done with clothes gave a special emphasis to what was being said. (a) People tore their garments as a sign of sorrow when they heard blasphemy (Matt. 26:65; Acts 14:14). Paul shook out his garments (18:6; cf. Neh. 5:13) to show that he no longer felt any responsibility for the hardened Jews of Corinth.

(b) In Mk. 11:7–8 the multitude used their garments as a saddle on the donkey and a carpet on the road of the divine rider in Jesus' triumphal entry. By this symbolic action Jesus was proclaimed king at his entry into Jerusalem. Jesus' kingship was mocked by the purple robe that the soldiers put on him (Jn. 19:2, 5).

2. (a) In Mk. 2:21–22 par., *himation* stands for the radical newness of Jesus' kingdom. The new cloth could not be used to patch old rags (the old way of life). In Heb. 1:11 (quoting Ps. 102:26), *himation* denotes the universe.

(b) The garment (*endyma*) is the symbol of the righteousness promised by God (Matt. 22:11–12). In the parable of the marriage feast, the wedding garment is a metaphor for forgiveness and the promised righteousness (cf. Isa. 61:10). Being clothed with this garment is thus a symbol of belonging to the community of the redeemed. In Rev. this eschatological dress takes the form of white garments (3:4, 5, 18) that are washed in the blood of the Lamb (7:14). White (→ *leukos*, *3328*) denotes purity.

See also *gymnos*, naked (*1218*); *dynō*, set, dress (*1544*).

| 2674 | Ἰορδάνης |

Ἰορδάνης (*Iordanēs*), the river Jordan (*2674*).

OT This was the Gk. name for the river that descended from Lake Huleh through the deepest valley depression on earth and ended in the Dead Sea. It was the principal river of Palestine. Of the OT incidents relating to the Jordan, its crossing by the Israelites was the most notable (Jos. 3:16). Its waters were also used in the miraculous healing of Naaman (2 Ki. 5:14).

NT In the NT, the celebrated river was the site of John the Baptist's ministry (Matt. 3:6; Mk. 1:5; Jn. 1:28; 3:26) and the place where Jesus was baptized (Matt. 3:13; Mk. 1:9; Lk. 4:1). Aside from references to Christ exercising his ministry on the far side of the Jordan (Matt. 19:1; Mk. 10:1) and returning on one occasion to the site of John's baptism spot (Jn. 10:40), there is no other NT passage that significantly involves the Jordan.

See also *thalassa*, sea, lake (*2498*); *pēgē*, spring, source (*4380*); *hydōr*, water (*5623*); *kataklysmos*, a deluge, flood (*2886*); *limnē*, lake (*3349*).

| 2675 | ἰός |

ἰός (*ios*), poison (*2675*).

CL & OT In cl. Gk. *ios* is used of a variety of poisons, esp. the poison of snakes. It is used also for rust on iron and for other chemical deposits, such as the patina on bronze statues. In the LXX *ios* means rust (Ezek. 24:6, 11–12) and poison (Ps. 140:3). It also occurs in Prov. 23:32 and Lam. 3:13, where it means an arrow.

NT In Rom. 3 Paul is concerned with the universality of sin. Quoting from Ps. 140:3 he writes, "the poison of vipers is on [sinners'] lips" (3:13). In his catena of quotations (3:10–18) Paul lays emphasis on the deadliness of wicked speech, referring to the throat, the tongue, the lips, and the mouth (feet and eyes are also mentioned).

James likewise finds "poison" an apt word for the untamed tongue, which is capable of all sorts of evil. The harm it causes makes it like "deadly poison" (Jas. 3:8). James uses the same word when he castigates the rich for their corroded gold and silver and sees the "corrosion" as something that will in due course eat them up (5:3). Gold and silver, of course, do not corrode, but James is speaking metaphorically, expressing forcefully the view that the treasures of the rich are tarnished and tainted.

2676 (Iouda, Judah), → *2677.*

| 2677 | Ἰουδαία |

Ἰουδαία (*Ioudaia*), Judea (*2677*); Ἰουδά (*Iouda*), Judah (*2676*); Ἰούδας (*Ioudas*), Judah, Judas, Jude (*2683*).

OT 1. *Iouda*, Judah, and *Ioudaia*, Judea (both for the Heb. *yᵉhûdâ*), occur as geographical terms for the mountainous desert region south of Jerusalem (Jos. 20:7; 21:11; Jdg. 1:16; Ps. 63:1). The tribe that settled there bore the name of Judah, the fourth son of Jacob and Leah (Gen. 29:35). The precise etymology is uncertain, though Gen. 29:35

suggests a link with *yādâ*, praise, in Leah's remark on the birth of her son, "'This time I will praise the LORD.' So she named him Judah."

2. The patriarch Judah seems to have held great influence among his brothers, as evidenced by their acquiescence to his wish that Joseph be sent to Egypt (Gen. 37:26–27) and by his acting as spokesman for them in Egypt (43:3–10; 44:16–34). Judah figures prominently in the blessing of Jacob, where he was promised a position of honor among his brothers as well as the prospect of sovereignty and dominion to be realized in a future king (49:10). The name Judah continued as the name of the tribe of which this son of Jacob was the progenitor.

3. The territory occupied by the tribe of Judah consisted mainly of the highland country in the area of Canaan westward from the Dead Sea. The territory extended to the Mediterranean Sea and was bounded on the north by the tribal territories of Benjamin and Dan. The Negev formed the southern boundary.

David, Israel's greatest king, came from the tribe of Judah. When the division of the united monarchy occurred, the southern kingdom became known as the kingdom of Judah, though elements in the tribe of Benjamin remained loyal to the house of David as well.

The kingdom of Judah's history was characterized by internal and external difficulties. Not all her kings were wise, though several made positive contributions to her welfare. During the reign of Uzziah (767–739 B.C.), the fortunes of Judah as well as of Israel were greatly enhanced by the quiescence of Assyria on the world scene. This period of affluence, however, belied an internal sickness, for the covenant stipulations were being violated, leading to societal wrongs that the 8th-cent. prophets warned would lead to her downfall.

Under Hezekiah (716–686 B.C.) a serious Assyrian incursion and siege of Jerusalem came to an end with the withdrawal of the Assyrian forces. While Hezekiah's foreign policy was, at times, unwise (Isa. 30:15), his contribution to the kingdom of Judah was generally commendable. Following Hezekiah's reign the fortunes of Judah began to suffer again. Nebuchadnezzar, king of Babylon, extracted tribute from Judah for some time after his rise to power in 605 B.C. After several rebellions against Babylon, successive attacks ultimately led to the end of Judah as a kingdom in 587 B.C.

NT 1. In Matt. 2:5–6, *Iouda* occurs in the sense of the territory of Judah (Judea), the place where Bethlehem was located (the quote from Mic. 5:2 determines that *Iouda* rather than *Ioudaia* be used). In Lk. 1:39 the virgin Mary heads to a town of *Iouda*, where Elizabeth lived. Since Lk. invariably uses *Ioudaia* for the Roman province of Judea, it seems likely that *Iouda* here is a town now unknown.

Heb. 7:14 makes reference to the descent of Christ from the tribe of Judah, a tribe with no priestly prerogatives. The point is made that the Levitical priesthood was unable to achieve perfection for its adherents, hence the need for another priest. This represents a change in the law (7:12), for Christ did not descend from the tribe of Levi, which, according to the law, was the tribe from which the priests were to be chosen.

In Heb. 8:8 the house of Judah is cited along with the house of Israel to represent the whole nation. The reference here is to the two kingdoms of the divided monarchy and occurs in a quotation from Jer. 31:31–34, where the new covenant is predicted.

In Rev. 5:5 Christ's descent from the tribe of Judah is reflected in the appellation "Lion of the tribe of Judah." In 7:5, the tribe of Judah is cited along with other tribes with whom the group numbering 144,000 is associated.

2. *Ioudas* occurs as the name of several individuals in the NT. (a) The name is used for the fourth son of Jacob (Matt. 1:2–3; Lk. 3:33–34; see OT, above).

(b) *Ioudas* was the name of another ancestor of Christ (Lk. 3:30), who was the son of a certain Joseph.

(c) One of the brothers of Jesus was named Judas (Matt. 13:55; Mk. 6:3). This Judas is considered by some to be the author of the NT letter of Jude (Jude 1:1). Most scholars think that this Judas was a child of Mary and Joseph, although a few scholars suggest he was the son of Joseph from a previous marriage or else a cousin of Jesus (taking *adelphos*, brother, in the general sense of relative).

(d) Judas son of James was one of the twelve apostles (Lk. 6:16; Acts 1:13). He was one of the group who engaged in prayer in the upper room after Jesus' ascension.

(e) The most well-known Judas is Judas Iscariot, who betrayed Jesus (Matt. 10:4; Mk. 3:19; Lk. 6:16). The meaning of Iscariot is not clear. It may have been a Hellenization of the Heb. "man of Qerioth." His betrayal of Jesus was decisively carried out after Jesus said to him, "What you are about to do, do quickly" (Jn. 13:26–30). After an unsuccessful effort to atone for his wrong by returning the money paid him for his treachery, Judas hanged himself (Matt. 27:5).

(f) A certain Judas, surnamed "the Galilean," participated in an insurrection during a tax census under Quirinius (Acts 5:37).

(g) Judas of Damascus gave Saul of Tarsus lodging after the latter's vision on the road to Damascus (Acts 9:11). It was there that Ananias was to go to find Saul.

(h) Judas Barsabbas was chosen by the Jerusalem council along with Silas to accompany Paul and Barnabas to Antioch (Acts 15:22) to substantiate the council's decision.

See also *Israēl*, Israel (2702); *Iakōb*, Jacob (2609).

2680 (Ioudaïkōs, Jewish), → 2702.

2681 (Ioudaios, Jew), → 2702.

2682 (Ioudaïsmos, Judaism), → 2702.

2683 (Ioudas, Judah, Judas, Jude), → 2677.

2692 (iris, rainbow), → 847.

2693	Ἰσαάκ		Ἰσαάκ (*Isaak*), Isaac (2693).

OT The son of Abraham's old age, whose name means "he laughs" (Gen. 17:17–19; 18:12–15; 21:6, 9). Isaac is a less colorful individual than the other patriarchs, but he has an important place as the child of promise in the theological development of the tradition. His birth (21:1–7) is the first step toward the fulfillment of the promise of 12:1–3 and a refutation of the human impatience that produced Ishmael.

The questions of faith in the promise and obedience to the God of the promise underlie the challenge of the sacrifice of Isaac (Gen. 22:1–19). The remaining Isaac narratives trace the next steps in the development of the promise—the marriage to Rebekah (24:62–67) and the births of Esau and Jacob (25:19–28). His success is viewed as a mark of God's special blessing (26:12–13, 29). In Amos 7:9, 16, Isaac is a synonym for the nation Israel.

NT In the NT Isaac occurs in genealogies (Matt. 1:2; Lk. 3:34) and in formal conjunction with other patriarchs (Matt. 8:11; 22:32; Mk. 12:26; Lk. 13:28; 20:37; Acts 3:13; 7:8, 32). Like Sarah he figures in the Pauline argument for the freedom of God's electing purpose (Rom. 9:7, 10), and like Hagar in the allegorical proof that Christians are the children of promise (Gal. 4:28). The letter to the Heb. follows the theological pattern of the Genesis traditions, seeing Isaac as heir to the promise (11:9), the testing ground for Abraham's faith (11:17–18), and the one who handed on the blessings of the promise to the next generation (11:20). Jas. uses the sacrifice of Isaac to demonstrate the necessity of works (obedience) as well as faith (belief) (2:21). The tendency to see in the sacrifice of Isaac a type of Christ's death is a feature of later Christian interpretation.

See also *Abraam*, Abraham (*11*); *Sarra*, Sarah (*4925*); *Hagar*, Hagar (*29*).

2694 (isangelos, like an angel), → 34.

2698	ἴσος

ἴσος (isos), equal, corresponding to (2698); ἰσότης (isotēs), equality, fairness (2699); ἰσότιμος (isotimos), of equal value (2700); ἰσόψυχος (isopsychos), of like soul or mind (2701).

CL & OT 1. (a) In cl. Gk. *isos* and *isotēs* in their earliest stage expressed a fundamental rule in the sharing of the booty of war, that there was not only an equality of quantity but also an equality of value of the objects divided up. From this, these two words came to denote numerical and physical equality (e.g., of number, value), substantial equality (e.g., of the copy with its original), and political and legal equality (e.g., Gk. democracy rested on the principle that all citizens possessed equal standing in society and enjoyed equal political and legal rights). By extension, *isos* became the expression for impartiality and meant essentially the same as *dikaios*, just.

(b) Behind the idea of legal equality and fairness lay fundamental philosophical convictions about the essential equality of all human beings. In Stoic ethics the thought of the homogeneity of humanity led to the leveling out of the natural differences in good or evil thoughts and deeds; good is good and evil is, without distinction, evil.

(c) As a principle of order *isotēs* meant cosmic harmony, the balancing of all forces. This cosmic principle is reflected in human striving for equality.

(d) This sense of equality, so strongly developed in Gk. intellectual life, led in Hellenism via the veneration of heroes to the doctrine of deification. In Gk. tragedies, for instance, heroes were believed to possess powers like the gods. An ideal of Gk. philosophy was to become as far as possible like god.

2. In the LXX *isos* and *isotēs* are infrequent. *isos* is used for the most part in comparisons such as similes (e.g., Job 5:14; 10:10; Ezek. 40:5–9). The Apocr. sometimes reflects the principle of equality of humanity through *isos* compounds: e.g., *isomoiros*, having an equal share (2 Macc. 8:30); *isopolitēs*, a full citizen with equal rights (3 Macc. 2:30). But there is nothing like the Gk. concept of equality between humans and the gods, because of the fundamental distance between God and his creatures. No mortal, for example, may dare wish to be God's equal (*isotheos*, 2 Macc. 9:12); not even the heavenly beings may be likened to him (*isoō*, Ps. 89:6).

3. Rab. Jud., with all its delight in the law and striving after faithfulness, championed the idea that, despite the different standards of fulfillment of the law in this life, in eternity all believers in the Messiah will receive equal rewards as a gift of grace. The Messiah will so lead his people that every member will be equal to all the others (*Pss. Sol.* 17:41–46).

NT In the NT the adj. *isos* occurs 8x, *isotēs* 3x, *isotimos* only in 2 Pet. 1:1, and *isopsychos* only in Phil. 2:20.

1. Some uses of *isos* remain within the framework of cl. Gk. The word marks equality of size (Lk. 6:34; Rev. 21:16) and conversely, at the trial of Jesus, the lack of unanimity in the evidence of the witnesses (Mk. 14:56, 59). In Phil. 2:20 Paul recommends Timothy to the congregation as a fully like-minded (*isopsychos*) and reliable colleague.

2. (a) The equality among Christians in salvation is experienced as a supernatural act, through one and the same experience of the Spirit, which removes all barriers between Jewish Christians and Gentiles (Acts 11:17; cf. 2 Pet. 1:1, *isotimos*, "as precious as," lit., "equal in value"). Jesus also notes a removal of differences with regard to the eschatological equality of Christians. All believers will receive the same reward (*misthos*, 3635) in heaven as a gift of grace, whether they entered the work in the vineyard early or late (Matt. 20:12).

(b) The existing social inequities of the members of the congregation, however, are not denied or simply removed. But the fellowship of poor and rich, of masters and slaves, receives new rules and standards through love as a new regulating principle of life among Christians. Thus masters should treat their slaves justly and with fairness (*isotēs*; Col. 4:1). They are no longer a possession subject to their master's caprice, but brothers in Christ. This principle of equality took concrete expression in the original community in Jerusalem in relations between the wealthy and the poor (Acts 2:44–45; 4:36–37). With these assumptions Paul appealed to the Corinthians to give of their own surplus to meet the economic lack of the community in Jerusalem, so "that there might be equality" (*isotēs*, 2 Cor. 8:13–14).

This new attitude of brotherly love means being free to love one's enemy. It surpasses the law of giving in order to get, which even sinners practice when they help one another, "expecting to be repaid in full [*isos*]" (Lk. 6:34).

(c) Though the word is not used, the apostle Paul makes it plain that the gifts of grace (*charismata*) are variously divided but have equality of value in Christ (Rom. 12:6–8; 1 Cor. 12:4–30; Eph. 4:16; cf. Matt. 25:14–15). The uniting force is love (1 Cor. 13).

3. Two passages speak of Jesus' equality with God. (a) In Jn. 5:16 Jesus has broken the Sabbath commandment. He defends himself by saying, "My Father is always at his work to this very day, and I, too, am working" (5:17). Thereupon the Jews try to kill him because by calling God his Father, he is "making himself equal with God"(5:18). In their own context they may have a point, but to Jesus, as the obedient Son, he is equal to the Father in the harmony of their will and their working (5:19–44).

(b) The hymn to Christ in Phil. 2:6–11 contains the assertion that Jesus "did not consider equality [*isa*] with God something to be grasped" (2:6). On the one hand, since this passage deals with historical sequencing in the life of Jesus, we should not treat this phrase in isolation, as if it were an ontological statement about equality with God possessed by the preexistent Jesus. The striking point is that the Preexistent One entered without reserve into the sphere of humanity, death, and historical existence in all its ambiguity. On the other hand, this passage is not just a statement of Jesus' exemplary obedience (2:8) or model humility, but objectively of incarnation from his status as "being in very nature God." Paul's message here involves Jesus' renouncing the glory of divine status and living under the conditions of a fully human existence.

See also *homoios*, like, of the same nature, similar (3927).

2699 (*isotēs*, equality, fairness), → 2698.

2700 (*isotimos*, of equal value), → 2698.

2701 (*isopsychos*, of like soul or mind), → 2698.

2702	Ἰσραήλ

Ἰσραήλ (*Israēl*), Israel (2702); Ἰσραηλίτης (*Israēlitēs*), Israelite (2703); Ἰουδαῖος (*Ioudaios*), Jew (2681); Ἰουδαϊσμός (*Ioudaïsmos*), Jew (2682); Ἰουδαϊκῶς (*Ioudaïkōs*), Jewish (2680); Ἑβραῖος (*Hebraios*), Hebrew (noun) (1578); Ἑβραΐς (*Hebraïs*), Hebrew (fem. adj.) (1579).

OT 1. The name "Israel" (Heb. *yiśrā'ēl*) is formed from the noun *'ēl* (God) and a verbal predicate. An explanation of it is given in Gen. 32:28 in the context of the story of Jacob's (→ *Iakōb*, 2609) wrestling with God: "Your name will no longer be Jacob, but Israel, because you have struggled with God and with men and have overcome" (cf. Hos. 12:4). Hence, the name has been interpreted to mean *He who strives with God* (the vb. being *śārar*, to rule, or *śārâ*, contend, fight). This interpretation is supported by the story. But since elsewhere *'ēl* is never the obj. in proper names, but is always the subj., the meaning *God strives* has also been put forward.

"Israel" thus began in the OT as a personal name (e.g., Gen. 50:2; Exod. 1:1; 1 Chr. 1:34). But it was also used as a tribal and national name: "the Israelites [lit., the sons of Israel]" (Lev. 1:2; Jdg. 2:4), "the house of Israel" (Exod. 40:38; 1 Sam. 7:2; Isa. 46:3), and a term specifically applied to the northern kingdom (1 Ki. 12:21; Hos. 5:1; Amos 5:1; Mic. 1:5), though it was also used as a title of honor for the southern kingdom (Isa. 5:7; Jer. 10:1). The earliest external reference to the Israelites outside the OT occurs in an inscription on a pillar set up by Merneptah, king of Egypt, ca. 1220 B.C., to celebrate his victories. In it he boasts: "Israel lies desolate; its seed is no more."

"Hebrew" (Heb. *ᶜibrî*; Gk. *Hebraios*) is an old word of uncertain meaning. Many scholars link this word with the Habiru, a people frequently mentioned in Babylonian, Ugaritic, and Egyptian texts of the mid-2d cent. There it seems to denote people of equal social standing who, not having a permanent home or possessions, entered the service of the settled population on a contractual basis (cf. 1 Sam. 14:21). In closely knit groups, the Habiru penetrated the arable land. The native Canaanites perhaps called them the *ᶜēber* people, because they had come from *ᶜēber*, from the (land) beyond (e.g., Gen. 14:13). Hence, the word "Hebrew" was sometimes used by other peoples in a derogatory manner, sometimes by Israel in dealings with foreigners in a self-deprecating manner (Gen. 40:15; 43:32; Exod. 1:15–19; 2:11–13; 3:18; 1 Sam. 4:6, 9; 13:3, 19; 29:3).

2. (a) After the twelve tribes of Israel occupied the promised land, a common religious center was set up at Shiloh (1 Sam. 1:3; 4:3–4). During the time of the judges, each tribe was responsible for defending its own territory. The pressure exerted by the Philistines made Israel desire a common defense under a single leader. Saul, having been installed as king (1 Sam. 9–12), demanded military service and united the tribes politically. This double basis in religion and politics set up a tension that was to run throughout and determine Israel's history.

After David's united kingdom was split following the death of Solomon, Israel (also called Ephraim, after the younger of Joseph's two sons [Gen. 41:50–52])—a term applied only to the northern kingdom—exercised autonomy in religion and politics for a good 200 years. The God of Israel was worshiped at the sanctuaries of Bethel and Dan. In 733 and 722 B.C. Assyria defeated Israel (cf. 2 Ki. 15–17). As the result of deportations and the mingling of the remainder of the inhabitants with newly settled people (which had the express intention of producing a cultural and religious syncretism), there arose the Assyrian province of Samaria (→ *samaritēs*, 4901).

Judah, the southern kingdom, survived the northern kingdom by about one and a half centuries, partly no doubt on account of its dynastic basis and its more skillful politics. Under Babylonian overlordship, things ended up better for Judah than they did for the northern kingdom under Assyria. Thus, under the Persians the exile of Judah could be reversed.

The southern kingdom also received important theological support. Isa. glorified the Davidic dynasty in Zion. By taking over the name Israel and all its traditional associations for the southern kingdom after the fall of the northern kingdom (cf. Isa. 24–28), Isa. defined theological hopes in accordance with actual political circumstances. The sphere of salvation was narrowed down to the remnant, Judah/Israel.

By contrast, Jer. retained the name Israel for the northern kingdom, though it had been destroyed a century earlier. Without prejudice to Josiah's attempt to restore the state of Israel (2 Ki. 23), Jer. proclaimed that the old Israel was finished. But God would one day recreate from it his people. They would be a community that would once again be stateless (cf. Jer. 3:11–18; 31; 37:7–11). On the pattern of the time of Moses, God would draw up a new covenant with them, this time writing the commandments in their hearts (31:31–34). These hopes for Israel meant, however, that Jeremiah had to announce judgment and destruction for the state of Judah, which he loved and for which he pleaded before God (Jer. 14–19).

(b) God's relationship to Israel is expressed in a variety of metaphors: He is father, king, savior, guardian, refuge, and comforter. Correspondingly, Israel is a son, bride, wife, possession, vineyard, and vine. These mostly personal terms indicate a relationship of partnership. God lets his beloved son know both what he does for him and what he requires of him (Deut. 10:12; Mic. 6:8). Through such instruction, Israel became a unique people (Num. 23:9), distinguished and separated from all others (Deut. 4:5–10). In the holy land of Israel this holy people was to live for the holy God in holiness (Lev. 11:44–45; 19:2; 20:26). Israel's election was at the same time a commission. Although the least significant of the peoples (Deut. 7:7), Israel still had to be for the nations a prince and a light, a witness to God by his very existence (Isa. 43:8–12).

Israel continually ran the risk of falling back into Canaanite cults and of wanting to be like the other peoples. This meant that the relationship of trust could be damaged from the human side, but not destroyed, for the covenant with Israel remained irrevocable for God's sake. To make this fact certain beyond all doubt, use was made of concepts taken from the realm of law: God would not abandon his legal claim on Israel (Amos 9:1–15), nor would he publish a bill of divorce (Isa. 50:1). Lest his name be blasphemed among the heathen for faithlessness, God remained true to the oath he had sworn to the fathers (Ezek. 20:9, 14, 22; cf. Deut. 7:8). Even judgment was a sign of his faithfulness.

Israel was warned, threatened, and comforted through God's servants the prophets of Israel (Ezek. 38:17). But in all this we encounter only different forms of the same invitation to repentance. God's own faithfulness to the covenant made it possible for Israel to be purified and the covenant relationship renewed. The hope of the restoration of the whole of Israel did not rest on Israel's righteousness but on God's love to the fathers (Exod. 32:11–14; Deut. 9:5), and on his freedom that chose Israel contrary to all expectations (Ezek. 16:59–63).

(c) Shortly after the return of the exiles from Babylon, the prophets announced a turning point in the coming of salvation (cf. Hag. 2:20–23; Zech. 6:9–15). But three generations later Ezra and Nehemiah saw in these semipolitical dreams a danger to Israel's continued existence. The latter left to the Persians the management of political relations and concentrated on the internal building up of the covenant community in Jer.'s sense, using Holy Scripture as a basis. What had hitherto been the privilege of the priests now became a common possession (cf. Neh. 8).

(d) The rest of Israel's history has been a continual struggle to retain its identity both politically and culturally. Religiously, it seemed able to remain separate, primarily through its synagogues, its adherence to the Hebrew Scriptures, and its observance of unique laws, such as circumcision, food restrictions, and keeping the Sabbath. Politically the people of Israel had a succession of overlords, from Alexander the Great (356–323 B.C.) to the Seleucids and Ptolemies, the Romans (see NT section), Arabs, Crusaders, Turks, and British—with only occasional moments of independence, such as with the Maccabees and Simon Bar Kokhba. Yet even under the most difficult conditions, remnant Jewish communities repeatedly migrated back. In 1948, after the horrific treatment of Jews during World War II and with the approval of world public opinion, there arose once again a state with the ancient name of Israel.

NT The intertestamental period and NT era witnessed an intense struggle over the identity of the true Israel in the face of foreign rule, competing groups within Jud., and the emergence of the church. Despite the many strata within it, Jud. was a relatively unified whole compared with the other peoples. As bearers of God's revelation in the struggle against the heathen, even the early followers of Jesus recognized themselves as belonging to Israel. Hence, the rise of the Christian church must be seen against the background of the competing groups within Jud. that were concerned with the identity and destiny of Israel.

1. *Israel in the context of foreign rule.* (a) In the Hel. environment, with its striving for cultural unity, it was possible for Jews to take over not only the Gk. language but also many Hel. manners, as long as they were not connected with a pagan cult and thus incompatible with Jewish religious principles. Through mission, which had its theological roots in the universal claim of the one God, who desires the salvation of all the nations (cf. Isa. 41–42; 49), the tension between Israel and the nations was removed by the anticipation of the reunion expected in the end time (cf. 1 Cor. 12:13; Gal. 3:28).

Thus postexilic Jud. became a missionary religion, ready to accept anyone who confessed Israel's God. Success was great, esp. among women (who were not circumcised, only baptized). About one in ten of the inhabitants of the Hel. Mediterranean world was a Jew, not necessarily by birth but by belief.

But this openness, which the nations found attractive in Jud., also gave rise to hatred and persecution. In times of crisis the position of Jews before the law worsened, and enmity led to pogroms (e.g., the persecutions under Trajan, A.D. 115–117). Jews were faced with the choice either of giving up their Jewishness and adopting the pagan gods and the cult of the emperor or of renouncing the privilege of cultural and political equality. As a result, those who remained faithful to their community withdrew into a kind of ghetto existence, involving a separation that was completely religious in character. As the theology of the Talmud shows, Pharisaism, based on Heb. Scripture, made the whole of Israel immune to the damaging influences of Hel. anti-Jewish culture and gave it a self-consciousness that supplied the power to survive as a community for thousands of years amid the hatred and persecution of a hostile environment.

(b) The use of the terms relating to the Jews was determined by these conflicts. The word *Hebrew* (noun and adj.) was the most neutral. It denoted the language and the script, then also the people who used them. In worship the Bible was read in the Heb. original and then translated into current Aram. in the form of the Targums. Where it is used without any special significance, Heb. frequently means the then-current Aram. (cf. Jn. 5:2; 19:13, 17, 20; 20:16; Acts 21:40; 22:2; 26:14; Rev. 9:11; 16:16).

Since language, education, and the structure of theology are largely determined by the fact of belonging to a particular cultural sphere, the word *Hebrew* (cf. Acts 6:1) could sometimes acquire an apologetic or polemical tone. Paul emphasized in 2 Cor. 11:22 and Phil. 3:5 his Heb.-speaking origins and affiliations as something positive.

The terms *Judah, Jew, Jewish,* and *Judaism* possess a political and sociological coloring. They denote not only the membership of the nation but also the people who turn to Jud. and live according to Jewish customs (cf. Gal. 2:14; Tit. 1:14). To this context belongs the noun first coined by the LXX, *Ioudaïsmos,* Judaism, as a way of life and faith (Gal. 1:13–14; cf. 2 Macc. 2:21; 8:1; 14:38; 4 Macc. 4:26). This usage was taken over by the Jews themselves, esp. in dealings with foreigners.

In the NT the word *Jew* is used of individuals and in the pl. of groups, occurring some 195x with almost every shade of meaning (79x are in Acts, 71x in Jn., 26x in Paul, but only 17x in the Synoptic Gospels). It was often used by Gentiles as a contemptuous term, for they did not understand the peculiarity and necessary separation of the Jewish people (Add. Est. 13:12–19). Because Jews did not take part in Gentile cults and social life, they were regarded as godless, haters of foreigners, and even as haters of humanity in general (3 Macc. 3:4–29). Contempt for Jews also resulted in a hatred that worked itself out in bloody persecution.

Intensified by such anti-Jewish attitudes, Jud.'s consciousness of itself as "Israel" developed. This is the most pregnant of the theological concepts consistently used within the community. *Israēl* occurs 68x in the NT, most often in Paul (17x) and Acts (15x). *Israēlitēs* occurs 5x in Acts (always as a form of address: 2:22; 3:12; 5:35; 13:16; 21:28), 3x in Paul (Rom. 9:4; 11:1; 2 Cor. 11:22), and once in Jn. (Jn. 1.47). Each time it refers to Jews as members of the people of God. The world was created for Israel's sake (2 Esd. 7:11). Israel is God's possession and his firstborn (*Pss. Sol.* 18:4). It owes its special character solely to the gift of instruction. God stands by his promises, and he will gather all those who have been scattered. They will possess the land (Matt. 5:5; → *klēros, 3102*), and all Israel has a share in the world to come.

2. *The struggle over Israel within Judaism.* (a) During the Hel. period, postexilic Jud. was divided geographically between the homeland and the Diaspora. Parallel with this was the cultural division between Hebrews and Hellenists. Some Diaspora Jews emphasized their connection with the Heb. (or Aram.) language and culture and separated themselves from those Jews who were more open towards Hel. culture (cf. synagogues of the Heb. in Rome and Corinth). But there were also in Jerusalem Jewish groups who in language and perhaps also in customs were those of Hellenists (2 Macc. 4:13; Acts 6:1; 9:29).

Jews who lived in the homeland retained close links with those who lived in the Diaspora. Jerusalem was supported materially by the latter in the form of the temple tax, while it remained a religious focal point with its pilgrim festivals (cf. Acts 2:5–11) and regularly sent out embassies to Jewish communities. Still, there was no common political action, either during the rebellions in Israel or the persecutions in the Diaspora.

From the sociological point of view Israel was divided into several classes: e.g., priests, Levites, Israelites, and proselytes. But because the question of how Israel could continue to exist before God in this period was interpreted in various ways, several groups arose, each of which maintained that it was the true community (e.g., Sadducees, baptists, apocalyptists, Pharisees, and Zealots). Membership in these groups no longer depended on origin but on the decision of an individual to accept a particular doctrinal opinion. The boundaries of the parties were fluid, and it was possible to transfer from one to another. Thus, for example, disciples of John the Baptist transferred their allegiance to the Jesus group (Jn. 1:38–40).

Some of these groups were divided further into subgroups. Thus, within the Pharisees there was a Zealot wing, hostile to foreigners, and a missionary wing, friendly towards Rome. Similar splits arose also among the followers of Jesus (1 Cor. 1:12; 3:4; 2 Cor. 11; Gal. 1–2).

The idea of election, the continued existence of Israel, and the formulation of instruction in purity were hammered out in continuous debate over points of doctrine and constant conflict. The passion with which the struggle for Israel's reality was fought is a sign of the vitality of the prophetic spirit in this period.

(b) The course of this conflict among the Jews was bitter—of a kind that could only come about among brothers disputing a common heritage. The fight had been going on for a long time before the Jesus movement arose and entered the debate.

The methods of polemic were various. Opponents were denounced in forthright language, as can be seen by the NT use of terms such as "hypocrite" (Matt. 23:13) and "brood of vipers" (3:7). Wholesale appeal was made to history, like Paul's comment about the behavior of the Jews, "who killed the Lord Jesus," as typical of their treatment of the prophets (1 Thess. 2:14–15). An opponent's positive points could be assertively transformed into negatives (e.g., the law in Paul, Rom. 4:13–15; Gal 3:10–13; the devil and lies instead of God and truth, Jn. 8:41–44; Rev. 3:9; cf. Paul's interpretation of current Jewish attitudes in the light of the Scriptures in 2 Cor. 3:4–18 and Gal. 4:21–31).

Such polemic had the air of prophetic denunciation: e.g., Israel was stubborn and godless, and God was hiding his face from Israel. In line with this, Paul, missionary to the Gentiles, took up the arguments of the Gentile-Jewish polemic (1 Thess. 2:14–16). We meet the sharpest form of the polemic in Jn., which seems to separate believers entirely from the Jews (see below).

Jewish writing remains so polemical that dangerous misunderstandings were unavoidable, where the different sides were considered in isolation. After the destruction of the temple, feelings were so intense that opposing positions were treated as nonexistent. Thus the Talmud is almost completely silent about its opponents. The last step was legal separation between Jews and Christians through the introduction in the 80s of the petition on heretics into the Eighteen Benedictions: "May the Nazarenes and heretics disappear in a moment; they shall be erased from the book of life and not be written with the faithful" (cf. Jn. 9:22; 12:42).

(c) The positive side of such polemic was an apologetic presentation of one's own position. Each individual group felt that it was the separated remnant of Israel that would lead to the eschatological community of the saved. It is striking, however, that everyone refrained from simply identifying his or her group with the eschatological total-Israel. Thus 1 Cor. 10:18 lacks a corresponding "Israel according to the spirit." The nearest approach to this is the "community of the new covenant" (cf. Lk. 22:20; 1 Cor. 11:25; 2 Cor. 3:6).

Even if primarily one's own group is intended, an open attitude towards a future gathered Israel was retained. Separation *from* Israel was election *for* Israel. The community of the remnant realized its commission to call the entire people to repentance. The community of the remnant was a light for the whole community. For their sakes the whole of Israel would be saved in the end (cf. Rom. 11:26). The clearest expression of hope for the whole of Israel occurs in prayers that frequently conclude with a reference to the whole of Israel (Gal. 6:16). The remnant of the elect in the NT also hoped for the salvation and the reestablishment of Israel as one people (Mk. 13:27; Lk. 24:21; Acts 1:6). The expected judgment would be carried out through the twelve disciples, whose number indicates the totality of Israel (Matt. 19:28; Lk. 22:30).

(d) All 1st-cent. groups of Jud. were united in the belief that Israel's hope would be realized in some individual figure who would usher in the eschatological salvation. God would reveal himself to them and lead them out of their obscurity and ambiguity. All such attempts at messianic realization found people ready to believe in them; all ended in apparent catastrophe: the Teacher of Righteousness at Qumran, John the Baptist, Jesus, the Zealot leaders, and Bar Kokhba. Only two groups survived the ultimate catastrophe of A.D. 70: the Pharisees, who excluded all messianic or Zealot tendencies at Jamnia; and the Jewish believers in Jesus, who stressed their eschatological, messianic beliefs over against the Pharisees. The messianic belief of the NT can, therefore, be considered representative of a typical Jewish outlook at the time of the second temple.

Each Jewish group took and applied key statements from the Jewish Scriptures to the person who, for them, represented all Israel. This representative was the elect one among the community of the elect, the righteous one among the righteous, the son among the sons, the servant among the servants (Isa. 53), who took Israel's suffering on himself. The son of man, the figure of judgment representing the people of Israel in Dan. 7:13, was now identified with the Messiah.

Specifically for the Christian movement, as God constantly spoke to Israel, he also spoke to the Christ. As Israel was enabled in a unique way to hear and to obey, so also was Christ (Jn. 5:19, 36; cf. Matt. 5:17; 11:27). Terms were therefore applied to him that in the Heb. Scriptures denoted Israel; e.g., the vineyard, the vine (Ps. 80:8–9; Jer. 2:21; 2 Esd. 5:23; Jn. 15:1–8), and the cornerstone (Ps. 118:22–24; Matt. 21:42; Mk. 12:10–11; Lk. 20:17; Acts 4:11; Eph. 2:20; 1 Pet. 2:6–8).

The Messiah and Israel stand inseparably together. Whoever does not decide for this elect one opposes him. Whoever refuses to trust him has thereby decided against Israel. Such a one has lost descent from Abraham (Jn. 8:39) and belongs to Satan's synagogue (Rev. 3:9). Nevertheless, both the one who evidences such trust (even though it should be proved false) and the one who refuses it stand within Jud.

Israel and its Scriptures were the critical principle by which every messianic pretender was to be judged: The messiahs of Qumran were expected to come from Aaron and Israel, and the Messiah Jesus from the patriarchs (Matt. 1:1–17; 11:2–6; Jn. 5:39; Rom. 1:3; 9:5). This was the only way in which Israel could protect herself against excess in spirit and prophecy, against the majority of messianic pretenders, and against overhasty solutions of the problems of her existence.

The NT witnesses also knew that the reality of Israel was the touchstone of Christology and thus clung passionately to Israel as the basic foundation of the Christ event. Consequently, there emerges from the NT sharp opposition to any abandonment of Israel (cf. Jn. 4:22; Rom. 9–11). Only in living union with Israel is Jesus the Christ. Apart from this historical reality he dissolves into an idea, a Gnostic myth, and a Docetic speculation.

Hence in the case of the Messiah Jesus, baptism and the Lord's Supper are the feasts of Israel. The cross he bore was a sharing in Israel's suffering. Although Jewish Christians engaged in the dialogue within Jud. found themselves cut off from their Jewish brethren because of him, the NT demonstrates that Jesus, the Jew and Hebrew, represents Israel completely in his person. He is bound up with Israel from first to last.

(e) This identification of Jesus, the bringer of salvation, with Israel entailed consequent missionary activity among Jews. As Jesus turned exclusively to the lost sheep of the house of Israel, his messengers were to go only into the towns of Israel (Matt. 10:5–6; 15:24). Paul, the Jewish missionary (1 Cor. 9:20), also demonstrated the priority of Jud. in salvation history (Rom. 1:16) by always going first of all to the Jews (Acts 13:14; 14:1), always acknowledging that he was a Jew (Acts 22:3; 2 Cor. 11:22; Phil. 3:5). Despite the failures of his Jewish mission he held fast to Israel, his people (cf. Acts 28:20). On the basis of the Jewish Scriptures Paul demonstrated in Rom. 9–11, in a kind of commentary of OT teaching, that just as Israel's present hardening was causing the message of Christ to come to the Gentiles, who were thus acquiring a share in Israel's salvation, in the end time, all Israel would be saved (11:26). An anticipatory sign of this undiminished faithfulness of God was Jewish Christianity, the faithful remnant of Jud., represented by Paul himself.

(f) The position of the various NT writers vis-à-vis Jud. is revealed in their use of terms. Thus in Paul *Jew* is used 26x, often in opposition to Greek, Gentile, and mostly in a positive sense. *Israel* (17x) stands for either the historic people or the eschatological whole of Israel, though not for Christian community (except perhaps Gal. 6:16). In the Synoptics, *Israel* stands for the people and the land (e.g., Matt. 26, 20), used in preference to Jew. *Jew* is used esp. in the phrase "king of the Jews" (e.g., Matt. 27:11; Mk. 15:2; Lk. 23:3; Jn. 18:33, 39), and the term appears almost without exception on the lips of Gentiles (cf. Matt. 2:2; 28:15; Mk. 7:3; Lk. 7:3). The use of the word *Israel* in general maintains the connection with the reality and hope of Israel.

In Acts *Israel* is used more frequently in the account of the Palestinian church, while *Jew* is used in the narrative of Paul's missionary journeys. This corresponds to Hel. usage. In Jn. it is clear from the few but fundamental passages where *Israel* is used (1:31, 49; 3:10; 12:13) that the writer is still within the sphere of the whole of Israel, even though his polemic is sharp. This is expressed in the Johannine use of *Jew* (71x), which can indeed be used neutrally of the people or the religious community (e.g., 4:9; 18:35) but with sharp rejection when it denotes the ruling classes (e.g., 1:19; 7:11; 18:12). In Rev. *Jew* has a positive sense, but it is not applied to the community that does not believe in Jesus (2:9; 3:9). Israel is the true eschatological people of God (2:14; 7:4; 21:12).

3. *From the Gentile mission to the Gentile Christian church.* Only when those to whom the Jewish mission was originally addressed overwhelmingly rejected the offer did the mission to the Gentiles arise (Acts 13:46). The tradition therefore had to be restated to meet the demands of missionary practice among Gentiles. The history of Israel, which had figured so prominently in addressing the Jews (Acts 2:14–36; 3:22–26; 7:2–53), was dropped from the instruction given, because the people did not have the preparation necessary to understand it. Nevertheless, God's encounter with the Gentiles remained rooted in the historical experience of Israel in the teaching of the Jewish missionaries to the Gentiles. The Jesus covenant is the extension of the Sinai covenant (cf. Rom. 9–11; 1 Cor. 11:25; 2 Cor. 3:6–18; Gal. 4:24–31; Heb. 8:8–13; 10:16–18). In terms of world history the Christ event became the inclusion of the nations in the Sinai event.

Due to mounting internal tensions and disappointment over the attitude of the Diaspora, the position of Jewish Christians in the land of Israel became continually more difficult. Step by step they were transformed from a competing Jewish group to the independent opponents of the Pharisees, who now represented orthodox Jud. From A.D.

70 on, Jewish Christians saw their own way of faith as something distinct from that of the synagogue in the Jewish community.

The path of Gentile Christianity turned from Jud. and eventually led into Gentile anti-Semitism, which increased after the destruction of Jerusalem. The OT prophets' criticism of Israel was construed as anti-Jewish and repeated irresponsibly. In place of living and healthy dialogue between the groups, there arose what was more like a dogmatizing monologue. Ignatius of Antioch, for example, a Gentile Christian, writing ca. A.D. 115, expressed the opinion that a Christian must necessarily be an opponent of the Jews (Ign. *Magn.* 8; 10:3). Somewhat later a Gentile Christian named Barnabas used the word *Israel* mostly in connection with his exegesis of the Bible against Israel, although he did not yet dare to take over this word for the church. Justin Martyr, by contrast, asserts boldly: "We are . . . the true spiritual Israel" (*Dial.* 11, 5). The way of Barnabas and Justin became the way of the church.

See also *Iakōb*, Jacob (*2609*); *Ioudaia*, Judea (*2677*).

2703 (*Israēlitēs*, Israelite), → *2702*.

2708 (*ischyros*, strong, powerful, mighty), → *2709*.

2709	ἰσχύς

ἰσχύς (*ischys*), strength, power, might (*2709*); ἰσχύω (*ischyō*), be strong, powerful; (*2710*) ἰσχυρός (*ischyros*), strong, powerful, mighty (*2708*); κατισχύω (*katischyō*), to be strong, be dominant, prevail (*2996*).

CL & OT 1. In cl. Gk. *ischys* denotes the strength and power possessed by living beings or by things. In the Gk. tragedies it was sometimes applied to deities. *ischyros* means strong either in body or mind and was also applied to deities, living creatures, or things. *ischyō* means to be able to do something, have the ability to, be strong, healthy. It can also mean to use force, exercise power, esp. physical power. In the legal sphere, this vb. acquired the meaning to be valid, be applicable, have value. *katischyō* means to be superior to others, be the victor, gain the upper hand, prevail.

2. (a) In the LXX *ischys* translates 30 different Heb. words. It can express one's physical strength (e.g., Jos. 8:3; Jdg. 16:5; Ps. 22:15; 31:10; Ezek. 30:21) or intellectual power (Prov. 8:14) but is used esp. for divine power (e.g., the Lord's bringing up his people from Egypt "by [his] power"; Num. 14:13; cf. Ps. 29:4; 147:5). As such it can be a gift of God to us (Mic. 3:8).

(b) *ischyō* in the LXX usually denotes becoming strong or being strong in a physical sense: of things (e.g., Isa. 28:22, "or your chains will become heavier"), and of human beings (e.g., Jos. 14:11, "I am still as strong today as the day Moses sent me out").

(c) *katischyō* denotes being superior in a physical sense. It is used of human beings (e.g., Jos. 17:13, "when the Israelites grew stronger"; Ezek. 30:24, "I will strengthen the arms of the king of Babylon"), of things (Isa. 54:2, "lengthen your cords"), and of God's power (1 Chr. 29:12).

(d) *ischyros* denotes strong: of persons (Num. 13:18 = LXX 13:19), animals (Prov. 30:30 = LXX 24:65), things (Isa. 8:7), or God (Deut. 10:17).

NT 1. This group of words is found in almost all NT writings and refers to the strength and power of living creatures (e.g., Heb. 11:34) or things (e.g., 6:18, strong consolation; 5:7, strong cries). The particular trans. depends on the nuances of the context. Peter (Mk. 14:37) must answer the question: "Could you not [lit., did you not have strength to] keep watch for one hour?" (cf. Matt. 26:40). We are called on to love God with all our "strength" (Mk. 12:30; Lk. 10:27). Salt that has lost its taste is "good for" nothing (Matt. 5:13). In Lk. 15:14 the famine is described as "severe." The prayer of a righteous man "is powerful" (Jas. 5:16). The gates of Hades "will not overcome" the church (Matt. 16:18). In a fig. sense people can be called "the healthy" in contrast with the sick (Mk. 2:17; cf. also Rev. 6:15). As a legal term *ischyō* means to avail, be valid (Heb. 9:17, of the validity of a will; cf. Gal. 5:6).

2. Some NT passages need special attention. The Synoptic tradition uses this group of words in a manner that implies approval of an action or quality; thus the strong man is safe unless a stronger man comes (Mk. 3:27). Since in Isa. 49:24–25 it is God who sets the prisoners free, Mk. 3:27 may be suggesting that God, the stronger one, has conquered Satan, the strong one, and cast him out of heaven. In Mk.'s context, however, the passage means that Jesus' victory over the demons proves him to be stronger than the strong, i.e., stronger than demons or the demon-possessed (cf. Acts 10:38).

Jesus' superiority is also seen vis-à-vis John the Baptist; the expected one is mightier than John and will demonstrate this by baptizing with the Holy Spirit and with fire (the fire of judgment; Matt. 3:11; Lk. 3:16), or with the Holy Spirit as a gift of salvation (Mk. 1:7–8). *ischyō* is also used in various places to depict Christ's superior power in contrast to the impotence of others, thereby emphasizing the greatness both of a miracle and of the one by whom it is done. In Mk. 5:4 the observation that no one had sufficient strength to subdue the demoniac prepares us to appreciate the greatness of Christ's miracle (cf. also Lk. 8:43; Rev. 18:10). Christ's opponents are inferior to him (Lk. 14:6; cf. 14:29–30; 20:26), their impotence merely throwing his superior power into sharper relief; the same superiority is evident in the infant church in Acts 19:20, and in the "wisdom [and] the Spirit" with which Stephen spoke (6:10) and died.

3. To defend himself against his opponents in Corinth, who were proud of their strength and their abundance of gifts (1 Cor. 4:10), Paul set weakness and impotence over against strength. "The weakness of God is stronger than man's strength," and God puts the strong to shame by choosing what is weak (1 Cor. 1:25–27). Paul himself had to suffer the reproach that, while his letters were "weighty and forceful [*ischys*]," he himself was weak (2 Cor. 10:10).

Still, Paul did not regard his own lack of strength as a disadvantage (cf. his comments on his "thorn in [the] flesh," 2 Cor. 12:7). He argues from the strength of God, which the unbeliever regards as foolishness, i.e., weakness (1 Cor. 1:18). Christ's power, like God's power, carries the day and is transmitted to those who live in him (Phil. 4:13). There is no power inherent in a human being; it can exist only when God's strength is displayed in human weakness (2 Cor. 12:9).

4. Eph. and 2 Thess. use the *ischyō* word group to express a somewhat different concept of strength and power. Eph. 1:9 and 6:10 speak of the power of God, not the power of Christ, and 2 Thess. 1:19 echoes Isa. 2:10, 19 in ascribing to the power of God the punishment of the ungodly at the last day.

5. In Rev. the grandeur of the imagery is conveyed by *ischys* and *ischyros*. "Strength" figures among the ascriptions addressed to the Lamb (Rev. 5:12) and to God (7:12; 18:8). It is also attributed to the angels (5:2; 10:1; 18:21; cf. 2 Pet. 2:11), whose voice is mighty (Rev. 18:2; cf. 19:6) and who are superior to the dragon (12:8). They belong to the heavenly kingdom and are thus closely associated with God; hence in the worship of heaven the hymn addressed to God may likewise be addressed to them.

See also *bia*, force, violence (*1040*); *keras*, horn (*3043*); *kratos*, power, might, rule (*3197*); *dynamis*, power (*1539*).

2710 (*ischyō*, be strong, powerful), → *2709*.

2715 (*ichthydion*, little fish), → *2716*.

2716	ἰχθύς

ἰχθύς (*ichthys*), fish (*2716*); ἰχθύδιον (*ichthydion*), diminutive of *ichthys*, little fish (*2715*); ὀψάριον (*opsarion*), fish for eating (with bread) (*4066*); κῆτος (*kētos*), sea-monster (*3063*).

CL & OT 1. In cl. Gk. *ichthys* was in general use as a word for fish. It appears as a metaphor for a "foolish man" in Plutarch. *kētos* is specifically a sea-monster, of the whale kind. *kētos* is also a constellation, and the supposition that sea-monsters inhabited the deep gave rise to *kētos* in the sense of "gulf."

2. In the LXX, *ichthys* describes all created life living in the water (e.g., 1 Ki. 4:33; Job 12:8), whether fresh (Exod. 7:18; Ezek. 29:4) or salt (Hos. 4:3) water. Fish are involved in the subservience of creation to the Creator (Ezek. 38:20) and by the Creator's will are under human domination (Gen. 1:26; 9:2; Ps. 8:8). Their commercial value is implied in Neh. 13:16 as well as by the provision of a "Fish Gate" (3:3, *ichthyēros*). With the rest of creation, fish fall under divine judgments on the human race (Exod. 7:18; Ps. 105:29), illustrate divine providential interventions (Isa. 50:2), and figure in the ideal future (Ezek. 47:9). The angler's art aptly denotes the inhumane treatment of humans (Hab. 1:14). Religiously, it is forbidden to make fish-like representations of the divine nature , a prohibition much to the point in the light of Assyrian representations of Ea in fish form and the fish costume of exorcist priests (Deut. 4:18; cf. Tob. 6:1–17).

The LXX uses *kētos* in Gen. 1:21 ("great creatures of the sea"; cf. Sir. 43:25) as well as Job 3:8 ("Leviathan") and 9:13; 26:12 ("Rahab"). In Job it has mythological overtones. Otherwise it is only used of the "great fish" in Jon. 1:17; 2:10 (= LXX 2:1, 11) and 3 Macc. 6:8.

NT The NT use of *ichthys* reflects the OT background. The whole Galilee narrative of the Gospels implies commerce in fish, but neither here nor throughout the OT is there any stress on different species of fish. The vocabulary of the LXX is increased by the occasional use of *opsarion* for fish prepared for food (Jn. 6:9, 11; 21:9–13). The word does not necessarily mean "small" fish, as Jn. 21:9–13 indicates.

The sole NT observation on zoology appears in 1 Cor. 15:39, but its interest is clearly theological—the subservience of all creation to the Creator's will and design. This truth receives vivid illustration in the nature miracles of Jesus, the two feedings of the crowds (Matt. 14:17; 15:36, with par.), the tribute money (17:27), and the miraculous catches of fish (Lk. 5:6; Jn. 21:6). The single thread of truth linking these narratives is that by the mere exercise of his will Jesus subdues creation to his plan in works of mercy for the well-being of people, and thus is manifested as the incarnate Creator.

kētos makes its only appearance in Matt. 12:40 with reference to the "huge fish" of Jonah. Both the LXX and NT have clearly made the correct word choice here, a sea-monster of undefined nature but undoubted size.

| 2731 | Ἰωνᾶς |

Ἰωνᾶς (*Iōnas*), Jonah (*2731*).

OT 1. *Iōnas* is a transliteration of Heb. *yônâ*—the OT prophet Jonah.

2. Four elements in the Jonah story relate to the NT. (a) What was the motive for Jonah's flight (Jon. 1:3–17)? Most scholars think that he was a religious particularist who did not want to see Israel's privileges shared with the heathen. It should be noted, however, that later Jewish opinion stressed the repentance of the Ninevites as an example that God's people were called to follow. This was the point Jesus sought to make.

(b) The book of Jonah records his own comment on his remarkable experience. In Jonah's prayer, the belly of the fish becomes "the depths of the grave [Heb. Sheol]" (Jon. 2:2). While recognizing that Sheol is frequently metaphorical for that which is dark and likely to end in death, the use of the metaphor here, coupled with the reference to "the pit" (2:6), forms part of the OT background to Jesus' use of the incident.

(c) The only thing the OT records regarding Jonah's preaching is coming judgment (Jon. 3:4). It was the force of his word and the recognition of the divine authorization that lay behind this word that motivated the Ninevites' repentance.

(d) The Ninevites heeded the call to repentance, and God expressed his satisfaction with this (Jon. 3:10–4:10).

NT The NT refers to Jonah only in passages in which Jesus alludes to him in the context of certain controversial exchanges with the Pharisees (Matt. 12:38–41; 16:4; Lk. 11:29–32). These references are both general to the career of Jonah and particular, in that they refer to him as a sign (→ *semeion, 4956*).

In speaking of the people of his day as "wicked and adulterous" (Matt. 12:39; cf. Lk. 11:29, which omits "adulterous"), Jesus undoubtedly intended to set up a parallelism between them and Nineveh (Jon. 1:2): "wicked" in heart and life, "adulterous" physically and spiritually. The Lord underlines their spiritual vacuity by his refusal of the sign they sought. Matt. 16:1 notes that the Pharisees and Sadducees wanted a "sign from heaven," presumably something unequivocally from God that would authenticate Jesus—primarily without his being involved in its performance. To Jesus (cf. Matt. 11:4) this was rank blindness in the face of his constant performance of his own works before their eyes. In this context he set up a threefold comparison.

1. He made an open comparison between himself and Jonah. In Matt. 16:4 Jesus leaves his hearers to their own interpretative devices. In Lk. 11:30, there is a significant change of tense: "As Jonah was . . . so also will the Son of Man be. . . ." That is, if the Jewish leaders review the story of Jonah, they can see that he was a divinely sent persuader, a heaven-sent opportunity that came once and did not return. Similarly, the Son of Man will, at some later point, make them aware that he too was sent from God and that in him they reached, for good or ill, a point of no return.

2. Jesus compared Jonah's experience of a three-day sojourn in the fish to his own coming sojourn "in the heart of the earth" (Matt. 12:40).To what Jesus was looking forward when he predicted a coming event in the light of which his own status as a Jonah-type sign would be clear? His resurrection from an unequivocal experience of death would be the "sign from heaven" that they had faithlessly sought and would not, even when it happened, be able to recognize (cf. Lk. 16:31). Matt.'s comparison between Jonah in a Sheol-like situation and Jesus "in the heart of the earth" is distinctly apt.

3. Note also the comparison between Jonah's preaching and its result, and Jesus' own preaching and its result (Matt. 12:41; Lk. 11:32). The comparison here is a fortiori. The ensuing judgment on the impenitence of the Jewish leaders would be greater because the one who calls to repentance is greater. Jesus is claiming here the honor due to his deity.

K *kappa*

2748 (*kathairō*, to clean, make clean), → 2754.

2751 (*katharizō*, cleanse, purify), → 2754.

2752 (*katharismos*, cleansing), → 2754.

2754	καθαρός

καθαρός (*katharos*), clean, pure (*2754*); καθαίρω (*kathairō*), to clean, make clean (*2748*); ἐκκαθαίρω (*ekkathairō*), clean out (*1705*); καθαρίζω (*katharizō*), cleanse, purify (*2751*); καθαρότης (*katharotēs*), cleanness, purity (*2755*); καθαρισμός (*katharismos*), cleansing (*2752*); ἀκάθαρτος (*akathartos*), unclean (*176*); ἀκαθαρσία (*akatharsia*), uncleanness (*174*).

CL & OT 1. (a) In cl. Gk. the family of words that go with *katharos* embraces the realms of physical, cultic, and ethical purity. *katharos* means clean in a physical sense, in the sense of being ritually pure, and in a moral sense. The cognate vb. *kathairō* means to clean, sweep, cleanse. The compound vb. *ekkathairō* intensifies the primary meaning, so that it means to sweep out, cleanse thoroughly. More common in Hel. Gk. is *katharizō*, to cleanse, in a physical, ritual, or moral sense. *katharotēs* means cleanness (lit. and fig.). The later Hel. term *katharismos* is found first as a technical term in agriculture, and then generally in the sense of physical or ritual cleaning.

(b) The negative words formed by adding the alpha-privative (*akathartos* and *akatharsia*) refer to the whole realm of uncleanness, ranging from menstruation to moral pollution through wrongdoing.

(c) In Gk. religion the system of purificatory and expiatory rites had nothing to do with penitence for sin or an inward purification of the heart. It was concerned rather with the warding off of demonic spirits by means of exorcism and ritual acts.

A woman after childbirth, as well as her child, were unclean. So too was a dead person. Those who touched either of these had to undergo purification, which removed the uncleanness that had come from without. A person who shed blood, even if done in the course of executing justice, had to be cleansed. The blood of an animal was poured over the hands of the person who had become unclean, so banishing death by death. Later these rites were given a deeper, ethical meaning. The credit for this goes to the Orphics and Pythagoreans, but above all to the mystery religions and the philosophers.

(d) The concept *pure* and its opposite *impure* are woven into the history of all religions. In primitive cultures, a supernatural force possesses dangerous powers that are conceived in material terms and are thought to be transferable by physical contact. In particular, birth, death, and sexual processes are associated with this force. A person wishing to approach the deity had to be careful not to offend the gods by uncleanness, which contradicts their nature. Thus arose a demand for cultic purification. The priest had to undertake purificatory rites, washing away what was unclean, in order to free the individual from evil and demonic influences. Not until later did purity receive an inward sense, thus freeing it from ritual and linking it instead to morality and ethics.

2. (a) In the LXX *katharos* usually denotes ritual purity, while *akathartos* and *akatharsia* mean ritual impurity (e.g., Lev. 5:3; 15:24). The distinction between clean and unclean goes back to an early period. Within the same realm of ideas are the concepts of holy (*hagios*, → *41*) and profane (*koinos*; → *koinōnia, 3126*).

(b) In the OT purity and impurity are spoken of chiefly in a cultic sense. The distinction between them is inseparably connected with Israel's belief in Yahweh, which was grounded on the presupposition that uncleanness and Yahweh are irreconcilable opposites. Purity is therefore regarded as the norm, qualifying one to take part in worship, while impurity separates one from worship and from God's people, so that it must be opposed and purged out as an abomination (Lev. 7:19–20 = LXX 7:9–10).

(i) Purity begins with the individual. Diseases, esp. leprosy, render a person unclean. One of the OT priest's duties was to pronounce a person who had contracted leprosy either clean or unclean (see Lev. 13:17, 44). Likewise, sexual processes made a person unclean (e.g., emission of semen, 15:16; menstruation, 15:19; adultery, 18:20; homosexuality, 18:22; sexual intercourse, 1 Sam. 21:5–6). A dead body is unclean in the highest degree; its uncleanness was transferred to every person present and also to open vessels (Num. 19:14–15). In general, cleansing with clear water was sufficient, but special cleansing water, previously mixed with the ashes of a red heifer, was necessary in cases of defilement by contact with a dead body (Num. 19).

(ii) Lev. 11 presents a catalogue of clean and unclean animals. These distinctions appear to guard against animal worship (occasionally practiced in the northern kingdom, 1 Ki. 12:28–32), to show Israel's rejection of animals symbolizing foreign religions (such as the pig in the Adonis-Tammuz cult), and to formulate health regulations. Foreign territory was likewise regarded as unclean, since foreign gods were worshiped there (Amos 7:17). Even Israel's own land and the temple could be defiled by idolatry (Jer. 2:7; 7:30). The temple, the altar, and the Most Holy Place, as the abodes of Yahweh, were the places of greatest purity and sanctity; because of the uncleanness of the Israelites, these places needed regular purification by the ritual of atonement (Lev. 16).

(iii) The prophets did not abandon the distinction between clean and unclean. Rather, they extended and spiritualized the concepts, for in criticizing cultic abuses they introduced a concept of purity that had to do with people and their behavior (Isa. 6:5; Jer. 2:23–25). The concept of impurity thus approached those of guilt and sin (33:8; Ezek. 39:24; cf. Ps. 51).

(c) Thus, when the OT distinguishes between clean and unclean, it is much more than a concern with merely cold, legalistic superficialities. Rather, we have here evidence of the dynamic struggle of Israel's religion with that of her neighbors.

3. (a) Beginning in intertestamental times, Jud. surrounded the laws of purity with many casuistic and sometimes grotesque prohibitions and commands, which made the regulations into laws that were difficult to fulfill. A Pharisee was defiled, for example, merely by sitting on the clothes of someone who could not read the Torah.

(b) The most common act of ritual purification was washing one's hands before the blessing at a meal (cf. Mk. 7:3–4; Jn. 2:6). This requirement applied also to the hours of prayer. Recitation of the Shema also became involved in ritual purification. Such regulations were meant as a guide for life, but they became a heavy burden in the sense of a legalistic system of casuistry.

4. The Essenes were even stricter than Pharisees on matters of purity and purification. Since they regarded themselves as the priestly, redemptive community of the end time, they made the Jewish rules for the priests binding on the whole community. Daily immersion was practiced in the pools that have been uncovered at Qumran. Anyone who offended in some way against the rules of the community was excluded temporarily or permanently from the purity of the many. At the same time, fig. language is used when an individual gives thanks that God has cleansed him from sin (1QS 3:4–12; 4:20–23).

NT In the NT *katharos* and its cognates occur in nearly all the writings, though references to purity are not as frequent as those to words derived from *hagios*, holy. We find these words used in a physical (e.g., Rev. 15:6), cultic (e.g., Matt. 8:2–4; Lk. 17:14), and spiritual (e.g., Matt. 5:8) sense. The concept of purity does acquire a new character through the preaching and person of Jesus.

1. (a) Jesus develops his doctrine of purity in his struggle against Pharisaism. In Matt. 23:25–26 he rejects the observance of ritual regulations on the ground that this kind of purity is merely external. Behind the practices of the Pharisees lurks the misguided notion that uncleanness comes from outside a person (cf. Matt. 15:11, 16–17; Mk. 7:15, 18). The opposite is true: What defiles a person comes from within, from the human heart (Mk. 7:15, 20–23). Jesus counters the Pharisaic emphasis on washing hands with a demand for purity of heart, as expressed in Matt. 5:8: "Blessed are the pure in heart, for they will see God."

For love that surrenders itself fully to God and to other people, there are no longer any unclean foods (Mk. 7:19c). Jesus sits down to eat with tax collectors and sinners (2:13–17). He does not repel lepers but heals them (Lk. 17:11–19). He talks to Samaritans (17:16c) and even Gentiles (Matt. 8:5–13; 15:21–28). By removing the dividing barriers of the ceremonial law and by demanding purity of heart and character, Jesus breaks through the innermost essence of Jud. and leaves it behind him.

(b) For the Christian community at Jerusalem, it was difficult to step across the barriers that Jesus had broken down, for as Jewish Christians they held on at first to the ceremonial law and temple worship. This difficulty is illustrated by the story of the conversion of the centurion Cornelius as a result of Peter's preaching (Acts 10:1–11:18). In a vision Peter becomes aware of the invalidity of the outward distinction between clean and unclean: "Do not call anything impure that God has made clean" (10:15). Granted, in the apostolic decree of the Jerusalem council, ritual requirements are laid on the Gentile church at Antioch (15:29), but at the same time the view prevails that God makes no distinction between Jews and Gentiles, but cleanses human hearts by faith (15:9).

2. (a) Paul is the first to recognize clearly that Christ has brought about the end of the law (Rom. 10:4), so that all cultic and ceremonial distinctions become obsolete. In the controversy between the strong and the weak, distinguished by differing attitudes toward eating meat used in pagan sacrifice, Paul comes down resolutely on the side of the strong: "All food is clean" (14:20; cf. also Tit. 1:15). For him the only reason to observe any kind of legalistic rules is regard for the weaker believer.

(b) In Jn.'s writings purity is brought through the saving death of Jesus. That is, Jn. gives purity a Christological foundation: "The blood of Jesus, his Son, purifies us from all sin" (1 Jn. 1:7; cf. 1:9). The story of Jesus washing the disciples' feet also shows that those who allow themselves to be served (as in baptism) by Jesus are clean (Jn. 13:10; cf. also Eph. 5:26). Purity is mediated by the word of Christ (Jn. 15:3). In Johannine thought, therefore, purity is not an ethical quality that one must work for, but an outworking of the fact that the church belongs to Christ.

(c) Heb. interprets the death of Jesus with the help of OT ritual concepts in order to demonstrate the superior quality of the new covenant over the old (9:13–14). In contrast to the purification of the OT temple by sacrifice, repeated every year (which the writer sees as an annual reminder of sin, 10:1–4), the purification effected by Christ's blood is valid once and for all. Moreover, it serves not only to bring outward purification, but also inner cleansing from sin (1:3; 10:22). Like 1 Jn., Heb. links the concept of purity with that of forgiveness (9:22).

(d) It is not until the Pastoral Letters as well as Jas. and 1 Pet. that the concept of purity gains in part an ethical character. The letters to Tim., in language formally similar to the preaching of Jesus, exhort purity of heart and conscience (1 Tim. 1:5; 3:9; 2 Tim. 2:22). Meanwhile, the focus shifts from the person of Jesus to didactic instruction: "The goal of this command is love, which comes from a pure heart and a good conscience and a sincere faith" (1 Tim. 1:5; cf. 1 Pet. 1:22).

Jas. shows a certain tendency to return to a concept of religious purity when he describes self-denial in the face of a sinful world as pure and undefiled religion (1:27). The nearest the NT comes to traditional Jewish thinking is in Rev., with its talk of purity in terms of physically clean linen garments (15:6; 19:8, 14) and the new Jerusalem of "pure [*katharos*] gold (21:18, 21).

3. It is significant that in the NT comparatively little use is made of the idea of purity in preaching Christ or Christian ethics. Preaching and teaching are dominated rather by words such as discipleship, obedience, sanctification, and love. But subsequent church history demonstrates how easy it is to fall back into a legalistic outlook. Again and again groups and sects have arisen that taught an ascetic purity as a distinguishing mark of Christian faith, seeking to impose this by rules and laws. This view of purity—which is, generally speaking, nearer to the radical Jud. of the Pharisees or Essenes—shows that in Christian proclamation the struggle between law and gospel must constantly be fought anew, in order that a Christ-centered doctrine of purity may be achieved, liberating us rather than bringing us back into legalism.

See also *hagnos*, pure, holy (*54*).

2755 (*katharotēs*, cleanness, purity), → *2754*.

2756 (*kathedra*, seat), → *2764*.

2757 (*kathezomai*, sit), → *2764*.

2761	καθεύδω

καθεύδω (*katheudō*), sleep (*2761*); κοιμάω (*koimaō*), sleep, fall asleep (*3121*); ὕπνος (*hypnos*), sleep (*5678*).

CL & OT 1. In cl. Gk. *katheudō* means exclusively sleep; *koimaō* (from *keimai*, lie) means lull (oneself), sink into sleep. In its mid. and pass. forms it can be used either of natural sleep or of dying. *hypnos* denotes natural sleep that refreshes or overcomes a person, causing one to forget the day's burdens. However, inasmuch as the Gks. identified life with our waking consciousness, sleep came to be seen as useless, degrading, and animal-like. The similarity between sleep and death led in mythology to the portrayal of *Hypnos* as the twin brother of the god *Thanatos*.

2. (a) In the LXX *katheudō* (35x) denotes natural sleep and never means to die. The same applies in general to the noun *hypnos*, though Jer. 51:39 (= LXX 28:39) refers to *hypnon aiōnion*, eternal sleep (see also Job 14:12; Ps. 13:3, *hypnoō*). *hypnoō*, sleep, occurs 25x in the LXX.

(b) *koimaō* (150x), meaning sleep (e.g., 1 Sam. 3:9), developed several nuances in the OT. In the Pentateuch esp., *koimaō meta* (e.g., Gen. 19:32–35) is used of sleeping together as a euphemism of sexual activity. In later parts of the OT, it acquired the meaning die, in the sense of an honorable death (e.g., "he slept with his fathers," 36x in 2 Ki. and Chr.; cf. also Isa. 43:17; Ezek. 32:19–32).

3. *katheudō* and *hypnos* are used by Philo and Josephus of sleep in the physical sense only. In intertestamental lit. we find the expression *hypnos aiōnios*, eternal sleep, from which the departed are to be awakened (cf. *T. Iss.* 9:9). The concept of an intermediate state finds further development in Jewish apocalyptic (e.g., *1 Enoch* 91:10; 92:3) and forms the background of NT teaching about death and resurrection.

NT *hypnos* (6x in the NT) and *katheudō* (22x) usually refer to the literal state of sleep (e.g., Matt. 1:24; Lk. 9:32; Jn. 11:13). Only in 1 Thess. 5:10 does it have the sense of having died (but cf. also Matt. 9:24 par.). In the scene in Gethsemane (Matt. 26:40; Mk. 14:37; Lk. 22:46) and in 1 Thess. 5:6–7 sleep has a negative connotation, indicating a lack of watchfulness. *koimaō*, on the other hand, is used 15x to mean die (only at Matt. 28:13; Lk. 22:45; Acts 12:6 does it have the sense of sleep).

It is chiefly Paul who uses *koimaō* in a fig. sense, emphasizing the close relationship between a sleeping person and death. He generally uses participial forms to describe deceased believers as those who have fallen asleep (see 1 Cor. 15:18, 20; 1 Thess. 4:13–15, both in connection with statements about the resurrection; cf. also Matt. 27:52).

In 1 Cor. 7:39; 15:6, 51, *koimaō* is used as an equivalent of die (cf. also Acts 7:60; 13:36; 2 Pet. 3:4). Jn. uses the ancient ambiguity of the vb. in Jn. 11:11–14, in the story of the raising of Lazarus, to show a misunderstanding on the part of the disciples. Jesus meant that Lazarus had died, but the disciples understood him to mean a sleep that would bring healing. Such language draws attention to Jesus' victory over the power of death. For him *thanatos* is no more than *hypnos*.

See also *apokteinō*, kill (*650*); *thanatos*, death (*2505*); *nekros*, dead, dead person (*3738*).

2762 (kathēgētēs, teacher, leader), → *4806.*

2764	κάθημαι

κάθημαι (*kathēmai*), sit (*2764*); καθέζομαι (*kathezomai*), sit (*2757*); καθίζω (*kathizo*), sit, cause to sit (*2767*); καθέδρα (*kathedra*), seat (*2756*); πρωτοκαθεδρία (*prōtokathedria*), best seat, place of honor (*4751*); πρωτοκλισία (*prōtoklisia*), best seat, place of honor (*4752*).

CL & OT 1. In cl. Gk. *kathizō* was originally a trans. verb, to cause someone to sit. But it acquired also an intrans. sense and became a synonym of *kathēmai* and *kathezomai*. Sitting was often a mark of honor or authority in the ancient world: A king sat to receive his subjects, a court to give judgment, and a teacher to teach.

2. Of the many different situations in which people sit in the OT, the following are significant. (a) In various contexts, sitting is a mark of honor and authority. The king sits on his throne. To sit at his right hand is a mark of the highest honor (e.g., 1 Ki. 2:19; cf. Ps. 110:1); in 1 Sam. 2:8 to sit with princes is a picture of exaltation. God, as king, also sits enthroned in heaven (1 Ki. 22:19; Ps. 29:10). The court, or judge, sits to give judgment (Exod. 18:13–14; Dan. 7:9–10, 26). A respected elder sits while others stand (cf. Job 29:7–8). A teacher sits among his pupils (2 Ki. 6:32; Ezek. 8:1). David "sat before the LORD" (2 Sam. 7:18)—a privilege apparently reserved for the king.

(b) To sit on the ground, by contrast, is a mark of abasement. It is a characteristic attitude of the sufferer (Job 2:8), mourner (Ps. 137:1), humiliated (Isa. 47:1), penitent (Ezra 9:3–4; Jon. 3:6), and suppliant (Jdg. 20:26; 2 Sam. 7:18).

(c) For most of the OT period it was normal to sit at a table (1 Sam. 20:5, 18, 25; 1 Ki. 13:20). The custom of reclining appears first in the Persian period (Est. 1:6; 7:8).

NT The NT also mentions people sitting in a wide variety of situations, including most of those listed above.

1. Kings sat on a throne (e.g., Acts 12:21; Rev. 18:7). God as king is also described in Rev. as the one who sits on the throne (e.g., 4:2–10; 5:1–13; 6:16; 7:10–17; 21:5). It is a mark of Christ's glory that he has been seated at God's right hand (e.g., Mk. 14:62; Eph. 1:20) or even shares the very throne of God (Rev. 3:21). Thus, having completed his work of redemption, he is now seated in the place of supreme authority until all opposition is finally destroyed (Heb. 1:3–4; 10:11–13).

2. As a remarkable extension of this idea, the believer, who is "in Christ," shares this exalted position. James and John asked for this place of honor as a personal right, but it was refused (Mk. 10:37–40). But the Christian's union with Christ means that "God raised us up with Christ and seated us with him [*synkathizō*] in the heavenly realms" (Eph. 2:6). He even offers us a place on the throne he shares with the Father (Rev. 3:21; cf. Matt. 19:28).

3. The seated position of the judge or court (Acts 6:15; 23:3; 26:30) leads to the trans. use of *kathizō* as a term for the appointment of judges (1 Cor. 6:4). In Jn. 19:13 this vb. can either be trans., that Pilate placed Jesus on the judgment seat as an act of mockery, or

intrans., that he sat on it himself. God (Rev. 20:11) and Christ in glory (Matt. 25:31) are described as sitting on thrones to give judgment.

4. Jesus customarily sat down to teach, whether in the open air (e.g., Matt. 5:1; 13:1–2) or in the temple court (26:55). In the synagogues it was customary for the preacher to stand to read the Scriptures and to sit to expound them (Lk. 4:16–21). The expression "Moses' seat" (Matt. 23:2) may therefore be fig., indicating the authority of the teacher who, like Moses, speaks in God's name.

5. The worshipers in the synagogue apparently sat (Acts 13:14), and Christian worship followed the same pattern (20:9; 1 Cor. 14:30). The most respected members of the synagogue congregation sat in the front seats (Mk. 12:39), a practice that led to unhealthy class distinction (cf. Jas. 2:2–4).

6. As in the OT, sitting on the ground was a mark of humiliation (Jas. 2:3). Mary's sitting by Jesus' feet (Lk. 10:39, *parakathezomai*) was a sign of humility. Sitting in sackcloth and ashes as a sign of penitence is still known (10:13), and beggars sit on the ground to ask for alms (Mk. 10:46; Jn. 9:8).

See also *klinō*, recline, sit down (*3111*).

2767 (kathizō, sit, cause to sit), → *2764.*

2770	καθίστημι

καθίστημι (*kathistēmi*), bring, appoint, put in charge (*2770*).

CL & OT *kathistēmi* has three main meanings: (a) lead or bring in; (b) appoint, esp. to an office or position; (c) bring to pass, become something, appear as. The usual meanings in the LXX are place somewhere and appoint to an office (cf. Deut. 17:15; 1 Sam. 8:1; Ps. 105:21).

NT Meaning (a) is found only in Acts 17:15: "(those) who escorted Paul"; (b) is found in 6:3 (of deacons); Tit. 1:5 (of elders); Heb. 5:1; 8:3 (of the high priest); Matt. 24:45 par. (of the controller of a household).

Meaning (c) occurs in Rom. 5:19; Jas. 4:4; 2 Pet. 1:8. Rom. 5:12–21 contrasts Adam and Christ. Adam's act of disobedience has binding results for all: "The many were made sinners." Through Christ's obedience, however, "the many will be made righteous" (5:19). In both cases, "were/will be made" is *kathistēmi*. Drawing on the language and ideas of the OT, Paul uses this vb. to describe God's judgment on humanity. But the decisive event is Christ's obedience even to death (cf. Phil. 2:5–11). Through that event it is now possible for all to stand as righteous before God.

See also *horizō*, determine, appoint (*3988*); *paristēmi*, place, put at the disposal of (*4225*); *procheirizō*, determine, appoint (*4741*); *tassō*, arrange, appoint (*5435*); *tithēmi*, put, place, set, appoint (*5502*); *prothesmia*, appointed date (*4607*); *cheirotoneō*, appoint (*5936*); *lanchanō*, obtain as by lot (*3275*).

2775 (kathoraō, look at), → *3972.*

2785	καινός

καινός (*kainos*), new (*2785*); καινότης (*kainotēs*), newness (*2786*); ἐγκαινίζω (*enkainizō*), make new, consecrate (*1590*); ἀνακαινόω (*anakainoō*), renew (*363*); ἀνακαίνωσις (*anakainōsis*), renewal (*364*).

CL & OT 1. In cl. Gk. *kainos* tends to denote what is qualitatively new as compared with what has existed until now, what is better than the old. *neos*, by contrast, is a temporal word for what has not yet been, what has just made its appearance. But the longer these words were used, the less strictly was this conceptual differentiation maintained.

2. In the LXX *kainos* often follows cl. Gk. by indicating something new, something previously not there (e.g., Deut. 20:5, a new house;

Jos. 9:13, new wineskins; 1 Ki. 11:29, a new cloak). The word finds its theological place in the eschatological message of the prophets, who question Israel's previous experience of salvation in history and announce God's new and saving activity in the future. This move of Yahweh's consists, according to Jer., in the establishment of a "new covenant" (31:31–34), in contrast to the covenant at Sinai; in this covenant Yahweh will put his will in Israel's heart in order to bring about a new obedience among his people.

Ezek. makes a similar promise of a "new heart and a new spirit" that Yahweh will create within his people (18:31; cf. 11:19; 36:26).

Isa. 43:18–19 presents the programmatic formulation of "forget the former things; do not dwell on the past. See, I am doing a new thing!" (cf. also 42:9; 48:6). The prophet understands Yahweh's activity in leading Israel back out of the Babylonian exile as a new creation, which will embrace the nation and the whole created order (43:16–21). In 65:17–18 he proclaims the creation of "new heavens and a new earth." The new thing that is awaited and promised in the prophetic proclamation as Yahweh's future act reaches from the inner parts of the human being all the way to the universal dimensions of a new world. The Israelite covenant community responds to these deeds of Yahweh with the "new song" (Ps. 33:3; 40:3; 144:9; 149:1).

NT 1. (a) The NT also follows the cl. Gk. usage of *kainos*. It occurs in the sense of unused (Matt. 9:17; 27:60; Mk. 2:21; Lk. 5:36; Jn. 19:41), unfamiliar, interesting (Mk. 1:27; Acts 17:19, 21), and novel (Matt. 13:52; 2 Jn. 5).

(b) But everything in the NT connected with Jesus' saving work is also characterized as new: a new covenant (Lk. 22:20; 1 Cor. 11:25; 2 Cor. 3:6; Heb. 8:8, 13; 9:15), a new command (Jn. 13:34; 1 Jn. 2:7–8), a new creation (2 Cor. 5:17; Gal. 6:15), the new existence of life in the Spirit (*kainotēs*, newness, Rom. 6:4; 7:6), the new self (Eph. 2:15; 4:24; cf. *anakainoō*, renew, 2 Cor. 4:16; Col. 3:10), a new heaven and a new earth (2 Pet. 3:13; Rev. 21:1), a new name (2:17; 3:12), the new Jerusalem (3:12; 21:2), and a new song (5:9; 14:3).

2. The following features emerge from an investigation of theological usage. (a) Most important is the use of *kainos* with *diathēkē* (covenant, → *1347*), in both the Synoptic and Pauline traditions of the Last Supper, in the words spoken over the cup: "This cup is the new covenant in my blood" (1 Cor. 11:25; cf. Lk. 22:20). These words signify that the blood, or death, of Jesus is the basis of the new covenant. This is an evident link with the promise of Jer. 31:31–34.

Elsewhere Paul interprets the new covenant as a covenant of the Spirit in contrast to the old covenant with its written code (2 Cor. 3:6). "We serve in the new way [*kainotēs*] of the Spirit, and not in the old way of the written code" (Rom. 7:6).

Heb. develops the new covenant theme further, contrasting the imperfect old covenant of Sinai with the perfect new one (8:6–7). The quotation from Jer. 31:31–34 is explained thus: "By calling this covenant 'new,' he has made the first one obsolete" (Heb. 8:13). Again and again the statements of this book circle around the newness of this covenant (9:15), which can also be called a "superior" (8:6) or "eternal" covenant (13:20). Through Jesus' death and mediating work "those who are called [will] receive the promised eternal inheritance" (9:15).

(b) The Synoptics use *kainos* from time to time with the same meaning as *neos* in order to distinguish the new that is an integral part of the appearance of Jesus from the old already in existence: e.g., in the parable of "new [*neos*] wine" that must be put into "new [*kainos*] wineskins" (Mk. 2:22). Similarly, 1:27 reports the strong impression that Jesus' teaching created: "a new [*kainos*] teaching—and with authority!" The nature of the newness is characterized by its contrast with the casuistic rab. method of teaching (1:22), by its authoritativeness, and by its power to effect what it says (as the context of the healing of the spirit-possessed man shows).

(c) In Gal. 6:15, Paul designates God's saving act in the cross of Christ "a new [*kainos*] creation" (cf. 6:14), setting it in opposition to the legalism advocated by the Judaizers, who claimed that God requires all male believers to be circumcised. For Paul, God's saving act is something fundamentally new. The new creation of God embraces not only humanity (1 Cor. 8:6) but the whole creation (Rom. 8:18–22; cf. Isa. 43:18–21).

Similar in meaning is 2 Cor. 5:17, where Paul declares: "Therefore, if anyone is in Christ, he is a new [*kainos*] creation; the old has gone, the new [*kainos*] has come!" Those who believe are transferred by faith into Christ and go from the present age into the age to come. This is indeed a new act of creation (*ktisis*, → *3232*) analogous to the original creative act by which the world came into being. The apostle is here taking up his earlier thought of God's new creative act in Christ in 4:6: "For God, who said, 'Let light shine out of darkness,' made his light shine in our hearts to give us the light of the knowledge of the glory of God in the face of Christ" (cf. Gen. 1:3).

In 2 Cor. 4:16 Paul continues this discussion of newness. Our salvation is not a matter of gaining some new psychological or ethical quality. It entails a daily process of renewal: "Though outwardly we are wasting away, yet inwardly we are being renewed [*anakainoō*] day by day." This takes place through the recreative power of the Spirit given by Christ, "in the new way [*kainotēs*] of the Spirit" (Rom. 7:6; cf. Tit. 3:5).

The existence of the new person thus involves a new way of life, which is hidden with Christ in God (Col. 3:3). Those who embark on it should hold fast to their new life and put on the new self, "since you have taken off your old self with its practices and have put on the new [*neos*] self, which is being renewed [*anakainoō*] in knowledge in the image of its Creator" (Col. 3:9–10; cf. Rom. 12:2; Eph. 4:23–24). The imperative does not invalidate the indicative; rather, the concealment of the existence of the new creation is itself the basis for the energetic imperative to the new way of life (cf. Gal. 5:25).

The two passages just mentioned (2 Cor. 4:16; Col. 3:10) are the only uses of *anakainoō* in the NT; in both cases it is in the pass. The corresponding noun *anakainōsis*, renewal, is also found only twice in the NT. In Rom. 12:2 believers are exhorted to let this renewal affect their social attitudes: "Do not conform any longer to the pattern of this world, but be transformed by the renewing [*anakainōsis*] of your mind." Tit. 3:5 sees salvation grounded in renewal: "He saved us, not because of righteous things we had done, but because of his mercy. He saved us through the washing of rebirth [→ *palingenesia*, *4098*] and renewal [*anakainōsis*] by the Holy Spirit."

(d) Jn. 13:34 speaks of the "new [*kainos*] command" of brotherly love: "A new command I give you: Love one another. As I have loved you, so you must love one another." The command is new because Jesus was the first to reveal fully what love means (cf. 1:17; 15:13). Here, too, the imperative to love is grounded in the indicative of Jesus' love. Because the Christian community has experienced the reality of the self-sacrificial love of Jesus, it is summoned at the same time to transform concern for self into concern for others. It is not a question of an ethical principle, but of becoming new in love by virtue of the new love of Christ.

In 1 Jn. the point at issue is likewise that of brotherly love (1 Jn. 2:7–11). The command is called, strikingly, old and new at the same time (2:7–8; cf. 2 Jn. 5). It is old in the sense that it goes back to the beginning of the Christian life. As to content, it is simply the new love for one's fellow believers that is in view, although the Christological foundation of Jn.'s Gospel is not explicitly expounded in this letter (1 Jn. 2:8–11).

(e) The vb. *enkainizō* occurs only 2x, both in Heb. In 10:20, believers have confidence to enter the sanctuary "by a new and living way opened [*enkainizō*] for us through the curtain, that is, his body" (cf. the use of this vb. in 1 Sam. 11:14; Ps. 51:10). The meaning of inaugurate is suggested for this vb. in Heb. 9:18: "Even the first covenant was not put into effect [*enkainizō*] without blood" (cf. Deut. 20:5; 1 Ki. 8:63; 2 Chr. 7:5).

(f) *kainos* plays an important role in the visions of Rev. Those who are victorious over their earthly temptations will receive "a white stone with a new name" (2:17; cf. 3:12). This stone may reflect the white stone used by jurors to signify acquittal, a token entitling one to free entertainment at royal assemblies (i.e., admission to the heavenly feast), or a white stone regarded as a mark of felicity (or even a combination of these or other images). The new name is not that of the bearer, but of the one giving authority to the bearer. The context of Rev. 1 suggests that the new name is that of Christ as Lord (cf. 1:8, 10–20; cf. Phil. 2:11), for he has conquered and has assumed lordship (cf. Rev.2:17; 5:5–11; 22:13, 20). He is the one who makes the new reality possible.

The heavenly community of the redeemed will strike up a "new song" in honor of the Lamb who was slain (Rev. 5:9; 14:3). When the great and final apocalyptic battle has been fought out against Satan and all the enemies of the Lamb have been defeated, the "new Jerusalem" will arise (21:2), and "a new heaven and a new earth" will be created (21:1; cf. 2 Pet. 3:13). Then there will be no more tears, suffering, pain, or death (Rev. 21:4). In Jesus Christ is the universal hope of all things being made new (21:5).

See also *neos*, new, young, fresh (*3742*); *prosphatos*, fresh, new, late (*4710*).

2786 (kainotēs, newness), → 2785.

2789	καιρός

καιρός (*kairos*), time, especially a point of time, moment (*2789*); εὐκαιρέω (*eukaireō*), have opportunity (*2320*); εὐκαιρία (*eukairia*), favorable opportunity, the right moment (*2321*); εὔκαιρος (*eukairos*), opportune (*2322*); εὐκαίρως (*eukairōs*), when convenient (*2323*); ἀκαιρέομαι (*akaireomai*), have no time, no opportunity (*177*); ἀκαίρως (*akairōs*), untimely, ill-timed, inopportune (*178*); πρόσκαιρος (*proskairos*), temporary, transitory, passing (*4672*); σήμερον (*sēmeron*), today (*4958*); νῦν (*nyn*) now (*3814*); νυνί (*nyni*), now (*3815*); ἄρτι (*arti*), now, just, immediately (*785*); εὐθύς (*euthys*), at once, immediately (*2317*); εὐθέως (*eutheōs*), at once, immediately (*2311*).

CL 1. (a) In cl. Gk. *kairos* originally denoted right measure, correct proportion, that which is convenient and appropriate; it can also have a locative sense, meaning right spot, suitable place. Used in a material sense, it can denote importance, norm, wise moderation. Used in a temporal sense, the word characterizes a critical situation, one that demands a decision. Positively, this implies opportunity, suitable time, right moment; negatively, danger. But *kairos* can also appear as a synonym with other temporal concepts and denote generally time (*chronos*, → *5989*), season of the year, hour (*hōra*, → *6052*), or the present moment (e.g., *nyn*, now, and *sēmeron*, today). Various words have been derived from *kairos* (see the lexical paragraph above for these words with their meanings).

(b) Further mention must be made of the adv. *nyn* and the synonymous intensive form *nyni*, now, at the present moment. Not infrequently *nyn* has a more material meaning as well as the temporal, such as in accordance with the present situation, as matters now stand. *nyn* is also frequently used adjectively, meaning present (e.g., *ho nyn chronos*, "the present time"), or even substantively (e.g., *to nyn*, "the present time").

(c) Synonymous with *nyn* is the temporal adv. *arti*, now, just, forthwith. With the preps. *heōs*, until, and *apo*, away from, *arti* turns the attention from the present moment to the past or future.

2. The presence of the two etymological word groups for time suggests that the Gks. distinguished individual points of time that can be affected by human decisions (*kairos*) from the stream of time, whose progress is independent of human influence (*chronos*). The will to seize the moment, which can also grasp the wrong thing (*kairos*-thinking), counteracts the danger of fatalism, which can grow out of *chronos*-thinking.

(a) *kairos*, *nyn*, and *sēmeron* mark those points of time that are of importance for an individual's life in the infinite onward flow of the stream of *chronos*. Where the Gks. showed an interest in the exploration of tangible reality, reflection on time led to prominence being given to smaller units of time.

(b) It is against the background of the swift passing of time (*chronos*) that the point of time that demands action (*kairos*), whether it is given by gods or by fate, gains its importance. In later times Kairos was even worshiped as a god. *kairos* is the space of time in which decisions are made for the individual, which one must dare to exploit. Those who miss or evade their *kairos* destroy themselves. It is important to take to heart the call to recognize the moment and in all one's activity to find the right moment.

OT In the OT, where time is essentially understood qualitatively from the point of view of the encounter between God and humankind, the use of a term to denote the right moment was important. It is therefore not surprising that *kairos* occurs about 300x in the LXX, three times more than *chronos*. It is primarily used to render the Heb. word for time *ʿēt* (198x). In some places, *kairos* appears more or less synonymously with other words for time (such as *chronos*, Eccl. 3:1; Dan. 2:21; 7:12; Wis. 7:18; 8:8; *hēmera*, day, Ps. 37:19; Jer. 50:27, 31 = LXX 27:27, 31; *hōra*, hour, Num. 9:3, cf. 9:7, 13).

1. While *kairos* often serves simply for precise (e.g., Gen. 17:23, 26) or more general (e.g., Jdg. 11:26; 1 Ki. 11:4; Ps. 71:9) temporal designations, in other passages it helps to illustrate the characteristic aspect of the OT understanding of time. For time is not an anonymous destiny. Yahweh has created the whole of time and fills it in accordance with his will, and also fixes the individual *kairoi* (cf. Gen. 1:14). He does this as the Lord of nature, who guides the heavenly bodies (Job 38:32), directs the weather (Lev. 26:4), and allots times and seasons for the biological growth of plants (Ps. 1:3) and animals (Job 39:1). The feasts and festivals in the context of the yearly cycle are special times of joy and rest given by Yahweh (Exod. 23:14–17).

As Lord of humanity, God also apportions one's life span (Sir. 17:2): he determines the hour of birth (Eccl. 3:2) and death (7:17 = LXX 7:18). All the elements of human existence in their tension-laden diversity are times from and in God's hands (cf. Ps. 31:15), as the song in praise of time stresses (Eccl. 3:1–8).

In times of affliction it is not easy to hold to this confession of Yahweh as the giver of times, but even then the Israelites who remain with the covenant do not allow their relationship with God to be broken (cf. Ps. 32:6; 37:19, 39). It is in times of distress that they hope for a time of pardon (102:13), for the *kairos* of God's help and redemption (cf. Isa. 33:2; Judith 13:5).

2. Such a trust in the particular moment (*kairos*) of a saving act of Yahweh is founded on the historical experiences of the people of Israel. Again and again in the stereotyped phrase "at that time [*kairos*]," attention is directed to the events of salvation history in the past, in the first instance to the time of Moses and the exodus from Egypt (cf. e.g., Deut. 1:9, 16, 18), but also to the that of prophetess Deborah (Jdg. 4:4), the reign of David (1 Chr. 21:28–29), or the building of Solomon's temple (2 Chr. 7:8). Esp. in the historical books of the OT, *kairos* is often found with this function of drawing attention to God's activity in the history of his people.

3. In the OT prophets and in later apocalyptic circles of Jud., a change took place from a focus on the fulfilled time of earlier generations and the patriarchal traditions to the expectation and hope of judgment and fulfillment in the future, which achieves the same significance for life in the present as past history had done before. The phrase "at that time" now takes on a future reference (e.g., Jer. 3:17; 4:11; Dan. 12:1; Joel 3:1) and points to an intervention by God in the near or distant future that will have the character of a comprehensive judgment. For the godless in and around Israel, that "day of the Lord" will be a time (*kairos*) of visitation (Jer. 6:15; 10:15), wrath (Sir. 44:17), and punishment (5:7; 18:24). But those who remain obedient and practice righteousness await everlasting salvation (Zeph. 3:16, 19–20; cf. Isa. 60:20–22; Dan. 12:1–2). Right up to the final day of

judgment, however, Yahweh gives time for repentance (cf. Sir. 18:21) and for acting uprightly. This comes about by a right use of the present *kairos* at any given time (cf. 51:30).

4. (a) In later Jewish writings both the chronological interest and the expectation of a final space of *kairos* are powerfully elaborated. The Jews prepared for an early end to the present time and hoped for a new age, conceived in temporal terms.

(b) The conception of time in the Dead Sea Scrolls has the strong imprint of deterministic thought. In the present ordering of time we must obey God's will (1QS 9:12–16), which consists in being separate from sinners in order to prepare the way for the last days (9:18–20). For God has preordained the moment of visitation (3:18), when an end will be put to wickedness and truth will come to light in the world forever (4:18–23).

NT In the NT, *kairos* occurs 85x, *eukaireō* 3x, and *eukairia, eukairos,* and *eukairōs* 2x each. *akairōs* and *akaireomai* are used once. *proskairos* occurs 4x, *sēmeron* 41x, *nyn* 147x, *nyni* 20x, *arti* 36x, *euthys* 51x, and *eutheōs* 36x. These words tend to be most prominent in the writings of Lk. and Paul.

1. The OT understanding of time stamps the NT use of the word group. In a whole range of passages *kairos* means the same or nearly the same as other words for time, denoting generally a particular time (e.g., the phrase "at that time," Matt. 11:25; 12:1; Acts 7:20). This should not be understood merely as a short point or moment of time (except in Lk. 8:13). *kairos* often refers to a longer or shorter time span (e.g., "the times of the Gentiles" in 21:24; "present sufferings" in Rom. 8:18). It can mean the times in the life of nature established in creation (Matt. 13:20; 21:34; Mk. 12:2), but any kind of nature idolatry is repudiated (Gal. 4:9–10), and the confession of God as the giver of fruitful times is given added strength (Acts 14:17).

2. The decisively new and constitutive factor for any Christian conception of time is the conviction that, with the coming of Jesus, a unique *kairos* has dawned, one by which all other time is qualified. Mk. 1:15 makes this clear in programmatic fashion: "The time [*kairos*] has come.... The kingdom of God is near. Repent and believe the good news." The time of grace for which the prophets hoped and waited has now been realized with Jesus Christ (cf. Rom. 3:21; 1 Pet. 1:10–11). Anyone who listens to him now in faith and obedience will have eternal life (Jn. 5:25; cf. 3:36). With the life and esp. the suffering and death of Jesus, the old age has passed away, and with the present time of divine righteousness (Rom. 3:26; 5:6) the fulfillment of the times has dawned. But this time also presents the church with the opportunity to serve one another, as Paul suggests in Phil. 4:10 (using the vb. *akaireomai*, have no time, no opportunity).

3. (a) As the physical presence of Jesus plunged every concrete "today" into the light of divine salvation (Lk. 13:32; 19:5, 9; 23:43; cf. 2:11), so his redeeming power can become effective in our lives from now on through our relationship of faith with the exalted God (cf. 22:69). Jesus' suffering and death is no mere fact of the past; it is, rather, present time. From Easter on, this is the proclamation that counts: "I tell you, now is the time [*kairos*] of God's favor; now is the day of salvation" (2 Cor. 6:2; cf. Isa. 49:8). By passing on this message of the *kairos*, the "now" of the offer of salvation keeps on becoming afresh the reality that demands a decision.

Just as the disciples obeyed when Jesus called them (Matt. 4:20, 22; Mk. 1:18), so each person is summoned today to respond to the missionary proclamation without delay and begin to follow Jesus. They are not to evade the decision by delaying the Today until Tomorrow and are certainly not to "harden" their hearts, i.e., to reinforce their will for an existence without God (cf. Heb. 3:7, 15; 4:7), lest they find themselves, like Jerusalem, standing under the verdict of a "woe" (cf. Lk. 19:44).

(b) If, therefore, *kairos* must be used initially for the fundamental decision of faith, those who are now reconciled (cf. Rom. 5:11; 13:11) must henceforth live by faith. The "once" or "formerly" of

idolatry is to be superseded by the "now" of true worship of God (Gal. 4:8–9; Eph. 5:8–9). Faith brings release from being the servile victim of time; it brings freedom from the burdensome past through the acceptance of the gift of forgiveness. At the same time, however, it does not absolve one from the ethical responsibility to make sensible use of the time at one's disposal (Gal. 6:10; Col. 4:5). Indeed, the opposite is true. Believers are assigned historical time with the imperative to make "the most of every opportunity" (Eph. 5:16).

This new life of faith is not, of course, without affliction. "This present time [*kairos*]" (Lk. 12:56; cf. Mk. 10:30), and therefore also the time of the church, is not a time of blessedness free from temptation but a time of struggle (cf. 1 Cor. 9:24–27; Eph. 6:12; 1 Tim. 6:11–15) and suffering (Rom. 8:18). Thus Christians must encourage each other to prevent a falling away (Heb. 3:12–13) in the moment of temptation (Lk. 8:13).

4. The fullness of divine glory will dawn only with "the last time" (1 Pet. 1:5, *kairos eschatos*), the precise date of which is unknown (Mk. 13:33; Acts 1:7; 1 Thess. 5:1–11) and that is sometimes expected as imminent (1 Cor. 7:29; Rev. 1:3; 22:10) and sometimes as more remote (2 Thess. 2:1–12). The NT is always pointing to this *telos* of final time (→ *telos*, goal, *5465*). The eschatological *kairos* is now understood Christologically as the time of Christ's return in glory (1 Tim. 6:14) and as the time of the final judgment (1 Cor. 4:5; 1 Pet. 4:17–18; Rev. 11:18; cf. Jn. 5:28–29), when the godless are punished and those who trust in God are rewarded (cf. Mk. 10:30; Gal. 6:9).

Thus with the pattern "once" and "now" there corresponds the "already" (confident in faith and hope) and "not yet" (full blessedness, cf. Rom. 8:18; Heb. 11:25–26; 1 Pet. 1:5–6). Jesus' lordship is still not completely visible or perceptible (Heb. 2:8). Satan is still allowed a period of time for his diabolical intrigues (Rev. 12:12). The Christian still comes up against the harsh realities of life (cf. 2 Cor. 4:18), esp. those of bad times (cf. Eph. 5:16; 2 Tim. 3:1; 4:3). The time between the appearance of the earthly Jesus and the Parousia thus remains a tension-laden time, which requires vigilant concentration (cf. Lk. 21:36; Eph. 6:18, by prayer) on the part of Christians. Such a time of probation, of course, stands clearly within the sign of the promise that embraces all times: "Jesus Christ is the same yesterday and today and forever" (Heb. 13:8).

See also *aiōn*, aeon, age, life span, epoch, eternity (*172*); *chronos*, time, period of time (*5989*); *hōra*, hour, time, point of time (*6052*).

| 2790 Καῖσαρ | Καῖσαρ (*Kaisar*), Caesar, emperor (*2790*). |

CL "Caesar" was originally a proper name, the family name of the Julian family, esp. of Julius Caesar, but also of Augustus (so Lk. 2:1). It developed a titular significance and became equivalent to "the emperor." This usage appears in all NT refs.

NT Insofar as *Kaisar* functions as a theological concept within the NT, it denotes the legitimate power of political authority. Thus, it is important for Luke that Paul can affirm his innocence not only with respect to the Jewish law and temple, but also with respect to Caesar (Acts 25:8); so too Paul is wholly justified in appealing to this civil power for protection against what amounted to religious persecution (25:11).

It is possible, however, for the authority of Caesar to be contrary to the authority of God in a false antithesis. Thus, according to Acts 17:1–9, the Jewish community in Thessalonica had apparently achieved a satisfactory balance between their religious and secular obligations and felt a threat to this equilibrium by the strong challenge of the Christian gospel (cf. 2 Thess. 2:5). That which was threatening their established way of life, they accused of threatening the law and order of society at large. The claims of the exalted and soon-to-return king Jesus on personal life and relationships were so far-reaching that they could be (and were) misrepresented as the claims of an earthly tyrant, and Jesus was portrayed as a rival to Caesar (Acts 17:7).

The possible conflict between the authority of God and that of Caesar must have been a real one for early Christians and is tackled in Mk. 12:13–17. The question put to Jesus concerned the poll tax that had been levied on the inhabitants of Judea, Samaria, and Idumea since A.D. 6. As tribute money to the occupying Roman power, the tax became a focus for intense national and religious feeling on the part of the Jews. The Zealots were esp. vehement and implacable in their hostility; God was their only ruler and king. The question whether it was lawful to pay the tax to Caesar was thus well chosen to trap Jesus on the horns of a dilemma: Either deny the authority of Caesar (rebellion) or deny the full authority of God (blasphemy).

Jesus clearly viewed the antithesis as false, for political and divine authority need not necessarily conflict. Paying taxes is a legitimate obligation within the network of human relations. Thus, the poll tax did not conflict with the higher authority of God. To pose Caesar and God as mutually exclusive authorities makes all human relationships antithetical to divine authority, for all relationships involve obligation of one kind or another. Human beings can live within human relationships of authority and obligation and still "give. . . to God what is God's."

There is, however, the possibility of real conflict between one's obligation to Caesar and obligation to God. Loyalty to Caesar can become an excuse for evading higher obligation to the truth (Jn. 18:38; 19:12–16). Those who limit their motives and aims to friendship with Caesar shut themselves off from an answer to the question, "What is truth?" Whoever affirms loyalty only to Caesar is thereby self-condemned (cf. Jn. 16:8–11).

See also *hēgemōn*, leader, commander, chief (*2450*); *anthypatos*, proconsul (*478*).

2798 (*kakia*, badness), → *2805*.

2800	κακολογέω

κακολογέω (*kakologeō*), speak evil of, revile, insult, execrate (*2800*).

CL & OT *kakologeō* is seldom used in cl. Gk. It means speak ill of, revile (a person or thing; see 2 Macc. 4:1). In the LXX *kakologeō* often means execrate (cf. Exod. 21:16; 22:28; Ezek. 22:7). The transition to this meaning has its explanation in the Jewish belief in the power of the spoken word. Certainly reviling can also include a curse.

NT *kakologeō* occurs 4x in the NT. In Matt. 15:4 and Mk. 7:10 it has the idea of curse. The biblical basis here is Exod. 21:17. Jesus takes issue with the Jewish interpretation of the biblical commandments, which softened their meaning and robbed them of their force (Matt. 15:5–6). In Mk. 9:39 Jesus forbids his disciples from restraining a strange miracle worker who was casting out demons in his name, for "no one who does a miracle in my name can in the next moment say anything bad about me." In Acts 19:9 *kakologeō* refers to unbelieving Jews who "publicly maligned the Way."

See also *anathema*, cursed, accursed (*353*); *katara*, curse, malediction (*2932*); *rhaka*, empty-head, fool (*4819*).

2801 (*kakopatheia*, suffering), → *4248*.

2802 (*kakopatheō*, suffer evil, endure hardship), → *4248*.

2803 (*kakopoieō*, do wrong, harm), → *2805*.

2804 (*kakopoios*, evildoer), → *2805*.

2805	κακός

κακός (*kakos*), bad, evil (*2805*); ἄκακος (*akakos*), guileless, innocent (*179*); κακία (*kakia*), badness (*2798*); κακόω (*kakoō*), harm, embitter (*2808*); κακῶς (*kakoō*), badly, with evil intent (*2809*); κακοποιέω (*kakopoieō*), do wrong, harm (*2803*); κακοποιός (*kakopoios*), evildoer (*2804*); κακοῦργος (*kakourgos*), evildoer, delin-

quent (*2806*); ἐγκακέω (*enkakeō*), become tired, lose heart (*1591*); φαῦλος (*phaulos*), bad, evil (*5765*).

CL & OT 1. In cl. Gk. *kakos* means bad in the sense of lacking something, always in contrast to *agathos*, good. It has four primary uses: (a) negligible, unsuitable; (b) morally evil; (c) weak, miserable; (d) harmful, unfavorable. *to kakon* and the pl. *ta kaka* mean evil, suffering, misfortune, ruin.

The Gk. world had two basic frameworks within which to understand the question of the meaning and origin of evil. (a) Evil was seen as a metaphysical principle. (b) Human ignorance is the source of all evil. An unenlightened and ignorant person does evil involuntarily, and this is the basis of ruin and corruption. Enlightenment leads to knowledge and frees one from evil, causing one to do good.

Plato synthesized these two basic concepts by developing a metaphysical dualism of spirit and matter, with its ethical expression in a dualism of soul and body. The cause leading to evil lies in the material and physical. In his old age Plato went a step further and assumed the existence of an evil world soul.

The basis of evil in the cl. world must not be regarded as personal guilt, for it is not the result of a free and responsible personal decision to do evil but of a lack, such as the lack of knowing divine providence.

2. In the LXX *kakos* is used predominantly for Heb. *raʿ* and *rāʿâ* (227x), which are also rendered by *ponēros* 226x (→ *4505*). There is a similar balance in the use of the vbs. *kakoō* (21x) and *ponēreuomai* (22x).

(a) *kakos* is primarily the evil that objectively hurts one's existence. (i) It is principally regarded as God's punishment (Deut. 31:17), which usually corresponds to the preceding sin. Yahweh brings evil back on one's head. Hence Amos 3:6b can say, "When disaster comes to a city, has not the LORD caused it?" (ii) Yet God grants protection to the pious in the midst of all evil (Ps. 23:4). God's "plans [are] to prosper you and not to harm you" (Jer. 29:11 = LXX 36:11). (iii) Behind the evil lies God's gracious purpose of visitation. His final purpose is "to give you hope and a future" (Jer. 29:11c). (iv) The OT reaches the climax of its search for the origin and purpose of evil when faced with God's all-sovereign goodness. Here all questioning is silenced. In Job the three friends seek to link Job's suffering with his sins. Job never denies his sinfulness, but the work as a whole makes no direct connection between his sinfulness and his sufferings. Suffering is not necessarily the result of sin; it may be training in faith and hence testing (Job 5:17–18; cf. also Ps. 73).

(b) Evil is also an aspect of moral behavior (cf. Ps. 28:3; 34:12–16; Jer. 7:24; Mic. 2:1). Note that the OT seldom speaks theoretically of evil. It describes it concretely.

(c) Some passage of the OT connect the concept of evil with an evil power opposed to God (cf. 1 Chr. 21:1).

3. According to the teaching of Qumran, God created at the beginning two spirits, the good spirit (the spirit of light) and the evil spirit (the spirit of darkness). According to God's eternal decree, all humans belong to one or other of these spirits, and this is revealed by their good or evil deeds (1QS 3:13–21).

4. Philo attributes the origin of good to God and evil to humanity. But human beings have the possibility of choosing the good, just as they choose between good and bad clothes. Evil is a reality opposed to God, but not a person opposed to him.

NT 1. *kakos* (50x in the NT, half in Paul) means evil, bad, destructive, unjust. Its derivative *akakos* means without suspicion, simpleminded (Rom. 16:18) or guiltless, untouched by evil (used of Christ in Heb. 7:26). The related adv., *kakōs*, occurs 16x, often in connection with diseases (Mk. 1:32, 34; 2:17). Jas. 4:3 uses this word to mean improper motives.

The noun *kakia* is often used synonymously with the neut. adj. *kakon* to mean evil, wickedness, and denotes the source of the behavior of a *kakos*, an evil person, or *kakopoios*, evildoer (cf. Acts 8:22; Rom. 1:29; 1 Cor. 5:8). In Matt. 6:34 it has the more general meaning of trouble, hardship, or misfortune.

The vb. *kakoō* means do evil, cause damage, or harm (1 Pet. 3:13; 5x in Acts); *kakopoieō* means behave badly, do wrong (1 Pet. 3:17; 3 Jn. 11), harm (cf. Mk. 3:4; Lk. 6:9). A change in meaning is evident with *enkakeō*. It no longer means behave badly, but become tired or careless (e.g., in prayer, Lk. 18:1; in doing good, 2 Thess. 3:13) or lose heart (2 Cor. 4:1, 16; Eph. 3:13). Weariness here is not physical but spiritual.

kakos and its derivations are of less importance in the NT than in the OT, since the NT prefers *ponēros* and *hamartia* (→ *281*) to express evil and personal guilt.

2. (a) The NT knows of no dualism in which evil has the same power as good. Equally rejected is the idea that the root of evil could lie in God, "for God cannot be tempted by evil" (Jas. 1:13). Evil comes rather from a person's heart in the form of evil thoughts that find expression in acts (Mk. 7:21–22 par.), such as love of money (1 Tim. 6:10) or the misuse of the tongue (Jas. 3:6–10; 1 Pet. 3:10).

(b) Evil may be God's righteous punishment, from which only repentance can deliver one (e.g., Lk. 13:1–5), or it can be borne and conquered by the experience of the love of God in Christ (Rom. 5:5; 8:35, 37–39).

(c) *kakos* is used attributively as a noun of persons (Matt. 21:41; 24:48; Phil. 3:2; Tit. 1:12; Rev. 2:2) and of things (Mk. 7:21; Rom. 13:3; 1 Cor. 15:33; Rev. 16:2). Otherwise it is always a neut. noun meaning evil or the evil in the sense of a misfortune, wrong, suffering (cf. Lk. 16:25; Acts 16:28; 28:5), or an evil act, a sin (cf. Matt. 27:23 par.; Acts 23:9).

(d) For Paul, the problem of evil lies in the fact that people often do evil against their will (Rom. 7:15, 17–19), which rules in them like a strange law (7:21, 23), and yet it is an expression of their existence and nature. One's evil nature shows itself in evil acts, separates one from God, and brings one under judgment. Since we constantly do the evil instead of the good we want to do and thus achieve death and not life, every hope of conquering evil by our own strength is demolished. The solution of this problem is found in Christ's victory over evil in his cross and resurrection. Note Paul's shout of salvation: "Thanks be to God—through Jesus Christ our Lord!" (Rom. 7:25).

(e) We must understand the apostolic exhortations to conquer, lay aside, and shun evil against this background of evil being stripped of its power (Rom. 12:17, 21; 16:19; 1 Cor. 10:6; Col. 3:5; 1 Pet. 3:11). Though every governing authority (Rom. 13:1, 3–4; → *exousia*, *2026*) should as God's representative hold down evil, the problem of evil is finally solved only by justification and sanctification. The one who has been justified is in the sphere of influence of the One who has conquered evil and who gives the Spirit. Hence no believer faces the powers of evil without strength (Rom. 13:10; 2 Cor. 13:7).

3. *phaulos* (6x in the NT) is a synonym of *kakos*. In Tit. 2:8 it is used in a judgment on people. Otherwise it is used for people's actions (Jn. 3:20; 5:29; Rom. 9:11; 2 Cor. 5:10; Jas. 3:16); its opposite is *agathos* (→ *19*).

4. In two NT passages we find *kakourgos*, evildoer, criminal. In Lk. 23:32, 33, 39, it is used for the criminals crucified with Jesus. In 2 Tim. 2:9 Paul uses it to refer to his imprisonment "like a criminal."

See also *ponēros*, sick, bad, evil (*4505*).

2806 (kakourgos, evildoer, delinquent), → *2805.*

2808 (kakoō, harm, embitter), → *2805.*

2809 (kakōs, badly, with evil intent), → *2805.*

2813	καλέω

καλέω (*kaleō*), call (*2813*); κλῆσις (*klēsis*), call, invitation (*3104*); κλητός (*klētos*), called, invited (*3105*); ἐπικαλέω (*epikaleō*), call, appeal to (*2126*); προσκαλέω (*proskaleō*), summon (*4673*).

CL 1. (a) *kaleō* means to speak to another person, either immediately or mediately, in order to bring that person nearer, either physically or in a personal relationship. Thus the word can mean invite (e.g., into a house, to a feast) The part. *klētos* means invited one, a guest, and *klēsis* means the act of inviting (even official summons by an authority). (b) *kaleō* (and *epikaleō*) and *klēsis* mean summon one's adversary or witnesses before a court of law—later, *proskaleō* and *prosklēsis* were used. (c) *kaleō* also means to name, either when a person is being addressed or when a name is bestowed. *kaloumenos* with the names of people or places means called, so-called.

2. *epikaleō*, usually in the mid., normally has the meaning of invoking. It is used either of the worship of the gods or, in legal language, of lodging an appeal.

3. *kaleō* and *klēsis* are seldom used of a divine call in cl. Gk. Such a use comes from the mystery religions, the influence of the LXX, and especially NT use. Various words besides *kaleō* were used to denote an individual's work in society (e.g., *ergon* or *ponos*); work was considered to be one's calling. Consciousness of vocation remained confined to priests and to some extent to those who devoted themselves to intellectual and administrative tasks.

OT With minor exceptions *kaleō* (ca. 300x), *epikaleō* (ca. 150x), and *proskaleō* (25x) are used in the LXX to render various forms of the Heb. *qārāʾ*. The LXX uses *klēsis* only in Jer. 31:6 (LXX 38:6); 3 Macc. 5:14; Jdt. 12:10. *klētoi* and the part. *keklēmenoi* are used for those invited (guests). The combination *klētē hagia* denotes the worshiping congregation at festivals (Exod. 12:16; Lev. 23:2–37 [11x]; Num. 28:25). The phrase is particularly used with reference to their calendar (see also *ekklēsia* [*1711*]).

1. (a) *kaleō* often means naming—of things (e.g., Gen. 1:5, 8–9; 2:19; Isa. 35:8; 56:7) or persons (e.g., Gen. 25:26, Jacob; 29:32–35; 30:6–24). When God promises to give his servants "another name" (Isa. 65:15), it implies a new existence. (b) *epikaleō* can also denote naming (e.g., Num. 21:3). The phrase "Your name is called (*epikeklētai*) over us" (Jer. 7:14 in LXX) implies a special degree of possession and protection.

2. *epikaleō* is the most important term in the LXX for calling on the Lord and worshiping him, and it has the special characteristic of confession (cf. Gen. 4:26; where a cry of need is involved, *krazō* may be used). Worship is addressed to God, to the God of Israel, to the Lord (1 Ki. 17:21), or above all to the name of God (Gen. 13:4; Isa. 64:7; Jer. 10:25), which is a strong tower (cf. Prov. 18:10). The purpose of the manifestation of God's presence is that we should turn to him in worship.

3. (a) For the most part *kaleō* and *proskaleō* describe a call from those higher in rank to individuals or groups under them, e.g., parents to children (Gen. 24:58), rulers to subjects (Exod. 1:18; Jdg. 12:1), and Moses to the elders (Exod. 12:21; 19:7). Such a call was always a summons or a command, never a mere invitation (Job 13:22). This call expects people to hear and answer, though they can refuse to obey God's call (Isa. 50:2; 65:12; Jer. 7:13; cf. 13:10). By contrast, God's commanding call creates order in the universe. He calls the stars (Isa. 40:26) and causes events to happen in history.

(b) Before a person can answer God's call, one must realize that the call has indeed come from God. The difficulty of this is shown dramatically in the story of Samuel's call (1 Sam. 3:4–10; *kaleō* appears 11x). God's call often leads to suffering for his sake. This shows that fundamentally his call is only bringing to light the election that preceded it. In Isaiah's Servant Songs we have the profoundest use of *kaleō* in the sense of service and dedication, linked with an exceptionally frequent appearance of *eklegomai*, choose (→ *1721*). God calls the elect one (Isa. 41:8; 43:10) in righteousness (42:6) and by name (43:1; 45:3). This individual is a type of all who have been called (41:2, 4).

4. This word group does not occur in the accounts of the call of the judges (Jdg. 6:13) and the prophets (cf. Isa. 6:1–8; 40:6–12; Jer. 1:4–9; Ezek. 2:1–8). This is because those calls are not described in Scripture with specific words but by content and form.

5. Within Jud. only the people of Qumran seem to have had a special sense of call. While election played a considerable part there, the

specific call of God is mentioned only 2x, though the expression "the called of God" is found a number of times.

NT In the NT *kaleō* is found 148x, *epikaleō* 30x, *proskaleō* 29x, *klēsis* 11x, and *klētos* 10x. Paul tends to use the word group often, whereas it occurs rarely in the General Letters and in Rev. Lk.'s infrequent use of it is probably due to his Greek background; he is the only NT writer to use more classical compounds such as *eiskaleō*, invite, *metakaleō*, have brought to oneself.

1. (a) In the NT *kaleō* can mean the giving of a name (Matt. 1:21; Jn. 1:42), the use of a title when addressing someone (Matt. 23:7–8), or the attribution of a particular rank (23:9, father; Lk. 6:46, Lord; 22:25, benefactor). Of special importance are the cases where God gives a name. By conferring the names "Jesus" (Lk. 1:31) and "John" (1:13), God expresses, as in the OT, his control over their lives.

(b) Frequently behind the pass. *kaleomai*, be named, be called, lies an expression of the character and existence of a person or thing. This is perhaps most clearly seen in Paul's remark that he does "not even deserve to be called an apostle" (1 Cor. 15:9). Often in such expressions OT ideas have been taken over, as in Mk. 11:17 par., where the temple is called "a house of prayer" (quoting Isa. 56:7). This usage is particularly important in Lk. 1:32, 35, where Jesus is called "the Son of the Most High," i.e., "the Son of God." Consequently, his followers will be called "sons of God" (Matt. 5:9; Rom. 9:26) and "children of God" (1 Jn. 3:1). These new names clearly express a new existence granted by an act of God.

2. (a) We meet the meaning "invite" for *kaleō* principally in the parables of the great banquet (Lk. 14:7–25 [11x]) and the marriage feast (Matt. 22:2–10 [5x]; cf. also Rev. 19:9). There is a hint of both privilege and command in these passages. Probably this is also how we should understand "I have not come to call the righteous, but sinners" (Matt. 9:13; Mk. 2:17; Lk. 5:32). When someone ignores the divine invitation, he or she is not only missing an opportunity, but may be squandering life and hope.

(b) The note of command in the verb comes through even more clearly in passages where rulers or officials call their subordinates: Herod (Matt. 2:7) and the owner of the vineyard (20:8). As a result, it would have been natural for Jesus to use it as a special term for the call of his disciples, though it occurs only in 4:21 and Mk. 1:20.

(c) It is striking that *proskaleō* is likewise not used for such a call. This word is used of a commanding call to an individual (Matt. 18:2; Mk. 15:44), an existing, fairly well-defined group like the disciples (Matt. 10:1; Mk. 6:7; 12:43; Acts 6:2), or the people in general (Matt. 15:10; Mk. 7:14). In Acts 13:2 the vb. indicates the heavenly call to Paul and Barnabas, which was to be realized in their earthly commissioning. In 16:10 a heavenly directive to Paul and his companions was communicated by a vision.

(d) The statement, "For many are invited [*klētoi*], but few are chosen" (Matt. 22:14), reflects on the relationship between God's call and election. It shows that, at least from the standpoint of human response, the circle of the called and of the elect cannot be taken as necessarily coinciding (→ *eklegomai*, choose [*1721*]).

3. (a) Paul uses *kaleō* (33x), *klēsis* (9x), and *klētos* (7x) almost always with the sense of divine calling. He understands calling as the process by which God calls those whom he has already elected and appointed out of their bondage to this world, so that he may justify and sanctify them (Rom. 8:29–30) and bring them into his service. This call is thus part of God's work of reconciliation and peace (1 Cor. 7:15). It reaches us only through the love of Christ directed toward us (Gal. 1:6, 15).

When Paul says that God's decision is not dependent on works but solely "by him who calls" (Rom. 9:12), he is stressing the unfettered choice of God, which is not influenced by human preconditions (cf. also Gal. 1:6; 1 Thess. 2:12; 1 Pet. 1:15). Rom. 4:17 shows that God's call means a new existence, equivalent to a new creation.

(b) God's call is mediated by the message of the gospel (2 Thess. 2:14), which comes through the witness of humans. It brings people into fellowship with Christ (1 Cor. 1:9) and with the other members of his body. Since the divine call is "as members of one body" (Col. 3:15), it is equivalent to entering the kingdom of God. The use of *klēsis* always indicates either that the call comes from God (Rom. 11:29; Phil. 3:14) or that one is brought into fellowship with the church as a whole (1 Cor. 1:26; Eph. 4:1). Baptism is both a visible sign of the call and of the obligation of the believer to live a life "worthy of the calling ... received" (Eph. 4:1; cf. 1 Thess. 2:12).

(c) Paul addresses church members as *klētoi*, called ones (Rom. 1:6–7; 8:28; 1 Cor. 1:2, 24—sometimes written as those "called as saints"). He stresses that both the existence of the church and individual membership in it are based solely on the will and work of God. In 1 Cor. 1:26 we see how Paul saw this calling as dependent on God and how it involves the church. In considering their calling, the Corinthians will realize what they once were and with what sort of people God has joined them in his church.

In 1 Cor. 7:15–24 the Christian's call does not necessarily change his or her social status. That is, it does not free the slave from a master or force the believer to change occupations. The change in relationships is reached not by revolution but by a change in one's inner attitude. In 1 Cor. 7:20 *klēsis* denotes a particular place or station in life.

(d) In rare cases Paul uses *klētos* of a personal commission. When in Rom. 1:1 and 1 Cor. 1:1 he declares himself to be *klētos apostolos* ("called to be an apostle"), he is stressing that he owes his office as apostle to a special call by God.

4. The use of the word group in 1 Pet. is essentially Pauline. Peter stresses in 1:15 and 5:10 that the call comes from God and that God has a purpose in his call (2:21; 3:9). Those called by him are to bear witness to the one who has called them out of darkness (2:9) by following the example of Christ (2:21); thus, they will inherit a blessing (3:9). Similar is Heb. 3:1 and 9:15, which speak of the heavenly call and a promised inheritance.

5. *epikaleō* (in the NT only in the mid. and pass.) is used with much the same nuance as *kaleō*. In the expression "[those] who bear my name" (lit., "over whom the name of God has been called," Acts 15:17; cf. Jas. 2:7), both God's assumption of power over his people and his simultaneous expression of care for them are brought out. Twice (Acts 4:36; 12:12) *epikaleō* is a virtual synonym for *kaleō*.

Paul uses *epikaleō* 6x in his appeal to Caesar (Acts 25–28). In addition, it is frequently used of calling on God or his name (cf. 7:59; 9:14; Rom. 10:12–14; 1 Cor. 1:2). It normally carries with it the thought of confessing God within the church. In 2 Cor. 1:23 we note an exception, for here God is being called on as a witness. Such expressions are based on OT language for the invocation of Yahweh.

2814 (kallielaios, cultivated olive), → *1778.*

2815 (kalodidaskalos, teaching what is good), → *1437.*

2818 (kalopoieō, do good), → *2819.*

2819	καλός

καλός (*kalos*), good, beautiful, noble (*2819*); καλοποιέω (*kalopoieō*), do good (*2818*); καλῶς (*kalōs*), well, beautifully (*2822*).

CL & OT 1. (a) In cl. Gk. the basic meaning of *kalos* is organically fit, suitable, useful, sound: e.g., a suitable harbor, a healthy body, pure gold, an unblemished sacrifice. Aesthetic judgments became attached to this meaning, so that *kalos* also came to mean the beautiful. Finally the concept was broadened again to mean morally good. Thus, the concept *kalos* achieved an inclusive meaning, denoting a state of soundness, wholeness, and order, both externally and internally.

(b) A Gk. ideal for life and education was expressed by the phrase *kalos kai agathos*, which showed the aristocracy how to live. An education based on the arts and exemplary behavior molded the nobleman in the ethics of his class. Socrates and Plato raised this chivalrous class ethic to be a general goal of all Gk. education. In their writings the *kalos kagathos* (as it came to be written) is someone who is respectful and fair, thoughtful and discreet, moderate and capable in the way he conducts his life.

(c) Finally, Plato raised the concept *kalos* in the sphere of philosophy and religion to the status of an eternal idea by linking it with the experience of *erōs* (love). The unremitting longing and striving of the soul is directed towards the *kalon*; *erōs* is the force that drives people to seek and recognize the *kalon* in this world. Earthly beauty partakes of the eternal archetype of the beautiful. The *kalon* thus links the divine and earthly realms and gives life meaning and an eternal dimension. This religious significance of *kalos* was retained in later Christian thought. True beauty is at one with the eternally true and good and is only found with God; everything on earth is a mere reflection of that divine beauty.

2. The meaning the Gks. gave to *kalos* scarcely penetrated the world of the OT or NT. In the LXX *kalos* occurs most often beside *agathos* and *chrēstos* as a translation of *ṭôb*. It means good—not so much in the sense of an ethical evaluation as in that which is pleasant, enjoyable, beneficial. *kalos* is what is pleasing to Yahweh, what he likes, or what gives him joy. Note esp. the use of *kala* as an expression of God's aesthetic judgment in Gen. 1:31. *kalos* means fair or beautiful in, e.g., 6:2; 12:14; 2 Sam. 11:2; 13:1.

It is striking that the OT shows no interest in the Gk. ideal of beauty as a motive for living and for education. Everything is directed toward God's will, which is expressed in the law; any ideal of self-perfection is thus excluded. Hence, *kalos* is frequently used as a synonym for *agathos* (cf. Isa. 1:17; Mic. 6:8; Mal 2:17; also Num. 24:1; Deut. 6:18; 12:28; 2 Chr. 14:2; Prov. 3:4). In the story of the fall, *kalos* is used in the description of "the tree of the knowledge of good and evil" (Gen. 2:9, 17).

NT 1. In the NT *kalos* is used 100x (almost the same as *agathos*, 102x; → *19*) to denote good. In the Synoptic Gospels, John the Baptist demanded from those who wanted to enter the fellowship of the kingdom "good fruit" (Matt. 3:10; Lk. 3:9). Jesus made the same demand (Matt. 7:17–19; 12:33; cf. Lk. 6:43–45). His parables speak of "good seed" (Matt. 13:24, 27, 38), "good fish" (i.e., people) who are caught in the net (13:48), and "good soil" in which the Word flourishes (13:23; Mk. 4:20; Lk. 8:15). It is in this sense that Jesus calls us to "good deeds" (Matt. 5:16), which are summed up in the maxim of 25:40: "Whatever you did for one of the least of these brothers of mine, you did for me." They remain connected with the works of love that served as directives for the practice of mercy in Jud. (cf. Isa. 58:6–7). At the same time, from good deeds is removed all thought of striving after reward (cf. Lk. 10:30–37).

In the story of the anointing at Bethany (Mk. 14:6), Jesus, aware of his imminent passion, places this "beautiful thing" done to him higher than his disciples' almsgiving. The opportunity for this act—the anticipatory anointing of his body and thus the affirmation of his path of suffering—only offered itself in this historical moment.

2. In Jn. Jesus is "the good [*kalos*] shepherd." Here *kalos* brings into focus his office as shepherd in all its uniqueness, in contrast to contemporary false claims to the office of shepherd (Jn. 10:11, 14). He is the good, the lawful, shepherd, because he opposes the wolf at the risk and cost of his own life. This pattern of Jesus must be seen against the OT background of Yahweh as shepherd (Gen. 49:24; Ps. 23; → *poimēn*, *4478*). In Jn. 10:32 Jesus speaks of his "many great [*kalos*] miracles" in the context of a controversy with the Jews. It is not the miracles themselves that are in dispute, but his messianic claim, the evidence for which is in these works.

3. In general Paul uses *kalos* as a synonym for *agathos*; it does not convey anything that could not be expressed by *agathos* (cf. Rom. 7:18, 21; 1 Cor. 7:1; 2 Cor. 13:7; Gal. 6:9). By contrast, the preference for *kalos* in the Pastorals is striking (cf., e.g., 1 Tim.3:1; 5:10, 25; 6:18; Tit. 2:7, 14; 3:8, 14), esp. in military imagery (cf. 1 Tim. 1:18;

6:12; 2 Tim. 2:3; 4:7). The reason for this usage may be because *kalos* was a favorite in popular Hel. speech and expressed a Hel. sense of values. Thus, it helped express more clearly for a second generation of Christians what is involved in Christian discipleship. *kalos* continues in the General Letters to describe desirable Christian conduct (e.g., Heb. 5:14; 10:24; Jas. 2:7; 3:13; 4:17; 1 Pet. 2:12; 4:10).

4. The adv. *kalōs* occurs 37x in the NT. It often bears the meaning to say something right or correctly (e.g., of the Scriptures, Matt. 15:7; Acts 28:25; of people, Mk. 12:32; Jn. 4:17). It can also be used to denote correct or appropriate conduct (e.g., 1 Tim. 3:4, 12–13; Heb. 13:18; Jas. 2:8).

See also **agathos**, good (*19*); **chrēstos**, pleasant, kind, good (*5982*).

2820 (kalymma, veil, covering), → 2821.

2821 καλύπτω

καλύπτω (*kalyptō*), cover, hide, conceal (*2821*); ἀνακαλύπτω (*anakalyptō*), uncover, unveil (*365*); κατακαλύπτω (*katakalyptō*), cover up, veil (*2877*); κάλυμμα (*kalymma*), veil, covering (*2820*); ἀκατακάλυπτος (*akatakalyptos*), unveiled (*184*).

CL & OT 1. *kalyptō*, to conceal, cover, occurs in cl. Gk. in both lit. and fig. senses. It is often used in the sense of burying someone by covering with earth. *katakalyptō*, to hide, cover up, put on a veil, is attested in cl. Gk. from Homer on, while *anakalyptō*, to uncover, remove a veil, is a later word. *kalymma*, veil, head-covering, is used in a variety of ways, such as the veil of a bride or the veil that a priest wore when he spoke on behalf of a deity.

2. (a) *kalyptō* in the LXX is used of the cloud that covered Sinai and of the darkness that covers the earth (Exod. 24:15; Isa. 60:2). In Ps. 32:5 the word is used of concealing sin, while in 85:2 it refers to God's covering of sin in forgiveness. The word is frequent in Ps. (e.g., 44:15; 69:7; 85:2) and Ezek. (e.g., 7:18; 16:8; 24:7–8).

(b) *anakalyptō* is related in meaning to *apokalyptō* (→ *636*). It is used in Job 12:22 of the uncovering of hidden depths shrouded in darkness and in 33:16 of the uncovering of the human mind. In Isa. 47:3 Babylon, addressed as a virgin, is threatened with the uncovering of her nakedness as a divine punishment, while in Jer. 13:22 Judah is similarly threatened with the lifting of her skirts (a symbol of humiliation).

(c) *katakalyptō* occurs in Exod. 26:34; Num. 4:5 of the covering of the ark with a curtain. In Isa. 6:2 the seraphim cover their faces and feet with their wings. Tamar in Gen. 38:15 veils her face, i.e., like a prostitute. The rare verbal adj. *akatakalyptos*, unveiled, occurs in Lev. 13:45.

(d) *kalymma* is used in Exod. 34:34–35 of the veil worn by Moses to cover his face. In Num. 4:6, 8, 12, etc., this word (along with *katakalymma*) is used of the cloths with which the holy objects like the ark of the covenant, the altar, and the altar vessels were kept from being touched or seen. To look at them or touch them could mean death (Num. 4:15, 20).

NT 1. (a) In the lit. sense *kalyptō* is found at Matt. 8:24 (the boat is covered by waves); Lk. 8:16 (no one hides a lit lamp in a jar); and 23:30 (people cry to the hills to cover them). (b) A fig. use is found in the general statement, "There is nothing concealed that will not be disclosed" (Matt. 10:26; cf. Lk. 12:2). The statement allows of various applications, but in the context it refers to the commission Jesus gave to his disciples. The word told to them in secret is to be proclaimed publicly from the rooftops (Matt. 10:27).

2. In 1 Cor. 11:1–6 Paul deals with the question of women's veils. This is the only place in the NT where the mid. *katakalyptomai*, to veil oneself (11:6–7), and the adj. *akatakalyptos*, unveiled (11:5, 13), are found. Paul requires women to wear a veil when praying or prophesying in church (11:4–5) and offers various arguments why. For one thing, this is in keeping with the strict Jewish practice of what is fitting and proper, according to which it would be unthinkable for a

woman to appear in public without a veil (11:13). Paul wants this custom to be observed not only in Corinth but also in the other churches as well (11:16).

The most puzzling ground for this ruling is the one given in 11:10: Women are to have a "sign of authority" (*exousia*) on their heads. Exactly what Paul means by this is unclear. Just as difficult are the words "because of the angels" in this verse. Are the angels guardians of the natural order (11:8–9; cf. Gen. 2:21–23)? Or is the veil a protection against fallen angels, who might wish to lead the women astray? The brevity of Paul's reference makes its interpretation difficult (→ *kephalē, 3051*, for more interpretative comments on 1 Cor. 11:2–16).

3. (a) The word *kalymma*, covering, occurs 4x in the NT, all in 2 Cor. 3:13–16. Here Paul refers to Exod. 34:33–35, where Moses puts a veil over his face because the Israelites feared the divine radiance coming from it (34:30; cf. Num. 4:15, 20). Paul disregards the fear motive. Rather, he suggests that Moses put on the veil in order that the Israelites might not see the end of his temporary radiance. One of Paul's main points here is the passing glory of the old covenant contrasted with the eternal glory of the new (2 Cor. 3:11). This veil remains unlifted up to the present day when the "old covenant" is read (3:14–15). It lies over the minds of the Jews who cannot grasp the true meaning of the old covenant as pointing to Christ. Just as Moses removed the veil when he went in to God (Exod. 34:34), so will the veil be removed from Israel when they are converted to the Lord, i.e., when they allow themselves to be ruled by the Spirit (3:16).

(b) The only NT instances of the vb. *anakalyptō*, to unveil, uncover, are also found in 2 Cor. 3:14, 18. Paul's statement in 3:14, which says that the veil remains over the reading of the "old covenant," is difficult to interpret, though Paul emphasizes that for Christians the veils that might prevent them from seeing "the light of the gospel of the glory of Christ" (4:4; cf. 4:6) have been removed. This is clear from 3:18, which expresses this assurance of Christian faith: "We [believers] ... with unveiled faces all reflect the Lord's glory." The beholders are changed by the Lord, who is the Spirit (3:17), into the likeness of the one whom they behold.

In Corinth there were opponents of the apostle who held that his gospel was veiled (cf. 2 Cor. 4:3, pass. of *kalyptō*), that is, obscure or contradictory. Paul throws back the criticism in his opponents' face by saying that it is veiled "to those who are perishing," that is, to those who cannot see the light of the gospel because Satan has blinded them (4:4). This judgment agrees with the remarks about the unbelieving Jews made in 2 Cor. 3:13.

4. In 1 Pet. 4:8 the readers are exhorted to love on the ground that "love covers over a multitude of sins." In Jas. 5:20 the same exhortation is given in order to bring back "a sinner from the error of his way." Probably what we have here is a catch phrase that had its origin in Prov. 10:12. This phrase may mean that love wins for those who practice it the divine forgiveness of sins. More likely, however, it means that love covers up, by means of human forgiveness, a multitude of sins in others.

See also *kryptō*, hide, conceal (*3221*).

2822 (*kalōs*, well, beautifully), → *2819*.

2834	κανών

κανών (*kanōn*), rule, standard, norm (*2834*).

CL & OT 1. In cl. Gk. *kanōn* is a loan word from Sem., where it meant reed, cane, stalk of grain. *kanōn* means anything that can be held against something else in order to stretch, roll up, or measure it. The idea of measurement became predominant, and eventually *kanōn* meant esp. a measuring line or rod, fixed rule, norm. In mathematics, astronomy, and history, *kanōn* means list or table; in art a guideline. In philosophy *kanōn* denotes a criterion of judgment.

In 4 Macc. 7:21 *kanōn* means a standard of judgment, while in Jdt. 13:6 it stands for something like a bedpost. In Mic. 7:4, an almost

unintelligible verse in the LXX, *kanōn* seems to be a meaningless conjecture with no Heb. equivalent.

NT 1. *kanōn* occurs 4x in the NT, only by Paul. It denotes both the rule for the individual Christian's life and the standard by which to judge others. "Peace and mercy to all who follow this rule [*kanōn*], even to the Israel of God" (Gal. 6:16). Paul is summing up here all he has previously said, esp. about the death of Christ on the cross, which gives a new relationship with God and a new basis for existence. The *kanōn* establishes a new scale of values, different from everything outside salvation in Christ. These values are to be applied in our everyday lives. To "follow this rule" means that the new being, shaped by Christ's saving work, manifests itself in thought and action. Whoever lives by the rule belongs to the "Israel of God."

2. *kanōn* occurs in some MSS readings of Phil. 3:16: "Only let us live up to [the same standard as] what we have already attained." In the context Paul speaks of being taken hold of by Christ, an experience that enables him to press toward the goal of his heavenly calling. If we adopt the word *kanōn* here, it has same sense as in Gal. 6:16.

3. *kanōn* is used three times in 2 Cor. 10, where it is translated "field" (10:13), "area of activity" (10:15), and "territory" (10:16). The NIV thus interprets *kanōn* in a geographical sense, i.e., the area of work measured out or allotted to Paul. Other interpreters understand *kanōn* here as the rule or pattern that Paul follows by preaching the gospel only in areas where it has not yet been proclaimed (see Rom. 15:20–21).

4. In later church usage the word *kanōn* designated the rule of faith and esp. the list of writings recognized by the church as documents of divine revelation. Regarding the OT, by the time of Jesus the authoritative books seem to have been widely agreed upon, namely, the books that we today accept as the OT Scriptures (not including the Apocr.). The NT quotes from or alludes to all books of the OT except Est. This body of writings seems to have been formally accepted by the Jews at Jamnia in about A.D. 90.

Regarding the NT, it was a matter of recognizing which books the Spirit was speaking through. The earliest list of NT writings that corresponds precisely to what we today accept as the NT canon was written in A.D. 367; this list and others that preceded it were often drawn up to guard the church against heretics and their writings. However, note that the authority of the four Gospels, Acts, and the letters of Paul was generally recognized early in the 2d cent. And even earlier than that, Paul could testify that when the Thessalonians "received the word of God, which you heard from us, you accepted it not as the word of men, but as what it actually is, the word of God, which is at work in you who believe" (1 Thess. 2:13). In 2 Pet. 3:15–16, Peter includes the "letters" of Paul along with "the other Scriptures."

See also *metron*, measure (*3586*).

2840	καρδία

καρδία (*kardia*), heart (*2840*); καρδιογνώστης (*kardiognōstēs*), knower of hearts (*2841*); σκληροκαρδία (*sklērokardia*), hardness of heart (*5016*).

CL & OT 1. In cl. Gk. *kardia* was used in lit. and fig. senses. Lit., it denoted the heart as a bodily organ and the center of physical life. Fig., it was regarded as the seat of the emotions, instincts, and passions, as well as the source of intellectual and spiritual life. The heart was the center of the human will and the seat of one's power of decision. Used in specific senses with reference to nature, it meant the pith of wood and the seed of plants.

2. The OT also uses heart with a lit. and a fig. meaning. The Heb. word *lēb* (also *lēbāb*) is most often rendered by *kardia*, sometimes by *dianoia* (mind) and *psychē* (soul). (a) Viewed as a bodily organ, the heart is the seat of strength and of physical life (Ps. 38:10; Isa. 1:5). When the heart is strengthened by food, the whole person is revived (Jdg. 19:5; cf. Gen. 18:5; 1 Ki. 21:7).

(b) In a fig. sense *kardia* is the seat of one's intellectual and spiritual life, one's inner nature. It is the seat of a person's emotions: joy (Deut. 28:47), pain (Jer. 4:19), tranquillity (Prov. 14:30), or excitement (Deut. 19:6). It is the seat of understanding and knowledge: of rational forces and powers (1 Ki. 3:12; 4:29), and of delusions and visions (Jer. 14:14). Folly (Prov. 10:20–21) and evil thoughts also operate in the heart. Finally, the will originates in the heart, with its carefully weighed intentions (1 Ki. 8:17) and decisions (Exod. 36:2). In a general sense, *kardia* is a comprehensive word for the total person (Ps. 22:26; 73:26; 84:2)

3. The idea of human responsibility is particularly related to the heart. Thus, the heart is also the organ through which a person is converted (Ps. 51:10, 17; Joel 2:12) and acts according to God's Word. It is the seat of awe and worship (1 Sam. 12:24; Jer. 32:40 = LXX 39:40); the heart of the godly inclines in faithfulness to the law of God (Isa. 51:7), while that of the ungodly is hardened and far from God (29:13).

4. Philo and Josephus use "heart" exclusively as a bodily organ, the central part of physical life, without clearly defining the seat of the inner life. Philo leaves open the question of whether one's controlling reason is to be found in the heart or in the brain, although he shows many echoes of OT usage. By contrast, rab. Jud. speaks of the heart as the center of life, even of life before God; good and evil thoughts live in the heart, and in the heart one worships God.

NT *kardia* occurs 156x in the NT. Its use of this term coincides with the OT, though the meaning of the heart as the inner life, the center of the personality, and the place in which God reveals himself is more clearly expressed in the NT than in the OT.

1. (a) *kardia* is the center of physical life and one's psychological makeup. This word seldom occurs in the sense of the bodily organ, the seat of natural life (cf. Lk. 21:34; Acts 14:17; Jas. 5:5). By contrast, it frequently denotes the seat of intellectual and spiritual life, the "inner self" in opposition to external appearance (1 Pet. 3:4, lit., "the hidden person of the heart"; cf. 2 Cor. 5:12; 1 Thess. 2:17). The powers of the spirit, reason, and will have their seat in the heart in the same way as the movements of the soul, feelings, passions, and instincts.

A striking feature of the NT is the closeness of *kardia* to the concept *nous*, mind (→ *3808*). Like *kardia*, *nous* also has the meaning of person, inner self. Heart and mind (*noēmata*, lit., thoughts) are parallel in 2 Cor. 3:14–15 or used synonymously in Phil. 4:7. In such cases the element of knowledge is more heavily emphasized with *nous* than with *kardia*, where the stress lies more on the emotions and the will.

(b) *kardia* is also the center of spiritual life. The most significant instances of *kardia* in the NT occur in those passages that speak of one's standing before God. The heart is that part in us that is addressed by God. It is the seat of doubt and hardness as well as of faith and obedience.

2. Sin marks, dominates, and spoils not only the physical aspects of the natural self, not only one's thinking, willing, and feeling, but also one's innermost being, the heart. If the heart has been enslaved by sin, the whole person is in bondage (cf. Jer. 17:9). Evil thoughts come from the heart (Mk. 7:21 par. Matt. 15:19). Shameful desires live in the heart (Rom. 1:24). The heart is disobedient and impenitent (2:5; 2 Cor. 3:14–15), hard and faithless (Heb. 3:12), dull and darkened (Rom. 1:21; Eph. 4:18). Referring to his opponents, Jesus quoted Isa. 29:13, "Their hearts are far from me" (Mk. 7:6; par. Matt. 15:8). Equally, he rebuked his disciples for their slowness of heart (Lk. 24:25). The Gentiles cannot excuse themselves before God, for they carry in their hearts the knowledge of what is good and right in God's sight (Rom. 2:15).

3. God alone can reveal the things hidden in the human heart (1 Cor. 4:5), examine them (Rom. 8:27), and test them (1 Thess. 2:4). Because corruption stems from the heart, that is where God begins his work of renewal, sometimes by piercing it (Acts 2:37; cf. 7:54, where "furious" lit. translates "furious in their hearts"). It is in the heart that conversion takes place, and it is a matter of the whole person. The heart is thus the seat of faith (Rom. 10:6–10), and Christ takes up residence there (Eph. 3:17).

Conversion of the heart is not achieved through the will or desire of the person (1 Cor. 2:9), but solely because God opens the heart (Acts 16:14) and lets his light illumine it (2 Cor. 4:6). God bears his witness to humankind by sending into the human heart the Spirit of his Son (2 Cor. 1:22). When this Spirit takes up his dwelling there, we are no longer slaves to sin but children and heirs of God (Gal 4:6–7). In short, God pours his love into our hearts (Rom. 5:5).

4. The human heart, however, is the place not only where God arouses and creates faith; here faith also proves its reality in obedience and patience (Rom. 6:17; 2 Thess. 3:5). The Word of God takes root in the heart (Lk. 8:15), and the peace of Christ begins its rule there (Col. 3:15). God's grace strengthens and establishes the heart (Heb. 13:9). The NT describes a heart directed unreservedly to God as a "pure" heart (Matt. 5:8; 1 Tim. 1:5). This purity is based solely on the fact that the blood of Christ cleanses it (Heb. 10:22; cf. 1 Jn. 1:7).

5. *kardiognōstēs* (unknown in cl. Gk.) occurs in the NT only in Acts 1:24 and 15:8. It describes God as the one who knows human hearts. As noted above, he sees, tests, and examines the hidden depths of the human heart (see also Lk. 16:15; Rev. 2:23). *sklērokardia* occurs in the LXX in Deut. 10:16; Jer. 4:4; Sir. 16:10. In the NT it occurs at Matt. 19:8; Mk. 10:5; 16:14; cf. Rom. 2:5 (see also *sklēros*, *5017*). Hardness of heart is the closedness of the self-centered person to God, his offer of salvation, and his demands, and also to one's fellow human beings. The natural person has a stony heart, turned against God and neighbor, until God's intervention gives that person a new, obedient heart (cf. Ezek. 36:26–27).

2841 (kardiognōstēs, knower of hearts), → *2840.*

2843	καρπός	καρπός (*karpos*), fruit (*2843*); καρποφορέω (*karpophoreō*),

bear fruit (*2844*); ἄκαρπος (*akarpos*), unfruitful, fruitless (*182*).

CL & OT 1. In cl. Gk. *karpos* is used both of the fruit from plants and of the offspring of animals. It also occurs in an extended sense for the result or outcome of an undertaking, whether good or bad.

2. Likewise in the LXX *karpos* means the fruit of plants (e.g., Deut. 1:25; Mal. 3:11), but also the fruit of the body, posterity (e.g., Gen. 30:2; Deut. 7:13; Ps. 21:10; Mic. 6:7), and, fig., the fruit of an action (e.g., Jer. 6:19; 17:10; Hos. 10:13).

In Jewish writings, the righteous bring forth good fruit, the unrighteous bad. Commercial language used *karpos* in the sense of interest (as the fruit of a transaction), as also did theology with its growing emphasis on belief in the beyond. Thus, in discussing sin a distinction was drawn between the original stock or capital (so-called original sin) and interest (individual sins). Punishment of the former was reserved for the beyond; the latter was punished here and now, partly through giving birth to ever new sins.

NT 1. (a) *karpos* occurs 66x in the NT. Its primary meaning denotes the fruit of plants (Matt. 13:8 par.; 21:19 par.; Lk. 12:17) or the produce of the earth (Jas. 5:7, 18; cf. Lk. 20:10). Passages such as Jas. 5 make it clear that people can prepare for and encourage the growth of fruit by their work but can expect and receive it only as a gift. The seed and harvest are bestowed on them. To what extent the growth of fruit is removed from human willpower is also shown by the fact that it ripens at its appointed time (Matt. 21:34; *kairos*, → *2789*).

The form of a fruit is not optional but is determined by the seed (cf. 1 Cor. 15:35–44), so that one may reason back from the fruit to the plant (Matt. 12:33 par.; cf. 7:16, 20). This applies not only to the species but also to quality. Matt. especially contrasts "good fruit" from good trees with "bad fruit" from bad trees (3:10; 7:17–19; 12:33). Fruit that does not come up to expectation is useless, and that which bears it (the tree, 7:19; Lk. 3:9; 13:6–9) is unusable.

(b) *karpos* in the sense of fruit of the body, offspring, is found only in Lk. 1:42; Acts 2:30.

2. The passages under 1 (a) are not concerned primarily with the processes of nature but with humans before God. This applies even more to the remaining passages, in which the idea of fruit is applied to one's life. These are often connected with the vbs. *poieō* (do) and *pherō* (bear, bring forth). The verbal compound *karpophoreō* (bear fruit) occurs 8x.

(a) When John the Baptist demanded good deeds from people as "fruit in keeping with repentance" (Matt. 3:8 par.), the use of *karpos* expressly indicates that it is not a question of deliberate, self-determined action on one's part. Rather, it is "fruit-bearing" that follows from one's turning to God and the power of the Spirit working in one's life. When Jesus taught that true disciples are recognized as such precisely by their fruit (7:16–20), which they bear in true discipleship, he means that their faith shows itself alive in their love. In receiving divine love, they will love; in receiving forgiveness, they will forgive. In short, the sanctification that has come to them and is going on in them is expressed by their giving God the honor.

At the same time they put at the disposal of others the benefit of the divine working in them through what they do and say. The graphic pronouncement that every tree without fruit will be condemned in the judgment of God (Matt. 3:10; 7:19; Lk. 13:9) also raises the question of the outworking of faith in those who have received God's word. Those who check the growth of fruit or even hold back others from enjoying it will receive a reward from God in keeping with their evil deeds.

(b) The expression *karpon pherō* (bear fruit) is used esp. in Jn. 15:2–16, where close fellowship of Jesus' disciples with their Lord is portrayed as the secret of the power to bear fruit. His death is the soil out of which rich fruit grows (12:24); his death on the cross brings about redemption. As the vine, he sends through his branches the life-giving power that is the prerequisite and means of faith.

True, humans can accomplish moral and technical achievements by their natural gifts. But the "fruit of the gospel" (Luther)—that which God expects from us—can grow only from the soil of obedience, which essentially consists in recognition of the bond between Creator and creature, established by the death of Christ. We no longer need to consider our own achievements. Freed from the anxiety of failure, we are capable of the highest endeavor ("more fruit," Jn. 15:2, 5, 8). Because the source of our capacity to bear fruit lies outside ourselves, the yield is certain. It counts and abides for eternal life (4:36; 15:16).

(c) Paul recognizes good deeds as the "fruit of righteousness" (Phil. 1:11; cf. Heb. 12:11; Jas. 3:18) and "the fruit of the light" (Eph. 5:9), produced by God himself, Jesus Christ, or the Holy Spirit. He sharply distinguishes it from striving in one's own strength to attain salvation (Gal. 5:22; Col. 1:10). Works or deeds (→ *ergon*, 2240)—a word that comes from the world of techniques and craftsmanship, signifying what one produces by one's own efforts—is seldom used in a positive sense. *karpos*, however, comes from the realm of natural growth and signifies that which grows by drawing on the life-giving power of the tree or soil.

But this growth as a sign of life does not lie at our disposal. In using this metaphor, Paul stresses that the fruit appears naturally in those who have been received into the body of Christ, in whom the Spirit of Christ is active, and who have a share in the gifts of this living fellowship (Gal. 5:22–23) because it is not something manufactured. While believers in Christ thus bring their fruit to God and live for him, the power of sinful desires can only bear fruit for death (Rom. 7:4–5).

(d) Where fruit is lacking, the NT uses the adj. *akarpos*, unfruitful, fruitless, unproductive (e.g., Mk. 4:19 par.; Tit. 3:14; 2 Pet. 1:8; Jude 12). *akarpos* describes the works of darkness (Eph. 5:11) and the state of the mind when prayer is made in tongues (1 Cor. 14:14).

(e) Paul also uses *karpos* for the results of his own missionary work (Rom. 1:13; Phil. 1:22). It can even be said that the apostles and, in particular, missionaries who are building up the churches have a right to make a living through that work (1 Cor. 9:7; 2 Tim. 2:6; cf. Matt. 21:41–43; Lk. 20:10). In these passages fruit means wages.

(f) *karpos* occurs twice in Rev. 22:2. The picture of the tree of life, "bearing ... fruit ... every month," represents the fullness of God's pervading presence in the new world, where shame and sin are overcome and all hindrances to the activity of the divine Spirit are removed.

See also *sperma*, seed (5065); *therismos*, harvest (2546).

2844 (karpophoreō, bear fruit), → 2843.

2846	καρτερέω

καρτερέω (*kartereō*), be strong, steadfast, persevere (2846); προσκαρτερέω (*proskartereō*), persevere with, persist in (4674); προσκαρτέρησις (*proskarterēsis*), persistence, steadfastness, perseverance (4675).

CL & OT In cl. Gk. *kartereō* (from *kratos*, strength) means to remain strong, steadfast, endure. It has the same sense in the LXX (cf. Job 2:9; Sir. 2:2; 12:15). The word is used in 4 Macc. for the patient endurance of Jewish martyrs (9:9, 28; cf. 10:1; 13:11; 14:9). The compound *proskartereō* has the same basic meaning, but gives greater emphasis to the time element: to persist, persevere with a person, persist in an activity (Num. 13:20 = LXX 13:21).

NT 1. In the NT *kartereō* is found only in Heb. 11:27, where it describes the faith of Moses. According to Heb. 11:1, 3, faith is a persuasion of invisible things. Moses is one of a number of OT saints who "persevered because he saw him who is invisible." The kind of endurance that clings tenaciously to the invisible God makes possible that attitude of faith exemplified by Moses, whom Christian readers are to emulate.

2. The vb. *proskartereō* occurs (10x) esp. in Acts (6x). (a) It is sometimes used in a nonreligious sense to indicate duration. Thus in Mk. 3:9 Jesus tells his disciples to keep a boat "ready" for him. Acts 8:13 and 10:7 refer to a prolonged or continuous stay with a person: After his baptism Simon Magus "followed Philip everywhere," while certain soldiers are permanent "attendants" of the centurion Cornelius. In Rom. 13:6 Paul says that as servants of God, rulers "give their full time" to their governing duties.

(b) Constancy and perseverance are esp. important in the Christian's prayer life. In Rom. 12:12; Col. 4:2, the apostle exhorts Christians to devote themselves to prayer (echoing Christ's teaching in Lk. 11:1–13; 18:1–8). Acts also uses *proskartereō* to denote the constant attitude of prayer that was a part of the early church leaders both before and after Pentecost (1:14; 6:4). The description of the church in 2:42 likewise makes use of this word: "They devoted themselves [*proskartereō*] to the apostles' teaching and to the fellowship, to the breaking of bread and to prayer," as does the notation in 2:46 that they "continued to meet together" in the temple.

3. The noun *proskarterēsis* occurs only in Eph. 6:18. Here too believers are encouraged to persevere in prayer and supplication, which is to be made in the Holy Spirit and must include the apostle (cf. also Col. 4:2–3). With these solemn words the apostolic injunction receives the emphasis its importance demands.

See also *anechomai*, bear, endure (462); *makrothymia*, patience, long-suffering (3429); *hypomenō*, be patient, persevere, endure, be steadfast (5702).

2848	κατά

κατά (*kata*), down from, concerning, according to (2848).

CL The primary local meaning of *kata* is down from, expressing vertical extension. That *kata* is closely related to *ana* is clear from the fact that "down" and "up" simply represent the same idea from opposite viewpoints.

NT 1. Examples of the spatial meaning of *kata* (with the gen.) include Matt. 8:32 (a herd of pigs rushing down a mountain) and Acts 27:14 (a strong wind swept "down from the island").

2. In 2 Cor. 8:2 is a clear example of the developed metaphorical sense: "extreme poverty" (lit., "poverty reaching down to [*kata*] the depths"). From the local meaning "down upon," there naturally arose the idea of hostile movement directed against someone or something, as in the charge against Stephen that he was speaking "against this holy place" (Acts 6:13).

In this regard 2 Cor. 13:8 does not mean that truth is its own defense ("for we cannot do anything against [*kata*] the truth"). Rather, to explain why he does not expect the Corinthians to discover him to be a false apostle or counterfeit Christian, Paul asserts that he would never be able to bring himself to propagate falsehood or to hinder the advance of the truth without first changing his identity as an apostle. In Col. 2:14 Paul speaks of God's obliteration, through the cross of Christ, of the signed acknowledgment of indebtedness "that was against [*kata*] us."

3. Two significant corresponding uses of this prep. are *kata sarka* (lit., "according to the flesh," → *4922*) and *kata pneuma* (lit., "according to the Spirit," → *4460*). *kata sarka* can mean simply with respect to physical descent (Rom. 1:3; 4:1; 9:3). Some commentators find in 2 Cor. 5:16b a Pauline disavowal of interest in the historical Jesus (i.e., not regarding Christ *kata sarka*). But *kata sarka* in this case means "from a worldly [or nationalistic] point of view" and qualifies "regarded," not Christ. Since his conversion Paul has ceased making superficial judgments based on external appearances (cf. 5:12), so that he regards the time-honored division of humanity into Jew and Gentile (5:16a) as less significant for him than the believer-unbeliever distinction (Rom. 2:28–29; 10:12–13; 1 Cor. 5:12–13; Gal. 6:10), which was based on a *kata pneuma* ("in light of the Spirit") or *kata stauron* ("in the light of the cross") attitude.

The opposition between *sarx* and *pneuma* is an important ingredient in Paul's theology (see, e.g., Gal. 5:16–24). The sense of Rom. 8:5 is that "those who live according to [*kata*] the sinful nature [*sarx*]" are earthly-minded or take the side of the flesh in the Spirit-flesh conflict, while "those who live in accordance with [*kata*] the Spirit" give their attention to spiritual matters or take the side of the Spirit. The contrast here is between two diametrically opposed determinative principles of action.

This contrast is given a different turn in Gal. 4:21–31. Here "the son born in the ordinary way [*kata sarka*]" (4:29a) refers to Ishmael as the son of the slave woman Hagar (4:23a) and then allegorically as the descendants of Abraham who do not believe in Jesus, while "the son born by the power of the Spirit [*kata pneuma*]" (4:29b) refers first to Isaac as the "son [born] by the free woman . . . as the result of a promise" (4:23b) and then to all those who share Abraham's faith as "children of promise" (4:28).

4. Often the noun that follows *kata* specifies the criterion, standard, or norm in the light of which a statement is made or is true, an action is performed, or a judgment is passed. In such cases *kata* will mean according to, in conformity with, corresponding to. This use is common in reference to the precise and impartial standard of judgment on the day of judgment (Matt. 16:27; Rom. 2:6; 1 Cor. 3:8; 2 Tim. 4:14; 1 Pet. 1:17; Rev. 2:23). Noteworthy too is the twice-repeated "according to [*kata*] the Scriptures" in 1 Cor. 15:3–4, which constitutes an appeal to certain OT prophecies of the death of Christ to atone for sins (Isa. 53:4–6, 10–12), and to the resurrection of Christ (Ps. 16:10; Isa. 53:10b, 11a; 54:7).

kata theon (God) may signify "in accordance with God's will" (Rom. 8:27), "like [i.e., in the image of] God" (Eph. 4:24; cf. Col. 3:10), "as God intended" (2 Cor. 7:9), "as God wants you to be" (1 Pet. 5:2), or simply "godly" (2 Cor. 7:10–11).

Sometimes the ideas of standard and reason merge, as in those "called according to his purpose" in Rom. 8:28. Here this phrase indicates either that God's calling is in accord with his purpose or that it is on basis of his purpose. Similarly in 1 Pet. 1:1–2, election is based on (*kata*) the foreknowledge of God the Father, is effected by (*en*, in, → *1877*) the sanctifying work of the Spirit, and aims at or achieves (*eis*,

unto, → *1650*) obedience and the constant sprinkling of the blood of Jesus Christ. In 1:3a *kata* expresses the idea that regeneration is the result of the Father's great mercy.

5. Finally, *kata* can have a distributive meaning. According to Acts 2:46, the early church in Jerusalem celebrated the Lord's Supper "every day" (lit., "according to each day"), and taught and proclaimed the good news "from house to house" (5:42; lit., "according to the house"). With regard to ecclesiastical polity, Paul and Barnabas appointed elders "in each church" of South Galatia (14:23; lit., "according to the church").

2849 (*katabainō*, descend), → *326*.

2850 (*kataballō*, throw or strike down, found, ground), → *2856*.

2851 (*katabareō*, burden, be a burden to), → *983*.

2856	καταβολή

καταβολή (*katabolē*), foundation, beginning (*2856*); καταβάλλω (*kataballō*), throw or strike down, found, ground (*2850*).

CL & OT 1. The vb. *kataballō* derives its basic meaning from its two roots *kata*, down, and *ballō*, throw. It thus means bring from an upright into a horizontal position (e.g., throw down, or, in a fig. sense, put down, reject). The related meaning lay a foundation, found, is derived from ancient building techniques and refers to the stacking of stones into the foundation trench or the rolling and pushing of the vital cornerstones of the building.

The noun *katabolē* chiefly takes up the fig. meaning. It can mean payment (laying out) of certain sums of money or the date of commencement for a building. Biologically, it can denote the depositing of seed in the ground or in a mother. Later writers use the phrase *apo* or *ek katabolēs kosmou*, since the beginning of the world.

2. *kataballō* in the LXX has no relationship to the idea of creation. Only once (2 Macc. 2:13) does it have the sense of found (a library). *katabolē* occurs only at 2 Macc. 2:29, where it indicates a master builder's concern "with the whole construction."

NT 1. *kataballō* is used only twice in the NT. In 2 Cor. 4:9, Paul refers to the fact that in his ministry he has frequently been "struck down, but not destroyed," while Heb. 6:1 refers to the foundation of one's faith, upon which one must build.

2. The noun occurs 11x. The expression "creation [lit., foundation] of the world" (Matt. 13:35, citing Ps. 78:2; Matt. 25:34; Rev. 13:8) is a fixed expression for the point from which historical dates are reckoned. When God's free activity is dated before this point in time (e.g., Jn. 17:24, where the obj. of God's love is Jesus; Eph. 1:4, where the obj. is the election of believers), the purpose is to declare the independence of God's providence from the absolute beginning he himself set for human history. This independence enables God to break into history in his loving purposes and to bring the course of salvation history to its completion, again in his love.

3. Two points stand out in all the texts that mention the foundation of the world. (a) It is always associated with a statement about humanity's destiny. (b) There is an implied connection between God's foreknowledge and predestination. Matt. 25:34 and Eph. 1:4 speak of election; Rev. 13:8 and 17:8 speak of reprobation. Lk. 11:50 (a lamentation of Jesus) and Heb. 4:3 speak of historical failure for which account must be rendered. Finally, Matt. 13:35; Heb. 9:26; and 1 Pet. 1:20 (cf. Jn. 17:24) refer to the unique, central position of Jesus Christ in the history of salvation. He reveals what has been hidden since the foundation of the world and thus fixes the end of time.

4. In Heb. 11:11, *katabolē* is linked with the cl. idea of depositing seed (i.e., begetting).

See also *ktisis*, creation (*3232*); *dēmiourgos*, maker (*1321*).

2857 (*katabrabeuō*, decide against, condemn), → *1092*.

2858 (*katangeleus*, proclaimer), → *33*.

2859 (*katangellō*, proclaim), → *33*.

2860 (*katagelaō*, laugh at, mock), → *1151*.

2861 (*kataginōskō*, condemn), → *3210*.

2865 (*katagōnizomai*, conquer, defeat), → *74*.

2868	καταδικάζω

καταδικάζω (*katadikazō*), condemn (*2868*); καταδίκη (*katadikē*), condemnation (*2869*).

CL & OT 1. In cl. Gk. the vb. *katadikazō* means to condemn, render judgment against; the noun *katadikē* denotes a legal sentence or judgment brought against someone.

2. *katadikazō* translates several Heb. verbs in the LXX. It means to condemn as guilty in Job 34:29; Ps. 37:33; 94:21; to subvert someone in a cause in Lam. 3:36 (NIV, "deprive . . . of justice"); and to inculpate and hence endanger one's life in Dan. 1:10 (Theod.). In Wis. 2:20; 11:10; 12:15; 17:11 it has the sense of formal condemnation. *katadikē* occurs in 12:27 of the condemnation pronounced on those who do not heed God.

NT *katadikazō* is used 5x in the NT, always in the sense of condemn, pass judgment against, find guilty. This is particularly clear in Matt. 12:37, where it is used in contrast with *dikaioō* (→ *dikaiosynē*, *1466*). In Lk. 6:37 *katadikazō* occurs 2x in connection with *krinō* (→ *krima*, *3210*), where it connotes the formal act of passing judgment. The same concept is evident in the metaphorical usage of the term in Jas. 5:6, where "you have condemned" represents a formal pronouncement of judgment before the execution of a sentence. The noun *katadikē* occurs only once in the NT (Acts 25:15) in the sense of a sentence of guilt and condemnation.

See also *krima*, dispute, decision, verdict, judgment (*3210*); *paradidōmi*, deliver up, give up, hand over (*4140*); *bēma*, judgment seat (*1037*).

2869 (*katadikē*, condemnation), → *2868*.

2870 (*katadiōkō*, search for, hunt for), → *1503*.

2873 (*katathema*, accursed thing), → *353*.

2874 (*katathematizō*, curse), → *353*.

2875 (*kataischynō*, to dishonor, disgrace, put to shame), → *158*.

2877 (*katakalyptō*, cover up, veil), → *2821*.

2878 (*katakauchaomai*, boast against, exult over), → *3017*.

2880 (*kataklaō*, break in pieces), → *3089*.

2883 (*kataklēronomeō*, give as inheritance), → *3102*.

2886	κατακλυσμός

κατακλυσμός (*kataklysmos*), a deluge, flood (*2886*).

CL & OT In cl. Gk. *kataklysmos* was used lit. and fig. to signify a deluge, a great flood. The LXX uses the word for the flood of Noah (e.g., Gen. 6:17; Ps. 29:10; Sir. 40:10); in Ps. 32:6; Sir. 21:13; 39:22, however, the references are fig.

NT The word occurs only 4x in the NT (Matt. 24:38–39; Lk. 17:27; 2 Pet. 2:5), referring each time to the devastation of Noah's deluge.

See also *thalassa*, sea, lake (*2498*); *pēgē*, spring, source (*4380*); *hydōr*, water (*5623*); *Iordanēs*, the river Jordan (*2674*); *limnē*, lake (*3349*).

2890 (*katakrima*, punishment, condemnation), → *3210*.

2891 (*katakrinō*, condemn), → *3210*.

2892 (*katakrisis*, condemnation), → *3210*.

2894 (*katakyrieuō*, rule over, conquer, be master of, lord it over), → *3261*.

2895	καταλαλέω

καταλαλέω (*katalaleō*), speak evil of, rail at, slander (*2895*);

καταλαλιά (*katalalia*), evil speech, railing, slander (*2896*); κατάλαλος (*katalalos*), slanderer, railer, defamer (*2897*); ψιθυρισμός (*psithyrismos*), gossip (*6030*); ψιθυριστής (*psithyristēs*), whisperer, gossiper (*6031*).

CL & OT *katalaleō*, to speak evil against, slander, is rare in cl. Gk. In the LXX this vb. expresses hostility of speech, whether against God (Num. 21:5, 7; Ps. 78:19; Hos. 7:13), against his servant Moses (Num. 12:8; 21:7), or against other people—e.g., when Job is reproached by his friends (Job 19:3) or when one's brother or neighbor is slandered (Ps. 50:20; 101:5). The noun *katalalia*, slander, is found only in the Bible (e.g., Wis. 1:11) or in texts depending on it. *katalalos*, slanderer, is found for the first time in the NT.

NT In the NT *katalaleō* is not used of blasphemy against God (→ *blasphēmeō*, *1059*). Slanderers (*katalalos*) are among the sinners whom Paul lists in Rom. 1:30 as typical examples of paganism. This word is linked with *psithyristes*, a whisperer, gossiper (1:29). The cognate nouns *psithyrismos*, gossip, tale-bearing, and *katalalia* are again linked in 2 Cor. 12:20 and 1 Clem. 30:3; 35:5. *katalalia*, slander, is among the sins that Paul fears he will encounter in the rebellious church of Corinth (2 Cor. 12:20); fellowship in the community is destroyed by this sin.

The Christian churches are themselves the victims of such evil speech; it is the result of the hostile attitude taken up toward them by the heathen world. Christians should, therefore, be much more concerned to show by their "good behavior in Christ" that the slanders against them are groundless (1 Pet. 3:16; cf. 2:12). As "newborn babies" (i.e., those born again, who know the kindness of their Lord), Christians should put away "slander of every kind," along with other sins (1 Pet. 2:1–3). The letter of Jas. also, with its particular censure of sins of the tongue (cf. 3:1–12), emphatically forbids Christians to indulge in slandering other believers (4:11–12), for such a sin is a slight to God's law and an affront to God himself as the one Lawgiver and Judge of all.

See also *blasphēmeō*, slander, defame, blaspheme (*1059*); *loidoreō*, insult, abuse, revile (*3366*); *oneidizō*, insult, denounce, rebuke (*3943*).

2896 (*katalalia*, evil speech, railing, slander), → *2895*.

2897 (*katalalos*, slanderer, railer, defamer), → *2895*.

2898 (*katalambanō*, seize, attain, make one's own, take possession), → *3284*.

2901 (*kataleipō*, leave, leave behind, leave over), → *3309*.

2903 (*katallagē*, reconciliation), → *2904*.

2904	καταλλάσσω

καταλλάσσω (*katallassō*), reconcile (*2904*); καταλλαγή (*katallagē*), reconciliation (*2903*); ἀπαλλάσσω (*apallassō*), set free, release (*557*); διαλλάσσομαι (*diallassomai*), become reconciled (*1367*); ἀποκαταλλάσσω (*apokatallassō*), reconcile (*639*); μεταλλάσσω (*metallassō*), to exchange (*3563*); ἀντάλλαγμα (*antallagma*), what is given or taken in exchange (*498*); ἀλλάσσω (*allassō*), change (*248*).

CL & OT 1. In cl. Gk. *katallassō* is a compound of *allassō*, to alter, exchange. Its original meaning is to change, exchange; transferred, it means to reconcile. It generally denotes the restoration of an understanding between people after hostility or displeasure. The vb. is rarely found in the sense of reconciliation in a religious setting. The corresponding noun is *katallagē*, reconciliation. From the same root is derived the noun *antallagma*, what is given in exchange, price of purchase.

2. *allassō* is used 30x in the LXX, meaning change (e.g., wages, Gen. 31:7; clothes, 35:2; 41:14; cf. 2 Ki. 5:5, 22–23), renew (Isa. 40:31; 41:1), exchange (Lev. 27:10, 27, 33), or, similarly, redeem (i.e., to exchange one sacrifice with another, Exod. 13:13).

The compounds of this group are rare in the LXX. *katallassō* is found only at Jer. 48:39 (= LXX 31:39, shattered, dismayed); 2 Macc. 1:5; 7:33; 8:29. *katallagē* occurs only at Isa. 9:4 (= LXX 9:5), where it differs from the Heb. text and is hard to understand, and at 2 Macc. 5:20. *diallassō* can mean remove (Job 12:20, 24), break, frustrate (5:12); similarly, *apallassō* can mean destroy (Job 9:34; cf. also Exod. 19:22; 1 Sam. 14:29; 22:1; 3 Macc. 6:30). *antallagma* means price (1 Ki. 21:2 = LXX 20:2; Jer. 15:13), a change (Ps. 55:19), a ransom price (Amos 5:12), or exchange (Ruth 4:7). Later rab. usage is anticipated in 1 Sam. 29:4, where *diallassomai* deviates from its usual sense to mean to make oneself acceptable. *katallassō* and its derivatives are not found in cultic and priestly contexts.

3. In Jud., confession of sins and repentance are means by which reconciliation with God is sought, i.e., the restoration of his favor. Thus *katallassō* appears with reference to God in 2 Macc. 1:5; 7:33; 8:29. When the fulfillment of the law becomes a means to the end of achieving righteousness before God, the thought of reconciliation can find itself in close proximity with that of reward. *katallassō* and cognates are not unfamiliar in such contexts, but occur infrequently.

NT 1. In the NT *katallassō* occurs only in the sense of to reconcile or (pass.) to be reconciled. It is used of the reconciliation of people with one another (1 Cor. 7:11; cf. *diallassomai* in Matt. 5:24) and of people with God (only in Paul: Rom. 5:10; 2 Cor. 5:18–20; cf. *apokatallassō* in Eph. 2:16; Col. 1:20, 22). *katallagē* also occurs in the sense of reconciliation (only in Paul: Rom. 5:11; 11:15; 2 Cor. 5:18–19).

apallassō occurs in the act., meaning to free (Heb. 2:15), and in the mid. or pass., to get free, be released, settle with (Lk. 12:58; Acts 19:12). Similarly, we find *metallassō* in its original sense (Rom. 1:25–26). *antallagma*, ransom money, is found only at Matt. 16:26; Mk. 8:37.

allassō (6x) means to change, sometimes in a natural sense (i.e., in Gal. 4:20 Paul wishes he could change his tone with the Galatians), but also in an eschatological sense (on the last day, "we will all be changed," 1 Cor. 15:51–52; cf. Heb. 1:12). In Rom. 1:23 Paul insists that those who worshiped idols knew God via general revelation but "exchanged the glory of the immortal God for images made to look like mortal man and birds and animals and reptiles."

2. *katallassō* and *katallagē* are among the basic concepts of Pauline theology. They serve to give greater theological precision to Christ and his work than the soteriological concepts found in the Synoptic Gospels and Acts (e.g., forgiveness). (a) The subject of reconciliation is God (2 Cor. 5:18–19). Note the contrast to pagan thought, which knew the deity only as the object of the reconciling work of humans. At the same time it is consistent with the OT message of God as the "compassionate and gracious" one, who reveals "love and faithfulness" as belonging to his very being (Exod. 34:6–7; cf. Ps. 103:8–18), and who promises forgiveness and restoration of the covenant as his sovereign work (Isa. 43:25; 54:7–10; Jer. 31:31–34).

The *katallagē* created by God is thus a completed act that precedes all human action. "For if, when we were God's enemies, we were reconciled [*katallassō*] to him through the death of his Son, how much more, having been reconciled [*katallassō*], shall we be saved through his life" (Rom. 5:10). Before the reconciliation took place, therefore, we were at enmity with God. But Jesus' resurrection is the guarantee of salvation and reconciliation. Human action, including repentance and confession of sins, is not a work we do to bring about and initiate reconciliation, to which God reacts. Rather, it is God's work, to which we must react.

That this is the state of affairs is confirmed by Paul's characteristic order of indicative followed by imperative, which starts out from God's act as the matter of primary importance and moves to the injunction to proclaim the good news of being reconciled to God. This is the basis of the believer's joy in God: "Not only is this so, but we also rejoice in God through our Lord Jesus Christ, through whom we have now received reconciliation [*katallagē*]" (Rom. 5:11). In 2 Cor. 5:20,

in which Paul expresses similar thoughts, he does not hesitate to follow up his description of reconciliation with: "We implore you on Christ's behalf: Be reconciled to God."

(b) The reconciliation has been effected by Christ's work in his death and resurrection. Reconciliation is an expression of the new situation that this work has brought about and that Paul usually indicates in terms like *dikaioō*, justify, *dikaiosynē*, righteousness (→ *1466*). The fact that *katallassō* and *katallagē* can be used in parallel with these terms (cf. Rom. 5:9 with 5:10; 2 Cor. 5:19 with Rom. 4:3–22) indicates the central place they have in the preaching and theology of Paul.

(c) Later in Rom. Paul probes the place of the Jewish nation in the divine economy of salvation. This explains why he is anxious to demonstrate from the OT that salvation has always been by grace through faith (cf. chs. 3–4) and to show that the role of the law was never intended to be a means of self-salvation. In Rom. 9–11 Paul asks whether God has forsaken Israel forever in view of their rejection of Christ. Part of his answer he gives in terms of reconciliation: "For if their rejection is the reconciliation [*katallagē*] of the world [i.e., the Gentiles], what will their acceptance be but life from the dead?" (11:15).

3. As God's unilateral act in Christ, reconciliation is his gift, and the ministry of reconciliation is spoken of in these terms in 2 Cor. 5:18–21. Having depicted the act of new creation that takes place when a person is "in Christ," Paul writes: "All this is from God, who reconciled us to himself through Christ and gave us the ministry of reconciliation: that God was reconciling the world to himself in Christ, not counting men's sins against them. And he has committed to us the message of reconciliation. We are therefore Christ's ambassadors, as though God were making his appeal through us. We implore you on Christ's behalf: Be reconciled to God. God made him who had no sin to be sin for us, so that in him we might become the righteousness of God."

Reconciliation here denotes the end of a relation of enmity and the substitution of one of peace and goodwill. The initiative for reconciliation was God's, who found through the death of his Son a way both for his love for the sinner and his wrath against sin to be accommodated. In this way, God remains righteous, but sinful humans can also be justified through faith in Jesus.

In 2 Cor. 5:19 reconciliation is understood as justification. It is expressed first of all negatively ("not counting men's sins against them") and then positively in 5:21, where Christ is said to have assumed our sin so that "we might become the righteousness of God." This is no legal fiction. For in Christ believers actually assume his righteousness, just as Christ assumed believers' sins as he hung on the cross.

But the ministry of reconciliation does not end with this. We are to proclaim it as "ambassadors" (2 Cor. 5:20; cf. Eph. 6:20; → *presbeuō*, *4563*). In 1 Cor. 1:18; 2:2, Paul defined his task in terms of preaching the word of the cross, the message of God's love for sinners and reconciliation (Rom. 5:8–11). What he calls "the message of reconciliation" in 2 Cor. 5:19 is the gospel itself, and the proclamation of the gospel is responsibility of the whole church. At the same time, note that the appeal to "be reconciled to God" (2 Cor. 5:20b) is addressed to the church. Both the church and the world (5:19) must enter into this reconciliation and live it out. The substance of this exhortation ("be reconciled to God") draws attention to the fact that reconciliation is incomplete until it is accepted by both sides.

The thought of both 2 Cor. 5:21 and Rom. 8:3 requires us to say that what Christ did on the cross comprehends and supersedes the OT sin offerings. In Gal. 3:13–14 Paul does not use the concept of reconciliation but expresses the atoning work of Christ on the cross in terms of the removal of the curse (→ *katara*, *2932*). Here again there is the thought of the benefit to others achieved by Christ in his death on their behalf. He is our vicarious substitute.

4. The substance of the reconciliation lies in the ending of the enmity between God and humanity (Rom. 5:10). Reconciliation results therefore in our having "peace with God," a phrase used in 5:1 for the

effect of justification. In this sense reconciliation is the precondition of our salvation (5:10b) and the basis for the all-embracing "new creation" (2 Cor. 5:17–21).

5. (a) Col. 1:20, 22 uses, instead of *katallassō*, the otherwise unknown vb. *apokatallassō* (cf. Eph. 2:16), but this links with the previously mentioned Pauline use of *katallassō* and has essentially the same meaning: "For God was pleased to have all his fullness dwell in him, and through him to reconcile [*apokatallassō*] to himself all things, whether things on earth or things in heaven, by making peace through his blood, shed on the cross. Once you were alienated from God and were enemies in your minds because of your evil behavior. But now he has reconciled [*apokatallassō*] you by Christ's physical body through death to present you holy in his sight, without blemish and free from accusation" (1:19–22).

This passage has many of the features of reconciliation we have seen in Rom. and 2 Cor.: estrangement caused by sin that has to be dealt with before God; God's offer to be reconciled with us; its initiation from God's side; Christ's death as the reconciling process, referred to in terms of his "blood" and "cross"; and the purpose of presenting us as righteous before God. The ground of this victory is the cancellation of the debt of the law on the cross, thus depriving the principalities and powers of their hold on us (Col. 2:13–15).

But the scope of reconciliation is given here a cosmic dimension. The text presupposes a cosmic catastrophe caused by the powers of evil. The one who is the creator and sustainer of all is the one who has triumphed over the powers of evil on the cross and is therefore the reconciler of all (Col. 1:16–20; cf. 2:15). Within this cosmic context is set the reconciliation of believers (1:21–22). But it should be noted that the reconciliation is conditional upon continuing in the faith (1:23).

(b) Eph. 2:16 sees the reconciliation in the context of its effect on the relationship of Jews and Gentiles before God. The Gentiles were at one time "separate from Christ, excluded from citizenship in Israel and foreigners to the covenants of the promise, without hope and without God in the world" (2:12). But they have been "brought near through the blood of Christ" (2:13). Christ's death has, however, not only reconciled the Gentiles; it has also reconciled the Jews, providing a way of salvation to them that they did not have before. At the same time the act of reconciling Jew and Gentile to God reconciles them to each other and creates a new humanity. Christ is our peace, having created "in himself one new man out of the two, thus making peace, and in this one body to reconcile [*apokatallassō*] both of them to God through the cross" (2:15–16).

6. Reconciliation on a human level is discussed in two important passages. (a) In 1 Cor. 7:10–11 Paul discusses the issue of divorce: "To the married I give this command (not I, but the Lord): A wife must not separate from her husband. But if she does, she must remain unmarried or else be reconciled [*katallassō*] to her husband. And a husband must not divorce his wife." The teaching is in line with Jesus' interpretation of the OT on this matter (cf. Matt. 19:3–12; Mk. 10:2–12; Lk. 16:18; cf. Deut. 24:1–4; Matt. 5:27–32) and hence may properly be said to be a charge from the Lord.

In contrast with 1 Cor. 7:13–16, where Paul deals with the question of whether divorce should take place on the grounds that one party is a believer and the other is not, Paul's judgment in 7:10–11 seems to refer to the question of divorce in general. The two courses open are either to separate and remain single or to be reconciled. In 7:13–16, however, Paul apparently recognizes that there are cases where there is no real alternative but for the breakup of a marriage. The fact that a believer may find himself or herself married to an unbeliever is no grounds for separation, as the believing partner consecrates the other partner and provides the possibility of saving him or her (7:12–16). Thus, Paul does not teach that a believer must inevitably separate from an unbeliever in a marriage.

(b) The unique vb. *diallassomai* occurs in Matt. 5:24: "Therefore, if you are offering your gift at the altar and there remember that your brother has something against you, leave your gift there in front of the altar. First go and be reconciled [*diallassomai*] to your brother; then come and offer your gift" (5:23–24). Jesus' teaching here is of a piece with his teaching on the two great commands and the parable of the good Samaritan, which lays down the responsibility to love God with all one's being and one's neighbor as oneself (Matt. 22:34–40; Lk. 10:25–37; cf. Lev. 19:18; Deut. 6:5). No sacrifice is acceptable to God without repentance and reconciliation.

The following saying (Matt. 5:25–26) is paralleled in Lk. 12:58: "As you are going with your adversary to the magistrate, try hard to be reconciled [*apallassō*] to him on the way, or he may drag you off to the judge, and the judge turn you over to the officer, and the officer throw you into prison." The need for human reconciliation is parabolic of our need for reconciliation with God (cf. also the parable of the unforgiving servant in Matt. 18:23–35). The adversary (or accuser) here may represent Jesus Christ, with his message of repentance in view of the coming of the impending judgment; for when judgment falls, it will be irrevocable (cf. the context of this passage: Lk. 12:54–57; 13:1–9). We must seek reconciliation with him before that occurs.

7. The act. of *apallassō* occurs in Heb. 2:15 and means to free, release, deliver. Jesus partook of our human nature and through his death destroyed the one who had the power of death, that is, the devil, and so was able to "free [*apallassō*] those who all their lives were held in slavery by their fear of death." In Acts 19:12 this same vb. is used for the curing of illnesses.

8. *antallagma*, that which is given in exchange, occurs only in Matt. 16:26 and Mk. 8:37: "What can a man give in exchange for his soul?" The context is that of the call for complete renunciation of self as the precondition of discipleship and acceptance with the Father: "For whoever wants to save his life will lose it, but whoever loses his life for me and for the gospel will save it" (8:35). We can give nothing in exchange for our life, and thus even to take up the cross in utter self-abandonment is far more important than gaining the whole world. Like the other sayings in the Synoptics, this one does not offer a theology of reconciliation in the Pauline sense. Rather, it states in the sharpest possible terms our *need* for reconciliation, while implying at the same time that reconciliation is available to those who are concerned enough to seek it.

See also *apokatastasis*, restoration (640); *hilaskomai*, propitiate, expiate, be gracious (2661).

2905 (kataloipos, what is left, the rest), → *3309*.

2906 (katalyma, lodging, guest room), → *3395*.

2907 (katalyō, destroy, demolish, abolish), → *3395*.

2909 (katamartyreō, bear witness against, testify against), → *3456*.

2917 (katanoeō, notice, observe, consider, contemplate), → *3808*.

2918	καταντάω

καταντάω (*katantaō*), come to, arrive at (*2918*); ἀπαντάω (*apantaō*), meet (*560*); ὑπαντάω (*hypantaō*), meet (*5636*); ἀπάντησις (*apantēsis*), meeting (*561*); ὑπάντησις (*hypantēsis*), meeting, coming to meet (*5637*).

CL & OT *katantaō* denotes movement towards a goal, primarily a place (such as a town). In a metaphorical sense it denotes the attainment of an objective. The word occurs infrequently in the LXX. It is used lit. in the sense of coming to Jerusalem or Tyre (2 Macc. 4:21, 44); it is used fig. of attaining to the status of high priest and of people reaching the full measure of sin (4:24; 6:14). In 2 Sam. 3:29 it is used of Yahweh's requiting blood guilt on the head of Joab.

NT 1. In the NT *katantaō* occurs 13x. In Acts it is used primarily in the sense of arrive (16:1; 18:19, 24). It occurs once in a metaphorical sense. In his address to Agrippa, Paul declared that the twelve tribes of Israel hope to "see fulfilled" the promise made by God to their ancestors (26:7).

2. This expression is related to Paul's usage that is always metaphorical. The ultimate goal of the Christian life is "to attain to the resurrection from the dead" (Phil. 3:11). Eph. 4:13 expresses the goal that all Christians should "reach unity in the faith and in the knowledge of the Son of God." In 1 Cor. 10:11 the apostle speaks of us "on whom the fulfillment of the ages has come (*katantaō*)" (cf. Heb. 9:26). Christ, who inaugurates the end of the ages, will begin a new world era and order of things. Admittedly, this is apparent only to believers. Nevertheless, the form of this world is passing away (1 Cor. 7:31). This movement that comes from God is also to be seen in the fact that the Word of God "has reached (*katantaō*)" the churches (14:36; cf. 1 Thess. 2:13).

3. *apantaō* (Mk. 14:13; Lk. 17:12) and *hypantaō* (e.g., Matt. 8:28; Lk. 8:27) mean meet, and the related nouns *apantēsis* (Matt. 25:6; Acts 28:15; 1 Thess. 4:17) and *hypantēsis* (Matt. 8:34; 25:1; Jn. 12:13) mean meeting.

The use of *apantēsis* in 1 Thess. 4:17 is noteworthy. The ancient expression for the civic welcome of an important visitor or the triumphal entry of a new ruler into the capital city is applied to Christ. "After that, we who are still alive and are left will be caught up together with them in the clouds to meet (*eis apantēsin*) the Lord in the air." The same thoughts occur in the parable of the ten virgins (Matt. 25:1).

See also *erchomai*, come, go (2262); *mellō*, be about to, intend, propose (3516).

2921 (*kataxioō*, deem worthy, consider worthy), → 545.

2922 (*katapateō*, trample), → 4344.

2923 (*katapausis*, rest, place of rest), → 398.

2924 (*katapauō*, bring to rest, rest, stop, resting), → 398.

2925	καταπέτασμα

καταπέτασμα (*katapetasma*), covering, veil, curtain (2925).

CL & OT *katapetasma* appears to have been a technical term for a temple curtain. With but few exceptions this word is used in the LXX for the curtain separating the Holy Place and the Most Holy Place in the tabernacle (Exod. 26:31–37; 27:21; Lev. 4:6, 17; Num. 4:5; 18:7) and the temple (2 Chr. 3:14). It is used sometimes for the curtain at the entrance of the tabernacle, but the regular word for that is *kalymma* (e.g., 1 Sam. 1:18; 9:22; 2 Sam. 7:6).

This inner curtain was made of fine linen interwoven with blue, purple, and scarlet wool; on it were the figures of two cherubs. It symbolized the separation between God and humankind. The high priest alone could enter the Most Holy Place only once a year to offer the atoning blood in the presence of God.

NT 1. It is debated whether "the curtain [*katapetasma*] of the temple" that was torn at the time of the crucifixion was the inner or outer curtain (Matt. 27:51; Mk. 15:38; Lk. 23:45). If it was the inner one, it symbolized the reality that Jesus' death opened the way for all humans to enter God's presence. This tearing, however, would not have been known to the public, since only the priests could enter the Holy Place. The early church fathers regarded the tearing as a prophetic sign of the destruction of the temple.

The writer of Heb. finds great assurance in knowing that Jesus, as the forerunner of all believers, entered God's presence within the inner curtain in the heavenly sanctuary (6:19–20), what was symbolized by the *katapetasma* of the tabernacle (9:3). Later he insists that Jesus opened the way for us to enter through this inner curtain (10:20). This may be an allusion to the tearing of the curtain when Jesus died, though no explicit reference is made to it.

2. *kalymma* is used in the NT only of Moses' veil (2 Cor. 3:13–16; cf. Exod. 34:33–35; → *kalyptō*, to hide, 2821).

2927 (*katapinō*, swallow, overwhelm), → 4403.

2928 (*katapiptō*, fall down), → 4406.

2932	κατάρα

κατάρα (*katara*), curse, malediction (2932); καταράομαι (*kataraomai*), curse (2933); ἀρά (*ara*), curse (725); ἐπικατάρατος (*epikataratos*), cursed (2129); ἐπάρατος (*eparatos*), accursed (2063).

CL & OT 1. *ara* and *katara* mean essentially the same thing, curse. *kataraomai* means curse someone (dat.) or execrate someone (acc.). In ancient thought the spoken word had intrinsic power, which was released by the act of utterance. The person cursed was thus exposed to a sphere of destructive power. It worked effectively against a person until the power within the curse was spent. Words of malediction and of benediction are thus more than evil or pious wishes.

2. In the LXX both *ara* (e.g., Ps. 10:7 = LXX 9:28; 14:3; 59:12) and *katara* occur. The latter is often given as the opposite of *eulogia* (→ 2330), blessing (Deut. 11:26–29; 30:1): "I have set before you life and death, blessings and curses" (30:19). *kataraomai* (e.g., Gen. 12:3; Num. 22:6–12), *araomai* (e.g., Num. 22:6, 11), and *epikataraomai* (e.g., Num. 22:17; 23:7) occur as vbs.

The Balaam story (Num. 22–24) shows how belief in the power of the curse, widespread in the ancient world, was prevalent in Israel. The Moabite king Balak charged Balaam to curse Israel so that he might become master of his mighty enemy. But God prevented Balaam from pronouncing the curse. Instead, he had to bless Israel.

The curse decreed by God or his messengers works irrevocably. The punishment with which Jer. threatens Jerusalem in 26:6 (= LXX 33:6) consists in her being delivered defenseless to the curse of the heathen (cf. 24:9). Likewise in Mal. 2:2, divine judgment consists in the blessing of the priests being changed by God into a curse. Only God himself can annul this curse.

NT In the NT *ara* occurs only in Rom. 3:14 (quoting Ps.10:7). It exhibits the sinfulness of those who live under the law. Heretics who entice unbalanced souls are "an accursed brood" (*katara* in 2 Pet. 2:14). Ground that, in spite of rain and cultivation, grows only thorns and thistles is said figuratively in Heb. 6:8 to be near to being cursed. The passage has in mind Christians who, in spite of the spiritual blessing they have received, fall away from the faith (6:4–10).

The vb. *kataraomai* is found in the story of the fig tree that Jesus cursed because it had no fruit on it (Mk. 11:21); the tree withered. This story is a fig. reference to the judgment of God (cf. Lk. 13:6–9). To Jesus those "who are cursed" (Matt. 25:41) are sinners condemned in the final judgment. Humans should not take an active part in the divine judgment; thus, believers are forbidden to curse (Rom. 12:14, 19). Rather, they should love their enemies and bless those who curse them (Matt. 5:44; Lk. 6:28). The warning given in Jas. 3:9–10 points in the same direction.

eparatos, accursed, is found only in Jn. 7:49. The Pharisees held that people who believed in Jesus were accursed because they did not know the law. This incident provides evidence of the enmity of the Pharisees against Jesus.

The verbal adj. *epikataratos* occurs twice in the NT (Gal. 3:10–13). Paul uses it as he interprets the relationship between the curse of the law and redemption through Christ. The curse of the law signifies being surrendered to the judgment and wrath of God. It affects all who do not abide in the commandments of the law (3:10), which essentially means the entire human race (cf. Rom. 1:18; 2:5; 3:23; also Lev. 18:5; Deut. 27:26).

Jesus, however, who hung on the cross as one cursed by God (cf. Deut. 21:23) and died the death of a criminal, took on himself the curse that lay on sinful humanity and with it the judgment of God (Gal. 3:13). Here Paul expresses the idea of substitution (cf. Rom. 3:25; 1 Cor. 1:30; 2 Cor. 5:21). Through his redemption the curse has been broken. In its place, the blessing of Abraham can now come to those who believe in Christ. As the redeemed who are called to divine sonship, they receive the fullness of salvation that is bound up with the promise of the Holy Spirit (Gal. 3:14; 4:5–7).

See also *anathema*, cursed, accursed (*353*); *kakologeō*, speak evil of, revile, insult (*2800*); *rhaka*, empty-head, fool (*4819*).

2933 (kataraomai, curse), → *2932.*

2934 καταργέω

καταργέω (*katargeō*), abolish, nullify(*2934*).

CL & OT Derived from *argos*, inactive, useless, *katargeō* is a late word that in cl. Gk. means to render inactive, put out of use, cancel. It only appears in the LXX in Ezra 4:21, 23; 5:5; 6:8, where it signifies hindering or interrupting the rebuilding of the temple.

NT Of its 27x in the NT, one is in a parable (the fig tree of Lk. 13:7 "uses up the soil" in the sense of making it unproductive); the rest are in theological contexts, all but one being in Paul.

1. God puts out of action through the cross and the *parousia* destructive powers that threaten our spiritual well-being. These include (a) the rulers of this age (1 Cor. 2:6, possibly human, but more likely demonic); (b) the law, which set Jew and Gentile at enmity and made both guilty before God (Eph. 2:15; cf. Rom. 7:2); (c) the sin-dominated nature that was ours in Adam (6:6); (d) the "lawless one" (2 Thess. 2:8); (e) all forces presently hostile to Christ (1 Cor. 15:24), including death, which has already been brought to nothing in principle through Jesus' resurrection (15:26; cf. 2 Tim. 1:10). The writer to Heb. adds (f) the devil (2:14).

2. God removes and displaces what is transient to make way for better and abiding things. Already displaced through the coming of the new order in Christ is the "glory," such as it was, of the Mosaic dispensation (2 Cor. 3:7, 11, 13), and the "veil" that was on Jewish hearts like Paul's (3:14). Being displaced, as God's plan goes forward, are "things that are" in this world—though grammatically neut., the phrase denotes people (1 Cor. 1:28). Due for displacement through the changes that the *parousia* will bring are (a) the belly and food (6:13: our present bodies will be changed) and (b) prophecies and conceptual knowledge (→ *gnōsis, 1194*), which, being at best partial, will be left behind, just as a grown person abandons childish things when he or she apprehends God directly by sight (13:8, 10, 11).

3. Humans attempt, wittingly or unwittingly, to contradict and cancel those principles and powers of divine working that bring salvation. To preach justification by circumcision or to seek justification by works of law is not only to cancel the offense of the cross (Gal. 5:11) but also to be "alienated" from Christ and his grace (5:4). But just as faith does not cancel the law (Rom. 3:31), the law does not set aside the covenant promises (Gal. 3:17), and Israel's unbelief does not nullify God's faithfulness (Rom. 3:3), so the gospel of grace will stand, despite human efforts to nullify it, and in the end it will triumph.

See also *atheteō* , set at naught, reject (*119*); *exoutheneō*, reject with contempt (*2024*).

2936 (katartizō, put in order, restore, make complete, prepare), → *787.*

2937 (katartisis, being made complete, completion), → *787.*

2938 (katartismos, preparation, equipment), → *787.*

2939 (kataseiō, shake down, motion the hand as a signal), → *4940.*

2941 κατασκευάζω

κατασκευάζω (*kataskeuazō*), make ready, prepare, build, construct, erect, equip, furnish (*2941*); παρασκευάζω (*paraskeuazō*), get ready, prepare (oneself) (*4186*); παρασκευή (*paraskeuē*), day of preparation (*4187*); ἀπαρασκεύαστος (*aparaskeuastos*), unprepared (*564*).

CL & OT 1. In cl. Gk. both compounds occur regarding setting up and decorating rooms and festal routes or making various kinds of preparations (e.g., dressing, meals, and battles on land or sea). *kataskeuazō* is also used in an inward sense, for the instruction of those who are learning and for preparation for religious rituals. This vb. also occurs in philosophical logic and geometry for the construction of positive arguments.

2. (a) The LXX uses *kataskeuazō* 30x. In Isa. 40:28; 43:7; 45:7, 9, the vb. refers to God's work of preparation in the context of creation. Equipping troops with arms and warships is mentioned in 1 Macc. 10:21; 15:3. The Apocr. also uses *kataskeuazō* in connection with the production of idols (Ep. Jer. 9, 45–46).

(b) *paraskeuazō* occurs 16x in the LXX. In Jer. 6:4; 50:42; 51:11 (= LXX 27:42; 28:11), it refers to preparation for battle; in Tob. 8:19; 2 Macc. 2:27; 6:21 it occurs in reports of the preparation of a meal.

(c) Both vbs. are used of other activities of preparation: construction of a building (Num. 21:27; 2 Chr. 32:5), tilling a field (Prov. 24:27 = LXX 24:42), spreading a net as a trap (29:5).

NT In the NT, *paraskeuazō* is found 4x and *kataskeuazō* 11x.

1. In Acts 10:10 *paraskeuazō* refers to the preparation of a meal, while in 1 Cor. 14:8, in a passage about the inadequacy of speaking in tongues, it occurs in the metaphor of preparation for battle. In 2 Cor. 9:2–3 it is used with regard to the Christians in Achaia, who "since last year . . . were ready to give" for the collection to Jerusalem. The next verse contains the only NT use of the adj. *aparaskeuastos*, of the possibility of their not being ready to do this after all.

2. (a) *kataskeuazō* is used 3x in connection with John the Baptist's function of preparing the way for the Lord's messenger (Matt. 11:10; Mk. 1:2; Lk. 7:27), and once of his function to make ready "a people prepared" (1:17). In each case Mal. 3:1 is cited (with echoes of Exod. 23:20; Isa. 40:3, both of which use *hetoimazō* [→ *hetoimos, 2289*]).

(b) *kataskeuazō* is used in 1 Pet. 3:20 (in connection with baptism) for the building of Noah's ark. All the other NT examples of this vb. are in Heb. and refer to the construction and furnishing of a building. The OT concept of God's all-embracing work of creation introduces the simile of the building of a house and concludes that God has built everything (3:3–4). The underlying thought here is of Christ as the builder of the church. Heb. 11:7 refers to Noah's building the ark in obedient faith, in order to prepare a way of escape for him and his family. In 9:2, 6, in a section about Christ's unique sacrifice, the author refers to setting up the tabernacle for worship according to God's instructions.

3. In cl. Gk. the noun *paraskeuē* means preparation in general, but the NT uses it always as a temporal expression to indicate the "day of Preparation" preceding a Sabbath or Passover festival: Matt. 27:62; Mk. 15:42; Lk. 23:54; Jn. 19:14, 31, 42.

See also *hetoimos*, ready, prepared (*2289*); *zōnnymi*, gird (*2439*).

2942 (kataskēnoō, live, dwell, perch), → *5008.*

2943 (kataskēnōsis, place to live, nest), → *5008.*

2958 (katasphragizō, to seal), → *5382.*

2961 (katatomē, mutilation), → *4362.*

2968 (kataphileō, to kiss), → *5797.*

2969 καταφρονέω

καταφρονέω (*kataphroneō*), despise (*2969*); περιφρονέω (*periphroneō*), despise (*4368*); καταφρονητής (*kataphronētēs*), despiser (*2970*).

CL & OT In cl. Gk. *kataphroneō* is a common word, which means showing contempt or disregard for someone or something. Whether it denotes a compliment or censure depends on who or what is being disparaged. *kataphronētēs* means one who despises, usually in a bad sense. *periphroneō* can be a synonym of *kataphroneō*, although its primary meaning is simply to think hard about something.

In the LXX, objects of *kataphroneō* include God (Hos. 6:7 = LXX 6:8), one's father (Gen. 27:12), one's mother (Prov. 23:22), and the ways of the law (19:16). Such contempt was, of course, profoundly impious. *periphroneō* has a good sense of despising distress (4 Macc. 6:9), torments (7:16), and pains (14:1). *kataphronētēs* signifies one who deals treacherously and unfaithfully (Hab. 1:5; 2:5; Zeph. 3:4).

NT *kataphroneō* occurs 9x in the NT. In the proverbial saying of Matt. 6:24 par. it is morally neutral; its sense is good in Heb. 12:2, where Jesus is said to have despised the shame of the cross. But it has a bad sense in the warnings against despising God's kindness (Rom. 2:4), his church (1 Cor. 11:22), Christ's little ones (Matt. 18:10), a youthful leader of the church (1 Tim. 4:12), and Christian masters (6:2). It is also bad when Peter censures heretics for despising "authority" (likely the lordship of Christ exercised through church officers, 2 Pet. 2:10; cf. Jude 8, which uses *atheteō*, reject).

periphroneō occurs only in Tit. 2:15, the sense of which is parallel to 1 Tim. 4:12. *kataphronētēs* appears only in Paul's citation of Hab. 1:5 at the end of his evangelistic sermon in Antioch of Pisidia (Acts 13:41), where it means "scoffers."

2970 (*kataphronētēs*, despiser), → 2969.

2977 (*kateidōlos*, full of idols), → 1631.

2980 (*katexousiazo*, exercise authority over, tyrannize), → 2026.

2989 (*katēgoreō*, accuse), → 2991.

2990 (*katēgoria*), accusation, → 2991.

2991	κατήγορος

κατήγορος (*katēgoros*), accuser (2991); κατήγωρ (*katēgōr*), accuser (2992); κατηγορέω (*katēgoreō*), accuse (2989); κατηγορία (*katēgoria*), accusation (2990).

CL & OT *katēgoros* means speaking against or accusing someone; as a noun, it means accuser. Satan is the great accuser in the OT, though humans also carry out his work (Dan. 6:5). The biblical foundation for this teaching is esp. Job 1–2 and Zech. 3. Satan as accuser is concerned with Israel, but he also accuses individual persons. He acts particularly when people accuse themselves, run into danger, or live carelessly. In the heavenly court he can appear when he wants to, and he is turned away only on the merits of the case. Michael is his opponent.

NT Rev. 12:10 is clearly based on Jewish concepts, and only here in the NT is Satan called *katēgōr*. He is said to accuse the children of God "day and night." After the exaltation of Jesus Christ, Satan was cast out of heaven (12:7–9). The same picture of the fall of Satan, but without the use of *katēgoros*, is found in Lk. 10:18; Jn. 12:31; and Rom. 8:33–34. Jesus, the intercessor, replaces the accuser. In other NT passages *katēgoros* refers to human accusers before earthly tribunals, as in the case of Paul's enemies before the Roman procurators (Acts 23:30, 35; 25:16, 18).

katēgoreō is derived from *katēgoros* and means to be an accuser, betray, make known. The enemies of Jesus spied on him to see whether he would heal on the Sabbath, so that they might accuse him of a breach of the Sabbath before the local Sanhedrin (Mk. 3:2; Lk. 6:7). The chief priests accused Jesus before Pilate (Mk. 15:3–4; Lk. 23:10, 14). The word appears more frequently in Acts because of the repeated accounts of attacks on Paul (22:30; 24:2; 25:5; 28:19). He defended himself by pointing out that his accusers could not prove their accusations (24:13, 19; cf. 25:5, 11, 16). He appealed to Caesar, but not because he wanted to accuse the Jews (28:19).

katēgoreō is used also in a nonlegal sense in Rom. 2:15: "their thoughts now accusing, now even defending them."

Jn. 5:45 refers to the last judgment. Jesus is not the one who will accuse the Jews who do not believe, but Moses, because those who do not believe in Jesus refuse also to believe in the law of Moses, which bears witness to Jesus (5:46).

katēgoria is derived from *katēgoros* and means an accusation in the legal sense. Pilate asked the chief priests what "charges" they brought against Jesus (Jn. 18:29). Timothy was instructed not to accept an accusation against an elder unless there were two or three witnesses (1 Tim. 5:19; cf. Deut. 19:15). One of the conditions that a candidate for eldership must fulfill is that his children are not open to the accusation of being wild or disobedient (Tit. 1:6).

See also *diabolos*, adj., slanderous; noun, slanderer, the devil (*1333*); *krima*, judgment (*3210*); *enkaleo*, accuse (*1592*).

2992 (*katēgōr*, accuser), → 2991.

2994	κατηχέω

κατηχέω (*katecheo*), inform, instruct (*2994*).

CL & OT 1. This word, rare in cl. Gk. and found only at a late date, meant originally to sound down from above, and so denotes the action of poets or actors who speak from a stage. In Plutarch the word has the general sense of to give information about something, report something. It is also found with the meaning to instruct, teach. A related noun *katechesis* is used in Stoic lit.

2. The word is absent from the LXX, and its usage in Philo and Josephus conforms to that of cl. Gk.

NT Paul and Lk. use this vb. 4x each. Lk.'s usage covers both normal meanings: to report something (Acts 21:21, 24) and to instruct someone (18:25). The meaning of the word in Lk. 1:4 is disputed as to whether Theophilus has been receiving reports about Jesus' life, death, and resurrection, or whether he has been formally instructed in these teachings of Christ. If the latter, the *katecheo* is here being used as a technical word for Christian instruction (see below).

Paul uses *katecheo* exclusively in the sense of to instruct someone regarding the content of the faith (see 1 Cor. 14:19; Gal. 6:6; in Rom. 2:18 the law is the subject of instruction), so that it may even be regarded as a technical term for "to instruct in the faith." This meaning seems particularly appropriate in 1 Cor. 14:19, where Paul asserts that he would rather speak five intelligible words "to instruct others" than ten thousand words in tongues, which after all may merely encourage self-glorification on the part of the speaker.

In Gal. 6:6 Paul enjoins that the one who is taught (*katechoumenos*, pres. pass. part. of *katecheo*) should supply the material needs of the teacher (*katechōn*, pres. act. part. of *katecheo*). This is the earliest evidence we have for a teaching office in the early church (cf. 1 Cor. 9:3–18); perhaps Paul himself introduced the term *katechōn* for the teacher of the gospel.

The use of *katecheo* as a technical term also occurs in Acts 18:25, if "the way of the Lord" refers to God's redemptive work in Christ and in history. By the time 2 Clem. 17:1 was written (mid-2d cent. A.D.), *katecheo* had become the normal term for giving baptismal instruction to catechumens. The process came to be called *katechesis* (from which we get the Eng. words "catechism" and "catechesis").

See also *didaskō*, teach (*1438*); *didaskalos*, teacher, master (*1437*); *didaskalia*, teaching, instruction (*1436*); *paideuō*, bring up, instruct, train, educate (*4084*); *paradidōmi*, to deliver, hand down (*4140*).

2996 (*katischyō*, to be strong, powerful, be dominant, prevail), → 2709.

2997 (*katoikeō*, inhabit), → 3875.

2999 (*katoikētērion*, dwelling place, habitation), → 3875.

3001 (*katoikizō*, settle), → 3875.

3004 (*katō*, below, downward, down), → 539.

3005	κατώτερος

κατώτερος (*katōteros*), lower (*3005*).

CL & OT *katōteros* is the comparative of *katō*, under. In the LXX it occurs mostly in the Ps. to denote any area in which life is threatened, or the realm of the dead itself (63:9; 86:13; 88:6; 139:15).

NT In the NT *katōteros* occurs only in Eph. 4:9: Christ "descended into the lower parts of the earth" (lit. trans.). The following questions arise: Is the comparative *katōteros* here used in the sense of the superlative ("into the lowest regions of the earth") or of the positive ("into the regions of the earth that lie below")? Is "of the earth" a gen. of apposition? If so, the expression would mean, "the lowest parts, namely, the earth." Or is it a partitive gen.? If so, the expression would mean "the lowest parts of the earth." Does *katōteros* correspond to the expression in the OT, "the depths of the earth," which can refer to the earth itself (Ps. 139:15) as well as to Hades (63:9; cf. Tob. 13:2)? According to a rab. tradition, one of the names for Gehinnom (→ *geenna*, *1147*) was lowest land, lowest earth.

Perhaps Eph. 4:9 is dependent on an older Jewish exposition of Ps. 68:18, in which Moses ascended into heaven to receive the Torah and then descended to earth to transmit it to humans; this exposition is then applied to Christ (→ *anabainō*, *326*, for another explanation). Or perhaps "he descended" and "the lower parts of the earth" refer to Jesus' death. Anyone who dies, according to the Jewish view, goes into the realm of the dead, and this realm of the dead lies under the earth (→ *hadēs*, *87*)—hence "descended."

Regardless of which view is correct, Jesus did become a human being in such a way that he took our final destiny, death, on himself. Light is thus thrown on the statement of Eph. 1:20–23. The "all in all" (lit. trans.) that he fills means the highest heights and the lowest depths (the realm of the dead). It also means that he has received power over all beings, esp. the spirits. Ultimately it matters little whether the earth itself or regions lying beneath its surface are meant in 4:9. What is important is that Christ, the exalted one, is conqueror of all powers and dominions and that as such he has given gifts to his church.

See also *abyssos*, abyss, pit, underworld (*12*); *hadēs*, Hades, the underworld, the realm of the dead (*87*); *geenna*, Gehenna, hell (*1147*); *tartaroō*, sent to Tartarus, hell (*5434*).

3008	καῦμα

καῦμα (*kauma*), heat, burning (*3008*); καυματίζω (*kaumatizō*), burn, scorch (*3009*); καῦσις (*kausis*), burning, heat (*3011*); καυσόω (*kausoō*), be on fire, burn (*3012*); καύσων (*kausōn*), heat (*3014*).

CL & OT 1. In cl. Gk. *kauma* means burning, heat, esp. sunburn or heat of the sun; in a transferred sense, fever heat, ardor of love, frostbite. *kaumatizō* means dry up by heat, and by extension, in the mid. form, suffer from fever. The rest of the words in this group all have to do with burning or intense heat.

2. In the LXX *kauma* serves most frequently as a translation of *ḥōreb* or *ḥōm* (each 4x) in its original sense of the heat of the sun, burning sun (cf. Gen. 31:40; Jer. 36:30 = LXX 43:30; cf. Sir. 43:3), but also in the transferred sense of fever heat (Job 30:30). Its use is, however, illuminating, as can be seen from the context in each case.

(a) Even in Jer. 36:30 the context should be noted. The fact that Jehoiakim's body is to be exposed to the heat of the sun and the frost of night is a sign of divine judgment on him because of his guilt. The same idea is conveyed by the complaint of Job, "My body burns with fever" (30:30). He sees in this a sign that God has become a cruel enemy (30:21).

(b) *kauma* is also used as a parable for affliction and trouble. Thus in Jer. 17:8 the one who trusts in the Lord is "like a tree planted by the water, [which] does not fear when heat comes; its leaves are always green." Similarly in Sir. 14:27 those who meditate on wisdom will be "sheltered by her from the heat." Looking forward to the coming reign of peace, Isa. prophesies that God's glory "will be a shelter and shade from the heat of the day" (4:6).

(c) *kausis* is used for natural fire: for baking bread (Isa. 44:16), on an altar (40:16), or on the golden lampstand (2 Chr. 13:11). *kausōn* denotes heat, esp. from the sun (Gen. 31:40; Isa. 49:10; Jon. 4:8).

NT 1. In the NT this word group occurs 4x in the Gospels, 5x in the General Letters, and 4x in Rev. (1) Rev. 16:8–9 speaks of divine judgment and wrath. The fourth bowl of wrath is poured on the sun, which "was given power to *scorch* [*kaumatizō*] people with fire. They were *seared* [*kaumatizō*] by the intense *heat* [*kauma*]."

2. Matt. 13:6 and Mk. 4:6 tell of the seed falling on rocky ground, which was "scorched" (*kaumatizō*) by the sun after germination. This parable refers to those who take offense at God's Word when tribulation and persecution arise.

3. In Rev. 7:16 God's people have come through great affliction and martyrdom and been raised to the heavenly glory: "Never again will they hunger; never again will they thirst. The sun will not beat upon them, nor any scorching heat [*kauma*]."

4. In 2 Pet. 3:10, 12, *kausoō* is used for the eschatological fire that will burn up the elements before the creation of the new heaven and earth. In Heb. 6:8, *kausis* is used for the burning of useless thorns and thistles—a symbol of God's ultimate destruction of those who have fallen away.

5. *kausōn* denotes the heat of the day because of the burning sun (Matt. 20:12; Lk. 12:55; Jas. 1:11). The last of these uses is fig. for the passing value of riches.

See also *pyr*, fire (*4786*).

3009 (*kaumatizō*, burn, scorch), → *3008*.

3011 (*kausis*, burning, heat), → *3008*.

3012 (*kausoō*, be on fire, burn), → *3008*.

3013	καυστηριάζω

καυστηριάζω (*kaustēriazō*), mark by a branding iron, brand (*3013*).

CL & OT In cl. Gk. this vb. means to burn with hot iron, to brand. The LXX does not have the vb., but 4 Macc. 15:22 has the related noun *kautērion* in the sense of branding iron.

NT The sole NT occurrence of *kaustēriazō* is 1 Tim. 4:2, where Paul refers to false teachers who have their consciences "seared." The condition of these heretics is perhaps that of men who are possessed by Satan and demonic forces. Alternatively, it may mean that their consciences have been made insensible to moral distinctions.

See also *stigma*, mark, brand (*5116*); *charagma*, mark, stamp, graven object (*5916*).

3014 (*kausōn*, heat), → *3008*.

3016 (*kauchaomai*, boast), → *3017*.

3017	καύχημα

καύχημα (*kauchēma*), boast, pride, object of boasting (*3017*); καύχησις (*kauchēsis*), boasting (*3018*); καυχάομαι (*kauchaomai*), boast (*3016*); ἐγκαυχάομαι (*enkauchaomai*), boast (*1595*); κατακαυχάομαι (*katakauchaomai*), boast against, exult over, triumph over (*2878*).

CL & OT 1. All of the above words occur in cl. Gk. *katakauchaomai* means vaunt oneself against someone, treat someone in a derogatory or contemptuous manner. *kauchēma* refers to the subj. of boasting (similarly, *kauchēsis*), to the words used by the boaster, and occasionally also to the act of boasting. Although the Gks. recognized legitimate pride in oneself, they drew a clear distinction between this and unwarranted bragging, which was pilloried by the satirists and others.

2. The OT also recognizes legitimate pride, e.g., of children in their fathers (Prov. 17:6) or of old men in their gray hair (16:31). Personal boasting, however, is reprehensible (1 Ki. 20:11 = LXX 21:11; Prov. 25:14; 27:1), an expression of sheer folly and ungodliness (cf. Ps. 52:1; 94:4). The theological basis for rejecting all self-praise lies in the fact that those who boast focus attention on themselves and no

longer look to God, the Creator and Redeemer. They trust in themselves instead of having confidence in God, praising his grace and faithfulness (Jer. 9:23–24 = LXX 9:22–23). Boasting in God and his acts, however, is always appropriate (Deut. 33:29; 1 Chr. 16:28–29; 29:11; Ps. 5:11; 32:11; 89:16–17; Jer. 17:14).

3. In Jud. this group of words has the same meaning as in the OT, except that the Mosaic law is added to the list of things truly worthy of praise (Sir. 39:8). In rab. theology, praise of Abraham has its basis in his fulfillment of the law. The rabbis also warned against arrogance and spiritual pride and encouraged humility. Moreover, suffering becomes a ground for boasting, as it is received by the believer at God's hand.

NT In the NT *kauchaomai* occurs 37x, *enkauchaomai* once, *katakauchaomai* 4x, and the nouns *kauchēma* and *kauchēsis* each 11x. Most occurrences are in Paul's letters. He uses these words to emphasize an idea central to his doctrine of justification, namely, that original sin consists in glorifying oneself and not giving God his due.

kauchaomai occurs with particular frequency in polemical passages. Just as Paul attacks the Jewish doctrine of justification by works, so he opposes the closely related habit of human self-praise, based on fulfillment of the law. The emptiness of such *kauchēsis* is revealed by the rhetorical question in Rom. 3:27: "Where, then, is boasting?" Through the principle of faith, all human glorying is made of no account.

This is clearly evident in Eph. 2:8–9: "For it is by grace you have been saved, through faith—and this not from yourselves, it is the gift of God—not by works, so that no one can boast." The worthlessness of human boasting, when based on the Mosaic law, is similarly exposed in the context of Rom. 2:23 (cf. also 4:2, where Abraham's works gave him nothing about which to boast before God; Gal. 6:13).

Paul attacks just as strongly the self-confidence of the Gks., who boast of their wisdom (1 Cor. 1:29; cf. also 3:21). All forms of boasting in the flesh (2 Cor. 11:18; Phil. 3:3–4) are wrong; they include such things as the arrogant attitude of Gentile Christians to non-Christian Jews (Rom. 11:17–18) and false bragging (1 Cor. 4:7; cf. 2 Cor. 5:12; 12:6; Jas. 3:14). Personal boasting is evil (4:16; cf. 1 Cor. 5:6), and it conflicts with an appropriate form of boasting, cited from Jer. 9:24 in 1 Cor. 1:31: "Let him who boasts boast in the Lord" (cf. 2 Cor. 10:17–18).

For Christians, therefore, the only fitting form of *kauchēsis* is to boast of God through Jesus Christ (Rom. 5:11; cf. Phil. 3:3) or, as Gal. 6:14 puts it, to glory in the cross of our Lord. The Christian's *kauchēsis* can include glorying in the acts of God to which the apostles bear witness, and also in those acts brought about in the course of apostolic ministry. In this sense Paul can boast of the authority that has been given to him (2 Cor. 10:8; cf. Rom. 15:17) in contrast to the false apostles (2 Cor. 11:12–30).

Paul also boasts of individual churches in which the fruit of faith can be seen (1 Cor. 15:31; 2 Cor. 1:14; 7:4, 14; 8:24; 2 Thess. 1:4; → *ergon*, 2240). In the context of Christ's return, he can describe the Thessalonians as "the crown in which we . . . glory" (1 Thess. 2:19). He writes also that the Philippians will be his *kauchēma* "on the day of Christ" (Phil. 2:16; cf. 1:26). He will have no one deprive him of this apostolic ground for boasting (1 Cor. 9:15).

Naturally, Paul knows where the limit comes (cf. 2 Cor. 11:16–30). Christians can really only boast of their weakness, because that is where God's strength becomes apparent (11:30; 12:5, 9). If we boast of our own behavior (1:12; cf. Gal. 6:4; Jas. 3:14), we should do so only insofar as we live in dependence on God and in responsibility to him (cf. 1 Cor. 9:16). Where the Lord is not the foundation and content of our *kauchēma*, boasting remains "in the flesh" and is therefore sinful. However, it is vital "to hold on to . . . the hope of which we boast" (Heb. 3:6; cf. Rom. 5:2).

3018 (kauchēsis, boasting), → 3017.

3026 (keleusma, signal, cry of command), → 3027.

3027	κελεύω

κελεύω (*keleuō*), command, order (*3027*); κέλευσμα (*keleusma*), signal, cry of command (*3026*).

CL & OT *keleuō* occurs widely in cl. Gk. It is generally used of verbal orders emanating from a person of superior rank or status. In the LXX its use is confined to the Apocr., where it is used of a variety of types of commands: from religious leaders, army officers, kings, prophets, and even God. The meaning of *keleusma* in cl. Gk. ranges from specific commands to terse orders and inarticulate cries; it is often used of the command of a god. In the LXX *keleusma* occurs only in Prov. 30:27 = LXX 24:62.

NT In the NT *keleuō* (25x) is confined mostly to Matt. and Acts. In Acts the word is used only of orders given by human authorities: the Sanhedrin (4:15), the Ethiopian eunuch (8:38), Gamaliel (5:34), Herod (12:19), the magistrates (16:22), the tribune (21:33; 22:24; 22:30; 23:10), the high priest (23:3), Felix (23:35), Festus (25:6, 17, 21, 23), and the centurion (27:43). In Matt. *keleuō* is also used of orders given by human authorities: e.g., Pilate (27:58; 27:64) and Herod (14:9). But on a few occasions it refers to orders given by Jesus (8:18; 14:19). In Lk. the vb. is used for Jesus' command to have a blind man brought to him (18:40).

keleusma is found only in 1 Thess. 4:16, where it denotes a shout of command at the onset of the Parousia, together with a call of the archangel and a trumpet sound. It is not clear who gives this *keleusma*—God, Christ, or the archangel.

See also *dogma*, decree, ordinance, command (*1504*); *entolē*, command, order (*1953*); *parangellō*, give orders, command (*4133*).

3029 (kenodoxia, desire for praise, conceit, vanity, illusion), → 1518 and 3031.

3030 (kenodoxos, desirous of praise, conceited, boastful), → 1518 and 3031.

3031	κενός

κενός (*kenos*), empty, fig. without content, truth, or power, without result or profit (*3031*); κενόω (*kenoō*), to empty, destroy, render void (*3033*); κενοδοξία (*kenodoxia*), desire for praise, conceit, vanity, illusion (*3029*); κενόδοξος (*kenodoxos*), desirous of praise, conceited, boastful (*3030*).

CL & OT 1. In cl. Gk. *kenos* means empty as opposed to *plērēs* (full). It is used mostly lit. of things (e.g., an empty jug, pit, or house), but also occasionally of persons (e.g., with empty hands). When used metaphorically in connection with things, *kenos* means either lacking content or a missing effect (esp. the expression *eis kenon*, in vain); with people, hollow, shallow, lacking in judgment, vain.

The vb. *kenoō* means to empty, in the sense of plunder or bring to nothing. *kenodoxos* means vainglorious, conceited. *kenodoxia* means either vanity, conceit, or error, delusion.

2. Heb. has no exact equivalent to *kenos*. The LXX uses this word to translate 19 different Heb. words. The most common of these is *rîq*, empty, worthless, vain. For the most part it means empty (e.g., Jer. 14:3, vessels; Deut. 15:13, empty-handed). But it also has a distinctive metaphorical sense; Jdg. 9:4; 11:3 speak of *andres kenoi*, worthless men, who are not counted among the people of Yahweh and who are willing to perform any kind of deed. The prophets spoke of turning away from Yahweh as giving oneself to vanity. The help Israel sought from the Egyptians was worthless and empty (Isa. 30:7). Israel has forgotten Yahweh and offers sacrifice to vanity or nothing, i.e., to idols (Jer. 18:15). By contrast, the Lord's chosen ones will not toil in vain (Isa. 65:23).

3. The word is found most frequently in the cries of Job. He resents the vain words (Job 27:12) and the empty comfort (21:34) of his friends. He sees not only the things around him but his own life sink into nothing. He laments the months of emptiness (7:3) and vain hope

(7:6), crying out: "Let me alone; my days have no meaning" (7:16). Unless Yahweh rescues him, he can only perish.

NT 1. *kenos* occurs in the parable of the vineyard, when the tenants send back the master's servants empty-handed (Mk. 12:3; Lk. 20:10–11). Most of the other NT occurrences of this word are in Paul, who gives it a distinctive sense, especially in the negative expression *mē eis kenon*, not in vain, where the accent is on fruitlessness and inefficacy. He uses it to suggest that under certain circumstances things such as grace (2 Cor. 6:1), preaching (1 Cor. 15:14), missionary work (1 Thess. 3:5), and his own activity as an apostle (Gal. 2:2; Phil. 2:16) are fruitless or in vain. As the work of God, Paul's mission is wrought in power, in contrast to the empty, ineffective words of paganism (Eph. 5:6).

2. Paul uses *kenodoxia* (Phil. 2:3) and *kenodoxos* (Gal. 5:26) each once, both with the nuance of conceit.

3. Similar to *kenos*, Paul uses the vb. *kenoō* negatively and also passively. He speaks of certain things that must not be made empty, i.e., made void. Among them are faith (Rom. 4:14), the cross of Christ (1 Cor. 1:17), and his boasting as an apostle (2 Cor. 9:3). The cross and faith form the central subject matter of the gospel and thus constitute its power. Hence, the offense of the cross, which both condemns and saves, should not be made void by words of worldly wisdom (1 Cor. 1:17). The saving way of faith should not be made void by justification through the law (Rom. 4:14).

4. The precise significance of *heauton ekenōsen* (Phil. 2:7) has been much discussed. The words mean lit. "he emptied himself." Most scholars regard Phil. 2:6–11 as a pre-Pauline hymn about Christ, which Paul quotes in the course of his argument in order to illustrate his point that Christians should be unselfish, humble, and outgoing in their relationships, and thus have the mind of Christ (2:5). Some scholars interpret Christ's emptying himself in the sense of his freely exchanging his preexistent, divine mode of being (2:6) for a common, human, earthly existence (cf. 2 Cor. 8:9). Others, however, suggest that the passage should be translated: "He poured out his life" (cf. Isa. 53:12), so that it refers not to Jesus' incarnation but to his self-surrender on the cross.

Phil. 2:7 has played an important part in the discussion of Christology. It has given rise to the doctrine of *kenōsis*, according to which Christ emptied himself of, and made no use of, at least some of his divine attributes during the period of his earthly life. Thus, he was not omnipresent, omniscient, or omnipotent in his incarnate state. Scholars appeal to the Gospels to show that Jesus was tired and had other bodily needs. He also disclaimed omniscience (Mk. 13:32). They then explain this in terms of a self-emptying of divine attributes, which they find implied in Phil. 2:7.

This Christology has been questioned on two levels. (a) It raises certain theological questions. The attributes of omniscience, omnipotence, and omnipresence are essential attributes of divinity. God would not be God without them. If Christ were divested of essential divine attributes, it is difficult to see how the doctrine of his divinity can still be maintained. It would make him, as the Arians believed, something less than God but more than human. Moreover, what became of the cosmic functions of the divine Word (cf. Jn. 1:1–5; Col. 1:17; Heb. 1:3) during the period of Jesus' incarnation? Did the Word abandon them (as *kenōsis* seems to imply)? Or was it rather that the divine Word that sustains the universe was both in him, living out the divine life in this human life, and also outside him?

To resolve this dilemma scholars have offered an analogy between the conscious mind's relationship to the unconscious mind and Jesus' relationship to the divine Word. The conscious mind is only partly aware of its own workings, yet it continues to work unconsciously. In a similar way, Jesus was aware only of what he needed to be aware of as God's Son and the servant of humankind.

(b) Does Phil. 2:7 really imply kenoticism? Neither the Gospels nor Phil. 2 presents the picture of the abandonment of any divine attributes. They do, however, show Jesus clearly accepting the status and role of a servant (Phil. 2:7; cf. Mk. 10:45; Lk. 22:27; Jn. 13:3–16;

15:20). The motive and guiding principle in all his actions was love, humility, and obedience to the Father (cf. Matt. 3:15; Jn. 5:19; 7:16; 15:10; 17:4; Gal. 4:4). As a servant, Jesus accepted the limitations that were the Father's will.

Phil. 2 sees Christ as having three states: a preexistent state, a state of humiliation as a servant in his life and death, and a state of exaltation in which he is universally acknowledged as Lord. It is usual to take the various descriptions in 2:7–8 as involving successive acts. But the emptying, the taking the form of a servant, and being born in the likeness of humankind are clearly not successive acts, for the birth is mentioned last. Similarly, the humbling and obedience are not stages that follow each other until they are replaced by the cross. Rather, these descriptions each apply to Christ's entire life, all of them culminating in the cross. Thus, the imagery of the passages makes use of both the picture of the preexistent Christ and the suffering servant. The emptying of 2:7 is the outpouring of Christ during his life and also on the cross.

See also *mataios*, empty, fruitless, useless (*3469*).

3033 (*kenoō*, to empty, destroy, render void), → *3031*.

3035 (*kentyriōn*, centurion), → *4483*.

3038 (*kerameus*, potter), → *3040*.

3039 (*keramikos*, belonging to the potter, made of clay), → *3040*.

3040	κεράμιον

κεράμιον (*keramion*), an earthenware vessel, jar (*3040*); κέραμος (*keramos*), clay, earthenware vessel, a roof tile (*3041*); κεραμεύς (*kerameus*), potter (*3038*); κεραμικός (*keramikos*), belonging to the potter, made of clay (*3039*); κεράννυμι (*kerannymi*), mix (*3042*); σκεῦος (*skeuos*), thing, object, vessel (*5007*).

CL & OT 1. (a) In cl. Gk. this group of words revolves around the potter's craft. From Homer on, *keramion* denotes vessels of clay, esp. earthenware jars for storing wine or water. The potter was a familiar figure in every village. The fragility of earthenware pots and the ease with which a potter's stock could be depleted through breakage gave rise to proverbs that suggest the potter was sometimes the butt of jokes: e.g., "to make a pot of the potter"; "the potter bears a grudge against the potter." *keramos* also came to designate in the pl. tile work, e.g., in the building of a temple or roof tiles of a house.

(b) The vb. *kerannymi*, to mix, blend, may originally have had something to do with mixing water and soil in order to prepare the potter's clay. But usually it is used of diluting wine with water.

2. (a) In the LXX *keramion* designates an earthenware pot or jar. In Isa. 5:10 God warns unresponsive Israel that a ten-acre vineyard will yield only one *keramion* of wine. Jars filled with wine signified prosperity and blessing. Conversely, God's judgment on Moab is pronounced in terms of emptying his vessels (*skeuos*) and smashing his wine jars (Jer. 48:12).

(b) *kerameus* means potter (e.g., 1 Chr. 4:23). Normally, the reference to the potter is lit. in the OT, although the potter's craft suggested a metaphor for God in his relationship to Israel and the nations (Ps. 2:9; Isa. 29:16; 41:25; Jer. 18:2–3, 6). Typical is the oracle of lament in Isa. 45:9, which pronounces woe on those who disbelieve in the deliverance God has promised. As inconceivable as it would be for a lump of clay to inquire of the potter what he was doing in the molding process, so is the folly of anyone who tries to argue that God is unable to accomplish what he has promised.

Keen observation of the potter is characteristic of Ben Sira. In a moving passage, he contrasts the wisdom of the scribe with the skill of the farmer, the gem cutter, the smith, and the potter—all who keep the fabric of the world stable (Sir. 38:24–34). He observes not only the potter at work at his wheel, but the importance of glazing and the cleaning of the kiln (38:29–30). The concentration of the potter on his work suggests an apt figure for God in pursuing his purposes among humanity (33:13 = LXX 36:13). Similarly, the effect of the kiln on the finished vessel furnishes a simile for the manner in which human reasoning tests individual character (27:5).

(c) In common with cl. Gk., the vb. *kerannymi* refers to the diluting of wine with water (Prov. 9:2, 5; Isa. 5:22; 19:14) and has no association with the potter's trade.

NT 1. *keramion* occurs 2x in the NT, both in connection with the arrangements for the Last Supper (Mk. 14:13; Lk. 22:10). The two disciples charged with the preparation were to follow a man in the city carrying a clay water jar, who would lead them to the house where the feast was to be celebrated. The device of a man carrying a water jar suggests a prearranged signal, for ordinarily women carried water in jars. Perhaps Jesus resorted to a means of recognition that required no exchange of words in the street because his enemies were looking for a way to arrest and kill him (cf. Jn. 11:47–54).

2. *keramos* occurs only in Lk. 5:19, where it means roof tiles. When four men were unable to break through a crowd with their paralyzed friend, they climbed a staircase on the side of the house to the flat roof and broke it open in order to lower the man before Jesus. Such a roof was made from light material coated with clay (cf. Mk. 2:4).

3. *kerameus* occurs 3x in the NT, two in the stylized phrase "the potter's field" (Matt. 27:7, 10), which refer to a field the chief priests purchased with the thirty pieces of silver Judas returned, to be used as burial ground for strangers who died in Jerusalem (27:3–10; cf. Acts 1:18). The field contained a pit where potsherds were discarded.

It also occurs in the parable of the potter in Rom. 9:19–29, where God's sovereign disposition over his own creation is affirmed on the analogy of the potter's determination to make from the same lump of clay one vessel (*skeuos*) of striking beauty and another destined for menial use (9:21). Paul uses the analogy in response to the charge that God is unjust in the administration of his judgment. He first appeals to Exod. 33:19, where God affirms, "I will have mercy on whom I have mercy." From this, Paul deduces that everything depends on God's mercy, which he extends or withholds according to his sovereign will (Rom. 9:15–18). But how God can hold an individual accountable for transgression if he himself assigns to each person his or her role (9:19)?

In his reply, Paul makes use of the parable of the potter (cf. Isa. 29:16; 45:9). As the clay cannot protest against the action of the potter, neither can the creature protest against the action of the creator (Rom. 9:20). Verse 21 recalls Jer. 18:6 (cf. Wis. 15:7), where God's right to make vessels designed for different purposes from the same lump of clay is affirmed. Rom. 9:22–29 contemplates the two categories of such vessels in terms of the sovereign disposition of the divine will. Implied in the discussion is a call for Israel to become open to God's grace expressed in Christ and to the experience of mercy.

4. In addition to its use in Rom. 9:21, *skeuos*, object, vessel, jar, occurs elsewhere in Paul and other NT writings. In 2 Cor. 4:7 Paul speaks of having the treasure of the knowledge of the glory of God "in jars of clay." In 2 Tim. 2:21 anyone who purifies oneself from what is ignoble "will be a instrument [*skeuos*] for noble purposes . . . useful to the Master." This reflects the language of Acts 9:15, where Ananias is told that Saul of Tarsus is "my chosen instrument to carry my name before the Gentiles and their kings and before the people of Israel."

skeuos can mean generally any object for any purpose (Mk. 11:16), goods, or property (Matt. 12:29; Mk. 3:27; Lk. 17:31). The addition of a qualifying phrase may define its nature more precisely, e.g., "everything [lit., all the vessels] used in its ceremonies" (Heb. 9:21; cf. also Rev. 18:12). In Acts 27:17 it seems to be an anchor, though it may be gear or sails (cf. also 10:11, 16; 11:5). For its meaning in 1 Thess. 4:4 and 1 Pet. 3:7, in the context of marriage relationships, → *gynē*, woman, *1222*.

5. The adj. *keramikos* occurs only once in the NT, in the pledge of shared power with Christ extended to faithful Christians at Thyatira (Rev. 2:27). Together they will rule the nations with an iron rod and "will dash them to pieces like pottery" (a quotation from Ps. 2:9). The new order must be preceded by the shattering of the old (cf. Rev. 11:15). This promise provides an assurance of vindication and a reversal of roles in which the humiliated people of God will share in the authority of their Lord.

6. As in cl. Gk. the vb. *kerannymi* is used of diluting wine with water. In Rev. 14:10 it carries the nuance of pouring out the wine of God's wrath "full strength." In 18:6 it describes the fate of Babylon, whose judgment is depicted as mixing a double portion of wine to make her reel from drunkenness and deprive her of all sense and capability (cf. Isa. 19:14; *Pss. Sol.* 8:14).

See also *ostrakinos*, made of earth or clay, earthenware (*4017*); *pēlos*, clay, mud, mire (*4384*); *phyrama*, a mixture, a lump (*5878*).

3041 (*keramos*, clay, earthenware vessel, a roof tile), → *3040*.

3042 (*kerannymi*, mix), → *3040*.

3043	κέρας

κέρας (*keras*), horn (*3043*).

CL & OT 1. In cl. Gk. *keras* is a common word for the horn of an animal; later it came to mean courage or stubbornness. In ancient religion, though probably not in Greece, horns symbolized the strength of gods and humans. Thus, Assyrian princes and Babylonian priests wore two-horned headdresses similar to those that normally adorned the gods. Alexander the Great was known as "The Horned One."

2. In the LXX *keras* is used in two different connections. (a) It denotes the horns of animals (Deut. 33:17) and is esp. frequent with this meaning in apocalyptic lit. (e.g., Dan. 7:7; 8:3; *1 Enoch* 90:9). In priestly and sacrificial contexts the word refers to the twisted horn-like corners or projections of the altar (Exod. 27:2; Lev. 4:7; Ps. 118:27).

(b) From these original connotations came the fig. use of *keras* to express the power and might of human beings and of Yahweh. As in the prophetic and symbolic act of Zedekiah (1 Ki. 22:11), the horn frequently denotes physical power and superiority (Mic. 4:13) as well as well-being in general (1 Sam. 2:1). When Yahweh is addressed as "the horn of my salvation" (2 Sam. 22:3; Ps. 18:2), he is considered to be the power that brings about salvation and preserves humans against hostile attacks.

NT 1. In the NT *keras* is found only in Lk. 1:69 and in Rev. In Zechariah's song of praise (Lk. 1:68–79), strongly reminiscent of Ps. and full of OT imagery, the phrase "horn of salvation" is taken over from Ps. 18:2 and means "saving power." The vb. "raised up" suggests that by his acts in history God brings about salvation. The addition of "in the house of his servant David," which goes back to 132:17, specifies the Messiah as the horn of salvation. Lk. 1:69 glorifies God as one who has demonstrated his power in history and who by sending the Messiah has raised up a power that brings salvation.

2. Rev. 9:13 refers to the horns of the golden altar before God. The fig. use of horns in Rev., where they have no organic connection with the animals concerned and so cannot in any sense be envisaged biologically, is connected with OT and Jewish apocalyptic. The Lamb bears seven horns (5:6). In accordance with the symbolic meaning of the number seven and of the metaphor of the horn, these horns express divine power.

The dragon and the beast each have ten horns (Rev. 12:3; 13:1; 17:3). Those of the beast are related to the ten horns of Dan. 7:7 as well as to their application (ten kings; cf. 7:24), who, according to Rev. 17:12–14, give over their power to the beast. They join with the beast in his war against the Lamb but are vanquished. Like most of Rev., the meaning of this vision is debated. Some interpret it as referring to the 1st cent., so that the beast represents Nero *redivivus* and the ten horns represent princes or Roman emperors. Others suggest that these horns represent all rulers and their subjects (cf. 19:17–21) who are linked with the Antichrist in the open battle against Christ.

See also *bia*, force, violence (*1040*); *ischys*, strength, power, might (*2709*); *kratos*, power, might, rule (*3197*).

3045 (*kerdainō*, to gain), → *3046*.

3046	κέρδος

κέρδος (*kerdos*), gain (*3046*); κερδαίνω (*kerdainō*), to gain (*3045*); ζημία (*zēmia*), damage, disadvantage, forfeit, loss (*2422*); ζημιόω (*zēmioō*), suffer damage, loss, forfeit (*2423*).

CL & OT 1. In cl. Gk. *kerdos* means gain, profit, advantage; sometimes clever advice, cunning attacks; in the pl. even deceit. The vb. *kerdainō* means to make a profit or gain an advantage; it can also mean to spare or avoid (cf. Acts 27:21), since avoiding loss brings a gain. The opposite of *kerdos* is *zēmia*, disadvantage, loss, and (occasionally) punishment. The opposite of *kerdainō* is *zēmioō*, suffer loss.

2. Neither *kerdos* nor *kerdainō* occurs in the LXX, though the concept of profit does. The OT refers to gains that are unjustly acquired (e.g., Gen. 37:26; Exod. 18:21; Ps. 10:3; 119:36; Isa. 33:15; 56:11; 57:17), using such words as *anomia*, lawlessness, *anoma*, lawless things (→ *nomos*, law, *3795*), and *adikia*, unrighteousness (→ *94*). Eccl. stresses that there is no true profit (*perisseia*; → *perisseuō*, abound, surpass, *4355*) under the sun (cf. Eccl. 1:3; 2:13; 3:9, 19; 5:15; 6:8).

zēmioō does occur in the LXX. It refers to some sort of legal punishment, such as a levied fine (Exod. 21:22; Deut. 22:19). In Prov. 17:26; 19:19; 21:11, it occurs as a generic word for punishment. In 2 Ki. 23:33 *zēmia* refers to a levy imposed by Pharaoh Neco on Judah; in Ezra 7:26, to the notion of confiscation of property; and in Prov. 27:12 to the loss a fool suffers by refusing to avoid danger.

NT 1. In the NT *kerdos* occurs only 3x (all in Paul); *kerdainō* occurs 17x. The NT opposes the normal economic orientation of profit insofar as profit is anticipated out of selfish motives. Tit. 1:11 is directed against teachers of false doctrine from Crete who were spreading ideas with an eye to "dishonest gain" (cf. also the warnings to church leaders in 1 Tim. 3:8; Tit. 1:7; 1 Pet. 5:2). Anyone whose view of life is dominated by the profit motive falls into an arrogant self-centeredness and thus into sin (Jas. 4:13). Matt. 16:26 (Mk. 8:36; Lk. 9:25) warns against finding one's life by means of self-preservation. One may need to lose one's life in order to gain it.

2. Paul develops a positive understanding of gain. The gain of Christ is the ultimate good. Death itself is thus a "gain" (Phil. 1:21), since it marks the end of the life of martyrdom and leads to life with Christ. In Phil. 3 Paul recounts his own privileges as a Jew and as a Pharisee, such as his circumcision and faithful adherence to the law. But what he at one time considered "profit" (*kerdos*) has become, for the sake of Christ, total "loss" (*zēmia*), because these things were bound by the law of human achievement and conferred none of the "righteousness that comes from God" (3:9). Paul, therefore, regards human gains as losses, in order to gain Christ and to be found in him.

3. Paul takes on the same language as he reflects on his missionary commission. His main goal is to "win" (*kerdainō*) as many as possible for the Lord by whatever means possible (1 Cor. 9:19–22). Likewise, Peter exhorts wives to win their unbelieving husbands by their godly behavior (1 Pet. 3:1). Jesus exhorts people to use effective pastoral care and concern to gain a fellow believer who has fallen into sin (Matt. 18:15). Jesus also uses *kerdainō* metaphorically in the parable of the talents, when he refers to those who have gained more talents by their wise use of what the master had given them (25:16–17, 20, 22).

See also *apodidōmi*, give away, give back, sell, recompense (*625*); *misthos*, pay, wages, reward (*3635*); *opsōnion*, wages, payment (*4072*).

3051	κεφαλή

κεφαλή (*kephalē*), head (*3051*); ἀνακεφαλαιόω (*anakephalaioō*), sum up, recapitulate (*368*).

CL & OT 1. In cl. Gk. *kephalē* means (a) the head of man or animal, the coping of a wall, the capital of a column, the source or mouth of a river, the beginning or end of a month, etc. (b) It also denotes what is decisive, superior. In Gk. anthropology the head takes precedence over all other members; in it lies the authoritative principle, reason. (c) It also stands for the life of an individual. As early as Homer it was used in a similar way to *psychē*. Thus, curses that name the head are directed against the whole person.

2. (a) In the LXX *kephalē* has the primary meanings we know from cl. Gk.: the head of a man (Gen. 28:11), the head of an animal (3:15), the top of a mountain (8:5) or tower (11:4).

(b) The head is particularly important in the language of gesture. It was shaven in times of grief (Ezek. 7:18); a man under a vow did not shave it (Num. 6:5; cf. Acts 18:18). It was covered (2 Sam. 15:30) or strewn with ashes (13:19) as a sign of penitence.

(c) Via expressions like "for each person" (Exod. 16:16; lit., "for each head") and "one by one" (Num. 1:2; lit., "head by head"), the use of *kephalē* in the LXX was extended to cover the life of the individual. The OT sees the human person as a unity, but in each case it singles out that part of the person that is significant. In this case it is the head as the source of life. The head can be used as the equivalent of the person and one's whole existence (e.g., 2 Ki. 25:27; Ps. 3:3; Ezek. 9:10; 33:4). In Isa. 43:4 *kephalē* stands for *nepeš* ("soul") and denotes a human life.

(d) By comparison with other nations Israel will be "the head, not the tail" (Deut. 28:13; cf. Isa. 9:14). Thus *kephalē* can denote the one who occupies a position of superiority in the community (cf. Jdg. 10:18).

3. Philo's use of *kephalē* was seminal. The *logos* (word) is the head of the universe that God has created, its source of life, overlord, ruler. In contrast to ANE mythology, which saw the whole cosmos encompassed in the head and body of the highest god (→ *aiōn*, *172*), Philo believed in God as the creator of the cosmos. In the gnostic use of *kephalē*, the term serves to denote not only the unity of the body, but also the controlling influence over it. The post-Christian *Odes of Solomon* speak of the head concept of the first man in a manner comparable with that in which the NT speaks of Christ.

NT 1. In the NT, *kephalē* appears 75x, primarily in its basic meaning of the head of a person (Matt. 14:8), animal, or demons (Rev. 17:3). It occurs most frequently in Rev. (19x), where it refers to those human and animal forms characterized by the shape or the ornament of their heads. The head bears the tokens of honor and dignity (4:4; 19:12; etc.), but also those of shame (13:1). Jesus' head is often mentioned in the passion narrative (Matt. 27:29–30, 37; Mk. 15:19, 29; Jn. 19:2, 30). The smiting of his head stands in marked contrast with an anointing of it (Matt. 26:7; Mk. 14:3; Lk. 7:46). The head of Jesus is also mentioned in the resurrection narratives (Jn. 20:7, 12). On the phrase *kephalēn gōnias*, head of the corner (Matt. 21:42; Mk. 12:10; Lk. 20:17; Acts 4:11; 1 Pet. 2:7), → *gōnia*, *1224*.

2. The head is mentioned in the NT also in connection with the customs of fasting and penitence (Matt. 6:17; Acts 18:18; Rev. 18:19). As we know from the LXX, the shaking of the head signifies that a claim and its consequences have been rejected (Matt. 27:39). With the phrase, "Your blood be on your own heads!" Paul placed on the Corinthian Jews the responsibility for their rejection of the Messiah (Acts 18:6; cf. Matt. 27:25).

The numbering of the hairs of the head (Matt. 10:30) and the saying that "not a hair of your head will perish" (Lk. 21:18) speak of God's promise to preserve those who commit themselves into his hands. In wanting to have his head washed (Jn. 13:9), Peter wanted his whole life to be cleansed. Jesus prohibited swearing by one's head

(Matt. 5:36; cf. *m. Sanh.* 3:2, where the rabbis refused to allow anyone to retract an oath by the life of the head).

3. In 1 Cor. 11:2–15 one notes a discussion of reasons why women should be required to veil their heads during public worship. The reference to a veil is to something that conceals the whole head, including the hair. In Jud. women were veiled in public. Paul's teaching here may have been influenced by the presence of Jews in Corinth, who maintained Jewish practices in their synagogue worship and who may well have looked with a critical eye on what was going on in the church. Note that immediately before the present passage Paul has urged that no offense be given to Jews, Greeks, or the church (10:32) and that the church should follow him in trying to please everyone and in being imitators of Christ (10:33–11:1).

The underlying problem in Corinth was one of freedom in the light of the new and equal standing of males and females before God. In his letter of 1 Cor., Paul reflects in several places on the importance of freedom to these new church members—often a form of freedom that had no restraints. He emphasizes a freedom that is linked with service to God and love for others. Thus, freedom can never be equated with license. The apostle is concerned not only with freedom but also with order in society. For him the role and relationships of the sexes, which are determined by creation, are not abolished by salvation. This must be reflected in public worship. Thus, Paul advances the following arguments for the subordinate role of women and for the veiling of the woman's head.

(a) The hierarchy of the order is God–Christ–man–woman, in which each of the first three members is the head of the following one (1 Cor. 11:3). Here *kephalē* should probably be understood not as ruler but as source or origin. The creation narrative of Gen. 2:21–23 assigns a priority to the male (cf. also Eph. 5:22–33; Col. 3:18–19; 1 Tim. 2:11–14). But the Christian knows that Christ has a greater priority as the archetypal man (cf. 1 Cor. 8:6; 15:46–49; Col. 1:16), and the head of Christ is God (cf. 1 Cor. 3:23; 8:6).

There is a transition from the sense of head in 1 Cor. 11:3 to its literal sense in 11:4–6, and from there on the text oscillates between the two senses. Paul argues that for a man to pray with his head covered is to dishonor his head (11:4, cf. 11:7), because it implies that he is abdicating the sovereignty and dignity given to him by the Creator. But for a woman to pray or prophesy with her head unveiled dishonors her head (11:5), for this is tantamount to a denial of her relation to man in the ordinances of creation. It is just as dishonorable as if her head were shaven, which was a commonly accepted sign of dishonor.

Paul's argument at this point has two premises: (i) the propriety of covering the head in the presence of a superior, and (ii) the constitutional relationship of man and woman, which gives a certain priority to the man. Given these two premises, the propriety of veiling the woman in worship (the most solemn occasion for recognizing the divine ordering of things) logically follows. However, in situations where the former premise is neither recognized nor understood, the validity of the conclusion no longer has the same weight as it did in Paul's day.

(b) Man has priority in the order of creation in relation to the glory of God (11:7–9, 12). The argument is now developed in relation to the concept of glory (*doxa*, → *1518*). Gen. 1:26–27 states that all humans (Heb. *ʾādām*; Gk. *anthrōpos*) were made in the image of God. Here in 1 Cor., however, Paul speaks only of the male (Gk. *anēr*). Perhaps he is reading Gen. 2:18–23 in the light of Gen. 1:26–27. But he also couples together here the concepts of image and glory in a way that goes beyond the Gen. narratives: "A man ought not to cover his head, since he is the image and glory of God; but the woman is the glory of man" (1 Cor. 11:7). Elsewhere Paul argues that humankind has fallen short of the glory of God (Rom. 3:23; cf. 1:21) and that the glory of God is revealed in the gospel in the face of Christ (2 Cor. 4:4–6), who restores the image of God in humanity (Col. 3:10).

In addition to the priority of the male in the created order and the significance of veiling, Paul here has two further premises implied in his conclusion. (i) The glory *of God* should not be veiled in the presence of God, for this would be a contradiction in terms. Hence, the man should not be veiled. (ii) Woman is the glory of man (for woman was made for man, cf. 1 Cor. 11:9). Hence, the glory *of man* should be veiled in the presence of God. Again, it should be said that the practical application drawn from these premises depends on how far they are recognized in a community.

(c) Paul then refers to the angels (1 Cor. 11:10): "That is why the woman ought to have authority [*exousia*] over the head, because of the angels" (lit. trans.). The veil was a sign of the woman's authority. In Christ a woman has an equal status with men before God. The veil was a sign of this new authority, which was denied her in the synagogue. As a woman she may pray or prophesy (11:5), but she must maintain due regard for her place in the created order. Whereas the man shows his authority by not being veiled, the woman shows hers by wearing a veil. The wearing of the veil manifests both the *liberty* and the *restraint* that belongs to the woman in Christ. The liberty derives from freedom in Christ; the restraint (as elsewhere) derives from the ordering of society, which has divine sanction.

What about the reference to angels? According to Rev. 8:3, angels are charged with the task of transmitting prayers to God. They are the sign of the divine presence. Therefore no offense should be given them. The major premise of the argument is that one should not give offense—in this particular case, to the angels. The minor premise (implied) is that the veil is a sign of a woman's status and authority in the Christian community. Thus, women should be veiled in worship. Again it may be noted that, although the guiding principles behind Paul's recommendation hold good, its continued application depends on the continued acceptance of all the premises of the argument. In a culture where the significance of veiling is no longer understood in the same way, the argument no longer has the same force.

(d) Next, Paul appeals to custom grounded in the natural order (1 Cor. 11:13–15). He shares the view that it is natural for men to have their hair short, though it may be grown longer on occasion in connection with a vow (Acts 18:18). The statement that a woman's long hair is "her glory ... given to her as a covering" (1 Cor. 11:15) does not imply that if she has sufficient hair, she need not be veiled. Rather, the veiling of the woman in worship is seen as consonant with nature. Paul's view of the woman's hair as "her glory" is perhaps taking up the thought that, just as in the presence of God the glory of man must be veiled (see above), so too must the "glory" of the woman. In each case Paul uses the same word, *doxa*.

(e) The argument concludes in 1 Cor. 11:16 by stating that this is the practice recognized by Paul and the other churches. The passage has been used in support of requiring women to wear hats in worship today. If this application were valid, the argument would support not the wearing of hats but full veils. However, the above discussion has shown that its force depends on the common understanding of certain premises valid in Paul's culture. Where these premises no longer obtain, the conclusions also no longer obtain, even though the motivating *principle* of maintaining freedom of the Spirit and restraint with regard to the order of nature and society still holds.

4. In Eph. 4 the head is contrasted with the body (→ *sōma, 5393*). Christ is the head of his body (4:15). The body is supplied from the head and grows because of it (4:16). To describe the relationship of the Lord to his people, the church, Eph. emphasizes that the church is to grow *eis andra teleion* (lit., "into the perfect or complete man," 4:13). In this picture, Christ is the head, and as head he sustains the whole body. Thus, in 4:15 the head determines the relationship of love and truth in the body of Christ, i.e., the fellowship of those who practice truth and through love grow up into him. The relationship of *kephalē* to *sōma* expresses the authority of Christ (cf. Col. 2:10) and the corresponding subordination of the church. It expresses the body's participation in and dependence on the head for the gift of life. The head is always the heavenly goal of the body, which cannot be attained except in a body sustained by faith and revelation.

Eph. 1:21–22 declares that all powers are now subject to Christ, who is the "head over everything for the church." The *archē*, the principality that previously was so important, is now one of the many subject to Christ. The application to Christ of *archē* ("beginning") in Col. 1:18 (where he is also said to be "the head of the body, the church") does not contradict this, for here the word stands in polemic juxtaposition to the *archai* (1:16; → *archē*, 794).

5. In Rom. 12:19 Paul urges believers not to avenge themselves, for vengeance belongs to the Lord (cf. Lev. 19:18; Deut. 32:35). He then backs this up with a quote from Prov. 25:21–22a: "If your enemy is hungry, feed him; if he is thirsty, give him something to drink. In doing so, you will heap burning coals on his head" (Rom. 12:20). While the imagery behind this thought is debated, it seems most likely that the coals represent an element of shame or contrition, not a form of punishment. Paul's main concern is that the life of the believer should be free from all thought of revenge, that the enemy might be convicted (though not necessarily converted—for that is God's work) by kindness, and that the way to overcome evil is not to repay in kind but to repay it with good.

6. The rare vb. *anakephalaioō* means to bring something to a *kephalaion*, to sum up, recapitulate. It is used in Rom. 13:9 of the individual commandments, which "are summed up in this one rule, 'Love your neighbor as yourself.'" In Eph. 1:10 it occurs in the statement of God's plan "when the times will have reached their fulfillment—to bring all things in heaven and on earth together under one head [*anakephalaiōsasthai*], even Christ." The thought of unity implied here has affinity with the use of the vb. in Rom. and is one of the great themes of Eph. (cf. 2:14–22; 4:3–4). But there may also be an overtone of renewal, which is in fact a condition of unity. Christ and his people, both Jew and Gentile, constitute the "one new man" (2:15; cf. 4:13). Moreover, this affects the entire created order. In his body, which represents the *plērōma* (fullness; → *plēroō*, 4444), the heavenly domain of his presence, Christ fills all in all (1:22–23; cf. 1:10).

3056 (*kēnsos*, tax, poll-tax), → 5088.

3060 (*kērygma*, proclamation, announcement, preaching), → 3062.

3061 (*kēryx*, herald), → 3062.

3062	κηρύσσω

κηρύσσω (*kēryssō*), announce, make known, proclaim (aloud) (3062); κῆρυξ (*kēryx*), herald (3061); κήρυγμα (*kērygma*), proclamation, announcement, preaching (3060).

CL & OT 1. (a) In cl. Gk. the noun *kēryx* denotes a man commissioned by his ruler or the state to make known, with a clear voice, some important news (a sort of town crier). The vb. *kēryssō* was formed from the noun to describe the activity of the herald, though it occurs less often than the noun. The noun *kērygma* was later formed to describe either the act of shouting aloud or the report or edict that was proclaimed.

(b) The precise meaning of these words depends on the function of the *kēryx* in the historical period in question. (i) In Homer *kēryx* is used of the attendants of a prince who performed duties in keeping with the role of senior court officials, whose task was to care for the personal well-being of the prince and his guests. They had the respect of the prince and a status similar to that of friends. The herald's staff, a kind of scepter, in their hands, made that clear as they carried out the commission (to inform or invite) authorized by the prince.

(ii) In the period of the *polis*, the democratic city-state, the institution was maintained, though in this age there were various types of heralds. Formally these men were servants of certain authorities, whose chief qualification for office was a loud and clear voice; but heralds also called the soldiers to battle and the full citizens to the assembly. They were responsible for good order in the assembly and opened it with prayers and sacrifices and announced its end. In public court hearings heralds announced the result of the drawing of lots for the

judges, called on the judges to cast their votes, and asked the people whether anyone had objections about procedure or the statements of the witnesses. Thus they were, so to speak, responsible for the maintenance of law and order.

There was also a certain sacredness to their position. When the *kēryx* appeared, weapons were stilled, e.g., when heralds from one city invited all Greece to a festival in honor of the gods. The herald who came to an enemy with a message in time of war was not to be touched, since that would incur the wrath not only of the one who sent him, but also that of the gods. It is probably because of this position that heralds occasionally functioned as political ambassadors.

(iii) The following general characteristics may therefore be listed. The *kēryx* was always under the authority of someone else, whose spokesman he was. He himself was immune from danger, since he conveyed the message and intention of his master. Since all he could do was announce, he had no liberty of his own to negotiate. He also proclaimed legal and judicial verdicts, and what he announced became valid by his act. The binding and settling nature of this proclamation distinguishes *kēryssō* and its cognates from *angellō* (→ 33) and its compounds, which refer primarily to the imparting of information.

(c) With the relaxation of the rigid order of the *polis*, the Stoics were provided with the opportunity for giving a quite different interpretation to the office of *kēryx*, after it had largely lost its significance for society. Epictetus saw the real *kēryx* of his day as the Cynic philosopher, who moved around the country as a messenger of the gods and guardian of the moral order. Without means of his own and totally dedicated to his task, he came to denounce the way of life of his contemporaries and to call them to repentance and reformation of life. These preachers of virtue prepared the stage on which later the messengers of the gospel of Jesus Christ were to stand. The Eleusinian mysteries also had their special heralds, who carried out liturgical functions in the cult, were responsible for announcements, and together with the priests exercised great influence.

2. (a) In striking contrast to Gk. lit., the noun *kēryx* occurs only 4x in the LXX (Gen. 41:43; Dan. 3:4; Sir. 20:15; 4 Macc. 6:4). In Gen. 41 and Dan. 3 the emphasis is on the vb. *kēryssō*, which appears in addition to the noun. In other words, a figure comparable to the Gk. *kēryx* was unknown in Israel. It is clearly not appropriate to describe the prophets in this way.

(b) The LXX uses the vb. *kēryssō* 30x. In Exod. 36:6 it is used for an announcement made throughout the camp by Moses; in 2 Chr. 36:22, throughout the kingdom by King Cyrus. In Hos. 5:8; Joel 2:1; Zeph. 3:14; Zech. 9:9, the vb. refers to a loud cry (a cry of alarm raised or accompanied by instruments, or the triumphant battle cry or shout of victory). In Prov. 1:21; 8:1, wisdom cries out with a loud voice.

If we leave aside the Prov. passages and Zeph. 3:14; Zech. 9:9, we may say that *kēryssō* is used only for three classic functions of the herald: (i) for the proclamation of a cultic festival (Exod. 32:5; 2 Ki. 10:20) or fast (2 Chr. 20:3; Joel 1:14; 2:15; Jon. 3:5, 7); (ii) for the orders of the military commander in the field or a decree of the prince (Exod. 36:6; 2 Chr. 24:9; 1 Esd. 2:2; 1 Macc. 5:49); (iii) for the proclamation of judgment (Hos. 5:8; Joel 3:9; Jon. 3:2, 4), of Yahweh's day of judgment (Joel 2:1), or of liberty to captives (Isa. 61:1). Note that in Mic. 3:5, *kēryssō* is used to render the false prophets' proclamation of peace.

The noun *kērygma* is found once in each of the above categories, describing the content of what is proclaimed (2 Chr. 30:5; Prov. 9:3; Jon. 3:2; 1 Esd. 9:3). Categories (i) and (ii) move within the familiar framework of orders given by human authorities, but the prophetic passages mentioned under (iii) speak of the proclamation of a judgment of Yahweh. The number of references is, however, relatively small. The *kēryx* word group never achieves central importance in the OT's proclamation of salvation; this purpose is served by other vbs. (e.g., *angellō*).

3. (a) In Jewish writings outside the OT, Josephus's use of *kēryx* corresponds to the cl. Gk. usage when he refers to the conveying of mil-

itary commands and to diplomatic missions. Philo, by contrast, uses the words for the utterances of the OT prophets. In rab. lit. both the noun and the vb. appear where an announcement or a judicial verdict is publicly proclaimed and also for the public announcement of rab. decisions on doctrine when these are relevant to the keeping of the law.

(b) At Qumran the vb. *sāpar*, to tell, recount, which sometimes comes close in meaning to the Gk. *kēryssō*, occurs fairly frequently in the Hymns. Here, of course, it is used of the congregation's, or the individual worshiper's, act of proclaiming praise to God and recording the wonderful works of Yahweh or his honor, majesty, patience, and mercy.

NT 1. The first noticeable feature in the NT is that, in keeping with the LXX, it uses the noun *kēryx* only 3x (1 Tim. 2:7; 2 Tim. 1:11; 2 Pet. 2:5). *kērygma*, too, is found relatively seldom. Paul uses it for the message of Christ that he proclaims (Rom. 16:25) or for his preaching generally (1 Cor. 2:4; 15:14; 2 Tim. 4:17; Tit. 1:3). In Matt. 12:41; Lk. 11:32, *kērygma* is used for the "preaching" of Jonah to Nineveh.

The vb. *kēryssō*, on the other hand, occurs 61x. An analysis of the grammatical obj. of the vb. reveals that in early works of Paul (Gal. 2:2; 1 Thess. 2:9; cf. Col. 1:23), and in some Gospel passages (Matt. 4:23; 9:35; 24:14; 26:13; Mk. 1:14; 13:10; 14:9), the obj. is *to euangelion*, the gospel. But in Acts 8:5; 9:20; 19:13; 1 Cor. 1:23; 15:12; 2 Cor. 1:19; 11:4, Phil. 1:15, the obj. is Christ (4x), Jesus (3x), or Christ Jesus. John the Baptist preached "a baptism of repentance for the forgiveness of sins" (Mk. 1:4; Lk. 3:3; cf. Acts 10:37). For Luke the *basileia*, kingdom (→ 993), is the obj. of proclamation (Lk. 9:2; Acts 20:25; 28:31; cf. Matt. 4:23; 9:35; 24:14).

2. (a) This evidence makes it clear that the NT writers, following other streams of Jud., avoided identifying themselves or the messengers of Jesus with the Gk. institution of the *kēryx*, open as it was to such a wide variety of interpretation. Only in the later NT passages (1 Tim. 2:7; 2 Tim. 1:11, leaving aside the description of Noah as a *kēryx* of righteousness in 2 Pet. 2:5) is the word used, and then in combination with *apostolos*, apostle (→ 693), which qualifies it. But even these two texts reveal the basic difference between the biblical viewpoint and that of the surrounding world: It is not the institution or the person to which importance is attached, but only the effective act of proclamation. This may be why the establishment of a definite, official position of "preacher" was avoided by not using that particular noun (e.g., it is not included in the listing of special ministry gifts in Eph. 4:11–12).

(b) A similar finding results from a study of the term *kērygma*, proclamation, in the NT. Where it is used (e.g., Matt. 12:41; Lk. 11:32 for the *kērygma* of Jonah), it undoubtedly includes the content of Jonah's message to Nineveh. But the emphasis lies much more on the carrying out by Jonah of a divine commission—the delivery of a message containing not only a threat of judgment but also an invitation to repentance and salvation.

In three texts of Paul (1 Cor. 1:21; 2:4; 15:14), this emphasis is even more obvious. The emphasis in *kērygma* has in mind the apostle's activity of preaching just as much as the content of his message. In Rom. 16:25 *kērygma*, message, is already becoming hypostasized: It is Christ-preaching, as carried out by Paul. Furthest of all along this line goes 2 Tim. 4:17, where the *kērygma* is the actual act of proclamation, which has need of the particular messenger only in order to complete it and give it concrete fulfillment (see also Tit. 1:3).

(c) The nouns of this group are thus used in the NT generally to express the form of an activity; *what* the *kērygma* is—i.e., what content it makes known—can be seen only from the context in each case. The NT is therefore as faithful to the original meaning of the word as is the OT. *kērygma* is the phenomenon of a call that goes out and makes a claim on the hearers; it corresponds to the life and activity of the prophets. It is not until the 4th cent. that Athanasius, after centuries in which the word had been used in a variety of ways, used the noun *kērygma* in the full sense of Christian or church doctrine.

3. (a) The NT's predominant conception of proclamation as a process and event, whose content can only be determined by closer definition, is confirmed by the greater frequency with which the vb. is used in comparison with the nouns. *kēryssō* is one of a number of formal verbs of telling and communication, which connote a certain means of communication but are not limited as to the content (e.g., *didaskō*, to teach [*1438*]; *angellō*, to report [*33*]; *legō*, to say [*3306*]; *homologeō*, to confess [*3933*]; *martyreō*, to bear witness [*3455*]; *euangelizō*, to preach [*2294*]). None of these vbs. gained a position of clear dominance in the NT or became a technical term (see, e.g., Lk. 4:43; 6:13; 9:6; Phil. 1:18; 1 Thess. 2:2, 9).

The nearest the NT comes to the classical figure of the herald is in Rev. 5:2, where the angel makes a proclamation with a mighty voice, and in 1 Pet. 3:19, where the voice of the crucified one rings out in Hades (here the vb. has no obj.). Perhaps also Matt. 10:27; Lk. 12:3, where proclaiming from the rooftops refers to the public revelation of what has hitherto been hidden, can be mentioned here.

(b) Traces of the original meaning of the word are also to be found here and there in Paul. In Rom. 2:21 he addresses those who make a demand that people should not steal and yet do it themselves: "You who preach [*kēryssō*] against stealing, do you steal?" Here *kēryssō* may be compared with the Stoic sense of proclamation of a definite command that demands obedience (see also 1 Cor. 9:27; Gal. 5:11).

Positively. Paul sees himself as one who proclaims the gospel of God (1 Thess. 2:9) among the Gentiles (Gal. 2:2), something that can be done only if it is accompanied by a total giving of his own person (1 Thess. 2:8). For Paul proclamation is not, as with Jonah, a once-for-all cry. The proclamation of the message of Christ requires unceasing pleading and wooing with a love that seeks and is accompanied by a constant care for the individual. It also involves exhortation (→ *parakaleō*, *4151*), warning, encouragement (→ *paramytheomai*, *4170*), and witness (*martyreō*, *3455*). In such a context *kēryssō* appears as the central act of proclamation, which is needed if the call of God is to be realized (1 Thess. 2:12).

The basis for this invitation (i.e., its content and origin) may be discovered from other passages in his letters where Paul uses *kēryssō*. It is Christ, a person, whom Paul proclaims in this way (1 Cor. 1:23; 15:12; 2 Cor. 1:19; 4:5; Phil. 1:15; cf. 2 Cor. 11:4). It is in fact the crucified Christ (1 Cor. 1:23; cf. 2:2) who is presented in this proclamation as the basis of life. It is the Christ in whom Paul sees all the previous promises of God as being fulfilled and taking concrete form (2 Cor. 1:20). It is the Christ to whom Paul bears witness on the basis of the tradition handed down to him (→ *paradidōmi*, *4140*), but also on the basis of his own experience (1 Cor. 15:3–8). The death of Jesus for the sin of others, as well as his presence and exaltation made possible only by this means (1 Cor. 15:1–2; cf. Phil. 2:8–11), formed the central content of what Paul preached as his saving and world-changing message (1 Cor. 15:12).

The act of proclamation is ultimately a prerequisite of faith, inasmuch as it has as its goal not simply the imparting of information or a formal allegiance, but a faith that involves self-surrender and trust (cf. 1 Cor. 15:11). Therefore, Paul sees proclamation as legitimate and possible only where a commission and authority has been given (Rom. 10:8–12; cf. 10:15 with Acts 13:3 and Isa. 52:7). This means that Christ is not merely an object of proclamation, but also the subject, who has authority over it. He himself is the one who commands the proclamation and who allows the hearers to experience him in and through such human proclamation (cf. Gal. 3:1).

(c) The Synoptic Gospels all use *kēryssō* for the activity of John the Baptist (Matt. 3:1; Mk. 1:4; Lk. 3:3), indicating, as the allusion to Isa. 40:3 also shows, that he is the last of the prophets. Mk. sums up his preaching as that of a "baptism of repentance for the forgiveness of sins." This phrase includes both the means and the end. Matt. and Lk. develop this further with some examples of his teaching. All three Gospels record, however, that the Baptist's preaching extended to the announcement of the coming stronger one, through whose Spirit-baptism a new order would begin (Matt. 3:11; cf. Jn. 1:26–27).

(i) Matt. inserts at this point (3:2), as the factor that legitimates and motivates John's preaching, the truth that " the kingdom of heaven is near." This means that John's call to repentance is set against the background of the promised lordship of Christ (cf. Jesus' almost identical words in 4:17), and is emphasized at 10:7 as the center of the message the disciples are to proclaim. Just as the prophets, represented by John, have pointed forward to Jesus' coming, so the disciples bear witness to its dawning. The content of the *kēryssō* remains the same— a proclamation of Christ's lordship.

Note that Matt. is the only evangelist to use the term *kēryssō* exclusively in reference to the ministry of John, Jesus, and the disciples expressly sent out by him. He thus underlines the binding, almost judicial and official character of the proclamation, which, in contrast to *didaskō*, to teach, takes place not only in the synagogues but also in the desert and the villages and even among the Gentiles (Matt. 24:14).

(ii) Likewise in Mark the line may indeed be followed from John (1:4, 7), through Jesus (1:38–39), to the commissioned disciples (3:14; cf. 6:12). But Mk. emphasizes the inner power and the necessity of proclamation rather than its official character. Even before the disciples have been commissioned, those who have been healed proclaim, despite being expressly forbidden to do so. Their encounter with Jesus, their experience of God's mercy, and their own recognition of the dawn of the new age in this Jesus (7:37, echoing Isa. 35:5) are enough to compel them to tell others.

(iii) Finally, Luke takes up in Lk. 4:18–19 the prophetic words of Isa. 61:1–2 in Jesus' sermon at Nazareth and his declaration that the word has been fulfilled by his coming. He describes Jesus as the one who both proclaims and carries through the work of God, and then sends out the disciples to proclaim it (Lk. 10:9). When they speak of Christ, they proclaim by that very act the kingdom—God's new ordering of the things in the world, taking place in and through Jesus (cf. Acts 8:5; 9:20; 20:25; 28:31). Conversely, the proclamation of the *basileia* is tied up with the words and teaching of Jesus (28:31).

The sermons recorded in Acts tend to have a general common structure and message. Jesus is described as the Son of God (9:20), who fulfilled the OT prophecies concerning the Messiah (cf. 2:25–35; 3:24–26; 10:43; 13:32–37). He went about doing good (10:37–38), was crucified but arose from the dead (e.g., 2:32; 4:10), and is now exalted at God's right hand (2:33; 3:21; 10:42). In his name alone forgiveness of sins can be realized (2:38; 3:19; 10:43). Acts 15:21 makes it clear that the proclamation refers also to binding principles of faith and life for the fellowship.

4. What is the particular nuance of *kēryssō* as compared with the other, synonymous words used for the passing on of the message of Christ? Both Luke and Paul prefer the vb. *euangelizō* when they want to describe the total activity of proclamation (in the case of Lk., *katangellō* also) and use *kēryssō* more often to denote Jesus Christ as the originator and the object of proclamation (e.g., Lk. 4:18–19, 44; 8:1; 1 Cor. 1:23; 15:12; 2 Cor. 4:5; Phil. 1:15). Lk. also uses *kēryssō* with reference to the particular message that God's rule has dawned in Christ (Lk. 9:2; cf. also 1:19; 2:10; 3:18; 9:2, 6; Acts 5:42; 8:4–6). In each case the proclamation has a personal character, and the one who proclaims must stake his or her existence on it.

At the same time, the conveying of the message of Christ does not consist solely in *kēryssō*, as Matt. makes clear. He describes the work of Jesus as "teaching . . . preaching . . . and healing" (Matt. 4:23; 9:35). The description of the disciples' work follows the same essential pattern (10:7–8), though the word for teaching does not appear in connection with the disciples until the great commission of Matt. 28:20. All this is to say that the event of proclamation is surrounded by objective instruction and by events and actions that make known the dawn and the power of the new age.

See also *angellō*, announce (33).

3063 (*kētos*, sea-monster), → 2716.

3064 (*Kēphas*, Cephas), → 4376.

3073	κινδυνεύω

κινδυνεύω (*kindyneuō*), be in danger (*3073*); κίνδυνος (*kindynos*), danger, risk (*3074*).

CL & OT Both vb. and noun are found widely in Hel. Gk. In the LXX the vb. is found in Isa. 28:13, where it describes the risk run by those who refuse to listen. In Ps. 116:3 *kindynos* describes a dire predicament from which the psalmist has been delivered. In Sir. 43:24 *kindynos* is used of the perils faced by mariners.

NT *kindyneuō* occurs 4x in the NT. In Lk.'s rendition of the stilling of the storm, he emphasizes the danger the disciples were in (Lk. 8:23), thus adding to the color and drama of the narrative. In 1 Cor. 15:30 Paul refers to the constant dangers attending his ministry; his argument is that to face these risks is pointless if there is no resurrection. In Acts 19:27 Demetrius and his fellow craftsmen are concerned at the danger posed to their trade by the activity of Paul; in 19:40 the town clerk warns of the perilous consequences of the Ephesians' rioting.

kindynos occurs 9x. In Rom. 8:35 peril is an element that cannot separate believers from Christ's love. In 2 Cor. 11:26 Paul uses the word 8x to describe difficulties that have beset his ministry. The perils include the elements (sea and storm) and hostility from other people (robbers, Jews, and Gentiles). These reflections form part of the apostle's attempt to demonstrate to the Corinthians the authenticity of his ministry.

3074 (*kindynos*, danger, risk), → 3073.

3080 (*klados*, branch), → 1285.

3081	κλαίω

κλαίω (*klaiō*), weep (*3081*); κλαυθμός (*klauthmos*), weeping (*3088*).

CL & OT 1. In cl. Gk. *klaiō* means intrans. to cry aloud, weep; trans. bewail. The word does not express remorse or sorrow, but physical or mental pain that is outwardly visible.

2. (a) In the LXX *klaiō* can express profound grief (1 Sam. 1:7; Lam. 1:16 = LXX 1:15) as well as deep sorrow in mourning for the dead (Gen. 50:1). But it may equally express supreme joy, as at the meeting of Jacob and Joseph (46:29). The whole personality is involved, as it is in the case of a crying child (21:16; Exod. 2:6). In the OT the person weeping often expresses dependence on God by addressing cries or complaints to him in prayer (e.g., Samson in Jdg. 15:18; 16:28; cf. Isa. 30:19). A further OT feature is the cultic lamentation of the whole people before Yahweh, usually accompanied by a general fast (Jdg. 20:23, 26).

(b) The noun *klauthmos* means weeping (e.g., Gen. 45:2; Deut. 34:8; Jdg. 21:2; Job 30:31; Isa. 15:2–3; 30:19).

NT 1. Similar to the OT, *klaiō* expresses violent emotion, e.g., when parting (Acts 21:13), when thinking of the enemies of Christ (Phil. 3:18), when facing dying and death (Mk. 5:38; Lk. 7:13, 32; Jn. 11:31, 33; Acts 9:39), or generally when face-to-face with affliction (Rom. 12:15; 1 Cor. 7:30). Tears of joy are not mentioned in the NT.

2. The third Beatitude of Lk., "you who weep now" (6:21), is contrasted with the rich who laugh now and of whom all speak well (6:25–26). The latter are self-righteous people "who do not need to repent" (15:7) and who think highly of themselves. Those who "weep now," however, live humbly in complete dependence on God, since they are conscious of their guilt (Matt. 26:75; Lk. 7:38) and therefore acknowledge that God's assessment of them is just. Christ's promise to them is: "You will laugh" (Lk. 6:21). His followers' weeping over their guilt and the sufferings of the present will give way, at the end of time, to the laughter of the children of the kingdom.

3. By contrast, those who laugh now are warned: "You will mourn and weep" (Lk. 6:25). Where *klaiō* has a future reference in the NT, it is connected with warnings of disaster. Those who now are godless and scornful will be put to shame in the final judgment. To intensify the severity of these statements *klaiō* is sometimes combined with another vb. of mourning (cf. also Jn. 16:20; Jas. 4:9; Rev. 18:9).

4. To avoid lamentation in the future (when it will be too late), James exhorts his readers to weep now (4:9–10). He is perhaps recalling Jesus' words in Lk. 6:25.

5. The noun *klauthmos*, weeping, occurs frequently in the NT in the expression "weeping and gnashing of teeth" (e.g., Matt. 8:12; 13:42, 50; 22:13; 24:51; 25:30; Lk. 13:28). Here the word describes the final remorse that those who have rejected their opportunity to believe in Jesus will experience. In Matt. 2:18 *klauthmos* is associated with loud lamentation in the quotation from Jer. 31:15, seen as fulfilled in the slaughter of the innocents at Bethlehem.

See also *koptō*, strike (*3164*); *lypeō*, inflict pain (*3382*); *brychō*, gnash (*1107*); *pentheō*, be sad, grieve, mourn (*4291*); *stenazō*, to sigh, groan (*5100*).

3082 (*klasis*, breaking), → *3089*.

3083 (*klasma*, broken piece), → *3089*.

3088 (*klauthmos*, weeping), → *3081*.

3089 κλάω

κλάω (*klaō*), break (*3089*); κλάσις (*klasis*), breaking (*3082*); κλάσμα (*klasma*), broken piece (*3083*); κατακλάω (*kataklaō*), break in pieces (*2880*); ἐκκλάω (*ekklaō*), break off (*1709*).

CL & OT 1. In cl. Gk. *klaō* is a general vb. for to break, break off, break into pieces. It was esp. used for the idea of pruning branches of a tree.

2. Words in this group occur infrequently in the LXX. In Jdg. 9:53 (except A), *klaō* refers to the breaking of the head of Abimelech, son of Gideon, by a millstone (termed a "*klasma* of a mill"; cf. also 2 Sam. 11:21, 23) dropped on him. In Jer. 16:7 this vb. is used in the expression of breaking bread. The word *klasma* refers to a cake (1 Sam. 30:12) or the broken pieces of a grain offering (Lev. 2:6; 6:21). *ekklaō* is used for the breaking of a bird's wings in preparation for an offering (Lev. 1:17). *kataklaō* refers to broken branches in a vineyard, symbolic of the Lord's judgment (Ezek. 19:12).

NT 1. In the NT *klaō* occurs 14x and always in the expression of breaking bread. In the 1st cent., it was the usual pattern to break bread with one's hands at the beginning of a meal rather than to cut it with a knife. Thus Jesus broke the bread before he fed it to the multitudes (Matt. 14:19; 15:36; note also Mk. 6:41; Lk. 9:16, which use *kataklaō*). Paul similarly broke bread in the presence of the storm-exhausted people on the boat headed to Rome (Acts 27:35).

2. But breaking bread takes on religious significance because of the fact that Jesus broke bread with his disciples in the upper room as he celebrated the Passover with them (Matt. 26:26; Mk. 14:22; Lk. 22:19; 1 Cor. 11:24), telling them to do this in remembrance of him. As the early church developed, breaking bread seems to have become a technical phrase for the Lord's Supper (Acts 2:42 [*klasis*], 46; 20:7, 11 [*klaō*]). Breaking and eating bread in a worship setting denoted "participation in the body of Christ" (1 Cor. 10:16). This breaking of bread evoked not only the memory of the Last Supper but also the fact that Jesus broke bread with his followers after he was raised from the dead (Lk. 24:30; cf. the use of *klasis* in 24:35).

3. The word *klasma* is used exclusively for the broken pieces of bread that were gathered by the disciples after Jesus' feeding miracles (e.g., Mt. 14:20; 15:37; Jn. 6:12–13).

4. Finally, Paul uses *ekklaō* in Rom. 11:17, 19, 20 in his discussion of how some branches of the "natural" olive shoot (Jews) have

been temporarily "broken off" so that branches from a "wild" olive shoot can be grafted in.

3090 κλείς

κλείς (*kleis*), a key (*3090*); κλείω (*kleiō*), to close, shut (*3091*).

CL & OT 1. The noun *kleis* means key; the vb. *kleiō*, to close or shut. *kleis* was also used in cl. Gk. in connection with heaven and the underworld: Certain celestial powers or deities had control over the keys to heaven (e.g., Dike) or the underworld (e.g., Persephone). The imagery of the key extended into everyday life, such as rest being cited as the most important key to deliberation or to war.

2. In the LXX *kleis* occurs only 5x. In OT times a key was probably so large that it had to be carried on a belt or even a shoulder (cf. Isa. 22:22); with such a key one could turn backward and forward the bolt of the door from the outside. One of the offices of the Levites was to administer the keys to the rooms and storerooms of the temple (1 Chr. 9:27). The announcement in Isa. 22:22 of the installation of Eliakim into his office, giving him the power of the keys to the house of David, originally had no messianic reference; it was interpreted as conferring teaching authority. Jn. interpreted it typologically and Christologically in Rev. 3:7 (→ *anoigō*, 487). *kleis* also occurs in Jdg. 3:25; Job 31:22; Bel. 12. The vb. *kleiō* occurs in various OT passages (e.g., Gen. 7:16; Jos. 2:5, 7; Jdg. 9:51; Neh. 6:10; 13:19; Isa. 24:10; 60:11; Ezek. 44:1–2).

NT *kleis* occurs 6x (4x in Rev.) and is used only fig. *kleiō* occurs 16x. It is used lit. of closed, shut, or locked doors in Matt. 6:6; 25:10; Lk. 11:7; Jn. 20:19, 26; Acts 5:23; 21:30. In Matt. 25:10 it illustrates that the time of opportunity is past, while in Lk. 11:7 it pictures the importance of persistence in prayer.

1. Lk. 4:25 refers to the time of Elijah, "when the sky was shut for three and a half years" (cf. 1 Ki. 17:1–18:1; Jas. 5:17–18). Jesus' point is that during this time Elijah was sent not to a widow in Israel, but to one in Zarephath. Thus, Jesus of Nazareth will pass over a rebellious Israel in favor of the Gentiles.

2. In Lk. 11:52 Jesus denounces the experts in the law for their hypocrisy and misguided legalism; they have taken away "the key to knowledge" and thus hindered people from entering the kingdom. The parallel saying in Matt. 23:13 refers specifically to the kingdom: "Woe to you, teachers of the law and Pharisees, you hypocrites! You shut the kingdom of heaven in men's faces."

3. Matt.'s account of Peter's confession culminates in the promise: "And I tell you that you are Peter, and on this rock I will build my church, and the gates of Hades will not overcome it. I will give you the keys of the kingdom of heaven; whatever you bind on earth will be bound in heaven, and whatever you loose on earth will be loosed in heaven" (16:18–19). Jesus' choice of twelve disciples, reflecting the twelve tribes of Israel, is closely bound up with his reconstitution of the people of God. The band of disciples anticipates the messianic community that is constituted by Christ's death. Even though he dies, the gates of death will not prevail against his community.

In this passage Christ is seen as the master of the house. He has the keys to that house, the kingdom of heaven. Just as in Isa. 22:22 the Lord gave the key to David's house to Eliakim, so Jesus commits to Peter the keys of his house and thereby sets him up as representative of all the apostles, as its administrator (cf. also Mk. 13:34; Lk. 12:42; 16:1–12; 1 Cor. 4:1; 1 Pet. 4:10). He must lead God's new people into the resurrection kingdom. In this he stands in contrast with the Pharisees, who purportedly had the key to the kingdom but did not use it to enter and even prevented others from entering (cf. above on Matt. 23:13). Peter and the others have a preaching mission to give people access to the kingdom. This role the apostles fulfilled in Acts (for Peter, see esp. Acts 2 [ministry to Jewish believers]; 10 [to Gentile believers]).

The words "bind" (→ *deō*, 1313) and "loose" (→ *lyō*, 3395) in Matt. 16:19 may refer to prohibit and permit, i.e., establish rules; but they may also be referring to putting under the ban and acquitting (note the implied connection with entry into the kingdom). The power to teach and to discipline cannot be sharply separated. As the disciples had already shared in the work of Christ in his earthly ministry (cf. Matt. 9:35–10:42; Mk. 6:7–13; Lk. 9:1–6; 10:1–24), so now they are to share in the highest office of the forgiveness of sins (cf. Jn. 20:23). However, the idea of binding may also refer back to the picture of the binding of the strong man (i.e., Satan), who must first be bound before his goods (i.e., those enthralled by him) may be plundered (Matt. 12:29; Mk. 3:27). Thus Peter is perhaps being promised the power to bind Satan and to liberate people; not even death, the power of Hades, can thwart it (see also *petra*, rock, *4376*).

This passage may be linked with Matt. 18:18, where the power to bind and loose is given to all the apostles (in the context of procedure in the church to deal with problems of discipline caused by one member sinning against another). This text confirms that in Matt. 16:16 Peter is being addressed as representative of all the apostles (cf. his confession in 16:16, which is the confession of all). Matt. 16:19 can also be related to Jn. 20:23, where Jesus gives a similar promise to his disciples about forgiving and retaining sins.

4. *kleiō* is used metaphorically in 1 Jn. 3:17: "If anyone has material possessions and sees his brother in need but has no pity on him [lit., closes his heart against him], how can the love of God be in him?" The phrase used here is unique (but cf. Ps. 77:9).

5. Access to God's kingdom is also the concern of those apocalyptic passages where the key of David is mentioned (Rev. 3:7–8). Jn. interprets Isa. 22:22 messianically: Just as Eliakim received the key to the house of David and was given the authority to decide admission to it, so Christ, the promised descendant of David, holds the perfect key in his hand to decide admission to and exclusion from the future regal city of God. As the crucified and risen Savior, he has the keys to the world of the dead (1:18), so that death has lost its final terror for the believer. Possessing the keys to the abyss (20:1), he is the Lord who governs the spirits of the underworld (20:3).

See also *anoigō*, open (*487*).

3091 (kleiō, to close, shut), → *3090.*

3095 (kleptēs, thief), → *3334.*

3096 (kleptō, steal), → *3334.*

3097 (klēma, branch), → *1285.*

3099 (klēronomeō, inherit), → *3102.*

3100 (klēronomia, inheritance), → *3102.*

3101 (klēronomos, inheritor, heir), → *3102.*

3102 κλῆρος	

κλῆρος (*klēros*), inheritance, lot (*3102*); κληρόω (*klēroō*), cast lots, determine by lot (*3103*); κληρονομέω (*klēronomeō*), inherit (*3099*); κατακληρονομέω (*kataklēronomeō*), give as inheritance (*2883*); κληρονομία (*klēronomia*), inheritance (*3100*); κληρονόμος (*klēronomos*), inheritor, heir (*3101*); προσκληρόω (*prosklēroō*), allot, assign; pass. join (*4677*); συγκληρονόμος (*synklēronomos*), fellow heir (*5169*).

CL & OT 1. Used from Homer on, *klēros* meant originally the fragment of stone or piece of wood used as a lot. Lots were also drawn to discover the will of the gods. Since land was divided by lot, *klēros* came to mean a share, land received by lot, and finally inheritance. Of the related vbs., *klēroō* means to draw lots, apportion by lot, and *klēronomeō*, to be an heir, inherit. *klēronomia* first meant the activity of dividing by lot, then the portion so divided, the inheritance. A *klēronomos* is an inheritor; *synklēronomos*, a fellow heir.

2. Lots (Heb. *gôrāl*) were also drawn in the OT to discover God's will. The high priest wore the Urim and Thummim in the breastplate of judgment attached to the ephod (Exod. 28:30; Lev. 8:8; Deut. 33:8) for that purpose (Num. 27:21; Ezr. 2:63; Neh. 7:65). Heathen and

magical oracles were an abomination to Yahweh and were denied to Israel by divine decree (Deut. 18:9–14). Guidance by lots was permitted only when carried out in obedience to God. But even then God could refuse to give an answer (1 Sam. 14:37; 28:6). God could also reveal himself to the heathen through the casting of lots and other means of divination (Jon. 1:7; Ezek. 21:21).

There are many examples of casting lots in Israel. In Jos. 7:14 and 1 Sam. 14:41 lots discovered the person under the ban. Saul was chosen as king by lot (10:20–21). In Chr. and Neh. lots were cast for priestly office and to choose who was to live in Jerusalem (cf. 1 Chr. 24:5–6; Neh. 11:1). Lots were cast over the goats on the Day of Atonement (Lev. 16:8) and were used in legal actions (Prov. 18:18). Captives and booty could be divided by lot among the victors (Ps. 22:18; Joel 3:3; Obad. 11; Nah. 3:10). When all is said and done, God controls the lot (Prov. 16:33).

3. Of special significance is the relationship of casting lots and the settlement of the land. Two different concepts intersect in the OT. (a) The land is Yahweh's inheritance (e.g. 1 Sam. 26:19; Ps. 68:9; 79:1; Jer. 2:7; Ezek. 38:16; Joel 1:6), in which he lives and should be worshiped (Exod. 15:17; Jos. 22:19). He brought his people out of Egypt and chose them from among the other peoples (Deut. 32:8–9; 1 Ki. 8:51, 53). Hence, not only the land but also Israel itself is God's heritage or inheritance (e.g., Deut. 9:26–29; 2 Ki. 21:14; Isa. 19:25; 47:6; Jer. 10:16; Mic. 7:18; Joel 2:17–18).

(b) The land is Israel's heritage, promised by God to Abraham and the patriarchs and given to Israel through conquest. Under Joshua, Israel took possession of the land and divided it by lot (e.g. Num. 26:52–56; Jos. 13:6; 21:43–45). The Levites also had their cities apportioned to them by lot (1 Chr. 6:54–81). Since the land is God's, his regulations should control it. Israel is thus called to obey God's commandments in order to live and remain in the land (Deut. 30:15–20; Jos. 22:1–5). This also explains the regulations for the sabbatical year and the Year of Jubilee (Lev. 25), which provided for the restoration of property and slaves, for the land is Yahweh's property and is therefore subject to his claims and regulations.

4. The recurring statement that the priests and Levites "have no share or inheritance among their brothers; the LORD is their inheritance" (Deut. 10:9; cf. 12:12; 18:1–2; Num. 18:20; Jos. 13:14, cf. Ezek. 44:28) calls for special attention. (a) The Levites receive a share in the offerings and gifts of the people. Through their example Israel is to learn that God's people must not seek safety and security through the land but only in the Lord and giver of the land, Yahweh.

(b) The affirmations that God is the strength and portion of the one who prays contain the same thought (Ps. 73:25–26; 142:5; Lam. 3:24). Note Ps. 16:5–6: "LORD, you have assigned me my portion and my cup; you have made my lot secure. The boundary lines have fallen for me in pleasant places; surely I have a delightful inheritance." Such statements of faith go back to the promise to Abraham, to whom God promised not merely descendants and land, but also himself as his "shield . . . [and] very great reward" (Gen. 15:1). This promise was fulfilled in the conquest, but was not exhausted by it.

(c) The message of the postexilic prophets links these two groups of statements, showing that God stands by his promises. Even though the people have been exiled, the land and its mountains remain theirs. The Lord will give it anew to his people (Ezek. 36–37), and it will once again be divided by lot (45:1; 47:13–14; 48:29; cf. Isa. 49:8). Aliens also will receive their portion (Ezek. 47:22–23).

5. Later on *gôrāl* came to be used for the individual's fate in the last day (cf. already Isa. 57:6; Dan. 12:13), more or less in the sense of the heritage of the righteous. The rabbis speak of inheriting the land (cf. Ps. 37:9, 22, 29), the coming age, future reward, the garden of Eden, and also Gehenna. Here we meet the thought of rewards.

6. In the Qumran writings *gôrāl* denotes the fate predestinated by God (1QS 2:17; 1QM 13:9), signifying either that one belongs to God, the sons of light, the spirits of knowledge, etc., or to Belial, the sons of darkness, and its spirits. Hence this word has the meaning of adher-

ents, party (1QS 2:2, 4–5; 1QH 3:22–25; 1QM 1:1, 5, 11). From this comes almost the meaning class, rank (1QS 1:10; 2:23; CD 13:12). "To cast the lot" often means to determine a person's fate or even to judge (1QS 4:26; 1QH 3:22).

NT   1. (a) *klēros* is used 6x in the lit. sense of lot, as when the soldiers cast lots for Jesus' garments at the crucifixion (Matt. 27:35; Mk. 15:24; Lk. 23:34; Jn. 19:24). Jn. sees this as a fulfillment of Ps. 22:18, which views such an activity as the ultimate degradation of a human being. But the psalmist also recognizes that God is in control and that he alone can give help (22:19). In Jesus' passion, by extension, God himself is behind the events (cf. Acts 2:23–24; 3:18–23; 4:28).

Acts 1:26 records the decision as to whether Joseph Barsabbas or Matthias should fill Judas's place among the twelve apostles. Both candidates met the necessary qualifications of being a member of the company who had followed Jesus throughout his earthly ministry and of being a witness to Jesus' resurrection (1:21–22). The lots were cast following the prayer: "Lord, you know everyone's heart. Show us which of these two you have chosen to take over this apostolic ministry, which Judas left to go where he belongs" (1:24–25). Matthias was chosen.

(b) In Acts 1:17, Judas is referred to as having been "one of our number and shared [*klēros* is part of this verbal expression] in this ministry." Here *klēros* is used in its other main sense—having a part or share in a ministry. In this verse too there is a profound sense of divine overruling (see next sec.).

2. With the meaning share, inheritance, *klēros* occurs 4x in the NT and *klēronomia*, 14x; *klēronomos*, heir, 15x; *synklēronomos*, fellow heir, 4x; *klēronomeō*, inherit, 18x. In Lk. 12:13 *klēronomia* has the basic secular sense of inheritance. *kataklēronomeō* occurs in Paul's review at Pisidian Antioch of salvation history in his reference to the seven Canaanite nations, whose land God gave Israel as an inheritance (Acts 13:19; cf. Deut. 7:1; Jos. 14:1). *prosklēroō* occurs only in Acts 17:4 (see below).

(a) The concept of inheritance has soteriological and eschatological dimensions. It is linked with God's historical saving acts. The idea of possession of the promised land passes beyond its first fulfillment in history to its later historical fulfillment in Christ and beyond that to the future final fulfillment at the end of time. The essential thought is that of inheriting the promise to which believers are called. According to various strata of the NT, the object of this inheritance is the kingdom of God (Matt. 25:34; 1 Cor. 6:9; 15:50a; Gal. 5:21; Eph. 5:5; Jas. 2:5).

In the Beatitudes, Jesus puts side by side the promise of the kingdom and that of inheriting the earth (*gē* [→ *1178*] in Matt. 5:5; cf. 5:10). By this he suggests that the promised land of the OT is replaced by the all-embracing concept of the kingdom of God. This kingdom embraces all those promises, the fulfillment of which is yet future. This is confirmed when we look at the other things promised as an inheritance in the NT: eternal life (Matt. 19:29; Lk. 18:18; Tit. 3:7); salvation (Heb. 1:14); the imperishable order (1 Cor. 15:50b); an imperishable inheritance, kept in heaven (1 Pet. 1:4); the blessing (Heb. 12:17; 1 Pet. 3:9); the promises (Heb. 6:12; cf. 10:36); the new heaven and new earth (Rev. 21:7; cf. 21:1). In these statements OT thought is both retained and transformed (Rom. 4:13–15; Heb. 6:17; cf. Acts 7:5; 13:19).

(b) This inheritance, however, is not merely future. It can be recognized already now in faith (Eph. 1:18). According to Heb. 11:7, Noah inherited the righteousness that comes by faith. In Eph. 1:11 we are told that in Christ "we were made heirs" (NIV text note) and in 1:13–14 that we have the guarantee of this inheritance in the Holy Spirit whom we have received. The first Beatitude suggests that the poor in spirit already possess the kingdom of heaven, even though its full realization, like that of the remaining Beatitudes, lies in the future (Matt. 5:3).

(c) The fact that salvation is future and yet present (already/not yet) comes from our being inheritors through Jesus Christ (Eph. 1:11–

12) and his death (Heb. 9:15). He who has come and will come again has brought us the inheritance. Indeed, he is the inheritance and the kingdom (cf. the OT statements about the heritage of the Levites and the expressions of faith in Ps.), and through him we are fellow heirs (Rom. 8:17).

The parable of the tenants of the vineyard (Matt. 21:33–41; Mk. 12:1–12; Lk. 20:9–19; cf. Isa. 5:1–7) shows Jesus as the heir and introduces the OT concept of the remnant. Yahweh has chosen Israel as his people—his vineyard and inheritance. He gave them the land, but they were disobedient. Now there was only a remnant. This remnant, repeatedly referred to by the prophets, is ultimately a single individual—Jesus, the Son. But through him the remnant grows into a great multitude of believers who are fellow heirs. Thus the rich young ruler should have become an heir with him of eternal life (Matt. 19:16–30; Mk. 10:17–30; Lk. 18:18–30).

Alongside the witness of the Synoptics is that of Paul, who gives special prominence to the connection between the promise to Abraham and the church as the heir in Christ. In Rom. 4:13 Paul declares that "through the righteousness that comes by faith" the promise to Abraham that he should inherit the world becomes ours. In the faith that we share in Christ we become heirs. If this depended on the law and not on Christ, "faith [would have] no value" (4:14). Those who are Christ's are Abraham's offspring and so his heirs (Gal. 3:29; cf. 4:1, 7; Tit. 3:7).

The author of Heb. stresses that by an oath to Abraham God promised salvation "to the heirs of what was promised" (6:17). They already have the future inheritance, but only in hope (6:18). They inherit it as did Abraham, "through faith and patience" (6:12). The one who has opened the way to this promise is Jesus (6:20); he is the Son and heir (1:2, 4). The stress is different here from Paul, though the essential concept is the same, for the future nature of the heritage and the need to hold fast to the promise are more strongly emphasized. In 11:7, as in Paul, faith is seen as believing and acting on God's Word. It is by this that Noah became an "heir of the righteousness that comes by faith" (cf. Rom. 4:3; Gal. 3:6; Gen. 15:6).

Jas. 2:5 echoes the teaching of the Synoptics. It treats the question of the heirs of the kingdom, even though the relationship to Jesus, through whom we become heirs, is not expressed. "Has not God chosen those who are poor in the eyes of the world to be rich in faith and to inherit the kingdom he promised those who love him?" There is a firm link between election, promise, and inheritance throughout the NT.

(d) Since Jesus is the heir and also the one who has given himself for us, we cannot have this inheritance except in relation to him. This involves practical obedience (Heb. 11:8) and demands patient endurance (6:12). Without it we will not inherit the kingdom of God (Gal. 5:21; 1 Cor. 15:50a). In his parable of the final judgment (Matt. 25:31–46), Jesus shows how this relationship to him and thus inheriting the kingdom involves love in our dealings with others, through whom he comes to us. Jesus' conversation with the rich young ruler also shows that eternal life can be inherited only in the obedience of faith (Matt. 19:29; cf. Mk. 10:29; Lk. 18:29).

Because Jesus has appointed us as his heirs, we are not merely fellow heirs with him (Rom. 8:17) but also fellow heirs with each other (1 Pet. 3:7), which involves our relationships with others (3:9). This obedience in faith is the concomitant of faith that is required to possess the salvation of God and his Son (cf. 1 Jn. 5:12; 2 Jn. 9). Although Col. 3:24 speaks of receiving the "inheritance . . . as a reward," this is not earned but rather a gift of God (cf. Gal. 3:18).

(e) Finally, the NT makes it clear that the inheritance of the promise is not only for God's chosen people Israel. Through Christ the Gentiles have become fellow heirs with them. Paul stresses again and again that in Christ all believers without distinction are children of God and inheritors of the promise (Gal. 3:23–29; cf. 4:30; Rom. 4:13–14). In Eph. 3:6 the Gentiles are fellow heirs in Christ through the gospel. Note in Eph. 1:3–14 the change of "we" (1:11–12) to "you" (1:13) and the stressed "also," suggesting Paul's identification of himself with the Jewish people and the inclusion of Gentile believers alongside Jewish believers in the Ephesian church.

According to Acts 26:15–18, Paul was commissioned by the risen Lord to open the eyes of the Gentiles, that they might turn from darkness to light and receive forgiveness of sins and an inheritance (NIV "place," *klēros*) "among those who are sanctified by faith" in Christ. In Col. 1:12, Paul affirms that the Gentile church in Colosse has a "share in the inheritance of the saints in the kingdom of light" (cf. Num. 18:20; Deut. 10:9; Ps. 15:5; 56:13; Isa. 2:5; 60:1–3). By contrast, in Acts 8:21 John and Peter deny Simon Magus "part or share in this ministry," i.e., the gospel. The expression is here a formula of excommunication.

In Acts 17:4 *prosklēroō* simply means that some of the Jews "joined Paul and Silas," along with a large number of Gentiles; yet behind this word is the thought that these Gentiles in Thessalonica have obtained a share in the promised heritage.

See also *meros*, part, share, portion, lot (*3538*).

3103 (klēroō, cast lots, determine by lot), → *3102*.

3104 (klēsis, call, invitation), → *2813*.

3105 (klētos, called, invited), → *2813*.

3109 (klinē, mat, bed), → *3111*.

3110 (klinidion, mat, bed), → *3111*.

3111 κλίνω

κλίνω (*klinō*), recline, lie down, incline (*3111*); ἀνακλίνω (*anaklinō*), recline, sit down (*369*); ἀνάκειμαι (*anakeimai*), recline, be seated (*367*); ἀναπίπτω (*anapiptō*), recline, sit down (*404*); κλίνη (*klinē*), mat, bed (*3109*); κλινίδιον (*klinidion*), mat, bed (*3110*); κράββατος (*krabbatos*), mat, bed (*3187*).

CL & OT 1. In cl. Gk. *klinō* means (act.) to make something slope, turn aside, sit down; (pass.) to lean, rest, lie down (at meals). *anaklinō* means to lean back or lie down. *anapiptō* means to fall back or, for soldiers in a battle, to give ground; thus, fig. it could mean to lose heart. *anakeimai* means to be laid up, set up (as a votive offering), also to depend on; in Hel. Gk. it took on the meaning to lie down, recline. The general practice at meals in the Greco-Roman world was not to sit on chairs but to recline on couches placed around three sides of the table. *klinē* is a bed or couch on which one lies; *klinidion* is a diminutive form.

2. *klinō* occurs frequently in the LXX with a variety of meanings. It can mean to kneel down (Jdg. 7:5), incline (one's heart, 9:3; Ps. 119:36); turn (one's ear, 49:4; 71:2); part (the heavens, 2 Sam. 22:10); plot (evil, Ps. 21:11); fall (46:6); to fade (of daylight, Jer. 6:4). *anapiptō* occurs in Gen. 49:9, where Jacob refers to Judah as a lion who "crouches" and lies down. One should note that for most of the OT period it was normal to sit at table (1 Sam. 20:5, 18, 25; 1 Ki. 13:20). The custom of reclining appears first in the Persian period (Est. 1:6; 7:8). *klinē* is the usual word in the OT for bed (e.g., Gen. 48:2; 49:33; Exod. 8:3; Ps. 6:6).

NT 1. In the NT *klinō* occurs 7x, *klinē* 9x, *klinidion* 2x, *krabbatos* 11x, *anaklinō* 6x, *anakeimai* 14x, and *anapiptō* 12x. Except for one occurrence of *klinō* in Heb. 11:34 ("routed") and *klinē* in Rev. 2:22, all these occurrences are in the Gospels. *klinē* invariably means one's mat or bed (e.g., Matt. 9:6; Lk. 8:16); it is synonymous with *klinidion* (Lk. 5:19, 24) and krabbatos (e.g., Mk. 2:4, 9; Jn. 5:8–11). *klinō* is used in the statement of Jesus that he has nowhere to lay his head (Matt. 8:20; Lk. 9:58). It is also used in an expression that means late in the day, i.e., the time when the sun goes down (9:12; 24:29).

2. *anakeimai*, *anaklinō*, and *anapiptō* all have to do with eating and refer to the custom in the NT of reclining at meals, particularly on more formal or festive occasions; the words for "sit" (→ *kathēmai*, *2764*) are never used in this connection. A "guest" at a meal is lit. "one who reclines" (cf. Matt. 22:10–11; Mk. 6:26). *anapiptō* and

anaklinō are also used in Jesus' feeding miracles, when he orders the people to "sit down" (Matt. 15:35; Mk. 6:39; Jn. 6:10).

3. As in the synagogue, the place assigned is a mark of the guest's importance, the closest to the host being the most prestigious (Lk. 14:7–10; cf. Mk. 12:39). Thus we should understand the significance of the position of "the disciple whom Jesus loved" at the Last Supper, "reclining next to him" (Jn. 13:23, 25; 21:20); this was the position on Jesus' right (the left elbow being used to support the body), the place of a trusted friend, which allowed confidential conversation.

See also *kathēmai*, sit (*2764*).

3120 κοιλία

κοιλία (*koilia*), belly (*3120*).

CL & OT The basic meaning of *koilia* is a hollow or cavity. In cl. Gk. it can mean belly, abdomen, bowels, stomach; the abdomen as the site of the sexual organs, the womb. In the LXX it can also metaphorically mean the inner person (→ *kardia*, *2840*).

NT Hence in the NT *koilia* means belly, stomach (Matt. 12:40; Rev. 10:9–10), the womb (Lk. 1:41–42; 2:21; 11:27; Acts 3:2), and the inner person (only in Jn. 7:38).

In Matt. 15:10–20 and Mk. 7:14–23 evil is said to come out of the heart (*kardia*) (7:21). That which enters a person from the outside enters the stomach (7:19). Thus, food cannot make someone unclean. Paul also argued against a false evaluation of stomach and food (1 Cor. 6:13). The linking of stomach and food shows that every effort to give food a religious value and make it subject to all kinds of ideologies is theologically improper and therefore to be rejected.

Paul uses *koilia* metaphorically in Rom. 16:18 and Phil. 3:19 ("their god is their stomach"). He rejects not only gluttonous and sexual excess, but also undue estimation of physical life (→ *sarx*, *4922*).

3121 (koimaō, sleep, fall asleep), → *2761*.

3123 (koinos, common, communal), → *3126*.

3124 (koinoō, make common or impure, defile, profane), → *3126*.

3125 (koinōneō, share, participate in), → *3126*.

3126 κοινωνία

κοινωνία (*koinōnia*), association, fellowship, participation (*3126*); κοινός (*koinos*), common, communal (*3123*); κοινόω (*koinoō*), make common or impure, defile, profane (*3124*); κοινωνέω (*koinōneō*), share, participate in (*3125*); κοινωνικός (*koinōnikos*), giving, sharing, liberal (*3127*); κοινωνός (*koinōnos*), companion, partner, sharer (*3128*); συγκοινωνός (*synkoinōnos*), participant, partner (*5171*); συγκοινωνέω (*synkoinōneō*), participate in with someone, share (*5170*).

CL & OT 1. (a) In cl. Gk. *koinos*, when applied to things, means common, mutual, public. Hence, *to koinon* means the community, common property; in the pl., public affairs, the state. When applied to people, *koinos* means related, a partner, impartial. The corresponding vb. *koinoō* means to have a share in, unite, communicate, also to profane. *koinōneō* means to possess together, have a share in; *koinōnia* means communion, participation, intercourse. As an adj., *koinōnos* means common; as a noun, companion, partner.

The word *koinōnia* could denote the unbroken fellowship between the gods and humans. It also denoted the close union and brotherly bond among human beings. It was taken up by the philosophers to denote the ideal to be sought, virtually having the sense of brotherhood. The word *koinos* could also depict gods from different cultures reigning together. It also testified to an ever-increasing cosmopolitanism.

(b) To people groaning under the oppression of the aristocracy, Hesiod's *Works and Days* proclaimed the myth of an earlier golden age, characterized by happiness, equality, justice, and brotherliness.

The doctrine of common property had a primeval aspect; early Athens was seen as a model. But whereas this looked back to a golden age, the sharing in the early church at Jerusalem is to be understood in the light of its eschatological experience. Moreover, the Stoics declared that friends must share and that possessions are the common property of friends. But they too based their demands on an ideal picture of a golden age, now lost forever in its original, pure form. The NT, by contrast, looks forward. The new age must break into the present, lost world.

2. The OT primeval history of Gen. records the rupture of fellowship with God, followed by the loss of unity among humans. But God's activity in forgiving, saving, and preserving did not cease. Instead, it found new ways (Gen. 8:21–22; 12:3). Abraham—and after him the people of Israel—stood in a saving relationship to Yahweh, the goal of which was to bridge the gulf between God and humankind.

God dealt with the Israelites as a community and fulfilled his promises to it. He gave them the land as an inheritance, which in the last analysis belonged to him (Lev. 25:23). The tribes, families, and esp. individuals were only tenants of the portions allocated to them. They had therefore no right to dispose of them. The judicial murder of Naboth (1 Ki. 21) should be judged in this light. Its background is the clash between the ancient Israelite right to land described above and the Canaanite doctrine of royal right, which Ahab wanted to exercise.

From here a line can be drawn to the attitude of the prophets in general. Just as Elijah denounced the breach of the ancient right, the prophets were opposed to all land speculation (cf. Isa. 5:8) and stood up for the interests of the community. This solidarity of God, the nation, and the land continued into the NT period. Israel could not envisage faith in God without entering the community and receiving the sign of circumcision.

3. The theological motif of broken fellowship with God, the problem of preserving the community according to God's will (cf. Isa. 5:8), and the role of the community in the ultimate, universal picture of salvation (cf. Gen. 12:3; Isa. 49:6) play a large part in the OT. It is therefore all the more striking that the *koinōnia* word group occurs almost exclusively in the later writings (Eccl., Prov., Wis., 1–4 Macc.), usually to translate words connected with the Heb. root *ḥābar* (unite, join together). In the OT stress was laid on the covenant and the individual's membership of the people. These were communal ideas. But in contrast to the quasi-egalitarian idea of *koinōnia*, these ideas stressed the unilateral role of Yahweh as the founder and guarantor of the community and its members. Where the *koinōnia* word group occurs in the LXX, it is used in a general sense (see Job 34:8; Prov. 21:9; 25:24; Eccl. 9:4).

4. The communal life of the Essenes was based on the idea of the equality of all its members. This is emphatically supported by the evidence of the Dead Sea Scrolls for the Qumran community, where each new member had to renounce and hand over his entire possessions to the estate of the community (1QS 1:11–12). The principal motive for this was not, as in ancient Greece, the ideal of brotherly communal possession, but the idea that possession of money was tainted with sin.

NT 1. The adj. *koinos* (Mk. 7:2, 5; Acts 10:14) and the vb. *koinoō* (Mk. 7:18; Acts 10:15; 21:28) mean respectively unclean, impure, and to defile, make impure. *Koinos* occurs in Mk. 7:2, 5 in the context of Jesus' teaching that it is not dirt or anything external that defiles a person but the thoughts of one's heart (see also Rom. 14:14). The vision to Peter in Acts 10, in which he was commanded to eat unclean creatures (*koinos* in 10:14, 28; 11:8), symbolized God's acceptance of the Gentiles and their inclusion in the new covenant. Paul was accused of defiling the temple by introducing Gentiles (Acts 21:28), although in fact he had refrained from giving offense in this way.

Koinoō refers to defilement under the old covenant in Heb. 9:13. But Heb. 10:29 speaks of defiling or profaning the blood of the covenant, spurning the Son of God, and thus being worthy of greater punishment than under the old covenant. Rev. 21:27 takes up the con-

cept and applies it in a moral sense, when it declares that "nothing impure will ever enter" the new Jerusalem, "nor will anyone who does what is shameful or deceitful, but only those whose names are written in the Lamb's book of life."

2. *koinōnia* is absent from the Synoptics and Jn. But it occurs 13x in Paul and is a typical Pauline term. The same is true of the vb. *koinōneō*. Elsewhere, *koinōnos* (Lk. 5:10; 2 Cor. 8:23; Phlm. 17) means partner, companion, sharer. In most cases, however, it is to be translated as an adj., sharing, participating in, or by a verbal phrase. *Koinōnikos* occurs only in 1 Tim. 6:18, where it means liberal. *Synkoinōnos* (participant, partner) and *synkoinōneō* (participate in with someone, share) occur only in Paul and Rev. 1:9; 18:4.

3. Acts 4:32–37 gives a picture of the communal sharing of goods practiced for a time in the early church. But it presupposed the continuance of private earning and the voluntary character of sacrifice and giving to the needy. There is no hint of either communal production or communal consumption. It was not organized and is not to be seen in economic categories. It rose out of the freedom from earthly care that Jesus preached and from his lofty scorn of goods (Matt. 6:25–34). It is to be seen as the continuance of the common life that Jesus led with his disciples (Lk. 8:1–3; Jn. 12:4–6; 13:29). The idea of equality is lacking.

The extraordinary actions of Barnabas (Acts 4:36–37) and of Ananias and Sapphira (5:1–11) are singled out for mention. But this does not mean that the community of possessions was general. This would not have been possible for the great majority of church members. Mention of the house of Mary (12:12) indicates that private ownership continued (cf. 5:4). Lk.'s general account of the Jerusalem church reflects the attitude of love that was intensified by an acute expectation of the end.

The *koinōnia* in Acts 2:42 can be taken in an absolute sense as an essential part of the life of worship: "They devoted themselves to the apostles' teaching and to the fellowship, to the breaking of bread and to prayer." Here *koinōnia* should probably be translated "communion" or "liturgical fellowship in worship." This word expresses something new and independent here. It denotes the unanimity and unity brought about by the Spirit. The individual was completely upheld by the community.

The early church doubtless had financial cares. The fishermen and peasants that had migrated from Galilee would find earning a living difficult in the capital city. Moreover, the economic state of Palestine deteriorated through famine and continued unrest. The collections that Paul brought to Jerusalem were a tangible expression of fellowship in the churches. The collection has a religious overtone in 2 Cor. 9:13: "your generosity in sharing [*koinōnias*] with them and with everyone else." For it arose out of the one gospel that unites Jew and Gentile and belongs to the same spiritual and material giving and taking of which Paul speaks in Rom. 15:26. There was real need in Jerusalem. The poor among the saints at Jerusalem were in the majority. The stream of "spiritual gifts" that flowed from Jerusalem was answered by a counterstream of "earthly gifts."

The example of the early church remained isolated. Copying its example was neither demanded nor acted upon. The integrity of private property was regarded as a matter of course in all the churches. Christianity brought a new outlook, not a new order of society.

4. Close analysis of the word *koinōnia* shows that Paul never uses it in a secular sense but always in a religious one. It is not to be equated with *societas*, companionship or community. It is not a parallel to *ekklēsia* and has nothing to do with the local congregation. (a) For Paul *koinōnia* refers strictly to the relation of faith to Christ: "fellowship with his Son" (1 Cor. 1:9), "the fellowship of the Holy Spirit" (2 Cor. 13:14), "partnership in the gospel" (Phil. 1:5), "sharing your faith" (Phlm. 6). In each case the obj. is in the gen. The "right hand of fellowship" (Gal. 2:9) given to Paul and Barnabas by James, Peter, and John was not just a handshake over a deal but mutual recognition of being in Christ.

Similarly, *koinōnia* in 1 Cor. 10:16 means "participation" in the body and blood of Christ and thus union with the exalted Christ. This fellowship with Christ comes about through the creative intervention of God. It is a result of our birth into a new existence, which is not a divinization in the sense of the mystery religions, but incorporation into Jesus' death, burial, resurrection, and glory. It denotes a new relationship based on the forgiveness of sins. Paul conveyed this in new expressions he coined and mixed metaphors using *syn* ("with") compounds, such as to "live with [Christ]" (Rom. 6:8); to "share in his sufferings" (8:17); to be "crucified with him" (6:6); to be "raised with him" (Col. 2:12; 3:1); to be "made . . . alive with Christ" (2:13; cf. Eph. 2:5); to "share in his glory" (Rom. 8:17); to be "co-heirs with Christ" (8:17); and to "reign with him" (2 Tim. 2:12).

(b) Apart from Matt. 23:30, where the Pharisees reject the charge that they had a share in the blood of the prophets, and those passages where it means partner or companion, *koinōnos* belongs to this area of Pauline usage. To eat meat that has been sacrificed to idols means to be a sharer in pagan sacrifice and to fellowship with demons, which excludes one from fellowship with the Lord's Supper and fellowship with Christ (1 Cor. 10:18). Conversely, 2 Cor. 1:7 and 1 Pet. 5:1 refer to the sharing by the apostle and the church in the suffering and glory of the risen Lord. Anyone who suffers oppression and persecution through following Christ may rest assured that he or she will, like the Lord, attain life through temptation and death. In the same connection, Heb. 10:33 speaks of being partners with those who are ill-treated and exhorts its readers to patience.

According to 2 Pet. 1:4, believers "participate in the divine nature," "through our knowledge of him who called us by his own glory and goodness" (1:3), and through patient endurance. Thus, we already have a share in a divine nature that is superior to all mundane existence. The same applies to passages where *synkoinōneō* and *synkoinōnos* occur. Participation in evil is rejected (Eph. 5:11; Rev. 18:4). But one can participate in suffering (Phil. 4:14) and the gospel and its hope (1 Cor. 9:23; Phil. 1:7). According to Rom. 11:17, believing Gentiles, who are like branches grafted into the olive tree of Israel, now share in its election and promises.

5. *koinōnia* in 1 Jn. 1:3, 6–7 does not refer to a mystical fusion with Christ and God, but to fellowship in faith. Its basis is in the apostolic preaching of the historical Jesus, in walking in the light, and in the blood of Jesus, which cleanses from all sin. It thus excludes the sectarian pride that denies the incarnation and misrepresents the character of sin.

See also *echō*, to have (*2400*).

3127 (koinōnikos, giving, sharing, liberal), → *3126.*

3128 (koinōnos, companion, partner, sharer), → *3126.*

3130	κοίτη

κοίτη (*koitē*), bed, marriage bed, intercourse (*3130*).

CL & OT 1. In cl. Gk. *koitē* connotes the marriage bed. It was used also of the den of an animal or the nest of a bird.

2. (a) In the LXX, *koitē* has a variety of meanings. It often translates the Heb. verb that means to lie down and can represent the bed as the place of sleep or rest (e.g., 2 Sam. 11:13; 1 Ki. 1:47; Mic. 2:1). It can mean the marriage bed (cf. Gen. 49:4), but it does not necessarily have sexual connotations (cf. Exod. 10:23; Isa. 56:10; Dan. 2:28–29 [Theod.]; 7:1), for it can mean the home of an animal, such as the sheepfold (Isa. 17:2), the den of a snake (11:8), a pasture (Mic. 2:12), and a lair (Job 37:8; Jer. 10:22). In Exod. 21:18 *koitē* means a sick bed (cf. also Job 33:19; Ps. 41:3).

In keeping with the notion of the act or place of lying, *koitē* can also refer to the laying of seed in a woman—a technical term for emission of semen (cf. Lev. 15:18; 19:20; Num. 5:13). In Lev. 15:16–17, however, the word denotes the emission of semen apart from coitus.

koitē also occurs in a number of instances where it is associated with sexual implications deriving from Levitical regulations relating to various forms of sexual impurity (Lev. 15:21, 23, 24, 26). In Prov. 7:17 the word is used of the prostitute's bed, thus connoting in an implicit sense sexual intercourse. It is used similarly in Isa. 57:7, where the prophet berates the people for setting their beds on the mountains. The reference there is to idolatry and hence is used also here in the sense of spiritual fornication. Similarly, in Wis. 3:13 *koitē* describes a sinful union; in 3:16 it is a reference to the offspring of unlawful coitus.

NT In the NT *koitē* occurs 4x. In Lk. 11:7 it means the bed as a place of rest. A man in Jesus' parable protests that he is unable to help someone who needs bread since he is already "in bed."

In Rom. 9:10 the word occurs in the expression that means coitus and, by expansion, conception and pregnancy. The theological point of the passage is that Rebekah conceived children by "one and the same father [*koitē*], our father Isaac." Yet before either of these male twins had done anything good or bad, God in his divine sovereignty had decreed that "the older will serve the younger" (9:12; cf. Gen. 25:23). The argument forms an important part of Paul's case demonstrating to Jewish readers the consistency of divine sovereignty in the inclusion of the Gentiles in the people of God.

In Rom. 13:13 *koitē* is used in the pl. in a list of sins, including orgies and debauchery; it denotes illicit sexual union. Believers are warned to avoid these sins, together with dissension and jealousy; instead, they are "to clothe [themselves] with the Lord Jesus Christ, and . . . not think about how to gratify the desires of the sinful nature" (13:14).

In Heb. 13:4 the word occurs in the sense of "marriage bed," as it does in the OT. The writer affirms that the marriage relationship should be kept honorable.

See also *gameō*, marry (*1138*); *moicheuō*, commit adultery (*3658*); *nymphē*, bride (*3811*); *hyperakmos*, past the peak, begin to fade; be overpassionate (*5644*).

3134 (kolazō, punish), → *3136.*

3136	κόλασις

κόλασις (*kolasis*), punishment (*3136*); κολάζω (*kolazō*), punish (*3134*).

CL & OT 1. *kolazō* and *kolasis* were fixed terms in Gk. sacral jurisprudence. In inscriptions there are references to the gods punishing violations of cultic laws. Plato suggested that those who punish aright do good and that punishment is a blessing since it frees one from a false frame of soul.

2. In the LXX, the two words occur chiefly in the Apocr. *kolazō* is found in such passages as 1 Esd. 8:24; Wis. 3:4; Sir. 23:21; 1 Macc. 7:7; 2 Macc. 6:14; 3 Macc. 3:26; *kolasis* occurs in such passages as Ezek. 14:3–4, 7; 43:11; Wis. 11:13; 2 Macc. 4:38.

3. Philo distinguished between the beneficent power of God with which he made the world and the judicial power by which he rules what is created. God's mercy is older than punishment, and God prefers to forgive rather than to punish. Both Josephus and Philo speak of *kolasis* as divine retribution.

NT 1. *kolazō* and *kolasis* each occur 2x in the NT. The vb. is found in Acts 4:21 of the Jewish leaders' treatment of Peter and John, when they "could not decide how to punish them." It is used of divine chastisement in 2 Pet. 2:9: "Then the Lord knows how to rescue godly men from trials and to hold the unrighteous for the day of judgment, while continuing their punishment."

2. (a) The noun occurs in 1 Jn. 4:18: "Perfect love drives out fear, because fear has to do with punishment." That is, continued existence in fear is a sign of an inadequate relationship with God, which is meant to exist on the plane of love. Moreover, those who live in

fear before God are already punished by this fear. The love in question involves both God's love for us and ours for him and for fellow believers. When people live on that level, they have "confidence on the day of judgment" (4:17).

(b) Matt. 25:46 raises the question of eternal punishment. At the end of the parable of the sheep and the goats, the Lord separates the blessed, who have manifested their righteousness in practical love, from those who have failed to do so. The latter are cursed and sent away from the presence of God into "eternal punishment," while the righteous receive eternal life (see also references to eternal judgment in 2 Thess. 1:9 and Heb. 6:2). Eternal punishment, like the idea of eternal fire, does not necessarily imply that those concerned go on being judged or continue to be consumed. If the metaphor of fire is to be pressed, it simply implies that the fire of righteousness continues to burn, but that what is consumed once is consumed for good. For more on the nature of "eternal" (*aiōnios*) in this phrase, → *aiōn, 172*.

See also *dikē*, justice, punishment, vengeance (*1472*).

3139 (kolaphizō, beat), → *3463.*

| 3140   κολλάω |

κολλάω (*kollaō*), join, cleave to, stick to (*3140*); προσκολλάω (*proskollaō*), cleave to, stick to (*4681*).

CL & OT 1. *kollaō* is a vb. related to *kolla*, glue, and means to glue in contrast to nailing, to join together tightly. It can be used of gluing a broken pot or gluing inlay work of gold and ivory, also of closing a wound. The compound *proskollaō* means to stick to.

2. (a) The LXX uses both words to mean cling, cleave to. In Job 29:10; Ps. 22:15; 137:6; Lam. 4:4, for example, the tongue cleaves to the gums for thirst. Similarly leprosy, pestilence, or diseases cleave to a person (Deut. 28:21, 60; 2 Ki. 5:27).

(b) It frequently means to join someone, to cleave to someone (e.g., Ruth. 2:8, 21; 2 Sam. 20:2; Job 41:9, 15 = LXX 41:8, 14; Ps. 101:3; 119:31; 1 Macc. 3:2; 6:21).

(c) *proskollaō* is used of the permanent relationship of man and woman (Gen. 2:24), who cleave to each other. As is shown by 1 Esd. 4:20, *kollaō* refers to more than the sexual union of man and wife, extending to the whole relationship. Because Solomon "held fast" (*kollaō*) to foreign wives (1 Ki. 11:2), he came under their religious influence. "The man who consorts with prostitutes" (Sir. 19:2) comes under an influence inconsistent with wisdom.

(d) The contrast is union with God. "Fear the LORD your God and serve him. Hold fast to him" (Deut. 10:20; cf. 6:13; 2 Ki. 18:6; Jer. 13:11; Sir. 2:3). The stress here is on inner union with God in contrast to the cultic and legal one of the context.

NT 1. The basic meaning of *kollaō* is found in Lk. 10:11, "the dust . . . that sticks to our feet"; cf. also Rev. 18:5 ("her sins are piled up to heaven" [cf. Jer. 51:9]).

2. The most common NT usage is to join someone or a group. The prodigal son joined himself to foreign citizens (Lk. 15:15); Philip joined the chariot of the Ethiopian (Acts 8:29); Paul tried to join the church (9:26); some who had joined Paul came to faith (17:34); though the people of Jerusalem held the Christians in high honor, no non-Christian ventured to join them (5:13); it was reprehensible for a Jew to "associate with" heathens (10:28), because they did not have the law.

3. Mk. 10:7 and Eph. 5:31 both quote Gen. 2:24 (with its *proskollaō*; cf. Matt. 19:5, which uses *kollaō*). (a) In Mk. 10:7–8, marriage is indissoluble, because in it two persons become one living being. This refers to the total relationship of the partners and not merely the sexual union.

(b) According to Eph. 5:31, Christ left his Father to be joined to his bride, the *ekklēsia*, and to become one flesh with her. As in Ezek. 16, the husband here comes as *sōtēr*, Savior (Eph. 5:23). His wife—the new people of God—is decked with imperishable riches (5:26–27;

cf. Ezek. 16:10–13). This marriage relationship of Christ and the church is a "profound mystery" (Eph. 5:32).

4. The believer's union with God necessitates that one must detest evil and "cling to what is good" (Rom. 12:9). Since with one's body a person is a member of the body of Christ, a man cannot become one body, a human unity, with a prostitute. For "he who unites himself with the Lord is one with him in spirit" (1 Cor. 6:17). He should live in this Spirit and perfectly imitate the actions and revelation of his Lord. But if he unites himself with a prostitute, he will become like her (6:16). Having sexual relations with a prostitute means a common existence with her. The spirit of the brothel and the Spirit of Christ mutually exclude one another.

| 3141   κολλούριον |

κολλούριον (*kollourion*), eye salve (*3141*).

CL Eye wash or salve was common in ancient times. It was used for various purposes, but esp. for applying to the eyes.

NT The sole use of *kollourion* in the NT is Rev. 3:18. Since the context is the letter to the church at Laodicea, it is assumed that the writer had in mind a preparation made from powdered Phrygian stone used at the medical school there. Its significance must be understood together with that of the gold, which calls to mind the prosperity of the city of Laodicea, and the white clothing, which contrasts with the famous black wool of that area. The three items represent a spiritual value that the church failed to realize was missing (3:17). Apparently this was a worldly and prosperous church whose members mistook both the nature and source of true well-being.

See also *horaō*, see (*3972*); *blepō*, look at, see (*1063*); *atenizō*, look at a person or thing intently, gaze on (*867*); *theatron*, theater, place of assembly, a spectacle (*2519*).

3154 (koniaō, whitewash), → *3328.*

3157 (kopetos, mourning, lamentation), → *3164.*

3159 (kopiaō, become weary, tired, work hard, toil), → *3160.*

| 3160   κόπος |

κόπος (*kopos*), trouble, difficulty, work, labor, toil (*3160*); κοπιάω (*kopiaō*), become weary, tired, work hard, toil (*3159*); πόνος (*ponos*), hard labor, toil, pain, distress, affliction (*4506*); μόχθος (*mochthos*), labor, exertion, hardship (*3677*).

CL & OT 1. *kopos* means a striking, beating. It then came to denote the physical consequences of a stroke, weariness, depression. Thus, everything that leads to toil, pain, and hardship can be called *kopos*. The same applies to the vb. *kopiaō*; it denotes not only the activity of exertion and toil and the process of becoming tired, but also the consequent fatigue and exhaustion. *ponos* is a virtual synonym for *kopos* and means work and toil.

2. In the LXX *kopos* means labor (Ps. 73:5), adversity (Jdg. 10:16), or trouble (Ps. 10:7, 14; 94:20). *kopiaō* means grow weary (Isa. 40:28, 30), be weary of (43:22), labor (Job 20:18; Isa. 49:4). The ideas give expression to the sober reality of pessimism and resignation: "What does man gain from all his labor (*mochthos*) at which he toils under the sun?" (Eccl. 1:3; cf. 2:18). Even the servant of the Lord laments his toil: "I have labored to no purpose; I have spent my strength in vain and for nothing" (Isa. 49:4).

Against this background the growth of eschatological hope is understandable. Humankind will not toil in vain (Isa. 33:24; 65:23) forever. Those weary (*kopiaō*) people returning from exile will receive renewed strength (40:29–31).

NT 1. In the NT *ponos* occurs 4x; *mochthos*, 3x (all in Paul). The *kopos* word group occurs 41x. *kopiaō* is used in the general sense of labor or toil in everyday work (Matt. 6:28; Lk. 5:5; Rom. 16:6; cf.

kopos in 1 Cor. 3:8). Jn. 4:38 and 2 Tim. 2:6 refer to working in the fields and harvesting—a picture of work in the kingdom of God. Work (*kopos*) in Rev. 2:2 and 14:13 refers to our work here as having eternal significance.

2. The *kopos* word group also denotes weariness. Jn. 4:6 speaks of weariness because of a journey. The church at Ephesus is praised for having borne much persecution without having become weary (Rev. 2:3). In Matt. 11:28 Jesus offers those who are exhausted by the claims of the law an enduring rest from their toil.

3. Paul uses *kopos* and *kopiaō* to describe his own manual labor (1 Cor. 4:12; 1 Thess. 2:9), which he performed in order to make himself financially independent. He also designates his missionary activity as a heavy burden (2 Cor. 6:5; 11:23, 27), which he sometimes feared might prove fruitless (Gal. 4:11). On the other hand, it involved the joy of encouragement (1 Cor. 15:10; Phil. 2:16). The goal of his labor was to present every person complete in Christ before God (Col. 1:29; cf. 1 Tim. 4:10).

Other missionaries labored together with Paul (Rom. 16:12; 1 Cor. 16:16; 1 Thess. 5:12) in "preaching and teaching" (1 Tim. 5:17) with the same goal and methods. It was a labor of love (1 Thess. 1:3).

See also *baros*, weight, burden (*983*).

3164	κόπτω

κόπτω (*koptō*), act., strike; mid., beat the breast (*3164*); κοπετός (*kopetos*), mourning, lamentation (*3157*).

CL & OT 1. *koptō* basically means to strike and was used for striking the breast in a time of sorrow. The derivative *kopetos* means lamentation for the dead. There is widespread evidence in antiquity for public mourning and lamentation for the dead. Smiting the breast and cheeks, loud wailing, and dirge singing were originally intended to drive away the spirits of the dead or to honor the dead. Various mourning customs, some of them violent, extend into the Hel. period. These customs became increasingly a general expression of grief at death.

2. The OT reflects numerous parallels to the burial customs of the surrounding world. *koptō* is used for lamentation in, e.g., Gen. 23:2; 1 Sam. 25:1; 28:3; Jer. 16:5–6. The Israelites had a variety of customs associated with mourning for the dead (Gen. 23:1–2; 37:34–35; 2 Sam. 3:31–34): cutting oneself, shaving off one's hair, eating mourning bread, drinking from the cup of consolation (Jer. 16:5–7), calling in mourning women (9:16–21), putting on sackcloth (Isa. 15:3), removing one's beard (7:20), beating one's breast (Nah. 2:7; cf. Jer. 31:19). The most prominent and abiding feature of mourning was wailing (Isa. 15:2; Jer. 22:18; 34:5; Amos 5:16) and the funeral dirge (2 Sam. 1:17–27; 3:33–34).

3. Mourning for the dead held a special place in the preaching of the prophets. While Lam. bewails and interprets the divine judgment that has already befallen Judah and Jerusalem, the prophets announce—often in the form of a lament for the dead—a catastrophe that lies in the future (Jer. 9:10; Ezek. 32:1–16; Amos 5:1–2, 16–17; Mic. 1:8). By doing this they aim to arouse the people and call them to repentance (Jer. 9:18; Ezek. 19; 27:30–34). It is characteristic of Israel's faith that again and again, even as the message of destruction rings in their ears, it changes into hope in God, who will deliver them and turn "wailing into dancing" (Ps. 30:11).

4. In Jud., heathen mourning practices were forbidden (Lev. 19:28; Deut. 14:1), but it was customary before or at a burial to wail and lament for the dead, to beat the breast, and so to fulfill one's loving obligations toward the deceased. In the Hel. period, attempts were made by the state to check the extravagances that had crept into mourning customs, though they met with little success. A marked feature of this period was the funeral song, used by men and women, relatives, and professional mourners.

NT 1. In the Synoptics *koptō* occurs 4x in the mid. to mean "mourn" (Matt. 11:17; 24:30; Lk. 8:52; 23:27) and 2x in Rev. (1:7; 18:9).

kopetos is used only in Acts 8:2. Jewish mourning customs in the time of Jesus are suggested by Jesus' parable of the children lamenting the dead when playing funeral (Matt. 11:17; cf. Lk. 7:32). The story of Jairus's daughter (Matt. 9:23; Mk. 5:38; Lk. 8:52) shows that immediately after a person's death, a lamentation was begun by a great crowd of relatives, neighbors, and mourning women. After the death of Lazarus (Jn. 11:17, 30) and four days after the burial, a great crowd of neighbors and acquaintances from Jerusalem gathered in Bethany, weeping (11:33) and consoling Mary and Martha (11:19, 31). Mourning women followed Jesus on the way to Golgotha (Lk. 23:27), and in the early church "godly men" came together after Stephen's death and "mourned deeply" over him (Acts 8:2).

2. Why did Jesus weep on the way to the grave of Lazarus (Jn. 11:35)? His tears express his compassion for people, subject as they are to death and all its woe. But he also weeps because of the faithless and hopeless lamentation for the dead with which he finds himself surrounded. He has come to take on himself human suffering and distress and become the conqueror of death. His saving, life-giving work puts an end to such lamentation (Lk. 7:13). His cross and resurrection manifest his victory over death. In our natural grief after the death of a loved one we are sustained by the hope of the resurrection of the dead.

3. Thus the characteristic of the Christian church is not lamentation for the dead, but the hope of life in Christ Jesus (Rom. 6:23). Since God's gift in Jesus is eternal life, lamentation for the dead belongs to those who are far from God, who are under the sentence of death, and who have no hope. Believers, by contrast, can look forward to the time when "there will be no more death or mourning or crying or pain, for the old order of things has passed away" (Rev. 21:4). By faith in the conqueror of death we enter into the truth of Christ's promise: "Your grief will turn to joy" (Jn. 16:20).

See also *klaiō*, weep (*3081*); *lypeō*, inflict pain (*3382*); *brychō*, gnash (*1107*); *pentheō*, be sad, grieve, mourn (*4291*); *stenazō*, to sigh, groan (*5100*).

3167	κορβᾶν

κορβᾶν (*korban*), corban, gift (*3167*); κορβανᾶς (*korbanas*), temple treasury (*3168*).

OT The Gk. word *korban* is transliterated from the Heb. noun *qorbān* and denotes a gift consecrated to God (Lev. 1:2; 22:27; 23:14; Num. 7:25; Ezek. 20:28; 40:43). The offerings mentioned include both sacrifices and gifts.

Later the word was used in a more technical sense. Josephus mentions those who "dedicate themselves to God, as a corban, which denotes what the Greeks call a *gift*" (*Ant.* 4.73). Release from the vow could be obtained by payment of an appropriate sum. Rab. practice was formulated in the Mishnah in the tractate Nedarim. The rabbis were divided over the extent to which a gift vowed as corban (also later termed *kōnām*) was binding. The school of Shammai apparently held that duty to one's parents constituted grounds for release from a gift vowed to God (*m. Ned.* 9:1). The school of Hillel took the more rigorist view: "If anyone expressly lays such a corban on his relatives, then they are bound by it and cannot receive anything from him that is covered by the corban" (*m. Ned.* 3:2). The context of these pronouncements shows that the question was not so much the handing over of certain things to God but their withdrawal from use by specified persons.

NT The rigorist position that permitted a man to neglect the care of parents on the grounds that the gift is dedicated to God as corban was denounced by Jesus in Mk. 7:11 (the par. in Matt. 15:5 uses *dōron*, gift, present; → *1565*). This act is condemned as an act of hypocrisy in the words of Isa. 29:13 (cf. Matt. 15:7–9; Mk. 7:6–7). Jesus characterizes the Pharisees' teaching on this point as "tradition" that nullifies the "word of God" (7:13). They had allowed obligation to something that was relatively trivial to take precedence over a fundamental, humanitarian command (in this case the fifth commandment, Exod. 20:12; Deut. 5:16).

korbanas (Matt. 27:6) denotes the temple treasury in which everything offered as *korban* (or the price of its redemption) was collected. The chief priests declined to put into it Judas's thirty pieces of silver on the grounds that they were "blood money."

See also *arrabōn*, down payment, pledge, earnest (*775*); *dōron*, gift, present (*1565*).

3168 (korbanas, temple treasury), → *3167*.

3175 (kosmeō, arrange, put in order, adorn), → *3180*.

3176 (kosmikos, earthly, worldly), → *3180*.

3177 (kosmios, respectable, honorable), → *3180*.

3179 (kosmokratōr, ruler of the world), → *3197*.

3180 κόσμος

κόσμος (*kosmos*), adornment, world (*3180*); κοσμέω (*kosmeō*), arrange, put in order, adorn (*3175*); κόσμιος (*kosmios*), respectable, honorable (*3177*); κοσμικός (*kosmikos*), earthly, worldly (*3176*).

CL 1. The noun *kosmos* denoted originally building and construction, but more esp. order, both generally and specifically (e.g., battle array, the regulation of life in human society, the constitution). It could also mean ornament and adornment (esp. of women). In Gk. philosophy *kosmos* came to be the basic term for the world order, the world system, the cosmos, the universe, and also the inhabitants of the earth, humanity.

The vb. *kosmeō* was used as a technical term, e.g., to marshal an army, to arrange battle formation, and also generally to organize, put in order, and frequently to adorn.

2. The concept of cosmos in Gk. philosophy may be seen against the background of the question: How is it possible that, with all the individual things conflicting with one another (heaven and earth; God, humans, and living beings), the world is not destroyed? The basic answer is that these are held together by an all-embracing order, designated by the word *kosmos*.

(a) Plato was the first to teach that the origin of the cosmos was due to a Demiurge (→ *dēmiourgos, 1321*), who fashioned the world according to the idea of the perfect living being. For him the cosmos is an animated body, a rational being, and thus a manifestation of God. The cosmos is not creature and not creation, but a copy.

(b) Aristotle conceived of the world as a spherical earth, surrounded by various heavenly spheres, which rests unmoved in the center of a spherical cosmos. The cosmos is the sum total of everything linked to space and time. Beyond that is the transcendent world of God, which leads an unchangeable and thus perfect life. God has not fashioned the world. He moves everything, but he himself remains unmoved and does not intervene in world events.

(c) To the Stoics, the cosmos does not owe its origin to a new beginning but is the restoration of that which once was. The disappearance of the cosmos in a universal conflagration is not its end; it arises anew in a cosmic rebirth.

(d) In Neo-Platonism the dualism that one finds in Plato reaches its climax. The intelligible world and the world of appearances are mutually opposed. Although the empirical world is the beginning of evil, Plotinus can boast of its size, order, and beauty; how much more praiseworthy, then, must be the true cosmos, the archetype of this world.

Gnosticism had conflicting statements about the cosmos. On the one hand, the separation between God and world had become absolute. The cosmos was a creation of demonic powers from the chaos of darkness; it had been rid of every element of divinity. It is purely material and fleshly, a fullness (→ *plērōma, 4445*) of evil. It is therefore a prison from which the preexistent human soul longs for liberation, for which the heavenly figure of light, the Son of God, gives help. On the other hand, the *kosmos* is also considered a mythological figure and is designated *inter alia* "Son of God."

OT 1. In the LXX *kosmos* can mean ornaments and decoration, but also the hosts of heaven (and earth), the stars (cf. Gen. 2:1; Deut. 4:19). The meaning "world" for *kosmos* occurs only in the Apocr. It probably adopted this meaning under the influence of Hel. Jud. (see below).

2. The OT has no *word* corresponding to the Gk. *kosmos*. It calls the universe "heaven and earth," later "all things" or "the all" (e.g., Ps. 103:19; Jer. 10:16). The OT also lacks the Gk. *concept* of the cosmos. It never regards the world and its elements as an independent entity in itself, but always in its relation to God, the Creator (→ *ktisis*, creation, creature, *3232*); they are only instruments of God. It is true that the account of creation in Gen. 1:1–2:4a is interested in cosmology, in that it speaks of the deep and the waters, the firmament, the heavenly ocean, and the stars. But its statements have the sole intention of witnessing to God as the Lord over everything, including chaos. The primary objective of Gen. 1 is clearly the creation of humans.

Humanity's vocation is to recognize its task in the world as accountable to God and to exercise rulership over the creation (Gen. 1:26, 28; 2:15, 19; cf. Ps. 8). Gen. 1 expresses God's lordship over the nations of the world and their history. When it states that "all that he had made . . . was very good" (1:31), it is not the world as such that is being praised but God, who made it and established his dominion over it for the salvation of the human race (cf. Ps. 33; 65; 136; 148; Amos 4:13; 5:8; 9:5–6).

3. The OT draws on contemporary oriental ideas, which it uses in its own particular way as the framework for its own proclamation. The world is thus represented as tripartite. (a) The "expanse" (RSV "firmament"; NRSV "dome") of heaven divides the waters above from the waters below (Gen. 1:6–20). This vault rests on "pillars" (Job 26:11; cf. Ps. 104:3), and the stars are set in it as luminaries (Gen. 1:14–17).

(b) The earth is sometimes pictured as a disc, whose middle point is the central sanctuary (Jdg. 9:37; Ezek. 38:12). It too rests on pillars (Job 9:6; cf. Ps. 104:5) or is suspended over nothing (Job 26:7). The waters above it and below it are restrained by God's providential care (Gen. 1:7; 7:11; 49:25; Exod. 20:4; Deut. 33:13).

(c) The underworld (Heb. *šeʾôl*; Gk. *hadēs, 87*) is the kingdom of the dead, from which there is no return (Job 10:21). In complete contrast with contemporary religions, the OT does not engage in speculative embellishment about the underworld.

4. Philo uses the word *kosmos* with strikingly greater frequency than the OT, but in statements that conflict with one another. He distinguishes between the *kosmos* that can only be apprehended by the mind and the *kosmos* that is apprehended by the senses (the "visible world"). Yet at the same time he can insist that there is only one cosmos. Philo also speaks of the cosmos as a living and animate being. Starting from the picture of God as the Father of the cosmos, he can even call it "son of God."

5. In Hel. Jud. *kosmos* acquired the spatial meaning of world, universe, world of humanity. Together with the Jewish apocalyptic doctrine of the two ages (→ *aiōn, 172*), this concept conditioned Jewish views of the world. "This world," like "this age," is under the domination of Satan, sin, and death. Such thinking led to a moral depreciation of the existing cosmos. But since Jud. never lost its belief in creation, it did not adopt a gnostic dualistic worldview.

NT 1. (a) In the NT, as in secular Gk. and Hel. Jud., the noun *kosmos* denotes the world. The sole exception is 1 Pet. 3:3, where it means adornment. It occurs 186x in the NT (78x in Jn., 24x in the Johannine letters, 47x in Paul, 15x in the Synoptics, and 22x in the rest of the NT). This frequent usage indicates both its theological importance and its point of confrontation. The concept of *kosmos* demands clarification when the gospel comes into contact with Gk. thought.

(b) The adjs. are rare, found only in the later NT writings: *kosmios*, honorable, virtuous (1 Tim. 2:9; 3:2); *kosmikos*, earthly, worldly

(Tit. 2:12; Heb. 9:1). The vb. *kosmeō*, put in order, decorate, adorn, occurs 10x (e.g., Matt. 12:44; 25:7; Tit. 2:10).

2. The use of the noun *kosmos* in the inclusive sense of "world" exhibits three nuances. (a) It can denote the universe (e.g., Acts 17:24) or the world as the sum total of created things (cf. Jn. 1:3). (b) It can also mean the world as the sphere or place of human life, the earth, the *oikoumenē* (→ *3876*). This usage takes precedence in the Synoptics (e.g., Matt. 4:8, "all the kingdoms of the world"; Mk. 8:36, "to gain the whole world"). The phrases to come "into the world" (e.g., Jn. 1:9), to be "in the world" (e.g., 1:10), and "to leave this world" (e.g., 1 Cor. 5:10) can also be understood in this sense. (c) Finally, *kosmos* can stand for humanity (cf. Jn. 3:19; 2 Cor. 5:19), where, especially in Paul and John, it designates the place and object of God's saving activity.

3. As early as Paul, the term *kosmos* is given a typically anthropological and historical stamp. (a) The course of the world is determined by humanity, through whose fall death "entered the world" and rules over it (Rom. 5:12–14). "The whole world" (i.e., human world) has become guilty before God (3:19). Even the created world (8:20–22, using *ktisis*) has been subjected to transience and longs for liberation. The *kosmos* is thus also the whole creation subject to futility.

This understanding of the world primarily finds verbal expression in Paul's references to "this world" as analogous to "this age" (e.g., 1 Cor. 3:19; Eph. 2:2; → *aiōn*, *172*). God passes judgment on the *kosmos* (Rom. 3:6), which belongs to the present age. The degree to which *kosmos* denotes the present world threatened by futility can also be seen in that the future redeemed world is never called *kosmos* in the NT, but the "kingdom of God" or "a new heaven and a new earth." There is no phrase such as "the coming world." God and *kosmos* are strictly disparate.

(b) But it is into this world as it is, a world that has fallen into the power of sin and destruction, that God has sent his Son in order to reconcile it to himself (2 Cor. 5:19–21). And in this cosmos, whose form is passing away (1 Cor. 7:31), the Christian church lives as a sign of Christ's presence. Believers must neither unconditionally surrender to nor deny the world. Because they live in the *kosmos* (5:10; Phil. 2:15), they must deal with it. But they must do so as if they had no dealings with it (1 Cor. 7:29–31). Moreover, the church can be assured that the world and everything in it belongs to them, yet they themselves belong not to the world but to Christ (1 Cor. 3:21–23). The world has thus become the field for obedience and maintenance of faith. Christians are free from the world and its regulations (7:20–24; cf. Matt. 17:24–27).

(c) Col. shows how early Christianity had to come to grips with confronting the *kosmos*. The principalities and powers have been defeated by Christ (2:15). Therefore the elements of the cosmos (2:8, 20a) cannot be the object of ritual celebration or veneration. Christians who through Christ have died to the elements of the world no longer live "in the *kosmos*" (2:20b), but have been completely freed from subjection to its precepts and constraints.

4. In Jn. *kosmos* almost always denotes the world of humans, esp. the world of sinful humanity that opposes God, resists the redeeming work of the Son, does not believe in him, and indeed hates him (Jn. 7:7). Out of love for this world (a completely un-Gk. thought!) God sent his Son (3:16), not to judge but to save the world (3:17; 12:47). As "the Lamb of God" he bears the sins of the world (1:29; cf. 1 Jn. 2:2). But the Son, who has come into the world to bring salvation, at the same time becomes its judgment (Jn. 3:19), since it does not know him and is blind to him (1:10).

The *kosmos* is ruled by its prince (Jn. 12:31; 16:11), the evil one (1 Jn. 5:19). Still, the Son remains the victor over the world (Jn. 16:33). This does not lead to the world's extinction but to its redemption, creating those who are not born "of the world" (15:19; 17:14, 16) but of God (1:12–13) and the Holy Spirit (3:5). These people endure much anguish in the world but are removed from its domination (16:33).

Even though believers are no longer conditioned by the world and its values, they are not taken out of the world (Jn. 17:15); they remain in the Son (15:4–7) and are able to demonstrate in the world their belief in and practice of the new commandment to love (13:34–35; 14:15, 23; 15:9–17). When the Christian church is warned to maintain its distance over against the world (e.g., 1 Jn. 2:15), we are concerned with the cosmos in its transience (2:17). The church is to keep itself free from its seductive power. For anyone who loves this world does not have any share in the love of God that reaches out to him, and is therefore incapable of love as instructed in the command of the Lord.

See also *gē*, earth, world (*1178*); *oikoumenē*, earth (*3876*); *agros*, field (*69*); *chous*, soil, dust (*5967*).

3187 (*krabbatos*, mat, bed), → *3111*.

3189	κράζω

κράζω (*krazō*), cry aloud (*3189*); ἐπιφωνέω (*epiphōneō*), call out, shout (*2215*); κραυγάζω (*kraugazō*), shout, cry out (*3198*).

CL & OT *krazō* originally reflected the raucous cry of the raven and then the noise of frogs. More commonly it is applied to human beings. Its religious connection is usually in the sphere of the demonic. Witches, for example, cry out magical incantations. *epiphōneō* means call out, proclaim, exclaim, or, in a weaker sense, tell of.

In the LXX *krazō* is flexible enough to cover the shout of war (Jos. 6:16 = LXX 6:15), the cry of childbirth (Isa. 26:17), the wild call of a raven (Job 38:41), and the braying of an ass (6:5). Humans cry to the Lord in individual or national distress, and God hears and delivers (Exod. 22:22–23; Jdg. 3:9; Ps. 22:5; 34:17). Although Yahweh invites such crying (cf. Isa. 40:3–26), he will not listen to the cry of the ungodly (Mic. 3:4). The crying depicted in the Psalms pulsates with assurances that God will answer (e.g., 4:3; 22:24; 55:16). Two distinctive uses deserve note: the worshipful crying of angels who stand in Yahweh's presence (Isa. 6:3–4), and the quietness of the servant of Yahweh (42:2).

epiphōneō is used 3x in the LXX in quasi-liturgical responses of the people (1 Esd. 9:47; 2 Macc. 1:23; 3 Macc. 7:13).

NT In the Synoptics, *krazō* is used mainly for cries of help springing out of need and/or fear (e.g., Matt. 9:27; 14:26, 30; 15:22–23) and for the cries of demons, whether articulate (8:29) or inarticulate (Mk. 5:5; Lk. 9:39). An element of praise is introduced by the personification metaphor of Lk. 19:40: The stones would cry out if Jesus were to hush the crowd. But more resonant are the cries of hate demanding Jesus' death (Matt. 27:23; Mk. 15:13–14; *epiphōneō* in Lk. 23:21). Jesus himself is quiet; Isa. 42:2 is fulfilled in him (Matt. 12:19, using *kraugazō*). When he does cry out (27:50), it is not an inarticulate sound (cf. Lk. 23:46), but a prayer to his Father, which brings his work on the cross to its blessed climax.

John customarily employs *kraugazō* where the Synoptists prefer *krazō* (e.g., Jn. 12:13; 18:40; 19:12). Likewise, Jesus calls forth Lazarus from his tomb (11:43). John's four occurrences of *krazō* bear the distinctive meaning of proclaim. Each refers to some facet of Christ's person or work: the Baptist's proclamation of the superiority of Jesus (1:15), and Jesus' crying out his message to the people (7:28, 37–38; 12:44–50).

Acts contains several references to the cries of Christians: e.g., in petition for others (7:60), in protest (14:14), and in public outcry (19:28). *epiphōneō* is used for the incoherent but denunciatory uproar against Paul (21:34; 22:24 [*kraugazō* in 22:23]), and for the people's cry in idolatrous worship of Herod (12:22).

Paul utilizes *krazō* 3x: in the sense of prophetic proclamation (Rom. 9:27), and in the Spirit's enabling the believer to cry "Abba, Father!" (Rom. 8:15; Gal. 4:6). In Jas. 5:4, injustice, or more explicitly, withheld pay, is personified and cries out to heaven. The personification is reminiscent of Lk. 19:40.

Rev. uses *krazō* for a call for help (6:10); a cry of jubilation (7:10); an angelic cry (10:3), command (7:2; 19:17), proclamation

(18:2), or address to the Son of Man (14:15); the wail of a woman in childbirth (12:2); and lamentation over fallen Babylon (18:2). The plethora of dramatic cries reinforces the thought that the end comes quickly and cataclysmically.

See also *boaō*, call, shout, cry out (*1066*).

3193 (*krataios*, strong, mighty), → *3197*.

3194 (*krataioō*, make strong, strengthen), → *3197*.

3195 (*krateō*, to be strong, to take possession of, hold, grasp, seize), → *3197*.

3196 (*kratistos*, most honorable, illustrious, excellent), → *3197*.

3197	κράτος

κράτος (*kratos*), power, might, rule (*3197*); κρατέω (*krateō*), to be strong, to take possession of, hold, grasp, seize (*3195*); κραταιόω (*krataioō*), make strong, strengthen (*3194*); κραταιός (*krataios*), strong, mighty (*3193*); παντοκράτωρ (*pantokratōr*), the Almighty (*4120*); κοσμοκράτωρ (*kosmokratōr*), ruler of the world (*3179*); κράτιστος (*kratistos*), most honorable, illustrious, excellent (*3196*).

CL & OT 1. (a) In cl. Gk. *krateō* can mean to be strong, possess might, be in control of, be master of, obtain victory over, or gain the upper hand over. This vb. can also indicate the act of seizing and esp. that of arresting, or it can express a continuous action, i.e., holding fast. In the legal sphere the word acquired the meaning to have the right of possession. (b) *kratos* denotes power and strength, such as the physical strength or power possessed by humans, rulers, or gods. This word is also a title of royalty and means rule, dominion, or victory. (c) *krataios* means mighty, full of power; it is sometimes found in combination with *cheir*, hand (i.e., "with strong hands").

2. (a) All the above-mentioned meanings of *krateō*, except the legal one, can be found in the LXX, where it occurs about 170x, frequently as a translation of *ḥāzaq* (hiph.). It can mean be strong (Jer. 20:7), rule (Prov. 16:32; 4 Macc. 1:5), take control (1 Macc. 10:52; 2 Macc. 4:27), seize (Jdg. 8:12; Ps. 137:9), and hold (Song 3:4). The expression to seize by the hand is found at Gen. 19:16; Isa. 42:6.

(b) *kratos* denotes the power and strength of humans and things (e.g., Ps. 89:9), and esp. the power of God (e.g., 62:11), which can be given to us (86:16).

(c) *krataioō*, to make strong, take courage, gain the upper hand over, is not found before the LXX (e.g., 2 Sam. 1:23; 11:23; Job 36:22; Ps. 105:4), where it occurs 64x.

(d) The LXX usually applies the adj. *krataios* to God (e.g., Deut. 7:21; Ps. 24:8; 71:7; Prov. 23:11). The adj. is combined with "hand" 31x, almost all of them referring to the mighty hand of God (e.g., Exod. 3:19; 13:3, 9, 14, 16; Deut. 7:8, 19, 21; Ps. 136:12).

(e) *pantokratōr*, the Almighty, occurs first in the LXX and is a title for deities, both secular and Yahweh. The LXX translates *ṣᵉbā'ôt* and *šadday* by *pantokratōr* (e.g., Job 5:17; 8:5; Hos. 12:5; Amos 3:13; 5:14–16; Zech. 1:3–17; 8:1–23; Mal. 1:4–14).

(f) *kosmokratōr*, ruler of the world, not found before the 1st cent. A.D., generally denotes the rulers of the universe on whom the fate of humanity depends.

(g) *kratistos* (a superlative adj.) is found several times in the LXX. It occurs 2x in Ps. 16:6 ("pleasant," "delightful") and is translated "better off" in Amos 6:2.

NT 1. (a) In the Synoptic tradition *krateō* is sometimes a technical term meaning to arrest or seek to arrest (Matt. 14:3; Mk. 6:17, on the arrest of John the Baptist; 12:12; 14:1, 44, on the plan to arrest Jesus; 14:46, on his actual arrest). Lk. seems to avoid the word with this meaning (except for Acts 24:6).

(b) *krateō* also means generally to take hold of: Jesus took hold of the dead child's hand (Matt. 9:25; Mk. 5:41; Lk. 8:54) and that of a sick woman (Mk. 1:31). Often a miracle worker touches a patient's hand in order that miraculous power may flow into the other's body.

Matt. mentions an owner's taking hold of a sheep that has fallen into a well on the Sabbath (12:11) and the disciples' taking hold of Jesus by his feet (28:9).

(c) Holding fast to Jewish tradition is called in question in Mk. 7:3–4, for such tradition often consists of human ordinances rather than God's command (7:8). In the course of time a Christian tradition developed, observance of which was laid down as binding (2 Thess. 2:15; Heb. 4:14; 6:18; Rev. 2:13, 25; 3:11); those who clung to false doctrines were opposed (2:14–15). Mk. 9:10 tells how the disciples kept the word of Jesus to themselves and did not pass it on. The OT and Jewish concept of sins being retained (cf. Matt. 16:19; 18:18) is expressed by *krateō* in Jn. 20:23.

(d) The Emmaus disciples saw Jesus but failed to recognize him; their eyes "were kept [*krateō*] from recognizing him" (Lk. 24:16). In Acts 2:24 death is said to have been unable to "keep its hold" on Jesus. The lame man, once he was healed, clung to Peter and John (3:11), showing that he owed his healing to them and ultimately to God. In 27:13, the sailors supposed they "had obtained" the wind they wanted. As these examples show, in Lk.'s use of *krateō*, he thinks of holding fast rather than of taking hold or arresting.

2. *kratos* is an attribute and honorific title for kings, emperors, and their households, but it is also applied to God (1 Pet. 5:11; Rev. 5:13) and to Christ (1 Tim. 6:16; 1 Pet. 4:11; Rev. 1:6; 5:13). Power that is not used directly on people, i.e., that is not soteriological in character, describes God's majesty and grandeur. The holding of the seven stars and the four winds (Rev. 2:1; 7:1, *krateō*) and the seizing of the dragon (20:2) are apocalyptic and symbolic ways of expressing power and might. Passages, however, that reveal the effects of God's power are anthropological: e.g., in the *Magnificat* God puts forth his strength in order to scatter the proud (Lk. 1:51).

Acts 19:20 describes God's power at work among humans: God's word (i.e., the gospel and its proclamation) has had a success that can only be ascribed to God. Eph. 1:19, although in the form of a doxology, teaches that "the working of [God's] mighty strength" (lit., "the working of the strength [*kratos*] of his might [*ischys*, → *2709*]") is seen in believers; similarly in 6:10, "his mighty power" is to become effective in those addressed (cf. Col. 1:11). The power of death, according to Heb. 2:14, has been taken from the devil.

3. *krataioō* is used in Lk.'s birth narratives to describe John the Baptist and the child Jesus growing and becoming strong in spirit (Lk. 1:80) and wisdom (2:40). Paul uses this vb. in his encouragement to the Corinthians to "be strong" (1 Cor. 16:13) and in his prayer to the Ephesians that God will "strengthen" them in their inner being (Eph. 3:16).

4. *krataios* occurs only in 1 Pet. 5:6: The hand of God, under which we are called to humble ourselves, is a "mighty" hand.

5. *pantokratōr*, the Almighty, the Lord of all, occurs both in connection with OT quotations (2 Cor. 6:18; cf. Isa. 43:6; Hos. 1:10) and independently (Rev. 1:8; 4:8; 11:17; 15:3; 16:7, 14; 19:6, 15; 21:22). In both cases the title serves to describe the immense greatness of God, who has power over all creation.

6. *kosmokratōr* occurs only in Eph. 6:12 (in the pl.), where it refers to the cosmic rulers, the evil spirits, against whom we are to wage war.

7. *kratistos*, most excellent, honorable, seems to be a warm, respectful form of address applied to Theophilus in Lk. 1:3. When applied to Felix and Festus, however (Acts 23:26; 24:3; 26:25), it is used in its official sense as a form of address applied to members of the equestrian order in Roman society.

See also *bia*, force, violence (*1040*); *ischys*, strength, power, might (*2709*); *keras*, horn (*3043*).

3198 (*kraugazō*, shout, cry out), → *3189*.

3200 (*kreas*, flesh, meat), → *4922*.

3203 (*kremannymi*, hang), → *5089*.

<table>
<tr><td>3210</td><td>κρίμα</td></tr>
</table>

κρίμα (krima), dispute, decision, verdict, judgment (3210); κρίνω (krinō), separate, judge, consider, decide (3212); ἀνακρίνω (anakrinō), investigate, examine (373); κρίσις (krisis), decision, crisis (3213); κριτής (kritēs), a judge (3216); συγκρίνω (synkrinō), compare, interpret (5173); κατάκριμα (katakrima), punishment, condemnation (2890); κατακρίνω (katakrinō), condemn (2891); κατάκρισις (katakrisis), condemnation (2892); καταγινώσκω (kataginōskō), condemn (2861); αὐτοκατάκριτος (autokatakritos), self-condemned (896); κριτικός (kritikos), able to discern and decide, critical (3217); ἀκατάκριτος (akatakritos), without a trial, uncondemned (185).

CL & OT 1. In cl. Gk. *krima*, judgment, is derived from *krinō*, to judge, which in its numerous compounds came to occupy a major place in legal terminology. (a) The original meaning of *krinō*, to separate, sift, came to be used in connection with human value judgments: to discriminate, distinguish, approve, prefer. Along with this came an assessment, so that *krinō* means (technically) to judge, pronounce judgment, decide, condemn. In the mid. and pass. it means to dispute, debate, or fight.

(b) The compound *synkrinō* reveals a similar process in its meanings to compare, judge, measure; also to explain, expound, and interpret (dreams). *anakrinō* expresses the questioning process that leads to a judgment: to examine, cross-examine, interrogate, inquire, and investigate.

(c) The noun *krima*, like *krinō*, embraces a variety of meanings: decision, verdict, controversy, dispute (human or divine); also condemnation or punishment. *krisis*, a derivative of *krima*, means decision (of a referee), crisis (in battle, sickness, etc.), also separation, dissension, dispute. The person making the decision is called *kritēs*: critic, judge, referee. A derivative adj. (*kritikos*) denotes a competent, experienced judge.

(d) The compound *katakrinō* means to condemn. Two nouns are related: *katakrisis*, condemnation, and *katakrima*, punishment, damnation. *autokatakritos* is a rare word, formed from the adj. *katakritos* and the prefix *auto*, self. It is a moral word that means self-condemned. A moral assessment is also expressed by *kataginōskō*, meaning to recognize as guilty, despise, condemn.

2. In the LXX *krinō* acquired a meaning beyond its general cl. Gk. usage, for the Heb. word underlying it, *dîn*, not only means to judge, but also to punish, vindicate, and obtain justice for a person (Gen. 15:14; 30:6; Deut. 32:36; 2 Sam. 19:9; Jer. 5:28). *šāpaṭ*, a frequent OT word, adds further shades of meaning to the Heb. concept, so that to judge comes to mean to rule (Exod. 2:14; 1 Sam. 8:20; 2 Sam. 15:4). One who judges brings salvation, peace, and deliverance, esp. to the persecuted and oppressed (cf. Deut. 10:18; Ps. 72:1–2). The judges in the book of Jdg. (LXX *kritai*), are deliverers or saviors raised up by God. They obtain justice for the tribes of Israel in the face of their enemies by annihilating or driving out their oppressors, thus bringing salvation, rest, and peace to the land (Jdg. 3:9, 15). *krima* can mean statute (Lev. 18:5; 20:22), and in Jer. 51:10 (= LXX 28:10) righteousness or vindication.

3. (a) In Israel justice was dispensed with a view to restoring peace within the community (the family, the tribe, or the nation). In difficult cases it meant removing an offending member. After the conquest justice was dispensed partly by the heads of families and tribal elders, and partly by the local community elders sitting in the gate of a town or village, all full citizens having the right to speak (Ruth 4:1–2). In Jerusalem certain officials were appointed as judges.

(b) In Israel all justice is ascribed to God: Yahweh is Lord and judge (Deut. 1:17). As such he helps his people (Jdg. 11:27; 2 Sam. 18:31). He never deviates from justice (Ps. 7:11) and will not suffer his honor to be brought into disrepute. Heaven and earth are often called upon to act as a tribunal (Isa. 1:2; Jer. 2:12; Mic. 6:1). Yahweh judges all the nations (Gen. 11:1–9; Ps. 67:4; Joel 3:2; Amos 1:2–2:3; Mal. 3:2–5), especially on the "day of the LORD," when he will destroy all ungodliness (Isa. 2:12–18; 13:9; Jer. 46:10; Ezek. 30:3; Zeph. 1:7–18). He comes to the aid of anyone suffering violence and injustice (Gen. 4:9–12), and one must submit to his inscrutable judgment (Job).

The Lord's judgments are just, i.e., they are in harmony with his faithfulness, whereby he espouses the cause of his chosen people, guides them, and ensures their safety. Thus God's judgment is motivated by love, grace, and mercy, and its outcome is salvation (Ps. 25:6–9; 33:5; 103:6–14; 146:7; Isa. 30:18).

(c) God's judgment on Israel receives the most attention in the judgment discourses of the prophets (Isa. 48:1–11; Jer. 2:4–9; Hos. 4:1; Amos 5:18; 6:8–14; Mic. 1). Since Israel is the elect nation, it will be judged (Ezek. 20:33–38; Amos 3:1–15). Moreover, Yahweh the judge is king of the universe and uses nations and powers as instruments of his judgment (Hab. 1). Ultimately, however, God will preserve his people.

(d) The description of God's judgment acquired certain apocalyptic features in the postexilic period. Its character as punishment is emphasized: God's enemies (either human or supernatural) will be dashed to pieces. The "congregation of wickedness" will be annihilated, while the "sons of light" will attain salvation (cf. 1QS 3–4; 1QM 3:9–19). The doctrine of retribution led people to regard any calamity as God's judgment on them; this in turn had an adverse effect on their social life and shook their faith in divine justice. Belief in a further judgment after death (*Pss. Sol.* 3:1ff.; *1 Enoch*) offered a way out of this mental anguish. Judgment would still fall, even though we might not live to see it. God or the Son of man is the judge of the world at the "last day" (2 Esd. 7).

NT 1. The NT contains much legal and semi-legal language where *krima, krinō,* and their derivatives are used with the same complex meanings as outlined above.

(a) *krinō* has a wide variety of meanings: to distinguish, give preference, esteem (Rom. 14:5); consider, regard as (Acts 13:46; 16:15; 26:8); speak or think ill of, decide, judge (Matt. 7:1–2; Lk. 7:43; Acts 4:19; 15:19; Rom. 14:3–4, 10, 13; 1 Cor. 4:5); decide, resolve (Acts 3:13; Rom. 14:13; 1 Cor. 2:2; Tit. 3:12). *synkrinō* means to interpret (1 Cor. 2:13; cf. 2 Cor. 10:12). *anakrinō* means to inquire (Acts 17:11; 1 Cor. 10:25, 27), examine, interrogate (Lk. 23:14; Acts 4:9; 12:19; 1 Cor. 9:3), form an estimate of (2:14).

(b) *krinō* and *krima* are often used in the NT in a strictly judicial sense. *krinō* means to judge; in the mid. to dispute; in the pass. to bring to trial, condemn, punish. People judge according to the law (Jn. 18:31; Acts 23:3). The apostles and the church judge (1 Cor. 5:12; 6:2–3). Paul is put on trial (Acts 23:6). On two occasions he asserted his rights as a Roman citizen to the Roman authorities that he should not be beaten apart from a trial (*akatakritos*; lit., uncondemned, 16:37; 22:25). The people cannot come to a right judgment (Lk. 12:57). People go to law to settle disputes (Matt. 5:40; 1 Cor. 6:6). The noun *krima* is used similarly: The disciples of Jesus should not judge, and with the judgment that one pronounces on others will oneself be judged (Matt. 7:1–2). The Christians in Corinth, unfortunately, have lawsuits with one another (1 Cor. 6:7). *krisis* can mean judgment by the authorities (Matt. 5:21), judgment passed either by one person on another (Jn. 7:24) or by the angels on the devil (2 Pet. 2:11; Jude 9). *kritēs* means the authorized (Matt. 5:25; Lk. 12:14, 58; 18:2) and unauthorized (Jas. 2:4; 4:11) judge—anyone who brings injustice to light (Matt. 12:27). *autokatakritos* (only in Tit. 3:11) is one who is self-condemned.

kataginōskō (Gal. 2:11; 1 Jn. 3:20–21) means to be recognized as guilty and condemned by one's own heart or conduct. Human condemnation is also expressed by *katakrinō*: The people of Nineveh will appear at the last judgment and condemn the present generation (Matt. 12:41; cf. Heb. 11:7). Note the similar use of this vb. in Jn. 8:10–11; Rom. 2:1; 8:34. Jesus is condemned to death (Matt. 20:18; 27:3; Mk. 14:64). The noun *katakrisis* occurs twice: "the ministry that condemns" (2 Cor. 3:9) and "not . . . to condemn you" (7:3).

LXX influence appears when *krisis* means justice (Matt. 12:18; 23:23; Acts 8:33) and when *krima* means rule. Authority to rule is given to the disciples and martyrs (Lk. 22:30; Rev. 20:4); the twelve apostles will rule over the twelve tribes (Matt. 19:28).

(c) God and Jesus judge (e.g., Jn. 5:22, 29–30; Acts 17:31). Each is called *kritēs*, judge (Acts 10:42; 2 Tim. 4:8; Heb. 12:23; Jas. 4:12; 5:9), and God's word is called *kritikos*, a discerner (Heb. 4:12). When the passive form is used, the reference is similarly to the activity of the divine judge (Rev. 11:18). Christ judges the living and the dead (2 Tim. 4:1; 1 Pet. 4:5–6), the secrets of humans (Rom. 2:16), the world (Acts 17:31), and everyone according to his or her deeds (1 Pet. 1:17; Rev. 20:12–13; cf. 2 Cor. 5:10).

The noun *krima* is used of divine judgment: Jesus brings judgment (Jn. 9:39), and God's activity as a judge begins with the church (1 Pet. 4:17); future and eternal judgment is in his hands (Acts 24:25; Heb. 6:2). Similarly, *krisis* can denote the judgment of God or of Christ (Jn. 5:30; 2 Thess. 1:5) or the day of judgment (Matt. 10:15; 2 Pet. 2:9; 3:7; 1 Jn. 4:17; Jude 6; Rev. 14:7). Divine judgment brings separation (Jn. 3:19) as well as destruction (Heb. 10:27). Those who hear Jesus' word and believe him do not come into judgment (Jn. 5:24). The dead who have done evil will arise to judgment (5:29).

Divine judgment often includes punishment (Jn. 3:17–18; Rom. 2:12; 3:6; 2 Thess. 2:12; Heb. 10:30; 13:4; Jas. 5:9). God's condemnation is just (Rom. 2:2–3; 3:8) and swift (2 Pet. 2:3). Thus, the prince of this world is condemned (Jn. 16:11). Divine condemnation is expressed by *katakrima* (Rom. 5:16, 18; 8:1) and *katakrinō* (God condemned sin in the flesh, Rom. 8:3; cf. also 14:23; 1 Cor. 11:32; 2 Pet. 2:6).

2. Just as in the OT all judgment is ascribed to God, so also in the NT all human judgment and punishment stands within the wider context of God's sovereign judgment, a principle expressed with the utmost clarity in Matt. 7:1: "Do not judge, or you too will be judged." The church of Christ has been entrusted with the task of judging in matters that affect its members (1 Cor. 5:12; 6:2). Measured by the standard of God's perfect righteousness, no one is righteous in his sight but all are under his wrath (Rom. 1–3). This is the reason why ultimately no human being has a right to judge another.

The unsearchable nature of God's judgments (Rom. 11:33) means that the doctrine of retribution can no longer be rigidly upheld. The human principle of "tit for tat" has no place in the divine judge's dealings with us (cf. Lk. 6:37; 13:1–5; Jn. 9:2–3). That God *is* judge is basic to the NT, but words like judgment and judge are incapable of expressing the unsearchableness of God, particularly when his unsearchable decrees reveal his love. This is the other side of God's character, displayed throughout the NT.

Jesus, like John the Baptist, preached by word and deed the nearness of divine judgment, which should stir us to hope and repentance (Lk. 13:6–9) but will bring woe on the unrepentant (Matt. 11:20–24; 12:41–42). Coming judgment means that all are advancing towards God's final verdict on them and their works. Before God nothing is forgotten, whether deed or word. The only way to escape condemnation is forgiveness.

Divine patience gives us time to repent and believe in Christ, who has been made "to be sin for us, so that in him we might become the righteousness of God" (2 Cor. 5:21; cf. Rom. 3:23–26; Gal. 3:13; Col. 2:13–15). Judgment already rests on unbelievers because they refuse the Savior, while believers escape condemnation (Jn. 3:16–18; 11:25–26). They can have confidence as they anticipate the day of judgment.

See also *paradidōmi*, deliver up, give up, hand over (*4140*); *bēma*, judgment seat (*1037*); *katadikazō*, condemn (*2868*).

3212 (*krinō*, separate, judge, consider, decide), → *3210*.

3213 (*krisis*, decision, crisis), → *3210*.

3216 (*kritēs*, a judge), → *3210*.

3217 (*kritikos*, able to discern and decide, critical), → *3210*.

3218	κρούω

κρούω (*krouō*), knock (*3218*).

CL & OT *krouō* is used in both cl. Gk. and the LXX (e.g., Song 5:2) for striking something, esp. knocking on a door.

NT To knock at a door is the strict meaning in all 9 NT instances of the vb. (Matt. 7:7–8; Lk. 11:9–10; 12:36; 13:25; Acts 12:13, 16; Rev. 3:20). Apart from the passages in Acts, the context is in each case metaphorical. The saying "Knock and the door will be opened to you" (Matt. 7:7; Lk. 11:9) is probably a common proverb since it is found also in Jud. This knocking does not mean seeking to enter the kingdom (cf. Matt. 7:13–14) but bringing one's petitions before the Lord; note that the situation presupposed in Lk. 11:5–8 is that of a persistent friend at midnight, who eventually gets what he asks for. Lk. refers the spiritual message of this parable ultimately to the gift of the Holy Spirit (11:13). Knocking in 12:36 and 13:25 is a detail of the parables of the returning master and of those excluded from entering the narrow door; the vb. here has eschatological significance.

Rev. 3:20 pictures the risen Lord standing at a door, knocking and inviting those inside to open and receive him. He is addressing the spiritually lukewarm church at Laodicea, and the anticipation of his return means victory and a place in the presence of his Father. This prediction of his confrontation with idle church people is both a disturbing warning that apathy will not go unheeded and a gracious encouragement that the Lord will not allow his people to remain ineffective, but intends rather to establish them in victorious living. The background to the image may be the Lord's Supper.

See also *aiteō*, ask, ask for, demand (*160*); *gonypeteō*, fall on one's knees, kneel down before (*1206*); *deomai*, ask, request, beseech, beg (*1289*); *proseuchomai*, to pray, entreat (*4667*); *proskyneō*, worship, do obeisance to, prostrate oneself, do reverence to (*4686*); *erōtaō*, ask, ask a question, request (*2263*); *entynchanō*, meet, turn to, approach, petition, pray, intercede (*1961*).

3220 (*kryptos*, hidden, secret), → *3221*.

3221	κρύπτω

κρύπτω (*kryptō*), hide, conceal (*3221*); ἀποκρύπτω (*apokryptō*), hide (*648*); κρυπτός (*kryptos*), hidden, secret (*3220*); ἀπόκρυφος (*apokryphos*), hidden (*649*); κρυφαῖος (*kryphaios*), hidden (*3224*).

CL & OT 1. In cl. Gk. *kryptō*, to hide, conceal, has a fig. meaning, to keep secret. The derivative *apokryptō* also means to keep secret. One cannot draw an absolute distinction between these vbs. and *kalyptō*, to hide. The adjs. *kryptos*, *apokryphos*, and *kryphaios* all mean hidden. Gk. and Hel. religion does not emphasize the hiddenness of the deity greatly, though there are occasional references to it. The biblical doctrine of God, with his transcendence and unapproachability, is largely foreign to the Gk. mind. The word *apokryphos*, however, plays a major role in describing the content of books of magic and astrology.

2. In the LXX *kryptō* is found both in the lit. sense of to hide (e.g., Gen. 3:8, 10) and the fig. sense of to keep secret (e.g., 18:17; 1 Sam. 3:17–18). *apokryptō*, to hide, usually has the fig. meaning (Isa. 40:27; Wis. 6:22). The adj. *kryptos* is used in both the lit. and the fig. senses (Deut. 29:29; 2 Macc. 1:16). *apokryphos* is used in Isa. 45:3; Dan. 11:43; and 1 Macc. 1:23 of secret treasures. The expression *en apokryphō*, in secret, is also found (e.g., Deut. 27:15; Ps. 10:9).

3. (a) The hiddenness and unapproachability of God is depicted impressively in the OT in the story of the call of Moses. Moses is not allowed to approach the God who has revealed himself to him in the burning bush, but turns his face away; he is afraid of God's face (Exod. 3:6). Similarly, the Israelites do not dare to approach God at Sinai; Moses alone dares to go forward into the darkness (20:21).

In later OT books, God hears his people's cry of distress in the secret place of thunder (Ps. 81:7). At the consecration of the temple Solomon declared that God dwells in darkness (1 Ki. 8:12). In a fig.

sense, the painful misfortunes of Israel are regarded as divine judgments in which his comfort remains hidden (Hos. 13:14). The God of Israel is a hidden God, though he remains the Savior. He hides his face in wrath, but he returns to his people with everlasting grace (Isa. 45:15; 54:8). Though Israel's way may be hidden from God, it is not cut off from the comfort of the Lord, who gives power and strength to the weary (40:27, 29).

(b) Although God hides himself from us, we cannot hide from him. He is the Lord who fills heaven and earth (Jer. 23:24). Everywhere we are surrounded by God's presence; God's eye sees even in the darkness, and nothing is hidden from him (Ps. 139:7–12, 15; Sir. 39:19). To flee from God, as the case of Jonah shows (Jon. 1:3), is therefore a hopeless quest. Above all, human sin is not hidden from God (Ps. 69:5; Jer. 16:17). There is no darkness where evildoers can hide and do their evil deeds (Job 34:22; Sir. 17:15, 20). To sinful people God is like a bear lying in wait or a lion in hiding (Lam. 3:10).

The awareness of personal guilt and distance from God finds strong expression in Ps. All the more urgent, therefore, is the plea made to God by the righteous: "Do not close your ears to my cry for relief" (Lam. 3:56). Nor can the sighing of the righteous remain hidden from God (Ps. 38:9). They therefore must stand before God with their sin and confess it; if they do not hide it, they can obtain God's forgiveness (32:5). The righteous also ask for this forgiveness for hidden faults (19:12). One effect of this attitude of faith and trust is the desire to hide God's commands in one's heart, i.e., to be their guardian (119:11, 19).

(c) The OT expresses in a variety of ways the tension between the hiddenness of God and his revelation. God reveals what is hidden, such as the hidden things that concern the future (Dan. 2:22; Sir. 42:19; 48:25). This opens up the way to Jewish apocalyptic lit., beginning with the book of Daniel. God is revealed in his judgments as the righteous Judge, who brings to light what is hidden (Eccl. 12:14; 2 Macc. 12:41; cf. Gen. 18:23–33).

3. In 1st-cent. Jud., the apocalyptic lit. that continues the tradition of the book of Daniel concerns itself with the hidden things, esp. insofar as they have to do with the future. In *1 Enoch*, for example, the chosen one intends to reveal all the treasures of what is hidden, and all secrets of wisdom will proceed from his mouth (46:3; 51:3). The Qumran texts speak of a secret knowledge of God's will that remains hidden to outsiders and is attainable only to the community (1QS 4:6; 9:17; 11:6; 1QH 5:24–25). Even in rab. Jud. the awareness of God's hiddenness and mysteries does not totally disappear, but it is balanced by the conviction of the pious Jew that the full and valid revelation of God has been given in the Torah.

NT   1. (a) In the NT *kryptō* occurs 18x; *apokryptō*, 4x; *kryptos*, 17x; *apokryphos*, 3x (Mk. 4:22; Lk. 8:17; Col. 2:3); *kryphaios* 2x (Matt. 6:18). Mk. 4:22 (cf. Matt. 10:26, which uses *kalyptō*, → *2821*; Lk. 12:2) reads: "Whatever is hidden [*kryptos*] is meant to be disclosed, and whatever is concealed [*apokryphos*] is meant to be brought out into the open." Thus, no clear line of distinction can be drawn between *kryptō* words and *kalyptō* words (cf. Lk. 23:30 with Rev. 6:16).

(b) The *kryptō* words are often used in a lit. sense. Matt. 13:44 mentions the treasure hidden in a field, while in the parable of the talents the unfaithful servant hides his money in the earth (25:18, 25). Similarly, the woman hides leaven in the flour (13:33, *enkryptō*). In a reference to Exod. 2, Heb. 11:23 records the hiding of the baby Moses after his birth.

2. Of theological significance are sayings in the Gospels that deal with the hiddenness of revelation and of the revelatory work of God. The revelation God gives through Jesus to babes remains hidden from the wise and prudent (Matt. 11:25 par. Lk. 10:21). The hiddenness of revelation corresponds to the hiddenness of the kingdom of heaven. This is the message of the parables of the leaven and of the hidden treasure (Matt. 13:33, 44). Just as the kingdom is hidden, so must the disciples' almsgiving, prayers, and fasting be done in secret; the

Father, who sees in secret, will reward them. Jesus emphasizes this in the face of a type of piety that seeks to display itself (Matt. 6:4, 6, 18). The passion predictions of Jesus indicate that for the disciples the divine plan remains for the present hidden; it will not be revealed to them until after the resurrection (Lk. 18:34). Similarly, Jerusalem has failed to recognize the salvation Jesus desires to bring her; the things that have been made for her peace remain hidden from her eyes (19:42).

In Matt. 10:26–27 Jesus commissions the disciples to spread his message; in this way what is "hidden" will "be made known." In Matt.'s rendition of the purpose of parables, they are intended to express what has been "hidden since the creation of the world" (Matt. 13:35; cf. Ps. 78:2). A city set on a hill cannot be hid, and a light is not placed under a bowl or hidden in a corner but is put on a lampstand so that all may see it (Matt. 5:14–16; cf. Lk. 11:33, *kryptē*).

Joseph of Arimathea is a secret (a form of *kryptō*) disciple for fear of the Jews (Jn. 19:38). In contrast to this, Jesus confesses at his trial before the high priest: "I said nothing in secret" (18:20). His task was to manifest the Father's name before others (17:6). In 7:8–10 Jesus says he does not plan to go up to Jerusalem for the Feast of Tabernacles (7:2–5). Later, however, he goes "in secret" (7:8, 10). On another occasion he hides from the Jews and leaves the temple when they try to stone him (8:59). He will give up his life at his own time, when his hour has come (7:8; 13:1; 17:1).

The hiddenness of Jesus exposes his lack of dependence on humans and his majesty and union with God. It does not mean that his revelation will remain hidden to all, for Jesus is the light of the world (Jn. 8:12). But it is given only to his disciples (Jn. 17); unbelievers are subject to the judgment of total blindness (9:39).

3. (a) Paul declares that his apostolic message is the "secret wisdom" of God, which he ordained from all eternity for our glory (1 Cor. 2:7). It has its origin in divine revelation (Rom. 16:25; 1 Cor. 2:10; Gal. 1:12). Its content is Christ, whom God has made wisdom for us (1 Cor. 1:30); that Spirit-inspired message brings us the deep knowledge of God (2:10–11).

(b) Eph. and Col. carry these ideas further. The message is "the mystery . . . kept hidden for ages and generations, but . . . now disclosed to the saints" (Col. 1:26) and to the holy apostles and prophets (Eph. 3:5). It proclaims to us the Christ present in Christians and his unsearchable riches (3:8; Col. 1:27). In this Christ "are hidden all the treasures of wisdom and knowledge" (2:3).

Moreover, Christ is also the hidden life of the Christian. Christians are buried with him in baptism and raised by faith to a new life (Col. 2:12). This life is "hidden with Christ in God" (3:3). Therefore, they can take no part in "secret and shameful ways" (2 Cor. 4:2), i.e., in works of darkness that take place in secret and yet cannot remain hidden (Eph. 5:12, *kryphē*; cf. 1 Tim. 5:25).

(c) In 1 Pet. Christian wives are called to a life of holiness, evident by not adorning themselves with costly outward finery, but by adorning "your inner [*kryptos*] self, the unfading beauty of a gentle and quiet spirit" (1 Pet. 3:4). The mark of this hidden, inner person is a life of hope, submission, and fear of God (3:2, 5–6).

4. (a) Paul describes true believers in Rom. 2:29 as Jews "inwardly" (lit., "in secret"). Through the Spirit they have received a circumcision of the heart, a circumcision made without hands (Col. 2:11–12; cf. Phil. 3:3)—which means baptism, through which they share in Christ's burial and resurrection (cf. Rom. 6:3–10). Thus, believers become the "Israel of God" (Gal. 6:16). By contrast, outward Jews rely mainly on the circumcision of the flesh.

(b) Rev. 2:17 speaks of the "hidden manna," a gift from the heavenly world. Manna was the secret food provided by God to the Israelites, which they received from heaven on their journey through the desert (Exod. 16:4). Jews expected that manna would be given to Israel anew at the end of the ages. Ultimately this hidden manna is Christ himself: He is the bread of God that comes down from heaven (Jn. 6:33–35).

5. (a) As to the future, God is the Judge, who will bring into judgment "men's secrets" (Rom. 2:16); he will also "bring to light what is hidden in darkness and will expose the motives of men's hearts" (1 Cor. 4:5), just as the Spirit of God already at work in Christians discloses "the secrets of [the] heart" (14:25).

(b) Rev. takes up OT prophecies (Isa. 2:10–11; Jer. 4:29; Hos. 10:8) and describes how on the judgment day the kings and great men of the earth will have to hide in caves and clefts of the rocks; they will cry out to the mountains and rocks, "Fall on us and hide us from the face of him who sits on the throne" (Rev. 6:16; cf. Lk. 23:30).

(c) The idea of judgment is only one side of NT expectation concerning the future. First and foremost the NT looks forward to the coming of the Lord, when Christ, the hidden life of Christians, will appear and they will appear with him in glory (Col. 3:3–4). Then the knowledge that is here enjoyed only in part and cannot lift the veil of God's hiddenness will no longer be obscure. It will no longer be a matter of seeing "a poor reflection as in a mirror" (1 Cor. 13:12), but will be turned into sight, face to face.

6. The English word *apocryphal* has passed into common usage because of the so-called apocryphal lit. These writings were secret, hidden writings, which were not to be read out in church. The way was paved for the appearance of this lit. by the fact that in the NT period the *authority* of the Scriptures was already established, but the question of which *writings* belonged to the canon had not yet been fully resolved. The specific term *Apocrypha* denotes those books included in the LXX that do not appear in the Heb. canon of the OT. These books were accepted by the Roman Catholic Church as canonical during the Council of Trent in 1546. Protestants in general have seen them as good and useful to read but not canonical.

See also *kalyptō*, cover, hide, conceal (*2821*).

3224 (*kryphaios̃*, hidden), → *3221*.

3228 (*ktēma*, property, possessions), → *5975*.

3231 (*ktizō*, create, produce), → *3232*.

3232	κτίσις

κτίσις (*ktisis*), creation, creature (*3232*); κτίζω (*ktizō*), create, produce (*3231*); κτίσμα (*ktisma*), created thing, creature (*3233*); κτίστης (*ktistēs*), originator, creator (*3234*).

CL & OT 1. In cl. Gk. *ktizō* early on took on the meaning bring into being, set in operation, colonize. *ktisis* means primarily the act of creation or the created thing (the result of this act); *ktisma* does not occur before the LXX and is generally synonymous with *ktisis*. *ktistēs* is most often a name for rulers in their function as founders and originators, in particular as restorers of the old order. Applied to a deity, it means creator.

2. LXX has two terms for create: *dēmiourgeō*, work on or with a material, manufacture; and *ktizō*, which expresses the decisive act of will that brings something into being. The latter is preferred as a description of God's creative activity. Nevertheless, the exclusiveness implied by the Heb. *bārāʾ* (see below) remains largely hidden in the LXX (esp. Pent. and Isa.), since *poieō*, make, is often used instead of *ktizō* (note that later versions of the OT, such as Theod., Aquila, and Sym., use *ktizō* in the Pent. and latter portions of Isa.). *ktizō* occurs 66x in the LXX.

(a) Heb. *bārāʾ* (trans. *ktizō* 16x) is a theological term whose subj. is always God. It is the word used to convey Israel's explicit faith in creation, expressed in Gen. 1 and the later chapters of Isa. *bārāʾ* expresses the incomparable creative activity of God, in which the word and act of creation are one (cf. Gen. 1; Ps. 148:5). It refers not only to God's activity in calling the world and individual creatures into being, but also to his actions in history that lie behind election, temporal destiny, human behavior, and even justification.

Referring to the original creative activity of God, *bārāʾ* is used of the creation of the heavens and earth (Ps. 148:5), the north and

south (89:12), the mountains and the wind (Amos 4:13), and humanity (Deut. 4:32; Ps. 89:47). It also expresses God's new work of creation extending into history. Thus Ps. 104:30, echoing Gen. 2, declares: "When you send your Spirit, they are created." In Eccl. 12:1 (lit., "Remember him who created you"), the reference is to the creation of the individual. A people yet to be created will praise God (Ps. 102:18). In the well-known text, "Create in me a pure heart, O God" (51:10), *bārāʾ* is again used in this sense. These last two references reveal the rift that runs through the original creation, which makes it necessary for God to intervene on behalf of his chosen people and the individual sinner.

The link between statements of God's original creation and those concerning his creative work in history becomes clear in Isa. 45:7, where God created not only light and darkness but also says, "I bring prosperity and create disaster." He who created the weapons that threaten has also created the destroyer of those weapons (54:16). The people whom God has created nonetheless profane the covenant (Mal. 2:10).

(b) *qānâ* (trans. *ktizō* 4x in LXX) means create, produce. Gen. 14:19, 22 speak of God Most High, in blessing and prayer respectively, as he who has made heaven and earth. Wisdom (Prov. 8:22), probably seen here as a heavenly being with a mediatorial role, exists before God's creation of the world.

(c) *yāṣar* (trans. *ktizō* 2x) means form, fashion (like a potter), plan. It can refer to the spontaneous action of God in history: He directs destinies (Isa. 22:11).

(d) *kûn* (trans. *ktizō* 2x) is used both of the original creation and of God's working in history. Thus precious stones were prepared (Ezek. 28:13), and Yahweh is the one who has established Israel (Deut. 32:6b).

(e) *ktizō* is used once for *yāsad* (Exod. 9:18); once for *ʿāmad*, stand forth at God's creative word (Ps. 33:9); and once for *šākan*, be established, of the tabernacle (Lev. 16:16).

3. In 39 occurrences of *ktizō*, there is no Heb. equivalent (most of these belong to the Apocr.). These uses give priority to the doctrine of creation over that of redemption. Confession, praise, and prayer to the Creator become the sole basis and content of faith (1 Esd. 6:13; Jdt. 13:18; Bel 5 [Theod.]; 3 Macc. 2:3, 9). God has created all things that they might exist (Wis. 1:14), and the world was created out of formless matter (11:17). He has created humanity for incorruption in the likeness of his own nature (2:23). God is called the "author of beauty" in connection with the creation of the stars (13:3).

Emphasis on the preexistence of the hypostasized figure of wisdom as the first created being accompanies a dehistoricizing of the concept of God. God becomes absolutely transcendent and exercises only mediate influence on present history. It also dehistoricizes creation (Wis. 10:1; Sir. 1:4, 9–10; 24:8–9). This reverses what happened with the emergence of an explicit doctrine of creation. History must now be seen from the viewpoint of creation, in which all is foreseen. From the beginning goodness is determined for the good. Winds, fire, hail, famine, and plague are created for punishment; and death, bloodshed, strife, sword, devastation, corruption, hunger, and tribulation for the ungodly (cf. Sir. 23:20; 39:21–30; 40:10).

One of the theological emphases of wisdom lit. is the extension of the doctrine of creation to include joy in the good things that have been made. Wine has been created to make us glad (Sir. 31:27 = LXX 34:27). Even tilling the soil is an ordinance of the Most High (7:15), and we have God to thank for doctors and medicines (38:1, 4, 12).

4. The noun *ktisis* has only 2 Heb. equivalents, each occurring 2x and meaning goods, wealth, possessions (Ps. 105:21; Prov. 1:13; 10:15); only in Ps. 104:24 does this word have the sense of creatures. Of more interest are the 15x that have no Heb. equivalent. Most of these underline the doctrine of creation in prayer (Ps. 74:18; Tob. 8:5, 15; Jdt. 9:12; 16:14; 3 Macc. 2:2, 7; 6:2). Since God is the Creator through his word, he can be taken at his word and addressed as the Lord of creation. God's power in history is no longer seen to be direct in its

operation but mediated by his creation. He arms the *ktisis*, for example, to bring vengeance on his enemies (Wis. 5:17; 16:24; 19:6).

The proper attitude of humanity to creation is to marvel at its wonders (Sir. 43:24–25), praise the Creator (Tob. 8:5, 15), and serve fellow humans (Jdt. 16:14). On the other hand, it is despicable to misuse the creation in order to gain purely selfish enjoyment, as the ungodly encourage one another to do (Wis. 2:6).

5. *ktisma* occurs only in the Apocr. In Wis. 9:2 the author prays for wisdom, which is seen as the instrument of creation. In Sir. 36:20 a prayer for God's intervention is based on the continuing interest of God in his creation. According to Wis. 13:5 and 14:11 (cf. Rom. 1:20), the greatness and beauty of created things enable us to draw conclusions regarding their Creator, but idols are an abomination within the created order.

6. The noun *ktistēs*, creator, used 9x (including 2 Sam. 22:32; Isa. 43:15 in Sym.), gives us a glimpse of the central position occupied by the doctrine of creation in the two centuries before Christ. The Creator of the universe is invoked in confession (2 Macc. 7:23; 4 Macc. 11:5). To him is committed in prayer the salvation of Israel (2 Macc. 1:24–29) and the outcome in holy war (13:14). The hypostasized figure of wisdom stands as mediator in direct relation to him (Sir. 24:8).

7. The Qumran sect brought a demonological and anthropological dualism to the doctrine of creation. God has created the spirits of light and darkness and based every work on them. The doctrine of double predestination corresponds to this in the historical creation of the righteous and the ungodly—the one intended for the day of favor, the other for the day of conflict. This dualistic thinking allows the seas and floods to have been created and not merely separated. The idea of the new, eternal creation after the breakup of the old is consistent with the eschatological future envisaged by the righteous.

NT 1. *ktizō*, create, produce, occurs 15x; *ktisis*, creation, created thing, 19x; *ktistēs*, creator, only in 1 Pet. 4:19. The latter concept is, however, expressed 8 times by a relative clause or a part. The limited occurrences of this group of words do not, however, exhaust the terminology of creation. Note also *poieō*, make; *plassō*, form; *kataskeuazō*, prepare (Heb. 3:4); *themelioō*, found; and *dēmiourgos*, artisan, shaper. Certain other statements directly refer to creation events (Rom. 4:17) or repeat phrases from the creation narratives (2 Cor. 4:6).

2. The NT presupposes the OT doctrine of creation, but it gains the historical power of faith in the God of creation as it proclaims God's kingdom at hand and dawning in Christ. A key text here is Matt. 6:24–34 (cf. esp. 6:33), which testifies to the vital link between a person's faith in historical salvation ("Seek first. . .") and in creation ("all these things will be given to you as well"). The same is true of the Lord's Prayer (cf. the first three petitions with the fourth).

In the preaching and actions of Jesus, people are brought to unbroken, healing confidence in the Creator. The Sabbath was made for humans (Mk. 2:27 par.). Foods do not defile a person (Matt. 15:11 par.). Fasting is not appropriate in the presence of Jesus (Mk. 2:18–20 par.). In his service there is no lack of life's necessities (Lk. 22:35). Monogamy and the indissolubility of marriage are based on the creation ordinance from the beginning (Mk. 10:6 par.), as against the practice of divorce, which arose later from hardness of heart. Jesus does not succumb to the temptation arbitrarily to use the creation in opposition to God's will (Matt. 4:1–11 par.).

Moreover, Jesus demonstrates his creative power in the so-called nature miracles (the feeding miracles, walking on the water, and stilling the storm). In his exorcisms, healings, and raising of the dead, his creative power is exercised for the benefit of those who belong to a fallen creation. Thus the whole creation needs the gospel of Christ (cf. Mk. 16:15).

3. It is therefore a necessary consequence of the self-revelation of God that the post-resurrection confession of faith should include worship of the ascended one, who now sits at God's right hand, as the original mediator of creation (Jn. 1:1–3; 1 Cor. 8:6; Col. 1:16; Heb. 1:2,

10). The whole creation was made through him and with him in view (Jn. 1:3, 9–12). It has its basis (Rev. 3:14) and its goal in him (Heb. 1:11–12).

4. References in Paul's letters to the doctrine of creation may be grouped into (a) those regarding the nature of the first creation, and (b) those that have as their subject the new creation, *kainē ktisis*, which has begun in Christ.

(a) The Creator alone is worthy of worship and veneration; the creature is limited by the fact that it is created. Where worship is nevertheless offered to creatures, God gives up those who have thus transgressed to their own evil ways (Rom. 1:24–28). Since the creation (*ktisis*) of the world, God's invisible nature has been clearly seen and recognized in his works (1:20; cf. Wis. 13:5), so that no one has an excuse. Yet all have failed to make use of this opportunity and are therefore dependent on God's free gift in the redemptive work of Jesus Christ (Rom. 3:21–26).

Everything created (*ktisma*) by God is good, and nothing that God has created is to be rejected. This includes foods, which are to be received with thanks (1 Tim. 4:3–4). However, because of human arrogance and rebellion the creation is in danger of becoming a temptation to humans and of separating them from the love of God in Christ (Rom. 8:39). Since humankind is the pinnacle of creation, the state of the created order is determined by them. All the hopes and longings of every created thing (*ktisis*) are therefore directed to them. But the created world has become subjected to futility, and it sighs and groans in its sufferings (8:19a, 20, 22).

In a polemical passage (1 Cor. 11:9), Paul bases his teaching on the behavior and role of women in worship on the principle of the original creation, whereby woman was made for man (Gen. 2:18). In Gal. 3:28, however, he declares the equality of the sexes in the unity that exists in Christ. While he ascribes to man an authority that he does not ascribe to woman, he nevertheless asserts their mutual dependence on each other and their joint dependence on God (1 Cor. 11:11–12).

(b) Because of what humans have done, all creatures are dependent on the restoration of a right relationship between God and humans in the created world, which can come about only through his intervention (see Rom. 8:19b). The hope of the final revelation of God's children is also the hope that looks for the liberation of all creatures from their bondage to decay (8:21). Believers are already hidden in Christ (Col. 3:3). Paul can therefore speak with full assurance that when a person belongs to Christ, new creation is a fact (2 Cor. 5:17). Former things that hitherto determined life have passed away.

In Christ the old privileges that people use to erect barriers between themselves (e.g., circumcision and uncircumcision) are no longer valid. Only belonging to him counts—the new creation; the past has been canceled by the cross. Therefore the world, as the embodiment of the old creation, is unable to make any claims on Christ. Christians cannot live in dependence on the world; they are dead to each other (Gal. 6:14–15.).

Similarly, in Eph. 2:15 the removal by Christ of the basic distinction among humans is regarded as the decisive act of reconciliation. "One new man" has been created in Christ, who now stands before God representing all humans, so we must see ourselves as his workmanship (2:10). We must "put on the new self, created to be like God" (4:24). Whereas the old self was characterized by acts that destroy fellowship with God and with other people, the new self is marked by a new knowledge emanating from God's will. This knowledge allows us to become truly an image of our Creator in acts of neighborly love (Col. 3:10–12). The new self accepts the rightness of God's gracious verdict on us, is separated for service to him in holiness, and lives in dependence on him who is the truth, i.e., Christ (Eph. 4:24).

5. The occasional references in the General Letters to the old creation and the new are essentially no different from Paul's. Christians are "the firstfruits of all [God] created," having been born again through "the word of truth" (Jas. 1:18). Heb. emphasizes God's eter-

nal creative power; someday, all his creatures will have to give account of their actions (4:13; cf. Rom. 1:20b). Heb. also stresses the infinite superiority of the new covenant over the old. The worship center for the old covenant belongs to this present created order; it is made with hands. The sphere of operation of the one heavenly high priest, Christ, is not subject to such limitation (9:11). Peter attributes the ability of Christians to put their life at God's disposal for good works, even if this means suffering, to the faithfulness of the Creator (1 Pet. 4:19).

The interpretation of *ktisis* in 1 Pet. 2:13 is debated. But seeing that *ktisis* can mean the act by which an authoritative body is created and hence also the result of that act, the word there probably means authority or institution. The Christian hope of the return of Christ is defended in 2 Pet. 3:4 against those who maintain that there is a perpetual continuity "since the beginning of creation" and use it to justify their self-assurance.

6. The language of Rev. depicts a visionary anticipation of the creation of the world to come. In hymns and acts of heavenly worship it proclaims what is already true in faith and will one day be objectively true forever (see 21:1–5). He who sits on the throne is worthy to receive glory, honor, and power, for he has created all things and they owe their existence to his will (4:11). Worship and praise from every creature (*ktisma*, 5:13; cf. 10:6) belong not only to him but also to the Lamb (the crucified and exalted one). Startling in its applicability to the present day is the vision of the death of a third of the creatures (*ktismata*) in the sea, when a mountain of fire is thrown into it (8:8–9).

See also *katabolē*, foundation, beginning (*2856*); *dēmiourgos*, maker (*1321*).

3233 (*ktisma*, created thing, creature), → *3232*.

3234 (*ktistēs*, originator, creator), → *3232*.

3236 (*kybernēsis*, administration), → *4565*.

| 3245 | κυλλός | κυλλός (*kyllos*), crooked, crippled, maimed (*3245*). |

CL & OT The background of *kyllos* was predominantly medical. It was used of crooked or disabled legs, bent outward by diseases such as rickets or disabled through badly reduced fractures or other forms of surgical accident; also of disabled feet or ears. *kyllos* does not occur in the LXX or other Gk. versions of the OT or Apocr.

NT *kyllos* occurs only 4x in the NT. Matt. 15:30–31 does not indicate the type of disability; the persons involved may have been congenitally afflicted or sustained crippling accidents. Matt. 18:8 and Mk. 9:43 describe the voluntary amputation of a hand as a means of forestalling sin from a source that is jeopardizing entry to eternal life. The severing of the hand at the wrist was an ancient oriental method of punishing thieves.

See also *chōlos*, lame, halt, maimed (*6000*).

3248 (*kyminon*, cummin), → *3303*.

3257 (*kyria*, lady, mistress), → *3261*.

| 3258 | κυριακός | κυριακός (*kyriakos*), belonging to the Lord, the Lord's (Supper *or* Day) (*3258*). |

OT *kyriakos*, belonging to the Lord, is an adj. derived from *kyrios*, Lord (*3261*). This word is not used in the LXX. It does occur in inscriptions and papyri from 68 B.C. with the meaning of belonging to or connected with a lord, a proprietor, or the emperor.

NT 1. *kyriakos* is used only 2x in the NT. In 1 Cor. 11:20 Paul refers to the *kyriakon deipnon*, the Lord's Supper, which presumably means "the supper instituted by the Lord" or "belonging to the Lord." It is impossible to partake of the Lord's Supper and thus receive food from him and at the same time to take part in pagan sacrificial meals, whereby one enters into communion with demons (10:19–22). In patristic writings this adj. is used of "the words" of Christ, the covenants, the people, the house, the cross, but most commonly of the Lord's Day.

2. The most likely meaning of the phrase "the Lord's Day" in Rev. 1:10 is the name that has come to be given to the first day of the week. This is definitely the meaning from the late 1st cent. on. It may be taken for granted that the adj. was used here to differentiate it from "the day of the Lord" (2 Thess. 2:2). But since this adj. had already been attached to the Lord's Supper, where it hinted at a special connection with Christ in its institution, it may well carry something of this meaning in Rev. 1:10.

3. If indeed "the Lord's Day" referred to the Christian Sunday, the first day of the week, in order to see its theological significance we must examine other passages that refer to the first day of the week. The earliest reference appears in 1 Cor. 16:2, where Paul asks the Corinthian Christians to lay something aside on each first day of the week. Although the laying aside was at home, the day's connection with Christian worship would make it easy to remember this duty. This suggests that the first day was becoming the regular day of worship.

In Acts 20:7 we find Paul meeting with the Christians at Troas to break bread, probably the Eucharist, on the first day of the week, even though he was with them for seven days. In the *Did.* (late 1st cent.), this day was the regular day of worship for the church. The strong emphasis on the first day of the week as the day on which Christ rose from the dead suggests that the theological reason for the change from the seventh to the first day was the resurrection of our Lord (Matt. 28:1; Mk. 16:2; Lk. 24:1; Jn. 20:1).

From the biblical data regarding the OT institution of the Sabbath with its humanitarian and spiritual advantages (→ *sabbaton*, 4879), of Christ's insistence that it was made for humanity, of Paul's insistence that no day in itself has any special sacredness, and of warnings against legalistic involvement in the Jewish ritual calendar, we may assume that the Christian church was guided by the Holy Spirit to attach the same privileges and blessings of one sacred day of rest in seven to the new Lord's Day.

See also *kyrios*, Lord (*3261*); *sabbaton*, Sabbath (*4879*).

3259 (*kyrieuō*, be lord, master, rule), → *3261*.

| 3261 | κύριος | κύριος (*kyrios*), lord, master, owner, Lord (*3261*); κυρία (*kyria*), lady, mistress (*3257*); κυριότης (*kyriotēs*), lordship, dominion (*3262*); κυριεύω (*kyrieuō*), be lord, master, rule (*3259*); κατακυριεύω (*katakyrieuō*), rule over, conquer, be master of (*2894*). |

CL & OT 1. (a) In cl. Gk. *kyrios* is an adj., having power, authoritative, derived from the noun *to kyros*, power, might. As a subst. *kyrios* meant lord, ruler, one who has control. *kyrios* always contains the idea of legality and authority. Anyone occupying a superior position can be referred to as *kyrios* and be addressed as *kyrie* (fem. *kyria*).

(b) In early Gk. *kyrios* was not used as a divine title. Although the term was applied to the gods, there was no general belief in a personal creator Lord. The gods were not creators and lords of fate but were, like human beings, subject to fate. The Gks. of this period did not feel dependent on a god or personally responsible to the gods. Only insofar as the gods ruled over particular spheres in the world could they be called *kyrioi*.

(c) The situation was different in the East. The gods created humans who were personally answerable to them. They could intervene in human lives to save, punish, or judge. They also established justice and law, which they communicated to human beings, e.g., through the king. Therefore they were called lords.

(d) Instances of the title *kyrios* in Hel. times with reference to gods or rulers do not occur until the 1st cent. B.C. *kyrios basileus*, "lord and king," is found often between 64 and 50 B.C. In 12 B.C. Emperor Augustus was called *theos kai kyrios*, "god and lord," in Egypt. *kyrios* was also used of Herod the Great (ca. 73–4 B.C.), Agrippa I (ca. 10 B.C.–A.D. 44), and Agrippa II (A.D. 27–ca. 100). Other high officials also received this title. *kyrios* was used of the gods who, in contemporary popular thought, were referred to as lords. Where *kyrios* was used of a god, the servant (→ *doulos*, *1528*) using the term stood in a personal relationship of responsibility to the god. Individual gods were worshiped as lords of their cultic communities and of the separate members of the fellowship. The worship of other lords was not excluded, however, for no god was worshiped as universal lord.

(e) The Roman emperors Augustus (31 B.C.–A.D. 14) and Tiberius (A.D. 14–37) rejected the title *kyrios* and all that it meant. But Caligula (A.D. 37–41) found the title attractive. During and after the time of Nero (A.D. 54–68), who was described in an inscription as "lord of all the world," the title *kyrios* occurs more frequently (one of the oldest instances is Acts 25:26). In and of itself the title *kyrios* does not call the emperor god, but when he is worshiped as divine, the title *lord* also counts as a divine predicate. It was against such religious claims that the early Christians rejected the totalitarian attitudes of the state.

2. (a) *kyrios* occurs over 9,000x in the LXX. It translates *ʾādôn*, lord, which refers 190x to men as the responsible heads of groups (e.g., 1 Sam. 25:10). It is used only 15x for *baʿal*, which means the owner of a wife or a piece of land (e.g., Jdg. 19:22–23). Yahweh is rarely called owner (Hos. 2:16), but more frequently Lord of the community belonging to him (cf. Ps. 123:2). *kyrios* can also mean commander or ruler.

(b) In over 6,000 instances, however, *kyrios* replaces the Heb. proper name of God, the tetragrammaton *YHWH* (Yahweh). The LXX thus strengthened the tendency to avoid the utterance of God's name and finally to avoid its use altogether. Where *kyrios* stands for *ʾādôn* or *ʾadōnay* as a word relating to God, there is genuine translation; but where it stands for Yahweh, it is an interpretative circumlocution for all that the Heb. text implied by the use of the divine name: Yahweh is Creator and Lord of the whole universe, of humans, Lord of life and death. Above all he is the Lord God of Israel, his covenant people. By choosing *kyrios* for Yahweh the LXX also emphasizes legal authority. Because Yahweh saved his people from Egypt and chose them as his possession, he is the legitimate Lord of Israel. As Creator Yahweh is also the legitimate Lord of the entire universe, with unlimited control over it.

(c) *kyrieuō* occurs more than 50x in the LXX, generally with the meaning to rule.

3. In post-OT Jewish lit. *kyrios* appears as a term for God in Wis. (27x; e.g., 1:1, 7, 9; 2:13), then esp. often in Philo and Josephus. Philo seems to have been unaware that *kyrios* stood for the tetragrammaton, for he used *theos* ("God") to indicate the gracious power of God, while *kyrios* describes God's kingly power.

NT Of the 717x in which *kyrios* occurs in the NT, the majority are found in Luke's writings (210x) and Paul's letters (275x). This one-sidedness can be explained by the fact that Luke wrote for, and Paul wrote to, people who lived in areas dominated by Gk. culture and language. On the other hand, Mk., more firmly based in Jewish Christian tradition, uses the *kyrios* title only 18x, and these mostly in quotations. The remaining occurrences of *kyrios* are spread over the other NT books. The uses of *kyrios* accords with its varied use in the LXX.

1. *The secular use of* kyrios. The *kyrios* stands over against the slave (Matt. 10:24–25; 18:25, 27; 25:19; Lk. 12:36–37, 46; Eph. 6:5, 9; Col. 3:22). *kyrios* means owner (Matt. 15:27; Mk. 12:9; Lk. 19:33; Gal. 4:1) or employer (Lk. 16:3, 5). The husband faces his wife as *kyrios*, i.e., as superior (1 Pet. 3:6). *kyrios* used as a form of address can emphasize the power of a superior over an inferior, but it can also

simply be politeness (Matt. 18:21–22; 25:20–26; 27:63; Lk. 13:8; Jn. 12:21; 20:15; Acts 16:30). The term is also used to address angels (10:4; Rev. 7:14) and the unknown in the heavenly vision outside Damascus (Acts 9:5; 22:8, 10; 26:15). A twice-repeated *kyrios* corresponds to Palestinian usage (Matt. 7:21–22; 25:11; Lk. 6:46).

2. *God as the* kyrios. God is frequently called *kyrios*, esp. in the many quotations from the OT in which *kyrios* stands for Yahweh, corresponding to the custom of pronouncing the title *kyrios* instead of the tetragrammaton in public reading (e.g., Rom. 4:8 = Ps. 32:2; Rom. 9:28–29 = Isa. 10:22 and 1:9; Rom. 10:16 = Isa. 53:1). In Lk.'s birth narratives *kyrios* frequently denotes God (e.g., 1:32; 2:9). In the gen. accompanying another word it corresponds to OT usage: e.g., the hand of the *kyrios* (1:66); the angel of the *kyrios* (Matt. 1:20); the name of the *kyrios* (Jas. 5:10); the Spirit of the *kyrios* (Acts 5:9); the word of the *kyrios* (Acts 8:25). The formula "says the *kyrios*" (e.g., Rom. 12:19 = Deut. 32:35) also comes from OT. The formula "our Lord and God" (Rev. 4:11) is reminiscent of the title adopted by Domitian.

Jesus is adopting Jewish forms of speech when he addresses God the Father as "*kyrios* of heaven and earth" (Matt. 11:25; Lk. 10:21). God is "the Lord of the harvest" (Matt. 9:38). He is the only ruler, the King of kings and the *kyrios* of lords (cf. Dan. 2:47), who will cause our *kyrios* Jesus Christ to appear (1 Tim. 6:15). God is the Creator and as such Lord of all (Acts 17:24). By acknowledging God as *kyrios*, the NT esp. confesses him as Creator—his power revealed in history and his just dominion over the universe.

3. *Jesus as the* kyrios. (a) The earthly Jesus as *kyrios*. This word applied to the earthly Jesus is first of all a polite form of address. This no doubt goes back to the title *Rabbi* (cf. Mk. 9:5 with Matt. 17:4; see also "sir" in Jn. 4:15; 5:7; 6:34). This address also implies recognition of Jesus as a leader and willingness to obey him (Matt. 7:21; 21:29–30). As Son of Man Jesus is also *kyrios* of the Sabbath; he has control over the holy day of God's people (Mk. 2:28–29). Even after his death and resurrection the words of the earthly Jesus have authority for the Christian community. Paul appeals to words of the *kyrios* to decide a question (1 Cor. 7:10, cf. 25; 1 Thess. 4:15; cf. Acts 20:35).

(b) The exalted Jesus as *kyrios*. The confessional cry used in worship, *kyrios Iēsous* ("Jesus [is] Lord") originated early in the Christian community. This confession is one of the oldest Christian creeds, if not the oldest. Note the Aramaic formula *Marana tha* (see 1 Cor. 16:22, NIV text note), which means "Lord, come," "Our Lord has come," or "The Lord will come"(cf. Rev. 22:20).

With this confession the NT community submitted itself to its Lord, but at the same time it also confessed him as ruler of the world (Rom. 10:9a; 1 Cor. 12:3; Phil. 2:11). God raised Jesus from the dead and "gave him the name that is above every name" (Phil. 2:9; cf. Isa. 45:23–24), i.e., the name *kyrios*, and with it the position corresponding to the name. The exalted *kyrios* rules over humanity (Rom. 14:9, *kyrieuō*). All powers and beings in the universe must bow before him. When that happens, God the Father will be worshiped (cf. Eph. 1:20–21; 1 Pet. 3:22).

Jesus Christ is called the ruler over all the kings of the earth, King of kings and Lord of lords (Rev. 17:14; 19:15–16). In this way he has received the same titles of honor as God himself (1 Tim. 6:15; cf. Dan. 2:47). According to contemporary Jewish thought, the different spheres of the world in nature and history were ruled by angelic powers. Since Christ has now been raised to the position of *kyrios*, all powers have been subjected to him and must serve him (Eph. 1:20–21; Col. 2:6, 10). When Christ has overcome every power (1 Cor. 15:25), he will submit himself to God the Father. Thus his lordship will have achieved its goal and God will be all in all (15:28). The one God and the one *kyrios* Jesus stand in opposition to the many gods and lords of the pagan world (8:5–6; Eph. 4:5–6).

Scriptural evidence for the exaltation of Jesus and for his installation as Lord was found in Ps. 110:1, the most quoted Ps. in the NT (cf., e.g., Matt. 22:44; 26:64; Acts 2:34; Eph. 1:20; Heb. 1:3, 13). The Jewish interpretation of this passage looked forward to the messianic future, but in the faith of the Christians this hope was transferred to the present. The lordship of the Messiah, Jesus, is a present reality. He is exercising in a hidden way God's authority and lordship over the world and will bring it to completion in the future. This faith was articulated in Thomas's confession (Jn. 20:28): "My Lord and my God." Early Christianity saw no infringement of monotheism in the installation of Jesus as Lord, but rather its confirmation (1 Cor. 8:6; Eph. 4:5; Phil. 2:11). It is God who exalted the Lord Jesus (Acts 2:36) and made him Lord of all things.

As far as we can establish, the NT church did not formally reflect on the relationship of the exalted Christ to God the Father as the church did later. Perhaps we can say that there is no developed doctrine of the Trinity in the NT, but that the writers thought in Trinitarian forms.

(c) *kyrios* and the Lord's Supper. *kyrios* figures frequently in expressions connected with the Lord's Supper. Note the phrases that are partly pre-Pauline: "the Lord's table" (1 Cor. 10:21), "the Lord's death" (11:26), "the cup of the Lord" (10:21; 11:27), "arouse the Lord's jealousy" (10:22), "the Lord's Supper" (11:20; → *kyriakos, 3258*), "judged by the Lord" (11:32), and "guilty of sinning against the body and blood of the Lord" (11:27). These expressions indicate that the Lord's Supper is the place where the Christian community submits itself in a special way to the saving work of the *kyrios* and receives a share in his body and power (see also *deipnon, 1270*).

(d) *kyrios* and Spirit. Paul taught the Christian community to distinguish between the one who is speaking in the Holy Spirit and the one who is not (1 Cor. 12:3). A person can only say "Jesus is Lord" if he or she is filled with the Holy Spirit. Anyone who, by acknowledging allegiance to Jesus as *kyrios*, belongs to the new covenant, belongs to the sphere of the Spirit and no longer to that of the old covenant and of the letter. Such a one stands in freedom: "Where the Spirit of the Lord is, there is freedom" (2 Cor. 3:17).

(e) *kyrios* in epistolary greetings. In the opening greetings of Paul's letters the "Lord Jesus Christ" is frequently mentioned beside God the Father (e.g., Rom. 1:7; 1 Cor. 1:3). The concluding greeting, with the phrase "the grace of the *kyrios* Jesus be with you," continued the pre-Pauline tradition that may have had its origin in the Lord's Supper (cf. 1 Cor. 16:23; 2 Cor. 13:14; Phlm. 25). The description of God as the "Father of our *kyrios* Jesus Christ" goes back to the early Christian community (Rom. 15:6; 2 Cor. 1:3; 11:31; cf. 1 Pet. 1:3). The formula was introduced into an originally Jewish context (the praise of God). Christian missionaries did not just call people to faith in God the Father but also to faith in the *kyrios* Jesus (Acts 5:14; 18:8).

4. *The lordship of the* kyrios. (a) The activity of the church before the *kyrios* Jesus. In every expression of its life the Christian community stands before the *kyrios* who has authority and exercises it over the community (1 Cor. 4:19; 14:37; 16:7). He causes the community to grow (1 Thess. 3:12–13), bestows authority on the apostles (2 Cor. 10:8; 13:10), and gives different ministries to the members of his body, the church (1 Cor. 3:5; 7:17; 12:5). The *kyrios* also gives visions and revelations (2 Cor. 12:1). The whole life of the Christian community is determined by its relationship to the *kyrios* (Rom. 14:8). The body, i.e., the complete earthly existence of the Christian, belongs to the *kyrios*; this precludes dealings with prostitutes (1 Cor. 6:13–17).

The *kyrios* gives to each one the measure of faith (1 Cor. 3:5; 7:17; Eph. 4:5). He is the *kyrios* of peace and gives peace (2 Thess. 3:16), mercy (2 Tim. 1:16), and insight (2:7). On the basis of faith in the *kyrios* Christ, even earthly relationships between masters and slaves take on a new aspect. Faithful service of earthly masters (*kyrioi*) is service of the *kyrios* of the church (Col. 3:22–24; cf. 1 Pet. 2:13).

(b) The formulae "through" and "in" the *kyrios*. The formula "through the [our] Lord Jesus [Christ]" occurs in the most varied contexts: e.g., thanksgiving (Rom. 7:25; 1 Cor. 15:57), praise (Rom. 5:11), and exhortation (15:30; 1 Thess. 4:2). In such phrases *kyrios* is used in order to claim the power of the exalted Lord for the life of the church and of the individual.

The phrase "in the Lord" occurs esp. in Paul and means the same as "in Jesus Christ," e.g., *in the Lord*: a door was opened for mission (2 Cor. 2:12), Paul affirms and exhorts (Eph. 4:17; 1 Thess. 4:1), Paul is convinced (Rom. 14:14), people are received (16:2; Phil. 2:29), and the church is to rejoice (3:1), stand firm (4:1), and greet one another (Rom. 16:22; 1 Cor. 16:19). Christians are to marry in the Lord (7:39), be strong in the Lord (Eph. 6:10), and walk in the Lord (Col. 2:6). People are chosen (Rom. 16:13) and loved (16:8; 1 Cor. 4:17) in the Lord; in him their work is not in vain (15:58). The whole of life, in both the present and the future, is determined by the fact of Christ expressed by this formula: Paul and his churches stand in the presence and under the power of the *kyrios*.

(c) Statements about the Parousia. At present Christians are separated from the *kyrios* and long to be with him (2 Cor. 5:6, 8). Those who are alive at the Second Coming will be caught up to meet the *kyrios* (1 Thess. 4:17). Thus, the NT church looks forward to the future, visible return of Christ and to a final union with the Lord of life and death. We read about the day of the Lord (1 Cor. 1:8; 5:5; 2 Cor. 1:14; 1 Thess. 5:2; 2 Thess. 2:2), "the coming [*parousia*] of our *kyrios*" (2 Thess. 2:1), and the "appearing [*epiphaneia*] of our *kyrios*" (1 Tim. 6:14). When he comes, the exalted *kyrios* is Judge (2 Thess. 1:9; 2:8) and Savior (Phil. 3:20).

5. *Derivatives of kyrios.* (a) *kyria* (fem. of *kyrios*) means lady, owner, mistress of the house. In the NT it occurs only in 2 Jn. 1, 5, where it refers to the church (cf. v. 13, where the churches are sisters and their members children). In addressing the church as "lady," the author is expressing his respect for it and honors it as a work of the *kyrios*.

(b) *kyriotēs*, lordly power or position, dominion. In the NT this word occurs in the pl. with reference to angelic powers (Eph. 1:20–21; Col. 1:16). The NT letters stress that the exalted Christ rules over these dominions. *kyriotēs* occurs in the sing. in Jude 8 and 2 Pet. 2:10, where the thought is not of angels but of God's dominion.

(c) *kyrieuō*, be a lord, act as master. In the NT this vb. occurs 7x. The rule of kings over their people is characterized by ambition (Lk. 22:25), because they misuse their power for selfish ends; the disciples are to seek rather to serve, as Jesus did (22:26–27). Paul uses *kyrieuō* to describe relationships of power. Because Christ has risen, death no longer has any power over him (Rom. 6:9). Christ died and rose in order that he might reign over the living and the dead (14:9). God is the ruler of those who rule (1 Tim. 6:15). Since Christians have been baptized into Jesus' death and have risen with him (Rom. 6:3–4), sin must not reign over them any longer (6:14). For they no longer stand under law but under grace (7:1, 6). Paul does not want to lord it over the faith of the Corinthians but to work with them for their joy (2 Cor. 1:24).

(d) *katakyrieuō*, rule over, conquer. The prefix *kata-* has a negative force. In the NT the word occurs 4x. It is a characteristic of Gentile rulers to exercise their rule to their own advantage and contrary to the interests and well-being of the people (Matt. 20:25; Mk. 10:42). The vb. also describes the man with an evil spirit who leaped on the seven sons of Sceva and "overpowered" them (Acts 19:16) as they attempted to imitate Christian exorcism. Finally, Peter exhorts elders not to exercise their office by lording it over the congregation, but to be examples to the flock (1 Pet. 5:2–3).

See also *theos*, God (*2536*); *Emmanouēl*, Immanuel (*1842*); *despotēs*, lord, master (of a house), owner (*1305*); *kyriakos*, belonging to the Lord, the Lord's (*3258*).

3262 (kyriotēs, lordship, dominion), → *3261.*

3263	κυρόω

κυρόω (*kyroō*), confirm, ratify, make valid (*3263*); προκυρόω (*prokyroō*), establish, confirm beforehand (*4623*).

CL & OT *kyroō*, from *kyros*, means authority or validity. It expresses the thought of ratifying and making firm in all sorts of contexts. In the

LXX this word occurs 3x, 2x times in the pass. voice of confirming possession (Gen. 23:20; Lev. 25:30; cf. also 4 Macc. 7:9).

NT In Gal. 3:15, 17, both *kyroō* and *prokyroō* appear in connection with the ratification of a will. In 2 Cor. 2:8 Paul uses the former word in his plea to the Corinthians to "reaffirm" their love for an errant brother.

See also *bebaios*, sure (*1010*); *themelios*, foundation (*2529*); *asphaleia*, firmness, certainty (*854*).

3266	κωλύω

κωλύω (*kōlyō*), hamper, hinder, prevent, restrain, forbid (*3266*).

CL & OT 1. In cl. Gk. *kōlyō* originally meant to cut short, then to hinder. There are familiar idioms connected with this vb., such as *ti kōlyei*, why not? and *ouden kōlyei*, proceed by all means.

2. The vb. occurs 33x in the LXX, of which 19 are in the Apocr. Its basic meaning is to hinder (cf. Job 12:15; Ezek. 31:15); it is used mostly in the sense of restrain, withhold. The subj. of the vb. can be God (1 Sam. 25:26; Ezek. 31:15) or people (e.g., Moses, Num. 11:28; the writer, Ps. 40:9; 119:101), while the obj. of the vb. can be people (Gen. 23:6; Num. 11:28; Ps. 119:101) and things (e.g., wind or water, Job 12:15; Eccl. 8:8; Ezek. 31:15). The contexts can be either secular (e.g., Gen. 23:6) or religious.

NT 1. *kōlyō* occurs 23x in the NT, most often in Lk.'s writings. Besides a purely secular use in connection with tax evasion (Lk. 23:2), he has also a theological use. (a) From the point of view of the object, the hindering relates mostly to people: Soldiers are prevented from killing Paul (Acts 27:43); children are prevented from coming to Jesus (Mk. 10:14); Paul was prevented from going to Rome (Rom. 1:13) and from continuing his mission (1 Thess. 2:16). In 1 Cor. 14:39 one notes an exception, since what is *not* to be prohibited is speaking in tongues.

(b) There are a variety of subjects of this vb.: a Roman centurion (Acts 24:23; 27:43), disciples (Mk. 10:14), a believer (Lk. 6:29), the Holy Spirit (Acts 16:6), circumstances (Rom. 1:13), or death (Heb. 7:23).

(c) Most frequently, the vb. relates to the preaching of the gospel (Acts 16:6; Rom. 1:13; 1 Thess. 2:16; in a wider sense, 1 Cor. 14:39). In Acts 16:6 Paul is prevented by the Holy Spirit from preaching the gospel in the Roman province of Asia. Here Luke demonstrates God's leading along the road toward Europe. In Lk. 11:52 Jesus condemns the experts in the law for hindering people from knowledge of the law (Matt. 23:13 has "kingdom of heaven" and *kleiō*, shut [see 3090], here).

2. It is striking that both Paul (implied in Rom. 1:13) and Luke (cf. Acts 16:6) see the ultimate origin of hindrances affecting Christians not in the actions of people but in God himself (or his Spirit, or Jesus). However, a disciple's own decisions and actions clearly affect whether his or her faith is able to grow and develop or whether it is constricted and hindered (cf. 1 Cor. 9:4, 7–18; 1 Pet. 3:7). The same applies to the church as a whole.

3. An important use of this vb. developed in the idea of withholding baptism. As early as the 1st cent., *kōlyō* became the technical term for refusing or not refusing baptism—due in part, perhaps, to this vb.'s being used in connection with baptism in the NT (Acts 8:36; 10:47; 11:17). Mk. 10:14 and par. Matt. 10:13; Lk. 18:15–16 were regularly used in arguments against scruples over infant baptism.

See also *enkoptō*, hinder, thwart (*1601*).

3273	κωφός

κωφός (*kōphos*), deaf, dumb (*3273*).

CL & OT *kōphos* has the general sense of blunt or dull in cl. Gk., but more specifically can mean either deaf or dumb. In Jewish usage *kōphos* means dumb in Wis. 10:21 and deaf in Exod. 4:11; Ps. 38:13; Isa. 43:8. A fig. use of this word is applied to idols in Hab. 2:18.

NT *kōphos* is found only in the Gospels. In Mk. 7:32, 37 the word must mean deaf since the text also uses the rare word *mogilalos* (having a speech impediment) and the miracle includes the gift of hearing (7:35). In 9:25 *kōphos* is used for a demon-possessed boy. This spirit was dumb (*alalos*, 9:17), and, in addressing it, Jesus also calls it *kōphos*, implying deafness. In Matt. 11:5; Lk. 7:22, part of the evidence demonstrating the reality of Jesus' messiahship to John the Baptist is the fact that the *kōphoi* hear.

But *kōphos* can also signify dumbness. In Matt. 9:32–33; 12:22; Lk. 11:14 the criticism that Jesus heals by devilish power is prompted by the healing of a man who was *kōphos* but who now speaks (cf. Matt. 15:30–31). In Lk. 1:22, Zechariah's vision in the temple renders him unable to speak (*kōphos*).

Λ lambda

3275	λαγχάνω

λαγχάνω (*lanchanō*), obtain by lot, draw lots for (*3275*).

CL & OT The basic cl. meaning of *lanchanō* is obtain something by lot. At Athens, both political offices and permission to bring suits in the law courts were awarded by lot. More broadly, the word denotes getting anything as if by lot, i.e., out of the blue—by chance rather than by one's effort. In the LXX the vb. is used of Saul's obtaining the monarchy, which he did by God's appointment (1 Sam. 14:47; cf. also Wis. 8:19; 3 Macc. 6:1).

NT In Jn. 19:24 *lanchanō* appears in the nonclassical sense of casting lots for Jesus' coat. Otherwise, it indicates divine appointment irrespective of personal quality. In Lk. 1:9 Zechariah obtains by lot the honor of offering incense in the Holy Place of the temple. In Acts 1:17 Peter refers to Judas's having obtained through Christ's choice a share in the apostolic ministry. In 2 Pet. 1:1 Peter addresses those (presumably Gentiles) who have obtained by grace "a faith as precious as ours."

See also *kathistēmi*, bring, appoint (*2770*); *horizō*, determine, appoint (*3988*); *paristēmi*, place, put at the disposal of (*4225*); *procheirizō*, determine, appoint (*4741*); *tassō*, arrange, appoint (*5435*); *tithēmi*, put, place, set, appoint (*5502*); *prothesmia*, appointed date (*4607*); *cheirotoneō*, appoint (*5936*).

3278 (*lailaps*, a tempestuous wind), → *847*.

3281 (*laleō*, to talk, chat, speak), → *3364*.

3284	λαμβάνω

λαμβάνω (*lambanō*), take, receive (*3284*); ἀναλαμβάνω (*analambanō*), take up, take to oneself (*377*); ἀνάλημψις (*analēmpsis*), reception (*378*); ἐπιλαμβάνομαι (*epilambanomai*), lay hold of, grasp, catch (*2138*); καταλαμβάνω (*katalambanō*), seize, grasp, attain, make one's own, take possession (*2898*); μεταλαμβάνω (*metalambanō*), receive a share (*3561*); μετάλημψις (*metalēmpsis*), sharing, receiving (*3562*); παραλαμβάνω (*paralambanō*), take to oneself, take with or along, take over (*4161*); προλαμβάνω (*prolambanō*), anticipate, take, get (*4624*); προσλαμβάνω (*proslambanō*), take, receive or accept into one's society (*4689*); πρόσλημψις (*proslēmpsis*), admission, acceptance (*4691*); ὑπολαμβάνω (*hypolambanō*), take up, think, assume, be of the opinion that (*5696*); ἀπολαμβάνω (*apolambanō*), receive, get back (*655*); ἀνεπίλημπτος (*anepilēmptos*), above reproach, without blame (*455*).

CL & OT 1. (a) In cl. Gk. *lambanō* originally meant to take or grasp. It can indicate both benevolent and hostile actions and have as obj. either people or things; e.g., take a wife, collect taxes, accept a verdict, take a road, and fig. take courage. Fear or terror can also seize a person. *lambanō* also came to mean to receive; it was used to embrace all areas of life, from simple things to spiritual benefit.

(b) The compounds strengthen or enlarge the basic meaning. *analambanō* means receive up (on) high, receive to oneself; the corresponding noun, *analēmpsis*, means lifting or taking up. *hypolambanō* means take up from below, take hold, and mentally apprehend, believe, hold an opinion. *epilambanō* means to lay hold of, occupy, assist; mid. obtain for oneself. *katalambanō* strengthens the original intention and means to seize, take a firm grip, attack; mid. seize for oneself; mental apprehension is basically appropriation and understanding. *metalambanō* means to gain a share in, get, receive; *metalēmpsis* denotes participation, acceptance. *prolambanō* means take in advance, forestall. *proslambanō* means to take in addition, draw in;

mid. take aside, admit; the corresponding noun is *proslēmpsis*, admission, acceptance. *paralambanō* means to draw someone to oneself, take over an office or a thing.

2. (a) *lambanō* and its compounds occur frequently in the LXX, mostly translating *lāqaḥ*; the act. meaning of take dominates: e.g., take a sword (Gen. 34:25) or a wife (4:19). In Exod. 15:15, trembling seizes the leaders of Moab. The pass. meaning of receive is rarer: e.g., receive presents, bribes (1 Sam. 8:3), or an office or reward (Ps. 109:8; Prov. 11:21).

(b) The following compounds may be mentioned. *analambanō* is used regularly in the LXX; it is theologically significant in the aor. pass. for the translation of Enoch (Sir. 49:14) and of Elijah (2 Ki. 2:11; Sir. 48:9; 1 Macc. 2:58). The LXX uses *epilambanō* in its basic meaning of holding or taking hold in 2 Sam. 13:11; Isa. 3:6; Jer. 31:32 = LXX 38:32; Zech. 14:13. *katalambanō* describes God's holding grip. God's hand takes hold of the world (Isa. 10:14). He traps humans (Job 5:13) and comprehends the incomprehensible (34:24). Humans ask how they are to conceive of God and lay hold of his righteousness and wisdom, i.e., make it their possession (Sir. 15:1; 27:8). The powers of destruction also clutch at humankind and attack them (Gen. 19:19; Num. 32:33). *proslambanō* denotes the way in which God draws his people or elect out of danger and destitution to himself (Ps. 18:16; 27:10; 65:4; 73:24; Wis. 17:11).

(c) *paralambanō* has a distinct meaning in Hellenism and Jud. It means to receive and indicates the way one takes over a tradition, whether the teaching and training of a philosopher or the mysteries and rites of the mystery religions. In Jud. tradition limited itself to the Torah and its exegesis (cf. Mk. 7:4). The rabbis, too, passed on certain subject matter in teaching under conditions of strict secrecy in order to prevent misunderstandings amongst the religiously impure.

NT 1. In the NT *lambanō* is attested 258x, esp. in Matt., John, and Rev. (a) This vb. has a broad range of meaning: to take (in an act. sense), e.g., bread, lamps, the tithe, and (fig.) one's cross upon oneself (Matt. 10:38) or the form of a servant (Phil. 2:7). It also means to remove or take possession of, e.g., remove money (Matt. 28:15), diseases (8:17, cf. Isa. 53:4), a crown (Rev. 3:11), peace from the earth (6:4). In a theological context Jesus has the power to take his life back again (Jn. 10:18). The enemy also has the ability to attack people's lives (cf. Matt. 21:35–39) or to seize the sick (Lk. 9:39). Emotions take control of people (5:26; 7:16). Further, *lambanō* has the sense of to admit someone into a house; also to receive Jesus (Jn. 1:12; 5:43; 13:20) or to receive his words (12:48; 17:8).

(b) In a more pass. sense *lambanō* means to receive: e.g., a bite, money, alms. It is important with theological objects: eternal life (Mk. 10:30), the Spirit (Jn. 7:39), grace (Rom. 1:5), condemnation (Mk. 12:40), forgiveness (Acts 10:43), and mercy (Heb. 4:16). *lambanō* is also used as a circumlocution for the pass.; e.g., receive edification, be edified (1 Cor. 14:5).

This vb. is theologically significant: God gives, and humans receive. (i) Jesus received his commission, the Spirit, and power (Jn. 10:18; Acts 2:33; Rev. 2:27). He is God's gift and lives by receiving. In taking the form of a servant (Phil. 2:7) and taking away our infirmities (cf. Matt. 8:17 with reference to Isa. 53), he took on himself the death of a sinner and fulfilled the commission he received from the Father (Jn. 10:18). So too in resurrection and exaltation: The crucified one is worthy to receive "power and wealth and wisdom and strength and honor and glory and praise" (Rev. 5:12).

(ii) Only when we receive do we find ourselves and stand within the God-given order and plan that Jesus Christ reveals. For those who hear the witness of Jesus, the acceptance of that word decides over life and death. At this point, Jn. distinguishes the various objects that are received, accepted, or laid hold of. Those who receive the *martyria*, the witness of Jesus, set their seal to this "that God is truthful" (Jn. 3:33). Those who accept Jesus' words gain knowledge of his revelation: Jesus comes from God and receives his life from God (17:8; cf. 1 Cor. 2:12). So Jesus himself, who is the Word of God, can become the obj. of believing acceptance. Those who receive him have a share of his inexhaustible grace and receive the Holy Spirit (Jn. 1:16; 7:39; 20:22). Those who do not accept him, i.e., do not recognize or acknowledge him, will be judged (12:48). That same word of Jesus will be judge on the last day.

(iii) For Paul *lambanō* means sharing in the fulfillment of the promise in Christ (Gal. 3:14), receiving the Spirit (Rom. 8:15), and receiving grace and the gift of righteousness (5:17), just as he himself received his apostleship as a special token of God's grace (1:5). Although poor in God's sight, those who receive are exceedingly rich (1 Cor. 4:7), for when they accept, they receive salvation, fellowship with Christ, and life in the future world (Phil. 3:12–14).

2. The compounds *analambanō* and *hypolambanō* develop the aspect of taking up. (a) *analambanō* means to take with or take up, take someone on board (Acts 20:13–14; 2 Tim. 4:11). Paul's command to "put on [take up] the full armor of God" it is a powerful picture of the active fight of believers against the powers of darkness (Eph. 6:13; cf. also 6:16). In the aor. pass. the vb. is used of the ascension of the resurrected one (Acts 1:11; 1 Tim. 3:16). *analēmpsis*, lifting up high, being taken up, is found in the NT only in Lk. 9:51 and is generally interpreted of Christ's ascension, but *analēmpsis* can also mean death, decease. Both ideas are implied in the NT expectation of Jesus' death, since the death includes the exaltation of the Lord.

(b) *hypolambanō* occurs 5x in the NT: e.g., Acts 1:9: "a cloud hid [took] him from their sight." This taking suggests a taking up from below. In 3 Jn. 8 the author exhorts that strangers are to be taken up, i.e., offered hospitality and cared for. When extended to mental processes *hypolambanō* can mean pick up someone's words (Lk. 10:30), imagine (Acts 2:15).

3. The compounds *epilambanomai* and *katalambanō* intensify the original meaning of the word and mean seize. (a) *epilambanomai* denotes both violent apprehension and trustful holding of the hand. For example, Paul is seized by his opponents (Acts 17:19; cf. 9:27; 16:19; 18:17; 21:30, 33; 23:19). Fig. *epilambanomai* means to catch somebody in speech, such as when Jesus' opponents attempt to catch him in his words (Lk. 20:20). Jesus touched the blind, children, and a man with dropsy (Mk. 8:23; Lk. 9:47; 14:4), and he stretched out his hand to Peter as he began to sink (Matt. 14:31). Paul finds *epilambanomai* the right word for characterizing the movement of faith as directed to eternal life: "Take hold of . . . eternal life" (1 Tim. 6:12). *anepilēmptos*, irreproachable (1 Tim. 3:2; 5:7; cf. 6:14), is a qualification for bishops and church members in their care of widows.

(b) *katalambanō* in the NT designates the attack of evil powers as well as the grip of Christ on people. The boy with epilepsy was attacked by a dumb spirit and dashed to the ground (Mk. 9:18). The darkness has not received the light, i.e., has neither accepted nor comprehended Christ (Jn. 1:5, cf. 1:11); darkness overtakes those who do not have Christ (12:35). Paul warns his readers against a false reliance on their faith in light of the coming day of the Lord (1 Thess. 5:4). On the positive side, *katalambanō* marks the hold of Christ on a believer. Paul has been apprehended by Jesus Christ; he is Christ's possession and therefore is stretching out toward the goal of the high calling (Phil. 3:12–13). Only someone who has been laid hold of strives to obtain the victor's imperishable crown of eternal life (1 Cor. 9:24). The mid. of *katalambanomai* denotes grasping truth, by which one may recognize God's hidden actions (Acts 4:13; 10:34; 25:25). In Rom. 9:30 the Gentiles attain righteousness, even though they have not pursued it, and in Eph. 3:18 the believer comprehends the extent of God's love.

4. *metalambanō* (7x) and *metalēmpsis* (only in 1 Tim. 4:3) indicate participation in physical and spiritual benefits. Food is taken and eaten (Acts 2:46; 27:33; cf. 2 Tim. 2:6); God created it to be "received with thanksgiving" (1 Tim. 4:3). The earth "receives the blessing of God" (Heb. 6:7). God waits for the Yes that responds to his offer, for the obedience and thankfulness that respond to the giver and his gifts. Heb. 6:4–8 includes the warning that a blessing that has been received is forfeited forever by an act of conscious apostasy from Christ. Every kind of discipline serves toward our participation in God's holiness (12:10).

5. In *prolambanō* the temporal significance of *pro* is retained, for the woman anointed Jesus with the jar of perfume in advance of his death (Mk. 14:8). Her action was a prophetic sign of his death and a substitute for anointing the entire body. In 1 Cor. 11:21 certain individuals were going ahead of others with their own meals at the Lord's Supper; Paul condemns their actions as unworthy. In Gal. 6:1 Paul encourages clemency toward a sinner, if one "is caught in a sin." The *pro* here suggests that the sinner has been forcibly laid hold of by sin without thinking. Thus, Paul requests gentleness and brotherly assistance.

6. *proslambanō* is found in the NT only in the mid. It means to take along (Acts 17:5), take (of food, 27:33, 36), and take aside to engage in an intense personal conversation (Mk. 8:32; cf. Matt. 16:22; Acts 18:26). This vb. has a theological importance when it means admit into fellowship: "God has accepted" someone who is weak in faith (Rom. 14:3). Paul exhorts the Romans to seek out those who have a weak faith, because strong and weak are equally accepted into fellowship with God through Christ's death (15:7). Even for Jews, who by their rejection of Christ are rejected from salvation, Paul anticipates their *proslēmpsis*, acceptance, by God (11:15).

7. In the Gospels and Acts *paralambanō* is frequently followed by the acc. of person, i.e., take someone with oneself, choose out from a large number, offer fellowship to a chosen one, or introduce a particular plan. Thus Jesus took to himself three disciples in order to reveal himself to them (Matt. 17:1; 20:17; 26:37; cf. Mk. 5:40). He "came to that which was his own, but his own did not receive him" (Jn. 1:11). But for believers there stands the promise: "I will come back and take you to be with me" (14:3).

Paul further uses *paralambanō* to denote the acceptance of mental and spiritual benefits and refers to the receiving of teaching and ethical traditions passed down to others, among which are the words of institution of the Lord's Supper (1 Cor. 11:23), the exhortation of Phil. 4:9, "the word of God" (1 Thess. 2:13), the "gospel" (1 Cor. 15:1–3), and Jesus Christ as Lord (Col. 2:6).

paralambanō is also used in the sayings about the two men in the field and the two women grinding at the mill—one being taken and the other left (Matt. 24:40–41; Lk. 17:34–35). The point of these sayings is to encourage the hearers to watch and be ready for the coming of the Son of Man (cf. Matt. 24:39, 44; Lk. 17:22–30), for no one knows the hour. Just as when the flood came only Noah and his family were prepared, so the coming of the Son of Man will find people engaged in identical activities, but some will be ready and others not. *paralambanō* is also used generally for taking someone along (e.g., Matt. 2:13–14, 20–21; 17:1; Lk. 9:28), including the spirit that took seven other spirits to help him (11:26).

8. *apolambanō* means: to receive (e.g., adoption, Gal. 4:5; rewards and punishments, Lk. 23:41; Rom. 1:27; Col. 3:24; 2 Jn. 8); to receive in return, get back (the same amount, Lk. 6:34; the lost son, 15:27); and to take aside (Mk. 7:33).

See also *dechomai*, take, receive, accept (*1312*).

3286 (lampas, torch, lamp), → *3290.*

3287 (lampros, beaming, bright, shining, radiant, gleaming, beautiful), → *3290.*

3288 (lamprotēs), brilliance, splendor, large-heartedness), → *3290.*

3289 (*lampros*, brilliantly, splendidly, sumptuously), → *3290*.

3290	λάμπω

λάμπω (*lampō*), shine (*3290*); λαμπάς (*lampas*), torch, lamp (*3286*); λαμπρός (*lampros*), beaming, bright, shining, radiant, gleaming, beautiful (*3287*); λαμπρότης (*lamprotēs*), brilliance, splendor, large-heartedness (*3288*); λαμπρῶς (*lamprōs*), brilliantly, splendidly, sumptuously (*3289*); ἐκλάμπω (*eklampō*), shine forth (*1719*); περιλάμπω (*perilampō*), surround with light (*4334*).

CL & OT 1. (a) In cl. Gk. *lampō* is generally intrans. and means to shine. In its lit. sense it refers to sources of light such as the sun, lightning, a torch, or a lamp. But it is frequently used fig. in reference to humans, e.g., eyes flashing with anger, shining faces, radiant beauty. The compound *perilampō* means to surround with light, while *eklampō* means to shine forth, e.g., of the sun. The noun *lampas* means a torch or a lamp (i.e., an oil-vessel with a wick). *lamprotēs*, by contrast, is abstract, meaning brilliance, or fig. large-heartedness. Finally, the adj. *lampros* means beaming, gleaming, shining white, and the adv. *lamprōs* means brilliantly, splendidly, sumptuously.

(b) While in its primary sense *lampō* describes the function of light (*phōs*) in illuminating darkness, used metaphorically it can refer to a shining hero striking fear into human hearts. Justice and certain virtues are also said to shine forth.

2. In the LXX *lampō* and *eklampō* can mean both to shine, illumine. *lampas* means torch (Gen. 15:17; Jdg. 7:16, 20; 15:4–5); it was used in the OT to describe something of brilliant or dazzling appearance, such as the undulating light in the midst of the four creatures (Ezek. 1:13; cf. Dan. 10:6). In Nah. 2:4 the word describes the gleaming of chariots; in Job 41:19, the exhalations of Leviathan; in Isa. 62:1, the visible manifestation of Israel's deliverance among the nations. In Zech. 12:6 the clans of Judah are likened to a flaming torch that ignites sheaves.

These words are important theologically since, in certain contexts, God manifests himself as light and hence as a source of illumination. For the most part the radiance of his glory (→ *doxa*, *1518*) is represented in terms of man-made or natural luminaries. Thus flaming torches indicate the presence of God (Gen. 15:17; Ezek. 1:13; cf. Exod. 19:18; 24:17). In Zech. 4:1–10 the vision of the seven-branched candlestick with lamps symbolizes the eyes of the Lord that survey the whole earth. Certainly the seven-branched lampstand (Exod. 25:31–40) is a symbol of life and light; to the godly, it points back to God as the source of all blessings. Even Job 41:10–34 fits this context of ideas, for Leviathan, pictured as a crocodile spitting out sparks of fire (41:19), is an impressive illustration of the power and greatness of the Creator.

Hence in the OT lightning, flaming torches, and lamps frequently accompany a theophany or draw attention to Yahweh's glory. There is also a close connection between flaming torches and divine judgment (cf. Num. 16:35), an association vividly portrayed in Zech. 12:6, where the princes of Israel, as instruments of divine justice, are compared to flaming torches ready to consume Israel's enemies (cf. Nah. 2:4). The future of the covenant people is radiant with light and life (cf. Ps. 36:9), while that of the godless is dark (Prov. 4:18–19).

NT 1. In the NT, words in this word group occur a total of 30x, mostly in Matt. and Rev. The words are used in their lit. sense to denote the shining of the sun (Acts 26:13; cf. 2 Cor. 4:6, where Paul stresses the creative act of God in causing light to break forth); also of lightning (Lk. 17:24; cf. Rev. 8:10) and of a light on a lampstand (Matt. 5:15–16). The pl. of *lampas* is used both for torches (Jn. 18:3; cf. Rev. 8:10) and for oil lamps (Matt. 25:1–4, 7–8; Acts 20:8).

2. The adj. *lampros* can denote the magnificence of a garment, indicating affluence or luxury (Jas. 2:2–3; cf. Lk. 23:11; Rev. 19:8). It also pictures the faded splendor of the prostitute of Babylon (18:14), or, adverbially, the luxurious living of the rich man in Lk. 16:19. In

these passages the words begin to have metaphorical significance, for true splendor comes only from heaven. Thus Paul, on his way to Damascus, is suddenly surrounded by a light "brighter than the sun" (Acts 26:13); similarly, in Lk. 2:9, the shepherds are surrounded with the radiance of angels, who appear as shining figures in a blaze of light (cf. Acts 10:30; 12:7; Rev. 15:6).

3. Supremely it is Jesus Christ himself who was so transfigured by divine radiance that his face shone (*lampō*) like the sun and his garments became gleaming white (Matt. 17:2; cf. Mk. 9:2–3; Lk. 9:29). John sees Jesus as the "bright Morning Star" (Rev. 22:16). As the lightning illuminates the whole sky, so will it be at Christ's Parousia (Lk. 17:24): "Then the righteous will shine like the sun in the kingdom of their Father" (Matt. 13:43, alluding to Dan. 12:3). Until then Christ's disciples have the task of shining like lights on a lampstand (Matt. 5:15–16; cf. Rev. 1:12, 20; 2:1), which is made possible only by sharing with Paul in the experience of 2 Cor. 4:6.

See also *lychnos*, lamp, light (*3394*); *phainō*, shine (*5743*); *emphanizō*, reveal, make known (*1872*); *phōs*, light, brilliance, brightness (*5890*).

3295	λαός

λαός (*laos*), people (*3295*).

CL & OT 1. In cl. Gk. *laos* first meant a number of men, a crowd, esp. an army, a military company. Later this meaning disappeared, and the word meant the common people, population; in the pl., the multitude of individuals out of whom the people is made up.

2. (a) In the LXX *laos* occurs about 2,000x. The pl. (approx. 140x) always means nations and so is synonymous with *ethnos* (→ *1620*). *laos* sometimes means the people in contrast to the ruler or ruling class (cf. Gen. 41:40; 47:21; Exod. 1:22; Jer. 23:34). Even the dead can be termed *laos* (Gen. 25:8; 49:33). Such passages are not, however, typical.

(b) To the translators of the LXX the term *laos*, infrequently used in the Gk. of their time, seemed ideally suited for expressing the special relationship of Israel to Yahweh. *laos* serves in the overwhelming majority of cases as a translation of the Heb. *ʿam* and means Israel as the chosen people of God, just as the Heb. *gôy* is used esp. for the Gentiles (*ethnē*).

In one of the oldest passages in the OT (the song of Deborah), the expression "the people of the LORD" means the army, the levy of the people as they march down to battle (Jdg. 5:11, 13; cf. also 2 Sam. 1:12, where the NIV translates *ʿam* by "army"). As the nation developed, however, the entire people became known as *laos*. About 10x Israel is called the "people of the LORD." In another 300x we find the phrase "my people," where "my" refers to Yahweh (e.g., Exod. 3:7, 10; cf. also "your people" in 5:23).

(c) In the prophetic crisis, when the relationship between Yahweh and the people has been broken (Isa. 1:3; 5:25), Yahweh turns in words of judgment and threats against "my people Israel" (Amos 7:8, 15; 8:2). To fall away and follow Baal is all the more serious to Yahweh, because for him Israel is "my people" (Hos. 4:6–12). Thus the exhortation addressed to them is, "Return to your God" (12:6). Hosea's third child is called *lōʾ-ʿammî* (LXX *ou-laos-mou*), "not my people," and the reason given by Yahweh is, "You are not my people, and I am not your God" (1:9); i.e., Israel has behaved as if she were not Yahweh's people. In contrast to this comes the promise, "You are my people" (2:23); i.e., when Yahweh turns again to Israel, she will again become "my people."

(d) One of the most important passages in the Pentateuch is Deut. 26:16–19, which records a mutual declaration between Yahweh and Israel in the style of an adoption ceremony: Israel is to be Yahweh's people, he will be their God, and they are to walk in his ways and obey him. Thus originated the formula, traced back to the time of Moses: "I will be your God and you will be my people" (Jer. 7:23; cf. 11:4; 24:7; 30:22; 32:38 = LXX 39:38; Ezek. 11:20; 14:11; Zech. 8:8).

(e) Since Israel is Yahweh's people, they are further defined as "the people of his inheritance" (Deut. 4:20), "his treasured possession" (7:6), "a people holy to the LORD" (e.g., 7:6; 14:2). The theme of Deut. is the people of God; the covenant formula is embedded in instruction for the keeping of the law (cf. 26:12–19). God's gracious approach to his people remains, however, the starting point (cf. Jer. 11:3–5). It appears again projected into the future in the promise of the "new covenant" (31:31–33; cf. 24:7; 32:38–40; Ezek. 36:26–38). Note that the promise of the prophets can also go beyond Israel and embrace the Gentile world, who will become "my people" (Zech. 2:11).

3. What makes Israel the *laos* is Yahweh's election and grace, not national, natural, or historical factors. This grace must be repeatedly confirmed by faithfulness and obedience. From an earthly point of view, unfaithfulness on the part of the people makes them lose everything that makes them God's people. They will then become like all the other nations, and indeed worse off (Deut. 28:58–64). But because Yahweh keeps faith with his people despite all apostasy and unfaithfulness, Israel remains God's *laos*. When all is said and done, they live not through any achievement of their own, but only because of Yahweh's faithfulness and grace.

4. (a) In the rab. literature and the Pseudepigrapha part of the foundation of all faith is that Israel is God's chosen people, his possession. Israel's special relationship with God is expressed in metaphors taken from family life: Israel is Yahweh's firstborn son (cf. 2 Esd. 6:58); the Israelites are God's brothers and kinsmen, royal children. As a special token of Yahweh's love it has been revealed to them that they are children of God. Israel is also called the bride, the betrothed, the spouse of God. Many other OT ideas are reflected in rab. literature.

(b) At Qumran *'am* often means Israel. The community there saw themselves as the people chosen from all peoples (1QM 10:9), with whom God made an eternal covenant (13:7) and whom he redeemed to be a people forever (13:9). They are God's redeemed people (14:5), whom he will not allow to be destroyed by other nations (1QpHab 5:3). The wicked among God's people he will destroy (5:5). They are the "saints of the covenant" (1QM 10:10), the "elect of the holy people" (12:1). The "people" is the army in the final conflict (9:1; 10:2). In the hierarchy of Qumran the "people" had third place after the priests and Levites (1QS 2:21; 6:8–9).

In other places, however, *'am* (and pl. *'ammîm*) mean the nations, the Gentiles. God is praised as the Creator, who has brought about the division of the nations (1QM 10:14). A sword is coming over all nations (16:1). Their heroes will be brought low by God (11:13), and their princes will be thrust down (1QSb 3:27; 5:27).

NT 1. *laos* occurs 142x in the NT (more than half of these are in Lk. and Acts). In many cases the language and concepts of the LXX exert an influence, though *laos* often follows a previous reference to *ochlos* (→ *4063*) and carries the same meaning (e.g., Lk. 7:24, 29; 8:42, 47; cf. Matt. 27:24–25; Mk. 14:2) or stands instead of *ochlos* in a parallel passage (cf. Lk. 19:48 with Mk. 11:18; Lk. 20:45 with Matt. 23:1). Used on its own, *laos* can mean also crowd, common people (e.g., Lk. 1:10; 7:1; 20:1, 9; Acts 2:47). Many of these passages refer to the activity of John the Baptist, Jesus, or the apostles, whose ministry was practically restricted to Israel (cf. Matt. 4:23; 26:5; 27:64), and Israel is, after all, the *laos* and not an *ethnos* (an exception is Jn. 11:50, where both words are used).

The pl. *laoi* is parallel to *ethnē* (→ *1620*) in Lk. 2:31–32 (cf. Isa. 40:5–6; 42:6); Rom. 15:11 (cf. Ps. 117:1); Rev. 10:11 (cf. Dan. 3:4). The great multitude (*ochlos*) standing before the Lamb comes from every *ethnos* and *laos* (Rev. 7:9; 11:9; 17:15), and here it means the whole of humanity.

The word *pas*, all, often precedes *laos* (e.g., "all the people" in Lk. 3:21; 7:29; Acts 3:9; 5:34). As in the LXX, *laos* can mean the people in contrast to the ruling classes (Lk. 22:2; 23:5; Acts 6:12), or in a cultic setting the broad mass of the people as opposed to the priest

(Heb. 5:3; 7:27), or again, the ordinary people as opposed to the few witnesses of the resurrection (Acts 10:41; 13:31).

2. In keeping with the LXX, Israel is described as the *laos* (e.g., Acts 4:10; 13:17) or "this/these people" (cf. OT quotations in Matt. 13:15 [cf. Isa. 6:10]; Matt. 15:8 [cf. Isa. 29:13]; Acts 28:26–27 [cf. Isa. 6:9–10]). The idea is also alluded to when the high priests, elders, or leaders of the *laos* are referred to (e.g., Matt. 2:4; 21:23; Lk. 19:47; Acts 4:8) and when it is said that Jesus will save his people from their sins (Matt. 1:21), that God has visited his *laos* by sending Jesus (Lk. 7:16; 24:19), or that he will not reject his *laos*, Israel (Rom. 11:1–2; cf. Ps. 94:14). Even an assembled synagogue can be called *laos* (Acts 13:15).

The same line of thought is present when Israel as the *laos* is set over against the Gentiles as *ethnē* (Acts 4:25–27; 26:23; Rom. 15:10). In the first of these, Pilate is identified with the *ethnē*, Herod and Israel with the *laoi*. Frequently qualifying phrases or the context show that *laos* means Israel (e.g., the parallel of "our people" in a list along with "our law" and "this place" in Acts 21:28, or in the comment in 10:2 that the God-fearing Gentile Cornelius had done much good to the *laos*).

3. (a) Finally, the honored title of Israel's being God's *laos* is transferred to the Christian church. God has taken from the *ethnē* a *laos* for his name (Acts 15:14). He has called a church from the Jews and the Gentiles (Rom. 9:24–26). This church (even as a local church, cf. Acts 18:10) is the temple and *laos* of God (2 Cor. 6:14–16, where quotations from Lev. 26:12; Ezek. 37:27 are applied to the Christian church). The description of Israel as "my/his treasured possession" (lit., "a people of my/his possession," Exod. 19:5–6; Deut. 7:6; 14:2) is likewise claimed for the Christian church (Tit. 2:14; 1 Pet. 2:9).

(b) In Heb. esp., the statements of the OT cultus, seen as types of Christ, are transferred to the church. The Son of God is a human being who atones for the sins of the *laos* (Heb. 2:17), which he sanctified with his blood (13:12). The church is the *laos* of God for whom a Sabbath rest remains (4:9). Similarly in Rev. 18:4 (cf. Jer. 51:45) and 21:3 (cf. Ezek. 37:27; Zech. 2:10) OT passages are applied to the church as the new people of God. By faith in Jesus Christ as Lord, the church becomes the people of God, irrespective of the national background of its members (cf. 1 Cor. 12:13; Gal. 3:26–29; Col. 3:11).

(c) That is not to say, of course, that in the NT the church has simply taken the place of Israel as the people of God, as if Israel has lost the priority given to her by God. This is a major problem that Paul wrestles with in Rom. He concludes that Israel remains God's *laos* and has not been rejected by God (cf. Rom. 9–11, esp. 9:4–5; 11:1–2, 25–26, 32).

See also *dēmos*, people, populace, crowd, popular assembly (*1322*); *ethnos*, nation, people, pagans, Gentiles (*1620*); *ochlos*, (throng of) people, crowd, mob (*4063*); *polis*, city, city-state (*4484*).

3301 (latreia, service or worship [of God]), → *3302.*

3302 λατρεύω	λατρεύω (*latreuō*), serve (*3302*); λατρεία (*latreia*), service or wor-

ship (of God) (*3301*); θρῆσκος (*thrēskos*), pious (*2580*); θρησκεία (*thrēskeia*), service of God, religion (*2579*).

CL & OT 1. In cl. Gk. *latreuō* meant to work for wages and then to serve without wages. It was originally used mainly for physical work, but then came to be used more generally and could include cultic service. *latreia* has the same meaning, i.e., work for wages, work, care, service. This word later had a cultic use, honoring of the gods, worship.

2. (a) *latreuō* occurs about 90x in the LXX, esp. in Exod., Deut., Jos., and Jdg. Almost everywhere it translates *'ābad*, serve, esp. where this vb. has a religious reference. Thus in Exod. 4:23; 8:1, 20; 9:1, Moses asks Pharaoh to let the people go that they may serve or "worship" their God. According to the OT, however, what constitutes true worship of the Lord is not primarily meticulously performed cultic

acts but obedience to his voice, in gratitude for what he has done for us in the history of salvation (cf. Deut. 10:12–13).

Hence, in the LXX *latreuō* is close to *leitourgeō* (serve, → *3310*) in meaning, though the latter is used exclusively for the service of the priests, while the former means the service of God by the whole people and by the individual, both outwardly in the cult and inwardly in the heart. The noun *latreia* is found only 9x in the LXX; with the exception of 3 Macc. 4:14 (where it means forced labor) it is used in the same way as the vb. In Exod. 12:25–26; 13:5 it refers to the sacred custom of the Passover (see also Jos. 22:27; 1 Chr. 28:13; 1 Macc. 1:43; 2:19, 22).

(b) As in the OT, Jewish writings express the relationship of humanity to God as service. Humans are servants or slaves of God. Thus, *ʿābad* and its derivatives can denote worship of the true God or of false gods. The meaning of worship has been perpetuated in the synagogue. But it is used also of the inner worship of the heart: With reference to Deut. 11:13 and Dan. 6:11, 16, it is said that to serve the Lord means prayer.

NT 1. (a) *latreuō* occurs 21x in the NT, all in a religious sense (e.g., Matt. 4:10; Lk. 4:8; Acts 7:7), including the worship of strange gods (Acts 7:42; Rom. 1:25). Its use throughout the NT is fixed by the OT. This is true of passages such as Lk. 1:74; 2:37 and those where the God of the fathers is mentioned, whom Paul (Acts 24:14) or the twelve tribes (26:6–7) worship. But by and large *latreuō* has lost its cultic connotation in favor of that of the inner worship of the heart by faith (cf. 24:14b) and prayer.

(b) Heb. shows the closest links with the OT. Of its six uses, four refer to worship in the temple/tabernacle (8:5; 9:9; 10:2; 13:10). There is no need, however, to restrict these passages to the priest's vicarious acts for the people in the sacrificial worship, for the people are included in the worship. Heb. 9:14; 12:28 emphasize that only the conscience that has been cleansed and brought to life by Christ, only the one who has been received into the true and eternal community of God, can worship God acceptably "with reverence and awe."

(c) When Paul wants to describe the Christian's daily walk with God, he uses *latreia* ("spiritual act of worship" in Rom. 12:1) and says of himself that he serves (*latreuō*) God with his whole heart as he preaches the gospel (1:9). Similarly in Phil. 3:3, he writes of those "who worship by the Spirit of God" or "who worship God in spirit." These passages give clear expression to Jesus' statement that true and genuine worship must be in Spirit and through the Spirit, for God himself is Spirit (Jn. 4:23–24; *proskyneō* is used 4x here for worship, → *4686*). Such worship is freed from all the restrictions of cultic rules, circumcision, and the struggle to attain righteousness through works. Those who have been reconciled and renewed carry out their worship of God through the Spirit by presenting their whole being to God.

2. *latreia*, apart from Rom. 12:1 (see above), is found only 4x more in the NT. In Rom. 9:4, Heb. 9:1, 6 it refers to OT cultic acts; in Jn. 16:2 it expresses the service that those who hate the gospel think they bring God whenever they persecute Christ's witnesses.

3. There is little difference between *latreia* and *thrēskeia*, which means worship of God (Jas. 1:26–27), worship of angels (Col. 2:18), and religion in general (Acts 26:5). Correspondingly the adj. *thrēskos* (Jas. 1:26) can be rendered pious or "religious."

See also *diakoneō*, serve, support, serve as a deacon (*1354*); *leitourgeō*, serve (*3310*).

| 3303 | λάχανον |

λάχανον (*lachanon*), herb, vegetable (*3303*); βοτάνη (*botanē*), plant (*1083*); ἄνηθον (*anēthon*), dill (*464*); ἡδύοσμον (*hēdyosmon*), mint (*2455*); κύμινον (*kyminon*), cummin (*3248*); πήγανον (*pēganon*), rue (*4379*).

CL & OT In cl. Gk. *lachanon* denotes garden herbs and vegetables as opposed to wild plants. *botanē* is used of pasture, herbs, weeds; *anēthon* means dill; *hēdyosmon* (this word lit. means sweet smell) is

mint; *kyminon* is cummin, an aromatic seed grown for flavoring dishes; and *pēganon* is rue, a culinary and medicinal herb.

Three of the above terms appear in the LXX, but with one exception only in the lit. sense. *lachanon* stands for edible herbs and vegetables (Gen. 9:3; Ps. 37:2). *botanē* means grass (Gen. 1:11; Jer. 14:5) or herbage in general (Exod. 9:22; Job 8:12). *kyminon* occurs in Isa. 28:25, 27.

NT 1. In the NT *lachanon* is consistently used for herbs (Lk. 11:42) and *chortos* for grass (Matt. 14:19) or the early grasslike blades of crops (13:26). Jesus deplores the Pharisees' concern for tithing insignificant herbs (*lachanon*) like mint (*hēdyosmon*), rue (*pēganon*), dill (*anēthon*), and cummin (*kyminon*), while neglecting the more important matters of the law (Matt. 23:23; Lk. 11:42).

2. In Rom. 14:2 Paul refers to certain converts from Jud. eating only vegetables (*lachanon*) because their feeble grasp of Christian liberty keeps them from disregarding either Jewish dietary laws or the possibility that meat sold in the marketplace has been associated with pagan sacrifices. In Heb. 6:7 responsive believers are compared to fertile land that produces good crops (*botanē*).

3306 (*legō*, collect, count, say), → *3364*.

3307 (*leimma*, remnant), → *3309*.

| 3309 | λείπω |

λείπω (*leipō*), leave, leave behind, lack (*3309*); λοιπός (*loipos*), remaining, other (*3370*); λεῖμμα (*leimma*), remnant (*3307*); καταλείπω (*kataleipō*), leave, leave behind, leave over (*2901*); περιλείπομαι (*perileipomai*), survive, leave behind (*4335*); ὑπόλειμμα (*hypoleimma*), remnant (*5698*); ὑπολείπω (*hypoleipō*), to be left remaining (*5699*); διαλείπω (*dialeipō*), to leave off, cease (*1364*); κατάλοιπος (*kataloipos*), the rest (*2905*); ἐγκαταλείπω (*enkataleipō*), abandon, desert (*1593*).

CL & OT 1. In cl. Gk. *leipō* means to leave, leave behind, leave over. As an intrans. act., it can assume the meaning of to be lacking. The compound *kataleipō* means to leave behind, leave remaining; *perileipomai*, to survive. Later derivatives are the adjs. *loipos*, remaining, and *kataloipos*, left over. The rare nouns *leimma* and *kataleimma* mean remnant, residue. Neither vbs. nor nouns acquired any special nuance or religious meaning.

2. (a) In the LXX *leipō* and its derivatives denote what is left or remains. The noun *leimma* occurs only once (2 Ki. 19:4), meaning remnant. The vb. *leipō* occurs 8x, and the adj. *loipos* more than 120x. Most frequent is *kataleipō* (300x), meaning to be left, to forsake. The adj. *kataloipos* usually means remnant (cf. Amos 9:12, quoted in Acts 15:17); the noun *kataleimma* (21x) also means remnant. *enkataleipō* (over 150x) can simply mean leave (2 Ki. 2:2, 4, 6), but also desert, abandon (tents, 7:7; God deserting his people, Neh. 9:17, 19, 28, 31). In a number of cases, God is praised for not abandoning his people (Ps. 9:10; 16:10; 37:25, 28) or, conversely, petitioned to show his care for those who feel abandoned (22:1 [see below]; 27:9; 71:9, 18). Less frequent is *hypoleimma*, remnant (9x).

(b) In general most of the words of this group describe a total destruction of things with nothing remaining (e.g., Exod. 10:15, 19) or refer to a remnant that survives (e.g., Isa. 10:19, where only a few forest trees remain; 44:17, 19, where what is left of a tree is fashioned into an idol).

(c) The terms "remnant" and "survive" describe the activity of Yahweh in preserving what he has created. Thus in the flood story we find the words: "Only Noah was left [*kataleipō*], and those with him in the ark" (Gen. 7:23). In 1 Ki. 19:18 it refers to the preserving activity of Yahweh in his promise to Elijah: "I reserve [*kataleipō*] seven thousand in Israel—all whose knees have not bowed down to Baal and all whose mouths have not kissed him."

3. (a) The first explicit mention of the idea of a remnant of Israel occurs in the early prophets. In Amos 5:15 the prophet says that

"perhaps the LORD God Almighty will have mercy on the remnant of Joseph." In Isa. the military concept of a remnant is given a theological content. In the context of the prophet's exhortation to King Ahaz not to be afraid (cf. Isa. 30:15) but to trust in Yahweh, we find reference to the prophet's son Shear-Jashub, meaning "a remnant will return" (7:3). The object of Isa.'s exhortation is to save God's people from a catastrophe in which, while they will not be totally destroyed, only a remnant will survive. Here the concept of the remnant serves to underline and confirm the dreadfulness of the catastrophe.

(b) During the time of the catastrophic downfall of the southern kingdom in 597 and 587 B.C., there is no mention of a remnant remaining in the land of Israel who could maintain the hope of a new beginning. Jer. testifies that Yahweh will let Judah be annihilated (19:11). He compares those who have been left in the land under Zedekiah to bad figs (24:8). The remnant of Judah under Gedaliah forfeits the possibility of remaining in the land when Gedaliah is murdered by Ishmael (40:11–41:3).

In Ezek., the concept of the remnant is either excluded (9:8; 11:13; 17:21) or used in an entirely different way. There is a remnant remaining in Jerusalem after the judgments of Yahweh, but the only purpose is to bring home to the exiles proof of the massive destruction of Jerusalem and its inhabitants. For Jer. and Ezek. alike, the true remnant is represented by the exiles, i.e., by those who survive the catastrophe through deportation. They are the ones, according to Ezek., to whom God appears.

(c) It was during the exile that the concept of the remnant acquired a fixed theological content, namely, the hope of Yahweh's preserving and saving work. Behind this was the discovery that, although in the national catastrophe Yahweh had executed a terrible judgment, even this judgment was limited by his will to maintain and preserve his people. We have a witness to this hope in Isa. 46:3–4, when Yahweh addresses the exiles as "you who remain of the house of Israel," whom he will "sustain," "carry," and "rescue." In the second half of Isa. we also find the concept of a remnant applied to the "fugitives from the nations" (45:20) who, embarrassed as a result of their idolatry, "take counsel together" before Yahweh (45:21).

(d) In the late exilic and postexilic periods, when the temple is rebuilt by the returned exiles, the concept of the remnant gains increasingly in importance (cf. Mic. 2:12–13; 5:7–8; 7:18; Zeph. 2:7, 9). In Obad. 17 we find the concept of the remnant linked with the hope for Jerusalem or Zion, and Zech. announces the return of Yahweh to Zion and awakes in the survivors the hope of the preservation of Jerusalem (8:3, 6, 11–12).

(e) In Joel 2:32 the concept of the remnant is linked to Zion. In the books of Ezr. and Neh. the idea of the remnant is applied several times to the exiles who have returned (Ezr. 9:8, 15; Neh. 1:2–3). The latter chapters of Zech. speak of a remnant that will be purified (13:8–9) and that will survive when the nations assemble to fight against Jerusalem (14:2, linked with apocalyptic ideas about the day of the Lord).

4. (a) In extracanonical apocalyptic writings, the remnant concept is occasionally applied to the whole creation: "And now, my son, arise and make a petition to the Lord of glory, since you are a believer, that a remnant may remain on the earth, and that he may not destroy the whole world" (*1 Enoch* 83:8). More frequent are the remnant sayings that refer to Israel or the synagogue: 2 Esd. 9:7–8 refers to "my salvation in my land and within my borders" in connection with those who have been saved (cf. 12:34; 13:48).

(b) The linking of the remnant concept to Israel led, in Palestinian Jud., to the making of exclusive claims for particular groups and consequently to an intensification of the idea. The Qumran community, for instance, saw in itself the holy remnant promised in the OT (CD 1:4–5), enjoying God's assistance (1QM 13:8; 14:8–9), while their enemies were utterly destroyed (1:6; 4:2; 14:5). Likewise, the Pharisees attempted, by voluntary submission to priestly ordinances regarding cleansing, to set themselves up as the holy remnant.

(c) In rab. Jud. the primary condition for belonging to the remnant was observance of the Torah. Those who survive will return to Zion, and those who have kept the Torah will remain in Jerusalem.

NT 1. In the NT the noun *leimma*, remnant, is found only once (Rom. 11:5), and the vb. *leipō*, to lack, be in want of, 6x (Lk. 18:22; Tit. 1:5; 3:13; Jas. 1:4–5; 2:15). The adj. *loipos*, remaining, other (mostly in the pl.) or adverbially ("finally"), occurs 55x—occasionally with a critical undertone, when it refers to those who are hardened (Lk. 8:10; Rom. 11:7), who do not believe (Mk. 16:13; 1 Thess. 4:13), who act as hypocrites (Gal. 2:13), or who do not repent (Rev. 9:20). *perileipomai* occurs 2x, both references to those who are left alive at the coming of the Lord (1 Thess. 4:15, 17).

As in the LXX, the most common compound is *kataleipō*, again with various meanings, such as to leave (a region, Matt. 4:13; father and mother, 19:5; cf. Gen. 2:24; possessions, Lk. 5:28), fall behind, neglect (Acts 6:2), and leave behind (someone, e.g., 18:19). The following appear once each: *kataloipos*, the rest (Acts 15:17; cf. Amos 9:12); *dialeipō*, to leave off, cease (Lk. 7:45); *hypoleipō*, to be left remaining (Rom. 11:3; cf. 1 Ki. 19:10, 14); and *hypoleimma*, remnant (Rom. 9:27; cf. Isa. 10:22).

2. (a) In the NT, the OT remnant concept is taken up only in Rom. 9–11. Here Paul deals with the fact that the majority of Jews refuse to believe in Christ. Indeed, a central theme of Rom. is the question of the standing of the Jewish people in relation to salvation in Christ alone. Rom. 1–8 deals with the basis of salvation, showing that the OT anticipates the way of salvation in Christ, while 9–11 deals with the position of the Jews as God's chosen people in the light of their rejection of Christ and God's overall purposes. What attitude should the early church, composed as it is of both Gentile and Jewish Christians, adopt toward this fact? Does this rejection of Christ mean that Israel's election no longer applies? Paul holds on to the special position of Israel among the nations. This special position, however, is based on God's free elective grace (9:11; 11:5), as is the calling of Gentiles into the community of the new people of God (9:24).

To show that the Gentiles are accepted as children of God, Paul cites Hos. 2:23 and 1:10 (Rom. 9:25–26). This is followed immediately (9:27) by the warning of Isa. 10:22–23, which speaks of the decimation of Israel down to a remnant that repents; but like the LXX, Paul does not say that "the remnant will return," but rather, "the remnant will be saved." In Rom. 9:29 Paul adds a citation of Isa. 1:9, where the LXX has already introduced a greater note of hope: for the Heb. *śārîd*, remnant (NIV "survivors"), both the LXX and Paul have *sperma* (lit., "seed," i.e., descendants).

This combination of OT citations displays clearly the direction of Paul's reinterpretation of the remnant. In setting a reference to the remnant of Israel alongside the prophecy of the Gentiles' acceptance as the children of God, Paul is altering the status of the former. The remnant in OT prophecy merges into the new people of God, constituted on the basis of faith in Christ. The remnant of Israel is not eliminated, but it stands alongside those Gentiles, who are called to be members of God's new people. The remnant (Isa. 1:9 MT), or the descendants (Isa. 1:9 LXX), are those whom God has called, together with the Gentiles, into the church of Christ.

In Rom. 11:3–5, the concept of the remnant is introduced by a reference to Elijah's complaint on Mount Horeb (1 Ki. 19:10) and Yahweh's reply (19:18). Paul uses this reference as evidence that God has not rejected Israel. The "remnant chosen by grace" is, however, based not on Israel's efforts, but on God's set purpose (Rom. 11:5), and it is characterized by faith in Christ. Paul's hope is that through this remnant, and through the Gentile Christians who with them form the church, the "fullness" (*plērōma*, Rom. 11:12; → *plēroō*, *4444*) of Israel can be won for Christ. Thus in the remnant of Israel, which confesses faith in Christ, there is a new beginning for all Israel. This remnant is a challenge to all the Jews.

(b) Paul uses the adj. *loipos*, remaining, 2x of those who mourn because they have no hope (1 Thess. 4:13) or those who are asleep in the sense that they are not expecting the Parousia (5:6). In Rom. 1:13 it is used of other nations, or Gentiles, in contrast to those being addressed in the letter, and in Gal. 2:13 it refers to other Jewish Christians who joined Peter in acting hypocritically in separating themselves from eating with Gentiles in Antioch. Otherwise Paul uses the adj. without any specialized meaning, like other NT writers.

loipos is used adverbially in various expressions of time: *(to) loipon*, from now on, henceforth (1 Cor. 7:29; 2 Tim. 4:8) or finally (Acts 27:20; 1 Cor. 1:16; Phil. 3:1; 4:8); *tou loipou*, from now on, in the future, finally (Gal. 6:17; Eph. 6:10).

3. In the Synoptics the adj. *loipos* sometimes describes those outside the rule of God. Thus in the parable of the royal wedding feast (Matt. 22:1–13), the pl. refers to "the rest" (22:6) who mock and kill the servants sent by the king to invite them; in 25:1–12 it refers to "the others [virgins]" (25:11), those excluded from the wedding feast. Jesus' cry of derelction from the cross is received by "the rest" with the words: "Now leave him alone. Let's see if Elijah comes to save him" (27:49). In Lk. 8:10 the "others" (those outside the band of the disciples, who do not understand the parables because they are hardened; cf. Rom. 11:7) stand in contrast with the disciples. The parable of the Pharisee and the publican (Lk. 18:9–14) is addressed to those who, in their own faithful observance of the law, despise "everybody else" (18:9; cf. "other men" used by the Pharisee, 18:11).

4. The vb. *leipō* occurs in Lk. 18:22 of the decisive shortcoming that hinders the rich man from the life of discipleship, namely, his riches: "You still lack [*leipō*] one thing. Sell everything you have and give to the poor, and you will have treasure in heaven. Then come, follow me." In Jas. 1:4–5 and 2:15 the vb. means to lack, have need of (cf. Tit. 3:13). In Tit. 1:5 it is used of the defects that Titus is to amend in the church in Crete.

5. (a) *enkataleipō* is used in Ps. 22:1, which Jesus quotes in his cry from the cross, "My God, my God, why have you forsaken me?" (Matt. 27:46; Mk. 15:34). The theological issue of how Jesus, who was both Son of God and God himself, could be forsaken by God is not directly addressed in the NT. Suffice it to say that through this cry, accompanied by the three hours of darkness, Jesus was suffering the ultimate punishment of sin. Some scholars think that while on the cross, Jesus may have quoted the entire psalm, which contains several messianic prophecies. If so, note that the psalm ends with a message of triumph.

(b) *enkataleipō* also occurs in Ps. 16:10, where David expresses the assurance that God will not leave his soul in Sheol. Peter sees in this verse a prophecy of the resurrection of Jesus; he notes that David remains buried in Jerusalem, but Jesus' body did not stay in the grave but was raised from the dead (Acts 2:27–31).

(c) This same vb. also occurs in Deut. 31:6, where God promises never to leave or forsake his people as they conquer the promised land. Heb. applies this same promise to Christians who are undergoing persecution for their faith (13:6). This same writer also encourages believers not to "give up meeting together," even though such meetings might expose them to danger (10:25).

6. In Rev. the adj. *loipos* is found 8x; in two cases it has a meaning reminiscent of the remnant idea. In 11:13 we read of the "survivors" of the judgment on the city who give glory to God; in 12:17 it is used in the context of the war waged by the dragon on the "rest" of the woman's offspring, "who obey God's commandments and hold to the testimony to Jesus" and against whom both the beasts fight (ch. 13). Although it is possible to see behind these sayings a wealth of Jewish apocalyptic material, these references are not to the remnant in the sense of a new beginning.

3310	λειτουργέω

λειτουργέω (*leitourgeō*), serve (*3310*); λειτουργία (*leitourgia*), service (*3311*); λειτουργός (*leitourgos*), servant (*3313*); λειτουργικός (*leitourgikos*), serving (*3312*).

CL & OT 1. (a) In cl. Gk. *leitourgeō* meant do public work at one's own expense. It was a political, almost legal, concept. *leitourgia* similarly meant service for the people. In the later cl. period it was as common a term as "taxes" today. We seldom find the noun *leitourgos* in cl. Gk.; where it does occur it usually means an artisan.

(b) In Hel. Gk. *leitourgeō* covers all kinds of service to the community that a person had to do because of the size of his income, though it could also be carried out voluntarily. The concept gradually expanded, esp. in Egypt, to cover every conceivable compulsory service for the state, often regulated by specific rules. Then it widened further to cover any sort of service. Beside this legal meaning in public life, there developed an entirely new, religious, and cultic use of the words.

2. (a) In the LXX *leitourgeō* occurs about 100x and *leitourgia* about 40x. They are used almost exclusively for the service of priests and Levites in the temple and occur esp. in those sections that describe priestly functions and ritual (e.g., Exod. 28–39; Num. 1–4; 8; 1 Chr. 23; Ezek. 40–46). These words were esp. suited for expressing the cultic service since the activities of the priests were public, fixed, and regulated by law, and the welfare of God's people depended on it. The LXX also used these words for heathen cultic worship (e.g., Ezek. 44:12).

(b) In intertestamental Jud., esp. as it was developed in the synagogue and in the Diaspora, we find a gradual spiritualizing of this concept of service, most notably in the interpretation of prayer as "sacrifice" (cf. Wis. 18:21).

NT 1. In the NT *leitourgeō* occurs only 3x, *leitourgia* 6x, *leitourgos* 5x, and *leitourgikos* only once. In Heb. and in some passages in Paul and Lk., the word group is used in its cultic-sacred sense. (a) In Lk. 1:23, *leitourgia* is used lit. for Zechariah's priestly service in the temple.

(b) Heb. seeks to make clear the unique meaning of the cross and exaltation by using the cultic concepts of the OT. In 8:2 Christ, as *leitourgos*, exercises the service of the high priest in the true, heavenly sanctuary. There he is the one, true high priest, who has obtained a superior "ministry" (8:6, *leitourgia*). Christ has accomplished through his suffering and death the one eternally valid sacrifice (cf. 10:10); by so doing he has shown that through the daily performance of the religious duties of the priest (10:11), no sins can be taken away. We find *leitourgia* again in 9:21 in reference to the OT cultic "ceremonies."

(c) Rom. 15:16 also presupposes cultic usage. Paul justifies the boldness of what he has written by pointing to the fact that by the grace of God, he had become Christ's *leitourgos* (i.e., minister) to the Gentiles, "with the priestly duty of proclaiming the gospel of God" so that the converted Gentiles may be brought as a sacrifice to God. By this Paul expresses not only his complete dedication to and dependence on God; he also redefines the nature of sacrifice and priestly service in terms of the gospel and its service and fruit. We should also add Phil. 2:17 here, where Paul sees himself as the messenger of Christ performing the "service" (*leitourgia*) of offering up the obedient faith of the Philippians to God. His own self-giving in martyrdom is seen as a libation on the sacrificial offering of their faith.

2. The use of *leitourgeō* in Acts 13:2 has a meaning derived from the LXX. Here the cultic meaning is spiritualized and applied to Christian worship in prayer.

3. There is no consensus as to how *leitourgeō* in Rom. 15:27 and *leitourgia* in 2 Cor. 9:12 are to be understood. Some commentators see the cultic use here also, so that the words denote the loving service in the collection for Jerusalem. If so, then Paul is stressing that this project is a religious service to God. Others interpret the words in terms of the cl. Gk. usage, which makes the collection the official and public aid to the Jerusalem community. We can no longer be certain whether Paul implied anything beyond general service in his use of these words. Note that in both Rom. 15 and 2 Cor. 8–9 this word group and the *diakoneō* word group (to serve, → *1354*) stand parallel.

4. Clearly there is no cultic background to the use of the *leitourgeō* word group in Phil. 2:25, 30. Epaphroditus had become a *leitourgos* (2:25), helper, when he served Paul during his hour of need. He rendered to Paul the "help" (*leitourgia*) that the church in Philippi, owing to circumstances, was unable to render (2:30). Similarly in Rom. 13:6, political authorities are God's "servants" (*leitourgos*); in 13:4 Paul uses the word *diakonos* for the same concept; no priestly functions are ascribed to the state.

In Heb. 1:7 *leitourgos* also lacks cultic connotation. Citing Ps. 104:4, this passage calls angels "servants"; in 1:14 they are called "ministering [*leitourgikos*] spirits." The angels stand in contrast to the immutability of Christ (1:8–9), for their form and function are controlled by God.

See also *diakoneō*, serve, support, serve as a deacon (*1354*); *latreuō*, serve (*3302*).

3311 (*leitourgia*, service), → *3310*.

3312 (*leitourgikos*, serving), → *3310*.

3313 (*leitourgos*, servant), → *3310*.

3319 (*lepra*, leprosy), → *3320*.

3320	λεπρός

λεπρός (*lepros*), leprous, chiefly used as a noun describing a leper (*3320*); λέπρα (*lepra*), leprosy (*3319*).

CL & OT 1. Cl. writers used *lepros* to describe anything rough, scabby, or scaly, including items made from roughly textured animal skins or hides. Hippocrates used the word to describe a leprous person, i.e., someone with a scaly skin affliction such as psoriasis. In Herodotus and the medical authors, *lepra* was a disease that gave a scaly or uneven texture to the skin. Another use of the word was for a whitish spot on the skin, the result of loss of pigmentation. The Gk. medical authors used the term *elephas* to describe a different and much more serious chronic disorder, which was found frequently in Egypt, the symptoms of which corresponded largely to those now associated with clinical leprosy.

2. (a) *lepros* occurs in the LXX in Lev. 13:44–45; 14:2–3; 22:4; Num. 5:2, etc. as a skin disease. It could describe any kind of skin eruption, of which clinical leprosy (Hansen's disease) was one form. Note that the instructions given in Lev. 13 to the priests to enable them to detect leprosy also suggest that skin afflictions other than clinical leprosy may be present. In other words, *lepros* was sufficiently flexible to include common dermatological conditions as *impetigo, psoriasis, eczema,* and *acne vulgaris.*

The Heb. *ṣāraʿat*, traditionally translated "leprosy," is an eruptive condition (forms of fungus or molds) that can appear on leather (Lev. 14:55), clothing (13:47, 59), and the walls of houses (14:44), in addition to human beings. Because of this variety of nuances, the ancient Heb. technical terms are difficult to understand.

(b) Preliminary symptoms of human *ṣāraʿat* included a swelling, a localized tissue crust on the epidermis, and a whitish-red swollen spot. Since any or all of these could presage clinical leprosy, sufferers had to present themselves to the priest for examination. If subcutaneous penetration was exhibited along with a whitening of the small local cuticular hairs, a malignant state was suspected and the patient was declared unclean. But if the skin tissue, while swollen, was not actually inflamed (13:4) or the hair discolored, the patient was quarantined for seven days. If on reexamination the swollen area of the whitish spot had not increased in size, a further seven days' quarantine could be followed by a priestly diagnosis of a benign skin condition.

If, however, there was a spreading of the eruption in the skin, it was diagnosed as leprosy (Lev. 13:8). A chronic state of leprosy was indicated by depigmented hairs and ulcerated tissue in an area of swollen white skin, rendering the sufferer unclean. But if the whole body was covered with patches of depigmented skin, the individual

who manifested this condition was pronounced clean (13:13). Differential diagnosis turned on the degree of cutaneous penetration of the disease. Scalp disease was treated in the same manner as other forms of skin eruptions, so that an itchy condition such as ringworm could be differentiated from more serious cutaneous diseases.

3. The development of Hansen's disease may exhibit three forms. (a) The nodular type produces lumps in the facial tissues and a form of cutaneous induration that results in a characteristic scabby appearance. Degenerative changes also occur in nose and throat membranes. (b) An anaesthetic variety attacks the nerves of the skin, producing depigmented areas in which there is no feeling. Blisters and ulcers frequently form on these patches, and it is common for the extremities of the arms and legs to be affected. In such cases necrosis occurs and the diseased part is rejected by the body, leaving a well-healed stump. (c) A third form of leprosy combines the symptoms of the first two kinds in varying degrees and is chronic in nature.

NT 1. *lepros* occurs 9x in the NT. Jesus heals lepers in Matt. 11:5; Mk. 1:40–42; Lk. 7:22; 17:12. Lk. 4:27 cited the OT miracle whereby Elisha healed the leprosy of Naaman (2 Kings 5:1–14). *lepros* was also used of Simon, formerly a leper, in Matt. 26:6; Mk. 14:3. This word was used in as broad a sense as its OT counterpart, and the fact that some clinical manifestations called for a priestly declaration of cleanness implies that the conditions described by *lepros* varied in severity.

2. *lepra* occurs 4x, only in passages apparently describing the same incident (Matt. 8:3; Mk. 1:42; Lk. 5:12–13). Lk. noted the advanced nature of the condition, but apart from this it is not easy to determine its true nature. The sufferer seems to have been moving around in society to some extent, although the possibility of an advanced case of clinical leprosy should not be discounted.

3321	λεπτός

λεπτός (*leptos*), small copper coin (*3321*).

CL & OT In cl. Gk. *leptos* means thin, slender, small, or delicate. In the LXX this word was used for the thin, emaciated cows that Pharaoh saw in his dream (Gen. 41). It was also used to describe the "thin" flakes of manna (Exod. 16:14). The word occurs frequently in connection with idolatry. Moses ground the golden calf "to powder" and threw the particles into the Israelites' drinking water (32:20; Deut. 9:21). Josiah did the same thing with the idols of his predecessors (2 Chr. 34:7). Isa. prophesies a day in which idols will be broken into pieces and ground to fine powder (27:9; 30:14, 22).

NT Coins were frequently minted and used throughout the Roman empire. In general Jews did not object to using coins with figures on them for secular purposes, provided that these symbols were inoffensive to Jewish sensibilities. Herod Archelaus (4 B.C.–A.D. 6), for example, introduced the grape cluster and the tall, double-crested helmet. Symbols on *lepta* employed by Roman governors were wheat ears or barley, palm branches, or palm trees. Pilate aroused considerable resentment when he tried to employ such cultic implements as an augur's wand or a *simpulum* (a type of ladle used in connection with Roman sacrifice). When Herod Agrippa I was installed as king (A.D. 37–44), he reverted to inoffensive types, such as triple ears of wheat.

While coins with pagan symbols would never have been allowed for use in worship in the temple, *lepta* with nondescript images seem to have been permitted. The most notable example of bronze coinage presented in the temple treasury is the contribution of two *lepta*, placed in the offering box, by a poor widow whom Christ commended (Mk. 12:42; Lk. 21:2). These coins may have been those from Roman government officials, though they may have gone back to the days of the Hasmoneans (e.g., John Hyrcanus II), which are common in Jewish burial sites throughout Israel even to this day. The *lepton* is also mentioned at Lk. 12:59, where Jesus warns the crowd to seek reconciliation with an adversary, lest they be thrown into prison by the magistrate: "You will not get out until you have paid the last penny" (the par. Matt. 5:26 has *kodrantēs*, the Roman quadrans).

3322 Λευί

Λευί (*Leui*), Levi (*3322*); Λευίτης (*Leuitēs*), Levite (*3324*); Λευιτικός (*Leuitikos*), Levitical (*3325*).

OT A Levite was any descendant of Jacob's third son, Levi (Gen. 29:34), but the term is seldom so used in OT. Normally it refers to the male descendants of Levi apart from the priests, the descendants of Aaron—i.e., to those entitled to serve in the sanctuary in a subordinate role.

In the course of time the Levites diminished in importance, largely for economic reasons. Num. 18:21, 24 gave the whole tithe to the Levites, who were expected to give a tithe (tenth) of it to the priests (18:26–32). It seems clear that as the priestly clans multiplied, the Levites were squeezed out of the more important roles, esp. after Josiah's reform, and did not continue to receive their share of the tithe. Thus few Levites returned from Babylonia with Zerubbabel and Jeshua (cf. Ezr. 2:40 with 2:36–39). In fact, Ezra had great difficulty in persuading any to accompany him (8:15–20).

Nehemiah restored the tithe position (Neh. 10:37–38), but later Josephus suggests that they were again taken from the Levites in favor of the priests. This is confirmed in rab. sources. The teaching function of the Levites was largely taken over by the scribes. Moreover, the lower ranks of temple servants gradually obtained the right to call themselves Levites. This helps explain the rarity of their mention in the NT.

NT 1. Levi occurs as a proper name 8x in the NT: the son of Jacob (Heb. 7:5, 9; Rev. 7:7); two ancestors of Jesus (Lk. 3:24, 29); and a son of Alphaeus, presumably Matthew (Mk. 2:14; Lk. 5:27, 29).

2. Levites are referred to 3x in the NT. (a) The leading Pharisees in Jerusalem ("the Jews") sent priests and Levites to question John the Baptist (Jn. 1:19). The choice was probably motivated by the fact that the tribe of Levi historically had the divinely given privilege of teaching (Deut. 33:10).

(b) A priest and a Levite are linked in the parable of the Good Samaritan (Lk. 10:31–32). Neither paid much attention to the wounded traveler.

(c) Barnabas, a native of Cyprus, was a Levite (Acts 4:36). It is impossible to establish whether he ever functioned in the Jerusalem temple.

3. Heb. 7:11a uses the expression "the Levitical priesthood." It stresses that the priests were of the tribe of Levi, unlike the priest forever "in the order of Melchizedek," who was of the tribe of Judah (7:11b–17). The fact that Melchizedek received offerings from Abraham and that Levi, at the time, could be said to be "in the body of his ancestor" Abraham (7:10) demonstrates the superiority of the Melchizedekian priesthood (which climaxed in Christ) to the Levitical.

3324 (Leuitēs, Levite), → 3322.

3325 (Leuitikos, Levitical), → 3322.

3328 λευκός

λευκός (*leukos*), white (*3328*); κονιάω (*koniaō*), whitewash (*3154*).

CL & OT *leukos* means light, bright, clear, white. In the LXX it means the color white (Gen. 49:12; Zech. 1:8), though it may include half-yellow. White is the color of God himself (Dan. 7:9). It also symbolizes the state of being purified from the defilement of sin (cf. *leukainō* in Ps. 51:7; Isa. 1:18). Thus, the priest's linen clothing is white. From the 1st cent. A.D. on, the dead were buried in white linen. This may be connected with the imagery of the garments of glory worn by the saints in their transfigured state (*1 Enoch* 62:14–16). On a negative note, white is also used in the diagnosis of leprosy (Lev. 13).

NT *leukos* occurs only in the Gospels, Acts, and Rev. It is used of the yellowish-white, ripe corn ready for harvest (Jn. 4:35), in a context that suggests that the eschatological harvest is at hand and the disciples are now being sent out as reapers (cf. Matt. 9:37).

White is an eschatological color in various other contexts, esp. in the description of garments. In the transfiguration of Jesus, his garments appeared brilliantly white (Matt. 17:2; Mk. 9:3; Lk. 9:29). So too was the appearance of the angels at the tomb (Matt. 28:3; Mk. 16:5; Jn. 20:12; cf. Lk. 24:4), and of the two men who addressed the disciples after Jesus had ascended (Acts 1:10).

White is also the color of the garments of the saints in the afterlife (Rev. 3:4–5, 18; 4:4; 6:11; 7:9, 13; 19:14). Here white is associated with eschatological and transcendent existence, not with Godhead as such. However, the throne of God is white (20:11), and in an earlier vision John has seen "one 'like a son of man'" seated on a white cloud, wearing a golden crown, and bearing a sharp sickle (14:14). The glorified Christ appeared with white hair like wool and snow (1:14), associating the risen Christ with the "Ancient of Days" (Dan. 7:9). Since white is the color of God himself, the white garments of the saints symbolize the holiness and purity that only God bestows. In keeping with this, the glorified Christ who comes in judgment is seen riding "a white horse" (Rev. 19:11), and the armies of heaven who follow him are clad in "fine linen, white and clean," riding "white horses" (19:14).

In the letter to the church at Pergamum, those who overcome are promised "hidden manna" and "a white stone with a new name written on it, known only to him who receives it" (Rev. 2:17). Various images may lie behind this. The white stone was used by Gk. jurors to signify acquittal. A rab. tradition taught that precious stones fell along with the manna in the desert. The tribes of Israel were represented by precious stones in the high priest's breastplate (Exod. 28:15–21). Perhaps John is combining some of these ideas with that of confessing the name of Christ as Lord (cf. Matt. 10:32; Mk. 8:38; Lk. 12:8; Rom. 10:9–13; 1 Cor. 12:3; Phil. 2:11).

All of this stands in contrast with the vb. *koniaō*, whitewash, which is used of the tombs that were whitewashed annually before the Passover, lest pilgrims inadvertently tread on them and so become defiled (Matt. 23:27; cf. Lk. 11:44). Jesus denounced the teachers of the law and the Pharisees as hypocrites, being "like whitewashed tombs, which look beautiful on the outside but on the inside are full of dead men's bones and everything unclean" (Matt. 23:27). Similarly, Paul denounced Ananias as a "whitewashed wall" (Acts 23:3, perhaps combining the idea of a tomb built into a wall and that of the whitewashed fragile wall in Ezek. 13:10–16).

3334 λῃστής

λῃστής (*lēstēs*), robber, highwayman, bandit, revolutionary (*3334*); κλέπτω (*kleptō*), steal (*3096*); κλέπτης (*kleptēs*), thief (*3095*).

CL & OT 1. In cl. Gk. *kleptō* emphasizes the secrecy, craft, and cheating involved in the act of stealing or embezzlement. By contrast, *lēstēs* includes the element of violence, though not necessarily of dishonesty: a soldier exercising his right to seize plunder can be termed *lēstēs*. The word usually meant robber, bandit, pirate.

2. In the LXX *kleptō* includes the sense of stealth. Theft is a sin against God, as is stated in the Decalogue (Exod. 20:15 = LXX 20:14; Deut. 5:19) and its echoes (Lev. 19:11; Jer. 7:9). What is stolen may include objects of value (Gen. 44:5; Exod. 22:6 = LXX 22:7), animals (Gen. 30:33), humans (40:15; Exod. 21:16 = LXX 21:17), things devoted to God (Jos. 7:11), household gods (Gen. 31:19), and genuine words of God, stolen by false prophets (Jer. 23:30). To be guilty of theft incurs punishment (Exod. 22:1–2; Deut. 24:7). Even when prompted by need or poverty, stealing dishonors God (Prov. 30:9 = LXX 24:32; cf. 6:30).

The noun *lēstēs*, which seldom occurs in the LXX, translates three Heb. words, all associated with violence (see Jer. 7:11; 18:22; Obad. 5). By referring to both bandits and Zealots as *lēstai*, Josephus and the rabbis reveal their opposition to the methods employed by these nationalists.

NT 1. The requirements of the Decalogue, including "do not steal" (*kleptō*), still apply in the Christian era. Jesus quotes this command to the rich young ruler (Matt. 19:18; Mk. 10:19; Lk. 18:20), as does Paul in Rom. 13:9; it is alluded to in 1 Cor. 6:10 and 1 Pet. 4:15. As the breaking of a divine command, theft is an offense against God's will and, in terms of human relationships, it betrays fellowship (Jn. 12:6). The positive fulfillment of this commandment, as of the others in the second table, is brought about by loving one's neighbor (Rom. 13:9–10; cf. Matt. 22:39). In practical terms, a thief must stop stealing and instead do honest work, so that such a person can serve not his or her own selfish ends but the needs of those who lack (Eph. 4:28).

2. Jesus also warns against reliance on accumulated wealth, for thieves can easily dig through house walls made of mud brick and steal one's property (Matt. 6:19–20). By contrast, treasures in heaven, i.e., what wins divine approval and reward in the coming kingdom, are beyond the reach of thieves or inflation.

Judas, who pilfered money, was a *kleptēs* (Jn. 12:6); Barabbas, who was implicated in violence, was a *lēstēs* (Jn. 18:40). In Matt. 27:64 the Jews fear that the disciples may quietly steal the body of Jesus, and in 28:13 they decide to put it about that this explains the empty tomb. The vb. *kleptō* and the noun *kleptēs* are used to describe the sudden arrival without warning of the messianic age. As an alert householder is able to forestall a thief approaching secretly, so the disciple needs to be on the watch for the Parousia of the Lord (Matt. 24:43–44; Lk. 12:39). The same simile illustrates the unexpected moment of the Lord's coming in 1 Thess. 5:2, 4; 2 Pet. 3:10; Rev. 3:3; 16:15.

The Fourth Gospel's discourse on the good shepherd opens with a description of a prospective sheep stealer as both *kleptēs* and *lēstēs*, i.e., using either stealth or force to get into the sheepfold (Jn. 10:1). Jesus goes on to use the pl. "thieves and robbers" in 10:8 to define all who came before him: false messiahs, such as Theudas and Judas the Galilean (cf. Acts 5:36–37). Such a *kleptēs* destroys life by furthering his own ends. By contrast, Jesus has come to give a full life, even at the expense of his own (10:10).

In the parable of the good Samaritan the plural *lēstai* (Lk. 10:30, 36) may not refer to bandits in the general sense, but bear the rab. meaning of Zealots. The victim is a Jew. But he is not killed, and his injuries may have been due to his resisting the attack. When Zealots robbed to raise supplies for themselves, they usually did not take more than was necessary from their own countrymen. If this is so, it adds to Jesus' response to the question from the teacher of the law about the neighbor, for the Pharisees were constantly pressing Jesus to declare his attitude towards this nationalistic movement (Matt. 22:15–22).

At the cleansing of the temple, Jesus charges the merchants trafficking there with making God's house of prayer (Isa. 56:7) into "a den of robbers [*lēstai*]" (Mk. 11:17; cf. Jer. 7:11). Apart from profiting by high prices, the Jews' market in the forecourt robbed the Gentile nations (Mk. 11:17) of the only area in the temple that was available to them as a place of prayer (Matt. 21:13; Lk. 19:46). If *lēstēs* also has the technical sense of Zealot, Jesus is saying that by their activities the temple authorities are opening the way for the building to be turned into a Zealot stronghold, as did happen in the revolt of A.D. 68–70.

At his arrest in Gethsemane, Jesus ironically demands to know whether his enemies, armed to the teeth, now take him for a *lēstēs*, a bandit or insurrectionist who would sell his life dearly (Matt. 26:55; Mk. 14:48; Lk. 22:52). The two men crucified with Jesus are described as *lēstai* (Matt. 27:38, 44; Mk. 15:27), probably bandits rather than revolutionaries in view of the use of *kakourgoi*, criminals, in Lk. 23:33. Paul includes *lēstai*, bandits, among the perils he faced on his travels (2 Cor. 11:26).

See also *sylaō*, plunder, rob (*5195*); *apostereō*, rob, defraud, deprive (*691*); *andrapodistēs*, slave-dealer, kidnapper (*435*); *spēlaion*, cave, den (*5068*).

3337   λίβανος

λίβανος (*libanos*), frankincense (*3337*); λιβανωτός (*libanōtos*), frankincense (*3338*); θυμίαμα (*thymiama*), incense (*2592*); θυμιάω (*thymiaō*), burn incense (*2594*); θυμιατήριον (*thymiatērion*), censer, altar of incense (*2593*).

CL & OT 1. In cl. Gk. *libanos* is the frankincense tree and, by extension, the tree's aromatic gum frankincense, for which *libanōtos* is also used. *thymiama* (incense) is the general term for fragrant substances burned with sacrifices or for fumigation purposes, or used in embalming. The vb. *thymiaō* means to burn so as to produce smoke, more particularly to burn incense or to fumigate. The related noun *thymiatērion* is the censer.

1. (a) Apart from two instances of *libanōtos* (1 Chr. 9:29; 3 Macc. 5:2), the LXX always uses *libanos* for frankincense. Brittle, glittering, and bitter to the taste, frankincense produced a gratifying if expensive fragrance when burned (Song 3:6; 4:6). Besides being an ingredient of a special incense constantly used in OT worship, pure frankincense was burned with bread of the Presence (Lev. 24:7) and grain offering (2:2).

(b) *thymiama* (incense) and its vb. *thymiaō* (make sacrifices smoke) occur frequently in the LXX. *thymiatērion* always means censer (2 Chr. 26:19; Ezek. 8:11; 4 Macc. 7:11). The holy incense was a special compound reserved for the divine service (Exod. 30:34–35) and used according to strict instructions (Lev. 16:12–13; cf. 10:1–11). Morning and evening the high priest burned incense before the veil of the Most Holy Place (Exod. 30:7–8). On the Day of Atonement he entered the Most Holy Place carrying burning incense, the fumes of which provided an atonement for him as he approached the atonement cover of the ark (Lev. 16:12–13; cf. Num. 16:46).

Rising incense smoke symbolized praise (Isa. 60:6) and prayer (Ps. 141:2), worship fragrant to God. In the messianic age converted Gentiles will gladly bring abundant incense to the temple (Isa. 60:6), indicative of their worship of God.

NT 1. In the NT *libanos* occurs only 2x (Matt. 2:11; Rev. 18:13) and has its lit. meaning of frankincense. In Rev. 8:3, 5 *libanōtos* uncharacteristically means not frankincense but censer, the vessel for carrying incense. *thymiaō* (burn incense) occurs only in Lk. 1:9–11, together with the noun *thymiama*. In the second temple ordinary priests took turns, chosen by lot, in the daily offering of incense. Zechariah was carrying out this duty for the only time in his life when he had his vision. *thymiatērion* appears only in Heb. 9:4, where it means altar of incense.

2. *libanos* (frankincense), brought to the infant Jesus (Matt. 2:11), symbolizes both his divinity and priestly office of intercession (Heb. 7:25). The bringing of frankincense by Gentiles to the Messiah was a Jewish hope (Isa. 60:6). In Rev. 8:3, 5 the association of one and the same censer (*libanōtos*) with intercession and judgment shows the potency of Christian prayer in fulfilling God's purposes. In Rev. 5:8; 8:3–4 *thymiama*, incense, represents the prayers of the saints in the heavenly temple.

See also *smyrna*, myrrh (*5043*).

3338 (*libanōtos*, frankincense), → *3337*.

3339   λιβερτῖνος

λιβερτῖνος (*libertinos*), freedman (*3339*).

CL & OT *libertinos* is a Gk. borrowing of the Lat. *libertinus*, found in cl. Gk. only in an inscription. The normal Gk. word here is *apeleutheros* (cf. 1 Cor. 7:22, → *eleutheria*, freedom, *1800*) or *exeleutheros*. The *libertinus* was a freed slave who after either buying or having been given freedom underwent manumission, a process whereby freedom was secured publicly. But such freedom did not amount to full citizen rights; e.g., such a person could not petition for legal action without permission or gain high military office. Some freedmen, however, as employees of the state or of wealthy patrons, amassed considerable wealth and wielded political power.

NT The only place in the NT where this word occurs is Acts 6:9, which talks about the "Synagogue of the Freedmen (as it was called)—Jews of Cyrene and Alexandria as well as the provinces of Cilicia and Asia," where Stephen debated about Jesus as the Christ. These were probably Jewish freedmen, but we do not know whether they had come from Cyrene, Alexandria, Asia, and Cilicia (cf. NIV) or whether they were different from the Cyrenians and the others (e.g., descendants of Jews brought to Rome by Pompey in 63 B.C. and later set free). Note that large towns often had more than one synagogue; this particular one in Jerusalem seemed to be for Hel. Jews whose ancestors had once been slaves.

See also *aichmalōtos*, captive, prisoner of war (*171*); *desmios*, bind (with bonds) (*1300*); *doulos*, slave (*1528*).

3342 (*lithazō*, to stone), → *3345*.

3343 (*lithinos*, of stone), → *3345*.

3344 (*lithoboleō*, to stone), → *3345*.

3345	λίθος

λίθος (*lithos*), stone (*3345*); λίθινος (*lithinos*), of stone (*3343*); λιθάζω (*lithazō*), to stone (*3342*); λιθοβολέω (*lithoboleō*), to stone (*3344*); μύλος (*mylos*), mill, millstone (*3685*); μυλικός (*mylikos*), belonging to a mill (*3683*); μύλινος (*mylinos*), belonging to a mill (*3684*).

CL & OT 1. In cl. Gk. *lithos* can be used for stones of every sort; *lithinos* means of stone. In particular one can distinguish building stones and precious stones.

2. (a) Usually the LXX translates the Heb. *'eben* by *lithos* (used 350x), though it translates other Heb. words that mean, e.g., millstones, boundary stones, piles of stones, precious stones, etc., usually without differentiating them. The most important of the occurrences of *lithos* are those in a theological context and are taken up in the NT. The vb. *lithazō* occurs only in 2 Sam. 16:6, 13, where it refers to pelting someone with stones. For the OT method of execution by stoning, the vb. *lithoboleō* is used (e.g., Lev. 20:2, 27; Deut. 13:10; Josh. 7:25).

(b) The word *mylos*, mill, occurring in cl. Gk. and the LXX (cf. Exod. 11:5; Deut. 24:6; Isa. 47:2), denotes two round, flat stones between which grain was placed and the husks removed by grinding. In Jdg. 9:53 Abimelech was killed by a millstone thrown by a woman as he besieged the tower at Thebez.

3. (a) In a threatening passage the prophet Isa. warns his people not to free themselves from the danger of an Assyrian invasion through self-sufficient and faithless exertions (Isa. 8:11–15). He testifies that the real danger for Judah is not the Assyrians but the proximity of God as their judge, who will become a "stone that causes men to stumble" (8:14). As someone might stumble over a stone in the middle of the night, God's people will be smitten unexpectedly by his judgment (see also *petra*, rock, *4376*).

(b) Isa. 28:16a uses the image of the building of a house and the foundation stone. In contrast to the Jerusalem rulers' policy of alliances against Assyria, a policy doomed to fail, Yahweh is laying in Zion a firm foundation stone, which gives a stable base for the walls and the whole building. Isa. 28:16b—"The one who trusts will never be dismayed"—interprets the foundation stone, on which the building of the nation and state is to be erected, as faith and trust in Yahweh's help, which makes a search for alliances superfluous (for more on this passage, → *gōnia*, cornerstone, *1224*).

(c) Likewise Ps. 118:22 cites what looks like a proverb about a cornerstone. The psalmist thanks Yahweh for the salvation he shares. He likens his existence, threatened by death, to a stone that the builders discarded as useless and his rescuing by Yahweh to a cornerstone or keystone of a building.

(d) Zech. makes several references to stone in his prophecy about the completion of the building of the postexilic temple by Zerubbabel: "'What are you, O mighty mountain? Before Zerubbabel you will become level ground. Then he will bring out the capstone [lit. in LXX, the stone of inheritance] to shouts of "God bless it! God bless it!"'... Men will rejoice when they see the plumb line [lit. in LXX, the tin stone] in the hand of Zerubbabel'" (Zech. 4:7–10). The thought here is that mountains of opposition to God's work cannot impede it. The completion of the temple is symbolic of the victory of God's Spirit (cf. 4:6). It is possible for the "tin stone" to refer to a plumb line, though plumb lines were usually made of lead. The cause of rejoicing is the placing of a final ceremonial stone on the height of the temple walls by Zerubbabel.

(e) Dan. 2:34–35 tells of Nebuchadnezzar's dream, in which he saw a stone break off from a mountain without any human agency and shatter the great image on its feet of iron and clay. The image was dispersed without trace. "But the rock that struck the statue became a huge mountain and filled the whole earth." In 2:44–45 the dream is interpreted as the establishment of God's kingdom, which will crush all other kingdoms of the earth.

4. In intertestamental and post-NT Jud. the various sayings about stones were given a messianic interpretation. Already in the LXX the phrase "in him" was added to "the one who trusts" in Isa. 28:16. Jud. expected a glorification or renewal of the temple. The Qumran community regarded itself as the eschatological Israel, as God's true temple, and cited Isa. 28:16 as evidence (1QS 8:7–8).

NT In the NT most instances of the word *lithos* are in the Synoptic Gospels, esp. Matt. It is used lit. of a millstone (Lk. 17:2), a boulder (Matt. 27:60; 28:2), or a precious stone (Rev. 18:12, 16; 21:11, 19). Its fig. use is chiefly in connection with various OT quotations, which receive a messianic interpretation.

1. (a) The saying about the stones crying out (Lk. 19:40) is to be understood against an OT and Jewish background, where we occasionally get references to the accusing cry of lifeless objects (Gen. 4:10; Hab. 2:11; 2 Esd. 5:5).

(b) John the Baptist's saying that "out of these stones God can raise up children for Abraham" (Matt. 3:9; Lk. 3:8) means that God can fashion a new Israel from those who can claim no qualifications (like descent) of their own (cf. Rom. 4:9–25).

(c) In the saying that no stone of the temple will be left standing on another (Mk. 13:2), Jesus is most likely looking ahead to the destruction of the temple in Jerusalem, which took place in A.D. 70. This need not, however, indicate that the Gospel of Mk. was written after the Roman victory, for Jesus presumably has the ability to predict future events.

2. (a) Occasionally Jesus is likened to a stone. Mk. 12:10; Lk. 20:17–18 cites Ps. 118:22 in connection with the parable of the husbandmen: The stone rejected by the builders has become the cornerstone or keystone. He who is rejected by humans is the one exalted by God. According to Acts 4:10–11, this exaltation has already taken place in Jesus' resurrection. Eph. 2:20–22 also makes Jesus the cornerstone or keystone, which holds the whole building together, while the apostles and prophets form the foundation (→ *gōnia*, corner, *1224*).

(b) On the other hand, Jesus is likened in Lk. 20:18 to a destroying stone that will crush its opponents, an allusion to Dan. 2:34. In Rom. 9:32 Paul quotes Isa. 8:14 and interprets the stone of offense as Christ, who has been the undoing of the Jews.

(c) In Rom. 9:33 and 1 Pet. 2:4–8 (cf. also Lk. 2:34) the positive interpretation of Jesus as the cornerstone or keystone is combined with the negative one of him as the destructive stone of offense by combining different OT quotations (→ *petra*, rock, *4376*). This serves to show the significance of Jesus as both gospel and law, as both salvation and disaster. It is the faith of individual people that decides whether Christ the stone has a vital (1 Pet. 2:4) or a fatal (Lk. 20:18) effect.

3. In 1 Pet. 2:5 Christians are likened to "living stones . . . built into a spiritual house" (cf. Eph. 2:20). The inanimate image of a building here is inadequate for the truth expressed. Because Christ lives, the foundation and thus the entire building is living; moreover, because Christians live through him they can be addressed as "living stones."

4. The word *mylos*, mill, figures in Jesus' warning about the suddenness of the Parousia and how unprepared some will be for it: "Two women will be grinding with a hand mill; one will be taken and the other left" (Matt. 24:41; cf. Num. 11:8). The fact that "the sound of a millstone will never be heard in you again" is a vivid way of expressing judgment on Babylon, i.e., godless civilization (Rev. 18:22). This follows 18:21: "Then a mighty angel picked up a boulder [*lithos*] the size of a large millstone and threw it into the sea, and said, 'With such violence the great city of Babylon will be thrown down, never to be found again.'" The judgment on Babylon recalls Jer. 51:60–64 (cf. 7:34; 16:9; 25:10), and the destruction by a stone is reminiscent of Dan. 2:34–35.

The millstone in Rev. 18:22 denotes a harmless and necessary activity, whereas the millstone in 18:21 becomes an instrument of destruction, as in Jesus' saying: "If anyone causes one of these little ones who believe in me to sin, it would be better for him to be thrown into sea with a large millstone tied around his neck" (Mk. 9:42; cf. Matt. 18:6; Lk. 17:1–2). The *mylos onikos* of Matt. and Mk. means lit. a "donkey stone"; Lk. has *lithos mylikos*, stone belonging to a mill, which signifies a large stone worked by donkey power. This was a serious warning for any who try to prevent the exercise of faith in Jesus' name; by graphic language it impresses the seriousness of the matter on the hearts of Jesus' listeners.

5. *lithazō* is used 9x in the NT and *lithoboleō* 7x, in each case referring to the act of execution or attempted execution via stoning (*lithazō* in Jn. 8:5; 10:31–33; Acts 14:19; *lithoboleō* in Matt. 21:35; Acts 7:58–59).

See also *petra*, rock (*4376*); *gōnia*, corner (*1224*); *margaritēs*, pearl (*3449*).

3349	λίμνη

λίμνη (*limnē*), lake (*3349*).

CL & OT In cl. Gk. *limnē* was used of a fresh- or saltwater pool or marsh; many Gk. poets used *limnē* for the sea. Gk. papyri used the word in the more modest sense of lake. *limnē* occurs occasionally in the LXX (e.g., Ps. 107:35; 114:8; 1 Macc. 11:35; 2 Macc. 12:16).

NT Lk. uses *limnē* for fresh-water lakes, being associated with the Sea of Galilee (Lk. 5:2; 8:22–33), also called the Lake of Gennesaret (5:1). Fig., *limnē* occurs in Rev. 19:20; 20:10–15; 21:8 for the lake of burning sulfur in which the ungodly will be destroyed.

See also *thalassa*, sea, lake (*2498*); *pēgē*, spring, source (*4380*); *hydōr*, water (*5623*); *kataklysmos*, a deluge, flood (*2886*); *Iordanēs*, the river Jordan (*2674*).

3350 (*limos*, hunger, famine), → *4277*.

3356	λογεία

λογεία (*logeia*), collection (of money), tax (*3356*).

CL & OT The use of *logeia* in the pre-Christian era is not attested apart from occurrences in the papyri and inscriptions from the 3d cent. B.C. on. Where it does occur, it means a collection of money. There are no uses of this word in the LXX.

NT 1. *logeia* occurs 2x in the NT, both in 1 Cor. 16:1–2. Possibly in answer to a question from the Corinthians concerning the collection for the Jerusalem saints that had been posed in a letter to Paul, the apostle repeats instructions he had given to the Galatian churches. Every Sunday each believer was privately to set aside and store up some money in proportion to the income of the previous week, so that collections would not be needed after Paul arrived.

While some Jerusalem Christians may have regarded this collection as a sort of tax on Gentile Christians that was the rightful due of the mother church in the holy city (analogous to the Jewish temple tax), Paul promoted it both as an act of service to God (2 Cor. 9:12–13) that would honor Christ (8:19) and as a spontaneous gesture of brotherly love (cf. Rom. 12:13; 15:31; 1 Cor. 16:3; 2 Cor. 9:1, 5; Gal. 6:10) that called for generous giving (2 Cor. 8:7, 24; 9:5–14). He emphasizes that this giving should be voluntary, an act of free will, a noncompulsory sharing of one's material possessions with no stipulated amount (→ *dekatos*, tithe, *1281*). The apostle also regarded it as a tangible expression by Gentile believers of their spiritual indebtedness to the church at Jerusalem (Rom. 15:19, 27).

2. Paul had earlier been involved in bringing money to Jerusalem for famine relief (Acts 11:27–30). His more systematic collection during his third missionary journey presumably began as an act of charity, motivated by the love of Christ. But as tensions increased between the Gentile mission led by Paul, with its more liberal attitude toward the law, and those at Jerusalem who clung to Jewish practices, the collection took on a Christological and soteriological significance. It became an expression of the solidarity of the Christian fellowship, showing that God had also called the Gentiles to faith. The high value the apostle placed on this collection in part explains his insistence on going to Jerusalem after his third missionary journey despite obvious dangers (20:3, 23; 21:4, 10–14). While we do not know the extent to which Paul accomplished his goals in the collection, his instructions have been immensely fruitful in formulating principles of Christian giving.

See also *statēr*, stater, a silver coin worth four drachmas (*5088*); *telōnion*, customs house, tax office (*5468*).

3357	λογίζομαι

λογίζομαι (*logizomai*), reckon, think, credit (*3357*); λογισμός (*logismos*), thought (*3361*).

CL & OT 1. In cl. Gk. *logizomai* means to count, collect, reckon, calculate; also consider, deliberate, draw a logical conclusion, decide. Accordingly *logismos* means a counting or calculation; reflection, argument, thought, plan; the ability to draw a logical conclusion. The concept implies an activity of the reason that, starting with ascertainable facts, draws a conclusion, esp. a mathematical one or one pertaining to business, where calculations are essential. Plato uses it for thought unaffected by the emotions.

2. *logizomai* in the LXX often means to think, account (e.g., Gen. 15:6; 31:15; Num. 18:27, 30). But the vb. receives a new and personal slant here, for it can mean to care for, plan, intend. The objective reckoning of the intellect is replaced in the meaning of this word by the feeling of the heart conditioned by individual personality (e.g., Ps. 140:2; Isa. 10:7; Zech. 8:17). The personal element is seen also in the reckoning of guilt or righteousness (e.g., Gen. 15:6; 2 Sam. 19:19), often in Ps. (e.g., 32:2) and in the cultic imputation of guilt or purification (e.g., Lev. 7:18 = LXX 7:8; 17:4).

logizomai is sometimes used for one's relationship to God and often for God's purposes with us, whether they are thoughts of peace (2 Sam. 14:14) or punitive judgments (Jer. 49:20 = LXX 29:20; 50:45 = LXX 27:45), or whether he will change them, if his people will only repent (26:3 = LXX 33:3; 36:3 = LXX 43:3). Hence, this concept, which in Heb. expresses the emotional and personal and in Gk. the objective understanding of calculation and evaluation, can express both sides of the biblical message. God's personal, righteous dealings with his people on the basis of his law alone enable them to believe and to count on God. God does not act in an arbitrary and incalculable fashion; he has revealed his purpose and plan of salvation through the prophetic word.

NT 1. *logizomai* occurs 40x in the NT, of which 34x are in Paul. He uses *logizomai* and *logismos* in relating the foundation of faith to the righteousness of God. Since the apostle associates righteousness with the facts of the cross and resurrection of Jesus, he never separates the concept of *logizomai* from the personal activity of God in Jesus Christ. For him, faith is not an objective observing from a neutral vantage point, but being conquered by the crucified and risen Lord.

(a) When Paul in Rom. 2:15 mentions the "thoughts" (*logismos*) that can accuse or defend a person, he is not thinking of unemotional, philosophical thought, but of that reckoning and deduction that separates the good from the evil in a person's conscience. According to Paul, it is the living God who bears testimony in the human heart. Behind all the strivings of the heathen lies a standard that God has fixed—the work of natural law written in a person's inner being. Failure to reach this standard is recognized as guilt by the conscience, and the thoughts of the heart reckon in practice with God's judgment.

Humans can, however, use their thoughts to fortify themselves against the knowledge of the true God and his claims to obedience (2 Cor. 10:4–5). Therefore, Paul is concerned in his missionary work to reveal the divine purpose and act in Christ, and in the full authority of God to take clever human thoughts prisoner, so that their proud arrogance should bow to Christ in conquered and liberated freedom (cf. 10:5). Even so, this obedient *logismos* remains partial until it is perfected in eternity (1 Cor. 13:12).

(b) When the *noēma*, the mind (→ *nous*, mind, *3808*), is so conquered, it grasps God's purpose and action in the cross; thereupon, the mind gladly acknowledges itself as conquered. Paul expresses this divine reckoning in 2 Cor. 5:19: "God was reconciling the world to himself in Christ, not counting [*logizomai*] men's sins against them." This does not mean that God does not take sin seriously. The reverse is true, but he deals with it in Christ. Since he does not impute sin to us, it has been truly removed (cf. Col. 2:13) in Christ and his work. Indeed, God "made him ... to be sin for us" (2 Cor. 5:21). Sin has been completely settled on the cross.

This completely trustworthy attitude of God, in which he acts in this way for the sake of his righteousness, has its background in the prophetic oracle: The servant of the Lord "was numbered [*logizomai*] with the transgressors" (Isa. 53:12), where the suffering of the servant of the Lord is foretold. The passive ultimately implies God and his will; he bruised or crushed his servant not because of his sin, but because of ours. God laid the punishment on him so that we might have peace. That is how Lk. 22:37 understands this passage.

The converse of this statement is the reckoning of faith as righteousness in Paul's letters, linking it with Gen. 15:6 in Rom. 4:3–6, 8, 10, 22–24, and in Gal. 3:6. Faith was a merit for many of the rabbis, but Paul wished to reckon as God did, who reckoned salvation and righteousness to Abraham on the basis of faith in him and his word. God reckons on the basis of his promise (Rom. 9:8), and what he promises he performs.

(c) Because of the foregoing, those reconciled through Christ may and should so reckon and think. Hence, Paul draws clear theological (Rom. 3:28) and practical conclusions for himself and his readers (2 Cor. 10:7; cf. Rom. 2:3). The standard for our *logizomai* is, therefore, because of the cross, not a principle but a fact, to which every act and thought should conform.

Paul, therefore, in Rom. 8:18 already reckons with the glory that at some future time will be revealed and that will reduce all present suffering with Christ to insignificance. As Christ's sufferings, death, and resurrection have led to glory, so the church's suffering with him will lead to being glorified together with him. Thus, we also may count confidently on the coming glory.

(d) The sharing of the *logizomai* through faith is not a case of merely holding something to be true but is also an inspiration and

activity. Thus, 1 Cor. 13:5 and Phil. 4:8 are to be expounded in the light of Zech. 8:17. This kind of thinking is not solely an intellectual construction, but can arrive at factual conclusions that demand corresponding actions (Rom. 14:14), just as word and act are one with God. Therefore, we should evaluate others and ourselves rightly, not by false standards, but as they and we stand in God's sight (1 Cor. 4:1; 2 Cor. 10:2; 11:5; 12:6; Phil. 3:13).

2. (a) John also writes of God's act on which faith is based (1 Jn. 1:1) and of the love revealed in this act (Jn. 3:16). But his purpose was not the same as Paul's. The latter was involved in conflict with Jud., and the unity of judgment and grace in the divine saving activity was the focus of his teaching. John's witness centers on the testimony that truth and life can be found only in Jesus Christ, who came in the flesh, died, and arose again. Hence, John found little use for the concept *logizomai*. He uses the word only in Jn. 11:50, in reporting the high priest Caiaphas's unconscious prophecy: "You do not realize [*logizomai*] that it is better for you that one man die for the people than that the whole nation perish."

(b) We find the word also in Acts 19:27; 1 Pet. 5:12, while Heb. 11:19 uses it in its full theological sense. Jas. 2:23 uses the quotation from Gen. 15:6 about the reckoning of faith as righteousness in his own way by pointing to Abraham's active obedience.

See also *dialogizomai*, ponder, consider, reason (*1368*); *dokeō*, trans. think, believe, consider; intrans. seem, appear (*1506*).

3358 (*logikos*, intellectual, rational, reasonable, spiritual), → *3364*.

3359 (*logion*, saying), → *3364*.

3360 (*logios*, eloquent, cultured), → *3364*.

3361 (*logismos*, thought), → *3357*.

3362 (*logomacheō*, to quarrel about words), → *3364*.

3363 (*logomachia*, quarreling about words), → *3364*.

3364	λόγος

λόγος (*logos*), word, utterance, meaning (*3364*); λέγω (*legō*), collect, count, say (*3306*); προλέγω (*prolegō*), say before, tell ahead of time (*4625*); λογικός (*logikos*), intellectual, rational, reasonable, spiritual (*3358*); λόγιον (*logion*), saying (*3359*); λόγιος (*logios*), eloquent, cultured (*3360*); ἄλογος (*alogos*), irrational, without speech (*263*); λαλέω (*laleō*), to talk, chat, speak (*3281*); λογομαχέω (*logomacheō*), to quarrel about words (*3362*); λογομαχία (*logomachia*), quarreling about words (*3363*).

CL 1. *Early usage.* Homer uses *logos* only 2x, both pl., as a synonym for *mythos* (myth) and *epos* (word, speech). Post-Homeric reserves *epos* for epic lit. based on the Homeric meter and *mythos* for fictitious stories (esp. of the gods), which have an inner content of truth. *logos* stays restricted to the meaning of discourse.

2. *Philosophical usage.* (a) The decisive change in the use of *logos* begins with Heraclitus (ca. 500 B.C.). For him *logos* can mean didactic discourse (teaching), word, and even reputation. But it can also denote proportion, meaning, universal law, and truth. Heraclitus was concerned with getting hold of the unity of the One and the All through the existence of the universal law of proportion that underlies continuous change. *logos* for him expresses both the thought process and its conclusion. Thus, *logos* originally had nothing to do with talking or speaking. Everything one sees is explored with the mind and is related together; this relationship is the *logos* of individual objects, contained in the objects themselves, and exhibits a law common to all existents.

Heraclitus's contemporary Parmenides combined *logos* with the idea of pure thought undisturbed by the senses. Thus he transplanted the realm of the *logos* to the other side of the deceptive world of appearances, in the world of pure being. Three things become evident for the first time in the *logos*-concept: antithetical argument, dualism, and the narrowing down of the concept of *logos* to the subjective sphere of the activity of thinking and the thought itself.

(b) For the Sophists (mid-5th cent.), philosophical reflection is directed toward humanity and toward the relationship between the individual and society. Through *logos*, discourse, people are able to play a sensible part in political life. In this scheme, *logos* takes on the meaning of the individual method of argument, the only important thing being to defend one's own proposition. Every *logos* contains a counter-*logos*, so that antithetical argumentation (good and bad; truth and falsehood) is recognized as the basic principle of debate. Thus people saw a great force in the *logos*; it had a pedagogic power by which the bad is reproved and the good praised.

(c) Socrates viewed discussion and debate as a community-producing activity as long as people were struggling for truth. Their purpose is not talking for talking's sake, but via reflection through dialogue to discover the *logos* of things.

(d) Plato, whose thought was concerned primarily with the concept of ideas or forms, added nothing decisively new to the understanding of *logos*. Even with Aristotle no new ground is broken; for him, humanity alone has *logos*, because their actions are determined by the word, and they are capable of speech and understanding.

(e) With the Stoics, a spiritualization of *logos* takes place. Their main question was not one of abstract truth but of ethics: How must I live in order to be able to be happy? The *logos* is the expression for the ordered and harmonious purpose of the world. It is equated with God; it is the constitutive principle of the cosmos, which extends through matter. For the Stoics truth derives from a specific point of origin in the Logos-God. There is a right *logos* or universal law that bestows on humans the power of knowledge and thus of moral behavior. In this connection a distinction is made between the inner *logos* (thinking), given by the God-Logos, and the *logos* ordained for articulation (speaking).

(f) In the post-NT era, *logos* thinking developed in Neo-Platonism, so that *logos* was conceived as a force that invests material objects with shape, form, and life, and is even bracketed together with life. In the mystery religions of this era, reflection did not focus on philosophical inquiry, but on cultic actions leading to purification and even deification. What one used for this was a sacred text (*hieros logos*), revealed by the founder of the cult or by those inspired by the divinity.

3. *Usage in grammar, logic, and rhetoric.* (a) Apart from its use in philosophical formulations, the word *logos* is used with striking precision in the field of grammar as a word, which is able to express everything that exists. Since a word is made up of various letters and words can be combined into a sentence, its possible uses are limitless. From this perspective developed grammar (the teaching of sentence analysis) and metaphysics (the teaching of the "logical" shape of the cosmos).

(b) Aristotle systematized this use of *logos* in that he first investigated the words in themselves before placing them in a meaningful context. The sentence gives the individual word its sense and defines its meaning, so *logos* came to mean the definition. Moreover, for Aristotle, *logos* means the conclusion, i.e., the final proposition of a line of syllogism. Finally, *logos* means the proof itself. As a result of this thinking, it becomes clear that the art of rhetoric works with the idea of *logos*, so that the *logos* becomes the stylistic form of orators.

OT 1. *Heb. terms for* word. Heb. has four terms for *word*: *dābār*, *ʾēmer*, *ʾimrâ*, and *millâ*. In the OT historical books *logos* is the primary rendering for *dābār*, while in the prophets *rhēma* (→ *4839*) predominates. Note that *dābār* means word, report, and command, but also thing, matter, affair. The vb. *legō* stands chiefly for *ʾāmar*, to speak, say. The expression "word of Yahweh" (*dᵉbar yhwh*) is found 241x in the OT and has three main nuances. It is primarily a technical term for the prophetic revelation of the divine word, but it also designates the divine commandment and will for justice (e.g., Exod. 34:28) and the creatively efficacious activity of God in creation (Gen. 1) and nature (Ps. 29; 33). For more on these three nuances, see secs. 3–5.

2. *Ancient oriental notion of the word of God.* In the ancient Orient a word could be used as an indicative bearer of meaningful content (the noetic aspect of the word), but it was esp. a power that was efficacious in incantations and magical spells, in blessings and curses, even in the spatial and material world. A curse, for example, could penetrate the affected person like some disintegrating substance and bring destruction by spreading outward from within (the dynamic aspect of the word). In Israel, the creative word of God was purified of magical understanding to become the word of the God who by claim and promise gives shape to the world and to history. Note that what God says even in a "gentle whisper" is more powerful than wind, earthquake, or fire (1 Ki. 19:9–14).

3. *The forms of the prophetic proclamation of the word of God.* The subject matter of prophetic proclamation is the word of God. It is not the prophet who avails himself of the word, but Yahweh's word that takes the prophet into its service. (a) The word of God is a word of vocation. The special nature of prophetic proclamation finds expression in accounts of calls where the authority of the prophetic word is grounded solely in the word of God that gives the prophet his commission. Two forms of call can be distinguished: a direct appointment by divine discourse, often with a reluctance to accept the assignment (e.g., Jer. 1:4–10), and a vision seen by the prophet, where the call is a result of a consultation of Yahweh with his council (e.g., Isa. 6; Ezek. 1). In both forms, the word is essential. Thus, when the Lord speaks, the prophet cannot help but prophesy (Amos 3:8).

(b) The word of God is the word of a messenger. One of the most striking marks of the prophetic proclamation throughout the OT is the introductory formula, "This is what the LORD says." This formula presupposes that the messenger has received a message; sometimes, in delivering his message, he may refer back to this occasion (cf. Gen. 32:4–6; 2 Ki. 18:19, 29, 31). The adoption of this messenger formula indicates that the prophet is passing on the entrusted word of God. In the case of Ezek., this is pictured as the prophet ingesting God's word prior to his speaking it (3:1–11). The words that are spoken can contain both information from the Lord or rebuke.

(c) The word of God is often a word of judgment. The prophet names the crime and announces Yahweh's judgment, which can be directed against an individual king (e.g., 1 Ki. 21:17–19) or against Israel or Judah as a whole (e.g., Isa. 8:5–8; Amos 4:1–3). In the writing prophets, judgment is also pronounced on nations other than Israel (e.g., Isa. 13–21; Jer. 46–51; Ezek. 25–30; Amos 1; Obad.). As a word of judgment, the word of the Lord has power. The story of the scroll in Jer. 36 shows that even if people want to burn Yahweh's word (36:23), it remains in force nonetheless (36:32).

(d) The word of God can also be a word of deliverance and salvation. Esp. in the exilic and postexilic prophets one finds sections in which the prophet sees God restoring his people and reestablishing them in the promised land (e.g., Isa. 40; Jer. 30–33; Ezek. 37; 40–48). Yahweh is, after all, sovereign over all nations, and his word creates history.

4. *The word of God as covenant commandment.* (a) God's specific commandments, the proclamation of God's will for justice, are called "the Ten Commandments [lit., words]" in Exod. 34:28 and described more precisely as "the words of the covenant." These words are God's will for justice among his people and are introduced in 20:1 by: "God spoke all these words." The proper response to God's words is obedience. Thus the people "responded with one voice, 'Everything [lit., all the words] the LORD has said we will do.'" To facilitate this obedience, Moses wrote down "everything [lit., all the words] the LORD had said" (24:3–4).

(b) Time and again, when the prophets speak their words of judgment, they come back to the old covenant regulations as the basis for what they say. The people have disobeyed the word of the Lord by oppressing the poor and perverting justice (Amos 2:7–8; 3:9–10). Because they have transgressed the covenant law, the Lord will abrogate his covenant (Hos. 4:2–6). In Jer.'s temple speech the people have their sin uncovered in a Decalogue-like array of justice (cf. the enumeration of stealing, murdering, committing adultery, and perjury, 7:9).

(c) In Deut. not only is the covenant commandment designated as (lit.) "the ten words" (4:13; 10:4), but the multiplicity of commandments are designated as "words" (e.g., 1:1; 4:10), and an individual commandment as a (lit.) "word" (e.g., 15:15; 24:18, 22). In fact, "word" can be used in the sing. to denote God's entire law (e.g., Deut. 4:2; cf. Jos. 1:13), and in consequence to express total human dependence on this word (cf. this word is "your life," Deut. 32:47).

5. *The word of God as the word of the creator.* (a) Yahweh's word in creation, by which he has called heaven into existence (Ps. 33:6), is at the same time the word of salvation (33:4–5). Note that the creation narrative of Gen. 1, in which God's word figures so prominently, is also the opening chapter of the history of the covenant. This association of the word of the creator with salvation history corresponds with Isa. 40–55.

(b) There is also a correlation of the word of the creator with God's word of law. In Ps. 147:15–19 the creative "word" of God is specifically linked with meteorological phenomena (e.g., snow and hail, 147:16–17). But this same word that holds sway over nature is none other than the word of the covenant law, by which Yahweh lays claim to Israel: "He has revealed his word to Jacob, his laws and decrees to Israel" (147:19). Israel understands God's word as one word, evident both in creation and in redemption.

6. (a) In the Dead Sea Scrolls *dābār* occurs with the meaning word (esp. in hymns or exegetical works) or thing, matter (esp. in legal stipulations). The human word and the faculty of speech are considered to be particular miracles of the divine creation (1QH 1:28–29). But *dābār* also means the word of God, his commandment (4:35), and his promise (1QS 2:13). With the meaning affair, concern, *dābār* is the object of consultations in the community (6:1, 4, 16).

(b) In Philo *rhēma* is overshadowed by *logos* and simply means word; in grammar it means verb. Sometimes it is used to distinguish a thought from a deed.

(c) In rab. lit., and in Heb. generally, *dābār* means both word and matter. Humans have received, as something unique to them, words in their mouths. The rabbis warned, however, against loquaciousness, which leads to sin. In the practice of teaching, the *dābār* is associated with the all-dominant Torah, though this word is also used for "words of the tradition" and the "words of the scribes." With the meaning matter or thing, *dābār* is often used as a general designation for legal cases. The formula "another matter" sometimes indicates things that one does not want to mention by name, such as idolatry or sexual intercourse.

(d) In Targums the Aram. *mēmrā*, word, is used as a periphrasis for the God who reveals himself.

NT 1. *The occurrence and significance of* logos *and* legō *in the NT.* *logos* occurs 330x in the NT, meaning such things as statement (Matt. 5:37), utterance (12:32), question (21:24), report (28:15), discourse (15:12), command (Lk. 4:36), matter (Mk. 9:10), word of Scripture (1 Cor. 15:54), motive (Acts 10:29), instruction (Lk. 4:32), and Jesus as the Word (Jn. 1:1, 14). *legō*, to say, occurs 2353x in the NT, usually without special significance. *laleō*, to speak, occurs 296x, primarily in Luke and Paul.

2. *The word of Jesus Christ.* (a) The proclamation of Jesus. At the center of Jesus' message stands the proclamation of God's nearness and the inauguration of his kingdom, already present in Jesus' person and words. His words thus announce neither simply the presence nor exclusively the future of God's kingdom. Rather, he spoke of a coming of the future kingdom, which was already present in his words. Jesus rarely uses *logos* to mean "the word of God" in an absolute sense (cf. Mk. 4:13–20, the parable of the sower).

(i) Nowhere does Jesus follow the OT prophets in prefacing his words with the formula, "This is what the Lord says." The only thing in the NT that bears similarity is Lk. 3:2: "The word of God came to

John." Lk. uses *rhēma* (word, → 4839) here of John the Baptist, the last of the prophets (cf. 16:16). Thus, Jesus' proclamation cannot be understood simply in prophetic categories. This is undoubtedly because of the close association of Jesus with God the Father and because Jesus himself is the Word (see below).

(ii) Jesus sets his message in contrast to that of the OT: e.g., "You have heard that it was said to the people long ago. . . . But I tell you . . ." (Matt. 5:21–47). Jesus modifies the statements of the past that were regarded as having divine authority, setting his own *I* in the place where, in the prophets, we find Yahweh's. Jesus is not here claiming to be merely the legitimate interpreter of God's law. Rather, he is setting himself and his words up directly alongside God and the word of God.

The same is true of the formula, "I tell you the truth" (e.g., Mk. 3:28; 8:12; → *amēn*, amen, truly, 297). This formula was normally used to strengthen someone else's words and was used in OT times to introduce words of blessing or cursing. But Jesus uses it without exception in order to preface and strengthen his own words, thereby characterizing them as something sure and trustworthy.

(iii) Jesus intends his word to take the place of the Torah. Note Matt. 7:24, where he insists that those who hear his words and obey them will be like a wise man who builds his house on a rock. He claims divine authority for what he says. This authority is also illustrated in his call to discipleship, when Jesus says to certain men, "Follow me" (Mk. 2:14; cf. 1:16–20). This call of Jesus requires obedience. The power of Jesus' word is further reflected in the response of the hearers: They either take offense at his words (10:22) or are amazed "because he taught as one who had authority, and not as their teachers of the law" (Matt. 7:29).

(iv) The power of Jesus' word is also shown in the stories of healing, which take place through his word (Matt. 8:8; Mk. 2:11) or command (9:25). Note the close connection between Jesus' word of forgiveness (2:5) and his word of healing (2:11). The word of the judge of the entire world, who has the power to forgive sins, is proved in the healing of a paralyzed man to be an effective and a creative word.

Jesus' healings may never be detached from his proclamation. In Lk. 4:18 Jesus relates the prophetic word of Isa. 61:1–2 to his own mission: God sent him to bring good news to the poor and to give sight to the blind. In this unity of word and deed, the superiority goes to the word, for his primary task is to "preach" (Mk. 1:38); the healings are physical expression of his word.

(b) The heart and soul of Jesus' message is that of his suffering and death. This probably explains why he forbids people to spread the news about his miracles (e.g., Mk. 1:43–45), since he does not want them to get to know him as the Messiah by hearing tales of miracles. The true mystery of his messiahship and the center of his story are revealed in his passion and crucifixion. When Jesus speaks in parables, he is veiling his message (4:10–12); when he tells his disciples about his coming death and resurrection, he is speaking "plainly" (8:32).

3. *The word concerning Jesus Christ.* (a) Paul calls the message he proclaimed to his congregation "the word of God" (1 Cor. 14:36; 1 Thess. 2:13) or "the Lord's message [*logos*]" (1 Thess. 1:8). (i) Paul insists that the word he proclaims is founded directly on the revelation of the Son of God (Gal. 1:1, 15–16), but he also stresses that his message and that proclaimed by the Jerusalem apostles are the same. Closely following an early church confession, Paul preaches the message of the Son of God, who, on the basis of the resurrection, has been designated Son of God in all his power (Rom. 1:3–4). In 1 Cor. 15:1–8, the apostle reminds the church in Corinth that his message is the one he has received—Christ died, was buried, rose again, and appeared to eyewitnesses. By this message people are saved.

(ii) Paul describes the center of his proclamation as "the message of the cross" (1 Cor. 1:18). He publicly proclaimed the crucified Christ in the Galatian congregations (Gal. 3:1) and made it the sole content of his preaching (1 Cor. 2:2). This word stands in absolute opposition to "the wisdom of the world" (1:18–2:16), in that it makes nonsense of the wisdom of this world and the boasting of those who claim superior knowledge (4:8). Thus, it stands in opposition to a theology of glory consonant with such a wisdom, where the cross and the crucified one no longer have any place (cf. 2:8). That word of the cross is at the same time "the word of life" (Phil. 2:16).

(iii) Paul calls the word of the cross "the message [*logos*] of reconciliation" in 2 Cor. 5:19. This word, which is passed on by the apostolic "ministry of reconciliation" (5:18), is founded on the event of reconciliation in Jesus' death, which took place "while we were still sinners" (Rom. 5:8–10). Reconciliation with God is available for all humans (cf. 2 Cor. 5:14, "one died for all"; also Col. 1:19–22). Still, this word of reconciliation must be distinguished from the reconciliation itself. Paul himself distinguishes between the historical event of the reconciliation of the world and the speaking event of the word concerning this event.

(iv) As Paul in Rom. 9:9 designates the word of election to Isaac as the word of God, so Christ, the "Yes" of God's promises (2 Cor. 1:19–20), makes the word of proclamation an unambiguous word of salvation (1:18). His representative death and the curse laid on him fulfills the word of promise given to Abraham (Gal. 3:6–14; cf. Gen. 12:3; 15:6; 18:18), which retains its validity for Israel, even though they rejected the Messiah. Thus, the question as to the validity of God's word in view of Israel's rejection of the Messiah becomes the keynote of Rom. 9–11: "It is not as though God's word had failed" (9:6). For Paul, the question of the fulfillment and the abiding validity of the OT word of promise means nothing less than that the whole perspicuity and trustworthiness of the word of reconciliation and justification are at stake. At times NT writers use *prolegō* to refer to God's message spoken beforehand through OT prophets (e.g., Rom. 9:29; Heb. 4:7; 2 Pet. 3:2).

(v) The word of God, which according to Paul is promulgated in the shape of a human word, might easily be confused with other human words. This is why Paul thanks God that the church at Thessalonica accepted what they heard from him "not as the word of men, but as it actually is, the word of God" (1 Thess. 2:13).

When Paul arrived in Thessalonica, he worked hard to earn his own living and proclaimed the word of God to the people there without any attempt to impress by appearances (2:9–10). He consciously avoided proclaiming the word of God like the wandering apostles of the day; he did not use enthusiastic speech or human power, did not draw on impressive words of wisdom, and did not falsify God's word (1 Thess. 2:5; cf. 1 Cor. 2:1, 4, 13; 2 Cor. 2:17; 4:2). Instead, and in order to legitimate the word of God, he pointed to his human weakness (cf. 10:10) and to his persecution as a disciple of the cross (Gal. 6:17). Knowing the humanity of the word of God, Paul also instructed the church to give precedence in worship to intelligible language rather than unintelligible indulgence of one's own possession of the Spirit (1 Cor. 14:9, 19).

(b) The author of Heb. begins by pointing out how God has spoken repeatedly and in various ways through the prophets. But in these last days he has spoken through his Son (1:1–4) as God's final word, which ushers in the turning point of the ages. As a word of promise directed toward a coming fulfillment, it is "living and active" and "sharper than any double-edged sword" (4:12). This word of God, which had its beginning in the words of Jesus (2:3), is grounded in the exaltation of Jesus to the right hand of God (1:5–13) and in his installation as eschatological high priest (7:1–8:2).

This installation into the authority of the high priest, grounded in the divine (lit.) "word of the oath" (Heb. 7:28), introduces us to "a better hope" (7:19), to God's decisive word of promise guaranteed by oath. That word of promise is also the effective summons to the church to "hold unswervingly to the hope we profess" (10:23). As a "word of exhortation" (13:22), Heb. itself is directed to the church, now grown weary in the face of the persecutions and sufferings.

(c) Acts uses, as a regular periphrasis for the apostolic preaching, the "word of God" (e.g., 6:2, 7; 13:5), "the word of the Lord" (e.g., 8:25; 13:49), or even simply "the word" (e.g., 8:4). This is linked with "the message [*logos*]" that God sent to the Israelites (10:36), which has for its content the word event of the historical Jesus (10:37–43). This apostolic proclamation of Christ (8:25; 13:5, 46), which God himself (17:30) proclaims, is "the message [*logos*] of salvation" (13:26), intended for both Jews and Gentiles. The word of God is commended to the church (20:32), is powerful (19:20), grows (6:7; 12:24), and spreads throughout the land (cf. 1:8). Acts closes (28:30–31) with Paul proclaiming the kingdom of God and the gospel of Jesus Christ in Rome.

4. *Jesus Christ as the Word.* (a) John's Gospel, like the Synoptics, identifies Jesus' preaching as the proclamation of the word of God. Jesus' words are those of the Father, in which the work of the Father is performed (14:24). Anyone, therefore, who hears Jesus' words and accepts them in faith hears God's word (5:24; 12:48–49; 14:24). Because Jesus' word is at the same time the word of the Father, it is therefore the word of life (5:24), salvation (8:51), and truth (17:17). But over and above the statement that Jesus' word is the word of God, Jesus is himself called "the Word" (Jn. 1:1, 14; 1 Jn. 1:1; Rev. 19:13).

(b) Many scholars consider the prologue to the Gospel of Jn. (1:1–18) to be a hymn to Christ, either written by John or picked up (and adapted) by him. It has four main themes: the divine existence of the Word and his function in creation (1:1–3); the function of this Word as light and life for the world of humanity (1:4–5, 9); the rejection of the Word and his work in the world both before and after his incarnation (1:10–11); and the event of the incarnation of the Word and its believing acceptance in the Christian community (1:14, 16).

This prologue stresses the preexistent being of the Word even before time began. The Word was not only with God, he was God. By this Word, the universe was created and humans have life and the benefit of light (Jn. 1:1–4). The Logos then came into the world, to whom John the Baptist bore witness (1:6–8). He was rejected by his people in an incomprehensible way (1:9–11), although some did come to faith and thus became children of God (1:12–13). Without surrendering his essential divinity, the Word became a mortal human (*sarx*, flesh, → 4922), took up residence among the human race, and, as the presence of God's glory, signified the gift of God's grace and covenant faithfulness to them (1:14, 16), surpassing the OT revelation of the word (1:17–18).

(c) The source of this concept of Jesus as the Logos continues to be a matter of scholarly debate. As has been noted in the cl. Gk. section (see above), *logos* became an increasingly important word in the Gk. philosophical tradition. But *logos* was also important in the OT (also see above)—though we should stress that the OT never uses that word as a person and certainly never as an incarnate divine being. Thus, Jn.'s concept transcends the OT concept of *logos*. In Jewish speculations on wisdom, wisdom participates in the creation of the world, is sent into the world by God, and rejected by humans (e.g., Prov. 8:22–36; Sir. 24:3–12). But note that the word *logos* is never used for this concept. This would argue against a direct derivation of Jn.'s *logos* concept from Jewish wisdom speculations. A derivation of the *logos* concept from Aram., rab., or gnostic sources is also doubtful.

Perhaps the most likely source for Jn.'s use of *logos* is Hel. Jud. In Wis. 18:14–19, for example, God's all-powerful *logos* comes down from heaven and brings judgment on the Egyptians. Esp. Philo's doctrine of the *logos* provides a strong contact with Jn.'s concept of the *logos*. In Philo not only is Jewish wisdom identified with the Logos (which Philo understands as a mediating power between God and the creation and to which he ascribes divine predicates), but he also combines OT statements of creation by the word with Stoic statements of the Logos as the world soul and Platonic elements of the Logos as the archetype of the created world.

Yet even here there are contrasts. In Philo, the divine Logos binds together the heavenly and earthly world and rules over and through both macrocosm and microcosm. In Jn. 1, however, the Logos no longer works "spiritually" but is found embodied in a mortal human. It no longer embraces the whole world in a simultaneous transcendence and immanence in order to mediate salvation through inspiration, but the Logos becomes one man and takes human sin on himself. As the Word, God himself (1:1–2) in his divine glory (1:14–15) assumes the full reality of historical objectivity, human transience, and human death. Jesus, the Logos, signifies the presence of God in the flesh. A religious or philosophical parallel to this statement has not been found.

5. *Cognates.* (a) Apollos is described in Acts 18:24 as a "learned [*logios*] man." Whether or not the Apollos faction in Corinth was attracted to him because of such learning cannot be known for sure (1 Cor. 1:10–12).

(b) *logion* (only in pl. *logia* in NT) is used in the LXX for an oracular saying (Num. 24:4, 16), an individual saying (Isa. 28:13), and the commandments (Deut. 33:9); but it is also used as a general statement about the word of God (e.g., Ps. 12:6; Isa. 5:24). Similarly, in Acts 7:38 Moses is said to have received "living words [*logia*]," i.e., the Torah or perhaps the Decalogue (cf. Deut. 32:46–47), while in Rom. 3:2 Paul lists among the advantages of the Jews the fact that they were entrusted with the "very words [*logia*] of God" (cf. 15:8). But these advantages did not turn out to be an abiding benefit, for the Jews did not use them for salvation. The readers of Heb. 5:12 are rebuked for needing instruction again in "the elementary truths of God's word [*logia*]," which suggests a failure to grasp not only the OT revelation but the word of God in Jesus Christ (cf. 1:2). In the context of an exhortation to use gifts for one another, Peter urges: "If anyone speaks, he should do it as one speaking the very words [*logia*] of God" (1 Pet. 4:11); i.e., no one should speak his or her own opinions but only what God has revealed, to his own glory.

(c) *prolegō*, speak ahead of time, in addition to referring to the OT prophets, is also used to refer to prophecies of Jesus (Matt. 24:25) and his apostles (Jude 17), as well as to warnings that Paul gave on earlier occasions to his churches (2 Cor. 13:2; Gal. 1:9; 5:21; 1 Thess. 4:6).

(d) *alogos* in Acts 25:27 has the sense of without reason, but in 2 Pet. 2:12 and Jude 10 it can mean either without reason or dumb.

(e) In 1 Pet. 2:2 the author writes: "Like newborn babies, crave pure spiritual [*logikos*] milk, so that by it you may grow up in your salvation." Although this Gk. word usually meant reasonable or rational in cl. Gk., it seems best to translate it as "spiritual" here. This meaning also suits Rom. 12:1, where Christian worship in the Spirit is set over against Jewish conceptions of religion. But *logikos* may have been chosen in both these places because of the ambiguity of both *spiritual* and *rational*. Paul, for example, may be emphasizing the need for charismatic worship to express itself in forms that were at once spiritual and rational rather than ecstatic and free-floating.

(f) The vb. *logomacheō* and the noun *logomachia* each occur once in the Pastoral Letters. Paul ends 1 Tim. with a warning about contentious teachers who have a craving for controversies and "quarrels about words," which disrupt and even destroy the church (1 Tim. 6:3–5). Similarly, Paul urges Timothy to warn God's people "against quarreling about words," which ruins the hearers (2 Tim. 2:14). These passages probably refer to the heretics in view in these letters, who occupy themselves with myths and endless genealogies (cf. 1 Tim. 4:3; 6:20; 2 Tim. 2:14–18; Tit. 1:14–16; 3:9). The precise nature of the teaching is obscure, though it would seem to be some form of early Gnosticism.

See also *glōssa*, tongue, language, speech (*1185*); *rhēma*, word, utterance, thing, matter, event, case (*4839*).

3366	λοιδορέω

λοιδορέω (*loidoreō*), insult, abuse, revile (*3366*); λοιδορία (*loidoria*), insult, abuse, railing (*3367*); λοίδορος (*loidoros*), railing, abusive, a reviler (*3368*); ἀντιλοιδορέω (*antiloidoreō*), abuse or revile in turn (*518*).

CL & OT 1. This word group is frequently found in cl. Gk., though generally not in a religious sense. Rather it was in the political and social life of the Gks. that importance came to be attached to slander,

insult, and disparagement of an opponent, e.g., as an orator's weapon in a political dispute. For a Gk. person one of the arts of life was to know how to insult others or how to bear insults against oneself.

2. In the LXX these words are similar to cl. Gk. They occur altogether only 21x. The vb. means to quarrel, accuse, rebuke (e.g., Gen. 49:23; Jer. 29:27 = LXX 36:27; 2 Macc. 12:14). *loidoria* means slander (e.g., Exod. 17:7; Num. 20:24; Prov. 10:18; 20:3). *loidoros* means strife, contention (Prov. 25:24; 26:21; 27:15; Sir. 23:8).

NT 1. In the NT these words occur only 10x. They retain the meaning they have in cl. Gk., although they are used chiefly in religious contexts. The suffering of slander and insults is part of the cross that the Christian disciple is called to bear (1 Cor. 4:12; 1 Pet. 2:23). This is more than simply imitating Christ. As those who have been freed in order to obey, we constantly encounter the unredeemed character of the world and share our Lord's suffering in it. We must maintain the faith in the form of love even toward our enemies (cf. *loidoria* in 1 Pet. 3:9). When reviling is answered with blessing, we manifest the power of Jesus Christ (cf. 2:23) and of the gospel to overcome the world, which has to be worked out in faith.

We therefore find *loidoros* twice in lists of sins, indicating conduct not becoming to the Christian (1 Cor. 5:11; 6:10). Nor should Christians themselves give any cause for evil gossip (1 Tim. 5:14), because their lives should be a testimony to our Lord. They will, however, have to endure reviling for their Lord's sake (cf. Jn. 9:28).

2. The case is different in Acts 23:4–5. *loidoreō* is here used in the same way as *blasphēmeō*. Paul utters a curse, pronouncing God's judgment on the high priest, because he was misusing the authority given to him by God. Paul's statement that he did not know he was addressing the high priest should probably be understood as ironical: Ananias was not behaving as a high priest in the way he executed his office. If he had been behaving in a proper manner, Paul's curse would have been blasphemy.

See also *blasphēmeō*, slander, defame, blaspheme (*1059*); *katalaleō*, speak evil of, rail at, slander (*2895*); *oneidizō*, insult, denounce, rebuke (*3943*).

3367 (*loidoria*, insult, abuse, railing), → 3366.

3368 (*loidoros*, railing, abusive, a reviler), → 3366.

3370 (*loipos*, remaining, other), → 3309.

3373 (*loutron*, bath, washing), → 3374.

3374	λούω

λούω (*louō*), wash (*3374*); ἀπολούω (*apolouō*), wash, wash away (*666*); λουτρόν (*loutron*), bath, washing (*3373*).

CL & OT 1. In cl. Gk. *louō* means wash, (mid.) wash oneself, take a bath; generally it indicates washing the whole body in contrast to *niptō*, which was used for washing parts of the body, and *plynō*, which was used of objects, especially clothes. *apolouō* is a strengthened form of *louō*. *loutron* means the place where one has a bath or simply the bath.

Washing for ritual purification was common among ancient peoples of the Orient. The origin of religious lustrations lies in animistic religion, when people believed that certain waters were impregnated with the power of deity and that this power was communicated to persons and objects plunged in them. Such washings safeguarded a person approaching a deity and seeking protection from demonic assaults. When the nature of religious belief changed, the lustrations were spiritualized and extended in their application. Thus, washing was required before prayer, in preparation for initiation into religious cults, and after bloodshed in war.

2. Similar phenomena may be traced in the OT, though with an emphasis more in keeping with the OT view of sin and uncleanness. When Aaron approached the holy God in the Most Holy Place on the Day of Atonement, he had to bathe his body in water, put on holy

garments (Lev. 16:4), offer a sacrifice (16:6), and burn incense in the sanctuary "so that he will not die" (16:13).

The processes of birth, sickness, and death all entail ritual uncleanness. Purification by washing in water is required after sexual emissions (Lev. 15:16–18), menstruation (15:19–30), birth (12:1–8), and contact with leprosy (13:1–14:32) or death (Num. 5:1–3; 19:11–22). The conviction of Israel's exclusive relationship with Yahweh possibly lent to these rites a polemic aspect. If Israel's neighbors resorted to magical rites to secure aid from the gods in the critical moments of life, the answer of Israel's priests was to urge cleansing from them all and to be exclusively devoted to Yahweh. In the last days God himself promised to sprinkle water on his people and to give them a new heart and a new spirit (Ezek. 36:25); he would open up a fountain to purify them from sin and uncleanness (Zech. 13:1), and he would purge them with fire and fuller's bleach (Mal. 3:1–4).

3. At Qumran, the sectaries stressed the necessity for repentance if the ritual bath was to be efficacious for religious cleansing.

NT 1. (a) *louō* occurs only 5x in the NT. In Acts 16:33 it has a non-religious meaning, but in Jn. 13:10 it relates to washing for purification and entails a contrast between washing the entire body (*louō*) and rinsing individual limbs (*niptō*). It is improbable that any reference to Christian baptism is intended in this passage.

(b) In Heb. 10:22, however, Christians have their "hearts sprinkled (*rhantizō*) to cleanse us from a guilty conscience" and their "bodies washed (*louō*) with pure water." We should not interpret this as a contrast between internal cleansing by the blood of Christ's sacrifice and external cleansing by baptism. If the sprinkling and the washing do not both refer to cleansing waters (as in Ezek. 36:25 and the Qumran writings), the cleansing blood of Christ is thought of as effective in baptism, just as the cleansing power of baptism is the shed blood of Christ (cf. Rom. 6:1–4).

(c) In Acts 22:16 *apolouō* undoubtedly relates to baptism. The similarity of language in 1 Cor. 6:11 indicates that it, too, has in view the cleansing of sins in baptism. One should note in both cases the aor. tense of the verbs, pointing to a single occasion of washing, sanctification, and justification. "In the name of Jesus Christ" reflects the use of Jesus' name in baptismal formulas; "by one Spirit" links the action of the Spirit with baptism (cf. Acts 2:38; 1 Cor. 12:13; etc.).

2. *loutron* appears twice in the NT, both in contexts that relate to baptism; they denote the act rather than the place of washing. Eph. 5:26 may allude to the ceremonial bath taken by a bride in preparation for marriage. For the bride of Christ (→ *nymphē*, *3811*), the counterpart to this bath is baptism, in which the members of the body are cleansed "by the washing with water through the word" (i.e., the confession that "Jesus is Lord" [Rom. 10:9]). In Tit. 3:5 baptism is "the washing of rebirth and renewal by the Holy Spirit." The "washing" is not that which effects the renewal. Rather, it is the occasion when the Spirit creatively works in the individual, just as he made the community of disciples the body of Christ at Pentecost (Acts 2:33) and at the end will produce a new creation (Matt. 19:28).

See also *baptizō*, baptize, immerse (*966*); *niptō*, wash (*3782*).

| 3382 | λυπέω | λυπέω (*lypeō*), inflict pain (*3382*); λύπη (*lypē*), sorrow, pain (*3383*). |

CL & OT 1. *lypē* denotes physical pain and emotional suffering. Joy and sorrow are part and parcel of human life. Hel. philosophy understood sorrow as the antithesis to the joy that is worth striving for. The Stoics held that a human being's task was to overcome sorrow through frugality and impassiveness. Only later, esp. in Gnosticism, was a more positive understanding of sorrow attained: Through accident, sickness, and pain humans are refined and brought to salutary repentance.

2. *lypeō* occurs approximately 50x in the LXX to denote physical hardship, pain, sorrow, grief, mourning, fear, displeasure, and anger (mainly in the later OT writings and the Apocr., esp. Dan., Prov., Sir., and Macc.). In the ANE emotions are a part of everyday life and are not subjected to any kind of theoretical analysis.

The explanation of sorrow and pain given in Gen. 3 is that *lypē* is sent by God as a result of the fall (3:16–19). Wisdom lit. speaks of the *lypē* that is present even in joy (Prov. 14:13) and has to be overcome (Sir. 30:21–23). When Isa. (1:5) says that the "whole heart" of the people is "afflicted" (lit., "in pain"), he means that they are in the worst state imaginable. Eschatological salvation is promised as a time without sorrow and sighing (35:10; 51:11); the age to come will know nothing but joy and glory (cf. 2 Esd. 7:13).

NT In the NT (as in the LXX) there are fewer references to mourning than to its opposite, joy. Specifically, *lypeō* occurs 26x and *lypē* 16x, whereas *chairō* (→ *5897*) and *chara* occur 74x and 59x respectively. While Matt. prefers the vb. *lypeō* and Jn. the noun *lypē*, both vb. and noun occur most frequently in 2 Cor., a fact that indicates Paul's profound personal understanding of "godly sorrow." The sufferings of this present time are regarded as contrary to the purpose of creation—hence the longing to be free of them.

1. In general *lypē* in the NT denotes both physical and emotional pain. Jesus experienced fear and dread before his death (Matt. 26:37–38). Paul was "grieved" (perhaps ill-treated) by a member of the Corinthian church (2 Cor. 2:5). In 2 Cor. 2:1–5 Paul hopes that the Corinthians will cause him no further grief. The OT expectation of salvation is reflected in the NT as future consolation and is promised to those now sorrowing. Rev. looks forward to a new heaven and a new earth from which pain and sorrow will be banished (cf. 7:17; 21:4).

2. Paul portrays *lypē* as an essential mark of the Christian life. In 2 Cor. 7:8–11 he contrasts "godly sorrow" with "worldly sorrow." The latter laments personal disappointment and the transitoriness of life, but godly sorrow brings one to see one's own guilt and leads to repentance (7:10). Within the framework of his theology of the cross, Paul speaks of himself as taking up the cross of Christ (cf. Gal. 6:14). This lays on his shoulders the cross of this world's sorrow and pain—hence the list of his sufferings in 2 Cor. 4:8–12 and 11:23–33. While non-Christians fear loss of their lives, Christians find new life (4:11; Phil. 3:10–11) in being crucified with Christ (Rom. 6:6). This leads to a paradox in the believer's experience, for all the normal values relating to life and suffering are reversed (cf. the antitheses of 2 Cor. 6:3–10).

3. What Paul describes as a paradox in Christian experience is set out in Jn. 16:20–22 as a temporal sequence. The church at the present time "grieves" because of Christ's departure and apparent absence, though for the "world" this is a cause for rejoicing. Jn. shows that the present lot of the church is to endure loneliness and the world's hatred. At the same time, however, the departing Christ promises his church joy at his return; this joy no one will take from her (16:22).

See also *klaiō*, weep (*3081*); *koptō*, strike (*3164*); *brychō*, gnash (*1107*); *pentheō*, be sad, grieve, mourn (*4291*); *stenazō*, to sigh, groan (*5100*).

3383 (*lypē*, sorrow, pain), → *3382*.

3386 (*lysis*, release, divorce), → *3395*.

| 3389 | λύτρον | λύτρον (*lytron*), price of release, ransom, ransom price (*3389*); ἀν- |

τίλυτρον (*antilytron*), ransom, ransom price (*519*); λυτρόω (*lytroō*), to ransom, redeem (*3390*); λύτρωσις (*lytrōsis*), redemption, deliverance, release (*3391*); ἀπολύτρωσις (*apolytrōsis*), redemption, deliverance, release (*667*); λυτρωτής (*lytrōtēs*), redeemer (*3392*).

CL & OT 1. *lytron* and *antilytron* (only postbiblical in secular Gk.) denote the means or money for a ransom. The pl. *lytra* is common. We find also the meaning of recompense. Among the Gks. a ransom was often paid to free slaves, but the word is seldom found in cultic contexts. *lytroō* means to free by a ransom, redeem. It is used only in act. in cl. Gk., but is mid. or pass. in biblical Gk. *lytrōsis* and *apolytrōsis*, synonyms meaning freeing, redeeming, are rare. *lytrōtēs*, redeemer, is found only in biblical Gk.

2 (a). In the LXX the sing. *lytron* is found only in Lev. 27:31; Prov. 6:35; 13:8; otherwise it is always in pl. *lytron* often translates Heb. *kōper*, which denotes the gift in exchange for a life, which according to the sacred law is forfeited or has come under the punishment of God (Exod. 21:30; 30:12). A ransom was not to be paid for a murderer (Num. 35:31–32). It is not usually clear whether God or those who represent him (i.e., priests) are the recipients of the ransom money. This use of *lytron* has included the notion of reconciliation (for more on the related vb. *kipper*, to reconcile, → *hilaskomai*, 2661).

(b) *lytron* is used for words derived from *pādâ*, ransom, redeem (cf. Lev. 19:20; Num. 3:46–51; 18:15). This has to be paid for those who by sacred law belong to God (e.g., a firstborn man or animal). It can be paid by animal sacrifice (Exod. 13:13, 15; 34:20) or money (30:13–16). Lev. 19:20 uses *lytra* for the ransoming of a slave girl.

(c) *lytra* also renders the noun *geʾullâ*, redemption (from the vb. *gāʾal*, redeem, act as kinsman; → *lyō*, 3395). The redeemer (*gōʾēl*) was originally the closest relative who, as the avenger of blood, had to redeem the blood of the murdered victim (Num. 35:19, 21, 24, 25, 27; Jos. 20:3, 5) as well as a family possession that had been sold (Lev. 27:13, 15, 19–20, 31), and even the person whose economic plight had caused him to sell himself to a non-Jew (25:48–49). In 25:26, 51–52 the *geʾullâ* is the price of redemption. In 25:24 it means redemption, while in 25:29, 31–32, 48; Ruth 4:6; Jer. 32:8 it signifies the right of redemption.

(d) The duties prescribed by these OT laws are understandable against the background of the covenant that made Israel Yahweh's unique possession (Exod. 19:5), among whom he dwelt (25:8). The land was Yahweh's and given to Israel through Yahweh's saving intervention as Lord of history. Therefore the land was not to be sold in perpetuity (Lev. 25:23), but rather to be redeemed (25:24). By being redeemed out of Egypt, Israel had become Yahweh's servants (25:38, 55; cf. Deut. 15:15); thus, the impoverished Israelite who had sold himself into slavery was either to be redeemed (Lev. 25:55) or to be released in the Year of Jubilee (25:50, 54).

3. The vb. *lytroō* occurs more frequently in the LXX than *lytron*. In most cases Yahweh is the subj. (e.g., Exod. 6:6; Deut. 7:8; 9:26; Neh. 1:10; Ps. 25:22; Isa. 51:11; Jer. 15:21; Hos. 7:13). The basic idea of making free by a ransom can be seen in Exod. 34:20; Lev. 19:20; 25:25. But in other places, *lytroō* no longer refers to a material price paid but simply to the redeeming activity of God, who freed Israel from slavery in Egypt. It is the use of his power in the service of his love and faithfulness that redeems from bondage. In Isa. the deliverance is in the first place the freeing of Israel from Babylonian captivity and the return of the people (41:14; 47:4). The foreign nations are to receive no ransom for them; in fact, God gives them as ransom for Israel (43:1–4; 45:13).

4. In the intertestamental period, since the dominion of foreigners over Israel continued, words in this group received a political and nationalistic connotation (*Pss. Sol.* 9:1; 12:6). The Qumran texts also stress this aspect (1QM 1:12–13; 14:5–6). Redemption was often conceived of in a wider sense. Especially in Ps. the thought is of the individual: God redeems a person from oppression and wrong (Ps. 31:5; 72:14), from destruction (103:4; Sir. 51:2), and from sin (Ps. 130:8).

5. In Lev. 25:29, 48 *lytrōsis* means the right of redemption of property that has been sold. Ps. 49:8 states that there is no ransom from death. In Isa. 63:4 the judgment on the heathen appears to Israel as "the year of my redemption." Ps. 111:9 thinks of Israel's redemption in general and 130:7 of redemption from sin. *apolytrōsis* is used in the LXX only in Dan. 4:34 of the freeing of Nebuchadnezzar from his madness. God is twice called *lytrōtēs*, redeemer (Ps. 19:14; 78:35).

6. Jud. reflected much on the OT statements about ransom money. Above all, the good deeds of the martyrs appeared as a ransom with atoning power (cf. 4 Macc. 6:28–29; 17:22). On the other hand, it is stressed that there is no ransom for the Gentiles in the final judgment (cf. *1 Enoch* 98:10). *gāʾal* is used only once in the Qumran texts as kinsman or protector (CD 14:16); *pādâ* is more important. In 1QH, for example, the author praises God for delivering him from his enemies (2:32, 35) and from destruction (3:19).

gāʾal is often used of the exodus deliverance in rab. lit. Both *gāʾal* and *pādâ* are frequent in the Mishnah in cases of legal and cultic redemption. *gāʾal* is also applied to Israel's future deliverance when all afflictions will be ended. The rabbis used *gōʾēl* for the coming Messiah, the redeemer of the glorious future.

NT 1. In the NT *lytron* is found only in the saying of Jesus in Matt. 20:28; Mk. 10:45: "The Son of Man did not come to be served, but to serve, and to give his life as a ransom [*lytron*] for many" (cf. also Lk. 22:27, which stresses the serving nature of Jesus, but does not include the ransom element). Mk. 10:45 has often been interpreted in the light of the suffering servant of Isa. 53 (esp. 53:10–12), where the sacrifice of one man is contrasted with the many, for whom it is made. Note that in Qumran "the many" is sometimes a technical term for the elect community. Thus, Mk. 10:45 seems to combine the substitutionary redemption of Isa. 53 by the one on behalf of many with the idea that the many are the elect community.

The reconciling significance of Jesus' passion, which in Mk. 10:45 is designated by the word *lytron*, corresponds to what in Heb. was expressed by the *kipper* word group (→ *hilaskomai*, reconcile, 2661). In the earliest form of NT proclamation it was expressed in the formula that "Christ died for [*hyper*] our sins according to the Scriptures" (1 Cor. 15:3). Whereas atoning value is ascribed to the sufferings of the Jewish martyrs in 2 Macc. 7:37; 4 Macc. 6:28; 17:21–22, this passage offers a parallel and a stark contrast. It affirms that atonement is made by suffering, but it implicitly denies that such atonement can be made by Jewish martyrs; rather, it is brought about by Jesus alone. The prep. *hyper* suggests that Jesus' suffering is a substitute suffering, in the place of those condemned to sin and death; by his suffering, he sets us free.

In other words, the ransom notion has not only an atoning but also a liberating aspect. The many are set free not only from guilt, but also from its consequences, death and judgment. In Mk. 8:37 Jesus asks: "What can a man give in exchange for his soul?" (→ *katallassō*, reconcile, 2904). The question finds its answer in Mk. 10:45. The same Jesus, who completes his service in giving up his life, is the Son of Man who will come in glory (Matt. 25:31). Jesus does not say who will receive the ransom. Since Mk. 8:33 pictures Satan as endeavoring to prevent Jesus' path of suffering, we can think only of God in this context.

2. The rare word *antilytron*, ransom, not found in the LXX, occurs in the NT only at 1 Tim. 2:6 in the context of an exhortation to prayer for all people, including kings and those in high positions: "For there is one God and one mediator between God and men, the man Christ Jesus, who gave himself as a ransom [*antilytron*] for all men . . ." (1 Tim. 2:5–6). The saying points back to Mk. 10:45. Whereas Mk. 10:45 speak of a *lytron anti* ("a ransom for"), Paul uses a noun that combines the noun *lytron* and the prep. *anti* in a single word, suggesting a ransom that has been completely paid. The use of *anti* may even accentuate the notion of exchange. The word "all" in "all men" denotes either that the effect of Jesus' death is available for all people or that he is a ransom for all kinds of people, including pagan rulers (cf. 1 Tim. 2:1), whom some Christians might deem to be beyond the pale. What is clear in 2:6 is that Paul extends the "many" of Mk. 10:45 to include not only the Gentiles who have actually responded to the gospel but to pagan rulers who at the time might be hostile.

Similar thoughts on Christ's death as a ransom given in love may be found elsewhere in Paul. His self-giving in death is grounded in love (Gal. 2:20; Eph. 5:2). Believers are bought with a price (1 Cor. 6:20; 7:23) that was paid to atone for sin and its consequences (Gal. 1:4; Eph. 1:7; Col. 1:14). Christ's death is a propitiation (Rom. 3:25) that brings about reconciliation (2 Cor. 5:18–21).

3. *lytrōsis*, deliverance, release, redemption, occurs twice in the birth and infancy narratives of Lk. and once in Heb. Zechariah, the father of John the Baptist, sang a song of prophecy after the birth of his son John, which begins: "Praise be to the Lord, the God of Israel, because he has come and has redeemed [*lytrōsis*] his people" (Lk. 1:68; cf. 1:69, which develops this theme further). Similarly, the prophetess Anna gave thanks to God on seeing the infant Jesus in the temple "and spoke about the child to all who were looking forward to the redemption [*lytrōsis*] of Jerusalem" (2:38; cf. also 24:21, where those on the road to Emmaus hoped that Jesus was going "to redeem" [*lytroō*] Israel). The idea of ransoming or purchasing does not stand out explicitly, but it cannot be discounted.

It is questionable how far the idea of ransoming is present in Heb. 9:12, although clearly atonement is here made by blood. The death, resurrection, and ascension of Jesus is here understood in terms of the Day of Atonement ritual of Lev. 16: Christ "entered the Most Holy Place once for all by his own blood, having obtained eternal redemption [*lytrōsis*]." The sacrifices of the Day of Atonement were not strictly speaking a *ransom*, although the shedding of blood made propitiation (→ *hilaskomai*, reconcile, *2661*).

4. *lytrōtēs* occurs only in Stephen's speech in Acts 7, where it is applied to Moses: "This is the same Moses whom they had rejected with the words, 'Who made you ruler and judge?' He was sent to be their ruler and deliverer [*lytrōtēs*] by God himself" (7:35; cf. Exod. 2:14). The point of the argument is to show that the Jews' treatment of Jesus is consistent with the Jews' attitude to divinely appointed leaders and deliverers down through the ages. Moses, whom the Jews regarded as the leader and deliverer par excellence, is a type of Christ in two ways here: He is a ruler and deliverer, and he was rejected by the Jews (cf. Acts 7:52).

5. *apolytrōsis* occurs 10x in the NT. In Paul's writings it figures largely to designate the deliverance from sin and its penalty brought about by the propitiatory death of Christ. In this sense it is a present reality grounded exclusively in Christ: We "are justified freely by his grace through the redemption [*apolytrōsis*] that came by Christ Jesus" (Rom. 3:24; see also 1 Cor. 1:30; Eph. 1:7; Col. 1:14).

But this redemption also has a future aspect, for its full realization will only come with the Parousia: "Not only so, but we ourselves, who have the firstfruits of the Spirit, groan inwardly as we wait eagerly for our adoption as sons, the redemption [*apolytrōsis*] of our bodies" (Rom. 8:23; cf. Lk. 21:28; Phil. 3:21). Similarly, Eph. 1:14 sees the present sealing by the Spirit as the guarantee of our inheritance until our final redemption.

Heb. 9:15 combines the Pauline association of redemption and the death of Christ with the characteristic theme in Heb. of the comparison of the new covenant with the old: Jesus is the mediator of a new covenant, and "he has died as a ransom [*apolytrōsis*] to set them free from the sins committed under the first covenant." In 11:35 *apolytrōsis* has the secular sense of "release" from one's captors (cf., perhaps, the story in 2 Macc. 7).

6. The vb. *lytroō* (3x, only in mid. and pass.) occurs in Lk. 24:21 (see comments under 3, above). Tit. 2:14 interprets Christologically the thought of Ps. 130:8 (cf. also Deut. 14:2; Ezek. 37:23); it describes the Christian life as renouncing irreligion and worldly passions and living in a godly way, awaiting the appearing of Christ, "who gave himself for us to redeem [*lytroō*] us from all wickedness." In 1 Pet. 1:18–19 *lytroō* refers both to that from which the believer is ransomed or redeemed and to the means of the ransom—"not with perishable things such as silver or gold [cf. Isa. 52:3] ... but with the precious blood of Christ [cf. Eph. 1:7; Heb. 9:12, 22; Rev. 1:5], a lamb without blemish or defect" (cf. Isa. 53:7). The Passover lamb and animal sacrifices were to be without blemish (Exod. 12:5; 29:1; Lev. 22:17–25; Ezek. 43:22–23).

See also *lyō*, to loose, untie, set free, release, annul, abolish (*3395*); *rhyomai*, rescue, deliver, preserve, save (*4861*); *sōzō*, save, keep from harm, preserve, rescue (*5392*); *sōtēr*, savior, deliverer, preserver (*5400*).

3390 (*lytroō*, to ransom, redeem), → *3389*.

3391 (*lytrōsis*, redemption, deliverance, release), → *3389*.

3392 (*lytrōtēs*, redeemer), → *3389*.

3393 (*lychnia*, candlestick, lampstand), → *3394*.

3394	λύχνος

λύχνος (*lychnos*), lamp, light (*3394*); λυχνία (*lychnia*), candlestick, lampstand (*3393*).

CL & OT 1. In cl. Gk. *lychnos* means light, lamp. Later it came to denote some form of oil lamp that was placed on a lampstand to diffuse the beam.

2. Among the Israelites, lamp and lampstand were important both as everyday objects (cf. 2 Ki. 4:10) and as a part of public worship (cf. esp. the seven-branched candlestick in the tabernacle and the temple, e.g., Exod. 25:31–40; Heb. 9:2).

NT In the NT *lychnos* occurs 14x, *lychnia* 12x. The importance of lights and lamps (e.g., for the household, Lk. 15:8) explains why Jesus used them to illustrate his disciples' function in the world: As a lamp on the lampstand lights up the surrounding darkness, so disciples are to have an illuminating effect on their environment (Matt. 5:15–16; Mk. 4:21; Lk. 8:16; 11:33). The eye is called "the lamp [*lychnos*] of the body" (Matt. 6:22; Lk. 11:34); its health determines whether the blessings of light come to us.

While Jesus described himself as light (Jn. 8:12; 9:5; → *phōs*, *5890*), his forerunner John the Baptist is likened to a burning and light-giving lamp (*lychnos*, 5:35). Similarly, the two witnesses are compared to two lampstands (Rev. 11:4, cf. Zech. 4:3, 11–14), and the seven churches are symbolized by seven golden lampstands (Rev. 1:12–13, 20; 2:1). The source of this light is indicated in 2 Pet. 1:19, where the word of prophecy is called "light" that looks forward to the glory of Christ. It is clear from Rev. 2:5 that the light of Christian witness can become dull and even go out, and that it can be renewed only by repentance (cf. Heb. 6:4–8, on the apostasy of "those who have once been enlightened").

Babylon is warned that when she sinks into ruin, "the light of a lamp will never shine in you again" (Rev. 18:23). But the heavenly Jerusalem will be illuminated by the glory of God (21:23), which makes all lamps superfluous (22:5), for God himself will be the sole light. Until then, Christians live in eschatological tension; we are to be watchful, as in the vivid metaphors of Lk. 12:35: "Be dressed ready for service and keep your lamps burning."

See also *lampō*, shine (*3290*); *phainō*, shine (*5743*); *emphanizō*, reveal, make known (*1872*); *phōs*, light, brilliance, brightness (*5890*).

3395	λύω

λύω (*lyō*), to loose, untie, set free, release, annul, abolish (*3395*); λύσις (*lysis*), release, divorce (*3386*); καταλύω (*katalyō*), destroy, demolish, abolish (*2907*); κατάλυμα (*katalyma*), lodging, guest room (*2906*); ἀκατάλυτος (*akatalytos*), indestructible (*186*); ἐκλύω (*eklyō*), become loose, become weary, become weak (*1725*).

CL & OT 1. In cl. Gk. *lyō* means to loose, make free. When used with a pers. obj. it means to set free, ransom, deliver, both lit. and metaphorically. The meaning to dissolve gives the further sense of to destroy. Already in Homer it was used of the deliverance that the gods give to humans, e.g., from difficulties and need, but without any recognizable link with sin.

2. The LXX uses *lyō* to translate a variety of Heb. vbs. It can mean to open (Gen. 42:27), free those in bondage (Ps. 105:20), draw off

(e.g., sandals, Exod. 3:5), loosen [knots], i.e., solve difficulties (Dan. 5:12), be pleased with, accept favorably (Isa. 40:2), lift up, take away [sins] (Job 42:9), and destroy (Ezr. 5:12).

katalyō is used 67x. It often means to lodge, pass the night, esp. in historical narratives (e.g., Gen. 19:2; 24:23; Num. 22:8; Ruth 4:14). It can also mean to break down (2 Ki. 25:10) or dissolve, abolish (2 Macc. 2:22).

eklyō commonly has the meaning of losing one's strength, letting one's heart become faint, or relaxing one's hands (e.g., Deut. 20:3; Jos. 10:6; 18:3; Isa. 13:7; Lam. 2:12, 19; Ezek. 7:17). However, in Job 19:25 it stands for *gōʾēl*, a participial form of a Heb. vb. that means redeem, act as a redeemer: "I know that my Redeemer [lit. in LXX, the one about to redeem me] lives." The *gōʾēl* in Heb. was the kinsman redeemer, who as the closest relative was responsible to redeem the blood of a murdered victim, to buy back family possessions, to redeem from bondage, and to take a kinsman's widow as wife (→ *lytron*, ransom, *3389*).

The meaning of Job 19:25 is notoriously difficult. Some regard the *gōʾēl* as "vindicator," for the context is not concerned with deliverance from Sheol but with the vindication of Job's name before other people. But others relate this verse to 16:19: "Even now my witness is in heaven; my advocate is on high." Job is thinking of God himself as his *gōʾēl* (cf. the use of this Heb. word with reference to God in Ps. 19:14, "my Redeemer"; LXX has *lytrōtēs* here). In both cases the emphasis is on vindication and help. Whether there is also an element of buying back depends on the degree to which it is possible to speak of this factor in the general idea of the *gōʾēl*. However, it seems implied that the *gōʾēl* rescues that which was forfeited and restores justice to those who are not in a position to help themselves.

NT 1. In the NT *lyō* is used in the lit. sense of untying the thong of a sandal (Mk. 1:7; Jn. 1:27; Acts 13:25), untying a donkey's colt (Matt. 21:2), unwrapping Lazarus from his grave clothes (Jn. 11:44), and removing Paul's bonds (Acts 22:30). In a weakened sense in 13:43 it denotes being dismissed from a synagogue.

2. The sense of setting free, untying, and thus loosing is applied to angels (Rev. 9:14–15) and Satan (20:3, 7; on this and the question of the millennium, → *chilias* [*5942*]). In 9:14–15, the sixth angel with a trumpet is commanded: "'Release the four angels who are bound at the great river Euphrates.' And the four angels ... were released," killing a third of human population. The river represents the boundary of Assyria and Babylon, the area from which invasions came in OT times. In Rev. Babylon represents the wicked world in its ongoing manifestations (see chs. 17–18). The number four probably represents completeness. The significance of the vision depends on how Rev. as a whole is interpreted—esp. whether the visions are consecutive or parallel. In any case, destruction and loss of life gives occasion for repentance, even though many do not take it (9:20–21).

3. Satan is mentioned in connection with binding and loosing in Lk. 13:16 in the description of a woman crippled for eighteen years: "Should not this woman, a daughter of Abraham, whom Satan has kept bound for eighteen long years, be set free [*lyō*] on the Sabbath...?" There is probably a play on *lyō* here that underlines the hypocrisy of Jesus' enemies, for they were complaining about Jesus' practice of healing on the Sabbath, yet they themselves would "untie" their animals to lead them to water on the Sabbath (13:15).

lyō is also used in the case of the healing of the deaf man with an impediment in his speech: "At this, the man's ears were opened, his tongue was loosened, and he began to speak plainly" (Mk. 7:35).

4. *lyō* can also have the sense of to break or destroy. In Rev. 5:2 the scroll of ongoing history, held by God who is seated on his throne, is sealed with seven seals, which no one is "worthy to break" and open. However, "the Lion of the tribe of Judah, the Root of David, has triumphed" and so is able to open the seals (5:5). Acts 27:41 tells of the breaking up of the stern of the ship on which Paul was bound for Rome. Likewise, Peter in 2 Pet. 3:10–12 describes the eschatological

conflagration, when "the elements [→ *stoicheion*, *5122*] will be destroyed [*lyō*] by fire" and there will be a new heaven and earth (cf. Matt. 19:28; Mk. 14:25; Lk. 22:30).

5. *lyō* also has the sense of loosing or freeing from sin (Rev. 1:5) and death (Acts 2:24). Rev. 1:5 relates remission of sin to the death of Jesus in that he "has freed us from our sins by his blood." The KJV reads *louō* (wash) rather than *luō* here; both ideas find parallels elsewhere in the book: washing robes in the blood of the Lamb (7:14), and ransoming people by his blood (5:9). But the context fits the idea of redemption as a new exodus of God's people. The Lamb of God frees us from slavery to sin, as typified in the Passover lamb. In Acts 2:24 *lyō* is applied to the resurrection of Jesus: God raised up Jesus, "freeing him from the agony of death" (on the imagery of the cords of Sheol and death, see 2 Sam. 22:6; Ps. 18:4–6; 116:3).

6. *lyō* is found in various senses in connection with the institutions of Jud. In each case the divine origin of the institution is recognized either explicitly or implicitly. But the coming of Jesus demands a fresh understanding in the form of either a renewed attitude to what stands or the realization that what was formerly regarded as valid and binding is now superseded.

(a) In his Sermon on the Mount Jesus says: "Do not think that I have come to abolish [*katalyō*] the Law or the Prophets; I have not come to abolish [*katalyō*] them but to fulfill them. I tell you the truth, until heaven and earth disappear, not the smallest letter, not the least stroke of a pen, will by any means disappear from the Law until everything is accomplished. Anyone who breaks [*lyō*] one of the least of these commandments and teaches others to do the same will be called least in the kingdom of heaven ..." (Matt. 5:17–19). The attitude Jesus expresses here is essentially the same as that found in Mk. 7:6–13; 10:1–12; 11:15–19; Lk. 11:45–52, in which he upholds the intention and spirit of the law in contrast with the scribal interpretations that stultify its demands. Note too the emphasis in Matt. on fulfilling the prophets (→ *plēroō*, *4444*).

The Gk. text in Matt. 5 contains a play on words between *katalyō*, destroy, abolish, and *lyō*, relax. In 5:17 Jesus emphatically states that he has not come to *katalyō* the Law and the Prophets; in 5:19 he gives dire warning to anyone who would *lyō* the least of these commands. This is related in 5:20 to the scribes and Pharisees, and Jesus proceeds to give examples of how commandments have been relaxed: e.g., murder and anger (Matt. 5:21–26; cf. Exod. 20:13; Deut. 5:17); adultery and lust (Matt. 5:27–30; cf. Exod. 20:14; Deut. 5:18); divorce and adultery (Matt. 5:31–32; cf. Deut. 24:1–4; Matt. 19:9; Mk. 10:11–12; Lk. 16:18); loving one's neighbor (Matt. 5:43–48; cf. Lev. 19:18; Prov. 25:21–22). In all these instances Jesus, far from relaxing the law, ratifies it and applies it to one's inner attitudes as well as outward acts. (For Jesus' teaching on the law elsewhere in Matt. see 7:12; 11:13; 22:40; for his denunciation of those who make a mockery of the law by their hypocrisy see 15:1–11; 23:1–39.)

A consistent picture emerges in Matt. Jesus is presented not only as one who upholds the law, but as one who insists that the law must be rightly interpreted and applied. To that extent the true disciple is also a teacher (23:34), but one who has to be "instructed about the kingdom of heaven," so that he might bring "out of his storeroom new treasures as well as old" (13:52; see also *thēsauros*, treasure, *2565*; *grammateus*, teacher, *1208*). The point is that not all interpretation and application are wrong. Jesus and the disciples engage in it. But it is wrong where it fails to bring out the true meaning of the law and when it substitutes human tradition for God's word. Misguided interpretation is seen as relaxing the commandments. Still, one's attitude to the commandments determines one's place in the kingdom; because of their fundamental lack of righteousness, many Jewish teachers are excluded.

(b) *lyō* is twice used in connection with the temple. In Jn.'s account of the cleansing of the temple the Jews ask for a sign of Jesus' authority. "Jesus answered them, 'Destroy [*lyō*] this temple, and I will raise it again in three days'" (Jn. 2:19). Jn. goes on to point out that the temple Jesus was referring to "was his body" (2:21), a point that the disciples understood after the resurrection (2:22). At his trial before the Jewish leaders, false witnesses claimed: "We heard him say, 'I will destroy [*katalyō*] this man-made temple and in three days will build another, not made by man'" (Mk. 14:58). *lyō* and *katalyō* are often used for the destruction of buildings (Matt. 27:40; Mk. 13:2; 14:58; 15:29; Acts 6:14). Jn. 2:19–22 implies that Jesus' own person has already replaced the temple as the divinely appointed place of meeting between God and humankind. It further implies that Jewish disobedience is directly responsible for the destruction of this temple, just as it was for the destruction of the first one (2 Ki. 25:9, 13–17).

Eph. 2:14 uses *lyō* to make a different point: "For he himself is our peace, who has made the two one and has destroyed [*lyō*] the barrier, the dividing wall of hostility." The dividing wall may refer to the inscription in the wall of the Jerusalem temple that forbade, on penalty of death, any non-Jew from going within the sanctuary. By contrast, with Jesus, the new temple, both Jewish and Gentile believers may now "become a holy temple in the Lord" (2:21). The dividing wall between Jewish and Gentile believers before God is gone as a result of the reconciling death of Jesus (2:15–16). Note that in contrast with the Gospels, where Jesus never actually says that *he* will destroy the temple, in Eph. 2:14 he is in fact the subject of the vb.

(c) In Jn. 5:18 *lyō* is used in a phrase about breaking the Sabbath: "For this reason the Jews tried all the harder to kill him; not only was he breaking [*lyō*] the Sabbath, but he was even calling God his own Father, making himself equal with God." The occasion was the healing of a paralytic man by the pool of Bethesda. Jesus defended his action on the basis that his Father continues to work (5:17). This answer is intended to show that there is a sense in which God is working on the Sabbath both in general in sustaining the world and in particular in the case of this healing, in which Jesus is cooperating with the Father.

(d) The same issue is taken up again, but this time with reference to the law, in Jn. 7:23: "Now if a child can be circumcised on the Sabbath so that the law of Moses may not be broken [*lyō*], why are you angry with me for healing the whole man on the Sabbath?" There is an irony between circumcision performed on the male sexual organ (which causes some suffering) and the healing of the whole body, which banishes suffering. Jesus' stance implies that just as in healing he was not breaking the Sabbath, so also he is not breaking the law. The point is extended to Scripture in general in 10:35–36, where Jesus insists that the Scriptures cannot be broken.

(e) The binding and loosing [*lyō*] with which Peter was authorized in Matt. 16:19 and that was given to the disciples and the church at large in 18:18 stands in contrast with rab. usage. The authority of the rabbis as teachers was shown by their being able to forbid or allow certain things. They were apparently even able to excommunicate, i.e., exclude a person from the synagogue. The authority given to the church, however, is independent of any Jewish notion, for it has its own God-given power. For more on this, → *deō*, bind (*1313*); *kleis*, key (*3090*).

(f) *lyō* and the unique noun *lysis* occur in 1 Cor. 7:27 in connection with divorce. The word *lysis* as used here is a somewhat untechnical word for divorce (in contrast to the words used in 7:10–11). Perhaps Paul was using a more general term that covers not only formal divorce but also separation. What he says here must be seen in light of "the present crisis" (7:26), whatever that may mean, and it should probably be read as advice, not as a strict ruling that all must obey. Nevertheless, it is not a sin for those who find themselves "unmarried" (lit., "free [*lyō*] from a wife") to marry (7:28).

7. Compounds of *lyō* are not infrequent in the NT (see also *apolyō* at *687*). (a) *katalyō* means to throw down, detach a stone from a building (Matt. 24:2) or destroy, demolish, (26:61; Mk. 14:58); metaphorically it can refer to Paul's demolition of the Jewish understanding of salvation and way of life (Gal. 2:18), to the destruction of the human body at death (2 Cor. 5:1), and to tearing down God's work in the church (Rom. 14:20) over questions of eating what is unclean. It can also mean to abolish, make invalid—of the law (Matt. 5:17), of the church (which Gamaliel said would fail if it was of humans, Acts 5:38–39)—and to halt (i.e., unharness the pack animals), hence to find lodging (Lk. 9:12; 19:7). *katalyma* means generally lodging, but more particularly a guest room or dining room (Mk. 14:14; Lk. 2:7; 22:11). *akatalytos* occurs only in Heb. 7:16, meaning indestructible or endless; it refers to Jesus as the eternal high priest.

(b) *eklyō* means to become loose, to become weak and weary; it is used of the hungry crowds in the desert (Matt. 15:32; Mk. 8:3), of a believer's certainty of reaping the harvest of well doing if one does not grow weary (Gal. 6:9), and of not losing one's courage in adversity, since discipline is a sign of being a child of God (Heb. 12:5, quoting Prov. 3:11).

See also *lytron*, price of release, ransom, ransom price (*3389*); *rhyomai*, rescue, deliver, preserve, save (*4861*); *sōzō*, save, keep from harm, preserve, rescue (*5392*); *sōtēr*, savior, deliverer, preserver (*5400*).

M *mu*

3404   μαγεία
μαγεία (*mageia*), magic (*3404*); περίεργος (*periergos*), meddlesome, curious, belonging to magic (*4319*); μαγεύω (*mageuō*), practice magic (*3405*); μάγος (*magos*), magus, magician (*3407*); φαρμακεία (*pharmakeia*), magic, sorcery (*5758*); φάρμακον (*pharmakon*), poison, magic potion, charm, medicine, remedy, drug (*5760*); φάρμακος (*pharmakos*), poisoner, magician (*5761*); γόης (*goēs*), sorcerer, juggler (*1200*); πύθων (*pythōn*), the Python, spirit of divination (*4780*); μαντεύομαι (*manteuomai*), foretell, utter oracles, prophesy (*3446*); βασκαίνω (*baskainō*), bewitch (*1001*); φάντασμα (*phantasma*), apparition, ghost (*5753*).

CL & OT 1. Magic is the technique of manipulating supernatural or supernormal forces to attain one's own ends. It may be a means of bending spirits of various grades to carry out one's wishes or of developing psychic powers so one can project an inner force onto some person or situation. Magic is invoked to deal with what cannot be controlled by known natural means. Evidence of magic dates back at least to Paleolithic culture, where, for example, cave art depicts animals stuck with darts with a view to causing the same thing to happen in a future hunt. The dividing line between magic and religion is often indistinct. A distinction is sometimes drawn between white and black magic, with the former being benevolent in intention (e.g., rain-making), whereas the latter is malevolent (loss of health or property, destruction, and death).

2. Common features of magic are: (a) the spell, i.e., the utterance of words according to a set formula; (b) the rite, i.e., a set of actions designed to convey the spell to the object concerned; and (c) the condition of the performer, who must not breach any relevant taboo and must be in the requisite emotional state to perform the prescribed actions.

Magic abounds in Gk. mythology, with various beings accredited with supernatural powers. The most renowned enchantress was Medea. Gk. and Lat. literary writers give pictures of magic and witchcraft. The growth in knowledge and progress of Gk. civilization led to the suppression of magic. Nevertheless, as secularization increased in the higher social levels during the 4th cent. B.C., there was a renewed outburst of interest in magic in the lower levels.

3. (a) Evidence of magic is found throughout the cultures that form the backdrop of the OT: e.g., Sumero-Akkadian and Canaanite religious lit. Behind it lies the belief that no single power has ultimate control over the universe. Even the gods must resort to powers they themselves do not possess.

(b) The reality of these occult powers is recognized in the OT. Deut. 18:10–14 lists the various practices of the surrounding peoples, but categorically prohibits the Israelites from any such practices: divination, sorcery, interpreting omens, witchcraft, casting spells, spiritism, and necromancy. Elsewhere in the OT are references to other occult phenomena, such as charms, enchanting, soothsaying, astrology, and stargazing.

(c) The OT saw any magic as a potential rival to the worship of Yahweh and a threat to the well-being of the people. It was forbidden by law, and those who practiced it were to be put to death (Exod. 22:18; Lev. 19:26, 31; 20:6, 27; cf. Mic. 5:12). As Deut. 18:10–14 shows, such practices were ranked with human sacrifice as an abomination to the Lord (cf. also 2 Ki. 17:17; 2 Chr. 33:6). The prophets denounced it as lies and deception (Isa. 44:25; 57:3; Jer. 27:9–10; Ezek. 22:28; Zech. 10:2; Mal. 3:5). Jezebel was condemned as a sorceress (2 Ki. 9:22), and Manasseh's apostate practices included various forms of magic, soothsaying, and human sacrifice (21:3–6). His grandson Josiah abolished all forms of the occult (23:24).

4. The most significant evidence of magic in the Hel. world is found in certain papyri from Egypt dating from the 3d and 4th cents. A.D. In addition numerous cursing tablets, inscriptions on thin sheets of lead known as *tabellae defixionum*, amulets, and ostraca have been found. Magic here was a fusion of the Gk. spirit with Egyptian influences. Among them were the belief that magic words gained additional power if written on a gem; belief in monstrous beings, half animal and half human; belief that while magic allows one to control the gods, it was at the same time a gift and revelation from the gods; and prominent figures such as Seth, Thoth, and Osiris. There was also a Persian influence, which included the idea of magic as a defense against evil spirits rather than as a means of manipulating the high gods.

Magical practices were also rife in Jud. Justin Martyr testifies to the use of the name of God in exorcism, and the use of *Iaō*, Sabaoth, Adonai, and Yahweh is common in the magical papyri. Apart from divine names, that of Moses appears with that of Thoth and Zoroaster, and Solomon was important. The Heb. language itself, as a sacred language, had a special use. Angels and demons figured esp. in Jewish magic. The normal magical ceremony consisted of two parts: the invocation to the gods and the ritual. The latter could take various forms involving the use of amulets, sacrifices, the mixing of special substances and potions, libations, and secret writing. Elaborate ceremonies could take several days.

NT 1. The NT names several magicians: (a) Simon, commonly referred to as Simon Magus (Acts 8:9–24), practiced spectacular magic in Samaria but professed conversion in response to Philip's preaching. He was astounded by the manifestations of the Holy Spirit that followed the laying on of hands by Peter and John and, being still under the influence of his old ideas, assumed that the apostles had some secret technique that he might acquire as a Christian magician. For this he was roundly rebuked by Peter. Christian writers of the 2d cent. speak of him as a heretic of gnostic type and as the founder of the Simonians.

(b) Bar-Jesus or Elymas (Acts 13:4–12), a magician on Cyprus in the employ of Sergius Paulus (the proconsul), resisted Paul and Barnabas but was struck with temporary blindness. The name Elymas is probably connected with the Arabic ʿalîm, wise, magician.

(c) Jannes and Jambres are named in 2 Tim. 3:8 as two of the Egyptian magicians who opposed Moses. They are not named in Exod., but they do occur in Jewish writings.

2. The following descriptive words are found in the NT. (a) *periergos*, "sorcery" (Acts 19:19). This text refers to the voluntary burning of books by those who had previously practiced various magic arts at Ephesus, an event seen as testimony to the growth and power of the word of the Lord (19:20), esp. since the value of the books was put at fifty thousand pieces of silver. *periergos* has the root idea of being concerned with other people's business and is translated "busybodies" in 1 Tim. 5:13 (→ *4318*).

(b) *magos*, magus, magician; *mageia*, magic; *mageuō*, practice magic. According to Herodotus, the Magi were originally Medians who became priests under the Persian empire. Like the Chaldeans of Dan. 1:4 and 2:2–12, 48, they merged their racial identity in their profession, and their name was applied to any practitioner, such as the *magos* Bar-Jesus (Acts 13:6, 8). The noun *mageia* and the vb. *mageuō* also occur in 8:9, 11 of the magic of Simon Magus. *magos* is also used of the Magi from the East, who saw a special star and came to Bethlehem sometime after the birth of Jesus (Matt. 2:1–16). In their search of holy books to interpret the appearance of that star, they must have come across Num. 24:17: "A star will come out of Jacob; a scepter will rise out of Israel."

It is clear that the Magi were neither crude practitioners of the occult arts nor ordinary astrologers. They believed that God showed signs in heaven and that a certain heavenly body (whether planet, star, comet, or supernova) indicated from its appearance and position that God had fulfilled a royal promise, of which they had doubtless heard from Jews in the East. The Pseudepigrapha (e.g., *T. Levi* 18:3–4) and other Jewish writings also testify to Num. 24:17 as messianic (cf. also 2 Pet. 1:19; Rev. 22:16).

(c) *pharmakos*, magician (Rev. 21:8; 22:15); *pharmakeia*, magic, sorcery (Gal. 5:20; Rev. 18:23). The root word *pharmakon* occurs in the NT only in 9:21, but its meaning of medicine, magic potion, or poison gives the underlying idea of the related words. Potions include poisons, but there has always been a magical tradition of herbs gathered and prepared for spells, and also for encouraging the presence of spirits at magical ceremonies. Such activity is classed among the works of the sinful nature in Gal. 5:20.

(d) *goēs*, sorcerer, juggler, occurs only in 2 Tim. 3:13. In cl. Gk. this word can mean a magician or wizard. In view of Jannes and Jambres in 3:8, some have translated *goēs* in this manner. But cl. Gk. also knows the meaning of imposter for this word, since spellbinders could make false claims for their powers. The NIV prefers this translation in 2 Tim. 3:13 in the light of the closing words of this verse.

(e) The word *pythōn* was connected with the oracle at Delphi, where Apollo slew the mighty serpent Python that guarded the oracle. Later on *pythōn* came to designate a spirit of divination or a ventriloquist, who was thought to have such a spirit inside his or her belly. In Acts 16:16 a girl at Philippi had a "spirit by which she predicted the future" (*pneuma pythōna*); the vb. *manteuomai* is used for her "fortune-telling." She probably had second sight fostered by a possessing spirit. This spirit was forced to admit the truth of the gospel, just as other spirits had confessed Jesus Christ during his earthly ministry (Matt. 8:29; Mk. 1:24; Lk. 4:34), but neither Jesus nor Paul accepted testimony from this source, and they cast out such spirits.

(f) *baskainō* can mean to cast a spell by what is called the evil eye. Paul uses the word of the deceived Galatians in Gal. 3:1 ("Who has bewitched you?"). Some believed that the effect of the spell, if the evil eye was detected at the time, could be averted by spitting, and some hold that this was in Paul's mind in his use of *ekptyō* in 4:14 (lit., spit out; NIV "scorn").

3. Whatever heresy Paul has in mind in Col. 2, much of what he says is applicable to practitioners of the occult. Paul's theme is the absolute supremacy and sufficiency of Christ. If Christians are linked to Christ, they share in his supremacy over the spirit world, good and bad, and, to say the least, one is foolish to think he or she can gain more power through intermediate spirit beings. Thus 2:8 and 20 speak of the Christian's deliverance from "the elemental spirits of the universe" (NRSV; *stoicheia*, → *5122*). In 2:15 there is the conquest of "the powers and authorities" (cf. Eph. 6:12) and Col. 2:18 refers to "the worship of angels" and induced visions. Finally 2:21–23 may be describing the rigorous ritual of the magician to produce and safeguard contacts with the spirits.

4. Mediumship (also called spiritualism) is an attempt to communicate with the departed, but there is no relaxation in the NT of the OT ban against such endeavors (e.g., Lev. 19:31; Deut. 18:10–11; 1 Chr. 10:13–14; Isa. 8:19–20). It may be true that the argument is from silence, but it is from significant silence. When Paul, for example, speaks of the departed, he assures Christians that their loved ones have not perished, but that they will meet them again (cf. 1 Cor. 15:17–19; 1 Thess. 4:13–18), for both they and the departed believers are "in Christ." He never suggests that Christian mediums can put the bereaved in touch with those who have passed on.

The NT shows that God may allow a departed spirit to return for purposes of his own: e.g., Moses and Elijah returned on the Mount of Transfiguration to reassert the testimony of the Law and the

Prophets to the sacrifice of Christ on the cross (Matt. 17:3; Mk. 9:4; Lk. 9:30–31).

There are two other references to spirits or ghosts in the NT. When Jesus walked on the water, the disciples thought they were seeing a *phantasma* (Matt. 14:26; Mk. 6:49), a general word used to describe an apparition. The more important reference is Lk. 24:37–41, where Jesus appeared to his disciples after his resurrection. Some thought he was a *pneuma*, a spirit or ghost. Jesus did not deny the existence of ghosts but demonstrated that his resurrection body was of a different order altogether from a spirit form.

5. Some have sought to relate Jesus' miracles, at least in part, to the principles of magic. The evidence for magical practices in the Gospels is slim, however. In the accounts of the healing of the woman with the issue of blood (Matt. 9:20–22; Mk. 5:25–34; Lk. 8:42–48), it is true that the woman may have had a certain magical sense in that she believed that she would be healed if only she could touch Jesus' clothes. But all three Evangelists avoid any support for connecting the healing with magic in giving Jesus' reply: "Your faith has healed you."

Moreover, whereas magicians used names in connection with spells, neither Jesus nor the apostles used secret rituals or esoteric signs to gain control over supernatural powers. Still less is there any trace of trying to coerce a reluctant God to further one's own ends. Although Jesus' enemies insinuated that Jesus cast out demons in the name of Beelzebub, the self-contradictory nature of the charge is at once evident in the light of the exorcisms that Jesus performed (Matt. 12:25–37; Mk. 3:23–30; Lk. 11:17–23). For Jesus the control over evil spirits was not an end in itself. He told his followers: "However, do not rejoice that the spirits submit to you, but rejoice that your names are written in heaven" (10:20).

3405 (*mageuō*, practice magic), → *3404*.

3407 (*magos*, magus, magician), → *3404*.

3408 (*Magōg*, Magog), → *4483*.

3411 (*mathēteuō*, to instruct, make disciples), → *3412*.

| 3412 μαθητής |

μαθητής (*mathētēs*), learner, pupil, disciple (*3412*); μαθητεύω (*mathēteuō*), to instruct, make disciples (*3411*); μανθάνω (*manthanō*), learn (*3443*).

CL & OT 1. (a) *manthanō* denotes the process by which one acquires theoretical knowledge. The word therefore plays an important role in speculative thought from Socrates on. When a person is learning something, one should penetrate deeply into the nature of everything and proceed beyond this insight to a knowledge of morality.

(b) A person is called a *mathētēs* when one binds oneself to someone else in order to acquire practical and theoretical knowledge. Such a person may be an apprentice in a trade, a student of medicine, or a member of a philosophical school. One can only be a *mathētēs* in the company of a *didaskalos*, master or teacher, for which a fee was usually paid. In contrast to the Sophists, Socrates refused any kind of payment from his pupils. From his time on *mathētēs* largely fell into disuse.

2. (a) *manthanō* in the LXX means grow accustomed to, make oneself familiar with, learn. In most of these passages the vb. has no special theological emphasis (e.g., "nor will they train for war anymore," Isa. 2:4; Mic. 4:3). A theological use of *manthanō* is clear in Deut., where Israel is in danger of forgetting Yahweh's goodness and of forfeiting its election and the divine promises of salvation (cf. 6:10–12; 8:17–18; 9:4–6; 11:2). They must learn again to fear the Lord and obey his will (4:10; 14:23; 17:19; 31:12–13). Learning means the process by which the past experience of God's love is translated by the learners into obedience to God's Torah (cf. 4:14). It means fully understanding the story of the saving actions of God's will.

Similarly in Ps. 119:7–8, 71, 73, the psalmist prays for a right attitude of learning the Torah, which is here understood as an all-embracing guide and direction. The goal of learning is action that corresponds to God's word (119:101). Among the objects of *manthanō* are a correct disposition (Isa. 1:17; Bar. 3:14), insight (Sir. 8:9), and wisdom (Wis. 6:9; 7:13).

(b) *mathētēs* is found in the LXX only in alternative readings of Jer. 13:21; 20:11; 46:9 = LXX 26:9. The lack of OT vocabulary for a learner is linked with Israel's consciousness of being an elect people, in which the individual mattered little. There was no disciple-master relationship among humans, for even the priest and the prophet did not teach on their own authority. Note that the attendants of Moses and the prophets are aides and servants, not pupils (Exod. 24:13; Num. 11:28; 1 Ki. 19:19–21; 2 Ki. 4:12). The vb. *mathēteuō* does not occur in the OT.

3. The situation is different in rab. Jud. The *talmîd* is one who is concerned with the entire Jewish tradition: the written and oral Torah. He belongs to his teacher, to whom he subordinates himself in almost servile fashion. Since the rabbi's knowledge gives one direct access to the Scriptures, which facilitates understanding, the rabbi becomes a kind of mediator between his pupils and the Torah. Learning is determined by the authority of a teacher and his interpretation of the Torah, not by a personal study of the Torah. In other words, the *talmîd* appropriates the knowledge of his teacher and examines it critically by comparing it against the Torah. Only one who has studied for an extensive period can become a *hākām*, one who can teach with authority.

NT *manthanō* occurs 25x in the NT—only 6x in the Gospels, where one would have expected it most as a mark of discipleship; much more common is *didaskō*, teach. *mathētēs* occurs 261x, exclusively in the Gospels and Acts. It indicates discipleship as total attachment to someone, not the cl. Gk. idea of pupil. Matt. 10:24 ("A student is not above his teacher, nor a servant above his master") and Lk. 6:40 does not contradict this, since the issue there is the relationship of a disciple to Jesus as master. *matheuō* occurs 4x.

1. (a) On some occasions *manthanō* reflects the specifically OT sense of learn the will of God or learn to devote oneself to that will (Matt. 9:13; Jn. 6:45; cf. Mk. 13:28 par.). Jesus is the only point of reference, from whom alone one can know God's will (Matt. 11:29). He does not introduce a new law to be learned. Instead, he restores God's law to its original function of enabling people to recognize his will and do it. In concrete terms, learning means putting one's faith in Jesus and following him in his work of compassion.

(b) *manthanō* has a similar meaning in the letters; it refers to the message or teaching of Jesus (Rom. 16:17; Eph. 4:20; Col. 1:7; 2 Tim. 3:14). To hold to the teaching that the recipients have received means to hold to their faith. Learning implies not only acquiring teaching about Christ, but also acceptance of Christ himself, beginning the new life of discipleship in him (cf. 1 Cor. 4:6; Phil. 4:9).

(c) The Hel. play on words in Heb. 5:8 is unique. It says that Jesus "learned obedience from what he suffered." Learning here means recognition of the Father's will in his suffering and affirmation of that will in acceptance of his suffering.

2. The main NT interest in this word group falls on the noun *mathētēs*. The Evangelists probably took it over from Hel. Jud. but gave it a new character through their association with Jesus. They also employed the word with a wider frame of reference in such expressions as the disciples of John the Baptist (Matt. 11:2 par.; Mk. 2:18 par.; Lk. 5:33; Jn. 1:35, 37), of Moses (9:28), and of the Pharisees (Matt. 22:16; Mk. 2:18).

(a) The disciples of John the Baptist formed a solid group. They were not far away when he was in prison (Matt. 11:2 par.) and later buried his body (Mk. 6:29 par.). They had their own form of prayer (Lk. 11:1) and fasting (Mk. 2:18 par.), and they became involved in controversy with the Jews (Jn. 3:25). In all these particulars they were no longer "pupils" like the *talmîdîm* of the rab. schools. Jn. 1:25–42 reports that Jesus' first two disciples originated from the Baptist's circle of disciples.

(b) The NT may have used *mathētēs* in connection with the Pharisees as an explanatory term to readers unfamiliar with the system of the *talmîdîm*. The Pharisees, like the teachers of the law, the Sadducees, and the high priests, were enemies of Jesus and together with their followers stand typically for the entire Jewish nation.

3. It is indisputable that the earthly Jesus called people to be his disciples and to follow him. From the Gospels we can list various characteristics of that discipleship.

(a) Clearly, Jesus appeared in many respects to be a rabbi. He taught and discussed like one (Mk. 12:18–40) and was asked to make legal decisions (Lk. 12:13–14). Even if he was not recognized as such by many, since he had not passed through a rab. school (Mk. 6:2; Jn. 7:15), he was certainly addressed as "Rabbi" by his disciples (Mk. 9:5; 11:21; Jn. 1:38; 4:31) and outsiders (cf. 3:2). Even here one can see a parallel with the rabbis of Jud. in that Jesus gathered a circle of disciples around him. But at several decisive points Jesus went beyond the recognized limits for a rabbi, which gives his disciple-master relationship its own distinctive coloring.

(b) Whereas in rab. circles and in Gk. philosophical schools one made a voluntary decision to join the school of his master and so become a disciple, Jesus' *call* was decisive (Mk. 1:17 par.; 2:14 par.; Lk. 5:1–11; cf. Matt. 4:18–22).

(c) Gk. pupils and the rab. students bound themselves personally to their master and looked for objective teaching, with the ultimate aim of themselves becoming a master or a rabbi. But Jesus' call to discipleship did not lead to eventually becoming a master (cf. Matt. 23:8). Following him as a disciple meant unconditional sacrifice for one's entire life (10:24–25, 37; Lk. 14:26–27; Jn. 11:16). To be a disciple meant to stay bound to Jesus and to do God's will (Matt. 12:46–50; cf. Mk. 3:31–35). The disciple literally had to "follow" Jesus (→ *akoloutheō*, 199).

(d) Unlike the rabbis, Jesus broke through the barriers that separated the clean from the unclean, the sinful from the obedient. Thus he summoned a tax collector who stood outside the worshiping community to abandon his old association for discipleship (Mk. 2:14), just as he did a Zealot (Lk. 6:15; Acts 1:13) and some fishermen (Mk. 1:16–20).

(e) It is important for understanding Jesus' discipleship to realize that the call to be a disciple always included the call to service (e.g., the call to be "fishers of men" in Mk. 1:17; cf. Lk. 5:10, a colloquial phrase that meant the disciples were to bring people into the kingdom by preaching the gospel and working in Jesus' name; cf. Matt. 16:15–19). When Jesus sent out the Twelve (Mk. 6:7–13 par.) and later the Seventy-Two (Lk. 10:1–17), they were to go out in pairs, healing, bringing salvation and peace, and proclaiming the kingdom of God. This service led the disciple into the same dangers as his master (cf. Mk. 10:32). A disciple could expect no better fortune than his Lord (Matt. 10:24–25; 16:24–25).

(f) In the Gospels we read about the disciples' lack of understanding. This applies not only to Jesus' message (Mk. 4:10–11 par.), activity (10:13–16, 48), and the goal of discipleship (10:35–45), but above all to Jesus' suffering (Matt. 16:22–23; Mk. 14:47; Lk. 18:34).

(g) The promised reward was fellowship with God through Jesus and thus a share in Jesus' authority. It was also the new and future life (cf. Matt. 16:25; Jn. 14:6).

(h) The *mathētai* are not simply the Twelve. The circle of the Twelve was not only a symbolic representation of the twelve tribes of Israel, and thus of the whole people of God, but also a section of the larger circle of disciples that Jesus summoned to discipleship from a still wider group of adherents. The disciples would have been a circle of immediate followers who were commissioned to particular service.

4. (a) As a rule, the Gospel passages that speak of following and of discipleship are already reflections on its meaning. Renunciation (Matt. 23:7–12), humility (18:1–4), poverty (19:23–30), and readiness to suffer (10:17–33) are all characteristics of discipleship. Decisive in understanding *mathētēs* is faith (Mk. 16:16; Lk. 17:5; 22:32) in Jesus himself (Matt. 18:5; esp. Jn. 2:11; 6:69; 11:45). Lk. 12:8–9 expresses

both the promise and the dangers of discipleship. The disciple's faithfulness to the Lord is crucial.

(b) Reflection on discipleship is particularly characteristic of Jn.'s Gospel. Not only do the categories of the narrower and wider circles of disciples point beyond themselves to the Christian community being addressed (cf. 6:60, 66), *mathētēs* is often simply a term for Christian (8:31; 13:35; 15:8) or for the gathered community. In Jesus' farewell discourses (Jn. 13–17), the disciples are no longer bound to the presence of the earthly Jesus. But through the Spirit they remain in full fellowship with him (14:15–17; 15:26–27), which finds its visible expression in the manner of their service. Everyone is to be able to recognize disciples of Jesus by seeing their love (13:34–35) and by their fulfillment of duty in being witnesses to the Lord (→ *martyria, 3456*).

(c) This becomes clearer from the way the word is used in Acts, where *mathētēs* simply means Christian, one who believes in Jesus and witnesses for him (cf. 6:1–2, 7; 9:1, 10, 19, 25–26, 38; 11:26, 29; 13:52; 14:20, 22, 28; etc.).

5. The vb. *mathēteuō* is primarily used of someone who has become a disciple (applied to Joseph of Arimathea in Matt. 27:57; of a large number of people in Acts 14:21). In Matt. 28:19, Jesus' parting instructions of his disciples was to "go and make disciples of all nations."

See also *akoloutheō*, follow (*199*); *mimeomai*, imitate, follow (*3628*); *opisō*, behind, after (*3958*).

3419	μαίνομαι

μαίνομαι (*mainomai*), rave, be mad, be out of one's mind (*3419*); μανία (*mania*), madness, frenzy (*3444*).

CL & OT Cl. Gk. used *mainomai* esp. for excited thought, being in ecstasy, raving: (a) rage, rave; (b) be intoxicated; (c) be passionately in love; (d) be mad (i.e., opposite of *sōphroneō, 5404*); (e) be entranced, as one possessed by the spirit of a god. This vb. became the technical term of the cult of Dionysus and of the inspired "mantic" divination, the best-known representatives of which were the Sibyls. *mania* was one of the oldest attributes of Dionysus. This god could also free a person of madness and allow him or her to return to quiet self-consciousness through an act of purification.

The LXX uses *mainomai* in Jer. 25:16 (= LXX 32:16) of the peoples who have drunk from God's cup of wrath. Yahweh threatens them all with the terror of war as punishment. In 29:26 (= LXX 36:26) "any madman" is placed beside "who acts like a prophet" in a context intended to bring Jer.'s prophetic opponents into discredit. In 4 Macc. 8:5; 10:13 Antiochus Epiphanes considers as madness the loyalty of the priest Eleazar and his sons to their faith, which led to their death as martyrs.

NT *mainomai* is found 5x and *mania* once in the NT. In Acts 12:15 Rhoda was told, "You're out of your mind," when she came with unbelievable news. Festus (26:24) believed that Paul was out of his mind in his enthusiasm to penetrate into the ultimate secrets. However, Paul placed the sober and reasonable truth (*sōphrosynē*) in antithesis to *mania* (26:25). In 1 Cor. 14:23 Paul used *mainomai* to describe the impression that speaking in tongues would make on invited or casual visitors to the church.

A good Jew was not allowed to listen to a demon-possessed man. In Jn. 10:20 unbelieving Jews reacted to Jesus' message by saying, "He is demon-possessed and raving mad." Therefore, since Jesus had lost his wits through the action of an evil demon (cf. Jn. 7:20; 8:52), they were absolved from the responsibility of listening further. Others, however, saw the healing of the blind man as God's vindication of Jesus' message. In other words, we have here a strong, religiously motivated repudiation of Jesus. The use of *mainomai* here reminds us of the madness in the cult of Dionysus.

See also *ekstasis*, distraction, confusion, ecstasy (*1749*); *ekplēssō*, amaze, astound (*1742*).

3420 (*makarizō*, call or consider blessed, happy), → *3421*.

3421	μακάριος

μακάριος (*makarios*), blessed, fortunate, happy (*3421*); μακαρίζω (*makarizō*), call or consider blessed, happy (*3420*); μακαρισμός (*makarismos*), blessing (*3422*).

CL & OT 1. *makarios* originally meant free from daily cares and worries. In poetic language it described the condition of the gods and those who share their happy existence. Later, it became a common word, like our "happy." The word most frequently occurs in the formalized language of blessing, *makarios hos(tis)*, "happy is he who...." People were congratulated on happy events, such as parents on their children, the rich on their wealth, the wise on their knowledge, the pious on their inward well-being, and initiates on their experience of God.

2. In the LXX *makarios* and *makarizō* generally translate the Heb. *ʾešer*, happiness, well-being; *ʾāšar*, pronounce happy; and *ʾašrê*, well-being to. Stylized blessings are found in the wisdom lit., irrespective of whether the reference is to earthly blessings (Ps. 127:5; Sir. 25:8), prosperity (Job 29:10–11), a wise life (Prov. 3:13; Sir. 14:20), or fulfilling God's commandment (Ps. 1:1; 41:1; 119:1). Psalms that have been influenced by the wisdom tradition pronounce as blessed those who trust in God (e.g., 2:12; 32:1–2; 34:8). A connection between religious happiness consisting in Yahweh's favor and earthly happiness through his gifts is basic in wisdom lit.

This formula always ascribes well-being to a human. That is, Yahweh himself is never called *makarios*. The benediction (→ *eulogia, 2330*), an authoritative and efficacious word, is much different.

3. In the later Israelite period (e.g., Sir. 25:7–10), more elaborate pronouncements of this sort and even whole series of them are found, especially in apocalyptic texts (Dan. 12:12; Tob. 13:14–16). Pronouncements of blessedness are often supplemented by a contrasting series of woes (2 Enoch 52:1–8; cf. 1 Enoch 103:5). In substance these pronouncements have the force of an eschatological consolation (see 58:2).

NT 1. In the NT *makarizō* occurs only 2x (Lk. 1:48; Jas. 5:11), *makarismos* 3x (Rom. 4:6, 9; Gal. 4:15; the former two suggest use of a formula). *Makarios*, however, occurs 50x, generally in the context of pronouncing someone or something blessed.

2. Stylistically the NT pronouncements follow the tradition of those in apocalyptic texts (see above). Corresponding to the Heb. style, the eschatological pronouncements in Jesus' preaching and the gospel records are made in the third person. Almost uniformly they are furnished with a reason or a description of the bliss ascribed (see sec. 3). Contrasting woes are explicitly set against the ascriptions of blessing in Lk. 6:20–26 and implicitly in the visions of Rev. 14:13; 16:15; 19:9. Paul aligns himself stylistically with the pronouncements of the wisdom tradition. A clearly Hel. usage is found in 1 Tim. 1:11 and 6:15, where God himself is pronounced blessed.

3. The pronouncements of the Sermon on the Mount (e.g., "Blessed are the poor in spirit, for theirs is the kingdom of heaven," Matt. 5:3) dominate the NT scene. These eschatological pronouncements are distinguishable from apocalyptic ones by their paradoxical statements (the kingdom belongs to the poor in spirit, the powerless, the sorrowful) and by the fact that this kingdom of God is bound up with the life and message of Jesus. They explain Matt. 11:5–6: The message of joy is brought to the poor.

Present and future are related to one another in these pronouncements. This is clearest in Lk.'s version of them in 6:20–26, where the word "now" is inserted 2x in 6:21, underlining this relationship: "Blessed are you who hunger now, for you will be satisfied. Blessed are you who weep now, for you will laugh." All the benefits praised in the OT are now eclipsed. Hence the pronouncement also applies to all those who share the experience of the arrival of God's kingdom (Matt. 13:16–17), who face this encounter in the right way

(16:17; Lk. 1:45; Jn. 20:29), and who are not offended at it (Matt. 11:6). They remain steadfast and faithful (24:46; Lk. 12:37–38; Jas. 1:12; Rev. 16:15). Although the pronouncements in the NT are varied, their futuristic character is not to be understood in the sense of consolation and subsequent recompense. The promised future always involves a radical alteration of the present.

See also *eulogia*, praise, blessing (*2330*).

3422 (makarismos, blessing), → *3421.*

3426 (makran, far), → *1584.*

3428 (makrothymeō, be patient, longsuffering), → *3429.*

3429	μακροθυμία

μακροθυμία (*makrothymia*), patience, longsuffering (*3429*); μακροθυμέω (*makrothymeō*), be patient, longsuffering (*3428*).

CL & OT 1. In cl. Gk. *makrothymia*, unlike other compounds of *thymos* (anger, wrath), is rare. It denotes a typically human virtue: the prolonged restraint of *thymos*, i.e., patience, longsuffering, for whereas the gods know nothing of affliction, humans must bear their lot in patience. There is always an element of resignation in the word, even when it describes the kind of endurance that one can only admire. Positively it expresses a persistence or unswerving willingness to await events rather than trying to force them. In ancient Greece *makrothymia* is concerned primarily with the molding of a person's inner character; it is not a virtue exercised toward one's fellow human beings.

2. In the LXX the related adj. *makrothymos* frequently denotes an attribute of Yahweh, namely, his being slow to anger (e.g., Num. 14:18; Ps. 86:15; 103:8; Joel 2:13; Nah. 1:3). It denotes, therefore, the idea of restrained wrath, forbearance being exercised for a limited period only. The Israelites make frequent reference to God's forbearance (e.g., Exod. 34:6) and even appeal to it when conscious of guilt (Wis. 15:1–2). They know that, being a God of forbearance, Yahweh is ready to bestow grace on his people.

Yet at the same time, the godly Israelite is aware of the tension between grace and wrath, for it is possible to exhaust God's patience and cause his anger to burst forth (Ps. 7:11–16). Even the obedient sometimes find it hard to acquiesce in God's forbearance (Jer. 15:15; Jon. 4:2), but patience increasingly becomes a virtue required of the wise (Prov. 19:11; Sir. 29:1–8) and is given prominence in wisdom lit. (Prov. 14:29; 16:32; 25:15).

NT In the NT forbearance is a characteristic both of God and of the person who is united with Jesus Christ. The noun is used only in NT letters. The subject is treated thematically in Heb. 6:9–15; Jas. 5:7–11; and to some extent in 2 Pet. 3:4–15.

1. The connection between divine and human patience is made clear in the parable of the unforgiving servant in Matt. 18:21–35 (note the use of *makrothymeō*, have patience, 18:26, 29). This parable follows Jesus' instructions on what to do if a fellow believer sins against you (18:15–20) and his command to Peter to be willing to forgive not only seven times but seventy-seven times—i.e., an unlimited number of times (the reverse of Gen. 4:24).

The parable of the unforgiving servant illustrates the divine attitude toward forgiveness and our dealings with our fellow human beings. The heavily indebted servant asks the king to "be patient" (*makrothymeō*) and he will repay everything (Matt. 18:26). But the king actually does more: He remits the entire amount. However, this servant does not act the same way toward a fellow servant who likewise asks for patience (again *makrothymeō*, 18:29); instead, he becomes harsh. On learning the true facts of the case, the king has the first servant put in prison "until he should pay back all he owed" (18:34). The parable concludes with the pronouncement: "This is how my heavenly Father will treat each of you unless you forgive your

brother from your heart" (18:35)—a verse that recalls the fifth petition of the Lord's Prayer (Matt. 6:12; cf. 6:14–15).

2. The contrast in the parable between a debt so enormous as to defy repayment and one that could easily be met out of normal income is a vivid way of expressing the incomparable greatness of God's longsuffering. At the same time longsuffering makes possible our entry into newness of life. In Rom. 2:4 Paul reminds us that God's "patience" leads us to repentance. The background in this passage is God's righteous anger, but his patience, being linked with kindness (*chrēstotēs*; → *chrēstos*, 5982), assumes the character of benevolence. Paul puts the matter clearly in 9:22: "With great patience" God bore with those who are appointed to wrath, in order to display his power and mercy in the salvation of the elect (cf. 1 Pet. 3:20).

In 1 Tim. 1:16 Paul speaks of the "unlimited patience" of Christ (cf. 2 Pet. 3:15) as an example to those who were to believe in him for eternal life. By following this example, Paul demonstrates divine patience, a proof of God's mercy to sinners. Timothy, in turn, should follow his example of "patience" (2 Tim. 3:10; 4:2).

3. In the parable of Matt. 18 human patience is related to, and dependent on, divine patience. God in his longsuffering holds open the door to newness of life, but such new life in believers is proved genuine by the fact that they practice forgiveness. Thus *makrothymia* comes into its own in the NT lists of virtues. Paul incorporates these lists in his practical exhortations, such as "the fruit of the Spirit" (Gal. 5:22; cf. Col. 1:11; 1 Thess. 5:14; 2 Tim. 3:10) or our living "a life worthy of [our] calling" (Eph. 4:1–2; Col. 3:12). *makrothymia* in the NT is not what Gk. humanism held it to be, namely, a virtuous attitude cultivated exclusively in one's own interests. Rather, it is something that makes a believer always prepared to meet a neighbor halfway and to share one's life with him or her. In other words, human patience or forbearance is not a character trait but a way of life. Indeed, it is a primary expression of love, for "love is patient [*makrothymeō*], love is kind" (1 Cor. 13:4).

4. James points out another aspect of the patience required of believers. In view of "the Lord's coming" (Jas. 5:7), he links together the forbearance we must extend to our fellow human beings and the patience needed to cope with all the trials and tribulations of this world. Thus, he exhorts his readers to be "patient" (5:7–8, 10). We must not grumble at each other, for the judge is standing at the door (5:9). We are to follow the example of the suffering and "patience" of the prophets (5:10) and be steadfast like Job (5:11; cf. Job 1:21–22; 2:10), remembering that the Lord is compassionate and merciful (Jas. 5:11; cf. Ps. 10:18; 111:4).

5. Patience is an aspect of faith and hope that was exhibited by Abraham, and it will likewise enable believers to inherit the promises of God: "We want each of you to show this same diligence to the very end, in order to make your hope sure. We do not want you to become lazy, but to imitate those who through faith and patience [*makrothymia*] inherit what has been promised" (Heb. 6:11–12). We should be like Abraham, who "after waiting patiently . . . received what was promised" (6:15; cf. Gen. 22:16–17).

6. In 2 Pet. 3 Peter discusses the apparent delay in the Parousia. This is not to be taken as an indefinite postponement but as a sign of God's patience to give people full opportunity to repent. The Lord "is patient with you" because he does not want anyone to perish, but everyone to reach repentance (3:9). A few verses later Peter relates this to Paul's teaching: "Bear in mind that our Lord's patience [*makrothymia*] means salvation, just as our dear brother Paul also wrote you with the wisdom that God gave him" (3:15).

7. The interpretation of Lk. 18:7 has been the subject of much discussion. This verse follows the parable of the unjust judge (18:1–6), which Jesus told in order to teach the disciples "that they should always pray and not give up" (18:1). In the parable the widow finally gets the judge to grant her justice because of her constant petitioning. Then Jesus asks: "And will not God bring about justice for his chosen ones, who cry out to him day and night? Will he keep putting them off

[*makrothymeō*]?" Most likely what this phrase means is: "Will not God be patient with their complaint?" A loving and kind God will be patient with his people and hear their cries.

See also *anechomai*, bear, endure (*462*); *karvereō*, be strong, steadfast, persevere (*2846*); *hypomenō*, be patient, persevere, endure, be steadfast (*5702*).

| 3433 μαλακία | μαλακία (*malakia*), weakness, softness, sickness (*3433*). |

CL & OT 1. In cl. Gk. *malakia* came to be used of effeminate men. In the medical writers it describes weakness or illness.

2. *malakia* occurs in the LXX as a general term for sickness (cf. Deut. 7:15; 28:61; Isa. 38:9; 53:3). Passages such as Deut. 7:15 emphasize the punitive function of illness, but this view is modified in the work of the divine servant (Isa. 53:4), who bore our diseases and carried our pains. Matt. 8:17 relates this passage to divine healing as an integral part of Christ's saving work.

NT This word occurs only 3x in the NT (Matt. 4:23; 9:35; 10:1) in the sense of weakness or sickness. The healing of physical conditions was for Matt. an important feature of the gospel of the kingdom.

See also *astheneia*, weakness, sickness, disease, timidity (*819*); *nosos*, illness, sickness (*3798*); *paralytikos*, paralytic (*4166*).

| 3440 μαμωνᾶς | μαμωνᾶς (*mamōnas*), money, wealth, property (*3440*). |

NT 1. (a) The Gk. word *mamōnas* is first found in the NT. It renders the emphatic state *māmônāʾ* of the Aram. *māmôn*. Most scholars link it with the vb. *ʾāman*, to believe in, trust, as "that in which one trusts," though it may also denote what is entrusted to humans. In Lk. 16:11 there is an apparent play on words with this root meaning: "So if you have not been trustworthy [*pistos*; → *pistis*, *4411*] in handling worldly wealth [*mamōnas*], who will trust [*pisteuō*] you with true [*alēthinos*; → *alētheia*, *237*] riches?" The three Gk. words *pistos*, *pisteuō*, and *alēthinos* all appear to translate words from the same Aram. root *ʾmn*, from which mammon is formed.

(b) The Aram. word is found in rab. writings, where it has the sense of profit or money, or, more generally, one's possessions. In itself the word may be neutral, but it acquired in negative contexts the connotation of possessions dishonestly gained, as in bribery.

2. *mamōnas* occurs 3x in sayings appended to the parable of the shrewd manager (Lk. 16:1–8). At the end of the parable "the master" (or perhaps "the Lord") commended the dishonest manager because of his shrewdness, "for the people of this world are more shrewd in dealing with their own kind than are the people of the light" (16:8). This parable is addressed to Jesus' disciples, teaching them prudence in handling this world's goods. They are to use the goods of this world in a way that is righteous and will benefit others. The manager's action in remitting various debts owed to his master achieved a double object. On the one hand, the master had been charging exorbitant interest, forbidden by the Mosaic law, and the manager was actually putting his master right in the eyes of the law. On the other hand, he was doing himself a favor by ingratiating himself with his master's debtors.

Lk. 16:9 then adds: "I tell you, use worldly wealth [*mamōnas*] to gain friends for yourselves, so that when it is gone, [they] will be welcomed into eternal dwellings." The injunction is not to befriend wealth but to use it for the benefit of others. In this verse "they" (NIV "you") may refer to those who have benefited from such use of wealth, it may be a Hebraism referring to God without actually mentioning his name, or it may refer to God and his angels. The point is that wealth itself does not endure, but it can be used to achieve something enduring. Mammon itself is material, but its use has personal dimensions.

Lk. 16:11 (see above) contrasts the relatively minor value of material things with true riches that exist on a higher and personal plain. Stewardship of material possessions is thus a probationary test for further stewardship (cf. the parables of the pounds [19:11–27] and the talents [Matt. 25:14–30]). Lk. 16:12 implies that worldly wealth is not something that one actually possesses but belongs, in fact, to someone else. The disciple has to prove to be a faithful and wise manager of this before he or she may be entrusted with something greater. But neither should one be the servant of Money, for Money (personified in 16:13) inevitably becomes our master if we try to make ourselves its master by acquiring it for its own sake. We are confronted by the stark choice: Serve either God or Money; we cannot do both.

3. The only other place in which *mamōnas* occurs is Matt. 6:24, which is verbally identical with Lk. 16:13 but set in the context of the Sermon on the Mount. The message is essentially the same: We cannot serve both God and Money.

See also *thēsauros*, treasure box, chest, storeroom, treasure (*2565*); *peripoieō*, save for oneself, acquire, gain possession of (*4347*); *ploutos*, wealth, riches (*4458*); *chrēma*, property, wealth, means, money (*5975*).

3443 (manthanō, learn), → 3412.

3444 (mania, madness, frenzy), → 3419.

| 3445 μάννα | μάννα (*manna*), manna (*3445*). |

OT Heb. *mān* is a name for the sap that is sucked from the manna-tamarisk in the Sinai desert in the rainy season by a kind of scale insect, which then drops in the form of small, sweet balls. These balls melt and disperse in the heat of the midday sun. That it was this phenomenon that the Israelites met in the desert as a helping miracle from God has been considered certain since Josephus and Origen. Exod. 16:15 offers a Heb. etymological explanation of the name, expressing the amazement of the people: *mān hûʾ*, which means, What is it? Manna was not, of course, the Israelites' sole source of food in the desert, for they brought flocks and herds with them out of Egypt (cf. 12:38) and found other food in oases (15:27) and from defeated enemies (Num. 31:25–47). But this does not diminish the OT's feeling for the miracle of food that kept Israel from perishing of hunger.

Exod. 16 and Num. 11 (the miracle of quail) are concerned only with the actual food. Deut. 8:3 uses the memory of the miraculous food to stress that "man does not live on bread alone but on every word that comes from the mouth of the LORD" (cf. Matt. 4:4; Lk. 4:4). The concept was increasingly spiritualized. Note Ps. 78:24–25, where *mān* is called "the grain of heaven" and "the bread of angels," and where it is used together with God's other gracious acts to his people as symbolic of divine salvation.

In later Jewish writings manna plays a considerable role. It is linked with the tradition that the Messiah will bring back the ark and its contents, which had been hidden by Jeremiah (2 Macc. 2:4–12); this would include the pot of manna stored by Moses in the ark (cf. Exod. 16:33). Moreover, manna is the heavenly bread that will come down from heaven to feed the believers who experience this age. Finally, the Messiah will parallel Moses in various respects, including the giving of manna.

NT Rev. 2:17 perhaps reflects the notion of the "hidden manna." Heb. 9:4 mentions the preservation of manna in the ark. In Jn. 6:31–34 the Jews refer to the belief that the miracle of the manna will be repeated in the messianic age. Jesus rejected this parallelism by pointing out that it was not Moses but God himself who had given bread in the desert.

In Jn. 6:49–51a the manna of the desert wanderings is contrasted with the true bread from heaven. The manna had not kept those who had eaten it from dying; true bread from heaven is that which alone can impart eternal life. This can be found only in the one who says, "I am the living bread that came down from heaven" (6:51).

See also *artos*, bread, loaf (*788*); *epiousios*, daily (*2157*); *deipnon*, meal, supper (*1270*).

3446 (*manteuomai*, tell fortunes, utter oracles, prophesy), → *3404*.

3448	μαράνα θά

μαράνα θα (*maranatha*), maranatha, i.e., "Our Lord has come!" "Our Lord is coming!" or "Our Lord, come!" (*3448*).

NT 1. *marana tha* is an Aram. phrase found in the NT only in 1 Cor. 16:22: "If anyone does not love the Lord—a curse be on him. Come, O Lord [*marana tha*]!" Its precise meaning is disputed, though it is certainly a combination of the Aram. *māran* or *māranā* ("our Lord") and the verb *'atā* ("to come"). The expression should thus be seen either as a perf. (*māran 'atā*), i.e., "Our Lord has come," or as an imperative (*māranā' tā*), i.e., "Our Lord, come!"

Apart from 1 Cor. 16:22, the phrase is found in the prayers associated with the Lord's Supper in the *Didache* (10:6; ca. A.D. 100), but all subsequent references are based on 1 Cor. 16:22. Where the phrase originated is a matter of debate, although most scholars regard the Jerusalem church as the most likely source. Both the ascription of lordship to Jesus in that church (e.g., Acts 2:36) and its presence in this Aram. formula suggest that it goes back to the early Jerusalem church.

2. (a) Both translations of the phrase are possible. By and large the church fathers understood it as a perf., though this interpretation may also include the present: "Our Lord has come and is now here." In this case, Phil. 4:5 ("The Lord is near") may allude to the phrase *marana tha*. The statement of 1 Cor. 16:22 is then a warning. The words, "If anyone does not love the Lord—a curse be on him," are being emphasized because the Lord is near. The same may be true of the call to repentance in *Did.* 10:6.

(b) The imperative, however, is the more likely interpretation. Appeal may be made to Rev. 22:20, where the words, "Amen. Come, Lord Jesus," appears to be a free rendering of the original Aram. prayer. Note the parallel with another Aram. word *'abbā*, "Father" (Mk. 14:36; Rom. 8:15; Gal. 4:6), which is likewise a prayer. It makes sense that these brief prayers should be passed on in their original form. No immediate connection with the context is essential.

3. Since in *Did.* 10:6 the phrase *marana tha* occurs in prayers associated with the Lord's Supper, the expression may be assumed to have been used in the liturgy of the Supper, perhaps from its very beginning. We know from 1 Cor. 11:26 that early on the Lord's Supper looked forward in hope to the Lord's coming (cf. also Matt. 26:29; Mk. 14:25). The prayers associated with the Supper in the *Did.* 9–10 show how alive this hope remained even at a later period. Thus *marana tha* is to be understood, in the light of Rev. 22:20, as a prayer for the coming of the Lord in the sense of the last advent.

This need not be the only thought, however, for just as Jn. 14:18 speaks of the risen Lord coming to his own, *marana tha* may also include this idea within its scope. Such a prayer is in fact partially answered whenever the church celebrates the Lord's Supper. The Lord comes in the elements of the bread and the cup.

See also *hēmera*, day (*2465*); *parousia*, presence, appearing, coming, advent (*4242*).

3449	μαργαρίτης

μαργαρίτης (*margaritēs*), pearl (*3449*).

CL & OT 1. In cl. Gk. *margaritēs*, pearl, is a rare phenomenon in the ancient world. Pliny describes how pearls originate as dewdrops falling into open oysters.

2. There are no certain references to pearls in the OT, and *margaritēs* does not occur in the LXX. The use of pearls for the gates of the new Jerusalem was a familiar messianic picture in Jewish lit. (e.g., *m. B. Bat.* 37:1; *Exod. Rab.* 15.114.4).

NT 1. In Matt. 7:6 Jesus urges discrimination in offering "what is sacred," that which stands in special relation to God, to the irrespon-

sible and unappreciative, an action that is tantamount to casting costly "pearls to pigs." Pearls are mentioned in 1 Tim. 2:9; Rev. 17:4 as extravagances of feminine finery, and in Matt. 13:45–46; Rev. 18:12, 16 as articles of merchandise.

2. In Matt. 13:45–46, a parable told by Jesus, a prudent merchant is prepared to sell all that he has to acquire a single pearl of great price. It is suggestive that of all the precious stones only the pearl results from an injury done to a living organism (the oyster). This precious pearl represents the church that Jesus purchased with his own blood (cf. Acts 20:28). Entrance into the Father's presence is only by way of the work of Jesus himself (Jn. 14:6)—hinted at in the use of pearls in Rev. for the gates of heaven.

3. Each gate of the heavenly city is a gigantic pearl, some 200 feet across (Rev. 21:21; cf. Isa. 54:12). On each gate is inscribed the name of one of the tribes of Israel (21:12). The large number of gates suggests free and ample access to the city. The names of the twelve tribes on the gates should be related with the names of the twelve apostles on the foundations (21:14). The implication is that the true children of God under both old and new covenants alike share in the heavenly city. The gates of the city are not intended to stand against assault—indeed, they are always open (21:25). The angels on duty (21:12) are not armed (cf. Gen. 3:24), but form a guard of honor.

See also *petra*, rock (*4376*); *gōnia*, corner (*1224*); *lithos*, stone (*3345*).

3455 (*martyreō*, bear witness, testify), → *3456*.

3456	μαρτυρία

μαρτυρία (*martyria*), testimony, testifying, attestation (*3456*); μαρτυρέω (*martyreō*), bear witness, testify (*3455*); μαρτύριον (*martyrion*), testimony, evidence, proof (*3457*); μαρτύρομαι (*martyromai*), testify, bear witness, affirm (*3458*); μάρτυς (*martys*), a witness (*3459*); διαμαρτύρομαι (*diamartyromai*), charge, adjure, bear witness to, testify of (*1371*); καταμαρτυρέω (*katamartyreō*), bear witness against, testify against (*2909*); συμμαρτυρέω (*symmartyreō*), testify in support, confirm (*5210*); ψευδομαρτυρέω (*pseudomartyreō*), bear false witness (*6018*); ψευδομαρτυρία (*pseudomartyria*), false witness (*6019*); ψευδόμαρτυς (*pseudomartys*), one who gives false testimony (*6020*).

CL & OT 1. (a) *martyria* means the making of an active appearance and statements as a witness (*martys*). From the 5th cent. B.C. come the derived vbs. *martyreō*, to bear witness, confirm something, testify that something is the case; *martyromai*, call someone as a witness; and the noun *martyrion*, evidence, proof. The gods can be invoked as witnesses in oaths, but humans can also be summoned as witnesses. *symmartyreō* means to testify in support, confirm evidence; *katamartyreō*, to give evidence against someone; *diamartyromai*, to call in as a witness, certify, or urge strongly, conjure. A *pseudomartys* is one whose statement does not accord with the truth but who twists or covers it up (cf. *pseudomartyria*, false testimony; *pseudomartyreō*, to bear false witness).

(b) The original setting of the word group in cl. Gk. is clearly the legal sphere. Witnesses give evidence in a trial concerning past events or formally provide substantiation for the future, e.g., for legal transactions or for confirmation in the finalizing and signing of agreements. The *martyria* in a trial is to be given freely, i.e., without constraint or against one's better knowledge (such could take place by torture). The invocation of the gods as witnesses has its place where human witnesses or given circumstances cannot be adduced.

(c) Esp. from the time of the Stoics, *martyria* entered the field of moral or philosophical convictions. The Stoic or Cynic philosopher regarded himself as a witness who was called to give evidence on behalf of divine truth and testified to his ideas and doctrines by living appropriately in spite of adverse circumstances. This kind of *martyria* is related to but not identical with the later Christian concept of martyrdom (related to the word *martys*).

2. (a) In the LXX the most common member of this word group is *martyrion* (nearly 300x). Most of these are in the Pentateuch, where it may refer to the "two tablets of the Testimony" (Exod. 31:18; 32:15), the "Tent of Meeting" (29:4, 10–11), or "the ark of the Testimony" (40:3). *martyrion* here accords with its later usage in cl. Gk., namely, a piece of evidence that calls to mind a particular event (e.g., the founding of the covenant or the law).

As to other uses of *martyrion*, in Gen. 31:44 Laban and Jacob set up a stone "as a witness between us" (cf. Jos. 22:27–28; 24:27). In Wis. 10:7, the desolation of Sodom and Gomorrah stands as "evidence of [human] wickedness" and God's ensuing judgment. In Ps. 119 (23x), this word refers to God's law or precepts as that which gives direction to the psalmist's way of life (e.g., 119:2, 14, 88, 119); it is the expression of the covenant and the means whereby one knows Yahweh.

(b) *martyria* occurs 12x in the LXX. In 1 Sam. 9:24 it means "occasion." In Prov. 12:19; 25:18; Sir. 31:23–24 (= LXX 34:23–24) this word describes the act of giving testimony, which can be characterized as truthful, lying, or unjust. *martys* (54x) is used in the cl. Gk. sense for one who gives testimony on the basis of observation or who in the legal sense is enlisted to confirm a state of affairs, an agreement (e.g., Ruth 4:9–11; cf. Deut. 19:15–18). In 1 Sam. 12:5, Samuel invokes Yahweh as witness that he has not taken any bribe (cf. Job 16:19 = LXX 16:20; Wis. 1:6). In the prophetic oracle of Jer. 29:23 (= LXX 36:23), Yahweh likewise comes forward as a witness against his people and their behavior. In Isa. 43:10, 12; 44:8, God calls the nation to come forward as witnesses to the uniqueness and righteousness of Yahweh.

(c) *martyreō* occurs only 16x: for legal testimony (Num. 35:30; Deut. 19:15, 18), but also for the commemorative function of a monument (Gen. 31:46–48) and the Song of Moses (Deut. 31:19, 21). *katamartyreō* (5x; e.g., 1 Ki. 21:10, 13 = LXX 20:10, 13; Prov. 25:18) denotes false evidence that leads to condemnation. *pseudomartyreō* means to bear deliberate false testimony (Exod. 20:16; Deut. 5:17 = LXX 5:20). *diamartyromai* can mean to call up or enlist someone as a witness (e.g., Deut. 4:26; 31:28; Mal. 2:14), but it is also used for the passing on of instructions received from Yahweh (Exod. 18:20; 19:10, 21). It can therefore have the sense both of to warn, testify on oath (e.g., in the name of God, Ps. 50:7), and to certify, promise (e.g., Zech. 3:6 = LXX 3:7).

(d) By and large the words of this group are essentially the same as in cl. Gk. One is a witness for something one has experienced, or one is enlisted as such for an event. It is something one has experienced or something that a person will testify to. Esp. where God is mentioned or invoked as witness, the partisanship of the witness for the right of the covenant is clearly felt. The OT does not know the subjective idea of testimony as what one presents on behalf of one's religious conviction (e.g., witnessing to the truth of God's Word).

(e) The thought of suffering involved in bearing witness to one's faith even to the point of death and the high esteem paid to martyrdom were widespread in Jud. (cf. esp. 4 Macc. 18:11–24). But we should note that terms like *martys*, *martyria*, or *martyreō* and even *martyrion* were never used for such heroes of faith.

NT This word group is esp. important in Acts and Johannine lit. *katamartyreō* occurs only in Matt. 26:62; 27:13; Mk. 14:60 in questions directed to Jesus as to whether he did not wish to answer the evidence presented against him. *symmartyreō* is used exclusively by Paul in Rom. 2:15; 8:16; 9:1, expressing a confirmatory, reinforcing, or accusatory cotestimony of the Spirit or of human conscience. *diamartyromai* occurs 15x (9x in Acts, where the vb. is used as a special expression for proclamation or warning; cf. 1 Thess. 4:6; 1 Tim. 5:21; 2 Tim. 2:14; 4:1).

1. The legal use of the word, common to cl. Gk. and the LXX, dominates the examples in the Synoptics (e.g., *martyria* in Mk. 14:55, 56, 59; Lk. 22:71; *martys* in Matt. 26:65; Mk. 14:63, each of which are related to false evidence produced against Jesus; cf. also Acts 6:13;

7:58). The citations of Deut. 19:15 (Matt. 18:16; Jn. 8:17) and Deut. 17:6 (Heb. 10:28) are to be understood in the same sense.

2. Paul's use of the words is also closely linked to LXX usage (e.g., *martyreō* in Rom. 10:2; 2 Cor. 8:3; Gal. 4:15; Col. 4:13). In Rom. 3:21 he calls "the Law and the Prophets" as that which testifies to God's righteousness. In 1:9; 2 Cor. 1:23; Phil. 1:8; 1 Thess. 2:5, 10, he calls on God as witness. But Paul is perhaps also the first to give *martyrion* a new meaning and content when he says in 1 Cor. 1:6: "because our testimony [*martyrion*] about Christ was confirmed in you." This word no longer means a piece of evidence or a recollection giving encouragement or warning; the word is used in the sense of the gospel, the proclaimed message of salvation in Christ (cf. 1 Cor. 2:1; 15:15; 2 Thess. 1:10).

3. The Synoptics also expand the conceptual area of witness above the legal usage noted above. The sacrifice of the healed man is offered "as a testimony [*martyrion*]," as documented proof that the healing has taken place (Matt. 8:4; Mk. 1:44; Lk. 5:14). The same expression occurs in Matt. 10:18 (the sending out of the Twelve), where the arrest and trial of the disciples will be "as witnesses" to the Jews and Gentiles. Such tribunals will provide opportunities for testifying to Christ in public.

4. In Acts, *martyreō* is sometimes used in the sense of human attestation regarding good conduct (6:3; 16:2; 22:5, 12) and *martys* of false witnesses brought against Stephen (6:13; 7:58). But *martyreō* occurs for the first time in 23:11 without an obj., meaning to testify in the sense of proclaiming Christ. This corresponds with the meaning of *martyrion* in 4:33, where the apostles testify to a message with great power; it also links with the word *martys*, witness, in Lk. 24:48 and Acts 1:8, where the risen Lord calls his apostles as his witnesses to the ends of the earth. This witness is more precisely defined in 1:22 as witness of the resurrection of Jesus (cf. 2:32; 3:15; 13:31; 26:16) and of his deeds. From this meaning it soon becomes clear that the way of a witness is a way of rejection, suffering, and possibly of death ("your martyr Stephen," 22:20). Luke likes to use *diamartyromai* for testimony to Jesus as the Christ (18:5) and the proclamation of the grace of God (20:24; cf. 2:40; 8:25; 28:23).

5. The concept of witness has a more central theological significance for Jn. than for all the other NT writers. He summarizes the content of the Christ event and of the gospel in the concept of the *logos* (word, → 3364) and adopts the vb. *martyreō* and the noun *martyria* in order to express the event of the divine communication of revelation in all its aspects. (a) John is aware, to be sure, of the cl. Gk. use of the word in the sense of human attestation or testimonial (see Jn. 2:25, where Jesus says he does not need human testimony to form an opinion about someone; 12:17, where people bear witness to the resurrection of Lazarus; 18:23, where Jesus challenges the temple guard who struck him to give proof of his improper speech; cf. also 3 Jn. 3, 6, 12).

(b) But it is precisely against this background that the specific character of Jn.'s concept of witness surfaces in three aspects of the meaning of witness as being specific testimony borne to Christ. (i) More strongly in Jn. than in the other Gospels John the Baptist is portrayed as the forerunner, the final prophet. His task was to point to or witness to the Coming One: "He came as a witness [*martyria*] to testify [*martyreō*] concerning that light, so that through him all men might believe" (Jn. 1:7; cf. 1:15, 32, 34; 3:26, 31–32; 5:33). Thus witness here is proclamation that points to Jesus as the revealer of God.

(ii) A central theme of Jn.'s Gospel is that Jesus testifies of himself. Against the Jewish leaders, who maintain that because he is testifying to himself, his *martyria* cannot be true (8:13, 17; cf. Deut. 19:15), Jesus sets his word in Jn. 8:14. When Jesus says something about himself, his *martyria* is true, because he knows where he has come from and where he is going. This is not self-glorification (cf. esp. 5:31, which is in tension with 8:14). Rather, his legitimation is: "The very work that the Father has given me ... testifies that the Father has sent me" (5:36; cf. 10:25). Moreover, the Father too is a witness to his

Son (5:32, 37; cf. 6:65; 10:32). In addition, in 5:39 the Scriptures are named as a witness. What is meant is finally expressed in the trial scene before Pilate: "For this I came into the world, to testify to the truth" (18:37). In short, Jesus himself is the mediator of the testimony, i.e., of the revelation of God to the world (8:14), which hates him and thus rejects his testimony (3:11, 32).

(iii) For those who have accepted the truth about Jesus and thus confirmed or certified the truth of God (Jn. 3:33), their message becomes testimony about Jesus. This happens first with the Samaritan woman, whose testimony led the way to the Samaritans to believe in him (4:39). In 15:26, Jesus promises that the Paraclete, the Spirit, will testify about him. He opens the world's eyes to the truth of God and the truth about itself. Jesus then expands this in the phrase, "you also must testify" (15:27). In 1 Jn. 1:2 the apostle emphasizes that he testified to the life, who has appeared (cf. 4:14; 5:10–11). Similarly, 5:6, speaking of the witness of the Spirit, takes up Jn. 15:26.

(c) This *martyria* concerning Jesus Christ as the revelation of the significance of Jesus, communicated and accepted in faith, is for the seer of Rev. identical with "the word of God" (1:2, 9; cf. 12:11). The *martyria* is more precisely qualified as "the spirit of prophecy" (19:10), which may mean testifying to what has been here revealed concerning the future. To be touched by the testimony of Jesus Christ places one in the service of witness. It obliges one to pass it on, though doing so almost inevitably means suffering and persecution (cf. 6:9; 12:17). But such people are also assured of victory (12:11; cf. 20:4).

In Rev. 1:5, Jesus is specifically called "the faithful witness" (cf. 3:14). Those who suffer and are killed because of their relationship with Jesus are likewise called faithful witnesses (see Antipas in 2:13; cf. 6:9; 11:3, 7). Note how the great prostitute, Babylon, is drunk with the blood of Jesus' witnesses (17:6). To be sure, what stands in the foreground is still not so much one's death but one's appearance as a trustworthy witness of Jesus.

6. Heb. is different from the other NT writings in that it uses the vb. *martyreō* exclusively in the pass. and chiefly in Heb. 11. The one who bears witness, confirming the faith of the one named, is God himself (11:2, 4, 5, 39). Those whose fate bears all the signs of the martyrdom of faith obtain a witness, i.e., are recognized by God. It is in accord with this that these people, who have been accredited on account of holding firm to the hope of their faith, are in 12:1 called a "cloud of witnesses" for the church of the present time.

7. What is the application of this theme for believers today? (a) The frequent use of the witness theme in the NT stresses the importance of the historical foundations of the Christian religion. The apostles, who were with Jesus from the beginning of his ministry, are eyewitnesses to vouch for the facts of Jesus' life, death, and resurrection. The Gospels testify to this, as does Paul in 1 Cor. 15:1–8. This is a powerful message in the light of those who reject the historicity of much of the Gospels.

In terms of the legal meaning of this word group, the Gospel of Jn. esp. provides the setting for the most sustained controversy in the NT. Here Jesus has a lawsuit with the world. His witnesses include John the Baptist, the Scriptures, the Father, his own words and works, and later the apostles and the Holy Spirit. They are opposed by the world, which is represented by the unbelieving Jews. John has a case to present, and for this reason he advances arguments, asks juridical questions, and presents his witnesses.

(b) In Rev. the stress falls on Christ, "the faithful and true witness" (3:14), who serves as the archetype for the faithful band of believers, who must maintain the same testimony even at the sacrifice of life itself (cf. also 1 Tim. 6:12–16). The faithful witness often entails suffering and persecution. Christians are about to enter a time of severe persecution, and some of them will be brought before courts and sentenced to death. For this reason the seer of Patmos encourages them to "hold to the testimony of Jesus" (Rev. 12:17; cf. 20:4). Thus it is not surprising that wherever Christians have faced opposition and hostile

law courts for the sake of their testimony, this book has been a source of inspiration.

3457 (*martyrion*, testimony, evidence, proof), → *3456*.

3458 (*martyromai*, testify, bear witness, affirm), → *3456*.

3459 (*martys*, a witness), → *3456*.

3463 μαστιγόω	μαστιγόω (*mastigoō*), whip, flog, scourge, chastise (*3463*);

μάστιξ (*mastix*), whip, lash, scourging, torment (*3465*); μαστίζω (*mastizō*), strike with a whip, scourge (*3464*); κολαφίζω (*kolaphizō*), beat (*3139*); δέρω (*derō*), beat (*1296*); πατάσσω (*patassō*), strike, hit (*4250*); πληγή (*plēgē*), blow, stroke, wound (*4435*); ὑπωπιάζω (*hypōpiazō*), strike under the eye, treat roughly, maltreat (*5724*); φραγέλλιον (*phragellion*), whip, lash (*5848*); φραγελλόω (*phragelloō*), flog, scourge (*5849*).

CL & OT 1. In cl. Gk. a variety of words denote physical violence, often distinguished by the manner in which the violence is inflicted. Of those that occur in the NT, *derō* originally meant flay or skin, but came to mean beat. *mastizō* and *mastigoō* refer to a more severe form of punishment and are later applied (together with the Lat. loan words *phragellion* and *phragelloō*) to the Roman punishment of scourging that accompanied capital offenses. *hypōpiazō* derives from the world of boxing (lit., strike under the eye; hence, treat roughly, maltreat). Some of these terms also developed fig. meanings (e.g., *plēgē* could mean a misfortune sent by a god).

2. The most frequent of the above words in the LXX are *plēgē*, *patassō*, and *mastigoō*. Besides their lit. usage, they are all applied fig. to the plagues and sorrows inflicted by God both on the nations and on his own people. *plēgē* is used of the plagues in Egypt (Exod. 11:1; 12:13) and of the suffering servant as "a man of sorrows" (Isa. 53:3). Gen. 8:21 uses the fut. of *patassō*: "Never again will I destroy all living creatures." Ps. 39:10 pleads, "Remove your scourge [*mastix* in pl.] from me." *derō* is found only in the sense of flay (Lev. 1:6).

NT 1. These various words are used in a lit. sense in the NT. (a) *derō* (Lk. 22:63), *phragelloō* (Matt. 27:26; Mk. 15:15), and *mastigoō* (Jn. 19:1) describe the scourging Jesus received. He was also struck by the soldiers (*rhapizō*, Matt. 26:67; *rhapisma*, Mk. 14:65; Jn. 19:3; Matt. and Mk. also have *kolaphizō*). *mastigoō* occurs in the passion predictions (Matt. 20:19; Mk. 10:34; Lk. 18:32). Jesus' parabolic teaching shows that he anticipated such treatment of himself (*derō* in Matt. 21:35; Mk. 12:3, 5; Lk. 20:10–11).

(b) Several texts refer to punishment from the Jews. The disciples can expect scourging (*mastigoō*, Matt. 10:17; 23:34) and beating (*derō*, Mk. 13:9). Acts 5:40 and 22:19 describe instances of beating by Jewish authorities. The example of those who were scourged for their faith is held up by Heb. 11:36.

(c) Punishment by civil magistrates is also mentioned, perhaps sometimes as a mode of examination under torture (Acts 16:23, 33; 2 Cor. 11:23–24, *plēgē*; Acts 16:37, *derō*; 22:24, *mastix*).

2. Some of these words are used in a fig. sense. (a) God corrects and chastises (*mastigoō*) his own people for their good (Heb. 12:6; cf. Prov. 3:12). Paul encourages believers to forestall this through self-discipline (1 Cor. 9:27, *hypōpiazō*; cf. 11:30–31).

(b) In Mk. 3:10; 5:29; Lk. 7:21 *mastix* denotes a bodily illness in the sense of suffering or affliction. It reflects the belief that illness was a chastisement from God, though Jesus denied any necessary connection between sickness and sin (Jn. 9:3).

(c) At the crucifixion the shepherd himself was smitten (*patassō*) by God (Matt. 26:31; cf. Zech. 13:7; Isa. 53:3–4) and thus shouldered God's judgment. In 1 Pet. 2:24 *mōlōps* expresses the paradox: by his wound(s) you have been healed.

(d) God inflicts judgment on all who have rebelled against him in order to lead them back to repentance. *plēgē* is repeatedly used in

Rev. for manifestations of God's wrath. When people fail to repent, they are finally destroyed (9:20–21; 11:6; 15:1).

(e) *kolaphizō* is used lit. in Matt. 26:67; Mk. 14:65; 1 Pet. 2:20; in 2 Cor. 12:7 it is used fig. of Paul's "thorn in [the] flesh, a messenger of Satan, to torment" him. Presumably this is some sort of physical affliction or possibly of those opposing him. In response to Paul's prayer three times for its removal, the reply is given, "My grace is sufficient for you, for my power is made perfect in weakness" (12:9).

See also *paideuō*, instruct, train (*4084*); *rhabdos*, rod, staff (*4811*).

3464 (mastizō, strike with a whip, scourge), → *3463.*

3465 (mastix, whip, lash, scourging, torment), → *3463.*

3467 (mataiologia, useless talk, empty prattle), → *3469.*

3468 (mataiologos, idle talker), → *3469.*

3469	μάταιος

μάταιος (*mataios*), empty, useless, worthless, futile (*3469*); ματαιότης (*mataiotēs*), emptiness, futility, worthlessness (*3470*); ματαιόω (*mataioō*), render futile (*3471*); μάτην (*matēn*), in vain, to no end (*3472*); ματαιολογία (*mataiologia*), useless talk, empty prattle (*3467*); ματαιολόγος (*mataiologos*), idle talker (*3468*).

CL & OT 1. In cl. Gk. *mataios* means null as both cause and effect. Hence it means both fallacious, fictitious, groundless, and in vain, ineffectual, aimless. This word and its cognates have as their background certain set values, moral standards, and religious realities. The conduct of anyone who ignores or transgresses these falls under the judgment of being *mataios*. One's life thus becomes a deceptive appearance, and such a person can be called a fool or even a criminal. The Gk. world counseled reflection and prudence to guard against such aberrations.

To check *mataiotēs*, Aeschylus coined the counter-idea *mē mataion*, which manifests itself in *sōphrosynē* (*5408*). The gods did not possess the power effectively to overcome negative *mataiotēs*. Evidently the conflict between *mataios* and *mē mataion*, between one's mere appearance and his or her being, slackened off in a later age.

2. The LXX used this word group to translate various Heb. words that denote different aspects of vanity, deception, or nothingness. Those who can be called *mataios* resist the reality of God in his revelation and claims on them. An example of Yahweh's uncompromising confrontation with vanity is the third commandment: "You shall not misuse the name of the LORD your God" (Exod. 20:7).

mataios occurs in the OT chiefly in three contexts. (a) Prophets who speak without being commissioned and utter the revelations of their imaginations as God's word speak vanity. Their words are lies and deception and are under God's judgment (cf. Jer. 23:16–32; Lam. 2:14; Ezek. 13:6–9; Zech. 10:2). Anyone who follows them falls prey to vanity. Zeph. 3:13 promises the eventual cessation of lies and vanity.

(b) *mataios* is often used as a designation of idols, of the making of idols, and of their worship. *ta mataia* (the empty things or vain things) is often used as a trans. for the names of gods of foreign peoples (2 Chr. 11:15; Isa. 2:20). They are "nothings."

(c) The godly person in the OT is not unaware of the futility and vanity of human life (Ps. 103:14–16; Job 14:1–6 and often elsewhere) and thought (Ps. 94:11). In Eccl. this awareness is intensified to the point of apparent skepticism: "All is vanity" (*mataiotēs*; NIV "meaningless"; Eccl. 1:2; cf. 2:1 and often). The Teacher's skepticism can understand neither God's government nor the meaning of his own life. There remains only the resignation of tragic existence, which has lamentation for the vanity of existence. This may be partly explained by the author's distance in time from God's mighty acts in history and by the absence of God's intervention in the course of the world in the present. Nevertheless, the Teacher is held back from plunging into nihilism by such affirmations of life as 2:25; 3:13; 7:14; 9:7–10.

NT In contrast to the frequent use of *mataios* in the prophets, this word and its cognates occur in the NT only 14x. Generally this word group denotes emptiness and futility. With the same sharpness as in the OT, the judgment *mataios* is passed on everything that is opposed to God and his commands, such as the presumption of human thought (Rom. 1:21; 1 Cor. 3:20), pagan idolatry (Acts 14:15), and a deceitful way of life (Jas. 1:26; 1 Pet. 1:18).

1. In 1 Cor. 3:20 Paul contends against worldly pseudo-wisdom. The cross of Jesus makes those who would be clever foolish before God and humanity. Paul finds confirmation of this in Ps. 94:11. The Lord "knows the thoughts of man; he knows that they are futile." The wisdom of the worldly wise stands in contrast to the foolishness of the cross, which is God's wisdom for those who believe (1 Cor. 1:24). The cross appears foolish, weak, and vain to natural thinking.

In 1 Cor. 15:17 Paul describes as vain a faith that denies the reality of the risen Christ. It is still under the power of sin and removes the basis of the kerygma, the message of Christ. Paul uses *kenos* (→ *3031*) 2x in 1 Cor. 15:14. However, because the resurrection of Jesus actually happened as the act of God, faith is not "futile" (*mataia*).

2. The prophetic attack on idols is continued in missionary preaching (Acts 14:15). The revelation of God in Christ does not permit foreign gods, humans, or images to be worshiped as divine. Through the preaching of the gospel people turn from these "worthless" nonentities (such as Zeus and Hermes, 14:12) to the living God.

3. The church's sanctified way of life is contrasted with the pagan way in 1 Pet. 1:14–18. Christ's sacrificial death brings about redemption from the futile way of life inherited from one's ancestors (1:18). The Gentile Christian would understand *mataios* here as the worship of idols, which was the root of the former unrestrained way of life. According to Jas. 1:26, one's religion is "worthless" if one is outwardly pious but at the same time devoted to unrestrained prattle (cf. 2 Pet. 2:18).

4. In Rom. 8:20 Paul sees the whole creation subject to *mataiotēs* ("frustration"). It is in bondage to decay (8:21). But this corruptibility also passes, because it is not self-elected but imposed on it by the Creator, so that he may reveal to it its future splendor. Thus there is not only sighing (8:22), but a well-founded waiting for redemption (8:19). According to Eph. 4:17, *mataiotēs* is the characteristic of the pagan way of thought and life. In ingratitude human beings forsake God, the fountain of life, and give themselves over to a life of immorality through "the futility of their thinking."

5. *mataioō* occurs in the LXX almost entirely in the pass. in the sense of being given over to vanity (cf. Jer. 2:5). Rom. 1:21 speaks of humans as being responsible for this (cf. comments on 8:20). They are given over to futility because they ungratefully deny God the honor that is justly his.

6. *matēn*, in vain, occurs in Matt. 15:9; Mk. 7:7; cf. Isa. 29:13. *mataiologia* (1 Tim. 1:6) means empty prattle, "meaningless talk." This comes about when people do not keep to what God has appointed for them: "love, which comes from a pure heart and a good conscience and a sincere faith" (1:5; cf. 2 Pet. 2:18). There are many "mere talkers" (*mataiologoi*, Tit. 1:10) and deceivers, especially among the circumcision party.

See also *kenos*, empty, without truth or power (*3031*).

3470 (mataiotēs, emptiness, futility, worthlessness), → *3469.*

3471 (mataioō, render futile), → *3469.*

3472 (matēn, in vain, to no end), → *3469.*

3479 (machaira, sword), → *4483.*

3480 (machē, battle, fighting, quarrels, strife, disputes), → *4483.*

3481 (machomai, fight, quarrel, dispute), → *4483.*

3483 (megaleios, mighty deed), → *3489.*

3484 (megaleiotēs, grandeur), → *3489.*

3486 (megalynō, make large, great, magnify), → *3489.*

3488 (megalōsynē, majesty), → *3489.*

3489	μέγας

μέγας (*megas*), large, great (*3489*); μεγαλύνω (*megalynō*), make large, great, magnify (*3486*); μεγαλειότης (*megaleiotēs*), grandeur (*3484*); μεγαλωσύνη (*megalōsynē*), majesty (*3488*); μεγαλεῖος (*megaleios*), mighty deed (*3483*); μείζων (*meizōn*), greater than (*3505*).

CL & OT 1. (a) *megas*, great, is the antonym of *mikros*, small (→ *3625*). Its use ranges from the measurement of physical shapes and spaces to designations of rank. According to the context, *megas* can mean fully grown, important, magnificent, powerful. Used as an epithet of honor, it occurs frequently in the formula of acclamation *megas theos* ("great god"), and in connection with the names of gods. *meizōn* is the comparative and *megistos* the superlative.

(b) The derived vb. *megalynō* means to make great and can be used fig. in the sense of to praise, glorify. *megaleiotēs*, grandeur, splendor, and *megalōsynē*, majesty, splendor, are not attested in pre-Christian lit. *megaleia*, good and mighty deeds, is the neut. pl. of *megaleios* used as a noun.

2. (a) In the LXX *megas* occurs about 820x in various OT writings; *megalynō* occurs 93x. *megas* translates a variety of Heb. words, which suggests that the translators were not trying to find a corresponding Gk. term for each Heb. word, but were generalizing.

(b) In contrast to the wide-ranging use of the adj., the derived nouns in the LXX have a clear denotation. In addition to two verses in the Apocr. (1 Esd. 1:5; 4:40), *megaleiotēs* is used in Jer. 33:9 (= LXX 33:9) and Dan. 7:27 in connection with the fact that God's activity in Israel will extend to all peoples on earth in power and glory. *megalōsynē* occurs 27x, mainly in expressions of God's surpassing greatness and power (e.g., 2 Sam. 7:23), evident esp. in his redemption of Israel. Similarly the word is used in 1 Chr. 17:19 and Ps. 150:2 to assert God's creative will and his lordship over history. There is a twofold emphasis here: (a) to describe God's greatness, and (b) to summon people to see and praise God's greatness, i.e., to glorify him.

(c) *megaleia* has the same almost exclusive reference to Yahweh's mighty acts (e.g., Deut. 11:2; Ps. 106:21). At times the OT presents Yahweh as greater than all gods (cf. Exod. 18:11; Ps. 77:13).

NT 1. The *megas* word group is attested over 200x in the NT. The adj. occurs esp. frequently in Lk.'s writings; it is also prominent in later NT letters, while the group rarely appears in the earlier Pauline writings. It is in Rev. that the greatest number of occurrences (80x) are found. The phrase "small and great," meaning all without distinction, is typical of Acts and Rev. (e.g., Acts 8:10; 26:22; Rev. 11:18; 20:12; cf. Gen. 19:11; 1 Sam. 30:2).

(a) *megas* is important in various Synoptic sayings of Jesus. These reveal his rejection of the rab. striving after piety as it was practiced in a world strictly divided into great and small, i.e., into people of higher and lower standing. The sayings concern rewards and true greatness in the kingdom of heaven. They cut across the Pharisaic attitude to commandments (Matt. 5:19–20), warn about human enmity, and call for love of one's enemies (cf. Lk. 6:23, 35, both using *polys*). Jesus' own attitude surfaces in his teaching on the Sabbath, which leads to the declaration that "one greater than the temple is here" (Matt. 12:6, *meizōn*), namely, the order of the kingdom of God, already present in the actions and person of Jesus.

(b) The instances of *megas* in Rev. are bound up with the apocalyptic form of the book (cf. also Matt. 24:21, 24, 31; Lk. 21:11, 23). It is used in the larger-than-life symbolism that characterizes the eschatological dimension of events, e.g., the day (Rev. 6:17), the earthquake (16:18), and the city (18:2, 10, 16, 18–19, 21). Particularly striking are the 21 occurrences of *phōnē megalē*, "a loud [lit., great] voice." This expression indicates the sovereignty of God, which drowns all other sounds of his messengers (e.g., Rev. 1:10; 5:2; 7:2; 10:3; 11:15; 16:1;

21:3). The note of divine sovereignty is also heard in the loud voice of the multitude praising him (5:12; 6:10; 7:10; 19:1). The phrase has a similar meaning in the Gospels, where it is used both of the cry of Jesus on the cross (Matt. 27:50; Mk. 15:37; Lk. 23:46) and of the demons' cry of terror (4:33).

2. *megaleiotēs* is used 2x for God's majesty, supremacy, and splendor (Lk. 9:43; 2 Pet. 1:16) and once for the presumed "divine majesty" of Artemis (Acts 19:27). *megalōsynē* occurs in Heb. 1:3; 8:1; Jude 25 as a surrogate for God, expressing his sublime majesty. *megaleios* occurs only in Acts 2:11 (pl.), where the Jews of the Diaspora visiting Jerusalem express amazement at hearing the followers of Jesus declaring "the wonders" of God in their own languages.

3. In Jn. the comparative *meizōn* brings into prominence Jesus' claims and the unique effectiveness of his work. In authority he is "greater" than Jacob, Abraham, or anyone else, for he brings life (4:12; 5:20, 36; 8:53). His works have been given him by the Father, who, despite the unity and equality that exist between the two, is "greater" than Jesus himself (10:29; 14:28). The commission with which the Father sends the Son is balanced by the Son's obedience in carrying out his work of love.

4. *megas* takes on special significance in a number of passages with particular theological importance. Jesus' teaching presents something new.

(a) In Matt. 22:36, 38 Jesus is asked a controversial question about the "the greatest [lit., great] commandment" (cf. Mk. 12:28). The use of the positive *megalē* instead of the superlative *megistē* is a Semitism. Some rab. teaching emphasized the equal importance of all commandments, but there was also a tendency in Jud. to seek a single principle. Jesus replies by referring to the double command to love God and one's neighbor. He thus makes an organic connection between Deut. 6:5 and Lev. 19:18, a connection rarely made in Jewish legal thought. Moreover, the works that Jesus does and the "greater works" the disciples will do are to be understood as combining this love for God and love for other people. According to Jesus, love in the form of service must underlie all our works (→ *agapē*, 27).

(b) In the parallel section in Lk., Jesus' answer is linked with the parable of the Good Samaritan (10:25–37). This makes clear how, in Jesus' understanding of love, a special standard for reckoning greatness and smallness applies. That story is the standard example for those who want to obey the twofold "greatest" commandment: A person shows love for God by loving his or her neighbor.

(c) Thus, as regards function, the "greatest commandment" goes hand in hand with the definition of greatness and smallness in the kingdom of heaven, as it appears in the passage where the disciples argue about personal precedence (Matt. 18:1–5; Mk. 9:33–37; Lk. 9:46–48). Jesus demonstrates the supremely valid guideline for his disciples. He puts a child in their midst and declares, "Whoever humbles himself like this child [i.e., acknowledges his own smallness] is the greatest in the kingdom of heaven" (Matt. 18:4).

(d) In this devaluation and revaluation of worldly orders of precedence, the structure of the Christian community, determined by the model of Christ, emerges as a fellowship based on service to others (cf. Lk. 22:26–27, where "the greatest" is used as a synonym of "the one who serves"; cf. Matt. 20:26; 23:11; Mk. 10:43–44). The discussions about the greatness or smallness of John the Baptist should be understood in the same way (Matt. 11:11; Lk. 7:28). Jesus, insofar as he ushers in the kingdom of God, performs the greatest work, while the Baptist still belongs to the previous era of expectation.

See also *mikros*, small, little (*3625*).

3493 (methermēneuō, translate), → *2257.*

3494 (methē, drunkenness), → *3501.*

3497 (methodeia, method, esp. scheming, craftiness), → *3847.*

3499 (methyskō, cause to become intoxicated), → *3501.*

3500 (methysos, drunkard), → *3501.*

| 3501 μεθύω | μεθύω (*methyō*), be drunk (*3501*); μεθύσκω (*methyskō*), cause to |

become intoxicated (*3499*); μέθυσος (*methysos*), drunkard (*3500*); μέθη (*methē*), drunkenness (*3494*); πάροινος (*paroinos*), given to drunkenness (*4232*).

CL & OT These words occur regularly in Hel. Gk. in connection with intoxication. In Gnosticism drunkenness is often linked with *agnōsia* in opposition to true *gnōsis* (cf. also *Odes Sol.* 11:8). In the LXX *methyō*, intoxicated with wine, is familiar enough (cf. Gen. 9:21; Isa. 19:14; 28:1; Joel 1:5). The word can also be used of the refreshment brought by rain to dry ground (Ps. 65:10; Isa. 55:10). *methē*, drunkenness, occurs in Prov. 20:1; Isa. 28:7; Ezek. 23:33. Sometimes *methyskō* is used fig., as in Isa. 34:5, where the sword of Yahweh drinks its fill, with blood as the intoxicating liquid (34:7; 49:26).

NT In the NT *methysos* and *methē* occur in lists of vices (Rom. 13:13; Gal. 5:21; 1 Cor. 5:11; 6:10); drunkenness is seen here as an element of the old way of life now abandoned. Typical of the Pauline attitude is 1 Thess. 5:6–7, where, with an awareness of the imminence of the end, the apostle issues a strong warning against the perils of drunkenness. The argument is based on the conviction that Christians now live in the light of Christ's new day. Since drunkenness is a nighttime experience, it is incompatible with authentic Christianity (cf. also Matt. 24:49; Lk. 12:45; 21:34).

This incompatibility can also be deduced from the fact that the Christian is Spirit-filled (Eph. 5:18; cf. Acts 2:15), a condition that shows itself not so much in ecstasies or mystical experiences, but in liturgical praise (Eph. 5:18–20) and in ethical commitment (5:21–6:9). The incongruity of drunkenness and Christian experience emerges clearly in the context of the Lord's Supper (1 Cor. 11:20–21). Perhaps the Dionysus cult, with its stress on religious intoxication, was affecting some Christians in Corinth.

In Rev. 17:2 idolatry is vividly depicted as a drunkenness with the wine of adultery, probably with direct allusion to the intoxicating and orgiastic character of some of the current cults. In 17:6 the woman, symbolizing power opposed to God within the world, is drunk with the blood of the saints.

paroinos is the distinctive word for drunkenness in the Pastoral Letters; in 1 Tim. 3:3 and Tit. 1:7 it is one of the disqualifying factors for the office of bishop. Two other words, *kraipalē*, intoxication (Lk. 21:34), and *oinophlygia*, drunkenness (1 Pet. 4:3), each occur once, both as a characteristic that is incompatible with Christian life.

See also *nēphō*, be sober (*3768*).

3505 (*meizōn*, greater than), → *3489*.

| 3506 μέλας | μέλας (*melas*), black (*3506*). |

CL & OT *melas* means dark, black, and in a transferred sense sinister, enigmatic. It occurs in the LXX as black (cf. Song 1:5; Zech. 6:2); Philo and Josephus use *melas* metaphorically as the sign of a stranger, of mourning, and of personal misfortune.

NT The neut. *to melan* means ink at 2 Cor. 3:3; 2 Jn. 12; 3 Jn. 13. *melas* is contrasted with *leukos*, white (→ *3328*), in Matt. 5:36: "And do not swear by your head, for you cannot make even one hair white or black." Here we have perhaps a complex of ideas. Swearing was sometimes made by the head, and in some cases the vow was symbolized by not cutting one's hair (cf. Jdg. 13:5; Acts 18:18). Moreover, several times disciples are assured that the hairs of their heads are all numbered and thus they will not perish (Matt. 10:30; Lk. 12:7; Acts 27:34). We have no control over the course of time; our vows cannot turn the clock back by turning white hair again to the black hair of youth. Nevertheless, we can trust in the Father's providential care that nothing will befall us without his will.

At Rev. 6:5 the rider of a black horse holds a balance, while a voice quotes high prices for food, probably a sign of famine sent as judgment. The apocalyptic image is derived from the four horses in Zech. 6:2, which represent the universal lordship of God. In Rev. 6:12 the sun becomes "black like sackcloth," a sign of mourning. The darkening of the sun is a recurrent eschatological symbol of the Lord's coming in judgment that the NT takes over from the OT (Isa. 13:10; 50:3; Ezek. 32:7; Joel 2:10, 31; Amos 8:9; Matt. 24:29; Mk. 13:24; Lk. 23:45; Acts 2:20; Rev. 6:12; 9:2).

3508 (*melei*, be concerned, be worried about), → *3533*.

| 3516 μέλλω | μέλλω (*mellō*), be about to, be on the point of, intend, propose (*3516*). |

CL & OT *mellō* is commonly followed by an infinitive, which denotes the intentions of the subject. Thus *mellō* means "I am able to, I can." With a future infinitive it denotes "I am about to, I intend to." When the action is regarded as compelled by the gods, fate, or some law, *mellō* denotes something inevitable and determined. When the action in question is delayed so that it never comes about, *mellō* means hesitate. The part. *mellōn* means the future, what is about to come.

In the LXX *mellō* is often used with a present infinitive, usually as the equivalent of the imperfect future form of the Heb. vb. Some LXX MSS of Isa. 9:5 (= LXX 9:6) have *patēr tou mellontos aiōnos* (Father of the age to come).

NT 1. In the NT *mellō* means the same as in cl. Gk: intend, have in mind (e.g., Matt. 2:13; Lk. 10:1; 19:4; Jn. 6:6, 15; 7:35; Heb. 8:5). It occurs frequently with the present infinitive (84x) and occasionally with the aor. infinitive. *ti melleis* (Acts 22:16) means, "What are you waiting for?"

2. *mellō* means must, have to, in the context of events that happen according to the will and decree of God. It occurs in statements about Christ's saving work, esp. his suffering and death. Thus, Jesus "told them what *was going to* happen to him" (Mk. 10:32); "the Son of Man *is going to* be betrayed into the hands of men" (Matt. 17:22). It occurs in the context of God's action in grace and judgment (Mk. 13:4; Acts 17:31; Rom. 4:24; 8:13; Gal. 3:23; 1 Thess. 3:4; Heb. 10:27; Rev. 1:19; 3:10). With this may be included prophetic utterances made with divine certainty (Acts 11:28; 24:15; 26:22).

3. Participial forms of *mellō* are used both as adjs. and nouns in the sense of coming, future (Lk. 13:9; Rom. 8:38; 2 Pet. 2:6). In this sense, it is incorporated in an important NT eschatological formula. The teaching of the two ages (→ *aiōn*, *172*) provides the foundation for the NT doctrine of the kingdom of God. The present age, which is passing away, has been broken into by the age to come (*mellōn aiōn*). This coming world (Heb. 2:5; cf. Eph. 1:21) is alone the realm of Christ. At present, believers have no abiding city; they seek a future (*mellousa*) one (Heb. 13:14), a heavenly city (11:16; 12:22), prepared by God. This new world is described in terms of future glory (Rom. 8:18; cf. 1 Pet. 5:1). It is already present with God and is ready to be revealed.

In light of the future, the sufferings of the present age are to be counted as nothing. But those who "live according to the sinful nature ... will die" (*mellete apothnēskein*, Rom. 8:13). This is the inevitable outcome of the coming judgment and God's wrath (Matt. 3:7; Acts 24:25). Christ is the coming Son of Man (Matt. 16:27) and judge (2 Tim. 4:1). Godliness is of value as it holds promise for the present life and the life to come (1 Tim. 4:8). It is possible to taste the powers of the age to come (Heb. 6:5). The law is only the shadow of the good things to come (10:1; cf. Col. 2:17).

See also *erchomai*, come, go (*2262*); *katantaō*, come to, arrive at (*2918*).

| 3517 μέλος |

μέλος (*melos*), member, part, limb (*3517*).

CL & OT In cl. Gk. *melos* means limb; also musical member, phrase, hence song or music to which a song is set. In pre-Socratic writers the pl. can mean members. The sing. is used later for a member of a body or a city (where the city is understood as an organism). In Hel. mystery religions and Gnosticism the idea of the body and its members has a religious application in creation mythology and especially in gnostic redemption myths. The redeemed are lost members of the redeemer's body, which have now been found.

melos occurs 12x in the canonical books of the LXX. In Exod. 29:17 it denotes the dismembered parts of the sacrifice; in Jdg. 19:29 it is used of the dismembered body of the Levite's concubine. Since the word is not used of the limbs of a living human body, there is no thought of the body and its members in a theological or a sociological sense. The OT is, however, interested in the function of individual parts of the body. The heart, for example, is mentioned 851x (rarely referring to the physical organ); it is associated with human thoughts and feelings, similar to the way in which we today associate the heart with our emotions (cf. Isa. 6:10; Lam. 2:11). The lower parts of the body, such as the liver and kidneys, are the emotional center of a person (Prov. 12:10; 26:22).

In combining Jewish thinking with Gk. philosophical thinking, Philo taught that the dismembered parts of the sacrificed animal have ontological significance. The apologetic intention is clear. The physiological fact derived from the OT, which saw the part in relation to the whole, conceals the philosophical principle that the parts receive their function from the whole and must work for the benefit of the whole.

In rab. lit. the number of members that make up the human body illustrates the totality and universality of the Mosaic law. The body has 248 members, which corresponds to the 248 positive commands of the Torah. (There were 365 negative commands, corresponding to the number of days in the year.) Elsewhere, rab. theologians relate their observations on the function of the individual members to assessments of their worth and mutual relations.

NT Most instances of *melos* in the NT occur in Rom. 6:13, 19; 7:5, 23; 12:4–5; 1 Cor. 6:15; 12:12–27. (See also Eph. 4:25; 5:30; Col. 3:5; Jas. 3:5 [sing.]; 3:6; 4:1.) It occurs only twice in the Gospels in the parallel sayings of Jesus in Matt. 5:29–30.

1. "If your right eye causes you to sin, gouge it out and throw it away. It is better for you to lose one part of your body [lit., one of your members] than for your whole body [*sōma*] to be thrown into hell" (Matt. 5:29; similarly in 5:30 regarding the hand). Jesus clearly did not intend the sayings to be taken literally. They apply rather to the evil functions of which the eye and hand are instruments—the lustful look and the malicious act. It is these that must cease. Evil must be rooted out if one's body (i.e., the whole person) is to be saved from judgment, and the whole body will be redeemed if just a single part is rooted out.

With the same eschatological sharpening and clarity, Jas. 3:5–6 describes the tongue as a little member that destroys like a devouring fire. Jas. 4:1 shows that passions can arise from all the members of the body, which can destroy the life of the church.

2. In describing the Christian's new life in Rom. 6, Paul writes: "Do not offer the parts of your body to sin, as instruments of wickedness, but rather offer yourselves to God . . . and the parts of your body to him as instruments of righteousness" (6:13, cf. 6:19). The test of whether we have this new life is whether we practice righteousness in our relationships in the world. At the same time, this reveals the tension between what we desire to do as Christians and the sinful nature that still remains with us (7:22–23, cf. 7:5). This tension remains as long as we live on earth (7:25).

The thought of the members of the body as instruments is renewed in 1 Cor. 6:15 and Col. 3:5. The former precludes prostitu-

tion for a Christian. Insofar as a man is a believer, his members are the members of Christ. To have sexual relations with a prostitute is to become one body with her (1 Cor. 6:16). In such a case, the members of Christ become the members of a prostitute.

3. Rom. 12 and 1 Cor. 12 teach that the church is the body (→ *sōma*, *5393*) of Christ in both reality and function. It is made a reality by the presence of the Holy Spirit, whose gifts are enjoyed and practiced by many individuals. But taken by themselves in isolation these gifts have no significance; they find their importance only in relation to the whole fellowship: "To each one the manifestation of the Spirit is given for the common good" (1 Cor. 12:7). In this extended sense of members (i.e., individual believers as members of the body of Christ), Paul's greatest concern is with the well-being of the body, the church as a whole (cf. also Eph. 4:25; 5:30).

See also *sōma*, body, (*5393*).

| 3519 Μελχισέδεκ |

Μελχισέδεκ (*Melchisedek*), Melchizedek, ancient Canaanite king of Salem (*3519*).

OT Melchizedek (Heb. meaning "king of righteousness" or "my king is righteous") was a Canaanite king. He emerges without warning in OT history (Gen. 14:18–20), following Abram's rout of the forces of Kedorlaomer. He is introduced as "king of Salem," presumably monarch of Jerusalem. As an expression of Near Eastern hospitality, Melchizedek supplies bread and wine for the refreshment of Abram and his victorious warriors. The Gen. narrative concludes with the remarkable observation that the Canaanite king blessed Abram and received a tenth of the spoils of battle from him, Abram thereby acknowledging the prominence of Melchizedek's priesthood.

The only other mention of Melchizedek in the OT occurs in Ps. 110:4, where the LORD (*Yahweh*) addresses David's Lord (*'ādôn*) with the acclamation: "You are a priest forever, in the order of Melchizedek." This verse thus suggests that the priest-king of messianic expectation will be installed in a new non-Aaronic order, patterned after that of Melchizedek. In both pre-Christian and early Christian eras this psalm was interpreted by the Jews in a messianic sense; the Jews dropped a messianic interpretation A.D. 50 and 250 (probably because of Christian interpretation). Rab. Jud. saw Melchizedek as Shem, as an incarnate angel who performs priestly functions, as the archangel Michael, or as an idealized high priest of the messianic age who would emerge alongside the Messiah.

Philo clothes the OT figure of Melchizedek in the garb of Platonic philosophy and allegorizes the historical features of the text. Melchizedek is royal Mind (*nous*), who, unlike despotic kings, decrees pleasing laws and offers to the soul the food of joy and gladness. He is priestly Reason (*logos*), who with the gift of wine releases the soul from earthly contemplation and intoxicates it with heavenly virtues. Thus through his offering of bread and wine Melchizedek mediates the soul's direct access to God.

In pre-Christian Samaritan tradition Melchizedek figured prominently in the establishment of the sanctuary of the sect, apparently as its first priest. Salem is identified with Shechem, and Mount Gerizim is named after Melchizedek, priest of God Most High.

Melchizedek occupies a prominent place in the 11QMelch Qumran scroll, which quotes Ps. 82:1–2 and transfers its meaning to Melchizedek. The king is depicted in the scroll as a heavenly angel standing in God's tribunal, who preserves the faithful and executes judgment on the perverse spirits.

NT Only the author of Heb. in the NT takes interest in the enigmatic figure of Melchizedek. The idea of the Melchizedekian priesthood of Christ is introduced in 5:6, 10, but its full explication is interrupted by a paraenetic digression (5:11–6:19) necessitated by the dullness and immaturity of the readers. Heb. 7 then contains a detailed development of the novel concept of priesthood "in the order of Melchizedek"

(7:1–10) and its application to the high priest of the new covenant (7:11–28).

According to Heb. 7:1–2a, Melchizedek's name ("king of righteousness") and title ("king of peace") points to the Messiah, whose person and ministry is characterized by righteousness (Isa. 32:1; Jer. 23:5–6; 33:15–16) and peace (1 Chr. 22:9; Zech. 9:10; Eph. 2:14–15). The writer then establishes Melchizedek as a fitting model of the radical nonlegal priesthood embodied by Jesus (Heb. 7:3; cf. Ps. 110:4). Since the OT lists no parentage for Melchizedek, his priesthood violates the conditions of the Aaronic order, which stipulate paternal descent from Aaron (Exod. 28:1; Num. 3:10; 18:1) and maternal descent from a pure Israelite (Lev. 21:7, 13–14; Ezek. 44:22). Melchizedek thus adumbrates the messianic high priest, who was descended from the tribe of Judah.

Melchizedek was symbolically what Christ is in reality: a ministrant who suddenly emerged from the distant reaches of eternity and who later vanishes into its depths equally as mysteriously. He exercises a priesthood of uninterrupted duration, since he neither succeeded another priest nor was himself succeeded in office.

Having sketched Melchizedek's similarity to Christ, the writer then argues Melchizedek's dissimilarity to Abraham (and hence to the Levites), thereby demonstrating Christ's superiority to the antiquated legal order (7:4–10). Melchizedek receives tithes from Abraham, which was a priestly right; hence, Levi (Abraham's grandson) is seen as giving tithes to this greater high priest. Moreover, the patriarch Abraham receives a blessing from this Gentile (Gen. 14:19–20), and Melchizedek "lives on" in Scripture, unlike the Levitical priests, who succumbed to death.

The remainder of the chapter (Heb. 7:11–28) delineates the merits of Christ as the Melchizedekian high priest. Using Ps. 110:1, the writer demonstrates that the high priest of the new covenant is vastly superior to the ministrants of the old order. Christ is high priest *forever* "in the order of Melchizedek." His priesthood is indissoluble (Heb. 7:16), inviolable (7:24), efficacious (7:25), and perfect (7:28).

See also *Salēm*, Salem, seat of Melchizedek's rule (*4889*).

3522 (memphomai, find fault), → 289.

3523 (mempsimoiros, fault-finding), → 289.

3524 (mempsis, reason for complaint), → 289.

3531   μένω

μένω (*menō*), remain (*3531*); ἐμμένω (*emmenō*), stay or remain in, persevere, abide by (*1844*); ἐπιμένω (*epimenō*), stay, remain, continue (in) (*2152*); παραμένω (*paramenō*), remain, stay on, continue in (*4169*); προσμένω (*prosmenō*), remain, stay with, remain longer (*4693*); περιμένω (*perimenō*), wait (*4338*); μονή (*monē*), staying, tarrying, dwelling place, room, abode (*3665*).

CL & OT 1. In cl. Gk. *menō* means to remain: in one place, at a given time, or with someone. Fig., it can mean to keep an agreement, remain in a particular sphere of life, or make a stand against difficult circumstances (e.g., illness or death). Hence *menō* can be used of what remains valid in law, e.g., a will. In religious language, it is used for the gods, or what is inspired by them (e.g., mind, ideas), as having continuing existence. As a trans. vb. (seldom used), it means to wait for, expect someone or something. The noun *monē* has various meanings, such as abiding, persistence, continuance, permanence.

2. In the LXX *menō* occasionally means to remain in one place (e.g., Exod. 9:28; Lev. 13:23). Sometimes it means to wait (e.g., Gen. 45:9; Job 36:2). Generally it is concerned with the existence or continuing validity of something. A vow is valid (Num. 30:4, 9) or invalid (30:5, 12). The wealth of the godless does not endure (Job 15:29), while the salvation of the righteous endures (remains) forever (Ps. 112:3, 9).

It is, therefore, particularly used of God. His relationship with humanity is not severed by him but endures (Ps. 112:3, 9), as does his

word (Isa. 40:8) and truth (Ps. 117:2). God waits to have mercy (Isa. 30:18). Esp. in Ps. and Isa., God's constancy is stressed as a characteristic in contrast to the changeability of false gods and the transitory nature of the world. We do not find this as a merely abstract theological statement but always in the living context of the worship and praise of God. God is the living one who endures forever (102:12; Dan. 6:26). Humans opposed to God perish under his judgment and wrath, but the new heavens, the new earth, and God's people remain (Isa. 66:22). Just as Yahweh abides, so does his name, plan, or counsel (Ps. 33:11; Isa. 14:24), his righteousness (Ps. 111:3), and his praise (111:10).

NT 1. *menō* occurs 118x in the NT (40x in Jn. and 27x in 1–2 Jn.). The cl. Gk. uses of the word are found in the NT. (a) Intrans., *menō* means to remain: e.g., to stay in a place (Lk. 19:5) or with someone (24:29; Matt. 26:38), to continue to exist for a specific time (11:23), to live (Jn. 1:38); metaphorically it means to hold fast, remain steadfast: e.g., in a teaching (2 Tim. 3:14; 2 Jn. 9), in fellowship with someone (Jn. 14:10), or in an unmarried state (1 Cor. 7:40); to stand firm, pass the test: e.g., when one's works are judged (3:14); to live on and not to have died (15:6). (b) Trans., *menō* means to wait for (Acts 20:5, 23).

2. Like the OT, the NT speaks of the unchanging character of God, who maintains his word (1 Pet. 1:23; cf. Dan. 6:26; 1 Pet. 1:25, quoting Isa. 40:8); he continues and carries through his plan of election in human history (Rom. 9:11). God's constancy has been made visible in the sending and life of Jesus, the Messiah, who continues forever (Heb. 7:24). Those who have been born anew receive from the Holy Spirit not only ecstatic experiences from time to time, but the power of God abides continually in them (1 Jn. 2:27). Those who confess that Jesus is God's Son in God, i.e., are bound to him by God's love (4:14–15). They do not seek for an enduring city here (Heb. 13:14), but have lasting possessions in heaven (10:34).

Paul points out that in contrast to the service by Moses, which was transitory, the new service of the Spirit and of righteousness is permanent (2 Cor. 3:7–11); along with them faith, hope, and love (1 Cor. 13:13) remain—but above all, love (cf. 13:8).

3. Since Christ will bring about the final and lasting state, human effort for change and self-fulfillment in this transitory life loses its attraction. With this new focus, Christians should give up personal social advancement as their goal in life and the expectation that marriage will fulfill every hope. It is best to remain quietly as they are. That is why Paul advises the Christians in Corinth, "Were you a slave when you were called? Don't let it trouble you" (1 Cor. 7:21). The unmarried and widows should remain unmarried unless they cannot exercise self-control (7:8–9). All their energies should be concentrated on the dawning kingdom of God, and all their efforts should be given to remaining in love and true faith (1 Tim. 2:15; 2 Tim. 3:14).

4. Jn.'s use of *menō en* ("remain in") is parallel to Paul's conception of Christ's dwelling in the believer (Rom. 8:9–11) and the believer's dwelling in Christ. In fact, it is expanded and strengthened. (a) *menō* expresses the closest possible relationship between Father and Son: "The Father, living in me, . . . is doing his work" (Jn. 14:10). The work of Jesus is therefore the work of God. Unlike a prophet, Christ has not been called for a particular task and a limited period; his whole person remains in a lasting and unique nearness to the Father (1:32), just as a son, in contrast to the slave, continues forever in his father's house (8:35). Christ acted in continual oneness with his Father.

(b) Jn. describes the closest possible relationship between Christ and the believer; Jesus calls us to remain in fellowship with him and guarantees that we also will remain in him (Jn. 15:4–5). This abiding of Jesus in believers is proclaimed in the promise that the Holy Spirit will remain in them (14:17; 1 Jn. 2:27).

The statement that Christ remains in the believer contains an indubitably mystical element; it creates an inner unity. One of Paul's ways of expressing this relationship is to use the picture of the body, but that is not found in Jn. This does not mean that God is absorbed into humanity; rather, Christ's abiding in his own is inseparably linked with the abiding of his word in them (Jn. 15:7; 1 Jn. 2:24; cf. Jn. 8:31) and with the acceptance of the reconciling power that flows from the death of Jesus. This is expressed above all in the words: "Whoever eats my flesh and drinks my blood remains in me, and I in him" (6:56). This concept expresses the real meaning of the Lord's Supper for Jn.

(c) Such a remaining in Christ makes us Christ's property right down to the depths of our being. It is not confined to a spiritual relationship, but denotes the present experience of salvation and hence life (Jn. 6:57). Therefore "whoever claims to live in him must walk as Jesus did" (1 Jn. 2:6). The indwelling Christ, or life through the word of Christ, forms a life in conformity to his spirit and nature and brings about sanctification: "The man who does the will of God lives [lit. remains] forever" (2:17).

Remaining in Christ is the same as bearing fruit (Jn. 15:5). If there is no fruit, it is a sign that the fellowship has already been interrupted (15:6; 1 Jn. 3:6). Wherever this is true, the wrath of God rests on such people (Jn. 3:36). Our relationship with God is ultimately determined by how we relate to the word of Jesus. To remain in Jesus also means that we will remain in love (cf. 15:9–17). Abiding in love becomes a reality in action (15:10), in the bearing of continuing fruit (15:16), which becomes visible in unbounded love of our fellow believers (1 Jn. 2:10; 3:14–15).

5. (a) *emmenō* occurs only 4x in the NT. After their initial missionary work, Paul and Barnabas returned to Lystra, Iconium, and Antioch, "strengthening the disciples and encouraging them to remain [*emmenō*] true to the faith" (Acts 14:22). Acts ends with Paul staying in Rome two whole years at his own expense, welcoming all who came to him and preaching the kingdom of God (28:30–31). *emmenō* has the sense of "continue to do" in Gal. 3:10, where Paul cites Deut. 27:26 to show the impossibility of keeping the law as a way of salvation. In Heb. 8:9 (citing Jer. 31:32) it has the sense of "remain faithful to" God's covenant. In its place, Yahweh promises a new covenant written on the heart (Heb. 8:10)—a covenant now established by Christ (8:6–13; 10:14–18).

(b) *epimenō*, stay, remain, is used in a lit. sense in Acts 10:48; 21:4, 10; 28:12, 14; 1 Cor. 16:7–8; Gal. 1:18. The reason for staying in a particular location is usually connected with Christian service. In Phil. 1:24 Paul, reflecting on his possible imminent execution, writes: "But it is more necessary for you that I remain [*epimenenō*] in the body." Hence, he is convinced that his life will be spared for the sake of continued service. Yet should he die, it would be gain (1:21) for that would bring release from earthly troubles and usher him into the immediate presence of Christ.

epimenō also has the fig. sense of continue, persist in, persevere. Thus, Peter continues knocking on the door after his escape from prison (Acts 12:16). In the story of the woman taken in adultery, the Jews keep on asking Jesus what to do until he says: "If any one of you is without sin, let him be the first to throw a stone at her" (Jn. 8:7; cf. Lev. 20:10; Deut. 13:10; 17:7; 22:20–22).

The fig. use of this vb. is used in the sense of continuing in sin in Rom. 6:1, which Paul rejects on the grounds that to desire to do so is utterly incompatible with dying and rising with Christ as represented by baptism. The freedom we have through justification by faith is not a freedom to sin but to live out the life of Christ. Later on in Rom. Paul discusses the status of the Jews as God's people with regard to his saving purposes, using the image of pruning and grafting into the olive tree. He encourages present believers to "continue in [God's] kindness" and assures them that if unbelieving Jews "do not persist in unbelief," they will be grafted back into the tree (Rom. 11:22–23). For the present, however, they are no longer the people of God, for the church is God's new people. Note too that the continuance of the Gentiles is also conditional on their continuing in God's kindness (cf. *epimenō* in Col. 1:23; see also the warnings in Heb. 3:15–4:13; 6:1–8).

In all these passages where *epimenō* is used in connection with salvation, there is a paradox: reconciliation and redemption are free

gifts of God, but they must be appropriated and lived out. Continuance and perseverance are essential features of the life of faith.

In 1 Tim. 4:16 Paul exhorts Timothy to "persevere" in life and doctrine in order to save both himself and his hearers. Here again there is stress on perseverance, but it is now expressly linked with teaching (*didaskalia*; → *didaskō, 1438*). Not only must believers persevere in personal faith, but also, in view of the false teaching and the dangers of the times, they must be guided by a defined body of truth.

(c) *paramenō*, remain, stay on, continue in, occurs 4x in the NT. Paul, faced with the prospect of execution, tells the Philippians that he would prefer to be with Christ but that it is more necessary to remain in the flesh on their account. "Convinced of this, I know that I will remain [*menō*], and I will continue [*paramenō*] with all of you for your progress and joy in the faith" (Phil. 1:25). Heb. 7 argues for the superiority of Christ's priesthood after the order of Melchizedek. In his discussion, the author contrasts Christ's permanent and continuing ministry with the temporary nature of the Levitical priesthood; death prevented them "from continuing in office" (7:23).

In the course of his argument that true believers should show their faith by good deeds, James argues that those who look into the perfect law, the law of freedom, "and continue to do this," will be blessed in what they do (Jas. 1:25). The vb. also occurs in 1 Cor. 16:6 in the sense of Paul's plans to physically stay in Corinth for some time.

(d) *perimenō*, expect, await, occurs only once in the NT, where it signifies waiting for the gift promised by the Father, i.e., the Holy Spirit (Acts 1:4). The disciples are to stay in Jerusalem until they receive it.

(e) *prosmenō*, remain, stay with, stay longer, occurs 7x in the NT. It is used of the crowds who have been with Jesus for three days (Matt. 15:32; Mk. 8:2; cf. also Acts 18:18; 1 Tim. 1:3). Barnabas exhorts the believers at Antioch "to remain true to the Lord" (Acts 11:23), while Paul and Barnabas urge their followers in the synagogue at Pisidian Antioch "to continue in the grace of God" (13:43). In 1 Tim. 5:5 Paul gives part of his description of the true widow: one who "continues night and day to pray."

(f) *monē* occurs 2x in the NT. In Jn. 14:2 Jesus refers to the many "rooms" that are being prepared for believers in his Father's house. In Jewish belief there were various compartments or dwelling places in heaven (e.g., *1 Enoch* 39:4–8). Our earthly state is transitory and provisional compared with the blessedness of being eternally with God. By contrast, *monē* in 14:23 refers to Jesus and the Father's coming to make their "home" with those who love him and obey his teachings (cf. the uses of *menō* in Jn., above).

See also *adialeiptos*, unceasing, constant (*89*).

3532   μερίζω

μερίζω (*merizō*), divide (*3532*); διαμερίζω (*diamerizō*), divide, separate (*1374*); διαμερισμός (*diamerismos*), division (*1375*); μερισμός (*merismos*), dividing, distribution (*3536*).

CL & OT 1. In cl. Gk. *merizō* means to divide something into parts or to distribute, while *merismos* denotes a partitioning or distributing. *diamerizō* also means to divide, but it has a fig. meaning of causing dissension (i.e., division in people's thinking).

2. *merizō* is used most frequently in the LXX for the dividing of spoils after battle (Exod. 15:9; 1 Sam. 30:24; Isa. 53:12) and the dividing of the land of Canaan by lot to the various tribes (Num. 26:54, 55–56; Jos. 13:7). But it could also be used for the dividing of people into factions (1 Ki. 16:21). *merismos* is used for tribal divisions (Jos. 11:23; Ezr. 6:18). *diamerizō* is basically a synonym (e.g., Gen. 10:25; Jdg. 5:30; Ps. 60:6; Zech. 14:1).

NT 1. The words in this group can have a lit. meaning. Jesus divided (*merizō*) the fish among the people in the feeding of the 5,000 (Mk. 6:41); he also divided (*diamerizō*) the cup among his disciples at the

Last Supper (Lk. 22:17). A young man once came to Jesus and asked him to make his brother divide (*merizō*) the inheritance with him (12:13). The soldiers at the cross divided up (*diamerizō*) Jesus' clothes (Matt. 27:35; Jn. 19:24). The early Christians shared (*diamerizō*) their possessions with those who were needy (Acts 2:45).

2. But the words in this group also take on a fig. meaning. In the Synoptic Gospels Jesus refers to the dividing of a kingdom against itself (Matt. 12:25–26; Mk. 3:24–26 use *merizō*; Lk. 11:17–18 uses *diamerizō*). Jesus also predicts a time of division within families because of the attitude of its members to him (12:51–53 uses both *diamerizō* and *diamerismos*). Paul employs *merizō* when he asks the question in the context of the factions in Corinth: "Is Christ divided?" (1 Cor. 1:13). Later in this letter he uses the same word for a husband's internal conflict between tending to the needs of his family and to the interests of Christ (7:34).

3. The NT also uses these words for God's actions. He has divided (*merismos*) his gifts among his people (Heb. 2:4; cf. also *merizō* in Rom. 12:3). He has also "assigned" each of us a place in life (1 Cor. 7:17; 2 Cor. 10:13). In a different vein, God's powerful word works "even to dividing [*merismos*] soul and spirit" (Heb. 4:12). While some use this last verse to differentiate the human soul from the human spirit, it is not at all certain that the writer of Heb. is trying to establish this point; the emphasis is rather on how the word of God penetrates our lives.

3533 μέριμνα

μέριμνα (*merimna*), care (*3533*); μεριμνάω (*merimnaō*), care, be anxious (*3534*); προμεριμνάω (*promerimnaō*), be anxious beforehand (*4628*); μέλει (*melei*), be concerned, be worried about (*3508*); ἀμέριμνος (*amerimnos*), free from concern (*291*).

CL & OT In cl. Gk. the noun *merimna* and the vb. *merimnaō* have the same range of meaning as the Eng. term *concern*. Thus *merimna* can denote either an anxious fear or a providing care, and *merimnaō* can mean either being anxious or worried or taking responsibility for someone or something. As seems obvious, these words are usually oriented to the future. *melei*, it concerns (someone) about, is the 3d pers. sing. of *melō*, be concerned about. It is usually used impers.

In the LXX these words appear infrequently and have the same range as in cl. Gk. The noun *merimna* (12x) means anxious care (e.g., Job 11:18; Dan. 11:26; 1 Macc. 6:10); the vb. *merimnaō* (9x) means be anxious (2 Sam. 7:10; 1 Chr. 17:9) or be troubled (2 Sam. 7:10; 1 Chr. 17:9). The same word is used in a weaker sense in Exod. 5:9, be concerned for. Wisdom lit. uses the vb. and the noun in the positive sense of caring, providing (e.g., Prov. 14:23; 17:12), although *merimna* can mean anxious care (e.g., Sir. 30:24; 42:9).

NT In the NT *merimna*, care, occurs 4x in the Synoptics, once in Paul, and once in 1 Pet.; *merimnaō*, be anxious, care for, occurs in Matt. (7x), Lk. (5x), and Paul (7x). Like the OT, the NT understands care chiefly as a natural human reaction to poverty, hunger, and other troubles that befall us in daily life. Oppressed by burdens, we imagine ourselves delivered to a fate before which we stand powerless. We try to protect ourselves as best we can from what confronts us.

1. The most comprehensive summary of the NT's witness on worry is found in the Sermon on the Mount (Matt. 6:25–34) or the Sermon on the Plain (Lk. 12:22–31). It is directed against the error that denies God's care and love by supposing that we can secure our own future by temporarily securing what we need for our daily lives. Worry is foolish because life is more than food (Matt. 6:25) and anxiety cannot make life secure (6:27). If *hēlikia* in 6:27 is translated as stature and not length of life (→ *2461*), then the folly of worry is emphasized by this reductio ad absurdum. For if something as unimportant as bodily size cannot be guaranteed by human worry, how much less life itself.

We can take the saying of Matt. 6:34 in the same ironic sense. The disciple who adds tomorrow's concerns to today's is acting

absurdly and is put to shame by secular wisdom, which has long recognized the fact. Besides being foolish, worry is also God-less because it impugns his care for humans. If God feeds the birds of the air and decks the transitory flowers of the field with beauty, he will do "much more" for creatures made in his image (6:26, 30). He is the Father who knows what his children need (6:32). Those who forget that and, in the weakness of faith, give way to worry are acting like Gentiles (6:32; → *mamōnas*, *3440*).

By contrast, the knowledge that the kingdom of God is dawning liberates us from anxiety and worry. Those who welcome this kingdom and the righteousness proclaimed in it with zeal and trust find that everything needful for life is provided by God (6:33). In his kingdom all our needs are put in their rightful place, because the Father's love supplies things great and small, daily needs and special ones. It is therefore superfluous to make anxious provision to secure one's life. Because God is concerned (*melei*) about us and cares for us, we can unload our cares onto him (1 Pet. 5:7).

2. Luke's picture of Mary and Martha (Lk. 10:38–42) exhibits the same contrast of attitudes as the Sermon on the Mount. The "many things" over which people worry in order to secure the necessities of life stand in contrast with the "one thing" that is necessary: the question concerning life's purpose, which Mary sees answered in Jesus' teaching. Worry is contrasted with zeal for God's kingdom. Similarly the parable of the sower sees the word imperiled by cares (Mk. 4:19 par.). Lk. 21:34 warns against being weighed down by "the anxieties (*merimnai*) of life," i.e., worries about our daily needs. Finally, Jesus assures us that we do not need to "worry beforehand about" (*promerimnaō*) what to say if we are brought to trial for our faith, since the Holy Spirit will give us the necessary words (Mk. 13:11).

3. *merimna* and *merimnaō* can also have a positive sense, such as showing concern for others whom God entrusts to us. Thus Paul views himself as one who must care for all the churches (2 Cor. 11:28). God has fashioned the church like a body so that "its parts should have equal concern for each other" (1 Cor. 12:25). Paul commends Timothy to the church in Philippi as someone who will care for their interests like no one else (Phil. 2:20). Such concern is a part of seeking the interests of Jesus Christ (2:21).

In 1 Cor. 7:32 Paul manifests his awareness of the dangers in caring about other people. Because he wants believers to be without worries (*amerimnous*), he recommends the unmarried not to marry in view of the eschatological situation (7:29, 31), and the married to live to the Lord (7:29).

In the exhortation of Phil. 4:6 ("Do not be anxious about anything"), *merimnaō* once again has the meaning anxious care. The reason for this freedom from care lies in the Lord's proximity (4:5) and in the church's privilege of being able to present all their requests in prayer to God with thanksgiving.

3534 (merimnaō, care, be anxious), → *3533*.

3535 (meris, part, portion), → *3538*.

3536 (merismos, dividing, distribution), → *3532*.

3538 μέρος

μέρος (*meros*), part, share, portion, lot (*3538*); μερίς (*meris*), part, portion (*3535*).

CL & OT 1. *meros* means a part, e.g., of the body, a landscape, a territory, and esp., in the pl., a locality. Metaphorically it means a share, a concern, a social class, a business. It often stands in adverbial phrases with prepositions (see NT uses).

2. In the LXX *meros* most frequently expresses locality: e.g., border (Exod. 16:35; Jos. 18:19–20), area of land (2:18; 1 Sam. 30:14), end, edge (Jos. 13:27; 15:2). When things are being described, *meros* means side (e.g., Exod. 26:26–27; 32:15), while in Prov. 17:2 it is a share in an inheritance, and in 2 Macc. 15:20 a place.

NT In the NT *meros* means a part of the body, an estate, or one's dress (Lk. 11:36; 15:12; Jn. 19:23), the side of a boat (21:6), a party (e.g., of Pharisees or Sadducees, Acts 23:6, 9). Often it denotes a district or place (Matt. 2:22; 15:21; 16:13). The meaning of "the lower, earthly regions [*merē*]" (Eph. 4:9) is uncertain. It means either Jesus' descent among the dead in his death or simply his coming down to the earth in his incarnation.

In Acts 19:27 *meros* means occupation or trade and in 2 Cor. 3:10; 9:3 case or matter. In the story of Jesus' washing his disciples' feet, the Lord says to Peter: "Unless I wash you, you have no part with me" (Jn. 13:8). This sharing is enjoyed by Christians, who are each a living "part" of the body, the church (1 Cor. 12:27; Eph. 4:16). One can also have one's "place" with the hypocrites and godless (Matt. 24:51; Lk. 12:46). It depends on the group to which one belongs whether one has a share in the first resurrection and the tree of life (Rev. 20:6; 22:19) or in the fiery lake, the second death (21:8).

meros is used adverbially with various prepositions. *apo merous* (Rom. 11:25) denotes that a "hardening in part" that has come on Israel. *apo merous* means "on some points" (15:15), "in part" (2 Cor. 1:14), and "to some extent" (2 Cor. 2:5), while *ana meros* means "one at a time" (1 Cor. 14:27). *ek merous* means "in part" or "imperfect" in 13:9–10, 12, where Paul stresses the incomplete, fragmentary, and transitory character of knowledge in contrast with love. When the perfect comes, the imperfect will pass away. *en merei* means "with regard to" (Col. 2:16), and *kata meros* (Heb. 9:5) "in detail."

meris means part, in the sense of a "district" in Acts 16:12, and share or portion in Lk. 10:42; Acts 8:21 (cf. Deut. 12:12); 2 Cor. 6:15 ("What does a believer have in common [*meris*] with an unbeliever?"); Col. 1:12.

See also *klēros*, inheritance, lot (*3102*).

3541 (*mesiteuō*, mediate, confirm, act as surety), → *3542*.

| 3542 μεσίτης | μεσίτης (*mesitēs*), mediator, intermediary, guarantor (*3542*); μεσιτεύω (*mesiteuō*), mediate, confirm, act as surety (*3541*). |

CL & OT 1. *mesitēs*, mediator, denotes a person who stands between two parties. Already in cl. Gk. *mesos* became a legal term meaning a neutral place between two parties in conflict, occupied by the arbitrator who sought to judge and settle. The *mesitēs* could be the conciliator or arbitrator in cases that had not yet come before a court of law, so as to prevent this happening. He was also the witness to legal business that had been settled, with the responsibility of guaranteeing that the decision would be carried out.

2. (a) There is no single term for a mediator in OT. The comprehensive Gk. term *mesitēs* is found in the LXX only in Job 9:33, but here it is not a question of arbitrating between the two parties, but of listening to accusation and defense and restoring the infringed law by dealing with the guilty party—unless, of course, the accusation was rejected. Thus the relationship between the parties was restored. Israel had no civil code that functioned by upholding a golden mean between conflicting interests. There was only divine law, which bound together the members of God's people as fellow citizens. It was ultimately God who chastened and judged (cf. Ps. 5:2). Hence there could hardly be any real difference between an arbitrator and an official judge in Israel.

(b) Where the concept of mediator appears in the OT, it means something different from that in the Gk. world. The priest and prophet were mediators between God and his people, but never in the role of a neutral third party. Still, two mediators stand out in Israel's history. Moses mediated salvation at the Red Sea (Exod. 14:15–18); he was the mediator of the covenant at Sinai (24:4–8) and, as such, of the law and of revelation (33:7–11). In Isa., the awaited Servant of Yahweh is the bearer of God's revelation (42:1–4) and salvation to the nations (49:1–6). He takes the guilt of humanity on himself and blots it out by his suffering (52:13–53:12).

3. In post-biblical Heb. and Aram. *sarsōr* means middle man, negotiator, interpreter. It acquires a theological meaning when applied to Moses, who was the mediator par excellence of the Torah. Philo uses *mesiteuō* to express the activity of the invisible God and of the Logos (Word), who is also called *mesitēs*.

NT *mesitēs* occurs only 6x in the NT. As applied to Christ, *mesitēs* is qualified by the gen. *diathēkēs*, of a covenant (of a better covenant, Heb. 8:6; of a new covenant, 9:15; 12:24), or by the gen. *theou kai anthrōpou*, "between God and men" (1 Tim. 2:5). The word also refers to another figure who once mediated the law (Gal. 3:19–20).

1. According to Gal. 3:19–20, the law was not given directly by God, but revealed to Moses by angels. The age of the law, and so of Moses and the angelic powers he represented, was brought to an end by Christ, who had been referred to in God's promise to Abraham 430 years earlier. Unlike Moses he is not a *mesitēs*, but its fulfillment. Hence the age of the mediator has passed and that of the Son has come (Gal. 4:4; cf. Jn. 1:17).

2. In Heb. *mesitēs* has a different meaning, that of guarantor. The author is concerned with the surety for our attaining to the heavenly land of rest. We have this right because of what God has done through Christ in his death. As *mesitēs*, Christ has procured and guarantees that right. On the one hand, this right is "founded on better promises" (8:6); on the other hand, it is the presupposition of the fulfillment of the promise (9:15) that was "confirmed" (*mesiteuō*) by God "with an oath" (6:17).

mesitēs thus denotes the one who guarantees us salvation, both as its creator and giver. As the ever-present high priest who has been exalted by his obedience, sufferings, death on the cross, and sacrifice accepted by God, Jesus has by his own blood transformed the right of vengeance into the right of forgiveness (cf. *mesitēs* in 12:24). Thus *mesitēs* in Heb. is similar to a term Paul uses regarding the Holy Spirit, *arrabōn* (→ 775).

3. One passage in the NT explicitly calls Jesus Christ a *mesitēs* "between God and men" (1 Tim. 2:5). This concept links directly with the fact that our whole salvation is found in the one man Jesus (cf. 2 Cor. 5:14; Gal. 3:12–19). God has provided no other mediator besides Jesus Christ.

4. While there is only one passage in the NT where Jesus Christ is called mediator in the full sense of the word, other passages contain the same concept. Note, for example, Jn. 14:6, "I am the way and the truth and the life. No one comes to the Father except through me" (cf. also Matt. 11:25–30). Furthermore, the figure of the high priest in the OT, who stood between the people and the Lord in a mediating role, is fulfilled in Jesus Christ as our eternal high priest who "always lives [in the presence of the Father] to intercede for [his people]" (Heb. 7:25).

See also *diathēkē*, covenant (*1347*); *engyos*, guarantor (*1583*).

| 3546 μεσότοιχον | μεσότοιχον (*mesotoichon*), dividing wall (*3546*). |

CL & OT *mesotoichon* is a combination of *mesos* (middle) and *toichos* (wall). It is found only a few times outside the NT, where it refers to a partition wall or barrier. Josephus uses the separate words (*meson toichon*) to refer to the partition between the Holy Place and the Most Holy Place in the temple.

NT *mesotoichon* occurs in the NT only in Eph. 2:14, where it may allude to the balustrade in the temple courtyard that separated the court of the Gentiles from the more sacred precincts, though no document is known where this word refers to that wall. That barrier carried warnings in Gk. and Lat., telling Gentiles that they could be killed if they crossed over. Although Ephesus was a Gentile city far from Jerusalem, Paul's allusion to the *mesotoichon* would have been clear to the Christians there. For Paul himself had narrowly escaped death two or three years before when it was rumored that he had violated that sacred space by taking the Gentile Trophimus, an Ephesian, into one of the inner courts (Acts 21:28–29). To Paul, this wall symbolized the enmity between Jews and Gentiles. It has been removed by the sacrifice of Jesus, so that through him we all now have access to the Father.

Another suggestion for the *mesotoichon* is the invisible wall of separation between God and humanity. The fall brought humans into enmity with God (Eph. 2:16); the cross of Christ reconciles us with the Father by removing the stain of our sin.

See also *phragmos*, fence, wall, hedge (*5850*).

3549 (*Messias*, Messiah), → *5986.*

3552 (*meta*, with), → *5250.*

3553 (*metabainō*, pass over), → *326.*

3561 (*metalambanō*, receive a share), → *3284.*

3562 (*metalēmpsis*, sharing, receiving), → *3284.*

3563 (*metallassō*, to exchange), → *2904.*

3564	μεταμέλομαι

μεταμέλομαι (*metamelomai*), change one's mind, regret, repent (*3564*); ἀμεταμέλητος (*ametamelētos*), not to be regretted, hence irrevocable (*294*).

CL & OT *metamelomai* is linked with the impers. *melei*, it concerns (someone). In cl. Gk. this vb. expressed a changed feeling towards a thing, but it cannot always be clearly distinguished from *metanoeō*, which implies that one thinks differently about a matter.

The LXX did not distinguish between *metanoeō* or *metamelomai*. The latter word occurs in Exod. 13:17 for purely human regret, while in Ezek. 14:22 it involves humble agreement with God's righteous judgment, for good or ill. When God is said in the OT to repent, there are two possibilities: God can reject humans because they have turned against him in disobedience (1 Sam. 15:11, 35); however, God can also turn again to them in grace and mercy (1 Chr. 21:15; Ps. 106:45; cf. Jon. 3:9–10). When the OT clearly stresses that God does *not* repent (Ps. 110:4; cf. Jer. 4:28), it is the guarantee that God will not deviate from the plan that he conceived at the first.

NT *metamelomai* occurs 6x in the NT. In Jesus' parable in Matt. 21:28–32 the father asks both of his sons to work in his vineyard. One refuses, but then regrets his answer and goes; the other agrees to go, but does not. Here the word can be translated "change one's decision." Jesus directed the parable at the high priests and elders of Israel. The first son changed his attitude to his father, just as the tax collectors and harlots had believed John the Baptist's message and had repented. The religious leaders, however, had continued in their unbelief and disobedience (*oude metemelēthēte*).

The example of Judas makes it clear that *metamelomai* and *metanoeō* are not simply interchangeable in the NT. When Judas recognized that Jesus had been wrongly condemned, he regretted (*metamelomai*) his betrayal (Matt. 27:3). However, he did not find the way to genuine repentance (*metanoia*). We find the same differentiation in 2 Cor. 7:8–10. Paul did not regret that he had written a sharp letter to the Corinthians, for the sorrow it caused had led its recipients to true repentance (*metanoia*), to an inner turning to God. Paul argues that there is no need to regret such a repentance, for it serves our salvation.

The oath that God will never regret serves both to guarantee the superiority of Jesus' high priesthood over that of the OT and to express the unchangeable faithfulness of God (Heb. 7:21, quoting Ps. 110:4).

The adj. *ametamelētos* occurs 2x; it refers to something of which God (Rom. 11:29) or a human (2 Cor. 7:10) will not repent, and hence means irrevocable.

See also *epistrephō*, turn, turn around, turn back, be converted (*2188*); *metanoia*, change of mind, conversion (*3567*); *prosēlytos*, proselyte (*4670*).

3565	μεταμορφόω

μεταμορφόω (*metamorphoō*), change into another form or image, transform (*3565*).

CL & OT 1. The idea of transformation from one appearance or form into another is presented in two Lat. works called *Metamorphoses*. Ovid's work is a series of tales involving supernatural beings as well as humans, who experience different kinds of transformations. Apuleius describes, in autobiographic style, being transformed into an ass and finally being restored by the power of the goddess Isis. This experience illustrates the concept of religious change and release, which was idealized in Hel. religion.

2. *metamorphoō* does not occur in the LXX. But the skin of Moses' face shone after his conversation with God on Mount Sinai (cf. Exod. 34:29–35, esp. as background to 2 Cor. 3:12–18). The vision of Dan. 10:5–6 does not involve a transformation, but it does provide an apocalyptic imagery useful in the study of the description of Jesus' transfiguration. Dan. 12:3 describes the shining of the "wise" in the future resurrection.

NT *metamorphoō* occurs 4x in the NT (Matt. 17:2; Mk. 9:2; Rom. 12:2; 2 Cor. 3:18) and is presumably avoided once. This omission is in Lk.'s account of the transfiguration of Jesus, for presumably he did not want to use a word that could invite comparison with the pagan ideas of transformation.

1. (a) In Matt. 17:2 and Mk. 9:2 *metamorphoō* describes the transformation of Christ's features and clothing during his transfiguration. Matt. 17:2 uses the image of the shining sun to express the transfigured radiance of Jesus' face. A comparison may be drawn with the radiance of Moses' face in Exod. 34, although it must be remembered that the LXX terminology is different. In Jesus' transfiguration, moreover, his clothing also was rendered brilliant: "white as the light" (Matt. 17:2), more dazzling than bleached cloth (Mk. 9:3), and "bright as a flash of lightning" (Lk. 9:29).

(b) This experience is called a *horama* (vision, Matt. 17:9; → *horaō*, *3972*), a word that denotes a thing of supernatural quality that becomes observable (cf. Acts 7:31; 9:10, 12; 10:3, 17, 19). Note how 2 Pet. 1:16–18 uses Jesus' transfiguration as evidence of the reliability of the Christian gospel. This event is thus ascribed a reality beyond that sometimes implied in our word *vision*.

(c) The meaning of the transfiguration is to be found in the biblical context. The imagery is that of Dan. 7:13–14 (note the elements in the narrative that suggest a glorified Son of Man motif, e.g., the cloud). This point of reference does not exhaust the meaning, however. For not only are there messianic motifs, but the imagery of the exodus is also prominent. In that OT event, God also made his presence known in a cloud. The six-day interval of Matt. 17:1 and Mk. 9:2 may recall the period of waiting when Moses ascended a mountain to receive God's commandments (Exod. 24:9–16). Moreover, a cloud was present at that time as well, both as a covering and as a vehicle for the manifestation of God's glory. The very fact that Moses appears with Jesus on the mount of transfiguration suggests that the exodus motif is prominent. Furthermore, Luke records that Moses and Elijah were discussing with Jesus the "departure" (Gk. *exodos*) that Jesus was about to accomplish at Jerusalem (9:31).

It is thus important to see this event from both a typological (exodus) and eschatological (Parousia) perspective. The latter is reinforced by the presence of that great Jewish figure of eschatological significance, Elijah (cf. Mal. 4:5). The essential meaning is, however, not centered in either a past or future event, but in the person of the one transfigured. This is made clear by the voice from heaven, which uses terminology from four Christologically important OT texts: Ps. 2:7, about the royal son; Gen. 22:2, about the beloved only son; Isa. 42:1, about the chosen servant; and Deut. 18:15 ("listen to him") about the prophet Moses. The transfiguration is to be understood, therefore, as an affirmation by God of the messiahship and unique sonship of Jesus, who will fulfill his mission as the suffering servant according to Mk. 8:27–9:1.

2. The other two occurrences of *metamorphoō* are related to the Christian experience. In Rom. 12:2 believers are to be characterized by a continuing process of transformation, which is accomplished by an inner renewal of the mind and by resisting the influence of the world (or age, *aiōn*, → *172*). A more detailed explanation of the Christian's transformation is given in 2 Cor. 3:18, where the experience of Moses in Exod. 34:29–35 serves as an imperfect model. The glory brought by the gospel is not temporary, like the radiance of Moses' face, but enduring. Believers have an open relationship with the Lord of glory, which has a transforming effect.

See also *metaschēmatizō*, change the form of a person or thing (*3571*).

3566 (*metanoeō*, change one's mind, repent, be converted), → *3567*.

3567	μετάνοια

μετάνοια (*metanoia*), change of mind, repentance, conversion (*3567*); μετανοέω (*metanoeō*), change one's mind, repent, be converted (*3566*); ἀμετανόητος (*ametanoētos*), impenitent (*295*).

CL & OT 1. Lit., *metanoia* means a change of mind about something. The word group is rare in cl. Gk.; the vb. and noun are more frequent in Koine Gk. However, Gk. society never thought of a radical change in a person's life as a whole.

2. The LXX uses *metanoia* only 5x, most notably in Wis. 11:23; 12:10, 19 with reference to God, who shows mercy and patience so that people will repent. The vb. *metanoeō* is used either of God (cf. 1 Sam. 15:29; Jer. 18:8; Joel 2:13–14; Amos 7:3, 6) or of humans (Jer. 8:6; 31:19 = LXX 38:19) as a trans. of the Heb. *niḥam*. The thought of turning round, preached by the prophets with the Heb. vb. *šûb*, is rendered by *epistrephō* in Gk. (Amos 4:6; Hos. 5:4; 6:1; → *2188*). The prophetic call to turn presupposes that the relationship of the people and the individual to God must be understood in personal terms. Sin and apostasy disturb and break this relationship. Turning means turning away from evil and returning to God.

3. The Qumran community continued the prophetic call to repentance by demanding that its members be converted from all evil and return to every commandment of the Mosaic law. Its members therefore called themselves the converts of Israel.

NT 1. The NT uses *metanoeō* to express the force of the Heb. *šûb*, turn round. The choice of *metanoeō* rather than *epistrephō* shows that the NT does not stress the concrete, outward turning implied in the OT use of *šûb*, but rather the thought, the will, the *nous*. The ideas of repentance and conversion come to the fore, stressing a decision by the whole person to turn around. Along similar lines, *ametanoētos* (Rom. 2:5) means impenitent.

2. The closest link with the prophetic call to repentance is found in John the Baptist, who called the people to repent and to "produce fruit in keeping with repentance" (Matt. 3:2, 8 par.). Corresponding to the OT pattern, this call was addressed to the entire people (cf. Acts 13:24; 19:4), including the pious, who believed that they did not need to repent (Matt. 3:7–12). But John based the urgency of his message on a different foundation from that of the prophets. In the OT motivation for repentance and returning to the true road of God's righteousness was linked with Israel's social unrighteousness and idolatry. For John it was that "the kingdom of heaven is near" (3:2). Hence, there can be only one way for people to escape judgment. They must repent, so that entire lives are changed and brought into a new relationship with God (3:10).

John linked his call to repentance with baptism as sign of the forgiveness of sins (Mk. 1:4 par.), having repentance as its goal (Matt. 3:11; cf. Acts 13:24; 19:4). Repentance was regarded both as an act open to humans and as a duty on them.

3. According to the Synoptics, Jesus' preaching resembled that of the Baptist. Indeed, Matt. 3:2 and 4:17 record the identical call, "Repent, for the kingdom of heaven is near." The clear difference between them is that Jesus did not, as did John, look for one to follow him (cf. 3:11). He saw in his own coming the beginning of God's decisive work (11:6; Lk. 11:20; 17:21), which explains the woes addressed to the towns that were not ready to repent (Matt. 11:20–24 par.). That is why the inhabitants of Nineveh will find it better in the day of judgment than will Jesus' contemporaries. The former repented at the preaching of Jonah, and "now one greater than Jonah is here" (12:41 par.). Repentance is now no longer obedience to a law but to a person. The call to repentance becomes a call to discipleship.

There are many passages in which the word *metanoeō* does not appear, but in which the thought of repentance is clearly present (e.g., see Matt. 5:3; 18:3, 10, 14; Lk. 14:33). Jesus did not come to call the righteous but sinners to repentance (Lk. 5:32). Conversion and repentance are accompanied by joy, for they mean the opening up of life for the one who has turned. The parables in Lk. 15 not only bear testimony to the joy of God over sinners who repent but also call on us to share this joy. To the repentant God promises life. Note the comment of the father in the parable of the prodigal son: "This son of mine was dead and is alive again" (Lk. 15:24; cf. 15:32).

4. Primitive Christian preaching continued the call for repentance (cf. Mk. 6:12 and the sermons in Acts). This missionary preaching linked with the call for repentance the elements already mentioned: faith (Acts 20:21; cf. 19:4; 26:18), the demand to be baptized (2:38), the promise of forgiveness of sins (Lk. 24:47; Acts 3:19; 5:31), and the gift of life and of salvation (11:18; 2 Cor. 7:9–10). Conversion is turning from evil (Acts 8:22; 2 Cor. 12:21; Rev. 2:21–22) to God (Acts 20:21; 26:20; Rev. 16:9). In Acts 3:19 and 26:20 *metanoeō* and *epistrephō* are placed side by side; *metanoeō* describes the turning from evil and *epistrephō* the turning to God.

5. The fact that this group of words occurs seldom in Paul's letters (only 6x) and not at all in Jn.'s Gospel or letters does not mean that the idea of conversion is not present there, but only that a more specialized terminology developed. Paul speaks of a person, through faith, as being in Christ, as dying and rising with Christ, as a new creation, or as putting on the new self. John represents new life in Christ as new birth, as a passing from death to life or from darkness to light, or as the victory of truth over falsehood and of love over hate.

6. The early church faced the issue of whether a person could turn repeatedly to God. A most difficult passage in Heb. (6:4–8) seems to reject the possibility of a second repentance. On the one hand, in keeping with the view of the rest of the NT, the possibility was rejected to stress the absoluteness of conversion over against a form of Christian faith that was lapsing into apathy or apostasy. On the other hand, it showed that conversion was not just a human act but that God must give a chance to repent (12:17). A person who deliberately sins after conversion incurs God's judgment (6:8; 10:26–27).

Such a heavy emphasis on the finality of conversion does not exclude God's all-embracing desire to save. He does not want "anyone to perish, but everyone to come to repentance" (2 Pet. 3:9). Rather, it stresses the absoluteness of God's mercy. God saves completely and finally, and thus conversion to God must be complete and final.

See also *epistrephō*, turn, turn around, turn back, be converted (*2188*); *metamelomai*, change one's mind, regret, repent (*3564*); *prosēlytos*, proselyte (*4670*).

3571	μετασχηματίζω

μετασχηματίζω (*metaschēmatizō*), change the form of a person or thing (*3571*).

CL & OT In cl. Gk. *metaschēmatizō* means to alter or transform the outward appearance of a person or thing. The word is also used in the field of astronomy with reference to the changing of the constellations.

In the LXX *metaschēmatizō* only occurs in 4 Macc. 9:22, where it refers to the transforming of martyrs upon their death into incorruptibility. In Sym.'s OT, this word denotes the disguise Saul used to make himself unrecognizable to the witch at Endor (1 Sam. 28:8).

NT 1. *metaschēmatizō* occurs 5x in the NT. In 1 Cor. 4:6, it has a general meaning of Paul's application of the preceding discussion about being faithful stewards of God's word to himself and Apollos. In a different application, Paul uses the word in Phil. 3:21 to describe the future transformation of our "lowly bodies" by the power of God. No detail is given of the exact nature of this transformation.

2. In 2 Cor. 11:13–15 *metaschēmatizō* occurs 3x. The thought is not that false apostles have actually transformed themselves into apostles, but that they have masqueraded as such. At this time people did not sharply define what constituted an apostle. Paul's opponents called themselves apostles and earnestly presented themselves in this manner. In the eyes of many, these opponents really were apostles, but to Paul they were impostors. Perhaps, however, Paul is ironically describing them as actually transforming themselves into apostles: They identified themselves with the apostles—but they were false apostles.

The same process applies to Satan (1 Cor. 11:14). He not only masquerades as an angel of light and plays at being such, he actually identifies himself with an angel of light and assumes the character of one. The interpretation that this is only an appearance is due not so much to the vb. *metaschēmatizō* as to the insertion of the word *hōs* ("as") in 11:15. Both Satan and his servants present themselves "as though" they were servants of righteousness.

See also *metamorphoō*, change into another form or image, transform (*3565*).

3572 (*metatithēmi*, to transfer, change the position of, turn away), → *773*.

3576 (*metechō*, share, participate in), → *2400*.

3580 (*metochē*, sharing, participation), → *2400*.

3581 (*metochos*, partaking, sharing, a partner, companion), → *2400*.

3582 (*metreō*, take the dimensions of, measure, give out, deal out, apportion), → *3586*.

3583 (*metrētēs*, measure [a unit of measure equal to ten gallons]), → *3586*.

3586	μέτρον

μέτρον (*metron*), measure (*3586*); ἄμετρος (*ametros*), without measure (*296*); μετρέω (*metreō*), take the dimensions of, measure, give out, deal out, apportion (*3582*); μετρητής (*metrētēs*), measure (a unit of measure equal to ten gallons) (*3583*).

CL & OT 1. In cl. Gk. *metron* means a measure, proportion, order, and measure in verse, while in philosophy it denotes the measure by which all things are measured; Plato identifies the measure with God. The vb. *metreō* means to measure, traverse, evaluate, judge.

2. In the LXX *metron* is used of the measurements of the tabernacle and temple (esp. Ezek. 40–48), weights and measures that stand under Yahweh's surveillance (Lev. 19:35; 1 Chr. 23:29; Prov. 20:10; Amos 8:5), the measures of the world in connection with creation (Job 11:9; 28:25; 38:5; Wis. 11:20), and standards used in pronouncements of judgment and salvation (e.g., 2 Ki. 21:13; Isa. 5:10; Lam. 2:8; Ezek. 4:11, 16).

NT 1. In the NT the noun and the vb. are found esp. in contexts of judgment and of the gift of grace allotted to believers. (a) Both words occur in Matt. 7:2: "In the same way you judge others, you will be judged, and with the measure you use, it will be measured to you." In other words, if you condemn others, you will exclude yourself from God's forgiveness. Jesus may have been quoting a common proverb to bring home a truth of judgment from which no one is exempt (cf. *m. Sotah* 7:1). It is the reverse of Jesus' exhortation to forgive (Matt. 6:14–15), and it is on a par with other exhortations in the Sermon on the Mount to leave everything to God—e.g., rewards (6:1–6), petitions in prayer (6:7–13), and concerns for worldly needs and cares (6:19–34).

(b) In the context of condemnation for shedding the blood of the prophets, Jesus declares: "Fill up, then, the measure of the sin of your forefathers" (Matt. 23:32). This may be an allusion to the Jewish view that the final judgment will come only after people have reached the absolute nadir of sinfulness.

2. (a) Jn. 3:34 states: "For the one whom God has sent speaks the words of God, for [he] gives the Spirit without limit." Although this may mean that the Son gives the Spirit to believers without measure, the most likely reference is that the Father gives the Spirit to the Son without measure (cf. also 14:26; 15:26).

(b) The noun *metrētēs*, a type of liquid measure, occurs only in the account of the Cana wedding, where each jar is said to contain between two and three measures. Most interpreters see a measure as equal to the Heb. *bat* (about ten gallons).

3. *metron* occurs 6x in Paul. (a) In Rom. 12:3 Paul instructs Christians not to think too highly of themselves but to think of themselves "with sober judgment, in accordance with the measure of faith God has given you." The phrase "measure of faith" probably means a standard by which a person can measure his or her Christian faith, namely, Jesus Christ. He is, after all, the norm for our faith.

(b) In Eph. *metron* occurs in connection with gifts: "But to each one of us grace has been given as Christ apportioned it [lit., according to the measure of Christ]" (4:7); "until we all reach unity in the faith and in the knowledge of the Son of God and become mature, attaining to the whole measure of the fullness of Christ" (4:13); "from him the whole body, joined and held together by every supporting ligament, grows and builds itself up in love, as each part does its work [in its measure; NIV does not translate *metron* here]" (4:16). The church is not a body in which every part is like every other part; rather, God has created variety in the church, and each individual is to function according to the task and ability God has given.

In 2 Cor. 10:13 *metron* is translated "field" (2x, once in connection with *kanōn*). Paul is stressing here the geographical spheres in which he ministers and his refusal to boast about work done in areas not assigned to him by God—in contrast to the infiltrators in Corinth, who try to boast about the great work they are doing in Paul's area. (For more on this passage, → *kanōn*, standard, *2834*.) The action of these opponents contrasts with Jesus' teaching on measuring. The adj. *ametros*, without measure, beyond limits, occurs 2x, only in 10:13, 15.

4. (a) In Rev. 11:1–2 Jn. is given a measuring rod like a staff and is told: "Go and measure the temple of God and the altar, and count the worshipers there. But exclude the outer court; do not measure it, because it has been given to the Gentiles." This vision takes up the theme of Ezek. 40–48, where the measuring was with a view to reconstructing the new temple after the destruction of the old, but here the people are measured in addition to the temple. The passage symbolizes the separation of the church, the new temple of God, from the rest of the world, with the implied promise that God will preserve it.

(b) Rev. 21:15–17 again takes up the measuring theme from Ezek. in connection with the dimensions of the new Jerusalem with its perfect proportions (→ *dōdeka*, twelve, *1557*).

See also *kanōn*, rule, standard, norm (*2834*).

3613	μήτηρ

μήτηρ (*mētēr*), mother (*3613*).

CL & OT 1. (a) A high estimation of motherhood can be traced everywhere in antiquity. The earth became the great mother who first gives everything and then in death takes everything back into herself. Thus in many regions the oldest figures of the gods are earth mothers. Veneration of them often led to cultic prostitution in order to gain an immediate share in their life-controlling powers. Yet the picture of the mother deity can also be spiritualized, detached from the highly erotic domain of the figure of Venus (e.g., the Egyptian goddess, Isis, the embodiment of the true wife and mother).

(b) In Gk. philosophy the mother concept is used in a fig. sense, as when Plato speaks of matter as the mother of all. Philo designates wisdom as the mother of the world and of the Logos.

2. In the LXX *mētēr* occurs more than 300x. (a) In the OT we find many traces of the mother deities of the heathen world. The prophets fought a ceaseless battle against the Canaanite Astarte cult. The worship of the goddess of fertility was bound up for the most part with cultic prostitution (cf. 1 Sam. 31:10; 2 Ki. 23:13). Such prostitution became a symbol of idolatry and apostasy from Yahweh (Hos. 4:13–18).

(b) By and large the world of the OT was patriarchal; e.g., a mother who has borne sons enjoys a special position of honor among mothers and women. A maternal judicial praxis perhaps still operates in formulations such as "your own mother's son" as a synonym for brother (Ps. 50:20; cf. Jdg. 8:19) and "her mother's household" (e.g., Gen. 24:28), or when the mother sought a wife for her son (21:21).

(c) Motherhood is also guarded in the fifth commandment (Exod. 20:12), and the death penalty rests on anyone who strikes or curses father or mother (21:15–17). In marriage, a man is to leave his father and mother and be united to his wife (Gen. 2:24).

(d) The concept was also carried over into the preaching of the prophets: The people of God are called the mother of Israel (Jer. 50:12 = LXX 27:12). In Hos. they become an adulteress (2:4, 7 = LXX 2:2, 5); in Ezek. 16:3, 15, a prostitute. In Isa. 50:1 Israel is the mother whom God divorces for the sins of her children. The picture of a mother is also used for the capital city Jerusalem, Mount Zion, about which the people cluster as children about their mother (2 Sam. 20:19; cf. Gal. 4:26).

NT 1. *Jesus.* In the NT *mētēr* occurs 83x, though this concept is never exalted to a religious symbol or used in mythological presentations. In the Gospels, besides explicit mention of many mothers, we find the whole gamut of the natural relationship between mother and child. (a) Jesus accepted the fifth commandment in all its absoluteness, even in respect of the consequences of its violation (Matt. 15:4; Mk. 7:10; cf. Exod. 20:12). A Pharisaic softening of the commandment is firmly rejected (Matt. 15:5–6). Nevertheless, as in the OT, the spousal relationship in marriage takes precedence over that to a mother (see Matt. 19:5; Mk. 10:7–8; cf. Eph. 5:31).

(b) Jesus clearly delineates the limits of parental power that deny the claims of God. For the sake of the kingdom of God adherence to the parental home must be put aside (Matt. 10:35; Lk. 12:53).

2. *Paul.* For Paul, respect for motherhood is an obvious manifestation of divinely given life (Rom. 16:13; cf. also 1 Thess. 2:7, which uses *trophos*, "mother"). He compares his pastoral passion for new Christians with that of a mother, just as he can also call himself a father to those whom he has begotten in the faith (Gal. 4:19; Phlm. 10). He praises Timothy's mother, Eunice, and grandmother, Lois (2 Tim. 1:5), and urges him to treat older women like mothers and younger ones like sisters (1 Tim. 5:2). Our mother is the Jerusalem that is above, a contrast to the present Jerusalem, which is in bondage (Gal. 4:26–27). On the other hand, Rev. 17:5 describes Babylon as "THE MOTHER OF PROSTITUTES AND OF THE ABOMINATIONS OF THE EARTH."

3. *The status of Jesus' mother.* (a) Mary's psalm, the Magnificat (Lk. 1:46–55), is set in the context of the annunciation of Jesus' birth (1:26–38) and the family relationship between Mary and Elizabeth, the mother of John the Baptist (1:5–25). It is significant that this song is part of recorded Scripture. Whereas Matt. records Joseph's reaction to Mary's pregnancy and the subsequent visit of an angel (1:18–25), the visit of the Magi to Bethlehem, and the flight into Egypt (2:1–23), Lk. records the birth in Bethlehem and the visit of the shepherds, including the fact that Mary pondered in her heart the things that she was experiencing (2:1–20).

(b) For all his respect for his mother (e.g., his remaining subject to her at age twelve, Lk. 2:51) and all his care for her (e.g., during the crucifixion, Jn. 19:26–27), there remains a clear distinction between Jesus and his mother (cf. Lk. 2:49). He prevents her when she would have hampered him in his messianic office (Matt. 12:46–50; Mk. 3:31–35; Lk. 8:19–21), and he appears to brush her aside at the time of the wedding at Cana (Jn. 2:4). Lk. 11:27–28 is also significant. Jesus turned the *personal* adulation for his mother into a *general* injunction: "Blessed rather are those who hear the word of God and obey it."

(c) The status of Mary in early Christendom is in accord with Jesus' attitude. After the resurrection the NT mentions her incidentally only once (Acts 1:14). Note that Mary found her salvation not in her position as Jesus' mother, but by her faith in Jesus and in her association with the church. The later adoration of the virgin Mary is a development subsequent to the NT.

See also *gynē*, woman (*1222*); *parthenos*, maiden, virgin (*4221*); *chēra*, widow (*5939*).

3620	μιαίνω

μιαίνω (*miainō*), defile (*3620*); μίασμα (*miasma*), defilement, pollution (*3621*); μιασμός (*miasmos*), defilement, pollution (*3622*); ἀμίαντος (*amiantos*), undefiled, pure (*299*).

CL & OT The basic meaning of *miainō* is to color something by painting or staining it. In this sense the word is morally neutral. But early on it was used metaphorically for causing oneself or other people or places to be "stained," i.e., unclean, so that they needed ritual cleansing. In a broader moral sense *miainō* was used for profaning religion and justice, sullying someone's fame, and polluting one's soul. *miasma*, defilement, and *miasmos*, the defiled state, have a corresponding range of meanings, while *amiantos* signifies freedom from defilement in both moral and religious senses.

In the LXX, *miainō* is used most frequently for ritual defilement in Lev., Num., and Ezek. In Lev. 13:3 *miainō* means pronounce unclean. Since the OT does not separate ritual and moral defilement, *miainō* is used also of the defilement that moral and spiritual transgressions cause (e.g., Isa. 47:6; Ezek. 14:11; Hos. 6:10 = LXX 6:11). Disregard for God's law, esp. sexual license, is highlighted as a source of defilement. In the canonical LXX *miasma* occurs 3x; in the Apocr. it is found 5x, *miasmos* 2x, and *amiantos* 5x (Wis. 3:13; 4:2; 8:20; 2 Macc. 14:36; 15:34).

NT In the NT *miainō* denotes the ritual uncleanness Jews feared from entering Gentile premises (Jn. 18:28), as well as the moral defilement of mind, conscience, and flesh that results from becoming a faithless libertine (Tit. 1:15; Jude 8). Heb. 12:15 expresses the fear that one apostate will defile others, presumably by drawing them to follow his bad example. *miasma* comes only in the phrase "corruption of the world" (2 Pet. 2:20); *miasmos* appears only in 2:10, in a phrase meaning "corrupt desire of the sinful nature," apparently referring to sexual and perhaps homosexual self-indulgence.

amiantos expresses the purity of Christ as high priest (Heb. 7:27), of our heavenly inheritance (2 Pet. 1:4), of sexual relations within marriage (Heb. 13:4), and of practical religion (Jas. 1:27); what it affirms in each of its applications is the absence of anything that constitutes guilt before God.

See also *molynō*, defile (*3662*).

3621 (*miasma*, defilement, pollution), → *3620*.

3622 (*miasmos*, defilement, pollution), → *3620*.

3625	μικρός

μικρός (*mikros*), small, little (*3625*); ἐλάσσων (*elassōn*), smaller, younger (*1781*); ἐλάχιστος (*elachistos*), very small, the least (*1788*); ὀλίγος (*oligos*), little, small, few (*3900*).

CL & OT 1. The adj. *mikros*, small, is the antonym of *megas*, great (→ *3489*). In evaluations and comparisons these two words express a quantitative or qualitative difference that can refer to things, living beings, and periods of time. *elassōn* (smaller, younger) is the comparative and *elachistos* (very small, the least) the superlative. *oligos* also occurs in cl. Gk. lit.; it designates a small quantity, a small number, a few people, or a few days.

2. (a) The LXX uses the words in this group about 190x to translate various concepts: e.g., little houses (Amos 6:11 = LXX 6:12), a small light (Gen. 1:16), something almost (lit., by a little) happened (Ps. 73:2), a small boy (1 Sam. 16:11; Isa. 11:6). The combination "small and great" has the sense of all (e.g., Deut. 1:17; Ps. 115:13 = LXX 113:21). The LXX also uses *oligos* (103x) for a few days (Gen. 29:20), a small number of Israelites (Deut. 4:27), a short life span, indicating God's punishment (Job 10:20; Ps. 109:8).

(b) The LXX also uses *mikros* and its derivatives to denote humility toward God. Gideon calls himself the least in his family, from the weakest clan (Jdg. 6:15). The language of Solomon's prayer after succession to the throne uses the courtly style of ancient oriental kingly formulas: "I am only a little child" (1 Ki. 3:7). Self-effacement before God on the part of God's elect enjoys his favor (cf. Isa. 60:22).

(c) The OT clearly emphasizes that Yahweh is frequently on the side of the very people who have little in the way of possessions (e.g., Ps. 37:16–17). He often helps by means of small things (e.g., "Nothing can hinder the LORD from saving, whether by many of by few," 1 Sam. 14:6).

NT 1. The lines laid down by the OT are continued in the NT. Thus *mikros* (46x) is used in such expressions as small of stature (Lk. 19:3), of little value (Jn. 2:10, *elassōn*), younger in age (Rom. 9:12; 1 Tim. 5:9, *elassōn*). The juxtaposition of small and great as a phrase for "all" also occurs (e.g., Acts 8:10; Heb. 8:11; Rev. 11:18; 13:16; 19:5, 18). *oligos* (40x) is similarly used. The reversal of values is theologically significant (e.g., Matt. 25:21, 23; cf. Lk. 19:17): God will not treat human faithfulness in matters of little importance with contempt, but will reward it.

2. The Pauline writings contain the word group relatively rarely. The proverb about the far-reaching effects of a little yeast are mentioned in 1 Cor. 5:6 and Gal. 5:9. The subst. *to mikron* and the superlative *elachistos* occur in contexts in which Paul speaks of himself in the same self-effacing manner as noted in the OT (e.g., 1 Cor. 15:9; 2 Cor. 11:1, 16; cf. also Eph. 3:8, with the special form *elachistoteros*—"less than the least of all God's people"), while 1 Tim. 4:8 declares that bodily training is of a little (*oligon*) value.

3. With one exception Jn. uses *mikros* only in a temporal sense, i.e., "a little while" (e.g., Jn. 12:35). The heaping up of the word in 16:16–19 denotes first of all the time between Jesus' discourse and his coming arrest in Gethsemane "in a little while," and then the short interval until his disciples meet him after his resurrection. An element of comfort is implied in this section (cf. also Heb. 10:37).

4. The Synoptics use *mikros* in one significant way that differs from Hel. and Jewish lit. Jesus' contemporaries undervalued the "little ones" and "children." Jesus, however, was esp. concerned for their protection. He sharply warns anyone who causes the least of those who believe in him to stumble (Mk. 9:42; Lk. 17:2). Conversely, those who do good to the least of these are promised eternal reward (Matt. 10:42; 25:40, 45).

The implications for the Christian community in Matt. 18:1–6, 10, 14 (cf. Mk. 9:33–34, 37, 42; Lk. 9:46–48; 17:1–2) clearly correspond to the character and ways of God. The kingdom of God is not attained by quarrels over precedence and lust for greatness but by being least, by self-effacing service, and by poverty, which rely entirely on the sufficiency of God's help.

The sayings about the little grain of mustard seed (Matt. 13:31–32; Mk. 4:30–32; cf. Lk. 13:18–19) that becomes a great tree, the little flock (Lk. 12:32), and John the Baptist's being less than the "least

in the kingdom of God" (7:28) are also to be interpreted from this standpoint. In the Christian community, and therefore before God, the only thing that counts is the renunciation of all the greatness that one has striven after.

See also *megas*, large, great (*3489*).

3628	μιμέομαι

μιμέομαι (*mimeomai*), imitate, follow (*3628*); μιμητής (*mimētēs*), imitator (*3629*); συμμιμητής (*symmimētēs*), fellow-imitator (*5213*).

CL & OT 1. *mimeomai* means imitate, mimic what one sees someone else doing; emulate, follow; represent reality by imitation (as in the arts). A *symmimētēs* is an imitator, esp. a performer or artist. The words were used ethically to express the modeling of a hero or the imitation of the good example of one's teacher or parents. In Platonic cosmology, the lower world of appearances is the imperfect, visible copy or likeness of the invisible archetype in the higher world of the Ideas. The phrase "to imitate god" means reflection on the image of the Idea that sticks in the memory; it is not an ethical expression.

2. The LXX only attests *mimeomai* and *mimēma* in the Apocr. (Wis. 4:2; 9:8; 15:9; 4 Macc. 9:23; 13:9; Ps. 31:6 in B¹ is an error). In rab. lit. we find the first expressions of imitating God in the sense of developing the image of God in us (see also *T. Ash.* 4:3; *Let. Aris.* 188, 210, 280–81).

NT In the NT *mimeomai* occurs 4x; *mimētēs*, 6x; and *symmimētēs* once. All uses have an ethical aim and are linked with the obligation to a specific kind of conduct.

1. The words are applied to particular persons as living examples of the life of faith. For example, when Paul puts himself forward as such a model (1 Cor. 4:16; 11:1; Phil. 3:17; 2 Thess. 3:7, 9), he does not offer himself personally as the embodiment of an ideal that must be imitated. In fact, just prior to the demand to imitate him, Paul deliberately places a confession of his own imperfection (Phil. 3:12). The reason for his life being an example is that it is in fellowship with Christ. To be an imitator of the apostle accordingly means to lay hold of Christ and let one's life be remolded by him (see 1 Cor. 4:16–17).

2. (a) On two occasions Paul specifically names Christ alongside himself as the one to be imitated. Believers share Christ's lot passively in what they suffer (1 Thess. 1:6) and actively by imitating him in his love (1 Cor. 11:1). When Paul refers to Christ here, he is not thinking so much of the earthly life of Jesus, but of the authority of the Exalted One present in his Word and Spirit and of the kind of behavior that would be consistent with the sphere of his lordship. Paul's appeal to imitate Christ is also conveyed by other expressions (Rom. 15:7; 2 Cor. 5:14; 8:9; 10:1; Eph. 5:2, 25; Phil. 2:5–13; cf. Mk. 10:45; Jn. 13:15).

(b) Heb. uses the word group much as Paul does. The attitude of faith evident in the OT saints (6:12) and the believers' own teachers (13:7) is exemplary of those who have finished their course and strengthens the conviction and confidence of believers who find themselves still en route.

(c) Eph. 5:1 is the first place where the idea appears that God should be imitated, though not as a metaphysical Being with certain attributes, but in his nature as revealed in Christ. What believers are to imitate is Christ's obedient adherence to the Father's will, shown in love and forgiveness (cf. Matt. 5:48 par.).

3. Imitation in the NT is thus not presented as the reproduction of a given pattern. It is the way of life of those who derive their being from the forgiveness of God. It is an attitude of thanks in response to the salvation that has been given to us. The summons to discipleship can only be fulfilled when one is grasped by Christ and undergoes the transformation that existence under the lordship of Christ involves.

See also *akoloutheō*, follow (*199*); *mathētēs*, learner, pupil, disciple (*3412*); *opisō*, behind, after (*3958*).

3629 (*mimētēs*, imitator), → *3628*.

3630 μιμνήσκομαι

μιμνήσκομαι (*mimnēskomai*), recall to mind, remember (*3630*); μνεία (*mneia*), remembrance, memory, mention (*3644*); μνήμη (*mnēmē*), recollection, memory (*3647*); μνημονεύω (*mnēmoneuō*), remember, mention (*3648*); μνημόσυνον (*mnēmosynon*), memory, recollection (*3649*); ἀνάμνησις (*anamnēsis*), reminder, remembrance (*390*); ὑπόμνησις (*hypomnēsis*), recollection (*5704*); ἀναμιμνήσκω (*anamimnēskō*), remind (*389*); ὑπομιμνήσκω (*hypomimnēskō*), remind (*5703*).

CL 1. In cl. Gk. words in the *mimnēskomai* word group mean essentially to recall to mind, remember. The simple and compound forms of both vbs. and nouns are used interchangeably, with no fundamental difference in meaning. The following principal meanings are attested: (a) to remind oneself or someone else; recollection, memory; (b) to mention (verbally or in writing), make known, warn; (c) to consider, think of, ponder; (d) to remember for good or ill, concern oneself with; (e) to be mindful of, take into account, comply with.

anamnēsis has special significance in Plato. Seeing that it is possible to probe behind the externals of things, events, etc., and to recall their "ideas," he deduces a bodiless, free, spiritual preexistence of the soul and its survival after death.

2. *mnēmē* is an idea central to Gk. and Hel. cults and religiophilosophical systems. (a) In Homer, Hades is the kingdom of *lēthē*, i.e., oblivion and forgetfulness; its inhabitants are silent and unremembered.

(b) In Orphism *mnēmē* is personified as a goddess *Mnēmosynē*; also, under the figure of water from a divine spring, it is a gift of the goddess, i.e., the immortality of the human soul. Here memory is not only a natural power but also the process that this power sets in motion.

(c) In Gnosticism the human soul has left its heavenly home and thus become separated from unity with the divine (→ *heis*, 1651). Its tendency is to forget that divine origin through contamination by earthly evil. Recollection is the soul's first step in returning to its heavenly home; this recollection is evoked by the arrival of a redeemer through a "call." This call is the magic formula that sets the process in motion.

(d) This line is carried further in the mystery cults, where the fortunes of the particular god being worshiped are recalled in sensual fashion by means of ceremonies frequently based on a mixture of mysticism and magic.

OT 1. (a) In the LXX words from *mnē-* group generally correspond to derivatives of the Heb. vb. *zākar* and are used as in ordinary Gk. meanings: to remember (e.g., Gen. 8:1; 40:23; Wis. 12:2); to consider (e.g., Isa. 47:7; Sir. 41:1–2); to remember for good or ill (e.g., Gen. 30:22; Deut. esp. has remembering as a central theme); to be mindful of (e.g., Deut. 15:15); to mention (Est. 2:23).

(b) But words of this group also have unique biblical nuances. (i) For example, people recall things in prayer to God or even call God to remembrance (e.g., Ps. 74:18; see below).

(ii) To proclaim, celebrate. The existence of Israel, their faith in Yahweh as Savior and Redeemer, their obedience to him as the sovereign Lord of history, their public worship—all these things are grounded in their experience of his gracious help in the past. Hence, at their festivals the people of God are publicly called upon to remember his deeds; as they do so, the same God addresses them once again in the present. In this way, the words spoken, sung, or heard take up redemptive history and turn it into something requiring present commitment.

(iii) To believe, obey, become converted. To remember God in this sense means to serve, adore, obey, and follow him, to recognize him as Creator and Lord (Num. 15:39–40; Tob. 1:11–12). The phrase "to remember God" can be a formula summing up one's religious standing (Jdt. 13:19; Tob. 2:2). Thus in Ps. 22:27–28 *mimnēskomai* refers to the act of turning in faith to the Lord (cf. *Pss. Sol.* 4:21).

(iv) To confess with praise and adoration, give adoring testimony. When used in this way, words of this group always include the idea of public confession or acknowledgment of God (e.g., Ps. 6:5; 30:4; 97:12; cf. Sir. 17:27–28).

2. In rab. Jud., the specifically biblical usage recedes. Remembrance for good or ill comes to be heavily rationalized. For example, in the midrash on Gen. 30:22 God's remembrance is interpreted as his recollection of Rachel's good works. Yet the biblical meaning to help, be gracious, lived on in Jewish liturgy. The use of '*azkārâ*, remembrance, can even stand in place of *hašēm*, the Name of God. In the Qumran texts God remembered the old covenant and gave the new covenant for his elect, while in the eschatological war he will remember the sons of light and help them against the sons of darkness.

3. The topic of memory and remembering is an important theological concept in the OT. (a) When the vb. is used of God, it often occurs in psalms of complaint in an indirect plea for mercy or for God to rise up and act on behalf of his people. In Ps. 79:8, for example, the psalmist cries out: "Do not hold [lit., remember] against us the sins of the fathers" ; in 74:18, "Remember how the enemy has mocked you, O LORD." Jeremiah is more direct in his address for Yahweh to remember him; he uses the imperative to call on God to take vengeance on his enemies: "Remember me and care for me. Avenge me on my persecutors" (15:15).

Other psalms, rather than using pleas or commands, employ the indicative for Yahweh's remembering his covenant faithfulness and promises (e.g., Ps. 98:3; 105:8, 42). This memory is not confined to past events; it is active in the present and will continue into the future (e.g., 103:14; 105:8; 111:5). In each case, memory serves as a source of comfort and encouragement to the psalmist of God's care and concern for him.

(b) But Israel also remembers. God's people have not been cut off from their redemptive history; rather, they encounter the same covenant God through a living tradition. Memory links the past and the present (cf. Deut. 7:18; 9:7; 25:17). Here the Sabbath plays an important part, for Israel observes the Sabbath in order to call to mind her slavery in Egypt and God's remarkable deliverance in the exodus (5:15). Memory is to shape Israel's actions in the present (cf. "do not forget" in 8:11–20).

In prophetic passages such as Mic. 6:5, an appeal to memory is characteristic of a defendant's speech in a law court. The present rupture with Yahweh stems from Israel's failure to understand his saving acts. In Isa. 43:18; 44:21; 46:9 we see both continuity and discontinuity with Israel's past. There is continuity because of the one purpose of God; there is discontinuity because of Israel's failure. God's people are to use the experiences of the past to shape their future. The prophet Ezekiel (e.g., 16:22, 61; 36:31) calls on God's people to remember their sins. The goal is the same: that they might "know that I am LORD" (6:10; 16:62; 20:44; 36:23) and adjust their lives accordingly.

Ps. contains the largest number of instances of Israel's remembering, often in psalms of complaint (e.g., 42:4; 77:3; 143:5). The psalmist can remember a situation quite different from the one he is in and uses this memory to call out to the Lord for aid. In Ps. 77, for example, the psalmist grieves that Yahweh has changed his attitude toward him. He remembers when times were different and cries out in bitter frustration (77:3–9), but his attitude changes when he "remembers the deeds of the LORD . . . [the] miracles of long ago" (77:11), and the rest of the psalm is a reflection on God's mighty deeds.

4. One important feature of memory in the OT is use of the memorial sign, the *zikkārôn* (23x in the OT). In the pass. sense it means a memorandum, a thing worthy to be remembered, such as a memorial written in a book that will serve to bring to mind the defeat of the Amalekites (Exod. 17:14). In the act. sense it means a memorial that calls something else to remembrance. Two onyx stones in the high priest's ephod with the names of the twelve tribes is a "memorial before the LORD" (Exod. 28:12); the Passover is a memorial festival so that generations to come might remember the great saving act of

their God (12:14; cf. also Jos. 4:7). Signs and memorials serve to maintain for each generation their eternal relationship with the Lord God. The cultic acts of Israel continually remind God of this eternal covenantal order.

5. The Gk. noun *anamnēsis*, remembrance, which features in the words of institution in the Lord's Supper, is comparatively rare in the LXX. In Lev. 24:7 it stands for *ʾazkārâ*, which was a memorial offering. This offering was evidently intended to be a perpetual reminder of the covenant, to be offered every Sabbath (24:8–9). The memorial aspect seems to be an appeal to Yahweh to remember his covenant faithfulness as well as to Israel to do the same. The fact that only the priests might eat this offering indicates its holy character and their representative role on behalf of the people. Similarly in Num. 10:10 *anamnēsis* is linked with offerings as "a memorial for you before your God."

The word *anamnēsis* also occurs in the titles to Ps. 38 and 70 (NIV, "a petition"). It is difficult to know precisely what the word means here; perhaps the psalmist is calling on God to remember him in his present crisis. In the Apocr. *anamnēsis* occurs only in Wis. 16:6; in recalling the incident of the biting fiery serpents and of the bronze serpent as a means of deliverance, the writer says: "They ... received a symbol of deliverance to remind [*anamnēsis*] them of your law's command."

NT 1. The majority of NT passages using this word group reflect normal Gk. usage. (a) To remember, call to mind. Thus, "Peter remembered [*mimnēskomai*] the word Jesus had spoken ... and he went outside and wept bitterly" (Matt. 26:75; cf. Mk. 14:72, which uses the pass. of *anamimnēskō*, remind; Lk. 22:61, which uses the passive of *hypomimnēskō*, remind). In 2 Tim. 1:6 Paul uses *anamimnēskō*: "For this reason I remind you to fan into flame the gift of God, which is in you through the laying on of my hands." In each case theological lessons are drawn. Peter's memory of Jesus' warning about his denial, for example, underlines the folly of his self-confidence. In the other passage, remembering plays an important part in sustaining the life of faith.

(b) To consider. "Remember [*mnēmoneuō*] Lot's wife" (Lk. 17:32). The example of Lot's wife in refusing to give herself totally to escaping the judgment on Sodom and Gomorrah was a warning for consideration in both Jewish and Christian teaching. Note also Heb. 10:32: "Remember [*anamnēskomai*] those earlier days ... when you stood your ground in a great contest in the face of suffering" (according to 12:4 this was probably a persecution that had stopped short of martyrdom). Remembering in the form of considering should play an important part in one's conduct of life (cf. also Lk. 16:25).

(c) To remember in a way that will benefit a person. Here the passages are either OT quotations or have strong OT overtones. Mary's song contains the following: "He has helped his servant Israel, remembering to be merciful" (Lk. 1:54; cf. *Pss. Sol. 10:4*). Zechariah's psalm blesses God for fulfilling his promises "to show mercy to our fathers and to remember his holy covenant" (Lk. 1:72; cf. Exod. 2:24; 6:5; Ps. 105:8). Heb. 8:12 also operates within the theology of the covenant, taking up the promise of Jer. 31:34: "For I will forgive their wickedness and will remember their sins no more." The plea of the penitent thief ("Jesus, remember me when you come into your kingdom") means essentially, "Save me!" (Lk. 23:42). Rev. 18:5 expresses the converse aspect of this kind of remembering in the oracles against Babylon: "For her sins are piled up to heaven, and God has remembered her crimes."

(d) To be mindful of. In most of these cases the translation "to remember" is too weak. Rather, the remembering is seen as a positive force that affects one's behavior. Thus Heb. 11:15 reads: "If they had been thinking [*mnēmoneuō*] of the country they had left, they would have had opportunity to return." When Abraham left Ur and sojourned in the promised land, he did not keep pining after the country he had left (Gen. 11:31–12:9). Peter instructs us "to recall the words spoken

in the past by the holy prophets and the command given by our Lord and Savior through your apostles" (2 Pet. 3:2). Similarly Timothy is exhorted: "Keep reminding [the people] of these things. Warn them before God against quarreling about words" (2 Tim. 2:14; cf. also 1 Cor. 11:2; 2 Tim. 1:5; Jude 5, 17).

(e) To mention. *hypomimnēskō* in 3 Jn. 10 means "I will call attention to," i.e., the elder will raise the question of the actions of Diotrephes before the church. In the vision of Rev. 16:19, "God remembered [i.e., arraigned] Babylon the Great and gave her the cup filled with ... his wrath."

2. About one-fourth of the NT uses of this word group reflect the unique biblical usage. (a) To mention in prayer, to remember in prayer. *mnēmoneuō* in 1 Thess. 1:3 means to intercede, pray for. In Acts 10:4 Cornelius the centurion is told by an angel of God, "Your prayers and gifts to the poor have come up as a memorial offering before God." Some scholars see in the use of *mnēmosynon* a "sacrificial efficacy" in Cornelius's conduct (cf. also 10:31).

(b) To proclaim. "So I will always remind [*hypomimnēskō*] you of these things, though you know them and are firmly established in the truth you now have. I think it right to refresh your memory [*hypomnēsis*] as long as I live in the tent of this body" (2 Pet. 1:12–13). Here the reminding is understood in terms of presenting again the known truth of the gospel. According to Jn. 14:26, such reminding is the work of the Holy Spirit. As Christ's hearers bring to mind the message they have heard from him, the Holy Spirit enables them to proclaim the Lordship of Christ in ways that are relevant to each succeeding generation. There are overtones of this sense of proclamation also in 1 Cor. 4:17. Similarly, the woman who anointed Jesus becomes part of the NT proclamation: "Wherever the gospel is preached throughout the world, what she has done will also be told, in memory [*mnēmosynon*] of her" (Mk. 14:9; cf. Matt. 26:13).

Exhortation in the form of *anamnēsis* or *hypomnēsis* is a marked feature of the Christian message. Note Tit. 3:1: "Remind [*hypomimnēskō*] the people to be subject to rulers and authorities, to be obedient, to be ready to do whatever is good."

(c) To believe. "Remember Jesus Christ [*mnēmoneue Iēsoun Christon*], raised from the dead, descended from David. This is my gospel" (2 Tim. 2:8). What is to be remembered is a short creedal statement.

(d) To confess. Referring to the sacrifices under the old covenant, Heb. 10:3 declares: "But those sacrifices are an annual reminder [*anamnēsis*] of sins." Here the allusion may well be to the Day of Atonement ritual (Lev. 16), which involved public acknowledgment of sins committed in the past year.

3. The only other NT instances of *anamnēsis* occur in Paul's and Lk.'s accounts of the Last Supper: "When he had given thanks, he broke it and said, 'This is my body, which is for you; do this in remembrance [*anamnēsis*] of me.' In the same way, after supper he took the cup, saying, 'This cup is the new covenant in my blood; do this, whenever you drink it, in remembrance [*anamnēsis*] of me'" (1 Cor. 11:24–25; cf. Lk. 22:19).

Traditionally, these words have been understood to mean that the Lord's Supper was Jesus' appointed means of being present in the hearts and minds of the assembled church. At one end of the scale is the Zwinglian interpretation, which sees the Lord's Supper as a kind of stimulus to the act of mental recollection of Jesus' atoning death. Zwingli believed that the physical body of Christ was risen, ascended, and seated at the right hand of the Father and therefore could not be present in the Lord's Supper. Moreover, he held that it is the Spirit that gives life (Jn. 6:63); thus, the access we have to Christ in remembering him is through the Spirit.

At the other end of the scale is the Catholic interpretation, which speaks of the real presence of Christ in the Eucharist, involving the doctrine of transubstantiation in which the substance of the bread and the wine is changed into the body and blood of Christ, though outwardly it remains bread and wine. The Protestant Max Thurian takes these words to mean: "with a view to my memorial, as the memorial of me." This memorial is not a simple subjective act of recollection but a liturgical action that makes the Lord and his sacrifice present to us. Jeremias understands "in remembrance of me" to mean: "that God may remember me."

Perhaps it is best to have a comprehensive view of the word *anamnēsis* in the Lord's Supper. The command to "do this in remembrance of me" may be paraphrased as follows: "Do this, by eating the bread and drinking the cup (i.e., by participating in my life and death), by the preaching of the word (1 Cor. 11:26), and the singing of praise."

4. The original meanings of the *mimnēskomai* word-group were entirely nonreligious, ranging from sexual desire to the heights of philosophy. However, as a result of their adoption into the LXX as renderings of Heb. equivalents, the Gk. words underwent a significant expansion of meaning, particularly along the lines of public worship. What makes this so significant is the fact that the Gk. of the NT possesses so many other words relating to public worship, yet the words of this group are introduced into early Christian vocabulary for use in this special area, with the result that what was a peripheral meaning in cl. Gk. becomes central.

Undoubtedly the main reason for this is that public worship of God belongs to the sphere of the historical, stretching from yesterday, through today, and on into the future—from Sinai to Calvary, from the OT covenant people to the church of Christ, then on to us, and eventually to the end of the age and God's eternal kingdom. In worship believers recall historical events. The biblical view of history is linear, not cyclical. This is true of proclamation, which aims to give outward expression to something that has happened in the past by removing it from the wrappings of memory or of oral or written tradition and so recalling it to our minds. The same applies to the Lord's Supper, instituted at a precise time and place to be a "remembrance" of Christ throughout the church's history "until he comes" again (1 Cor. 11:26).

God's remembrance of his people (expressed in preaching) dovetails with his people's remembrance of him in praise and testimony. Within the context of revelation, God's remembrance is expressed verbally (i.e., it is addressed to our minds and is personal), but it is not mere words. God's remembering is a creative event. Thus it can bring blessing (Gen. 30:22) or judgment (Rev. 16:19). Our response is similarly remembrance, expressed not only verbally in the ordinance of public worship, but in a manner that involves the whole person as only eating and drinking can do, i.e., in the Lord's Supper; and, over and above all this, expressed tangibly in collecting money for the poor (see Gal. 2:10).

3631	μισέω

μισέω (*miseō*), hate (*3631*).

CL & OT 1. *miseō* in cl. Gk. means hate, abhor, reject. It connotes not only antipathy to certain actions, but also a permanent and deepseated human hostility toward others or even toward deities. It is further used of the gods' abhorrence of the base aspects of human nature and of divine hatred of those who are unrighteous.

2. In the LXX *miseō* can mean several things. (a) It can denote hate as an emotional impulse. Joseph's brothers hated him because he was his father's favorite (Gen. 37:2–4). Wisdom teaches that hatred (*misos*) stirs up strife, but love covers all offenses (Prov. 10:12). Yahweh forbids hatred against fellow members of Israel and commands that love be extended to them as to oneself (Lev. 19:17–18).

(b) The pass. *miseomai*, especially the part. *misoumenē*, can also be used of a wife who is not loved (Gen. 29:31, 33; Deut. 21:15–17; 22:13–16; Isa. 60:15). The transformation of strong desire into utter loathing is portrayed in 2 Sam. 13.

(c) The word haters is often a synonym for enemies (Deut. 7:15; 30:7; 2 Sam. 22:18; Ps. 18:17)—also where the reference is to God's enemies (Num. 10:35; Ps. 68:1; 139:21). Similarly one's enemies are those whom one hates (Ezek. 16:37; 23:28).

(d) Those who hate God are also those who are disobedient to him (Exod. 20:5; Deut. 5:9; 7:9–11). They hate anyone who reproves them in the name of Yahweh (1 Ki. 22:8; Amos 5:10), right knowledge (Prov. 1:22, 29), and the righteous or godly (Ps. 34:21; 69:4, 14; Prov. 29:10).

(e) God hates wickedness (Jer. 44:3–4 = LXX 51:3–4; Zech. 8:17; Mal. 2:16, divorce) and those who do it (Ps. 5:5, an aphorism; Prov. 6:16–19; Jer. 12:8; Hos. 9:15). Israel therefore is also to hate wickedness (Amos 5:15; cf. Ps. 26:5, the company of evildoers; 119:104, the way of lying; Ps. 139:21, those who hate God).

(f) To hate oneself is folly (Prov. 15:32 = LXX 16:3; cf. 29:24).

3. Ancient Jud. recognized the destructive power of hatred. Baseless hatred destroyed the second temple, for hatred is more serious than immorality, idolatry, and the shedding of blood put together (*b. Yoma* 9a). At the same time there is a hatred that is commanded: "Hate the Epicureans [free-thinkers], those who seduce and mislead, and likewise those who betray" (*'Abot R. Nat.* 16; cf. Ps. 139:21–22).The Qumran community spoke in a similar vein. Its members were to "do what is good and righteous before him [God] as he commanded by the hand of Moses and all his servants the prophets . . . [to] love all the sons of light, each according to his lot in God's design, and hate the sons of darkness, each according to his guilt in God's vengeance" (1QS 1:2–3, 9–11; cf. 9:21–23).

NT 1. According to Jesus, God now accepts his enemies as sons (Matt. 5:43–48; cf. Lk. 15:11–32). Hence it no longer makes sense for the righteous to hate "the sons of darkness." Rather, with the authority of God Jesus demands: "You have heard that it was said, 'Love your neighbor and hate your enemy.' But I tell you: Love your enemies" (Matt. 5:43–44), and "do good to those who hate you" (Lk. 6:27). It is, of course, right for the Christian church, just as it is for "the Son" (Heb. 1:9), to hate evil and evil deeds (Rev. 2:6; cf. also Jude 23; Rev. 3:4). But within the church, "anyone who claims to be in the light but hates his brother is still in darkness" (1 Jn. 2:9), and "anyone who hates his brother is a murderer" (3:15; cf. 4:20). Still, in the last days there will be hatred even within the church (Matt. 24:10), though this is the mark of non-Christian humanity (Tit. 3:3).

2. Jesus' radical command to love one's enemies brings the disciples into line with God's action toward both good and evil people (Matt. 5:45–48; Lk. 6:35). But Jesus also stated: "If anyone comes to me and does not hate his father and mother, his wife and children, his brothers and sisters—yes, even his own life—he cannot be my disciple" (14:26; cf. Jn. 12:25). Comparison with Matt. 10:37 suggests the meaning here for "hate" is "love less." Like God himself (Deut. 13:6–11), Jesus requires that obedience to God must take precedence over all human obligations.

The world, however, like everyone who does evil, hates the light (Jn. 3:20). It hates Christ without cause (15:25), because he bears witness that its works are evil (7:7). This hatred is directed also against Jesus' disciples (Matt. 10:22; Mk. 13:13; Lk. 21:17; Jn. 15:18–25; 17:14; 1 Jn. 3:13). They are counted blessed when people hate them (Lk. 6:22) for Christ's sake (Matt. 5:11).

3. Paul uses *miseō* in two difficult passages. (a) In Rom. 7:15 he says of those under the law: "I do not understand what I do. For what I want to do I do not do, but what I hate I do." The reference is not to one's inability to become righteous in terms of God's law (as Phil. 3:6 shows), but one's inability to discern the outcome of an attempt to fulfill the law. We do not attain to life, as we want, but to death, which we hate, since sin is able to make use even of the law for its own ends.

(b) In Rom. 9:13 Paul cites Mal. 1:2–3: "Jacob I loved, but Esau I hated." Even before the two sons of Isaac could give any grounds for acceptance or rejection, God chose the younger one, Jacob, as the heir of his promise, and rejected Esau, the older brother, in order to show that his salvation rests on his promise alone, not on natural descent or similar prerogatives (Rom. 9:7–8, 11–12).

4. *miseō* is used in a sense completely in line with the OT at Lk. 1:71 (of enemies) and Rev. 18:2 (of unclean birds, loathed by God).

See also *echthros*, hostile, hated, enemy (*2398*).

3632 (misthapodosia, recompense), → *3635*.

3633 (misthapodotēs, one who pays wages, a rewarder), → *3635*.

3634 (misthios, hired servant), → *3635*.

3635	μισθός

μισθός (*misthos*), pay, wages, reward (*3635*); μισθόω (*misthoō*), hire (*3636*); μισθωτός (*misthōtos*), hired servant (*3638*); μίσθωμα (*misthōma*), contract price, rent (*3637*); μίσθιος (*misthios*), hired servant (*3634*); μισθαποδοσία (*misthapodosia*), recompense (*3632*); μισθαποδότης (*misthapodotēs*), one who pays wages, a rewarder (*3633*).

CL & OT 1. In cl. Gk. the noun *misthos* denotes reward or pay for work. It occurs mainly in industrial or commercial contexts. More rarely, examples can be found of good fortune being given to humans as a reward for their ethical endeavors. But *misthos* is not used in cl. Gk. in a religious sense, since Gk. religion did not rest on the basis of rewards. In general, what a person received in the afterlife was based on honor or virtue.

From Hel. times on, the idea of reward penetrated religious thought. Belief in rewards and punishments in the next life begins to play a decisive role in the religions of Serapis-Isis and of Mithras. In Roman religion the commercial conception of payment and of reward expanded to include the relationship of humans to the gods, illustrated by the basic phrase *do ut des*, I give (to you) so that you can give (to me). The concept of reward is linked here with the language of sacrifice.

2. (a) In the LXX the noun *misthos* translates a variety of Heb. words and means hire, wages, or reward, depending on context (e.g., Gen. 15:1; 30:18, 28, 32–33; 31:8; Exod. 2:9; 22:14 = LXX 22:13; Num. 18:31; Ezek. 27:15; Tob. 2:12, 14; Wis. 2:22; 5:15). The vb. *misthoō* normally translates verbal forms derived from *śākar*, to hire (Gen. 30:16; Deut. 23:5 = LXX 23:4; Jdg. 9:4; Neh. 6:12; 13:2; Isa. 7:20; 46:6). *misthios* means a hired servant (Lev. 19:13; 25:50; Sir. 7:20); *misthōma*, hire (Hos. 2:14 = LXX 2;12; Mic. 1:7); *misthōtos*, hired servant (Exod. 12:45; Lev. 19:13; 22:10; 25:6; Isa. 28:1, 3; 1 Macc. 6:29).

(b) Reward in the OT is primarily used in its secular sense summoning Israelites to social action. Laborers are to be paid their wages daily in order to avoid possible want or starvation (Deut. 24:14; Jer. 22:13).

(c) Semitic and Israelite thought is largely determined by the connection between human dealings and fortunes. Earthly rewards and punishments are part of the obvious makeup of OT faith. Leah receives her son Issachar as a reward from God (Gen. 30:18; cf. Ps. 127:3), while Yahweh punishes the Amalekite crimes by putting them under a ban and destroying them (1 Sam. 15:2–3). The negative aspect of punishment and retribution tends to stand out. Note esp. Amos 1:3–2:16, which connects the bleak fate of Israel and the other nations with God's judgment. Ezek. replaces the concept of wholesale recompense by that of punishment, and takes note of more individual offenses (18:20), while Deut. unfolds a positive understanding of reward, linking together obedience and blessing (cf. 28:1–14), and their antithesis, disobedience and curse (cf. 28:15–68).

But it is in the wisdom lit. that the concept of reward receives its distinctive stamp. Here for the first time a systematized pattern is developed, possessing authority for the whole of life; there is reward for the righteous and punishment for the godless (cf. Prov. 11:18, 21, 31). Job's attack on the theology of his friends (cf. Job 8:4–6) is a protest against this theory of retribution for good and bad, because it does not do justice to the suffering of the godly. The Preacher also

reveals his dissatisfaction with an over-neat correlation of rewards and punishments (Eccl. 8:14).

(d) But note how different the concept of divine reward is from our own human concepts. God is a sovereign Lord who rules his servants but is not obliged to reward the amount of work they do. Redemption is a gift that he gives, a royal bounty, which far exceeds in value any service from his subjects (see esp. Ps. 127:3, where the reward from God is not payment for services or remuneration for achievement but a free gift from a generous king). The blessings of salvation and the reward of God are generally understood in earthly terms (cf. Deut. 28:3–14; 30:15).

3. In intertestamental Jud., a reward from God was considered as having significance beyond this life. But hand in hand with this development went a fateful modification in the understanding of reward—that one could earn God's grace through good behavior. Good works became the means of attaining grace and the precondition of the expected reward. The Mosaic law ceased to be the fence that held Israelites inside the saving boundaries of the covenant and became instead a ladder and a means of acquiring salvation, now thought of as lying in the future. Yahweh's covenant became a starting position for self-justification instead of something one aimed to fulfill in its own right; yet one could never be certain whether enough had been credited to one's account. Eschatological expectation can never become a matter of certain hope where a concept of reward has been perverted into a system of merit and achievement.

NT 1. In the NT *misthos* appears 15x in the Gospels (esp. Matt.) and 6x in Paul . Two surprising compound words are found only in Heb.: *misthapodosia*, reward or recompense (3x), and *misthapodotēs*, one who rewards or recompenses (once).

(a) *misthos* is a basic part of Jesus' preaching concerning the coming kingdom of God. Some references give the impression that Jesus took over the prevalent Jewish conception of reward. If you sell all your possessions, you will win a treasure in heaven (Matt. 19:21, though not using *misthos*), while God will not withhold the reward for godliness if it is directed to him (6:1). Jesus placed all human action and existence under the coming judgment, but this raises the question whether this does not open the flood-gates to "works-righteousness."

The parable of the workers in the vineyard (Matt. 20:1–16) answers this. Note that the landowner is entirely free and under no external constraint (20:15), a characteristic made even clearer in the parable of the talents (25:24). The reason why those who worked only an hour were paid the same wage as the others who had "borne the burden of the work and the heat of the day" (20:12) is not that their work was of a higher quality or that God reckoned their small efforts worth the same pay. Rather, payment is made on the grounds of freedom and generosity rather than reward.

God not only repays far beyond any merit (cf. Lk. 19:17, 19); payment of reward is independent of a worker's achievements. Its root lies in God's sovereign generosity: "Don't I have the right to do what I want with my own money? Or are you envious because I am generous?" (Matt. 20:15). Every claim to one's deserts must fall silent in the face of the demand for total obedience: "So you also, when you have done everything you were told to do, should say, 'We are unworthy servants; we have only done our duty'" (Lk. 17:10). Nevertheless, even the smallest act of service in the kingdom of God will not go unrewarded (Matt. 10:42; cf. Mk. 9:41).

(b) Jesus' polemic against the false piety of the Pharisees is also instructive (Matt. 6:1–18). A Pharisee who is putting his piety on show is not looking for God's acceptance and honor but for compliments from other people. If they admire him and his virtues, his reward has already been paid out to him (6:2, 5, 16). The genuinely pious, however, do everything for God's sake; hence God will reward them in his judgment. Faith that stands on the side of God, ready to suffer for Jesus' sake, results in a reward in heaven (5:11–12). Profession of faith in the Lord is not only verbal; it also means accepting "the least of these brothers of mine" in his name (25:40; cf. 10:42; 25:45). Such an attitude is rewarded insofar as a person occupies the place in the kingdom of God that has been prepared.

Thus, our works have no intrinsic moral value that can accrue merit with God. Rather, they are integral parts of faith and of our confession of Christ. Even the reward is based solely on our acceptance by the eschatological judge (Matt. 10:32); it includes full salvation and eternal life (Mk. 8:36; 10:29–30; cf. Matt. 19:29; Lk. 18:29–30). In making the concept of reward subsidiary to the prior category of the coming kingdom of God, Jesus makes a clean break with the Jud. of his day.

2. (a) Paul was well acquainted with the thought of judgment based on works (cf. Rom. 2:6; 2 Cor. 5:10). But with him the rab. Jewish concept of merit is replaced by his doctrine of justification by faith. How is this to be understood? The nature of *misthos* is explained by the use of other concepts: The righteous man receives "praise" (Rom. 2:29), "glory, honor and immortality" (2:7), and the "prize for which God has called me heavenward" (Phil. 3:14) in the judgment. What we have earned is death; life is what God gives us by his grace (Rom. 6:23). He does not owe us this reward (4:4).

(b) This does not mean that the *misthos* has no place in a Christian's activity. There is the prize that beckons the victor into the race (cf. 1 Cor. 9:24; Phil. 3:14). The wise master-builder of the community will receive a reward (1 Cor. 3:14), but there can only be a question of reward when it is given for something done voluntarily. Paul felt under obligation to preach the gospel (9:16), but he freely waived the church's obligation to maintain his upkeep, lest he be regarded as under obligation to others (9:15). Although Paul speaks to the Corinthians of his reward, his understanding of it is paradoxical. For it turns out that the reward he seeks is not something that he covets for himself, but to make the gospel free of charge (9:17–18). He wants no obstacle in the way of the gospel (9:12). It is a further aspect of his conduct as a skilled builder (3:10) and an apostle who is content to suffer (4:9–13).

(c) In connection with *misthos*, Paul distinguishes between the builder and one's work, which, if unserviceable, will be burned up in the fire of judgment. God's grace does not allow such a person to be lost (1 Cor. 3:15) even though the work is. Note too Eph. 2:10, that even the good deeds we do perform are a gift of God's grace. It is God "who works in you to will and to act according to his good purpose" (Phil. 2:13). All personal vainglory is excluded.

3. Heb. reveals by its choice of vocabulary that reward can be spoken of only in terms of the sovereign act of God. According to 10:35–36 it is the blessing of the promise that richly rewards us (*misthapodosia*, which denotes here the bestowal of eternal life; cf. 11:6). No human action can in any way counterbalance this in value. Rather, this gift is intended for those who seek God with a bold faith. Faith is indeed bound up with patience and not giving "up meeting together" (10:25), but there is never any mention of merit that leads to salvation.

True, Heb. contains repeated warnings against despising the grace of God and the day of opportunity (e.g., 3:7–19; 4:1–13; 6:4–8; 10:35–39; 12:3–6, 15–17, 25–27). There comes a point of no return from sin. But believers have not come to Mount Sinai and all its terrors of judgment, but "to Mount Zion . . . to the spirits of righteous men made perfect, to Jesus the mediator of a new covenant . . ." (Heb. 12:22–24). The prospect of judgment for the faithful is not a petty reckoning up of human values and achievements, but a joyful hopefulness (10:35). Moses is an example of such faith, for "he regarded disgrace for the sake of Christ as of greater value than the treasures of Egypt, because he was looking ahead to his reward [*misthapodosian*]" (11:26).

4. In Jn. 4 Jesus' discourse with the disciples after his conversation with the Samaritan woman indicates that the "harvest," the eschatological age of salvation, has already broken in. Indeed, the "reaper" is already drawing "his wages [*misthon*], even now he harvests the crop for eternal life" (4:36; cf. Lev. 26:5; Deut. 28:33; Jdg. 6:3). The

thought of wages here is not a matter of merit. The "work of God" that has eternal life as its consequence is faith (Jn. 6:29). It is in this sense that 2 Jn. 8 speaks of the *misthos* of faith: "Watch out that you do not lose what you have worked for, but that you may be rewarded fully."

5. The OT and the NT together testify that eternal life is a gift that comes from outside ourselves, from God himself who, as our judge, pronounces us righteous despite ourselves. All rewards lie in his gift. Yet there is a connection between the anticipated reward and our conduct. God rewards those who serve him without thought of reward. Whatever reward we receive is a further token of the free grace of God that enables us to act in the first place.

See also *apodidōmi*, give away, give back, sell, recompense (*625*); *kerdos*, gain (*3046*); *opsōnion*, wages, payment (*4072*).

3636 (*misthoō*, hire), → *3635*.

3637 (*misthōma*, contract price, rent), → *3635*.

3638 (*misthōtos*, hired servant), → *3635*.

3640 Μιχαήλ	Μιχαήλ (*Michaēl*), Michael (*3640*).

OT The name probably means "who is like God?" Michael appears in the OT only in Dan. Like Gabriel, he is a celestial being, but he has special responsibilities as the champion of Israel against the rival angel of the Persians (10:13, 20), and he leads the heavenly armies against all supernatural forces of evil in the last great battle (12:1).

This military patronage is frequently attested in other late Jewish writings, and his name as protector of Israel is also on the shields of one division of the Sons of Light at Qumran. Michael also has an intercessory role and was considered to be the recording angel. He was therefore the intermediary between God and Moses at Sinai.

NT In the NT Michael appears on two occasions. Jude 9 refers to a dispute between Michael and the devil concerning Moses' body. The theme of Dan. 12:1 is taken up in Rev. 12:7, which presents Michael as the vanquisher of the primordial dragon, identified as Satan and representing the supernatural forces of evil.

3644 (*mneia*, remembrance, memory, mention), → *3630*.

3645 (*mnēma*, tomb), → *2507*.

3646 (*mnēmeion*, memorial, tomb), → *2507*.

3647 (*mnēmē*, recollection, memory), → *3630*.

3648 (*mnēmoneuō*, remember, mention), → *3630*.

3649 (*mnēmosynon*, memory, recollection), → *3630*.

3655 (*moichalis*, adulteress, prostitute), → *3658*.

3656 (*moichaō*, commit adultery), → *3658*.

3657 (*moicheia*, adultery), → *3658*.

3658 μοιχεύω	μοιχεύω (*moicheuō*), commit adultery (*3658*); μοιχεία (*moicheia*), adultery (*3657*); μοιχός (*moichos*), adulterer (*3659*); μοιχαλίς (*moichalis*), adulteress, prostitute (*3655*); μοιχάω (*moichaō*), commit adultery (*3656*).

CL & OT 1. In cl. Gk. *moicheuō* means to commit adultery, sometimes to seduce a woman, violate. Adultery was punishable in law codes going back to the 2d millennium B.C. Every form of sexual relationship outside marriage was forbidden to the wife, for she was the real guarantor of the integrity of the family and clan; by adultery she broke her own marriage. A man, by contrast, committed adultery only by sexual relationships with a married woman, i.e., when breaking into another's arrangement. Traces of older concepts from different cultures can be detected here as well: (a) Adultery with a married woman involved an offense against a man's property, and (b) the woman committing adultery opened the clan to the influence of evil powers.

The punishment of adultery (death, ill-treatment, or the payment of a fine) was normally left to the initiative of the wronged husband or his clan.

2. In the LXX adultery, as in other societies, covered every extramarital sexual relationship by a married woman, and the extramarital sexual relationship of a man with a married or engaged woman (Gen. 38:15–16; Lev. 19:20–22; Deut. 22:28–29). Adultery was punishable by death, normally by stoning (but cf. Gen. 38:24) both parties (Lev. 20:10; Deut. 22:22–27; Ezek. 16:40; cf. Jn. 8:5). In contrast to society outside Israel, adultery offended not only the personal rights of marriage and family but also the law of God (Exod. 20:14) and so threatened the basis of the people's existence (Deut. 22:22b). Hence, the punishment had to be inflicted by the community. If a woman was suspected of adultery, a test of guilt or innocence was prescribed to be carried out by the priests (Num. 5:11–31).

3. Marriage and adultery are used symbolically for the relationship between Yahweh and his people in Hos. (→ *gameō*, *1138*). When Israel began to sacrifice to strange gods, the nation acted as an adulteress who leaves her husband and plays the prostitute with other men (2:2). Yahweh will severely punish this adultery (5:7–15), though the goal of this is not the destruction of the adulteress but her repentance (3:5). This picture is later taken up by Jer. (cf. 2:2; 3:1–10; 5:7; 13:22, 26) and Ezek. (cf. 16:1–63; 23:37–45).

4. The serious warnings against adultery in wisdom lit. (cf. Prov. 6:20–35; Sir. 25:2) show a weakening of strict marriage morality in the course of Israel's history (cf. esp. Prov. 6:35; Mal. 2:14–16). It is the mark of the fool to be led astray by a prostitute. His action brings disgrace and ruin (cf. also Prov. 2:16–19; 7:5–27; 30:20). The serious social consequences of adultery were also a cause for concern.

NT 1. This word group is used in the NT with the same meanings as outlined above. In several places the NT quotes Exod. 20:14 (e.g., Matt. 19:18; Mk. 10:19; Lk. 18:20; Jas. 2:11). At the same time, however, the NT's understanding of marriage and adultery is carried forward to a position known neither to cl. Gk. nor the OT. (a) Adultery on the man's part is unreservedly measured by the same standards as in the woman (Matt. 5:32; Mk. 10:11–12; Lk. 16:18).

(b) The desire, i.e., the willingness, to commit the act is equivalent to adultery itself (Matt. 5:27–28).

(c) Since the NT considers marriage to be indissoluble (Mk. 10:8), remarriage following divorce, permitted by the OT on the grounds of the hardness of human hearts, enters the realm of adultery (Matt. 5:31–32). In 19:9, Jesus applies the statement equally to the man who divorces his wife, marries again, and so commits adultery. Matt. does recognize an exception that permits divorce (→ *porneuō*, *4519*).

(d) Adultery is incompatible with the hope of life in the kingdom of God (1 Cor. 6:9–10) and is under God's judgment (Heb. 13:4). Thus, a destructive libertinism (2 Pet. 2:14) goes hand in hand with doubts about the return of Christ and the judgment to follow (3:3–7).

2. Jesus' severe condemnation of adultery does not exclude God's mercy to the repentant sinner, whose conversion he desires (Lk. 18:9–14; cf. 1 Cor. 6:9–11). Thus the adulteress in Jn. 8:3–11, who had earned the death penalty, had her guilt forgiven while the apparently guiltless multitude had a mirror held up to their hypocritical self-righteousness. However, all impenitent sinners are excluded from the kingdom (1 Tim. 1:10; Heb. 13:4; Rev. 21:8; 22:15).

3. The theme of adultery is used in the NT, as in OT prophecy, in a metaphorical sense (cf. Jas. 4:4, where adulterers are considered lovers of the world). Similarly the Jewish people are called "a wicked and adulterous generation," esp. as exemplified by their religious representatives: Pharisees, teachers of the law (Matt. 12:39), and Sadducees (16:4). A metaphorical explanation is most likely here. This contemporary generation, a people shown to be disloyal to God by their rejection of Jesus (cf. Mk. 8:38), is characterized by its desire for a sign when there is already enough proof of God's love present in Jesus.

See also *gameō*, marry (*1138*); *nymphē*, bride (*3811*); *koitē*, bed, marriage bed, intercourse (*3130*); *hyperakmos*, past the peak, begin to fade; be overpassionate (*5644*).

3659 (*moichos*, adulterer), → *3658*.

| 3662 | μολύνω |

μολύνω (*molynō*), defile, befoul (*3662*); μολυσμός (*molysmos*), defilement (*3663*).

CL & OT The lit. meaning of *molynō* is besmear, soil, by applying mud or other filth. It is used in ethical and religious contexts for actions that demean and pollute oneself and/or others, esp. in sexual matters. *molysmos* has a comparable range of meaning.

In the LXX, *molynō* occurs 19x, used both lit. (dirtying feet and clothes, Gen. 37:31; Song 5:3; Isa. 59:3) and fig. (causing defilement before God, 65:4; Jer. 23:11). *molysmos* occurs only in Jer. 23:15; 1 Esd. 8:82; 2 Macc. 5:27.

NT *molynō* is used in its metaphorical sense 3x in the NT: in 1 Cor. 8:7, of a weak conscience that is defiled, i.e., made to feel guilty, through doing things about which one has scruples; in Rev. 3:4; 14:4, of not lapsing into impure, disobedient ways. *molysmos* appears only in 2 Cor. 7:1 for the defilement that comes from a pagan lifestyle.

See also *miainō*, defile (*3620*).

3663 (*molysmos*, defilement), → *3662*.

3665 (*monē*, staying, tarrying, dwelling place, room, abode), → *3531*.

3666 (*monogenēs*, only), → *3668*.

3667 (*monon*, only), → *3668*.

| 3668 | μόνος |

μόνος (*monos*), alone, only (*3668*); μονογενής (*monogenēs*), only (*3666*); μόνον (*monon*), only (*3667*).

CL & OT 1. In cl. Gk. *monos* means only, lonely, alone; in an extended sense it means unique. The adv. *monōs* or *monon* (neut.) means only, solely. The uses of the adj. and the adv. run into one another.

2. In the LXX *monos* can mean in separation from or in solitude from. To be alone implies a troubled mind and restlessness (e.g., Isa. 49:21; Jer. 15:17, where the prophet, bent down by God's hand and cut off from human contact, sits alone). This sense is also found in Gen. 2:18, where God says that "it is not good for the man to be alone. I will make a helper suitable for him."

monos is frequently used for God's uniqueness (e.g., Deut. 32:12; Job 9:8). It occurs in confessional statements in 2 Ki. 19:15, 19; Isa. 37:16. It occurs frequently in Ps. (e.g., 4:8; 51:4; 148:13) and is thus used in statements about the exclusive worship of the one God (e.g., Exod. 22:20; Ps. 71:16). Ezek. 14:16 shows that the righteous alone will be delivered. Exod. 24:2 uses *monos* to stress Moses' uniqueness. *monos* can be intensified. Thus in 1 Ki. 19:10, 14, Elijah, persecuted by Jezebel, says in his despondency that he has survived being *monōtatos*, utterly alone, as the Lord's prophet.

NT 1. *monos* is found 48x in the NT and *monon* (neut. used as adv.) 66x. (a) The adv. means "only" (Matt. 9:21; 1 Cor. 15:19); "not only ... but also" (Matt. 21:21); "not only ... but now much more" (Phil. 2:12). (b) The adj. can mean alone, unaccompanied (Matt. 17:8; Jn. 8:16; Rom. 11:3); alone, by oneself (Mk. 4:10; Lk. 9:18); single (Jn. 12:24); without any help (Lk. 10:40). (c) With a noun or pron. *monos* means only in the sense of exclusively (e.g., Matt. 12:4; Heb. 9:7; Rev. 15:4). (d) The word can also denote the one and only God (Jn. 17:3; Jude 4, 25).

2. *monos* becomes theologically significant when it is used in the confession of the one and only God, esp. in doxologies (Jn. 5:44; Rom. 16:27; 1 Tim. 1:17; 6:15–16). It is significant that the confession of the one holy God in Rev. 15:4 is found in the song of the mar-

tyrs who "had been victorious over the beast" (15:2). Similarly in Jn. 17:3, *monos* is linked with "true," presumably in contrast to the deceptive appearance of all other gods and revealers; in 5:44 it stands in contrast to the false praise of the world, which does not seek the true praise (*doxa*, → *1518*) of the one and only God.

3. There is a dialectic use of *monos* in regard to Jesus. On the one hand, the earthly Jesus is not "alone" even if all forsake him, since the Father is with him (Jn. 8:16, 29; 16:32). On the other hand, in Jude 4 Jesus is called without qualification "our only Sovereign and Lord" (cf. Jn. 20:28; Rom. 9:5; Tit. 2:13).

4. *monogenēs* (lit., of a single kind) is found as a Christological title only in Jn. This word marks out Jesus as unique, above all earthly and heavenly beings, yet the soteriological meaning is more strongly stressed than that of ontology or origin (Jn. 1:14, 18; 3:16, 18; 1 Jn. 4:9). It reflects what the OT says of Isaac (Gen. 22:2, 12, 16; cf. Heb. 11:17, where *monogenēs* is used). Jesus as *monogenēs* is the only one who can say, "I and the Father are one" (Jn. 10:30). Included in the uniqueness of God, Jesus does not disappear in history and the historical, but stands over them as Lord.

See also *hapax*, once (*562*); *heis*, one (*1651*).

3671	μορφή

μορφή (*morphē*), form, outward appearance, shape (*3671*); σύμμορφος (*symmorphos*), having the same shape, similar in form or appearance (*5215*); συμμορφίζω (*symmorphizō*), be conformed to, take on the same form as (*5214*); μόρφωσις (*morphōsis*), embodiment, formulation, outward form, appearance (*3673*); μορφόω (*morphoō*), form, shape (*3672*).

CL & OT 1. (a) By and large in cl. Gk. *morphē* denotes form in the sense of outward appearance. It can also mean the embodiment of the form, the person insofar as he or she comes into view. Gk. philosophy was concerned with the question of matter and form. Plato presents Socrates as saying that an exact description of the nature of the soul will enable us to see "whether she be single and the same, or, like the *morphē* of the body, multiform" (*Phaedr.*, 271). Aristotle worked out a more precise set of concepts. He distinguished matter (*hylē*) from form (*morphē*, also *eidos*). Matter has within itself a great number of possibilities for becoming a form and thus becoming manifest as a form.

These concepts do not imply that form and matter are separable, as husk and kernel are. Rather, they represent different principles and ways of looking at the same object. The outward appearance cannot be detached from the essence of the thing; the essence of the thing is indicated by its outward form.

(b) Similarly, *morphōsis* means embodiment, receiving form; *symmorphos*, having the same form; *symmorphizō*, to take on the same form; and *metamorphoō*, to be transformed (→ *3565*).

(c) Of special interest is the use of *morphē* in the lit. of Gnosticism and the Hel. mystery religions. The main issue here is the transformation of a human into divine form. It is not merely the external appearance that is changed. Rather, the external can recede behind that of essential character. The external appearance is undoubtedly meant not as an antithesis to the essential character, but as the expression of it. Thus the Hel. mystery religions contain a great number of stories about transformations. The initiate is transformed by dedication and rites into divine substances and so is deified.

2. *morphē* occurs 12x in the LXX (e.g., Job 4:16; Isa. 44:13; Dan. 3:19). The OT spoke of God in anthropological terms. Inevitably humans have to speak of God in this way. Gen. 18:1–2 may be taken to mean that God appeared to Abraham in the form of three men, although the LXX never uses *morphē* to speak of the form of God.

3. Jewish apocalyptic expected a transformation of the present world at some point in the future. According to *2 Bar.* 51:1, when that appointed day has passed, the appearance of sinners is transformed, so that those who have acted righteously appear glorified.

NT *morphē* and its cognates occur only rarely in the NT. *morphē* occurs only 3x. By and large the words in this group are confined to Paul's writings.

1. It is a matter of debate whether Phil. 2:6–11 forms a single unit and whether Paul incorporated into his letter an already existing hymn. Nevertheless, there is a virtual consensus that these verses do constitute a hymn about Christ in which the expressions *en morphē theou* ("in the form [NIV, very nature] of God") and *morphēn doulou* ("the form [NIV, very nature] of a servant") occur. The prep. *en* does not mean that the essential nature of Christ was different from the form, as if it were an outer shell or a part played by an actor. Rather, it means that the essential nature of Christ is defined as a divine nature, which is thought of as existing "in" divine substance and power.

Regarding this divine mode of existence, the hymn says that Christ existed in it in the past ("being," 2:6). The word used here for "being" (*hyparchō*) suggests Christ's preexistence prior to his incarnation. *en morphē theou* characterizes, therefore, that existence before his earthly life. But then he "emptied himself" (NIV, "made himself nothing"), taking the *morphēn doulou* ("form of a servant"). Some interpreters see this as a new form that replaced the "form of God," that is, that Christ's mode of being was essentially changed from a divine one to a human, servant one. Most evangelicals, however, regard Christ as adding on a human form (nature) without divesting himself of his divine form or nature. (For further comments, → *kenos, 3031*.)

Christ's new mode of existence in his earthly life is described as that of a "servant." This has been interpreted in various ways. According to some, Christ entered into a mode of existence that was under bondage and serfdom to the rule of cosmic powers and the elements of the world. It is perhaps best, however, to see this as a title of honor, corresponding to the Servant of the Lord in Isa. 53, who suffered on our behalf.

2. Phil. 3:21 contains the word *symmorphos*, in that Christ, by his power, will some day "transform" (on this word, → *schēma, 5386*) our bodies so that they "will be like his glorious body." The thought here is not that of clothing, in the sense that Christ covers over our essential character, but that of the essential transformation of the lowly body into a completely different glorified body. *symmorphos* does not mean becoming like, similar, or equal. Rather, it signifies an existence in Christ whose own mode of body permeates us without dissolving our own persons. Christ and ourselves are not sharply separated individuals according to the modern understanding of personality. We have our existence in the realm of the power of Christ.

In addition, Rom. 8:29 declares that "those God foreknew he also predestined to be conformed to the likeness (*symmorphous tēs eikonos*) of his Son, that he might be the firstborn among many brothers." This passage presupposes that Christ is the image of God, that in Christ God is really present. Again, *symmorphos* means here that we will not only be similar to or like Christ but that we will come into the same realm of power as he is in. We will be identified with the same substance and enter into the same essential nature as Christ. Nevertheless, within this relationship Christ retains separate identity ("the firstborn among many brothers"; cf. also 2 Cor. 3:18).

Phil. 3:10 relates the word *symmorphizō* to Christ's death: "I want to know Christ and the power of his resurrection and the fellowship of sharing in his sufferings, becoming like him (*symmorphizomenos*) in his death." The thought here is not that Paul might through martyrdom become like Jesus on the cross but that in his suffering he sees the death of Christ becoming a reality in his own death. The death of Christ acquires a *morphē* in the death of the apostle. The death of Jesus is not simply a historical datum of the past for Paul. It is a present event. Still, here too Paul and Christ remain two separate personalities.

3. In Gal. 4:19 Paul speaks of being "in the pains of childbirth until Christ is formed (aor. pass. of *morphoō*) in you." Paul's thought is that of coming into the world as a child comes into the world through conception and birth. Christ himself is to be formed in the Galatians in the reality of their being.

4. Rom. 2:20 refers to the Jew as "an instructor of the foolish . . . because you have in the law the embodiment (*morphōsis*) of knowledge and truth." This may be a reference to a Jewish work of propaganda that contained the word *morphōsis* in its title. Knowledge and truth are contained in the law and are really present in it.

5. The passages cited above may reflect the religious background of Gnosticism and the mystery cults, but that is not the case of the remaining passages. In 2 Tim. 3:5 Paul speaks of those "having a form (*morphōsis*) of godliness but denying its power." Here *morphōsis* means "appearance." The heretics are not really pious; they are only apparently devout.

6. In the longer ending of Mk. Jesus is reported to have appeared "in a different form (*morphē*)" (16:12). If, as seems likely, this refers to the incident recorded in Luke 24:13–32, the two people on the way to Emmaus did not recognize Jesus until he broke the bread. But Mark does not raise or answer the question as to how Jesus' form was in fact different from the pre-resurrection Christ.

See also *eidos*, form, outward appearance, sight (*1626*); *schēma*, outward appearance, form, shape (*5386*); *hypostasis*, substantial nature, essence, confidence (*5712*).

3672 (morphoō, form, shape), → *3671.*

3673 (morphōsis, embodiment, outward form, appearance), → *3671.*

3677 (mochthos, labor, hardship), → *3160.*

3679 (myeō, initiate, instruct), → *3696.*

3680	μῦθος	μῦθος (*mythos*), myth, story (*3680*).

CL & OT 1. (a) Homer uses *mythos* of any kind of speech and even of unspoken thought, a plan conceived in the mind. More particularly he uses this word of a story, whether true or false. In this usage there is no distinction between *mythos* and *logos* (→ *3364*). Gradually, however, a distinction appeared between *mythos*, fiction, and *logos*, factual narrative.

(b) When philosophical debate leads Plato so far on his quest that he cannot proceed further, the poet in Plato takes over and expresses in the form of an imaginative story or parable (*mythos*) the insight that is the goal of his quest. *mythos* was also a technical term in cl. Gk. for the plot of a tragedy or comedy. The *mythos* was a sacred story involving the gods, and the *drama* was the ritual enactment of the story.

2. The term *myth* has been frequently used in studies of the OT, esp. to describe what are perceived as religious rituals of Near Eastern culture adapted in the Heb. religious practices. But this word has nothing to do with the use of *mythos* in the LXX. In fact, *mythos* rarely occurs in the LXX, and only in the Apocr. In Sir. 20:19 an ungracious man is compared to "an inappropriate story [*mythos*] . . . on the lips of the ignorant." In Bar. 3:23 "the story-tellers [*mythologoi*] and the seekers for understanding have not learned the way to wisdom." The word here has its most general sense of story.

NT 1. In NT *mythos* is found only in the Pastoral Letters and 2 Pet., always in a disparaging sense. Timothy is told to forbid "certain men" at Ephesus from devoting "themselves to myths and endless genealogies" (1 Tim. 1:4). The context suggests a Jewish element in these myths (cf. a similar injunction in Tit. 3:9). Presumably the heresy here warned against was a mixture of Jewish and incipient gnostic speculation. The "godless myths and old wives' tales" of 1 Tim. 4:7 are probably of the same sort, as are the "myths" into which hearers with "itching ears" are led astray by false teachers (2 Tim. 4:3–4) or the "Jewish myths" that the Cretan Christians must be admonished to refuse to hear (Tit. 1:14).

These myths are subversive of sound faith and are set in contrast to "the truth." The gospel belongs to a different category. It is a record

of fact, for "we did not follow cleverly invented stories [*mythos*] when we told you about the power and coming of our Lord Jesus Christ, but we were eyewitnesses . . ." (2 Pet. 1:16).

2. The term *myth* became popular in NT studies with R. Bultmann's so-called program of demythologizing the NT. He felt that the gospel, if it is to make proper impact in contemporary society, must be freed from those features that belong to the worldview of the culture in which it was first preached: e.g., the three-stage universe (cf. Phil. 2:10), the concept of our world as open to invasion by transcendent powers, the preexistent Christ, his virgin birth, his historical resurrection, and the personal activity of the Holy Spirit. While his aim of making Christianity relevant in the modern world may have been noble, he had to deny much of what the Bible presents as fact, esp. anything miraculous. In our post-modern world, people are much more ready to accept the active intervention of God in the world of space and time.

Quite different is the approach of C. Williams, C. S. Lewis, and others, who maintain that in Christianity the ancient myths have come true; in other words, when God became a human being, as Lewis put it, "Myth became Fact," so that the aspirations and insights of the human soul that have from ancient times found mythological expression have been given a satisfying answer in the historical events of the gospel.

3683 (mylikos, belonging to a mill), → *3345.*

3684 (mylinos, belonging to a mill), → *3345.*

3685 (mylos, mill, millstone), → *3345.*

3693 (myron, ointment, perfume), → *5043.*

3696	μυστήριον	μυστήριον (*mystērion*), mystery, secret (*3696*); μυέω (*myeō*), initiate, instruct (*3679*).

CL & OT 1. (a) In cl. Gk. *mystērion* comes from *myō*, to shut (the mouth), and means that which must not or cannot be said. The pl. is almost exclusively a technical term for festivals such as those that took place in Eleusis from the 17th cent. B.C. on and were widespread during the Hel. period as the mysteries associated with Isis, Attis, Mithras, etc. grew. The mystery celebration gave a ceremonial and dramatic representation of the deity suffering and overcoming death. The initiated attained salvation and deification by sharing in the deity's fortunes through sacramental acts such as baptism, cultic feasts, and ceremonies of death and resurrection. The cultic acts and symbols were kept strictly secret. *myeō* meant originally to initiate into the mysteries and then took on the meaning of to instruct, teach.

(b) As early as Plato, ideas and terms from the mystery cults were transferred to philosophy. He describes the path of knowledge for immutable being as the path of true initiation. In later mystic philosophy, esp. in Neoplatonism, *mystērion* is that which by its very nature cannot be put into words. Mystic speech is the negation of speech.

(c) In Gnosticism the *mystēria* become secret revelations granted only to the "perfect" (*teleioi*), with a view to the redemption of their souls.

2. (a) In the LXX *mystērion* occurs only in later writings, i.e., those belonging to the Hel. period; the same is true of *apokalypsis*, revelation (→ *apokalyptō*, reveal, *636*), in its theological sense of the revelation of a mystery. In general the OT stresses that God's words and deeds in history are openly manifest in that they take place before the eyes of the whole world. Numerous passages demonstrate this. For example, God does not speak in secret (Isa. 45:19; 48:16). Amos 3:7 would likewise take issue with the concept of "mystery" in the mystery religions: "Surely the Sovereign LORD does nothing without revealing his plan to his servants the prophets."

(b) When *mystērion* does occur in the LXX, mystery terminology can sometimes refer to heathen cults (Wis. 14:23). Nevertheless, in 2:22; 6:22 the way to divine wisdom is described approvingly in terms of mysteries. But even here (6:22) the authentic OT note is still sounded in that the way of wisdom is faithfully and uncompromisingly set forth.

(c) Dan. uses the word *mystērion* in a definite theological sense, that of "eschatological secret," the vision of what God has decreed will take place in the future (2:28). When given in the form of a dream, it can be interpreted only by a Spirit-inspired seer (4:6, 18), for the revelation of mysteries belongs to God alone (2:28–29).

(d) In writings other than Wis. and Dan., *mystērion* occurs with secular meanings, such as the secret plans of a political leader (Tob. 12:7; Jdt. 2:2), military secrets (2 Macc. 13:21), or secrets shared among friends (Sir. 22:22; 27:16–17, 21).

3. The use of *mystērion* in Dan. serves as a transition to the special use of the term in intertestamental Jewish apocalyptic, where *mystēria* can denote eschatological events: e.g., the judgment and punishment of sinners (*1 Enoch* 38:3), the reward of the righteous (103:2–4), and the cosmic upheaval at the denouement of world history (83:7). Future events, insofar as they belong to the divine decrees, are present realities in the heavenly sphere and are revealed in vision to the apocalyptic seer. He knows even now about "the approach of the ages" (*2 Bar.* 81:4), and what must, of divine necessity, come to pass in the last days. But what he beholds remains a secret in that he may pass it on only in symbolic, oracular language and for the exclusive benefit of a given circle of initiates (2 Esd. 12:36–38).

4. (a) In rab. lit. there are also references to "secrets" in connection with the interpretation of the written and oral tradition. The secrets of the Torah reveal the inner workings of the Lawgiver's mind and, being also "the secrets of creation," throw light on his purposes for the world (cf. *3 Enoch* 11:1). Such secrets are part of an esoteric scheme of doctrine reminiscent of Gnosticism.

(b) In true apocalyptic tradition the Qumran texts speak of the secrets that God has prepared for humans, frequently in stereotyped association with wonders or miracles. The "wondrous secrets" are God's decrees, according to which, in strictly dualistic and predestinarian fashion, he has set apart one section of humankind, the sons of righteousness, for the way of light (1QS 3:20), and the other section, the sons of evil, for the way of darkness (3:21). Certain people are given the ability to interpret these mysteries. The secrets give information about God's purposes for the world from its beginning to its end: about his creation, his deeds in history, and cultic arrangements, interpreted along the lines of Qumran observance. All this is arrived at through a kind of spiritual exegesis of the written tradition, with correction and reinterpretation of existing prophecies.

NT In the NT *mystērion* is comparatively rare, occurring only 28x. It is significant that it is found most frequently (21x) in Paul, perhaps because it is here that the mystery cults and Gnosticism were most prominent. *mystērion* occurs in the pl. in Matt. 13:11; Lk. 8:10; 1 Cor. 4:1; 13:2; 14:2; everywhere else it is sing.

1. Mk. emphasizes that with Jesus, the kingdom of God has arrived (1:14–15). In 4:11, Jesus stresses that "the secret" of his kingdom and its appearing are expressed in his parables. The meaning of the parables, i.e., Christ's teaching as a whole, has to do with his way to the cross. Only this will usher God's kingdom into the world. One of the ideas basic to Mk.'s Gospel is that neither the people nor the disciples realized until after the resurrection that this way to the cross was according to God's will (cf. 3:35), even though the Twelve had received clear teaching on the matter (see 8:32–38; 9:31–32; 10:33–34). Only the evil spirits knew from the beginning that the turning point of the ages had come (1:24).

In Matt. 13:11 and Lk. 8:10 (the par. to Mk. 4:11), the pl. "secrets" is used. This pl. does not stress the messianic secret, but rather indicates that the decrees of God concerning Christ and his church, latent in the OT but now explainable to the disciples, are at last being fulfilled (cf. the frequent references to the fulfillment of OT

prophecies: e.g., Matt. 2:17, 23; 3:3). Christ's way of suffering and that of his church are a matter of divine necessity (24:26) and will issue in the glory of heaven (cf. 23:43; Acts 7:55).

2. The mystery with which Paul firmly confronts his opponents in 1 Cor. is that of the cross of Christ, revealing as it does God's redemptive decree for the world. Paul is concerned to set before humans only Jesus Christ and him crucified (1 Cor. 2:2; cf. 1:23). This is the essence of "the *mystērion* of God" (2:1; NIV reads *matryrion*, testimony [→ *matryria*, 3456], though *mystērion* is a well-attested variant). Although the apostle uses terminology of the "mystery" religions (*teleioi*, "perfect," NIV "mature," 2:6; *en mystēriō*, "in a mystery," NIV "secret," 2:7; *psychikos* "physical," NIV "without the Spirit," and *pneumatikos*, "spiritual," 2:14–15), he interprets this "mystery" in an eschatological manner.

Before the beginning of time God in his wisdom, through the prophets, predestined the cross of Christ to our glory, i.e., with a view to our glorification at the end of time (1 Cor. 2:7; cf. Rom. 16:25). That which has already been prepared in heaven and promised in OT prophecy has now taken place in time and history (1 Cor. 1:19 quotes Isa. 29:14; 1 Cor. 2:9 quotes Isa. 64:4). The rulers of this age have not known the secret of the divine decree (1 Cor. 2:6); but those who have been enlightened by the Spirit (2:12) now acknowledge it in humble submission. Paul is left speechless before its unfathomable depth (1:23; 2:3), yet his grasp of it is sufficient to bind him irresistibly to its service for life (9:16) and to rule out all boasting of self (1:31; 3:21).

Only thus, in weakness and humility, are the apostles, as servants of the crucified Christ, "entrusted with the secret things [*mystēria*] of God" (1 Cor. 4:1). They submit to the "administration [*oikonomia*, → 3873] of this mystery" (Eph. 3:9). Their sole ground of boasting is that in spite of all their weakness and insufficiency, God can still use them as instruments of his grace (1 Cor. 1:26–27; 2 Cor. 1:12).

3. In most cases, wherever *mystērion* occurs in the NT, it is found with vbs. denoting revelation or proclamation, i.e., the *mystērion* is something that is revealed. In a sense, it is no longer secret, for it is now being revealed; it may have been hidden in the past, but today it is something dynamic and compelling.

This is vividly expressed in Col. By his office Paul discloses (Col. 1:26) or proclaims the mystery of Christ (4:3). By bearing in his own body that which "is still lacking in regard to Christ's afflictions" (1:24), Paul gives practical expression to the "mystery" and carries it on toward its final consummation. The riches of the mystery (1:27) are summed up as "Christ in you, the hope of glory" i.e., the worldwide church with Christ as its head, having reconciled humanity to himself through his death (1:18, 20). This was concealed from earlier generations (1:26), but now people have been appointed to proclaim it to all (1:28), so that all may share in the power of the firstborn from the dead (1:18) and be incorporated into his resurrection body (1:28).

In Eph. also the mystery of Christ is essentially the fact that through Christ the Gentiles have been given access to the Father of all creation (3:15; cf. 2:18; also Rom. 16:25). They are members of the worldwide church of Jews and Gentiles, described in Eph. 1:22–23 as a body whose "head" is the pivot of all creation and in 2:20–21 as a building whose "chief cornerstone" is Jesus Christ. This mystery was God's will before time began (3:9; cf. 1:9) and was all part of his great purpose and plan (3:6). It was kept secret in the past, but now, since the time is fulfilled (1:10), God has made known his will to those who proclaim the gospel (3:8), that through them his purpose may come to fulfillment (1:9–10). This mystery is now being proclaimed throughout the whole world, though it is meeting with much opposition along the way (6:19).

The only other Christological passage with the word *mystērion* is 1 Tim. 3:9, 16, where the "deep truths [*mystērion*] of the faith" and "the mystery [*mystērion*] of godliness [*or* our religion]" both refer to the confession of Christ and his redeeming work; i.e., *mystērion* here is a paraphrase for a formulated confession of faith.

4. The same divine economy that directs the course of history toward its predestined goal also concerns itself with the destiny of Israel. In Rom. 11:1 the apostle is appalled at the thought that God may have rejected his people, even though their present hardness of heart might lend color to the idea. Against all the dictates of reason and experience (11:9–19, 25a), he unfolds "the mystery" of God's final acceptance of his chosen people. Israel has been stricken with blindness only for a limited period, in order that the gospel may have free course among the Gentiles and that their fullness (*plērōma*; → *pleroō*, to fulfill, *4444*) may come in. Believing Gentiles, knowing that they are now God's elect people, are to respond not with pride or arrogance but with reverent, adoring fear (11:20). They are also to be humbled by the fact that the Jews who at present are hard of heart will one day be saved. Truly the mystery of free grace is unfathomable (11:33–36)!

5. (a) In 1 Cor. 14 Paul warns against too high an estimation of speaking with tongues. In his judgment it is subordinate to preaching, for to outsiders it is not intelligible of itself and does not serve to build up the church (14:2, 16). The "mysteries" uttered in ecstatic, unintelligible sounds need to be interpreted (14:13), and in any case no such ecstatic experience of divine mysteries can bear comparison with love (13:2).

(b) Paul writes 1 Cor. 15:51 in the light of the imminence of Christ's Parousia. He reveals to the Corinthians "a mystery," namely, that on the day of resurrection, which is imminent, all those still living will be changed into imperishable bodies (cf. Phil. 3:20–21).

(c) In Eph. 5:32 Paul uses *mystērion* with reference to his interpretation of Gen. 2:24, that ultimately it refers to the relationship between Christ and his church. The apostle's phrase "I am talking about" excludes other interpretations.

(d) The context of 2 Thess. 2:7 deals with the events that are to precede the Parousia. Before Christ returns, there will come a period of apostasy, in which the "man of lawlessness" will gain the upper hand (2:3–4). At present there is a power that hinders his appearing, but already "the secret power [*mystērion*] of lawlessness" is working and the day of Antichrist is dawning (2:7).

6. In Rev. *mystērion* is used for apocalyptic events that, occurring in a time of distress, will precede the return of the Lord. These mysteries are presented in the form of OT symbols and metaphors that require interpretation. But God reveals them to his church through the mouth of the prophets (10:7) and through Jn., the seer (17:7; cf. 1:9). The victory is God's (18:2; 19:6), and this knowledge comforts his church as it passes through severe affliction and persecution.

Rev. 1:20 introduces the seven letters by referring to the "mystery" of the seven churches and their angels. As the mystery unfolds, these churches are enlightened as to their true standing in the eyes of God, who sees through all pretense of virtue and goodness, and they are exhorted to repent.

3701 (mōrainō, make foolish, pass. be foolish), → 3702.

| 3702 μωρία |

μωρία (*mōria*), foolishness, folly (*3702*); μωραίνω (*mōrainō*), make foolish, pass. be foolish (*3701*); μωρός (*mōros*), foolish, stupid (*3704*); μωρολογία (*mōrologia*), foolish talk (*3703*); ἄφρων (*aphrōn*), foolish, senseless (*933*); ἀφροσύνη (*aphrosynē*), lack of sense, folly, foolishness (*932*).

CL & OT 1. (a) In cl. Gk. *mōros* means foolish, stupid; *mōria*, foolishness; and *mōrainō*, to be foolish, act foolishly, make foolish. The word group denotes inappropriate behavior, thought, or speech, both of single lapses as well as a permanent attribute. It is concerned equally with lack of knowledge and lack of discernment. Sometimes these words are used for a state of mental derangement or for one's behavior when acting under the influence of one's desires.

(b) *aphrōn*, senseless, foolish, and *aphrosynē*, lack of sense, foolishness, indicate lack of insight and reason, esp. deficient perception of value and truth.

2. (a) The Heb. words for fool, foolish, and folly (from *kāsal*) are usually rendered in the LXX by *aphrōn* (used 134x total in the LXX) or *aphrosynē* (36x). *nābāl*, also common, is rendered by *aphrōn* mainly in Job and Ps., but by *mōros* in Deut. and Isa. The instances based on *nābāl* are unequivocal in insisting that foolishness is not lack of knowledge but rebellion against God. Hence, a fool is one who denies God, a blasphemer (cf. Ps. 14:1; 53:1; Isa. 32:5–6; Sir. 50:26). Such a person also destroys fellowship with other humans (see Ps. 39:8; Isa. 32:6; Jer. 17:11).

(b) For the Qumran community the one who remains outside the fellowship is counted a fool (CD 15:15). Wisdom and folly lie struggling together in the human heart (1QS 4:24). Folly is listed as one of the major sins (4:9–11), which will be annihilated at the end of time (4:12–14).

NT In the NT the *aphrōn* word group is found 15x, whereas the *mōria* group numbers 22x. The latter occur esp. in Matt. and in Paul's letters.

1. *Synoptic Gospels.* (a) The picture of salt becoming insipid (*mōrainō*, Matt. 5:13; Lk. 14:34) may have its background in Jesus' promise that the gospel, like salt, must never lose its force. The saying is shaped as a warning to take care that we do not let the gospel become insipid in our lives.

(b) The meaning of the term of abuse "you fool [*mōros*]!" in Matt. 5:22 is disputed (see also *rhaka, 4819*). The best interpretation still appears to be the association of this word with the word "godless" (cf. Matt. 23:17).

(c) *mōros* is used in parables by Matt. as an opposite to *phronimos*, wise (7:24–27; 25:1–13; → *phroneō*, to think, *5858*). Here, too, the associated sense deriving from the OT plays a role: Foolishness is not stupidity but rebellion against God. People prove themselves foolish when they decline God's offer and fall into judgment. Obedience is the prudence of believers (cf. the parable of the rich fool, *aphrōn*, Lk. 12:20).

2. *Paul's letters.* (a) Paul uses *mōria* and *mōros* to characterize the preaching of the cross over against the wisdom of the world, which rejects the cross of Christ (1 Cor. 1:23); in Corinth this is part of the theology of the Corinthian spiritual party, which despised the lowliness of the apostle. To Paul, God has turned this sort of wisdom into foolishness through Christ's death on the cross (1:20; 3:19; see also *sophia*, wisdom, *5053*).

The preaching of the cross, which appears so foolish, is in fact foolish merely from a worldly standpoint. After all, where else is power best displayed in weakness? Paul, therefore, contradicts the Corinthian spiritual party by explaining that the "foolishness [*mōron*] of God [i.e., his freely chosen way of dealing with the world in the cross of Christ] is wiser than man's wisdom, and the weakness of God is stronger than man's strength" (1 Cor. 1:25). To share in the folly of degradation of the cross means to share in the power of God (1:18), for God's "power is made perfect in weakness" (2 Cor. 12:9). This is why Paul can offer the paradoxical advice that one should become foolish in order to become wise (1 Cor. 3:18) and why he can call himself and the apostles "fools for Christ" (4:10).

(b) Paul uses *aphrōn* and *aphrosynē* in 2 Cor. 11–12 to define his boasting, which he feels forced into because of his opponents, who wished to be wise (*phronimos*, 11:19; cf. 11:1, 16–17, 21; 12:11 for *aphrōn* and *aphrosynē*). If it is appropriate, in a foolish way, to boast, the apostle can go along with them; but he decides to boast of his weakness (2 Cor. 11:30; 12:9).

(c) Paul calls on the believers in Ephesus not to be foolish but to inquire after the will of the Lord (Eph. 5:17). *aphrōn* stands here close to *asophoi*, unwise (5:15); obviously Christians should guard themselves from undisciplined behavior. In 5:4 Paul warns the believers to avoid "foolish talk" (*mōrologia*), which is out of place for them.

(d) In 2 Tim. 2:23 Paul warns against "foolish [*mōros*] and stupid arguments," that is, unprofitable discussions over hair-splitting minutiae such as genealogies and the law (Tit. 3:9), which only lead to senseless quarrels.

3. In 1 Pet. 2:15 Peter urges the congregation, by its good deeds, to "silence the ignorant talk of foolish men" and so to do God's will.

See also *sophia*, wisdom (*5053*); *philosophia*, love of wisdom, philosophy (*5814*).

3703 (*mōrologia*, foolish talk), → *3702*.

3704 (*mōros*, foolish, stupid), → *3702*.

3707	Μωϋσῆς

Μωϋσῆς (*Mōysēs*), Moses (*3707*).

OT 1. The Gk. form of the name *Moses* (from the LXX on) perhaps originates from Egyptian sources. The Bible describes this man's life in great detail. He lived 120 years (Deut. 34:7), forty years each in Egypt, Arabia, and the desert (cf. Acts 7:23, 30, 36).

2. The book of Exod. sets Moses' birth in the context of the history of the Israelites, who went to Egypt during a famine and remained there after Joseph's death. Whereas they had once been favored on his account, "a new king, who did not know about Joseph, came to power in Egypt" (1:8). Fearing the growth of this nation, this king subjected them to slavery, forcing them to work on the store cities of Pithom and Rameses (1:11). When Moses was born, there was a decree commanding the death of all male Israelites at birth (1:16, 22). Moses, however, was saved by being hidden in a basket among the reeds along the bank of the Nile and by being found and adopted by Pharaoh's daughter (2:1–10). His name is explained in 2:10 from the vb. *māšâ*, draw out, for she said, "I drew him out of the water." His own mother served as his nurse.

As a young man, Moses killed an Egyptian beating a fellow Israelite and then fled for his life to Midian in the Arabian Peninsula (Exod. 2:11–15), where he adopted a nomadic way of life, marrying Zipporah, the daughter of Reuel or Jethro (cf. 2:18 with 3:1), a priest of Midian; she bore Moses a son, Gershom (2:16–22). When Yahweh heard the groaning of his people in Egypt (2:23–25), he revealed himself to Moses in the theophany of the burning bush at Horeb, the mountain of God, declaring his name and commissioning Moses to lead his people out of Egypt "into the land of the Canaanites, Hittites, Amorites, Perizzites, Hivites and Jebusites—a land flowing with milk and honey" (3:17).

Initially Moses was to ask Pharaoh to let the people go three days' journey into the desert to sacrifice to Yahweh. When Moses hesitated to assume this daunting task, he was given signs (Exod. 4:1–9) and was permitted to let Aaron, his brother, be his spokesman (4:10–17). Moses returned to Egypt and, together with Aaron, delivered Yahweh's call to the people of Israel, who responded in faith (4:27–31). They then confronted Pharaoh with the request to let the people go into the desert to sacrifice to Yahweh. Pharaoh responded by doubling the burdens of the Israelites (5:1–23). Then follows the ten great plagues sent on Egypt (7:14–12:30). The final one was the slaying of every firstborn son throughout Egypt (11:1–12:30), though Israelite families were spared as they celebrated the Passover for the first time (12:1–28). At this point Pharaoh relented and the exodus commenced (12:31–42).

The Israelites were guided by a pillar of cloud by day and a pillar of fire by night. After the miraculous crossing of the Red (or Reed) Sea, the people headed out into the desert. They frequently grumbled for want of food and water; they were supplied with quail and manna (Exod. 16) and with water from a struck rock (17:1–7). The Israelites eventually arrived at Mount Sinai, where Moses and the people prepared to receive a fresh revelation (19:1–13). They received the Ten Commandments (19:14–20:17) and various other laws for the community (21:1–23:33), and Moses renewed the covenant between Yahweh and Israel (24:1–18). Details of the tabernacle and its contents were given to Moses by God (25:1–31:18).

While Moses was with Yahweh on Mount Sinai, the people turned back to the worship of other gods, symbolized in the golden calf made by Aaron, which Moses destroyed after his return from Mount Sinai (Exod. 32). Moses' indignation led him to break the tablets of the law (32:19). Moses went back up the mountain, where Yahweh revealed his glory to Moses, though he was not allowed to see the Lord's face directly (33:12–23), and then renewed the tablets of the law (34:1–4). When Moses returned, he covered his shining face with a veil (34:28–35). The rest of Exod. tells how Moses superintended the building of the tabernacle (35:1–40:38).

In Num. 1:1–54 Moses is charged with numbering the people; 2:1–34 gives their camping and marching orders. In 10:11, the journey to the promised land continues. When the Israelites arrived at its border, spies were sent out, the majority of which inspired fear into the people that they would not be able take the land because of its walled cities and giants. As a result the people sought to return to Egypt. The Lord punished this rebellious nation by requiring them to wander in the desert for forty years until that unbelieving generation had died (13:1–14:35). Num. records several other rebellions by the Israelites, plus the abortive attempt of Balak to make Balaam curse Israel (22:1–24:25).

Deut. is presented as the renewal of the covenant with the Lord as the Israelites are once again on the border of Canaan. Deut. concludes with Moses' song (32:1–43), blessing (33:2–29), and death (34:1–12). He is permitted to see the promised land from Mount Pisgah, but not to enter it (34:4) because of his sin at Meribah (Num. 20:12). Deut. concludes with the declaration: "Since then, no prophet has arisen in Israel like Moses, whom the LORD knew face to face, who did all those miraculous signs and wonders . . ." (34:10–11).

The authorship of the Pentateuch has traditionally been ascribed to Moses, except of course the account of his own death. However, only the following passages are explicitly ascribed to him: the historical and legal narrative of Deut. 1:1–31:23, the song of Moses (32:1–43), and the blessing of Moses (33:1–29; cf. also Ps. 90). Note too the places where Moses writes what God tells him to write: Exod. 17:14; 20:1–17; 24:4, 7; Num. 33:2; Deut. 31:9.

3. In the Hel. world, information about Moses is found almost without exception in anti-Jewish utterances. Moses was regarded as lawgiver, organizer of the nation, and founder of the Jewish state, its capital, and temple. He was seen as the scorner of every cult or as a magician and a deceiver—his name was often used in magical formulas. Hecataeus and Posidonius alone spoke of Moses in terms of admiration.

Hel. Jud. produced its apologies in reply. Since the Hel. world regarded Egyptian culture as the most ancient, the apologists attributed this to the patriarchs and also extolled Moses as the discoverer of writing. Various other legends grew up surrounding Moses.

4. Throughout Palestinian Jud. Moses was the revealer without equal. For the rabbis, the prophets were simply the bearers of the oral tradition that Moses had received at Sinai, as were their successors, the scribes or teachers of the law (Matt. 23:2). Moses and his age were counted as the pattern of the messianic age, with a second exodus marking the inauguration of salvation. As Moses suffered, so also the redeemer will suffer. Moses was also named and celebrated as a lawgiver of Israel at Qumran.

NT Moses is the most frequently mentioned OT figure in the NT (80x; Abraham, 73x). Jesus shook the foundations of contemporary Jud. by coming forward as a revealer like Moses—not as his interpreter, as the OT prophets had been—preaching and living in the name of the final arrival of the kingdom of God. The NT tradition presents the relationship between Moses and Christ in differing ways.

1. *Mark.* Moses is recognized as lawgiver (Mk. 1:44). His law establishes the resurrection of the dead, contra the Sadducees (12:19, 26), and the commandment of Exod. 20:12, as against scribal tradition (Mk. 7:10–11; note that in 7:14–15 Jesus reveals his own new authority). At the transfiguration, Elijah and Moses appear; they had both

suffered (as did Jesus) under the hatred of their own people (9:4–5). Peter misunderstands the heavenly appearance, thinking that it is an earthly one and that the new period in the desert has begun, since Moses, Elijah, and the Messiah are here united.

2. *Matthew* sees a close correspondence between Jesus and Moses. Just as the Israelites were called out of Egypt, so was Jesus (cf. Matt. 2:15 with Hos. 11:1; → *plēroō, 4444*). Jesus stayed in the desert for forty days without food and drink, as did Moses on Mount Sinai (Matt. 4:1–2; cf. Exod. 34:28). Above all, Jesus is the new lawgiver (cf. Matt. 5:1 with Exod. 19–20), who, like Moses, dispenses blessings (Matt. 5:3–11) as well as curses (23:13–36). The Mosaic teaching office of the scribes is recognized (23:2–3) but at the same time superseded in that, under the guidance of Jesus, one is to display a better righteousness than that of the Pharisees (5:17–20).

3. *Luke* sees Jesus' connection with Moses as given in the function of the prophet. Acts 3:22 and 7:37 quote Deut. 18:15 (cf. 18:18): "a prophet like me [Moses]." As Moses was mighty both in word and deed (Acts 7:22), so Jesus was a mighty prophet before God and the people (Lk. 24:19; cf. 4:24; 7:16; 13:33). Like Moses, Jesus gives a share in his power and Spirit (10:1, 17–19) to his disciples, to the seventy-two, and to the whole church. Just as Moses suffered (Acts 7:25–29) and was disowned by the people, even though God had sent him as a ruler and redeemer (7:35), so Jesus had to be consigned to death by the chief priests and teachers of the law and raised by God to be ruler (Lk. 24:27, 44; cf. Acts 26:22; 28:23). Thus anyone who does not listen to Moses and the prophets will also not believe the one whom God resurrected (Lk. 16:29–31).

Despite accusations to the contrary, Stephen (Acts 6:11–14) and Paul (21:20–21; cf. also 18:18; 21:24–29) did not preach a regression from the customs of Moses. In fact, freedom from the requirement of circumcision was demanded by Paul, with Peter's concurrence, only for the non-Jews (15:1–21; cf. 16:3). But the righteousness of faith, which Jesus gives as a gift, Moses' law cannot bring (13:38).

4. *Paul* places Moses and Christ in antithesis to one another. As lawgiver (Rom. 5:14; 1 Cor. 9:9), Moses gives only the letter. The one who fulfills the righteousness of the law will live by it (Rom. 10:5), but true righteousness can only come by faith (10:6). Moses' "ministry that brought death" possesses only a fading glory (2 Cor. 3:7; cf. Gal. 3:17–25). By way of contrast, the "ministry that brings righteousness" (2 Cor. 3:9) possesses the Spirit and a permanent glory. To this day the Jews have a "veil" over their hearts "when Moses is read" (3:15). But the new Israel beholds the glory of the Lord "with unveiled faces" and is transformed from one degree of glory to another. All this comes from the Lord, who is the Spirit (3:17–18). If Jews open their hearts to the Lord, the veil will disappear (3:16), and Moses will be recognized as a witness to the true righteousness of God.

God chooses solely on the basis of his promise, not on the basis of human zeal (Rom. 9:15–16). Indeed, the calling of the Gentiles shows that Israel's law creates no privilege in God's sight (10:19). Baptism into Moses was a promise, not a natural law. Those baptized did indeed receive the gifts of the Spirit, but since they did not remain within the promise, they perished (1 Cor. 10:2–5).

5. *John* stands starkly opposed to Jud. The teaching of Jesus comes directly from God (Jn. 7:15); anyone who wants to do God's will should know that his teaching is from God (7:17). Yet none of the Jews truly keep the law, for they base their lives on its letter and not, as the law itself demands, on God and his revealer (7:19). In the end, Moses' law is surpassed by Jesus (1:17).

The people rightly recognize that Jesus is the promised prophet (Jn. 6:14), but in trying to make him king they fail to understand that his kingdom is not of this world (6:15; 18:36). The leaders of the people call themselves Moses' disciples, but in untruth (9:28–33). Jesus is the true bread of life, while those who ate the bread Moses gave them died (6:32–35, 48–51). Likewise, Moses lifted up the serpent in the desert to preserve people's earthly lives, but when Jesus is "lifted up," everyone who believes in him will have *eternal* life (3:14–15).

6. *Hebrews* stresses that the pattern given by Moses has been surpassed and fulfilled in Christ. Jesus' faithfulness is greater than Moses', because he, as the Son, came from God's high heaven and is not merely, like Moses, a servant in God's house (Heb. 3:2–6). Jesus is the high priest in the heavenly sanctuary, which Moses once saw and after which he patterned an earthly copy (8:5). The church of Christ is not led to Mount Sinai, which terrified Moses and the people with its fire, smoke, lightning, and thunder (12:18–19). Rather, we can approach the Lord with confidence. Yet we must not refuse him who is speaking (12:25), for judgment awaits those who spurn God. Moses is pictured in 11:23–29 as a pattern for faith, even in suffering.

7. There are three final isolated references in the NT to Moses. In Rev. 15:3 the passing through the sea is a pattern for the deliverance of the saints from suffering in the last days. Jude 9 is based on post-OT traditions preserved in the apocryphal *Assumption of Moses*, which said that Satan fought with Michael over the body of Moses. In 2 Tim. 3:8, Jannes and Jambres are the names tradition assigned to the Egyptian magicians who imitated Moses' miracle of turning a staff into a serpent (cf. Exod. 7:11).

N *nu*

<table>
<tr><td>3716</td><td>Ναζαρηνός</td></tr>
</table>

Ναζαρηνός (*Nazarēnos*), Nazarene, from Nazareth (*3716*); Ναζωραῖος (*Nazōraios*), Nazarene, from Nazareth (*3717*).

NT 1. Since many in the 1st cent. had the name *Jesus* (→ *Iēsous*, *2652*), it was necessary to distinguish among them with an additional appellation. Thus, Jesus is sometimes called in the Gospels "the son ... of Joseph" (Lk. 3:23; 4:22; Jn. 1:45; 6:42) or even "Mary's son" (Mk. 6:3, evidently after Joseph's death). In addition the designation of Jesus as *Nazarēnos* or *Nazōraios* achieved importance and lasting significance. In the NT textual tradition these two words are sometimes given as alternates. This compels the conclusion that the writers and copiers saw no difference in meaning between them.

2. (a) Mk. consistently uses *Nazarēnos* (1:24; 10:47; 14:67; 16:6). Lk. 4:34 no doubt depends on Mk. 1:24 with its *Nazarēnos*; otherwise, Luke (except for Lk. 24:19) consistently uses *Nazōraios* (18:37; Acts 2:22; 3:6; 4:10; 6:14; 22:8; 26:9) and by this procedure expresses the fact that for him the two words mean the same. Matt. (2:23; 26:71) and Jn. (18:5, 7; 19:19) have only *Nazōraios*. Neither word occurs anywhere else in the NT. In most of these uses, the writers are communicating that Jesus came from Nazareth in Galilee.

(b) As a term to denote Christians in Gk. areas (Acts 24:5), *Nazōraios* ("the Nazarene sect") seems to have disappeared early in favor of *Christianos* (11:26), while it was retained in this sense in Jewish areas and survives today in Heb. *noṣrî* as a designation for one who believes in Jesus.

3. A word needs to be said about "Nazarene" in Matt. 2:23. Matt. sees Jesus' being brought up in Nazareth as a fulfillment of "what was said through the prophets: 'He will be called a Nazarene.'" Note first that there is no specific prophecy to this effect in any single OT text. But it seems clear from Jn. 1:46 ("Can anything good come from [Nazareth]?") that the town of Nazareth had undertones of dissociation and contempt (cf. 7:42, 52). There are several OT passages that clearly prophesy that the coming Messiah would be a man of contempt and lowliness (e.g., Ps. 22:6–8; 69:8, 20–21; Isa. 49:7; 53:2–3). Thus, the town of Jesus' upbringing led to the fulfillment of such prophecies, for he was considered without status or prestige in the surrounding world.

See also *Iēsous*, Jesus (*2652*); *Christos*, Christ (*5986*); *Christianos*, Christian (*5985*).

3717 (*Nazōraios*, Nazarene, from Nazareth), → *3716*.

<table>
<tr><td>3724</td><td>ναός</td></tr>
</table>

ναός (*naos*), temple, shrine, sanctuary (*3724*).

CL & OT 1. (a) The noun *naos* originally meant a dwelling, esp. the dwelling of a god, a temple, or the innermost area of such. In the Hel. period heaven, as the dwelling of the gods, could also be described as *naos*. *naos* must consequently be distinguished from *temenos* (cf. Lat. *templum*, Eng. *temple*), which is older in terms of religious history but is not found in the NT. This word meant a space fenced in, or at least clearly marked, as being an area where a theophany once occurred and was expected again on the ground of tradition. It was usually a place marked out by nature: e.g., a grotto, rock cleft, or holy grove. In the special place, not made by human hands, the god appeared as a revealer, healer, or giver of fertility, though he did not dwell there.

(b) For the sake of clarity *naos* can thus be translated temple. Such temples are found, in the earliest days of human buildings, in various forms, such as temple towers, pillared temples, round temples, and even portable ones.

2. In the LXX *naos* is used 61x, 55 of which translate the Heb. *hêkāl*, palace, temple. As a building constructed as a dwelling for the gods, it is used for sacrifice, worship of the gods (idols), and oracles, and hence it requires a local priesthood. In 1 Chr. 28:11; 2 Chr. 8:12; 15:8; 29:7, 17, *naos* designates the temple porch.

(a) Even in the OT one may observe a distinct reserve in the use of the term *hêkāl*. The tower of Babel (Gen. 11), the places where the Philistines sacrificed (Jdg. 16:23–30), and the shrines at Bethel and Dan are never called by this word. The OT refers much more often to the temple by means of the simple Heb. term *bayit* (Gk. *oikos*), house. When religious sites are in view, only Solomon's edifice in Jerusalem (1 Ki. 6–7), and before that the shrine at Shiloh (1 Sam. 1:9; 3:3), from which the ark of the covenant was finally brought to Jerusalem (2 Sam. 6), are described as *hêkāl*.

(b) Whereas the OT thus uses its terminology to distinguish true worship from false, the LXX (except for Ps. 45:15) never uses *naos* where the Heb. *hêkāl* means palace; it uses *oikos* instead (e.g., 2 Ki. 20:18; Isa. 13:22). Thus, *naos* becomes a purely cultic term for the true temple of God. After the desecration of the temple in Jerusalem by Nebuchadnezzar, the ruins are never called *naos* (cf. Ezr. 6:5). In Ps. 45:15, where the king's palace is called *naos*, the LXX seems to have adopted a symbolic interpretation of this ancient love song: The community is Yahweh's bride.

Ps. tends to focus attention on the temple not so much as a place of sacrifice and hence of the priesthood, but as the place above all others that is longed for (27:4), to which a cry for help (28:2) or an individual's worship is directed (5:7; 138:2), and hence where comfort (65:4), God's response (18:6), and God's might (68:28–29) can be found.

(c) In postexilic times, rather than being a national sanctuary, the temple gained a new significance for the prayers of the faithful, and as the symbol of the nation's longing it also became the sign of the new thing promised by God. This new view may have arisen because of the dangers that were apparent in the false sense of security that the preexilic Israelites saw in the existence of the Jerusalem temple. We cannot draw this distinction absolutely, however, for even before the exile, the temple was used for the prayers of the faithful, and after the exile sacrifices were offered there. Note also the high estimation of God's house to which the design of the new temple in Ezek. 40–43, the work of Hag., and the books of Macc. bear witness. The splendor of the new building erected by Herod the Great mainly between 19 and 9 B.C. was also an object of pride.

Yet as early as the 2d cent. B.C. a group of priests separated themselves from the temple because they regarded it as polluted by sin (CD 1:5–11). In doing so they clearly continued the prophetic tradition of criticism of the cult, and they founded in the desert of the Dead Sea at Qumran a community that regarded itself as the true sanctuary of God (cf. 1QS 8:5; 9:6). The place of the Jerusalem cultus was now taken by the chosen community, which lived in strict obedience to the Torah, awaiting the revelation of God's righteousness.

NT In the NT *naos* is found most frequently in Rev. (16x) and Paul (8x). The Synoptics use it for the most part only in the passion narrative (16x; esp. Matt., 9x), and the Johannine writings (apart from Jn. 2:19–21) do not use it at all.

1. Paul stands clearly on the basis of Jewish tradition when he speaks of the *naos*: The redeemed community is the temple of God (1 Cor. 3:16–17), and God's Spirit dwells in her (6:19; cf. 1 Ki. 8:16–17, where God's name dwells in the temple). If, however, the church allows itself to be led astray, the adversary dwells within her (2 Thess.

2:4). To be the community in which God makes his dwelling implies separation from the ungodly (2 Cor. 6:16). In Eph. 2:21 this concept is developed further.

In Acts 17:24 Paul declares to the Athenians that "the God who made the world and everything in it is the Lord of heaven and earth and does not live in temples [*naos*] built by hands." Acts 19:24 refers to "a silversmith named Demetrius, who made silver shrines [*naos*] of Artemis," which brought much business to Ephesus; he accused Paul of turning many people away by his preaching and teaching (19:26). Here *naos* refers to pagan temples.

2. The return to the language of the OT and Jud. is clearly evident in Rev. Those who conquer will be preserved and will adorn the heavenly temple (3:12; cf. Ps. 144:12). Indeed, just as Ezekiel's temple was measured (Ezek. 40–42), so the eschatological community will be (Rev. 11:1–2). The Apocalypse speaks often of the heavenly temple (7:15; 11:19; 14:15–17; 15:5–8; 16:1, 17). Yet in 21:22 it is expressly stated that in the new Jerusalem there will no longer be a *naos*, since God himself will be the temple for the community. God himself is the dwelling place of his people; the community and the temple are coextensive (21:3). Thus the central idea of the covenant promise "I will be your God, and you will be my people" will be fulfilled (→ *diathēkē*, covenant, *1347*).

3. (a) In contrast to Paul and Rev., the Synoptics use *naos* with reference to the Jerusalem temple, which will be subject to eschatological criticism (cf. the destruction of the temple in A.D. 70, Mk. 11:15–17; 13:1–2) or at least in need of purification (Lk. 19:45–48). True, the Synoptic writers speak mostly of the *hieron* (→ *2639*), but in several passages that reveal the influence of the OT they also use *naos*, temple. In Mk. 14:58 special importance is attached to a saying attributed to Jesus that he would destroy the temple and build it in three days (cf. Jn. 2:18–21); this statement (which presumably showed disrespect for the temple) was used as false evidence against him during his trial.

In Mk. 15:29, however, the saying is taken up by the mockers at the foot of the cross, and its secret meaning is revealed. It is not a matter of saving the physical body of Jesus, but rather of God's new creation, before which the old must pass away, i.e., a matter of death and resurrection. In keeping with this Matt., in his polemic against the Pharisees, attacks with particular severity the Jewish practice of swearing by the temple (Matt. 23:16–21): God does not want casuistry, but honesty and obedience.

(b) Luke places the temple in the setting of the history of salvation. The period before Jesus was a period of priestly service in the temple (*naos*), as Lk. 1:9, 21–22 illustrate with the narrative about Zechariah. It is true that Jesus repeatedly went to the temple (cf. Lk. 20–21) in order to teach there; but he kept to the outer courts (*hieron*), which were open to all Israelites, as did also the early Christian church at first (Acts 3:1–10, etc.). Not surprisingly Lk. also gives the greatest prominence to Jesus' teaching in the synagogues, where all Jews could assemble. This practice was continued in Acts, insofar as the apostles typically began their preaching in the synagogue.

See also *hieron*, temple (*2639*).

3738	νεκρός

νεκρός (*nekros*), dead, dead person (*3738*); νεκρόω (*nekroō*), put to death (*3739*); νέκρωσις (*nekrōsis*), death, deadness (*3740*).

CL & OT 1. As a noun *nekros* means dead person, corpse; as an adj., dead. The vb. *nekroō*, kill, put to death (more often used passively, die) and the noun *nekrōsis*, the process of dying or the state of being dead, are Hel. forms from the medical sphere; they indicate the mortification of a part of the body because of illness.

2. Stoic writers use *nekros* esp. in a fig. sense. They distinguish three criteria: (a) What is *nekros* is what is not controlled by the *psychē*, soul, or *nous*, mind. (b) *nekros* is the physical part of humans, i.e., the *sōma*, body—the part that one has in common with the animal world and that separates one from what is divine. (c) *nekros* describes that which does not accord with one's own standards of judgment, determined by *nous*. In sum, whatever does not come under the control of *nous* is dead.

3. In the LXX *nekros* occurs about 60x, both as a noun and as an adj. It usually means one who has died, a dead person, a corpse. It is consistently used of people who are in the state of death (e.g., Abraham's wife, Gen. 23:3–15). The dead are to be buried (Tob. 2:8; 12:12); it is regarded as a terrible punishment if they are left uncovered, to be eaten by animals (Deut. 28:26; Jer. 7:33; 19:7).

Num. 19 draws a boundary between the sphere of death and that of life. Those who come directly or indirectly in contact with the dead are unclean, i.e., separated from Yahweh. The dead know and see nothing (Eccl. 9:5; Isa. 26:14; cf. Ps. 88:4–5). God has no more dealings with them (88:10), and they do not praise him (115:17 = LXX 113:25). There is no hope for them (143:3; Wis. 13:10), and so "a live dog is better off than a dead lion" (Eccl. 9:4). This marks off Israel's religion sharply from the cult of the dead and the oracles of the dead that were so common in the surrounding world. Not until the exile do we find the clear beginnings of a hope for resurrection. This hope at first takes the form of a confidence that even death cannot separate from Yahweh (cf. Isa. 26:19; Sir. 48:5; cf. also Ezek. 37:9).

4. The lit. of Qumran does not depart from OT usage. But in rab. lit. a metaphorical use is occasionally found. The ungodly can be described as dead. In the Eighteen Benedictions mention is made of God, "who makes the dead to live."

NT 1. In the NT *nekros*, dead person, corpse, occurs 129x, both as an adj. and as a noun. *nekroō*, kill, is found 3x (Rom. 4:19; Col. 3:5; Heb. 11:12); *nekrōsis*, death, putting to death, occurs only at Rom. 4:19 and 2 Cor. 4:10. In Rom. 4:19 Paul makes use of the latter two words to indicate the ending of Abraham's and Sarah's capacity to have children (cf. Heb. 11:12). In 2 Cor. 4:10 *nekrōsis tou Iēsou*, the "death [dying] of Jesus," which the apostle speaks of carrying about in his own body, refers to the symptoms of a loss of strength and suffering marked by death. It is, as it were, a sharing in the passion of Christ that takes place in this life.

2. The NT use of *nekros* differs from both cl. Gk. usage and the OT. Death is no longer a final state for humans but must be viewed in the light of Jesus' resurrection. No less than 75x *nekros* is the obj. of *egeirō*, awaken, *anastasis*, resurrection, or cognate words. In addition to this are combinations with such words as *zōopoieō*, make alive (e.g., Rom. 4:17), and *prōtotokos*, firstborn (e.g., Col. 1:18; Rev. 1:5).

(a) This association of terms gives expression to a set of doctrines underlying them. The basis of the Christian proclamation lies in the fact that God raised Jesus from the dead (e.g., Acts 3:15; 4:10; 10:40–41; 13:30, 34), that he is the "firstborn from among the dead" (Col. 1:18), and that he is "the Living One" (Rev. 1:18). This testimony is most extensively developed in 1 Cor. 15:3–57.

(b) In the OT it was still necessary to say that God was God not of the dead, but of the living, i.e., the dead no longer had a relationship with God (cf. Lk. 24:5). When, however, the statement is taken up in the mouth of Jesus at Mk. 12:27 par., it is put into the context of the expectation of the general resurrection. It is thus changed in light of Jesus' death and resurrection. He is "Lord of both the dead and the living" (Rom. 14:9), "the one whom God appointed as judge of the living and the dead" (Acts 10:42; cf. 1 Pet. 4:5). Death is no longer a realm inaccessible to God and beyond the range of his power. It has been conquered by Jesus.

The Gospel accounts of Jesus' raising the dead to life (Matt. 9:23–25; Lk. 7:11–15; Jn. 11:1–44; 12:1, 9) provide graphic backing for this assertion. When Jesus provides a prophetic background of his miracle-working power as proof to John the Baptist of his messiahship (see Matt. 11:5 par.), he adds "the dead are raised" to the formulas from Isa. 35:5–6; 61:1–2. Jesus grants the same power to his disciples in Matt. 10:8, and resurrection miracles are recorded for both Peter and Paul (Acts 9:36–43; 20:9–12).

3. In only a few places does *nekros* occur apart from a resurrection context in the lit. sense of corpse. Rev. 11:18; 20:5, 12–13 speak of the dead in the final judgment. Matt. 8:22 par. sets the word in its lit. sense alongside a figurative usage: "Let the dead bury their own dead." In 28:4 and Mk. 9:26, *nekros* is used in a simile. In Acts 5:10 it refers to the dead body of Sapphira.

4. (a) As in the Stoic writers, the NT can use *nekros* in a fig. sense. In the parable of the prodigal son, Luke calls the one son "dead" (15:24, 32): as far as the father was concerned, the son had left the company of the living. Paul uses *nekros* in sacramental language concerning the doctrine of baptism at Rom. 6:11, 13, where he exhorts Christians to consider themselves "dead to sin" and to give themselves to God as "those who have been brought from death to life" (cf. also 8:10). In Eph. 2:1, 5; Col. 2:13, the state of being *nekros* is grounded in our transgressions and sins.

(b) In Heb. 6:1; 9:14, human attempts, apart from Christ, to obtain life are described as *nekros*, dead. Jas. 2:17, 26 goes a step further and characterizes even faith as dead if it does not result in outward manifestations of life.

See also *apokteinō*, kill (650); *thanatos*, death (2505); *katheudō*, sleep (2761).

3739 (nekroō, put to death), → *3738.*

3740 (nekrōsis, death, deadness), → *3738.*

3741 (neomēnia, new moon, first of the month), → *4943.*

3742	νέος

νέος (*neos*), new, young, fresh (*3742*); νεότης (*neotēs*), youth (*3744*); νεόφυτος (*neophytos*), newly planted (*3745*); ἀνανεόω (*ananeoō*), renew (*391*).

CL & OT 1. In cl. Gk. *neos* generally denotes a temporal sense of new, fresh; in a fig. sense it can be used of persons with some recently gained honor or position. *neos* is most commonly used (esp. in the comparative *neōteros*) to designate the age range of youths between 20 and 30 years old as distinct from the *presbyteroi* (older people) or *gerontes* (old people), although it can also denote an inexperienced person, a novice. There is little differentiation between *neos* and synonymous adjs. *kainos* (→ *2785*) and *prosphatos* (→ *4710*).

2. The LXX uses *neos* chiefly in the comparative *neōteros*, for a younger or even youngest person (see, e.g., Gen. 9:24; 19:31, 34–35; Jdg. 8:20; 2 Chr. 13:7; Job 24:5). In Num. 28:26 the word "firstfruits" is *ta nea* (lit., "the new things"); similarly, the month Abib, which is the first month of the liturgical year, is lit. "the month of the new things" (Exod. 13:4; 23:15; 34:18; Lev. 2:14) because it is the month of the ripening of grain.

3. In the Apocr. and intertestamental lit. *neos* comes increasingly to denote youthful inexperience, immaturity, and susceptibility (e.g., Tob. 1:4; Sir. 9:10; 1 Macc. 6:17; 11:54, 57; 4 Macc. 2:3).

NT 1. The uses of *neos* in the NT, though not as frequent as *kainos*, are scattered in various writings. The temporal aspect is dominant, marking out the present moment as compared with a former: "new batch" of dough (1 Cor. 5:7), freshly prepared and not yet blended with leaven; "new wine," still fermenting (Matt. 9:17; Mk. 2:22; Lk. 5:38); the "new self" (Col. 3:10); the "new covenant" as contrasted with the old covenant broken by God's people (Heb. 12:24). In some of these references, *kainos* is used in the context to denote the same thing.

neos, when it means a young(er) person, is mainly used in the comparative in the NT (Lk. 15:12; Jn. 21:18; Acts 5:6; 1 Tim. 5:1–2, 11, 14; Tit. 2:4, 6; 1 Pet. 5:5). In some cases, as in the LXX, the comparative *neōteros* can mean "the youngest" (Lk. 22:26). *neotēs* means youth (Mk. 10:20; Lk. 18:21; Acts 26:4; 1 Tim. 4:12), while *neophy-*

tos, newly planted, refers to one who is a "recent convert" and thus should not serve as a church leader (1 Tim. 3:6).

2. *neos* thus characterizes the new thing that Jesus brought to us both as gift and as task, the new life that commences at his coming and that will be completed at his return. *neos* stands in opposition to that which was old (cf. Heb. 1:1; → *palai, 4093*). The old self is the autonomous self under sin (Rom. 7:6), which is laid aside (Eph. 4:22) and must be purified from the old leaven of unregenerate ways. God himself has declared that the earlier worship of his people is obsolete (Heb. 8:13) and that his will is that believers serve him in the newness of the Spirit (→ *kainos, 2785*).

3. Both *neos* and *kainos* denote the new salvation Christ has brought and the new life of faith in him. The picture of new wine and old wineskins (Matt. 9:17; Mk. 2:22; Lk. 5:38) makes a sharp distinction between the new (the person and preaching of Jesus) and the old (Jud. and John the Baptist's followers). Jesus calls for a clean break between old and new, since both can only be linked together with resultant mutual disadvantages. The new, fresh wine at the wedding feast at Cana also shows that the new is better than the old (Jn. 2:1–11), even though "new" and "old" are not used in the account.

4. The picture of the congregation as a "new batch" of dough that is separated from "the yeast of malice and wickedness" takes the thought a step further (1 Cor. 5:7–8). Just as the old yeast had to be purged annually at the Passover (Deut. 16:3–4) and a fresh start made, so nothing of the old life should be allowed to corrupt the new. In context Paul is referring to the boasting of the Corinthians regarding their recent case of gross immorality (1 Cor. 5:1–6). He goes on to urge them to celebrate the festival "with bread without yeast, the bread of sincerity and truth" (5:8), for the church has entered a new era: "Christ, our Passover lamb, has been sacrificed" (5:7).

5. The vb. *ananeoō* occurs only at Eph. 4:23, where it signifies that our inner nature or attitudes must "be made new" (cf. *anakainoō* in Col. 3:10). Eph. 4:24 adds that we must "put on the new [*kainon*] self, created to be like God in true righteousness and holiness."

See also *kainos*, new (2785); *prosphatos*, fresh, new, late (4710).

3744 (neotēs, youth), → *3742.*

3745 (neophytos, newly planted), → *3742.*

3749 (nephelē, cloud), → *847.*

3753	νεωκόρος

νεωκόρος (*neōkoros*), temple keeper (*3753*).

CL *neōkoros* is derived from *neōs* (the Attic form of *naos*, temple) and *koreō*, to sweep. From "temple sweeper" it came to mean "temple keeper" and became a title for cities in Asia Minor that had built a temple in honor of their patron god or the emperor. The word does not occur in the LXX.

NT In Acts 19:35 this title is ascribed to Ephesus, where a temple was built in honor of the goddess Artemis.

3758	νήπιος

νήπιος (*nēpios*), infant, minor (*3758*).

CL & OT The noun *nēpios* denotes an infant, child, or minor in cl. Gk; it also often carries overtones of helplessness, inexperience, simplicity, and even foolishness. Gk. philosophers who wanted to communicate true knowledge of the world and the life of reason dismissed with biting sarcasm the unperceptive person with no experience of life as *nēpios*, a fool.

The LXX uses *nēpios* to translate 5 different Heb. words (e.g., 1 Sam. 15:3; Prov. 23:13; Isa. 11:8; Ezek. 9:6; 45:20). In these contexts the most important characteristics of the *nēpios* are the weakness, helplessness, and submission of the child to the adult (cf. Lam. 1:5). Hos. 11:1 represents the origins of Israel (i.e., the exodus from

Egypt) as the people's youth (*nēpios*). By contrast with the period of apostasy in Canaan, Israel followed Yahweh with undivided loyalty. The LXX also uses *nēpios* in Ps. 19:7, where it denotes the person with a simple faith (cf. also 116:6; 119:130), who stands under God's protection and pays attention to his instruction.

NT 1. (a) Matt. 21:16 quotes Ps. 8:2 in the account of Jesus' cleansing of the temple. Jesus answers the indignation of the chief priests and teachers of the law at the Hosanna of the children with the question, "Have you never read, 'From the lips of children (*nēpioi*) and infants you have ordained praise'?" This OT quotation had undisputed authority for his opponents, so that their accusations immediately lost all substance.

(b) Matt. 11:25 and Lk. 10:21 are both placed after the woes pronounced on Chorazin, Bethsaida, and Capernaum: "I praise you, Father, Lord of heaven and earth, because you have hidden these things from the wise and learned, and revealed them to little children." *nēpioi* here draws a contrast with the wise and learned and refers either to children who, by comparison with adults, are usually considered immature and unwise (cf. 1 Cor. 14:20), or generally to the simple, without any emphasis being laid on the age of the "children."

2. (a) Paul also refers to the child/adult contrast in 1 Cor. 13:11. Just as an adult thinks differently from a child, one's knowledge in the coming age will be transformed. But faith, hope, and especially love hold good now and will abide in the age to come (13:13). In Rom. 2:20 the child/adult contrast is applied to the teacher/pupil relationship. Jews, who have the law, are conscious of being in the role of teacher, who instructs the *nēpios*. But their failure to see their own hypocrisy in the light of the law undermines this role and brings dishonor to God (2:22–24).

In 1 Cor. 3:1 the spiritual is contrasted with the fleshly and childish. The "not yet" (3:2) and the "in Christ" with *nēpios* stand in contrast to the development that should take place, as the further metaphor of milk and solid food indicates. What is at issue here is not a pre-Christian stage in contrast to the Christian life, but Christian life that has begun but still needs to develop. Childishness is a transitional phase that one should grow out of (see also Heb. 5:13–14).

Paul uses a similar picture in Eph. 4:14: "Then we will no longer be infants (*nēpioi*), tossed back and forth by the waves, and blown here and there by every wind of teaching and by the cunning and craftiness of men in their deceitful scheming." The apostle is not distinguishing between Christians and non-Christians, but referring to those Christians who are as easily led astray as immature children. His concern is about their growing (4:15) and becoming complete (4:13).

(b) Paul's argument in Gal. 4:3 is different from the above passages. Here he uses legal and temporal categories. The pre-Christian period (i.e., the time before Jesus' coming, 4:4) was the *nēpios* period of immaturity and slavery. The *nēpioi* were held bound "in slavery under the basic principles of the world." But Christ has come "to redeem those under law, that we might receive the full rights of sons" (4:5, → *huios*, 5626) The two periods stand in clearly marked contrast.

See also *pais*, child, young man, son, servant (*4090*); *teknon*, child (*5451*); *huios*, son (*5626*).

3763 (*nēsteia*, fasting, fast), → *3764*.

| *3764* νηστεύω |

νηστεύω (*nēsteuō*), to fast (*3764*); νηστεία (*nēsteia*), fasting, fast (*3763*); νῆστις (*nēstis*), not eating, fasting (*3765*).

CL & OT 1. In cl. Gk. this word group means generally to abstain from food (usually for a limited period), sometimes to starve. Fasting was most frequently undertaken as a religious ritual. Fear of demons, for example, led to fasting; it was considered an effective means of preparing oneself for an encounter with the deity, for it created an openness to divine influence. The mystery religions used fasting as part of the initiation ritual for novices. In magic and with the oracles

fasting was regarded as a preparation necessary for success. The custom of fasting following a death was widespread. It was believed that there was a danger of demonic infection in eating and drinking while the soul of the dead person was still near. Fasting was also required in certain fertility rites. Fasting for ethical motives (asceticism) was uncommon in the ancient world.

2. (a) In the LXX the words in this group generally translate only the Heb. verb to fast. A conceptually related Heb. expression meaning to afflict oneself (lit., to humble one's soul) as a purification rite (in which fasting played a part) is translated by *tapeinō* (e.g., Lev. 16:29, 31; 23:27, 32; Isa. 58:3). We also read of occasions when there was no eating of bread or drinking of water (e.g., Exod. 34:28).

(b) Fasting took place in Israel as a preparation for meeting God (Exod. 34:28; Deut. 9:9; Dan. 9:3). An individual might fast when oppressed by great cares (2 Sam. 12:16–23; 1 Ki. 21:27 = LXX 20:27; Ps. 35:13; 69:10). The entire nation fasted in times of imminent danger (Jdg. 20:26; 2 Chr. 20:3; Est. 4:16; Jdt. 4:9, 13; cf. Jon. 3:4–10), during a plague of locusts (Joel 1–2), for success of the return of exiles (Ezr. 8:21–23), as an expiatory rite (Neh. 9:1), and in connection with mourning the dead (2 Sam. 1:12).

Fasting and prayer belonged together (Ezr. 8:21, 23; Neh. 1:4; Jer. 14:11–12). A fast usually lasted from morning to evening (Jdg. 20:26; 1 Sam. 14:24; 2 Sam. 1:12), although Est. 4:16 speaks of a three-day fast. In Ps. 109:24 the description of the torments of fasting during the period of accusation are at the same time a reflection of the inward torments suffered by the suppliant.

The Israelite law ordained fasting (lit., afflicting oneself) only on the Day of Atonement (Lev. 23:27–32; Num. 29:7). After the destruction of Jerusalem (587 B.C.) four fast days were laid down as days of remembrance (Zech. 7:3–5; 8:19).

3. In the course of time the deeper meaning of fasting—as an expression of one's humility before God—was lost for Israel. Increasingly it came to be regarded as a pious achievement. The struggle of the prophets against this depersonalization and emptying of the concept was without success (cf. Isa. 58:3–7; Jer. 14:12). By the time of Jesus those earnest about their religion, esp. the Pharisees, were required to keep two fast days each week (cf. Lk. 18:12). The disciples of John had a similar rule (cf. Mk. 2:18).

NT In the NT *nēsteuō* occurs 20x, all in the Synoptic Gospels and Acts. *nēsteia* occurs 5x (3x in Lk. and Acts, 2x in Paul), and *nēstis* 2x (Matt. and Mk.).

1. The entirely new view brought by the NT to the question of fasting is most clearly expressed in the words of Jesus, "How can the guests of the bridegroom fast while he is with them?" (Mk. 2:19 par.). The advent of God's kingdom, the presence of the Messiah, the good news of salvation not dependent on good works—all this means joy, something excluded by fasting in the Jewish sense. In the light of the Messiah-centered preaching of Jesus, such fasting is a thing of the past, belonging to a bygone era.

In the Gospels the answer to the question about fasting is linked to the parables of the new patch on the old garment and the new wine in the old bottles (Mk. 2:21–22 par.). In other words, fasting has been superseded by Jesus.

2. A number of passages, however, raise questions about the consistency of this picture. (a) According to Matt. 4:2, Jesus himself fasted for 40 days and 40 nights before beginning his public ministry. It can be argued, of course, that this took place on the threshold of the coming of salvation.

(b) In Matt. 6:16–18 Jesus does not condemn fasting as such, merely ostentatious fasting. Fasting is not to be practiced before other people but before God, who is unseen and "sees what is done in secret." Here, however, Jesus may be addressing not the community of his disciples, but the Jews.

(c) According to Matt. 17:21, there are certain conditions of demonic enslavement from which a person can only be released "through prayer and fasting." Many NT MSS, however, omit this verse (see NIV note; cf. also Mk. 9:29).

(d) In Acts 13:3 and 14:23 we read that occasionally in the Christian church, prayer was backed up by fasting.

We may thus conclude that fasting does have a value, but only if it is voluntary. The early Christian churches, esp. predominantly Jewish-Christian ones, retained the practice of fasting in order to demonstrate that their prayers were in earnest (cf. Acts 13:3; 14:23). In those passages that concentrate on the ascetic tendencies of some (Rom. 14 and Col. 2), however, fasting is not mentioned. The two occasions of "fasting" mentioned in Paul's letters (2 Cor. 6:5; 11:27) are autobiographical and may refer only to "hunger."

3765 (nēstis, not eating, fasting), → *3764.*

3767 (nēphalios, temperate), → *3768.*

3768	νήφω

νήφω (*nephō*), be sober (*3768*); νηφάλιος (*nēphalios*), temperate (*3767*); ἐκνήφω (*eknēphō*), become sober, come to one's senses (*1729*); ἀνανήφω (*ananēphō*), become sober (*392*).

CL & OT This word group carries the idea of sobriety, the opposite of intoxication (→ *methyō, 3501*). In Hel. Gk. the words can be used lit. of a state of abstinence from wine, but also fig. to indicate complete clarity of mind and its resulting good judgment.

NT For the NT writers, the fig. sense is also prominent. *nephō* occurs 2x in 1 Thess. 5:6–8, denoting the alertness required in light of an imminent Parousia, and once in the Pastoral Letters (2 Tim. 4:5), where it indicates the clarity of mind able to resist the subtle attractions of deviant mythologies (cf. also the use of *eknephō* in 1 Cor. 15:34). Likewise, in 1 Pet., *nephō* points to the appropriate frame of mind for the imminent appearance of Jesus (1:13) and for prayer in the end time (4:7). The ferocious hostility of the devil is evident in these days, making an alertness able to resist essential (5:8).

nēphalios occurs only in the Pastorals and denotes the abstemious lifestyle required of bishops (1 Tim. 3:2), women (3:11), and elders (Tit. 2:2). The main point here is the self-control necessary for effective ministry. *ananephō* occurs only in 2 Tim. 2:26 and indicates the clarity of mind demanded of a teacher if opponents are to be silenced.

See also *methyō*, be drunk (*3501*).

3771	νικάω

νικάω (*nikaō*), be victorious (*3771*); νῖκος (*nikos*), victory (*3777*); νίκη (*nikē*), victory (*3772*); ὑπερνικάω (*hypernikaō*), be more than victorious (*5664*).

CL & OT 1. In Gk. lit. *nikaō* frequently means to be victorious, both in military and legal combat. The vb. expresses visible superiority in the natural rivalry that takes place among people or, occasionally, among the gods. The vb. can also be translated surpass, overcome, be stronger. It presupposes achievement in physical or spiritual combat. The corresponding noun is *nikē*, victory or the power that confers victory. *Nikē* is also the name of a Gk. goddess, who is often represented in art as a symbol of personal superiority. The gods assist humans in their conflicts and give the victory to the side of their choice.

2. In the LXX *nikaō* occurs 26x and *nikē* 11x. By far the majority are to be found in Macc. The rest typically render the Heb. vb. *nāṣaḥ*, to defeat, have control of, or noun *nēṣaḥ*, splendor, endurance.

The OT is familiar with the phenomenon of human rivalry (e.g., between Hagar and Sarah, Gen. 16:1–16; Joseph and his brothers, 37:2–35), but *nikaō* is used in the LXX almost exclusively to denote victory over hostile powers. Here the real victor is God, who has power over his own enemies and those of his people and of the righteous (cf. 1 Chr. 29:11, where NIV translates *nēṣaḥ* as "majesty"). The people's victory does not primarily depend on the strength of their soldiers but on whether God has delivered the enemy into the hands of the Israelite armies (cf. Jdg. 7; 1 Macc. 3:19). For this reason the rallying cry for the Maccabean "holy war" was "Victory with God!" (2 Macc. 13:15). Finally, the faith of Israel waits and prays for the time when God will defeat all their enemies.

In the wisdom lit. this word group acquired a spiritualized meaning. The wise man does not allow himself to be conquered by the beauty of an adulteress (Prov. 6:25), but rather reason overcomes instinct (4 Macc. 3:17; 6:33).

NT The NT usage of this word group generally presupposes the conflict between God or Christ and opposing demonic powers. *nikaō* occurs most frequently in Rev. and 1 Jn. *nikē* occurs only in 1 Jn. 5:4; *hypernikaō* only in Rom. 8:37. The terms occur seldom in Paul, but when they do, they have particular theological significance.

1. In the Synoptic tradition the word group appears only in Matt. 12:20 in a quotation from the first Servant Song (Isa. 42:1–4: "he leads justice to victory") and in Lk. 11:22, where the stronger man overcomes, disarms, and despoils the armed strong man. The metaphor explains Jesus' superiority over the demonic powers: "If I drive out demons by the finger of God, then the kingdom of God has come to you" (11:20). The earthly Jesus demonstrates by his actions that he is the hidden victor over the forces opposed to God, though it is not until the resurrection that he achieves the final victory over sin, death, and the devil.

2. In 1 Cor. 15 Paul speaks forcibly about overcoming the world and death through the redemptive work of Jesus Christ. Jesus' death on the cross and resurrection mean that no power in the world can finally have the victory. "Death has been swallowed up in victory. 'Where, O death, is your victory?'" (1 Cor. 15:54–55). As children of God, believers are included in this victory. Our victory is not an achievement or reward, but is given us (15:57). We are thereby placed in a position in which we ourselves can overcome evil (Rom. 12:21).

In this life we are often oppressed by trouble, anxiety, danger, persecution, and hunger. But these forces have lost their controlling power. Our struggle against the rule of these demonic forces is conducted under the promise of victory and thus takes on the character of overcoming: "No, in all these things we are more than conquerors through him who loved us" (Rom. 8:37).

3. John sums up the forces opposed to God in the term *kosmos* (world). Jesus' coming, suffering, and return to the Father signify victory over the world. The evil one, the ruler of this world, has had his power restricted by Jesus, the stronger man who has freed his people from the dominion of the evil one. The battle has thus been decided, even if it is not yet over. By faith Christians participate in this victory and are thus placed in a position to overcome the world for themselves. Faith is the victory over the world (1 Jn. 2:13–14; 4:4–5; 5:4–5).

4. The seven letters of Rev. 2–3 are directed to troubled churches in Asia Minor suffering under persecution. Each letter concludes with a call to overcome, introduced by the formula "he who overcomes" or "to him who overcomes" (2:7, 11 etc.). The conflict and the trials of this present life in the world and in the church are not final. The church's anticipated victory has its foundations laid in the victory already won by Jesus. The promise of an inheritance is to those who overcome (cf. 21:7).

The end, however, will be preceded by an apocalyptic conflict between God and the demonic powers, the theme of Rev. The world powers often gain victories in this conflict (6:2; 11:7; 13:7), but they are only fleeting. In the end the Lamb will prevail. Christians have followed him and have poured out their blood in martyrdom (11:7–12). In the middle of the picture of the plagues and the wrath of God John sees the victors standing, singing a hymn of praise (15:2–4). Thus the victory the Lamb has won and has promised to his people is already secure, despite confrontations with the demonic powers, for the Lamb is the King of all kings and the Lord of all lords (17:14). This is the origin of the Christian symbol of the Lamb with the banner of victory.

See also *athleō*, compete (*123*); *agōn*, fight (*74*); *brabeion*, prize (*1092*); *thriambeuō*, lead to a triumphal procession (*2581*).

3772 (*nikē*, victory), → *3771*.

| 3774 | Νικολαΐτης |

Νικολαΐτης (*Nikolaitēs*), Nicolaitan (*3774*); Νικόλαος (*Nikolaos*), Nicolas (*3775*).

NT 1. The Nicolaitans were members of an early Christian sect, apparently formed from the personal name Nicolas or Nicolaus. The word occurs in the NT only at Rev. 2:6, 15, in the letters to the churches in Ephesus and in Pergamum. The first passage commends the church's rejection of them without specifying the nature of their teaching. It is an open question whether they are to be identified with the false apostles of 2:2.

The more explicit context of Rev. 2:15 must be the basis for any interpretation of the tenets of the group. There the Nicolaitans are equated in some sense with Balaam. Although this man's evil counsel is never explicitly recorded in the OT, the inference from comparing Num. 31:16 with 25:1–3 is that he was responsible for contriving the sin of Israelite men marrying the daughters of Moab—thus encouraging both their "eating food sacrificed to idols and . . . sexual immorality" (Rev. 2:15). These same sins are ascribed to the teaching of "Jezebel" at Thyatira (2:20), though she is never called a Nicolaitan. Both passages concern errors of practice rather than of speculative doctrine, although the phrase "Satan's so-called deep secrets" (2:24) may suggest some kind of gnostic background for Jezebel's teaching. In other words, Nicolaitanism was, to some extent, a libertarian or antinomian movement.

Note that Balaam is unexpectedly prominent in Jewish tradition. He represented a type of lawless wickedness and was the antagonist of Moses the lawgiver. Jude 11 and 2 Pet. 2:15 contain references to controversies involving Balaam's name. So perhaps a polemical use of the name was already current in the milieu of the Asian churches (cf. the messianic use of Balaam's prophecy in Num. 24:17, echoed in Rev. 2:26–28). Balaam's advocacy of eating food sacrificed to idols and of sexual immorality also recalls the terms of the apostolic decree of Acts 15:20, 29, which itself echoes Num. 25:1–2 and to which Paul assented. Paul was, of course, sensitive to the charge of antinomianism (Rom. 6:1–2). In Rev. John rejects the application of the term "Balaam" to Christians, turning the word against a perversion to which the gospel of faith apart from works was open.

2. The value of later references in the church fathers to Nicolaitans is debatable. Irenaeus regards them as the earliest exponents of the error of Cerinthus and ascribes to them a gnostic cosmology. This may, however, be an inference from 1 Tim. 6:20, to which Irenaeus seems to refer in his discussion of this heresy.

3. The churches of Asia Minor do appear to have been under severe pressure to secure their earthly position by accommodation either to Jud. or to pagan society. The Nicolaitans (and Jezebel) are mentioned in connection with churches in those three cities where pagan compromise seems to have been most insistent. The temptation to idolatry at Thyatira may be connected with the strength of the pagan trade guilds in that city; Christians who valued their livelihood were under pressure to participate in the idolatrous feasts of the guilds. At Ephesus was the power of the Artemis cult. Pergamum was the provincial center of the imperial cult, and a new rigor of enforcement of that cult by Domitian faced the church with an acute dilemma. Safety might be assured only by what John saw as amounting to apostasy. The Nicolaitans and their kind were plausible advocates of the pagan compromise.

3775 (*Nikolaos*, Nicolas), → *3774*.

3777 (*nikos*, victory), → *3771*.

| 3780 | Νινευΐτης |

Νινευΐτης (*Nineuitēs*), Ninevite (*3780*).

CL & OT 1. Nineveh (Gk. *Ninos*) is cited frequently in cl. Gk. historians such as Xenophon, Herodotus, Cassius Dio, Diodorus, and Strabo. Josephus refers often to the city, attributing its founding to Assyras.

2. Nineveh is mentioned 17x in the OT. According to Gen. 10:11–12, Nimrod founded the city; in 2 Ki. 19:36 (see also Isa. 37:37), Sennacherib returned to his royal residence at Nineveh after his failure to conquer Jerusalem. The city figures most prominently in Jonah's prophecy (1:2; 3:2–7; 4:11), where its wickedness is described as the cause for its threatened destruction. The three days' journey required to cross it (3:3) possibly refers to the administrative district of Nineveh. The preaching of the prophet Jonah led to repentance on the part of its citizens, so that the impending catastrophe was averted (3:10).

Nineveh also figures prominently in Nahum's prophecy, an oracle dealing solely with the destruction of Nineveh (cf. 1:1; 3:7). The reference to the opening of the river gates (2:6) may picture the inundation of part of the city by a coalition of Medes, Babylonians, and Scythians, who conquered Nineveh in 612 B.C. This city is also cited in Zeph. 2:13, where its destruction is mentioned along with others in an oracle about God's judgment on Israel's enemies and Israel's eventual vindication.

Nineveh is mentioned in cuneiform sources from the reigns of Gudea (ca. 2200 B.C.) and Hammurabi (ca. 1750 B.C.). Archaeological excavation at the site of ancient Nineveh has revealed occupation from prehistoric times. With the restoration of Assyria's fortunes under Shalmaneser I (ca. 1260 B.C.), Nineveh gained in importance and became one of his royal residences. The Assyrian king who made the greatest contribution to Nineveh was Sennacherib, who rebuilt its defenses and constructed a system of dams and canals.

After the death of Ashurbanipal (669–627 B.C.), the Assyrian empire declined and Nineveh was eventually destroyed. Thereafter the city became a symbol of Assyria's utter collapse. In its day, Nineveh was the crystallization of the culture and power of that kingdom. As such, it represented to the OT prophets the seat of the cruelty and oppression that the Assyrian empire brought to bear on Israel.

NT Jesus refers to Nineveh in his saying about the sign of the prophet Jonah: "The men of Nineveh will stand up at the judgment with this generation and condemn it; for they repented at the preaching of Jonah, and now one greater than Jonah is here" (Matt. 12:41; Lk. 11:32). The point of this saying and the accompanying one about the Queen of the South's visit to Solomon is to contrast the responsiveness of outsiders to God's message with the faithless response of God's chosen people, whom Jesus calls "this generation." Not content with what Jesus had already said and did, the Jews sought a sign (cf. also Matt. 16:1; 1 Cor. 1:22). Jesus replied that "a wicked and adulterous generation asks for a miraculous sign! But none will be given it except the sign of the prophet Jonah. For as Jonah was three days and three nights in the belly of a huge fish, so the Son of Man will be three days and three nights in the heart of the earth" (Matt. 12:39–40; cf. Lk. 11:29).

This pericope is enigmatic, for the Ninevite generation was not judged but the prophet himself was (cf. Jon. 1:4, 10, 12, 15). But it also suggests that death will not be the end of the Son of Man, just as being thrown into the sea was not the end of Jonah. Jesus' vindication will come soon. Then follows the reference to the citizens of Nineveh, who responded to Jonah's preaching that the Lord intended to destroy their city (cf. 3:1–10). The contrast between Jonah and Jesus in Matt. 12:41 (Jesus is "greater than Jonah") challenges Jesus' hearers to think for themselves as to who he is and what their relation should be to the kingdom of God.

| 3782 | νίπτω |

νίπτω (*niptō*), wash (*3782*).

CL & OT In cl. Gk. *niptō* means to wash, when the obj. is part of the body (→ *louō*, *3374*). In religious contexts *niptō* is commonly used of the ceremonial washing of hands (e.g., before prayer or sacrifice).

A similar use of *niptō* appears in the LXX, both in a secular sense (e.g., Gen. 18:4) and for religious washings (Exod. 30:18–21). The prescriptions relating to priests washing their hands amidst religious duties was extended to a demand that Jews generally rinse their hands before meals (see Mk. 7:3).

NT The Pharisees criticize the disciples of Jesus for eating with "unwashed" (*aniptos*), i.e., ceremonially unclean, hands (Mk. 7:2–3). In his disciples' defense Jesus not only rejects the tradition that included the custom (7:5–13), but denies several fundamental presuppositions concerning uncleanness that it involves (7:14–23).

The narrative of the foot-washing may contain a reference to current Jewish teaching on purification: "A person who has had a bath needs only to wash his feet; his whole body is clean" (Jn. 13:10). That is, the action of Jesus in washing the disciples' feet represented a complete bath (*louō*). If 13:7 hints that more is involved in the act than a lesson in humility (13:13–17) and that it cannot be understood until after the crucifixion, it is likely that we are to interpret Jesus' foot-washing as an acted parable regarding the Lord's humiliation unto death.

See also *baptizō*, baptize, immerse (*966*); *louō*, wash (*3374*).

3783 (*noeō*, apprehend, perceive, understand, gain insight into), → *3808*.

3784 (*noēma*, thought, mind), → *3808*.

3785 (*nothos*, born out of wedlock), → *2302*.

3788 (*nomikos*, pertaining to the law, hence legal expert, lawyer), → *1208*.

3789 (*nomimōs*, conforming to the law, according to rule), → *3795*.

3791 (*nomodidaskalos*, teacher of the law), → *1437*.

3792 (*nomothesia*, law-giving, legislation), → *3795*.

3793 (*nomotheteō*, make laws, legislate, ordain, enact), → *3795*.

3794 (*nomothetēs*, lawgiver), → *3795*.

3795	νόμος

νόμος (*nomos*), law, norm (*3795*); νομίμως (*nomimōs*), conforming to the law, according to rule (*3789*); νομοθεσία (*nomothesia*), law-giving, legislation (*3792*); νομοθετέω (*nomotheteō*), make laws, legislate, ordain, enact (*3793*); νομοθέτης (*nomothetēs*), lawgiver (*3794*); ἀνομία (*anomia*), lawlessness (*490*); ἄνομος (*anomos*), lawless, unlawful (*491*); ἀνόμως (*anomōs*), apart from the law (*492*); ἔννομος (*ennomos*), under law, orderly (*1937*); παρανομέω (*paranomeō*), break the law, act contrary to the law (*4174*).

CL 1. (a) The noun *nomos* is formed from the vb. *nemō*, distribute, assign, esp. in the sense of assigning property. In other words, this vb. refers to processes essential for humans to live together in a community. Relationships to earthly possessions must be determined in a legally binding fashion, so that private and communal ownership may become a reality. Thus *nemō* covers shades of meaning from merely handing something over for a given period of time to transferring something, once and for all, to the ownership of another. (b) The fig. sense of the vb. has the idea of to watch over, protect; also to esteem, respect.

2. In the same way, the word *nomos* originally referred to distributing something and what followed from it. It meant that which was laid down or ordered—esp. the results of this, namely, arrangements that become regularized and attain the status of tradition. The word thus denotes custom, statute, law, esp. in the distribution of goods and in law and order.

The legal, ethical, and religious meanings of *nomos* are inseparable in antiquity, for all goods were believed to come from the gods, who upheld order in the universe and in relations among humans. Hence comes the universal conviction that law is linked to the divine. The close interrelationship between the worship of the gods, the customs of the time, and one's duty to the state was expressed in the charge leveled at Socrates, namely, that he failed to reverence the gods

officially worshiped by the city, or at least that he did not worship them as everyone else did.

3. Used in a political context, *nomos* was regarded as the most essential feature of the *polis* or city-state, i.e., the judicial norm, legal custom, the "law of the land." From the 5th cent. B.C. on, *nomos* was written down as *nomoi* (pl.), thereby acquiring the meaning of specific written laws, the constitution, which had to be obeyed on pain of punishment. Many Gk. tragedies rest on the fact that one law stands over against another, both claiming validity but being mutually incompatible. Hence, people are caught in the midst of such conflict. Indeed, *nomos* is sometimes disparaged as a human exaggeration as compared with *physis* (nature) or universal law.

4. Gk. philosophy kept alive the awareness that since human laws are often fallible, humans cannot exist unless they conform to cosmic, universal law. Only when one is inwardly in harmony with the universe does one have peace of mind amid the vicissitudes of life. Whereas the Sophists criticized the absolute validity attached to *nomos*, Plato and Aristotle (each in his own way) connected it with the *nous*, the human spirit, and thereby once again with the divine.

OT 1. In the LXX *nomos* occurs about 430x. About half have no Heb. equivalents; for the rest, the commonest equivalent is *tôrâ*. In the canonical OT, *nomos* is concentrated most heavily in the Pentateuchal books other than Gen. Next come Ezr. and Neh., then Ps. (40x, of which 27 are in Ps. 119). The frequent use of the word in the Apocr. (100x in the books of the Macc., 30x in Sir.) indicates the importance of law in the Jewish thought of the last two centuries B.C.

2. This section deals with passages in the LXX where *tôrâ* is translated by *nomos*. Note first that *tôrâ* frequently does *not* mean law in the modern sense of the term. The Jews, in a manner similar to the Gks., viewed law as the transcript of an eternal norm. (a) Originally *tôrâ* meant an instruction from God, a command for a given situation. Instruction for given situations was also given by the prophets (e.g., Isa. 1:10; 5:24; Jer. 6:19; Mic. 4:2), the priests (Deut. 17:9, 11–12; Jer. 2:8; Ezek. 7:26; Hos. 4:6), or a judge (Deut. 17:9, 11–12). The prophets threatened judgment on priests and prophets who issued their own instruction without having received it from Yahweh (Jer. 2:8; 8:8; Ezek. 22:26; Zeph. 3:4).

(b) Human counsel given by a teacher of wisdom was also called *tôrâ* and hence *nomos* (Prov. 13:14; 28:4, 7, 9).

(c) Also called *nomos* are the specific instructions for the different kinds of offerings (Lev. 6), for priestly procedure (Num. 5:29), or for the Nazirites (6:13, 21).

(d) After the reform of Josiah, after which the book of Deut. became prominent, phrases such as "the law of the LORD" became widespread, epitomizing the laws in general and without any further qualification (Jer. 8:8 and passim; cf. 2 Ki. 10:31; Amos 2:4). Deut. is itself called "this Book of the Law" (Deut. 28:61; 30:10; 31:26; cf. also 29:20), and after the exile the whole Pentateuch is called this (Neh. 8:3). Corresponding to this is the formula "written in the Law," found in the postexilic lit. (8:14; 10:35, 37 = LXX 10:34, 36; Dan. 9:11; cf. 2 Chr. 23:18), where the law is seen as a written norm.

(e) The vbs. used in connection with *tôrâ* indicate whether the latter is conceived of as oral instruction or as written law. Oral instruction is implied by such expressions as to teach instruction (Exod. 18:20), to hear it (Isa. 42:24), to forget it (Hos. 4:6), or to despise it (Isa. 5:24). Other phrases indicate written law: to observe or keep the law (Ps. 119:34, 44; Prov. 28:4), or to walk in it, i.e., to order one's life by it (Exod. 16:4; 2 Chr. 6:16; Ps. 78:10).

3. *ḥōq* (another Heb. word translated by *nomos*) can refer to: (a) Yahweh's sacrificial requirement, his right to receive sacrifice (Lev. 6:15); or (b) the legal system proclaimed in the cult, to which Israel is bound (Jos. 24:25). The fem. *ḥuqqâ* means: (a) creation ordinances, laws of nature (Jer. 31:35); (b) the ordinance of the Passover (Exod. 12:43; Num. 9:3, 14); (c) statutes regulating everyday life (Lev. 19:19, 37); or (d) sacrificial ordinances (Jer. 44:23).

4. The equivalent *dāt* occurs only in the late OT writings, always denoting a written law—either God's law (Ezr. 7:12, 14, 21, 25, 26; Dan. 6:6; Est. 3:8) or that of the king (Ezr. 7:26; Est. 1:8, 13, 15, 19; 3:8; 4:16).

5. This survey is sufficient to show that we cannot speak simply of "the law in the OT" as if it expressed a uniform concept, much less of the OT itself as law. There are essentially three types of "law" to be distinguished:

- *casuistic law*, which denotes legal custom. It has its setting "in the gate," where the law was administered. Large sections of the Book of the Covenant (Exod. 21:1–23:19) contain such lists of laws, each with the characteristic "if . . . , then . . ." form.
- *apodictic law*, set out in series of ten or twelve for ease of memorizing: "anyone who . . . shall surely be put to death" (Exod. 21:12, 15–17); or "I am the LORD . . . you shall not . . ." (as in the Decalogue, Exod. 20:2–17). Here the setting is the worshiping community, esp. at the feast of covenant renewal. In the OT, incidentally, the Ten Commandments are never called "law."
- *cultic regulations*, to be carried out and expounded by the priests.

The laws inherent in such passages were part and parcel of the covenant. It was the rule of life for those who had been redeemed (see Exod. 20:1–2), and God's people were expected to obey them. The law thus had a prophetic character. In the postexilic period, the law came to be viewed more as a set of rigid rules, instead of serving the community as an ordinance of salvation.

6. (a) In the Jud. of the last two centuries B.C. and at the time of Jesus, the law was an absolute in itself and was independent of the covenant. Fulfillment of the law determined one's relationship to God. Israel no longer saw her special status as the result of Yahweh's living self-revelation in the course of her history, but considered this status to rest on the obedience of those who were righteous in terms of the law. Observance of the law distinguished true Israel both from non-Jews and from the godless Jewish masses. In other words, the law had assumed a dominant role as mediator between God and humanity. The whole of life was regulated by the law.

In Hel. Jud., the law came to stand alongside wisdom, which had likewise come to be seen as having a hypostasis. In this respect the law became separated from its original setting, namely, the covenant as given by God. In addition, it could now be presented as universal law, i.e., as universally valid. Further, its universality was extended backward in time. The patriarchs, it was claimed, already knew it; in fact, it antedated the whole of creation. In this manner, Hel. Jews were able to give the law a rational basis and proclaim it as a superior philosophy. The method they adopted was to allegorize it, which involved cutting it loose from its historical roots.

(b) Similarly, rab. Jud. no longer saw God's self-revelation as tied to the covenant, but rather to the Torah as a covenant ordinance. Thus the Torah came to occupy the place of a "canon within the canon," even before the latter was finally determined. The Torah became normative over against the Prophets and the Writings, which were held merely to develop what was already germinally present in the Torah. The Torah (= the Pentateuch) had been delivered by God to Moses. God had committed himself to it, but not only so, he is eternally committed to it. Human life and death hang upon fulfilling its commands (cf. Lk. 18:9–14). As an aid toward this goal, use was made both of casuistry and of summaries of the law in the form of a few commands or even of one basic command.

NT In the NT the noun *nomos* (194x) occurs most often in Paul (119x). It does not occur in Mk., in the General Letters apart from Jas., or in Rev. Its infrequent appearance in the Synoptics should not blind us to the fact that Jesus dealt intensively with the whole issue of the law (cf. Mk. 2:23–28; 10:1–12).

1. The summaries of Christ's work as given in Jn. 1:17 and Eph. 2:14–18 also apply to his preaching. In all that he said and did, Jesus removed the law from its mediatorial position and opened up immediate access to God (cf. the parables in Lk. 15; 18:9–14; also Matt. 11:28–30).

(a) In Matt. 11:7–19, John the Baptist is Elijah come again (11:14), who brings one divine dispensation to an end and proclaims the arrival of a new one, the kingdom of God (cf. Mal. 4:5; Matt. 17:10–13; Lk. 1:17; Jn. 1:21). Thus the teaching of the Prophets and the Law reaches its goal (Matt. 11:13) and comes to an end. "The Prophets and the Law" here are regarded to some extent as constituent parts of the OT, but the primary reference is to their content as salvation history. The wording draws attention not only to the precedence accorded to the Prophets over the Law, but also to the dynamic view of both: They proclaim, preach, and prophesy. From now on the kingdom of God is proclaimed directly, like the news of great victory (→ *basileia*, 993).

Similarly, in the antitheses of the Sermon on the Mount (Matt. 5:21–48) Jesus put an end to all self-satisfaction at having kept individual commands of the law (5:20, 46). At root God's law required absolute conformity to the requirements of his divine majesty in thought as well as in deed (5:20, 48). Thus Jesus made the unprecedented claim that what was said in the law (5:21, 27, 31, 33, 38) is now made out of date by himself: "But I tell you . . ." (5:22, 28, 32, 34, 39, 44). To those who did not acknowledge him as bringing in God's kingdom or recognize his teaching as being the new rule of life, this claim must have made his condemnation for seeking to abolish the law (5:17) a foregone conclusion.

(b) Jesus makes it clear, however, that his claim was not leveled against the law as such (Matt. 5:17–19), but against a person's self-righteous attitude to the law (5:19–20; cf. Paul in Rom. 7:12). Jesus set himself to fulfill in detail the law's demand for a life of utter obedience to God (Matt. 5:17; cf. 3:15), as he had done already from his circumcision on and continued to do until his death on the cross. Even his condemnation was in accordance with established Jewish law (cf. Jn. 19:7). The inviolability of the law (Matt. 5:18) likewise determined Christ's attitude in conversation with the teachers of the law (*nomikoi*, specialists in ethical interpretation of the law) and the theological leaders of the Pharisees. Jesus shared the view that the law could be summed up in two great commandments (Matt. 22:34–40; cf. Lk. 10:25–28), but he rejected the Pharisees' gradations within the double commandment. In his repeated cries of "Woe to you!" (Matt. 23:13–16, 23, 25, 27, 29) he condemned their failure to recognize the basic intent of the law, namely, justice, mercy, and faith (23:23).

(c) In the words of Jesus his reference to *nomos* is generally to the whole law as a part of Scripture, without any further delineation of content. Thus Jesus referred to "the Law" (Matt. 5:18), "the Law or the Prophets" (5:17; cf. 7:12), "Moses and all the Prophets" (Lk. 24:27), and "the Law of Moses" (24:44).

2. Paul, confronted as he was by his own Pharisaic past and by his Jewish and Jewish-Christian opponents, developed a theology of the law connected historically with the promise and on a personal level with Christ. His teaching remains within the limits previously laid down by Jesus; he merely brings out the basic significance of Christ's work, now completed in the cross and resurrection. As Lk. 10:25–37 shows, it is possible to keep the law fully (10:37) only by being in fellowship with Christ, listening to his loving voice, and following him. In the same way, after his resurrection, it is those who are "in Christ" who can keep the law, not with any thought of works-righteousness, but rather out of gratitude and in the liberty of one set free to love and obey.

Paul also follows Jesus in denying both the absoluteness of the law and the idea that it is the way to salvation. He takes this position, however, not because of any emotional complexes arising from his being a converted Pharisee (cf. Phil. 3:5–11), but because he saw the uniqueness and newness of Christ. As the apostle to the Gentiles, he has the prophetic insight to realize that without a comprehensive theology of law, the universal claims of the gospel lack all credibility (see Rom. and Gal.).

Paul uses *nomos* for the Pentateuch (Rom. 3:21b; Gal. 4:21) as well as for the whole of Scripture (Rom. 3:19; 1 Cor. 14:21, citing Isa. 28:11–12; Deut. 28:49), but esp. for the Mosaic law, and the Decalogue in particular (Rom. 2:14a, 17; 3:28; 7:12; Gal. 5:3), with its demand for unconditional obedience from the Jews. Rom. 2:14b is to be translated, "The Gentiles are law for themselves," for God has given them the law in another way (cf. 2:15). Paul also uses *nomos* to indicate a part of the law (e.g., 7:2b) and in the metaphorical sense (e.g., 3:28, divine commands in the widest sense). Paul often personifies the law, in that it speaks (3:19; 7:7), works (4:15), and rules (7:1). He is not here subscribing to the idea of law as a hypostasis, but he means that the law is the mouthpiece of the living God.

Paul views the law against the background of the cross of Christ. (a) In his death on the cross Jesus upheld the law's condemnation of all humanity. He became a curse (Gal. 3:13; cf. Deut. 21:23). He was made sin, yet only as the representative for the sins of others (2 Cor. 5:21; cf. Lk. 22:37, quoting Isa. 53:12). These statements indicate a deliberate, vicarious act by Jesus on our behalf.

(b) At the same time Christ fulfilled all the obedience required by the law (Phil. 2:8), so that now that he has fulfilled the law, salvation rests not on our meeting certain conditions, but on the simple fact that the law has now been fulfilled (Rom. 3:31).

(c) Because they believe in Jesus, Christians are no longer under the law (1 Cor. 9:20b). They are free to be as people "not having the law [*anomos*] ... so as to win those not having the law [*anomois*]" (9:21). They are also free to fulfill the law in love (Rom. 13:10b; Gal. 5:14, 22), to be as those under the law in order to win those under the law, i.e., the Jews (1 Cor. 9:20). The author and inspirer of such love is the Holy Spirit, who brings believers from the realm of the law and flesh with its resulting sin and death (Rom. 8:4; Gal. 5:18, 22).

(d) Since Christ is the end and goal (*telos*) of the law for believers (Rom. 10:4), Paul can look back from his vantage point, as it were, and describe the law both as having no more role to play in salvation and at the same time as possessing a valid function apart from Christ (Rom. 5:20–21; Gal. 3:19–29). The law, which is holy and good (Rom. 7:12), was one of God's gifts to Israel (9:4, here *nomothesia* means giving of the law). It came in "so that the trespass might increase" (5:20; cf. 7:8–13; 1 Cor. 15:56b) and so that people might be "held prisoners by the law" and sin, with no prospect of escape until Christ should come (Gal. 3:22–23)—a dreadful thought, were it not for God's superabundant grace (Rom. 5:20b) and his gift of sonship (Gal. 3:25–29)!

(e) Those who stand before God "under the law" (Rom. 2:12b, i.e., the Jews) must reckon with the following consequences: The law demands entire obedience (Gal. 3:10, quoting Deut. 27:26); only those who *do* the law will live and be justified (Gal. 3:12b, quoting Lev. 18:5), while those who do not obey are condemned (Rom. 2:12b; Gal. 3:10). No one is justified before God merely by hearing or knowing the law (Rom. 2:12–13a). To be justified one must be made alive, which is precisely where the law fails (7:9–10; Gal. 3:21). Indeed, only those who have faith in Christ are made alive (3:26–27). Thus law is linked with sin, and faith with promise. But the law is not contrary to the promise (3:17) but has an educational part to play, both within redemptive history and in individual experience, driving us to Christ and to faith in him.

The law is a *paidagōgos*, a custodian or tutor (Gal. 3:24–25). A *paidagōgos* was usually a slave whose duty it was to take the pupil to school and to supervise his conduct (→ *paideuō*, 4084). The law produces a startling realization of sin that does not save (Rom. 3:20; 7:7); it calls forth a cry for help in one's lost condition (7:24), a cry that can be answered effectively only by Jesus Christ (7:25).

(f) Even those "who sin apart from the law" (*anomōs* in Rom. 2:12a), i.e., before Christ came or outside the bounds of Christianity, do not conform to God's will (3:23). Outside the law people are judged by God according to what they have done (2:6–7), for the Gentiles can know what is good, the work of the law being "written on their hearts, their consciences also bearing witness" (3:15; cf. 1:32). Deep within themselves they know they are sinners. Thus whether a people live within the Jewish law or outside of it, both Jews and Gentiles will meet the same judgment, without respect of persons (2:11–12, 16), according to their works.

Destruction and death await everyone (Rom. 3:23, 27; 6:23; 7:10, 11c, 13), for no one has put into practice his or her knowledge of what is good (3:23; 7:18–19, 21). All humans, therefore, depend for salvation on Christ's work, which has to be appropriated by faith (3:25–26, 29–30), apart from observing the law (3:28).

(g) This indicates the fundamental weakness of the law, namely, that its only answer to sin is to forbid and condemn it. The law cannot overcome sin, since it depends on the cooperation of the flesh (NIV, "sinful nature"), which is weak (Rom. 8:3). Here "the flesh" (*sarx*, → 4922) means would-be autonomous human nature, incapable of obedience. The law is part of the fabric of this world (→ *stoicheion*, 5122) and thus cannot lead us beyond it. What the law demands can be wrought only by the Spirit on the basis of the work of Christ (8:4). The law is essentially a letter that kills, while the life of the new covenant is the Spirit who makes alive (7:6; 2 Cor. 3:6).

(h) The commandment to love, which can be fulfilled in the Spirit, can now be called the "law of Christ" (Gal. 6:2; cf. 1 Cor. 9:21). It is the Torah of the Lord, which he himself has lived out. On raising us to spiritual life, he can require of us its fulfillment.

(i) Occasionally the law is invoked as a secondary authority, in order to provide scriptural support for Paul's injunctions to the church. In 1 Cor. 9:8–12 Paul uses Deut. 25:4 to back up his claim that, as an apostle, he had the right to be materially supported by the church. In 1 Cor. 14:21 he combines quotations from Deut. 28:49 and Isa. 28:11–12 in order to regulate speaking in tongues. Basically, however, the life of the church is controlled not by the principle, "Anything contrary to the law is sin," but rather, "Everything that does not come from faith is sin" (Rom. 14:23).

3. Eph. and the Pastorals contain statements in complete accord with Paul's theology of the law, but they also have other statements that indicate that a controversy had arisen over the law's function and that uphold the law as a regulative principle. (a) Eph. 2:15 is fully in line with Paul's doctrine of the law (see above 2 [b]).

(b) Within the struggle against libertinism and asceticism 1 Tim. 1:8 repeats the assertion of Rom. 7:12 that the law is good. But whereas Rom. develops the role of the law in provoking and convicting of sin, 1 Tim. 1:9–10 enumerates various categories of sin condemned by the law. Tit. 2:14 adds that Christ appeared "to redeem us from all wickedness [*anomia*, lawlessness]" (quoting Ps. 130:8). The "righteous" in 1 Tim. 1:9 no longer appear to be (as in Rom.) people justified by faith (cf. Rom. 1:17; Gal. 3:11). Nor did Paul say in Rom. that "the law is good *if one uses it properly* [*nomimōs*]" (1 Tim. 1:8). The false teachers of the law (*nomodidaskaloi*, 1 Tim. 1:7) are those who preach antinomianism as well as those who lead the church astray with their ascetic demands (4:1–3). This passage is thoroughly Pauline in its exhortation to receive God's good gifts of creation in a spirit of faith and thanksgiving and not to stand aloof from them in the interests of ascetic regulations. Like 1 Tim., Tit. 3:9 recommends the avoidance of quarrels about the law.

In 2 Thess. 2:1–12 the fact that Christ's return has not yet occurred is explained that the "man of lawlessness [*anomia*]" (2:3) or the "lawless one [*ho anomos*]" (2:8) must first appear, and the "secret power of lawlessness [*anomia*]," although already at work, is not yet revealed (2:7; cf. Matt. 24:12).

4. The writer of Heb. sees the law, esp. the sacrificial law, as a manifestation of the old covenant, inferior to and now superseded by the new covenant (8:13; 10:9b). Heb. contains extensive passages proving the superiority of the single, once-for-all sacrifice of Christ, the great high priest, over the offerings of the OT priests—a sacrifice, moreover, in which he himself is both offering and offerer (4:14–5:10;

7:1–10, 18). Thus in working out his teaching on inferiority and superiority, the writer puts *nomos* in the negative part of his comparisons (e.g., cf. 7:5 with 7:6–8; 7:12 with 7:13–15; 7:16a with 7:15–16b; 8:4–5a with 8:5b–6; 9:19–22 with 9:24–28; 10:1 with 10:2b; etc.).

The vb. *nomotheteō*, to give laws, is used to present the same antithesis: The people of the old covenant received the law under the Levitical priesthood (7:11); Christ is the mediator of a better covenant, legally instituted on the basis of better promises (8:6).

Christ's overcoming of lawlessness (*anomia*) is the ground on which the new covenant is based. The Son has hated lawlessness (Heb. 1:9, quoting Ps. 45:7), and the Holy Spirit, speaking through the prophets, promised that one day sin would be finally forgiven; that day has now come (10:17, quoting Jer. 31:34). Since the new covenant is now a reality, the writer can state that the law never made anything perfect (Heb. 7:19; 10:1) and that the OT sacrifices are finished (cf. 10:18).

5. In the Gospel of Jn. Christ and the Jews clash vehemently over the question of the law. Jesus claims personally to reveal God, whereas they represent the rebellious "world." They measure him by the law (7:23, 52; 8:5; 12:34, quoting various OT passages treated as law), and he in return measures them by the law. He has an absolute knowledge of it, expounds it, and uses it to expose their hypocrisy (7:19; 8:17; 10:34; 15:25; in the last two passages Ps. 82:6 and 35:19 are called "law").

The Gospel of Jn. develops the basic thesis (1:17) that, as compared with the law given through Moses, the knowledge and truth revealed in Jesus Christ bring the full revelation of God. Christ's repeated use of "your own Law" (8:17; cf. 10:34) and "their Law" shows that the Son is not subject to the law. He charges the Jews with appealing to Moses merely in self-justification; none of them keeps the law (7:19; cf. Rom. 2:17–24). When it comes to healing and forgiveness, Jesus cuts through the pedantry and complacency with which the leaders treat the law (Jn. 7:23; 8:5–7). He uses the OT writings to support his testimony to himself (cf. 8:17 with Deut. 19:15; Jn. 10:34 with Ps. 82:6). The Jews, by contrast, are prevented from recognizing God's present revelation in Christ, since the Scriptures are nothing but rules and regulations to them (Jn. 5:39; 12:34).

The extent to which the handling of the law had become a matter for the specialists and thus something to be exploited is shown by the debate in the Sanhedrin after an abortive attempt to arrest Jesus. "This mob . . . knows nothing of the law" (Jn. 7:49), say the Pharisees, while one of their number, Nicodemus, points out their own disregard of the law (7:51).

The last legal debate (before Pilate) over the fate of Jesus demonstrates the utter paradox of his opponents' enslavement to the law. As an occupied people, the Jews were not permitted to carry out the death penalty laid down in Exod. 20:7; Lev. 24:16 (cf. Jn. 5:18). By demanding that Christ's accusers should judge him according to their own law, Pilate adroitly extracts from them admission of their hatred and also of their impotence (Jn. 18:31). Only by appealing to their own law, that of Moses (19:7), can the Jews get their prisoner put to death, albeit by a method that treats their law with contempt. But by thus rejecting the revelation of Christ, they make his willing sacrifice a reality. At the same time the judgment of the law falls not only on him, but on them (15:2–6).

6. In 1 Jn. 3:4 the equation of sin with lawlessness or transgression of the law (*anomia*) occurs twice. This does not imply some new legal ethic but combats what many scholars regard as the gnostic heresy of sinlessness (see 1:8, 10; cf. 2 Pet. 2:1–2). To counteract this teaching, 1 Jn. distinguishes between "sin that leads to death" (5:16b), which is apostasy from true faith in Jesus, the Son of God (5:1–12), and "sin that does not lead to death" (5:16a, 17), which can be confessed and forgiven (1:9). Those who remain in the true faith acknowledge that they need forgiveness for transgressions against the law (*anomia*) and that such forgiveness is available to them. Everything depends on abiding in Christ (2:1b; 3:6); such people then do what is pleasing to God (3:22–24).

7. On two occasions James uses the seemingly contradictory phrase "the law that gives freedom" (1:25; 2:12), both times in connection with his peculiar emphasis on not merely hearing but doing the word (1:22). This phrase probably comes from the Jewish-Christian Diaspora and refers primarily to those collections of Christ's sayings, such as the Sermon on the Mount (Matt. 5–7), that were regarded as the rule of the Christian life. Anyone putting them into practice was thereby set free from a literal observance of OT law. On both occasions James asserts a reward of blessedness to those who obey the law that gives freedom.

The preceding context and Jas. 2:13 make it clear that mercy is the chief element in this law of liberty, which Jas. also calls the "royal law" (2:8). It can be summarized in the command to love one's neighbor. Those who keep this command are free from the fear of having to keep the whole of the Jewish law by a minute observance of every single command (2:10–11; cf. Gal. 3:10). It remains true, however, that those who ride roughshod over this royal law by showing partiality will finally fall under "judgment without mercy," exactly as if they had not kept the OT law (2:13a).

Like many of James's other sayings, the prohibition of slander and judging (Jas. 4:11–12) has its origins in both the OT (Lev. 19:16) and NT (Matt. 7:1–5; cf. Rom. 2:2). Regardless of its source, the import remains the same. To speak ill of a fellow believer is to speak ill of the law and to sit in judgment on it. Again, God wants us to observe the law, but the Lawgiver (*nomothetēs*) and Judge are one, and one who judges another has ultimately to do with him whose judgment is final (Jas. 4:12; cf. Rom. 14:4). The twofold use of "one" for the divine name in Jas. 4:12 enables the reader to identify the "Lawgiver" as both the Father and the Son. (On the attitude of James and Paul to justification, faith, and works, → *pistis, 4411*.)

8. Acts provides a vivid picture of the controversies over the law that arose in the early church. Many Jewish Christians remained true to the law, but there were also Hel. Christians who thought in universal terms. With the exception of 15:5 and 23:29, all references to the law are found in discourses, which accords well with the author's historical approach and bring both persons and situations into sharp relief. There is a striking parallel between the accusations and prosecution that the Hel. Christian leaders had to face and the treatment meted out to Jesus. To that extent the disciples are indeed not above their master (Matt. 10:23–25).

The charges leveled against Christians were as follows: speaking against the temple and the law (Acts 6:13; cf. 6:11); persuading people to worship God in "ways contrary to the law" (18:13, against Paul in Corinth); teaching "all men everywhere" against the people, the temple, and the law (21:28, against Paul in Jerusalem; cf. 21:21). In the course of his defense, Stephen asserts that the temple is not God's dwelling place (7:48–49) and goes so far as to charge the Jews with not keeping the law (7:53; cf. Jn. 7:19; Rom. 3:19–20). This so provokes the Jews that he is immediately stoned (7:57–60). Paul, on the other hand, when defending himself against his Jewish accusers before Festus, opens his speech with the assertion that he has committed offense neither against the law of the Jews nor against the temple (25:8).

This is in line with the policy Paul had adopted ever since his arrival in Jerusalem. Having welcomed him to the city with joy, Jewish Christians pointed out that they had remained zealous for the law (Acts 21:20) and referred to the unfavorable reports about him in circulation, esp. that he taught Jews to forsake Moses, circumcision, and Jewish customs. Since his life was in danger, they advised him to show the Jews and Jewish Christians that he was true to the law (21:24) by financing the discharge of four destitute Nazirites, an act of charity considered particularly pious among the Jews. This advice to Paul and the fact that they insisted again that Gentile Christians should observe the so-called apostolic decree (cf. 15:28–29) show the efforts undertaken by the Jerusalem church leadership to maintain the utmost loyalty to the Jews and at the same time not to lose contact with Gentile Christianity as promoted by Paul.

Paul complied with the Jerusalem church's request and behaved as a devout Jew (Acts 21:26), but being recognized again by Jews from Asia Minor who protested publicly against his missionary activities (21:27–28), he was nearly killed. The tribune of the Roman forces, however, permitted Paul to address the people after his arrest, whereupon he emphasized his upbringing in the law (22:3) and also Ananias's loyalty to the law (22:12). The high priest, who had him struck during interrogation, was accused by Paul of violating the law even while administering it (23:3).

This positive attitude toward the law is explained by Paul's freedom from the law (cf. 1 Cor. 9:19–20). Paul knew that he was in the service of the *gospel* and thus saw no inconsistency between his present attitude and his insistence that in God's purposes of salvation the law has now come to an end (Rom. 10:4; cf. 11:13–14). The picture of Paul that emerges from Acts is of an apostle who opposed Jewish-Christian demands that Gentile converts be obliged to practice circumcision and keep the law (15:8), but who also delivered the terms of the apostolic decree to the churches (16:4; cf. 15:28–29), and even had his (half-Jewish) assistant Timothy circumcised out of regard for the Jews (16:3). Indeed, when preaching in the synagogue at Pisidian Antioch, Paul presented Christ as completing the justification left unfinished by the law (13:38).

It is noteworthy that the Roman authorities tended to reject the charge of illegality leveled against the preaching of the early Christians and treated such matters as mere controversies over Jewish law (e.g., Gallio, Acts 18:15; Claudius Lysias, 23:29).

See also *ethos*, usage, custom (*1621*); *stoicheion*, elements, rudiments (*5122*); *entolē*, command (*1953*); *grammateus*, teacher of the law, scribe (*1208*).

3796 (noseō, to be ill, be ailing), → 3798.

3798	νόσος

νόσος (*nosos*), illness, sickness (*3798*); νοσέω (*noseō*), to be ill, be ailing (*3796*); ἄρρωστος (*arrōstos*), sick, ill (*779*).

CL & OT 1. (a) In cl. Gk. *nosos* and *noseō* carry primarily the meaning of illness, to be ill. *nosos* can be used specifically for calamity, torment, and madness. But it can be used in a fig. sense for a plague afflicting a city, chronic disease of the state, weakness of character, or depravity. *noseō* occurs more frequently than *nosos* in general contexts and in fig. expressions.

(b) Like many in the ancient world, the Gks. drew a connection between sickness and attacks of invisible deities, whose wrath they sought to appease through sacrifice and other ritual practices. This conclusion was later modified by critical reflection from the philosophers, who explained disease in anthropological terms, i.e., the outward disease corresponds to an inward suffering, which consists of ignorance. Medicinal therapy and philosophical instruction and virtue are thus closely related.

2. (a) In the LXX *nosos* occurs only 13x and *noseō* 2x. Sickness is also rendered by the nouns *malakia* (→ *3433*) and *arrōstia* (not in NT). The fact that a general word for illness is not often found in the LXX may be due to the OT tendency to be concerned less with generalities than with concrete manifestations (e.g., specific skin diseases, cf. Lev. 13–14). Israel may have found it difficult to come to terms with the fact of disease, for there is scarcely any recognition of a fig. or spiritualized understanding of illness.

(b) The OT view of sickness fits into the pattern of the general understanding of disease in the ANE in that, like sexual discharges and death, it belongs to the sphere of the unclean (→ *katharos*, *2754*). When healing takes place, there has to be a corresponding purificatory rite (cf. Lev. 13–14; Lk. 17:12–14). Moreover, often sin and disease are linked together (e.g., Ps. 32:1–5; 38:3–8, 18). The prophets compare Israel's sin to a person who is mortally ill (Isa. 1:5–6; Jer. 30:12–

13). The recognition that disease is ordained, or at least permitted, by Yahweh leads the OT believer to see it as a divine judgment on sin (2 Sam. 12:15–19; 24:10–15; cf. esp. the friends of Job). Recovery, by contrast, leads to thanksgiving for forgiveness (Ps. 103:3; Isa. 38:16–17).

(c) In Jud. the dogma of retributive suffering reaches its most consistent extreme (cf. Jn. 9:2), for the rabbis were able to name the sin that corresponded to every disease. At the same time, however, the Jews developed the concept of discipline imposed out of love; with this came encouragement to visit, pray for, and help the sick, since God is esp. near to those who are ill.

NT 1. In the NT *nosos* (11x) and *arrōstos* (5x) occur mostly in the Gospels and Acts. The single occurrence of *noseō* (1 Tim. 6:4) has a fig. meaning. The NT thus retains the realism of the OT: The problem of disease is primarily that which concerns its concrete manifestations. Other elements taken over from the OT are the idea of the influence of demonic powers (Lk. 13:11, 16; Rev. 16:2) and the connection between disease and sin (Jn. 5:14; 1 Cor. 11:30).

2. Although the NT occasionally views sickness as divine punishment or judgment (e.g., 1 Cor. 11:32; Rev. 6:8), it also addresses the beneficial chastening that results from God's love (Heb. 12:4–13; cf. Prov. 3:11–12). The primary insight of the NT, however, is that disease and disease-bringing demons, even if they are permitted by God to act (Acts 12:23; 2 Cor. 12:7–9), have to do with the power of hostile forces that oppose God's rule (Mk. 1:23–24; 3:27). Jesus' battle against disease accords with this. He broke the terrible connection of sin and disease (Mk. 2:5–12) by his assurance of forgiveness and brought in the dawn of God's kingdom by casting out demons and healing the sick (Mk. 5:1–13; esp. Lk. 11:20; → *iaomai*, to heal, *2615*).

3. (a) In Matt. 9:12–13 sinners are described in a parabolic saying as those who are sick (cf. Isa. 1:5–6). Jesus' commission in coming to the earth is to transform our plight by his call to repentance and his works of healing.

(b) Matt. 8:17 uses Isa. 53:4 to summarize Jesus' ministry of healing: "He took up our infirmities [*astheneia*] and carried our diseases [*nosos*]." Matt. interprets this verse as referring to the removal of disease by the power of Jesus. For both Isa. and Matt. sin was the root cause of disease.

(c) In Jn. 9:2–3 the disciples' question about the cause of a man's blindness is dismissed as inappropriate and replaced by an indication of its purpose: "that the work of God might be displayed in his life."

(d) Paul regards his own infirmity (2 Cor. 12:7–10; cf. Gal. 4:13–14; → *skolops*, thorn, *5022*), along with persecutions and other troubles (cf. 2 Cor. 11:23–28), as part of the suffering laid on the followers of Christ (cf. 1:5–7), in which by a dialectic process God's power becomes apparent: "For when I am weak, then I am strong" (12:10).

(e) The use of *noseō* in 1 Tim. 6:4 corresponds to the Hel. usage of the vb. Craving for controversy and disputes about words point to a sick condition in the inner self. The comparison of the spreading nature of false teaching with the progress of a cancerous tumor (2 Tim. 2:17) likewise belongs to the realm of Hel. thought.

See also *astheneia*, weakness, sickness, disease, timidity (*819*); *malakia*, weakness, softness, sickness (*3433*); *paralytikos*, paralytic (*4166*).

3803 (notos, south wind), → 847.

3804 (nouthesia, admonition, warning, instruction), → 3805.

3805	νουθετέω

νουθετέω (*noutheteō*), warn, advise (*3805*); νουθεσία (*nouthesia*), admonition, warning, instruction (*3804*).

CL & OT 1. In cl. Gk. *noutheteō* and *nouthesia*, derived from *nous* (mind) and *tithēmi* (put), describe exertion of influence on the *nous*. By means of admonition, advice, warning, reminding, teaching, and exhorting, a person can be redirected from wrong ways so that one's behavior is corrected. In contrast to *didaskō* (teach, → *1438*), which is concerned with the development and guidance of the intellect, *noutheteō* has to do with a person's will and feelings.

2. Except for 1 Sam. 3:13, the LXX uses *noutheteō* only in the wisdom lit. (e.g., Wis. 11:10; 12:2, 26, warn). The noun occurs only in Wis. 16:6, where the plague of serpents during Israel's desert wanderings was God's "warning" for the people. In the book of Job the vb. has the act. sense of instruct (Job 4:3). But it can also be used in a negative sense (30:1). The more unusual pass. meaning, to let oneself be taught, is also found in Job (23:14; 36:12; 37:14; 38:18).

NT In the NT *noutheteō* is found only in Paul's letters and Acts 20:31, where Luke reports a speech of the apostle; the noun occurs only at 1 Cor. 10:11; Eph. 6:4; Tit. 3:10.

In Ephesus Paul worked as a faithful and exemplary church leader with constant zeal for the continued life of the church, showing concern for every individual and "warning [them] with tears" (Acts 20:31). Elsewhere he warns the church leaders in Corinth as his "dear children" (1 Cor. 4:14). Even if he has to write to them in a correcting and critical vein, it is done out of his love for them and for their own good.

Col. 1:28 and 3:16 use *noutheteō* with *didaskō* in reference to the proclamation of Christ. Warning and teaching belong inseparably together, as the constant counterpart of knowledge and action. The aim of this teaching and warning ministry is that believers might become mature in Christ.

An important task of apostles, church leaders, and elders is to admonish the members of the church; on its part, the church should accept and recognize this ministry in love (1 Thess. 5:12). Admonition as a form of spiritual counseling is also the task of the whole church toward one another (Col. 3:16), provided that it is spiritually fit to do so (cf. Rom. 15:14). Individual members, when disobedient, must also be corrected by the church, so that they may be made aware of the wrongness of what they are doing and won back again (1 Thess. 5:14; 2 Thess. 3:15). Failure to respond to such admonition can under certain circumstances lead to a total rejection of the one being warned (Tit. 3:10).

According to Eph. 6:4, the right way to bring up children is "in the training [*paideia*] and instruction [or correction, *nouthesia*] of the Lord." Such activity is not determined by the use or nonuse of certain educational helps, but by whether it is directed toward the Lord. These two words used are close in meaning. It is not the educational method, but the purpose for which it is used, that characterizes Christian upbringing. In 1 Cor. 10:11 *nouthesia* is used (as in Wis. 16:6) in the sense of warning. The list of punishments that befell the Israelites because of their sins should serve as a warning to the readers.

See also *parakaleō*, summon, invite, exhort, encourage (*4151*); *epitimaō*, rebuke (*2203*).

3808	νοῦς

νοῦς (*nous*), mind, intellect, understanding, reason, thought (*3808*); νοέω (*noeō*), apprehend, perceive, understand, gain insight into (*3783*); νόημα (*noēma*), thought, mind (*3784*); ἀνόητος (*anoetos*), unintelligent, foolish (*485*); ἄνοια (*anoia*), folly (*486*); διανόημα (*dianoēma*), thought (*1378*); διάνοια (*dianoia*), understanding, intelligence, mind, thought (*1379*); δυσνόητος (*dysnoetos*), hard to understand (*1554*); ἔννοια (*ennoia*), thought, knowledge, insight (*1936*); κατανοέω (*katanoeō*), notice, observe, consider, contemplate (*2917*).

CL 1. (a) The Gk. word *nous* has a variety of meanings: disposition, resolve, understanding, insight, reason, mind. Along with feeling and will, understanding belongs, like the ability to think, to the inner powers of a person. *nous* can also denote a moral attitude determined by the reflection of one's mind.

(b) In Gk. philosophy and religion *nous* came to mean reason or mind as the organ of thought that comprehends the world and human existence. It perceives, orders, and controls everything. In Plato *nous* denotes the ruling principle of pure thought, the highest of the three parts of the soul. True and divine reason rules in a human and in the universe, in the microcosm as well as in the macrocosm. Reason comprehends truth. In one's reason lies one's awareness of God.

Aristotle set understanding above the powers of the soul. He distinguished a theoretical *nous* from a practical *nous*. This reason, the most important part of the human mind, is immortal and divine. This linking of *nous* and the divine is also characteristic of Stoicism. Reason is the essence of God.

2. A whole group of words is derived from the root *nous*. *dianoia*, the act or faculty of thinking and reflection, is the special philosophical power of thought in contrast to sensory perceptions and feelings. *dianoia* also means way of thinking, disposition, intention, purpose, design. *ennoia* meant originally the act of thought, then the result: thought, realization, insight, disposition. In Gk. philosophy *ennoia* means idea, concept (e.g., the concept of time, the idea of the beautiful). *noēma* is that which is thought, also concept, plan. The meaning of *dianoēma* is similar: thought, notion, resolve, plan; it can also mean ulterior motive. *anoia* means folly, lack of understanding. Plato distinguished two kinds of lack of understanding: that resulting from madness and that resulting from lack of teaching.

3. Corresponding to these nouns is a group of vbs. that give expression to the process of thinking and to thought itself. *noeō* originally meant to perceive with understanding, including both sensory and mental impressions. In the philosophy of Parmenides, thought and being are made almost identical. A strengthened form of *noeō* is *katanoeō*, to direct one's mind toward something, to notice it. Thus it can mean to observe, test, comprehend, understand.

4. The verbal adj. *noētos* means intelligible; its opposite is *anoētos*, unintelligible, unimaginable; also senseless, foolish, indicating a lack of understanding and judgment. *dysnoētos* means difficult to understand.

OT 1. (a) In comparison with the central role played by the *nous* in the world of Gk. thought, it is surprising how little use is made of this group of words in the LXX. The most common word is *dianoia* (75x), whereas *nous* and *noeō* each occurs only about 35x, and the other derivatives even less. This sparing use of these words in the LXX is linked to the fact that the Heb. has no term equivalent to the Gk. *nous*. The Heb. *lēb* or *lēbāb* is translated in the LXX 6x by *nous* (e.g., Exod. 7:23; Isa. 10:7b) and 38x by *dianoia* (e.g., Gen. 8:21; Exod. 35:22; Isa. 35:4), but the rest of the time (about 800x) by *kardia*, heart (→ *2840*). In other words, in OT thought the heart was the seat of intellectual processes. This implies that understanding lies within the realm of moral decisions. An unusual use of *nous* is its translation of *rûaḥ*, spirit (Isa. 40:13).

(b) *ennoia* (13x) render various Heb. words, esp. in Prov. (1:4; 2:11; 3:21; 4:1; 5:2; 8:12; 16:22; 18:15; 19:7; 23:4, 19; 24:7; Wis. 2:14). All the Heb. equivalents mean understanding, wisdom, knowledge; thus, *ennoia* retains its sense of reflection, insight, perception, wisdom, though not the theoretical meaning of concept.

(c) *noēma* (3x) appears in the LXX in the sense of evil intention, plot (Sir. 21:11; Bar. 2:8; 3 Macc. 5:30). *dianoēma* can mean wise thought, insight (Prov. 14:14; 15:24; Isa. 55:9) or that element in the wicked that decides to worship idols (Ezek. 14:3-4).

(d) *anoia* (14x) means lack of understanding, folly, esp. in a moral sense (Prov. 14:8; 22:15), or even wickedness (2 Macc. 4:6, 40; 14:5; 15:33).

(e) OT anthropology knows nothing of the Gk. division of the soul into three parts, so human understanding does not become pushed into the foreground. Understanding belongs with the will and aims less at theoretical contemplation than at right conduct. The intellectual sphere is thus anchored more firmly in the whole person, body and soul, than in Gk. thought.

While words in the *nous* word group are more frequent in wisdom lit., they come into their own in the Gk. writings of the LXX (esp. Macc.). In other words, the Gk. concept of *nous* did not enter the OT tradition until the Apocr., which can speak of keeping in mind (2 Macc. 15:8), an understanding mind (4 Macc. 1:35; 2:16), and an innocent mind (Wis. 4:12). *dianoia* in intertestamental lit. means spirit, mind, consciousness, disposition, esp. in a moral sense. Philo writes of *dianoia* in the same way as he does of *nous*—the divine element in humankind, which makes us immortal.

2. (a) The intellectual element of the word group is displayed clearly in the use of the vb. *noeō*, for it goes back to the Heb. *bîn*, to understand, perceive, observe (e.g., Prov. 20:24; Jer. 2:10), or *śākal*, understand, have insight (e.g., Prov. 1:3; Jer. 10:21). Insight and understanding mean in the OT the process of judging and exploring the relation of things to one another. The difference from Gk. thought is that this insight is not regarded as an independent achievement of using one's critical faculties, but as a gift of Yahweh. All true knowledge comes from God.

(b) *katanoeō* (30x) is used in the LXX in the sense of to notice, regard, look at (e.g., Exod. 19:21; Ps. 22:17; Isa. 5:12). It can also mean spy, watch (e.g., Ps. 37:32). Philo uses it in the sense of meditative reflection, in referring to the beauty of an idea.

(c) *anoētos* means foolish, without sense (Deut. 32:31; Prov. 15:21; 17:28; Sir. 21:19; 42:8). It occurs alongside *mōros* (→ *mōria*, 3702) in a moral and religious sense: senseless, foolish (Sir. 21:19–20; 42:8).

3. (a) In Philo's writings we find all the elements of the Gk. concept of *nous*. The mysterious element of thought and understanding comes in, however, for stronger emphasis here than in cl. Gk. God is the reason behind all things, the perfect world-reason. Because reason is inspired by God, it leads to the knowledge of God. More important for Philo than knowledge of God gained by reason is an ecstatic knowledge of God, conveyed by God's Spirit.

(b) For the Qumran community understanding and insight belong only to God and the children of light. The mysteries of the insight and wisdom of God will bring wickedness to an end at the appointed time (1QS 4:18–19). Those who would join the community must first be tested for their insight (CD 13:11). The Qumran hymns praise God, who has lent to his own the insight to recognize his wonders and mighty deeds (1QH 11:22–23; 12:13; 13:9).

NT 1. If one goes strictly by statistics, the *nous* group of words in the NT does not play a central role. *nous* is found only 24x, *noeō* and *katanoeō* 14x each, and the other words even less. This statistical survey gives, however, a false impression. True, the concept of *nous* has only a peripheral place in the Gospels (but cf. Luke–Acts, which uses *katanoeō* 8x) and in the general letters of the NT. But we find this Hel. terminology more frequently in Paul (*nous* occurs 21 of the 24x). The apostle was not only the historical link between the early church and its Hel. environment, but also thought out the fundamental theological relationship between faith and knowledge. Although he adopted concepts and ways of formulating problems from Hellenism, he rejected Gk. attempts at solving them and relegated reason to its proper and inalienable place, both limiting and freeing it by means of the Christian faith.

All in all, it may be said that the NT gives this word group its own interpretation. All these words are associated more firmly with the will, and the understanding spoken of is an understanding of God and his will in salvation, an understanding of the word in Scripture and preaching. Understanding itself becomes a disposition, an attitude, and thus a standpoint of faith.

2. (a) The noun *nous* means mind, faculty of judgment, insight (e.g., 2 Thess. 2:2). But this understanding is a religious understanding, a religious faculty of judgment, set alongside the conscience (Tit. 1:15). *nous* is a term parallel to faith, which in the Pastorals means the same thing as religion: The false teachers are corrupt in their religious

discernment and not to be trusted in matters of Christian religion (2 Tim. 3:8; cf. also 1 Tim. 6:5).

In Rom. 7:23 Paul writes: "I see another law at work in the members of my body, waging war against the law of my mind [*nous*]." In 7:25 he goes on: "So, then, I myself in my mind [*nous*, i.e., understanding] am a slave to God's law, but in the sinful nature a slave to the law of sin." This *nous* is the same thing as the inner person or *egō*, the real self, which can distinguish between good and bad. The self agrees with the law that it is good; it wishes to fulfill the law. But against this law, the law of religious understanding, there fights the other law of sin. *nous* is here the religious knowledge and insight that honors and recognizes God's law.

Understanding, i.e., the faculty of religious discernment, is what is meant in Eph. 4:18 by *dianoia*. Here we read about the darkening of one's understanding—parallel, incidentally, to the futility of the *nous*. On the positive side we read of the gift of understanding, the ability to recognize religious truth, which from the hand of Christ Christians are enabled to discern him who is true, namely, God (1 Jn. 5:20).

(b) *dianoia* comes close in meaning to *nous* and means the ability to think, faculty of knowledge, understanding; then mind, and particularly disposition. NT usage is different from that of Gk. philosophy but close to that of the LXX. This is shown by citations of the OT in which *dianoia* stands in parallelism to *kardia*, heart (Heb. 8:10; 10:16, from Jer. 31:33; → *kardia*, 2840; see also Lk. 1:51). In the sense of understanding or mind, *dianoia* is counted among the inward powers of a human (Matt. 22:37). Yet *dianoia* can in some contexts mean the power of the disposition or the will and thus acquire a religious flavor. It is the spiritual consciousness, the disposition, the attitude of faith. It can be sincere (2 Pet. 3:1), but it can also be hostile (Col. 1:21). It can be fig. girded up, like one's loins (1 Pet. 1:13).

(c) Similarly, the NT uses *ennoia* in the sense of one's attitude. It is found alongside *enthymēsis*, thoughts (→ *thymos*, 2596), with the gen. "of the heart" (Heb. 4:12). Peter exhorts believers to arm themselves with the same thought with which Christ was filled when he suffered (1 Pet. 4:1).

(d) *noēma* is found only in Paul (5x in 2 Cor., once in Phil.). Even here we find a religious sense: the understanding of the divine will concerning salvation or thinking concerned with this topic. This thinking can be corrupted, so that it no longer concerns itself simply with Christ (2 Cor. 11:3). It can be hardened and made inaccessible to God's Word and the understanding of Scripture (3:14). It can become blind, so that it no longer perceives the illumination that comes from the gospel of the glory of Christ (4:4). The apostle, in the authority of his position and his commission, makes it his business to take every thought captive, so that it will submit, not to him, but to Christ (10:5). *noēma* is thus the general faculty of judgment, which takes decisions and pronounces verdicts right or wrong, depending on the influences to which it is exposed. In 2:11 the pl. refers to the designs of Satan.

At the climax of Phil. the apostle urges his readers to continual rejoicing, forbearance, and freedom from anxiety by committing everything to God in prayer. He then adds: "And the peace of God, which transcends all understanding, will guard your hearts and your minds [*noēma*] in Christ Jesus" (4:7).

(e) *dianoēma* appears only in Lk. 11:17, where it refers to hostile thoughts. The par. in Matt. 12:25 uses *enthymēseis*, thoughts, and refers to the Pharisees (cf. 9:4).

(f) *anoia* is lack of understanding, the absence of *nous* and *dianoia*. Those without understanding have no comprehension of Jesus' action toward a sick man on the Sabbath (Lk. 6:11). They do not understand the saving work of God in Christ. The folly of false teachers will come to light (2 Tim. 3:9).

3. (a) The vb. *noeō* means to perceive, recognize in a religious sense, with special reference to God, his acts, and his will. The juxtaposition of *noeō* and *kardia*, heart, in the quotation from Isa. 6:10 shows that *noeō* is regarded as an activity of the heart, a spiritual recognition (Jn. 12:40). According to Paul, through visible creation, "God's

invisible qualities—his eternal power and divine nature—have been clearly seen" (Rom. 1:20; cf. Wis. 13:4–5). Ultimately this recognition depends on faith. That the world was created by the word of God, only faith can "understand" (Heb. 11:3).

The parenthetical expression, "let the reader understand" (Matt. 24:15), calling the reader to understand the text aright, uses *noeō* in the sense of an understanding of the divine plan of salvation. In Eph. 3:4, Paul trusts that the church will have the spiritual understanding (*noeō* with *synesis*; → *5304*) of the divine, secret plan that he proclaims in his writings.

(b) The use of *katanoeō*, see and perceive, inspect, follows a similar pattern. The speck in the brother's eye is seen, but the log in one's own eye should be paid "attention to" (Lk. 6:41; cf. Matt. 7:3). Lk. 20:23 shows that *katanoeō* includes what goes on behind the scenes. In the same way, Heb. 3:1 stresses that it is not the outward figure of Jesus that we should look to, but who he really is, the emissary of God, the true high priest, the proper object of Christian faith. We are exhorted to focus our attention on our standing as Christians, working in love, good works, and mutual fellowship (10:24).

(c) The *anoētos* is the person who lacks understanding, knowledge, and spiritual insight; such people are "the foolish" (Rom. 1:14), the opposite of the *sophos*, wise. The Galatians, who do not understand the freedom that their salvation has given them, are *anoētoi*, foolish (Gal. 3:1, 3). So are the disciples who do not understand God's plan of salvation, embracing as it does the death of Jesus (Lk. 24:25); they do not understand the OT and its promises about the Messiah.

(d) *dysnoētos*, hard to understand, occurs only once in the NT (2 Pet. 3:16), where it refers to difficult passages in Paul's letters.

4. (a) The understanding of one's *nous* has particular reference to the OT Scriptures. The risen Christ opened the minds of the disciples that they might understand the Scriptures (Lk. 24:45). Those with understanding know its real meaning and the ways in which God manifests himself there; in other words, they know the secrets of the divine plan (Rev. 13:18; 17:9). Here *nous* and *sophia*, understanding and wisdom, are interchangeable terms. Divine wisdom has been given to those who are spiritual.

(b) Rom. 11:34 speaks about the *nous* of God, about his plan of salvation: "Who has known the mind of the Lord?" (cf. Isa. 40:13–14). In 1 Cor. 2:16 we read again of the *nous* of the Lord, of his plan to save the human race (also quoting Isa. 40:13). After this quotation Paul adds: "We have the mind of Christ." This is in keeping with 1 Cor. 2:12, that Christians have received the Spirit from God in order that they may know what God has given them.

In this context we should also consider Paul's remarks about speaking in tongues. The one who speaks in tongues is filled with the Spirit. Thus one's spirit prays, but the "mind [*nous*] is unfruitful" (1 Cor. 14:14). Paul also contrasts speaking with the mind and speaking in tongues (14:19). Note, of course, that speaking with the mind is also the work of the Spirit. Even where the Spirit and the mind are separated (14:14), it is only a matter of two different modes of the Spirit's operation. What is described in 14:24, the conviction of the outsider when he comes into the Christian assembly, is a conscious experience, the result of the comprehensible prophetic charisma.

(c) *nous* in the sense of right understanding leads to a right attitude of mind. The heathen have a foolish attitude of mind because they lack right knowledge (Eph. 4:17). Christians, by contrast, must be renewed in the spirit of their mind (4:23). The Spirit upholds and fills the mind of the Christian. The hortatory part of Rom. begins with the command to be transformed by the renewing of the mind (12:2), so that everyone may be convinced in his or her decisions and knowledge (14:5). Paul appeals to the Corinthians, beset by divisions, to continue in one mind and opinion (1 Cor. 1:10).

See also *phronēsis*, way of thinking, frame of mind, intelligence, good sense (*5860*); *synesis*, faculty of comprehension, understanding, insight (*5304*); *epistamai*, know, understand (*2179*).

3811	νύμφη

νύμφη (*nymphē*), bride (*3811*); νυμφίος (*nymphios*), bridegroom (*3812*); νυμφών (*nymphōn*), wedding hall, bride chamber (*3813*).

CL & OT 1. In cl. Gk. *nymphē* means the bride or betrothed. The term can be applied to a virgin, a young woman, a bride at a wedding, or a young wife. Similarly *nymphios* means the betrothed, a bridegroom, or a young husband. *nymphē* is also a term for feminine deities of lower rank.

In Hellenism, and esp. in Gnosticism, the picture of bridegroom and bride is used for the relationship of the *sōtēr*, savior, to humanity, and is taken into the concept of a sacred marriage. This prepared the way for religious eroticism and sacred prostitution.

2. The OT occasionally refers to customs that preceded the wedding (e.g., Gen. 24:59–67; Jos. 15:18–19; Jdg. 14; Isa. 61:10; Song). A girl was capable of marriage at age twelve, a young man at fifteen. While personal choice probably played some role, an agreement made between their families was essential. *nymphē* could also, therefore, mean daughter-in-law.

In the foreground of the OT passages mentioning bride and bridegroom stands the joy that they have in one another. This finds its finest expression in Song of Songs, which many Jews saw as an allegory of the relationship between Yahweh and his people (cf. also Isa. 61:10; 62:5; Jer. 7:34; 16:9). This joy is applied metaphorically to the relationship between Yahweh and Israel, esp. to the worship in which the congregation rejoiced in Yahweh as the eternal king and founder of the kingdom of peace in Zion (cf. Ps. 45; Isa. 60:1–9). This picture corresponds to the title of Israel as bride of Yahweh (Isa. 49:18; 62:5; Jer. 2:2).

NT *nymphē* is used almost exclusively as a metaphor in the NT. In Matt. 10:35 and Lk. 12:53 it means, as in Jewish usage, daughter-in-law. The bride can also be called *gynē* ("woman," → *1222*), because by Jewish laws of marriage the engaged woman was already regarded as wife (see Matt. 1:20, 24; Rev. 19:7; 21:9). *nymphios* in the NT is bridegroom, lit. and fig. (Matt. 25:1, 6; Jn. 2:9; 3:29; Rev. 18:23). The "guests of the bridegroom" were indispensable for the carrying through of the festive ceremonial (Matt. 9:15; Mk. 2:19–20; Lk. 5:34).

1. The wedding period is, as in the OT, a time of joy. In Matt. 9:15; Mk. 2:19–20; Lk. 5:34 Jesus rejects the need to fast at the present time. The time of the Messiah's presence was commonly compared to a wedding (Isa. 62:5); with Jesus the messianic age has dawned. Thus, the disciples were filled with joy. The parable of the ten virgins (Matt. 25:1–13) belongs also in this setting, though it is also a parable of judgment stressing the need for being awake and waiting. The OT parallelism of bride and bridegroom, symbolizing Israel and Yahweh, is here applied to the church and Jesus.

2. In Jn. 3:29–30 the relationship of John the Baptist to Jesus is described as that of the bridegroom's "friend," whose part was that of the best man. The final age begins with Jesus, but the friend prepares the way for him and has no greater joy than in seeing the wedding take place.

3. The picture (though not the vocabulary) of the bridegroom and bride applies to Christ and the church in 2 Cor. 11:2. Paul presents believers "as a pure virgin" to her one husband, to Christ (→ *parthenos*, *4221*). But he fears that they might be led astray from pure devotion, just as Eve was (11:3). The picture of marriage is also applied to Christ and the church in Eph. 5:22–32 (→ *gameō*, *1138*).

4. In Rev. 19–22, which describes the final consummation, we find the church-bride waiting for her heavenly bridegroom, here called the Lamb of God. Joy again stands in the foreground (19:7, 9). The church rejoices and adorns herself so as to welcome Christ as her Lord (21:2, 9–21). She is the heavenly Jerusalem, the eschatological church, who longs like a bride for the final fulfillment of her existence and calls out, "Come, Lord Jesus" (22:17, 20).

See also *gameō*, marry (*1138*); *moicheuō*, commit adultery (*3658*); *koitē*, bed, marriage bed, intercourse (*3130*); *hyperakmos*, past the peak, begin to fade; be overpassionate (*5644*).

3812 (*nymphios*, bridegroom), → *3811*.

3813 (*nymphōn*, wedding hall, bride chamber), → *3811*.

3814 (*nyn*, now), → *2789*.

3815 (*nyni*, now), → *2789*.

3816	νύξ

νύξ (*nyx*), night (*3816*).

CL & OT *nyx*, night, means the period without sunlight that is divided into 3 or 4 watches. In a fig. sense it means darkness, obscurity, blindness, powerlessness, death. In cl. Gk. *nyx* is only occasionally seen positively (i.e., as the time of refreshment in sleep). In general, night is ominous and brings fear.

In the OT *nyx* can simply indicate time (e.g., Gen. 7:4; Jon. 1:17 = LXX 2:1). But it can also be the hour of terror (cf. *nykterinos* in Ps. 91:5) and the time of drunkenness (Gen. 19:33), thieves (Jer. 49:9 = LXX 29:9), sexual misdeeds (Jdg. 19:25), murder (Neh. 6:10), and occult practices (1 Sam. 28:8). At night one is particularly prone to worry and to the attacks of the evil one (Job 7:3; Ps. 6:6). Yet *nyx* is also God's time, when he shows the way by a pillar of fire (Exod. 13:21) and makes himself known in dreams (Gen. 20:3) and visions (Dan. 7:2; Zech. 1:8). At the last day, when salvation is fulfilled, there will be no more night (14:7).

NT *nyx* occurs 61x in the NT, usually as an indication of time. In the 4th watch of the night Jesus walked on the water (Matt. 14:25). He spent the night praying (Lk. 6:12, *dianyktereuō*). Nicodemus chose the quietness of night for his visit with Jesus (Jn. 3:2). *nyx* is also the hour of escape (Acts 9:25), betrayal (Jn. 13:30), and denial (Matt. 26:34). Particularly in Acts, *nyx* is the time for the activity of divine powers: when angels perform their services (5:19; 12:6–7; 27:23; cf. Lk. 2:8–9), when God speaks in visions (cf. Acts 16:9; 18:9; 23:11), and when he instructs in dreams (cf. Matt. 2:12, 22).

Metaphorically, *nyx* can have the meaning of *skotia*, darkness, describing estrangement from God or Christ (Jn. 9:4; 11:10). In a similar vein, Paul contrasts *nyx* with *hēmera*, day, in connection with the era of salvation that has dawned in Jesus Christ (1 Thess. 5:5–7; see also Rom. 13:12). Those who cling to Christ are no longer under the curse of night (1 Thess. 5:5) but are awake (5:6; cf. 1 Cor. 16:13; 1 Pet. 5:8). When the last day breaks in "like a thief in the night" (1 Thess. 5:2; cf. Lk. 17:34), night will end (Rev. 21:25), "for the Lord God will give [his people] light" (22:5).

See also *skotos*, darkness, gloom (*5030*).

3820	Νῶε

Νῶε (*Nōe*), Noah (*3820*).

OT 1. Noah was the tenth in line of descent from Adam (Gen. 5:28–29) and figures as the hero of the flood narrative (6:11–9:19), as an outstandingly righteous man (6:9; 7:1) who "found favor in the eyes of the LORD" (6:8), and as the first man to plant a vineyard (9:20). With his wife, his three sons, and their wives, he survived the flood in the ark he constructed at God's command and became the ancestor of a new world.

Ezek. 14:14, 20 affirms that if Noah were living in Jerusalem in the period preceding its destruction by the Babylonians, his righteousness would avail to deliver himself alone. On a more cheerful note, on the eve of return from the exile, Jerusalem is assured that Yahweh's steadfast love for her will be as irrevocable as his covenant with the human race in "the days of Noah" (Isa. 54:9–10; cf. Gen. 9:8–17).

2. Jewish wisdom writers found in Noah an example of true wisdom. Because he "was found perfect and righteous . . . a remnant was left to the earth when the flood came" (Sir. 44:17). Again, "when the earth was flooded . . . wisdom again saved it, steering the righteous man in a paltry piece of wood" (Wis. 10:4). Philo notes that Noah is the first man recorded in Scripture as righteous. Various Jewish apocalyptic writings reflect on Noah, esp. on the fall of the angels in Gen. 6:1–4 that led to the flood.

NT 1. Jesus used the flood of Noah's day, like the destruction of Sodom and the other cities, as a pattern of the judgment that will overtake the world at the coming of the Son of Man, esp. in its swiftness and suddenness (Lk. 17:26–27; cf. Matt. 24:37–39).

2. Heb. 11:7 emphasizes Noah's faith, the quality of which was shown by his obedience to the divine command (Gen. 6:22). Thus "he condemned the world" (i.e., exposed the perversity of those who refused to believe God) and was justified by faith.

3. In 1 Pet. 3:19–20 is a reference to the spirits imprisoned because of their disobedience "when God waited patiently in the days of Noah while the ark was being built. In it only a few people, eight in all, were saved through water." To these spirits Christ is reported to have made proclamation—presumably of his triumph that ultimately sealed their doom. The relevance of the flood narrative to 1 Pet. lies in its providing an OT counterpart to Christian baptism, which the readers of the letter were "now" receiving (3:21).

4. In 2 Pet. 2:4–5 the preservation of Noah "and seven others" is set in antithesis to the imprisonment in Tartarus (→ *tartaroō*, *5434*) of the rebel angels until the final judgment (cf. Jude 6)—a guarantee of God's power to preserve the godly and punish the wicked. Noah is here called "a preacher of righteousness." In 2 Pet. 3:5–7 the destruction by water of "the world of that time" is viewed as a harbinger of the destruction of the present world by fire.

5. The absence of any mention of Noah in Paul's letters is noteworthy. Although Noah was the second father of the human race, he is not treated as a typical figure, as Adam is (Rom. 5:12–21). Nor does Paul make any reference to the "Noachian decrees" (Gen. 9:1–7), which were held in rab. teaching to be binding on all of Noah's descendants, Gentiles as well as Jews. Paul, instead, regarded the ungodliness of the pagan world (Rom. 1:18–32) as disobedience to God's *creation* ordinances.

The "Noachian decrees" may be reflected in the apostolic ruling of Acts 15:20, 29; 21:25, esp. in the Western text, where its emphasis on food restrictions gives a mainly ethical requirement that Gentile converts to Christianity should abstain from idolatry, sexual immorality, and "blood" (it is left uncertain whether this means eating meat with blood in it or shedding human blood).

Ξ *xi*

3825 (*xenia*, kindness to strangers, lodging), → *3828*.

3826 (*xenizō*, receive as a guest, entertain; think it strange),
→ *3828*.

3827 (*xenodocheō*, show hospitality), → *3828*.

3828	ξένος

ξένος (*xenos*), adj., strange, foreign; noun, stranger, alien (*3828*);
ξενίζω (*xenizō*), receive as a guest, entertain; think it strange (*3826*);
φιλοξενία (*philoxenia*), hospitality (*5810*); φιλόξενος (*philoxenos*),
hospitable (*5811*); ξενοδοχέω (*xenodocheō*), show hospitality (*3827*);
ξενία (*xenia*), kindness to strangers, lodging (*3825*).

CL & OT 1. (a) In primitive society strangers were generally seen as
enemies, because they were unknown. People were afraid of aliens
and those around them. Thus, they were often outlawed and either
killed or driven away. They had no rights. Later, however, a pattern of
relationship with strangers emerged, which originally developed out
of fear. The alien was seen as a messenger of the gods and out of fear
was given a helping hand and hospitality. The stranger thus came
under the protection of religion and the law.

(b) Homer saw the stranger and the beggar as coming from Zeus;
hence strangers must be treated with respect. For the Gks. in general
it was a sign of barbarity if aliens were treated as though they had no
rights and were mistreated. Strangers stood under the protection of
Zeus and the Dioscuri. Anyone who injured an alien was subject to the
wrath of the Erinyes. Conversely, those who honored the gods also
honored strangers. Hence temple and altar assumed the role of an asylum for the stranger who desired refuge there or sought the protection
of the priests. The first hospices for aliens sprang up in the vicinity of
holy places in the 4th cent. Worshipers came from far and wide and
needed to be housed and fed.

(c) Through close contact with non-Gk. cities and nations from
the time of the Persian wars, changes set in. The foreigner was simply
someone who did not belong to one's own cultic community or *polis*.
This did not prevent agreements from being made with strangers. Only
if trouble developed could they be banished. But the situation in religion was ambivalent. On the one hand, people were opposed to "new"
and "strange" gods, since they did not belong to the nation and endangered morals. On the other hand, the doors were opened wide to innumerable foreign cults.

(d) In Rome up to the imperial period the stranger in theory had
no rights. Only those who had a patron had any chance of lodging and
protection of the law. The expulsion of a troublesome alien was always
a possibility.

(e) The custom of regular hospitality to strangers persisted into
late antiquity. The motive of both Gks. and Romans was not only fear
of the gods but also love of humankind. In ancient catalogues of vices,
injustice to foreigners is ranked immediately after godlessness and
irreverence to parents. The ethics of popular philosophy exhorted
everyone to show friendship to the stranger. On their part, resident
aliens had obligations toward the state, such as payment of taxes and
military service.

(f) Gk. philosophy from the 4th cent. on developed the thought
of one's being a stranger. The soul was seen as an alien in the world,
since its true home lay beyond the material sphere. Being a *xenos*
became an anthropological category. The human body, like the world,
was only a temporary lodging for the soul.

2. *xenos* occurs 21x in the LXX. (a) In the OT, hospitality was a
self-explanatory practice and duty (Gen. 18:1–8; 19:1–11; 2 Sam.

12:4; Job 31:32). Thus Jael's action was a serious breach of the right
of a guest (Jdg. 4:17–21), which could only be justified by the extremity of God's people in their struggle for survival. Israel's law forbade
affliction of aliens, because the nation itself had been an alien in Egypt
(Exod. 22:21; 23:9; Deut. 24:14). Like the Israelites, aliens were to
enjoy the Sabbath rest (Exod. 20:10). Yahweh also loves and protects
them (Deut. 10:18). At the consecration of the temple Solomon inter-
ceded for aliens, that they might honor Yahweh and that he might hear
them (1 Ki. 8:41–43).

(b) The people of Israel were themselves "aliens" in the land of
Canaan (Lev. 25:23). The land did not belong to them; it was Yahweh's
property and could not be sold permanently. But since they were God's
possession, they enjoyed his protection (1 Chr. 29:15; Ps. 39:12; 61:4–
5; 119:19). Ultimately the Israelites were aliens in the world (Est.
3:13; but cf. already Num. 23:9), a view based on the recognition that
Yahweh himself is not an immanent power within the world. Rather,
as its Creator and Lord he stands over it, and his acts can be "strange"
and "alien" (Isa. 28:21).

(c) It was a great misfortune whenever foreigners conquered the
land that God had given his people as a dwelling place (Lam. 5:2). It
was seen as the Lord's punishment as they were led away into foreign countries out of the land God had given them (e.g., Deut. 29:28;
Jer. 5:19).

(d) The protection afforded to an alien in Israel was not extended
to foreign religions. Such cults were condemned and punished as idolatry (Deut. 4:25–28; Jos. 24:23; 1 Ki. 11:4–6; Jer. 5:19).

(e) Yahweh is Lord over all the nations (cf. Amos 9:7). Hence the
prophets spoke of the coming proclamation of God's glory among the
heathen (Isa. 42:6–7; 66:19) and promised their turning to Yahweh
(14:1; 45:14–24; 56:1–8; Ezek. 47:22–23; Zech. 14:16). The godless
were threatened with annihilation (Jer. 46–51; Ezek. 25–32). In practice after the exile there was a strict segregation from the heathen (Neh.
13:1–9). Mixed marriages were prohibited and dissolved (Ezra 9–10;
Neh. 13:23–28).

3. Rab. Jud. held hospitality in high esteem. Those who practiced were promised a rich reward in the age to come. It is of great significance for subsequent ages that the LXX never (apart from Job 31:32)
translated the Heb. *gēr* (stranger) by the Gk. word *xenos*, but almost
always by *prosēlytos* (→ *4670*) or *paroikos* (→ *4230*). This led to the
OT regulations and commands concerning hospitality to aliens being
applied only to full proselytes. Some Gk. practices did penetrate Jud.
through the Hel. Diaspora: regular hospitality (Tob. 5:6) and the establishment of inns (cf. Lk. 10:34). The Essenes kept hospices in every
city for strangers.

4. For part of the Hel. period there was considerable danger of
Israel's being swamped by foreign practices even in the sphere of religion (1 Macc. 1:11–15). The Maccabean reaction and revolt were
directed against this. Those loyal to the law restricted trade with the
heathen. They refused fellowship and marriage with them. They were
afraid of entering Gentile houses for fear of defilement. But the rabbis also zealously took up missionary work, sometimes with considerable success in making proselytes (cf. Matt. 23:15). Philo and
Josephus strove to refute the charge of hostility to strangers, which
was leveled against Jews.

NT 1. *xenos* occurs in the NT 14x. In Matt. 25:31–46 (4x), care of
the *xenos* is equivalent to care of Jesus himself; refusal to provide hospitality to a stranger is to exclude Jesus. According to 27:7, with the
"blood money" flung down by Judas the high priests bought the potter's field for the burial of strangers, i.e., non-Jews.

398

2. The Gospel records show Jesus as a frequent recipient of hospitality in his public ministry (e.g., Mk. 1:29–31; 2:15–17; Lk. 7:36–50; 10:38–42). Hospitality also figures in the parables of Jesus (e.g., 10:33–35; 11:5–8). God's summons to his kingdom is depicted as a banquet (13:29; 14:16–24). Jesus sent out his disciples to proclaim the kingdom, expecting that they would enjoy hospitality in the towns and villages (Matt. 10:11–14; Lk. 10:5–11). Note that in Jud. hospitality was urged especially toward rabbis.

3. Missionaries enjoyed the hospitality of the early church (e.g., Acts 10:6; 16:15). In Rom. 16:23 Gaius appears as a *xenos*, i.e., as Paul's host. In 3 Jn. 5 another Gaius is praised for what he has done for believers from abroad. *xenia* (2x) denotes the lodging where Paul entertained people in Rome (Acts 28:23) and the kind reception Paul hoped soon to receive from Philemon (Phlm. 22).

4. On occasion, the idea of God as a stranger to someone occurs without the word *xenos* actually being used (Jn. 8:19; cf. Acts 17:23; cf. 17:20). Christ is "not of this world" and so is alien in this sense (cf. Jn. 8:14, 25–29; 9:29–30).

5. Eph. 2:19 says that, before their call to faith in Christ, Gentile Christians were *xenoi* ("foreigners") and *paroikoi* ("aliens"; → *4230*). As such, they had no part in Israel's call to be God's people and were excluded from his promises. But now in Christ they are "fellow citizens with God's people," i.e., Jewish Christians, and "members of God's household." As Christians thus become citizens in God's sight, they have their citizenship in heaven (Phil. 3:20; cf. Gal. 4:26; Eph. 2:6; Heb. 11:15–16; 12:22–23; 13:14). The patriarchs provide the pattern for this. They did not receive the promises but saw them from afar, thereby showing that they lived as *xenoi* ("aliens") and *parepidēmoi* ("strangers"; → *4215*) on the earth (11:13). Christians are thus put under a new divine law of life, which shields them from the vices of the heathen, who regard them as strange (*xenizō*, 1 Pet. 4:4).

6. The Athenians supposed that Paul wanted to preach "foreign gods" (Acts 17:18). Anyone living in Athens (both Athenians and "the foreigners") were eager for what was new (17:21). But Paul preached "strange ideas" (part. of *xenizō*) to their ears (17:20). By contrast, the church is warned in advance against being led astray by "strange (*xenos*) teachings" (Heb. 13:9). The sufferings that befall the church are not "something strange" but belong to the Christian's lot (1 Pet. 4:12).

7. *philoxenia* (hospitality) is expected from the whole church (cf. 1 Pet. 4:9). It is recommended as a virtue to Christians (Rom. 12:13; Heb. 13:2). It is even connected with a promise: Because some have practiced hospitality (*xenizō*), they have entertained angels without knowing it (13:2; cf. Gen. 18:3; 19:2–3). In the NT many a door was opened to a messenger of the new covenant and the host was thus blessed. Cornelius received Peter, and Publius took in Paul and his companions (Acts 10:23; 28:7). Paul also requested Philemon to have a guest room (*xenia*) ready for him (Phlm. 22). The Pastoral Letters indicate the importance set by hospitality in the young church. It is not only the bishop who should be hospitable (*philoxenos*, 1 Tim. 3:2; Tit. 1:8), but even the true widow was expected to show hospitality to strangers (1 Tim. 5:10).

See also *allotrios*, alien, hostile (*259*); *diaspora*, dispersion (*1402*); *parepidēmos*, staying for a while in a strange place; stranger, resident alien (*4215*); *paroikos*, stranger, alien (*4230*).

3830	ξηραίνω

ξηραίνω (*xērainō*), dry up (*3830*); ξηρός (*xēros*), dried up (*3831*).

CL & OT In cl. Gk. *xērainō* generally occurs in the pass. Both the vb. and noun are normally used in a lit. sense: of plants or of dry land, but sometimes of human ailments. In the LXX an act. form of *xērainō* occurs in Isa. 42:15 with reference to plants (cf. Jer. 51:36 = LXX 28:36). The pass. is more usual, however, and occurs in connection with trees (Ezek. 17:24; Joel 1:12), water (Gen. 8:7; 1 Ki. 17:7; Isa.

19:5–6), and Jeroboam's withered hand (1 Ki. 13:4). *xēros* often means dry land (e.g., Gen. 1:9); it can also be used of a sea that has been dried up (Jon. 1:9; 1 Macc. 8:23, 32). In Hos. 9:14 it is used of milk-less breasts.

NT In the NT *xērainō* occurs in the act. only in Jas. 1:11, where it refers to the scorching effect of the sun's heat on grass. This effect is likened to the transience of a rich man's wealth.

The pass. form occurs in the story of Jesus' cursing of the fig tree (Matt. 21:19–20; Mk. 11:20–21), which illustrates Jesus' perception of the Jud. of his day—a leafy appearance of righteousness but without the fruit. In Matt. the tree withers at once, while in Mk. it happens overnight. Judgment is also central in Jn. 15:6, where a severed and withering branch is fit only for burning. In Lk. 23:31, set in the crucifixion narrative, dry wood (*xēros*) symbolizes times of testing and difficulty; a fearsome fate will overtake those guilty of the crucifixion in the less propitious times that are coming.

The parable of the sower uses the vb. of plants that lack good roots and therefore cannot withstand the heat of the sun (Matt. 13:6 par.). Here again a judgment motif is central, for the coming of the kingdom does not meet with universal recognition. In 1 Pet. 1:24 (a quotation from Isa. 40:7), the idea of withering stresses the fleeting nature of human existence in contrast to the permanence of God's Word. In Rev. 14:15 the vb. must be understood as to be ripe (or possibly overripe), i.e., fruit ready for harvesting.

The drying up of the Euphrates (Rev. 16:12) also appears in a prominently judgmental context; this is a prelude to the final battle between God and his adversaries. In Heb. 11:29 the word refers to the drying up of the Red Sea. When Jesus refers to the proselytizing activity of the Pharisees in Matt. 23:15, *xēros* is used of land in general.

Several occurrences of both words can be found in connection with the healing ministry of Jesus: a man with a withered hand (Matt. 12:10 par., likely a form of paralysis; cf. "paralyzed" in Jn. 5:3), the woman with the flow of blood (Mk. 5:29), and the condition of rigidity to which an evil spirit reduces a young boy (9:18).

3831 (xēros, dried up), → *3830*.

3833	ξύλον

ξύλον (*xylon*), wood, pole, gallows, tree, cross (*3833*).

CL & OT 1. *xylon* is commonly used in cl. Gk. for wood as a building material, fuel, and that from which utensils and cultic objects are made. *xylon* as a tree is rare.

2. *xylon* is mentioned in the LXX (over 200x) as fuel (Gen. 22:3), building material (6:14; Exod. 25:10–13; 1 Ki. 6:15), and an instrument of torture (shackles, Job 33:11). Unlike cl. Gk., the meaning *tree* is common, denoting fruit trees, cypresses, and trees planted by running water (Gen. 1:11; Ps. 1:3; Isa. 14:8).

In the Garden of Eden, the tree of life represents the fact that all life comes from God as a gift; the tree of the knowledge of good and evil symbolizes the benevolent character of God's commands (Gen. 2:9). In setting the tree of knowledge as a limit, God lets humankind know that he both gives to them and requires obedience. But disobedience turns a created thing into a god, and the tree becomes a cultic object and the carving an idol. The prophets condemned Israel's apostasy as "adultery with stone and wood" (Jer. 3:9; cf. Isa. 40:20; 44:13–14; Ezek. 20:32).

Wood is rarely mentioned in the LXX as an instrument of torture and execution. However, executed criminals were "hung on a tree" (Deut. 21:22–23; cf. Jos. 10:26).

NT 1. The NT mentions *xylon* as a weapon (Matt. 26:47; Mk. 14:43) and as building material (Rev. 18:12). Jesus asked figuratively: "For if men do these things when the tree is green, what will happen when it is dry?" (Lk. 23:31). In other words, if Jesus himself was not spared divine judgment, how much more will Israel burn like dead wood in the fire of judgment?

In 1 Cor. 3:12 wood is mentioned metaphorically in the context of a series of materials ranging from gold to straw. There is only one possible foundation for the church—Christ. But we may build a variety of structures on this foundation, all of which will be tested by fire. Those that are perishable, like wood and straw, will be consumed, though the foundation will remain. One's work may be burned up, but the person will be saved, yet only as through fire (3:13–15).

2. The concepts of the tree (cross) as a curse and the tree of life are theologically more central. Peter accused the Jewish leaders of killing Jesus "by hanging him on a tree" (Acts 5:30; cf. 10:39). This expression, reminiscent of Deut. 21:23, stresses the shame of the crucifixion. As someone hanged on a tree, Jesus stood under the curse of God (see Gal. 3:13). He took on himself in our place and for our benefit the curse of the law, and by his death he has destroyed it (cf. 2 Cor. 5:21). Alluding to Isa. 53:4, 12, Peter declares: "He himself bore our sins in his body on the tree, so that we might die to sins and live for righteousness" (1 Pet. 2:24). The tree is the place at which Christ's body, laden with our sin, was killed. Through his death on the cross, sin was annulled.

The tree of life reappears in Rev. 2:7. What was forbidden to Adam and Eve after their sin is available in the new Jerusalem, where that tree grows on either side of the river of life (22:2). The righteous alone have access to this tree (22:14, 19). It symbolizes life and presents a contrast with the cross as the wooden instrument of death. But the significance of the cross is retained, for it is the place where God bears and overcomes suffering and death, so that he may give life to a world overcome by sin and death (22:14).

See also *stauros*, cross (*5089*); *dendron*, tree (*1285*).

O omicron

3838 (*ogdoos*, eighth), → 3893.

3842 (*hodēgeō*, to lead, guide), → 3847.

3843 (*hodēgos*, leader, guide), → 3847.

3847	ὁδός

ὁδός (*hodos*), way, road, highway, way of life (*3847*); μεθοδεία (*methodeia*), method, in biblical and Christian literature only in an unfavorable sense, i.e., scheming, craftiness; (pl.) tricks (*3497*); εἴσοδος (*eisodos*), entrance, access (*1658*); ἔξοδος (*exodos*), departure, exit (*2016*); ὁδηγός (*hodēgos*), leader, guide (*3843*); ὁδηγέω (*hodēgeō*), to lead, guide (*3842*); εὐοδόω (*euodoō*), to lead on a good road, succeed (*2338*).

CL & OT 1. (a) In cl. Gk. *hodos* denotes a walk, journey, or voyage by land or sea; in a spatial sense, the path or road where one goes, drives, or marches; also the passage a ship takes. The term is used early on in a fig. sense for the means and way of reaching or carrying out something, measures, procedure, the style in which one lives. Life is occasionally compared to a way.

(b) *eisodos* denotes entering, going into, entry; in the spatial sense the entrance or access to a place or building, the door (also fig.). *exodos* is the opposite: going out, departure; exit, door; fig., disappearing, the outcome of an event, end. In the sense of the end of life (death), it is rare. Anyone who does not know the way needs a *hodēgos*, a leader, to show the way (*hodēgeō*). Sometimes this vb. can mean to lead in the context of the journey of the soul to heaven.

(c) In Gk. lit. one often encounters the picture of the two ways: *aretē* (virtue) and *kakia* (badness). Whoever decides for virtue must be ready to undertake hard work and exertion. The motif of the two ways is frequently used in Hel. times with reference to the ethical decisions of humankind.

2. In the LXX *hodos* occurs nearly 900x, in both lit. and fig. senses. In most cases it translates Heb. *derek*, way. (a) God led his people by a way—out of Egypt, forty years in the desert, and then into the promised land. The way through the desert was a testing ground (Deut. 8:2).

(b) *hodēgeō*, to lead, occurs 44x, always with reference to God (e.g., Exod. 13:17; 15:13), mostly in Ps. in confessions of God's leading in an individual's life (e.g., 23:3) and in requests for his care and leading (e.g., 5:8). In Isa. 43:16, 19; 51:10, God is the one who makes the *hodos*, but wisdom replaces God in this leading in wisdom lit. *hodēgos*, leader, is found in a few late texts; only in Wis. 7:15 does it refer to God. *exodos* sometimes refers to Israel's departure from Egypt (e.g., Exod. 19:1; Num. 33:38; Ps. 105:38); elsewhere it is combined with *eisodos* in the sense of going in and out, which denotes continuous fellowship or all one's activities (e.g., 1 Sam. 29:6; Ps. 121:8).

(c) The expression "the way of God" often denotes the saving activity of God (Ps. 67:2; 145:17). His ways surpass human ways and cannot therefore simply be apprehended by people (Isa. 55:8–9). It is a different matter, however, with the ways God appoints as he bids us to walk in his commandments (e.g., Gen. 18:19). The frequent expression "to walk in the ways of God" means to act according to his will revealed in his law (1 Ki. 2:3; 8:58). That law is called "the way of the LORD" (Jer. 5:4), for which the prophets have to struggle to see that it is observed, because Israel repeatedly succumbs to the temptation to evade his demands (Exod. 32:8; Mal. 2:8). Other related expressions were also used: e.g., "way of your testimonies," "way of truth," "way of your commandments" (Ps. 119; cf. "[wisdom's] ways" in Prov. 3:17).

(d) Human life as a whole or in its individual aspects can be called a way (Isa. 53:6; cf. Ps. 119:105). God's eyes see all our ways (Jer. 16:17; 32:19 = LXX 39:19); he has them in his hand (Dan. 5:23,

Theod.). Thus it is good to entrust our ways to him (Ps. 37:5) and not go "in the way of sinners" (1:1). When we die, we go "the way of all the earth" (1 Ki. 2:2).

(e) The way by which God leads his people has salvation as its goal. The same applies to the ways he enjoins on us (Deut. 30:15–16), which is "the path [way] of life" (Ps. 16:11; Prov. 5:6). Turning from these ways leads to destruction and God's judgment (cf. Deut. 30:17–18). Wisdom maintains that wise conduct leads to a successful life, but foolishness leads to death (Ps. 1).

3. (a) Philo's use of *hodos* is influenced by general philosophical usage. The important lines of OT usage (i.e., "ways of God") are not found in him. The "royal" road that leads to God, the king of the universe, is equated with Wisdom, by which the spirit reaches its goal, knowledge of God. Asceticism plays an important role here. Philo also speaks of the necessity of a leader, since humanity does not know the way. It is the Logos, above all God himself, who, as the compassionate redeemer, leads the *nous*, the mind, on the right way.

(b) The rest of Jewish lit. shows the effect of the OT view. How God wants us to walk finds absolute expression as "the way" (2 Esd. 14:22). The way of the Lord is the way of the law or of righteousness. Probably the earliest attested reference to the expression "the two ways" in Jewish writing is *T. Ash.* 1:3: the way of light and the way of darkness. Likewise, the Qumran community speaks of two ways: that of truth and of wickedness. The children of righteousness walk in the ways of light; the children of error walk in the ways of darkness (1QS 3:17–21).

NT 1. (a) *hodos* in the lit. sense is found 55x in the NT, mostly in the Synoptics. The roads Jesus took are not mentioned, although he was often *en tē hodō*, i.e., en route with his disciples (e.g., Matt. 5:25; 15:32; Mk. 8:3; 10:52), and events happened along the way (e.g., Matt. 20:30; Mk. 10:46). "The way of a day" (lit., Lk. 2:44) is the distance one can cover in one day, a day's journey. "A Sabbath day's walk" (Acts 1:12) denotes the distance a Jew was allowed to walk on the Sabbath without transgressing Exod. 16:29 (about a half mile).

(b) *hodos* occurs 46x in a fig. sense, spread over the whole NT. It stands in part, like the OT usage, for God's deeds and saving activity (e.g., Rom. 11:33; Heb. 3:10; Rev. 15:3) or will (e.g., Matt. 22:16; Mk. 12:14; Lk. 20:21), often in OT quotations and phrases (Acts 2:28; cf. Ps. 16:11), and for one's way of life (Acts 14:16; Rom. 3:16; Jas. 1:8; 5:20). A further peculiarity in the NT is the absolute use of "the Way" in Acts as a designation for the Christian community and its preaching (see below).

(c) *eisodos*, entrance, access, approach, occurs 5x in the NT (Acts 13:24; 1 Thess. 1:9; 2:1; Heb. 10:19; 2 Pet. 1:11). *exodos* occurs 3x (Lk. 9:31; Heb. 11:22; 2 Pet. 1:15).

2. (a) Matt. 3:3; Mk. 1:3; Lk. 3:4 quote Isa. 40:3 with the call to "prepare the way" for the Lord. John the Baptist, the forerunner of Jesus, did so by announcing Jesus' coming and by calling people to repent and be baptized.

(b) In his Sermon on the Mount Jesus gives the double picture of the two ways and the two gates (Matt. 7:13–14). As in cl. Gk., the goals to which the two ways lead are brought into view. But here it is not the ethical problem of conduct, but the question of life or death, salvation or destruction, that is put before the hearers. The picture of the two ways figures in both Jewish and early Christian writings, though this saying is most closely related to Deut. 30:19.

(c) In connection with the conception of Jesus' high priesthood, Heb. 9:8 and 10:19–20 speak of the "way" or "entrance into the sanctuary," whereby *hodos* almost acquires the sense of *eisodos*, access. Jesus, the author of our salvation (12:2), has opened a previously nonexistent and living way of access for us to God through his sacrificial death. What separates us from God is sin; through Jesus' death we are freed from a guilty conscience (10:22). The underlying imagery here is the Day of Atonement ritual (cf. Lev. 16), in which the high priest entered the Most Holy Place once a year by means of sacrificial blood. Under the old covenant only the high priest had access to Yahweh; now we all do.

(d) In John's Gospel *hodos* is applied to the person of Jesus in a manner unique in the NT (14:1–6). Jesus there reveals himself to his disciples as the only way that leads to the Father: "I am the way and the truth and the life. No one comes to the Father except through me" (14:6). The goal of this way is fellowship with the Father.

(e) In Acts *hodos* occurs 20x. In addition to other uses as already discussed, Acts uses "the Way" as a designation for the Christian religion (e.g., 9:2; 19:9, 23; 22:4; 24:14). Perhaps this comes from such expressions as the Christian proclamation being termed "the way to be saved" (16:17), "the way of the Lord" (18:25), and "the way of God" (18:26). When Paul admits that he persecuted "the followers of this Way" (22:4), he means the Christian community and its message of the resurrection of the Crucified One. Included in this expression is the fact that this message also comprises a particular walk of life.

(f) The "most excellent way" of which Paul speaks in 1 Cor. 12:31b means living a life governed by love, *agapē* (→ 27), which is ranked above any aspirations after spiritual gifts (cf. 1 Cor. 14:1; Phil. 2:1–5). Note also 1 Cor. 4:17, where Paul uses the expression "my way of life in Christ." There he is dealing with conformity with Christ, and he summons the congregation to be his "imitators," i.e., to walk in that way.

(g) In 2 Pet., in order to combat heresy, Christianity is called "the way of truth" (2:2) and "the way of righteousness" (2:21). It is viewed from the angle of the new morality that it brings, which distinguishes it from paganism. The false teachers, by contrast, left the "straight way" and followed the "way of Balaam" (2:15; cf. Num. 22–24), thus bringing Christianity into disrepute. This and the similar expression in Jude 11 ("way of Cain"; cf. Gen. 4:3–8) should be understood from the viewpoint of later Jewish tradition, which saw Cain and Balaam as the originators of all libertines and heretics.

3. (a) The noun *hodēgos*, leader, guide, is found only 5x in the NT. In Acts 1:16 the word is used lit. of Judas, who guided those who arrested Jesus. In Matt. 15:14; 23:16, 24, Jesus refers to the Jewish leaders as "blind guides." Similarly, in Rom. 2:19, Paul characterizes the Jew who is instructed in the law as one who presumes to be "a guide for the blind."

(b) *hodēgeō*, to lead, guide, also occurs 5x. In Matt. 15:14; Lk. 6:39, it is used in Jesus' statement about the blind leading the blind. But it is used in Jn. 16:13 with reference to the Spirit of truth, who will "guide . . . into all the truth," and in Rev. 7:17 of the Lamb who, as a shepherd, will "lead" those who have been made perfect to springs of living water. In Acts 8:31, this vb. is used fig. for guiding someone in understanding the Scriptures.

(c) *methodeia* occurs only 2x in the NT, both in the negative sense of scheming or cunning devices (Eph. 4:14; 6:11)—threats to which Christians are exposed.

(d) *euodoō* means to lead along a good road; in the NT it is always fig., i.e., to prosper, succeed (Rom. 1:10; 1 Cor. 16:2; 3 Jn. 2).

See also *anastrephō*, to overturn, turn back, turn round; fig. behave, conduct oneself, live (418); *peripateō*, go about, walk (4344); *poreuomai*, go, to journey, to travel, to walk (4513).

3857	οἶδα

οἶδα (*oida*), know, understand (3857).

CL & OT *oida* is a defective perf. of the stem *eid-*, to see, with a pres. meaning, to know. In other words, if one has seen something, one knows it. The emphasis here, however, is on intellectual or theoreti-

cal knowledge (i.e., "I have perceived" = "I know"). *ginōskō*, by contrast, tends to stress the acquisition of knowledge (to come to know; → 1182).

As time went on, however, esp. in the development of Hel. Gk., *ginōskō* and *oida* became virtually synonymous. For example, in Isa. 59:8 ("the way of peace they do not know"), the LXX has *oida* and a variant reading has *ginōskō*. Note also Sir. 34:9–10 (= LXX 31:9–10): "An educated person knows [*ginōskō*] many things . . . an inexperienced person knows [*oida*] few things" (NRSV).

NT 1. *oida* occurs well over 300x in the NT, about 100x more than *ginōskō*. Paul uses *oida* 103x, Jn. uses it 84x in his Gospel and 16x in 1 and 3 Jn., the Synoptics use it 70x. One is hard-pressed to find any significant difference in Koine Gk. between these two words. In scholarly circles, however, the latter tends to get more attention, probably because of the relationship of *ginōskō/gnōsis* to the philosophical movement called Gnosticism (see further, *ginōskō, 1182*). When biblical writers appear to have an early form of this movement in mind in the context of their writing, they tend to use *ginōskō* rather than *oida* (though this is less true of Jn.).

2. On the similarities in use between *ginōskō* and *oida*, note such par. passages as Matt. 16:3 (*ginōskō*) and Lk. 12:56 (*oida*), "know how to interpret." Both Jn. in Jn. 7:27 and Paul in 2 Cor. 5:16 use the two vbs. synonymously in virtually identical phrases. Note also the various places where *oida* serves as a textual variant for *ginōskō* (e.g., 1 Cor. 8:2; Phil. 2:22) and vice versa (e.g., Lk. 6:8; Jn. 21:4; Rom. 15:29).

3. Briefly, as far as uses of *oida* are concerned, the subj. of the vb. is generally a person (e.g., Mk. 11:33) or a spiritual being (e.g., 1:24, 34). Regarding the obj. of one's knowing, one can know (or not know) God (Jn. 8:19; 1 Thess. 4:5; 2 Tim. 1:12) or another person (Matt. 25:12; 26:72, 74; Mk. 1:24; Jn. 1:31)—in the sense of either recognizing who that person is or knowing him or her personally. Esp. prominent is the knowing of facts or teachings (e.g., Mk. 10:19, the commandments; Rom. 2:2, God's judgment; 2 Tim. 3:15, the Scriptures); in such cases *oida* is often followed by *hoti*, that ("I know that . . . ," e.g., Jn. 5:32; Rom. 5:3). One can also know how to do something (e.g., Matt. 7:11, how to give good gifts; Phil. 4:12, know how to handle poverty and plenty). Paul uses this vb. in the sense of remember (1 Cor. 1:16).

Jesus had the ability to know a person's thoughts (Matt. 9:4; 12:25; Mk. 12:15), though the Son does not know the day or the hour set by the Father for his return (13:32). The disciples sometimes had difficulty understanding what Jesus was trying to communicate—e.g., in his parables (4:13) or in his reference to leaving for a little while and then returning (Jn. 16:18).

See also *ginōskō*, know (1182); *epistamai*, know, understand (2179).

3858 (*oikeios*, belonging to the house, member of the household), → 3875.

3860 (*oiketēs*, slave, household servant), → 3875.

3861 (*oikeō*, dwell, inhabit), → 3875.

3864 (*oikia*, dwelling, house), → 3875.

3866 (*oikodespoteō*, be master of a house, rule one's household), → 1305.

3867 (*oikodespotēs*, the master of a house), → 1305.

3868	οἰκοδομέω

οἰκοδομέω (*oikodomeō*), build, build up (3868); οἰκοδομή (*oikodomē*), the process of building, a building (3869); ἐποικοδομέω (*epoikodomeō*), build on something, build further (2224); ἀνοικοδομέω (*anoikodomeō*), rebuild (488); συνοικοδομέω (*synoikodomeō*), build together with (5325).

CL & OT 1. In cl. Gk. *oikodomeō* means to build, build up, and is used in many ways both lit. and fig. *oikodomē*, building up, building, originally meant the process of building.

2. In the LXX *oikodomeō* occurs almost 350x, mostly in the lit. sense for the erection of a building. *oikodomē*, on the other hand, occurs rarely and mostly in later writings. The fig. use of *oikodomeō*, which occurs esp. in Jer., is interesting. To "plant" and to "build" go together (24:6); they are God's work and have their opposites in God's judgment to "uproot" and to "destroy" (1:10). God himself will rebuild Israel (31:4; 33:7 = LXX 38:4; 40:7) by putting his words in the mouths of the prophets (cf. 1:9–10). He leads the nations into the fellowship of Israel and thus builds them up (12:14–16). This OT use of the concept particularly influenced Paul's usage (→ *oikos*, 3875).

NT 1. The opposites build (*oikodomeō*) and destroy (*katalyō*) were used in the accusation against Jesus at his trial (Matt. 26:61; Mk. 14:58; cf. also Jn. 2:19–20); the passages speak of destroying the temple with hands and in three days building another, not made with hands. Jn. 2:19–22 interprets this in terms of Jesus' resurrection and even uses *egeirō*, to raise, rather than *oikodomeō*. Mk. 14:58, however, can be understood perfectly well as a prophecy of the erection of the new fig. temple, i.e., the eschatological community. Such an interpretation agrees with the promise about building the church in Matt. 16:18. In any event, both passages ultimately refer to the believing community as the eschatological building of God.

2. The use of this word group in Acts must likewise be seen against its OT background. *anoikodomeō* in Acts 15:16 refers to Amos 9:11 and perhaps to Jer. 12:15–16 and promises the eschatological restoration of the people of Israel.

3. The most important passages for understanding this concept occur in Paul's letters, where almost all the occurrences of the noun are found (though the verbal use is more important). *oikodomē* has the meaning of a building only in 1 Cor. 3:9 and 2 Cor. 5:1; otherwise it denotes the process of building and has the same meaning as the vb.

(a) *oikodomē* describes Paul's apostolic activity (2 Cor. 10:8; 12:19; 13:10) against the background of OT models (cf. Jer. 1:10; 24:6; esp. the opposites of "destroy" and "build up"). In 1 Cor. 3:5–17 Paul combines the two images of planting and building in order to illustrate the process of building the temple of God (i.e., the Christian community, 3:16).

(b) Apart from the activity of the apostle, *oikodomeō* and *oikodomē* describe the inner growth and outer expansion of the community through the Spirit. There is one rule that applies to everything that takes place within the church: It must serve to build up the community (Rom. 14:19; 15:2; 1 Cor. 14:12, 17, 26; Eph. 4:29; 1 Thess. 5:11). Thus the gifts of grace and offices are judged according to what they contribute to that building up (1 Cor. 14:3–5; Eph. 4:12). Paul scolds the Corinthians: "Knowledge puffs up, but love builds up" (1 Cor. 8:1). The enthusiasts in Corinth perhaps had a slogan, "Knowledge builds up," which Paul here corrects. Similarly in 10:23 Paul corrects the Corinthian slogan that "everything is permissible" by urging people to ask themselves whether their actions are conducive to building up the community.

(c) The positive use of *oikodomeō* always refers to the community. Paul uses sharp words to criticize anyone who speaks in a tongue simply to edify (*oikodomei*) himself or herself (1 Cor. 14:4). Edification not aimed at serving others is self-centered and pointless.

4. In Eph. 4:12, 16, the image of the body of Christ appears alongside that of building. This leads to the thought that the building grows (like an organism). The same idea of a building growing (the cornerstone of which, Jesus Christ, has indeed already been put in position) appears in Eph. 2:19–22 (cf. also Matt. 21:42; Acts 4:10–11; 1 Pet. 2:7). To be built into this growing building means to be put in as "living stones" (1 Pet. 2:5). All these passages are concerned with the unity and holiness of the Christian community.

5. *oikodomē* is used as an anthropological term in an individualistic perspective only in 2 Cor. 5:1. The transient tent of the earthly body is contrasted with an eternal *oikodomē*, prepared by God, not made with hands.

6. *synoikodomeō* (build together; pass. be built into, Eph. 2:22) and *epoikodomeō* (build on something) underline again the idea of fellowship contained in the concept of "building up." Believers are rooted and built up in Christ (Col. 2:7). The Christian community is also built up together through the cooperation of all the participants (1 Cor. 3:10–14) and in unity with the apostles and prophets (Eph. 2:20), to become the one holy community of the Lord.

See also *oikos*, house, dwelling place (*3875*); *oikonomia*, management, office (*3873*).

> 3869 (*oikodomē*, the process of building, a building), → 3868.
>
> 3872 (*oikonomeō*, manage, administer, plan), → 3873.

3873   οἰκονομία

οἰκονομία (*oikonomia*), management, office (*3873*); οἰκονόμος (*oikonomos*), steward (*3874*); οἰκονομέω (*oikonomeō*), manage, administer, plan (*3872*).

CL & OT 1. In cl. Gk. *oikonomia* referred primarily to the management of a household, but was extended to the administration of the state and then to any kind of activity resulting from the holding of an office. *oikonomos* was used of people and has a more concrete meaning. It denotes the house steward and by extension the managers of individual departments within a household (e.g., porter, head cook, accountant, who were domestic officials recruited from among the slaves). Similarly, *oikonomeō* means to manage as a house steward, order, regulate.

2. The use of these words in the LXX does not give much help toward understanding the NT concept. *oikonomia* occurs only in Isa. 22:19, 21, where it means administration, office. *oikonomos* appears more frequently and is likewise used in the technical sense of a court official, chiefly the royal palace governor (e.g., 2 Ki. 18:18, 37; 19:2; Isa. 36:3, 22; 37:2). *oikonomeō* is used in Ps. 112:5 to describe how one "conducts" one's affairs (cf. also 2 Macc. 3:14; 3 Macc. 3:2).

NT This word group does not appear frequently in the NT: *oikonomia* occurs 9x, *oikonomos* 10x, and *oikonomeō* only once (Lk. 16:2). Nevertheless, a specific NT usage has been established that has two main different aspects.

1. (a) The words are used in their technical sense, both lit. and fig., to denote household and state managers and their tasks (Lk. 12:42; 16:1–8; cf. its use as a title with the name Erastus, Rom. 16:23). Also belonging in this category is Gal. 4:2, where *oikonomos* describes humanity's being like a minor child prior to the coming of Christ, but it also serves within the metaphor as the designation of an occupation, in order to clarify a legal concept: "He is subject to guardians [*epitropous*] and trustees [*oikonomous*] until the time set by his father." In Lk., the only Gospel in which *oikonomos* and *oikonomia* appear, *oikonomos* may be used alternately with *doulos*, slave (12:42–47; but cf. 16:1–8). Admittedly both of these passages are parables, so one can on this ground speak in a certain sense of a fig. use of the words.

(b) This use of the word group is found elsewhere in the NT. For example, in 1 Cor. 4:1 Paul uses *oikonomos* to describe his apostolic task and then names faithfulness as an essential requirement in a steward (4:2). Likewise, Tit. 1:7 requires that "an overseer . . . entrusted with God's work [*oikonomos*] . . . must be blameless." In 1 Pet. 4:10 one reads that all the members of the community, as recipients of the gifts of grace, are administrators of God's grace.

(c) To understand the concepts of this word group we must note that its root lies in the concept of the house, *oikos* (→ *3875*). God's people, God's community, form his house, which he builds up through those whom he has called to the task and to whom he has entrusted its administration. Such people must regard these household affairs as their own; they are merely stewards of the gifts entrusted to them and will have to give an account of their activities (Lk. 16:2; cf. Matt. 25:14–30; Lk. 19:11–27, which describe the same concept though without the word *oikonomos*). In addition to the gifts of the Spirit

(1 Pet. 4:10), it is esp. the gospel that is entrusted to stewards. Thus Paul refers to himself and his fellow workers as "servants of Christ and as those entrusted with the secret things of God" (1 Cor. 4:1). Likewise in 9:17 Paul calls the preaching of the gospel a "trust" that has been committed to him (his *oikonomia*), from which he cannot withdraw. Eph. 3:2 and Col. 1:25 perhaps belong here as well. In all these passages the divine office committed to the apostle is under discussion.

2. The NT use of *oikonomia* moves in a second direction in the sense of God's plan of salvation. This meaning, related to salvation history, could have arisen on the basis of the breadth of meaning of the Gk. word. In Eph. it is used for God's plan of salvation, hidden from eternity in God (3:9) but now, in the fullness of time, realized in Christ (1:10).

3. The two meanings of the term are not completely independent. Because God allows his plan of salvation to be proclaimed through human beings (1 Cor. 4:1; Eph. 3:9), the work of the *oikonomos* is rooted in the divine *oikonomia*. Since time has its function in God's plan, a definite period of time is given to the steward, even though he or she may not himself know how long it is (Lk. 12:46). At the end one must render account. Thus in God's plan of salvation time itself is a gift entrusted to us, to be used (Eph. 5:15–16; Col. 4:5) and managed responsibly.

See also *oikos*, house, dwelling place (*3875*); *oikodomeō*, build, build up (*3868*).

3874 (oikonomos, steward), → *3873.*

3875   οἶκος

οἶκος (*oikos*), house, dwelling place (*3875*); οἰκία (*oikia*), dwelling, house (*3864*); οἰκέω (*oikeō*), dwell, inhabit (*3861*); κατοικέω (*katoikeō*), inhabit (*2997*); κατοικητήριον (*katoikētērion*), dwelling place, habitation (*2999*); κατοικίζω (*katoikizō*), settle (*3001*); ἐνοικέω (*enoikeō*), live in, dwell in (*1940*); οἰκεῖος (*oikeios*), belonging to the house, member of the household (*3858*); οἰκέτης (*oiketēs*), slave, household servant (*3860*).

CL & OT 1. In cl. Gk. *oikia* originally denoted the specific dwelling place, *oikos* the whole house, the premises, the family property, and even the inhabitants of the house. Later, esp. after the LXX, the distinctions were not maintained and the words became synonyms. In popular speech *oikos* meant any kind of house, but frequently a particular house, even a temple. In such cases the divine name attached to *oikos* indicated the god to whom the temple was dedicated. The vb. *oikeō*, used intrans. means to have one's dwelling, dwell; trans. to inhabit, occupy.

2. *oikos* and *oikia* appear frequently in the LXX, both denoting a building (house, palace, or temple). But because Heb., like Gk., has no word for the small social unit we call the family, *bayit* (and hence *oikos*) also acquired the meaning of household (those bound together by sharing the same dwelling place); in a broader sense, family and clan; and even still bigger, tribal unit (e.g., the house of Judah). When Ps. 127:1 states that God must build the house if it is to endure, it refers both to those who live under one roof and to their heirs and descendants (2 Sam. 7:11–29), who must give one another unconditional protection.

3. (a) Used with God's name, *oikos* means the temple, the sanctuary. Beside criticism of the idea that anyone could build God a house (2 Sam. 7:5–6; 1 Ki. 8:27; Isa. 66:1), we find sincere expressions of joy at the privilege of being in the house of the Lord, esp. in Ps. (e.g., 23:6; 26:8; 27:4; 84:4, 10; 122:1). To this feeling corresponds the longing for God's house on the part of those who are prevented from being there (cf. 42:4).

(b) It is doubtful whether the idea of the "house of God" is transferred from the temple to the congregation worshiping in that place in the same way as *oikos* meant both house and family. All the statements about the house of God remain firmly attached to the earthly

sanctuary. The only verse that expressly lies behind the NT understanding of the congregation as the "house of God" (Num. 12:7 = Heb. 3:2, 5) does not refer directly to the temple but to the land in which Yahweh (through his people) has settled and therefore reigns. Most likely an extended use of "house of David" for the people of God prepared the way for the idea that the community was "God's house" and "God's building."

4. In the Qumran documents "house" denotes the Qumran community, which understood itself as a temple or sanctuary (1QS 8:9; 9:6; CD 3:19).

NT   *oikos* and *oikia* are virtually synonymous in the NT and have the same range of meaning as in cl. Gk. and the LXX. Nevertheless, they occur in a number of characteristic phrases peculiar to the NT. In these *oikos* appears more frequently.

1. The most frequent use of both *oikos* and *oikia* is in the lit. sense of house (e.g., Matt. 2:11; 7:24–27; 9:7; Mk. 7:30) and in the simple metaphorical sense of family, household (e.g., Matt. 13:57; Mk. 6:4; Jn. 4:53; 1 Cor. 1:16; 16:15; 2 Tim. 1:16; 4:19).

2. Passages that use *oikos theou* ("house of God") for the temple are self-explanatory (e.g., Mk. 2:26; 11:17; Jn. 2:16–17). The only question has to do with Acts 7:46–50, whether Stephen is here criticizing Solomon's building of a house for God (7:47) in contrast with David's request to be allowed to make God a dwelling place (*skēnōma* in 7:46; → *skēnē, 5008*). The statement, illustrated by the allusion to Isa. 66:1 that "the Most High does not live in houses made by men" (7:48), may support such an interpretation. In any case, Stephen's words had a blasphemous ring for the Jews.

3. Passages that speak of "the house of Israel," "the house of Jacob," or "the house of Judah" (e.g., Lk. 1:33; Acts 7:42; Heb. 8:8, 10) are linked with the metaphorical sense of house, family, race (cf. "house . . . of David" Lk. 1:69; 2:4), which they extend in the direction of the people of God. In this they are following the OT example.

4. (a) The NT designation of the Christian community as the house of God goes beyond the OT model (Heb. 3:2–6; 10:21; 1 Pet. 2:5; 4:17). Behind this, perhaps, lies the OT concepts of God's proprietary rights over his people (expressed there, admittedly, more through the images of the vine, the vineyard, and the plantation, Ps. 80:8–16; Isa. 5:7; Jer. 2:21; Hos. 10:1; cf. 1 Cor. 3:6–9), but which apply equally in the case of the house. Further, note that Qumran documents also see the community as a holy house, built on the foundation of truth (1QH 7:8–9).

(b) In its exposition of Num. 12:7, Heb. 3:1–6 is linked to the OT in its terminology, but it extends the thought. Moses and Christ are contrasted: Moses was "faithful in all God's house" as a servant, while Christ was the "son" and "builder" of the house and thus superior. Whatever sense "house" may have had in Num. 12:7 (Israel as God's people or God's royal household), for the writer of Heb. it meant that the Christian community is "God's house," as 3:6b concludes: "We are his house, if we hold on to our courage and the hope of which we boast."

(c) What is important in this connection is not only that God or Christ is regarded as the builder of the house, but also that the Christian community as a whole is designated as a house. Moreover, Paul's references to the body as the temple of the Holy Spirit (1 Cor. 3:16; cf. 6:19), an idea undoubtedly connected with the idea of the house of God, are to be understood as the Christian community and the problems that arise from the fellowship.

(d) Eph. 2:19–22 shows that the ideas contained in the terms "household" of God and "temple" of God naturally run into one another. Here, no less than six different derivatives of *oikos* (though not *oikos* itself) are used to describe the spiritual reality of the community under the metaphor of the temple and of a building. In 1 Pet. 2:4–5 the images also overlap. Christians should allow themselves to be built up as spiritual stones into a spiritual house (→ *oikodomeō, 3868*), in order to present spiritual sacrifices to God as (here the picture changes) a spiritual priesthood. When 4:17 reckons that the judgment will begin with "the family [*oikos*] of God," the natural assumption is the Christian community. Similarly, 1 Tim. 3:15 expressly identifies "God's household [*oikos*]" with "the church of the living God, the pillar and foundation of the truth."

(e) Given the fig. use of the terms, it was inevitable that numerous related concepts and images would be introduced to elucidate the truth concerning the Christian community as God's house. There is the idea of the foundation (1 Cor. 3:10–12; Eph. 2:20; 2 Tim. 2:19), of Christ as the capstone or cornerstone (Acts 4:11; Eph. 2:20; 1 Pet. 2:4), of Christians as living stones (1 Pet. 2:5), of pillars (1 Tim. 3:15), and above all of the temple (1 Cor. 3:16–17; 6:19; 2 Cor. 6:16; Eph. 2:21).

5. (a) The idea of the church as the family of God came into being in the early Christian community through the house churches. The household as a community (the family included slaves) formed the smallest unit and basis of the congregation. The house churches mentioned in the NT (Acts 11:14; 16:15, 31, 34; 18:8; 1 Cor. 1:16; 2 Tim. 1:16; 4:19; Phlm. 2) no doubt came into being through the use of the homes as meeting places. The gospel was preached in them (Acts 5:42; 20:20), and the Lord's Supper was celebrated there (2:46). The conversion of the head of the house brought the whole family into the congregation and—however it is to be understood—into the faith (16:31, 34; 18:8).

The NT also speaks of the baptism of whole households in the same way (Acts 16:15; 1 Cor. 1:16; cf. Acts 16:33; 18:8). For the question whether one may conclude from this that the early church practiced infant baptism, → *baptizō, 966.*

(b) The formation of the house churches was of the greatest significance for the spreading of the gospel. With them the early church took over the natural order of life without falling into idealization of the house churches. The way in which the Gospels take up Micah's prophecy of the end times (Mic. 7:6; see Matt. 10:35–36; Lk. 12:53) indicates that the Christian community had to reckon with the disruption of the family for the sake of the gospel. Those who believe in Jesus are promised "in this present age ... homes, brothers, sisters, mothers, children" (Mk. 10:30 par. Matt. 19:29; Lk. 18:29–30). The place of the disrupted family is taken by the new family of God, the Christian community.

6. Jesus in Jn. 14:2 promises his disciples "many rooms" in his "Father's house," into which the disciples will be received when the Lord returns to establish God's kingdom. Most likely behind this lies the notion of Christ's followers as forming a house or family.

7. (a) The vb. *oikeō*, live, occurs in the NT both in a lit. and fig. sense. Belonging to the former category is 1 Cor. 7:12–13, which deals with marriages of Christians and non-Christians, while 1 Tim. 6:16—God "lives in unapproachable light"—stands on the borderline between lit. and fig. meanings. In a fig. sense *oikeō* describes the inner processes in humans; for example, the phrase "sin living in me" (Rom. 7:20, cf. 7:18) depicts the old self, while the truth about the new self is reflected in the confession of faith, "the Spirit of God lives in you" (8:9; cf. 8:11; 1 Cor. 3:16). *katoikizō* occurs in the same sense in Jas. 4:5.

(b) The compound *katoikeō* occurs more frequently in the NT than *oikeō*. Beside the widespread use of the word in its lit. meaning, it is also used for the possession of a person by God, by Christ, or by ungodly powers. Demons "live" in a person (Matt. 12:45). To believers God's purpose is "that Christ may dwell in your hearts through faith" (Eph. 3:17). Col. 2:9 can declare that in Christ "all the fullness of the Deity lives in bodily form" (cf. 1:19; → *plēroō, 4444*). The noun *katoikētērion*, dwelling place, home, occurs in connection with the great picture of the Christian community as the spiritual building and temple (Eph. 2:19–22).

(c) Another compound, *enoikeō*, dwell in, indwell, is only used in the fig. sense in the NT, similarly to *katoikeō*. God himself will live among us (2 Cor. 6:16), and the Holy Spirit now lives in believers (Rom. 8:11; 2 Tim. 1:14). But the word of Christ (Col. 3:16) and faith

(2 Tim. 1:5) are also said to dwell in us. On the other hand, the same may be said of sin (Rom. 7:17, *oikeō*).

(d) The adj. *oikeios* is only used as a substantive meaning member of the household. The lit. meaning appears in 1 Tim. 5:8. In the other two passages it denotes the congregation as the household of God. Eph. 2:19 assures the Gentiles that they are no longer strangers but have been accepted into full fellowship of the house of God. Gal. 6:10 reminds Christians of their duty to do good to everyone, but to begin with "those who belong to the family of believers."

(e) *oiketēs* is a word sometimes used only 4x for a household servant, far less frequently than *doulos* (→ *1528*). Lk. uses it in Lk. 16:13 in the phrase that "no servant can serve two masters" (Matt. 6:24 simply uses "no one" in the par. passage). The household servants in Acts 10:7 are called by this term; Peter instructs slaves to submit to their masters (1 Pet. 2:18).

See also *oikodomeō*, build, build up (*3868*); *oikonomia*, management, office (*3873*).

3876	οἰκουμένη

οἰκουμένη (*oikoumenē*), earth (*3876*).

CL & OT *oikoumenē* (with *gē* understood) is the pres. pass. part. of *oikeō*, inhabit. It means the inhabited (earth) and was used first for the world inhabited by Gks. in contrast to those lands inhabited by "barbarians," then for the entire inhabited world (as opposed to unsettled areas). In the Roman period, it became more of a political concept than a cultural one, denoting the Roman empire.

The LXX uses the word 46x, especially in Ps. and Isa. In Ps. it often occurs in confessional expressions: "He will judge the world in righteousness" (9:8; cf. 67:4; 96:13; 98:9); "to the ends of the world" (19:4; cf. 72:8); "all the people of the world" (33:8; cf. 49:1). In Isa. it appears esp. in the oracles against the nations (e.g., 13:5, 9, 11; 14:17, 26; 23:17). Throughout the OT, the word means the inhabited world (e.g., Exod. 16:35, where Canaan is defined as "a land that was settled").

NT *oikoumenē* is found 15x in NT. The political and imperial usage is clearly the main one in Lk. 2:1, where Emperor Augustus ordered a census of the whole *oikoumenē*, i.e., the territories over which he ruled. The entire population of the *oikoumenē* suffers under satanic powers for religious, but primarily political, reasons (cf. Rev. 3:10; 12:9; 16:14). In the story of Christ's temptation, Lk.'s use of *oikoumenē* in 4:5 (cf. *kosmos* in Matt. 4:8) suggests a strong political connotation, even though "the kingdoms of the world" prevents a direct identification with the Roman Empire. In Lk. 21:26; Acts 11:28; Rev. 3:10 it is used in apocalyptic prophecies. In Acts 17:6 the enemies of the apostles attack them by insisting that evangelism was a political crime directed against the emperor by those "who have caused trouble all over the *oikoumenē*" (cf. also 19:27; 24:5).

It is striking that the term is not used by Paul except in Rom. 10:18, where he quotes Ps. 19:4. Perhaps Paul saw the state in a friendlier light than Luke and Rev. and thus avoided using for it an expression with negative overtones. The believers' place of fellowship is the *ekklēsia* (*1711*), not the *oikoumenē*. The church, however, lives in the *oikoumenē*, and she claims it for her Lord, who has been brought into the *oikoumenē* as God's firstborn (Heb. 1:6) and who therefore is its ruler.

See also *gē*, earth, world (*1178*); *agros*, field (*69*); *chous*, soil, dust (*5967*); *kosmos*, adornment, world (*3180*).

3880	οἰκτιρμός

οἰκτιρμός (*oiktirmos*), compassion, pity (*3880*); οἰκτίρω (*oiktirō*), have compassion, show pity or mercy (*3882*); οἰκτίρμων (*oiktirmōn*), compassionate (*3881*).

CL & OT 1. In cl. Gk. the root word *oiktos* means to lament or regret a person's misfortune or death, then metaphorically to show sympathy, pity. *oiktirmos* was originally a poetic form of *oiktos*. *oiktirmōn*, compassionate, seldom occurs. The vb. *oiktirō* means to have compassion, pity, in the sense both of mere feeling and of merciful action; it is often a synonym of *eleeō* (→ *eleos, 1799*).

2. The words of this group occur about 80x in the LXX and with the same range of meaning as in cl. Gk. They translate the same Heb. words as *eleos* and its derivatives. They are found most frequently in Ps. (e.g., 2 Sam. 24:14; Ps. 25:6; 40:11; 51:1; Isa. 63:15).

NT 1. Words in this word group occur 10x in the NT, far less than the *eleos* words. Since God is "the Father of compassion" (lit., "mercies") and as such shows mercy to humans (2 Cor. 1:3), Paul can use "God's mercy" in Rom. 12:1 as the bridge between doctrine and moral exhortation. Just as this phrase sums up God's saving acts and plan of salvation as outlined in Rom. 11, so also that same mercy is the presupposition—the grounds of the "therefore" (12:1)—for the Christian life. Because of God's compassion, believers should likewise be compassionate in their dealings with each other (Phil. 2:1; Col. 3:12). Heb. 10:28–29 points out that the punishment of someone who has "insulted the Spirit of grace" and has "trampled the Son of God under foot" will be less merciful (hence, more severe) than that meted out to a violator of the law of Moses.

2. The vb. *oiktirō* is found only in Rom. 9:15 (a quotation of Exod. 33:19), where it is parallel to *eleeō*, have compassion.

3. The adj. *oiktirmōn* in Jas. 5:11 (alluding to Ps. 103:8; 111:4) expresses "mercy" as a quality of God. In the Sermon on the Plain (Lk. 6:20–49) Jesus calls for us to be merciful (6:36), putting God's merciful attitude as the measure of human action.

See also *eleos*, compassion, mercy, pity (*1799*); *splanchnon*, inward parts, hence as the seat of emotion, the heart, love (*5073*).

3881 (*oiktirmōn*, compassionate), → *3880*.

3882 (*oiktirō*, have compassion, show pity or mercy), → *3880*.

3884 (*oinopotēs*, wine-drinker), → *306*.

3885 (*oinos*, wine), → *306*.

3886 (*oinophlygia*, drunkenness), → *306*.

3893	ὀκτώ

ὀκτώ (*oktō*), eight (*3893*); ὄγδοος (*ogdoos*), eighth (*3838*).

NT Eight, like six in Lk. 13:14, is occasionally involved in the significance attached to seven, but is rarely important in itself. Thus "eight days" is just inclusive reckoning for a "week" (9:28; Jn. 20:26). The Jewish male child was circumcised on the eighth (*ogdoos*) day (cf. Gen. 17:12; Lev. 12:3; Lk. 1:59; 2:21; Phil. 3:5).

A difficulty is raised by two much debated passages, 1 Pet. 3:20 and 2 Pet. 2:5. In the latter case "Noah the eighth" (lit. trans. of *ogdoos*) gives the sense "Noah . . . and seven others." It is parallel, then, with 1 Pet. 3:20 ("only a few people, eight in all, were saved"), and the two passages have a similar reference. Peter's emphasis is on the small number of those saved from the flood. The concepts of 3:20 were the subject of allegoric interpretation in Justin Martyr (2d cent. A.D.), where the eight persons stand for the eighth day of resurrection and salvation.

3897	ὄλεθρος

ὄλεθρος (*olethros*), destruction, ruin, death (*3897*); ὀλοθρευτής (*olothreutēs*), destroying (*3904*); ἐξολεθρεύω (*exolethreuō*), destroy utterly (*2017*); ὀλοθρεύω (*olothreuō*), destroyer (*3905*).

CL & OT *olethros* means destruction, ruin, death; it can also refer to that which brings destruction. It often connotes sudden destruction, esp. destruction of life. In some cases it can mean the loss of things. *exolethreuō*, the intensive form of *olothreuō*, means destroy utterly, annihilate.

In the LXX, words of this group often carry the meaning of an eschatological destruction as a result of God's judgment (e.g., Jer. 5:6; 22:7; 25:36 = LXX 32:22; Ezek. 6:14; 14:16; Hag. 2:22 = LXX 2:23). The

vb. *exolethreuō* is used in Deut., Jos., and Ps. to describe punishment by God. It expresses his wrath over human sin and the disobedience of his people Israel.

NT In the NT *olethros* occurs only 4x, all in Paul; *olothreuō*, *olothreutēs*, and *exolethreuō* are used one time each. In comparison with *apōleia* (→ *724*), this seldom-used word group is used only for the destruction of persons.

1. *exolethreuō* occurs in Acts 3:23 in connection with a quotation of Deut. 18:15, 18–19, which is actually made more severe with this word. While Deut. 18:19 only says that God will "call [the sinner] to account" for disobedience to the words of the prophet, the actual punishment is now named: This person will be "completely cut off from among his people" (cf. Lev. 23:29). Peter probably modifies this OT text in order to bring home to his hearers the seriousness of their situation and the need for repentance. The same object may lie behind Paul's use of *olothreutēs* in 1 Cor. 10:10, where he warns the Corinthians about "the destroying angel" in the desert. This is likewise the significance of *olothreuōn*, destroyer, in Heb. 11:28, again in the context of a message from OT history (cf. Exod. 12:12–13, 23; Wis. 18:25).

2. In 1 Thess. 5:3 *olethros* refers to eschatological destruction suddenly breaking into a situation of apparent security and taking people unawares, like labor pains coming on a pregnant woman. Special candidates for this final destruction are the rich, whose end will be *olethros* and *apōleia* (1 Tim. 6:9). They, of course, are only one group among the ungodly, who will all suffer "everlasting destruction" (2 Thess. 1:9; cf. Ps. 37:17).

3. The context of 1 Cor. 5:5 suggests that the judgment of *olethros* may even fall within the province of the church. The Corinthian church has apparently countenanced a case of gross immorality, and Paul urges that the offender be "put out of your fellowship" (5:2). The goal behind this judgment is "to hand this man over to Satan, so that the sinful nature (*sarx*) may be destroyed (*eis olethron*) and his spirit saved on the day of the Lord" (5:5). Paul here envisions expulsion from the church (cf. 1 Tim. 1:20; also Rom. 6:6) into the realm dominated by "the god of this age" (2 Cor. 4:4). The offender in question is to be excluded from the sphere of grace and its promises, as mediated by the Word and sacraments, in the hope that he will be driven back to God in penitence. This expulsion is to take place at a formal meeting of the church (1 Cor. 5:4). Paul's recommendations suggest the proceedings laid down in Matt. 18:15–20, where the church is given power to bind and loose in heaven and on earth when gathered in the name of Jesus.

Elsewhere in Scripture, Satan is portrayed as one who in God's providence is permitted to afflict the flesh for the ultimate benefit of a person. Satan was allowed to afflict Job; despite every trial, however, Job retained his faith and integrity (Job 2:3–10). Paul's own "thorn in [his] flesh, a messenger of Satan" (2 Cor. 12:7), made him realize that God's strength is made perfect in human weakness (12:9). In 1 Cor. 5:5, however, the word *olethros* and the circumstances of the offense suggest that this case is so serious that the judgment of exclusion from the church and thus from the realm of grace are necessary. Paul's stated goal is that the person might suffer some severe illness or even succumb to physical death, as did Ananias and Sapphira (Acts 5:1–11; cf. 1 Cor. 11:30). To be cut off from the body of Christ (1 Cor. 12:12–26) is to be exposed to the reign of evil and death. The destruction of God's temple invites destruction by God (1 Cor. 3:17).

At the same time, Paul's expressed intention is that this man's "spirit [may be] saved on the day of the Lord" (1 Cor. 5:5; cf. 1:8; 3:13; 15:22–28). The destruction here envisaged is not the ultimate and complete outworking of God's wrath (as in 2 Thess. 1:9; 1 Tim. 6:9). The body may waste away, but the self will be clothed in life (2 Cor. 4:16; 5:4). Perhaps this man will be saved, "but only as one escaping through the flames" (1 Cor. 3:15). Or maybe Paul hopes that some temporal judgment will bring about in the man the "godly sorrow" that "brings repentance that leads to salvation" and not the "worldly sorrow" that "brings death" (2 Cor. 7:10). Some see Paul's remarks in 2 Cor. 2:5–11 as relating to the same situation as 1 Cor. 5, though this is by no means certain.

See also *apōleia*, destruction (*724*); *phtheirō*, destroy, ruin (*5780*); *exaleiphō*, wipe away, blot out (*1981*).

3900 (oligos, little, small, few), → *3625.*

3901 (oligopsychos, fainthearted, timid), → *6034.*

3902 ὀλιγωρέω	ὀλιγωρέω (*oligōreō*), despise (*3902*).

CL & OT *oligōreō* in cl. Gk. means think little of, make light of. In the LXX, it is used only in Prov. 3:11, which contains a warning against despising God's *paideia*, training.

NT The warning of Prov. 3:11 is quoted in Heb. 12:5 as an admonition from the heavenly Father to his persecuted children telling them to see their sufferings as a providential means of sanctifying them for the life God has in store for them.

3904 (olothreutēs, destroying), → *3897.*

3905 (olothreuō, destroyer), → *3897.*

3906 (holokautōma, whole burnt offering), → *2604.*

3915 (ombros, rainstorm), → *847.*

3920 (homichlē, mist, fog), → *847.*

3923 ὀμνύω	ὀμνύω (*omnyō*), swear (*3923*); ὅρκος (*horkos*), oath (*3992*);

ὀρκίζω (*horkizō*), adjure, implore (*3991*); ἐνορκίζω (*enorkizō*), adjure, cause someone to swear (*1941*); ἐπιορκέω (*epiorkeō*), swear falsely, commit perjury, break one's oath (*2155*); ἐπίορκος (*epiorkos*), perjured, perjurer (*2156*); ὀρκωμοσία (*horkōmosia*), asserting on oath, taking an oath (*3993*).

CL & OT 1. (a) In cl. Gk. *omnyō* is a parallel form to *omnymi*, both of which mean to hold fast and hence to swear. *horkos* meant originally the staff that was grasped and raised in swearing, thus oaths in general. The corresponding vb. *horkizō* means to put on oath, adjure. The compound *enorkizō* is a stronger form and means to adjure. *epiorkeō* means to swear falsely, commit perjury or break an oath; correspondingly *epiorkos* means perjurious. The noun *horkōmosia* is infrequent and means asserting on oath.

(b) The original idea behind the oath lay in guaranteeing one's word. An undoubtedly higher court of appeal was frequently provided by calling upon a deity. The formula of the oath had the character of conditionally cursing oneself if a statement should prove not to correspond to the truth. One can distinguish between assertive oaths, which are concerned with past and present events and are taken primarily in court, and promissory oaths, which promise a future activity and play an important part in religious as well as private life.

(c) The Gks. applied oaths to many areas, for many reasons, and in many forms. Their original setting was a cultic one, but the practice of swearing oaths found a place in politics and law with oaths for officials, citizens, and judges. Even the appropriate deities were fixed by the legislator, so that the oath in public life received religious sanction. Oaths were also used in contracts whose reliability might be guaranteed by the pledging of valuable property (children, the marriage bed, or weapons). The Gks. also used oaths in medicine: The Hippocratic oath is generally attributed to Hippocrates (ca. 460–ca. 357 B.C.), a physician who was a native of the island of Cos.

(d) In earlier times people almost always swore by the gods. In the Hel. period, oaths by deities were supplemented or replaced by those involving kings or emperors, either the person or the entire dynasty of the ruler of the day. It was the custom among the Romans

for those who took oaths to take a stone in the hand and ask to be hurled forth like this stone if they broke their word.

(e) The increasing frequency of oaths led to a decline in their power and authority, and some ancient sources (esp. Roman) offer evidence of an attempt to ban the oath. For example, the Pythagoreans prohibited their disciples from using oaths. Plutarch declares that an oath, being a constraint on the spirit of a free person, was an indignity. These efforts to abolish oaths met with no success in Greece.

2. (a) The LXX usually translates the niph. of *šābaʿ* by *omnyō*, the hiph. by *horkizō*. The original meaning of *šābaʿ* is to come under the influence of seven things (cf. *šebaʿ*, seven). Gen. 21:30–31 offers evidence that in early times an oath was ratified by the sacrifice of seven animals (cf. 15:10).

(b) An ancient form of oath involved the practice of calling Yahweh to witness between two partners: "God is a witness between you and me" (Gen. 31:50; cf. 1 Sam. 20:12). Special weight is given to an oath by the ancient practice of invoking a curse on oneself if the oath is broken: "May the LORD deal with me, be it ever so severely, if . . ." (1 Sam. 20:13). The most frequent form is the phrase, "As the LORD lives" (20:3); this could be varied into an oath by the life of the king (17:55) or of the person addressed (1:26; 20:4).

(c) In treaties (between Abraham and Abimelech, Gen. 21:23; Jacob and Laban, 31:50) and bequests by father to son (Jacob and Joseph, 47:31), the oath had its original promissory function: The partners placed themselves under the power and judgment of Yahweh, who was invoked and recognized as witness for the validity of the promise. Thus the OT oath contained by implication a confession of faith in Yahweh (Deut. 6:13; 10:20). Therefore, to swear falsely is tantamount to a misuse of Yahweh's name (Exod. 20:7; Lev. 19:12). The OT does not know the assertive oath of a witness before a law court; instead it has the so-called oath of purification in which the accused, in the absence of pertinent witnesses, asserts innocence before Yahweh and corroborates this with curses if perjury is committed (Num. 5:11–28). Since perjury can rarely be detected, the person guilty of it is generally assigned to the judgment of God (1 Ki. 8:31–32).

(d) Whereas in Gen. we read chiefly of oaths taken by human beings, other places in the Pentateuch speak of Yahweh's oath. Yahweh swears by himself, and the form of oath is: "As surely as I live . . ." (Num. 14:21; Deut. 32:40). Yahweh guarantees with an oath the truth of his word, so that his oath is tantamount to a corroboration of his promise. He swore to give the land of Canaan to the patriarchs (1:8; 6:10, 18, 23) and sealed with an oath the covenant he made with the "forefathers" of Israel (4:31; 7:8, 12; 29:12–15). The basic elements contained in Yahweh's promises to the patriarchs (people [Gen. 12:2], land [13:15], and covenant [17:7]), are taken up again in the exhortations of Deut. and their validity is reinforced by references to Yahweh's oath (8:1, 18).

(e) Yahweh's oath also takes the form of a curse with which he punishes the disobedience of his people. Thus the grumbling Israelites will die in the desert (Num. 14:21, 28; Deut. 1:34–35; 2:14); Moses will not enter the promised land (4:21); the guilt of Eli will not be expiated (1 Sam. 3:14). The double-sided nature of Yahweh's oath, serving as it does both as corroboration of his promise and curse of disobedience, corresponds to the structure of blessing and curse (cf. Deut. 28; 30:19).

3. In rab. Jud. the practice of oath-taking became widespread. We read of the following types of oath: corroborative oath, oath of testimony, oath under pledge, judge's oath, rabbinical oath, and perjurious oath. As in Hel. culture, there were efforts to limit the excessive use of oaths (Sir. 23:9–11). Philo, like the Stoics, advocates the abolition of oaths. In his opinion it is best not to swear, second best to swear truly, but the worst thing of all is to commit perjury. The most radical rejection of oath-taking is found among the Essenes, who instead prized the plain word, though they did have oaths of initiation.

NT 1. (a) *omnyō* occurs 26x in the NT, most often in Matt. and Heb. The corresponding vb. *horkizō* occurs only in Mk. 5:7 and Acts 19:13, *enorkizō* only in 1 Thess. 5:27, *epiorkeō* only in Matt. 5:33, *epiorkos* only in 1 Tim. 1:10, and *horkōmosia* only in Heb. 7:20–21, 28.

(b) Matt. 5:33–37, in the Sermon on the Mount, contains Jesus' decisive pronouncement on oaths. It is joined to the OT prohibition of perjury (Lev. 19:12) and the commandment to keep one's vows (Num. 30:3–4; Deut. 23:23). In contrast to the OT, Jesus pronounces a total prohibition: "Do not swear at all" (Matt. 5:34). In order to exclude any misunderstanding that might water the teaching down, four explanatory phrases are added to give sharpness and clarity: not by heaven, earth, Jerusalem, nor one's own head is one permitted to swear (5:34–36). This constitutes an attack on the contemporary Jewish practice of oath-taking, in which an attempt was made to avoid misusing God's name in numerous oaths by means of circumlocution.

According to the Mishnah, swearing by the heavens and the earth was not binding on witnesses (*m. Sheb.* 6:13). Such an oath would thus be ambiguous and indeed a contradiction in terms. In Matt. 5:35 "by Jerusalem" means "toward Jerusalem" and may reflect the rab. view that a vow made "by Jerusalem" is nothing unless it is sworn while facing in the direction of Jerusalem. An oath "by your head" is referred to in *m. Sanh.* 3:2; a person's head is determined by God. In invoking these other authorities, in other words, one still had God to reckon with, for he is the Lord of all of them.

(c) Jesus' third woe against the teachers of the law and Pharisees (Matt. 23:16–22) attacks with like severity their casuistic attitude to oaths and vows. Those who swear by the altar, the temple, or heaven include in their oaths him who has given these things their authority, namely, God. In this way the hair-splitting rules governing the Jewish practice of oath-taking are reduced to absurdity. With these explanations, it is impossible to be in any doubt about the universal validity of Jesus' prohibition: Jesus forbids every oath, whether made in the religious sphere, court, everyday life, or private. For the oath adds nothing to the simple affirmation or negation.

(d) In view of the freedom with which oath-taking is presupposed and practiced in the OT, why does Jesus prohibit swearing? The oath was developed to combat lying and demands total truthfulness in what one says; indirectly it presupposes lying in everyday human speech. Lying, however, creeps into even the taking of oaths in the form of perjury and the misuse of God's name. Jesus therefore prohibits swearing in order to fight against lying. His aim is stated in the last sentence of the teaching: "Simply let your 'Yes' be 'Yes,' and your 'No,' 'No'; anything beyond this comes from the evil one" (Matt. 5:37; cf. also Jas. 5:12). The follower of Jesus is by no means released from responsibility before God. On the contrary, not only isolated statements, but one's whole speech takes place in the presence of the all-knowing God. Each word is to be nothing but the truth. Since an oath casts a shadow of doubtfulness over all one's other words, it is therefore "from the evil one."

(e) The words of Jesus are frequently introduced by the formula (lit.): "Truly [*amēn*, Amen, → 297] I say to you" (Matt. 5:18; cf. the Gospel of Jn.). This is not a form of oath, but rather the underlining of Jesus' words by the authority of his person (cf. Matt. 5:22, 28, 32, 34, 39, 44). He is "the truth" (cf. Jn. 14:6), and his words are therefore true. As Paul notes, "For no matter how many promises God has made, they are 'Yes' in Christ. And so through him the 'Amen' is spoken by us to the glory of God" (2 Cor. 1:20). Granted, before the Sanhedrin Jesus was pressed to state on oath that he was the Son of God, but Jesus refused the oath and simply affirmed what the high priest had asked: "Yes, it is as you say" (Matt. 26:63–64).

(f) Matt. 14:7–9 (cf. Mk. 6:23) provides an example of the rash practice of oath-taking. Herod, intoxicated at his birthday feast, casually swore to grant whatever his step-daughter might ask. Her mother, Herodias, took the opportunity to demand the head of John the Baptist, who had been imprisoned by Herod for denouncing Herod's liaison with Herodias. In his denial scene, Peter maintained that he did not know Jesus and corroborated this lie with an oath and curses on himself (Matt. 26:72–74; Mk. 14:71; cf. Lk. 22:60). Such an incident shows the danger of using oaths, as Jesus had earlier discussed.

2. No forms of oath are found in Paul's writings, only asseverations to underline the sincerity of his words. Particularly in his battle for the churches in Galatia and Corinth, he calls God to witness for the truth of his life story (Gal. 1:20) and his actions (2 Cor. 1:23). In Rom. Paul asserts the truth of his gospel (1:9) and stresses beyond all doubt his concern for his own nation: "I speak the truth in Christ—I am not lying, my conscience confirms it in the Holy Spirit" (9:1).

3. As in the OT, so in the NT we read of God's oath. In Lk. 1:73; Acts 2:30; Heb. 6:13, the oath of God means no more than his promises given to Abraham and David. Heb. even carries over the negative divine oath, God's curse on the disobedient Israelites in the desert (3:11, 18; 4:3; cf. Num. 14:21–23, 26; Deut. 1:34), in order to add a warning exhortation to obedience and zeal for the promised rest of God's people (Heb. 4:9–11). Heb. 6:16–17 alludes to the practice of oath-taking in order to contrast human oaths by someone or something greater with God's plain oath by himself.

Heb. 7:20–22 (*horkōmosia*) goes still further, drawing a distinction between God's plain word and his word under oath. In contrast to the appointment of the Levites as priests, which was made without an oath, God swore with an oath in Ps. 110:4 to demonstrate confidently that Christ's priesthood is better and unchangeable.

4. Rev. 10:6 echoes Dan. 12:5–7, in which an angel announces the end with an oath.

See also *exorkistēs*, exorcist (*2020*).

3924	ὁμοθυμαδόν

ὁμοθυμαδόν (*homothymadon*), unanimous, of one mind (*3924*).

CL & OT 1. In cl. Gk. *homothymadon* means unanimous, with one accord, though the word is later weakened simply to mean together. In the political sphere it is used esp. for the visible, inner unity of a group faced by a common duty or danger. This unanimity is not based on common personal feelings but on a cause greater than the individual.

2. The LXX uses this word 36x. In the canonical books, *homothymadon* generally has the weaker meaning of together (e.g., Exod. 19:8; Job 2:11; Jer. 5:5). In the Apocr. it has both the earlier sense of unanimity (e.g., Jdt. 4:12; 15:2, 5; Wis. 10:20) and the weaker sense of together (e.g., 18:5; 3 Macc. 4:4).

NT 1. Apart from Rom. 15:6, *homothymadon* is used only in Acts (10x). In Acts 12:20 it means no more than that Tyre and Sidon join in sending envoys to King Herod Agrippa I. In the other cases a unanimity is indicated: the eleven with the women and Mary in prayer (1:14), the growing church worshiping in the temple (2:46–47; 5:12), the prayer after the release of Peter and John (4:24), the sending of Judas and Silas with the decisions of the Jerusalem meeting (15:25). There is unanimity even in the close attention paid to Philip's message (8:6) and in the hatred of the Jews (7:57; 18:12–13) and Hellenists (9:29) when faced with the message of the crucified and exalted Jesus.

Thus Acts manifests a double kind of unanimity—of the church and of its enemies. The cause is the same, the preaching of Christ as Savior and Lord. The reaction can be either faith and worship or hatred and rejection. The church's enemies are united when they reject the claims of Christ, for they see either their religious traditions or their commercial interests threatened. In a similar manner, the church's unanimity is not based on the sharing of the same human or religious feelings and convictions, but on the reality of Christ, who has brought together Jews and Gentiles (cf. Acts 15:11).

When the local church lives and works *homothymadon*, it is in harmony with its origin. If Lk. plays down most of the elements that militate against such unanimity in his picture of the early church (Acts 6:1–6; 15:37–40; cf. 8:1), it is hardly because he wants to idealize it. It does have its tensions and controversies (cf., e.g., 1 and 2 Cor.,

Gal.). Rather, Lk. wants to show the essential unity of the church, an expression of its nature and thus a pattern for later generations. As a unified body, it carries out its work of witness (Acts 1:8) in a world that rejects the salvation offered to it.

2. Paul envisages the same goal, the unanimous praise of God with one voice, in Rom. 15:5–6. He prays to God for "one heart" in service that comes from Christ and that surmounts all differences in understanding and knowledge.

3926 (homoiopathēs, with the same nature), → 3927.

3927	ὅμοιος

ὅμοιος (*homoios*), like, of the same nature, similar (*3927*); ὁμοίως (*homoiōs*), likewise, so, similarly, in the same way (*3931*); ὁμοιόω (*homoioō*), make like, compare (*3929*); ὁμοιότης (*homoiotēs*), likeness, similarity, agreement (*3928*); ὁμοίωμα (*homoiōma*), likeness, image, copy, appearance (*3930*); ὁμοίωσις (*homoiōsis*), likeness, resemblance (*3932*); ὁμοιοπαθής (*homoiopathēs*), with the same nature (*3926*); παρόμοιος (*paromoios*), like, similar (*4235*); παρομοιάζω (*paromoiazo*), be like (*4234*); ἀφομοιόω (*aphomoioō*), make like, similar (*926*).

CL & OT 1. The adj. *homoios* has four different though related meanings: (a) Of the same kind or condition, referring to persons and things. When linked with *isos* (→ *2698*), *homoios* tends to emphasize similarity of kind rather than sameness. (b) Of the same character, endowed with the same rights (fellow member of a party, likeminded companion). Thus *hoi homoioi* means one's peers, the citizens who possessed the same right of access to office. (c) What is divided equally to all. (d) In geometry similar figures in the sense of equal.

2. (a) The vb. *homoioō* remains within this range of meaning. It means (act.) to make someone like a person or thing, hold in similar regard, compare; (pass.) to be like, resemble. (b) The nouns *homoiotēs, homoiōsis,* and *homoiōma* are virtually synonymous, meaning likeness, resemblance. (c) *homoiopathēs* means lit. suffering the same, then generally of similar disposition. (d) The rare *paromoios* means similar in the sense of almost the same (with minor differences). *paromoiazo*, to be similar, occurs first in the NT (Matt. 23:27). (e) *aphomoioō* means to make like, to copy; to become like.

3. In the LXX *homoios* is used in comparisons of the same or similar types, e.g., of animals in Lev. 11:14–22. *homoioō* means to be like; the nouns *homoiōsis* and *homoiōma*, pattern, shape, image (e.g., Exod. 20:4; Deut. 4:16–18), likeness. In Ezek. 1:5, 16, 22, 26; 2:1; 8:2–3; 10:1, 8, 10, 21–22; 23:15 *homoiōma* denotes the mysterious forms that the prophet saw. *homoioō*, as in cl. Gk., occurs often in the introduction to illustrations and parables (e.g., Ps. 144:4; Song 2:17; 7:8 = LXX 7:7; Sir. 13:1). It also features in statements about Yahweh's incomparability; e.g., "To whom will you compare me?" (Isa. 46:5).

In contrast to Yahweh's incomparability, Gen. 1:26 states that God created humans "in our image [→ *eikōn, 1635*], in our likeness [*homoiōsis*]." Humanity is here accorded a special creaturely worth and even has a special glory (Ps. 8:5). But the primary focus of this statement is not on how humans look but on the purpose for which the image is given, namely, to be God's authorized agents on this earth.

NT The majority of NT occurrences of the adj., adv., and vb. are in the Gospels, though *homoios* also occurs 21x in Rev. Most of the instances of the nouns, by contrast, are in the Pauline writings and Heb. *homoioō* and *aphomoioō* occur once each in Heb., while *homoiopathēs* occurs once each in Acts and Jas.

1. In the Gospels *homoios* and *homoioō* are found mostly in the introductory formula to Jesus' parables, esp. in Matt.: e.g., "the kingdom of heaven is like . . ." (13:24, 31, 33, 44, 45, 47; 18:23; 20:1; 22:2). The point of comparison is not, e.g., in 13:45 the merchant but the pearl; in 22:2 it is not the king but the wedding feast, etc.

2. In other passages *homoios* is found in varied connections. (a) In Matt. 22:39, in the double commandment, love for one's neighbor

is placed beside love for God as its necessary counterpart and illustration. According to Jn. 8:55, Jesus would be a liar like his opponents if he were to be silent and avoid giving offense.

(b) *homoios* also occurs in connection with the polemic against the worship of false gods. In Acts 17:29 the idea that God cannot be depicted physically struck a chord among educated Gks., but it was to such people that Paul's speech before the Areopagus sought to present an apology for Christianity as the model of the only true worship of the "UNKNOWN GOD" (17:23). Rom. 1:23 also belongs to the polemic against the worship of false gods. Through their images the heathen have "exchanged the glory of the immortal God for images made to look like [*en homoiōmati*] mortal man and birds and animals and reptiles." Thereby the revelation of the true God is negated.

In Acts 14:11 the crowd thought that their gods, Zeus and Hermes, had taken on "human form" (*homoioō*) in Barnabas and Paul. The apostles protested, indicating that they too were ordinary humans "like" (*homoiopathēs*) the people of Lystra and mere messengers of the living God (14:15). *homoiopathēs* also occurs in Jas. 5:17, where Elijah is cited as a mortal person "just like us."

(c) Christians can expect that we will be "like" (*homoioi*) Jesus at his Parousia because we will see him as he is (1 Jn. 3:2). For the present we are instructed to seek the true knowledge of Christ in his Word, which only allows us a token knowledge of his true being (cf. 1 Cor. 13:12). At the Parousia, however, an unimpaired relationship will be possible. Yet the writer does not intend this isolated remark to be a speculative description of future likeness to God.

In Rev. 1:13 and 14:14 the "someone 'like a son of man'" is to be interpreted within the framework of Son of Man Christology (→ *huios tou anthrōpou* under *huios, 5626*). The "son of man" of Dan. 7:13, the divinely appointed, kingly judge of the world, is the exalted Christ, the coming Messiah.

(d) *homoios* occurs elsewhere in comparisons without having any particular stress of its own: e.g., see "and the like" in Gal. 5:21; cf. also the comparisons in Rev. 2:18; 4:3, 6–7; 9:7, 10, 19 in symbolic comparisons; *homoiōma* is used of a comparison in 9:7.

3. *homoiōma* plays an important role in the Christological statements of Rom. and Phil. to express both the divinity of the Preexistent One and the humanity of the Incarnate One. (a) Rom. 5:14 asserts that humankind as a whole, like Adam, has been subjected to the rule of death, even if it has not sinned in exactly the same way "as did Adam." Adam is the type of Christ, the last Adam (cf. 1 Cor. 15:45). What Christ brings about by grace surpasses by far the equivalent effect of the fall of the first man.

(b) Rom. 6:5 presents certain exegetical difficulties: "If we have been united with him like this [*homoiōma*] in his death, we will certainly also be united with him in his resurrection." The interpretation depends on whether one understands *homoiōma* here concretely as a picture (i.e., the symbolic representation of something else) or as the actual realization of an event by means of a symbolic representation. If one prefers the second alternative, the text then means: "In the act of baptism, the death of Jesus Christ is present, although in a different form from that on Golgotha," and we are "received into the same saving event."

(c) Rom. 8:3 also presents difficulties: "For what the law was powerless to do in that it was weakened by the sinful nature, God did by sending his own Son in the likeness [*homoiōma*] of sinful man to be a sin offering. And so he condemned sin in sinful man." This text is difficult because of the theological problem of grasping conceptually the incarnation, i.e., the paradox of how Christ can be fully God and fully human, and applying it to the justification of the sinner. But by remaining obedient under the form of our bodily existence and bearing its burden, Jesus became in a unique way a sign of God's righteousness.

(d) Similarly in Phil. 2:7 the Incarnate One is described as "being made in human likeness [*homoiōma*]." He took on human form and became like a human being. Rather than understand this verse as reflecting only an apparent rather than a real likeness (which tends to Docetism) or as ethical (Jesus' coming into human flesh is merely a model for the obedience of faith), this passage applies unequivocally what has just been mentioned regarding Rom. 8:3: Christ has in fact taken a historically unique, unambiguously human form. He was in fact delivered to death, the curse of sinful humanity (cf. Gal. 3:13), even though he himself was sinless (cf. Heb. 4:15). Thus at a specific point in time he broke the power of sin and death.

4. (a) Heb. likewise uses *homoioō, aphomoioō,* and *homoiotēs* in connection with Christological statements. Christ "had to be made like [pass. of *homoioō*] his brothers in every way" (2:17). Hence he was tempted "in every way, just as [*homoiotēs*] we are" (4:15). That Christ took flesh and blood and was thus placed in the situation of humanity before God is seen in the light of theological reflection as a matter of necessity. For only thus can the sentence of death, which hangs over humanity, be averted.

(b) In Heb. 7 the Son of God is compared with Melchizedek in the form of type and antitype. Melchizedek is said to be "like [*aphomoiōo*] the Son of God" (7:3). His priesthood is not limited in time. No genealogy is given for him, and his birth and death find no mention in the OT. Hence he possessed a special being and office. Thus, when Christ is installed in his priestly office "like [*homoiotēs*] Melchizedek" (7:15), he has both an office not limited in time and a share in "the power of an indestructible life" (7:16), to which he has opened the way of access (cf. 10:19–22) for us as our pioneer or originator (12:2).

5. The only verse in which *homoiōsis* occurs (Jas. 3:9) warns against sins of the tongue. The tongue is capable of contradictory opposites: blessing God and cursing humans, who have been created "in God's likeness" (cf. Gen. 1:26). In short, to curse humans is indirectly to curse God.

6. The term *homoousios* ("of the same substance," not used in the NT) became crucial in the history of Christian doctrine in view of its central importance in the Arian controversy. Arius and his followers denied Christ's divinity—specifically, he was not of the same substance as the Father. At the Council of Nicea (A.D. 325) *homoousios* was inserted into the creed to express the faith of the church. That initiated a debate as to whether *homoiousios* ("of a similar substance") might not express better the relationship between the Father and the Son. But nearly sixty years later, at the Council of Constantinople (A.D. 381), *homoousios* was reaffirmed. For more on this topic, see books on the history of Christian doctrine.

See also *isos*, equal, corresponding to (*2698*).

3928 (*homoiotēs*, likeness, similarity, agreement), → *3927*.

3929 (*homoioō*, make like, compare), → *3927*.

3930 (*homoiōma*, likeness, image, copy, appearance), → *3927*.

3931 (*homoiōs*, likewise, so, similarly, in the same way), → *3927*.

3932 (*homoiōsis*, likeness, resemblance), → *3927*.

3933 ὁμολογέω

ὁμολογέω (*homologeō*), promise, confess, declare, praise (*3933*); ἐξομολογέω (*exomologeō*), promise, confess, praise (*2018*); ὁμολογία (*homologia*), confession (*3934*).

CL & OT 1. *homologeō* and *homologia* are compounds of *homos*, the same, similar, and *legō*, say. Hence *homologeō* means say the same thing, i.e., agree in one's statements; *homologia* means agreement, consent. The legal connotation is dominant. The religious use of the words is probably derived from the use of the word in the language of treaties and law courts. Those who bind themselves by an oath (*homologeō*) enter into a treaty relationship with the deity. The meaning of solemn confession of wrongdoing before a law court led to use of this word as the confession of sin to the deity.

2. In the LXX *homologeō* is used in the language of vowing and swearing. More common, however, is *exomologeō* (120x), praise, confess. It is sometimes used along with *psallō*, sing praises, or *aineō*, thank. The subject of a confession of praise is God's majesty and power (1 Chr. 29:12–13), his mighty acts in history (Ps. 105:1–6), his gracious goodness (118:1–4), his saving of people from distress (107:1, 8, 15, 21, 31), and his deliverance from enemies (9:1). The LXX also uses this word group for the confession of an offense to God (Jos. 7:19; 1 Ki. 8:33–36; 2 Chr. 6:24–27). The association of confession of sin and praise of God may seem strange to us (though note that we do use the word "confess" both for a confession of faith and of sin).

In Israel praise of God is linked with a definite past action of God, with a saving event in history, or even with an act of judgment. When the one praying confesses in thanksgiving that God is right and so recognizes one's own fault and the rightness of the subsequent punishment, the lawsuit against this person is closed. This gives a clue to the understanding of passages such as Jos. 7:19, where Achan is called on to give glory to God before his execution.

NT *homologeō* is found 26x in the NT with a wide range of usage; the same is true of *exomologeō*, which occurs 10x. The noun *homologia* (6x), however, is confined to the Christian confession (2 Cor. 9:13; 1 Tim. 6:12–13) and is used with a fixed liturgical connotation (cf. Heb. 3:1; 4:14; 10:23).

1. Herod promises with an oath to carry out his step-daughter's wish (*homologeō*, Matt. 14:7); Judas bound himself with an oath to betray Jesus (*exomologeō*, Lk. 22:6). In both cases the "confessing" is tantamount to promising or swearing (cf. also Acts 7:17). Heb. 11:13 means either that on the threshold of the promised land the patriarchs "admitted" that they were only strangers on the earth or that they were in effect proclaiming that.

2. *homologeō* and *exomologeō* can both have the LXX meaning of praise. Jesus praised God's actions by gladly accepting his plan for his life (Matt. 11:25; Lk. 10:21). Praise to the glory of God begun in Christ is to be taken up and continued by the Gentiles (Rom. 15:9). Heb. 13:15 calls on the church to praise the name of God through Christ.

3. This word group is used most often in the sense of confess, state openly. (a) Paul, on trial before Felix, openly acknowledged that he worshiped Israel's God through his involvement with the Christian Way (Acts 24:14). Similarly, John the Baptist confessed openly that he was not the one the Jews were awaiting (Jn. 1:20).

(b) In 1 Jn. 1:9, *homologeō* means a confession and acknowledgment of sins. Those who acknowledge their faults honestly experience God's faithfulness and justice in the forgiveness of their sins. Confession is a sign of repentance and thus a mark of the new life of faith. Note Mk. 1:5 par., where public confession of sins means also being set free from them (cf. also Acts 19:18; Jas. 5:16).

(c) Believers respond to the saving act of God in Jesus Christ by publicly acknowledging Jesus Christ as Lord and affirming his resurrection (Rom. 10:9–10, which undoubtedly reflects an early Christian confessional formula; cf. 1 Tim. 6:12, which may refer to baptism). When belief and confession, heart and mouth, are in unison, there is a promise of justification and salvation for eternity. Obedience to one's confession leads to practical loving action (2 Cor. 9:13; cf. Tit. 1:16).

An integral part of true faith is the public confession of the incarnate Son of God (1 Jn. 4:2; cf. Jn. 1:14); fellowship with God is dependent on it (1 Jn. 2:23; 4:15). It is a mark of true Christology in the face of heretical movements that denied that Jesus is the Christ (2:22; 4:2–3). In Jn. 9:22; 12:42, the apostle relates that anyone who openly confessed Jesus as the Messiah was put out of the synagogue. He calls on the church to distinguish in its meetings between true and false confessions (cf. 1 Jn. 4:1–2).

When *homologeō* stands in contrast to its opposite, *arneomai*, deny (Jesus) (→ *766*; cf. Lk. 12:8–9; Jn. 1:20; Tit. 1:16; 1 Jn. 2:22–23), the eschatological aspect of the confession is esp. emphasized. The decision made determines how God will act in judgment (Matt. 10:32–33; Rev. 3:5, 8; cf. Mk. 8:38). Thus believers who confess Jesus before other people are making that confession, as it were, before

God's judgment seat. Confession here includes not only what one says but also whether one is obedient to the will of God. Lack of total obedience is equivalent to denial; Jesus "will tell [such people] plainly" (*homologeō*) on the day of judgment, "I never knew you" (Matt. 7:23). In the end, however, every power and might will have to confess Jesus as the Christ, i.e., recognize and do homage to him (Phil. 2:11).

3934 (homologia, confession), → *3933*.

3941	ὄναρ

ὄναρ (*onar*), dream (*3941*).

CL & OT *onar* occurs widely in cl. Greek, but not in the LXX, where *enypnion* is used for dream. In the ANE generally, dreams were understood to contain messages from the divine (Job 33:14–18), particularly dreams experienced by kings and priests. Dreams with divine content often occurred at sanctuaries (e.g., Jacob at Bethel [Gen. 28:12–17], Samuel at Shiloh [1 Sam. 3], Solomon at Gibeon [1 Ki. 3:4–15]). In Gen. dreams are a regular means of divine communication (e.g., 20:3; 28:12; 31:11). The dream was also a medium by which truth was conveyed to a prophet (Num. 12:6), while the dreams of old men are a part of the contact with God to be experienced in the latter days (Joel 2:28; quoted in Acts 2:17).

In most cases the content of the divine message is conveyed to the dreamer clearly and unambiguously (e.g., Gen. 20:3; 31:10–13; 1 Ki. 3:4–15). But in two cycles of stories, the skills of professional interpreters are required: the Joseph stories (Gen. 37:5–10; 40:5–13; 41:1–32) and the Daniel narratives (Dan. 2). These special skills are God-given (Gen. 40:8; Dan. 2:27–28) and involve an ability to read the pattern of future events in the various symbolic features of the dream.

Still, dreams and their interpretations were not accepted uncritically by everyone. The polemic against false prophecy in Jer. contains scathing criticism of lying dreamers (23:32; 27:9); Zech. offers similar criticism (10:2). A dreamer whose word encourages apostasy is to be put to death (Deut. 13:2–6). Qoheleth's skepticism extends to the dream world (Eccl. 5:7), and witness to its fleeting, insubstantial character is found in Job 20:8; Ps. 73:20; 90:5.

NT *onar* is found only in Matt., 5x in Jesus' birth narrative: to Joseph, explaining through an angel Mary's pregnancy (1:20); to the wise men, warning them not to return to Herod (2:12); to Joseph, telling him through an angel to flee with his family to Egypt (2:13); to Joseph, telling him to return from Egypt (2:19); to Joseph, warning him against settling in Judea (2:22). This means of communication and guidance conveys God's particular provision for the infant Jesus in the face of various uncertainties and threats. It serves to reinforce a theme in Matt. that this Jesus is God's chosen and anointed one.

The only other occurrence of *onar* is in Matt. 27:19, where, at the trial of Jesus, Pilate's wife reports a disturbing dream she has suffered on Jesus' account. In Acts Paul often receives direction and encouragement in visions of the night (Acts 16:9; 18:9; 23:11; 27:23–24), but *onar* is not used.

3943	ὀνειδίζω

ὀνειδίζω (*oneidizō*), insult, denounce, rebuke (*3943*); ὀνειδισμός (*oneidismos*), insult, disgrace (*3944*); ὄνειδος (*oneidos*), disgrace (*3945*); ἐμπαίζω (*empaizō*), mock, ridicule (*1850*).

CL & OT 1. In cl. Gk. the primary sense of the *oneidizō* word group is disgrace, shame, reproach. Much of the ancient world was shaped around what has been called an "honor-shame" culture (still prevalent in the Middle East). One of the worst things a person can do is to bring dishonor or shame to oneself or one's family by doing what is immoral or against the law. Conversely, in interpersonal conflicts a person might try to heap shame or insult on an enemy.

2. (a) The LXX notes how humans are often subject to insult, shame, and disgrace. At times it comes as a result of a person's situation. Not to be married, for whatever reason, brings disgrace (Isa. 4:1), as does not having children (Gen. 30:23). When Nahash intended to gouge out the right eye of the men of Jabesh Gilead, he did so with the intent of bringing disgrace (1 Sam. 11:2). In a more general sense, "sin is a disgrace [*elassonousi*] to any people" (Prov. 14:34).

(b) Goliath insulted God's people with his defiant taunts (1 Sam. 17:10, 36), as did the field commander of Sennacherib (2 Ki. 19:4). Evil people can also taunt God-fearing individuals (e.g., Ps. 42:10; 44:16; 69:9). It is equally possible to defy or insult God (Isa. 65:7). In the future, God will avenge the insults brought against him (Zeph. 2:8, 10) and bring shame to such people by exposing their nakedness (Isa. 47:3). In doing so, he will also take away our reproach (54:4).

NT 1. *oneidizō* occurs 9x in the NT, *empaizō* 13x, *oneidismos* 5x, and *oneidos* only in Lk. 1:25, where it deals with the notion of social disgrace: the barrenness of Elizabeth, which was removed through the birth of John the Baptist. In Lk. 14:29–30, Jesus tells the parable of a man who begins a major building project but is unable to complete it; such an individual is subject to ridicule.

2. *oneidizō* is used twice for reproaches from Jesus: on the cities who refused to believe in him (Matt. 11:20) and on those disciples who refused to believe that he was risen from the dead (Mk. 16:14).

3. Insults and mockery were heaped upon Christ as he hung upon the cross. *empaizō* is used of the general crowd's mockery of Jesus (e.g., Matt. 20:19; 27:29, 31, 41); *oneidizō* is used for the mockery of the two robbers hanging with Jesus (27:44; Mk. 15:32). In fact, Jesus' very crucifixion can be termed as his bearing disgrace (Heb. 13:13).

4. In several places words in the *oneidizō* group have to do with the insults and disgrace that believers experience from the unbelieving world. Jesus knew that this would occur and told his followers that they should consider themselves blessed when it does (Matt. 5:11; Lk. 6:22). Both Heb. and 1 Pet. were written to people experiencing such abuse (Heb. 10:23; 13:13; 1 Pet. 4:14). In a proleptic sense, Moses "regarded disgrace for the sake of Christ as of greater value than the treasures of Egypt" (Heb. 11:26).

See also *blasphēmeō*, slander, defame, blaspheme (*1059*); *katalaleō*, speak evil of, rail at, slander (*2895*); *loidoreō*, insult, abuse, revile (*3366*).

3944 (oneidismos, insult, disgrace), → *3943*.

3945 (oneidos, disgrace), → *3943*.

3950	ὄνομα

ὄνομα (*onoma*), name (*3950*); ὀνομάζω (*onomazō*), to call, name (*3951*); ἐπονομάζω (*eponomazō*), call by a name, give a surname (*2226*); ψευδώνυμος (*pseudōnymos*), bearing a false name (*6024*).

CL & OT 1. In cl. Gk. *onoma* means name. Derived from the noun are two vbs.: (1) *onomazō*, name, specify, designate, tell; and (2) *eponomazō*, apply a word as a name, give a second name or nickname. *pseudōnymos*, formed from the addition of *pseud-*, false, means bearing a false name; or incorrectly, inappropriately named.

(a) In the thought of virtually every people group one's name is inextricably bound up with the person, whether of a human, a god, or a demon. Anyone who knows the name of a being can exert power over that being. In magic the potential energy that resides in the name can be translated into effective power if the name is mentioned or used in an oath.

(b) Gk. philosophy struggled with the relationship between the name and the thing named. To Plato, for example, words are phonetic symbols, which receive their meaning through custom and are thus of little relevance for true knowledge. For the Stoics, by contrast, words represented things in accordance with their nature; as regarded content, the spoken word, the concept, and the object itself are all alike.

(c) The names of the gods also entered into these discussions. Hesiod tried to find the key to the nature of the gods from the etymology of their names. Others insisted that the higher a god stood, the more names he had. The Stoics tried to overcome polytheism by transferring all the many names to one god, Zeus; here, the plurality of names expressed fullness of being. The magical formulas found on the papyri of late antiquity reveal the belief in the power and effectiveness of the names of gods and demons.

2. The Heb. *šēm* appears 770x in the OT; the Gk. *onoma* occurs over 1000x in the LXX. (a) The Israelites were well aware of the significance of personal and proper names. The best-known example is that of Nabal, who is a fool, as his name suggests (1 Sam. 25:25). In this context belong also the numerous etymological interpretations that are offered where people and places are given names: e.g., Eve, "the mother of all the living" (Gen. 3:20); Babel, "because there the LORD confused the language of the whole world" (11:9). To give a name means to exercise lordship and dominion: e.g., Adam's naming of the animals in 2:19–20. As the one who gives names to the stars, Yahweh is their Creator and Lord (Ps. 147:4).

(b) Name changes also testify to their significance (Gen. 41:45; 2 Ki. 23:34). Yahweh can change someone's name when he gives that person a new importance for the present or the future. Thus Abram becomes Abraham, the father of many nations (Gen. 17:5); Jacob becomes Israel, because he fought with God (32:28).

3. (a) Of primary significance is the name of Yahweh, which he himself made known in his revelation (Exod. 3:14; 6:2; cf. Gen. 17:1; → *theos*, *2536*). An essential feature of the biblical revelation is the fact that God is not without a name; he has a personal name by which he can and is to be invoked. When people appeal to Yahweh, he comes near and makes his promise true: "Wherever I cause my name to be honored, I will come to you and bless you" (Exod. 20:24; cf. Num. 6:24 –26). Priests and Levites, even the king, bless in the name of Yahweh (6:27; Deut. 10:8; 2 Sam. 6:18). The name of Yahweh, indeed, is such a powerful expression of his personal rule and activity that it can be used as an alternative way of speaking of Yahweh himself (Lev. 18:21; Ps. 7:17; Amos 2:7; Mic. 5:4).

(b) Yahweh's historical dealings with people in the past (Exod. 3:6, 13, 15), present (20:7), and future (Ezek. 25:17; 34:30) are inextricably bound up with his name. Misuse of this name in magic or in false oaths is forbidden (Exod. 20:7). The name of Yahweh is committed in trust to Israel; the heathen do not know it (Ps. 79:6). Israel has the task of hallowing his name, which takes place in the cult, at sacrifice, in prayer, in blessing and cursing, and also in holy war (29:8)— in other words, in serving Yahweh, and him alone, and in obeying his commands. To take part in the worship of another god, therefore, profanes the name of Yahweh (Lev. 18:21).

(c) According to Deut., Yahweh lives in heaven, but he chooses on earth a place where he causes "his Name" to dwell (12:11; 14:23– 24; 16:2, 6, 11; cf. 2 Sam. 7:13; 1 Ki. 3:2; 5:3). In that his name dwells in the temple, Yahweh's presence is itself guaranteed, but only in such a way that even if the temple is profaned, Yahweh's transcendence remains preserved (cf. 8:13, 27–28). Yahweh's name, like he himself, remains sovereign.

(d) Thus, Yahweh's name assumes a powerful and independent existence of its own, although it is naturally still closely linked with Yahweh himself. Through its mighty sway, the godly experience Yahweh's protection and help (cf. Ps. 54:6; Prov. 18:10; Mal. 1:11). His name almost becomes a hypostasis of Yahweh himself (cf. Ps. 54:1; 89:24; 118:10–12).

(e) In later OT writings Yahweh's name is frequently used in the sense of his "praise" or "glory" (Isa. 26:8; 55:13). Phrases like "the LORD Almighty is his name" (e.g., 51:15; Jer. 10:16; Amos 4:13) indicate Yahweh's claim to sovereign glory in the world and among nations to whom Israel makes it known (Isa. 12:4).

4. (a) The Heb. expression *bᵉšēm* ("in the name") occurs frequently in the OT. Linked with the names of places or people it can mean by name (Jos. 21:9), after the name of (Jdg. 18:29), in the name of (1 Ki. 21:8; Est. 3:12), and on behalf of (1 Sam. 25:9). The phrase

appears most often in association with the name of Yahweh, with the primary meaning of calling on Yahweh by his name, i.e., worshiping him (cf. Gen. 4:26; 12:8). The formula is also used in order to swear, since by the use of the expression, Yahweh's might is called on to interpose (Deut. 10:8; 2 Sam. 6:18; 2 Ki. 2:24). The appeal of false prophets to Yahweh is illegitimate, for they have received neither their commission nor his words from him (Deut. 18:20; Jer. 14:14–15; 23:25; 29:9).

5. (a) It is possible that Josephus, a priest, knew the Heb. name Yahweh, but he never uses it. He does not even use the Gk. *kyrios*, Lord, which the LXX used to translate Yahweh. This shows the extent to which fear of uttering the name of God had gone. Instead, he uses *onoma* and has a predilection for *prosēgoria*, address, appellation, title, even where Yahweh's name is under consideration. In his rendering of Exod. 3, he adds that he is not allowed to say anything about God's name. Israel's temple bears God's name, like heathen temples that bear the names of their gods.

(b) Qumran writings follow the same paths as the OT as far as the use of God's name is concerned.

(c) God's name is important in rab. tradition. One may pass on a doctrine or tradition only if one names the authority from whom one has received it. Still, the name of Yahweh is avoided if at all possible, in order to keep from disobeying the third commandment (Exod. 20:7). Yahweh's name was still used in the high priest's blessing on the Day of Atonement, but in scriptural quotations *Yahweh* came to be replaced by *šēm* (Heb. "name"). So the tetragrammaton YHWH ceased to be used, and its pronunciation was forgotten. Thus, the name of God became a secret name used as a means of magical power, esp. in the piety of the lower strata of society.

NT In the NT *onoma* (which can mean reputation [Mk. 6:14; Rev. 3:1] and person [Acts 1:15; Rev. 3:4; 11:13]) occurs 231x, most commonly in Lk. (34x in Lk.; 60x in Acts). *onomazō* occurs 10x, while *eponomazō* is found only in Rom. 2:17, and *pseudōnymos* is used only in 1 Tim. 6:20.

1. *Names of humans and other beings.* (a) The names of the twelve apostles on the foundation stones of the new Jerusalem (Rev. 21:14) and the names of the twelve tribes of Israel on its gates (21:12) proclaim the final unity of the old and the new people of God. Jesus proves himself to be the good shepherd by calling his sheep by name and knowing them personally (Jn. 10:3). In giving his disciples new names, he draws them in a special way into his service (Matt. 10:2– 4; Mk. 3:16–19; Lk. 6:14–16): Jesus gives to Simon the name Peter (→ *petra*, *4376*); Mk. 3:17 mentions that to James and John, sons of Zebedee, "Jesus gave the name Boanerges, which means Sons of Thunder." The fact that the names of the disciples are written in heaven (Lk. 10:20) means that they belong to God and to his kingdom (Rev. 3:5). The new name that the one who overcomes receives expresses one's inalienable fellowship with Christ himself (2:17).

(b) Evil spirits have names also, which predicate something of their nature or power. In Mk. 5:9, Jesus discovers that the name of a multitude of demons is "Legion," and he gains power over them. The "beast" in Rev. 13:1 bears blasphemous names—he is given names and honorific titles that belong to God or to Christ. His name is contained in a number (13:17–18), which his adherents also bear (13:17; 15:2). The name of the "great prostitute" (17:1, 3) is "BABYLON THE GREAT, THE MOTHER OF PROSTITUTES AND OF THE ABOMINATIONS OF THE EARTH" (17:5); she stands in contrast to the woman of Rev. 12, who bears the male child and is the mother of all the faithful.

2. *The name of God.* God's name belongs with his revelation. He reveals himself as the loving Father, and he glorifies his name in Jesus' saving work (Jn. 17:12, 26). Thus Jesus, and he alone, reveals the name of God as the Father (17:6). In 12:28 "Father," "glorify," and "name" are closely bound together. That the disciples are kept in the name of God indicates that they live in the sphere of an effective power, which protects them from ruin and unites them with each other

(17:11–12). The goal of proclaiming the name of God as Father is that the love of the Father for the Son is also to be found in believers (17:26). In these affirmations of Jn.'s Gospel, and above all in the high priestly prayer of Jesus (17:1–26), we have the Christological interpretation of the OT affirmations concerning the name of Yahweh.

Jesus thus acts in the name of and on behalf of God in fulfillment of his will and as proof of his sonship (Mk. 11:9–10; Jn. 10:24–25). At his Parousia he will come "in the name of the Lord" (Matt. 23:39). When the name of God is conjoined with that of the Son and of the Holy Spirit, it assumes the character of completeness and fullness (28:19); this is Trinitarian thought, even if a precise Trinitarian formula is lacking. The first request of the Lord's Prayer concerns hallowing God's name (6:9), presumably through our own lives. A person who despises God's will and commands, or a Christian slave who is disobedient to his master, is in effect slandering God's name (Rom. 2:24; 1 Tim. 6:1).

3. *The name of Jesus.* (a) The significance of Jesus' life and activity is evident in his name (Matt. 1:21; → *Iēsous*, *2652*; *Emmanouēl*, *1842*). He bears the sublime name of Son (Heb. 1:4–5). His name is "the Word of God" (Rev. 19:13; cf. Jn. 1:1), and God's name of Lord also becomes his name (Phil. 2:9–10; Rev. 19:16). Above and beyond this, he bears a name that he alone knows (19:12). The name "Jesus" can be replaced simply by "the Name" (Acts 5:41; 3 Jn. 7). The whole content of God's saving truth revealed in Jesus is comprised in his name (Acts 4:12; 1 Cor. 6:11). To believe in the name of the Son (Jn. 3:18) is God's command (1 Jn. 3:23; 5:13). Anyone who believes in his name receives forgiveness of sins (Acts 10:43; 1 Jn. 2:12), has eternal life (Jn. 20:31; 1 Jn. 5:13), and escapes the judgment (Jn. 3:18). A Christian's whole life is to be dominated by the name of Jesus (Col. 3:17).

Jesus' name is the basis of the proclamation of the gospel to all nations (Acts 8:12; 9:16; Rom. 1:5). The authorities at Jerusalem prohibited the apostles from preaching "in the name of Jesus" (Acts 5:40). Faith and proclamation include confession of that name (Rev. 2:13; 3:8) and readiness to suffer for its sake (Matt. 10:22; 24:9). The name of Christ contains the implication of glory, so that 1 Pet. 4:14 declares: "If you are insulted because of the name of Christ, you are blessed, for the Spirit of glory and of God rests on you" (cf. Isa. 11:2). Moreover, whoever calls on the name of the Lord belongs to the church (Acts 9:14; 1 Cor. 1:2) and is saved (Acts 2:17–21; Rom. 10:13; cf. Joel 2:32). Believers were called Christians because of the name of Christ (Acts 11:26; cf. 26:28; 1 Pet. 4:16; → *Christianos*, *5985*). One of the gifts of final perfection is that the victors will bear the name of the Lamb (Rev. 3:12; 14:1; 22:4).

(b) The formula "in the name of Jesus." God gives the Holy Spirit in the name of Jesus (Jn. 14:26). Thanks are given in that name (Eph. 5:20). The nations place their hope in it (Matt. 12:21; cf. Isa. 42:4), and in that name the congregation prays (Jn. 14:13–14; 15:16); this is the reason why their prayers are heard. Since the disciples are sent out by Jesus, they can perform miracles and acts of compassion in his name (Lk. 10:17; cf. Mk. 9:38–39). After Easter, the name of Jesus continued to maintain its power (Acts 3:6; 4:10). Jesus himself gives help in his name (9:34), though not if unbelievers try to misuse it in magical exorcisms (19:13–16). Statements such as this show that the OT manner of speaking of the name of Yahweh has been transferred to Jesus and his name.

(c) Baptism "in the name of Jesus." Baptism symbolically assigns the person baptized to Christ for forgiveness of sins (Acts 8:16; 19:5; 1 Cor. 1:13, 15; cf. Matt. 28:19). The fullness of Christ's saving work is contained in his name (as Yahweh's saving work was in his name) and is present in the church. This is symbolized by an individual's baptism, since he or she has been caught up into Jesus' death and resurrection (Rom. 6:1–11; Col. 2:12; cf. 2 Cor. 4:10).

4. The vb. *onomazō* occurs 10x in the NT. The name and service of an apostle are traced back to Jesus (Lk. 6:13). A man who bears the name of brother but lives unworthy of it is to be denied fellowship (1 Cor. 5:11). The congregation is so detached from sin that it is not even to be named in it (Eph. 5:3; cf. 2 Tim. 2:19). God names every fam-

ily in heaven and on earth and so is the Father of all (Eph. 3:15). *eponomazō*, to name after, give a second name, occurs only in Rom. 2:17: "if you call yourself [*eponomazē*] a Jew." Here "Jew" is a title of honor, signifying an heir to the legacy described in 2:17–20. Paul attacks the inconsistency of claiming to be a Jew and at the same time countenancing sin. Jews stand under the same divine judgment as Gentiles.

5. *pseudōnymos* occurs only at 1 Tim. 6:20: "Turn away from godless chatter and the opposing ideas of what is falsely called [*pseudōnymou*] knowledge." Here Paul warns against a movement that gives the lie to its name and leads one into error (cf. 6:21).

3951 (*onomazō*, to call, name), → *3950*.

3954 (*oxos*, wine vinegar), → *5958*.

3957 (*opisthen*, from behind), → *3958*.

3958	ὀπίσω

ὀπίσω (*opisō*), behind, after (*3958*); ὄπισθεν (*opisthen*), from behind (*3957*).

CL & OT *opisō* is an adv. of place, meaning behind, to the rear. *opisthen* also means from behind and is equivalent to *opisō*. Each occurs as an adv., noun, and prep.

1. In the LXX these words indicate following behind, as in processions after the ark (cf. Jos. 3:3; 6:9 = LXX 6:8), following in war (1 Sam. 11:7), political allegiance (Jdg. 9:3–4; 2 Sam. 2:10; Ezek. 29:16), following as a prophet's servant (1 Ki. 19:20–21), devotion to a lover (Ruth 3:10; fig. in Jer. 2:5; Hos. 2:5, 13), following after spiritual objects (2 Ki. 13:2; Isa. 65:2; Jer. 3:17), and dedication and obedience to a god/God (Deut. 13:4; Jdg. 2:12–13; 1 Ki. 19:21; Jer. 2:23; 7:6, 9; Ezek. 20:16).

2. As a rab. expression, following after someone refers to the state of being a pupil, largely with respect to the shared life with the teacher (→ *mathētēs*, *3412*).

NT *opisō* can be used as a time preposition meaning after (e.g., Matt. 3:11; Jn. 1:15, 27, 30) and as a phrase indicating attachment (e.g., Lk. 21:8; Jn. 6:66; 12:19; Acts 5:37; 20:30; Rev. 13:3). It is mostly used in the NT with the gen. of persons. Those passages where the gen. *opisō mou* refers to Jesus (e.g., Matt. 10:38; Mk. 1:17 par.; 8:34 par.) are particularly significant. *opisō* here takes on the meaning of *akoloutheō*, follow, go behind someone (cf. Mk. 2:14). Mk. 1:17 has this call to discipleship in its simplest form: (lit.) "Come after me (*opisō mou*), and I will make you to become fishers of men."

"Going behind" means having a share in the fellowship of Jesus' life and suffering (Matt. 10:38 par.; 16:24 par.; cf. Lk. 23:26). According to Matt. 16:23, it is precisely this pattern of suffering that Peter does not understand. In discipleship, Jesus goes on ahead and prescribes the way. Looking back is out of the question for one who is fleeing persecution (Lk. 17:31–32 par.), who is plowing (9:62), or who, as a runner, has one's eye on the goal (Phil. 3:13–14). One ought not look back at associations that have been left behind or on past achievements.

See also *akoloutheō*, follow (*199*); *mathētēs*, learner, pupil, disciple (*3412*); *mimeomai*, imitate, follow (*3628*).

3959 (*hoplizō*, equip, arm), → *4483*.

3960 (*hoplon*, weapon), → *4483*.

3965 (*optasia*, vision), → *3972*.

3969 (*horama*, sight, vision), → *3972*.

3970 (*horasis*, vision, appearance), → *3972*.

3971 (*horatos*, visible), → *3972*.

3972	ὁράω

ὁράω (*horaō*), see (*3972*); ἰδού (*idou*), see! behold! look! (*2627*); ὁρατός (*horatos*), visible (*3971*); ἀόρατος (*aoratos*), invisible (*548*); ὅραμα (*horama*), sight, vision (*3969*); ὅρασις (*horasis*), appearance, vision (*3970*); ὀπτασία (*optasia*), vision (*3965*); ἐποπτεύω (*epopteuō*), observe (*2227*); καθοράω (*kathoraō*), look at (*2775*); θεάομαι (*theaomai*), behold (*2517*); θεωρέω (*theōreō*), watch (*2555*); ὀφθαλμός (*ophthalmos*), eye (*4057*).

CL & OT 1. (a) The vb. *horaō* is only found with the root *hor-* in the pres. stem and in the perf. act stem. The fut. mid. (dep.) *opsomai* and the fut./aor. pass. *ōphthēn* are derived from the Gk. root *op-*, and the aor. act. *eidon* from the root *id-*. The vb. is common and in the act. means to see, look, perceive, observe; it also often means to look toward something. Already by Homer's time it had the meaning of to conceive or experience, and even to be present at or participate. In a fig. sense it means to understand, recognize, consider, attend to. From the pass. used with an intrans. sense it came to mean appear, become visible.

(b) The verbal adj. *horatos* and the negative form *aoratos* mean, respectively, visible and invisible. Three important nouns formed from *horaō* are *horasis*, vision, appearance; *horama*, what is seen, view, vision; and *optasia*, view, sight, vision.

(c) Compound vbs. include *prooraō*, to foresee the future, see something that one has seen before; and *kathoraō* and *epopteuō*, to look at, regard, observe.

(d) The noun *ophthalmos*, eye, derived from the root *op-*, can have a specialized use in the poetic sense of the eye of heaven, the sun and the moon, as well as expressing the ideas of light, well-being, and that which brings comfort. In general the eye is the highest means of contact with the world around. It is the organ of perception. Fig. *ophthalmos* means that which is dearest and most loved (cf. the apple of the eye). The eye is often associated with a person's relation to God, to one's fellow humans, and to the world around. In Gk. the "eye of the soul" gains insight into the cosmos. Moral concepts are associated with the eye (e.g., to look covetously, to cast jealous glances).

(e) *theaomai* means to view, behold, watch. *theōreō*, also to watch, look at something, has the fig. meanings of reflect on, notice, understand, comprehend; in the pass. it means become visible or be looked at.

(f) The Gk. vbs. of seeing or beholding have religious and philosophical significance, for Gk. religion, like that of antiquity in general, was a religion of seeing. Jud., by way of contrast, emphasized the role of hearing. Insight into the cosmic order and the rationale of this world was understood religiously. That applied both to the world on the grand scale, in the sense of the macrocosm, and to the world on a small scale, in the sense of the microcosm. The "eye of the soul" is particularly significant here.

Human actions were governed by this insight into the cosmos. In Plato God is more an object than a subject and being seen is predicated of him. From that Plato arrives at the concept of the vision of the ideas (→ *eidos*, form, appearance, *1626*), which denote the knowledge of supernatural things achieved by the spirit: pattern, idea, essence.

In general the Gk. deity is regarded as invisible. Yet from Homer on we find the notion of the gods going about in bodily form (anthropomorphism). They "appear" in human disguise and have human qualities and propensities. But in general their invisibility is still emphasized. The "vision of god" serves as the way to be like the immortals.

2. (a) *horaō* (with its 2d aor. *eidon*) occurs some 1450x in the LXX. Generally it means to see with one's own eye, become aware (Gen. 27:1). Fig. it can denote perceive intellectually or spiritually; notice, become conscious (Ps. 34:8); experience, suffer (e.g., see death, 89:48). It also means to regard (e.g., misfortune, 106:44), attend to, know (Deut. 11:2), or be concerned about something (Gen. 37:14). Seeing in the OT can refer also to perception by means of other senses, e.g., hearing (Jer. 33:24 in MT) or understanding (1 Sam. 12:17; 1 Ki. 20:7 = LXX 21:7). In the pass. it is used for letting oneself be seen; here the idea is of true perception in contrast to the imagination. God let himself be seen, disclosed, or revealed in visions (*horama*). Through

this action the one who sees as well as the hearer is encouraged or commissioned (Gen. 15:1; 46:2).

(b) Seeing can also refer to prophetic perception. Prophetic seeing, which sometimes assumes the character of a vision, occurs frequently in the OT. Hence the prophet can also be designated a seer (Heb. *ḥōzeh*; LXX *horōn*; 1 Chr. 21:9; 2 Chr. 9:29). The seer's visions generally have a twofold reference: the thing seen, the vision (*horama*), or the appearance of the vision (Exod. 3:3; Dan. 7:1); and the effect on the seer, who is encouraged, chosen, shocked, pardoned, etc. (Gen. 15:1; Dan. 7:13). This prophetic vision involves primarily a revelation of God and his word, and only then a visual impact: God lets it be known what he wants or what he is going to do and "shows" it to someone whom he has chosen.

(c) It is simply assumed in the OT that God sees and watches humans. He sees injustice (Lam. 3:34–36, 50, 59–60), the death of his prophet (2 Chr. 24:22), and the distress of his own (Exod. 3:7). He looks for faithfulness (Ps. 101:6) and for trust (Jer. 5:3). He also has his eyes on the sinful kingdom (Amos 9:8). No one can hide from him (Ps. 139:3, 7, 16). God sees into our innermost being (1 Sam. 16:7).

(d) Even though the OT speaks of God's becoming visible in visions (theophanies), it contains no inquisitive speculation into his form. God appears to Abraham, Isaac, Jacob, and Moses (Num. 12:8) face to face and in human form. Several passages extend this bodily imagery (Gen. 3:8; Exod. 33:23; Isa. 6:1–4; Amos 9:11–15). Through these modes of manifestation OT saints recognized and understood God's nature. Fire, gale, clouds, and the like are mentioned as important elements in these manifestations.

In a theophany God's glory (Gk. *doxa*, → *1518*) is revealed (Exod. 33:18; Num. 14:22; Ezek. 1:28 = LXX 2:1). Heaven opens (1:1), and the transcendent breaks through and is visible. Supernatural brightness (Ps. 18:12; 50:2; Hab. 3:4), the likeness of sunrise (Hos. 6:3), and storm and tempest (Job 38:1; Nah. 1:3) are mentioned as concomitant phenomena for God's presence.

(e) In the context of the theophanies God's face denotes his very person (→ *prosōpon*, face, *4725*). It reveals something of God's nature (Gen. 32:30–31). The parts of God's form that are mentioned (the eye, ear, and hand) illustrate his faithfulness and care. It is significant that qualities like those attributed to the Gk. gods (e.g., sexuality) are not ascribed to God in the OT. The OT seeks instead to disclose God's nature, not to provide a concrete visual image of him. God's holiness and majesty prevent humans from seeing his face. Our consciousness of guilt leads to a consciousness of distance (Isa. 6:5). Seeing God's glory can kill a person (cf. Exod. 33:20).

The OT theophanies express God's partnership with humanity. People in the OT see themselves as God's creatures and at the same time know themselves as his partners. The OT God is one who meets us, consorts with us, and is known as such.

(f) In the OT the future constantly appears in visions. In view are the coming redemption, conquest of one's enemies, and establishment of God's kingdom (1 Chr. 29:11; Ps. 22:28–29; Isa. 11:6–9; 57:19). The goal is to see God face to face (Ps. 42:2), perhaps in a future life. However, this last point is not unambiguously attested in the OT (cf. 17:15). The promise of Matt. 5:8 and the confident assertion of 1 Jn. 3:2 have no direct OT parallels.

3. In Jud. of the intertestamental period seeing gave way to hearing, esp. in Philo. Seeing is frequently separated from the grasping of sense-perceptions. *horaō* and its derivatives came to mean attaining knowledge and, occasionally, seeing God. Philo held that the world (creation) should lead to a knowledge of God (cf. Rom. 1:20, *kathoraō*).

NT 1. *Survey of words.* This group of words occurs frequently in the NT: *horaō* and the fut. *opsomai* occur ca. 110x, the aor. *eidon* 336x. Generally they have the same sense as in cl. Gk. and the OT. (a) *horaō*, *opsomai*, and *eidon* generally mean see, perceive (e.g., Matt. 28:7; Mk. 16:7; Jn. 16:16). These vbs. can be used fig. for perceiving, recalling, ascertaining, realizing (e.g., Matt. 13:14) as well as for a vision of the spirit or intellect (Lk. 2:30, seeing salvation; Acts 2:17; 26:16, seeing visions or appearances).

(b) The verbal adjs. *horatos* and *aoratos* mean visible and invisible, respectively. They emphasize God's invisibility (Rom. 1:20; Col. 1:15–16; 1 Tim. 1:17).

(c) The nouns *horasis, horama,* and *optasia* are used in the same sense as in the OT. *horasis* means appearance (Rev. 4:3) or vision (Acts 2:17; Rev. 9:17) and *horama* the thing seen, the vision (Matt. 17:9; Acts 18:9), including the vision seen in a dream (16:9). In keeping with the OT perspective, the NT represents its effects on the visionary as pardoning, encouraging, or commissioning (9:10, 12; 10:3). *optasia*, the appearance of the vision, is found in Lk. 1:22; 24:23 of the appearances of angels, and in 2 Cor. 12:1 probably of ecstatic experiences.

(d) There are various *horaō* compounds. *kathoraō* means to perceive; thus in Rom. 1:20 it refers to the invisible, which is perceived in the external and visible. *epopteuō*, to look at, is used in 1 Pet. 2:12; 3:2 with reference to a Christian's manner of life that the Gentiles will notice. For *prooraō*, foresee, see ahead, → *4632*.

(e) *theaomai* means to visit (Rom. 15:24), look at (Matt. 22:11), and notice something (Lk. 23:55). *theōreō*, to look at, behold, but also experience (Matt. 27:55; Lk. 14:29), is also used of intellectual seeing (Jn. 4:19; Acts 4:13). In the pass. it means become visible.

(f) *ophthalmos*, eye, occurs 100x in the NT, whereas the ear is mentioned only 36x. It often occurs in conjunction with moral concepts, esp. in the Synoptics: to look enviously (Matt. 20:15; Mk. 7:22) or ingenuously or with evil (Matt. 6:22–23). It can be the occasion of taking offense or inciting to sin (5:29; 2 Pet. 2:14). It is also the organ of understanding and knowing. Eph. 1:18 speaks of "the eyes of your heart." Rarely does the NT refer to God's eyes (Heb. 4:13; 1 Pet. 3:12).

(g) The use, esp. in the Synoptic Gospels, of *idou* or *kai idou* (adapted from the OT but not found in cl. Gk.), is also noteworthy. This construction is used to attract attention, esp. at the beginning of a conversation (Mk. 3:32; 10:28). Matt. and Mk. also use it with a predicate, to advertise something surprising or new (Matt. 12:2; Mk. 2:24). This formulation also occurs in the context of the proclamation of salvation (Lk. 2:34), while at other times it draws attention to the fulfillment of a promise (Matt. 12:41; Mk. 14:41–42; Jn. 4:35) and assures the fulfillment of what has been announced (Mk. 10:33; Jn. 16:32). These two words serve a kerygmatic purpose, addressing the hearer, before whose eyes the message is proclaimed.

2. *Jn.'s concept of seeing.* In Jn. the vbs. of seeing take on a special significance. He loves to use *horaō* for that which the preexistent Son saw when he was with his Father (Jn. 3:11, 32; 6:46; 8:38). *theaomai* is used of seeing Jesus' *doxa*, glory (1:14), and of the Spirit's descending (1:32).

(a) Jn. uses the vbs. of seeing in a threefold sense. (i) They are used in connection with seeing earthly things and events that are taking place (Jn. 1:38, 47; 9:8). (ii) They denote the perception of supernatural elements, which only certain people enjoy. Hence, John the Baptist sees the Spirit descending in the form of a dove (1:32–34). (iii) Jn. also thinks of seeing as the perception of a revelatory event. This is a spiritual act of seeing, the sight of faith. The disciples see the Son's glory (1:14), which is also revealed to them in his signs (cf. 2:11).

The real nature of the Son, his *doxa*, is disclosed to those who believe. That which in the OT was proclaimed and appeared only symbolically now has become a historical reality in the incarnate Word. Faith, discerning it through hearing and seeing, responds to God's revelation in Jesus Christ. It also discerns Jesus Christ's *doxa* in the signs (2:11). Unbelievers do not discern it; they are spiritually blind (cf. 9:39–41). The believer perceives in the Son the Father who sent him (12:45; 14:9). Those who see the Son also see the Father.

(b) Although the seer is only occasionally important in the NT (cf. Jn. on Patmos, Rev. 1:9), there is a stronger emphasis in Johannine literature on the eyewitness (cf. "the man who saw it" in Jn. 19:35), whose testimony is valid (1 Jn. 1:1; cf. Lk. 1:1–4).

(c) Jesus' own seeing is important in the event of revelation (Jn. 12:45; 14:9). He sees the Father (1:18). This is characteristic of Jesus' special relationship with him and is the basis of his message. He sees what is in us and discloses it. He sees Nathanael under the fig tree (1:48) and the thoughts and inner nature of a person (cf. 2:25).

(d) Hearing and seeing can be used interchangeably in relation to faith (cf. Jn. 5:24; 8:45; with 5:37–39; 6:40), and the concept of eternal life is associated with seeing. Seeing as well as hearing again and again provide the impetus to faith (2:11; 20:8), lead to knowledge (14:9), and minister to inner perception (e.g., "I can see that you are a prophet," 4:19). Faith recognizes the coming Messiah. Seeing is thus an encounter with Jesus. However, faith based on seeing has no advantage, for Jesus pronounces a special blessing on those who believe without seeing (20:29).

3. *The theological meaning of these words in the rest of the NT.* (a) One's eyes and ears are not just for physical perception; they are symbols of spiritual perception. They see God and hear him speak.

(b) Spiritual perception as a function of seeing comes to mean make the acquaintance of (Lk. 23:8), meet (Acts 20:25), watch or look out for (cf. Mk. 13:33; Phil. 3:2). Spiritual seeing is at the same time an experience (Lk. 2:26; Jn. 8:51) or the conceiving of or experiencing of God's love (1 Jn. 3:1).

(c) Seeing acquires a new perspective with reference to faith. In the Synoptic Gospels it is used to express obtaining a share in salvation (Lk. 2:26). Hence, seeing takes on the character of a decision (Matt. 21:32; Mk. 8:18); the unbeliever does not perceive (Matt. 13:13–14; Mk. 4:12).

(d) Theophanies do not occur in the NT, though appearances of angels are mentioned in connection with Jesus' coming (Lk. 2:13), the temptation (Matt. 4:11), the passion (Lk. 22:43), and the resurrection (Matt. 28:2, 5). There are also occasionally revelatory dreams (e.g., Matt. 1:20; 2:13, 19). There are various accounts of visions of the risen Christ (*horama* and *optasia*), given by God, who causes his Son to be seen (Acts 9:10, 12; 10:3). They have a dramatic effect on those who see them.

4. For the NT God is utterly invisible (Jn. 6:46; Col. 1:15; 1 Tim. 1:17; 6:16), though the resurrection narratives stress that the risen Christ is visible. There he is encountered as a person and recognized by his actions (Matt. 28; Lk. 24), esp. that of eating. The Gospels use a rich vocabulary to describe these visible encounters with him in the body (Matt. 28:17; Lk. 24:31, 36–37; Jn. 20:14–29). That the risen Christ is seen is an event of revelation. In Jn. 20:25 the disciples come to believe through seeing the risen Christ ("We have seen the Lord"). These encounters lead to faith, commitment, witness, and sending.

Paul attests that the risen Christ was seen or appeared with the aor. pass. of *horaō* (1 Cor. 15:5–8). The appearances are never only visual, but are always bound up with hearing the word of the risen Christ; yet hearing should not be stressed at the expense of seeing. Thus the Easter message is summed up in Jn. 19:35: "The man who saw it has given testimony, and his testimony is true. He knows that he tells the truth, and he testifies so that you also may believe."

5. The vbs. of seeing are also used in the NT with respect to the future. The promise for the future contains three essential elements: (a) seeing God's glory (Jn. 17:24); (b) seeing God's kingly rule (3:3); and (c) supremely, seeing God (Matt. 5:8; 1 Jn. 3:2) and living in fellowship with him (Rev. 21:3). The angels already see God's face (Matt. 18:10). In the coming era of fulfillment, God will restore the fellowship with us that was broken by sin. He does not put himself at our disposal, nor does he give himself up to human clutches, but he does open the way to fellowship with himself. Now we still wait in faith, yet the watching community knows that the day is coming when we will see God (Matt. 5:8).

See also *kollourion*, eye salve (*3141*); *blepō*, look at, see (*1063*); *atenizō*, look at a person or thing intently, gaze on (*867*); *theatron*, theater, place of assembly, a spectacle (*2519*).

3973 ὀργή

ὀργή (*orgē*), anger, wrath (*3973*); ὀργίζω (*orgizō*), be or become angry, make angry (*3974*); ὀργίλος (*orgilos*), inclined to anger (*3975*); παροργίζω (*parorgizō*) enrage, make angry (*4239*); παροργισμός (*parorgismos*), anger (*4240*); παροξύνω (*paroxynō*), provoke to anger (*4236*); παροξυσμός (*paroxysmos*), sharp disagreement (*4237*).

CL & OT 1. *orgē*, a cognate of *orgaō* (be puffed up, swell, be excited), means a natural impulse, disposition; anger, wrath. A word in the gen. following it indicates the subj. of the anger or the occasion of the anger. The obj. of the anger is usually designated by the prepositions *eis*, *pros*, or *epi* with the acc.

(a) In the main, *orgē* is seen in humans as a character defect that one should strive to lay aside. Anger as the expression of unrestrained passion stands in contradiction to reason and conflicts with the image of the wise person. Its only appropriate human use is for a judge in the pursuit of righteousness.

(b) But *orgē* is also a prominent characteristic of the Gk. deities, directed either against other gods or against human beings. It is provoked as a rule by violating one of the fundamental demands of life, morals, or law. In the Roman world the idea of wrathful gods and their punitive judgments, afflicting individuals with sickness, suffering, and natural catastrophes, is even more strongly historicized. The great historical writers often allude to divine anger as the effective cause of historical incidents.

2. (a) The OT speaks frequently of God's anger and of human anger. At least 7 different Heb. words are translated in the LXX with either *thymos* or *orgē*.

(b) In parts of the OT both *orgē* and *thymos* designate a human reaction in a neutral or even a positive sense. Zebul's anger (Jdg. 9:30), for example, is thoroughly justified. Still more legitimate is David's anger with the rich man in Nathan's fable (2 Sam. 12:5). Moses' indignation at the sin of the people dancing round the golden calf is even presented as a holy anger, in which Moses places himself on the side of God (Exod. 32:19; cf. 16:20; 1 Sam. 11:6; Job 32:2–3; Jer. 6:11).

But elsewhere in the OT outbursts of anger are depicted as a vice (cf. Job 36:13; Ps. 37:8) and are rejected (cf. Gen. 49:7, where anger is cursed). It is not only cruel (Prov. 27:4) but leads to quarreling and wrangling (cf. 30:33). It disunites people (1 Sam. 20:30) and can lead to bloody acts (Gen. 49:6). By anger one shows oneself to be unwise (Prov. 29:8), for it is a mark of fools (12:16; 27:3). We should avoid it at all costs (Job 36:18).

(c) The role of the divine anger in the OT is of greater significance. Yahweh is repeatedly described as a jealous and angry God. His anger can be presented in drastic terms (Ps. 2:5; Isa. 13:13; 30:27–28; Jer. 30:23–24 = LXX 37:23–24). A human encounter with the holy could be dangerous (Gen. 32:25–31; Exod. 4:24–26; 19:9–13; Isa. 6:5), for the anger of Yahweh expresses his holiness and righteousness. It points to the living, personal nature of God, whose ways are beyond humans (Exod. 4:24; 1 Sam. 26:19; 2 Sam. 16:10–12; 24:1).

The behavior of specific individuals can provoke divine anger (Exod. 4:14; Num. 12:9; Deut. 29:18–21; 2 Sam. 6:7; 2 Chr. 19:2; 25:15; cf. Sir. 47:20; Pr. Man. 9–10), but most often it is provoked by the apostasy, unfaithfulness, and disobedience of God's covenant people (Num. 25:3; 32:10; Deut. 29:25–28; Jdg. 2:14, 20; Ps. 78:21). The prophets (esp. Amos, Hos., Isa., and Mic.) referred to divine wrath as an appropriate reaction to the people's way of life, social and economic attitudes, political behavior, and particularly cultic practice. Within the framework of covenant theology Yahweh's wrath is an expression of rejected and wounded love. This is the deepest root of wrath, and in this light one can fully understand the overwhelming force of the message.

Yahweh's anger can equally be directed against the nations (Isa. 10:25; 13:3; Jer. 50:13 = LXX 27:13; Ezek. 30:15; Mic. 5:15), although never without prior warning (cf. Exod. 22:23–24; 32:10; Deut. 6:13–15). "The nations that have not obeyed [him]" (Mic. 5:15; cf. Jer.

42:18 = LXX 49:18; Lam. 3:42–43), who did not walk in accord with the divine ordinances (Ezek. 9:8–10; 22:31), are punished. God passes judgment on whole nations (including his own), sending sword, hunger, and pestilence (6:11–14), trampling under foot (Isa. 63:6; Hab. 3:12), annihilation (Deut. 29:22 = LXX 29:23), devastation (Jer. 25:37–38 = LXX 32:37–38), and burning of the land (Isa. 9:18–19; 30:27). He treads the nations in his winepress (63:1–3) and gives them the cup of his fury to drink (51:17; cf. Jer. 25:15–16).

But God's anger will not last forever. The "moment" of anger is spoken of repeatedly (cf. Ps. 30:5; Isa. 26:20; 54:7–8); behind it shines grounds for hope (cf. 2 Sam. 24:16; Isa. 40:2; 51:22; 54:8–10; Hos. 14:4), which is nourished on observation that God's saving will prevails again and again (Ps. 78:38; 103:6–13). People are able to hold to this hope if they humble themselves (cf. 2 Chr. 12:12; 32:26), turn to God in penitent prayer (Exod. 32:12, 14; 2 Sam. 12:13; Ps. 6:2; Dan. 9:15–16; Hab. 3:2), and reaffirm the covenant in obedience (Num. 25:6–11; Jos. 7:1–26; cf. Jon. 3:7–10). Then God's anger has fulfilled its task and has brought about restoration (Isa. 42:25; Jer. 4:4; 36:7 = LXX 43:7).

3. In Jud. and Qumran some passages deal with justified anger (directed against sinners). But the negative judgment on anger as a vice incompatible with wisdom is forcefully exemplified (Wis. 10:3; Sir. 27:30). The rich (28:10) and rulers (47:20–21; 2 Macc. 14:27) appear to be esp. susceptible to anger. In every case anger and rage are an abomination that the godless pursue (Sir. 27:30). But God's wrath is directed against the godless (Wis. 11:9; 19:1; Sir. 5:7; 16:6–7). This must be taken as seriously as his compassion (16:12). It is an admonition to genuine repentance (5:7).

Jud. also spoke of an ultimate day of wrath, when God will sit in judgment (cf. Ezek. 7:19; Dan. 8:19; Zeph. 2:2–3). This day is presented in strong apocalyptic colors as "a day of trouble and ruin, a day of darkness and gloom" (Zeph. 1:15), as a day of "the fierce anger of the LORD" (2:2). Then the righteous and unrighteous will be divided according to how they have walked (Ezek. 7:3). God will accept those who turn to him in penitence, but his righteous anger will destroy the others.

NT In the NT the noun *orgē* occurs 36x and relates both to human and divine anger. All the other cognate words speak only of human anger: *orgizō*, be angry (8x); *orgilos*, angry (only in Tit. 1:7); *paroxynō*, become angry (Acts 17:16; 1 Cor. 13:5); *parorgizō*, make angry (Rom. 10:19; Eph. 6:4); *parorgismos*, anger (Eph. 4:26); *paroxysmos*, strong disagreement (Acts 15:39) or ardent incitement (Heb. 10:24).

1. As a human passion, *orgē* is by and large synonymous with *thymos*. The latter tends to be preferred for depictions of sudden outbursts of anger (Lk. 4:28; Acts 19:28), whereas in *orgē* there is an occasional element of deliberate thought. Yet both words are condemned as vices, in some cases in the same breath (Eph. 4:31; Col. 3:8).

Though perhaps the anger of the king in the parable of the wedding feast (Matt. 22:7; cf. Lk. 14:21) is justified, the anger of the elder brother in the parable of the prodigal son (15:28) is certainly not. A prohibition of anger directed against a fellow human is clearly expressed in the Sermon on the Mount (Matt. 5:22).

In most of the rest of the NT, statements on human anger move within these same lines. In Eph. 6:4 fathers are enjoined not to provoke their children to anger (*parorgizō*). Jas. 1:19–20 lays down a general rule: "Everyone should be quick to listen, slow to speak and slow to become angry, for man's anger does not bring about the righteous life that God desires." When someone becomes angry (whether for good or bad reasons), that person should not let the sun set on the anger (*parorgismos*) and so give the devil a foothold in one's life (Eph. 4:26–27). Further, prayer is incompatible with anger (1 Tim. 2:8).

It is understandable, therefore, why anger is repeatedly named in NT lists of sins (Eph. 4:31; Col. 3:8; Tit. 1:7). *orgē* is among those things on account of which God's wrath "comes on those who are disobedient" (Eph. 5:6; cf. Col. 3:6). Note Eph. 4:32: "Be kind and compassionate to one another, forgiving each other, just as in Christ God forgave you." Love is the attitude and lifestyle that Christians should adopt (Col. 3:14; cf. 3:8). Being *orgilos* ("quick-tempered," Tit. 1:7) disqualifies a man from being a bishop (*episkopos*).

2. However, in a few places human anger is not evaluated negatively. Eph. 4:26, quoting Ps. 4:4, may be paraphrased: "You may be angry, only do not sin." The anger of the king with those who refused his invitation (Matt. 22:7; cf. Lk. 14:21), and even more clearly that of the king with the unforgiving servant (Matt. 18:34), may thus appear thoroughly justified. Perhaps in these cases anger is understood as human participation in God's anger. The reality of Jesus' anger (Mk. 3:5) suggest this possibility, even if the words themselves do not always occur (e.g., against Peter, Matt. 16:23; Mk. 8:33; the Pharisees, Matt. 23; or where God's honor is insulted, Matt. 21:12; Mk. 11:15–17; Lk. 19:45–46; Jn. 2:14–17).

Paul can even regard the ruler of the secular state as "God's servant, an agent of wrath to bring punishment on the wrongdoer" (Rom. 13:4). Believers must not avenge themselves, "but leave room for God's wrath, for it is written, 'It is mine to avenge; I will repay,' says the Lord" (12:19; cf. Lev. 19:18; Deut. 32:35; Heb. 10:30).

3. (a) As in the OT, the NT also uses the *orgē* word group to illustrate the character of God. The future wrathful judgment of God plays an important role in the preaching of John the Baptist (Matt. 3:7; Lk. 3:2–17) and Jesus (Lk. 21:23; cf. Matt. 22:7). Only those who repent (→ *metanoia*, 3567) will be able to escape that wrath; merely appealing to being children of Abraham does not suffice (cf. Jn. 8:31–41).

(b) The future wrath of God is unfolded on a massive scale in Rev., which speaks of the anger of the nations (11:18) and of the anger of the dragon, a power opposed to God (12:17). That wrath will finally culminate in judgment, and those who destroy the earth will be brought to destruction (11:18; cf. 6:16). The descriptions of the judgment include the pictures of the rod of iron and "the winepress of the fury of the wrath of God Almighty" (19:15; cf. 14:19), and the "cup of his wrath" (14:10), from which those who worship the beast and also Babylon must drink (16:19; cf. 17:4; 18:3).

4. While attention is thus forcibly drawn to the awful wrath of God in the future, it is viewed in Pauline theology on the horizon of an eschatology that is already being realized in the course of history from the time of Christ's coming. By nature, as children of this world, humans stand under God's wrath (Eph. 2:3; cf. Rom. 1:18–3:20). That wrath does not merely await them on the day of judgment (cf. Jn. 3:36), although Paul can also speak of it as a future event (Rom. 2:5; cf. Eph. 5:6; Col. 3:6).

God's wrath is first directed against the unrighteous, law-breakers, irreverent (→ *sebō*, 4936), and those who disdain the Creator (Rom. 1:18, 21–32). But his anger is also aroused by the attitude of the so-called pious, who through their observance of the law allow themselves to be driven into a feeling of their own self-esteem. No one can satisfy the Mosaic law; therefore, the law brings wrath (4:15). The lost situation of all humans as prisoners in sin and thus under God's anger has now been revealed by God through the sending of Jesus Christ. That is the central statement of Rom. 1:18. In him God shows the world his righteousness (*dikaiosynē*), which embraces both his wrath (*orgē*) and his grace (*charis*) and compassion (*eleos*).

On account of the two aspects of this revelation people are placed in a situation that inescapably demands a decision. On the one hand, they may persist as "objects of his wrath" (Rom. 9:22), as—to Paul's sorrow—do most of the Jews of his time (1 Thess. 2:16). On the other hand, they may turn to Jesus Christ and allow him to save them from God's wrath in the realm of his love (Rom. 5:8–9; 1 Thess. 1:10). Thus, the coming of Jesus Christ does not simply mean "cheap grace" for all. If God has destined us to be "objects of his mercy" (Rom. 9:23) "to receive salvation" (1 Thess. 5:9), the offer of salvation requires acceptance. This comes about through faith. Only those who believe in the Son need no longer fear God's judgment, for only

to them is the promise of eternal life given. In both Jn. and Paul, eternal life describes the contrast between destruction, the fruit of the divine anger, and compassion, the fruit of the divine mercy (Jn. 3:36; Rom. 2:7).

See also *thymos*, anger (2596).

3974 (*orgizō*, be or become angry, make angry), → 3973.

3975 (*orgilos,* inclined to anger), → 3973.

3977	ὀρέγω

ὀρέγω (*oregō*), strive (3977); ὄρεξις (*orexis*), desire (3979).

CL & OT *oregō* means stretch oneself, stretch out. It is used esp. with a metaphorical meaning. *orexis* denotes striving of the heart and mind, or (relatively seldom) of bodily desire. The Stoics gave it the special sense of a striving of the soul, following on a deliberate decision of the will guided by human reason.

oregō does not occur in the LXX, *orexis* only in the Apocr. It is used in a good sense in Wis. 16:2–3, where God satisfies the desire of Israel in the desert with quails. In a bad sense it is found in Sir. 18:30 and 23:6, where Ben Sira warns against perversions at banquets.

NT *oregō* occurs 3x in the NT and *orexis* once. In 1 Tim. 3:1 and Heb. 11:16 the words have a good sense. The latter speaks of the desire of faith for a better and heavenly homeland, a home with God. Such desire does not come from within a person but from response to God's promise (cf. 11:9, 13, 15). It manifests itself in reliance on the promise and the obedience of faith (11:8, 17). In 1 Tim. 3:1, *oregō* refers to the appropriate desire one may have for church office.

In a bad sense, when the goal of our striving is not salvation, we fall victim to destructive powers, such as the love of money (1 Tim. 6:10). In Rom. 1:27 *orexis* is used in Paul's attacks on perverted forms of sexual desire, such as homosexuality.

See also *epithymia*, desire, lust (2123); *hēdonē*, pleasure, (2454).

3978 (*oreinos*, hilly, mountainous), → 4001.

3979 (*orexis*, desire), → 3977.

3980 (*orthopodeō*, walk uprightly, act rightly, be straightforward), → 3981.

3981	ὀρθός

ὀρθός (*orthos*), upright, straight, right (3981); ὀρθῶς (*orthōs*), rightly, correctly (3987); διόρθωσις (*diorthōsis*), improvement, reformation, new order (1481); ἐπανόρθωσις (*epanorthōsis*), correcting, restoration, improvement (2061); ὀρθοτομέω (*orthotomeō*), cut straight, lead in a straight way, rightly handle (3982); ὀρθοποδέω (*orthopodeō*), walk uprightly, act rightly, be straightforward (3980).

CL & OT 1. In cl. Gk. *orthos* means standing upright, continuing in a straight direction; fig., right, true. It often denotes ethically correct behavior. Both in the cl. period and for the Stoics, the word refers to an objective quality or virtue. *diorthōsis* denotes straightening what has become disordered or right treatment; fig., correction of a mistake. *epanorthōsis* means restoration (e.g., of what has been destroyed); fig., improvement (e.g., of laws).

2. In the LXX *orthos* is also used in the sense of walking upright (Mic. 2:3). It has a special use in the wisdom lit., where it means right, correct, true (e.g., Prov. 8:6, 9, right words; 11:6, an upright person; 16:25, a right way). Thus *orthos* refers to the kind of right attitude, speech, and action that accords with a proper relationship to Yahweh. It does not describe a virtue so much as a relationship.

NT 1. In the NT letters none of the words occurs more than once or twice. In the Gospels only the adv. *orthōs* occurs, where it is used to confirm the correctness of a speech or answer (Lk. 10:28; 20:21). In Acts 14:10 *orthos* is found with its lit. sense, where Paul heals a lame man by calling, "Stand up [upright] on your feet." Heb. 9:10 speaks of the time of a right and better order (*diorthōsis*), which has begun with Christ's coming and is contrasted with the provisional nature of the OT covenant.

2. Other instances of this word group belong to the sphere of NT ethics and exhortation. (a) Heb. 12:13 exhorts a church that has become weary not to lose sight of the risen Lord and the goal toward which it is moving. The "level paths" (quoting Prov. 4:26) refer to the proper ethical direction set for God's people. Thus *orthos* is here used in the sense of an appropriate alignment for the Christian church.

(b) Gal. 2:14 deals with the delicate question of Peter's behavior (*ouk orthopodeō*, "not acting in line") toward the Gentile Christians of Antioch, for when people from James came from Jerusalem, Peter changed courses. By right behavior or walking uprightly, Paul means obedience to the gospel of Christ in its freedom from the law.

(c) In 2 Tim. 3:16 Paul lists the uses of Holy Scripture in ethical and didactic categories. They serve progressively to convert, to restore and improve (*epanorthōsis*), and to instruct in righteousness.

3. *orthotomeō* (cf. LXX at Prov. 3:6; 11:5 for cutting a path in a straight direction) occurs only at 2 Tim. 2:15: "Do your best to present yourself to God as one approved, a workman who does not need to be ashamed and who correctly handles [*orthotomeō*] the word of truth." Some suggest this means to guide the word of truth along a straight path, like a road that goes straight toward its goal. Others suggest it means to teach the word aright, expound it soundly, shape it rightly, and preach it fearlessly.

See also *axios*, of like value, fit, worthy, worth (*545*); *artios*, suitable, complete, capable, sound (*787*).

3982 (*orthotomeō*, cut straight, lead in a straight way, rightly handle), → *3981*.

3987 (*orthos*, rightly, correctly), → *3981*.

3988	ὁρίζω

ὁρίζω (*horizō*), determine, appoint (*3988*); ἀφορίζω (*aphorizō*), separate, set apart, appoint (*928*).

CL & OT *horizō* originally meant set bounds; hence, establish, determine. The gods establish laws or determine human fate. Later authors transfer the force of the vb. to temporal relationships. The compound *aphorizō* means separate, choose, determine.

horizō is found 21x in the LXX. It means set a boundary (Num. 34:6; Jos. 13:27; 15:12; 18:20); bind oneself by a vow (Num. 30:3–12, 9x); and separate, decide between (Prov. 18:18). *aphorizō* is found over 50x in the LXX, always with the connotation of separating, cutting off (cf. Gen. 10:5, "peoples spread out"; Lev. 13:4; Deut. 4:41).

NT 1. In the NT *horizō* (8x) means determine, establish, appoint. Jesus' messianic claim and his death on the cross were irreconcilable opposites for the Jews. Peter counters this offense by showing that Jesus was crucified by blinded Jewry as a result of God's "set" plan and purpose (Acts 2:23). Similarly in Lk. 22:22 the Son goes the way "decreed" by God for him, "but woe to that man who betrays him." This Jesus has been "appointed" by God as judge of all humanity (Acts 10:42).

In Paul's speech to the Areopagus, he observes that after God had "determined" allotted periods and boundaries for the human race so that they should seek him, he "appointed" a man to judge the world on his set day (Acts 17:26, 31). Heb. 4:7 declares that after the day of testing in the wilderness (3:8), God "set" another day, a new period of salvation beginning with Christ, that offers the opportunity to repent.

In Rom. 1:3–4 Paul may be quoting an early Christian creed when he states that the man Jesus, a descendant of David, "was declared with power" to be God's Son by the resurrection. This does not mean that Jesus was first installed Son of God after his resurrection, for Paul holds that Jesus was his Son from all eternity (cf. 8:3). *horizō* here means being determined beforehand and now publicly declaring.

In one place alone (Acts 11:29) the vb. has humans as subject: The disciples "decided" to send relief to their fellow Christians in need.

2. *aphorizō* occurs 10x, meaning separate, choose for, determine. The good are separated from the evil (Matt. 13:49; 25:32). Unbelievers exclude the believers (Lk. 6:22), and conversely the church withdraws from unbelief (Acts 19:9; 2 Cor. 6:17). In Gal. 2:12 Paul accuses Peter of separating himself from meal fellowship with Gentile Christians after Jewish Christians had come from Jerusalem to Antioch; this act made Paul angry, since Peter was recognizing the validity of Jewish dietary laws and thereby breaking apart the unity of the church.

Paul knows himself to have been "set apart" for the service of the gospel (Rom. 1:1; Gal. 1:15). He did not appoint himself as an apostle, but God did (Acts 13:2).

See also *kathistēmi*, bring, appoint (*2770*); *paristēmi*, place, put at the disposal of (*4225*); *procheirizō*, determine, appoint (*4741*); *tassō*, arrange, appoint (*5435*); *tithēmi*, put, place, set, appoint (*5502*); *prothesmia*, appointed date (*4607*); *cheirotoneō*, appoint (*5936*); *lanchanō*, obtain as by lot (*3275*).

3991 (*horkizō*, adjure, implore), → *3923*.

3992 (*horkos*, oath), → *3923*.

3993 (*horkōmosia*, asserting on oath, taking an oath), → *3923*.

4001	ὄρος

ὄρος (*oros*), mountain, mountain chain or region (*4001*); ὀρεινός (*oreinos*), hilly, mountainous (*3978*).

CL & OT 1. The Mesopotamians were conscious of the height and power of mountains, and the Gks. viewed Mount Olympus as the supreme home of the gods. In the Ras Shamra texts, Zaphon, a hill north of Ras Shamra, is the abode of Baal.

2. In the LXX *oros* generally translates *har*. Mountains and ravines could be an obstacle to communication (2 Ki. 19:23; Isa. 37:24). Growth of grass on them for pasture is a sign of God's love (Ps. 147:8). Most of the hills in Palestine do not rise above 3,000 ft. and so could be used for beacons. The beacon as a signal of invasion is used in an oracle of judgment (Isa. 13:2; cf. 30:17). The view Moses had from the top of Pisgah was a revelation of all that God would give Israel (Deut. 34:1–4), though Moses was not allowed to set foot in the promised land. Prophecy and parable were delivered from mountains (Jdg. 9:7), and people were addressed from them (2 Chr. 13:4; cf. 2 Sam. 2:25–26). Mountains could be places of refuge (Jdg. 6:2; Ps. 11:1).

3. Mountains are frequently associated with Yahweh's presence. Isaac was to be offered on a mountain (Gen. 22:2). During the battle with the Amalekites Moses prayed on top of a hill (Exod. 17:9–10). Elijah went to the top of Mount Carmel to pray (1 Ki. 18:42), and later received a theophany on Mount Horeb (19:8–18). Blessings and curses were invoked from Mount Ebal and Mount Gerizim (Deut. 11:29; 27:12–13). The ark was set on a hill in the promised land (1 Sam. 7:1; 2 Sam. 6:3), and sacrifices were offered on high places (1 Sam. 9:12–14, 25; 1 Ki. 3:4). David captured the elevated Jebusite fortress at Jerusalem (2 Sam. 5:6–10), which subsequently became the site of the temple erected by Solomon.

4. Esp. in Ps. and the prophetic writings mountains demonstrate Yahweh's power. He made them and was before them, and he has power to destroy them even though they are rooted in the earth (Job 28:9; Ps. 65:6; 83:14; 90:2; 95:4; Hab. 3:6).

5. Mountains also figure in eschatological expectation. They will drip with wine as a symbol of plenty (Joel 3:18; Amos 9:13). The leveling of hills and valleys is a symbol of God's overruling in return from exile (Isa. 40:4; 45:2). The Mount of Olives, overlooking the temple, will be split (Zech. 14:4). Mount Zion (→ *Ierousalēm*, Jerusalem, *2647*) will be higher than other hills, and the Gentile nations will stream to it (Isa. 2:2–4; Mic. 4:1–3). Zion is here the focal point

of meeting with Yahweh. The Gentiles will be included with Israel, and the earth will enjoy universal peace.

NT 1. *oros* ranges from a simple geographical location, including several references to the Mount of Olives, to passages of great theological significance. Jesus apparently often sought the isolation of rugged elevated locations in order to pray or to be alone with his disciples (Matt. 14:23; Mk. 3:13; 6:46; Lk. 6:12). The identification of the mount of transfiguration is unknown. Mount Tabor was occupied by a fortress in Jesus' day, and Mount Hermon seems too far away both for the great crowd at its base, which included some teachers of the law (Mk. 9:14), and for the reference to the return trip being "through Galilee" (9:30). The highest mountain in Galilee was Mount Meron (3,926 feet), which fits the description of Matt. 17:1; Mk. 9:2.

2. The adjective "high" (*hypsēlos*; → *hypsos*, high, *5737*) modifies *oros* 4x in the NT: once to describe the mount of temptation (Matt. 4:8; cf. Lk. 4:5), 2x in reference to the mount of transfiguration (Matt. 17:1; Mk. 9:2), and once to describe a vantage point to which the seer John was taken (Rev. 21:10).

3. Most important is the theological symbolism of mountains. Certainly the associations with Mount Sinai are strong in the transfiguration narrative: e.g., the appearance of Moses, the cloud, reference to tabernacles, and mention of Jesus' approaching "departure" (Lk. 9:31, Gk. *exodos*, lit., exodus). Likewise, the mountain on which Jesus gave his sermon with its authoritative comments on the law (Matt. 5–7) may represent a new Sinai (→ *Sina*, *4982*), though this association rests on assumptions regarding Matt.'s intention to establish an exodus motif in his narrative (a matter of debate).

4. Lk.'s references to the leveling of mountains and hills at the coming of the Lord (Lk. 3:4–6) and his omission of the Mount of Olives in 21:5–7 (cf. Matt. 24:1–3) have raised the question whether he envisions an eschatological landscape without mountains. It seems more reasonable to assume that he shares the biblical view of God's sovereignty over even the majestic mountains. As the Lord brings "salvation" (3:6), everything must make way for his coming. Flight to the mountains in time of eschatological distress (Matt. 24:16; Mk. 13:14; Lk. 21:21) is a normal reference to hills and their caves as places of refuge.

5. The saying about the power of faith to remove a mountain (Matt. 17:20; Mk. 11:23) may well have as its background a proverbial expression for overcoming difficulties (cf. Isa. 40:4; 49:11; 54:10), but in context "this mountain" may signify the mount of the transfiguration (Matt. 17:1, 9). In view of this association, the power ascribed to faith to remove "this mountain" is all the more striking. Through that power, Jesus' followers will have the ability to do incredible works for the kingdom of God (cf. Phil. 4:13).

6. The Sermon on the Mount contains the statement: "A city on a hill cannot be hidden" (Matt. 5:14b). It is preceded by, "You are the light of the world" (5:14a), and followed by the saying about putting a lamp on a lampstand and the exhortation to let one's light shine before others (5:16). This saying focuses on the raison d'être of the disciples. Because of their calling, they cannot remain obscure; the character of their lives should be such that others will have cause to glorify God through their witness (cf. Isa. 2:2, 5). Perhaps too we must see here the fulfillment of the promise that in Abraham and his seed all the nations of the earth will be blessed (Gen. 12:3; 18:18; 22:18; 26:4; 28:14; cf. Acts 3:25; Gal. 3:8). As the light is manifested in the community of disciples as the people of God, so the nations will come to them as the new Jerusalem to receive blessing and glorify God.

7. Rev. 8:8 perhaps alludes to the eruption of Vesuvius in A.D. 79, seen as a fulfillment of Jer. 51:25. Rev. 17:9 takes up into the symbolism of world powers the seven hills on which Rome was founded, while 6:14 and 16:20 go beyond the OT expectation of the leveling of the mountains; they will disappear, heralding a new heaven and earth (cf. 20:11; 21:1).

See also *erēmos*, abandoned, solitary, desolate, deserted (*2245*); *Sina*, Sinai (*4892*).

| 4003 ὀρφανός | ὀρφανός (*orphanos*), orphan (*4003*). |

CL & OT 1. In cl. Gk. *orphanos* as an adj. means without parents, or more generally, bereaved; as a noun, orphan. Careful provision was made in ancient Greece for orphan children. A guardian, usually a near relative, was appointed, who was responsible for the orphan's maintenance and education. Any assets the children inherited were protected until they came of age. Orphans were exempted from the regular taxes. *orphanos* was also used fig. of disciples left without a master.

2. In the LXX an *orphanos* is someone who has lost a father, regardless of whether a child's mother has died (cf. Job 24:9). Without the father, "the father's house," the primary unit of family life, ceases to exist and the remaining members of the household become vulnerable to abuse. This is why orphans and widows are often grouped together (e.g., Deut. 10:18; Ps. 146:9). Because the orphans are so helpless—they are "wandering beggars" (109:10)—there can be nothing more wicked than to exploit them (Deut. 27:19; Job 6:27; 22:9; 24:3, 9; Ps. 10:18 = LXX 9:39; Jer. 5:28; Ezek. 22:7).

Thus, the OT law code demanded that the rights of orphans be upheld and their needs met. Orphans were to have a share in the special tithe (Deut. 14:28–29; 26:12–15) and were to be included in the annual feasts (16:11, 14). The sheaves, olives, and grapes that remain after the harvest were to be left for "the alien, the fatherless [*orphanos*] and the widow" (24:19, 21). The repentance and moral renewal called for by the prophets must include care for orphans (Isa. 1:17; Jer. 7:6; 22:3; Zech. 7:10).

Behind this insistence on provision for orphans lies the conviction that it is ultimately Yahweh himself who "defends the cause of the fatherless" (Deut. 10:18; cf. Exod. 22:22–24; Ps. 146:9; Prov. 23:10–11; Hos. 14:3 = LXX 14:4). He is "a father to the fatherless" (Ps. 68:5; cf. 10:14 = LXX 9:35).

Concern for orphans is also apparent at Qumran (CD 6:16–17; 14:14). One of the nonbiblical psalms of that community gives praise to the Lord, who has not "forsaken the orphan" (1QH 13:20). Philo uses the image of the orphan as a collective symbol of the people of God. Rab. Jud. continued to safeguard the rights of orphans, to legislate for their welfare, and to regard their care as meritorious. Until an orphan boy or girl marries, he or she is to be maintained from charity funds. Deserving of special praise and reward is the one who cares for an orphan in his or her home.

NT 1. *orphanos* occurs 2x in the NT. In Jas. 1:27, James enjoins practical concern for those least able to help themselves: "orphans and widows." He follows the OT in mentioning the two groups together, more fundamentally in insisting that claims to be religious are futile unless the one who makes them exercises justice and compassion.

2. In Jn. 14:18, Jesus says, "I will not leave you as orphans." Here *orphanos* is used in a fig. sense, recalling the use of the term in cl. Gk. to describe the feelings of disciples bereft of their teacher. But the image draws its force from the OT estimate of the family as primarily "the father's house," a household living a single corporate life whose center and source is the father. With the father's death the house is no more, and thus the desolation of the orphan is the loss of all by which he lives. The relationship of Jesus to his disciples is presented here as that of a father to his children (cf. 13:3). His death will make them "orphans."

But they will not be left in this pitiable situation. He will come to them. The time for this return is most likely the resurrection (rather than at the coming of the Spirit or at the Parousia), for orphans, unless intervention is swift, have little hope of survival. Easter will end the disciples' bereavement and their fear of being left as orphans.

4008 ὅσιος

ὅσιος (*hosios*), holy, devout, pious (*4008*); ὁσιότης (*hosiotēs*), holiness, devoutness, piety (*4009*); ἀνόσιος (*anosios*), unholy (*495*).

CL & OT 1. In cl. Gk. the earliest form of word from this group is *hosiē*, which stood for what was in accordance with divine direction and providence. *hosios* could mean the obligations laid on a person in ritual and ceremonies, e.g., burial rites. It then came to have the general sense of sanctioned or allowed by divine or natural law, but did not denote something inherently sacred. Used of people, *hosios* means pious, religious; of actions, pure, clean.

2. *hosios* by and large translates Heb. *ḥāsîd*, which denotes the one who readily accepts the obligations that arise from the people's relationship to God, the loyal, the pious one. This Heb. word occurs most frequently in the pl. and means the congregation gathered for worship (e.g., Ps. 50:5; 85:8) and serving God (79:2). The Gentile nations are not *ḥāsîd*, and within the people of God the *ḥᵃsîdîm* are contrasted with those declared guilty (Ps. 15). Even in the context of strict observance of the law, *ḥāsîd* can have the sense of trusting (e.g., 32:6; cf. 52:9–10). The Hasidim as the name of a particular group within Jud. does not occur until the time of the Maccabees (1 Macc. 2:42; 7:13; 2 Macc. 14:6). This group seems to have strictly observed the Torah. The absence of the word in the Qumran documents is, however, striking.

3. God is several times described as *hosios* in the LXX (see Deut. 32:4; Ps. 145:13, 17). He supports the fallen, satisfies the hungry, and is near to those who pray. God takes *hosiotēs* as an invincible shield (Wis. 5:19; cf. Rev. 15:4). *ta hosia* (Deut. 29:19) are the kindnesses that one expects from God, and in Isa. 55:3 the successes that David could expect from God.

NT 1. In the NT *hosios* is a rare word (8x, of which 5 are in quotations); *hosiotēs* and *anosios* both occur 2x. The most important OT use (*hosioi*, the congregation) does not appear. Rather, the members of the Christian community are called "the chosen" (*eklektoi*; → *eklegomai*, *1721*) and saints (*hagioi*, → *41*). In Lk. 1:75, *hosiotēs* is used of Jewish piety, and in 1 Tim. 1:9 the negative *anosios* refers to the law laid down for the unholy (cf. 2 Tim. 3:2). Eph. 4:24 mentions *hosiotēs* as one of the qualities of the new person in Christ.

2. God is twice called *hosios* in quotations. The hymn of Rev. 15:3–4 goes back to Ps. 145:17 and its context. Rev. 16:5 recalls Deut. 32:4: God is equally *dikaios* (just) and *hosios* (holy) in judgment when he condemns evildoers.

3. The use of *hosios* in Heb. 7:26 is unique. It is used absolutely in the way in which elsewhere it can be used only of God. As high priest, Christ is completely *hosios*, completely sinless and utterly pure, so that his offering is sufficient, once for all. Acts 2:27 and 13:35 (quoting Ps. 16:10) refer to God's promise not to let his Holy One (*hosios*) see destruction—a promise not fulfilled in David but only in Christ. By virtue of the resurrection Jesus is the true Holy One, even though he was condemned by the religious authorities as a religious criminal.

See also *hagios*, holy, sacred (*41*); *hieros*, holy (*2641*).

4009 (*hosiotēs*, holiness, devoutness, piety), → *4008*.

4011 ὀσμή

ὀσμή (*osmē*), smell, scent (*4011*); εὐωδία (*euōdia*), fragrance, aroma (*2380*).

CL & OT 1. In cl. Gk. *osmē* means smell, scent. Antiquity conceived of smell in strongly material terms, so that the trunk of a tree was said to receive new life and vitality from the scent of water (cf. Job 14:9). Smell contained a life-giving force. This materialistic idea of smell as something charged with energy also appears in the sphere of religion. In the revelation of deity the smell proceeding from it is important as the bearer of divine life.

2. Some passages of the OT refer to the power of physical smell: The bridegroom in the Song of Songs sings of the ravishing fragrance of his beloved (e.g., Song 4:10); the smell of fresh hide indicates to Isaac the presence of his firstborn son, a strong, virile hunter (Gen. 27:27). In a fig. sense the power of Moab is compared with that of mature wine and its "aroma" (Jer. 48:11 = LXX 31:11). Wisdom is said to diffuse fragrance (Sir. 24:15), while 39:14 calls the praise of God by his people a sweet smell. But the materialistic background is still present here, in that the fragrance diffused by wisdom and godliness contains a life-giving power.

In the OT religious sphere, offerings are made to the Lord for a "pleasing aroma" (Gen. 8:21; Lev. 2:12; cf. 1:9; 13, 17; Num. 28:1–2). But note Lev. 26:31 and Amos 5:21, which show that God is not dependent on offerings or their smell.

NT 1. *osmē* is found only 6x in the NT, two of which are in the combination *osmē euōdias* (Eph. 5:2; Phil. 4:18; lit., "scent of an aroma"; NIV "fragrant offering"). Elsewhere *euōdia* occurs only in 2 Cor. 2:15, between two verses each containing *osmē*.

2. In the story of the anointing at Bethany (Jn. 12:3), the house is said to have been filled with the fragrance of the ointment. In addition to the lit. sense, there is doubtless symbolism here: As the fragrance of the ointment filled the house, so the fragrance of the gospel will fill the whole earth. In Eph. 5:2 *osmē euōdias* describes Christ's death as a sacrifice that is "a fragrant offering . . . to God." The fig. usage is esp. apparent in Phil. 4:18, where Paul calls the financial aid sent to him by the Philippians "a fragrant offering." The idea here is not simply that of a sacrifice in the strict sense of the word; rather, the Philippians' gift is a symbol of every gift we bring to God.

3. The idea of *osmē* as a life-giving or death-giving force is prominent in 2 Cor. 2:14–16. The fragrance of the knowledge of God is being diffused by the work of the apostle; indeed, Paul himself is the bearer of the fragrance of Christ. This fragrance has a twofold effect: To those who obey the gospel it brings divine life, while to those who refuse the message it brings eternal death. That is, the gospel divides humans, calling for individual decision and emphasizing the divine power inherent in the gospel.

Moreover, the apostle stresses here that in all his weakness, suffering, and lack of acclaim and in his message of the cross, he is like the stench of death to those who only see defeat and a morbid message. But in reality, his sacrificial service for the gospel of Christ's sacrifice is sweet, recalling the sweet savor of the OT sacrifices (cf. Gen. 8:21; Exod. 29:18; Lev. 1:9; Num. 15:3; Ezek. 6:13; Dan. 4:34). The apostles, in other words, are the smoke that arises out of the sacrifice of Christ to God, diffusing as it spreads out the knowledge of God communicated in the cross.

4017 ὀστράκινος

ὀστράκινος (*ostrakinos*), made of earth or clay, earthenware (*4017*).

CL & OT 1. In cl. Gk. *ostrakeus* meant a potter. In the cl. and Hel. periods, the sing. noun *ostrakon* denotes either a clay vessel or a fragment of such a vessel, a potsherd. From the practice at Athens and elsewhere of using potsherds for voting on the banishment of a citizen, the vb. *ostrakizō* was coined to speak of the ostracizing of someone. The adj. *ostrakinos* was used in Hel. Christian writings to describe as useless and lifeless the terracotta images of pagan idols.

2. (a) In the LXX the adj. *ostrakinos* simply identifies the material from which a vessel was made as clay (Lev. 6:28; 11:33; 14:5, 50; Num. 5:17; Jer. 32:14 = LXX 39:14). Pleasant speech concealing an evil heart is compared to a clay jar covered by silver glaze (Prov. 26:23, *ostrakon*). The humiliated sons of Zion, who were "once worth their weight in gold," are considered of no more value by their captors than common earthenware (Lam. 4:2). In Dan. 2:33, 34, 41–42 *ostrakinos* describes the great image Nebuchadnezzar saw in a dream, whose feet were partly of iron and partly of clay.

The related meaning, potsherd, also occurs in the LXX. Judgment is pronounced on Israel's unbelief in terms of the ruthless smashing of a potter's vessel into small fragments (Isa. 30:14). The familiar sight of shards of pottery bleached by the scorching sun provided an image for the parched sufferer who complains that his strength is dried up "like a potsherd" (Ps. 22:15, *ostrakon*). Both nuances of the word are evident in the instruction given to Jer. to purchase an earthenware flask from the potter but to smash it before the elders to represent what will happen to Jerusalem for her sins (19:1, 11). In Sir. 22:7, futility is pictured as gluing together a smashed pot (*ostrakon*).

NT 1. *ostrakinos* occurs 2x in the NT. In 2 Cor. 4:6 Paul describes the gospel as "the light of the knowledge of the glory of God in the face of Christ," but in 4:7 he maintains that this treasure has been committed to jars "of clay," a metaphor that compares the apostle and his colleagues to common clay pots. The striking contrast between the splendor of the treasure and the ordinary nature of the vessel in which it is stored directs attention away from preachers to the glory of their message. It was not unusual in the ancient world to conceal valuable treasures in clay urns. Paul's detractors had described his bodily appearance as weak and had dismissed his words as inconsequential (10:1, 10; 11:6). His self-description as *ostrakinos* attests that human weakness presents no barrier to the accomplishment of the divine intention when it is undergirded by God's power.

2. Paul also uses *ostrakinos* when he urges Timothy to separate himself from false teachers such as Philetus and Hymenaeus, who have subverted the faith of some at Ephesus (2 Tim. 2:14–19, 22–26). But why are there disloyal persons in the congregation? Paul responds by comparing the church to a large house in which it is normal to find vessels of differing material serving differing functions (2:20). As the presence of wood and clay (*ostrakinos*) vessels devoted to disreputable use occasions no surprise, so base leadership in the church can be anticipated. But whether a vessel is made of gold, silver, or clay, it may be clean in order to be ready for honorable service. By separating himself from false teachers and cleansing himself from their disreputable actions, Timothy will be prepared for any task to which God calls him.

See also *keramion*, an earthenware vessel, jar (*3040*); *pēlos*, clay, mud, mire (*4384*); *phyrama*, a mixture, a lump (*5878*).

4026 οὐαί

οὐαί (*ouai*), woe, alas (*4026*).

CL & OT *ouai* is an onomatopoeic exclamation of pain or anger, infrequently used in cl. Gk. It occurs 69x in the LXX, usually representing the Heb. *hôy*. *ouai* can express grief (Prov. 23:29), despair (1 Sam. 4:8), lamentation (1 Ki. 13:30), dissatisfaction (Isa. 1:4), pain (Jer. 10:19), and fear in the face of a threat (Ezek. 16:23). The Heb. *hôy* is also used simply to attract attention (Isa. 55:1, untranslated in the LXX).

NT In the NT *ouai* expresses primarily condemnation, though in some cases the idea of sympathetic sorrow is also apparent.

1. (a) In Matt. 11:21; Lk. 10:13 Jesus cries condemnatory woes on Korazin and Bethsaida (later Capernaum, the base of Jesus' ministry, cf. 4:13; 11:23–24) for their utter lack of response to his message and miracles. Jesus compares these cities' lack of response with the reaction that Tyre and Sidon would have had (repentance) if these notoriously wicked cities (Isa. 23) had been given similar opportunities to witness God's mighty signs. Matt. 18:7 ("Woe to the world!") offers a warning for those who cause esp. the weak and unsuspecting to sin. Such sin is culpable.

(b) The seven woes Jesus pronounces on the teachers of the law and Pharisees in Matt. 23:13–29 are denunciatory. These leaders' casuistry makes it virtually impossible for people to devote themselves to the fidelity that leads to the kingdom of heaven. Sympathetic sorrow is present here as well, as is clear from Jesus' closing lament over Jerusalem (23:37–39).

The first woe (Matt. 23:13) is directed against the lawyers, who block the way to the kingdom of heaven by their misinterpretation of

Scripture. The second (23:15) condemns the lengths to which these men go to secure converts from among Gentiles, but only to their own sectarian brand of Pharisaism. The third woe (23:16–22) exposes the casuistry that subverts morality: even after an oath people need not tell the truth if the oath was not made in a particular way. The fourth woe (23:23–24) refers to Pharisaic scrupulousness in the application of the law of tithing (Lev. 27:30–33; Deut. 14:22–29). The fifth woe (23:25–26) condemns the punctilious observance of ritual purifications in the kitchen to the neglect of plain moral obligations. In the sixth (23:27–28), whitened tombs appear clean and attractive on the outside, but their interiors are full of foulness; such were the Pharisees. Finally, the seventh woe (23:29–33) condemns the Pharisees' hypocrisy in building fine tombs to honor prophets murdered by their ancestors, while plotting to do away with Jesus, the living prophet in their midst.

(c) Jesus utters four woes in Luke 6:24–26, both to warn those who do not follow him and to express his sadness at what he knows is their inevitable end. Such people may be rich in worldly terms, but in what really matters, things of the Spirit, they are empty.

(d) Jesus' woe on the fate of Judas (Matt. 26:24; Mk. 14:21; Lk. 22:22) combines divine wrath and intense sorrow, for Judas is putting himself outside God's mercy.

(e) In Jude 11 the writer utters a prophetic woe on heretical teachers, whom he describes in terms of the sins and fates of Cain, Balaam, and Korah, the classic examples of what happens to those who are jealous, greedy, and proud. In NT times Cain was not only a murderer, but also as a personification of selfishness, self-sufficiency, and power over the lives of others for evil. Balaam reflects the unprincipled character known in Hel. Jud. as the prototype of mercenaries who shrink from nothing for financial gain. Korah is someone who took others with him in his blasphemous insubordination (Num. 16).

2. In Matt. 24:19 (Mk. 13:17; Lk. 21:23) *ouai* expresses primarily pity and compassion for those who on account of family responsibilities will be hindered in their escape from the doomed city of Jerusalem.

3. In 1 Cor. 9:16 Paul offers a special use of *ouai*. In this context he stresses his personal decision not to accept support from the Corinthian church while ministering there. But in one respect he has no liberty: Preach he must. The compulsion he feels to proclaim the gospel of Christ is both an inward divine constraint and an outward burden pressing on him (cf. Isa. 8:11; Jer. 20:9). *ouai* for him if he does not do so. The meaning is not that God will punish him, but that for Paul to be unfaithful to the trust given to him would be the greatest misery imaginable.

4. Rev. includes *ouai* 14x. In 8:13 the threefold warning of *ouai* from an eagle corresponds to three trumpet blasts about to be sounded in succession by three angels who announce drastic judgments to fall on an unbelieving world (9:12; 11:14). In 12:12, after the devil is expelled by Michael and his angels, the inhabitants of heaven rejoice, but a loud *ouai* warns that heaven's deliverance means a redoubling of the devil's wrath against the earth. In 18:10, 16, 19 *ouai* is a cry of self-pity by national leaders (18:9), traders (18:11), and merchant sailors (18:17; cf. Ezek. 27:29–36) on the spectacular collapse of the mighty commercial but self-seeking and sinful city of Babylon; they know that their source and means of financial profit have been swept away.

4039 (*ouranios*, heavenly), → *4041*.

4040 (*ouranothen*, from heaven), → *4041*.

4041 οὐρανός

οὐρανός (*ouranos*), heaven (*4041*); οὐράνιος (*ouranios*), heavenly (*4039*); ἐπουράνιος (*epouranios*), heavenly (*2230*); οὐρανόθεν (*ouranothen*), from heaven (*4040*).

CL *ouranos* embraces everything and is thus divine. In Gk. mythology Uranos derived from the earth, Ge, which he impregnated in a holy marriage. He was castrated and deposed as a god by Kronos, the son of Uranos and Ge. In Homer, heaven rests on pillars that Atlas carries. In it dwell the gods, esp. Zeus.

As the ancient mythological concepts dissolved, *ouranos* became simply the firmament, and *ouranios* (what is in heaven, heavenly) was applied to phenomena appearing in this firmament. In Plato heaven was equated with the all, the cosmos. The starry heavens, the dwelling place of the gods, became the starting point for the investigation of existence and absolute knowledge. Hence Plato used *ouranios* to denote what really is and what is truly coming to be. The Stoics understood heaven as the outermost layer of the ether and then also as the directing world principle. The expression "earth and heaven" denoted the whole world.

OT 1. *OT concepts of heaven.* (a) The OT concepts of heaven contain certain echoes of ancient cosmology. The underworld, the earth, and heaven together form a cosmic building. Several OT references suggest the picture of the earth as a flat disc, surrounded by the ocean, above which heaven or the firmament forms a vault like an upturned bowl; above this is the heavenly ocean (Gen. 1:8; Ps. 148:4–6). According to the ancient cosmology, there are many other heavenly spheres beyond the firmament, which is visible from the earth. Such concepts are echoed in the expression "the highest heavens" (Deut. 10:14; 1 Ki. 8:27; Ps. 148:4).

The OT uses poetic imagery that reflects the language of the ancient myths to describe heaven. Heaven has windows (Gen. 7:11; 2 Ki. 7:2), through which waters restrained by the firmament can pour. Above the firmament are the storehouses of snow, hail (Job 38:22), wind (37:9; Ps. 135:7; Jer. 49:36), and waters (Job 38:37; Ps. 33:7), which return to heaven after it has rained (Job 36:27; Isa. 55:10). Heaven rests on pillars (Job 26:11) or on foundations (2 Sam. 22:8). It is like a pitched tent (Ps. 104:2; Isa. 40:22; 44:24). It is an unrolled scroll and can be torn (64:1). Together with the earth and the water under it, the heavens make up the universe (cf. Exod. 20:4; Ps. 115:15–16 = LXX 115:23–24). It is compared to a house in which the heavens are like a loft (104:3; Amos 9:6).

(b) In the sense of horizontal expanse it is possible to speak of the four ends of heaven (Jer. 49:36 = LXX 25:15; Dan. 7:2; Zech. 6:5). Humans cannot ascend to heaven (Deut. 30:12; Prov. 30:4 = LXX 24:27), and to attempt to do so is folly (cf. the Tower of Babel story, Gen. 11:4–9).

(c) Heaven is the embodiment of permanence (Deut. 11:21; Ps. 89:29), though prophetic preaching also refers to catastrophic judgment on the heavens (Isa. 13:13; 34:4; 50:3; 51:6; Jer. 4:23–26). Isa. speaks of the creation of a new heaven (65:17; 66:22).

(d) The "heavenly array" or "heavenly host" means the stars (Deut. 4:19; cf. Gen. 2:1) or supernatural beings (1 Ki. 22:19; Job 1:6–2:2). The latter is under a commander (cf. Jos. 5:14) and has fiery horses (2 Ki. 2:11; cf. 6:17). In the OT, however, heaven is never accorded a ruling function. Even the stars in the firmament are mere lights to divide up the calendar (Gen. 1:14), not gods. The ancient worldview has, in this respect, been demythologized. Astrological ideas that elsewhere in the ANE were richly developed appear only on the periphery (Deut. 18:9–13; Isa. 47:13; Jer. 10:2). But under foreign influence "the starry hosts" became an object of worship, a practice against which the prophets protested (e.g., 2 Ki. 17:16; 21:3).

(e) The OT reflects a correspondence between the heavenly and the earthly, esp. in the things that have a sacral value. Thus, the tabernacle was built following a heavenly model (Exod. 25:9, 40). Ezek. speaks of a scroll that preexisted in heaven (2:9–3:2). The eschatological order of salvation is prefigured and has happened in heaven, so that it precedes the earthly event (Zech. 2–3).

2. *Yahweh and heaven.* (a) More important for faith than these cosmological concepts is the statement that Yahweh created the heavens and the earth, i.e., the whole universe (Gen. 1:1; cf. Ps. 33:6; Isa. 42:5). Like the whole creation, the firmament and the heavens praise Yahweh (Ps. 19:1). The heavenly beings praise Yahweh because of his acts, for everything that happens on earth reveals his glory (29:9).

(b) The main concern of the OT writers was not with where Yahweh lives but on his dealings with Israel and the nations. Thus Yahweh can dwell either on Mount Sinai (e.g., Deut. 33:2; Jdg. 5:4–5) or on Mount Zion (Isa. 8:18; Amos 1:2). In 1 Ki. 8:12–13 Yahweh is said to dwell in the darkness of the Most Holy Place, i.e., in the temple. By contrast, several verses later (8:27) Solomon says that "even the highest heaven" cannot contain him. Neither the visible nor the invisible world can enclose Yahweh, for both were created by him.

(c) Numerous passages describe Yahweh as the God or king of heaven (Ezr. 5:11–12; 6:9–10; 7:12, 21, 23; Dan. 2:28, 37, 44; cf. Gen. 11:5; 24:3; Ps. 29:10). He rides on the clouds (Deut. 33:26; Ps. 68:4; Isa. 19:1) and has built his palace on the heavenly ocean (Ps. 104:3). Yahweh is enthroned in heaven, surrounded by heavenly beings and taking counsel with them (1 Ki. 22:19–22; Job 1:6–12; Ps. 82:1; Isa. 6:3–8; Dan. 7:9–10). The gods of the Canaanites become Yahweh's servants, and he is the only God in heaven and on earth (Deut. 4:39; 10:14).

(d) According to the theology of Deut., Yahweh lives in heaven and speaks from there (4:36; 26:15). Only his "Name" dwells on earth (12:5, 11, 21). The eternal word of God has its place in heaven (Ps. 89:2; 119:89). The godly, praying in their need, complain that Yahweh is hidden (Lam. 3:1–9) and ask him to rend the heavens and come down (Isa. 64:1 = LXX 63:19). In prayer, suppliants raise their hands to heaven (Exod. 9:29, 33).

(e) It is possible for Yahweh to take chosen people to himself in heaven (2 Ki. 2:11; cf. Gen. 5:24; Ps. 73:24). This is a particular favor and honor, for on the OT view heaven is not otherwise the place where the dead or souls go.

3. *The LXX and Judaism.* (a) With few exceptions, *ouranos* in the LXX (667x) always translates *šāmayim*. It is in the pl. 51x (partly because the Heb. word is a pl. form, i.e., dual). In later writings the frequency of the pl. increases, indicating that the ancient oriental conception of several heavens began to have an effect (Tob. 8:5; Wis. 9:10; 2 Macc. 15:23; 3 Macc. 2:2).

In Jud. the tendency to avoid the use of God's name became increasingly stronger (cf. Exod. 20:7). In its place substitutes were used, among them "heaven" (1 Macc. 3:18–19; 4:10–11; 12:15). *ouranios* only occurs 9x in the LXX—for the God of Israel (1 Esd. 6:15), his power (Dan. 4:23, Theod.), the angels as a heavenly army (4 Macc. 4:11; cf. Lk. 2:13), and the children of God (2 Macc. 7:34). *epouranios* only occurs 7x in the LXX.

(b) Contact with the intellectual climate of the ANE resulted in a variety of cosmological speculations in pseudepigraphic and rab. writings. In them apocalyptists and rabbis undertake journeys to heaven and give revelations about things on the other side, but no generally binding doctrines about these things were ever arrived at. Some apocalyptic writings know of only one heaven (*1 Enoch, 4 Esd., 2 Bar.*). Others speak of three (*T. Levi* 2–3) or five heavens (*3 Bar.*); *2 Enoch, T. Ab.,* and rab. tradition speak of seven heavens. A further result of Eastern influence is the doctrine that everything corresponds to an archetype and pattern in heaven and that all earthly events are prefigured in heaven (→ *anō, 539*).

(c) In certain writings Paradise is located in heaven, either in the 3d (*2 Enoch* 8:1–8; *Assum. Mos.* 37), or esp. in rab. tradition in the 7th. Even hell (→ *geenna, 1147*) can be located in heaven. After death the righteous go to heavenly dwelling places. Satan can also be found in heaven. In connection with OT traditions he is viewed as the accuser of humans before God (cf. Job 1–2) as well as an evil power opposed to God. Jewish traditions about heavenly treasure-houses are important. In them are kept the good works of people and the fate of earthly beings. Also recorded are the rewards and punishments that await the last judgment.

(d) Philo combined Gk. and OT ideas. The *ouranos noētos*, the immaterial heaven of conceptual thinking present only in idea, must be distinguished from the *ouranos aisthētos*, the tangible heaven, which must not be deified. Heaven actualizes the unity of the cosmos. Philo spoke of the heavenly person as *ouranios*, a copy of God. Insofar as every person is a part of him, every person is also an inhabitant of heaven.

NT In the NT *ouranos* occurs 273x, most frequently in Matt. (82x), esp. in the phrase "the kingdom of heaven." Apart from Matt., it occurs mostly in the sing. *ouranios* occurs 9x, of which 7 are in Matt. in the phrase "your/my heavenly Father" (5:48; 6:14, 26, 32; 15:13; 18:35; 23:9). *epouranios* is found 19x in the NT, clearly preferred over *ouranios*. Occasionally *ouranos* means "sky" (Lk. 4:25; Rev. 11:6), but usually it has more theological nuances.

1. *General statements.* (a) Rev. makes the most statements about heavenly beings and objects, though the interest is not cosmological but theological and soteriological. There is no attempt, as in certain rab. writings, to give definitive instruction about the geography of heaven. It is striking that there is no mention of several heavens in Rev. but only of one. One NT passage speaks of three heavens (2 Cor. 12:2–4), but we are not given any more precise information. As in the OT, the expression "heaven and earth" means the universe (e.g., Matt. 5:18, 34–35; 11:25). Occasionally a reference to the sea is added, giving rise to a tripartite formula (Acts 4:24; 14:15; Rev. 14:7).

Since, according to this world picture, heaven is "above" (→ *anō, 539*), people raise their hands or their eyes toward it (Mk. 6:41; 7:34; Lk. 18:13; Jn. 17:1; Acts 1:11; 7:55; Rev. 10:5). The air can also be called heaven (Matt. 6:26; 8:20; 16:2; Mk. 4:32; Lk. 8:5; Acts 10:12; 11:6; → *aēr, 113*). In heaven, i.e., the firmament, are set the stars, which in eschatological discourse about the Parousia fall to the earth (Mk. 13:25; Lk. 21:26; Rev. 6:13; 8:10; 9:1; 12:4). Portents are seen in heaven (12:1, 3; 15:1).

(b) There are angels in heaven, who serve as God's messengers and servants (Matt. 18:10; Mk. 12:25; 13:32; Eph. 3:15; Rev. 12:7; 19:1, 14). They come from and return to heaven (Matt. 28:2; Lk. 2:15; 22:43). They appear in the visions of John (Rev. 10:1; 18:1). Satan is thrown out of heaven as the consequence of Christ's saving work so that he may no longer accuse Jesus' disciples (Lk. 10:18; Jn. 12:31; Rev. 12:12). At this, heaven and the martyrs in heaven rejoice (5:13; 11:12; 18:20). Thus, everything dark and evil vanishes from heaven, so that it becomes a world of pure light. Where evil powers in heaven are mentioned, the reference is primarily to the air or to the firmament (Acts 7:42; Eph. 2:2; 3:10; 6:12). Their sphere of influence, therefore, is entirely on this side of God's realm of light.

(c) In agreement with the OT it is stated that God created heaven and earth (Acts 4:24; 14:15; 17:24; Rev. 10:6; 14:7) and that he will recreate them (2 Pet. 3:13; Rev. 21:1). The present heaven will pass away like the earth (Mk. 13:31; Heb. 12:26; 2 Pet. 3:7, 10, 12; Rev. 20:11), but Jesus' words will remain (Mk. 13:31). God is Lord of heaven and earth (Matt. 5:34; 11:25; Acts 7:49; 17:24; cf. Isa. 66:1).

(d) God is said to dwell "in heaven," but there is no reflection on difficulties inherent in this statement. Occasionally God is referred to by the OT expression "God of heaven" (Rev. 11:13; 16:11). Heaven itself is God's throne (Matt. 5:34; Acts 7:49; Heb. 8:1; Rev. 4–5). It follows from this that heaven can be used as a substitute for God (Matt. 5:10; 6:20; Mk. 11:30; Lk. 10:20; Jn. 3:27), esp. in Matt.'s expression "the kingdom of heaven."

It is more important theologically that God is called "Father in heaven" (Matt. 5:16, 45; 6:1, 9; 7:11, 21; 10:32–33; 12:50). Because God is in heaven his revelation takes place from there (11:27). At Jesus' baptism and at other crises in his earthly ministry God's voice was heard from heaven (Mk. 1:11; Jn. 12:28; cf. Heb. 12:25). The seer heard voices from heaven (Rev. 10:4, 8; 11:12; 14:13; 18:4; cf. 21:3), and the Holy Spirit came down from heaven (Mk. 1:10; Acts 2:2; 1 Pet. 1:12). In the same way God's wrath goes forth from heaven (Lk. 17:29; Rom. 1:18).

(e) Acts 14:17 states that God gives rain and fruitful seasons *ouranothen*, "from heaven," implying both the physical and the spiritual source. The only other occurrence of this word is in 26:13, where it is an alternative to *ek tou ouranou* ("from heaven," 9:3).

(f) The NT also speaks of treasures of salvation in heaven (Matt. 6:20). Rewards are in heaven (5:12), and the names of the disciples are recorded in heaven (Lk. 10:20; cf. Heb. 12:23). Their inheritance is there as well (1 Pet. 1:4). Christians have a building (2 Cor. 5:1–2) and their citizenship or home in heaven (Phil. 3:20). There is mention of a heavenly Jerusalem, which is the Christians' true home (Gal. 4:26; Heb. 12:22; Rev. 3:12; 21:2; 10), and even of a temple in heaven (11:19; but cf. 21:22).

2. *Christological statements.* (a) The statements about heaven are particularly important when they stand in relation to Jesus Christ. At his baptism the heavens opened, the Holy Spirit descended on him, and God the Father acknowledged him (Matt. 3:16–17). Heaven was open above him because he himself was the door of heaven and of God's house on earth (Jn. 1:51; cf. Gen. 28:12). Jesus taught his disciples to pray for God's will to be done on earth as in heaven (Matt. 6:10). When Jesus gave authority to Peter or to the disciples, their actions were valid in heaven, i.e., with God (16:19; 18:19).

Jesus of Nazareth will sit at God's right hand and will come with the clouds of heaven (Mk. 14:62; cf. Ps. 110:1; Dan. 7:13). At the Parousia the sign of the Son of Man will appear in heaven (Matt. 24:30), at which time he will gather his elect from one end of heaven to the other (Mk. 13:27). All power in heaven and on earth has been given to the Risen One (Matt. 28:18). He is Lord (→ *kyrios, 3261*), and to him everything on earth and in heaven will pay homage (Phil. 2:10). He bestows the Holy Spirit from heaven and displays wonders and signs in heaven (Acts 2:17–20, 32–36). The Christian community's task is to wait for him to come to judge and to save (Phil. 3:20; 1 Thess. 1:10; 4:16; 2 Thess. 1:7), not to look up into heaven (Acts 1:10–11).

As the Lamb who has been exalted to God's throne, Christ has the authority to open the sealed book and thus to set in motion the final phase of the world's history (Rev. 5:3–6:1). Thus, the whole of creation praises him (5:11–14). This means, moreover, that Christ does not belong to the realm of the world, but to the realm of God. As the one who has come from heaven and returned there, Jesus Christ reveals himself as the true bread from heaven, by means of which God bestows eternal life (Jn. 6:31–33, 38, 41–42, 50–51; cf. Exod. 16:4, 13–15).

(b) As in the OT (Exod. 25:9), the earthly sanctuary in Heb. is a copy of the heavenly one. But it is only a shadow; the heavenly sanctuary is the only true and real one. This heavenly sanctuary is still, eschatologically speaking, to come (Heb. 8:5; 9:23–24). Since Christ has entered the heavenly sanctuary, he has shown himself to be the true high priest (8:1–2). The Christian's calling to faith is also *epouranios* (3:1; cf. Phil. 3:14), as are the gifts, the salvation that Christians have tasted (Heb. 6:4; cf. 9:28). The homeland of the pilgrim people of God (11:16) and their Jerusalem, viewed as an eschatological goal, are likewise *epouranios* (12:22).

According to Heb., Jesus' exaltation (1:3; 8:1) signifies the fulfillment of his high priestly office. He has passed through the heavens and has been raised higher than they (4:14; 7:26; 9:11, 23–24), since he has reached the very throne of God. There he performs his real, true priestly service (8:1–2), at the same time fulfilling and surpassing that of the OT.

(c) Certain special emphases are found in Eph. and Col. Christ existed before anything created came to be, and he himself was not created (Col. 1:16). He is the instrument, the agent, and the goal of creation; without him nothing can exist (cf. also Jn. 1:3). Special emphasis is laid on the fact that everything, including the heavenly powers, has been created "in Christ" and is reconciled through him (Col. 1:15–23). Christ is head over all principalities and powers.

The exalted Christ has penetrated all the heavenly spheres and come down to earth. He has broken through the barrier erected by the evil powers that isolated humans from God (Eph. 1:10; 4:9). Similarly 1:23 and 4:10 apply to Christ the OT statement that Yahweh fills heaven and earth. This is a consequence of the thought of 1:10 (cf. Col. 1:16, 20) that every created thing has its goal to be united in Christ and has no independent existence apart from him. Creation is strictly related to the Redeemer and to redemption.

3. (a) In Jn. *ouranos*, heaven, occurs only in the sing. God's will to save and the salvation effected by Jesus Christ determine the statements about heaven. Jesus comes from heaven and returns there. In principle the Son of Man, who has come down from heaven, has much to say about heavenly things (*epourania*) and the plans of God concealed there. But not everyone can believe and understand these things, so Jesus concentrates on God's present activity on earth (Jn. 3:12–13, 31–32).

(b) Paul refers to the bodily form of heavenly beings—either stars or angelic powers—in 1 Cor. 15:40. Christ, the preexistent, risen, and coming one, is the heavenly man, whose image, i.e., whose bodily form, Christians will receive at the Parousia (15:48–49). God has seated Jesus "at his right hand in the heavenly realms" (*ta epourania*, a circumlocution for heaven) and thus blessed Christians with spiritual blessing (Eph. 1:20; cf. 1:3). Spiritually we have already risen with Christ and been exalted to heaven (2:6; cf. Ps. 110:1). The manifold wisdom of God will be made known to the principalities and powers in heaven (Eph. 3:10); the saving work of Christ thus has cosmic significance. According to 2 Tim. 4:18, Christ's kingdom is *epouranios*, i.e., it possesses heavenly authority and glory, and is therefore superior to every temptation and persecution the apostle has to suffer.

See also *anabainō*, go up, mount up (*326*); *anō*, above, upward (*539*).

4045 (ousia, substance, property), → *5975*.

4050 (opheiletēs, debtor), → *4053*.

4051 (opheilē, obligation), → *4053*.

4052 (opheilēma, what is owed, a debt), → *4053*.

4053	ὀφείλω

ὀφείλω (*opheilō*), owe, be indebted to (*4053*); ὀφείλημα (*opheilēma*), what is owed, a debt (*4052*); ὀφειλέτης (*opheiletēs*), debtor (*4050*); ὄφελον (*ophelon*), O that, would that, if only (*4054*); ὀφειλή (*opheilē*), obligation (*4051*).

CL & OT 1. (a) The word group formed from the stem *opheil-* belongs originally to the sphere of law. When linked with an obj., *opheilō* means to owe someone something, e.g., money; when used with an infinitive, to owe in the sense of being indebted. An *opheiletēs* is a debtor or someone under an obligation to achieve something. *opheilē* (rare) and the more common *opheilēma* denote a debt, esp. of a financial nature. *ophelon* (originally an aor. part. of *opheilō* with *estin* [is] added) became the set expression for the optative, "O that," "would that," "if only."

(b) There are also moral obligations in respect of people or of state laws. Thus a culprit may be punished by being required to pay compensation to an injured party. Infringement of divine regulations and thanks owed in return for benefactions of the gods make humans debtors, requiring from them some cultic penance or act.

2. (a) In the LXX *opheilō* occurs only 22x (10x in the Apocr.), either in the optative formula *ophelon* (e.g., Num. 14:2 = LXX 14:3; 20:3) or in connection with the law of debt (e.g., Isa. 24:2; Ezek. 18:7). In Deut. 15:2 loans are regulated in such a way that for sacral law in Israel, as distinct from other nations of the ANE, monetary debts were not permanently enforced for life. Every seven years they were to be remitted by the creditor. The stipulation concerning a pledge (*opheilēma*) in Deut. 24:10 has a pronounced humanitarian character (cf. 1 Macc. 10:43; 13:39).

(b) The OT does not make use of the concept of legal debt in order to depict obligation to Yahweh. This was due to the fact that a

person's relationship with God in the OT was not yet conceived on the analogy of a business agreement between partners, but as obedience to his will (cf. *dei*, *1256*).

The situation is different in intertestamental Jud., where *opheilō* eventually meant to come off badly (from what is demanded of one), i.e., to be guilty, liable to punishment; and (positively) to be indebted. *opheilēma* referred to arrears in payment, a debt, obligation. In this context, sin is no longer conceived of as intrinsic disobedience but as an outstanding debt, for which one can compensate by appropriate means.

NT *opheilō* is used mainly in two sets of contexts: to designate our relationship with God (in the Gospels, esp. Matt.), and as a paraenetic concept (in the letters, esp. Paul's).

1. From a formal point of view Jesus spoke of humans as debtors to God, just as Jud. did. The difference lies in the fact that, unlike Jud., Jesus took the business relationship to be not the reality, but a parable of our relationship to God. Thus, the concept of debt (*opheilēma*) is linked by Jesus not with achievements or demands concerning payments of arrears, but with forgiveness (*aphesis*; → *aphiēmi*, *918*).

(a) Both these differences are made clear in the parable of the unmerciful servant (Matt. 18:23–35). The picture of the creditor and the debtor (*opheiletēs*) reveals our dependence on and responsibility to God, who will settle accounts with his servants (18:23). The fantastically high sum of money that is owed (10,000 talents, i.e., a debt that one cannot hope to pay) is from the outset an illusion. Only through the compassion of the creditor can it be remitted. But the parable also reveals our duty (18:33; *dei*, *1256*). By virtue of the great debt that has been remitted by God, we ought to forgive one another the small debts owed to us.

(b) A certain parallel is offered in the parable of the two debtors, which Lk. has woven into the narrative of the sinful woman (Lk. 7:41–43), in order to point out the connection between the greater or lesser degree of love and the greater or lesser degree of debt forgiven (cf. also 16:5–7).

(c) In Matt. 6:12 *opheilēma* means debt in the sense of sin. This fifth request of the Lord's Prayer stresses the correspondence between divine forgiveness of debts and human readiness to forgive. Human forgiveness is an echo and an obligation of the forgiveness received (cf. 6:14–15).

2. In the NT letters *opheilō* predominantly denotes the positive sense of responsibility that arises out of our belonging to Christ. In Rom. 13:8 Paul uses the double meaning of *opheilō* to exhort his readers to a love that is both a task and a debt to one's neighbor that can never be paid. In 15:1–3 the connection between ethical obligation and Christ's foundation work becomes particularly clear: "We who are strong ought [*opheilomen*] to bear with the failings of the weak, and not to please ourselves. . . . For even Christ did not please himself. . . ."

In 1 Cor. 11:7, 10 Paul speaks of the duty of discipline in the congregation; in 2 Thess. 1:3; 2:13, of the duty of gratitude for the spiritual growth of the congregations; and in 2 Cor. 12:14, of responsible parenthood. In 1 Jn. 4:11 John speaks similarly of brotherly love; in 3:16, of the sacrifice of one's life. These thoughts are summarized in 2:6: "Whoever claims to live in him must [*opheilei*] walk as Jesus did." Heb. uses *opheilō* in parallel to *dei* and *prepei*, in order to underline the divine purpose in what befell Christ (2:17; cf. 2:1, 10; see also 5:3).

3. The optative particle *ophelon* is found only in Paul (1 Cor. 4:8; 2 Cor. 11:1; Gal. 5:12) and in Rev. 3:15. *opheilē* denotes monetary debt in Matt. 18:32, civil dues in Rom. 13:7, and the command to marital sexual intercourse in 1 Cor. 7:3. *opheiletēs* denotes a debtor (Matt. 6:12) and one under obligation (Paul in Rom. 1:14) to world mission. In Gal. 5:3 it expresses the obligation to keep the whole law if one practices circumcision. By contrast, Rom. 8:12 speaks of believers who "have an obligation—but it is not to the sinful nature," and 15:27 of what Gentile believers owe Jewish believers.

See also *ananke*, compulsion (*340*); *dei*, it is necessary, one must (*1256*); *prepō*, be fitting, seemly or suitable (*4560*).

4054 (*ophelon*, O that, would that, if only), → *4053*.

4057 (*ophthalmos*, eye), → *3972*.

4058	ὄφις

ὄφις (*ophis*), snake, serpent (*4058*).

CL & OT 1. The attitude of people toward the snake has always been ambivalent. On the one hand, it has been regarded as a strange and threatening animal, dangerous to life and full of cunning, deceit, and evil. On the other hand, because of its nearness to the earth and the subterranean waters, it has been linked with the subterranean gods and their powers to give and renew life. It was also a symbol of the gods who grant healing. Thus, it became a symbol of the earth itself, which both gives life and then receives it back.

2. *ophis* is found 37x in the LXX. In Gen. 3, it is introduced as an exceptionally clever, sly animal, which led humankind into disobedience. This recondite figure conveys the mystery of the breaking in of evil into the world, which God created good. In Num. 21 the Israelites' murmuring against God and Moses is punished by a plague of snakes. But Yahweh turns again in grace to his people: Anyone who looked to the symbol of a bronze snake was saved. According to 2 Ki. 18:4, this bronze snake survived until the time of Hezekiah, who destroyed it because the people were burning incense to it.

In later Jewish writings the snake became an established instrument of the devil or was even identified with him. Occasionally it was identified with the Angel of Death. These writings contain speculations about the motives that moved the snake in Paradise to attack humankind, such as envy, sexual desire, or desire for world rule.

NT Jesus' condemnation of the teachers of the law and the Pharisees in Matt. 23:33 (cf. 3:7) calls them "snakes" in view of their evil and unwillingness to repent, possibly indicating their link with Satan. He threatens them with the judgment of *geenna* (→ *1147*). In his call to prayer in faith, Jesus stressed that no father would give his son a snake instead of the fish he had asked for (7:10; Lk. 11:11), i.e., something evil and dangerous instead of food. How much more will God give that which is good when asked by the disciples. Gen. 3:1 and Song 5:2; 6:9 lie behind the paradoxical exhortation to wisdom and innocence in Matt. 10:16.

Because Satan has been cast down, the disciples have obtained authority to tread on snakes and scorpions, the instruments of the Evil One (Lk. 10:19; cf. Ps. 91:13; Mk. 16:18; cf. also Acts 28:1–6, which uses *echidna*, viper).

In Rev. 9:19 the horses of the demonic cavalry have tails like snakes, by which they do harm. In 12:9; 20:2 the snake recalls Gen. 3 and is identified with Satan (→ *drakōn*, *1532*). The Gen. story is also recalled in 2 Cor. 11:3, where the church is warned against listening to Satan's whispered suggestions and so being led astray from sincere devotion to and trust in Christ. Jn. 3:14–15 looks back to Num. 21:8–9: Just as looking at the bronze snake that had been lifted up on the pole brought salvation, so faith saves the one who looks to the Son of Man exalted on the cross and on the throne of God.

See also *drakōn*, dragon (*1532*).

4063	ὄχλος

ὄχλος (*ochlos*), (throng of) people, crowd, mob (*4063*).

CL & OT 1. In cl. Gk. *ochlos* means a crowd, throng; the public, in contrast to individual people; and esp. in contrast to the nobility or people of rank, a mob or insignificant mass. In the military world the word means a company, troop, army.

2. In the LXX *ochlos* occurs about 60x, with the meaning crowd (1 Ki. 20:13 = LXX 21:13), army (Num. 20:20; Ezek. 17:17), people (Jer. 38:1 = LXX 45:1; Dan. 3:4), throng (Jer. 31:8 = LXX 38:8), or mob

(Ezek. 16:40; 23:24). It is sometimes combined with synonyms, such as *laos* (→ *3295*) or *ethnos* (→ *1620*).

NT In the NT *ochlos* occurs 174x. Of these 4 are in Rev., and all the others in the Gospels and Acts. In Mk. 14:43 the word means the armed crowd at the arrest of Jesus, but usually it is an unorganized crowd of people with no particular characteristics. A crowd comes to hear John the Baptist (Lk. 3:7, 10) or Jesus (Matt. 4:25; 5:1). It is esp. to these people, who have nothing particular to offer, that Jesus directs his teaching and his compassion (9:33) and his provision of food (14:19; Lk. 9:16; Jn. 6:5). The contrast to these is provided by the ruling classes, the Pharisees and teachers of the law, who despised the *ochlos* as the ignorant masses who did not keep the law. To them the masses were accursed (Jn. 7:31, 48–49).

In Jn. 7:49 *ochlos* doubtless refers to "the people of the land." In the preexilic age the people of the land denoted full citizens who were liable to military service. But in the postexilic age it denoted the foreign or mixed population as distinct from the returned exiles. It became a term of abuse, connoting ignorance of and a lax attitude toward the law. Jesus and later Paul were accused of leading the *ochlos* astray (Jn. 7:12; Acts 19:26).

Herod Antipas hesitates to kill John the Baptist because he fears the *ochlos* (Matt. 14:5). The ruling class similarly fear the *ochlos* and do not dare to lay hands on Jesus (21:26, 46), but they later stir up the *ochlos* against him (27:20). Pilate acts under pressure from the *ochlos* (Mk. 15:15). Jesus tells parables to the *ochlos* (Matt. 13:34). He has a whole *ochlos* of disciples (Lk. 6:17; cf. Acts 1:15). A great *ochlos* goes to Bethany to see Jesus and Lazarus (Jn. 12:9). Before the throne of God and of the Lamb stands an innumerable *ochlos* (Rev. 7:9); in 17:15 nations are meant.

See also *dēmos*, people, populace, crowd, popular assembly (*1322*); *ethnos*, nation, people, pagans, Gentiles (*1620*); *laos*, people (*3295*); *polis*, city, city-state (*4484*).

4066 (*opsarion*, fish for eating), → *2716*.

4069 (*opsimos*, late [rain]), → *847*.

4072	ὀψώνιον

ὀψώνιον (*opsōnion*), wages, payment (*4072*).

CL & OT *opsōnion* refers to the cash one needs to buy food (1 Esd. 4:56). In the pl., it refers esp. to a soldier's maintenance allowances, which he received above and beyond natural provisions. Finally, it means wages in general (1 Macc. 3:28; 14:32), occasionally the salary of government officials. *opsōnion* thus denotes what one is entitled to receive. It is a minimum subsistence wage rather than an appropriate reward for work carried out.

NT 1. *opsōnion* occurs 4x in the NT. John the Baptist advises the soldiers to be satisfied with their wages (Lk. 3:14).

2. In 1 Cor. 9:7 Paul uses the pl. to refer to the support to which he was entitled from the various congregations as remuneration for his missionary work (cf. 2 Cor. 11:8). This is not only an allusion to soldiers' pay, comparing his missionary work with military service; it also implies the legal claim of the apostle on the congregations. Paul's waiving of his *opsōnion* underlines that God's gift of grace costs nothing, just as it is offered to all in the apostolic preaching without any conditions.

3. According to Rom. 6:23, sin pays out wages, which is death. Sin promises life and gives death. This death does not just begin at the end of our temporal lives; it is the current payment we already receive. It is the only right to which we can lay claim as sinners. But over against this right stands God's gift of grace, which we receive in service under him (3:23b). Yet no one in God's service can claim anything as a right; he or she receives eternal life as a free gift from God.

See also *apodidōmi*, give away, give back, sell, recompense (*625*); *kerdos*, gain (*3046*); *misthos*, pay, wages, reward (*3635*).

Π *pi*

4077 (*pathēma*, suffering, affliction, misfortune), → *4248*.

4078 (*pathētos*, subject to suffering, capable of suffering), → *4248*.

4079 (*pathos*, suffering, passion), → *4248*.

4080 (*paidagōgos*, custodian, guide, guardian), → *4084*.

4081 (*paidarion*, little boy, child, youth), → *4090*.

4082 (*paideia*, upbringing, training, instruction, discipline), → *4084*.

4083 (*paideutēs*, instructor, teacher), → *4084*.

4084	παιδεύω

παιδεύω (*paideuō*), bring up, instruct, train, educate (*4084*); παιδεία (*paideia*), upbringing, training, instruction, discipline (*4082*); παιδευτής (*paideutēs*), instructor, teacher (*4083*); παιδαγωγός (*paidagōgos*), custodian, guide, guardian, the man (usually a slave) who took boys and youths to and from school and generally superintended their conduct (*4080*).

CL & OT 1. (a) The underlying root of this word group is *pais*, child, boy (→ *4090*). *paideuō* thus lit. means to be together with a child, hence, to bring up, educate, instruct, teach. Derived from this is the noun *paideia*, which is found as early as the 6th cent. B.C. in the sense of education and which connotes the process of education, development of culture. Later the word was extended to cover adult education as well and was used generally of scientific training. Other derivatives are *paidagōgos*, one in charge of boys, custodian, tutor (usually referring to slaves), and *paideutēs*, teacher, educator.

(b) Though the word *paideuō* was not used, education and the ideals of education of each new generation to moral and legal traditions through example and imitation were important. The Sophists were probably the first to emphasize consistently the equality and hence educability of all people. They thus held courses of lectures, which anyone who paid might attend. In contrast to the formal principle of the Sophists, Socrates maintained the concrete principle of the *agathon*, the good, which could be brought to light by an individual's study and growth in wisdom and knowledge through mind-guiding conversation.

In Plato education is the only possible way to overcome injustice and to create a true, just state. The basis for this is education in music and gymnastics. Since children belong to the state rather than to their parents, school should be compulsory. For the elite who are fit to govern, there is also a gradual introduction to philosophical thinking, the object of which is to arouse in the individual the memory, already present, of the ideas, the archetypes of reality. Aristotle took as his aim in education the aesthetically and ethically cultured citizen. Exhortation and habit both played a part. Aristotle did not include the sciences as a part of education. In the Hellenism of the NT period, the Stoic ideal of the leader who is responsible to himself and to reason, standing above the people, is of crucial importance in cultured circles.

To summarize, wherever the concept of education prevailed, the central position was occupied by humans, since they are creatures endowed with reason and thus capable of being educated. The aim of education is the complete person, i.e., the person who exercises mastery over *aretē* (virtue). By and large the Gks. never understood the principle of education in a perfectionist sense. Concepts like fate, deity, and (later) chance and personal freedom had too much influence on Gk. thought for that.

2. *paideuō* (84x in the LXX) is used 41x for the Heb. *yāsar* (mostly piel), to chastise, discipline, correct. The noun *paideia* (103x in the LXX) occurs 37x for *mûsār*, chastisement, discipline. The words are found esp. often in Ps., Prov., and Sir.

(a) The OT bears witness to God's self-revelation to Israel and intervention in the lives of his chosen people. In response to his love and care for them, God expects trust and obedience, reflecting his holiness. The trouble that God has with his people forces him to severe disciplinary measures or chastening (*yāsar/mûsār*). But God does not educate in order to achieve an ideal; he watches over his people's faithfulness, which should flow from trust and from a constant readiness to hear and truly listen that arises from obedience to his Word.

Originally Israel as a nation was seen as being subject to God's discipline (Deut. 4:36; 8:5; Hos. 7:12; 10:10); but later, in proverbial wisdom, it was more a matter of God's education of the individual (Prov. 3:11; 15:33 = LXX 16:4; Sir. 18:14). This education, which Israel was ever trying to escape, is shared equally by all members of the nation. Thus there is no *independent* religious education of the young. It is God who educates, and the upbringing of children takes place within the sphere of this God, who instructs in love and punishes because of the recalcitrance of his own people.

The Heb. words *yāsar/mûsār* refer primarily to the chastisement that a father must inflict on his son (Deut. 21:18; Prov. 13:24; 19:18; 23:13; 29:17) and that God allows to be inflicted on his servant for the sake of his people's salvation (Isa. 53:5). Thus in Deut. 11:2 the *paideia* of the Lord is his guidance, his educational dealings with Israel in history. Because of sin he chastises and corrects (Lev. 26:18, 28), but always "with justice" (Jer. 10:24; 46:28 = LXX 26:28). We are able to accept or despise, love or hate this education (Ps. 50:17; Prov. 12:1; Jer. 5:3).

In Prov. one observes a gradual change from the process of discipline to its effect, namely, "instruction," which has to be learned (1:2), bought, and kept (23:23). But God, not the child or an ideal, is always central and forms its content. His educational aim is to lead his people to the realization that they owe their existence to the saving will of Yahweh alone and therefore owe obedience to their divine instructor (Deut. 8:1–6).

How then does the education of the young proceed in Israel? God commands that they obey their parents, who are next to him in importance. The father acts like a priest to the family, handing on the tradition as well as God's law to the family (cf. Deut. 6:6–9). He can do so in response to the questions of his children (Exod. 12:26–27), and his answer is a confession of God's saving activity of Israel. The children are told of this not only in words but also by means of impressive signs in the form of monumental stones (Jos. 4:6–7, 21–24). The OT has no theory of education, no special educational institutions, but the young become accustomed to the life of the nation, which stands under God's loving discipline. Watching and listening, they enter into the inheritance of their ancestors. Those who hear aright will obey.

In wisdom lit. we find a moralizing and humanizing tendency. The aim of education here is wisdom (Prov. 1:7; 8:33), which recognizes at the bottom of things a prevailing order to which the wise submit. In the LXX the vb. *paideuō* remains nearer in meaning to the OT vb. "chasten," although the noun *paideia* tends more in the direction of the Hel. idea of instruction. But even though now an educational ideal has developed in Israel, the point of reference remains God's revelation and commandments. In summoning Israel to keep God's commands as they enter the promised land, Deut. 11:2 calls on them to reflect on Yahweh's past dealings with them, and in so doing provides the expression *paideia kyriou*, "the discipline of the Lord."

In Palestinian Jud. education was still closely associated with the OT: Its aim was to produce a person who obeyed God's will, esp.

as determined in the law. In the period following the exile, this goal became more and more an absolute, standing over Israel as a timeless demand and forming the basis of the people's relationship to God. This notion of education had its classic expression in the rab. schools, where the Torah was taught. In Hel. Jud., by contrast, education was more strongly influenced by Gk. ideas. Typical of this are the philosophical schools of Alexandria, with Philo as the main representative.

NT 1. Words of this group occur 24x in the NT. (a) *paideuō* is used 2x with the meaning of to teach, instruct: Moses was instructed in Egyptian wisdom (Acts 7:22), and Paul was educated by Gamaliel (22:3).

(b) *paideuō* is also used 2x in the sense of to scourge, whip, punish (Lk. 23:16, 22). It is no longer possible to determine whether here, as in so many parts of the passion narrative, allusion is being made to an OT prophecy (Isa. 53:5) or whether *paideuō* here is taken simply from popular Gk. usage.

2. (a) The concept of education by God underwent decisive further development in Jud., with the idea that God's teaching and therefore loving hand was to be experienced in suffering (e.g., Jdt. 8:25–27; 2 Macc. 6:12–17; *Pss. Sol.* 3:4; 13:9). Hints of this idea are found even in the OT (e.g., Deut. 8:5; 11:2; 2 Sam. 7:14–15).

(b) This view of chastening as God's loving action in order to preserve people from the final judgment is taken over in Heb. 12:5–6 (which cites Prov. 3:11–12). "The Lord's discipline" is a sign of his love and is not therefore any ground for losing courage. This scriptural quotation is followed by a discussion in Heb. 12:7–11. God is the one who educates his people. His method of education is illustrated by human upbringing, which is a weak reflection of the former. God is the Father who chastens because he loves, in order to keep us in the status of being his children and to cause his children to turn around and come home. We can resist this discipline, defy God, and doubt his fatherly love (12:6), although in doing so we are rejecting divine sonship; for it is precisely in discipline that God's fatherly activity is experienced.

If in the bringing up of a family the status of a true son is to be recognized by the fact that his father educates and "disciplines" him, how much more so with regard to God. Human fathers exercise discipline without ultimate insight and are open to mistakes, but the Lord does so with the ultimate object of making us share in his holiness (Heb. 12:10). The aim of this discipline is peace with God (12:11), which is also the starting point for God's educative activity, education in divine sonship. Although the Stoics talked in similar terms, the peak of their education is found in the self-perfection of a person.

In this context Heb. 12:9 uses the comparatively rare word *paideutēs*, instructor, teacher, one who disciplines. The same word is also found in Rom. 2:20 of the Jew who sets himself up as a teacher of the law, oblivious to his own failings in the light of the law.

(c) The idea that it is precisely in discipline that God's love becomes visible is found also in Paul, in connection with his exhortations about the Lord's Supper (1 Cor. 11:32). Christians are not spared illness and death caused by sin. Here discipline overlaps with God's judgment. But since this judgment has the nature of discipline, believers are graciously spared God's final judgment over the world (11:32b; see also Rev. 3:19). Paul knows from his experience in carrying out his apostolic commission (2 Cor. 6:9) that discipline does not contradict God's love, but is rather to be understood on the basis of it.

(d) The NT view of education through discipline is, however, fundamentally different, not only from the Gk. concept of education (i.e., toward an ideal), but also from the rab. teachings, which accord to suffering as a result of chastening an expiatory power. In the NT discipline at God's hand is a practical necessity in order that believers can recognize that they are in a proper position of sonship.

(e) A different kind of education is brought about by God's Word in the OT (2 Tim. 3:16). Since here too God himself is really the one who is speaking, the NT church finds in the OT instruction as to God's

will and is thus trained up to live a sanctified life pleasing to God. Tit. 2:11–13 speaks even more directly of God's educative grace: Everything flows together into the message of the cross (2:13–14). Here too education is an outworking of grace; the language in both these passages is Hel., but the basic thought belongs to the OT.

(f) Finally, Paul also speaks of the educative function of the law (Gal. 3:24–4:7). The law is the *paidagōgos*, custodian or taskmaster, that leads us to Christ. The *paidagōgos* and the *didaskalos* (teacher, → *1437*) were differentiated. Whether Paul was thinking of the slave to whom boys were entrusted and who sometimes beat them, or whether he was thinking in more positive terms, cannot be determined. In any case he means the person who keeps the boys in order.

The purpose of God's law was broader, however: to uphold his order and reveal human disobedience. The law itself was good and holy (Rom. 7:12). With the coming of Christ, who introduces and brings in the new age, this function has ended (Gal. 3:25). Through faith in Christ a young person becomes a mature child of God (4:1, 4–7). The apostle is here speaking in terms of salvation history. Humanity in their sinful state cannot keep the God-given law; when they recognize the validity of the commandment and thus their own guilt, they are driven to Christ. But those who are in Christ are free from the Mosaic law and are under the law of the love (Rom. 13:10b; cf. 10:4).

3. In 1 Tim. 1:20 Paul refers to those who have been delivered to Satan for punishment. What we have here is an act of church discipline (probably a form of excommunication), in which Satan embodies God's wrath, afflicting with illness and death those who are destroying God's church. Even this chastening, however, is not directed toward the final destruction of sinners, but rather toward bringing them to their senses and to repentance (1:20b).

4. Education is also a human activity. Paul's exhortation that children are to respect their parents is followed in Eph. 6:4 by a word to fathers, that they should bring up their children "in the training [*paideia*] and instruction of the Lord." The phrase "of the Lord" may mean that God is behind human upbringing (obj. gen.), or the reference may be to education that has to do with the Lord (subj. gen.). In any case, the Christian who declares with Paul that "Jesus is Lord" (1 Cor. 12:3) must renounce the demands of all other masters and be totally faithful to him. Like other aspects of life, the sphere of education is, for believers, under the lordship of Jesus and can proceed in the faith that overcomes the world (1 Jn. 5:4–5).

See also *didaskō*, teach (*1438*); *didaskalos*, teacher, master (*1437*); *didaskalia*, teaching, instruction (*1436*); *katecheō*, inform, instruct (*2994*); *paradidōmi*, to deliver, hand down (*4140*).

4086 (paidion, very young child, infant), → *4090*.

4087 (paidiskē, servant girl), → *4090*.

4090	παῖς

παῖς (*pais*), child, young man, son, servant (*4090*); παιδίσκη (*paidiskē*), servant girl (*4087*); παιδίον (*paidion*), very young child, infant (*4086*); παιδάριον (*paidarion*), little boy, child, youth (*4081*); βρέφος (*brephos*), unborn child, embryo, baby, infant (*1100*).

CL & OT 1. *pais* usually means son, though it can also denote a daughter in relation to descent. It normally denotes a child between seven and fourteen years, as distinct from a little child or a youth. *pais* also suggests the child's lowly position in society and ancient function as a slave. The word could therefore also mean servant or slave. *paidion* and *paidarion*, both diminutives of *pais*, denote a little child up to seven years or a young slave, although occasionally a young man. Finally, *brephos* denotes an unborn or newborn child, infant.

2. In the LXX *pais* occurs some 500x and stands for 10 different Heb. words (esp. *ʿebed*, slave, servant; → *doulos*, *1528*). Its breadth of meaning is the same as in cl. Gk. *paidion* and *paidarion* in the LXX, as in secular Gk., denote baby (Gen. 21:7), little child (21:14), lad (22:5, 12), and young man (Jdg. 8:14). This word group frequently emphasizes

the serving capacity of young people as companions (Gen. 22:5), messengers (Jdg. 7:10 = LXX 7:9), armor-bearers (9:54; 1 Sam. 14:1), or servants (Ruth 2:5–6; Neh. 13:19).

3. The phrase *pais theou*, servant of God, has a specialized meaning in the LXX. (a) Of the 870 occurrences of ʿ*ebed* in the Heb. OT, *pais* is used 340x, *doulos* 327x (also used are *therapōn*, servant, attendant, 46x; and *oiketēs*, household slave, 36x). In Jdg. to 2 Ki. *pais* is used of the free servant of the king and *doulos* for enforced bondage.

doulos is used in religious contexts to identify oneself or others as servants of God, thus expressing the great difference between humans and God. In the other OT books the religious idea of the *doulos* is prominent as well, but in Job it can be replaced by *therapōn* and in Isa. by *pais*. Although the "Servant" passages of Isa. are mostly rendered with *pais* and may be collectively interpreted, a messianic figure seems to have been discerned behind Isa. 52:13–53:12.

(b) *pais theou* occurs seldom in the lit. of Gk.-speaking Jud., since it was overshadowed by the *doulos* concept. But where it was used, it usually meant servant of God and referred to Moses (cf. Bar. 1:20; 2:28), the prophets (2:20), or the righteous (Wis. 9:4–5). Less often *pais* means child of God (cf. 2:13; 12:7, 20; 19:6). In 2 Esd. 13:32, 37, 52; 14:9 and *2 Bar.* 70:9 we find an apocalyptic tradition that refers to the Messiah as son, child, youth, or servant. Behind these translations lies the older ʿ*ebed* tradition transmitted by *pais theou*. Older prophecies involving the destiny of Israel and the nations are used here, but the revelation of God's elect is the central idea. Apocalyptic accentuates the element of transcendence in the ʿ*ebed* tradition.

Hel. Jud. understood the ʿ*ebed* passages in Isa. collectively of the people of Israel (cf. 42:1) or of the righteous (Wis. 2:13). No agreement has been reached as to whether the "Servant" passages in Isa. were messianically interpreted in Palestinian Jud. in pre-Christian times. The references to Isa. 53 are not always obvious. The passages could also be derived from the concept of the atoning death of the righteous, which was widespread in late Jud. Qumran continued the OT tradition in referring to the prophets as "God's servants." It is striking how the Teacher of Righteousness adopts the title of "God's servant" in the Qumran hymns.

In any event, at least prior to A.D. 200 official Jud. had not interpreted Isa. 53 in terms of a suffering Messiah. On the contrary, perhaps influenced by anti-Christian polemic, Jud. had eradicated or drastically reinterpreted any statements there about his suffering. The idea of a suffering Messiah only appears late in Jewish writings.

NT 1. The centurion's servant is called a *pais* (Matt. 8:6, 13; Lk. 7:7) and the children in the market place are *paidia* (Matt. 11:16; Lk. 7:32). Matt. uses *pais* of Herod's servants (14:2) and *paidion* (14:21; 15:38) in the great feedings (the number given excluded women and children). *paidiskē* occurs 13x in the NT, always for a female servant (Matt. 26:69; Acts 12:13; Gal. 4:22–23).

Lk. is the only Evangelist to use *brephos*, chiefly in the infancy narratives, of the unborn child (Lk. 1:41, 44) and the newborn baby (2:12, 16; cf. Acts 7:19). In using *brephos* instead of *paidion* in 18:15 (though not 18:16–17; cf. Matt. 19:13–14; Mk. 10:13–15), Lk. was perhaps thinking esp. of babies. But *pais* also occurs in Lk. 2:43 of the twelve-year-old Jesus; in 8:51, 54 of a girl; and in 12:45; 15:26 of servants. He uses *paidion* in 1:59 of a child at a circumcision and in 11:7 of children in the parable of the friend at midnight.

Jn. also uses *pais* (Jn. 4:51), *paidion* (4:49), and *huios* (son, 4:50) of the same child. He uses *paidion* of the newborn child (16:21) and *paidarion* (6:9, the only NT occurrence of the word) of the lad with five loaves and two small fishes.

In 1 Cor. 14:20 Paul warns against being childish ("stop thinking like children" [*paidia*]). Thus the picture of the child is here used negatively (contrast Mk. 10:15). Otherwise, the word group occurs in Paul only in Gal. 4:22–23, 30–31, in the comparison of the bondage of Jud. with Sarah's female slave (*paidiskē*; cf. Gen. 16:15; 21:2, 9–12). Heb. uses *paidion* 3 times (2:13–14; 11:23). *brephos* appears in

2 Tim. 3:15 (*apo brephous*, "from infancy") and 1 Pet. 2:2 ("Like newborn babies, crave pure spiritual milk, so that by it you may grow up in your salvation"). The latter passage speaks of newborn children in a metaphorical sense.

2. With the exception of *paidiskē* in Gal. 4:21–31 (Paul's allegory of Sarah and the slave woman Hagar; → *Hagar*, 29; *Sarra*, Sarah, 4925), in the above passages no special theological significance attaches to *pais*, *paidiskē*, and *paidion*. But in three groups of passages children are related to God's kingdom. (a) Matt. 19:13–15; Mk. 10:13–16; and Lk. 18:15–17 relate the incident of Jesus' blessing the children despite the protests of his disciples. Their reluctance to allow adults to bring children to Jesus has been attributed to a concern that Jesus was tired. But perhaps there was also the feeling that children were too young to make a responsible commitment. Certainly they would not be of the age of accountability at which they could take on themselves the yoke of the Mosaic law.

Jesus replied that children should come to him, for the kingdom of God belongs "to such as these." Jesus then took the children in his arms, blessed them, and laid his hands on them (Mk. 10:14–16). The phrase "such as these" may suggest "these and other actual children" or "these and others who, though not literally children, share the characteristics of children." (On the role of children in the divine order see Ps. 8:2; Matt. 11:25; 21:15–16.) But Mk. 10:15 suggests that the second interpretation is the better one, so that Jesus is reversing the apparent understanding of the disciples. The reason why the kingdom belongs to children is not because of any subjective qualities that they may have; rather, it lies in their objective helplessness (cf. Jn. 3:1–8, Jesus' discourse with Nicodemus comparing entry into the kingdom with rebirth).

Some have seen implications of infant baptism in this story. There is no solid evidence, however, for inferring that Jesus or the early church linked this event with baptism. On the other hand, Jesus' categorical statement that the kingdom belongs to such does suggest that they may be full members of the church and thus fit subjects to receive the sacrament of incorporation.

(b) A similar saying occurs in Matt. 18:3–4 in the course of a dispute among the disciples regarding who would be the greatest in the kingdom. Jesus set a child (*paidion*) in their midst and said: "Unless you change and become like children, you will never enter the kingdom of heaven. Therefore, whoever humbles himself like this child is the greatest in the kingdom of heaven." This passage stresses the need to become humble like little children in order to enter the kingdom (on humility, see 5:3; 20:26; 23:11).

(c) Mk. 9:37 (see also Lk. 18:17) reads: "Whoever welcomes one of these little children in my name welcomes me; and whoever welcomes me does not welcome me but the one who sent me." This underlines again the role that children have in their own right in God's kingdom. But it is also related to a theme that finds recurrent expression in the Gospels: Jesus is present (albeit incognito) in those who are his. This is said of appointed witnesses to Christ (Matt. 10:40; Lk. 10:16; Jn. 13:20), of children (in the present passage), of those in need (Matt. 25:35–45; cf. Mk. 9:41), and of those in prayer and service (Matt. 18:20; cf. Jn. 15:4–7). These passages carry with them the corollary that those who maltreat representatives of Christ bear a terrible responsibility.

3. (a) The NT uses the title *pais theou* 5x of Jesus (Matt. 12:18; Acts 3:13, 26; 4:27, 30). It is noteworthy how it is used in an OT quotation early in Acts (cf. 3:13 with Exod. 3:16; Isa. 52:13; and Acts 4:27 with Ps. 2:2–3). In Acts 4:27, 30 the meaning "servant" is confirmed by 4:25, where David is called God's "servant" (*pais*) and not his "child." (For the interchange of *doulos* and *pais*, cf. Lk. 7:2–3, 7–8.)

(b) But the influence of the title *pais theou* in its application to Jesus is not to be limited to the occurrences of this particular phrase. The *doulos* concept in Mk. 10:44 has certainly been molded by Isa. 53:10; i.e., behind it stands the ʿ*ebed* (*pais* in LXX) of the Servant

Songs, who was interpreted as a servant by ancient tradition and thus related to Jesus. Perhaps the *ʿebed* of Isa. 42:1 also lies behind the *huios*, son, of Matt. 3:17 par. (Jesus' baptism) and 17:5 par. (Jesus' transfiguration). Certainly in Johannine literature (though *pais* is not used of Jesus) the motif of Jesus as a servant appears in Jn. 13:4–17 (the washing of feet was one of the most menial jobs of a slave). In 1:29, 36 the servant of Isa. 53 undoubtedly lies behind the reference to the Lamb of God.

Moreover, the *ʿebed* of Isa. 53 seems also to lie behind the *hyper* formula, esp. the phrase *hyper pollōn*, "for many" (Mk. 14:24; → *polys*, *4498*); note also the *anti pollōn*, "for many" (Matt. 20:28; Mk. 10:45), and *peri pollōn*, "for many" (Matt. 26:28). One might also add the formulaic use of *paradidōmi*, deliver over, in the pass. voice in Rom. 4:25; 1 Cor. 11:23; that of *didonai heauton*, give oneself, in Gal. 1:4; 1 Tim. 2:6; and that of *tithenai tēn psychēn*, lay down one's life, in Jn. 10:11, 15, 17–18. All these may be based on Isa. 53:12.

(c) Without doubt the Servant concept exercised a considerable influence on the developing theology of the early church, esp. in traditional formulations of doctrine. As the most obvious statement of the death and vindication of God's Servant in the OT, it is highly probable that the reference to Christ's death "according to the Scriptures" (1 Cor. 15:3–4) conceal allusions to Isa. 53. The Servant figure can even be seen in the old hymn of Phil. 2:6–11. Allusions to Isa. 53:12 may also be present in Rom. 8:34; Heb. 7:25; 9:28.

The pervasiveness of these allusions to the Servant figure of Isa. prompts the question as to whether Jesus himself gave the impulse to the church to interpret his person and work in this way. Whether or not *huios* replaces an original *pais* in Mk. 1:11, the baptismal narrative certainly contains an allusion to Isa. 42:1–4 ("with you I am well pleased"). In Lk. 22:37 Jesus quotes Isa. 53:12, and in Lk. 4:18–19 he relates Isa. 61:1–2 to himself (a passage that some Jewish traditions saw as a Servant passage). These references strongly suggest that Jesus saw his vocation as the Son of Man in terms of the suffering and humiliation of the Servant of Yahweh.

(d) The NT, however, does not restrict the title *pais theou* to Jesus. It is used of Israel in Lk. 1:54, a hymn built up of OT quotations, and of David in 1:69 and Acts 4:25. The use of the title for the people of Israel and for David is in line with the usage that had been current since the times of Isaiah.

(e) *pais theou* is not used of Christians in the NT, but such a differentiation is only significant in Gk.-speaking areas. Paul is certainly conscious of being God's servant in accordance with Isa. 49:1 (Gal. 1:15); this shows the variety of ways in which the NT uses this concept. Paul also uses it with a wider sense when he calls himself (Rom. 1:1), his fellow workers (Phil. 1:1; Col. 4:12), and all Christians (1 Cor. 7:22) *douloi*, servants, of Christ (cf. also Jas. 1:1; Rev. 1:1).

Here too the effects of the biblical concept of faith as service are to be seen, but now this service is concentrated esp. in the relation of Christians to Christ. A fundamental distinction can be drawn between the new filial relationship and the old servile one (Rom. 8:14–17; Gal. 4:1–7). This attachment to Christ does not alter this biblical perspective of faith as service, but it does lift it clear of the servile nature of the pre-Christian existence. The servant task is also reflected in the mission of the church in Acts 13:47 (Isa. 49:6); Rom. 10:16 (Isa. 53:1); and Rom. 15:21 (Isa. 52:15).

See also *nēpios*, infant, minor (*3758*); *teknon*, child (*5451*); *huios*, son (*5626*); *doulos*, servant, slave (*1528*).

4093 πάλαι

πάλαι (*palai*), formerly, earlier (*4093*); παλαιός (*palaios*), old (*4094*); παλαιότης (*palaiotēs*), age, obsoleteness (*4095*); παλαιόω (*palaioō*), grow old, make or treat as old (*4096*).

CL & OT 1. In cl. Gk. the original meaning of *palai* focuses on the earlier or past in contrast with the present. Thus it means old: (a) pos-

itively, as existing for a long time and hence venerable; (b) negatively, as obsolete, worn out, and hence worthless. It is a synonym of *archaios*, though this latter word is used almost always positively.

2. In the LXX *palaios* usually has the meaning of old, last year's, antiquated (cf. Lev. 25:22). *palaioō* can mean (trans.) cause to pass away (Job. 9:5), and (intrans.) pass away, fall into decay (14:18), reach old age (21:7). *palaioō* is used metaphorically in the exilic and postexilic writings of the OT for the transience and wasting away of one's life and work, and also of heaven and earth (e.g., 13:28; Isa. 50:9). By giving the whole creation over to decay and corruption, God passes judgment on the sin and fall of humankind (Ps. 102:26; Isa. 51:6).

NT 1. In the NT *palai* points to something that lies in the recent or remote past: e.g., God spoke "in the past" (Heb. 1:1); they would have repented "long ago" (Matt. 11:21; cf. Jude 4); "past" sins (2 Pet. 1:9); Pilate asked if Jesus had "already" died (Mk. 15:44).

2. In *palaios* and *palaiotēs* the old, obsolete past stands in contrast with the completely new (→ *kaino*, *2785*; *neos*, *3742*). The salvation of God in Jesus Christ has broken into this present age and made it obsolete, together with its institutions and practices (2 Cor. 5:17). The final fulfillment is still awaited. With the coming again of the Lord this age will be brought to an end and world history will be completed (2 Pet. 3:13).

(a) The parabolic sayings of Matt. 9:14–17; Mk. 2:18–22; Lk. 5:33–39 are probably to be understood in this context. Jesus here stresses that the age of the old world has passed and that of salvation has begun. Thus the old age is compared to an old garment (Mk. 2:21) and old wine (2:22). A garment (→ *himation*, *2668*) and wine (→ *ampelos*, vine, *306*) were traditional symbols of the cosmos or the age of salvation. In the Synoptic context the passage can also mean that the new excludes the old; the new age of salvation demands a new manner of life that cannot be inserted in the old customs, such as fasting and mourning. The old is fulfilled in the new (cf. Matt. 5:17).

The proverb of Lk. 5:39 in this context is evidently ironical: "No one after drinking old wine wants the new, for he says, 'The old is better.'" It implies that some (i.e., those who cling to Jewish traditions) are incorrigibly attached to the old ways.

In Matt. 13:52 Jesus says, "Every teacher of the law who has been instructed about the kingdom of heaven is like a owner of a house who brings out of his storeroom new treasures as well as old [*palaia*]." This saying stands at the conclusion of Matt.'s account of seven parables. The "teacher of the law" is one who knows both the old, the message of the OT Scriptures, and their fulfillment in the new, the message and person of Jesus. These teachers expound the OT Scriptures as they have been fulfilled by Jesus (5:17–18). Note that they are not first of all trained in the law; rather, they are trained in the kingdom and thus are able to bring out old and new treasures. In this respect they stand in contrast with those teachers trained in "the tradition of the elders" (15:2), who for the sake of human tradition make void the word of God (15:6–7).

(b) In Paul and Heb. the opposition between old and new is to be understood in the same way as in the Synoptic Gospels. Baptism represents the death of the old self and the birth of the new. In the picture of the old and new self we no doubt have part of early Christian baptismal exhortation (Rom. 6:6; Eph. 4:22; Col. 3:9). The "old" means everything connected with the fall of the human race and with our subjection to the distress and death of a transitory life, separated from God. In this concept we hear undertones of God's wrath and the wages of sin. At the same time we are pointed to the completely new, to that healing and salvation given to us when we are crucified with Christ and raised with him (Rom. 6:3–10).

palaiotēs, age, obsoleteness, that which is outdated, occurs only at Rom. 7:6, where Paul emphasizes the incompatibility of the old and the new as ways of salvation and life: We serve in the newness of the Spirit and not in the oldness of the letter. Paul has been using the analogy of divorce: A woman is bound to her husband by law as long as he lives and is only free to marry someone else if he dies. By dying to the law "through the body of Christ" (7:4), we have died "to what once bound us [and] have been released from the law" (7:6a). We are therefore free to serve "in the new way of the Spirit." Life comes as something new apart from the law and thus makes the letter of the law old (in that it came first) and obsolete (in that it is superseded by the Spirit of Christ) (cf. Rom. 7:6 with 8:5–11; also 2 Cor. 3:6; → *nomos*, law, *3795*).

Because Jesus is the new man and those who believe in him are born again to a new life, the old life, alienated from God, is dead. The old self is without power or rights, so it must daily be given over to death. In 1 Cor. 5:7–8 Paul alludes to an OT command (cf. Exod. 12:19; 13:7; Deut. 16:3–4). Just as the last remnants of the old yeast had to be eliminated before the Passover, so the evil and crookedness of the old life, the old yeast of sin and disobedience, must be cleared out to make room for the new life of sincerity and obedience. Jesus' message and work bring the new that is promised in the OT and fulfills the old or deprives it of power.

Heb. 8:13 takes up the promise of the "new covenant" of Jer. 31:31–34: "By calling this covenant 'new,' he has made the first one obsolete [*palaioō*]; and what is obsolete [*palaioō*] and aging will soon disappear." This is entirely God's work. In Christ the first covenant is regarded as old and fulfilled (2 Cor. 3:14). Indeed, it may be said that the NT speaks of the old only from the standpoint of the new and for the sake of the new.

3. *palaios* is used in another sense only in 1 Jn. 2:7. The writer is not communicating a "new command" to his readers, but the "old command" they had known "since the beginning," i.e., since their conversion. In the context of 2:1–6 "old" refers to the early Christian tradition, not to Lev. 19:18.

4094 (palaios, old), → *4093*.

4095 (palaiotēs, age, obsoleteness), → *4093*.

4096 (palaioō, grow old, make or treat as old), → *4093*.

| 4098 παλιγγενεσία | παλιγγενεσία (*palingenesia*), rebirth, regeneration (*4098*). |

CL & OT 1. *palingenesia* is a compound noun from *palin* (again) and *genesis* (birth, origin). In everyday speech it denotes various kinds of renewal: the return or restoration of something, termination of captivity, restoration to health following a birth or illness. The Stoics used the word in a cosmic context. The cosmos would periodically perish through a world conflagration and then arise anew in a rebirth (*palingenesia*). But for the Stoics, the cosmos did not attain to a new mode of being or quality through the rebirth; the world that has passed away was there once again. *palingenesia* was also used to express the rebirth of individuals in a new cosmic age.

The idea of rebirth occupied a significant place in the Hel. mystery religions. All of the mystery religions spoke about a deity who died and awoke to new life. In the cultic rites this was not taught as a doctrine, but represented in a dramatic way in which the initiate shared in the life-giving and renewing power of the deity. Rebirth was a renewal to a higher, divine existence.

2. *palingenesia* does not occur in the LXX. The closest phrase that one finds is *heōs palin genōmai*, a free rendering of Job 14:14: "If a man dies, will he live again?" There is no thought here of the rebirth of an individual in a new age, as in the NT. There is, however, the thought of eschatological renewal in Ezek. 11:19, where God promises his people a new heart and spirit (cf. Isa. 60:21; Jer. 24:7; 31:18, 33). This change is proclaimed as a future blessing of salvation that the Lord himself will bring about; the people are not themselves capable of such a change (Gen. 6:5; 8:21; Jer. 13:23). Therefore the person of faith prays to God: "Create in me a pure heart, O God, and renew a steadfast spirit within me" (Ps. 51:10).

One should also note the promises of a restoration of Israel (e.g., Isa. 11:11–6; Ezek. 36:24–38; Mic. 4:6–7), the establishment of a

new covenant (Jer. 31:31–32; Ezek. 34:25), the building of a new Jerusalem (Zech. 14:10–11, 16), and the creation of a new heaven and a new earth (Isa. 65:17). The NT idea of rebirth or regeneration thus appears to have its roots in the OT prophecy of restoration and renewal in the messianic age.

In Hel. Jud. *palingenesia* occurs frequently. Philo uses it to denote the renewal of the world after the flood and also of individuals. Josephus describes the revival of Israelite national life after the exile as the *palingenesia* of the land. In contrast to the Stoics, regeneration is unique and does not occur in cycles.

NT 1. *palingenesia* occurs only 2x. (a) Matt. 19:28 refers to the "renewal (*palingenesia*) of all things, when the Son of Man sits on his glorious throne." This is an eschatological term denoting the renewal of the world. Both the title of majesty "Son of Man" and the reference to judgment connect the regeneration with the end time (cf. Rev. 21:1–5). It may also denote the new lifestyle of those who participate in God's reign.

(b) Tit. 3:5 declares: "He saved us, not because of righteous things we had done, but because of his mercy. He saved us through the washing of rebirth (*palingenesias*) and renewal (*anakainōseōs*) by the Holy Spirit." *palingenesia* denotes a saving act of God, performed on humans but not by them (cf. 3:3–4). The imagery suggests baptism (cf. Eph. 5:26), in which believers receive the Holy Spirit (Acts 2:38; → *baptizō*, *966*). The washing and the reception of the Spirit are here seen as a unity (cf. Jn. 3:5). Those born again live in the hope that, in the righteousness of God that has been promised to them, they will be heirs of and participants in future life. In this renewal a new lifestyle, opposite the former one (Tit. 3:3), becomes possible. Regeneration does not, however, bring sinless perfection. Rather, it leads to daily renunciation of worldly passions and to sober, upright, godly living in this world (2:12).

2. Alongside and linked in meaning to *palingenesia* and the corresponding vb. *anagennaō* (→ *gennaō*, *1164*) are *anakainoō* (renew) and *anakainōsis* (renewal); on these, → *kainos*, *2785*.

See also *gennaō*, beget, become the father of, bear (*1164*); *ginomai*, be born, become, happen (*1181*); *ektrōma*, miscarriage (*1765*); *tiktō*, bring forth, bear, give birth to (*5503*); *eugenēs*, well-born, noble in descent or character (*2302*).

4110 (panoplia, full armor, panoply), → *4483*.

| 4111 πανουργία | πανουργία (*panourgia*), craftiness, cunning (*4111*); πανοῦρ- |

γος (*panourgos*), crafty, cunning, knavish (*4112*).

CL & OT The word group derives from the two roots *pan-* (all) and *erg-* (work), giving the basic meaning "capable of all work." In cl. Gk. its connotation is usually pejorative, an unprincipled "capable of doing anything." In the few instances where the word bears a positive sense, there is a hint of arrogance or perhaps deceptive evaluation.

In the LXX, the word group can mean crafty, sly (e.g., Jos. 9:4; Job 5:12), but in Prov., where it occurs most frequently, it takes on an unconditionally positive nuance: prudent, clever (1:4; 8:5; 12:16; 13:1; 21:11; 28:2). *panourgia* has been invested with new meaning, probably due in part to the belief that the person who fears God and is blessed by him can indeed successfully accomplish any task.

Positive uses continue in the Apocr. (e.g., Sir. 6:32; 21:20), where *panourgia* derives from wisdom springing from divine revelation. When, however, *panourgia* throws off this restriction, it degenerates to *panourgia* in the negative sense (21:12; cf. 19:25). In both Josephus and Philo, the term is consistently negative and heads a long list of vices.

NT In light of this background, it is perhaps surprising that *panourgia* is used only negatively in its 5 NT appearances. The scribes and chief priests are guilty of "duplicity" in their question to Jesus (Lk.

20:23). God catches the wise in their "craftiness" (1 Cor. 3:19), since one's ability to reason cannot stand up against divine sovereignty. Opponents of the truth are accused of deceptively distorting God's Word (2 Cor. 4:2; Eph. 4:14); therefore Paul fears that the minds of the Corinthian converts might be led astray from purity of devotion to Christ, as the serpent by his "cunning" deceived Eve (2 Cor. 11:3). The one occurrence of *panourgos* in the NT bears the added weight of irony (12:16): Paul claims he is "crafty," meaning, however, that he is not.

4112 (panourgos, crafty, cunning, knavish), → *4111.*

4120 (pantokratōr, the Almighty), → *3197.*

4123	παρά

παρά (*para*), beside, alongside (*4123*).

CL This is one of the few Gk. preps. that occurs in all three cases. In the gen. it means (in general) from the side of, in the dat. at the side of, and in the acc. to the side of.

NT 1. *Basic sense.* In the NT *para* occurs with all three cases. With the acc. (60x) it generally designates movement to a position beside (Mk. 4:4; Acts 4:35); with the gen. (78x), movement from beside (Jn. 1:6); with the dat. (50x), rest or position beside (Lk. 9:47; Jn. 8:38; 19:25).

2. *Extended meaning.* By transference from the local sense this prep. bears with the gen., *para* with the acc. came to mean "beyond," then "contrary to." Thus, when Paul anathematized anyone who preached a gospel "other than" (*para*) the gospel he proclaimed and the Galatians had received (Gal. 1:8–9), he implies that Judaistic teaching was not conforming to the apostolic norm. The opposite of *para* in this sense is *kata* (in accordance with, → *2848*).

para can also mark a comparison by indicating that one thing lies beyond and therefore is superior to something else (e.g., Rom. 14:5, "one man considers one day more sacred than [*para*] another"). When this comparison is heightened, the sense is not merely one of preference ("more than") but of exclusiveness ("instead of"). One aspect of Paul's indictment of humankind in Rom. 1:18–32 is that they worshiped and served created things "rather than" the Creator (1:25). In Lk. 18:14 the tax collector went home justified "rather than" the Pharisee.

The phrase *para* [*tō*] *theō* (lit., "in the sight [judgment] of God"; Rom. 2:13; 1 Cor. 3:19; 7:24; Jas. 1:27; 1 Pet. 2:20) indicates the ultimate standard—the purity of the divine life and the clarity of the divine vision—by which all aspects of thought and conduct, whether human or angelic, should now be assessed and will in the end be judged.

3. *In the Gospel of Jn.* Here *para* figures prominently in denoting the relation of the Son to the Father, where "is from [beside]" (6:46; 7:29; 9:33) means "came from [beside]" (16:27–28; 17:8). In 1:14, "from [*para*] the Father" (following "the One and Only") denotes that the Son's mission can be traced back to God the Father. Note also that not only Jesus (9:33) but also John the Baptist came "from" God (1:6). Similarly, 15:26 explains that Christ sent the Spirit "from [*para*] the Father," just as the Son himself came forth "from [*ek*, → *1666*] God" (8:42).

4124 (parabainō, go aside, turn aside, transgress), → *4126.*

4125 (paraballō, throw alongside, compare), → *4130.*

4126	παράβασις

παράβασις (*parabasis*), overstepping, transgression (*4126*); παραβαίνω (*parabainō*), go aside, turn aside, transgress (*4124*); παραβάτης (*parabatēs*), transgressor (*4127*); ἀπαράβατος (*aparabatos*), unchangeable (*563*); ὑπερβαίνω (*hyperbainō*), overstep, transgress (*5648*).

CL & OT 1. (a) In cl. Gk. the vb. *parabainō* lit. means to walk beside, go beside, pass by, and refers both in its spatial and fig. senses to deviation from an original and true direction. Trans. the vb. means

to transgress, neglect. It takes as its objects those words that the Gks. used to indicate the standard and norm by which they regulated their lives: e.g., righteousness, law, oath, morals, etc. Later *parabainō* was used absolutely to mean sin, usually some obligation that is not kept. It was also used in a religious context in the sense of ceasing to reverence the gods.

(b) *parabasis* is found with the same objects as *parabainō*; it is seldom used absolutely. It is used either spatially or fig. of deviation, trespassing, transgressing. Almost nowhere does *parabatēs* occur in a fig. sense. It means a bystander, comrade, companion. *aparabatos*, a rare word, means that which cannot be superseded, thus unchangeable, inviolable, eternal.

(c) *hyperbainō* follows the many senses of its prefix. Lit. it means to step over, go over the bank, thence injure, transgress, err, but also presume, pass over someone in silence.

2. This group of words is not common in the LXX; where they do occur, the fig. sense predominates. *parabatēs*, transgressor, evildoer, occurs only in Sym. (Ps. 17:4; 139:19; Jer. 6:28). *parabainō* occurs ca. 80x and has such meanings as pass on, cross over, turn aside, deviate. The objects associated with *parabainō* are such things as God's words (Num. 14:41; Deut. 1:43), the word of the Lord (1 Sam. 15:24), legal demands (1 Esd. 1:48), and esp. often the covenant (Jos. 7:11; Ezek. 16:59; 17:15–19; Hos. 6:7 = LXX 6:8; 8:1). The noun *parabasis* is associated with more general concepts (way, word, covenant) rather than with individual commandments. Thus its basic meaning in the LXX is to neglect God, break the covenant, fail to maintain an obedient relationship with God (see 2 Ki. 2:24; Ps. 101:3; Wis. 14:31; 2 Macc. 15:10).

NT The NT's use of these concepts follows on from that of the OT. While *adikia* (→ *94*) and *anomia* (→ *nomos,* law, *3795*) are conceived of in general terms and refer to injustice in the sense of antisocial and unlawful actions, and while *asebeia*, irreverence (→ *sebō,* to revere, *4936*), and *hamartia* (sin, *281*) are oriented toward the person of God, *parabasis* is related to God's gracious ordinances, such as his covenant (Heb. 9:15) and law (Rom. 2:23–27; 4:15; Jas. 2:9–11), his commands and tradition (Matt. 15:2–3). Since those OT ordinances of God appear in a completely new light on account of the Christ-event, *hamartia* becomes the essential idea of sin, while *parabasis* decreases sharply in importance.

1. (a) In Matt. 15:1–6 *parabainō* is associated with *paradosis*, tradition, and *entolē*, command. Jesus is attacking the superficiality of the Pharisees' observance of the law. He turns the charge of *parabasis* back on them and shows that when the kingdom arrives, it is not the Pharisaic law that will matter but the new dispensation (e.g., as described in the Sermon on the Mount). The OT law is not abandoned (cf. 5:17–18), but in the light of this new dispensation the *paradosis* of the Pharisees is shown to be but a human ordinance.

(b) The original spatial meaning of these words is still recognizable in Acts 1:25. Judas's sin consisted in abandoning his place or position of service in order to go his own way. Judas has abandoned his discipleship.

2. Almost all the instances of the nouns *parabasis* and *parabatēs* occur in Paul's letters. (Jas. 2:9–11 is an exception; sin is here understood as transgression of the law.) As in Matt. 15, so also in Paul the law is no longer central in the Christian faith. It has been displaced from its function as a way of salvation by faith, which is made possible through the coming, death, and resurrection of Jesus Christ. Thus the concept chiefly appears in Paul where he is involved in argument with Jewish law theology.

(a) By their transgression of the law the Jews stand before God as sinners, just as the Gentiles do (Rom. 2:17–29). They are ostensibly striving to obtain God's righteousness, but their actions show that they fall far short of it. Nevertheless, God's claim on both Jew and Gentile is binding (2:14–15). God is still the judge who demands good works, even of Christians (1:18–3:20; 2 Cor. 5:10).

(b) Faith in Christ does not replace the law, but it provides a way to righteousness even for those who do not know the law and therefore cannot transgress it. By faith they can become children of Abraham (Rom. 4:13–16) and receive a share in the promise. Therefore *parabasis* can no longer be the main content of the concept of sin, as it was for the Jews. Sin is measured by God himself and no longer by the law alone. Only in 4:14–20 is sin as a universal fact referred to as a "transgression" (*parabasis*). This is because Adam is a type of sin as the transgressing of God's commandment.

(c) Christ renders the way of the law as a way of salvation powerless and replaces it with faith in him. From faith comes righteousness (Gal. 3:22–25). What part does the law now play? Paul's answer in 3:19 is that the law's purpose in the history of salvation lies in its function of showing sin to be sin. It stirs us up to transgression (cf. Rom. 5:20) and so leads us to sin; in this process, it ultimately leads us to Christ (7:7–12).

3. (a) In 1 Tim. 2:14 Paul amplifies Rom. 5:14 in the light of the narrative of Gen. 2–3 (on the role of Eve, → *Heua*, *2293*). In these passages human sin is presented as a rebellion against God and his commandment.

(b) Heb. 2:2 and 9:15 speak of *parabasis* in the context of the OT period. The allusion to the punishing of *parabasis* and disobedience in the OT serves to underline the warning in 2:2 against neglecting the salvation given in Christ; 9:15 stresses the significance of Jesus' death as redemption from the transgressions committed under the first covenant.

4. *aparabatos*, unchangeable, occurs only in Heb. 7:24, where it retains a clear echo of the lit. meaning. The OT priesthood, which was tied up with the law and thus was liable to violation and transgression (7:11), is contrasted with Jesus' priesthood, which is eternal and unchangeable; it is not exposed to any *parabasis*.

5. *hyperbainō* occurs only in 1 Thess. 4:6, where Paul instructs believers not to "wrong" each other.

See also *adikia*, wrongdoing, unrighteousness, injustice (*94*); *hamartia*, sin (*281*); *paraptōma*, transgression, trespass, false step, sin (*4183*).

4127 (parabatēs, transgressor), → *4126*.

4130	παραβολή

παραβολή (*parabolē*), type, figure, parable (*4130*); παραβάλλω (*paraballō*), throw alongside, compare (*4125*); αἴνιγμα (*ainigma*), riddle, indistinct image (*141*); ἀλληγορέω (*allēgoreo*), speak allegorically (*251*).

CL & OT 1. In cl. Gk. *parabolē* is derived from *paraballō*, to place alongside, compare. It has such meanings as comparison, meeting, venture. (a) In cl. rhetoric *parabolē* became the technical term for a specific form of speech alongside other figures of speech, such as metaphors, comparisons, images, illustrative stories, and allegories. In these what is unknown is compared with what is known to the listener, in order to help that person grasp a certain truth. In general, the imagery is drawn from life.

(b) In rhetoric allegory is clearly distinguished from the other forms. The vb. *allēgoreo* probably originated in Hel. times and means to speak allegorically or to allegorize. Allegorizing has always played an important role in sacred writings. When they become antiquated, a new, contemporary content is injected into them by means of allegorical explanations so that their canonical authority is preserved.

(c) *ainigma*, dark or puzzling saying, riddle, is the opposite of a plain, straightforward, or simple word. Though it may use the literary form of metaphor, it should be understood as a wise saying. The riddle was considered, therefore, as a touchstone of wisdom.

2. In the LXX *parabolē* is always the equivalent of the Heb. noun *māšal* or the vb. *māšal*. The Heb. noun denotes a saying that contains a comparison or taunt or a wise saying, perhaps in parabolic form. The Heb. vb. means to speak or tell a *māšal*.

(a) The vb. *māšal* acquired a broad semantic field. It was used first of all as a technical term for various types or forms of comparisons. Thus the noun *māšal*, in popular speech, means a proverb (→ *paroimia*, *4231*), which often contains a comparison (1 Sam. 10:12; 24:14; Ezek. 18:2). If the saying makes fun of a person or disparages one as a bad example, it denotes a taunt (Isa. 14:4; Hab. 2:6).

(b) Later *māšal* became a technical term among the wise and meant a wise saying, rich in comparisons (cf. Prov. 26:7, 9) and the instruction of the wise. In the LXX the superscription to Prov. and the collections within it carry the word *paroimia* (1:1) or *paideia* (25:1; → *paideuō*, *4084*) as the translation of *māšal*. The wise person in the OT loves the enigmatic, dark saying. In this context *māšal* approaches the Heb. word *ḥîdâ*, riddle, for which it can even be used as a synonym (1:6).

(c) The LXX translates *ḥîdâ* appropriately by *ainigma*, i.e., riddle, dark saying. The riddle (1 Ki. 10:1; 2 Chr. 9:1) was part of the cult of wisdom at Solomon's court and has its place in the wisdom lit. (Prov. 1:6). The only OT riddle given word for word is in Jdg. 14:12–20. An *ainigma* requires explanation. God speaks to humans—though not to Moses—in *ainigma*-type language (Num. 12:8); prophetic speech also is enigmatic (Ezek. 17:2).

(d) In the realm of prophecy (→ *prophēteia*, *4735*) *māšal* has its place. On the one hand, it occurs as proverb and taunt (see above). On the other hand, although the word is not present, various parabolic forms occur in prophecies. The later prophets used more developed forms of *māšal* in order to clarify, strengthen, and lend urgency to their messages. Allegory, too, aims at urgency, but goes about it another way: through a certain veiling of the truth, it seeks to attract the attention of the listener. In the latest OT books, actual allegorical visions occur (e.g., Dan. 2; 4; 7; 8; Zech.; 2 Esd. 9:26–13:56). The symbolic actions of the prophets, whose meaning is called *māšal*, stand in close relationship to the prophetic parables.

NT In the NT *parabolē* occurs only in the Synoptic Gospels (48x) and in Heb. (2x); *ainigma* only in 1 Cor. 13:12; and *allēgoreō* only in Gal. 4:24. *parabolē* in the NT has the following meanings.

1. The ritual of the tabernacle is seen as a *parabolē* ("illustration") of the time of salvation (Heb. 9:9), and the restoration of Isaac as a picture of the resurrection ("figuratively speaking, he did receive Isaac back," 11:19). In Matt. 15:15; Mk. 7:17 *parabolē* means a saying, and in Lk. 4:23 a proverb. In all other occurrences in the NT it has the meaning of parable in one or other of its various senses, as listed below.

(a) In *figurative sayings* image and reality are placed together without a comparative adv. (as), so that the image (the known) may elucidate the reality (the unknown): e.g., "You are the light of the world" (Matt. 5:14). This type of saying takes on the character of a metaphor.

(b) The *metaphor* is a fig. expression in which a name or descriptive term is applied to some object to which it is not literally and properly applicable. It often involves the transference of the concrete to the abstract: e.g., "Enter through the narrow gate" (Matt. 7:13), where access to the kingdom is viewed as that which requires effort and difficulty. Similarly, the mission of the church is viewed as a harvest (9:37–38). Metaphor places the image not beside the reality, as in the figurative saying, but in place of the reality. One has to know beforehand what reality lies behind the metaphor or it remains unintelligible.

(c) The *simile* is a sentence in which reality and image are placed beside one another by means of a comparative adv., e.g., "as" or "like." In this case there is only one principal point of comparison: e.g., "Be as shrewd as snakes and as innocent as doves" (Matt. 10:16). Similes are not frequent, since often the concept has passed over into a metaphor.

(d) The *parable* is a story that has developed out of a simile or a figurative saying. Two similar things, events, or situations are compared, so that the known can elucidate the unknown. The image depicts a typical event or circumstance, and there is, strictly speaking, only one main point of comparison: e.g., "The kingdom of heaven is like yeast . . ." (Matt. 13:33).

(e) The *parabolic story* differs from the pure parable only in that its picture, which is a fictional story, is recounted as if it had once happened. Thus, the parabolic story of the unjust judge begins: "In a certain town there was a judge . . ." (Lk. 18:2–5).

(f) The *illustrative story* is a freely invented story that gives an example, a model case, that has to be generalized by the hearer. Thus the story of the good Samaritan ends with Jesus saying: "Go and do likewise" (Lk. 10:37). Conversely, the illustrative story of the Pharisee and the tax collector in the temple ends with a statement about who will be justified (18:10–14). It is noteworthy that the NT illustrative stories occur only in Lk.

(g) An *allegory* is a freely invented story that says something other than it appears to say on the surface by heaping metaphor on metaphor. It is a continuous metaphor: e.g., "The kingdom of heaven is like a king who prepared a wedding banquet for his son . . ." (Matt. 22:2–10). Like metaphor, allegory rests on convention. It is only intelligible when the metaphors are known, for they have to be translated step by step, and when the matter they depict is known. It is a literary form intelligible only to the initiated. Ezek. 17:12–21 offers a model exposition. Allegories of this kind occur in the NT, but they are designated *parabolē*, not *allēgoria* (e.g., Matt. 22:1).

2. In the interpretation of parables, several general principles should be kept in mind. (a) In parables and the related forms a distinction may be drawn between the image and the reality. The purpose of the parable comes where these two halves intersect, the point of comparison.

(b) The story portion of the parable is usually told as concisely and simply as possible. Irrelevant emotions and motives are not disclosed. In most instances there are no more than three characters or groups of characters in a parable and never more than two actors in one scene. If the conclusion is self-evident, it may be omitted.

(c) In general, the drama of the parable is recounted from only one point of view, though there are exceptions to this rule.

(d) For the expositor the stress comes at the end of the parable.

(e) The material for the drama is taken from the world of the hearer and reflects his or her experiences and thoughts. Frequently a parable is told in response to a question, which draws the listener into the parable and may even find him or her portrayed in the parable.

(f) Still, many parables have acquired new addressees in the course of their transmission, so that a parable originally directed to, e.g., an expert in the law (Lk. 10:25–37) becomes relevant to the disciples and even to believers today.

3. The NT parables contain the same Christological significance as the miracle narratives. There are two main groups of themes, the kingdom of God and repentance. (a) The parables of growth belong to the first group (Matt. 13; Mk. 4; Lk. 8; 13:18–21) as do the parables that speak of God and his activity (Matt. 20:1–16; 25:14–30; Lk. 15:11–32). (b) The second group enjoins the urgency of repentance (12:16–21; 13:6–9), which demands decisive (16:1–8), radical (Matt. 13:44–46) and watchful action (24:42–25:13), because the kingdom is near. The parables that speak of action towards one's neighbor also belong to this group (18:23–35; Lk. 10:30–37).

4. A number of parables are contained in *Gospel of Thomas*, a 4th-cent. Coptic document found around 1945. This work is a collection of 114 sayings attributed to Jesus. Some parables are substantially the same as those contained in the canonical Gospels: e.g., the sower (No. 9), the mustard seed (No. 20), the rich fool (No. 63), and the great supper (No. 64). Some parables appear to have a significantly different thrust from the canonical Gospels (e.g., the parable of the lost sheep, No. 107, the thrust of which is the love of the shepherd for the one lost sheep more than all the others), and some parables are entirely new (e.g., No. 97, about a woman who carries a jar of meal a long way but inadvertently loses all of its contents by the time she reaches home).

5. One of the most puzzling elements in the interpretation of parables is their expressed purpose as stated in Mk. 4:10–11 (cf. Matt. 13:10–15; Lk. 8:9–10). One might gather from this that Jesus told parables to confuse people rather than to enlighten them. Several comments can be made here. (a) The "so that" (*hina*) clause of Mk. 4:12 can be understood as a result clause rather than as a purpose clause. In other words, for those who do not care to delve into the personal meaning of a parable, the result is that they will understand the story but not its eschatological meaning.

(b) In Mk. 4:12 the *hina* clause introduces an OT quotation (Isa. 6:9–10). Through Jesus' telling parables, he is fulfilling the prophecy given in the time of Isaiah, that to people hardened by unbelief, all preaching falls on deaf ears. In view of this general statement about the way God works, Mk. 4:12 deals not only with Jesus' parables but with his preaching in general.

(c) We should also recognize that, if considered by themselves, the meaning of the stories told in the parables is not always clear (e.g., if a preacher today told, as the entire sermon, a really good story, then sent the people home, they might wonder, "What's the point?"). Jesus wanted his dedicated followers to probe further the significance of his stories and to ask him about them, precisely as the disciples did (Mk. 4:10). This process separated the dedicated followers of Jesus from the merely curious, who came to be entertained by Jesus' story-telling ability. The truth about God and humankind cannot be learned as if it were a series of mere facts that involves no personal commitment.

6. Apart from the use of *parabolē* and the numerous instances of verbal parables in the Gospels, one may also speak of the parabolic *actions* of Jesus. Just as OT prophets sometimes performed symbolic acts that were in themselves a message from Yahweh to those with eyes to see (e.g., Hosea's marriage to an adulteress [1:2–3:5], Jeremiah's purchase of a field [32:7–15]), so also some of Jesus' actions may be construed as unspoken parables. Such actions might include his characteristic reception of outcasts (Lk. 15:1–2; 19:5–6), his endorsement of the disciples' plucking of grain on the Sabbath (Matt. 12:1–8; Mk. 2:23–28; Lk. 6:1–5), his choosing of twelve disciples (patterned on the twelve tribes of Israel [→ *dōdeka*, *1557*]), his entry into Jerusalem (Matt. 21:1–9; Mk. 11:1–10; Lk. 19:29–38), and the Last Supper (→ *deipnon*, *1270*).

7. The vb. *allēgoreō* occurs only in Gal. 4:24. Note first of all that "allegory" here is not related to "allegory" as defined in 1(g), above. There an allegory is a continuous metaphor that includes within itself the intention of having more than one point and has the various characters and elements in the story each representing something. What we are discussing in this paragraph is the allegorical interpretation of sacred writings (cf. the cl. Gk. section, above). The Scriptures have undergone a long history of allegorical interpretation, beginning already with Philo's method of interpreting the Jewish law in terms of the Hellenistic philosophy (ca. 20 B.C.–ca. A.D. 50). In this process, the OT is "found" to contain hidden, spiritual meanings that are often significantly different from the apparently intended or historical ones. Such meanings are read into a story in a way alien to its original intention.

Does Paul use allegory in this sense in Gal. 4:24–31? In this passage the apostle relates Hagar to the old covenant delivered at Mount Sinai. He goes on to compare Mount Sinai with the present Jerusalem, symbolizing bondage to the law, which contrasts with the Jerusalem that is above, which is free and is "our mother." Though the passage may appear somewhat fanciful, a strong case can be made that Paul is here dealing with typology (→ *typos*, *5596*), not allegory, as it came to be understood in the history of the church.

What about a passage like 1 Cor. 9:9, where Paul appeals to Deut. 25:4 in support of his contention that apostles have the right to be supported by the church (cf. 1 Tim. 5:18)? Some have charged Paul with inappropriate allegory here. But one should note that there is a common principle here underlying the original OT pronouncement and the application Paul draws: Those who labor on anything (whether a human or animal) have the right to sustenance for their work. This applies to the quotation from Deut. 25:4 and to all the other illustrations that Paul adduces in support of the point.

8. The riddle or dark saying (*ainigma*) is not a NT literary form. The word occurs only at 1 Cor. 13:12 in the NT. In the context Paul is contrasting knowledge with faith, hope, and love (13:13) and points out (lit.), "For now we look through a glass in a riddle." Looking glasses were made at Corinth, and the fact that they do not give a direct vision of reality underlines Paul's point about the limitations of knowledge. The preposition *dia* (through) is to be explained by the fact that the image in the mirror appears to lie on the further side. "In a riddle" may be based on Num. 12:8, where God says that he will speak to Moses "face to face, clearly and not in riddles," (i.e., not obscurely). For Paul what we apprehend in the present life is like a riddle; it is obscure and enigmatic. It contrasts with knowledge in the future state, when "we shall see face to face" and "know fully, even as [we are] fully known" (1 Cor. 12:12; cf. Matt. 5:8).

See also *paroimia*, proverb, wise saying; dark saying, riddle (*4231*).

4132 (*parangelia*, order, command, precept, advice), → *4133*.

4133	παραγγέλλω

παραγγέλλω (*parangellō*), give orders, command, instruct, direct (*4133*); παραγγελία (*parangelia*), order, command, precept, advice (*4132*).

CL & OT *parangellō* (vb.) and *parangelia* (noun) mean order or command. These words were used by persons of different kinds of authority, such as military commands, the instructions of the philosophers, and even the instructions of a god. The essential element is that someone is put under an obligation.

The noun does not occur in the LXX (though 1 Sam. 22:14 has *parangelma*). The vb. is used of the military proclamations of kings and generals (1 Sam. 15:4; 23:8), the command of leaders (Jos. 6:7 = LXX 6:8; 2 Chr. 36:22), etc. The instructions of Daniel and Judas Maccabaeus also had a religious character (Dan. 2:18; 2 Macc. 13:10). However, Nebuchadnezzar's command to worship the image of his cult was opposed to God (Dan. 3:4).

NT 1. Both words are used in the NT in a general sense, such as the command given by the authorities at Philippi to imprison Paul and Silas (Acts 16:23–24; see also 4:18; 5:28, 40; 23:22, 30). In the early church were Jewish Christians who claimed that Gentile Christians should be "circumcised and *required* to obey the law of Moses" (15:5).

2. In the Gospels only the vb. is used and exclusively for Jesus' commands. In the feeding of the four thousand, for example, Jesus commanded the crowd to sit down on the ground (Matt. 15:35; Mk. 8:6; see also Lk. 5:14; 8:29, 56; 9:21; Acts 16:18). The statements in Matt. 10:5 and Mk. 6:8 refer to the instructions the Lord gave to the disciples when he sent them out. The risen Christ commanded his disciples not to leave Jerusalem before Pentecost (Acts 1:4). The authority of Jesus continued in the apostolic preaching, which stood under the command of Jesus and through which God commands everyone to repent (10:42; 17:30).

3. The apostolic letters present the same picture. Paul based his prohibition of divorce on the "command" of the Lord (1 Cor. 7:10). Here he distinguished between Jesus' authority and his own, showing that the commands he gave "from the Lord" were binding for the church (7:25; cf. also 1 Thess. 4:2). Apostolic authority lay behind the directions for the behavior of women in worship and the exhortations to Christians to behave respectably in a pagan world and to work in peace and eat their own bread (1 Cor. 11:17; 1 Thess. 4:11; 2 Thess. 3:12). Regardless of whether the instructions were written or oral, the apostle expected the church to comply with them. They were to keep away from anyone who did not walk according to such commands (2 Thess. 3:4, 6, 10–15).

In 1 Tim. 6:13–14 Paul commanded (*parangellō*) Timothy, "Keep this command [*entolē*] without spot or blame until the appearing of our Lord Jesus Christ." Earlier he writes, "The goal of this command (*parangelia*) is love, which comes from a pure heart and a good conscience and a sincere faith" (1:5). Timothy is therefore charged to wage a good warfare (1:18) and to "command certain men not to teach false doctrines any longer" (1:3). The solemn appeal to God and Christ makes clear the nature of authority behind the apostolic commands (6:13–14).

See also *dogma*, decree, ordinance, command (*1504*); *entolē*, command, order (*1953*); *keleuō*, command, order (*3027*).

4136 (*paradeigmatizō*, expose to public disgrace, make an example of), → *1259*.

4137	παράδεισος

παράδεισος (*paradeisos*), garden, park, paradise (*4137*).

CL & OT 1. In cl. Gk. *paradeisos*, a loanword from the Middle Iranian, means a garden, park, or paradise. Myths from many nations speak of a land or a place of blessedness in primeval times or on the present edge of the known world, where the gods lived and where distinguished mortals were carried away after death.

2. In the LXX the word is found 46x, mostly as trans. of Heb. words meaning garden. Of these passages it occurs 13x in Gen. 2–3, 4x in Ezek., and 3x in Isa. In each case the reference is to the garden of God, present or future. In Neh. 2:8; Eccl. 2:5; Song 4:13 it means orchard, forest.

(a) Though there is no full description of *paradeisos* in the OT, a few common motifs appear: the tree of life, the tree of knowledge, the water of life (Gen. 2–3; 13:10; Ezek. 28:13; 31:8–9). Paradise is conceived of as a lovely orchard in which both the tree of life and the tree of knowledge stood. Here God walked and handed over the garden to humankind for cultivation. As a result of the first sin, Adam and Eve were driven out of paradise. Return to it is impossible, since a cherub guards all access.

(b) Later Jewish writers wrote numerous speculations about the paradise of Gen. 2–3. For example, because of Adam's sin it was removed and hidden at the edges of the earth, on a high mountain, or in heaven. With the infiltration of the Gk. doctrine of the immortality of the soul, paradise became the dwelling place of the righteous during the intermediate state. Pious imagination increasingly embellished the conception of paradise: It had walls and gates, angels watched over it, light shone on the righteous, the tree of life was within it, and fragrant streams flowed through it.

In a renewed creation paradise will emerge from its concealment. God or the Messiah will bring it to a renewed earth, to Palestine, near Jerusalem. The righteous will study the Torah there, and God will prepare for them a messianic meal. Above all, they may then enjoy the fruit of the tree of life.

NT 1. In the NT *paradeisos* occurs only 3x. (a) Lk. 23:43 may reflect contemporary Jewish conceptions that refer to the hidden and intermediate abode of the righteous. Jesus promises the criminal on the cross fellowship with him "today . . . in paradise" and thus allows him to share in forgiveness and blessedness. The intermediate state thereby becomes essentially fellowship with Christ (cf. Acts 7:56; 2 Cor. 5:8; Phil. 1:23).

(b) In 2 Cor. 12:4 Paul speaks of a personal experience in the Spirit in which he was "caught up to paradise" and there heard words that a person is "not permitted to tell." This statement is parallel to what he says in 12:2 about being "caught up to the third heaven." Paul's reference to this experience "fourteen years ago" underlines the fact that it occurred long before the foundation of the Corinthian church. That this visionary experience took place either "in the body or out of the body" (he is not sure) rules out the Damascus road experience, for Paul did not regard this as a vision.

Ancient cosmology pictured three, five, seven, or ten heavens, three being a commonly accepted number. Paul's use of "the third heaven" and "paradise" may reflect a widely accepted image for something that by his own account is indescribable (cf. 2 Cor. 12:4). The idea of hearing "inexpressible things" is possibly related to the idea of a sealed revelation found in the OT (Isa. 8:16; Dan. 12:4; cf. Rev. 14:3), though similar language is found also in the mystery religions and in apocalyptic writings of Paul's day. In all this the apostle is using contemporary images of the transcendent world to describe an ecstatic experience that was evidently far more impressive than anything of which his opponents could boast. But this experience was something for his own private, personal edification. What a Christian should boast about is one's weaknesses, that God may be glorified in and through him or her.

(c) In Rev. 2:7 the Spirit promises to the church of Ephesus: "To him who overcomes, I will give the right to eat from the tree of life, which is in the paradise of God." This takes up the thought of Gen. 3, where after the fall humanity was barred from the tree of life. Those who overcome the trials and temptations of this world are promised not only restoration of what Adam lost but access to life in a way that Adam never had. Note also Rev. 22:1–2, 14, which gives a final vision of the tree of life in the new Jerusalem, which though not called paradise in Rev., is related to paradise in other pseudepigraphical writings.

2. In the course of church history many extrabiblical motifs, pictures, and ideas have been absorbed into the conception of paradise, in order to paint the state of the blessed after death in bright colors. Jesus' statement to the criminal (Lk. 23:43) was generalized and referred to every believer. Moreover, with the increased popularity of the doctrine of the immortality of the soul, theologians insisted that the soul receives judgment after death and attains to paradise (thought of as other-worldly), whereas sinners go to hell. In such doctrinal works, the images of Rev. 21–22 are used to describe heaven and paradise.

4140	παραδίδωμι

παραδίδωμι (*paradidōmi*), deliver up, give up, hand over; to hand down, pass on, transmit (*4140*); παράδοσις (*paradosis*), tradition (*4142*).

CL & OT 1. (a) In cl. Gk. *paradidōmi* denotes all aspects of deliberate giving or giving over: to deliver up, give away, offer, hand over, betray. As a legal term, it means to bring before a court, deliver up a prisoner. It extends from the handing over of a captive to the reprehensible act of betrayal, whereby a free man of good repute, who may well be innocent, is ruined.

(b) The vb. can also have a positive sense of hand down, pass on instruction from teacher to pupil. In the Hel. mystery religions the word is used in connection with the delivery of a holy teaching.

(c) The noun *paradosis* denotes (actively) a handing down, (passively) that which is handed down, tradition.

2. (a) The LXX uses *paradidōmi* about 200x. Roughly 150x it translates the Heb. *nātan*, to give, hand over, deliver. The formula "to deliver into someone's hands" stems ultimately from the wars of Yahweh. The subject of this vb. is almost always God, and that in most cases implies handing over to ruin, defeat, or death. Before a battle began, a priest or a prophet would consult the Lord; if all was well, Yahweh would deliver the enemy into Israel's hand. But if Israel was disobedient, Yahweh would deliver them into the hands of their enemies (Jdg. 2:14; 6:13; Isa. 65:12; Jer. 32:4 = LXX 39:4). In Deut. the formula came to mean the annihilation of the earlier inhabitants of the land (e.g., 1:8). Note esp. the analogous use of this vb. in Isa. 53:6, 12, where the Lord delivered over his servant to death for our sins.

(b) In the other use of *paradidōmi*, the handing down of sagas, narratives, laws, and lists of names (tradition properly so-called) came into being when Jud. was confronted with aggressive Hellenism in the last two centuries B.C. and with Christianity in the 1st cent. A.D. The Heb. word *māsar*, translated *paradidōmi*, refers to the strictly regulated process of handing down received expositions of the law. Josephus characteristically uses the expression "the tradition [*paradosis*] of the fathers"

for the scribes' oral exposition of Torah. The Heb. equivalent is *māsōret*, which occurs in the OT only in Ezek. 20:37. Much later this led to the term "Masoretic," the officially handed-down text of the OT.

NT In the NT *paradidōmi* occurs 119x; *paradosis* 13x (Matt. 15; Mk. 7, and 5x in Paul, all in the sense of the transmission of doctrine).

1. The most common meaning of *paradidōmi* in the NT is to deliver up to judgment and death. (a) John the Baptist's being delivered up (Matt. 4:12) signifies his imprisonment leading to his execution. The adversary delivers to the judge (5:25), and the judge to the officer (Lk. 12:58). Jesus' followers will be delivered to the council (Matt. 10:17) and to synagogues (Lk. 21:12) and exposed to persecution and oppression (Matt. 24:9). Brother will be delivered up by brother to death (Mk. 13:12; cf. also Acts 8:3; 12:4; 22:4).

(b) Most of the passages in which *paradidōmi* occurs, however, refer to Jesus' being betrayed or delivered up "into the hands of men" (Matt. 17:22), to the high priests and scribes (20:18), to the Gentiles (20:19), to Pilate (27:2), and to crucifixion (26:2; cf. also 1 Cor. 11:23). Judas, the person who delivered him up, is the betrayer. This frequent use of *paradidōmi* in the NT reflects its technical legal use.

(c) The vb. is occasionally used for deliverance to something other than a human court, such as to "the sinful desires of their hearts" (Rom. 1:24). The Gentiles "have given themselves over to sensuality," which in itself is a judgment (Eph. 4:19); likewise, God gave Israel "over to the worship of the heavenly bodies" (Acts 7:42). In 1 Cor. 5:5 and 1 Tim. 1:20 Paul delivers men to Satan, the executor of the divine judgment.

(d) Finally, *paradidōmi* is found in the context of giving up one's life (Jn. 19:30), risking one's life (Acts 15:26), and Jesus' giving himself up for us (Gal. 2:20; cf. Eph. 5:25).

2. In a number of passages, however, *paradidōmi* occurs in a context other than that of judgment and death. (a) It can denote Jesus' messianic sovereignty, in the sense of things having been committed to him by his Father (Matt. 11:27; Lk. 10:22; cf. 1 Cor. 15:24). But the devil also asserts he can grant power to whomsoever he will, since it has been placed at his disposal (Lk. 4:6). In Acts 14:26 Paul and Barnabas in Antioch are "committed to the grace of God," i.e., placed under its protective power.

(b) The vb. also conveys the idea of handing down tradition, both in Jewish and Christian circles. In Mk. 7:13, the obj. of *paradidōmi* is the rab. exposition of the law. Similarly, in Acts 6:14 false witnesses testify against Stephen that the Jesus whom he preaches will change the customs Moses "handed down."

(c) In Acts 16:4 Luke uses *paradidōmi* in connection with the decisions of the apostolic council that Paul handed over to the churches in Lycaonia and elsewhere. The use of this vb. in Lk. 1:2 is significant. Its obj. is the account of those who from the beginning were eyewitnesses of Jesus' life. The story of Jesus is now a tradition handed down.

(d) In Rom. 6:17, the subj. of a pass. form of *paradidōmi* is a teaching handed down to believers. In 1 Cor. 11:2, 23; 15:3 the obj. of the vb. is Christian doctrines—both those handed down to Paul and those that he handed on to the Corinthians. In 11:23 he names the "Lord" as the source of the tradition: "For I received from the Lord what I also passed on to you." The phrase "from the Lord" expresses Paul's belief that, as the ensuing words of institution of the Lord's Supper derive from the Lord himself, *his* word is of supreme authority (cf. 9:14). Though 15:3 does not locate the source of the tradition, most likely Paul is referring to the earliest church tradition.

(e) Likewise in 2 Pet. 2:21 ("the sacred command that was passed on to them") and Jude 3 ("the faith that was once for all entrusted to the saints"), traditions that must be preserved and passed on to others are in view.

3. (a) Regarding the noun *paradosis*, in Mk. 7:3, 5 (par. Matt. 15:2), the phrase "the tradition of the elders" means Jewish tradition of the law that is not laid down in the Bible and which Jesus in the same

context (7:8) calls "the traditions of men." According to Mk. 7, this rab. exposition of the law is in conflict with God's true will (cf. the use of *paradosis* in Gal. 1:14).

(b) In 1 Cor. 11:2 and 2 Thess. 2:15 Paul's "teachings" are called *paradoseis*. The word here does not refer to a fixed canon of writings handed down and supplemented by oral tradition but to Paul's written and oral admonitions to the church, which the church has duly accepted (cf. 2 Thess. 3:6).

(c) In Col. 2:8, the phrase "human tradition" does not mean Jewish exposition of the law as in Mk. 7:8, but is a polemical way of referring to the "hollow and deceptive" teachings that Paul's Colossian opponents regarded as revelations of "the basic principles of this world" (→ *stoicheion*, 5122). The Colossian believers are not to receive such traditions, since they have already "received Christ Jesus as Lord" (2:6).

See also *krima*, dispute, decision, verdict, judgment (*3210*); *bēma*, judgment seat (*1037*); *katadikazō*, condemn (*2868*).

4142 (*paradosis*, tradition), → *4140*.

4148 (*paraiteomai*, ask for, request, excuse, refuse), → *160*.

4151	παρακαλέω

παρακαλέω (*parakaleō*), summon, invite, exhort, encourage, (*4151*); παράκλησις (*paraklēsis*), encouragement, exhortation, appeal, comfort (*4155*).

CL & OT 1. In cl. Gk. *parakaleō* basically means to call in. From this follow the other meanings, which are often hard to distinguish from one another: to ask (sometimes used of invoking the gods), exhort, request, and speak consoling words (esp. in cases of bereavement).

2. In the LXX *parakaleō* frequently means to be moved to comfort (e.g., Gen. 37:35; Ps. 119:50). To bring comfort is part of a prophet's task (cf. Isa. 40:1). But this word can also mean to be sorry, have compassion (e.g., Jdg. 2:18; Ps. 135:14), encourage, strengthen (Deut. 3:28; Job 4:3), lead astray (Deut. 13:6), or lead along (Exod. 15:13). In 1st-cent. Jud. the "consolation of Israel" (cf. Lk. 2:25) means "the fulfillment of the messianic hope."

It is striking that more is heard of asking and exhortation in the Hel. world, while the emphasis is on comfort where the influence of the OT is felt. Perhaps this reflects the lack of comfort that burdened Hellenism and the consolation hoped for in the world of the OT.

NT *parakaleō* occurs 109x in the NT and means (1) to summon, invite, ask, implore; (2) to exhort; (3) to comfort, encourage. The noun *paraklēsis* means exhortation, encouragement, appeal, request, comfort, consolation.

1. The sense of summon (or ask) is found in Acts 28:20. In 28:14 it should be translated in the special sense of invite. In all the strands of the Synoptic tradition *parakaleō* means to ask or implore, in the context of needy people who come with their requests to Jesus (e.g., Matt. 8:5, 31; 18:29; Lk. 15:28). Only at Matt. 26:53 is it said of Jesus himself that he could request from his Father angelic assistance. In Acts 16:9–10 (cf. also 8:31; 13:42) the reference is to a request for missionary ministry.

2. Obviously prior to Paul, exhortation had its place in the life of the church, esp. as the task of the early Christian prophets. Thus in 1 Cor. 14:30–31. Paul sees the need of requiring the local prophets to speak one after another in order, so that all may be exhorted. In Acts 15:32 the prophets Judas and Silas are said to have exhorted and strengthened the church. Exhortation is an almost stereotyped part of the church's life (cf. 16:40). Paul sends Timothy, among other things, to exhort the church (1 Thess. 3:2; cf. Rom. 12:8). This ministry of exhortation, attested as it is from the earliest Christian period, is probably the setting for the hortatory passages found at the end of Paul's letters. The apostle sees it as his duty to exhort the community (12:1; Phil. 4:2; 1 Thess. 4:1).

Theologically, however, Paul gives to exhortation a specific basis. He does not give his readers direct moral instruction, but addresses them "through" (*dia*) God or Christ, so that the apostle thinks of his admonition as mediated, for example, "in view of God's mercy" (Rom. 12:1; cf. 12:3), "by our Lord Jesus Christ and by the love of the Spirit" (15:30), or "by the meekness and gentleness of Christ" (2 Cor. 10:1; cf. also 1 Thess. 4:1; 2 Thess. 3:12).

Consideration of the special basis for exhortation in Paul leads us to the fundamental and much wider problem of ethics and the imperative in Paul. This imperative can only be properly understood when it is viewed in the light of the indicative. The believer's life is a gift from God, which leads in turn to a believer's desire to live as God would have us live. Thus Paul exhorts the Corinthians not to receive God's grace "in vain" (2 Cor. 6:1), which would be the case if they did not prove themselves in their lives. The apostle can describe himself as their example in view of his "way of life in Christ" (1 Cor. 4:17; cf. 1 Thess. 2:12; 4:1, 10; 5:11).

Luke also offers a strong emphasis on right conduct in this life. Now is the time when it is important to prove oneself. Therefore John the Baptist, Judas, Silas, and others exhort people to walk aright (cf. Lk. 3:18; Acts 15:32). It is necessary to warn them to remain faithful to the Lord (11:23) and to the faith (14:22), and to save themselves (2:40). The necessity of mastering the present leads further in Eph. 4:1, the Pastoral Letters, Heb., and 1 Pet. to the exhortation to "live a life worthy of [our] calling."

3. The sense of "comfort," which connotes friendly speech as much as exhortation (e.g., Acts 16:39), is found with special frequency in 2 Cor. 1:3–6. Here Paul sets consolation over against tribulation, suffering, and death, identifying his own sufferings with those of Christ and at the same time sharing in Christ's comfort. This line of thought is carried further by the application of the apostle's suffering and his experience of comfort to the situation of his readers. In 7:4–7 the tribulation and comfort theme is again taken up. Paul is now comforted by Titus and what he has to tell of the situation in Corinth (cf. also 1 Thess. 3:7).

The comfort promised to the mourners in Matt. 5:4 is paralleled by the woes promised to the rich in Lk. 6:24. Suffering is met by God's consolation. Luke presents the alternative: Those who are rich in this life cannot expect the consolation of God in the life to come (cf. also 16:25). Finally, comfort (along with hope, Rom. 15:4; 2 Thess. 2:16) is part of Christian experience in this world (Heb. 6:18; 12:5).

See also *noutheteō*, warn, advise (*3805*); *epitimaō*, rebuke (*2203*).

4155 (*paraklēsis*, encouragement, exhortation, appeal, comfort), → *4151*.

4156	παράκλητος

παράκλητος (*paraklētos*), helper, intercessor, advocate (*4156*).

CL & OT *paraklētos* is a cognate of the vb. *parakaleō*, which in cl. Gk. meant call in, summon, exhort, encourage, comfort. The noun *paraklētos* is derived from the verbal adj. and means called (to one's aid). Its first occurrence in a legal context (in the court of justice) means legal assistant, advocate.

This word appears in the LXX only in Job 16:2 (Aquila, Theod.), where it designates Job's "comforters." One might ask whether there is a correspondence between the "comforters" and Satan (cf. Job 1:6–2:7, 11–12). They are ostensibly friends who come to admonish Job but are unable to do so. Philo used the word in the sense of intercessor and adviser or helper. Rab. Jud. used the word as a loanword in the sense of advocate, counsel, defender, especially of humans before God. Only later did the meaning of "comforter" penetrate early Christian lit. through its connection with *parakaleō* (exhort, → *4151*).

NT The passages in which *paraklētos* occurs in the NT show that the pass. sense of someone called in to help is alien to its meaning. The *paraklētos* is not called in by people but sent by God (Jn. 14:26; 15:26;

16:7), given, and received (14:16–17). He does not merely put in a good word, but brings active help. The sense of helper and intercessor is suitable in all the occurrences of the word. In 1 Jn. 2:1–2 the word has a soteriological character in calling "Jesus Christ, the Righteous One" both "one who speaks . . . in our defense" (*paraklētos*) and the "atoning sacrifice [*hilasmos*] . . . for the sins of the whole world" (→ *hilaskomai*, reconcile, make atonement for, *2661*).

The descriptions of the *paraklētos* in Jn.'s Gospel go beyond the task of an intercessor. He will "convict the world of guilt in regard to sin and righteousness and judgment" (16:8; cf. also 16:9–11; → *elenchō*, convict of guilt, *1794*). He will "teach you all things and will remind you of everything I have said to you" (14:26). Although the world will not know the *paraklētos*, the disciples "know him, for he lives with you and will be in you" (14:17). He will "testify about" Jesus (15:26).

All this indicates that the role of the *paraklētos* is to continue the revealing work of Jesus. The Spirit of truth "will guide you into all the truth. He will not speak on his own; he will speak only what he hears, and he will tell you what is yet to come. He will bring glory to me by taking from what is mine and making it known to you" (Jn. 16:13–14). His purpose is not to satisfy our curiosity about the future, but to continue the work of the historical Jesus in the Christ proclaimed by the church. These sayings led to a stage in early Christian history that Luke treats in his description of the bestowal of the Spirit (Acts 1; 2; 10). The Spirit honors Jesus and gives prominence to his work. At the same time, the church has the gift of the Spirit and thus stands in continuity with Jesus.

Only Jesus together with the Spirit is called *paraklētos* in the NT (Jn. 14:16; 1 Jn. 2:1). This restriction of the title requires a theological interpretation that is at the same time polemical. Only these two—and not the multitude of non-Christian revealers and helpers—are real paracletes. This accounts for the repeated and stressed connection with the Father. On the one hand, it is Jesus who sends the *paraklētos* from the Father (Jn. 15:26). On the other hand, the Father sends the *paraklētos* at the request of Jesus (14:16, 26). According to 14:16, 26, Jesus himself is a *paraklētos*, who is distinct from the other *paraklētos* whom the Father will send in his name.

It is striking that the term *paraklētos* is only found in the Johannine writings, and apart from 1 Jn. 2:1 occurs only in Jesus' farewell discourses (Jn. 14:16, 26; 15:26; 16:7; cf. 16:12–15). Still, the other Evangelists express aspects of this teaching in other ways. Matt., for example, speaks of Christ's continued presence and help in a way that does not involve his physical presence (Matt. 18:20). This presence is linked with the Father and the Holy Spirit (28:19–20; Lk. 24:48–49). Furthermore, Jesus promised the assistance of the Holy Spirit in enabling his followers to speak under trial (Matt. 10:20; Mk. 13:11; cf. Lk. 21:15). Matt. and Lk. speak of a commitment of Jesus to his followers in such a way that those who receive them receive him and him who sent them (Matt. 10:40; Lk. 10:16; cf. Jn. 13:20). This presence of Jesus in those who are his forms the basis of the conviction of the nations in judgment (Matt. 25:31–46). In other words, what in Matt. and Lk. is depicted as the continuing presence and work of Jesus in the post-resurrection church is depicted by Jn. as the activity of the *paraklētos* of Jesus.

The trans. of *paraklētos* into Eng. presents obvious difficulties. The word "advocate" reflects the early Christian Lat. equivalent (*advocatus*) with all its legal connotations, as does the trans. "Counselor" (RSV, NIV), though the latter may also have overtones of giving advice. While this trans. may well fit Jn. 16:7–11 and 1 Jn. 2:1, the legal connotation seems to be absent from the other passages. The trans. "Comforter," which goes back to Wycliffe, is weak and misleading, unless one reads into it an etymological sense (Lat. *con* with; *fortis* strong). This leaves either the Gk. loanword "paraclete" or "helper." "Paraclete" has the advantage of being neutral, but it is essentially meaningless, unless the Gk. background is known. "Helper" is the one English word that is both meaningful and fits all the passages in which *paraklētos* occurs in the NT.

See also *pneuma*, spirit (*4460*).

4157 (*parakoē*, disobedience), → *201*.

4158 (*parakoloutheō*, accompany, understand), → *199*.

4159 (*parakouō*, fail to hear, take no heed), → *201*.

4161 (*paralambanō*, take to oneself, take with or along, take over), → *3284*.

4165 (*paralogizomai*, cheat, deceive, delude), → *4414*.

4166	παραλυτικός

παραλυτικός (*paralytikos*), paralytic (*4166*); παραλύω (*paralyō*), to loose from the side, release, set free (*4168*).

CL & OT This word is infrequent in cl. Gk. and appears only once in the papyri. When paralytic disability is described, medical authors prefer the perf. part. pass. of *paralyō*; this was a chronic condition with organic degeneration. *paralytikos* does not occur in the LXX; *paralyō* has a variety of meanings, such as experience judgment (Gen. 4:15), plan (Isa. 23:9), expose (Ezek. 25:9), and tremble (Isa. 35:3; Ezek. 7:27; 21:7).

NT In the NT, *paralytikos* occurs only in Matt. 4:24; 8:6; 9:2, 6; Mk. 2:3–10. In Matt. 8:6, the paralysis is perhaps a disease that begins in one's legs and proceeds quickly to the arms and neck, generally being fatal within three weeks. The paralysis of 9:2 was probably some form of paraplegia, in which paralysis affects the lower half of the person's body. Lk. uses the perf. part. pass. of *paralyō* instead of *paralytikos* (cf. Lk. 5:18, 24; Acts 8:7; 9:33). In Heb. 12:13 *paralyō* alludes to Isa. 35:3 in its call for strengthening "weak" knees by depending on the plan and power of God.

See also *astheneia*, weakness, sickness, disease, timidity (*819*); *nosos*, illness, sickness (*3798*); *malakia*, weakness, softness, sickness (*3433*).

4168 (*paralyō*, to loose from the side, release, set free), → *4166*.

4169 (*paramenō*, remain, stay on, continue in), → *3531*.

4170	παραμυθέομαι

παραμυθέομαι (*paramytheomai*), encourage, cheer up, console (*4170*); παραμυθία (*paramythia*), encouragement, comfort, consolation (*4171*); παραμύθιον (*paramythion*), encouragement, consolation (*4172*).

CL & OT *paramytheomai* has the general meaning of speaking to someone in a positive, benevolent way. It also means encourage, exhort, comfort, soothe.

Heb. has no direct equivalent to *paramytheomai*. The LXX uses the word in the sense of comfort, console, encourage (2 Macc. 15:8–9; cf. Wis. 3:18). The OT mentions various kinds of comfort and comforting (→ *parakaleō*, *4151*), but not with the sentimental overtones that the word has acquired in our language. Isa. 57:17–18 speaks first of God's anger and punishment; then God alters his plan and brings healing and comfort. The Word of God has life-giving power and thus brings comfort in affliction (Ps. 119:50).

NT Paul uses *paramytheomai* in conjunction with *parakaleō*, exhort, in 1 Thess. 2:12. He reminds his readers that when he visited Thessalonica, he comforted them "as a father deals with his own children" (2:11) and urged (*martyromai*) them "to live lives worthy of God." In 5:14 he urged the entire church to "encourage [*paramytheomai*] the timid."

Encouragement is an outworking of love, forming one of the foundations of church life as lived out in the sphere of Christ (Phil. 2:1). Thus at Corinth those with the gift of prophecy were expected to build up, encourage, and console (*paramythian*) the church (1 Cor. 14:3–4). In other words, giving comfort was part of the apostle's missionary activity and of the life of the young church. Such comfort was extended both to individuals and to the church as a whole.

In Jn. 11:19, 31 *paramytheomai* is a technical term for expression of sympathy.

See also *tharseō*, be of good courage, take heart (*2510*).

4171 (*paramythia*, encouragement, comfort), → *4170*.

4172 (*paramythion*, encouragement, consolation), → *4170*.

4174 (*paranomeō*, break the law, act contrary to the law), → *3795*.

4176 (*parapikrainō*, embitter, make angry, provoke), → *4394*.

4177 (*parapikrasmos*, rebellion), → *4394*.

4178 (*parapiptō*, fall beside, go astray, err, sin), → *4183*.

4183 παράπτωμα | παράπτωμα (*paraptōma*), transgression, trespass, false step, sin (*4183*); παραπίπτω (*parapiptō*), fall beside, go astray, err, sin (*4178*).

CL & OT 1. In cl. Gk. *parapiptō* means to fall at the side; thence, accidentally bump into something; (later) to turn out amiss, miss one's way or the truth, fail in one's duty. Used absolutely it means make a mistake, err, meaning an accidental and excusable oversight. Correspondingly the noun *paraptōma* means oversight, error, mistake (unintentional).

2. In the LXX both the noun and the vb. are found most frequently in Ezek. *parapiptō* means to commit acts of unfaithfulness (e.g., 14:13; 15:8; 18:24; 20:27). *paraptōma* expresses conscious and deliberate sinning against God (rebellion, Job 36:9; Ezek. 14:11; 18:22; injustice, 3:20; 18:26). There are only isolated instances of its meaning of unintentional sins committed in weakness (Ps. 19:12) and negligence in official duties (Dan. 6:4).

NT 1. *parapiptō* occurs in the NT only in Heb. 6:6. It means to fall away, be unfaithful (similar to *aphistēmi* [fall away, → *923*] in 3:12 and the expression used in 10:26). This is certainly not meant in the sense of a single lapse but rather expresses the abandonment of the Christian truth. This would, of course, manifest itself in specific behavior. The idea is one of a person's self-rejection by one's rejection of the grace of God continually being offered.

2. Apart from Paul's writings, *paraptōma* is only found in Matt. 6:14–15; Mk. 11:25. As in the OT, it is used as one of several words for sin, but it emphasizes strongly the deliberate act (only in Rom. 5:20 is it used of a universal fact) with its fateful consequences. Hence, it means an action through which one falls and loses the position granted by God. Thus trespasses committed by one individual against another directly affect one's relation to God and in the final judgment provide the standard by which a person is judged. Consequently, we must help to put any failure right (Gal. 6:1).

The sinful act of Adam (Rom. 5:15–18; cf. Wis. 10:1 = LXX 10:2) brought in its train a mass of sin and woe (Rom. 5:18, 20) and even death (5:15, 17–18), so that even before physical death a person is in the power of death (Eph. 2:1, 5; Col. 2:13). Thus Christ died (Rom. 4:25) in order that we might receive forgiveness for our sins (2 Cor. 5:19; Eph. 1:7; Col. 2:13). According to Rom. 11:11–12, Israel's fall consists in its rejection of the gospel.

See also *adikia*, wrongdoing, unrighteousness, injustice (*94*); *hamartia*, sin (*281*); *parabasis*, overstepping, transgression (*4126*).

4184 (*pararreō*, flow past, drift away, let slip), → *4835*.

4186 (*paraskeuazō*, get ready, prepare [oneself]), → *2941*.

4187 (*paraskeuē*, day of preparation), → *2941*.

4190 (*paratēreō*, watch [closely], observe), → *5498*.

4191 (*paratērēsis*, observation), → *5498*.

4205 (*pareimi*, be present, have come), → *4242*.

4209 (*pareiserchomai*, come in, step in), → *2262*.

4212 (*paremballō*, throw up a palisade), → *4483*.

4213 (*parembolē*, fortified camp, barracks), → *4483*.

4215 παρεπίδημος | παρεπίδημος (*parepidēmos*), adj., staying for a while in a strange place; noun, a stranger, alien, exile (*4215*).

CL & OT *parepidēmos* is derived from *dēmos* (people) and is found only twice in the LXX (Gen. 23:4; Ps. 39:12). It means someone who lives in a foreign place as an alien.

NT *parepidēmos* occurs 3x in the NT. In 1 Pet. 1:1 and 2:11 this word is applied to believers, calling them "strangers." In the latter it stands in parallel to *paroikoi* (aliens, → *4230*), pointing back to Gen. 23:4 and Ps. 39:12. Because our true home is in heaven (cf. Phil. 3:20), we as God's elect have been drawn out of all natural ties and relations. We now live on earth as exiles.

This call and vocation give rise to the warning to abstain from sinful desires (1 Pet. 2:11). Rather, we are to live according to the decrees and laws of our true homeland. Heb. 11:13 depicts Abraham and the patriarchs as patterns for the Christian. Abraham looked toward the future city (11:10), living as a stranger and exile on the earth.

See also *allotrios*, alien, hostile (*259*); *diaspora*, dispersion (*1402*); *xenos*, foreign; stranger, alien (*3828*); *paroikos*, stranger, alien (*4230*).

4216 (*parerchomai*, go by, pass by), → *2262*.

4217 (*paresis*, letting pass, passing over), → *918*.

4220 (*parthenia*, virginity), → *4221*.

4221 παρθένος | παρθένος (*parthenos*), maiden, virgin (*4221*); παρθενία (*parthenia*), virginity (*4220*).

CL & OT 1. As in many centers of culture, virginity was esteemed highly among the Gks. In religion virginity is a characteristic of many goddesses; e.g., the Gk. goddess Athene or Parthenos (whose Athenian temple was called the Parthenon) was not born of a woman. In apparent variance with virginity, these goddesses, esp. Artemis, were often the guardians of birth, motherhood, and the fertility of the land and animals. Here the emphasis lies less on chastity than on youthful vitality with its magical power.

2. Heb. has two main words for maiden (ʿalmâ and bᵉtûlâ). *parthenos* (64x in LXX) is used primarily to translate bᵉtûlâ (44x), which means an untouched maiden. Like a young man, she is the embodiment of hope (cf. Amos 8:13), so the word can serve as a designation of Israel (5:2), Jerusalem, (Lam. 1:15), and Zion (2:13). ʿalmâ denotes a young girl or a woman from the age of puberty (cf. Prov. 30:19) until she gives birth to her first child. Only twice is this word translated by *parthenos* (Gen. 24:43; Isa. 7:14). In Gen. 24:43 ʿalmâ refers to a virgin (cf. 24:16), though it is debated whether the word itself carries this meaning. In Isa. 7:14 it may likewise be questioned whether a virgin as such is implied, for otherwise bᵉtûlâ would most likely have been used (see further, *Emmanouēl*, Immanuel, *1842*). It is interesting to note that other Gk. translations (e.g., Theod., Aquila, Sym.) have *neanis* (young girl, a word not used in the NT) instead of *parthenos* here.

NT 1. *parthenos* occurs 15x in the NT. It carries a general meaning in the parable of the ten virgins (Matt. 25:1, 7, 11). In Acts 21:9 unmarried daughters are meant. Lk. 2:36 speaks of Anna living with her husband seven years after her *parthenia* (i.e., her marriage and its subsequent loss of virginity).

2. (a) In Rev. 14:4 *parthenos* probably means those who, in contrast to the promiscuous and idolaters, are able to devote themselves entirely to the Lamb. In 2 Cor. 11:2 Paul hopes that he may be able to present the church to the coming Lord as a "pure virgin," i.e., people who have not cast about for another Savior.

(b) The precise meaning of *parthenos* in 1 Cor. 7:25, 28 is debated. Some scholars think that the term refers to married women whose spiritual ideals cause them to live as virgins; but since Paul describes this situation in 7:1–7 and does not use *parthenos* there, that interpretation is unlikely. In 7:25–38, the couples in question are not married. More likely Paul has in mind the relation of a man to his betrothed, who is a virgin in the ordinary sense.

(c) Where the NT speaks of Mary as a virgin, it has in mind the period up to the birth of Jesus. Statements regarding Jesus' supernatural conception are limited to the nativity narratives in Matt. 1 and Lk. 1. Jesus' divine sonship is based on a miracle that went beyond the experience of Elizabeth (Lk. 1:36). Matt. adds a quotation from Isa. 7:14 and indicates Jesus' conception as fulfilling OT prophecy. Matt.'s genealogy denotes Mary's legal relation to Joseph, since for the sake of his Davidic sonship Jesus must pass legally for a son of Joseph (1:16; cf. Lk. 3:23). In spite of its importance in Christian theology, Paul makes no explicit reference to the virgin birth (see Rom. 1:3; Gal. 4:4, for his references to the birth of Jesus).

See also *gynē*, woman (*1222*); *mētēr*, mother (*3613*); *chēra*, widow (*5939*).

4225	παρίστημι

παρίστημι (*paristēmi*), place, put at the disposal of, present (*4225*).

CL & OT The basic meaning of *paristēmi* is (trans.) place beside, (intrans.) stand beside, and (mid.) place before oneself. Various nuances developed, such as: (trans.) put down, place at someone's disposal, bring (a sacrifice); (intrans.) approach (the emperor or an enemy), help someone, wait on (as a servant), be present.

The word is used in the LXX about 100x. It could refer to a foreigner entering God's service (Isa. 60:10), a servant standing before a master (a position of honor, cf. 1 Sam. 16:21; 2 Ki. 5:25), and angels (Job 1:6) and martyrs (4 Macc. 17:18) standing before God. The word also expresses God's standing by someone to reveal himself (Exod. 34:5), to help that person (Ps. 109:31), or to charge someone with sin (50:21).

NT 1. In the NT *paristēmi* is used intrans. of Paul's standing before Caesar (Acts 27:24) or humanity's standing before God's judgment (Rom. 14:10). God supported Paul by standing at his side (2 Tim. 4:17), an angel stood beside Paul (Acts 27:23), and Phoebe was to be supported by the local church (Rom. 16:2). Gabriel stands before God (Lk. 1:19) (note that in heaven, only God sits; all created beings must stand before him).

2. The trans. use is found primarily in Acts and Paul's letters. In Lk. 2:22 it denotes the presentation of Jesus to the Lord in the temple (cf. Exod. 13:2). Passages where *paristēmi* is used in the sense of make or present are of special importance. Col. 1:22 implies that because of Jesus' death, a new, holy community is being presented to God. Since Christ is perfect, the church can also be presented perfect to God (1:28). Just as Jesus presented himself as alive after Easter to his apostles in various appearances (Acts 1:3), so God will present believers raised to a new life with Jesus in his presence (2 Cor. 4:14). By his self-sacrifice Christ has presented the church in the splendor of a bride (Eph. 5:27; cf. 2 Cor. 11:2; Col. 1:22). Similarly, we should do our best to present ourselves as approved to God (2 Tim. 2:15).

Neither the supposed freedom of those who think themselves strong nor the scrupulous self-denial of those weak in faith will "bring us near to God" (1 Cor. 8:8). Rather, the members that were once yielded to impurity are now to be offered to God in the service of righteousness (Rom. 6:13–19). Those who have been justified by faith "offer" their bodies to God as living sacrifices (12:1). Paul may be adopting Hel. sacrificial terminology here for Christian service to Jesus as Lord.

See also *kathistēmi*, bring, appoint (*2770*); *horizō*, determine, appoint (*3988*); *procheirizō*, determine, appoint (*4741*); *tassō*, arrange, appoint (*5435*); *tithēmi*, put, place, set, appoint (*5502*); *prothesmia*, appointed

date (*4607*); *cheirotoneō*, appoint (*5936*); *lanchanō*, obtain as by lot (*3275*).

4228 (*paroikeō*, inhabit as a stranger, live beside), → *4230*.

4229 (*paroikia*, the stay of a noncitizen in a strange place), → *4230*.

4230	πάροικος

πάροικος (*paroikos*), stranger, alien (*4230*); παροικέω (*paroikeō*), inhabit as a stranger, live beside (*4228*); παροικία (*paroikia*), the stay of a noncitizen in a strange place (*4229*).

CL & OT 1. *paroikos* is a compound of *para* (by) and *oikos* (house). It was originally an adj. but was later used as a noun meaning neighbor, noncitizen, one who lives among citizens without having citizen rights yet enjoying the protection of the community. The vb. *paroikeo* means to live beside, inhabit as a stranger. *paroikia* means sojourning.

2. In the LXX *paroikos* occurs over 30x, translating *gēr* and *tôšāb*, both words meaning an alien or stranger. *paroikeō* occurs over 60x, esp. as the equivalent of *gûr*, to sojourn. *paroikia* is found 16x. Words in this group designate non-Israelites who lived in Israel (2 Sam. 4:3; Isa. 16:4). The Israelites had definite obligations to resident aliens. For example, an adequate living should be made possible for them (Lev. 25:35–47). They were allowed to share the food of the Sabbath year (25:6), although they were prohibited from eating the Passover lamb (Exod. 12:45) or the sacrificial gift (Lev. 22:10). They had the right of asylum (Num. 35:15), and, like widows and orphans, they stood under the protection of the law (cf. Exod. 22:21). The devout, even if aliens, could live in the tent of Yahweh (Ps. 15) and so experience fellowship with him. Ezek. 47:22–23 promises the equality of Israelites and resident aliens. Still, resident aliens also had obligations. For example, they were required to keep the Sabbath (Exod. 20:10).

Repeated stress in the OT was laid on the fact that the patriarchs were aliens (Gen. 12:10; 17:8; 19:9; 20:1; 23:4; 35:27; 47:4; Exod. 6:4). Moses was an alien in Midian (2:22), as was the entire nation of Israel in Egypt. Israel's attitude toward aliens was to be motivated by this fact (cf. 22:21; 23:9). In one sense the Israelites were always aliens, even when they lived in the promised land (1 Chr. 29:15; Ps. 39:12; 119:19, 54; 120:5; 3 Macc. 7:19). The earth and soil of Palestine, as indeed the whole earth (cf. Ps. 24:1), belongs to Yahweh. For this reason the land could not be sold (Lev. 25:23).

3. For Philo, the godly man is a *paroikos*, for he lives far off from his heavenly home. Philo combined the ancient world's denial of the world with OT ideas.

NT The words of this group are found only in Lk., Acts, Eph., Heb., and 1 Pet. Each passage contains a quotation or reference to the history of Israel (cf. Acts 7:29 with Exod. 2:15; Acts 7:6 with Gen. 15:13). In Acts 13:16–17 Paul recalls Israel's *paroikia* in Egypt, while Heb. 11:9–10 stresses that Abraham lived as an alien in the promised land as in a foreign country, since by faith he was a citizen of the heavenly city. The same thought occurs in the use of *xenos* (→ *3828*) and *parepidēmos* (→ *4215*) in 11:13. In Jesus Christ Gentile believers are no longer *xenoi* and *paroikoi*, but fellow citizens with the saints and members of God's household. Consequently, the promises made to Israel and the call to the kingdom of God are also valid for them (Eph. 2:19).

From this point of view, Christians are also in a new sense *paroikoi* and *parepidēmoi* here on earth—hence the warning to abstain from sinful desires (1 Pet. 2:11). They are to live in their time of sojourning in the fear of God (1:17). *paroikeō* means "live" only in Lk. 24:18. Perhaps even here the thought is that the "visitor" in question is a member of the Jewish dispersion living at Jerusalem, or that he is a pilgrim temporarily staying in the city to attend the Passover.

See also *allotrios*, alien, hostile (*259*); *diaspora*, dispersion (*1402*); *xenos*, foreign; stranger, alien (*3828*); *parepidēmos*, staying for a while in a strange place; stranger, resident alien (*4215*).

4231 παροιμία	παροιμία (*paroimia*), proverb, wise saying; dark saying, riddle (*4231*).

CL & OT 1. In cl. Gk. a *paroimia* states an accepted truth in a short and pointed form, expressing general timeless truth (e.g., a proverb). Its popular and traditional form distinguishes it from the aphorism and the maxim (*gnōmē*; → *ginōskō, 1182*). Aristotle linked it with metaphor because of its vivid imagery; others, with fable.

2. In the LXX *paroimia* occurs only 7x (Prov. 1:1; 25:1; Sir. 6:35; 8:8; 18:29; 39:3; 47:17; see also the title to Prov.). In these two books it is virtually a technical term for instruction by the wise. Philo uses it with the meaning proverb.

NT 1. The Gospels contain many sayings of Jesus that are similar to the OT instruction of the wise (e.g., Matt. 5:13–15; Mk. 9:50). Proverbs are also quoted in some of the NT letters (e.g., Rom. 12:20, quoting Prov. 25:21–22; Heb. 12:5–6, quoting Prov. 3:11–12). In 1 Cor. 15:33 Paul actually quotes a secular proverb from Menander's lost comedy *Thais*: "Bad company corrupts good character." But in none of these instances is *paroimia* used. The only occurrence of this word in that sense is in 2 Pet. 2:22, where Peter quotes two "proverbs . . . 'A dog returns to its vomit,' and, 'A sow that is washed goes back to her wallowing in the mud.'" Both are intended to demonstrate the contemptible conduct of false teachers.

2. In Jn. *paroimia* occurs in the sense of fig. saying or riddle (Jn. 10:6; 16:25, 29). This meaning reflects the Heb. equivalent *māšāl* and the consequent approximation to *parabolē* (→ *4130*). In retrospect Jesus' discourse on the shepherd (10:6) and, indeed, his discourses in general (16:25), are characterized as fig., somewhat obscure sayings. They stand in contrast to the later, clear revelatory sayings (16:25, 29). The former are not difficult to understand because words are difficult, but because the hearer tries to understand them intellectually rather than in the light of Jesus and his kingdom. Those who have a relationship with Jesus understand his words "plainly" or "clearly" (16:25, 29; → *parrēsia, 4244*).

See also *parabolē*, type, figure, parable (*4130*).

4232 (*paroinos*, given to drunkenness), → *3501*.

4234 (*paromoiazo*, be like), → *3927*.

4235 (*paromoios*, like, similar), → *3927*.

4236 (*paroxynō*, provoke to anger), → *3973*.

4239 (*parorgizō*, enrage, make angry), → *3973*.

4240 (*parorgismos*, anger), → *3973*.

4242 παρουσία	παρουσία (*parousia*), presence, appearing, coming, advent (*4242*);

πάρειμι (*pareimi*), be present, have come (*4205*).

CL & OT 1. In cl. Gk. *pareimi* covers both the pres. tense idea of "being there" and the perf. idea of "having come." *parousia* means, therefore, both presence or (in a more neutral sense) property, fortune, military strength; and arrival, someone's coming in order to be present. Technically the noun was used for the arrival of a king, emperor, or ruler (the corresponding Lat. term is *adventus*). From this it is an easy step to speak of an appearing of the gods on behalf of human beings. Such a *parousia* is not thought of merely as future, but is experienced as a reality in the present.

2. The Greek translations of the OT use the vb. *pareimi* for seven different Heb. words, most of which mean to come (e.g., Num. 22:20; 1 Sam. 9:6; 2 Sam. 5:23; 13:35; Isa. 30:13; Lam. 4:18). The noun *parousia* is virtually absent from the LXX (Jdg. 10:18; 2 Macc. 8:12; 15:21; 3 Macc. 3:17; it occurs in some MSS. of Neh. 2:6). Nevertheless, the idea is there, for from the earliest times the OT speaks of the coming of God: God manifests himself in victory (Jdg. 5:4), in dreams (Gen. 20:3), in his Spirit (Num. 24:2), with his hand (1 Ki. 18:46), in

his word (2 Sam. 7:4), and in the last days (Isa. 2:2; → *hēmera, 2465*). God also comes as king of the world (Exod. 15:18; Ps. 24:7–10; 95:3–4). There are also references to the coming of the anointed one (Zech. 9:9–10).

Important for the NT view is the expectation of God's coming in the Jewish apocalyptic texts (whose present texts may have Christian influence). Note, for example: "A king shall arise out of Judah and shall establish a new priesthood for all the Gentiles after the fashion of the Gentiles. And his appearing is greatly desired as a prophet of the Most High, of the seed of Abraham our father" (*T. Levi* 8:14–15; see also *T. Jud.* 22:2; *1 Enoch* 38:2; 49:4). Josephus uses *parousia* to mean the presence of God in the Shekinah, which is revealed to his people and even to the pagan governor, Petronius. Philo says virtually nothing about a coming of Yahweh or the Messiah.

NT 1. (a) Paul uses *pareimi* with the meaning to be present. He distinguishes his personal, bodily absence (*apeimi*) from his being present (*pareimi*) in spirit (1 Cor. 5:3); the latter also refers to his presence in Corinth (2 Cor. 10:2, 11; 11:9; 13:2, 10) and among the Galatians (Gal. 4:18, 20; cf. Jn. 11:28; Acts 10:33; 24:19; Rev. 17:8). In Col. 1:6 the apostle refers to the gospel "that has come to you." Similarly in Jn. 7:6 the time has not yet come (→ *kairos*, opportunity, *2789*). In Heb. 12:11 the vb. is used in an expression that means "at the time," that is, for the present moment.

(b) The noun *parousia* occurs 24x in the NT, of which 14 are in Paul. It denotes generally presence and arrival, though Paul is the only NT writer to use it in this way. He rejoices over the presence of Stephanas (1 Cor. 16:17); he is comforted by God through the arrival of Titus (2 Cor. 7:6–7); he speaks of his coming to Philippi (Phil. 1:26; 2:12) and suffers the reproach of being strong in his letters but weak in his personal presence and speech (2 Cor. 10:10).

2. In its special NT sense, *parousia* is linked with NT eschatology. Jesus proclaimed the kingdom of God as imminent and his *parousia* (Matt. 24:3, 27, 37, 39) as having a decisive effect on how we are to live now in the light of this coming event (cf. also Mk. 13:26; Lk. 17:23–24). Though the present and the future are viewed as a chronological succession, the future affects the present, not in the sense of being already realized in the present, but in the sense that we make our decisions as those who must give account at the imminent appearing of the kingdom of God.

With Jesus' death and resurrection, the idea of the *parousia* becomes bound up with the church's expectation of Christ's appearing at the end of the age. Where Christ's presence and the present experience of salvation are stressed (e.g., Gal. 2:20), the *parousia* may be relativized to some degree in that its blessings are already being experienced here and now (cf. Jn. 6:39–40; 11:24, 26). It is true that the delay of the *parousia* led to difficulties in the church, but believers remained confident in Christ's salvation and agreed that his *parousia* would come suddenly (cf. Lk. 17:23–24; 1 Thess. 5:1–11). Note that other words are also used to describe the *parousia* of Christ (e.g., *hēmera*, day, *2465*; *epiphaneia*, appearance, *2211*).

The earliest NT passage that speaks of the *parousia* is 1 Thess. 4:15: "According to the Lord's own word, we tell you that we who are still alive, who are left till the coming [*parousia*] of the Lord, will certainly not precede those who have fallen asleep." Paul's reference to "the Lord's own word" may have in view Matt. 24:30–31, an otherwise unknown saying of Jesus, a private revelation to Paul (2 Cor. 12:1–4; Gal. 1:12), or a statement of what the apostle believes accords with the mind of Christ (cf. 1 Cor. 2:16; 7:10, 12). Here resurrection and *parousia* are closely intertwined, for when the latter occurs believers who have previously died will have no disadvantage, nor will the living enjoy any advantage.

Paul expresses a similar thought in 1 Cor. 15:23, where he reflects on the decisive moment: "But each in his own turn: Christ, the firstfruits; then, when he comes [lit., at his coming, *parousia*], those who belong to him." The *parousia* will involve different categories of people, but it does not follow that the apostle has in mind two resurrections of the dead, an intervening millennial kingdom, or a systematic, chronological sequence of eschatological events. Paul breaks with traditional apocalyptic ideas by insisting that eschatology is already being worked out: Believers are to live not in sadness but in hope (1 Thess. 4:13; 5:23). And although separated from the Thessalonian church, Paul can still describe this church as his "hope," "joy," and crown of boasting "in the presence of our Lord Jesus when he comes" (1 Thess. 2:19).

In 2 Thess. we see a different situation. A tension is apparent here between the presence of Christ experienced right now and the *parousia* at some future date (2 Thess. 2:2). Evidently some claimed that "the day of the Lord has already come," purporting to have communication from Paul to this effect (2:2). Others made the imminence of the return of the Lord an excuse for idleness, to which Paul replied: "For even when we were with you, we gave you this rule: If a man will not work, he shall not eat" (3:10). The letter thus attacks those who claimed a present experience of events that in reality were still future. This leads Paul to give a vehement warning about Satan and the *parousia* of the lawless one, which will take place before the *parousia* of Christ (2:7–12).

3. The delay in Christ's *parousia* led people to question whether that day would ever come. In this situation Jas. 5:7–8 calls for patience "until the Lord's coming." After using the example of a farmer patiently waiting for a harvest, James goes on: "Be patient and stand firm, because the Lord's coming is near." Likewise, in 2 Pet. 1:16 and 3:4–12 believers are urged to continue expecting the *parousia* despite the fact that so far nothing has happened.

Matt. presents a dialectical tension. On the one hand, Jesus is present whenever his church assembles (18:20) and is with his people to the end of the age as they spread the gospel (28:20). On the other hand, the coming of the Son of Man is still future (24:39), its date being unknown to anyone (24:36). His coming will occur suddenly, when people are living entirely for the present (24:27, 37–38). This tension between the already and the not yet permeates much of the NT teaching about the *parousia* (→ *aiōn*, age, *172*).

See also *hēmera*, day (*2465*); *marana tha*, maranatha (*3448*).

4244	παρρησία

παρρησία (*parrēsia*), openness, confidence, boldness, frankness (*4244*); παρρησιάζομαι (*parrēsiazomai*), speak out, speak openly, speak boldly (*4245*).

CL & OT 1. In cl. Gk. *parrēsia* referred to freedom of speech. In practice this freedom encountered opposition from time to time, so the word acquired the further meaning of boldness, frankness. A negative overtone is also perceptible in some cases where freedom of speech has been misused to the point of bluntness and shamelessness. In an extended sense *parrēsia* can mean confidence and joyfulness. The corresponding vb. *parrēsiazomai* means to speak openly or boldly, and to have confidence.

2. (a) In the LXX this word group occurs rarely (*parrēsia*, 12x; *parrēsiazomai*, 6x), and in most cases there is no corresponding Heb. word. The concept is used both of God and of those who stand over against him. It is used of God in Ps. 94:1, where *parrēsiazomai* translates a Heb. vb. meaning shine forth: God is called on to shine forth as the avenger and requite the ungodly of their wickedness. A link between such a manifestation of God and divine utterance is given in Prov. 1:20, where the LXX reads, "In the broad places of a city [wisdom] acts with confidence."

(b) *parrēsia* occurs in Job 27:10, where the LXX reads: "Or when trouble comes upon him, has he any confidence [*parrēsia*] before [God]?" The vb. features in 22:26: "Then you will have confidence before the Lord and look up to heaven with cheerfulness." The remaining instances of *parrēsia* occur at Lev. 26:13; Est. 8:13; Prov. 10:10;

13:5; Wis. 5:1; Sir. 25:25; 1 Macc. 4:18; 3 Macc. 4:1; 7:12; 4 Macc. 10:5; of *parrēsiazomai* at Ps. 12:5; Prov. 20:9; Song 8:10; Sir. 6:11.

NT *parrēsia* occurs 31x in the NT; *parrēsiazomai*, 9x. The two words vary in meaning from the equivalent of *eleutheria*, freedom, to *elpis*, hope.

1. In Jn. *parrēsia* is used in the unique sense of openly, in public: "Here he is, speaking publicly, and they are not saying a word to him" (7:26; cf. 11:54; 18:20; also Mk. 8:32). In each of these passages in Jn. the word refers to Jesus' boldness in teaching in public. In Jn. 7:4, Jesus' brothers urge him to do something in public in order to convince them of his power. By contrast 7:13 reports that no one spoke of Jesus openly for fear of the Jews.

When Jesus spoke openly in public, *parrēsia* can also mean that he spoke unambiguously and plainly, not in allusions (Jn. 11:14; cf. 10:24–25) or veiled parables (16:29). But Jesus spoke so freely only for believers (16:25, 29), while to the world he spoke in parables (→ *paroimia*, *4231*), which could not be understood without faith. Hence, there is a tension between *parrēsia* and *paroimia*, which corresponds to the Johannine dualism of life and death, truth and the lie, etc., which demands a decision and can only be resolved in faith.

2. Corresponding to the *parrēsia* of Jesus, there is the open and authoritative testimony of the apostles. Again and again Acts reports how fearlessly Peter, Paul, and others stand before the Jews or Gentiles and proclaim the works of God (*parrēsia* in Acts 2:29; 4:13, 29, 31; 28:31; *parrēsiazomai* in 9:27–28; 13:46; 14:3; 18:26; 19:8; 26:26). This boldness evokes astonishment (4:13), division (14:3–4), and persecution (9:27). It is not something that one has under one's control; rather, it is the fruit of the Holy Spirit (4:31) that has to be sought again and again (4:29).

3. This is the view of the *parrēsia* of the witness taken by Paul. It characterizes effective preaching of the mysteries of God (Eph. 6:19) and the honoring of Christ in life and death (Phil. 1:20). Since perseverance is demanded of the disciple (cf. Eph. 6:20), *parrēsia* has here also the sense of boldness and courage (1 Thess. 2:2). Such courage is not a human quality; it comes from God (2:2) and Christ (Phlm. 8).

We should approach the future not in fear of judgment but in full confidence, in openness to God, and in the hope of the fullness of God's glory (cf. 2 Cor. 3:11–12). We should abide in Christ (Heb. 3:6; 10:35; 1 Jn. 2:28), who has already triumphed over the principalities and the powers in "public" (Col. 2:15) and made possible access into the Most Holy Place (Heb. 10:19; cf. 4:16). Those who persevere in faith hold to Christ in love (cf. 1 Jn. 4:17; cf. also the emphasis laid on *assurance* gained through faithful service, 1 Tim. 3:13), and those who are not condemned by their own hearts will have "confidence" in prayer (1 Jn. 3:21; 5:14). Moreover, they will also "be confident and unashamed before him at his coming" (2:28). Thus, *parrēsia* contains the ideas of trust in God, certainty of salvation, power to pray, and hope for the future.

4245 (parrēsiazomai, speak out openly, speak boldly), → *4244*.

4246	πᾶς

πᾶς (*pas*), each, all, the whole (*4246*); ἅπας (*hapas*), all, the whole (*570*).

NT *pas* as an adj. in the sing. (a) without the art., means each; (b) before a noun with the art., means all (e.g., "all Judea" in Matt. 3:5); (c) between the art. and noun, means the whole, all (e.g., "the entire law" in Gal. 5:14). Here the stress lies on the sum total as opposed to the parts, the complete as opposed to the separated portions. *pas* in the pl. means all.

pas as a noun means each, everyone; linked with *tis* it means any. *to pan* means all, the whole, the main point. The neut. pl. *panta* means all, *ta panta*, all this (2 Cor. 4:15), all things (Rom. 11:36; Col. 1:16–17). *hapas* is a strengthened form of *pas*, often used with the same but sometimes with an intensive meaning: the whole, all, everybody.

1. The concept of *pas* expresses a collective totality; *polys* (→ *4498*) often bears a similar meaning. For the Jews, God alone is one. The world remains a plurality, showing many differences, and is unified only by the creative sovereignty of God over it. This understanding is based on the OT, as 1 Cor. 8:6 shows: "For us there is but one God, the Father, from whom all things (*ta panta*) came and for whom we live; and there is but one Lord, Jesus Christ, through whom all things came and through whom we live." All comes from God and returns to him. God is the beginning and the end, origin, and goal; he has made himself known in his Son.

2. Paul expresses the same point in Rom. 11:36: "For from him and through him and to him are all things (*ta panta*)" (cf. Isa. 44:24). This witness to the uniqueness and universality of God is fully aware of the first commandment and rejects every power (except, of course, that of Jesus Christ; cf. 1 Cor. 8:6; Col. 1:15–16) that claims to have shared in God's work of creation. Christ is the executor of God's will (1:19–20). All beings exist because he exists, live because he lives, and are under God's rule because he rules them (Jn. 1:3; Col. 1:16–18). Those who separate themselves from the Son cut themselves off from the root of his life.

3. The exaltation of the Son confirms that all authority (→ *exousia, 2026*) has been given to him (Matt. 28:18). His office as ruler embraces the fullness and majesty of God. Hence, he has authority in heaven, and on earth nothing has power apart from him (Jn. 1:3; Col. 1:15–18; cf. Matt. 11:27).

Our Lord's power over the entire cosmos was not there merely to comfort the disciples. They were to proclaim it in all the world to every creature (Matt. 28:18–20; Mk. 16:15; Col. 1:23). This power gives motive and success to the apostolic preaching, to mission and evangelism. The church is to reach its fulfillment in Christ (Eph. 1:22; Col. 3:11). Eventually the whole creation will recognize and acknowledge Christ as Lord (Phil. 2:9–11). If all authority had not been given him, the proclamation of the gospel would be a fruitless venture. But Christ lifts people from striving after security for their own existence and raises them to participate in the work of the creation.

See also *polys*, many (*4498*).

4247	πάσχα

πάσχα (*pascha*), Passover (*4247*).

OT *pascha* is the Gk. transliteration of the Aram. *pashā'*, which corresponds to the Heb. *pesaḥ*. The meaning is not completely clear. Exod. 12:13, 23, 27 indicate a connection with the Heb. *pāsaḥ ʿal*, pass over, spare. The Gk. word has in origin nothing to do with *paschō*, to suffer, although a kinship was postulated in the patristic age.

1. In OT and Jewish lit. *pascha* is used in various senses. It can mean (a) the Passover festival (Exod. 12:11; Num. 9:2), which took place between Nisan 14 and 15 (Lev. 23:5); (b) the animal killed at this festival (Exod. 12: 21; Deut. 16:2); and, in Jud., (c) the seven-day Feast of Unleavened Bread (Lev. 23:6–8).

2. In the OT the Passover festival is associated with the events of Israel's exodus from Egypt (Exod. 12:21–23) and is dedicated as a memorial of this event in the history of God's salvation of his people (12:11–14; Deut. 16:1). The way in which it was observed underwent changes in the course of time, the most radical of which was in connection with the religious reforms of Josiah (621 B.C.). Josiah seems to have nationalized a festival that had earlier been celebrated locally by the individual clans, linking it with the temple worship in Jerusalem (Deut. 16:1–8; 2 Ki. 23:21–23).

3. (a) In NT times the Passover was the chief festival of the year. Thousands of pilgrims from the entire Jewish world streamed to Jerusalem (cf. Lk. 2:41; Jn. 11:55). The Passover meal took place in houses and, because of the great number of those taking part (more than 100,000), also on roofs and in courtyards. It was held in small groups of at least 10 persons and began after sunset on Nisan 15. The killing of the lambs in the inner forecourt of the temple, which was carried out

by representatives of the individual groups (the only duty of the priests was the sprinkling of the blood of the lambs on the altar of burnt offering), and the preparation of the Passover meal took place the previous afternoon. The meal itself was eaten reclining.

(b) Numerous traditions developed as to the liturgy of celebration. (i) To begin with, the head of the household spoke a word of dedication over a first cup of wine, from which he and after him all the members of the household drank. Then a preliminary dish was eaten (various herbs with a sauce of fruit purée). After this the main meal (Passover lamb, unleavened bread, bitter herbs, and purée, together with wine) was brought in, and a second cup of wine poured out. (ii) Neither of these was touched, however, before the next event of the Passover liturgy took place. The head of the family related the story of Israel's exodus from Egypt (cf. Deut. 26:5–11) and explained the meaning of the special items in the meal (the lamb, the unleavened bread, and the bitter herbs). Then followed communal singing of Ps. 113 and/or 114 (the first part of the Passover Hallel). (iii) The main meal was then eaten, the head of the family introducing this with a prayer over the unleavened bread and ending it with a prayer over a third cup of wine. (iv) The end of the feast, which was not to continue beyond midnight, was formed by singing Ps. 114–117 or 115–118 (the second part of the Passover Hallel) and by a blessing pronounced by the head of the family over a fourth cup of wine.

(c) This feast served in ancient Jud. as a reminder of the redemption of the people from the slavery of the Egyptians and the joy over the freedom thus attained. In addition, it was an occasion for looking forward to the coming redemption to be brought by the Messiah. Passover time, particularly during the Roman occupation of Palestine, was always a time of increased messianic expectation (cf. Mk. 15:7; Lk. 13:1–3; Jn. 6:15).

NT In the NT *pascha* has the same range of meanings as in contemporary Jud. Its chief meaning is for the Feast of the Passover, including the Feast of Unleavened Bread (e.g., Matt. 26:2; Lk. 2:41; 22:1; Jn. 2:13, 23; 6:4; 11:55; 12:1; Acts 12:4). But the word can also refer to the Passover lamb (Matt. 26:17; Lk. 22:7–8; Jn. 18:28; 1 Cor. 5:7). The expressions "to prepare the Passover" and "to eat the Passover" could also refer to the entire main part of the feast.

1. (a) The only NT reference to the event of the original Passover is at Heb. 11:28. Moses believed God's promise to spare the people on the basis of the Passover blood, and he showed his faith by keeping the Passover.

(b) The Passover background plays a special part in the Passion narrative. All four Gospels record that Jesus' Last Supper, arrest, trial, and condemnation took place at Passover time (Matt. 26–27; Mk. 14; Lk. 22–23; Jn. 18–19). According to the Synoptics, the Last Supper was itself a Passover meal (Mk. 14:12–26 par.), and Jesus was arrested, tried, and condemned on the Passover night and crucified the next day. According to Jn., however, these events happened 24 hours prior to the Passover (cf. 18:28; 19:14), so that the death of Jesus took place at the time when the Passover lambs were killed (the afternoon of Nisan 14).

Some regard John's record as a later alteration of the date, perhaps occasioned by the comparison, found elsewhere in the NT (e.g., 1 Cor. 5:7; 1 Pet. 1:19; cf. Rev. 5:6, 9, 12), of Jesus with the Passover lamb. Others, however, hold that different Jewish groups in the 1st cent. followed different calendars and that John follows a different calendar from the Synoptics.

2. Apparently the early church continued to celebrate the Passover (see Acts 20:6). As in Jud., the feast took place on the evening following Nisan 14 and in expectation of eschatological redemption. As we can see from 1 Cor. 5:7–8 and 1 Pet. 1:13–19, the early church regarded itself as the people of God redeemed in the eschatological Passover. The baptized are exhorted, as were those involved in the first Passover, to live holy lives in readiness to depart (1:13, 17), redeemed "with the precious blood of Christ, a lamb without blemish

or defect" (1:19; cf. also 1 Cor. 5:7, "Christ, our Passover lamb"). Likewise, the church receives the call to "keep the Festival" and to cleanse itself from the old yeast, "that you may be a new batch without yeast" (5:7–8). The eschatological Passover feast has begun with Good Friday, and its fulfillment in the return of Christ is awaited at any time in the Passover night.

3. This form and interpretation of the Passover festival disappeared early in the history of the church. During the 2d cent. the celebration of Easter on a Sunday became general, with its emphasis on remembering the sacrificial death of Jesus, the true Passover lamb. This process gives clear expression both to the break between Jud. and Christianity and to the decline of eschatological expectation within the early church.

See also *heortē*, feast, festival (*2038*); *deipnon*, supper, banquet (*1270*).

4248 πάσχω

πάσχω (*paschō*), suffer, endure (*4248*); κακοπάθεια (*kakopatheia*), suffering (*2801*); κακοπαθέω (*kakopatheō*), suffer evil, endure hardship (*2802*); συγκακοπαθέω (*synkakopatheō*), endure hardship together with someone (*5155*); συμπαθέω (*sympatheō*), have compassion, sympathize with (*5217*); συμπάσχω (*sympaschō*), suffer the same thing as, suffer together with, sympathize with (*5224*); πάθημα (*pathēma*), suffering, affliction, misfortune (*4077*); παθητός (*pathētos*), subject to suffering, capable of suffering (*4078*); πάθος (*pathos*), suffering, passion (*4079*).

CL & OT 1. The basic meaning of *paschō* is that of experiencing something that stems from outside oneself but that affects me, either for good or ill. (a) This vb. originally meant nothing more than to be affected by; how one was affected was expressed by additional words, e.g., *kakōs paschō*, to be in a bad situation; *eu paschō*, to be in a good situation. But since such additions tended to be negative, the vb. itself gradually came to have a negative meaning, unless there were clear indications to the contrary. In most cases it is a matter of being delivered up to an adverse fate or to malevolent gods and humans.

(b) The situation is similar with the noun *pathos*; it means that which is passively experienced. But for the most part *pathos* describes the emotions of the soul, i.e., human feelings and impulses one does not produce within oneself but finds already present and by which a person can be carried away. *pathos* acquired a predominantly negative meaning, that of passion, esp. among the Stoics.

(c) At an early period questions were asked concerning the purpose and meaning of suffering. Salutary lessons can be learned from one's own suffering and that of others; trials can make a person wise, according to Hesiod. The Gk. tragedies teach the profound truth that through suffering we can learn who we are and what station befits us in life.

(d) The Stoics extended the idea of suffering into something universal and cosmological: All nondivine beings are subject to suffering, i.e., are affected by external influences and emotions. But such emotions hinder true knowledge and the practice of virtue, so the passions must be overcome in order that the ideal of "dispassionateness" (*apatheia*) may be attained.

2. *paschō* occurs only 22x in the LXX and means to feel compassion (Ezek. 16:5; Zech. 11:5) or to be affected, impressed (Amos 6:6). In spite of its infrequency, however, the ideas expressed by this vb. and its derivatives are clearly present in the OT, where the question of suffering is approached from various angles.

(a) The cause of suffering lies mostly in the inherent causality of an evil deed, which brings its own retribution by virtue of its consequences and so produces suffering. In some cases, the suffering caused by an evil deed can affect a group of people (Gen. 20:3–7; 1 Sam. 14:24–46) or even an entire nation (Jos. 7). But usually the suffering is restricted to the individual, esp. in the wisdom poetry (e.g., Prov. 26:27). Each individual is personally responsible for the moral decisions he or she makes and for any consequences.

(b) These two ideas, however, are not mutually exclusive but indicate that whenever the Israelites were called upon to suffer, they always tried to understand what Yahweh was doing. Since Yahweh is a living God, both good and evil come from him (Job 2:10; Amos 3:6), although he may use secondary causes as well. The OT therefore leaves little room for suffering that is fortuitous (Jdg. 9:23; 1 Ki. 22:19–23; Job 1:1–2:10). Suffering is not regarded anthropologically with a view to obtaining a deeper insight into one's own existence but is instead a matter of God's providence. The story of Joseph, for example, is seen ultimately as God's directing of painful affairs for the ultimate good of his people (cf. Gen. 50:20).

(c) The fact that there is no tension between the problem of suffering as such and the problem of one's own individual suffering is indicated by the psalms of lament, which show the psalmist overwhelmed with every conceivable kind of trouble (e.g., Ps. 22). Such psalms are not biographies of the psalmist, nor do they give allegorical accounts of his spiritual experiences; rather, they are liturgical formularies for common use within the OT community. Important for the psalmist is not the analysis of his personal sufferings but his experience of comfort from the priestly oracle or from seeking refuge in Yahweh (e.g., 17:8).

3. The issue of the purpose of suffering is one that emerges only in the course of time. (a) Prov. 12:1; 13:1 refer to its educational value: Suffering improves character.

(b) The book of Job in particular is radical and uncompromising in its attitude toward suffering. In his own case Job sees no causal connection between guilt and suffering (6:24) but recognizes that humans cannot enter into litigation with Almighty God (9:32–33). Thus, the book ends with a hymn in which God declares his own omnipotence; his inscrutable wisdom reduces humankind to silence even in the face of unaccountable suffering (38:1–42:6). For who can claim to understand the mysteries of human life or presume to give God counsel or reproof? Thus this book challenges us not to offer blind allegiance to a theological scheme linking sin with suffering, but rather to submit to God.

(c) A further aspect of the suffering of the innocent is the exemplary suffering endured by chosen individuals (e.g., Moses, Num. 11:11; Elijah, 1 Ki. 19; Hosea, Hos. 1–3; Jeremiah, Jer. 15:10; 18:18; 20:14–18), men whose very office exposed them to suffering. The Israelites refused the prophet's message and thus rejected the God from whom the message came. Hence the fate experienced by the prophets demonstrates Israel's hostility to Yahweh. In other words, Yahweh's own suffering as a result of his people's sin is exemplified in the suffering of certain chosen individuals.

(d) The concept of vicarious suffering comes to a climax in Isa.'s message concerning the suffering servant (→ *pais*, son, servant, *4090*). His suffering is seen as punishment for the sins of others (53:4–6).

(e) In Wisdom of Solomon the educational aspect of suffering once again emerges (12:22). Israel's enemies suffer by way of punishment and warning (12:20, 25–27). When God's children suffer, God is carefully leading them to repentance (12:19, 21). However, the educational aspects of suffering receive less emphasis than its teleological and redemptive aspects. According to 2 Macc., even the God-fearing suffer as punishment for their sins (7:18, 32), though joy comes from suffering as a martyr "in the fear of God" (6:30).

4. (a) Josephus frequently deals with this subject. He sees the possibility of pious Jews suffering any extreme for their law. *paschō* in his writings usually has the sense of to endure, suffer punishment, or even suffer death.

(b) But not all suffering leads to death. In rab. Jud., esp. after the destruction of Jerusalem and the consequent cessation of the sacrifices, atoning power was attributed to all suffering for sin; since suffering was intended to lead the sinner to repentance, one could only thank God for it. Further, the rabbis developed a doctrine of vicarious suffering and of meritorious suffering. In fact, earthly sufferings could mitigate retribution in the world to come (cf. 1 Pet. 4:1). Thus the righteous could actually see God's love at work in their sufferings, while the unrighteous, having no sufferings to bear, were deprived of the chance to make amends. *Gen. Rab.* 44:6 on Gen. 15:1 contains the statement (perhaps directed against Christianity) that in every generation there is one righteous man who makes atonement for sin through his sufferings.

NT 1. (a) The vb. *paschō* is used 42x in the NT, most often in the Synoptic Gospels, Acts, Heb., and 1 Pet. The noun *pathēma* occurs 16x (in Paul, 1 Pet., and Heb.). *synkakopatheō* (2 Tim. 1:8; 2:3) and *kakopatheō* (2:9; 4:5) occur with reference to suffering as followers of Christ; in addition, *kakopatheō* is used more generally in Jas. 5:13. The adj. *pathētos* occurs only in Acts 26:23 (Christ was subject to suffering), while *sympatheō* is used 2x, that the exalted Christ (Heb. 4:15) and his people (10:34) are able to exercise compassion. *pathos* occurs only in Rom. 1:26; Col. 3:5; 1 Thess. 4:5.

Since the Synoptic Gospels are, in a sense, passion accounts extended both backward and forward in time, it is striking how little use they make of *paschō* and *pathēma*. In Jn. the whole life of the incarnate Logos is presented as his passion (cf. 1:5, 11), through which he is glorified. Despite this emphasis, however, Jn. makes no use of this word group, so that the importance of the passion idea in the NT cannot be inferred from mere statistics of specific words.

(b) There are only a few places where *paschō* and its derivatives are used in a general sense. Pilate's wife is badly frightened by a dream (Matt. 27:19), and the woman with the issue of blood has suffered a great deal at the hands of many physicians (Mk. 5:26; cf. also Lk. 13:2; Acts 28:5; Gal. 3:4). In the main, however, the word group serves to describe the suffering of Christ and of his disciples.

2. *The suffering of Christ*. (a) *paschō* has a twofold use in reference to Jesus' passion. (i) It can refer exclusively to his death, esp. in phrases in which, although death is not explicitly mentioned, his suffering stands alongside something else, such as his resurrection (Lk. 24:46; Acts 3:18; cf. 3:15; 17:3), his entrance into glory (Lk. 24:26), or his showing himself alive (Acts 1:3). In such passages his suffering is *pathēma tou thanatou* (Heb. 2:9, lit., "suffering of death"), i.e., death itself (13:12).

(ii) In the statements where the forthcoming sufferings of Christ are first announced (e.g., Mk. 8:31; 9:12), the phrase "suffer many things" probably refers to those sufferings prior to his trial before the high priest and not to his death. Note how Jesus' being killed receives separate mention as the third element of the four mentioned. Lk. 17:25, however, has only "suffer many things" and "be rejected." Matt. extends the scope of "suffer many things" to include Christ's sufferings up to and including his death, for Jesus is to suffer these things "at the hands of the elders, chief priests and teachers of the law" (16:21).

(b) The NT strongly insists that Christ's passion is no accident but is of divine necessity (→ *dei*, it is necessary, *1256*; cf. Matt. 16:21; Lk. 13:33; 17:25; 24:26; Acts 17:3) and has been predicted in the OT (Mk. 9:12; Lk. 24:26; Acts 3:18; 1 Pet. 1:11). Thus, the author of Heb. says that, like the OT sin offering (Lev. 16:27), Jesus suffered outside the gate of Jerusalem (Heb. 13:11–13).

(c) Christ's suffering acquires its soteriological significance from the fact that it is substitutionary in character: He is the atoning sacrifice for our sins (Heb. 13:12; 1 Pet. 2:21). This is proved by quotations from Isa. 53 (cf. 1 Pet. 2:22, 24 with Isa. 53:9, 5). Thus through his death (Heb. 2:9–10), Christ becomes the author (*archēgos*; → *archē*, *794*) of our salvation (*sōtēria*, salvation, → *5401*).

(d) The uniqueness of Christ's sufferings follows from this, as is shown by the fact that in the Synoptics Christ uses *paschō* only to refer to his own coming passion. Heb. also uses the vb. only in connection with Christ (but cf. the noun in 10:32) and emphasizes the uniqueness, all-sufficiency, and completeness of his atoning sacrifice (see 7:27; 9:12; cf. Rom. 6:10; 1 Pet. 3:18).

(e) Christ's vicarious suffering does not mean for his followers, however, deliverance *from* earthly suffering but deliverance *for* earthly

suffering. He has suffered and been tempted as we are (Heb. 2:18), yet he was without sin (4:15); indeed, since Christ has shared in all his people's experiences, he is able as the exalted one to "sympathize with [their] weaknesses" (*sympatheō*, 4:15). His suffering was a test that he was called on to undergo and in which he learned obedience (5:8). Having been tested by suffering, he is our pattern and example (1 Pet. 2:21). His suffering requires us as his followers to walk a similar path (Heb. 13:12–13; 1 Pet. 2:21).

(f) Christ is described as *pathētos*, subject to suffering, only in Acts 26:23. As suffering and resurrection are mentioned together, the thought here is similar to that in Lk. 24:26 and Acts 17:3. Hence, the question is not whether Christ, being God, could suffer. This was a post-NT discussion inspired because of the heresy of Docetism, which argued from his deity that Jesus was unable to suffer. Such thinking never became a part of orthodox Christianity.

3. *The suffering of Christ's people*. (a) Suffering and fellowship. The idea of suffering is inseparable from the NT concept of *koinōnia* (fellowship, → *3126*). Thus, those who arm themselves with the mind Christ must suffer in the flesh (1 Pet. 4:1; cf. 2 Cor. 11:23–29). To suffer "as a Christian" (1 Pet. 4:16) means to share in the sufferings of Christ (Phil. 3:10; 1 Pet. 4:13), to suffer with him (*sympaschō*, Rom. 8:17). Indeed, such a mystic union exists between Christ and his body that the sufferings of believers may be identified as one and the same (2 Cor. 1:5). Different churches are united by the bonds of common suffering (1 Thess. 2:14; 1 Pet. 5:9), and the same applies to any individual church. If the members of a fellowship are to show not merely sympathy with one another but active and practical compassion (*sympaschō*), then true unity in the faith is required (1 Cor. 12:26; Heb. 10:34).

Fellowship in suffering can also exist between the apostle and the local church (2 Cor. 1:6–7) or the apostle and an individual disciple (2 Tim. 1:8; 2:3). The great example of this process is Jesus Christ (1 Pet. 2:21), not only for an apostle himself as a "witness of Christ's sufferings" (1 Pet. 5:1), but also for those who follow an apostle (2 Tim. 3:10–11) or who are called on to imitate an apostle (1 Cor. 11:1). Just as the prophets were good examples of how to endure unjust suffering (*kakopatheia*, Jas. 5:10), so now the apostles set a good example. Their sufferings are part of their ministry (→ *diakoneō*, serve, *1354*) and serve to identify the true servants of the church (cf. 2 Cor. 11:23–29). What Paul suffers for the church is not redemptive but missionary (Col. 1:24).

But not all suffering is fellowship with the sufferings of Christ. For suffering to be in this category, the apostles and the church must suffer for the sake of their office or of their Christian calling; i.e., they must suffer as Christians (1 Pet. 4:16), unjustly (2:19–20), and not as evildoers or murderers (4:15; cf. Lk. 23:32–33)—who suffer justly. True suffering in this sense is called suffering "according to God's will" (1 Pet. 4:19), "for [the] name" of Jesus Christ (Acts 9:16; Phil. 1:29), "for the gospel" (2 Tim. 1:8), "for what is right" (1 Pet. 3:14), and for "the kingdom of God" (2 Thess. 1:5).

(b) The eschatological aspect of suffering. Just as Christ's suffering was not an end in itself but a means to a great end, perfection (Heb. 2:10), the same applies to his people (1 Pet. 5:9). The goal for which Christians suffer is that of God's kingdom. Compared with the hope of "eternal glory," this present period of suffering shrinks to "a little while" (5:10). In Rom. 8:18 Paul emphasizes that the sufferings of the present bear no comparison with future glory, so that even suffering may be regarded as a precious gift (Phil. 1:29; 1 Pet. 2:19) from "the God of all grace" (5:10).

Paul speaks of the aim of his new life as being to enter experimentally into the knowledge (first) of the power of Christ's resurrection, and (only then) of the fellowship of his sufferings (Phil. 3:10). Again and again in the NT suffering and glory (Rom. 8:17; 1 Pet. 5:1, 10), as well as suffering and patience (2 Thess. 1:4–5; Heb. 10:32), are mentioned in the same breath. Indeed, Paul can take the idea of suffering as being temporary because it is advancing toward final glory, and he extends it to cover the whole of creation (Rom. 8:18–25). Thus believers await not the *end* of suffering but its *goal*.

4250 (patassō, strike, hit), → 3463.

4251 (pateō, tread, trample), → 4344.

4252	πατήρ

πατήρ (*patēr*), father (*4252*); πατριά (*patria*), family, clan (*4255*); πατρίς (*patris*), fatherland, homeland, home city (*4258*); ἀπάτωρ (*apatōr*), fatherless (*574*).

CL & OT 1. In cl. Gk. *patēr* means not only father but also the patriarch of a family or (in the pl.) ancestors generally. In a fig. sense *patēr* is used as a title of respect for a venerable old man. It also denotes intellectual or spiritual fatherhood, so that a philosopher may be called the "father" of his followers, and in the mystery religions the one who conducts the ceremony of initiation can be described as "father" of the newly initiated.

patria, lineage, clan, indicates descent from the same father and ancestral patriarch (cf. Lk. 2:4; Acts 3:25; Eph. 3:15); *patris* means fatherland (cf. Jn. 4:44; Heb. 11:14) or home city (cf. Matt. 13:54, 57; Lk. 4:23); and *apatōr* means fatherless (see Heb. 7:3). The last term is used of orphans, children born out of wedlock, outcasts, and outlaws. Whenever gods are described as "fatherless," the word denotes their miraculous origin.

2. (a) The use of the title "father" for a deity in the religions of the ancient world is based on mythical ideas of an original act of begetting and the natural, physical descent of all humans from God. Thus the god El of Ugarit was called "father of humankind," and the Gk. Zeus "father of humans and gods." In Egypt the pharaoh was regarded as the son of the deity in a physical sense. The term *father* denotes above all the absolute authority of one who can demand obedience, but at the same time his merciful love, goodness, and care. People should respond by recognizing their own powerlessness and dependence on the deity and should trust and love him.

(b) The idea of the fatherhood of God is given a philosophical interpretation in Plato and the Stoics. The former, in his cosmological elaboration of the father idea, emphasizes the creator relationship of God, the "universal father," to the entire cosmos. According to Stoic teaching, Zeus's authority as father pervades the universe; he is the creator, father, and sustainer of human beings.

(c) In the ancient mystery cults the regeneration and deification of the initiate is seen as an act of begetting by the deity; hence the latter is invoked in prayer as "father."

(d) The gnostics also describe the supreme God as the father or first father. Here, however, the personal relationship between the deity and humankind disappears.

3. The LXX uses the word *patēr* (Heb. *ʾāb*) almost exclusively (ca. 1180x) in a secular sense. Both the OT and the lit. of ancient Palestinian Jud. have a marked reserve in the use of this word in a religious sense. Diaspora Jud. tended to use "Father" in reference to God more frequently.

(a) *Secular usage.* Physical fatherhood is the gift and command of the Creator (Gen. 1:28). As bearer of the divine blessing (cf. Gen. 27), the father is head of the family and an authority that must be respected under all circumstances (Exod. 20:12; 21:15, 17; Prov. 23:22). Not only is it his task to feed, protect, and educate his family, but, more important, he is the family priest (Exod. 12:3–11) and teacher (12:26–27; 13:14–16; Deut. 6:7; 32:7, 46; Isa. 38:19). The father is responsible for seeing that family life is in accordance with the covenant and that the children receive religious instruction. Even servants may address a master as "my father" (2 Ki. 5:13).

Earlier generations of Israel are called "fathers" (Ps. 22:4; 106:7), as are outstanding men of God of previous ages (Sir. 44:1–19)—particularly the patriarchs Abraham, Isaac, and Jacob, the bearers and mediators of the covenant promises of God (Jos. 24:3; 1 Chr. 29:18).

Father is also used as a title of honor for a priest (Jdg. 17:10; 18:19) or prophet (2 Ki. 6:21; 13:14). In rab. Jud., *father* was frequently used of respected scribes, and the metaphor of father and child is occasionally applied to the relationship between a teacher of the Torah and his pupil.

(b) *Religious usage.* (i) God as Father in the OT. Apart from comparisons with an earthly father (Ps. 103:13; Prov. 3:12; cf. Deut. 1:31; 8:5), the word "father" is used of God only 15x in the OT—13x as an epithet and 2x directly in prayer (Jer. 3:4, 19).

God as Father in the OT refers only to his relationship with the people of Israel (Deut. 32:6; Isa. 63:16 [2x]; 64:8; Jer. 31:9 = LXX 38:9; Mal. 1:6; 2:10) or, more specifically, with the king of Israel (2 Sam. 7:14; 1 Chr. 22:10; 28:6; Ps. 89:26; cf. 2:7), never to humankind in general. The basic difference between this and the views of the fatherhood of the deity held by Israel's neighbors is that in the OT God's fatherhood is not understood in a biological or mythological sense, but in a soteriological one. To be God's child is grounded in the miracle of divine election and redemption (cf. Exod. 4:22; Deut. 14:1–2; Hos. 11:1–4). Even where the language of divine begetting is used, the reference is to the historical, elective action of God.

When God, the one who elects and redeems, is described as Father, expression is given both to his merciful, forgiving love (Jer. 31:9, 20 = LXX 38:9, 20; cf. Hos. 11:8) and to his claim to respect and obedience (Deut. 32:5–6; Jer. 3:4–5, 19; Mal. 1:6). Because the Israelites share in being children of God, they have a special obligation to be loyal to one another (2:10). If the individual sees God as Father, it is because of that person's status as a member of the people and because he or she has experienced the work of God in a way corresponding to his redemption of Israel (Ps. 68:5 in the context of 68:4–10).

(ii) God as Father in Palestinian Judaism. As in the OT, in Palestinian Jud. before the birth of Christ the description of God as Father is rare (e.g., Tob. 13:4; Sir. 51:10; *Jub.* 1:24–25, 28; 19:29); the Qumran texts provide but a single example (1QH 9:35–36). In rab. Jud. of the 1st cent. A.D. the use of *Father* became more widespread, but it was still far less frequent than other descriptions of God. God is known as "Father in heaven," the addition of "in heaven" indicating the distance between God and humankind. But in contrast to the OT, any individual worshiper can speak of God as his or her "Father in heaven." The indispensable condition for this personal relationship is obedience to God's commandments (cf. Sir. 4:10).

As an invocation of God, we find in the 1st cent. A.D. the expression "our Father, our King." But this is only in liturgical prayers of the whole congregation, not in the normal spoken Aram., but in the Heb. language of worship—thus drawing attention both to the fatherhood of God and to his majesty. We have yet to find an example of an individual addressing God as "my Father." Sir. 23:1, 4 appears in the Gk. text as "Lord, my Father," but the Heb. original has "God of my father" (cf. Exod. 15:2).

(iii) God as Father in Diaspora Judaism. The Greek-speaking Jews of the Diaspora were more frequent and less reserved than the Jews of Palestine in their use of the term *father* as a description of God (3 Macc. 5:7; Wis. 2:16). Philo and Josephus both reveal the influence of the Gk. concept of the universal father. In the Diaspora even individuals could address God as "Father" (cf. 3 Macc. 6:3, 8; Wis. 14:3).

NT The range of meaning of *patēr*, father, in the NT corresponds to that of *ʾāb* and *patēr* in the OT. In contrast to the OT, however, the number of examples of *patēr* in the religious sense (245x) far exceeds the number of those in a secular sense (158x).

1. *The secular use of* patēr. (a) According to the Synoptic tradition, Jesus specifically emphasized the binding validity of the commandment to honor one's parents (Mk. 7:9–13 par.; 10:19 par.; cf. Exod. 20:12). Even more important, however, is the obligation Jesus makes to follow him (Matt. 10:37; Lk. 14:26). The family rules laid

down in Eph. and Col. likewise underline the commandment of obedience toward father and mother, but they also point to the human and spiritual responsibility of a father toward his children (Eph. 6:1–4; Col. 3:20–21).

(b) The close connection between Israel and the church, which receives extended treatment in Rom. 9–11, is the basis of Paul's words in 1 Cor. 10:1, when he speaks of God's people of the OT as "our forefathers," even though he is addressing Gentile Christians (cf. also Rom. 9:10; Heb. 1:1).

(c) The idea of spiritual fatherhood appears in 1 Cor. 4:14–15 and also indirectly where spiritual sonship is mentioned (1 Tim. 1:2, 18; 2 Tim. 1:2; 2:1; Tit. 1:4; Phlm. 10; 1 Pet. 5:13). The apostle is regarded as "father" of those Christians who owe their faith to his preaching, but Matt. 23:9 forbids the use of the term *father* as a title of honor.

(d) Among the derivatives of *patēr*, *apatōr* (without father, Heb. 7:3) deserves special mention. The author of Heb. describes Melchizedek as "without father or mother, without genealogy, without beginning of days or end of life." The writer arrives at this remarkable conclusion with the help of the rab. principle, "What is not mentioned in the Torah does not exist." In the silence of the OT (Gen. 14:18–24) about the descent, parentage, birth, and death of Melchizedek, he finds a cryptic reference to the miraculous, heavenly origin of the priest-king and to his eternal priesthood. As a heavenly being (cf. 11QMelch), Melchizedek is superior to the Levitical priests, for whom priestly descent is a precondition for service (Neh. 7:63–64; cf. Lev. 21:13–23). Hence he is for the writer of Heb. a prophetic prefiguring of the preexistent Son of God and eternal high priest Christ, who is similarly not descended from the tribe of Levi (Heb. 7:13–14).

2. *God as Father.* In the concept of the fatherhood of God we see one of the central ideas of early Christian theology (see also *abba*, 5; *hyios*, 5626).

(a) Jesus uses the title "Father" for God nearly 150x. Note that Jesus never calls God the "Father of Israel." He speaks of God as "my Father" and as the father of the disciples ("your Father"). But he never joins with them together in a common "our Father." (The Lord's Prayer is a prayer he gave to the disciples to use!)

Jesus' reference to God as his Father is based on a unique revelation of God given him from above and on his incomparable status as Son (Matt. 11:25–27; Lk. 10:21–22). In the mission of Jesus, in whose word and works the kingdom of God is dawning, God reveals himself as Father.

Insofar as Jesus spoke to his disciples about God as "your Father," he did not teach the idea that God is the Father of all human beings. Rather, he linked the fatherhood of God to one's relationship to him. God shows himself to be the Father of the disciples in his mercy (Lk. 6:36), goodness (Matt. 5:45), forgiving love (Mk. 11:25), and care (Matt. 6:8; 6:32 par.; Lk. 12:30). He gives them the gifts of the age of salvation (Matt. 7:11) and is preparing for them full salvation at the close of the age (Lk. 12:32). The disciple's experience of God's fatherly love places one under a special obligation to treat one's fellow human beings properly (see Matt. 5:44–45; Lk. 6:36).

Except for Jesus' cry from the cross in Matt. 27:46 and Mk. 15:34, where he quotes Ps. 22:1 ("my God"), Jesus always addresses God in his prayers with the words "(my) Father." Insofar as this appellation was new in Palestine, it must have seemed nothing short of outrageous.

(b) Other NT witnesses, especially Paul and John, are unanimous in making the fatherhood of God rest on a basis of Christology and soteriology.

Paul describes God as Father 40x, normally in liturgical formulas (blessings: Rom. 1:7; 1 Cor. 1:3; 2 Cor. 1:2; doxologies: Rom. 15:6; 2 Cor. 1:3; Eph. 1:3; creeds: 1 Cor. 8:6; Eph. 4:6; prayers: Eph. 5:20; Col. 1:12). When he uses the phrase "the God and Father of our Lord Jesus Christ," as he frequently does (e.g., Rom. 15:6; 2 Cor. 1:3; cf. 11:31), he is emphasizing that God has revealed himself as Father

in Jesus Christ and can hence be recognized as such only in him. The fatherhood of God is not a fact of nature, but an eschatological miracle (cf. Rom. 8:14–17; Gal. 4:1–7).

John stresses Jesus' unique relationship to the Father (Jn. 6:57; 10:30; 14:10–11). As the Son who has been accorded a complete knowledge of God (3:35; 10:15a; 16:15a), he reveals the Father (1:18; 8:26–29; 14:7, 9). He thus imparts to his own the status of children of God, which can only be attained through him (1:12; 14:6; 17:25–26) and can only be received as a gift of divine love (1 Jn. 3:1–2).

Only 3x in the NT does a concept of God's fatherhood possibly appear without a Christological anchor. In Eph. 3:14–15 God in his capacity as Creator of the world is called "the Father, from whom all fatherhood [*patria*] in heaven and on earth derives its name" (NIV note; cf., however, "from whom his whole family" in NIV text). In Heb. 12:9 in his capacity as the Creator of human souls God is called "Father of spirits" (NRSV). In Jas. 1:17 as Creator of the stars, he is called "Father of the heavenly lights."

See also *abba*, father (5).

4255 (*patria*, family, clan), → 4252.

4258 (*patris*, fatherland, homeland, home city), → 4252.

4266 (*pachynō*, thicken, make insensitive), → 5017.

4272 (*peitharcheō*, obey), → 4275.

4273 (*peithos*, persuasive), → 4275.

4275 πείθω

πείθω (*peithō*), convince, persuade; (mid. pass.) believe, obey (*4275*); πεποίθησις (*pepoithēsis*), trust, confidence (*4301*); πειθός (*peithos*), persuasive (*4273*); πειθαρχέω (*peitharcheō*), obey (*4272*); πεισμονή (*peismonē*), persuasion (*4282*); ἀπειθέω (*apeitheō*), be disobedient (*578*); ἀπειθής (*apeithēs*), disobedient (*579*); ἀπείθεια (*apeitheia*), disobedience (*577*); πιθανολογία (*pithanologia*), persuasive speech, art of persuasion (*4391*).

CL & OT 1. (a) In cl. Gk. the stem *peith-* has the basic meaning of trust. Trust can refer to a statement (i.e., to put faith in) or to a demand (i.e., to be persuaded, hence to obey). The original intrans. act. *peithō* (trust) became trans., to convince, persuade, and the meaning of trust was taken over in the pass. *peithomai*. Only the 2d perf. *pepoitha* retains in the act. the original intrans. meaning (strictly, to have taken hold of trust with the effect continuing into the present); it has the present meaning of trust firmly, rely on. The mid. pass. of the 1st perf. *pepeismai* likewise means to be convinced.

(b) *apeitheō* (be disobedient) and *apeitheia* (disobedience) are derived from *apeithēs* (disobedient).

(c) The act. meaning convince, persuade, is especially characteristic of Gk. thought. It is significant that Peitho is regarded as a goddess. But *peithō* can also extend the meaning of persuade to include lead astray, corrupt.

2. (a) Heb. has no word for persuade, convince. In the few places where tenses other than the perf. of *peithō* and *peithomai* occur in the LXX (chiefly in 2 and 4 Macc. and Tob.), there is no Heb. equivalent.

(b) It is otherwise in the case of the perf. *pepoitha*, which occurs about 80x for the Heb. *bāṭaḥ*, trust, rely upon. This Heb. word and its derivatives are translated almost as often by *pepoitha* as by the vbs. *elpizō* and *epelpizō* and the noun *elpis* (→ *1828*). *pepoitha* serves to draw attention to the object and ground of Israel's hope and refuge, especially in Isa. 10:20, Jer., proverbial wisdom, and (together with the more common *elpizō*) in psalms expressing trust (cf. Ps. 25:2; 57:1). This trust lies in God's covenant fidelity, election, and promise, and it is to be distinguished from trust in humans, idols, and material goods (cf. Ps. 118:8; Isa. 17:7–8; 32:3; 36:6; Jer. 7:4). The noun *pepoithēsis* occurs in the LXX only in 2 Ki. 18:19.

(c) *apeitheō* and *apeithēs* are used to characterize the people who disobey God, esp. in Deut. and Isa. (e.g., Deut. 1:26; 9:23–24; Isa. 3:8).

NT *peithō* (including the mid. pass. *peithomai* and the 2d perf. *pepoitha*) are common in the NT; they occur most frequently in Paul (22x) and Acts (17x). Paul, like the LXX, used the act. (nonperf.) forms rarely (2x), but the perf. forms of *pepoitha* most often. The noun *pepoithēsis* is found 6x in Paul. *peitharcheō* occurs only in Acts (3x) and Tit. 3:1.

The negative forms occur less frequently: *apeitheō* occurs 13x (5x in Rom., 4x in 1 Pet.), the noun and the adj. are each found 6x.

1. The range of meaning of the vb. may be ascertained by looking at its tenses with regard to the beginning, end, and duration of the action concerned. (a) The act. form of *peithō* in the aor. (e.g., Matt. 27:20; cf. Acts 12:20; 14:19; 19:26) always has the meaning of persuade, induce, and even to mislead or corrupt. It has no special theological significance. By contrast, the imperf. expresses the attempt to influence a person to adopt a particular attitude or action. Acts uses the vb. to describe Paul's preaching to the Jews and Greeks. He was not trying to evince faith in the one God, but to persuade them of the newly given grace in Christ (Acts 13:43) through teaching (18:4; → *dialogizomai*, 1368). The same applies to the pres. part. In 19:8 Paul argues for three months in the synagogue, attempting to convince the Jews of the kingdom of God.

(b) The pres. ind. denotes not only the duration of the action but the fact that it is taking place at the present time. Here the context determines the meaning. In three texts the meaning is disputed. Some see King Agrippa in Acts 26:28 as acknowledging that he has come within a hair's breadth of conversion. Others, however, insist that Agrippa's words indicate just how far he was from taking the step, as if to say, "Do you think in such a short time you can persuade me to become a Christian?" (cf. NIV). There is no consensus on interpretation here. In any case, Agrippa sees himself in a dilemma. If he says that he rejects the prophets (26:27), his reputation for orthodoxy will be damaged. But if he agrees with Paul's reasoning, he realizes that he is being maneuvered into a position of public agreement with Paul.

In 2 Cor. 5:11 and Gal. 1:10 Paul admits he has to defend himself against the claims of spurious authorities who have been working against him. In 2 Cor. 5:11 he says: "Since, then, we know what it is to fear the Lord, we try to persuade men." In Gal. 1:10 he asks: "Am I now trying to win the approval of men, or of God?" In these two passages the apostle is stressing the fact that he strives to convince people by argument, not because it is necessary for his personal authority, but for the sake of the gospel.

(c) The fut. act. comes close to the aor. in meaning to persuade. It also means to reassure. The thought of corruption seems to be in the background of Matt. 28:14. In 1 Jn. 3:19 ("This then is how we know that we belong to the truth, and how we set our hearts at rest [*peisomen*] in his presence"), it is a question of true self-knowledge. The point is a double one. On the one hand, it is a question of being in the truth or not, which is shown by whether love is shown in action. On the other hand, it is a question of whether God will condemn us. These two points are not simply parallel. Those who are merely of the truth can still condemn themselves before God, although this does not inevitably follow (cf. 3:21). If one's heart drives a person to it, he or she may still reassure it before God. For God knows better than ourselves not only about our guilt, but also that which he has newly created in us.

2. The mid. and pass. dep. *peithomai* stresses the result and outcome of being influenced. This applies to the aor., imperf., and fut., which occur only in Luke's writings in the NT. (a) The aor. occurs 3x. Acts 17:4 shows the success of Paul's teaching in the synagogue of Thessalonica (cf. 17:2), while 5:40 refers to the council of Jewish leaders being persuaded by Gamaliel. Luke uses the same form of the vb. in both passages and in 23:21, a warning against being influenced by false advice. The dat. following the vb. refers to the persons exerting influence. The following are possible meanings: to be persuaded by someone, to yield to (cf. 23:21), to listen to in the sense of obey.

(b) Similarly, the imperf. means to heed, to pay attention to someone's words or actions so that one is influenced by them. According to Acts 27:11, the centurion "followed the advice" of the pilot and the owner of the ship rather than "listening to" Paul's advice. With reference to the behavior of the Roman Jews, 28:24 expresses a contrast: "Some were convinced [*epeithonto*] by what he said, but others would not believe [*ēpistoun*]." *peithomai* here has the meaning of believe (Paul's words). The vb. can also denote followers of a leader, as in the case of Theudas and Judas the Galilean (5:36–37).

(c) In the only passage in the fut. (Lk. 16:31), *peithomai* means to be convinced: "If they do not listen to Moses and the Prophets, they will not be convinced even if someone rises from the dead." Whereas in Acts Paul seeks to convince the Jews by arguments that any Jew must accept, Lk. 16:31 expresses the corollary, that where agreement to such argument is refused, nothing will convince such a person.

(d) The pres. has no particular theological significance in Acts 21:14 and 26:26, where it simply means to be convinced, and in Heb. 13:18 ("we are sure"). In other places it means to obey or follow (Gal. 5:7; Heb. 13:17; Jas. 3:3). In Rom. 2:8 disobedience (→ *apeitheō* below) to the truth is seen as being grounded in subjection to unrighteousness, which is abolished by faith. But where there is a renewed regard for the law, disobedience to the truth necessarily follows (cf. Gal. 5:7; *peismonē* below).

(e) The perf. always denotes a situation in which the act of examining and weighing up has been concluded and a firm conviction has already been reached (cf. Lk. 20:6; Rom. 8:38; 14:14; 15:14; 2 Tim. 1:5, 12; Heb. 6:9). This can refer to convictions concerning facts or people as well as to the all-embracing, unshakeable certainty that has been attained in faith (Rom. 8:38–39).

3. The 2d perf. *pepoitha* with the prep. *epi* or *en* always means to depend on, trust in, put one's confidence in. It indicates a conviction as the basis for further thought and action. Thus it can refer to one's trust in one's own righteousness or one's own flesh (Lk. 18:9; 2 Cor. 1:9; Phil. 3:3–4). But it can also refer in a good sense to trust that can be placed in someone. Thus Paul expresses confidence in the church (2 Cor. 2:3; 2 Thess. 3:4, "in the Lord"; cf. Gal. 5:10; Phil. 1:25; 2:24). However, in both the former passages the vb. can be understood in relation to the following *hoti*, so that, as in other passages, *pepoitha hoti* can be translated to be confident that. *epi*, like *eis* in Gal. 5:10, means "in view of." Thus the confidence would refer not so much to the persons as to the circumstances brought about by God in which Paul trusts "in the Lord," such as God's faithfulness in completing the work he has begun. In any case, the trust is ultimately in the Lord himself.

Confidence is also expressed by forms of *pepoitha* followed by the infin. "If anyone is confident [*pepoithen*] that he belongs to Christ [*einai* plus gen.], he should consider again that we belong to Christ just as much as he" (2 Cor. 10:7; cf. Rom. 2:19). When followed by the dat., the vb. means simply to trust, believe in (Phil. 1:14; Phlm. 21). The entrusting of oneself to God that is characteristic of Ps. finds direct expression only in OT quotations that are applied to Jesus (see Matt. 27:43; Heb. 2:13; cf. Isa. 8:17). Trust in God now coincides with faith in Jesus Christ. This also applies to 2 Cor. 1:9, where trust in God who raises the dead comes from faith in the risen Christ.

4. The noun *pepoithēsis*, confidence, has the same meaning in Phil. 3:4 as the vb. in 3:3–4. It is likewise connected with *en sarki*, "in the flesh," and refers to the self-confidence that grows out of observance of the law. On the other hand, 2 Cor. 3:4 refers to the confidence that grows out of the apostolic commission (cf. 3:5–6), which leads Paul to describe the Corinthian church as his letter of commendation, written by God's Spirit on hearts of flesh (3:3). Confidence in human beings (8:22, where the prep. *eis* is used for "in"; cf. Gal. 5:10) is set in the context of confidence in God (*pros ton theon*, 2 Cor. 3:4), while the confidence expressed in 1:15 is to be understood in the light of the hope of 1:13–14. The confidence of 10:2 is grounded in Paul's commission as an apostle (see above on 3:4), which enabled him to risk

coming into violent conflict with certain people. In Eph. 3:12 this boldness of approaching God is further defined by the words "with . . . confidence."

5. In 1 Cor. 2:4 there is a textual question as to whether Paul is using the adj. *peithos* (persuasive) or the noun *peithō* (persuasiveness). The meaning of the text remains the same in either case, for Paul is clearly stating that the Corinthians did not come to faith through human wisdom and its ways of persuading. The latter are described in Col. 2:4 as *pithanologia* ("fine-sounding [but false] arguments"), by which people are deceived.

6. The noun *peismonē* in Gal. 5:8 ("persuasion") may be understood actively in relation to *peithō*. But there may be here a play on words with *peithesthai* in the preceding verse, which means to obey: "Who . . . kept you from obeying the truth? That kind of persuasion does not come from the one who calls you." The result of this persuasion that did not come from God would thus be that the Galatians are no longer allowing themselves to be persuaded by the truth.

7. The vb. *peitharcheō* (obey) is used for obedience both to God (Acts 5:29) and to other humans (27:21; cf. *peithomai* in 27:11). In Tit. 3:1 it is identified with being submissive to rulers and authorities.

8. (a) *apeithēs* (disobedient) occurs in Acts 26:19 in the form of a double negative that is designed to stress Paul's obedience: "So then, King Agrippa, I was not disobedient to the vision from heaven." In Rom. 1:30 and 2 Tim. 3:2 the word occurs in catalogues of vices in connection with disobedience to parents.

(b) In all other passages where *apeithēs*, the noun *apeitheia* (disobedience), and the vb. *apeitheō* (be disobedient) occur, the context suggests disobedience to God, mostly in contrast with faith. This is the sense of the LXX (cf. Lk. 1:17, which speaks of Elijah being sent to turn "the disobedient to the wisdom of the righteous"; cf. Mal. 4:6). It is exemplified by Jn. 3:36; Acts 14:2; 19:9 (of disbelieving Jews); Rom. 15:31; Eph. 2:2; 5:6 (contrast "those who are disobedient," i.e., non-Christians, with the "children of light," 5:8); and Tit. 1:16. A distinctive use is offered in the way 1 Pet. qualifies disobedience as disobedience to the word or the gospel (2:8; 3:1; 4:17). It also speaks of the defective obedience of people before the flood despite the patience of God (3:20).

Heb. 3:18 and 4:6 hold up to Christians (cf. 4:11) the behavior of the Israelites in the desert as a warning example. Those who stop their ears to God's instructions for the present time will come to grief; they are not ready to receive the future from the hands of God in utter trust. Because of her faith Rahab the harlot was unlike those people, and she did not meet with the destruction that came on the disobedient citizens of Jericho (11:31). The Gentile Christians were themselves once likewise disobedient (Rom. 11:30; cf. Tit. 3:3). But now, through the *apeitheia* of Israel, in which God's covenant people as a whole did not wish to enter the new covenant in Jesus Christ (cf. Rom. 10:21), Gentiles have received mercy. Israel's disobedience is intensified through their opposition to the mercy that has come on the Gentiles (11:31). But in turn they may through all this now receive mercy.

The climax of the argument of Rom. 9–11 shows that this lack of trust, obedience, faith, and acceptance of God's will is the normal situation of the human race (11:32). Only God himself can save us by having mercy on us and granting us faith.

See also *pistis*, faith (*4411*).

4277	πεινάω

πεινάω (*peinaō*), hunger (*4277*); διψάω (*dipsaō*), to thirst (*1498*); δίψος (*dipsos*), thirst (*1499*); λιμός (*limos*), hunger, famine (*3350*).

CL & OT 1. (a) The range of meaning of the above words is not limited to physical hunger or thirst, but extends to the intellectual and spiritual life. They express a passionate longing for something without which one cannot live, e.g., freedom, honor, fame, wealth, praise, enlightenment. Hunger and thirst are often bracketed together.

(b) The ancients attributed famine to the wrath of the gods. Vegetation gods were thus supposed to guarantee the provision of food. In the mystery religions these old fertility gods satisfied human hunger for enduring eternal life. It was the task of rulers (e.g., the pharaohs of Egypt) to protect their subjects against hunger. But every case of hunger and thirst presented an obligation to help whoever was in need.

(c) Gk. philosophers generally attempted to educate their adherents to free themselves from enslavement to bodily needs. Thus the Stoics sought to make themselves independent of all the vicissitudes of life by the practice of asceticism, and the gnostics to free themselves from a sensual attachment to the world through the denial of the body in order to attain to the realm of the spirit.

2. While *peinaō* and *dipsaō* or *dipsos* each occurs about 50x in the LXX, *limos* occurs over 100x. Hunger and thirst are the worst forms of lack, and of the two thirst is more distressing in the sun-drenched East. Among the causes is failure of the rains, with consequent failure of the harvest (1 Ki. 17:1), so that one can even speak of the thirst of the land. Hunger and thirst are also connected with war, wanderings in the desert (Ps. 107:5), idleness (Prov. 19:15), and esp. godlessness (Ps. 34:10; Isa. 65:13; Sir. 40:9). God sends hunger and thirst as judgment and as a means of humbling the godless attitudes of people (Deut. 32:24; 2 Sam. 24:13; Ezek. 5:15–16).

During times of famine Israel sought help in more fertile Egypt (Gen. 12:10; 41:53–57; 42:1–5). But it was in such times of need (both during the wandering in the desert and in the land of Canaan) that Israel learned that God was her real Savior from need (Exod. 16:3–18; 17:3–7; cf. 1 Ki. 8:37–40). Yahweh takes up the cause of the hungry who belong to the dispossessed poor (1 Sam. 2:5). Judgment is pronounced on those who are filled, but there is the promise of salvation for the hungry (Ps. 107:36–42; 146:7; Isa. 65:13). God demands from the devout a corresponding attitude to the poor (58:7, 10; Ezek. 18:7, 16), among whom even their enemies must not be overlooked (Prov. 25:21).

3. (a) This word group is occasionally used fig. of thirst for God (Ps. 42:2; 63:1; 143:6) and of striving after wisdom (Sir. 51:24). Amos 8:11–13 speaks of a hungering after the word of God alongside an actual famine: God can in the end withhold everything as a punishment. Several passages meant for the Jewish people during the Babylonian exile have particular significance. Though at present discouraged (Isa. 40:27–31) and poor (41:17–18; 49:9–10; 55:1), they will be allowed by God to return home. He will transform the arduous route through the desert into an oasis journey (41:18; 43:20; 48:21), and their wasted homeland itself into a garden of salvation (Ezek. 34:29; cf. Isa. 35:1, 6–7). This material well-being includes the idea of salvation (44:3; Jer. 31:12 = LXX 38:12).

(b) In *Pss. Sol.* 5:1–12; 10:1–6; 13:7–10, hunger and thirst serve as inducements to better keeping of the law.

NT *peinaō* occurs 23x in the NT, mostly in the Synoptics (esp. Matt.). *dipsaō* occurs 16x and *limos* 12x. Both OT and NT take human physical needs seriously. But it is not only the stomach but the whole person that needs to be satisfied. External well-being and inner salvation are most closely related. This explains the fact that many NT statements about hunger and thirst show a peculiar ambiguity, making it scarcely possible to distinguish the literal from the metaphorical.

1. Like the OT, the NT speaks of famines (Lk. 4:25; Acts 7:11). These are among the terrors of the end time (Matt. 24:7; Rev. 6:8; 18:8) and the occasion of special measures of assistance (Acts 11:28). Hunger can move a person to conversion, where questions about food raise questions about faith (Lk. 15:14, 17).

2. (a) Luke esp. depicts Jesus as the advocate of the poor and hungry (Lk. 1:53; 6:21), understanding hunger in the broadest sense. Believers should not fear hunger, for in the coming order God will act on behalf of the needy. Thus, Jesus calls them blessed already in view of the coming day of God. For those who can expect nothing from this world and direct all their hope toward God, there will be no more

hunger (6:21). There is no promise, however, for those who are satisfied in this world. Instead, they are threatened with the prospect of mourning and weeping (6:25).

(b) In contrast to Lk., the beatitude of Matt. 5:6 understands hunger as "hunger and thirst for righteousness," a longing to be right with God and to live right (cf. 6:10). Those who hunger are the same as those who believe and long for the kingdom of God (6:33). Their promised filling begins with the coming of Jesus and continues until everything else is theirs.

(c) Hunger and thirst in the Johannine writings have a double meaning. Natural thirst (Jn. 4:13) and physical hunger (6:1–13) convey the longing for life in general. Jesus seizes upon this longing in order to show that it is only through contact with himself, the giver of life, that it is satisfied (4:14–15; 6:35; 7:37). But what is promised in all the sayings about the satisfaction of hunger and thirst is only fully received in God's new world, when all physical and spiritual needs will end (Rev. 7:16; 21:6; 22:17).

3. The description of Jesus himself having to suffer hunger and thirst demonstrates his humanity. After his forty days of fasting, the devil used Jesus' hunger to tempt him to use his authority as Son of God to satisfy his own need through a miracle (Matt. 4:2; Lk. 4:2). Only by obeying God's Word was he able to stand firm, for "man does not live on bread alone, but on every word that comes from the mouth of God" (Matt. 4:4; cf. Lk. 4:4; Deut. 8:3). Jesus cursed the fig tree that did not satisfy his hunger for fruit (Matt. 21:18–19) and thereby demonstrated in parabolic fashion how a curse will fall on all who do not bear the fruit of righteousness. On the cross he thirsted, though he offered himself as the living water to satisfy all thirst (Jn. 19:28).

4. The disciples shared Jesus' poverty. He defended their action of plucking ears of grain on the Sabbath (Matt. 12:1–8; Mk. 2:23–28; Lk. 6:1–5). Hunger and thirst were also among the deprivations Paul underwent for the crucified Christ, in contrast to the enthusiasts in Corinth, who believed they already enjoyed full possession of all the good things of the coming world (1 Cor. 4:8, 11; 2 Cor. 11:27). When they assembled for worship, these enthusiasts pitilessly took no notice of the hungry among them (1 Cor. 11:21, 34).

Hunger and thirst are not necessarily signs of God's disfavor. They may afflict, but they cannot separate us from the love of God (Rom. 8:35). Yet if Paul was able to overcome them, he did so not on the basis of asceticism or superior knowledge, but through Christ alone (Phil. 4:12).

5. Hunger and thirst are occasions for the exercise of love. Their satisfaction is reckoned among the works of mercy that will serve as a basis of judgment (Matt. 25:35, 37, 42) and that should include one's enemy (Rom. 12:20). We must remember also that in those who hunger and thirst Jesus Christ himself meets us incognito (Matt. 25:37, 42).

See also *brōma*, food (*1109*); *geuomai*, taste, partake of, enjoy, experience (*1174*); *esthiō*, eat (*2266*); *pinō*, drink (*4403*).

4278 (*peira*, attempt, trial, experiment), → *4280*.

4279 (*peirazō*, try, test, put on trial, tempt), → *4280*.

4280   πειρασμός

πειρασμός (*peirasmos*), test, trial, tempting, temptation (*4280*); πεῖρα (*peira*), attempt, trial, experiment (*4278*); πειράω (*peiraō*), try, attempt, endeavor (*4281*); πειράζω (*peirazō*), try, test, put on trial, tempt (*4279*); ἐκπειράζω (*ekpeirazō*), put to the test, try, tempt (*1733*); ἀπείραστος (*apeirastos*), without temptation, untempted (*585*).

CL 1. The noun *peira*, attempt, and the vb. *peiraō*, to test, try, together with the intensive form (rare in cl. Gk.) *peirazō*, to tempt someone, put to the test, are related to *peraō*, to drive across, pass through, to strive to get through, and express an intention that includes a certain element of resolution. Thus *peiraō* and *peirazō* convey the

general sense of to try, and in view of the effort required, to exert oneself, strive. Referring to competition against other persons, *peiraō*, usually in mid. or pass., means to measure oneself against someone, strive for someone's favor, lead into temptation (esp. in the sense of unchastity), and then to get to know by experience.

Along the same lines as the vbs., the noun *peira* means attempt, trial, test, risk, attack, experience. *peirasmos* means a medical test; *ekpeirazō* and *apeirastos* are lacking in cl. Gk.

2. (a) In the LXX *peirazō* and *peirao* stand exclusively for *nāsâ* in the piel form of the vb. (e.g., Gen. 22:1; Exod. 15:25; 16:4; Isa. 7:12; Dan. 1:12, 14). They also occur in the Apocr. and some canonical writings without Heb. equivalent (e.g., Dan. 12:10; Tob. 12:14; Wis. 1:2; 2:17, 24). Similarly, *ekpeirazō* always translates *nāsâ* in the piel (Deut. 6:16; 8:2, 16; Ps. 78:18), while *peirasmos* usually stands for the cognate noun *massâ* (Exod. 17:7; Deut. 4:34; Ps. 95:8), and has no Heb. equivalent in Sir. 2:1; 27:5, 7; 1 Macc. 2:52.

(b) These words are found in their purely secular senses: to try to do something (Deut. 4:34; 28:56), try something out (Eccl. 2:1; 7:23 = LXX 7:24; Dan. 1:12), put to the proof (1 Ki. 10:1); the noun *peirasmos* means trial in Deut. 7:19; 29:2 = LXX 29:3.

(c) In the OT, esp. in Deut. and the Deuteronomic history, the ideas of tempting and putting to the test become religious concepts. (i) Yahweh may put his people to the test. Their obligations to him are defined in such words as to fear God, love him, worship him, be faithful to him, listen to his voice, obey his word, walk after his commands, etc. Thus when the OT speaks of Yahweh testing his covenant people, it means that he arranges a test to find out whether they will remain faithful to the covenant. The classic example is the testing of Abraham, when God commanded Abraham to offer the covenant son of promise, Isaac (Gen. 22; for other tests of individuals, see Deut. 33:8 [Levi]; Jdt. 8:26 [Isaac]). As for testing his entire covenant people, in Exod. 16:4 Yahweh tells Moses of his decision to let bread rain down from heaven for the people, who are to gather only enough for each day, to "test them and see whether they will follow my instructions" (cf. also 20:20; Deut. 8:2; Jdg. 2:22).

(ii) Unbelief, disobedience, and murmuring among God's people constitute a challenge to Yahweh, putting him to the test. Note that when the OT refers to Israel's testing of a divine being, it is always Yahweh and never a pagan god. "Tempting God" is the inexplicable way for God's people to behave. Still, it occurred and is described in such passages as Num. 14:22; Ps. 78:40–41; Isa. 7:12; Mal. 3:15. The classic instance for tempting God was at Massah (which the LXX translates *peirasmos*, testing) in the desert (Exod. 17:2, 7; Deut. 6:16; 9:22; 33:8; Ps. 95:8–9; in the last two instances Massah is linked with Meribah).

(iii) Religious testing is also something that God's people on occasion ought to do. Deut. 13:1–5 admits the possibility of false prophets performing wonders in order to lead the people astray. The people are to test such people, not by questioning whether the wonder has actually occurred but by asking whether their teaching agrees with the commands that Israel has received.

(d) Testing is one of the means by which God carries out his saving purposes. Those tested often do not know until afterward whether or why God has been testing them, i.e., only after they survive the tribulation with a stronger faith, having been preserved, proved, purified, disciplined, and taught. Abraham later became an oft-quoted example of someone kept through great testing (e.g., *Apoc. Ab.*; *Jub.* 17–19). Israel also knew about defeat that resulted from failing the testing, when it caused them to go astray and fall away from God. God is the one who works in everything, and therefore he is the one who tests. At times, of course, he allows Satan to do the testing (cf. Job 1:11–12; 2:6–7; → *diabolos*, devil, *1333*).

3. (a) Rab. lit. exhibits a tendency of Satan to become independent in his role as tempter. He is depicted as the head of a kingdom opposed to God, which tries to frustrate God's saving purposes by leading humankind into sin and accusing them before God (e.g., *Tanḥ.*

40b; *b. Sanh.* 89b). In this he makes use of the evil impulse already present in humans, which now becomes the gate through which temptation makes its inroads (e.g., *m. B.Bat.* 16).

(b) The independence of the evil one is even more strongly marked in the Apocr. and Pseudepigrapha. Suffering and evil are now experienced as so oppressive and devilish that it was felt inappropriate to link them in any way with God.

NT In the NT the intensive form *peirazō* occurs 38x—not only for the temptation of Jesus by Satan or Jesus' opponents, but also for the temptation of Christians. In addition, the word can have a secular sense of to try, attempt. *ekpeirazō* is used 4x (Matt. 4:7; Lk. 4:12; 10:25; 1 Cor. 10:9), and *peiraō* once (Acts 26:21). New to the NT is the verbal adj. *apeirastos*, incapable of temptation (Jas. 1:13). The noun *peirasmos*, temptation, trial, occurs 21x; *peira*, attempt, trial, is found only in Heb. 11:29, 36.

1. Examples of the secular sense of this word group are: to make an attempt (Heb. 11:29), get experience of (11:36), attempt (Acts 9:26; 16:7; 24:6), and test (2 Cor. 13:5; Rev. 2:2). Four passages contain the OT ideas of testing God (Acts 5:9; 15:10; 1 Cor. 10:9; Heb. 3:8–9).

2. The world of ideas behind the NT use of *peirasmos* in the religious sense is generally dependent on the OT. Believers are constantly being tempted to fall away from God. They must protect themselves with spiritual armor (Eph. 6:10–17) against the attacks of the "prince of this world" (Jn. 12:31; 14:30; 16:11; cf. Eph. 2:2) and stand firm or be watchful (1 Pet. 5:8), always with prayer (Eph. 6:18). Thus the willing spirit controls the weak flesh, so that the beleaguered entry gate for satanic temptations may remain closed (Mk. 14:38).

What entices us into temptation is the weakness of the human nature, also described as desire (*epithymia*, Jas. 1:14; → *2123*), so that the power of the evil one closes over us like a trap (1 Tim. 6:9). Satan uses all sorts of devices to lead us into temptation (1 Cor. 7:5; 1 Thess. 3:5). In fact, almost anything can become a temptation (1 Cor. 10:13; Gal. 6:1). Paul admits in 4:14 that his situation when he arrived in Galatia (whatever that was; perhaps his "thorn in [the] flesh"? 2 Cor. 12:7) could have been a "trial" to them, but they brushed it off and received the apostle as "an angel of God."

3. To have to suffer as a Christian is a form of testing. But it can also be a mark of true discipleship and therefore a ground for joy (1 Pet. 1:6; 4:12), esp. when one knows, by looking back to the great examples of Abraham and Job, that it is possible to emerge from temptation approved and preserved in patience (Jas. 1:2). At the end of the testing God never turns out to be an enemy, but one who rewards.

In stark opposition to any attempt to hold God responsible for human failures, Jas. maintains that God, who is himself *apeirastos*, incapable of being tempted by the evil one, tempts no one (Jas. 1:13). Rather, he helps and rescues from temptation (1 Cor. 10:13; 2 Pet. 2:9). The question of the origin of temptation is left open. At most we can say, as noted above, that God allows the evil one to send us trials, which may tempt us to turn our backs on him.

Jesus commanded his disciples to pray against temptation (Mk. 14:38) and taught them to ask the Father, "Lead us not into temptation, but deliver us from the evil one" (Matt. 6:13). Here God, having been asked for the forgiveness of sins, is asked not to allow his church to come into the kind of satanic temptation that might lead them to fall away, but to rescue them from the power of the evil one and so let his kingdom come. The ultimate coming of God's rule cannot be separated from the present fight against the kingdom of the tempter. But with God's help, we can endure the hour of trial and overcome (Rev. 2:10; 3:10). And we can be sure that our Savior is praying for us during times of severe trial (cf. Lk. 22:28–34).

4. (a) Jesus was the subject of temptation throughout his life. This is brought out esp. by Lk. (4:13; 22:28) and Heb. (2:18; 4:15). For this very reason he can help his followers in their temptations. Jesus was without sin, so Satan constantly attacked him in many forms, trying to break down his resistance. When his opponents tried to take

him in with trick questions, it was only a covering action (Matt. 22:35; Mk. 10:2; 12:15; Lk. 10:2; Jn. 8:6). Because of false, human expectations among the people, the Pharisees and the disciples were ever seeking to divert Jesus from his life's task. They are thus temptations and hindrances for the Messiah, who remained obedient to God (Matt. 16:1; Mk. 8:11; Lk. 11:16). In the struggle in Gethsemane Jesus even asked the Father to remove the cup from him (Mk. 14:35–39).

(b) The nature of the constant temptations in Jesus' life is epitomized in the story of the temptations that preceded his public ministry (Matt. 4:1–11; Lk. 4:1–13). The Spirit led Jesus into the desert, where he was tempted by Satan. That scene recalls the testing of Israel as God's son in the desert wanderings prior to their entry into the promised land (cf. Deut. 6–8). There is indeed a parallel between the forty years of desert wandering and the forty days of Jesus in the desert.

(i) The first temptation is not merely an invitation to perform a spectacular miracle for selfish ends by turning stones into bread. Rather, it must be seen against the background of OT promises of how Yahweh provides food for his children (cf. Deut. 2:7; 28:1–14; Neh. 9:21; Ps. 23:1; 33:18–19). Yahweh gave his people manna and quails, but once their immediate needs were satisfied, they grumbled about what God had given them and wanted something better (Exod. 16:2–12; Num. 11:4–6, 33–34; 21:4–5; Deut. 8:2–3; 9:22; 29:5; Ps. 78:18–22, 26–32).

Jesus' reply to Satan's first temptation comes from an OT passage that recalls the desert wanderings and Yahweh's provision of manna (Deut. 8:3; cf. Matt. 4:4; Lk. 4:4). Israel did not withstand this temptation; the people were seized with craving, discontent, doubt, and unbelief, grumbling because they wanted a different kind of food. The tempter wants to entice Jesus into this same sin. It is not without significance that the Sermon on the Mount records the saying: "Which of you, if his son asks for bread, will give him a stone?" (Matt. 7:9).

(ii) The second temptation in Matt.'s account and the third in Lk.'s is set on the pinnacle of the temple (see also *pterygion*, wing, edge, *4762*). Its background may be the promises of divine protection for Israel in their desert wanderings (e.g., Exod. 19:4–6; Deut. 1:31; 32:10–14). But God's promised protection was not confined to the desert generation. The temple was the place par excellence where this protection could be expected, for there the divine presence was concentrated. It was an inviolable place of sanctuary (cf. Ps. 36:7–8; 61:4).

This perspective is particularly true of Ps. 91, which the rabbis associated with both the temple and the desert wanderings. Satan issues the temptation to Jesus to cast himself from the wing of the temple on the basis of 91:11–12: "For he will command his angels concerning you to guard you in all your ways; they will lift you up in their hands, so that you will not strike your foot against a stone" (cf. Matt. 4:6; Lk. 4:10–11). There is probably a play on words between the "wing" (*pterygion*) of the temple and the clause "under his wings [*pterygas*] you will find refuge" (Ps. 91:4). This temptation is not simply a demand, like that of the Pharisees, for a spectacular sign. Rather, Satan wants Jesus to tempt God, i.e., to demand from God some token that he is a God who keeps his covenantal promises.

But this temptation is rejected by a quotation, which (like the previous one) is taken from Deut.: "Do not put the Lord your God to the test" (Matt. 4:7; Lk. 4:12; cf. Deut. 6:16). To put God to the test in this way breaks the great commandment to love God above all (Deut. 6:4–5). Note also how later on, the power of the disciples over the demons is noted as a sign that God is honoring the promises of Ps. 91, for Lk. 10:19 quotes Ps. 91:13, where the disciples' power over the enemy is seen as a fulfillment of the Ps. and evidence of Satan's fall.

(iii) In the third temptation in Matt. the devil takes Jesus to a high mountain, shows him all the kingdoms of the world, and says to him, " 'All this I will give you . . . if you will bow down and worship me'" (Matt. 4:8–9; cf. Lk. 4:5–7, where it is the second temptation). This passage is rich in OT associations. Moses went up to the top of Mount Pisgah, where Yahweh showed him the promised land (Deut. 34:1–4). Note that in many OT contexts, mountains are the scene either of revelation (e.g., Sinai, Exod. 19:3; 34:2–3) or of idolatrous worship (Deut. 12:1–3). Deut. also stresses that the riches of the promised land should not lead Israel to forget Yahweh and follow other gods (6:10–12; cf. 8:10–20)—a warning that follows the command to love Yahweh above all and precedes the command not to put him to the test (6:16). This connection with Deut. is confirmed by the fact that Jesus resists Satan's third temptation by citing Deut. 6:13: "Worship the Lord your God, and serve him only" (Matt. 4:10; cf. Lk. 4:8).

Whereas Israel as God's son succumbed to this temptation to worship other gods (and hence, Satan, Deut. 32:15–17), Jesus as God's Son overcomes it through living by God's word, just as Israel should have done. By rejecting the false promise of the riches of the land that Satan promises, Jesus is able to enter into his true inheritance as God's Son, although this comes by the way of the cross. In this sense Jesus lives by the third beatitude, "Blessed are the meek, for they will inherit the earth" (Matt. 5:5). The fulfillment of the promise lies in a way different from that envisaged by Satan. While rejecting the temptation leads to hardship and suffering for Jesus, ultimately it spells Satan's defeat. Note esp. Matt. 4:11: "Then the devil left him, and angels came and attended him."

By resisting these temptations, Jesus gains victory over Satan and thus makes it possible for his people to inherit God's promises. By placing the temptation concerning the kingdoms of the world at the climax of the temptations, Matt. sees the victory here in the light of the triumph of the kingdom of heaven over the kingdom of this world. Note too how this Gospel ends with the words of the risen Christ to the effect that Jesus now legitimately has the authority Satan promised deceitfully: "All authority in heaven and on earth has been given to me" (28:18). In Mk., even though the writer does not describe Jesus' temptations (1:12–13), he assumes that Jesus resisted Satan here, for throughout the rest of the book, Jesus manifested complete power over demons and evil spirits (e.g., 1:21–26; 5:1–20; 9:14–29).

See also *dokimos*, tested, approved, genuine, esteemed (*1511*).

4281 (peiraō, try, attempt, endeavor), → *4280*.

4282 (peismonē, persuasion), → *4275*.

4287 (pempō, send), → *690*.

4288	πένης

πένης (*penēs*), poor (*4288*); πενιχρός (*penichros*), poor (*4293*).

CL & OT 1. In cl. Gk. *penēs* is linked with *ponos*, burden, trouble. It refers to the person who cannot live from one's property, but has to work with one's hands. Hence the *penēs* is not like the *ptōchos* (→ *4777*), who is poor enough to be a beggar and needs help. A *penēs*, therefore, is only relatively poor—the opposite of *plousios*, wealthy (→ *ploutos*, *4458*). It includes the handworker and small peasant. Although at one time property was considered the best guarantee of a virtuous life and *penia*, poverty, the root of moral offenses, the Gks. eventually came to accept that *penia* could lead to virtue, which is the true ideal in life. A life in poverty can be rich and free. No religious value was attributed to poverty.

2. (a) In the LXX *penēs* is used about 75x; *penichros*, 3x (Exod. 22:25; Prov. 28:15; 29:7). Normally *penēs* denotes the economically and legally oppressed (e.g., Ps. 72:4, 13; 86:1; Amos 2:6; 4:1; 5:12; 8:4, 6). It is virtually synonymous for *ptōchos*, perhaps because in the Israelite concept of property and social order, poverty ultimately was created by unrighteousness, i.e., by a failure of the community to obey God and his law.

(b) In Hel. Jud. writers such as Philo tend to follow the cl. Gk. meaning of *penēs* (*ptōchos* does not occur in Philo, even in quotes where it appears in the LXX). By so doing he uses the less offensive, more polite term for poor, thus making the Bible more suitable for Gk. ears.

NT The NT follows OT thought about the poor but not the LXX's choice of words. *penēs* occurs only in 2 Cor. 9:9, a quotation from Ps. 112:9; the normal NT word for "poor" is *ptōchos*. *penichros* is found only in Lk. 21:2, of the widow at the temple treasury, who was visibly poor (the par. in Mk. 12:42 uses *ptōchos*).

See also *ptōchos*, poor (*4777*).

4291	πενθέω

πενθέω (*pentheō*), be sad, grieve, mourn (*4291*); πένθος (*penthos*), grief, sadness, mourning (*4292*).

CL & OT 1. *pentheō* means to lament or mourn, usually for someone; *penthos* has the sense of mourning or sorrow. It is used esp. of the external signs of mourning, as when mourning for the dead.

2. In the LXX *pentheō* connotes the act of mourning, usually as a result of realized or impending misfortune. It can be used fig. of inanimate objects such as the earth, the land, or parts of the structure of cities on which catastrophe has come or is yet to come (cf. Isa. 3:26; 19:8; 24:4; 33:9; Jer. 4:28; 23:10; Lam. 2:8; Hos. 4:3). It is also used of mourning over the death of an individual (Gen. 23:2; 50:3; 2 Sam. 14:2; 1 Chr. 7:22), of remorse in general (Neh. 8:9), and of the sorrow experienced during the absence of a loved one (2 Sam. 13:37; 19:1). In Isa. 16:8 it denotes the languishing of fields.

The noun *penthos* denotes mourning (e.g., Gen. 27:41; 50:10; Amos 5:16; 8:10).

NT 1. *pentheō* occurs in Matt. 9:15 in the sense of sorrow over the absence of a loved one, and in Mk. 16:10 of those who mourned the death of Christ. Paul uses it of the sorrow he may have to experience when he learns that some have not repented of their sins (2 Cor. 12:21). In Lk.'s account of the Beatitudes *pentheō* occurs as the antithesis of laugh (Lk. 6:25), describing the eventual mourning of those who laugh now. Those who are not contrite will later experience the results of their lack of contrition. In Matt. 5:4 *pentheō* refers to sorrow in a general sense.

In Rev. 18:11, 15, 19, the judgment on Babylon is mourned by those who trafficked with her. The deep sense of loss at the destruction of their source of wealth pervades the description of their reaction.

Paul and James use *pentheō* in a sense closely paralleling the concept of godly sorrow or repentance. In 1 Cor. 5:2 the vb. describes the attitude that should characterize the Corinthian Christians relative to the immorality among them. He describes their present attitude over an incestuous man as "proud" and indicates that they should rather be "filled with grief" over the situation. James exhorts sinners to "mourn and wail" as an aspect of their humbling themselves before God (Jas. 4:9).

2. James uses the noun *penthos* in Jas. 4:9 similarly to the vb., i.e., in the sense of godly sorrow. He calls on sinners to draw near to God, cleanse their hands, purify their hearts, and to change their laughter "to mourning." The section closes with an exhortation to humble themselves before the Lord, for he will then exalt them.

In Rev. 18:7–8 *penthos* describes sorrow as a result of catastrophe and loss. Mourning will come on Babylon at her fall. By contrast 21:4 uses the word for sorrow in general, the removal of which will lead to the joy experienced by those who will inhabit the new Jerusalem.

See also *klaiō*, weep (*3081*); *koptō*, strike (*3164*); *lypeō*, inflict pain (*3382*); *brychō*, gnash (*1107*); *stenazō*, to sigh, groan (*5100*).

4292 (penthos, grief, sadness, mourning), → *4291*.

4293 (penichros, poor), → *4288*.

4297	πέντε

πέντε (*pente*), five (*4297*).

NT Five is common and natural as a round number wherever the decimal system is used (e.g., Matt. 25:20; Lk. 12:52; 14:19; 16:28).

There is no clear evidence that this number should be given any symbolic meaning in the NT. The "five months" of Rev. 9:5, 10 are just a limited period of chastisement.

| 4300 πεντηκοστή | πεντηκοστή (*pentēkostē*), Pentecost (*4300*). |

OT 1. *pentēcostē* is a fem. noun formed from the numeral *pentēkostos*, 50th, which occurs in cl. Gk. In Jewish and Christian lit. the word stands for *hē pentēkostē hēmera*, the 50th day, referring to the festival celebrated on the 50th day after Passover (Tob. 2:1; 2 Macc. 12:32). In Deut. 16:10 it is called "the Feast of Weeks."

Pentecost was the second great feast of the Jewish year, a harvest festival, when the firstfruits of the wheat harvest were presented to Yahweh. It was celebrated seven weeks after the beginning of the barley harvest (hence "Feast of Weeks"), fifty days after the Passover (hence "Pentecost"; see Exod. 23:16; 34:22; Lev. 23:15–21; Num. 28:26–31; Deut. 16:9–12).

2. Jewish thinking about Pentecost developed during the period before and after Jesus. In *Jub.* 6:17–21 (ca. 100 B.C.) Pentecost is noted as the feast of covenant renewal (probably also at Qumran). This meant a link between Pentecost and the covenant of Sinai; Exod. 19:1 specifies "the third month" (the month during which Pentecost was celebrated) as the time of the arrival of the Israelites at Sinai. In rab. Jud. Pentecost thus became associated with the giving of the law. But this link between Pentecost and Sinai is not documented before the 2d cent. A.D.

NT 1. Although Luke may have been aware of an association established in Jud. between Pentecost and the law giving at Sinai, it plays no role in his narrative in Acts 2 or elsewhere.

2. (a) To the early Christian community, Pentecost meant the outpouring of the Spirit promised by God for the end time. Charismatic and ecstatic manifestations attributed to God's Spirit were a distinctive feature of both Palestinian and Hel. Christianity (cf. Matt. 3:11; Jn. 7:38–39; Acts 2:38; 6:3–5; 8:14–17; 10:44–48; 19:1–7; Rom. 8:9, 14–15; 1 Cor. 12:13; Eph. 4:8). In particular, Pentecost was seen as the fulfillment of Joel 2:28—"in the last days" (Acts 2:17); the language of Joel 2:28 ("pour out") has stamped itself on early Christian talk about the Spirit (Acts 2:17–18, 33; 10:45; Rom. 5:5; Tit. 3:6). Acts 20:16 even hints that the Jerusalem church observed Pentecost as the anniversary of the Spirit's outpouring (cf. 1 Cor. 16:8).

(b) The first Christian Pentecost was an ecstatic experience involving vision (sound like wind, tongues as of fire) and glossolalia (Acts 2:1–13). It resulted in an enthusiastic community, bound together by their common loyalty to the risen Jesus and by their common experience of the Spirit (3:19–20). The resurrection of Jesus and the gift of Spirit constituted the start of the end-time harvest of final resurrection (Rom. 8:23; 1 Cor. 15:20, 23). They doubtless regarded themselves as the eschatological Israel (cf. Matt. 16:18–19; 19:28; Acts 1:6, 21–22).

The first Christians experienced the Spirit primarily as the prophetic Spirit, in accordance with Jewish expectation (see Joel 2:28). This was the privilege of all and not just the prerogative of a few (Acts 2:1, 4, 17–18, 38–39). The link between Pentecost, covenant renewal, and the giving of the law perhaps prompted the first believers to interpret their experience of the Spirit as the fulfillment of the promise of a new covenant, as the law written in their hearts (Deut. 30:6; Jer. 31:31–34; Ezek. 36:26–27; 37:14; cf. 1 Cor. 11:25; Heb. 10:15–16, 29). But the implications of this insight for continuing faith and conduct were not recognized and elaborated until Paul (Rom. 2:28–29; 7:6; 2 Cor. 3:4–18; Gal. 3:1–4:7; Phil. 3:3; Col. 2:11; 1 Thess. 4:8).

(c) The outpouring of the Spirit was attributed to the exalted Jesus, as implied by John the Baptist's predictions (Matt. 3:11; Acts 1:5; 11:16) and by Acts 2:33. Yet the relationship between the exalted Jesus and the Spirit did not receive much analysis prior to Paul and John.

3. (a) For Luke Pentecost is the fulfillment of the divine promise (Lk. 24:49; Acts 1:4; 2:33, 38–39). Thus it is also the fulfillment of covenant promise (2:39; 3:25; 13:23, 32; 26:6), with Pentecost being the institution of the new covenant. For Luke Pentecost is the birthday of the church (2:38, 41–47), and the Spirit of Pentecost is preeminently the prophetic Spirit, the inspirer of speech (2:4, 18; 4:8, 31; 6:10; 10:46; 13:9; 19:6).

(b) Luke also presents Pentecost as the beginning of world mission, as prophesied by Jesus in Acts 1:8. The gospel begins in Jerusalem, branches out to Judea and Samaria, and goes "to the ends of the earth" (note how the book of Acts ends in Rome, the capital of the empire). Those who bear witness to the effects of the Spirit's outpouring and hear the gospel proclaimed by Peter represent "every nation under heaven" (2:5), while the appended list of nationalities embraces a wide sweep of the eastern Mediterranean (2:9–11). The glossolalia is identified as the languages spoken by these foreign Jews (2:4, 6, 8, 11). Finally, Peter's sermon ends with an open invitation and offer of the promised Spirit to "all who are far off" (2:39).

(c) Luke plays down the eschatological dimension of Pentecost-engendered enthusiasm. Pentecost is not so much the precursor of the end as the beginning of a whole new epoch of salvation history. It becomes most explicit in the sharp distinction that Luke draws between the epoch of Jesus, ended by resurrection appearances and ascension, and Pentecost, the beginning of the epoch of the Spirit. The two are separated by a period of ten days when neither the risen Jesus nor the inspiring Spirit are in evidence and the election of Matthias has to revert to the old epoch's use of lots (Acts 1:26).

4. Jn. 20:22 has sometimes been called "the Johannine Pentecost," not because John is contesting Lk.'s dating of the outpouring of the Spirit, but because he wishes to bring out other theological aspects. (a) John esp. emphasizes that the gift of the Spirit is not to be separated from the event of Jesus' death, resurrection, and ascension; it is the immediate and direct result and consequence of Jesus' "glorification" and "ascending" (6:62–63; 19:30; cf. 19:34 with 7:38–39).

(b) John also affirms the immediate continuity between Jesus and the Spirit. The Spirit is the *other* Counselor (14:16–17), whose coming fulfills Jesus' promise to return and live in his disciples (14:18–24). The Spirit given by the ascended Jesus enables the believer to share in the life of the risen, glorified Christ (4:14; 6:62–63).

(c) John brings out the epochal significance of the Pentecostal Spirit even more clearly than Luke by the word "breathed" in 20:22. Clearly echoing the same word in Gen. 2:7; Ezek. 37:9; Wis. 15:11, John presents the act of Jesus as a new creation.

(d) Finally, the earlier emphasis on mission is retained by bracketing 20:22 with 20:21 and 23; forgiveness or retention of sins is a charismatic authority and a part of Pentecostal mission; "the disciples" thereby commissioned are not "the twelve" or "the apostles" (never in John) but those gathered round Jesus during his passion (including women), who represent all who believe in Jesus (7:37–39).

4301 (pepoithēsis, trust, confidence), → *4275.*

| 4309 περί | περί (*peri*), about, around (*4309*). |

CL & OT The basic, local sense of *peri* is around or encircling; it can also mean concerning, in connection with. Generally the LXX renders the Heb. phrase translated "for a sin offering" with *peri hamartias* (lit., "in connection with sin"; e.g., Lev. 16:5; Ps. 40:6b). With this abbreviated phrase one should understand the word "offering," i.e., "the offering that relates to sin."

NT 1. The local sense of *peri* occurs in Acts 22:6 (a bright light flashed "around" Paul). In a derived, fig. meaning, *peri* designates a center of activity around which something or someone revolves. Thus *hoi peri Paulon* (13:13; lit., "those around Paul") marks out the apostle as a sun with several satellites. Standing absolutely at the beginning of a sentence, *peri (de)* means "(now) concerning" and marks a new section of thought (e.g., 1 Cor. 7:1, 25; 8:1; 12:1; 16:1), a point of importance for the reconstruction of the Corinthian letter to Paul (1 Cor. 7–16).

2. In Heb. 10:6, 8 (citing Ps. 40:6, LXX) and probably in Heb. 13:11 (cf. Lev. 16:27) the phrase *peri hamartias* (see above) means "sin offering." It is possible that the same phrase in the pl. has this nuance in Heb. 5:3b (*peri* occurs 2x) and 1 Pet. 3:18, but not in Heb. 10:18, 26; 1 Jn. 2:2 (where the phrase is dependent on a noun meaning sacrifice). In Rom. 8:3 *peri hamartias* can mean "in reference to sin" (i.e., "to atone for sin"), but, given OT usage, the rendering "to be a sin offering" (NIV) or "as a sacrifice for sin" seems more appropriate.

| 4318 περιεργάζομαι | περιεργάζομαι (*periergazomai*), meddle, be a busybody (*4318*); περίεργος (*periergos*), meddlesome, curious, belonging to magic (*4319*). |

CL & OT *periergazomai* combines the prep. *peri* (around, beyond) and *ergazomai* (work). Thus, its root meaning is to do superfluous work. It does occur in a good sense (investigate thoroughly), but more often it has a bad connotation (take more pains than necessary, be a busybody). The derived adj. *periergos* has the same range.

In the LXX *periergazomai* appears in a positive sense in Wis. 8:5 (S¹ only) to describe how wisdom works or accomplishes all things, in a negative sense for meddling in Sir. 3:23. In addition, the vb. appears in two alternative readings in Sym., where it means to seek diligently (2 Sam. 11:3; Eccl. 7:30).

NT *periergazomai* is used only in 2 Thess. 3:11, where there is a deliberate wordplay on *ergazomai*. Paul condemns those who are not working but instead are busybodies. *periergos* refers to young women on the church widows' register who become busybodies through having nothing constructive to do (1 Tim. 5:13). In Acts 19:19 it has a semi-technical sense of sorcery (NIV) or magic arts (see further *3404*).

4319 (*periergos*, meddlesome, curious, belonging to magic), → *3404* and *4318*.

4320 (*perierchomai*, wander), → *2262*.

4322 (*perizōnnymi*, gird with, gird around), → *2439*.

4326 (*perikatharma*, filth, offscouring), → *4370*.

4330 (*perikephalaia*, helmet), → *4483*.

4334 (*perilampō*, surround with light), → *3290*.

4335 (*perileipomai*, survive, leave behind), → *3309*.

4338 (*perimenō*, wait), → *3531*.

4342 (*periousios*, chosen, special), → *4347*.

| 4344 περιπατέω | περιπατέω (*peripateō*), go about, walk (*4344*); ἐμπεριπατέω (*emperipateō*), go about, walk (*1853*); πατέω (*pateō*), tread, trample (*4251*); καταπατέω (*katapateō*), trample (*2922*). |

CL & OT 1. In cl. Gk. *pateō* and its compounds denote a stepping movement of the feet: trans. to tread, set foot on, trample down; fig. to treat contemptuously, maltreat, plunder; intrans. to go, walk. *katapateō* denotes complete crushing or trampling down, often fig. to treat disdainfully, despise. *peripateō* occurs only with the lit. meaning of strolling; not until the 1st cent. B.C. does one find the meaning to live.

2. In the LXX *peripateō* is found 34x, most often in the wisdom lit.; *emperipateō* occurs 9x. In general these two vbs. mean simply to go or to walk about (e.g., Exod. 21:19; 1 Sam. 17:39). Several times God's walking about is spoken of anthropomorphically (Gen. 3:8, 10; Ps. 104:3), as also is Satan's (Job 1:7; 2:2). Occasionally *peripateō* denotes fig. a way of life (e.g., 2 Ki. 20:3; Eccl. 11:9). The LXX prefers to use *poreuomai*, to go, in combination with *hodos*, way, to express that one should conduct one's way of life in the paths indicated by God.

3. According to the Dead Sea Scrolls, God has set two spirits for humans to walk in until the time of their visitation, namely, the spirits of truth and of perversity (1QS 3:18–21). The sons of righteousness walk in the ways of light (i.e., according to the will of God, 5:10); the sons of wickedness walk in the ways of darkness (3:20–21).

NT 1. In the NT *peripateō* occurs 95x, half of which are lit. and half fig. In the Gospels, Acts, and Rev., the vb. usually means to go, walk about. In 1 Pet. 5:8 it is applied to the devil, who is compared to a lion walking about seeking whom he may devour. In Rev. 2:1; 3:4; 21:24, *peripateō* denotes walking in the perfection and light of the heavenly Jerusalem. *emperipateō* occurs only in 2 Cor. 6:16 (cf. Lev. 26:12), of God's covenant relationship with his people, in which he walks among them; this now applies to the church. The simple form *pateō*, tread, trample, is found at Lk. 10:19; 21:24; Rev. 11:2, in each case with overtones of judgment and power. *katapateo* means to tread underfoot (Matt. 5:13; 7:6; Lk. 8:5; 12:1), despise (the Son of God, Heb. 10:29).

2. In the fig. sense of to conduct one's life *peripateō* is found mainly in Paul's and Jn.'s writings (though cf. Mk. 7:5; Acts 21:21; Heb. 13:9, where it refers to observing Jewish customs and traditions). The vb., in itself neutral, is more precisely fixed by designating positively or negatively that to which one conforms one's life.

(a) In Paul two ways of life stand opposed to one another: the (former) heathen way of life (Eph. 2:2, walking in "the ways of this world"; cf. Rom. 8:4; 1 Cor. 3:3), and the (present) walk in Christ (Rom. 8:4, walking "according to the Spirit"; cf. Gal. 5:16; Eph. 5:8; Col. 2:6; NIV often translates as "live"). Since the Christian message involves leading a person dominated by a self-seeking "I" (Gal. 5:16) into a new life (Rom. 6:4) dominated by God and his will, "how to live in order to please God" (1 Thess. 4:1) is a part of this preaching.

(b) Paul starts from the position that humans under the law are under bondage and thus unable to fulfill God's will. By faith in Christ we are promised freedom from these compulsions (Eph. 2:1–10), so that we can now serve God and our neighbor (Rom. 7:6). But we must again and again be exhorted to live in this new reality, because as believers we still live "in the flesh" (2 Cor. 10:3 KJV) and thus remain open to the temptation to living "like mere men" (1 Cor. 3:3), i.e., in a self-seeking way.

As Christians who walk "by faith, not by sight," we must try to please the Lord (2 Cor. 5:7–9; cf. Eph. 5:8–10, 15) and so conduct our lives in a way that corresponds with our holy calling (4:1; 1 Thess. 2:12). This also means an attitude that is sensitive to those who do not belong to the congregation and to what they think about believers (Col. 4:5; 1 Thess. 4:12). In 2 Thess. 3:6 the Thessalonians are urged to keep away from those who are "idle and [do] not live according to [Paul's] teaching."

emperipateō, walk about, move, occurs only in 2 Cor. 6:16, which quotes the promise of Lev. 26:12 that God will walk among his people. Paul sees this covenant promise fulfilled in the Christian community, which is now "the temple of the living God."

(c) In Jn.'s writings *peripateō* occurs in both lit. and fig. senses. In Jn. 11:9–10 Jesus speaks about walking in daylight or at nighttime, but this verse has a fig. implication for the life of faith versus the life in unbelief. The expressions "walk in the light," "walk in the truth," and "walk in darkness" do not refer to moral or immoral behavior, but existence governed either by God or the world. To walk in the light means to live with one's face turned to God, by faith in Jesus Christ (12:35–36), while to walk in darkness means to have one's life closed to God. Those whose lives are closed to God miss real life (12:35; 1 Jn. 2:11). Jesus, however, has come as the light of the world so that we may find life through him (Jn. 8:12).

Walking in the light (1 Jn. 1:7; 2 Jn. 4; cf. 3 Jn. 3–4) has an ethical side, as the letters of John show. Not mere words, but the whole way one lives, will lead to fellowship with God (1 Jn. 1:6–7). This is the way Jesus himself walked (2:6; cf. 2 Jn. 6), which serves as our example (Jn. 13:14; 1 Jn. 4:11, 19). Living in the light also leads to fellowship with one another (3:16–17). By way of contrast, walking in darkness means having no fellowship with God (1:6); such a life is not determined by love, but by hate (2:11).

See also *anastrephō*, to overturn, turn back, turn round; fig. behave, conduct oneself, live (418); *hodos*, way, road, highway, way of life (3847); *poreuomai*, go, to journey, to travel, to walk (4513).

4346 (peripiptō, fall into, among), → *4406.*

4347	περιποιέω

περιποιέω (*peripoieō*), save for oneself, acquire, gain possession of (*4347*); πεπιποίησις (*peripoiēsis*), gaining, obtaining, acquisition, a possession, property (*4348*); περιούσιος (*periousios*), chosen, special (*4342*); ἴδιος (*idios*), one's own, possessions, property (*2625*).

CL & OT 1. In cl. Gk. *peripoieō* means to cause to save up, procure, keep for oneself. The noun *peripoiēsis* means keeping safe, preservation, gaining possession of. *periousios* means having more than enough, rich, wealthy.

2. *peripoiēsis* occurs in Hag. 2:9 (= LXX 2:10), where (in a LXX addition) the writer speaks of a peace of mind that is acquired by those who work hard to raise the temple. The word is also in Mal. 3:17, where God's chosen people are his treasured "possession." In a similar phrase, *periousios* is used of God's chosen people at Exod. 19:5; Deut. 7:6; 14:2; 26:18. The idea behind *periousios* is not just that of Israel as God's property but that of his rich possession.

NT 1. In the NT *peripoieō* (3x) and *peripoiēsis* (5x) are preferred to *periousios* (once). The idea of salvation stands in the background. The vb. occurs at Lk. 17:33 ("Whoever tries to keep [*peripoieō*] his life will lose it"); Acts 20:28 ("Be shepherds of the church of God, which he bought [*peripoieō*] with his own blood"); and 1 Tim. 3:13 ("Those who have served well gain [*peripoieō*] an excellent standing and great assurance in their faith").

peripoiēsis occurs in Eph. 1:14, where the Spirit is said to be "a deposit guaranteeing our inheritance until the redemption of those who are God's possession [*peripoiēseis*]." In 1 Thess. 5:9 Paul assures his readers that God has destined us "to receive [*peripoiēsis*] salvation through our Lord Jesus Christ"; in 2 Thess. 2:14 it is the glory of the Lord Jesus that we "share." Heb. 10:39 refers to those who believe and "are saved" (lit., "for the preserving [*peripoiēsis*] of the soul"; cf. Lk. 17:33). Finally, 1 Pet. 2:9 takes up the thought of Exod. 19:5, where one of Peter's phrases for God's people is "a people belonging [*peripoiēsis*] to God."

2. *periousios* occurs only in Tit. 2:14, which describes the work of Christ, who redeems us from all wickedness and purifies for himself "a people that are his very own [*periousios*], eager to do what is good." As in the OT, we see the idea of God's treasured people (cf. Exod. 19:5; Deut. 14:2), but it is applied to the church not to Israel. Paul draws attention to the kind of deeds that God's people should be zealous to perform.

3. The adj. *idios* (113x in the NT) means own and is used in a variety of contexts and meanings: e.g., each according to one's own ability (Matt. 25:15), each receiving wages according to one's own work (1 Cor. 3:8), one's own (private) interpretation (2 Pet. 1:20), his own sheep (Jn. 10:3–4), each in turn (1 Cor. 15:23), with our own hands (4:12). As an adv. *idia* means by oneself, privately (Matt. 14:13; 1 Cor. 12:11).

The neut. pl. (*ta idia*) means one's home or one's things. In the NT it appears to mean "home" in Jn. 16:32. In 1:11 we read: "He came to that which was his own, but his own did not receive him." The first "his own" is neut. pl., whereas the second "his own" is masc. pl. The first perhaps refers to the world that Christ created and everything in it (a concept prominent in the context), whereas the masc. pl. almost certainly means the Jewish people, who by and large rejected Jesus as the Messiah.

Lk. 18:28 follows the story of the rich young ruler, who refused to sell all he had to give to the poor and follow Jesus. *ta idia* here may be translated as homes or possessions: "Then Peter said, 'Look, we have left our homes [*ta idia*] and followed you'" (NRSV; the par. in Matt. 19:27 and Mk. 10:28 have *panta*, all things). In response, Jesus assures that those who have put him ahead of "home or wife or brothers or parents or children" will receive much in this age and eternal life in the age to come (Lk. 18:29–30).

See also *thēsauros*, treasure box, chest, storeroom, treasure (2565); *mamōnas*, money, wealth, property (3440); *ploutos*, wealth, riches (4458); *chrēma*, property, wealth, means, money (5975).

4348 (peripoiēsis, gaining, acquisition, possession, property), → *4347.*

4353 (perisseia, surplus, abundance), → *4355.*

4354 (perisseuma, abundance, fullness), → *4355.*

4355	περισσεύω

περισσεύω (*perisseuō*), be more than enough, be left over, be abundant, abound, excel (*4355*); περισσός (*perissos*), exceeding the usual number or size, extraordinary, abundant (*4356*); περισσότερος (*perissoteros*), greater, more (*4358*); περισσοτέρως (*perissoterōs*), adv. more (*4359*); περισσῶς (*perissōs*), exceedingly, beyond measure (*4360*); ὑπερπερισσεύω (*hyperperisseuō*), increase all the more (*5668*); ὑπερπερισσῶς (*hyperperissōs*), beyond all measure (*5669*); ὑπερεκπερισσοῦ (*hyperekperissou*), beyond all measure (*5655*); περισσεία (*perisseia*), surplus, abundance (*4353*); περίσσευμα (*perisseuma*), abundance, fullness (*4354*).

CL & OT 1. In cl. Gk. *perisseuō* is used intrans. in the sense of to be over and above, go beyond, be more than enough, remain over. *perissos* means beyond the regular number or size, out of the common, extraordinary, more than sufficient, excessive. *perissōs* means extraordinarily, exceedingly.

2. *perisseuō* and its cognates are not common in the LXX. (a) *perisseia* occurs only in Eccl., usually in the sense of gain, advantage: "What does man gain from all his labor at which he toils under the sun?" (1:3). The wise man like the fool (2:14b; 6:8) and humanity like the animal world (3:19) must leave this world and be forgotten. God freely bestows earthly goods (6:2), so we should enjoy them in gratitude and not haggle with God over the place allotted to us (6:9–10). Such wisdom that recognizes the freedom of the Creator is real gain (7:12, 19).

(b) *perisseuō* means to have precedence (1 Macc. 3:30), posterity (1 Sam. 2:33, 36), but elsewhere to have abundance (Sir. 11:12). According to 19:24, the one who is too sure of wisdom stands in greater danger of transgressing the law.

(c) *perissos* denotes what is over, the remainder (Exod. 10:5; 2 Ki. 25:11), that which is superfluous and useless (Eccl. 2:15). But it also denotes what is extraordinary and outstanding (Dan. 5:12, 14, Theod.).

3. Certain books of intertestamental Jud. expected in the end time an abundance and blessed profusion of all desirable goods: numerous offspring, possessions, superabundant crops (*1 Enoch* 10:17–11:2; *2 Bar.* 29:5–8), as well as joy (*1 Enoch* 51:5), righteousness, and wisdom (48:1).

NT In the NT *perisseuō* occurs 39x; *perissos* and its comparative and adverbial forms 38x; *perisseuma* 5x; *perisseia* 4x; and forms with the prefix *hyper*- 6x. All the words occur mainly in the Pauline writings and the Gospels. An element of excess and fullness that overflows the set bounds is inherent in all the words. The existing standards and rules are transcended, and what was comparable becomes incomparable.

1. (a) In the Gospels *perisseuō* and its cognates are found with the primary meaning to have abundance, have many goods. Thus Mk.

12:44 tells of the widow who gave all that she possessed, whereas others gave of their *abundance*. Lk. 12:15 warns of misplaced trust in the abundance of possessions. The proverbial utterance in Matt. 12:34 declares: "For out of the overflow of the heart the mouth speaks." The more Jesus commanded people not to tell of his healing work, "the more" (*mallon perissoteron*) they proclaimed it (Mk. 7:36). The secret of his person exerted pressure on others to proclaim it openly in view of his mighty acts. The people "were overwhelmed" (*hyperperissōs*) with amazement (7:37), and likewise the disciples were "completely" (*ek perissou*) amazed at Jesus' walking on the water and quieting the storm (6:51).

(b) As the one who prepared the way for Jesus, John was more than a prophet (Matt. 11:9). But the victorious breaking in of the kingdom with Jesus showed that John stood at the threshold of a new era. This is brought out strikingly in the accounts of the feeding of the four thousand (Matt. 15:32–39; Mk. 8:1–10) and the five thousand (Matt. 14:13–21; Mk. 6:30–44; Lk. 9:10–17; Jn. 6:1–13). All the accounts mention the quantities of bread that were left over (e.g., 7 baskets "left over" [*perisseumata*], Mk. 8:8). Those who belong to Jesus have life and have it "to the full" (*perisson*, Jn. 10:10). The prodigal son reflected that his father's servants had bread enough and to spare (Lk. 15:17). All this shows that the father has abundant grace that he holds out to the lost.

(c) Corresponding to the offer of abundant grace is the requirement that the disciples' righteousness must exceed greatly (*perisseusē . . . pleion*) that of the scribes and Pharisees (Matt. 5:20; cf. 5:47). Jesus' radical expectation raises the anxious question as to who can be saved (19:25; Mk. 10:26; Lk. 18:26). The NT precludes all self-security, riches in their widest sense (Matt. 19:24), and Pharisaic casuistry (5:37; 15:4–5). Faith should rely on the fact that with God all things are possible (19:26), and therefore God can make obedience possible to faith.

The two great commandments to love God with one's entire self and one's neighbor as oneself are the foundation of the Law and the Prophets (Matt. 22:37–40). There are no greater (*perissoteron*) commandments than these (Mk. 12:33). By contrast, those who devour widows' houses and for a pretence make long prayers will receive the greater (*perissoteron*) condemnation (12:40; Lk. 20:47). Those who receive more from the Lord will be asked to give "much more" (*perissoteron*, 12:48; cf. Matt. 13:12).

2. (a) Paul uses *perisseuō* and its cognates in Rom. when he speaks of God's justifying grace. Thus he explains, "The law was added so that trespass might increase. But where sin increased, grace increased all the more (*hypereperisseusen*)" (5:20). The glory of the law now seems to have no glory because of the "surpassing glory" of the ministry of Jesus, inasmuch as "the ministry that condemns men" is surpassed by "the ministry that brings righteousness" (2 Cor. 3:9–10). As sin gained dominance in Adam, so grace abounded (*eperisseusen*) in Christ (Rom. 5:15; cf. 10:4). Because the abundance (*perisseia*) of grace cannot be exhausted, there can be no place for reliance on fulfilling the law (3:20). The advantage (*perisson*) of the Jews (3:1) consists in the fact that they were entrusted with the oracles of God. But their denial cannot hinder the victorious course of grace. Rather, it brings about the fact that whatever humankind does enhances God's glory (3:7). Moreover, it means that God's grace has now come to the Gentiles (11:11).

Jew and Gentile alike are utterly dependent on grace (cf. Rom. 11:32). In view of this, Paul prays: "May the God of hope fill you with all joy and peace as you trust in him, so that you may overflow (*perisseuein*) with hope by the power of the Holy Spirit" (15:13). Eph. 3:20 states that by the power at work in us God is able to do "immeasurably more" (*hyperekperissou*) than what we can ask or imagine, while 1:7–10 defines the riches of his grace that "he lavished" (*eperisseusen*) on us as "redemption through his blood, the forgiveness of sins." Being rooted and built up in Christ, believers should live in him, "overflowing (*perisseuontes*) with thankfulness" (Col. 2:7).

(b) Just as Paul, prior to conversion, was obsessed (*perissōs*) with persecuting the church (Acts 26:11) and the traditions of the law (Gal. 1:14), he pursued with the same zeal the saving work of Christ in the building up and sanctification of the churches (cf. 1 Cor. 15:58; Phil. 1:9, 26; 1 Thess. 3:12; 4:1, 10; in each case the vb. *perisseuō* appears). In 3:10 Paul states that he prayed "most earnestly" (*hyperekperissou*) day and night that he might be with the Thessalonian church to supply what was lacking in their faith (cf. 2:17). He urged the Corinthians to use their gifts for building up the church, so that they might "excel" (1 Cor. 14:12).

The apostle knows how to be in need and how to "have plenty" (*perisseuein*), according to whether the former is commanded or the latter given (Phil. 4:12; cf. 4:18). He has striven more and suffered more (*perissoteros*, 1 Cor. 15:10; 2 Cor. 11:23; 12:15). He thus had more cause for boasting than his opponents (1:12; 10:8). But his way is to be satisfied with the power that proves itself in weakness (12:9). Hence, imprisonment and suffering arouse in him more courage to bear witness (Phil. 1:14).

(c) In 2 Cor. *perisseuō* is featured in a particular way in connection with the collection for the Jerusalem church. Paul is concerned with more than the money that is brought in. It is a test of love for the churches, which shows whether it corresponds to Christ's self-sacrifice (8:8–9). Thus he praises the churches of Macedonia that "out of the most severe trial, their overflowing (*perisseia*) joy and their extreme poverty welled up (*eperisseusen*) in rich generosity" (8:2). The apostle expresses his conviction that "God is able to make all grace abound (*perisseusai*) to you, so that . . . you will abound (*perisseuēte*) in every good work" (9:8). Perhaps a further play on words is intended by his introductory remark that "there is no need (*perisson*) for me to write to you about this service for the saints" (9:1). The collection represented and established a key link between the Jerusalem church and the Gentile churches: "This service . . . is also overflowing (*perisseuousa*) in many expressions of thanks to God" (9:12).

3. Heb. warns the church, threatened by persecution, to keep its eyes on its goal and to pay more careful (*perissoterōs*) attention to the teaching it has been given (Heb. 2:1). When God desired to make "very clear" (*perissoteron*) to the heirs of promise his unchangeable character, he interposed with an oath (6:17). Finally, the character of Christ's priesthood becomes "even more (*perissoteron*) clear" (7:15) in view of the testimony of Ps. 110:4 to being a priest forever in the order of Melchizedek.

See also *gemō*, to load, be full (*1154*); *plēthos*, number, multitude, crowd (*4436*); *plēroō*, fill, complete, fulfill, accomplish, carry out (*4444*); *chortazō*, to feed, fatten, fill (*5963*); *chōreō*, have or make room, give way, go (*6003*).

4356 (*perissos*, extraordinary, abundant), → *4355*.

4358 (*perissoteros*, greater, more abundant), → *4355*.

4359 (*perissoterōs*, adv. more, greater), → *4355*.

4360 (*perissōs*, exceedingly, beyond measure), → *4355*.

4361 (*peristera*, dove), → *4374*.

4362	περιτέμνω

περιτέμνω (*peritemnō*), circumcise (*4362*); περιτομή (*peritomē*), circumcision (*4364*); ἀπερίτμητος (*aperitmētos*), uncircumcised (*598*); κατατομή (*katatomē*), mutilation (*2961*); ἀκροβυστία (*akrobystia*), foreskin, uncircumcision, hence Gentiles (*213*).

CL & OT 1. *peritemnō* means lit. cut round. From cl. times on it was used as a technical term for the separation or removal of the male prepuce or of the female clitoris. *peritomē* was the technical term for circumcision. *aperitmētos* means unmutilated, uncircumcised. In secular Gk. this word group with its religious associations was used only with reference to foreign peoples, esp. the Egyptians, for the Greeks did not practice circumcision.

2. The words of this group are of great theological importance in the OT, where they are used exclusively to identify circumcision as a cultic practice. (a) Circumcision gained significance through its connection with faith in Yahweh and its obligatory role as a distinguishing mark of membership in the covenant. It is first described in Gen. 17:1–14, where Yahweh commanded it as the sign and seal of his covenant with Abraham.

Circumcision was evidently not practiced among adult males at certain periods in Israel's history (Jos. 5:2–7). But its mandatory use is clearly reflected by the ordinances in Gen. 17:12; 21:4; and Lev. 12:3. Not merely the children of Jewish parents, but also slaves, whether born in the house or bought, were to be circumcised (Gen. 17:12–13). This applied also to the foreigner who came to believe in Yahweh (cf. Exod. 12:48). Only the circumcised might eat the Passover meal (12:43–48). Anyone refusing circumcision was in breach of the covenant and was to be cut off from the people (Gen. 17:14).

(b) In addition to the physical meaning of circumcision, the OT knows a spiritualized sense. Only the man who lets his heart be circumcised (i.e., who humbles himself before God, accepts the punishment of his iniquity [Lev. 26:41], and so repledges his loyalty to the covenant) is really circumcised "to the LORD" (Jer. 4:4; cf. 9:25; Ezek. 44:9). The recognition that physical circumcision could in some circumstances cause false confidence led to the use of this deepened meaning of the concept as a call to Israel to repent: "Circumcise your hearts, therefore, and do not be stiff-necked any longer" (Deut. 10:16). Paul's thought coincides with this understanding of circumcision as a new noncultic, but complete surrender to God (cf. Rom. 2:25–27).

3. In Hel. and Roman periods circumcision was a confessional sign of Jud. Antiochus IV Epiphanes (176–163 B.C.), for example, threatened those who circumcised their children with the same penalty as murder (1 Macc. 1:48–50). But Jewish women preferred death to abandoning God's holy law, refusing to have their children circumcised (1:60–61). For the Jews apostasy, renunciation of faith, and breach of the covenant were expressed by the word *epispasmos*, the surgical replacement of the foreskin. The spiritual interpretation of circumcision is found in Qumran.

NT *peritemnō*, circumcise, is found 17x in the NT; *peritomē*, 36x. It has three main meanings: circumcision itself, the fact of being circumcised (e.g., Phil. 3:5), and a euphemism for the Jews (e.g., Tit. 1:10). *aperitmētos*, uncircumcised (Acts 7:51), and *katatomē*, mutilation (Phil. 3:2), are each found once. The opposite of *peritomē* (*akrobystia*) occurs 20x in the NT, mostly in Paul. Like *peritomē*, it means the foreskin, the fact of being uncircumcised (e.g., Rom. 4:10), and the Gentiles (e.g., 3:30).

1. In the Gospels, circumcision is used only in its physical meaning. Lk. 1:59 and 2:21 tell of the naming of John the Baptist and of Jesus on the occasion of their circumcision on the eighth day after birth (cf. Acts 7:8; Phil. 3:5). Jn. 7:22–23 assumes the Jewish custom and its position in the law in order to throw doubt on the rab. concepts of how the Sabbath was to be hallowed. The contradiction lay in the fact that, when the eighth day fell on a Sabbath, circumcision, far from profaning it, was actually commanded. Yet the Jews were angry with Jesus "for healing the whole man."

2. The word group is important chiefly in the Pauline letters and Acts, where it illustrates the tension between Paul and the circumcision party. Early Christian communities saw a tension between believers from among the circumcised (i.e., Jewish Christians; Acts 10:45; cf. 11:2; Rom. 3:30; Gal. 2:12; Col. 4:11; Tit. 1:10) and those called the uncircumcision (i.e., Gentile Christians; Eph. 2:11; cf. Acts 11:3; Rom. 4:10; 1 Cor. 7:18). These two groups constantly clashed, because the Jewish Christians insisted that circumcision was necessary for salvation: "Unless you are circumcised, according to the custom taught by Moses, you cannot be saved" (Acts 15:1; cf. 15:5).

James and the elders of the Jerusalem church held discussions with Paul, the apostle to the Gentiles, because they had heard rumors that he taught that not merely Gentile Christians but also Jewish Christians were free from the law of circumcision (Acts 21:21). After all, Paul made freedom from the law through Christ's death and resurrection a central point in his proclamation. He stressed that the gospel for the uncircumcised (the Gentiles) had been entrusted to him, even as that for the Jews (the circumcised) had been to Peter (Gal. 2:7). This clearly implied freedom from the law of circumcision. This freedom had been supported at the Apostolic Council (Acts 15:19–20; cf. Gal. 2:6–10) and had included his fellow workers like Titus (2:3).

Is there a contradiction, then, in Paul's circumcision of Timothy (Acts 16:3)? Not at all. According to Jewish law, Timothy was a Jew and so should have been circumcised; thus Paul was only making good what should have been done years before. Moreover, since Paul claimed to "have become all things to all men so that by all possible means I might save some" (1 Cor. 9:22), this included becoming as a Jew in order to win Jews (cf. 9:20). Paul's witness in the synagogues would have been seriously curtailed and damaged had he left the Jew Timothy uncircumcised (cf. also Acts 21:17–26).

If Paul had a "sharp dispute and debate" with the Jewish Christians about circumcision (Acts 15:2), it was not that he was concerned merely with a cultic act. The issue was linked with the whole question of law and freedom, for anyone who accepted circumcision obligated himself to keep the whole law. That is why he was so intransigent and why he took Peter's vacillation on the matter so seriously (Gal. 2:11–14). Jews believed that circumcision made one a member of the covenant people once and for all. Using Jewish arguments, Paul took an extreme position on the relationship of circumcision and the Mosaic law, stressing that only for those who did the will of God without reserve was circumcision a true sign of the covenant. Breaking the law meant that circumcision becomes uncircumcision (Rom. 2:25; cf. also Phil. 3:2). To keep the law completely by one's own unaided power is impossible. Life must be lived by the grace revealed in Christ, for "Christ is the end of the law" (Rom. 10:4; cf. also Gal. 3).

For the church, therefore, circumcision can never have the importance it had in Jud. For Paul, believers "are the circumcision, we who worship by the Spirit of God, who glory in Christ Jesus, and who put no confidence in the flesh" (Phil. 3:3; cf. 3:5; Gal. 6:13–14). In Rom. 3:1–2 Paul speaks of a relative value attached to circumcision because of the promises connected with it. But he means only to stress that the fulfillment of the promises is solely dependent on faith, irrespective of circumcision. For God "will justify the circumcised by faith and the uncircumcised through that same faith" (3:30).

Rom. 4:7–12 shows that from the standpoint of eternity it is immaterial whether or not a man is circumcised. There Paul calls Abraham as his chief witness for his concept of the equal value of Jewish Christian and Gentile Christian faith. Abraham is equally "father" of both groups (4:11–12). If in 15:8 Paul can warn the Gentiles against pride by pointing out that, historically speaking, Christ "has become a servant of the Jews [lit., circumcised]" for the sake of God's trustworthiness and faithfulness, it has to be understood in the context of 11:17–24 (cf. 15:5–13).

Fundamentally neither circumcision nor uncircumcision have any decisive value in God's sight. The main question is how one reacts to the total claim of God. We may reject it, as, to Paul's grief, many circumcised did, or we may put our faith in Jesus and allow it to become effective through love (cf. 1 Cor. 7:19; Gal. 5:6; 6:15; Col. 3:11). Theologically, the question of circumcision turns on whether one is circumcised in heart through the Spirit (Rom. 2:29; cf. Acts 7:51). Jesus Christ has made the circumcised and the uncircumcised one (Eph. 2:14–22), a new creation (Gal. 6:15).

This new nature is put on in the act of baptism, which is depicted in Col. 2:11–12 as spiritual circumcision. When the old nature is put off and the new one put on, old contrasts are suspended by a new reality. Now "there is no Greek or Jew, circumcised or uncircumcised . . . but Christ is all, and is in all" (3:11).

4364 (*peritomē*, circumcision), → *4362*.

4368 (*periphroneō*, despise), → *2969*.

4370 περίψημα

περίψημα (*peripsēma*), filth (*4370*); περικάθαρμα (*perikatharma*) filth, offscouring (*4326*).

CL & OT From *peripsaō*, wipe round, rub clean, *peripsēma* means that which is wiped off, refuse, scum; or that which effects cleansing (lit., bath towel; fig., expiatory sacrifice). Communities often placated angry gods by offering a human sacrifice as a scapegoat. For such sacrifices the "scum" of society (e.g., criminals, paupers, deformed persons) were regularly recruited; thus the pejorative sense of *peripsēma* was reinforced. *perikatharma* is almost synonymous with *peripsēma*: a guilt-laden expiatory sacrifice, particularly a human one, and a term of contempt for the victims (human rubbish).

In the LXX *peripsēma* occurs only in Tob. 5:18, meaning a sacrifice or ransom in virtue of which God will protect Tobias's life. *perikatharma* occurs only in Prov. 21:18, where God in his providence expends the wicked in order to preserve the upright (cf. Isa. 43:3–4); note how this pattern was reversed in Christ's cross (cf. 1 Pet. 3:18).

NT In the NT, both words occur once only, in 1 Cor. 4:13, as Paul's ironic description of the apostles as those who, by throwing away their lives, were bringing benefit to others (see 2 Cor. 4:10–17; 6:10; Phil. 2:17; Col. 1:24).

See also *rhypos*, dirt (*4866*); *skybalon*, refuse, dung (*5032*).

4374 πετεινόν

πετεινόν (*peteinon*), bird (*4374*); περιστερά (*peristera*), dove (*4361*).

CL & OT The adj. *peteinos*, able to fly, winged, as a subst. means bird. In the Greco-Roman world some birds were held as sacred and could even represent the deity.

Among those animals created by God are "every winged bird" (Gen. 1:21; cf. Ps. 78:27). The OT law distinguishes between clean and unclean birds (Lev. 11:13–19; Deut. 14:11–20); generally speaking, the latter are birds of prey. Numerous references to hunters, fowlers, and traps suggest that birds were eaten for food (Lev. 17:13; Job 18:8–10; Ps. 124:7; Prov. 6:5; Jer. 5:27; Hos. 7:12; Amos 3:5). Doves and pigeons were offered in sacrifice (Lev. 1:14–17; cf. Gen. 8:20). On the birth of a child the mother was to offer a lamb for a burnt offering and a young pigeon or turtledove for a sin offering to make atonement; in cases of poverty two turtledoves or two young pigeons were sufficient (Lev. 12:6–8). The fact that the parents of Jesus offered the latter is an indication of their poverty (Lk. 2:24).

Birds often took on a fig. significance in the OT. Referring to the exodus, Moses reminds the people how Yahweh bore them "on eagles' wings" and brought them to himself (Exod. 19:4; cf. Ps. 103:5; Jer. 49:22; Obad. 4). The eagle also appears as one of the four living creatures in Ezek. 1:10 and in contexts of judgment (Deut. 28:49; Jer. 49:16; Hab. 1:8; cf. Lam. 4:19; Hos. 8:1). In Job 39:27–30 the eagle represents the unfathomable wisdom of God.

Birds can depict desolation (Ps. 102:6–7; Isa. 34:11; Zeph. 2:14). But they can also be the object of God's care (Job 38:41; Ps. 84:3; 147:9). By way of contrast, the flitting of the sparrow and swallow illustrates the ineffectuality of a causeless curse under the providence of God (Prov. 26:2). Birds can also serve humans (Gen. 8:6–12). Elijah subsisted for a time on the food brought by ravens (1 Ki. 17:4–6). Flocks of quail providentially provided Israel with food in their desert wanderings (Exod. 16:13; Num. 11:31–32; Ps. 105:40).

NT As in the OT, birds in the NT illustrate the workings of divine providence. Apart from Peter's denial of Jesus three times before the rooster crowed (Matt. 26:34, 75; Mk. 14:30, 72; Lk. 22:34, 61; Jn. 18:27), virtually all the other allusions to birds have a theological sig-

nificance. Jesus urged his disciples not to be anxious about the necessities of life. God provides for the birds, who know nothing of anxious toil, and humans have more value than they (Matt. 6:26; Lk. 12:24). Jesus' comment that foxes have holes and birds have nests but that the Son of Man has nowhere to lay his head (Matt. 8:20; Lk. 9:58), is a summons to utter trust and abandonment to the providence of the Father.

The question "Are not two sparrows sold for a penny? Yet not one of them will fall to the ground apart from the will of your Father" (Matt. 10:29; cf. Lk. 12:6) underlines the stark realities of the situation. The birds were not sold as pets but as food for the poor. This saying follows a warning not to fear those who kill the body and can do no more, but to fear him who has power to kill and to cast into hell. The saying, therefore, does not promise being spared from suffering and death but gives assurance of God's love and providential ordering in life and death. It expresses poignantly what Paul expressed in his exultant celebration of God's providence in Rom. 8:28–39.

Birds feature in the parables of the sower and the mustard seed. In the former they depict the activity of the devil in removing the seed of the word that is not understood (Matt. 13:4, 19; Mk. 4:4, 15; Lk. 8:5, 12). In the latter, the fact that birds can make nests in the branches of a tree emphasizes the sureness of the growth of the kingdom from apparently insignificant beginnings (Matt. 13:32; Mk. 4:32; Lk. 13:19).

One of the most striking sayings in the Gospels is Matt. 23:37–39, where Jesus expresses his love over Jerusalem in terms of a hen and her chicks, but also his judgment for their refusal to accept his care. He is addressing the crowds, commenting harshly on the teachers of the law and the Pharisees (cf. 23:1–36). Far from being a source of light and refuge, the religious leaders have been misleading the people and persecuting the prophets of God—both in the past and in Jesus' own day. The temple, which should have been the true sanctuary of God for the people, was not fulfilling that role. Thus, Jesus may be implying that he is the true sanctuary and assuming the role of both the temple and Yahweh as the refuge of the people.

The context in Matt. 23:37–39 also suggests a wider application. Jesus' saying follows the denunciation of these who build the tombs of the prophets and upon whom will come the blood of the righteous from Abel to Zechariah (Matt. 23:29–36; cf. Lk. 11:45–52). Jesus' desire to protect the children of Jerusalem in his earthly ministry is but the climax of the same divine desire throughout history. Thus Jesus makes it clear that the day of opportunity is irrevocably lost. Judgment on the house of Israel is now inevitable. At the same time it will vindicate Jesus, whose messianic return will be welcomed.

The dove became a symbol of virtues for the early Christians. This finds expression in the saying: "Be as shrewd as snakes and as innocent as doves" (Matt. 10:16). At Jesus' baptism the Holy Spirit appeared "like a dove" (3:16; Mk. 1:10; Lk. 3:22; Jn. 1:32). The symbolism here may recall the Spirit of God brooding on the waters (cf. Gen. 1:2), suggesting the guiding presence of the Creator Spirit in the new creative work about to begin through Christ (cf. Jn. 1:1–10; 2 Cor. 4:6 for passages that link Christ's work with that of creation).

Peter's vision of a great sheet containing all kinds of animals, reptiles, and birds (Acts 10:12; 11:6), which he was commanded to kill and eat, symbolized that God has now accepted what was hitherto unclean. The way was open to receive Gentiles into the fellowship of the church, since they had already received the Holy Spirit.

4376 πέτρα

πέτρα (*petra*), rock (*4376*); πέτρος (*petros*), stone, rock, Peter (*4377*); Κηφᾶς (*kēphas*), Cephas (rock, the Aram. name given to Peter) (*3064*); πετρώδης (*petrōdēs*), rocky (*4378*).

CL & OT 1. In cl. Gk. *petra* means rock, boulder, and stone as material; by the 5th cent. B.C. it could denote hard-heartedness. *petros* means a (broken off) piece of rock, stone. A strict distinction of meaning cannot be maintained, however, for *petros* can mean rock, and *petra*, stone.

2. In the LXX *petros* is found only at 2 Macc. 1:16 and 4:41, in the sense of stone; *petra*, rock (occurring about 100x), usually translates the Heb. *ṣûr,* rock, or *selaʾ,* rock, crag, cliff (e.g., Exod. 17:6; Num. 20:8). Rocks provide a refuge for animals (Ps. 104:18; Prov. 30:26 = LXX 24:61) and for humans (1 Sam. 13:6). On the day of Yahweh people will creep into the clefts of the rocks to escape from the terrible majesty of God (Isa. 2:19). Since a rock affords protection and thus also strength, God himself is described as David's "rock" (2 Sam. 22:2; cf. Gen. 49:24). The LXX avoids the word *petra* in Gen. 49:24 and instead makes use of a circumlocution (cf. also Ps. 31:4; 62:7).

A rock is also the scene of divine revelation (Jdg. 6:20–21; 13:19). The numinous character of the divine revelation is evident in the way rocks are torn apart by God or by his word (1 Ki. 19:11; Jer. 23:29; Nah. 1:6). The memory of the miracle recorded in Exod. 17:1–6, Num. 20:1–13, where Moses brought water out of the rock by striking it at God's command, is reflected in such passages as Neh. 9:15; Ps. 78:15–16. A similar miracle, the feeding of the people with honey from the rock, is recorded at Deut. 32:13; Ps. 81:16. In a transferred sense the rock is also a symbol of firmness and resolution (Isa. 50:7; Ezek. 3:9) and of stubborn resistance (Jer. 5:3).

The rabbis, taking up Isa. 51:1–2, describe Abraham as a rock. The Qumran community is compared to a building with foundations on the rock; the image of the cornerstone is likewise present in Qumran writings.

NT 1. In the NT *petros* occurs 155x, all but Jn. 1:42 as a second name for Simon. *petra* occurs 15x. In the parable at the end of the Sermon on the Mount Jesus refers to those who hear and do his word as those who build a house on a rock, i.e., on a firm, sure foundation (Matt. 7:24–25; cf. also Deut. 28:15, 30). The parable of the sower speaks of the seed that falls on the rock (Lk. 8:6, 13); Matt. 13:5, 20; Mk. 4:5, 16 speak of "rocky ground" (*petrōdēs*). According to Matt. 27:51, the death of Jesus is accompanied by earthquakes and the splitting of rocks; Joseph of Arimathea laid Jesus' corpse in a tomb hewn out of the rock (27:60; Mk. 15:46). According to Rev. 6:15–17 people will hide themselves in the caves and rocks of the mountains; behind this description lies not only Isa. 2, but a recollection of Hos. 10:8.

2. Three sets of passages require particular attention: Rom. 9:33 and 1 Pet. 2:8; 1 Cor. 10:3–4; and Matt. 16:18.

(a) Rom. 9:33 and 1 Pet. 2:8 refer to "a rock that makes [men] fall," which is interpreted Christologically (a quotation from Isa. 8:14). This is further developed in Isa. 28:16 to that of the cornerstone (→ *gōnia, 1224*), which, according to Ps. 118:22, was rejected by the builders. Isa. 8:13–15 promises that Yahweh will be a sanctuary to those who fear him, but those who disdain him will break themselves on him.

Paul sees a fulfillment of Isa. 8:14 in the Jewish rejection of Christ, esp. because Israel pursued a righteousness based on law and works and not on faith (Rom. 9:33; cf. 9:31–32). But the Gentiles who did not pursue righteousness have found it through faith (9:30). In 1 Pet. 2:8 the Isa. passage underlines the contrast between the disobedient (i.e., the old Israel, who rejected Christ) and the "spiritual house" of God, the "holy priesthood" that offers spiritual sacrifices (2:5; i.e., the church, cf. 2:7).

(b) In 1 Cor. 10:3–4 Paul refers to the miracles of Exod. 17 and Num. 20: The fathers in the desert "all ate the same spiritual food and drank the same spiritual drink, for they drank from the spiritual rock that accompanied them, and that rock was Christ." Regarding these two OT passages, Jewish rabbis had concluded that the rock that provided the water kept following the Israelites on their journey, though they did not give a messianic interpretation of the passage. Paul also interprets the OT miracle in the light of the Lord's Supper, which is spiritual food and spiritual drink having its origin in Christ. This OT narrative is a type foreshadowing the Christ event (cf. also Jn. 6:35–58; 7:37).

(c) (i) In Matt. 16:18 Jesus calls Peter the rock on which he will build his church: "And I tell you that you are Peter [*petros*], and on this rock [*petra*] I will build my church, and the gates of Hades [*hadēs, 87*] will not overcome it." The basis here is a play on the words *petros* and *petra*. According to Mk. 3:16 and Jn. 1:42, Jesus gave Simon the name Peter. Jn. 1:42, the only place in the NT where the noun *petros* is used in its normal sense, states that *Kēphas* (Cephas) means *petros*. Both the Aram. transliteration and the Gk. translation, *kēphas/petros*, can mean rock, and thus *petra* in Matt. 16:18 can be translated as rock. The assonance of the words makes it immediately evident that Peter is the "rock-man," the foundation on which Jesus will build his church. Normally one would expect *petra* in both halves of Matt. 16:18, but since *petra* is a fem. noun, the NT chooses the less usual masc. Gk. word *petros*, which is Peter's name.

(ii) But in what sense is Peter the rock? Note that as early as the beginning of the 3d cent. A.D. the Roman pope began using Matt. 16:18–19 to support his claim to be head of the church, asserting that this position had been given to him by Christ as the successor of Peter. The Gospel account, however, makes no mention of Peter's successors. Furthermore, the follow-up comment about binding and loosing is extended to all the apostles in 18:18. Peter, therefore, is in 16:18 a representative of all the apostles, who together formed and laid the foundation of the church (see Eph. 2:20; Rev. 21:14).

For many evangelicals, however, this interpretation is not satisfactory. In Matt. 16:18 Jesus is not speaking of the laying of foundations, but of building the church. Note how Paul, who acknowledges Peter's apostleship (Gal. 2:8), states clearly in 2:14 that "the truth of the gospel" stands as the norm binding on all apostles, even on Peter. It is this truth that underlies the conferring of apostolic authority on Peter in Matt. 16:18. It is implied in the confession that Jesus is the Christ, for like the gospel itself this confession is based on divine revelation (Matt. 16:17; Gal. 1:12). This confession, which is the source of all apostolic authority, points us to Christ as the true foundation of the church (1 Cor. 3:11).

Understood in this light, the words of Matt. 16:18 are simply an interpretation of Peter's confession of Christ in 16:16. This view accords with that of the Reformers. They did not see the church as founded on the person of Peter, certainly not on his subjective act of faith; for them the rock foundation on which Christ built his church was the eternal, unchangeable truth of Peter's confession about Christ. The church founded on this rock is covered by Christ's promise even today, that the gates of hell will not prevail against it.

(iii) Even if Peter himself is seen as the rock, the passage gives no grounds for thinking that Jesus gave the name Cephas because of his stable character. In fact, his vacillation under pressure gives a certain irony to the name (cf. Matt. 26:31–35, 69–75; Gal. 2:11–21). It would appear, therefore, that Peter is the rock in the sense that he is the first member of the church proper. He is the first to confess Jesus as the Christ, the Son of the living God. As such, he is informed and assured that flesh and blood has not revealed this to him but the Father in heaven (Matt. 16:16–17).

In the mission outreach of the church, Peter uses the keys of the kingdom (Matt. 16:19; cf. Isa. 22:22; Rev. 1:18; 3:7; → *kleis*, key, *3090*) in opening the church first to the Jews (Acts 2) and then to the Gentiles (Acts 10) by proclaiming the gospel to them. He exercises leadership in the appointment of Matthias to the apostolic band as a replacement for Judas (1:15–26) and discipline in the case of Ananias and Sapphira (5:1–11). He figures prominently in the early days of the church in bearing witness before the Jews and their leaders (4:8–22; 5:15, 29; 9:32).

However, once the church is thereby opened and established, Peter's foundational role is essentially over. After his imprisonment (Acts 12) he begins to occupy a less prominent place. Peter's work is confined to the Jewish mission (Gal. 2:8). In the first great council of the church recounted in Acts 15 it is James, the Lord's brother, who presides (15:13–21). Although Peter plays an important part in the debate (15:7–11), James delivers the decisive judgment. Moreover, nowhere in the NT does Peter lay claim to primacy. In the opening verses of the two epistles of Peter, the author describes himself simply as an apostle, and this is how Paul views him (1 Cor. 9:5).

There apparently were tensions in the apostolic church centering on personalities, which may explain certain passages in which Paul counterbalances possible claims by a Petrine faction. In 1 Cor. 1:12 he rebukes those who claim to belong to Paul, Cephas, or Apollos. Baptism into Christ precludes any such factious divisions (1:13), while in 3:11 Paul may even be countering a partisan understanding of Peter's foundational role: "For no one can lay any foundation other than the one already laid, which is Jesus Christ" (→ *themelios*, foundation, *2529*). Paul's subsequent remarks may also be influenced by this: his warning about what one builds on the foundation that will be tried by fire (3:12–15), and the reminder that believers form God's holy temple and God's Spirit lives in them (3:16–17).

In Gal. 2:9 there is a certain irony in the allusion to James, Cephas, and John, who were "reputed to be pillars," since Paul goes on to discuss Peter's vacillation in the face of the Jewish circumcision party (2:11–14). Eph. 2:20 allows a foundational role to the apostles and prophets but insists with the Gospels that Christ is the cornerstone. Similarly the new Jerusalem in Rev. 21:14 is built on the foundation of the apostles. This theme is taken up by Peter himself when he describes believers as "living stones . . . being built into a spiritual house" (1 Pet. 2:5). There is no hint of the foundation of Peter continuing right through the building. Peter never claims primacy for himself or any successors.

While it seems probable that Peter visited Rome and probably even died there (cf. 1 Pet. 5:13), there is no evidence that Peter was ever bishop of Rome. Indeed, the primary document for the church at Rome in the subapostolic age is 1 Clem., but this letter reflects little of the primacy of a bishop at Rome. Rather, the church of Rome at that time seems to be governed by a college of presbyters. The letter was sent in the name of the church and is attributed to the individual Clement only by a variant ending preserved in some later manuscripts.

See also *gōnia*, corner (*1224*); *lithos*, stone (*3345*); *margaritēs*, pearl (*3449*).

4377 (*petros*, stone, rock, Peter), → *4376*.

4378 (*petrōdēs*, rocky), → *4376*.

4379 (*pēganon*, rue), → *3303*.

4380 πηγή	πηγή (*pēgē*), spring, source (*4380*); ποταμός (*potamos*), river, stream (*4532*).

CL & OT 1. In cl. Gk. *pēgē* designates the source of streams or rivers. *potamos* denotes flowing water, esp. dangerous rivers or streams. In popular Gk. belief, rivers and springs were personified as inferior divinities.

2. (a) For Israel rivers possessed special significance in geographical and political respects. Settlements were established by rivers, which were often bitterly fought over as boundaries and providers of water. The rivers most frequently mentioned are the Nile, the Jordan, the Euphrates, and the Kebar (Ezek. 1:1).

(b) Springs and rivers, together with the sea (→ *thalassa*, *2498*), belong to the mass of water created by God, on which he founded the earth (Ps. 24:2) and over which he rules (Exod. 7; Ps. 78:44). But while the role of the sea is viewed mainly in negative terms, springs and rivers are viewed positively as that which makes human, animal, and plant life possible (though cf. 18:15; 124:4–5). Yahweh causes springs to flow, and human beings and animals to quench their thirst (104:10–11); the river of God waters the land and provides nourishment and prosperity (65:9). Important decisions are often made at a well (e.g., Gen. 24:11–18; 29:1–4). By bathing in the Jordan, Naaman is healed of leprosy (2 Ki. 5:1–19). By the Kebar River Ezekiel

receives his call (Ezek. 1:1–2:8) and message (3:15–21). As creations of Yahweh, rivers join in praising their creator (Ps. 98:8).

(c) Several times Israel experienced Yahweh as the Lord of the springs and the rivers and gratefully testified to these facts of its salvation history (Ps. 66:6, the miracle of the Red Sea and the crossing of the Jordan). God's provision of water from a spring in the rock (Exod. 17:5–6) is often praised (Ps. 74:15; 78:16). The hope of thirst-quenching water in plentiful abundance forms an essential part of statements concerning the coming reign of peace (e.g., Isa. 12:3; 30:23–25; 35:7).

(d) Spring water is also part of the OT conception of Paradise. Gen. 2:10–14 states that the river that rises in Eden divides into the four branches: Pishon, Gihon, Tigris, and Euphrates. Since the last days are depicted in terms analogous to the original state (though excelling it), the eschatological speculations of OT and Jewish lit. attach themselves to this river in Eden. The river rising in the eschatological temple and banked by trees of life (Ezek. 47:1–12) serves for purification and irrigation (Joel 3:18; cf. Zech. 13:1–2; 14:8). Various OT prophecies refer to the irrigating and thirst-quenching function of rainfalls, rivers, and streams in the last days (e.g., Isa. 12:3; 43:19–21; 44:3; cf. Sir. 24:30–33).

(e) Springs and rivers also have a fig. use. God's blessings flood his people and land as an irrigating river (Isa. 66:12), and the God-given peace of the righteous is like a peacefully flowing river (48:18). Yahweh himself is a spring of living water (Jer. 2:13). The compassionate person is compared with a well-watered garden and a never-failing spring of water (Isa. 58:11). But note also that God's wrath comes "like a pent-up flood" on his enemies, sweeping them away with elemental power (59:19).

NT 1. *potamos*, river, as a purely geographical designation, is found for the Jordan (Matt. 3:6), the Euphrates (Rev. 9:14; 16:12), and the little stream on whose banks was the place of prayer in Philippi (Acts 16:13).

2. (a) NT theological statements about springs and rivers reflect the OT background. God has not only created heaven, earth, and sea, but also the fountains of water (Rev. 14:7). God has full right of disposal over rivers and fountains, so that in the end times he can either revoke the blessing and gift of drinking water (8:10; 16:4) or cause rivers to dry up (16:12). Jesus reveals himself to the Samaritan woman at Jacob's well (Jn. 4:5–15). Using the water in the well as a starting point Jesus refers her to the water of life, which is eternally brimming over. The Jordan is the place for the prophetic symbolic action of the Baptist (Matt. 3:6) and thus also the scene of Jesus' baptism (3:13) and God's self-revelation in Spirit and in Word (3:16–17).

(b) The experience of the dangerous threat to life caused by swollen rivers (Matt. 7:25, 27) leads to regarding streams of water as the instrument of demonic powers (Rev. 12:15–16). Thus the dragon attempts to do away with the woman who gave birth to the male child and who symbolizes the mother of Jesus and the church.

(c) Eschatological speculation, linking on to prophetic promises (e.g., Ezek. 47:1–12; Joel 3:18), is vitally interested in the healing character of the river that surpasses the river of Paradise in Gen. 2:10–14 and will at the end of time both quench thirst and spread abroad life, salvation, and purity (Rev. 22:1–2, 17). The throne of God and of the Lamb (22:1) takes over the place of the temple of Ezek. 47:1 as the source of this river: God himself pours out in Christ the water of life (21:6). Jn. 7:37–38 should be similarly understood, which interprets Ezek. 47:1 of Jesus (cf. also Isa. 44:3; 55:1; 58:11). This water of life quenches thirst for all time and, as a spring of life, flows out from the one who has previously drunk it (Jn. 4:13–14). Note that 7:39 expounds the streams of living water expressly in terms of the Spirit, which passes from Jesus to those who believe in him.

See also *thalassa*, sea, lake (*2498*); *hydōr*, water (*5623*); *kataklysmos*, a deluge, flood (*2886*); *Iordanēs*, the river Jordan (*2674*); *limnē*, lake (*3349*).

<table>
<tr><td>4384</td><td>πηλός</td></tr>
</table>

πηλός (*pēlos*), clay, mud, mire (*4384*).

CL & OT 1. In cl. Gk. *pēlos* means mud, muck, dung, or clay. It denotes dust or soil mixed with some fluid, esp. water, with the result that the material becomes soft and pliable. The word commonly designates the clay or earth used by masons and potters. The skill of the potter in molding clay suggested an image for describing humans as clay figurines. In the Hel. period the thought of a human as a piece of clay is common. In the Roman period there is some evidence for the use of mud or clay in medical procedures.

2. The LXX uses *pēlos* for mud or mire (e.g., 2 Sam. 22:43; Ps. 69:14), loam or clay (e.g., Isa. 29:16; 41:25; Jer. 18:6). It is esp. the work of a potter in preparing and shaping the clay that suggested lines of thought that were theologically important.

(a) The account that God formed the first man out of dust (Gen. 2:7; 3:19) finds a distinct echo in the book of Job, where people are described as those "who live in houses of clay" (4:19). Job chides God for having fashioned him "like clay," then turning about to destroy him (10:8–9). The fragility of clay provides an apt figure for Job's powerlessness when overcome by affliction and impending death.

The image of God fashioning humans as a potter forms clay vessels becomes explicit in Isa. 29:16, where those who believe they can conceal their plans from the Lord are cautioned not to confuse themselves with God, who made them, "as if the potter were thought to be like the clay." A rebellious person who strives with God is like clay that disputes with the potter (45:9; cf. Sir. 33:10–13 = LXX 36:10–13).

(b) Jer. found in the action of a local potter working at his wheel an object lesson that illumined the sovereign judgment of God on the nation (18:1–12). When the recalcitrant clay refused to conform to the potter's purpose and the intended vessel was spoiled, he reworked the clay into another vessel. So God remains master of the clay (i.e., Israel as a nation), and he will shape it to his intended purpose (18:6).

(c) In the preparation of clay for his trade, a potter kneads the clay by treading on it with his feet (cf. Nah. 3:14). This common practice furnished Isa. with a vivid image for the ruthless treatment Babylon can expect from an invader who will approach from the north (41:25). As a potter treads on the clay, this conqueror will trample under foot his enemies.

(d) In Wis. 15:7–17 the writer focuses on a pagan potter who makes his living from the manufacture and sale of terracotta figurines. From the same lump of clay he molds "counterfeit gods" (15:9) and sewer tiles (15:7). Here the biblical motif of God as creator and humankind as clay are mockingly combined with a defense of the second commandment, which prohibits the fashioning of graven images (15:13).

NT 1. The NT uses *pēlos* in two ways. In Jn. it designates the mixture of dirt and spittle that Jesus applied to the eyes of a man born blind (Jn. 9:6–15), a practice that was widespread in Jewish healing arts. The repeated reference to the claylike mixture (5x in Jn. 19:6, 11, 14–15) suggests a deeper level of meaning. By his action on this man, Jesus performs a creative activity that provides humans with sight and thus demonstrates that he is the light of the world (cf. Jn. 1:4–9; 8:12; 9:5).

2. In Rom. 9:20–21 Paul draws on the common OT image of God as the potter who exercises sovereign control over his creation. In the context humans are described as molded clay and God as the one who molds it for his own purposes. The rhetorical question, "Does not the potter have the right to make out of the same lump of clay some pottery for noble purposes and some for common use?" is indebted to Isa. 29:16; 45:9. The imagery underscores God's freedom and sovereignty in relationship to us as his creatures, and we must not confuse our claims with the divine prerogative.

See also *keramion*, an earthenware vessel, jar (*3040*); *ostrakinos*, made of earth or clay, earthenware (*4017*); *phyrama*, a mixture, a lump (*5878*).

4391 (*pithanologia*, persuasive speech, art of persuasion), → *4275*.

4393 (*pikrainō*, make bitter, embitter), → *4394*.

<table>
<tr><td>4394</td><td>πικρία</td></tr>
</table>

πικρία (*pikria*), bitterness (*4394*); πικρός (*pikros*), bitter (*4395*); πικρῶς (*pikrōs*), bitterly (*4396*); πικραίνω (*pikrainō*), make bitter, embitter (*4393*); παραπικραίνω (*parapikrainō*), embitter, make angry, provoke (*4176*); παραπικρασμός (*parapikrasmos*), rebellion (*4177*).

CL & OT In cl. Gk., *pikros* means pointed, sharp, pungent, bitter tasting, and in a transferred sense painful, angry, relentless, embittered. This word group occurs often in the LXX, occasionally with a lit. sense (e.g., Exod. 15:23; Jer. 23:15), but mostly with a metaphorical sense (see Deut. 29:18; Prov. 5:4; Lam. 3:15, 19; cf. Amos 6:12 = LXX 6:13), such as the bitterness associated with grief, disappointment, and anger—both in God (e.g., Isa. 28:21 [trans. "strange" and "alien"]) and in humans (e.g., Ruth 1:20; Lam. 3:15, 19). *parapikrainō* is often used in the LXX for provoking God to anger (e.g., Jer. 32:29; 44:3 = LXX 29:29; 51:3).

NT In Heb. 12:15 ("bitter root," lit., "root of bitterness"; cf. Deut. 29:18) bitterness (*pikria*) is associated with anger as in the OT. Rom. 3:14 (a quotation of Ps. 10:7) associates the word with cursing; Paul uses the verse to show that both Jews and Gentiles are "under sin" (Rom. 3:9). In Acts 8:23 Peter accused Simon Magus of being "full of bitterness and captive to sin" after he tried to purchase the Holy Spirit. *pikria* comes first in a list of vices that the Christian is called upon to put away (Eph. 4:31).

The adj. *pikros* is found only at Jas. 3:11 (bitter water as a symbol of the evil that issues from the tongue) and 3:14 (bitter envy). Such conduct is incompatible with a Christian profession and must be done away with. The adv. *pikrōs* is found only at Matt. 26:75 and Lk. 22:62, where Peter acknowledged his denial and "wept bitterly."

Husbands are not to be harsh or bitter (*pikrainō*) toward their wives (Col. 3:19). In Rev. 8:11 *pikrainō* means to make water bitter through wormwood (cf. OT). It describes one of the afflictions of humankind in the vision of the angels and trumpets. In 10:9–10 the vb. describes the scroll that the angel commanded John to eat, which was sweet in his mouth but made his stomach bitter. The image suggests the anguish that the prophetic message caused him.

parapikrainō is found only at Heb. 3:16 (see Ps. 95:7b–11). The noun *parapikrasmos*, rebellion, occurs in Heb. 3:8, 15 (both from Ps. 95:8). The OT text refers to the exodus rebellion (cf. Exod. 15:23; 17:7; Num. 14; 20:2–5), and the author of Heb. cites this incident as a warning against disobedience.

4395 (*pikros*, bitter), → *4394*.

4396 (*pikrōs*, bitterly), → *4394*.

4398 (*pimplēmi*, fill, complete, fulfill), → *4444*.

<table>
<tr><td>4403</td><td>πίνω</td></tr>
</table>

πίνω (*pinō*), drink (*4403*); ποτίζω (*potizō*), water, give to drink (*4540*); ποτήριον (*potērion*), cup (*4539*); πόμα (*poma*), a drink (*4503*); πόσις (*posis*), drinking, a drink (*4530*); πότος (*potos*), drinking, i.e., revelry (*4542*); καταπίνω (*katapinō*), swallow, overwhelm (*2927*).

CL & OT 1. (a) In cl. Gk. *pinō* means to drink. The related vb. *potizō* has the trans. meaning, to enable someone to drink, to give to drink, to water (of animals). *posis* denotes the act of drinking or what is drunk, the drink; *poma* and *poton* both mean drink. *potērion* is the drinking vessel, the cup or goblet.

(b) Drinking satisfies thirst and refreshes. In popular opinion drinking was considered a pleasure, and it could become a passion. In philosophical discussions a life of drinking too much runs up against criticism. Drinking had a special place in the mystery religions, esp. in sacral meals.

2. In view of frequently occurring shortages of water, thirst (Exod. 17:1–7; → *peinaō*, *4277*) and drinking (1 Ki. 17:3–4) are esp. significant in the OT world. Rain transforms the land into a watered garden (cf. Isa. 55:10), while lack of it causes vegetation to wither and results in catastrophic famines (1 Ki. 18:2–6). Closely connected with the shortage of water is the presence of bad and undrinkable water (Exod. 15:23).

3. The ability to satisfy thirst is attributed to God: "You care for the land and water it; you enrich it abundantly. The streams of God are filled with water to provide the people with grain" (Ps. 65:9). Drink is a gift that is continually received anew from God and is a cause of thanksgiving. Correspondingly, thirst that cannot be quenched is understood as God's anger and punishment (Isa. 5:13). When the quenching of thirst is taken for granted, God has been forgotten (Jer. 2:6).

4. Fig., drinking can stand for the way God's judgments or gifts come to humans: "the cup of his wrath" (Isa. 51:17; cf. Ps. 75:8; Jer. 25:15–29) or his "cup of salvation" (Ps. 116:13; cf. Isa. 55:1). Amos 8:11 speaks of thirst for the word of God that can be quenched only if God wills.

NT 1. The NT speaks of drinking and eating in a variety of connections. (a) Like eating (→ *esthiō*, *2266*), drinking is referred to lit., though eating and drinking, like dress, are relativized (Matt. 6:25–27, 31). Life itself is more important than either of these, and we can rely on God to take care of these matters. Seeking the kingdom of God and his righteousness (Matt. 6:33; cf. Lk. 12:31) should take priority, and then the matters of daily living will settle themselves.

(b) Observing the distinction between clean and unclean foods belongs to the old covenant (Acts 10:14). Peter's vision symbolizes the abolition of Jewish exclusiveness and the inclusion of the Gentiles into the people of God.

(c) The materialistic attitude that looks no further than this life is rejected (1 Cor. 15:32; cf. Lk. 12:19). Those given to eating and drinking and fail to recognize their responsibility toward God (Matt. 24:48–51; Lk. 12:19) will be called to account (Matt. 24:38–39; cf. Lk. 17:27–30).

2. (a) Thus, eating and drinking are not to be seen as ends in themselves or as pleasures for the self-indulgent, but in the light of one's responsibility to God and other people. Paul saw the problem in terms of the church. Although believers have complete freedom to eat and drink what they like (1 Cor. 9:4), they must take account of their fellow believers (Rom. 14:21). The question is seen Christologically in Matt.: In the poor to whom a drink is given (*potizō*) Christ himself is encountered (25:37, 42).

(b) The problem was understood eschatologically by John the Baptist. The seriousness of imminent events cast its shadow over the present age (Mk. 1:5–6). Therefore John neither ate nor drank beyond a minimum sustenance (Matt. 11:18).

(c) The behavior of the Son of Man is depicted as a direct contrast to this, for he both ate and drank (Matt. 11:19). A number of stories refer to his eating and drinking with sinners (Mk. 2:16; cf. Lk. 5:30, 33), perhaps anticipating the messianic banquet. Jesus did not come "to call the righteous, but sinners to repentance" (Lk. 5:32).

3. (a) Drinking takes on a deeper significance when, along with eating, it expresses the unity that exists among those who share a meal. On the day of judgment, some, in order to claim a place at his side, will recall that they have eaten and drunk with Jesus (Lk. 13:26). But he will reply that he never knew them (13:27; cf. Matt. 7:21–23; 25:41; Lk. 6:46), for the relationship was merely formal. By contrast, the disciples are promised that they will eat and drink at Jesus' table (22:30).

(b) The request of the sons of Zebedee to sit at Jesus' side in eternity has an apocalyptic-eschatological character (Matt. 20:20–21; Mk. 10:35–37; cf. Lk. 22:24–30), but it is striking that Jesus' answer

points rather to his death: The cup is understood as the cup of suffering, the baptism as the baptism of death (Matt. 20:22; Mk. 10:38). The "cup" of suffering is mentioned later in the Gospels, where Jesus requested his Father to let that cup (*potērion*) pass from him but submitted himself to God's will (Matt. 26:39; Mk. 14:36; Lk. 22:42).

4. (a) Drinking is referred to fig. in 1 Cor. 10:4 (cf. Exod. 17:6; Num. 20:11). It is not certain how this drinking from Christ is to be understood. Some think Paul may be alluding in 1 Cor. 10:3–4 to the Lord's Supper as a saving event already anticipated in the time of Moses (cf. the use of "spiritual," i.e., pertaining to the Spirit, in 10:4). If so, there is a real identity between the ancient and the new saving events. Others, however, look at the passage typologically, that the rock from which the Israelites drank in the desert pointed forward to Jesus Christ as the one who gives living water.

(b) In 1 Cor. 10:16, Paul, using language of the early Christian tradition, calls the cup (*potērion*) "a participation in the blood of Christ." Through the communion cup, believers are united with Christ in his death. Note also Paul's words in 11:23–26, where eating the bread and drinking the cup unites us with the body and the blood of the crucified and risen Lord (see also *pascha*, *4247*).

(c) *katapinō* is used fig. for the fact that death will be "swallowed up in victory" at the resurrection on the last day (1 Cor. 15:54; cf. 2 Cor. 5:4). By contrast, Satan prowls around, looking for some prey to "devour" (1 Pet. 5:8).

5. Jn. 4:10–15 raises the question of the water of life (4:11). Ordinary water quenches the thirst only for the time being (4:13), but the water Jesus gives bestows eternal life (4:14). One must therefore come to Jesus (7:37; cf. Isa. 55:1), i.e., have faith in him. While the gift here is Jesus himself (cf. also Jn. 6:51–58), in 7:39 it is related to the Spirit as the Spirit of Christ.

See also *peinaō*, hunger (*4277*); *brōma*, food (*1109*); *geuomai*, taste, partake of, enjoy, experience (*1174*); *esthiō*, eat (*2266*).

4405 (pipraskō, sell), → *4797.*

4406	πίπτω

πίπτω (*piptō*), fall (*4406*); ἐκπίπτω (*ekpiptō*), fall off or from, lose one's way (*1738*); ἐπιπίπτω (*epipiptō*), fall on (*2158*); καταπίπτω (*katapiptō*), fall down (*2928*); περιπίπτω (*peripiptō*), fall into, among (*4346*); πτῶμα (*ptōma*), that which has fallen, corpse (*4773*); πτῶσις (*ptōsis*), falling, fall (*4774*).

CL & OT 1. In cl. Gk. *piptō* has the basic meaning to fall (from a height or an upright position); it can also mean to fall in battle but also to fall into life (i.e., to be born). In a fig. sense *piptō* means to fly into a rage, to fall into misfortune, shame, and the like; also to be ruined. The nouns *ptōsis*, act of falling, and *ptōma*, that which has fallen, signify misfortune or disaster. *ptōma* also denotes a corpse, esp. of one killed violently.

ekpiptō means to fall out of something, e.g., lose the way, give up hope; in the pass., to be driven out, excluded. As a technical naval term it means to be driven off course, to be cast ashore, because of inability to follow the course on which one has set out. *peripiptō* means to fall around. It is also used of events that befall one.

2. The LXX mostly uses *piptō* to translate forms of *nāpal*. These words exhibit here the same broad range of meaning as they do outside the Bible. *piptō* has a fig. meaning for the most part in the OT wisdom lit., i.e., to have a mishap through no fault of one's own (Ps. 37:24; Prov. 24:16; Eccl. 4:10); to go to ruin, be destroyed (Job 18:12, *ptōma*; Prov. 24:17; Sir. 5:13, *ptōsis*). The Heb. manner of expression remains concrete even in metaphorical use: "The wicked are brought down by [lit., fall into] their own wickedness" (Prov. 11:5; cf. Isa. 8:14–15; Jer. 8:4; Mic. 7:8). The NT sense of losing one's salvation has no parallel in the OT (though cf. Prov. 11:28; Sir. 1:30; 2:7).

NT 1. Words of this group are found most often in the lit. sense: of the collapse of buildings (Lk. 13:4; Heb. 11:30); of things falling down

(Matt. 13:4–8 par.; 15:27; Jn. 12:24), esp. the falling off of dead flowers as an image of the shortness of life (Jas. 1:11; 1 Pet. 1:24; cf. Isa. 40:7); the falling of animals (Matt. 10:29); and the unintentional falling of humans (15:14; cf. Mk. 9:20; Acts 20:9).

2. Even abstract things such as fear and darkness can be said to fall on someone. The word here conveys the idea of suddenness and inescapability. Usually a heavenly vision or some other manifestation of God brings this about (Lk. 1:12; Acts 13:11; 19:17; Rev. 11:11). God's Spirit also falls on people; it comes with irresistible power, silencing all opposition and doubt (Acts 10:44; 11:15; cf. 8:16; 1 Sam. 18:10).

3. The *piptō* words also appear in idiomatic sayings. When a person's love is aroused, he has the urge to fall on someone's neck, i.e., "embrace" that person (Lk. 15:20; Acts 20:37; cf. Gen. 45:14; 46:29). The "falling" of the lot indicates a decision having nothing to do with human choice, a divine verdict (Acts 1:26; cf. Ps. 16:6; Jon. 1:7). "Not a hair will fall from your head" (Acts 27:34, lit. trans.) means "No evil will befall you."

4. Like the OT (Jos. 23:14; 1 Sam. 3:19; 2 Ki. 10:10), the NT says that God's word does not (lit.) "fall to the ground," but retains its validity and efficacy (Lk. 16:17; Rom. 9:6; cf. 1 Pet. 1:24). Neither will love "fail" (1 Cor. 13:8), since faith, hope, and love form the three unchanging gifts of God's grace (13:13).

5. To fall on one's face before someone (Jn. 11:32; cf. Gen. 17:3, 17; 44:14; Ruth 2:10) is an expression of deferential greeting. Slaves do this to indicate subjection to their master (Matt. 18:26). It can be done to make a request (18:29; Mk. 5:22; Lk. 5:12) or give thanks (17:16). It is the humblest posture for prayer (Matt. 26:39) and the attitude of self-abasing reverence (before a king, 2:11; a supernatural being, 4:9; Acts 10:25; Rev. 19:10; 22:8; God and Christ, 1 Cor. 14:25; Rev. 4:10). It can be the effect of a revelation from God (Matt. 17:6; Lk. 5:8; Acts 9:4; 16:29; cf. Mk. 5:33; Jn. 18:6; Rev. 1:17; → *gonypeteō* [1206] and *proskyneō* [4686]).

6. *piptō* can also mean to fall down dead, be killed (Lk. 21:24; Acts 5:5, 10; 1 Cor. 10:8; Rev. 17:10). *ptōma*, corpse, is used of human corpses (Matt. 14:12; Mk. 15:45; Rev. 11:8–9) and perhaps also animal carcasses in Matt. 24:28. It marks the place where the vultures gather.

7. Words in this group are used in various ways in the portrayal of apocalyptic horrors of the end times. Everything that is makeshift will collapse in a flood-like catastrophe (Matt. 7:25, 27), and great parts of cities (Rev. 11:13), even whole cities (16:19), will become heaps of ruins. The great world power, hostile to God, will be overthrown (14:8; 18:2; cf. Isa. 21:9; Jer. 51:8). In their terror at the desolation of the last days, people will cry out in their longing to die for a great earthquake, which will make mountains with their rocks fall on them (Lk. 23:30; Rev. 6:16).

In a cosmic upheaval stars will fall from heaven like meteorites (Matt. 24:29; Mk. 13:25; Rev. 6:13; cf. Isa. 34:4). These stars can also stand for political powers, since in Isa. 14:12 the expression is used of the fall of a powerful ruler. The fall of great stars from heaven makes the water on which life depends unusable and unleashes the powers of darkness (Rev. 8:10; 9:1). The picture of Satan's fall from heaven in Lk. 10:18 is intended to show that the end has come for the devil's dominion. The mighty ruler who up until now has terrorized the world has lost his power and his position as accuser before God in a fall as rapid as a flash of lightning.

8. The Gospels, Paul, Heb., and Rev. use a fig. sense of *piptō* peculiar to the NT. Apart from Rev. 2:5 and perhaps Rom. 11:11, 22, all the following passages speak of incurring guilt and the consequent loss of salvation. It is a catastrophic fall, which means eternal ruin. If it were not so, the warnings against falling lose their threatening urgency.

(a) It lies in the background of images like that in Matt. 7:25, 27 of total human downfall and in 15:14 of the blind leading the blind (cf. Lk. 6:39). In Lk. 2:34 Christ is the stone on which many will meet their doom, while 20:18 describes the annihilating effect of this stone on all who reject the claim and the person of Jesus. Either they will fall over the stone or the stone will fall on them (i.e., Christ will shatter his enemies).

(b) Paul uses the metaphor of standing and falling (cf. Prov. 24:16; Jer. 8:4; Amos 5:2; 8:14) in Rom. 14:4, where he alludes to the ancient law whereby a slave is subject to his master's jurisdiction, who alone decides whether his performance of a task is satisfactory or whether he must be condemned. In the same way the Christian is responsible to no one but his Lord, who alone decides whether one has done well or failed. The same idea is present in 1 Cor. 10:12, with its warning to guard against false security. As long as the eschatological tribulation with its satanic power has not run its full course, the possibility of falling must not be forgotten (*piptō* here echoes 10:8).

(c) "To fall from grace" is an expression arising from the concept of grace as the new sphere of life given to the Christian, into which the believer has "gained access" (cf. Rom. 5:2). Those who depart from it deny God's unconditional mercy, the redeeming work of Christ (Gal. 5:4). Christians must abide in this state of grace and not fall prey to any false teaching (2 Pet. 3:17). In Rom. 11:11, 22 *piptō* is again used of falling into destruction. The fall of Israel (despite God's gracious desire not to give up his people) demonstrates the severity of his judgment. In Heb. 4:11 falling (i.e., apostasy) is the result of disobedience. According to 10:31, the apostate faces a terrible future (see also *aphistēmi*, 923).

(d) Rev. 2:5 reminds a church of the love in which it stood at first. But it has moved quickly downwards and has fallen a long way. A return is nonetheless still possible, for the corruption has not yet gone too far.

See also *aphistēmi*, cause to revolt, go away, depart (*923*).

4409 (*pisteuō*, believe), → *4411*.

4411	πίστις

πίστις (*pistis*), faith (*4411*); πιστεύω (*pisteuō*), believe (*4409*); πιστός (*pistos*), pass. trustworthy, faithful; act. trusting, believing (*4412*); πιστόω (*pistoō*), rely, convince (*4413*); ἀπιστία (*apistia*), unbelief (*602*); ἀπιστέω (*apisteō*), disbelieve (*601*); ἄπιστος (*apistos*), unbelievable, faithless, unbelieving (*603*).

CL 1. (a) In cl. Gk. *pistis* denotes the trust that someone may place in other people or in the gods, credibility, credit in business, guarantee, or something entrusted. Similarly, *pisteuō* means to trust something or someone; it can refer to and confirm legendary tales and mythical ideas. With reference to people, *pisteuō* means to obey; the pass. means to enjoy trust. The adj. *pistos* means trusting or being trustworthy. The vb. *pistoō* has the meaning of binding someone or oneself to be faithful.

Apistia, by way of contrast, means mistrust, unreliability, and incredibility; *apisteō*, to be mistrustful, disbelieve, be disobedient; *apistos*, distrustful, undependable.

(b) Very early the words in this group also denoted faithfulness and fidelity. For example, in order to obtain a pause in battle, it was necessary to make agreements pledging fidelity while negotiations took place.

(c) The word group also had religious overtones at an early date. The gods vouch for the validity of an alliance or treaty. The words were also applied directly to the divinity in cases of the trustworthiness of an oracle. Unquestioned obedience to the will of the gods was required of humans.

2. (a) In the Hel. period, during the struggle with skepticism and atheism, *pistis* acquired the sense of conviction as to the existence and activity of the gods. The didactic element now emerged as the general and basic meaning. *pistis* as faith in God stood for theoretical conviction. But stress was laid on the belief that life was constituted in accordance with this conviction. To that extent *pistis* could assume the practical features of the older *eusebeia* (piety). Neo-Platonism had a

materialized concept of faith that called for a definite, intellectualistic conviction, which was conditioned by tradition.

(b) The Stoic understanding of *pistis* is particularly important. Here the philosopher expressed his recognition of the divine ordering of the world, the center of which was himself as an autonomous moral person. *pistis* reveals the essence of humankind. Fidelity to one's moral destiny leads to fidelity towards others.

(c) In the mystery religions faith denotes abandonment to the deity by following his teaching and by putting oneself under his protection. Besides Jud. and Christianity, the mystery religions stand out in their demand of faith in their divinities and in the revelations and teaching delivered by them. In this way salvation (equated with divinization in the mystery religions) was promised to the believer.

OT 1. *The concept of faith.* (a) In Heb. the root *ʾāman* in the niph. means to be true, reliable, faithful. It can be applied to humans (e.g., Moses, Num. 12:7; servants, 1 Sam. 22:14; prophets, 3:20; a witness, Isa. 8:2; a messenger, Prov. 25:13) and to God, who keeps his covenant and gives grace to those who love him (Deut. 7:9). Particular stress is laid on God's word preserving its dependability and being confirmed by subsequent action (1 Ki. 8:26; 1 Chr. 17:23–24). In many passages *ʾāman* acquires the meaning of to be entrusted with (e.g., Num. 12:7; 1 Sam. 3:20; Hos. 12:1). In an ancient strand of tradition going back to an original promise, the Davidic dynasty is called an "established" house (2 Sam. 7:8–16). This state of being confirmed does not rest on the qualities of the members of the dynasty or on human measures, but on the action of God initiated by his promise (2 Sam. 7:16; cf. 1 Sam. 25:28).

A related idea is expressed by the root *bāṭaḥ* (→ *peithō*, convince, *4275*; *elpis*, hope, *1828*), with the meaning to trust, rely on. The negative evaluation of such action is dominant: humans trust in false security (Hab. 2:18) or set their hope on something false (Hos. 10:13). But it was also early on applied to Yahweh, the true ground of security (2 Ki. 18:30; Jer. 39:18).

(b) Later the root *bāṭaḥ* was assimilated in meaning to the root *ʾāman*. Basic for the OT idea of faith are the statements of Exod. 4:1–9, 27–31. The question is how will Moses assert his authority as the one sent by God before the people. In reply to Moses' objection that the people will doubt his commission, God promises three miracles through which they will believe in his mission and the coming redemption. Faith is here related to a mission expressly confirmed by divine authentication.

(c) The absolute use of *ʾāman* in Isa. is important. In a confrontation with Ahaz in view of the political threat, Isaiah dares to say: "If you do not stand firm in your faith, you will not stand at all" (7:9). The survival of the people lay alone in firm trust in the eternal God. Political action was called for that corresponded to this trust. Thus Isa. 28:16 states, "See, I lay a stone in Zion, a tested stone, a precious cornerstone for a sure foundation; the one who trusts will never be dismayed." In the coming catastrophe only the believer can be sure of divine protection. The prophet himself is an example of believing trust: "I will wait for the LORD, who is hiding his face from the house of Jacob. I will put my trust in him" (8:17). The prophets stood in the midst of national catastrophe as spokesmen for the God who had placed them in an almost hopeless situation. The faith that is set before the people is the way of deliverance from catastrophe to a future beyond the disaster.

(d) Gen. 15:6 is also critical for the connection between the OT and the NT (cf. Rom. 4:3, 9, 22–23; Gal. 3:6; Jas. 2:23). The passage speaks of Abraham's faith as his readiness to lay hold of God's rich promises. The crediting of faith constituted a declaratory act, which was formerly customary with the priests. God treats this trust of Abraham as the behavior appropriate to the covenant relationship. In fellowship with God lies a claim one fulfills when he or she trusts. The statement in Gen. 15:6 does not describe Abraham's entire relationship with God. But in view of a particular situation God's gracious, overarching judgment was pronounced over him.

(e) The prophetic context of Hab. 2:3–4 is also important for the Jewish and Christian traditions. The vision granted by God is confirmed and preserved for the end; it will not fail to appear. Those who are "puffed up" are condemned by God's word, but life is promised to the "righteous" in view of their faithfulness (the arrogant stand on the side of the hostile world power, the "righteous" on that of the people of Judah). "Faithfulness" and "faith" stand here close together in the Heb. word *ʾemûnâ*. The idea is that of unwavering hold of God's word against all contrary appearances. The sense is changed by the promise in the LXX translation: "The righteous will live by my faithfulness [*ek pisteōs mou*]."

(f) Later in the OT, the trustworthiness of the commandments is firmly underlined (Ps. 119:66). Through them the godly receive instruction in God's will; they know they receive wisdom and knowledge from them and can rely on them in the temptations of life. Postexilic Jewish piety cannot be called legalistic without qualification. The law and God's word were living entities received by the godly in obedience and trust, and were praised with thanksgiving and testimony.

To sum up, *heʾemîn* and *ʾemûnâ* describe a living act of trust in the OT as well as the dimension of human existence in a historical situation. Special stress is laid on the future. The past was the starting-point but not the goal of trust. The whole emphasis falls on overcoming the opposition of the ungodly and the realization of the divine purpose. Above all, it is clear in the prophets that faith must pass through extreme need and judgment before it attains its goal in the salvation that lies in the future.

2. *The influence of the terms in later Judaism.* (a) In later Jud. the main emphasis falls on the behavior of the individual. *Sotah* 48b preserves an aphorism of R. Eliezer b. Hyrcanus: "If anyone has bread in his basket and says, what shall I eat tomorrow? he belongs to those who are small in trust." One knows that faith is frugal (Prov. 30:8) and one must overcome anxiety about possessing too much. "Small in faith" becomes a deprecatory word-picture that represents failure. The expression "men of faithfulness" (*ʾanšê ʾamānâ*) in rab. lit. is the mark of definable, exemplary conduct.

Faith is taught and inculcated in the manner of the wisdom lit. Because of its identity with faithfulness, faith remains the most important feature of righteousness. The celebrated "Song of Faith" in *Mek. Exod.* 14:31, which begins with the words "Great is faith," is concerned with the teaching of Exod. 14:31: faith in God and his servant Moses. Those who believe in the shepherd of Israel believe in God himself, who spoke and called the world into being. There follows praise of faith and its reward in the style of the wisdom writings. The "reward" is understood as the Holy Spirit, who praises the saving acts of God in hymn and confession (Exod. 14:31; 15:1).

(b) At Qumran the basic passage Hab. 2:4 was interpreted of all doers of the law—thus of the members of the community. God will save them from the house of judgment on account of their suffering and their faithfulness to the teacher of righteousness (1QpHab 8:1–3). The doing of the law is the supreme and decisive idea. Faithfulness to the teacher means holding to the knowledge revealed to him.

(c) The idea of faith played a particular role in later apocalyptic lit., because expectation of the future made a radical demand of faith. In such apocalyptic circles the concept of faith drew a dividing line between the true community and their opponents.

(d) In Hel. Jud., faith as the confession of the OT revelation stood in opposition to the surrounding pagan world. The contrast between the "godless" and the "righteous" and their differing views of life is typical of wisdom lit. (Wis. 2:1–3:19). Faith in wisdom belongs to the teaching about righteousness and wisdom (1:2; 3:9). It is expressed in fixed formulas such as *hoi pepoithotes*, those who trust (→ *peithō*, *4275*); *hoi pistoi*, the faithful; *hoi eklektoi*, the elect (→ *eklegomai*, *1721*). Faith enters the realm of philosophical interpretation and becomes an outlook and a virtue.

In Philo also faith in God can be trust and the presupposition of all human existence and conduct. In his or her relation to God the wise person is the "believer." For his part God bestows trust through his promises. As formerly in Jud. at large, faith is regarded as the source and sum of every other attitude.

NT The call to believe in the name of God as he has revealed himself in Christ is the special mark of the Christian missionary preaching in the ancient world. Yet there are several stages in the early Christian tradition that should not be overlooked. John the Baptist set repentance, not faith, at the center of his preaching. Still, his overthrow of all contrived security (Matt. 3:9) is reminiscent of the tension between godly ʾāman and false bāṭaḥ. Moreover, the mission of the Baptist raises the question of its legitimacy and thus also of faith (expressed in 21:25, 32). Yet not until Jesus do we hear the specific call: "Repent and believe the good news" (Mk. 1:15). In time the good news became a fixed tradition of teaching that was to be accepted by every hearer. This development is examined in the following survey.

The NT use of the *pistis/pisteuō* word group involves the development of the OT and Jewish tradition. The frequent use of *pisteuō eis*, believe in (e.g., Jn. 1:12; 3:18; Gal. 2:16), is a striking departure from ordinary Gk. and from the LXX. *pisteuō hoti* sentences (believe *that* ...), which relate faith to a particular event in the history of Jesus (Rom. 10:9; 1 Thess. 4:14) or to a Christological statement (Jn. 20:31), are significant for the linguistic usage of the NT church. They involve the incorporation of a specific, historical content into the Christian confession. "Repentance from acts that lead to death" and "faith in God" were important elements in the teaching of the early Christian catechism (Heb. 6:1). More important is the pointed use of *pistis* in Paul's writings to denote the reception of Christian proclamation and the saving faith that was called forth by the gospel (Rom. 1:8; 1 Thess. 1:8). For Paul *pistis* is indissolubly bound with proclamation.

1. *Jesus and the Synoptic tradition.* The miracle stories often contain reference to the faith of the sick or of those around them (Matt. 8:10; Mk. 2:5; 5:34, 36; 10:52). What is meant here is trust in Jesus' mission and his power to deliver from trouble. These saving acts were performed in the service of his commission and were intended to confirm an existing faith. Jesus not only sought to deliver people from physical need, but also to make them witnesses of his saving work. Faith was not a condition on which he acted; rather, Jesus was concerned with a goal beyond the physical process: to be a helper in God's name. He was therefore more concerned to ask for faith than to demand it. Human trust presented the possibility for God to do his work.

Mk. 6:5–6 contains an account of the opposition in Nazareth, Jesus' hometown. Refusal to believe was so strong that he could perform no miracles there. He confined himself to helping a number of sick individuals. If his saving work was bound up with faith, refusal to believe likewise brought conflict with him, though the Evangelists did not intend to convey the impression that it was *absolutely* impossible for Jesus to do miracles here because of the unbelief of the Nazarenes.

The Gospel writers record several sayings of Jesus that appear to go beyond the specific situation in which they occur (Matt. 17:20; Mk. 9:23–24; 11:22–24; Lk. 17:5–6). The distinctive feature of these sayings about faith lies in the fact that they present the believer with unlimited possibilities and that Jesus expressly summons his disciples to this sort of boundless faith. The pictures of faith moving mountains (Mk. 11:23) and uprooting a fig tree (Lk. 17:6) confirm the word of power that is able to transform the created order. The instructions to the disciples in Mk. 11:23–24 show the connection in Jesus' teaching between the promise that rests on the word of power and supplication. The supplication is the prerequisite of the word of power.

Faith in God means for Jesus being open to the possibilities that God presents (cf. Mk. 11:22: "have faith in God"), and Jesus encouraged others to follow his example. Such faith also involves a reckoning with God that is not simply content with the thing given and the events that have come about. Expressions like "have faith in God" and "increase our faith" (Lk. 17:5) denote a special kind of faith. The

antithesis between small and great (17:6; cf. Matt. 17:20) presents a contrast between the human attitude and the greatness of the promise. That is, what takes place in a human being is small compared with the greatness that comes from God.

However, Jesus spoke of a boundless faith as if of something new. He did not build on something that was already there. Yet his teaching was distinct from wild enthusiasm, because it was not divorced from constant wrestling with God and speaking with him. It stood within the circle of trust and knowledge. Jesus turned to the individual, because his people as a whole were summoned to the decision of faith (cf. Lk. 19:42).

Statements about faith in the Synoptic tradition are always qualified. Every summons and statement of Jesus contain the elements of faith, trust, knowledge, decision, obedience, and self-direction. Jesus' faith was deeply involved in the act of living and was on a completely different plane from hypothetical abstractions.

2. *Paul and the Pauline tradition.* Paul's teaching presupposes a continuity with the teaching of the Palestinian Jewish and the Hel. church. His calling by the risen Lord led him to grapple with the particular questions raised by these churches. Paul addressed his readers as believers (*hoi pisteuontes*, Rom. 1:16; 3:22; 4:11; 1 Cor. 1:21). Their turning to God is described as "believing" (1 Cor. 15:2, 11). "Faith" means receiving the message of salvation and conduct based on the gospel (Rom. 1:8; 1 Cor. 2:5; 15:14, 17). It is explicitly a saving faith, based on the death and resurrection of Jesus (15:3–4).

This unique event is the divinely appointed norm that determines every theological statement and every aspect of Christian conduct. The righteousness received by faith is a gift of grace. It contradicts all human boasting and undermines any attempt to base one's relationship with God on keeping the Mosaic law (Rom. 3:27–31; Gal. 3:10–14, 23–25). The new covenant supersedes the old both in its historical form and its effect on humans (2 Cor. 3:6; Gal. 3:23–4:7, 21–31). Faith recognizes the eschatological saving event anticipated in the call of Abraham (Rom. 4:9–15; Gal. 3:17–18); it finds its goal in the Gentile mission (Rom. 4:17–18; Gal. 3:26–29). Paul stressed historical facts and our eschatological goal (2 Cor. 5:7). Since faith contains the element of being sustained (Heb. ʾāman), as well as trust (Heb. bāṭaḥ), it merges into hope (Rom. 8:24; 1 Cor. 13:13).

Of special importance is the way Paul links together the triad of faith, hope, and love (1 Cor. 13:13; Col. 1:4–5; 1 Thess. 3:5, 8). These three are different aspects of the Christian life and form the basis of the life of the church. The transforming eschatological prospective reveals what is unique here: Faith and hope come to fulfillment, while love alone determines the new aeon (1 Cor. 13:13; → *aiōn*, 172).

The Pauline triad of faith, hope, and love must not be regarded as charismatic gifts, for they are distinct from the latter. They are the practical application of the gospel itself and are obligatory for all members of the church, without exception. Charismatic gifts have a different structure (→ *charis*, 5921). At the same time, however, Paul's endeavor to set out the fullness of gifts in his doctrine of the Spirit led him to include faith as a gift along with the others (1 Cor. 12:9). Justifying faith is not meant here. Nor perhaps is the faith that can move mountains (13:2). What is clear is that it is distinct from "the message of wisdom" and "the message of knowledge" (mentioned in 12:8).

There is a tension between the invisible and the visible. This points to the fact that we do not have the future at our disposal. There is a contrast between what is accessible to us and what is accessible to God alone (cf. 2 Cor. 4:18; 5:7). The invisible mentioned here is not a Platonic immaterial world, but the goal of Christian existence perceived in faith and trust. The cross of Christ is always the focal point of attack against legalism (Gal. 2:21) and speculative wisdom (1 Cor. 1:17). The resurrection opens the way to the gift of a new existence through baptism (Rom. 6:4; 2 Cor. 5:17).

Thus Gal. 5:6 teaches: "For in Christ Jesus neither circumcision nor uncircumcision has any value. The only thing that counts is faith expressing itself through love" (cf. also 1 Cor. 7:19; Gal. 6:15). Through baptism a new law that transcends all the previous differences has come into operation. God's will, expressed in the demands of the law, finds its eschatological fulfillment in love. This solution that Paul stresses places faith in the context of eschatological transformation. It thus corresponds directly with Paul's doctrine of the Spirit. His teaching on faith and the gift of the Spirit are brought together in baptism.

Another important element of Paul's teaching is his understanding of the life of faith, characterized by the tension between indicative and imperative. Believers who are justified must become what they are, yet they find themselves in a struggle between the Spirit and the sinful human nature (Rom. 8:4–13; Gal. 5:16–25). We must not evade the tasks of the Spirit or avoid living according to the fruit of the Spirit. Without such obedience, faith does not gain the power required in this conflict (1 Cor. 2:4).

The idea of being "weak" in faith (Rom. 14:1) introduces a particular discussion bound up with making critical judgments. For Paul there is such a thing as growing in faith (2 Cor. 10:15), being steadfast in faith (1 Cor. 15:58), and self-critical examining whether one's attitude springs from faith (cf. Rom. 14:23). All these exhortations starkly show how faith is not only exposed to critical judgment, but submits itself repeatedly to it. The fact that the gospel finds its ultimate expression and foundation in the cross of Christ means that faith must constantly measure itself by this norm. Faith is dynamic movement that involves adjustment and self-adjustment. In this respect also the situation corresponds to Paul's doctrine of the Spirit.

Eph. 4:3 calls believers to maintain "the unity of the Spirit." Despite diversity of groups and differences of opinion, postapostolic tradition tried to maintain a general outlook. Eph. 4:5 speaks of "one faith" together with "one Lord" and "one baptism," as if this triad reflected the baptismal act. The common outlook conferred by baptism is a process directed towards a goal (4:13) and guided by Christ himself.

3. *The Johannine tradition.* Here, as in the OT, the vb. comes to the forefront. The noun is found only occasionally in the letters (1 Jn. 5:4) and Rev. (2:13, 19; 13:10; 14:12). The adj. *pistos* can be applied to Jesus, his witnesses, and the church (Jn. 20:27; 1 Jn. 1:9; Rev. 1:5; 2:10, 13). The link with Sem. thought is clear esp. in Rev. Faith and the act of believing assume the character of fidelity. Rev. also contains didactic lists of qualities and actions in which "deeds" predominate (2:2, 19); *pistis* here comes close to being the motive of faithfulness (2:19). It is basic for the Johannine tradition that the attitude of faith should be modeled on and formed by the testimony recognized by the church, notably, eyewitness testimony.

The thought forms are different from elsewhere in the NT. Faith arises out of testimony, authenticated by God, in which signs also play a part. It is addressed to all (Jn. 1:7). Faith and knowledge (6:69), knowledge and faith (17:8; 1 Jn. 4:16), are not two entities distinct from each other, but instructive coordinates. Faith alone receives the testimony and possesses knowledge; those who know the truth are pointed to faith. The hearer should understand that acceptance of the testimony and personal response conforming to the testimony are both involved in salvation. The distinction in Jn. 4:42 is important.

Faith and life are intimately connected. Those who believe in the Son have the promise that they will not perish but have eternal life (Jn. 3:16–18; 11:25–26). The promise points to a fulfillment already in the present. The world's enmity toward God is not a metaphysical one; it is a reaction to the one sent by God (3:20; 7:7; 15:18, 23). Even the disciples are drawn into it. Believers are able to endure this conflict with the world through no longer being subject to its motive power and by seeking the will of God (1 Jn. 2:15–17).

The blessing pronounced on those who believe and love the Lord even though they have not seen him (Jn. 20:29; cf. 1 Pet. 1:8) is particularly relevant to certain questions raised by the Easter tradition. The original saving event belongs in the past. Faith and love represent further instruction for new situations in life that developed out of baptismal teaching (cf. 1 Tim. 2:15; 4:12; 6:11; 2 Tim. 2:22).

4. *The understanding of faith in the rest of the NT.* The linguistic usage of Acts often points back to formulas and expressions drawn from the terminology of mission. People come to faith in God (Acts 16:34) or in the Lord (5:14; 18:8). Exhortations to faith are directly connected with the promise of salvation (16:31). There is also a new trust in Christian circles in what is "written" (24:14; 26:27). There thus grew up a way of looking at salvation history analogous to Jewish Hel. piety.

The book of Heb. represents an independent tradition of teaching. It makes extensive use of OT motifs and draws on the history of the patriarchs in connection with words of the *pistis*-group. Thus in its exhortation, Heb. takes up the promise of faith as well as the warning against unbelief (10:37–38 = Hab. 2:3–4). Above all, Heb. 11:1 presents an instructive definition that combines OT and Hel. motifs: "Now faith is being sure of what we hope for and certain of what we do not see." This is not a comprehensive summary of all the elements in faith, but of those that were fundamental for a church under persecution. The future and what is hidden from view are closely connected here.

This definition introduces the survey of patriarchal history in Heb. 11 and the picture of the church in 12:1–11. Jesus Christ appears as the "author and perfecter of our faith" (12:2). He has been made perfect by God and can now bring the struggle for perfection to its conclusion. As those given the promise, God's people are charged with acting on faith. The next world is the goal promised by the word of God. The tension between the here and now and the beyond finds new expression.

The essence of Paul's thought reappears in the Pastoral Letters. But it is restated in a context that is opposed to wild enthusiasm and false teaching. Thus 1 Tim. 1:5 puts forward the thesis: "The goal of this command is love, which comes from a pure heart and a good conscience and a sincere faith." A tendency opposed to enthusiasm may be detected here. The command to love is reformulated so as to include faith. Soundness in faith (Tit. 1:13; 2:2) sets a new standard that distinguishes the Christian life from all false teaching. We now get a reference to "the faith," an established body of Christian truth (1 Tim. 3:9; 4:1, 6; 5:8; Tit. 1:4, 13; 3:15). The overtones of philosophy and wisdom strengthen the self-awareness of a church that is consolidating itself.

As in the paraenetic tradition elsewhere, Jas. is conscious of the need to prove one's faith (1:3; cf. 1 Pet. 1:7). He demands renunciation of all conduct that conflicts with living faith and one's confession (Jas. 1:6–8). For him, faith and obedient conduct are indissolubly linked. Faith understood merely as trust and confession of certain elemental truths is not able to save. Only through obedience (→ *hypakoē*, *5633*) and conduct that fulfills God's commands does faith come to completion (Jas. 2:22). The opponents that the author has in mind do not attack the Christian faith but exempt themselves from obedience.

Some scholars hold that the teaching of Jas. stands in conflict with that of Paul, esp. on the question of justification. But Jas. is responding to those who have apparently taken Paul's doctrine of justification by faith out of context, concluding that Paul's repudiation of works as the ground of justification relieved them of the need for good works and a changed life (Paul deals with this issue in Rom. 6:1–22; 12:1–2; Gal. 5:15–26).

It is striking that Jas. 2:23 quotes Gen. 15:6 (as does Paul) and illustrates the argument by referring to Abraham's example. But whereas Paul appeals to Abraham's belief in the promise of God that was the occasion of the verdict of justification in Gen. 15, Jas. appeals to the story in Gen. 22, which shows Abraham's willingness to sacrifice Isaac. Jas. 2:22 draws the conclusion: "You see that [Abraham's] faith and his actions were working together, and his faith was made complete by what he did." For both Paul and Jas. *justify* means to declare righteous. However, in the case of Paul, it is God who declares believers righteous. In the case of Jas., our works declare us to be righteous by showing that we are people of faith (cf. 2:17).

5. *The act, structure, and content of faith.* Christianity is a unique faith-event; this gave the most powerful expression to its understanding of the historical situation and its outlook in view of the claims of the gospel. The act of faith, together with the thought-forms and structures bound up with it (i.e., the gospel, the kerygma, the word of God), has a special significance in Christianity. It is only in relation to the gospel and the claims of God's word that faith can declare what it has to say. Christians know that they have received grace and are summoned to follow a particular path towards a goal. The saving act of God goes before them. The basis of faith is God's revelation of himself. Faith remains subordinate to knowledge, but knowledge belongs to the substance of faith.

See also *peithō*, persuade (*4275*).

4412 (*pistos*, pass. trustworthy, faithful; act. trusting, believing), → *4411*.

4413 (*pistoō*, rely, convince), → *4411*.

4414	πλανάω

πλανάω (*planaō*), lead astray, cause to wander, mislead (*4414*); πλάνη (*planē*), wandering, delusion, error (*4415*); πλανήτης (*planētēs*), wandering (*4417*); πλάνος (*planos*), leading astray, deceitful, deceiver, imposter (*4418*); ἀποπλανάω (*apoplanaō*), go astray, wander away (*675*); ἀπατάω (*apataō*), trick, deceive (*572*); ἐξαπατάω (*exapataō*), trick, deceive (*1987*); ἀπάτη (*apatē*), deception, trickery, deceitfulness (*573*); παραλογίζομαι (*paralogizomai*), cheat, deceive, delude (*4165*).

CL & OT 1. (a) In cl. Gk. *planaō* in the act. means to lead astray, esp. by one's behavior or words; in the mid. and pass., to go astray, be led astray. It can refer to a person's judgment or to actions in the realm of morals. *apoplanaomai*, to wander from or roam about, can be used of humans, powers, animals, rumors, and even of blood or breath pulsing through the body; it does not always have a negative undertone. In a transferred sense the vb. can mean to wander off course, miss the mark in thought, speech, or action. Here again the word carries no implication of guilt.

(b) In Gk. tragedy one's mistakes are seen as a fate laid on a person by the gods. In Plato the way to right insight leads through error. The gnostics and the mystery cults used the word for a person's entanglement in the world from which one must be released.

(c) Similar meanings characterize the other derivatives of this group of words. *planos* means going astray, roaming; also unsteady, deceiving; as a noun it means deviation or imposter. *planē* means vacillation and error as characteristics of human life.

(d) *apataō*, *exapataō*, and *apatē* are sometimes synonymous with words from the root *plan-*. The basis for deceit and trickery here, however, is not ignorance so much as *epithymia* (→ *2123*), desire. *apatē* accordingly comes to mean pleasure, enjoyment. A negative sense was not at first attached to it, though this develops later.

(e) *paralogizomai* is a negative form of *logizomai*, which means to calculate, reckon, or consider. It connotes deception, cheating by false reasoning.

2. The cl. meaning of *planaō* is taken over in the LXX. The spatial sense of the vb. is found in the context of leading the blind astray (Deut. 27:18), and it is also the basic concept behind the description of people staggering as a result of drinking wine (cf. Isa. 19:13–14; 28:7).

planaō is frequently used in combination with *hodos*, way, to denote Israel's way of life as wandering sheep (Ps. 119:176; Isa. 13:14; 53:6; cf. Deut. 22:1). The wandering of the people in the desert is a punishment of God for their disobedience (Num. 14:29, 33; cf. also Deut. 2:14). The people go astray by ignoring God's commands and practicing idolatry (cf. 13:6 = LXX 13:5). What leads them astray are idols (Amos 2:4), false prophets (Jer. 23:32), and unfaithful kings (2 Chr. 33:9). Even God himself appears as one who leads astray (Job

12:24–25; Isa. 63:17; Ezek. 14:9). Turning from this erroneous path and salvation are necessary. Thus this basic relationship to God is aptly expressed by the picture of sheep who cannot exist without a shepherd (→ *probaton*, → *4585*).

3. *apataō* means to deceive, seduce, lead astray. The deception can be used as a human stratagem to dupe others (e.g., Samson in Jdg. 14:15; 16:5). Gen. 3:13 speaks of the serpent's deception in enticing Eve to eat the forbidden fruit. The prophet Micaiah in a vision sees a spirit who offers, in Yahweh's royal council, to become a lying spirit and to entice King Ahab and his prophets (1 Ki. 22:20–22). By contrast, note the psalmist's testimony: "I sought God . . . and I was not deceived" (Ps. 77:2, LXX).

4. In the intertestamental period some important elements are added to the concept of being led astray. The agents are often spirits or powers (e.g., sons of God [Gen. 6:1–4] and the devil). Apocalyptic lit. predicts the *planē* as a precursor of the end of the world, the day of the Messiah. The Qumran texts speak of a wandering astray of the children of light, brought about by evil spirits (1QS 3:21; CD 2:17; 3:4, 14), and of those who have appeared as deceivers of the community (20:11; 1QH 2:14, 19; 4:7, 12).

NT 1. (a) *planaō* and *apoplanaō* in the act. are used mostly in an apocalyptic context (e.g., Matt. 24:4–5, 11, 24; Rev. 2:20; 12:9; 20:3, 8, 10) and of false teachers who lead others astray (2 Tim. 3:13; 1 Jn. 1:8; 2:26; 3:7). The nouns also often appear in this context (e.g., 2 Thess. 2:11; 2 Pet. 2:18; Jude 11, 13; 2 Jn. 7). The spatial sense is seen most clearly where the picture of sheep is offered (Matt. 18:12–13; 1 Pet. 2:25). There is always a theological meaning associated with its use.

The mid. *planaomai* and *apoplanaomai* have the sense be wrong, be led astray, err (Matt. 22:29; Mk. 12:24; 1 Tim. 6:10; Tit. 3:3; Heb. 3:10; 5:2; Jas. 5:19). The formula *mē planasthē* means, "Do not be deceived" (e.g., Gal. 6:7). The noun *planē* refers to a specific mistake (Matt. 27:64; 2 Pet. 3:17; Jude 11) or to more general confusion, error, lack of discipline, and restraint (Rom. 1:27; Eph. 4:14; 1 Jn. 4:6).

(b) *planētēs* occurs in Jude 13 in the sense of a wandering star or planet, with which Jude compares the false teachers. The apparently irregular movement of the planets, which seems to violate the order of the heavens, is attributed to the disobedience of the angels controlling them. *planos* is used both as an adj. (of deceitful spirits, 1 Tim. 4:1) and as a noun (deceiver, imposter; Matt. 27:63; 2 Cor. 6:8; 2 Jn. 7).

(c) *apataō*, *exapataō*, and *apatē* occur in 2 Cor. 11:3 and 1 Tim. 2:14 with reference to the fall, the archetype of deception and disobedience as a result of desire; in 2 Thess. 2:3; Eph. 5:6; Col. 2:8 in connection with false teachers; and in Matt. 13:22; Rom. 7:11; 2 Thess. 2:10; Heb. 3:13; 2 Pet. 2:13 in the ethical sense of enticement to sin. *apataō* in Jas. 1:26 refers to a person who "deceives himself."

(d) *paralogizomai* occurs only at Col. 2:4 and Jas. 1:22, meaning to delude or to deceive oneself (by being merely a hearer and not a doer of the word).

2. The NT takes up the OT picture of a sheep that wanders and gets lost (Matt. 10:6; 12:11–12; 18:12; 26:31; Lk. 15:4; Jn. 10; 1 Pet. 2:25). Most places where *planaō* words are used may be interpreted in terms of this background, even if it is not expressly mentioned. Jesus is the way (*hodos*) and the truth (Jn. 14:6); to be removed from him, the shepherd, means to wander about without guidance or protection and so be in danger of getting lost.

Where we read of nations going astray (Rev. 18:23), of people having wandered from the right way (Jas. 5:20; 2 Pet. 2:15), or God's people going astray (Heb. 3:10; 5:2), the underlying shepherd image is sometimes coupled with the desert wanderings of Israel. It is also implicit in passages where mention is made of false teachers who lead astray (e.g., Matt. 24:4–11; Jn. 7:12; 1 Jn. 3:7; Rev. 20:8–10).

3. Life prior to becoming a Christian is described as *planē*, error and being deceived (Rom. 1:27; Eph. 4:14; cf. Tit. 3:3; 1 Pet. 2:25). People are without the guidance and support of a Lord and shepherd.

To wander away from the faith (1 Tim. 6:10) or the truth (Jas. 5:19–20) or to have one's heart go astray (Heb. 3:10, 13) is sinful and incurs guilt (cf. also 2 Thess. 2:10). Riches are seductive (Matt. 13:22; Mk. 4:19; 1 Tim. 6:10), but there are also other desires lying in wait to deceive the believer (Rom. 16:18; Eph. 4:22; 2 Pet. 2:13).

In the background are dark powers, such as the spirit of deception (1 Tim. 4:1; 1 Jn. 4:6), the Antichrist (2 Jn. 7), and ultimately Satan himself (Rev. 12:9; 20:10).

4. The danger for Christians is deceiving themselves (1 Cor. 3:18; 1 Jn. 1:8), which can lead to falling away from right doctrine. Hence the need for the warning "Do not be deceived" (1 Cor. 6:9; 15:33; Gal. 6:7; Jas. 1:16; cf. 2 Thess. 2:3). Those not firmly grounded in the faith are in danger of missing the true knowledge, since numerous false teachers threaten the church (Eph. 4:14; Col. 2:8; 1 Thess. 2:3; 2 Thess. 2:3; 2 Tim. 3:13; 2 Pet. 2:18; 3:17; 1 Jn. 2:26; 3:7; 4:6). To be led astray by false teaching and to be led astray into definite acts of sin go hand in hand. On the opposite side is the truth (Jas. 5:19–20), which must be held firmly by faith in him who is the truth.

5. Jesus was hated and persecuted by the Jews because they saw him as one who led the people astray (Matt. 27:63; Jn. 7:12, 47). In the eyes of those who did not believe the apostles were imposters (2 Cor. 6:8), although they were servants of the truth. In the struggle to uphold the truth the church is pointed to him who himself experienced human weaknesses (Heb. 5:2) and who can therefore provide support. Faith in him is the yardstick of truth and error. Seen in this light, the church's opponents turn out to be deceivers who themselves have been deceived, and the Pharisees are those who really lead the people astray (Matt. 22:29; Mk. 12:24, 27; cf. 2 Tim. 3:13).

6. The final demonstration of the truth lies in the future, in the final revelation of Jesus Christ at his second coming. In the meantime, the era of the church is the era of fighting for the truth. The apostles' testimony is proclaimed to all nations (Matt. 28:18–20), but at the same time the powers increasingly bring in confusion and error (24:4–5, 11, 24; Rev. 20:3, 8). It is against the background of this final climax of the struggle that most of the texts containing the terms we have been considering are to be understood. When the Lord returns, he will end all *planē*, deception (2 Thess. 2; 2 Pet. 3; Rev. 12:9; 13:14).

4415 (planē, wandering, delusion, error), → *4414.*

4417 (planētēs, wandering), → *4414.*

4418 (planos, leading astray, deceitful, deceiver, imposter), → *4414.*

4424	πλάτος

πλάτος (*platos*), breadth, width (*4424*); πλατύνω (*platynō*), make broad, enlarge, open out (*4425*); πλατύς (*platys*), broad, wide (*4426*).

CL & OT The vb. *platynō* means (act.) widen; (pass.) to grow wide, be opened; and in a transferred sense, open (the heart) and expand (the understanding). *platys*, wide or level, in an extended sense can mean widespread, strong (oaths), brackish, or flat (of the sea).

NT In Eph. 3:18 *platos*, width, occurs together with length, height, and depth, an idiom that represents the universe of experience known in God. In Rev. 21:16 (2x) the word simply denotes width. In 20:9, the NIV translates "the breadth of the earth." This phrase, as used in Dan. 12:2 LXX ("dust of the earth"), denotes the place of the dead awaiting everlasting life or everlasting contempt.

platynō in Matt. 23:5 may refer to ostentatious wearing of wider phylactery straps by the teachers of the law and the Pharisees or to large leather cases containing texts (cf. Exod. 13:16). In 2 Cor. 6:11, 13, Paul uses this vb. to demonstrate and appeal for a show of generous, expansive affection.

platys is found only in Matt. 7:13, where it refers either to a road (and thus means wide or level) or to a gate (and thus means wide; for background on the road to destruction see Ps. 1:6; Prov. 13:15; 14:12;

Sir. 21:10). Jesus stresses the need for believers to separate from the masses who follow the easy way that leads to destruction.

4425 (platynō, make broad, enlarge), → *4424.*

4426 (platys, broad, wide), → *4424.*

4429	πλεονάζω

πλεονάζω (*pleonazō*), to be or become more or great, to grow, to increase (*4429*); ὑπερπλεονάζω (*hyperpleonazō*), to be present in great abundance (*5670*).

CL & OT 1. *pleonazō* is formed from *pleon* (more, comparative of *polys*) and the ending *-azō*; it means to be or become (too) much or many. The augmented form *hyperpleonazō*, to be present in excessive quantity, is rare. Its developed meaning (intrans.) is to exceed the correct amount and thus become presumptuous, to overflow (of a sea or a river), to become (too) numerous (e.g., the Jews in Rome), to be present in plentiful abundance, to be rich in something, to have more than is necessary. Trans. *pleonazō* means to make rich, to increase or multiply, or to cause to grow. In ethical contexts this vb. denotes in a censorious way that which violates the ideal of moderation, reason, and wholeness.

2. In the LXX *pleonazō* (27x) generally means to be surplus, to be or become many: e.g., of goods (Exod. 16:18, 23), people (1 Chr. 4:27; 5:23; Jer. 30:19 = LXX 37:19), money (2 Chr. 24:11; 31:5; Sir. 35:1 = LXX 32:1), and sins (23:3).

NT In the NT *pleonazō* occurs 9x; *hyperpleonazō* only in 1 Tim. 1:4. The vb. expresses a process of growing, multiplying, or increasing. It stands in contrast with *perisseuō* (→ *4355*), which expresses (often in an eschatological sense) the element of the abundance that far exceeds all measurement and of the fullness that overflows all previously fixed boundaries. *pleonazō*, on the other hand, renders more the idea of development, the growth process of something: "that grace may increase" (Rom. 6:1); "love . . . is increasing" (2 Thess. 1:3); "in increasing measure" (2 Pet. 1:8).

1. In Rom. 5:20 Paul is formulating the relationship between law and grace. Through the law (→ *nomos, 3795*) sin increases (*pleonazō*) to its full extent and exposes the hopelessness of humanity in the face of death. But grace has abounded all the more (*hyperperisseuō*) in the new age. The more hopelessly we entangle ourselves in increasing sin, the greater is God's liberating act in granting pardon. This view of the relationship between sin and grace apparently led to a misunderstanding, which Paul addressed in Rom. 6:1–22. In 6:1 he uses *pleonazō* with reference to grace, not, as one might have supposed, *perisseuō*. Paul is concerned with the process of grace becoming greater; it cannot be stimulated by a conscious persistence in sin.

2. Paul links *pleonazō* with *charis* (grace) in 2 Cor. 4:15, explaining that as grace extends to more and more people, thanksgiving overflows (*perisseuō*) to the glory of God.

3. In Phil. 4:15–17 Paul uses language from the world of business (e.g., the settlement of giving and receiving, 4:15). With reference to the contribution of the Philippians the apostle says, "Not that I am looking for a gift, but I am looking for what may be credited [*pleonazonta*, from *pleonazō*] to your account." Paul's use of *perisseuō* in 4:18 ("I have received full payment and even more") shows again the thrust of *pleonazō*.

4. Paul prays that the Lord will grant the Thessalonians the ability to grow (*pleonazō*) and overflow (*perisseuō*) in love for one another (1 Thess. 3:12). *pleonazō* is thus intensified by *perisseuō*.

5. *pleonazō* occurs in the sense of *perisseuō* in the OT quotation (Exod. 16:18) in 2 Cor. 8:15: "He who gathered much did not have too much," i.e., had no more than was necessary.

See also *auxanō*, grow, cause to grow, increase (*889*).

4430 (pleonekteō, take advantage of, cheat), → *4432.*

4431 (pleonektēs, one who is greedy, covetous person), → *4432.*

4432 πλεονεξία	

πλεονεξία (*pleonexia*), greediness, avarice, covetousness (*4432*); πλεονεκτέω (*pleonekteō*), take advantage of, defraud, cheat (*4430*); πλεονέκτης (*pleonektēs*), one who is greedy, a covetous person (*4431*).

CL & OT Etymologically, *pleonexia* combines *pleon* (more) and *echō* (to have). Cl. Gk. writers used the word not only for a covetous desire for more material possessions, but also for immoral lust for power and inappropriate sexual desire. There was no room for *pleonexia* in a just society. Together with *philotimia* (ambition), it was a decisive force in human action and the progress of history. The Cynics and Stoics repudiated all desire, for possessions of any kind meant attachment to what is empty.

In the LXX this word group appears chiefly in the prophetic denunciations and warnings about dishonest gain and the enrichment by violence of the politically powerful (Jer. 22:17; Ezek. 22:27; Hab. 2:9; 2 Macc. 4:50). The emphasis thus falls on the ungodly character of covetousness.

NT 1. Except for *pleonexia* in Mk. 7:22; Lk. 12:15; 2 Pet. 2:3, 14, in the NT this word group is found only in Paul. The action denoted by these words is always judged negatively, and except in 2 Cor. 2:11 it is always directed towards material gain.

2. In Paul's catalogs of vices *pleonexia* is a mark of a life that lacks knowledge of God (Rom. 1:29; 1 Cor. 6:10–11), faith, and obedience (5:10–11; Eph. 5:3). Where the bond between creature and Creator is severed, human society falls into disorder. Those who no longer have God as their goal or focus seek fulfillment in themselves, their possessions, and their acquisitiveness. Ultimately they make themselves into an idol that strives to subject everything to itself. For that reason Col. 3:5 identifies covetousness with idolatry (→ *eidōlon, 1631*).

Similarly, in Matt. 6:24 and Lk. 16:13 "Money" (→ *mamōnas, 3440*) is an idol that holds in its sway those who seem to control it. Thus 1 Thess. 4:6 lays down the rule that no one should "wrong his brother or take advantage [*pleonekteō*] of him." It is not clear whether this rule refers to sexual relations outside marriage (as the prior context suggests) or to business conduct.

3. Christians should not associate with a greedy person in the church (1 Cor. 5:11). By *pleonexia* such people exclude themselves from it and ultimately from the kingdom of God (6:10; Eph. 5:5). Like immorality and impurity, covetousness must be kept out of the life of the church (5:5). Col. 3:5 urges believers to "put to death . . . whatever belongs to your earthly nature: sexual immorality, impurity, lust, evil desires and greed, which is idolatry." This recalls Matt. 5:29–30 and urges that the physical nature enslaved in sin be subjected to the rule of the new spiritual life, with its transforming liberating power revealed in Christ (→ *sarx, 4922*; *pneuma, 4460*).

4. False teachers are characterized by their greed for material gain (2 Pet. 2:3, 14). Along the same lines, Paul's opponents "peddle the word of God for profit" (2 Cor. 2:17). Against this Paul can point out that as a rule he earned his keep with his own hands (Phil. 4:15; 1 Thess. 2:9) and that even in Corinth he and his coworkers did not try to enrich themselves by their service (2 Cor. 7:2; 12:17). But with regard to the collection for Jerusalem, Paul could ask in urgent terms for a liberal gift (2 Cor. 8–9).

See also *philargyria*, love of money, avarice (*5794*).

4435 (plēgē, blow, stroke, wound), → *3463*.

4436 πλῆθος	

πλῆθος (*plēthos*), number, multitude, crowd, throng, assembly, people (*4436*); πληθύνω (*plēthynō*), increase, multiply, grow (*4437*).

CL & OT 1. *plēthos* (linked with the root *plē-*, full) means a crowd or multitude in contrast to a small number or an individual. It can be used for a great number of things and, in connection with time, dura-

tion. With persons, it means a multitude, crowd; as a military term, a mass of troops; from a sociological standpoint, the mass that lacks culture and moral understanding; in a democracy, the total number of voters, the majority that turns the scales in political decisions, or the assembly (e.g., of the citizens of Athens); in religious communities, the body of members, the congregation. The pl. can be used to give emphasis (crowds, flocks). The vb. *plēthynō* means increase, enlarge, multiply; intrans. to be full, to increase in number.

2. In the LXX *plēthos* is found nearly 300x; *plēthynō*, about 200x. Most often it translates words related to the root *rābâ*, be or become much, many, great. The various forms are used to describe the abundant fullness of God's giving: in the blessing of creation (Gen. 1:22, 28); in the promise to the patriarchs and the people of God of great posterity (17:2, 4; 22:17; Exod. 1:7, 20; 32:13); in the bestowal of rich blessings (Deut. 28:11) and salvation (Ps. 5:7; 31:19; 51:1). God's fullness of glory (Exod. 15:7) and majesty (Ps. 150:2) is to be praised. Humans, by contrast, should not trust in the abundance of their strength (33:16), nor should God's people trust in the multitude of their warriors (Hos. 10:13) or sacrifices (Isa. 1:11). We stand before the great God with an abundance of guilt (Gen. 6:5; Amos 4:4; Sir. 5:6; 23:3, 16).

NT *plēthos* occurs 31x in the NT; *plēthynō*, 12x—most are in Luke's writings. The words can describe the fullness of God's giving. This is illustrated by passages from the OT that refer to the growth of God's people in fulfillment of the divine promises (Acts 7:17 = Exod. 1:7; Heb. 6:14 = Gen. 22:17; Heb. 11:12 = Gen. 15:5). *plēthynō* also occurs in the formula of greeting that prays that grace and peace (1 Pet. 1:2; 2 Pet. 1:2), or mercy, peace, and love (Jude 2) may "be yours in abundance."

Jas. 5:20 and 1 Pet. 4:8 (= Prov. 10:12) declare that the love that brings back a sinner from the error of his or her ways and the mutual love practiced in the community cover "a multitude of sins." This expression is not so much concerned with the number of sins committed, as if they were counted up in some divine bookkeeping, but with the effect of love that shows itself to be all the greater in undoing sin. Similarly, 2 Cor. 9:10 (cf. Isa. 55:10; Hos. 10:12) promises that God will see to it that no gift of love will make a person poor, but will "increase" rich blessings.

Luke frequently uses these words to describe the great impact made by Jesus and the gospel on the populace (Lk. 8:37; Acts 14:4; 21:36), which caused a large crowd to follow him (Lk. 6:17 par.; Mk. 3:7; Lk. 23:27; Acts 5:14, 16; 14:1; 17:4). Peter's apostolic missionary work and the harvest of the gospel among the Gentiles is anticipated by the great catch of fishes (Lk. 5:6; Jn. 21:6). The vb. *plēthynō* esp. is used to indicate the increase of the church through the spreading of God's Word (Acts 7:17; 9:31; 12:24; reminiscent of the OT increase of the people of God as a sign of blessing).

Lk. also makes a literary use of *plēthos* to focus attention on a small group of individuals alongside the anonymous multitude: the priest and the multitude (Lk. 1:10), the angel of the Lord and the heavenly host (2:13), the disciples and the people (6:17), and the Twelve and the great body of the church (Acts 6:2, 5). It means company or assembly in Acts 4:32; 14:4; 23:7, and underlines the corporate character of the action of the group in Lk. 19:37; 23:1; Acts 4:32; 25:24. In Lk. *plēthos* can also mean a religious assembly: participants in worship (Lk. 1:10; Acts 19:9), the company of believers (4:32), and the great body of the church (6:2, 5; 15:12, 30).

Matt. 24:12 speaks of the increase of wickedness in the end times. The disciples are not to lose their zeal under the pressure of such events, esp. when anti-Christian forces gain control even in the church and the widespread rejection of God's law makes life unbearable.

See also *gemō*, to load, be full (*1154*); *perisseuō*, be more than enough, abound, excel (*4355*); *plēroō*, fill, complete, fulfill, accomplish, carry out (*4444*); *chortazō*, to feed, fatten, fill (*5963*); *chōreō*, have or make room, give way, go (*6003*).

4437 (*plēthynō*, increase, multiply, grow), → 4436.

4441 (*plērēs*, full, filled, complete), → 4444.

4442 (*plērophoreō*, bring in full measure, fulfill, fully persuade), → 4444.

4443 (*plērophoria*, fullness, full assurance), → 4444.

4444	πληρόω

πληρόω (*plēroō*), fill, complete, fulfill, accomplish, carry out (4444); πλήρης (*plērēs*), full, filled, complete (4441); πλήρωμα (*plērōma*), that which has been completed, fullness (4445); ἀναπληρόω (*anaplēroō*), fill up (405); πληροφορέω (*plērophoreō*), bring in full measure, fulfill, fully persuade (4442); πληροφορία (*plērophoria*), fullness, full assurance (4443); πίμπλημι (*pimplēmi*), fill, complete, fulfill (4398); ἐμπίμπλημι (*empimplēmi*), fill full, fill up, satisfy (1855).

CL & OT 1. (a) Most of these words contain the common root *plē-*, full, fullness. *plēroō*, as well as *empimplēmi*, means lit. to fill a vessel, so that the result can be described by *plērēs* or *plērōma*. It is used in an extended sense of fulfilling a wish, hearing a prayer, satisfying a desire, stilling wrath and anger, meeting an obligation, and carrying out work. It has the further sense of bringing to full measure, delivering a reward or tribute, filling a gap, and enlarging. It is used in a temporal sense in the pass. of expiring, coming to an end, e.g., a full (*plērēs*) year, a full number (*plērōma*) of years.

(b) Just as a person can be full of pain, joy, love, and virtue, he or she can also be filled with God, i.e., possessed and inspired by God (e.g., it is applied to those who uttered oracles). Elsewhere in Gk. thought is the notion that God fills or permeates the universe. According to Plato, the transcendent God fills the universe by his presence and working.

2. (a) *plēroō* and *pimplēmi* are almost equally common in the LXX. They have the same range of meaning as in cl. Gk.: e.g., the lit. sense (Gen. 21:19; 2 Ki. 4:4); of the divine ordinance to fill the earth (Gen. 1:28; 9:7). In an extended sense, *plēroō* and its derivatives are used of hearing prayers (Ps. 20:5), finishing work (1 Ki. 7:51), paying tribute (2 Macc. 8:10), confirming the words of someone else (1 Ki. 1:14), and bringing a punishment to full measure (Wis. 19:4).

(b) *plēroō* is used frequently in the LXX (*pimplēmi* less so) in connection with expressions of time: to make a time full, mainly in the pass. in the sense of expiring, coming to an end. The idea implies a definite amount of time that must inevitably come to an end, because nature (Gen. 25:24), a vow (Num. 6:5), the law (Lev. 8:33), or God's word (Jer. 25:12; cf. 2 Chr. 36:21) decrees or determines it. The OT also speaks about the filling up of sins, such as the iniquity of the Amorites being not yet complete (Gen. 15:16; cf. also 2 Macc. 6:12–16). The attainment of the full measure of sins means the end of the dominion of the four godless kingdoms (Dan. 8:23).

(c) There is a specific OT use of the term when the word of God spoken by the prophets is said to be fulfilled (cf. 1 Ki. 2:27; 2 Chr. 36:21–22; 1 Esd. 1:57). Yahweh himself is the one who executes what has been prophesied in his name (1 Ki. 8:15, 24).

(d) There are numerous references to being filled (*empimplēmi*) by the Spirit of God. It is the distinguishing mark of the prophets (Sir. 48:12) and can be transmitted by the laying on of hands (Deut. 34:9). Skilled craftsmen are also said to be filled by a spirit, that of knowledge and craftsmanship (Exod. 28:3; 31:3). Being filled by the Spirit is also given to those who seek the Lord and study the law (Sir. 39:6–10).

The statement of Wis. 1:7 that "the spirit of the Lord has filled the world" is not to be understood in a pantheistic sense; rather, it is a confession that God hears and knows everything and punishes sin (see the context). Similarly, the rhetorical question of Jer. 23:24, "Do not I fill heaven and earth?" means that God sees all things. The statement that God's glory fills the earth (cf. Num. 14:21; Ps. 72:19; Isa.

6:4) means that God will reveal himself in full measure. Originally this glory was confined to the tabernacle (Exod. 40:34–35) and the temple (1 Ki. 8:10–11; 2 Chr. 5:14; 7:1; Hag. 2:8). But in the end time, "the earth will be filled with the knowledge of the glory of the LORD, as the waters cover the sea" (Hab. 2:14).

3. The Qumran writings mainly use the idea of filling to denote the completion of a period of time (cf. 1QS 7:20, 22), as well as in the eschatological sense that all existence and events are fulfilled according to a firm plan already fixed by God (3:16; 1QM 17:9). In the time of salvation expected at the end God will fill his land with the rich bounty of blessing and all the wealth of the nations will be brought together at Jerusalem (12:12–16; cf. 14:4).

NT The NT usage of these terms is in line with the foregoing. *pimplēmi* (24x) and *empimplēmi* (5x) remain close to the lit. meaning. Both are used most often by Luke, the former to denote endowment by the Spirit, pictured in a physical and visual manner, the latter to denote satisfying with physical food (Lk. 1:53; 6:25; Acts 14:17).

plēroō is more significant, not only because it is more frequent (86x), but also because it is virtually a technical term used in connection with the fulfillment of Scripture as well as with the fulfillment of time in an eschatological sense. *plērēs* is used lit. in the Synoptic Gospels, although it is also used for one full of the Holy Spirit, full of faith, or full of good works (cf. Acts 6:3, 5; 9:36). *plērophoreō* and *plērophoria* (10x total) come close in meaning to the vb. *perisseuō* (→ 4355). *plērophoria* can mean lit. fullness and fig. also full assurance, conviction. It is difficult to determine whether *plērōma* (a favorite Pauline word) focuses on the process of filling or the fact of being filled. In the rest of this article, we will focus on the more theological uses of these words.

1. *Fulfillment of OT Scripture.* (a) The NT church was conscious that it lived in continuity with the OT. It found its strength in the OT, and not merely in the way it made use of the OT in authenticating its apologetic and mission vis-à-vis Jud. Right from the beginning, going back to Jesus himself, the church felt the need to base its life on the OT. It appealed to the OT with a sometimes surprising self-confidence in a manner characterized by the key concept of fulfillment. The usual term was *plēroō*, although *anaplēroō* and *pimplēmi* occur once each in this connection (Matt. 13:14; Lk. 21:22).

(b) The fulfillment is often introduced by the conjunctions *hopōs* or *hina* ("so that"). This is esp. true of those fulfillment quotations that have their origin in the church's understanding of its faith (e.g., Jas. 2:23) or episodes in the life of Jesus that were seen as the fulfillment of the divine plan of salvation revealed in the OT. In this sense writers speak of the fulfillment of the Scriptures. The entire OT can be in mind (e.g., Lk. 24:44), though the prophetic writings stand out (e.g., Matt. 26:56). Hence, writers may speak of the fulfillment of prophecy (13:14) or of the words of the prophets (Acts 13:27).

Sometimes the prophets are named whose words are cited as Scripture (e.g., Isa. in Matt. 4:14; 8:17; Jer. in Matt. 2:17; cf. 16:14). At other times the reference is simply to "the prophet" (1:22; 2:5, 15; 21:4). Matt. expressly characterizes the prophet's activity as a subordinate one with the preposition *dia*, through ("through the prophet," 10x). Behind the Scripture stands the true author, God himself (cf. 1:22; 2:15). He is the one who declared it beforehand (Acts 3:18).

(c) Just as God is the originator, he is also the fulfiller of the word spoken by him. This finds expression in the frequent circumlocution using the pass. voice, to be fulfilled. Although God brings about fulfillment (Acts 3:18; 13:33), this does not preclude human participation. By their failure to understand the utterances of the prophets the inhabitants of Jerusalem fulfilled Scripture (13:27).

The NT also speaks of the fulfillment of the words of an angel (Lk. 1:20) and of Jesus (Jn. 18:9, 32). In any case, the process of evaluating scriptural proofs cited in the NT starts from the eschatologically understood present and reaches back to the OT Scripture (cf. the frequent *kathōs gegraptai*, "as it is written," e.g., Mk. 9:13; Lk. 2:23).

Generally it is the wording of the LXX and not the Heb. text that is referred to. Certain passages are understood as mysteriously presaging the present advent of the final events (→ *apokalypsis, 637*). Faith discovers in the OT the promise of the salvation that is now coming to pass.

One can sometimes note in such passages a striking freedom in dealing with the wording of the OT. Jesus' attitude to the wording of the OT was already discriminating (cf. Matt. 5:17; Mk. 10:2–9). Paul also distinguished between the Spirit and the letter (2 Cor. 3:6–11). Sometimes he expounded the OT in an allegorical manner (Gal. 4:21–31; cf. also 1 Cor. 9:9; 1 Tim. 5:18 with Deut. 25:4). The author of Heb. used the form of a homily in which he expounded on a connected string of OT passages step by step.

It is sometimes suggested that the apologetic interest of the NT writers led them to wrest OT passages out of their original contexts in order to give them a Christological interpretation. Thus the quotation of Hos. 11:1 ("and out of Egypt I called my son") by Matt. 2:15 appears in its context to have nothing to do with the infant Jesus returning from Egypt. Rather, it refers to the original exodus of the people of Israel. Similarly, the Immanuel prophecy of Isa. 7:14, quoted in Matt. 1:23, appears to lose its point for Isaiah's time if the fulfillment did not occur until the birth of Jesus. If these and other OT quotations are regarded as direct predictions of events that did not happen until Jesus, then the NT writers cannot be exonerated of the charge of taking texts out of context, displaying indifference to the original meaning of the text.

But we should understand these NT passages from the standpoint of an eschatological present. The OT passages are treated not so much as predictions as anticipations. From the standpoint of the Israelite living at the time of the original prophecy, the utterance was about something significant in the history of the Jewish people. Matt.'s idea of fulfillment says, in effect, that the event that the Jews thought was significant turns out to be an anticipation of an event of a similar kind but ultimately more significant in God's purposes for the salvation of humankind. It is in this sense that the latter fulfills the former.

2. *The fulfillment of time*. (a) In a general sense, the expression of the fulfillment of time (e.g., Lk. 1:23, 57; 2:6, cf. 43; Acts 7:23) refers to a certain period of time coming to an end. It is always pass. in the NT.

(b) The idea of fulfillment in Lk. 21:24 is significant. The execution of divine judgment on Jerusalem will go on "until the times of the Gentiles are fulfilled." There is more emphasis here than in (a) above on the thought that God determines the times and the seasons, since God is the implied subj. in these pass. constructions. Time (→ *aiōn, 172*) has a function in God's plan of salvation. Similarly, 9:51 speaks of the fulfillment of the time for Jesus' being taken to heaven, and Acts 2:1 of the day of Pentecost being fulfilled (both using *symplēroō*).

(c) According to Mk. 1:15, Jesus' first public preaching began with the notion that the time appointed by God and awaited by Israel has come. This may be compared with Jesus' declaration in the synagogue at Nazareth after reading from Isa. 61:1–2 (Lk. 4:18–19): "Today this scripture is fulfilled in your hearing" (4:21). By way of contrast, Jesus declares in Jn. 7:8, "The right time has not yet come (*peplērōtai*)." Although the time of God's intervention in Christ has already come, the events of Jesus' earthly life are still fully in the hands of God. No one, not even Jesus himself, can control them (cf. 2:4; 7:30; 8:20). The proper time is only revealed to Jesus later (12:31; 13:1; 17:1).

(d) In this connection, Paul makes use of the noun *plērōma*: "But when the time had fully come, God sent his Son, born of a woman, born under law, to redeem those under law, that we might receive the full rights of sons" (Gal. 4:4–5). This does not mean only that an appointed time has come. Rather, it means that in the divine economy of salvation time has reached its full measure. Similarly in Eph. 1:10 Paul links God's plan of salvation with the times reaching their fulfillment (*plērōma*). He wishes to stress that the Christ event does not lie in the realm of human factors and possibilities but in the counsel of God (1:9).

3. *The fulfillment of God's law*. (a) The NT discussion of fulfillment of the law is always concerned with the basic thought that "love is the fulfillment (*plērōma*) of the law" (Rom. 13:10, cf. 13:8). Similarly in Gal. 5:14 Paul says, "The entire law is summed up in a single command: 'Love your neighbor as yourself'" (quoting Lev. 19:18). Concretely, this can mean: "Carry each other's burdens, and in this way you will fulfill (*anaplērōsete*) the law of Christ" (Gal. 6:2).

(b) In his Sermon on the Mount Jesus said that he had not "come to abolish the Law and the Prophets [i.e., the OT Scriptures in which God has made his will known] but to fulfill them" (Matt. 5:17). However one attempts to resolve the tension between 5:18–20 and 5:21–48, it is clear that fulfillment is not to be understood in a formal way. Here too the basic motive is love. Jesus shows this love from the start in fulfilling "all righteousness" (3:15).

(c) Although the righteous demand of the law still remains, the sting of death is removed. Through the righteous act of Christ, righteousness has come to us (Rom. 5:18). The sending of God's Son and the condemnation of sin in the flesh (8:3) effect what the law could not do, "in order that the righteous requirements of the law might be fully met (*plērōthē*) in us, who do not live according to the sinful nature but according to the Spirit" (8:4).

4. *Being filled with the Spirit*. In this connection *pimplēmi* and *plēroō* are used only in the pass., since God is always thought of as the giver. The adj. *plērēs* also occurs. The thought is specifically Lukan. Paul develops his doctrine of the Spirit in a different way.

(a) John the Baptist is said to be "filled with the Holy Spirit" from his mother's womb (Lk. 1:15). Likewise, John's parents, Elizabeth (1:41) and Zechariah (1:67), are full of the Holy Spirit in their prophesying.

(b) Mk. 1:12 offers a dynamic view of Jesus' relationship with the Sprit: The latter drives (*ekballei*) Jesus into the desert as a personal power (cf. the temporary endowment by the Spirit of the charismatic leaders in the book of Jdg., e.g., 6:34; 11:29; 14:19). Lk., however, presents the concept of a special act of bestowing the Spirit in baptism, which endows the recipient with an enduring, miraculous power, so that Jesus returns from his baptism "full of the Holy Spirit" (Lk. 4:1).

(c) What until Pentecost, the decisive date for the universal church, was the privilege of only a few individuals, is from that day forward the most important characteristic of the Jewish and subsequently the Gentile church (cf. Acts 10). According to 2:4, *all* of the believers present "were filled with the Holy Spirit." This was manifested in the gift of tongues. This connection between being filled and speaking also comes out in 4:8, 31 (cf. 13:9). This filling is not an end in itself, but the condition for speaking with boldness in the missionary situation (cf. esp. 4:31). Although being filled with the Spirit appears to be a mark of the Christian in general, it is esp. stressed in the case of certain individuals, such as Stephen (6:5; 7:55), Paul (9:17), and Barnabas (11:24).

(d) Acts 6 shows that various gifts were apparently bestowed together with the gift of the Spirit: wisdom (6:3, 10), faith (6:5), grace, and power (6:8). Without the Spirit one can be filled with bad qualities, such as wrath (Lk. 4:28; Acts 19:29), fury (Lk. 6:11), and jealousy (Acts 5:17; 13:45). Peter, filled with the Spirit, unmasked their originator as Satan (5:3; 13:9). There is evidently no neutral position for a person between Christ and Satan (Lk. 11:23).

(e) Paul saw humans as standing between these two alternatives: bringing forth "the fruit of the Spirit" or living according to "the acts of the sinful nature" (Gal. 5:19, 22; → *karpos, 2843*, and *sarx, 4922*). To be filled with the power of the Spirit (cf. Eph. 5:18) means to "live by the Spirit" (Gal. 5:25), to be "in Christ," or to "have the mind of Christ" (1 Cor. 2:16). All of these mean that one has the fullness of the gifts of grace that flow through oneself as a member of the body of Christ.

5. *The fullness of Christ.* A few passages in the NT speak of "the fullness" (*plērōma*) of Christ. It is not easy to attribute a single, unambiguous meaning to this noun. In Rom. 11:12 it means full inclusion; in 11:25, "full number"; in 15:29, "full measure"; and in 13:10, "fulfillment" in the act. sense.

(a) Jn. 1:16 says that the incarnate Word possesses a "fullness," which has already been referred to in 1:14, where the Logos is described as being "full of grace and truth." This fullness denotes, like the glory in 1:14, revelation. Humanity can see the fullness and have a part in this glory.

(b) According to Col. 2:9, "in Christ all the fullness (*plērōma*) of the Deity lives in bodily form." This fullness, described in Col. 1:15–18, is related to Christ's cross (1:20), death (1:22), and resurrection (1:18). For this reason believers also have this fullness in Christ (2:10). By his cross, death, and resurrection they are reconciled through faith (2:12–14), renewed, and made to participate in his triumph. Many scholars see this doctrine of Christ as the fullness as an answer to the so-called Colossian heresy, which apparently taught that one could attain fullness with the Deity through some sort of angelic hierarchy (a sort of incipient Gnosticism).

(c) Believers "have been given fullness (*peplērōmenoi*) in Christ" (Col. 2:10). But the fact of their salvation does not exclude their own contribution to this fullness. Eph. 3:19 contains the prayer that the readers may "know this love [of Christ] that surpasses knowledge—that you may be filled to the measure of all the fullness of God." It is clear that such knowledge is not given automatically. It depends on the building up of the church as the body of Christ. Christian service must contribute to the realization of the unity of faith and the knowledge of the Son of God. This in turn leads "to the whole measure of the fullness of Christ" (4:13), in which believers are no longer carried about by every wind of doctrine (4:14). This faith-knowledge is assured by Christ and is given to the church, "which is his body, the fullness of him who fills everything in every way" (1:23).

6. *The filling up of the measure of sin.* We noted in the OT section that the filling up of the measure of sin in the OT was applied to the Gentile nations. Tob. 14:5 restricts it to them and argues that God will protect the people of Israel against it. But in Matt. 23:32 Jesus says expressly to the Jewish leaders: "Fill up, then, the measure of the sin of your forefathers." This implies that they are sinning just as much as their fathers did, or that they fill out what was still lacking in sins. Paul likewise turns the expression against the Jews in 1 Thess. 2:15–16: The Jews killed the Lord Jesus and the prophets, drove the Christian missionaries out, and displeased God by keeping them "from speaking to the Gentiles so that they may be saved. In this way they always heap up their sins to the limit (*anaplērōsai*). The wrath of God has come upon them at last."

7. *Filling a need.* In the Pauline letters *anaplēroō*, *antanaplēroō*, and *prosanaplēroō* are linked with *hysterēma*, lack (both in sing. and pl.), in the sense of filling a lack that someone has. Thus, the coming of Stephanas, Fortunatus, and Achaicus made up for Paul's being separated from the Corinthian church (1 Cor. 16:17). Epaphroditus served Paul as the representative of the Philippian church in their stead (Phil. 2:30).

Most important is Col. 1:24, where Paul declares: "Now I rejoice in what was suffered for you, and I fill up in my flesh what is still lacking in regard to Christ's afflictions, for the sake of his body, which is the church." The sufferings of the church are not to be separated from those of Christ, so that one can speak of Christ's still being afflicted (→ *thlipsis, 2568*)—not that these sufferings make satisfaction for sin, only that they are edificatory both for oneself and for the church. Note how in Acts 9:4 the Lord asks the persecuting Saul, "Saul, Saul, why do you persecute *me*?" Not all persecution fell to the historical Jesus; a part remains for the members of his body, the church. Paul, the servant (Col. 1:23, 25), felt that the great suffering that was his lot was in a certain measure suffering for the body of Christ. He thus rejoiced in his suffering.

8. *Complete joy.* In Jn. and the Johannine letters there is a frequent connection between joy as a subject and the vb. *plēroō* in the pass. This joy is the joy of Jesus (Jn. 15:11; 17:13), which he brings through his coming (3:29), his words (15:11; 17:13), and his return (16:22) to his disciples (15:11; 17:13). It replaces the sorrow that fills their hearts (16:16, 20). Thus Christ's joy becomes their joy (15:11; 16:24; cf. 1 Jn. 1:4). This joy characterizes the life of the disciples in their walk with Jesus, and it becomes complete (Jn. 3:29; 15:11; 16:24; 17:13; 1 Jn. 1:4; 2 Jn. 12). The pass. underlies the fact that it is God who completes this joy.

See also *gemō*, to load, be full (*1154*); *perisseuō*, be more than enough, abound, excel (*4355*); *plēthos*, number, multitude, crowd (*4436*); *chortazō*, to feed, fatten, fill (*5963*); *chōreō*, have or make room, give way, go (*6003*).

4445 (*plērōma*, that which has been completed, fullness),
→ *4444*.

4446	πλησίον

πλησίον (*plēsion*), neighbor (*4446*).

CL & OT *plēsios* basically means near, nearby. The noun derived from it, *ho plēsion*, means the one standing near, one's neighbor or fellow human being. In the vast majority of cases *plēsion* in the LXX represents *rēaʿ*, which can represent every form of human relationship: someone belonging to my surroundings and life (without any reference to blood relationship or nationality), or one with whom I have to do, such as my neighbor (Exod. 11:2), friend (2 Sam. 13:3), or fellow human being (Prov. 6:1, though *plēsion* is not used in the latter two cases).

The appearance of *rēaʿ* in legal texts is ambiguous. In the law of love (Lev. 19:18) only members of the covenant community are in view; the alien is not mentioned until 19:33–34. This suggests that the concept of *rēaʿ* developed in the history of Israel. At first it meant only those incorporated in the covenant people. But later it came to mean simply one's fellow humans. By choosing *plēsion* the LXX arrayed itself with the wider interpretation. In stricter Jewish circles, only Jews and full proselytes were included under *plēsion*; in the Qumran community the word was confined to its members.

NT The NT clearly adopts the wider meaning of the LXX. This is seen esp. in Matt. 5:43–47 and Lk. 10:29–37, which form the basis for the interpretation of the command to love. Jesus did not agree with restricting Lev. 19:18 to the brother and friend. He demanded the inclusion of even the enemy.

Jesus placed the law of love under the gospel. The statement "Anyone in need is always my neighbor" is subordinate to the statement "My neighbor is the one who shows me mercy" (cf. the good Samaritan in Lk. 10:37). The question as to whom I am to love is foolish, because the Samaritan, the former enemy, has become my neighbor by his compassionate treatment of me and so challenges me to act in love. In other words, the experience of being loved comes before the challenge, the encouragement before the claim, the gospel before the command. Jesus himself is the key to the parable. The phrase "he took pity on him" (10:33b; → *splanchnon, 5073*), which in the Gospels is applied generally only to Jesus, indicates that Luke saw Jesus shining through the Samaritan.

The NT combines the two OT commands of love to God (Deut. 6:5) and love to one's neighbor (Lev. 19:18) into a double command (Matt. 22:37–40 par.; cf. Rom. 13:9; Gal. 5:14; Jas. 2:8). It sees them embodied together in Christ. Jesus awakens love for himself in us bruised and miserable humans. His call to "go and do likewise" (Lk. 10:37) demands action that is capable of awakening love in my neighbor. Christ meets me in the other person, whether he is brother or enemy, helper or beggar. He gives me his love and fills me with it, so that it flows over to the other. This moves love to my neighbor out of the dangerous region of new legalism and puts it under the sway of love, which both takes and gives. It opens up a wide sphere of Christian action (Eph. 4:25–5:2) and creates new fellowship and service to God (Mk. 12:28–34; cf. Hos. 6:6).

See also *adelphos*, brother (*81*); *hetairos*, companion, friend (*2279*).

4454 (plousios, rich, a rich man), → *4458.*

4455 (plousiōs, richly), → *4458.*

4456 (plouteō, be rich, become rich), → *4458.*

4457 (ploutizō, make rich), → *4458.*

4458	πλοῦτος

πλοῦτος (*ploutos*), wealth, riches (*4458*); πλούσιος (*plousios*), rich, a rich man (*4454*); πλουσίως (*plousiōs*), richly (*4455*); πλουτέω (*plouteō*), be rich, become rich (*4456*); πλουτίζω (*ploutizō*), make rich (*4457*).

CL & OT 1. (a) In cl. Gk. this word group initially meant abundance of earthly possessions. Later its meaning divided into two directions: riches in a technical and material sense, and riches in a more general sense, used in such phrases as riches of wisdom, honor, mercy, etc. All the words in this group can bear this double meaning.

(b) In Homer external wealth and virtue are not separated; *rich* is a comprehensive term for a fortunate life blessed by the gods. Plato and Aristotle judge riches by their effect on society, i.e., if they do not serve the community, they are to be rejected. The Cynics despised material possessions because they brought commitments and anxieties with them. The Stoics believed that the chief danger of riches lay in the creation of a feeling of false security, but they also recognized their value because of the opportunities of developing one's personality. In Gk. culture riches did not seem to have the sociologically divisive influence as they did in other cultures. At the same time, the idea did not develop that riches should be shared with the poor.

2. In the LXX the words in this word group translate a variety of Heb. words, esp. from the root ʿšr. Riches in the earlier parts of OT are seen as having positive value. They consisted mainly of flocks and herds, children and slaves (e.g., Gen. 13:2; 30:43), and were a gift from God. In the nomadic or semi-nomadic period riches presented no problem, for there were no blatant differences between rich and poor. At the conquest of Canaan Yahweh gave everyone a share. Since the land belonged to God, he extended protection to the individual's property (cf. the laws in Exod. 23:1–19, expanded in Deut.).

The period of the monarchy saw the development of royal cities and courts. With the growth of commerce and trade a major social differentiation developed. There was a small upper class of the rich and influential, who, as may be seen in the prophets (Isa. 5:8–12; Jer. 5:26–28; 34:8–11; Amos 2:6–7; 5:10–12; Mic. 2:1–2), destroyed God's people by injustice and violence and so brought deserved judgment on the nation.

In the OT wisdom lit., where the word group is most frequent, we often find unaffected praise of riches (e.g., Prov. 10:4, 15). But there are also references to their relative value (e.g., Ps. 49:16; Prov. 22:1) and their power to lead people astray (e.g., Ps. 49:6; 52:7). At the same time we find in Job and Ps. the problem of vindicating the divine rule (esp. Job 21; Ps. 37; 49; 73).

3. The members of the Qumran community adopted "the poor" as a title of honor. They practiced community of possessions (→ *ptōchos*, *4777*). For Enoch the end will bring with it a complete reversal of all earthly possession and fortune (*1 Enoch* 96:4; 100:6; 103:4–5). Among the Pharisees only the righteousness derived from keeping the law had real value, although riches enabled one to do good works, carrying with them corresponding obligations. All circles where eschatological hopes were earthly or nationalistic had a high opinion of riches.

NT 1. *Occurrences. ploutos* is found in the Gospels only in Matt. 13:22; Mk. 4:19; Lk. 8:14, where it means wealth in terms of earthly goods (cf. 1 Tim. 6:17; Jas. 5:2; Rev. 18:17). The word is linked with God (Rom. 9:23), Christ (Eph. 3:8), and churches (2 Cor. 8:2). *plousios*, as adj. or noun, describes persons rich in this world's goods (e.g., Matt. 19:23–24; 27:57; Mk. 12:41; Lk. 6:24; 12:16; Jas. 1:10–11; 2:6; Rev. 3:17; 13:16). Followed by the dat., it expresses the riches of God (Eph. 2:4) or of the Christian (Jas. 2:5). In 2 Cor. 8:9 and Rev. 2:9 it means those rich in spiritual possessions.

The vb. *plouteō* is used absolutely in Lk. 1:53; 1 Tim. 6:9; Rev. 18:15 in the reference to earthly possessions, and in 1 Cor. 4:8; 2 Cor. 8:9; Rev. 3:17–18 of spiritual possessions. Rom. 10:12 indicates that God's riches are available for all. *ploutizō* means make rich, enrich. God makes the church rich in all things (1 Cor. 1:5); the Christian passes on those riches given by God so as to make others rich (2 Cor. 6:10; 9:11). The adv. *plousiōs* occurs only at Col. 3:16; 1 Tim. 6:17; Tit. 3:6; 2 Pet. 1:11, each of which has a spiritual sense of God's rich grace.

2. *Theological significance.* (a) Matt. exhibits no ascetic rejection of possessions and riches. Granted, he stresses the dangers inherent in them that may hinder the kingdom of God, but they are not basically satanic (cf. 27:57). If Jesus mercilessly attacks attachment to earthly possessions (13:22; 19:23–24), his denunciation applies to riches in exactly the same way as it does to every human self-contrived security and obsession that make it impossible for us to see the kingdom of God. The seed that falls among thorns is choked by worry and "the deceitfulness of wealth" (13:22). Anxiety is a characteristic of this age (cf. 6:25–32), and every kind of riches is deceitful when it so appeals to people that they are hindered from hearing the message of the kingdom. By contrast, poverty in the Beatitudes means being open for the kingdom of God.

We find the same theme in Matt. 19:23–24, where "hard" is explained by Jesus' answer in 19:26. The reaction of the disciples in 19:25 shows that more is meant by "rich man" than economic standing, for they realized that they were being included. In other words riches are a characteristic of the inner self. In all this teaching Jesus entertains no possibility of someone attaining the kingdom of God (i.e., life) as one stands. The new righteousness, which carries life within it, comes alone from God's power. We must receive it in repentance and faith. In other words, Jesus' view of riches cannot be separated from the crucial hour of decision.

(b) In Mk. the judgment on riches is expressed more mildly. By speaking of "the desires for other things" (4:19) Jesus expresses the danger in terms of a subjective threat to the individual psyche. Riches encourage confidence in oneself and so become a great obstacle on the way to the kingdom of God (10:23–25).

(c) The rich landowner in Lk. 12:16–20 represents rich people in general, who often forget that God is the giver of what they have and thus put their confidence in their riches, or who give themselves up to unrestrained enjoyment of riches and so miss God's purpose for their lives (cf. 16:19–31). The Pharisees scoffed at Jesus' warning against money (16:13–14; → *mamōnas*, *3440*), for they were lovers of wealth (cf. 1 Tim. 6:10; 2 Tim. 3:2; → *thēsauros*, *2565*). The general verdict and context of the passages in which Lk. deals with the rich suggest the possibility that the term is used for Jesus' enemies, or that they are collectively identified by that name. As a result, there is a complete rejection of the rich.

God's kingdom brings with it the reversal of all earthly relationships (Lk. 1:53; 6:24–25; 16:25). Those who reject Jesus and his message because they are enslaved by the present age and its deceitful riches lose the future in their attempt to secure the present. Salvation comes to those who are liberated by the gospel and know that their riches lie in the future, which is even now dawning. The reversal of all earthly values, which will become evident at the end of the age, will confirm that only those riches that have been stored up with God have lasting value and bring salvation (16:9). Zacchaeus's behavior (19:8) and the admonition of 14:12–14 are models for this.

(d) The selfish rich are completely rejected in Jas., which echoes the judgment of the OT prophets and depicts the rich as the unrighteous

(2:6; 5:1–6), who can only expect calamity in the coming transformation of the world (1:10–11; 5:1–6; cf. Isa. 40:6–8). By contrast, it is the poor, the rich in faith, whom God has chosen (Jas. 2:5).

(e) Paul is not interested in the material understanding of the term *riches*. He gives it a deeper meaning by applying it to God, Christ, and the church. Fullness marks out God, the only truly rich one, e.g., in glory (Rom. 9:23; Eph. 3:16) and grace (1:7; 2:7). The church shares in these riches (1 Cor. 1:5; Eph. 1:7, 18). To be rich is a spiritual gift unconnected with material possessions. Though the apostle is himself poor, he makes many rich by his preaching (2 Cor. 6:10). Seeing that Christ could make us rich only by emptying himself and becoming poor (8:9; cf. Phil. 2:5–11), the Christian's pathway through the world is one of self-emptying and helping fellow believers (2 Cor. 8:2; 9:10–15). Israel's rejection of Christ means riches for the Gentiles, for the message of salvation is now directed to them (Rom. 11:12). The eschatological nature of these riches is missed if they are used as the justification for self-praise within the church (1 Cor. 4:8).

(f) In 1 Tim. earthly riches are not rejected, but the rich are warned against putting their confidence in that which is transient; they are called on instead to become rich in good works by a right use of their possessions (1 Tim. 6:17–19). Heb. 11:26 has a Pauline flavor: Transient abuse became riches for Moses as he looked to the future reward, and his sufferings for God's people anticipates the sufferings of Christ (→ *thēsauros*, *2565*).

(g) Rev. contains a double message: (i) The rich are unable to stand before the wrath of the Lamb (6:15–16), and those who have been enriched by Babylon fall together with it (18:3, 15, 17, 19). (ii) The church in Smyrna, perhaps because it is persecuted for the sake of the faith, is truly rich (2:9). By contrast, Laodicea is poor, because it thinks itself spiritually rich. It is called on to become rich by turning to the Lord (3:17–18). Riches are mentioned in 5:12 in the praise offered to the Lamb.

See also *thēsauros*, treasure box, chest, storeroom, treasure (*2565*); *mamōnas*, money, wealth, property (*3440*); *peripoieō*, save for oneself, acquire, gain possession of (*4347*); *chrēma*, property, wealth, means, money (*5975*).

4460	πνεῦμα

πνεῦμα (*pneuma*), spirit, wind (*4460*); πνέω (*pneō*), to blow (*4463*); πνοή (*pnoē*), wind, breath (*4466*); ἐκπνέω (*ekpneō*), breathe out (*1743*); ἐμπνέω (*empneō*), to pant (*1863*); πνευματικός (*pneumatikos*), spiritual (*4461*); πνευματικῶς (*pneumatikōs*), spiritually (*4462*); θεόπνευστος (*theopneustos*), God-breathed, inspired by God (*2535*).

CL & OT 1. (a) The Gk. root *pneu-* denotes dynamic movement of the air. Of its derivatives, *pneō* means to blow (of wind and air generally, also on a musical instrument); breathe; emit a fragrance; radiate heat, anger, courage, benevolence, and the like. *pnoē* refers to blowing, breathing (esp. panting), inspiration (by a deity), steam, evaporation. *ekpneō* means to breathe out, blow out, stop breathing (i.e., die), get out of breath. *empneō* means to breathe (in), be alive, blow on or into something, inspire.

(b) *pneuma*, spirit, denotes the result of the action of breathing, namely, air set in motion, with an underlying stress on its inherent power. It thus can mean wind or breath, but increasingly it took on the functions of related concepts, so that by the Hel. period it was a term of some importance, though still with a somewhat materialistic connotation.

The air that we breathe was considered to be the bearer of life. From the 5th cent. on Gk. physicians drew a distinction between one's inward, innate *pneuma* and the air one breathed. In Aristotle this *pneuma* was the formative power that, beginning already in the embryo, gradually produced the mature individual and then became the instrument whereby the soul controlled the body.

pneuma, in other words, approached the meaning held by *psychē*, soul (→ *6034*), the distinction being that the latter was a purely functional term, while *pneuma* was regarded as a substance. In Stoic philosophy, however, *pneuma* took over the functions of *psychē* in relation to the senses and to thought and speech (some even identified *pneuma* with *nous*, the human power of intellect, → *3808*). Stoicism also regarded *pneuma* as an elemental principle that gave coherence to the different entities in creation, while at the same time differentiating them from each other. Thus, it arranged the world in terms of a descending scale, without which the world's existence would be impossible. It came to be regarded as the fifth element (along with air, fire, water, and land).

Probably under Stoic influence, *pneuma* came to denote inspiration, a material substance that filled a human and enabled one to prophesy. This prophetic *pneuma* was ecstatic, visionary, demonic, holy, even divine. It played an active role in popular religion (always given to magic and soothsaying). Finally, *pneuma* is also found in the sense of spirit or demon in Hel. inscriptions and papyri.

(c) The adj. *pneumatikos* shares the meanings of *pneuma* and is used from the pre-Socratic school on. *theopneustos* (inspired by God) is rare, not being used before the Hel. period and then only with reference to divination.

2. In the LXX the Heb. equivalent of *pneuma* is almost always *rûaḥ*. Of the 377x *rûaḥ* occurs in the MT, 264 are translated by *pneuma* (the next most frequent rendering is *anemos*, wind, 49x; → *astrapē*, lightning, *847*). The idea behind *rûaḥ* is the extraordinary fact that something as intangible as air can move; at the same time it is not so much the movement per se that excites attention, but the energy manifested by such movement.

(a) In roughly one third of all occurrences, *pneuma* is used for the wind, which has God as its immediate cause (e.g., Gen. 8:1; Ps. 104:4; Amos 4:13). In this same connection, *rûaḥ* takes on two special senses: the direction of the wind (e.g., Ezek. 37:9; 42:16–20) and fig., because of the wind's ephemeral nature (cf. Ps. 78:39), nothingness (e.g., Eccl. 5:15, LXX *anemos*).

(b) The same phenomenon occurs in the breath, both of humans (Ezek. 37:8, 10) and of animals (Eccl. 3:19, 21). It denotes the life-force of the individual (Jdg. 15:19) and of the group (Num. 16:22), that which is lacking in idols (Jer. 10:14) but not in God (Ps. 33:6) or the Messiah (Isa. 11:4). God gives (42:5) and protects it (Ps. 31:6) but is free to take it back again (104:29), whereupon it returns to God (Eccl. 12:7). As a life-force it manifests itself in varying degrees of intensity, the dominant idea being that of its vitality. It can be adversely affected by emotions ranging from anxiety (Gen. 41:8) and grief (26:35) to utter despair (Job 17:1). It is heightened by jealousy (Num. 5:14) or anger (Jdg. 8:3), while there is a clear echo of the word's basic meaning in the vivid phrase expressing God's wrath: "the blast [*pneuma*] of your nostrils" (Exod. 15:8).

This reveals the manner in which the OT speaks of the human being: not clinically, with human attributes neatly classified, but concretely; in other words, the OT writers take humans as they find them and assess their behavior toward others and the attitude displayed toward God's law. So concrete is the OT's approach that the terms it uses are taken from the ordinary and tangible phenomena of the world about us. The thought implicit in *rûaḥ* is that breathing, with the movement of air that this involves, is the outward expression of the life-force inherent in all human behavior.

This is true of behavior requiring a greater or a lesser degree of energy: behavior in which energy has to be directed along certain channels (e.g., Ezr. 1:1, to stir up one's spirit, i.e., bring a person to a decision), in which case *spirit* may be synonymous with *plan* or *intention* (Isa. 19:3); behavior toward others, whether humble or proud (Prov. 16:19; Eccl. 7:8 = LXX 7:9), patient or impatient (Eccl. 7:8 = LXX 7:9; Prov. 14:29); behavior toward God, guileless (Ps. 32:2), steadfast (51:12; 78:8), broken in penitence (34:18; 51:17), or disobedient (Isa. 29:24; Hos. 4:12).

(c) *pneuma* frequently stands alongside "heart" (e.g., Exod. 35:31–35), the ideas behind these two words being similar. The difference is that the heart dwells within a person, having indeed been created by God; it is not a fleeting, oscillating gift like the breath of a person's spirit. The heart denote one's aims, resolves, and courage, while one's spirit denotes the direction in which one's vitality flows, the self-expression involved in one's behavior—including ecstatic behavior.

(d) *pneuma* is never used for that higher quality in a person that distinguishes him or her from animals. Rather, just as the wind comes from God and the human spirit is God's gift, spirit is essentially of God. About 100x it is expressly called the Spirit of God (e.g., Gen. 1:2) or of Yahweh (e.g., Isa. 11:2), while in 31:3 *spirit* is the power of God contrasted with the impotence of mere creatures; such power is inescapable and universally present (Ps. 139:7).

God's *pneuma* can come mightily on a person (Jdg. 14:6, 19; 1 Sam. 16:13–16), "clothe" someone (Jdg. 6:34), enter into someone (Ezek. 2:2), descend on someone (2 Ki. 2:9; Isa. 11:2), and impel someone (Jdg. 13:25). All these indicate the powerful operation of God on a person, enabling him or her to perform some supernatural deed (e.g., the salvation of Israel by the judges; Jdg. 3:10; 6:34; 11:29; 1 Sam. 11:6; 16:13), or the office and utterances of the prophets (Num. 11:25–27; 1 Sam. 18:10; Ezek. 3:12; 8:3; 11:1, 24). God's Spirit is also the source of poetic utterance (e.g., 2 Sam. 23:2), of the craftsman's skill involved in the building of the tabernacle (Exod. 31:3), or indeed of any outstanding ability (Dan. 6:3).

(e) Even destructive evil is a spirit sent by God, for, as far as the OT is concerned, there is no power of evil independent of him (1 Sam. 16:14–16, 23; Isa. 29:10).

3. The writing prophets have a clearly delineated doctrine of the Spirit. According to Isa. 32:15–20 (cf. 44:3), God will conclude his judgment of the proud and complacent by pouring out from on high his Spirit, which, like rain, will bring about fertility, i.e., righteousness, peace, and security. This salvation will be wrought by David's offspring (11:1–8), who, being ordained by God's Spirit, will exercise a dominion of perfect integrity and righteousness amid conditions of heavenly peace.

Through the process of judgment and salvation, God heals his people's idolatry and backsliding (Hos. 4:12; cf. Isa. 29:24), giving a new spirit of godliness not only to the nation at large (Ezek. 11:19–20; 18:31; 36:26–27; 39:29), but also to the individual (Ps. 51:10). Ezekiel declares this to be nothing less than Israel's resurrection from the dead—their death having been caused by unbelief (Ezek. 37:1–14, a vision which, as the whole prophecy indicates, refers to the restoration of God's people as a whole).

The later chapters of Isa. proclaim the same message: The servant of the Lord extends the blessings of his rule to include Gentiles (42:1–4; 49:1–6), the covenant promise being fulfilled in God's irrevocable gift of his Spirit (59:21; cf. Joel 2:28–29). Similarly in the past, the period of salvation at the exodus was marked by the gift of the Spirit to Moses; indeed, that whole national deliverance took place in the power of the Spirit (Isa. 63:11–14). The postexilic prophets see this promise fulfilled in the reestablishment of Israel in Jerusalem (cf. Hag. 2:5 = LXX 2:6; Zech. 4:6: "Not by might nor by power, but by my Spirit"). God's almighty, all-pervasive but intangible Spirit is linked with the covenant, for the latter reveals that God works not only for the salvation of his people but brings their lives into active conformity with his holy will.

4. In Jud. under the influence of its Hel. environment, *pneuma* was a vital force divinely breathed into humankind and forming a distinct part of one's being; it was not distinguished from the "soul" as far as terminology was concerned, but was contrasted rather with the body: The body is of the earth, the spirit stems from heaven (Wis. 15:11). In Palestinian Jud. the body was never the prison house of the soul or its seducer into sin. Philo, on the other hand, called the flesh a "burden," which weighed down *pneuma* and confined it in earthly fet-

ters; hence its appetites must be denied for the sake of the spirit. Palestinian Jud. also differed from its Hel. counterpart in regarding the spirit not as part of a divine substance but rather as something divinely created and therefore to be clearly distinguished from its Creator. It possessed immortality (12:1) and at a later stage was also credited with preexistence.

5. At Qumran, the spirit manifested its presence when a person conducted life wisely and with a view to pleasing God (1QS 5:21, 24), while apostasy of spirit led to sinful conduct (7:18, 23); in other words, *spirit* expresses the basic orientation of a person's life. We find references to a "broken" (8:3) or "apostate" (8:12) spirit; the word could also be used collectively of "the spirit of the fellowship of [God's] truth" (13:7–8). This spirit was either an eschatological gift or something eternally predestinated.

6. Although in the OT God is never said to dwell among spirits, this pl. came to be used throughout Jud. as a collective term for heavenly beings (e.g., *1 Enoch* 15:4, 6). "Spirits" (with or without the epithet "evil") also denoted the demons so familiar to Jud. (e.g., 15:6–10). Linked with this and found throughout apocalyptic lit. was the belief in Satan and his evil spirits, God's adversaries who tempt humans to sin.

The Qumran texts also developed the theory of two spirits, one of "righteousness" or "light," the other of "iniquity" or "darkness." As the principles of good and evil that God had established, these two are locked in perpetual conflict in this world (1QS 3:13–4:26). Each had a retinue of virtues or vices respectively, likewise described as spirits.

7. The "Spirit of God," the "divine Spirit," and the "holy Spirit" sometimes meant the God-given Spirit living in humans. But it esp. meant that spiritual reality that performed God's work on earth, e.g., creation (Wis. 1:7; 12:1) and esp. prophecy (Sir. 48:12). The rabbis believed this Spirit spoke in the Scriptures. Stress was laid on Isa.'s promise of a Messiah who would have a special endowment of the Spirit and on Joel's prophecy (Joel 2:28–29) about the pouring out of the Spirit on the godly in the last days.

NT *pneuma* occurs 379x in the NT. As in Jewish thought, it denotes the power that humans experience that relates them to the spiritual realm, the realm of reality that lies beyond ordinary observation and human control. Within this broad definition *pneuma* has a wide range of meaning. By far its most frequent reference is to the Spirit of God, the Holy Spirit (250x).

1. *The human spirit.* At one end of *pneuma*'s spectrum of meaning is the human spirit, or perhaps better, the human person insofar as he or she belongs to and interacts with the spiritual realm. In this sense *pneuma* occurs in the NT nearly 40x. Thus the human spirit is that aspect of a person through which God most immediately encounters him or her (Rom. 8:16; 1 Cor. 2:11; Gal. 6:18; Phil. 4:23; 2 Tim. 4:22; Phlm. 25; Heb. 4:12; Jas. 4:5), that dimension whereby human beings are most immediately open and responsive to God (Matt. 5:3; Lk. 1:47; Rom. 1:9; 1 Pet. 3:4), that aspect of human awareness most sensitive to matters of the spiritual realm (Mk. 2:8; 8:12; Jn. 11:33; 13:21; Acts 17:16; 2 Cor. 2:13; 7:13).

It is not clear whether the language refers to the spirit of a person, to a particular force that one experiences through this dimension of one's being, or to a spirit or power from without. Hence, scholars differ over certain passages as to whether the reference is to the human spirit or the Spirit of God (e.g., Mk. 14:38; Lk. 1:17, 80; Rom. 8:15; 11:8; 1 Cor. 4:21; 6:17; 14:14, 32; Gal. 6:1; Eph. 1:17; 4:23; 2 Tim. 1:7; Rev. 22:6).

The NT writers can speak of the (human) spirit as though it was something possessed by the individual, but this does not mean that they envisaged it as a divine spark incarcerated, as it were, in the physical body. This language is more a natural and easy way of speaking about the human person as he or she belongs to the spiritual realm and that relates one to the beyond (e.g., Lk. 8:55; Rom. 8:16; 1 Cor. 2:11;

5:5; 7:34; 16:18; 2 Cor. 7:1; 1 Thess. 5:23). Here too persists the ancient Hebraic idea of *pneuma* (*rûaḥ*) as the breath of God (2 Thess. 2:8; cf. Jn. 20:22), the breath of life (Rev. 11:11; 13:15).

So also death as a giving up of one's spirit (Matt. 27:50; Lk. 23:46; Acts 7:59) is to be interpreted not so much as the release of one's soul from the body but in terms of the physical body ceasing to be the embodiment of the whole person. At death a human being ceases to exist *both* in the realm of the physical *and* in the realm of the spiritual, and continues existing instead *only* in the spiritual; the physical body, ceasing to be the embodiment of the whole person in the observable world, becomes merely a corpse (Jas. 2:26). In Paul's terms, the danger confronting humans in the world is that they live *solely* on the level of the physical world ("according to the sinful nature [lit., flesh]") and not also and predominantly on the level of the spirit ("according to the Spirit," Rom. 8:4), so that when the body dies the whole person dies in the destruction of the flesh (cf. 1 Cor. 15:42–50), a danger Paul evidently seeks to counter in 1 Cor. 5:5.

From this it follows also that a dead person can be thought of simply as a *pneuma*, as belonging wholly to the spiritual realm (Lk. 24:37, 39; 1 Tim. 3:16; Heb. 12:23; 1 Pet. 3:18–19; 4:6). Paul also seems to have thought that a human being was able, while still in this life, to leave the body temporarily and project oneself through the spiritual realm into heaven (2 Cor. 12:2–4, though Paul did not know how to understand this experience) or into the presence of others (1 Cor. 5:3; Col. 2:5, though these two passages may simply be earnest expressions of empathetic concern and feeling).

2. *Evil spirits and good spirits.* (a) It was natural in the worldview of the 1st cent. that the mysterious powers that afflict people should be thought of as evil spirits and demons (more than 40x, mainly in the Synoptic Gospels and Acts; e.g., Matt. 8:16; Mk. 1:23, 26–27; Lk. 4:36; Acts 19:12–16; cf. 1 Tim. 4:1; Rev. 16:13–14; 18:2). The evil spirit can also be depicted as a spirit that dominates the world of humankind, the spirit or god of this world (1 Cor. 2:12; Eph. 2:2; cf. 2 Cor. 11:4; 1 Jn. 4:6). These evil forces are understood as personal forces from the spiritual realm, evil or unclean because they injure and hinder one's full relationship with God and one's fellow human beings.

But at no time do NT writers give way to a dualism, where the evil that thus manifests itself is as strong as God. Rather, the evil spirits are inferior to God and subject to the power of his Spirit operating through his agents (e.g., Christ and the apostles). Indeed, it was precisely this effective power over evil spirits in his ministry of exorcism that Jesus saw as proof that the end-time kingdom was already present, since it indicated that the final rout of Satan had already begun (e.g., Lk. 10:17–18; 11:19–20).

(b) Other forces operating on the human world from the spiritual realm are considered to be good spirits or angels (Acts 23:8–9; Heb. 1:7, 14; 12:9). But esp. Paul and John recognize the ambiguity of such experiences of spirits and the need for a discernment of spirits to distinguish good from evil (see 1 Cor. 12:10; 14:12; 2 Cor. 11:4; 1 Thess. 5:19–22; 2 Thess. 2:2; 1 Jn. 4:1, 3, 6).

3. *Jesus and the Spirit.* (a) If we are to understand Jesus' teaching on the Spirit as fully as possible, we must recall that his ministry follows that of John the Baptist. John is a prophet of judgment (Matt. 3:7–12; Lk. 3:7–9, 15–18); his proclamation centers on the imminent coming of one who will administer God's final judgment. In particular, the coming one will baptize "with the Holy Spirit and with fire" (3:16). The coming one's baptism is in some sense a promise to those who accept John's baptism of repentance.

John's metaphor about the baptism Jesus administers is perhaps best understood as a variation on a prominent theme within intertestamental apocalyptic expectation: the belief in the messianic woes, the conviction that the new age will be inaugurated only after a time of affliction and suffering (e.g., Dan. 7:19–22; *2 Bar.* 25–30). Thus "fire" denotes judgment and purification (e.g., Amos 7:4; Mal. 3:1–2; 4:1), as does *pneuma* (e.g., Isa. 4:4; Jer. 4:11–12), and the river or flood

vividly portray overwhelming calamity (Ps. 69:2, 15; Isa. 43:2). Notice how these three elements are combined in Isa. 4:4; 30:28; Dan. 7:10.

John's baptism in the Jordan (presumably by immersion) was a potent symbol of the end-time tribulation. Those who acknowledge their liability to judgment by submitting to John's baptism will experience the messianic woes as a cleansing by a spirit of judgment and by a spirit of burning (Isa. 4:4). Those who deny their guilt and do not repent will experience the coming one's baptism in Spirit and fire as the bonfire that burns up the unfruitful branches and chaff.

(b) Jesus' understanding of his mission in terms of the Spirit comes to clearest expression primarily at two places: his explanation for his success as an exorcist and his consciousness of inspiration. (i) Jesus' statements in Matt. 12:24–29; Mk. 3:22–29; Lk. 11:14–22 embody a claim to exorcise by God's power. In Matt. 12:28 ("But if I drive out demons by the Spirit of God, then the kingdom of God has come upon you"), the emphasis in the Gk. falls on two phrases: "Spirit of God" and "kingdom of God."

The significance of this saying is twofold. First, the presence of the kingdom of God (the distinctive note in Jesus' proclamation) is defined in terms of the effective power of the Spirit. The end-time rule of God can be said to be already operative, because the end-time power is evidently at work conquering demonic power. Second, Jesus is claiming a unique empowering by the Spirit. There were other exorcists, but their work did not bear the same significance (Matt. 12:27; Lk. 11:19). Jesus' exorcisms were so effective that he was able to conclude that his was the power of the end-time rule of God; he was beginning the final battle with Satan.

(ii) Jesus' consciousness of inspiration is clearly implied in his astonishingly authoritative claims ("But I tell you . . . ," Matt. 5:22, 28, etc.) and in his understanding of himself as a prophet (esp. 13:57; Mk. 6:4). Since the Spirit was principally regarded as the Spirit of prophecy in the Jud. of that time, Jesus' claim was in effect a claim to be inspired by the Spirit. And since the rabbis taught that the Spirit had been withdrawn from Israel since Malachi and would be given again only in the last days, Jesus was in effect claiming to be the eschatological prophet (see esp. Deut. 18:15, 18–19; Isa. 61:1–2). In fact, Jesus himself regarded Isa. 61:1–2 as fulfilled in his own ministry (Lk. 4:16–21). This understanding of his mission as a Spirit-anointed proclamation of good news to the poor is clearly implied in the first of the Beatitudes (Matt. 5:3–6; Lk. 6:20–21) and in Matt. 11:5; Lk. 7:22.

There are several key points here: Jesus attributed his ministry and its effectiveness to an anointing with the end-time Spirit (presumably at Jordan, as the Gospels affirm). Thus, in his ministry the hopes for the new age were already being realized; the Spirit was so bound up with Jesus that he himself was part of the offense of his own ministry (Matt. 11:6).

(c) Jesus thus also saw his ministry in relation to the Spirit in terms more of eschatological blessing than of judgment. His response to the Baptist in Matt. 11:5; Lk. 7:22 seems deliberately to pick up the promise of blessing in Isa. 29:18–19; 35:3–5; 61:1–2 and to ignore the threat of judgment in these three passages. But Jesus did not reject the Baptist's message outright, for he did see his ministry also in terms of dispensing fiery judgment (Mk. 9:49; Lk. 12:49–53), and the parallelism of 12:49–50 suggests that Jesus anticipated his own death as a fiery baptism, i.e., as a suffering of the messianic woes (cf. Mk. 10:38–39; 14:27, 36; cf. also Isa. 53; Dan. 7).

Did Jesus see himself as dispenser of the Spirit, as a baptizer in the Spirit? Note first how Lk. has "Holy Spirit" where Matt. has "good gifts" (Matt. 7:11; Lk. 11:13). Certainly Jesus saw his disciples as receiving the Spirit during times of persecution and trial (Mk. 13:11). Moreover, Jesus' words in Acts 1:5, 8 foretell his outpouring of the Spirit on the day of Pentecost. Finally, the Paraclete promises of Jn. 14–16 also refer to his dispensing of the Spirit to his disciples (e.g., 15:26; 16:7–11).

(d) The Gospel writers have no doubt that Jesus was the unique man of the Spirit. Jesus' conception was effected by the power of the

Spirit without the agency of a human father (Matt. 1:18–25; Lk. 1:35; cf. also Isa. 7:14). At the Jordan Jesus was anointed with the Spirit and thus entered his messianic role (Matt. 3:16; Mk. 1:10; Lk. 3:22; Jn. 1:33; cf. 3:34). Jesus also went forth to his temptations at the instigation of the Spirit (Matt. 4:1; Mk. 1:12; Lk. 4:1). Moreover, his ministry was effective by the power of the Spirit (see Matt. 12:18 [Isa. 42:1]; Lk. 4:18 [Isa. 61:1]; see also Acts 10:38). Jesus' post-resurrection ministry is also characterized in terms of the Spirit (1:2), with his outpouring of the Spirit explicitly referred to in Jn. 20:22 and Acts 2:33.

In Luke–Acts, Jesus, in his relation with the Spirit, provides a bridge between the old age of Israel and the new age now recognized as the age of the church. Thus the conception and birth of Jesus by the Spirit's power take place in the context of a sporadic reappearance of the Spirit of prophecy (Lk. 1:15, 17, 41, 67; 2:25–27), a last flare-up of the spiritual power and vitality of the divine revelation of the OT era before Jesus alone fills center stage. As a result of the descent of the Spirit on Jesus at his baptism, Jesus, already the Son of God (1:35; 2:49), enters a higher stage of his messianic mission as God's Son (3:22, citing Ps. 2:7; Acts 10:38). But only with his ascension does he enter the fullness of sonship and messianic office (2:36; 13:33), and only then does he become Lord of the Spirit, the one who dispenses the Spirit to others not only by virtue of his own anointing, but by virtue also of his death and exaltation (2:33).

4. *The Spirit in the earliest Christian communities and in Acts.* The Holy Spirit, through his supernatural power, works through and directs believers. This is nowhere more evident than in Acts, where the Spirit is presented as a tangible force, visible in its effects. This power of the Spirit manifests itself in three main areas in Luke's account of the early church.

(a) The Spirit is a transforming power in conversion. Christianity dates from the earliest experiences of the Spirit after Jesus' death and resurrection. Luke locates the outpouring of the Spirit in Jerusalem at the first Pentecost after Jesus' resurrection. It was a dramatic experience and ecstatic in nature (including visionary elements and prophetic speech). It transformed the disciples into a confident and dynamic group of believers, keen to propagate and live out their faith in Jesus as Messiah and as the returning Son of Man. In Acts 2–5 Luke has caught much of the atmosphere of excitement of these early days.

This first experience of the Spirit set a pattern for the reception of the Spirit thereafter (cf. Acts 11:15–16). The Spirit was the eschatological gift par excellence, and its possession was *the* mark of one who belonged to the messianic community of the last days (hence the promise of the Spirit as the climax to the first sermon of Peter, 2:38–39). Moreover, reception of the Spirit was indicated by the visible transformation of the individual, usually reckoned in manifestations of ecstasy, such as in prophecy and speaking in tongues (cf. 4:31). Consequently, at critical or problematic moments of the early mission, what was looked for above all else was the reception or possession of the Spirit (9:17; 11:15–16; 15:8; 19:1–2) as testified by clear-cut manifestations of spiritual power or ecstasy (8:15–19; 10:44–47; 19:6).

Luke links the Spirit with ecstatic manifestations to such an extent that the presence of the Spirit cannot be assumed in the absence of such tangible effects. Indeed, it is precisely their absence in the cases of the Samaritans in Acts 8:12–16 and the Ephesians in 19:1–5 that leads the apostles to conclude that the Spirit has not yet been given to them, and it is the obvious presence of the Spirit in Cornelius and his company (10:44–48) and Apollos (18:25) that proves that they *already* belong to the new Christian community (cf. 11:15–18).

(b) The Spirit is the Spirit of prophecy. For the earliest Christians, the Spirit was most characteristically a divine power manifesting itself in inspired utterances. The same power that had inspired David and the prophets in the old age (Acts 1:16; 4:25; 28:25) has now been poured out in all its fullness, as Joel had foretold (Acts 2:17–21; cf. Joel 2:28–32). Moses' ancient hope had been fulfilled, that all the Lord's people were prophets, that the Lord *had* put his Spirit on them (Num. 11:29;

cf. Acts 2:17–18, 38–39; 4:31). What indicated the coming of the Spirit was inspired utterance (2:4; 10:44–48; 19:6).

Beyond conversion, this power was experienced as a surge of inspiration in moments of crisis and relief, providing both words and boldness of speech (Acts 4:8, 13, 29–31; 7:55; 13:9). More generally the Spirit was understood as the power enabling effective testimony and teaching (5:32; 6:10; 18:25). But while this Spirit was given to all and all experienced his filling, there also arose a recognition that certain individuals had a fuller bestowal of the prophetic Spirit, or at least were more regularly inspired to prophesy—hence the appearance of both resident and wandering prophets in the earliest communities (11:27–28; 13:1; 15:32; 20:23; 21:4, 9–11).

The Spirit of prophecy, a gift known sporadically in the old age (Lk. 1–2), has become in the new age the prerogative of all ("and they will prophesy" in the Joel quotation in Acts 2:18). Luke does not link the Spirit specifically with any of the miracles performed in Acts (although such a link may be implied in 2:19, 43; 4:30–31; 6:8), perhaps because the link with prophecy is so dominant.

(c) The Spirit is the director of mission. The Spirit pervaded the early community and gave its early leadership an aura of authority that could not be withstood (Acts 4:31; 5:1–10; 6:10; 8:9–13; 13:9–11). With the movement out from Jerusalem after Stephen's death, the Spirit becomes much more regularly understood as the power of mission (cf. 1:8), directing the apostles and other believers into the new developments that continually opened up before them (8:29, 39; 10:19; 11:12; 13:2, 4; 15:28; 16:6–7). In this expansion visions also played a significant role (esp. 9:10; 10:3, 7, 10–16; 16:9–10; 22:17–18), though these are not specifically linked to the Spirit (despite 2:17).

In Luke's presentation this compulsion to mission and outreach characterized the earliest community's understanding of the Spirit from the first (cf. Acts 1:8; 2:5–11). So also the more formally structured leadership of presbyters or overseers is attributed specifically to the Spirit in 20:28 (cf. 15:28). However, the fundamental theological question as to the relation between the exalted Christ and the Spirit is not clarified: Christ introduces "the last days" by dispensing the Spirit (2:33), but thereafter the two are brought together only in the enigmatic reference to "the Spirit of Jesus" in 16:7.

5. *The Spirit in the Pauline letters.* Of the NT writers, Paul most deserves the title "the theologian of the Spirit," for he gives a more rounded and integrated teaching on the Spirit than we find in any other of the NT books or the apostolic fathers.

(a) The Spirit as the fundamental mark of belonging to Christ. As with the early church, so with Paul, the gift of the Spirit makes us members of Christ (Rom. 8:9; cf. 1 Cor. 2:12; 2 Cor. 11:4; 1 Thess. 4:8) and unites us with him (1 Cor. 6:17), so that we share in his sonship (Rom. 8:14–16; Gal. 4:6). The Spirit is, as it were, the exalted Lord's steward taking possession of his property on his behalf (1 Cor. 3:16; 6:19–20). It is the reception of the Spirit through faith that marks the beginning of the Christian life (Gal. 3:2–3), a gift that fulfills the promise to Abraham and is therefore another name for justification (1 Cor. 6:11; Gal. 3:14). Alternatively expressed, it is by being baptized in the one Spirit that individuals become members of the one body of Christ (1 Cor. 12:13).

For Paul it is precisely the gift of the Spirit that distinguishes Christian from Jew, the new age from the old (Rom. 2:29; 7:6; 2 Cor. 3:6–8; Gal. 4:29; Phil. 3:3). The Spirit constitutes that immediacy of personal relations with God that Moses had fitfully enjoyed (2 Cor. 3:13–18) and that Jeremiah had only foreseen from afar (3:3, referring to Jer. 31:33–34; cf. Eph. 2:18). In all this, "Spirit" is almost synonymous with "grace" in the sense of God's action in reaching out to us and establishing a positive relation with us (see, e.g., Rom. 3:24; 1 Cor. 15:10; 2 Cor. 6:1; Gal. 1:15; Eph. 2:8).

It is important to realize that for Paul too the Spirit is a divine power whose impact on a life is discernible by its effects. In some cases this manifestation was charismatic utterance and act (1 Cor. 1:4–7; Gal. 3:5), but in others it was evidently an overwhelming experience of being accepted by God (Eph. 1:7–8), of being swamped by divine love (Rom. 5:5), or of experiencing a joy that made light of affliction (1 Thess. 1:6). In still others it was an experience of illumination as to the significance of Jesus (1 Cor. 2:10–13; 2 Cor. 3:14–17; 4:6; Gal. 1:12, 15–16; cf. Eph. 1:17; 3:5), of liberation from the deadening effect of the law and of sin's power (Rom. 8:2; 2 Cor. 3:17), or of moral transformation dramatic in its suddenness (1 Cor. 6:9–11). The Spirit is like a seal affixed to goods or documents to indicate ownership (2 Cor. 1:22; Eph. 1:13; 4:30).

(b) The eschatological Spirit. As for Jesus so for Paul, the Spirit is the power of the new age that has already broken into the old, not to bring the old to an end or render it ineffective, but to enable believers to live in and through the old age in the power and in the light of the new. In Tit. 3:5 the Spirit is the power of regeneration and renewal poured out by Christ (cf. Jn. 3:5–8; Acts 2:33); he is also called the down payment and guarantee (→ *arrabōn*, 775) that God will complete the work begun in us through the Spirit (2 Cor. 1:22; 5:5; Eph. 1:13–14). The Spirit is the "firstfruits" of God's harvest at the end of time (Rom. 8:23), the first installment of the believer's inheritance in the kingdom of God (8:15–17; 14:17; 1 Cor. 6:9–11; 15:42–50; Gal. 4:6–7; 5:16–24).

This means also that (i) the gift of the Spirit is only the beginning of a lifelong process of being saved, of sanctification, of being conformed to the image of Christ (2 Cor. 3:18; 2 Thess. 2:13; cf. Rom. 8:28; 15:16; Gal. 6:8; Eph. 3:16–17).

(ii) Our lives in the present are characterized by a tension and even warfare between the old age and the new, between the desires of the flesh and those of the Spirit, between the powers of death and of life at work in us, each seeking to gain mastery over us (Rom. 7:14–25; 8:10–13; Gal. 5:16–17).

(iii) The final consummation of God's redemptive activity is the completion of what he has already begun in the gift of the Spirit and is achieved when the Spirit takes full control over the whole person, i.e., in the resurrection of the body, when we become spiritual bodies, wholly belonging to the new age, wholly like Christ, wholly under the Spirit's direction (Rom. 8:11, 23; 1 Cor. 15:44–49; 2 Cor. 5:1–5; Eph. 1:14).

(iv) Therefore, there is no foundation in Paul for a distinctively second or third gift of the Spirit, since the Spirit always has the essential character of that power that *begins* the process of salvation and carries it through to completion. Nor is there room in Paul for a gift of the Spirit in this life that sets the believer free from the eschatological tension and warfare between flesh and Spirit. On the contrary, the Spirit's activity in the present age is marked more by *hope* than by fulfillment or complete victory (Rom. 5:5; 8:18–25; 15:13; Gal. 5:5; Eph. 1:17–18), and prayer in the Spirit is at the same time the inarticulate groaning of this-worldly weakness (Rom. 8:26–27).

(c) Life in the Spirit. For Paul, believers have a responsibility to live in the power of the Spirit. In general terms that means we must be molded by God according to the pattern of Jesus Christ—not as something we achieve for ourselves, but as something that by attentive openness to God he allows the Spirit to produce through us ("fruit," 2 Cor. 3:18; Gal. 5:18–23; cf. Rom. 8:28; 9:1; 14:17; 15:13, 30; 2 Cor. 6:6; Gal. 6:1; Col. 1:8). In particular, it means that one's daily conduct is a walking or living by the Spirit, a being led by the Spirit, an ordering of one's life by the Spirit (Rom. 8:4–6, 14; Gal. 5:16, 18, 25; cf. Rom. 8:13; Gal. 6:8).

The apostle contrasts this experience of daily guidance with the sort of dependence on the rule book of the law that characterized his previous religious practice (Rom. 7:6; 2 Cor. 3:6; Gal. 5:16). That is to say, he experienced the Spirit precisely as the fulfillment of the prophetic hope that the law would be written on the heart, not just on tablets of stone, so that we will know God for ourselves and be able to discern his will immediately without having to refer to the Scriptures and the case-law of tradition (cf. Rom. 12:2; 2 Cor. 3:3; cf. Jer. 31:31–34). Similarly worship and prayer are not a matter of liturgical rote or outward form. Worship is characterized as worship in or by the Spirit of God (Rom. 2:28–29; Phil. 3:3; cf. Eph. 2:18, 22), and prayer as prayer in the Spirit (6:18).

(d) The charismatic Spirit. It is important for Paul that the Spirit is a shared gift; it is a centripetal force drawing believers together into the one body of Christ. Thus, on the one hand, the corporate life of Christians arises out of their shared experience of the Spirit. That is, they are constituted the one body of Christ by their common participation in the one Spirit (1 Cor. 12:13; 2 Cor. 13:14; Eph. 4:3–4; Phil. 1:27; 2:1). On the other hand, the existence and unity of a church depends on sharing that Spirit, who creates community by seeking to manifest himself in the gifts of grace that build up the community to full maturity in Christ (Rom. 12:4–8; 1 Cor. 12:14–26; 14:12, 26; Eph. 4:11–16).

For Paul these manifestations of the Spirit are given, not achieved; expressions of divine energy, not human talent; acts of service that promote the common good, not talents for personal edification or aggrandizement (cf. 1 Cor. 12:4–7). These spiritual gifts may be individual acts or utterances (e.g., Rom. 1:11; 1 Cor. 12:8–11; 14:26) or more regular ministries (e.g., Rom. 12:6–8; 1 Cor. 12:28; Eph. 4:11).

In 1 Tim. 4:1 the Spirit was the inspirer of prophecy in the period prior to these "later times." The Spirit also preserves tradition as well as leads into new truth (2 Tim. 1:14). But he esp. seeks to express himself today in prophecy, which builds up the church most effectively (Rom. 12:6; 1 Cor. 14:1–5, 13–19; see also 2:13–14; 7:40; 12:3), just as speech inspired by the Spirit is most effective to convict and convert the unbeliever. The importance Paul places on the gifts of the Spirit explains his concern lest they be restricted in their range or expression (Eph. 4:30; 5:18–19), but he is equally concerned lest they be abused by overemphasis on some or by failure to exercise critical discernment (Rom. 12:3; 1 Cor. 2:12–14; 1 Thess. 5:19–22).

(e) The Spirit of Christ. Most significant, the Spirit for Paul has been stamped with the character of Christ. Christ by his resurrection entered wholly upon the realm of the Spirit (Rom. 1:4; 8:11). He is mentioned in the liturgical formula of 1 Tim. 3:16 as the mode of Jesus' exalted life. Indeed, Paul can conclude that Christ by his resurrection became "a life-giving Spirit" (1 Cor. 15:45). That is to say, the exalted Christ is now experienced in, through, and as the Spirit. Christ cannot be experienced apart from the Spirit; the Spirit is the medium of union between Christ and the believer (6:17), so that those who belong to Christ have the Spirit and are led by the Spirit (Rom. 8:9, 14). Conversely, the Spirit is now experienced as the power of the risen Christ. It is the confession of Jesus' lordship that marks out that inspiration that is the Spirit's (1 Cor. 12:3).

It is precisely the reproduction of Jesus' own distinctive *Abba*-prayer that marks out the Spirit as the Spirit of the Son (Rom. 8:15–16; Gal. 4:6), and the transformation of the believer's character into the character of Christ marks out the eschatological Spirit (2 Cor. 3:18). The Spirit is now nothing less and nothing more than the Spirit of Christ (Rom. 8:9; Gal. 4:6; Phil. 1:19; cf. 2 Thess. 2:8). The more formless and impersonal power that characterized the Spirit in the old age has been given sharper definition and personality. Only that which makes an individual or the church more like Christ can claim fully to be an expression of the Spirit of Christ.

6. *The Spirit in the Johannine writings.* The Spirit is also of considerable importance in John's theology. (a) His understanding of the Spirit overlaps with that of other NT writers. In particular, the new life of the Spirit is presented through vigorous metaphors such as birth from above (Jn. 3:5–8; 1 Jn. 3:9), new creation (Jn. 20:22, the vb. echoing Gen. 2:7; Ezek. 37:9; Wis. 15:11), life-giving water and bread (Jn. 4:14; 6:63; 7:38–39), and anointing (1 Jn. 2:20, 27). In the Johannine letters as elsewhere in the NT the Spirit is detectable by the effects of his coming (Jn. 3:8), so much so that the immediacy of the Spirit's indwelling is one of the tests of life (1 Jn. 3:24; 4:13).

(b) More distinctive of John's theology of the Spirit is the way in which he expresses the relation between the Spirit and Christ.

(i) Although his Christology is high (Jesus as the incarnate Logos), John clearly mentions Jesus' being anointed with the Spirit at the Jordan (Jn. 1:32–33; 3:34).

(ii) He links Jesus' gift of the Spirit closely to Jesus' death, in that to receive the Spirit of the ascended Jesus is to eat his flesh given for the life of the world (Jn. 6:51–58, 62–63); it is the crucified Jesus who "gave up his spirit" (19:30), and it is Christ newly risen and ascended who bestows the Spirit on the disciples (20:22).

(iii) The unity of Christ and the Spirit in personality and mission is neatly expressed by identifying the Spirit as "another Counselor" (Jn. 14:16), where Jesus is by implication the first Paraclete (cf. 1 Jn. 2:1), so that the Paraclete continues the presence and work of the Son once he has departed (Jn. 14:16–28; → *paraklētos, 4156*) or, stated differently, that the Spirit becomes the seed of sonship, the Spirit of the Son (1 Jn. 3:9, 24; 4:13). As in Paul, the Spirit is conformed to Christ's character and work and only that Spirit that displays Jesus' character and testifies to him as the Christ can to be recognized as the Spirit of God (1 Jn. 4:1–3, 6; 5:6–8).

(c) The chief role attributed to the Paraclete is that of witness, revealer, and interpreter; this embraces both recalling the teaching originally given (Jn. 14:26; 15:26; 16:14; cf. 1 Jn. 5:6–8) and leading into new truth (Jn. 16:12–13; cf. Isa. 42:9; 44:7; 1 Jn. 2:27). That is, new revelation and original teaching are held in tension for John, so that the Spirit's role is never simply that of repeating the original teaching or that of revealing new truth unrelated to the old, but rather that of reinterpreting the old to give it contemporary significance and of revealing the new in a way that is consistent with the old. This balance between the freedom of present inspiration and the constraint of earlier revelation is present in the description of true worship in Jn. 4:23–24: As God is Spirit in his communion with us, so we must worship in the liberty of the Spirit and in accordance with his definitive revelation in Christ.

(d) Finally, we may note the Spirit's role in mission in Jn. 16:8–11. Together with 1 Cor. 14:24–25, this is the only passage that talks of the Spirit's role in convicting of sin. Note that for John the chief sin is failure to recognize the real significance of Jesus, that he has conquered the prince of this world. But when people respond to the Spirit-inspired mission of the disciples, their sins are forgiven (Jn. 20:22–23).

7. *The Spirit in other NT writings.* The Spirit is not as prominent in the rest of the NT. (a) Heb. recalls the charismatic vitality of the early Christian mission (2:4), and conversion is still understood as sharing in the Spirit and in the illumination and eschatological powers by which he manifests himself. The statements of 3:7; 9:8; 10:15 reflect the traditional view of the Spirit as the inspirer of Scripture, which is thus the voice of the Spirit. More distinctive is the fierceness of the warning that the new relation of grace can be so abused that the Spirit of grace can be lost (6:4–8; 10:29), and the author's assertion that Christ was enabled to offer himself up in death by the power of the eternal Spirit (9:14).

(b) Jas. 4:5 is not at all clear. To what Scripture does James refer? Is he referring to the human spirit as the breath of God, as in ancient Heb. thought (cf. Gen. 6:3; Job 33:4), or of the divine Spirit as given in conversion, as more regularly in the NT?

(c) Peter's understanding of the Spirit is typical of the NT: the Spirit of prophecy (1 Pet. 1:11), the inspirer of mission and the power of the gospel (1:12), the power that sets us apart for God (1:2) and changes us into the image of God's glory through suffering and persecution (4:14), the mode of existence in life beyond death (3:18; 4:6). In 2 Pet. 1:21 one encounters a view of inspiration that involves the prophets' complete surrender of mind and will to the overpowering Spirit.

(d) Jude 19–20 is Pauline in character: Believers are those who by definition have the Spirit, whereas those who boast of their spirituality give evidence of their lack of spirituality (cf. 1 Cor. 2:12–3:4). Jude alone outside Paul's letters exhorts his readers to pray in the Spirit (cf. 1 Cor. 14:15; Eph. 6:18).

(e) The seer of Rev. attributes his inspiration and visions to the Spirit (1:10; 4:2; 14:13; 17:3; 21:10; 22:17) and writes to the seven churches at the Spirit's dictation (2:7, 11, 17, 29; 3:6, 13, 22). The author is probably referring to the Spirit of God under the symbolism of the seven spirits (1:4; 4:5), esp. as he implies they form the Spirit of the exalted Jesus (3:1; 5:6). Perhaps his most interesting reference is to "the testimony of Jesus" as "the spirit of prophecy" (19:10), presumably an affirmation that prophecy must be understood in relation to Jesus Christ. Note also 11:11, where *pneuma* is the breath of resurrection life, a divine power that the antichrist tries to ape in order to deceive (13:15).

8. *Spiritual. pneumatikos*, the adj. formed from *pneuma*, conveys the sense of belonging to the realm of spirit/Spirit and embodying or manifesting spirit/Spirit. Within the NT it is almost exclusively a Pauline word (though cf. 1 Pet. 2:5). More than half of the occurrences of this word are in 1 Cor. Where the word is introduced at key points in that letter (2:13–3:1; 12:1; 14:1, 37; 15:44–46), Paul may be both taking over and reformulating the language of his opponents, thus meeting the challenge of what may be characterized as an incipient Gnosticism expressing a perfectionist spirituality.

Paul uses the word in three ways. (a) As an adj., a spiritual something. Whatever gift (*charisma*) Paul shares with the Romans will be spiritual, from the Spirit and expressing the life and power of the Spirit (Rom. 1:11). The law is spiritual in the sense that it derives from the Spirit (i.e., given by revelation and inspiration) and was intended to achieve a fruitful encounter between the divine Spirit and the human spirit (7:14). The resurrection body is spiritual in that it embodies the Spirit (1 Cor. 15:44, 46). The spiritual (body) does not precede the natural; rather, the spiritual (body) succeeds the natural (body). It is in some sense a re-creation of the natural, and so is not yet (→ *psychē*, soul, *6034*). According to Eph. 1:3, the blessings are spiritual in that they derive from the Spirit and take their character from the Spirit (cf. also 5:19; Col. 1:9; 3:16; 1 Pet. 2:5).

In 1 Cor. 10:3–4, *pneumatikos* is best understood as a midrash with allegorical elements (cf. 2 Cor. 3:7–18; Gal. 4:22–31). The "rock" that accompanied the people in the wilderness in a Jewish legend is interpreted as equivalent to Christ in his presence with his people; the manna and water from the rock are to be taken as pictures of the Christian's supernatural sustenance. In this case *pneumatikos* is used in a slightly extended sense, almost equivalent to "allegorical" (cf. also 1 Pet. 2:5; Rev. 11:8, where *pneumatikōs* denotes a spiritual reality or conveys a spiritual meaning).

(b) As a masc. noun, spiritual person. Both Paul's opponents and the apostle himself claim that some Christians are "spiritual" and others are not—i.e., some are possessed by and manifest the Spirit of God more than others (1 Cor. 2:13, 15; 3:1; 14:37; Gal. 6:1). But whereas for Paul's opponents this higher spirituality is marked out by superior wisdom and speech and divisive self-concern, for Paul the spiritual person is marked out by love and concern for others, by a lack of self-conceit and envy, and by an ability to distinguish what is loving from what is merely lawful, what is of God from what is merely inspired, what is for the benefit of the whole community from what merely edifies the individual (1 Cor. 2:13–15; 14:37).

(c) As a neut. noun, spiritual things. In Rom. 15:27 and 1 Cor. 9:11 "spiritual [things]" denotes the whole range of activities, attitudes, experiences, etc. that ultimately depend on and derive from the Spirit and that draw their significance from the Spirit—in contrast to the merely material or to those activities, attitudes, etc., that derive from the sinful human nature (→ *sarx*, flesh, *4922*) and draw their significance from what is merely physical and worldly. In 1 Cor. 12:1; 14:1 (and probably 2:13) *pneumatika* is used in a more restricted sense with reference to spiritual gifts, more or less equivalent to *charismata*. Of the two words the latter seems to be Paul's preferred choice (cf. Rom. 1:11; 12:6; 1 Cor. 1:7). His use of *pneumatika* in Eph. 6:12 in reference to evil spirits confirms that *pneumatika* is more ambiguous than *charismata* in Paul's mind and underlines the ambiguous nature of "spiritual things" that necessitates that discernment (1 Cor. 2:13–15; 14:37).

9. *Other words used in connection with the Spirit.* (a) The noun *pnoē*, wind, occurs in the description of the "violent wind" as a manifestation of the Spirit at Pentecost (Acts 2:2). The account recalls the moving of God's Spirit over the waters in creation (Gen. 1:2), and possibly the wind that preceded God's speaking to Elijah (1 Ki. 19:11). In both cases the movement of the wind precedes the utterance of the word of God. In Acts 17:25 *pnoē* means breath (cf. Gen. 2:7) in the proclamation that the God who made all things does not live in shrines and "is not served by human hands, as if he needed anything, because he himself gives all men life and breath and everything else."

(b) The cognate vb. *pneō* occurs in the parable of the houses built on the rock and the sand, signifying the day of reckoning (Matt. 7:25, 27), in the saying about the south wind (Lk. 12:55), in the account of the storm (Jn. 6:18; cf. Acts 27:40), in the vision of the four winds held back by the angels (Rev. 7:1), and in the description of the movement of the Spirit that humans cannot discern (Jn. 3:8).

(c) *ekpneō* means to breathe out, breathe one's last, expire (Mk. 15:37, 39; Lk. 23:46).

(d) *empneō* means to breathe on and is used fig. of Saul's threats of murder against the disciples of the Lord (Acts 9:1).

(e) Using *theopneustos*, God-breathed, inspired by God, Paul writes in 2 Tim. 3:16–17: "All scripture is God-breathed [*theopneustos*] and is useful for teaching, rebuking, correcting and training in righteousness, so that the man of God may be thoroughly equipped for every good work." The adj. *theopneustos* does not imply any particular mode of inspiration, such as divine dictation, nor does it imply the suspension of the human authors' normal cognitive faculties. Yet it is something different from mere poetic inspiration. The sacred Scriptures express the mind of God, but they do so with a view to their practical outworking in life.

4461 (pneumatikos, spiritual), → *4460.*

4462 (pneumatikōs, spiritually), → *4460.*

4463 (pneō, to blow), → *4460.*

4464 (pnigō, strangle), → *4465.*

4465	πνικτός

πνικτός (*pniktos*), strangled (*4465*); ἀποπνίγω (*apopnigō*), strangle (*678*); πνίγω (*pnigō*), strangle (*4464*); συμπνίγω (*sympnigō*), strangle (*5231*).

CL & OT *pnigō* and related vbs. mean strangle, choke, cause choking, harass; in the pass. they mean drown. The adj. *pniktos*, strangled, means steamed, stewed. In the LXX this word group is rare (1 Sam. 16:14–15; Nah. 2:12); *pniktos* does not occur.

NT 1. In the story of the demoniac at Gerassa the herd of pigs *drowned* in the lake (Mk. 5:13; Lk. 8:33). In the parable of the sower thorns *choked* the seed (Matt. 13:7; Mk. 4:7; Lk. 8:7). The unforgiving servant *choked* his fellow servant to force him to pay his debt (Matt. 18:28), while in Lk. 8:42 we are told hyperbolically that the multitude *choked* Jesus ("the crowd almost crushed him").

2. The adj. *pniktos* is of theological importance in Acts 15:20, 29; 21:25. The context is a command about food, which the Jewish Christians imposed on Gentile Christians and which is closely linked to the prohibition against eating blood. The command goes back to Lev. 17:13–14 and Deut. 12:16, 23. An animal should be so slaughtered that its blood, in which is its life, should be allowed to drain out. If the animal is killed in any other way, it has been "strangled." The reason behind the prohibition was possibly that among the heathen, animals were often killed by being strangled, especially in the sacrificial cultus. Presumably such customs are here being forbidden.

4466 (pnoē, wind, breath), → *4460.*

4472	ποιέω

ποιέω (*poieō*), do, make (*4472*); ποίησις (*poiēsis*), doing, working, deed (*4474*); ποίημα (*poiēma*), what is made, work, creation (*4473*); ποιητής (*poiētēs*), one who does something, maker, doer (*4475*).

CL & OT 1. In cl. Gk. *poieō* is the basic term for all activity, both of gods and of human beings. Regarding the gods, the word can take on the meaning of to create, generate, give shape to. Human doing and making can refer to any kind of activity. The noun *poiēsis* means both directed action and the manufacture of objects. *poiēma* denotes the finished work. It is executed by a *poiētēs*, a doer, an author (also a poet).

2. The LXX *poieō* can occur as an independent vb. (e.g., Exod. 30:25), but it is also used many times to help formulate a thought with a determinative noun: e.g., to do the commandment (Jos. 22:5), to do work (Exod. 20:9–10), to do good or evil (Ps. 34:14; Jer. 2:13), to make peace (Isa. 27:5), to construct an idol (44:9; 46:6).

(a) As far as God's work is concerned, the Heb. uses both ʿāśâ and bārāʾ (this latter word is used exclusively for the work of Yahweh, esp. creation). Both can be translated by *poieō* (e.g., Gen. 6:7), though *ktizō* (→ *ktisis*, creation, *3232*) is often used for *bārāʾ*. But Yahweh also acts in history, esp. directing the fortunes of his people Israel. He does wonders (Exod. 15:11; Jos. 3:5), makes the days (Ps. 118:24), and does great things (Job 5:9).

(b) The use of *poieō* for human actions branches out in many directions. It can simply denote what a person does (e.g., Abraham holds a feast, Gen. 21:8; Jacob will work for Laban, 30:31), but also obedience to God's will and law (e.g., Deut. 29:29 = LXX 29:28; Ps. 40:8; Isa. 44:28). The pious Jew recognized in his or her deed the required seriousness of moral or cultic acts.

NT 1. In the NT *poieō* occurs 568x, mostly in the Gospels. (a) The NT reaffirms the OT statements of God as Creator (e.g., Mk. 10:6; Acts 4:24; Rev. 14:7). *poiēma* (Rom. 1:20; Eph. 2:10) means the works of God's creation and new creation. NT statements concerning God's activity of salvation history also belong here. The NT writers speak confidently of God's mighty historical acts (e.g., Rom. 4:21; 1 Thess. 5:24; Rev. 21:5).

(b) The loving dealings of God are revealed in Jesus' work and deeds (e.g., Acts 2:22). Again and again the question crops up as to the motivation, justification, and significance of Jesus' work. He fully performed the will and the works the Father gave him as Son to do (Jn. 5:19; 6:38; 8:53; 10:37–38). According to Eph. 2:14–15, Jesus' work consisted in "making peace" between God and humankind by his death on the cross. The author of Heb. also describes Jesus' saving work with *poieō*. He "provided purification for sins" (1:3) and "sacrificed for . . . sins once for all" (7:27). According to Rev. 1:6 and 3:12, believers are "made" kings and priests, and pillars in the future temple of God.

2. (a) Purely secular human activity is not particularly stressed in the NT, though *poieō* can be used for various activities (e.g., Mk. 11:3, 5; Jn. 19:12; Acts 9:39; Jas. 4:13).

(b) More decisive is the assessment of human action in God's sight. Human work is never neutral; it is either obedience or disobedience before (1 Cor. 10:31). This expectation is expressed emphatically in Jesus' parables (e.g., Matt. 5:36; 20:11–15; 21:31; Lk. 12:17–18). Human actions are subject to Jesus' claim to lordship (cf. Lk. 6:46; Jn. 7:17). They reveal their worth when they are performed in love for one's neighbor (Matt. 25:40, 45). Because of the central significance of such actions, there is a frequent summons in the gospel of Jesus and the apostles to put God's word into practice (Matt. 7:24–26; Jn. 14:12; Phlm. 21).

(c) The discourses of Jn.'s Gospel stress right action, grounded in the Lord (13:15) and made possible by his Spirit. Without Christ believers can "do nothing" (15:5). Jn. 8:34–44 deals with the contrasting attitude in committing sin, which is of the devil and does not stem from God and his truth. In 1 Jn. 2:29 (cf. 2:17; 3:7–10; 5:2), the author emphasizes the imperative of right action.

3. (a) As to *poiētēs*, the NT calls us to be doers of the word and the law (Rom. 2:13; Jas. 1:22, 23, 25). Only Acts 17:28 uses this noun in the secular Gk. sense of poet.

(b) *poiēsis* occurs only in Jas. 1:25. For a discussion of two Gk. words that combine *agathos*, good, and *poieō*, → *agathos* (19).

See also *ergazomai*, work, be active (2237); *prassō*, accomplish, do (4556).

4473 (*poiēma*, what is made, work, creation), → *4472*.

4474 (*poiēsis*, doing, working, deed), → *4472*.

4475 (*poiētēs*, one who does something, maker, doer), → *4472*.

4477 (*poimainō*, to herd, tend), → *4478*.

4478   ποιμήν

ποιμήν (*poimēn*), shepherd (*4478*); ποίμνη (*poimnē*), flock (*4479*); ποίμνιον (*poimnion*), flock (*4480*); ποιμαίνω (*poimainō*), to herd, tend (*4477*); ἀρχιποίμην (*archipoimēn*), chief shepherd, over-shepherd (*799*).

CL & OT 1. (a) In cl. Gk. *poimēn*, herdsman, shepherd, is a word that is frequently used in fig. senses: leader, ruler, commander, even lawgiver. *poimainō* means to be a shepherd, tend; fig., to care for. *poimnē* or *poimnion* is the herd, esp. a flock of sheep. Plato calls attention to the religious use of the word when he compares the rulers of the city-state to shepherds who care for their flock.

(b) In the ANE, shepherd at an early date became a title of honor applied to divinities and rulers alike, both in Sumerian king lists and in Babylonian texts. The custom seems to have been followed throughout antiquity. Pastoral terminology was much in vogue throughout the Hel. world.

2. (a) Before Israel settled in Canaan, various ethnic groups depended on constant wandering with their herds and flocks. The patriarchs (cf. also Job) were nomads who owned sheep and goats along with cattle. The shepherd's task was undertaken preferably by family members, by daughters only in the immediate vicinity of the dwelling (cf. Exod. 2:16). The shepherds and the servants who worked with them were expected to show caution, patient care, and honesty. In the dry summer on poor soil it was not easy to find new pasture as the flocks passed through lonely regions or to balance properly grazing, watering, rest, and travel. The shepherd had to care tirelessly for these animals (cf. Ezek. 34:1–6). Devotion to duty was proved in the nightly guarding of the flock against wild animals and thieves. In this respect hired shepherds frequently disappointed their employers.

(b) By *poimnion* the LXX means a herd of small livestock, esp. a flock of sheep (cf. Gen. 29:2–3; 30:40). In NT times such a herd would consist of from 20 to 500 animals (Lk. 15:4 refers to 100 sheep). Sheep and goats grazed together but were separated in the evening, for the goats spent the night in the center of the pen or the walled enclosure, where it was warmer (cf. Matt. 25:32).

(c) Even after the occupation of Canaan the raising of livestock played a dominant role, alongside cultivation, as a means of earning a living. Still, the memory of the classical nomadic days of ancient Israel before the occupation, when the people lived as aliens in tents, remained alive, because God's activities in salvation history were bound up with it. For this reason the Levites did not receive any arable land at the occupation but remained herdsmen (Jos. 21). The sect of the Recabites held fast in prophetic times to the pastoral way of life as an example (Jer. 35).

3. (a) Yahweh is the only shepherd of his people, Israel (see Gen. 48:15; 49:24). In certain Psalms and prophetic writings, the fig. idea of the shepherd comes into great prominence (e.g., Ps. 23; 78:52–53; 80:1; 95:7; Isa. 40:10–11; 49:9; Jer. 23:2; 31:10; Ezek. 34:11–12; Mic. 4:6–7; 7:14). The acknowledgment that Yahweh was Israel's shepherd grew out of the living religious experience of the people and is thus to be distinguished from the cold courtly style of the ANE. In

invocation, praise, and prayer for forgiveness, but also in temptation and despair (Ps. 73), worshipers knew that they were safe in the care of God, the faithful shepherd. At the same time the recognition of God's unlimited sovereignty over his flock is not absent. Rather, it coexists in creative tension with the overwhelming consciousness of God's spontaneous love.

(b) The people are Yahweh's flock (cf. Ps. 79:13; 95:7; 100:3; Isa. 40:11; Jer. 13:17; Ezek. 34:31; Mic. 7:14; Zech. 10:3). As God's chosen people, Israel applied the metaphor of Yahweh's flock only to themselves. Sir. 18:13 is the sole instance of the metaphor being applied universally to all people, who at the end of time will be gathered together into one flock.

The shepherd theme is also applied to Israel's leaders (e.g., to David in 2 Sam. 5:2; 1 Chr. 11:2; Ps. 78:71–72). But by and large, in the light of God's faithfulness, they failed as shepherds. The prophets denounced the political and military shepherds in unquestionably negative terms; these had all failed because of their arrogance and disobedience to God (cf. Isa. 56:11; Jer. 2:8; 3:15; 10:21; 22:22; 23:1–5; 25:34 = LXX 32:34; 50:6 = LXX 27:6; Ezek. 34:2–10; Zech. 10:3; 11:5–6).

In Isa. 44:28 God calls Cyrus, king of Persia, "my shepherd." In accordance with God's will, he was concerned for the well-being of the returning exiles and the rebuilding of Jerusalem and of the temple. In a different manner Jer. 25:34–38 threatens the shepherds, the rulers, of the foreign nations with judgment and destruction (cf. Nah. 3:18).

4. When national disaster was breaking loose, the title of shepherd suddenly appeared as a designation of the future Davidic Messiah. At first the references were to "shepherds" (pl.), but these prophecies pointed to the figure of a single shepherd (Jer. 3:15; 23:4; Ezek. 34:23; 37:24). This figure of a future messianic ruler remained mysterious. The shepherd, described as Messiah or David, was particularly emphasized in postexilic times in Zech. 13:7 (cf. 12:10).

5. Intertestamental Jud. drew distinctions between shepherds. After the exile the Pharisaic rabbis prompted a striking devaluation of the shepherd occupation in Palestinian Jud. According to their writings, in a time of poor pay, shepherds were suspected of dishonesty. The pious were forbidden to buy wool, milk, or meat from them. At Qumran, however, the Overseer of the Camp functioned as a shepherd with his sheep (CD 13:7–9).

NT 1. *poimēn* occurs 18x in the NT; *poimnē* and *poimnion* each 5x; *poimainō*, 11x. Jesus' contemporaries despised the shepherd, but this view is not taken over into the NT. Rather, the shepherd's devotion to duty is painted in glowing colors (cf. Lk. 15:4–6; Jn. 10:3–4; cf. Matt. 18:12–14). Jesus used the metaphor to glorify God's love for sinners and to reveal his opposition to Pharisaic condemnation of them (cf. Lk. 15:4–6). Only in Lk. 2:8–20 do actual shepherds play a role in the NT; elsewhere they appear only in parables and figures of speech.

2. The Synoptic parable of the lost sheep speaks of God as shepherd (Matt. 18:12–14; Lk. 15:4–7). The shepherd's joy at finding a lost sheep after an anxious search is compared to God's joy over one repentant sinner in contrast to ninety-nine supposedly righteous people. Elsewhere Jesus is the messianic shepherd promised in the OT, referred to in three ways.

(a) Jesus begins to fulfill this messianic role by gathering the lost sheep of the house of Israel (Matt. 9:36; 10:6; 15:24; cf. Lk. 19:10 with Ezek. 34:15). This marks the dawning of the era of salvation announced by the prophets. Jesus is the ruler of Israel, promised in Mic. 5:3–5, who gathers the shepherdless flock (Matt. 2:6; 9:36; Mk. 6:34; cf. Ezek. 34:5). But this does not mean any abandonment of the nations, for he is also the universal shepherd (cf. Jn. 10:16).

(b) But Jesus must first die for his flock and rise again (Matt. 26:31–32; Mk. 14:27–28). Jesus takes up the words of Zech. 13:7 and claims to be the promised shepherd anticipated in the OT, the shepherd whose representative death ushers in the time of salvation (cf. also Isa. 53).

(c) The era of salvation during which the flock, the people of God, is gathered under the good shepherd reaches its climax in the day of judgment. When all the nations are gathered around his glorious throne, Jesus will separate the sheep from the goats (→ *probaton*, sheep, *4585*). He will sit in judgment, an event that will bring to an end the era of world mission, in which, since his death and resurrection, his flock has been called together from out of every nation (Matt. 25:32).

3. (a) The good shepherd of Jn. 10:1–30 is contrasted with both the thief and the stranger. The shepherd enters through the door; his sheep know him and follow him willingly. In typically Johannine fashion the unique relationship between this shepherd and his flock is expounded—a relationship elsewhere expressed in other metaphors (e.g., the vine and the branches in Jn. 15).

This relationship is made possible by the shepherd's voluntary laying down of his life, the special contribution of Jn. 10 to the theme of Jesus as shepherd (esp. 10:17–18). The hireling will not do this, for he flees in the hour of danger. The links with the OT are obvious (cf. Ezek. 34). Most scholars see Jesus' statements in the light of the OT background.

(b) As the shepherd stands for their Lord (→ *kyrios*, *3261*), so the flock (*poimnē*, Jn. 10:16), the sum total of his sheep, stands for his people. This is one of several powerful images Jn. uses in his Gospel for the church. The risen Christ gathers his flock like a "good shepherd" (10:10–11). They know him as he knows them, and no one can snatch them out of his hand (10:27–28). Jesus unites all his followers, including Gentiles, into one great flock (10:16).

4. In Paul's speech to the elders at Ephesus, he juxtaposes *poimainō* and *poimnion* with *ekklēsia* (Acts 20:28). In his letters, however, he uses the shepherd theme only twice: in 1 Cor. 9:7, where he compares his claim on the church for hospitality with the shepherd's claim on the produce of his flock, and in Eph. 4:11, where he refers to certain church leaders as "pastors" (see below).

Peter, however, looks back to the image of the shepherd and his flock (1 Pet. 2:25); Jesus is "the Shepherd and Overseer" of human souls. Later Peter exhorts the elders to "be shepherds [*poimainō*] of God's flock." That is, they are not to be self-seeking masters over the Christian community, but examples of service to it, so that they may pass the test when Jesus, the chief shepherd (*archipoimēn*), appears (5:3–4). In Heb. 13:20 Christ is the "great Shepherd" who, in accordance with the theme of the letter, has surpassed all prototypes, including Moses himself. According to Rev. 7:17, "the Lamb" (*arnion*; → *amnos*, sheep, *303*) will be the shepherd of his flock, and the sheep will gladly follow him (cf. 14:4).

5. In the list of church leaders in Eph. 4:11 we find the phrase "pastors [*poimēn*] and teachers [*didaskalos*, → *didaskalia*, teaching, *1436*]." Since *pastor* is by no means an official title yet, the emphasis here is on function, not on title. Pastors are to care for the spiritual welfare of the flock (Jn. 21:15–17; Acts 20:28; 1 Pet. 5:2–4) as well as seek the wandering and lost (cf. Matt. 12:30; 18:12–14; Lk. 11:23). In these cases the leaders have to prove themselves worthy examples to the flock. This is the background of Peter's appointment to pastoral office by the risen Christ to "take care of [*poimainō*] my sheep" (Jn. 21:16), a passage that suggests a special responsibility given to Peter for the whole flock, the whole church.

See also *amnos*, sheep (*303*); *probaton*, sheep (*4585*).

4479 (*poimnē*, flock), → *4478*.

4480 (*poimnion*, flock), → *4478*.

4482 (*polemeō*, make war, fight), → *4483*.

4483	πόλεμος

πόλεμος (*polemos*), war, battle, fight, strife, conflict, quarrel (*4483*); πολεμέω (*polemeō*), make war, fight (*4482*); στρατεία (*strateia*), expedition, campaign (*5127*); στράτευμα (*strateuma*), army, detachment, troops (*5128*); στρατεύομαι (*strateuomai*), serve

as a soldier (*5129*); στρατηγός (*stratēgos*), general, chief magistrate, praetor (*5130*); στρατιά (*stratia*), army (*5131*); στρατιώτης (*stratiōtēs*), soldier (*5132*); στρατολογέω (*stratologeō*), gather an army, enlist soldiers (*5133*); στρατόπεδον (*stratopedon*), camp, body of troops, army (*5136*); ἑκατοντάρχης (*hekatontarchēs*), centurion (*1672*); κεντυρίων (*kentyriōn*), centurion (*3035*); μάχαιρα (*machaira*), sword (*3479*); μάχη (*machē*), battle, fighting, quarrels, strife, disputes (*3480*); μάχομαι (*machomai*), fight, quarrel, dispute (*3481*); Ἁρμαγεδών (*Harmagedōn*), Armageddon (*762*); Γώγ (*Gōg*), Gog (*1223*); Μαγώγ (*Magōg*), Magog (*3408*); ὅπλον (*hoplon*), weapon (*3960*); ὁπλίζω (*hoplizō*), equip, arm (*3959*); πανοπλία (*panoplia*), full armor, panoply (*4110*); θώραξ (*thōrax*), breastplate (*2606*); θυρεός (*thyreos*), shield (*2599*); περικεφαλαία (*perikephalaia*), helmet (*4330*); βέλος (*belos*), arrow, dart (*1018*); ῥομφαία (*rhomphaia*), a large, broad sword (*4855*); παρεμβολή (*parembolē*), fortified camp, barracks, army in battle array, battle line (*4213*); παρεμβάλλω (*paremballō*), throw up a palisade (*4212*).

CL & OT Note that the basic cl. Gk. definitions are given in the NT section.

1. The works of Homer testify to the close link between war and the rule of the gods in the ancient world, though it is an open question whether one can speak of gods of war. True, Hesiod reports how Athene rejoiced in war and battle. But Ares, the so-called god of war, was never elevated to the status of an Olympian deity. Alongside the glorification of heroism in war is a detestation of the lack of fidelity that causes war through breach of a treaty. More championed than war was peace; note how the great *pax Romana* instituted by Augustus led to emperor worship.

2. War was a common experience in the OT. Israel, like the surrounding nations, knew few periods of real peace, and the OT is filled with accounts of war from Gen. 14 to 2 Ki. 25. The main theological interest of the OT centers on God's role in war. Deut., Jos., Jdg., and Sam. describe Yahweh, the divine warrior (cf. Exod. 15), taking the initiative and instructing his people on how to participate for what has been called "holy war." They are to prepare themselves as they would for worship, and they are to take neither booty nor prisoners. For Yahweh's role in war, note the common phrase used of the exodus: "with a mighty hand and an outstretched arm" (e.g., Deut. 5:15; 1 Ki. 8:42; Ps. 136:12).

The practice of holy war ceased during the reign of David. With the consolidation of the state and the established authority of the king, war changed more to a defensive rather than an offensive mode in the promised land. While the practice of holy war changed, the ideas that had supported it did not die. The view of God as the divine warrior (cf. Ps. 24:8) continued in the title "Lord of hosts." Yahweh was the commander of all the supernatural powers as well as the armies of Israel.

Prophets were consulted before joining battle (cf. 1 Ki. 20; 22). They also spoke about Yahweh's control of world politics. God would judge the nations through wars that he controlled and used (e.g., Isa. 13–23; Jer. 46–51; Ezek. 25–32; Amos 1–2). The prophets challenged Israel's right to continue claiming the status of holy war. They even announced that Yahweh, the divine warrior, would direct battles against Israel and bring about their downfall (cf. Amos 2:6–16).

Israel's relation to war changed after the exile. Except for the brief Hasmonean period of independence after 165 B.C. and the revolts against Roman rule in A.D. 70 and 132, there was no opportunity for military experience. But the ideology of the divine king and warrior did not fade. Yahweh ruled the powers of heaven and exercised authority over those of history. With the birth of apocalyptic thinking, holy war and the concept of the divine warrior came into their own again, depicting God's triumph over all his enemies on behalf of his people.

The theology of war played a great role in the Qumran community, as evidenced by the War Scroll, a work that draws inspiration from Dan. 11:40–12:3 and describes the eschatological battle between the "sons of light" (the Qumran community) and "the sons of darkness, the army of Satan" (1QM 1:1). The two sides are evenly matched, but by God's intervention, the wicked are vanquished.

NT 1. *polemos* means war, battle; fig. strife, conflict, quarrel. (a) It stands for a single battle in Rev. 9:7, 9; 12:7; 16:14; 20:8. In 1 Cor. 14:8 Paul asks: "If the trumpet does not sound a clear call, who will get ready for battle?" The context is a discussion of speaking in tongues (cf. 14:6), and he uses this and other illustrations to describe unintelligibility, which has no practical value to the hearer. Tongues are useless if there is no interpreter (cf. 14:11–12, 23–24, 27–28).

(b) Heb. 11:34 alludes to great military events in Israelite history, describing people who through faith "became powerful in battle and routed foreign armies" (e.g., Joshua in Jos. 6:1–27; Gideon in Jdg. 6:15–7:25). Victory was in the last analysis the work of Yahweh (1 Sam. 14:6), and the battle was his (2 Chr. 20:15). One man could therefore put a thousand to flight and two ten thousand (Deut. 32:30; Jos. 23:10).

(c) Jesus foretells wars and rumors of wars in his eschatological discourse (Matt. 24:6); they precede the final judgment. This theme is also taken up by Rev., where war is made on the saints (11:7; 12:17; 13:7). Among the features of the ultimate conflict in Rev. is the battle at Armageddon (16:16), a transliteration of the Heb. *Har Magedōn*, the mountains of Megiddo (cf. Zech. 12:11; 14:2). The gathering of the kings here takes up the picture of Ezek. 38–39 with its reference to Gog and Magog (cf. also Rev. 20:7–10), where Gog is the prince of Magog. Jewish apocalyptic writers use Gog as a term for the nations generally, who combine in assault on Israel. But the enemies of God's people will be destroyed by fire from heaven, and the devil will be thrown into the lake of fire with the beast and the false prophet.

(d) *polemos* is used in the fig. sense of strife, conflict, quarrel in Jas. 4:1: "What causes fights [*polemos*] and quarrels [*machē*] among you? Don't they come from your desires that battle [*strateuomai*] within you?"

2. (a) The cognate vb. *polemeō* means to fight, make war (Rev. 2:16; 12:7; 13:4; 17:14; 19:11). These passages possess strong symbolic overtones, and the subject can be either the opponents of the church or believers, the Spirit of Christ or the exalted Christ. *machomai* is used in the lit. sense of fight (between two persons) in Acts 7:26 (cf. Exod. 2:11–15; fig., *theomachos* means one who fights against God, Acts 5:39).

(b) *polemeō* is used of disputes among Christians in Jas. 4:2. *machomai* is also used fig. in this verse (see also Jn. 6:52).

3. *strateia* means an expedition or campaign, though in 2 Cor. 10:4 it means warfare: "The weapons [*hoplon*] we fight with [lit., of our warfare, *strateia*] are not the weapons of the world. On the contrary, they have divine power to demolish strongholds." The picture is that of a siege engine attacking an embattled position. Paul's opponents had evidently accused Paul of operating in a worldly way (cf. 1:17), whereas they themselves were "spiritual" (cf. 1 Cor. 3:1). Paul turns the tables on his opponents, implying that pseudo-spirituality is an obstacle to the knowledge of God.

The cognate vb. *strateuomai*, do military service, serve as a soldier, occurs in 2 Cor. 10:3. Both the noun *strateai* and the vb. occur again in 1 Tim. 1:18, where Timothy is urged to fight the good fight. God is presumably the commander-in-chief.

4. In addition to 2 Cor. 10:4, *hoplon*, weapon, also occurs in Rom. 13:12: "The night is nearly over; the day is almost here. So let us put aside the deeds of darkness and put on the armor [*hoplon*] of light." This mixed metaphor picks up the twin ideas that armor is worn during the daytime when battles were fought, implying that the Christian is to take the offensive and also that the Christian should wear armor appropriate to the light, in contrast to darkness. In 2 Cor. 6:7 Paul speaks of "the weapons [*hoplon*] of righteousness" in the context of a discussion of Christian virtues and attitudes in the face of adversity. *hoplon* is used lit. of weapons in Jn. 18:3; in Rom. 6:13 it means a tool.

The cognate vb. *hoplizō* is used in 1 Pet. 4:1: "Therefore, since Christ suffered in his body, arm yourselves also with the same attitude." Christians are to follow Christ who has died, is risen, and has ascended (3:18–22). We belong to him and thus to a different way of life from the ungodly (cf. 3:13–17; 4:2–7).

5. (a) In 1 Cor. 9:7 Paul asks rhetorically: "Who serves as a soldier [*strateuomai*] at his own expense?" Along with other analogies, Paul is demonstrating that Christian workers have a right to be supported by the church. In 2 Tim. 2:3–4 the same imagery occurs in an exhortation to single-hearted devotion: "Endure hardship with us like a good soldier [*stratiōtēs*] of Christ Jesus. No one serving as a soldier [*strateuomai*] gets involved in civilian affairs—he wants to please his commanding officer [*stratologeō*]." The vb. *strateuomai* is used of the Christian struggle against "sinful desires, which wage war [*strateuomai*] against your soul" (1 Pet. 2:11).

(b) Elsewhere *stratiōtēs* occurs in the lit. sense for Roman soldiers (e.g., Matt. 8:9; 27:27; 28:12; Acts 10:7). *strateuma* means an army (Rev. 19:14, 19), a detachment (Acts 23:10, 27), and troops (Matt. 22:7; Lk. 23:11; Rev. 9:16). *stratēgos* is used both for the chief magistrates in the Roman colony of Philippi (e.g., Acts 16:20, 22) and the captain of the temple (Lk. 22:4, 52; Acts 4:1; 5:24). *stratia*, army, is used for the heavenly host of angels (Lk. 2:13) and the host of heaven as an object of idolatrous worship (Acts 7:42). *stratopedon* means lit. a camp, and then a body of troops, an army (Lk. 21:20).

6. The Roman centurion (an officer in charge of a hundred soldiers) generally appears in a positive light in the NT. Two main words are used: *hekatontarchēs* (e.g., Matt. 8:5, 8, 13; Acts 10:1, 22; 27:1, 31) and the transliterated *kentyriōn* (Mk. 15:39, 44–45). Note Jesus' comment about the centurion at Capernaum: "I tell you, I have not found such great faith even in Israel" (Lk. 7:9). This man had drawn an analogy between his own authority and that of Jesus and felt unworthy to receive Jesus under his roof. The Jews, by contrast, sought signs and argued with Jesus. The comment of the centurion by the cross, "Surely this man was the Son of God" (Mk. 15:39), likewise stands in marked contrast with that of the chief priests and teachers of the law (15:31–32).

7. *parembolē* means a camp, esp. a fortified camp (e.g., Exod. 29:14; Lev. 4:12, 21). It has this sense in Heb. 13:11, 13, where the author alludes to Lev. 16:27 and draws an analogy to the crucifixion of Jesus outside Jerusalem. The present Jerusalem is no "enduring city" (Heb. 13:14); it is in fact a "camp" (13:13). It is therefore better to suffer rejection with Christ and be part of the true pilgrim people of God. Elsewhere *parembolē* means the barracks or headquarters of the Roman troops in Jerusalem (Acts 21:34, 37). *paremballō* means to throw up a palisade and is used in Jesus' pronouncement of judgment on Jerusalem (Lk. 19:43).

8. Various weapons and items of armor are mentioned in the NT, esp. in connection with defense against spiritual attack. The breastplate as "faith and love" and the helmet as "the hope of salvation" (1 Thess. 5:8) are elaborated in Eph. 6:10–17 in a comprehensive description of the Christian's warfare and weapons in the fight against the supernatural powers of evil. The "full armor [*panoplia*] of God" is needed in order to stand against the devils' schemes (6:11).

The loins are to be girded with truth (Eph. 6:14). The breastplate (*thōrax*) is the metal breastplate that protects the soldier's chest. To Paul it is either righteousness (6:14) or faith (1 Thess. 5:8). In view of the link between righteousness and faith, the same piece of armor can be viewed from complementary perspectives, for righteousness is the gift of God appropriated by faith. Eph. 6:15 speaks of the believer's feet being "fitted with the readiness that comes from the gospel of peace." The "shield [*thyreos*] of faith" is designed to quench "the flaming arrows [*belos*] of the evil one" (6:16). For the Roman soldier, this shield had an iron frame and several layers of leather soaked in water that would extinguish any flaming arrows. Finally, the believer must take "the sword [*machaira*] of the Spirit, which is the word of God" (6:17). The word of God comes from the Holy Spirit and is the weapon he provides.

machaira occurs 29x in the NT (e.g., Matt. 10:34; 26:47; Acts 12:2; Heb. 4:12; Rev. 6:4). It denotes a short sword, in contrast to the *rhomphaia*, which denotes a large, broad sword (see Rev. 1:16; 2:12). The latter is used lit. in 6:8; 19:15, 21 and fig. for anguish and pain in Lk. 2:35. Heb. 4:12 speaks of the word of God as "sharper than any double-edged sword [*machaira*]." Jesus' response to the disciples in Lk. 22:38 about two swords is no doubt ironical. His initial remark about going out to buy a sword (22:36) is probably an intimation of what is about to take place. The sudden appearance of two swords may suggest that some of the disciples had links with the zealots or at least were ready to resort to arms. The words, "It is enough," may imply that that is enough of that kind of talk.

| 4484   πόλις |

πόλις (*polis*), city, city-state (*4484*); πολίτης (*politēs*), citizen (*4489*); συμπολίτης (*sympolitēs*), fellow citizen (*5232*); πολιτεύομαι (*politeuomai*), be a citizen, take part in government, live, conduct one's life (*4488*); πολιτεία (*politeia*), rights of a citizen, commonwealth, state (*4486*); πολίτευμα (*politeuma*), commonwealth, state, colony, citizenship (*4487*); πολιτάρχης (*politarchēs*), politarch, civic magistrate (*4485*).

CL & OT 1. (a) In cl. Gk. *polis* means a city, state, and *politēs* a citizen. *politeuomai* means to be a citizen or administer the state. The abstract noun *politeia* means citizen's rights, the condition or way of life of citizenship, also civil policy, constitution. The closely related noun *politeuma* had originally the same meaning. It was then used for individual political acts or measures, or for the constitution and acts of public administration. Still later the word meant political commonwealth or the state generally.

(b) The development of the city-state in Greece is a typically Gk. phenomenon. The rule of warrior kings was effective primarily during times of war. There arose an increasing desire for concentration of the political will in individual, overseeable territories or districts. In the 8th and 7th centuries B.C. there arose a large number of settlements, mostly dependent on those already in existence. The concentration of political life within the new framework enabled the nobility, as the assistants of the king, to strengthen their own power and finally to supplant the monarchy. During the period that followed, the city-state or *polis* became the expression of Gk. culture, to which the free citizen gave total allegiance. This formation of independent city-states hindered the unification of larger areas of the Gk. mainland. But with the rise of the Macedonians and the spread of their superstate, the ancient *polis* came to an end.

2. (a) In the LXX *polis* occurs about 1,600x, in most cases meaning city (e.g., Gen. 4:17; 10:11–12; 11:4–5, 8) or town (e.g., Jos. 15:9, 13, 15–16). In Israel the city had a different function from the *polis* in Greece. Israel's constitution was tribal, which distinguished them from the Canaanite city-states with their monarchy. In the OT, therefore, every fortified height could be called a "city." The city afforded its inhabitants protection against enemies and enabled them to withstand attackers. Often cities are spoken of when the inhabitants are meant. Thus the city was to a considerable extent, as in Greece, a community of persons (cf. 1 Sam. 4:13; Isa. 40:9).

(b) Of particular importance as a city is Jerusalem. It is sometimes referred to simply as "the city" (Ezek. 7:23). Yahweh has chosen it (2 Chr. 6:38) and makes his name dwell there (cf. Deut. 12:5; 14:23). Prayers and sacrifices may be offered there. Jerusalem is the "city of God" (cf. Ps. 46:4; 48:1, 8; 87:3), the "city of the Great King" (48:2), the "holy city" (cf. Isa. 48:2; 52:1). When its citizens did not live up to the character God expected, prophets called them to repentance (e.g., Ezek. 22:2–4). In latter days a new Jerusalem, more in keeping with its original calling, is expected (Isa. 1:26; 32:18; Jer. 31:38 = LXX 38:28; Joel 3:17).

3. The nouns derived from *polis* are found primarily in the books of Macc. (a) *politēs* generally denotes one's neighbor (e.g., Prov. 11:9, 12; 24:28 = LXX 24:43; Jer. 31:34 = LXX 38:34). In the sense of citizen, it occurs only at 2 Macc. 9:19; 3 Macc. 1:22. (b) *politeia* (9x in 2–4 Macc.) usually means devout way of life (2 Macc. 8:17; 4 Macc. 17:19); in 3 Macc. 3:21, 23, citizens' rights. (c) *politeuomai* always means to live in a certain manner (Est. 8:12; 2 Macc. 6:1; 11:25; 3 Macc. 3:4; 4 Macc. 2:8, 23; 4:23; 5:16). (d) *politeuma* occurs only at 2 Macc. 12:7, where it means community.

NT In the NT *polis* is found 162x: in Luke, 39x; Acts, 42x; Matt., 27x; and Rev., 27x. It always means city, in the sense of an enclosed settlement or its inhabitants (Matt. 8:34; 21:10; Mk. 1:33). The distinction between it and *kōmē*, village (27x), often disappears. In keeping with OT and Jewish usage Jerusalem is called the "holy city" (Matt. 4:5; 27:53; Rev. 11:2). This city kills the prophets (Matt. 23:37) and Jesus (Rev. 11:8; cf. Lk. 13:33). Her downfall is certain (Matt. 24:2–25; Lk. 21:6–24).

1. (a) Over against the "present city of Jerusalem" stands "the Jerusalem that is above," the free Jerusalem, the mother of Christians (Gal. 4:25–26; → *parabolē*, *4130*, for comments on allegory and typology here).

(b) Heb. esp. contrasts the present and the future Jerusalem. Even the patriarchs knew of this new city and set their hope on it. Compared with it all earthly cities are temporary tent-camps. For the sake of this coming city the patriarchs regarded themselves as strangers and aliens (11:10, 16). This city is "Mount Zion" and "the city of the living God" (12:22). It awaits the Christians, who have here no continuing city (13:14; cf. Rev. 3:12; 22:14). The earthly Jerusalem is only a copy and a shadow (Heb. 8:5; 10:1) or an "illustration" (9:9) of the city that is to come and that is already present in heaven. In this new city those who conquer in times of persecution have citizens' rights (Rev. 3:12). The new Jerusalem will come down on the new earth (21:2, 10–27).

2. *politēs*, citizen, occurs only 4x in the NT. It has political emphasis only in Acts 21:39, where Paul says that he is a citizen of Tarsus. Perhaps Paul was born at Tarsus, where his father, liberated, became a Roman citizen. The other instances of *politēs* occur at Lk. 15:15; 19:14; Heb. 8:11 ("neighbor," quoting Jer. 31:34).

3. *sympolitēs*, fellow citizen (Eph. 2:19), indicates that Gentile Christians share through Christ in the calling of Israel, God's people, as fellow-citizens.

4. *politeia* in Acts 22:28 reflects on the Roman citizenship of Paul. In Eph. 2:12 it means the privileged position of Israel in salvation history, to which Gentile Christians now have access by faith in Jesus Christ.

5. *politeuma* occurs only at Phil. 3:20, where Paul contrasts Christians with those who are "enemies of the cross of Christ" (3:18): "But our citizenship [*politeuma*] is in heaven. And we eagerly await a Savior from there, the Lord Jesus Christ." This translation stresses *politeuma* as the present status of the believers. Others, however, → *politeuma* as reflecting a political entity (i.e., a city) that keeps its citizens on a register. Note that the second half of the verse requires a place to be meant here, in order to make sense of the remark that "from there [or it]" we await a Savior. It is also significant that Philippi was a Roman military colony directly under Rome's control. As Roman subjects, the Philippian Christians owed allegiance to the far-off capital city of Rome. At the same time, they had "another king, one called Jesus" (Acts 17:7). Hence, on earth they were resident aliens, living in a foreign country but with their capital and homeland elsewhere (cf. Jas. 1:1; Heb. 11:13; 1 Pet. 1:1; 2:11).

6. *politeuomai* is found only at Acts 23:1 and Phil. 1:27, where (as in LXX) it means to walk or live in a way in keeping with the faith.

7. *politarchēs* is a civic magistrate, a politarch. In Macedonian cities and occasionally elsewhere, a number of politarchs formed the city council. There were five or six in Thessalonica before whom the Jews dragged Jason (Acts 17:6, 8), accusing him of harboring "these men who have caused trouble all over the world" and "defying

Caesar's decrees." But the politarchs dismissed the charge, thereby putting the Jews in a bad light and the Christians and authorities in a good one. Yet to keep the peace, they required (through a bond posted by Jason) that Paul and Silas had to leave the city.

See also *dēmos*, people, populace, crowd, popular assembly (*1322*); *ethnos*, nation, people, pagans, Gentiles (*1620*); *laos*, people (*3295*); *ochlos*, (throng of) people, crowd, mob (*4063*).

4485 (*politarchēs*, politarch, civic magistrate), → *4484*.

4486 (*politeia*, rights of a citizen, commonwealth, state), → *4484*.

4487 (*politeuma*, commonwealth, state, colony, citizenship), → *4484*.

4488 (*politeuomai*, be a citizen, take part in government, conduct one's life), → *4484*.

4489 (*politēs*, citizen), → *4484*.

4498 πολύς	πολύς (*polys*), much, many; often in the pl. (*polloi*), the many (*4498*).

CL & OT *hoi polloi* in secular Gk. means the most, the majority. But in the LXX it often represents the Heb. *rabbîm*, which tends to mean "all." Hence while the Gk. use drew a distinction between a majority as contrasted with a minority, Heb. use is capable of an inclusive meaning, denoting the many individuals forming a totality (cf. Deut. 7:1; 15:6; 28:12; Isa. 52:14–15; Ezek. 39:27).

Used in this way, *rabbîm* in the OT occurs with *ʿammîm* or *gôyîm* of non-Israelite peoples. Many peoples stream to Zion to come under God's protection and enter his service (Isa. 2:2–5); the Servant of God bears the sins of the many (53:11–12).

NT The interpretation of this word in the NT depends on its grammatical position. Three usages may be distinguished.

1. As a noun with the art. *hoi polloi* is twice used with the meaning of "the most" (Matt. 24:12; 2 Cor. 2:17). Elsewhere the phrase has the summarizing meaning of the OT (cf. "many" in Mk. 6:2, where Lk. 4:22 has "all"; similarly Mk. 9:26).

In Rom. 5:15–21 "the many" in the sense of "all" are contrasted with the one who puts an end to the dominating power of sin and death. Just as through one man (Adam) sin and death came to all, so also through one individual man, Jesus, righteousness and life was brought to all. That *hoi polloi* has here a summarizing meaning can be seen from the context (cf. 5:15 with 5:12 and 1 Cor. 15:22, which have *pantes*, meaning all; cf. Rom. 5:19 with 5:18, which has *pantes*). In addition, the section has clear references to Isa. 53:11–12, which makes an interpretation in the Heb. sense more likely. Paul contrasts here the totality of Adam's descendants with the totality of believers. He leaves an open question here whether the totality of believers will ever include the whole of humankind.

Rom. 12:5 and 1 Cor. 10:17a speak of the many (*hoi polloi*) as being one body in Christ, referring to all the members of the church (cf. *pantes* in 1 Cor. 10:17b; 12:13). In Heb. 12:15 the reference to "many" suggests that the whole congregation might be defiled through the bitterness of some.

2. As a noun without the art. The question arises whether *polloi* without the art. or used as an adj. is used with a summarizing meaning in the sense of "all." The question is important in cases like Matt. 22:14, "Many are invited, but few are chosen"; Mk. 10:45 (Matt. 20:28), "The Son of man [came] . . . to give his life as a ransom for many"; Mk. 14:24 (Matt. 26:28), "This is my blood of the covenant, which is poured out for many"; Heb. 9:28, "Christ was sacrificed once to take away the sins of many people."

It is doubtful whether *polloi* has the summarizing meaning in Matt. 22:14. The many who have come together to hear God's word are in fact called, but their mere presence is no guarantee that they are

the chosen for the world to come. Therefore, the "many" here means a majority in contrast with the "few," a minority who have true fellowship with God (cf. 7:21–23). The other passages, however, do reflect the summarizing meaning, for they all look to Isa. 53, where "the many" means all the nations of the world. Jesus, the Servant of God, gives his life as a ransom for all and sheds his blood for the reconciliation of the whole world (cf. *hoi polloi* in Heb. 12:15). This does not imply, however, that all people have in fact been reconciled to God through Christ.

3. As an adj. In Rom. 5:16 and Lk. 7:47 *polloi* is linked with sins and transgressions. In Rom. 5:16 a summarizing meaning may be deduced from the context: God's free gift of grace covers not only the majority of transgressions but all of them in bringing justification. The Gk. of Lk. 7:47 says lit.: "Her sins, the many, are forgiven." This implies the totality: "All her sins—and they are many—are forgiven."

See also *pas*, all (*4246*).

4499 (*polysplanchnos*, sympathetic, compassionate), → *5073*.

4503 (*poma*, a drink), → *4403*.

4504 (*ponēria*, evil, badness, wickedness), → *4505*.

4505 πονηρός	πονηρός (*ponēros*), sick, bad, evil (*4505*); πονηρία (*ponēria*), evil, badness, wickedness (*4504*).

CL & OT 1. In cl. Gk. *ponēros* and *ponēria* are often used as synonyms of *kakos* and *kakia*. In a pass. sense it designated something laden with toil, full of suffering, unfit, miserable. The act. force is also found in the sense of bad, causing disaster, dangerous, esp. in the political and social arena, where it describes an enemy of the state. This leads to the moral concept of ethically reprehensible, bad.

2. In the LXX *ponēros* frequently represents Heb. *raʿ* (→ *kakos*, 2805), evil, bad, of little value. When used of animals it can mean dangerous, harmful (Gen. 37:20). It can also mean damaging to a person's reputation (e.g., Deut. 22:14) or evil in relation to the human spirit (e.g., 1 Sam. 16:14–16). Ethically *ponēros* means evil, worthless, depraved, corrupt, whether of persons (cf. Gen. 13:13; Isa. 9:17) or of things (cf. 3:9). Like *kakos*, *ponēros* has not merely a moral but also a religious connotation. It implies separation from and opposition to God and his will (Amos 5:14–15). In contrast to the NT, the LXX never uses this word to denote the devil. The expression "good and evil" (*kalos kai ponēros*) in Gen. 3:5, 22 means in the widest sense everything.

The noun *ponēria* shares many of the meanings of the adj. Unlike *kakia*, which can refer to the harm or calamity that God brings on humanity (e.g., Isa. 45:7; Jer. 2:3), *ponēria* and its cognates are restricted to the evil that humans do against God or their fellow human beings (Jdg. 11:27; Neh. 6:2).

NT 1. *ponēros* is used 78x in the NT. It is used physically of the eyes in Matt. 6:23 and Lk. 11:34. It is probably used here in an ethical sense, but even if it refers to sickness of the eye, the parable intends for us to understand it in a metaphorical sense. In Matt. 18:32 *ponēros* refers to worthless servants. It is used of trees and useless fruit in 7:17–18.

2. *ponēros* is used ethically in the sense of being opposed to God. (a) Jesus uses it as an adj. of humans in general, whom he calls evil (cf. Matt. 7:11 par.). God alone is good (cf. Mk. 10:18). The Pharisees were evil in the sense of being hardened (Matt. 12:34), just as the Jews were the evil generation (12:39; 16:4; Lk. 11:29), who showed their character in their opposition to Jesus. Anyone who decides against Jesus is evil (cf. 2 Thess. 3:2; 2 Tim. 3:13). Out of the evil treasure of one's heart one brings forth evil (Matt. 12:35 par.).

Thoughts too can be evil (Matt. 15:19). In Col. 1:21 and 2 Tim. 4:18 it is used with *ergon* ("work, deed" [→ *2237*]) to denote evil human actions. *ponēros* can also be used in connection with boasting, words, insults, conscience, the name of Christian (Lk. 6:22), the present age (Gal. 1:4), and the present day (Eph. 6:13). John's contrast of *ponēros* with God's light, work, and word is particularly striking (Jn. 3:19; 17:15; 1 Jn. 2:13; 3:12; 5:18–19; 2 Jn. 11; 3 Jn. 10).

(b) When used as a noun, *ponēros* has a double meaning. (i) It can mean a bad person (e.g., Matt. 5:39; 22:10). Matt. 13:49–50 states that in the final judgment the *ponēroi* will be separated out by God and condemned (cf. 22:13–14). The church should exclude the evil person from its midst (1 Cor. 5:13). But the goodness of God is available even for the evil as long as they live on earth. Hence Christians should show them love (Lk. 6:35).

(ii) *ho ponēros*, standing absolutely, is the evil one (i.e., Satan; see Matt. 13:19 [note par. Mk. 4:15, Satan; Lk. 8:12, the devil]; cf. also Jn. 17:15; Eph. 6:16). It is used noticeably often in 1 Jn. (cf. 2:13–14; 3:12; 5:18–19). Interpreters are divided over the meaning of this expression in the Lord's Prayer (Matt. 6:13b): "Deliver us from the evil one" (NIV) or "deliver us from evil." Arguments pro and con are equally divided among scholars. If 6:13a refers to protection against the testing of God through false prophets and false saviors, then we must understand *ponērou* in 6:13b as masc. It is a prayer to be snatched out of this power.

See also *kakos*, bad, evil (*2805*).

4506 (*ponos*, hard labor, toil, distress), → *3160*.

| *4513* πορεύομαι | πορεύομαι (*poreuomai*), go, to journey, to travel, to walk (*4513*); |

τρέχω (*trechō*), run, move quickly (*5556*); συντρέχω (*syntrechō*), run together (*5340*); δρόμος (*dromos*), course, race (*1536*); πρόδρομος (*prodromos*), running before, forerunner (*4596*).

CL & OT 1. In cl. Gk. *poreuomai*, to go, journey, travel, march, denotes by contrast with *peripateō* (→ *4344*) going in a particular direction or with a particular intention. It is rarely used fig. (e.g., traveling along the path of life). *trechō* means to move quickly, run, esp. at a contest in a stadium. This vb. is also found in statements that express effort or achievement in respect of mental and spiritual matters.

2. In the LXX *poreuomai* occurs some 750x, chiefly for Heb. *hālak*, to go. (a) It often has the lit. sense of journeying, traveling (e.g., Gen. 12:4–5; Deut. 1:19, 33). It can take on the fig. sense of following (i.e., obeying) someone (e.g., of David following God, 1 Ki. 14:8). It can also denote departure from life (2:2), and in later times the journey to Sheol or Hades (e.g., Job 10:21; 16:22 = LXX 16:23; Eccl. 9:10).

(b) This vb. often stands in the LXX in the fig. sense of way of life (e.g., 1 Ki. 3:14), esp. in the characteristic combination with *hodos*, way. To travel in the "ways of God" (i.e., his commandments; e.g., Deut. 8:6; 10:12; Jer. 7:23), can also be called "walking before God" (1 Ki. 8:25). Other phrases and terms can also modify *poreuomai*, such as "the law of the LORD" (Ps. 119:1), "righteousness" (Isa. 33:15), and "truth" (Prov. 28:6).

(c) *trechō*, to run, occurs 60x in the LXX, mostly for lit. running (e.g., Gen. 18:7; 1 Ki. 18:46). It does appear in a fig. sense for living according to God's commands (e.g., Ps. 119:32), taking delight in lies (62:4), and for "running the course toward immortality" (4 Macc. 14:5).

NT 1. *poreuomai* occurs 153x in the NT. (a) It mostly has the lit. sense of to go (e.g., Matt. 28:19; Lk. 7:8), travel, journey (e.g., 9:53). In 22:22 it means going in the sense of dying; in Jn. 14:2–3 it denotes Jesus' departure to return to the Father (cf. also Acts 1:10–11). It can also mean departing into the eternal fire at the final judgment (Matt. 25:41).

(b) *poreuomai* rarely has the sense of walking in the commandments and regulations of the Lord (cf. Lk. 1:6; Acts 9:31; for this, *peripateō* is usually used). In 1 Pet. 4:3; 2 Pet. 2:10; 3:3; Jude 11, 16, 18 the vb. occurs in statements concerning a bad way of life.

2. *trechō*, to run, occurs in the NT in the lit. sense, including those running to or from the empty tomb (e.g., Matt. 28:8; Lk. 24:12;

Jn. 20:2, 4). In 2 Thess. 3:1 it is used of the word of the Lord spreading rapidly. Paul usually uses this vb. in a fig. sense to express how the Christian life as a whole is directed toward a goal (Gal. 2:2; 5:7; Phil. 2:16). Using an athletic analogy, Paul stresses that what matters most is applying maximum effort and holding out to the end (1 Cor. 9:24–26; cf. Heb. 12:1). But he also points out that when all is said and done it is not our "effort" (running) but God's mercy that counts (Rom. 9:16). *syntrechō*, run together, occurs in Mk. 6:33; Acts 3:11 (of people); 1 Pet. 4:4 (fig. of people plunging together into debauchery).

3. (a) In 2 Tim. 4:7 Paul uses *dromos*, race, fig. for his career and work as an apostle. In Acts 13:25, it refers to the course of John the Baptist's life and in 20:24 to the complete course of Paul's ministry. (b) *prodromos*, forerunner, occurs only at Heb. 6:20, where Jesus is seen as a forerunner, having become a high priest forever and having entered the inner sanctuary, i.e., the immediate presence of God, on our behalf. As a priest after the order of Melchizedek, Jesus belongs to an order superior to that of the Levitical priests, who as mortals had to perform the rite annually.

See also *anastrephō*, to overturn, turn back, turn round; fig. behave, conduct oneself, live (*418*); *hodos*, way, road, highway, way of life (*3847*); *peripateō*, go about, walk (*4344*).

4518 (*porneia* unchastity, prostitution, immorality), → *4519*.

| *4519* πορνεύω | πορνεύω (*porneuō*), practice prostitution or sexual immorality |

(*4519*); πόρνη (*pornē*), prostitute (*4520*); πόρνος (*pornos*), immoral person, fornicator (*4521*); πορνεία (*porneia*) unchastity, prostitution, immorality (*4518*).

CL & OT 1. *porneuō* means (trans.) to prostitute. It is usually used in the pass. for a woman: to prostitute oneself, become a prostitute. But it is also used of the man, meaning commit sexual immorality. *pornē* means a woman who is for sale, a prostitute; *pornos*, one who has sexual intercourse with prostitutes, also an immoral man, male prostitute; *porneia*, prostitution, unchastity (including homosexual activity).

This word group describes various extramarital sexual modes of behavior insofar as they deviate from accepted social and religious norms (e.g., homosexuality, promiscuity, pedophilia, and esp. prostitution). Cultic prostitution was often included as part of ancient fertility rites, under the belief that performance of sexual intercourse in the sanctuary would ensure the fertility of everything living in the land and prevent the loss of the procreative and generative faculties. Evidence of cultic prostitution is first found in Babylon. Noncultic sexual activity outside of marriage, such as with one's own slave girls and with prostitutes, was accepted in many cultures in the ANE.

2. The *pornē* word group in the LXX generally stands for the Heb. *zānâ*, to engage in prostitution, whereas *moicheuō*, to commit adultery (→ *3658*), regularly represents *nā'ap*. (a) Prostitution was not unknown in Israel, though in the beginning it does not appear to have been considered a serious moral problem (cf. Gen. 38:15; Jdg. 16:1; 1 Ki. 3:16). Thus in certain circumstances both female prostitution and extramarital intercourse on the part of the man (e.g., with a maid—Gen. 16:1–2; 30:1–13) were sanctioned.

(b) Prostitution became a serious problem through Israel's confrontation with the fertility cults, particularly the Baal cult. Male devotees had sexual intercourse with a prostitute in the sanctuary, which was supposed to bring him into cosmic harmony; this had a strong attraction for the educated Israelites. The bitter struggle of the prophets was directed against the belief of many in Israel that they owed the blessings of the land to the rites of the Baal cult, the spirit of prostitution, which had gained acceptance in the Yahweh cult. Israel "has not acknowledged that I [Yahweh] was the one who gave her the grain, the new wine and oil, who lavished on her the silver and gold—which they used for Baal" (Hos. 2:8).

In other words, what shocked the prophets was Israel's lack of personal faithfulness. The priests disregarded the tradition of Yahweh's word and lost their orientation (cf. Hos. 4:4–19). Cultic prostitution had taken on disgusting forms (cf. Jer. 3:1–9; 5:7–17; Ezek. 16; 23). Thus, prostitution became a figure used for Israel's apostasy from Yahweh. As a result, there arose in Israel a sharp rejection of any kind of prostitution.

3. Rab. Jud. frowned on any kind of prostitution or extramarital sexual intercourse. Incest and all kinds of unnatural sexual intercourse were viewed as *porneia*. One who surrenders to it shows ultimately that he or she has broken with God (cf. Wis. 14:27–28). *The Book of Jubilees* goes so far as to call *porneia* an unforgivable sin (33:13, 18). In order to avoid fornication, early marriage was recommended. In the so-called lists of vices of Hel. Jud., adultery and prostitution are found alongside idolatry, sorcery, and murder. The Dead Sea Scrolls give frequent warnings against sexual immorality.

NT In the NT the main weight of this word group (used 55x) falls in Paul (21x) and in Rev. (19x). In other words, the question of *porneia* comes up for discussion esp. in the confrontation with the Gk. world and in the context of the final judgment.

1. Prostitution existed in Israel at the time of Jesus. But whereas, according to Jewish law, prostitutes and tax collectors were excluded from the community of God and thus from salvation, Jesus proclaimed to them God's forgiveness on the basis of their faith and offered them salvation (Matt. 21:31–32; cf. Heb. 11:31; Jas. 2:25). The faith they displayed is held up as an example for the self-confident priests and elders of the people. But this in no way softens Jesus' rejection of prostitution (Mk. 7:21 par.).

It is not clear whether *porneia* in the so-called "exceptive clause" (Matt. 5:32; 19:9) is to be understood simply as extramarital sexual intercourse in the sense of *moicheia* or as including prostitution. Most interpreters tend to favor the former interpretation. In this clause, Matt. is apparently dealing with a vital question that Mk. and Lk. do not consider, namely, the question of *remarriage* after divorce for marital unfaithfulness. Note that Matt. 19:9; Mk. 10:11; and Lk. 16:18 agree in abrogating the permission to divorce that is implied in Deut. 24:1–4. The Mosaic law was not concerned with divorce for adultery (for which death was the prescribed penalty, see 22:22), so it did not need to consider the question of remarriage in such an event. Jesus, therefore, felt a need to give God's will on this issue (see also *apostasion*, 687).

2. The *porne* word group denotes any kind of illegitimate sexual intercourse in Paul's letters. *porneia* was particularly an issue in the church at Corinth (the word group appears 14x in 1 Cor.), in part because that city had a significant number of temple prostitutes and because, as an important port city, it was open to the syncretism of the ancient world and was stamped with sexual licentiousness in the slums around the harbor. From 1 Cor. 1:26 and 2 Cor. 12:21, we can deduce that many members of the Corinthian church came from precisely that area. Moreover, certain elements in the Corinthian community boasted of their freedom in the Spirit to live as they pleased (cf. "everything is permissible," 1 Cor. 6:12; 10:23). They appear to have held to a dualism that maintained that what believers did with their bodies did not affect them spiritually.

It is against this background that the problem of incest must be seen (intercourse of a son with his step-mother, 1 Cor. 5:1–13). Paul maintains that if the congregation does not separate from such immoral persons, the whole church is endangered (5:9–11) and is subject to God's judgment (→ *olethros*, 3897). Since the dualism prevalent in Corinth saw the human body as something that would perish anyway, sexual needs could be expressed freely and spontaneously. Paul passionately resisted this outlook (6:9–20). The human body is not intended for immorality (6:13). Because a human does not have a *sōma* (body) but is *sōma*, what he or she does with the body matters a great deal (6:15–17; cf. Heb. 12:16). One must flee from sexual immorality and honor God with one's body (1 Cor. 6:18–20).

3. In Rev. unbridled sexual excess is mentioned among the chief sins of the pagans (9:21), just as the sexually immoral are mentioned among the sinners who are threatened by the second death (21:8; 22:15). In the fig. sense Babylon (chs. 17–19, probably a symbol of Rome), the great prostitute, is named as the embodiment and the personification of enmity to God. Prostitution is meant both lit. and fig. (as a reference to Rome's wooing for political and economic favors).

4520 (porne, prostitute), → *4519.*

4521 (pornos, immoral person, fornicator), → *4519.*

4525   πορφύρα

πορφύρα (*porphyra*), purple (4525); πορφυροῦς (*porphyrous*), purple (4528).

Purple (*porphyrous*, Rev. 17:4) symbolizes wealth and luxury (18:16; cf. Lk. 16:19). The noun *porphyra* originally meant the purple shell-fish (murex), then the dye obtained from it, and finally cloth, clothing (cf. Acts 16:14, *porphyropōlis*). It is used of the garment that the Roman soldiers put on Jesus (Mk. 15:17, 20; Jn. 19:2, 5), mocking him as a king.

4528 (porphyrous, purple), → *4525.*

4530 (posis, drinking, a drink), → *4403.*

4532 (potamos, river, stream), → *4380.*

4539 (potērion, cup), → *4403.*

4540 (potizō, water, give to drink), → *4403.*

4542 (potos, drinking, i.e., revelry), → *4403.*

4547 (pragma, deed, matter, thing, task, lawsuit, dispute), → *4556.*

4548 (pragmateia, activity, occupation, undertaking), → *4556.*

4549 (pragmateuomai, do business, trade), → *4556.*

4551 (praktōr, officer), → *4556.*

4552 (praxis, act, action, deed, function), → *4556.*

4556   πράσσω

πράσσω (*prassō*), accomplish, do (4556); πρᾶξις (*praxis*), act, action, deed, function (4552); πρᾶγμα (*pragma*), deed, matter, thing, undertaking, task, lawsuit, dispute (4547); πραγματεία (*pragmateia*), activity, occupation, undertaking (4548); πραγματεύομαι (*pragmateuomai*), do business, trade (4549); πράκτωρ (*praktōr*), officer (4551).

CL & OT 1. (a) In cl. Gk. *prassō* means to accomplish, do something. In monetary contexts, *prassō* means collecting or exacting payment of taxes or debts. Intrans., *prassō* means to act. It is often met in the formula "to do and to say." Linked with an adv., it expresses the condition or state of a person (e.g., *eu prassō*, I am doing [feel] well). It is rarely used of gods. In contrast to *poieō* (→ 4472), which tends to signify more concrete deeds, *prassō* is used where a philosopher seeks to assess human action in general.

(b) The meanings of *praxis* and *pragma* overlap. *praxis* denotes acting, activity, and can refer to some completed act or work, the way an activity is carried out, or a planned action. It can also mean a business or an undertaking. *pragma* means deed, act, business, task, but also a general matter or thing, or even a lawsuit, trial.

2. (a) In comparison with *poieō* in the LXX, *prassō* occurs infrequently. When it is used, it often describes human behavior, either bad (e.g., Gen. 31:28; Job 27:6) or good (e.g., 4 Macc. 3:20).

(b) *pragma* occurs approximately 125x in the LXX, *praxis* only 23x. Whereas the latter refers only to human acts, *pragma* can be used for divine acts (e.g., Isa. 25:1; 28:22).

NT 1. *prassō* occurs 39x in the NT. It never refers to divine, creative activity. Rather, it often denotes negative and more or less abstractly conceived human action; in some places it is used for positive dealings or has a neutral value. (a) In connection with money matters, John the Baptist instructs tax collectors not to "collect" more than they should (Lk. 3:13; cf. also 19:23). In 12:58 *praktōr* is an officer in charge of the debtor's prison.

(b) *prassō* refers to the human condition in Eph. 6:21; linked with the adv. *eu* it has the sense of doing well in Acts 15:29. The shout to the jailer in Philippi is also intended to serve personal well-being: "Do yourself no harm!" (lit., 16:28).

(c) Finally, *prassō* has a neutral sense in 1 Thess. 4:11, where it means one's own affairs. Acts 5:35 speaks generally of human action, which can turn out either well or badly.

2. *prassō* often has religious or ethical overtones. (a) It indicates a deed that can stand neither in the regular earthly courts (cf. Lk. 23:41; Acts 17:7; Rom. 13:4) nor before God (cf. Jn. 5:29; Rom. 2:2–3). Formulaic phrases speak of offenses that deserve death (e.g., Lk. 23:15; Acts 25:11, 25; Rom. 1:32). An individual, concrete deed (unchastity) is named in 1 Cor. 5:2; *prassō* also refers primarily to sexual sins in 2 Cor. 12:21.

(b) In Acts 19:19 the vb. is used of those who "practiced" sorcery. It also refers to Jesus' betrayal (Lk. 22:23), the killing of Jesus brought about in ignorance by the people (Acts 3:17), and Saul's hostilities directed against the name of Jesus (26:9).

(c) In Rom. 7:14–25 *prassō* and *poieō* are used alongside each other in connection with doing evil. Temptation must be resisted, for anyone who does evil hates the light (Jn. 3:20), and anyone who does the deeds of the sinful nature (Gal. 5:21) will not inherit God's kingdom. In the old covenant, it was important to act in accordance with the law (Rom. 2:25), but in Acts 26:20 Paul enjoins his hearers to prove their repentance by their deeds, which gives *prassō* a positive significance (cf. also Phil. 4:9).

The notion that right action has its reward receives clear expression in 1 Cor. 9:17. The definition of the relationship between human action and its eschatological valuation is developed in Jn. 5:29 in the form of general validity, in both positive and negative directions. One day the dead will leave their graves, those who have done (*poieō*) good deeds will receive the resurrection of life, while those who have done (*prassō*) evil, the resurrection of judgment.

3. (a) *praxis* occurs 6x in the NT. The word has a neutral and abstract meaning in Rom. 12:4, where Paul writes that not all the members of Christ's body have the same function. In Matt. 16:27 *praxis* should be understood ambivalently: The deeds that will be judged at the Parousia can be good or bad. In the other 4 places *praxis* refers to obviously evil actions (Lk. 23:51; Acts 19:18; Rom. 8:13; Col. 3:9).

(b) *pragma* (11x) has a wider range of nuances. It has neutral value in Matt. 18:19, where it is used of a prayer request, and in Rom. 16:2, where it refers to Phoebe's affairs. In 1 Thess. 4:6 it probably refers to some business transaction. It is used of judicial proceedings in 1 Cor. 6:1, and it has the sense of historical events in Lk. 1:1. Acts 5:4 and 2 Cor. 7:11 are concerned with a concrete offense (cf. Jas. 3:16). In 2 Tim. 2:4 *pragmateia* means the affairs of everyday life, whereas the vb. *pragmateuomai* means to do business, trade (Lk. 19:13).

(c) The use of *pragma* in Heb. provides a striking contrast. In 6:18 *pragma* means two "things" (the promise and oath of God) by which God declares his truth, while 10:1 contrasts the shadow of the good things to come contained in the law with "the realities" (pl.) themselves. Faith relates to these things, even when it cannot see them (11:1).

See also *ergazomai*, to labor, be active, work, bring about (*2237*); *poieō*, do, make (*4472*).

4557 (praupathia, gentleness), → *4558.*

| 4558   πραΰς |

πραΰς (*praus*), gentle, humble, considerate, meek (*4558*); πραΰτης (*prautēs*), gentleness, humility, considerateness, meekness (*4559*); πραϋπαθία (*praupathia*), gentleness (*4557*); ἐπιεικής

(*epieikēs*), mild, yielding, gentle, kind, forbearing (*2117*); ἐπιείκεια (*epieikeia*), mildness, forbearance, gentleness, graciousness (*2116*).

CL & OT 1. In cl. Gk. *praus* means friendly, mild, gentle; the noun *prautēs* means gentleness, mild friendliness. The virtually synonymous *epieikēs* and its noun *epieikeia* mean the proper way of life, or later, forbearance, mildness. Words from the *praus* group are used of things (e.g., mild words, soothing medicine), animals (tame), and people (benevolent). It is a quality shown by friends, while stern harshness may be expected from an enemy. *epieikēs* came to be used for a considerate, thoughtful attitude in legal relationships, which was prepared to mitigate the rigors of justice, in contrast to the attitude that demands rights to be upheld at all costs.

Both concepts are opposed to unbridled anger, harshness, brutality, and self-expression. They represent character traits of the noble-minded, the wise who remain meek in the face of insults, the judge who is lenient in judgment, and the king who is kind in his rule. Hence these words appear often in pictures of the ideal ruler and in eulogies on men in high positions.

2. (a) *epieikeia* is found 10x in the LXX and *epieikēs*, including the adv., 6x. They describe God's gracious gentleness in his rule (1 Sam. 12:22; Ps. 86:5; Wis. 12:18), and also the actions of a king (2 Macc. 9:27), a prophet (2 Ki. 6:3), and the pious (Wis. 2:19).

(b) *praus*, found 17x in the LXX, translates ʿānî (3x), poor, afflicted, humble, defenseless; and more generally its later variant ʿānāw, poor, humble, meek (cf. Ps. 25:9). The poor were those in Israel who had no landed property. They were wrongfully restricted, disinherited, and deprived of the fullness that God willed (→ *penēs*, *4288*). They were often the victims of unscrupulous exploitation (Job 24:4; cf. Ps. 37:11, 14; Isa. 32:7).

(c) Yahweh, however, takes the part of the ʿānî in the Mosaic law (Exod. 22:21–24; Deut. 24:14–15), the prophets (Isa. 3:14–15; Amos 2:7; 8:4; Zech. 7:10), and wisdom lit. (Prov. 14:21; 22:22; 31:9, 20). He hears and comforts those who find no mercy among their fellow Israelites (Job 36:15; Isa. 29:19) and will finally reverse all that is not now in their favor (Ps. 37:11; 147:6; Isa. 26:6). Hence ʿānî (and esp. ʿānāw) changes its meaning from those who are materially poor to those who, in deep need and difficulty, humbly seek help from Yahweh alone (e.g., Ps. 40:17; Isa. 41:17; 49:13; 66:2; Zeph. 2:3; 3:12) so that the word is sometimes used with the meaning meek, humble, modest (Num. 12:3; Eccl. 6:8).

(d) In the messianic passages of the OT God's king is depicted as the helper of all who have been deprived of their rights and of all the needy (Ps. 45:4; 72; Isa. 11:4; 61:1). The term ʿānî is never applied to God, but in Zech. 9:9 it is a title of honor given to the promised Messiah. As he rides the donkey, the animal used by the socially insignificant, rather than the horse, his way leads to the poor and those deprived of their rights and offers them peace.

NT 1. Both *prautēs* and *epieikeia* are marks of Christ's rule. In contrast to the representatives of a political messianism, Jesus repudiates the use of force to bring about God's rule. His activity on earth is that of the OT king who brings salvation without using force or war (Matt. 11:29; 21:5; cf. Zech. 9:9). Matt. 11:29 stresses the human humility of the Messiah. In 2 Cor. 10:1 Paul mentions *prautēs* and *epieikeia* as characteristics of Jesus' attitude toward humans during his life on earth and holds them out as an example to the church.

2. These words express an attitude demanded of Christians, though they are applied also to non-Christians (Acts 24:4, where the Jewish spokesman Tertullus uses *epieikeia* in addressing Felix; cf. 1 Pet. 2:18, of masters). These words also stand in lists of virtues as expressions of Christian love (Col. 3:12; 1 Tim. 6:11; 1 Pet. 3:4), of "the wisdom that comes from heaven" (Jas. 3:17), and of the fruit of the Holy Spirit (Gal. 5:23). They state the rule for the way in which Christians and non-Christians should live together (Phil. 4:5; Tit. 3:2). They also apply in dealing with Christians who have committed sins

(1 Cor. 4:21; Gal. 6:1; 2 Tim. 2:25) and in living in the midst of enmity and persecution (1 Pet. 3:15). Christians, esp. bishops (1 Tim. 3:3), should set an example of this (Jas. 3:13).

3. The relationship between *praus* and *ʿānî* may help explain Matt. 5:5: "Blessed are the meek, for they will inherit [*klēronomeō*] the earth." Since the vb. to inherit appears in Deut. 4:1; 16:20; Ps. 37:11; 69:35 with reference to possessing the land of Israel, Jesus' thought here is of possessing or inheriting the new promised land. Just as obedience and righteousness were the conditions of entering Canaan, so humble obedience to his teaching is the condition of entering the new land of God's kingdom. Those who are now oppressed and despised and have nothing to call their own (like Israel prior to the conquest of Canaan) will enter the inheritance of God's rule on earth. At the same time Matt. 5:5 is a veiled statement about Jesus himself.

See also *tapeinos*, lowly, humble (*5424*).

4559 (*prautēs*, gentleness, humility, meekness), → *4558*.

4560	πρέπω

πρέπω (*prepō*), be fitting, seemly or suitable (*4560*).

CL & OT *prepō* in cl. Gk. usually occurs in the impers. forms *eprepen*, it was fitting, and *prepei*, it is fitting. Whereas *dei* and *opheilō* relate to necessity and obligation, *prepō* expresses what is proper and appropriate. It is found in the LXX in Ps. 33:1; 65:1; 93:5. In the Apocr. it occurs in Sir. 33:28; 32:3 = LXX 30:27; 35:3; 1 Macc. 12:11; 3 Macc. 3:20, 25; 7:13, 19.

NT In the Gospels *prepei* occurs only in Matt. 3:15 in Jesus' reply to the protestations of John the Baptist at his request for baptism: "Let it be so now; it is proper [*prepon*] for us to do this to fulfill all righteousness." In discussing the question of the veiling of women in worship, Paul asks: "Judge for yourselves: Is it proper [*prepon estin*] for a woman to pray to God with her head uncovered?" (1 Cor. 11:13). Eph. 5:3 asserts that no hint of immorality, impurity, or covetousness should exist among believers, as is proper (*prepei*) for God's people.

The Pastoral Letters give direction for appropriate conduct for women and Christian teachers. Women should adorn themselves "with good deeds, appropriate [*prepei*] for women who profess to worship God" (1 Tim. 2:10). Titus is urged to "teach what is in accord [*prepei*] with sound doctrine" (Tit. 2:1).

Finally, Heb. makes two observations on the appropriateness of Jesus' actions. First, "It was fitting" (*eprepen*) that in order to bring many to glory, Jesus should be made perfect through suffering (2:10). God also had to produce a high priest who could meet (*eprepen*) our needs, one who was holy, blameless, and pure (7:26).

The common factor in all these instances of *prepei* is the absence of external constraint and absolute necessity. In each case the person concerned could have acted otherwise. However, righteousness and the exigencies of the situation made the conduct specified not only appropriate but imperative.

See also *ananke*, compulsion (*340*); *dei*, it is necessary, one must (*1256*); *opheilō*, owe, be indebted to (*4053*).

4561 (*presbeia*, embassy, ambassador), → *4565*.

4563 (*presbeuō*, be older, be an ambassador, rule), → *4565*.

4564 (*presbyterion*, council of elders, rank of elder or presbyter), → *4565*.

4565	πρεσβύτερος

πρεσβύτερος (*presbyteros*), older, elder, presbyter (*4565*); πρεσβεύω (*presbeuō*), be older, be an ambassador, rule (*4563*); πρεσβυτέριον (*presbyterion*), council of elders, rank of elder or presbyter (*4564*); πρεσβύτης (*presbytēs*), old man (*4566*); πρεσβεία (*presbeia*), embassy, ambassador (*4561*); προΐστημι (*proistēmi*), be

at the head of, rule, be concerned about (*4613*); κυβέρνησις (*kybernēsis*), administration (*3236*).

CL 1. *presbys*, old, *presbyteros*, older, and *presbytatos*, oldest, first denoted a person's age relative to others; then, greater importance; and finally, more honored. In ancient Gk. society older people received respect and authority on the grounds of their experience and wisdom. This meaning determines the use of the other words from this root. Thus the noun *presbytēs* denotes age, rank, or an older man who is no longer a *neaniskos* (young man) and is probably over 50 years old. The fem. *presbytis* means old woman. The vb. *presbeuō* means to be older; later, to take the first place

Hence the words from this root came to be used for institutional functions in society, for which the wisdom of age is regarded as a prerequisite. *presbeuō* is used for the activity of an ambassador, who represents the people who send him and negotiates for them. *presbeia* means embassy, ambassador. Older people often had an advisory role within the political community. Hence, the vb. could mean command, and *presbyteros* could be the title of an office of state. In Egypt, the pl. *presbyteroi* appears as the title for members of associations or religious bodies, or elected agents of village councils, who had judicial and administrative duties.

2. *proistēmi* means (lit.) to set before or over someone or something. It could refer to the functions of leadership in an army, state, or party, positions that required guarding or protecting. Thus the verb could also mean support, care for.

3. *kybernaō* was originally used of the action of a ship helmsman. Later, the derivative noun came to designate a leading statesman. Divine guidance and rule were also described by cognate words of this group.

OT 1. In the LXX words derived from the root *presb-* are used in three primary areas. (a) *presbytēs* occurs 30x to designate someone older in years (e.g., the old man Eli, 1 Sam. 2:22); *presbyteros* occurs 50x with this meaning (e.g., Gen. 18:11). *presbeion* denotes advanced age as well as the right of the eldest as firstborn (43:33; Ps. 71:18).

(b) *presbyteroi* (usually pl.) denotes a group of men within a tribe, family, people, or community of settlers who have some leadership role (see below).

(c) *presbeutēs* and *presbys* are used in rare instances in the cl. sense of ambassador, envoy, negotiator (e.g., 2 Chr. 32:31; Isa. 57:9).

2. *proistēmi* occurs only 8x, meaning to be head of a household (2 Sam. 13:17; Amos 6:10), govern the people (1 Macc. 5:19), and even take trouble (Isa. 43:24).

3. *kybernēsis* is a function of rulers (Prov. 1:5; 11:14). But *kybernaō* is also used of the wily plans of the wicked (12:5).

4. In the OT there is no *theological* significance in age except in the case of the rights of the firstborn. But the existence of elders *as an institution* was of considerable significance in the life of ancient Israel and the Jewish synagogue community. They were an established part of the patriarchal clan and tribal system, where authority belonged to the heads of families.

(a) In Exod. 12:21–27, all the elders of Israel (the LXX translates this by *gerousia*, council of elders) are called together and given instructions about the Passover celebrations within their families. These men have authority over these communities.

(b) In the rest of the Pentateuch the elders are representatives of all Israel. Moses must inform them of Yahweh's resolve to deliver his people, and they are to be witnesses of his plea at Pharaoh's court (Exod. 3:16, 18; 4:29). They see the miracle of the spring at Horeb (17:5) and take part in the feast with Jethro (18:12). They witness the punishment of Dathan and Abiram (Num. 16:25).

A considerable number of men receive the title *presbyteros*, for Moses twice chooses out 70 "*of* the elders of Israel" to form a body representative of the representatives (see Exod. 24:1; Num. 11:16–30). The original ethnic office of elder took on a new function within the framework of the Mosaic covenant (cf. Exod. 18:13–26; Deut. 1:9–18, though admittedly the men assigned juridical duties are not described as elders; but cf. Isa. 24:23). This fact was later seen as a type of the rab. ordination, as is clear from the number 70 in the constitution of the Sanhedrin (see below).

(c) After Israel settled in the promised land, the elders controlled the local communities as a kind of patrician class (cf. Jos. 20:4; Jdg. 11:5–11; Ruth 4:2–11; 1 Sam. 16:4; 30:26). They were responsible for judicial, political, and military decisions within the towns. Their task, together with that of the judges, was to make sure that the requirements of the Mosaic law were kept (Deut. 21:2; 25:8, etc.).

At the same time, the title of *elder* also continued to be applied to the ruling class of the individual tribes (cf. 2 Sam. 19:11). They made the decision to send the ark against the Philistines (1 Sam. 4:3) and demanded the introduction of a monarchy (8:4). How much the kings depended on their goodwill is demonstrated by Saul's pleas to Samuel (15:30), David's ascent of the throne (2 Sam. 3:17; 5:3), Absalom's threat to it (17:4, 15; 19:12 = LXX 19:11), etc. (see 1 Ki. 12:6–24; 20:7–8 = LXX 21:7–8; 21:8, 11 = LXX 20:8, 11; 2 Chr. 10:6–13).

Finally, elders appear as representatives of the entire people at Solomon's dedication of the temple (cf. 1 Ki. 8; 2 Chr. 5), along with the heads of the tribes and families. Their critical, occasionally conspiratorial, attitude towards the monarchy is doubtless due not least to the threat that the formation of a royal civil service and the growth of dynastic power posed to their influence.

(d) The deeply rooted position of the elders is demonstrated by what happened after the monarchy ended and large portions of the population went into exile, for the elders once again appear as the guardians and representatives of the Jewish community (see Jer. 29:1 = LXX 36:1; Ezek. 8:1–12). But a change also took place during this period. Influential families supersede the clans and gain a position of eminence among the people as a whole. The heads of these families become an aristocratic ruling class (cf. Ezr. 8:1–14).

(e) At the end of the 3d or the beginning of the 2d cent. B.C., under the Seleucid king Antiochus III, we have evidence of a council of elders consisting of 70 (or 71) members, the Sanhedrin. At first, all the members generally are spoken of as *presbyteroi*. But the word is used more and more to designate the lay members of the Sanhedrin, who probably came from the patrician families of Jerusalem (cf. the NT, "the chief priests and the elders," Matt. 27:3, 12, 20). The "teachers of the law," who were increasingly taking over the actual leadership, were mainly orthodox Pharisees.

(f) After the destruction of Jerusalem (A.D. 70), the newly constituted Sanhedrin of Jamnia, whose function is restricted to the exposition and application of the Mosaic law, consists solely of teachers of the law. Consequently, the term *elder* came to be used as a title of honor for outstanding theologians. It implies, if not membership of the council, as least ordination. At the same time the presidents of the Jewish synagogues are also called *presbyteroi*. They preserve the traditional order with disciplinary powers.

NT 1. (a) *presbeia* occurs only in Jesus' parables (Lk. 14:32; 19:14) in the sense of a political delegation, embassy. The vb. *presbeuō* is used 2x by Paul: In 2 Cor. 5:20 it expresses the official character of the message of reconciliation that believers bring as "Christ's ambassadors" (see also Eph. 6:20). *presbytēs* refers simply to older men (Lk. 1:18; Tit. 2:2; Phlm. 9; cf. *presbytis*, "older women," in Tit. 2:3). *presbyterion* in Lk. 22:26; Acts 22:5 refers to the Jewish Sanhedrin, while in 1 Tim. 4:14 it means office of elder, which is conferred by laying on of hands.

(b) *proistēmi* occurs only in the writings of Paul. In 1 Thess. 5:12 it refers to those who labor in the church and "are over you in the Lord," i.e., a group exercising church leadership. In Rom. 12:8, one who exercises "leadership . . . [must] govern diligently." Insofar as this person is listed alongside those who teach, exhort, show mercy, and the like, this word seems to designate an activity rather than an office.

In the Pastoral Letters, *proistēmi* is used mostly in a general sense for those who "devote themselves" to good works (Tit. 3:8, 14). Behind 1 Tim. 3:4, 5, 12 is the picture of a patriarchal head of the household or father of the family. If one manages this role well, one fulfills a vital qualification for being a church leader (*episkopos* [→ *2176*] or *diakonos* [→ *1354*]). In 1 Tim. 5:17 the participle *proestōtes* is closely linked with *presbyteroi*. This passage refers to presiding elders; it appears by this time that the church had an organized system of offices.

(c) *kybernēsis* (referring to those with gifts of administration) is used in 1 Cor. 12:28 in a list beginning with apostles, prophets, and teachers, and progressing to various charismatic gifts. The position of *kybernēseis* after the "gifts of healing" and "those able to help others" and before "different kinds of tongues" suggests that it denotes a mediating function of keeping order within the whole life of the church (cf. *kybernētēs* in the sense of helmsman in Acts 27:11; Rev. 18:17).

2. *presbyteros* is found 65x in the NT and is used in four main senses. (a) In Acts 2:17 (a quotation from Joel 2:28) the old as opposed to the young are meant (see also Lk. 15:25; Jn. 8:9; 1 Tim. 5:2; Heb. 11:2; 1 Pet. 5:1, 5).

(b) In general in the Synoptic Gospels and at the beginning and end of Acts, *presbyteros* designates the lay members of the Jewish Sanhedrin (cf. above). They are regularly listed after the "chief priests" (→ *hiereus, 2636*), which shows their close association with and dependence on the latter. The priestly members of the Sanhedrin are the real agents and instigators of Jesus' crucifixion (→ *stauros, 5089*).

Matt. emphasizes the close association of the chief priests and elders, generally with no mention of the teachers of the law (→ *grammateus, 1208*), while Mk. tends to mention the teachers of the law but not the elders. The choice of terms denotes the viewpoint of each writer. Mk. seeks to underline the part played by the teachers of the law in Jesus' passion, while Matt. emphasizes more heavily those who represent all Israel. He is the only one to use the expression "elders of the people" (21:23; 26:3, 47; 27:1). John speaks merely of Jesus' opponents as "the Jews."

In Mk. 7:3, 5, the tradition of "the elders" refers to the teachers and interpreters of the law (the Pharisees). In this case, *presbyteros* is a title of honor for the *grammateus*. In Lk. 7:3 *elders* refers to the members of the presiding body of the local synagogue, who approach Jesus on behalf of a Roman officer.

(c) Lk. is the first not only to use the term *Christianoi* (Acts 11:26), but also to introduce the *presbyteroi* in the same context as those who exercised leadership in the church at Jerusalem (11:30; cf. 21:18). On the analogy of the Sanhedrin, this presupposes a *gerousia*, a council of elders, in which the apostles (→ *690*) play the leading role. Both are mentioned together in Acts 15:2, 4, 6, 22–23; 16:4. Lk. thus cites a continuity between the old covenant and the new in the structure of the church. He also uses the term in describing the Pauline churches (cf. 14:23; 20:17).

In Paul's description of the church offices in 1 Tim. 5:17, 19 and Tit. 1:5, *presbyteros* has become the title of honor for those who care for the members and the spiritual life of the church. Mention of them in conferring the gift of prophecy suggests the collegiate character of their work (1 Tim. 4:14). From this body those who "direct the affairs" of the church, along with preachers and teachers, are drawn (5:17). Here we find the root of the present-day presbyterian system of church government.

Tit. 1:5, 7 implies that the terms *presbyteros* and *episkopos* are interchangeable (cf. Acts 20:17, 28). Besides meeting general personal and moral requirements, they have the special tasks of exhorting and refuting objectors. In other words, they continue the juridical role of synagogue elders in the form of a presiding group (see also Jas. 5:14). Insofar as Titus is to appoint elders in individual churches (Tit. 1:5), we see the beginnings of a more hierarchical church structure.

The writer of 2 and 3 Jn. refers to himself as *presbyteros* (v. 1 in both cases). This may be a title of honor for one who bears and delivers the apostolic tradition, but more likely it refers to a man valued and respected widely in the churches of the day. This person's authority lies solely in the importance of what he says, in the power of truth and of the Spirit.

(d) Finally, *presbyteroi* are mentioned 12x in the visions of Rev., always as a group of 24 men (4:4–10; cf. 7:11). They wear white clothes and are crowned. They sit around the throne of the Almighty, separated from it only by the four heavenly creatures. They praise God for his saving acts in history (4:10–11; 5:6–14; 11:16–18) or are present when others sing God's praises (14:3). Occasionally one of them comes forward to say something (5:5; 7:13).

Although these visions suggest the idea of a heavenly counterpart of the office of elders in the earthly churches, thus elevating that office to a higher plane, it is not possible to verify this suggestion. The number 24 is probably derived from the leaders of the 24 divisions of Jewish priests (1 Chr. 24:7–18) or of the temple singers (25:9–31), who were called "elders" in later Jud. They may also represent the twelve patriarchs and the twelve apostles whose names are written on the gates and foundations of the holy city (Rev. 21:12–14).

See also *episkopos*, overseer (*2176*).

4566 (presbytēs, old man), → 4565.

4585	πρόβατον

πρόβατον (*probaton*), sheep (*4585*).

CL & OT 1. In cl. Gk. *probaton* in its widest sense denotes all four-footed animals (esp. domestic ones) as opposed to swimming and creeping animals. In mixed herds the *probata* were the small livestock (esp. the sheep). At first the word was used only in the pl. (i.e., of a flock or herd), but later the sing. appeared for a specific sheep. The word could be used metaphorically as a term of abuse for anything inferior or stupid or as a positive descriptive word for someone who needed guidance.

2. *probaton* in the OT means primarily the sheep as a useful and gregarious animal (Gen. 30:38; Isa. 7:21; Amos 7:15) and less as a sacrifice (Lev. 1:2; for this the more frequent word is *amnos*, → *303*). *probaton* (usually in the pl. *probata*) metaphorically denotes God's people (Ps. 74:1; 77:20; 78:52), under the king as *poimēn* (→ *4478*), shepherd (2 Sam. 24:17). The essential point is the sheep's need of protection. Without the shepherd's guidance the flock is scattered (Ezek. 34:5–6), as each sheep goes its own way (Isa. 53:6). Since sheep wander about and fall victims to the dangers of the desert (Ezek. 34:5–6), they need to be guided by a skillful shepherd to the right pastures, if they are to survive (Ps. 23). Hence, the people of Israel in the desert, without a leader, are "like sheep without a shepherd" (Num. 27:17). The individual also, without God's guidance, has "strayed like a lost sheep" (Ps. 119:176).

Yahweh provides for his scattered flock by appointing shepherds such as the messianic king (Jer. 23:1–4; Ezek. 34:22–23), Moses (Ps. 77:20; Isa. 63:11). God himself acts as shepherd of his people (Ps. 78:52–53; 80:1; Isa. 40:11). By repeatedly calling themselves God's sheep, the people of Israel were acknowledging that, left to themselves, they were defenseless and that they needed to trust the guidance of their good shepherd, Yahweh himself (Ps. 23; 95:7; 100:3).

NT 1. *probaton* occurs 39x in the NT, mostly in Matt. (11x) and Jn. (19x). From the use Jesus makes of sheep in his parables and teaching, it is clear that his contemporaries understood how utterly lost a sheep is if left to itself without a shepherd's care (Lk. 15:4). A sheep's great need is loving, unselfish protection (Matt. 12:11). Without a shepherd a sheep is "harassed and helpless" (9:36), goes "astray" (1 Pet. 2:25), and is "lost" (Matt. 10:6; 15:24).

Following OT usage and likening his people to a flock of sheep without a shepherd (Mk. 6:34; cf. Num. 27:17; 1 Ki. 22:17), Jesus stresses that they are heading for certain destruction unless deliverance is forthcoming. In the same way Christians in 1 Pet. 2:25 are reminded

that before their conversion they, like sheep, were hopelessly lost and at the mercy of false shepherds (cf. Ezek. 34:5). But Jesus is the "great Shepherd of the sheep" (Heb. 13:20), who is sent first to "the lost sheep of Israel" (Matt. 15:24).

2. The word *sheep* is also applied in Matt. to the exclusive band of disciples gathered by Jesus. As he sends them forth to preach (10:16), Jesus likens them to defenseless sheep sent by the shepherd into the midst of ferocious wolves. The sheep are under the constant threat and specter of dispersal by their enemies: "I will strike the shepherd, and the sheep of the flock will be scattered" (26:31; Mk. 14:27). This quotation from Zech. 13:7 is interpreted Christologically, with the implication that Jesus' followers are the true Israel and that it is God who will smite Jesus. The "sheep," who consciously or unconsciously have done God's will, will not be finally separated from the goats until the shepherd himself separates them on the day of judgment (Matt. 25:32–33).

3. In Jn. *probaton* denotes Christ's elect people, "his own" (Jn. 10:4). The sheep know the voice of their shepherd, hear his call, and follow him. As the good shepherd, Jesus knows his sheep, calls them, guards them from the wolf, and lays down his life for them (10:1–11). The shepherd comes forth from God in order to reveal him, while the flock is the church listening to his voice. When there is "one flock and one shepherd" (10:16; cf. 17:20–21), i.e., when at last Jews and Gentiles are gathered into one church under one Lord, then the purpose of Christ's saving work is achieved.

4. As in the OT, *probaton* hardly ever means a sacrificial animal (only in Jn. 2:14; Acts 8:32), this idea being expressed in the NT mainly by *amnos* and *arnion*.

See also *amnos*, lamb (*303*); *poimēn*, shepherd (*4478*).

4589	προγινώσκω

προγινώσκω (*proginōskō*), know beforehand, know in advance (*4589*); πρόγνωσις (*prognōsis*), foreknowledge (*4590*).

CL & OT 1. In cl. Gk. *proginōskō* (*pro*, before, with the vb. *ginōskō*, perceive, understand, know) means to know or perceive in advance, to see the future. The corresponding noun *prognōsis* (attested as a medical technical term since Hippocrates and continuing even today) denotes the foreknowledge that makes it possible to predict the future.

The early Gks. understood *prognōsis* as nonverbal foreknowledge of a dream-like kind, which can however be apprehended and communicated by those who are clever enough to do so. It belongs to the realm of destiny. It is often both hidden from humans and open to them. It is capricious, like the gods themselves. Both gods and humans are subject to it. Its power controls the rise and fall of gods and nations.

Hel. thinkers, especially the Stoics, transformed the concept and understood it in a pantheistic way as an expression of the purposefully creative order of the divine world-force that includes both nature and humankind. Fate itself is subject to this order and can be a factor in the order. Divinity, destiny, order, and necessity become identical. Everything is arranged rationally and harmoniously, or at least in the direction of a development toward a harmonious consummation.

2. In the OT these two words occur only in the Apocr. *proginōskō* occurs only 3x. Two of these occurrences concern *sophia* (wisdom), conceived in personal terms: Wisdom knows in advance those who desire her (Wis. 6:13), and Wisdom has foreknowledge of signs and wonders (8:8). The other reference concerns the foreknowledge that the Israelites in Egypt were given of the destruction of the Egyptian firstborn (18:6). *prognōsis* occurs only 2x: Jdt. 9:6, of God's foreknowledge decreeing the fall of the Egyptians; and 11:19, of prophetic foreknowledge.

NT 1. In the NT the vb. *proginōskō* occurs 5x. Two occurrences are in Paul (Rom. 8:29; 11:2). Acts 26:5 speaks of people who "have known" Paul for a long time (cf. 1 Pet. 1:20; 2 Pet. 3:17). The noun *prognōsis*, foreknowledge, occurs in Acts 2:23; 1 Pet. 1:2.

2. In Paul *proginōskō* demonstrates the character of God's activity among humans. It assumes a personal relationship with a group of people that originates in God himself. Rom. 8:29 declares that those whom "God foreknew he also predestined to be conformed to the likeness of his Son." In 11:2 the vb. expresses God's election and love of Israel, which opposes the idea of a final rejection of Israel.

3. According to 1 Pet. 1:20, Christ "was chosen before the creation of the world." In 1:2 the noun *prognōsis* denotes "the foreknowledge of God," which is said to be the ground of election for the Christians scattered throughout the world. Membership of the community in a differently orientated and partly hostile environment is thus grounded in the relationship that God takes up with his people as their Father.

In 2 Pet. 3:17 the apostle speaks of the advance knowledge of believers. They are aware that the Parousia is coming, despite its delay. The point at issue here is misunderstandings and disagreements over statements of Paul (cf. 3:15–16). They are, therefore, urged to watchfulness to counteract the danger of apostasy. Human foreknowledge thus gains a theological stress in paraenesis here.

4. In Acts 2:23 *prognōsis* characterizes the events surrounding Jesus of Nazareth before and up to his execution: He was "handed over to [his enemies] by God's set purpose and foreknowledge."

5. In sum, both the vb. and the noun speak primarily of God's action toward Christ or toward humans, witnessing to that activity as planned and directed. Any interpretation in terms of an impersonal constraint (e.g., destiny, fate, or doom) or of an autonomy that removes itself from the normal course of world events contradicts the NT use of these words.

See also *pronoeō*, perceive beforehand, foresee, provide, care for (*4629*); *prooraō*, see in advance, foresee (*4632*); *proorizō*, decide on beforehand, predestine (*4633*); *protithēmi*, mid. display publicly, plan, propose (*4729*).

4590 (*prognōsis*, foreknowledge), → *4589*.

4592 (*prographō*, to write beforehand, set forth publicly), → *1210*.

4596 (*prodromos*, running before, forerunner), → *4513*.

4598 (*proelpizō*, hope in advance), → *1828*.

4600 (*proepangellō*, announce before, promise before), → *2039*.

4601 (*proerchomai*, go forward, advance), → *2262*.

4602 (*proetoimazō*, prepare beforehand), → *2289*.

4603 (*proeuangelizomai*, announce the good news beforehand), → *2295*.

4606 (*prothesis*, presentation, display, plan, purpose, resolve), → *4729*.

4607	προθεσμία

προθεσμία (*prothesmia*), appointed date (*4607*).

CL & OT Derived from *thesmos* (law in the sense of what is laid down), *prothesmia* signifies a time limit appointed in advance for completing legal, financial, or political transactions.

NT *prothesmia* occurs in Gal. 4:2, where "by his father" suggests a special guardianship of a child operating during the father's lifetime, which ended automatically when he reached a "set" age.

See also *kathistēmi*, bring, appoint, (*2770*); *horizō*, determine, appoint (*3988*); *paristēmi*, place, put at the disposal of (*4225*); *procheirizō*, determine, appoint (*4741*); *tassō*, arrange, appoint (*5435*); *tithēmi*, put, place, set, appoint (*5502*); *cheirotoneō*, appoint (*5936*); *lanchanō*, obtain as by lot (*3275*).

4611 (*proïmos*, early [rain]), → *847*.

4613 (*proïstēmi*, be at the head of, rule), → *4565*.

4615 (*prokatangellō*, announce, proclaim beforehand, foretell), → *33*.

4616 (*prokatartizō*, get ready, arrange in advance), → *787*.

4620 (*prokopē*, progress, advancement, furtherance), → *889*.

4621 (*prokoptō*, go forward, advance, make progress, prosper), → *889*.

4623 (*prokyroō*, establish, confirm beforehand), → *3263*.

4624 (*prolambanō*, anticipate, take, get), → *3284*.

4625 (*prolegō*, say before, tell ahead of time), → *3364*.

4628 (*promerimnaō*, be anxious beforehand), → *3533*.

4629	προνοέω

προνοέω (*pronoeō*), perceive beforehand, foresee, provide, care for (*4629*); πρόνοια (*pronoia*), forethought, foresight, provident care (*4630*).

CL & OT 1. (a) *pronoeō* (*pro*, before, with the vb. *noeō*, observe, notice) meant initially to observe in advance, notice beforehand, foresee. But in most cases it had the meaning of care, attend to, make provision for. For the noun *pronoia*, the temporal meaning of foresight or foreknowledge was likewise rare. The predominant meaning was foresight in the sense of forethought, care, providence.

(b) In Herodotus, however, *pronoia* designated divine providence, and a generation later it became a philosophical technical term. Even later, in Stoic philosophy, it became an important concept for describing the emanation of the purposeful operations of a world-force possessing divine status and working for the benefit of humankind as well as the perfection of nature. This word thus gained a religious significance and became an expression of religious piety. In fact, among the Stoics it was raised to the level of an indisputable dogma. Chance is ruled out, because everything runs its course according to an implanted divine law of development, which is itself divine.

The characteristics of this understanding of providence are twofold. (i) Providence is implanted as a law, as the divinity of nature, humanity, and history. Thus, the imperative is understood as an indicative. (ii) Everything evolves automatically in line with this providential power; everything repugnant is excluded.

2. In the LXX the vb. *pronoeō* occurs only 11x, mostly in the Apocr. Only in Wis. 6:7 is the vb. used of God: "He takes thought for all (small and great) alike." The noun *pronoia* occurs 9x, almost exclusively in the Apocr. The hoped-for human assistance of King Seleucus IV is spoken of in 2 Macc. 4:6. All the other passages speak either of God's care or provision: God's care steers the ship (Wis. 14:3); by God's provision the jaws of the lions remain shut (Dan. 6:19 = LXX 6:18; cf. 3 Macc. 5:30; 4 Macc. 9:24). The word also refers to God's eternal (Wis. 17:2), omniscient (4 Macc. 13:19), or divine providence (17:22), which redeems the nation through the blood of the martyrs as a way of propitiation.

3. This word for providence, therefore, has no corresponding equivalent in the Heb. OT. Similarly, the idea of providence did not take on any distinctive didactic stamp in the OT. Rather, the idea itself and its didactic expression stem from Gk.-Hel. thought.

4. The acceptance of the Hel. idea of providence into Jewish thought becomes particularly evident in Philo and Josephus. The attestations for *pronoeō* and *pronoia* are numerous. God's providence and provision become clear in the ruin of a persecutor of the Jews and in God's care for the world.

NT In the NT the vb. *pronoeō* is found only in Rom. 12:17; 2 Cor. 8:21; 1 Tim. 5:8. All three instances refer to human endeavor in goodness, honesty, and sincerity (probably with ref. to the LXX wording of Prov. 3:4: "And provide for good things in the presence of God and men"). The noun *pronoia* (Rom. 13:14) also means concern or forethought. In this case it refers to refusing to think about how to gratify the desires of the flesh. In Acts 24:2 the advocate Tertullus flatters Felix for his caring provision. Thus, neither vb. nor noun is used of God's caring activity.

The fact that *pronoia*, in the sense of a divine wisdom of the world, does not appear in the NT despite its representation as a central concept of the surrounding world is not accidental. It is a sign that the NT speaks an equally eloquent language by avoiding some Hel. concepts, as it does by accepting and recoining others (e.g., *agapē*, love).

See also *proginōskō*, know beforehand, know in advance (*4589*); *proorao*, see in advance, foresee (*4632*); *proorizō*, decide on beforehand, predestine (*4633*); *protithēmi*, mid. display publicly, plan, propose (*4729*).

4630 (pronoia, forethought, provident care), → 4629.

4632	προοράω

προοράω (*proorao*), see previously, see in advance, foresee (the future) (*4632*).

CL & OT 1. The vb. *proorao* (*pro*, before, with the vb. *horao*, see, notice, *3972*) is attested in the spatial sense of seeing in front of someone since Homer and in the sense of foreseeing or knowing the future in advance (first in Pindar).

2. In the LXX *proorao* is found only in Ps. 139:3 ("you are familiar with all my ways") of God's forward-reaching sight and knowledge; in 16:8 of keeping the Lord before one's eyes; in Gen. 37:18 of Joseph being seen from a distance by his brothers; and in 1 Esd. 5:63 of those who had seen the former house of God.

Philo used the word largely in the temporal sense of foreseeing dangers and in combination with *pronoia*, the providence of God, by which God foresees what is coming. In Josephus we find the added meaning to make provision for.

NT In the NT *proorao* occurs 4x. In Gal. 3:8 Paul says, with reference to Gen. 12:3, that the Scripture (here personalized) "foresaw that God would justify the Gentiles by faith." The three other passages are in Acts. In 2:25, Peter quotes Ps. 16:8 (cf. above). In Acts 21:29, the vb. refers to what the Jews had "previously seen" when they saw Paul in the temple with Trophimus. In 2:31, Peter says that David spoke with foresight or foreknowledge about the resurrection in Ps. 16:10. The vb. is thus not used in the NT to describe the activity of God.

See also *proginōskō*, know beforehand, know in advance (*4589*); *pronoeō*, perceive beforehand, foresee, provide, care for (*4629*); *proorizō*, decide on beforehand, predestine (*4633*); *protithēmi*, mid. display publicly, plan, propose (*4729*); *horao*, see (*3972*).

4633	προορίζω

προορίζω (*proorizō*), decide upon beforehand, predestine, foreordain (*4633*).

CL & OT The compound *proorizō* (*pro*, before, with the vb. *horizō*, to ordain, determine) means to preordain in cl. Gk. It is not found in the LXX.

NT The NT uses *proorizō* 6x to speak exclusively of God's decrees.

1. Paul uses the vb. in Rom. 8:29 together with *proginōskō*, foreknow (→ *4589*) and *prothesis*, plan, decision (→ *4729*), in order to ground God's call in his prior decree. In 8:30 *proorizō* is taken up again in order to specify the end to which God's dealings with humans are directed, namely, to justify those who are called and to give them a share in his glory. In 1 Cor. 2:7 Paul speaks of God's wisdom that he himself "destined for our glory." God's predestination is thus described as an activity of his directed towards the fellowship of humans with him.

2. Essentially on the same lines is Eph. 1:5, which describes how our sonship shared in Christ is grounded in God's predetermining love. In 1:11 the vb. is again used with *prothesis* in order to characterize the inheritance that Christians themselves are and that Christ has made possible. All of this derives from God's will, who "works out everything in conformity with the purpose of his will."

3. In Acts 4:27–28 expression is given to the conviction that Herod, Pontius Pilate, the nations, and people of Israel were only able to do to Jesus what God had previously determined. *proorizō* is thus here intended to underline that even the sinful actions of people are drawn into the realization of the divine plan of salvation.

See also *proginōskō*, know beforehand, know in advance (*4589*); *pronoeō*, perceive beforehand, foresee, provide, care for (*4629*); *proorao*, see in advance, foresee (*4632*); *protithēmi*, mid. display publicly, plan, propose (*4729*).

4639	πρός

πρός (*pros*), to, toward (*4639*).

CL In cl. Gk. this prep. took all three cases. In its basic spatial sense *pros* denotes motion from the presence of when followed by the gen. case, near when followed by the dat. case, and direction toward when followed by the acc. case.

NT 1. In the NT *pros* occurs only once with the gen. (Acts 27:34) and 6x with the dat., but 691x with the acc. It can have a spatial sense (e.g., Matt. 26:57; 1 Thess. 3:6), but the developed sense of mental direction or tendency followed naturally, referring to friendly (e.g., Jn. 6:37; 2 Cor. 3:16; Gal. 6:10; Eph. 3:14) or hostile (e.g., 1 Cor. 6:1; Col. 2:23) relationships. This notion of psychological orientation led to the use of *pros* to express the ideas of estimation (Matt. 19:8), purpose (1 Cor. 10:11), conformity (Lk. 12:47), and reference (18:1).

2. *John 1:1b*. Jn. 1:1a speaks of the pretemporality of the Logos, but even more so John implies the eternal preexistence of the Word, whose true sphere is not time but eternity. Having defined the relation of the Word to time, John specifies his relation to the Father, that "the Word was with [*pros*] God." Two meanings seem possible here. *pros* with the acc. can be regarded as equivalent to *para* (beside, → *4123*) with the dat., denoting position: "with." Support for this view may be found in the NT parallels where *pros* with the acc., often following the verb to be, denotes not linear motion but punctiliar rest (e.g., Matt. 26:18; Mk. 6:3; 9:19; 1 Cor. 16:6–7, 10; Phlm. 13). This usage reflects the blurring of the notions of movement and rest in Hel. Gk., and the reduction of the dat. case and the extension of the acc. case in Hel. Gk. But one should note that elsewhere John uses *para* to express the proximity of one person to another (e.g., Jn. 1:39; 4:40).

Perhaps a better view is the sense that "the Word was (in active communion) with the Father." This seems to be the import of John's statement, whether or not *pros* bears a dynamic sense, for when *pros* describes a relationship between persons it connotes personal intercourse rather than simply spatial juxtaposition. Used of divine persons, *pros* would point to eternal intercommunion (though we should not read all of later Christology into this one verse).

3. *2 Corinthians 5:8*. In 2 Cor. 5:6 Paul states that as long as he continues to dwell in a mortal body he is (spatially) absent from the Lord. Therefore, he prefers to leave his present form of embodiment and take up residence "with [*pros*] the Lord" (5:8). The prep. phrase may simply mean being in the presence of the Lord, for in itself *pros* contains no idea of reciprocal action. But if a believer's future destiny may be summed up as being "with Christ" (Phil. 1:23), something more is likely signified than simply a spatial proximity to Christ. An eternal human-divine relationship is being depicted in 2 Cor. 5:8, so that *pros* implies dynamic interpersonal communion, a settled mutual fellowship.

4. *1 John 5:16–17*. In the context these two verses identify a prayer of intercession that is "according to [God's] will" and thus will be answered (1 Jn. 5:14–16; cf. 3:21–22), i.e., prayer for a fellow believer who has sinned. But John places one restriction on the scope of such prayer: He does not counsel intercession for a person who has committed a sin "that leads to [*pros*; lit., toward] death," since the granting of pardon or life to such a person is contrary to God's will. This prep. phrase may be rendered either "tending to death" or "issuing in death." It is difficult to understand "life" and "death" here as referring

to eternal life and eternal death, since eternal life can scarcely be said to be given to an erring believer as a result of vicarious intercession, and John likely did not think some sins would not "result in" eternal death. It is best here to understand death as physical death, regarded as a penalty administered not by human beings (cf. Num. 18:22; Deut. 22:25–26) but by God (see 1 Cor. 11:30–32; cf. Acts 5:1–10).

On this view the apostle is encouraging intercession for any believer whose sin has not met with immediate divine judgment. As a result of intercessory prayer God will grant such a person the boon of further physical life and of renewed spiritual life—in spite of his or her own, willful sin. But he discourages intercession for any believer who has experienced God's judgment of death. Such prayer for the dead is contrary to his will. As for the identification of the "sin that leads to death," it may be the open and deliberate rejection of Christ (1 Jn. 2:22; 4:2–3; 2 Jn. 7; i.e., apostasy), blasphemy against the Holy Spirit (Mk. 3:28–30), or deliberate, defiant sin (cf. Heb. 10:26–31; also Num. 15:30–31), such as premeditated murder or persistent hatred.

4656 (prosdeomai, need [in addition or further]), → *1289.*

4657 (prosdechomai, receive, welcome), → *638.*

4659 (prosdokaō, wait for, look for, expect), → *638.*

4660 (prosdokia, expectation), → *638.*

4665 (proserchomai, go to, approach), → *2262.*

4666 (proseuchē, prayer), → *4667.*

4667	προσεύχομαι

προσεύχομαι (*proseuchomai*), to pray, entreat (*4667*); εὔχομαι (*euchomai*), request, vow (*2377*); εὐχή (*euchē*), prayer, oath, vow (*2376*); προσευχή (*proseuchē*), prayer (*4666*).

CL & OT 1. In cl. Gk. *euchomai* is a technical term for invoking a deity and so covers every aspect of such invocation: request, entreat, vow, consecrate; in a word, to pray. In Gk. culture prayer was often accompanied by an offering in order to make the gods favorably disposed. Here prayer takes the form of supplication. In earlier Gk. writings, the vb. is used almost exclusively with reference to tangible benefits; later the words have in view spiritual and ethical values or denote prayer for preservation from spiritual or moral harm. Characteristically, any assurance of being heard is lacking, for the Gks. did not hold to an omnipresent divine being. In the Hel. mystery religions, the person at prayer could experience the nearness of the deity; at such times prayer was replaced by silent rapture.

2. In the OT prayer is all-important because of that which characterizes and constitutes the nation of Israel, one's relation to God. The whole history of Israel is therefore permeated and borne along by prayer. At all important points God's people converse with him, even if specific words for prayer are not heard. Expressions like to speak, call, or cry out are often used instead. To indicate intense emotional involvement, vbs. such as to groan, sigh, or weep occur.

However urgently they prayed, people in the OT never forgot that they were addressing the holy, almighty God—an utter impossibility apart from his kindness and grace. This is shown by the frequent prostrating of oneself before God, which may indicate a customary posture in prayer (although there is also evidence of prayer being offered from a standing position). The parallel expression, to fall down on one's knees, is also used. Such phrases indicate the humility of mind that must characterize a person as he or she prays. In addition, the OT contains many expressions for prayers of praise and thanksgiving, along with other expressions such as to shout with joy, exult, and sing.

In the LXX *proseuchomai* occurs many times to translate various Heb. vbs. that mean to pray (e.g., Gen. 20:7, 17; 1 Sam. 1:10; 2:1; 1 Chr. 17:25; Ezr. 10:1; Ps. 5:2; Isa. 16:12; Jer. 7:16). *proseuchē* translates corresponding Heb. nouns for prayer (e.g., 2 Sam. 7:27; 1 Ki. 8:38, 45; Neh. 1:6, 11; Ps. 4:1; Prov. 28:9; Jon. 2:8; Hab. 3:1).

3. Prayer in the OT is characterized by being directed to the one true God, who is both the God of Israel and the Lord of the nations and of the whole earth, having revealed himself as such to his people (1 Ki. 8:22–53; 2 Ki. 19:15). Therefore, the Israelite always prays first as a member of the people, not as an individual (Ps. 35:18; 111:1), and knows what to expect of God. God's people know that he hears their prayers and answers them if they are in agreement with his will (3:4; 18:6; 65:2; Jer. 29:12). They thus pray with firm confidence in God (Ps. 17:6–7). They experience temptation and doubt, to be sure, but these are possible only against the background of such confidence.

The Israelites also know that in the eyes of a holy God there can be no question of their prayers counting as pious works that God must honor with his blessing (cf. the prayer of Elijah, Yahweh's prophet, with that of the priests of Baal, for whom it is nothing more than a technique aimed at manipulating their god, 1 Ki. 18:26, 29). They also know that God is a person, so they pray in a thoroughly personal and specific fashion, aware that they are actually speaking to God, not merely invoking some lifeless deity (cf. Gen. 18:22–33; 1 Sam. 1:10–11; Ps. 77:1–11). Such speaking to God can become a veritable wrestling with God, esp. in the case of intercession on behalf of others (Exod. 32:11–14; Num. 14:13–19; Deut. 9:26–29; Neh. 1:4–11). The suppliants may refer to God's promises, remind him of his saving deeds in the past and of his election of Israel, and appeal to his honor and his nature, which is of forbearance, grace, and mercy. In addition, the suppliants thank God for the miracles he has wrought in the history of his people (Ps. 105; 106) and ask for further guidance and continued deliverance from all possible distresses. Prayer and thanksgiving can cover all the material and spiritual needs of both the individual and the community.

As an aid to prayer mention is sometimes made of fasting (Ezr. 8:23; Neh. 1:4; Jer. 14:12; Joel 1:14; 2:12, 15), probably as an expression of that humble penitence before God that should lie at the root of all prayer.

4. Prayer is not restricted to any special place of worship but can take place anywhere (Gen. 24:26–27, 63), though of course it is esp. fostered in the early sanctuaries and later in the temple at Jerusalem.

5. The OT distinguishes between true and false prayer. True prayer is of the heart, i.e., it involves the whole person and means that one comes before God with one's whole being and in an attitude of humble submission (Jer. 29:12–14). False prayer, by contrast, is offered merely with the lips, i.e., with words and phrases that have no self-surrender, do not offer one's heart and life to God (except perhaps as a pure formality), and show no intention of fulfilling God's revealed will (Isa. 1:15–16; 29:13; Amos 5:23–24).

The OT also speaks of hindrances to prayer, which make an answer difficult or even impossible to obtain: e.g., disobedience (Deut. 1:43–45; Isa. 1:15–17; 59:1–2), lovelessness toward others (58:3–10), and injustice (Mic. 3:1–4).

6. Prayer also played a large part in the piety of rab. Jud. Of all devout exercises, fasting and praying were the most prominent, although the texts of prayers found at Qumran indicate a great variety of prayers, both as regards form as well as content. Pharisaic orthodoxy had been extending its systematization, from the closing years of the 1st cent. B.C. on, to include the piety of prayer. This applied not merely to public prayers offered in the synagogue, which included the ancient Shema (Deut. 6:4–5) and the Eighteen Benedictions, but also to private prayer. The prayers handed down from individual rabbis prove to be remarkably uniform. The idea of achieving righteousness dominated the Pharisees' piety and left its imprint on prayer.

NT In the NT, *proseuchomai* occurs 85x and *proseuchē* 36x, both esp. frequent in Acts. The simple vb. *euchomai* is found only 7x in the NT, *euchē* 3x.

1. *The nature and scope of prayer.* (a) NT prayer reflects the prior development of the OT. It is modeled, however, on the praying of Jesus, to which there are repeated references and which in its turn

draws on OT prayers and ideas. NT prayer is addressed to God or to Jesus, now called Lord (see *kyrios*, *3261*), esp. in passages with the vb. *proskyneō*, worship (→ *4686*). But *proseuchomai* itself can also relate to Jesus (e.g., Acts 1:24). In this way the early church shows that it regarded Jesus Christ as its Lord and living head. Consequently one can enter into personal contact with him, talking with him just as one did when he was on earth (cf. Acts 9:10–16; 2 Cor. 12:8–9).

It follows that genuine prayer is not monologue but dialogue, in which the person praying is often silent in order to listen to Jesus. As in the OT, therefore, prayer is personal and specific, a genuine conversation with God or Jesus Christ. In addition, since the NT believer knows God as Father with even greater clarity than any OT saint, praying proceeds from a childlike trust, as expressed in the typical NT form of address "Abba" or "Father" (Matt. 6:6–9; Lk. 11:2; Rom. 8:15; Gal. 4:6; Eph. 3:14–15). It is precisely at this point that NT prayer contrasts most sharply with that of rab. Jud. (→ *patēr*, father, *4252*).

(b) The suppliant's assurance that his or her prayers are heard (→ *aiteō*, *160*) is even stronger in the NT than in the OT, being grounded in the experience of God's fatherly love in Jesus Christ. Jesus explicitly strengthens this assurance, which comes from faith, by promising that prayer will be heard (e.g., Mk. 11:24). Even if it seems as if God does not answer prayers, we must not doubt his fatherly love or the power of prayer (cf. Jesus in Gethsemane [e.g., Matt. 26:36–46], where his passion is the Father's will).

(c) True prayer has great power. It expresses that faith whereby the sinner is justified (Lk. 18:10, 14). It is answered with the gift of the Holy Spirit (11:13), clarifies the way ahead (Mk. 1:35–39), and enables the suppliant to receive and put on the whole armor of God (cf. Eph. 6:18). We should surround all activities with prayer, esp. for the perseverance of the saints and for bold and faithful witness (6:19–20). True prayer overcomes anxieties (Phil. 4:6). But at the same time it is a fight with the powers of evil and darkness (Rom. 15:30; Col. 4:12; cf. Matt. 6:13).

Nevertheless, the NT, like the OT, warns of hindrances that can make prayer ineffectual: licentiousness and lovelessness (1 Pet. 3:7; Jas. 4:3), unbelief and doubt (1:5–7), or an unforgiving spirit (Matt. 6:14–15; Mk. 11:25).

(d) NT prayer can be about anything, from the smallest matter to the greatest, from the affairs of today to those of eternity. The best example is the Lord's Prayer (Matt. 6:9–13; Lk. 11:2–4). Here the prayer for daily bread, which includes all our daily needs, is flanked on the one side by prayer for the coming of God's kingdom and for his will to be done on earth, and on the other by prayer for forgiveness of sin, for preservation in temptation, and for deliverance from all evil. But it is important to note that the prayers that refer to God, his will, his kingdom, and his name stand first. The Lord's Prayer is embedded in longer discourses about true prayer (Matt. 6:5–15; Lk. 11:1–13), which must be marked by simplicity, concentration, discipline, patient confidence—and obedience.

(e) In addition to supplication, the NT, like the OT, notes the following types of prayer: intercession (e.g., Rom. 15:30; 1 Thess. 5:25; 2 Thess. 3:1; Jas. 5:14–18), which ought to embrace everyone, even enemies (Matt. 5:44); and praise, thanksgiving, and adoration, which is addressed exclusively to God, apart from his gifts (cf. esp. Rev. 4:8–11; 5:8–14; 7:9–17; 11:15–18; 15:2–4; 16:5–7; 19:1–8; 22:3, 9). The NT frequently insists that prayer should be constant (Lk. 18:1–8; Acts 12:5; 1 Thess. 5:17). That is, Christians ought always to live in the presence of their Lord and in communication with him, and should constantly be looking to him (Col. 4:2).

The posture in prayer was either kneeling (Lk. 22:41; Acts 21:5; Eph. 3:14–16), in which case the forehead might touch the ground (Matt. 26:39), or standing (Mk. 11:25; Lk. 18:11, 13), sometimes with uplifted hands (1 Tim. 2:8).

Communal prayer appears to have been customary in the early church, both in public worship (1 Cor. 11:4–5; 14:13–17) and smaller gatherings (Matt. 18:19, where Jesus attaches a special promise to communal prayer; see also Acts 2:42; 12:12), although private prayer is the fountainhead of prayer in general (Matt. 6:6); note also that Jesus frequently prayed alone (e.g., 14:23; Mk. 1:35; Lk. 5:16; 6:12; 9:18).

2. *The form of the Lord's Prayer*. Set prayers certainly existed, but even here there was no rigidity, as can be seen from the fact that the Lord's Prayer has been handed down in two variant forms (Matt. 6:9–13; Lk. 11:2–4). Certain MSS have with the text of Matt. an addition such as: "For yours is the kingdom and the power and the glory forever. Amen" (see NIV note). But these are all relatively late and probably not original. This praise ascription was probably composed to adapt the prayer for liturgical use in the early church (perhaps on the model of 1 Chr. 29:11).

There are also differences between the version of the Lord's Prayer in Matt. and in Lk. For example, Lk. begins with the address "Father," reflecting the Gk. *patēr* and the Aram. *ʾabbāʾ* ("Dear Father"), whereas Matt. gives the pious and more reverent form of Palestinian invocation ("Our Father"). One should note that the shorter form of Lk. is completely contained in the longer form of Matt. It seems most likely that the Matthean form is an expanded one, for in general liturgical texts grew by expansion. Moreover, no one would have dared to shorten a sacred text like the Lord's Prayer and leave out two petitions if they had been part of the original tradition. Yet both Matt. and Lk. have the same basic order, which puts God first and humanity and human needs second. This also reflects the order of the two great commandments and the Shema (cf. Matt. 22:34–40; Mk. 12:28–34; Lk. 10:25–28).

In Matt. 6:9–13 the prayer consists of two halves, each consisting of three petitions: three for the honor of God and three for our needs. Some argue that Matt. sees the prayer in the context of a new Sinai, since he records it in the Sermon on the Mount, where Jesus is the new lawgiver. Each half of the Lord's Prayer opens with a petition recalling the book of Exod. The first petition is a Christian restatement of the third commandment (Matt. 6:9; cf. Exod. 20:7; Deut. 5:11), stating it positively. In so doing it not only precludes taking the name of God in vain, but it also secures what is implied in the first and second commandments concerning other gods and graven images (Exod. 20:3–6; Deut. 5:7–10).

The petitions for God's kingdom to come and for his will to be done extend and supersede the fourth commandment's teaching concerning the Sabbath (Exod. 20:8–11; Deut. 5:12–15). Commandments five through ten are directed at personal relationships (e.g., honoring one's parents; prohibitions against murder, adultery, stealing, bearing false witness, and coveting, Exod. 20:12–17; Deut. 5:16–21); these are reflected in the fifth and sixth petitions for forgiveness and avoidance of temptation. These themes are interwoven with the history of Israel in general and with the desert wanderings in particular.

The fourth petition does not reflect any of the ten commandments, but it does recall the coming to Sinai in God's provision of the manna (Matt. 6:11; Lk. 11:3; cf. Exod. 16:15; Num. 11:4–9; Deut. 8:3; Ps. 78:24–25; on the significance of "daily" bread, → *epiousios*, *2157*). It implies provision for one's immediate needs, as in the desert wanderings, and also provision in the coming kingdom symbolized by the messianic banquet. Note esp. Deut. 8:2–3, which tells how God humbled the Israelites in the desert, then fed them with manna in order to teach them that "man does not live on bread alone but on every word that comes from the mouth of the LORD" (cf. Matt. 4:4; Lk. 4:4).

In other words, the Lord's Prayer applies the themes by which ancient Israel lived to the life of the new Israel. It is thus a fulfillment of the ten commandments and the exodus themes (cf. Matt. 5:17–18). At the same time, it transforms the themes from external commandments into petitions with which the one who prays personally identifies. Thus the law may be said to be written in one's heart (cf. Jer. 31:33).

3. *Prayer in individual NT writers*. (a) The frequent use of *proseuchomai* in Lk.'s writings is striking. For Lk. prayer is a basic expression of Christian faith and life, and Jesus is the model of how

to pray aright (Lk. 11:1). All the important points in the lives of Jesus, his apostles, and the members of his church are marked by prayer to God, and all important decisions are made with prayer (3:21–22; 6:12–13; 9:18, 28–29; 22:44–46; Acts 1:14, 24–25; 6:6; 9:11; 10:9; 13:3). That prayer was experienced as genuine conversation with God is clear from the fact that those praying often receive definite instructions from God (e.g., Acts 10:9–16, 30–32; 13:2).

(b) In Jn. the *euchomai* word group is absent (except for *euchomai* in 3 Jn. 1:2, which is more of a wish than a prayer). In referring to Christ's prayers, Jn. uses the ordinary words for speaking and talking, qualifying them only with statements about Jesus lifting up his eyes to heaven (e.g., Jn. 11:41; 17:1). Moreover, it is noticeable that Jesus almost always speaks to his heavenly Father in the immediate situation (see esp. 12:27–28). In this way Jn. indicates Jesus' continual fellowship with God; for him praying did not require a special act, since his whole life was one of prayer.

(c) Paul stresses that true prayer is wrought by the Spirit (Rom. 8:15, 26; Gal. 4:6). In Rom. 8:15; Gal. 4:6, Paul uses *krazō* (to cry, *3189*) in order to express that freedom, joy, and confidence in prayer that spring from our awareness of being God's children. Such prayer does not originate in any power we possess and can never be considered a meritorious work. Like faith itself, from which it stems and with which it is practically identical, prayer is a gift from above (cf. Eph. 6:18). To Paul, prayer is ultimately the indwelling, energizing Spirit speaking with God himself, who "is the Spirit" (2 Cor. 3:17; cf. Jn. 4:23–24). Thus prayer is not dependent for its efficacy on human eloquence. Rather, assurance of salvation is the result of Spirit-wrought prayer (Rom. 8:15–16; cf. also "through Jesus Christ" in Paul's prayers, 1:8; 7:25).

Paul likewise refers to a kind of Spirit-filled prayer that transcends the limitations of human speech and understanding: the so-called speaking in tongues or praying in the Spirit (1 Cor. 14:14–16). Yet he considers prayer that is intelligible to the hearers to have greater value than prayer offered in tongues (14:19), because only when others can give assent is the church edified as a body. Note that Jn. also regards Spirit-wrought prayer as the new departure in Christian praying (see Jn. 4:23–24).

According to Paul, prayer contains various elements: (i) doxology (e.g., Rom. 1:21); (ii) praise (e.g., 14:11; 15:9–11); (iii) blessing (e.g., 1:25; 9:5); (iv) worship (e.g., 1 Cor. 14:25); (v) hymns, community singing, psalms, etc. (e.g., 14:26; Eph. 5:19; Col. 3:16); (vi) thanksgiving (e.g., Rom. 1:8–10); (vii) boasting in Christ or before God (e.g., 5:2–3, 11); (viii) petition for self (e.g., 1:10; 7:24); (ix) intercession for others (e.g., 1:7b; 9:1–3).

By far the largest element among these nine is intercessory prayer. Paul sees himself as a mediator and intercessor before God, esp. for the needs of others. An important feature here is the wish prayer, a desire that God may take action regarding the person(s) mentioned in the wish. Thus, for example, Paul writes in Rom. 15:13: "May the God of hope fill you with all joy and peace as you trust in him, so that you may overflow with hope by the power of the Holy Spirit" (cf. also 15:5–6; 1 Thess. 3:11–13). Also revealing are the prayer reports, where at the beginning of most of his letters Paul assures his readers not only of his thanksgivings for them, but also of his intercessions on their behalf (e.g., Rom. 1:9–10; Phil. 1:4–6, 9–11). Such prayer reports may also occur in the body of letters (e.g., Rom. 9:3; Col. 1:29–2:3).

Paul's prayers were grounded in the gospel of Christ and infused by warm personal feeling and expectation. His awareness that we are living in the last days and will soon stand before the judgment seat of Christ adds urgency to his prayer life. But his prayers also indicate concern for mutual intercession, reconciliation, and unity throughout the church. Sometimes his prayers are characterized by a tension between confident thanksgiving and anxious supplication, but invariably they lead back to thanksgiving in view of mercies already given.

(d) Jas. 5:13–18 merits special mention. On the one hand, it teaches that a Christian's whole life, the good times as well as the bad,

should be lived in an atmosphere of prayer—i.e., that believers should lay before God everything that happens to them, so that each experience is suffused with prayer. On the other hand, in cases of sickness, prayer is to be accompanied by the laying on of hands, anointing, and confession of sins. Here the laying on of hands (implicit in the phrase "pray over him") and the anointing with oil are considered to be tangible expressions of prayer for the benefit of the sick individual, while confession of sins is made in order to remove any hindrances to prayer.

4. Finally, in one passage only (Acts 16:13, 16) *proseuchē* means a place of prayer.

See also *aiteō*, ask, ask for, demand (*160*); *gonypeteō*, fall on one's knees, kneel down before (*1206*); *deomai*, ask, request, beseech, beg (*1289*); *proskyneō*, worship, do obeisance to, prostrate oneself, do reverence to (*4686*); *erōtaō*, ask, ask a question, request (*2263*); *krouō*, knock (*3218*); *entynchanō*, meet, turn to, approach, petition, pray, intercede (*1961*).

4670 προσήλυτος

προσήλυτος (*prosēlytos*), proselyte (*4670*); φοβούμενος τὸν θεόν (*phoboumenos ton theon*), God-fearer (*5828* + *2536*); σεβόμενος τὸν θεόν (*sebomenos ton theon*), God-fearer (*4936* + *2536*).

OT 1. *prosēlytos* (from *proserchomai*, approach) occurs only in Jewish and Christian lit. In LXX *prosēlytos* (trans. of Heb. *gēr*) designates a non-Israelite who has permanently settled in the land. Such people usually worked under Israelite masters as citizens without full rights, but in contrast to slaves they had personal freedom. They were not allowed to own or acquire landed property. But they did enjoy privileges in the land (e.g., they received legal protection, cf. Exod. 22:21), and they also had responsibilities, such as keeping the Sabbath according to God's law (20:10; 23:12).

Later, when Israel separated itself more and more from everything non-Jewish, the *gērîm* were to an increasing degree drawn into national life. They were given a share in the law, as in the sacrifices and great festivals (Num. 15:15–16, 30). If they accepted circumcision, they could even celebrate the Passover and were then fully integrated into the people (Exod. 12:48).

2. During the intertestamental period, *prosēlytos* acquired its more traditional meaning of a pagan who became a full-fledged Jew through conversion, circumcision, baptism, and a sacrifice in the temple. An intensive missionary movement began in the Hel. Jewish Diaspora. On the one hand, this movement was effective because of its concept of the transcendent, invisible God, who was incapable of representation by an image. On the other hand, it was limited by circumcision as an act of complete adherence.

3. Proselytes must be distinguished from non-Jews who took part in synagogue worship and kept the law to some extent, but who did not accept circumcision. The latter were required only to keep the Sabbath and food laws, together with the moral code, and to acknowledge the one God. These were called God-fearers (Gk. *phoboumenoi ton theon* [→ *5828*] or *sebomenoi ton theon* [→ *4936*]).

NT In the NT *proselyte* and *God-fearer* appear only in Acts (except for Matt. 23:15), the book that describes the coming into being of the young church on the mission field or among the Jews of the Diaspora.

1. *prosēlytos* occurs only 4x. In Matt. 23:15 Jesus is not attacking the missionary zeal of the Pharisees as such but the fact that they convert pagans to their own legalistic understanding of the law and thus make twice as much a "son of hell." In Acts 2:11 the various national groups are summed up as Jews (by birth) and proselytes (NIV, "converts to Judaism"). In 6:5 Nicolaus, one of the seven, is called "a convert to Judaism," since in contrast to the others, he was born a pagan. In 13:43 we find a more precise definition, "devout converts to Judaism" (*sebomenōn prosēlytōn*), designating full worshiping proselytes.

2. The phrase *phoboumenos* or *sebomenos ton theon* occurs only in Acts. Paul preached in the synagogues before Jews and "God-fearing

Gentiles" (Acts 13:26; cf. 13:16, "you Gentiles who worship God").
It was among such people that he found a powerful hearing. Lydia, a
seller of purple cloth in Philippi (16:14), and Titius Justus in Corinth
(18:7) are specifically mentioned as God-fearers. It was because Paul
did not demand circumcision but only faith in Christ that the *sebomenoi
ton theon* attached themselves to him. As a result, he came into conflict with the Jews, who accused him before Gallio of persuading
people to worship God contrary to the law (18:13).

The same type of conflict first surfaces in the story of the centurion, Cornelius (Acts 10:1–11:18), who is described as *phoboumenos
ton theon* (10:2, 22). Peter was attacked by the Jerusalem church
because he had not avoided contact with the uncircumcised, regardless
of how pious the centurion may have been, as was commanded in the
law of Moses. Rather, he actually baptized this man and his house as
believers in Christ.

See also *epistrephō*, turn, turn around, turn back, be converted (*2188*);
metamelomai, change one's mind, regret, repent (*3564*); *metanoia*,
change of mind, conversion (*3567*).

4672 (*proskairos*, temporary, transitory, passing), → *2789*.

4673 (*proskaleō*, summon), → *2813*.

4674 (*proskartereō*, persevere with, persist in), → *2846*.

4675 (*proskarterēsis*, persistence, steadfastness, perseverance),
→ *2846*.

4677 (*prosklēroō*, allot, assign, [pass.] join), → *3102*.

4681 (*proskollaō*, cleave to, stick to), → *3140*.

4682	πρόσκομμα

πρόσκομμα (*proskomma*), stumbling, offense, obstacle (*4682*);
προσκοπή (*proskopē*), occasion for taking offense or making a false
step (*4683*); προσκόπτω (*proskoptō*), strike, beat against, stumble,
be offended (*4684*); ἀπρόσκοπος (*aproskopos*), without offense, giving no offense, blameless (*718*).

CL & OT 1. In cl. Gk. *proskoptō* means trans. to strike or knock
against; intrans. to knock oneself against, trip, or fall. Metaphorically
it means either to give or to take offense. *proskomma* means the cause,
the process, and the results of the offense, and thus an obstacle, fall,
or destruction. *proskopē* means the offense or the reason for taking
offense. The verbal adj. *aproskopos* means both giving no offense
(i.e., being blameless) and taking no offense (i.e., being unhurt).

2. The OT is clear that sin causes a fall. Though the God of Israel
guards a person from tripping and falling (Ps. 91:11–12) and is "the
Rock" of Israel's strength and salvation (Deut. 32:15; Isa. 17:10), he
can become "a stone that causes men to stumble" (8:14), so that they
fall and perish. The God of Israel humbles those who do not fear him
(cf. Ps. 18:26). Hence he warns his people against worshiping heathen gods and fellowshipping with the godless inhabitants of the land,
who are a snare to them (Exod. 23:33; 34:12).

NT The words in this group follow the OT and have in the background the idea of tripping over a stone and falling. Four uses may be
distinguished.

1. Christ remains obedient to God and true to his task. Thus, neither Satan, who (alluding to Ps. 91:11–12) says that Jesus as God's Son
will not strike (*proskoptō*) his foot against a stone (Matt. 4:6; Lk. 4:11),
nor the threat of death by the Jews (Jn. 11:7–10), who were planning
to stone him should he come to Jerusalem, could cause him to stumble and nullify his messianic mission.

2. Christ is both the stone that serves as the foundation (→ *themelios*, *2529*) for the church and the stone over which one can fall (Rom.
9:33; 1 Pet. 2:8, both referring to Ps. 118:22; Isa. 8:14; 28:16). This
explained why many Jews were not coming to salvation. Whoever
refuses Jesus and his message finds eternal destruction (cf. Lk. 2:34).
Lk.'s version of the saying about the cornerstone presses the picture

further: "Everyone who falls on that stone will be broken to pieces, but
he on whom it falls will be crushed" (20:18). The background here is
Isa. 8:14–15, which declares that Yahweh will become "a stone that
causes men to stumble and a rock that makes them fall.... Many of
them will stumble; they will fall and be broken." What was said of
Yahweh by Isa. is said of Jesus in Lk. Humans will be either broken
on Christ now, as he shatters their preconceived plans for their lives,
or they will be broken by him in judgment.

3. Whether the disciple of Christ may cause offense to others is
another matter. Paul expressly forbids the strong to cause the weak to
stumble and to hurt their conscience (Rom. 14:13, 20–21; 1 Cor. 8:9).
Their freedom, though justified in itself, must not cause others to fall.
This is the law of love. Those who hurt the conscience of another create an obstacle for the gospel (cf. 1 Cor. 9:12–13, 19–20). Paul
enlarges the circle still further when he says, "Do not cause anyone to
stumble, whether Jews, Greeks or the church of God" (10:32).

4. The day of Christ makes it imperative that the Christian should
be without offense. Paul prays for the Christians in Philippi that they
"may be pure and blameless [*aproskopoi*] until the day of Christ"
(Phil. 1:10). Paul is not referring only to external and ethical behavior but also to the nature of our relationship to Christ (1:9); his prayer
is also a warning to the church. In his defense before Felix, Paul rebuts
the accusations of Tertullus when he declares, "So I strive always to
keep my conscience clear [*aproskopon*] before God and man" (Acts
24:16); in other words, Paul wants a conscience undefiled by sin.

See also *skandalon*, offense (*4998*).

4683 (*proskopē*, occasion for taking offense or making a false
step), → *4682*.

4684 (*proskoptō*, strike, beat against, stumble, be offended),
→ *4682*.

4686	προσκυνέω

προσκυνέω (*proskyneō*), worship, do obeisance to, prostrate
oneself, show reverence (*4686*); προσκυνητής (*proskynētēs*), a worshiper (*4687*).

CL & OT 1. In cl. Gk. *proskyneō* is a technical term for the adoration of the gods, meaning to fall down, prostrate oneself, adore on
one's knees. Often this took place by casting oneself on the ground to
show homage to a deity. Later the vb. was used in connection with the
deification of rulers and the Roman emperor cult. *proskyneō* can also
denote an inward attitude of reverence and humility.

2. In the overwhelming majority of cases in the LXX *proskyneō*
means to bow down; it is used both of bowing down before humans
and before God (e.g., Gen. 18:2; 19:1; 22:5; 23:7, 12; Exod. 4:31;
20:5). The noun *proskynēsis*, worship, which is absent from the NT,
occurs only in Sir. 50:21; 3 Macc. 3:7. Although in cl. Gk. *proskyneō*
is generally used trans., it hardly ever takes an acc. in the LXX, being
followed instead by a prep. phrase (e.g., *epi* [Gen. 18:2], *enantion*
[23:12], *enōpion* [Ps. 22:27], *pros* [5:7]). This Hebraism marks off
the adoration of Yahweh from pagan worship, in which the worshiper
has no sense of having to keep a distance from the deity. The God of
Israel is worshiped without images and thus is not within the grasp of
the worshiper.

proskyneō retains its physical sense of bending, except that this
is understood as bowing to the will of the exalted one (cf. Exod.
12:27–28). Just as folding or crossing the hands and arms denotes
the suppliant's mental concentration, and as lifting up outstretched
hands expresses the fact that one is making a request, so the physical
act of bending indicates one's readiness to bow to God's will. When
proskyneō refers to human beings, it indicates reverence shown to a
person superior in position or power (2 Sam. 18:21). But that certain
limits were observed in this matter is shown by Est. 3:2, 5, where a
Jew, at the peril of his life, refuses to prostrate himself before a heathen prince.

NT 1. In the NT the *proskyneō* occurs 60x (24 in Rev., 11 in Jn., and 13 in Matt.). The OT sense is further developed, except that now it denotes exclusively worship addressed (or which should be addressed) to God or to Jesus Christ (even in Matt. 18:26 the king is a symbolic figure for God). Acts 10:25–26; Rev. 19:10; 22:8–9 note that worship is to be offered to God alone, not to an apostle or even to an angelic being. Therefore, whenever obeisance is made before Jesus, the idea is either explicit or implicit that he is king (Matt. 2:2), Lord (8:2), the Son of God (14:33), or one who can act with divine omnipotence (e.g., 14:33; Mk. 5:6; 15:19).

For this reason obeisance is often linked with an earnest request for help. It intensifies the request and is a sign of faith in the divine helper and redeemer, a faith certain of being heard (e.g., Matt. 8:2; 9:18; 15:25). In Jn. 9:38 obeisance is nothing less than the outward reflex action of faith: To believe means to adore Jesus, to recognize him as Lord, to render him homage as king. Thus, obeisance is esp. appropriate before the risen and exalted Lord (Matt. 28:9, 17; Lk. 24:52).

When Satan, reversing the true order of things, suggests obeisance from Jesus (Matt. 4:9; Lk. 4:7), he demonstrates himself as God's great adversary, who wants to usurp what is due to God alone (Matt. 4:10; Lk. 4:8) and so overthrow all the good purposes and ordinances of God.

2. In this context obeisance is a sign of humankind's fundamentally religious nature. One's worship shows who one's god is: the true God, idols, demons, or even Satan himself (cf. Rev. 9:20; 13:4, 8, 12). For a person's relation to God is expressed principally in worship, and above all in prayer. The call to conversion can thus be put in the form: "Worship God!" i.e., recognize him in all his power and glory as creator and judge, and acknowledge his exclusive sovereign rights and claim on you (Rev. 14:7; 22:9).

3. When *proskyneō* is used absolutely, it means to participate in public worship, to offer prayers (e.g., Jn. 12:20; Acts 8:27; 24:11). Hence in Rev., *proskyneō* comes to denote a particular kind of prayer, namely, adoration. Its characteristic features find expression in the various hymns of adoration found throughout this book (4:8–11; 5:8–10, 12–14; 7:10–12; 11:15–18; 12:10–12; 15:3–4; 16:5–7; 19:1–8). These hymns are addressed to God himself (or to Jesus Christ) and are concerned with his being and his works in a worldwide context. They use varied language and ideas, constantly finding new titles of dignity with which to praise God and ascribing to him the most exalted merits and attributes (eternity, omnipotence, honor, wisdom, holiness, power, etc.). This often takes the form of royal acclamation: "You are worthy" (4:11; 5:9, 12) and "Salvation!" (7:10), interspersed with exclamations such as "Hallelujah!" "Amen!" (7:12; 19:1, 3, 4). Through such hymns runs a gloriously universal strain, and in the face of such adoration, human petitions and thanksgivings fade away into silence.

4. The noun *proskynētēs*, worshiper, occurs only in Jn. 4:23 in the context of Jesus' reply to the woman of Samaria that the time has come during which "true worshipers will worship the Father in spirit and truth" (cf. also 4:24). Earlier the woman had declared that her ancestors had worshiped on Mt. Gerizim (4:20). Jesus had countered this woman's assertion of her Samaritan faith by stating that "a time is coming when you will worship the Father neither on this mountain nor in Jerusalem" (4:21).

There is a dispute among scholars as to whether "in spirit and truth" refers to the human spirit or God's Spirit. If the former, Jesus' words are referring to the need to take up a correct personal attitude in worship in contrast to mere custom and ritual. But if the Spirit of God is meant here, the phrase may be a hendiadys meaning "Spirit of truth." This option does fit better the train of thought, for in the context, both "this mountain" and "Jerusalem" have come to stand for ways in which humans have seen fit to worship God in ways that are not acceptable to him. But in the coming age people will worship God in the true way, which he himself has chosen and provided, i.e., in and through himself (note Jn.'s teaching on the Spirit in Jn. 1:32–33;

3:5–8, 34; 6:63; 7:39; 11:33; 13:21; 14:16–17, 26; 15:26; 16:7, 13; 20:22).

See also *aiteō*, ask, ask for, demand (*160*); *gonypeteō*, fall on one's knees, kneel down before (*1206*); *deomai*, ask, request, beseech, beg (*1289*); *proseuchomai*, to pray, entreat (*4667*); *erōtaō*, ask, ask a question, request (*2263*); *krouō*, knock (*3218*); *entynchanō*, meet, turn to, approach, petition, pray, intercede (*1961*).

4687 (proskynētēs, a worshiper), → 4686.

4689 (proslambanō, take, receive or accept into one's society), → 3284.

4691 (proslēmpsis, admission, acceptance), → 3284.

4693 (prosmenō, remain, stay with, remain longer), → 3531.

4705 (prostassō, command, appoint), → 5435.

4710	πρόσφατος

πρόσφατος (*prosphatos*), fresh, new, late (*4710*); προσφάτως (*prosphatōs*), lately, recently (*4711*).

CL & OT In cl. Gk. this word was originally a sacrificial term: *pros* and *phatos* (a verbal adj. related to the noun *phonos*, slaughter); it meant just slaughtered and hence fresh or new. In the LXX this word occurs in Num. 6:3, where it means fresh grape juice; in Deut. 32:17, where it refers to new gods (cf. also Ps. 81:9); and in Eccl. 1:9, where the Teacher says that there is "nothing new under the sun" (cf. "new" in 1:10, which shows that *prosphatos* is a synonym for *kainos*). The adv. *prosphatōs*, "soon," occurs in Deut. 24:5; Ezek. 11:3; Jdt. 4:3, 5; 2 Macc. 14:36.

NT The adv. *prosphatōs* occurs without theological significance in Acts 18:2, where Lk. notes that Aquila and his wife, Priscilla, had "recently" come from Italy because of the command of Claudius that all Jews had to leave Rome.

The adj. *prosphatos* occurs only in Heb. 10:20, where it refers to the "new" (fresh) and living way of immediate access to the Father that has been opened for us through the physical death of Jesus Christ. That death is here associated with "the curtain," relating Jesus' sacrifice to the OT Day of Atonement, in which the high priest went behind the curtain into the Most Holy Place to enter the presence of God, symbolized by the ark of the covenant. Since the death and resurrection of Jesus and his position as our "great high priest over the house of God" (10:21), we no longer need the ceremonial system of the old covenant. Insofar as our ability to draw near to God is related to the "new [*kainos*] covenant" (8:8; 9:15), *prosphatos* is a synonym of *kainos*.

See also *neos*, new, young, fresh (*3742*); *kainos*, new (*2785*).

4712 (prospherō, offer, sacrifice), → 2604.

4714 (prosphora, offering, the act of offering), → 2604.

4717 (proschysis, pouring or sprinkling [of blood]), → 1772.

4719 (prosōpolēmpteō, show partiality, give a biased judgment), → 4725.

4720 (prosōpolēmptēs, biased, taking sides), → 4725.

4721 (prosōpolēmpsia, partiality, bias), → 4725.

4725	πρόσωπον

πρόσωπον (*prosōpon*), face (*4725*); προσωπολημψία (*prosōpolēmpsia*), partiality, bias (*4721*); προσωπολημπτέω (*prosōpolēmpteō*), show partiality, give a biased judgment (*4719*); προσωπολήμπτης (*prosōpolēmptēs*), biased, taking sides (*4720*); ἀπροσωπολήμπτως (*aprosōpolēmptōs*), unbiased (*719*).

CL & OT 1. In cl. Gk. *prosopon* means face, actor's mask, and then (fig.) the part played by the actor. When used of things it means surface, either the top or the one facing the observer. It is occasionally used for the face of the gods.

2. *prosōpon* is found about 900x in the LXX, mostly as a translation of *pānîm*. (a) It is used for someone's face (Gen. 31:2) or appearance (4:5), also as a paraphrase for the whole person (Deut. 7:10). The frequent expression "to turn the face" means to greet respectfully. It is sometimes also used for the faces of animals (Ezek. 1:10).

(b) It can denote the face (surface) of the earth (Gen. 2:6).

(c) It is also used with various preps. to express relationships, e.g., "before the face of," meaning before, into, in front of, opposite.

(d) It is used above all for the "face" of God. Where the LXX uses this phrase, it is often referring to some relationship of God to human beings, e.g., his gracious turning to them or his disappointed turning away from them. If God lifts up or causes his face to shine on the Israelites, they receive peace (i.e., salvation; see Num. 6:25–26). When God hides or turns away his face, it implies the withdrawal of grace (cf. Ps. 13:1; 104:29). Seeing God's face is mentioned as the most exceptional possibility (Gen. 32:30, Peniel, the face of God; cf. also 16:13; Exod. 24:9–11; Deut. 4:12; Jdg. 6:22–23). This is always a dangerous experience, for if sinful people see the holy God, they must die (Exod. 33:20; cf. Isa. 6:5).

(e) When God's face is mentioned in connection with the temple, the language is cultic. Extrabiblical usage may have had an influence here. Among the nations surrounding Israel, the face of the deity was seen and worshiped in its temple. Since Israel had no image of God in the temple, the expression of seeking God's face has a metaphorical sense, denoting prayer (Ps. 24:6; 42:2; Zech. 8:21–22; Mal. 1:9) or the seeking of God's fellowship (Ps. 105:4).

(f) In rab. Jud. a human's highest hope is to see the face of God or the Shekinah, either in the hour of death and in the world to come after the days of the Messiah or even during the days of the Messiah.

NT The NT follows the OT usage in its use of *prosōpon*.

1. (a) It can be used lit. of a person's face (Matt. 6:16–17; 2 Cor. 11:20). (b) It is used in various metaphorical expressions: e.g., "to fall on one's face" is a sign of respect and subjection (Matt. 17:6; Lk. 5:12; 1 Cor. 14:25), and "Jesus resolutely set out for [lit., set his face to go to] Jerusalem" (Lk. 9:51) expresses his immovable decision to head for Jerusalem. (c) *prosōpon* can stand for the whole person (2 Cor. 1:11). (d) It is also frequently combined with preps., mostly in lit. reproductions of Sem. expressions: e.g., "ahead of you [lit., before your face]" (Mk. 1:2), "in the sight of" (Lk. 2:31). (e) Face is also used to refer to the surface of the earth (Lk. 21:35; Acts 17:26) and the appearance of the sky (Matt. 16:3) and of plants (Jas. 1:11).

2. *prosōpon* is further used of the face of God and of Christ. The angels of the "little ones . . . see the face of [God] in heaven" (Matt. 18:10), a circumlocution for God's care for the humble. In the heavenly sanctuary Christ appears for us "in God's presence" (lit., "before the face of God," Heb. 9:24). Thereby the heavenly sanctuary replaces the earthly temple.

For believers the glory of God (→ *doxa*, *1518*) has appeared "in the face of Christ" (2 Cor. 4:6). Paul is writing here about the glorified Lord. Thus, *prosōpon* as used here recalls the face of God in the OT. Christ "is the image of God" (4:4; cf. Jn. 12:45; 14:9), God's turning to us and his final revelation. The reference of the whole context to Exod. 34 makes this certain. The glory on Moses' face, derived from his meeting with God, was transient (2 Cor. 3:13). Hence he covered his face with a veil. Paul expands the picture to cover the whole OT. The veil that hid Moses' transient glory covers the whole OT, so that Israel cannot see the glory of the promise and fulfillment in Christ (3:14–15). Only when there is faith in Christ is the veil removed (3:16). All present knowledge by faith is only an imperfect anticipation of the future knowledge, "face to face" (1 Cor. 13:12). God's servants will not see his face until they are in the new Jerusalem (Rev. 22:4).

3. *prosōpon* is also used in the compound words *prosōpolēmpsia, prosōpolēmptēs, prosōpolēmpteō*—all compounded with a form of the verb *lambanō* (lit., take). This translates the Heb. *nāśāʾ*, to lift up the face of one who has bowed humbly in greeting, i.e., to acknowl-

edge that person. God does not allow himself to be influenced by appearances or respect of persons (Deut. 10:17). He is impartial (*ouk estin prosōpolēmptēs*, Acts 10:34) and acts with impartiality (*aprosōpolēmptōs*, 1 Pet. 1:17). Likewise, the earthly judge must refrain from all partiality (Lev. 19:15; Deut. 1:17; 16:19; cf. also Mk. 12:14; Gal. 2:6; Jude 16). *prosōpolēmpsia* means partiality or bias (Rom. 2:11; Eph. 6:9; Col. 3:25; Jas. 2:1). In Jas. 2:9 *prosōpolēmpteō* means to show partiality.

4728 (*proteros*, beforehand), → *4755*.

4729	προτίθημι

προτίθημι (*protithēmi*), mid. display publicly, plan, propose, intend; act. set before as a duty (*4729*); πρόθεσις (*prothesis*), setting forth, presentation, display, plan, purpose, resolve (*4606*).

CL & OT 1. The vb. *protithēmi* (*pro*, before, with the vb. *tithēmi*, set, place; → *5502*) possesses the basic meaning to set before, but also means to resolve, propose, determine. The noun *prothesis* can denote the public lying in state of the dead, public announcements, and later, an intention.

2. In the LXX *protithēmi* (used 19x) is used 5x in the sense of laying before or laying on (e.g., Exod. 40:4 of the bread of the Presence). In Ps. 86:14 it describes a conscious refusal to turn to God (cf. also 101:3, where it denotes not setting evil before one's eyes). The noun *prothesis* (19x) is used 13x as a technical term for the bread of the Presence (e.g., Exod. 39:36 = LXX 39:18) and is thus to be translated *presentation*. The meaning of intention, purpose, plan is found only in 2 Macc. 3:8; 3 Macc. 1:22; 2:26; 5:12, 29.

NT 1. In the NT *protithēmi* is found 3x. It means to resolve in Rom. 1:13 (cf. Paul's intention to visit Rome), to put forward in 3:25 (God "presented [Christ] as a sacrifice of atonement"; → *hilaskomai*, *2661*), and to set forth in Eph. 1:9 (God set forth his purpose in Christ). The noun *prothesis* occurs 12x, 4 of which refer to the "consecrated bread," i.e., the bread of the Presence (e.g., Matt. 12:4; Heb. 9:2). Human objectives are mentioned in Acts 11:23; 27:13; 2 Tim. 3:10 ("purpose").

2. By contrast with the nontheological use of the word in the LXX, Paul uses *prothesis* 2x in order to describe the primal decision of God. In Rom. 8:28 God's *prothesis* (resolve, purpose) is stated to be the foundation of the Christian's call. Our hope and certainty are based on and upheld by God's previous activity, not by any human capacity for decision making. Paul uses the word similarly in 9:11 (cf. Gen. 25:23). The election of Jacob was already laid down in God's resolve before the birth of the twins. Here also *prothesis* serves to characterize God's activity as free and grounded in his will alone. It is thus independent of human prerogatives. The keeping of the promise is always God's free act both in Israel and in the church.

3. In Eph. 1:11 the existence of the church is described as the result of a decision made by God. This decision is both in time and in all aspects a *preceding resolve*. As in Rom. 8:28–30, there is an accumulation of words that emphasize the priority of God's will. In Eph. 3:8–11 Paul discusses the realization of God's saving plan in Christ. *prothesis* in 3:11 serves to characterize God's activity in Christ as the fulfillment of an "eternal purpose." It is one in which we do not have a say, either in time or in its intentions. In 2 Tim. 1:9 Paul is concerned with the redeeming and calling activity of God. Once again, its assumptions do not lie in the area of prior human achievement but of God's own decision.

See also *proginōskō*, know beforehand, know in advance (*4589*); *pronoeō*, perceive beforehand, foresee, provide, care for (*4629*); *prooraō*, see in advance, foresee (*4632*); *proorizō*, decide on beforehand, predestine (*4633*).

4735 (*prophēteia*, prophetic activity, gift, word, or saying), → *4737*.

4736 (*prophēteuō*, make prophetic revelations, prophesy), → *4737*.

| 4737 προφήτης |

προφήτης (*prophētēs*), prophet, proclaimer (*4737*); προφῆτις (*prophētis*), prophetess (*4739*); προφητεύω (*prophēteuō*), make prophetic revelations, prophesy (*4736*); προφητεία (*prophēteia*), prophetic activity, prophetic gift, prophetic word, prophetic saying (*4735*); προφητικός (*prophētikos*), prophetic (*4738*); ψευδο-προφήτης (*pseudoprophētēs*), false prophet (*6021*).

CL 1. *prophētēs* (from *pro-*, before, and *phē-*, to say) essentially means one who proclaims openly or states publicly. The vb. *prophēteuō* has a similar meaning. Often behind this word is a note of authority. The rest of the words in this group are derived from the same root.

2. From cl. Gk. lit. we can ascertain the place of the prophet in Gk. public life. The words of this group are tied up with the Gk. oracle, the most famous being that at Delphi, presided over by Apollo. In this connection we meet these words in two senses.

(a) The Pythia at Delphi was called *prophētis*, but had the further title of *promantis*. She was an elderly woman who sat on a tripod over a cavity in the earth, from which an "oracular spirit" in the form of smoke arose and gave her inspiration. This was enhanced by the chewing of bay leaves (Apollo's plant). She would burst out with enigmatic inarticulate sounds, similar to speaking in tongues. Her messages concerned future events and had a direct connection with the person consulting the oracle, who came to it baffled by a problem and sought help in the form of instruction. The person consulting would present in writing a question that had arisen in his or her life—a question of business, religion, politics, ethics, or education.

(b) Since the Pythia's reply was usually incomprehensible to the visitor, other officials at the shrine were responsible to translate the utterance into a saying that could be understood and remembered. This task was carried out by wise and respected old men, called to this position by the oracle and likewise known as *prophētai*. They did not work by direct inspiration but rather by reason and understanding. They received the Pythian oracles, tested them, interpreted them, and formulated the final saying. Thus they never spoke on their own initiative, but only after a visitor had presented a question and the Pythia had uttered the oracle.

(c) From the preceding discussion we note the following features: (i) The prophet received a message indirectly from the god or the inspired soothsayer. Direct inspiration was a privilege reserved for the Pythia. Indirect inspiration came through her inarticulate utterances or through such things as the blowing of the wind, the rustling of the sacred oaks, the clanging of cymbals, or the shaking of an image of a god borne by priests.

(ii) The prophet did not give advice until asked. The initiative was the questioner's alone, not the god's or the prophet's.

(iii) For this reason the words of the Gk. prophet were always addressed to a unique, historical situation in the life of the client. The advice given embraced a whole range of counseling help that was called for by human troubles and needs.

3. In early times the Gk. poet also had the title of prophet, since he achieved in his poetry something unique. He derived his wisdom from the gods.

OT 1. The Heb. word for prophet (*nābî'*) is probably derived from a vb. that means to call, proclaim. This can be understood either in an act. sense (a prophet is someone who calls out, proclaims), or in a pass. sense (someone called or appointed by God). From this noun the vb. *nābā'* is derived, which means to show, present, or express oneself, to speak as a prophet (1 Sam. 10:5f., 10ff.; 19:20; 1 Ki. 22:10, 12).

(a) The noun *nābî'* occurs 309x in the OT. In the historical books the pl. signifies groups of prophets; the sing. in early texts denotes widely varying types of people, while in later texts it denotes one who speaks on behalf of Yahweh. In earlier texts, the prophet can also have the title "man of God"—a title of distinction given to great leaders such as Moses (Deut. 33:1), David (Neh. 12:24, 36), but above all Elisha

(29x) and the unnamed prophet of Judah in 1 Ki. 13:1–31 (15x)—or "seer" (i.e., someone who through visions has the ability to reveal hidden secrets and future events [1 Sam. 9:6–20]).

(b) Various figures in the history of Israel were given the title of *nābî'*. They include Abraham (Gen. 20:7), Moses (Deut. 34:10), and Aaron (Exod. 7:1). Miriam received the title of prophetess (Exod. 15:20), which is doubtless linked with the Song of Moses at the Red Sea.

2. Before the fully-fledged prophecy of the writing prophets took shape, certain earlier forms are found in the OT. (a) One of these is the groups of ecstatics who moved freely about the country, putting themselves by the use of musical instruments into a state of trance and in such a condition babbling out their messages. This ecstasy was infectious, so that Saul also came to be counted "among the prophets" (1 Sam. 10:11; 19:24). The prophets of Baal were also ecstatics (1 Ki. 18:19–40). In Num. 11:10–30, seventy elders were seized by the Spirit of God and went into an ecstasy. Joshua was critical of them, but Moses replied: "I wish that all the LORD's people were prophets and that the LORD would put his Spirit on them!" (11:29).

(b) Another early form is the groups of prophets in monastic communities. These groups formed themselves around a prominent figure (e.g., Elisha, 2 Ki. 2:3–18; 4:38; 6:1), whom they addressed as "master" or "father," at whose feet they sat and learned, and with whom they lived in communal dwellings. Such groups are linked with a sanctuary (1 Ki. 13:11, Bethel; 2 Ki. 2:1, 4, 5, Gilgal, Jericho). Ecstasy has here a markedly reduced role. Instead, the gift of the Spirit seems to be manifested by the working of miracles (2:19–25; 4:1–7, 8–37). But note too that Elisha was also a man of God's word, who gave both spiritual (4:1–7, 8–37; 5:1–14) and political counsel (13:14–20).

(c) A third early form involved the cultic prophets employed as officials at the national sanctuary. These men had a place along with the priests in the cult. Their task was to give oracles in answer to communal laments, esp. to the king. For this reason they had great influence in the royal court (1 Ki. 1:8), where they spoke as men of God (22:24–28), sometimes with remarkable severity (cf. Nathan in 2 Sam. 12:1–14). The cultic prophets were feared, because their powerful word could bring success or disaster (1 Sam. 16:4; 1 Ki. 17:18). Among the cultic prophets we may count Shimei (1 Ki. 1:8), Zedekiah (22:24), and Nathan (2 Sam. 12:1–14; 1 Ki. 1:8–45), who worked in close association with the court and yet enjoyed an astonishing degree of independence.

3. Prophecy in the traditional sense associated with the prophetic lit. of the OT began in Israel with the monarchy. Ecstasy, soothsaying, and miracle-working fade into the background, and the word of Yahweh comes increasingly to the fore. Ties with the cult, with institutions, and with the monarchy also become progressively looser. In fact, these prophets were often critical of the cult (e.g., Isa. 1:10–17; Jer. 7:1–15; Mic. 3:9–12). The word was the predominant means of proclamation. The only actions of the prophets were symbolic actions, acting out the content of the word (e.g., Isa. 7:3; 8:3–4; 20:2; Jer. 16:2, 5, 8; Hos. 1:2, 4, 6, 9; 3:1–5).

The cl. prophets were active during three periods: the dissolution of the northern kingdom (around 721 B.C.), the destruction of the southern kingdom (around 597–587 B.C.), and the return from exile (around 539 B.C.). Their message had a horizontal dimension (messages regarding Israel and the nations) and a vertical dimension. Often their messages included warnings, where the future is linked with the present situation of the hearer. Their themes include the following:

(a) Prophecies of judgment. Esp. before the exile, the prophets warned the people about approaching judgment. This could take various forms, such as droughts, earthquakes, and wars. But since the prophets were also responsible for exhorting and counseling the people with a view to repentance, the threat of judgment was accompanied by an explanation of its reason. Judgment was a result of the sins of the nation, the king, or a group within the nation. For the prophets, sin is human behavior that is out of accord with God's character and will. In Isa. this meant that the people were not trusting in Yahweh alone; in Amos and Mic., that the people were disobeying the law of Yahweh; in Hos., Jer., and Ezek., that the people were unfaithful by worshiping idols.

(b) Prophecies of salvation. These prophecies, which were based on the loving will of God, included promises of God's future help (Isa. 41:17–20; Jer. 31:31–40) and descriptions of the salvation that God would bring about (cf. Isa. 11:1–9; Zech. 8:4–5). Prophecies of salvation predominated during and after the exile. Salvation would become a reality in the renewal of the relationship between Israel and God, in the eschatological king (the Messiah), in the new ordering of the cult, and in the political liberation of the nation. A majestic representation of salvation was generally followed by an explanation of the ground on which it was based: not the faithfulness, holiness, or zeal of the people, but the faithfulness, holiness, and unconditional love of God.

4. At least two of the later canonical prophets (Dan. and Zech.) wrote in the style of Jewish apocalyptic. Apocalyptic is not a straightforward continuation of prophecy, though both share the element of future expectation. Thus in Zech.'s seven visions of the night (1:7–6:8), the prophet becomes a seer to whom the eschatological future of the nations and of Israel is revealed (cf. Isa. 24–27; Ezek. 38–39; Joel). The rabbis saw in apocalyptic the legitimate successor of prophecy. The cessation of prophecy is indicated by Ps. 74:9 and 1 Macc. 9:27 (cf. 4:46; 14:41).

5. The Qumran community treasured the OT prophetic writings to an extraordinary degree. They applied the prophecies to the events of their own day, which they saw as the end time. The Teacher of Righteousness reveals the secrets of the prophetic words (1QpHab 7:1–5) and so takes on the role of an actual prophet. The Qumran community awaited the coming of "the Prophet and the Messiahs of Aaron and Israel" (1QS 9:11).

NT 1. (a) In the NT *prophētēs* is found 144x (most frequently in Matt. and Luke–Acts). It means a prophet, one who proclaims and expounds divine revelation. In most cases it refers to OT prophets, but it is also applied to John the Baptist, Jesus, and others who proclaim the kingdom of God or Christ, and to those believers who possess the gift of prophecy. Only in one place (Tit. 1:12) does a pagan (the poet Epimenides) receive the title of prophet; he was also regarded as a prophet by Gk. writers in the ancient world. As well as referring to a person, the word *prophētēs* is also used of the OT prophetic writings (e.g., Matt. 5:17; Jn. 6:45; Rom. 3:21).

(b) The title *prophētis* (prophetess) is given in the NT only to Anna, the daughter of Phanuel, because she proclaimed Christ (Lk. 2:36), and to Jezebel, the type of the woman who led astray into idolatry and who called herself a prophetess (Rev. 2:20).

(c) The abstract noun *prophēteia* occurs only 19x in the NT (9x in Paul and 7x in Rev.). It refers to the prophetic word of an OT (e.g., Matt. 13:14) or of a Christian prophet (e.g., 1 Cor. 14:6). Only Paul uses it as a term for the gift of prophecy (e.g., Rom. 12:6). At Rev. 19:10 it probably means prophetic word, while at 11:6 it signifies prophetic activity.

(d) The vb. *prophēteuō* is found 28x in the NT (11x in Paul, all in 1 Cor.). The basic meaning is to proclaim divine revelation (e.g., Matt. 7:22). This can be understood in an ethical, hortatory sense (e.g., 1 Cor. 14:3, 31), in a revelatory sense (e.g., Matt. 26:68), or as pointing to the future (e.g., 15:7).

(e) The late word *pseudoprophētēs* is found 11x in the NT. It denotes a person who makes a false claim to being a prophet (e.g., Matt. 7:15). Since such people proceed to preach what is not true, the name is applied to anyone who does this (1 Jn. 4:1). The adj. *prophētikos* occurs only in Rom. 16:26 and 2 Pet. 1:19.

2. The NT term *prophet* is used in five ways. (a) It can mean the OT prophet, who is a spokesperson for God (Acts 3:18, 21). God is behind the pass. construction in Matt. 2:17, 23, etc. In Heb. 1:1 the prophet is likewise an instrument of God who makes an open proclamation. Often the focus of the OT prophet's message is on predictions that are fulfilled in Jesus Christ (e.g., Matt. 1:22–23; 2:5–6, 15, 17–18, 23; for more on this, → *plēroō*, fulfill, *4444*). Matt. does not cite these prophets in an attempt to prove their authority as prophets; rather, the texts are quotations intended to prove that Jesus Christ is the promised Messiah. The direction of the argument is thus the opposite to that of a proof text that establishes the truth of Scripture.

A striking feature is the frequency of NT references to the violent deaths of the prophets (Matt. 23:31; Acts 7:52). In early Christianity martyrdom was related to the concept of the prophet. Jesus presented himself as one who stood in the long line of rejected prophets; his own rejection marked the climax of evil and brought open judgment on Jerusalem (Matt. 21:33–44). He was also the culminating figure of those who were martyred for their righteousness (23:35; Lk. 11:51). Abel (Gen. 4) was the first; Zechariah, the son of Jehoiada, is mentioned toward the end of the last book of the Heb. canon (2 Chr. 24:20–22).

(b) John the Baptist is consistently given the title of prophet. This is justified since he takes up and makes even more radical the prophetic preaching of judgment and repentance (Jer. 7:3–29; 26:1–19; Amos 9:7–15; Mic. 3:12). His preaching was aimed at moral improvement and at shaking the religious self-confidence of the Jews. His baptism was a testimony of conversion and formed a seal of salvation. It is not surprising that many Jews therefore regarded John as the expected eschatological prophet who would bring in the age of salvation (cf. Deut. 18:15–18). The NT, however, portrays him as the forerunner (e.g., Matt. 3:1–12; 11:11–12; 14:2–5; 16:14; 17:13) or witness of Jesus (Jn. 1:6–9), who points in his preaching to Jesus Christ, the true eschatological prophet.

(c) Only occasionally in the NT is Jesus Christ called a prophet and generally only by the people (Matt. 16:14; 21:11, 46; Mk. 6:15; Lk. 7:16; 24:19; Jn. 4:19; in Lk. 13:33, Jesus alludes to himself as a prophet). He stands in the succession of the OT prophets, though he is greater than them (Matt. 12:41), since he not only announced but also brought salvation (Lk. 10:24; 1 Pet. 1:10–11). Jesus is presented as a prophet in the sense of Deut. 18:15: "The LORD your God will raise up for you a prophet like me [Moses] from among your own brothers. You must listen to him" (cf. Acts 3:22–23; 7:37; see also Jn. 6:14; 7:40).

(d) In the nativity narrative of Lk., and only here, we find people who have been specially commissioned and equipped by God to proclaim prophetic messages given to them by the Holy Spirit. Of these only Anna has the title of prophetess (Lk. 2:36). Zechariah's song is described as a prophecy inspired by the Holy Spirit (1:67). Elizabeth (1:41–42) and Simeon (2:25) speak by the Holy Spirit, which implies a prophetic gift.

(e) The early Christian church had believers who possessed the gift of prophecy. They were regarded as a sign that the Spirit was present in the church. It appears as if this charismatic gift became institutionalized, and prophets were then seen as the holders of a spiritual office. They had their own standing in the community on a par with apostles and teachers (Lk. 11:49; 1 Cor. 12:28–29; Eph. 2:20; 3:5; 4:11), next to teachers (Acts 13:1), or next to saints and apostles (Rev. 18:20).

(i) In the worship at Corinth prophets had the task of exhorting, comforting, and edifying the church (1 Cor. 14:3, 24–25, 31), and of communicating knowledge and mysteries (13:2). Paul instructed them to do this in words that could be understood (14:15–16, 23–24), not in a state of ecstasy. There was evidently a danger that the prophetic spirit might break out in uncontrolled, ecstatic power so that several would be prophesying at the same time (14:31). Paul ruled that the spirits of prophets should be subject to the prophets (14:32), by which he meant submission to order and the peace of God (14:33a). The prophet must also be able to remain silent.

(ii) In Eph. 2:20 the prophets together with the apostles form part of the "foundation" of the church, with Jesus Christ being the chief cornerstone. Traditionally these prophets have been understood to be OT prophets, but most scholars today acknowledge that Paul probably means NT prophets (cf. the order, "apostles and prophets"). The image used suggests that when the period in which the laying of the foundation of the church was over, the prophetic office would be over (→ *themelios*, foundation, *2529*).

(iii) Warnings against false prophets in the Synoptic Gospels (Matt. 7:15, 22–23; 24:24) suggest that there must have been a great number of Christian prophets in the area of Syria and Palestine, some of whom were pretenders and not genuine prophets.

(iv) Acts gives considerable information about prophets. One sign of the superabundant outpouring of the Holy Spirit is the recognition that all Christians are given prophetic inspiration (2:17–18; 19:6). In fact, Lk. gives the names of certain early Christian prophets (11:27–28; 13:1; 15:32; 21:9–11), such as Agabus, who predicted a widespread famine (11:28) and Paul's arrest (21:10–11), and the four daughters of Philip, who prophesied (21:9). The vb. *prophēteuō* is always used in Acts of Christians. Although Peter is not called a prophet, he has the marks of one, which include knowledge of human hearts (5:3; 8:21–23). He also had experience of visions and dreams, fulfilling the prophecy of Joel (cf. also Acts 10:10–20). Others had these prophetic experiences as well (9:10; 16:9; 22:17–21; 27:23; cf. Num. 12:6).

What distinguishes the prophets in Acts? Certain functions are reminiscent of the OT prophet: prediction of future events (11:28; 20:23, 25; 27:22), declaration of divine judgments (13:11; 28:25–28), and the employment of symbolic actions (21:11). There is also, as in the OT, a link between prophecy and exhortation. Judas and Silas, "who were themselves prophets, said much to encourage and strengthen the brothers" (15:32; → *parakaleō*, encourage, *4151*). The interpretation of Scripture, usually in the synagogues, is a central feature of the mission of the prophets, though it is not confined to them (2:14–36; 3:12–26; 4:8–12; 7:2–53; 9:20–22; 13:5, 16–41).

(v) In Rev. prophets are mentioned in 10:7; 11:10, 18; 16:6; 18:20, 24; 22:6, 9. The author regards himself as a prophet who has received from the exalted Lord a revelation of the meaning of the events of history (1:1; 22:9). This is embodied in a series of seven sets of visions, which constitute the substance of his book. He is called to console and exhort (cf. above). Although the words *parakaleō* and *paraklēsis* do not occur, the letters to the seven churches in chs. 2–3 (and indeed the whole work) are messages of consolation and exhortation that carry the authority of the exalted Christ, speaking through the Spirit (22:18–19).

(vi) For a time prophecy continued to have a place in the church. Prophets are known in the *Didache* (end of 1st cent.), though the author shows some nervousness about false prophets and those who outstay their welcome (10:7; 11:7–12; 13:1–7). Prophets featured in Montanism in the 2d and 3d centuries, but Montanist abuse led to the gradual discrediting and disappearance of prophecy in the church.

4738 (prophētikos, prophetic), → *4737*.

4739 (prophētis, prophetess), → *4737*.

| 4741 προχειρίζω | προχειρίζω (*procheirizō*), determine, appoint (*4741*). |

CL & OT *procheirizō* means prepare something or someone for a purpose; the mid. usually means prepare for oneself, keep something at one's disposal; determine, nominate, elect. It was used for the election of leaders of the people or the appointment of a prosecutor by the general assembly. It was also used of the allotment of land, of legions to a general, or of the resolutions of a legislative or executive body. It became a common term in legal language of the inscriptions and papyri.

In the LXX *procheirizō* occurs 6x. It means the choice and commissioning of someone by God (Exod. 4:13) or leaders (Jos. 3:12; Dan. 3:22) to carry out a particular task, esp. one of a political or military nature (2 Macc. 3:7; 8:9; 14:12).

NT This vb. is found only 3x, all in Acts. In 26:16 it is used in the words of the risen Christ to Paul, whom he appointed as a minister and witness to what he had seen and would be shown (cf. 16:9–10; 22:17–21; 23:11). Ananias's words (22:14) are to be similarly understood: The God of Israel had "chosen [Paul] to know his will and to see the Righteous One and to hear words from his mouth." Paul's calling rested on this event. In 3:20 Peter urges repentance "that [God] may send the Christ, who has been appointed for you."

See also *kathistēmi*, bring, appoint (*2770*); *horizō*, determine, appoint (*3988*); *paristēmi*, place, put at the disposal of (*4225*); *tassō*, arrange, appoint (*5435*); *tithēmi*, put, place, set, appoint (*5502*); *prothesmia*, appointed date (*4607*); *cheirotoneō*, appoint (*5936*); *lanchanō*, obtain as by lot (*3275*).

4742 (procheirotoneō, appoint beforehand), → *5936*.

4750 (prōteuō, be first), → *4755*.

4751 (prōtokathedria, seat of honor), → *2764*.

4752 (prōtoklisia, place of honor, best seat), → *2764*.

4754 (prōton, first of all), → *4755*.

| 4755 πρῶτος | πρῶτος (*prōtos*), first (*4755*); πρῶτον (*prōton*), first of all (*4754*); πρωτεύω (*prōteuō*), be first (*4750*); πρότερος (*proteros*), beforehand (*4728*). |

CL & OT 1. *prōtos* is the superlative of *pro*, before, and the ordinal number corresponding to *heis*, one. In late Koine Gk. it was also used for *proteron* (earlier). It was originally used as an adj. or noun, meaning first in time or space; then in the neut., *prōton*, as an adv. meaning first, at first. *prōtos* further connotes first in order or succession, and first in rank or worth. In Gk. philosophy *ta prōta* means the basic elements; in logic, the primary, unprovable propositions. In Aristotle *prōtē philosophia* means that which is of the highest order (i.e., metaphysics), or alternatively, the philosophy of the ancients. In mathematics the prime numbers are called *prōtoi arithmoi*.

2. In the LXX *prōtos* (240x) usually represents, as does *archē* (beginning), the Heb. *rōʾš*; also *ʾehād* (17x), first, one; and *qedem* (9x), forward. Generally speaking, the meanings of *prōtos* correspond to those in cl. Gk., though they are confined to the nonphilosophical senses.

(a) *prōtos* can have a spatial sense: in front, toward the East (i.e., the first in rank of the directions, "toward the sunrise," Num. 2:3); in the front, above (1 Sam. 9:22). (b) In the temporal sense (most frequent) it means first (Deut. 13:9; Ruth 3:10), in earlier times (2 Sam. 16:23), first of all (Tob. 5:9, S); as a noun in neut. pl., former things in contrast to later things (Eccl. 1:11). (c) As an ordinal it denotes order or succession: first (Gen. 32:17; Exod. 12:18; 1 Sam. 14:14). (d) Finally, it denotes rank and worth of both persons (e.g., the chief priest or high priest, 1 Ki. 2:35; the king's closest friend, 1 Chr. 27:33; the lead singer, Neh. 12:46) and things (the most valuable, 1 Sam. 15:21; the most precious, Amos 6:6).

Theologically, *prōtos* can be used to designate God as "the first"—a special characteristic of the preaching and theology of Isa. (cf. 41:4; 44:6; 48:12). God is *prōtos* as the Creator; he is also the last. The whole creation is directed toward his acts. It is true that the temporal sense is present here as well, since the Creator is the Eternal One before (and after) all creation. But in the first instance *prōtos* here expresses the position of God as the Lord of the world.

3. In interpreting Gen. 2:7, Philo distinguished two kinds of humans. The "first" is from heaven and spiritual, while the "second" is Adam, the forefather of the human race; note how Paul reverses the order: "The first man Adam became a living being; the last Adam, a life-giving spirit" (1 Cor. 15:45). Occasionally God is called *prōtos kai monos*, the first and only one (→ *monos*, *3668*); both terms express his uniqueness.

NT 1. In the NT *prōtos* occurs 155x (95x as adj. or noun, 60x as adv.). It is used in much the same way as it is in the LXX. (a) It is used in a spatial sense in such passages as Acts 12:10; Heb. 9:2, 6, 8.

(b) It is also used in a temporal sense: first, first of all, to begin with, previously (Matt. 5:24; Lk. 9:59, 61); in the pair of opposites *ta prōta—ta eschata*, "first [condition]"—"final condition" (Lk. 11:26). An element of evaluation is contained in the contrast between *hē prōtē* and *hē kainē diathēkē*, the first and the new covenant (Heb. 8:7, 13; cf. 8:6, 8). The first or old covenant has been superseded by the new and is no longer valid (*archaios* is used in 2 Cor. 5:17 and 2 Pet. 2:5; *palaios* in 2 Cor. 3:14).

(c) In a succession or order, *prōtos* means first in a series, followed possibly by *deuteros, tritos*, second, third, or else by *heteros*, the other (Matt. 22:25; Lk. 14:18; Jn. 19:32). It is used adverbially as the first (20:4).

(d) As a designation of rank and office, *prōtoi* ("leading men," Mk. 6:21) stands alongside *megistanes* and *chiliarchoi* as a title. It draws attention to the value of a special garment ("best robe," Lk. 15:22). In the *prōtoi* and *eschatoi* of Matt. 19:30 there is an element of evaluation: The *prōtoi* are those who have been accepted, the last, those who have been rejected. Used adverbially in this sense, it denotes priority perhaps to the exclusion of others (Mk. 7:27), in the first place or first of all (Rom. 1:16; 2:9–10), so also probably in 1 Tim. 1:16, where Paul as the first is a typical representative of God's grace.

(e) *prōteuō* also denotes privilege: to take the first place, be preeminent (Col. 1:18; see here *prōtotokos, 4758*).

2. The frequent NT use of *prōtos/prōton* as an expression of order or sequence (69x) demonstrates the significance of order in God's plan and revelation, however important the free, unpredictable Spirit may be. This is partly accounted for by the influence of the OT and Jud. and the importance they attached to a devout, believing, well-ordered life (Lk. 11:38; Jn. 7:51). Jesus insisted on priorities in his new, messianic order. Thus, before bringing your sacrifice, first be reconciled to your fellow believer (Matt. 5:24); seek first the kingdom of God (6:33); first take the beam out of your own eye, then set about removing the splinter from your neighbor's (7:5). God has even ordered various events in the course of salvation history (e.g., Mk. 9:11 par.; 1 Thess. 4:16; 2 Thess. 2:3; 1 Pet. 4:17).

The early church drew inferences from this divine ordering of events that it applied to the ordering of worship (1 Cor. 14:30; cf. 14:33, 40) and the ordering of offices in the church (12:28). But the order of the church of Christ must not be made into a hierarchy. To be the first is not, and never becomes, an institution. It always remains a function: Those who want to be first in the church must become its servants and so follow the example of Jesus.

Jesus is the only servant (*diakonos*) in the full sense, and thus the only one who is "first" (Matt. 20:27–28). God made Jesus the Lord of this order by making him the *prōtos kai eschatos* (a title of God, Isa. 44:6; 48:12; cf. Rev. 1:17; 2:8; 22:13). As the First and the Last, he is also the unique one, and his mission is unrepeatable. Hence Jesus alone has the authority to make the last first and the first last (Matt. 20:16). Thus he confirms Israel's abiding preeminence (Mk. 7:27; cf. Rom. 1:16; 2:9–10; but see also Matt. 8:11; Lk. 13:28–30). Yet for the moment Christ is giving the Gentiles preference over his own people (to be understood in the temporal sense, cf. Rom. 11:25–32), in order to make them jealous and move them to return to him.

See also *prōtotokos*, firstborn (*4758*).

| 4758 | πρωτότοκος | πρωτότοκος (*prōtotokos*), firstborn (*4758*). |

CL & OT *prōtotokos* is a late derivative from *prōtos* (first) and the aor. root *tek*- (born). As an act. form *prōtotokos* means bearing one's firstborn; as a pass. form *prōtotokos* is first found in the LXX, about 130x.

1. In the LXX *prōtotokos* is used (a) in its lit. sense both of humans and animals, often as a noun in the neut. sing. with the accompanying phrase "of every womb" (lit., "which opens the womb," e.g., Exod. 13:2). The following expressions are confined to humans: *prōtotokos hyios*, firstborn son (cf. Gen. 25:25, Esau), and *prōtotokos* as a noun joined to the proper name (e.g., "Nadab the firstborn" in Num. 3:2). In the ANE the firstborn was generally believed to inherit his father's strength (cf. Gen. 49:3), which gave him a special position in law (cf. Deut. 21:15–17). For this reason it was normal for him to receive his father's special love.

(b) In a transferred sense, *prōtotokos* is used to express a special relationship with one's father, especially with God. Here the two roots from which it is derived no longer play any role in the meaning (e.g., Exod. 4:22). In Ps. 89:27 the thought is of "adoption," i.e., the bestowal of special legal rights and honors; here the king is not born "my firstborn," but "appointed." It is to be noted that while *prōtotokos* is used in the OT as a title of honor for the chosen, that is, those who have received grace, it is not found in an eschatological or soteriological sense.

2. In rab. Jud. the Torah is described in a comment on Prov. 8:22–23 as the first created thing, the firstborn of the way of Yahweh, and the earliest of his works. The same description is applied to the sanctuary with reference to Jer. 17:12. In both cases the term is used in a fig. sense to express the special love of God for the Torah and the sanctuary.

NT *prōtotokos* appears 8x in the NT.

1. In the lit. sense, *prōtotokos* describes the birth of Jesus as Mary's firstborn in Lk. 2:7. "Firstborn" possibly conveys the implication that Jesus was the first of several children (cf. Mk. 6:3). Or it may emphasize, in view of the mention in Lk. 1:27, 34 of her virginity, that Mary had borne no previous children. In any case, however, *prōtotokos* does not preclude further children of Mary.

2. In the fig. sense, as a title of honor for Jesus, *prōtotokos* is comprehensible only if seen as the derived definition of this word in the LXX. This must not be forgotten when we encounter shades of meaning in the NT that go beyond its use in the LXX.

(a) It is used in Col. 1:15 as a title for the mediator of creation, as is demonstrated by parallel sayings in 1:16, "by him all things were created . . . all things were created by him and for him"; and 1:17, "He is before all things, and in him all things hold together." These statements are a confession of the supreme rank of the preexistent Christ as the mediator in the creation of all things.

(b) It is used in an eschatological sense in Heb. 1:6 to qualify *hyios*, son (1:5), as a title given to Jesus at his ascension, i.e., the heavenly enthronement of the risen Lord. According to Ps. 2:7 (cited in Heb. 1:5), Christ's exaltation represents the perfection of Jesus, and he will be followed by others. Since the exalted Christ is one step ahead of his followers on the way to consummation, he is already *prōtotokos*. Rom. 8:29 refers to the eschatological transfiguration, when those who have been foreknown and chosen out are made like him (by the resurrection of the dead), although they will never be completely like him, for he remains their Lord. Col. 1:18 and Rev. 1:5 connect the title *prōtotokos* with the resurrection: Jesus is the first to be raised by God (→ *prōtos, 4755*), so that "in everything he might have the supremacy" (Col. 1:18).

As a title of honor for Jesus, *prōtotokos* expresses more clearly than almost any other the unity of God's saving will and acts: "the firstborn over all creation" (Col. 1:15), "the firstborn from among the dead" (1:18), and "the firstborn among many brothers" (Rom. 8:29; cf. Heb. 12:23). Creator and Redeemer are one and the same, the all-powerful God in Jesus Christ, "the First and the Last, the Beginning and the End" (Rev. 22:13), who binds his own to himself from all eternity and is their surety for salvation, if they remain in him. This goes beyond the limits of what can be logically asserted: The man Jesus of Nazareth is the mediator of creation; he who was executed on the cross as a criminal is the first to experience resurrection and the one who leads us into life. In the man Christ Jesus, the *prōtotokos*, God has brought his divine power and glory to its climax (Col. 1:19–20), and he has given a share in this to the church.

3. The pl. *prōtotokoi* refers to the church in Heb. 12:23 ("the church of the firstborn, whose names are written in heaven"). Is this concept be taken literally? This would mean that Christians are here set directly alongside Christ in an unparalleled and almost dangerous manner. Doubtless the author sees the Son and the sons (chs. 1–2) as closely related: They are all "of the same family" (2:11). But these *prōtotokoi*, as "brothers" of Christ, do not possess the rank of firstborn as an inalienable right, as Christ does, but receive it like heirs, only on the ground that Christ is the *prōtotokos* and as such "the author of their salvation" (2:10).

See also *prōtos*, first (*4755*).

4762 πτερύγιον

πτερύγιον (*pterygion*), end, edge (4762).

CL & OT *pterygion* is the diminutive of *pteryx*, wing, and designates the tip or extremity of anything. On a building a *pterygion* may designate a turret or battlement or a pointed roof. Both *pterygion* and *pteryx* are used in the LXX to translate the Heb. *kānāp*, wing.

NT The devil took Jesus to the *pterygion* of the temple and urged him to jump, in order to demonstrate that he would be miraculously protected by divine power (Matt. 4:5–7; Lk. 4:9–12). Probably this refers to the southeast corner of the temple area, where one could look straight down from the roof of Solomon's porch into the Kidron Valley far below. There may be a play on words in this passage, for the word *pteryx*, wing, occurs in the same psalm that Satan quoted about the angels taking care of Jesus. In Ps. 91:4 we read: "He will cover you with his feathers, and under his wings [*pteryx*] you will find refuge."

Eusebius preserves a story of Hegesippus, which tells how the Jewish leaders set James, the brother of Jesus, on the pinnacle of the temple in order to speak to the Passover crowds and persuade them not to go astray after Jesus. But when James testified to Jesus instead, the leaders cast him down and stoned him.

4773 (*ptōma*, that which has fallen, corpse), → *4406*.

4774 (*ptōsis*, falling, fall), → *4406*.

4775 (*ptōcheia*, poverty), → *4777*.

4776 (*ptōcheuō*, be poor, beg), → *4777*.

4777 πτωχός

πτωχός (*ptōchos*), poor (4777); πτωχεύω (*ptōcheuō*), be poor, beg (4776); πτωχεία (*ptōcheia*), poverty (4775).

CL & OT 1. (a) In cl. Gk. *ptōchos* signifies utter dependence on society. As an adj. it means begging, poor, dependent on the help of strangers; as a noun it means beggar. This word stands in contrast to *plousios*, rich, owning property. It is also used as a metaphor for meager, inadequate, scanty. Derived from it are *ptōcheuō*, beg, live the life of a beggar, be destitute, and *ptōcheia*, begging, destitution, poverty.

(b) In early Gk. thought poverty was not considered to have religious value. Charity, esp. by the propertied classes to those impoverished by the blows of fate, was considered a virtue because it was useful to society, but it was not regarded as a religious or ethical act. There was no public care for the poor. In later Gk. philosophy poverty was regarded by some as a favorable precondition for virtue.

2. In the LXX *ptōchos* (some 100x) generally translates one of five different Heb. words. In most cases it is synonymous with *penēs* (poor, *4288*). (a) *ptōchos* has various connotations. It can mean the socially poor, those without land, the peasants as poor, needy, and unimportant. It can also denote the physically weak. Finally, it refers

to beggars and the homeless. In general, *ptōchos* here has widened its cl. Gk. meaning, esp. in social, economic, and religious spheres.

(b) Because Israel's land is Yahweh's land, God commanded that there be no continuing poverty among his people. Hence the Book of the Covenant (Exod. 20:22–23:19) lays down several stipulations that in principle were always valid in Israel, even if they were seldom carried out. (i) Any Israelites who as a result of economic need had to sell themselves into slavery in payment of debt were to be freed in the sabbatical year (21:2). (ii) In the sabbatical year, when the ground was allowed to lie fallow, its produce belonged to the poor (23:10–11). (iii) It was forbidden to exploit or oppress the poor (22:22–27). (iv) The law may not be perverted against the poor (23:6–8). Yahweh himself was their protector (22:27b), and he reminded Israel of how he had freed them from slavery in Egypt (22:21; 23:9).

(c) Under the monarchy the economy changed from a predominantly barter economy to one using some form of money. As a result, many of the farmers became financially dependent on business people. This impoverishment of a wide stratum of the population was felt not merely as a major social problem but also as a religious one, for it involved a breach of the divine law. The 8th-cent. prophets esp. attacked social injustice in the name of Yahweh, threatening God's judgment on the rich, who were responsible (e.g., Isa. 3:14–15; 5:8–9; Amos 2:7; 4:1; 5:11; 8:4; Mic. 2:2; 3:2–4).

Only in this setting can we understand the meaning of "poor" and "needy" in Ps. The poor are those who suffer injustice; they are poor not because of disobedience or laziness but because others have despised God's law. Thus they turn, helpless and humble, to God in prayer, aware that ultimately it is a question of God's glory (e.g., 25:16; 40:17; 69:29; 86:1; 109:22). Through this process there gradually developed the specific connotation of "poor" as all those who turn to God in great need and seek his help. God is praised as the judge of Israel and the protector of the poor (e.g., 72:2, 4, 12–13; 132:15), who procures justice for them against their oppressors (cf. Ps. 9; 10; 35; 74; 140).

Ezek. saw the coming destruction of the kingdom of Judah as Yahweh's punishment for their oppression of the poor and needy (22:29). The misery of the exile led to the use of "poor" and "needy" as collective terms for the people; these words are found in a number of hopeful eschatological promises about the future of the people (e.g., Isa. 29:19; 41:17; 49:13; 51:21–23; 54:11–15; 61:1–4).

(d) Pronouncements in wisdom lit. on the poor are much less religious in tone. They vary from explanations of poverty as the fault of those who suffer it (e.g., Prov. 6:6–11; 23:21) and warnings against it (Sir. 40:28), to the praise of the poor and a call to improve their lot (Prov. 14:31; Sir. 10:30).

3. All the main lines of OT thought occur again in rab. Jud., both concerning material poverty and its alleviation and its spiritualization and religious classification. (a) The Pharisees, Essenes, and the Hel. Jews of Jerusalem had their special forms of charitable work (e.g., feeding the poor, clothing the naked).

(b) The synagogue communities had an excellent organization of care for the poor, which went as far as founding hospices. It was rooted in the law of the OT and was made possible by the temple tax, and after the destruction of Jerusalem by weekly public alms. In fact, clear norms were laid down for contributions expected from synagogue members. The poor themselves were expected to contribute in order to demonstrate their religious equality, though they were the first to profit from care of the poor. Priests and Levites without estates, foreigners, widows, and orphans received tithes for the poor paid at the end of every third year (cf. Deut. 14:29; 26:12).

4. A considerable variety of opinion is found in the spiritual judgments on poverty. (a) *Pss. Sol.* esp. reserves the word "poor" for those who have experienced divine acts of deliverance and are hence identical with the righteous (cf. 5:2, 11; 10:6; 15:1; 18:2). Heavy material burdens and martyrdom are generally included.

(b) The community of the "poor" in Qumran rejected private property and built up a well-organized community life in expectation

4777 (ptōchos)

of eschatological salvation. They chose the term "poor" for themselves. Their writings attacked the priests who exploited the poor.

(c) Rab. theology ultimately denied that poverty had theological value. It even saw it as the result of lack of knowledge of the Torah, the one real poverty. This led to a feeling of moral superiority over the poor. In striking contrast, however, was a form of popular eschatology that saw the poor as the primary objects of divine mercy. Such belief led to the danger of idealizing poverty.

NT *ptōchos* occurs 34x in the NT, mostly in the Gospels; *ptōcheia*, 3x; *ptōcheuō*, only in 2 Cor. 8:9.

1. *The Gospels.* (a) *ptōchos* occurs in its lit. sense in the Synoptics. Jesus told the rich man who wanted to inherit eternal life: "Go, sell everything you have and give to the poor" (Mk. 10:21; cf. Lk. 18:22). In Mk. 12:41–44 (cf. Lk. 21:1–4) Jesus says that the apparently negligible gift of the poor woman, entitled to support, is far greater than those of the rich. Only in Jesus' anointing by a woman (Matt. 26:11; Mk. 14:7; cf. Jn. 12:8) do we read that almsgiving must take second place, but here it is a question of one final opportunity for an extravagant act of love to Jesus before his death.

(b) Jesus speaks of the poor in Matt. 11:5 and in the first beatitude (5:3; Lk. 6:20). Neither passage uses "poor" in the general social meaning. Rather, the enlarged form that Matt. uses ("the poor in spirit") brings out the true nuance, based on OT and Jewish background, that people in affliction have confidence only in God. Lk. indicates that the poverty of the beatitudes is a poverty caused by discipleship: Those who believe in the Son find all that God's promises for the poor, the miserable, and the humble (e.g., Isa. 57:15; 61:1) are fulfilled in him.

(c) Lk. 4:18 records Jesus' quotation of Isa. 61:1 ("to preach good news to the poor") at the beginning of his ministry. In Lk. this dominant theme of poverty is linked with a sharp attack on the rich (6:24–26). Jesus told the man who had invited him to a meal (14:12–14) to invite the poor and others from whom no repayment could be expected and promised him an eschatological reward for so doing. Similarly, the poor are among the first substitute guests at the great banquet (14:21). Lazarus is the type of poor whom God receives (16:20, 22), and the anonymous rich man who fails in his duty to him is the type of those condemned by God (cf. 12:13–21). When Zacchaeus promises to give half of his goods to the poor after his conversion (19:8), his gratitude shows itself in concern for the poor, and he is saved (19:10).

(d) The Synoptic Gospels depict Jesus' way of life as one of self-chosen poverty. Note esp. Jesus' reply to a would-be disciple: "Foxes have holes and birds of the air have nests, but the Son of Man has no place to lay his head" (Matt. 8:20). The disciples left all in order to follow him (4:18–22; Jn. 1:35–51). Jesus demanded that the rich young ruler sell his possessions and pursue a life of discipleship in poverty as the precondition of eternal life (Matt. 19:16–22; Lk. 18:18–24). When Jesus sent out his disciples, they were to go without possessions or provisions (Matt. 10:1–16; Lk. 9:1–6). In this way of life was a double separation: from possessions and from family ties (Matt. 10:37–39; Lk. 14:25–33).

The lifestyle that Jesus adopted for himself and called his disciples to embrace was one exemplified in the Sermon on the Mount, esp. the Beatitudes. Jesus' way of life was a conscious identification with the poor and the OT concept of poverty. In itself this was an act of loving compassion. At the same time it was a life that deliberately chose to cast itself on the care of the Father. But in doing so, Jesus was also putting to the test the people of Israel.

2. *James.* James vigorously attacks the attitude of the rich both in public and in church services (2:2–3, 6–7) and demands equal esteem for the poor. He bases his position on the fact that God "has ... chosen those who are poor in the eyes of the world" (2:5) and the knowledge that mercy toward others will be the criterion in the final judgment (2:13; cf. Matt. 25:31–46).

3. *Revelation.* In the letters to the churches of Smyrna (2:9) and Laodicea (3:17) the contrast between poor and rich shows the difference between a human estimate and that of the glorified Lord (1:9–18). In 13:16 John describes how all social and economic classes, rich and poor alike, are captured by the hypnotic power of the beast from the abyss.

4. *Paul's letters.* Paul makes only occasional use of the concept, although he is deeply concerned for the poor. (a) Paul refers to the poor in a lit. sense in connection with his collection for the church in Jerusalem. "The poor in Jerusalem" was perhaps a name these believers had acquired (cf. Rom. 15:26, where "of the saints" is added; cf. also Gal. 2:10). In Rom. 15:26 Paul speaks of "a contribution" that the churches of Macedonia and Achaia were making: "They were pleased to do it, and indeed they owe it to them. For if the Gentiles have shared in the Jews' spiritual blessings, they owe it to the Jews to share with them their material blessings" (15:27). Paul himself was going to Jerusalem with this contribution prior to a prospective mission trip to Spain (15:24–25).

(b) In 1 Cor. 16:1–4 Paul had given various recommendations about the collection to the churches of Galatia, suggesting that they put something aside on the first day of each week (16:2) and proposing on his arrival to send "the men you approve ... to Jerusalem" (16:3); if it seems advisable, he will go himself as well (16:4).

It appears as if the Corinthians did not follow these instructions, for Paul returns to the issue in 2 Cor. 8–9 with strong encouragement to finish the project. Evidently a year had elapsed and the collection had not advanced much (8:10). Paul, therefore, sends Titus to help them in this regard (8:6, 16–17, 23). Paul writes not as a command (as he had done in 1 Cor. 16:1–2), but "to test the sincerity of your love by comparing it with the earnestness of others" (2 Cor. 8:8). In addition, he sets before them the example of Christ: "For you know the grace of our Lord Jesus Christ, that though he was rich, yet for your sakes he became poor [*ptōcheuō*], so that you through his poverty [*ptōcheia*] might become rich " (8:9). Christ's leaving heaven to come to this sinful earth has practical application for Paul. His becoming poor is the paradoxical ground of the true riches of the believer (cf. also Phil. 2:6–11).

In 2 Cor. 9:1–4 Paul expresses the hope that his boasting about the Corinthians to the churches of Macedonia and Achaia will not prove vain in view of the possibility of a meager response. He reminds them that "whoever sows sparingly will also reap sparingly, and whoever sows generously will also reap generously. Each man should give what he has decided in his heart to give, not reluctantly or under compulsion, for God loves a cheerful giver" (9:6–7; cf. Prov. 22:9). This is further reinforced by a quote from Ps. 112:9.

(c) In Gal. 2:10, the poor are mentioned in relation to Paul's meeting with the "pillars" of the Jerusalem church, where he was recognized as the apostle to the Gentiles while they would go to the Jews. The only stipulation was that Paul and company "should continue to remember the poor, the very thing I was eager to do." The need of material relief at Jerusalem is evident from the story of the appointment of the seven to serve in the daily distribution to Gk.-speaking widows (Acts 6:1–6). The situation was no doubt aggravated for the church by Jewish hostility (cf. 5:17–41; 7:54–8:3; 9:1–2; 12:1–5). Acts 11:27–30 tells how the Christian prophet Agabus foretold the terrible famine that took place under the emperor Claudius. The church at Antioch responded by sending relief to Jerusalem through Barnabas and Saul.

(d) Paul develops the theme of poverty further in relation to the apostles, who, among other things, are described as "poor, yet making many rich" (2 Cor. 6:10). The paradoxical nature of the apostolic ministry follows the pattern set by Christ, who is himself the ground and pattern for all Christian life and giving.

(e) The cosmic spirits (→ *stoicheion*, 5122) worshiped by the heathen, including formerly the Galatian believers, are called "weak and miserable [*ptōchos*]" (Gal. 4:9; cf. 4:3). The word translated "miserable" here is the same word translated "poor" at 2:10. In other words,

504

the *stoicheia* have nothing at all to offer but enslavement. But by listening to the Judaizers with their insistence on the necessity of circumcision for salvation and the other legal observances (4:10), the Galatian Christians are in danger of returning to their former enslavement, whereas through Christ and the Spirit they can live as sons and heirs of God himself (4:1–7).

See also *penēs*, poor (*4288*).

4780 (pythōn, the Python, spirit of divination), → 3404.

4783	πύλη

πύλη (*pylē*), gate, door (*4783*); πυλών (*pylōn*), gate, gateway, entrance (*4784*).

CL & OT 1. In cl. Gk. *pylē* is used, mostly in the pl., to mean the gates of a town, although it can also mean the door of a house. In a general sense it may designate any entrance or opening (e.g., a geographical pass or straits). The gates of Hades was a common expression for the other world, the realm of the dead. *pylōn* means a gateway.

2. In the LXX *pylē* refers to (a) the gate of a city, building, farm, or village; (b) the area immediately inside a city gate; and (c) the gate(s) of death (Job 38:17; Ps. 107:18), of Sheol or the abode of the dead (Isa. 38:10; Wis. 16:13; 3 Macc. 5:51; cf. *Pss. Sol.* 16:2), and of heaven (Gen. 28:17). *pylōn* denotes an entrance or doorway.

NT 1. In the NT *pylē* can denote (a) a city gate (Lk. 7:12; Acts 9:24; 16:13). Jesus suffered outside the gate of Jerusalem (Heb. 13:12; cf. Lev. 16:27), which emphasizes that his suffering represents the true offering of the Day of Atonement and that, in his death, he is classified with lawbreakers, who were stoned outside the camp (24:14; Num. 15:35). (b) It can also mean a gate of the temple (Acts 3:10; cf. 3:2, which uses *thyra*), and (c) a prison gate (12:10).

2. (a) *pylē* is used fig. of the narrow gate through which one must pass to enter life (Matt. 7:13–14; cf. Lk. 13:24, which uses *thyra*). This image indicates an entrance that is difficult to find and hence ignored by many. These words form an appeal to decide to follow Christ and face all the consequences that obedience entails.

(b) *pylē* is used of "the gates of Hades" in Matt. 16:18. This image reflects the commonly held ancient idea that the underworld was secured by strong gates that prevented escape and barred access to invaders. It is improbable that Jesus uses this expression for the ungodly powers of the underworld assailing the rock, for Hades (→ *hadēs*, 87) was not regarded as the abode of evil powers who emerge to attack humans (the word for that abode is *geenna*, hell, → *1147*). In the light of the Jewish background, Jesus is affirming in Matt. 16:18 that death, in spite of its unconquerable power, will not win control over the *ekklēsia* built on the rock; that is, death will not vanquish the Messiah who builds the church or the members of his community.

pylōn denotes (a) the gateway or porch of a house (Matt. 26:71; Lk. 16:20; Acts 10:17; 12:13–14), and (b) the gate(s) of a city (14:13), in particular, the gates of the New Jerusalem (Rev. 21:12–13, 21, 25; 22:14).

See also *thyra*, door, entrance (*2598*).

4784 (pylōn, gate, gateway, entrance), → 4783.

4786	πῦρ

πῦρ (*pyr*), fire (*4786*); πυρόω (*pyroō*), to set on fire, burn (*4792*); πύρωσις (*pyrōsis*), burning, being burnt (*4796*); πύρινος (*pyrinos*), fiery, of fire (*4791*); πυρράζω (*pyrrazō*), be red (*4793*); πυρά (*pyra*), pile of combustible or burning material (*4787*); πυρετός (*pyretos*), fever (*4790*); πυρέσσω (*pyressō*), suffer with a fever (*4789*).

CL 1. Great importance has been attached to fire in human existence, in both a positive and a negative sense: as a life-giving and as a life-destroying force. It is used by people at the center of the home (the hearth, which is thus, like sacrificial fire, regarded by many people as something holy). It is also used as a weapon in fighting and war.

As to the environment of the OT and Jud., the fire cult of the Persian religion is of particular importance. Fire and a serpent represent the contraries truth and falsehood in the Mazda teaching of Zoroastrianism. In the conflict between the good and evil basic principles, human beings should place themselves on the side of the good, to which fire belongs. Fire is the protector of the good, divine order of life. Since fire is revered as the element of purity, it must not be allowed to become contaminated. In the final judgment fire will be the means employed for the last test.

2. In the Gk. world fire was used in both secular and religious spheres. Metaphorically it described the most diverse human experiences, such as intensity of passion, wickedness, or the heat of battle. In Gk. religion Prometheus and Hermes are said to have brought fire to the human race. Fire was used as a means of ritual cleansing (e.g., purificatory offering after childbirth or a death, and the various feasts of purification). Although corpses were burned in funeral rites, it was believed that the soul could not be affected by the fire or cut off from its future existence. Fire played an important part in the mystery religions, both for purification and in the representation of the divine and of the new nature of the initiated.

In Gk. philosophy fire is one of the four (or five) basic elements of all things. According to Heraclitus, the world is a movement of fire, which is undergoing a constant process of change and is identical with the deity (or *logos*). In this pantheistic system, God, the fiery universe, universal reason, and the human spirit are all regarded as one. Heraclitus held that a great world era will come to its end when everything is burned up and returns to the primal fire; then a new world will be produced out of the primal fire. The Stoics likewise saw fire as the active world principle, the world soul that guides everything according to purpose, holding all things together and controlling them by law and reason. The human soul is part of the godhead and thus fiery in nature; it will return to primal fire when the world disappears in flames.

OT 1. In the LXX *pyr* is used over 350x. Fire is used for several purposes in the home (Exod. 12:8; 2 Chr. 35:13; Isa. 44:16; Jer. 7:18) and in craftwork, especially metal work (Isa. 44:12–17; Jer. 6:29; Sir. 38:28). In war it is a means of destruction (cf. Deut. 13:16; Jdg. 20:48; Amos 1:4). No fire may be kindled on the Sabbath (Exod. 35:3). Among natural phenomena, lightning is the "fire of God" (2 Ki. 1:10–14). In a metaphorical sense, fire stands for various human activities: slander and quarreling (Prov. 26:20–21), anger (Sir. 28:10–11), the shedding of blood (11:32; 22:24), the passion of love and debauchery (9:8; 23:16), and adultery (Job 31:12; Prov. 6:27–28).

Fire also serves in the OT as a means of purification (cf. Lev. 13:52, 55; Num. 31:23; Isa. 6:6). The only corpses that are burned, however, are those of criminals (Gen. 38:24; Lev. 20:14; 21:9; Jos. 7:15), so that they may have no place in the grave of their ancestors.

In worship the sacrificial fire is used for burning gifts on the altar and incense in the censer (Lev. 1:7–17; 3:5; 6:9–13; 16:12–13). No sacrifice may be offered by fire that does not come from the altar (10:1; Num. 3:4). Heathen customs are forbidden, such as the burning of children to Molech (Lev. 20:2; Deut. 12:31; 18:10; cf. 2 Ki.16:3; 17:17; 21:6). We do not know the purpose and nature of this custom, or the extent to which it was practiced in ancient Israel.

Since Yahweh is present among his people as the Judge who delivers as well as punishes, the fire that accompanies him becomes the expression of two different aspects of his activity. (a) It is the mark of divine judgment (Gen. 19:24; Exod. 9:24; Lev. 10:2; Num. 11:1; 16:35; 2 Ki. 1:10; Amos 1:4, 7). (b) It is also a sign of Yahweh's grace, in that he displays by means of fire his acceptance of a sacrifice (Gen. 15:17; Lev. 9:23–24; Jdg. 6:21; 1 Ki. 18:38; 1 Chr. 21:26; 2 Chr. 7:1). In addition, fire is also a sign of divine guidance (cf. the pillars of cloud and of fire, Exod. 13:22; Num. 14:14). Yahweh speaks out of the fire (Deut. 4:12, 15, 33). Elect persons can even be taken to him with fiery manifestations (2 Ki. 2:11).

Yahweh himself is a devouring fire who watches over obedience to his will with fiery zeal (Deut. 4:24; 9:3; Isa. 33:14). His word can also be described as a devouring fire (Jer. 23:29).

Regarding a theophany, when Yahweh appears, he is accompanied by fire (Gen. 15:17; Exod. 3:2–3; 19:18; Num. 14:14; Jdg. 6:21; 13:20; Isa. 4:5; Ezek. 1:27). This does not mean, however, that he is thought of as the god of fire, for Israel drew a distinction between Yahweh himself and the phenomena that accompany his appearance. Fire is one of Yahweh's servants, an instrument in his hand (1 Ki. 19:11–12; Ps. 50:3; 104:4). Fire is a symbol of Yahweh's holiness as judge of the world, also of his divine power and glory (Exod. 24:17; Isa. 6:1–4; Ezek. 1:27–28). According to Dan. 7:10, a stream of fire issues from beneath Yahweh's throne, a concept that plays an important part in Jewish and Christian cosmology and apocalyptic.

In the postexilic period it was expected that Yahweh would appear to bring history to its consummation, and fire is the token announcing the day of Yahweh (Joel 2:30). His enemies will be destroyed by fire and the sword (Isa. 66:15–16; Ezek. 38:22; 39:6; Mal. 4:1). According to Isa. 66:24, the effects will be far-reaching: Those condemned in the judgment will be continuously tormented by fire.

2. In Jewish apocalyptic fire is the mark of the heavenly world. The heavenly house in which Yahweh lives is surrounded by fire (*1 Enoch* 14:9–22). Fire is the means of punishment in hell (91:9; 100:9; 2 Esd. 7:38), and the final judgment is by fire (*1 Enoch* 102:1; 2 Esd. 13:10–11). The community of Qumran also expected the ungodly to be judged by fire in the final judgment (1QS 2:8; 4:13).

NT In the NT *pyr* occurs 71x. It is part of everyday life (Mk. 9:22; Lk. 22:55), including its use as an instrument of torture (Heb. 11:34; Rev. 17:16) and in war (18:8). It appears in a fig. sense in Jas. 3:5–6 (the tongue as a corrupting fire) and Lk. 12:49 (the fire of discord). Similarly the vb. *pyroō*, burn, be inflamed, is used of the heat of emotions, such as sexual desire (1 Cor. 7:9) and indignation over another's hurt (2 Cor. 11:29). Several derivative words (see the lexical section) also occur in the NT.

1. Fire has theological significance as a sign of heavenly, divine glory. The exalted Christ has eyes like flames of fire (Rev. 1:14; cf. Ezek. 1:27; Rev. 2:18; 19:12). The angel in 10:1 has legs like pillars of fire. Before God's throne burn seven lamps of fire (4:5; 15:2). The Holy Spirit, being of heavenly origin, appears in tongues as of fire (Acts 2:3, cf. Jn. 3:8), and fire accompanies the appearance of God (Acts 7:30).

2. Fire is also used in various metaphorical expressions. In the proverbial sayings in 1 Pet. 1:7 (cf. Prov. 17:3), faith is tested by suffering in this world as gold is tested in fire. Sufferings are a *pyrōsis*, burning, which come upon Christians in order to test or prove them. This is also a sign of the end times (1 Pet. 4:12; cf. 4:7). In Rev. 3:18, gold's being refined by fire represents true Christian faith that can stand the test. In the passage about the spiritual armor of the Christian (Eph. 6:16), the shield of faith serves to ward off "all the flaming arrows of the evil one."

3. Fire is also a picture of divine judgment (Matt. 3:10; 7:19; Lk. 3:9; Jn. 15:6). (a) Even in this age God can use fire as a means of judgment: The sons of Zebedee want Jesus to give them permission to call down fire on the inhospitable Samaritan village (Lk. 9:54; cf. 2 Ki. 1:10, 12). Rev. 9:17–18 depicts horses coming out to execute judgment, with smoke and sulfur issuing from their mouths. This marks them out as a scourge, bringing destruction with them. Similarly the riders' breastplates, "fiery red," point to the dawning of the judgment. The final powers to array themselves against God, Gog and Magog, will be destroyed by divine fire (20:9). The two witnesses are able to destroy their enemies with fire (11:5): God's power of judgment is at their disposal (cf. 2 Sam. 22:9). But the false prophet also, empowered by Satan, can call down fire from heaven (Rev. 13:13).

(b) In Lk. 12:49–50 Jesus' mission is presented as a fulfillment of John the Baptist's prophecy, but now in the sense that he who baptizes in spirit and fire must himself suffer. His way of bringing the judgment is to take it upon himself, so that the eschatological judgment is taken up in the present, historical sufferings of Jesus. In Mk. 9:49 salt and fire are linked together in a riddle. Salt has power to purify, preserve, and give flavor, and fire is an image of the divine judgment. Those who want to find fellowship with God must give up the old self to judgment by denying themselves. Any who refuse to do so are liable to the eschatological judgment of wrath.

In 1 Cor. 3:13 we find recorded the traditional notion of an eschatological judgment by fire, in which every person's work will be tested. Bad workmanship will be burned up, though the builder will narrowly escape, like a stick being pulled out of a burning woodpile. In 2 Thess. 1:7 the Parousia is described as Jesus' revelation "in blazing fire" (cf. Exod. 3:2; Isa. 66:15). In Rom. 12:20 Paul cites Prov. 25:21–22, making the metaphor refer to the final divine judgment. Only in one NT passage (2 Pet. 3:7–12) does the ancient idea of a world conflagration appear, combined with a recollection of the flood catastrophe recorded in the OT.

(c) Fire appears in Matt. 13:42; 18:8–9; 25:41 par.; Mk. 9:43–49 as the opposite of the "kingdom of God" and life (→ *zōē*, *2437*). The "hell of fire" (→ *geenna*, *1147*) in Mk. 9:48 recalls Isa. 66:24. Contemporary Jewish ideas of the present punishment by fire of the people of Sodom and Gomorrah are suggested by Jude 7. Burning sulfur indicates eternal damnation in hell at the end of time (Rev. 14:10; 19:20; 20:10, 14; 21:8).

See also *kauma*, heat, burning (*3008*).

4787 (*pyra*, pile of combustible or burning material), → *4786*.

4789 (*pyressō*, suffer with a fever), → *4786*.

4790 (*pyretos*, fever), → *4786*.

4791 (*pyrinos*, fiery, of fire), → *4786*.

4792 (*pyroō*, to set on fire, burn), → *4786*.

4793 (*pyrrazō*, be red), → *4786*.

| 4794 | πυρρός | πυρρός (*pyrros*), red (as fire) (*4794*). |

CL & OT *pyrros* is connected with *pyr*, fire (→ *4786*), and *pyroō*, burn. It can mean red, yellow, yellow-gray, or tawny. The LXX uses *pyrros* for red in Gen. 25:30; Num. 19:2; 2 Ki. 3:22; for "ruddy" in Song 5:10. Red horses figure in the vision of Zech. 1:8; 6:2, symbolizing the east.

NT The word occurs only at Rev. 6:4 and 12:3, though *Pyrros*, Pyrrhus, occurs as a proper name in Acts 20:4. The rider of the fiery horse (Rev. 6:4) is a war-monger, the color signifying slaughter. Most interpreters interpret the four riders as agents of destruction, sent out or simply permitted by God. The red dragon (12:3) denotes Satan but recalls the evil Leviathan (Isa. 27:1) associated with Egyptian power (Ezek. 29:3). The color might stand for bloodthirstiness (Rev. 12:4) or for evil (cf. 17:3; cf. Isa. 1:18).

4796 (*pyrōsis*, burning, being burnt), → *4786*.

| 4797 | πωλέω | πωλέω (*pōleō*), sell (*4797*); πιπράσκω (*piraskō*), sell (*4405*); |

ἐμπορεύομαι (*emporeuomai*), trade (*1864*).

CL & OT In cl. Gk. *pōleō* and *pipraskō* can both mean sell as in normal trade, but also betray or sell for a bribe. *pipraskō* was the word normally used for selling captives or slaves. *emporeuomai* began as a general term for travel, but later meant travel on business, trade.

In the LXX *pōleō* and *pipraskō* are used for selling either things or people (e.g., Gen. 41:56; Exod. 21:8). The latter word was also applied fig. to sin and its consequences (i.e., God "sells" his people [Isa. 50:1], and an individual can "sell oneself" to do what is evil [2 Ki. 17:17; cf. 1 Macc. 1:15]). *emporeuomai* normally means trade (e.g., Gen. 42:34; Amos 8:6). Once it is used fig. of trading in wisdom (Prov. 3:14).

NT   Both *pōleō* and *pipraskō* occur in the NT as commercial terms for selling commodities (Mk. 10:21 par.; Lk. 12:33; Acts 4:34). Only *pipraskō* is used of selling a person: once lit. in a parable (Matt. 18:25),

and once fig. in Rom. 7:14 ("sold as a slave to sin"). *emporeuomai* occurs 2x in the NT: in Jas. 4:13 it means engage in trade; in 2 Pet. 2:3 it is used fig. to convey the idea of exploitation.

See also *agorazō*, buy (60).

4800 (*pōroō*, harden, become hard), → *5017*.

4801 (*pōrōsis*, hardness), → *5017*.

P rho

| 4806 | ῥαββί |

ῥαββί (*rhabbi*) (from Heb. *rabbî*, "my lord"), rabbi (*4806*); ῥαββουνί (*rhabbouni*) (from Aram. *rabbûnî*, "my lord"), rabbi, my master (*4808*); καθηγητής (*kathēgētēs*), teacher, leader (*2762*).

OT The Sem. *rab* means many or great. In the latter sense we find it both inside and outside Israel as a designation for chief officers (e.g., Est. 1:8; Jer. 39:13; 41:1; Dan. 1:3; Jon. 1:6, of a sea captain), and it has come down to us in the titles of certain Assyrian and Babylonian officials (e.g., 2 Ki. 18:17; Jer. 39:13).

NT 1. *Rabbi* was a title of respect given to teachers of the law, such as the Pharisees (Matt. 23:7–8), as well as to any teacher. Gradually it became a technical term for one who had received ordination (*sᵉmîkâ*), i.e., who had received authority to act as judge in religious matters. This was conferred on the recipient by the laying on of hands.

2. John the Baptist's disciples addressed John by this title (Jn. 3:26). It was applied to Jesus a number of times: by Nicodemus (3:2), by Nathanael (1:49), by Peter (Mk. 9:5; 11:21), and by Judas (Matt. 26:25, 49; Mk. 14:45). The Aram. *rhabbouni* is found in the mouth of Bartimaeus (Mk. 10:51) and Mary Magdalene (Jn. 20:16).

3. In the Gospels the most common form of address for Jesus is *didaskale*, i.e., teacher (→ *didaskalos*, *1437*); Lk. uses the synonym *epistata* 7x (5:5; 8:24 [2x], 45; 9:33, 49; 17:13). Jesus is also often called *kyrie* (i.e., lord, master; → *kyrios*, *3261*). This is often no more than a mark of respect (e.g., Matt. 13:27), though it also does acknowledge that Jesus was regarded as a teacher. The Aram. title *rhabbouni* was normally avoided in Gk.-speaking circles as unfamiliar (cf. Jn. 20:16). Matt. also tends not to use *didaskalos* (*rhabbi*) for Jesus, since being in sharp conflict with the Jewish rabbis, he wishes to avoid the too-frequent ascription of their title to Jesus.

Note esp. Matt. 23:8, where Jesus instructs his disciples not to be called *rhabbi*, since they really have only one *didaskalos*, Jesus Christ himself (cf. 23:10, where NIV "teacher" and "Teacher" is *kathēgētēs*, a word that occurs only there in the NT).

4808 (*rhabbouni*, rabbi, my master), → *4806*.

4810 (*rhabdizō*, beat with a rod), → *4811*.

| 4811 | ῥάβδος |

ῥάβδος (*rhabdos*), rod, staff (*4811*); ῥαβδίζω (*rhabdizō*), beat with a rod (*4810*); ῥαπίζω (*rhapizō*), strike (*4824*); ῥάπισμα (*rhapisma*), a blow with a club, rod, or whip (*4825*).

CL & OT Along with other words, *rhabdos* refers to a rod or staff, esp. that carried by kings as a hereditary emblem of authority and by heralds and public speakers. Roman magistrates bore the *rhabdoi* as a badge of their authority. *rhabdizō* denotes beating with a stick or rod, generally as a punishment for minor offenses by slaves or children. *rhapizō* indicates striking with the hand.

In the LXX *rhabdos* denotes a shepherd's club (Mic. 7:14), Aaron's rod (Num. 17), the ruler's scepter (Ps. 45:6), a rod as a means of punishment (Exod. 21:20), and a traveler's staff. Several passages containing the *idea* of a staff (e.g., Gen. 49:10; Num. 24:17) became important in later Jewish messianic interpretation. In addition, the Qumran Isa. commentary applies the *rhabdos* of Jesse from Isa. 11:1 to the kingly Messiah.

NT *rhabdos* occurs 12x in the NT; *rhabdizō* 2x (Acts 16:22; 2 Cor. 11:25); *rhapizō* 2x (Matt. 5:39; 26:67); and *rhapisma* 3x (Mk. 14:65; Jn. 18:22; 19:3).

1. Jesus was struck by the soldiers (*rhapizō*, Matt. 26:67; *rhapisma*, Mk. 14:65; Jn. 19:3; Matt. and Mk. also have *kolaphizō*). In keeping with his earlier teaching not to retaliate against those who strike with the hand (*rhapizō*, Matt. 5:39), Jesus neither defended himself against nor struck back at those who beat him. Like his Lord, Paul was beaten by civil magistrates (*rhabdizō*, 2 Cor. 11:25).

2. *rhabdos* is used of a traveler's staff in Jesus' sending forth of the Twelve (Matt. 10:10; Mk. 6:8; Lk. 9:3; cf. also Heb. 11:21). In Matt. and Lk. they are to take no staff; in Mk. a staff is permitted. *rhabdos* is also used for a rod of authority or chastisement (see Acts 16:22, where the magistrates beat [*rhabdizō*] Paul and Silas with rods). This last sense of *rhabdos* is applied fig. in 1 Cor. 4:21.

rhabdos is also used several times to denote divine majesty, rule, and power, particularly in connection with the final overthrow of evil. In this connection, some of the OT passages where the scepter was already explained messianically in Jud. are applied to Christ. For example, God has entrusted absolute authority to the Son (Rev. 2:27; 12:5). The one who will smite (*patassō*) the nations and rule them with a rod of iron (19:15; cf. Ps. 2:9) is the Lamb who was himself slain (Rev. 5:8–9; 12:11; 19:7, 9, 13).

References to *rhabdos* in Heb. illustrate further the theme of the scepter of authority in the NT's exegesis of the OT. The superiority of the unique Son to the angels is reinforced by an appeal to a series of OT testimonies, including Ps. 2 and 45 (a royal marriage psalm that invokes the righteous king as "God," cf. Heb. 1:8). Heb. 9:4, which contrasts the temporary character of the OT sanctuary with the eternal new covenant, alludes to the rod of Aaron that budded and was preserved (Num. 17:10); this emblem of the Levitical priesthood has now been superseded.

See also *mastigoō*, beat, flog (*3463*).

| 4819 | ῥακά |

ῥακά (*rhaka*), empty-head, fool (*4819*).

CL & OT The origin of *rhaka* is uncertain. Derivations from Aram., Heb., and Gk. have been suggested. Perhaps the best option is as the transcription of the Aram. term of abuse *rêqāʾ*, empty-head, blockhead.

NT *rhaka* appears only in Matt. 5:22: "But I tell you ... anyone who says to his brother, 'Raca,' is answerable to the Sanhedrin. But anyone who says, 'You fool (*mōre*)!' will be in danger of the fire of hell." *rhaka* is here compared with *mōre*, the term of abuse that was more commonly used. *mōre* is more drastic and is best rendered by idiot or fool. In 5:22 are thus assembled the two everyday terms of abuse prevalent in Jesus' day.

With the expression "but I tell you," Jesus introduces a divine law that is a development of the OT. Not only does actual murder place people under punishment of death; the heart inflamed with a destructive mental attitude, from which springs the damning word or act, merits the same judgment. God's judgment on sin is radical and far-reaching. It not merely covers the accomplished deed; it exposes the motive behind it. Sins of thought and tongue are on the same level as physical murder.

See also *anathema*, cursed, accursed (*353*); *kakologeō*, speak evil of, revile, insult (*2800*); *katara*, curse, malediction (*2932*).

| 4822 | ῥαντίζω |

ῥαντίζω (*rhantizō*), sprinkle (*4822*); ῥαντισμός (*rhantismos*), sprinkling (*4823*).

CL & OT *rhantizō* is rare in cl. Gk. and infrequent in the LXX. It is distinguished from *niptō*, to rinse part of a body (→ *3782*); *louō*, wash the whole body (→ *3374*); and *baptō/baptizō*, immerse (→ *966*). Gk. lit. attests sprinkling for religious cleansing.

Oil mixed with the blood of sacrifice was sprinkled on Aaron and his sons to consecrate them (Exod. 29:21), but sprinkling was primarily for cleansing, whether by the blood of sacrifice or by water. On the Day of Atonement the sanctuary and its sacred objects were cleansed by sprinkling the blood of a bull and of a goat offered as sin offerings (Lev. 16:11–19). The sprinkling of the Israelites with the "blood of the covenant" at the making of the Sinai covenant (Exod. 24:8) had a different purpose, namely, to bring Israel into a unity of fellowship with Yahweh and to seal the covenant.

Sprinkling was performed esp. for cleansing from defilement incurred through contact with leprosy (Lev. 14:6–7, 51) and with the dead (Num. 19:9–21). In Ps. 51:7 the ceremony of cleansing of the leper and his house provides the inspiration for the symbolic language of a divine inner cleansing by sprinkling. As a leper was cleansed by blood sprinkled from a sprig of hyssop and by water, so the self-confessed sinner seeks spiritual cleansing from God. In Ezek. 36:25 sprinkling with water symbolizes an eschatological cleansing of God's people in the end times, which is tantamount to a new creation.

NT The book of Heb. frequently recalls the OT sprinkling with sacrificial blood in order to show the superior power of Christ's blood to cleanse (e.g., 9:13–14, 18–28). In 10:22 cleansing by sprinkling (presumably of Christ's sacrificial blood) is parallel with washing with pure water. The cleansing power of Christ's sacrifice is known in baptism, even as the believer becomes one with Christ in his dying and rising (cf. Rom. 6:1–10).

The noun *rhantismos*, sprinkling, has not been found outside the Bible. Its occurrence in Heb. 12:24 is instructive, for though it is set in parallelism with Abel's blood, the latter was not sprinkled. The phrase "sprinkled blood" was therefore a current expression. In contrast to the cry of Abel's blood for vengeance (Gen. 4:10), the sprinkled blood of Christ assures forgiveness.

4823 (rhantismos, sprinkling), → *4822.*

4824 (rhapizō, strike), → *4811.*

4825 (rhapisma, a blow with a club, rod, or whip), → *4811.*

4835	ῥέω

ῥέω (*rheō*), flow, stream (*4835*); ῥύσις (*rhysis*), a flowing river, stream (*4868*); παραρρέω (*pararreō*), flow past, drift away, let slip (*4184*).

CL & OT 1. This word group commonly refers to the flow of a stream or river, but it is also applied to the run-off from melted snow, the "running" of milk and honey (equivalent to prosperity), or, with respect to blood, a hemorrhage. In addition, a city or area may stream with people or gold. Solid objects liquefy and "melt away." Thus it is not surprising that this word group takes on the meaning of fall, drop off (e.g., of hair or ripe fruit).

2. The LXX reflects an equally wide variety of usage. These words are most often applied to the promised land as flowing with milk and honey (Exod. 3:8; 13:5; Lev. 20:24; Num. 14:8; Deut. 6:3) or to some discharge or hemorrhage (esp. in Lev. 15). Water flowed from the smitten rock (Ps. 78:20; 105:41).

The word group was also used in connection with the descent of precipitation at the divine command (Job 36:28; 38:30; Ps. 147:18 = LXX 147:7; Prov. 3:20), the falling of tears (Jer. 9:18), and wafting of perfume by the wind (Song 4:16). Joel uses *rheō* 2x to refer to the flow of water and milk from Judah's hills when the Spirit of the Lord is poured out and blessings abound (3:18). Zech. uses the vb. more ominously by picturing flesh decaying and eyes "rotting out" of their sockets, fitting retribution for those who war against Jerusalem (14:12). The disappearance of hope among ungrateful people is

likened to the flowing away of water and the melting of hoar frost (Wis. 16:29).

NT *rheō* occurs only once in the NT: "Streams of living water will flow from within" the believer (Jn. 7:38). Here believers are viewed as channels for the outflowing of the Spirit to others (cf. 15:26–27). The 3 NT occurrences of *rhysis* all occur in connection with the "flow of blood" = "bleeding" (Mk. 5:25 = Lk. 8:43–44), endured by a woman for twelve years. The compound *pararreō* (lit., "flow past") is used fig. in Heb. 2:1 with reference to "what we have heard [i.e., the gospel], so that we do not drift away."

4839	ῥῆμα

ῥῆμα (*rhēma*), word, utterance, thing, matter, event, case (*4839*).

CL & OT 1. In cl. Gk. *rhēma* means that which is stated intentionally: a word, an utterance. In Plato *rhēma* denotes an individual word but also a sentence. In grammar *rhēma* means a vb. as distinct from a noun.

2. In the LXX *rhēma* usually translates Heb. *dābār*, word, thing, which is chiefly rendered by *logos* (word, → *3364*). *rhēma* is used mostly in prophetic books, though it is found 147x in the Pentateuch as well as in other historical books. The double meaning of *dābār* as word or thing has colored the use of *rhēma*, which can mean both word, utterance as well as matter, event.

(a) *rhēma*, word, utterance, is often synonymous with *logos* (cf. the alternation of both words in Exod. 34:27–28; 2 Sam. 14:20–21). Frequently *rhēma* relates to a word from God: a single utterance (Exod. 19:6), a command (Deut. 4:1), the creative word (8:3), or a directive oracle (1 Sam. 3:1). The pl. occasionally denotes the commandments in general (Deut. 28:58), the Ten Commandments (Exod. 34:1), and the teachings of wisdom (Sir. 39:6; Wis. 6:25). *rhēma*, word, can also be used for the process of inspiration (e.g., Num. 23:5, 16, where God puts the word into the mouth of the pagan Balaam) and in the phrase "the word of the LORD came to . . ." (e.g., 1 Sam. 15:10; 1 Ki. 17:2, 8), but *logos* is mainly used for this in the historical books.

(b) *rhēma*, thing, matter, is more specifically defined by the context as an action (Gen. 22:16; Deut. 15:10; 23:10 = LXX 23:9), legal case (Exod. 18:26; Deut. 1:17), event (4:32), or thought (15:9). The narrative portions of the Pentateuch sometimes use *rhēma* in the construction "after these things" (e.g., Gen. 15:1; 22:1).

NT In the NT the term *rhēma* occurs 68x. It usually means word rather than matter, esp. because the NT does not have much legal material. Whereas *logos* often designates the Christian proclamation as a whole in the NT, *rhēma* usually relates to individual words and utterances: e.g., we will have to render account for every unjust word we speak (Matt. 12:36); Jesus answered Pilate without a single word (27:14).

1. For Lk. a basic principle is: "Nothing [lit., not a thing] is impossible with God" (Lk. 1:37; cf. *rhēma* in Gen. 18:14); he may have understood *rhēma* as the word of promise, which never remains unfulfilled (cf. Lk. 2:29). The Christmas message (2:17), proclaimed by an angel, is God's word, to which one bows in trust and obedience and the realization of which one lives to see (2:15, 19). The preaching of John the Baptist makes this clear. Whereas prophecy was extinct for the rabbis, Lk. applies a typical OT formula to John ("the word of God came to John," 3:2; cf. 7:26–27).

In this sense even the words of Jesus are designated by the noun *rhēma* in Lk. Anyone who believes and obeys him and, like Peter, throws out the net in response to his word sees its fulfillment (Lk. 5:5–8). True, Jesus' word is not always immediately understood (2:50), esp. predictions of his suffering (18:34), but later realization awakes the memory and discloses the connection between word and event (24:8; Acts 11:16).

2. In Acts the pl. *rhēmata* relates to Stephen's critique of law and temple, condemned as blasphemous (6:11, 13), and positively to the apostolic witness of the Christ event proclaimed in the speeches

(2:14; 5:20; 10:22, 44; cf. 26:25). The individual events of the Christ event are also denoted as *rhēmata* (5:32; 13:42).

3. In Jn.'s Gospel the unity of Jesus' word and God's word is expressly established: Jesus speaks "the words of God" (Jn. 3:34; cf. 8:47; 14:10; 17:8); his words are spirit and life (6:63), i.e., they are inspired and give eternal life (6:68) to those who accept them (17:8) and who keep them in themselves (15:7). The divine authority of these words rests on the sending of Jesus (3:34), esp. on his sonship (3:35; 17:8).

4. In the NT letters, this equation of Jesus' words and God's word is matched by the correlation between gospel and OT prophecy (Rom. 1:2–4). What was said in Deut. 30:12–14 concerning the *rhēma* of the Torah points to the message of justification through Christ: it is, for the believer, the word that is near and that saves (Rom. 10:8). But like the song of praise of the spheres, this word is carried into the furthest corners of the earth (10:18; cf. Ps. 19:4). Paul can designate the glad tidings of the gospel as the *rhēma* of Christ (Rom. 10:17). Peter also identifies the gospel and the OT by relating Isa. 40:8 ("the word of the Lord stands forever") to the gospel (1 Pet. 1:24–25; cf. also 2 Pet. 3:2; Jude 17).

5. As to the meaning of thing or matter, *rhēma* appears in Lk. 2:15, 19 for the Christmas events. Several times the NT refers to the legal provision of Deut. 19:15, whereby a legal matter (*rhēma*) is to be binding on the basis of the evidence of two or three witnesses. Whereas in Matt. 18:16 this provision is impressed on the church as a community rule and is applied by Paul to his judicial decisions in community affairs (2 Cor. 13:1), John relates it to proclamation as witnessed by Jesus and God (Jn. 8:17).

See also *glōssa*, tongue, language, speech (*1185*); *logos*, word, utterance, meaning (*3364*).

4844 (rhiza, root), → *1285.*

4845 (rhizoō, take root), → *1285.*

4847 (rhipizō, blow), → *847.*

4855 (rhomphaia, a large, broad sword), → *4483.*

4861 ῥύομαι	ῥύομαι (*rhyomai*), rescue, deliver, preserve, save (*4861*).

CL & OT 1. (a) *rhyomai* is a mid. dep. vb. found in cl. Gk. and in inscriptions and papyri. It is used of deliverance by both the gods and humans. Such deliverance extends not only to individuals in battle, but to various dangers and afflictions, even to protection of property.

(b) On the human level the vb. is applied to the action of princes in delivering cities and countries as well as women and children. It can even be used of inanimate objects. Thus, walls, helmets, and armor are said to protect. On the other hand, Odysseus cannot save his comrades who have destroyed themselves by sin, and there are cases where not even the gods can save.

2. In the LXX *rhyomai* translates mostly various forms of *nāṣal*, to rescue, deliver (90x). It is used 12x to translate *gāʾal*, redeem, buy back, deliver (→ *lyō, 3395*) as well as several other vbs. with the same general nuance. There appear to be two main groups of passages: those that correspond to cl. Gk. usage, except that Yahweh fulfils the role that in Gk. lit. is ascribed to the gods, and a distinctive OT usage.

(a) The psalmists sing of divine deliverance from persecutors (Ps. 7:1), wicked neighbors (34:4), and evil men (43:1); from murder (18:29), the sword (22:20), death, and famine (33:19); from sin and its consequences (39:8; 40:13). But the Torah, prophetic, historical, and wisdom writings celebrate Yahweh's deliverance of his people both as a whole (Exod. 6:6; 14:30; Isa. 36:15; Ezek. 13:21, 23) and as individuals (2 Sam. 22:18, 44, 49; Job 5:20; 22:30). Sometimes this is related to the specific saving acts of God, esp. the exodus (Exod. 6:6; 14:30) and the settlement in Canaan (Jdg. 8:34).

The OT, like cl. Gk. lit., knows of human deliverers. But these people act in the name and power of Yahweh. Thus Moses saved the daughters of the priest of Midian (Exod. 2:17, 19), and Gideon is called a savior of Israel (Jdg. 9:17). The king saves Israel (2 Sam. 19:9). It is the task of the judge to deliver (Ps. 82:4). In Sir. 40:24 a brother or companion may be a savior.

(b) A distinctive OT emphasis occurs in passages where a theocentric understanding replaces the anthropocentric understanding of secular Gk. Deliverance is no longer determined by the laws of being that obtain for both gods and humans but by the sustaining word of Yahweh, for whom the deliverance of the people is part of salvation history. He delivers according to his mercies (Neh. 9:28) and his name's sake (Ps. 79:9). In the later part of Isa. Yahweh is celebrated as the one who delivers his people from bondage—his name is "our Redeemer" (63:16; cf. 44:6; 47:4).

Deliverance in the OT has nothing magical about it. Because it has to do with historical situations, it occurs in history. However, deliverance comes in Yahweh's good time. Such deliverance is often linked to faith on the part of the people: "In you our fathers put their trust; they trusted and you delivered them" (Ps. 22:4). Unbelief amounts to a denial that the Lord can save (Isa. 36:14–20; Wis. 2:18). But he delivers those who fear him and hope in his steadfast love (Ps. 33:18–19; Ezek. 14:20), who consider the poor (Ps. 41; cf. Sir. 40:24), and who, out of an individual awareness of guilt, offer a heartfelt cry for deliverance from transgression (Ps. 39:8; 40:13; 79:9). Salvation is grounded in Yahweh's mercy (31:1; 71:2; 86:13).

NT 1. The vb. occurs only 15x in the NT, seven of which are in quotations or allusions to the OT; in each case God is the deliverer. The taunt of the bystanders at the crucifixion echoes Ps. 22:8: "He trusts in God. Let God rescue him now if he wants him, for he said, 'I am the Son of God'" (Matt. 27:43). The mockers take the sufferings of Jesus and the failure of God to deliver him as conclusive disproof of his claims. But Matt. sees the allusion to Ps. 22:8 as proof of a deeper working of God. Although God does not deliver Jesus from death in the way that might have been expected, he delivers him in a deeper sense in the resurrection. The song of Zechariah in Lk. 1:74 sees the promised deliverance from the hand of Israel's enemies to serve God without fear as a fulfillment of God's promise to Abraham (cf. Gen. 22:16–17).

In dealing with the question of whether God has finally rejected Israel (Rom. 9–11), Paul argues that the present hardening is merely a temporary element of God's purpose and that Isa. 59:20–21 has yet to be fulfilled: "So all Israel will be saved, as it is written: 'The deliverer will come from Zion; he will turn godlessness away from Jacob'" (Rom. 11:26; cf. also Ps. 14:7).

Paul uses *rhyomai* 3x in his account of his afflictions in Asia, expressing language that recalls the psalmist's praise of Yahweh's deliverance from death: "He has delivered us from such a deadly peril, and he will deliver us. On him we have set our hope that he will continue to deliver us" (2 Cor. 1:10). Paul may be alluding here to the riot in Ephesus (Acts 19:23–40), to a serious illness (cf. 2 Cor. 12:7), or even to a more serious danger in Asia not recorded in Acts 19.

As to other uses of the vb. in Paul, his prayer to be "delivered from wicked and evil men" (2 Thess. 3:2) recalls OT language (cf. Ps. 140:1; Isa. 25:4). In view of 1 Thess. 2:15–16, this may refer to opposition from the Jews (cf. Acts 17:5–15). OT language is again found in 2 Tim. 3:11, where Paul refers to his sufferings at Antioch, Iconium, and Lystra (cf. Acts 13:14–14:20; 16:1–5), from which "the Lord rescued me." In 2 Tim. 4:17–18 Paul presumably describes a preliminary hearing of his case at Rome. Although friends of a defendant often appeared in court to give support, no one stood by Paul. "But the Lord stood at my side and . . . I was delivered [*rhyomai*] from the lion's mouth. The Lord will rescue [*rhyomai*] me from evil attack." Paul's situation recalls Dan. 6:20 and Ps. 22:21, but doubtless refers also to the Roman practice of exposing criminals to wild beasts in the arena. Paul's expectation of future deliverance looks forward to deliverance through death and whatever terrifying circumstances may attend it.

Peter in 2 Pet. 2:9 uses several OT stories to illustrate the exhortation: "The Lord knows how to rescue godly men from trials." The examples he cites are Noah and the flood (2:5; cf. Gen. 6:1–8:22), and the judgment on Sodom and Gomorrah (6; cf. Gen. 19:24) and the rescue of Lot (2 Pet. 2:7; cf. Gen. 19:16, 29). In each case the righteous are saved from a judgment that befalls the ungodly; this is both an encouragement and a warning.

2. Only once is *rhyomai* used with a clear reference to the deliverance that believers have already experienced: "He has rescued us from the dominion of darkness and brought us into the kingdom of the Son he loves" (Col. 1:13; cf. Eph. 2:5–8, where *sōzō*, save, *5392*, is used). Paul may be alluding to baptism, esp. if we look at baptism in the light of the cross and the Christian experience of life in Christ (Col. 2:12–15; 3:1–4). In 1:14 this deliverance is related to redemption (*apolytrōsis*; → *lytron*, ransom price, *3389*) and the forgiveness of sins.

3. There has been considerable debate on the interpretation of Rom. 7:24, esp. on the question of whose cry this is: a redeemed person, an unredeemed person, or even a redeemed person looking back at the time when he or she was not redeemed: "What a wretched man I am! Who will rescue me from this body of death?" This person is subject to death because of sin (5:12, 21; 6:23). The answer to the question is given in 7:25: "Thanks be to God—through Jesus Christ our Lord! So then, I myself in my mind am a slave to God's law, but in the sinful nature a slave to the law of sin." The believer's life in this world remains one of conflict. The answer is further developed in ch. 8. What the law was powerless to do God has done by sending his Son to fully meet God's law and by giving us the Spirit, who comes to live in us.

4. The Lord's Prayer contains the petition: "But deliver [*rhyomai*] us from the evil one" (Matt. 6:13). Jesus instructs us to pray for release from the power that dominates this age and constantly threatens us. But there is also an eschatological note: the thought of eternal salvation as the goal of deliverance (cf. also Rom. 11:26; 1 Thess. 1:10). The latter passage expresses our Christian hope as waiting for God's "Son from heaven, whom he raised from the dead—Jesus, who rescues [*rhyomai*] us from the coming wrath."

See also *lyō*, to loose, untie, set free, release, annul, abolish (*3395*); *lytron*, price of release, ransom, ransom price (*3389*); *sōzō*, save, keep from harm, preserve, rescue (*5392*); *sōtēr*, savior, deliverer, preserver (*5400*).

4862 (*rhypainō*, make filthy), → *4866*.

4864 (*rhyparia*, filthiness), → *4866*.

4865 (*rhyparos*, dirty), → *4866*.

4866	ῥύπος

ῥύπος (*rhypos*), dirt (*4866*); ῥυπαρία (*rhyparia*), filthiness (*4864*); ῥυπαρός (*rhyparos*), dirty (*4865*); ῥυπαίνω (*rhypainō*), make filthy (*4862*).

CL & OT In cl. Gk. *rhypos* is used of literal dirt, liquid and solid. *rhyparos* and *rhyparia* carry both lit. and fig. meanings; with *rhypainō* the fig. meaning, to mess up (one's life and character), seems primary. *rhypos* appears 2x in the LXX for lit. dirt (Job 9:31; 11:15) and 2x for defilement before God (14:4; Isa. 4:4). *rhyparos* is used in Zech. 3:4–5 of dirty clothes.

NT *rhypos* occurs once, of physical dirt (1 Pet. 3:21); *rhyparia* once, of moral filthiness (Jas. 1:21). *rhyparos* is used 2x, once of dirty clothing (2:2) and once of a morally unclean person (Rev. 22:11). *rhypainō* appears in 22:11, where the meaning is "let him who is vile [*rhyparos*] continue to be vile [*rhypainō*]."

See also *peripsēma*, filth (*4370*); *skybalon*, refuse, dung (*5032*).

4868 (*rhysis*, a flowing river, stream), → *4835*.

Σ *sigma*

4878 (*sabbatismos*, Sabbath-rest), → 4879.

| 4879 | σάββατον |

σάββατον (*sabbaton*), Sabbath (4879); σαββατισμός (*sabbatismos*), Sabbath-rest (4878).

OT 1. *sabbaton* transliterates the Heb. *šabbāt*. It is found in the sing. and the pl. (*sabbata*) for a single Sabbath day. Presumably the word derives from the Heb. vb. *šābat*, to cease, pause (cf. Gen. 2:2–3, where this vb. is used for God's resting on the seventh day; cf. also Exod. 20:8–11). There seems to be no difference in meaning between the sing. and pl. forms of the Gk. equivalent in the LXX.

2. The Sabbath is mentioned in numerous parts of the law (e.g., Exod. 20:8–11; 23:12; 31:12–17; 35:1–3; Lev. 23:1–3). No other commandment is so strongly emphasized, showing its great importance in Israel's history. It carried the death penalty for infringement (Exod. 31:14; cf. 35:3; Num. 15:32–36). The rite of circumcision was performed on the Sabbath if it fell on the eighth day after the boy's birth (Lev. 12:3; cf. Jn. 7:22). The special day may go back to a pre-Mosaic period and have been known to the Israelites when they were in Egypt or even earlier.

Sabbath observance is strongly emphasized in both versions of the Decalogue, though in a slightly different form and with a different reason suggested. In Exod. 20:8–11, its observance is based on the seven days of creation in Gen. 1:1–2:3. After creating humankind, God blessed the seventh day and set it apart as holy. In Deut. 5:12–15, observance is linked with redemption from bondage in Egypt. God's people had been slaves there, but God mightily delivered them; thus, the day was to be kept holy. In both cases the Sabbath was established for the benefit of humanity and for calling to one's mind the fact that we owe everything to God. The emphasis on resting from labor shows that its main purpose was the cessation of ordinary work for one day in seven. In Exod. 31:17 the Sabbath is a covenant sign between God and Israel.

Lev. 23:1–3 includes the Sabbath in the feasts of the Lord, which were commemorative days set apart so that Israel might spend time in meditation on different aspects of God's good hand over the nation. Included in their observance were sacred assemblies, public acts of worship. Both for the individual and the community the Sabbath was thus to be a day of public worship as well as an opportunity for a joyful observance of the day in the home. This was so in preexilic times (Isa. 1:13; Hos. 2:11; Amos 8:5). It was also a suitable time for consulting a prophet (2 Ki. 4:23).

On the Sabbath special sacrifices were offered (Num. 28:9), and with them the renewal of the Bread of the Presence (Lev. 24:8), thus linking Sabbath with the official ritual of tabernacle and temple. It seems special Sabbath psalms were also appointed (cf. the title of Ps. 92). The insistence on laying aside work, even in the busiest times of plowing and harvest (Exod. 34:21), and the infliction of the death penalty for its breach (31:14; Num. 15:32) show the supreme importance attached to this command in the life of Israel. Yet the Sabbath was to be regarded not as a burden, but as a delight, "the LORD's holy day" (Isa. 58:13). Special blessings were attached to its observance (56:2).

After the exile, in the disordered state of the nation, one naturally finds a reemphasis on this day in Nehemiah's reforms (Neh. 10:32; 13:15–22).

3. During the intertestamental period Jud. gradually began to divide into two types. In Palestine and Mesopotamia a more legal attitude emerged, while in other parts of the Diaspora a more liberal atti-

tude prevailed. Both sections insisted on the observance of Sabbath as a divine institution and regarded it, with circumcision, as one of the signs of the covenant. Synagogue worship on the Sabbath was a regular feature of both types.

Hel. circles took a more mystical and spiritual attitude to the Sabbath. Philo insisted that it should be dedicated to the study of the spiritual. On that day the slave became a free person. With the translation of the OT into Gk., although the Heb. word itself was transliterated in Gk., its meaning was given as *anapausis* (rest, → 398).

Palestinian Jud. tended toward a more lit. and rigid attitude. Traditions of how it was to be observed began to crystallize. Even the rescue of an animal from death on the Sabbath was forbidden at Qumran (CD 10:14–11:18). To protect it from Gentile influences, a stereotyped code of what could or could not be done on the Sabbath came into existence (→ *Jub.* 2:17–33). These traditions later became codified in the Mishnah tractate *Shabbat*. Yet even here, under certain circumstances the Sabbath law could be superseded. These included the service of the priests in the temple, the saving of life in emergency, and circumcision on the eighth day.

In spite of these burdensome regulations the Sabbath was welcomed with joy. It was to be celebrated at home as rest and refreshment, corporately in public worship. On the day before the Sabbath, the day of preparation (*paraskeuē*; → *kataskeuazō*, prepare, *2941*), everything was to be made ready and the lamps lit, since the Sabbath commenced at sunset. A meal extra to the normal two was added and the best clothes worn. Guests were often invited (cf. Mk. 14:3).

NT 1. *The Gospels.* The Palestinian attitude to Sabbath observance is clear in the Gospels. One of Christ's conflicts with the Jews, mentioned in all four Gospels, centers on what was or was not permissible on the Sabbath. All but one of these involves healing on the Sabbath day. The exception is when the disciples plucked the ears of grain as they passed through a field.

Was Jesus abrogating the day of rest or merely challenging the restrictions that the rabbis had imposed for the Sabbath? Let us examine the six recorded confrontations of Jesus with the Jews over the Sabbath question. (a) Matt. 12:1–8 (Mk. 2:23–28; Lk. 6:1–5) relates the incident of the plucking of ears of grain on the Sabbath day. According to the Pharisees, this was breaking the law. Jesus claims, however, that as was the case with David and his men (cf. 1 Sam. 21:1–6), human need overrides ritual law (cf. Exod. 23:12; Deut. 5:14). The law itself is not challenged, but Jesus claims an overriding factor.

(b) Matt. 12:9–14 (Mk. 3:1–6; Lk. 6:6–11) describes Jesus' healing of the man with a withered hand. Before healing him, Jesus asks the Jewish leaders whether it is lawful on the Sabbath day "to do good or to do evil, to save life or to kill?" (Mk. 3:4). Again, Jesus does not challenge the law itself; in fact the wording assumes its relevance. The right use of the law, the healing of the whole person, is the object behind that law, and thus the healing is justified.

(c) Lk. 13:10–17 relates the story of a woman bent over with infirmity. She comes into the synagogue, and Jesus restores her on the Sabbath, which rouses the anger of the synagogue ruler. Jesus' response includes two points. What he did was an act of mercy such as the leaders would have allowed to an animal. It was also the destruction of a work of Satan. There is no hint that the principle of a day of rest is being questioned, but merely the proper use of the day.

(d) In Lk. 14:1–6 Jesus again opens the discussion by asking the Pharisees whether it is right to heal on the Sabbath day or not. They offer no reply. This is an esp. important incident, since the question is addressed to experts in the law. Jesus proceeds to heal a man suffering from dropsy and then explains that healing the sick is in fact just as much an act of mercy as pulling an animal out of a well. The fact that the experts offer no reply suggests that they agree that Jesus is not challenging the Sabbath law.

(e) In Jn. 5:1–9, 16–17; 7:22 Jesus chooses the Sabbath day to heal a man crippled for 38 years, telling him to take up his bed and walk. When the Jews persecute Jesus for this, he replies, "My Father is always at his work to this very day, and I, too, am working" (5:16). That is, Jesus is continuing the work the Father has been doing all the while. He is not annulling the Sabbath here, for he goes on to stress how the law of circumcision overrides the law of the Sabbath. Had he been annulling the Sabbath law, he would not have argued in this way. Moreover, "to this very day" suggest that while the Sabbath command was in force, God in fact kept working. In other words, the Sabbath command does not mean to do nothing, but to do the work of God. This was what Christ was doing in healing the infirm man.

(f) In the case of the man born blind (Jn. 9), Christ does not defend his action. But in the initial answer to the disciples' question in 9:2, Christ claims the Sabbath healing was "that the work of God might be made displayed in his life" (9:3).

(g) We should also note Lk. 4:16, where Lk. notes that Jesus attended the synagogue "as was his custom." That is, Jesus followed the ordinary habits of Jewish worship on the Sabbath day, a pattern evident in his boyhood (2:22, 41). It may be significant that at his trial (e.g., Matt. 26:57–68; Jn. 18:12–24), there is no mention of his annulling of the Sabbath law.

(h) Christ's statement that his followers should pray, in view of the coming destruction of Jerusalem, that their flight not occur in the winter or on the Sabbath, implies that he foresees his followers continuing to observe the Sabbath but that it will be hard to get help or buy what is needed on a Sabbath day in the vicinity of Jerusalem (Matt. 24:20).

(i) In Mk. 2:27–28 we find Christ's positive statement about the Sabbath. He insists that the Sabbath was made for humanity's good, probably an indirect reference to Gen. 2:2–3. If so, the Sabbath ordinance was not merely for Israel, but had a pre-Israelite, worldwide, humanitarian implication. Moreover, Jesus is "Lord even of the Sabbath." In other words, he has the authority to decide about its observance. Far from suggesting that it is to be annulled, this saying suggests that the manner of its observance is under the control of Christ himself.

2. *Acts.* The decrees of the Jerusalem Council in Acts 15 make no mention of the Sabbath. This presumably was not a point of contention between Jewish and Gentile Christians. On his missionary journeys Paul seized every opportunity to preach in the synagogues on the Sabbath day (13:5, 14, 42–44; 14:1; 16:13; 17:2, 16; 18:4; 19:8). Yet we also find him meeting with the Christians on the first day of the week (20:7; cf. 1 Cor. 16:2; → *kyriakos*, Lord's day, *3258*).

3. *The NT letters.* Three significant passages in Paul's letters explore the Christian attitude toward the Sabbath. (a) Rom. 14:5–6 has no direct reference to the Sabbath but touches on this theme. It deals with the weak Christian, one who still is influenced by the letter of the law. In the case of days, instead of thinking of one day as being esp. sacred, the strong Christian considers all days as God's days, to be lived to God. No day *in itself* has any special sanctity.

(b) In Gal. 4:10 Paul addresses Gentile converts who, after their conversion, were turning to a scrupulous observance of Jewish ritual, special days, new moons, and feasts, i.e., taking on themselves the Jewish law. Paul will not countenance a reversal to Jewish practices for Gentile Christians.

(c) In Col. 2:16 Paul argues that the legal demands of the Jewish law have been cancelled in Christ's death (2:14); thus, Jewish food regulations and religious days are not binding on the Christian. Included in this ritual is the Jewish Sabbath. These observances, Paul claims, point to a spiritual reality fulfilled in Christ.

(d) Heb. 4:9 is unique in passages on the Sabbath: "There remains, then, a Sabbath-rest [*sabbatismos*] for the people of God."

Here the rest typified by the Sabbath is seen as the rest of the heart, provided in Christ (cf. Matt. 11:28)—to be realized partially now and fully in the life to come.

4. *Theological insights.* Just as God's rest after creation included the idea of the Sabbath day each week, the rest of the heart remaining to God's people includes the foretaste of the final rest in the weekly rest day. We have seen that the Sabbath concept includes both a national aspect as part of the covenant relationship with the Jews and a universal aspect as a spiritual and humanitarian benefit for humankind as a whole. The end of the Sabbath, as a sign of the covenant with Israel, does not necessarily mean the abolition of the concept of a weekly day of rest. Mk. 2:27 suggests that such an outward enjoyment of a Sabbath rest was an integral part of the inward heart rest, of which the Sabbath under the old covenant had been a shadow. The fact that an analogous day for Christians, the Lord's Day, had already come into being suggests that this is the right solution of the problem.

See also *kyriakos*, the Lord's (day) (*3258*).

4881 Σαδδουκαῖος	Σαδδουκαῖος (*Saddoukaios*), Sadducee (*4881*).

NT 1. This noun is not found in cl. Gk. or the LXX. In the NT it is always found in the pl. (*Saddoukaioi*). It designates a group or party within Palestinian Jud. before and during the 1st cent. Usually it is assumed that the term goes back to the name Zadok (LXX *Saddouk*), the name of several priests, one as early as David's reign (2 Sam. 15:24–36; 17:15; 19:11), who gained control of the high priesthood and temple under Solomon (1 Ki. 2:35; 1 Chr. 29:22; cf. also the "descendants of Zadok" in Ezek. 44:15). However, this identification is by no means certain.

2. In fact, information about the Sadducees with any claim to authenticity is found only in Josephus, the NT, and the Mishnah. (Talmudic references to the Sadducees are late, confused, and unreliable.) (a) Josephus first mentions the Sadducees in connection with the reign of John Hyrcanus (135–105 B.C.), but he assumes that they were a well-established group by that time. They were rude in their conduct, few in number, and held the confidence of the wealthy alone. Josephus usually refers to the Sadducees in the context of their continued controversy with the Pharisees. The Sadducees rejected the oral law and did not believe in continued existence, bodily resurrection, rewards and punishments after death, or predestination.

(b) In the NT, Matt. 3:7–10 and 16:1–12 name the Sadducees along with the Pharisees as leaders of the Jewish people rebuked by both John the Baptist and Jesus. In Mk. 12:18–27 the Sadducees, "who say there is no resurrection," present Jesus with a situation that they believe makes the resurrection look ridiculous. Jesus, however, silences them with an argument based on the written law.

Acts places the Sadducees among the opponents of the early Christians. In 4:1 they are associated with, but distinguished from, the priests; in 5:17, the high priest and his associates are specifically identified as "the party of the Sadducees." In 4:2 the opponents of the Christians were "greatly disturbed because the apostles were teaching the people and proclaiming in Jesus the resurrection from the dead," while 23:6–9 describes an uproar in the Jewish Council when Paul, perceiving the presence of both Sadducees and Pharisees, identifies himself with the latter. Lk. explains, "The Sadducees say that there is no resurrection, and that there are neither angels nor spirits, but the Pharisees acknowledge them all" (23:8).

(c) References to the Sadducees in the Mishnah describe them almost entirely in terms of their differences with the Pharisees on ritual, ceremonial, and judicial matters. These issues relate to such matters as the date and observance of certain feasts, Sabbath-keeping, the way sacrifices were to be offered and temple ritual performed, the conduct and penalties in criminal cases, and procedures relating to ceremonial defilement and cleanliness.

3. In sum, the Sadducees came into existence during the intertestamental period, probably assuming their definitive stance after the Hasmonean priest-rulers gained firm control. They were closely associated with the priestly aristocracy and hence deeply involved in politics. Like the priests, the Sadducees seem to have given at least some support to foreign influences (Hellenism) and powers (the Romans) present in Jewish Palestine in order to maintain their own position.

Their religious and theological views resulted from a conservative, lit. handling of the OT law. The Sadducees were bitter opponents of the Pharisees, for whom oral tradition attempted to interpret, update, and apply the written law in the face of changing circumstances. The Sadducees maintained their own traditions and hermeneutical methods that accepted only the written law (i.e., the Pentateuch) as authoritative. Hence they refused the mass of postbiblical developments associated with Pharisaism, including belief in the imminence of divine activity and life after death. The Sadducees were essentially secularists. This doubtless resulted from their exclusion of God from human history and their limitation of humanity's existence and blessing to this life.

Political motives stirred the Sadducees to oppose Jesus and the Jewish church. Jesus' preaching and public ministry posed a threat to the political status quo and the dominance of the priestly party within it (cf. Jn. 11:47–50). His emphasis on the spiritual realm, his attacks on the external religion of Jewry, and the popular acceptance accorded him and his followers endangered their already precarious position. To make matters worse, Christianity was in agreement with much in the position of the Sadducees' enemies, the Pharisees. Still, the Sadducees found one emphasis of Christian doctrine even more objectionable than any Pharisaic teaching, namely, that the resurrection is a present reality accomplished in Jesus (cf. Acts 4:2).

| 4888   σαλεύω |

σαλεύω (*saleō*), shake, cause to waver or totter, unsettle, drive away (*4888*); σάλος (*salos*), rolling or tossing motion (*4893*); ἀσάλευτος (*asaleutos*), unshakable, firm, enduring (*810*).

CL & OT 1. In cl. Gk. *saleō* means to rock, vibrate (sea, ground), loosen (tooth, nail), roll, toss (of ships in stormy seas); fig. it means to be in distress, be unstable, shake (because of sickness or age). Hence, life in the world beyond is *asaleutos*, not subject to trouble or disturbance. *asaleutos* also refers to the calmness of the sea, or fig. of the mind. *salos* means tossing motion, earthquake, rolling swell of the sea; perplexity, restlessness (political or personal).

2. In the LXX *saleō* appears 77x, translating a variety of Heb. words. Frequently in Ps. it denotes the godly person who is not moved in the face of enemies (e.g., 15:5; 16:8; 112:6). *salos* occurs 8x and denotes a slipping of the feet (66:9), the tumult of the waves (89:9), the raging of the sea (Jon. 1:15), and a storm (Zech. 9:14). *asaleutos* occurs in Exod. 13:16; Deut. 6:8; 11:18 in reference to the immovability of the symbols that were to be worn on hands and forehead as a reminder of Yahweh and his Word. It is from these verses that the Jewish practice of wearing phylacteries arose (Matt. 23:5).

NT 1. *saleō* is used of the shaking caused by wind and storm, as in the parable of the two men whose houses, built on sand and rock respectively, faced a violent storm with dramatically different consequences (Lk. 6:48). After the release of Peter and John from prison, the house where the Christians in Jerusalem had met to pray was shaken as in an earthquake as a sign of divine approval (Acts 4:31; cf. 2:2; also Exod. 19:18; Isa. 6:4; 2 Esd. 6:15–16, 29). At Philippi, the foundations of the prison were shaken by an earthquake (Acts 16:26). The swaying building perhaps unlatched the doors and momentarily opened up the rough mortar between the stones, thus causing the staples holding the prisoners' chains to fall out.

2. After answering messengers from John the Baptist, Jesus took occasion to speak about John's character and mission. A reed "swayed"

by the wind (Matt. 11:7; Lk. 7:24) may be a collective sing., referring to the cane grass growing on the banks of the Jordan. People went to the desert not to gaze at the beauty of the cane grass being swayed about in the wind, but to look for a man with a message. This swaying cane grass may also be a metaphor for a fickle person, which John the Baptist was not. *saleō* is also used fig. to express abundant giving, just as full volume is obtained by shaking together the contents of a grain measure (6:38); to be thoroughly unsettled in mind (2 Thess. 2:2); to incite a mob (Acts 17:13); and to shake out of a sense of security and happiness (Acts 2:25, quoting Ps. 16:8).

3. After the tribulation, the Son of Man's return will be accompanied by unmistakable cosmic portents. These are described in the Synoptic Gospels in the traditional terminology of Jewish apocalyptic, commonly used to symbolize political upheaval and the end of the world (Isa. 13:10; 34:4; Ezek. 32:7; Amos 8:9; 2 Esd. 13:1–13, 30–38). According to Matt. 24:29; Mk. 13:25; Lk. 21:26, the powers of the heavens—either the heavenly bodies or the forces that control them—will be shaken. This disruption of nature involves a tumult of the elements, so that the universe loses its equilibrium and becomes unhinged. This will signal the reappearance of the Son of Man.

4. The noun *salos* occurs only at Lk. 21:25, where the rolling swell of the sea is one of the eschatological signs that will distress the nations (cf. Hag. 2:6). The image of roaring waves often symbolizes turbulent conditions in the life of the nations (Ps. 65:7).

5. Lk. tells how, when the crew of Paul's storm-tossed ship ran the vessel ashore, the bow stuck fast in the mud and "would not move" (*asaleutos*, Acts 27:41). The only other use of *asaleutos* is in Heb. 12:28, where the writer says that the divine kingdom "cannot be shaken" and is thus eternal, in contrast to the fate of the material creation, however solid that has appeared in the past (12:26, quoting Hag. 2:6).

See also *seiō*, shake, cause to quake, agitate (*4940*); *ektinassō*, shake out, shake off (*1759*).

| 4889   Σαλήμ |

Σαλήμ (*Salēm*), Salem, seat of Melchizedek's rule (*4889*).

OT 1. Salem is associated from earliest times with Jerusalem. As a place name *šālēm* occurs only 2x in the OT: Gen. 14:18 and Ps. 76:2 (a poetic abbreviation of Jerusalem). In the mind of the psalmist, Salem is the dwelling place of God, parallel to Mount Zion. According to Josephus the priest-king Melchizedek renamed that city Jerusalem.

2. *šālēm*, a common OT cognate of *šālôm* ("wholeness," "peace") bears the meaning peaceful in the MT in the sense of a covenant of peace among humans (Gen. 34:21). More frequently it signifies the concept of perfect devotion or blamelessness as a description of our spiritual relation to God (1 Ki. 8:61; 11:4; 15:3; 2 Chr. 16:9).

NT In the NT *Salēm* occurs only in Heb. 7:1–2. After identifying Melchizedek as "king of Salem" (cf. Gen. 14:18), the writer quickly unfolds the deeper spiritual meaning implicit in Melchizedek's royal title. To the eyes of faith the "king of Salem" is "king of peace" (→ *eirēnē*, *1645*). Heb. reflects little interest in the geographical location of Salem. Rather, from the etymology of Salem the letter deduces a principal characteristic (i.e., peace) of the reign of the end-time priest-king.

See also *Melchisedek*, Melchizedek (*3519*).

4893 (*salos*, rolling or tossing motion), → *4888*.

| 4894   σάλπιγξ |

σάλπιγξ (*salpinx*), trumpet, trumpet call (*4894*); σαλπίζω (*salpizō*), sound the trumpet, give a blast of the bugle (*4895*); σαλπιστής (*salpistēs*), trumpeter (*4896*).

CL & OT 1. In the ancient world the trumpet was used to give signals in war (e.g., to change guard, prepare for attack or retreat, or terrify or deceive the enemy). In times of peace it was used at trials, before prayer, by shepherds, in funeral or festal processions, and at athletic contests.

2. In the LXX the *salpinx* was sounded at burnt offerings and fellowship offerings (Num. 10:10; 2 Chr. 29:27–28), at feast times (Lev. 25:9), at royal coronations (2 Ki. 9:13), and at dedications (2 Chr. 5:12; Ezr. 3:10), as well as in war to mark the beginning of a battle (Job 39:24–25; 1 Macc. 9:12–13) or to warn of an invasion (Amos 3:6). Trumpets played an important part in the taking of Jericho (Jos. 6:4–21) and Gideon's defeat of the Midianites (Jdg. 7:18–22).

NT 1. Occurring 11x in the NT, *salpinx* denotes both the instrument itself (1 Cor. 14:8) and the sound it emits (15:52). *salpizō* occurs 12x, all but two (Matt. 6:2; 1 Cor. 15:52) in Rev. 8–11. *salpistēs* occurs only once.

2. (a) The injunction of Jesus not to "announce … with trumpets" the giving of alms (Matt. 6:2) prohibits ostentatious giving that is designed to gain human attention and praise (6:1–4). Jesus may be alluding to a practice (not elsewhere attested) of blowing a trumpet in the temple when alms were being collected for some special relief project or in the synagogue when notable gifts were given, to encourage other generous donations and to bring the donors to God's attention. But *salpizō* here may well be fig.

(b) Paul observes that only a distinct bugle blast rouses troops for battle. Similarly, only clear, intelligible communications should have a place in corporate worship (1 Cor. 14:8–9).

(c) Although the sound of a trumpet may be one of the concomitants of a theophany (Heb. 12:18–19), sometimes the authoritative and indescribable voice of God or Christ is itself said to sound "like a trumpet" (Rev. 1:10; 4:1). As in the OT, a trumpet call announces divine judgment (8:2–9:21; 11:15–19; cf. Joel 2:1–2; Zeph. 1:14–16), the resurrection of the dead (1 Cor. 15:52; 1 Thess. 4:16; cf. 2 Esd. 6:23–24), and the gathering of the elect from the four corners of the earth (Matt. 24:31; cf. Isa. 27:13).

(d) Only in Rev. 18:22 is there a reference to the trumpet as an instrument of music, played by trumpeters (*salpistēs*).

4895 (*salpizō*, sound the trumpet, give a blast of the bugle),
→ *4894*.

4896 (*salpistēs*, trumpeter), → *4894*.

4899 (*Samareia*, Samaria), → *4901*.

4901 Σαμαρίτης	Σαμαρίτης (*Samaritēs*), Samaritan (*4901*); Σαμάρεια (*Samareia*), Samaria (*4899*).

OT 1. The Gk. word *Samareia* stands for the Heb. *šômᵉrôn* and designates originally the capital city of the northern kingdom founded by Omri in 876 B.C. It later came to designate the area of the northern kingdom as an administrative unit of several successive empires. In the NT *Samareia* always denotes the territory of Samaria (e.g., Lk. 17:11; Jn. 4:4; Acts 1:8; 8:1; 9:31; 15:3). *Samareitēs* (first used in 2 Ki. 17:29; in the LXX only here; also *Samaritēs*), denotes the inhabitants of Samaria, both the city and the territory. In the NT *Samaritēs* applies only to the latter.

Samaritēs is both a geographical/ethnic term and a religious designation (cf. *Ioudaios*, Jew; → *Israēl*, Israel, *2702*). The ethnic identity of the Samaritans is a point of dispute between the Jews and the Samaritans. The anti-Samaritan polemic of Jud. assumed a total deportation of the population of the northern kingdom. But the religious community centered on Shechem, or Mount Gerizim, saw itself as a religious group within Israel, standing in unbroken continuity with the northern tribes, esp. of Ephraim and Manasseh.

2. The origins of the Samaritan community lie in obscurity and are covered over by the mutual polemic of the Jews and Samaritans. The political and religious tension between the northern and southern tribes and between the northern and southern kingdoms doubtless forms part of the antecedents of the schism. But tracing it to the Assyrian colonization as recorded in Jewish polemics (based on 2 Ki. 17:24–41, which also influenced the Christian view of the Samaritans) is questionable. But neither can we accept the Samaritan attempt to date their origin as early as the time of Eli. Even the conflict between the Persian administration in Samaria, headed by the house of Sanballat, and the leaders of the restoration in Jerusalem (Nehemiah and Ezra) should be regarded as only one contribution to the growing alienation between Judea and Samaria (cf. Ezr. 4; Neh. 4; 13:28).

The most important single event in the history of the rise of the Samaritan community was probably the construction of the temple to Yahweh on Mount Gerizim towards the end of the 4th cent. B.C. According to Josephus, the initiative came from the priests who had been excluded from Jerusalem because their marriages had been rejected as mixed marriages. They were settled by Sanballat in Shechem. Permission to build the temple presumably was granted by Alexander the Great in gratitude for military support by Sanballat. In the mouth of Josephus this is a credible and historically plausible tradition, because the erection of a temple was in any case an act of state (cf. Ezr. 1:1–8).

This was not the only temple to Yahweh erected outside Jerusalem in the postexilic period (cf. the temple at Elephantine in Upper Egypt in the 5th cent. B.C.). However, the Gerizim temple alone became a real challenge to the Jerusalem temple, since it represented a considerable political faction and because sooner or later the claims of Deut. about the sole, legitimate cultic center came to be related to it. It is entirely likely that the participants in the founding of the sanctuary saw the Gerizim temple as an act of restoration (cf. Jos. 24:2, esp. LXX), since Shechem and Gerizim had ancient Israelite traditions on their side (cf. Deut. 27:4).

The next conflict that opened up deep wounds and that was perhaps decisive for the ultimate schism arose through the opportunist policy of Shechem under Antiochus IV Epiphanes (175–ca. 164 B.C.). Josephus reports that the Samaritans requested in 167/166 that their temple on Mount Gerizim be dedicated to Zeus Hellenios. They did not intend thereby to implement any change of cultic practice. Rather, they were suggesting that their own deities could also be identified with Gk. gods and worshiped under their names. As a result, the Samaritans escaped persecution, while in Judea the Maccabees and their followers resisted the policy of cultural and religious Hellenization at the price of their lives. Thus, it was only natural that the success of the Maccabean revolt led not only to the expansion of Judea (cf. 1 Macc. 10:38; 11:34, 57), but also to the destruction of the temple on Mount Gerizim by John Hyrcanus in 129/128.

Pompey ended Judean dominance over Samaria in 63 B.C. This explains the good relations of the Samaritans to the Romans, which lasted until A.D. 67, and to the house of Herod, which was closely tied to Rome. This was interrupted only by a bloodbath precipitated by Pontius Pilate, which cost him his office, and a trial for breach of peace in A.D. 52, when the Samaritans, who were supported by the procurator Cumanus, came into violent conflict with the Jews. Following the trial in Rome, the leading Samaritans were executed and Cumanus banished.

NT 1. *Samaria* and the *Samaritans* occur in various places in the NT. Within the framework of the commissioning of the disciples, Matt. 10:5–6 contain the saying peculiar to Matt.: "Do not go among the Gentiles or enter any town of the Samaritans. Go rather to the lost sheep of Israel." The parallelism between "the Samaritans" with "the Gentiles" and their juxtaposition with "Israel" show unmistakably that the Samaritans are not recognized as Israelites here. The saying is closely linked to 15:24, where Jesus says to the Canaanite woman: "I was sent only to the lost sheep of Israel." Matt. 10:5–6 is not to be understood as a purely geographical limitation of the mission of the disciples to Galilee; rather, "Israel" indicates that all members of the people of Israel are included, *wherever they live*. In the light of this, it is questionable whether "town of the Samaritans" here means the province of Samaria. Rather, a distinction must be drawn between the journey through the province of Samaria and specific entry into a Samaritan town or village (cf. Jn. 4:5).

Historically Matt. 10:5–6 stands in connection with the conception of a mission solely to Israel (cf. also 10:23). But we should not understand the negations of 10:5 as directed against a Samaritan or Gentile mission that was beginning at the time this Gospel was being written, in view of the fact that the charge was clearly directed to the Twelve in 10:5–6. Their role, after all, was related to the twelve tribes of Israel even after Pentecost (cf. 19:28; Gal. 2:7–10).

2. (a) The narrative in Lk. 9:51–56 fits perfectly into our picture of the mutual attitudes of the Jews and Samaritans of the 1st cent. A.D. The reaction of James and John, the sons of Zebedee (9:54), takes up the Elijah tradition of 2 Ki. 10:10–14 and recalls the judgment on the people of Sodom (Gen. 19; cf. Lk. 10:12). The astonishing feeling of power of the two disciples is perhaps to be understood as an anticipation of 10:17–20. Jesus' rebuke (9:55) serves as a repudiation of false notions of the character of his messianic way (9:51, 53; cf. Matt. 16:22–23) and the apostolic commission (cf. Lk. 10:3–16).

(b) The parable of the Good Samaritan (Lk. 10:30–37) is a Lukan amplification of the pericope on the two great commandments (10:25–28), giving an illustration in the form of a narrative and expounding Lev. 19:18. The introductory question to the parable ("And who is my neighbor?") stands in tension with the point of the parable drawn out in Lk. 10:36–37 ("'Which of these three do you think was a neighbor to the man who fell into the hands of robbers?' The expert in the law replied, 'The one who had mercy on him.' Jesus told him, 'Go and do likewise'").

The fact that the positive figure in the narrative is a Samaritan serves to detach the love command from all previous relationships with a person in need. In the context of the priest and Levite (cf. Jn. 1:19), it contains an element of criticism of official Jud. (cf. 4:1–45). Attention is not drawn to any particular qualities of the Samaritan.

(c) The description of the grateful Samaritan in Lk. 17:11–19 as a "foreigner" can in itself be intended in an unpolemical way: "Was no one found to return and give praise to God except this foreigner?" (17:18). For the Samaritans could occasionally describe themselves as being an independent nation. Jewish polemics referred to an independent Samaritan nation by stressing their alleged non-Israelite origin. Another possible background for calling the Samaritans a foreign people is the use of Deut. 32:21 in anti-Samaritan polemics (cf. Sir. 50:25–26).

The intention of Lk. 17:11–19 is comparable not only with 10:30–37 but also with Matt. 8:5–13 (par. Lk. 7:1–10), where a heathen puts the whole of Israel to shame with his faith. In such a text the later way of mission (cf. Acts 8; 10–11) is anticipated in paradigmatic cases in the pre-Easter history of Jesus (cf. Jn. 4:1–42).

3. (a) Acts 1:8 contains the promise and commission: "But you will receive power when the Holy Spirit comes on you; and you will be my witnesses in Jerusalem, and in all Judea and Samaria, and to the ends of the earth." The fact that "Samaria" in 1:8 is attached to "Judea" without repetition of the preposition and article in the Gk. makes the phrase "in all Judea and Samaria" appear to be a single concept and not the designation of two consecutive stages in the history of the mission. This corresponds to the common administration of Judea and Samaria by a Roman procurator from A.D. 6 on.

(b) Acts 9:31 concludes the account of Paul's conversion and first preaching with the statement: "Then the church throughout Judea, Galilee and Samaria enjoyed a time of peace. It was strengthened; and encouraged by the Holy Spirit, it grew in numbers." The mention of Galilee between Judea and Samaria does not conflict with the above interpretation, for in 1:8 and 8:1 Galilee was probably included in the notion of Judea, which would correspond to the religious orientation of Galilee around Jerusalem. From a geographical standpoint the statement in 1:8 has therefore three parts: Jerusalem, the land of

Israel, and finally the whole world are to be the scene of the disciples' testimony.

(c) In order to understand the account of Philip's missionary success in Samaria (Acts 8:4–25), we must grasp the geographical aspect. One immediate question is which "city in Samaria" (8:5) Philip went to. The logical possibilities would be the former capital Sebaste, Neapolis, or Sychar (cf. Jn. 4:5, where the same expression is used of the latter). The reference to Simon the sorcerer suggests not a Roman city in Samaria but some town in the middle of the province, for Philip goes to a place where Simon's power dominates the religious scene (cf. Acts 8:10).

4. (a) Jn. 4:1–42 is one of the prominent references to the Samaritans in the NT. Sychar (4:5) was "near the plot of ground Jacob had given to his son Joseph" (cf. Gen. 48:22). Here was located a spring or well (Jn. 4:6, 11–12), one not mentioned in the OT. The sole tradition about a well associated with Jacob's name is found in Gen. 29:2–10, where the place is given as Haran. But the Jewish haggadah (commentary on nonlegal OT passages) compressed this tradition into the picture of a single miraculous spring that "accompanied" both the patriarchs and Moses on their wanderings (cf. 1 Cor. 10:4). The Samaritan concentration of the most diverse patriarchal traditions on Shechem and its environment (cf. Jn. 4:20) led logically to the local tradition of the well of Jacob.

The woman's amazement and Jn.'s explanatory comment (Jn. 4:9) refer to Jesus' request for water, which indicates a kind of meal fellowship. This is distinguished from the Pharisaic conception, according to which the vessels of the Samaritans were considered unclean and could not be used by the Jews. The symbolism of the living water (4:10–15) does not relate to the once-and-for-all reception of the Spirit (cf. 7:37–39), but rather to the continued working of the words of Jesus (cf. 6:63). The allusion to the life of the Samaritan woman in the course of the conversation (4:16–19) focuses on Jesus' special gift of seeing inside a person (cf. 2:25) and elicits a corresponding confession about his being a prophet (cf. 1:49; 4:19).

Allegiance to Mount Gerizim as the sole legitimate place of worship was the distinctive point of the Samaritan creed. The way in which the Samaritan woman introduces the theme (Jn. 4:20) is an excellent expression of the Samaritan standpoint: The age-old Israelite practice is set in opposition to the Jewish claims in favor of Jerusalem. According to Samaritan tradition, a long chain of important biblical figures from Adam to Joseph knew and recognized Gerizim as a holy place. Jesus' position on the problem of the right cultic center (4:21–24) exhibits different lines of thought. The essentially futuristic pronouncements of 4:21 and 23–24 relativize the question of place in favor of stressing the dimension of Spirit and truth in which God will be worshiped. In 4:22, however, Jesus speaks in the present and clearly adopts the Jewish standpoint and thus condemns the Samaritan one.

Jesus' comment that "salvation is from the Jews" (Jn. 4:22) fits into the context of the chapter (cf. 4:9 and 42) and of the entire Gospel (cf. 1:11; 4:43–44; 12:37–41). Jesus is a Jew, and Judea is his actual domain; it is this reality that gives his conflict with the Jews its particular sharpness. Yet an evident concern of Jn. is to present the Spirit as the decisive power of the new age inaugurated by Jesus (cf. 1:32–33; 3:3–8; 6:63; 20:22).

The reproach in Jn. 4:22 ("You Samaritans worship what you do not know") recalls Acts 17:23 and fits in well with the tendency in Jud. to place the Samaritans on the same level as the Gentiles on cultic questions. This was particularly pronounced in the 1st cent. A.D., esp. in light of the Samaritan request to Antiochus Epiphanes to represent their sanctuary on Mount Gerizim as dedicated to Zeus. The Maccabees and the Hasidim, of course, understood these maneuvers of Samaritan politics as a desertion of Yahweh into Gk. religion.

The woman's testimony to belief in the coming Messiah (Jn. 4:25) relates to the Jewish expectation of salvation, endorsed by Jesus in 4:22. The idea of a Messiah is lacking in Samaritan texts; to their ears it was probably too closely tied to the ideal of the Davidic king.

The openness of the woman to a Messiah should probably be understood as the consequence of the impression made on her by Jesus' prophetic knowledge (4:19). This line is continued in her receptivity to his messianic claims (4:29; cf. 4:26).

The present wording of Jn. 4:25–26 hardly provides a basis for the frequently expressed opinion that Jesus is here shown as the fulfillment of a Samaritan messianic expectation. The Samaritans did indeed expect that their Taheb (coming one, restorer, who was an eschatological figure) would reveal truth. But in its context (and in contrast to 4:25) this is not to be understood in terms of proclamation, but as the realization of the divinely willed state of affairs (cf. 2 Esd. 6:27–28), in particular the restoration of worship on Mount Gerizim. Furthermore, the dating of the Taheb expectation is disputed. Note too that the beginnings of Samaritan eschatology lie in obscurity. Thus, Jn. 4:25c should probably be understood from the context of the Fourth Gospel as the expression of a Christology that gives strong prominence to the element of proclamation and teaching as the mission of Jesus (e.g., 1:18; 6:68; 18:37).

The final confession of the Samaritans in Jn. 4:42 ("We no longer believe just because of what you said; now we have heard for ourselves, and we know that this man really is the Savior of the world.") cannot be demonstrated as the expression of contemporary Samaritan theology. The title "Savior of the world" is a synonym for the title of Messiah or Christ. It is in Jn. that the office of Savior is applied to the whole world for the first time (cf. 4:14). This extension is probably connected with the Johannine preexistence Christology, which binds the Messiah closely with the concept of God and at the same time allots him a cosmological function (cf. 1:1–18).

(b) In Jn. 8:48, in the context of a violent controversy, the Jews put to Jesus the question: "Aren't we right in saying that you are a Samaritan and demon-possessed?" Jesus' reply gives an explicit answer only to the second part of the question: "I am not possessed by a demon . . . but I honor my Father, and you dishonor me" (8:49). Both the question and Jesus' answer have been variously understood. Two main lines of thought may be noted. (i) For most exegetes (the more likely interpretation) the two halves of the question in 8:48 are materially related or even mean the same thing, so that the answer in 8:49 reflects the fact that Samaria was considered to be a demon-possessed land. (ii) Other scholars stress the difference between the two halves of the question in 8:48 and Jesus' refusal to address the accusation of being a Samaritan in 8:49.

4920 (*sarkikos*, after the manner of the flesh, fleshly), → *4922*.

4921 (*sarkinos*, consisting of flesh, fleshly), → *4922*.

4922	σάρξ

σάρξ (*sarx*), flesh (*4922*); σάρκινος (*sarkinos*), consisting of flesh, fleshly (*4921*); σαρκικός (*sarkikos*), after the manner of the flesh, belonging to the domain of the flesh, fleshly (*4920*); κρέας (*kreas*), flesh, meat (*3200*).

CL *sarx* (in Homer nearly always in the pl.) means the flesh of a human as distinct from his or her bones, sinew, etc. From Hesiod on it also denotes the flesh of an animal, and in a wider development (also now in the sing.) the flesh of fishes and small animals, as well as of fruits. The body (*sōma*) consists of bones, blood, sinews, flesh, and skin. Occasionally *sarx* denotes the entire physical body.

Transitoriness is a particularly characteristic mark of *sarx*. When vital energy (*psychē*, soul) and desire (*thymos*) pass away, flesh and bones disappear. Unlike human and animals, the gods have no *sarx*, but are *nous* (mind), *epistēmē* (insight), and *logos* (word, reason). In this vein a person's imperishable nature is increasingly contrasted with perishable flesh. Our flesh dies and is buried, but our real being lives on.

According to Epicurus, the start and root of all good is wellbeing, the *hēdonē* (desire) of the belly. When flesh cries out, "Do not hunger, do not freeze, do not thirst," the soul heeds this reminder. Since the *dianoia* (understanding) knows the end and the limit of the

sarx, Epicurus certainly does not invite people to a life of luxury; on the contrary, he invites them to an utterly controlled and temperate life. For not only present but also future *hēdonē* is essential to good fortune.

These ideas were caricatured by Platonists in a form that depicted Epicureans as favoring evil desires. To them, the cravings and lusts of the body defile the soul, which has a share in the divine. Epicurus was obliged to defend himself against the imputation of approving appetite, bodily desire, fornication, and intemperance. This anti-Epicurean polemic was widely spread in Hellenism and penetrated deeply into Jud.

OT The most frequent Heb. equivalent of *sarx* is *bāśār* (though *bāśār* is also rendered by *kreas*, denoting mostly flesh as an item of food). *sarx* has a wider meaning. It can even denote humanity (Isa. 40:5–6).

1. (a) *bāśār* denotes flesh as food for people (e.g., Gen. 41:2; Num. 11:33; 1 Sam. 2:13, 15). Flesh ("meat") and wine are food for good times (Dan. 10:3).

(b) Likewise, *bāśār* denotes human flesh. God took one of the ribs of the first man and closed up its place with flesh (Gen. 2:21). Daniel and his friends remained, in spite of a reduced diet, (lit.) "fatter in flesh" and therefore in good bodily condition (Dan. 1:15). Ezek. 37:6, 8 mentions together sinews, flesh, skin, and spirit, and Job 10:11 refers to skin, flesh, bones, and sinews. In a specific sense the penis is called the naked flesh (Exod. 28:42) or the flesh of the foreskin (Gen. 17:11–25; Lev. 12:3).

(c) *bāśār* can also denote the human body in its entirety, specifying the part for the whole. When in deep sleep a word from Yahweh is heard, the hair of the flesh stands up (Job 4:15). The flesh is, however, not merely the body but the whole person: "O God, you are my God, earnestly I seek you; my soul thirsts for you, my body [lit., flesh] longs for you" (Ps. 63:1). Here the flesh denotes one's self. In Job 19:25–26 one possible explanation is that Job is hoping for vindication after death while existing in some physical form.

(d) The self does not stand alone, however. A relative is "my own flesh and blood" (Gen. 29:14). Joseph's brothers admit that he is "our own flesh" (37:27). Still more comprehensively all flesh means all humankind (see Job 34:15) or everyone (Isa. 66:23). Finally, the phrase can include humanity and the animal world, as in Gen. 6:17–19; 9:11–12.

(e) From the foregoing the anthropological differences between the OT and Gk. lit. are clear. In the OT flesh denotes the human as a whole. According to the Gk. conception, however, a human has flesh but *is not* flesh.

The same distinction shows itself in the understanding of transitoriness. In the OT the flesh denotes a person in his or her transitoriness as one who suffers sickness, death, fright, etc. Thus Isa. says: "All men [flesh] are like grass, and all their glory is like the flowers of the field. The grass withers and the flowers fall" (40:6–7). Sennacherib's Assyrian horde is called "the arm of flesh," which is puny compared with God (2 Chr. 32:8). God "remembered that they [Israel] were but flesh, a passing breeze that does not return," so he forgave their iniquity (Ps. 78:38–39). One should not depend "on flesh for his strength" but on the Lord (Jer. 17:5).

2. *šeʾēr* (another Heb. word translated by *sarx* in the LXX) means flesh to eat (Exod. 2:10; Ps. 78:20, 27), human flesh (Jer. 51:35; Mic. 3:2–3), or a blood relative (Lev. 18:6; 20:19; 25:49; Num. 27:11).

3. Jud. in its various forms closely connected one's carnality with one's sin, but without identifying flesh as the actual cause of sin. It referred to OT statements that describe dependence on the flesh not merely as folly but also as sin (Isa. 31:3). "All flesh" is humankind, and to strive after evil is inherent in a human being (Gen. 8:21).

(a) Some of the Qumran teachings about inherent evil in a human fully accord with the OT (cf. Ps. 51:5). But elsewhere in their writings, humans are seen as belonging to the community of wickedness because they are mere flesh. The counterpart to flesh is not, however, spirit. For side by side with the spirit of holiness is found the spirit of wickedness and of the flesh. It is always God or his justifying righteousness that stands over against the flesh.

(b) Rab. usage evidences two characteristic departures from the OT. Humanity in its transitoriness is now called "flesh and blood." Even more important is the frequent replacement of the OT *bāśār* by *gûp*. Behind this doubtless stands a new anthropological conception of the body as a vessel that at any time can be possessed by a different spirit. In this way the body is not devalued, since in the final judgment God will fetch the soul, place it in the body, and judge the two together. But the body no longer denotes a human being as a whole. A Hel. oriental influence is to be found here.

(c) Hel. Jud. showed its peculiarity in two characteristic alterations made in the LXX as compared with the MT. In Ezek. 10:12 it does not speak of the flesh of the cherubim, and in Num. 16:22; 27:16 it translates the Heb. phrase "God of the spirits of all flesh" by "God of the spirits *and* of all flesh." Elsewhere, the appraisal of flesh is also quite different. According to *1 Enoch* 17:6 (Gk. text), Hades is the place where no flesh goes, and according to *L.A.E.* 43:4 and 2 Esd. 7:78, 100, the soul in death detaches itself from the body. But in *Apoc. El.* 5:32 (which probably dates from the 2d or 3d cent. A.D.), physical flesh is discarded and a spiritual flesh is put on.

(d) Philo's works include statements inclining in the direction of cosmological dualism. For him God is a being without flesh or body. For the human soul the body (i.e., the flesh) is a burden or a coffin. Freedom from the flesh through asceticism is thus important, for otherwise the soul is hampered in its upward flight. Guilt begins with the soul's steadfast continuance in the flesh.

NT Just as in 1st-cent. Jud., the different authors of the NT vary in their appraisal of the flesh. The division can be shown statistically: 91 of the 147x of *sarx* are found in the Paul's writings, above all in Rom. and Gal. The adjectives *sarkikos* (7x) and *sarkinos* (4x) also occur primarily in Rom. and 1 and 2 Cor. *kreas* occurs in the NT only 2x in Paul in the sense of flesh as a food item. Note that the NIV uses a wide variety of expressions to translate *sarx*: e.g., "flesh" (33x), "sinful nature" (23x), "body" (20x), "human" (3x), "people" (3x), and "sinful man" (3x). For the most part we will use the word *flesh* in this article.

1. Paul uses *sarx* so frequently that only the most essential passages for its understanding can be discussed.

(a) As mere flesh (of people, animals, birds, fishes), *sarx* occurs only in 1 Cor. 15:39. Occasionally it denotes the *human body* (as in 2 Cor. 12:7, a thorn in the flesh probably means sickness; Gal. 4:13–14, illness of the flesh, probably again sickness). But *sarx* can also denote humanity generally. According to 2 Cor. 7:5, (lit.) "our flesh" (i.e., we) had no rest because there were fightings without and fears within (about the stability of the Corinthian church). In marriage the flesh suffers troubles (1 Cor. 7:28), because now it is the last time and persecutions threaten (7:29–31). When Paul says that before he began to preach the gospel he did not confer with flesh and blood (Gal. 1:16), he means he did not confer with other people. If flesh and blood will not inherit the kingdom of God (1 Cor. 15:50), it means that, according to OT anthropology (Prov. 5:11), in death the whole self must disappear and a new *sōma* come into existence (→ *5393*).

(b) *sarx* also denotes relationships that have a temporary significance. Thus according to the flesh, Jesus is a son of David (Rom. 1:3), but only from the resurrection onward is his *divine* sonship declared by the Spirit of holiness (1:4). "Israel after the flesh" (lit., 1 Cor. 10:18) is the nation descended from Abraham (Rom. 4:1; cf. 11:14). From him Paul's kinsmen according to the flesh are descended (9:3), and from his descendants comes the Messiah (9:5, 8). *sarx* also means common humanity in Phlm. 16. Paul uses "all flesh" for "humankind" only in the fundamental expression of his theology: "No one [lit., no flesh] may boast before [God]" (1 Cor. 1:29).

(c) *sarx* is used not only to indicate physical kinship; it can be used also generally in reference to what is human. Thus "the wise after the flesh" (lit.) are the wise according to human standards (1 Cor. 1:16; cf. 2:6, "wisdom of this age"). The weapons Paul uses in his campaign are no longer of human invention, but are made effectual by God (2 Cor. 10:3–4). In contrast to him stand those who wish to make themselves agreeable to the church by human means (Gal. 6:12), so that in human ways they can glory in the circumcision of a Christian church (6:13). Paul might have every reason to glory in descent, circumcision, and zeal for the law. But that would be to have confidence in a human reckoning (the flesh), which does not count with God (Phil. 3:3–4). With God only the righteousness of Christ, received by faith, is of any consequence (3:8–11).

(d) This leads to the use of the phrase *kata sarka*, according to the flesh. Even though Paul lived as a man "in the flesh," he did not carry on his fight in the light of human standards (2 Cor. 10:2–3; cf. 1:17). This principle applies even to seemingly "religious" matters. To glory in visions is as foolish as to glory in circumcision (11:18), and even Jesus Christ himself must be seen with new eyes rather than simply in accordance with old pre-Christian expectations and values (5:16).

Similarly, Christians are no longer in the grip of the self-centered, self-justifying standards of secular humanity. They do "not live according to the sinful nature (*kata sarka*) but according to the Spirit (*kata pneuma*)" (Rom. 8:4). Therefore, the new life in the Spirit is paralleled by a renunciation in principle of human efforts at self-justification.

(e) The flesh, i.e., one's existence apart from God, has therefore a drive that is opposed to God. It not only occasions sin but also becomes entangled in it. Accordingly, Paul can draw up a catalogue of vices that he characterizes as "acts of the sinful nature [*sarx*]" or "the desires of the sinful nature [*sarx*]" (Gal. 5:16, 19; cf. Rom. 13:14). Above all, in Gal. 5:17 Paul is able to say, "The sinful nature [*sarx*] desires what is contrary to the Spirit, and the Spirit what is contrary to the sinful nature. They are in conflict with each other, so that you do not do what you want." This is not the flesh of the anti-Epicurean polemic, but the human self, insofar as it gives itself to aims in opposition to God.

Hence, the law also is weak through the flesh, because it can be used by the flesh as a means of self-assertion against God (Rom. 8:3). Therefore, God sent his Son in the likeness of a human being (*sarx*) determined by sin so that in this most Godlike of all humans he might bring sin into judgment and thus achieve righteousness. Consequently, believers are already dead in respect to the ambitions and drives that mold life apart from God. In this sense they are no longer in the flesh (8:9), for they now live according to God's life. They desire to achieve what is good, i.e., true life. However, the problem is that they achieve instead the evil that they do not desire (i.e., death), because they do not allow God to care for them. Paul writes, "So then, I myself in my mind (*nous*) am a slave to God's law, but in the sinful nature [*sarx*] a slave to the law of sin" (7:25b). Although Paul adopts here a typically Gk. manner of speaking, his understanding is completely different. Even the *nous*, the rational power of mental comprehension, is unable to find out what is good, since the true meaning of life remains hidden from it by sin.

(f) On the one hand, Paul can say that believers no longer live in the flesh (Rom. 7:5; 8:8–9; Gal. 5:24). But on the other hand, as a believer, Paul still lives in the flesh (2 Cor. 10:3; Gal. 2:20; Phil. 1:22–24). The contradiction is resolved in 1:22–24. To be in the flesh is for Paul something that has been so vanquished that for him it makes no difference whether he lives or dies. Life is to exist in and for Christ. Even death, as departure and being with Christ, is much better. But for the sake of the future of God's kingdom it is more important for him to remain in the flesh.

In the combination "body of the flesh" Col. seems to show Hel. influence. *sarx* is here the material of which the body (*sōma*) is composed (Col. 1:22; 2:11). Hence, "the uncircumcision of the *sarx*" in 2:13 means the time before the putting off in baptism of the body of the flesh (2:11). *sarx* is not corporality but understanding oneself as flesh. Its meaning is shown in 2:18. "The mind of the flesh" ("unspiritual mind") is preoccupied with angelic powers to whom as *sarx* the human race appears to be in subjection. But believers hold fast to the Head (2:19), in whom the whole fullness of Deity dwells bodily (2:9). Thus, living in the flesh, they are not in subjection to these powers, but in the flesh they already share in the life of Christ (1:24).

Eph. pursues a related idea. In its desires the flesh is open to the powers and influences of this world, which themselves are not flesh and blood (2:2–3; 6:12). In 2:11–12 *sarx* appears as that which is temporary. The wall of partition that existed between circumcision in the flesh and uncircumcision in the flesh Jesus broke down by his death in the flesh, thus abolishing the law of commandments and ordinances.

Flesh in 1 Tim. 3:16 (presumably an early creedal formulary) means human, physical life: Jesus "appeared in a body."

2. (a) The non-Pauline uses of *sarx* are, as might be expected, quite different. From the OT heritage comes Matt. 16:17, where flesh and blood, i.e., humans, are contrasted with God. The same holds good for Acts 2:31 (cf. Ps. 16:10). Christ was not left in Hades and his flesh did not see corruption, for here "flesh," being parallel to Christ, stands for the whole person. In Lk. 24:39 the risen Jesus makes it known that he is not a spirit because he has flesh and bones. The saying in Mk. 14:38 that "the spirit is willing, but the *sarx* is weak" is not an OT quotation, but is perhaps inspired by Num. 27:16; Isa. 31:3. In 2 Pet. 2:10 (cf. also Jude 7) there is the more Heb. thought, that one should not in any way hanker after the flesh, because such hankering brings defilement.

In the same way 1 Pet. 2:11 speaks of the fleshly (*sarkikos*) desires that wage war against the soul. Christ has suffered in his flesh. Only those who suffer in the flesh in the same spirit as Christ are free from sin (4:1–3) and escape the depravities of the flesh (4:4–5). Christ was indeed put to death in the flesh but was made alive in the spirit (3:18). Accordingly, one interpretation of 4:6 declares that the gospel was preached to the dead so that like all human beings in the flesh, they might receive their sentence. In their case, since they were already dead, this has already come about. But behind this is the intention that they might live according to God's will in the spirit. Hence baptism also serves not for cleansing the flesh, but for cleansing the spirit in a good conscience (3:21).

Alternate interpretations of 1 Pet. 4:6 suggest that it refers to the proclamation of the gospel by the preincarnate Christ to people in OT times, which may also be related to 3:20. Or perhaps it refers simply to those in the present age who have received the gospel and since died. The verse would then mean that, although they share the common destiny of sinful humankind in death, nevertheless they live now in the spirit.

Heb. makes use of *sarx* as the human nature that Christ assumed. Christ for a while was made lower than the angels and so shared in flesh and blood (2:14). These were "the days of his flesh" (lit., 5:7). Through his flesh he made for us a way into the heavenly sanctuary; the sphere of flesh is the curtain that separates us from it, and by death Jesus passed through it (10:20). He cleanses the conscience and not merely the flesh, as the offerings of rams and bulls did (9:13–14). The "external regulations" (lit., "regulations for the flesh," 9:10) are therefore statutes only for the purification of the flesh.

sarkinos (Heb. 7:16) refers to the physical descent of the Levitical priesthood in contrast to the priesthood of Melchizedek and Christ.

sarx mia (Matt. 19:5b) has a special significance as the translation of the Heb. *bāśār ʾeḥād* (one flesh) of Gen. 2:24. The union of man and woman creates a new relationship. "One flesh" does not in the first instance mean sexual intercourse, although it includes it. It signifies primarily the coming into being of a unitary existence, a complete partnership of man and woman that cannot be broken without damage to the partners in it, a partnership toward which husband and wife should strive. This is the meaning of marriage granted by God (19:6).

(b) In many respects, Jn. appears to stand near to the OT. He speaks of all flesh in the OT sense (Jn. 17:2). The declaration that people should not judge Jesus according to the flesh (8:15; cf. "by mere appearances" in 7:24) is in accord with Matt. 16:17. One should judge him not by his human circumstances but by his mission, for that which is born of the flesh is flesh, and that which is born of the Spirit is spirit (3:6). That which is born of the flesh comes from itself or the world, but that which is born of the Spirit is a completely new humanity insofar as it comes from God (1:13). It is not surprising, then, that the flesh profits nothing; it is the spirit indeed that gives life (6:63). We cannot comprehend Jesus on a merely human level, but we may do so by receiving his words, which are spirit and life.

Alongside all this, there is another fact for Jn.: The Word, which was *theos* and was in the beginning with God, became flesh (1:14). The entry of the Word as flesh among all flesh reveals how estranged flesh is from the Word and so from true life, which it does not have. Jn. 6:51–58 should be understood against this background. Those who eat the flesh of the Revealer not only confess that only the coming of the Word in the flesh can redeem them; they also confess that there is nothing in the flesh (i.e., the world) to help. In receiving the incarnate Word they are in the world but not of the world.

In 1–3 Jn. the confession that Jesus is come in the flesh separates belief from unbelief (1 Jn. 4:2; 2 Jn. 7). Jn.'s opponents no longer wished to associate the Revealer with the flesh they had rejected. Jn., however, asserts the historicity of the incarnation.

3. Since the meaning of *sarx* varies radically from context to context, we will draw here a brief summary of this concept in the Bible. (a) In some contexts, esp. in the OT, *sarx* emphasizes human *creatureliness and frailty*—i.e., people as a whole are fallible and vulnerable. The biblical writers draw at least four distinct lessons from this basic datum. (i) They warn against any false hope and consequent disillusionment brought about by putting undue confidence and trust in such fallible and frail creatures. (ii) They also call attention to a person's creatureliness before God and distance from him in his otherness and transcendence. (iii) In at least one passage one's very weakness is a ground of God's loving compassion and restraining patience (Ps. 78:38–39). (iv) In times of oppression or persecution, the believer is encouraged not to fear an enemy who is mere flesh.

(b) In other contexts *sarx* is used simply to denote the *physical* part of a human and does not offer an evaluation of a person as a whole. (i) Especially in Johannine thought this relates to the incarnation: "The Word became flesh" (Jn. 1:14). (ii) Similarly the physical nature of *sarx* has positive significance in terms of the bodily obedience of the Christian. Here Paul's use of flesh overlaps with that of *sōma*, body (2 Cor. 4:10). Believers still live "in" the flesh (*en sarki*) but not "according to" the flesh (2 Cor. 10:3).

(c) To assess a truth or a phenomenon "in accordance with the flesh" is to reach a verdict on the basis of purely *human, external,* or *natural considerations.* It is an assessment that leaves spiritual dimensions out of account.

(d) A quite different use of *sarx* appears in the major theological passages of Paul, such as Rom. 8:5–8. Here the mental outlook of the flesh is hostile to God. It is *the outlook orientated toward the sinful self, that which pursues its own ends in self-sufficient independence of God.* At the same time, *sarx* admittedly also characterizes a human being as a sinner in one's rejection of the law. Moreover, in at least two passages Paul outlines the close relationship between flesh and death (8:13; Gal. 6:8). Here death is the inevitable fruit that grows out of a fleshly way of living.

4925 Σάρρα	Σάρρα (*Sarra*), Sarah (*4925*).

OT This is the personal name of the wife of Abraham and mother of Isaac. In Gen. 17:15 her name is changed from Sarai to Sarah, and all subsequent references conform to this. The name is generally understood to mean princess, but there may be a connection with the Heb. root *śārâ* (to strive), the root underlying the name Israel.

In the Gen. traditions Sarah emerges as the beautiful wife who is all but lost to a foreign ruler (12:10–20; 20:1–18), the resolute adversary of Hagar and her offspring (16:1–14; 21:8–21), and the mother of Isaac (18:1–15; 21:1–7). All three stories are part of a narrative complex that traces the somewhat tortuous course by which the promise of 12:1–3 moved towards fulfillment. To later Jews Sarah was to be appreciated, along with Abraham, as the rock from which Israel was hewn (Isa. 51:2).

NT Sarah has a place in two important Pauline arguments. In his theology of justification her barrenness is the context in which Abraham's justifying faith is demonstrated (Rom. 4:19). In addition, the conception of Isaac as the heir of promise over against Ishmael is cited as evidence of the free sovereignty of God's electing purpose (9:9; cf. also the argument of Gal. 4:21–31).

The authors of Heb. and 1 Pet. treat Sarah as a model of faith and submission. Her faith is one that accepts the unseen as real and takes nothing to be impossible (Heb. 11:11). In 1 Pet. 3:6 her obedient attitude to her husband establishes the pattern that Christian wives should follow.

See also *Abraam*, Abraham (*11*); *Hagar*, Hagar (*29*); *Isaak*, Isaac (*2693*).

4928 (Satanas, the adversary, Satan), → *1333.*

4931 σβέννυμι	σβέννυμι (*sbennymi*), quench, extinguish, quell (*4931*).

CL & OT 1. In cl. Gk. *sbennymi* means to extinguish by drowning with water, as opposed to smothering; also, to allay or subdue. When applied to liquids, it means to dry up, evaporate. In the pass. the word is occasionally used of people becoming extinct, while in medical lit. it describes the disappearance of inflammation.

2. In the LXX this word has its normal lit. meaning of extinguish, quench (e.g., Lev. 6:5–6 = LXX 6:12–13; 2 Sam. 14:7; 2 Ki. 22:17; Isa. 1:31; 34:10; Amos 5:6), though a metaphorical usage occurs in Song 8:7 (the quenching of love) and 4 Macc. 3:17 (the quenching of passion).

NT *sbennymi* is used in the NT in both a lit. sense (Matt. 12:20; 25:8; Mk. 9:48; Eph. 6:16; Heb. 11:34) and a metaphorical sense (1 Thess. 5:19). In Eph. 6:16 believers are urged to shield themselves behind an all-embracing faith so they can deflect and extinguish the evil temptations that would sear and consume the personality. The shield in this armor of faith is the old wooden *scutum* of the Romans, which protected most of the body. Its leather covering soaked in water effectively stopped and extinguished darts dipped in pitch, which were used as fiery missiles.

In 1 Thess. 5:19 Paul warns the church against quenching the Spirit, whose advent was marked by fiery tongues (Acts 2:3), by living in a manner contrary to Christ's will. This verse does not apply specifically to quenching speaking in tongues but to refusing to allow the exercise of any of the Spirit's gifts within the community, all of which have been given to build up the church (cf. 1 Cor. 12:7; 14:26).

The expression in Matt. 12:19–20 that the Messiah will not cry out, break a bruised reed, or "snuff out" a smoldering wick is part of a quotation from Isa. 42, which occurs in the context of the application of the servant song of 42:1–4 to Jesus (Matt. 12:15–21). In refusing to argue with the Pharisees or to allow his messiahship to be openly asserted, Jesus does not wrangle or cry aloud. Rather, his goal is to nurture the fragile faith and hope of people through announcing the arrival of his universal rule.

The description of punishment in Mk. 9:48 ("their worm does not die, and the fire is not quenched") comes from Isa. 66:24. This seems to be an early description of eternal punishment (cf. also Jdt. 16:17; Sir. 7:17). The picture is taken from the Valley of Hinnom (→ *geenna*,

hell, *1147*), where human sacrifice had been offered during the monarchy (2 Ki. 23:10; Jer. 7:31; 32:35). Later this area became Jerusalem's rubbish dump, and unclean corpses that could not be buried were burned there.

The mention of the heroes of old who by faith "quenched the fury of the flames" (Heb. 11:34) is probably an allusion to Shadrach, Meshach, and Abednego, who were delivered from the fiery furnace after they refused to worship Nebuchadnezzar's golden image (Dan. 3). The readers of this letter might themselves soon face a fiery ordeal.

See also *asbestos*, inextinguishable, what cannot be quenched (*812*).

4933 (sebazomai, show religious reverence, worship), → *4936.*

4934 (sebasma, object of religious reverence, holy thing, sanctuary), → *4936.*

4936 σέβω	σέβω (*sebō*), to reverence, shrink back in fear, worship (*4936*);

σεβάζομαι (*sebazomai*), show religious reverence, worship (*4933*); σέβασμα (*sebasma*), object of religious reverence, holy thing, sanctuary (*4934*); εὐσεβέω (*eusebeō*), reverence, be devout (*2355*); εὐσέβεια (*eusebeia*), devoutness, piety, fear of God, religion (*2354*); εὐσεβής (*eusebēs*), God-fearing, devout, pious (*2356*); εὐσεβῶς (*eusebōs*), godly, in a godly manner (*2357*); θεοσέβεια (*theosebeia*), fear of God, reverence for God, devoutness (*2537*); θεοσεβής (*theosebēs*), devout, God-fearing (*2538*); ἀσέβεια (*asebeia*), impiety, godlessness (*813*); ἀσεβής (*asebēs*), godless, impious (*815*); σεμνός (*semnos*), honorable, worthy of reverence, venerable, holy (*4948*); σεμνότης (*semnotēs*), honorableness, dignity, holiness (*4949*).

CL & OT 1. (a) In cl. Gk. the root *seb-* meant originally to step back from someone or something, maintain a distance. From this spatial meaning developed the metaphorical idea of trepidation ranging from shame, through wonder, to something approaching fear. This attitude is evoked by that which is sublime and majestic or by the risk of failure. The word *theosebeia*, which conveys the restricted idea of one's attitude towards deities, is essentially the same as *eusebeia*. *sebasma* is an object of religious reverence, an idol; in the pl. it often means the cult.

Words deriving from this stem frequently convey the idea of devoutness, although this attitude does not entail—as it does in the Bible—a committed obedience to a single, personally conceived God. Those worthy of reverence are above all the members of one's own family (including one's ancestors), the gods, and the laws ordained by them. In religious usage there is an easy transition to the reverence of the cult. *eusebeia* is one of the virtues of one who is righteous and acceptable to the gods. Later this basic idea of *seb-* fades, and *sebō* can assume the meaning to bless or congratulate.

(b) The negative *asebeia* likewise has an ethical and religious content. Because of the close connection between the ordinances of the Gk. city-state and the worship of the gods, the *asebēs* is often named side by side with the *adikos* (wicked); want of reverence for the gods and neglect of cultic obligations were considered antisocial. In the case of a someone who was a misfit in the community, *adikia* was that aspect of his (immoral) behavior that was against the ordinances, while *asebeia* described the aspect that was against the gods. In Greece the worship of the gods declined more and more in favor of a philosophical ideal and an ethical-moral attitude. That is, a philosopher could actually be an atheist (*atheotēs*) while still being *eusebēs*, and Christians also were described in this way because they did not reverence the old gods.

(c) *semnos* and *semnotēs* denote that which is sublime, majestic, holy, evoking reverence. The difference between these words and the *seb-* words is that they contain a stronger aesthetic element; thus a royal throne, an ornament, or sublime music can be so described. The adj. and the noun often denote the majesty of deity, but sometimes also the solemnity, serious purpose, and grandeur of a human.

2. (a) These ideas and words rarely appear in the LXX, since the basis of OT piety differs from that of Gks. The Creator God lays claim to a person's service in thought, word, and deed; he requires active obedience, not merely devout trepidation to which lip-service is paid just on fixed occasions in cultic homage or in the sphere of intellectual rhetoric. This active obedience, together with worship, is the characteristic feature of the fear of God (→ *phobos*, 5832), which is essentially the OT idea of piety. Thus, in the few cases where *eusebeia* and its cognates are used, it usually renders words from the Heb. root *yārē'*, to fear.

(b) Only in the wisdom lit. and in the Apocr. (esp. 4 Macc.) do *eusebeia* and its related words occur more frequently—an indication of Hel. influence. The same is true of the *semnos* word group. This adj. describes that which is sublime, holy, and thus worthy of God; in contrast with *hagios* (holy), therefore, the aesthetic element predominates.

(c) The LXX uses the negative compound *asebēs*, impious, synonymously with *adikos*, unrighteous, unjust, wicked, and describes both an individual action and a general human attitude of departing from God. An human injustice is at the same time an offense against God and his commandments. Thus *asebeia* and *adikia* stand close to *hamartia* (sin, 281); social order and social justice are inseparable from worship.

NT 1. This word group is found rarely in the NT. Apart from the OT quotation in Mk. 7:7 par. Matt. 15:9 (= Isa. 29:13 LXX), *sebō* occurs only in Acts, usually in its adjectival form as a technical term to denote the Gk. adherents of Jud. (→ *prosēlytos*, 4670). In Acts 17:23 and 2 Thess. 2:4 *sebasma* is the heathen object of worship. *sebazomai* appears only in Rom. 1:25, where it means to show religious reverence. The vb. *eusebeō* (2x), the adj. *eusebēs* (3x), the adv. *eusebōs* (2x), and the noun *eusebeia* (15x) are, apart from 4x in Acts, confined to the Pastorals and 2 Pet.

Like *hosios* (holy), which frequently stands alongside *dikaios* (righteousness), *eusebēs* and *eusebeia* denote a moral attitude in the Gk.-speaking world. Both ideas occur frequently in Hel. Jud. They are almost entirely lacking in the earlier NT lit., though much in evidence in the Pastorals. This is best explained by supposing that early Christianity used these words at first for non-Christian piety and that only later the apostles gave them Christian content. Exceptions are the negative forms *asebeia*, godlessness, and the adj. *asebēs*, ungodly.

2. Whilst *latreuō* (→ 3302) is a neutral word for cultic worship and thus appears in various parts of the NT, *sebō* retains the anthropological emphasis of typical Gk. piety, i.e., deference to that which is sublime and exalted. It is difficult to use such language in relation to God and Christ, because the Christian is in personal union with them, a union in obedience and trust.

In Rom. 1:18 Paul describes the pagan as enslaved by *asebeia* and *adikia* ("godlessness and wickedness") and states that the wrath of God rests on such people for giving divine honors to the creature rather than the Creator (1:25). He thus pronounces judgment on all contemporary religious activity, for being wise in its own eyes, it fails to make any contact with the one true God and his holy purpose either in the realm of worship or in that of interpersonal relationships. Here, as in the LXX, there is no longer a sharp distinction between *asebeia* and *adikia* because in the light of Christ's revelation both are sin (*hamartia*, 281). This latter word gained ascendancy over *asebeia*, as indeed over all other terms that denote the outworkings of the power of evil.

As in the OT, *hamartōlos* and *asebēs* can stand side by side in Paul to describe the sinner whom Christ makes righteous (cf. Rom. 4:5; 5:6, 8). The Pastorals take over this association (1 Tim. 1:9; cf. 1 Pet. 4:18), though here *asebeia* is the antithesis of the much used *eusebeia* (cf. 1 Tim. 3:16; Tit. 2:12).

3. *theosebēs* is used in Jn. 9:31. True piety consists in doing God's will. In Acts 10:2 the fear of God is described by the combination of *eusebēs* and *phoboumenos*: God is revered in that human beings

fear him, i.e., offer him veneration, worship, and sacrifice. At the same time the appropriate distance is maintained, because humans are sinners. This also explains the technical term *sebomenos* in Acts, which denotes those Gentiles who worshiped the God of the Jews without wholly belonging to his people, i.e., without circumcision and minute observance of the law (13:43, 50; 16:14; 18:7). This word group is naturally used for Gentile veneration of the gods (cf. 17:23; 19:27).

4. The Pastoral Letters use the relevant Gk. vocabulary more freely than the other NT writings, the probable reason being that faith is here more of a virtue and now means primarily a Christian attitude to life. Only on that account can the OT phrase "fear of the LORD" be rendered so consistently by the Hel. *eusebeia*, though to be sure the attitude of the believer—"to live a godly life [*eusebōs*] in Christ Jesus" (2 Tim. 3:12)—is based on faith in Christ (1 Tim. 3:16; cf. 6:3). The NT devout person now understands himself or herself as a follower of Jesus Christ. Consequently, devoutness becomes one in a series of Christian virtues (1 Tim. 6:11; Tit. 1:1; 2:12).

Thus *pistis*, faith, takes on a special coloring as compared with its use elsewhere in the NT. Good works are definitely included in it (1 Tim. 2:10; 5:4), not, however, in the sense of justification by works (4:7–8; 6:5–6; 2 Tim. 3:5). Faith is rather seen as something ethical and related to this world; only once is it defined in relation to its ultimate goal, the coming kingdom of God (1 Tim. 4:8).

5. The use of the *semnotēs* group (noun 3x, adj. 4x) also fits into this framework. It occurs in Phil. 4:8 ("noble"), where Paul gives directions to Christians for the conduct of their everyday lives. Otherwise it occurs almost exclusively in the Pastorals. *semnotēs* differs from *eusebeia* in that it indicates, without direct reference to God, an ethical and aesthetic outlook resulting in decency and orderliness. Seriousness both of doctrine and of life is expected of the leaders of the church. By ruling their own families well and setting a good example, they are to bring up their children to be obedient and to lead honorable lives (1 Tim. 2:2; 3:4, 8; Tit. 2:2, 7).

6. In Jude and 2 Pet. Christians are described as the righteous who live, like Noah and Lot, in the midst of *asebeis*, ungodly men (2 Pet. 2:5–6; 3:7; Jude 4, 15, 18). Here *eusebeia* is seen as the Christian manner of life, which keeps Christ's return constantly in view (2 Pet. 3:11–12). The Christian who lives with this expectation strives after knowledge and is preserved from temptation (1:3–8; 2:9).

See also *eulabeia*, fear, awe, piety (2325).

4939 (seismos, shaking, commotion, earthquake), → *4940.*

4940	σείω

σείω (*seiō*), shake, cause to quake, agitate (4940); σεισμός (*seismos*), shaking, commotion, earthquake (4939); ἀνασείω (*anaseiō*), stir up, incite, excite (411); διασείω (*diaseiō*), shake violently, intimidate (1398); κατασείω (*kataseiō*), shake down, motion, shake or wave the hand as a signal (2939).

CL & OT 1. In cl. Gk. *seiō* means to shake, move to and fro (e.g., a poised spear, a door, the head [as a sign of discontent], the ground); fig. it means to agitate, disturb, upset; accuse falsely, spitefully; extort (shake out) hush money, blackmail. *seismos* means shaking, shock, earthquake, blackmail; *anaseiō*, shake back (hair from head), swing to and fro, brandish, threaten; *diaseiō*, shake violently, wag (a tail), shake off (people), throw into confusion; *kataseiō*, shake down, throw down; fig. listen carefully by throwing back the ears; be dead drunk (thrown on the floor); signal with the hand.

2. (a) *seiō* occurs 37x in the LXX, usually meaning to shake, move to and fro. In the Song of Deborah the earth is said to have been shaken (Jdg. 5:4). This depiction of the divine presence occurs frequently in the OT, esp. when God comes in judgment, the anticipation of which causes a shaking or trembling among the peoples (Ezek. 38:19–20). When Judah is threatened, the whole land is said to tremble (i.e., with fear) in anticipation of the thundering horses of the invader (Jer. 8:16).

In its day, the terror of Babylon causes other nations to tremble (Isa. 14:16). Paradoxically, her end produces a similar effect (Jer. 50:46 = LXX 27:46). Nebuchadnezzar's heavy chariots and wagons driving into the city (Ezek. 26:10) will cause the walls of Tyre to shake or vibrate both lit. and fig., the latter because the strength of a city, symbolized by its wall, has been destroyed, and no one knows what the enemy will now do to a defenseless people.

(b) *seismos* occurs 15x in the LXX. It means an earthquake, lit. or fig., in Isa. 29:6; Jer. 10:22; 23:19; Ezek. 3:12–13; 38:19; Amos 1:1; Zech. 14:5; the rumbling of wheels in Nah. 3:2; the rattling of chariots in Jer. 47:3 = LXX 29:3; trembling for fear in Isa. 15:5; the rattling of dry bones in the valley as they come together in Ezek. 37:7.

(c) *diaseiō* is used of intimidation, esp. to extort money (3 Macc. 7:21). In Job 4:14 it describes a great shaking of bones caused by a fearful nightmare. *kataseiō* occurs 2x. Daniel's servants sprinkled (*kataseiō*) ashes over the floor of Bel's temple to betray the footprints of the nightly intruders (Bel 14); in 1 Macc. 6:38 *kataseiō* denotes horsemen being placed in position on either wing of an army.

NT 1. *seiō* occurs 5x in the NT. It is a powerful word to describe the effect on the people when Jesus entered Jerusalem seated on a donkey: "The whole city was stirred" (Matt. 21:10), shaken to its foundations; his deliberate fulfilling of the prophecy of Messiah's entry (Zech. 9:9) was unmistakable. At the resurrection the guards at the tomb "shook" violently at the sight of the angel (28:4).

Heb. 12:26 refers to the giving of the law on Sinai, when the divine voice shook the earth. The earthquake at the time (Exod. 19:18) was an event that Israel never forgot (Ps. 68:7–8). At the end of the present world order God will shake (*seiō*, as in Hag. 2:16, quoted in Heb. 12:26) not only earth but heaven as well. The opening of the sixth seal leads to cataclysmic events of cosmic proportions, including stars falling to the earth, like so many figs being shaken off the tree by a gale (Rev. 6:13; cf. Isa. 34:4).

2. In Matt. 8:24 *seismos* describes the violence of the sudden storm that threatened to engulf Jesus and the disciples on the lake. The other 13 occurrences of *seismos* in the NT all refer to earthquakes and always as divine interventions: at the moment of Jesus' death (Matt. 27:54), which symbolizes his shattering of the power of death; at the resurrection, where it is linked with the rolling back of the stone (28:2); at Philippi, when Paul and Silas sang God's praises in prison (Acts 16:26). Together with the subsequent resurrection of a number of saints in the holy city, the earthquake at Calvary foreshadows the eschatological earthquakes as a sign of the end times (Matt. 24:7; Mk. 13:8; Lk. 21:11; Rev. 6:12; 8:5; 11:13, 19; 16:18), the general resurrection, the destruction of the present earth, and the formation of the new (21:1).

3. *anaseiō* occurs only at Mk. 15:11, where the chief priests incite the crowd to ask for Barabbas, and at Lk. 23:5, where they insist that Jesus has been inciting people to rebellion all over Judea. *diaseiō* appears in Lk. 3:14, where John the Baptist tells the soldiers who responded to his preaching not to use their position to intimidate anyone, i.e., not to extort money. They were probably not Roman soldiers but a Jewish paramilitary force used to support tax collectors. *kataseiō* is used 4x, only in Acts: of Peter (12:17), Paul (13:16; 21:40), and Alexander (19:33) motioning with their hands to gain people's silent attention before speaking to them.

See also *saleuō*, shake, cause to waver, unsettle, drive away (*4888*); *ektinassō*, shake out, shake off (*1759*).

4943 σελήνη

σελήνη (*selēnē*), moon (*4943*); σεληνιάζομαι (*selēniazomai*), be moon-struck, have seizures (*4944*); νεομηνία (*neomēnia*), new moon, first of the month (*3741*).

CL & OT 1. Cl. Gk. writers often refer to *selēnē*, the moon, in its lit. sense. Commonly in view is the moon's specialized function of marking time by waxing and waning. The religious festivals of many ancient societies, including the Israelites, were determined by the lunar calendar (see esp. Sir. 43:6–8). Cl. writers refer to Selene, the moon goddess. The moon with its unique cycle of phases, its growth and decline, its effect on the tides, though a lesser light, is more prominent in pagan mythology and religion than is the sun. Because the ancients observed what they thought was a relationship between the phases of the moon and human behavior, *selēniazomai* means to be a lunatic.

2. The OT frequently refers to the moon. It is never mentioned alone; only twice do we read about the moon apart from the sun, and in both instances it is associated with the stars (Job 25:5; Ps. 8:3). Some OT references to the moon have a fig. sense (e.g., Song 6:10 = LXX 6:9; Sir. 27:11; 50:6). (a) The moon provides nocturnal light (136:9) and demonstrates the fixed order of God's creation (Jer. 31:35 = LXX 38:35), its beauty (Ps. 8:3), and its permanence (72:5, 7).

(b) Since the Heb. calendar was a lunar calendar, each new moon (*neomēnia*) was a festival to the Lord (Num. 10:10; 1 Sam. 20:5, 18). However, worship of the moon, as of the sun and the stars, is prohibited (cf. Deut. 17:3; 2 Ki. 23:5).

(c) A specialized reflection of popular belief in the preternatural power of the moon is the promise that under Yahweh's protection the moon will not smite one by night (Ps. 121:6). The vb. *selēniazomai*, however, does not occur in the LXX.

(d) As with the sun, the prospect of eschatological judgment and blessing affects the light of the moon. In judgment it will be darkened (Isa. 13:10; Ezek. 32:7; Joel 2:10), "abashed" (Isa. 24:23), turned into blood (Joel 2:31), or held up in its course (Hab. 3:11; 2 Esd. 5:4). In blessing its light will be as the light of the sun (Isa. 30:26), and the moon will no longer function as a luminary at night (60:19–20).

NT 1. In the NT *selēnē* occurs only in association with *hēlios*. Only two occurrences are not apocalyptic in tone: a reference to the glory of the moon as distinct from sun and stars in Paul's argument about the resurrection body (1 Cor. 15:41), and the fig. reference in the description of the woman who has the moon under her feet (Rev. 12:1). The cognate vb. *selēniazomai* (Matt. 4:24; 17:15) reflects the popular connection of demon-possession with the moon (cf. the English word "lunacy"). The latter passage describes symptoms of something like epilepsy, a malady there attributed to an evil spirit.

2. The cosmic phenomena associated with eschatological happenings regularly include references to the moon. (a) In passages where judgment is in view, the apocalyptic language of the LXX is used. As the sun will be darkened, so "the moon will not give its light" (Matt. 24:29; Mk. 13:24). The par. in Lk. simply indicates that there will be signs in the sun, moon, and stars (21:25). The quotation of Joel 2:31 in Acts 2:20 speaks of the moon being turned into blood; Rev. 6:12 similarly says that at the opening of the sixth seal "the whole moon turned blood red." When the fourth angel blew his trumpet in 8:12, the moon, together with the sun and stars, was darkened by one third.

(b) The only other reference to *selēnē* concerns the eschatological era of blessing: The holy city, the new Jerusalem, is said to need no moon to shine on it since the glory of God is its light (Rev. 21:23).

3. The only NT use of *neomēnia* is in Col. 2:16, where Paul encourages believers not to feel judged for ignoring certain old covenant rituals, including observance of the New Moon (cf. Neh. 10:32–33; Isa. 1:13–14; Hos. 2:11; 1 Macc. 10:34).

See also *hēlios*, sun (*2463*); *astēr*, star (*843*).

4944 (selēniazomai, be moon-struck, have seizures), → *4943.*

4948 (semnos, honorable, worthy of reverence, holy), → *4936.*

4949 (semnotēs, honorableness, dignity, holiness), → *4936.*

4956 σημεῖον

σημεῖον (*sēmeion*), sign, wonder, miracle (*4956*).

CL & OT 1. (a) The basic meaning of *sēmeion* is a sign by which one recognizes a particular person or thing, an authenticating mark or token. Among the nuances is the omen that announces coming events. As distinct from *teras* (→ 5469), *sēmeion* does not necessarily have the character of the miraculous.

(b) When a *sēmeion* has the character of the marvelous, the word acquires the meaning of miraculous sign. It then denotes in general a miracle, worked by a deity or a miracle worker, that contradicts the natural course of things. Note the phrase *sēmeia kai terata*, "signs and wonders," first attested in Polybius.

2. *sēmeion* occasionally translates the Heb. *môpēt* (Exod. 11:9–10), i.e., that which by its remarkable nature excites wonder and attracts attention. But for the most part it translates *>ôt*, which means (a) sign, mark, token; (b) miraculous sign, miracle.

(a) Whether directly or by authorized agents, whether unrequested (e.g., 1 Sam. 10:1–9) or in answer to prayer (e.g., Jdg. 6:17), Yahweh grants and works signs, which accompany his word and vouch for its validity and reliability. Thus the sign of Cain (Gen. 4:15) vouches for the promise of divine protection, and the blood on the Israelite houses (Exod. 12:13) vouches for the promised exemption. Just as the rainbow guarantees God's covenant promise (Gen. 9:8–17), so circumcision (17:11) and Sabbath (Exod. 31:13, 17) are also "signs of the covenant" that express and seal the relationship between Yahweh and Israel (cf. also 3:12; Jdg. 6:16–37; 1 Sam. 10:1–9; Isa. 7:10–14).

Yahweh's messengers can authenticate their mission and message by signs performed (Exod. 4:1–17) or predicted (1 Sam. 10:1–9; 2 Ki. 19:29). The symbolic actions of the prophets are a way of making visible the word of God (1 Ki. 11:29–39; Isa. 8:1–10; 20:1–6; Jer. 19:1–13; 27:1–7; Ezek. 4–5; Hos. 1–3). They are not simply pictorial illustrations of the oral proclamation but, like the prophetic word itself (cf. Isa. 55:10–11), tokens of the power that shapes history. Even the prophet, as a witness of the message, can himself become a "sign" (8:18; Ezek. 12:3–6; 24:24, 27).

(b) Alongside such signs, which are either ordinary incidents or ones where the aspect of the marvelous does not lie in the sign itself but in the prophetic prediction, there are others that possess a thoroughly miraculous character. In this category belong the signs worked by Moses (Exod. 4; 7–12; 14; 17; Deut. 34:11) and those granted to Gideon (Jdg. 6) and Hezekiah (2 Ki. 20:8–11; cf. Isa. 38:7–8). The phrase *sēmeia kai terata*, "miraculous signs and wonders" (no essential distinction between the two words), is found primarily in those texts that describe the time of Moses as a time of Yahweh's marvelous action in history (Exod. 7:3; cf. Deut. 4:34; 6:22; 7:19; 29:2 = LXX 29:3; Neh. 9:10; Ps. 78:43; 105:27; 135:9; Jer. 32:20–21 = LXX 39:20–21).

The OT also records numerous miracles in which God works directly or through specially chosen people (e.g., Gen. 17:17; 18:11; Jos. 3; 6; 10; 1 Ki. 17–18; 2 Ki. 6–7). Every such event goes back to God; nothing is impossible for him (Gen. 18:14). All signs are pointers to Yahweh himself, a revelation of his might and glory. Through them Israel—indeed, all the nations of the world—are to encounter Yahweh and recognize that he alone is God (cf. Deut. 4:34–35; 1 Ki. 18:36–39; Ps. 86:10, 17). Since the goal of signs is the universal glorification of the divine name (72:18–19), unbelief and disobedience are expressions of an incomprehensible hardness of heart (Num. 14:11, 22; Ps. 95:8–11).

(c) Miraculous signs are not uniformly distributed throughout the OT. They are largely grouped in three main periods, each of which was marked by a life-and-death struggle for God's people and which put Yahweh's saving power and will to the proof: (i) the redemption of God's people from Egypt and their establishment in Canaan; (ii) the conflict with pagan religion under Elijah and Elisha; and (iii) the time of Daniel during the exile, when the supremacy of Yahweh and the faithfulness of Daniel and his companions is vindicated. The same can be said for the fourth period of miraculous signs, the time of Jesus and the gospel age.

Some of the miraculous events in the OT need not have involved suspension of natural causes. The locusts that plagued Egypt were

blown there by a strong east wind and were blown away by a strong west wind (Exod. 10:13, 19). The arrival of the quails coincided with the spring migration (16:13). The parting of the Red Sea was caused by a strong east wind blowing all night (14:21). In such instances the event is a providential ordering of natural causes for the benefit of God's people. Similarly, the fire falling on Elijah's sacrifice on Mount Carmel (1 Ki. 18:38) may have been a thunderbolt. Nevertheless, these events were remembered as indicative of Yahweh's providential help.

3. According to Exod. 7–8, the Egyptian magicians had the power to perform miracles by secret magical arts, but they were inferior to the miracles of Yahweh. Likewise in Deut. 13:2–5 the false prophet who wishes to seduce Israel to apostasy from Yahweh has an apparent power to perform signs and wonders. These are recognized as opposed to God in that the word they authenticate separates one from him rather than binds one to him. Hence, even though a prophet may perform such signs, he is to be tested by his teaching. If his teaching leads to other gods, he is to be rejected.

4. The apocalyptic signs of the end of time (cf. 2 Esd. 4:51–52; 6:11–12; 8:63) are partly concerned with horrible and frightening portents, which indicate that the last days are dawning. Insofar as these portents are convulsions of a cosmic nature, they announce the transformation of the world: the dissolution of the old creation and the reconstitution of the whole of nature.

5. Rab. lit. speaks often of miraculous signs or miracles, God's miracles, the miraculous workings of great men of God and of the rabbis, and the miracles of the messianic age. A prophet must prove his identity by means of signs and wonders (cf. Matt. 16:1; Jn. 6:30). Miracles are equally regarded as divine confirmatory signs for the proclamation of a rabbi.

NT *sēmeion* is found 77x in the NT, predominantly in the Gospels (48x) and Acts (13x). As in the LXX, *sēmeion* means either a sign (= mark, signal; Matt. 26:48; Lk. 2:12; 2 Thess. 3:17), or a miraculous sign (= miracle; Jn. 2:11, 18, 23; Acts 4:16, 22; 8:6; 1 Cor. 1:22). The phrase *sēmeia kai terata*, "signs and miracles," occurs 16x (e.g., Mk. 13:22; Jn. 4:48; Acts 2:19, 22, 43; Rom. 15:19; Heb. 2:4). The apocalyptic meaning of the signs of the end is also found (e.g., Matt. 24:3; Mk. 13:4; Lk. 21:11, 25).

1. It is the OT conception of the prophet as Yahweh's sign that underlies Jesus' being the God-given sign (Lk. 2:34) by which the rise or fall, the salvation or ruin, of every human being is decided. In this connection Jesus also rejects a demand for signs (Matt. 16:1, 4; Mk. 8:11–12; Lk. 11:16), which is linked in Matt. 12:38–39; 16:1–4; Lk. 11:16, 29–30 with mention of the sign of Jonah. Jesus unmasks the demand for signs as a subterfuge concealing a refusal to repent. Anyone who does not believe God's final word going forth in him will not be brought to repentance even by miracles (cf. Lk. 16:27–31). The only sign God gives to the unrepentant generation is that of Jonah: As Jonah once came back from the dead, so at the Parousia (→ 4242) the Son of Man will come in judgment (cf. Matt. 24:30).

The parabolic actions of Jesus that demonstrate the dawn of the age of salvation (Mk. 2:18–22; 3:13–15) are to be compared with the prophetic symbolic actions of the OT. Thus, Jesus' table fellowship with sinners (Matt. 9:9–13; Mk. 2:13–17; Lk. 5:27–32; 19:1–10) is a prophetic sign, an anticipation of the acquittal of the final judgment and a practical illustration in advance of the messianic meal in the age of salvation.

2. Alongside miracles performed directly by God (e.g., Acts 5:19; 12:3–10; 16:25–28) one can also distinguish the following uses of *sēmeion* in the NT: (a) Jesus' miracles; (b) the miracles of his witnesses; and (c) the miraculous power of elements hostile to God.

(a) The Gospels record many healing miracles of Jesus, three cases of people being raised from the dead (Jairus's daughter, Matt. 9:18–26; the widow of Nain's son, Lk. 7:11–17; Lazarus, Jn. 11:1–44), and eight so-called nature miracles (the stilling of the storm, Matt. 8:18, 23–27; the feeding of the 5,000, 14:13–21; the feeding of the

4,000, 15:32–39; Jesus' walking on the water, 14:22–33; the cursing of the fig tree, 21:18–19; the coin in the fish's mouth, 17:24–27; the catch of fishes, Lk. 5:1–11; and water changed into wine, Jn. 2:1–11). The essential characteristic of the effective work of Jesus is seen in the combination of proclamation and healing (cf. Mk. 1:38–39; Lk. 9:11; 10:23–24; 13:32).

There do exist accounts of miracles of Jewish and pagan miracle workers of antiquity. A comparison of these accounts with those of the Gospels shows that the NT miracle traditions have adopted certain narrative forms and motifs from their milieu, but it also draws attention to the particularities of the Gospel witness. With Jesus magic, conjuration, cursing of people, and spells are all absent. He performed miracles by his authoritative word, to which he sometimes added a gesture (e.g., Mk. 1:31, 41; 5:41). Jesus carried out no miracles of punishment (cf. Lk. 9:51–56). He declined to perform miracles in order to rescue himself (Matt. 4:1–7; 26:51–54; 27:39–44) and rejected demonstrations of power designed to prove his divine sending (4:5–7; 16:1–4).

Moreover, Jesus forbade those whom he had healed to relate his miracles to others (e.g., Mk. 5:43; 7:36; Lk. 8:56); in the case of the healed leper the man was to show himself "to the priest and offer the sacrifices that Moses commanded" (Mk. 1:44; cf. Lev. 13:49; 14:2–22). It was not personal gain but thanks to God that Jesus looked for from those who experienced his miraculous help (Lk. 17:11–19). By and large the accounts pay little attention to the miraculous process as such; they concentrate instead on the encounter of Jesus with the whole person in his or her physical and spiritual needs.

In Matt. 9:2–8 forgiveness of sins is linked with healing. Healing becomes a turning point in the life of the one healed (cf. 20:34; Mk. 5:18–20; 10:52; Lk. 18:43). Anyone who experiences a miracle of Jesus is thereby placed on the road of discipleship, in the same way that miracles in general are related to faith. Only faith, i.e., trust in the power of Jesus that transcends all human possibilities, can receive miracles (Mk. 2:5; 5:34; 7:29; 9:23–24; cf. Jn. 4:50; 11:40); unbelief is denied miracles (Matt. 13:53–58; Mk. 6:1–6). Note that Jesus' miracles often presuppose faith; they do not first create it. Note also that miracles silence all opposition; if believers see God at work, the verdict of Jesus' opponents is that he is in league with Satan (Matt. 12:24; Mk. 3:22).

What finally and radically distinguishes Jesus' miracles from those of the Jewish and Hel. narratives is their eschatological reference. As Matt. 11:2–6; Lk. 7:18–24; 11:20 clearly reveal, miracles are signs of God's kingly rule, the dawn of which Jesus announced in his proclamation (Matt. 4:23; 9:35; Mk. 1:39; 6:6; Lk. 4:14–15, 44). His words and works are the beginning of the age of salvation, his miracles a foreshadowing and a promise of the coming universal redemption.

Ultimately, then, it is in this eschatological context that the accounts of Jesus' miracles are to be read. The casting out of demons signals God's invasion into the realm of Satan and its final annihilation (Matt. 12:29; Lk. 10:18; Jn. 12:31; Rev. 20:1–3, 10); the raising of the dead announces that death will be forever done away with (1 Cor. 15:26; Rev. 21:4; cf. Isa. 25:8); the healing of the sick testifies to the cessation of all suffering (Rev. 21:4); the miraculous provisions of food are tokens of the end of all physical need and of the messianic banquet (7:16–17; 19:9); the stilling of the storm points to complete victory over the powers of chaos that threaten the earth (21:1).

The eschatological reference of Jesus' miracles is esp. expressed in Jn.'s Gospel, which stresses the historical reality of the events. At the same time, the miracles are signs pointing beyond themselves to the one who performs them. They prove Jesus' identity as the Christ, the Son of God (Jn. 20:30), who brings the fullness of salvation (2:1–11; wine was a symbol of the age of salvation in the OT, cf. Isa. 25:6), offers the bread of life (6:1–14), grants resurrection and eternal life (11:1–44), and banishes darkness (9:1–7). In his miracles Jesus reveals his glory (2:11; 11:4), which is the glory of God himself (1:14). Granted, miracles have this power of statement only for those whose eyes God himself opens (12:37–41; cf. Isa. 6:10; 53:1), so that in faith

they become aware of Jesus' glory (Jn. 2:11; 11:40). Those who are unenlightened, by contrast, react to Jesus' miracles with sham faith (2:23–25) or unbelief (12:37–43).

The NT writers agree that Jesus' miracles also express his uniqueness: his compassionate love as well as his divine authority (cf. Acts 10:38). In him God himself "has come to help his people" (Lk. 7:16).

(b) According to the Synoptics, Jesus also sent out his disciples to preach and to perform miracles (Matt. 10:7–8; Mk. 3:14–15; Lk. 9:1–2; 10:9). Similarly, Acts frequently mentions the correlation of apostolic proclamation and apostolic miracle-working (4:29–30; cf. 3:1–10; 4:16, 22; 5:12; 6:8; 8:6–8; 9:32–43; 15:12; 20:7–12). The miracles are coordinated with the preaching; they are accompanying signs, by which Christ confirms the word of the witnesses (14:3). As in the authoritative word (6:10), so in the signs is manifested the power of the Holy Spirit promised to the disciples (1:8).

Likewise for Paul word and deed, preaching and signs, belong together; in both Christ is at work through the power of the Holy Spirit (Rom. 15:18–19). Signs and wonders accompany the proclamation that takes place in "demonstration of the Spirit's power" (1 Cor. 2:4; cf. 1 Thess. 1:5). They are marks of the divine legitimization and the authority of the apostolic office and work (2 Cor. 12:12). To those who listen to the preaching the Spirit also mediates miraculous powers (Gal. 3:5). That is why, alongside the gifts of proclamation, the charisma of healing and the power to perform miracles belong to the living gifts of the Holy Spirit to the church (1 Cor. 12:8–11, 28).

Finally, Heb. also maintains that God confirms the preaching of salvation by signs and wonders (2:3–4), which, as "powers of the coming age" (6:5), foreshadow complete salvation. Kerygma and charisma, preaching and miracles thus belong together. In both Jesus Christ proves himself to be the living Lord, present in his church in the Holy Spirit.

(c) Like the OT, the NT reckons also with signs and wonders worked by false prophets and pseudo-messianic figures (Matt. 24:24; Mk. 13:22; Rev. 13:11–14; 16:14; 19:20), by whom people will be seduced into apostasy from God. The Antichrist is expected to perform signs and wonders in the power of Satan (2 Thess. 2:3–12).

See also *thauma*, object of wonder, wonder, marvel, miracle (*2512*); *teras*, miraculous sign, prodigy, portent, omen, wonder (*5469*).

4958 (*sēmeron*, today), → *2789*.

4967	σιγάω

σιγάω (*sigaō*), to be quiet, be silent (*4967*); σιγή (*sigē*), silence (*4968*).

CL & OT 1. In cl. Gk. *sigaō* means to be silent, keep still, say nothing. The noun *sigē*, silence, was a favorite word of the mystery religions, that humans should remain in silence before the gods.

2. (a) In the LXX *sigaō* has various nuances. In Eccl. 3:7 it is used in the Teacher's time passage to contrast simply "a time to be silent and a time to speak." But the vb. can also mean more than just being silent. It is used several times to refer to an agonizing silence. In Ps. 32:3 *sigaō* denotes the inner turmoil the psalmist feels before he confesses his sin before God, and in 39:2 the psalmist uses every ounce of his energy to keep silent in the presence of the wicked. In God's judgment in Amos 6:10 (= LXX 6:11), a survivor pleads with a relative, "Hush! We must not mention the name of the LORD," while in Lam. 3:49 the poet refuses to be silent as he pours out his soul in pain.

(b) This word can also be used in connection with Yahweh. In Ps. 50:21, the Lord decides to remain silent while the wicked persist in their ways. But the time is soon coming when God will rebuke them and tear them to pieces. In 107:29, the Lord commands the raging storm at sea to be calm, and "the waves of the sea were hushed" by him. In Exod. 14:14, Moses assures the people on the edge of the Red Sea that they do not need fear: "The LORD will fight for you; you need only to be still."

NT 1. *sigaō* occurs 10x in the NT, and *sigē*, 2x. These two words are used frequently of the silence of either an individual or a group of people. Lk. uses it for the silence of Jesus' enemies after he had given a brilliant answer to their question about paying taxes to Caesar (Lk. 20:26). The disciples were silent about their experience with Jesus on the Mount of Transfiguration (9:36). The crowd in 18:39 told a blind beggar, calling out to Jesus for help, "to be quiet." Peter motioned for the believers "to be quiet" so that he could tell them about his miraculous escape from prison (Acts 12:17). Those gathered at the council of Jerusalem were silent as they listened to Barnabas and Paul tell about the marvelous things the Lord had done through them among the Gentiles (15:12). When Paul motioned to the angry crowd in Jerusalem, "they were all silent," and he addressed them (21:40).

2. Paul uses *sigaō* in his instructions regarding proper church order in 1 Cor. 14. With regard to speaking in tongues, if no interpreter is present, then the speaker "should keep quiet" (14:28). Regarding prophecy, if one person is prophesying and a revelation comes to someone else, the first speaker "should stop." Finally, in a passage that has prompted much scholarly discussion, the apostle instructs women to "remain silent" in the churches. Among the numerous suggestions that have been made on this passage, Paul certainly cannot mean that women may say nothing in church, since in 11:5 he implies that women have a right to pray and prophesy in public.

3. In Rom. 16:25 Paul uses *sigaō* to refer to the mystery that God had kept "hidden" for centuries, about how he would someday include the Gentiles in his plan of salvation. God did give hints in the prophets to this effect, and in the NT era he made plain what his goal for the nations was (→ *mysterion, 3696*).

4. Finally, John uses *sigē* in Rev. 8:1 for the great half-hour silence in heaven immediately after the opening of the seventh seal. This silence was followed by the blowing of the seven trumpets.

See also *hēsychia*, quiet, quietness, rest, silence (*2484*); *echos*, sound, noise, report (*2491*); *siōpaō*, to be quiet, be silent (*4995*); *phimoō*, to quiet, muzzle (*5821*); *phōnē*, sound, noise, voice, language (*5889*).

4968 (sigē, silence), → *4967.*

| 4970 σίδηρος | σίδηρος (*sideros*), iron (*4970*); σιδηροῦς (*siderous*), made of iron (*4971*). |

CL & OT 1. This Gk. word meant not only iron but also anything made of iron and a place for selling iron. In Homer's time iron was highly valued and pieces were given as prizes. Hesiod considered the Iron Age in which he lived to be the epitome of human evil. The word is used symbolically by Homer to mean hard, stubborn, merciless.

2. In the LXX this word occurs frequently, translating Heb. *barzel*. Deut. mentions "the iron-smelting furnace" (4:20). Iron metallurgy was probably developed by the Hittites during the 2d millennium B.C. Hittite iron was brought to Palestine by merchants from Tyre and later by the Philistines, who monopolized the blacksmith's art (1 Sam. 13:19–20). The Canaanites possessed chariots of iron (i.e., with iron fittings) in the period of the judges (Jos. 17:16; Jdg. 1:19; 4:3). By the time of David iron was used for nails (1 Chr. 22:3), though bronze was still being used in large quantities. The OT uses iron as a symbol of strength (Ps. 2:9; Jer. 1:18), endurance, hardness (Job 19:24; Mic. 4:13), and cruelty (Dan. 7:7, 19; Amos 1:3). In Nebuchadnezzar's image (Dan. 2) iron with clay represented the last human kingdom before God's kingdom filled the earth.

NT Rev. 2:27; 12:5; 19:15 allude to Ps. 2:9, about God's Anointed One (i.e., Christ) reigning in judgment with an iron scepter. This scepter may have been a short-handled battle mace. In Rev. 9:9 the locusts who appeared after the sounding of the fifth trumpet had "breastplates like breastplates of iron." Rev. 18:12 refers to iron as an item of merchandise, and Acts 12:10 speaks of the iron gate of

Jerusalem that opened by itself when Peter and his delivering angel walked through it.

4971 (siderous, made of iron), → *4970.*

| 4982 Σινά | Σινά (*Sina*), Sinai (*4982*). |

OT The indeclinable proper name *Sina* is derived from the Heb. *sînay* (see Exod. 16:1; Deut. 33:2; Jdg. 5:5; Ps. 68:8, 17; Sir. 48:7). Sinai is the name of the sacred mountain before which Israel encamped when Yahweh made them his covenant people (Exod. 19–24). Moses ascended the mountain to speak with God (19:3, 20; 24:9) and came down to communicate God's word to the people (19:25). After concluding the covenant Moses went up another forty days and nights (24:18; cf. 32:1). In revealing his presence to the people, Yahweh did so with thunders and thick cloud, with trumpet blast to warn the people not to touch the mountain (19:16–24). This is the setting of the Ten Commandments (Exod. 20; cf. Deut. 5). After the golden calf incident, Moses went up the mountain again to replace the tablets broken at the foot of the mountain.

The exact site of Mount Sinai (also called Horeb) has been much debated. Traditionally it is located at Jebel Musa among the high mountains at the apex of the Sinai peninsula, although alternate sights have also been suggested.

NT Sinai is mentioned 2x each in Acts and Gal. and is alluded to in Heb. 12.

1. The speech of Stephen prior to his martyrdom summarizes Israel's history. The Lord God, perhaps through an angel, spoke with Moses at the burning bush in the desert near Mount Sinai (Acts 7:30; cf. Exod. 3:1–2) and again when he gave the law (Acts 7:38; cf. Exod. 19). Sinai thus played a prominent part in Israel's salvation history. But according to Stephen, the present Jewish leaders have failed to understand God's workings.

2. In Gal. 4:21–31 Paul identifies the present stubborn and disobedient Israel with Hagar (Gen. 16:15) and Mount Sinai, symbols of standing outside the covenant promises and being in bondage to the law, respectively. Together they are typified by the present Jerusalem, which is in bondage, as contrasted with the believing church, "the Jerusalem that is above," which is "free" and "our mother" (Gal. 4:26).

3. In Heb. 12:18–29 Mount Sinai (although not mentioned by name) is contrasted with Mount Zion, representing the old and new covenants respectively. The description of the former, drawn from Exod. 19–20, stresses its holiness and inaccessibility for ordinary people, whereas that of the latter stresses that believers have come to "the church of the firstborn, whose names are written in heaven" (12:23), "to Jesus the mediator of a new covenant" (12:24). We, therefore, must listen to God (12:25), for we have a kingdom that cannot be shaken (12:28).

See also *erēmos*, abandoned, solitary, desolate, deserted (*2245*); *oros*, mountain, mountain chain or region (*4001*).

4994 (Siōn, Zion), → *2647.*

| 4995 σιωπάω | σιωπάω (*siōpaō*), to be quiet, be silent (*4995*). |

CL & OT 1. In cl. Gk. *siōpaō* means to be still or silent, also to keep secret. The imperative can mean "Hush!" Both Socrates and Plato kept silent before the jury when they were on trial for their lives.

2. *siōpaō* has a variety of nuances in the LXX. (a) It can mean physical silence. A husband whose wife has made a vow and who, when he learns of it, says nothing cannot later annul the vow, for he was silent about it (Num. 30:10–15). Job says that people used to sit silent before him and listen to his wise counsel (Job 29:21). The Israelites did not answer the field commander of the Assyrians because the king had told them to be quiet (Isa. 36:21). The four lepers knew

that they should not keep silent about the fact that the enemy camp of the Arameans had been deserted (2 Ki. 7:9).

(b) Silence (or the impossibility of it) can also denote pain and agony. Even if Job remains silent, that does not mean his pain has gone away (Job. 16:6 = LXX 16:7). In fact, the churning inside him never grows quiet (30:27). The elders of Israel sit on the ground in silence after the destruction of Jerusalem (Lam. 2:10), and the eyes of the people are given no respite from tears (2:18). In Amos 5:13, those who grieve at injustice in Israel keep quiet, for if they were to speak, they too would become liable to some form of oppression. The prophet Jer. writhes in pain and cannot keep silent (4:19).

(c) *siōpaō* is used of the call to the Israelites to be silent before the Lord so that they can listen to his word (Deut. 27:9). In a similar vein, when Nehemiah commands the people after the reading of God's law to rejoice and not to mourn or weep, the Levites go through the city and tell the people: "Be still, for this is a sacred day" (Neh. 8:11).

(d) Finally, *siōpaō* is used for the silence of God. After a time, while the enemies of his people were destroying the nation (mostly because he had been fed up with their wickedness) the Lord said, "I have kept silent, I have been quiet [both *siōpaō*] and held myself back" (Isa. 42:14; cf. 64:12). But now the Lord will not longer be silent (62:1) for the sake of Zion, for he will show her his salvation. Nor will he be silent with the enemies of his people, but will pay them back in full (65:6).

NT 1. *siōpaō* occurs 10x in the NT, all but once in the Gospels. It is used of the physical silence of the human voice. Gabriel told Zechariah that he would "be silent" until the birth of his son (Lk. 1:20). The crowd told the two blind men "to be quiet" and stop shouting out for Jesus to have mercy on them (Matt. 20:31). The disciples kept quiet before Jesus out of embarrassment of what they had been discussing (Mk. 9:34). Jesus refused to instruct his followers to be silent at his triumphal entry into Jerusalem, for otherwise the stones would cry out (Lk. 19:40). Jesus' enemies remained silent when he asked them whether it was appropriate to do good or to do evil (Mk. 3:4), and Jesus himself remained silent before his accusers (Matt. 26:63; Mk. 14:61).

2. In a vision given to Paul, the apostle was told to keep preaching and to "not be silent" in Corinth, for the Lord had many people in that city whom he wanted to call to himself through Paul.

3. The main theological use of this vb. is in the command Jesus gave to the wind and the waves on the storm of the sea of Galilee: "Quiet!" (Mk. 4:39). Note that only Mark gives the direct words of Jesus here (see also *phimoō*, to quiet, muzzle, *5821*). This saying links back to a similar command of the Lord to the stormy seas in Ps. 107:29, though the LXX uses *sigaō* (→ *4967*) there rather than *siōpaō*.

See also *hēsychia*, quiet, quietness, rest, silence (*2484*); *ēchos*, sound, noise, report (*2491*); *sigaō*, to be quiet, be silent (*4967*); *phimoō*, to quiet, muzzle (*5821*); *phōnē*, sound, noise, voice, language (*5889*).

4997 (skandalizō, give offense, lead astray), → *4998*.

| 4998 σκάνδαλον | σκάνδαλον (*skandalon*), offense (*4998*); σκανδαλίζω (*skandali-zō*), give offense, lead astray (*4997*). |

CL & OT 1. *skandalon* was originally the piece of wood that kept open a trap for animals; a related word (not found in the NT) means (fig.) a trap set through questions. No nonbiblical example of the vb. *skandalizō* has been found.

2. Both words have been shaped by biblical language. The LXX uses *skandalon* fig. to denote a snare to destroy a person (1 Sam. 18:21; Ps. 141:9) or to cause one to sin (Jos. 23:13; Jdg. 2:3; 8:27; Ps. 106:36). It can also mean an obstacle in the way of the blind (Lev. 19:14), fig., a cause of misfortune (Ps. 119:165) or of troubled conscience (1 Sam. 25:31). Hos. 4:17 uses this word to refer to idols. *skandalizō* occurs in Dan. 11:41; Sir. 9:5; 23:8; 32:15 (= LXX 35:15) with the meaning of stumble, be led astray.

3. In Qumran writings, the Heb. words translated by this word group are a metaphorical expression for sinning or for leading someone to sin.

NT The NT usage is fixed essentially by the OT. It is often based directly on OT passages (e.g., Matt. 13:41 on Zeph. 1:3 [Sym.]; Matt. 24:10 on Dan. 11:41; Rom. 9:33 and 1 Pet. 2:8 on Isa. 8:14 [Aquila, Sym., Theod.]). The vb. is used 29x (14x in Matt., 8x in Mk.). The noun occurs 5x in Matt. and 4x in Rom., as well as several times in other books.

1. The original concept of a bait or trap is found only in Rom. 11:9 (quoting Ps. 69:22). Otherwise *skandalon* is used with the thought of a stone or obstacle over which one can trip and fall. It is used in parallel with *proskomma* in Rom. 9:33; 1 Pet. 2:8 (→ *4682*). When the sense is to cause people to sin, the connotation of trap is still present (cf. Rev. 2:14).

2. (a) *skandalon* denotes a temptation to sin, an enticement to apostasy and unbelief (e.g., Matt. 16:23; 18:7; Rom. 9:33; 14:13; 16:17; 1 Pet. 2:8; Rev. 2:14). It is then used as that which causes offense or scandal or hinders faith (e.g., Matt. 13:41; 1 Cor. 1:23; Gal. 5:11; 1 Jn. 2:10).

(b) Correspondingly *skandalizō* means to lead into sin, give offense (e.g., Matt. 5:29–30; 18:6; 1 Cor. 8:13). In the pass. it means to take offense, fall away, be misled (e.g., Matt. 13:21; 24:10; Jn. 16:1; 2 Cor. 11:29). It can also mean to offend, provoke, raise dissensions (e.g., Matt. 15:12; 17:27; Jn. 6:61).

3. (a) The NT stresses that Jesus constantly becomes an offense. Thus the idea of being repelled by or taking offense at, is always linked with him. The disciples took offense at his prophesied sufferings (Matt. 26:31), because they were incompatible with their preconceptions about the Messiah (see also 11:6; 13:57; 26:33; Mk. 6:3; Lk. 7:23). When Peter took offense in Matt. 16:22, his protestation was rejected by Jesus as a satanic suggestion. Jesus also became an offense for John the Baptist (11:6; Lk. 7:23), because John had expected him to reveal himself as Messiah in a different way. The Pharisees took offense at Jesus' teaching (Matt. 15:12), for it contradicted their concept of the law and of one's cooperation with God's grace. The depth of their offense is seen from Jesus' comparison of them with weeds to be rooted up (15:13).

(b) The basis of the offense caused by Jesus is the cross (1 Cor. 1:23), which nullifies all human wisdom and excludes all human cooperation in salvation (cf. Gal. 5:11). As a result, the preaching of Christ crucified is a *skandalon* to the Jews (it was a sign of God's curse, 3:13; cf. Deut. 21:23) and foolishness to the Gentiles. This infuriating offense must remain, otherwise the gospel will cease to be the message of salvation.

(c) The foundation of the offense caused by Christ is God's decree (see Paul's quote of Isa. 8:14; 28:16 in Rom. 9:33; see also 1 Pet. 2:8). This OT passage explains why the Jews are excluded at first from salvation, though not forever (Rom.), and why in general unbelief rejects Jesus (1 Pet.). In the offense we see an aspect of God's election (cf. in 1 Pet. 2:8, "what they were destined for").

(d) Jesus and his gospel become the cause of sin only when unbelief rejects the salvation he brings, for as he presented it, it did not correspond with human expectations. While those who believe in him will not be put to shame (Rom. 9:33; 1 Pet. 2:6), those who do not believe stumble at him (2:8). It is human blindness that makes Jesus an occasion for destruction. That is true both of the Pharisees (Matt. 15:14) and of those who walk in darkness because they do not love their fellow believers (1 Jn. 2:11). Those who love their fellow believers, on the other hand, find no cause for stumbling (2:10). Many disciples found Jesus' saying about his body being life-giving food "a hard teaching" and so took offense and drew back (Jn. 6:60–61, 66). Such behavior made the disciples guilty, for they saw nothing more than flesh in Jesus ("the flesh counts for nothing," 6:63).

(e) In his eschatological discourse Jesus speaks esp. of the offenses of the last days. That is, because of tribulation, many "will turn away from the faith [*skandalizō*]" and deny their Lord (Matt. 24:10). This will reveal the identity of true believers. Matt. 13:41 should be understood in a similar vein: "The Son of Man will send out his angels, and they will weed out of his kingdom everything that causes sin [*skandalon*] and all who do evil." Those who cause others to sin are "sons of the evil one" (13:38), who will someday be separated from all contact with the kingdom of God.

In his farewell discourse Jesus declares: "All this I have told you so that you will not go astray [*skandalizō*]" (Jn. 16:1). He is referring here particularly to the promise of the Paraclete (15:18–27), but also to his preaching as a whole (cf. 6:63).

4. While there is an offense inherent in the gospel that must not be removed, there is a human offense that must be avoided. Such offenses are inevitable (Matt. 18:7b; Lk. 17:1). They belong to the world and make it ripe for condemnation, but woe to those through whom they come. This is esp. true of those who offend the "little ones" who believe in Jesus (Matt. 18:6). Jesus was probably thinking both of children and of those who need special help from the body of believers. It is easy to give such people an occasion for straying away from Jesus. But those who do are subject to judgment. That is why the strong are exhorted not to cause the weak to stumble (Rom. 14:13, 21; 1 Cor. 8:13), for it destroys the work of God (Rom. 14:20).

We must also beware ourselves of separating ourselves from God by actions (Matt. 5:30) or by looking (5:29). The cutting off of part of the body is not to be taken lit. One should also beware of offenses caused by false doctrine and avoid those who create them (Rom. 16:17).

See also *proskomma*, stumbling, offense, obstacle (*4682*).

5007 (skeuos, thing, object, vessel), → *3040.*

5008	σκηνή

σκηνή (*skēnē*), tent, tabernacle, dwelling (*5008*); σκῆνος (*skēnos*), tent (*5011*); σκήνωμα (*skēnōma*), tent, dwelling (*5013*); σκηνοποιός (*skēnopoios*), leather worker, tentmaker (*5010*); σκηνόω (*skēnoō*), live, dwell, encamp (*5012*); ἐπισκηνόω (*episkēnoō*), take up one's abode with (*2172*); κατασκηνόω (*kataskēnoō*), live, dwell, perch (*2942*); κατασκήνωσις (*kataskēnōsis*), place to live, nest (*2943*); σκηνοπηγία (*skēnopēgia*), booth, tabernacle (*5009*).

CL & OT 1. In cl. Gk. *skēnē* originally denoted a tent covering made of branches or poles with a matted roof and sides constructed from straw, leaves, or skins. The term was also used of the raised stage of a theater, the cover of a wagon, or the cabin of a ship. Because of the nature of a tent, it came to signify transitoriness.

2. (a) In the LXX *skēnē* (430x) and *skēnōma* (80x) are used synonymously, meaning tent, dwelling, or perhaps a matted booth or shed. *skēnē* is used for the tabernacle, the tent of meeting, the appointed place where God meets his people (cf. Exod. 26:36; Lev. 1:3) or where Yahweh resides. It was also called the "tabernacle of the Testimony" (cf. Acts 7:44; Rev. 15:5) because it contained the covenant tablets. *skēnos* is found only in Wis. 9:15: "A perishable body weighs down the soul, and this earthy tent burdens the thoughtful mind."

The tent is the customary dwelling of nomadic or seminomadic peoples. The Hebrew patriarchs were tent-dwellers (e.g., Gen. 12:8; 13:3; 26:25), as were the Israelites during their desert wanderings (Num. 16:27). Later, when celebrating the Feast of Tabernacles each year, the Israelites lived in tents for seven days to recall their journey from Egypt to Canaan (Lev. 23:34, 42–43). During the time of Jeremiah the simplicity and independence of the nomadic tent life was idealized by the Rechabites (Jer. 35:6–10 = LXX 42:7–10). Even when sedentary life became the norm (cf. Heb. 11:9–10), tents were used by shepherds (Isa. 38:12) or herdsmen (Jdg. 6:5) and by armies (2 Ki. 7:7–8).

(b) The tabernacle continued to be used long after Israel's entry into Canaan. Under the judges it was at Shiloh (Jos. 18:1) and during

Saul's reign at Nob (1 Sam. 21) and Gibeon (1 Chr. 16:39). According to 1 Ki. 8:4, Solomon had it brought into the temple. Its structure and contents are described in Exod. 25–30; 35–38. The two interior compartments were divided by a veil or curtain. The first room, called "the Holy Place," was twenty cubits deep; the second, the "Most Holy Place" (Lev. 16:2–3; cf. Heb. 9:12; 10:19), was entered by the high priest on the annual Day of Atonement (Lev. 16).

In the Most Holy Place stood the ark (Exod. 25:10–22), a slab of gold with a cherub at each end resting on top. This article was termed the *kappōret* (LXX *hilastērion;* → *hilaskomai,* reconcile, *2661*), the "atonement cover" or "mercy seat." The high priest sprinkled it with blood on the Day of Atonement. The altar of incense or the golden altar stood in the Holy Place in front of the curtain (30:1–10; 37:25–28); on the north side was the table of the bread of the Presence (25:23–30) together with various vessels and instruments. On the south side stood the lampstand (25:31–40; 37:17–24; 40:24). The tabernacle stood in a courtyard one hundred cubits by fifty cubits, with its door facing east (27:9–19; 38:9–20). The altar of burnt offering stood on the eastern side of the court (27:1–8; 38:1–7); between the altar and the tabernacle door stood the basin for the priests' washing (30:17–21; 38:8; 40:30–32). The later temple was modeled after the tabernacle.

NT 1. *Luke's writings.* In Lk. 16:9 Jesus encourages the diplomatic use of wealth so that when it collapses (either at an individual's death or the end of the world), the benefactor may be welcomed into "eternal dwellings [*skēnē*]." At Jesus' transfiguration Peter offered to construct "three shelters [*skēnē*]" for Jesus and the two heavenly visitors, Moses and Elijah (9:33). Peter wanted to perpetuate his experience of the unveiled glorious personal presence of God in Christ.

As he summarized the findings of the Jerusalem council (Acts 15:13–21), James appealed to Amos 9:11–12 (LXX). He recognized the rebuilding of "David's fallen tent" (possibly alluding to a matted hut in which David lived or held audience when he was on military expeditions) in the resurrection and exaltation of Christ and the rise of the church as the new Israel. It was precisely because of this restoration that Gentiles were seeking the Lord (Acts 15:17–18). Therefore, the Gentile mission was not illegitimate (15:19).

Acts 18:3 indicates that Aquila and Paul were "tentmakers" (*skēnopoios*) by trade. While this term originally meant tentmaker, it came to be used of leather workers in general. The articles that Paul made for sale probably included furnishings as well as tents (which in antiquity were often made of leather). By such manual labor Paul avoided being dependent on any congregation in which he was currently ministering.

The vb. *kataskēnoō* is used intrans. in the NT for to live, settle, dwell (of birds; cf. Ps. 104:12; Matt. 13:32; Mk. 4:32; Lk. 13:19; cf. also *kataskēnōsis,* a place to live, a nest in Matt. 8:20; Lk. 9:58). *kataskēnoō* occurs in a quotation from Ps. 16:9c, which is seen as being fulfilled in the resurrection of Jesus: "My body also will live in hope" (Acts 2:26).

2. *John's writings. skēnoō* is found only in Jn.'s writings. In the body of Jn.'s Gospel Jesus is pictured as the new temple (Jn. 2:19–22), but in the prologue he is the tabernacle ("made his dwelling" in 1:14 uses *skēnoō*), the locus of God's presence among humans on earth (cf. Exod. 25:8–9). Where Christ is, there is God's dwelling.

Rev. 7:15 pictures one of the elders before God's throne informing John that God "will spread his tent" (*skēnoō*) over those who have come out of the great tribulation; that is, he will live with them continuously within his temple. With the arrival of the new Jerusalem "prepared as a bride beautifully dressed for her husband," God will live with humans (21:2–3, where both *skēnē* and *skēnoō* are used). He himself will be personally and permanently present in the midst of his people, who will witness the final fulfillment of the oft-repeated promise of Yahweh to his covenant people: "I will be their God, and they will be my people" (Exod. 6:7; Lev. 26:12; Jer. 32:38; Ezek.

37:27; Zech. 8:8; 2 Cor. 6:16). Elsewhere in Rev. (12:12; 13:6) *skē-noō* is used of the permanent inhabitants of heaven.

skēnopēgia is found mostly as a technical term in Jewish religion for the building of tents or booths, i.e., the Feast of Booths or Tabernacles (e.g., Deut. 16:16; 31:10; Zech. 14:16, 18–19; 2 Macc. 1:9). It was celebrated in the month of Tishri 15–21 (i.e., October), when booths were made from branches of trees. Jn. 7:2 refers to this feast: "when the Jewish Feast of Tabernacles was near." Jesus rejected his brothers' plea to go to the feast in Jerusalem, do miracles there, and win popular acclaim (7:3–9). But he went during the middle of the feast after all (7:14). Then, on "the last and greatest day of the Feast," Jesus stood up and issued his invitation: "If anyone is thirsty, let him come to me and drink. Whoever believes in me, as the Scripture has said, streams of living water will flow from within him" (7:37–38). That is, those who come to believe in Jesus will have fulfilled in them what the Scriptures prophesy about the activity of the Holy Spirit (cf. Isa. 58:11; Jn. 7:39).

There may have been a significant connection between these utterances of Jesus and the Feast of Tabernacles. According to Jewish tradition, on the seven days of the feast a golden flagon was filled with water from the pool of Siloam and used for libations. Jesus may well have been contrasting this water with the living water he gives. Similarly, his pronouncement about being the light of the world (Jn. 8:12) may be an allusion to the lights used in the feast.

3. *Paul.* The two NT uses of *skēnos* are in 2 Cor. 5:1, 4, where a believer's earthly body is described as a temporary tent, in contrast to the heavenly body that will form one's eternal dwelling. This *skēnos* concept remains near the foreground of the apostle's thought throughout 5:1–7. This word suggests the impermanence and frustrating limitations of mortal embodiment (5:2, 4, 6) and the Christian's pilgrimage of faith to the promised land of Christ's immediate presence (5:6–8). Although Paul honored the human body (cf. 1 Cor. 6:19), he was painfully aware of its inadequacy as an organ for either the human spirit or the Holy Spirit when compared to the resurrection body. In 2 Cor. 12:9 Paul uses *episkēnoō*, to take up one's abode, in his declaration: "Therefore I will boast all the more gladly about my weaknesses, so that Christ's power may rest on [*episkēnoō*] me." The passage concludes his discussion of his "thorn in the flesh."

4. *Hebrews.* Ten of the 20 NT uses of *skēnē* are in Heb., eight occurring in chs. 8–9. Heb. contrasts the heavenly and true *skēnē* pitched by God (8:1–2; 9:11) with the earthly tabernacle erected by Moses at divine direction (8:5; cf. 9:24). It is evident from Exod. 25:40 (cited in Heb. 8:5) that the earthly tabernacle was a precise model of a heavenly prototype visible to Moses. In 9:2–3, 6–8 the writer draws a distinction between a front or outer *skēnē* ("first room") and a rear or inner ("second") *skēnē*, i.e., between the Holy Place and the Most Holy Place. This distinction highlights the severe restrictions placed on human access into the Most Holy Place under the old covenant (for the various religious objects in the tabernacle, → *hieron*, temple, 2639).

Later in this book (Heb. 11:9, 13), tent nomadism is associated with being strangers and exiles. Finally, in 13:10 the expression "those who minister at the tabernacle" probably does not refer to Christian believers, as if their worship were focused on some fig. altar in the heavenly sanctuary, but to all the worshipers belonging to the old order to whom the sacrifice of Christ ("an altar," by metonymy) seemed superfluous.

5. *Peter.* In 2 Pet. 1:13–14 mortal existence and physical embodiment are equated with dwelling in a tent (*skēnōma*), death with the laying aside (or perhaps dismantling) of that tent (cf. Job 4:21). However, because the concept of laying aside such a tent (2 Pet. 1:14) refers more appropriately to a body than to a tent or dwelling, some prefer to render *skēnōma* in both these verses by "body" (NIV renders the second one as "it"). This putting aside marks departure from earthly life (1:15) and entrance into the eternal kingdom of Jesus Christ (1:11). Note also that in Stephen's speech (Acts 7:46) *skēnōma* is applied to the habitation that David wished to build for the God of Jacob.

5009 (*skēnopēgia*, booth, tabernacle), → *5008*.

5010 (*skēnopoios*, leather worker, tentmaker), → *5008*.

5011 (*skēnos*, tent), → *5008*.

5012 (*skēnoō*, live, dwell, encamp), → *5008*.

5013 (*skēnōma*, tent, dwelling), → *5008*.

5014 σκιά

σκιά (*skia*), shade, shadow, overshadowing (*5014*); ἐπισκιάζω (*episkiazō*), overshadow, cover (*2173*); ἀποσκίασμα (*aposkiasma*), shadow, darkness (*684*).

CL & OT 1. (a) In cl. Gk. the noun *skia* has both a proper and a transferred meaning. It can mean a lit. shadow, thrown by an object (e.g., a tree or a rock) or a person. But it can also assume the meaning of *skotos* and indicate the sphere of darkness (→ *5030*). A particularly important example of this is in the expression *skia thanatou*, shadow of death. *skia* here underlines the suggestion of threat already contained in the concept of death. This noun can also be used to signify the vanity of human actions and of humanity in general. Occasionally it can be translated image, reflection. Plato used *skia* alongside *eikōn* almost as a synonym (→ *1635*), both of which describe a mere likeness of the true and eternal realities.

(b) The Platonic distinction between shadowy image and real form, which is ultimately equivalent to that between appearance and reality, plays an important part in Philo's religious philosophy. He describes God's works of creation as *skia*, so that we can draw conclusions from the visible world about the invisible God. The Logos, which has in addition a mediating function, can also be called *eikōn* and *skia*. Philo makes a conscious distinction between the exceptional, mediatorial role of Moses, and that of the prophets, attributing to Moses a knowledge of God *en eidei*, in form, while the prophets know him only *en skia*, in a shadow.

(c) *episkiazō* means to overshadow, cover, which is an intensive form of *skiazō*, to shade. The noun *aposkiasma* occurs nowhere in pre-Christian lit.; it signifies a darkening caused by the movements of constellations.

2. (a) In the LXX *skia* means shadow. Most frequently it is found in a concrete sense: the shadow of mountains (Jdg. 9:36), plants (Ezek. 17:23; 31:6; Jon. 4:6), a booth (4:5), and a sundial (2 Ki. 20:9–11; Isa. 38:8).

(b) There is no mention in the OT of a human shadow; but the idea is in the background of Isa. 51:16, with its mention of "the shadow of [God's] hand" (cf. 49:2) and in places where the "shadow of the Almighty" is mentioned (Ps. 91:1; cf. 57:1). In Exod. 40:34–35 is a reference to the cloud whose shadow is a demonstration of God's authority. Paradoxically, words of this group assume a positive meaning akin to that of *phōs*, light, in passages where "shadow" refers to the sphere of God's protection and shelter rather than some sinister darkness.

(c) The negative sense of *skia* is retained in places where, in poetic lit., *skia* is linked with *thanatos*, death (e.g., Job 3:5; 12:22; 28:3; Ps. 23:4; 107:10, 14; Isa. 9:2). In these contexts *skia* denotes the realm of darkness, which threatens life. The metaphor of shadow is a favorite one for describing the short and transitory nature of human life. For "man is like a breath; his days are like a fleeting shadow" (Ps. 144:4; cf. 1 Chr. 29:15; Job 14:2).

(d) In the Apocr. "shadow" is used chiefly to demonstrate the nothingness of human life (cf. Wis. 2:5; 5:9) and effort (cf. Sir. 34:2 = LXX 31:2). But the lit. meaning is also found (cf. Wis. 19:7; Bar. 5:8, both using *skiazō*); *skia* can also refer to an (earthly) empire (cf. Bar. 1:12).

NT 1. In the NT *skia* occurs 7x, the vb. *episkiazō* 5x, and *aposkiasma* once. At Mk. 4:32 we find the lit. meaning: Birds will be able to nest in the shadow of the mustard plant when it has grown into a tree. The shadow of a shrub affording shelter to birds indicates a place of security such as is offered by nature.

2. In all 5 uses of *episkiazō*, God is ultimately the cause of the overshadowing, which demonstrates his power and glory. The sphere of God's rule is characterized in the Synoptic Gospels by use of the OT image of the bright cloud that overshadowed (*episkiazō*) Jesus and his disciples during his transfiguration (Matt. 17:5; Mk. 9:5; Lk. 9:34). Here the cloud's shadow symbolizes God's gracious presence.

In Lk. 1:35 the specific image of a cloud throwing its shadow is lacking. Instead, there is a more abstract and yet direct reference to the divine subject of *episkiazō* when Mary is told: "The Holy Spirit will come upon you, and the power of the Most High will overshadow you." The vb. here recalls the Shekinah presence of Yahweh.

Acts 5:15, which speaks about the sick who were carried out on to the street "so that at least Peter's shadow might fall on some of them as he passed by," points to the healing power of God, whose sphere of operation is in this case identified with Peter.

3. As in the OT, *skia* in the NT can also refer to the sphere of darkness in which people find themselves before they come to the light. By nature humanity lives in the land and the shadow of death (cf. the citation of Isa. 9:2 in Matt. 4:16 and the words about John the Baptist at Lk. 1:79). Here death and darkness are intensified to mean the darkness of separation from God and from his Messiah.

4. It is not only the transitoriness of human life, however, with its threatened termination by death, that is expressed by *skia*. As in Philo, *skia* plays an important part in the distinction drawn between real and unreal existence in Col. and Heb. In Heb. *skia* stands with *hypodeigma*, copy (Heb. 8:5, → *5682*), and *parabolē*, likeness (9:9, → *4130*), in stark contrast to *typos*, pattern (8:5, → *5596*), and *eikōn*, form (10:1, → *1635*). Unlike Philo, the author of Heb. understands this contrast Christologically. That is, in comparison with the high-priestly work of Jesus Christ, who is in the heavens, all earthly worship, as conducted in the tabernacle, takes on secondary importance. Thus the Mosaic law may not be regarded as absolute in its validity, for it belongs to the "shadow of the good things that are coming" (Heb. 10:1; cf. 8:5).

Col. 2:17 asserts that questions of food and drink, festival, New Moon, and Sabbaths "are a shadow [*skia*] of the things that were to come; the reality, however, is found in Christ." The person who belongs to Christ, the bearer of true reality, does not have to submit to the judgment of others in such matters. It is not that the ordinance has been suspended. Rather, it is made clear that the direct relation to God established by faith in Christ has priority, since it links humanity with genuine reality, with God in Christ.

5. Before this God all that is earthly, including certain religious and cultic formalities, cannot but appear transient. Earthly things are marked by the characteristics of the shadow: change and darkening. With God, on the other hand, the Father of lights, there is no "change like shifting shadows [*aposkiasma*]" (Jas. 1:17); that is, the processes of change and darkening, such as occur among the constellations, are excluded in the case of God.

5016 (sklērokardia, hard-heartedness), → *2840*.

5017 σκληρός

σκληρός (*sklēros*), hard, rough (*5017*); σκληρότης (*sklērotēs*), hardness (*5018*); σκληρύνω (*sklērynō*), to be, become, hard (*5020*); σκληροτράχηλος (*sklērotrachēlos*), stiff-necked, obstinate (*5019*); πωρόω (*pōroō*), harden, become hard (*4800*); πώρωσις (*pōrōsis*), hardness (*4801*); παχύνω (*pachynō*), thicken, make insensitive (*4266*).

CL & OT 1. (a) In cl. Gk. *sklēros* means dry, hard, rough; *sklērotēs*, hardness. The vb. *sklērynō* was originally a medical term meaning to harden (act.) or to grow hard (pass.). *sklērotrachēlos* means stiff-necked, stubborn, obdurate. (b) *pōroō* (derived from *pōros*, porous stone) means to harden, form a callous, and thus petrify or become hard. (c) *pachynō*, from *pachys* (thick, fat) originally meant to thicken, fatten, then by extension to make impervious (to water). Hence fig. it came to mean to make insensitive; in the pass., to be insensitive.

2. Hardening, according to the OT, results from the fact that people persist in shutting themselves to God's call and command. A state then arises in which they are no longer able to hear and are therefore irretrievably enslaved. Alternatively, God makes the hardening final, so that the people affected by it cannot escape from it.

(a) In the oldest OT narratives it is always non-Israelites who are hardened. The most important is that of the hardening of Pharaoh (Exod. 4–14). After every appeal by Moses and every plague we read, "Yet Pharaoh's heart became hard" (7:13, 22; 8:15, etc.). It was God who hardened Pharaoh's heart. Whole peoples could be hardened by God (e.g., the Canaanites, Jos. 11:20). Non-Israelites were hardened, therefore, only when they came into contact with Israel, for the hardening of the peoples was one of the means God used to fulfill his purpose for Israel.

(b) Not until the appearance of the great prophets do we see Israel as a hardened people. This is expressed most strongly in Isa.'s writings. God's word had come to the priests and the prophets in Jerusalem, but they did not want to listen. Consequently, that word became a word of judgment against them, "so that they will go and fall backward, be injured and snared and captured" (28:13). On the occasion of his call Isaiah received the command, "Make the heart of this people calloused [*pachynō*]; make their ears dull and close their eyes" (6:10). One of God's judgments on his people is not that he no longer speaks to them. Granted, God's word is still proclaimed with utter clarity. But because the people have not wanted to listen, from now on they will be unable to do so. The vineyard that did not want to bear fruit is now unable to bear, because God has forbidden the clouds to rain on it (5:1–7).

(c) The claim that God himself is the one who mercilessly hardens Israel is an extreme statement. The later prophets do not speak with the same severity. Jer. speaks of hardening, but he no longer names God as its cause (6:28). For Jer. the cause is the obstinacy of the people who give heed to the false prophets. The decisive new element is the promise of God's new covenant. Then Israel will hear and recognize the Lord (31:33–34), and people will receive a new, no longer hard, heart and a new spirit (Ezek. 36:26–27).

(d) In the wisdom lit. the godless are often characterized as hardened (e.g., Prov. 28:14; 29:1). Here attention is directed more to the guilt occasioned by such hardness. Hardening is the continually mounting refusal to listen to God's law. It is not, however, inevitable. There is room, therefore, for the appeal, "Today, if you hear his voice, do not harden your hearts" (Ps. 95:7–8). For God's judgment takes place as a result of hardness.

NT 1. (a) *sklēros* is used in a metaphorical sense of things: e.g., "strong" winds (Jas. 3:4), or a "hard [unacceptable] teaching" of Jesus (Jn. 6:60). God will punish the ungodly because of all the "harsh" things they have spoken against him (Jude 15, quoting *1 Enoch* 1:9). *sklēros* is also used of people: The master in the parable of the talents is described in Matt. 25:24 as "a hard [hard-hearted] man." The word is used absolutely in Acts 26:14: "It is hard [difficult] for you to kick against the goads."

(b) *sklērotēs* occurs in Rom. 2:5 to describe a human characteristic. Specifically, by the Jews' "stubbornness" and unrepentant hearts, they were storing up for themselves the wrath of the coming judgment.

(c) *sklērynō* is used trans. with a human subject: "Do not harden your hearts" (Heb. 3:8, 15; 4:7). The appeal of Ps. 95:8 is repeated three times; the community must not forfeit God's promise. Heb. 3:13 takes up the appeal of 3:8 in the pass., that no one "may be hardened" by the deceitfulness of sin. God is subject of the hardening in Rom. 9:18: "He hardens whom he wants to harden." The hardening of Pharaoh in Exod. 4:21 is doubtless in the background here. God punishes by abandoning people to their sin (cf. Rom. 1:24, 26, 28). Acts 19:9 records that some Jews in Ephesus, "obstinate" at Paul's preaching in the synagogue, refused to believe.

(d) *sklērotrachēlos* occurs only in Acts 7:51. In his speech Stephen calls the Jews "stiff-necked . . . with uncircumcised hearts and ears." Like their fathers and unwilling to listen to God, they always resist the Holy Spirit and instead kill his prophets.

2. (a) *pōroō* is used metaphorically in all five passages where it occurs. Mk. 6:52 and 8:17 use the word of the hardening of Jesus' disciples so that they do not understand who the Lord is. In Jn. 12:40 *pōroō* refers to the Jews at whose hand Jesus met with rejection (quoting Isa. 6:10). In two passages of Paul it also refers to the Jews: "The others [i.e., the non-elect] were hardened" (Rom. 11:7); "their minds were made dull" (2 Cor. 3:14).

(b) Two passages also apply the verbal noun *pōrōsis* to the Jews. Jesus is grieved at their "stubborn hearts" (Mk. 3:5; cf. Matt. 19:8; Mk. 10:5, *sklērokardia*, → *kardia*, 2840), while Paul states that "a hardening in part" has come on Israel (Rom. 11:25). In Eph. 4:18 the apostle says that Gentiles have no understanding and are separated from God because of "the hardening of their hearts."

3. Both passages where *pachynō* occurs (Matt. 13:15; Acts 28:27) quote from Isa. 6:10.

4. All these words are used in a metaphorical and theological sense and denote the same idea: the reluctance of humans to respond to God. In the NT those who do not open themselves to the gospel are described as hardened—Jews, Gentiles, and even Jesus' disciples when they do not understand the coming cross. The prophetic idea that God hardens people is taken over from the OT (e.g., Rom. 11) without for a moment losing sight of the notion of personal responsibility (2:5). The inability to hear renders a person liable to judgment. The appeals in Heb. not to harden our hearts are meaningful only because hardness is broken down with the promise of forgiveness and a new beginning (cf. 8:9–10). With the gospel God also gives the ability to understand it.

God gave people over to their sin (Rom. 1:24), but in Christ he gives a new opportunity of hearing through his Spirit. He thus fulfills the promises of the OT. Over against hardening, the inability to receive God's word, stands faith as the obedient reception of the word. Still, Paul grapples with the question of whether, despite Christ's coming, the Jews will remain hardened in his exposition of God's plan of salvation in Rom. 9–11.

5018 (sklērotēs, hardness), → *5017.*

5019 (sklērotrachēlos, stiff-necked, obstinate), → *5017.*

5020 (sklērynō, to be, become, hard), → *5017.*

5022	σκόλοψ

σκόλοψ (*skolops*), thorn (*5022*).

CL & OT This word is not common in secular Gk. Originally it meant a pointed stake that was used in defense or as that on which the head of an enemy could be stuck. But it is also well-attested as a word for a thorn or splinter.

skolops is used metaphorically in the LXX. In Num. 33:55 it identifies those whom, if the Israelites failed to drive them out of the land, would become "barbs [lit., thorns] in your eyes." In Ezek. 28:24, when the Lord gathers his people back from exile, their neighbors will no longer be "painful briers" or "sharp thorns (*akantha*)" (see also Hos. 2:8 = LXX 2:6; Sir. 43:19).

NT *skolops* is used only once in the NT, for Paul's "thorn in [his] flesh" (2 Cor. 12:7). In the prior context Paul refers to his own "visions and revelations" (12:1) in reply to those at Corinth who were vaunting their own spiritual experiences and decrying Paul's foolishness and weakness (11:16–21). Whereas his opponents made much of power, Paul refrains from boasting, "so no one will think more of me than is warranted by what I do or say" (12:6). He goes on: "To keep me from becoming conceited because of these surpassingly great revelations, there was given me a thorn [*skolops*] in my flesh, a messenger of Satan, to torment me."

Various theories have been offered as to what this thorn was. Perhaps it was a temptation to hate or to covet. Some scholars take "flesh" in the broadest sense as the sphere of physical existence, so that

Paul need not be referring to a physical ailment but perhaps to his opponents or Satan's work behind them. Note that physical ailments are not implied in the OT uses of the word.

Still, the context suggests some definite weakness or hardship (12:9–10; cf. 11:23–30). Epilepsy or some form of eye trouble are possible explanations if the expression refers to a bodily ailment. In support of the latter some commentators refer to Gal. 4:13–15, where Paul refers to an "illness" and reminds the Galatians that "you would have torn out your eyes and given them to me." The theory of eye trouble may be supported by the reference to the "large letters" Paul wrote with his own hand (6:11). Likewise, the reference to bearing in his body "the marks of Jesus" (6:17) may refer to some physical illness or to afflictions suffered in the course of preaching the gospel. Luke the physician's attendance on Paul may have been due to Paul's ailments.

The exact nature of the thorn in the flesh remains obscure. In any case, the affliction that may have been severe is seen to be ultimately trivial. The case illustrates the role of intercessory prayer. Paul did not regard it as wrong to pray for himself for alleviation. But in answer to his prayer the Lord said to him, "My grace is sufficient for you, for my power is made perfect in weakness" (2 Cor. 12:9). Paul did not regard the Christian life as a life free from weakness and hardship. In response Paul declares: "I will boast all the more gladly about my weaknesses, so that Christ's power may rest on me. That is why, for Christ's sake, I delight in weaknesses, in insults, in hardships, in persecutions, in difficulties. For when I am weak, then I am strong" (12:9–10).

See also *akantha,* thorn (*180*); *tribolos,* thistle (*5560*).

5025	σκορπίζω

σκορπίζω (*skorpizō*), scatter, disperse, distribute (*5025*); διασκορπίζω (*diaskorpizō*), scatter, disperse, waste (*1399*); διαλύω (*dialyō*), break up, dissolve, disperse (*1370*); διασπείρω (*diaspeirō*), scatter (*1401*).

CL & OT 1. In cl. Gk. *skorpizō* means to scatter, disperse, as do *diaskorpizō* and *diaspeirō*. In the Christian era it is sometimes used in the pass. of churches. *dialyō*, which generally means break up, dissolve, can be used of the dispersing of a crowd.

2. In the LXX *diaspeirō* appears approximately 60x, *diaskorpizō* 50x, *skorpizō* 21x, and *dialyō* 12x. These verbs are used intrans. of those who disperse themselves and are scattered; e.g., a people (Gen. 11:4; Num. 10:35; 1 Sam. 11:11; 13:11; Ezek. 46:18) or a flock (34:5; Zech. 13:7). They are also used trans. to mean shatter a people (Jer. 13:14; 51:23 = LXX 28:23); cast loosely about, spread (e.g., Mal. 2:3); rout enemies (Isa. 41:16; Jer. 15:7; Ezek. 5:2); or disperse nations (Lev. 26:33; Ezek. 5:10; 6:5; 30:26).

NT *skorpizō* occurs only 5x in the NT. In Jn. it occurs in connection with the persecution of Christians (Jn. 16:32) and in the allegory in which "the wolf attacks the flock and scatters it" (10:12). Both Matt. and Lk. draw attention to the missionary principle enunciated by Jesus: "He who is not with me is against me, and he who does not gather with me scatters" (Matt. 12:30; Lk. 11:23). Jesus here takes the theme of gathering and scattering applied in the OT to the people of God (Isa. 40:11; 49:6; Ezek. 34:13, 16) and applies it to his own significance in the end time. The comparable inverted form of this saying—"whoever is not against us is for us" (Mk. 9:40; cf. Lk. 9:50)—occurs in the context of casting out demons. These are not contradictory, however, for the former was spoken to the indifferent about themselves, the latter to the disciples about another adherent of Jesus. Paul uses *skorpizō* once in a quotation from Ps. 112:9 in his argument for a benevolent offering for the poor in Jerusalem (2 Cor. 9:9).

diaskorpizō (9x in NT) can refer to the squandering of resources, either one's own or those entrusted by someone else (Lk. 15:13; 16:1). The vb. also highlights the persecution and dispersion of the messianic community, for the "shepherd" will be smitten and the "sheep" scattered (Matt. 26:31; Mk. 14:27; cf. Zech. 13:7). Lk. uses the vb. in

Mary's song to express her confidence in God's ability to turn tables on the lofty (Lk. 1:51). A striking instance of the scattering of the proud appears in the case of Judas the Galilean, whose followers dispersed when he was discredited as a messianic pretender (Acts 5:37). Matt. twice contrasts "scattering" and "gathering" in the parable of the talents (25:24, 26). John sees Jesus' mission as embracing the "scattered children of God" (i.e., Gentiles) as well as Jews, in order that he might "bring them together and make them one" (Jn. 11:52).

The verb *dialyō* appears in the NT only when Gamaliel draws attention to the futility of the revolt led by Theudas and the subsequent dispersal of his followers (Acts 5:36).

The vb. *diaspeirō* is used 3x of the dispersion of the early Christians through persecution (Acts 8:1, 4; 11:19). The beneficent result of such circumstances was the proclamation of the Christian message in new areas; that is, persecution paved the way for missionary advance. On the related noun *diaspora*, → *1402*.

See also *synagō*, gather (*5251*).

5027 (*skoteinos*, dark, obscure), → *5030*.

5028 (*skotia*, darkness, gloom), → *5030*.

5029 (*skotizomai*, darken), → *5030*.

5030	σκότος

σκότος (*skotos*), darkness, gloom (*5030*); σκοτία (*skotia*), darkness, gloom (*5028*); σκοτόω (*skotoō*), darken (*5031*); σκοτίζομαι (*skotizomai*), darken (*5029*); σκοτεινός (*skoteinos*), dark, obscure (*5027*).

CL & OT 1. Both *skotos* and *skotia* mean essentially the same: darkness, gloom. Likewise, *skotoō* and *skotizomai* mean darken, become dark. Darkness applies primarily to the state characterized by the absence of light. Uses of the word concentrate on the effect of darkness on humanity. In the dark humans grope around uncertainly, since their ability to see is limited. They may not know which way to turn. Thus, darkness appears as a place of danger and anxiety. Since all anxiety ultimately derives from the fear of death, the ominous character of darkness culminates in the darkness of death, which no one can escape. Darkness is therefore also Hades, the world of the dead.

Freed from their temporal sense, the words of this group can describe human ways of life and behavior. They can describe one's seclusion or obscurity. They can also indicate the secrecy, furtiveness, or deceitfulness of one's activity, as well as one's lack of enlightenment, insight. and knowledge.

2. In Gnosticism, darkness becomes an independent force, seen as the unlimited ruler of the earthly world. In contrast to this world of darkness shines the transcendent world. Humanity has been endowed with a soul, coming from a spark of light. By means of *gnōsis* (knowledge) people can attain to enlightenment; *agnoia*, ignorance, keeps one from salvation. The contrast between the world of light and of darkness results in a call to *metanoia*, repentance (conversion), the decision to turn from the darkness of the earth-bound and bodily to the light and life.

3. The key to the OT view of light and darkness is faith in God as Creator, who stands above both. He is not only the Lord of light; darkness also bows before him. Darkness is first mentioned in connection with the primeval chaos (Gen. 1:2). God creates both light and darkness (Isa. 45:7), and he causes day to follow night (Ps. 104:20; Amos 5:8; cf. Gen. 1:4–5, 18). In his saving activity he can make use of darkness, as when he sent darkness on Egypt (Exod. 10:22; Ps. 105:28).

The fact that God is Lord over darkness does not automatically diminish the threat of this force hostile to humankind. Darkness is a symbol of limitation, restraint, and affliction (Isa. 9:1 = LXX 9:2). Humans belong to this sphere by nature (8:22; cf. 60:2). Even the righteous are exposed to the terrors of darkness (Job 19:8; 30:26; Ps. 88:6). When people separate themselves from God by disobedience, darkness

remains (107:10–11). Conversely, God illumines the darkness for those who fear him. Those who walk through the valley of deep darkness need not fear (Ps. 23:4; cf. 112:4; Isa. 50:10; Mic. 7:8), for darkness is not dark to God (Ps. 139:11–12) and to those led by him (Isa. 42:7, 16; 49:9).

God promises that the people who walk in darkness will see a great light (Isa. 9:2). But sinners, who hide themselves from the light of God (29:15), are heading for that day when God will bring the darkness of sin into the light (Job 12:22) and hold a terrible judgment (34:23–24). Hence the prophets proclaim that the day of Yahweh will not be, as the people expect, a day of joy for Israel but rather a day of darkness and calamity (Joel 2:2, 10; Amos 5:20; 8:9)—unless they repent (Joel 2:12–17). Eschatological darkness means the final and eternal destruction of the faithless and disobedient.

4. Later Jewish writings develop the concept of eschatological darkness and damnation in the world beyond (cf. *Jub.* 5:14; *1 Enoch* 17:6; 63:6; 108:11–14). The purpose of such teaching is to bring about enlightenment and a decision to follow the way of light. Qumran lit. frequently refers to humanity caught in the tension between light and darkness. Darkness seeks to lead them astray, but they can extricate themselves from the power of darkness by deciding to enter the covenant as a child of light.

NT 1. The NT uses the word darkness in a lit. sense to indicate time in connection with night setting in or departing (Jn. 6:17; 20:1). Metaphorically but without negative allusion attaching to night, *skotia* and *phōs* (light) are used in Matt. 10:27 and Lk. 12:3.

2. The *skotia* word group connotes a clearly negative sense in those passages that contrast a sound eye in a body full of light with an evil eye in a body full of darkness (Matt. 6:22–23; Lk. 11:34–36). At Jesus' arrest (22:53) and still more in his hour of death (Matt. 27:45; Mk. 15:33; Lk. 23:44), the power of darkness gave the impression of having won a victory. But at Easter the divine power of light triumphed once and for all over the satanic powers of darkness. It is in the light of this victory that darkness is mostly seen and evaluated in the NT.

3. The natural abode for human beings is in darkness. People live in darkness (cf. Isa. 9:2, quoted in Matt. 4:16) and cannot avoid the darkness of death (Lk. 1:79). In this sphere the power of Satan holds sway (Acts 26:18; cf. Eph. 6:12), which impels humans to do the evil works of darkness (Jn. 3:19; Rom. 13:12; Eph. 5:11); "their foolish hearts [are] darkened" (Rom. 1:21). This includes Jews, whose strict adherence to the law can cause them to become blind leaders of the blind (Matt. 8:12; 15:14; cf. Rom. 2:19). In fact, darkness can be so dominating that Paul writes that the Ephesians once *were* darkness (Eph. 5:8).

4. Darkness is not, of course, a power equal with God. He is in control of it; for example, he blinded the magician Bar-Jesus by a word of the Spirit spoken by Paul (Acts 13:11). Just as in creation, God now causes light to shine in human hearts out of darkness (2 Cor. 4:6). He is Lord over darkness, a lordship displayed above all in Jesus Christ, whom he has sent into the world to call his people out of darkness into his wonderful light (1 Pet. 2:9), into the kingdom of the Son of his love (Col. 1:13).

This theme is particularly prevalent in John, who often uses the metaphor of light and darkness. Thus in the prologue of his Gospel he writes: "The light shines in the darkness, and the darkness has not overcome it" (Jn. 1:5, cf. NIV note). Light and darkness are mutuallly exclusive elements (cf. 2 Cor. 6:14), and we must make a decision for one or the other, for God or against him—or to be more precise, for Jesus Christ, who is "the light of the world" (Jn. 12:46; cf. 8:12). Those who believe in him (12:46) and follow him no longer walk in darkness (8:12).

5. It is not enough merely, however, to confess allegiance to the light with one's lips. No one can have fellowship with God and at the same time walk in darkness; such people are liars (1 Jn. 1:6). Refusal to love others means living in darkness (2:9–11; cf. Jn. 12:35). Such

people have not understood that darkness is passing away and that the one true light is already shining (1 Jn. 2:8).

For those people who stubbornly reject the light, who refuse to acknowledge Jesus Christ as Lord, and who perform the works of darkness—here false teachers come in for special mention (2 Pet. 2:17; Jude 13)—a day of deepest darkness is coming, God's judgment. On that day the Lord will "bring to light what is hidden in darkness and will expose the motives of men's hearts" (1 Cor. 4:5). Such people will be cast out into the gloomy place of eschatological destruction (cf. Matt. 8:12; 22:13; 25:30).

This judgment is expected at the second coming of Christ, which will be accompanied by manifestations of darkness, when "the sun will be darkened, and the moon will not give its light" (Matt. 24:29; Mk. 13:24; cf. Isa. 13:10; Ezek. 32:7). Thus, Paul can strongly exhort Christians to watchfulness and soberness in the light of the Parousia, which will suddenly overtake them (1 Thess. 5:4–6).

See also *nyx*, night (*3816*).

5031 (skotoō, darken), → 5030.

5032	σκύβαλον

σκύβαλον (*skybalon*), refuse, dung (*5032*).

CL This depressing word means rubbish and muck of many kinds: excrement, rotten food, bits left at a meal as not worth eating, a rotting corpse. Nastiness and decay are the constant elements of its meaning. It is a coarse, ugly word implying worthlessness and repulsiveness. *skybalon* occurs once in the LXX, signifying moral uncleanness (Sir. 27:4).

NT The only NT usage of *skybalon* is in Phil. 3:8, where Paul writes that all the natural and religious privileges that once seemed sweet and precious to him as a Pharisee he now considers "rubbish." Now that Paul is a believer, they no longer have any value to him.

See also *peripsēma*, filth (*4370*); *rhypos*, dirt (*4866*).

5043	σμύρνα

σμύρνα (*smyrna*), myrrh (*5043*); σμυρνίζω (*smyrnizō*), mix with myrrh (*5046*); μύρον (*myron*), ointment, perfume (*3693*).

OT Myrrh is a gum from a low, thorny tree that grows primarily in Somaliland, Ethiopia, and Arabia. The gum exudes from the trunk and branches, giving a pleasant fragrance. The LXX uses *smyrna* to translate Heb. *mōr* or *môr*. In Exod. 30:23 it is an important ingredient in the anointing oil used in the consecration of the tabernacle and priests. In Ps. 45:8 its fragrance is mentioned in connection with the oil of gladness with which God anoints his chosen king (see also Song 3:6; 4:6, 14; 5:1, 5, 13; Sir. 24:15).

NT *smyrna* was among the gifts brought to the infant Jesus by the Gentile Magi (Matt. 2:11). Here and elsewhere outside the Bible it is mentioned together with incense. These gifts may have been understood as a fulfillment of Ps. 72:10–11 (cf. also Isa. 60:6).

Nicodemus brought a mixture of myrrh and aloes weighing a hundred pounds to the burial of Jesus (Jn. 19:39). This large amount was probably an expression of honor. Jn. 19:40 indicates that spices were usually laid between the clothes in which the body was wrapped (cf. also Mk. 16:1; Lk. 23:56; 24:1). This attempt to preserve Jesus' body suggests that none of those involved expected an immediate resurrection.

The pass. part. of *smyrnizō* occurs in Mk. 15:23 in the reference to the "wine mixed with myrrh" that was offered to Jesus by the soldiers prior to the crucifixion. This is often taken to be an anodyne given to condemned prisoners to blunt their consciousness, though it may have been nothing more than a drink given by the soldiers to the exhausted.

myron is probably best translated as ointment or perfume (Matt. 26:7, 9, 12; Mk. 14:3–5; Lk. 7:37–38, 46; 23:56; Jn. 11:2; 12:3, 5; Rev. 18:13).

See also *libanos*, frankincense (*3337*).

5046 (smyrnizō, mix with myrrh), → 5043.

5048	Σολομών

Σολομών (*Solomōn*), Solomon (*5048*).

OT Solomon was the son (by Bathsheba) and successor of David, the last king of a united Israel. His reign (ca. 961–ca. 922 B.C.) was peaceful and prosperous, except for some economic difficulties and abortive revolts toward the end of it. It was without doubt the most splendid era in Israel's history. Building on the foundations laid by David, Solomon organized an efficient administration, developed industry and commerce, and established harmonious relationships with neighboring states. His most lasting achievement was the building of the temple in Jerusalem.

At birth, he was named both Solomon and Jedidiah (2 Sam. 12:24–25). The meaning of *Solomon* is not certain—"his [i.e., Yahweh's] peace, well-being" is possible, but most probable is "his compensation," i.e., God's compensation to David for the death of Bathsheba's firstborn. He was by no means David's oldest son, and thus it was not without rivalry and intrigue that he came to the throne, first as coregent with David (1 Ki. 1). He quickly and ruthlessly consolidated his position (1 Ki. 2) and then took appropriate steps to strengthen his kingdom and empire. In the face of external foes, Jerusalem and other strategic cities were fortified and garrisoned with a powerful chariot force (9:15–19; 10:26). Solomon attempted to strengthen the internal structures of Israel by breaking down the old tribal pattern and replacing it with a system of administrative districts (4:7–19).

Solomon established good relations with neighboring states, esp. Tyre and Egypt (1 Ki. 3:1; 5:12; but cf. 9:12). These alliances not only provided military security but also encouraged the development of commerce, both overland and maritime (cf. 10:22, 25). The trade was boosted by the exploitation of Israel's resources, esp. the copper mines in the Negev.

In all these cases Solomon displayed vision, statesmanship, and skill; the divine promise of wisdom, made at the start of his reign, was thus amply fulfilled (1 Ki. 3:12). The wisdom for which his name became a byword was two-fold. (1) It was a practical wisdom; statecraft and the administration of justice were above all the areas in which it was needed and demonstrated (3:9, 16–28). (2) It was an academic and didactic wisdom; in a world already famed for its wise men, Solomon showed himself outstanding, making major contributions to the collection of proverbial and related material (4:29–34). His name is linked with the books of Prov. (1:1), Song of Songs (1:1), and (by implication) Eccl. (1:1), and we may see him as the founder and patron of a great deal of literary activity in Israel. He may well have established "wisdom schools" in Israel.

Solomon's shrewdness and sagacity were not, however, unalloyed. Many of his ventures were excessive and expensive, so that he gradually impoverished the country. In time, heavy taxation and forced service caused deep resentments, which eventually broke up his kingdom (cf. 1 Ki. 12:1–20). His diplomatic marriages were but the beginning of a vast and expensive harem. His personal piety also lapsed into a measure of apostasy and idolatry (11:1–10). Ironically, the man who built the temple was the first one to adulterate its worship.

In later lit., beginning at least with Josephus, many legends and legendary features became attached to the OT's more realistic information. In particular, the story of the Queen of Sheba's visit (1 Ki. 10:1–13) attracted many such accretions. Solomon's wisdom, magnificence, and pious attachment to the law of Moses were heightened and extolled while his faults were glossed over. Strangely, the weight of later Jewish criticisms of Solomon centered on something of which he was not historically guilty, namely, the development of magical practices.

NT Solomon figures little in the NT; he is neither exalted nor denigrated. In Matt. 1:6–7 he appears in his appropriate place in the genealogy of Christ. Matt. 6:29 and Lk. 12:27 mention his splendor, Matt. 12:42 and Lk. 11:31 his wisdom. Finally Acts 7:47 recognizes him as the builder of the temple.

These widely separated references both acknowledge Solomon's achievements but also highlight their lack of finality in God's purposes. Solomon was great David's son, but he was not the promised Messiah, merely his progenitor (Matt. 1:6–7). Solomon had indeed built a majestic temple in God's honor; but the whole burden of Stephen's speech in Acts 7 is to depreciate any temple "made by men" (7:48). Solomon's temple and the second temple after it became centers of apostasy and unbelief. Both Acts 7:50 and Matt. 6:29 turn the reader's attention from human achievement such as Solomon's to the glories of the Creator. Finally, 12:42 expressly states that Solomon in all his wisdom has been eclipsed by Christ. This verse, which is primarily attacking Jewish unbelief, suggests that Solomon is as a type of Christ.

5053 σοφία

σοφία (*sophia*), wisdom (*5053*); σοφός (*sophos*), wise (*5055*); σοφίζω (*sophizō*), make wise, teach, instruct; mid. to reason out, devise craftily (*5054*).

CL & OT 1. In cl. Gk. *sophos* and *sophia* denote an attribute, not an activity. They indicate unusual ability and knowledge, either in the practical sphere or in theoretical knowledge. In some cases *sophia* was held to be an *innate* sense of wisdom and discernment; the Sophists, however, viewed it as knowledge that could be taught and acquired. Socrates' wisdom consisted in the fact that he knew that he knew nothing. All authoritarian wisdom is in reality no wisdom. In Plato wisdom is related to his view of eternal forms or ideas. For Aristotle, *sophia* and *philosophia* were identical. With the Stoics theory and practice coincide; wisdom is realized knowledge.

2. (a) As a rule, this word group occurs in the LXX to render words from the stem *ḥkm*, the majority of which are in wisdom lit. (Job, Ps., Prov., Eccl.; also Sir. and Wis.). This word group has a wide breadth of meaning. *sophia* denotes specialist knowledge in a particular field, such as a handicraft or art (Exod. 36:1–2), but also economic shrewdness (cf. Prov. 8:1, 18, 21), the art of governing (8:15), and education (1 Ki. 4:29–34). Moreover, the OT is concerned with wise behavior that enables one to master life (Prov. 8:32–36), which depends on right conduct in obedience to God's will rather than on theoretical insight. Wisdom is thus integrally connected with the fear of Yahweh (9:10; cf. 1:7; 15:33 = LXX 16:4; Job 28:28; Ps. 111:10).

(b) The OT is aware of wisdom in the surrounding nations (e.g., in Babylon, Jer. 50:35; 51:57; Egypt, 1 Ki. 4:30). There are astonishing parallels between certain Egyptian texts and Heb. wisdom lit. (e.g., between Prov. 22:17–23:11 and the Egyptian *Wisdom of Amenemope*). But even as they adapted these texts, Israel brought them firmly into line with its own religious convictions. Also, just as in Egypt wisdom texts served in the training and education of future palace officials, so at Solomon's court such texts were collected for the training and education of the rising generation of royal advisers. Daniel and his companions also belong to these courtly circles (Dan. 2:48; 5:11–12).

(c) Over all acquired and transmitted wisdom, however, stands the wisdom given as a gift by God to King Solomon (1 Ki. 3:5–14), which finds expression in judicial shrewdness (3:16–28) and leads, in later minds, to admiring recognition by Israel's neighbors (4:31, 34; 10:1–9). Here is founded the longing of later generations for the splendor and security of Solomon's reign. It is equally comprehensible that wisdom was expected in the hoped-for messianic king (Isa. 11:2).

(d) The concept of wisdom is pervasive in postexilic times. Wisdom, now conceived in personal terms, becomes the mediator of revelation and a teacher (Prov. 8:1–21), who summons (1:20–21; 8:32–34) and invites us into her presence (9:1–6). Created prior to all the works of creation (8:22–31), wisdom discloses the original order inherent in creation. She thus gains the role of a divine principle implanted in the world.

3. (a) In Hel. Jud. wisdom is identified with the law (Sir. 24:8–34; cf. also Josephus). The student of wisdom follows her like a lover and wins all the bliss of living with her (14:20–27). Wisdom was not only present at the creation but is herself creator as the "mother" of all good things and innumerable riches (Wis. 7:12). She sits by the throne of God (9:4), mediating God's salvation (7:27). Similar ideas are found in Philo. For rab. Jud., wisdom and scriptural erudition are essentially identical.

(b) In the Dead Sea Scrolls wisdom is influenced by the dualism of the sect's theology. God's all-embracing plan for the world, the goal of which is the annihilation of the wicked, is determined by wisdom (1QS 4:18). The elect are allotted wisdom by the Spirit of truth (4:21–22).

NT In the NT terms from this word group are found mostly in 1 Cor. 1–3 (26x) and Paul's later writings, whereas the Gospels and other books seldom use them.

1. *Gospels.* (a) The use of these words in the Gospels is generally tied to the traditional OT and Jewish conception, where wisdom is a person's approach to life, arising out of life in the covenant bestowed by God and so must be regarded as the gift of God. Thus, the twelve-year-old Jesus grew in wisdom and insight and distinguished himself by his exceptional knowledge of the law (Lk. 2:40, 52). Mk. 6:2 depicts the later astonishment of the inhabitants of Nazareth at the wisdom given to Jesus (cf. Matt. 13:54). In Acts Stephen is similarly represented as a man equipped by God with the Spirit and wisdom, whose testimony cannot be contradicted for this reason (6:3, 10; cf. also the promise of wisdom for defense speeches during the coming final days, Lk. 21:15).

(b) The Jewish tradition of a personally understood wisdom who calls people to her may lie behind the remarkable statement that "wisdom is proved right by her actions" (Matt. 11:19). Jesus and John his witness are understood as the mouths of wisdom, who brings salvation. Note that God's word of wisdom in Lk. 11:49 is cited as a word of Jesus in Matt. 23:34–35; Jesus is wisdom come to earth, someone "greater than Solomon" (12:42). It therefore seems justifiable to speak of a *sophia*-Christology (cf. also *logos* in Jn. 1; → *3364*).

2. *Paul's earlier letters.* (a) In a fundamental and far-reaching exposition that develops his theology of the cross, Paul contrasts the wisdom of the world with the message of the cross. God has turned the wisdom of the world into foolishness (1 Cor. 1:20; cf. 3:19), not through words or arguments, but through an action, namely, Christ's death. Since in God's will "Christ the power of God and the wisdom of God" (1:24; cf. 1:30) has been revealed, worldly wisdom that rejects the cross is proved to be that which it always was: foolishness (→ *mōria, 3702*, i.e., rebellion against God), in the form of human self-exaltation and boasting (1:29, 31).

Humans have closed their minds to God's wisdom as they encountered it in the works of creation and instead have attempted to create their own wisdom (1 Cor. 1:21; cf. Rom. 1:18–23). However, God has chosen to save those who believe through the foolishness of the preaching of the cross. Thus every attempt to demand a proof for the truth of God (1:22) is as condemned to failure as is every attempt to boast of oneself (3:18–21).

Both the character of the Corinthian congregation and the manner of Paul's preaching confirm this interpretation of the salvation event. God's election of the foolish, the weak, and the despised—who formed the church in Corinth—shows that God puts to shame those who are considered wise by human standards (1 Cor. 1:26–29). God's will, announced in the OT as judging human pride (1:19, 31; 3:19–20), is thereby fulfilled. Paul's renunciation of "superior wisdom" (2:1) serves the sole saving work of the cross, which may not be emptied of its power (1:17). Paul can still say that he speaks wisdom "among the mature," but it is God's wisdom, hidden in the mystery (2:6–7). This is probably due to the fact that Paul takes up ideas of his opponents (who believed in a spiritual, nonsuffering Christ) and puts to a positive use in his own theology.

(b) In the hymn that concludes his exposition of the mystery of Israel's election, Paul praises "the depth of the riches of the wisdom and knowledge of God" (Rom. 11:33). God's wisdom is revealed in his inscrutable judgments and ways (cf. Isa. 40:13–14) and is thus not to be extolled in speculation, but experienced in history. This salvation history reference, along with the reminiscences of Prov. 8, allows us to understand wisdom here as the work of the creator, who is at the same time the Lord and perfecter of history.

(c) That Paul can use *sophos* in its ordinary nontechnical sense is shown by 1 Cor. 3:10, where he describes himself as an "expert builder" of the community, and possibly also by the question in 6:5, where Paul asks rhetorically if there is in the community no wise person able to render judgment, in order to keep members from bringing lawsuits in heathen courts.

3. *Paul's later letters.* Wisdom is understood as a gift of God's grace (Eph. 1:8, 17; Col. 1:9), in which believers may grow. The content of this teaching of wisdom revealed by the Spirit is the mystery of God—Christ, "in whom are hidden all the treasures of wisdom and knowledge" (2:3). The Christology developed here links to the OT and Jewish conception of wisdom hidden in God before the creation of the world (Prov. 8; Sir. 24). This wisdom will be revealed in the fullness of time in Christ through the church (Eph. 3:9–10).

4. *Other NT books.* (a) Jas. 3:13 teaches that wisdom is shown in good behavior by works of kindness. This letter deals with opponents who (like those in Corinth) claim for themselves wisdom "from above," but cause strife here on earth (3:15–16). James describes this wisdom as peaceable, full of compassion, and without hypocrisy (3:17). To get such wisdom one must pray to God (1:5).

(b) In Rev. *sophia* is praised in two hymns: as an attribute of God (7:12) and of the slain Lamb at his exaltation (5:12). The exalted Christ has the same power and wisdom as God has. In 13:18; 17:9, *sophia* is the secret knowledge of Christians, on the basis of which they can interpret the apocalyptic mysteries and events of their time.

5. *sophizō* occurs 2x in the NT. Its use in 2 Tim. 3:14–15 is similar to that of Ps. 19:7; 105:22; 119:98: God's word is able to make us "wise for salvation through faith in Christ Jesus." Its use in 2 Pet. 1:16, where reference is made to "cleverly invented" stories in contrast to the historical truth of Jesus, is similar to the negative nuance of this vb. in Eccl. 7:16; Sir. 7:5; 32:4 (= LXX 35:4).

See also *mōria*, foolishness, folly (*3702*); *philosophia*, love of wisdom, philosophy (*5814*).

5054 (*sophizō*, make wise, teach; mid. to reason out, devise craftily), → *5053*.

5055 (*sophos*, wise), → *5053*.

5062 (*speirō*, sow), → *5065*.

5064 (*spendō*, pour out [a drink offering]), → *1772*.

5065 σπέρμα

σπέρμα (*sperma*), seed (*5065*); σπείρω (*speirō*), sow (*5062*); σπόρος (*sporos*), seed (*5078*); φυτεύω (*phyteuō*), to plant (*5885*).

CL & OT 1. In cl. Gk. the *sperma* group is often used in the lit. sense of sowing seeds and fig. of producing offspring. Pindar refers to the pure, divine seed of the god. *speirō* had wide currency in ethical "sowing–reaping" maxims, highlighting the inevitable consequences of willful deeds.

2. (a) In the LXX *sperma* and *speirō* occur 217x and 52x times respectively, often referring to sowing seed, either in the ground (Gen. 47:23; Isa. 55:10) and of male semen (Lev. 15:16; 22:4; Jer. 31:27 = LXX 38:27). This word group is used fig. of offspring or posterity, either individually (Gen. 4:25; 21:13) or collectively (e.g., seed of Abraham, 15:5; 17:7–8; 22:18; seed of Noah, 9:9; seed of the patriarchs, Deut. 1:8), thereby highlighting the cohesion of the elect community. In later interpretations *seed* in Gen. 3:15 included a collective

and an individual sense. Collectively the word foreshadows the spiritually renewed posterity of Adam who strive with Satan, while ultimately it refers to Christ, the paramount seed who seals Satan's doom. Ps. 22:30 refers to the *sperma* (i.e., spiritual progeny) of the Messiah.

(b) *speirō* is used fig. of Yahweh's sowing Israel in the land (Hos. 2:23) or into dispersion (Zech. 10:9) and of the chosen nation's bearing fruit (Jer. 31:27 = LXX 38:27; Ezek. 36:9). The imagery of sowing seed is employed in injunctions to ethical action (Hos. 10:12; Jer. 4:3) and in warnings against evil practices (Job 4:8; Prov. 22:8).

3. (a) In Jewish writings the ethical idea of sowing and harvest (→ *therismos*, *2546*) occurs in an apocalyptic context. The present evil world is like a field sown with corrupt seed, which can only bear fruit (→ *karpos*, *2843*) after its kind (2 Esd. 9:17). Unless the produce of this seed is gathered in, the beneficent age to come cannot be inaugurated. The image of sowing seed was also used of the implantation of the law in the children of Israel (9:31).

(b) In Philo *sperma* is the starting point of the universe and of all that exists. The body originates from human seed, but the soul from divine seed. God sows every chaste virtue in the soul, while wisdom, the daughter of God, sows knowledge and discernment. But humans possess the capacity of sowing both good and evil seed.

NT 1. *sperma* (43x in the NT) and *speirō* (52x) occur frequently in Jesus' parables, where the familiar imagery of seed sown in a field conveys profound teaching about the kingdom of God. (a) In the parable of the sower (Matt. 13:1–9; Mk. 4:1–9; Lk. 8:4–8) emphasis rests on the act of sowing the seed, which Jesus identifies with the proclamation of the word of God. Jesus' later interpretation of the parable (Matt. 13:10–23; Mk. 4:10–20; Lk. 8:9–15) emphasizes the four kinds of soils on which the word was sown, thus illustrating the diversity of response to the word. The seed sown along the path symbolizes the stubborn, secular person. That sown on rocky ground characterizes the shallow hearer. The seed sown among thorns depicts the selfish recipient. The seed cast on good soil represents the saved, who by embracing the proclaimed word participate in the eternal increase of the kingdom. The parable extends the promise of an overflow of a spiritual harvest, thus encouraging persistence in preaching.

(b) In the parable of the seed growing secretly (Mk. 4:26–29), the seed deposited in the earth develops successively into the blade, the ear, and finally the full head of grain, symbolizing the growth of the life of the Spirit in the believer promoted by the secret power of God. Lacking the life of the kingdom, humanity is like the flower of the grass that fades and comes to naught (Jas. 1:10–11). The parable of the wheat and weeds (Matt. 13:24–30), in which the Son of Man sows the seed of wheat and the devil the seed of weeds, affirms the simultaneous growth of good and evil during the present age. Finally, in the parable of the mustard seed (Matt. 13:31–32; Mk. 4:30–32; Lk. 13:18–19) the growth of a tiny seed into a magnificent shrub highlights the contrast between the insignificant beginnings of the kingdom and its final manifestation in majesty.

2. (a) The NT frequently uses *sperma* in the sense of offspring or posterity. The word often occurs in citations of OT promise texts that foretell the future blessing of the descendants of, e.g., Abraham (Lk. 1:55 [cf. Gen. 17:7; 18:18; 22:17; Mic. 7:20]; Acts 7:5–6 [cf. Gen. 12:7; 17:8]) and Isaac (Rom. 9:7 and Heb. 11:18 [cf. Gen. 21:12]).

(b) Paul's use of *sperma* occasionally transcends the basic physical relation to include the spiritual descendants of OT believers. Consequently, the NT expression "Abraham's seed" is not restricted to the generic house of Israel, but includes all who possess the same kind of faith as the patriarch had (Gal. 3:29). The OT promise to the patriarchs thus includes the ultimate spiritual blessing of all who believe, Jew or Gentile (Rom. 4:16–18). In Rev. 12:17 the seed ("offspring") of the woman represents the NT community that becomes the focus of Satan's attack.

(c) Paul ultimately interprets the OT promise of a seed in terms of Christ, the paramount offspring of Abraham (Gal. 3:16–19; cf. Gen.

12:7). As head of the corporate community (Gal. 3:29), Christ is identified as the ultimate fulfillment of the divine promises to the patriarchs and later to David (Acts 13:23, 33–37).

Paul's exegesis in Gal. 3:16–19 has sometimes been criticized for its artificiality. Note that the pl. of the Heb. word for "seed" generally means grain or crops (e.g., 1 Sam. 8:15); thus the Heb. of Gen. 12:7 must have been sing., even though God's promise to Abraham was not confined to a single individual but extended to his posterity. Yet Paul's argument in Gal. 3:16–19 is not grammatical but theological. In the first instance, the *seed* refers to the people of Israel, the posterity of Abraham. Although the children of Ishmael also descended from Abraham, there was only one covenant people (seed) descended from him, the line that came through Isaac. Christ as the ultimate seed represents the covenant line through Isaac.

Moreover, Paul is making use here of the notion of corporate solidarity, where a single individual represents an entire people (cf. the Adam–Christ typology in Rom. 5:12–21). Esp. since Paul is fully aware that physical descent is no guarantee of spiritual relationship (9:6–7), he is able to use the collective sing. in Gal. 3:29: "If you belong to Christ, then you are Abraham's seed, and heirs according to the promise." The Messiah, as the true descendant of Abraham and the true representative of his people, and in him his elect ones, as sharers in his experiences and his benefits, are seen as the legitimate heirs of God's promises. While the Judaizers at Galatia may have insisted that the promises made to Abraham and his seed involved the Jewish people as a whole, Paul finds a deeper application of this principle.

(d) Philo's concept of the divine seed receives a Christian interpretation in 1 Jn. 3:9, where *sperma* signifies the divine principle of life (the Spirit?) in the believer, which renders continuance in sin incongruous. As the physical *sperma* was the generator of life in the physical order, so the divine *sperma* becomes the fount and origin of life in the new order of recreated humanity.

(e) Paul uses the figure of a seed sown in the earth (cf. Jn. 12:24) to illustrate the burial and resurrection of the bodies of deceased believers (1 Cor. 15:36–44). As the bare grain of wheat sown in the soil unfolds into a full-grown ear, so the seed of spiritual life deposited in the ground will be raised into a glorious new body animated by the Spirit. Just as there is continuity as well as discontinuity between the seed that is sown and the plant that emerges, so there is continuity and discontinuity between the body that is buried and the resurrected body.

(f) Paul uses *speirō* (and its correlate *phyteuō*) in the context of the material maintenance of the gospel preacher. Like the servant who plants a vineyard (1 Cor. 9:7), the one who sows the seed of spiritual fruit is entitled to reap the reward of a decent living (9:11). To underscore the church's responsibility for the financial support of the preacher, Paul in 2 Cor. 9:6 asserts that the liberality with which one sows determines the spiritual and material benefits one reaps.

(g) Paul also uses *phyteuō* in 1 Cor. 3:6–8 to describe his work of evangelism in contrast to Apollos's follow-up work of nurturing believers who have made a commitment to Christ. Paul plants the seed, whereas Apollos waters it. But the credit for any fruit that comes through that process belongs to God alone. Elsewhere in the NT, *phyteuō* usually refers to physical planting and occurs mostly in parables of Jesus (e.g., Matt. 21:33; Mk. 12:1; Lk. 13:6; 20:9).

(h) In Gal. 6:7–8 this theme of sowing and reaping is developed into an ethical proverb familiar to secular antiquity and the OT (cf. Prov. 11:30; 13:2). Paul, however, focuses attention on the old and new natures as the two spheres in which ethical action is sown. A sowing to the sinful human nature yields a harvest of moral corruption, while a sowing to the Spirit produces eternal life. James adds that the divine standard of ethical conduct is achieved only by those possessors of heavenly wisdom who sow in gentleness, humility, and peace (Jas. 3:18).

See also *therismos*, harvest (*2546*); *karpos*, fruit (*2843*); *dendron*, tree (*1285*).

| 5068 | σπήλαιον |

σπήλαιον (*spēlaion*), cave, den (*5068*).

CL & OT *spēlaion* means cavern, grotto. The LXX uses *spēlaion* for a cave as a place of refuge (Gen. 19:30; Jos. 10:16; 1 Sam. 22:1), as a tomb (Gen. 23:9), or as a robber's hideout (Jer. 7:11).

NT In Matt. 21:13 (par. Mk. 11:17; Lk. 19:46) Jesus, as the Lord of the temple (Matt. 12:6), protests that the Jerusalem authorities have degraded God's house of prayer (Isa. 56:7) into a den (*spēlaion*) of thieves (→ *lēstēs*, *3334*), robbing the helpless while themselves enjoying the safe refuge of privilege. Their trading activities betrayed an insensitivity to the holiness of the outer court and denied Gentiles access to the only part of the temple area permitted to them for quiet worship. Jer. 7:11, alluded to here, had correctly forecast the destruction of the land in Jeremiah's day.

The sale of animals in the temple forecourt was apparently a recent innovation by the high priest Caiaphas (ca. A.D. 30), competing against the four traditional markets on the Mount of Olives. So unpopular among ordinary Jews was the temple trading, because of the greed of those in charge, that a popular uprising three years before Jerusalem was destroyed in A.D. 70 swept away these bazaars. Heb. 11:38 and Rev. 6:15 describe refugees seeking shelter in *spēlaia*, caves, a feature of the limestone rocks of Palestine (cf. 2 Macc. 6:11; 10:6). Natural caves could also be adapted as burial places, as in the case of Lazarus (Jn. 11:38).

See also *lēstēs*, robber, highwayman, bandit, revolutionary (*3334*); *sylaō*, plunder, rob (*5195*); *apostereō*, rob, defraud, deprive (*691*); *andrapodistēs*, slave-dealer, kidnapper (*435*).

5072 (splanchnizomai, have pity, show mercy, feel sympathy), → *5073.*

| 5073 | σπλάγχνον |

σπλάγχνον (*splanchnon*), almost always in the pl. *splanchna*, inward parts, entrails, hence as the seat of emotion, the heart, love (*5073*); σπλαγχνίζομαι (*splanchnizomai*), have pity, show mercy, feel sympathy (*5072*); πολύσπλαγχνος (*polysplanchnos*), sympathetic, compassionate (*4499*); εὔσπλαγχνος (*eusplanchnos*), tenderhearted, compassionate (*2359*).

CL & OT 1. In cl. Gk., *to splanchnon*, used almost entirely in the pl., originally meant the inward parts or entrails (of a sacrificial animal), esp. the more valuable parts: the heart, lungs, liver, spleen, and/or kidneys. Since immediately after killing the animal these parts were removed, roasted, and eaten in a sacrificial meal, the word came to mean the sacrificial meal itself. Starting in the 5th cent. B.C., we find *splanchna* used also for the human entrails—esp. the male sexual organs and the womb—as the site of the powers of conception and birth, Hence children were sometimes called *splanchna*. Since the intestines were regarded as the site of the natural passions (e.g., anger, fretful desires, love), the word came to have the fig. meaning of heart (as the organ of feelings and emotions), or the sense of premonition; finally, it came to mean affection and love.

The vb. *splanchneuō* originally meant to eat the entrails or prophesy from the entrails. The later form *splanchnizomai*, with the metaphorical meaning to have mercy on, feel pity or compassion for, is found only in the writings of Jud. and the NT.

2. The LXX uses the noun 15x, the vb. 2x, mostly in the Apocr. In Prov. 12:10 the noun means kindness, mercy; in 26:22, inner parts, belly. In 2 Macc. 9:5; 4 Macc. 5:30; 10:8, it means intestines; in 15:23, 29, mother love; in 2 Macc. 9:6, heart. In the Pseudepigrapha the words contain the predominant meaning merciful (e.g., *T. Zeb.* 7:3; 8:2, 6).

NT 1. The vb. *splanchnizomai* occurs only in the Synoptic Gospels. (a) Jesus was filled with compassion when he saw various human needs, such as sick people who needed healing (Matt. 14:14; 20:34;

Mk. 1:41), the masses who were like sheep without a shepherd (Matt. 9:36; Mk. 6:34), the widow at Nain who mourned the death of her only son (Lk. 7:13), and the crowds who were hungry (Matt. 15:32; Mk. 8:2). In Mk. 9:22 a father asks Jesus to "take pity" on him and his demon-possessed son.

(b) In the parables of the unforgiving servant (Matt. 18:23–35) and the prodigal son (Lk. 15:11–32), *splanchnizomai* expresses the strong feeling of a merciful master (Matt. 18:27) or a loving father (Lk. 15:20). In both parables this vb. makes the unbounded mercy of God visible. In the parable of the good Samaritan (Lk. 10:30–37) the vb. expresses the Samaritan's willingness to use all means—time, strength, and life—for saving the wounded traveler (10:33; note the contrast with the priest and Levite, 10:31–32). Such action reflects the "mercy" (*eleos*, → *1799*) that Jesus expects of us (10:37). Humanity and neighborliness are not qualities but action.

2. The noun *splanchna* (pl., as in OT) denotes the "tender mercy" of God in Lk. 1:78 (with *eleos*, → *1799*). Elsewhere this noun is generally used (mostly in Paul) to refer to the whole person in his or her capacity to love. The frequent translation "heart" is suitable if we understand the heart as the center of loving and kind action. In 2 Cor. 6:12 Paul accuses his readers of showing him little affection, while in 7:15 he says of Titus that his heart went out to the Corinthians. In Phil. 1:8 Christ is the source of the love that embraces and lays claim to the apostle's personality.

splanchna occurs 3x in Phlm., which shows Paul's inner participation and personal concern in the matter of the runaway slave, Onesimus. In v. 7 Paul praises Philemon for his love and kindness, which have "refreshed the hearts of the saints," while in v. 20 Paul hopes that his own "heart" will be refreshed by Philemon's actions regarding the slave. In v. 12 the word can be rendered "as a piece of me" (NIV, "my very heart").

3. In Acts 1:18 the intestines in the physical sense are meant. In 1 Jn. 3:17 *splanchna* means the heart that expresses "pity" for someone in need.

4. Jas. 5:11 links *polysplanchnos* with *oiktirmōn* (→ *oiktirmos*, *3880*) in a phrase that means the "compassion and mercy" of God. *eusplanchnos*, compassionate, tenderhearted, is found in lists of Christian virtues in Eph. 4:32 and 1 Pet. 3:8.

See also *eleos*, compassion, mercy, pity (*1799*); *oiktirmos*, compassion, pity (*3880*).

5078 (*sporos*, seed), → *5065*.

5079 (*spoudazō*, to be zealous), → *5082*.

5080 (*spoudaios*, zealous), → *5082*.

5081 (*spoudaiōs*, eagerly), → *5082*.

5082	σπουδή

σπουδή (*spoudē*), zeal (*5082*); σπουδαῖος (*spoudaios*), zealous (*5080*); σπουδαίως (*spoudaiōs*), eagerly (*5081*); σπουδάζω (*spoudazō*), to be zealous (*5079*).

CL & OT 1. In cl. Gk. the words in this group denote quick movement in the interests of a person or cause: i.e., *spoudazō*, to hasten oneself; *spoudaios*, quick, hasty; *spoudē*, haste or speed. From there the words went on to suggest inner movement, e.g., for the vb., to be zealous, seek to do, be concerned for; for the adj., busy, active, industrious; for the noun, zeal, industry, effort. When used in contrast to play and joking, these words stress serious preoccupation with something. When used with a moral connotation *spoudē* means willingness, good will; *spoudaios* implies a person concerned with the good, a virtuous individual. In religious contexts the vb. means to involve oneself wholeheartedly.

2. *spoudē* and its cognates are normally used in the LXX with the meaning of urgency and haste (e.g., Gen. 19:15; Exod. 12:11, 33). Only in later OT writings does *spoudē* mean zeal (e.g., Wis. 14:17; Sir. 27:3).

NT 1. In the NT *spoudē* can mean haste (e.g., Lk. 1:39). In Lk. 7:4 *spoudaiōs* stresses the intensity of the request by which opposition should be overcome, and in 2 Tim. 1:17 it brings out the diligence of the search to overcome obstacles (cf. Tit. 3:13). In 1 Thess. 2:17 the vb. underlines the intensity of Paul's efforts to see the Thessalonian believers again. In 2 Pet. 1:15 the vb. and in Jude 3 the noun are used in connection with the writing of an important letter.

2. For Paul *spoudē* is a necessary expression of the life of the Christian community; it is a gift of God that must be developed. Its power should be seen in a solid "effort" to maintain unity (Eph. 4:3), to aid other Christians (Gal. 2:10; 2 Cor. 8:7, 8, 16), to make good of a wrong done (7:11–12), and to exercise leadership in the church (Rom. 12:8). All believers are expected to give themselves completely (12:11), and a zealous example can prove infectious (2 Cor. 8:8).

3. In later writings of the NT *spoudē* has a more general meaning. Our whole conduct of life must be molded by it, if we are not to lose what we have received (2 Tim. 2:15; Heb. 4:11; 6:11; 2 Pet. 1:5, 10; 3:14).

See also *zēlos*, zeal (*2419*).

5088	στατήρ

στατήρ (*statēr*), stater, a silver coin worth four drachmas (*5088*); δίδραχμον (*didrachmon*), a double drachma, two-drachma piece, worth about half a shekel among the Jews (*1440*); κῆνσος (*kēnsos*), tax, poll-tax (*3056*); δηνάριον (*dēnarion*), denarius, a day's wage (*1324*); φόρος (*phoros*), tax, tribute (*5843*).

CL & OT 1. In cl. Gk. the *statēr* was a silver (later gold) coin of a certain weight. The *drachma* was a coin of much less value, comparable to a Roman *denarius*. Three Gk. words could be used to indicate a tax or tribute: *kēnsos*, *telos* (→ *telōnion*, customs house, tax office, *5468*), and *phoros* (a tribute paid by foreigners to a city state).

2. The LXX uses both *drachma* (e.g., Gen. 24:22; Exod. 38:26 = LXX 39:2; NIV "beka") and *didrachma* (e.g., Gen. 20:16; 23:15–16; NIV "shekel") for Israelite currency, but it also uses a transliterated word *siklos* for the Heb. *šeqel* (shekel). Before the exile there were no real coins; metals were fashioned into lumps of recognized weights. Various forms of shekels are mentioned (e.g., "by the royal standard," 2 Sam. 14:26; "the sanctuary shekel," Lev. 5:15). Exod. 30:11–16 states that when the Israelites were subjected to a census in the desert, Moses ordered each man to pay half a shekel as ransom money to prevent the plague spreading among the people. The money raised in this way was spent on the tabernacle (30:16; 38:25–28).

When Solomon built the first temple, he raised heavy taxes and used forced labor (1 Ki. 4:6; 5:13–14; *phoros*), both of which were resented (12:4). In 2 Ki. 12:10 we read of a collection box for the upkeep of the temple, but 2 Chr. 24:6, 9 refers to what was levied by Moses as something that was to be perpetuated. Neh. 10:32 speaks of this tax as a third of a shekel (LXX *didrachma*), but it was evidently raised to half a shekel later. Every Israelite male over twenty had to pay. It was paid as long as the temple stood. The Romans evidently recognized this as a Jewish religious obligation. Jews of the Diaspora contributed, and the bullion trains required strong protection. After the destruction of the temple, Vespasian decreed that the tax should still be paid, not to the Jewish temple, but to Jupiter Capitolinus.

NT 1. The temple tax lies in the background of Matt. 17:24–27. Tax collectors approach Peter as a representative disciple of Jesus and ask him whether his leader has ever paid the standard contribution (*didrachma*) to the support of the temple as required in Exod. 30:11–16. Since Jesus and his followers constantly moved from one place to another, it was difficult for tax agents to make contact with them. But now that they are back in Capernaum, this matter can be dealt with.

After Jesus makes the point that as the Son of God it is not really appropriate for him to pay a tax to his own Father, he directs Peter nevertheless to secure the money for payment by going down to the lake, casting in his fish line, and pulling up the first fish to strike his bait. In its mouth he will find a *statēr* (Matt. 17:27)—probably a *tetradrachma* (i.e., a four-drachma coin; already in Ptolemaic times the term *statēr* was applied to the four-drachma piece, thus sufficient to pay the tax for Jesus and Peter). Most likely this coin was a Tyrian shekel. Because of its high silver content and standardized weight, the Tyrian shekel was generally preferred in Palestine, despite the paganism of its symbols.

In the context of Matt. this story illustrates the distinction Jesus draws between his own followers as the true people of God and the Jewish nation. The disciples are the true sons of God who do not need to pay tribute to aliens. But to avoid giving offense the tax is paid.

2. The best-known discussion of any coin in Scripture occurs when Jesus is questioned as to whether it is lawful to pay taxes to Caesar (Mk. 12:13–17). His enemies feel they have him on the horns of a dilemma. If he answers that it is acceptable to pay tribute to Rome, this will offend the religionists who oppose any support to a pagan power; but if he declares himself opposed to paying of such taxes, he can incur the charge of fomenting sedition and be immediately turned over to the Roman authorities.

In answer to their craftiness, Jesus simply asks the Jewish leaders to produce a silver *dēnarion* from their own pockets. Holding it up before them he points out that the portrait on the obverse is that of the Roman emperor and that the inscription bears Caesar's name. They obviously have no compunctions about using this money, with all of its advantages of protection for law-abiding citizens and the safeguarding of their financial security. The leaders also have no scruples about accepting Roman law and order and military defense against marauding invaders. Therefore, their pious question concerning the legitimacy of paying taxes to the government is nothing more than arrant hypocrisy. Thus Jesus answered: "Give to Caesar what is Caesar's [the money and support necessary for a strong, efficient government] and to God what is God's [not only their tithes and temple taxes, but also the worship of their hearts and the faithful obedience to his revealed will]" (Mk. 12:17).

3. In Rom. 13:6–7 Paul also adopts the same attitude of Jesus with regard to payment of taxes to the Roman state: "This is also why you pay taxes [*phoros*], for the authorities are God's servants.... Give everyone what you owe him. If you owe taxes [*phoros*], pay taxes; if revenue [*telos*], then revenue." The premises of Paul's position are that "there is no authority except that which God has established" (13:1; cf. 1 Pet. 2:13–14), that these have been instituted for the well-being of the human race (Rom. 13:2–3), and that to resist what God has appointed is to resist God and thus provoke divine wrath (13:4–5).

See also *logeia*, collection (of money), tax (*3356*); *telōnion*, customs house, tax office (*5468*).

5089	σταυρός

σταυρός (*stauros*), stake, cross (*5089*); σταυρόω (*stauroō*), hang upon a cross, crucify (*5090*); ἀνασταυρόω (*anastauroō*), crucify (*416*); συσταυρόω (*systauroō*), crucify with (*5365*); κρεμάννυμι (*kremannymi*), hang (*3203*).

CL 1. *stauros* is an upright, sometimes pointed stake. It may serve for fencing, a foundation, and a palisade. Similarly, *stauroō* means drive in stakes or erect a palisade. Both the noun and vb. have a more specific meaning in connection with punishment, though this occurred in a variety of ways. The vb. is more common in the compound *anastauroō*, which means hang up, impale, apparently always in public. Corresponding to the vb., *stauros* can mean a stake on which an already executed criminal was publicly displayed in shame as a further punishment. But *stauros* can also itself be an instrument of execution in the form of a vertical stake and a cross-beam of the same length.

2. In order to determine the exact technical form and significance of execution as conveyed by *stauros* and (*ana*)*stauroō*, one needs to know in what region and under what authority the execution was carried out. It is also necessary to know the standpoint of the writer who uses these terms.

(a) The East and West had a fundamental difference over the question of execution and its means. The East hanged and impaled bodies that were already executed, sometimes by decapitation. But this form of punishment was not practiced in the West. Hanging or fastening to a stake, beam, or cross was itself a means of execution. In this method, a more or less quick death was effected by strangulation, although hanging could also be long and painful for the victim. Execution by crucifixion was known in Greece and Carthage.

(b) In Judea at the time of Jesus sentencing to crucifixion and execution was entirely in the hands of Roman authorities. As with the Gks. and probably throughout the East, freedmen with Roman citizenship were exempted from crucifixion. This method of execution, therefore, was reserved for slaves, foreigners, and inhabitants of foreign provinces. As a rule, it was used only in cases of serious crimes, such as treason. It is understandable that in Palestine crucifixion constituted an important punitive weapon in the hands of the Roman occupying power, by which it sought to deal effectively with any resistance to its authority. This method of death was intended more as a deterrent than as a means of retribution. This explains why a cross was set up in an open place. Contemporary writers condemned this form of execution as excessively cruel.

There were two possible ways of erecting the *stauros*. The condemned man could be fastened to the cross lying on the ground at the place of execution, then lifted up. Alternatively, the stake would already be implanted in the ground before the execution. The victim was tied to the crossbeam, hoisted up with the horizontal beam, and tied fast to the vertical stake. The cross was probably not much higher than the height of a man.

According to Roman practice, there was first a legal conviction. If the execution was to take place somewhere other than the place of sentencing, the condemned man carried the crossbeam to the spot of crucifixion, usually outside the town. At that place the victim was stripped and scourged. He was then tied or nailed with outstretched arms to the crossbeam and hoisted on to the stake with the crossbeam. Death came slowly after extraordinary agony, probably through exhaustion and/or suffocation. The body could be left on the scaffold to rot or provide food for predatory animals and carrion crows. Occasionally the body was given to relatives or acquaintances for burial.

3. Oriental ways of execution were known in ancient Israel and were in part followed. In Joseph's interpretation of the dream of an Egyptian court official, Pharaoh would behead the baker and dishonor him by leaving his body hanging on a stake (Gen. 40:18–19). The body of Saul was beheaded by the Philistines and then hung to a wall (1 Sam. 31:9–10). Darius made a decree that anyone infringing an edict of Cyrus should have a beam pulled from his house and be impaled on it (Ezr. 6:11). The regulation in Deut. 21:22–23 clearly shows that penal procedure in Israel followed general oriental practice. The penalty is applied here to capital offenses, but a specific limitation is also made: The corpse was not to remain on the tree overnight, lest the land be defiled (cf. Jos. 8:29; 10:26).

4. The LXX never uses the noun *stauros*. The vb. *stauroō* occurs only in Est. 7:9; 8:13; possibly Lam. 5:13; these usages are somewhat ambiguous. Josephus records that the Jewish ruler Alexander Jannaeus (103–76 B.C.) ordered a mass execution by hanging men alive on stakes. This violent attack was an unusual procedure, detested and not normally practiced in Jud.

NT In the NT *stauros*, *anastauroō* and *stauroō*, and *systauroō* occur essentially in three sets of textual and theological complexes: (1) in the passion narratives of the Gospels (Matt. 27:1–2, 11–61; Mk. 15:1–47; Lk. 23:1–56; Jn. 18:28–19:37; cf. also Matt. 20:19; Lk. 24:20; Acts 2:36; 4:10; Rev. 11:8); (2) in the theological reflection of Paul's letters (some 20x); (3) in Jesus' sayings about bearing one's cross (Matt. 10:38; 16:24; Mk. 8:34; Lk. 9:23; 14:27).

1. *The crucifixion of Jesus as a historical and theological question.* Paul speaks of Christ's cross in numerous places, but he gives no details about the event. However, 1 Thess. 2:15–16 is important in view of the fact that he sees the church of his day threatened by persecution from the Jews in a parallel situation to Jesus: They "killed the Lord Jesus and the prophets and also drove us out" (cf. also Matt. 23:34).

The Jews and their representatives similarly appear in Mk. as the driving force behind the crucifixion. It is at their instigation that Jesus is arrested (14:43–49), tried, and sentenced to death by the Sanhedrin (14:53–64). Pilate recognizes their motives but finds no legal grounds for this condemnation. Finally for political reasons, he gives in to the people, who have been stirred up by the Jewish leaders to demand Jesus' crucifixion. The theologically significant insults heaped on the crucified Jesus come from the lips of passing Jews and those who represent the Jewish nation and its theology (15:29–32).

The other Evangelists include other material that likewise implicates the Jews. Pilate's wife urges her husband not to have anything to do with Jesus, "for I have suffered a great deal today in a dream because of him" (Matt. 27:19). Pilate washes his hands and declares, "I am innocent of this man's blood. . . . It is your responsibility," which the crowd accepts (27:24–25). Lk. records the saying, "Daughters of Jerusalem, do not weep for me; weep for yourselves and for your children" (Lk. 23:28). He expresses the Evangelists' typical attitude in the words of Peter addressed to the Jews at Pentecost: "this Jesus, whom you crucified" (Acts 2:36).

(a) Any historical reconstruction must be based on the following. (i) In Judea in the NT era, capital jurisdiction belonged to the imperial representative alone. (ii) Pilate's judicial decision for the *stauros* was decisive. (iii) If he used any justification to crucify Jesus, it would have been on the basis of Jesus being an agitator, not a blasphemer. (iv) The execution was carried out by the Romans according to their practice. (v) Jesus died on the cross as an instrument of torture, probably slowly through suffocation or exhaustion. (vi) Known Roman practice authenticates the account of Jesus' scourging, the removal of his clothing, and the guard of Roman soldiers at the place of execution. (vii) Jesus bore the crossbeam to the place of execution outside the city (Mk. 15:20b–21).

(b) Exegetical and theological considerations also demand close scrutiny of the historical question. Matt. and especially Lk. exhibit differences from Mk.'s account; Jn. deals with the passion narrative quite differently. In each case a writer's theological motives can be ascertained. The oldest tradition of the crucifixion of Jesus, used by Mk., shows a definite tendency to see the relationship of these events to Ps. 22 (cf. Ps. 22:1 [Matt. 27:46; Mk. 15:34], 6–7 [Matt. 27:39, 43; Mk. 15:29; Lk. 23:35], 8 [Matt. 27:43], 18 [Matt. 27:35; Mk. 15:24; Lk. 23:34b; Jn. 19:24], 22 [Heb. 2:12]). Attempts to harmonize the account should not be allowed to obscure such theological intentions.

Passages like Heb. 2:14–18; 3:14; 4:14–15; 5:7–10 indicate additional reasons for the early church's interest in the story of the crucifixion and suffering of its Lord. Basic is its confession of the crucified Jesus as the one exalted to God in the sense of a cosmic, saving act. When the church saw itself attacked, persecuted, and suffering as a consequence of this confession, its interest in the earthly career of its Lord came to the fore. The Savior led the way as an obligatory pattern of suffering for his followers.

The basis of Jewish opposition to Jesus is stated as envy (Matt. 27:18; Mk. 15:10); Jn. presents the actions of Caiaphas as being motivated by expediency (Jn. 11:49–50). But there was a genuine theological zeal that was present in the Jews' attitude to Jesus and their reaction to the early church. The repudiation of the craving for legitimization of "the message of the cross" by "miraculous signs" (1 Cor. 1:18–25) is reflected in the crucifixion narrative of Matt. 27:39–43; Mk. 15:29–32; Lk. 23:35–39.

The historical question of responsibility for the crucifixion must be discussed without prejudice. But equally the question of guilt transcends the time of Jesus. This aspect is shown by Heb. 6:6, where those who commit apostasy are said to be "crucifying [*anastaurountas*, pres. part.] the Son of God all over again and subjecting him to public disgrace." The question of guilt for the cross of Christ remains a contemporary one, wherever one's righteousness is presented as grounded in the grace of God, demanding self-surrender in faith.

2. *The theological significance of the crucifixion of Jesus.* (a) Paul's earlier letters. The use of the *stauros* word group in a theological sense occurs most frequently in Paul's earlier letters (17x): *stauros*, 7x; *stauroō*, 8x; *systauroō*, 2x. All these statements see the cross of Christ as the saving event that radically transforms the world.

The gospel embraces "the message of the cross," i.e., the saving proclamation based on the cross of Christ (1 Cor. 1:17–18; cf. 2:1–2; Rom. 1:16; Gal. 3:1). That cross is not an isolated event in history but the act of God; that is, the transcendent God acts as the cross of Christ is proclaimed, his liberating message to humankind. That proclamation did not paint the historic details of the crucifixion before the eyes of its hearers. Instead, it publicly proclaimed Jesus Christ as the Crucified One, portraying him as God's saving event in terms of the law (cf. Gal. 3:1).

The message of the cross brings *sōtēria*, salvation (→ *sōzō*, 5392). This is indeed only to those who believe (1 Cor. 1:21), who submit to God's verdict in the cross of Christ, even though it may appear foolishness. This condemnatory and at the same time liberating message of salvation is folly and scandalous not only to the Jews and Greeks (1:18–25). It is also this to any perverted form of Christianity, whether it is enamored of its own religious experiences (like the Corinthian church) or whether it falls back into a legalism that effectively denies the cross of Christ (like the Galatians).

This identification of the gospel with the cross of Christ is underlined by Phil. 2:8. Most scholars regard Phil. 2:6–11 as an early hymn about Christ's emptying of himself of his heavenly glory and humiliating himself by becoming obedient to death (which Paul incorporated into his argument to urge Christians to have the mind of Christ). But Paul was not satisfied merely with the statement in the hymn about the death of Christ; he added the words "even death on a cross."

This focus on the theology of the cross coincides with Paul's particular emphases. For example, 1 Cor. 1:13 shows how he used the traditional interpretation of the death of Jesus (cf. 15:3) to respond to the disunity among the Corinthians: "Was Paul crucified for you?" Paul had not brought about salvation; the Corinthians were not his property. Thus, there was no basis for dividing the church as the body of Christ on his account. Paul uses here the preposition *hyper* in connection with *stauroō* in a way that was characteristic of the early church's sacrificial and representative theology. Moreover, the whole argument of Rom. reveals how Paul thinks of Christ's death as a representative sacrifice bearing the punishment of sin on behalf of others (cf. Paul's use of *hyper*, instead of, in the place of, in connection with the death of Christ in such crucial passages as 1 Cor. 15:3 and Gal. 3:13; cf. Rom. 5:10–11, 18; 1 Cor. 11:24–25; Eph. 1:7; 1 Tim. 2:6).

Morever, Paul's theology of the cross has its own special emphases. Paul saw all humans as unredeemed, not simply because of an uncleanness brought about by the accumulation of individual acts of sin, but because of a basic, depraved, self-seeking hostility to God that rejects God's offer to liberate us. This appears in the presumptuous demand that God's message should be validated by miraculous proofs and that the gospel of God should conform to worldly wisdom (see 1 Cor. 1:22). In effect, we judge God and discount the cross and its proclamation for our justification and salvation (1 Cor. 1:19–29; Gal. 2:19–21).

For Paul, it is not enough to speak simply of "Christ." For "Christ" could be understood as a glorified Christ, removed from the world and removing us from the world. Paul sets alongside the word *Christos* the unambiguous *estaurōmenos* (crucified, 1 Cor. 1:23; Gal. 3:1). He speaks with special emphasis in 1 Cor. 2:2: "I resolved to know nothing while I was with you except Jesus Christ and him crucified." This intensification reflects his experience in Corinth and in general (Gal. 3:1). The cross of Christ alone is Paul's ground for boasting and confidence (cf. Gal. 6:14). In practical terms, this means that Paul boasted most gladly of his weaknesses (2 Cor. 12:9–10).

The practical significance of the resurrection is implied in Paul's teaching about the cross. He presents Christ crucified as the decisive act of God in salvation. The risen Christ does not simply cancel out or supersede the crucified Christ. Through the exaltation his self-humiliation and obedient death are raised in power as the sign of salvation (Phil. 2:8–11). Christ, who took on himself this weakness and was thus crucified, now lives by reason of the creative power of God, who raises the dead (2 Cor. 13:4). Believers enter this resurrection life that comes from God, an act that conquers death in the believers' existence under the cross. This teaching forms the basis of the apostle's existence under the cross (1 Cor. 15:30–32). Without the resurrection Paul's life would be the most pitiable self-deception imaginable (15:19).

The cross of Christ and the crucified Christ are alone the power and wisdom of God (1 Cor. 1:18–24). They form Paul's answer to a church that was preoccupied with power, fame, and wisdom and was thus dividing the body of Christ (1:10–4:21). They also apply to renunciation of one's rights (6:1–11) and even to one's proper freedom for the sake of others (8:1–11:1). In addition, Paul also refers to an astonishing extent to his own mode of life and preaching. They represent the way of life controlled by the cross of Christ (1:17, 23; 2:1–5; 3:5–15; 4:6; cf. also the exhortations to imitate Paul, which occasionally round off the longer sections, 4:16; 11:1).

The fundamental pattern here is Christ, especially his renunciation of his rights (1 Cor. 11:1) and his humiliation to death on the cross for the sake of others (Phil. 2:1–11). To this also belongs Heb. 12:2. The afflicted are exhorted to look to Jesus, who endured the cross, despising its shame because of the joy that was set before him.

Paul speaks of some people as "enemies of the cross of Christ" (Phil. 3:18) in the context of a call to imitate the example of himself and others (3:17). These enemies are those who strive after earthly things and whose lives are not shaped by the message of the cross (3:18–19). They are those who have not sought salvation in Christ crucified. They have not, like Paul, left their legalistic existence behind them, sought to know the sufferings of Christ, or be conformed to his death (3:7–11).

What Paul says about the preaching of the cross in 1 Cor., about humility in Phil. 2, about justification in Phil. 3, and in all three places about imitation and its practical application, he also develops in relation to baptism (Rom. 6; cf. Gal. 2:20). Christ has died (Rom. 6:10), and thus Christians have also died with him (6:2). They have been thereby, like him, freed from the guilt and power of sin (6:10). Baptism into Christ means baptism into his death (6:3). Baptism thus represents the all-encompassing event of Christ's death. Believers are thus crucified with Christ (*systauroō*, Rom. 6:6; Gal. 2:20).

At the same time, through the cross of Christ the compelling power of the world has been crucified for the benefit of the believer's inner self. Those who have become Christ's possession have crucified the sinful nature "with its passions and desires" (Gal. 5:24). In this they are not merely passive; it is something they do themselves. The continuing role of the cross of Christ in the believer brings about a radical transformation of daily living (cf. 6:14).

(b) Col. and Eph. adopt a somewhat different approach from Paul's other letters (*stauros* alone occurs, 3x). Col. does continue the earlier Pauline teaching that in Rom. 6 relates dying with Christ to baptism (Col. 2:12; cf. 3:3), a process that liberates us from the enslaving, cosmic powers (2:20; → *stoicheon, 5122*). Paul's exhortation to put to death what is earthly in us (3:5–9) is the outworking of the decisive saving event of the death of Christ (cf. Gal. 5:24). Eph., by contrast, speaks only of the believer's being made alive in Christ (2:1; cf. 1:20; 2:6; Col. 3:1). Neither Col. nor Eph. make any specific reference to a believer's being crucified with Christ. The development of soteriological ideas is correspondingly less rigorous than in the earlier letters (cf. Col. 2:12 with Rom. 6:6).

However, Col. and Eph. develop a theology of the cosmic significance of the Christ event that is not found in the earlier letters. With Christ's "blood . . . shed on the cross" as its basis, reconciliation of all things to God has taken place through Christ's exaltation and assumption of authority (Col. 1:19–20). Eph. 2:16 develops this thought in a specific direction, declaring that God's purpose was to "reconcile both [Jew and Gentile] to God through the cross, by which he put to death their hostility."

Col. 2:14–15 further develops the cosmic significance of the cross, in that God "canceled the written code, with its regulations, that was against us and that stood opposed to us; he took it away, nailing it to the cross." Two pictures are combined here. (i) There is the picture of debt, drawn from the ancient business world. This represents the ordinances of the Jewish law and the dictates of the false teachers; its accusing testimony is canceled. (ii) There is also the picture of a public, official decree that has been posted (cf. the sign typically posted on a cross, giving the reason for a criminal's punishment). Taken together these pictures show that Christ himself made the cross into a public declaration, proclaiming the cancellation of our sins and the end of all claim to legalism.

3. *The sayings about bearing the cross.* These sayings occur 5x in the Synoptic Gospels (Matt. 10:38; 16:24; Mk. 8:34; Lk. 9:23; 14:27). Jesus emphasizes that if believers want to gain life, they will not be exempted from a life of self-renunciation, perhaps even martyrdom. The way of Christ is also the way for Christians. These sayings, in other words, are the equivalent of Paul's theology of the cross.

Jesus became increasingly aware that because of the attitude of the religious leaders of his day, he would be put to death at the hands of the Romans through crucifixion. He also knew of the practice of a condemned man bearing the crossbeam of the cross. Whatever fate awaited him would also await those who followed him. The sayings about bearing the cross form part of his warning to his disciples to count the cost (see the context of Matt. 10:38; Lk. 14:27). Note also Jesus' warning that a servant is not above his or her master (Matt. 10:24; cf. Lk. 6:40; Jn. 13:16; 15:20).

See also *xylon*, wood, tree (*3833*).

5090 (stauroō, hang on a cross, crucify), → *5089.*

5098 (stemma, garland), → *5109.*

5099 (stenagmos, sigh, groan, groaning), → *5100.*

5100 στενάζω

στενάζω (*stenazō*), to sigh, groan (*5100*); στεναγμός (*stenagmos*), sigh, groan, groaning (*5099*).

CL & OT 1. *stenazō* in cl. Gk. means sighing or moaning. *stenagmos* connotes a sighing or groaning.

2. In the LXX *stenazō* has various meanings. In Isa. 19:8 it denotes the general concept of mourning. On several occasions it means to sigh or groan, suggesting grief as a result of physical suffering, loss, or distress (24:7; Lam. 1:8, 21; Ezek. 21:6–7). It can also describe the groaning of the wounded (28:19).

In Isa. 59:11 *stenazō* describes the roaring of a bear. In Job 31:38 it is used fig. for the crying out of the land, in 24:12 for the crying out of the wounded, and in 30:25 for a personal grief for the poor.

3. The noun *stenagmos* has the same flavor of meanings. In Exod. 2:24; 6:5; Jdg. 2:18 it is used of groaning as a result of physical affliction and distress. In Ps. 38:8 it describes the groaning of the psalmist in distress, while in Jer. 4:31 it describes the anguish of a woman in labor. In Gen. 3:16, however, the noun bears a metaphorical meaning for pregnancy.

NT *stenazō* in Mk. 7:34 describes the general sense of sighing as an expression of inward emotion. Paul uses the term exclusively of sighing in the sense of deeply longing for something (Rom. 8:23; 2 Cor. 5:2, 4). In Heb. 13:17, however, it stands as the antithesis of "joy" and means "burden." James uses the vb. to instruct believers not to "grumble against each another" (Jas. 5:9).

The noun *stenagmos* occurs 2x in the NT. In Acts 7:34 it describes the groaning of the Israelites in their slavery in Egypt. In Rom. 8:26 it refers to the interceding Spirit's "groans that words cannot express." There is a progression in the context where Paul moves from the groaning of the creation (8:22) to the groaning of the Christian (8:23). Such groaning is shared by the Holy Spirit and the believer. The Spirit utilizes these deep groanings in intercession for believers. They are in turn observed by the one who "searches our hearts" (8:27). The deep emotive elements in *stenagmos* should be retained here (for more on this passage, → *entynchanō*, *1961*).

See also *klaiō*, weep (*3081*); *koptō*, strike (*3164*); *lypeō*, inflict pain (*3382*); *brychō*, gnash (*1107*); *pentheō*, be sad, grieve, mourn (*4291*).

5102 (*stenochōreō*, crowd, cramp, confine, oppress), → *2568*.

5103 (*stenochōria*, straits, distress, affliction, difficulty), → *2568*.

| 5109   στέφανος |

στέφανος (*stephanos*), wreath, crown (*5109*); στεφανόω (*stephanoō*), crown (someone) (*5110*); στέμμα (*stemma*), garland (*5098*); διάδημα (*diadēma*), diadem, crown (*1343*).

CL & OT 1. (a) *stephanos* was used originally of anything that encircles, such as a besieging army or the wall around a city. It developed into its usual meaning of crown or wreath, esp. the victor's wreath of leaves at athletic games. The *stephanos* in fact bore diverse connotations: of victory, festivity, worship, public office or honor, kingship, or royal visitation. *stephanos* and the vb. *stephanoō* were often used fig. to denote an object of pride.

(b) *stemma* was used esp. of the laurel wreath of a sacrificing priest.

(c) *diadēma* was the band around the tiara of the Persian king, worn also by Alexander and later kings, and so generally denoted a crown as a badge of kingship.

2. (a) In the LXX *stephanos* usually refers to a royal crown (e.g., 2 Sam. 12:30) and is used as a figure for honor, victory, or pride. *diadēma* is applied in Est. 1:11; 2:17 to the royal crown of Persia, but occurs more frequently in the Apocr. (also there with metaphorical senses; e.g., Wis. 5:16; Sir. 47:6).

(b) The crown was a frequent image in later Jud. The expectation of a "crown of glory" appears in *T. Benj.* 4:1. There were said to be three crowns: of Torah, priesthood, and royalty.

NT 1. *diadēma* occurs 3x in the NT and signifies the kingship of the dragon (Rev. 12:3), of the beast (13:1), and of Christ (19:2). *stemma* is used only in Acts 14:13 of the "wreaths" brought by the pagan priest who was planning to offer sacrifices to Paul and Barnabas at Lystra.

2. *stephanos* occurs 18x. It is used of Jesus' "crown of thorns" (Matt. 27:29; Mk. 15:17; Jn. 19:2, 5). To the soldiers it meant mock royalty, to the Evangelists it constituted testimony to the true kingship of Christ over a spiritual kingdom, while perhaps also implying his forthcoming victory over death.

This same word is used for the prize of athletic victory and as a metaphor for the eternal reward of the faithful (1 Cor. 9:25; 2 Tim. 2:5; 4:8; Jas. 1:12 ["crown of life"]; 1 Pet. 5:4 ["crown of glory"]; Rev. 3:11; 4:4, 10). In two cases the believer's eternal hope is set against the transience of perishable wreaths (1 Cor. 9:25; 1 Pet. 5:4). In 2 Tim. 4:8 Christ at his Parousia will bestow on his people "a crown of righteousness."

Paul calls the church at Philippi his *stephanos*, that is, his pride or glory (Phil. 4:1). The Thessalonians (1 Thess. 2:19) are Paul's joyful tribute to the coming Christ. The imagery used here may link with an ancient practice in which a ruler was presented with a crown as a token of one's allegiance (cf. 1 Macc. 13:37; 2 Macc. 14:4).

The phrase "crown of life" in Rev. 2:10 (cf. Jas. 1:12) is of special interest. The gen. here is best taken as epexegetical, that is, the prize "that consists in life." The term was particularly appropriate in Smyrna, where a crown or wreath was a pervasively common numismatic emblem. Eternal life, untouched by the threat of spiritual death, will be the prize of all those faithful who endure persecution to the suffering of death. Such people will share the experience of him "who died and came to life again" (Rev. 2:8).

3. *stephanoō* in Heb. 2:7, 9 is used in a messianic application of Ps. 8:5. While some see a reference here to the transfiguration or Christ's crown of thorns, the words probably refer to his future glory (cf. Phil. 2:9).

5110 (*stephanoō*, crown [someone]), → *5109*.

5113 (*stērigmos*, steadfastness), → *5114*.

| 5114   στηρίζω |

στηρίζω (*stērizō*), make fast, establish, strengthen (*5114*); ἐπιστηρίζω (*epistērizō*), strengthen (*2185*); στηριγμός (*stērigmos*), steadfastness (*5113*); ἀστήρικτος (*astēriktos*), unstable (*844*).

CL & OT 1. In cl. Gk. *stērizō* means primarily to fix something so that it remains stable and secure, such as supporting a vine with a stake. In a fig. sense, it came to mean to confirm or establish. In the field of medicine it could mean to gain bodily strength, to strengthen.

2. In the LXX *stērizō* at times denotes physical support, such as the ladder that Jacob saw in his dream resting on the earth (Gen. 28:12) and Moses' hands being supported by Aaron and Hur (Exod. 17:12). Likewise, *epistērizō* is used of the pillars that supported the Philistine temple (Jdg. 16:26, 29). *stērizō* also denotes food that strengthens and refreshes a person (Jdg. 19:5, 8).

Often the words in this group describe giving moral or spiritual support. In 2 Ki. 18:21 Sennacherib's field commander uses *stērizō* in a warning to Hezekiah that leaning on Egypt for aid will prove ineffective. By contrast, David prays for God to sustain him with a willing spirit (Ps. 51:12). The psalmist in Ps. 111:8 affirms that God's laws are dependable, and in 112:8 that because he trusts in the Lord, his heart is secure. *epistērizō* is used in Ps. 71:6 for the psalmist's reliance on God since birth.

Finally *stērizō* is used 10x in Ezek. for God's command to the prophet to "set" his face against Israel and other nations and to prophesy judgment against them.

NT 1. *stērizō* occurs 13x in the NT, *epistērizō* 4x (all in Acts); *stērigmos* and *astēriktos* occur only in 2 Pet. (once and 2x respectively). In the parable of the rich man and Lazarus, Abraham stresses that the gulf between heaven and hell "has been fixed" (Lk. 16:26). In a phrase similar to Ezek., Lk. 9:51 says that Jesus resolved (lit., "set his face") to go to Jerusalem.

2. Far more frequent are the fig. uses of this word group. All four uses of *epistērizō* stress the strengthening of churches through the word of the Lord (Acts 14:22; 15:32, 41; 18:23). In Rom. 1:11 Paul hopes that his visit to Rome will "make [them] strong" (in this sense, *stērizō* is similar to *parakaleō*, encourage, → *4151*). On several occasions Paul prays that God will strengthen believers (Rom. 16:25; 1 Thess. 3:2, 13; 2 Thess. 2:17; 3:3; cf. 1 Pet. 5:10), esp. in the context of the opposition they are facing.

3. Peter uses *stērigmos* in 2 Pet. 3:17 to encourage believers to be on their guard against heretics and instead to remain steadfast in their faith. *astēriktos*, by contrast, is used to describe the instability of these heretics (3:16) and their protégés (2:14).

| 5116   στίγμα |

στίγμα (*stigma*), mark, brand (*5116*).

CL & OT 1. In cl. Gk. *stigma* is related to the vb. *stizō*, to prick, mark with a pointed instrument, hence, to brand, tattoo. *stigmata* (pl.)

were used to mark cattle and other animals as a protection against theft. *stigmata* applied to the human body were a sign of disgrace, used on deserters. Criminals were marked as a punishment, and esp. slaves suffered this penalty if they ran away and were caught or broke the law in some other way. The imperial period saw the branding of slaves as a mark of ownership; the mark was usually placed on the forehead. Stigmata could also be used as a sign of devotion to the gods.

2. The LXX has *stigmata* only once, and then with an insignificant meaning (Song 1:11 for earrings "studded" with silver). Nonetheless, the idea behind the word is present in several cases: when slaves were marked as a badge of ownership (Exod. 21:6; Deut. 15:16–17), when Cain was given a mark as a sign of Yahweh's preservation of his life (Gen. 4:15), when the remnant of the Israelite faithful were marked with the Heb. letter *tāw* as a pledge of their safety against the day of judgment (Ezek. 9:4), and esp. when Yahweh's people are bidden to inscribe his name on their hands as a promise of fidelity (Isa. 44:5).

Real *stigmata* (cuts on the body and "tattoo marks") were expressly forbidden in Israel, according to Lev. 19:28 (the related Gk. word used here, *stikta*, does not occur in the NT). Only in her apostate days did Israel borrow this practice from the Gentile nations (Jer. 16:6; 41:5; cf. 47:5; 48:37). True Yahwism is thus differentiated from the practices of the nations (1 Ki. 18:28), but 20:41 may be an exception if the prophet had Yahweh's "mark" on his forehead.

In the intertestamental period Jews were branded by their captors (*Pss. Sol.* 2:6), and slaves were branded to prevent their escape. The Hel. persecution of Jews took the form of the forcible imposition of pagan symbols, and Philo regarded the willing acceptance of a brand as a hallmark of apostasy. Jews regarded circumcision as the effective antidote to the desire to be tattooed, since a loyal Jew had this badge of his membership of the elect race and needed no other religious marking. Marks on bodies (in a fig. sense) and on grave sites in a literal fashion suggest a protective claim to belong to Yahweh (cf. *Pss. Sol.* 15:6–9). The sign of the *tāw* on Jewish tombs and ossuaries was a development of Ezek. 9:4.

NT The single NT occurrence of *stigma* is in Gal. 6:17. Perhaps Paul is referring to his claim to ownership by the Lord Jesus, whose slave Paul is. Or he may be implying some badge of protection that none of his enemies in Galatia can ignore with impunity (the Galatians would be familiar with the idea of a religious teacher being under the care of the gods and so immune from attack). Or perhaps the *stigmata* serve as a Christian counterpart to Jewish circumcision, a sign of eschatological fulfillment marking out the new Israel (6:16) as the true circumcision (cf. Phil. 3:3).

These *stigmata* are not to be seen as deliberately marked symbols (e.g., as though Paul had tattooed the sign of the cross or the name of Jesus on his flesh). Rather, they are scars and wounds received in his missionary service on behalf of the Gentiles (Eph. 3:1, 13; Col. 1:24).

See also *charagma*, mark, stamp, graven object (*5916*); *kaustēriazō*, mark by a branding iron, brand (*3013*).

5122	στοιχεῖον

στοιχεῖον (*stoicheion*), element; usually pl. *stoicheia*, elements, rudiments (*5122*); στοιχέω (*stoicheō*), be in line with, hold to (*5123*); συστοιχέω (*systoicheō*), stand in the same line, correspond to, conform to (*5368*).

CL & OT 1. The root *stoichos* means row, rank, line, esp. battle line. The vb. *stoicheō* thus means to be in a row, remain in a line, march in rank and file, or (metaphorically) step into line. The noun *to stoicheion* denoted the shadow on a sundial or (fig.) a part of a word (i.e., a letter, a syllable), a component of the universe (i.e., beginning, foundation, etc.).

2. In the LXX *stoicheion* occurs only in the Apocr. (3x, always pl.). In Wis. 7:17; 19:18 it means "elements of the universe" or "mat-

ter," and in 4 Macc. 12:13, "the substance of human life." *stoicheō* is found only in Eccl. 11:6, in the sense to succeed, to prosper.

NT 1. In the NT *stoicheō* occurs only 5x. Acts 21:24c gives the clearest sense: (lit.) "you too are in the ranks as one who keeps the law." In other words, it refers to leading a closely regulated life, to living according to definite rules. This is also shown by Phil. 3:16: "Only let us live up [*stoichein*] to what we have already attained." In Gal. 6:16 Paul uses the word *kanōn* to describe the rule just given in 6:15 and links it with the vb. *stoicheō*: "follow this rule." Gal. 5:25b should thus be paraphrased: "conduct our lives in conformity with the Spirit" (cf. also Rom. 4:12, when the vb. is translated "walk").

The compound *systoicheō* (Gal. 4:25) interprets the meaning of one of the two lines of descent from Abraham in 4:22–25, that of slavery: Hagar belongs to the same line (*systoichei*) as the present city of Jerusalem. Sinai, the mountain on which the law was given, is here linked with *stoicheō*, just as "law" is in Acts 21:24.

2. The noun is used 7x in the NT letters (always in the pl.; 4x in Paul, once in Heb., and 2x in 2 Pet.). The uses in 2 Pet. 3:10, 12, are the simplest to interpret. The reference to "the elements" (3:10) means earth, water, and air, of which only the first is named explicitly. When the world is consumed, these elements will melt and be destroyed (3:10, 12) in the primeval element, fire.

The meaning of Heb. 5:12 is also clear because of the presence of *archē*, beginning. The linking of these two words ("elementary truths" or "first principles") carries a derogatory ring, which is further emphasized by the reminder that the readers need milk and not solid food. The recipients of Heb. are not familiar with even the basic teachings of the faith (cf. 6:1–4).

In the case of Gal. 4:3, 9 and Col. 2:8, 20 many scholars hold that the *stoicheia* are angels, demons, and gods, i.e., personified forces as taught by a certain gnostic heresy. Others take Gal. 4 to refer to the Torah with its statutes and the world of false gods that the readers once served. In Col. the expression refers to religion before and outside Christ. But the interpretation is relatively unimportant, since the hierarchy of beings taught by Gnosticism, while partly syncretistic, was in fact the product of a current philosophico-religious view of the world.

The important point is that in Gal. 4:1–11 Paul has nothing positive to say about "the basic principles of the world," since he knows they have been overcome by Christ. Compared with him they are "weak and miserable" (4:9) and not the gods (4:8) the Gentiles believed them to be before conversion. Even the law is reckoned as among these principles and hence is declared null and void. Thus "the basic principles of the world" cover all the things in which humans place trust apart from the living God revealed in Christ; they become gods, and humans become their slaves.

In Col. 2:8, human tradition and "the basic principles of this world" both come under the heading of "hollow and deceptive philosophy," which seeks to prey on humankind. Such philosophy has long since been defeated by Christ and has appeared as a captive in his triumphal procession (2:10–15). As in Gal. 4:3, 5 "the basic principles of this world" are disapprovingly linked with "rules," which may be Jewish legal requirements. Note that later Gnosticism had significant links with the OT. Those who have died with Christ (Col. 2:20) should have nothing further to do with them; they are freed from the burdens imposed by the *stoicheia* on their day-to-day lives (2:21–23; cf. 3:1–17).

See also *ethos*, usage, custom (*1621*); *nomos*, law, norm (*3795*).

5123 (*stoicheō*, be in line with, hold to), → *5122*.

5127 (*strateia*, expedition, campaign), → *4483*.

5128 (*strateuma*, army, detachment, troops), → *4483*.

5129 (*strateuomai*, serve as a soldier), → *4483*.

5130 (*stratēgos*, general, chief magistrate, praetor), → *4483*.

5131 (*stratia*, army), → *4483*.

5132 (*stratiōtēs*, soldier), → *4483*.

5133 (*stratologeō*, gather an army, enlist soldiers), → *4483*.

5136 (*stratopedon*, camp, body of troops, army), → *4483*.

5138 (*strephō*, turn, change), → *2188*.

5146 στῦλος	στῦλος (*stylos*), pillar, support (*5146*).

CL & OT *stylos* is a common Gk. word used for different kinds of pillars, columns, and other supports. In the LXX *stylos* is used for various Heb. words, esp. the posts in the tabernacle (Exod. 27:10–17; 36:36 = LXX 37:4) and the pillars in the temple (1 Ki. 7:15–45). It is also used for the pillar of cloud and of fire that represented God's guidance in the desert (Exod. 13:21; Ps. 99:7). Fig. it refers to the structure of the house that wisdom builds for the God-fearing person (Prov. 9:1).

NT *stylos* is used with reference to the temple in Rev. 3:12, where the Spirit of Jesus promises that those who overcome will become pillars in the temple of God. This metaphor probably refers to the two pillars that adorned the porch of Solomon's temple. The same word is used fig. of the leaders of the Jerusalem church, James, Cephas, and John (Gal. 2:9), and of the church of the living God as the foundation of truth (1 Tim. 3:15).

5155 (*synkakopatheō*, endure hardship together with someone), → *4248*.

5169 (*synklēronomos*, fellow heir), → *3102*.

5170 (*synkoinōneō*, participate in with someone, share), → *3126*.

5171 (*synkoinōnos*, participant, partner), → *3126*.

5173 (*synkrinō*, compare, interpret), → *3210*.

5176 (*synchairō*, rejoice with), → *5897*.

5182 (*syzaō*, live with), → *2437*.

5183 (*syzeugnymi*, yoke together, join together), → *2433*.

5187 (*syzygos*, yokefellow, comrade), → *2433*.

5188 (*syzōopoieō*, make alive with), → *2437*.

5190 συκῆ	συκῆ (*sykē*), fig, both the tree and the fruit (*5190*); σῦκον (*sykon*), fig (*5192*).

CL & OT The forms *sykea* and *sykē* are both found in cl. Gk. and can refer to the resin of the pine or fir, as well as to the fig tree.

sykē is widely used in the LXX for the Heb. *tᵉʾēnâ* for the fig tree, its fruit, and its leaves (Gen. 3:7; Num. 13:24), esp. as characteristic of the fruitfulness of the promised land (Deut. 8:8). *sykē* has wide parabolic (cf. Jdg. 9:10) and fig. extensions. It represents ease and prosperity (cf. 1 Ki. 4:25), esp. in the messianic age (Mic. 4:4; Zech. 3:10 = LXX 3:11); it affords comparisons for that which is intrinsically desirable (Hos. 9:10), for renewal (Joel 2:22), and for that which fades (Isa. 34:4), and it is easy to capture (Nah. 3:12). It is also a description of disappointed hopes (Hab. 3:17).

The destruction of the fig tree, like that of other trees and crops, is a picture of judgment (Isa. 34:4; Jer. 8:13; Hos. 2:12; Joel 1:2–12). In Hos. 9:10 and Jer. 24 *sykē* symbolizes the nation that otherwise is generally pictured as a vine. Mic. 7:1–3 depicts the corrupt state of the nation that is full of bitterness, mutual hostility, and bloodshed in metaphorical terms of the absence of the fig when sought.

NT The reference to Jesus seeing Nathanael under the fig tree (Jn. 1:48, 50) is presumably to be taken lit. The remaining NT references all have fig. and symbolic aspects.

1. Particular problems attend the interpretation of Jesus' cursing of the fig tree (Matt. 21:18–22; Mk. 11:12–14, 20–25). As it stands, this event is not only the sole destructive miracle in Jesus' ministry, but it is also an acted parable in which Jesus depicted the judgment about to fall on Jerusalem. Most difficult is the statement, "it was not the season for figs [*sykon*]" (Mk. 11:13). (a) For Jesus to seek figs where he knew there could be none supplies the element of the incongruous, which calls attention to the presence of a metaphorical meaning or a parable.

(b) "Season" (*kairos*, → *2789*) should be understood as in Mk. 12:2 of the time of ingathering. Jesus is thus reported to have come by the tree when, by its show of leaves, it ought to be in fruit, and, inasmuch as the harvest had not been gathered, the fruit should be showing on the tree.

(c) In addition, the explanatory clause, "it was not the season for figs," should not be attached to the foregoing words, "he found nothing but leaves," but to the words before that, "to find out if it had any fruit." Surely if the stones would cry out to greet the Messiah (Lk. 19:40), a fig tree could bear fruit out of season! After all, fruit should be continually in season during the messianic age, and Jesus' triumphal entry into Jerusalem (Mk. 11:1–10) had, in fact, pointed to the inauguration of the messianic age.

(d) One should also note the OT precedents for the association of the destruction of fig trees with judgment and the symbolic representation of Israel by the figure of figs. The attitude of the Jewish leaders to Jesus and the impending betrayal of Judas are best summed up in Mic. 7:1–6. The spiritual state of the nation and its leaders is uppermost in Jesus' mind at this period (cf. Mk. 11:1; Lk. 19:41–46). The cursing of the fig tree is, therefore, not an isolated event, but an integral part of the symbolic acts of Jesus' final visit to Jerusalem. It symbolizes judgment on the nation for its barren state and is of a piece with the cleansing of the temple that occurred at the same time.

2. Lk. does not record the cursing of the fig tree but contains a parable that presents a counterpart. In Lk. 13:6 the fig tree planted in a vineyard symbolizes Israel, which, despite tending, has so far failed to produce fruit. The master in the parable has sought fruit for the past three years (the period of Jesus' ministry?). But the caretaker of the vineyard asks for it to be spared one final year to give it a chance to bear fruit. If not, he will cut it down. This time of sparing corresponds to the time in which Israel is spared the final calamity of judgment, thus giving it one last chance to bear fruit. Note the context in which Jesus warns his hearers: "Unless you repent, you too will all perish" (13:5).

3. In Matt. 24:32–33; Mk. 13:28; Lk. 21:29 the growth of the fig tree is seen as a sign of the approaching summer, the climax of which will be the time when the figs are ripe for gathering. This is the time when the Son of Man will gather the elect (Mk. 13:27; cf. Matt. 24:31; Lk. 21:28) and come to take account (Mk. 13:34–37; cf. Matt. 24:36–51; Lk. 21:34–35). If the references to the fig tree in the ministry of Jesus are connected, then this reference is also a picture of Israel as it moves inevitably to the time when fruit will be sought and none found, reminiscent of the fig tree that was cursed.

4. Expectation of fruit also underlies Jas. 3:12, where the picture is one of natural (and, by analogy, moral) consistency between the one bearing fruit and the type of fruit produced. In Rev. 6:13, the picture suggests that which falls easily in judgment.

5192 (*sykon*, fig), → *5190*.

5194 (*sylagōgeō*, rob, carry off as booty or captive), → *5195*.

5195 συλάω	συλάω (*sylaō*), plunder, rob (*5195*); συλαγωγέω (*sylagōgeō*), rob, carry off as booty or captive (*5194*).

CL & OT *sylaō* means to strip off the arms from a fallen enemy; to take a bow out of its case or the lid off a quiver; to despoil secretly, i.e., cheat. In the LXX *sylaō* occurs only in Ep. Jer. (Bar. 6:18), referring to burglary, for fear of which priests bolt and bar their temples.

NT *sylaō* occurs only at 2 Cor. 11:8. By a bold military metaphor Paul dramatizes the fact that his ministry at Corinth was at no cost to the Christians there, because he had, as it were, plundered other churches by accepting financial support from them, rather than expecting the Corinthians to give money to him for his personal needs.

sylagōgeō, rob, carry off as booty, occurs for the first time in the NT. In Col. 2:8 the vb. is used fig. of drawing someone away from the truth of Christ into the slavery of error. Paul warns the converts at Colosse against the threat of being seduced from the Lord. His vb. gives the picture of prisoners being led away with a rope around their necks, like the long strings of captives portrayed on Assyrian monuments.

See also *lēstēs*, robber, highwayman, bandit, revolutionary (*3334*); *apostereō*, rob, defraud, deprive (*691*); *andrapodistēs*, slave-dealer, kidnapper (*435*); *spēlaion*, cave, den (*5068*).

5197	συλλαμβάνω

συλλαμβάνω (*syllambanō*), seize, conceive, assist (*5197*).

CL & OT In cl. Gk. *syllambanō* meant collect together as its primary meaning; it could also mean: put together, close; lay hands on, seize; grasp (of the mind); conceive, become pregnant; take part with another, assist.

In the LXX, *syllambanō* often means conceive, either lit. (e.g., Gen. 4:1, 17; 1 Sam. 1:20) or fig. (Ps. 7:14). It can also mean seize, arrest, capture, either lit. (e.g., Num. 5:13; Deut. 21:19; Jdg. 15:4) or fig. (e.g., the snatching away of sinners before their time by an act of God's judgment, Job 22:16; Ps. 9:16; the snaring of the unsuspecting by the wicked, Jer. 5:26; cf. Eccl. 7:27).

NT *syllambanō* occurs 16x in the NT.

1. Lk. uses it to mean conceive in his account of the births of John the Baptist and Jesus (Lk. 1:24; 31, 36; 2:21), while Jas. 1:15 uses the imagery of conception and birth fig.

2. The vb. can also mean seize or capture. It is used in all four Gospels to describe the seizing of Jesus in the Garden of Gethsemane (Mk. 14:48 par.; Jn. 18:12; cf. Acts 1:16). Lk. also uses it in his narrative of the arrest of Peter (Acts 12:3) and in the account of the attempt by the Jews to lynch Paul outside the temple at Jerusalem (23:27). In Lk. 5:9 the same word describes a huge catch of fish.

3. The vb. appears 2x in the mid. voice, meaning take hold of together, assist. In Lk. 5:7 those in Simon's boat call for assistance (NIV, "help") when their nets break under the strain of a miraculous catch; in Phil. 4:3 Paul uses *syllambanō* to appeal to an unknown church member to "help" Euodia and Syntyche resolve their differences.

5198 (*syllegō*, gather up), → *5251*.

5203 (*symbasileuō*, share the rule), → *995*.

5205	συμβουλεύω

συμβουλεύω (*symbouleuō*), advise (*5205*); σύμβουλος (*symboulos*), adviser (*5207*); συμβούλιον (*symboulion*), advice, council (*5206*).

CL & OT Words associated with the stem *symboul-* refer to the giving of advice by one person to another, either in private or in public affairs. In the LXX, *symbouleuō* generally means advise. *symboulos* is used once of a person who might give advice to God (Isa. 40:13), the thought, however, being the inappropriateness of such an attempt.

NT *symbouleuō* is used of the evil plots of the Jews against Jesus and the early church (Matt. 26:4; Jn. 18:14; Acts 9:23), but also of the good advice given by Christ to the church at Laodicea (Rev. 3:18). A *symboulion* can be the panel of advisers employed by a Roman governor (Acts 25:12). Matt. uses *symboulion lambanō* for the machinations of the Jewish authorities against Jesus (12:14; 22:15; 27:1, 7; 28:12); *symboulion didōmi* (Mk. 3:6) conveys the same meaning. *sym-*

boulion poieō (15:1) can mean reach a decision or hold a meeting; the phraseology leaves it uncertain whether this refers to a second, morning meeting of the Sanhedrin. *symboulos* occurs in a quotation of Isa. 40:13 in Rom. 11:34; the rhetorical question stresses the transcendent and incomprehensible character of God's wisdom.

See also *synedrion*, council, Sanhedrin (*5284*).

5206 (*symboulion*, advice, council), → *5205*.

5207 (*symboulos*, adviser), → *5205*.

5210 (*symmartyreō*, testify in support, confirm), → *3456*.

5213 (*symmimētēs*, fellow-imitator), → *3628*.

5214 (*symmorphizō*, be conformed to, take on the same form as), → *3671*.

5215 (*symmorphos*, having the same shape, similar in form or appearance), → *3671*.

5217 (*sympatheō*, have compassion, sympathize with), → *4248*.

5224 (*sympaschō*, suffer together with, sympathize with), → *4248*.

5231 (*sympnigō*, strangle), → *4465*.

5232 (*sympolitēs*, fellow citizen), → *4484*.

5249 (*sympsychos*, of the same mind or spirit), → *6034*.

5250	σύν

σύν (*syn*), with (*5250*); μετά (*meta*), with (*3552*).

CL In cl. Gk. *syn* meant including, with the aid of, while, and *meta* means in company with. In Hel. Gk., however, these two words become virtually synonymous. *syn* has not survived in modern popular Gk.

NT 1. *syn* occurs 128x in the NT, of which 74 are in Luke–Acts. *meta* is more common (364x) than *syn*, but the latter is rarely used in compound verbs. Both preps. are used in connection with Christian discipleship, fellowship meals, and eschatology.

2. In spite of the general interchangeability of these two preps., it is significant that Paul regularly ends his letters with the prayer that God's grace might be "with" (*meta*, never *syn*) his addressees, whereas he depicts the Christian life as one of identification with (*syn*) Christ and the Christian's destiny as living "with him" (*syn*, e.g., 2 Cor. 13:4). This suggests that of the two preps., *syn* was the more suited to express intimate personal union (e.g., Col. 3:4) and *meta* the more suited to denote close association or attendant circumstances (e.g., 1 Thess. 3:13).

The more dominant expression in Paul regarding our present relationship with Christ is that we are "in [*en*, → *1877*] him." But when we die, there is an added dimension: We go to be "with [*syn*] Christ" (Phil. 1:23). *syn* here signifies more than mere spatial juxtaposition and even more than coexistence. Our destiny after death is active communion with Christ. Moreover, after the Parousia, our being "with [*syn*] the Lord" (1 Thess. 4:17) denotes the added dimension of our sharing in the eschatological blessings of the kingdom enjoyed by Christ since his resurrection.

5251	συνάγω

συνάγω (*synagō*), gather (*5251*); ἐπισυνάγω (*episynagō*), gather together (*2190*); συλλέγω (*syllegō*), gather up (*5198*); τρυγάω (*trygaō*), gather in (*5582*); συστρέφω (*systrephō*), gather together (*5370*); ἀθροίζω (*athroizō*), gather together (*125*); συναθροίζω (*synathroizō*), gather together (*5255*); ἐπισυναγωγή (*episynagōgē*), gathering together (*2191*); ἐπαθροίζω (*epathroizo*), be gathered even more (*2044*).

CL & OT In cl. Gk. *synagō* is used of bringing together, collecting, or convening, even in a hostile sense of joining battle. It can also refer to uniting in marriage or forming a conclusion from certain premises. Sometimes it speaks of gathering together stores or crops (Xenophon).

In the LXX *synagō* occurs about 350x and stands chiefly for the Heb. *ʾāsap*. It is used of collecting things, esp. fruits (Exod. 23:10; Lev. 25:3, 20; Isa. 17:5), but also ears of grain (Ruth 2:7), quails (Num. 11:32), money (2 Ki. 22:4; 2 Chr. 24:11), and the ashes of a red heifer (Num. 19:9). More important, the vb. may refer to gathering together persons, nations, or armies (Exod. 3:16; 4:29; Num. 21:16, 23; 2 Sam. 10:17; 12:29). It also refers to being gathered to one's people in Sheol (2 Ki. 22:20) and gathering those slain in battle in order to bury them (Jer. 9:22; Ezek. 29:5).

A diff. Heb. verb (*qābaṣ*), also translated by *synagō*, is used of collecting grain or grapes (Gen. 41:35, 48; Isa. 62:9), booty (Deut. 13:16), money (2 Chr. 24:5), birds (Isa. 34:16), animals (Ezek. 39:17), and people (Deut. 30:3–4). It is used esp. of God's recalling and assembling the exiles (Isa. 40:11; 43:5; 56:8) and his gathering the nations for judgment (66:18; Mic. 4:12).

NT In the NT *synagō* appears 59x. In the Synoptics it refers to the gathering of people (e.g., crowds, Matt. 13:2; wedding guests, 22:10) or things (food, 6:26; fish, 13:47; vultures, 24:28). It is contrasted with *skorpizō* (scatter; → *5025*) in connection with the mission of the church (12:30; 25:24, 26). Matt. frequently records an assembling of the religious leaders (2:4; 22:34, 41; 26:3, 57; 27:17, 62; 28:12), and once uses *synagō* to refer to the whole Roman cohort gathering in the Praetorium before Jesus' crucifixion (27:27). The nations will be gathered together at the last judgment (25:32), and the Messiah will gather the wheat into his barn (3:12; cf. 13:30, where the reapers are angels sent by the Son of Man). Wherever several believers gather in Christ's name, he will be in their midst (18:20). In 25:35, 38, 43 *synagō* means invite in, receive as a guest.

In Jn. the fragments from the feeding of the five thousand are gathered up (Jn. 6:12–13). Christian workers gather fruit unto life eternal (4:36), and Christ's mission is to gather and to make into one the children of God scattered abroad (11:52). Fruitless branches, however, are gathered and burned (15:6). Jesus often gathers his disciples to Gethsemane (18:2), and the chief priests and Pharisees convene a council (11:47).

In Acts the early church gathers for prayer (4:31), instruction (11:26), information (14:27; 15:30), consultation (15:6), and the breaking of bread (20:7–8). On the other hand, just as Herod and Pilate assembled against Jesus (4:26–27), so do the Jewish religious leaders against the church (4:5). In Pisidian Antioch practically the whole city gathers to hear the word of God (13:44).

The only instance of *synagō* in Paul occurs in 1 Cor. 5:4, where believers will assemble to deal with a case of incest requiring excommunication. In Rev. we read of a gathering for the great eschatological battle (16:14, 16; 19:19; 20:8) and for the great supper of God (19:17).

episynagō is used in Jesus' lament over rebellious Jerusalem (Matt. 23:37; Lk. 13:34), in eschatological passages speaking of the gathering of the elect (Matt. 24:31; Mk. 13:27), and in connection with crowds gathering about Jesus (1:33; Lk. 12:1). In Lk. 17:37 *episynagō* is used in a warning: "Where there is a dead body, there the vultures will gather."

syllegō is used for collecting grapes (Matt. 7:16; Lk. 6:44), good fish (Matt. 13:48), and weeds for destruction (13:28, 29, 30, 40, 41). *trygaō* appears as a stylistic variation for *syllegō* in Lk. 6:44. In Rev. 14:18–19 *trygaō* speaks of gathering the clusters of the vine, a fig. use in which the winepress of God's wrath is in view.

Several other words are used sparingly for gathering together: (1) *systrephō* in Acts 28:3, of Paul's gathering a bundle of sticks (cf. Matt. 17:22); (2) *athroizō* in Lk. 24:33, of the eleven apostles and others gathered together in Jerusalem; (3) *synathroizō* in Acts 12:12, of the believers assembled in the home of John Mark's mother (cf. 19:25); (4) *epathroizō* in Lk. 11:29, of crowds gathered.

episynagōgē in 2 Thess. 2:1 refers to believers "being gathered" together to Christ at the Parousia; in Heb. 10:25 to the regular gathering together of believers in worship and instruction.

See also *ekklēsia*, assembly, meeting, congregation, church (*1711*); *skorpizō*, scatter, disperse, distribute (*5025*).

5252 (*synagōgē*, assembly, synagogue), → *1711*.

5253 (*synagōnizomai*, fight along with, help), → *74*.

5254 (*synathleō*, contend with), → *123*.

5255 (*synathroizō*, gather together), → *5251*.

5257 (*synaichmalōtos*, fellow prisoner), → *171*.

5258 (*synakoloutheō*, follow), → *199*.

5259 (*synalizō*, to assemble with, eat [salt] with), → *229*.

5271 (*synapothnēskō*, die together with someone), → *2505*.

5278 (*syndesmos*, that which binds together, bond, fetter), → *1300*.

5280 (*syndoxazō*, glorify together), → *1518*.

5281 (*syndoulos*, fellow servant), → *1528*.

5283 (*synegeirō*, raise with), → *1586*.

| 5284 | συνέδριον | συνέδριον (*synedrion*), council, Sanhedrin (*5284*). |

CL & OT *synedrion* is related to *synedros* (*syn* + *hedra*), one who sits with somebody else (in a council), and *synedreuō*, sit in council. Originally it meant the place where a council met, then the body of councilors, or their actual meeting. It was used of various official bodies (including courts).

The word is used a dozen times in the LXX, but with no fixed significance. Josephus uses it for various councils and courts, but esp. as a technical term for the supreme Jewish council. The body that guided Jewish affairs in Jerusalem after return from the exile was an aristocratic council of priests and lay leaders. Later, scribes of the Pharisaic party gained seats on it. The earliest use of *synedrion* in this sense occurs in a decree of Gabinius (57–55 B.C.), which mentions five such bodies in different areas of Palestine. Somewhat later the Jerusalem council gained authority over the whole country and was regularly called *synedrion*, even by the Jews, who took the word over into the Heb./Aram. as *sanhedrîn*.

This council was composed of 71 members, with the high priest as chairman. It included the heads of the priestly families, leaders of the lay aristocracy (the elders), and a number of scribes; the first two groups stood together as the Sadducean party, while the third group was Pharisaic in outlook. Membership appears to have been self-perpetuating. The Sanhedrin was essentially a court charged with the maintenance of Jewish customs. It could impose the death sentence, but (except in rare circumstances) the Romans retained the right of actually inflicting the penalty (Jn. 18:31). We do not know how it functioned in NT times, since the rules for procedure contained in the Mishnah reflect Pharisaic ideals rather than the actual Sadducean practice.

There were also smaller Jewish courts known by the same name outside Jerusalem, who exercised jurisdiction among Jewish communities in Palestine and the Diaspora. The Mishnah lays down a membership of 23 persons for them.

NT Christians are warned that they may be summoned to bear witness before such local courts and might even be sentenced to scourging by them (Matt. 10:17 par.). Jesus said that a person who is angry with his brother is liable to judgment by the *synedrion*, thus indicating metaphorically that anger is as culpable as murder (5:21–22).

The majority of references to the Sanhedrin are in connection with its proceedings against Jesus and the early church. At a particular point in Jesus' ministry the Sanhedrin determined that he had to be put away (Jn. 11:47), and it seized the opportunity given by Judas at the Passover to arrest Jesus and try him (Mk. 14:55; 15:1; Lk. 22:66). This opposition continued toward the early church (Acts 4; 5:17–41; 6:8–7:60; 22:30–23:10, 20, 28; 24:20), though according to Acts the Pharisees took a more favorable position.

See also *symbouleuō*, advise (5205).

| 5287 συνείδησις |

συνείδησις (*syneidēsis*), consciousness, conscience (5287); σύνοιδα (*synoida*), perf. with pres. meaning, be conscious of, have a conscience about (5323).

CL & OT 1. In cl. Gk. *synoida* can mean share the knowledge of (e.g., as witness in court), be privy to, be conscious of. *syneidēsis* and *syneidos* (used synonymously) mean the faculty of memory, consciousness, and conscience.

(a) Originally *syneidēsis* focused on knowledge, specifically the capacity to relate to oneself by looking back at one's past. This activity included evaluations and judgments about good and evil. Hence, the word acquired the moral meaning of conscience. In this context writers spoke of a good (*agathē* or *orthē*) or a bad (*deinē* or *ponēra*) conscience. The good conscience is generally at peace, whereas the bad conscience makes itself painfully felt by relentlessly troubling its owner.

(b) It is striking that pre-Christian Gk. lit. speaks almost exclusively of a bad conscience, whereas the Romans often spoke of a good or clear conscience (used esp. regarding performance of expected duties). Later writers saw the conscience as a watchman bestowed by God to guide a person to live according to nature and to direct one's moral progress. The ground was thus laid for conscience to become a normative guide.

2. The OT has no special word for the conscience. In the LXX *syneidēsis* occurs only in several late passages (Eccl. 10:20; Wis. 17:11; Sir. 42:18), where it does take on the Gk. notion of this human phenomenon. For the Israelites the question of one's attitude toward oneself was less significant than that of one's attitude toward God. God's people were to be more concerned with their accountability before him than with exploring self-consciousness.

This does not mean that the OT knows nothing of a tormented conscience but that the voice of conscience possesses no intrinsic value. It is the voice of the divine Judge that counts, demanding from people an account of their dealings. The function of conscience is attributed to the human heart. Thus David's heart smote him to remind him of his guilt (1 Sam. 24:5; 2 Sam. 24:10) and summoned him to penitence and regret (cf. Ps. 51:10). The idea of a clean heart points forward to the NT notion of a good conscience.

3. The correspondence between the OT idea of the heart and the Gk. notion of conscience is developed in Philo. For him conscience is a normative entity in a human shaped by the law of God. Its task is to convict of sin and reprove and thus bring one to repentance. Otherwise, it will continue to trouble the sinner. The ultimate goal of conscience is to drive the sinner into the arms of a merciful God.

NT 1. In the NT the vb. *synoida* occurs only 2x. In 1 Cor. 4:4 it is reflexive: "My conscience is clear." Acts 5:2 suggests a shared knowledge: "With his wife's full knowledge [Ananias] kept back part of the money."

2. The noun *syneidēsis*, however, occurs 30x. In Rom. 2:15 it stands alongside *kardia* (heart) and *logismoi* (thoughts) as a critical human organ. All three elements enable Gentiles to conduct lives that correspond to those of the Jews, who live according to God's revealed law. Conscience is assigned the role of awakening awareness of the law that is written on the human heart. It appears, as it were, as a court of appeal that cannot promulgate any statutes (for only God himself can do this) but is able to deliver judgment on the cases before it.

The thought of conscience as a court of appeal is clear in the passages in which Paul deals with the Corinthians' question of the propriety of eating meat sacrificed to idols (1 Cor. 8:7–13; 10:25–11:1). He makes two points: Christians are free from regimentation by an alien conscience, yet they must show regard for the more sensitive or "weak conscience" of others.

Paul rejoices in the testimony of his own conscience that has been formed by God (2 Cor. 1:12). Likewise, he hopes that the consciences of those who are open to God will recognize the sincerity of his missionary life and work (4:2; 5:11). Therefore, the avoidance of a bad, accusing conscience is worth aspiring after, yet it is even more important to have a good conscience that confirms the correspondence of faith and life. Appealing to such a conscience that is in line with God's will, Paul can also demand obedience to those in authority "because of conscience" (Rom. 13:5; cf. 1 Pet. 2:19). Acts 24:16 lays down what is virtually a rule of conduct: "I [Paul] strive to keep my conscience clear before God and man" (cf. 23:1).

3. The Pastoral Letters lay great emphasis on a good conscience. They refer to the corrupt and unbelieving, whose "minds and consciences are corrupted" (Tit. 1:15), and to "hypocritical liars, whose consciences have been seared" (1 Tim. 4:2). By contrast, Christians are to hold "to faith and a good conscience" (1:19; cf. 1 Pet. 3:16) and "to serve ... with a clear conscience" (2 Tim. 1:3). Alongside a "pure heart" and a "sincere faith," 1 Tim. 1:5 names "a good conscience" as the source of love in action. In short, the conscience can be regarded as the place where the "deep truths of the faith" are kept (3:9). That is why "the pledge of a good conscience toward God," which is the essence of baptism (1 Pet. 3:21), is so important.

4. Heb. stresses the Christological basis of the NT understanding of conscience when it declares that "the blood of Christ" purifies the conscience "from acts that lead to death, so that we may serve the living God" (9:14). Using the symbolism of the Day of Atonement ritual, in which the high priest entered the sanctuary once a year, 10:22 urges believers to enter and to draw near themselves "with a sincere heart in full assurance of faith, having our hearts sprinkled to cleanse us from a guilty conscience and having our bodies washed with pure water." It is only because of the high priestly sacrifice of Christ that "we are sure that we have a clear conscience" (13:18).

5. In this way the Christian understanding of conscience is transformed by faith in the forgiving power of Christ. The Gks. saw conscience as something bad, operating retrospectively, whereas Christians came to see conscience as being made clean through faith. Its purity lay in the believer's knowledge of his or her standing in Christ. The fact that it was directed by the Word of God gave the believer a heart to serve God in love.

5300 (*synergeō*, to work together, cooperate, aid), → 2237.

5301 (*synergos*, working together with, fellow worker, assistant), → 2237.

5302 (*synerchomai*, come together, assemble), → 2262.

| 5304 σύνεσις |

σύνεσις (*synesis*), faculty of comprehension, understanding, insight (5304); συνίημι (*syniēmi*), perceive, comprehend, understand (5317); συνετός (*synetos*), quick at apprehending, understanding, intelligent (5305); ἀσύνετος (*asynetos*), senseless, foolish (852).

CL & OT 1. In cl. Gk. the vb. *syniēmi* originally meant to bring together, a meaning not found in the NT. Fig., *syniēmi* means to perceive, take notice of, understand, comprehend. The noun *synesis* originally meant a joining (e.g., of rivers); then, in a transferred sense, the faculty of judgment, apprehension, understanding, insight, comprehension. Neither vb. nor noun acquired any great philosophical importance. The adj. *synetos* means quick at apprehending, clever; also intelligible. The opposite is *asynetos*, stupid or unintelligible.

2. In the LXX both noun and vb. occur about 100x each, the adj. 53x, the negative adj. only 12x. As one might expect, these words are found most frequently in the wisdom lit. Words in this group often

occur in connection with sayings about wisdom. *synesis*, understanding, insight, and *sophia*, wisdom (*5053*), are used together (Job 12:13; Prov. 1:7; Isa. 11:2; 29:14; Sir. 1:19–20). The object of this knowledge is the fact that the Lord is God (e.g., Jer. 9:24). Fear of the Lord, justice and righteousness, right and wrong are named as the objects of insight (1 Ki. 3:9, 11; Prov. 2:5, 9). Thus, insight is not open to everyone. Since the knowledge of God is always associated with his revelatory activity, insight can ultimately be understood only as a gift that God imparts in response to our request (1 Ki. 3:9; Dan. 2:21) but can also withdraw because of disobedience (Isa. 29:14).

NT *syniēmi* occurs only in the Synoptic Gospels and Acts, in quotations from the LXX at Rom. 3:11; 15:21, and otherwise in 2 Cor. 10:12; Eph. 5:17. *synesis* occurs 7x times (once in a quotation). The OT idea that insight is a gift of God and is linked with his revelation reappears in the NT usage. In many cases the NT passages in question are quoting from or alluding to the OT (e.g., Isa. 6:9–10 in Matt. 13:14–15; Deut. 6:5 in Mk. 12:33; Ps. 14:2 in Rom. 3:11).

1. In the Synoptics the most important passages are those that deal with the theme of the so-called "messianic secret." (a) Mk. records the disciples' lack of understanding regarding Jesus' words and actions (6:52; 8:17, 21; in 8:18 with direct reference to Isa. 6:9–10 or Jer. 5:21). That is, the closeness of the disciples to Jesus was not alone sufficient to guarantee understanding. His work can only be understood in the light of Easter.

Mk. 4:10–12 makes this point clear. Here Jesus stresses that his works become revelation to those who believe. Therefore, believers are the ones who receive the secret of the kingdom of God; to "those on the outside" everything comes in parables. Because they do not understand the parables, they are unable to turn and be saved (cf. Isa. 6:9–10 again).

(b) Matt. has a different emphasis from Mk., for he stresses the disciples' understanding. Matt. shows how the disciples did in fact come to understand, though he does stress that such understanding is a divine gift (cf. 16:16–20; 17:5–13). At the end of the parabolic discourse, for example, Jesus asks the disciples, "Have you understood all these things?" They reply, "Yes" (13:51). The statement of Mk. 6:52, which attributes their lack of insight to hardness of heart, is replaced by an exclamation of worship, praising Jesus as the Son of God (Matt. 14:33). The discussion of yeast in Mk. 8:14–21, which ends with the accusing question, "Do you still not understand?" leads in Matt. 16:5–12 to the final understanding of the disciples.

(c) In Lk. 18:34 the disciples' lack of understanding is emphasized particularly in regard to Jesus' passion prediction. In 2:47 the insight of Jesus at twelve years of age is the subject of amazement, and there is no doubt that such insight is regarded as a gift from God. Conversely, his parents' failure to understand (2:50) must be seen as the opposite. In addition, it is the risen Christ who enables the downcast disciples on the Emmaus road to understand the Scriptures and to grasp the fact that his sufferings were foreordained by God (24:45).

Acts 28:26–27 cites Isa. 6:9–10 as the explanation for the unwillingness and inability of the Jews in Rome to understand the gospel (cf. Jn. 12:40, where *noeō* is used instead of *syniēmi*). Although insight is a gift of God, the fault for lack of insight lies within ourselves.

2. In Paul the use of these words is again affected by OT concepts, esp. since in most cases they occur in quotations from the OT or allusions to OT phrases (Rom. 3:11 = Ps. 14:2; Rom. 10:19 = Deut. 32:21; Rom. 15:21 = Isa. 52:15; 1 Cor. 1:19 = Isa. 29:14). Whether lack of insight is being condemned (Rom. 3:11), or God's wrath is pronounced over the arrogance of those who believe themselves to be wise (1 Cor. 1:19), or the subject is the universality of the message of salvation (Rom. 10:19; 15:21), insight is always seen as a gift of God and lack of insight as not merely a chance lack of knowledge. Rather, as Rom. 1:21 stresses, lack of insight must be regarded as culpable behavior. *asynetos*, having no insight, "foolish," appears among the list of evils in Rom. 1:31.

3. In the later Pauline letters we find not only the familiar ideas (insight as a gift, 2 Tim. 2:7), but also a new emphasis as a result of the connection of these words with the concept of mystery. Fullness of understanding is given in the revelation of the secret of God in Christ, in whom all the treasures of wisdom and knowledge lie hidden (Col. 2:2–3). We may compare Eph. 3:4, where the content of the mystery of Christ is, in keeping with the wider context of this letter, associated with the church.

See also *phronēsis*, way of thinking, frame of mind, intelligence, good sense (*5860*); *nous*, mind, intellect, understanding, reason, thought (*3808*); *epistamai*, know, understand (*2179*).

5305 (*synetos*, quick at apprehending, understanding, intelligent), → *5304*.

5313 (*synthaptō*, bury with), → *2507*.

5317 (*syniēmi*, perceive, comprehend, understand), → *5304*.

5323 (*synoida*, be conscious of, have conscience about), → *5287*.

5325 (*synoikodomeō*, build together with), → *3868*.

5333 (*synteleia*, completion, close, consummation), → *5465*.

5334 (*synteleō*, complete, carry out, fulfill, accomplish), → *5465*.

5340 (*syntrechō*, run together), → *4513*.

5347 (*synypokrinomai*, act insincerely, join in hypocrisy), → *5693*.

5365 (*systauroō*, crucify with), → *5089*.

5368 (*systoicheō*, stand in the same line, correspond to, conform to), → *5122*.

5370 (*systrephō*, gather together), → *5251*.

5372 (*syschēmatizō*, to mold, form after; pass. be formed like, be conformed to), → *5386*.

5381 (*sphragizō*, to seal), → *5382*.

5382	σφραγίς

σφραγίς (*sphragis*), seal, signet (*5382*); σφραγίζω (*sphragizō*), to seal (*5381*); κατασφραγίζω (*katasphragizō*), to seal (*2958*).

CL & OT 1. (a) In cl. Gk. *sphragis* means the tool that seals (e.g., a signet ring), the stone set in it (the gem), or the engraving on it (an image or name). Seals were widely used in the ANE by both private persons and authorities, esp. in Mesopotamia but later in the whole Mediterranean area. The importance of the seal was legal: An owner put his mark on his possessions, his animals, and his slaves in order to guard them against theft. It was thus a protecting sign or a guarantee. When used with documents (wills, deeds of sale, etc.) the seal served as a signature to authorize what was written there. Things sealed were at the disposal of the possessor of the seal and symbolized authority.

(b) Seals were also important in religious life. For instance, an animal could be attested as ritually pure and thus suitable for a sacrificial victim. People showed themselves to be the possession of their deity by the imprint of their seal. More tangibly one could seal houses, etc., to guarantee that they were preserved, or documents, to keep their contents a secret. Hence, one could also say that the mouth or words are sealed; what one has experienced must remain secret and in safekeeping. This applied esp. to secrets of the mystery religions.

2. In the LXX *sphragis* and *sphragizō* are used lit. and fig. In this way they approximate to nonbiblical usage. (a) A seal engraved by a maker of signets (Sir. 38:27) can leave its impress in clay (Job 38:14). It has a legal use; by means of a seal a document (e.g., a marriage contract, Tob. 7:14; a deed of sale, Jer. 32:10–11, 44 = LXX 39:10–11, 44) becomes valid. All who affix their seals to a document are bound to abide by its contents (Neh. 10:1). To give one's seal to another implies the transference of authority and power (Gen. 41:42; 1 Ki. 21:8 = LXX

20:8; Est. 3:10; 8:8, 10). Hence, one of the means by which the dying Antiochus Epiphanes appointed his friend Philip as regent over his kingdom was to hand over his seal to him (1 Macc. 6:15).

The LXX also speaks of a seal used as a fastening (for a purse, 2 Ki. 22:4; Tob. 9:5; a pit, Dan. 6:17; a fountain, Cant. 4:12). Thus the act of sealing is also equivalent to keeping something secret (e.g., a book, Dan. 12:4; Isa. 29:11; cf. 1 Esd. 3:8). The seal is necessary in both private and public life. The seal of the state (Jerusalem, 2 Esd. 10:23) is carefully guarded (Tob. 1:22). Signet rings are precious (Isa. 3:21; Sir. 32:5–6) and are regarded as valuable spoil (Num. 31:50).

(b) The fig. use of the concept is found esp. with the sense of concluding or shutting up. One can, e.g., ask for a seal to be set on one's lips that one may not sin in speaking (Sir. 22:27; cf. Ps. 141:3). God seals the stars (Job 9:7) by shutting them up so that they no longer shine, and he seals people, preventing them from working, so that they may recognize their dependence on him (37:7 LXX). Several times sins are said to be sealed (in a bag, 14:17; cf. Hos. 13:12). A revelation that is sealed remains hidden (Dan. 12:9), and one can learn as little of its contents as of those of a sealed book. The end of life is sealed in that it is unalterable (Wis. 2:5).

(c) The application of sealing to a religious context plays some part in the LXX. These precise words are not used, but their meaning is present. Isa. 44:5 presupposes the custom of having a seal with the words "The LORD's," i.e., Yahweh's property, tattooed on the hand. Ezek. 9:4–6 is also relevant here: God orders one of his servants to mark a sign on the foreheads of his children to protect them in the judgment. The seal is thus God's protective mark for his property (cf. *Pss. Sol.* 15:6–9).

3. The affixing of seals is also frequently mentioned in rab. Jud. For example, letters are sealed (*m. Ohal.* 17:5; cf. *m. Shab.* 8:5). In the temple was a room where four kinds of seals for victims were kept (*m. Sheqal.* 5:3–4). A seal can be made of metal or coral (*m. Kelim* 13:6). The Mishnah also uses the word in a metaphorical sense (e.g., *m. Sanh.* 4:5).

Sealing often occurs in the sense of signing, esp. in the tractate *Gittin* (1:1, 3), where two witnesses are said to "seal" a bill of divorce. Circumcision is called the seal of the holy covenant (*y. Ber.* 9:3) or the seal of Abraham (*Exod. Rab.* 19:5), since he was the first to receive this sign (Gen. 17:11). The noun and the vb. occur only infrequently in the Qumran texts.

NT 1. *sphragis* occurs 16x in the NT, *sphragizō* 15x, and *katasphragizō* once. (a) Twice *sphragizō* is used of actual physical sealing: the stone in front of Jesus' grave (Matt. 27:66; cf. Dan. 6:17) and the pit into which the devil is thrown (Rev. 20:3). In both cases this is done to prevent the one enclosed within from leading people astray (Matt. 27:63–64; Rev. 20:3).

(b) In Rom. 15:28 Paul says that he is "sealing" (NIV, "made sure") the collections from Macedonia and Achaia for the Jerusalem church. Paul is either saying that he has "sealed" the collections as one seals a purse (cf. Tob. 9:5) so that the contents may be kept safe, or that he has finished the collection.

2. (a) Jn. uses *sphragizō* in the sense of confirm, authenticate. Those who receive God's witness thus certify that God is true (Jn. 3:33), while 6:27 says that God has put "his seal of approval" on the Son of Man. By doing so he attests that the eternal food that the Son of Man gives is true spiritual food; by his seal God authenticates the Son of Man's work. Some think Jn. is reflecting here on baptism as a sealing; others think that this seal is the miracle of the feeding of the five thousand (6:1–15) or the testimony of holy Scripture (5:39).

When Paul in 1 Cor. 9:2 calls the Corinthian community the seal of his apostleship, he means that the existence of this community in the world confirms the legitimacy of his apostolic authority and that they are at the same time his letters of recommendation (cf. 2 Cor. 3:1–3).

(b) Three times Paul connects sealing with the Holy Spirit. This sealing, as he sees it, is symbolized by baptism, which he associates

with the gift of the Spirit (1 Cor. 6:11; 12:13; cf. Acts 2:38; 10:47). While Eph. 1:13 relates being sealed with the Holy Spirit (cf. 4:30) to the whole baptismal event, 2 Cor. 1:21–22 looks on baptism as an anointing in Christ and associates it with the receiving of the pledge of the Spirit (*arrabōn*, → 775). As Christ was anointed with the Spirit at his baptism (cf. Lk. 3:22; 4:18), so also are believers at theirs. The Spirit is a pledge until the day of redemption (Eph. 1:14; 2 Cor. 1:22; cf. 5:5). In sealing believers with his Spirit, God makes them his own possession.

It is not certain that Paul used the word *seal* in Rom. 4:11 in connection with Abraham's circumcision because he thought of baptism as a "seal" (cf. also Col. 2:11–12, which mentions a circumcision not performed by human hands, which comes through Christ). This idea did become explicit at a later stage (e.g., 2 Clem. 7:6; 8:6). Rom. 4:11 most likely means that by the seal of circumcision God confirmed that Abraham was justified even before God made his covenant with him (Gen. 17:10–14), a covenant whose sign is circumcision. Thus, circumcision here represents God's confirmatory sign, given as a seal to Abraham.

(c) In 2 Tim. 2:19, Paul speaks of a firm foundation that is fixed (cf. Isa. 28:16) and bears an inscription: "'The Lord knows those who are his,' and, 'Everyone who confesses the name of the Lord must turn away from wickedness.'" The word *sphragis* here means the inscription on a seal (Exod. 28:36 = LXX 28:32). The question is what is meant by the foundation on which this mark is stamped: Is it Christ (cf. 1 Cor. 3:10–11), the church (cf. 1 Tim. 3:15), the apostolic witness (cf. Eph. 2:20), or the truth in contrast to what is taught by the false teachers (2 Tim. 2:15, 18)? In any case, through his seal God guarantees the firmness of the foundation, for he knows his own and does not tolerate unrighteousness. The two inscriptions probably depend on Num. 16:5.

3. More than half of the uses of this word group occur in Rev. (a) In 22:10 the seer is forbidden to seal the words of the prophecy; he must not keep them secret since the time of their fulfillment is near (cf. the opposite in Dan. 12:4). By contrast, Rev. 10:4 reads: "Seal up what the seven thunders have said and do not write it down." This reflects the idea that what is sealed up is hidden (cf. Isa. 29:11). The message of the thunders, which ushers in the beginning of the final judgment, is only for the seer's ears and is not to be communicated to anyone else.

(b) Rev. 5:1 tells us how Jn. sees in the right hand of him who sits on the heavenly throne a scroll written on both sides, which has seven seals. No one but the Lamb can open it (5:2–10). The contents of the scroll are so voluminous that they cover both sides (cf. Ezek. 2:9–10). But it is still secret, even for the seer (cf. Dan. 12:4, 9). The number seven recalls the Roman custom of sealing a will with seven seals, but the more likely reason for seven seals is to be derived from the use of this number in Rev. itself (→ *hepta*, seven, *2231*).

It is difficult to imagine what the scroll looks like, since a part of the final cataclysm is revealed with the opening of each individual seal (Rev. 6:1, 3, 5, 7, 9, 12; 8:1), despite the fact that the contents of ancient documents were disclosed only after the opening of *all* the seals. But the writer is not interested in this idea itself, but in emphasizing that only the Lamb is worthy of setting the final events in motion.

(c) Finally Rev. 7:1–8 refers to the "seal of the living God" (7:2), which is imprinted on the foreheads of believers before the four angels of judgment are allowed to begin their work. These seals will protect them from the judgment that is coming on the world (9:4; cf. Ezek. 9:4; *Pss. Sol.* 15:6–9). The seal is here a sign of ownership and thus also of the one who protects; God keeps his own from the judgment. That 12,000 of each tribe receive the seal means that God's entire people will be spared from judgment (→ *chilias*, thousand, *5942*). The imprinting of the seal that bears God's name (cf. 14:1; 22:4) will distinguish believers from those who bear the "mark of the beast" on their hands and foreheads (13:16–17; 14:9, 11). God's sign protects one from judgment; the mark of the beast brings it upon one (9:4; 14:9–11). It is easy to discern here a word of consolation to a community living through the trials of persecution.

| 5386 | σχῆμα |

σχῆμα (*schēma*), outward appearance, form, shape (*5386*); συσχηματίζω (*syschēmatizō*), to mold, form after; pass. be formed like, be conformed to (*5372*).

CL & OT 1. In cl. Gk. *schēma* means (1) form, shape, figure; (2) appearance, as opposed to reality; (3) bearing, air; (4) fashion, manner; (5) character. Gk. thought did not sharply distinguish between the external and the internal. *schēma* denotes the form that is seen. It could thus denote the role played by an actor, which includes its essential character. But the outward form can also be deceptive and appearance a sham. *schēma* can thus mean mere appearance as opposed to reality. One must beware of the modern perspective, however, which tends to relate *schēma* merely to external things, implying that the essential character is something different. To the Gk. mind, the observer saw not only the outer shell but the whole form with it.

syschēmatizō means not only to conform to the external form, but to assume the form of something, to identify oneself essentially with someone else. A similar vb., *metaschēmatizō* (→ *3571*) indicates the process by which an object or a person is transformed and changed.

2. In Isa. 3:17 *schēma* refers to the proud bearing of women. Words of this group do not appear elsewhere in the LXX.

NT 1. *schēma* and *syschēmatizō* each occurs 2x in the NT. In Phil. 2:7, in the Christian hymn incorporated into this letter, Paul refers to Jesus Christ as "being found in appearance as a man" (*schēma*). This refers primarily to the way in which Jesus' humanity appeared, the way in which anyone could see him (for more on this passage, → *morphē, 3671,* and *kenos, 3031*).

2. (a) In 1 Cor. 7:31 Paul shows how real the *schēma* was for him when he declares: "This world in its present form is passing away."

(b) In Rom. 12:2 Paul warns us not to "conform" (*syschēmatizō*) to this age, that is, not to be absorbed by it, surrender oneself to it, and fall prey to it. To do so is to yield oneself to its power (cf. 1 Pet. 1:14).

See also *eidos*, form, outward appearance, sight (*1626*); *morphē*, form, outward appearance, shape (*3671*); *hypostasis*, substantial nature, essence, confidence (*5712*).

| 5387 | σχίζω |

σχίζω (*schizō*), split, tear, divide, separate (*5387*); σχίσμα (*schisma*), split, tear, division (*5388*).

CL & OT 1. In cl. Gk. *schizō* is generally used lit. of dividing into parts or breaking into pieces; only rarely is it used in the fig. sense of a division of opinion. The rare noun *schisma* denotes a slit, cleft, or clique.

2. *schizō* occurs 11x in the LXX in reference to cutting wood (Gen. 22:3), splitting rocks (Isa. 48:21) or mountains (Zech. 14:4), or dividing water (Exod. 14:21). *schisma* is not found in the LXX. A related noun *schismē* is, but it is used in a lit. sense (Isa. 2:19, 21; Jon. 2:6).

NT 1. (a) At the baptism of Jesus, the heavens were "torn open" (Mk. 1:10), a sign of divine disclosure at a crucial point of history (cf. Jn. 1:51; Acts 7:56; 10:11; perhaps an allusion to Isa. 64:1; Matt. 3:16 and Lk. 3:21 use *anoigō*, open; → *487*).

(b) In each of the Synoptic Gospels the story about the failure of Jesus' disciples to fast is followed by a parable about patching clothing (Matt. 9:16; Mk. 2:21; Lk. 5:36). No one ever sews a piece of newly woven, unshrunk cloth into an old garment because the added patch would tear away (*schizō* in Lk.) some of the garment and make a worse tear (*schisma* in Matt. and Mk.). Jesus is stressing the incompatibility of mixing his new era with the old era of Jud.

(c) Jesus' death was marked by the tearing of the inner curtain of the temple "in two from top to bottom" (Mk. 15:38; cf. Matt. 27:51; Lk. 23:45), the curtain that separated the Holy Place from the Most Holy Place (Exod. 26:31–35; 40:21). This symbolized the opening up of direct access into God's presence that Christ's sacrifice secured (Heb. 6:19–20; 9:8; 10:19–20). Matt. 27:51 mentions an earthquake that "split" the rocks (cf. Isa. 48:21).

(d) In the decision of the soldiers "not [to] tear" Jesus' tunic but to cast lots for it, Jn. sees a fulfillment of Scripture (Jn. 19:24, citing Ps. 22:18). A few days later, in the miraculous catch of 153 fish, Jn. writes that "the net was not torn" (Jn. 21:11). On three occasions Jn. notes that the Jews "were divided" (*schisma*) regarding Jesus; the points at issue were Jesus' identity (7:43), his miraculous cure of the man born blind (9:16), and his teaching about the good shepherd (10:19).

2. Paul's preaching is twice said to have prompted a division of opinion: once with the people of Iconium (Acts 14:4), and once with the Sanhedrin (23:7). In the Corinthian church there was not only squabbling (1 Cor. 1:11) but also a tendency to form "divisions" (1:10; 11:18), probably on the basis of sociological groupings or personal preferences for one church leader over another (see 1:12; 3:4; 11:17–22, 33–34). Such divisions, Paul insists, constitute a denial of their allegiance to one Lord (1:10, 13) and their membership of one body (12:12–26), where no division should occur (12:25).

See also *chōrizō*, divide, separate (*6004*).

5388 (*schisma*, split, tear, division), → *5387.*

| 5392 | σώζω |

σώζω (*sōzō*), save, keep from harm, preserve, rescue (*5392*); σωτηρία (*sōtēria*), salvation, deliverance, preservation (*5401*); διασώζω (*diasōzō*), bring safely through, save, rescue (*1407*).

CL & OT 1. (a) In cl. Gk. both *sōzō* and *sōtēria* basically denote rescue and deliverance in the sense of averting some danger threatening life. This can be deliverance from war or from danger in the sea, but it can also be deliverance from an illness. Where no immediate danger is mentioned, the words can mean to keep or preserve, even a safe return home. In religious contexts the gods save humans from various perils of life. They are regarded as saviors and protectors.

(b) For Gnostics knowledge given by divine revelation frees the soul from the power of death. In the mystery religions deliverance comes through the initiate's sharing in the experience of the dying and rising god through the actions of the mystery cult. The initiate participates in the divine being and thus attains a life that extends beyond death.

(c) In the philosophical sphere, *sōzō* and *sōtēria* can denote the divine preservation of all things. Plato expressed belief in such an ordering. In the Hel. period, when belief in fate replaced that of a divine harmony, the gods were seen as having power to save and keep people from an inscrutable destiny. Marcus Aurelius, the Stoic philosopher-emperor of the 2d cent. A.D., took comfort from the thought of a higher divine ordering and preservation (*sōtēria*) of life.

2. In the LXX *sōzō* translates at least 15 Heb. vbs., the most important of which are *yāšaʿ* (hiphil), to deliver and save; and *mālaṭ* (niphal), to slip away, escape, or (piel) to deliver, save. *sōtēria* stands for six different Heb. formations, most related to *yāšaʿ*.

(a) Deliverance may come about through humans (e.g., judges and kings, Jdg. 8:22; 13:5; 2 Sam. 3:18; 14:4; 2 Ki. 6:26), though this does not necessarily exclude Yahweh's ultimate agency. In some cases deliverance may lack theological significance (e.g., 1 Sam. 23:5). It may be the relief of a besieged city (11:3) or help in battle (Jdg. 12:2–3). The king was also a deliverer of the poor, needy, and oppressed within the nation (Ps. 72:4, 13).

The OT gives repeated reminders about human limitations. Often humans are powerless to save (Jer. 14:9). God did not want Gideon to think that his victory came as a result of human hands (Jdg. 7:2). Moreover, astrologers are powerless to save (Isa. 47:13), as are idols (45:20; 46:7; Jer. 2:27–28) and the nations (Hos. 14:3 = LXX 14:4). Rather, victory over one's enemies is by the power and name of Yahweh alone (Ps. 33:16–17; 44:3, 6–7). Thus Isa. 30:15 counsels: "In repentance and rest is your salvation, in quietness and trust is your strength." It is important to do Yahweh's work by Yahweh's appointed means.

(b) Regarding yāšaʿ, while Yahweh employs human agents, the pious Israelite is fully aware that deliverance comes ultimately from Yahweh himself. This vb. is esp. prominent in the Psalms, where people look both back to past and ahead to future deliverance from enemies and trouble (e.g., 12:1; 20:9; 28:9; 60:5). Deliverance or salvation is the work of God, but its precise content varies according to context and circumstances. In 74:12 sōtēria denotes the victory over the powers of chaos at the creation, but it can also denote victory over historical enemies (60:11; 144:10).

The theme of salvation and deliverance is by no means confined to Ps., although both there and elsewhere it has often cultic associations. At the climax of Moses' review of Yahweh's dealings with the tribes, Israel is seen as a unique nation, "saved by the LORD ... your shield and helper and your glorious sword" (Deut. 33:29; cf. Exod. 15:2; 1 Sam. 11:13; 14:39). Conversely, Israel's failure to trust Yahweh's saving power provokes his wrath (cf. Num. 10:9; Deut. 20:4; Ps. 78:22; Isa. 17:10; Hab. 3:13). When Yahweh is absent or the people turn to other gods, they are not saved (Jdg. 10:12–14; 1 Sam. 4:3). According to the historical writings and the prophets, victory comes from Yahweh (Isa. 33:2; Jer. 14:8; 15:20; 17:14; Zeph. 3:17).

Solomon prays at the dedication of the Jerusalem temple that priests may be "clothed with salvation" (2 Chr. 6:41; cf. Ps. 132:9, 16) and thus be instruments of the divine blessing, which is pure and holy and at the same time brings deliverance to the people (cf. 2 Chr. 6:36–39). There may be here an underlying allusion to the function of the priests as the givers of oracles of salvation. They are to lead the people into the ways of righteousness, which bring deliverance from trouble (see also Isa. 61:10).

Another expression with cultic overtones is "the cup of salvation" (Ps. 116:13; cf. 16:5). This "cup" may be a drink offering of wine that was part of the thank offering (cf. Num. 28:7), though it may also stand in contrast to the cup of Yahweh's wrath (cf. Isa. 51:17; Jer. 25:15). Similarly in Exod. 14:13 Israel's role in order to receive "the deliverance the LORD will bring" is that of trusting response; the exodus provides a pattern.

Here the salvation in question is earthly and historical. Indeed, many OT references to salvation speak of a material deliverance accompanied by spiritual blessings. But certain passages in the prophets have an eschatological dimension. For example, in the last days Yahweh will bring full salvation for his people (e.g., Isa. 43:5–13; Jer. 31:7 = LXX 38:7; Zech. 8:7). Then Israel "will draw water from the wells of salvation" (Isa. 12:3); the whole world will share in this salvation (45:22; 49:6).

Finally, we should note that yāšaʿ appears in certain proper names that celebrate Yahweh as the deliverer: e.g., Isaiah (which means "salvation of Yah[weh]"). Most noteworthy is Joshua (Heb. yᵉhôšuaʿ, later yēšûaʿ, "Yah[weh] is salvation"), not only the name of Moses' successor (Exod. 17:9–14; Deut. 1:38; Jos. 1:1) but also the name from which Jesus derives (→ Iēsous, 2652).

(c) Regarding the vb. mālaṭ, the fathers of Israel testify that they trusted in God to save them (Ps. 22:5; cf. 8, 21). Job's comforter, Eliphaz the Temanite, argues that God will save the downcast (Job 22:30). The message of this book is that suffering is not necessarily the direct effect of sin and that God's ways are more marvelous than we can comprehend. In the end God does deliver Job and restores to him more than he had at first.

Many OT texts warn against turning for deliverance to that which, in worldly wisdom, we would naturally expect to save us from calamity: an army or the strength of a war horse (Ps. 33:16–17), a

mighty foreign state (Isa. 20:6), wealth (Job 20:20), or one's own understanding (Prov. 28:26). In the coming deliverance prophesied by Isa. 49:24–25, captives will be delivered from those who held them captive. In the last days those who call on the name of the Lord will be saved (Joel 2:32). In Dan. 12:1 those whose names are written in the book of life will be saved.

3. In the Apocr. sōzō is seldom used of one person rescuing another (though see 1 Macc. 6:44; 9:21). It is more often found in the mid. and pass. of being saved through flight (e.g., 2:44; 9:9; 10:83; 11:48). Moreover, the author of 4 Macc. stresses that deliverance cannot be found by abandoning the law (9:4; 15:2, 8, 27). The vb. is always used in the context of dire threat to life. Most occurrences have to do with God's rescuing of the godly (Wis. 9:18; 16:7; 18:5; 1 Macc. 3:18; 4:9, 11). Conversely, the heathen gods cannot save (Ep. Jer. 49). The idea of an eternal salvation that comes from God, as contrasted with an earthly one that comes from humans, is present in 4 Macc. 15:3.

In 1 Enoch 106:16 the idea of being saved occurs in reference to the flood. But the idea occurs most frequently in statements to the effect that the ungodly have no salvation or hope of salvation (5:6; 98:10, 14; 99:1; 102:1). Elsewhere salvation is applied to the individual in both temporal deliverance (T. Reu. 3:9; T. Jos. 10:3) and eternal salvation (T. Benj. 4:1; T. Ash. 5:2). Over against the eternal salvation stands eternal punishment, in which the wicked are cast into the fire. The godly individual attains salvation by prayers and piety and by God's help. But T. Jud. 22:2; T. Ash. 7:3; T. Benj. 10:5 also speak of the eschatological salvation of Israel in which even the nations participate.

4. Josephus generally uses both the noun and the vb. in the sense of rescuing someone from death, a city from an enemy, or the land and the temple from destruction. Similarly, Philo uses them frequently in the sense of rescuing from danger or preservation in a temporal sense, though his main interest lies in the relationship between God and the godly person. God is the savior (sōtēr) who not only preserves order but also saves and helps in the struggles of the soul against the passions. Qumran lit. frequently refers to God's saving and helping in the history of Israel (1QM 4:13; 11:3; 14:4–5; 18:7; CD 5:19; 1QS 1:18–19). But God's saving also figures in the personal life of the godly. Regarded eschatologically, it is not the individual but God's people as a whole who are the objects of salvation.

NT   1. The vb. sōzō is found 106x in the NT, diasōzō 8x, and the noun sōtēria 45x. The meaning of deliverance from physical danger to life is comparatively rare. It occurs, e.g., in the account of Paul's shipwreck (Acts 27:20, 31, 34). Note that five occurrences of diasōzō come in accounts of how Paul escaped various dangers (23:24; 27:43, 44; 28:1, 4); the other three uses of this vb. refer to the sick who touched Jesus' garment being made well (Matt. 14:36), the plea of the centurion to heal his slave (Lk. 7:3), and the eight souls, including Noah, who were "saved through water" (1 Pet. 3:20). The last instance refers to physical danger but has soteriological overtones and is cited as a parallel to baptism, with its symbolism of cleansing and death and resurrection (3:21).

A number of passages use sōzō in the sense of saving from death, but there are often implications of divine deliverance (cf. Matt. 8:25; 14:30). These are esp. prominent in uses of this vb. in events surrounding Jesus' crucifixion. One criminal on the cross railed at Jesus to "save yourself and us," thinking of physical salvation (Lk. 23:39). But the other one sought salvation in terms of repentance and mercy and was promised by Jesus to be with him that day in paradise (23:43). Jesus himself asked whether he should pray, "Father, save me from this hour." No, he replied, "it was for this very reason I came to this hour" (Jn. 12:27; cf. also Heb. 5:7). Such passages show that saving in the NT transcends physical saving.

2. In the Synoptic accounts of Jesus' miracles of healing, sōzō is used 16x and diasōzō 2x (see above). The healing in these stories is

always of the whole person. The faith of the person is of great importance for its achievement, making effective Christ's saving power: "Your faith has healed [*sōzō*] you" (Mk. 10:52; Lk. 8:48; 17:19; 18:42). Here *sōzō* has the sense of delivering from physical affliction. Jesus' acts of healing were continued by the apostles, carried out in the name of Jesus Christ (Acts 4:10); they presupposed faith as necessary for healing (14:9; cf. Jas. 5:15).

The particular theological and soteriological significance of the word group is largely latent in the Synoptic tradition. Zechariah's psalm at the birth of his son, John the Baptist, makes three references to the salvation that the child will herald, but he does so in terms of OT thought. He blesses God for raising up "a horn of salvation for us" (Lk. 1:69; cf. also 1:71, 77; cf. Mal. 4:5; Mk. 1:4). This salvation is construed as being saved from one's enemies. In the OT cleansing from sin was a precondition of physical salvation from one's enemies, but this song suggests that it is the precondition of light and peace (Lk. 1:78–79 cf. Isa. 9:2), now understood in terms of a personal relationship with God in Christ. Matt. 1:21 explains the name Jesus: "He will save his people from their sins."

Certain passages in the Synoptics imply eschatological salvation. In a saying following his challenge to take up one's cross, Jesus declares: "For whoever wants to save his life will lose it, but whoever loses his life for me and for the gospel will save it" (Mk. 8:35; par. Matt. 16:25; Lk. 9:24). Jesus first envisions people standing in a human court where a denial of association with him brings release, whereas admitting such association brings martyrdom. But in the hereafter, the situation is reversed, and those who yield their lives in loyalty to Jesus safeguard it in a deeper sense. Following the saying about the camel and the eye of a needle, the disciples ask, "Who then can be saved?" (Mk. 10:26). Jesus replies: "With man this is impossible, but not with God; all things are possible with God" (10:27). Only the sovereign God can bring one into his eternal kingdom.

This salvation becomes a present fact through the actions of Jesus that bring forgiveness of sins. It is stressed in Lk.'s account of the change that came over Zacchaeus: "Jesus said to him, 'Today salvation has come to this house, because this man, too, is a son of Abraham. For the Son of Man came to seek and to save what was lost'" (19:9–10).

3. In the proclamation of the early church, *sōzō* and *sōtēria* gain a central importance through their application to Christ as the basis, content, and goal of the gospel. They sum up the essential characteristic of his mission. Note esp. Acts 4:12, where Peter declares to the assembled religious leaders that "salvation is found in no one else, for there is no other name under heaven given to men by which we must be saved." *sōtēria* here embraces both healing and salvation, for the occasion is Peter's defense after being arrested for healing the lame man in the temple in the name of Jesus Christ of Nazareth (3:6–8; cf. 4:9–10). Peter took the opportunity to preach Jesus as the servant foretold by the prophets, whom God raised up as Savior from sin (3:12–26). Acts 4:12 makes an absolute and universal claim for the Christian message of salvation.

The apostolic preaching, addressed first to the Jews (Acts 13:26) and then to the Gentiles (16:17), excludes every other way of salvation (13:38; 15:10–11), for salvation can be gained only by faith in Christ (16:31). The salvation given to those who believe consists in the forgiveness of sins (10:43; cf. 26:18) and a new relationship with God.

In Acts, statements about salvation frequently focus on the immediate present. The offer of salvation is linked with the demand, "Save yourselves from this corrupt generation" (2:40). But 2:21, alluding to Joel 2:32, refers to future salvation: "Everyone who calls on the name of the Lord will be saved." The Joel prophecy refers to the end time, and its use here implies that the end time has now arrived. Note that "the name" for Joel was that of Yahweh, whereas in Acts it is applied to Jesus. In him God is personally present in a saving way.

4. Paul frequently uses *sōzō* and *sōtēria* exclusively for the saving activity of God. The message of saving grace comes to us through the gospel message. It brings salvation (Eph. 1:13). "It is the power of God for the salvation of everyone who believes" (Rom. 1:16; cf. 1 Cor. 1:21). The word of the cross is God's power for those who are being saved (1:18). We have obtained deliverance (15:2); we have been saved by the grace of God through faith (Eph. 2:8).

Eph. 1:13 presents a comprehensive picture of the process of salvation: The believers addressed here heard the gospel before their deliverance; they came to faith and were sealed with the Holy Spirit. Paul's statements about the goal of his missionary activity correspond to this. He was intent on bringing the good news of salvation to as many Jews and Gentiles as possible through the preaching of the gospel (Rom. 1:15; 11:14; 1 Cor. 9:22; 10:33; 1 Thess. 2:16). Those who have been saved through faith are contrasted with those who are perishing (1 Cor. 1:18; 2 Cor. 2:15). The apostle testifies that salvation is a present reality through the divine means of grace offered to people, and he adds to his quotation of Isa. 49:8 the words, "Now is the day of salvation" (2 Cor. 6:2).

From Rom. 8:24 we see how strongly Paul was conscious of the inner relation between present and future salvation. The fact that we have already been saved makes the expectation of final eschatological salvation the greater reality, when the final verdict is passed (1 Cor. 3:15; 5:5; cf. 2 Cor. 5:10). This future salvation, which is "nearer now than when we first believed" (Rom. 13:11), is the goal toward which Christians press. All present discipline and punishment have as their purpose that we should not forfeit this salvation (cf. 1 Cor. 9:24–27). Accordingly, in Phil. 2:12 those who have been saved by God's grace are exhorted to work out their future salvation by a sanctified life in fear and trembling.

According to God's plan of salvation, all Israel will share in the future salvation after the fullness of the Gentiles has come into the church of God (Rom. 11:25–26). In this final salvation (1 Thess. 5:8–9; 2 Thess. 2:13) we are concerned first with deliverance from the coming wrath of God (Rom. 5:9; 1 Cor. 3:15; 1 Thess. 1:10) and then with the granting of the divine glory. Then Christians will be fully conformed to the image of God's Son and so God's activity will reach its conclusion (Rom. 8:29; 2 Thess. 2:13–14).

5. In the Pastoral Letters there is a whole series of statements about salvation that shows a comprehensive understanding of it: past, present, and future. (a) God desires the salvation of everyone (1 Tim. 2:4). The task of Jesus was to save sinners; that is why he came into the world (1:15; cf. 2 Tim. 1:9). Paul himself had experienced the saving power of grace, even though he felt he was the chief of sinners.

(b) Regarding the present experience of salvation, God calls us with a holy calling (2 Tim. 1:9). We are saved not because of deeds we have done, but in virtue of his own mercy (Tit. 3:5). Here salvation is linked with baptism and renewal of life through the Holy Spirit (see further *palingenesia*, 4098). According to 2 Tim. 3:14–15, knowledge of the Scriptures can bring salvation through faith in Jesus Christ (cf. Jn. 5:39; 2 Cor. 3:14; Heb. 4:2).

(c) In 2 Tim. 4:18 Paul speaks of the coming salvation; he is confident that the Lord will rescue him into his kingdom. In 2:10 Paul affirms that his sufferings are a necessary service for the elect, so "that they too may obtain the salvation that is in Christ Jesus, with eternal glory." In 1 Tim. 4:16 the future perfection of salvation is promised both to Timothy and his hearers, provided he shows discipline and faithfulness in teaching and life. In 2:15, Paul points out that women will be saved through faith, love, and holiness without abandoning their role as mothers (the meaning of being "saved through childbearing" is not easy to ascertain and is probably lost to us).

6. In 1 Pet. the apostle uses *sōtēria*, along with a number of other expressions, to express final salvation. Christians are guarded by God's power through faith for this salvation, which is already there but will be revealed only in the last time (1 Pet. 1:5). Christians "grow up in [their] salvation" through the spiritual food they receive through preaching and teaching (2:2), so that finally they reach "the goal of [their] faith, the salvation of [their] souls" (1:9). Already the OT prophets pondered on and prophesied about it (1:10).

In 1 Pet. the vb. *sōzō* is found only in 4:18 (quoting Prov. 11:31) and 3:21. In the latter passage baptism expresses the saving power of God; it saves now because of the resurrection of Jesus Christ from the destruction to which humans become subject because of their sins. In this sense baptism is an antitype of God saving Noah and his family "through water" (3:20). It is noteworthy that although 1 Pet. repeatedly mentions present salvation, the apostle seldom uses this word group; instead, he employs such terms as "you were redeemed" (1:18) and "he [God] has given us new birth" (1:3).

In 2 Pet. 3:15 the readers are exhorted to take God's forbearance, the main reason for the delay in the Parousia, as motivation to be concerned with their final salvation, which is sure only if they do not give up their efforts for sanctification. Eschatology and ethics are, as with Paul, closely linked.

7. In Heb. Christ is the "author" and the "source" of our salvation (2:10; 5:9). At his first coming Jesus laid the foundation for the future saving activity of God by his atoning sacrifice. As the one who lives forever, he "is able to save completely those who come to God through him" (7:25). At his second coming Christ will appear as the one who "brings salvation to those who are waiting for him" (9:28). In all aspects salvation is the goal of God's activity with us. This salvation is perfect and eternally valid (5:9). The saving activity of God in Christ began already with Christ's proclamation (1:1–2). From him it came to the hearers of his word, who passed it on, while it was confirmed by God by signs, wonders, various miracles, and by gifts of the Holy Spirit (2:3–4). We should therefore not ignore it (2:3).

8. Jas. uses *sōzō* to mean deliverance in the final judgment, except in 5:15, where it means to heal. The same is true of Jude, where both the noun (v. 3) and the vb. (v. 23) are found. In v. 5 the rescue of Israel from Egypt is the subject.

9. The word group is little represented in the Johannine writings, which speak more of "eternal life." *sōtēria* is found only once in the Gospel in the remark to the Samaritan woman that "salvation is from the Jews" (4:22). *sōzō* in the sense of salvation occurs 4x. In 3:17 and 12:47 Jesus says that he has come not to judge but to save the world; in 5:34 the word is applied to the Jews, in 10:9 to believers. The Son of God is the true and only mediator of salvation. (In 11:12 and 12:27 *sōzō* has the general meaning of being delivered from physical and emotional need.)

In Rev. only the noun is found (3x), in liturgical passages of worship. In 7:10 the great multitude attributes salvation to God and the Lamb (cf. 12:10; 19:1). These songs of triumph and victory proclaim that now, after the conquest of all enemies of God, salvation, glory, and power belong to God alone.

See also *lyō*, to loose, untie, set free, release, annul, abolish (*3395*); *lytron*, price of release, ransom, ransom price (*3389*); *rhyomai*, rescue, deliver, preserve, save (*4861*); *sōtēr*, savior, deliverer, preserver (*5400*).

5393	σῶμα

σῶμα (*sōma*), body (*5393*); σωματικός (*sōmatikos*), bodily (*5394*); σωματικῶς (*sōmatikōs*), in a bodily form (*5395*).

CL 1. In cl. Gk. *sōma* originally meant the corpse of a human or the carcass of an animal. In the 5th cent. B.C., it began to be used in the sense of torso, the whole body, and by extension the whole person. As the idea developed in Gk. philosophy of the soul alongside the body, *sōma* came to mean that which is mortal as distinct from the immortal soul. In Plato, the body is the abode of the preexistent soul; death frees the soul from the body. The picture of the body was also extended to the cosmos, which is ruled and directed by the divine soul. Aristotle held that the body is primarily that by which the soul becomes something particular. The bond between body and soul is thus indissoluble. He also used *sōma* in the sense of an organism to explain the character of the state.

The Stoics continued to maintain the traditional dichotomy of body and soul. The soul is the animating principle, whose seat can be

the head just as much as the heart. The soul permeates the entire body and conveys its sense impressions. However, the basic idea of wholeness in *sōma* remained decisive. The Stoic philosopher Marcus Aurelius spoke of a human as *sōma*, *pneuma* (spirit, soul), and *nous* (mind, reason). The further development of these thoughts together with neo-Platonic ideas led to a devaluation of the body as opposed to the soul.

2. The OT has no dualism corresponding to the Gk. idea of body and soul. In the LXX *sōma* denotes the entire range of ideas conveyed by the Heb. *bāśār*, flesh, signifying a human in his or her individual corporeality. This is distinct from *sarx*, flesh, which denotes humanity in its creatureliness. *sōma* can mean corpse (1 Sam. 31:10, 12) and even back (1 Ki. 14:9). But its basic meaning is the body in the sense of the whole person (cf. Lev. 15:11, 16, 19; 16:4; 19:28; etc.). It has virtually the sense of person, though this is not to be confused with personality. Even angels have *sōmata* (Ezek. 1:11, 23; Dan. 10:6 Theod.).

3. Depreciation of the body as the seat of passion first occurs in Sir. 23:16–18; 47:19. The books of Macc. reflect Hel. influence in the distinction drawn between body and soul (cf. also Wis. 9:15). A good soul and an undefiled body belong together (8:20). But the dominant thought is that of the soul as the particular gift of God. Hence, the body can be given up in persecution.

4. In later Jewish lit., the significance of death stands out in light of the connection between body and soul, for death separates body and soul. The body remains on earth and the soul is taken up to heaven (2 Esd. 60). Rab. lit. confirms the double aspect of the concept of body common in the NT period: In one sense the body is the person; in another, a distinction is drawn between body and soul, spirit, or mind.

5. The notion of the body played a central role in Gnosticism (→ *ginōskō*, *1182*). One's inner self must be set free from the material world of the flesh and the human body; this comes about through redemption. This idea of redemption was also applied to the cosmos. In general, however, Gnosticism postdates NT Christianity.

NT 1. (a) *sōma* in the NT reflects the wide range of meaning that it had in Gk. generally as well as in OT thought. It means corpse (e.g., Matt. 27:52; Lk. 17:37) and is used of the body of Jesus (Matt. 27:58; Mk. 15:43; Lk. 23:52, 55; Jn. 19:31). The thought that a dead body can be raised to life (Matt. 27:52) stands behind the expression "temple . . . [of] his body" (Jn. 2:21). This is the only instance in the Johannine writings where *sōma* does not mean dead body or slave (cf. Rev. 18:13). Paul sheds new light on the body of Christ in Col. 2:9, for he stresses that all the fullness of the Deity lived in Christ "in bodily form" (*sōmatikōs*).

(b) The physical aspect of the body is uppermost in Mk. 5:29 and Jas. 2:16. Matt. 6:22 speaks of the eye as the lamp of the body (cf. 5:29), while 6:25 speaks of the body as being more than clothing. These passages in Matt. point beyond the body as a mere physical organism to the *sōma* as signifying the self.

(c) Heb. 10:10 contrasts "the sacrifice of the body of Jesus Christ once for all" with the temple sacrifices. *sōma* here and in 1 Pet. 2:24 denotes not only Jesus' physical body but the total giving of himself in death. It thus contrasts with the merely physical bodies of animals in the sacrificial system.

2. (a) In Paul *sōma* has a specialized meaning in the sense of person. Human existence (even in the sphere of the *pneuma*, spirit) is a bodily, somatic existence. Passages such as Rom. 6:12 and 12:1 clearly show that the *sōma* is not merely an outer form but the whole person.

In a series of Pauline passages *sōma* denotes the general physical body (e.g., 1 Cor. 5:3; 7:34). In only one passage (1 Thess. 5:23) does Paul speak of humankind in a tripartite way: "May your whole spirit [*pneuma*], soul [*psychē*] and body [*sōma*] be kept blameless at the coming of our Lord Jesus Christ." Rom. 12:4–5 and 1 Cor. 12:12–26 take up the issue of the relation of the body to its members (→ *melos*, *3517*). The "marks of Jesus" that Paul bears in his body are perhaps the scars from wounds received in service to Jesus (Gal. 6:17; cf. 2 Cor. 11:24–27). In 1 Cor. 9:27 Paul speaks of disciplining his body, and in 13:3 he may have had in mind the most painful form of self-immolation (burning), which would be worthless without love. To Timothy Paul emphasizes that bodily or "physical" (*sōmatikos*) training has only limited value (1 Tim. 4:8).

The body is mentioned in connection with sexual relations in Rom. 4:19 and 1 Cor. 7:4. But the warnings against unchastity and immorality (Rom. 1:24; 1 Cor. 6:13–20) show a wider significance here than the merely physical. Bodily acts affect not only the individual act of sin but the whole person to one's innermost being. This is underlined by Paul's questions: "Do you not know that your bodies are members of Christ himself? . . . . Do you not know that your body is a temple of the Holy Spirit, who is in you, whom you have received from God? . . . . Therefore honor God with your body" (1 Cor. 6:15, 19–20).

(b) The body is not something external to a human being that is, as it were, added to one's essential self or soul. *sōma* denotes the whole person. The *sōma* can be the object of an action or the subject of an action. Regarding the former, when Paul speaks of treating his "body" roughly, he means treating himself roughly. Similarly, 1 Cor. 13:3 shows how one can immolate one's self, not just one's body. Moreover, we can sacrifice ourselves in the service of God by presenting our bodies "as living sacrifices, holy and pleasing to God" (Rom. 12:1).

The *sōma* can also be the subject of an action: "If by the Spirit you put to death the misdeeds of the body, you will live" (Rom. 8:13). These misdeeds (i.e., living "according to the sinful nature," 8:12–13) suggest action by one's body. Body here is equivalent to the self, the human "I" in its sinfulness. Similarly, Christians should not be led by the desires of their bodies (6:12), which can be dominated by the power of sin. The desires of the body and the desires of the sinful nature are synonymous (Gal. 5:16–21, 24).

Paul's understanding of *sōma* as "I," as a "person," as distinct from the *sarx* (flesh) is illustrated by Rom. 7:14–25. "I am unspiritual [*sarkinos*], sold as a slave to sin" (7:14). The body is open to two possibilities, desire and obedience. When Paul cries: "Who will rescue me from this body of death?" (7:24), he is thinking of the shattered character of human existence as it finds expression in the body. He sees in his existence the powers of sin and the Spirit, which can mean either destruction or life. One's bodily existence does not in itself denote something either good or bad. Rather, the body is the concrete sphere of existence in which one's relationship with God is realized.

(c) In this light, it is understandable why Paul in 1 Cor. 15 stresses the resurrection of the body over against his Corinthian opponents. His understanding of resurrection is influenced by Jewish anthropology. Human life is thinkable only in a body. Thus, any division of the person into soul and body along the lines of Gk. anthropology is precluded (cf. also 2 Cor. 5:1–10).

In this discourse Paul contrasts an earthly or "natural body" and a "spiritual body" (1 Cor. 15:44). The former represents his earthly existence and the latter his post-resurrection life. These images are presented in spatio-temporal terms, although a spiritual body cannot be conceived in terms of matter. Paul's aim here is to express a person's essential being, which is characterized by existence in a body. The body in the sense of the "I," the person, will survive death through the creative act of God (15:38, 42, 44).

The continuity between the earthly body and the heavenly body does not rest on a transformation. If that were the case, Paul would have stressed the temporal aspect of his concept of the "spiritual body" (15:44). The thought would then be of a body consisting of a substance known as *pneuma*. But Paul is not concerned with the description of such a spiritual substance. His concern is with the fact that God determines this *sōma* through the Spirit as a power of God (cf. 15:50). Thus, after the resurrection this *sōma* is no longer subject to sin and death. It is no longer a divided self. One's personhood is, therefore, not something at one's disposal. It is not founded on oneself. It remains a gift.

(d) Over and above this, *sōma* has a specific meaning in Paul that no longer refers to an individual but to a group. He speaks of the *sōma* of Christ (Rom. 12:5; 1 Cor. 12:27; Eph. 4:12; etc.). Paul uses the picture of the body to express the essential character of the Christian church. In 1 Cor. 12:12–30 his exposition takes up the Gk. thought of the organism, basing the necessity of the different functions of the members on the unity of the body. But the essential character is not based on the Gk. image. The members do not constitute the whole. Rather, it is the *task* of the members that highlights their corporate nature in their diverse functions.

The body constitutes the unity and in this sense can be described as the body of Christ. It is based on Christ himself. The description of the church as the body of Christ means that he constitutes the existence of the individual as a member of his body. The bestowal of the Spirit is connected with baptism (1 Cor. 12:13). The church has an eschatological character. It exists by the promise of God in Christ for the future.

The Lord's Supper is rooted in the concept of the body as a community (Matt. 26:26–29; Mk. 14:22–25; Lk. 22:17–20; cf. 1 Cor. 10:16–17; 11:23–26). Christ's death gives the Lord's Supper its meaning. That death is the decisive saving act "for you" (11:24) and is proclaimed by the Lord's Supper (11:26). In the center stand not the elements or substance of bread and wine but the action of the fellowship as the body of Christ. To be guilty of the body and blood of the Lord (11:27) signifies an act of one believer against another. The giving of Christ's body in death is the authentic sign of his church, which understands itself as the body of Christ.

(e) Col. and Eph. develop a picture of the body of Christ that is distinct from that in the other Pauline letters. In Col. 1:15–20, the cosmic dimension of Christ's saving act is particularly clear, for through his death Christ has reconciled all things to himself (cf. also Rom. 11:36; 1 Cor. 15:24–28; Eph. 1:22–23 for the cosmic significance of Christ). A redemption is offered here that holds good even in the face of the cosmic powers. Christ is the head of the world, and his body is the church, in which obedience to his lordship is proclaimed for realization in the world. Thus, the church and the world are not two great fixed entities set in permanent opposition. The church recognizes the real possibilities for the world under the lordship of Christ and the freedom to live in the world.

The concept of the body as the church of Christ is clear in Eph., where Christ is the head of that body (4:15–16). Believers grow up into him and become mature, building up the church in love. Those who are hesitant and misguided (called "infants" in 4:14) are carried about by every wind of doctrine. These people were perhaps gnostic-type individuals, who boasted of their own knowledge and not of their relationship with Christ. In addition, Paul here provides a definitive understanding of the church. By stressing Christ as the head, he is stressing both lordship and promise. The church is held and sustained by the power of Christ, and he protects it, through the truth recognized by those who are mature and the love practiced by them, from false teaching and schisms.

See also *melos*, member (*3517*).

5394 (*sōmatikos*, bodily), → *5393*.

5395 (*sōmatikōs*, in bodily form), → *5393*.

| 5400 | σωτήρ |

σωτήρ (*sōtēr*), savior, deliverer, preserver (*5400*); σωτήριον (*sōtērion*), salvation, deliverance (*5402*); σωτήριος (*sōtērios*), saving, delivering, bringing salvation (*5403*).

CL & OT 1. In cl. Gk. the noun *sōtēr*, formed from the vb. *sōzō* (save, → *5392*), includes the connotations of *sōzō* and *sōtēria*. It is applied almost exclusively to the gods or humans. (a) The gods are saviors from the dangers of life and also protectors and preservers of humans. The title was accorded to numerous gods, but esp. to Zeus. Isis and Serapis were also frequently called saviors. In the Hel. period Asclepius was regarded as a savior of the sick.

(b) Humans could also be called saviors if they healed or saved others from trouble and danger. Plato called the ideal ruler who governed and preserved the state a *sōtēr* in the sense of a protector. The term could also be applied to philosophers. It was widely applied to statesmen and rulers, such as Philip of Macedon, who was hailed by the inhabitants of Thessaly as friend, benefactor, and savior.

In the Hel. ruler cult *kyrios* ("lord") became part of the official title of kings, and divine honors were accorded them. *theos sōtēr* ("god savior") was also regularly incorporated into the Ptolomaic and Seleucid royal titles. This development reached its strongest expression in the Roman imperial cult. The expression "savior of the inhabited world" was applied to Augustus Caesar. However, *sōtēr* was not incorporated into the *official* titles of the Roman rulers, and an emperor rarely allowed himself to be called *sōtēr* on coins. But in inscriptions an emperor could be called a *sōtēr*, designating him as a benefactor linked with a golden age of peace, order, and prosperity. Although the emperor was called a savior only in a this-worldly sense, he had been empowered by the gods or divine providence.

(c) The adj. *sōtērios*, saving, delivering, bringing safety to, is found in cl. Gk. applied both to humans (e.g., someone bringing safety to the state) and to the gods.

2. *sōtēr* occurs in the LXX 35x for nouns or participles related to the Heb. vb. *yāšaʿ*. (a) In Jdg. 3:9, 15 *sōtēr* ("deliverer") may be taken as a technical term for the Israelite judges (cf. 12:3). Note 2:16: "Then the LORD raised up judges, who saved [*sōzō*] them out of the hands of these raiders" (cf. also Neh. 9:27). Still, Jdg. 2:18 stresses that Yahweh was the ultimate source of the saving. Samuel took the desire for a king as a rejection of "your God, who saves you" (1 Sam. 10:19, LXX "who is your *sōtēr*").

3. *sōtēr* is applied above all to Yahweh. Isa. 45 contrasts the mysteries of Yahweh's working with the impotence of the idols. Yahweh has anointed the Persian king Cyrus to liberate Israel from captivity in Babylon (45:1). Yahweh promises the wealth of the nations to captive Israel. The prophet cries: "Truly you are a God who hides himself, O God and Savior of Israel" (45:15). Israel is saved by Yahweh "with an everlasting salvation" (45:17). Turning to those who carry idols, Yahweh insists that "there is no God apart from me, a righteous God and a Savior." Yahweh is the only God who can save anywhere to the "ends of the earth" (45:21–22; see also such passages as Deut. 32:15; 1 Chr. 16:35; Ps. 24:5; Mic. 7:7; Hab. 3:18; often the LXX speaks of "God my Savior" whereas the Heb. speaks of "the God of my salvation").

The coming Messiah is not called *sōtēr*, even though the promised king in Zech. 9:9 is described by the part. *sōzōn* ("saving one") in the LXX. In Isa. 49:6 the servant of Yahweh's task is to bring Yahweh's "salvation to the ends of the earth."

In the Apocr. the title *sōtēr* is limited to God (Wis. 16:17; Sir. 51:1; Bar. 4:22; 1 Macc. 4:30; 3 Macc. 6:29, 32; 7:16). Josephus uses it only for human saviors; Philo saw God as the Savior of his people, the sustainer of the race and the cosmos, and the Savior of the soul in its struggle with the passions. Apart from one isolated instance in rab. writings, the Messiah is not called a Savior. Elsewhere, God and Messiah are described by the Heb. word *gōʾēl*, redeemer (→ *lytron*, *3389*).

NT *sōtēr* occurs 24x in the NT; 16x it refers to Christ, the remaining 8x are applied to God. Since it is never used of ordinary people, it occurs much less often than either *sōzō* or *sōtēria*.

1. (a) The angel who announced the birth of Jesus to the shepherds told them not to be afraid, for "today in the town of David a Savior has been born to you; he is Christ the Lord" (Lk. 2:11). The use of *sōtēr* here takes up the descriptions given to the national leaders and to God in the OT and Jud. In Lk. the word occurs elsewhere only in Mary's Magnificat, where it is applied to God (1:47; cf. Hab. 3:18). Some think that the use of *sōtēr* in Lk. may reflect the Christian response to the emperor cult (cf. above): Jesus is the true bringer of peace (note the reference to Augustus in 2:1).

(b) In the proclamation of the early church to the Jews, Jesus is presented as the Savior of Israel: "God exalted him to his own right

hand as Prince and Savior that he might give repentance and forgiveness of sins to Israel" (Acts 5:31; cf. 13:23). This preaching clearly draws a distinction between Jesus and God. At the same time, it draws attention to the uniqueness of Jesus as the divinely appointed and empowered one whom God chose as the instrument of salvation. It was precisely this that was the point of conflict between the church and the Jews.

(c) In Jn. it is left to the Samaritans to conclude: "We no longer believe just because of what you [the Samaritan woman] said; now we have heard for ourselves, and we know that this man really is the Savior of the world" (Jn. 4:42). Earlier Jesus had drawn attention to the futility of Samaritan worship and that salvation came from within Jud. (4:22). Paradoxically, however, 4:42 brings out salvation's universal aspect. There is also the further paradox implied by Jn. that the Samaritans have seen this and responded to it in the person of Jesus, whereas the Jews have not.

2. (a) In Paul's letters to churches *sōtēr* is found only twice. Phil. 3:20 reminds its readers of their expectation in the midst of the trials that "we eagerly await a Savior . . . the Lord Jesus Christ," who will return, change us, and take us to himself. Eph. 5:21–33 exhorts husbands and wives to mutual love and respect within marriage, based on the relationship between Christ and his church: "For the husband is the head of the wife as Christ is the head of the church, his body, of which he is the Savior" (5:23). Christ is the Savior because he gave himself up to death for his church and cleansed her by the washing of water and the word, in order to present her for himself pure and glorious (5:25–27).

(b) In the Pastoral Letters *sōtēr* occurs more frequently than in any other NT writings: 6x for God and 4x for Christ. This title for God links with the usage of the LXX (e.g., Ps. 25:5; 27:9; Hab. 3:18; Sir. 51:1). (i) The statements in the Pastorals about God as Savior show that God's offer of salvation is universal. The true and living God is "the Savior" of all people (1 Tim. 4:10), and he has instituted preaching so that the message of salvation might become known to all and that all might believe (Tit. 1:3). We must live lives that "will make the teaching about God our Savior attractive" (2:10). In the next verse, Paul declares that the grace of God is revealed above all in its power, bringing "salvation [that] has appeared to all men." In 1 Tim. 1:1, Paul also calls God "our Savior."

(ii) Passages that speak of Christ as our Savior furnish an all-embracing picture of God's activity for our salvation. To the world God has manifested his purpose to save the human race, planned "before the beginning of time" but now "revealed through the appearing of our Savior, Christ Jesus," who has destroyed death and brought life and immortality to light (2 Tim. 1:10). In this Savior have appeared God's goodness and kindness (Tit. 3:4), qualities praised in Hel. rulers but here transferred to God.

Through God's free purpose, decided before eternal ages, and through his grace revealed in Christ, believers are already saved. Through his cleansing and regeneration, not through our own works, God has saved us according to his mercy. The pouring out of the Holy Spirit has come richly "through Jesus Christ our Savior" (Tit. 3:5–6). As those justified by grace, believers await the fulfillment of their hope (3:7), which they will receive through "the glorious appearing of our great God and Savior, Jesus Christ" (2:13). This translation, while not accepted by all scholars, seems most in line with the patterns of the use of the Gk. article, even though elsewhere Paul distinguishes between God and Christ. Note esp. that *epiphaneia*, appearing (→ *2211*), is nowhere else in the NT used of God, only of Jesus.

The expression "Jesus Christ our Savior" cannot be derived directly from the OT, for there the Messiah is never called Savior. Nor did Jesus ever call himself *sōtēr*. The designation of Jesus as *sōtēr* is found mainly in the Hel. environment, perhaps partly in answer to the imperial cult. This does not explain everything, however, since the references to Jesus as one who saves his people from their sins (Matt. 1:21) occur in writings linked with the Jewish Christian church, and it is only a short jump from there to actually calling Jesus "Savior." The title Savior was necessary to help the Gks. understand what the title Messiah implied for the Jews.

3. Peter uses *sōtēr* in 2 Pet., linking it with the title *kyrios* (Lord; → *3261*). This letter is addressed "to those who through the righteousness of our God and Savior Jesus Christ have received a faith as precious as ours" (1:1). The apostle goes on to exhort his readers to confirm their calling and election, so that "you will receive a rich welcome into the eternal kingdom of our Lord and Savior Jesus Christ" (1:11). Later in the letter he warns believers against being enslaved to the passions after "they have escaped the corruption of the world by knowing our Lord and Savior Jesus Christ" (2:20). He also seeks to stimulate them to wholesome thinking in order "to recall . . . the command given by our Lord and Savior through [the] apostles" (3:2).

The letter of 2 Pet. closes with a command that takes up again the theme of knowledge (cf. 1:2–3, 5–6, 8): "But grow in the grace and knowledge of our Lord and Savior Jesus Christ. To him be glory both now and forever! Amen" (3:18; cf. a similar closing in Jude 25).

4. *sōtērios* is used as an adj. only in Tit. 2:11: "For the grace of God that brings salvation has appeared to all men." Elsewhere it is used in the neut. (*sōtērion*) as a noun, a synonym for *sōtēria* (salvation; → *sōzō*, *5392*) in Lk. 2:30; 3:6; Acts 28:28; Eph. 6:17.

See also *lyō*, to loose, untie, set free, release, annul, abolish (*3395*); *lytron*, price of release, ransom, ransom price (*3389*); *rhyomai*, rescue, deliver, preserve, save (*4861*); *sōzō*, save, keep from harm, preserve, rescue (*5392*).

5401 (*sōtēria*, salvation, deliverance, preservation), → *5392*.

5402 (*sōtērion*, salvation, deliverance), → *5400*.

5403 (*sōtērios*, saving, preserving, bringing salvation), → *5400*.

5404 (*sōphroneō*, be of sound mind, be reasonable, prudent), → *5408*.

5406 (*sōphronismos*, self-discipline), → *5408*.

5407 (*sōphronōs*, reasonably, with restraint, soberly), → *5408*.

5408	σωφροσύνη

σωφροσύνη (*sōphrosynē*), prudence, self-control (*5408*); σωφρονέω (*sōphroneō*), be of sound mind, be reasonable, prudent (*5404*); σωφρονισμός (*sōphronismos*), self-discipline (*5406*);

σωφρόνως (*sōphronōs*), reasonably, with restraint, soberly (*5407*); σώφρων (*sōphrōn*), prudent, sensible, self-controlled (*5409*).

CL & OT 1. Although the *sōphrosynē* word group can be found earlier in cl. Gk., it became esp. important in philosophical circles. The word was consolidated in Plato into the doctrine of the four cardinal virtues: wisdom (*sophia*), courage (*andreia*), prudence (*sōphrosynē*), and justice (*dikaiosynē*). In the relationship of the three classes of the state to one another, the lower ones particularly must exercise self-control. Among the Stoics and in popular philosophy prudence (*sōphrosynē*) also occurs in the scale of the cardinal virtues and was expanded into a series of subordinate virtues (e.g., discipline, obedience, decency, propriety, modesty, temperance, self-control). Some philosophers related *sōphrosynē* specifically to control of the sexual instincts and to chastity.

2. There is no Heb. equivalent for *sōphrosyne*. The noun is found chiefly in 4 Macc. In Wis. 8:7 *sōphrosynē* is one of the four cardinal virtues (the same four as in Plato), which those who love righteousness and wisdom practice. According to Philo, a person ought to suppress one's desires by means of prudence.

NT In the NT *sōphrosynē*, prudence, self-control, is found only in Acts 26:25 and 1 Tim. 2:9, 15; *sōphronismos*, self-discipline, occurs only in 2 Tim. 1:7. *sōphroneō*, *sōphronōs*, and *sōphrōn* occur in Mk. 5:15; Lk. 8:35; Rom. 12:3; 2 Cor. 5:13; 1 Pet. 4:7; and the Pastoral Letters (1 Tim. 3:2; Tit. 1:8; 2:2, 5, 6, 12). The NT does not contain a formal scheme of the four cardinal virtues, even though the paraenetic sections make use of the language and forms of the Hel. environment. The Pastoral Letters in particular stand within the Hel. tradition and thus adopt the admonition to be prudent in the correspondingly general sense of moral formulas (1 Tim. 3:2; Tit. 1:8; 2:2). *sōphrōn* in Tit. 2:5, where the women are addressed directly, has the meaning of chaste, pure (cf. 1 Tim. 2:9). Being prudent is here cited as a Christian virtue.

Thoughtful and prudent action is to be grounded in faith (Rom. 12:3). Paul thus appeals for an attitude that perceives both its own limitations and other people in their humanity, and that determines its action towards others accordingly. Prudence is a necessary element of a love that maintains the tension between commitment and reflective distance.

See also *enkrateia*, self-control, self-restraint, abstinence (*1602*).

5409 (*sōphrōn*, prudent, sensible, self-controlled), → *5408*.

T *tau*

5415	ταλαιπωρέω

ταλαιπωρέω (*talaipōreō*), experience distress, endure hard labor (*5415*); ταλαιπωρία (*talaipōria*), strenuous work, suffering, hardship (*5416*); ταλαίπωρος (*talaipōros*), wretched, distressed (*5417*).

CL & OT 1. Cl. authors used *talaipōreō* for those who endured hard work or suffered distress, perhaps to the point of being worn out physically or emotionally. *talaipōria* varied from the concept of regular exercise or normal usage to that of hard work, hardship, or suffering, the latter including pain caused by physical diseases. *talaipōros* describes people and circumstances that are wretched and miserable.

2. In the LXX *talaipōreō* is found mainly in prophetic lit. (e.g., Isa. 33:1; Jer. 4:13, 20; 10:20), usually in its ordinary physical sense, meaning to assail, distress, deal violently with. *talaipōria* is common in the LXX (e.g., Job 5:21; Hos. 9:6; Mic. 2:4) and describes troubles and difficulties (lit. or fig.) that are of a serious nature. *talaipōros* occurs mostly in the Apocr. to describe the persecutions of the Maccabean period (e.g., 2 Macc. 4:47).

NT *talaipōreō* occurs in the NT only in Jas. 4:9, a call to penitence and humility that exhorts readers to "grieve." *talaipōria* occurs only 2x in the NT: in Rom. 3:16, where Isa. 59:7 is quoted, and in Jas. 5:1, where it means "misery." *talaipōros* is also found only 2x (Rom. 7:24; Rev. 3:17), both describing a miserable, wretched condition of humanity.

See also *basanos*, torture, torment (*992*); *mastigoō*, whip, flog, scourge, chastise (*3463*); *ōdinō*, to travail as in giving birth (*6048*).

5416 (*talaipōria*, strenuous work, suffering, hardship), → *5415*.

5417 (*talaipōros*, wretched, distress), → *5415*.

5424	ταπεινός

ταπεινός (*tapeinos*), lowly, humble (*5424*); ταπεινόω (*tapeinoō*), make low, humble (*5427*); ταπείνωσις (*tapeinōsis*), abasement, humiliation (*5428*); ταπεινόφρων (*tapeinophrōn*), humble-minded (*5426*); ταπεινοφροσύνη (*tapeinophrosynē*), lowliness of mind, humility (*5425*).

CL & OT 1. (a) *tapeinos* was originally used with the sense of low-lying, although fig. uses were soon developed: (i) low socially, poor, powerless, unimportant; (ii) despondent, downcast; (iii) in ethical teaching, one should avoid the two extremes of arrogance and pride (*hybris*), and of groveling and servile behavior. (iv) Occasionally the word is used with a positive connotation in individual, social, ethical, and religious contexts; there it means unassuming, obedient, conforming one's behavior to the righteous laws of the gods.

(b) The vb. *tapeinoō* represents the various shades of meaning of the adj.: to level, humble (socially, politically, economically), make small, discourage, be obedient, etc. The reflexive form with *heauton* and the mid., meaning humble or demean oneself, is used normally in a derogatory sense. In some occasions, however, it could mean humbling oneself before the gods by covering one's head during sacrifice and prayer.

(c) *tapeinōsis* suggests the process of humiliation or being made low. *tapeinophrōn* and *tapeinophrosynē* generally have a depreciatory connotation: e.g., to think poorly, ill; to be ill-disposed, faint-hearted, or weakly; to have a servile mind.

2. In the Gk. world, with its anthropocentric view of humanity, lowliness was looked on as shameful, something to be avoided and overcome by act and thought. But in the OT and NT, with its theocentric view of humans, the words have a positive thrust, since they describe those events that bring a person into a right relationship with God and one's fellow human beings.

3. *tapeinos* and its cognates are found approximately 270x in the LXX. It uses the full range of meaning of this word group and adds a few variants of its own; e.g., to humble a woman in a sexual sense (Deut. 21:14; 2 Sam. 13:12; Ezek. 22:10–11), to rape (e.g., Gen. 34:2), to fast (e.g., Lev. 16:29; Isa. 58:3). But above all the words occur in expressions of belief in what Yahweh has done, in that he brings down the proud and arrogant and rescues the humiliated. This recognition is expressed in a number of ways. (a) The prophets express it in warnings of judgment (e.g., Isa. 2:9, 11, 17; 5:15; 10:33–34; 14:32; Zeph. 2:3) and in promises (Isa. 49:13; Zeph. 3:12).

(b) The historical books see it in events. This is shown in their theological attitudes and in their corresponding choice of language (e.g., in Hannah's prayer and song, 1 Sam. 1:11, 16; 2:7; in the promise given to David, 1 Chr. 17:10).

(c) Ps. and Lam. repeat it in prayers (e.g., Ps. 10:17–18; 25:18; 31:7). There is frequent parallelism with the poor. The relationship between Ps. 82:3 and 5–7 shows that the gods are incapable of giving justice to the lowly, so God himself must judge.

(d) Prov. speaks of humility as the fruit of experience and as a rule for life (e.g., Prov. 3:34; 11:1–2; 15:33 = LXX 16:1; 16:19; 18:12).

4. The members of the Qumran sect called themselves the poor, and in the Community Rule virtuous humility is mentioned along with lovingkindness, truth, right thinking, faithfulness, unity, and patience as the great virtue of the community (1QS 2:24; 4:3; 5:3, 25). This attitude stands alongside a hatred for the ruling sons of darkness (9:22; 11:1–2). Humility is the proper attitude before God as humans submit to his chastisement (1QH 17:22).

5. For the rabbis, humility also had a high place in the scale of virtues that people should attain, a humble spirit being the characteristic sign of the Jew. Jesus' teaching indicates a wide discrepancy between this high ideal and actual Pharisaic practice (Matt. 23:1–7; Lk. 18:9–14). They were humble among themselves but considered ignorance of the law to be a result of either sin or God's disfavor.

NT 1. Words of this group are found 34x in the NT. In Matt. and Lk. the words are closely linked with the proclamation of the eschatological breaking-in of the kingly rule of God. This is the new element in the frequent use of OT texts. Lk. introduces the theme in the opening chs. of his Gospel. The mother of Jesus praises the grandeur of God in OT phrases: "For he has been mindful of the humble state of his servant" (Lk. 1:48; cf. 1 Sam. 1:11; Ps. 113:5–9); "He has . . . lifted up the humble" (Lk. 1:52; cf. 1 Sam. 2:7; Job 5:11; Ps. 75:7). The work of John the Baptist is then presented as preparing for the coming of God, in accordance with the prophecy of Isa. 40:3–5, "every mountain and hill [shall be] made low" (Lk. 3:5).

Jesus himself went the way of humility (Matt. 11:29). He could, therefore, warn against desire for status (Lk. 14:11; cf. also Matt. 18:4; 1 Pet. 5:5) and promise that those who humble themselves will be exalted by God (Matt. 23:12; Lk. 18:14). In the same verses he threatens the proud with the last judgment.

2. The foundation of this promise and warning is found in Jesus' own way of life as expressed in his invitation in Matt. 11:28–30. He is "gentle [*praus*] and humble [*tapeinos*] in heart." The two thoughts stand in parallelism and show that Jesus was submissive before God, dependent on him, and devoted to him, and at the same time humble before human beings, whose servant and helper he came to be (Matt. 20:28; Mk. 10:45; Lk. 22:27). That is why he could call those who are weary and burdened to himself and offer them rest as they follow him.

Matt. 18:1–5 shows that Jesus' call to discipleship, with its teaching on humility, should not be confused with ethical attainment. The demand to humble oneself like the child that was placed among the disciples does not mean that one should make oneself lower than one actually is. Rather, one should know, like the child, how lowly one really is. Humility is to know how lowly we are before God. Such humility and lowliness bring joy and bliss, for they permit one to share in the royal rule of heaven.

3. (a) The central position of the Savior's invitation in Matt. corresponds to that of the hymn to Christ in Phil. 2:6–11. In Paul's description of Jesus' work from his self-emptying (→ *kenos*, *3031*), through his self-humbling (2:8), and to his exaltation by God, all the main lines of the OT proclamation of God's sovereign control of history come into focus as they find their fulfillment. Here God stands by his word. At the same time the self-humiliation of Jesus Christ inaugurates the new life under his rule (cf. 2:10–11). The meaning of self-humiliation is doubly defined in Jesus Christ. On the one hand, Jesus became obedient unto death, even the uttermost shame of the cross. On the other hand, he had no other support than the incredible promise of the faithfulness of God (cf. Ps. 22; 25:18; 31:17; 119:50, 92, 150; esp. Isa. 53:7–12).

(b) Acts 8:35 expounds Isa. 53:7–8, referring to the humiliation (cf. *tapeinōsis* in Acts 8:33) and exaltation of Jesus Christ.

(c) Paul understood his own apostolic service to be one of following the Lord, who gave him strength through his own exaltation won through self-humiliation. Hence Paul knew "what it is to be in need" (*tapeinoō*), i.e., being hungry and suffering want and affliction (Phil. 4:12–13; cf. 2 Cor. 11:23–29; 12:7–10). This experience may also include the physical work that, his enemies insinuated, was a penance for some hidden sin, but which Paul defended on the grounds that it enabled him to proclaim the gospel without charge (11:7).

Lk. faithfully conveys Paul's understanding of his apostolic service in the statement, "I served the Lord with great humility and with tears" (Acts 20:19). Paul recognized God's action both in humbling him through his failures (2 Cor. 12:21), which were manifest in the continuing strife and immorality of the Corinthians (12:20–21), and in comforting those who were humbled by strife and inner fears (7:5–6; cf. Isa. 49:13). In the midst of the difficulties of his service, Paul was supported by the hope that the coming Lord would transform "our lowly bodies" (lit., "our body of humiliation," Phil. 3:21) and make it like his glorious body.

(d) In three passages in Paul's letters words from this group are used in their original derogatory sense—in each case ironically in a polemical context. In 2 Cor. 10:1 Paul quotes the taunt of his opponents that he was so "timid" (*tapeinos*) when he was with them but bold when far away. In Col. 2:18, 23 he warns against the opponents who take pleasure in "false humility" (*tapeinophrosynē*), worship of angels, and asceticism.

(e) Paul's exhortation to humility is also rooted in the effective reality of Christ. Rom. 12:16 warns against haughtiness and recommends either, "Be willing to associate with people of low position," or, "Be willing to do menial work" (see NIV note). Similarly Eph. 4:2 and Col. 3:12 enjoin being humble (both passages using *tapeinophrosynē* parallel to *prautēs*; → *praus*, *4558*), which unites the church and holds it together.

4. The exhortations in Jas. and 1 Pet. do not add anything new to the OT and Paul's calls to humility. Jas. 1:9–10 speaks of the socially low, the poor, who can boast of their exaltation, while the rich, paradoxically, should boast of their low position (*tapeinōsis*), i.e., of their being subject to death. Jas. 4:6 and 1 Pet. 5:5 both quote Prov. 3:34, which promises God's favor to the humble, and both draw the conclusion: "Humble yourselves before the Lord, and he will lift you up" (Jas. 4:10; cf. 1 Pet. 5:6). In 1 Pet. 5:5 one also sees the metaphor of putting on clothing: "All of you, clothe yourselves with humility [*tapeinophrosynē*]" (cf. Jn. 13:4).

5. Gradually the concept of "humility" in the church changed from an eschatological expectation and a manner of life to a term describing an inclination to penance and fasting.

See also *praus*, gentle, humble, considerate, meek (*4558*).

5425 (*tapeinophrosynē*, lowliness of mind, humility), → *5424*.

5426 (*tapeinophrōn*, humble-minded), → *5424*.

5427 (*tapeinoō*, make low, humble), → *5424*.

5428 (*tapeinōsis*, abasement, humiliation), → *5424*.

5429	ταράσσω

ταράσσω (*tarassō*), shake together, stir up, disturb, unsettle, thrown into disorder (*5429*); τάραχος (*tarachos*), commotion, confusion, disturbance (*5431*).

CL & OT 1. In cl. Gk. *tarassō* means to shake something out of inertia and throw it into confusion, i.e., to disturb, upset, confound, agitate (from the stirring up of the sea or movement of the air to violent emotional agitation); hence it can mean to confuse, also to shake. There is a corresponding use of the pass.: to be disturbed, agitated, confused, even become alarmed. *tarachos* connotes agitation, confusion, tumult.

2. The LXX uses *tarassō* on the whole in the same way as cl. Gk., to render various Heb. equivalents (cf. Ezek. 32:2, 13, to trouble water; Ps. 46:6, of the nations in uproar; Isa. 8:12, to be dismayed, alarmed).

NT 1. In the NT *tarassō* occurs 17x and *tarachos* 2x. The meaning is essentially the same as in cl. Gk. (a) *tarassō* is used of the stirring of the water in the pool of Bethesda (Jn. 5:7). This water was perhaps disturbed from time to time by an intermittent spring, but popular belief supposed that at such times an angel endued the water with healing properties. The pool was more than 50 feet deep, with no shallow end, so a disabled person would have had to be carried and held all the time.

(b) *tarassō* is also used in a fig. sense to express the stirring up of spiritual or emotional excitement or confusion, e.g., as when the Jews stirred the emotions of the crowds in Acts 17:8, 13, or when false teachers brought the churches into confusion (15:24; Gal. 1:7; 5:10; cf. Acts 12:18, *tarachos*). The part. *hoi tarassontes* in Gal. 1:7 likely means that as the result of another, adulterated gospel, the churches of Galatia have become confused in their understanding and thus also in their actions—a confusion that may be fatal, since it destroys the living organism of the church. The sing. in 5:10 refers to the same false teachers as a unit. These people will have to answer before the judgment seat of God for the confusion they have sown.

(c) The pass. can sometimes have a negative sense, connoting emotional disturbance: to become terrified, be afraid or overawed. This form of the vb. occurs 5x in the Synoptic Gospels (Matt. 2:3; 14:26; Mk. 6:50; Lk. 1:12; 24:38). In each case the reference is to an emotional shock that is brought about not by any human action, but by an action of God—including Matt. 2:3, where Herod and Jerusalem are shaken at the report of the Messiah's birth.

(d) A different thought is contained in the expression in Jn. 14:1, 27: "Do not let your hearts be troubled." In this formula (cf. Ps. 55:5; 143:4), the heart stands for the self. Since the disciples will soon be left alone in a world in which there is conflict between the powers of this world and God's revelation, they will undergo inward shock and anxiety. This anxiety will be overcome, however, by faith in God, which is identical with faith in Jesus, since this faith knows of a home (14:1) where death has been conquered. Believers need not remain in a condition of fear and anxiety, since they have the promise of eschatological peace (14:27; cf. also 1 Pet. 3:14).

(e) Jesus too is at times troubled. At Jn. 11:33 *tarassō*, together with *embrimaomai* (be deeply moved), denotes the wave of anger that came over him when confronted with so much lack of faith and hope, although life itself was present within his person at the tomb of Lazarus. At 12:27 Jesus' words "my heart is troubled" do not refer simply to an emotional experience. The fear and anxiety he experienced shows that he has humbled himself to the utmost in order to take on himself our lost human condition and in this very condition to glorify the Father.

2. *tarachos* denotes the stir caused by Christians in both its occurrences (Acts 12:18; 19:23).

5431 (tarachos, commotion, confusion, disturbance), → 5429.

5434	ταρταρόω

ταρταρόω (*tartaroō*), send to Tartarus, hell (*5434*).

CL & OT *tartaroō,* to send or hurl into Tartarus, is a vb. dependent on Gk. mythology. Tartarus was a dark abyss, deep below Hades, to which rebellious gods and disobedient humans were sent for torment and punishment. It was surrounded by a brazen wall and encircled by impenetrable darkness. Specifically, the Cyclopes and Titans were imprisoned there by Uranos, Kronos, and Zeus (→ *ouranos, 4041*). Jewish apocalyptic writers in the intertestamental period adopted this language as another term (in addition to *geenna*) for where the ungodly were punished (e.g., *1 Enoch* 20:2, Gk. MSS). Although the vb. does not occur in the LXX, the noun *tartaros* does (e.g., see Job 41:31 = LXX 41:23, where it refers to the depths of the sea that Leviathan plays in; Prov. 30:16 = LXX 24:51, where it translates *šᵊʾôl*, one of the aspects of reality that is never satisfied).

NT In the NT *tartaroō* occurs only in 2 Pet. 2:4, which adopts the Jewish apocalyptic view of *tartaros* as the place where the disobedient angels were sent after they rebelled against the Lord. This place, however, is not the actual place of punishment for these angels. Rather, they are being "held" in the "gloomy dungeons" of *tartaros* for punishment later—presumably in *geenna* (→ *1147*). By being held there, God limits their ability to wreak havoc on the earth.

This is one of the only biblical passages that alludes to the fall of the angels, an event that presumably preceded the temptation of Adam and Eve in the Garden of Eden. Many scholars, however, see a reference here to Gen. 6:1–4, which in Jewish apocalyptic writers was frequently understood as a time when angels ("the sons of God") stepped out of their bounds and sinned against God by cohabiting with human women ("the daughters of men"), producing a rebellious race of humans, who were subsequently destroyed in the flood.

See also *abyssos,* abyss, pit, underworld (*12*); *hadēs,* Hades, the underworld, the realm of the dead (*87*); *geenna,* Gehenna, hell (*1147*); *katōteros,* lower (*3005*).

5435	τάσσω

τάσσω (*tassō*), arrange, appoint (*5435*); προστάσσω (*prostassō*), command, appoint (*4705*); διατάσσω (*diatassō*), command, order (*1411*); διαταγή (*diatagē*), ordinance, direction (*1408*); ἐπιτάσσω (*epitassō*), command, order (*2199*); ἐπιταγή (*epitagē*), order, injunction (*2198*).

CL & OT 1. *tassō* is common in cl. Gk. Its first meaning is military: draw up troops (or ships) in battle array. From this the vb. came to mean direct or appoint someone to a task, arrange, set up, put things or plans in order. *prostassō, diatassō,* and *epitassō* mean mostly command, order, arrange. The corresponding nouns have the same import. All these vbs. and nouns imply an acknowledged authority and power residing in the person from whom decisions or directives issue.

2. In the LXX the words in this word group are used with both God and humans as the arranging or directing agents. *tassō* is used far more frequently than any of the other three vbs. *diatagē* is used only in Ezr. 4:11 and *epitagē* in Dan. 3:16; Wis. 14:16; 18:16; 19:6; 1 Esd. 1:18; 3 Macc. 7:20.

NT 1. *tassō* is used 8x and means some order or arrangement that has been made. It denotes God's appointment of "the authorities that exist" (Rom. 13:1), of a career of service "assigned" for Paul (Acts 22:10),

and of individual persons "appointed" for eternal life through believing the gospel (13:48). In the mid. voice it means to make a mutual arrangement (28:23).

2. *prostassō,* with its official sense of command, occurs 7x and is used with the angel of the Lord (Matt. 1:24), Moses (8:4; Mk. 1:44), and Peter (Acts 10:48). In Acts 10:33 it refers to God's charge to Peter, and in 17:26 to God's setting of definite epochs in history.

3. *diatassō* occurs 16x and refers to various types of orders and commands. Jesus gave various directives to his disciples when he sent them out (Matt. 11:1; cf. 1 Cor. 9:14). God too can give orders (e.g., to Moses, Acts 7:44). But so can humans, such as the emperor Claudius (18:2) and Felix, the governor of Judea (23:31; 24:23). The apostle Paul did not hesitate to give orders to those churches he had started, such as his command to the ones in Galatia to participate in the collection for Jerusalem (1 Cor. 16:1) and his directives to the church in Corinth (7:17; 11:34). He also made assignments for Titus to carry out on Crete (Tit. 1:5). *diatagē* occurs only 2x in the NT. In Acts 7:53 it refers to the law put into effect through angels, and in Rom. 13:2 it refers to government leaders as being instituted by God.

4. *epitassō* occurs 10x. Like the other words in this group, it refers to various sorts of commands or orders. Several times it refers to orders that Jesus gave to evil spirits, who obeyed him (Mk. 1:27; 9:25; Lk. 4:36; 8:31). He also ordered the wind and waves to become calm (8:25). Humans in positions of power can give orders (Mk. 6:27; Acts 23:2). Paul believes he can order Philemon to take Onesimus back, but decides to appeal to him instead (Phlm. 8). *epitagē* occurs 7x, all in letters of Paul. It is used 5x in the expression *kat' epitagē,* according to command (e.g., a command from God, 1 Cor. 7:25; 1 Tim. 1:1; Tit. 1:3). In 1 Cor. 7:6 Paul insists that his word is not to be taken as a command but as advice. In 2 Cor. 8:8 he resorts to exhorting the Corinthians on the collection rather than commanding them again (in contrast to 1 Cor. 16:1–2). Titus is to preach "with all authority [*epitagē*]" (Tit. 2:15).

See also *kathistēmi,* bring, appoint, (*2770*); *horizō,* determine, appoint (*3988*); *paristēmi,* place, put at the disposal of (*4225*); *procheirizō,* determine, appoint (*4741*); *tithēmi,* put, place, set, appoint (*5502*); *prothesmia,* appointed date (*4607*); *cheirotoneō,* appoint (*5936*); *lanchanō,* obtain as by lot (*3275*).

5438 (taphē, burial), → 2507.

5439 (taphos, tomb), → 2507.

5446	τεῖχος

τεῖχος (*teichos*), wall around a city (*5446*); τοῖχος (*toichos*), wall of a house (*5526*).

CL & OT 1. In cl. Gk. *teichos* means a wall, esp. around a city. *toichos* is the wall of a house, temple, enclosure, side of a tent.

2. *teichos* occurs 193x in the LXX and generally means a town or city wall (e.g., Isa. 22:10), occasionally of other buildings (Lam. 2:7), and fig. of a chaste maiden difficult to approach (Song 8:9–10). *toichos* is used 88x and means the wall of a house or a room (Amos 5:19), the temple (1 Ki. 6:5), or occasionally a vineyard (Num. 22:25).

NT 1. In the NT *teichos* consistently means city wall. The local disciples lowered Saul of Tarsus in a basket through a window in the city wall to allow him to escape from Damascus (Acts 9:25; 2 Cor. 11:33). In Heb. 11:30 *teichos* is used for the walls of Jericho collapsing before Joshua's army.

In Rev. 21 *teichos* occurs 6x for the high city wall of the new Jerusalem (21:12), which symbolizes the eternal security of the inhabitants and excludes those outside (22:15). The twelve foundations of the city and its twelve gates are inscribed with the names of the twelve apostles and the twelve tribes of Israel, respectively, signifying the completeness of the number of the people of God under the two covenants. The measuring of the wall by an angel (21:17) not only draws attention to its extraordinary height but also alludes to its divine protection. The wall is said to be built of jasper and adorned with twelve different jewels, each gate being made of a single pearl (21:17–21).

2. *toichos* appears only in Paul's rebuke of the high priest Ananias as a "whitewashed wall" (Acts 23:3). The one dispensing justice ought to be a wall firm and true, supporting the house of Israel, its laws, and all who live within its shelter. The fig. of a *whitewashed wall*, on the other hand, suggests a structure whose precarious condition has been disguised by generous coats of whitewash (cf. Ezek. 13:10–16).

See also *mesotoichon*, dividing wall (*3546*); *phragmos*, fence, wall, hedge (*5850*); *charax*, pointed stake, palisade, rampart, mound (*5918*).

| 5447 | τεκμήριον | τεκμήριον (*tekmērion*), proof (*5447*). |

CL & OT In cl. Gk. *tekmērion* almost always means strict proof. In Aristotelian logic it denotes a compelling sign. This sense is suggested in the LXX (Wis. 5:11; 19:13; 3 Macc. 3:24).

NT *tekmērion* occurs only at Acts 1:3, where Lk. refers to many "convincing proofs" as infallible evidence of the resurrection of Christ. Lk. did not view Jesus' appearances as mere visions, since Jesus ate and drank with his disciples in his resurrected body (e.g., Lk. 24:41–43; Acts 1:4; 10:41).

See also *deiknymi*, show, explain, prove (*1259*).

5448 (*teknion*, little child), → *5451*.

5449 (*teknogoneō*, bear children), → *5503*.

5450 (*teknogonia*, childbearing), → *5503*.

| 5451 | τέκνον | τέκνον (*teknon*), child (*5451*); τεκνίον (*teknion*), little child (*5448*). |

CL & OT *teknon* denotes a child in relation to one's parents and ancestors. In the LXX it is used both of a child still unborn (Gen. 3:16; 17:16) and an elder son (27:13); it does not distinguish sex. In addition to the broader meaning of descendant (30:1), the word is also used metaphorically as an intimate form of address (43:29) or for a pupil in relationship to his master (1 Sam. 3:16; 26:17). In Ps. 34:11 wisdom calls out: "Come, my children, listen to me." *teknion*, diminutive of *teknon*, is a nursery term and denotes the little child (no occurrences in the LXX).

NT 1. In the Gospels, *teknon* describes the relationship of parents to their children (Matt. 18:25; 21:28; Mk. 13:12; Lk. 15:31; cf. Acts 21:5) and pictures our relationship with God (Matt. 7:11; Lk. 11:13). Note its use in Jesus' lament over Jerusalem (Matt. 23:37; Lk. 13:34) and in the generic sense of descendant (Matt. 3:9; Lk. 3:8; cf. also Jn. 8:39; Rom. 9:7–8; Gal. 4:31). Jesus uses the word as a form of address (Matt. 9:2; Mk. 2:5; 10:24).

There are several NT references to parent-child relationships. The obedience of children to their parents (Eph. 6:1; Col. 3:20) should be reciprocated by the kindness of parents towards their children (Eph. 6:4; Col. 3:21; cf. 1 Thess. 2:7). The parent's task includes warning; in a similar vein, Paul warns the church (2:11). He compares his flock to children (1 Cor. 4:14; 2 Cor. 6:13; Gal. 4:19) and saw his relationship to Timothy and Titus as a father-child relationship (1 Cor. 4:17; Phil. 2:22; 1 Tim. 1:2; 2 Tim. 1:2; 2:1; Tit. 1:4). The Pastoral Letters lay great stress on orderly family relationships (1 Tim. 3:4, 12; Tit. 1:6). *teknion*, little child, is used only in the Johannine writings, and then only as a form of address to the disciples or the church (Jn. 13:33; 1 Jn. 2:1, 12, 28; 3:7, 18; 4:4; 5:21).

teknon can, however, also describe characteristics of a particular group: those who have fallen under God's wrath (NIV, "objects [*tekna*] of wrath, " Eph. 2:3); "children of light" (5:8); the obedient (1 Pet. 1:14); those who stand under a curse (2 Pet. 2:14; cf. also 2 Jn.

1, 4, 13; 3 Jn. 4). Arndt regards most of these as Hebraisms, together with the expression children of wisdom (i.e., those who attach themselves to wisdom and are led by her, Lk. 7:35) and the designation of the inhabitants of a city as its *tekna* (Matt. 23:37; Lk. 13:34; 19:44; Gal. 4:25; cf. Joel 2:23; Zech. 9:13; 1 Macc. 1:38).

2. Paul's starting point is the promise that those who belong to Israel stand under God's blessing (Rom. 9:4–5; Gal. 4:21–22). But who belong to Israel? Not the natural descendants (*tekna*) of Abraham (Rom. 9:6–7; Gal. 4:23), but those who believe (see 3:7; cf. Rom. 8:13). It is not a question, therefore, of a natural relationship as children to God, but of a legal acceptance by adoption of believers as God's children and as heirs of the promise. The gift that establishes the relationship (adoption, *huiothesia*; → *huios*, *5626*) is the Spirit, who cries Abba, Father, leads us into freedom, and engenders in us the hope of sonship (Rom. 8:13–17, 19–23; cf. Gal. 4:5–6).

Jn. sees being children of God in terms of begetting and birth, as a new being mediated by initiation. The child (*teknon*) of God is born of God (Jn. 1:12–13; 1 Jn. 2:29; 3:2). Children of God and children of the devil stand opposed (3:10). Love for God and love for fellow believers characterize God's children (cf. 4:21). John uses *huios* (son) for Jesus Christ as the one and only Son of God (Jn. 3:16; 20:31), but *tekna* of those who receive him and so become his children (see 1:12–13; 1 Jn. 3:2). In Eph. 5:1 the church is called to be *mimētai tou theou*, imitators of God, and as such are *tekna agapēta*, dearly loved children. This expresses the call to discipleship.

Discipleship may, however, entail under certain circumstances the abandonment of all by the disciple, even one's children (Mk. 10:29–30; cf. Lk. 14:26). The horror of the end is depicted, among other things, in terms of a father set against his child and a child against the parents (Matt. 10:21; Mk. 13:12; cf. Lk. 21:16).

See also *nēpios*, infant, minor (*3758*); *pais*, child, young man, son, servant (*4090*); *huios*, son (*5626*).

5452 (*teknotropheō*, bring up children), → *5503*.

| 5454 | τέκτων | τέκτων (*tektōn*), builder (*5454*); ἀρχιτέκτων (*architektōn*), master builder (*802*); τεχνίτης (*technitēs*), craftsman (*5493*); τέχνη (*technē*), art, skill, trade (*5492*). |

CL & OT In cl. Gk. *tektōn* means a craftsman or builder in wood, stone, or metal; *architektōn* means a head builder, contractor, or director of works; *technitēs* means a craftsman, artisan, or designer; and *technē* means an art, craft, trade, or professional skill.

In the LXX all of these words appear in their cl. meaning. It is noteworthy that, unlike the more intellectual and aristocratic societies of Greece and Rome, the Jews had a high regard for manual work and a deep respect for those who did it well, whose ability was seen as a gift of God's Spirit (Exod. 35:30–36:2).

NT *tektōn* appears in the NT only in the identification of Jesus by the people of Nazareth as "the carpenter" (Mk. 6:3), "the carpenter's son" (Matt. 13:55). Though carpenter is the common rendering here, *tektōn* can also mean mason; perhaps Joseph and Jesus were builders, so that both carpentry and masonry were among their skills.

architektōn occurs only in Paul's description of himself as "an expert builder" (cf. the LXX of Isa. 3:3) who laid the foundation of the Corinthian church (1 Cor. 3:10). Paul identifies this foundation with Christ: i.e., Christ as set forth in the doctrines Paul preached, the teaching of reconciliation through the cross and the new community created thereby.

technitēs bears its ordinary sense of craftsman in Acts 19:24, 38; Rev. 18:22, but in Heb. 11:10 the word is applied to God as the craftsman who has built the heavenly city for which his people hope.

technē has its ordinary sense of skill or trade in Acts 17:29; 18:3 (where Paul and Aquila are identified as tentmakers or leather-workers); and Rev. 18:22.

5455 (*teleios*, complete, perfect), → *5465*.

5456 (*teleiotēs*, perfection, maturity), → *5465*.

5457 (*teleioō*), bring to completion, complete, accomplish, finish, fulfill, make perfect), → *5465*.

5459 (*teleiōsis*, perfection, fulfillment), → *5465*.

5460 (*teleiōtēs*, perfecter), → *5465*.

5462 (*teleutaō*, come to an end, die), → *650*.

5463 (*teleutē*, end, euphemism for death), → *650*.

5464 (*teleō*, bring to an end, finish, complete, carry out, accomplish), → *5465*; *teleō*, (to pay what is owed), → *5468*.

5465	τέλος

τέλος (*telos*), end, conclusion, close, goal (*5465*); τελέω (*teleō*), bring to an end, finish, complete, carry out, accomplish (*5464*); τελειόω (*teleioō*), bring to completion, complete, accomplish, finish, fulfill, make perfect (*5457*); τέλειος (*teleios*), complete, perfect (*5455*); τελειότης (*teleiotēs*), perfection, maturity (*5456*); τελείωσις (*teleiōsis*), perfection, fulfillment (*5459*); τελειωτής (*teleiōtēs*), perfecter (*5460*); συντέλεια (*synteleia*), completion, close, consummation (*5333*); συντελέω (*synteleō*), bring to an end, complete, carry out, fulfill, accomplish (*5334*).

CL & OT 1. (a) In cl. Gk. the noun *telos* meant a turning point, the culminating point at which one stage ends and another begins; later the goal, the end. Marriage is in this sense a *telos*, as also is death. *telos* can mean the completion of physical and/or intellectual development, as the use of the word *teleios* also makes clear. *telos* can have also dynamic character, as in the ratification of a law. This dynamic character is also clear in the religious sphere, where sacrifices and religious rites are called *telē*; their goal is to bring people nearer to God. Also of significance is the religious description of God as the *archē kai telos*, the beginning and end of all things, who embraces totality.

(b) Anything that has reached its *telos* is *teleios*, complete, perfect. One brings something to completion, perfection (*teleioō*). The pass. of *teleioō*, to be made perfect, to reach perfection, is used equally of human adulthood and of fully grown plants. The rare noun *teleiotēs* denotes a state of completeness or perfection.

(c) In Gk. philosophy *telos* has the primary meaning of goal. For the pre-Socratics the goal of life was delight in the beautiful, contentment, and contemplation. In Plato and Aristotle the *telos* to which one aspires is an ethical goal and ultimately happiness and bliss. Thus in the realm of ethics Plato can equate the concept of the perfect (*teleios*) with that of the good (*agathos*). In Gnosticism "perfection" is a technical term in the myth of the "redeemed Redeemer." He is the "perfect man." Anyone who is saved by him through true knowledge is the "perfect" gnostic.

2. (a) *telos* occurs more than 150x in the LXX, chiefly in adverbial combinations. *eis telos* (15x) means forever (e.g., Job 20:7; Ps. 9:6; Hab. 1:4) or utterly (e.g., 2 Chr. 12:12). It is also important to note that *telos* repeatedly translates Heb. words meaning end, border, boundary. In such cases it means conclusion, end (cf. 2 Sam. 15:7; 2 Ki. 8:3).

(b) *teleō* is found 28x in the LXX, usually meaning to bring to an end, to fulfill (e.g., Ruth 2:21; Ezr. 9:1). It occurs in the pass. as a religious term: to consecrate oneself (e.g., to the service of Baal Peor, cf. Num. 25:3, 5; Ps. 106:28).

(c) *teleios* (21x) usually means complete, sound; the stress lies on being whole, perfect, intact. It is used of the heart that is wholly turned toward God (1 Ki. 8:61; 11:4) and of the one who is bound wholly to God (Gen. 6:9; cf. Deut. 18:13). The thought of totality is also shown in the mention of a total depopulation (Jer. 13:19) and in the fact that whole offerings can be called *teleiai* (Jdg. 20:26; 21:4).

(d) *teleioō* (25x) has likewise the idea of being perfect and whole: to show oneself perfect, i.e., blameless (2 Sam. 22:26); to make beauty perfect (Ezek. 27:11). It is used 9x times in the Pentateuch as a religious term meaning to consecrate for the cult (e.g., Exod. 29:9, 29). But this word also means to bring to its conclusion (2 Chr. 8:16; Neh. 6:16).

(e) *teleiotēs* (only 6x) signifies perfection or integrity (Jdg. 9:16, 19; Prov. 11:3).

(f) *teleiōsis* (17x) occurs mainly in connection with cultic usage, occurring chiefly in connection with the consecration of priests.

3. (a) The OT apocalyptic lit. uses *synteleia*, end, completion (e.g., Dan. 8:19; 11:27; Heb. *qēṣ*), although the word is also used frequently elsewhere. In this eschatological sense *qēṣ* in rab. lit. refers chiefly to the days of the Messiah's coming that were ordained before the end of the world.

(b) In Qumran the term "perfect" is colored by the OT. Those who are perfect are those who keep God's law wholly and so walk perfectly in his ways (cf. 1QS 1:8; 2:2). In a narrower sense the members of the community are called "the perfect" (8:20).

(c) Philo has a double *telos* in a person's life: wisdom (*sophia*; i.e., the perfect and direct understanding of God that comes about by learning) and virtue (*aretē*), attained by practice. He has three stages on the way to perfection: beginners, advanced, and perfect. Repentance holds second place to perfection (*teleiotēs*). Both Philo and Josephus make use of the comprehensive description of God as *archē kai telos*, beginning and end.

NT In the NT the words of this group occur fairly often: *telos* 40x, *teleō* 28x, *teleios* 19x, *teleioō* 23x, *teleiotēs* 2x, *teleiōtēs* once (Heb. 12:2), and *teleiōsis* 2x. *telos* occurs frequently in the Synoptic Gospels and Paul, *teleō* particularly in the Synoptics and in Rev., whereas *teleios* and its derivatives are most common in Heb.

1. *The letters of Paul.* (a) Paul uses *telos* to mean end result, ultimate fate. Rom. 6:21–22 speaks of the alternatives that face a person as a result of his or her conduct: death or life (cf. Ps. 73:17). According to Phil. 3:19, the enemies of the cross of Christ will find their ultimate fate in eternal destruction (cf. also 2 Cor. 11:15). There is a debate on the meaning of *telos* in Rom. 10:4. Many consider it to mean that in Christ the law has ceased to be the way of salvation. But others argue that *telos* here denotes the logical end or goal of a process, its consummation (cf. 1 Tim. 1:5, "the goal of this command is love"). In this meaning, "Christ is the end of the law" in the sense of its climactic development, which in turn implies the end of the validity of the OT law.

In 1 Cor. 10:11 Paul refers to "the fulfillment [*telos*] of the ages" that have come over us; by this Paul means that we are living in the last days (cf. 7:29, 31). In 15:24 *telos* refers to the conclusion of the eschatological events (cf. Mk. 13:7 par.), the point of time when Christ hands over the kingdom to his Father. Finally, in a different vein, in Rom. 13:7 *telos* means tax (cf. 13:6, *teleō*, pay taxes; → *telōnion*, customs house, tax office, *5458*).

(b) *teleō* twice means to achieve one's object: of the power of Christ in the weakness of the apostle (2 Cor. 12:9), and of the desires of the flesh (Gal. 5:16). In two other places this vb. means to bring to an end: of fulfilling the law (Rom. 2:27) and of completing one's course (2 Tim. 4:7). Acts 20:24 uses *teleioō* in this sense (cf. 13:25).

(c) *teleios* occurs 5x meaning mature, adult: 1 Cor. 2:6; 14:20; Eph. 4:13; Phil. 3:15; Col. 1:28. Twice this word denotes that which is wholly in accord with God's will (Rom. 12:2; Col. 4:12). In 1 Cor. 13:10 "perfection" means the future world, in which everything imperfect (13:9), which distinguishes our present world, is overcome. Col. 3:14 calls love the "perfect unity," for by it the gifts given to the church (3:12–13) are fitted together into a whole.

2. *The Synoptic Gospels.* (a) In the eschatological discourses of Jesus *telos* is used as a technical term for the end of the world (Matt. 24:6, 14; Mk. 13:7; Lk. 21:9; cf. *synteleia [tou] aiōnos*, the consummation of

the age, Matt. 13:39–40, 49; 24:3; 28:20). It also occurs several times in the prep. combination *eis telos*, which probably refers to the end of the world (Matt. 10:22; 24:13). In Lk. 18:5 *eis telos* simply means finally.

The phrase *telos echein*, to have an end, occurs 2x. In Mk. 3:26 a kingdom in which division dominates will cease to stand (cf. on this Lk. 1:33, where the reign of Christ has no end). Lk. 22:37 attributes to Jesus the statement that "what is written . . . is reaching its fulfillment," for the words of Scripture (Isa. 53:12) were being fulfilled in him. *telos* as outcome is found in Matt. 26:58 and as tax in 17:25.

(b) Characteristic of Matt. is his use of *teleo* in the formulaic ending of Jesus' five great discourses and the resumption of narrative ("when Jesus had finished . . . ," 7:28; 11:1; 13:53; 19:1; 26:1). Lk. 12:50 and Matt. 10:23 (the disciples will not have come to the end of the towns of Israel before the Parousia breaks on them) also have the sense of carrying through to the end. Lk. uses the vb. 2x in the pass. for fulfillment of Scripture (18:31; 22:37; cf. Acts 13:29) and once in the act. for fulfilling the law (Lk. 2:39).

(c) Among the Synoptics, the adj. *teleios* occurs only in Matt. In 5:48 is the summons to be perfect, as the heavenly Father is perfect. In the light of the context, this is a command to be compassionate, to love friend and foe (cf. Lk. 6:36). To serve God with an undivided heart can also mean to sell one's possessions and give them to the poor (Matt. 19:21).

(d) Lk. is the only Synoptic writer to use the vb. *teleioo*. When the Passover feast "was over," the boy Jesus stayed behind at Jerusalem (2:43). Jesus told the Pharisees to tell Herod that "on the third day I will reach my goal" (13:32). Despite Herod Antipas's threats of murder Jesus intended to continue his work for salvation "today and tomorrow." What his completion on the third day signifies is not entirely clear. Does it mean that God will put an end to his work on the third day? Or does Jesus mean that whatever violence is inflicted on him, he will go on working, for "on the third day" he will be completed notwithstanding, i.e., rise from the dead (cf. 9:22; 18:33; 24:7, 46)?

3. *James and 1 Peter.* (a) In Jas. *teleios* (5x) has the basic meaning of "whole." One is perfect, i.e., not lagging behind in any point (1:4), when one is patient and forbearing. Jas. calls the law of freedom, by which he means the commandment to love one's neighbor (2:8), "perfect" (1:25), because this alone makes us really free (cf. Jn. 8:31–32; Gal. 5:13). That God's gifts can be called "perfect" (Jas. 1:17) goes without saying. According to Jas., the person who does not offend in words is "perfect" and not "at fault" (3:2). *teleioo* accordingly means to become whole: Only through works is faith brought to wholeness (2:22, cf. 2:17, 20). Elsewhere Jas. also uses *telos* as outcome (5:11; cf. Matt. 26:58) and *teleo* as to fulfill (a law, 2:8; cf. Lk. 2:39).

(b) *telos* is used in 1 Pet. 4x: as a goal (1:9), as an eschatological term (4:7; cf. Matt. 24:6), as one's ultimate fate (1 Pet. 4:17; cf. Rom. 6:21–22), and as meaning "finally" (1 Pet. 3:8; cf. the adv. *teleios*, meaning entirely, fully, in 1:13).

4. *Hebrews.* This word group occurs with the greatest frequency, relatively speaking, in Heb. (18x); only the vb. *teleo* is lacking. (a) By contrast with its use in the rest of the NT, *teleioo* is here attested 9x, nearly always with cultic overtones (cf. OT discussion above). It means to make perfect in the sense of consecrate, sanctify, so that, like the OT priest, one can come before God. Heb. uses the vb. to differentiate Christ—the high priest perfected through suffering (2:10) and made eternally perfect (7:28), who was thus able to be the source of eternal salvation for his people (5:9)—from the priests of the old covenant, who were subject to weaknesses (7:28) and whose sacrifices could not perfect their consciences (9:9; cf. also 10:1). Christ alone was able to perfect his people by a single sacrifice (10:14). The law (7:19), i.e., the Levitical priesthood, has completely failed to bring about "perfection" in anyone (*teleiōsis*, 7:11). Thus Heb. calls Christ's heavenly sanctuary "more perfect" (9:11) in contrast with the earthly one.

teleioo is used 2x without cultic reference. Heb. 11:40 means that the witnesses to faith under the old covenant (11:39) did not reach

perfection, for this was given only by Christ (cf. 10:14). Now, however, God's people share in that perfection (12:23).

(b) *teleios*, mature, occurs in 5:14. *teleiotēs*, "maturity" (6:1) means that part of Christian doctrine intended for adults; it is the opposite of *archē*, the beginning teachings (5:12; 6:1). In 12:2 *teleiotēs* stands alongside *archēgos*: Jesus is the beginner and perfecter of faith. He has not only maintained faith right to the end (5:7–8; 12:3), but he has also laid the foundation of faith (cf. 1:3).

(c) *telos* occurs in two prep. combinations: *mechri telous*, "till the end" (3:14) and *achri telous*, "to the very end" (6:11; see also the uses of *telos* in 6:8; 7:3).

5. *The Johannine writings.* (a) In Jn. 4:34; 5:36; 17:4, Jesus uses *teleioo* to denote the works of the Father that he must accomplish. Then on the cross he can say that they have been accomplished (*tetelestai*, "it is finished," 19:30, cf. 19:28). In his high priestly prayer Jesus asks that his own people be perfected in unity (17:23), so that the world will believe that the Father has sent the Son (cf. 17:21). In 19:28 *teleioo* is used of Scripture being fulfilled. Jn. uses *telos* to denote the full extent of Jesus' love or his love to the very end (13:1).

(b) In 1 Jn. the pass. of *teleioo* is used 4x with reference to love. Love of God reaches its completion when people keep his word (2:5) and love their neighbors (4:12). This love attains its goal in that they are liberated from fear on the judgment day (4:17; cf. 2:28). One who knows fear is not perfectly determined by this love, for "perfect [*teleios*] love drives out fear" (4:18).

(c) Rev. has *teleo* 8x, usually meaning to finish or to be finished. Rev. 11:7 refers to the completion of a testimony, while 15:1 announces the seven last plagues on the world in which God's wrath is brought to completion (cf. 15:8). Rev. 20 speaks 3x of the end of the thousand-year reign (20:3, 5, 7), while 10:7 and 17:17 deal with the mystery of God or the words of God being fulfilled.

Regarding *telos*, the formula "beginning and end" (cf. Isa. 41:4; 44:6; 48:12) expresses the power of God (Rev. 21:6) and of Christ (22:13), which embraces time and creation. Just as God is the beginning and the end (cf. 1:8), the creator and perfecter of all things, so also is the exalted Christ (cf. 1:17; 2:8). Thus in 2:26 Jesus exhorts his church to hold fast continually the works of Christ "to the end."

6. In summing up the theological function of this word group in the NT, a distinction can be drawn between an eschatological and an anthropological aspect. The two are bound up with the general areas of meaning associated with *telos* and *teleios*.

(a) First and foremost is the eschatological function of *telos*. The dynamic, goal-directed character of the noun is further underlined by the frequent use of the vb. *teleo*. This aspect stands out with particular clarity in passages concerned with the future consummation in the Synoptics (e.g., Mk. 13), Paul's letters (e.g., Phil. 3:19), and Rev. (e.g., 20:1–7). The important point here is that the end is not understood simply as the mechanical cessation of movement but rather as the consummating conclusion of a dynamic process, the goal of which manifests the realization of its meaning and its intentions.

(b) Connected with the idea of the end as the completion and realization of a goal is the sense of *teleios* as that which has reached its goal and is thus completed and perfected. To the extent that the whole is achieved only at the end, *teleios* may be applied in its fullest sense only to God (Matt. 5:48) and Christ (cf. Heb. 7:28). In the context of individual human development *teleios* applies to humans who have reached maturity, the grown persons who have come of age (esp. in Paul). The NT does not speak of an ideal of ethical perfection that is to be realized by degrees. Rather, when viewed against the background of the OT, *teleios* signifies the undivided wholeness of a person in one's behavior. When applied to humankind and ethics, therefore, *teleios* denotes not the qualitative end point of human endeavor, but the anticipation in time of eschatological wholeness in actual present-day living. Christian life in the NT is not projected idealistically as a struggle for perfection, but eschatologically as the wholeness a person is given and promised.

See also *engys*, near (*1584*); *eschatos*, last, end (*2274*).

5467 (*telōnēs*, farmer of taxes, tax collector), → *5468*.

5468	τελώνιον

τελώνιον (*telōnion*), customs house, tax office (*5468*); τελώ-νης (*telōnēs*), farmer of taxes, tax collector (*5467*); ἀρχιτελώνης (*architelōnēs*), chief tax collector (*803*); τέλος (*telos*), toll, customs duty, revenue (*5465*); τελέω (*teleō*), to pay what is owed (*5464*) (for other meanings of *telos* and *teleō*, → *telos*, end, goal, *5465*).

CL & OT 1. (a) The *telōnēs*, tax farmer, was a notorious figure at ancient Athens. The system of farming out sources of government revenue from taxes, tolls, property, land, mines, etc., goes back to the Gk. city states. Their *polis* constitutions did not provide for long-term civil servants. But by the tax-farming system the city was guaranteed a known income without the need for a complex financial administration. The privilege of farming taxes was auctioned annually. The successful individual or group had to have acceptable backers underwriting prompt payment, who then had to pay a first installment before being allowed to collect dues from the public. For the actual collection the tax farmers used employees, who in turn had to extract a sum over and above that required by their masters in order to provide an income for themselves. From the public's point of view it was a hated system, open to abuse.

The Romans operated a somewhat similar system, where the business of collecting taxes was left to certain leading officers, called *publicani*, chiefly belonging to the equestrian order. They paid an agreed sum to the government. These *publicani*, who were wealthy individuals, sublet the tax-collecting to agents (*magistri*), and the agents engaged local officials (*portitores*) to collect the dues. It was these *portitores* who are referred to in the NT as *telōnai*. The *telōnai* had to belong to the native population in order to be aware of local ways and to run less risk of being deceived. Indeed, they themselves almost invariably succeeded in deceiving and fleecing the tax-paying public.

(b) *telōnion* means a custom house, tax office; later, customs duty. *telos*, which usually means end, fulfillment (→ *5465*), can also denote duty for the state, payment of toll or tax. Similarly, *teleō* generally means to carry out, execute a plan, but also to pay what one owes, esp. in dues and taxes.

2. In the LXX *telos*, when meaning tax, translates *mekes*, tax collected for Yahweh from war booty (Num. 31:28, 37–41). It also translates other Heb. words to mean the redemption price of a field in the year of Jubilee (Lev. 27:23) as well as a general tribute imposed by King Artaxerxes (Est. 10:1). *teloneō*, to impose taxes, occurs in 1 Macc. 13:39, of tolls exacted from the Jews by the Syrians. In 1 Macc. 10:31; 11:35 *telos* means customs duty. *teleō* does not appear in the LXX with the meaning of render or pay.

3. (a) The first reference to tax farming in Palestine dates from the time of Ptolemy II Philadelphus in the 3d cent. B.C. Josephus refers to the collecting of taxes from the Jews during the Seleucid period. The capture of Jerusalem by Pompey in 63 B.C. led to the imposition of Roman taxation. But in 30 B.C. Augustus allowed Herod the Great to control his own finances, collecting taxes directly through royal slaves.

(b) Jewish sources distinguish two classes of tax officials: those responsible for income tax and poll tax, and customs officers stationed at bridges and canals and on state roads. During the time of Roman rule, taxation remained constant, but at a harsh level. The province of Judea alone had to find 600 talents annually. Tacitus mentions that in A.D. 17 the provinces of Syria and Judea begged for a reduction in taxes. There was some relief from A.D. 37 when the governor Vitellius remitted the market duty on crops.

According to the Mishnah, a Jew entering the customs service cut himself off from decent society. He was disqualified from being a judge or even a witness in court and was cast out of the synagogue. His family members were considered equally tarnished. Because of their exactions and extortions, customs officials were relegated to the same legal category as murderers and robbers. Money handled by tax collectors was tainted and could not be used, even for charity.

NT 1. The *telōnai* are mentioned only in the Synoptic Gospels. They themselves are not the holders of the tax-farming contracts, who are usually foreigners, but subordinates hired from among the native population. Herod Antipas adopted the farming system for Galilee and Perea, but as an imperial province, Judea paid taxes not through tax farmers but directly to the imperial treasury (Mk. 12:14). The responsibility for collection was imposed on the Sanhedrin, under the supervision of the Roman procurator.

The prevailing method of tax collection afforded collectors many opportunities for greed and unfairness. Hence *telōnai* were hated and despised as a class. Strict Jews were also offended by the fact that the tax collector was rendered unclean through continual contact with Gentiles and because his work involved breaking the Sabbath. Contemporary public opinion is accurately reflected in the disagreeable associations expressed in the NT: *telōnai* are linked with sinners (Matt. 9:10), pagan Gentiles (18:17), prostitutes (21:31), and extortioners, imposters, and adulterers (Lk. 18:11).

2. (a) Jesus teaches that for Christians to fail to include their enemies and persecutors in their love is to leave themselves on no higher a moral and spiritual plane than the most despised classes: tax collectors and pagan Gentiles (Matt. 5:46–47). Lk., writing to a wider audience, uses the more general term "sinners" (Lk. 6:33).

(b) Jesus' summons to the tax collector Matt. to join him (Matt. 9:9) must have outraged and bewildered public opinion. For Matt. himself (called Levi by Mk. and Lk.) the call of Jesus entailed great sacrifice, for he left everything (Lk. 5:28). Fishermen could return to their boats (Jn. 21:3), but a *telōnēs* who gave up his occupation had no prospect of another job, even with the skills he undoubtedly possessed (e.g., being multilingual and experienced in keeping records).

Matt.'s toll house (*telōnion*) at Capernaum commanded both the sea route from east and north of the Sea of Galilee and also the land road that led from Damascus to the Mediterranean Sea (Matt. 4:15). Customs would be levied on all goods carried by ship or caravan. In Matt.'s case the duty would be collected not on behalf of the Roman government but for the tetrarch Herod Antipas. This fact would, however, not make Matt.'s calling or class any less unpopular.

(c) Jesus' presence at the farewell banquet Matt. arranged for his old associates (Lk. 5:29) inevitably drew criticism from the teachers of the law and Pharisees. In answer to the accusation that by eating with such people he was defiling himself, Jesus uses a current proverb to equate tax collectors with the sick. Jesus associates with these people not for his own sake (because, unlike the Pharisees, they are sympathetic to him and receptive to his message), or even (as his enemies might hint) because birds of a feather flock together. Rather, just as a doctor must get near to patients in order to treat them, so Jesus shares the company of the outcasts of society, for he knows that they are spiritually sick and needy (Matt. 9:12; Mk. 2:17; Lk. 5:31).

(d) Jesus speaks of the refusal of the Pharisees to respond either to the Baptist or to himself. John was criticized for his asceticism and Jesus for exuberance in the company of tax collectors and sinners (Matt. 11:19; Lk. 7:29, 34). Often the spiritual response of the despised put their religious betters to shame (Matt. 8:2, 8–9; 9:9–13; 15:28; 21:32), but as a category of people tax collectors could still be referred to as those who were uninterested in spiritual matters. If an offending Christian brother refuses to heed the local congregation, he is to be regarded as putting himself outside the religious community, i.e., joining the same class as Gentiles and tax collectors (18:17).

3. Light is thrown on the parable of the unmerciful servant (Matt. 18:23–35) when it is seen against the background of tax farming. The two debtors and the other servants are ministers (*douloi*) of the king and probably engaged in the collection of taxes. The vast sum due to the king from the first minister is not necessarily hyperbolic (Josephus refers to one tax farmer who owed 16,000 talents). The minister's

plea for time is genuine, and the king releases him from immediate liability. When later the same minister's own hard-heartedness is exposed, the king delivers him to the torturers, who by severe examination will extract information from him about his personal assets.

4. Since *architelōnēs* is found only once (Lk. 19:2), Zacchaeus's official position is not clear. Probably he was the equivalent of the Roman *magister*, the intermediary between the *publicani* and the *portitores*. Jericho was a likely post for a tax officer of some standing, and one who would inevitably become rich. That city was an important customs station at the main ford of the Jordan, some seventeen miles from Jerusalem, and on the major route between Judea and lands east of the river. Zacchaeus's undertaking to recompense anyone he had defrauded (19:8) need not imply his own use of extortion. As the leading member of a company of *publicani*, he was responsible for and tainted by the actions of his subordinates. By inviting himself to this man's house, Jesus gently put pressure on his host's conscience. His initiative accomplished what many must have regarded as a miracle no less astonishing than any of his supernatural actions.

See also *logeia*, collection (of money), tax (*3356*); *statēr*, stater, a silver coin worth four drachmas (*5088*).

5469	τέρας

τέρας (*teras*), miraculous sign, prodigy, portent, omen, wonder (*5469*).

CL & OT 1. In cl. Gk. *teras* referred to terrible appearances that elicited fright and horror and that contradicted the ordered unity of nature. This gave rise to the meaning of *teras* as a miraculous sign or portent, which often came from the gods, esp. in the sense of an uncanny omen requiring interpretation by a seer.

2. In the LXX *teras* is different from the cl. Gk. usage. It is true that the character of the unusual also belongs to the word in the OT, but this is based on the fact that God created the world and controls nature, so that in essence these are not contrary to nature but works of God. Essential for *teras* is a reference to the self-revelation of Yahweh. The word thus designates a prophet who is made a sign (Isa. 8:18; 20:3; Ezek. 12:6, 11; 24:24, 27), and further, a man who becomes a manifestation of God's wrath and a horrible "portent" (Ps. 71:7; cf. 31:12). An event that announces future judgment can also be called a sign of horror (1 Ki. 13:3, 5). In apocalyptic contexts *teras* in Joel 2:30 is a baneful sign of the end (→ *sēmeion*, *4956*). Finally, the word can denote miracles in general (Exod. 7:9; 11:9; 2 Chr. 32:31, esp. when linked with *sēmeion*; cf. 32:24).

NT In the NT *teras* occurs 16x, always in the pl. and only in combination with *sēmeion* (→ *4956* for comments on *sēmeia kai terata*).

See also *thauma*, object of wonder, wonder, marvel, miracle (*2512*); *sēmeion*, sign, wonder, miracle (*4956*).

5475	τέσσαρες

τέσσαρες (*tessares*), four (*5475*).

CL & OT 1. The symbolic significance of the number four (*tessares*) is derived from the four points of the compass and the four directions of the wind (whereby the earth is pictured as a four-cornered disc), also from the four seasons and the corresponding constellations. In Babylonian mythology the four signs of the zodiac (Taurus, Leo, Scorpio, and Aquarius) appear as powerful figures that support the firmament of heaven by its four corners, or as the four beasts of burden of the four-wheeled heavenly chariot. The number four thus symbolizes the totality of earth and universe.

2. The OT uses *tessares* in this traditional sense, but without taking over the mythical connotations (e.g., Ezek. 1:4–18). Thus, in accord with ancient geography, four streams of Paradise encircle the four quarters of the globe (Gen. 2:10–14). In Zech. 1:18–21 the four horns represent four empires; in 6:5 the four spirits or winds denote

Yahweh's omnipotence. The four winds or corners of the earth are mentioned in Isa. 11:12 and Jer. 49:36 (= LXX 25:15; → *forty* as a multiple of four, *tesserakonta*, *5477*).

NT In the NT the number four occurs in the purely numerical sense (e.g., Mk. 2:3; Jn. 11:17; 19:23, where the division of Jesus' clothes into four presupposes that number of soldiers; Acts 21:9, 23; 27:29). In Peter's vision of the sheet with four corners containing clean and unclean animals (denoting God's acceptance of the Gentiles), the imagery may suggest the four corners (10:11; 11:5) of the vault of heaven. The four horns of the altar are mentioned in Rev. 9:13 (cf. Exod. 30:1–3).

Esp. in apocalyptic texts, the number four occurs with a symbolic meaning. But in most cases, the apocalyptic or mythological background is not decisive for the meaning. Thus the idea of gathering the elect from "the four winds" (Matt. 24:31; Mk. 13:27) is comparable with saying from all quarters. In Rev. 4:6, 8; 5:6, 8, 14; 6:1, 6; 7:11; 14:3; 15:7; 19:4 (cf. Ezek. 1:5–22), the imagery of the ancient world is formally adopted but with a transformed significance. The four living creatures, perhaps alluding to figures of the zodiac supporting the vault of heaven, become (by analogy with Isa. 6:2–3) creatures who praise God's holiness by day and by night. The four angels at the "four corners of the earth" who hold the winds (Rev. 7:1) and then later let them go (9:14–15) are creatures who serve God.

5477	τεσσεράκοντα

τεσσεράκοντα (*tesserakonta*), forty (*5477*).

OT Periods of forty days occur repeatedly in the OT (e.g., Gen. 7:4; 8:6; Exod. 24:18). Forty years was the duration of Israel's desert wanderings (16:35). Perhaps the number forty is a round number designating a generation. Forty is often associated with long periods of human endurance and the duration of successive developments of God's redemptive acts. In apocalyptic lit., forty days is the proper period for a term of instruction (*2 Bar.* 76:4; cf. *4 Ezra* 14:23). At Qumran, the war of the Sons of Light and the Sons of Darkness was to last forty years (1QM 2:6).

NT In keeping with forty as an important number in God's redemptive acts, Jesus was forty days in the desert (Matt. 4:2; Mk. 1:13; Lk. 4:2) and remained with his disciples forty days after the resurrection (Acts 1:3). There are several references in Acts and Heb. to the forty-year period of Israel in the desert, and it seems to have been a theme of early Christian preaching (Acts 7:36, 42; Heb. 3:9, 17; cf. Acts 7:23, 30; 13:21).

The Jews were scrupulously careful not to exceed the maximum of forty stripes in a flogging (Deut. 25:3; 2 Cor. 11:24).

5492 (technē, art, skill, trade), → *5454.*

5493 (technitēs, craftsman), → *5454.*

5498	τηρέω

τηρέω (*tēreō*), preserve, keep (*5498*); τήρησις (*tērēsis*), observance (*5499*); παρατηρέω (*paratēreō*), watch (closely), observe (*4190*); παρατήρησις (*paratērēsis*), observation (*4191*).

CL & OT 1. In cl. Gk. *tēreō* means: (a) have in view, perceive, observe; then (act.) wait for (the right opportunity); (mid.) be on one's guard; (b) guard, watch over, preserve (things, persons, or ethical values); (c) pay attention to, obey, comply with. The derivative noun *tērēsis* means: (a) guard, custody, detention; (b) prison; (c) observance, obedience. The compound *paratēreō* is identical with the simple vb.; *paratērēsis* is used only for observance of legal demands.

2. In the LXX *phylassō* has the same basic meaning and is much more common (over 400x) than *tēreō* (38x), which occurs mostly in wisdom lit. The predominant meaning of *tēreō* is that of religious observance, relating either to God's commands (1 Sam. 15:11; Prov. 19:16) or those of wisdom (3:1). Note the parallelism between *phylassō*

and *tēreō* in Prov. 13:3: "He who guards [*phylassō*] his lips guards [or preserves, *tēreō*] his life" (see also 16:17; 19:16). In Dan. 9:4, God keeps (*tēreō*) his covenant with all who obey (*phylassō*) him.

3. *tērēsis* is found in the LXX only in the Apocr. In Wis. 6:18, Sir. 32:23 (= LXX 35:23) it is used for the result of the love of wisdom or of the commandments. Otherwise it is used for the guarding of persons or of a city. *paratēreō* (6x) means lie in wait for; *paratērēsis* is found only as a variant reading (Aquila) in Exod. 12:42.

NT 1. In the NT *phylassō* (→ *5875*) occurs 31x, whereas *tēreō* is found 70x. Thus, the NT prefers the word less used in the LXX. In the NT *tēreō* means: (a) guard, keep watch (e.g., Matt. 27:36; Acts 16:23); (b) keep (e.g., Jn. 2:10; 12:7; 2 Pet. 2:4); (c) keep blameless, uninjured (e.g., 1 Cor. 7:37; 1 Thess. 5:23; 1 Tim. 5:22); (d) protect (e.g., Jn. 17:15); (e) hold fast (e.g., Eph. 4:3; Rev. 16:15); (f) follow, obey (e.g., the law, Jas. 2:10; the Sabbath, Jn. 9:16; traditions, Mk. 7:9; commands of Jesus, Jn. 14:15, 21; 15:10).

2. About half of the occurrences in the NT have this last-mentioned meaning. In contrast to *phylassō*, with only a few exceptions (e.g., Mk. 7:9; Jn. 9:16; Jas. 2:10), *tēreō* does not refer to keeping Jewish or Judaizing (Acts 15:5) traditions rejected by Christians (cf. the polemical use of *paratēreō* in Gal. 4:10 as it is applied to observing Jewish customs) but to keeping new Christian traditions (e.g., 1 Tim. 6:14; 2 Tim. 4:7). This is set out clearly in Christ's final command (Matt. 28:20), where he commands the church to "obey" the new righteousness he had taught during his ministry. The same use is found in 1 Cor. 7:19, where keeping (*tērēsis*) the commands of God is to be understood in terms of Christian ethics.

In Rev., linked with *logos* (word), *entolē* (command), and *pistis* (faith), *tēreō* has the force of holding fast a confession, both in facing false doctrine and in meeting a martyr's death (2:26; 3:3, 8, 10; 12:17; 14:12). All the Johannine passages—whether they deal with a church's or an individual's keeping of Jesus' words or commands (e.g., Jn. 8:51; 15:10; 1 Jn. 2:3; 3:22), or with God's or Christ's keeping of the church (Jn. 17:11, 15; 1 Jn. 5:18)—have to do with remaining in the church or in Christ. In Jn. 14:15, 21, 23–24, in the setting of Christ's farewell discourse, love to Christ is defined in terms of keeping his commands.

The reference of *paratērēsis* ("careful observation") in Lk. 17:20 cannot be established with certainty. Probably the word is used of the observation of apocalyptic signs. There is, however, the possibility that a keeping of the law is intended. *paratēreō*, apart from Gal. 4:10 (see above), is found only with the meaning of watch closely, lie in wait for (Mk. 3:2; Lk. 6:7; 14:1; 20:20; Acts 9:24).

See also *phylassō*, guard, preserve, keep (*5875*); *grēgoreō*, watch, be on the alert, be watchful (*1213*); *agrypneō*, keep or be awake, keep watch, guard (*70*).

5499 (*tērēsis*, observance), → *5498*.

5502	τίθημι

τίθημι (*tithēmi*), put, place, set, render, appoint (*5502*).

CL & OT *tithēmi* is a common Gk. word for put, used in both lit. (put something in a place) and metaphorical (put something into a category) senses. With a predicate in apposition it means cause to be or regard as.

NT In the NT *tithēmi* occurs 100x with a wide range of meanings. In the act. voice it signifies God destining someone for something, e.g., in Heb. 1:2 (he "appointed" the Son heir of all things) and in various OT texts quoted in the NT: Ps. 110:1, "until I *put* your enemies under your feet" (see Matt. 22:44; Mk. 12:36; Lk. 20:43; Acts 2:35; 1 Cor. 15:25; Heb. 1:13; 10:13); Gen. 17:5, "I have *made* [Abraham] a father of many nations" (see Rom. 4:17); Isa. 49:6, "I have *made* you a light for the Gentiles" (see Acts 13:47); Isa. 28:16, "I *lay* in Zion a stone" (see Rom. 9:33; 1 Pet. 2:6).

In the mid. voice God sets times (Acts 1:7), makes certain people overseers (20:28), arranges parts of the body (1 Cor. 12:18), appoints gifted people in the church (12:28), appoints Christians to obtain salvation (1 Thess. 5:9), appoints Paul to his ministerial work (1 Tim. 1:12) or to an apostolic role (2:7; 2 Tim. 1:11), and commits the word of reconciliation into his hands (2 Cor. 5:19). The thought of God settling what will be by his sovereign decision runs through these passages.

See also *kathistēmi*, bring, appoint (*2770*); *horizō*, determine, appoint (*3988*); *paristēmi*, place, put at the disposal of (*4225*); *procheirizō*, determine, appoint (*4741*); *tassō*, arrange, appoint (*5435*); *prothesmia*, appointed date (*4607*); *cheirotoneō*, appoint (*5936*); *lanchanō*, obtain as by lot (*3275*).

5503	τίκτω

τίκτω (*tiktō*), bring forth, bear, give birth to, produce (*5503*); τεκνογονέω (*teknogoneō*), bear children (*5449*); τεκνογονία (*teknogonia*), childbearing (*5450*); τεκνοτροφέω (*teknotropheō*), bring up children (*5452*).

CL & OT In cl. Gk. *tiktō* means beget (of the father), give birth to (of the mother); bear young, breed (of animals); produce (of the earth); generate, engender.

In the LXX *tiktō* is used 215x and stands almost exclusively for the Heb. *yālad* (bear). The word was used predominantly of the woman (male begetting is usually expressed by *gennaō*, → *1164*). The word often denotes the physical act of labor that comes as something over which one has no control (Isa. 13:8; 26:17–18). (On Isa. 7:14 [cf. Matt. 1:23], → *Emmanouēl*, *1842*, and *parthenos*, *4221*.) *tiktō* can also be applied to animals (Gen. 30:39).

tiktō is also used in a metaphorical, although somewhat negative, sense in the LXX in speaking of the nation of Israel (Num. 11:12; Isa. 66:8) and of bearing mischief (Ps. 7:14; Isa. 59:4). The picture here is of a hidden, irresistible power breaking out of a person. *tiktō* is never used of the Lord himself, though *gennaō* is (Deut. 32:18; Ps. 2:7).

NT 1. *tiktō* occurs chiefly in the birth narratives of Jesus and John the Baptist. It also occurs in Rev. 12:2, 5, in the heavenly vision of the birth by a woman of a child who is appointed to be Lord and Redeemer of the world and who is immediately caught up to God from the power of the dragon. *gennaō* is used more in a general sense, e.g., in the announcement to Elizabeth and Mary of the impending birth of their sons (Lk. 1:13, 35) and the report of Jesus' birth (Matt. 1:16), whereas *tiktō* expresses more the physical reality of giving birth (Lk. 2:6–7, 11). It appears in passages that bring home the reality of labor (Jn. 16:21; Rev. 12:2) or the shame of the woman who cannot give birth because she is barren (Gal. 4:27; see also *genea*, *1155*).

tiktō and its cognates are used exclusively of the woman in the NT. Thus, 1 Tim. 2:15 reinterprets the judgment pronounced on Eve about pain in childbearing (Gen. 3:16), suggesting that this judgment does not mean that women are eternally condemned: "Women will be saved through bearing children [*dia tēs teknogonias*]—if they continue in faith, love and holiness, with propriety." Widows should marry and bear children (*teknogoneō*), thus giving the enemy no opportunity to revile the church (5:14). Widows should not be enrolled under the age of sixty, and among other things they should be known for having brought up children (*teknotropheō*, 5:10).

2. *tiktō* occurs twice in a metaphorical sense: of the earth bearing useful plants (Heb. 6:7) and of desire that gives birth to sin (Jas. 1:15). Here the vb. expresses the necessary connection between conception and birth. Where there is rain, there is fruit. Where there is desire, there is sin and death. Jas. 1:15, 18 also contain the word *apokyeō* (bring forth), which is likewise used in a metaphorical sense. It expresses the end result, in the one case of desire and in the other case of God's will.

See also *gennaō*, beget, become the father of, bear (*1164*); *ginomai*, be born, become, happen (*1181*); *ektrōma*, miscarriage (*1765*);

palingenesia, rebirth, regeneration (*4098*); *eugenēs*, well-born, noble in descent or character (*2302*).

5506 (*timaō*, set a price on, honor), → *5507*.

| 5507 τιμή |

τιμή (*timē*), price, value, honor, respect (*5507*); τιμάω (*timaō*), set a price on, honor (*5506*); τίμιος (*timios*), precious, valuable (*5508*); τιμιότης (*timiotēs*), wealth (*5509*); ἀτιμία (*atimia*), shame, dishonor, disgrace (*871*); ἄτιμος (*atimos*), despised, dishonored (*872*); ἀτιμάζω (*atimazō*), dishonor, treat shamefully (*869*); ἔντιμος (*entimos*), respected, honored, valuable (*1952*).

CL & OT 1. (a) In cl. Gk. *timē* means worship, esteem, honor (used of people); worth, value, price (of things); compensation, satisfaction, penalty. *timē* denotes the proper recognition one enjoys in the community because of one's office, position, wealth, etc., and then the position itself, the office with its dignity and privileges. The *timē* of a person, state, or deity must be distinguished from that of another; it is a personal possession. Slaves had no *timē*.

(b) Every deity was shown honor because of the sphere of influence he or she controlled by sacrifice and hymns of praise. On their part the gods "honored" humans by giving them their earthly positions of honor and good fortune.

(c) Shame and dishonor (*atimia*) put a person outside the community. *atimia* was the technical term for the deprivation of a citizen's rights.

2. (a) In contrast to its use of *doxa* (→ *1518*) the LXX seldom uses *timē* for God's honor. Normally *timē* applies to human honor, although both words could render Heb. *kābôd*. Humankind has a position of honor in the creation (Ps. 8:3–8). Honor and position of office belong together (139:17, *timaō*). Honor should be shown to parents (Exod. 20:12; Sir. 3:3–16), the elderly (Lev. 19:32), and kings (Dan. 2:37). The rabbis stressed the honor due to a teacher of the law, one's neighbor (cf. Prov. 14:21; Sir. 10:23), and Jewish slaves.

(b) A person marked out by honor might expect a corresponding position, wealth (Gen. 31:1; Isa. 16:14, both *doxa*), and influence (Job 30:4, 8). A worthy appearance (Isa. 53:3), fitting speech (Sir. 5:13; cf. Job 29:21–25), and generosity (Prov. 22:9) also went with it.

(c) The godless experience *atimia* (Isa. 10:16; Jer. 23:40; cf. Dan. 12:2). The people did not grasp where the deepest dishonor lay, i.e., in faithlessness to God (Jer. 6:15), and this had to be recognized (Ezek. 16:63).

(d) The godly in the OT struggled with the problem of how dishonor could come to them (Job 10:15; 30:1–12). Only the Servant of the Lord bears shame patiently (Isa. 53:3) and leaves his cause in God's hand. Jud. ascribed an atoning value to the death of the martyrs and regarded it as honorable (4 Macc. 1:10; 17:20; Josephus, *J.W.*, 2.151). The pious rejected the scorn of the godless as something derived from a false outlook because the true basis of honor is not earthly prosperity but virtue and wisdom (Wis. 3:14–5:5).

NT 1. The word group is not strongly represented in the NT. *timē* is found 41x, *timaō* 21x, *timios* 13x, and *timiotēs* once (Rev. 18:19). Only Paul uses *atimia*. (a) Only the positive forms are used in the sense of price, sum of money: e.g., *timē* (price) in 1 Cor. 6:20; *timaō* (to set a price on) in Matt. 27:9; and *entimos* (precious) in 1 Pet. 2:4, 6.

(b) The meaning of *timaō* in the sense of show honor is rare (e.g., Acts 28:10). It is not clear whether *timē* should be rendered honor or honorarium in 1 Tim. 5:17.

(c) Generally *timē* represents the recognition of the dignity of an office or position in society (e.g., the authorities, Rom. 13:7; cf. 1 Pet. 2:17; owners of slaves, 1 Tim. 6:1; a wife, 1 Pet. 3:7; the sexes in general, 1 Thess. 4:4). The honoring of God is uppermost in the doxologies, where both *doxa* and *timē* occur (1 Tim. 1:17; 6:16; Rev. 4:11), but honor should be shown to everyone (1 Pet. 2:17).

(d) *timē* and its cognates are used for exaltation in the ultimate eschatological salvation (Jn. 12:26; Rom. 2:7, 10; 1 Pet. 1:7; 2:7).

(e) *timios*, an important NT word, occurs in a variety of contexts. It is used 6x in Rev. for "precious stones" (e.g., 17:4; 18:12, 16) or "costly wood" (18:12; cf. also 1 Cor. 3:12). Peter talks about the "precious" blood of Christ (1 Pet. 1:19) and the "precious" promises of God's word (2 Pet. 1:4). For Paul, life had no "worth" unless he was able to complete the task the Lord had assigned to him (Acts 20:24). The author of Heb. instructs us that marriage should be held in honor by everyone (13:4).

2. (a) The negative aspect sometimes receives less stress with *atimos*. It can mean without honor, unhonored, less honorable (1 Cor. 12:23). In 4:10, however, the connotation is stronger and means despised.

(b) *atimazō* means to handle shamefully, with or without physical maltreatment: e.g., what happened to those whom the owner of the vineyard sent (Mk. 12:4; Lk. 20:11), to apostles by the Sanhedrin (Acts 5:41), and to the poor by church members (Jas. 2:6).

(c) *atimia* is generally translated in the NT by dishonor or disgrace, e.g., of a man's long hair (1 Cor. 11:14), of the dead body (15:43), of the apostles' "glory and dishonor" (2 Cor. 6:8), and of "ignoble" purposes for household articles (2 Tim. 2:20).

(d) None of the uses deviates from secular Gk. A deepening ethical sense can be found in Rom. 1:26, where under the OT influence *atimia* means "shameful."

3. (a) As in Gk. society and the OT, *timē* is also used in the context of the social order decreed by God. *timē* is respect for the standing and task of a person who has a place in God's world of human beings, animals, and things. The resultant order and grades of honor must be respected not only by the one placed lower, but also by the one placed higher. For example, while the wife is placed below her husband, she is to receive full honor from her husband (1 Pet. 3:1, 7). Elsewhere the subjection of the wife is counterbalanced by the love of the husband, which becomes a reciprocal subjection (Eph. 5:21–33; Col. 3:18–19). Things and animals have no honor. In the ancient world this was true also of slaves, because they had no right to direct their lives, though both the Stoics and the NT judge otherwise.

(b) The biblical teaching about natural relationships—e.g., man and wife, parents and children, the authorities—was developed from this. The same principle was applied to church life. Honor was to be shown the elders (1 Tim. 5:17), widows (5:3), and the responsible leaders of the congregation in general (Phil. 2:29). It is noteworthy, however, that this hierarchical line is crossed by a person offering honor to those on a lower level. Those who carry out the lowest services should be shown particular honor (1 Cor. 12:23–24); note also the admonition to show mutual honor (Rom. 12:10).

(c) Humanity's intrinsic honor is based on their position of dominion in creation (Ps. 8:5–8). To that extent it is conferred by their status in the structure. However, it is also derived from having been formed in the image of God. All humans should be honored (1 Pet. 2:17; cf. Rom. 12:10). Hence slaves were members of the church (1 Cor. 7:22–23; 12:13; Eph. 6:9), just as much as non-Israelites. In the church the restoration of the image of God has once more become universally possible (Col. 3:10–11).

(d) According to the NT, therefore, the Christian must not despise any class of humans. They must, however, be willing to bear personal dishonor. In contrast with the early Israelites, material possessions and wealth no longer constitute a basis for honor. Hence to lose things is in itself nothing to be ashamed of. Nevertheless, the NT does not reduce the ground for honor, as did the Stoics, to an inner quality, such as virtue or wisdom. Dishonor, through being despised or suffering physical violence, must be borne for the sake of love after the pattern shown by Christ (Isa. 53:3–8; Heb. 12:2; 1 Pet. 2:23–24). It is to be endured by the power of God (2 Cor. 6:7–8) and is made less bitter by the hope of eternal life and glory (1 Cor. 15:43; 2 Cor. 4:17; Heb. 12:2; 1 Pet. 1:7). All this presupposes that it is as a righteous person that one suffers shame (3:13, 17).

(e) The dishonor caused by sin, disgrace, and degradation is quite different (Rom. 1:24, 26). Sin of this kind is not regarded simply as a moral lapse. The shame lies essentially in the fact that humans have fallen from the honor given them by God in creation and have misused their bodies.

See also *doxa*, glory, radiance (*1518*).

5508 (*timios*, precious, valuable), → *5507*.

5509 (*timiotēs*, wealth), → *5507*.

5526 (*toichos*, wall of house), → *5446*.

5528	τολμάω

τολμάω (*tolmaō*), be brave, dare, risk (*5528*); τολμηρός (*tolmēros*), confident, bold, audacious (*5529*); τολμητής (*tolmētēs*), arrogant (*5532*).

CL & OT With a basic sense of doing or bearing that which is fearful or difficult, the vb., adj., and noun embrace the related ideas of patience, submissiveness, courage, and daring (in a good sense of brave enough and in a bad sense of rash or foolhardy). In the LXX, the vb. appears 7x (e.g., Est. 1:18; 7:5; Job 15:12), the adv. 3x (Sir. 8:15; 19:2–3), always in a negative sense

NT The single occurrence of *tolmetēs* is clearly in the bad sense: the "bold . . . men" of 2 Pet. 2:10 brook no restriction on self-will and recognize no authority to which they will answer. The comparative adv. in Rom. 15:15, however, is used in a good sense: Paul is confident because of God's grace in him.

The vb. swings freely between these two usages, but for the most part it moves in the realm of the moral rather than the physical. It describes the courage of Joseph in asking for the body of Jesus (Mk. 15:43), the cowardice of those who shrank from joining the early church (Acts 5:13), the moral propriety of Moses who dared not gaze on God (7:32) and of Paul as he courageously asserted his convictions in relation to Corinthian opponents (2 Cor. 10:2; cf. Jude 9), and the moral impropriety of questioning the unimpeachable evidence of the resurrection (Jn. 21:12) or of taking a fellow Christian to law (1 Cor. 6:1).

Moral and physical courage are both involved in Matt. 22:46 par., a meaning combining both "did not have the face to" and "did not have the gall to." It has the strongest sense of putting oneself at risk in Rom. 5:7, and a weak but similar sense in 15:18; 2 Cor. 10:12; 11:21, where it is little more than venture to do something.

See also *parrēsia*, boldness (*4244*).

5529 (*tolmēros*, confident, bold, audacious), → *5528*.

5532 (*tolmētēs*, arrogant), → *5528*.

5544 (*trapeza*, table), → *1270*.

5552	τρεῖς

τρεῖς (*treis*), three (*5552*); τρίς (*tris*), three times (*5565*).

NT 1. The number three is common throughout the biblical lit., but great caution is called for in evaluating significant usages. Three is a common and natural rhetorical number, and threefold repetition or grouping occurs often where the number itself is not mentioned. Many repetitive narratives and parables have three elements. Many basic concepts are readily formalized on a tripartite pattern: i.e., beginning, middle, end; past, present, future; body, soul, spirit. Diverse examples are numerous: three enduring gifts in 1 Cor. 13:13, three witnesses in 1 Jn. 5:8, and the threefold titles of Christ and God in Rev. 1:4; 4:8.

2. A period of three days is common in the OT. It is often the length of a journey or of an interlude before a crisis (cf. Gen. 30:36; 40:12–19; Exod. 3:18). Note the easy transition to the phrase "the third day" (e.g., Gen. 40:20; → *tritos*, *5569*) and to the fuller expres-

sion "three days and three nights" (1 Sam. 30:12; Jon. 1:17). As the ancients reckoned inclusively, this may denote a period much shorter than seventy-two hours.

Some of these OT phrases are taken up significantly in the NT with reference to Jesus' death and resurrection. This is particularly striking in the allusion to Jonah (Matt. 12:40), a figure elsewhere prominent in the Gospels (Matt. 16:4; Lk. 11:29–32; see also Matt. 26:61; 27:40, 63; Mk. 8:31; 14:58; 15:29; Jn. 2:19–20).

3. Although three has widely been thought a sacred number, specifically religious uses of it in the Bible are relatively few. In the OT it is frequent in cultic contexts (e.g., Exod. 23:14, 17). In Rev. it is not as noteworthy as might be expected. Sometimes the structural pattern seven in Rev. divides into four and three (e.g., 8:13), and twelve is composed of four threes (21:13). There is, however, no reason to think that religious symbolism there attaches to three itself.

4. Yet the number three assumes peculiar importance indirectly in connection with the concept of the Trinity. There are threefold formulas listing the three persons in such passages as Matt. 28:19; Jn. 14:26; 15:26; 2 Cor. 13:14; 1 Pet. 1:2. There seems to be no precursor of this idea in any significant usage of the numerical concept in the OT, nor can we connect it with the occurrence of triads of deities in ANE paganism.

5556 (*trechō*, run, move quickly), → *4513*.

5560	τρίβολος

τρίβολος (*tribolos*), thistle (*5560*).

CL & OT 1. The root idea of this word is "three-pointed," and *tribolos* is first of all a weapon with three spikes, then a spiked water plant, then a similar land plant or a burr. It was metaphorically transferred to "sharp" tastes like vinegar and to sharp instruments, such as threshing machines.

2. *tribolos* appears in Gen. 3:18 with *akantha*; in 2 Sam. 12:31 "iron *triboloi*" are "iron picks." In Prov. 22:5 *triboloi* makes the path of the wicked hazardous.

NT *tribolos* occurs only twice in the NT. In Matt. 7:16 it illustrates consistency in nature, applied fig. to the moral life; in Heb. 6:8, an unchanged heart.

See also *akantha*, thorn (*180*); *skolops*, thorn (*5022*).

5565 (*tris*, three times), → *5552*.

5569	τρίτος

τρίτος (*tritos*), third (*5569*).

NT 1. *tritos* occurs 23x in Rev., more often than any other ordinal and much more than the cardinal *treis* (→ *5552*). In 14 cases it represents the fraction 1/3, referring to disasters in which a "third" part is destroyed (e.g., 8:10–12; cf. Ezek. 5:2, 12).

2. The uses of *tritos* in the Gospels and elsewhere are different. Of 25x it occurs outside Rev., 13 refer to the resurrection of Christ "on the third day." This was evidently a characteristic motif of the early Christian preaching (Acts 10:40; 1 Cor. 15:4). The Scripture to which the latter passage alludes is evidently Hos. 6:2, which speaks of the restoration of the apostate kingdom of Israel (see also *tris*, three, *5552*).

3. In 2 Cor. 12:2 Paul speaks of "the third heaven." While some Jewish writings refer to seven heavens, the apostle here seems to suggest that he was carried to the highest heaven. In 12:4 "paradise" is linked with this heaven (→ *paradeisos*, *4137*).

5582 (*trygaō*, gather in), → *5251*.

5595 (*typikōs*, as an example, typologically), → *5596*.

5596	τύπος

τύπος (*typos*), form, likeness, model, type (*5596*); τυπικῶς (*typikōs*), as an example, typologically (*5595*); ἀντίτυπος (*antitypos*), copy, image, antitype (*531*); ὑποτύπωσις (*hypotypōsis*), pattern, model, example, prototype, standard (*5721*).

CL & OT 1. (a) In cl. Gk. *typos* refers first of all to a concrete object (e.g., the shape of a loaf, relief, coin) and then the impression of a form (i.e., what an object leaves behind when pressed against another, e.g., a trace, scar, impress of a seal, a letter of the alphabet, etc.); still more generally, it can mean a likeness (→ *eikōn*, image, *1635*).

(b) The word is often found in the abstract sense of general form or type, such as the form of a style or a doctrine. From this follows a wider abstraction, such as the form that stamps and the form that is stamped. *typos* thus denotes: (i) an original, a pattern—e.g., a prototype or model, and the ethical sense of example; (ii) a copy (also *antitypon*).

2. In the LXX *typos* occurs only 4x. It Exod. 25:40 it refers to the original heavenly model for the tabernacle. In Amos 5:26 it means an image or idol, while in 3 Macc. 3:30 *typos* denotes the form or style of writing, and in 4 Macc. 6:19 a religio-ethical example.

3. (a) The word is a favorite of Philo, who uses it entirely in accord with cl. Gk. usage. It can denote both the original pattern as well as a copy or imitation. God conceived of the original tabernacle, which he gave as a *typos* or *paradeigma*, model, to the spirit of Moses.

(b) *typos* was also used among the rabbis as a loanword with the meaning, as in cl. Gk., of a form, model, and then the more general meaning of type.

NT 1. *typos* occurs 15x in the NT. The concrete meaning of the impression of a form is found in Jn. 20:25 for the mark of the nails in the hands of the risen Christ.

2. In Acts 23:25 *typos* has the abstract sense of the gist or content of a letter; in Rom. 6:17 it is the expression of teachings the Roman believers have received. In the latter reference, the original meaning of the form that stamps can still be strongly felt. The message of Christ is the factor that stamps and determines the life of the Christian.

3. The most common meaning for *typos* in the NT is the form that stamps. (a) The double meaning of *typos* as the form of both pattern and copy is found in Acts 7:43 (a quote from LXX of Amos 5:26), where it means the images of false gods, and Acts 7:44, which quotes Exod. 25:40 and denotes by *typos* the heavenly original, on the basis of which Moses erected the tabernacle (cf. also Heb. 8:5). The relationship of the original heavenly pattern (*typos*, 8:5; *eikōn*, 10:1) to the earthly copy (*antitypon*, 9:24; *hypodeigma*, copy, 8:5 [→ *5682*]; *skia*, shadow, 8:5 [→ *5014*]) is inserted into the scheme of the past and future blessings of salvation. Through Christ the heavenly patterns enter history and show the copies and shadows as perishable.

(b) Alongside *typos* and *hypotypōsis*, with the meaning of example, stand words such as *hypodeigma* or *hypogrammos* (example, → *5681*). These latter represent Christ's ministry of self-sacrifice (Jn. 13:15) and his suffering (1 Pet. 2:21), not simply as an ethical example, but as the saving work that the community may appropriate and so use to follow Christ (cf. 2:21b). *typos* with the meaning example is used solely with reference to Paul (Phil. 3:17; 2 Thess. 3:9), the officials of the congregation (1 Tim. 4:12; Tit. 2:7; 1 Pet. 5:3), or the congregation itself (1 Thess. 1:7). These passages are not simply admonitions to a morally exemplary life; rather, they call for obedience to the message (2 Thess. 3:6). It stamps those who proclaim it and gives them authority. Moreover, the shaping power of a life lived under the Word has, in turn, an effect on the community (1 Thess. 1:6), causing it to become a formative example.

4. Besides this common Gk. usage, *typos* also appears in the NT for the first time to denote historical events. It becomes a hermeneutical concept in the interpretation of OT tradition, esp. the historical experiences of Israel, with the present eschatological event of salvation.

(a) In 1 Cor. 10:6, 11, Paul uses *typos* and *typikōs* to interpret the events in the Corinthian church in the light of Israel's experiences in the desert. The punishment of God's ancient people, which followed their disgraceful practices, prefigures judgment on those who abuse the Lord's Supper. It carries a specific warning to the "strong" at Corinth not to abuse the sacrament. The typological method developed by Paul thus consists in expounding the analogous relationship of concrete historical OT events, in the sense of the past prefiguring present or future happenings.

This introduces a vital theological concern of Paul. God's activity in history is expounded in order to show how God is bound to his promises. It is God himself who creates this "typical" relationship, insofar as his Word of revelation (the Scriptures) fulfills it (cf. Rom. 4:23–24; 1 Cor. 10:11). In this prefiguration of saving events in OT history, witness is born to the community's participation in Christ's saving work. As against some supposed metaphysical misinterpretation, salvation history is interpreted as the self-fulfilling activity of God in concrete human history.

(b) Paul's argument in Rom. 4 and Gal. 3 is also typological in this sense, although the word *typos* does not occur. The same typological argumentation is present in 1 Pet. 3:21. Noah's deliverance through the flood waters is a prefiguration and type of the saving event of baptism, which thus becomes the *antitypon*, the antitype (in the sense of being an image).

(c) The *typos* concept produces a tension that breaks through the typological method in Rom. 5:14. The figures of Adam and Christ are compared and contrasted in their significance and effectiveness for "all." Adam is designated a "pattern [*typos*] of the one to come." This gives rise to an Adam-Christ typology. But since Adam cannot really count as a faithful prefiguration of Christ, and since there is no other known occurrence of *typos* meaning a contrasting picture, Paul here may be using the *typos* concept with the precise polemical intention of rejecting a traditional Adam-Messiah typology. It is a matter of the radical abrogation of the old by the new; the new only becomes actual when the old is overcome. Paul thus shows that this paradoxical relationship of the radical opposition and yet profound association of old and new is the reality in which the community is already living in the present.

In spite of this contrasting picture, however, Paul may also be using *typos* to designate a parallel in overall pattern between Adam and Christ. That is, just as Adam functioned as a representative for the entire human race in his decision to eat the forbidden fruit and so involved everyone in his decision, so Jesus also functions as a representative for the entire human race in satisfying God's judgment against sin through his sacrifice on the cross, so that any who come to him may be declared righteous in God's eyes. God's principle of operation remains the same in that he works through representative people.

See also *eikōn*, image, likeness, form, appearance (*1635*); *hypodeigma*, proof, example, model (*5682*); *hypogrammos*, outline, copy, example (*5681*); *charaktēr*, impress, stamp, representation, form (*5917*); *parabolē*, type, figure, parable (*4130*).

5603	τυφλός

τυφλός (*typhlos*), blind (*5603*); τυφλόω (*typhloō*), to blind (*5604*).

CL & OT 1. *typhlos* means blind. It is used lit. of humans and animals and fig. of other senses and the mind. The barbaric custom of blinding for revenge or punishment is well attested.

2. Blindness has always been common in the Near East. The brightness of the sun, dust, and dirt all encourage inflammation of the eyes, which may lead to blindness. The helplessness of the blind was proverbial in the OT (Deut. 28:29; Isa. 59:10; Lam. 4:14). They were the weakest and most needy members of society (cf. 2 Sam. 5:6–9). Consequently, the blind were under the special protection of the Mosaic law (Lev. 19:14; Deut. 27:18) and are expressly mentioned in the promise of release from bondage (Jer. 31:8). The pious Israelite helped the blind (Job 29:15).

The proper functioning of the senses is a gift from God; he decides whether a person sees or is blind (Exod. 4:11). Only in Deut. 28:28–29, in the context of the curse on those who do not obey the law, is blindness mentioned as a punishment in the OT. Blindness was a cultic blemish. The blind could not function as priests (Lev. 21:18), and blind animals were not to be offered as sacrifices (22:22; Deut. 15:21).

Blindness is also used fig. in the OT. Bribes make one blind (Exod. 23:8; Deut. 16:19), so that one no longer sees injustice. God can blind the disobedient, so that they no longer see what is right and true (Isa. 6:10; 29:9–10). In 42:19 the prophet calls those who pay no attention to the word of the Lord blind (both *typhos* and *typhloō* are used) and deaf.

3. Later in Jud. blindness came to be regarded as God's punishment for human sin because it prevented study of the law. The benediction on seeing a blind man was "Blessed be the truthful Judge," which implies that the blindness was a just judgment either on the person's own sins or on those of his or her parents (cf. Jn. 9:2). The Qumran community excluded the blind and others with physical defects from their membership. There was, however, no discrimination of the blind in the Jewish synagogue.

NT 1. The view of blindness changes in the NT. Jesus received the physically blind into his fellowship and gave them a share in the kingdom of God. He instructed the man who had invited him to a meal that he should invite the poor and blind (Lk. 14:13, 21).

2. The many cases in which Jesus healed the blind were messianic signs (Matt. 9:27–31; 12:22; 15:30; 21:14; Mk. 8:22–25; 10:46–52 par.; Lk. 7:21). Thus when John the Baptist grew doubtful and sent disciples to question him, Jesus answered, among other things, "The blind receive sight" (7:22), pointing him to Isa. 29:18; 35:5. Jesus'

appearance and ministry meant that the promised time of redemption had become a present reality. The new age, in which there will be no more blindness, had broken in.

When Jesus healed the man born blind (Jn. 9:1–34), he rejected the question that seemed so obvious to others: Who was responsible for his blindness? Jesus' concern was, "What is the purpose of this blindness?" In response, Jesus insisted that God's redemptive work was the ultimate factor: "Neither this man nor his parents sinned . . . but this happened that the work of God might be displayed in his life" (9:3). God's work is done in this man and at the same time God reveals Jesus as the light of the world.

3. Acts 13:11 tells of a man temporarily blinded as the result of a curse. The story makes clear the superiority of the Christian servant over the heathen magician.

4. (a) Blindness is used fig. in Matt. 15:14, where Jesus calls the Pharisees "blind guides" of the blind. He is alluding to the phrase that Jews versed in the law called themselves: *hodēgoi typhlōn* (guides of the blind, cf. Rom. 2:19)—a title of honor. As bringers of light, they offered truth and understanding. Jesus saw these leaders differently. He felt no sympathy for them in their blindness but rather condemned them, for it showed that they had become hardened (cf. also Matt. 23:16–17, 19, 26). In fact, in Jn. 12:40 Jesus applies Isa. 6:10 to these unbelieving Jews, suggesting that God has judged them by blinding (*typhloō*) their eyes and deadening their hearts.

(b) Elsewhere in the NT, Paul calls the blinding of unbelievers as something that Satan, the god of this age, has done (2 Cor. 4:4). Jn. says essentially the same thing, though he writes that "the darkness has blinded" them (1 Jn. 2:11).

5604 (typhloō, to blind), → 5603.

5614 (hybrizō, act arrogantly, ill-treat), → *5615.*

5615	ὕβρις

ὕβρις (*hybris*), insolence, arrogance, insult, ill-treatment (*5615*); ὑβρίζω (*hybrizō*), act arrogantly, ill-treat (*5614*); ὑβριστής (*hybristēs*), violent, insolent man (*5616*); ἐνυβρίζω (*enybrizō*), despise, insult (*1964*).

CL & OT 1. In cl. Gk. *hybris* originally meant excess weight or power; then also ill-treatment, abuse, insult; and arrogance, insolence, brutality. The word appears objectively as an infringement of the order of justice established by Zeus, which enabled community life in the Gk. city state to be maintained. Cl. Gk. tragedy contrasted *hybris* to *sōphrosynē*, modesty (→ *5408*), which respects the limits laid down for humans. Thus *hybris* is not, strictly speaking, directed against the gods. What the malefactor harms is good order.

2. *hybris* is used for various Heb. words meaning arrogance (e.g., Lev. 26:19; Job 35:12; 37:4; Prov. 8:13; 14:3; Isa. 13:11; 16:6; Ezek. 30:6, 18; Amos 6:8). It can also denote arrogant or boasting speech (Prov. 1:22; Jer. 13:17) and insolence (Prov. 11:2; 13:10; Ezek. 7:10). *hybrizō* is used in 2 Sam. 19:43; Isa. 13:3; 23:12; Jer. 48:29 (= LXX 31:29); 2 Macc. 14:42; 3 Macc. 6:9. *hybristēs* occurs 10x (e.g., Prov. 15:25; 27:13; Isa. 16:6; Sir. 8:11).

NT 1. In contrast with the OT, the abstract use of *hybris* in the sense of pride is absent from the NT. In 2 Cor. 12:10, it is used alongside *diōgmos*, persecution, so that the word clearly has in mind the *action* of ill-treatment (cf. Acts 27:10, 21, where it means hardship and damage caused by the elements). Paul's description of himself before Christ as a *hybristēs* (1 Tim. 1:13) likewise means a violent, insolent man. Similarly the vb. *hybrizō* regularly has the meaning of to mistreat or insult (Matt. 22:6; Lk. 11:45; 18:32; Acts 14:5; 1 Thess. 2:2).

2. In Rom. 1:30 *hybristēs* refers to a violent, insolent person who pays no attention to God's wrath and willingly offends his honor. Paul presents the catalog of vices listed in 1:29–31 as the outcome of idolatry and as a judgment by God (cf. 1:28).

3. The compound *enhybrizō*, to insult, outrage (with "the Spirit of grace" as its obj.) is used in Heb. 10:29, in parallel with *katapateō*, to trample underfoot (obj. "the Son of God," → *peripateō*, walk, *4344*), and with a Gk. phrase meaning to treat as profane ("the blood of the covenant"). The author has in mind here the OT difference between deliberate and involuntary sin (12:26). Religious apostasy belongs to the former category, and it is a serious sin, even perhaps unforgivable (see 6:4–8). He explicitly alludes to Exod. 24:8; Deut. 17:2–6; 32:35–36; Isa. 26:11, arguing a fortiori from instances of judgment in the OT to the present situation of his readers.

See also *hyperēphanos*, proud (*5662*).

5616 (hybristēs, violent, insolent man), → *5615.*

5617 (hygiainō, make well again, cure), → *5618.*

5618	ὑγιής

ὑγιής (*hygiēs*), healthy, well (*5618*); ὑγιαίνω (*hygiainō*), make well again, cure (*5617*).

CL & OT 1. In cl. Gk. *hygiēs* means (lit.) healthy (in body), strong, active, sound; (fig.) of good understanding, sensible, shrewd, sober, of good judgment. Likewise *hygiainō* means to be healthy, to be of sound mind, to be shrewd or sensible. These two words (frequently in conjunction with *logos*) were commonly used to describe an idea or opinion as judicious, sensible, i.e., "healthy" as opposed to being false or "sick."

2. In the LXX *hygiēs* and *hygiainō* (about 50x) are used only in a direct sense (e.g., Gen. 37:14; Isa. 38:21). The vb. form *hygiaine* sometimes stands for the Heb. *šālôm*, a greeting in the sense, "Peace be to you" (e.g., 1 Sam. 25:6; 2 Sam. 20:9; cf. 2 Macc. 9:19).

NT 1. Most of the 23x in which *hygiēs* or *hygiainō* are used in the NT occur in the Gospels and Pastoral Letters. In the Gospels and Acts *hygiēs* and *hygiainō* are used primarily in the sense of healthy, well. (a) Generally the well-being is the result of a healing miracle performed by Jesus (Matt. 12:13; 15:31; Lk. 7:10; Jn. 5:9–15) or the disciples (Acts 4:10). Faith occasions the saving act and thus the healing. Note the words of Jesus in Mk. 5:34: "Daughter, your faith has healed you. Go in peace and be freed [*hygiēs*] from your suffering."

In all of its uses here, however, *hygiēs* and *hygiainō* do not denote merely a physically healthy condition. Those healed by Jesus are healed in their entire beings by the word of the Messiah (Jn. 7:23), i.e., are also saved from sin (cf. Lk. 5:21–25). In the healing of the lame, the blind, and the deaf (Matt. 15:31; cf. Mk. 7:37; 8:23), the promise of God's coming (Isa. 35:4–6) is fulfilled. Good health, therefore, is not the result of medical treatment but indicates a more profound healing; i.e., it is a sign that the age of salvation has dawned.

(b) As in the above passages, the use of *hygiainō* ("safe and sound") in Lk. 15:27 does not mean merely physical well-being (cf. 15:24). Having returned from his period of alienation and come home to his father's house, the prodigal is reinstated to his original status as son, i.e., he has now become well. In Jesus and his healing word we see the Father running to meet us and restore us to full health. Thus, when faced with objections to his mingling with the outcasts of society, Jesus justifies his mission with the aphorism: "It is not the healthy [*hygiainontes*] who need a doctor, but the sick" (Lk. 5:31). Jesus is probably speaking ironically here when he calls the Pharisees and teachers of the law "healthy" (cf., e.g., 5:17, 21, 30).

2. The metaphorical meaning is found in the Pastoral Letters, where *hygiainō* and *hygiēs* are characteristic terms for soundness in faith and doctrine (1 Tim. 1:10; 6:3; 2 Tim. 1:13; 4:3; Tit. 1:9, 13; 2:1–2, 8). In these letters, the word *faith* (*pistis*, → *4411*) has the basic idea of a fixed body of doctrine rather than a subjective experience in the believer. Problems of heresy are to be solved by an appeal to the fixed norms of Pauline doctrine. Teachings that do not conform to the doctrinal tradition, and thus are not "healthy" or "sound," must be rejected. Hence, to be "sound in faith" (Tit. 2:2) means to hold the received apostolic doctrine as normative.

See also *therapeuō*, heal, cure (*2543*); *iaomai*, cure, restore (*2615*).

5623	ὕδωρ

ὕδωρ (*hydōr*), water (*5623*).

CL & OT 1. In cl. Gk. *hydōr* designates water.

2. *hydōr* is used 460x in the LXX. (a) Drinking water is a vital necessity for humans and cattle, also for irrigating vegetation (cf. the high esteem of rain in Deut. 11:11; 1 Ki. 18:41–45). Water is a precious gift from Yahweh, who turned the previously dead earth into fertile land by means of surging spring water, just as the abundance of water, indicated by the four-branched river of Paradise, characterizes the orchard of Eden (Gen. 2:10–14). From the period of desert wandering Israel gratefully acknowledges Yahweh's miraculous provision of water (Exod. 17:6), which is remembered again and again in paraenesis (e.g., Deut. 8:15; Ps. 78:15–16) and songs of praise (e.g.,

74:15). An abundance of sweet fresh water is of decisive significance for Israel's life in the promised land (cf. Num. 24:7; Deut. 8:7; 11:11).

(b) But *hydōr* is also viewed under the negative demonic aspect of something threatening. In the roar of the sea and the waves of rushing rivers, Israel discovered deadly powers that God can use when he causes the annihilating flood to cover his adversaries (cf. Gen. 6–8; Exod. 14–15; cf. Ezek. 26:19–20).

(c) Water is in the OT, as in the whole of the ancient world, the most preferable means of washing. Ablutions are part of the consecration rites for priests and Levites before entering on their vocation (Exod. 29:4; Num. 8:5–22). The high priest must wash on the Day of Atonement (Lev. 16:4, 24). After sexual discharge (15:1–33), after a birth (12:1–8), and after skin diseases (14:8–9), water baths erase the impurity (cf. also Num. 19:11–12). For the final future of their nation the prophets hoped for an eschatological sprinkling of God's purifying water, which would cleanse both land and people, set idolatry aside, and put a new Spirit in their hearts (Isa. 44:3; Ezek. 36:25–32; Zech. 13:1). Here water has become a picture for the Spirit of the Lord.

3. Hel. and apocalyptic Jud. continued the prophetic spiritualization of cleansing. Philo and Josephus interpreted purification by water as a symbol for the purification of the soul and the conscience. The Qumran community stressed the superiority of the converted way of life to the special water bath (1QS 3:4–12). By contrast, the Pharisees built up the OT prescriptions of Lev. 11–15 into a complicated system of ritual lustrations.

NT 1. *hydōr* occurs 76x in the NT, often in connection with *potamos*, river, or *pēgē*, spring (→ *4380*). (a) The NT reflects the OT use of this word. Drinking water remains a highly treasured commodity (Mk. 9:41). Giving a drink to the thirsty, therefore, counts as a work of particular compassion (Matt. 25:35, 42). The use of water for secular cleaning is also attested (Lk. 7:44; cf. Jn. 13:5). The preciousness of water and its vital necessity for life suggest various pictorial uses of the word (Jn. 4:7, 13–14; Rev. 7:17).

(b) That God created water is obvious in the NT. Rev. 14:7 names the fountains of water as God's creation (cf. also the cosmology of 2 Pet. 3:5; cf. Gen. 1:2, 6, 9; Ps. 24:2). Heaven and earth derived their existence, through God's word, out of water and by water, until the then-existing world perished in the waters of the flood.

(c) As in Jud., angelic or demonic powers shelter under the waters (Rev. 16:5). The healing power of individual springs or pools is the gift of these supernatural beings (Jn. 5:4, 7). The picture of "rushing waters" is the seer's description of the numinous power of heavenly voices (Rev. 1:15; 14:2; 19:6). Peter's walk on the waters (Matt. 14:28–31) is possible only as long as he maintains faith to share in Jesus' victory over the demonic powers personified in the water and wind (14:30). By contrast, the demon throws the possessed lad into fire and water in order to injure him (17:15), and the demons plunge pigs into the water—as it were, their own particular element—drowning the animals in which they have gone to live (8:32).

2. (a) The significance of water as a Jewish means of lustration is also familiar in the NT (Jn. 2:6). Water esp. serves for the ritual washing of the hands (Mk. 7:3–4) and vessels (Matt. 23:25–26). Pilate's symbolic washing of his hands is also in keeping with OT custom (27:24–25; cf. Deut. 21:6; Ps. 26:6). The baptism of John, carried out with the water of the Jordan (Matt. 3:6, 13–17), despite its ethical intention, retains formal affinities with proselyte baptism.

(b) Whereas Jesus absolved his disciples from the Pharisaic prescription of hand-washing before and after meals (Matt. 15:1–20), and even changed the water of Jewish purification into wine (Jn. 2:1–11), the baptismal practice of John the Baptist found its continuation in Christian baptism. It, too, takes place in water (Acts 8:36–39), and its effect is described as cleansing (Eph. 5:26; Heb. 10:22). The cleansed person receives God's Spirit (cf. Acts 2:38). Baptismal water is symbolized by Israel's walk through the Red Sea (1 Cor. 10:1–2) and by the Noachian flood (1 Pet. 3:20–21).

(c) Jn. sees the decisive significance of water esp. in its Christological and pneumatic aspects. Jesus washed his disciples' feet as an example for them to follow (Jn. 13:1–17). The Lamb leads us to springs of living water (Rev. 7:17), which rise from the throne of God and of the Lamb (22:1, 17; cf. 21:6). Christ pours out this water (Jn. 4:10–15; 7:37–38), which is God's Holy Spirit (7:39). For all who believe and are baptized, the river of the water of life is already flowing now—free of charge (Rev. 21:6; 22:17).

See also *thalassa*, sea, lake (*2498*); *pēgē*, spring, source (*4380*); *kataklysmos*, a deluge, flood (*2886*); *Iordanēs*, the river Jordan (*2674*); *limnē*, lake (*3349*).

5624 (hyetos, heavy shower), → *847*.

5625 (huiothesia, adoption), → *5626*.

5626 υἱός

υἱός (*huios*), son (*5626*); υἱοθεσία (*huiothesia*), adoption (*5625*).

huios in General

CL & OT 1. (a) *huios* denotes son in the widest sense, both son of human parents and the offspring of animals and plants. *huios* can also mean descendant in general. Moreover, the idea of family relationship can recede completely and give way to one of relationship of interest, e.g., a teacher-pupil relationship. Closely connected with this is the fact that membership of a particular group can be expressed by the word *son*. Finally, *huios* with the gen. (cf. Heb. *ben* in the construct) can denote that certain things and concepts are dependent on one another and belong together (e.g., sons of light, of darkness, etc.).

(b) In ancient Gk. society, children (esp. sons) were the pride of the family. They were a welcome help at work and inherited the honor and the duties of their father. Deformed children, however (esp. girls), were sometimes left to die. Later generations with an individualistic outlook on life tended to limit the number of children.

(c) *huiothesia*, adoption, occurs seldom in cl. Gk.

2. (a) In the OT the child, esp. the son, was a gift of God (Gen. 1:28; Deut. 28:4–11; Ps. 127:3–5; 128:3; Isa. 54:1), although both the burden of pregnancy and the pain of childbirth were understood as God's punishment (Gen. 3:16). To have no children was a disgrace (30:1–2; 1 Sam. 1:11) and a sign of a lack of blessing (Gen. 33:5). Children needed upbringing ("discipline," Prov. 22:15), so parents were to exercise their responsibility toward their children (Deut. 6:7). For their part, children were to respect their parents (Exod. 20:12); violence against one's parents merited the death penalty (21:15). The idea of the original innocence of children, widespread among us, is foreign to the OT (Jer. 6:11; 44:7). Children were considered unwise and helpless.

(b) On the notion of the Israelites as children (sons) of God, see the section below on "*ho huios tou theou*, the Son of God."

NT 1. (a) *huios* can denote the relationship of a son (→ *prōtotokos*, *4758*) to his father (Mk. 10:46), to his mother (Matt. 1:21), to both (Lk. 1:13), or to his physical ancestors (Matt. 1:20; Lk. 19:9). From this arises the more general meaning of descendant (Matt. 23:31).

(b) *huios* is used metaphorically to denote membership of a particular group of people (e.g., "heirs [lit., sons] of the prophets," Acts 3:25; "son of a Pharisee," 23:6). "Son of man" can denote membership in the human race (Mk. 3:28; Heb. 2:6; see "*ho huios tou anthrōpou*, the Son of Man," below). *huios* can denote participation in a greater whole: "children of the resurrection" (Lk. 20:36), "sons of the kingdom" (Matt. 13:38), "sons of light" (Jn. 12:36; cf. 1 Thess. 5:5), "sons of the evil one" (Matt. 13:38), "child of the devil" (Acts 13:10), and "Sons of Thunder" (Mk. 3:17).

(c) The parent-child relationship is set in a new light by Jesus' call to discipleship. On the one hand, ties of blood pale into insignificance in the light of the call (Matt. 10:37; Lk. 14:26–27) and in the events of the end time may even be transformed into enmity

(Mk. 13:12). On the other hand, they regain the significance they had lost at the hands of the Pharisees (7:9–13). In the NT letters children have a place in the directions about social and family relationships (Eph. 6:1–4; Col. 3:20–21).

2. (a) Of special significance are those passages that speak of our relationship to God as his children (cf. *huioi theou*; *huiothesia*, 5x in Paul). Through the power of the Spirit, believers acknowledge God as their Father (Rom. 8:14–15). In Gal. 4:5, Paul speaks of our receiving "the full rights of sons" through adoption (cf. Eph. 1:5); this is linked with baptism in Gal. 3:26–27, though baptism in the NT is never treated as a rite separable from faith (cf. Rom. 6:3–11; Gal. 2:20; 3:5–9, 23–25).

Paul takes the idea a stage further in that he understands sonship not just as a present condition (like his predecessors) but also as the goal of hope, still to be fulfilled (Rom. 8:23; cf. also Jas. 1:18; 1 Pet. 1:23). Thus the concept takes on a peculiar double aspect. Paul places adoption as God's children within his own framework of salvation history. Those who belong to Christ by faith are "children of Abraham" (Gal. 3:7, 29), which guarantees salvation. Christians have entered into their inheritance, because they are heirs of Christ and of God (Rom. 8:17; Gal. 4:4–7).

(b) In the seventh beatitude, Jesus promises that peacemakers "will be called sons of God" (Matt. 5:9; cf. Rom. 9:26). The beatitude is all the more significant in view of the fact that throughout Matt. Jesus is called the Son of God either explicitly or by implication (see 2:15; 3:17; 4:3, 6–7; 8:9, 29; 11:25–27; 14:33; 16:16; 17:5; 21:37–38; 26:63; 27:40, 43, 54). Against this background, there is the double implication in the beatitude: Israel as such is not the son of God but only those in Israel who are peacemakers, and we may become, by being disciples of Jesus, what he is in himself.

Matt.'s use of Hos. 11:1 ("Out of Egypt I called my son," cf. Matt. 2:15) reinforces this conclusion. He sees the return of the holy family from Egypt as a fulfillment of this prophecy. This is not to be understood in the sense of a simple prediction, for Hos. is clearly talking about the exodus and not about the infant Jesus' coming from Egypt. It is, however, fulfillment in the deeper sense that Jesus, not the nation of Israel, is God's true Son and that the original event of which Hos. spoke was only a foreshadowing of an apparently insignificant event that would turn out to be the most significant event for humankind.

(c) Lk. 20:36 speaks of "children of the resurrection." The expression is a Hebraism for God's people in the hereafter. Several NT passages make the metaphor explicit by relating resurrection and rebirth. Matt. 19:28 speaks of the "renewal" or regeneration (*palingenesia*) "of all things," suggesting a cosmic event. The only other NT use of this word relates it to baptism and personal renewal as a present reality (Tit. 3:5), while 1 Pet. 1:3 speaks of being given "new birth into a living hope through the resurrection of Jesus Christ from the dead." Here there is an element of realization in the present, and the resurrection in this instance is Christ's and not ours, but it has a future aspect (cf. 1:4, 23; 3:21–22; 5:10; cf. Col. 3:1–4).

The discussion of Jesus with Nicodemus on rebirth is usually taken to refer to present spiritual experiences, but it may well have overtones of the connection between resurrection, rebirth, and spiritual sonship. For that which is born of the flesh cannot enter the kingdom of God, but only that which is born of the Spirit (Jn. 3:5; cf. 1 Cor. 15:50). Sonship is connected with rebirth in Jn. 1:12–13 (where the Gk. word is *tekna;* see *5451*). But Jn. prefers to keep the term Son of God for Jesus (20:31; cf. 17:1), and his stress falls on the present reality of new life (cf. 3:16–21; 15:7–8).

ho huios tou anthrōpou, the Son of Man

OT 1. *The philological problem in the OT and Judaism.* The antecedents of the concept *ho huios tou anthrōpou* are found exclusively in the OT and in Jud., esp. in apocalyptic writings; in the LXX

the phrase goes back to the Heb. and Aram. words for *child* (*huios*) and for *man* (→ *anthrōpos,* 476).

(a) In biblical Heb. *ʾādām* or *ʾenôš* is a collective term for human(kind); thus an individual person is called *ben ʾādām,* son of a man, and a number of them are called *benê ʾādām,* sons of men. The use of "son of man" as an address in Ezek. is striking (ca. 90x). Here the prophet is not addressed by his own name but as an individual creature drawn from the genus human being and contrasted with God. God himself condescends to consort with his servant (cf. also Dan. 8:17).

The way in which the phrase "son of man" appears in elevated speech is thus important, esp. in parallel phrases: "God is not a man, that he should lie, nor a son of man (*ben ʾādām*), that he should change his mind" (Num. 23:19); "What is man (*ʾenôš*) that you are mindful of him, and the son of man (*ben ʾādām*) that you care for him?" (Ps. 8:4). The stark contrast between the God who offers reassurance and the people whom he addresses, who perish like grass, is plain in Isa. 51:12. In other words, the contrast between God and "man"/"son of man" is a definite Heb. idiom.

(b) In biblical Aram. we must note Dan. 7:13, which has become a fundamental problem in apocalyptic studies: "There before me was one like a son of man (*kebar ʾenāš*), coming with the clouds of heaven." In contrast to the beasts that have been described previously, there comes onto the stage one who is like a son of man (i.e., a member of the genus human being).

(c) Ps. 80:8–15, with its picture of the vine and the vineyard (referring to God's dealings with Israel), is particularly important. It leads to a prayer for the king, the "man at your right hand" (cf. Ps. 110:1) and "the son of man [whom] you have raised up for yourself" (80:17–18). Here the "son of man" (*ben ʾādām*) is used of that specific elect man, the king.

2. *The development of the tradition within apocalyptic.* (a) The basic starting point for the apocalyptic tradition is the vision of Dan. 7:13–14. As the beasts are being rendered powerless, the one like a son of man ascends with the clouds of heaven to the Ancient of Days. This vision apparently refers to the theocracy of Israel, which is conscious of being fundamentally different from other kingdoms and nations. Dan. 7:18 refers to the imminent crisis of history and the transference of power to the hitherto humbled people of Israel; hence the traits of the one like a son of man are transferred to Israel itself (cf. the Qumran community, which regarded itself as the eschatological Israel and as a fellowship between saints on earth and powers in heaven).

(b) (i) The son of man appears once again as an eschatological figure, the object of the expectation of a corresponding community, in the Similitudes of *1 Enoch* (37–71). The Elect One, the Righteous One, is the representative of God's righteousness and wisdom, who mediates this blessing to his community. He is "hidden before him" and exists before the creation of the world. However, he also takes on the messianic struggle with kings and powers and emerges victorious. The features of this delineation are gleaned from an exegesis of Ps. and the prophets (esp. Dan. 7:9–10).

One main question is whether Christian influence has produced this distinctive son of man tradition in *1 Enoch*. While the main document can be dated somewhere between 40–38 B.C. and A.D. 70, it is entirely possible that the Similitudes were not part of the original book but a later insertion. If so, the "son of man" tradition in that portion may indeed reflect Christian thinking.

(ii) The exaltation of Enoch to be son of man and his translation to be with the Lord of spirits (70–71) is especially important. These last two chs. of the Similitudes are remarkable for the problems they present as to their relation both to one another and to the book as a whole. Enoch is greeted as the "son of man," who is born to righteousness. That is, he is invested with the eschatological function of the son of man. What we have here is an exegetical development of the Enoch tradition of Gen. 5:21–24 and the "son of man" references in Dan. 7:13. Apparently the Jewish sect represented here had a son of man tradition linked with an apocalyptic exaltation of the teacher and preacher of repentance. This has many points of contact with NT motifs.

(iii) In the Similitudes, the vision of the son of man of Dan. 7 is interpreted of a *messianic figure* without the phrase "son of man" becoming a messianic title. In *1 Enoch* 70–71 the Enoch tradition is united with Dan. 7 to describe a representative of righteousness who bestows peace and salvation on his community.

(c) The connection of the "Apocalypse of Ezra" (2 Esd. 13) with the vision to Daniel is fundamentally different from that of the Enoch tradition, in that the destiny of the nation as a whole is more emphasized. It upholds a form of religion that is based more on the Torah (13:54). The real problem is posed by the discrepancy between the tradition and the motifs used: Son of man and messiah, apocalyptic vision and messianic expectation are joined in an unequal union, to the detriment of both elements. In apocalyptic terms the "man come up from the heart of the sea" (13:25) is described as "he whom the Most High has been keeping for many ages, who will himself deliver his creation [and] direct those who are left" (13:26, NRSV). However, messianic motifs are added: Humankind gathers to fight against the man who has risen from the sea, but unarmed he wages war with the stream of fire that issues from his lips. Then he descends from the mountain to gather a peaceable host out of the midst of the scattering or the great affliction (13:1–13). It is important to note that this "man" is at the same time the "son" or the "servant" through whom the Most High reveals himself (13:32, 37, 52). Until now he has been hidden, but when his day comes he is made manifest (13:52). This passage differs from Dan. 7 in its more fantastic imagery and the more active role given to the messianic man.

(d) It is also important to note how the "one like a son of man" and the "heavenly one" assume concrete historical features: Abel, Enoch, and Melchizedek appear in apocalyptic lit. as God's elect, who represent his righteousness and exercise his authority to judge. OT exegesis reveals their particular qualifications for this, but only Melchizedek is endowed with messianic traits (cf. Ps. 110). At Qumran, Melchizedek is thought of as a heavenly being who executes judgment on the godless. The motif of the son of man does not explicitly appear in this context, but it is clear that certain decisive functions of the Son of man can similarly be applied to angels or heavenly beings.

(e) Attempts to shed greater light on the meaning of the Son of man concept from pagan mythology have produced nothing conclusive. Almost certainly the background of the concept is to be found in the OT, where the Son of man is to be understood collectively of Israel as the heir of Adam. Although destined to rule, the Son of man undergoes loss of dominion and suffering, but he will finally be vindicated by God. Beyond that, what seems most apparent is a series of independent exegetical uses of Dan. 7 by the authors of 2 Esd. and *1 Enoch*, not a continuous developing Son of man tradition.

NT 1. *The designation of Jesus as the Son of Man and the oldest tradition.* (a) Statements in which Jesus speaks of himself as the Son of Man indicate his possessing a certain authority (e.g., Mk. 2:1–12) or his treading a path of suffering appointed for him (e.g., 8:31–38; 9:31; 10:33–34). But we also find statements about the coming Son of Man, which reflect an apocalyptic tradition (e.g., 13:24–27; 14:62). The Gk. phrase *ho huios tou anthrōpou* is derived from the LXX trans. of the Aram. *bar nāšāʾ*. This shows that the Evangelists attached a messianic significance to the Gk. trans.

(b) The church fathers in general saw in the phrase *ho huios tou anthrōpou* a reference to Jesus' humanity. But if one goes back to the Heb. or the Aram. equivalents of this phrase, the distinctiveness of "this man" as opposed to all other humans is prominent. It is advisable neither to discard completely any connection with apocalyptic nor to concentrate exclusively on Dan. 7 or the Enoch tradition as its religio-historical provenance. Jesus seems to have put his own stamp on this expression. "Son of man" refers to a unique historical course leading

from humiliation to exaltation. Undoubtedly the idea contains both the present lowliness of his being human and his striving after his vindication and authorization by God.

(c) One should never separate the "kingdom of God" sayings (including their messianic potential) from the "Son of Man" sayings. Neither set of sayings excludes the other; they stand together. Nor should one confuse the messianic motif with the idea of the Son of Man. Messianic elements concern Israel, as the OT shows, but the idea of the Son of Man concerns the fulfillment of humanity's goal. It is no coincidence that the concept of the Son of Man is not only associated with a particular, historical vocation, but also at times involves a separation from other humans.

(d) It is not a sound historical method to deny Jesus the use of the expression "the Son of Man" and to relegate this problem to later stages of the Christian community. In the Synoptic tradition the expression is used solely of Jesus by himself; it is neither a mode of address to him nor a confession of him. "Son of Man" was neither a name nor a title but the mark of a particular eschatological role. Yet there is a connection between the present sayings of Jesus (see below) and the future sayings (Mk. 8:38; Lk. 12:8 par.).

It is important to note that Jesus' path through suffering to exaltation has its parallels in the apocalyptic tradition: Abel's authority to judge (*T. Ab.* 13:2–3), the exaltation of Enoch, and the translation of Elijah and of the Servant of God (Isa. 53) all provide abundant fuel for the hope of being exalted by God on one's way through suffering (Lk. 22:69). Jesus thus follows the path of the Son of Man up to the Ancient of Days (Dan. 7:13) and does not come down from heaven to earth.

2. *Present statements in the Synoptic Gospels.* We now begin an analysis of the "Son of Man" sayings in the Gospels. (a) In Mk. 2:10 Jesus makes the claim that as "the Son of Man" he has power to forgive sins on earth; he can act with a unique authority in this eschatological hour. The phrase "the Son of Man" here also serves to bring the conflict with the hostile teachers of the law to a head. Matt. 9:8 may imply that Jesus grants a share in this "authority to men," to his community. Hence this material has a place in discussions between the Christian community and Jud.; it raises the issue whether Jesus approaches too closely to divine prerogatives.

(b) In Matt. 11:18–19 Jesus contrasts the coming of the Baptist with the coming of the "Son of Man." These two witnesses appear in different ways. The Son of Man eats bread and drinks wine (Matt. 11:19; Lk. 7:34). Note that it is not just any man who eats and drinks, but that eschatological Man sent from God; hence there can be no substitute for the phrase "the Son of Man" as a polemical designation of him.

(c) The position is complicated in Matt. 8:20. Most likely the homeless "Son of Man" means Jesus himself as he steels his disciples for discipleship and homelessness. It is a question here, not of the existence of a human being, but of the eschatological fate that characterizes the existence of the "Son of Man."

(d) While Mk. 2:27–28 could be regarded as a comment by Mk. to his readers, more likely Jesus here expresses his own authority as the leader of God's people to whom the Sabbath has been given.

(e) Matt. 16:13 ("Who do people say the Son of Man is?") gives a striking rendering of the simpler question of Jesus recorded by Mk. Here the phrase "the Son of Man" is probably a pure self-designation of Jesus that has lost any eschatological reference. At any rate, it comes remarkably close to being a periphrasis for "I."

3. *Announcements of the "Son of Man's" path of suffering.* It is striking how firmly rooted the idea of "the Son of Man" is in the general predictions of suffering (Mk. 8:31; 9:31; 10:33) and in the apocalyptic sayings of 9:12 and Lk. 17:25. The firm roots of the concept of "the Son of Man" here must owe something to motifs in Isa. (the "ransom" for Israel, Isa. 43:3–7; the Lord's making "his life a guilt offering," 53:10). It must be presupposed that "the Son of Man" has to contend with the opposition of his people (a tradition attached to the designation *bar nāšāʾ*).

Jesus' suffering presents special problems to scholars: Did it come as a surprise when he found himself caught up without warning in conflict and suffering in Jerusalem? Or did Jesus deliberately enter on the course of suffering laid on him by his Father? If, as seems likely, the second is the case, then the conflict that awaited him and the suffering enjoined on him must be exegetically substantiated.

(a) Mk. 9:31 betrays an Aram. or Heb. play on words ("Son of Man . . . men"), which can certainly be traced back to Jesus himself. God himself consigned him (the Son of Man) into the hands of men (cf. Lk. 9:44). While this text only mentions his being "betrayed into the hands of men "(without his being killed), it is probable that we have to do with a twofold utterance: God gave him up—men delivered him over to death.

(b) Mk. 8:31; 9:12; Lk. 17:25 record another "Son of Man" saying that, on the one hand, speaks of the divine decree (dei, must, Mk. 8:31; Lk. 17:25) and, on the other, emphasizes the combination of "suffer many things and be rejected by the elders, chief priests and teachers of the law" (Mk. 8:31, alluding to rejection by the "builders" of Ps. 118:22).

The OT conceived of the life of the "righteous" or of the "Servant of God" (Isa. 53:8, 10; Wis. 2:17, 20) as ending not in suffering but in an eschatological answer from God. The righteous will be raised up (Deut. 18:15) or exalted (Isa. 52:13). In order to understand Jesus we must, as far as possible, look for the Heb. or Aram. equivalents.

(c) Lk. 22:21–23 and 48 stand out among Jesus' prophetic announcements of suffering. Behind both passages we must assume an Aram. or Heb. version that emphasized betrayal by the table companion or "friend." The phrase "Son of Man" gives these words a solemn and emphatic ring; they point to the most abject humiliation possible in the area of human trust and friendship.

(d) In interpreting Mk. 10:45, we must bear in mind its close relationship to Lk. 22:27. These texts emphasize Jesus' service and point out in context how two elements of service and the surrender of one's life should be normative for discipleship. God is the pattern, for he himself serves his people instead of making them serve him (Isa. 43:22–24); neither must we discount the reference here to the Servant of God who surrendered up his life in death (53:12).

4. *The resumption of the apocalyptic "Son of Man" tradition.* (a) In some respects the distinction between the self-authenticating "I" and the corresponding apocalyptic "Son of Man" in Matt. 10:32–33; Mk. 8:38; Lk. 12:8–9 spans the present and the future statements. This presupposes the creation of a community that is subject to the prophetic law of discipleship. The earthly event is determinative for the future of those who confess and those who deny. The "Son of Man" is a future entity that is taken for granted as an object of confession. The disciples here are faced with afflictions that call for uncompromising resolution. Jesus himself takes part in this affliction and faces each individual disciple with a decision.

(b) Matt. 10:23, which goes closely with 10:5–6, has to do with a persecution of Jesus' followers within Palestine. Nevertheless, the mission must be confined to the cities of Israel, and no mission to Hel. settlements is anticipated. These texts offer consolation to Jesus' disciples in a time of eschatological persecution.

(c) Lk. 18:8 forms the conclusion to a parable and asks the question: "When the Son of Man comes, will he find faith [faithfulness] on the earth?" That is, will the covenant the Son of Man has made with his own people be preserved in faithfulness, harmony, and humility? In one tradition, Abraham sees the sins on the earth and has power to execute judgment; still, he cannot exercise it, lest he destroy the creation (cf. T. Ab. 12). So it seems that, according to one Jewish view, each generation had one "righteous one" to whose lot it fell to decide their fate. We should note perhaps how close this perspective is to the parable of Lk. 12:36: If the master comes and knocks, he wants to find his servants keeping watch.

(d) The paraenetic warning of Lk. 21:36 reveals the "Son of Man" as an eschatological figure possessing full authority to judge. To be sure, the material of 18:8 and 21:36 could derive from Jesus, though some scholars see them as coming from the tradition of the community like that which developed 1 Enoch (see above).

(e) Jesus' saying during his trial ("From now on, the Son of Man will be seated at the right hand of the mighty God," Lk. 22:69) bears relationship to the apocalyptic "Son of Man," like the righteous people of the old covenant (Abel, Enoch, Noah, Abraham, Melchizedek), exalted to be with God. He is the righteous one of the end times and the last in the series of witnesses.

(f) As to other occurrences of the phrase "Son of Man" in the Synoptics, in some cases the usage may be due to the work of the Gospel writers. Matt. 13:37–43 is generally thought to be Matt.'s own interpretation of the parable of the weeds. In addition, in 16:28 Matt. seems to have rephrased the difficult saying in Mk. 9:1 in order to clarify it for his readers. In Lk. 6:22, where Jesus speaks of the possibility of persecution "because of the Son of Man," the Matthean parallel offers "because of me" (Matt. 5:11); presumably Lk. has retained the original form of a statement in which Jesus referred to himself as a figure of rejection and called his disciples to be ready to face the same fate.

The saying about blasphemy and the Son of Man (Matt. 12:31–32; Lk. 12:10; cf. Mk. 3:28–29) is particularly difficult to understand (→ diabolos, 1333). In Mk., Jesus in effect says that humans can be forgiven every sin except blasphemy against the Spirit, whose power is displayed in the gracious acts of Jesus. In Lk. 12:10, blasphemy against the Son of Man (Jesus) is excusable, but not deliberate blasphemy against the manifest activity of the Spirit. This saying stands in tension with 12:8–9, where the Son of Man is a glorious figure who could hardly be blasphemed with impunity; perhaps the sayings were spoken on different occasions.

Lk. 19:10 adds to the picture of the present authority of the Son of Man by assigning to him the task of a shepherd who seeks out and rescues the lost sheep (cf. Matt. 18:11, NIV note). Other sayings refer to the Son of Man's activity in the future (i.e., from the temporal standpoint of Jesus). The saying comparing the Son of Man with Jonah (Matt. 12:39–40; Lk. 11:29–30) should probably be taken as a comparison between Jonah's miraculous deliverance from death and God's vindication of Jesus by raising him from the dead (as Matt. makes explicit).

Matt. 24:37–44 and Lk. 17:22–37 contain references to the day or the coming of the Son of Man, which is compared to the flood and the destruction of Sodom and Gomorrah, both of which came unawares on those who failed to prepare themselves for what lay ahead. Yet Jesus' disciples should not be unprepared. They will be longing for the consummation (17:22), and it should be clearly recognizable when it comes. Still, there is the danger of being misled by false prophets or of growing weary in waiting, so the disciples must be vigilant and not diverted by worldly concerns.

The expectation of the coming of the Son of Man, presupposed in these sayings, finds expression in the apocalyptic tradition, particularly in Dan. 7:13. Clear references to this text are to be found in Mk. 13:26 and 14:62; the latter text combines Ps. 110:1 and Dan. 7:13 in order to depict the vindication of the Son of Man by God and his coming to judgment (there may also be some influence from Zech. 12:10). In Mk. 14:62 the point of the saying is to show how Jesus reinterprets messiahship in terms of the Son of Man of Dan. 7:13 (cf. Mk. 8:29–31). In 13:26 the coming of the Son of Man is associated with the gathering of God's people and their deliverance from earthly tribulation.

(g) Two things are clear in the light of the Synoptic material: (i) We must not interpret the concept of "Son of Man" in too narrow a Christological sense; rather, it serves to establish the eschatological righteousness. (ii) Early Christian teachers and prophets have worked out various patterns in which the "Son of Man" plays a role. Hence, Dan. 7 is not the only decisive factor in determining the significance of these texts.

5. *The Son of Man in the Fourth Gospel.* (a) Jn.'s Gospel, one of the last books of the NT to be written, seems to reflect a development

in Son of Man theology. This development should be regarded not only as the expression of a certain ideology but also as the result of the church's internal and external struggles. This Gospel presents Jesus as the one who is "sent" from heaven and who represents God as both the "Son of God" and the "Son of Man."

As far as tradition is concerned, Jn. 13:16, 20 uses Synoptic material (Matt. 10:24, 40). Both verses speak of the execution of a commission that comes from God. Even the predicate granted to Jesus, "Son of God," is guarded from blasphemous claims by the reference to the OT tradition about such commissions (Jn. 10:34–36; cf. Ps. 82:3, 6).

(b) The concept of the "Son of Man" contains apocalyptic elements, but it itself is given a kerygmatic revaluation. God's commission determines his "descent" and "ascent" (Jn. 3:13, 31; 6:62). This sending determines his "way" and forms the destiny of him who, at the commission of the one who sent him, goes along this way himself and takes others with him along it. The apocalyptists spoke of a journey to heaven and the gnostics of an ascent into the heavenly world; for Jn., however, the decisive question is who gives true testimony, who is authorized to bring this message, and who has the right to be exalted to be with God. The "ascent" corresponds to being exalted, the "descent" to the incarnation (cf. Jn. 3:13 with 3:14; also 1:14; → *hypsoō*, *5738*). That Jesus has come into the flesh (1 Jn. 4:1–3; 2 Jn. 7) are anti-gnostic confessions that emphasize the unique nature of Jesus' sending. The Johannine concept of the "Son of Man" is thus seen to be a theological testimony of Jesus to himself.

The promise of Jn. 1:51 has an early Jewish-Christian sound; it recalls the story of Jacob (Gen. 28:10–17). Rab. tradition took the words "angels of God were ascending and descending on it" to refer either to the ladder or to Jacob himself. Now the Son of Man replaces the ladder, as Jn. apparently sees the Son of Man as replacing Jacob: Either Jacob becomes an eschatological symbol for the Son of Man or the Son of Man is identified with the true Israel. In the history of salvation, the Son of Man embraces the earthly Israel and now represents it.

(c) Jn. 5:27 tells us that the Father gave the Son authority to execute judgment because he is "the Son of Man" (the absence of the article here reflects proper Gk. grammar). It is an open question whether this text refers to the unique human existence of Jesus or to the rank referred to in Dan. 7:10, 14. Perhaps *T. Ab.* is connected with this material, for there it is explicitly denied that God himself judges, on the grounds that humans should be judged by humans (13:3). This is to be understood in the light of the idea that certain righteous men are chosen as judges.

(d) The heavenly messenger of Jn. is the counterpart of Moses. This Gospel is interested in Jesus' commission and authority, not in the idea of revelation. As the one who comes from heaven, he surpasses Moses (Jn. 1:17; 5:45). It was Moses who ascended and descended when he came from Sinai (Exod. 24:12; 34:29). Jesus ascended and descended in another way, and so bore another glory than that of Moses. The antithesis of Moses and Jesus contains a polemic against the rab. concept of salvation.

This antithesis is particularly clear in the passage on the bread from heaven in Jn. 6. This section contains three "Son of Man" sayings, which reveal the structural division of the passage (6:27, 53, 62); the authority of the Son of Man is made explicit in 6:27b. The dualistic predicates, "heavenly/earthly" or "imperishable/destined to perish," mold the figure of the messenger and his gifts. There is a radical change in the eschatological way of thinking, for Christ as the heavenly messenger, the Son of Man, imparts abiding food, which brings eternal life. His message is true.

(e) With the words "I am" (esp. Jn. 8:58), the heavenly messenger announces himself in the manner of the OT God (cf. Exod. 3:14; Isa. 43:25). As God's representative, the Son of Man assumes the attributes of God and Yahweh. His path is a unique part of the course of salvation history; gradually we will recognize the truth (Jn. 3:14; 8:28; 12:23; 13:31). This process, which is rooted in history and yet molds history anew, depends on the idea of the Son of Man. As far as the

unbelieving crowd is concerned, a claim to messianic status and the raising up of the Son of Man seem to be mutually exclusive (12:34). Jn., however, knows that that which "abides" and the process of salvation history are not mutually exclusive, but rather presuppose each other.

(f) The Son of Man sayings in Jn. pose various problems when they are considered in relation to the Synoptic tradition. At several points the title is used in the same way as in the other Gospels with reference to Jesus' death and exaltation (Jn. 3:14; 8:28; 12:23, 34; 13:31–32) and to his activity as judge (5:27; cf. 9:35–39). But the vocabulary with which these statements are expressed differs. Jesus is to be "lifted up" on the cross, a word that refers both to his being physically lifted up to die and to his being "exalted" by God in his death and in his resurrection. As the Son of Man who died on the cross, Jesus is the source of eternal life (6:27, 53).

Other passages, however, emphasize that the Son of Man came down from heaven (Jn. 3:13; 6:62); this thought of preexistence is absent from the Synoptic sayings, and it raises the question whether or not Johannine thought has been influenced from other directions. Though some writers have related this concept to gnostic speculation, it is important to note that the materials for the Johannine picture of the Son of Man can largely be found in the OT and the Christian tradition. (i) "Son of Man" is a title of majesty in Dan. 7 and the Synoptic Gospels. (ii) The descent of the Son of Man is probably implicit in Dan. 7. (iii) Jn.'s description of the exaltation of the Son of Man is presented in terms of the Servant of Yahweh (Isa. 52:13) and in light of the resurrection. (iv) Jn. emphasizes the present anticipatory fulfillment of eschatological expectations. These four elements largely account for the distinctive Johannine use of the title.

6. *The concept of the "Son of Man" in the rest of the NT.* (a) In the Pauline tradition we find the idea of "the man from heaven" as the antitype of the "earthly man" (1 Cor. 15:47–48) or, exegetically, the "last Adam" as the antitype of the "first Adam" (15:45). Perhaps here also, as was the case with the Son of Man idea, an originally apocalyptic and temporal concept has been adapted to the form of a doctrine of salvation based on the figure of the *anthrōpos*. We can detect traces of the older apocalyptic Son of Man tradition in the use of Ps. 8:6 in 1 Cor. 15:27. Yet note how Paul avoids this apocalyptic idea amidst his Hel. surroundings. He is concerned rather to set the new humanity in their setting within the saving event rather than under sin and death (cf. also Rom. 5:12–21). His view of history here takes on metaphysical and ontic features.

(b) Heb. 2:6–10 uses Ps. 8:4–6 to prove that "man" and "son of man" must undergo a process in the history of salvation before they can reign over the world to come. The connection of "man" and "son of man" is necessary here; it points to the various stages of Jesus' life and thus emphasizes that his final goal has not yet been reached (Heb. 2:8). As in Jn. 1:51, "son of man" here embraces the community of believers.

Heb. 2:5–9 provides the first evidence of the dissolution of the connection between the Messiah and angelic powers, which had developed in apocalyptic. That is, the Son of Man and humankind are in salvation history, but are on a different level than the angels. New light is also shed on Ps. 8:5–7. A statement in the OT that delimited the dignity of creaturely humanity by reference to God's creative power here refers to the glory that is paradoxically ascribed to the One who is humiliated.

(c) Although the Son of Man idea is firmly entrenched in Lk.'s Gospel in sayings about judgment and the Parousia, the same is not true of the corresponding sayings in Acts. Hence, Stephen's testimony in Acts 7:56, that the Son of Man is standing (not sitting) at God's right hand is all the more notable. It clearly shows that in Hel. circles the idea of the Son of Man was also interpreted in apocalyptic terms.

Five ways of interpreting Acts 7:56 have been offered: (1) Jesus stood to receive Stephen into heavenly glory; (2) Jesus stood up as Stephen's advocate or witness in the heavenly court (cf. Lk. 12:8); (3) Jesus stood up to take possession of his messianic inheritance; (4) Jesus was originally thought of as standing (just like the angels) before God; or (5) Jesus stood up, as God stands up, to face his enemies (cf. Ps. 3:7; 7:6; Isa. 14:22).

(d) The linguistic usage of Rev. 1:13; 14:14 reveals affinities to Dan. 7:13. Both passages speak of "one like a son of man" walking ("among the lampstands") or sitting on the clouds of heaven. Note too how Rev. differs from the Gospels in leaving out the article. This is apparently an imitation of the text of Dan. 7:13: The apocalyptic "son of man" is the figure found already in Dan. 7:13, but now as a glorified ruler and judge. He is in all respects like an angel (Dan. 10:5; cf. Rev. 1:13; 14:15).

ho huios tou theou, the Son of God

CL 1. In cl. Gk. *huios* is found in references to "sons of Zeus" and of other gods. Ancient Gk. mythology portrayed the world of the gods as one great family. Zeus is the "father of men and gods," and it was thought obvious that gods should cohabit with mortal women and thus produce children.

2. Even more important was the Egyptian ruler-cult, which influenced Alexander the Great. He was hailed in the Libyan desert as "son of Ammon," or, in Gk. terms, "son of Zeus." His successors, esp. the Ptolemies, adopted the Gk. version of that title. Under the Roman Empire, the idea of the son of God spread everywhere, but it now had its foundation in Roman political theory. After Caesar had been murdered in 44 B.C. and been declared divine, Octavian let it be known that, on the basis of his adoption in 45 B.C., he was *divi filius*, son of the divine. This nomenclature slowly established itself as that part of the name that indicated the genealogical succession. That remained true of all the emperors.

3. Particular guilds boasted of an attachment to a particular god and could thus call themselves *huioi*, sons, or *paides tou theou*, children of the god (e.g., doctors are "sons of the god" Asclepius). It was particularly easy for the Stoics to think of humans as children of gods, for they upheld the ultimate unity of God and humankind. A characteristic expression of Stoic thinking is the possibility of realizing the freedom and bliss offered by Zeus. It spoke of a world order and its destruction; the Christian message spoke of the woe that had come upon humanity and the world, and of redemption from it.

4. A separate problem involves the use of *theios* or *theos* to describe men whose acts or endowment surpass those of normal men. This is especially true of poets or seers, but also of commanders like Lysander, whose divine charisma or divine qualities were celebrated. Legends thus came to surround the births of famous men. Apollonius of Tyana in particular was furnished with all the characteristics of a divine endowment, and divine sonship also seems to have been part of this endowment.

5. Nevertheless, the significance of the Gk. and Hel. background for the NT should not be overestimated. Naturally, early Christian thinkers could not help being influenced by their Hel. environment, but it was primarily their OT and Jewish environment that provided them with the concepts and vocabulary with which to develop their understanding of the person of Jesus. Most admit that the use of *theios* with people endowed with superhuman qualities carries no essential relationship to the concept of Jesus as the Son of God.

OT 1. *Israel and sonship*. A foundational element of the OT tradition is that Israel has been chosen (→ *eklegomai, 1721*) and so is in a position of sonship. This gives expression, on the one hand, to the subordination of the son and the legal claim of God as Father (→ *patēr, 4252*) (Mal. 1:6), and on the other hand, to the care and love extended to Israel as God's "firstborn son" (Exod. 4:22–23; Jer. 31:9). Only in this context do the prophets' messages of judgment and the recognition of God's chastisements make sense. Israel provides a historical pattern for election and for a concept of sonship that is not interpreted in purely natural categories.

Yet we must not forget that Gen. 6:2, 4 speaks of "sons of God" who took to themselves "daughters of men" and fathered the "Nephilim" (cf. also heavenly "sons of God" in Job 1:6; 2:1; 38:7; Ps. 29:1; 82:6; 89:7). Here is evidence of the pictorial idea of a heavenly court. However, the idea of "sons of God" is replaced by other phrases, such as "sons of heaven," "holy ones of heaven." Human instruction in all art and science is traced back to the angels (*1 Enoch* 6–8). Their fall is the real disaster of history.

2. *The king as God's son*. Decisive for the later messianic hope (→ *Christos, 5986*) is Nathan's prophecy in 2 Sam. 7:12–16: God will establish a house and eternal kingdom for David. God will be a father to David's son, who will be a son to God. The dynastic changes within the house of David were thus authorized by the divine legitimation of the succession. The original covenant between the people and their king was replaced by one that God himself gave, which was between him and the royal house.

Ps. 89 takes up this divine legitimation, to which the psalmist appeals in interceding for the king, the firstborn, the most exalted of the kings born on earth (89:27–28). There was also a coronation ritual based on 2 Sam. 7:12–16, and the king could begin his rule only after Yahweh had recognized the king as his son (Ps. 2:7) and invested him with the royal crown (2 Ki. 11:12; Ps. 21:3) and scepter (110:2). The shout of joy in Isa. 9:6 ("To us a child is born, to us a son is given") perhaps arose out of the divine formula of acknowledgment (cf. Ps. 2:7).

Isa. 9:2–7; 11:1–9 describe the enthronement of the coming king of salvation and the equipment of the new shoot of David's line with the gifts of the Spirit of God. At his exaltation to sonship, he receives names that promise salvation and describe its constituents. The king is none other than God's representative on earth. With his coming, humanity's history of woe is at an end; he will bring salvation to the whole world.

3. *The special effects of these OT beginnings in later Judaism.* (a) The description of the eschatological event put on God's lips in *Jub.* 1:22–25 presupposes Israel's apostasy; his people return in all sincerity, with wholehearted heart and soul. God himself circumcises their hearts and bestows upon them a holy spirit. "I will be your father and you will be my children. And they all will be called children of the living God, and all angels and spirits will know, yes, they will know that they are my children and I am their father in truth and in righteousness, and that I love them" (cf. 2:20; 19:29).

In Qumran this eschatological process is given a distinctive form. Specifically, attachment to the community of the elect is described as sonship (sons of light: 1QS 1:9; 2:16; sons of favor: 1QH 4:32–33; son of grace: 7:20). In Israel the returning and transformation of God's people take place in a community that claims for itself the fulfillment of OT promises.

In 2 Esd. 7:28–29; 13:32, 37, 52; 14:9 we find the phrase "my son," which can be traced back to a Gk. *pais* (→ *4090*) or Heb. *ʿebed* tradition. These references fit in with Ps. 2:7; Isa. 11; their main emphasis is on the apocalyptic struggle with the nations.

(b) The Jewish wisdom tradition places great value on the life of the individual righteous person. Sir. 4:1–10 (Heb. text) concludes with the promise, "and God will call you his son, and he will be gracious to you and rescue you from the pit." The picture of the righteous person also lies behind Wis. 2:13–18. He claims a special knowledge of God and calls himself God's child and God his Father. His way of life is different from that of others, and he can be regarded as God's servant in the sense of Isa. 53. In 5:5 the righteous one is reckoned among God's children and receives a portion among the saints (cf. Isa. 53:12; Dan. 7:18).

(c) Hel. Jud. held fast to God as Creator and Father and saw in history the evidence of his providence, goodness, and righteousness. Josephus believed, for example, that God was "Father of all," i.e., he did not recognize any people as being God's sons in a special way. He did see the patriarchs as arising from God himself, as examples of his special working.

Philo was definitely interested in philosophical and exegetical problems, to which he gave a speculative interpretation. In his thinking, for example, the Logos is the oldest son of God and the cosmos the youngest. Abraham is not only God's friend, from whom nothing is hidden, but also God's child (*huios*). He is of noble birth because he has chosen God as his Father and is the only one to have been adopted by him as son.

NT 1. (a) The early Christian confession of Jesus as Son of God is in fundamental agreement with Jesus' manner of addressing God (Aram. *ʾabbāʾ*, Father; Mk. 14:36; Rom. 8:15; Gal. 4:6; → *proseuchomai, 4667*). It is something new when Jesus addresses God as "my Father"; this mode of address in prayer derives from the language of the family circle. Thus, understandably, Jesus speaks of himself as the "Son" and claims for himself a special knowledge of the Father (Matt. 11:27; Lk. 10:22). These statements involve election, knowledge, and revelation.

(b) "Son of God" is the essential confessional phrase of early Christianity. It is firmly rooted in baptism, preaching, and confessions (Acts 9:20; 13:33; Rom. 1:3–4) and points back to the founding of the community and the Easter event. Its close connection with the confession of Jesus as Messiah suggests that this sonship refers back to 2 Sam. 7:12, 14. Thus, the messianic element in Jesus' preaching is traceable back to the Davidic tradition.

On the other hand, Lk. 4:18–19 (cf. Isa. 61:1–2) shows that the messianic element in Jesus' message is also related to a special endowment with the Spirit. This tradition is associated with Ps. 2 and Isa. 11:1–10, two texts that left their mark on the preaching of the Baptist. The gifts of the Spirit have an immediate point of contact with 11:2: The Messiah is fully endowed with God's Spirit. Then the tradition divides: (1) The Messiah will judge by the breath of his mouth or by fire (11:4); (2) Jesus conceived of himself as God's Servant, on whom the Spirit of the Lord rests (in the sense of 42:1; 61:1–2).

Both the messianic and the adoptionist element of Ps. 2:7 and the tradition in Isa. 42:1; 61:1–2 concerning the Servant and the Spirit is important in NT Christology. Jesus is "Son" in his unique relation to God and his unique life of prayer; he is the Servant of God as the bearer of the message of the heavenly voice that called him. Both concepts designate a function and a task, a being in the presence of God.

2. *The concept of sonship in the tradition of Matt. 11:25–27; Lk. 10:21–22.* In Matt. 11:25–27; Lk. 10:21–22 we have a thanksgiving prayer of Jesus that consists of praise and a word of revelation. The middle section (Matt. 11:27; Lk. 10:22) suggests that the Father has handed over to the Son the full revelation that just as only a father really knows his son, so only a son really knows his father. That is, the Son alone is in the position to mediate this knowledge to others. The logion has its parallels in apocalyptic (Dan. 2:20–23; 1QS 11:15–20).

The content of this logion is Sem. The knowledge it presupposes is neither speculative nor mystic but personal. Note too the use of parallel clauses to express a reciprocal relationship; Sem. languages lack the reciprocal pronoun, "one another." The conceptual background can be found in Jewish wisdom teaching, which in turn is based on the OT (cf. Exod. 33:12–13; Job 28:25–28; Prov. 8:22–30; Sir. 1:1–10; Wis. 8:3–4). The saying grounds Jesus' right to be the mediator of knowledge of God to humanity in the exclusive relationship that a son has with his father, and thus implicitly Jesus claims a unique filial status. It fits in well with Jesus' other references to God as his Father.

The evidence for Jesus' own use of the specific term "Son" is comparatively small (mainly Matt. 11:27 par.). The title is generally found in statements addressed by others to Jesus, such as the heavenly voice (Mk. 1:11; 9:7) and evil powers (Matt. 4:3, 6; Mk. 3:11; 5:7). In the temptation story, Jesus refuses to misuse his relationship with God for his own ends.

3. *The voice at Jesus' baptism (Mk. 1:11 par.; Lk. 3:22).* The words of God recorded in all the Gospels in their accounts of the baptism (Mk. 1:11 par.) seem to form the real source of all the statements about the Son, the Servant, the Beloved, or the Elect One. Here Jesus was being called, chosen, and selected for a special task. It is important that the heavenly voice is associated with the gift of the Spirit. If the *ʿebed* tradition is present here, then the Heb. *ʿebed* in Isa. 42:1 is represented by *huios*, and *bāḥîr* by *agapētos*, beloved (note, however, that the LXX of 42:1 has *pais*, servant, child, and *eklektos*, elect one; → *eklegomai, 1721*). Jesus' baptism was a token of his death, which he undertook for the sins of the whole nation.

At the same time, we should not forget that also behind the baptism saying is Ps. 2:7 (see also Acts 13:33; Heb. 1:5), which favors the Son tradition. From the beginning the text confirmed God's recognition of Jesus as his Son as well as his Servant.

4. *The parable of the wicked tenants (Mk. 12:1–12 par.).* This parable acknowledges the appearance of the Son in contrast to the earlier sending of servants (the prophets). After sending several, the owner sends his son to the rebellious tenants. But their resistance is stiffened; they seize the son, kill him, and throw him out of the vineyard. Since the servants' commission was indistinguishable from that of the son, the parable's meaning undoubtedly lies in the extreme crisis of the historical situation when Jesus first told the parable, though Jesus also undoubtedly had a deeper meaning in mind.

Jesus' day saw the revolutionary temper of the Galilean peasants towards their foreign landlords (note that the owner lived abroad). The tenants had in mind the legal enactment that, under certain conditions, the estate of a deceased man was regarded as property without an owner, which anyone might appropriate; hence those who first seized possession had the prior claim. Jesus was contending against the tenants of the vineyard and the leaders of the nation, saying that they had again and again acted rebelliously against God and were even rejecting the final messenger of God.

5. *Jesus' birth stories (Matt. 1:18–2:18; Lk. 2:1–20).* Though Lk. refers to Jesus as "Son of the Most High," he concentrates on Jesus as the son of David, fulfilling 2 Sam. 7:12–16 (Lk. 1:32–33). Matt. calls the messianic child the "Son of God," quoting Hos. 11:1 (Matt. 2:15). The Redeemer, as a second Moses, must come out of Egypt (→ *plēroō, 4444*). Both Matt. and Lk. introduce the idea of Jesus' divine sonship with his being begotten (→ *gennaō, 1164*) by God without any earthly father.

6. *Pre-Pauline traditions and the Pauline message.* We must distinguish between the "Son of God" preexisting formulas that Paul quotes or adopts (Rom. 1:4; 8:3, 32; Gal. 2:20; 4:4–5; 1 Thess. 1:10) and his own formulations (Rom. 1:3, 9; 5:10; 8:29; 1 Cor. 1:9; 15:28; 2 Cor. 1:19; Gal. 1:16; 4:6). Statements involving "Christ" or "Lord" (*kyrios*) predominate. Still, the Son statements imply Jesus' legitimation, his relation to God, and his representation of God as his envoy. Behind these statements is the OT and Jewish background of the "Son" as the one who carried out the divine purpose.

(a) The twofold statement of Rom. 1:3–4 speaks of an *enthronement* and presupposes Ps. 2:7 and 110:1. Resurrection and enthronement thus coincide in history. Both forms of existence mentioned in this text, "descendant [son] of David" and "Son of God," describe life on earth and in heaven; the second form transcends the first.

(b) The statements about the *sending* of Jesus in Rom. 8:3 and Gal. 4:4–5 also seem to be pre-Pauline. One can discern here a formal scheme that can also be detected in the Johannine lit., although in a modified form (Jn. 3:17; 1 Jn. 4:9, 10, 14). The subsequent final clauses (*hina*, so that) specify the main purpose of the sending. Behind this lies the coming messenger who will surpass Moses (Deut. 18:15; Jn. 17:3).

(c) The *delivering up* of the Son (Rom. 4:25; 8:32; → *paradidōmi, 4140*) probably also belongs to pre-Pauline material. *paradidōmi* in this context may well be interpreted on the basis of the Passion story as an alternate sending formula ("deliver" meaning "send"). The example of Abraham, the patriarch who did not withhold his son (Gen. 22:12, 16), may also have played a part here. We have here a *kērygma* still influenced by Sem. ideas of the rights of a messenger. It is concerned with

God's decisive action as he commissions and authorizes his Son to suffer—an expression of his fatherly love.

(d) The summary of the old Gentile-Christian *kērygma* in 1 Thess. 1:9b–10 also appears to be pre-Pauline. It is probably built on a call to repentance and an expectation of salvation; it recalls elements of the Baptist's preaching of impending wrath (Matt. 3:7; cf. Rom. 5:9). The resurrection serves as a pledge of future salvation.

(e) Pre-Pauline material is likewise found in 1 Cor. 15:23–28. Passages such as Ps. 8:6 and 110:1 form the basis of the Christological affirmations here. The absolute use of "the Son" is key, as is his assumption of features that elsewhere are attributed to "son of man" (cf. Ps. 8). What is important here is the Son's obedience towards the "Father."

(f) These pre-Pauline statements concerning the Son of God lead us not only to the heart of old creedal formulations but also to the *kērygma* of the Christian mission in the Diaspora. Paul himself not only handed down earlier statements but also gave them a soteriological interpretation and subordinated them to his preaching of the cross.

(g) The only two references to the Son in Acts (9:20; 13:33 [Ps. 2:7 LXX]) both associate the term with the preaching of Paul. Clearly Lk. regarded it as distinctive of Paul's Christology. Paul used it to climax his theological statements and to demonstrate the close bond between Jesus and God in virtue of which Jesus is the mediator of salvation. Thus it is the Son who is the theme of the gospel (cf. Rom. 1:3, 9), and it is by means of this title that Paul emphasizes the supreme value of the death of the one who stood closest to God as the means of reconciling humankind with God (5:10; 8:32; Gal. 2:20; Col. 1:13–14). Note that for Paul Jesus was God's Son during his earthly life, and that it was as God's Son that he died. Consequently, Jesus did not cease to be divine in his earthly existence, and his self-emptying cannot mean that he gave up his divine nature to assume human nature (cf. Phil. 2:5–8).

It is, then, all the more remarkable that Paul can speak of Christians as the "sons of God" (Rom. 8:14, 19; 9:26; 2 Cor. 6:18; Gal. 3:26; 4:6–7) and claim that their destiny is conformity to the likeness of God's Son (Rom. 8:29). They are to share the glory of the exalted Son and must pattern their lives on his holy, sinless life.

7. *The Son of God in the Johannine literature.* The statements about the Son of God in Johannine lit., esp. in the letters, are important. In the Fourth Gospel, the sending of Jesus is a firm foundation for the doctrine of salvation. One believes and recognizes God and him whom he has sent (Jn. 17:3; cf. Num. 16:28). This statement about his being sent has its explicit purpose in showing Jesus' status as God's Son. It is a matter of God's decisive act in commissioning and authorizing his Son—but the Son therefore makes the same claims and has the same rights as the Father (Jn. 5:23).

(a) Jn. 3:35 describes the Son's authority to teach and to act. The Father loves him (i.e., chooses him) and has placed all things in his hands. This authority (→ *exousia*, 2026) belongs to one who is commissioned and executes justice. The Son can do nothing by himself but always looks at what the Father is doing (5:19; 7:18). His work is the execution of a commission from which he does not deviate in the least. The authority of the Father is, on the one hand, a once-for-all act in the past and, on the other hand, a continuous activity in the present; the main emphasis lies on the latter, for Jn. 6:40 expressly says that God's purpose is to draw all humanity into an encounter with the Son and so to faith. Only thus is true life achieved.

(b) Jn. reflects the early church's baptismal confession that "Jesus is the Christ, the Son of God" (Jn. 20:31; cf. Acts 8:37 in NIV note). This baptismal confession is also in view when Jn. speaks of faith "in the name of God's one and only Son" (Jn. 3:18; cf. 1:12). Part of faith is the deliberate saying of Jesus' name as a confession and a testimony (see also 1 Jn. 4:15; 5:5). The absolute use of "the Son" is typical of Jn. (e.g., Jn. 3:36), though he also uses "his Son" (e.g., 1 Jn. 1:3, 7), meaning "the Son of the Father." The expression "having the Son" (Jn. 3:36, lit.) is an oriental way of expressing participation in the being of God.

(c) The title "Son of God" is clearly fundamental in John's Christology and expresses a number of basic convictions about Jesus. (i) This title expresses the metaphysical or essential relationship between Jesus and his Father. So close is the link between them that to deny the Son is to deny the Father (1 Jn. 2:22–23). Father and Son belong inseparably to each other (Jn. 1:18; 5:23; 1 Jn. 1:3; 5:20). The Son is preexistent (Jn. 3:17; 11:27; 1 Jn. 3:8; 4:9–14). He is God's "only" Son, a term that expresses the special love between the Father and Jesus.

(ii) The NT in general does not speculate on the origin of the Son, and the use of the terminology of sonship is not designed to encourage such speculation, but to draw out the nature of the relationship between Jesus and God: a relationship of mutual love (Jn. 3:35; 5:20) and of filial obedience (5:19).

(iii) The Son shares the functions of the Father, esp. as the judge and the bringer of life (Jn. 5:17–30).

(iv) The Son mediates between God and humankind. He was given by the Father in order that we might be saved (Jn. 3:16). While in the world, he remains in constant communion with the Father (1:18; 3:13; 8:29; 16:32) and is thus able to reveal the Father to us. The title "Son" expresses above all the fact that Jesus is the Savior. In 1 Jn. "the Son" stands close in meaning to "Messiah," but for Jn. Jesus is the Savior particularly because of his metaphysical relationship with God (Jn. 11:41; 12:27–28; 17:1). This is why Jn. is so concerned to emphasize the real nature of the incarnation (2 Jn. 7–11).

(d) Jn. also refers to believers as "sons of God" or "children [*tekna*] of God." It is only in the Hel. tradition that the distinction arises between the "Son" of doctrinal statements and the children who become such through faith and baptism. Jn. 1:12 speaks of the "right" to become God's children (*tekna theou*), and 1 Jn. 3:1 of the gift of being "children of God." From this gift proceeds our "being" ("and that is what we are"). This right or gift of childhood is presented in terms of a birth process (Jn. 1:13; 3:3; 1 Jn. 2:29; 3:9–10; 4:7; 5:1, 4, 18), which is the product of the "Spirit" or the receiving of baptism ("water and the Spirit," Jn. 3:5). Those so born live a life of obedience and righteousness.

8. *The Son of God in Hebrews.* We meet the absolute use of the name "Son" in Heb. (1:2, 5, 8; 3:6; 5:8; 7:28). We also meet "Son of God" as an official rank, where the early Christian baptismal confession has left its mark (4:14; 6:6; 7:3; 10:29). Surprisingly, this book is reticent about God's position as Father (cf. 1:5; 12:7, 9).

Heb. 1:1–4 juxtaposes historical and metaphysical elements about Jesus the Son. He has been appointed heir (→ *klēros*, 3102) of all and was the mediator of creation, and he is now the "exact representation" of the invisible God (cf. also Col. 1:15–16). The historical process is described in the aor. tense and the metaphysical in the pres.

9. *The Son of God in Revelation.* In Rev. the concept "Son of God" appears only in 2:18, where it is Christ's name for himself. According to 2:23 he shares in God's activity of judgment (→ *krima*, 3210; cf. Jer. 17:10); Christ grants believers a share in his dominion over the nations (Rev. 2:26–27; cf. Ps. 2:8–9). It is significant that the authority of the Son of God is described in OT terms.

10. *The Trinitarian formula.* The triadic confessional formula of Matt. 28:19 ("name of the Father and of the Son and of the Holy Spirit") recalls the absolute use of the name Son. The entire formula is a brief summary of the saving event, of catechesis, and of the authorization for the baptism of the nations. Matt. presents a practice of baptism that has the highest authority.

In sum, the self-designation "the Son" is particularly important among the Christological statements because it traces back the call, the election, and the claims of Jesus to God himself and thus authenticates them.

huios Dauid, Son of David

OT 1. "Son of David" is a NT predicate of Jesus that has a long tradition behind it in the OT and in the traditions of Jud. (a) Nathan's promise in 2 Sam. 7:12–16 is fundamental: the raising up of a successor to David from his offspring and the confirmation of his "house" and kingdom forever. It is the basis for Ps. 2:7; 89:4; 132:11 (covenant-making and oath).

(b) Some of the OT prophets also presuppose this promise to David and give it a future interpretation in terms of Israel's messianic hope (see Isa. 9:6–7; 11:1–10). Just as God's Spirit once rested on David, so the new ruler, a second David, will be equipped with Yahweh's Spirit. His wisdom and understanding are stressed, and justice and righteousness are the results of the appearance of this king. Jer. 23:5 expressly mentions the "righteous Branch" of David, who will act in wisdom, justice, and righteousness (30:9; 33:15).

Ezek. 34:23 makes use of the shepherd image for their prophetic description: "I will place over them one shepherd, my servant David, and he will tend them" (cf. 37:24). Isa. 55:3 refers to an "everlasting covenant" and the realization of the gifts of grace promised to David; thus it gives an answer full of promise to the nation's complaint that its history is no longer favored by God's gracious care (Ps. 89). This everlasting covenant is also the beginning of salvation for the nation. Zech. 3:8 promises "my servant, the Branch," who "will branch out from his place and build the temple of the LORD" (6:12). The blessing of the house of David and the inhabitants of Jerusalem are here joined together (12:8, 10; 13:1).

(c) A messianic sense is clear in Gen. 49:9–10 (lion of Judah) and Num. 24:17 (star of Jacob), yet the connection with the promise of the "kingdom of the son of David" is at best indirect. Note that Isa. 11:1–10 and Mic. 5:1–5 presuppose that Yahweh once more starts his messianic work anew; both prophets look to the family from which David came and expect a completely new start in place of the ruling descendants of David.

2. Later, Jud. also took up the promise of a son of David in order to enable it to put up with its political oppression and its distress through its relationship to God.

(a) In wisdom lit., Sir. 47:11 and 1 Macc. 2:57 allude to the permanency of the throne or the throne fixed for eternity. More important is *Pss. Sol.* 17, which uses "Son of David" as a fixed messianic expression (cf. 2 Sam. 7:1; Ps. 2:9; Isa. 9:6; 11:1, 10). During a period when the Hasmoneans were making messianic claims for themselves and were appropriating the glory of the priesthood, the old Davidic promises were being revived. It was a time of affliction. The one who offered this prayer directed his prayer to God and held him to his promise. He expected a change in which the dominion of the Gentiles would be broken and the pollution of sinners would be done away with. The Messiah's appearance would mark the beginning of the gathering of a holy nation, a dominion over the Gentiles, and the establishment of righteousness.

Pss. Sol. 17 discloses the viewpoint of the Pharisees prior to 63 B.C. The "Son of David" is to renew David's dominion but in the way in which the Pharisaic party think of the coming of the messianic age: "But he rules over them as a righteous king, instructed by God, and in his days no injustice shall be done among them for they are all holy and their king is the Lord's Anointed" (17:35–36).

(b) Although messianic claims could be made for men of non-Davidic origin, the rabbis not only emphasized "the king, the Messiah," but also the "Son of David."

(c) The Qumran sect expected three future persons who would bring salvation: a prophet (Elijah or Moses), the Davidic Messiah, and a priest, who seems to have had first place in this trio. The coming shoot of David will appear with the interpreter of the law and will establish David's tent (interpreted elsewhere as the books of the law). In the Qumran lit. we see a similar messianic tradition to that of *Pss. Sol.*

(d) It is possible that the title "son of David" was understood particularly in terms of the character of Solomon, who had a reputation for wisdom as well as for power over evil spirits (→ *T. Sol.*). The evidence is sparse, but it does help explain why the title "son of David" is linked with exorcisms and healings in the Gospels.

NT On a number of occasions, the NT presupposes that Jesus of Nazareth belongs in terms of genealogy to the line of David and that this descent from David was a messianic element in his history.

1. The creedal formulas of Rom. 1:3–4 and 2 Tim. 2:8 presuppose that descent from David and divine sonship, based on his resurrection from the dead, are two stages in an early Christology. As indicated previously in the "Son of God" section, in Rom. 1:3–4 Paul quotes a confession handed down to him from the Palestinian community. The gospel concerns the "Son" (Mk. 1:11; 9:7), who descended from the seed of David according to the flesh, but who has been installed as "Son of God" in power according to the Spirit of holiness through the resurrection from the dead. This describes two consecutive episodes in Jesus' history according to God's plan of salvation: On earth he appears as the Son of David; by the resurrection, he is enthroned as the heavenly Messiah (see Ps. 110:1).

2. The speeches in Acts distinguish between David who died and the "Holy One" who has been raised from the dead and does not see corruption (Acts 2:27; 13:37, quoting Ps. 16:10). The quotation from Amos 9:11–12 in Acts 15:16–18 refers to the restoration of "David's fallen tent" and a new era of salvation for the remnant of Israel. The promise of the Son of David is presupposed here, though it is not explicitly mentioned.

3. (a) The structure of Mk.'s Gospel corresponds to the confession of Rom. 1:3–4: The Messiah (i.e., the Son of David) is the "Son of God" to whom the Evangelist bears witness. Mk. 12:35–37 par. records a discussion that raises the question of the relation of the "son of David" to David's Lord (according to Ps. 110:1; → *kyrios, 3261*). The answer accords with Rom. 1:3–4: The Son of David must be exalted. That Mk. sees Jesus as David's Son is shown by the mode of address in Mk. 10:48. Mk. 12:35–37 juxtaposes two apparently conflicting statements based on Scripture and asks how they are to be reconciled. The answer? The Messiah can be both a descendant of David and David's Lord by virtue of his exaltation; that is, the Messiah is not merely a descendant of David but also the Son of God (cf. 2 Sam. 7:12–16), or possibly the Son of Man.

(b) Matt. gives special weight to Jesus' Davidic descent and heightens the way in which he is thus addressed and acclaimed (9:27; 12:23; 15:22; 20:30; 21:9, 15; 22:42, 45). In his preface Jesus is described as "Christ" (*Christos*, i.e., Messiah), "son of David," and "son of Abraham" (1:1); this indicates that both Jesus' origin and his position in salvation history are a theme of the book.

In Matt. 1:20 Joseph also, the father of Jesus, "the husband of Mary" (1:16), is called "son of David." This shows that the genealogical sense of the phrase has not been relinquished. In Jud. it had above all a legal significance: Recognition by the father sets forth the succession. The degree to which the genealogy sets forth Jesus' claim to a place in salvation history is shown by the structure of the family tree with its three groups of fourteen members. Matt. deliberately fits Jesus' messianic status into Israel's history and thereby emphasizes his claims.

(c) Lk.'s birth narrative presupposes the tradition of Jesus' Davidic sonship ("descendant [house] of David," 1:27, 69; 2:4; "town of David," 2:4, 11; "throne of ... David," 1:32). That Lk. admits it genealogically is clear from the family tree (3:31). It is striking how Jesus is acclaimed as "king" by the lips of the Jewish people (19:38; 23:2); this draws out the full implications of the motif of Davidic sonship (cf. Jn. 12:13).

4. The Johannine tradition puts Jewish messianic questions to the tradition about Jesus: (a) "When the Christ comes, no one will know where he is from" (Jn. 7:27); (b) "the Christ will come from David's family and from Bethlehem, the town where David lived" (7:42). Objections such as these leveled by Jud. can appeal to the OT (origins in Bethlehem, Mic. 5:2) or to a given tradition (the hiddenness of the Messiah). It is not that the traditions are false, but the statements of the tradition cannot adequately accommodate the Christ whom Jn. confesses. The title "Son of David" does not occur in Jn.'s

Gospel in so many words; the confession of Jewish Christianity rather refers to the "King of Israel" (1:49; 12:13; 19:19; cf. 18:37).

5. There is an archaic ring about Rev. 5:5 (cf. Gen. 49:9–10; Isa. 11:1, 10) and Rev. 22:16 (cf. Num. 24:17; Isa. 11:1, 10), which is reminiscent of the Messiah as the Son of David. Note also Rev. 3:7, where Christ holds the key of David (cf. Isa. 22:22) that controls entry to the heavenly banqueting hall.

6. The title "Son of David" thus sums up the NT confession of Jesus as a descendant of David who fulfills the promise of the coming anointed king and who is the glorious antitype of both David and his son, Solomon. This messianic hope is fulfilled in Jesus' birth as the adopted son of Joseph at Bethlehem, in his works of mercy and healing, and in his entry into Jerusalem. The title is inadequate to convey the high status of the one who is David's (and everyone's) Lord, but it remains a fitting title for the exalted Son of God in whose possession is the key to the heavenly banquet.

See also *nēpios*, infant, minor (*3758*); *pais*, child, young man, son, servant (*4090*); *teknon*, child (*5451*).

5630 (hymneō, celebrate, praise, sing), → *5631.*

5631	ὕμνος

ὕμνος (*hymnos*), song, song of praise, hymn, ode (*5631*); ὑμνέω (*hymneō*), celebrate, praise, sing (*5630*).

CL & OT 1. In. cl. Gk. *hymnos* is something sung, a song. It includes varied poetical forms, both recited and sung. In general, this word refers to songs to the gods, esp. a song in praise of the divinity, as distinct perhaps from *epainos*, praise given to humans (→ *aineō*, to praise, *140*). *hymneō* means to sing of, celebrate, in poetry or prose; to discuss, tell repeatedly, recite; (pass.) ring (in one's ears).

2. In the LXX *hymneō* is found 69x and *hymnos* 28x. Both noun and vb. translate a variety of Heb. words for praising and singing. The Hallel psalms (Ps. 113–118) occupied an outstanding position in the rites of the individual feast already when the first temple was standing, and they continued to do so in the later worship of the synagogue. In the Passover the slaughtering of the lambs was accompanied by the repeated singing of these psalms. At the Passover meal itself, the first half of the Passover Hallel followed the Passover meal itself, the Haggadah, and the second half followed the final prayer of the meal and the drinking of the third cup (→ *pascha*, Passover, *4247*).

3. Noncanonical collections of hymns have also come down to us from various Jewish circles in Palestine; from the Qumran sect we have the great collection of *Hodayot*, the hymns of praise, and from Pharisaic circles the *Psalms of Solomon*.

NT 1. *hymnos* occurs in the NT only in Eph. 5:19 and Col. 3:16; *hymneō* only in Matt. 26:30; Mk. 14:26; Acts 16:25; Heb. 2:12. (a) The aor. part. of *hymneō*, "when they had sung a hymn" (Matt. 26:30; Mk. 14:26) is generally understood as referring to the singing of the Hallel psalms at the close of the Passover meal prior to drinking the fourth cup; this view in part depends on whether Jesus' last meal with the disciples was in fact a celebration of the Passover (→ *deipnon*, supper, meal, *1270*).

(b) Acts 16:25 records how, after being beaten and imprisoned at Philippi, "Paul and Silas were praying and singing hymns [*hymneō*] to God." The story shows how they could praise God despite their difficult circumstances. Their action was at the same time a testimony to their fellow prisoners. God vindicated them, not so much by the earthquake (which they did not use as an occasion for escape), but by the conversion of the jailer and their subsequent honorable release.

(c) Heb. 2:12 provides to Ps. 22:22 a Christological significance as an illustration of the solidarity of the speaker with God's people: "In the presence of the congregation I will sing your praises [*hymneō*]." Jesus cites this same psalm on the cross (Matt. 27:46; Mk. 15:34). In

fact, in the early church the entire first part of this psalm was seen as a *testimonium* of the crucifixion of Christ (cf. Ps. 22:18 with Mk. 15:24; Jn. 19:24). Thus, it was only natural that the second half of this psalm would also be seen as the voice of the exalted Christ (note that "congregation" in the LXX of Ps. 22:22 is *ekklēsia*, the standard word for "church" in the NT, → *1711*). Thus, the Son of God is pleased to call the members of the church his "brothers" (Heb. 2:11).

2. On the use of *hymnos* in Eph. 5:19 and Col. 3:16, → *ōdē*, song (*6046*).

See also *psalmos*, a sacred song, psalm (*6011*); *ōdē*, song, ode (of mourning, complaint, or joy) (*6046*).

5633 (hypakoē, obedience), → *5634.*

5634	ὑπακούω

ὑπακούω (*hypakouō*), listen, obey (*5634*); ὑπακοή (*hypakoē*), obedience (*5633*); ὑπήκοος (*hypēkoos*), obedient (*5675*).

CL & OT *hypakouō*, to listen to, answer, obey (derived from *akouō*, → *201*) was used in cl. Gk. with the dat. of the person or thing, sometimes with the gen. of the person. The noun *hypakoē*, obedience, is rare, while the adj. *hypēkoos*, obedient, is attested from the 5th cent. B.C.

In the LXX, *hypakouō* denotes obedience shown to humans (Gen. 16:2; 22:18), to wisdom (Sir. 4:15; 24:22), and to God (e.g., Jer. 3:13, 25). In several places, the vb. means to answer (Isa. 50:2; 65:24; 66:4), *hypakoē* also means an answer (2 Sam. 22:36). *hypēkoos* is used in Deut. 20:11 of subject peoples, and in Prov. 4:3; 13:1 of a son's obedience to his father.

NT 1. *hypakouō* occurs 21x in the NT; *hypakoē*, 15x; *hypēkoos*, 3x. In Acts 12:13 the vb. means to open in the sense of answering the door. Elsewhere the word group denotes obedience. The pattern of this obedience is Jesus Christ, who was "obedient [*hypēkoos*] to death" on the cross (Phil. 2:8). Through his obedience, which stands in contrast to Adam's disobedience, "the many" have been made righteous (Rom. 5:19). Heb. has a similar thought. Through his suffering Jesus learned obedience; thus he became the source of eternal salvation to those who obey him (5:8–9, both noun and vb. used). His obedience to his Father does not exclude his being Lord, whom demonic powers and the forces of nature obey (Mk. 1:27; 4:41).

2. Paul preached the good news "so that all nations might believe and obey" (Rom. 16:26; cf. 15:18; 16:19). Obedience to Christ includes submission to the apostle through whom Christ speaks (2 Cor. 7:15; 10:5–6; cf. Acts 6:7). He found in the Philippians an obedient attitude (Phil. 2:12), and he warned the Thessalonians to have nothing to do with those who would not obey his apostolic instructions (2 Thess. 3:14; cf. Rom. 10:16; 2 Thess. 1:8). Obedience to his preaching brings righteousness (Rom. 6:16–17). Heb. 11:8 identifies Abraham as an example of believing obedience (cf. Gen. 12:1–8). Christians are "obedient children" (1 Pet. 1:14), and this obedience must embrace their whole lives. This includes submitting willingly to earthly authorities, such as parents and masters; these in turn must acknowledge Christ as the highest authority (Eph. 6:1–9; Col. 3:20–22).

3. The use of the noun *hypakoē* corresponds to that of the vb. The apostle Paul sought to bring every thought captive in obedience to Christ (2 Cor. 10:5; cf. Rom. 16:26). Beneath all this lies the understanding of faith as an act of obedience to Christ (1:5). Such obedience cannot be separated from obedience to his messengers and the message they proclaim (15:18; 2 Cor. 10:6; Phlm. 21). Christians are hindered in their obedience because of the sinful passions of the body (1 Pet. 1:14, 22; cf. Rom. 6:12).

See also *akouō*, hear, listen, attend, perceive by hearing (*201*).

5636 (hypantaō, meet), → *2918.*

5637 (hypantēsis, meeting, coming to meet), → *2918.*

5638 (hyparxis, property), → *5975.*

5639 (ta hyparchonta, what belongs to someone, property, possessions), → *5975.*

| 5642 ὑπέρ |

ὑπέρ (*hyper*), over, above, for (*5642*).

CL & OT The original local sense of *hyper* (over, above) is found in cl. Gk. and occasionally in the papyri, but not in the LXX or NT. Its most common Hel. meaning (on behalf of) seems to have arisen from the image of one person standing over another to protect him or her, or of a shield lifted over the head that suffers the blow instead of the person. The use of *hyper* in the sense of exchange or substitution is rare in cl. Gk., but it does occur more frequently in the LXX (e.g., Deut. 24:16; Isa. 43:3–4; Jdt. 8:12).

NT 1. With the acc. case, *hyper* in the NT has the sense of surpassing over and above, beyond (e.g., 2 Cor. 1:8; Eph. 1:22; Phlm. 16; Heb. 4:12). In 1 Cor. 4:6 the *to* (neut. art.) that precedes "Do not go beyond [*hyper*] what is written" is a clue that the phrase in question is probably a quotation of a Pauline slogan or (conceivably) Paul's repudiation of a Corinthian watchword.

2. When *hyper* is used with a pers. noun or pronoun in the gen. case, it expresses some advantage or favor that accrues to persons and thus mean "on behalf of" (representation) or "in the place of" (substitution). When the benefit is gained by things, the meaning will be "for the sake of," which approaches a causal sense ("because of").

To act on behalf of a person often involves acting in that person's place. Hence *hyper* not infrequently has the sense of *anti* (instead of); in fact, in the NT period, *hyper* encroaches more and more into the meaning of *anti*. For example, of Onesimus Paul says to Philemon: "I would have liked to keep him with me so that he could take your place [*hyper sou*] in helping me while I am in chains for the gospel" (Phlm. 13). Paul wants Onesimus as a helper in place of the help that Philemon might otherwise want to give.

In Jn. 11:50, Caiaphas remonstrates with the Jewish leaders: "You do not realize that it is better for you that one man die for [*hyper*] the people" (Jn. 11:50; cf. 18:14). It is clear that *hyper* here denotes substitution, not simply benefit or representation, since Caiaphas remarks that such a death "for the people" would ensure that "the whole nation" did not perish (11:50b). That is, politically the death of the one (as a scapegoat) would be a substitute for the death of the many. As Jn. saw it (10:51–52; 18:14), Caiaphas unwittingly expressed a theological profundity here: Christ's suffering was vicarious and redemptive. Similar is Paul's affirmation that "one died for all" (2 Cor. 5:14–15). The death of Christ was the death of all, because he was dying their death. In becoming the object of divine wrath against human sin, Christ was acting vicariously, in our place (cf. 5:21; Gal. 3:13).

In some places, however, where "to die" or its equivalent occurs with *hyper*, it is difficult to determine whether or not the prep. denotes substitution (e.g., Rom. 8:32; Gal. 2:20; Eph. 5:2, 25; 1 Thess. 5:10; Tit. 2:14). In Rom. 14:15 for [*hyper*] whom" does not appear to have any substitutionary notion, since a parallel in 1 Cor. 8:11 uses the prep. *dia*. It is striking that, in addition to affirming that Christ died for (*hyper*) persons (Rom. 5:6, 8; 2 Cor. 5:14–15; 1 Thess. 5:10; 1 Tim. 2:6), Paul can say that he died or gave himself "for [*hyper*]" our sins (1 Cor. 15:3; Gal. 1:4; cf. Heb. 5:1; 7:27), i.e., with reference to our sins or to expiate our sins. That Paul never uses *anti* with respect to Christ's death is probably because *anti* was losing it popularity as a prep. and also because *hyper* could simultaneously express both representation and substitution.

3. Most puzzling is the use of *hyper* with the vb. *baptizō* (to baptize) in 1 Cor. 15:29 ("baptized for the dead"). Any interpretation of this passage must meet two requirements: (a) *hyper* should not be given a sense unparalleled in the Greek Bible, and (b) the resultant meaning of the verse must contribute to Paul's argument in 1 Cor. 15. Consequently, it seems probable that some baptized Corinthians had

a semimagical view of baptism and were being rebaptized vicariously for certain deceased Corinthians who were thought to be at a disadvantage because they had not been baptized before being overtaken by death. On this interpretation Paul is using an ad hominem argument (as in 15:30–32) in support of a conclusion already established (namely, that the dead in Christ will rise) and is appealing to an aberrant practice (otherwise unknown to us in the 1st cent.), without giving it his approval.

| 5644 ὑπέρακμος |

ὑπέρακμος (*hyperakmos*), past the peak, overripe, begin to fade; or, overwhelmingly strong, overpassionate (*5644*).

CL & OT The word is formed from *hyper*, beyond, and *akmē*, peak, which is used in the sense of the peak or high point in human development. Thus, the word denotes a person, either male or female, who is past one's prime, past marriageable age. The word does not occur in the LXX.

NT *hyperakmos* occurs only at 1 Cor. 7:36, where it has two possible explanations. The subject of the verse has traditionally been taken to refer to the father of a virgin daughter, who does not want her to go past the age in which she might normally be married (*hyperakmos*; → *gameō, 1138*). As far as Paul is concerned, such a man does not do wrong if he gives his virgin daughter away in marriage (the vb. *gamizō*, used 2x in 7:38).

But 1 Cor. 7:35–38 may also refer to a man who is in some kind of liaison with a virgin. It may imply a betrothal in which marriage has been put off on the grounds of the spiritual considerations Paul is urging in this passage. It may even refer to a spiritual marriage that has not been consummated physically, though evidence for such marriages is later than the NT. In this case the verse is saying, "If anyone thinks that he is not behaving properly to his virgin and he be overpassionate [*hyperakmos*] . . . let them marry." Or one can still take the subject of this verse to be the man but refer *hyperakmos* to the virgin, i.e., the man should go ahead and marry her on the grounds of her age.

In any case, the general tone of Paul's recommendations remains clear. It is not a sin to marry; out of personal humanitarian considerations it may be right to do so. But the present times make celibacy preferable.

See also *gameō,* marry (*1138*); *moicheuō,* commit adultery (*3658*); *nymphē,* bride (*3811*); *koitē,* bed, marriage bed, intercourse (*3130*).

5647 (hyperauxanō, grow abundantly), → *889.*

5648 (hyperbainō, overstep, transgress), → *4126.*

5655 (hyperekperissou, beyond all measure), → *4355.*

5659 (hyperentynchanō, plead, intercede), → *1961.*

5661 (hyperēphania, pride), → *5662.*

| 5662 ὑπερήφανος |

ὑπερήφανος (*hyperēphanos*), proud (*5662*); ὑπερηφανία (*hyperēphania*), pride (*5661*); ἀλαζών (*alazōn*), boastful (*225*); ἀλαζονεία (*alazoneia*), boastfulness (*224*).

CL & OT 1. (a) The cl. Gk. vb. *hyperēphaneō* means to be proud, arrogant. Later it was used trans.: to treat arrogantly, despise. The adj. *hyperēphanos* usually means arrogant, proud; it also has a positive use: magnificent. The noun *hyperēphania* means pride, arrogance, contempt.

(b) The *alazōn*, the wandering charlatan or braggart, was a favorite comedy character. A wandering sophist was also scornfully nicknamed *alazōn*. The corresponding abstract noun, *alazoneia*, means boastfulness, imposture.

2. (a) In the OT a central theme of the prophetic message (e.g., Isa. 13:11) and of the wisdom lit. (e.g., Prov. 3:34) is that God's judgment destroys all human pride. The number of Heb. words translated

by the four words mentioned above (plus *hybris*, *5615*) is large, though more than half are derivatives of the root *gāʾâ*, be exalted. The fact that *hybris* and *hyperēphaneia* are synonyms suggests that the LXX translators saw no fundamental distinction between them.

(b) *hyperēphania* occurs in such passages as Ps. 17:10; 31:18, 23; Prov. 8:13; Isa. 16:6; Amos 8:7. *hyperēphanos* occurs in Ps. 119:21, 51, 69, 78, 122; Prov. 3:34; Isa. 29:20; Wis. 14:6; Sir. 3:28. For the adv. *hyperēphanōs*, see 1 Macc. 7:34; 2 Macc. 9:4.

(c) *alazoneia* is found in Wis. 5:8; 17:7; 2 Macc. 9:8; 15:6; 4 Macc. 1:26; 2:15; 8:19; *alazōn* in Job 28:8; Prov. 21:24; Hab. 2:5.

3. (a) In wisdom lit. those who are *hyperēphanos* form a distinct group, contrasted with the righteous and the humble. *hyperēphanos* is never used of Israel in wisdom lit. According to the LXX of Prov. 3:34, "God resists the proud, but gives grace to the humble." Just as the fear of the Lord is the beginning of wisdom, to forsake the Lord is the beginning of pride (Sir. 10:12). Therefore, those who pray cleanse themselves from the suspicion of pride (Est. 4:17 LXX) and indicate their own lowliness as they anticipate God's help (Jdt. 6:19).

(b) The prophetic message, by contrast, accuses Israel itself of pride (using words from this group, Ezek. 7:20; 16:56; Amos 8:7; in general, cf. Hos. 5:5; 7:10; Amos 6:8; Zeph. 2:10) and thus takes up a position in the sharpest opposition to deeply ingrained conceptions.

NT 1. *hyperēphania* occurs only in Mk. 7:22; *hyperēphanos* occurs 5x. (a) The context of Lk. 1:51 is poetic (Mary's Magnificat, a song based on Hannah's song in 1 Sam. 2:1–10): "He [God] has performed mighty deeds with his arm; he has scattered those who are proud in their inmost thoughts." The verse also echoes Ps. 89:10 (where the LXX has "you have humiliated him as a wounded proud man"). The Magnificat itself expresses Mary's joyous gratitude for her personal blessing (Lk. 1:46–48), God's graciousness to all who revere him (1:49–50), and his special love for the lowly (1:51–53) and for Israel (1:54–55).

(b) The remaining instances of the *hyperēphan-* word group occur in paraenetic contexts, where they are included in lists of vices used in early Christian instruction. For example, Jesus uses *hyperēphania* in a list of things that he declares come out of the human heart, which must be dealt with at that level and cannot be cured by external washings (Mk. 7:21–22): "For from within, out of men's hearts, come evil thoughts, sexual immorality, theft, murder, adultery, greed, malice, deceit, lewdness, envy, slander, arrogance [*hyperēphania*] and folly." Similar lists of virtues and vices are also found in intertestamental lit. (e.g., Wis. 14:25–26; *T. Reu.* 3:3–6; *T. Jud.* 16:1). The NT writers continued this OT wisdom tradition (see, e.g., 1 Cor. 5:10–11; 6:9–10; Gal. 5:19–21; Eph. 5:3–5; 1 Pet. 4:3).

(c) In Rom. 1:30 *hyperēphanos* occurs in a catalog of vices that Paul sees as the outcome of idolatry, which is itself an expression of God's judgment (cf. 1:28). In this list are included the "insolent [*hybristēs*], arrogant [*hyperēphanos*] and boastful [*alazōn*]." In 2 Tim. 3:2 the haughty are included in a list describing the characteristics of the godless in the last days: "People will be lovers of themselves, lovers of money, boastful [*alazōn*], proud [*hyperēphanos*]...." Paul urges Timothy to "have nothing to do" with such people (3:5).

(d) Prov. 3:34 (from the LXX) is cited 2x in paraenetic passages of the NT that exhort humility (Jas. 4:6; 1 Pet. 5:5). The former passage is concerned with worldliness, the latter with relationships within the church in the wider context of living in the end times.

2. *alazōn* and *alazoneia* each occur 2x in the NT. (a) *alazōn* occurs in the catalogs in Rom. 1:30 and 2 Tim. 3:2 (see above). It denotes those who try to impress others with big claims. The *alazōn* is the braggart or the charlatan. Such people often delude themselves that they are greater than they really are.

(b) Jas. 4:16 takes up the thought of 4:6 (noted above): "As it is, you boast and brag [lit., in your arrogance, *alazoneia*]. All such boasting [*kauchēsis*, → *kauchēma*, *3017*] is evil." Jas. uses the pl. here, perhaps suggesting numerous instances of confidence in one's own

cleverness, luck, strength, or skill that have brought material advantage. The context deals with laying plans for material gain without regard to God. The author counters this with the remedy of saying, "If it is the Lord's will," before we do this or that (4:15). Moreover, if we know what is good and do not do it, we sin (4:17).

(c) *alazoneia* also occurs in 1 Jn. 2:16: "Everything in the world—the cravings of sinful man, the lust of his eyes and the boasting [*alazoneia*] of what he has and does—comes not from the Father but from the world." *alazoneia* here implies a lust for advantage and status. The expressions used here are not so much a classification of the kinds of evil that stem from fallen humanity as they are Jn.'s attempt to lay bare the world's self-centered, grasping structure, which can only be overcome by love (see 2:15).

See also *hybris*, insolence, arrogance, insult, ill-treatment (*5615*).

5664 (*hypernikaō*, be more than victorious), → *3771*.

5668 (*hyperperisseuō*, beyond all measure), → *4355*.

5669 (*hyperperissōs*, beyond all measure), → *4355*.

5670 (*hyperpleonazō*, to be present in great abundance), → *4429*.

5671 (*hyperypsoō*, raise above all heights), → *5738*.

5675 (*hypēkoos*, obedient), → *5634*.

5676 (*hypēreteō*, serve, render service, be helpful), → *1354*.

5677 (*hypēretēs*, servant, helper, assistant), → *1354*.

5678 (*hypnos*, sleep), → *2761*.

5679	ὑπό

ὑπό (*hypo*), under, by (*5679*).

CL The basic meaning of this prep. in cl. Gk. is under. But it was also used after a pass. voice to denote the pers. agent who carried out the action (in contrast to an impers. agent, which was usually expressed by the dat. of means or instrument).

NT 1. There are several ways in which agency is expressed in the NT: *hypo* (Matt. 4:1 [2x]), *dia* (through, 2 Cor. 1:19; → *1328*), *apo* (from, 3:18; → *608*), *ek* (out of, by, Gal. 4:4; → *1666*), *en* with the dat. (in, Matt. 9:34; → *1877*), or the simple dat. (Matt. 6:1).

2. Where *dia* and *hypo* are both used and can be distinguished, *dia* marks intermediate agency and *hypo* ultimate or original agency. Thus in Matt. 1:22, the Lord as the ultimate author (*hypo kyriou*, lit., "by the Lord") of the prophetic word is distinguished from the prophet Isa., who acted as a mediate agent ("through [*dia*] the prophet") in speaking the divine word.

3. Similarly to *dia*, sometimes *para* (from the side of, → *4123*) occurs where one might expect *hypo*. In Lk. 1:45, in the phrase "what was said to her by [*para*] the Lord" (lit.), *para* may allude to the intermediate agency of the angel. Whereas *para* traces an action back to its point of departure or source, *hypo* relates an action to its ultimate cause.

4. The opposite nuance occurs with respect to *apo* and *hypo* (→ *apo*, from, *608*).

5681	ὑπογραμμός

ὑπογραμμός (*hypogrammos*), outline, copy, example (*5681*).

CL & OT This word is late. Philo uses it in the sense of outline. Its most common use is for the faint outlines of letters that pupils traced over while learning to write, then also of the sets of letters written at the top of a page to be copied repeatedly by the learner on the rest of the page.

NT *hypogrammos* is applied metaphorically in 1 Pet. 2:21 to the example left by Christ for his disciples to follow, esp. in his patient endurance of undeserved suffering.

See also *eidōlon*, image, idol (*1631*); *eikōn*, image, likeness, form, appearance (*1635*); *charaktēr*, stamp, representation, outward appearance, form (*5917*); *apaugasma*, radiance, effulgence, reflection (*575*); *hypodeigma*, proof, example, model (*5682*); *typos*, type, pattern (*5596*).

| 5682 ὑπόδειγμα | ὑπόδειγμα (*hypodeigma*), proof, example, model (*5682*). |

CL & OT In Hel. Gk. *hypodeigma* means an example, with a transferred sense of demonstration, sample, or model (*typos* is a synonym). It is used in either the good sense of a model to copy or as warning of an example to avoid. Philo has an important discussion of the Levitical tabernacle as a model of the divine plan that Moses glimpsed and Bezalel constructed. The occurrences of this noun are in Ezek. 42:15 ("temple area," where LXX has the "ground-plan of the house"); Sir. 44:16 (Enoch was "an example of repentance"); 2 Macc. 6:28, 31 (the Maccabean martyrs are a "noble example").

NT The NT usage divides between the two meanings given in the LXX. It can mean a figure or copy. The Levitical furnishings and service are a "copy" of their heavenly counterparts, which alone have substantial reality (Heb. 8:5; 9:23). *hypodeigma* can also mean "example," either in a call to imitation (Jn. 13:15; Jas. 5:10) or in the bad sense of serving as a warning (Heb. 4:11; 2 Pet. 2:6).

See also *eidōlon*, image, idol (*1631*); *eikōn*, image, likeness, form, appearance (*1635*); *charaktēr*, stamp, representation, outward appearance, form (*5917*); *apaugasma*, radiance, effulgence, reflection (*575*); *hypogrammos*, outline, copy, example (*5681*); *typos*, type, pattern (*5596*).

| 5693 ὑποκρίνομαι | ὑποκρίνομαι (*hypokrinomai*), answer, pretend, dissimulate |

(*5693*); ὑπόκρισις (*hypokrisis*), pretense, hypocrisy (*5694*); ὑποκριτής (*hypokritēs*), pretender, hypocrite, a godless man (*5695*); συνυποκρίνομαι (*synypokrinomai*), join in hypocrisy (*5347*); ἀνυπόκριτος (*anypokritos*), unfeigned, genuine (*537*).

CL & OT 1. *hypokrinō* (usually in the mid.) is a compound verb based on *krinō*, judge. Its basic meaning is to reply, expound, interpret (e.g., dreams). In cl. Gk. words in this group had primary reference in the world of the theater. A *hypokritēs* appeared on stage and turned the speeches of the chorus into dialogue, or he explained to the audience what was going on. *hypokrisis* means reply, interpretation, play-acting, then also appearance, hypocrisy. *anypokritos* was someone inexperienced as an actor, and in a metaphorical sense unfeigned, genuine, simple.

2. In the LXX the vb. occurs rarely and mostly in late writings (Sir. 1:29; 33:2 = LXX 36:2; 2 Macc. 5:25; 6:21, 24; 4 Macc. 6:15, 17). *hypokritēs* means someone estranged from God (only in Job 34:30; 36:13); such people have God "on their lips," but keep him "far from their hearts" (Jer. 12:2). Job 36:13 describes an angry and taciturn man who is too proud to call for help when he needs it. Such a man should not be in a position of authority, because he directs all his efforts to the oppression of his subjects (34:30).

A rab. saying stated that 90 percent of all the world's hypocrisy was to be found in Jerusalem. This was one of the chief sins denounced in Jud., the Pharisees falling under special condemnation.

NT The NT uses the words in this group exclusively in the metaphorical sense of hypocrisy. They occur mainly in the Synoptics. *hypokrinomai* occurs only in Lk. 20:20, *synypokrinomai* only in Gal. 2:13. The noun *hypokrisis* is used 6x, *hypokritēs* 17x (mostly in Matt.). *anypokritos* occurs 6x.

1. *hypokrinomai* in Lk. 20:20 means to act or pretend; spies sent out to Jesus "pretended to be honest," but they were in fact trying to find grounds to accuse him. Similarly in Gal. 2:13, *synypokrinomai* describes how Pet. did not remain true to what he knew was right. He had been eating with Gentiles freely, but when "certain men came from James," Pet. decided to separate himself from the Gentiles and thus became a hypocrite.

2. Jesus calls his opponents' attempts to trap him with crafty questions "hypocrisy" (*hypokrisis*; Mk. 12:15; cf. Matt. 23:28). It involves a deliberate pretense, similar to that of a stage performance. Exhortations in the NT letters (e.g., 1 Tim. 4:2; 1 Pet. 2:1) list *hypokrisis* alongside lying and slander. It denotes attempts to cover up sin by putting oneself in a favorable light at the expense of truth.

3. (a) The noun *hypokritēs* is found exclusively on the lips of Jesus. In Matt. 15:7–9 he quotes Isa. 29:13 as prophetic of the Pharisees and the teachers of the law: "You hypocrites! Isaiah was right when he prophesied about you: 'These people honor me with their lips, but their hearts are far from me'" (cf. Mk. 7:6–7). These leaders are prime examples of unbelief (cf. Lk. 12:56). Outwardly they appear to be godly, but in reality they are sinners, guilty in God's sight since they do everything possible to repel the salvation that comes in Jesus. Jesus pronounces against these "hypocrites" a series of seven severe "woes" (Matt. 23:1–32).

(b) These Jewish leaders, however, are not the only ones so addressed. Jesus applies the word to any who seek to put forth an outward show of religion without having a heart truly devoted to God. For example, in the Sermon on the Mount a *hypokritēs* is someone who tries to remove a speck from someone else's eye while having a log in his or her own eye (Matt. 7:3–5; cf. Lk. 6:41–42). Again, anyone who prays in public primarily to be seen by others rather than to enter a relationship with God is a *hypokritēs*. People should rather pray in secret and give alms in secret (Matt. 6:2–6).

4. *anypokritos* is found only in the NT letters. It is used 3x to qualify love: *agapē* (Rom. 12:9; 2 Cor. 6:6) and *philadelphia* ("love for . . . brothers," 1 Pet. 1:22). Such love comes from an open and genuine heart that has no ulterior motives to hide; it does not deliberately put on a show. The same is said of faith in 1 Tim. 1:5; 2 Tim. 1:5. Faith is not affected by considerations of expediency but grows spontaneously out of the union of the Christian with the living Christ and finds its expression in a transparent life. This is also true of wisdom that comes from above (Jas. 3:17).

See also *pseudomai*, lie, deceive by lying (*6017*).

5694 (*hypokrisis*, pretense, hypocrisy), → *5693*.

5695 (*hypokritēs*, pretender, hypocrite, a godless man), → *5693*.

5696 (*hypolambanō*, take up, think, assume, be of the opinion that), → *3284*.

5698 (*hypoleimma*, remnant), → *3309*.

5699 (*hypoleipō*, to be left remaining), → *3309*.

| 5702 ὑπομένω | ὑπομένω (*hypomenō*), be patient, persevere, endure, be steadfast |

(*5702*); ὑπομονή (*hypomonē*), patience, steadfastness, endurance (*5705*).

CL & OT 1. In cl. Gk., *hypomenō* means to wait, remain behind, stand one's ground, survive, remain steadfast, persevere. It is used frequently in military contexts and at first is ethically neutral. Later the noun *hypomonē* came into use, and from then on both words imply value judgments in both a positive and a negative sense. Positively, among the noblest of virtues are steadfastness, constancy, and perseverance; a proud Gk. freeman endures burdens or difficulties solely for the sake of his honor. Negatively, there is the dishonorable attitude of passive resignation in the face of degradation, abuse, ostracism, slavery, or tyranny.

2. The LXX uses *hypomenō* predominantly in the sense of wait and await. This personal expectation appears to be grounded in the covenant relationship, for often Israel as a nation is called to wait on God (Ps. 27:14; 33:20), while God, who rules over all the nations, is called the "Hope of Israel" (Jer. 14:8; cf. 17:13; also Ps. 52:9; 130:5). Israel's endurance has none of the resigned attitude of a slave but reaches out to God and draws strength from him (Isa. 40:31). Thus

hypomonē expresses the attitude of the person living in the light of the last days (Dan. 12:12 Theod.; Hab. 2:3; Zeph. 3:8).

Job and later biblical writers use *hypomenō* in its Gk. sense of being steadfast, holding one's ground, persevering in distress (Job 6:11; Sir. 22:18). This use runs through the Jewish intertestamental lit. (esp. 4 Macc.) and is taken up in the NT by Paul.

NT 1. *The Synoptic Gospels.* *hypomenō* occurs in the lit. sense of staying (e.g., young Jesus stayed behind in Jerusalem, Lk. 2:43) and in Jesus' teaching about endurance as a prerequisite of salvation: "He who stands firm to the end will be saved" (Matt. 24:13; Mk. 13:13; the par. in Lk. 21:19 uses the noun instead of the vb.). The context is the eschatological discourse of Jesus, where the disciples have just been warned of numerous trials and persecutions, including being hated by all for the name of Jesus. The severity of the situation calls for endurance. A similar warning occurs in Matt. 10:22, where Jesus is sending out his twelve disciples. They will be hated by all, "but he who stands firm to the end will be saved." The blessedness of those who endure recalls Dan. 12:12.

Lk. uses the noun in the parable of the sower, where the good seed represents those who hear the word and retain it, "and by persevering produce a crop" (Lk. 8:15; cf. Matt. 13:23; Mk. 4:20). The cares of the world, riches, and pleasure may prevent us from producing a fruitful life; thus, we need patient endurance in order to bear the fruit of the word.

2. *Paul.* (a) Both the noun and the vb. figure in the argument of Rom. *hypomonē* is a quality required of humans if their lives are to be pleasing to God: "To those who by persistence [*hypomonē*] in doing good seek for glory, honor and immortality, he will give eternal life" (2:7). Both the act. sense of steady persistence in doing good and the pass. sense of patient endurance under difficulties are possible here. In Rom. 5 Paul shows how justified believers can turn even suffering to good account. They not only rejoice in the hope of sharing God's glory (5:2) but also develop their character through, among other things, "perseverance" (*hypomonē*; 5:3–4).

In Rom. 8:25 hope is characterized as waiting "patiently" for what we do not see. The context here is the groaning and frustration of the created order, "as we wait eagerly for our adoption as sons, the redemption of our bodies" (8:23). The concept occurs also in the practical exhortations at the end of Rom.: "Be joyful in hope, patient [*hypomenō*] in affliction, faithful in prayer" (12:12; cf. the connection between *hypomonē* and *thlipsis* [persecution, → 2568] here, as in 5:3). The purpose of the Scriptures is to promote "endurance" (*hypomonē*), which reflects the character of God (15:4–5; note the reiteration of the themes of 2:7; 5:3–4).

(b) Whereas *hypomonē* is a characteristic of hope in Rom., it is a characteristic of love in 1 Cor., since love "always perseveres" (13:7). In 2 Cor. Paul develops the theme of endurance, esp. in one's service for the church. His own affliction and comfort have occurred in order to help produce in the Corinthians "patient endurance of the same sufferings we suffer" (1:6), while 6:4; 12:12 allude to Paul's own apostolic endurance.

(c) "Endurance" (*hypomonē*) and "patience" (*makrothymia*, → 3429) are qualities for which Paul prays to be developed in the Colossian Christians (Col. 1:11). In 1 Thess. 1:3 the "endurance inspired by hope" of the Thessalonians is a cause for particular thanksgiving, and in 2 Thess. 1:4 Paul writes of his boast of their "perseverance and faith" among the churches of God. In 3:5 the apostle prays that the Lord may direct their hearts "into God's love and Christ's perseverance" (cf. Heb. 12:2–3).

(d) In the Pastoral Letters "endurance" is mentioned as a quality required of Christian workers (1 Tim. 6:11; cf. 2 Tim. 3:10) and of older men (Tit. 2:2). It is necessary to "endure [*hypomenō*] everything for the sake of the elect" (2 Tim. 2:10). Endurance is also a precondition of reigning (2:12), as in Paul's quotation of a hymn in this letter, which includes the words: "If we endure, we will also reign with him."

3. The theme of perseverance and falling away is a central theme of Heb. (cf. the use of Ps. 95:7–11 in Heb. 3:7–11, 15; 4:3–11; also the argument of ch. 12). Both *hypomenō* (10:32; 12:2–3, 7) and *hypomonē* (10:36; 12:1) figure in the exhortations to persevere. This stands in contrast with shrinking back (10:39). The author urges endurance in the light of his readers' past endurance, which included the loss of earthly goods (10:32, 34). They must endure to do the will of God and so "receive what he has promised" (10:36); such endurance is evidence of sonship (12:7), as Jesus himself demonstrated, "who for the joy set before him endured the cross, scorning its shame, and sat down at the right hand of the throne of God. Consider him who endured such opposition from sinful men, so that you will not grow weary and lose heart" (12:2–3).

4. The noun (Jas. 1:3–4; 5:11) and the vb. (1:12; 5:11) both feature in the letter of Jas. Here the role of "perseverance" in producing Christian character (1:3–4) may be compared with Paul's argument in Rom. 5:3–5 and 2 Pet. 1:6. Persevering under trial is necessary to receive the crown of life (Jas. 1:12; cf. Rom. 2:7; 8:25). Jas. 5:11 holds up the example of the perseverance of Job (cf. Job 1:21–22; 2:10).

5. Suffering for the sake of Christ is contrasted with enduring punishment rightly inflicted for a crime in 1 Pet. 2:20. There is no credit for the latter kind of endurance, and believers should not render themselves liable for such punishment. Pet. argues that earthly obligations such as submitting to government officials and (for slaves) obeying masters still hold good, since these people have been appointed by God. Moreover, in submitting without reviling, believers have the example of Christ before them (2:21–25). In 2 Pet. 1:6 *hypomonē* occurs 2x in a list of virtues in a way that recalls Rom. 5:3–5 and Jas. 1:3–4.

6. In Rev. patient endurance is the lot of Jn. himself in his exile on Patmos "because of the word of God and the testimony of Jesus" (1:9). Likewise, the churches of Ephesus and Thyatira are commended by the Spirit for their "perseverance" (2:2–3, 19), and the church at Philadelphia is encouraged: "Since you have kept my command to endure patiently [*hypomonē*], I will also keep you from the hour of trial that is going to come upon the whole world to test those who live on the earth" (3:10). The conflict with the beast gives rise to several exhortations: "This calls for patient endurance and faithfulness on the part of the saints" (13:10; cf. 14:12).

See also *anechomai*, bear, endure (462); *kartereō*, be strong, steadfast, persevere (2846); *makrothymia*, patience, longsuffering (3429).

5703 (*hypomimnēskō*, remind), → *3630*.

5704 (*hypomnēsis*, recollection), → *3630*.

5705 (*hypomonē*, patience, steadfastness, endurance), → *5702*.

5712	ὑπόστασις

ὑπόστασις (*hypostasis*), (1) substantial nature, substance, essence, actual being; (2) confidence, conviction, steadfastness (*5712*).

CL & OT 1. *hypostasis* has a wide range of meanings in both secular Gk. and the LXX. (a) In cl. Gk. it is used concretely for the basis of something; the bottom under water on which one can get a foothold; the value of property or land; life's starting point; substance; essence.

(b) As a human attitude the noun means putting oneself between, holding one's ground, enduring; a bold venture, enterprise; entering a risky undertaking; constancy.

(c) In philosophy *hypostasis* can denote the immanent Logos (word) in matter, giving it form. Here the *hypostasis* is distinguished from the *hypokeimenon*, the basic primary matter that has not yet been formed. Thus God, as the world-logos, is the *hypostasis* of the world. Without *hypostasis* there can be nothing empirical and no real being, for it actualizes a body. *hypostasis* is substantial, concrete being between the merely actual but contingent and the realities that are merely mental. Thought and appearance have existence (*hyparxis*), but not reality (*hypostasis*).

2. In view of the preceding the following basic elements in this word emerge: (a) that which is permanently constituted; (b) the enduring relationship of the particular thing to reality; (c) virtually the same as essence (*ousia*), esp. among the Stoics.

3. The LXX shows how in the Hel. period a complex word like *hypostasis* had become a fashionable term comparable with the word *existence* today. *hypostasis* occurs 20x, representing 15 different Heb. equivalents, which differ considerably in meaning.

(a) In a more general sense the word means the ground under water on which one can stand (Ps. 69:2); living being (Deut. 11:6); duration of life (Ps. 39:5; 89:47); food or sustenance (Jdg. 6:4); load, pack (Jer. 10:17); outpost (1 Sam. 14:4); pillar (Ezek. 26:11); a woven embryo (Ps. 139:15); arrangement (Ezek. 43:11).

(b) *hypostasis* is used in a more philosophical sense meaning council, group of intimates (Jer. 23:22); burden (Deut. 1:12); expectation, hope (Ruth 1:12; Ps. 39:7; Ezek. 19:5). This last meaning gives *hypostasis* a new focus within the compass of Scripture. The elements of hope and confidence are important for understanding NT usage.

NT *hypostasis* occurs only 5x in the NT. The reason for this may well be that, up to the time of the author of Heb., NT writers were not interested in philosophical trains of thought.

1. In 2 Cor. 9:4 Paul expresses the hope that the Corinthians will take part in the collection. Otherwise, if some Macedonians come with him and Paul finds that the believers in Corinth are not willing to participate, he will feel ashamed "of having been so confident" (lit., in this *hypostasis*). He uses the same word in 11:17, where in Paul's speech as a fool it translates lit., "in this confidence of boasting." But it may be asked whether the meaning in both passages should not be "enterprise" or "venture."

2. Compared with Paul, the use of *hypostasis* in Heb. is more theologically significant. (a) The term is important in Christology in 1:3, which states that Christ reflects God's glory and the "exact representation of his being [*hypostasis*]." The Son is not merely like the Father; rather, the substance of God is truly in Christ. What God essentially is has been made manifest in Christ. *hypostasis* here means "substance" or "real essence" in contrast to what merely appears to be.

(b) Heb. 3:14 states: "We have come to share in Christ if we hold firmly till the end the confidence [*hypostasis*] we had at first." The thought of the passage is that of confidence, similar to that of patience in 6:12 and perseverance in 12:1.

(c) From these two cases it seems clear how different the uses of *hypostasis* are in Heb. The most debated meaning of this word occurs in 11:1: "Now faith is being sure [*hypostasis*] of what we hope for and certain [*elenchos*] of what we do not see." The following explanations of this verse should be considered as possibilities.

(i) Confident trust in things hoped for. The gen. in "of things hoped for" is understood in this case as an obj. gen. In favor of this interpretation is Heb. 10:38–39, where faith and shrinking back are contrasted.

(ii) Pledge, security, guarantee, assurance. In other words, faith is a confident assurance that we will experience the reality of what we hope for.

(iii) Realization, actualization, substance. According to this meaning, faith already grasps the substance of what is promised. The problem with this interpretation, however, is that if faith gives a present existence to what is only hoped for in the future, faith becomes virtually identical with illusion.

Of these three options, the second one is the best. Heb. 11 proceeds to pile up a series of examples of what it means to live by faith. Faith not only grasps an event, an act of God such as the creation (11:3); it also shows itself in events. The more pleasing sacrifice and walk of Abel; the construction of the ark by Noah; Abraham's obedience in leaving his homeland, his life as a sojourner, and his near-sacrifice of Isaac; the blessing of the patriarchs; Moses' severance with the Egyptians; the saving of the firstborn of Israel by the Passover blood; the crossing of the Red Sea; the conquest of Jericho; the rescue

of Rahab—these were all saving acts of God in Israel's history, something new and unique on earth. Admittedly, the goal or fulfillment of all the hope still lay ahead. The people in the account were guarantees of their ultimate realization for the people of God. For this reason those addressed are exhorted not to neglect meeting together (10:25) and to remain with the people of God, in whom faith brings about a new reality and through whom God's deeds are wrought.

Note too how in 11:1 that "being sure of what we hope for" is set parallel with "[being] certain [*elenchos*] of what we do not see." This parallel would not work if *hypostasis* meant mere confidence. We should interpret *hypostasis* in the light of *elenchos*.

Throughout Heb. 11 faith is qualified by the instrumental dat. ("by faith"). This faith is seen as the relationship to the commands and promises of God that made possible the acts and behavior of the person concerned. Faith enabled what was hoped for to become a reality piece by piece. In other words, the phrase "things hoped for" is not an obj. gen., as if the things hoped for became real. Rather, it is a subj. gen., in that the things hoped for work through faith and produce action and attitudes. Thus Abraham hoped for a future city and so chose the life of a sojourner.

5717 (hypotagē, obedience, submission), → *5718.*

| 5718 ὑποτάσσω | ὑποτάσσω (*hypotassō*), submit, be in subjection (*5718*); ὑποταγή (*hypotagē*), obedience, submission (*5718*). |

CL & OT 1. *hypotassō* is a Hel. Gk. word that denotes subordination or subjection. In the act. voice it means to put things in a proper order, i.e., to subordinate. In the pass. voice it usually means to be subject to someone, which often implies obedience. In the mid. voice the vb. means either to subject oneself to someone or to become subservient; this can occur voluntarily or out of fear.

2. The meaning of *hypotassō* in the LXX is essentially the same as in Hel. Gk. The Lord subdued nations under David (act. voice: Ps. 18:47; 144:2; cf. 47:3; pass. voice: 1 Chr. 22:18; Ps. 108:9 [LXX lit., "foreign nations have been subjected to me"]). God placed all things in subjection to humans (8:6), and as punishment for disobedience, God subjected his people to their enemies (3 Macc. 2:13). In all these examples, these subjects had little choice.

The mid. voice, however, along with some uses of the aor. and fut. pass., often implies a voluntary element. For example, David's officers and mighty men submitted themselves to his son Solomon (1 Chr. 29:24). Ps. 37:7a reads in the LXX: "Be subject to the Lord and beseech him." Similarly, 62:1 reads: "Shall not my soul be subject to the Lord? For from him comes my salvation" (cf. 62:5). According to 2 Macc. 9:12, on his deathbed Antiochus Epiphanes IV said, "It is right to submit oneself to the Lord and not to think that a mortal is equal to God." These verses obviously imply a human role in submission to the Lord.

NT 1. Every NT use of *hypotassō* and *hypotagē* involves some sense of hierarchy, but as with the LXX, only context can determine whether the subordination is compulsory or voluntary. For example, children are expected to be obedient to their parents (1 Tim. 3:4 uses *hypotagē*; cf. Tit. 1:6; cf. also Eph. 6:1; Col. 3:20, both of which use *hypakouō*, obey, → *5634*). Yet when Lk. writes that Jesus "was obedient" (pass. of *hypotassō*) to his parents (Lk. 2:51), we should not understand that he was forced into obedience against his will, as it were. Rather, the Son of God was voluntarily submissive to his earthly parents.

2. Forms of *hypotassō* in the act. voice occur in Rom. 8:20 ("the one who subjected" creation); 1 Cor. 15:27 ("God ... put everything under Christ"); 15:28 (lit., "the one who has subjected all things to him"); Eph. 1:22 ("God placed all things under his [Jesus'] feet"); Phil. 3:21 ("to bring everything under his control"); Heb. 2:5 ("it is not to angels that he has subjected the world to come"); 2:8 ("put[ting] everything under him"). In all cases, God is the expressed or implied doer of the action, and in all but Rom. 8:20 the theme is that all things

have been made subject to the exalted and cosmic Christ, including angelic powers and death (1 Cor. 15:27–28; 1 Pet. 3:22).

3. In Lk. 10:17, the disciples report that demons submitted themselves to them (probably involuntarily). According to Paul, the sinful mind does not submit itself to God's law (Rom. 8:7). Likewise, the Jews who refused God's provision of salvation in Christ "did not submit to God's righteousness" (10:3). These last two verses imply a voluntary refusal to submit.

4. The rest of the uses (mid. and pass.) of *hypotassō* involve Christian behavior in the context of established authority structures. Thus all believers should voluntarily "submit to the Father" (Heb. 12:9). They should also be submissive to governing authorities, both secular (Rom. 13:1, 5; Tit. 3:1; 1 Pet. 2:13) and in the church (5:5). Similarly, Christian slaves should freely serve their masters (Tit. 2:9; 1 Pet. 2:18), and wives should be submissive to their husbands (Eph. 5:24; Col. 3:18; 1 Pet. 3:1, 5).

Since this last topic is set in Eph. 5:22–24 in the context of all Christians "submit[ting] to one another out of reverence for Christ" (5:21), the emphasis here must be on mutual submission: Just as husbands are called to love their wives with a self-sacrificing love (5:25–28), so wives are called to put aside their own agendas in submission to their husbands. The ideal, of course, is that this will be mutually voluntary. Only then will the Christian home function as God's wants it to.

5. The interpretation of *hypotagē* in 1 Tim. 2:11 is highly debatable. Is Paul establishing a universal principle or offering a particular instruction as he calls for women in the church to learn in quietness and "full submission" and to be silent before men in the church? And does Paul have in mind here the home situation (so that *anēr* means husband rather than man, → *467*), or is he referring to men generally? A complete understanding of this text and its cultural context, along with its parallel in 1 Cor. 14:34–35, will probably continue to elude us.

5721 (*hypotypōsis*, pattern, model, example, prototype, standard), → *5596*.

5724 (*hypōpiazō*, strike under the eye, maltreat), → *3463*.

5728 (*hystereō*, to come too late, miss, fail to reach; be in need of, lack; be less than, inferior to), → *5731*.

5729 (*hysterēma*, need, want, deficiency, lack, shortcoming), → *5731*.

5730 (*hysterēsis*, need, lack, poverty), → *5731*.

5731 ὕστερος

ὕστερος (*hysteros*), what is behind, after, later (*5731*); ὑστερέω (*hystereō*), to come too late, miss, fail to reach; be in need of, lack; be less than, inferior to (*5728*); ὑστέρημα (*hysterēma*), need, want, deficiency, lack, shortcoming (*5729*); ὑστέρησις (*hysterēsis*), need, lack, poverty (*5730*).

CL & OT 1. (a) In cl. Gk. *hysteros* means what is behind or after, esp. in reference to time. The adv. *hysteron* means secondly, after, later. *hystereō* was coined from the adj. and means to come after or too late. From this primary sense a fig. use of the verb developed, meaning to lag behind or to be inferior, and a secondary nuance, signifying failure in something. In the Hel. period *hystereō* means to lack something.

(b) The noun *hysterēma*, want, lack, need, first appears in the LXX. One ancient Hel. writer states that no titles were spared Caesar, i.e., what any single title lacked as a complete expression of honor was supplied by what the others contributed.

2. (a) In the LXX *hysteros* (4x) and *hysteron* (14x) are always used in a temporal sense: after, later, then. *hystereō* occurs 21x and means primarily to lack, have a need. In the year of release the prosperous Israelite is to lend generously to a poor fellow Israelite who has a need (Deut. 15:8). The Israelites of the desert generation were sustained by God and lacked nothing (Neh. 9:21; cf. Eccl. 6:2). The heart of a fool, however, lacks sense (10:3). Belshazzar's kingdom was

weighed in God's balances and found to be deficient (Dan. 5:27 Theod.). Ben Sira reflects on the person who works hard but finds he or she remains in want (Sir. 11:11–13).

Closely related to the concept of experiencing a lack is that of coming too late or failing. Those who fail to observe the Passover will be cut off (Num. 9:13). Although the fulfillment of what God has promised appears to delay, Israel must confidently wait for God to act (Hab. 2:3).

(b) The noun *hysterēma* occurs 6x in the LXX, where it means lack or need. A good land is a place where there is no lack of anything (Jdg. 18:10). According to Eccl. 1:15, what is lacking cannot be numbered. In two cases *hysterēma* shades into the meaning of want or poverty: "those who fear [the LORD] lack nothing" (Ps. 34:9); "haste leads to poverty" (Prov. 21:5 Theod.).

NT 1. *hysteros* is used primarily in the NT in the neut. sing. as an adv., later (Matt. 21:29; 25:11; Jn. 13:36), finally, last of all (Matt. 4:2; 21:37; 22:27; 26:60). Heb. 12:11 says that all parental discipline at the time it is administered is painful but "later on" produces a harvest of righteousness. Only once is *hysteros* used as an adj.: In 1 Tim. 4:1 it means "in later times"—a parallel to the eschatological formula "in the last days" (cf. 2 Tim. 3:1).

2. *hystereō* occurs 16x in the NT and has a broad range of nuances. (a) The basic sense is to come too late through one's own fault and so to be excluded from privilege. After referring to the desert generation, which forfeited its place in the promised land through rebellion and unbelief (Heb. 3:7–19), the writer of Heb. pleads with his readers to take care lest any of them, through lack of faith in God's word, should fall short of attaining God's promised rest (4:1). Near the end of the letter the author repeats this admonition, employing the parallel expression "misses the grace of God" (12:15). Paul concludes in Rom. 3:23 that all humans "fall short" of participation in the divine glory; God's grace is our only hope for eternal life.

(b) With reference to circumstances, *hystereō* means to lack. In Matt. 19:20 a wealthy young man affirms to Jesus that he has kept God's commandments and asks, "What do I still lack?" He is unaware of an absolute lack that will exclude him from eternal life but only of some unfulfilled remainder that he can yet complete. In the parallel account in Mark 10:21, Jesus is the one who speaks of a deficiency: "One thing you lack.... Go, sell everything you have ... come, follow me." The one thing the man lacks is the self-sacrificing devotion that characterizes every true disciple of Jesus.

(c) The most common idea of this vb. in the NT is expressed in the contrast between abundance and lack. When famine struck, the lost son experienced lack and was hungry (Lk. 15:14; cf. Phil. 4:12). Although Jesus sent out his disciples on their preaching mission without purse or provisions, they did not lack anything (Lk. 22:35). The Corinthians were enriched through God's grace so that they did not lack anything in the realm of spiritual gifts (1:5–7). When Paul was in Corinth and experienced need, what he lacked was provided by the generosity of believers in Macedonia (2 Cor. 11:9). Paul can speak of having learned the secret of enjoying abundance or experiencing lack with contentment (Phil. 4:12).

(d) Finally, the vb. occurs in the derivative sense to be less than, inferior to. Paul affirms that he is "not ... in the least inferior to" the super-apostles (2 Cor. 11:5; 12:11); that is, he needs nothing to compensate for some deficiency exhibited by a comparison with them. In comparing the church to a human body Paul observes that God has so adjusted the body that greater honor is bestowed on "the parts that lacked it" (1 Cor. 12:24).

3. (a) The cognate nouns *hysterēma* and *hysterēsis* are interchangeable (cf. Mk. 12:44 with Lk. 21:4). Jesus contrasts the gifts to the temple treasury of the wealthy, who give from their abundance, with the gift of an impoverished widow, who gives everything she has. In this context either noun means want in general, i.e., poverty (cf. a similar contrast in 2 Cor. 8:14; 9:12). The general sense of need or

lack is evident in Paul's response to the gift he received from Philippi. He does not complain of "living . . . in want," for he has learned the secret of self-sufficiency in every circumstance (Phil. 4:11–12).

(b) *hysterēma* occurs twice in the stylized expression "to fill up the lack of someone," where some absence is compensated for by representing other(s) who could not be present. A visit from the elders of Corinth has made up for the absence of the Corinthians, for whom Paul feels both affection and concern (1 Cor. 16:17). The Christians at Philippi were also genuinely concerned for Paul, but it was their emissary Epaphroditus who supplied what had been lacking to the community (Phil. 2:30).

(c) On two occasions Paul uses *hysterēma* in the pl. (i) He writes to the Thessalonians about his deep desire to return to Thessalonica in order to complete the work he had begun there (1 Thess. 2:17–3:13). He prays earnestly night and day that he may see them once again so that he may supply "what is lacking" in their faith (3:10). The pl. here embraces specific areas in which their faith needs to be matured (cf., e.g., 4:13–5:11, 14). In lieu of a visit, the apostle uses his letter to address these deficiencies in the experience of faith.

(ii) Col. 1:24 is difficult and its meaning continues to be debated. As Paul reports on his share in Christ's reconciling work, he affirms that he rejoices in the sufferings he has endured, for he is completing "what is still lacking" in Christ's afflictions for the sake of his church. This deficiency cannot refer to Christ's own vicarious sufferings on the cross in the accomplishment of redemption. Paul makes it clear that reconciliation has been truly and validly achieved through Christ's death (cf. 2:11–14).

The key to the interpretation is in the phrase "Christ's afflictions," which occurs only here in the NT. This phrase seems to be referring to a certain limitation on the messianic woes that has been determined by God (cf. Mk. 13:5–27; cf. *1 Enoch* 47:1–4). Once that measure has been attained, the old aeon, characterized by sin and suffering, will pass away and the new age will dawn. For the present, however, something is still lacking in those appointed sufferings. In Paul's experiences as the apostle to the Gentiles, he is doing his part to complete what is lacking in these messianic afflictions. Thus, he is bringing closer the dawning of the new age in which Christ will return in glory (Col. 1:28–29; 3:4). It is this prospect that accounts for Paul's joy.

See also *chreia*, need, necessity, lack, want (*5970*).

5734 (*hypsēlos*, high, exalted, proud), → *5737*.

5736 (*hypsistos*, highest, most exalted), → *5737*.

5737	ὕψος

ὕψος (*hypsos*), high (*5737*); ὑψηλός (*hypsēlos*), high, exalted, proud (*5734*); ὕψωμα (*hypsōma*), height, the exalted (*5739*); ὕψιστος (*hypsistos*), highest, most exalted (*5736*).

CL & OT 1. (a) In cl. Gk. *hypsos* denotes primarily extension upward in space, height (only of things, not of people); fig. it means the superiority and exaltation of one thing or person over another. In the case of people this term can take the negative sense of pride. In conjunction with *bathos*, it denotes the complete dimensions and aspects of an object. (b) The adj. *hypsēlos* was also originally spatial in meaning (e.g., high buildings, plants, position); it was used fig. in both a positive (sublime) and a negative (pompous, high-sounding) sense. (c) *hypsōma* is always used in fig. senses, e.g., as an astrological term for the closest approach of a star to the zenith.

2. (a) In the LXX *hypsos* is used lit. to denote the height of an object (e.g., a mountain, 2 Ki. 19:23; Ps. 95:4; the temple, Ezr. 6:3; a tree, Ezek. 31:14). Used absolutely, it often denotes the heavenly realm or the realm of God (Ps. 68:18; 102:19; Isa. 40:26). It is thus the opposite of *bathos* (that which is separated from God, → *958*). In fact, both *hypsos* and *hypsistos* (e.g., Gen. 14:18–19; Ps. 18:13) can be simply a substitute for God himself. In relation to humans, *hypsos* in Isa. 2:17

stands for human pride; in 1 Macc. 10:24 it has the sense of encouragement.

(b) The adj. *hypsēlos* occurs in the LXX in a variety of meanings. Used as a noun, it is more emphatic than *hypsos* to denote the realm of God (Ps. 93:4; cf. Lam. 1:13), the place where God lives (Isa. 33:5, 16; 57:15). The Spirit from on high (32:15) is God's Spirit. But in a remarkable reversal of this usage, the word is also used for Canaanite shrines and pagan high places (2 Chr. 14:3; 17:6; Jer. 19:5; Ezek. 6:3).

NT 1. *hypsos* in the spatial sense occurs only in Rev. 21:16 in the measurements of the new Jerusalem. In a similar way *hypsēlos* is used lit. in Matt. 4:8; 17:1; Mk. 9:2 and Rev. 21:10, 12 of mountains and walls. In these contexts the dimensional aspect is uppermost, although there are symbolic overtones.

2. (a) In accord with OT usage, both *hypsos* and *hypsistos* denote the realm of God or his dwelling (Lk. 1:78), to which Jesus is exalted (Eph. 4:8, citing Ps. 68:19; → *anabainō*, *326*), in order to sit at God's right hand and to intercede for us (cf. Heb. 9:24). Even with the fig. meaning the spatial concept still remains in the background (→ *ouranos*, *4041*).

In Heb. 7:26, *hypsēlos* denotes the place to which Jesus ascended, which is beyond what humans can conceive. Gnostic systems used *hypsos* for the place beyond the heavenly spheres that is filled with angels and powers. Compare this with Heb. 9–10, where Christ's exaltation is pictured in terms of the Day of Atonement ritual (cf. Lev. 16). Having penetrated these heights, the high priest Jesus Christ has been installed to exercise his sovereignty after his once-for-all sacrifice on the cross. The crucial moment is his going up to heaven, which corresponds to the high priest's going into the Most Holy Place. In other words, the sacrifice on the cross opens to the new high priest the way to heaven.

(b) Lk. 24:49 speaks of power from on high. Here also *hypsos* is a periphrasis for God. The same is true of *hypsistos*, "the Most High" (e.g., Lk. 1:32, 35, 76; Acts 7:48). Acts 13:17 also reflects OT ideas (cf. Exod. 6:6). The "exalted arm" (NIV, "mighty power") is an expression of the might and power of God. Describing this arm as *hypsēlos*, raised, stretched out, is a vivid way of expressing the idea that God's power is not in repose but in action.

3. (a) In Jas. 1:9 *hypsos* appears in contrast with *tapeinos* (→ *5424*) and is therefore appropriately rendered "high position." The passage refers to the salvation already given and yet still to come in Christ, which paradoxically reverses all human relationships. The poor person (which in Jas. is virtually synonymous with the Christian) must hold fast here and now to this eschatological exaltation by faith.

(b) Since this exaltation is not something Christians earn but is Christ's gift to them, Paul commands them not to think of themselves as *hypsēlos* ("arrogant," Rom. 11:20) but to associate with the lowly (12:16). Exaltation is God's work; thus, every personal desire for exaltation is an abomination to him (Lk. 16:15).

4. The NT use of *hypsōma* probably denotes cosmic powers. Rom. 8:39 and 2 Cor. 10:5 are both concerned with powers directed against God, seeking to intervene between God and us. They may be related to the *stoicheia tou kosmou*, the elemental powers of this world (cf. Col. 2:8, 20). However high and mighty they may seem, they are to be strenuously resisted (2 Cor. 10:5) in the knowledge that not even they can separate the Christian from Christ (Rom. 8:39).

See also *bathos*, depth (*958*); *hypsoō*, exalt, raise (*5738*).

5738	ὑψόω

ὑψόω (*hypsoō*), exalt, raise (*5738*); ὑπερυψόω (*hyperypsoō*), raise above all heights (*5671*).

CL & OT 1. The idea of exaltation played an important role in the myths that formed a part of the OT cultural background. (a) The Babylonian creation epic, *Enuma Elish*, describes exaltation as a work of the gods. The Babylonian god Marduk struggles with the gods of chaos (the sea-dragon, Tiamat, and the usurper of divine sovereignty,

Kingu). After defeating them Marduk creates the material world out of the divided halves of Tiamat (the sea-dragon), and humans out of Kingu's blood. Marduk is then exalted to a position of sovereignty over the world, whereupon he raises his earthly representative, Hammurabi, and installs him as ruler.

(b) The Babylonian myths of Adapa and Etana refer to human attempts at self-exaltation. Adapa is a man who works his way up to heaven but cannot obtain the food of life there. The enterprise founders on the punitive justice of the gods, who reduce him to the confines appointed to him. Etana tries in vain to reach Ishtar's throne in heaven on the back of an eagle, hoping to achieve immortality without dying.

2. *hypsoō* occurs over 150x in the LXX. The basic meaning is exalt (e.g., Ps. 18:46; Ezek. 28:2), be high (Ps. 89:13); then by extension stretch out, be loud (i.e., raise the voice, Isa. 37:23; 52:8), grow (Ezek. 31:4, 10), and praise (Ps. 107:32). In the OT God alone has the right to exalt (and also to bring low, 1 Sam. 2:7, 10). Humans run the risk of over-reaching themselves by self-exaltation. Thus in a few passages *hypsoō* means to be proud, haughty, presumptuous, arrogant (Ps. 37:20; 131:1; Ezek. 28:5). The following LXX usages are theologically significant.

(a) *The exaltation of the righteous*, that is, of all those who in their extreme need through poverty, oppression, or deprivation of rights seek help from Yahweh alone (cf. Ps. 37:34; 89:17). The righteous who encounter God experience exaltation by him in their everyday circumstances, lifting their lives to a new plane. Thus the righteous are promised a positive transformation of their present situation through Yahweh's intervention.

(b) *The exaltation of God* by the individual worshiper or the congregation. Such exaltation is a liturgical formula by which worshipers pay homage to God (e.g., Ps. 99:5, 9), and in which they acknowledge their loyalty to him as the Lord above all other gods (cf. 97:9). A pious person likewise uses this liturgical formula: "Glorify the LORD with me; let us exalt his name together" (34:3). In the OT the exaltation of Yahweh includes the exaltation of his people.

(c) *Self-exaltation*, that is, the exaltation that a person seeks to bring about independently from God, who desires obedience and provides for people's needs (cf. Ps. 75:4–5). By exalting oneself and in self-gratification relying on one's own strength, a person places himself or herself in opposition to God and calls forth his humbling intervention (75:7; Isa. 2:11, 17).

3. The post-canonical apocalyptic writings were more receptive to mythological ideas. Recalling Moses' ascent up the mountain of God, temporary exaltation became the vehicle of divine revelations (cf. *1 Enoch* 39:3; 52:1; 89:52; 2 Esd. 14:9, 49). The righteous are promised a place in heaven at a final exaltation (cf. Dan. 7:22; *2 Bar.* 13:3). As a son of man Enoch is exalted to the highest heaven (1 *Enoch* 70:1–4).

The way of the righteous as it is described in Wis. 2:10–20; 3:7–10; 4:10; 5:1–5 is also worth mentioning. The ungodly do violence to the righteous because the latter know God. The righteous are ill-treated and killed so that God may demonstrate whether they are his children. In the end, God exalts them. At the final judgment they will oppose their adversaries to their terror and will receive the kingdom of glory.

NT 1. *hypsoō* occurs 20x in the NT. It means to make great, "prosper" (Acts 13:17) or to exalt.

2. The theologically important passages are those in which *hypsoō* denotes the exaltation of Jesus (Jn. 3:14; 8:28; 12:32, 34; Acts 2:33; 5:31) and the exaltation of the humble.

(a) Behind Jesus' sayings on self-abasement and self-exaltation (Matt. 23:12; Lk. 14:11; 18:14) lies the basic form of the two-part OT saying (cf. Job 22:29; Prov. 29:23; Sir. 3:18). The righteous, humble, and suffering person is promised exaltation as a reward. This teaching acquires a new significance in the context of Jesus' message. Jesus puts all of human life once more on the basis of obedience toward God. Insofar as the Pharisees ascribed respect and honor to themselves (Lk. 18:9–12), they were denying God the obedience of service. The true disciple must be ready to follow Jesus along the path of humility to suffering (cf. 14:27), in order selflessly to serve the despised. Such people are promised exaltation at the resurrection (14:13–14) and the fulfillment of God's promises at the final judgment (Matt. 5:1–12).

But the immediate present already takes on a new form for the disciple in anticipation. Those who exalt themselves will lose their lives in God's judgment (cf. Lk. 17:33; cf. also 1:52; 10:12, 15). In their exhortations, therefore, 1 Pet. 5:6 and Jas. 4:10 warn Christians to submit to God in order that they might share in exaltation in the future glory.

(b) The early Christological statements in Acts clearly see the resurrection and exaltation of Jesus together (see 2:33; 5:31). That exaltation signifies the completion of God's action in his Anointed and the beginning, the continuance, and the expected fulfillment of Christ's Lordship over church and world (cf. 2:36).

(c) The idea of Jesus' exaltation also occurs in the hymn quoted by Paul in Phil. 2:5–11 (see esp. *hyperypsoō* in 2:9). Jesus' humiliation (2:6–8) is contrasted with his exaltation (2:9–11), which is the consequence of his obedience in suffering and consists in his designation as sovereign over the entire universe. In granting Jesus the new name of "Lord" (see *kyrios, 3261*), believers acknowledge his victory (cf. Col. 1:19–20). Similar statements expressed in different language occur elsewhere in the NT (e.g., Rom. 1:4; 1 Tim. 3:16).

(d) The concept of exaltation plays an important part in the Christology of Jn., where it is used in parallel with glorification, *doxazō* (e.g., Jn. 17:5; → *doxa, 1518*). In Jn. there is only *one* exaltation, that of Christ (3:14; 8:28; 12:32, 34). If Jesus used the expression "Son of Man" in order to embrace the double nature of his activity as of this world in humiliation and suffering (cf. "son of man" in Ezek.) and as exalted in full authority and glory (cf. "son of man" in Dan. 7:13), then Jn. uses this idea consistently. Note esp. how he describes Jesus' crucifixion as his exaltation (3:14; 8:28; cf. 12:34). He is lifted up on the cross, but at the same time he is lifted up to his heavenly glory as the Son of Man. At the very moment that his enemies think that they are passing judgment on him, he becomes their judge. Jesus' exaltation on the cross, however, does not discount the possibility of his final ascent to his Father (20:17).

See also *bathos*, depth (*958*); *hypsos*, high (*5737*).

5739 (hypsōma, height, the exalted), → *5737*.

Φ *phi*

5743	φαίνω

φαίνω (*phainō*), (act.) shine; (mid.) shine, appear, become manifest, come into view (*5743*).

CL & OT The act. of *phainō* means to shine (e.g., of the sun, the moon, or a lamp), while the mid. and pass. more frequently mean to appear, come into view.

NT 1. The act. of *phainō* occurs 9x in the NT, 7 of which are in the Johannine writings. It generally refers to the light of natural luminaries such as celestial bodies (Phil. 2:15), the sun (Rev. 1:16; 21:23; cf. 8:12), and the moon (21:23), but may also refer to the light of a lamp (Jn. 5:35; 2 Pet. 1:19; Rev. 18:23). In all these passages, the light concerned is contrasted with a stronger source of light; e.g., the sun and the moon will be superfluous when the glory of God illumines the heavenly Jerusalem (21:23). Only in two places does *phainō* refer to the "true" light, i.e., Christ (Jn. 1:5; 1 Jn. 2:8).

2. *phainō* in the mid. and pass. occurs 22x in the NT, of which 17 are in the Synoptics. It is used for the appearing of a star (Matt. 2:7) and of weeds among the wheat (13:26). *phainō* also occurs for angels appearing in dreams (1:20; 2:13, 19), for Elijah's rumored appearance (Lk. 9:8), and for the appearances of the risen Christ (Mk. 16:9). Certain phenomena will appear when he returns (Matt. 24:27, 30). The idea of becoming visible is present in 9:33 (of Christ's deeds); Jas. 4:14 (of a mist, to which one's brief life is compared); and 1 Pet. 4:18 (of the ungodly at the last judgment). Matt. 6:5, 16, 18 and 23:27–28 take what people are or do in secret and contrast this with outward appearances (cf. 2 Cor. 13:7). Mk. 14:64 and Lk. 24:11 refer to the way something "appears" to a person (cf. Rom. 7:13).

Heb. 11:3 is theologically significant. Here the prime cause of "what is seen" is said to be God's creative word. In this way the doctrine of *ex nihilo* creation is safeguarded against the error of materialism, which teaches that material things have evolved from *phainomena*, "what was visible."

See also *lampō*, shine (*3290*); *lychnos*, lamp, light (*3394*); *emphanizō*, reveal, make known (*1872*); *phōs*, light, brilliance, brightness (*5890*).

5745 (phaneros, visible, clear, open, evident), → *2211.*

5746 (phaneroō, reveal, make known, show, manifest), → *2211.*

5747 (phanerōs, openly), → *2211.*

5748 (phanerōsis, revelation, manifestation, disclosure), → *2211.*

5751 (phantazō, make visible), → *2211.*

5753 (phantasma, apparition, ghost), → *3404.*

5757	Φαρισαῖος

Φαρισαῖος (*Pharisaios*), Pharisee (*5757*).

OT *Pharisaios*, the Hel. form of an Aram. word meaning "the separated ones," denotes the representatives of an influential religious group in Jud. The designation is only attested in Hel. Jud. up till the time of the NT (though not in the LXX). The first occurrences of the word are from the time of Hyrcanus I (ca. 135 B.C.). From the 1st cent. B.C. on, however, the Pharisees were in the public esteem, the most respected and thus the leading group of Jud.

1. (a) Josephus, himself a Pharisee, came to speak of the movement in differing ways. He called them one of the many Jewish "philosophies" (along with, e.g., the Essenes and Sadducees). Since representatives of this group never called themselves by the name *Pharisee* but spoke of themselves rather as the *ḥᵃbērîm* (the comrades

of a *ḥᵃbûrâ*, a society), it is appropriate to ask whether the designation *Pharisaios* is perhaps a nickname that opponents gave to the exponents of that piety.

(b) The name of this group does imply separation, but separation from what? There are three possibilities. (i) The group is related in some way to the Hasidim, those separated from Judas Maccabeus (cf. 1 Macc. 2:42; 7:13), esp. when the Hasmoneans began to claim political domination. (ii) They separated themselves from the rest of the people who did not keep the law in order to follow exactly the individual prescriptions of the law. (iii) The name is a pun on the distinctions they made between the individual prescriptions of the law. Of these, probably (ii) is the best explanation.

2. The following are the characteristics of Pharisaism. (a) The legal prescriptions of the OT were observed with minute attention to detail (e.g., tithing all goods, attending to all the purificatory regulations, etc.). The Halakah (i.e., the body of legal decisions that interpreted the law; often called the oral Torah, since these were not written down by Moses) was considered equally as binding as the biblical tradition. The Pharisaic experts in the Scripture, the "teachers of the law," gave binding interpretations to the laws by way of casuistic exegesis. This casuistry led in part to controversial debates between individual scholars (esp. between the school of Shammai and that of Hillel). The Pharisees set the people a good example in keeping the law, in that they themselves adhered to the strict purificatory rites that were otherwise only binding for priests.

(b) In contrast to the Essenes, who emphasized the complete helplessness of the human will over against God, and the Sadducees, who stressed the unlimited freedom of the will, the Pharisees held firm to a conditional freedom of human will. Humans may not be able to frustrate the will of God, but within the frame of the divine plan they are able to do good or evil.

(c) The Pharisees adhered to the concept of the resurrection, of a judgment after death, and of supernatural beings such as angels and the devil. The Sadducees rejected these ideas as being irreconcilable with Scripture (cf. Acts 23:8).

(d) From the downfall of the Hasmoneans, the Pharisees, unlike the Zealots, renounced all use of force. God himself, through his intervention, would give the decisive turn and liberate his people.

(e) The Pharisees awaited the Messiah, whereas the Sadducees did not.

In that Pharisaism was sufficiently flexible to adjust itself to the conditions of a changed way of life, it was the most spiritually formative power in Jud. during the time of Jesus and was mainly responsible for reorganizing Jud. after the destruction of the temple in A.D. 70. But with its preoccupation over the fulfillment of the laws, Pharisaism was in fact an intensely narrow and rigid formalism.

NT 1. In the NT the Pharisees are named 98x: in the Gospels, Acts, and once in Paul (Phil. 3:5). In Pharisaism Jesus met Israel as it strove for true faith and obedience to God, but which had become totally hardened in formalism and thus barred itself from precisely that for which it was searching: to please God. In general Jesus and the Pharisees are depicted in Matt., Mk., and Jn. as embittered opponents (cf. Matt. 12:14; 24; Mk. 3:6; 12:13; Jn. 7:45–52; 11:46–47, 57).

2. It is a striking fact that Lk. does not generally represent the Pharisees as inimical to Jesus. Jesus was a guest of distinguished Pharisees and ate food at table with them (Lk. 7:36–37; 11:37; 14:1), and 13:31 even reports that Pharisees warned Jesus of Herod's attempts on his life. Pharisees were members of the Christian community (Acts 15:5). Some have questioned whether the Pharisees would have invited

to a meal a wandering preacher who violated their purificatory regulations so blatantly (Lk. 11:38). But individual Pharisees (such as Nicodemus in Jn. 3) were attracted to Jesus, though their background prevented them from extending the formal rites of fellowship and acceptance to one who stood outside their number. Thus, it is not unlikely that some of them did interact with Jesus in a dinner setting without full acceptance.

3. (a) The equation of oral tradition with the OT law led to serious divergences. The nature of the differences becomes clear only in the light of the two opposing understandings of God. For the Pharisees God is primarily one who makes demands; for Jesus he is gracious and compassionate. The Pharisee does not, of course, deny God's goodness and love, but for him these were expressed in the gift of the Torah and in the possibility of fulfilling what is there demanded. The Pharisee saw adherence to the oral tradition as the way to the fulfillment of the Torah (cf. Matt. 12:2–5; 15:1–2; Mk. 7:3, 5). By contrast, in Matt. 12:7 Jesus cites Hos. 6:6 ("I desire mercy, not sacrifice") and thus grounds the entire interpretation of the law in the command of love (cf. Matt. 22:34–40; Mk. 12:28–34; Lk. 10:25–28).

(b) Jesus repudiated the Pharisees' exclusion of the uneducated and notorious sinners (cf. Matt. 9:11; Mk. 2:16; Lk. 5:30) as lack of love. The Pharisees were ostensibly concerned about God's judgment, forgiveness, and the holy nation of Israel, but their attitude was the negative one of separation and concern for the minutiae of the law. Jesus, on the other hand, sought to heal the injuries of his people by bringing God's love to the helpless and the sick (cf. Matt. 9:12–13; Mk. 2:17).

(c) This segregation essentially led the Pharisees into a conflict between what the Torah demanded and what they actually performed (see Matt. 23). Their casuistic exegesis of the law, with its consequent dissociation from everything impure, led to a distinctly merit-based system of thought (→ *misthos*, *3635*). They drew on themselves the accusation of hypocrisy (→ *hypokrinomai*, *5693*) and pride (cf. Matt. 6:5, 16; 23:13, 15, 23, 25, 27, 29; Lk. 18:9–14).

The Pharisees' understanding of God and the law made them blind to the true offer and claim of God's meeting them in Jesus (cf. Matt. 23:26). The real tragedy was that the Pharisees earnestly sought God, but because a particular view of God had hardened in their tradition, they decided against Jesus and thus against God (cf. Matt. 12:24–32; Lk. 11:43–54).

5758 (pharmakeia, magic, sorcery), → *3404.*

5760 (pharmakon, poison, magic potion, charm, medicine, drug), → *3404.*

5761 (pharmakos, poisoner, magician), → *3404.*

5765 (phaulos, bad, evil), → *2805.*

5771	φεύγω

φεύγω (*pheugō*), escape, flee, avoid (*5771*); ἀποφεύγω (*apopheugō*), flee from, avoid (*709*); φυγή (*phygē*), flight (*5870*).

CL & OT From the time of Homer on, words in this word group most commonly meant flee, take flight, whether absolutely or from someone or something. Because a person may flee his or her country, the articular part. is used to refer to exiles or fugitives, and the verb itself may take on the force of be banished, be expelled. Similarly *phygē* came to mean exile, banishment. In legal terminology, the *pheugōn* is a defendant (opposed to the *diōkōn*, the prosecutor), and *pheugein graphēn* means to be put on trial. Thus, to escape one's prosecutors means to be acquitted.

In the LXX the *pheugō* word group is not used as a legal idiom but offers more instances of flight in a moral context: e.g., flight from an unbearable friend (Sir. 22:22) or from sin (21:2), flight to the Lord or to the altar (1 Ki. 2:29), or flight based on fearful ungodliness (Prov. 28:1). *pheugō* is usually avoided when the Heb. original means something less than rapid flight. The noun *phygē* always means flight or escape, although in Ps. 142:4 the thought is close to refuge.

NT 1. Joseph was ordered to flee to Egypt with Mary and the infant Jesus (Matt. 2:13). The disciples when persecuted in one city were to flee to the next and continue their ministry (10:23). There is no shame in the flight of the sheep from false shepherds (Jn. 10:5) nor in the escape from the sword accomplished by people of faith (Heb. 11:34). Indeed, believers in Jesus' day were commanded to flee to the mountains when Jerusalem appeared in danger (Matt. 24:16 par.; cf. 24:20, the only occurrence of *phygē* in the NT).

Fear is attached to the flight of the swine herds (Mk. 5:14 par.) and to the escape of Moses (Acts 7:29); cowardice to the hirelings (Jn. 10:12); irresponsibility and unbelief to the sailors manning the boat that conveyed Paul toward Rome (Acts 27:30); and shame to the total abandonment of Christ by the disciples in the Garden of Gethsemane (Mk. 14:50, 52 par.). The devil will flee from us if he is resisted (Jas. 4:7).

2. Both John the Baptist and Jesus warn us to flee from the coming wrath and from the judgment of hell (Matt. 3:7 par.; 23:33). Repentance thus becomes evidence of such flight.

3. Related to this is the epistolary exhortation to flee from moral evil. The Corinthians are told to flee from fornication (1 Cor. 6:18) and idolatry (10:14); Timothy to flee youthful lusts (2 Tim. 2:22) and various vices (1 Tim. 6:11) and to pursue such virtues as righteousness, godliness, faith, and love. *apopheugō* is used in 2 Pet. 1:4; 2:18, 20 in the sense of escape, rather than flee, the escape being from the corruption of the world.

4. *pheugō* is used metaphorically in the majestic apocalyptic panoramas of Rev. Thus the woman flees to the desert (12:6). When people seek death, it flees from them (9:6). The islands flee and the mountains disappear in God's fierce wrath (16:20); indeed, in the face of his majesty, heaven and earth flee away (20:11).

5778 (phthartos, perishable, mortal), → *5780.*

5780	φθείρω

φθείρω (*phtheirō*), destroy, ruin, corrupt, spoil (*5780*); φθαρτός (*phthartos*), perishable, mortal (*5778*); φθορά (*phthora*), ruin, destruction, perdition, corruption (*5785*); ἀφθαρσία (*aphtharsia*), incorruptibility, immortality (*914*); ἄφθαρτος (*aphthartos*), imperishable, incorruptible, immortal (*915*); διαφθείρω (*diaphtheirō*), spoil, destroy, ruin (*1425*); διαφθορά (*diaphthora*), destruction, corruption (*1426*).

CL & OT In cl. Gk. *phtheirō* means ruin, corrupt, destroy, kill. The term has various shades of meaning: to corrupt morally, bring down the state of laws, bribe, seduce a woman, and defile a virgin. In the pass. it means go to ruin, perish, be corrupted, destroyed. *phthartos* means mortal, corruptible; *phthora*, destruction, corruption. The compound *diaphthora* can mean destruction, murder, disorder; *diaphtheirō* to frustrate attempts to help or change one's mind.

In the LXX the words of this group can mean kill people (2 Sam. 24:16), lay waste a stretch of country (1 Chr. 20:1) or a city (1 Sam. 23:10), or destroy weapons (Isa. 54:16). In Gen. 6:11 and Hos 9:9 *phtheirō* describes a sinful and fallen world. God is the one who can redeem life from destruction (*phthora*, Ps. 103:4). A sacrificial animal not free of blemish is described as "deformed" (*phthartos*, Lev. 22:25).

NT In the NT words of this group are used mostly in a Hel. environment, with various shades of meaning: from the use of *diaphtheirō* in Lk. 12:33 for moths destroying clothes to Rev. 11:18, where the word expresses the extermination of people via God's judgment.

1. (a) In dealing with the moral shortcomings at Corinth, Paul writes: "If anyone destroys [*phtheirei*] God's temple, God will destroy [*phtherei*] him" (1 Cor. 3:17). The divine penalty is announced in the form of a legal judgment. In this way God protects his church. Paul, for his part, can claim, "we have wronged no one, we have corrupted [*phtheirō*] no one" (2 Cor. 7:2). He is therefore in a position to require the church in Corinth to make room for him and his message. He later fears that just as Eve was deceived by the serpent, so the church will

be led into rebellion by his opponents and their "minds may somehow be led astray [*phtharē*] from your sincere and pure devotion to Christ" (2 Cor. 11:2–3).

To demonstrate that false teaching and apostasy are not without their effect on human relationships, Paul refers to a Gk. saying that had become proverbial: "Bad company corrupts [*phtheirō*] good character" (1 Cor. 15:33). Paul uses the saying to warn the Corinthians not to consort with those who deny the resurrection.

(b) According to 2 Pet. 2:12, heretics are "like brute beasts" who are "born only to be caught and destroyed [*eis ... phthoran*]"; "like beasts they too will perish [*phtheirō*]" (cf. Jude 10). Those who serve Christ, however, are "to put off your old self, which is being corrupted [*phtheirō*] by its deceitful desires" (Eph. 4:22). Believers can thereby "escape the corruption [*phthora*] in the world" and live a new life in Christ's power (2 Pet. 1:4). Elsewhere Paul warns the church not to sow to the sinful nature, for those who do so will reap destruction (*phthora*, Gal. 6:7–8).

(c) In Rev. the harlot Babylon is the epitome of apostasy against God; she has "corrupted [*phtheirō*] the earth by her adulteries." But now she is judged. In other words, God's victory over the sin of the world has been made manifest (19:2).

2. By contrast, Pet. emphasizes that our salvation was not gained through "perishable things" (*phthartos*) such as silver or gold but with Christ's precious blood (1 Pet. 1:18). Just a few verses later he rephrases the same idea by saying that we have been born again not through "perishable" (*phthartos*) seed but through the imperishable, living, and enduring word of God (1:23).

3. (a) *aphthartos*, immortal, describes the character of God. In the doxology of 1 Tim. 1:17 the church praises him as "the King eternal, immortal, invisible, the only God." The sin of the heathen is that they exchange "the glory of the immortal God for images made to look like mortal man" (Rom. 1:23).

(b) Immortality is also attributed to Christ as Lord. In Eph. 6:24 peace is pronounced on all those who "love our Lord Jesus Christ *en aphtharsia*." The NIV translates this phrase "with an undying love," but others prefer the trans. "in his immortality." As the Exalted One, Jesus shares fully in the immortality of the Father. It is this Christ whom the church confesses, declaring that Christ "has destroyed death and has brought life and immortality [*aphtharsia*] to light through the gospel" (2 Tim. 1:10). In spite of the delay of the Parousia, the church lives in the knowledge that her salvation is something present and already given. She has been taken up into Christ's immortality.

Thus believers already possess an "inheritance that can never perish [*aphthartos*], spoil or fade" (1 Pet. 1:4). Pet. also instructs us to love one another, seeing that we have been born again of "imperishable [seed], through the living and enduring word of God" (1:23). This should be apparent even in outward things. Gentleness and quietness, not outward adornment, are the "unfading" (*aphthartos*) qualities of the Christian (3:3–4).

(c) In 1 Cor. 9:24–27 Paul compares the Christian life with an athletic contest (cf. Rom. 9:16; Gal. 2:2; 5:7). In both there is a victory to be striven for; both demand utter dedication and self-denial. The victor is beckoned by the prize, which for the athlete is one that "will not last" (*phthartos*), but for the believer is a crown "that will last forever" (*aphthartos*), namely, to be with God for eternity (cf. Rom. 2:7).

3. (a) In 1 Cor. 15:42–54 Paul uses the illustration of the seed sown in the ground to contrast mortality (*phthora*) and immortality (*aphtharsia*). There is no coming to life without a previous dying; i.e., only when the seed disintegrates in the earth is it changed into a new form (15:35–42a). It is the same with the resurrection of the dead, and yet it is quite different. "The body that is sown is perishable, it is raised imperishable" (15:42b), a spiritual body (15:44). Paul thus guards against the idea that there is anything intrinsically imperishable about human bodies. Everything passes away, because human beings are subject to sin and hence to death (Rom. 6:23); "outwardly we are wasting away" [*diaphtheirō*] (2 Cor. 4:16). Resurrection is a new existence, one that is gained by being raised to immortality, for "the perishable [*phthora*] [cannot] inherit the imperishable [*aphtharsia*]" (1 Cor. 15:50). Instead, "the perishable [*phthartos*] must clothe itself with the imperishable [*aphtharsia*]" (15:53).

(b) Paul emphasizes the same truth when he speaks of those who have died at the time of the Parousia. They do not simply continue their life in immortality; they will be changed (1 Cor. 15:52). It is just as true for them as for the dead, that mortality cannot attain immortality. When the end comes, the great transformation will come for all. Thus the illustration is used of putting on new clothes (→ *endyō*, *1907*): "the perishable must clothe itself with the imperishable" (15:54).

(c) Jesus is the first to have been resurrected by God and is thus vindicated as Messiah. His body did not "see decay" (*diaphthora*, Acts 2:31; 13:35–37), a quotation from Ps. 16:10. The defeat of death through Christ's victory affects the whole cosmos. That is, the redemption of humanity means also the redemption of creation, which will be "liberated from its bondage to decay [*phthora*]" (Rom. 8:21).

See also *apōleia*, destruction (*724*); *olethros*, destruction, ruin (*3897*); *exaleiphō*, wipe away, blot out (*1981*).

5783	φθονέω

φθονέω (*phthoneō*), be envious (*5783*); φθόνος (*phthonos*), envy (*5784*).

CL & OT In secular Gk., *phthoneō* can mean to bear ill-will of a general kind, but more often it expresses specifically the envy that makes a person grudge something that someone else owns. The noun *phthonos* is used in a similar way. Frequently it appears with *zēlos*, jealousy, though several cl. writers distinguish between these two synonyms.

phthoneō appears in the LXX only in Tob. 4:7, 16 in the sense of begrudging the giving of alms. *phthonos* occurs in 1 Macc. 8:16 and Wis. 2:24 (where the coming of death into the world is attributed to the devil's *phthonos*).

NT In the NT *phthoneō* is found only in Gal. 5:26, where "envying each other" is set in sharp contrast to living by the Spirit. *phthonos* occurs 9x.

1. In the NT letters *phthonos* features in several lists of bad qualities that characterize the unredeemed life. It is one of the "acts of the sinful nature" that are opposed to the "fruit of the Spirit" (Gal. 5:19–23; cf. Rom. 1:29). It is a feature of life before conversion (Tit. 3:3), to be put away by those who "grow up in [their] salvation" (1 Pet. 2:1–2). It is symptomatic of pseudo-Christian teaching that trades on controversy and wordy disputes (1 Tim. 6:4).

2. The phrase *dia phthonon*, "out of envy," describes the evil motives of those who delivered Jesus to Pontius Pilate (Mk. 15:10 par.). The same expression reappears in Phil. 1:15 (bracketed with *eris*, "rivalry," and contrasted to *eudokia*, "goodwill") to expose the motivation of those who preached the gospel from a desire to undermine Paul's evangelistic reputation, rather than share his gift.

3. Jas. 4:5 may provide the only example of *phthonos* used in a good sense, but the trans. of this verse is notoriously difficult. Following the NIV note, God "jealously (*pros phthonon*) longs for the spirit that he made to live in us." The description of God as the jealous lover who cannot brook a rival is prominent in the OT, but the LXX word used to translate the Heb. *qin'â* in this context is *zēlos* (→ *2419*), not *phthonos* (cf. Zech. 1:14). The NIV main text prefers to take the (human) spirit as the subject of the sentence in Jas. 4:5, giving *phthonos* its more usual bad sense of envy.

5784 (phthonos, envy), → *5783.*

5785 (phthora, ruin, destruction, perdition, corruption), → *5780.*

5789 (philadelphia, love for brother or sister), → *81* and *5797.*

5790 (philadelphos, loving one's brother or sister), → *81* and *5797*.

5792 (philanthrōpia, love for humankind, hospitality), → *5797*.

5794	φιλαργυρία

φιλαργυρία (*philargyria*), love of money, avarice, miserliness (*5794*); φιλάργυρος (*philargyros*), lover of money, (*5795*).

CL & OT In cl. Gk. *philargyria* means love of money, covetousness, miserliness; various authors considered this a vice. These two words appear infrequently in the LXX: *philargyria* only in 4 Macc. 1:26; 2:15 (S¹); and *philargyros* only in 2:8. The vb. *philargyreō* also occurs in 2 Macc. 10:20, where it means money-hungry.

NT 1. In 1 Tim. 6:10 *philargyria* (love of money) is described as "a root of all kinds of evil." What is said in this text comes of experience, for the dream of wealth and happiness can gain a demonic hold over a person or a nation. Even the ancient Gks. had a proverb that expressed a negative philosophical judgment on desire for material things.

This text gets its point through its application to one's relationship with God. Selfish amassing of material possessions has its prototype in Adam and Eve's grasping of the forbidden fruit in the garden of Eden. It is an indication that life, limited as it is by time, circumstance, and the vital interests of others, is no longer accepted thankfully from God's hand. Love of money erects a selfish dividing wall against God and our neighbors. It drives those who are possessed by it into utter isolation. Thus striving after wealth is the germ of total alienation from God.

2. Lk. notes that the Pharisees were lovers of money (Lk. 16:14). Paul warns Timothy that such people will become prevalent "in the last days" (2 Tim. 3:1–2).

See also *pleonexia*, greediness, avarice, covetousness (*4432*).

5795 (philargyros, lover of money), → *5794*.

5797	φιλέω

φιλέω (*phileō*), be fond of, love (*5797*); φίλος (*philos*), a relative, friend (*5813*); φιλία (*philia*), friendship, love (*5802*); καταφιλέω (*kataphileō*), to kiss (*2968*); φίλημα (*philēma*), a kiss (*5799*); φιλαδελφία (*philadelphia*), brotherly love (*5789*); φιλάδελφος (*philadelphos*), loving one's brother or sister (*5790*); φιλανθρωπία (*philanthrōpia*), love for humankind, hospitality (*5792*).

CL & OT 1. In cl. Gk. *phileō* is a regular word for showing affection, love, hospitality, etc. It also means be accustomed to, be in the habit of. There are many words compounded from *phil-*, such as *philoxenia*, hospitality, and *philadelphia*, brotherly love. *philos* originally was an adj. meaning dear, expensive, valuable, but became the ordinary word for a friend or relative; *philē* similarly means a female friend. *philia* is a later abstraction meaning friendship, love, devotion, favor; *philēma* is a love token, a kiss.

2. *phileō* rarely occurs in the LXX (on this, → *agapaō*, 26). When it is used, like *agapaō* it translates Heb. *'āhēb* (e.g., Gen. 27:4, 9, 14; Isa. 56:10, Prov. 8:17; 21:17). *philia* occurs only 38x; *philos* (181x) is more common.

NT In the NT the vb. *phileō* occurs in Matt. (5x) and Jn. (13x); elsewhere it appears only 7x. A distinction from *agapaō* is not strictly adhered to. The nouns *philos* (28x) or *philē* (once) are used for friends as well as for people bound together in faith. *philēma*, kiss, appears in the NT letters as a Christian form of greeting. The noun *philia* only appears in Jas. 4:4.

1. (a) A typical example for the original meaning of *phileō* is Matt. 6:5: The hypocrites "love" to pray at street corners (cf. also 23:6; Lk. 20:46). The use of *agapaō* in Lk. 11:43 and *phileō* in 20:46 shows how the difference between these two words is not always maintained. Note also Matt. 10:37, where the starting point is the natural love among relatives: "Anyone who loves [*ho philōn*] his father or mother more

than me is not worthy of me; anyone who loves [*ho philōn*] his son or daughter more than me is not worthy of me." (Note, of course, the transition to a theological meaning here, for the phraseology points implicitly to a love for Jesus, elsewhere described as *agapē*.) But clearly, when the kingdom of God breaks in, even usual family ties may be dissolved for the benefit of the new fellowship of the family of God.

(b) Jn. characterizes love according to whether the world (→ *kosmos*, *3180*) is viewed as God's creation or as the sphere of enmity toward God. In the case of the former, natural creaturely love has its legitimate place. Thus Jn. 11:3, 36 speak of Jesus' bond of friendship with Lazarus. But Jn. also sees the *kosmos* as the sphere of darkness that opposes God. Viewed thus, a person's love (*phileō*) for the world is the same as hatred for God's revelation (15:19; cf. Jas. 4:4). In 1 Jn. 2:15 Jn. expresses a similar idea, though the word *agapaō* (→ *26*) is used: "Do not love the world or anything in the world." God so loves the creation that hates him that he saves it (Jn. 3:16, *agapaō*), so the other imperative also holds: "Whoever loves God must also love his brother" (1 Jn. 4:21, both *agapaō*).

The scene with Peter in Jn. 21:15–19 clinches the fact that *phileō* and *agapaō* cannot always be distinguished. Initially 21:15–16 distinguish the *agapaō* in Jesus' mouth from the *phileō* in Peter's, but in 21:17 this distinction ceases. Nor is it possible to draw any exegetical consequences from this scene. Jn. 5:20 and 16:27 are the only places where *phileō* is predicated of God. Both times it is God the Father who is spoken of.

(c) There is a single, yet important, Pauline example of the use of *phileō*, in 1 Cor. 16:22: Love for the Lord is a condition of salvation. The whole history of the word would have led one to expect *agapaō* here. Thus again the impossibility of a rigid distinction is clear. *phileō* in Tit. 3:15, too, can only be correctly understood when it is born in mind that through God's love in the revelation of the Son, human love understood as love in faith requires a new interpretation. Note also the varying translation of Prov. 3:12 in Heb. 12:6 (*agapaō*) and Rev. 3:19 (*phileō*).

2. *philos* is also used in the NT for a friend to whom one is under a basic obligation (cf. Lk. 7:6; 11:5–6; 14:10, 12; 15:6, 9, 29; 23:12; Jn. 11:11; Acts 10:24; 19:31; 27:3). Relatives and friends are often mentioned alongside each other, but on other occasions, relatives are included in the *philoi*. In Lk. 16:9, people are linked by some relationship; Jesus here advises people to win friends for themselves by giving away their worldly wealth. A similar point is made when Pilate is threatened in Jn. 19:12 with losing his honorary title of "friend of Caesar." By contrast, *philos* can express God's love for the godless. In Matt. 11:19 and Lk. 7:34 Jesus is called a "friend of tax collectors and 'sinners.'" He loves them, although they are enemies, just as God loves the world that hates him.

That is also what is meant when Jesus addresses his disciples as "friends" (Lk. 12:4; Jn. 15:14–15). They come to Jesus as sinners and become his friends through his sacrificial love (15:13). They now belong to the family of God, in which they are brothers and friends of Jesus and children of the Father (Lk. 21:16; cf. also Jas. 2:23, where Abraham because of his faith is called "God's friend"). Brothers and sisters in faith can therefore be greeted as *philoi* (3 Jn. 14).

3. *philēma* is a kiss. For the vb. to kiss, *phileō* and *kataphileō* are both used in the NT. The kiss was a common courtesy greeting among rabbis, and Judas's kiss was of this nature (Matt. 26:48; Mk. 14:44; Lk. 22:47). In the story of the woman who was a sinner (Lk. 7:36–50), the kiss was a sign of respect.

The kiss in the ancient world was both a friendly sign of greeting and an emotional token of farewell (Lk. 15:20; Acts 20:37). In the early Christian congregations it became a "holy kiss." Those who have been incorporated into the fellowship of God's love are holy (→ *hagios*, *41*) and can greet one another as such (Rom. 16:16; 1 Cor. 16:20; 2 Cor. 13:12; 1 Thess. 5:26; 1 Pet. 5:14).

4. There are at least 24 words in the NT that have the root *phil-* in them (in addition are seven names, such as Philemon and Philip; for

all *phil-* words, → *5787–5819*). Chief among these is *philadelphia*. The writers of the NT letters exhort all believers, who are brothers and sisters in Christ, to love one another as family members (Rom. 12:10; 1 Thess. 4:9; Heb. 13:1; 1 Pet. 1:22; 2 Pet. 1:7; cf. the related *philadelphos* in 1 Pet. 3:8). *philanthrōpia*, love for humanity, is ascribed both to God in his kindness in sending our Savior (Tit. 3:4) and to the islanders in the hospitality shown to the shipwrecked passengers on the island of Malta (Acts 28:2; cf. also *philanthrōpōs*, kindly, in Acts 27:3).

See also *agapaō*, love (*26*).

5798 (*philēdonos*, lover of pleasure), → *2454*.

5799 (*philēma*, a kiss), → *5797*.

5802 (*philia*, friendship, love), → *5797*.

5810 (*philoxenia*, hospitality), → *3828*.

5811 (*philoxenos*, hospitable), → *3828*.

5813 (*philos*, a relative, friend), → *5797*.

5814	φιλοσοφία

φιλοσοφία (*philosophia*), love of wisdom, philosophy (*5814*); φιλόσοφος (*philosophos*), philosopher (*5815*).

CL & OT 1. In cl. Gk. *philosophia* (a compound of *philos*, friend, and *sophia*, wisdom) means love of wisdom, the sciences, or aspiration toward it. (a) Among the pre-Socratics *philosophia* meant striving toward any kind of scientific activity. It was then narrowed down to the question about the origin of the world from a single primary substance.

(b) For Socrates the whole weight falls on the first half of the word. Philosophy became the aspiration to wisdom—generally, of course, though combined with the knowledge that one never attains to this. According to Plato, philosophy is the knowledge of reality, the eternal and immortal ideas. To him the Sophists were those who believed that they possessed wisdom and pretended to be able to teach it. The true *philosophos*, however, is the modest man who knows that he knows nothing, but is seized by love for wisdom and searches after it his whole life long without ever entirely attaining to it. The word *sophos*, wise, befits the gods alone. Aristotle understood philosophy in the narrowest sense to mean metaphysics, investigation of the cause and principles of things or of the world of appearances.

(c) In Hel. philosophy *philosophia* acquired an almost religious significance. Its goal is happiness. This the Stoics and Epicureans propagate. For the Stoics, philosophy consists in striving for theoretical and esp. practical excellence, that is, for virtue. The Epicureans define *philosophia* as the pursuit of happiness by means of, and allowing the possibility of, reason. Here practical philosophy (ethics) dominates, to which rationality (logic) and the physical sciences are made subservient.

(d) In the mystery religions and Gnosticism *philosophia* is no longer concerned with a rational understanding of the world but depicts reality from the religious viewpoint. It thus runs into metaphysical speculation. True philosophy is defined as the quest for religious knowledge. Philosophy should, therefore, fulfill the function of spiritual worship.

2. (a) *philosophia* (as well as the vb. *philosopheō*) is found in the LXX only in 4 Macc. (e.g., 1:1; 5:10–11, 22; 7:9, 21). *philosophos* occurs in Dan. 1:20, where, judging by the context, conjurers must be meant (see also 4 Macc. 1:1; 5:35; 7:7).

(b) Hel. Jud. presented itself as philosophy. For Philo *philosophia* is synonymous with religion. The Mosaic law is the ancestral philosophy, and Philo calls all Jews philosophers. For Josephus likewise the Jewish religion and philosophy are identical. The same can be said for 4 Macc., where the tyrant Antiochus ridicules Jud. as "foolish philosophy" (4 Macc. 5:11); the martyrs, nevertheless, appear as the representatives of "divine philosophy" (7:9).

NT 1. In the NT *philosophia* occurs only in Col. 2:8, where Paul warns against it. To him, philosophy depends on human traditions and on "the basic principles [*stoicheia*, → *5122*] of this world," not on Christ. These principles of the world dealt not with natural components of being, in the sense of scientific analysis and philosophical knowledge of the laws of the world, but with personal powers (cf. 2:18), which constrained people under fixed precepts. To these Colossian heretics, Christ embodied these *stoicheia* and thus endorsed legalism and asceticism. The background of this philosophy is a gnosticized Jud.

Paul combats this Colossian philosophy in his letter, because its adherents were looking for salvation and fulfillment in the elements of the world, not in the saving deeds of Christ. Thus his warning against philosophy in 2:8 does not refer to cl. Gk. philosophy, but to a speculative doctrine that came to full expression in Gnosticism.

2. The noun *philosophos* is used only in Acts 17:18 in the setting of Paul's speech before the Areopagus. The "Epicurean and Stoic philosophers" confronted Paul about his ideas and the new gods he seemed to proclaim ("Jesus and the resurrection"). After Paul's speech, however, it appears as if both groups rejected what he had to say (17:32).

See also *mōria*, foolishness, folly (*3702*); *sophia*, wisdom (*5053*).

5815 (*philosophos*, philosopher), → *5814*.

5816 (*philostorgos*, tenderly loving, affectionate), → *26*.

5821	φιμόω

φιμόω (*phimoō*), to quiet, muzzle (*5821*).

CL & OT 1. In cl. Gk. *phimoō* is related to *phimos*, which is a muzzle, an instrument keeping the mouth of an animal closed. The vb. thus means to muzzle or gag. From this there developed a metaphorical meaning of keeping a person silent, whether by physical means or by threats.

2. In the LXX, the vb. *phimoō* occurs in Deut. 25:4, in the command of the Lord, "Do not muzzle an ox while it is treading out the grain." Presumably the reason for this command is that while the ox is working, it has a right to eat.

NT 1. *phimoō* occurs 7x in the NT. Paul quotes the command of Deut. 25:4 in 1 Tim. 5:18, applying the OT principle given for animals to those elders who preach and teach in the church; such people have a right to earn wages for their work.

2. Jesus gave a direct command to the wind and waves on the storm of the sea of Galilee: "Be still!" (Mk. 4:39; see also *siōpaō*, to silence, *4995*). This saying links back to a similar command Yahweh gave to the stormy seas in Ps. 107:29, though the LXX uses *sigaō* (→ *4967*) there rather than *phimoō*.

3. *phimoō* is used twice for Jesus' command to an evil spirit to be quiet and to come out of the person in whom it lived (Mk. 1:25; Lk. 4:35).

4. After Jesus had silenced the Sadducees with his wise answer concerning marriage and the resurrection, the Pharisees came to Jesus with a question (Matt. 22:34). In a similar vein, Pet. encourages us to "silence the ignorant talk of foolish men" by doing good, so that they will have nothing evil that they can say about us (1 Pet. 2:15).

See also *hēsychia*, quiet, quietness, rest, silence (*2484*); *ēchos*, sound, noise, report (*2491*); *sigaō*, to be quiet, be silent (*4967*); *siōpaō*, to quiet, be silent (*4995*); *phōnē*, sound, noise, voice, language (*5889*).

5828 (*phobeomai*, to be afraid, fear, have reverence, respect for), → *5832*.

5829 (*phoberos*, fearful, terrible, frightful), → *5832*.

5832	φόβος

φόβος (*phobos*), terror, fear, alarm, fright, reverence, respect, awe (*5832*); φοβέομαι (*phobeomai*), to be afraid, fear, have reverence, respect for (*5828*); φοβερός (*phoberos*), fearful, terrible, frightful (*5829*).

CL & OT 1. In cl. Gk. *phobos* means panic, fright, fear, awe, reverence. Sometimes these words denote fear of the gods, holy awe. But in general, the attitude of reverence before the deity is denoted by *sebō* (→ *4936*) and the related words *eusebeia* (godliness) and its opposite, *asebeia* (ungodliness, impiety).

2. In addition to the above, fear in the OT can also mean someone or something that is to be feared. It may even be applied to God (Gen. 31:42, 53; Isa. 8:13). The vb. *phobeomai* is used in the LXX and the NT only in the mid. (apart from Wis. 17:9). It is used intrans. with the prep. *apo* in the sense of "be afraid of" (Lev. 26:2; Deut. 1:29). It is used trans. with a pers. or impers. object meaning "to fear" (Lev. 19:3, parents; Prov. 13:13, a command; 24:21, the king; Num. 14:9, a foreign people). The adj. *phoberos* (fearful, terrible) is applied esp. to God in his works (e.g., Ps. 66:5).

There is a significant difference between Israel's relationship with God and the religious attitude of the Gks. The Israelite can stand before God in fear and love. Granted, God is great, mighty, and terrible (Deut. 10:17–18; cf. 1 Chr. 16:25), but he is gracious to humans (Deut. 6:5, 13). Thus we often read the address to God's people: "Do not be afraid" (e.g., Gen. 15:1; Jdg. 6:23; Isa. 44:2). God's grace and favor do not abolish the solemnity of the address. It demands total obedience (Hos. 6:6; Amos 5:6–7). Love is not mere feeling; it has to be proved in action, just as God's love is proved (e.g., Isa. 41:13).

Nevertheless, the motive of fear predominates. The fear of God is the first essential motive in the laws of the Pentateuch (Lev. 19:14, 32; Deut. 13:11; 17:13). It is the decisive religious factor in OT piety (e.g., Ps. 103:11–17; Prov. 1:7; 23:17; Sir. 1:11–30). On the other hand, those who trust in God do not need to fear enemies, adversity, or danger (e.g., Ps. 27; 46).

NT 1. The NT notes various causes of fear: the appearance of angels (Matt. 28:4; Lk. 1:12; 2:9), the catastrophes in the end times (21:26), death (Heb. 2:15), rulers (Rom. 13:3), and the Jews (Jn. 7:13; 20:19). Fear in the sense of anxiety is denoted by the expression *phobos kai tromos*, fear and trembling, which occurs already in the LXX (e.g., Exod. 15:16; cf. 1 Cor. 2:3; 2 Cor. 7:15; Phil. 2:12).

phobos and its cognates are used in the sense of fear, awe, and reverence before God (e.g., Acts 9:31; 2 Cor. 7:1; Col. 3:22). Reverence should be shown to masters (Eph. 6:5; 1 Pet. 2:18), husbands (3:2), and those outside the church (3:15). *phobeomai* may be followed by *apo* (e.g., Matt. 10:28; Lk. 12:4). But it may also be used trans. with a person or a thing as its obj. (Matt. 14:5, the people; Heb. 11:23, the king's edict). In such cases the object of fear is some power behind the immediate object. The vb. is used in the weakened sense of "to be afraid that" in Acts 23:10 and Gal. 4:11.

The term *phoboumenos ton theon*, a God-fearing person (Acts 10:2, 22; 13:16, 26), is a designation for a non-Jew who has connections with the synagogue (→ *prosēlytos*, *4670*). The adj. *phoberos* (fearful, terrible) occurs in Heb. 10:27, 31; 12:21.

2. Fear and reverence of God and of Christ (Eph. 5:21) provide both the motive for and the manner of Christian conduct (Lk. 18:2, 4; Acts 9:31; 1 Pet. 2:17; Rev. 11:18). Jesus himself impressed on his disciples the absolute necessity to fear God, who can destroy both body and soul in hell (Matt. 10:28; Lk. 12:5, → *geenna*, *1147*). Jesus' warning, like the teaching of the apostles (2 Cor. 5:11; 1 Pet. 1:17), points unambiguously to the prospect of judgment. Paul could exhort the Philippians to "work out your salvation with fear and trembling" (Phil. 2:12). But this is only one side of the motivation, for he immediately adds: "it is God who works in you to will and to act according to his good purpose" (2:13).

3. The fear that overtakes people when they encounter God or his messengers may be seen in the accounts of the miracles of Jesus and the apostles and also in the appearances of Christ and the angels. But

here, as in the OT, we repeatedly find the command, "Do not be afraid!" It occurs in the accounts of Jairus's daughter (Mk. 5:36; Lk. 8:50), Peter's catch of fish (5:10), the appearance of the angels to Zechariah and Mary (1:13, 30), Paul's visions (Acts 18:9; 27:24), John's vision on Patmos (Rev. 1:17), and the prophecy fulfilled on the first Palm Sunday (Jn. 12:15; cf. Isa. 41:10, 13; Zech. 9:9–10). It occurs in the pl. in the nativity story (Lk. 2:10), Jesus' walking on the water (Matt. 14:27; Mk. 6:50), the transfiguration (Matt. 17:7), and the angel's and Jesus' words at the empty tomb (28:5, 10).

4. The exhortation not to fear is also found frequently with regard to what is around us. We need not fear those who can only kill the body (Matt. 10:26, 28; Lk. 12:4–5). The little flock need not fear want (Lk. 12:32), while Christians should not fear their opponents (cf. Phil. 1:28) or suffering (1 Pet. 3:14; Rev. 2:10). Fear of other people is taken away from us by our sense of security in God (Matt. 10:30–31; Heb. 11:23, 27; 13:6).

5. The NT letters present the real ground for overcoming fear. Christ has appeared to "free those who all their lives were held in slavery by their fear of death" (Heb. 2:15). "God did not give us a spirit of timidity, but a spirit of power, of love and of self-discipline" (2 Tim. 1:7). Finally, "There is no fear in love. But perfect love drives out fear, because fear has to do with punishment. The one who fears is not made perfect in love" (1 Jn. 4:18; cf. 5:3). Thus, the NT presents a tension between fear and love. In a paradoxical way they exist together.

5843 (phoros, tax, tribute), → *5088*.

5844 (phortizō, to burden, load), → *983*.

5845 (phortion, burden, load), → *983*.

5848 (phragellion, whip, lash), → *3463*.

5849 (phragelloō, flog, scourge), → *3463*.

5850	φραγμός

φραγμός (*phragmos*), fence, wall, hedge (*5850*); φράσσω (*phrassō*), to fence in, stop, close (*5852*).

CL & OT 1. In cl. Gk. *phragmos* means a fencing in, hence a fence, enclosure. The corresponding vb. *phrassō* means to fence in, hedge around, esp. for protection or defense; fortify.

2. In the LXX, *phragmos* occurs 18x. It can refer to the wall of the city of Jerusalem (1 Ki. 11:27; cf. Ps. 144:14). A thorny hedge was used around vineyards to keep animals out, such as jackals and foxes (cf. Song 2:15). Fig. *phragmos* can refer to the "wall of protection" that God gives his people (Ezr. 9:9; cf. Isa. 5:2, 5; 58:12). In Ps. 62:3 a fragile person being assaulted by enemies is called a "leaning wall" (cf. a similar reference to the entire nation of Israel in 80:12).

phrassō occurs 8x in the LXX with a variety of meanings. In Prov. 21:13 it means to stop up (the ears), i.e., refuse to listen. In Song 7:2 it means to surround. In Job 38:8 Yahweh tells Job that he is the one who shuts in the sea. In Prov. 25:26 *phrassō* means to stop a well.

NT 1. *phragmos* is used in Matt. 21:33; Mk. 12:1 for the fence or hedge set up to protect the vineyard in the parable of the wicked tenants (cf. Isa. 5:2). This and the other precautions taken by the owner underline his care for his vineyard and his proprietary rights over it.

The messianic age will be inaugurated with a banquet (cf. Isa. 25:6). In Jesus' parable alluding to this great feast, the master, after being rebuffed by those originally invited (i.e., Jews), instructs his servant to go out to the highways and hedges (*phragmous*, Lk. 14:23; NIV "country lanes"; i.e., Gentiles) and persuade all he finds to come to the banquet.

In Eph. 2:14 *phragmos* refers to the ethnic "barrier" that stood between Gentiles and Jews, which has been removed by Christ.

2. *phrassō* occurs 3x in the NT. Paul concludes that one purpose of Scripture is to show that all people, both Jew and Gentile, stand condemned before God, so that every mouth "may be silenced" (Rom. 3:19). That is, no one can give any excuse or justification for his or her

way of life when viewed against the standards required by a holy and perfect God. In 2 Cor. 11:10 Paul declares that no one will prevent him from boasting: a metaphor drawn from damming a river or barricading a road. Heb. 11:33 refers to those who by faith "shut" the mouths of lions (e.g., Dan. 6:22; 4 Macc. 16:3, 21; 18:13), thus transmuting their natural instincts.

See also *teichos*, wall around a city (*5446*); *charax*, pointed stake, palisade, rampart, mound (*5918*).

5852 (*phrassō*, fence in, stop, close), → *5850*.

5858 (*phroneō*, think, judge, give one's mind to, set one's mind on, be minded), → *5860*.

5859 (*phronēma*, way of thinking, mentality), → *5860*.

5860	φρόνησις

φρόνησις (*phronēsis*), way of thinking, frame of mind, intelligence, good sense (*5860*); φρονέω (*phroneō*), think, judge, give one's mind to, set one's mind on, be minded (*5858*); φρόνημα (*phronēma*), way of thinking, mentality (*5859*); φρόνιμος (*phronimos*), intelligent, discerning, sensible, thoughtful, prudent (*5861*).

CL & OT 1. In cl. Gk. the words listed above by and large have their ordinary meanings. *phronēsis* frequently has the fuller sense of discernment, judicious insight.

2. All these words appear in the LXX of the OT. Various meanings are possible; e.g., in Job 5:13 *phronēsis* stands for cunning, craftiness, while *phronimos* has a corresponding sense in Gen. 3:1. In Prov. 24:5 *phronēsis* means a peasant's knowledge of his job; in Theod.'s trans. of Dan. 1:4; 5:12 it means intellectual acuteness, either as a qualification for training in the palace of the Persian king or in the interpretation of dreams.

These words occur mostly in wisdom lit., where they usually suggest discernment. Both noun and adj. are regularly used with reference to human beings, though *phronēsis* can denote the creative understanding of God (e.g., Prov. 3:19; Isa. 40:28; Jer. 10:12). In the LXX, one can detect a tendency to fill out the meaning of these words in accordance with the OT doctrine of wisdom (→ *sophia*, *5053*).

NT 1. In the NT the vb. occurs more frequently (26x) than the nouns or adj. (*phronēma*, 4x, all in Rom. 8; *phronēsis*, 2x; *phronimos*, 14x). The vb. tends to retain its ordinary meaning; it is, so to speak, more neutral and requires a context to indicate its true sense. Note also the use of *phroneō* in Acts 28:22; 1 Cor. 13:11; Phil. 1:7; 4:10, where it refers not so much to the process of thinking as to the content of what is thought.

This is even clearer when *phroneō* is used absolutely; it acquires its proper meaning only from its immediate context: e.g., from the use of *phroneō* words that have prefixes—such as *hyperphroneō*, "think ... more highly" (Rom. 12:3) and *sōphroneō* (12:3, "think ... with sober judgment"; → *sōphrosynē*, *5408*)—or that have the object *ta hypsēla* (lit., "do not think high things," i.e., "do not be arrogant," 11:20). These words and phrases indicate direction (upward or downward) and impart to *phroneō* its specific meaning in a given context.

2. In other words, there is no such thing as neutral thinking. Humans are always aiming at something; striving and endeavor are part of our nature. This is the idea behind *phronēma*, which means "mind" in Rom. 8:6 [2x], 7, 27. In this chapter Paul is describing the new life in Christ as life in God's Spirit. One's mind is set on certain things, and what these are depends on whether a person is controlled by the "sinful man" or "by the Spirit." Thus, "those who live according to the sinful nature" (8:5) set their minds on "what that nature desires." That is, their thinking and striving are directed toward those things that are human and transitory. But those "who live in accordance with the Spirit of God have their minds set on what the Spirit desires" (8:5). To them that are thus minded there is a promise of "life and peace" (8:6).

To focus one's mind on the sinful nature means death, not simply because there is an inevitable connection between the two (cf. Rom. 5:21; 6:23), but also because such thinking is rebellion against God and cannot submit to his law (8:7). In other words, the way we think is intimately related to the way we live, whether in Christ (i.e., in the Spirit and by faith) or in the sinful human nature (i.e., in sin and in spiritual death).

This close interrelationship between life and thought is echoed by the use of *phroneō* in Mk. 8:33 (cf. Matt. 16:23). There Pet. is reproved by Jesus because his thought and will are taking the side not of the things of God but of human things (which are opposed to God). It is God's will that Jesus be offered as a sacrifice, and by opposing that divine will in suggesting Jesus should not suffer and die, Pet. is furthering the cause of God's enemies (hence the sharp rebuke, "Get behind me, Satan!").

3. What should a Christian strive toward? What kind of thinking is fitting? The answer that seems most obvious—that one should strive for high ideals—is at first sight attractive to Christians. After all, God has given us gifts that we can seek to perfect and use for exalted purposes. But such striving can lead to jealousy, disappointment, and schisms in the church, as is seen in Corinth. That is why the apostle exhorts all Christians to "think ...with sober judgment, in accordance with the measure of faith God has given" (Rom. 12:3), for "everything that does not come from faith is sin" (14:23).

In Rom. 12:16 Paul warns: "Do not be proud, but be willing to associate with people of low position." The proud are under God's judgment: "God opposes the proud but gives grace to the humble" (1 Pet. 5:5, quoting Prov. 3:34). Whether Paul is warning "charismatic" believers to beware of spiritual pride (perhaps the context of Rom. 12:16) or censuring Gentile Christians for arrogance toward Jews (cf. 11:20), the message to Christians is clear: We must aim not higher but lower, seek to identify with the lowly and humble, and strive for the unity of the church.

4. Moreover, a Christian's aims are closely intertwined with the motives underlying them. Thus, Paul frequently exhorts believers to be of one mind or of the same mind (Rom. 12:16; 15:5; 2 Cor. 13:11; Gal. 5:10; Phil. 2:2; 4:2). Such exhortations, which are linked often with warnings against arrogance, do not spring simply from a pragmatic outlook that puts church unity above all else; rather, they are based on Christ, since he is the one on whom the church is built. This is esp. prominent in the Christ hymn of Phil. 2:6–11 and in 2:5, which introduces this hymn. This verse is best understood as meaning: "Have the same thoughts among yourselves as you have in your communion with Christ Jesus," rather than simply seeing Jesus' own attitude as a model for us to follow.

If this is so, then Paul's call to unity is based on the fact that the church possesses new life under the lordship of Christ (cf. Phil. 2:10–11), new life that springs from his life of self-abasement. This interpretation is supported by Phil. 4:2, where church members are required to "agree ... in the Lord" (lit., "think [*phroneō*] the same thing in the Lord"). "In the Lord" here is a formula for the believer's new life in Christ. Among other passages where the apostle calls for a harmonious attitude of mind, note his prayer in Rom. 15:5, where "a spirit of unity ... as you follow Christ Jesus" is lit. "to think the same according to Jesus Christ." In other words, God has given us the opportunity of achieving unity and harmony in Christ. Our new standing in Christ both creates and demands a new mentality, which comes to concrete expression in the unity of the church.

5. Similar considerations underlie Paul's injunction in Col. 3:2: "Set your minds on things above, not on earthly things." "Things above" refer not to anything humanly exalted but to that heavenly sphere where the exalted Christ exercises his lordship (cf. 3:1). He frees us from all that would hold us down (contrast Phil. 3:19, where Paul accuses his opponents of having "their mind ... on earthly things" and of making a god out of their "stomach").

6. (a) In the Gospels the adj. *phronimos* is confined to parables or fig. language; it refers to the wise, judicious behavior that should characterize people in God's kingdom. The examples offered are taken from everyday life: The wise man (*phronimos*) builds his house on the rock (Matt. 7:24); the five wise virgins have a supply of oil (25:1–9); a wise and faithful steward watches and is ready at the coming of his master (24:45); the unrighteous steward acts wisely (Lk. 16:8); and the wisdom of serpents is held up as an example to Christ's disciples (Matt. 10:16). Insofar as such wise thinking is contrasted with *mōros*, foolish thinking (→ *mōria*, 3702), the OT idea of wisdom is involved: The wise are those who do the will of the Lord (Matt. 7:24), whereas the foolish are those who refuse obedience.

(b) Paul's uses of *phronimos* arises from a slogan in circulation among the "charismatic" Corinthians who think they are "so wise in Christ" (1 Cor. 4:10), a claim Paul controverts (cf. 10:15; 2 Cor. 11:19). The wisdom claimed by such people is a purely human wisdom, which because of their arrogance jeopardizes the unity of the church. So Paul counters it both with a reference to his own suffering as an apostle and with the warning, supported by the OT, that those who regard themselves as wise fall under God's judgment (Rom. 11:25; 12:16).

7. The noun *phronēsis* comes closest to the OT concept of wisdom. In Eph. 1:8 it means discernment, insight. In Lk. 1:17 it may mean simply mental attitude, but since it occurs in a context strongly reminiscent of the OT, it means "the wisdom of the righteous." Such wisdom, however, is not merely rational discernment but is the result of God's people being turned to the obedience of faith, in accordance with OT prophecy.

See also *nous*, mind, insight, reason (*3808*).

5861 (*phronimos*, intelligent, discerning, sensible, prudent), → *5860.*

5864 (*phroureō*, guard, keep in custody), → *5875.*

5870 (*phygē*, flight), → *5771.*

5871 (*phylakē*, watch, guard, prison), → *5875.*

5873 (*phylaktērion*, phylactery), → *5875.*

5874 (*phylax*, guard, sentry), → *5875.*

5875	φυλάσσω

φυλάσσω (*phylassō*), guard, preserve, keep (*5875*); φυλακή (*phylakē*), watch, guard, prison (*5871*); φύλαξ (*phylax*), guard, sentry (*5874*); φρουρέω (*phroureō*), guard, keep in custody, preserve (*5864*); φυλακτήριον (*phylaktērion*), phylactery (*5873*).

CL & OT 1. In cl. Gk. *phylassō* means, intrans.: (a) be sleepless, watch, keep guard; (b) serve as garrison (for or in a city). This leads to the trans. use: (c) guard, preserve—originally of things, property, persons, and then fig. of love, loyalty, respect; (d) watch over, store (in safekeeping); (e) obey (an order, oath, law), attend to. *phroureō* means to pay attention to something; when used trans. it has the same meaning as *phylassō*.

2. In the LXX *phroureō* is found only 4x, all in the Apocr. *phylassō* (guard, watch, keep; follow, obey) is found over 400x, with no distinct difference in meaning between the act. and the mid. It usually denotes obedience to and keeping of the law, cultic regulations, the word of God in general, or the covenant. The subj. of the vb. can be the whole people of Israel, groups within it, or individuals (Exod. 12:24; Lev. 18:4; Deut. 5:1; Ps. 78:10; Prov. 19:16; Ezek. 11:20).

In general, the concept of *phylassō* developed in the OT from this original thought of fulfilling covenant obligations (positive or negative) to the intertestamental idea of keeping the law as the way to salvation (cf. Dan. 9:4; then also 1 Macc. 2:53; 8:26, 28; 4 Macc. 5:29; 6:18; 15:10; 18:7). At the end of this development God's covenant loyalty is regarded as dependent on the community's keeping of the law. The other cl. meanings of *phylassō* are also found in the LXX but much more rarely. To be stressed is the usage found esp. in Ps., of God's protecting actions for his people or the pious (cf. 12:7; 17:8; 145:20).

NT 1. In the NT *phylassō* occurs 31x, much less often than *tereō* (→ *5498*). It means: keep watch (Lk. 2:8); guard (e.g., Acts 12:4; 23:35); protect (by God or Christ: Jn. 17:12; 2 Thess. 3:3; 2 Tim. 1:12; 2 Pet. 2:5; Jude 24; by humans: Jn. 12:25); observe (e.g., the law, Gal. 6:13; God's commandments, Mk. 10:20; the words of Jesus, Jn. 12:47; or the decisions of the apostles, Acts 16:4). In the mid. it can mean beware of, abstain from (Lk. 12:15; Acts 21:25; 2 Tim. 4:15; 2 Pet. 3:17; 1 Jn. 5:21).

2. Matt. and Mk. use *phylassō* once each (Matt. 19:20; Mk. 10:20). In both cases it denotes keeping the law (see above on OT). Although in these two passages and in Lk. 18:21 there is no direct criticism of Jewish observance of the law, the radical demand made by Jesus on the rich young ruler is indirectly a complete rejection of it.

Paul uses *phylassō* only in its Jewish sense, but the context can give it a particular nuance. In Rom. 2:26 it is anti-legal; in Gal. 6:13, anti-Judaistic. The same connotation is found in Acts 7:53, where Stephen in his defense denies that the Jews had ever kept the law; in other words, the Jewish conception of how the law should be kept was rejected from the standpoint of early Christianity. Acts 21:24 approves of the Jewish observance, because the Jewish Christians also did so.

The Jewish legacy to early Christianity is found in a much more important form when *phylassō* is used with tradition, the handing on of the Christian message and teaching. In Acts 16:4 Paul and Timothy delivered to the churches of Asia Minor the decisions of the council of Jerusalem (cf. also a similar meaning in 1 Tim. 5:21; 6:20; 2 Tim. 1:14). The future of the church depends on believers guarding, working out, and making real the inheritance received from the apostles. Note 2 Tim. 1:12, where the Lord himself guards it. This step of stressing tradition was necessary for the development of the early church. *phylassō* is found in its lit. meaning frequently in Lk. (2:8; 11:21; 12:15) and Acts (12:4; 23:35; cf. also Jn. 12:25; 2 Tim. 4:15; 2 Pet. 2:5).

In Jn. 12:47 the expression about not keeping Jesus' words means simply not to believe in him as the Revealer sent by God. Belief and keeping Jesus' words are defined in terms of each other.

3. In 2 Thess. 3:3 Paul deals with preserving the church's faith: God is the one who protects (*phylassō*) the church from the evil one. The basic thought here is eschatological; the concrete background is the threat of a rising false doctrine within the church. The position is similar in Jude 24 and Phil. 4:7 (where *phroureō*, guard [cf. 2 Cor. 11:32], is used; cf. also 1 Pet. 1:5), passages in which the church is commended to God's protection in its fight against false doctrine. In 1 Jn. 5:21 believers must be on guard against idols. Jn. 17:11–12 is concerned with the maintenance of the unity of the church and its exclusive relationship to Christ. Here *phylassō* and *tereō* are used together as synonyms. *phroureō* is used in Gal. 3:23 in a special sense for the role of the law in the history of salvation.

4. (a) The noun *phylakē* means guard or watch (of the shepherds over their flocks in Lk. 2:8); also, the place of guarding or prison (Matt. 5:25; 14:3, 10; 18:30, where it is a picture of judgment); Lk. 21:12 (in the context of warnings about what will happen to Christ's disciples). In 1 Pet. 3:19 "the spirits in prison" presumably denote the underworld or place of punishment in hell. In Rev. 2:10 believers at Smyrna will be put in prison and are exhorted to remain faithful unto death so that they may receive the crown of life; in 20:7 Satan is released from his prison for a short time after the millennium and prior to his ultimate subjection. *phylakē* can also mean guard, sentinel (Acts 12:10); watch of the night, reflecting the Roman practice of dividing the time between 6 P.M. and 6 A.M. into four periods (Matt. 14:25; Mk. 6:48). *phylax* also denotes a guard or sentry (Acts 5:23; 12:6, 19).

(b) The related word *phylaktērion* (lit., a safeguard, means of protection) denotes a small box containing Scripture texts bound on the forehead and arm during prayer (Matt. 23:5; cf. Exod. 13:9, 16; Deut. 6:8; 11:18). Jesus refers to phylacteries in the context of his warnings against the Pharisees for merely external righteousness. They were regarded as a mark of devotion to the law as well as a protection against demonic influence.

See also *tēreō*, preserve, keep (*5498*); *grēgoreō*, watch, be on the alert, be watchful (*1213*); *agrypneō*, keep or be awake, keep watch, guard (*70*).

5876	φυλή

φυλή (*phylē*), tribe, clan, nation (*5876*).

CL & OT 1. In. cl. Gk. *phylē* derives from *phyō*, to bring forth, produce, be born. In the Athenian state the *phylē* became an important, if artificially constructed, unit of political organization. At first, it was limited to a group bound together by common descent, but the element of blood relationship almost disappears to mean simply a political subdivision of the people.

2. In the LXX *phylē* occurs over 400x, most frequently for the Heb. *maṭṭeh* and *šebeṭ*. Apart from Isa. 19:13, which refers to the tribes of Egypt, these two Heb. nouns apply only to Israelite tribes (though both words also denote a rod or staff). The other Heb. word that *phylē* sometimes translates is the word for clan, *mišpāḥâ* (this word is usually trans. by *dēmos*, people, → *1322*). The tribe was divided into a number of clans and the clans into families (see, e.g., Jos. 7:14).

The general meaning of *phylē* is a body of people united by kinship or habitation. In the OT it is used not only as a technical term for the twelve tribes of Israel (Num. 34:18–28), but it also applies to the nations of the world, as in the blessing of Abraham (Gen. 12:3). Later Jewish writings invariably mention tribes only in connection with OT texts, the number twelve, or the related hope of a regathering of all Israel. The Qumran community likewise speaks of the future restoration of a kingdom of twelve tribes.

NT 1. *phylē* occurs 31x in the NT, more than half of these in Rev. It can refer to the historic tribes of Israel (7:4–8, 13x) or universally to the tribes of the earth, i.e., peoples and nations (1:7). (a) "The twelve tribes of Israel" is used of eschatological Israel in Matt. 19:28; Lk. 22:30; Rev. 7:4; 21:12, i.e., the regenerated elect gathered out of the twelve tribes of historical Israel down through the ages (cf. Rom. 11:26). The promise in Matt. 19:28 that the twelve apostles will sit on twelve thrones, judging the twelve tribes of Israel, is a reward for their loyalty to Jesus. They will be given positions of royal authority and honor in the new world as judges, i.e., rulers (the sense of judge as in the book of Jdg.). In Lk. 22:29–30 Jesus speaks of assigning royal power to them.

(b) The phrase "the twelve tribes scattered among the nations" is used fig. of Christians as the true people of God in Jas. 1:1. The word "Israel" is first clearly equated with the Christian church by Justin Martyr (ca. A.D. 160). The nearest NT parallel is Gal. 6:16, where Paul prays for peace and mercy "to all who follow this rule, even to the Israel of God," i.e., all Christians, both Jewish and Gentile, who glory in the cross as the sole basis of their standing with God (→ *Israēl*, Israel, *2702*).

2. (a) In Rev. 21:12 there are twelve gates to the heavenly Jerusalem, corresponding to the number of the tribes of Israel, and the names of the tribes are inscribed on the gates (cf. Ezek. 48:30–34; also the Temple Scroll at Qumran). More grandly, rab. Jud. thought in terms of 144 gates in the city wall, twelve for each tribe. The number twelve implies completeness: the whole regenerate people of God, the whole apostolic band (→ *dōdeka*, twelve, *1557*).

(b) All twelve tribes are listed in Rev. 7:5–8, except Dan is replaced by Manasseh, which was actually a section of the tribe of Joseph. The change is probably deliberate, although we do not know why. Irenaeus held, based on an interpretation of Gen. 49:17, that Dan was omitted because the Antichrist was to come from this tribe. Rab. tradition consistently associated Dan with idolatry, deducing from 1 Ki. 12:28–29 that only Dan responded to the lure of the golden calf of Jeroboam I. The prince of Dan is said to be Satan in *T. Dan* 5:6.

Although Reuben was the firstborn son of Jacob (Gen. 35:23), Jn. puts Judah at the head of his list of the twelve tribes. This is no doubt because Jesus was of that tribe (Heb. 7:13–14; Rev. 5:5), in accordance with messianic expectation (Gen. 49:9).

3. Many Jews in NT times were either from proselyte families or the descendants of those forcibly converted to Jud. during Maccabean times. Thus only a minority of 1st-cent. Jews could genuinely trace their genealogy back to one of the twelve tribes of Israel. Even fewer Jews were able to do so after Herod the Great, who (according to tradition) burnt many Jewish family registers. Examples like Anna of the tribe of Asher (Lk. 2:36; cf. Gen. 30:13) and Paul of the tribe of Benjamin (Rom. 11:1; Phil. 3:5) show that where tribal origin was known, the pedigree was treasured. To be able to trace one's ancestral line back to a tribe was to have a sure claim on the covenant promises that the God of Israel made to his people. When Paul became a Christian, however, he willingly discarded the proudest of human links with the past, considering it to be so much "rubbish" in comparison with knowing Jesus (Phil. 3:7–8).

5877 (phyllon, leaf), → 1285.

5878	φύραμα

φύραμα (*phyrama*), a mixture, a lump (*5878*).

CL & OT 1. In cl. and Hel. Gk. *phyrama* describes something mixed or kneaded, like dough. Not until Plutarch is there a clear instance of this word being used for the dough-like mixture from which a potter molds wares.

2. In the LXX *phyrama* is unrelated to the potter's craft. It denotes the kneading bowls in which dough is prepared (Exod. 8:3), the dough itself (12:34), or the coarse flour to be worked into dough (Num. 15:20–21). The cognate vb. *phyraō* describes the mixing of unleavened flour with oil (e.g., Exod. 29:2, 40; Lev. 2:4–5; 1 Chr. 23:29) or the action of kneading (Gen. 18:6; 1 Sam. 28:24).

NT *phyrama* occurs 5x in the NT; 4x it refers to a lump of dough (Rom. 11:16; 1 Cor. 5:6, 7; Gal. 5:9). In Rom. 9:21, however, *phyrama* denotes the dough-like mixture of clay from which a potter may make one vessel for honored use and another to serve a menial purpose. Similarly, God has fashioned humans as vessels of mercy and of wrath. In the context it is clear that God's wrath stands in the service of his mercy and is designed to draw attention to the extent of his mercy toward all who receive by faith the righteousness provided in Christ (9:22–33).

See also *keramion*, an earthenware vessel, jar (*3040*); *ostrakinos*, made of earth or clay, earthenware (*4017*); *pēlos*, clay, mud, mire (*4384*).

5879 (physikos, natural), → 5882.

5880 (physikōs, naturally, by instinct), → 5882.

5882	φύσις

φύσις (*physis*), nature, condition, kind (*5882*); φυσικός (*physikos*), natural (*5879*); φυσικῶς (*physikōs*), naturally, by instinct (*5880*).

CL & OT 1. (a) *physis* is a word from the Gk. world of ideas. Its meanings are many and varied and kept changing, depending on which philosopher used it.

(b) *physis* denotes source, commencement, origin, also the lineage of adults or children. Aristotle regarded *physis* as the primal substance of the elements. From this basic understanding, *physis* denotes natural condition, quality, or state (e.g., of the air); outward form and appearance; and stamp or character. When set alongside *ethos*, custom, and *logos*, reason, it means (human) nature or the imperishable—and perishable—nature of the gods. *physis* can be used both for the bodily physique of individuals and for the institutions and constitutions of states.

(c) *physis* can further denote the creation, i.e., the world of nature. It is the efficacious generative power that causes plants to appear and hair to grow. Nature is endowed with reason and determined by its end; it produces nothing without purpose. Aristotle distinguishes nature (*physis*) both from *tychē*, fate, and from *technē*, skill. In the natural order of things, all humans are similar despite their individual and national differences. Nature is self-sufficient and strong. Our lives are determined by the twin forces of nature and laws; this order fixes the natural end of life.

(d) Among the Stoics, *physis* became a god of the universe, as is indicated in a famous quotation from Marcus Aurelius: "O Nature, from you comes everything, in you is everything, to you goes everything." Of importance for the Stoics is the assertion that one should live by following nature. Nature is here conceived of as that which is in harmony, good in itself and resting, and thus distinguished from the field of morals and ethics.

2. The Heb. lacked the Gk. conception of nature. This is connected both with the fact that all existing things are referred to the creation or to the Creator God, and also with the stronger historical thought of the OT. Thus in the LXX *physis* occurs only in the Apocr., where the Hel. influence is most evident: in Wis. (3x), 3 Macc. (once), and 4 Macc. (8x).

(a) *physis* is used in the sense of endowment and character (4 Macc. 13:27); it can also indicate a quality, such as the power of love for one's children (16:3). In 5:25 we read of the law being adapted to our nature, for the Creator of the world feels for us according to our nature. In 15:25, *physis* stands alongside *genesis*, creation, and *philoteknia*, filial love, to denote the regular order of nature. Nature is a dispenser of good things. Thus Antiochus seeks to convince elderly Eleazar to eat pork with the words, "When nature has granted it to us, why should you abhor eating the very excellent meat of this animal?" (5:8, NRSV).

(b) In 3 Macc. 3:29 *physis* means created beings, the whole world of creation, including humankind. In Wis. 7:20 it refers to species of living beings, but also (with reference to material objects) the fire-extinguishing property of water (19:20b). By nature, fundamentally, all human beings are foolish (13:1).

3. Philo is the first known Jewish writer to take over the word consciously. But he also modified it as he sought to expound the Jewish faith in its strength and breadth. (a) For him God stands in the foreground. Philo, in fact, ascribes to *physis* much of what, from the OT point of view, is the work of God. Like wisdom (cf. Prov. 8), *physis* is a power that participated in God's work of creation, though God himself stands outside nature.

(b) This *physis* is that which brings forth, e.g., all humanity. It is immortal. It teaches the division of time into day and night, waking and sleeping, and it also creates space, which remains confined to three dimensions. It reveals us to be people who dispose over plants and animals; it has given us speech and sexual relations.

(c) The law is the true word of nature, for the law follows nature and the prescriptions of the law are in agreement with nature. That is why one must follow nature and its developments. Nature ratifies the law. Philo also regarded nature as capable of receiving virtue; conscience makes use of it, because it hates evil and loves good. To nature belong godliness and love of humankind.

4. (a) Josephus similarly took over and adopted the Gk. concept of *physis* to his Jewish outlook. *physis* stands for the condition and characteristics of animals and humans and of natural self-love. It is almost synonymous with character. *physis* can also denote the being of God, of all things, or of the elements.

(b) At times *physis* means nature as a whole, the whole created world, or natural instincts. Thus a person can be active by nature or naturally freedom-loving. By contrast, sexual deviations are contrary to nature.

(c) *physis* can denote natural qualities. Thus suicide is foreign to the common nature of all living beings. *physis* can also mean the regular order of nature and its laws or the juxtaposition of divine and natural law.

NT *physis* in the NT occurs mostly in Paul, esp. Rom. (7x; the adj. *physikos* occurs 2x). Elsewhere the word occurs only in isolated passages. It has various shades of meaning, which correspond to the previous usage of the word.

1. In Gal. 2:15 *physis* means "by birth," i.e., one's line of descent. Corresponding to this is Rom. 2:27, where Paul refers to those who remain "physically" uncircumcised; one's line of descent is the reason why someone has not been circumcised. But Paul also says that such a man can fulfill the law and so perform God's will without belonging to Israel.

God will not spare the wild olive shoot (the Gentile Christians) if he did not spare "the natural branches" (the Jews) that belonged to the rich olive tree (Rom. 11:21). In Paul's parable here, the wild olive shoot is cut from a wild olive tree, to which it belongs "by nature," and is grafted "contrary to nature" into the cultivated olive tree. Paul's argument concludes: How much more can the "natural" olive branches that belong to the rich olive tree be grafted back (again) into their own olive tree (11:24). Paul is here following Hel. linguistic usage with his reference to the distinction between Jews and non-Jews. As transgressors of the first commandment the heathen are "by nature" (i.e., by descent) objects of wrath (Eph. 2:3; cf. Wis. 13:1). But this situation is ended by the grace of Christ in the lives of those whom God has made alive (Eph. 2:5–10).

2. *physis* stands further for the regular order of nature, which determines the distinction between the sexes. God has given up on the idolaters, with the result that they have exchanged "natural [*physikēn*] relations" between men and women for "unnatural ones" (Rom. 1:26; lit., "contrary to nature"). Yet some heathen do not have the Torah but do "by nature" what the law demands (2:14). It is not as if they read off the law from the natural order; rather, we are dealing here with the typically Stoic thought of the moral law founded in nature, which was taken over by Jud. and applied to the Torah. In this way the Mosaic law becomes the universal and perfect expression of the moral law founded in nature. In a similar way, Paul insists that "the very nature of things" teaches that it is degrading for a man, but a source of pride for a woman, to have long hair (1 Cor. 11:14).

3. In 2 Pet. 1:4, the apostle speaks of believers as those who "participate in the divine nature," which is a result of the "knowledge of our Lord Jesus Christ" (1:8) and our "calling and election" (1:10). The thought is not that of a metamorphosis into quasi-deity, for the results of this participation are expressed in positive human qualities. It is rather that to be truly human, one needs an enabling that comes from God himself. This teaching is comparable with Paul's instructions on the new creation and Jn.'s on being born again. Participation in the divine nature and its outworking in life are prerequisite for entrance "into the eternal kingdom of our Lord and Savior Jesus Christ" (1:11).

In contrast to participation in the divine nature stands the use of the adj. *physikos*, which is applied to humans in their natural state: "But these men . . . are like brute beasts, creatures of instinct [*physika*], born only to be caught and destroyed" (2 Pet. 2:12). The corresponding adv. (*physikōs*) occurs in a closely related passage: "Yet these men speak abusively against whatever they do not understand; and what things they do understand by instinct [*physikōs*], like unreasoning animals—these are the very things that destroy them" (Jude 10).

4. Jas. 3:7 uses *physis* twice in the sense of "kind": "All kinds [*physis*] of animals, birds, reptiles and creatures of the sea are being tamed and have been tamed by [humankind]." The thought corresponds with the conception of a regular order of nature. The point of the allusion is to emphasize, by contrast, the fact that "no man can tame the tongue. It is a restless evil, full of deadly poison" (3:8).

5884 (phyteia, plant), → 1285.

5885 (phyteuō, plant), → 5065.

5888 (phōneō, make a sound, call, summon), → 5889.

5889	φωνή

φωνή (*phōnē*), sound, noise, voice, language (5889); φωνέω (*phōneō*), make a sound, call, summon (5888).

CL & OT 1. In cl. Gk. *phōnē* signifies an audible sound made by a living creature, covering the whole range of animal noises or human sounds. As applied to human beings, it means voice, speech, or statements. A deity was thought to have an extraordinary *phōnē* (cf. Acts 12:21–22). *phōneō* can denote the sound of a musical instrument, person, or animal.

2. In the LXX *phōnē* generally denotes any audible sound, from the clap of thunder (Exod. 19:16) to the twittering of birds (Ps. 104:12), but not the organ of speech or speech itself. In several psalms (e.g., Ps. 29:3–4; 104:7) God's revelatory voice is described as thunder. To hear (i.e., obey) God's voice was the essence of Israel's religion (1 Sam. 12:14; cf. Jos. 24:19–24). By the 1st cent. the rabbis had a developed view of an echo of a heavenly voice that was audible on earth and proclaimed divine messages.

phōneō occurs 26x in the LXX: for human speech (Ps. 115:7 = LXX 113:15; 3 Macc. 2:22), animal cries (Zeph. 2:14), and a trumpet blast (Amos 3:6).

NT 1. As in the LXX, so in the NT *phōnē* describes any noise or sound, whatever its source: e.g., the wailing of Rachel (Matt. 2:18), the rustling of wind (Jn. 3:8), or the tumult of a crowd (Rev. 19:1). It occurs 139x in the NT.

2. Not all human voices sound alike (Jn. 3:29; Acts 12:14), and each person has more than one "tone" (Gal. 4:20). Speaking in a loud voice is something humans can do (Lk. 23:23; Acts 7:57, 60; 14:10; 26:24), including the souls of martyrs (Rev. 6:9–10). Unclean spirits (Mk. 1:26; 5:7; Lk. 4:33; Acts 8:7), angels (Rev. 5:12; 14:7, 9), and the archangel (1 Thess. 4:16) may also speak this way. Particularly noticeable is the close association of this idea with (a) the praise of God by angels (Rev. 5:11–12) or humans (Lk. 17:15–16; 19:37–38; Rev. 7:9–10); (b) the power of Jesus to raise the dead by his voice (Jn. 11:43; cf. 5:25, 28–29); and (c) the cry of Jesus at his death (Matt. 27:46, 50; Lk. 23:46).

3. The loud voice from heaven that figures so prominently in Rev. (e.g., 1:10; 4:1; 10:8; 11:12) or that dialogues with Pet. regarding Jewish food laws (Acts 10:9–16) is the personal voice of God (Rev. 16:17), Christ (Acts 10:13–15; 11:7–9), an angel (Rev. 18:1–2), or some heavenly inhabitants (11:15). Linking together the Synoptic records of Jesus' baptism (Matt. 3:13–17; Mk. 1:9–11; Lk. 3:21–22) and transfiguration (Matt. 17:1–8; Mk. 9:2–8; Lk. 9:28–36) is the "voice . . . from heaven" (Mk. 1:11) or "from the cloud" (9:7). The words "my Son" in this messianic confirmation clearly indicate that the voice belongs to God the Father.

4. For Jn., to hear (i.e., obey) the voice of Jesus (Jn. 10:3, 16, 27; 18:37) is to gain eternal life (5:24–25; 6:68; 10:27–28).

5. Paul too heard a voice from heaven during his conversion experience (Acts 9:4; 22:7; 26:14); his companions heard the voice but did not understand what was being said (9:7; 22:9).

6, Not infrequently the content of a *phōnē* is a solemn declaration of confession of faith (Acts 13:27; 19:34; 22:14; 24:21; 2 Pet. 1:17).

7. *phōneō* occurs 43x in the NT, only in the four Gospels, Acts, and Rev. 14:18. In some cases (e.g., Lk. 8:8; 16:24; Acts 10:18) it means the same as *krazō* (to cry out, → *3189*), esp. when *megalē phōnē* (lit., "loud voice") is added (e.g., Mk. 1:26). It sometimes denotes an urgent request (Matt. 27:47) or a powerful command (Lk. 8:54; Jn. 12:17), and not infrequently an authoritative summoning (e.g., Mk. 9:35; Lk. 16:2) or a polite invitation (e.g., 14:12; Jn. 1:48). In Palestine the cock would crow (*phōneō* in Matt. 26:34, 74) during the third watch (i.e., between midnight and 3 A.M.).

See also *hēsychia*, quiet, quietness, rest, silence (2484); *ēchos*, sound, noise, report (2491); *sigaō*, to be quiet, be silent (4967); *siōpaō*, to be quiet, be silent (4995); *phimoō*, to quiet, muzzle (5821).

5890	φῶς

φῶς (*phōs*), light, brilliance, brightness (5890); φωτίζω (*phōtizō*), light up, illumine, bring to light (5894); φωτισμός (*phōtismos*), illumination, enlightenment (5895); φωτεινός (*phōteinos*), shining, bright, radiant (5893); φωστήρ (*phōstēr*), luminary, brightness (5891); φωσφόρος (*phōsphoros*), bearing light, morning star (5892).

CL & OT 1. (a) In cl. Gk. the basic meaning of *phōs* is light, brightness; it also covers nuances such as sunlight, daylight, torch, fire, eyesight. Fig. *phōs* means the light of life, i.e., life itself, which is highly valued as something bright. One who brings salvation or victory is also referred to as *phōs*. The vb. *phōtizō*, almost always trans., means to light up, illumine, make visible. Its corresponding noun *phōtismos* denotes brilliance, radiance, revelation. The adj. *phōteinos* means shining, bright. A further derivative is *phōstēr*, luminary or brightness; from Euripides on the morning star (the planet Venus) is termed *phōsphoros*.

(b) Relatively early in Gk. usage *phōs* came to mean the sphere of ethical good, whereas misdeeds were said to take place in darkness. Hence the task of a judge is to bring hidden things "to light." In Plato, *phōs* increased its range of connotation; that is, it could stress the illuminating qualities of knowledge. Light possesses powers essential to true life. Hence "to be in the light" came to mean simply "to live," whereas to be in Hades (→ *hadēs*, 87) was to be in darkness.

(c) In many ancient religions the metaphor of light was important. The gods lived in a world of brightness, and torch races were held as part of their cultic veneration. In some mystery cults the cleansing and refining effect of fire played no small part. Gnosticism marked the climax of this process. It saw an essential difference between light and darkness, which stood against each other as hostile powers. Human beings, who by nature are in darkness, must liberate the elements of light within their own souls and free them from earthly matter so that they may be reunited with the supernatural world to which they really belong and so attain to true life. Light and life are inseparably connected.

2. (a) The OT frequently refers to light and its effects. The primeval light (Gen. 1:3) has pride of place over all the other lights; even the stars are only light-bearers. The sun, being the brightest heavenly body, is assigned to the day (Gen. 1:14–18; Sir. 43:2–5), and each new day begins with the ushering in of morning light (2 Sam. 23:4). The moon and stars seek to penetrate the darkness of the night (Gen. 1:16; Sir. 43:6–10). In a culture filled with astrological beliefs, the Israelites stressed the creation of light in order to render abortive any attempt to deify it. There is only one God, Yahweh. He creates light and darkness, and since he is Lord also of the darkness, he is able to turn darkness into light (Ps. 139:11–12).

(b) The OT frequently refers to light as a kind of attribute of God; light is his garment (Ps. 104:2). His nearness and presence are indicated by light (cf. Exod. 13:21–22; Neh. 9:12; Isa. 60:19–20; Dan. 2:22; Hab. 3:4). Light is esp. a feature of God's self-manifestation (Ps. 4:6; 43:3; 89:15).

For humanity the light of Yahweh means salvation, an idea expressed in Ps. 27:1: "The LORD is my light and my salvation—whom shall I fear?" (cf. Job 22:28). The light that comes from God sets the bounds of every person's life and arises on everyone (cf. 25:3; Sir. 42:16). Yet each person must turn to the light and consciously acknowledge its source.

The light of the ungodly is worthless. It goes out (Job 18:5–6) or is taken from them (38:15). They grope in darkness (cf. 12:25; Prov. 4:19), and even after death darkness will still surround them (Ps. 49:19), while God will redeem the soul of the righteous "from the grave" (49:15).

(c) Yet during their earthly lives, the godly enjoy the light of the living (Ps. 112:4; cf. Job 33:30; Prov. 4:18; 13:9). They experience God's saving power when they open their hearts to the light of God's Word (Ps. 119:105; cf. Prov. 6:23; Wis. 7:10, 26). In God's light we see light

(Ps. 36:9). Only when enlightened by God does the nature of reality dawn on us. Our lives must be lived in the light, i.e., in concrete obedience to God's commandments. Just as the "pillar of fire" marked Israel's route at the time of their exodus from Egypt (Exod. 13:21–22), so the law shows us how to walk in the light (cf. the exhortation of Isa. 2:5).

The prophets esp. stress the importance of walking in holiness and righteousness. Those who walk in the light themselves become a light for others (said of the Servant of the Lord, Isa. 42:6; 49:6). This missionary outlook is marked by a worldwide hope even in the OT for the truth of Yahweh will go forth as "a light to the nations" (51:4), who will flock to God's light (60:3). In the OT wisdom lit. we see the antithesis of light and darkness as the respective spheres of the God-fearing and the ungodly (e.g., Prov. 4:18–19).

3. (a) This dualism of light and darkness receives radical treatment in Qumran texts. The "sons of light" (i.e., members of the Qumran community) are locked in a conflict with the "sons of darkness" (1QS 1:9, 18, 24; 2:5, 16, 19; 3:13). This confrontation corresponds to a similar one in the metaphysical world of spirits, where the Prince of Light (3:20; CD 5:18; 1QM 13:10) is opposed as lord of the world by the Angel of Darkness (1QS 3:20–21). The sons of light are subject to attacks from the Angel of Darkness and his evil spirits, and their situation would be desperate apart from the help of the "God of Israel." He limits the power of darkness, for he created the spirits of both light and darkness.

(b) In Philo wisdom and knowledge are called the light of knowledge, i.e., they cast true light on the whole question of existence. Since he viewed salvation in terms of light, it is easy to see why he used the metaphor of light for epistemological concepts. The *logos* is light, as is the human *nous* or understanding. By describing conscience as *phōs*, Philo indicates the connection between knowledge and ethical behavior. Pride of place among the virtues is piety and love for God. He is the one and only God, living in a heaven of brightness and light.

NT In the NT *phōs* occurs 73x, of which 33 are in the Johannine writings; *phōtizō* occurs 11x; *phōtismos* 2x (2 Cor. 4:4, 6); *phōteinos* 5x; *phōstēr* 2x (Phil. 2:15; Rev. 21:11); *phōsphoros* only once (2 Pet. 1:19).

1. (a) The original meaning of *phōs* is found in reference to the light of the sun (Rev. 22:5), which is absent at night (Jn. 11:10); the light of lamps (Lk. 8:16; 11:33; Acts 16:29; Rev. 18:23; 22:5); and the warm glow of a fire (Mk. 14:54; Lk. 22:56).

(b) The "bright cloud" used by God in the transfiguration of his Son (Matt. 17:5) points beyond itself to God, whose appearing is inevitably accompanied by effulgence. The Son, too, is surrounded by radiance: "His face shone like the sun, and his clothes became white as the light" (17:2). Here light is a manifestation of God's presence; in several other places it indicates the appearing of the exalted Christ (Acts 9:3; 22:6, 9, 11; 26:13), and in still others the coming of angels as messengers from God himself (12:7; cf. Matt. 28:2–3).

The disciples are also described as light or light-bearers (Matt. 5:14, 16; Lk. 11:35; cf. Eph. 5:8; Phil. 2:15), since it is their task to pass on the divine light they have received. That which they heard from Jesus in the intimacy of his closed circle of friends they are to proclaim fearlessly "in the daylight" (i.e., in public; Matt. 10:27; cf. Lk. 12:3). As missionaries of Christ, they are to shine out into the world, not with their own light but with the light of heaven, God's dwelling-place (1 Tim. 6:16), or even with the light of God himself (1 Jn. 1:5).

2. Jn. portrays Jesus Christ as light breaking in upon the darkness of the world. Already in Jn. 1:4, light and life are linked together, i.e., Christ is the only remedy for those who by nature are in darkness (cf. 8:12). John the Baptist is a witness to the light (1:6–9; 5:35–36). "The true light that gives light to every man" came into the world in the person of Jesus Christ (1:9).

This same note of exclusiveness is sounded in one of Christ's celebrated "I am" sayings: "I am the light of the world. Whoever follows me will never walk in darkness, but will have the light of life" (Jn. 8:12; cf. 9:5; 12:46). By making the world bright, we as humans are able to see. Simply recognizing the way is not sufficient, however. We must walk in it, for he who is the light and the way does not want mere admirers but believing followers. Thus Jesus challenges us: "Put your trust in the light . . . so that you may become sons of light" (12:36).

An admonition such as this is necessary because the natural self loves darkness rather than light (Jn. 3:19). Even though since the coming of Jesus Christ "the darkness is passing " (1 Jn. 2:8), the Christian who comes to the light still needs to be urged to keep the commandment of brotherly love (2:8–10), for "whoever loves his brother lives in the light" (2:10; cf. 1:6–7). To do this, we must be in communion with him who is the light of the world, Jesus Christ.

3. Though using these words less frequently than Jn., Paul gives them a similar theological content. Light and darkness are as incompatible as righteousness and lawlessness (2 Cor. 6:14). The content of light is Christological. The god of this world has blinded unbelievers "so that they cannot see the light of the gospel of the glory of Christ." But God, "who said, 'Let light shine out of darkness,' made his light shine in our hearts to give us the light of the knowledge of the glory of God in the face of Christ" (2 Cor. 4:4, 6; cf. Gen. 1:3; 2 Tim. 1:10). Through him we share "in the inheritance of the saints in the kingdom of light" (Col. 1:12). Thus, believers are "children of light" and "light in the Lord" (Eph. 5:8; cf. 1 Thess. 5:5).

Such sonship, however, makes ethical demands on its recipients: "The fruit of the light consists in all goodness, righteousness and truth" (Eph. 5:9). Thus we must walk according to the light—and all the more so since Christians bear a missionary responsibility for the world about us, a responsibility we can only meet if we "shine like stars [*phōstēr*] in the universe" (Phil. 2:15; cf. Acts 13:47), even though this may involve them in conflict (Heb. 10:32).

In this world Christians live their lives, so to speak, between God and Satan. The latter can even disguise himself as "an angel of light" (2 Cor. 11:14). Hence Christians must put on "the armor of light" (Rom. 13:12). Only those who have fought a good fight in this armor have no need to fear the day when "the Father of the heavenly lights" (Jas. 1:17) brings to light what is hidden (1 Cor. 4:5).

4. Like the OT and 1st-cent. Jud., the NT describes the future of the ungodly in terms of eschatological darkness that symbolizes perdition. But believers have a hope that enables them to see the end of time differently. This too can be depicted in terms of light. In the new Jerusalem there will no longer be sun, moon, or created light, "for the glory of God gives it light, and the Lamb is its lamp [*lychnos*, → *3394*]. The nations will walk by its light" (Rev. 21:23–24; cf. 22:5). While the ungodly are excluded (21:8, 27; 22:3, 11, 18–19), there is an echo here of the Gentiles' coming to the light alongside Israel, which is featured in the eschatological proclamation of Isa. 2:2–5; 24:23; 60:1, 19.

In 2 Pet. 1:19 the apostle admonishes: "You will do well to pay attention to [the word of the OT prophets], as to a light shining in a dark place, until the day dawns and the morning star [*phōsphoros*] rises in your hearts." Stars are messianic symbols (→ *astēr*, *843*; cf. Num. 24:17; Lk. 1:78; Rev. 22:16). The thought of Christ as the morning star in 2 Pet. 1:19 presents a marked contrast with Isa. 14:12, where "morning star, son of the dawn" is a title applied to the king of Babylon, whose fall Isa. proclaims. Christ will claim the final victory.

See also *lampō*, shine (*3290*); *lychnos*, lamp, light (*3394*); *phainō*, shine (*5743*); *emphanizō*, reveal, make known (*1872*).

5891 (phōstēr, luminary, brightness), → *5890.*

5892 (phōsphoros, bearing light, morning star), → *5890.*

5893 (phōteinos, shining, bright, radiant), → *5890.*

5894 (phōtizō, light up, illumine, bring to light), → *5890.*

5895 (phōtismos, illumination, enlightenment), → *5890.*

X chi

| 5897 χαίρω |

χαίρω (*chairō*), be glad, rejoice (*5897*); χαρά (*chara*), joy (*5915*); συγχαίρω (*synchairō*), rejoice with (*5176*).

CL & OT 1. *chairō* means be glad, rejoice; *chara*, joy. The pres. imperative frequently occurs in the greeting, *chaire* (sing.), *chairete* (pl.), "Hail!" At the opening of a letter the infinitive *chairein*, is often used; the same formula is used at parting, "Farewell!" *chara* denotes both the state and the object of the joy. Also to be noted is the connection with *charis* (grace), which has not always been clearly distinguished in meaning from *chara*.

2. In the LXX *chara* appears primarily in the later writings (e.g., Wis. and 1–4 Macc.). There is no clear distinction between *chairō* and *euphrainō* (*2370*), which translate the same Heb. words (Est. 8:17; Prov. 29:6; Lam. 4:21). *chairō* covers both the subjective feeling and the objective cause of joy. Of all the words in this group, it thus comes closest to the Heb. *šālôm*, peace, salvation, and in fact is used to translate this in Isa. 48:22; 57:21. The vb. and the noun do not often appear in the context of joy in worship (Ps. 30:11); *agalliaō* and *euphrainō* are used here.

3. A nonspecific use as a greeting occurs particularly in 1–4 Macc. The general meaning to be glad, be pleased, is found in Gen. 45:16; Isa. 39:2. In the OT there is no apology for joy in the good things of life, such as health (Sir. 30:16), wise children (Prov. 23:25), eating and drinking (1 Ki. 3:1), or peace in the land (1 Macc. 14:11, *euphrainō*). But Prov. also warns that joy can be transitory and is threatened by the vicissitudes of life, for after laughter comes weeping (14:13).

4. God is the giver of all joy and blessings (1 Ki. 8:66). He gives and keeps his gracious word (8:56), which far outweighs transitory blessings. This word comforts and strengthens in times of temptation and distress (Jer. 15:16). It enables us to endure until such time as God turns mourning into joy (Ps. 126:5). The fear of the Lord is thus a source of joy (Sir. 1:12). As a result, *chairō* serves also to describe eschatological joy, rejoicing over ultimate salvation and peace (Isa. 66:10, 14; Joel 2:21, 23; Zech. 10:7).

5. Rab. Jud. emphasized joy in the law. Reading the Pentateuch is described in this way. In Philo divine wisdom is a source of joy. In Qumran joy springs from knowledge of the truth (1QH 11:30), but here it is the knowledge of God's election and mercy toward his elect. There is a decisive contrast between present sadness in affliction and chastisement (9:24) and the joy of final victory (e.g., 1QM 13:12–14; 14:4), when the sons of light will be brought to everlasting joy (1QH 13:6).

NT In the NT *chairō* occurs 74x, *chara* 59x, and *synchairō* 7x, mostly in the Gospels and Paul's letters. It is no accident that the words appear esp. in which eschatological fulfillment in Christ, being in him, and hope in him are mentioned. But note that the whole NT message as the proclamation of God's saving work in Christ is a message of joy.

1. The general use as a greeting needs only brief mention. *chairein* is used at the beginning of a letter in Acts 15:23; 23:26; Jas. 1:1. In Matt. 28:9 the risen Christ makes himself known to his disciples by using the familiar, everyday greeting, *chairete*. In 2 Jn. 10 those addressed are warned not to "welcome" teachers of heretical doctrine, so as to avoid involvement in their evil deeds. When in Matt. 26:49; 27:29, par. Jesus is saluted in derision as "Rabbi" or "King of the Jews," there is a concealed irony since he is unwittingly given the title that is his due. In Lk. 1:28, Mary is startled not so much by the *chaire* as by the message that follows.

2. According to the Synoptics, the coming of Jesus brings in a time of joy (cf. Matt. 9:15; Mk. 2:19; Lk. 5:34). The fact that he brings in the final salvation distinguishes him from John the Baptist and the OT prophets. The effect of his work and preaching is to bring joy (19:6). Even when he becomes an offense and the way of those who walk in his footsteps leads to suffering and persecution, the joyful assurance of salvation should not be lost: "Rejoice [*chairete*] and be glad, because great is your reward in heaven!" (Matt. 5:12).

Jesus is the coming judge of the whole world. Hence those who remain faithful to Christ's commission and receive the word with no mere ephemeral joy (Matt. 13:20 par.) will hear one day the welcoming summons to the joyous banquet of his Lord (cf. 25:21, 23; cf. Rev. 19:7, 9). When the disciples met the risen Christ, they were seized not only with fear but also with great joy (Matt. 28:8; cf. Mk. 16:8; Lk. 24:9).

3. (a) Lk.'s Gospel has joy as one of its basic themes, beginning with the birth narratives. Zechariah is promised joy and gladness; many will rejoice at the birth of his son (1:14) because of what God is about to do on behalf of his people (cf. 2:15). When Elizabeth meets the mother of the Savior, the child leaps for joy in her womb (*agalliasis*, 1:44). Jubilant praise of God, in the majestic language of the OT psalms, is expressed in the Magnificat of Mary (1:47) and in the hymn of Zechariah (1:68–79). The basis and content of this great joy is the Christmas message that in Jesus God has visited and redeemed his people (1:68) and has taken care of lost humanity.

Joy is an important result of Jesus' miracles (Lk. 13:17). The 70 disciples may share in his power over evil spirits and be filled with joy and pride (10:17), but joy in God's electing love counts for still more: "Rejoice that your names are written in heaven" (10:20; cf. Matt. 7:22–23). God deals mercifully with the lost, and there is joy in heaven over one sinner who repents (Lk. 15:7, 10, 32). Indeed, the whole of Lk. 15—with its parables of the lost sheep, the lost coin, and the lost son—presents Jesus as calling on us to rejoice with him over the lost returning to the Father (15:6, 9 [*synchairō*], 32 [*chairō*]). The conclusion of Lk. is remarkable for its amazement and overflowing joy (24:41, 52). This message is to be carried beyond Israel and preached to all nations.

(b) This process is repeated in Acts in expressions of joy over the irresistible worldwide expansion of the church. There is first the apostles' joy in suffering shame and persecution for Christ's sake (5:41; cf. Matt. 5:11–12). Believers experience such joy through the enabling of the Holy Spirit (Acts 13:52; cf. 7:55). There is also joy over the ingathering of the Gentiles (11:23; 13:48; 15:3). When the gospel is preached to them and they are baptized, the persons concerned are filled with joy (8:8, 39; 15:31).

4. Jn. in his Gospel features complete joy or fullness of joy (cf. 1 Jn. 1:4; 2 Jn. 12). It occurs as early as Jn. 3:29, where John the Baptist's joy is full on account of the "bridegroom," the promised revealer of heavenly truth (cf. Matt. 9:14–15 par.). The eschatological hour of joy has now arrived, in which continuous sowing exists side by side with harvest time (Jn. 4:35–36), and in which Jesus is already accomplishing the work he was given to do (cf. 4:34). Abraham in heaven joins in the rejoicing over this day (8:56). The perfect joy that Jesus has, because he is in full communion with the Father (14:20) and does his will (4:34), is to be given to the disciples as well (15:11). This he asks from the Father (17:13) and therefore exhorts his own to abide in him and in his love (15:4, 9). His work of love is completed as he lays down his life for his "friends" (15:13); it will only be fully revealed, however, when he goes away from them (16:20).

The world cannot take away this joy and consolation any more than it can take away the peace that Jesus gives (Jn. 14:27; 16:33), for they do not belong to this world. His disciples can expect the world's hatred and persecution (15:19; 16:2). But fear is banished because

Jesus has overcome the world (16:33; cf. 1 Jn. 1:4). Present sadness will be turned into joy (Jn. 16:22).

5. The Pauline letters testify to the paradox that Christian joy can be found only in the midst of sadness, affliction, and care. Indeed, this is precisely where it gives proof of its power. (a) This joy has its source beyond mere earthly, human joy. It is joy in the Lord. This is why Paul constantly exhorts his readers to manifest such joy (Rom. 12:12; 2 Cor. 6:10; Phil. 3:1; 4:4, 10). It is "joy in the faith" (Phil. 1:25; cf. Rom. 15:13); that is, it has its basis in the hope and confidence of faith, which despite all troubles and fear is certain of justification through Christ (Rom. 8:31–32; 2 Cor. 7:4) and looks forward to his return. Joy is also a fruit of the Spirit (Gal. 5:22; cf. Rom. 14:17; 1 Thess. 1:6). It is thus a spiritual gift, and in this respect approximates to *charis*, grace. Because faith and its consequent joy do not come from ourselves, Paul can be confident and rejoice even when Christ is preached with base motives. The important thing is that God is doing his gracious work and that as many as possible share in the gospel (Phil. 1:5–6, 15–18).

(b) In 2 Cor. Paul places joy in direct contrast to *thlipsis*, affliction (→ *2568*), by which he means not only the distress caused by outward trials, but also the necessary sorrow aroused by his apostolic rebukes. He protests to the Corinthians that "we work with you for your joy" (1:24). He wrote a harsh letter to them so that his joy might be shared by all (2:3). The lives of the Corinthians must be ruled not by passive resignation or the worldly grief that produces death (7:10), but by the joy of a purified faith. Having sharply rebuked them earlier, Paul has regained his confidence in them, and he now has even stronger grounds for rejoicing (7:9, 13).

(c) Paul wrote the letter to the Philippians from prison (possibly in Ephesus), at a time when he was still uncertain of the outcome of his trial. There is evidence that Paul felt lonely (Phil. 2:20–21) and that the faithful preaching of the gospel was in jeopardy (1:15–18; 2:21). Yet there were also grounds for thankfulness and unmitigated joy: thankfulness for the participation of the Philippians in the gospel enterprise (1:5), and joy over the continuing proclamation of Christ (1:18). Thus, constrained by the gospel and by Christ himself, Paul exhorts his readers to rejoice together with him (*synchairō*, 2:17–18), to cast care behind them (4:6), and to be of one mind in the fellowship of the Spirit (2:1–2). All Paul cares is that Christ be magnified in his body (1:20). Above all his joy is in the Lord (4:4).

(d) The present period of trial and distress is limited, for the Lord is at hand (Phil. 4:5; cf. 1 Thess. 5:2–3). Hence joy is based primarily on the hope that after suffering together we will be glorified together (Rom. 8:17). This joyous and confident waiting for the day of Christ puts our present experience into true perspective. It enables us to sympathize with others (12:15), and it reminds us that our present joys and sorrows belong to this life only and are not our final lot (1 Cor. 7:30; 2 Cor. 6:10).

6. (a) This Pauline teaching about joy in affliction and temptation proved its value when the later NT letters were being written. By this time, the persecution of Christians was so severe as to threaten the very existence of the church (1 Pet. 4:12–13). Still, being robbed of material goods could not deprive them of their joy (Heb. 10:34). Granted, persecution brings real distress (12:11). Thus, believers must exercise patience (10:36) and continue obediently in sound doctrine (12:17). Christ voluntarily gave up his own joy and took on himself the shame of the cross. Only looking to him can we obtain patience and endurance in temptation (12:2; cf. 1 Pet. 1:8–9).

(b) Jas. 1:2 comes close to teaching Christians to rejoice in martyrdom (cf. Acts 5:41). In the course of the church's history, however, this has at times degenerated into virtually seeking martyrdom for its own sake.

See also *agalliaō*, exult, rejoice greatly, be overjoyed (22); *euphrainō*, gladden, cheer (up) (2370).

5898 (chalaza, hail), → 847.

5901	χαλεπός

χαλεπός (*chalepos*), hard, difficult (*5901*).

CL & OT *chalepos* can be used of words that are difficult to bear, or of humans and animals that are hard to deal with and thus dangerous. Sometimes this word has moral implications, meaning bad or evil (cf. Wis. 3:19; 17:11; 19:13). In Isa. 18:2 it is used of a nation, probably in the sense of harsh. In Sir. 3:21, it is used of intellectual difficulty—that which is too difficult for a student.

NT *chalepos* occurs only 2x in the NT. In Matt. 8:28 it indicates the devilish ferocity of the two demoniacs from the country of the Gadarenes. In 2 Tim. 3:1 it denotes the character of the last days: times of hardship when self-interest is a decisive factor in human relationships.

5906 (chalkeus, coppersmith), → 5910.

5908 (chalkion, a copper vessel or implement), → 5910.

5909 (chalkolibanon, bronze), → 5910.

5910	χαλκός

χαλκός (*chalkos*), copper, bronze, a copper coin (*5910*); χαλκίον (*chalkion*), a copper vessel or implement (*5908*); χαλκεύς (*chalkeus*), coppersmith (*5906*); χαλκοῦς (*chalkous*), bronze, (*5911*); χαλκολίβανον (*chalkolibanon*), bronze (*5909*).

CL & OT 1. Since copper was the first metal to be worked in Greece, *chalkos* became the word for metal in general and applied at first also to iron. Later it also included bronze: copper to which a small amount of tin had been added.

2. (a) In the LXX copper is first mentioned, together with iron, in connection with Tubal-Cain, who made cutting instruments (Gen. 4:22). This notation draws attention to an important development in the history of humankind. Copper weapons, mace heads, helmets, and axe blades were developed in the Early Bronze Age. A cache of 450 copper objects found at Nahal Mishmar in the Judean desert in 1961 has pushed back into the 4th millennium the achievement of high technical standards. Bronze probably made its appearance ca. 2000 B.C., but copper remained in use for objects that did not need to be cast. Both metals became much more common from this time on. A hard cutting edge was achieved on this soft metal by hammering.

(b) The altar of sacrifice in the tabernacle was bronze-covered (Exod. 38:2), whereas its carrying rings were cast (38:5). Solomon imported Hiram from Tyre to oversee the lavish bronze and copper work connected with the temple (1 Ki. 7:13–47). Copper smelting was carried out as early as 4000 B.C. at Timnah, a mining site about 15 miles north of Elath. Mines found here have been explored. The deepest workings are several hundred feet below the surface and are supplied with ventilation by air channels, roughly the diameter of a thumb. A description of mining is given in Job 28:1–11.

NT The words in this group occur 10x in the NT. *chalkos* means copper coin (Matt. 10:9; Mk. 6:8; 12:41), a commodity of merchandise (Rev. 18:12), and a clanging "gong" (1 Cor. 13:1), such as was used in various cults (here symbolizing the emptiness of speaking in tongues when devoid of understanding and love). *chalkous* denotes the material from which an idol is made (Rev. 9:20). In Mk. 7:4 *chalkion* is translated "kettle," a vessel used for cooking. A *chalkeus* is a metalworker (2 Tim. 4:14). The compound *chalkolibanon* (Rev. 1:15; 2:18) describes an alloy, the exact nature of which is not known.

5911 (chalkous, bronze), → 5910.

5915 (chara, joy), → 5897.

5916	χάραγμα

χάραγμα (*charagma*), mark, stamp, graven object (*5916*).

CL & OT 1. In cl. Gk. the vb. *charassō*, from which *charagma* is derived, means to cut to a point, to sharpen. Later it developed a technical sense of inscribing on wood, stone, or brass. Then, in a special-ized meaning, it was used for the casting of a die and so the minting of coins. In the Hel. papyri ownership of property is secured by the brand mark (*charagma*), while documents are validated as true by the imposition of a stamp or seal (*charagma*). Imperial decrees are shown as genuine by the same token. Currency carries the impress (*charagma*) as a sign of its genuineness.

2. *charagma* does not appear in LXX, but the cognate vb. *charassō* occurs in 1 Ki. 15:27; 2 Ki. 17:11; Sir. 50:27. In 3 Macc. 2:29 it is used for Jewish markings with pagan cult symbols.

NT 1. Rev. 13:11–18 seems to refer to the imperial priesthood under the figure of the second beast, who requires that universal recognition and homage be given the "first beast" (the imperial line). All trading is possible only by those who have the "mark" (*charagma*) of the first beast on their right hand or forehead. That "mark" is identified with the beast's name or number (13:18).

Being marked was common in the ancient world (→ *stigma*, *5116*), denoting ownership and preservation. Repeatedly in Rev. the mark of the beast denotes subservience to anti-Christian powers (16:2; 19:20; 20:4). This mark is countered by a "seal" (*sphragis*, → *5382*) from God on his own people (7:1–8), and God's wrath is threatened to all who bear the mark of the beast (14:9, 11). Those who do not accept the satanic mark are promised the right to judge the evil powers (20:4).

2. In Acts 17:19 *charagma* is used in the sense of handiwork produced by an artist or craftsman in the production of a heathen god.

See also *stigma*, mark, brand (*5116*); *kaustēriazō*, mark by a branding iron, brand (*3013*).

5917 χαρακτήρ

χαρακτήρ (*charaktēr*), impress, stamp, reproduction, representa-tion, outward appearance, form (*5917*).

CL & OT In cl. Gk. *charaktēr* means one who sharpens or scratches, and later one who writes in stone, wood, or metal. Thence it came to mean an embosser and a stamp for making coins, and from this the embossed stamp made on the coin. Finally, it came to mean the basic bodily and psychological structure with which one is born, which is unique to each person and cannot be changed by education or by devel-opment. Hence *charaktēr* also means individuality, personal charac-teristics. In Philo the human soul is called the *charaktēr* of divine power and the Logos is entitled the *charaktēr* of God.

This concept cannot really be found in the OT, though it is rem-iniscent of passages about the image of God. The word is found in the LXX (e.g., Lev. 13:28), but there it means "scar."

NT *charaktēr* is found only in Heb. 1:3, where Christ is defined as "the exact representation [*charaktēr*] of his [God's] being," i.e., the one on whom God has stamped or imprinted his being. In other words, the NT use is entirely different from our modern concept of one's per-sonal character. The Son possesses the very stamp or substance of God's nature; those who see and recognize him, see and know the Father (Jn. 14:7–10). The word *charaktēr* expresses this truth even more emphatically than *eikōn* (→ *1635*).

The context of Heb. 1 makes it clear that the writer's purpose is to stress the glory of the Son who has entered history and the uniqueness of the revelation of God in the unique One. In 1:3 we perhaps have an early hymn (as in Phil. 2:6–11; 1 Tim. 3:16). The Son, who controls the beginning and the end (Heb. 1:2), stands in a unique relationship to God, whose "radiance" (→ *apaugasma*, *575*) and "exact representation" (*charaktēr*) he is. Jesus also stands in a unique relation to the universe, which he upholds, and to the church, which he has purified from sins. This letter is concerned equally with the preexistent, the historical, and the glorified Christ, in whom we have our true high priest.

See also *eidōlon*, image, idol (*1631*); *eikōn*, image, likeness, form, appearance (*1635*); *apaugasma*, radiance, effulgence, reflection (*575*);

hypodeigma, proof, example, model (*5682*); *hypogrammos*, outline, copy, example (*5681*); *typos*, type, pattern (*5596*).

5918 χάραξ

χάραξ (*charax*), pointed stake, palisade, rampart, mound (*5918*).

CL & OT 1. In cl. Gk. *charax* means a pointed stake, esp. a wooden support for vines; by extension, it denotes the timber used in con-structing a palisade around a city or camp.

2. *charax* occurs 14x in the LXX. Hezekiah is promised deliver-ance from the Assyrians threatening Jerusalem; against the city the enemy will not build up a "siege ramp" (Isa. 37:33; cf. also Jer. 33:4 = LXX 40:4; Ezek. 4:2). In Ezek. 21:22 *charax* is used for a "battering ram." The Assyrians raised up artificial mounds against the walls of cities as a platform, from which they could employ battering rams to greater advantage against the upper and weaker portion of the wall. In Deut. 20:19 instructions are given to the people of Israel that when besieging an enemy city, they were not, in a manner of speaking, to "besiege" the local fruit trees, i.e., not to attack and destroy them.

NT *charax* occurs only at Lk. 19:43, where Jesus laments over Jerusalem's coming fate. Her enemies will surround the city and cast up a *charax* about her: a protection for themselves and a site from which to launch their attacks. Forty years later the prophecy was ful-filled when the Roman army surrounded the city with siege works, which must have contained much timber, for the Jews destroyed them with fire. The Roman general Titus then replaced the *charax* with an earthen wall, from which he completed the siege.

See also *teichos*, wall around a city (*5446*); *phragmos*, fence, wall, hedge (*5850*).

5919 (*charizomai*, show favor or kindness, be gracious to some-one, pardon), → *5921*.

5921 χάρις

χάρις (*charis*), grace, graceful-ness, graciousness, favor, thanks, gratitude (*5921*); χάρισμα (*charisma*), gift given out of goodwill, spiritual gift (*5922*); χαρίζομαι (*charizomai*), show favor or kind-ness, give as a favor, be gracious to someone, pardon (*5919*); χαρι-τόω (*charitoō*), endue with grace (*5923*).

CL & OT 1. Words formed from the Gk. root *char-* indicate things that produce well-being. Included in this word group is *chara* (joy), which is the individual experience or expression of this well-being. (a) From this basic meaning of the root the individual meanings of *charis* are derived: e.g., grace, favor, beauty, thankfulness, gratitude, delight, kindness, benefit; in the pl., debt of gratitude, recompense, thanks. *charis* can describe both the attitude of the gods and of human beings (e.g., the emperor's dispensations). In Gk. mythology personifications of *charis* occur: Charis is the exceedingly beautiful wife of Hephaestus; *hai Charitēs*, the Graces, are the creators and bestowers of charm.

(b) The derived noun *charisma*, gracious gift, donation (only from God to humans) is found in pre-Christian lit. only in one LXX version of Sir. 7:33 (S); 38:30 (B¹); and Ps. 31:22 (Theod.); elsewhere only in Philo, *Leg.* 3, 78; *Sib. Or.*, 2.54.

(c) Outside the NT, the vb. *charizomai* does not occur with God as its subj. until the 2d cent. A.D., when it means to give graciously. When applied to human dealings with one another, it means to do something pleasant for someone, to be kind or gracious, to oblige or gratify someone. It is also used in the sense of courting a god's favor by sacrifice. In the context of ethics and law the vb. means to grant, remit, forgive, or pardon. In the perf. and plupf. pass. the vb. means to be pleasant, agreeable, or desired.

(d) The vb. *charitoō* occurs only in a few LXX and extracanoni-cal passages (Sir. 18:17; Ps. 17:26, Sym.; *Let. Aris.* 225; *T. Jos.* 1:6), always with reference to divine blessing. Otherwise it is confined to the NT and late post-Christian secular lit.

2. The LXX uses *charis* about 190x, of which only 75 have a Heb. equivalent (mostly the noun *hēn*, 61x). It usually means favor, inclination; less commonly beauty, charm (e.g., Ps. 45:2). Occasionally it is used as an adj. (Prov. 1:9; 4:9; 5:19).

(a) The use of *hēn* clarifies the biblical meaning of *charis* as "grace" in history and actions. It denotes the stronger coming to the help of the weaker. The stronger party acts by a voluntary decision, though moved by the dependence or request of the weaker party. A typical expression used to describe such an event is the formula "to find favor in someone's eyes," i.e., to acquire that person's favor, liking, benevolence, or understanding. The action itself is what makes the weaker party acceptable: e.g., Jacob to Esau (Gen. 32:5); the Egyptians to Joseph (47:25); Ruth to Boaz (Ruth 2:2, 10, 13). This acceptance is desired (Zech. 4:7) or experienced (Eccl. 9:11) as fortune or salvation. Often it can only be understood as the result of the special intervention of God, who supplies grace to the weak (Gen. 39:21; Exod. 3:21; 11:3; 12:36).

(b) *hēn* seldom denotes the activity of God, but when it does, it is mostly in the sense of God's undeserved gift in election. Noah is chosen out of a human race sentenced to destruction (Gen. 6:8). The choice of this one person allows us to recognize mercy in the midst of judgment. Moses, the chosen mediator, reminded Yahweh of his electing gift (Exod. 33:12–13a) and thus requested a renewed gift from him (33:13b, 16), recognizable as Yahweh's care in history for his covenant people and renewed on account of Moses' intercession (33:17). David also surrendered himself in moments of crisis to God's providence (2 Sam. 15:25). Bowing before God, humility and petition appear here not as necessary preconditions of God's merciful gift, but as the way open to humankind. Wisdom lit. recognized the relationship between a person's humility and divine grace (Prov. 3:34; cf. 1 Pet. 5:5).

(c) Even the postponement in history of punishment is a gracious act of God (cf. 2 Ki. 13:23). Various writers on OT theology rightly point out that, over and above the occurrences of the concept of grace, the OT teaches that all creatures live by Yahweh's grace, which produces everything that furthers life. Note how the increase of sin is often followed by a greater increase of grace: The flood is followed by the Noahic covenant (esp. Gen. 8:21–22); the tower of Babel is followed by the Abrahamic covenant for the blessing of all people (Gen. 10, 12).

3. (a) In addition to the established OT concepts, the Apocr. speaks of grace as a reward for good works, which include benevolence (Sir. 12:1; 17:22; 40:17), renunciation, and self-denial, esp. that of the martyr (Wis. 3:14). On the grace of martyrdom, see 4 Macc. 11:12.

(b) The Qumran texts betray a distinctive theology of grace: a theology that, within the bounds of covenant grace (1QM 12:3) and in confession and prayer, expresses hope for the gift of God reserved for the individual (e.g., 1QS 11:13–14 ["by his showing favor shall he provide my justification"]). The divine pleasure works as providence and foreknowledge, which make possible knowledge and a change for the good (10:6; 11:18). Through obedience and sacrifice this good pleasure can be influenced (9:4–5; 1QM 2:5).

(c) Rab. lit. contains more than a one-sided doctrine of justification by works. Grace can be procured by human behavior, for rewards are given only for deeds (e.g., 2 Esd. 8:31–33, 36). Yet there is also the belief that grace is necessary for every action; it initiates and completes even the actions of the elect. Thus, the divine reward is a reward of grace.

NT The NT uses the term *charis* 155x, mostly in Paul's letters (100x); it occurs 17x in Acts, 10x in 1 Pet., and 8x in Heb. In the Gospels it occurs only 12x (Lk. and Jn.). With the exception in 1 Pet., *charisma* is an exclusively Pauline concept (16x). *charizomai* occurs only in Paul (16x) and the writings of Lk. (7x); likewise *charitoō* (once each in Paul and Lk.).

1. The concept of *charis* in the sense of God's undeserved gift does not occur in Jesus' teaching. But the theme of his teaching and his acts as a whole reflect the central message of grace: God's condescension to the weak, poor, hopeless, and lost (Matt. 11:5, 28–30; Mk. 10:26–27; Lk. 15). Immeasurable remission of debt (Matt. 18:21–34), gracious reward in God's kingdom (20:1–16), and pardon leading to a new life (Lk. 7:36–50; 13:6–8; 19:9–10) are central themes in his ministry.

2. (a) In the few places where Lk. includes Jesus' references to *charis*, it means reward in the last day, payment for something taken as a matter of course (Lk. 6:32–34; 17:9); thus, it has a meaning almost the opposite of its usual meaning. In 4:22 "the gracious words" seem to include the astonishing rhetorical force of Jesus' words, his authority, the boldness of his claims, and the content of his teaching. Elsewhere Lk. uses *charis* in its OT sense to express the favor and the acceptability of Mary or the child Jesus before God (1:30; 2:40) and other human beings (2:52, quoting 1 Sam. 2:26). In the history of doctrine, of special significance is the angel's greeting to Mary, "Greetings, you who are highly favored!" (Lk. 1:28). This does not exalt Mary in her essential being over the rest of humankind (cf. a similar statement about Stephen in Acts 6:8). Rather, Mary is promised as a special favor of God a unique role in the history of God's saving purposes, of being "the Lord's servant" (1:38).

(b) In Acts *charis* denotes the power that flows from God or the exalted Christ and that accompanies the activity of the apostles, giving success to their mission (6:8; 11:23; 14:26; 15:40; 18:27). Paul's message of grace is identical with the gospel (13:43; 20:24), and the Lord himself confirmed it by miraculous signs (14:3). It is what enables people to believe (18:27) and builds them up (20:32). Even where the sense "favor of all the people" is present (2:47; cf. 4:33), God's initiative is the decisive factor. It occurs exclusively in the sense of human favor only in 24:27; 25:3, 9. Paul's view of law and grace is echoed in Pet.'s speech in 15:10–11, which contrasts the "yoke" (*zygos*, → *2433*) of circumcision with "the grace of our Lord Jesus." *charizomai* in Acts denotes granting someone's life to a third party (3:14; 27:24) and handing over someone (25:11, 16).

3. In Jn. *charis* occurs 4x, only in the prologue, where it is perhaps influenced by Paul's thought. The antithesis of law and grace (1:17) is typically Pauline. In 1:14, 17 the Evangelist has linked *charis* with one of his favorite concepts, truth (cf. Exod. 34:6). As in Paul, the event of Christ is identified with grace (seen esp. in Jesus earthly life, 1:14), and grace is regarded as the essence of "his glory" (→ *doxa*, *1518*). Grace is poured out in overflowing fullness (1:16). In the teaching of Jn. as a whole, the gifts that the Revealer brings, such as "life" and "light" (1:4–5), are identified with Jesus Christ himself (cf. his "I am" sayings) and can only be understood as gifts of his grace.

4. For Paul *charis* is the essence of God's decisive saving act in Jesus Christ, which took place in his sacrificial death, and also of all its consequences in the present and the future (Rom. 3:24–26). Therefore, the use of this word at the beginning and end of Paul's letters is much more than a polite cliché. "Grace" is not just a good wish for salvation; it is qualified as "the grace of the Lord Jesus Christ" (2 Cor. 13:14).

(a) Paul unfolds the reality and power of *charis* in a stubborn conflict with rab. ideas of justification by works and synergism. This leads him to set up and then contrast two antithetical, mutually exclusive series of ideas: grace, gift, the righteousness of God, superabundance, faith, gospel, and calling on the one side; and law, reward, sin, works, accomplishment owed, one's own righteousness, honor, worldly wisdom, and futility on the other side. The person and work of God's Son has made it possible for justice in the Judge's pardon not to conflict with grace (Rom. 3:21–26; 8:32; Gal. 2:20–21; Phil. 2:8–13). In Christ, therefore, God's grace is given as a precious gift (1 Cor. 1:4). Apart from him there can be no talk of grace (cf. 1:30–31; see also Jn. 1:14, 16–17). But this also means that grace can never become a quality that someone possesses in one's own right.

(b) The following extracts from Paul's letters outline the above summary. *charis* occurs in a central position or serves as the climax of the argument. Frequently it is defined by means of a contrast.

(i) *Rom. 3:21–31*. We are justified by God's grace as a gift through the redemption that is in Christ Jesus (3:24). Here grace is pardon by the divine Judge, who reckons to the sinner the righteousness of Christ.

(ii) *Rom. 4:2–25*. The ideas of grace and debt (i.e., a reward for work accomplished) are mutually exclusive. "Therefore, the promise comes by faith, so that it may be by grace and may be guaranteed to all Abraham's offspring—not only to those who are of the law but also to those who are of the faith of Abraham" (4:16). Only the free gift of God ensures the extension of the saving promise to all people.

(iii) *Rom. 5:15–21 and 6:1*. Rom. 5:15 declares that "the gift [*charisma*] is not like the trespass [*paraptōma*, → *4183*]." Here *charisma* is used in the sense of *charis*, the gift of life, which as "God's grace and the gift that came by the grace of . . . Jesus Christ, overflow[ed] to the many" (5:15; cf. 5:20b). But grace is not given to let us go on sinning (6:1). It does not owe its origin to sin, nor can it be manipulated by us. It is a new reality, a dominion established once and for all by Jesus Christ. Its ground is the new righteousness of Christ, and its goal is eternal life (5:21).

(iv) *Rom. 6:12–23*. This section carries this thought further, as 6:14–15 argues that those who have died with Christ and now live in him (cf. 6:11) no longer live under the dominion of sin (*hamartia*, → *281*), but under that of grace; 6:15 guards against any misunderstanding (as in 6:1–2). God's gracious gift (*charisma*) of eternal life has made the power of death as the wages of sin something that belongs to our past (6:21–23).

(v) *Rom. 11:5–6*. Being "chosen by grace" and a life based on "works" have nothing in common; otherwise, "grace would no longer be pure grace." It would be compromised by the rab. principle of accomplishment and achievement.

(vi) *2 Cor. 1:12*. To the Jewish desire for control of one's fate through works of law corresponds the Greek striving for autonomy by means of "worldly wisdom" (cf. also 1 Cor. 1:18–25). Grace opposes the pride of both as the sole source of power for the apostolic mission and for the Christian's life (cf. 1 Cor. 1:30–31).

(vii) *Gal. 2:21*. Here Paul formulates the climax of his theology of grace: "I do not set aside the grace of God, for if righteousness could be gained through the law, then Christ died for nothing!"

(viii) *Gal. 5:1–6*. Paul accuses the Galatian churches (5:4) of doing what he repudiated for himself in 2:21, i.e., of wanting by implication to be justified through the law. By doing this, he writes, they have become "alienated from Christ" and "have fallen away from grace." They have plunged into the abyss of their own righteousness and thus of bondage.

(c) Apart from the antithetic use of *charis* and law (*nomos*, → *3795*), Paul employs the concept of grace in various other connections. (i) Paul praises the gracious acts of God with the exclamation "thanks [*charis*] be to God" (Rom. 6:17; 7:25; 1 Cor. 15:57; 2 Cor. 2:14; 9:15; cf. 8:16; 1 Tim. 1:12; 2 Tim. 1:3) at crucial points in his letters. (ii) Those who partake in that which is by nature good without a load on the conscience do it "with thankfulness" (1 Cor. 10:30). (iii) The spiritual song is understood as "gratitude" to God (Col. 3:16). (iv) In 1 Cor. 16:3 and 2 Cor. 8:6, 7, 19, *charis* is the technical term for the gift of gratitude and love Paul was collecting for the Jerusalem community.

(d) Arising out of God's basic act of pardon and legal acquittal (Rom. 8:31–39), Paul understands the whole movement of the Christian life from beginning to end as grace (Rom. 5:2; 2 Cor. 6:1–9; cf. also Jn. 1:16). It is guaranteed by being anchored in God's purpose (Rom. 8:28). Human weakness, not self-determination, is its sphere of activity (2 Cor. 12:9). The grace of God makes the new self what he or she is (1 Cor. 15:10). This is as true of the apostolic mission in particular (Rom. 1:5; 12:3; 15:15; 1 Cor. 3:10; Gal. 2:9; Phil. 1:7) as it is of the Christian life in general (Rom. 12:3, 6; 1 Cor. 1:4–9; 2 Cor. 4:15; 6:1; 8:1; 9:8, 14; Phil. 1:7). The relationship with Christ is frequently expressed by *dia*, through. When grace is said to be given, to overflow,

etc., the intent is to acknowledge its reality in human life, not to imply that it is a thing or an object.

(e) The manifold outworking of the one grace in individual Christians through the one Spirit Paul calls a *charisma*, a personal endowment with grace. This is the specialized use of *charisma* as distinct from the general (see above on Rom. 5:15–16; 6:23). In Rom. 12:3–8 and 1 Cor. 12 Paul develops the meaning of this special endowment for service to the community. It has both inward- and outward-looking aspects: prophecy as a gift of proclamation, service, teaching, spiritual exhortation, leadership in the congregation, beneficence, and compassion. In 1 Cor. 12:9–10, 28–30, Paul adds faith, the gift of healing, special authority to distinguish between spirits, speaking in tongues, the interpretation of tongues, and, as first in the order of functions, the service of the apostle (12:28).

It is inconceivable to Paul that there should be any Christian without some *charisma*. At the same time, a single person may be characterized by more than one gift of grace. Paul himself had, beside his apostleship (2 Cor. 1:11), the gift of celibacy (1 Cor. 7:7), which did not belong of necessity to the apostolate (9:5). He also possessed the gift of tongues (14:18), and no doubt also prophecy, teaching, and administration. Capacity for spiritual service is determined by one's present *charisma*. It must not be overstepped through ambition (Rom. 12:3–5; 1 Cor. 12:11–27; cf. also 1 Pet. 4:10). Yet Paul also encouraged eager desire for the best gifts (1 Cor. 12:31), which can be attained not through achievements, but only through prayer and obedience. Rom. 11:29 designates as *charismata* the abiding privileges of Israel in salvation history (cf. 9:4–5).

(f) The vb. *charizomai*, like *charis*, is used primarily in connection with the decisive, gracious gift of God. Rom. 8:32 speaks of the all-embracing gift of God in giving his Son (cf. Jn. 3:16). God's Spirit leads to the knowledge of what God has bestowed (1 Cor. 2:12). Already in the old covenant the free gift of God is linked only with the promise (Gal. 3:18), not with the law. Readiness to suffer for Christ's sake is, like faith, given by God to the church by grace for Christ's sake (Paul uses the pass. of this vb. in Phil. 1:29, presumably to avoid using the divine name). Through Philemon's prayers the imprisoned Paul hopes God will enable him to come to that church as a guest (Phlm. 22).

Another meaning of *charizomai* is to forgive (e.g., 2 Cor. 2:7, 10; cf. also Eph. 4:32; Col. 2:13; 3:13). Christians are to forgive each other, since God in Christ (or the Lord) has forgiven them. In 2 Cor. 12:13 the vb. is used almost ironically to mean excuse.

5. In Eph. *charis* occurs 12x. It is used (as elsewhere in Paul's letters) in an antithetical connection: "[God] made us alive with Christ even when we were dead in transgressions—it is by grace [*chariti*] you have been saved" (2:5): "by grace [*chariti*] you have been saved, through faith . . . the gift of God," in contrast to "not from yourselves . . . not by works, so that no one can boast" (2:8–9). In contrast to Paul's earlier letters, *charis* is here connected with *sōzō*, save (→ *5392*), not with *dikaioō*, justify (which does not occur in Eph. and Col.). The emphasis is thus shifted from forensic justification to effective salvation. Hence grace is connected with *charitoō*, to favor, bless, freely give (Eph. 1:6). It looks forward to exaltation (1:6–7; 2:7), though it is still related to "redemption through his blood" (1:7; cf. 2:15; 4:9).

The cognitive aspect of grace that comes to humans in the gospel is stressed in Col. 1:6. Grace and truth belong together (1:5b; cf. Jn. 1:14). In Eph. 4:7—"But to each one of us grace [*charis*] has been given as Christ apportioned it"—*charis* is used in the sense of *charisma*, since a list of the ministry gifts to the church follow (4:11).

6. In the Pastorals 1 Tim. 1:12–16 alludes autobiographically to Rom. 5:20b. In 2 Tim. 1:9 Paul builds the connection of God's purpose and the grace of Christ (cf. Rom. 8:28, 32) and gives with Tit. 2:11 a doxology of joy over the present revelation of grace. As in Eph., grace and salvation are connected in 2:11: Grace works to train us away from the world and toward our eschatological hope.

In Tit. 3:7 grace has a double connection. It refers back to the Savior Jesus Christ, who pours out the renewing Holy Spirit (cf. 3:5–6). At the same time, it is related to justification in the truly Pauline sense ("justified by his grace"). Christ's grace brings about (also forensically) the appointment of heirs to future life. The Pastorals say nothing more about individual gifts of grace, but only speak of grace for office (2 Tim. 2:1). *charisma* is passed on through the laying on of hands (1 Tim. 4:14; 2 Tim. 1:6).

7. Of the remaining NT letters 1 Pet. and Heb. come nearest to Paul's understanding of grace. (a) Like Eph. and Col., 1 Pet. does not specifically link grace and justification. It speaks of God's grace that is given through Christ (1:10, announced by the prophets), the future revelation of which determines conduct and hope (1:13), and as stewards of which, in its manifold forms (4:10; 5:10), Christians should live. Grace also permits the endurance of undeserved suffering to be understood as approved by God (2:19–20; cf. 5:10). In the concluding message the standing of the addressees in grace is confirmed as true (5:12).

(b) Heb. 2:9 portrays *charis* as God's care in salvation history, which is made effective in Jesus' substitutionary death. Therefore the throne on which Christ sits to rule is "a throne of grace" (4:16). Here forgiveness can be received from the one who can sympathize with the weak, for he has identified himself with them as high priest. The remaining texts in Heb. are concerned with the problem of cheap grace. To abuse the spiritual gift by one's way of life is worse than transgressing the Mosaic law (10:29); grace once abandoned cannot be regained (12:15–17). But firmness of heart remains, in spite of all exhortations, a gift of God and not the result of keeping special regulations (13:9).

(c) The danger of falling away occurs in Jas. 4:6; the Spirit's offer of gifts outweighs his yearning demands (there follows a quotation from Prov. 3:34; cf. 1 Pet. 5:5). In 2 Pet. 3:18 the author paradoxically exhorts us to grow in grace, in contrast to falling from our own firm position (cf. Gal. 5:4 with 1 Cor. 12:31). Jude 4 warns against the misuse of grace to satisfy our passions, a danger Paul had already repulsed in Rom. 6:1.

5922 (*charisma*, gift given out of goodwill, spiritual gift), → *5921*.

5923 (*charitoō*, endue with grace), → *5921*.

| 5931   χείρ |

χείρ (*cheir*), hand (*5931*); δάκτυλος (*daktylos*), finger (*1235*); χειροποίητος (*cheiropoiētos*), man-made, made by human hands (*5935*).

CL & OT   1. In cl. Gk. *cheir* is the hand, the member of the human body that we put to the most active use, serving us both in our work and in defense of ourselves. Our strength and energy are made effective through our hands. In the pl. *cheires* and *dynameis* (power[s]) can be used as synonyms. When linked with a personal name, *cheir* stands as a substitute for the person.

2. The OT speaks of a person's activity as the work of one's hand. The hand is a symbol of human power. Thus, to fall into someone's hand means to come into their power (Gen. 32:11; Jdg. 2:14; Jer. 27:6–8 = LXX 34:6–8). In 2 Sam. 18:18 *cheir* means a mark or monument (cf. Isa. 56:5).

This word is also a symbol for divine omnipotence (2 Chr. 20:6; Ps. 89:21). God's hand created heaven and earth, and with his hand he controls them (Isa. 48:13). For Israel God's hand means salvation and release; but for their enemies, destruction and ruin (Exod. 7:4; 9:3; 1 Sam. 7:13). The hand of the Lord is used to express both God's righteous punishment (5:6, 11), and his loving care (Ezr. 7:6; Job 5:18; Ps. 145:16; Isa. 49:16) and divine protection (51:16).

3. Both in fig. language about God and with reference to humans the two hands do not have equal status. A higher value is placed on the right, because it is the one that is active (Exod. 15:6, 12; Ps. 118:15–16; Isa. 41:13; cf. Matt. 5:30; → *dexios, 1288*). Hands can serve to express displeasure and passionate excitement (Num. 24:10),

but also humble supplication (2 Chr. 6:12–13; Ps. 28:2), joy (47:1), sorrow (Jer. 2:37), solemn oath (Gen. 14:22; 24:2, 9; 47:29; Ezr. 10:19), and loyal citizenship (Prov. 6:1–5; 22:26). The "sign on your hand" (Exod. 13:9, 16; Deut. 6:8; 11:18) is a picturesque way of expressing constant remembrance of God's saving acts and of his commands. To fill someone's hand means to install him to priestly office (Num. 3:3). Washing the hands not only fulfills the laws concerning purification (Exod. 30:18–21) but also signifies an affirmation of innocence and a clear conscience (Deut. 21:6; Ps. 26:6; cf. Job 17:9; Ps. 24:4; Matt. 27:24).

NT   1. *cheir* occurs 177x in the NT. It is often used lit. in the combination *podes kai cheires*, feet and hands (Matt. 18:8; 22:13; Lk. 24:39; Jn. 11:44; Acts 21:11). The phrase *dia cheiros tinos* (also pl.), through someone, by someone (e.g., Mk. 6:2; Acts 5:12; 7:25; 11:30), is a Semitism representing the Heb. *bᵉyād*, by, with. The hands can stand for a person (17:25). *cheir* is used 25x times in connection with the laying on of hands (→ *epithēmi, 2202*).

2. As in the OT, the hand of the Lord denotes the embodiment of divine power. It is applied to Christ in Jn. 3:35; 10:28; 13:3. God's hand works in creation (Acts 7:50; Heb. 1:10) and in his plan of salvation (Acts 4:28). It expresses God's righteous punishment (13:11; Heb. 10:31) and the special care (Lk. 1:66), security, and protection (23:46; Jn. 10:29) he grants to all who trust him. God's hand indicates his wonder-working power with which he accompanies the apostolic proclamation of the gospel (Acts 4:30; 11:21). God can operate "through [an] angel" (lit., "by the hand of an angel, " 7:35). God's hand also indicates his hidden wisdom with which he leads his people on earth through suffering (1 Pet. 5:6). Hand, finally, can be a periphrasis for a hostile power, into whose control a person is delivered (esp. Matt. 17:22; 26:45; Acts 21:11), but from whose hand one can also be set free (12:11; 2 Cor. 11:33).

3. *cheir* is frequently used in connection with the verb *ekteinō*, to stretch out. Thus Jesus commanded a sick man to stretch out his hand (Matt. 12:13; Mk. 3:5; Lk. 6:10). He stretched out his own hand to heal (Matt. 8:3; Mk. 1:41; Lk. 5:13; cf. Acts 4:30). Stretching out the hand can be an orator's gesture (Matt. 12:49; Acts 26:1). It can happen with hostile intent (Lk. 22:53) or refer indirectly to a disciple's death by crucifixion (Jn. 21:18).

4. The Jewish practice of ceremonially washing one's hands before meals (Mk. 7:1–4) is condemned by Jesus as an instance of scrupulous observance of an outward human ordinance, practiced to the neglect of God's Word (7:6–13; cf. Isa. 29:13; Matt. 15:8–9) and the failure to realize that evil comes from the heart (Mk. 7:14–23; cf. Matt. 15:10–20). Pilate's act of washing his hands before the crowd (27:24) was a public gesture disclaiming responsibility. Although the crowd accepted responsibility for Jesus' blood, the gesture was empty, for moral responsibility cannot be disposed of by outward gestures.

5. The human finger (*daktylos*) is mentioned in Matt. 23:4; Mk. 7:33; Lk. 11:46; 16:24; Jn. 8:6; 20:25, 27. The expression "finger of God" (Lk. 11:20) is paralleled in Matt. 12:28 by "Spirit of God." Since this phrase is similar to one in Exod. 8:19 concerning God's power in the events of the exodus, presumably Jesus here is defining his own mission in terms of the exodus (cf. esp. *exodos* as used in Lk. 9:31; → *3847*).

6. *cheiropoiētos*, made by human hands, underlines the distinction between God's action and those of humans (Mk. 14:58; Acts 7:48; 17:24; Eph. 2:11; Heb. 9:11, 24). It is esp. used to contrast the building of a dwelling-place for God done by humans (e.g., tabernacle or temple) with the dwelling place he has built for himself (e.g., the heavenly sanctuary).

See also *dexios*, right, right hand, right side (*1288*); *aristeros*, left, left hand (*754*); *epitithēmi*, to put on, lay on (*2202*); *cheirotoneō*, choose, appoint (*5936*).

5935 (*cheiropoiētos*, man-made, made by human hands), → *5931*.

5936 χειροτονέω

χειροτονέω (*cheirotoneō*), appoint (*5936*); προχειροτονέω (*procheirotoneō*), appoint beforehand (*4742*).

CL & OT *cheirotoneō*, from *cheir*, hand, and *teinō*, stretch, means to vote or elect by a show of hands, as was regularly done in the Athenian assembly. From this the verb came to mean appoint, and its *pro*-compound means appoint beforehand.

NT In 2 Cor. 8:19 *cheirotoneō* refers to the churches' appointment of a representative to accompany Paul to Jerusalem to deliver the collection; in Acts 14:23 it refers to Paul's and Barnabas's appointment of elders in the Galatian churches. In 10:41 *procheirotoneō* signifies God's appointment of the apostles, prior to Jesus' resurrection, to be witnesses of that event.

See also *kathistēmi*, bring, appoint, (*2770*); *horizō*, determine, appoint (*3988*); *paristēmi*, place, put at the disposal of (*4225*); *procheirizō*, determine, appoint (*4741*); *tassō*, arrange, appoint (*5435*); *tithēmi*, put, place, set, appoint (*5502*); *prothesmia*, appointed date (*4607*); *lanchanō*, obtain as by lot (*3275*).

5938 χερούβ

χερούβ (*cheroub*), cherub (*5938*).

OT *cheroub* is a transliteration of the Heb. word *kᵉrûb* (pl. *kᵉrûbîm* or *kᵉrūbîm*), a winged heavenly messenger sometimes associated with the seraph (cf. Isa. 6:2–6). Cherubim guarded the way to the tree of life (Gen. 3:24) and either support or flank God's throne (Ps. 80:1; 99:1; Isa. 37:16). Their swiftness in flight is likened to the wind (2 Sam. 22:11; cf. Ps. 18:10). Two wooden replicas of cherubim, gold covered and with wings outspread, were placed over the atonement cover of the ark, protecting the holy things and forming a pedestal for Yahweh's throne (Exod. 25:17–21; 37:7–9; cf. Num. 7:89). Cherubim adorned the inmost curtains of the tabernacle and the veil that separated off the Most Holy Place (Exod. 26:1, 31); they symbolized the heavenly hosts of the Lord (1 Sam. 4:4; 2 Sam. 6:2; 2 Ki. 19:15; 1 Chr. 13:6). In descriptions of Solomon's temple emphasis is placed on the size of the cherubim, whose wings spanned the width of the sanctuary (1 Ki. 6:23–28; 2 Chr. 3:10–13).

Among the prophets only Ezek. mentions the word (apart from Isa. 37:16). The golden cherubim on which had rested the glory of the God of Israel were deserted (Ezek. 9:3), and the Lord was to be found among living cherubim, who carried out his every wish (10:1–20; cf. also 1:5–24). Cherubim also guard the presence of God (cf. 28:14–16).

Later Jud. meditated much on Ezek.'s chariot throne, but speculation was discouraged by the rabbis, and the Mishnah prohibited liturgical use of Ezek.'s chapters on the chariot. In a fragment from Qumran the cherubim utter blessings, accompanied by a still small voice (cf. 1 Ki. 19:12) as they move their wings. A similar interest in the heavenly throne is found in *1 Enoch* (14:11, 18; 20:7).

NT *cheroub* occurs only in Heb. 9:5, where the phrase "the cherubim of the Glory" is used in a description of the Most Holy Place. The book of the Rev., without using the word, describes in terms reminiscent of both cherubim and seraphim (4:6–8) the living creatures who worship the one on the throne. Cherubim are specifically associated with God's throne, whether in heaven or in its earthly counterpart. They stand guard, support the throne, and act as swift messengers of the Lord of hosts, whom they worship.

See also *angelos*, angel (*34*).

5939 χήρα

χήρα (*chēra*), widow (*5939*).

CL & OT 1. In cl. Gk. *chēra* is fem. of the adj. *chēros*, deprived, and means a woman deprived (of her husband), i.e., a widow.

2. (a) In the LXX *chēra* connotes not only a woman who has lost her husband but also the accompanying ideas of loneliness, abandonment, and helplessness. Widows are regarded in a special way as in need of protection, mentioned often in association with orphans and aliens (e.g., Exod. 22:22, 24; Deut. 10:18; 24:17–21). Their difficult condition had its basis in the social and legal status of women (→ *gynē*, woman, *1222*), esp. with regard to certain regulations of the law of inheritance.

(b) Yahweh receives widows to himself. They should put their trust in him (Jer. 49:11 = LXX 29:11), for he executes justice for them (Deut. 10:18; Ps. 68:5; Prov. 15:25; Mal. 3:5) and upholds them (Ps. 146:9). Therefore, his people also are called to maintain the widows' rights and to have compassion on them. Otherwise, they will bring down his wrath upon themselves (Deut. 27:19; cf. also Exod. 22:22–24; Isa. 1:17–23; 10:2; Jer. 7:6; 22:3; Zech. 7:10).

(c) Accordingly, in the OT various laws are given to ease the condition of widows. Their clothes should not be taken in pledge (Deut. 24:17); in the third year the tithe should be for their benefit (14:29; 26:12–13); and the gleanings of the field should be left for them, among others (24:19–21). Widows are to be invited to the sacrificial meals and to the feasts (16:11, 14) and thus have their place in the congregation. According to Lev. 22:12–13, the widowed daughters of priests have a share of the offering if they return childless to their fathers (cf. also 2 Macc. 3:10; 8:28, 30). Nevertheless, complaint about the unjust and merciless treatment of widows pervades the OT (e.g., Isa. 1:23; Ezek. 22:7; Mal. 3:5; Wis. 2:10).

(d) A plethora of legal questions, above all about the right of inheritance, arises when the remarriage of widows is considered. There are two restrictions. (i) A high priest may not marry a widow (Lev. 21:14). (ii) From the earliest times there are indications that a widow could be made an heiress to properties (cf. Ezek. 22:10; also Gen. 35:22; 2 Sam. 16:20–22; 1 Ki. 2:13–22).

(e) Isa. 47:8 uses *chēra* in a metaphorical sense for Babylon (cf. Rev. 18:7). But for Israel there stands, as the new divine covenant, the promise that the reproach of her widowhood (i.e., the exile) will no more be remembered (cf. Isa. 54:4).

NT 1. The Gospels speak of difficult circumstances for a widow: e.g., her need for persistent legal action (Lk. 18:1–5), the abuse of her trust (Mk. 12:40), and her poverty (12:41–44).

2. The NT churches also recognized their responsibility for the widow. The strongest expression occurs in Jas., where all outward veneration of God in worship is contrasted with the care of widows and orphans (1:27). In the church at Jerusalem there was at an early date an organized provision for widows. The murmuring of the Hel. group that their widows were being put at a disadvantage to Aram.-speaking widows led to the choice of seven men from the Hel. section to take charge of care for these widows (Acts 6:1–6).

3. In the later NT period, a distinction is drawn between ordinary widows and "widows who are really in need" (1 Tim. 5:3–16). For the latter category, if the widow is truly left alone (5:5), the church should provide for her (5:16); but if she has relatives, they are duty-bound to care for her (5:4, 16). The real widows were included in an official list of widows (5:9) and seem to have held some sort of office in the church. They had to be over sixty years old and to have been the wife of only one man (5:9). They also had to be "well known for . . . good deeds" (5:10), such as bringing up orphans, hospitality, and readiness for humble service. Those enrolled seem to have taken a decision not to marry again.

Younger widows, by contrast, were not to be put on the list of widows, for they would be ensnared too easily by laziness and become busybodies (1 Tim. 5:13). Rather, they were to be encouraged to remarry (5:14).

See also *gynē*, woman (*1222*); *mētēr*, mother (*3613*); *parthenos*, maiden, virgin (*4221*).

5941 (*chiliarchos*, commander), → *5942*.

5942 χιλιάς	χιλιάς (*chilias*), a thousand (*5942*); χίλιοι (*chilioi*), a thou-

sand (*5943*); χιλίαρχος (*chiliarchos*), commander (*5941*).

CL & OT 1. Both nouns are in cl. Gk. and the LXX, although *chilias* (250x) is more frequent in the LXX, esp. in Num. and the historical books. *chiliarchos* in cl. Gk. denotes a leader of a thousand soldiers; it was used in Roman times of the *tribunus militum*, the military tribune.

2. The number 1,000 frequently occurs in the numbering of the tribes (e.g., Num. 1:23–46; 2:4–32; 1 Chr. 7:2–40). The OT historical books display an interest in the thousands involved in battles (Jdg. 1:4; 3:29; 4:6–14; 1 Sam. 4:2, 10; 6:19; 2 Sam. 10:6, 18; 24:9, 15; 1 Chr. 12:20–37) and in the numbers involved in building Solomon's temple (1 Ki. 5:11–16; 2 Chr. 2:2–18). There is, however, a strong case for thinking that in many contexts "thousand" (Heb. ʾelep) does not lit. mean a thousand but was a term for a considerably smaller unit or perhaps meant ʾallûp, captain of a band; this would make feasible the apparently large numbers in many OT records. Ezek. is concerned with the measurement and proportions of the land, representing the perfect ordering of the people of God (45:1–6; 48:8–35).

3. The pl. *chiliades* is often used for large numbers that cannot be counted. God shows steadfast love to thousands of those who love him and keep his commands (Exod. 20:6; cf. 34:7; Deut. 5:10; 7:9; Jer. 32:18 = LXX 39:18). His power is described in terms of mighty chariots, "tens of thousands and thousands of thousands" (Ps. 68:17). The greatness of Yahweh is also expressed in 90:4: "For a thousand years in your sight are like a day that has just gone by, or like a watch in the night" (cf. 2 Pet. 3:8). What to us seems a great age is as a moment to Yahweh. Note also the confession of the psalmist: "Better is one day in your courts than a thousand elsewhere" (Ps. 84:10).

4. In intertestamental lit. innumerable hosts figure in the apocalyptic writings of *1 Enoch* 14:22; 40:1. The notion of thousands features in eschatological expectation: e.g., the thousands of children of the righteous and the superabundance of wine (10:17, 19). The number also features in speculations about the duration of the world and the new aeon, which include the idea of a cosmic week of seven millennia followed in some instances by a new era, an eighth millennium (*T. Ab.* B 7:16). The length of the messianic age varies from 1,000 years to 7,000 years.

5. One thousand features in the military structure of the Qumran community (CD 13:1–2; 1QS 2:21–22). Each thousand had its commander to lead it into battle (1QM 4:2; 1QSa 1:14, 29). The community believed that those who kept God's law would live a thousand generations (CD 7:6; 19:1–2; cf. Deut. 7:9).

NT 1. Various multiples of 1,000 occur in the NT. *dischilioi* (2,000), was the approximate number of the Gerasene swine (Mk. 5:13). About 3,000 (*trischilioi*) souls were added to the church at Pentecost (Acts 2:41). About 5,000 men heard and believed the word (4:4). The same number were fed by Jesus (Matt. 14:21; Mk. 6:44; 8:19; Lk. 9:14; Jn. 6:10); on another occasion it was 4,000 (Matt. 15:38; Mk. 8:9, 20). Acts 21:38 mentions the revolt of the Egyptian who led 4,000 men.

In dealing with the question whether God has rejected Israel for good, Paul recalls the remnant of 7,000 who did not bow the knee to Baal (Rom. 11:4; cf. 1 Ki. 19:18). This instance is at the same time a reminder that God is the one who preserves the remnant and that those who are saved are "chosen by grace" (Rom. 11:5); the alternative is salvation "by works" (11:6). In 1 Cor. 10:8 Paul recalls how 23,000 of the desert generation fell in a single day through idolatry (cf. Num. 25:1–18).

The military sense of a thousand is perhaps present in Jesus' question whether a king should first take counsel before meeting with 10,000 men his adversary who is coming against him with 20,000 (Lk. 14:31). Confronted by overwhelming odds, the first king sends an embassy and asks for peace. The illustration implies not only the need

to count the cost of discipleship but also the impossibility of finding an alternative way out.

2. In NT times, a *chiliarchos* commanded a cohort of about 600 men (e.g., Jn. 18:12; Acts 21:31–37; 22:24–29; 23:10, 15–22; 25:23). The word is used of a high ranking officer generally in Mk. 6:21; Rev. 6:15; 19:18.

3. *chilioi* occurs 2x in 2 Pet. 3:8 with reference to Ps. 90:4, where the readers are urged: "But do not forget this one thing, dear friends: With the Lord a day is like a thousand years, and a thousand years are like a day." The context is concerned with human indifference and sin in the light of the apparent delay of the day of the Lord. But God is not bound by the time scale of the physical world. The reason for the delay of the Parousia is God's patience, "not wanting anyone to perish, but everyone to come to repentance" (2 Pet. 3:9).

4. The remaining nine uses of *chilioi* are found in Rev. (11:3; 12:6; 14:20; 20:2–7). In addition, *chilias* occurs 19x in this book (5:11; 7:4–8; 11:13; 14:1, 3; 21:16), representing an apocalyptic interpretation of OT themes. (a) Rev. 5:11 takes up the picture in Dan. 7:10, of the heavenly hosts numbering "thousands upon thousands ... ten thousand times ten thousand," praising God. In contrast to the OT, this picture receives a Christological interpretation, for the object of their praise is the Lamb (Rev. 5:12–14).

(b) Rev. 7:4 gives the number of the sealed as "144,000 from all the tribes of Israel" (cf. 14:1–2). Rev. 7:5–8 enumerate the tribes by name, specifying "12,000" out of each tribe. The numbers used symbolize the final perfection of the people of God, based on the concept of the twelve tribes of Israel (→ *dōdeka, 1557*) and asserting historical continuity with Israel. Note that when Jn. hears the number, he hears these round numbers. But when he actually sees the multitude, the numbers are replaced by a countless host of all nations: "After this I looked and there before me was a great multitude that no one could count, from every nation, tribe, people and language, standing before the throne and in front of the Lamb" (7:9).

(c) Rev. 11:3; 12:6 mention a period of "1,260 days." This corresponds to the 42 months of 11:2; 13:5 and the "time, times and half a time" of 12:14. In 11:3 it is the period of prophecy, while in 12:6 it is the period of persecution. Both passages refer to the same period: the age of the church, which is one of prophetic witness and at the same time one of persecution. In light of eternity it is a comparatively short period, though when expressed in terms of days it may seem lengthy. In the background stands Dan. 7:25; 12:7, a period that is half of seven, the perfect number, comprising severe affliction, which continues until God accomplishes the end of all things. This affliction is described in Rev. 11:7–10 (cf. 12:2–6); it will culminate in the judgment of civilization (11:13). The 7,000 who perish in the earthquake represent the complete judgment on godless, secular society; the rest who are terrified and give glory to God represent those who respond to the witness and God's judgments.

(d) Rev. 14:20 depicts judgment on the civilized world in terms of the sack of a city: "They were trampled in the winepress outside the city, and blood flowed out of the press, rising as high as the horses' bridles for a distance of 1,600 stadia" (i.e., approx. 200 miles). This number is a square number, comparable with the 144,000 and the dimensions of the Jerusalem (cf. 7:4; 14:1; 21:16). It suggests the area of the four parts of the earth, i.e., the whole earth; the passage refers to the last judgment (cf. 19:11–21).

(e) By contrast, the area of the holy city, the new Jerusalem, is also square, which again indicates completeness: "The city was laid out like a square, as long as it was wide. He measured the city with the rod and found it to be 12,000 stadia in length, and as wide and high as it is long" (Rev. 21:16). The number twelve goes back in this case to the twelve tribes and the 12,000 from each tribe. Thus, the completeness of the new Jerusalem corresponds to the completeness of the people of God.

(f) Rev. 20:2–7 contains six references to a period of 1,000 years, the period commonly called the millennium: a thousand-year age of restoration in which evil is banished. The idea of a messianic kingdom, preceding the end and the coming reign of God, is attested in various Jewish apocalyptic documents (e.g., *1 Enoch* 91:12–13; 93:1–14; *2 Esd.* 7:28–29; *2 Bar.* 29:3; 30:1–5; 40:3). It extends the older idea of a Davidic king restoring the monarchy by combining it with that of universal judgment, resurrection, and the new aeon. The number 1,000 is probably connected with the idea of the cosmic week and Ps. 90:4.

In the early church belief in some form of a literal millennium is attested by, e.g., Papias, Irenaeus, Justin Martyr, and Tertullian. It was attacked by Origen and rejected by Augustine. In addition to apocalyptic ideas, Rev. 20 draws on Ezek. 36–48 with its visions of the resurrection of Israel, the conflict with Gog and Magog, and the promise of a new Jerusalem.

In modern times three main schools of thought have emerged concerning Rev. 20. The *premillennialists* treat the passage as future prophecy, in which Christ's second coming precedes the millennium. Satan will be bound for 1,000 years, the martyred dead will be raised, and Christ will reign as King of kings and Lord of lords from Jerusalem. The millennium will end with the final rebellion of Satan, but this will itself be put down. The resurrection and judgment of the wicked dead will precede the creation of the new heaven and earth. *Postmillennialists* see the second coming of Christ and the events of Rev. 20 as coming in the last thousand years of the present age. *Amillennialists* see the whole passage essentially as a symbolic description of the present age, in which Satan is already bound and the dead in Christ are already reigning with him.

The interpretation of Rev. 20 depends partly on how this vision is seen in relation to the entire book of Rev. Those who see the different visions as successive tend to see the millennium as the last of a series: a unique event immediately prior to the creation of a new heaven and a new earth. But a strong case can be made for seeing the book as structured into seven series of visions, each looking at the church in the gospel age. The visions are thus seven sets of parallel visions of the church and its tribulations between the two advents of Christ. On this view the period of a thousand years refers to the present era, culminating in a final outburst of satanic activity prior to the final destruction of all the evils that afflict humankind.

According to this interpretation, the vision of the binding of Satan has its roots in the saying of Jesus about the binding of the strong man, who must first be bound before his goods may be plundered (Matt. 12:29). The activity of Jesus is itself evidence of the binding of Satan. Furthermore, the gospel is being spread among the Gentile nations, which previously had been deceived by Satan (cf. Rev. 20:3). There is also a sense in which Satan has already fallen in power, evidenced by the power of the disciples over demons (Lk. 10:17–18; cf. Jn. 12:31; Col. 2:15). The first resurrection refers to the reign of the saints with Christ now (cf. Rev. 4:2–10; 5:6–13; 7:9–17; 12:5; 14:3, 5; 19:4–5).

This interpretation is in harmony with that of Jesus and Paul, neither of whom speak of a period of 1,000 years and into whose teaching such a period cannot easily be inserted (Matt. 24:4–36; 1 Cor. 15:20–28; 1 Thess. 5:1–11; 2 Thess. 2:1–12). Moreover, nowhere does Scripture speak clearly of two second comings of Christ: one before the millennium and one after. It seems best, therefore, to recognize the symbolic character of the apocalyptic language of Rev. 20 and see an eschatology in process of realization.

5943 (chilioi, a thousand), → *5942.*

5946 (chiōn, snow), → *847.*

5950 (chliaros, lukewarm), → *6037.*

5954 (choikos, made of soil), → *5967.*

5958	χολή

χολή (*cholē*), gall, bile (*5958*); ὄξος (*oxos*), wine vinegar (*3954*).

CL & OT *cholē* appears to refer first of all to the color of bile, from which it came to be used of gall or bile itself. The impressive thing was clearly its bitter taste. The word was also used for bitter anger or wrath. *oxos* was a wine vinegar popular among the lower ranks of society; it relieved thirst more effectively than water.

In the LXX *cholē* translates a variety of Heb. words and can mean gall (Deut. 32:32; Ps. 69:21; Prov. 5:4; Lam. 3:15) or venom (poison) (Job 20:14). On occasion it refers to a plant (e.g., Deut. 29:18; 32:32), but it remains uncertain which plant is meant. *oxos* occurs several times in the LXX, including Num. 6:3 (as one of the fermented drinks forbidden to the Nazirites) and Ps. 69:21 (see NT).

NT *cholē* is used in a lit. sense of the gall mixed with wine that was offered to Jesus as the soldiers prepared to crucify him (Matt. 27:34). In view of the parallel in Mk. 15:23, it seems that the word here refers to myrrh. This drink was perhaps a narcotic in order to dull Jesus' senses and alleviate pain, but he refused the sedative and heroically endured his sufferings to the end. Later Jesus did receive wine vinegar (*oxos*) in order to alleviate thirst (Matt. 27:48; Mk. 15:36; Lk. 23:36; Jn. 19:29–30). Both drinks may be seen as a fulfillment of Ps. 69:21.

cholē is also used metaphorically, which is important for understanding Acts 8:23. Simon Peter charged Simon Magus with being (lit.) "in the gall (*cholē*) of bitterness" when he offered the apostle money for the gift of conferring the Holy Spirit by the laying on of hands. To have such a complete misunderstanding of Christianity was not simply to be pleasantly mistaken; rather, it was to find oneself in a situation that must be described as bitterness. Simon had an inkling of what Christianity was all about. He had welcomed the gospel and accepted baptism. It is an exceedingly bitter thing when a man of whom so much might well have been expected proves to be so completely out of harmony with the gospel. He was caught in a bitter bondage to sin.

5963	χορτάζω

χορτάζω (*chortazō*), to feed, fatten (*5963*); χόρτασμα (*chortasma*), used mostly in pl., fodder (*5964*); χόρτος (*chortos*), enclosed pasturage, fodder (*5965*).

CL & OT 1. In early Gk. *chortazō* was used uniformly of animals, but in the exaggeration of comedy it was applied to humans feasting. Under the influence of colloquial use, it became virtually the equivalent of *esthiō*, to eat. *chortos*, feeding place, fodder for animals, implies primarily grass or hay for horses and cattle, though it could be used poetically for food in general.

2. In the LXX *chortazō* carries the basic idea of satisfying with food (Ps. 37:19; 59:15; 132:15). By extension, the ground is satisfied with rain (Job 38:27), the trees with water (Ps. 104:16), and the earth with the fruit of God's works (104:13). On two occasions disillusion is expressed (Jer. 5:7; Lam. 3:15, 30), but more often the depth of satisfaction goes beyond that of mere food to that of seeing and knowing God (Ps. 17:15; 81:16; 107:9).

chortasma denotes "fodder" (Gen. 24:25, 32; 43:24; Jdg. 19:19) and "grass" once (Deut. 11:15). *chortos* (used 50x) translates a variety of Heb. words for grass and plants, which include human food (e.g., Gen. 1:29; 2:5; 3:18; Ps. 37:2; Isa. 15:6). Because grass grows in Palestine only during the period of the winter and spring rains and withers immediately when the heat comes, it is a ready illustration of the brevity and transitory nature of human life, esp. in the poetic books (Job 13:25; Ps. 37:2; 102:4, 11; 103:15; Isa. 37:27; 40:6–7). Defeated enemies are like down-trodden grass (2 Ki. 19:26).

NT In the NT *chortazō* almost invariably means to eat or to satisfy with food, as in the accounts of the feeding of the five and four thousand (Matt. 14:20; 15:33; Mk. 6:42; 8:4, 8; Lk. 9:17; Jn. 6:26). The Evangelists all stress that the crowds not only ate but were satisfied, so taking up the sense of *chortazō* in the LXX of Ps., and Jesus promises the same in the Beatitudes (Matt. 5:6; Lk. 6:21). That all distinction between this vb. and *esthiō* has vanished is clear from Mk. 7:27–28, where *esthiō* is used for the pet dogs and *chortazō* for the children. The only other occurrences of the verb are in Lk. 16:21, Phil. 4:12; Jas. 2:16; Rev. 19:21.

chortasma occurs once only in the sense of food (Acts 7:11). *chortos* is used of growing plants (Matt. 13:26; Mk. 4:28) and of grass in general (6:39; Jn. 6:10; Rev. 8:7; 9:4). The short life of the grass of the field is used by Jesus in an assurance that God will clothe his children (Matt. 6:30; Lk. 12:28). Jas. and Pet. both quote from Isa. 40:7–8 (Jas. 1:10–11; 1 Pet. 1:24), emphasizing the shortness of human life. *chortos* also illustrates living a Christian life with works that do not glorify God but serve one's own interests (1 Cor. 3:12); people who live this way may be saved, but their life's work will go up in the flames of God's judgment (3:13–15).

See also *gemō*, to load, be full (*1154*); *perisseuō*, be more than enough, abound, excel (*4355*); *plēthos*, number, multitude, crowd (*4436*); *plēroō*, fill, complete, fulfill, accomplish, carry out (*4444*); *chōreō*, have or make room, give way, go (*6003*).

5964 (*chortasma*, fodder), → *5963*.

5965 (*chortos*, enclosed pasturage, fodder), → *5963*.

5967	χοῦς

χοῦς (*chous*), soil, dust (*5967*); χοϊκός (*choikos*), made of soil (*5954*).

CL & OT *chous* is used by the cl. historians Herodotus and Thucydides to describe excavated or heaped up soil. This same word, in the sense of "dirt" or "dust," is used extensively in the LXX to translate the Heb. *ʿāpār*. In similes it often signifies a tiny or worthless object (e.g., Ps. 35:5; Isa. 17:13; cf. Neh. 4:10). Enemies lick up *chous* in humiliation, while the penitent and bereaved pour it over their heads in grief (Jos. 7:6; Lam. 2:10). Significantly, it was out of *chous* that God made the first man (Gen. 2:7; Ps. 102:14), and it is to *chous* that humans return when they die (Eccl. 3:20; 12:7).

NT *chous* appears twice in the NT, where it refers to the dust of the road (Mk. 6:11) and to dirt thrown on one's head as a sign of mourning (Rev. 18:19). *choikos* is used 4x, all in 1 Cor. 15:47–49, where Paul distinguishes "the first man" as God created him (cf. Gen. 2:7) from Jesus, "the second man," whose origin is heavenly.

See also *gē*, earth, world (*1178*); *oikoumenē*, earth (*3876*); *agros*, field (*69*); *kosmos*, adornment, world (*3180*).

5970	χρεία

χρεία (*chreia*), need, necessity, lack, want (*5970*); χρή (*chrē*), there is a need, it is necessary (*5973*); χρήζω (*chrēzō*), to have need of (*5974*).

CL & OT 1. (a) In cl. Gk. *chreia* has the basic sense of need, want, necessity. The proverb that necessity is the mother of invention stems from a statement of Euripides that "necessity teaches wisdom even to the sluggish." From this primary notion of need developed the derivative ideas of office, duty, service, business. This same range of nuance occurs in the Hel. period, where *chreia* designates need or necessity. But the noun also signifies now occasion of need.

(b) The vb. form *chrē*, it is necessary, one must or ought to, is common in cl. Gk. In Hel. Gk. it recedes into the background and is almost totally displaced by *dei*. The parallel vb. *chrēzō* occurs throughout the period with the meaning to want, lack, have need of something. From the Hel. period we find the observation that those who drink wine need much discretion as well as the ethical injunction that if you have nothing to give to a person in need, show compassion.

2. The noun *chreia* is rare in the canonical books of the LXX but occurs frequently in the Apocr. (20x in Sir. alone). Its primary meaning is necessity or need, often denoting a need for something or someone. Thus the Medes have no need of gold (Isa. 13:17); a fool has no

need of wisdom (Prov. 18:2); God has no need of sinful humans (Sir. 15:12). The secondary meaning of office, duty, service also occurs in the Apocr., where we read of service in the temple (1 Esd. 8:17; 1 Macc. 10:42), fulfillment of duty (Sir. 32:2 = LXX 35:2), administration of public affairs (1 Macc. 10:37; 2 Macc. 7:24), or holding an office (1 Macc. 13:15). From this last nuance it was easy to shift the focus from the office to the officials, also termed *chreia* (12:45; 13:37).

chrē occurs only once in the LXX (Prov. 25:27; cf. 4 Macc. 8:26 A), while the more usual Hel. *chrēzō* occurs 2x (Jdg. 11:7 B; 1 Sam. 17:18 A).

NT 1. (a) In the primary sense of need, lack, want, we read of David, who was in need and was hungry (Mk. 2:25), of distribution made to anyone in Jerusalem "as he had need" (Acts 2:45; 4:35), and of seeing one's fellow believer "in need" (1 Jn. 3:17). Epaphroditus is described as the one who supplied Paul's need (Phil. 2:25; cf. 4:16, 19). In the pl. the noun designates needs or necessities (Acts 20:34; 28:10; Rom. 12:13; Tit. 3:14).

(b) In combination with the vb. "to have," *chreia* functions as an act. verb "to need" (lit., "to have need of"). The healthy have no need of a physician (Mk. 2:17); the owner has need of his animals (11:13); the court has no further need for witnesses (14:63). The church of Laodicea boasts, "I am rich . . . and do not need a thing" (Rev. 3:17).

(c) The secondary meaning of office, duty, service is found in the NT only in reference to the seven Hel. leaders: "We will turn this responsibility over to them" (Acts 6:3).

2. The rare term *chrē* occurs only once in the NT, in a comment of Jas. that "this [to both bless and curse from the same mouth] should not be" (3:10). The more usual *chrēzō* occurs 5x (Matt. 6:32; Lk. 11:8; 12:30; Rom. 16:2; 2 Cor. 3:1). When speaking of need, the NT writers usually use the phrase "to have a need [*chreia*]."

See also *hysteros*, what is behind, after, later (*5731*); *dei*, it is necessary (*1256*).

5973 (*chrē*, there is a need, it is necessary), → *5970*.

5974 (*chrēzō*, to have need of), → *5970*.

5975	χρῆμα

χρῆμα (*chrēma*), property, wealth, means, money (*5975*); κτῆμα (*ktēma*), property, possessions, (esp. in later usage) landed property (*3228*); ὕπαρξις (*hyparxis*), property (*5638*); τὰ ὑπάρχοντα (*ta hyparchonta*), what belongs to someone, property, goods, possessions (*5639*); οὐσία (*ousia*), substance, property (*4045*).

CL & OT 1. In cl. Gk. *chrēma* (derived from *chrē*, it is necessary) stands for what is necessary, then goods and riches (mostly pl.). In the sing. it normally means quantity of, also money. *ktēma* (derived from *ktaomai*, buy, gain) means that which has been gained. It is used for possessions of every kind but later was confined to landed property. *hyparxis* means existence, then property, riches.

2. *chrēma* in Job 27:17; 2 Chr. 1:11–12 means money (in the latter together with *ploutos*, → *4458*), while in Dan. 11:24, 28 it is the rich booty taken in war. *ktēma* in Job 20:29 has the general meaning of possessions or heritage, but in Prov. 12:27 it denotes riches as a reward for wisdom and hard work. *ta hyparchonta* (e.g., Gen. 13:6; 31:18; Prov. 6:31; Eccl. 5:19 = LXX 5:18; 6:2) means what one has, riches, possessions. In general the OT shows no hesitation regarding the mention of riches as good and as a blessing from God (Prov. 8:21; Eccl. 5:19; 6:2). But with *hyparxis*, as with *ploutos*, there is found, esp. in Prov., a critical outlook on wealth or the dangers bound up with it (cf. Job). Possessions are not the highest good. They are trivial compared with honor (Prov. 6:35), and they deceive one into seeking protection and security in them (18:10–11; cf. also 11:28; 28:6, 11; Sir. 11:18–19; 27:1–3; 31:3–11).

NT 1. With the exception of Mk. 10:23 and Lk. 18:24 (Matt. 19:23 has *plousios*), *chrēma* is found only in Acts 4:37; 8:18, 20; 24:26 and should be translated money. The sing. of *ktēma* is found only in Acts 5:1 and means a piece of land. The pl. *ktēmata* are the estates that in Acts 2:45 are distinguished from other possessions (cf. Matt. 19:22; Mk. 10:22; Acts 5:1). The pl. part. *hyparchonta* (e.g., Matt. 19:21; 25:14; Lk. 8:3; 11:21; 12:15; Acts 4:32; 1 Cor. 13:3; Heb. 10:34) is more common than the noun *hyparxis* (used only in Acts 2:45; Heb. 10:34). It means lit. the things that belong (to someone), and thus possessions.

Occasionally other words that have their primary reference elsewhere are used to denote possessions. For *bios*, which usually means life, → *1050*. One's means of subsistence and thus property, worldly goods, is also borne out in *ousia*, substance (related to the vb. *eimi*, to be) in the sense of wealth in its sole NT occurrence (Lk. 15:12–13; cf. Tob. 14:13; 3 Macc. 3:28).

2. Jesus demanded from the rich young ruler a complete renunciation of his possessions for the sake of God's kingdom: "Sell your possessions [*ta hyparchonta*] and give to the poor" (Matt. 19:21). His riches were preventing him from following Jesus' call, for he had "great wealth [*ktēmata*]" or many estates (19:22). The fetters of possessions are so strong that a rich person can only with difficulty enter the kingdom of God. But when they are rightly used, goods can be used for good works, as in the case of the women who provided for Jesus and his disciples (Lk. 8:3) and the case of Zacchaeus (19:8; cf. also 12:33).

Lk.'s critical attitude towards wealth is shown by his being the only Evangelist to give the parables of the rich landowner (12:16–21; → *thēsauros*, *2565*) and of the rich man and Lazarus (16:19–31). Covetousness (12:15) seeks security in life from material possessions and so leads a person to destruction (→ *pleonexia*, greed, *4432*). It is one of the worst vices in a person freed by God.

3. Partially motivated by Jesus' instructions on possessions (cf. Lk. 12:33), but esp. by the expectation of the imminent Parousia, individual members of the early church in Jerusalem renounced their right to private property (Acts 2:45, *ktēma* and *hyparxis*; 4:32, *hyparchonta*), sold it when there was need (2:45), and gave the money to the apostles for distribution (4:36–37; 5:1–2). Ananias and Sapphira were judged not because they had kept back the proceeds of the property they had sold, but because they had lied to the Holy Spirit in pretending to give all to the church (5:3). What the sin of Achan (Jos. 7) was in the OT, theirs was in the NT. Note that Mary, the mother of John Mark, retained possession of her house and allowed it to be used as a meeting place (12:12). Local churches outside of Jerusalem apparently did not adopt the same community of goods.

4. In 1 Cor. 13:3 Paul uses love as the only valid criterion for evaluating good actions for our fellow believers involving possessions. If one's willingness to give away one's possessions to the poor is not an expression of love, the giver has no gain from the action.

In an exhortation to perseverance Heb. 10:34 reminds its readers that "you . . . joyfully accepted the confiscation of your property [*ta hyparchonta*], because you knew that you . . . had better and lasting possessions [*hyparxis*]." This may refer to the expulsion of Jews from Rome by the emperor Claudius in A.D. 49, among whom were Priscilla and Aquila (cf. Acts 18:2) and doubtless other Christian Jews who would have suffered eviction and looting. The allusion to possessions is further illustrated by the examples of Abraham (Heb. 11:16) and Moses, who preferred to suffer reproach for the sake of the Anointed One than to possess the treasures of Egypt (11:24–26; → *thēsauros*, treasure, *2565*). It contrasts with the attitude of Esau, who forfeited his birthright for immediate material well-being (12:15–17; cf. Gen. 25:29–34).

See also *thēsauros*, treasure box, chest, storeroom, treasure (*2565*); *mamōnas*, money, wealth, property (*3440*); *peripoieō*, save for oneself, acquire, gain possession of (*4347*); *ploutos*, wealth, riches (*4458*).

5976	χρηματίζω

χρηματίζω (*chrēmatizō*), impart a revelation, injunction, or warning; bear a name, be called or named (*5976*); χρηματισμός (*chrēmatismos*), a divine statement or answer (*5977*).

CL & OT In cl. Gk. the vb. *chrēmatizō*, related to *chrēma*, property, wealth, money (→ *5975*), means to handle a matter, deal with something. In the language of government and business in the Hel. world it came to denote officially handling something or giving an official answer. It could denote a deity giving an answer. In the LXX *chrēmatizō* is used by Elijah to suggest sarcastically to the prophets of Baal on Mount Carmel that perhaps Baal is on official business (1 Ki. 18:27). In Jer. 26:2 (= LXX 33:2) *chrēmatizō* denotes what the Lord reveals to the prophet to "tell" the Israelites who come to God's house (cf. also 29:23; 30:2 = LXX 36:23; 37:2).

chrēmatismos in cl. Gk. means money-making, although it is also a term for an official instruction or decree or for a divine answer in Hellenism. In the LXX it means dispatch (2 Macc. 11:17), oracle (Prov. 31:1 = LXX 24:69), and divine direction (2 Macc. 2:4).

NT 1. In the NT *chrēmatizō* has 2 distinct senses. It may be connected with *chrēsmos*, oracle, and with *chrēmata*, business. (a) In the infancy stories of Jesus, it is used of the instruction of people by revelations. It is usually in the pass., and the recipient is regarded as an instrument of God. Thus the wise men are warned in a dream not to return to Herod (Matt. 2:12). Joseph is likewise warned not to go to Judea where Archelaus ruled and so withdraws to Galilee (2:22). It was "revealed" to Simeon by the Holy Spirit that he would not see death before he had seen the Messiah (Lk. 2:26).

In a similar way, in the account of the opening of the church to the Gentiles, an angel "told" Cornelius to send for Peter to come to his house in order to speak to him (Acts 10:22). Heb. 11:7 speaks of how Noah responded "when warned about things not yet seen," and 12:25 encourages professing Christians not to ignore any message from God, for the Israelites did not escape a less serious message from Moses, "who warned them on earth" (cf. also the use of this vb. for the warning given to Moses in 8:5).

(b) In two instances *chrēmatizō* means to appear as something, bear a name. Thus in Antioch the disciples "were called Christians" for the first time (Acts 11:26). In Rom. 7:3, a woman "is called an adulteress" if she lives with another man while her husband is still alive.

2. *chrēmatismos* occurs in the NT only at Rom. 11:4: "And what was God's answer [*chrēmatismos*] to [Elijah]? 'I have reserved for myself seven thousand who have not bowed the knee to Baal'" (cf. 1 Ki. 19:18). Thus, Paul argues, "at the present time there is a remnant chosen by grace" (Rom. 11:5). God has not rejected altogether his ancient people, the Israelites/Jews, and God's way of working now is the same as it was under the old covenant.

See also *apokalyptō*, uncover, disclose, reveal (*636*); *dēloō*, reveal, make clear, explain, give information, notify (*1317*); *epiphaneia*, appearance, revelation (*2211*).

5977 (*chrēmatismos*, a divine statement or answer), → *5976*.

5980 (*chrēsteuomai*, show kindness), → *5980*.

5982	χρηστός

χρηστός (*chrēstos*), mild, pleasant, kind, good (*5982*); χρηστότης (*chrēstotēs*), goodness, kindness, friendliness (*5983*); χρηστεύομαι (*chrēsteuomai*), show kindness (*5980*).

CL & OT 1. In cl. Gk. *chrēstos* originally denoted usefulness and thus anything that appeared good, suitable, proper. The word soon broadened to include moral excellence and perfection, in which inner greatness was linked with genuine goodness of heart. So *chrēstos* meant morally good and honorable, the capacity to show kindness to everyone. Used as a noun, *to chrēston* meant a friendly nature, kindness; in the pl. (*ta chrēsta*), kind actions. Similarly *chrēstotēs* acquired the meaning of friendliness, kindness, mildness, and was used in inscriptions as a title of honor for rulers and important public figures.

2. In the LXX the Heb. word *tôb* in its many shades of meaning is translated by *chrēstos*, along with *agathos* and *kalos*. There is little contemplation in the OT of the goodness of God in and of itself. On

the other hand, God's benevolent activity is constantly sung and recognized in hymns of praise. *chrestos* and *chrestotes* are favorite, although not the only, words for expressing the abundance of good that God in his covenant faithfulness displays to his own people and to everyone.

God's constant mercy and readiness to help is one of the essential themes of Ps. (e.g., 25:7–8; 31:19; 65:11). But *chrestos* also occurs in prophetic texts (e.g., Jer. 33:11 = LXX 40:11; cf. 24:2–5). This picture of God's kindness grows deeper in the face of a bewildering recognition of the enduring nature of sin. Yet he still remains kind! Nor could the fate of the nation after the exile, with its conviction that God's dealings are incomprehensible, suppress the acknowledgment that Yahweh is kind (cf. 2 Macc. 1:24).

3. The Qumran documents continue the same train of thought. Just as the OT expected the pious to show kindness, which should reflect the kindness they received from God, the sect also expected its members to show gracious kindness to one another (e.g., 1QS 2:24–25; 4:3; 5:4, 25; 8:2). But in unexpected juxtaposition to the demand for gracious kindness toward one another stands the command for "eternal hatred" of the sons of wickedness (4:17). Here the limitation of the OT command to love or show kindness did not include love of one's enemies.

NT 1. In the NT *chrestos* occurs 7x; *chrestotes*, 10x, and *chresteuomai* only in 1 Cor. 13:4. As in secular Gk., *chrestos* is used of things, to denote their goodness (e.g., Lk. 5:39, good wine).

2. *chrestos* is used in Lk. to widen the scope of the OT command to love (Lk. 6:35). Since God's kindness embraces even the ungrateful and the wicked (obstinate sinners), we are called to love our enemies unconditionally. Jesus invited those who had become exhausted by the legalistic piety of the Pharisees to take on themselves his "easy" yoke (Matt. 11:30). After experiencing his kindness, people are to be like him in showing kindness toward others (11:29).

3. Paul makes striking use of *chrestos* together with the noun *chrestotes*. In his attack on self-righteous Jewish piety he shows that the goodness of God is no cheap, convenient grace. It should lead to a horror of one's unwillingness to repent so that God's aim of converting others to himself may be achieved (Rom. 2:4).

Esp. in his use of the noun *chrestotes* the apostle makes repeated use of the idea of God's incomprehensible kindness. God does not desire the death of sinners but their salvation (Rom. 11:22; Eph. 2:7; Tit. 3:4). His purpose in saving people is to show the meaning of kindness in their lives. Kindness and gentleness thus belong to the visible gifts of the Spirit (Gal. 5:22). Love itself (→ *agape*, 27) manifests itself as kindness (1 Cor. 13:4).

Because kindness is one of the chief aspects of the Spirit-filled life, it becomes the subject of the exhortation of Col. 3:12: "As God's chosen people ... clothe yourselves with compassion, kindness." This completes the circle from the original kindness of the Creator God, who remains kind despite our sin and wickedness, to the revelation of his incomprehensible kindness in Jesus Christ in the fullness of time. In Jesus Christ God's fatherly kindness can be seen as in a mirror. Moreover, the members of the Christian community, the church, must choose as their path in the world the way of kindness. At the same time they choose that path in a world that often betrays little sign of it.

See also *agathos*, good (*19*); *kalos*, good, beautiful, noble (*2819*).

5983 (*chrestotes*, goodness, kindness, friendliness), → *5982*.

5984 (*chrisma*, anointing, unction), → *5987*.

5985 Χριστιανός	Χριστιανός (*Christianos*), Christian (*5985*).

NT The identification of the Messiah with Jesus of Nazareth brought the disciples the name *Christianoi*. Compared with other names for the followers of Jesus (e.g., disciple or believer), the word is rare in the NT.

It is a word that defines the one to whom it is applied as belonging to the party of a certain *Christos*, much as *Herodianos* is a technical term for the followers of Herod (Mk. 3:6; 12:13). Its use also presupposes that *Christos* had taken on the meaning of a proper name, a process that would have been facilitated by the resemblance to the name *Chrestos*, pronounced *Christos*.

According to Acts 11:26, *Christianos* was first used for Christians in Syrian Antioch. This verse, like the two others in which the word occurs in the NT (26:28; 1 Pet. 4:16), suggests that, being applied to Christians by outsiders, it contained an element of ridicule, similar to the word *Nazarenos* or *Nazoraios* (→ *3716*). But it soon became a name that those called by it felt honored to bear.

See also *Iesous*, Jesus (*2652*); *Nazarenos*, Nazarene, from Nazareth (*3716*); *Christos*, Christ (*5986*).

5986 Χριστός	Χριστός (*Christos*), Christ (*5986*); Μεσσίας (*Messias*), Messiah (*3549*).

CL & OT 1. In cl. Gk. *chrio* means to rub lightly, spread (over something); it requires more precise information about what is used, e.g., oil. The word has no sacral undertones. Naturally, then, this is true for the verbal adj. *christos*, which characterizes an object or a person as rubbed or smeared with whitewash, cosmetics, paint, etc. It is anything but an expression of honor. Where it refers to people, it even tends toward the disrespectful.

This is certainly why in non-Christian circles *Christos*, in its reference to Jesus, was soon confused with the Gk. name *Chrestos*, and why the Jewish translator of the OT, Aquila, thought it right to render *masiah* or *mesiha'*, not by *christos* but by *eleimmenos* (from *aleipheo*, which always means to anoint). Nevertheless, the meaning of the root *chrio* as rub (oil) on was essential for *christos* being used of Jesus of Nazareth and quickly acquired the character of a proper name.

2. *Christos*, used already in LXX, corresponds to the Heb. *masiah* and denotes someone who has been ceremonially anointed for an office. The Gk. transliteration of *mesiha'* is *Messias*, which (like *Iesous*) is made declinable by the added -*s* (not used in the LXX). But the NT authors were clearly taking over a word and concept that were already current in the pre-Christian period.

3. (a) In the OT two office-bearers are expressly described as *masiah* i.e., as anointed (with oil): the high priest (the one responsible for the official cult) and the king (→ *chrio*, anoint [*5987*]). In both cases the anointing, corresponding to its character as a legal act, was essential for the conferring of the authority connected with the office and for the resulting responsibility before God. However, in Jewish OT interpretation only the figure of the king was reckoned as messianic in the sense of specific messianic expectation.

(b) This expectation was ultimately related to the idea of the kingship and the sovereign kingly rule of God. The varying judgments on the monarchy in 1 Sam. 8–11 notwithstanding, the institution of the monarchy binds on the king a special responsibility for the things of God. This is clear from the censures that the OT historians passed on individual kings of Israel and Judah, according to whether or not they had ruled consistently with faith in Israel's God.

The crucial factor in being a *masiah* is one's responsibility before God on the basis of transferred power and authority. This must be so if, after the Davidic kings (to whom must be ascribed considerable significance for the development of the messianic expectation), a foreigner such as the Persian king Cyrus can be described as God's *masiah* (Isa. 45:1; see below). Cyrus was a chosen instrument of God in the pursuit of God's universal aim of the salvation of all people through the nation he had chosen. Recognition of the divine freedom implied here is all the more essential, as the expectation of a messianic, kingly savior figure was associated from an early date with the tribe of Judah (Gen. 49:8–12).

(c) A far-reaching influence on the development of the idea of the Messiah as a historical figure of increasingly supernatural dimensions was the memory of the magnificent and successful period of David's rule, the first king from Judah (cf. Isa. 9:2–7; 11:1–9; Mic. 5:2–6). A secondary motif here may be the association of the Messiah, especially in later Jud., with the pre-Davidic priest-kings of Jerusalem (such as Melchizedek), which David captured and made his capital (2 Sam. 5:6–10; 6:1–19).

(d) It is important to emphasize this kingly basis to Messiah because, with respect to the practice of anointing in Israel, both the king and high priest were anointed. But even though both anointings were similar in form, their life-setting was entirely different. The anointing of the kings of Judah was associated with the gift and the ritual transfer of authority, power, and honor. It gave the one anointed a position of power as well as the right to exercise it. The anointing of the priests, however, was a cultic purification, with the goal of enabling the priests to conduct valid worship.

4. (a) In this context we must consider further the description of the Persian king Cyrus as the anointed of God (Isa. 45:1), though he had clearly not been anointed as king in accordance with Judaic custom. We see here a sublimation of the concept, which makes it independent of the external act by transferring the entire weight onto God's appointment of the one designated by the anointing. In this case the anointed one is the one chosen in a special way by God and placed under his command, to do God's bidding and fulfill his plan in obedience to his will.

This helps to explain why the Judean kings, together with the OT Jewish Messiah, never themselves acquired divine features even in the so-called Enthronement Psalms (e.g., Ps. 2; 110). As the Lord's anointed, they remained in their kingship as dependent on God and responsible to him (cf. on David, 1 Sam. 16:1–13; 2 Sam. 19:22 = LXX 19:21; 23:1). At the same time, it follows that at any given moment the king, i.e., the actual reigning monarch of Judah from the house of David, could be introduced in Ps. as God's anointed without further special explanation (18:50; 20:6; 28:8; 84:9; 89:38, 51; 132:10, 17). This also explains how David (cf. 2 Sam. 3:18; 7:5) and his successors (e.g., Solomon, 1 Ki. 3:7–9; 8:28), and even a postexilic claimant like Zerubbabel (Hag. 2:23; cf. Zech. 3:8), are called the servants of God. Son (Ps. 2:7; 89:26–27) and servant, insofar as they describe the relationship of the anointed one to God, are not mutually exclusive. From God's point of view they belong inseparably together.

(b) It is difficult to give a precise answer to the question whether or not the Servant Songs (Isa. 42:1–4; 49:1–6; 50:4–9; 52:13–53:12) refer to a kingly figure as Messiah. Many scholars are not inclined to allow here an essential connection with the expectation of a future savior king. Yet there is a basis for it in the idea of responsibility under the claims of God, if even a prophet like Elisha (1 Ki. 19:16; cf. also Isa. 61:1) could appear in the ranks of the anointed.

5. The OT does not appear to exhibit any clear development of the messianic expectation. All that can be demonstrated is the presence of the expectation in the passages already referred to and in others extending, via Jer. 23:5–8 and Ezek. 34:23–24, to Hag. and Zech. Until this point they exhibit a strange uniformity. It is not until the Hel. period that this is overtaken by a sharp materialization of the concept in the direction of the expectation of an ideal eschatological Jewish national ruler who would nonetheless transcend national frontiers. It seems that the details, at least in part, were taken from the picture of the Maccabees and Hasmoneans and introduced into the older expectation oriented toward the memory of David.

We see this most clearly in *Pss. Sol.* 17:21–40; 18:3–9. Here the specific concept of the Messiah also appears in fixed form. Significantly its association with the Davidic tradition did not have the result that the Messiah could only be imagined as coming from the line of David. A notorious example of one who was no descendant of David is Simeon ben Kosebah, whom no less a person than Rabbi Akiba greeted as Bar Kokhba, the "star out of Jacob" promised in Num.

24:17, and thus identified him as messiah (ca. A.D. 132). Bar Kokhba's collapse, which severely shook messianism, may nevertheless have contributed to the fact that in Jud.'s liturgical texts, the hope of a Messiah from the line of David has persisted to this day.

NT 1. Wherever the NT is concerned with Jesus, it is concerned with him as Christ, i.e., as Messiah. In other words, for the whole of the NT, messianism no longer stands under the sign of expectation but under that of fulfillment. The Christ event is spoken of in the perf. or past tense. True, the writings do look into the future, sometimes intensively. But the One who is awaited is the One who has already come.

2. It is significant that the essential unity of the proclamation of Christ using the title Messiah is established, objectively as well as subjectively, with the least amount of ambiguity in the witness of Jn., one of the later NT books. The transliterated word *Messias* occurs only 2x in the Gk. NT, both in Jn. (1:41; 4:25); both times it is translated as *Christos*. Both passages lead to the conclusion that we must ascribe to Palestinian Jews the fact that in the Messiah the central concept in Jewish messianic expectation became the possession of the developing Hel. church. It found its way into the language of their worship and preaching.

No doubt the transference of this faith and language came about through the transmission of confessional summaries about Jesus. These were originally formulated in Aram. or Heb. in the Palestinian church and subsequently translated into Gk. as the church's mission extended beyond Palestinian Jewry. The best illustration of this process lies in 1 Cor. 15:1–7. Here Paul records the gospel he transmitted to the Corinthians, which he himself had previously received. Along with everything else we find *Christos* without the art., which seems to stem from the usage of contemporary Palestinian Jews. In the Gk. churches, therefore, the word *christos*, when linked with Jesus, completed relatively quickly the transition from an adj., which it is essentially, to a proper name. In the process it retained its traditional reference to Jesus' status.

3. The occurrence of *Christos* in this early Christian confession (1 Cor. 15:3–5) testifies to the fact that very early, believers saw no contradiction between Jesus' violent death on the cross and the name of Christ ascribed to him. This is remarkable because it seemed natural to the contemporaries of the early Christians that the collapse of a messianic pretender by crucifixion was decisive proof of the spuriousness both of his claims and of the hopes centered on him by his followers (cf. Acts 5:36–37 with Mk. 15:29; also 1 Cor. 1:23).

We find the same situation in other pre-Pauline passages incorporated by the apostle into his own proclamation: e.g., Rom. 4:25 (where "delivered over" refers to the death of Jesus, not to Judas's betrayal), or 3:25 (with its reference to Jesus' blood as a sacrifice of atonement). The same line is followed by all four Evangelists when they take over as part of the kerygma (most clearly in Jn. 18:36–37; 19:19–22) the inscription on the cross (cf. Matt. 27:37; Mk. 15:26; Lk. 23:38). This was intended to expose Jesus as pseudo-king of the Jews, i.e., as pseudo-Messiah, but the Evangelists make it an involuntary proclamation of Jesus as Messiah by his enemies, because that was what God willed. Jesus, because he was the Messiah, had to suffer and die (cf. Mk. 8:31; Jn. 3:14, where, however, this concept is linked with "the Son of Man"; also esp. Lk. 24:26).

The clear impression we receive from all such passages is that, when it represented itself as the community of Jesus, the early church presented itself simply as the messianic community. For in its preaching of Jesus as Messiah it was at the same time interpreting itself messianically in relation to its life, its historical origins, and its aims. If at a relatively early date Christians began to consider themselves as the Israel of God (Gal. 6:16), i.e., the true Israel as distinct from Israel according to the flesh (1 Cor. 10:18), the spiritual roots for this lie in the messianism that has just been outlined. Paul attests the same messianism when in 15:25 he leaves the last event before the end the kingly rule of the Christ/Messiah.

The most surprising fact is the part played by Jesus' messiahship in the Gospel of Jn. The crucial question throughout the book is that of a correct understanding of Jesus' kingship, beginning with the conversation between Jesus and Nathanael (1:47–50) to the dialogue between Pilate and Jesus (18:33–38) and that between Pilate and the chief priests (19:21–22). In Jesus' discussion with the Samaritan woman he discloses his messiahship (4:25–26). One recognizes in the solemn *Iēsous Christos*—lit, "Jesus is the Christ"—the confessional formula of Jn.'s own church (17:3; cf. further 1 Jn. 2:22; 4:2; 5:1; 2 Jn. 7). Here the early Christological inheritance is preserved in all its splendor and without any contraction.

4. Naturally the messianic element in the NT faith in Christ and in the NT confession of Christ is inseparable from the resurrection of Jesus from the dead. His resurrection is reckoned as his resurrection as Christ/Messiah (cf. Acts 2:31 with 1 Cor. 15:4; also Rom. 1:4). It appears everywhere as something done by God to the crucified and buried Jesus (cf. Acts 2:36) and moreover as his vindication by God (cf. Rom. 6:7–10; 1 Tim. 3:16). It is fully consistent, then, that in Jesus' statements about his suffering, the announcement of his impending death is always accompanied by that of his resurrection. This is not so much intended to discredit the opponents who refused to believe him and thus delivered him up to death on the cross so as to secure his messiahship, which seemed to be disproved by his death on the cross (cf. Lk. 24:26 with 19–21; cf. above).

What Paul writes in Rom. 9–11 about the relation of the church to Jud. presupposes a confident reliance on the messiahship of Jesus, which God legitimated just as much as does the expectation of a new heaven and a new earth (cf. esp. Rev. 5:1–5; 22:16). This is linked to the risen and exalted Jesus (cf. 1:5, 18), or the certainty that the coming of the kingdom of God is linked with Jesus as the Christ (Acts 28:31). To this extent the whole of Christian preaching has its source and its center everywhere in the messiahship of Jesus confirmed by God.

5. Finally, the formula *Iēsous Christos* leads to the question whether the linking of Jesus' name with the title of messianic dignity goes back to Jesus himself. This poses the issue of Jesus' messianic consciousness. A few comments here are appropriate.

(a) Many scholars argue that Jesus himself had no messianic consciousness. To support this view they point not only to the kerygmatic character of the accounts of his defense (e.g., before the Sanhedrin), but also to the fact that the so-called sayings source Q contains nothing that attributes messiahship to Jesus.

With respect to both reasons, however, we must recommend caution. First, Q remains a working hypothesis, not a document of historical fact. Second, there is still the need to explain how the kerygma by itself arrived at the idea of having Jesus represent himself to the Sanhedrin as the Messiah if he did not regard himself as such during his lifetime. Still, it is true that Jesus did not refer to himself in any clear form as Messiah. The most he permitted was for people to attribute to him messianic titles like "Son of David" (Mk. 10:47–48; → *huios*, 5626), without adopting an attitude of agreement or of denial toward them.

Furthermore, the picture of Jesus in the Gospels suggests that he conformed to none of the traditional messianic descriptions. He called in question by his person any notion of himself as a political savior-king and did not allow his own followers to address him as such. Even an event like Peter's confession at Caesarea Philippi (Matt. 16:13–23; Mk. 8:27–33; Lk. 9:18–22), if one accepts its historical reliability, does not take us fundamentally beyond this conclusion. Certainly the events connected with his passion and Easter would appear quite differently in the tradition if at any point in time Jesus had given precise information about himself as far as his messiahship was concerned. Finally, Jesus did not triumph over death and the grave as the man he was, but, in the case of his resurrection, was the object of a mysterious direct action on the part of God. The result is a fairly unanimous picture, which scholars describe, imperfectly and in an unbalanced fashion, by the ambiguous phrase "the messianic secret." Still, the phrase points in a direction in which the answer to the question posed at the outset is to be found.

(b) The problem of the messianic secret can only be properly understood when we realize that Jesus' whole ministry was deliberately concentrated with his disciples. The Twelve were, after all, the interpreters of Jesus. Granted, they did not achieve a full recognition of Jesus as Messiah until after the Easter events (cf. Lk. 24:25–27). Nevertheless, the view they proclaimed had to be consistent with what they had known about Jesus during his earthly ministry, so that they could then associate what he had said and done with the use of the category of Messiah. The new situation of the resurrection did not encourage the development of ideas but led to final personal decisions and corresponding actions. This could only come about if the picture of the risen Jesus and that of the earthly Jesus were not contradictory but mutually interpretative on the grounds of their connection with him.

In other words, it was the mystery of the person of Jesus that was responsible for the disciples' feeling themselves confronted by the question of the Messiah in the earthly Jesus. On the basis of their encounters with the risen Jesus, the disciples ultimately answered it with the confession that he was the Messiah and that in him God had fulfilled his promise to the house of David and to Israel of salvation for the whole of humanity in a manner that was nevertheless only accessible to faith.

(c) Naturally the name *Jesus Christ* means more to Christianity than the messianic status of a certain Jesus of Nazareth, in whom God fulfilled his promises to the fathers. Every aspect of the salvation God has bestowed on the world is bound up in Jesus insofar as he is the Christ. In Jesus as the Christ "all the fullness of the Deity lives in bodily form" (Col. 2:9) for the salvation of all those who put their trust in him and appropriate to themselves the fruit of his death and resurrection (Rom. 4:24–25). Yet to express all of this in a single title like Messiah or Christ is not sufficient. Thus, when the NT kerygma expounds the salvation bound up in Christ, it makes use of other titles of honor, which emphasize the side of Jesus' person or work on which the particular title depends—titles such as Son of God, Lord, Savior, and mediator.

Still, if "Christ" has been transformed from a title of honor to a part of Jesus' name, this corresponds to the essential feature in Jesus' historical appearance that at the same time must be reckoned as the condition of his whole work as mediator of salvation: his obedient submission to God's will as manifested in the process of God's self-revelation in the history of the people of Israel. To this extent Jesus' affirmation of his messiahship, whether or not it was ever explicitly announced, is for the whole kerygma the presupposition of his path to the cross. It is equally the presupposition of his resurrection and exaltation on God's part.

This element in Jesus' messiahship, central for Christology, is represented nowhere in the NT as clearly and at the same time as comprehensively as in the Christological hymn that Paul introduced into his letter to the Philippians (Phil. 2:5–11). Here he describes Jesus' path via the incarnation, the life of obedience, the death of obedience on the cross, the resurrection, and the exaltation at God's side as the path of that Messiah who is identical with Jesus of Nazareth.

See also *Iēsous*, Jesus (2652); *Nazarēnos*, Nazarene, from Nazareth (3716); *Christianos*, Christian (5985); *chriō*, anoint (5987).

5987 χρίω	χρίω (*chriō*), anoint (5987); χρῖσμα (*chrisma*), anointing, unction (5984).

CL & OT 1. In cl. Gk. *chriō* means simply to rub lightly, spread (over something). The word in no way specifies what is being rubbed. It can be done with oil, as for example with a human body after bathing, but also with poison (as in the preparation of arrows for battle), paint, whitewash, or even cosmetics.

2. *chriō* occurs 60x in the LXX. Apart from Deut. 28:40 and Ezek. 16:9, it translates the Heb. *māšaḥ*, to smear, anoint with oil or ointment. Unlike *aleiphō*, *chriō* is used basically in the symbolic ritual sense. Likewise, *chrisma* is used consistently of ritual anointing (Exod. 30:25; 40:9; etc.).

(a) From the petty states of the Canaanites in the region of Syria and Palestine, Israel adopted the institution of the monarchy, and with it probably also the anointing of kings (Jdg. 9:8, 15; 1 Sam. 9:16; 10:1; 16:3, 12–13). The OT tradition concerning the anointing of the king is not, however, uniform. In one place the anointing was performed by "the elders of Israel" on the basis of a contract between the king and these representatives of the twelve tribes (2 Sam. 5:3). Elsewhere it took place at the direct command of Yahweh and by the hand of a prophet (9:16). Whether it was Yahweh or the people who "made" the king, his anointing became a sacred act as part of the ceremony of enthronement, which took place in a holy place before Yahweh.

The anointing gave the new king the legal right to rule over Israel (→ *Christos*, *5986*). It was done from a special vessel, a horn kept in the temple (1 Ki. 1:39), using olive oil mixed with spices, which was poured over the king's head as appropriate words were said (2 Ki. 9:3, 6). The anointing formed the first part of the coronation ceremony in the temple and was followed by the acclamation by the people, "Long live the king!" (11:12), and finally the ascent of the throne in the royal palace (11:19).

(b) The anointing signified communication of *kābôd*, the gift of authority, strength, and honor (cf. Ps. 45:7–8). The descendants of David were regarded as his successors to the throne (2 Sam. 7), as Yahweh's anointed, without having in every instance been symbolically anointed by a prophet. Anointing by Yahweh is sometimes coupled with the gift of the Spirit and Yahweh's special protection (e.g., 1 Sam. 16:13; 24:6–11; 26:9–23). Thus, the anointed one stood in direct contact with God and was regarded as inviolate.

(c) The high priest was also anointed (Exod. 29:7), as were other priests (40:15). This anointing took place during the seven-day-long consecration of the priests, after the preparation of the sacrifice (29:1–3), the ritual cleansing (29:4), and the enrobing (29:5–6) at the entrance of the sanctuary (29:7; cf. 28:41; 29:29; 40:13). Anointing made the priests sacrosanct, separating them from the sphere of the unclean (30:29–30). This same process of sanctification could also apply to holy objects, such as the tabernacle (40:9), the altar (40:10), the vessels used in the sanctuary, and the ark (30:26–29).

3. In passages like Isa. 61:1 and Ezek. 16:9, the anointing is to be understood fig., since in Israel ritual anointing was only available to kings and priests. Isa. 61:1 should be regarded as the testimony of the prophet, who is here speaking of his charismatic endowment with authority. In the NT this text is applied to Jesus (Lk. 4:18); he has been anointed by God to be the promised prophet.

NT In the NT *chriō* (apart from the form *Christos*, Christ, → *5986*) occurs only 5x and *chrisma* only 3x (all in 1 Jn.). Both words are used exclusively in a fig. sense, corresponding to their use in the LXX. Anointing is a metaphor for the bestowal of the Holy Spirit, special power, or a divine commission.

1. Jesus was anointed by God (Lk. 4:18 [quoting Isa. 61:1]; Acts 4:27; 10:38; Heb. 1:9 [quoting Ps. 45:7]). The first three texts indicate a special endowment by the Holy Spirit with supernatural power, which probably recalls what happened at Jesus' baptism. On that occasion Jesus received the royal and priestly anointing that made him the *Christos*, the Messiah. Jesus of Nazareth was thereby declared the instrument of the gospel of peace. According to Lk. 4:18, Jesus read out the Isa. passage in order to proclaim that the period that begins with him is the period of salvation.

Heb. 1:9 does not refer to Jesus' baptism but to the ceremonial act of enthronement in heaven (cf. 1:3–4). On account of his obedience and endurance of suffering (2:9), Jesus was anointed and elevated at his ascension to the rank of eschatological ruler (1:8) and high priest (5:9–10).

2. The remaining instances of *chriō* and *chrisma* refer to the anointing of Christians. Some exegetes suggest the existence of an act of anointing before baptism. Perhaps 2 Cor. 1:21 and 1 Jn. 2:20, 27 refer to baptism, but we have no evidence of anointing as an independent rite within the baptismal ceremony. For Jn. the *chrisma* is the Spirit of truth, who gives believers the power of understanding so that they do not need any other teacher (2:27). The Spirit brings to mind what Jesus has said (cf. Jn. 14:26; 15:26; 16:13–14). By continuing in Jesus (1 Jn. 2:28) and through the power of the preached word as it works in the church, believers share in Jesus' messianic anointing. They receive the Holy Spirit, who is able to discern the spirits (4:1–6).

It is difficult to determine the meaning of *chriō* in 2 Cor. 1:21–22. Those exegetes are probably right who regard the three vbs. used here (stand firm, anoint, set his seal) as three different aspects of what happens in baptism. By their spiritual anointing, Christians are made rightful members of the covenant of promise. Paul's language here possibly implies a reference to a term in the gnostic mysteries, from which he thus dissociates himself. It is not our choice and decision that leads us through a mystic anointing to higher knowledge of the other world and to the way of redemption. It is the decision made by God for humankind in Christ Jesus, which operates through faith.

See also *aleiphō*, anoint (*230*); *Christos*, Christ, (*5986*).

5988 (*chronizō*, take time, linger, delay), → *5989*.

5989 χρόνος

χρόνος (*chronos*), time, period of time (*5989*); χρονίζω (*chronizō*), take time, linger, delay (*5988*); χρονοτριβέω (*chronotribeō*), spend, lose, or waste time (*5990*).

CL & OT 1. (a) In cl. Gk. *chronos* denotes a space of time, whose duration is not as a rule precisely determined, but at most is characterized by additional adjs. as longer (e.g., *polys*, much) or shorter (e.g., *oligos*, little). In the face of wasted time, *chronos* takes on the meaning of loss of time. With reference to people, *chronos* often means age, years, or time of life, and thus comes close to *bios*, life (→ *1050*). *chronos* is also used adverbially. In the gen. it means for a considerable time; in the dat. in (the course of) time, gradually, late; in the acc. for a set time.

(b) The older vb. *chronizō* means to be a long time coming, fail to appear, linger, remain, hesitate, put off doing something. The rare vb. *chronotribeō* means to spend, lose, or waste time.

(c) The Gks. experienced time as a power that inescapably determined life. On the one hand, time appeared to them to be an endless quantity. On the other hand, they were painfully aware that the time allotted to a person was all too short. One felt the advance of time, whose "omnipotence" overthrows all but the gods; it is always threatening life. Growing old in time as quickly as a shadow warns us of our transience. If youth is able to overlook this, that perspective disappears with age.

(d) "All-seeing time" was further felt to be a kind of judge, bringing everything to light. Time reveals the truth, esp. in respect of a person's real worth. If there are already echoes here of the positive functions of time, this is even more clearly the case where time is spoken of as that which gives healing forgetfulness; it erases everything.

(e) But even though it is the healer of wounds, time cannot save anyone from death. The Gks. reflected on human temporality and the necessity of one's own death. In this context, some aspired to make the fullest possible use of time; others sought to break through the limitations of time and achieve a life that would transcend death through a personal legacy.

(f) The Gks. also reflected philosophically on the nature and the origin of time. Such reflection reached its first great peak in Plato.

chronos was created at the same time as the starry heavens; moreover, time will also pass away together with them. In the world of finitude time has become an image of the infinite one in the form of an endless sequence of particulars. In being and becoming, time corresponds to the incessant circular movement of the planets. It thus describes in turn cycles of natural becoming and passing.

Aristotle's analytic formulation of this question shifted the interest from the problem of being to the analysis of existence, that is, reality. Aristotle saw in change the sole possibility of discovering reality. The sequence of movement can be measured by number. He thus defined time as the continuous quantity of successive movement; time is deduced from place and movement, a process typical of the Gk. way of expressing things visually.

2. The OT does not reflect abstractly on time. There is therefore no unified biblical word for time, but rather several concepts that are expressed in the Heb. (or Gk. equivalents of) words, such as day, hour, eternity, age, end, decisive moment, now, today. In contrast to other words on time (see, e.g., *kairos, 2789*), *chronos* occurs only about 100x, concentrated in Job, Isa., Dan., and Macc. *chronos* may sometimes be used synonymously with *hōra* (hour, *6052*) and *kairos* to denote a point of time (e.g., Jer. 38:28 = LXX 45:28). In general, however, it means an expanse of time. Esp. noteworthy is the formula *eis ton aiōna chronon*, "into eternal time" (e.g., Exod. 14:13; Isa. 9:7). The thought is here partly of the whole human life span, partly of a long period of time, but never of a timeless, otherworldly eternity.

(a) For Israelites, time and history were inseparably connected. That is, time interested them only insofar as it was qualified by a particular event. This was esp. the case with regard to Yahweh's dealings with his people. Certain periods of salvation history are accordingly described as the time of the fathers (1 Esd. 8:76), of Noah (Isa. 54:9), of Abraham (Gen. 26:1), of Joshua (2 Macc. 12:15), of Samuel (1 Esd. 1:20), etc.

Fundamental is the faith that the eternal, i.e., the "everlasting" God (cf. Ps. 90:1; cf. Exod. 15:18; Isa. 40:28; Dan. 12:7), is the Lord of time and that he gives all human time its content and meaning. If it was customary in ancient Israel to look more to the saving occasions of the past, the prophets fixed their eyes on future times. In Isa. this occurs through the use of *chronos*. Isa. saw that for long periods of time the enemies of Zion would be exposed to divine punishment (13:20; 14:20). Zion, by contrast, without being spared times of visitation (cf. 54:7; Jer. 29:8), will stand firm for all time (Isa. 33:20; cf. 34:17; 51:8), for Yahweh will establish an everlasting kingdom of peace (9:7).

(b) The problem of the elapse of a person's life span, which so oppressed the Gks., also comes up in the later strata of the OT. In Job, for example, the fact that humankind has only a short life (Job 14:1), though one would like to live for a long time (29:18), becomes a source of temptation. But Job and others find comfort in the knowledge that God prescribes the individual's allotted times (14:5, 13). Hence, even one who dies early can fill long spaces of time in a way that pleases the Lord (Wis. 4:13). All the same, from the perspective of this outlook, an extension of one's life span is regarded as a particular grace of God (Isa. 38:5).

(c) In wisdom lit. one finds the beginnings of a philosophical treatment of the question of time. But it is supported by a belief that it is God who, through wisdom (Eccl. 8:8), gives insight into the beginning, end, and middle of the times. The net result here is that God, who prepared the earth for eternal times (Bar. 3:32) and created the constellations to mark the time (Sir. 43:6), allots everything its time in nature, individual life, and national history (Eccl. 3:1). This is esp. true of times and opportunities for repentance (Wis. 12:20).

3. (a) Times of repentance with clearly defined limits played an important role in the Qumran community (1QS 7), whose consciousness of time was clearly formed by eschatological and apocalyptic ideas. Great emphasis was placed on the observance of special festive seasons (1:14–15; 10:1–5). In every period of time members of their fellowship were "to praise their Creator" (9:26), for only thus

would they survive the fires of wrath of the last days and the raging of the angel of darkness (3:23).

(b) In his reflections on time, Philo takes over Plato's cosmic understanding of time. He seeks to combine a philosophical view of the origin of time with OT faith in God the creator. It is he who has created, out of nothing, the heavenly bodies with their harmonic movement without thereby standing in need of time. Everything goes back to his creativity.

NT 1. In the NT *chronos* occurs 54x, *chronizō* 5x, and *chronotribeō* once (Acts 20:16). Like the other temporal terms, *chronos* serves initially for the formal designation of a space or point of time. Thus the longer or shorter duration of a condition or an activity is frequently described by phrases with *chronos* (cf. Lk. 8:27, 29; Jn. 5:6; Heb. 11:32). Often, esp. in Acts, the details of any actual or projected length of stay at various places are given by *chronos* (e.g., 14:3; 15:33; 19:22; cf. 1 Cor. 16:7). As in the OT, *chronos* can also denote a person's lifetime (Acts 1:21; 1 Cor. 7:39). Finally, it can also describe a short time span (Jn. 7:33; 12:35) and can even be found with the meaning of *kairos* and *nyn*, in a moment (Lk. 4:5).

2. Theologically more significant than the general indications of time are passages that speak of *chronos* in connection with specific events. Such passages occur esp. in Lk.'s writings. Lk. 1:57 mentions the *chronos* of Elizabeth's delivery. In Acts 13:18 the word denotes a period of forty years of salvation history. The climax of the *chronos*-pronouncements is reached in a whole series of Christological statements. For with Jesus Christ, something new and unique has happened in time. Nevertheless, the NT writers are not interested in speculative questions about the origin and the nature of time. Their thoughts center on Jesus Christ, who has given time and history a new significance. This is expressed by Paul in Gal. 4:4–5, where he refers to the coming of the Messiah as having occurred "when the time [*chronos*] had fully come."

(a) One is able, of course, to speak of an end of time only against the background of the eschatological and apocalyptic messianic expectations of contemporary Jud. With the coming of Christ this time of expectation has come to an end for the NT (cf. 1 Pet. 1:20). His appearance means the end of the old age.

(b) But Jesus also opens up a new epoch, for with him begins God's reign over the world. In light of the incarnation of God in his Son and his entering into historical time, several scholars refer to the "center of time" in relation to Lk.'s perspective. For with the appearance of Jesus, the kingdom of God has come among us (Lk. 17:21). The Christ-event becomes the criterion of all historical time, both backward and forward. Now that "the times of ignorance" are past (Acts 17:30, lit. trans.), one can accordingly, in the light of "the revelation of the mystery hidden for long ages past" (Rom. 16:25), understand the past as a time of preparation. In retrospect it can be seen as standing under the sign of the promise and the "grace ... given us in Christ Jesus before the beginning of time [*chronos*]" (2 Tim. 1:9; cf. Tit. 1:2; 1 Pet. 1:20).

3. (a) But the time of salvation was by no means past with Jesus' death. Jesus himself had spoken clearly of the coming end of the world (e.g., Mk. 13; Matt. 24–25) and thus assigned the believers into an interim period that stretches from Easter to the Parousia. Again and again the NT authors concern themselves with the remainder of the time (1 Pet. 4:2) and the events of the end. But they do not seek to predict that time of the end. Certain signs (e.g., the appearance of heretics and scoffers, Jude 18), are mentioned, but these serve only to encourage Christians to be watchful rather than to invite them to speculate about dates. God is the Lord of time, and it is his privilege to decide on the final hour for the consummation of his kingdom (Acts 1:6–7). Neither the angels nor Jesus himself know when the day of the Lord will break (Mk. 13:32). It will come suddenly, like a thief in the night (1 Thess. 5:1–11). Many early Christians were initially of the opinion that it would probably be only a short while until the Parousia; gradually, however, they adjusted themselves to a longer expanse of time.

(b) For all those who have not yet encountered God in Christ, who avoid him, or who (like the false prophetess Jezebel) resist him, this interim period is a "time to repent" (Rev. 2:20–21). But this time of decision will not be prolonged indefinitely. At the consummation of the divine mysteries time will cease to exist (10:6). Those who in faith recognize Christ as Lord are to use the time given them in the interim period for growing and maturing in their knowledge of the faith (cf. Heb. 5:12–13).

Pet. stresses further the ethical accountability of Christians, who are no longer to behave as they used to in earlier times in the manner of the heathen, but who are to live now by God's will (1 Pet. 4:2). According to 1:17, the interim period is defined as a "time [*chronos*] of exile" (lit. trans.) that leads us through much darkness, hours of temptation, and persecution. Comfort during this time is granted by the hope of God's future and the eventual restoration of the original order of creation.

See also *aiōn*, aeon, age, life span, epoch, eternity (*172*); *kairos*, time, esp. a point of time, moment (*2789*); *hōra*, hour, time, point of time (*6052*).

5990 (*chronotribeō*, spend, lose, or waste time), → *5989*.

5992 (*chrysion*, a piece of gold, gold coin), → *5996*.

5996	χρυσός

χρυσός (*chrysos*), gold (*5996*); χρυσίον (*chrysion*), a piece of gold, gold coin (*5992*); χρυσόω (*chrysoō*), adorn with gold (*5998*); χρυσοῦς (*chrysous*), golden (*5997*).

CL & OT 1. This word is borrowed from Sem. languages of the ANE (e.g., Heb. *ḥārûṣ*). This may reflect the fact that gold was rare in Greece before Alexander the Great captured Persia's stores of gold. In Egypt, West Arabia, the mountains of Armenia, and Persia gold was widely used and the goldsmith's art perfected from the 3d millennium B.C.

2. In the LXX *chrysos* and *chrysion*, which became interchangeable, translate five different Heb. words for gold. These probably indicated differing degrees of purity in the gold, which was often mixed with varying percentages of silver (cf. Gen. 2:11–12). In ancient times, there were three ways of working gold. It could be melted and cast into molds to form solid figures (Exod. 32:4), beaten into sheets with which objects could be covered (25:11), or beaten into a particular shape (25:31).

Besides the cultic associations of gold in both the tabernacle and the temple, in countries around Israel gold was made into idols (Exod. 20:23). It was frequently used for jewelry (Gen. 41:42; Jdg. 8:26), and at a comparatively early date was used for currency (2 Ki. 18:14; 23:33). Since royalty throughout the ages used gold for crowns, thrones, cups, and drinking bowls (1 Ki. 10:18, 21; Est. 1:7), it became an appropriate gift for a king (Ps. 72:15). In Dan.'s interpretation of Nebuchadnezzar's dream the Babylonian king is the head of gold (Dan. 2:38). Because gold is indestructible, it became a symbol for great value and enduring worth (Prov. 8:18–19).

NT The NT makes extensive use of the word group for gold. *chrysos* occurs 10x; *chrysion*, 12x; *chrysoō*, 2x, and *chrysous*, 18x. More than half of these uses are in the book of Rev.

Gold was used in the NT as an exchange of currency. When Pet. and Jn. encountered a crippled man as they were entering the temple, Pet. said, "Silver or gold I do not have" (Acts 3:6). Pet. did not have money to give to this man, but he did have the power of Jesus to make him walk. Similarly, when Jesus sent out the Twelve on their mission journeys, he instructed them, "Do not take any gold or silver or copper in your belts" (Matt. 10:9); rather, they were to be dependent on the people with whom they stayed for physical needs.

Gold was also used as a precious metal for a wide variety of purposes, both decorative and religious. It could be used as a commodity in its own right (Rev. 18:12), for jewelry (1 Tim. 2:9; 1 Pet. 3:3), for royal crowns (Rev. 9:7) and garments (17:4, 18:16), for valuable articles in one's home (2 Tim. 2:20), for various articles used in the service of God in the temple or heaven (Matt. 23:16–17; Heb. 9:4; cf. also Rev. 1:12, 20; 2:1; 8:3; 9:13), and for idols (Acts 17:29; Rev. 9:20). It is probably because of its great value and its association with royalty that the wise men presented gold as one of their gifts to "the king of the Jews" (i.e., the infant Jesus, Matt. 2:11).

Gold takes on symbolic value in several passages of the Scriptures. Pet. reminds us, for example, that saving faith has far greater value than gold, for through it we receive an imperishable inheritance, whereas gold can perish (1 Pet. 1:7; cf. Jas. 5:3, where Jas. refers to the "corrosion" of gold). Furthermore, the precious blood of Jesus is worth far more than perishable gold, for that blood redeems us from an "empty way of life" to a full and rich life in Jesus (1 Pet. 1:18). When Paul uses picturesque language to refer to building fruitful, enduring lives on the foundation of the church, which is Jesus Christ, he talks about using "gold, silver, costly stones," in contrast to those who build with elements that will not stand the test of God's fire of judgment: "wood, hay or straw" (1 Cor. 3:12).

This last verse touches on another metaphorical use of the topic of gold, namely, the fact that in order to be useful it has to be refined (though the Scriptures refer more frequently to the refining of silver than of gold; → *argyrion*, 736). To the lukewarm church in Laodicea Jesus gives counsel that if they want to be truly rich (i.e., rich with eternal, lasting treasure; cf. Matt. 6:19–21, 24), they ought to "buy from me gold refined in the fire," a euphemism for eternal, spiritual wealth available through faith in our Lord (Rev. 3:18; cf. 1 Pet. 1:7).

Finally, the new Jerusalem is described as a "city of pure gold," whose "great street [is] . . . of pure gold" (Rev. 21:18, 21; contrary to popular assumption, Rev. does not say that *all* the streets of the city will be paved with gold, only the "great street"). These references show both the perfection of that city and the inestimable value of trying to attain to it.

5997 (*chrysous*, golden), → *5996*.

5998 (*chrysoō*, adorn with gold), → *5996*.

6000	χωλός

χωλός (*chōlos*), lame, halt, maimed (*6000*).

CL & OT 1. In cl. Gk. *chōlos* describes a lame condition in the legs or feet that produces a halting or limping gait. In a later period the word was used to designate a deformed or impaired condition of the hand.

2. In the LXX *chōlos* means lame with respect to one's feet (2 Sam. 9:13; 19:26). Whether congenital or acquired, this condition disqualified a man from holding office as a priest in Israel (Lev. 21:18). This prohibition formed part of the concept of holiness for the nation and was esp. important for those participating in the sanctuary rituals, of whom a high standard was required. Whatever approached God or was offered up to him must be perfect, so that priests had to be free from both ceremonial impurity and physical defects (21:1–23; Deut. 15:21). In the same way sacrifices had to be without blemish (Lev. 22:19–22), to symbolize the offering of the very best of human productivity to God. Otherwise punishment would result (cf. Mal. 1:7–14). In Isa. 33:23; 35:6; Jer. 31:8, and elsewhere, the lame are mentioned in connection with the promised future.

NT *chōlos* occurs 14x in the NT. In Matt. 11:5; 15:30–31; 18:8; Mk. 9:45; Lk. 7:22; Acts 3:2; 14:8; Heb. 12:13, the reference is either implicitly or explicitly to impairment of the legs and feet. Of a more indeterminate nature is the use of *chōlos* in Matt. 21:14; Lk. 14:13, 21; Jn. 5:3; Acts 8:7. In the NT the lame, the maimed, or the crippled were invariably regarded as underprivileged members of society and thus objects of charity, whether of a secular (cf. Lk. 14:13) or Christian (cf. Acts 3:2–10) nature.

See also *kyllos*, crooked, crippled, maimed (*3245*); *paralytikos*, paralytic (*4166*).

6001 (*chōra*, country, region), → *6003*.

| 6003 χωρέω |

χωρέω (*chōreō*), have or make room for, give way, go (*6003*); χώρα (*chōra*), country, region (*6001*).

CL & OT 1. *chōreō* is a verbal derivative of *chōros* or *chōra*, an open space, a land, country, region. (a) Intrans. it means to give room, to be in motion from one place to another. When applied to persons, it can mean to give ground in battle, to tackle and carry out something, or to come to regret an action. When applied to things, its meaning includes to move things, to spread news or commands, to undertake something, e.g., a war. (b) Trans. it means to be able to take up, hold something; in an extended sense, to be able to put up with someone.

2. *chōra* is a frequent word in the LXX, occasionally for the land of Canaan (Gen. 15:7; Isa. 2:7) but much more often for other lands and territories (e.g., Gen. 10:20; Num. 32:1; Ps. 105:44). *chōreō* is rare in the LXX, being used in connection with the capacity that cultic vessels have to hold something (e.g., 1 Ki. 7:38). In the writings of Hel. Jud. outside the LXX *chōreō* is relatively common: (a) intrans., of war spreading, of human wickedness increasing and spreading; (b) trans., often of one's incapacity to grasp the knowledge of God presented to one or to bear the word of God.

NT 1. *Intransitive use.* The expression "everyone to come [*chōreō*] to repentance" (2 Pet. 3:9) corresponds to the use of *chōreō* in the sense of tackling something and carrying it out. The thought is probably that of a single act that is possible, since God is delaying the last judgment. The phrase "goes [*chōreō*] into the stomach" (Matt. 15:17) corresponds to the description of physiological processes in medicine. It suggests a certain independence of the natural processes of the mind and the will. *chōreō* in Jn. 8:37 means to spread or make progress. It is applied to the failure of Jesus' word to make progress in the hearts and minds of his Jewish opponents. In the context of 8:30, Jesus is apparently speaking to Jews who have heard his teaching with approval, yet without letting it take effect.

2. *Transitive use.* *chōreō* is used to denote the capacity to hold: of water jugs (Jn. 2:6), of a place (Mk. 2:2, "no room left"), and the world, which does not "have room for" all the books that could be written about Jesus (Jn. 21:25). It also means to receive or "accept" the apocalyptic teaching of Jesus (Matt. 19:11–12, contained in 19:9 or 10). Jesus is indirectly exhorting a group of people who have been given an insight or a gift for something to make use of it. The meaning corresponds to understanding and grasping the teaching of the parables (cf. 13:11, 16–17, 19, 23). In both instances Matt. stresses the understanding of the disciples.

Paul's plea to "make room for us" (2 Cor. 7:2) takes up his earlier plea to the Corinthians to extend themselves (6:13) and corresponds to the assurance that "we are not withholding our affection from you, but you are withholding yours from us" (6:12). They are to recognize Paul in his apostolic ministry as he has given himself to them (2 Cor. 1–6), so that they can be proud of one another on the day of the Lord Jesus (1:14).

3. As in the LXX, *chōra* can refer to the land of the Jews (Acts 8:1), but much more often for other countries and territories (Matt. 2:12; 8:28; Lk. 19:12; Acts 16:6). It is also the word commonly used for fields (Jas. 5:4). The shepherds of Bethlehem were out in the fields at night when angels visited them, announcing the birth of Jesus (Lk. 2:8); in Samaria, Jesus looked out and saw fields white for harvest (Jn. 4:35).

See also *gemō*, to load, be full (*1154*); *perisseuō*, be more than enough, abound, excel (*4355*); *plēthos*, number, multitude, crowd (*4436*); *plēroō*, fill, complete, fulfill, accomplish, carry out (*4444*); *chortazō*, to feed, fatten, fill (*5963*).

| 6004 χωρίζω |

χωρίζω (*chōrizō*), divide, separate; (pass.) depart, be separated, divorced (*6004*); ἄγαμος (*agamos*), unmarried (*23*).

CL & OT 1. Cl. Gk. authors use *chōrizō* to denote such separation as the freeing of the soul from the body at death or the dividing of opposing military forces. Fig. the vb. often indicates a separation in thought, i.e., logical distinctions or observable differences.

2. In the LXX *chōrizō* denotes spatial separation of persons (Lev. 13:46; Jdg. 4:11) or things (1 Esd. 4:44, 57), departure (Jdg. 6:18; 2 Macc. 10:19; 12:12), exclusion from office (1 Esd. 5:39), or separation from evil (Ezr. 9:1; Neh. 9:2; 1 Esd. 7:13). The vb. was often used in the papyri and Hel. Gk. in the pass. as a technical term for marital separation, esp. divorce.

NT 1. *chōrizō* may signify a physical separation of persons (Phlm. 15, "he was separated from you") or departure from a city or locality (Acts 1:4; 18:1–2).

2. (a) In a fig. sense, so convinced was Paul of the constancy of God's love that he could list—and then dismiss as impotent—all potential obstacles to the continued flow of that love in Christ to the believer (Rom. 8:35–39). To his question "Who shall separate us from the love of Christ?" (8:35a) comes the answer that nothing in all creation can (8:39).

(b) If the phrase "set apart from sinners" in Heb. 7:26 is construed with what precedes ("holy, blameless, pure"), it refers to Christ's sinlessness. If, on the other hand, it is taken with what follows ("exalted above the heavens"), it refers to his withdrawal from the world of evil. Perhaps the author intends us to understand Christ's separation as both moral and spatial.

3. In Matt. 19:6; Mk. 10:9; 1 Cor. 7:10–11, 15, *chōrizō* is used for divorce. (a) Matt. 19:3–9 (cf. Mk. 10:2–9) records an incident in which the Pharisees try to get Jesus to take sides in the contemporary dispute between the schools of Shammai and Hillel concerning permissible grounds of divorce: "Is it lawful for a man to divorce [*apolyō*; → *apostasion*, divorce, *687*] his wife for any and every reason?" (Matt. 19:3). In reply Jesus appeals to the divine ordinance in Gen. 2:24 that predates any Mosaic legislation (Deut. 24:1–4), in which God's ideal is that the two partners "become one flesh." We must not undo God's work by trying to "separate" what God has joined together (Matt. 19:6; see below for more on this).

(b) In 1 Cor. 7 Paul addresses an aberrant situation at Corinth in which a group of ascetics seem to be enjoining either celibacy (cf. 7:1–2, 8–9) or celibacy within marriage (cf. 7:3–7), or even the dissolution of marriages, whether Christian (cf. 7:10–11) or mixed (cf. 7:12–16). Paul appeals in 7:10–11 to Christ's prohibition of divorce (Matt. 19:6; cf. 5:32; 19:9); he has no need to express his own opinion (cf. 7:12, 25): "A wife must not separate from her husband," nor should "a husband . . . divorce [*aphiēmi*; → *918*] his wife" (7:10b, 11b). Parenthetically the apostle adds (7:11a) that if a separation does take place on the wife's initiative (owing either to her husband's adultery or to his ascetic tendencies), she should remain unmarried or else seek reconciliation. Her option might possibly imply his guilt.

However, with regard to mixed marriages Paul knows of no relevant word from Christ (1 Cor. 7:12a). His judgment is that separation is permissible only "if the unbeliever leaves" (7:15a, probably on the basis of religious incompatibility). In such circumstances, the believing partner need not feel bound to persist in seeking reconciliation since God's calling is to peace, not discord (7:15b), and there is no assurance that the unbelieving spouse will come to faith (7:16).

4. *Divorce, separation, and remarriage.* (a) In principle Paul regards the marriage bond as lifelong (1 Cor. 7:10–11, 39; cf. Rom. 7:1–3). He pictures the marriage union as an image of Christ and the church (Eph. 5:21–33), grounded in the creation ordinance of Gen. 2:24 (Eph. 5:31). The "one flesh" relationship can take place outside marriage, but then it is adulterous. In 1 Cor. 6:12–20 Paul discusses

relations with prostitutes and stresses that no believer should join himself to become one body with such a woman. "Do you not know that he who unites himself with a prostitute is one with her in body? For it is said, 'The two will become one flesh.' But he who unites himself with the Lord is one with him in spirit" (6:16–17). Since sexual acts establish relationships through the body, Paul distinguishes sexual immorality from all other sins (6:18).

In 1 Cor. 5 Paul deals with a case of incest: a certain man's cohabitation with his father's wife; in such a case excommunication is imperative (5:5, 13). The prescribed punishment for incest or adultery in the OT was the execution of the offending parties (Lev. 20:10–12; Deut. 22:22; cf. Jn. 8:1–11). But in the NT excommunication replaces execution. Just as certain acts affected the community in the OT and had to be purged, Paul urges that offender be removed from the NT community. The immoral and adulterers have no place in the kingdom of God (1 Cor. 5:9–11; 6:9–11). However, 6:11 shows that such sins are not beyond the grace of Christ and that the truly penitent can take their full place in the fellowship of the church (cf. also Jn. 8:11).

It is against this background that Paul discusses separation and divorce issues in 1 Cor. 7. The foundation of his teaching is a frank recognition of human needs and the fact that marriage is God's appointed way of avoiding the sins he has just been dealing with (7:2). Moreover, spouses should give each other their conjugal rights, for each rules over the other's body (7:3–4). They are to refrain from normal married relations in which intercourse plays a part only in order to devote themselves to prayer—and then only temporarily—lest Satan tempt them through a lack of self-control (7:5). Some have the gift of celibacy, which enables them to devote themselves to the things of the Lord and to be spared the troubles that beset the married, esp. in view of the times (7:7, 26, 29–35).

In 1 Cor. 7:25–29 Paul writes about "virgins" (7:25; *parthenos*, → *4221*), i.e., the "unmarried" (*agamos*; cf. 7:8, 11, 32). *agamos* is a broader category than *parthenos*, since it includes those who have been married and are now unmarried (7:11) as well as those who have never been married. What Paul says in this section applies equally to single people, widowers, widows, and the divorced. He begins by insisting that his observations are not based on a specific command of the Lord. If a person is currently married, he or she should not seek divorce; if a person is presently single, he or she should not seek marriage, though if anyone does want to get married, that person has not sinned.

Paul is mainly concerned about two things as to whether marriage should take place: the "present crisis" in which we live, coupled with the fact that marriage necessarily brings a division of loyalties (1 Cor. 7:26–35). But there is also a question of the kind of people we are, with our basic human needs and gifts (7:2–9, 36–38). In Paul's opinion this second factor is the decisive one, for if we do not have the gift of celibacy, the unmarried state can be more of a hindrance than a help (7:2, 5, 9, 36–38). It can mean less devoted service and even expose one to great moral danger. Getting married is no sin.

As far as marriage itself is concerned, Paul considers it to be permanent: "A woman is bound [*deō*, bind, → *1313*] to her husband as long as he lives" (1 Cor. 7:39; cf. Rom 7:2–3). Paul offers the following principles: (i) Marriage is intended by God to be lifelong. (ii) Remarriage after the death of a partner is permissible, though not mandatory. (iii) Sexual relations outside the marriage constitute adultery and are thus forbidden. (iv) In such cases divorce is permissible and the so-called innocent party free to remarry; yet grace and reconciliation are available in Christ for those who seek them (1 Cor. 6:9–11) and are preferable.

(b) Paul's teaching is not in conflict with that of Jesus. The question that the Pharisees raised with him deals with the interpretation of Deut. 24:1–4 in the light of existing marriages (Matt. 19:1–12; Mk. 10:1–12; cf. Lk. 16:18). The so-called "exception clause" in Matt. 5:32 and 19:9 permit divorce and remarriage on the grounds of *porneia*

("marital unfaithfulness"), a term that includes adultery (*moicheia*; → *moicheuō*, commit adultery, *3658*) as well as any kind of illegitimate sexual intercourse (→ *porneuō*, commit fornication, *4519*).

The OT law provided for divorce by the husband on the grounds of existing unchastity discovered after the marriage had taken place (Deut. 24:1–4). All he had to do was to give his wife a bill of divorce and send her away. She was then free to marry, but not to return to him as his wife after being married to someone else even if the second husband were to die. The question raised by the Pharisees arose out of the way in which this basis for divorce had been extended and trivialized. The stricter school of Shammai allowed divorce only in cases of adultery, whereas the more lenient school of Hillel extended it to incompatibility on various grounds. While the OT law did permit divorce in certain cases, in the case of adultery *after* marriage the penalty was the execution of the offending parties (Lev. 20:10; Deut. 22:22; cf. Gen. 38:24; Ezek. 16:38–42). The practice of stoning offenders was still an issue in Jesus' lifetime, though it was not always carried out and was stopped under Roman rule (Jn. 8:1–11).

Jesus' teaching went behind the Mosaic permission to the creation ordinance of Gen. 2:24: "For this reason a man will leave his father and mother and be united to his wife, and they will become one flesh." In so doing, he was basing his reply not on the provision made by the law for what a man might do if he found something "displeasing to him" (Deut. 24:1) in the wife he had married but on God's original goal for marriage. The "one flesh" relationship constitutes the essence of marriage and distinguishes that relationship from all others. On the basis of Gen. 2:24, a husband and wife "are no longer two, but one" and should not be separated (Mk. 10:8–9). Jesus goes on to ascribe the Mosaic regulation in Deut. 24:1 to the fact that "your hearts were hard" (Matt. 19:8; Mk. 10:5).

The culminating pronouncement Jesus made is double-edged: "Therefore what God has joined together, let man not separate" (Matt. 19:6b; Mk. 10:9b). The Pharisees had tried to maneuver Jesus into making a statement on a controversial issue in order to force him to take sides and possibly even to contradict the law (Matt. 19:3; Mk. 10:2). Jesus expanded the entire issue by relating it to any party that served to cause the breakdown of a marriage: husband, wife, or even a third party. In fact, as Jesus said in Matt. 5:27–30, even an adulterous look is a step in the direction of a marital separation, and either partner who actually commits adultery is de facto putting the marriage asunder.

The Synoptic Gospels all record Jesus' statement that the man who divorces his wife and marries another commits adultery (Matt. 19:9; Mk. 10:11; Lk. 16:18a). The Pharisees may have asked their initial question about divorce in the context of Herod Antipas, who divorced his own wife and married Herodias, the wife of his half-brother, Philip (Matt. 14:3–4; Mk. 6:17–18; Lk. 3:19). This situation had been denounced by John the Baptist and ultimately led to his death, and perhaps the Pharisees were hoping a similar perspective from Jesus would have the same result. The question would have added poignancy, since Jesus had just entered the territory of Antipas "across the Jordan" (Matt. 19:1; Mk. 10:1).

Moreover, in Mk. 10:12 Jesus denounces as adultery the case of the woman who divorces her husband in order to marry another. This too would fit the case of Herodias (though Jesus said this to his disciples in private). The key element in God's sight is not the formalities of a divorce but the action that constitutes the breakup of the marriage relationship. What is condemned as adulterous is what causes the breakup of a marriage for the sake of a new liaison.

What about the exception clause, which occurs in Matt. 5:32; 19:9, but not in Mk. or Lk.? Some scholars regard this clause as an addition by Matt. to soften the rigorous teaching of Jesus. Others, however, argue that Mk. and Lk. have abbreviated their sources. Clearly abbreviation has taken place in the case of Lk., who gives only the pronouncement with no background or prior discussion. Still others believe that Matt. has added material but see it as an editorial clarification expressing the mind of Jesus in the light of the historical situation.

We should also draw attention to the parallel between the teaching of Matt. 19:10–12 and Paul's teaching on gifts in relation to marriage and celibacy (1 Cor. 7:1–9, 36–38). The response of Jesus' disciples to his teaching on this issue is similar to that of the spiritual party at Corinth, that perhaps the best course for a follower of Jesus to follow is to refrain from sexual relations altogether, including marriage: "If this is the situation between a husband and wife, it is better not to marry" (Matt. 19:10). The implication is that the only safe course is to try to live without sexual relations. Jesus' reply crystallizes their thought by explicitly referring to "eunuchs." But Jesus distinguishes between those who are such by nature and those who are capable of living as such for the sake of the kingdom (19:12). In other words, as Paul said, both marriage and celibacy are gifts. Deliberately to avoid marriage for fear of not being able to stay married is an unrealistic solution. It all depends on the gifts one has been given: "The one who can accept this should accept it" (19:12).

See also *schizō*, split, tear, divide, separate (*5387*); *apostasion*, divorce (*687*).

Ψ *psi*

6010 (*psallō*, sing [a hymn or praise]), → 6011.

<table>
<tr><td>6011   ψαλμός</td></tr>
</table>

ψαλμός (*psalmos*), a sacred song, psalm (*6011*); ψάλλω (*psallō*), sing (a hymn or praise) (*6010*).

CL & OT 1. In cl. Gk. *psallō* originally meant to pluck (hair), to twang a bow-string, and then pluck a harp or any other stringed instrument. The noun *psalmos* refers in general to the sound of the instrument or to the actual production of the sound.

2. (a) In the LXX *psallō* and *psalmos* generally refer to the individual psalms in the book of Psalms. It often occurs in various headings, e.g., "A psalm of David." It seems apparent that, at least during the OT period, the singing of Ps. was always accompanied by musical instruments. *psalmos* can also mean any spiritual song, whether or not an instrumental accompaniment is mentioned (cf. Ps. 33:2). The phrase "play the harp" in 1 Sam. 16:16, 18 is *psallein en kinyra* (lit., "to sing with a lyre"). Finally, *psalmos* can refer to profane songs, such as the drunkards' songs of 69:12.

(b) The particular significance of "psalms" (nearly always meaning those of David, but also later poems up to and including the psalms of Qumran) is that, by and large, they constituted the backbone of Jewish synagogue worship. Individual psalms provided a daily form of prayer for the faithful Jew.

NT 1. In the NT two basic meanings can be ascertained. (a) *psalmos* can denote the OT book of "Psalms" or even the entire so-called Writings, the third division of the Heb. Bible, of which Ps. was first in this division (see Lk. 20:42; 24:44; Acts 1:20; 13:33). (b) More generally *psalmos* can mean a hymn of praise; *psallō*, to sing a spiritual or sacred song (→ *psalmos* in 1 Cor. 14:26; Eph. 5:19; Col. 3:16; *psallō* in Rom. 15:9; 1 Cor. 14:15; Eph. 5:19; Jas. 5:13).

2. It is remarkable not only that these words occur only 4x in Lk., 7x in Paul, and once in Jas., but also that they are used by Lk. only in the first sense and by the other writers only in the second. But the reason for this is not so much theological as that the vocabulary is influenced by the respective contexts. Lk., for instance, emphasizes the continuity of salvation history in Jud. and Christianity.

3. The meaning "hymn of praise" or "to sing a spiritual or inspired song" can be further subdivided as follows. (a) A hymn of praise (*psalmos*) or the singing of praises is a typical manifestation either of the Spirit of God in his present activity in the community of the baptized (Eph. 5:18–19; Col. 3:16), or of God himself (1 Cor. 14:25–26). This includes free compositions, repeated liturgical fragments, and new Christian songs (which may well have been modeled on the psalms of the OT and of Jud.), such as we know from the wording of the various songs of Rev. (cf. 5:9–13; 7:12; 11:15, 17–18; 12:10–12; 15:3–4; 19:1–2, 6–8).

In 1 Cor. 14:15 Paul also regards singing as a manifestation of the Spirit, being a higher activity than speaking in tongues on the grounds that it is more edifying: "I will sing with my spirit, but I will also sing with the mind." The contrast in the context of 14:14 is not between "with [or in] the spirit" (either the speaker's or more probably the Holy Spirit) and "with [or in] the mind," but between being in the Spirit unintelligibly and therefore unedifyingly (in tongues) and being in the Spirit intelligibly (cf. 14:16–19).

A similar meaning underlies Jas. 5:13, albeit in a less explicit sense: "Is any one of you in trouble? He should pray. Is anyone happy? Let him sing songs of praise." This answer is given in response to the question: How should a devout Christian react to adversity and pros-

perity? Our feelings must be expressed in an intelligible form and should be directed to God.

(b) *psallō* has the sense to sing hymns of praise in God's honor in Rom. 15:9, where Ps. 18:49 and 2 Sam. 22:50 are seen as finding fulfillment in the coming of Christ and the response to that among the Gentiles: "so that the Gentiles may glorify God for his mercy, as it is written, 'Therefore I will praise you among the Gentiles; I will sing hymns [*psallō*] to your name.'"

See also *hymnos*, song, song of praise, hymn, ode (*5631*); *ōdē*, song, ode (of mourning, complaint, or joy) (*6046*).

6012 (*pseudadelphos*, false brother), → *81*.

6013 (*pseudapostolos*, false apostle), → *690*.

6014 (*pseudēs*, deceitful, mendacious, a liar), → *6017*.

6015 (*pseudodidaskalos*, false teacher), → *1437*.

<table>
<tr><td>6017   ψεύδομαι</td></tr>
</table>

ψεύδομαι (*pseudomai*), lie, deceive by lying (*6017*); ψευδής (*pseudēs*), deceitful, mendacious, a liar (*6014*); ψεῦδος (*pseudos*), a lie (*6022*); ψεύστης (*pseustēs*), a liar (*6026*); ἀψευδής (*apseudēs*), guileless, truthful (*950*).

CL & OT 1. The noun *pseudos* means a lie, the antithesis of the truth (*alētheia*; → *237*). The OT proclaims that God is truthful. He and his word can be trusted. "God is not a man, that he should lie. . . . Does he speak and then not act? Does he promise and not fulfill?" (Num. 23:19; cf. 1 Sam. 15:29).

2. Humans, however, have fallen prey to a lie; they have dissociated themselves from God and do not acknowledge him as Lord. The prophets accuse God's people of falling prey to a lie. Instead of trusting their Lord, they rely on their own strength and political alliances. They listen to false prophets (Jer. 5:31; Ezek. 13:19) who flatter them, give false prophesies of salvation, and whitewash over sin (Ezek. 22:28; cf. Hos. 10:13). The most serious accusation is that the people put their faith in idols instead of in God, which the prophets call lies (Isa. 28:15; 59:13; Jer. 5:12; Ezek. 13:8; Amos 2:4). Lying, in the eyes of the prophets, is not so much an ethical offense as a basic moral attitude that turns its back on the one true God. Only a remnant will survive God's judgment: those who "speak no lies, nor will deceit be found in their mouths" (Zeph. 3:13).

3. Similarly in Ps. those who turn from God are described as liars: "Even from birth the wicked go astray; from the womb they are wayward and speak lies" (58:3). "In my dismay I said, 'All men are liars'" (116:11). But the devout hold firm to God and do not "turn aside to false [*pseudeis*] gods"(40:4). God will make an end of all liars (5:6).

4. In the OT laws the Lord states explicitly, "Do not lie. Do not deceive one another" (Lev. 19:11). Notable is the command in the Decalogue not to give false testimony (Exod. 20:16; cf. Lev. 19:12; Prov. 21:28). Such a thing is reprehensible because in ancient Israel judgment could be given solely on the basis of the evidence of two or three witnesses (Num. 35:30; Deut. 17:6–7; 19:15–21).

5. Rab. texts likewise declare that God has nothing to do with lies. Four groups of people will not see God: scoffers, hypocrites, liars, and slanderers. To bear false witness against one's neighbor is to bear false witness against God. In the Qumran writings, lies belong on the side of God's adversary and to the powers of darkness. They are the mark of the godless, whereas members of God's community are called "sons of truth." Belial uses lies to lead the godly astray; thus, the godly

person confesses: "I will not keep Belial within my heart, and in my mouth shall be heard no folly or deceitful lie" (1QS 10:22).

NT In the NT 15 different words contain the root *pseud-* (false; *6012–6026*), occurring esp. in Johannine and Pauline writings. Besides the words listed in the head paragraph are the following:

- *pseudadelphos*, false brother (2 Cor. 11:26; Gal. 2:4)
- *pseudapostolos*, false apostle (2 Cor. 11:13)
- *pseudodidaskalos*, false teacher (2 Pet. 2:1)
- *pseudologos*, liar (1 Tim. 4:2)
- *pseudomartyreō*, to give false witness (5x; e.g., Matt. 19:18; Mk. 14:56)
- *pseudomartys*, one who gives false witness (Matt. 26:60; 1 Cor. 15:15)
- *pseudomartyria*, false testimony (Matt. 15:19; 26:59)
- *pseudoprophētēs*, false prophet (11x; e.g., Matt. 7:15; 24:11, 24; Rev. 16:13; 19:20)
- *pseudochristos*, false Christ (Matt. 24:24; Mk. 13:22)
- *pseudōnymos*, bearing a false name (1 Tim. 6:20)
- *pseusma*, falsehood (Rom. 3:7)

1. (a) The NT takes up the OT witness to the truthfulness and truth of God. Tit. 1:2 speaks of God as one "who does not lie [*apseudēs*]." God keeps faith with his promises in history, for his decrees are unchangeable. The writer of Heb. stresses how God's keeping his promises and swearing an oath indicate that "it is impossible for God to lie" (6:18). Since the God who raised Jesus from the dead is the source of truth, Paul defended himself by claiming in the last resort that God knows that he is not lying (2 Cor. 11:31; Gal. 1:20).

(b) The revelation of God's truth in Jesus Christ lets the other side of the picture come to light—the lies of humans, who have "exchanged the truth of God for a lie, and worshiped and served created things rather than the Creator" (Rom. 1:25). The revelation of God's wrath against human wickedness (1:18–3:20) leads in 3:4 to the confession: "Let God be true, and every man be liar. As it is written: 'So that you may be proved right when you speak and prevail when you judge'" (cf. Ps. 51:4).

2. (a) Jn.'s Gospel presents a dualism of God and the devil in terms of truth and lie. The devil is "a liar and the father of lies" (Jn. 8:44); it is his "native language." Lying and death stand opposed to the truth and life of the Revealer. Lying here is not simply telling untruths; rather, it connotes the will directed against God, unbelief, and resulting futility (see 8:41–47, where Jesus accuses his opponents of lying). Such lying happens everywhere that humans seek their own glory and put up barriers to resist Christ's revelation.

(b) This thought is expanded in 1 Jn. People "make [God] out to be a liar" when they claim that they have not sinned (1:10; cf. 5:10). This letter is also directed against false teachers who preach lies (2:22), denying Jesus as the Christ (cf. Rev. 2:2). In the Johannine literature *lie* is used in the widest sense to mean hatred of Christ and thus life without God.

3. (a) The antithesis of truth and lie is not only the determining factor that distinguishes between Jesus' disciples and his enemies. It also operates within the church in the responses of obedience and disobedience to the word of truth. Peter asks Ananias, "How is it that Satan has so filled your heart that you have lied to the Holy Spirit?" (Acts 5:3). Ananias's sin was not that he withheld his property but that he lied to God in professing to have given it all to the church while retaining something for himself (5:4).

(b) In 1 Jn., the false evaluation that human beings give themselves in relation to God (see above) means that any contradiction between one's confession of faith and one's life as a member of the church involves him or her in a lie. Three examples of such behavior include: to profess fellowship with Christ while walking in darkness (1:6); to profess knowledge of Christ while disobeying his commands (2:4); to profess love for God while hating one's brother (4:20). Here,

too, it is apparent that for 1 Jn. lying is not only a moral offence but also the manifestation of life without God.

(c) The admonitions in Eph. and Col. have individual faults in mind when their readers are told to throw off falsehood and to speak the truth to each other (Eph. 4:25; Col. 3:9). Paul can make this command because Christians have put off "the old self" and may put on "the new self" (Eph. 4:22–24; cf. Col. 3:9–10) and are therefore in the position to stop lying.

(d) Rev. likewise understands lying in specific terms: No liar (*pseudēs*) or perpetrator of horrible deeds will enter the new Jerusalem (21:8, 27; 22:15). Those who belong to the Lamb stand opposed to liars: "No lie was found on their mouths" (14:5). As in Jn. and 1 Jn., lying and falsehood stand in fundamental opposition to God. Thus the Jews at Philadelphia are described as "the synagogue of Satan, who claim to be Jews . . . but are liars" (3:9).

See also *hypokrinomai*, answer, pretend, dissimulate (*5693*).

6018 (pseudomartyreō, bear false witness), → *3456*.

6019 (pseudomartyria, false witness), → *3456*.

6020 (pseudomartys, one who gives false testimony), → *3456*.

6021 (pseudoprophētēs, false prophet), → *4737*.

6022 (pseudos, a lie), → *6017*.

6023 (pseudochristos, false Christ), → *532*.

6024 (pseudōnymos, bearing a false name), → *3950*.

6026 (pseustēs, a liar), → *6017*.

6030 (psithyrismos, whispering, gossip), → *2895*.

6031 (psithyristēs, whisperer, gossiper), → *2895*.

6034 ψυχή

ψυχή (*psychē*), soul, life (*6034*); ψυχικός (*psychikos*), pertaining to the soul or life, and thus physical (in contrast to spiritual), unspiritual (*6035*); ἀνάψυξις (*anapsyxis*), refreshing (*433*); ἀναψύχω (*anapsychō*), to refresh, cheer (*434*); δίψυχος (*dipsychos*), double-minded (*1500*); εὐψυχέω (*eupsycheō*), to cheer (*2379*); ὀλιγόψυχος (*oligopsychos*), fainthearted, timid (*3901*); σύμψυχος (*sympsychos*), of the same mind or spirit (*5249*).

CL 1. Early in cl. Gk. *psychē* was impersonal: the breath that gives life to humankind. Linked with *psychē* was *thymos*, which denoted the warm flow of blood, the life force, hence, emotion. Together the two words connoted a psycho-physical entity. But when the dependence of the conscious soul (*thymos*) on the unconscious (*psychē*) became recognized in Gk. thinking, the meaning of *psychē* was broadened to include *thymos*. Thus the *psychē* became the bearer of conscious experiences. Later the *psychē* was regarded as the permanent part of the person, an independent soul in contrast to the body.

2. (a) In ancient Gk. lit., the soul is conceived as combined with the body as two parts forming one person. When it leaves the body, the body loses its life. Thus the soul can simply stand for life. A person may release one's soul, and so one's life, from oneself. *psychē* can even come to mean things as dear as life, e.g., money and children.

(b) *psychē* can also refer to the inward part of a person, i.e., one's personality. Here the soul becomes equivalent to the person. The *psychē*, bound as it is to the body, is so much a personal force that it can be used instead of the pers. pron. (i.e., "my soul" is equivalent to "I"). If a human being is anything at all, he or she is soul.

The actual power of the soul is seen first of all in the movement that it imparts to the body in which it lives. It becomes the character and disposition of the person. According to Aristotle, the soul fills and moves a person and describes it as fire and warmth; Plato suggests that the soul can be robbed of its body.

The soul is the seat of perception, of desire and pleasure, and of enjoyment. *psychē* can be used generally in place of emotion. The soul, not the body, is the seat of love and desire, hunger and thirst. The powers of reason and will are, however, also part of the soul. Thus the soul finds a place alongside thought and judgment; its tasks are to care, rule, and advise. In all this, the soul remains incorporeal.

With the Stoics, however, the view develops that the soul is material, nourished by material substances and filling the body. It is correlated to the body. The substance of the soul is the *pneuma*, breath. Like the body, it results from procreation. Emotions are the greatest enemies of the soul and are in a position to rob it of liberty.

The essential characteristic of the soul consists in the fact that it can set itself in motion. Among all animate beings, the human being is the one in whom the deity has implanted the most powerful soul. Furthermore, it has a share in divinity, since the divine power rules in humankind by means of the soul. The soul can be trained. The most important thing is to cultivate or take care of it rather than to pursue wealth or happiness. For virtue does not result from wealth; on the contrary, the acquisition of wealth and of other good things both in private and in public life are the fruit of virtue. One can say that here for the first time we find the concept of the care of souls. The human reaches harmony by gaining full mastery over oneself; the soul is enabled to govern the body.

(c) Gk. lit. speaks both of the departure of the soul (i.e., the loss of life) and of an abode of souls. It is a likeness of the person concerned, but it is not that person himself or herself. The soul is thus represented as an entity in its own right as opposed to the body; it joins itself to its body and leaves it again. Related to this in thought is the concept of a journey of the soul into the world beyond and its return to the earth, or of its descent from the realm of light into the body and its return to the heavenly world by means of a cycle of births. Another concept is that of a gathering of the souls in a field in the underworld, to hear the judgment as to whether they will partake in the eternal symposium or lie in the mire of the underworld. The driving force behind these ideas about the soul is the religious movement of Orphism.

Plato provides us with the idea that the soul is immortal and that it can be deprived of its body; in fact, the soul does not come fully into its own until it has been separated from the body. He argues for the necessity of the soul's immortality on the ground that a lifetime is too short a period for the moral struggle in humankind. A person must therefore be able to collect and assess experiences from several incarnations of one's soul. It has knowledge of the forms of ultimate reality, which it acquired in prephysical existence. The body is clothing for the soul or a kind of prison. Liberation from this prison may be achieved by Bacchic ceremonies, by the grace of gods who provide redemption, or by ascetic renunciation of earthly existence. The immortal souls are led into the underworld by Hermes.

In a fig. sense, *psychē* can also be used of the inspiring force in the constitution of a state. Gk. writers can refer to the soul of the city or even that of Greece. The thought of a world soul as the life principle of the cosmos is found in the Stoic writer Chrysippus.

OT 1. In the LXX, *psychē*, soul, occurs over 900x and is distributed fairly equally among the various books. Most often it stands for the Heb. *nep̄eš* (breath, life, soul), but also 25x for *lēb* (heart, inner person) as well as a few times for several other Heb. words.

(a) *nep̄eš* denotes that which makes a body, whether of a human or an animal, into a living being. When *nep̄eš* is translated as *psychē*, it signifies what gives life to a person (e.g., Gen. 2:7). Note 1:20, which speaks of "living souls" (NIV, "living creatures"). A dying person breathes out the soul (Jer. 15:9) or pours it out (Lam. 2:12), though it can also return to a person's body (1 Ki. 17:21). "Soul for soul" means "life for life" (Exod. 21:23). Blood, as the seat of life, can be practically identical with *psychē* (Gen. 9:4–5; Lev. 17:11, 14).

(b) *psychē*, rendering *nep̄eš*, is the sensitive part of the life of the ego, the seat of the emotions: e.g., love (Song 1:7), longing (Ps. 63:1), and gladness (86:4). The *psychē* reveals its life in movement and

the various expressions of the emotions. It is the uniting factor for the inner powers of a person—hence the phrase "with all your soul" (Deut. 13:3). Within the soul dwell the desire for food (12:20, 21), the lust of the flesh (Jer. 2:24), and the thirst for murder and revenge (Ps. 27:12). The soul expresses its feelings: It weeps (119:28), is poured out in tears (Job 30:16), and experiences patient endurance (6:11). But knowledge and understanding (Ps. 139:14), thought (1 Sam. 20:4), and memory (Lam. 3:20) have their seat in the soul as well. So much does the soul sum up the whole self of a person that "soul" can be equivalent to the self (cf. 1 Sam. 18:1). When the people are numbered, counting is by "souls" (Exod. 1:5; Deut. 10:22).

Living creatures likewise can be described as souls: everything that lives, all living things, usually in a collective sense (Lev. 11:10). A clear indication of how unfamiliar the OT is with the concept of a soul separate from the body (e.g., at death), is the fact that it can speak of a corpse as the soul of a person, meaning by this phrase the dead person in his or her corporeality (Num. 6:6).

(c) Whereas in Qumran texts this word remains totally within the OT framework, Hel. influence is more clearly discernible in the Apocr. While elsewhere the OT does not reflect on the relationship between body and soul, the Apocr. contrasts these two elements. A perishable body weighs down the soul (Wis. 9:15), and the souls of the righteous are in the hand of God (3:1). Pollution of souls is also mentioned (14:26). It is esp. bad when no healing can be found for the soul, so that it must perish eternally (16:9).

2. (a) For Josephus, *psychē* is primarily the seat of outward, earthly life. It is the sense of the inner person with its various powers as contrasted with the body. It is the locus of the will and the virtues, the seat of the emotions and various personal qualities. Josephus also contrasts immortal souls with human bodies. The soul, not being subject to corruption, can pass over into another body. The evil soul will, however, suffer eternal punishment. From these concepts it is clear that Josephus moves in the world of Hel. thought concerning the immortality of the soul and its true life, separated from the body, in eternal fellowship with God.

(b) For Philo the soul is the side of human existence that has been equipped with divine powers and possibilities; it belongs to the divine Spirit, and its first power is that of glorifying God. Of particular concern for Philo is the governing principle of souls, the *nous*, understanding (→ *3808*). The essence of this governing part is the Spirit of God. Philo also knows *psychē* in the sense of life; its whole being is in the blood and thus includes what is mortal. But in striking contrast to the OT, Philo takes it for granted that there are bodiless souls (i.e., angels). As in Gk. philosophy, the soul finally leaves the mortal part belonging to it behind and goes into the world of things imperishable and incorruptible. It is at home in the divine world; in the body it finds itself in an alien.

(c) Hel. influences are also discernible in Jewish lit. For example, 4 Macc. demonstrates this with its conception of an immortal soul that separates itself from the body in death (14:6); the victor's prize for virtue is everlasting life for the soul (cf. 17:12). In the hour of death, the souls of the righteous are received by the patriarchs (cf. 5:37; 13:17). Rab. lit. contains similar ideas. For example, in the midrash on Eccl. 3:21–22a the souls of both the righteous and the ungodly rise at death to the heavenly height in order to receive the judgment.

These views may be in the background of Lk. 16:23 (Lazarus in Abraham's bosom and the rich man in the place of torment) and of 23:43 (Jesus' saying, "Today you will be with me in paradise"). At the end of time, God will bring soul and body together and judge both. According to 2 Esd. 7:78–101 souls are judged directly after death and are sent to a place of refreshment, peace, and sevenfold joy, or to a place of torments and roaming in sevenfold pain.

NT 1. In the NT, by way of contrast to the frequent use of *psychē* in the LXX, this word occurs only 102x, the majority of which are in the narrative portions of the NT.

(a) *psychē*, soul, is the seat of life or life itself, as in the well-known saying: "Whoever wants to save his life [*psychē*] will lose it, but whoever loses his life for me . . . will save it" (Mk. 8:35; cf. Matt. 16:25; Lk. 9:24). The principle that the person who gives up one's life will truly find it becomes clear from the example of Jesus himself and his death and resurrection: True life is ever only won through sacrifice.

psychē also means life in the saying of Matt. 20:28; Mk. 10:45, where Christ's mission is stated as his giving his life as a ransom for many. So too at Lk. 14:26, to hate one's *psychē* means hating one's "own life" (cf. 9:23). The counterpart of 14:26 is Rev. 12:11, which speaks of those who have not loved their lives.

psychē embraces the whole natural being and life of a human being for which one concerns oneself and of which one takes constant care. Thus Matt. 6:25 speaks of being anxious for one's *psychē*, i.e., for its food. Life (*psychē*) and body (*sōma*) are God's handiwork; thus, they are of more importance than the food and clothing about which we are so concerned. In Lk. 12:19 the rich man addresses his *psychē*, i.e., he speaks to himself. What he does not realize is his *psychē*, i.e., his life, can be taken from him at any moment. The citation of Ps. 16:10 in Acts 2:27 also speaks of the *psychē*—again, the seat of life—as being left by God in Hades, i.e., left dead in the grave. Even for Paul, to think little of the soul means to think little of one's life (Phil. 2:30).

Jn. 10:11 speaks of Jesus laying down his *psychē* for the sheep. This is why the Father loves the good shepherd (10:17). The same expression is used in 13:37–38, where Pet. offers to lay down his *psychē* for Jesus. People can also risk their lives for others (Rom. 16:4) or "for the name of our Lord Jesus Christ" (Acts 15:26).

psychē is also found in the NT in recording numbers of people (e.g., "Jacob and his whole family, seventy-five [souls] in all" [Acts 7:14]; "276 [souls]" shipwrecked on Malta [27:37]; "a few people [*psychē*], eight in all," were saved in Noah's ark [1 Pet. 3:20]) as well as in the phrase "every soul," which means "everyone" (Acts 2:43; cf. 3:23; 27:22; Rom. 2:9; 13:1).

The expression "every living thing [soul]" (Rev. 16:3; cf. 8:9) is also to be understood in the OT sense. At creation the dust of the ground was made into a "living soul" by the breathing in of the divine breath (cf. Gen. 2:7). Paul takes up this idea in 1 Cor. 15:45 in order to contrast Adam as a created "living being [soul]" with the life-giving Spirit present in Jesus Christ.

(b) *psychē* means the inner life of a person, equivalent to the ego or personality, and has various powers. In 2 Cor. 1:23 Paul pledges his "soul" in a solemn oath (lit., "I call on God as my witness, upon my soul"). The reference here is not only to Paul's life but to his whole person, with all that he believes, hopes, and strives for. Similarly in 1 Thess. 2:8, Paul writes concerning himself and his coworkers that they have given their "souls," i.e., their living powers of energy, working day and night in their care of the churches. Jesus speaks of souls that are in need of rest and peace (Matt. 11:29), since, in the depth of one's inner soul sorrow is experienced (26:38; Mk. 14:34; cf. Ps. 42:6).

In Lk. 1:46 soul is used in parallel with spirit. Both have here the meaning of the whole inner person in contrast to the outward aspect of lips and speech. Above all, the soul is spoken of here in a sense that goes beyond the world of Gk. thought. It is the seat of the religious life and of one's relationship to God. It is this religious root in human existence that is referred to in 2:35, contrasted directly with the sword that wounds the body outwardly. We have here to do with a hidden, inward experience of the soul. The religious life of a person is also the subject of 3 Jn. 2: lit., "it is well with your soul."

(c) Of some interest is the contrast of soul (*psychē*) and spirit (*pneuma*, → *4460*) as expressed in 1 Thess. 5:23, with its tripartite division of a human: spirit, soul, and body. The "spirit" in this context, as in Philo and Platonism, means the higher side of a person (cf. Heb. 4:12). "Soul" thus means life, i.e., the fact of being alive, and the human aspect that has to do with willing and with emotion. In a similar way, in 1 Cor. 2:14 Paul contrasts *psychikos* and *pneumatikos*. The former is the animate person, filled with soul in the sense of life-

force ("a living being," Gen. 2:7; cf. 1 Cor. 15:45); the latter is spirit: that aspect of the individual that is enlightened by God's Spirit.

The adj. *psychikos* is used again in Paul's discussion of the nature of the resurrection in 1 Cor. 15:44–46, where the body of this life is contrasted with the resurrection body. The former is *psychikos*; the latter is *pneumatikos*. Through this distinction Paul counters the objection against the absurdity of thinking of the resurrection as the resuscitation of our corpses. The NIV rightly brings out the contrast between life under the conditions of space and time and the resurrection life by translating *psychikos* here by "natural." In Jas. 3:15, on the other hand, *psychikos* is best translated as "unspiritual." Here the contrast is worldly wisdom and divine wisdom. Finally, in Jude 19 the NIV translates this word as those who "follow mere natural instincts." In each case, the emphasis falls on a person in oneself without the new life of God.

In Heb. 6:19 ("an anchor for the soul"), "soul" again means the whole inner life of an individual with the powers of will, reason, and emotion. In this connection, mention should also be made of the use of *psychē* to mean insight, will, disposition, sensations, and moral powers of humankind (cf. also Matt. 22:37; Mk. 12:30; Lk. 10:27; cf. Deut. 6:5).

(d) In terms of Gk. phrases, *ek psychēs*, "from your heart" (Eph. 6:6; Col. 3:23), should be understood as the inner disposition of a person. Similarly we find the phrase *mia psychē*, "as one man" (Phil. 1:27), resulting from our standing firm "in one spirit." The background here is probably the notion that the church is the body of Christ, which, like a human body, is filled with a soul, showing itself as real and alive when it completes the unity of the body by bringing about a unity of inner powers within the church. Likewise, in Acts 4:32 the common "mind" is meant, so that the church is united with one heart and one soul. This inner power of the church members is also the target of the exhortation in Heb. 12:3 not to "lose heart." Souls that are not firmly established can be enticed and led astray (10:39). Souls can also be activated in wrong and evil ways; they can be poisoned (Acts 14:2).

(e) Hel. Jud. is familiar with the concepts both of the soul's corruption and of the soul's salvation. These lines of thought appear in the later letters of the NT, but nowhere does the NT refer to an immortal soul as the guarantee or substance of eternal life. Although certain passages show traces of Hellenism, they are nonetheless brought to a different level by biblical tradition, basic eschatological insights, and the Christian experience of faith in the risen Lord. It is the task of the church leader, for example, to "keep watch over your souls [NIV, you]," which are destined for eternity (Heb. 13:17).

Jas. 1:21 and 5:20 speak of the salvation of a soul that is in danger. The death from which it is said that the soul will be saved is eternal death.

The salvation of souls is the goal of faith and the content of God's saving activity, in which he gives all those who are baptized a share (1 Pet. 1:9). It is probably for this reason that 1:22 speaks of the purification of the soul, i.e., the inner life (NIV, "yourselves"). It is a matter of the soul in its relationship to God. The soul, as the part of us that believes and is sanctified, is destined to an inheritance in God's future kingdom. Thus here the contrast is not between spirit, soul, and body, but between the soul and the lusts of the sinful nature. It is souls in this sense that are meant in 2:25, their "Shepherd and Overseer" being Jesus Christ himself. "Soul" is used again in the same sense of being destined for eternal life and victory over death when Christians are exhorted in 4:19 to entrust their souls to God in time of persecution, for he will preserve us for eternity.

Matt. 10:28 (cf. Lk. 12:5) also falls into this category. The soul is directed to God alone, who "can destroy both soul and body in hell." The soul in this sense only exists because it is called by God and because it allows itself to be called and filled with divine power. God alone has power over it. He can let it live, and he can destroy it. Similarly in Rev. 6:9 and 20:4 mention is made of "the souls" of those who have been slain, who are under the altar of God in heaven. The martyrs, who have shed their blood for Christ's sake, are compared with sacrifices; that is why their souls are under the altar. The dominant thought here is that the souls that have been won by God, have been saved, believe in him, and have sacrificed themselves for him are preserved in his keeping.

2. The NT contains several other compounds related to *psyche*. (a) *anapsyxis* occurs only at Acts 3:19 in the phrase "times of refreshing," i.e., the age of salvation, which is promised to the nation of Israel if it repents. Although many Jews were converted (2:41; 4:4; 5:14; 21:20), the Israel Lk. describes in Acts is one in which large numbers of Gentiles are incorporated and from which many of the old Israel remain aloof.

(b) The cognate vb. *anapsychō* has a trans. meaning at the only place where it occurs in the NT, as compared with its intrans. sense in the LXX, where it means to refresh oneself (Exod. 23:12; Jdg. 15:19; 1 Sam. 16:23). In 2 Tim. 1:16 Paul mentions how Onesiphorus often refreshed him while he was in prison. It is not clear whether this refers to physical refreshing or spiritual encouragement, or both.

(c) The term *dipsychos*, "double-minded," occurs in Jas. 1:8. Perhaps it means with a divided heart. At any rate Jas. makes the twofold point that such a person is unstable and that cannot presume on the goodness of God, for prayer and devotion require a wholehearted attitude to God. In 4:8, Jas. calls on doubters to purify their double-minded (*dipsychos*) hearts (cf. also *haplotēs*, sincerity, *605*).

(d) The rare word *oligopsychos* means timid or discouraged (1 Thess. 5:14). Such persons are to be encouraged, though the idle are to be admonished.

(e) *sympsychos*, harmonious, united in spirit, occurs in Phil. 2:2, where Paul exhorts the church to complete his joy by being "one in spirit," love, and purpose.

(f) In Phil. 2:19 Paul expresses the hope that he "may be cheered" (*eupsycheō*) when he receives news of the Philippians, which no doubt implies the hope that they will have taken to heart his admonition in 2:1–18.

6035 (*psychikos*, pertaining to the soul or life), → *6034*.

6036 (*psychos*, cold), → *6037*.

6037	ψυχρός

ψυχρός (*psychros*), cold (*6037*); ψῦχος (*psychos*), cold (*6036*); ζεστός (*zestos*), boiling, hot (*2412*); χλιαρός (*chliaros*), lukewarm (*5950*); θερμαίνω (*thermainō*), warm, keep warm (*2548*); θέρμη (*thermē*), heat (*2549*).

CL & OT *psychros* (and the noun *psychos*, cold) are commonly used of lit. cold, often of liquids, but also fig., to mean ineffectual or cold-hearted. *zestos*, boiling, is usually lit., but may be applied fig. to human passions. *chliaros* refers mostly to liquids or food. *thermos*, hot, pas-

sionate, and its cognates are common in both lit. and metaphorical senses, often as the antithesis of *psychros*.

In the LXX *psychos* and the *thermē* group are freely used of temperature. The latter group is also occasionally fig.: in particular, *thermainō*, warm, used commonly of fire, may be applied to the heart (Ps. 39:3; Hos. 7:7; cf. Deut. 19:6).

NT 1. In Matt. 10:42 *psychron*, used alone, means cold water. *psychos* (Jn. 18:18; Acts 28:2; 2 Cor. 11:27) denotes cold temperature. *thermē* (once) and *thermainō* (6x) are used in two of the above passages, where Pet. and Paul respectively warm themselves at the fire (Mk. 14:54, 67; Jn. 18:18, 25; cf. Acts 28:2). To be warmed, filled with food, and clothed are the basic necessities of the destitute (Jas. 2:16; cf. 1 Tim. 6:8), and Jas. insists on a practical faith that will supply them to a fellow believer in need.

2. Words in this group are also used metaphorically. (a) The verbal form *psychō* is applied to one's spiritual state (love grows cold, Matt. 24:12; cf. *zeō*, to be fervent, in Acts 18:25; Rom. 12:11).

(b) The main significance of the word group attaches to *chliaros*, *psychros*, and *zestos* in Rev. 3:15–16. Here all three are used metaphorically and absolutely of personal character. The passage has usually been understood to refer to levels of spiritual fervor, which accords with the exhortation in 3:19 to be earnest.

The interpretation is, however, open to question. Rev. 3 presents the notions of cold and hot indifferently, as though both were desirable conditions; indeed, cold twice precedes hot. Note that the Lord does not say, "It is better to be hot or *even* cold, i.e., better *even* stony indifference than halfhearted support."

The present usage is better seen as an image referring to the water supply of Laodicea, which was derived from a pipeline bringing water that was lukewarm and so impure as to have an emetic effect. The words *hot* and *cold* were applicable to the waters of the two neighboring cities, Hierapolis and Colosse (cf. Col. 4:13). The *hot* water, which produced the celebrated petrified cascades of Hierapolis, was medicinal, being used for the eyes by local people even today (cf. Rev. 3:18b); the *cold* perennial stream at Colosse made that city the earliest natural settlement of the valley.

Lukewarmness should thus probably be understood as ineffectiveness, the inadequacy of human effort as a substitute for diverse manifestations of God's giving. Effective service hinges on one's response to Christ, not on human endeavor. The Laodicean Christians are characterized as those whose wealth and self-sufficiency prompted them to work by their own resources rather than to recognize their need of Christ. The point is reinforced by a series of images derived from notable industries and achievements of their city. They have "wealth and do not need a thing," but they must do their business with Christ if they are to obtain the real spiritual goods. In a city that sold eye ointments, the church is spiritually blind; Christ alone can supply it with vision.

Ω omega

6046 ᾠδή

ᾠδή (*ōdē*), song, ode (of mourning, complaint, or joy) (*6046*); ᾄδω (*adō*), to sing (*106*).

CL & OT 1. (a) In cl. Gk. *adō* means to sing; to produce all kinds of vocal sounds (e.g., the hoot of the owl or the croaking of a frog); to produce the sound of a plucked string or any other similar sound; to celebrate, praise, or honor in the cult. (b) The noun *ōdē* occurs in Gk. tragedy with these meanings: a song of mourning or lamentation, a song of joy or praise, poetry in general, and singing in general (whether of humans or birds).

2. (a) In the LXX the vb. occurs 66x, rendering chiefly the Heb. *šîr*, sing (e.g., Exod. 15:1, 21; Num. 21:17; Jdg. 5:1, 3). The noun *ōdē* occurs 87x, mainly for *šîr* and *šîrâ* (e.g., Exod. 15:1; Deut. 31:19, 21–22, 30; 32:44). Except for Deut. 31:30, where *ōdē* is spoken, singing is always indicated. Sometimes musical accompaniment is mentioned (e.g., 1 Chr. 16:42), and sometimes both music and dancing (2 Sam. 6:5). *adō* can also be used in parallel with other words for singing and rejoicing (e.g., 1 Chr. 16:9; Ps. 98:4).

(b) Often the joyous nature of an *ōdē* is stressed. The new song was a song for festive occasions. But Amos 8:10 gives a dire warning to those who self-confidently await the day of Yahweh: "I will turn your religious feasts into mourning and all your singing into weeping." In 1 Chr. 25 the Chronicler writes of the role of the temple singers and music in the cult.

(c) Music is mentioned in various connections in the OT: at a family gathering (Gen. 31:27), the acclamation of heroes (Jdg. 11:34; 1 Sam. 18:6), the king's enthronement and martial occasions (Jdg. 7:18–22; 2 Ki. 11:14; 2 Chr. 13:14; 20:28), harem and court music (2 Sam. 19:35; Eccl. 2:8), feasts (Isa. 5:12; 24:8–9), dirges and laments (2 Sam. 1:17–18; 2 Chr. 35:25), cultic occasions (Exod. 28:35; Jos. 6:4–20), and occupational songs (Num. 21:17–18; Jdg. 9:27; Isa. 16:10).

NT 1. In the NT *ōdē* and *adō* occur only 4x in Paul's letters and 8x in Rev., with both noun and vb. together in Rev. (cf. Eph. 5:19; Col. 3:16; Rev. 5:9; 14:3; 15:3). Rev. 5:9 suggests that it is always a song that is sung. In this book, the entire creation—in heaven, on earth, and below the earth—acknowledges, as of right, the lordship of the Lamb in their eschatological paean of praise. The "song of Moses" in 15:3 transposes the song of Moses in Exod. 15:1 and includes words from Ps. 145:7, giving them a Christological significance. As Moses once sang God's praises after crossing the Red Sea, so those who have gained freedom through the Lamb sing of God's saving deeds.

2. (a) Songs clearly formed a central part of early Christian liturgy, just as they had the worship of the OT community and of the temple. Paul twice alludes to songs in his discussion of the spiritual activity of believers. Rather than being drunk with wine, Christians are urged to "be filled with the Spirit. Speak to one another with psalms, hymns and spiritual songs [*ōdē*]. Sing [*adō*] and make music [*psallō*] in your heart to the Lord, always giving thanks to God the Father for everything, in the name of our Lord Jesus Christ" (Eph. 5:18–20). These songs would no doubt include OT psalms that the NT writers often freely quote, but Christian hymns as well.

(b) Rev. 5:9–10, 12–13; 12:10–12; 19:1–2, 6–8 are among the oldest of Christian songs. Perhaps the earliest Christian hymn is contained in Phil. 2:6–11, which Paul cites in support of his plea to the Philippians to have the mind of Christ. This may have been a pre-Pauline hymn or something that Paul composed himself and that was also known to his readers. Other possible Christological hymns are

the Prologue of Jn.; Eph. 2:14–18; Col. 1:15–20; 1 Tim. 3:16; Heb. 1:3; and 1 Pet. 3:18–22.

(c) Lk.'s account of the birth and infancy narratives contains psalms like the Magnificat, expressing Mary's praise for God's saving mercies (Lk. 1:46–55); the Benedictus, Zechariah's thanksgiving for his son, the future John the Baptist (1:68–79); and the Nunc Dimittis, Simeon's psalm on seeing the infant Jesus in the temple (2:29–32). These psalms are all couched in terms of Yahweh's saving acts against the background of OT expectation.

(d) Elsewhere music is mentioned in the NT in various connections: dirges (Matt. 9:23), prophetic passages (24:31; 1 Cor. 15:52; 1 Thess. 4:16; Heb. 12:19), the music of merrymaking at the return of the lost son (Lk. 15:25), and in a fig. sense (Matt. 6:2; 11:17; Lk. 7:32; 1 Cor. 13:1; 14:7–8).

(e) Singing is an expression of Christian joy; it is at the same time an edifying expression of the Spirit-filled life. Note Col. 3:16: "Let the word of Christ dwell in you richly as you teach and admonish one another with all wisdom, and as you sing psalms [*psalmos*], hymns [*hymnos*] and spiritual songs [*ōdē*] with gratitude in your hearts to God." Although it may be impossible to differentiate exactly between the three terms used here, taken together they express the full range of singing prompted by the Spirit. Psalms probably designates the OT psalms (→ *psalmos, 6011*), hymns were festive songs of praise (→ *hymnos, 5631*), and spiritual songs were songs in which God's acts were praised and glorified.

3. Liturgy, including liturgical singing, involved the entire congregation of the early church. Songs edified those present by building them into a community in Christ. It is interesting to note that the first attacks that the Roman state directed against the church were not so much against holding particular Christian beliefs but against liturgy, that is, against how those beliefs were expressed in the worship of the church. Next to the preaching of the Word and participation in the sacrament, the heart of worship was spiritual singing, a festive recognition of God in Jesus Christ as the Lord of the church and of the world. In this context, the use of *psallō* in parallel to *exomologeō*, confess, in Rom. 15:9 is esp. important: Even singing psalms is a confession of faith before God.

See also *hymnos*, song, song of praise, hymn, ode (*5631*); *psalmos*, a sacred song, psalm (*6011*).

6047 (*ōdin*, pain of labor), → *6048*.

6048 ὠδίνω

ὠδίνω (*ōdinō*), to travail as in giving birth (*6048*); ὠδίν (*ōdin*), pain of labor (*6047*).

CL & OT 1. The cl. authors used *ōdinō* to describe labor pains, esp. of women but also of animals. The word claimed a wide fig. usage for great anguish, hard physical work, emotional or mental strain, or ardent frustrated longing. The noun *ōdin* constitutes a late literary form of the cl. Gk. word *ōdis* and occurs mainly in the LXX and the NT; its meanings are similar to the vb.

2. In the LXX *ōdinō* occurs esp. in Isa. (e.g., 23:4; 45:10; 51:2) to describe the pangs of childbirth, usually used in a fig. sense. *ōdin* occurs frequently in the LXX (e.g., 13:8; 37:3; Jer. 6:24), sometimes describing the agonies of death (e.g., 1 Ki. 22:6; Ps. 18:4), but often used in the context of childbirth. While it is sometimes used fig., the lit. interpretation was strongly represented.

NT *ōdinō* occurs 3x in the NT. It is used lit. at Gal. 4:27 (citing Isa. 54:1) and Rev. 12:2. The only fig. sense is found in Gal. 4:19, where

Paul speaks of giving birth to the believers in Galatia. *ōdin* occurs in 1 Thess. 5:3, where the inevitable fact of labor in a pregnant woman is used fig. of the inescapable prospect of Christ's return. What is stressed is the suddenness of its coming. As a metaphor of intense suffering, *ōdin* occurs in Matt. 24:8; Mk. 13:8. In Acts 2:24 labors pains are associated with the agony of death, reflecting the phraseology of Ps. 18:5–6 ("cords [*ōdin*] of . . . death"). The thought that the Messiah could remain in the grip of death is inconceivable.

See also *basanos*, torture, torment (*992*); *mastigoō*, whip, flog, scourge, chastise (*3463*); *talaipōreō*, experience distress, endure hard labor (*5415*).

6052 ὥρα

ὥρα (*hōra*), hour, time, point of time (*6052*); ὡραῖος (*hōraios*), at the right time, seasonable, ripe, hence beautiful, fair, pleasant (*6053*).

CL & OT 1. (a) In cl. Gk. the noun *hōra* denotes a particular division of time, esp. an hour. But it can also mean year, day, and moment, or even designate a season (e.g., spring or summer) or a stage of life (e.g., youth). In Homer and other poets *hōra* marks the customarily appropriate time for certain activities, e.g., the evening meal, going to sleep, or sexual enjoyment. There is also the personification of the Horae, the goddesses of the seasons, who guard the gates of Olympus. Contemplation of nature and specifically of spring can arouse one's consciousness of transience and direct one's thoughts to "the last hour." In contrast to this, there is the summons to act in conformity with one's age and so to make use of the given "hour."

(b) The related adj. *hōraios* means appropriate to the season, at the right time. In connection with the timely occurrence of happy events, *hōraios* can take on the meaning of agreeable, lovely, and beautifully formed.

2. *hōra* occurs some 50x in the LXX, chiefly for the noun *ʿēt*, time. (a) It serves initially to indicate a somewhat indeterminate period of time (similar to *hēmera*, day, e.g., Dan. 12:13). Even where *hōra* is accompanied by an ordinal number, it can scarcely be an hour of sixty minutes that is in question. Dividing day and night into hours was unknown in ancient times, so only general expressions were used, such as morning, midday, and evening (e.g., Gen. 3:8; 18:1; 1 Sam. 11:11). A sundial is mentioned for the first time in 2 Ki. 20:9–11 (par. Isa. 38:8). In Exod. 18:22, 26, "at all times" (lit., "at every hour") simply means at any time.

(b) More frequently than periods of time *hōra* denotes a more or less restricted point of time. The prep. phrase *en autē tē hōra* (lit., "in that hour") has the meaning of immediately, on the spot (e.g., Dan. 5:5). Similarly, this formula can express temporal connection (Est. 8:1) or action following without delay (9:2). Various formulas express details of time: e.g., "at this time [*hōra*] tomorrow" (Exod. 9:18; 10:4) and "about this time [*hōra*] next year " (Gen. 18:10). In Rom. 9:9, where this last passage is quoted, *hōra* is replaced by the materially synonymous *kairos* (→ *2789*).

(c) Characteristic for the OT understanding of time and thus for the use of *hōra* is faith in God as the creator and Lord of time in all its dimensions. It is Yahweh who sees to it in nature that everything takes place at its appointed hour: e.g., rain comes at the proper season (Deut. 11:14; Job 36:28; Zech. 10:1), and grain is ripe for harvest (Job 5:26). God is Lord of the hour of birth (cf. Gen. 18:10, 14; 2 Ki. 4:16–17) and of death (cf. 2 Sam. 24:15; Job 5:26). The praise of the divine apportionment of time for natural processes sounds out in various passages (e.g., Sir. 39:33–34).

(d) Esp. important for the Israelites are God's mighty acts in history, such as when he strikes the enemies of his people at some particular hour (Exod. 9:18; 10:4; Jos. 11:6) or when he suddenly strikes terror into Belshazzar with the mysterious writing on the wall (Dan. 5:5). God's word is fulfilled punctually at the predetermined hour (cf. Gen. 21:1–2 with Gen. 18:10, 14). The remembrance of God's saving activity in history is to be kept alive at fixed festal hours in the cult

(Exod. 13:10). The children of Israel are thus to keep the Passover "at the appointed time [*hōra*]" (Num. 9:2). The chronological concept of hours, which played a large role in Christian liturgy, is approached most closely by the mention of "the time of the evening sacrifice" (Dan. 9:21). But in the OT as a whole, the temporal sense of *hōra* recedes behind that fullness of content that is effected by Yahweh or related to God in the cult.

3. *hōra*, like other temporal concepts, acquired a strong eschatological and apocalyptic stress in later Jewish writings. Like the "day of the Lord," phrases such the *hōra kairou*, "hour of time" (Dan. 8:17, 19, LXX), refers to the events of the last days when God will come with accompanying cosmic phenomena in order to punish the godless in the judgment and to lead the righteous to everlasting salvation. Thus Sir. urges: "Before judgment comes, examine yourself; and at the time [*hōra*] of scrutiny you will find forgiveness" (18:20, NRSV). For the individual's hour of death there is the promise of God's blessing and hope (11:22).

NT 1. By comparison with the LXX *hōra* is used twice as often in the NT (106x). *hōraios* occurs only 4x. (a) Linked with ordinal numbers *hōra* serves to fix events chronologically in the course of the day (e.g., Matt. 20:3, 5–6, 9; Jn. 1:39; 4:6; Acts 2:15). This is esp. true of particular points of time within the Passion narrative of Jesus (e.g., Matt. 27:45; Mk. 15:25, 33–34; Jn. 19:14) and in connection with Jewish times of prayer (Acts 3:1; 10:3, 9, 30). Alongside precise indications of time of this sort, *hōra* can also be used in accord with the ancient division of the day for more imprecise designations (e.g., lit., "at a late hour [of the evening]" in Matt. 14:15; Mk. 6:35). More generally still, *hōra* is used in phrases like "to this very hour" (1 Cor. 4:11), "at that very hour" (Matt. 8:13), or "from that moment" (9:22) to place an event in relationship to something before, simultaneous, or after.

The allusions to the point in time of the Parousia are similarly generalizing (cf. Matt. 24:36; 25:13; Mk. 13:32). Esp. vivid is the contraction of time (with the word *hōra*) to a single moment, embedded within greater periods of time, in the apocalyptic vision of Rev. 9:15: "And the four angels who had been kept ready for this very hour and day and month and year were released to kill a third of mankind."

(b) So far we have been dealing with more or less exact indications of time that are given by the word *hōra*, partly in the sense of *kairos* (→ *2789*). In another group of passages the word serves to describe limited time spans. Analogously with temporal concepts such as year, month, and day, *hōra* can means the length of time of a measurable hour. "Are there not twelve hours of daylight?" (Jn. 11:9). The last of the laborers to be hired worked only one hour (Matt. 20:3, 5, 9, 12). The disciples could not stay awake "one hour" (26:40). In general, an hour is felt to be relatively short. This is also shown in places where the thought is obviously not simply of a space of time sixty minutes in length (e.g., Jn. 5:35; 1 Thess. 2:17; Phlm. 15). Now and then in connection with *hōra* longer periods of time can be in mind (e.g., 1 Cor. 15:30).

2. (a) Like other biblical temporal concepts, *hōra* acquires its decisive importance from its content, from the event that has been, is being, or will be enacted at a particular hour. Granted, it is by no means irrelevant to the authors of the NT when something takes place, but even more significant for them is what invests the particular unit of time with its essential quality. This is already the case in the general human context. In a woman's life it is the sudden change from pain to joy that gives its own value to the hour in which she gives birth to a child (Jn. 16:21).

(b) More far-reaching in their force of statement are the individual hours within Jesus' lifetime. Again and again the Gospel writers point to particular periods of time in which things happen to or through Jesus that reveal his incomparable majesty and authority. There is, for instance, the hour in which Jesus legitimates himself for the benefit of the doubting John the Baptist by means of healing miracles (Lk. 7:21–23; cf. Matt. 8:13; 9:22; 15:28; 17:18).

It is esp. Jn. who stresses over and over again that such miraculous signs are not intended to serve Jesus' self-glorification but to point to God the Father. For the glory of God to shine out, Jesus must wait for the right hour, the *kairos*. This is true of his miraculous actions (cf. Jn. 2:4) as it is of his suffering (cf. 7:30; 8:20; 13:1). Thus when the "hour" (*hōra*) of Jesus' arrest, death, and return to the Father is impending (e.g., 12:23, 27; 13:1), Jesus uses the remaining time for table fellowship with his disciples in order to express his love in the symbolic action of the foot-washing and the farewell discourse.

3. (a) In addition to the general temporal and Christological passages, eschatological conceptions of time play an important role in the NT. From the Gospels to Rev. what becomes apparent, alongside belief in the hour that is filled with meaning by Christ, is the expectation of a still-awaited "last hour," which, after eschatological terrors (cf. Jn. 16:2, 32; Rev. 3:10), will run into the final hour of judgment (14:7; cf. Jn. 5:24–30). No one, not even Jesus, can provide an exact indication of "that day and hour" (Mk. 13:32), for it will break in suddenly like a thief (Lk. 12:39–40, 46; Rev. 3:3). But for this very reason one must stay awake, be ready (Rom. 13:11), and be careful to increase one's vigilance for the "signs of the times" (Matt. 16:3; cf. Lk. 12:56).

(b) Jn. can even say that the "last hour" has come (1 Jn. 2:18). When it became clear that the Parousia was being delayed, there still remained the task of handling every particular present hour correctly, grasping it as time given by God and realizing the possibilities that lay within it. This was the case both in the ethical responsibility of everyday life (cf. Rom. 13:11–14) and in the testing of times of persecution, for which Jesus prepared his disciples (Jn. 16:1–4). To those who will answer for their faith in court Jesus promised the assistance of his Spirit (Matt. 10:19), so that even the hour of their trial can serve to glorify God.

See also *aiōn*, aeon, age, life span, epoch, eternity (*172*); *kairos*, time, esp. a point of time, moment (*2789*); *chronos*, time, period of time (*5989*).

6053 (*hōraios*, at the right time, seasonable; hence beautiful, fair), → *6052*.

6057 ὡσαννά	ὡσαννά (*hōsanna*), hosanna (*6057*).

OT This Greek word is a transliteration from Aram. *hôšaʿ nāʾ* (Heb., *hôšîʿâ nāʾ*), meaning "O, save." The Heb. expression is found in Ps. 118:25, which the LXX translated as *sōson* (save [us]). Ps. 118 is most likely a liturgy for the Feast of Tabernacles. "Blessed is he who comes" (118:26) is likely the Davidic king, in his role as the Melchizedek priest, leading his people in procession to Yahweh's house. In this context "O, save" suggests an imploring cry to Yahweh to bring to reality that which the liturgy has depicted. Later Jewish thought applied this great cry to the expectation of the messianic king.

NT By NT times Hosanna had become a full "cultic cry." The Gk. of Matt. 21:9; Mk. 11:9; Jn. 12:13 transliterates but does not translate. The sight of Jesus fulfilling the kingly prophecy of Zech. 9:9, coupled with the strewing and waving of branches reminiscent of the ceremonial fronds that characterized the Feast of Tabernacles, prompted the shout appropriate to that occasion; unwittingly, the people greeted the true David, the true King of Israel, with the Davidic welcome.

See also *hallēlouia*, hallelujah (*252*); *amēn*, amen (*297*).

6066 (*ōpheleia*, advantage), → *6067*.

6067 ὠφελέω	ὠφελέω (*ōpheleō*), help, benefit, be of use (*6067*); ὠφέλεια (*ōpheleia*), advantage, value (*6066*); ὠφέλιμος (*ōphelimos*), useful, profitable (*6068*).

CL & OT In cl. Gk. the words in this group describe that which is helpful, serviceable, valuable, or beneficial to people. This meaning is continued in the LXX. For example, a messenger bringing good news "refreshes" those who have sent him (Prov. 25:13). In many cases, however, the OT writers tells us what is *not* useful. For example, wealth is of no benefit in a time of danger or disaster (11:4). According to Isa. 30:5, forming an alliance against God's will with an evil nation is "useless" to God's people and will bring them no "advantage." Isa. points out that esp. idols are "worthless" (44:9; 57:12).

NT 1. Some uses of this word group in the NT are on a human level. The woman with the twelve-year flow of blood had spent much money on doctors but to no avail (Mk. 5:26). Pilate saw that his attempt to release Jesus "was getting nowhere" (Matt. 27:24). Paul emphasizes to Timothy that physical training has only limited "value" (1 Tim. 4:8).

2. As in the LXX, many occurrences of this word group tell us what is *not* beneficial or advantageous to us. Circumcision, for example, has no intrinsic value (Rom. 2:25; cf. 3:1), and for those who seek it "Christ will be of no value" (Gal. 5:2). Nor does eating ceremonial foods have any ultimate spiritual value (Heb. 13:9). If we do amazing works supposedly for the Lord but do not have Christian love in our hearts, we "gain nothing" (1 Cor. 13:3). With regard to gaining life, the flesh "counts for nothing" (Jn. 6:63), and it will do us no "good" to gain the whole world if in the process we forfeit the soul (Matt. 16:26; Mk. 8:36; Lk. 9:25).

3. So, then, what does have value? Obviously, love for Christ and his people does. So does combining the message of the gospel with faith (Heb. 4:2) and with God's grace (13:9). Note also that "godliness has value for all things" (1 Tim. 4:8), as does devoting ourselves to "doing what is good" (Tit. 3:8). Finally, Paul stresses that "all Scripture is God-breathed and is useful [*ōphelimos*] for teaching, rebuking, correcting and training in righteousness, so that the man of God may be thoroughly equipped for every good work" (2 Tim. 3:16–17).

6068 (*ōphelimos*, useful, profitable), → *6067*.

Subject Index

This subject index is not a complete subject index to every occurrence of particular English words and concepts in this abridgment of *The New International Dictionary of New Testament Theology*. Rather, it is an index to the definitions of Greek words, where major discussions of a wide variety of concepts occur. For example, if you wanted to make a study of "love" in the New Testament, this index directs you to the discussions of the Greek words *agapaō* (and related words) on pp. 5ff., of *philadelphia* (and related words) on pp. 15ff., of *splanchnon* on pp. 535ff., and of *phileō* (and related words) on pp. 590ff. You should read each of these entries in its entirety. This index does not, however, show every place where God's love for us, our love for God, or love in the Christian community is briefly mentioned or alluded to. Note too that only the first page of the defined Greek word is given.

Scripture Index

Proverbs

Luke

Goodrick-Kohlenberger to Strong

In the Strong field:

@ = same word, but differences in spelling
+ = GK is a combination of more than one Strong word
& = GK is equivalent to more than one individual Strong word
* = GK has no equivalent in Strong

GK	Strong	GK	Strong	GK	Strong	GK	Strong	GK	Strong	GK	Strong	GK	Strong
1	1	82	81	163	157	244	232	325	304	406	379	487	455
2	2	83	82	164	4256@	245	233	326	305	407	4238@	488	456
3	3	84	83	165	159 & 158	246	234	327	306@	408	380	489	457
4	4	85	84	166	157@	247	235	328	307	409	381	490	458
5	5@	86	85	167	160	248	236	329	308	410	382	491	459
6	6@	87	86	168	161	249	237	330	309	411	383	492	460
7	7	88	87	169	162	250	*	331	310	412	384	493	453@
8	8@	89	88	170	163	251	238	332	311	413	385	494	461
9	9	90	89	171	164	252	239	333	508@	414	386	495	462
10	10	91	90	172	165	253	240	334	312	415	387	496	463
11	11	92	91	173	166	254	241	335	313	416	388	497	464
12	12	93	92	174	167	255	2087@	336	314	417	389	498	465
13	13@	94	93	175	168	256	242	337	315	418	390	499	466
14	14	95	94 + 2923	176	169	257	243	338	316	419	391	500	467
15	18 + 2041	96	94	177	170	258	244	339	317	420	*	501	468
16	15	97	95	178	171	259	245	340	318	421	392	502	469
17	16	98	689@	179	172	260	246	341	319@	422	393	503	470
18	17	99	96	180	173	261	247	342	320	423	394@	504	472@
19	18	100	97	181	174	262	248	343	321	424	395	505	473
20	19	101	98	182	175	263	249	344	322	425	510	506	474
21	20	102	99	183	176	264	250	345	323	426	396	507	475@
22	21	103	100	184	177	265	251	346	324	427	397	508	476
23	22	104	101	185	178	266	252	347	325	428	398	509	477
24	23	105	102	186	179	267	253@	348	326	429	399	510	478
25	24	106	103	187	180@	268	254	349	327	430	400	511	479
26	25	107	104	188	180	269	255	350	328	431	401	512	480
27	26	108	105	189	181	270	1@	351	329	432	402	513	481@
28	27	109	106	190	182	271	256@	352	330	433	403	514	482@
29	28@	110	107	191	183	272	257	353	331	434	404	515	483 & 471
30	29	111	108	192	184@	273	258	354	332	435	405	516	484@
31	30	112	*	193	185	274	259	355	333	436	406	517	485
32	31	113	109	194	85@	275	260	356	334	437	407	518	486
33	518@	114	110	195	186	276	261	357	335	438	408	519	487
34	32	115	2288 + 1	196	187	277	262	358	336	439	409	520	488
35	30@	116	111	197	188	278	263	359	337	440	507 + 2821	521	489
36	34	117	112	198	189	279	264	360	338	441	410	522	490
37	35	118	113	199	190	280	265	361	339	442	411	523	491
38	36	119	114	200	191	281	266	362	340	443	412	524	492
39	37	120	115	201	191	282	267	363	341	444	413	525	493
40	38	121	116	202	192	283	268	364	342	445	414@	526	494
41	40 & 39	122	117	203	193	284	*	365	343	446	415	527	495@
42	41	123	118	204	194	285	269	366	344	447	448@	528	496
43	42	124	119	205	195	286	270	367	345	448	416	529	497
44	43	125	4867@	206	196	287	271	368	346@	449	417	530	498@
45	44	126	120	207	196@	288	272	369	347	450	418	531	499@
46	45	127	121@	208	198	289	273	370	348	451	419@	532	500
47	46	128	122	209	199	290	274	371	349	452	420	533	501
48	47	129	123	210	200	291	275	372	*	453	421	534	502
49	48	130	124	211	201	292	276	373	350	454	422	535	503
50	49	131	125	212	202	293	277	374	351	455	423@	536	504
51	50	132	126	213	203	294	278	375	617	456	424	537	505
52	51	133	127	214	204	295	279	376	352	457	425	538	506
53	52	134	128	215	205	296	280	377	353	458	426	539	507
54	53	135	129	216	206	297	281	378	354@	459	427	540	509
55	54	136	130	217	207	298	282	379	355	460	428	541	510
56	55	137	131	218	208	299	283	380	242	461	429	542	511
57	56	138	132	219	209	300	284	381	356	462	430	543	512@
58	57	139	133	220	210	301	*	382	357	463	431	544	513
59	58	140	134	221	217@	302	285	383	358	464	432	545	514
60	59	141	135	222	211	303	286	384	355	465	433	546	515
61	60	142	136	223	211	304	287	385	359	466	434	547	516
62	61	143	137	224	212	305	880	386	360	467	435	548	517
63	62	144	2056@	225	213	306	288	387	361	468	436	549	2456@
64	63	145	138	226	214	307	289	388	362	469	437	550	518
65	64	146	139	227	215	308	290	389	363@	470	438	551	519@
66	65	147	140	228	216	309	291@	390	364	471	439	552	520
67	66	148	141	229	217	310	292	391	365@	472	440	553	521
68	67	149	142	230	218	311	906@ + 293	392	366	473	441	554	522
69	68	150	143	231	219	312	293	393	367@	474	442	555	523
70	69	151	144	232	220	313	294@	394	368	475	443	556	524
71	70	152	145	233	221	314	294	395	369	476	444	557	525
72	71 & 33	153	146	234	222	315	295	396	370	477	445	558	526
73	72	154	147	235	223	316	296	397	371	478	446	559	527
74	73	155	148	236	224	317	297@	398	372	479	447	560	528
75	74	156	150 & 149	237	225	318	298	399	373	480	448	561	529
76	75	157	151	238	226	319	*	400	374	481	449	562	530
77	76	158	152	239	227	320	299	401	376@	482	450	563	531
78	77	159	153	240	228	321	300	402	375	483	451@	564	532
79	78	160	154	241	229	322	301	403	450@	484	452@	565	533
80	79	161	155	242	230	323	302	404	377	485	453	566	575 + 737
81	80	162	156	243	231	324	303	405	378	486	454	567	534

568....535	668....630	768....721	868....817	968....909	1068....995	1168....1084
569....536	669....631@	769....722	869....818	969....910	1069....996	1169....1085
570....537	670....5278@	770....723	870....818@	970....911	1070....997	1170....1086@
571....782	671....632	771....724	871....819	971....920@	1071....998	1171....1086
572....538	672....633	772....725	872....820	972....912	1072....999@	1172....1087
573....539	673....575 + 3992	773....726	873....821	973....913	1073....999	1173....1088
574....540	674....634	774....727	874....822	974....914	1074....1000	1174....1089
575....541	675....635	775....728	875....823	975....915	1075....1001	1175....1090
576....1890	676....636	776....730	876....824	976....916	1076....1002	1176....1091
577....543	677....637	777....731	877....825	977....917	1077....1003	1177....1092
578....544	678....638	778....732@	878....826	978....918	1078....1003@	1178....1093
579....545	679....639	779....732	879....827	979....919	1079....1004	1179....1094
580....546	680....640	780....733	880....828	980....920	1080....1005	1180....1095
581....547	681....641	781....730	881....829	981....920	1081....1006	1181....1096
582....548@	682....642	782....734	882....830	982....921@	1082....1007	1182....1097
583....549@	683....643	783....735	883....831	983....922	1083....1008	1183....1098
584....550@ & 561	684....644	784....736	884....832	984....923@	1084....1009	1184....1099
585....551	685....645	785....737	885....833	985....924	1085....1010	1185....1100
586....552	686....646	786....738	886....834	986....925	1086....1011	1186....1101
587....553	687....647	787....739	887....835	987....926	1087....1012	1187....1102
588....554	688....3848@	788....740	888....836	988....927	1088....1013	1188....1103
589....555	689....648	789....741	889....837	989....928	1089....1014	1189....1104
590....556	690....649	790....742	890....838	990....929	1090....1015	1190....1105
591....557	691....650	791....743	891....837@	991....930	1091....1016	1191....1106
592....558	692....651	792....744	892....839	992....931	1092....1017	1192....1107
593....559	693....652	793....745	893....840	993....932	1093....1018	1193....1110@
594....560	694....653	794....746	894....841	994....934 & 933	1094....1019	1194....1108
595....561	695....654	795....747	895....842	995....935	1095....1020	1195....1109
596....562	696....655	796....748	896....843	996....936	1096....1021	1196....1110
597....563	697....656	797....749	897....844	997....937	1097....1022	1197....1111
598....564	698....657@	798....3027@	898....845	998....937@	1098....1023	1198....1112
599....565	699....658	799....750	899..846 & 847 & 848	999....938	1099....1024	1199....1113
600..568 & 566 & 567	700....659	800....751	900....1888@	1000....939	1100....1025	1200....1114
601....569	701....660	801....752	901....849	1001....940	1101....1026	1201....1115
602....570	702....661	802....753	902....3166@	1002....941	1102....1690@	1202....1116
603....571	703....662	803....754	903....850	1003....942	1103....1027	1203....1117
604....573@	704....663	804....755	904....851	1004....943	1104....1028	1204....1118
605....572	705....664	805....*	905....852	1005....944	1105....1029	1205....1119
606....573	706....665	806....757 & 756	906....853	1006....945@	1106....1030	1206....1120
607....574	707....666	807....758	907....854	1007....946	1107....1031	1207....1121
608....575	708....667	808....759	908....855	1008....947	1108....1032	1208....1122
609....576	709....668	809....760	909....856	1009....948@	1109....1033	1209....1123
610....577	710....669	810....761	910....857	1010....949	1110....1034	1210....1124
611....578	711....670	811....760@	911....858	1011....950	1111....1035	1211....1125
612....579	712....671	812....762	912....859	1012....951	1112....1036	1212....1126
613....580	713....672	813....763	913....860	1013....952	1113....1037	1213....1127
614....581@	714....673	814....764	914....861	1014....953	1114....1038	1214....1128
615....582	715....674	815....765	915....862	1015....954	1115....1039	1215....1129
616....583	716....675	816....766	916....*	1016....955@	1116....1040	1216....1130
617....584	717....676	817....767	917....*	1017....4476@	1117....1041	1217....1130@
618....585	718....677	818....768	918....863	1018....956	1118....*	1218....1131
619....586@	719....678@	819....769	919....864	1019....957@	1119....1042	1219....1132
620....586	720....679	820....770	920....865	1020....958@	1120....1043	1220....1133
621....587	721....681 & 680	821....771	921....866	1021....958	1121....1044	1221....1134
622....588	722....682	822....772	922....867	1022....959	1122....1045	1222....1135
623....589	723....683@	823....773	923....868	1023....960	1123....1046	1223....1136
624....590	724....684	824....774	924....869	1024....961	1124....1048	1224....1137
625....591	725....685	825....775	925....870	1025....*	1125....1047	1225....*
626....592	726....686	826....776	926....871	1026....1007@	1126....1049	1226....1138
627....593	727....687	827....777	927....872 & 542	1027....1007@	1127....1050	1227....1139
628....594	728....688	828....778	928....873	1028....962	1128....1051	1228....1140
629....595	729....*	829....779	929....874	1029....963	1129....1052	1229....1141
630....596	730....689	830....780	930....875	1030....962@	1130....1053	1230....1142
631....597	731....729@	831....781	931....876	1031....964	1131....1054	1231....1143
632....598	732....690	832....782	932....877	1032....964@	1132....1055	1232....1144
633....599@	733....691	833....783	933....878	1033....965@	1133....1056	1233....1145
634....600@	734....692	834....784	934....879	1034....966	1134....1057	1234....1146
635....600	735....693	835....785	935....650@	1035....966@	1135....1053@	1235....1147
636....601	736....694	836....786	936....880	1036....967	1136....1058	1236....1148
637....602	737....695	837....787	937....881	1037....968	1137....1059	1237....1149
638....603	738....696	838....4565@	938....882	1038....*	1138....1060	1238....1150
639....604	739....693@	839....788	939....883	1039....969	1139....1061@	1239....1151
640....605	740....697	840....789@	940....884	1040....970	1140....1061	1240....1152
641....606	741....698	841....790	941....881@	1041....971	1141....1062	1241....1153
642....607	742....699@	842....791	942....886	1042....972	1142....1063	1242....1154
643....608	743....700	843....792	943....885@	1043....973	1143....1064	1243....*
644....609	744....701	844....793	944....887	1044....974	1144....2802@	1244....1155
645....610	745....702@	845....794	945....888	1045....974	1145....1065	1245....1156
646....611	746....703	846....795	946....889	1046....975	1146....1066	1246....1157
647....612	747....*	847....796	947....890	1047....976	1147....1067	1247....1155
648....613	748....704	848....797	948....891	1048....977	1148....1068@	1248....1158
649....614	749....705	849....798	949....892	1049....978	1149....1068@	1249....1156@
650....615	750....706	850....799	950....893	1050....979	1150....1069	1250....1157
651....615@	751....707@	851....800	951....894@	1051....980	1151....1070	1251....1159
652....616	752....708	852....801	952....894	1052....981	1152....1071	1252....1160
653....617	753....709	853....802	953....895	1053....982	1153....1072	1253....1138@
654....2980@	754....710	854....803	954....*	1054....983	1154....1073	1254....1161
655....618	755....711	855....804	955....896	1055....984	1155....1074	1255....1162
656....619	756....712	856....805	956....897	1056....985	1156....1075	1256....1163
657....620	757....713	857....806	957....898	1057....985@	1157....1076	1257....1164
658....621	758....714	858....807	958....899	1058....986	1158....1077@	1258....1165
659....5277@	759....715@	859....808	959....900	1059....987	1159....1077@	1259....1166
660....622	760....715	860....809	960....901	1060....988	1160....1077	1260....1166
661....623	761....716	861....810	961....902@	1061....989	1161....1078	1261....1167
662....624	762....717	862....811	962....903	1062....990	1162....1079	1262....1168
663....625@	763....689@	863....812	963....904	1063....991	1163....1081@	1263....*
664....626	764....718	864....813	964....905@	1064....992	1164....1080	1264....1169
665....627	765....719	865....814	965....906	1065....993@	1165....1081	1265....1170
666....628	766....720	866....815	966....907	1066....994	1166....1082	1266....*
667....629	767....*	867....816	967....908	1067....1003@	1167....1083	1267....1171

1268 ... 1172	1367 ... 1259@	1467 ... 1344	1567 ... *	1665 ... 1486@	1765 ... 1626	1865 ... 1711
1269 ... *	1368 ... 1260	1468 ... 1345	1568 ... 1436	1666 ... 1537	1766 ... 1627	1866 ... 1712
1270 ... 1173	1369 ... 1261	1469 ... 1346	1569 ... 1437	1667 ... 1538	1767 ... 1628	1867 ... 1713
1271 ... 1173@	1370 ... 1262	1470 ... 1347	1570 ... 1437 + 4007	1668 ... 1539	1768 ... 1629	1868 ... 1714
1272 ... 1175	1371 ... 1263	1471 ... 1348	1571 ... 1438	1669 ... 1540	1769 ... 1630	1869 ... 1715
1273 ... 1174@	1372 ... 1264	1472 ... 1349	1572 ... 1439	1670 ... 1541@	1770 ... 1631	1870 ... 1716
1274 ... 1176	1373 ... 1265	1473 ... 1350	1573 ... 1440	1671 ... 1542	1771 ... 1537 + 5455	1871 ... 1717
1275 ... 1177	1374 ... 1266	1474 ... 1351	1574 ... 1441	1672 ... 1543	1772 ... 1632	1872 ... 1718
1276 ... 1176 + 1803@	1375 ... 1267	1475 ... 1352	1575 ... 1442	1673 ... 1543@	1773 ... 1632@	1873 ... 1719
1277 ... 1176 + 2532 + 3638	1376 ... 1268	1476 ... 1353	1576 ... 1443@	1674 ... 1831@	1774 ... 1633	1874 ... 1720
1278 ... 1178	1377 ... 1269	1477 ... 1354	1577 ... 1444	1675 ... 1544	1775 ... 1634	1875 ... 1721
1279 ... 1179	1378 ... 1270	1478 ... 1355	1578 ... 1445	1676 ... 1545	1776 ... 1635	1876 ... 5455@
1280 ... 1180	1379 ... 1271	1479 ... 1356	1579 ... 1446	1677 ... 1816@	1777 ... 1636	1877 ... 1722
1281 ... 1182 & 1181	1380 ... 1272	1480 ... 2735@	1580 ... 1447	1678 ... 1546	1778 ... 1637	1878 ... 1723
1282 ... 1183	1381 ... 1273	1481 ... 1357	1581 ... 1448	1679 ... 1547	1779 ... 1638	1879 ... 1724
1283 ... 1184	1382 ... 1274	1482 ... 1358	1582 ... 1449	1680 ... 1548	1780 ... 1639	1880 ... 2177@
1284 ... 1185	1383 ... 1275	1483 ... 1359	1583 ... 1450	1681 ... 1549	1781 ... 1640	1881 ... *
1285 ... 1186	1384 ... 3859	1484 ... 1360	1584 ... 1451	1682 ... 1550	1782 ... 1641	1882 ... 1725
1286 ... 1187@	1385 ... 1276	1485 ... 1361@	1585 ... 1452	1683 ... 1551	1783 ... 1642	1883 ... 1726
1287 ... 1187	1386 ... 1277	1486 ... 1362@	1586 ... 1453	1684 ... 1552	1784 ... 1640	1884 ... *
1288 ... 1188	1387 ... 1278@	1487 ... 1362	1587 ... 1454	1685 ... 1553	1785 ... 1643	1885 ... 1727
1289 ... 1189	1388 ... 1279	1488 ... 1363	1588 ... 1455	1686 ... 1554	1786 ... 1644	1886 ... 1756@
1290 ... 127@	1389 ... 1280	1489 ... 1364	1589 ... 1456	1687 ... 1555	1787 ... 1645	1887 ... 1728
1291 ... 1190	1390 ... 1281	1490 ... 1417 + 3461	1590 ... 1457	1688 ... 1556	1788 ... 1646 & 1647	1888 ... 1766@
1292 ... 1191	1391 ... 1282	1491 ... 1365	1591 ... 1573@	1689 ... 1557	1789 ... 1648	1889 ... 863@
1293 ... 1192	1392 ... 1284@	1492 ... 1366	1592 ... 1458	1690 ... 1558	1790 ... 1653@	1890 ... 1729
1294 ... 1193	1393 ... 1284@	1493 ... 1367	1593 ... 1459	1691 ... 1559	1791 ... 1650@	1891 ... 1730
1295 ... 2359@	1394 ... *	1494 ... 1368@	1594 ... 1460	1692 ... 1560	1792 ... 1649	1892 ... 1731
1296 ... 1194	1395 ... 1283	1495 ... 1369	1595 ... 2620	1693 ... 1561	1793 ... 1650	1893 ... 1732
1297 ... 1195	1396 ... 1284	1496 ... 1370	1596 ... 1461	1694 ... 1562	1794 ... 1651	1894 ... 1733
1298 ... 1196	1397 ... 1285	1497 ... 1371	1597 ... 2623@	1695 ... 1563	1795 ... 1652	1895 ... 1734
1299 ... 1197	1398 ... 1286	1498 ... 1372	1598 ... 1462	1696 ... 1564	1796 ... 1653	1896 ... 1735@
1300 ... 1198	1399 ... 1287	1499 ... 1373	1599 ... 1463	1697 ... 1565	1797 ... 1654	1897 ... 1736
1301 ... 1199	1400 ... 1288	1500 ... 1374	1600 ... 1464	1698 ... 1566	1798 ... 1655	1898 ... 1737
1302 ... 1200	1401 ... 1289	1501 ... 1375	1601 ... 1465	1699 ... 1567	1799 ... 1656	1899 ... 1738
1303 ... 1201	1402 ... 1290	1502 ... 1376	1602 ... 1466	1700 ... 2214@	1800 ... 1657	1900 ... 1739
1304 ... 1202	1403 ... 1291@	1503 ... 1377	1603 ... 1467	1701 ... 1568	1801 ... 1658	1901 ... 1740@
1305 ... 1203	1404 ... 1292	1504 ... 1378	1604 ... 1468	1702 ... 1569	1802 ... 1659	1902 ... 1741
1306 ... 1204	1405 ... 1293	1505 ... 1379	1605 ... 1469	1703 ... 2296@	1803 ... 1660	1903 ... 1742
1307 ... 1205	1406 ... 1294	1506 ... 1380	1606 ... 1470	1704 ... 1570	1804 ... 1661	1904 ... 1743
1308 ... 1206	1407 ... 1295@	1507 ... 1381	1607 ... 1471	1705 ... 1571	1805 ... 1662	1905 ... 1744
1309 ... 1208@	1408 ... 1296	1508 ... 1381@	1608 ... 1472	1706 ... 1572	1806 ... 1662@	1906 ... 1745
1310 ... 1207	1409 ... 1297	1509 ... 1382	1609 ... 1473 & 1691 & 1698 & 170	1707 ... 1573	1807 ... 3395@	1907 ... 1746
1311 ... 1208	1410 ... 1298	1510 ... 1383	1610 ... 1474	1708 ... 1574	1808 ... 1663	1908 ... 1739@
1312 ... 1209	1411 ... 1299	1511 ... 1384	1611 ... 1475	1709 ... 1575	1809 ... 1664	1909 ... 1747
1313 ... 1210	1412 ... 1300	1512 ... 1385	1612 ... 1476	1710 ... 1576	1810 ... 1665	1910 ... 1748
1314 ... 1211	1413 ... 1301	1513 ... 1386	1613 ... 1477	1711 ... 1577	1811 ... 1666@	1911 ... 1749
1315 ... 5081@	1414 ... 1302	1514 ... 1387	1614 ... 1478@	1712 ... 1578	1812 ... 1666	1912 ... 1750
1316 ... 1212	1415 ... 1303	1515 ... 1388	1615 ... 1479@	1713 ... 1579	1813 ... 1667 & 1507	1913 ... 1751
1317 ... 1213	1416 ... 1303	1516 ... 1389	1616 ... 1480	1714 ... 1580	1814 ... 1668	1914 ... 1752
1318 ... 1214	1417 ... 1304	1517 ... 1390	1617 ... 1481	1715 ... 1464@	1815 ... 1669	1915 ... 1752
1319 ... 1215	1418 ... 1305	1518 ... 1391	1618 ... 1482	1716 ... 1581	1816 ... 1670	1916 ... 1768@
1320 ... 1216	1419 ... 1306	1519 ... 1392	1619 ... 1483	1717 ... 1582@	1817 ... 1671	1917 ... 1769@
1321 ... 1217	1420 ... 1307@	1520 ... 1393	1620 ... 1484	1718 ... 1583	1818 ... 1672	1918 ... 1753
1322 ... 1218	1421 ... 1307	1521 ... 1394	1621 ... 1485	1719 ... 1584	1819 ... 1673	1919 ... 1754
1323 ... 1219	1422 ... 1308	1522 ... 1395	1622 ... 1486	1720 ... 1585	1820 ... 1674	1920 ... 1755
1324 ... 1220	1423 ... 1309	1523 ... 1190@	1623 ... 1487	1721 ... 1586	1821 ... 1675	1921 ... 1756
1325 ... 1221	1424 ... 1310	1524 ... 1396	1624 ... 2397@	1722 ... 1587	1822 ... 1676	1922 ... 1757
1326 ... *	1425 ... 1311	1525 ... 1397	1625 ... 3708@	1723 ... 1588	1823 ... 1677@	1923 ... 1758
1327 ... 1222	1426 ... 1312	1526 ... 1398	1626 ... 1491	1724 ... 1589	1824 ... 1677	1924 ... 1759
1328 ... 1223	1427 ... 1313	1527 ... 1399	1627 ... 1493	1725 ... 1590	1825 ... 1678@	1925 ... 1782@
1329 ... 1224	1428 ... 1314	1528 ... 1401 & 1400	1628 ... 1494	1726 ... 1591	1826 ... 1678	1926 ... 1760
1330 ... 1225	1429 ... 1315@	1529 ... 1401	1629 ... 1496	1727 ... 1592	1827 ... 1679	1927 ... 1761
1331 ... 1226	1430 ... 5512@	1530 ... 1402	1630 ... 1495@	1728 ... 1593	1828 ... 1680	1928 ... 1762
1332 ... 1227	1431 ... 1316@	1531 ... 1403	1631 ... 1497	1729 ... 1594	1829 ... 1681	1929 ... 1763
1333 ... 1228	1432 ... *	1532 ... 1404	1632 ... 1500@	1730 ... 1595	1830 ... 1682	1930 ... 4178@
1334 ... 1229	1433 ... *	1533 ... 1405	1633 ... 1501	1731 ... 1596	1831 ... 1683	1931 ... 1764
1335 ... 1230	1434 ... 1317	1534 ... 1406	1634 ... 1502	1732 ... 1597	1832 ... 1684	1932 ... 1765
1336 ... 1231	1435 ... 1318	1535 ... 1407	1635 ... 1504	1733 ... 1598	1833 ... 1685	1933 ... 1767
1337 ... 1232	1436 ... 1319	1536 ... 1408	1636 ... 1505	1734 ... 1599	1834 ... 1686@	1934 ... 1769
1338 ... 1233	1437 ... 1320	1537 ... 1409	1637 ... 1528@	1735 ... 1537 + 4053	1835 ... 1686	1935 ... 1770
1339 ... 1234	1438 ... 1321	1538 ... 1410	1638 ... 2229 + 3375	1736 ... 1600	1836 ... 1687	1936 ... 1771
1340 ... 1235	1439 ... 1322	1539 ... 1411	1639 ... 1510 & 1488 & 1498 & 151	1737 ... 1530@	1837 ... 1688	1937 ... 1772
1341 ... 1236	1440 ... 1323	1540 ... 1412	1640 ... *	1738 ... 1601	1838 ... 1689	1938 ... 1722 + 3551
1342 ... 1237	1441 ... 1324	1541 ... 1413	1641 ... 1752	1739 ... 1602	1839 ... 1690	1939 ... 1773@
1343 ... 1238	1442 ... 1325@	1542 ... 1414	1642 ... 1512@	1740 ... 1603	1840 ... 1692	1940 ... 1774
1344 ... 1239	1443 ... 1325	1543 ... 1415	1643 ... 1513@	1741 ... 1604	1841 ... 1693	1941 ... 3726@
1345 ... 1240	1444 ... 1326	1544 ... 1416	1644 ... 1514	1742 ... 1605	1842 ... 1694	1942 ... 1775
1346 ... 1241	1445 ... 1760@	1545 ... 1417	1645 ... 1515	1743 ... 1606	1843 ... 1695@	1943 ... 1776
1347 ... 1242	1446 ... 1831@	1546 ... 1419	1646 ... 1516	1744 ... 1607	1844 ... 1696	1944 ... 1777
1348 ... 1243	1447 ... 1327	1547 ... 1420	1647 ... 1517	1745 ... 1608	1845 ... 1722 + 3319	1945 ... 1778
1349 ... 1244	1448 ... 2058@	1548 ... 1420@	1648 ... 1518	1746 ... 1609	1846 ... 1697@	1946 ... 1779
1350 ... 1245@	1449 ... 1328	1549 ... 1421	1649 ... 3004@	1747 ... *	1847 ... 1699	1947 ... 1780
1351 ... 1245	1450 ... 1329	1550 ... *	1650 ... 1519	1748 ... 1610	1848 ... *	1948 ... 1781@
1352 ... 1246	1451 ... 1330	1551 ... 1422	1651 ... 1520 & 3391	1749 ... 1611	1849 ... 1701	1949 ... 1782
1353 ... 1781@	1452 ... 1331	1552 ... 1423	1652 ... 1521	1750 ... 1612	1850 ... 1702	1950 ... 1783
1354 ... 1247	1453 ... 1332	1553 ... 1424	1653 ... 1522	1751 ... 4982@	1851 ... 1703	1951 ... *
1355 ... 1248	1454 ... 1333	1554 ... 1425	1654 ... 1523	1752 ... 1613	1852 ... 649@	1952 ... 1784
1356 ... 1249	1455 ... 1334	1555 ... 987@	1655 ... 1524	1753 ... 1614	1853 ... 1704	1953 ... 1785
1357 ... 1250	1456 ... 1335	1556 ... 1426	1656 ... 1525	1754 ... 1615	1854 ... 1705@	1954 ... 1786
1358 ... 1251@	1457 ... 1336@	1557 ... 1427	1657 ... 1528@	1755 ... 1616	1855 ... 1705	1955 ... 1787
1359 ... 1252	1458 ... 1337	1558 ... 1428	1658 ... 1529	1756 ... 1618	1856 ... 1714@	1956 ... 1788
1360 ... 1253	1459 ... 1338	1559 ... 1429	1659 ... 1530	1757 ... 1619 & 1617	1857 ... 1705@	1957 ... 1789
1361 ... 1254	1460 ... 1339	1560 ... 1430	1660 ... 1531	1758 ... 1620	1858 ... 1705	1958 ... 1790
1362 ... 1255	1461 ... 333@	1561 ... 1431	1661 ... 1532	1759 ... 1621	1859 ... 1714@	1959 ... 1791
1363 ... 1256	1462 ... 1340	1562 ... 1432	1662 ... 1533	1760 ... 1622	1860 ... 1706	1960 ... 1792
1364 ... 1257	1463 ... 2613@	1563 ... 1433	1663 ... 1534	1761 ... 1623	1861 ... 1707	1961 ... 1793
1365 ... 1258	1464 ... 1341	1564 ... 1434	1664 ... 1535	1762 ... 1624	1862 ... 1708	1962 ... 1794
1366 ... *	1465 ... 1342	1565 ... 1435		1763 ... 1625	1863 ... 1709	1963 ... 1795
	1466 ... 1343	1566 ... 1248		1764 ... 1790@	1864 ... 1710	1964 ... 1796

1965....1797	2065....1885@	2165....1976	2265....2067	2365....2160	2465....2250	2565....2344
1966....1798	2066....1885@	2166....1977	2266....2068 & 5315	2366....2161	2466....2251	2566....2345
1967....*	2067....*	2167....3982@	2267....2068@	2367....2162	2467....2253	2567....2346
1968....1800	2068....1886	2168....1978	2268....2069@	2368....2163	2468....2255	2568....2347@
1969....1801	2069....1887	2169....1979	2269....2072	2369....2164	2469....2256	2569....2348@
1970....1802@	2070....1888	2170....1980	2270....2073	2370....2165	2470....2256@	2570....2349
1971....1803@	2071....1889	2171....643@	2271....*	2371....2166	2471....2259	2571....5182@
1972....1804	2072....1890	2172....1981	2272....2074@	2372....2167	2472....2260@	2572....2350
1973....1805	2073....1891	2173....1982	2273....2274@	2373....2168	2473....2261	2573....2351
1974....1806	2074....1892	2174....1983	2274....2078	2374....2169	2474....2262	2574....2352@
1975....1807	2075....1893	2175....1984	2275....2079	2375....2170	2475....2263	2575....2352
1976....1808	2076....1894	2176....1985	2276....2080	2376....2171	2476....2264@	2576....2353
1977....1809@	2077....1895	2177....1986	2277....2081	2377....2172	2477....2265@	2577....2354
1978....1810	2078....1896	2178....4687@	2278....2082	2378....2173	2478....2266@	2578....2355
1979....1811	2079....1966@	2179....1987	2279....2083	2379....2174	2479....2267@	2579....2356
1980....1812	2080....1897	2180....1999	2280....2084	2380....2175	2480....2268@	2580....2357
1981....1813	2081....1898	2181....1988	2281....2085	2381....2176	2481....2269	2581....2358
1982....1814	2082....1904@	2182....1989	2282....2086	2382....*	2482....2276@	2582....2359
1983....1815	2083....1899	2183....*	2283....2087	2383....2177	2483....2270	2583....2360
1984....1816	2084....1900	2184....1990	2284....2088	2384....2178	2484....2271	2584....2361
1985....1817	2085....1901	2185....1991	2285....2089	2385....2179	2485....2272	2585....2362
1986....455	2086....1902	2186....1992	2286....2090	2386....2180	2486....2273	2586....*
1987....1818	2087....1903	2187....1993	2287....1681@	2387....2181	2487....2274@	2587....2363
1988....1819	2088....1904	2188....1994	2288....2091	2388....2182	2488....2275	2588....2364
1989....1820@	2089....1905	2189....1995	2289....2092	2389....2183	2489....2276@	2589....2365
1990....1821	2090....1906	2190....1996	2290....2093	2390....2184	2490....2278	2590....2366
1991....*	2091....1907	2191....1997	2291....2094	2391....2185	2491....2279	2591....2367
1992....1822	2092....1908	2192....1998	2292....2095	2392....2186	2492....2279@	2592....2368
1993....1823	2093....1909	2193....1976	2293....2096@	2393....1896@	2493....2279@	2593....2369
1994....1824	2094....1910	2194....1999	2294....2097	2394....2187@	2494....*	2594....2370
1995....1825	2095....1911	2195....2000	2295....2098	2395....2188	2495....3134@	2595....2371
1996....1826	2096....1912	2196....2001	2296....2099	2396....5504@	2496....5008@	2596....2372
1997....1832@	2097....1913	2197....2002	2297....2100	2397....2189	2497....2280	2597....2373
1998....1827	2098....1914	2198....2003	2298....2101	2398....2190	2498....2281	2598....2374
1999....1828	2099....1915	2199....2004	2299....2102	2399....2191	2499....2282	2599....2375
2000....1829	2100....1916	2200....2005	2300....2103	2400....2192	2500....2283@	2600....2376
2001....1830	2101....1917	2201....2006	2301....2095@	2401....2193	2501....2284	2601....2377
2002....1831	2102....1918	2202....2007	2302....2104	2402....*	2502....2285	2602....2378
2003....1832	2103....1919	2203....2008	2303....2129@	2403....*	2503....2286	2603....2379
2004....1833	2104....1920	2204....2009	2304....2105	2404....2194	2504....2287	2604....2380
2005....1810@	2105....1921	2205....2010	2305....2106	2405....2195	2505....2288	2605....2381
2006....*	2106....1922	2206....2233@	2306....2107	2406....2196@	2506....2289	2606....2382
2007....1834	2107....1923	2207....2011	2307....2108	2407....4518@	2507....2290	2607....*
2008....1835	2108....1924	2208....2012	2308....2109	2408....2197	2508....2291	2608....2383@
2009....1836	2109....1925	2209....2013	2309....2110	2409....2198	2509....2292	2609....2384
2010....1837@	2110....1926	2210....2014	2310....2111	2410....4570@	2510....2293	2610....2385
2011....1838	2111....1927	2211....2015	2311....2112	2411....2199	2511....2294	2611....2386
2012....1839@	2112....1928	2212....2016	2312....2113	2412....2200	2512....2295	2612....2387
2013....1839@	2113....1929	2213....2017	2313....2114	2413....4801@	2513....2296	2613....2388@
2014....1839	2114....1930	2214....2018	2314....2115	2414....2201	2514....2297	2614....2389@
2015....1840	2115....1931	2215....2019	2315....2115@	2415....2202	2515....2298	2615....2390
2016....1841	2116....1932	2216....2020	2316....2116	2416....2203	2516....2299	2616....2391@
2017....1842@	2117....1933	2217....2021	2317....2117	2417....2204	2517....2300	2617....2392
2018....1843	2118....1934	2218....*	2318....2117	2418....2206@	2518....2301	2618....2393
2019....1844	2119....1935	2219....2022	2319....2118	2419....2205	2519....2302	2619....2394
2020....1845	2120....1936	2220....2023	2320....2119	2420....2206	2520....2303	2620....2395
2021....1846	2121....1937	2221....2024	2321....2120	2421....2207 & 2208	2521....2304	2621....*
2022....1847	2122....1938	2222....2025	2322....2121	2422....2209	2522....2305	2622....*
2023....1847	2123....1939	2223....2017@	2323....2122	2423....2210	2523....2306	2623....2396
2024....1848	2124....2380@	2224....2026	2324....2123@	2424....2211	2524....*	2624....2397
2025....1848@	2125....1940	2225....2027	2325....2124	2425....*	2525....2307	2625....2398
2026....1849	2126....1941@	2226....2028	2326....2125	2426....2212	2526....2308	2626....2399
2027....1850	2127....1942	2227....2029	2327....2126	2427....2213	2527....2309	2627....2400
2028....*	2128....1943	2228....2030	2328....2127	2428....2214	2528....2310@	2628....2401
2029....1851	2129....1944	2229....2031	2329....2128	2429....2215	2529....2310	2629....2402
2030....1852	2130....1945	2230....2032	2330....2129	2430....4667@	2530....2311	2630....2403@
2031....1853	2131....2027@	2231....2033	2331....2130	2431....2216@	2531....2312	2631....2404
2032....1854	2132....2770@	2232....2034	2332....2131	2432....2217	2532....2312'	2632....2405
2033....1855	2133....2778@	2233....2035	2333....2132	2433....2218	2533....2313	2633....2406
2034....1856	2134....1946	2234....4179	2334....2133	2434....2219	2534....2314	2634....2407
2035....1857	2135....1947	2235....2037	2335....2134	2435....2220	2535....2315	2635....2408@
2036....1503@	2136....*	2236....2045@	2336....2135	2436....2221	2536....2316	2636....2409
2037....1858	2137....1948	2237....2038	2337....2136	2437....2222	2537....2317	2637....2410@
2038....1859	2138....1949	2238....2039	2338....2137	2438....2223	2538....2318	2638....1494@
2039....1860	2139....2989	2239....2040	2339....2145@	2439....2224	2539....2319	2639....2411
2040....1861@	2140....1950	2240....2041	2340....2138	2440....2224	2540....2320	2640....2412
2041....1862	2141....1951@	2241....2042	2341....2139@	2441....2225@	2541....2321	2641....2413
2042....1863	2142....1952	2242....2043	2342....2139	2442....2226@	2542....2322	2642....2414
2043....1864	2143....621@	2243....2044	2343....2140	2443....2227@	2543....2323	2643....2415
2044....1865	2144....1953	2244....2047	2344....2141	2444....*	2544....2324	2644....2416
2045....1866	2145....1954	2245....2048	2345....2142	2445....2228	2545....2325	2645....2417
2046....1867	2146....1955	2246....2049	2346....2143	2446....2229	2546....2326	2646....2418
2047....1868	2147....1956	2247....2050	2347....2144	2447....2229 + 3375	2547....2327	2647....2419@
2048....1869	2148....1957	2248....2051	2348....2145	2448....2230	2548....2328	2648....2420
2049....1870	2149....1958	2249....2052	2349....2146	2449....2231	2549....2329	2649....2421
2050....1871	2150....1959	2250....2053	2350....2148@	2450....2232	2550....2330	2650....2422
2051....1872	2151....1960	2251....2054	2351....2147	2451....2233	2551....*	2651....2423
2052....1873	2152....1961	2252....2055	2352....2148	2452....2234 & 2236	2552....2331	2652....2424
2053....1874	2153....1962	2253....2056	2353....2149	2453....2235	2553....2332	2653....2425
2054....1875	2154....1963	2254....2057	2354....2150	2454....2237	2554....2333	2654....2426
2055....1876	2155....1964	2255....2058	2355....2151	2455....2238	2555....2334	2655....2427
2056....1877	2156....1965	2256....1328@	2356....2152	2456....2239	2556....2335	2656....2428
2057....1878@	2157....1967	2257....2059	2357....2153	2457....2240	2557....2336	2657....2429
2058....1879	2158....1968	2258....2060	2358....2154	2458....2241	2558....2337	2658....2430
2059....1880	2159....1969	2259....2061	2359....2155	2459....2242	2559....2338	2659....2431
2060....1881@	2160....1971	2260....2062	2360....807@	2460....2243	2560....2339	2660....2432
2061....1882	2161....1972	2261....2063	2361....2156	2461....2244	2561....2340	2661....2433
2062....1883	2162....1973	2262....2064	2362....2157	2462....2245	2562....2341	2662....2434
2063....1944@	2163....1974	2263....2065	2363....2158	2463....2246	2563....2342	2663....2435
2064....1884	2164....1975	2264....2066	2364....2159	2464....2247	2564....2343	2664....2436

G-K	Strong	G-K	Strong	G-K	Strong	G-K	Strong	G-K	Strong	G-K	Strong	G-K	Strong
2665	2437	2765	2596 + 2250	2865	2610	2965	2702	3065	*	3165	2876	3265	2966
2666	2438	2766	2522	2866	2611	2966	2703	3066	2787	3166	2877	3266	2967
2667	2439	2767	2523	2867	2612	2967	2704	3067	2788	3167	2878	3267	2968
2668	2440	2768	2524	2868	2613	2968	2705	3068	2789	3168	2878	3268	2969
2669	2441	2769	2525@	2869	1349@	2969	2706	3069	2790	3169	2879@	3269	2970
2670	2442	2770	2525	2870	2614	2970	2707	3070	2791	3170	2880	3270	2971
2671	2443	2771	2526	2871	2615	2971	2019@	3071	2791	3171	2881	3271	2972
2672	2444	2772	2526'	2872	2616	2972	2708	3072	2792	3172	2882	3272	2973
2673	2445	2773	2527	2873	2652@	2973	2709	3073	2793	3173	2883	3273	2974
2674	2446	2774	2528	2874	2653@	2974	2710	3074	2794	3174	2884	3274	*
2675	2447	2775	2529	2875	2617	2975	4785@	3075	2795	3175	2885	3275	2975
2676	2448	2776	2530	2876	2618	2976	2711	3076	2796	3176	2886	3276	2976
2677	2449	2777	2531	2877	2619	2977	2712	3077	2792@	3177	2887	3277	2977@
2678	2450@	2778	2509@	2878	2620	2978	2713	3078	2797	3178	2887@	3278	2978
2679	2451	2779	2532	2879	2621	2979	2714	3079	5531@	3179	2888	3279	2997@
2680	2452	2780	2533	2880	2622	2980	2715	3080	2798	3180	2889	3280	2979
2681	2453	2781	2534	2881	2623	2981	2716	3081	2799	3181	2890	3281	2980
2682	2454	2782	2535	2882	2624	2982	2718	3082	2800	3182	2891@	3282	2981
2683	2455	2783	2536@	2883	2624@	2983	2719	3083	2801	3183	2891	3283	2982
2684	2456	2784	2536	2884	2625	2984	2719@	3084	2802@	3184	2892	3284	2983
2685	2457	2785	2537	2885	2626	2985	2720	3085	2802	3185	2893	3285	2984
2686	2456@	2786	2538	2886	2627	2986	2127@	3086	2803	3186	2894	3286	2985
2687	2458@	2787	2757@	2887	2628	2987	2721@	3087	2804	3187	2895@	3287	2986
2688	2459	2788	2539	2888	2629	2988	2722	3088	2805	3188	2895	3288	2987
2689	2460	2789	2540	2889	2630	2989	2723	3089	2806	3189	2896	3289	2988
2690	2461@	2790	2541	2890	2631	2990	2724	3090	2807	3190	2897	3290	2989
2691	2462	2791	2542	2891	2632	2991	2725	3091	2808	3191	2898	3291	2990
2692	2463	2792	2543	2892	2633	2992	2725@	3092	2809	3192	2899	3292	2991
2693	2464	2793	2544	2893	2596 + 2955	2993	2726	3093	2810@	3193	2900	3293	2993
2694	2465	2794	2545	2894	2634	2994	2727	3094	2811	3194	2901	3294	2994
2695	2466	2795	2546	2895	2635	2995	2728	3095	2812	3195	2902	3295	2992
2696	2469@	2796	2547	2896	2636	2996	2729	3096	2813	3196	2903	3296	2995
2697	2469	2797	2548	2897	2637	2997	2730	3097	2814	3197	2904	3297	2996
2698	2470	2798	2549	2898	2638	2998	2731	3098	2815	3198	2905	3298	2996@
2699	2471	2799	2550	2899	2639	2999	2732	3099	2816	3199	2906	3299	2997
2700	2472	2800	2551	2900	2640	3000	2733	3100	2817	3200	2907	3300	2998
2701	2473	2801	2552	2901	2641	3001	2730@	3101	2818	3201	2908@	3301	2999
2702	2474	2802	2553	2902	2642	3002	2734@	3102	2819	3202	2909 & 2908	3302	3000
2703	2475	2803	2554	2903	2643	3003	2735	3103	2820	3203	2910	3303	3001
2704	2466@	2804	2555	2904	2644	3004	2736	3104	2821	3204	2911	3304	3002
2705	2476	2805	2556	2905	2645	3005	2737	3105	2822	3205	2912	3305	3003@
2706	*	2806	2557	2906	2646	3006	2736	3106	2823	3206	2913	3306	3004 & 2036 & 2046 & 448
2707	2477	2807	2558	2907	2647	3007	2802@	3107	2824	3207	2914	3307	3005
2708	2478	2808	2559	2908	2648	3008	2738	3108	2825@	3208	2915	3308	3006
2709	2479	2809	2560	2909	2649	3009	2739	3109	2825	3209	2916	3309	3007
2710	2480	2810	2561	2910	2650	3010	2739@	3110	2826	3210	2917	3310	3008
2711	2481	2811	2562	2911	2651	3011	2740	3111	2827	3211	2918	3311	3009
2712	2482	2812	2563	2912	2652	3012	2741	3112	2828	3212	2919	3312	3010
2713	2483	2813	2564	2913	2653	3013	2743@	3113	2829	3213	2920	3313	3011
2714	2484@	2814	2565	2914	2654	3014	2742	3114	2830	3214	2921	3314	621@
2715	2485	2815	2567	2915	2655	3015	2743	3115	2831	3215	2922	3315	*
2716	2486	2816	2568@	2916	2656	3016	2744	3116	2832	3216	2923	3316	2982@
2717	2487	2817	2552@	2917	2657	3017	2745	3117	2833	3217	2924	3317	3012
2718	2488@	2818	2569	2918	2658	3018	2746	3118	2834	3218	2925	3318	3013
2719	*	2819	2570 & 2566	2919	2659	3019	2584@	3119	2835	3219	2926@	3319	3014
2720	2489@	2820	2571	2920	2660@	3020	2747	3120	2836	3220	2927	3320	3015
2721	2489 & 2490	2821	2572	2921	2661	3021	2748@	3121	2837	3221	2928	3321	3016@
2722	2491	2822	2573	2922	2662	3022	2748	3122	2838	3222	2929	3322	3017
2723	*	2823	2574	2923	2663	3023	2749	3123	2839	3223	2930	3323	3018@
2724	2492	2824	2574@	2924	2664	3024	2750	3124	2840	3224	2927@	3324	3019@
2725	5601@	2825	2575	2925	2665	3025	2751	3125	2841	3225	2931@	3325	3020@
2726	2455@	2826	2576	2926	*	3026	2752	3126	2842	3226	2927@	3326	3021
2727	2493	2827	2577	2927	2666	3027	2753	3127	2843	3227	2932	3327	1039@
2728	2491@	2828	2578	2928	2667	3028	*	3128	2844	3228	2933	3328	3022
2729	2494@	2829	2579	2929	2668	3029	2754	3129	*	3229	2934	3329	3023
2730	2494	2830	2580@	2930	2669	3030	2755	3130	2845	3230	2935	3330	3024
2731	2495	2831	2581@	2931	2670	3031	2756	3131	2846	3231	2936	3331	3028@
2732	2496	2832	2581	2932	2671	3032	2757	3132	2847	3232	2937	3332	3025
2733	2497@	2833	2582	2933	2672	3033	2758	3133	2848	3233	2938	3333	3026
2734	2498	2834	2583	2934	2673	3034	2759	3134	2849	3234	2939	3334	3027
2735	2499	2835	2584	2935	2674	3035	2760	3135	2850	3235	2940	3335	3028
2736	2500	2836	2585	2936	2675	3036	2761	3136	2851	3236	2941	3336	3029
2737	2501	2837	2586	2937	2676	3037	2762	3137	2858@	3237	2942	3337	3030
2738	2501@	2838	2587	2938	2677	3038	2763	3138	2857@	3238	2944@	3338	3031
2739	2502	2839	603@	2939	2678	3039	2764	3139	2852	3239	2943	3339	3032
2740	2503	2840	2588	2940	2679	3040	2765	3140	2853	3240	2944	3340	3033
2741	*	2841	2589	2941	2680	3041	2766	3141	2854	3241	2945	3341	3032@
2742	943@	2842	2591	2942	2681	3042	2767	3142	2855	3242	2946	3342	3034
2743	2504	2843	2590	2943	2682	3043	2768	3143	2856	3243	2946@	3343	3035
2744	943@	2844	2592	2944	2683	3044	2769	3144	2858	3244	2947	3344	3036
2745	2505	2845	2593	2945	2684	3045	2770	3145	2857	3245	2948	3345	3037
2746	2506	2846	2594	2946	2685	3046	2771	3146	2859	3246	2949	3346	3038
2747	2507	2847	2595	2947	2686	3047	2772	3147	2860	3247	2950	3347	3039
2748	2508	2848	2596	2948	2687	3048	2773	3148	2861	3248	2951	3348	3040
2749	2509	2849	2597	2949	2688	3049	2774	3149	2862	3249	2952	3349	3041
2750	2510	2850	2598	2950	2689	3050	2775	3150	2863	3250	2953	3350	3042
2751	2511	2851	2599	2951	2690	3051	2776	3151	2864	3251	2954	3351	3043
2752	2512	2852	925@	2952	2691	3052	2775	3152	2865	3252	2955	3352	3044@
2753	4027@	2853	2600	2953	2692	3053	2777	3153	2866	3253	2956@	3353	3045
2754	2513	2854	2601	2954	2693	3054	*	3154	2867	3254	2956	3354	3046
2755	2514	2855	*	2955	2694	3055	5392@	3155	2868	3255	2957	3355	3047
2756	2515	2856	2602	2956	2695	3056	2778	3156	2869	3256	2958	3356	3048@
2757	2516	2857	2603	2957	2695	3057	2779	3157	2870	3257	2959@	3357	3049
2758	2596 + 1520	2858	2604	2958	2696	3058	2780	3158	2871	3258	2960	3358	3050
2759	2517	2859	2605	2959	2697	3059	2781	3159	2872	3259	2961	3359	3051
2760	2511@	2860	2606	2960	2698	3060	2782	3160	2873	3260	2958@	3360	3052
2761	2518	2861	2607	2961	2699	3061	2783@	3161	2874	3261	2962	3361	3053
2762	2519	2862	2608	2962	2700	3062	2784	3162	2874@	3262	2963	3362	3054
2763	2520	2863	1125@	2963	2701	3063	2785	3163	2874@	3263	2964	3363	3055
2764	2521	2864	2609	2964	826@	3064	2786	3164	2875	3264	2965		

3364	3056	3463	3146	3563	3337	3663	3436	3763	3521	3863	3613	3963	3699
3365	3057	3464	3147	3564	3338	3664	3437	3764	3522	3864	3614	3964	3700
3366	3058	3465	3148	3565	3339	3665	3438	3765	3523	3865	3615	3965	3701
3367	3059	3466	3149	3566	3340	3666	3439	3766	3524@	3866	3616	3966	3702
3368	3060	3467	3150	3567	3341	3667	3440	3767	3524	3867	3617	3967	3703
3369	3061	3468	3151	3568	3342	3668	3441	3768	3525	3868	3618	3968	3704
3370	3063@ & 3062 & 3064	3469	3152	3569	3343	3669	3442	3769	3526	3869	3619	3969	3705
3371	3065	3470	3153	3570	3344	3670	3443	3770	3527	3870	3620	3970	3706
3372	3066	3471	3154	3571	3345	3671	3444	3771	3528	3871	3618@	3971	3707
3373	3067	3472	3155	3572	3346	3672	3445	3772	3529	3872	3621	3972	3708
3374	3068	3473	3156	3573	3344@	3673	3446	3773	3530	3873	3622	3973	3709
3375	3069	3474	3157	3574	*	3674	3447	3774	3531	3874	3623	3974	3710
3376	3070	3475	3158	3575	3347	3675	3448	3775	3532	3875	3624	3975	3711
3377	3071	3476	3159	3576	3348	3676	3451	3776	3533	3876	3625	3976	3712
3378	3072	3477	3160	3577	3349@	3677	3449	3777	3534	3877	3626@	3977	3713@
3379	3073	3478	3161	3578	3350	3678	3452	3778	3535@	3878	3626	3978	3714
3380	3074	3479	3162	3579	3351	3679	3453	3779	3535	3879	3627	3979	3715
3381	3075@	3480	3163	3580	3352	3680	3454	3780	3536@	3880	3628	3980	3716
3382	3076	3481	3164	3581	3353	3681	3455	3781	3537	3881	3629	3981	3717
3383	3077	3482	3166	3582	3354	3682	3456	3782	3538	3882	3627	3982	3718
3384	3078	3483	3167	3583	3355	3683	3457	3783	3539	3883	3633	3983	3719
3385	3079	3484	3168	3584	3356	3684	3458@	3784	3540	3884	3630	3984	3720
3386	3080	3485	3169	3585	3357	3685	3458	3785	3541	3885	3631	3985	3721
3387	3081	3486	3170	3586	3358	3686	3459	3786	3542	3886	3632	3986	3722
3388	3082	3487	3171	3587	3359	3687	*	3787	3543	3887	3633	3987	3723
3389	3083	3488	3172	3588	3360	3688	3460	3788	3544	3888	3634	3988	3724
3390	3084	3489	3173	3589	3360@	3689	3461	3789	3545	3889	*	3989	3733@
3391	3085	3490	3174	3590	3361	3690	3462	3790	3546	3890	3635	3990	3725
3392	3086	3491	3175@	3591	3361 + 1065	3691	3463	3791	3547	3891	3636	3991	3726
3393	3087	3492	3176	3592	3365	3692	3463@	3792	3548	3892	3637	3992	3727
3394	3088	3493	3177	3593	3366	3693	3464	3793	3549	3893	3638	3993	3728
3395	3089	3494	3178	3594	3367	3694	3460@	3794	3550	3894	3644@	3994	3729
3396	3090	3495	3179	3595	3368	3695	3465	3795	3551	3895	3645@	3995	3730
3397	3091	3496	3179	3596	3369	3696	3466	3796	3552	3896	3639@	3996	3731
3398	*	3497	3180	3597	3370	3697	3467	3797	3553	3897	3639	3997	3732
3399	3092@	3498	3181@	3598	3365@	3698	3468	3798	3554	3898	570@	3998	3733
3400	3093@	3499	3182	3599	3367@	3699	3469	3799	3555	3899	3640	3999	3734
3401	3093	3500	3183	3600	3371	3700	3470	3800	3556	3900	3641	4000	*
3402	3094	3501	3184	3601	3372	3701	3471	3801	3502@	3901	3642	4001	3735
3403	717@	3502	3396@	3602	3373	3702	3472	3802	3557@	3902	3643	4002	3736
3404	3095	3503	3396@	3603	3374	3703	3473	3803	3558	3903	3689@	4003	3737
3405	3096	3504	3186	3604	3375	3704	3474	3804	3559	3904	3644	4004	3738
3406	3095	3505	3187 & 3185	3605	3376	3705	3475	3805	3560	3905	3645	4005	3739
3407	3097	3506	3189 & 3188	3606	3377	3706	3475	3806	3561	3906	3646	4006	3740
3408	3098	3507	3190@	3607	3379	3707	3475	3807	3562	3907	3647	4007	3739 + 1065
3409	3099	3508	3199@	3608	3361 + 4225	3708	*	3808	3563	3908	3648	4008	3741
3410	3149@	3509	3191	3609	3380	3709	3476	3809	3564@	3909	3649	4009	3742
3411	3100	3510	3192	3610	3381	3710	3477	3810	3564	3910	3650	4010	3743
3412	3101	3511	3193@	3611	3382	3711	3478@	3811	3565@	3911	3651	4011	3744
3413	3102	3512	3193@	3612	3383	3712	3478@	3812	3566	3912	3652	4012	3745
3414	3156@	3513	3193	3613	3384	3713	3478@	3813	3567	3913	3653	4013	3746
3415	3158@	3514	3194	3614	3385 & 3387	3714	3478	3814	3568	3914	3654	4014	3747
3416	3159@	3515	3194@	3615	3386	3715	3478	3815	3570	3915	3655	4015	3748 & 3755
3417	3103@	3516	3195	3616	3388	3716	3479	3816	3571	3916	2442@	4016	3747
3418	3104	3517	3196	3617	3389	3717	3480	3817	3572	3917	3656	4017	3749
3419	3105	3518	3197	3618	3389	3718	3481@	3818	3573	3918	3657	4018	3750
3420	3106	3519	3198@	3619	3390	3719	3481	3819	3574	3919	3658	4019	3751@
3421	3107	3520	3199	3620	3392	3720	3482	3820	3575	3920	*	4020	3752
3422	3108	3521	3200	3621	3393	3721	3483	3821	3576	3921	3659	4021	3753
3423	3109	3522	3201	3622	3394	3722	3497@	3822	3577	3922	3660@	4022	3754
3424	3110	3523	3202	3623	3395	3723	3484	3823	*	3923	3660	4023	3757
3425	3111	3524	3437@	3624	3396	3724	3485	3824	837@	3924	3661	4024	3756
3426	3112	3525	3303	3625	3398 & 3397	3725	3486	3825	3578	3925	3662	4025	3758
3427	3113	3526	3104@	3626	3399	3726	3487	3826	3579	3926	3663	4026	3759
3428	3114	3527	*	3627	3400	3727	3488	3827	3580	3927	3664	4027	3760
3429	3115	3528	3304@	3628	3401	3728	3489	3828	3581	3928	3665	4028	3761
3430	3116	3529	3304	3629	3402	3729	3490	3829	3582	3929	3666	4029	3762
3431	3117	3530	3305	3630	3403@	3730	3491	3830	3583	3930	3667	4030	3763
3432	3118	3531	3306	3631	3404	3731	3492	3831	3584	3931	3668	4031	3764
3433	3119	3532	3307	3632	3405	3732	3493	3832	3585	3932	3669	4032	3762@
3434	3120	3533	3308	3633	3406	3733	3494	3833	3586	3933	3670	4033	3765
3435	3121	3534	3309	3634	3407	3734	3495	3834	3587	3934	3671	4034	3766
3436	3122	3535	3310	3635	3408	3735	3496@	3835	*	3935	3672	4035	1695@
3437	3123	3536	3311	3636	3409	3736	3496	3836	3588 & 5120	3936	*	4036	3767
3438	3124	3537	3312	3637	3410	3737	3497	3837	3589	3937	3673	4037	3768
3439	3125	3538	3313	3638	3411	3738	3498	3838	3590	3938	3674	4038	3769
3440	3126	3539	3322@	3639	3412	3739	3499	3839	3591	3939	3675	4039	3770
3441	3127	3540	3314	3640	3413	3740	3500	3840	3592	3940	3676	4040	3771
3442	3128	3541	3315	3641	3414	3741	3561@	3841	3593	3941	3677	4041	3772
3443	3129	3542	3316	3642	3415	3742	3501	3842	3594	3942	3678	4042	3773
3444	3130	3543	3317	3643	3416	3743	3502	3843	3595	3943	3679	4043	3774
3445	3131	3544	3318	3644	3417	3744	3503	3844	3596	3944	3680	4044	3775
3446	3132	3545	3319	3645	3418	3745	3504	3845	3597	3945	3681	4045	3776
3447	3133	3546	3320	3646	3419	3746	3505	3846	3598 + 4160	3946	3682	4046	3777
3448	3134@	3547	3321	3647	3420	3747	*	3847	3598	3947	3683	4047	3778 & 5023 & 5025 & 502
3449	3135	3548	3322	3648	3421	3748	3506	3848	3599	3948	3684	4048	3779
3450	3136	3549	3323	3649	3422	3749	3507	3849	3600	3949	3685	4049	3780
3451	3137	3550	3324	3650	3423	3750	3508@	3850	3601	3950	3686	4050	3781
3452	3137@	3551	3325	3651	3424@	3751	3509	3851	3602	3951	3687	4051	3782
3453	3138@	3552	3326	3652	3424	3752	3510	3852	3604@	3952	3688	4052	3783
3454	3139	3553	3327	3653	3425	3753	3511	3853	3605	3953	3689	4053	3784
3455	3140	3554	3328	3654	3426	3754	3512	3854	3606	3954	3690	4054	3785
3456	3141	3555	3329	3655	3428	3755	3513	3855	3607	3955	3691	4055	3786
3457	3142	3556	3330	3656	3429	3756	3514	3856	3608	3956	3692	4056	3787@
3458	3143	3557	3331	3657	3430	3757	3515	3857	1492@	3957	3693	4057	3788
3459	3144	3558	3332	3658	3431	3758	3516	3858	3609	3958	3694	4058	3789
3460	3145	3559	3333	3659	3432	3759	3517	3859	2322@	3959	3695	4059	3790@
3461	3149@	3560	3334	3660	3433	3760	3518	3860	3610	3960	3696	4060	856@
3462	3145	3561	3335	3661	3434	3761	3519	3861	3611	3961	3697	4061	3791@
		3562	3336@	3662	3435	3762	3520	3862	3612	3962	3698		

4062....3792	4162....3881	4262....3971	4362....4059	4462....4153	4561....4242	4660....4329
4063....3793	4163....3882	4263....3972	4363....4060	4463....4154	4562....4246	4661....4330
4064....*	4164....3883	4264....3973	4364....4061	4464....4155	4563....4243	4662....4331
4065....3794	4165....3884	4265....3974	4365....4062	4465....4156	4564....4244	4663....4332
4066....3795	4166....3885	4266....3975	4366....4063	4466....4157	4565....4245	4664....4333
4067....3796	4167....3885@	4267....3976	4367....4064	4467....4217@	4566....4246	4665....4334
4068....3798@	4168....3886	4268....3977	4368....4065	4468....4158	4567....4247	4666....4335
4069....3797	4169....3887	4269....3978	4369....4066	4469....3537@	4568....4248	4667....4336
4070....3798	4170....3888	4270....3979	4370....4067	4470....4159	4569....4249	4668....4337
4071....3799	4171....3889	4271....3979@	4371....4068	4471....4169@	4570....4250	4669....4338
4072....3800	4172....3890	4272....3980	4372....4069	4472....4160	4571....4251	4670....4339
4073....*	4173....3913@	4273....3981	4373....4070	4473....4161	4572....4252	4671....4286@
4074....3802	4174....3891	4274....3981@	4374....4071	4474....4162	4573....4249@	4672....4340
4075....3803	4175....3892	4275....3982	4375....4072	4475....4163	4574....4253	4673....4341@
4076....697@	4176....3893	4276....4091@	4376....4073	4476....4164	4575....4254	4674....4342
4077....3804	4177....3894	4277....3983	4377....4074	4477....4165	4576....4255@	4675....4343
4078....3805	4178....3895	4278....3984	4378....4075	4478....4166	4577....4256	4676....4344
4079....3806	4179....3896	4279....3985	4379....4076	4479....4167	4578....4257	4677....4345
4080....3807	4180....3897@	4280....3986	4380....4077	4480....4168	4579....4258	4678....4346@
4081....3808	4181....3898	4281....3987	4381....4078	4481....4169	4580....4259	4679....4347@
4082....3809	4182....3899	4282....3988	4382....4079	4482....4170	4581....4260	4680....4346
4083....3810	4183....3900	4283....3989	4383....4080	4483....4171	4582....4261	4681....4347
4084....3811	4184....3901	4284....3990	4384....4081	4484....4172	4583....4262	4682....4348
4085....3812	4185....3902	4285....*	4385....4082	4485....4173	4584....4263@	4683....4349
4086....3813	4186....3903	4286....3991	4386....4456@	4486....4174	4585....4263	4684....4350
4087....3814	4187....3904	4287....3992	4387....4457@	4487....4175	4586....4264	4685....4351
4088....3812@	4188....4368@	4288....3993	4388....4083	4488....4176	4587....4265	4686....4352
4089....3815	4189....3905	4289....3994	4389....4084	4489....4177	4588....4266	4687....4353
4090....3816	4190....3906	4290....3995	4390....4085	4490....4178	4589....4267	4688....4354
4091....3817	4191....3907	4291....3996	4391....4086	4491....4179	4590....4268	4689....4355
4092....3818@	4192....3908	4292....3997	4392....3981@	4492....4184@	4591....4269	4690....*
4093....3819	4193....3909	4293....3998	4393....4087	4493....*	4592....4270	4691....4356
4094....3820	4194....3910	4294....3999	4394....4088	4494....4180	4593....4271	4692....4356
4095....3821	4195....3911	4295....4000	4395....4089	4495....4181	4594....4272	4693....4357
4096....3822	4196....3912	4296....4001	4396....4090	4496....*	4595....4273	4694....4358
4097....3823	4197....3913	4297....4002	4397....4091@	4497....4182	4596....4274	4695....4359
4098....3824	4198....3913@	4298....4003	4398....4130	4498....4183 & 4118 & 4119	4597....4302@	4696....4360
4099....3825	4199....3914	4299....4004	4399....4092	4499....4184	4598....4276	4697....*
4100....3824@	4200....3915	4300....4005	4400....4093	4500....4185	4599....4278	4698....4361
4101....3826	4201....2710@	4301....4006	4401....4093@	4501....4186	4600....4279@	4699....4362
4102....3827	4202....3916	4302....4007	4402....4094	4502....4187	4601....4281	4700....4363
4103....3828	4203....3917	4303....*	4403....4095	4503....4188	4602....4282	4701....4364@
4104....3829@	4204....4332@	4304....4012 + 2087	4404....4096	4504....4189	4603....4283	4702....4365
4105....3830@	4205....3918	4305....4008	4405....4097	4505....4190 & 4191	4604....4284@	4703....4366
4106....3829	4206....3919	4306....4009	4406....4098	4506....4192	4605....4285	4704....4366@
4107....3830	4207....3920	4307....4010	4407....4099	4507....4193	4606....4286	4705....4367
4108....3831	4208....3921	4308....4011	4408....4099@	4508....4194	4607....4287@	4706....4368
4109....3832	4209....3922	4309....4012	4409....4100	4509....5117@	4608....4288	4707....4369
4110....3833	4210....3923	4310....4013	4410....4101	4510....4195	4609....4289	4708....4370
4111....3834	4211....3924	4311....4014	4411....4102	4511....4196	4610....4290	4709....4371
4112....3835	4212....4016@	4312....681@	4412....4103	4512....4197	4611....4406@	4710....4372
4113....3826@	4213....3925	4313....4015	4413....4104	4513....4198	4612....4407@	4711....4373
4114....3837@	4214....3926	4314....4016	4414....4105	4514....4199	4613....4291	4712....4374
4115....3836	4215....3927	4315....4017	4415....4106	4515....4197@	4614....4292@	4713....4375
4116....3837	4216....3928	4316....4018	4416....4107@	4516....4200	4615....4293	4714....4376
4117....3838	4217....3929	4317....4019	4417....4107	4517....4201	4616....4294	4715....4377
4118....3839@	4218....3930	4318....4020	4418....4108	4518....4202	4617....4284@	4716....4370@
4119....3840	4219....3931	4319....4021	4419....4109	4519....4203	4618....4295	4717....4378
4120....3841	4220....3932	4320....4022	4420....4110	4520....4204	4619....4296	4718....4379
4121....3842	4221....3933	4321....4023	4421....4111	4521....4205	4620....4297	4719....4380
4122....3843	4222....3934@	4322....4024	4422....4112	4522....4206	4621....4298	4720....4381
4123....3844	4223....3935	4323....4024@	4423....4113	4523....4207	4622....4299	4721....4382
4124....3845	4224....3936@	4324....4025	4424....4114	4524....4208	4623....4300	4722....4380
4125....3846	4225....3936	4325....4026	4425....4115	4525....4209	4624....4301	4723....4381
4126....3847	4226....3937	4326....4027	4426....4116	4526....4210@	4625....4302 & 4277 & 4280	4724....4382
4127....3848	4227....3938	4327....4776@	4427....4117	4527....4211	4626....4303	4725....4383
4128....3849	4228....3939	4328....4028	4428....4120	4528....4210	4627....4304	4726....4384
4129....3851@	4229....3940	4329....4029	4429....4121	4529....4212	4628....4305	4727....4385
4130....3850	4230....3941	4330....4030	4430....4122	4530....4213	4629....4306	4728....4387 & 4386
4131....3851	4231....3942	4331....4031	4431....4123	4531....4214	4630....4307	4729....4388@
4132....3852	4232....3943	4332....4032@	4432....4124	4532....4215	4631....4308	4730....4389@
4133....3853	4233....3944	4333....4033	4433....4125	4533....4216	4632....4308 & 4275	4731....4390
4134....3854	4234....3945	4334....4034	4434....4126	4534....4217	4633....4309	4732....4391
4135....3855	4235....3946	4335....4035@	4435....4127	4535....4458@	4634....4310	4733....4392
4136....3856	4236....3947	4336....621@	4436....4128	4536....4219	4635....3962@	4734....4393
4137....3857	4237....3948	4337....4036	4437....4129	4537....4218	4636....4311	4735....4394
4138....3858	4238....5237@	4338....4037	4438....4131	4538....4220	4637....4312	4736....4395
4139....3859	4239....3949	4339....4038	4439....4132@	4539....4221	4638....4313	4737....4396
4140....3860	4240....3950	4340....4039	4440....4133	4540....4222	4639....4314	4738....4397
4141....3861	4241....3951	4341....4040	4441....4134	4541....4223	4640....4315	4739....4398
4142....3862	4242....3952	4342....4041	4442....4135	4542....4224	4641....4316	4740....4399
4143....3863	4243....3953	4343....4042	4443....4136	4543....4225	4642....4317	4741....4400@
4144....3864	4244....3954	4344....4043	4444....4137	4544....4226	4643....4318	4742....4401
4145....3865	4245....3955	4345....4044	4445....4138	4545....4227	4644....4319	4743....4402
4146....3866	4246....3956	4346....4045	4446....4139	4546....4228	4645....4319@	4744....4403
4147....3867	4247....3957	4347....4046@	4447....4140	4547....4229	4646....4320	4745....4404
4148....3868	4248....3958	4348....4047	4448....4141	4548....4230	4647....4355@	4746....4405
4149....3869@	4249....3959	4349....*	4449....4142	4549....4231	4648....4321	4747....4406
4150....3869	4250....3960	4350....*	4450....4143	4550....4232	4649....4321	4748....4407
4151....3870	4251....3961	4351....4048	4451....1708@	4551....4233	4650....4322	4749....4408@
4152....3871	4252....3962	4352....4049	4452....4144	4552....4234	4651....4323	4750....4409
4153....3872	4253....3963	4353....4050	4453....4144@	4553....4235@	4652....4317@	4751....4410
4154....3873	4254....3964	4354....4051	4454....4145	4554....4236@	4653....4324	4752....4411
4155....3874	4255....3965	4355....4052	4455....4146	4555....4237	4654....4317@	4753....3144@
4156....3875	4256....3966	4356....4053	4456....4147	4556....4238	4655....4325	4754....4412
4157....3876	4257....3967	4357....4054	4457....4148	4557....4239	4656....4326	4755....4413
4158....3877	4258....3968	4358....4055	4458....4149	4558....4239	4657....4327	4756....4414
4159....3878	4259....3969@	4359....4056	4459....4150	4559....4240	4658....1929@	4757....4415
4160....3879	4260....3964@	4360....4057	4460....4151	4560....4241	4659....4328	4758....4416
4161....3880	4261....3970	4361....4058	4461....4152			4759....4412@

4760....4417	4860....4505	4960....4595	5060....4685	5158....4780	5258....4870	5358....4950@
4761....4418	4861....4506	4961....4596	5061....4686	5159....4781	5259....4871	5359....4951
4762....4419	4862....4510@	4962....4597	5062....4687	5160....4782	5260....4871@	5360....4952
4763....4420	4863....4510@	4963....4598	5063....4688	5161....4783	5261....4900@	5361....4953
4764....4421	4864....4507	4964....4599	5064....4689	5162....*	5262....4872	5362....4954
4765....4422	4865....4508	4965....4600	5065....4690	5163....4784@	5263....4873	5363....4955
4766....4423	4866....4509	4966....4525@	5066....4691	5164....4785@	5264....4874@	5364....4956
4767....4424	4867....4510	4967....4601	5067....4692	5165....4873@	5265....4875	5365....4957
4768....4425	4868....4511	4968....4602	5068....4693	5166....4786	5266....*	5366....4958
4769....4426	4869....4512	4969....4603	5069....4694	5167....4787	5267....4876	5367....4959
4770....4427	4870....4513	4970....4604	5070....4696	5168....4788	5268....4877	5368....4960
4771....4428	4871....4514	4971....4603@	5071....4695	5169....4789	5269....4878	5369....4961
4772....4429	4872....4515	4972....4605	5072....4697	5170....4790	5270....4879	5370....4962
4773....4430	4873....4516	4973....4606	5073....4698	5171....4791	5271....4880@	5371....4963
4774....4431	4874....4517	4974....4607	5074....4699	5172....4792	5272....4881	5372....4964
4775....4432	4875....*	4975....4608	5075....4700	5173....4793	5273....4882	5373....4965
4776....4433	4876....4518@	4976....4609	5076....4701	5174....4794	5274....4883	5374....4966
4777....4434	4877....4519	4977....4610	5077....4702	5175....4795	5275....4884	5375....4967
4778....4435	4878....4520	4978....4611	5078....4703	5176....4796	5276....4871@	5376....4968
4779....*	4879....4521	4979....*	5079....4704	5177....4797	5277....4885	5377....4969
4780....4436@	4880....4522	4980....4612	5080....4705 & 4706 & 4707	5178....4798	5278....4886	5378....*
4781....4437	4881....4523	4981....4613	5081....4709 & 4708	5179....4797	5279....4887	5379....4970
4782....4438	4882....4524	4982....4614@	5082....4710	5180....4799	5280....4888	5380....4971
4783....4439	4883....4525	4983....4615	5083....4711	5181....2010@	5281....4889	5381....4972
4784....4440	4884....4526	4984....4616	5084....4712	5182....4800	5282....4890	5382....4973
4785....4441	4885....4527	4985....4617	5085....4713	5183....4801	5283....4891	5383....4974@
4786....4442	4886....4528	4986....4596@	5086....4955@	5184....4802	5284....4892	5384....4974
4787....4443	4887....4529	4987....4577@	5087....4714	5185....4803	5285....*	5385....4975
4788....4444	4888....4531	4988....4618	5088....4715	5186....4804	5286....*	5386....4976
4789....4445	4889....4532	4989....4621@	5089....4716	5187....4805	5287....4893	5387....4977
4790....4446	4890....4530@	4990....4619	5090....4717	5188....4806	5288....4894	5388....4978
4791....4447	4891....4533	4991....4620	5091....4718	5189....4807	5289....4895	5389....4979
4792....4448	4892....4534	4992....4621	5092....4719	5190....4808	5290....4896	5390....4980
4793....4449	4893....4535	4993....4965@	5093....4720	5191....4809@	5291....4897	5391....4981
4794....4450	4894....4536	4994....4622	5094....4721	5192....4810	5292....4898	5392....4982@
4795....*	4895....4537	4995....4623	5095....4722	5193....4811	5293....4899	5393....4983
4796....4451	4896....4538	4996....2977@	5096....4723@	5194....4812	5294....*	5394....4984
4797....4453	4897....4539	4997....4624	5097....4724	5195....4813	5295....4900	5395....4985
4798....4454	4898....4672@	4998....4625	5098....4725	5196....4814	5296....4901	5396....4986
4799....4455	4899....4540	4999....4626	5099....4726	5197....4815	5297....4862 + 1985	5397....4987
4800....4456	4900....4540@	5000....2469@	5100....4727	5198....4816	5298....4934@	5398....4988
4801....4457	4901....4541@	5001....2469@	5101....4728	5199....4817	5299....4902	5399....4989
4802....4459	4902....4542@	5002....4627	5102....4729	5200....4818	5300....4903	5400....4990
4803....4458@ & 4452	4903....4543	5003....4628	5103....4730	5201....4819	5301....4904	5401....4991
4804....*	4904....4544	5004....4629	5104....4731	5202....4820	5302....4905	5402....4992
4805....4460	4905....4545	5005....4630	5105....4732	5203....4821	5303....4906	5403....4992@
4806....4461	4906....*	5006....4631	5106....4733	5204....4822	5304....4907	5404....4993
4807....4462	4907....4546	5007....4632	5107....4734	5205....4823	5305....4908	5405....4994
4808....4462	4908....4547	5008....4633	5108....4736@	5206....4824	5306....4909	5406....4995
4809....4462@	4909....4548	5009....4634	5109....4735	5207....4825	5307....4910@	5407....4996
4810....4463	4910....4549	5010....4635	5110....4737	5208....4826	5308....4911	5408....4997
4811....4464	4911....4550	5011....4636	5111....4738	5209....4827	5309....4912	5409....4998
4812....4465	4912....4551@	5012....4637	5112....4739	5210....4828	5310....4913	5410....*
4813....*	4913....4552@	5013....4638	5113....4740	5211....4829	5311....4914	5411....4999@
4814....4466@	4914....4553	5014....4639	5114....4741	5212....4830	5312....4915	5412....5000
4815....4467	4915....4554	5015....4640	5115....4746@	5213....4831	5313....4916	5413....5001
4816....4468	4916....4555	5016....4641	5116....4742	5214....4833@	5314....4917	5414....5002
4817....911@	4917....4556@	5017....4642	5117....4743	5215....4832	5315....4918	5415....5003
4818....4481@	4918....4557	5018....4643	5118....4744	5216....4833	5316....4919	5416....5004
4819....4469	4919....4558	5019....4644	5119....4745	5217....4834	5317....4920	5417....5005
4820....4470	4920....4559	5020....4645	5120....4746	5218....4835	5318....4921	5418....5006
4821....4471@	4921....4560	5021....4646	5121....4770@	5219....4836	5319....4921	5419....5007
4822....4472	4922....4561	5022....4647	5122....4747	5220....4837	5320....4920@	5420....5008
4823....4473	4923....4562	5023....4648	5123....4748	5221....4838	5321....4922	5421....5009
4824....4474	4924....4563	5024....4649	5124....4749	5222....4839	5322....4923	5422....3569
4825....4475	4925....4564	5025....4650	5125....4750	5223....4840	5323....4894@	5423....5010
4826....4486	4926....4565@	5026....4651	5126....4751	5224....4841	5324....4924	5424....5011
4827....4476	4927....4566@	5027....4652	5127....4752	5225....4842	5325....4925	5425....5012
4828....4469@	4928....4567	5028....4653	5128....4753	5226....*	5326....4926	5426....5391@
4829....4477	4929....4568	5029....4654@	5129....4754	5227....4843	5327....4927	5427....5013
4830....4478	4930....4569	5030....4655	5130....4755	5228....4844	5328....4894@	5428....5014
4831....4479	4931....4570	5031....4656	5131....4756	5229....4098@	5329....*	5429....5015
4832....4480@	4932....4572	5032....4657	5132....4757	5230....4845	5330....4928	5430....5016
4833....4481	4933....4573	5033....4658	5133....4758	5231....4846	5331....4952@	5431....5017
4834....4481@	4934....4574	5034....4659	5134....4759	5232....4847	5332....4929	5432....5018
4835....4482	4935....4575	5035....4660	5135....4759@	5233....4848	5333....4930	5433....5019
4836....4484	4936....4576@	5036....4661	5136....4760	5234....4849@	5334....4931	5434....5020
4837....4485	4937....4577	5037....4662	5137....4761	5235....4849	5335....4932	5435....5021
4838....4486	4938....4577@	5038....4663	5138....4762	5236....4850	5336....*	5436....5022
4839....4487	4939....4578	5039....4664	5139....4763	5237....4851	5337....4933	5437....5024
4840....4488	4940....4579	5040....4665	5140....4764	5238....4852	5338....4934@	5438....5027
4841....4486	4941....4580	5041....3395@	5141....4765	5239....4851@	5339....4935	5439....5028
4842....4489	4942....4581	5042....3395@	5142....4766	5240....4833@	5340....4936	5440....5029
4843....4490	4943....4582	5043....4666	5143....4766	5241....4853	5341....4937	5441....5030 & 5032 & 5033
4844....4491	4944....4583	5044....4667	5144....4767	5242....4854	5342....4938	5442....5031
4845....4492	4945....4584	5045....4668	5145....4768	5243....4855	5343....4939	5443....5034
4846....4493	4946....4584@	5046....4669	5146....4769@	5244....4856	5344....4940	5444....5036 & 5035
4847....4494	4947....4585	5047....4670	5147....4770	5245....4857	5345....4941	5445....5037
4848....4495	4948....4586	5048....4672	5148....4771 & 4571 & 4671 & 467	5246....4858	5346....4795@	5446....5038
4849....4496	4949....4587	5049....4673	5149....4772	5247....4859	5347....4942	5447....5039
4850....4497	4950....4588	5050....4674	5150....4773	5248....4860	5348....4943	5448....5040
4851....4498	4951....4562@	5051....4676	5151....4773@	5249....4861	5349....4944	5449....5041
4852....4499	4952....4562@	5052....4677	5152....4774	5250....4862	5350....4945	5450....5042
4853....4500	4953....4589	5053....4678	5153....4775	5251....4863	5351....4949@	5451....5043
4854....4481@	4954....4590	5054....4679	5154....4776	5252....4864	5352....4946	5452....5044
4855....4501	4955....4591	5055....4680	5155....4777	5253....4865	5353....4947	5453....*
4856....4493@	4956....4592	5056....4681	5156....4778@	5254....4866	5354....4948	5454....5045
4857....4502	4957....4593	5057....4682	5157....4779	5255....4867	5355....4949@	5455....5046
4858....4503	4958....4594	5058....4683		5256....4868	5356....4949	5456....5047
4859....4504	4959....4612@	5059....4684		5257....4869	5357....*	

5457....5048	5545....5133	5633....5218	5721....5296	5809....5380	5897....5463	5985....5546
5458....5049	5546....5134	5634....5219	5722....5297	5810....5381	5898....5464	5986....5547
5459....5050	5547....5135	5635....5220	5723....5298	5811....5382	5899....5465	5987....5548
5460....5051	5548....5136	5636....5221	5724....5299	5812....5383	5900....5466	5988....5549
5461....5052	5549....5137	5637....5222	5725....5300	5813....5384	5901....5467	5989....5550
5462....5053	5550....5138	5638....5223	5726....*	5814....5385	5902....5468	5990....5551
5463....5054	5551....5139	5639....5225 & 5224	5727....5301	5815....5386	5903....5469	5991....5552
5464....5055	5552....5140	5640....5226	5728....5302	5816....5387	5904....5468@	5992....5553
5465....5056	5553....5140 + 4999	5641....5227	5729....5303	5817....5388	5905....5470	5993....5554
5466....5058@	5554....5141	5642....5228	5730....5304	5818....5389	5906....5471	5994....5555
5467....5057	5555....5142	5643....5229	5731....5306 & 5305	5819....5390	5907....5472	5995....5556
5468....5058	5556....5143	5644....5230	5732....*	5820....5391	5908....5473	5996....5557
5469....5059	5557....5169@	5645....5231	5733....5307	5821....5392	5909....5474	5997....5552@
5470....5060	5558....5144	5646....784@	5734....5308	5822....5417@	5910....5475	5998....5558
5471....*	5559....5145	5647....5232	5735....5309	5823....5393	5911....5470@	5999....5559
5472....5061	5560....5146	5648....5233	5736....5310	5824....5394	5912....5476	6000....5560
5473....5062	5561....5147	5649....5234	5737....5311	5825....5395	5913....5477@	6001....5561
5474....5063	5562....5148	5650....5235	5738....5312	5826....5396	5914....5478	6002....5523@
5475....5064	5563....5149	5651....5236	5739....5313	5827....5397	5915....5479	6003....5562
5476....5065	5564....5150	5652....5228 + 1473	5740....*	5828....5399	5916....5480	6004....5563
5477....5062@	5565....5151	5653....5237	5741....5314	5829....5398	5917....5481	6005....5564
5478....5063@	5566....5152	5654....5238	5742....5341@	5830....5399	5918....5482	6006....5565
5479....5066	5567....5153	5655....5240	5743....5316	5831....5400	5919....5483	6007....*
5480....5067	5568....5154@	5656....5240@	5744....5317	5832....5401	5920....5484	6008....5566
5481....5068	5569....5154	5657....5239	5745....5318	5833....5402	5921....5485	6009....*
5482....5069	5570....5155	5658....5240@	5746....5319	5834....5403	5922....5486	6010....5567
5483....5070	5571....5156	5659....5241	5747....5320	5835....4949@	5923....5487	6011....5568
5484....5071	5572....5157	5660....5242	5748....5321	5836....5404	5924....5488	6012....5569
5485....5072	5573....5158	5661....5243	5749....5322	5837....5405	5925....5489	6013....5570
5486....5073	5574....5159	5662....5244	5750....5323	5838....5406	5926....5490	6014....5571
5487....5073@	5575....5160	5663....5244	5751....5324	5839....5407	5927....5491	6015....5572
5488....5074	5576....5161	5664....5245	5752....5325	5840....5408	5928....5492	6016....5573
5489....5075	5577....5162	5665....5246	5753....5326	5841....5409	5929....5493	6017....5574
5490....5076	5578....5159@	5666....5237@	5754....5327	5842....5410@	5930....5494	6018....5576
5491....5077	5579....5163	5667....5247	5755....5328	5843....5411	5931....5495	6019....5577
5492....5078	5580....5164	5668....5248	5756....5329	5844....5412	5932....5496	6020....5575@
5493....5079	5581....5165	5669....5249	5757....5330	5845....5413	5933....5497	6021....5578
5494....5080@	5582....5166	5670....5250	5758....5331	5846....5414	5934....5498	6022....5579
5495....5081	5583....5167	5671....5251	5759....5332	5847....5415@	5935....5499	6023....5580
5496....5082	5584....5168	5672....5252	5760....5331@	5848....5416	5936....5500	6024....5581
5497....*	5585....5169	5673....5253	5761....5333@	5849....5417	5937....5501	6025....5582
5498....5083	5586....5170	5674....5254	5762....5334	5850....5418	5938....5502@	6026....5583
5499....5084	5587....5171	5675....5255	5763....5335	5851....5419	5939....5503	6027....5584
5500....5085	5588....5172	5676....5256	5764....5336	5852....5420	5940....5504	6028....5585
5501....5086	5589....5173	5677....5257	5765....5337	5853....5421	5941....5506	6029....5586
5502....5087	5590....5174@	5678....5258	5766....5338	5854....5422	5942....5505	6030....5587
5503....5088	5591....5175	5679....5259	5767....5339	5855....5423	5943....5507	6031....5588
5504....5089	5592....5176	5680....5260	5768....5340	5856....5424	5944....5508	6032....5589@
5505....5090	5593....5177	5681....5261	5769....5341	5857....5425	5945....5509	6033....5589
5506....5091	5594....5178	5682....5262	5770....5342	5858....5426	5946....5510	6034....5590
5507....5092	5595....5179@	5683....5263	5771....5343	5859....5427	5947....5516@	6035....5591
5508....5093	5596....5179	5684....5263@	5772....5344	5860....5428	5948....5511	6036....5592@
5509....5094	5597....5180	5685....5264	5773....5345	5861....5429	5949....5512	6037....5593
5510....5095	5598....5181	5686....5265	5774....5346	5862....5430	5950....5513	6038....5594
5511....5096	5599....*	5687....5266	5775....1310@	5863....5431	5951....5514	6039....5595
5512....5097	5600....5182	5688....5267	5776....5347	5864....5432	5952....5515	6040....5596
5513....5098	5601....5183	5689....5268	5777....5348	5865....5433	5953....5516@	6041....5597
5514....5099	5602....5184	5690....5269	5778....5349	5866....5434	5954....5517	6042....5598
5515....5101	5603....5185	5691....5270	5779....5350	5867....5435	5955....5518	6043....5599
5516....5100	5604....5186	5692....*	5780....5351	5868....*	5956....5519	6044....5601
5517....2459@	5605....5187@	5693....5271	5781....5352	5869....5436@	5957....5520	6045....5602
5518....5102	5606....5188	5694....5272	5782....5353	5870....5437	5958....5521	6046....5603
5519....5103	5607....5189	5695....5273	5783....5354	5871....5438	5959....5522	6047....5604
5520....5104	5608....5190	5696....5274	5784....5355	5872....5439	5960....5523	6048....5605
5521....5105	5609....*	5697....2985@	5785....5356	5873....5440	5961....5524	6049....5606
5522....5105	5610....5191	5698....2640@	5786....5357	5874....5441	5962....5525	6050....5608
5523....5106	5611....5192	5699....5275	5787....5358	5875....5442	5963....5526	6051....5609@
5524....5107	5612....5193	5700....5276	5788....5359	5876....5443	5964....5527	6052....5610
5525....5108	5613....5194	5701....5277	5789....5360	5877....5444	5965....5528	6053....5611
5526....5109	5614....5195	5702....5278	5790....5361	5878....5445	5966....5529	6054....5612
5527....5110	5615....5196	5703....5279@	5791....5362	5879....5446	5967....5522@	6055....5613
5528....5111	5616....5197	5704....5280	5792....5363	5880....5447	5968....5530	6056....5613 + 302
5529....5112@	5617....5198	5705....5281	5793....5364	5881....5448	5969....5531	6057....5614
5530....5112	5618....5199	5706....5282	5794....5365	5882....5449	5970....5532	6058....5615
5531....5112@	5619....5200	5707....5283	5795....5366	5883....5450	5971....5533	6059....5616
5532....5113	5620....5201	5708....5299@	5796....5367	5884....5451	5972....5533	6060....5617
5533....5114@	5621....5202	5709....5284	5797....5368	5885....5452	5973....5534	6061....5618
5534....5115	5622....5203	5710....5285	5798....5369	5886....5453	5974....5535	6062....5619
5535....5116	5623....5204	5711....5286	5799....5370	5887....5454	5975....5536	6063....5620
5536....5117	5624....5205	5712....5287	5800....5371	5888....5455	5976....5537	6064....5621@
5537....5118	5625....5206	5713....5288	5801....5372@	5889....5456	5977....5538	6065....5621
5538....5119	5626....5207	5714....5289	5802....5373	5890....5457	5978....5539	6066....5622
5539....5121	5627....5208	5715....5290	5803....5374	5891....5458	5979....5540	6067....5623
5540....5122	5628....5211	5716....5291@	5804....5375	5892....5459	5980....5541	6068....5624
5541....3694@	5629....5212	5717....5292	5805....5376	5893....5460	5981....5542	
5542....5123@	5630....5214	5718....5293	5806....5377	5894....5461	5982....5543	
5543....5131	5631....5215	5719....5294	5807....5378	5895....5462	5983....5544	
5544....5132	5632....5217	5720....5295	5808....5379	5896....*	5984....5545@	

Strong to Goodrick-Kohlenberger

In the GK field:

+ = Strong is a combination of more than one GK word
& = Strong is equivalent to more than one individual GK word
* = Strong has no equivalent in GK

Strong	GK	Strong	GK	Strong	GK	Strong	GK	Strong	GK	Strong	GK	Strong	GK
1	1 & 270	84	85	167	174	250	264	333	355 & 1461	416	448	499	531
2	2	85	194 & 86	168	175	251	265	334	356	417	449	500	532
3	3	86	87	169	176	252	266	335	357	418	450	501	533
4	4	87	88	170	177	253	267	336	358	419	451	502	534
5	5	88	89	171	178	254	268	337	359	420	452	503	535
6	6	89	90	172	179	255	269	338	360	421	453	504	536
7	7	90	91 & 916 & 917	173	180	256	271	339	361	422	454	505	537
8	8	91	92	174	181	257	272	340	362	423	455	506	538
9	9	92	93	175	182	258	273	341	363	424	456	507	539
10	10	93	94	176	183	259	274	342	364	425	457	508	333
11	11	94	96	177	184	260	275	343	365	426	458	509	540
12	12	95	97	178	185	261	276	344	366	427	459	510	425 & 541
13	13	96	99	179	186	262	277	345	367	428	460	511	542
14	14	97	100	180	187 & 188	263	278	346	368	429	461	512	543
15	16	98	101	181	189	264	279	347	369	430	462	513	544
16	17	99	102	182	190	265	280	348	370	431	463	514	545
17	18	100	103	183	191	266	281	349	371	432	464	515	546
18	19	101	104	184	192	267	282	350	373	433	465	516	547
19	20	102	105	185	193	268	283	351	374	434	466	517	548
20	21	103	106	186	195	269	285	352	376	435	467	518	33 & 550
21	22	104	107	187	196	270	286	353	377	436	468	519	551
22	23	105	108	188	197	271	287	354	378	437	469	520	552
23	24	106	109	189	198	272	288	355	379 & 384	438	470	521	553
24	25	107	110	190	199	273	289	356	381	439	471	522	554
25	26	108	111	191	200 & 201	274	290	357	382	440	472	523	555
26	27	109	113	192	202	275	291	358	383	441	473	524	556
27	28	110	114	193	203	276	292	359	385	442	474	525	557
28	29	111	116	194	204	277	293	360	386	443	475	526	558
29	30	112	117	195	205	278	294	361	387	444	476	527	559
30	31 & 35	113	118	196	206	279	295	362	388	445	477	528	560
31	32	114	119	197	209	280	296	363	389	446	478	529	561
32	34	115	120	198	208	281	297	364	390	447	479	530	562
33	72	116	121	199	209	282	298	365	391	448	447 & 480	531	563
34	36	117	122	200	210	283	299	366	392	449	481	532	564
35	37	118	123	201	211	284	300	367	393	450	403 & 482	533	565
36	38	119	124	202	212	285	302	368	394	451	483	534	567
37	39 & 420	120	126	203	213	286	303	369	395	452	484	535	568
38	40	121	127	204	214	287	304	370	396	453	485 & 493	536	569
39	41	122	128	205	215	288	306	371	397	454	486	537	570
40	41	123	129	206	216	289	307	372	398	455	487 & 1986	538	572
41	42	124	130	207	217	290	308	373	399	456	488	539	573
42	43	125	131	208	218	291	309	374	400	457	489	540	574
43	44	126	132	209	219	292	310	375	402	458	490	541	575
44	45	127	133 & 1290	210	220	293	312	376	401	459	491	542	927
45	46	128	134	211	222 & 223	294	313 & 314	377	404	460	492	543	577
46	47	129	135	212	224	295	315	378	405	461	494	544	578
47	48	130	136	213	225	296	316	379	406	462	495	545	579
48	49	131	137	214	226	297	317	380	408	463	496	546	580
49	50	132	138	215	227	298	318	381	409	464	497	547	581
50	51	133	139	216	228	299	320	382	410	465	498	548	582
51	52	134	140	217	221 & 229	300	321	383	411	466	499	549	583
52	53	135	141	218	230	301	322	384	412	467	500	550	584
53	54	136	142	219	231	302	323	385	413	468	501	551	585
54	55	137	143	220	232	303	324	386	414	469	502	552	586
55	56	138	145	221	233	304	325	387	415	470	503	553	587
56	57	139	146	222	234	305	326	388	416	471	515	554	588
57	58	140	147	223	235	306	327	389	417	472	504	555	589
58	59	141	148	224	236	307	328	390	418	473	505	556	590
59	60	142	149	225	237	308	329	391	419	474	506	557	591
60	61	143	150	226	238	309	330	392	421	475	507	558	592
61	62	144	151	227	239	310	331	393	422	476	508	559	593
62	63	145	152	228	240	311	332	394	423	477	509	560	594
63	64	146	153	229	241	312	334	395	424	478	510	561	584 & 595
64	65	147	154	230	242	313	335	396	426	479	511	562	596
65	66	148	155	231	243	314	336	397	427	480	512	563	597
66	67	149	156	232	244	315	337	398	428	481	513	564	598
67	68	150	156	233	245	316	338	399	429	482	514	565	599
68	69	151	157	234	246	317	339	400	430	483	515	566	600
69	70	152	158	235	247	318	340	401	431	484	516	567	600
70	71	153	159	236	248	319	341	402	432	485	517	568	600
71	72	154	160	237	249	320	342	403	433	486	518	569	601
72	73	155	161	238	251	321	343	404	434	487	519	570	602 & 3898
73	74	156	162	239	252	322	344	405	435	488	520	571	603
74	75	157	163 & 166	240	253	323	345	406	436	489	521	572	605
75	76	158	165	241	254	324	346	407	437	490	522	573	604 & 606
76	77	159	165	242	256 & 380	325	347	408	438	491	523	574	607
77	78	160	167	243	257	326	348	409	439	492	524	575	608
78	79	161	168	244	258	327	349	410	441	493	525	576	609
79	80	162	169	245	259	328	350	411	442	494	526	577	610
80	81	163	170	246	260	329	351	412	443	495	527	578	611
81	82	164	171	247	261	330	352	413	444	496	528	579	612
82	83	165	172	248	262	331	353	414	445	497	529	580	613
83	84	166	173	249	263	332	354	415	446	498	530	581	614

582......615
583......616
584......617
585......618
586......619 & 620
587......621
588......622
589......623
590......624
591......625
592......626
593......627
594......628
595......629
596......630
597......631
598......632
599......633
600......634 & 635
601......636
602......637
603......638 & 2839
604......639
605......640
606......641
607......642
608......643
609......644
610......645
611......646
612......647
613......648
614......649
615......650 & 651
616......652
617......375 & 653
618......655
619......656
620......657
621......658 & 2143 &
   3314 & 4336
622......660
623......661
624......662
625......663
626......664
627......665
628......666
629......667
630......668
631......669
632......671
633......672
634......674
635......675
636......676
637......677
638......678
639......679
640......680
641......681
642......682
643......683 & 2171
644......684
645......685
646......686
647......687
648......689
649......690 & 1852
650......691 & 935
651......692
652......693
653......694
654......695
655......696
656......697
657......698
658......699
659......700
660......701
661......702
662......703
663......704
664......705
665......706
666......707
667......708
668......709
669......710
670......711
671......712
672......713
673......714
674......715
675......716
676......717
677......718
678......719
679......720
680......721

681......721 & 4312
682......722
683......723
684......724
685......725
686......726
687......727
688......728
689......98 & 730 & 763
690......732
691......733
692......734
693......735 & 739
694......736
695......737
696......738
697......740 & 4076
698......741
699......742
700......743
701......744
702......745
703......746
704......748
705......749
706......750
707......751
708......752
709......753
710......754
711......755
712......756
713......757
714......758
715......759 & 760
716......761
717......762 & 3403
718......764
719......765
720......766
721......768
722......769
723......770
724......771
725......772
726......773
727......774
728......775
729......731
730......776 & 781
731......777
732......778 & 779
733......780
734......782
735......783
736......784
737......785
738......786
739......787
740......788
741......789
742......790
743......791
744......792
745......793
746......794
747......795
748......796
749......797
750......799
751......800
752......801
753......802
754......803
755......804
756......806
757......806
758......807
759......808
760......809 & 811
761......810
762......812
763......813
764......814
765......815
766......816
767......817
768......818
769......819
770......820
771......821
772......822
773......823
774......824
775......825
776......826
777......827
778......828
779......829
780......830

781......831
782......571 & 832
783......833
784......834 & 5646
785......835
786......836
787......837
788......839
789......840
790......841
791......842
792......843
793......844
794......845
795......846
796......847
797......848
798......849
799......850
800......851
801......852
802......853
803......854
804......855
805......856
806......857
807......858 & 2360
808......859
809......860
810......861
811......862
812......863
813......864
814......865
815......866
816......867
817......868
818......869 & 870
819......871
820......872
821......873
822......874
823......875
824......876
825......877
826......878 & 2964
827......879
828......880
829......881
830......882
831......883
832......884
833......885
834......886
835......887
836......888
837......889 & 891
   & 3824
838......890
839......892
840......893
841......894
842......895
843......896
844......897
845......898
846......899
847......898
848......898
849......901
850......903
851......904
852......905
853......906
854......907
855......908
856......909 & 4060
857......910
858......911
859......912
860......913
861......914
862......915
863......918 & 1889
864......919
865......920
866......921
867......922
868......923
869......924
870......925
871......926
872......927
873......928
874......929
875......930
876......931
877......932
878......933
879......934

880......936 & 305
881......937 & 941
882......938
883......939
884......940
885......943
886......942
887......944
888......945
889......946
890......947
891......948
892......949
893......950
894......951 & 952
895......953
896......955
897......956
898......957
899......958
900......959
901......960
902......961
903......962
904......963
905......964
906......965
907......966
908......967
909......968
910......969
911......970 & 4817
912......972
913......973
914......974
915......975
916......976
917......977
918......978
919......979
920......971 & 980
   & 981
921......982
922......983
923......984
924......985
925......986 & 2852
926......987
927......988
928......989
929......990
930......991
931......992
932......993
933......994
934......994
935......995
936......996
937......997 & 998
938......999
939......1000
940......1001
941......1002
942......1003
943......1004 & 2742
   & 2744
944......1005
945......1006
946......1007
947......1008
948......1009
949......1010
950......1011
951......1012
952......1013
953......1014
954......1015
955......1016
956......1018
957......1019
958......1020 & 1021
959......1022
960......1023
961......1024
962......1028 & 1030
963......1029
964......1031 & 1032
965......1033
966......1034 & 1035
967......1036
968......1037
969......1039
970......1040
971......1041
972......1042
973......1043
974......1044 & 1045
975......1046
976......1047
977......1048

978......1049
979......1050
980......1051
981......1052
982......1053
983......1054
984......1055
985......1056 & 1057
986......1058
987......1059 & 1555
988......1060
989......1061
990......1062
991......1063
992......1064
993......1065
994......1066
995......1068
996......1069
997......1070
998......1071
999......1072 & 1073
1000......1074
1001......1075
1002......1076
1003......1067 & 1077
   & 1078
1004......1079
1005......1080
1006......1081
1007......1026 & 1027
   & 1082
1008......1083
1009......1084
1010......1085
1011......1086
1012......1087
1013......1088
1014......1089
1015......1090
1016......1091
1017......1092
1018......1093
1019......1094
1020......1095
1021......1096
1022......1097
1023......1098
1024......1099
1025......1100
1026......1101
1027......1103
1028......1104
1029......1105
1030......1106
1031......1107
1032......1108
1033......1109
1034......1110
1035......1111
1036......1112
1037......1113
1038......1114
1039......1115 & 3327
1040......1116
1041......1117
1042......1119
1043......1120
1044......1121
1045......1122
1046......1123
1047......1125
1048......1124
1049......1126
1050......1127
1051......1128
1052......1129
1053......1130 & 1135
1054......1131
1055......1132
1056......1133
1057......1134
1058......1136
1059......1137
1060......1138
1061......1139 & 1140
1062......1141
1063......1142
1064......1143
1065......1145
1066......1147
1067......1147
1068......1148 & 1149
1069......1150
1070......1151
1071......1152
1072......1153
1073......1154
1074......1155
1075......1156

1076......1157
1077......1158 & 1159
   & 1160
1078......1161
1079......1162
1080......1164
1081......1163 & 1165
1082......1166
1083......1167
1084......1168
1085......1169
1086......1170 & 1171
1087......1172
1088......1173
1089......1174
1090......1175
1091......1176
1092......1177
1093......1178
1094......1179
1095......1180
1096......1181
1097......1182
1098......1183
1099......1184
1100......1185
1101......1186
1102......1187
1103......1188
1104......1189
1105......1190
1106......1191
1107......1192
1108......1194
1109......1195
1110......1193 & 1196
1111......1197
1112......1198
1113......1199
1114......1200
1115......1201
1116......1202
1117......1203
1118......1204
1119......1205
1120......1206
1121......1207
1122......1208
1123......1209
1124......1210
1125......1211 & 2863
1126......1212
1127......1213
1128......1214
1129......1215
1130......1216 & 1217
1131......1218
1132......1219
1133......1220
1134......1221
1135......1222
1136......1223
1137......1224
1138......1226 & 1253
1139......1227
1140......1228
1141......1229
1142......1230
1143......1231
1144......1232
1145......1233
1146......1234
1147......1235
1148......1236
1149......1237
1150......1238
1151......1239
1152......1240
1153......1241
1154......1242
1155......1244 & 1247
1156......1245 & 1249
1157......1246 & 1250
1158......1248
1159......1251
1160......1252
1161......1254
1162......1255
1163......1256
1164......1257
1165......1258
1166......1259 & 1260
1167......1261
1168......1262
1169......1264
1170......1265
1171......1267
1172......1268
1173......1270 & 1271
1174......1273

1175......1272
1176......1274
1177......1275
1178......1278
1179......1279
1180......1280
1181......1281
1182......1281
1183......1282
1184......1283
1185......1284
1186......1285
1187......1286 & 1287
1188......1288
1189......1289
1190......1291 & 1523
1191......1292
1192......1293
1193......1294
1194......1296
1195......1297
1196......1298
1197......1299
1198......1300
1199......1301
1200......1302
1201......1303
1202......1304
1203......1305
1204......1306
1205......1307
1206......1308
1207......1310
1208......1309 & 1311
1209......1312
1210......1313
1211......1314
1212......1316
1213......1317
1214......1318
1215......1319
1216......1320
1217......1321
1218......1322
1219......1323
1220......1324
1221......1325
1222......1327
1223......1328
1224......1329
1225......1330
1226......1331
1227......1332
1228......1333
1229......1334
1230......1335
1231......1336
1232......1337
1233......1338
1234......1339
1235......1340
1236......1341
1237......1342
1238......1343
1239......1344
1240......1345
1241......1346
1242......1347
1243......1348
1244......1349
1245......1350 & 1351
1246......1352
1247......1354
1248......1355 & 1566
1249......1356
1250......1357
1251......1358
1252......1359
1253......1360
1254......1361
1255......1362
1256......1363
1257......1364
1258......1365
1259......1367
1260......1368
1261......1369
1262......1370
1263......1371
1264......1372
1265......1373
1266......1374
1267......1375
1268......1376
1269......1377
1270......1378
1271......1379
1272......1380
1273......1381
1274......1382

Strong's	G/K
1275	1383
1276	1385
1277	1386
1278	1387
1279	1388
1280	1389
1281	1390
1282	1391
1283	1395
1284	1392 & 1393 & 1396
1285	1397
1286	1398
1287	1399
1288	1400
1289	1401
1290	1402
1291	1403
1292	1404
1293	1405
1294	1406
1295	1407
1296	1408
1297	1409
1298	1410
1299	1411
1300	1412
1301	1413
1302	1414
1303	1415 & 1416
1304	1417
1305	1418
1306	1419
1307	1420 & 1421
1308	1422
1309	1423
1310	1424 & 5775
1311	1425
1312	1426
1313	1427
1314	1428
1315	1429
1316	1431
1317	1434
1318	1435
1319	1436
1320	1437
1321	1438
1322	1439
1323	1440
1324	1441
1325	1442 & 1443
1326	1444
1327	1447
1328	1449 & 2256
1329	1450
1330	1451
1331	1452
1332	1453
1333	1454
1334	1455
1335	1456
1336	1457
1337	1458
1338	1459
1339	1460
1340	1462
1341	1464
1342	1465
1343	1466
1344	1467
1345	1468
1346	1469
1347	1470
1348	1471
1349	1472 & 2869
1350	1473
1351	1474
1352	1475
1353	1476
1354	1477
1355	1478
1356	1481
1357	1482
1358	1482
1359	1483
1360	1484
1361	1485
1362	1486 & 1487
1363	1488
1364	1489
1365	1491
1366	1492
1367	1493
1368	1494
1369	1495
1370	1496
1371	1497
1372	1498
1373	1499
1374	1500
1375	1501
1376	1502
1377	1503
1378	1504
1379	1505
1380	1506
1381	1507 & 1508
1382	1509
1383	1510
1384	1511
1385	1512
1386	1513
1387	1514
1388	1515
1389	1516
1390	1517
1391	1518
1392	1519
1393	1520
1394	1521
1395	1522
1396	1524
1397	1525
1398	1526
1399	1527
1400	1528
1401	1528 & 1529
1402	1530
1403	1531
1404	1532
1405	1533
1406	1534
1407	1535
1408	1536
1409	1537
1410	1538
1411	1539
1412	1540
1413	1541
1414	1542
1415	1543
1416	1544
1417	1545
1418	*
1419	1546
1420	1547 & 1548
1421	1549
1422	1551
1423	1552
1424	1553
1425	1554
1426	1556
1427	1557
1428	1558
1429	1559
1430	1560
1431	1561
1432	1562
1433	1563
1434	1564
1435	1565
1436	1568
1437	1569
1438	1571
1439	1572
1440	1573
1441	1574
1442	1575
1443	1576
1444	1577
1445	1578
1446	1579
1447	1580
1448	1581
1449	1582
1450	1583
1451	1584
1452	1585
1453	1586
1454	1587
1455	1588
1456	1589
1457	1590
1458	1592
1459	1593
1460	1594
1461	1596
1462	1598
1463	1599
1464	1600 & 1715
1465	1601
1466	1602
1467	1603
1468	1604
1469	1605
1470	1606
1471	1607
1472	1608
1473	1609
1474	1610
1475	1611
1476	1612
1477	1613
1478	1614
1479	1615
1480	1616
1481	1617
1482	1618
1483	1619
1484	1620
1485	1621
1486	1622 & 1665
1487	1623
1488	1639
1489	1623+1145
1490	1623+1254+3590+1145
1491	1626
1492	3857
1493	1627
1494	1628 & 2638
1495	1630
1496	1629
1497	1631
1498	1639
1499	1623+2779
1500	1632
1501	1633
1502	1634
1503	2036
1504	1635
1505	1636
1506	1637
1507	1813
1508	1623+3590
1509	1623+3590+5516
1510	1639
1511	1639
1512	1642
1513	1643
1514	1644
1515	1645
1516	1646
1517	1647
1518	1648
1519	1650
1520	1651
1521	1652
1522	1653
1523	1654
1524	1655
1525	1656
1526	1639
1527	1651+2848
1528	1657
1529	1658
1530	1659 & 1737
1531	1660
1532	1661
1533	1662
1534	1663
1535	1664
1536	1623+5516
1537	1666
1538	1667
1539	1668
1540	1669
1541	1670
1542	1671
1543	1672 & 1673
1544	1675
1545	1676
1546	1678
1547	1679
1548	1680
1549	1681
1550	1682
1551	1683
1552	1684
1553	1685
1554	1686
1555	1687
1556	1688
1557	1689
1558	1690
1559	1691
1560	1692
1561	1693
1562	1694
1563	1695
1564	1696
1565	1697
1566	1698
1567	1699
1568	1701
1569	1702
1570	1704
1571	1705
1572	1706
1573	1591 & 1707
1574	1708
1575	1709
1576	1710
1577	1711
1578	1712
1579	1713
1580	1714
1581	1716
1582	1717
1583	1718
1584	1719
1585	1720
1586	1721
1587	1722
1588	1723
1589	1724
1590	1725
1591	1726
1592	1727
1593	1728
1594	1729
1595	1730
1596	1731
1597	1732
1598	1733
1599	1734
1600	1736
1601	1738
1602	1739
1603	1740
1604	1741
1605	1742
1606	1743
1607	1744
1608	1745
1609	1746
1610	1748
1611	1749
1612	1750
1613	1752
1614	1753
1615	1754
1616	1755
1617	1757
1618	1756
1619	1757
1620	1758
1621	1759
1622	1760
1623	1761
1624	1762
1625	1763
1626	1765
1627	1766
1628	1767
1629	1768
1630	1769
1631	1770
1632	1772 & 1773
1633	1774
1634	1775
1635	1776
1636	1777
1637	1778
1638	1779
1639	1780
1640	1781 & 1784
1641	1782
1642	1783
1643	1785
1644	1786
1645	1787
1646	1788
1647	1788
1648	1789
1649	1792
1650	1791 & 1793
1651	1794
1652	1795
1653	1790 & 1796
1654	1797
1655	1798
1656	1799
1657	1800
1658	1801
1659	1802
1660	1803
1661	1804
1662	1805 & 1806
1663	1808
1664	1809
1665	1810
1666	1811 & 1812
1667	1813
1668	1814
1669	1815
1670	1816
1671	1817
1672	1818
1673	1819
1674	1820
1675	1821
1676	1822
1677	1823 & 1824
1678	1825 & 1826
1679	1827
1680	1828
1681	1829 & 2287
1682	1830
1683	1831
1684	1832
1685	1833
1686	1834 & 1835
1687	1836
1688	1837
1689	1838
1690	1102 & 1839
1691	1609
1692	1840
1693	1841
1694	1842
1695	1843 & 4035
1696	1844
1697	1846
1698	1609
1699	1847
1700	1609
1701	1849
1702	1850
1703	1851
1704	1853
1705	1854 & 1855 & 1857 & 1858
1706	1860
1707	1861
1708	1862 & 4451
1709	1863
1710	1864
1711	1865
1712	1866
1713	1867
1714	1856 & 1859 & 1868
1715	1869
1716	1870
1717	1871
1718	1872
1719	1873
1720	1874
1721	1875
1722	1877
1723	1878
1724	1879
1725	1882
1726	1883
1727	1885
1728	1887
1729	1890
1730	1891
1731	1892
1732	1893
1733	1894
1734	1895
1735	1896
1736	1897
1737	1898
1738	1899
1739	1900 & 1908
1740	1901
1741	1902
1742	1903
1743	1904
1744	1905
1745	1906
1746	1907
1747	1909
1748	1910
1749	1911
1750	1912
1751	1913
1752	1641 & 1914 & 1915
1753	1918
1754	1919
1755	1920
1756	1886 & 1921
1757	1922
1758	1923
1759	1924
1760	1445 & 1926
1761	1927
1762	1928
1763	1929
1764	1931
1765	1932
1766	1888
1767	1933
1768	1916
1769	1917 & 1934
1770	1935
1771	1936
1772	1937
1773	1939
1774	1940
1775	1942
1776	1943
1777	1944
1778	1945
1779	1946
1780	1947
1781	1353 & 1948
1782	1925 & 1949
1783	1950
1784	1952
1785	1953
1786	1954
1787	1955
1788	1956
1789	1957
1790	1764 & 1958
1791	1959
1792	1960
1793	1961
1794	1962
1795	1963
1796	1964
1797	1965
1798	1966
1799	1967
1800	1968
1801	1969
1802	1970
1803	1971
1804	1972
1805	1973
1806	1974
1807	1975
1808	1976
1809	1977
1810	1978 & 2005
1811	1979
1812	1980
1813	1981
1814	1982
1815	1983
1816	1677 & 1984
1817	1985
1818	1987
1819	1988
1820	1989
1821	1990
1822	1992
1823	1993
1824	1994
1825	1995
1826	1996
1827	1998
1828	1999
1829	2000
1830	2001
1831	2002 & 1446 & 1674
1832	1997 & 2003
1833	2004
1834	2007
1835	2008
1836	2009
1837	2010
1838	2011
1839	2012 & 2013 & 2014
1840	2015
1841	2016
1842	2017
1843	2018
1844	2019
1845	2020
1846	2021
1847	2022 & 2023
1848	2024 & 2025
1849	2026
1850	2027
1851	2029
1852	2030
1853	2031
1854	2032
1855	2033
1856	2034
1857	2035
1858	2037
1859	2038
1860	2039
1861	2040
1862	2041
1863	2042
1864	2043
1865	2044
1866	2045
1867	2046
1868	2047
1869	2048
1870	2049
1871	2050
1872	2051
1873	2052
1874	2053
1875	2054
1876	2055
1877	2056
1878	2057
1879	2058
1880	2059
1881	2060
1882	2061
1883	2062
1884	2064
1885	2065 & 2066
1886	2068
1887	2069
1888	900 & 2070
1889	2071
1890	576 & 2072
1891	2073
1892	2074
1893	2075
1894	2076
1895	2077
1896	2078 & 2393
1897	2080
1898	2081
1899	2083
1900	2084
1901	2085
1902	2086
1903	2087
1904	2082 & 2088
1905	2089
1906	2090
1907	2091
1908	2092
1909	2093
1910	2094
1911	2095
1912	2096
1913	2097
1914	2098
1915	2099
1916	2100
1917	2101
1918	2102
1919	2103
1920	2104
1921	2105
1922	2106
1923	2107
1924	2108
1925	2109
1926	2110
1927	2111
1928	2112
1929	2113 & 4658
1930	2114
1931	2115
1932	2116
1933	2117
1934	2118
1935	2119
1936	2120
1937	2121
1938	2122
1939	2123
1940	2125
1941	2126
1942	2127
1943	2128
1944	2063 & 2129
1945	2130
1946	2134
1947	2135
1948	2137
1949	2138
1950	2140
1951	2141
1952	2142
1953	2144
1954	2145
1955	2146
1956	2147
1957	2148
1958	2149
1959	2150
1960	2151
1961	2152
1962	2153
1963	2154
1964	2155
1965	2156
1966	2079

2662....2922
2663....2923
2664....2924
2665....2925
2666....2927
2667....2928
2668....2929
2669....2930
2670....2931
2671....2932
2672....2933
2673....2934
2674....2935
2675....2936
2676....2937
2677....2938
2678....2939
2679....2940
2680....2941
2681....2942
2682....2943
2683....2944
2684....2945
2685....2946
2686....2947
2687....2948
2688....2949
2689....2950
2690....2951
2691....2952
2692....2953
2693....2954
2694....2955
2695....2956 & 2957
2696....2958
2697....2959
2698....2960
2699....2961
2700....2962
2701....2963
2702....2965
2703....2966
2704....2967
2705....2968
2706....2969
2707....2970
2708....2972
2709....2973
2710....2974 & 4201
2711....2976
2712....2977
2713....2978
2714....2979
2715....2980
2716....2981
2717....[Omitted by Strong]
2718....2982
2719....2983 & 2984
2720....2985
2721....2987
2722....2988
2723....2989
2724....2990
2725....2991 & 2992
2726....2993
2727....2994
2728....2995
2729....2996
2730....2997 & 3001
2731....2998
2732....2999
2733....3000
2734....3002
2735....1480 & 3003
2736....3004 & 3006
2737....3005
2738....3008
2739....3009 & 3010
2740....3011
2741....3012
2742....3014
2743....3013 & 3015
2744....3016
2745....3017
2746....3018
2747....3020
2748....3021 & 3022
2749....3023
2750....3024
2751....3025
2752....3026
2753....3027
2754....3029
2755....3030
2756....3031
2757....2787 & 3032
2758....3033
2759....3034
2760....3035

2761....3036
2762....3037
2763....3038
2764....3039
2765....3040
2766....3041
2767....3042
2768....3043
2769....3044
2770....2132 & 3045
2771....3046
2772....3047
2773....3048
2774....3049
2775....3050 & 3052
2776....3051
2777....3053
2778....2133 & 3056
2779....3057
2780....3058
2781....3059
2782....3060
2783....3061
2784....3062
2785....3063
2786....3064
2787....3066
2788....3067
2789....3068
2790....3069
2791....3070 & 3071
2792....3072 & 3077
2793....3073
2794....3074
2795....3075
2796....3076
2797....3078
2798....3080
2799....3081
2800....3082
2801....3083
2802....1144 & 3007 & 3084 & 3085
2803....3086
2804....3087
2805....3088
2806....3089
2807....3090
2808....3091
2809....3092
2810....3093
2811....3094
2812....3095
2813....3096
2814....3097
2815....3098
2816....3099
2817....3100
2818....3101
2819....3102
2820....3103
2821....3104
2822....3105
2823....3106
2824....3107
2825....3108 & 3109
2826....3110
2827....3111
2828....3112
2829....3113
2830....3114
2831....3115
2832....3116
2833....3117
2834....3118
2835....3119
2836....3120
2837....3121
2838....3122
2839....3123
2840....3124
2841....3125
2842....3126
2843....3127
2844....3128
2845....3130
2846....3131
2847....3132
2848....3133
2849....3134
2850....3135
2851....3136
2852....3139
2853....3140
2854....3141
2855....3142
2856....3143
2857....3138 & 3145
2858....3137 & 3144
2859....3146

2860....3147
2861....3148
2862....3149
2863....3150
2864....3151
2865....3152
2866....3153
2867....3154
2868....3155
2869....3156
2870....3157
2871....3158
2872....3159
2873....3160
2874....3161 & 3162 & 3163
2875....3164
2876....3165
2877....3166
2878....3167 & 3168
2879....3169
2880....3170
2881....3171
2882....3172
2883....3173
2884....3174
2885....3175
2886....3176
2887....3177 & 3178
2888....3179
2889....3180
2890....3181
2891....3182 & 3183
2892....3184
2893....3185
2894....3186
2895....3187 & 3188
2896....3189
2897....3190
2898....3191
2899....3192
2900....3193
2901....3194
2902....3195
2903....3196
2904....3197
2905....3198
2906....3199
2907....3200
2908....3201
2909....3202
2910....3203
2911....3204
2912....3205
2913....3206
2914....3207
2915....3208
2916....3209
2917....3210
2918....3211
2919....3212
2920....3213
2921....3214
2922....3215
2923....3216
2924....3217
2925....3218
2926....3219
2927....3220 & 3224 & 3226
2928....3221
2929....3222
2930....3223
2931....3225
2932....3227
2933....3228
2934....3229
2935....3230
2936....3231
2937....3232
2938....3233
2939....3234
2940....3235
2941....3236
2942....3237
2943....3239
2944....3238 & 3240
2945....3241
2946....3242 & 3243
2947....3244
2948....3245
2949....3246
2950....3247
2951....3248
2952....3249
2953....3250
2954....3251
2955....3252
2956....3253 & 3254
2957....3255

2958....3256 & 3260
2959....3257
2960....3258
2961....3259
2962....3261
2963....3262
2964....3263
2965....3264
2966....3265
2967....3266
2968....3267
2969....3268
2970....3269
2971....3270
2972....3271
2973....3272
2974....3273
2975....3275
2976....3276
2977....3277 & 4996
2978....3278
2979....3280
2980....654 & 3281
2981....3282
2982....3283 & 3316
2983....3284
2984....3285
2985....3286 & 5697
2986....3287
2987....3288
2988....3289
2989....2139 & 3290
2990....3291
2991....3292
2992....3295
2993....3293
2994....3294
2995....3296
2996....3297 & 3298
2997....3279 & 3299
2998....3300
2999....3301
3000....3302
3001....3303
3002....3304
3003....3305
3004....1649 & 3306
3005....3307
3006....3308
3007....3309
3008....3310
3009....3311
3010....3312
3011....3313
3012....3317
3013....3318
3014....3319
3015....3320
3016....3321
3017....3322
3018....3323
3019....3324
3020....3325
3021....3326
3022....3328
3023....3329
3024....3330
3025....3332
3026....3333
3027....798 & 3334
3028....3331 & 3335
3029....3336
3030....3337
3031....3338
3032....3339 & 3341
3033....3340
3034....3342
3035....3343
3036....3344
3037....3345
3038....3346
3039....3347
3040....3348
3041....3349
3042....3350
3043....3351
3044....3352
3045....3353
3046....3354
3047....3355
3048....3356
3049....3357
3050....3358
3051....3359
3052....3360
3053....3361
3054....3362
3055....3363
3056....3364
3057....3365

3058....3366
3059....3367
3060....3368
3061....3369
3062....3370
3063....3370
3064....3370
3065....3371
3066....3372
3067....3373
3068....3374
3069....3375
3070....3376
3071....3377
3072....3378
3073....3379
3074....3380
3075....3381
3076....3382
3077....3383
3078....3384
3079....3385
3080....3386
3081....3387
3082....3388
3083....3389
3084....3390
3085....3391
3086....3392
3087....3393
3088....3394
3089....3395
3090....3396
3091....3397
3092....3399
3093....3400 & 3401
3094....3402
3095....3404 & 3406
3096....3405
3097....3407
3098....3408
3099....3409
3100....3411
3101....3412
3102....3413
3103....3417
3104....3418 & 3526
3105....3419
3106....3420
3107....3421
3108....3422
3109....3423
3110....3424
3111....3425
3112....3426
3113....3427
3114....3428
3115....3429
3116....3430
3117....3431
3118....3432
3119....3433
3120....3434
3121....3435
3122....3436
3123....3437
3124....3438
3125....3439
3126....3440
3127....3441
3128....3442
3129....3443
3130....3444
3131....3445
3132....3446
3133....3447
3134....2495 & 3448
3135....3449
3136....3450
3137....3451 & 3452
3138....3453
3139....3454
3140....3455
3141....3456
3142....3457
3143....3458
3144....3459 & 4753
3145....3460 & 3462
3146....3463
3147....3465
3148....3465
3149....3461 & 3461 & 3466
3150....3467
3151....3468
3152....3469
3153....3470
3154....3471
3155....3472
3156....3414 & 3473

3157....3474
3158....3415 & 3475
3159....3416 & 3476
3160....3477
3161....3478
3162....3479
3163....3480
3164....3481
3165....1609
3166....902 & 3482
3167....3483
3168....3484
3169....3485
3170....3486
3171....3487
3172....3488
3173....3489
3174....3490
3175....3491
3176....3492
3177....3493
3178....3494
3179....3495 & 3496
3180....3497
3181....3498
3182....3499
3183....3500
3184....3501
3185....3505
3186....3504
3187....3505
3188....3506
3189....3506
3190....3507
3191....3509
3192....3510
3193....3511 & 3512 & 3513
3194....3514 & 3515
3195....3516
3196....3517
3197....3518
3198....3519
3199....3508 & 3520
3200....3521
3201....3522
3202....3523
3203-3302....[Omitted by Strong]
3303....3525
3304....3528 & 3529
3305....3530
3306....3531
3307....3532
3308....3533
3309....3534
3310....3535
3311....3536
3312....3537
3313....3538
3314....3540
3315....3541
3316....3542
3317....3543
3318....3544
3319....3545
3320....3546
3321....3547
3322....3539 & 3548
3323....3549
3324....3550
3325....3551
3326....3552
3327....3553
3328....3554
3329....3555
3330....3556
3331....3557
3332....3558
3333....3559
3334....3560
3335....3561
3336....3562
3337....3563
3338....3564
3339....3565
3340....3566
3341....3567
3342....3568
3343....3569
3344....3570 & 3573
3345....3571
3346....3572
3347....3575
3348....3576
3349....3577
3350....3578
3351....3579
3352....3580
3353....3581

3354....3582
3355....3583
3356....3584
3357....3585
3358....3586
3359....3587
3360....3588 & 3589
3361....3590
3362....1569+3590
3363....2671+3590
3364....4024+3590
3365....3592 & 3598
3366....3593
3367....3594 & 3599
3368....3595
3369....3596
3370....3597
3371....3600
3372....3601
3373....3602
3374....3603
3375....3604
3376....3605
3377....3606
3378....3590+4024
3379....3607
3380....3609
3381....3610
3382....3611
3383....3612
3384....3613
3385....3614
3386....3615
3387....3614
3388....3616
3389....3617 & 3618
3390....3619
3391....1651
3392....3620
3393....3621
3394....3622
3395....1807 & 3623 & 5041 & 5042
3396....3502 & 3503 & 3624
3397....3625
3398....3625
3399....3626
3400....3627
3401....3628
3402....3629
3403....3630
3404....3631
3405....3632
3406....3633
3407....3634
3408....3635
3409....3636
3410....3637
3411....3638
3412....3639
3413....3640
3414....3641
3415....3642
3416....3643
3417....3644
3418....3645
3419....3646
3420....3647
3421....3648
3422....3649
3423....3650
3424....3651 & 3652
3425....3653
3426....3654
3427....1609
3428....3655
3429....3656
3430....3657
3431....3658
3432....3659
3433....3660
3434....3661
3435....3662
3436....3663
3437....3524 & 3664
3438....3665
3439....3666
3440....3667
3441....3668
3442....3669
3443....3670
3444....3671
3445....3672
3446....3673
3447....3674
3448....3675
3449....3677
3450....1609
3451....3676

From	To
3452	3678
3453	3679
3454	3680
3455	3681
3456	3682
3457	3683
3458	3684 & 3685
3459	3686
3460	3688 & 3694
3461	3689
3462	3690
3463	3691 & 3692
3464	3693
3465	3695
3466	3696
3467	3697
3468	3698
3469	3699
3470	3700
3471	3701
3472	3702
3473	3703
3474	3704
3475	3705 & 3706 & 3707
3476	3709
3477	3710
3478	3711 & 3712 & 3713 & 3714 & 3715
3479	3716
3480	3717
3481	3718 & 3719
3482	3720
3483	3721
3484	3723
3485	3724
3486	3725
3487	3726
3488	3727
3489	3728
3490	3729
3491	3730
3492	3731
3493	3732
3494	3733
3495	3734
3496	3735 & 3736
3497	3722 & 3737
3498	3738
3499	3739
3500	3740
3501	3742
3502	3743 & 3801
3503	3744
3504	3745
3505	3746
3506	3748
3507	3749
3508	3750
3509	3751
3510	3752
3511	3753
3512	3754
3513	3755
3514	3756
3515	3757
3516	3758
3517	3759
3518	3760
3519	3761
3520	3762
3521	3763
3522	3764
3523	3765
3524	3766 & 3767
3525	3768
3526	3769
3527	3770
3528	3771
3529	3772
3530	3773
3531	3774
3532	3775
3533	3776
3534	3777
3535	3778 & 3779
3536	3780
3537	3781 & 4469
3538	3782
3539	3783
3540	3784
3541	3785
3542	3786
3543	3787
3544	3788
3545	3789
3546	3790
3547	3791
3548	3792
3549	3793
3550	3794
3551	3795
3552	3796
3553	3797
3554	3798
3555	3799
3556	3800
3557	3802
3558	3803
3559	3804
3560	3805
3561	3741 & 3806
3562	3807
3563	3808
3564	3809 & 3810
3565	3811
3566	3812
3567	3813
3568	3814
3569	5422
3570	3815
3571	3816
3572	3817
3573	3818
3574	3819
3575	3820
3576	3821
3577	3822
3578	3825
3579	3826
3580	3827
3581	3828
3582	3829
3583	3830
3584	3831
3585	3832
3586	3833
3587	3834
3588	3836
3589	3837
3590	3838
3591	3839
3592	3840
3593	3841
3594	3842
3595	3843
3596	3844
3597	3845
3598	3847
3599	3848
3600	3849
3601	3850
3602	3851
3603	4005+1639
3604	3852
3605	3853
3606	3854
3607	3855
3608	3856
3609	3858
3610	3860
3611	3861
3612	3862
3613	3863
3614	3864
3615	3865
3616	3866
3617	3867
3618	3868 & 3871
3619	3869
3620	3870
3621	3872
3622	3873
3623	3874
3624	3875
3625	3876
3626	3877 & 3878
3627	3879 & 3882
3628	3880
3629	3881
3630	3884
3631	3885
3632	3886
3633	3883 & 3887
3634	3888
3635	3890
3636	3891
3637	3892
3638	3893
3639	3896 & 3897
3640	3899
3641	3900
3642	3901
3643	3902
3644	3894 & 3904
3645	3895 & 3905
3646	3906
3647	3907
3648	3908
3649	3909
3650	3910
3651	3911
3652	3912
3653	3913
3654	3914
3655	3915
3656	3917
3657	3918
3658	3919
3659	3921
3660	3922 & 3923
3661	3924
3662	3925
3663	3926
3664	3927
3665	3928
3666	3929
3667	3930
3668	3931
3669	3932
3670	3933
3671	3934
3672	3935
3673	3937
3674	3938
3675	3939
3676	3940
3677	3941
3678	3942
3679	3943
3680	3944
3681	3945
3682	3946
3683	3947
3684	3948
3685	3949
3686	3950
3687	3951
3688	3952
3689	3903 & 3953
3690	3954
3691	3955
3692	3956
3693	3957
3694	3958 & 5541
3695	3959
3696	3960
3697	3961
3698	3962
3699	3963
3700	3964
3701	3965
3702	3966
3703	3967
3704	3968
3705	3969
3706	3970
3707	3971
3708	1625 & 3972
3709	3973
3710	3974
3711	3975
3712	3976
3713	3977
3714	3978
3715	3979
3716	3980
3717	3981
3718	3982
3719	3983
3720	3984
3721	3985
3722	3986
3723	3987
3724	3988
3725	3990
3726	1941 & 3991
3727	3992
3728	3993
3729	3994
3730	3995
3731	3996
3732	3997
3733	3989 & 3998
3734	3999
3735	4001
3736	4002
3737	4003
3738	4004
3739	4005
3740	4006
3741	4008
3742	4009
3743	4010
3744	4011
3745	4012
3746	4013
3747	4014 & 4016
3748	4015
3749	4017
3750	4018
3751	4019
3752	4020
3753	4021
3754	4022
3755	4015
3756	4024
3757	4023
3758	4025
3759	4026
3760	4027
3761	4028
3762	4029 & 4032
3763	4030
3764	4031
3765	4033
3766	4034
3767	4036
3768	4037
3769	4038
3770	4039
3771	4040
3772	4041
3773	4042
3774	4043
3775	4044
3776	4045
3777	4046
3778	4047
3779	4048
3780	4049
3781	4050
3782	4051
3783	4052
3784	4053
3785	4054
3786	4055
3787	4056
3788	4057
3789	4058
3790	4059
3791	4061
3792	4062
3793	4063
3794	4065
3795	4066
3796	4067
3797	4069
3798	4068 & 4070
3799	4071
3800	4072
3801	3836+1639 +2779+2262
3802	4074
3803	4075
3804	4077
3805	4078
3806	4079
3807	4080
3808	4081
3809	4082
3810	4083
3811	4084
3812	4085 & 4088
3813	4086
3814	4087
3815	4089
3816	4090
3817	4091
3818	4092
3819	4093
3820	4094
3821	4095
3822	4096
3823	4097
3824	4098 & 4100
3825	4099
3826	4101 & 4113
3827	4102
3828	4103
3829	4104 & 4106
3830	4105 & 4107
3831	4108
3832	4109
3833	4110
3834	4111
3835	4112
3836	4115
3837	4114 & 4116
3838	4117
3839	4118
3840	4119
3841	4120
3842	4121
3843	4122
3844	4123
3845	4124
3846	4125
3847	4126
3848	688 & 4127
3849	4128
3850	4130
3851	4129 & 4131
3852	4132
3853	4133
3854	4134
3855	4135
3856	4136
3857	4137
3858	4138
3859	1384 & 4139
3860	4140
3861	4141
3862	4142
3863	4143
3864	4144
3865	4145
3866	4146
3867	4147
3868	4148
3869	4149 & 4150
3870	4151
3871	4152
3872	4153
3873	4154
3874	4155
3875	4156
3876	4157
3877	4158
3878	4159
3879	4160
3880	4161
3881	4162
3882	4163
3883	4164
3884	4165
3885	4166 & 4167
3886	4168
3887	4169
3888	4170
3889	4171
3890	4172
3891	4174
3892	4175
3893	4176
3894	4177
3895	4178
3896	4179
3897	4180
3898	4181
3899	4182
3900	4183
3901	4184
3902	4185
3903	4186
3904	4187
3905	4189
3906	4190
3907	4191
3908	4192
3909	4193
3910	4194
3911	4195
3912	4196
3913	4173 & 4197 & 4198
3914	4199
3915	4200
3916	4202
3917	4203
3918	4205
3919	4206
3920	4207
3921	4208
3922	4209
3923	4210
3924	4211
3925	4213
3926	4214
3927	4215
3928	4216
3929	4217
3930	4218
3931	4219
3932	4220
3933	4221
3934	4222
3935	4223
3936	4224 & 4225
3937	4226
3938	4227
3939	4228
3940	4229
3941	4230
3942	4231
3943	4232
3944	4233
3945	4234
3946	4235
3947	4236
3948	4237
3949	4239
3950	4240
3951	4241
3952	4242
3953	4243
3954	4244
3955	4245
3956	4246
3957	4247
3958	4248
3959	4249
3960	4250
3961	4251
3962	4635 & 4252
3963	4253
3964	4254 & 4260
3965	4255
3966	4256
3967	4257
3968	4258
3969	4259
3970	4261
3971	4262
3972	4263
3973	4264
3974	4265
3975	4266
3976	4267
3977	4268
3978	4269
3979	4270 & 4271
3980	4272
3981	4273 & 4274 & 4392
3982	2167 & 4275
3983	4277
3984	4278
3985	4279
3986	4280
3987	4281
3988	4282
3989	4283
3990	4284
3991	4286
3992	4287
3993	4288
3994	4289
3995	4290
3996	4291
3997	4292
3998	4293
3999	4294
4000	4295
4001	4296
4002	4297
4003	4298
4004	4299
4005	4300
4006	4301
4007	4302
4008	4305
4009	4306
4010	4307
4011	4308
4012	4309
4013	4310
4014	4311
4015	4313
4016	4212 & 4314
4017	4315
4018	4316
4019	4317
4020	4318
4021	4319
4022	4320
4023	4321
4024	4322 & 4323
4025	4324
4026	4325
4027	2753 & 4326
4028	4328
4029	4329
4030	4330
4031	4331
4032	4332
4033	4333
4034	4334
4035	4335
4036	4337
4037	4338
4038	4339
4039	4340
4040	4341
4041	4342
4042	4343
4043	4344
4044	4345
4045	4346
4046	4347
4047	4348
4048	4351
4049	4352
4050	4353
4051	4354
4052	4355
4053	4356
4054	4357
4055	4358
4056	4359
4057	4360
4058	4361
4059	4362
4060	4363
4061	4364
4062	4365
4063	4366
4064	4367
4065	4368
4066	4369
4067	4370
4068	4371
4069	4372
4070	4373
4071	4374
4072	4375
4073	4376
4074	4377
4075	4378
4076	4379
4077	4380
4078	4381
4079	4382
4080	4383
4081	4384
4082	4385
4083	4388
4084	4389
4085	4390
4086	4391
4087	4393
4088	4394
4089	4395
4090	4396
4091	4276 & 4397
4092	4399
4093	4400 & 4401
4094	4402
4095	4403
4096	4404
4097	4405
4098	4406 & 5229
4099	4407 & 4408
4100	4409
4101	4410
4102	4411
4103	4412
4104	4413
4105	4414
4106	4415
4107	4416 & 4417
4108	4418
4109	4419
4110	4420
4111	4421
4112	4422
4113	4423
4114	4424
4115	4425
4116	4426
4117	4427
4118	4498
4119	4498
4120	4428
4121	4429
4122	4430
4123	4431
4124	4432
4125	4433
4126	4434
4127	4435
4128	4436
4129	4437
4130	4398
4131	4438
4132	4439
4133	4440
4134	4441
4135	4442
4136	4443
4137	4444
4138	4445
4139	4446
4140	4447
4141	4448
4142	4449
4143	4450
4144	4452 & 4453
4145	4454

4146....4455	4246....4562 & 4566	4345....4677	4445....4789	4541....4901	4639....5014	4739....5112
4147....4456	4247....4567	4346....4678 & 4680	4446....4790	4542....4902	4640....5015	4740....5113
4148....4457	4248....4568	4347....4681 & 4679	4447....4791	4543....4903	4641....5016	4741....5114
4149....4458	4249....4569 & 4573	4348....4682	4448....4792	4544....4904	4642....5017	4742....5116
4150....4459	4250....4570	4349....4683	4449....4793	4545....4905	4643....5018	4743....5117
4151....4460	4251....4571	4350....4684	4450....4794	4546....4907	4644....5019	4744....5118
4152....4461	4252....4572	4351....4685	4451....4796	4547....4908	4645....5020	4745....5119
4153....4462	4253....4574	4352....4686	4452....4803	4548....4909	4646....5021	4746....5115 & 5120
4154....4463	4254....4575	4353....4687	4453....4797	4549....4910	4647....5022	4747....5122
4155....4464	4255....4576	4354....4688	4454....4798	4550....4911	4648....5023	4748....5123
4156....4465	4256....164 & 4577	4355....4647 & 4689	4455....4799	4551....4912	4649....5024	4749....5124
4157....4466	4257....4578	4356....4691 & 4692	4456....4386 & 4800	4552....4913	4650....5025	4750....5125
4158....4468	4258....4579	4357....4693	4457....4387 & 4801	4553....4914	4651....5026	4751....5126
4159....4470	4259....4580	4358....4694	4458....4535 & 4803	4554....4915	4652....5027	4752....5127
4160....4472	4260....4581	4359....4695	4459....4802	4555....4916	4653....5028	4753....5128
4161....4473	4261....4582	4360....4696	4460....4805	4556....4917	4654....5029	4754....5129
4162....4474	4262....4583	4361....4698	4461....4806	4557....4918	4655....5030	4755....5130
4163....4475	4263....4584 & 4585	4362....4699	4462....4807 & 4808 & 4809	4558....4919	4656....5031	4756....5131
4164....4476	4264....4586	4363....4700	4463....4810	4559....4920	4657....5032	4757....5132
4165....4477	4265....4587	4364....4701	4464....4811	4560....4921	4658....5033	4758....5133
4166....4478	4266....4588	4365....4702	4465....4812	4561....4922	4659....5034	4759....5134 & 5135
4167....4479	4267....4589	4366....4703 & 4704	4466....4814	4562....4923 & 4951 & 4952	4660....5035	4760....5136
4168....4480	4268....4590	4367....4705	4467....4815	4563....4924	4661....5036	4761....5137
4169....4471 & 4481	4269....4591	4368....4188 & 4706	4468....4816	4564....4925	4662....5037	4762....5138
4170....4482	4270....4592	4369....4707	4469....4819 & 4828	4565....838 & 4926	4663....5038	4763....5139
4171....4483	4271....4593	4370....4708 & 4716	4470....4820	4566....4927	4664....5039	4764....5140
4172....4484	4272....4594	4371....4709	4471....4821	4567....4928	4665....5040	4765....5141
4173....4485	4273....4595	4372....4710	4472....4822	4568....4929	4666....5043	4766....5142 & 5143
4174....4486	4274....4596	4373....4711	4473....4823	4569....4930	4667....2430 & 5044	4767....5144
4175....4487	4275....4632	4374....4712	4474....4824	4570....2410 & 4931	4668....5045	4768....5145
4176....4488	4276....4598	4375....4713	4475....4825	4571....5148	4669....5046	4769....5146
4177....4489	4277....4625 & 4597	4376....4714	4476....1017 & 4827	4572....4932	4670....5047	4770....5121 & 5147
4178....4490 & 1930	4278....4599	4377....4715	4477....4829	4573....4933	4671....5148	4771....5148
4179....2234 & 4491	4279....4600	4378....4717	4478....4830	4574....4934	4672....4898 & 5048	4772....5149
4180....4494	4280....4625 & 4597	4379....4718	4479....4831	4575....4935	4673....5049	4773....5150 & 5151
4181....4495	4281....4601	4380....4719 & 4722	4480....4832	4576....4936	4674....5050	4774....5152
4182....4497	4282....4602	4381....4720 & 4723	4481....4818 & 4833 & 4834 & 4854	4577....4937 & 4938 & 4987	4675....5148	4775....5153
4183....4498	4283....4603	4382....4721 & 4724	4482....4835	4578....4939	4676....5051	4776....4327 & 5154
4184....4492 & 4499	4284....4604 & 4617	4383....4725	4483....3306	4579....4940	4677....5052	4777....5155
4185....4500	4285....4605	4384....4726	4484....4836	4580....4941	4678....5053	4778....5156
4186....4501	4286....4606 & 4671	4385....4727	4485....4837	4581....4942	4679....5054	4779....5157
4187....4502	4287....4607	4386....4728	4486....4826 & 4838 & 4841	4582....4943	4680....5055	4780....5158
4188....4503	4288....4608	4387....4728	4487....4839	4583....4944	4681....5056	4781....5159
4189....4504	4289....4609	4388....4729	4488....4840	4584....4945 & 4946	4682....5057	4782....5160
4190....4505	4290....4610	4389....4730	4489....4842	4585....4947	4683....5058	4783....5161
4191....4505	4291....4613	4390....4731	4490....4843	4586....4948	4684....5059	4784....5163
4192....4506	4292....4614	4391....4732	4491....4844	4587....4949	4685....5060	4785....2975 & 5164
4193....4507	4293....4615	4392....4733	4492....4845	4588....4950	4686....5061	4786....5166
4194....4508	4294....4616	4393....4734	4493....4846 & 4856	4589....4953	4687....2178 & 5062	4787....5167
4195....4510	4295....4618	4394....4735	4494....4847	4590....4954	4688....5063	4788....5168
4196....4511	4296....4619	4395....4736	4495....4848	4591....4955	4689....5064	4789....5169
4197....4512 & 4515	4297....4620	4396....4737	4496....4849	4592....4956	4690....5065	4790....5170
4198....4513	4298....4621	4397....4738	4497....4850	4593....4957	4691....5066	4791....5171
4199....4514	4299....4622	4398....4739	4498....4851	4594....4958	4692....5067	4792....5172
4200....4516	4300....4623	4399....4740	4499....4852	4595....4960	4693....5068	4793....5173
4201....4517	4301....4624	4400....4741	4500....4853	4596....4961 & 4986	4694....5069	4794....5174
4202....4518	4302....4625 & 4597	4401....4742	4501....4855	4597....4962	4695....5071	4795....5175 & 5346
4203....4519	4303....4626	4402....4743	4502....4857	4598....4963	4696....5070	4796....5176
4204....4520	4304....4627	4403....4744	4503....4858	4599....4964	4697....5072	4797....5177 & 5179
4205....4521	4305....4628	4404....4745	4504....4859	4600....4965	4698....5073	4798....5178
4206....4522	4306....4629	4405....4746	4505....4860	4601....4967	4699....5074	4799....5180
4207....4523	4307....4630	4406....4611 & 4747	4506....4861	4602....4968	4700....5075	4800....5182
4208....4524	4308....4631 & 4632	4407....4612 & 4748	4507....4864	4603....4969 & 4971	4701....5076	4801....2413 & 5183
4209....4525	4309....4633	4408....4749	4508....4865	4604....4970	4702....5077	4802....5184
4210....4526 & 4528	4310....4634	4409....4750	4509....4866	4605....4972	4703....5078	4803....5185
4211....4527	4311....4636	4410....4751	4510....4862 & 4863 & 4867	4606....4973	4704....5079	4804....5186
4212....4529	4312....4637	4411....4752	4511....4868	4607....4974	4705....5080	4805....5187
4213....4530	4313....4638	4412....4754 & 4759	4512....4869	4608....4975	4706....5080	4806....5188
4214....4531	4314....4639	4413....4755	4513....4870	4609....4976	4707....5080	4807....5189
4215....4532	4315....4640	4414....4756	4514....4871	4610....4977	4708....5081	4808....5190
4216....4533	4316....4641	4415....4757	4515....4872	4611....4978	4709....5081	4809....5191
4217....4467 & 4534	4317....4642 & 4652 & 4654	4416....4758	4516....4873	4612....4959 & 4980	4710....5082	4810....5192
4218....4537	4318....4643	4417....4760	4517....4874	4613....4981	4711....5083	4811....5193
4219....4536	4319....4644 & 4645	4418....4761	4518....2407 & 4876	4614....4982	4712....5084	4812....5194
4220....4538	4320....4646	4419....4762	4519....4877	4615....4983	4713....5085	4813....5195
4221....4539	4321....4648 & 4649	4420....4763	4520....4878	4616....4984	4714....5087	4814....5196
4222....4540	4322....4650	4421....4764	4521....4879	4617....4985	4715....5088	4815....5197
4223....4541	4323....4651	4422....4765	4522....4880	4618....4988	4716....5089	4816....5198
4224....4542	4324....4653	4423....4766	4523....4881	4619....4990	4717....5090	4817....5199
4225....4543	4325....4655	4424....4767	4524....4882	4620....4991	4718....5091	4818....5200
4226....4544	4326....4656	4425....4768	4525....4883 & 4966	4621....4989 & 4992	4719....5092	4819....5201
4227....4545	4327....4657	4426....4769	4526....4884	4622....4994	4720....5093	4820....5202
4228....4546	4328....4659	4427....4770	4527....4885	4623....4995	4721....5094	4821....5203
4229....4547	4329....4660	4428....4771	4528....4886	4624....4997	4722....5095	4822....5204
4230....4548	4330....4661	4429....4772	4529....4887	4625....4998	4723....5096	4823....5205
4231....4549	4331....4662	4430....4773	4530....4890	4626....4999	4724....5097	4824....5206
4232....4550	4332....4204 & 4663	4431....4774	4531....4888	4627....5002	4725....5098	4825....5207
4233....4551	4333....4664	4432....4775	4532....4889	4628....5003	4726....5099	4826....5208
4234....4552	4334....4665	4433....4776	4533....4891	4629....5004	4727....5100	4827....5209
4235....4553	4335....4666	4434....4777	4534....4892	4630....5005	4728....5101	4828....5210
4236....4554 & 4557	4336....4667	4435....4778	4535....4893	4631....5006	4729....5102	4829....5211
4237....4555	4337....4668	4436....4780	4536....4894	4632....5007	4730....5103	4830....5212
4238....407 & 4556	4338....4669	4437....4781	4537....4895	4633....5008	4731....5104	4831....5213
4239....4558	4339....4670	4438....4782	4538....4896	4634....5009	4732....5105	4832....5215
4240....4559	4340....4672	4439....4783	4539....4897	4635....5010	4733....5106	4833....5214 & 5216 & 5240
4241....4560	4341....4673	4440....4784	4540....4899 & 4900	4636....5011	4734....5107	4834....5217
4242....4561	4342....4674	4441....4785		4637....5012	4735....5109	4835....5218
4243....4563	4343....4675	4442....4786		4638....5013	4736....5108	4836....5219
4244....4564	4344....4676	4443....4787			4737....5110	4837....5220
4245....4565		4444....4788			4738....5111	

Strong	G/K	Strong	G/K	Strong	G/K	Strong	G/K	Strong	G/K	Strong	G/K	Strong	G/K
4838	5221	4936	5340	5035	5444	5134	5546	5234	5649	5332	5759	5432	5864
4839	5222	4937	5341	5036	5444	5135	5547	5235	5650	5333	5761	5433	5865
4840	5223	4938	5342	5037	5445	5136	5548	5236	5651	5334	5762	5434	5866
4841	5224	4939	5343	5038	5446	5137	5549	5237	4238 & 5653 & 5666	5335	5763	5435	5867
4842	5225	4940	5344	5039	5447	5138	5550	5238	5654	5336	5764	5436	5869
4843	5227	4941	5345	5040	5448	5139	5551	5239	5657	5337	5765	5437	5870
4844	5228	4942	5347	5041	5449	5140	5552	5240	5655 & 5656 & 5658	5338	5766	5438	5871
4845	5230	4943	5348	5042	5450	5141	5554	5241	5659	5339	5767	5439	5872
4846	5231	4944	5349	5043	5451	5142	5555	5242	5660	5340	5768	5440	5873
4847	5232	4945	5350	5044	5452	5143	5556	5243	5661	5341	5742 & 5769	5441	5874
4848	5233	4946	5352	5045	5454	5144	5558	5244	5662 & 5663	5342	5770	5442	5875
4849	5234 & 5235	4947	5353	5046	5455	5145	5559	5245	5664	5343	5771	5443	5876
4850	5236	4948	5356	5047	5456	5146	5560	5246	5665	5344	5772	5444	5877
4851	5237 & 5239	4949	5351 & 5355 & 5356 & 5835	5048	5457	5147	5561	5247	5667	5345	5773	5445	5878
4852	5238	4950	5358	5049	5458	5148	5562	5248	5668	5346	5774	5446	5879
4853	5241	4951	5359	5050	5459	5149	5563	5249	5669	5347	5776	5447	5880
4854	5242	4952	5331 & 5360	5051	5460	5150	5564	5250	5670	5348	5777	5448	5881
4855	5243	4953	5361	5052	5461	5151	5565	5251	5671	5349	5778	5449	5882
4856	5244	4954	5362	5053	5462	5152	5566	5252	5672	5350	5779	5450	5883
4857	5245	4955	5086 & 5363	5054	5463	5153	5567	5253	5673	5351	5780	5451	5884
4858	5246	4956	5364	5055	5464	5154	5568 & 5569	5254	5674	5352	5781	5452	5885
4859	5247	4957	5365	5056	5465	5155	5570	5255	5675	5353	5782	5453	5886
4860	5248	4958	5366	5057	5467	5156	5571	5256	5676	5354	5783	5454	5887
4861	5249	4959	5367	5058	5466 & 5468	5157	5572	5257	5677	5355	5784	5455	1876 & 5888
4862	5250	4960	5368	5059	5469	5158	5573	5258	5678	5356	5785	5456	5889
4863	5251	4961	5369	5060	5470	5159	5574 & 5578	5259	5679	5357	5786	5457	5890
4864	5252	4962	5370	5061	5472	5160	5575	5260	5680	5358	5787	5458	5891
4865	5253	4963	5371	5062	5473 & 5477	5161	5576	5261	5681	5359	5788	5459	5892
4866	5254	4964	5372	5063	5474 & 5478	5162	5577	5262	5682	5360	5789	5460	5893
4867	125 & 5255	4965	4993 & 5373	5064	5475	5163	5579	5263	5683 & 5684	5361	5790	5461	5894
4868	5256	4966	5374	5065	5476	5164	5580	5264	5685	5362	5791	5462	5895
4869	5257	4967	5375	5066	5479	5165	5581	5265	5686	5363	5792	5463	5897
4870	5258	4968	5376	5067	5480	5166	5582	5266	5687	5364	5793	5464	5898
4871	5259 & 5260 & 5276	4969	5377	5068	5481	5167	5583	5267	5688	5365	5794	5465	5899
4872	5262	4970	5379	5069	5482	5168	5584	5268	5689	5366	5795	5466	5900
4873	5263 & 5165	4971	5380	5070	5483	5169	5557 & 5585	5269	5690	5367	5796	5467	5901
4874	5264	4972	5381	5071	5484	5170	5586	5270	5691	5368	5797	5468	5902 & 5904
4875	5265	4973	5382	5072	5485	5171	5587	5271	5693	5369	5798	5469	5903
4876	5267	4974	5383 & 5384	5073	5486 & 5487	5172	5588	5272	5694	5370	5799	5470	5905 & 5911
4877	5268	4975	5385	5074	5488	5173	5589	5273	5695	5371	5800	5471	5906
4878	5269	4976	5386	5075	5489	5174	5590	5274	5696	5372	5801	5472	5907
4879	5270	4977	5387	5076	5490	5175	5591	5275	5699	5373	5802	5473	5908
4880	5271	4978	5388	5077	5491	5176	5592	5276	5700	5374	5803	5474	5909
4881	5272	4979	5389	5078	5492	5177	5593	5277	659 & 5701	5375	5804	5475	5910
4882	5273	4980	5390	5079	5493	5178	5594	5278	670 & 5702	5376	5805	5476	5912
4883	5274	4981	5391	5080	5494	5179	5595 & 5596	5279	5703	5377	5806	5477	5913
4884	5275	4982	1751 & 5392	5081	1315 & 5495	5180	5597	5280	5704	5378	5807	5478	5914
4885	5277	4983	5393	5082	5496	5181	5598	5281	5705	5379	5808	5479	5915
4886	5278	4984	5394	5083	5498	5182	2571 & 5600	5282	5706	5380	5809	5480	5916
4887	5279	4985	5395	5084	5499	5183	5601	5283	5707	5381	5810	5481	5917
4888	5280	4986	5396	5085	5500	5184	5602	5284	5709	5382	5811	5482	5918
4889	5281	4987	5397	5086	5501	5185	5603	5285	5710	5383	5812	5483	5919
4890	5282	4988	5398	5087	5502	5186	5604	5286	5711	5384	5813	5484	5920
4891	5283	4989	5399	5088	5503	5187	5605	5287	5712	5385	5814	5485	5921
4892	5284	4990	5400	5089	5504	5188	5606	5288	5713	5386	5815	5486	5922
4893	5287	4991	5401	5090	5505	5189	5607	5289	5714	5387	5816	5487	5923
4894	5288 & 5323 & 5328	4992	5402 & 5403	5091	5506	5190	5608	5290	5715	5388	5817	5488	5924
4895	5289	4993	5404	5092	5507	5191	5610	5291	5716	5389	5818	5489	5925
4896	5290	4994	5405	5093	5508	5192	5611	5292	5717	5390	5819	5490	5926
4897	5291	4995	5406	5094	5509	5193	5612	5293	5718	5391	5426 & 5820	5491	5927
4898	5292	4996	5407	5095	5510	5194	5613	5294	5719	5392	3055 & 5821	5492	5928
4899	5293	4997	5408	5096	5511	5195	5614	5295	5720	5393	5823	5493	5929
4900	5261 & 5295	4998	5409	5097	5512	5196	5615	5296	5721	5394	5824	5494	5930
4901	5296	4999	5411	5098	5513	5197	5616	5297	5722	5395	5825	5495	5931
4902	5299	5000	5412	5099	5514	5198	5617	5298	5723	5396	5826	5496	5932
4903	5300	5001	5413	5100	5516	5199	5618	5299	5708 & 5724	5397	5827	5497	5933
4904	5301	5002	5414	5101	5515	5200	5619	5300	5725	5398	5829	5498	5934
4905	5302	5003	5415	5102	5518	5201	5620	5301	5727	5399	5828 & 5830	5499	5935
4906	5303	5004	5416	5103	5519	5202	5621	5302	5728	5400	5831	5500	5936
4907	5304	5005	5417	5104	5520	5203	5622	5303	5729	5401	5832	5501	5937
4908	5305	5006	5418	5105	5521 & 5522	5204	5623	5304	5730	5402	5833	5502	5938
4909	5306	5007	5419	5106	5523	5205	5624	5305	5731	5403	5834	5503	5939
4910	5307	5008	2496 & 5420	5107	5524	5206	5625	5306	5731	5404	5836	5504	2396 & 5940
4911	5308	5009	5421	5108	5525	5207	5626	5307	5733	5405	5837	5505	5942
4912	5309	5010	5423	5109	5526	5208	5627	5308	5734	5406	5838	5506	5941
4913	5310	5011	5424	5110	5527	5209	5148	5309	5735	5407	5839	5507	5943
4914	5311	5012	5425	5111	5528	5210	5148	5310	5736	5408	5840	5508	5944
4915	5312	5013	5427	5112	5529 & 5530 & 5531	5211	5628	5311	5737	5409	5841	5509	5945
4916	5313	5014	5428	5113	5532	5212	5629	5312	5738	5410	5842	5510	5946
4917	5314	5015	5429	5114	5533	5213	5148	5313	5739	5411	5843	5511	5948
4918	5315	5016	5430	5115	5534	5214	5630	5314	5741	5412	5844	5512	1430 & 5949
4919	5316	5017	5431	5116	5535	5215	5631	5315	2266	5413	5845	5513	5950
4920	5317 & 5320	5018	5432	5117	5536 & 4509	5216	5148	5316	5743	5414	5846	5514	5951
4921	5318 & 5319	5019	5433	5118	5537	5217	5632	5317	5744	5415	5847	5515	5952
4922	5321	5020	5434	5119	5538	5218	5633	5318	5745	5416	5848	5516	5947 & 5953
4923	5322	5021	5435	5120	3836	5219	5634	5319	5746	5417	5849 & 5822	5517	5954
4924	5324	5022	5436	5121	5539	5220	5635	5320	5747	5418	5850	5518	5955
4925	5325	5023	4047	5122	5540	5221	5636	5321	5748	5419	5851	5519	5956
4926	5326	5024	5437	5123	5542	5222	5637	5322	5749	5420	5852	5520	5957
4927	5327	5025	4047	5124	4047	5223	5638	5323	5750	5421	5853	5521	5958
4928	5330	5026	4047	5125	4047	5224	5639	5324	5751	5422	5854	5522	5967 & 5959
4929	5332	5027	5438	5126	4047	5225	5639	5325	5752	5423	5855	5523	5960 & 6002
4930	5333	5028	5439	5127	4047	5226	5640	5326	5753	5424	5856	5524	5961
4931	5334	5029	5440	5128	4047	5227	5641	5327	5754	5425	5857	5525	5962
4932	5335	5030	5441	5129	4047	5228	5642	5328	5755	5426	5858	5526	5963
4933	5337	5031	5442	5130	4047	5229	5643	5329	5756	5427	5859	5527	5964
4934	5298 & 5338	5032	5441	5131	5543	5230	5644	5330	5757	5428	5860	5528	5965
4935	5339	5033	5441	5132	5544	5231	5645	5331	5758 & 5760	5429	5861	5529	5966
		5034	5443	5133	5545	5232	5647			5430	5862	5530	5968
						5233	5648			5431	5863	5531	3079 & 5969

We want to hear from you. Please send your comments about this book to us in care of zreview@zondervan.com. Thank you.

ZONDERVAN.com/
AUTHORTRACKER
follow your favorite authors